For further reading

Friedman, Milton and Rose. *Free to Choose: A Personal Statement.* New York: Harcourt, Brace, Jovanovich, 1979.

Gilder, George. *Wealth and Poverty.* New York: Basic Books, Inc., 1981.

Heilbroner, Robert L. *The Worldly Philosophers: The Lives, Times, and Ideas of the Great Economic Thinkers.* New York: Simon and Schuster, 1953.

Kennedy, Charles R., Jr. *Managing the International Business Environment: Cases in Political and Country Risk.* Englewood Cliffs, N.J.: Prentice Hall, 1991.

Krugman, Paul. *The Age of Diminished Expectations: U.S. Economic Policy in the 1990s.* Cambridge, Mass.: The MIT Press, 1992.

North, Douglass C., and Roger LeRoy Miller. *The Economics of Public Issues.* New York: Harper and Row, 1976.

Smith, Adam. *The Money Game.* New York: Vintage Books, 1976.

FOR FURTHER READING

Follow up what you've learned

Glossary

Exchange rate

absolute advantage. The ability to use fewer resources to produce an item.

aggregate demand. A country's demand for all goods and services; equals the total of planned expenditures by firms, households, and government.

aggregate supply. The total of goods and services provided by all of a country's producers.

GLOSSARY

Review key terms and phrases

TESTS, HOMEWORK, & PROJECTS

Learn strategies for success

Economics

Tests, homework, and projects

Laying the groundwork
One nice thing about economics is that it is all around you. You can't open a newspaper, turn on a television, or even walk down a street without being exposed to situations in which economics plays a rol

Strategies for success
Most economics professors derive their homework and exam questions from "real world" situations. You can start thinking in economic terms after only a few weeks in an economics class. As you come into

Slope is an important concept in economics. The term is used to describe the steepness of a line, just as we might describe the steepness of a skier's hill. The slope of Hill A is greater (steeper) than the slope of Hill B.

ILLUSTRATIONS & PHOTOS

See examples of important points

CHARTS & GRAPHS

Fill in the facts

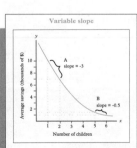

Variable slope

A
slope = -3

B
slope = -0.5

A curved line has a slope that varies. The slope along section A is (10-7)/(1-2) = -3, while section B is (1.5-1)/(5-6), which is -0.5. Note that the steeper section of the line has a larger slope in absolute values.

Student Handbook

College and University Edition

Including

What Happened When

Volume **4**

Student Handbook

College and University Edition

Including

What Happened When

THE SOUTHWESTERN COMPANY
Nashville, Tennessee

Contents

English Composition 28–115

Calculus 116–213

Contents

Economics 214–263

History of Western Civilization 264–313

Contents

Business Administration

314–363

Natural Sciences
Science, Measurement, and Math

Biology

Contents

Natural Sciences
Chemistry 390–407

Natural Sciences
Geology 408–423

Contents

Natural Sciences
Physics 424–439

Social Sciences
Psychology 442–457

Contents

Social Sciences
Sociology 458-473

Social Sciences
Political Science 474–487

Contents

Social Sciences
Cultural Anthropology 488–505

Study Skills 506–543

College Entrance Exams 544–569

Contents

19

Thinking About College 570–595

What Happened When

Editorial development of *Student Handbook, College and University Edition,* was directed by
Kidd & Company, Inc., Nashville, Tennessee 37215

Executive editor	Ronald Kidd
Administrative editor	D. Fran Morley
Production editor	Dorian Hastings
Calculus copy editor	Marjorie Seachrist
Proofreaders	Kerry Pappas
	Bitite Vinklers
	Jeannie Crawford–Lee
Typesetting, design, and production	Schatz+Schatz
Additional typesetting	Laurie Beers
	Dale Sprenkle
Photo research	Lisa Hartjens/Imagefinders, Inc.
	D. Fran Morley
Index	Schroeder Indexing Services

Subject editors
   English Composition   D. Fran Morley
   Calculus   Gloria E. Langer
   Economics   Luanne C. Bole–Becker
   History of Western Civilization   Susan Romeo
   Business Administration   Robert A. Weinstein
   Chemistry, Physics   Margaret Kuntz
   Social Sciences   Cynthia A. Hill
   Study Skills, College Entrance Exams,
      Thinking About College   Robert A. Weinstein

AUTHORS

English Composition	Steven Lynn, Ph.D. Associate professor University of South Carolina with Jennie Ariail
Calculus	LuAnn Malik, M.A. Mathematics faculty Aurora Community College with Chuck Smith
Economics	Catherine A. Melfi, Ph.D. Research scientist, econometrician Indiana University
History of Western Civilization	Edward A. Gosselin, Ph.D. Professor California State University, Long Beach
Business Administration	Gayle Baugh, Ph.D. Assistant professor University of West Florida with Robert A. Weinstein
Chemistry, Physics	Margaret Kuntz Science writer
Psychology	Charles A. Levin, Ph.D. Assistant professor Baldwin–Wallace College
Sociology	John W. King, Ph.D. Assistant professor Baldwin–Wallace College
Political Science	Ronald J. Busch, Ph.D. Associate professor Cleveland State University
Cultural Anthropology	Paul L. Aspelin, Ph.D. Associate professor Cleveland State University
	Barbara G. Hoffman Assistant professor Cleveland State University
Study Skills, College Entrance Exams, *Thinking About College*	Barbara C. Greenfeld, M.S. Director of admissions and testing services Howard Community College with Robert A. Weinstein

Student Handbook

College and University Edition

Including

What Happened When

English Composition

- Basic considerations
- Getting ready to write
- Writing the paper
- Preparing the final copy
- Writing about literature
- Other assignments
- Grammar review
- Rules and superstitions
- Improving your style
- The research paper

English Composition

The material presented in this chapter is designed to supplement whatever materials you are using in your writing classes. It provides a condensed version of what most textbooks tell you, but it also comments on that advice and offers some additional tips and shortcuts.

First, you'll find a discussion of the most essential task for college composition: writing an argumentative essay. Next, this chapter deals with writing specifically about literature. You'll find simple and direct discussions of some problems that bother most students, and you'll find some strategies explained that should help you think of lots of things to say about literature—of whatever sort.

Other kinds of writing assignments are then covered, followed by a whirlwind review of grammar. You'll get some advice about improving your style that, if you apply it, can make a dramatic difference in your writing options. Most students at some point have to do a research paper, so that topic is covered briefly here. And everyone has to handle in-class essay tests, homework, and projects. You'll find suggestions for dealing more effectively with those.

Concluding the chapter are a usage guide, providing quick reference for common writing questions, and a list of books for further reading.

Basic considerations

Why writing is so important. All the subjects you will study are of course important, especially when you consider that the average college student changes his or her major three times: any subject you study might determine your career, and all of them will likely change your life in some way. But composition has a special importance. In fact, one could argue that writing, for a number of reasons, is the single most important subject you will study, whatever your major.

Consider, for starters, how much writing you'll need to do when you graduate. One survey has revealed that engineering majors (at least some of whom chose engineering because they did not particularly enjoy literature and composition) will spend roughly a fifth to a fourth of their time writing! An engineer, in other words, can expect to spend about one day a week writing. People in most other fields probably spend as much if not more time "composing" in some sense— reports, letters, memorandums, speeches, talks, instructions, complaints, responses, inquiries, and all sorts of other things.

Further, as you gain responsibility and rank, the importance of writing for your work will increase. If you have been thinking that you'll be so rich and powerful that your secretary can do all your writing, or at least clean up the writing you scribble out, then you should think again. Writing is a powerful tool; you'll want to be able to wield it yourself. And the way you say something is often as important as what you say. If someone else controls your writing, then that person controls your image and your effectiveness.

Additionally, writing is much more than polishing up preexisting ideas—merely translating your brilliant thoughts into clean prose. Writing is in itself a way of learning, a mechanism for discovery and for thinking things through. There's often no better way to figure something out than to write about it. Thus, the clarity and imagination that are called for in writing apply to your personal as well as to your professional life. Most of us often solve our biggest problems by talking things over with a friend. Writing allows you to express your ideas in private, and also to record them in a more precise and detailed way—more effectively than most of us can manage in conversation.

Of course, writing is also important for your success in college. Even in your freshman year, you will find that being able to express yourself fluently and effectively will be very helpful (to understate the matter considerably).

You may have begun reading this section with some vague idea that, yes, writing is fairly important, and yes, you would like to do well in your English classes. But writing is crucially important: it is not an exaggeration to say that it is the key to your success.

Why writing is so difficult. Perhaps
the most important thing beginning writers should know (and we are all beginning in some sense) is that writing is not easy, even for the best professionals. If writing *is* easy for you, then at least one of two things is true: you are a great genius, blessed with an uncanny ability to express ideas, or you're not doing it right. Occasionally, to be sure, a writer will find a patch of smooth-running water and the prose will slide right across it effortlessly. More often, the writer inevitably faces crosscurrents, eddies, rapids, undertows, and gashing boulders, requiring concentration and sustained effort to overcome.

Why? Why does writing seem like negotiating a twisting mountain river? There are two reasons, both important for you to know about:

1. Writing is not natural. Children learn how to talk by observing other people and imitating them. Although we may encourage children to talk, we gen-

erally don't teach them in any formal way. Talking seems to come naturally. But learning to write generally calls for more explicit and extensive instruction. Writing is an invention, more difficult in some important ways than speaking, employing complexities and multitudinous conventions of committing language to paper (or stone, monitor screen, billboard, sky—whatever). You shouldn't feel discouraged if you find writing difficult and complicated. *It is*. It is, perhaps, the most amazing thing human beings do.

2. Writing is difficult because it usually demands more coherence, precision, and thoroughness than speech. When we talk with someone, we have many

clues other than the words themselves to tell us what is meant—tone, facial expression, body language. Most people would rather conduct important business in person for just this reason. The writer can't tell where a particular reader will be confused, or unconvinced, or bored, and so the writer has to anticipate what various readers may want at any moment. Good writing often sounds like speech—without all the repetition, delays, wandering around, and feedback that make up talking. But to remove everything we don't need in order to make sense, and to add all we do need, is hard work.

When to write.
There are reasons to wait until the very last minute to begin any writing task: you may enjoy the adrenaline rush of panic and anxiety; you may want to avoid wasting effort in case you are hit by lightning and don't have to turn in the assigned paper; or you may be trying to flunk out of school in order to begin your work career immediately.

There are better reasons to start as soon as possible—to begin writing immediately when an assignment is given. Obviously, the sooner you start, the more time you will have, but this initiative does not necessarily mean that if you start sooner, you will have to do more work. In fact, the contrary is likely to be the case.

How's that? How will starting sooner make for less effort and yet a better result? Long before Freud, human beings have been well aware of the unconscious mind and its incessant but hidden activity. We

have all tried in vain to solve a problem only to realize the answer when we have stopped thinking about it. How did the solution suddenly occur to you when you were taking a shower, playing tennis, standing on the sidewalk thinking about nothing in particular? The solution occurred because your subconscious mind continued to work on the problem even while your conscious mind went on to other things.

So, you should begin to write as soon as you can. If you engage your mind in the assigned task, you can then go for a walk or to a movie and still have some part of your brain working on the project—as if you hired some co-writers. If you start early, you will also be able to work in small chunks of time, staying fresh and taking breaks.

A certain amount of delay and procrastination is inevitable in writing. Writing is difficult, as we have noted, and everyone's mind naturally resists hard labor. As Newton said, objects at rest tend to stay at rest. But if you can get your mind in motion, you will find your delays and daydreams are often productive, for as Newton also said, objects in motion tend to stay in motion.

Get your mind in motion as soon as possible, and you'll find yourself picking up speed and momentum as you go along. And don't worry too much if your mind wanders off while you're trying to write. It happens to everyone. Indeed, such daydreams may lead you to useful ideas. Just keep returning your attention periodically to the task at hand, and keep those ideas rolling.

English Composition

Where to write. Although it might seem obvious that to write, one should seek out a quiet, well-lit place without distractions, interviews with writers and self-reports, surprisingly enough, suggest otherwise. Some writers work with music or even television on; some like to have their children playing around them; others like to sit in a restaurant or café. I know of two detective story authors who meet almost every morning at McDonald's and write together for several hours in their regular booth. Some research has, in fact, indicated that people tend to concentrate better with some background noise, perhaps because the noise forces them to focus more intently on the task.

In other words, you should not think you need to wait to write until you're in the library, or until your roommate is gone or asleep, or until you've solved every other problem that might distract you. Good writing has been done under just about any circumstance you can imagine. You will likely find that some circumstances work better than others for you, and most writers do like to work in the same place with the same materials, if possible. The point here is that you do want to find out where you write best, but you also don't want to be too fussy about it. You can probably write anywhere, if you put your mind to it.

Materials for writing. If you are going to write, part of thinking like a writer includes arranging to secure the materials a writer needs. You can build a brick wall with a kitchen knife and a yardstick, but it would be so much easier and probably more effective to use a brickmason's trowel and a tapeline. I have seen more than one writer, including students and professionals, struggle needlessly with a project because they simply did not have adequate materials for writing.

Although a writer can work just about anywhere at just about any time, many writers do prefer to work with certain materials, and it may be helpful to consider what materials are ideal even at the risk of being obvious.

First, a writer needs a desk or a table or some surface to work on. I know that Thomas Wolfe supposedly used the top of a refrigerator to write while standing (he was tall), and Mickey Spillane reportedly writes sometimes in his boat with his typewriter on his knees, but if you are writing an essay or anything that requires research, you'll be amazed how quickly papers multiply. If you have a surface large enough to spread out your papers and books, you'll find it much easier to stay organized. This surface ideally should be devoted to writing. If you use the kitchen table (and

Find a place to write where you can comfortably spread out all your resource materials.

A computer may make writing easier, but you still need sufficient time and a good place to work.

many people do), then you're continually clearing off your materials (or eating off the floor).

You do not need a computer to write well or quickly. Anthony Trollope and Samuel Johnson wrote thousands of well-crafted words in a few hours long before disk drives. But a computer is useful in preparing a final copy because it allows you to revise without retyping. If you don't already own a computer, don't think you can buy one right before you need to start writing and find it immediately helpful. You need to know how to type (some people neglect to consider this fact)—unless you have a computer that reads your handwriting. And you need to be familiar with whatever software program you plan to use, which may take days or weeks, depending on your computer literacy and available time. Computers are wonderful tools, but they aren't magical (see the next section), and you can write well without one.

Lined paper and index cards are essential, even if you write at a computer. Put bits of information and separate ideas on the cards, and use the paper for drafting, outlining, brainstorming, and diagramming. If you write with a pencil, you will find plastic erasers are a great tool (they erase better with less mess). If you use a pen, you may find that a fountain pen is a good investment, especially if your handwriting is bad: fountain pens have a way of making one's chicken scratches look elegant.

You'll need good lighting. An architect's lamp that combines fluorescent and incandescent light is ideal, providing the full spectrum of light that is much easier on the eyes. To help you keep track of what you've been able to see so clearly, the little plastic flags or removable notes are great. You just pop one on the page marking a passage, perhaps copying it later on your index cards.

For keeping books propped open, with the proper

page marked, I have found nothing better than clothespins, which mark better than even expensive leather bookmarkers. Keeping books open at a comfortable reading angle is a constant problem, especially if you are writing about a text or doing research. If you're working at the Folger Library in Washington or the British Library in London (having flown in on your personal jet, perhaps), you will find a very nice wood and brass bookstand. If you don't happen to have such a bookstand, you can use a cookbook stand or stack bricks to hold your books open.

I would apologize for covering such apparent trivialities as the materials you need, especially in such detail, except I know what a difference the right materials can make. Of course, what is right for one writer may be wrong for another. Perhaps you need a stand-up desk, or an italic fountain pen, or yellow legal pads. The important thing to note here is that the materials you use do make a difference. Give some thought to the question of what will be best for you.

Save time, avoid aggravations.

There are some simple but very useful tips that will help make your writing go faster and smoother.

Skip lines on your drafts, whether you are writing by hand, typewriter, or computer; and employ one-inch margins on all sides. You might even triple-space, because the idea is to give yourself room to make corrections and revisions. It is difficult and even irritating to try to delete and rewrite when you don't have enough room to work. The proofreaders' marks, discussed later in this chapter, will help you make changes efficiently, but you'll need space to use them.

If you write by hand, use only one side of the page. It's more legible and convenient. You may find as you are revising that you want to save only one passage on a page; rather than copying the passage over, you can simply cut it out and tape or paste it on another sheet—if you've written only on one side. Likewise, if you put information on index cards, you can insert them into your draft just by pasting or taping them where they go. Indeed, do anything to your draft pages that will make putting them together faster and easier. Too many students treat their manuscripts with reverence, reluctant to cut and paste, strike out, insert, tape together, and so forth. When you are famous, of course, your manuscripts will be precious—but they'll be much more interesting if you've actually worked on them!

Make copies of your work, anticipating and thereby avoiding disaster. Teachers as a rule don't lose student papers, but life is full of accidents; Ernest Hemingway lost an entire book manuscript—it was left in a taxi in Paris. Although it is some trouble to make copies, it is certainly much easier than rewriting a paper.

Getting ready to write

Analyzing the assignment. If you were in London and someone told you to drive to Bath, it is unlikely that you would immediately hop in a car and start driving in whatever direction seemed best. Instead, you would carefully consider where you wanted to go, and where you were, and map out a course. Then you'd start out, adjusting your route as the trip developed, and road conditions, weather, and other factors emerged.

But many students do the compositional equivalent of hopping in and driving off when given a writing assignment. Let's say that a student in an American history class is given the following assignment: "Discuss the causes of the Civil War."

The student has been fascinated by Abraham Lincoln's character and his resolve to keep the United States together. And so the student immediately begins to talk about Lincoln—reasonably enough, perhaps, since Lincoln's strength did play some major role in leading the nation to war. In order to help the reader understand Lincoln's character, the student discusses Lincoln's birth and childhood, his education and early career, his writings and ideas, his campaign for the presidency, and finally his role in the war.

No matter how well the student conducts this essay, it is of course on the wrong road. There is some very interesting scenery, but the journey won't get us to the causes of the Civil War. Now you may think this example is unrealistic, but let me assure you that it is not: the most fundamental problem of student writing,

most teachers will say, is a failure in some way to carry out the assigned task.

To help you focus on the assignment and execute it successfully, consider three aspects of your task.

The verb. Every assignment should have a verb that names the action your essay should undertake. In the example below, the verb is *discuss*, which offers you less specific directions than some others. *Discuss* could mean just about anything, from "talk about for a while" to "analyze" or "compose" or "support" or "refute" or something else. Whenever you encounter *discuss*, you need to consider what you're really being asked to do.

If the assignment asks you in some way to describe a series of events, for example, then it is likely that a narrative structure will be appropriate. An assignment calling for narration might ask you "to trace the development of x" (the Civil War, the exploration of the moon, or the collapse of communism). If the assignment asks you to explain what a key term means, then you are being asked to define and classify; the assignment may even use those terms—"define a civil war," for instance, or "classify the Crimean War as a kind of military engagement."

Here are some verbs you will commonly find in assignments, along with a brief discussion of their implications for your response:

Assignments that ask you to *agree or disagree* may seem to imply that only one response is correct. Oftentimes, however, a good case can be made either

---

Be sure to use clear, direct sentences that outline the structure of the piece being analyzed.

This is an open-ended word. You could use any writing strategy successfully.

Write a **well-organized** essay **discussing** the **similarities and differences** in both **theme and style** of the following **two poems**.

Be sure to consider both of these elements in your discussion.

Make sure you give equal time to both pieces being discussed.

Look for several examples of how the pieces being analyzed are alike and different.

Here's how one assignment might be analyzed.

When teachers assign an essay, they are usually more interested in getting you to think than in having you take a particular viewpoint.

way, and the teacher genuinely wants students to think for themselves. The important thing, usually, is not whether you agree or disagree, but how well you support your position. And don't assume that your position has to be simple: few issues are black and white; so even if you essentially agree (or disagree), you should acknowledge the good points of the opposing position.

In assignments that ask students to *analyze x*, the key activity involves breaking the object of attention, the "x," into its parts. Often there will be at least one obvious way to take apart and display the "x," but this strategy may not necessarily be most effective. You simply need to consider the purpose of your analysis. For example, if you are asked to analyze a luxury sedan, you might naturally break it down into the engine and drive train, brakes and tires, seating, sound system, and so forth, explaining each part. But let's imagine that the audience for your analysis is a potential buyer of the luxury sedan. Then your analysis might proceed differently—into, say, value, safety, reliability, and so forth. "Discuss the causes of the Civil War" could be treated as an *analyze* assignment, asking you to identify and explain the causes.

An assignment that asks you to *classify* is, like an analysis assignment, asking you to organize data. A classification system groups related items together. You might be given, for instance, fourteen causes of the Civil War and then asked to classify them. As with analysis, the way you group the causes together should depend on both your own logic and your purpose in classifying.

The kinds of assignments asking you to *consider how*

actually want you to explain the development of an entity, as in "Consider how the Civil War began." How is this assignment different from "discuss the causes of x" or "analyze x"? In a sense, teachers are trying to find different ways to ask students the same thing over and over again: you simply need to know enough about the causes of the Civil War to discuss them intelligently, whatever kind of discussion is called for. *Consider how* does suggest a chronological orientation, implying you should trace a sequence of events (rather than classify the kinds or analyze the different factors).

To *evaluate* means to compare one thing with another, or compare one thing with an ideal. If an assignment directs you to evaluate two different explanations of how the Civil War came about, your response will attempt to show which explanation better accounts for what happened. An ideal explanation would account for every fact, so you would not only be comparing one explanation to the other, but you would also be comparing each explanation to a hypothetical ideal one. Take care in such assignments that you don't oversimplify, offering only positive or only negative comments.

Occasionally an assignment may ask you to *persuade* your reader. In all writing tasks it is important to keep the audience in mind and shape the argument accordingly; but in an assignment that asks you to "persuade," such considerations are especially important.

Assignments that ask you to *refute or support* a given idea generally call for the same strategies as *agree or disagree*.

Ideally, with any assignment, the student is able to *summarize*—that is, select which information to use and which to leave out. If you're forced to employ every bit of information that you can possibly think of on a topic, then you may not have studied enough. Successful summaries necessarily omit information, requiring the student to demonstrate an understanding of a topic by intelligently condensing it. Suggestion: Think in terms of an outline, omitting the lower-level items.

The topic. The second aspect of the assignment to consider carefully is the subject. It's not a bad idea to circle the noun or noun phrase that names the subject of the assignment, just to focus your attention upon it. Notice any qualifiers or specifiers: If the assignment says "Discuss the causes of the Civil War," for instance, then it's obviously crucial to focus on the *causes*, not just the Civil War in general.

The audience. If you're lucky, the assignment will specify a particular audience. For instance, "For an issue of the *Weekly Reader*, read by sixth-grade students across the U.S., write a discussion of the causes of the Civil War," or "In a speech to the Daughters of

English Composition

the American Confederacy, discuss the causes of the Civil War." Obviously your discussion for these two audiences would be substantially different. The *Weekly Reader* audience would require background information that the Daughters would not; and the Daughters might want justification of some points that other audiences would readily accept. The vocabulary and wording would be different. If you believe that Southern antebellum culture nurtured an independent spirit that sometimes bordered on arrogance, you'll need to be careful how you put this opinion, avoiding offending the Daughters or confusing the sixth graders.

Classroom assignments are often especially tricky because the audience is unclear: if no audience is designated, are you supposed to write for the teacher? If you think of the teacher as the only audience, then you're often in the odd position of giving the audience information it already possesses. Ordinarily you'd be careful to acknowledge this prior awareness. But here the best strategy is to imagine an intelligent reader who is uninformed on the particular assignment topic but is well educated otherwise. You will be aware of course that your teacher *is* the audience in the end, but you are not trying to communicate exclusively with him or her; rather, imagine that your teacher will be judging your ability to communicate with an uninformed reader—and not your ability to repeat information to someone who already has that information.

Basic invention strategies.
Often, when faced with an assignment, everything you may have known about the subject immediately flies out of your mind. However, there are a number of ways you can generate new ideas and explore the knowledge you already have on a subject before you begin writing.

Freewriting. Freewriting is a popular strategy for generating ideas. It is based on the realization that we often limit and even block our creativity by focusing on grammar, phrasing, logic, neatness, and all sorts of minute particulars. In ancient times, classical rhetoricians made invention a separate stage of composing, distinct from arrangement and style, because they perceived the ways that attention to logic and style can siphon off energy from spontaneous creativity.

So how do you engage in freewriting? You simply concentrate on your subject and write as fast as you can, without censoring, without rephrasing, without editing, without evaluating. Just put your mind in gear and let it go—wide open—for a set period of time. Ten minutes for freewriting is a good idea. (This technique is also useful if part of your assignment is to find your own subject.)

This sounds ridiculously easy, and it often is. But you may find your attention wandering from your sub-

---

List of invention strategies

Freewriting. Write without stopping for ten minutes. Rest and repeat.

Looping. Identify promising passages in your freewriting and write quickly, developing those passages.

Cubing. Explore a topic from six perspectives: describe, compare, associate, trace, apply, and evaluate.

Brainstorming. Throw out ideas without censoring them. Record the information and look for the connections.

Asking questions. Generate questions, then later try to answer them.

Pro and con thinking. Construct a conversation enacting opposing sides of a subject.

Commonplace book. Write down useful and/or striking quotations or ideas.

---

ject, in which case you shouldn't be frustrated: just focus again on the topic. If you find yourself with nothing to say, simply say something dumb, or write "I have nothing to say; I don't know what to say" until something comes to mind. You can even speculate on why you have nothing to say. The important thing is to keep the pen moving.

Looping. Looping means returning to material you've written and focusing on some part of it in another session of writing. As you read over your freewriting or your draft, you'll probably find that some ideas seem useful and others don't. You might want to circle those words, phrases, sentences, or paragraphs that seem to be heading in the right direction and ignore the rest. Then use the circled passages as the basis for further freewriting and drafting.

It's always possible that as you "loop" back over your work, you won't find anything you like. Don't be discouraged, and don't crumple the paper and practice your rebound shot—just write some more. You may find, as you go along, that these rejected materials actually contain something valuable. And it's always possible—in theory, anyway—that in looping, you'll find your draft is just perfect.

If you have trouble deciding which materials to keep as you're looping, here's a tip: If you've written something that surprised you as you thought of it, that you really didn't expect to say when you began writing, then that material is probably good. Loop on it and see what happens.

Cubing. Cubing is a kind of directed freewriting that lets you quickly explore a topic from six different perspectives (a cube has six sides). These six different perspectives are: describe, compare, associate, trace, apply, and evaluate.

Freewriting example

Assignment: In a letter to your local newspaper, express your opinion on the appropriateness of media investigations into the private lives of political candidates.

Freewriting

Is a politician's private life really private? Is this a dumb question? Don't the basic rights and privileges of our country apply to all its citizens, including politicians? So private life has to be private, right? On the other hand, politicians are (or aspire to be) public servants, don't they? In offering to be our leaders, don't politicians in effect expose themselves to our scrutiny?

I don't know. I'm hungry. Both sides of this issue seem plausible to me. So how can it be decided? I think the public has the right to know, and I think the politician has the right to privacy. Something's gotta give here.

So, let's try to press beyond this dilemma. How? Maybe we could ask which of these valid concerns has more weight? One could argue that if one person's rights are violated, then the whole system is called into question. But that really isn't true, is it? Individuals' rights have been violated in the past and the system is still in place. On the other hand, should a truly evil person attain a position of power, our system might possibly be in jeopardy. At the least, harm could be done more serious than the violation of privacy. So at least I know what position I want to take. I would like to know everything about a politician's character, including anything in his or her private life that might conceivably affect on-the-job performance. Anyone who offers to run should, in my view, realize they surrender some privacy.

English Composition

Each perspective brings different questions into play. Focus on the questions for each side and freewrite for three to five minutes in response to the question for that side. After going through all six sides, which shouldn't take more than half an hour, you should have a good bit of material to work with. To address these questions, one obviously must view the subject as a static thing, which may seem an odd stance but nevertheless one that is often illuminating.

Visualize the six sides of a cube when you explore a topic from different perspectives in your cubing exercises.

Example

Let's say you decide to try cubing on a speech to your school's board of trustees about starting a football program.

How would you *describe* the features of the subject? What are its parts? What is its appearance? Form? Color? Thickness?

Football can be divided into the team and the fans. If we think of it as an object, through much of the week football is a fairly small entity, involving a hundred or so people at any school. On Saturdays, however, football swells quickly for a few hours to involve thousands of people. And throughout the week, thousands not directly involved will discuss the team. So, football as an entity is more than coaches and players; it extends itself throughout the community.

How does the subject *compare* to other subjects? What is it like? What is it not like? What does it have in common with other subjects?

Football seems most like soccer. You have a ball and two teams and two goals. Soccer is more important internationally, but football has just about displaced baseball as the American sport. Football is, in my opinion, much more exciting than soccer, requiring more teamwork and precise timing and more set plays and strategies. The action, to be sure, is just about continuous in soccer, but the scoring is usually low. Football is certainly more violent. Soccer is often a rough sport, admittedly, and the players don't wear pads. But football involves many collisions in every play: at any given moment, the object of the game for one side is to knock a player on the other side to the ground. In fact, football is so violent and brutal, one might wonder if it's really healthy—psychologically or physically.

What do you *associate* with this subject? What can you connect to this subject if you let your mind wander? What unexpected, creative links can you make between this subject and something else?

I associate football with tailgate parties and with getting dressed up. A football team would probably stimulate takeout food sales and clothing sales in the fall. Perhaps those merchants would like to help support football?

Being more creative, I see some likeness between football games and worship services: crowds of people come together once a week to sit together, raise their voices, and then go home. But football seems sometimes to be taken more seriously? More passionately, anyway?

Can you *trace* the progress of the subject? How did it begin? How did it develop? What will it become?

Fifty years or so ago, football players wore helmets that were just leather caps. Today they wear high-impact, lightweight plastic polymers with extensive padding; the face masks for some players look like cages, and some even have Plexiglas shields to protect their faces entirely. Shoulder pads have undergone a similar evolution. Indeed, every piece of equipment has been improved to allow stronger, faster, heavier players to crash into each other with incredible force. But the pads have not evolved enough to protect the players entirely, for in any given game, injuries abound. Are these injuries worth it?

In what ways can you *apply* the subject? What is its use? What problems can it be used to solve?

Football can be used to raise money. It can increase school spirit. It can teach lessons about teamwork and dedication and effort. Football can also stimulate a local economy: construction,

Looping example

Assignment: Imagine that the board of trustees at your school is beginning to consider whether to begin a football program. They have asked for student input in this process, and you have been selected as the student representative. Write the brief statement you will make to the board.

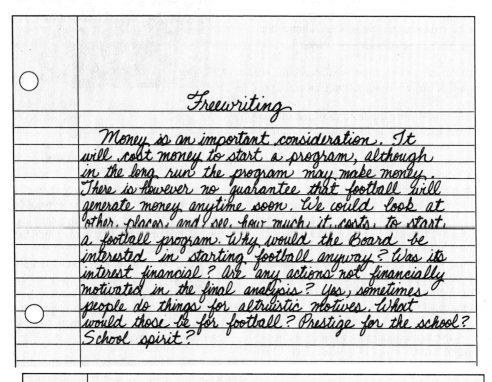

Freewriting

Money is an important consideration. It will cost money to start a program, although in the long run the program may make money. There is however no guarantee that football will generate money anytime soon. We could look at other places and see how much it costs to start a football program. Why would the Board be interested in starting football anyway? Was its interest financial? Are any actions not financially motivated in the final analysis? Yes, sometimes people do things for altruistic motives. What would those be for football? Prestige for the school? School spirit?

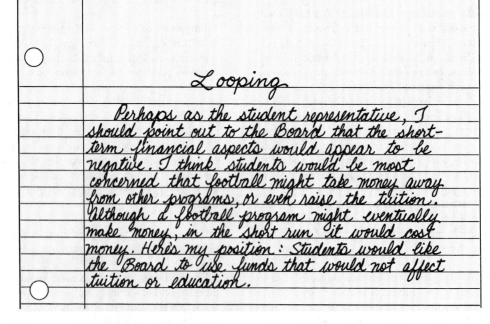

Looping

Perhaps as the student representative, I should point out to the Board that the short-term financial aspects would appear to be negative. I think students would be most concerned that football might take money away from other programs, or even raise the tuition. Although a football program might eventually make money, in the short run it would cost money. Here's my position: Students would like the Board to use funds that would not affect tuition or education.

restaurant, and lodging businesses may all benefit. Football may also provide an outlet for aggression, both for participants and spectators. It may encourage some students to continue their education in order to play.

How can you *evaluate* the subject? Is it good? Is it bad? What can be said in its favor? What can be said against it? How does its present state compare to its ideal?

Football can be a positive force, contributing to personal growth and stimulating economic growth for a school and a community. Football can also cause serious, sometimes even fatal injury to participants, even at the high school level and below. Football can promote physical fitness, to be sure. And most injuries are not serious. Like any sport, football can distract its participants from other (more important) activities.

★　★　★

Brainstorming. Brainstorming is another activity designed to help writers explore a topic quickly. It can be used by one person or a group, and it seems to be particularly popular with business executives, perhaps because it allows a group of people to share ideas in a nonjudgmental, nonthreatening way. Brainstorming is like freewriting: there are no wrong suggestions; anything you want to say is fine. But instead of freely writing in sentences, in brainstorming you can use single words or phrases.

The ideas suggested can be listed, or they can be written down as a network, with lines drawn to show connections. Just set a brief time limit (ten to fifteen minutes) and throw out ideas, writing them all down without censoring or judging. There's no telling what will turn out to be useful.

Asking questions. Cubing is valuable because it offers a prescribed set of questions you can rely upon to generate material. Questions are vital to any project; they are often more important and harder to find than answers. You are not, of course, limited to the questions presented in cubing, and you will find it helpful to spend some time, if possible, just thinking of questions related to any assignment.

Don't worry about answers at this point. The idea is to free up your creativity, to generate lines of inquiry. Therefore, you can even pose questions that are (or seem to be) impossible to answer. You can come at a problem that is already solved from a different angle: often we stop with the first answer when a better one

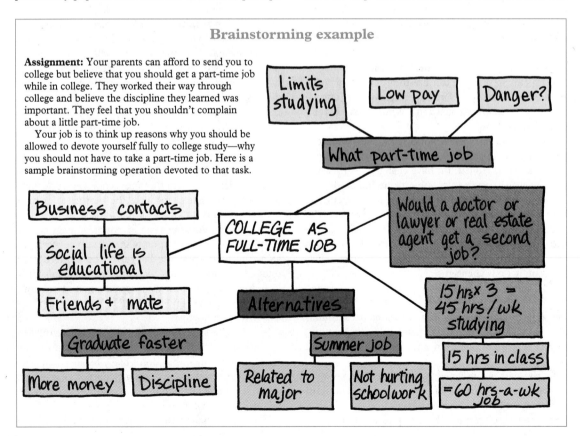

Brainstorming example

Assignment: Your parents can afford to send you to college but believe that you should get a part-time job while in college. They worked their way through college and believe the discipline they learned was important. They feel that you shouldn't complain about a little part-time job.

Your job is to think up reasons why you should be allowed to devote yourself fully to college study—why you should not have to take a part-time job. Here is a sample brainstorming operation devoted to that task.

Limits studying — Low pay — Danger?

What part-time job

Business contacts

Social life is educational

Friends + mate

COLLEGE AS FULL-TIME JOB

Would a doctor or lawyer or real estate agent get a second job?

15 hrs x 3 = 45 hrs / wk studying

Alternatives

Graduate faster

More money — Discipline

Summer job

Related to major — Not hurting schoolwork

15 hrs in class

= 60 hrs-a-wk job

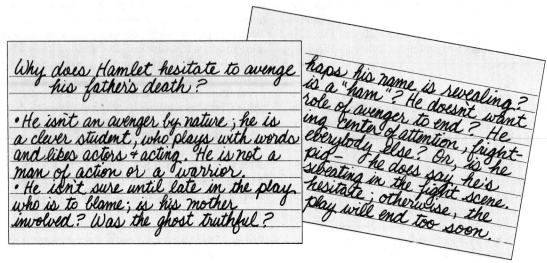

Why does Hamlet hesitate to avenge his father's death?

• He isn't an avenger by nature; he is a clever student, who plays with words and likes actors + acting. He is not a man of action or a warrior.
• He isn't sure until late in the play who is to blame; is his mother involved? Was the ghost truthful?

haps his name is revealing? is a "ham"? He doesn't want role of avenger to end? He[?] ing center of attention, frightening everybody else? Or, is he pig – he does say he's sweating in the fight scene. hesitate; otherwise, the play will end too soon.

As you ask questions, it's often helpful to write them on notecards along with answers.

might emerge with more consideration. Shift your attention from the obvious aspects and look elsewhere. You may have heard the story of the truck that got stuck under an overpass: just as the engineers were going to blowtorch the top of the truck, a bystander suggested letting the air out of the tires. Removing the truck top (where the problem was) certainly would have worked, but letting the air out of the tires (seemingly not where the problem was) was certainly much easier.

As you might imagine, there are other strategies besides cubing that you can use to prompt your questions. One of the most familiar, employed by journalists, asks the following questions: Who? What? Where? When? Why? How?

Another strategy involves displacing your subject in space or time. Imagine the subject, for instance, in one hundred years. How will it have changed? How will it be perceived? Imagine the subject one hundred years before now. Or imagine the subject in another culture: how will it change, or how will it be perceived?

You can also ask questions about the name of the subject: What is the history of its name? What words are associated with it? Has the name changed? Have the connotations changed?

You can elicit questions from your friends, asking them what they would like to know about the subject. Or you can imagine people from various backgrounds and conjure up the questions they would ask. You can, in fact, get questions from anywhere; the important thing is to collect them.

As you gather questions, try writing each one at the top of a card or on a slip of paper. I recommend large notecards or half of a regular sheet of paper, which is large enough to respond to the question but not as imposing as a full sheet. As you have ideas or even answers about the questions, or as you do research to find the answers, fill out the cards. These cards then become materials for your paper. You will be amazed how much more fun your writing is when you have material to work with and you are not scrambling for something to say.

Pro and con thinking. It is not uncommon in a discussion for one party to play "devil's advocate," as it is usually called. The purpose of such role-playing (in most cases) is to help the parties explore more aspects of the subject than would likely emerge in a one-sided discussion. Having an opponent is a useful stimulus to the process.

Our legal system is, in fact, based on the effectiveness of such an adversarial system. The prosecution tries to prove the accused guilty. The defense tries to show that the accused is innocent. Neither side is asked to determine guilt or innocence ahead of time; their jobs are instead to make the best case for their respective sides.

Pro and con thinking as an invention strategy can be envisioned as a conversation with a devil's advocate, or as a trial with opposing lawyers. You explore your topic by offering first one view and then its opposition. You don't have to limit your conversation to only two voices, but you will find it helpful to keep two antithetical views prominent.

Some writers have considerable trouble with this invention strategy because it forces them to make arguments in which they don't really believe. Just keep in mind that you are making a hypothetical case: no one will force you to endorse any position you maintain in a pro and con exercise.

We don't assume that a lawyer who defends an

English Composition

accused murderer is in favor of murder. Besides, if you do believe passionately in either the pro or the con, making the opposing case will help you to anticipate objections and counterarguments, making your own case stronger in the long run. See the example below of pro and con thinking on the subject of the SAT.

Example

Speaker 1: A student's college career shouldn't be determined by one test; therefore, we ought to do away with the SAT.

Speaker 2: The SAT is an effective predictor of past and future academic achievement; therefore, we ought to keep it.

Speaker 1: The SAT often keeps good students from going to the college of their choice; it may keep some students from going to college at all.

Speaker 2: Do you believe that all students should be allowed to go to college? College isn't for everybody.

Speaker 1: But this system positions one test over the recommendations of teachers and the record of a student's academic career. I know a student who didn't study at all in high school (his grades were mostly Cs), but because he did very well on the SAT, he received a full scholarship to Columbia University. His best friend, who had a grade point average of 3.7 and was highly recommended by his faculty, did not even get into Columbia.

(This discussion could be continued, of course.)

*   *   *

Commonplace book. A *commonplace* is a wise or memorable saying, and a commonplace book is a notebook in which a writer collects quotations along with facts, figures, questions, and anything else that might be of future use. Set aside a special notebook and keep it handy. As you read, when you come upon a passage or phrase or fact that is especially striking or important, jot it down.

You can also use your commonplace book to list new words and to meditate on their meanings. You can summarize what you've learned in class lectures or discussion (a really effective way to increase your learning). You can respond to reading assignments. But, mainly, you can copy or paraphrase quotations, storing up materials for future use. You can record what's going on in your life and use the space to write about its meaning and significance. Virtually all writers keep some kind of commonplace book to keep track of their ideas, a space to work things out on paper.

Focusing on a thesis. Once you have a
number of good ideas about what to write, you need to decide how you are going to present your ideas.

Any written argument has a thesis—an assertion that is its main point.

A thesis is a kind of sentence. In most cases, the thesis is explicitly stated, often near the beginning of the argument; but a thesis can appear anywhere in an essay, and it can even be implied. The purpose of an argument (almost always, anyway) is to persuade the audience to agree with the thesis. This goal should determine where the thesis appears, or if it appears at all. If the audience will automatically oppose the thesis, or be at the onset unable to understand the thesis, then it makes sense to hold the thesis until later in the argument when a foundation for accepting or understanding it has been built. If your audience will be strongly opposed to the thesis, no matter how it is introduced or supported, then the best strategy may be

---
Possible thesis sentences
Evaluate these sentences as thesis statements:

Lincoln's role in the Civil War was crucial.

This isn't a good thesis because it would be so readily accepted. Anyone who knows anything about the Civil War knows Lincoln's role was crucial, so there's no point in arguing it. You can argue that Lincoln's role wasn't as important as is usually thought, or that his role was actually more important than is usually thought.

Litchfield Beach is on an extraordinarily beautiful stretch of the coast of South Carolina.

Not a good thesis; it is a fact. One could argue, I suppose, that it is not "extraordinarily beautiful," since that is a matter of taste, but the thesis does not seem promising.

Satan is the real hero of Milton's Paradise Lost.

A good thesis. This argument has, in fact, been plausibly made by William Empson and plausibly refuted by, among others, Shelby Foote.

I like chocolate.

It is difficult to say whether this assertion would make a good argument or not. If the essay supports my love of chocolate in a persuasive way, then the real thesis is something like "Chocolate is good for you." If the essay merely asserts that I like chocolate, it would be very difficult to argue with me. How can anyone else say I don't like chocolate?

Chocolate is beneficial to the diet as an aid in combating depression.

A good thesis: controversial and arguable.

---

to leave it unstated, allowing your readers to come to that conclusion on their own.

In any case, explicitly stated or implied, a thesis is first of all a sentence. You cannot argue "taxes on the middle class." That is a subject. You can argue "we should increase (or lower, or abolish) taxes on the middle class."

A thesis is also a sentence that makes an arguable assumption. It would be difficult, if not impossible, to argue "the middle class pays 85 percent of the taxes in the United States." That statement is either a fact or it is incorrect. It would be tough to argue the point: we simply need to do some research and see. But we can argue that "the most effective tax increase would target the middle class because they pay most of the taxes." This point, while it might seem self-evident to some people, is arguable. One could disagree, for instance, by questioning the meaning of effective: effective in what sense? While the middle class already pays most of the taxes, and might therefore appear the logical place to raise taxes, one could argue that more taxes on the middle class will harm the economy by reducing the spending power of those who purchase most of the goods and services. Or one could make any number of opposing statements.

So, as you generate ideas and draft your essay, stay on the lookout for a central idea, an assertion that is arguable as a thesis. If everyone would agree with your main point, then you need a more controversial thesis; there's no point in arguing what is either obvious or a statement of fact. The most valuable thesis is probably one that seems questionable or even implausible as your essay begins, but becomes persuasive and even accepted by the argument's end.

Does it have to be narrow? Most textbooks will tell you that a thesis should be narrowed down. For instance, if you begin with the topic "trees," most textbooks say you should limit your discussion in the following fashion:

trees
↓
tree diseases
↓
American tree diseases
↓
catastrophic hardwood disease
↓
Dutch elm disease

The logic behind the advice is that you shouldn't take on a large, general, or abstract topic; you should limit your essays to topics you can handle: small, specific, concrete. Instead of an essay on the problem of evil, you should write on sudden infant death syndrome, narrowing down the topic like this:

In a sense, this advice is reasonable. It might be tough to write an essay on trees or on the problem of evil, but such essays might also be extremely valuable. You couldn't cover everything about trees in a three-page essay, but you couldn't cover everything we know about Dutch elm disease, either. The key to a successful essay is not whether your topic is large or small, but rather whether your theme is focused, interesting, and arguable. If you wanted to argue that "trees are the most valuable plants on earth" or that "trees are capable of emotional response," it would be unfortunate to settle for an explanation of Dutch elm disease.

A thesis doesn't have to be narrow, at least in the sense that it has to deal with a small topic. But it does have to make an arguable assertion.

How the audience affects the thesis. This section has already mentioned how your audience ought to affect the placement and the articulation of your thesis. But the nature of your audience can affect your thesis in even more fundamental ways. To understand this relationship between the audience and the thesis, let's think about three conditions that a good thesis should satisfy:

1. The thesis should be news. That is, the audience does not accept the thesis as common knowledge, or as a matter of fact accepted by most intelligent and informed people. Obviously, the audience in this regard is crucial: it would seem entirely unnecessary to argue, for instance, that the earth circles the sun unless your audience consisted of primitive tribesmen, the Flat Earth Society, or thirteenth-century Italian popes.

2. A thesis must be understandable. For the book I wrote on Samuel Johnson, I presented my argument to eighteenth-century scholars, to students, and to my family. My thesis for all three was in some sense the same, but the wording was different so as to constitute, in another sense, three different theses.

3. A thesis must also be supportable. Here, the audience again plays a determinative role, because the thesis must be a claim for which viable support can be presented. If your thesis depends on support from the Koran, for instance, and your audience is the Southern Baptist Convention, you really do not have a supportable thesis because the Koran, for that audience, is not an authority.

702

Of servile custom cramp her gen'rous pow'rs?
Would sordid policies, the barb'rous growth
Of ignorance and rapine bow her down
To tame pursuits, to indolence and fear?
Lo! she appeals to nature, to the winds
And rolling waves, the sun's unwearied course,
The elements and seasons: all declare
For what th'eternal maker has ordain'd
The pow'rs of man: we feel within ourselves
His energy divine: he tells the heart
He meant, he made us to behold and love
What he beholds and loves, the gen'ral orb
Of life and being; to be great like him
Beneficent and active. Thus the men
Whom nature's works can charm, with God himself
Hold converse; grow familiar day by day,
With his conceptions; act upon his plan;
And form to his the relish of their souls.

                    Pl. of Imagn. B.3. v. 568.
———————
                    ——— On my strain
Perhaps ev'n now, some cold fastidious judge
Casts a disdainful eye; and calls my toil,
And calls the love and beauty which I sing
The dream of folly. Thou grave censor! say,
Is beauty then a dream, because the glooms
Of dulness hang too heavy on thy sense
To let her shine upon thee?

                    id. v. 443.

Te flagrantis atrox hora Caniculae
Nescit tangere: tu frigus amabile
Fessis vomere tauris
Praebes, et pecori vago.
Fies nobilium tu quoque fontium.

                    Hor. L. 3. ode. 13.

Writing the paper

Arranging your ideas. Now that you have a good, understandable, supportable thesis, your paper is one third of the way finished. Your next task is to think about how your thesis and supporting statements can best be presented.

The shapes of paragraphs. Paragraphs, like people, come in all shapes and sizes. Although there is an average size for paragraphs, it would be wrong to suggest that all paragraphs should come close to that average. If you have read or been told that a paragraph should have, say, six to eight sentences, you should forget that advice immediately. Some paragraphs are longer, some shorter than average. Good writers vary paragraph size for the same reasons they vary sentence length and structure: to avoid monotony, and to shape the material in an effective way. A very short paragraph, like a very short sentence, can be striking.

And a very brief paragraph stands out—like this one.

That's because paragraphing is another form of punctuating, allowing you to vary the rhythm of your prose and impose a form on your material. Wherever a new paragraph begins, the reader is being cued to consider the following material as a new unit. The indentation of a paragraph is, thus, a kind of pause, encouraging the reader to collect the ideas in the preceding paragraph and begin to look for its relationship to the following paragraph. Good writers usually provide explicit cues to the nature of that relationship.

Although a paragraph marks the end of one unit of thought, there is no requirement that every paragraph have a topic sentence stating its main idea. In fact, in a random sample of paragraphs from all sorts of texts, a study found that less than one fifth contained topic sentences. Why do so few paragraphs have topic sentences (even though students so often are told that every paragraph should have one)? For the most part, I suspect, this is because two or more paragraphs often function as a unit, unfolding an idea, and because sometimes topic sentences (like thesis sentences) are implied rather than expressed. If a paragraph has a topic sentence, it can appear anywhere: beginning, end, or middle. Your common sense, paying attention to the flow of your argument and the needs of your audience, will usually suggest the most effective placement.

If there are no hard and fast rules regarding the size of paragraphs or the position of topic sentences, there is still one principle regarding the shape of paragraphs. Effective writers almost all consistently use paragraphs that alternate general and specific statements, moving from abstraction to detail or vice versa. It is at least as important to vary your levels of generality and specificity as it is to vary the length and structure.

Why studying English composition pays off
Reason #1: Academic success

Obviously you'll do better in your English classes if you study for them, but you'll also do better in your other classes. If you can say clearly, without distracting errors, and with a little life and energy, what you know about the Treaty of Versailles, your in-class history essay is going to get a better grade. In all college classes, even in the sciences, good writing can play an important role.

Example

Paragraph 1:

The union leaders are not being cooperative. The plant managers are being even less helpful. The whole mess seems headed for disaster. No viable solution has been offered.

Paragraph 2:

The union leaders are not being cooperative. They refuse to negotiate any of their demands. The plant managers are being even less cooperative, for they will not even attend the joint meetings or talk to the union leaders. The whole mess seems to be headed for disaster: the plant will close, or the union will be broken, and some violence may break out. No viable solution has been offered, although some unworkable ideas, such as having the union purchase the plant or reducing the managers' pay to the level of the average worker, have been put forth.

Paragraph 2 is better, telling us more because it moves from general to specific. All abstractions or all details would be much less effective than a mixture.

* * *

The shapes of essays. The shape of an essay should depend on its purpose: What is the essay supposed to do? Who is the audience, and what presentational form would be most effective?

Although virtually all college writing textbooks in recent years have advised against it, some students still come to college believing that good essays follow a certain prescribed format. In particular, a surprising number of students believe that an essay should begin with an opening paragraph that has the intellectual shape of an inverted pyramid, beginning with a broad generalization and narrowing down to a specific thesis.

English Composition

Rhythm is as important in writing as it is in music.

Then the model essay should have three paragraphs that support the thesis, each paragraph beginning with a thesis sentence. And an essay should conclude with another pyramid, this one right-side up, beginning with a specific point, then developing a broad concluding statement, opening up the implications of the essay.

There are several problems with this advice. For one thing, it is almost impossible to find published essays that follow such a form. It is an artificial formula, found almost exclusively in schoolroom writing. For another thing, this format almost inevitably produces an essay that seems awkward, unnatural, and ineffective. The essay seems formulaic, like an exercise, and not like a real effort to say something to someone.

To replace this tenacious writing formula, here are three other ways to think about the form of essays. First, think about the way an essay develops. (The sections below discuss six common methods of development; the logical structure of your essay will obviously affect its shape.)

Second, think in terms of an opening, a body, and a closing. As categories, these are very loose: there is no formula for opening, for instance, that you can always follow successfully. One can, however, talk about some sample strategies for opening, or closing, or developing an essay, keeping in mind that these are only samples, not prescriptions. If you understand the kinds of things writers do in order to open a particular essay, then you will be in a better position to invent an opening for your particular essay. Discussions of both openers and closers appear later in this chapter.

Third, think about the shape of essays in terms of a spectrum, ranging from logical to associational. An associational essay presents a cluster of points that are not necessarily in any particular order. It is as if the writer says, "Think about this, and then think about this, and then about this." Taken together, the writer's observations will add up to something, but one point is not really dependent upon a preceding point. The advantage of such a shape is that it seems more like thinking: readers move along with the writer in the act of thinking, and they are allowed to put the bits of information together for themselves. Such a shape can be very engaging and intriguing, drawing the reader in.

Then again, the writer may want to be more explicitly directive, telling the reader precisely how to process what is presented. In an essay that presents a tightly logical shape, one point leads logically to another, and the relationship is explicitly stated. The reader should see readily why the material is in the order it is in. For types of logical shapes that are available, see the next section, which is called "Kinds of development."

Openers. We all know how crucial first impressions are in real life, and writing is about as real as life gets. We do sometimes get a chance to correct a bad first impression, but it is altogether possible your reader will turn away if the opening of your essay isn't promising. And even if your reader is obligated to read the rest of the essay, a poor beginning is likely to influence the perception of the rest of your essay. Obviously, you want to start well. But what is a good opener?

A good opener's most important quality, of course, is that it keeps the reader reading. But don't think that your opening therefore has to be cute or shocking or dramatic. You want to avoid any impression that your beginning is just a trick to keep readers reading. Instead, you want to give the impression that the essay is beginning quickly, providing important information immediately, and that the point of the essay will be worthwhile. Thus, you want to start fast, and move directly to the point.

Of course, if you believe your audience will not be receptive to the point you want to make, or will be unlikely to understand your point, then you'll want to move as quickly as possible to the information that will make your point understandable or acceptable. Just

Checklist for openers
- Does your audience need to be prepared to accept or understand your argument?
- If not, then does your essay start fast?
- Does the essay provide necessary information as soon as possible?
- Does the essay give the impression of moving immediately toward an engaging point?
- Does the essay's opening employ an anecdote, or image, or question, or quotation, or some other drawing-in device?

about the worst thing you could do would be to offer some broad generalization or abstract observation that is slowly whittled down to a specific point.

Example

Compare these two openings, both taken from student papers written about George Eliot's often-taught novel *Silas Marner*.

Writer A:

In this passage from *Silas Marner*, George Eliot draws a distinct contrast between "old leisure" and "new leisure," praising the former and condemning the latter.

Writer B:

Literature has done many things in its time, giving entertainment, education, and examples of how the world has changed. One of the greatest writers of such literature was George Eliot. In this selection she did all three of these, but her view on the changing world is the most important. She described successfully her views of "old leisure" and "new leisure," and she represents the kind of literature that existed in her time.

Writer B's opening is better only if the writer is being paid by the word or is attempting to solve the reader's insomnia. After four sentences, B still has not said anything useful about Eliot's comparison of the two kinds of leisure. We can see that B may be inching toward some kind of assertion, having begun with the broadest of comments—"Literature has done many things in its time." But Writer A immediately says something specific about Eliot's treatment: old leisure is praised and the new leisure is condemned. A stance is taken in this opening sentence, and we can easily imagine how the essay would develop in defense of this position. I think any reasonable person would much rather read the rest of Writer A's work instead of Writer B's.

Notice also how Writer A quickly lets the reader know what the essay is about, naming the subject explicitly—Eliot and her novel, and the view of leisure it offers.

*   *   *

Starting quickly does require you to overcome the fear that you won't have enough to say. The best way to do that is to spend time inventing. Generate enough material in your drafting stages that you feel pressed to get it all in.

What other useful methods are there besides the quick start? You might try beginning with a quotation, if you can find one that is engaging and takes you to

George Eliot

A Victorian novelist whose technique of psychological analysis became a standard in modern fiction, George Eliot (pseudonym of Mary Ann Evans) shows in her work a strong influence of her religious upbringing, centering on concepts of love and duty.

Her first novel, *Adam Bede*, was published in 1859; immediately she became one of England's leading writers. Her other works include *The Mill on the Floss* (1860), *Silas Marner* (1861), and  *Romola* (1862–1863), but *Middlemarch* (1871–1872) is considered her masterpiece. After her death, her reputation declined as reading tastes changed; however, in 1948, the critic F. R. Leavis reassessed her work, praising both the intelligence and sensitivity of her books.

your starting point. Or you can consider starting with a little story, an anecdote that illustrates where you want to begin. You can begin with an image, a picture. You can begin with a question. You might also try occasionally a dramatically brief sentence, one that makes a striking observation or claim. It's always possible to begin by defining the terms of your topic, but that approach has been used so often that it rarely seems fresh: most English teachers have read a huge stack of papers that begin by telling the reader how Webster defines this word or that word, and they are tired of it.

Kinds of development.

There are a number of ways your paper can progress. The most common kinds of development are: definition, classification, description, narration, compare and contrast, and cause and effect.

Definition. In a freshman writing course, it's likely that you will be asked to write a definition paper. And in other kinds of essays, definition often plays a crucial role. So it's important for you to understand how defining works—or rather, how defining can work for you.

In most textbooks, if defining is explained in detail, a formal definition is usually presented as having three components:

A equals B minus C

A is the entity being defined; B is a category into which A falls; C refers to the features that differentiate A from B.

5. Not hasty; not viciously eager or impetuous.
    Too industrious to be great,
Nor *patient* to expect the turns of fate,
They open'd camps deform'd by civil fight.   *Prior.*

PA'TIENT. *n. s.* [*patient*, Fr.]
1. That which receives impressions from external agents.
    Malice is a passion so impetuous and precipitate, that it often involves the agent and the *patient*.   *Gov. of the Tongue.*
        To proper *patients* he kind agents brings,
    In various leagues binds disagreeing things.   *Creech.*
    Action and passion are modes which belong to substances: when a smith with a hammer strikes a piece of iron, the hammer and the smith are both agents or subjects of action; the one supreme, and the other subordinate: the iron is the *patient* or the subject of passion, in a philosophical sense, because it receives the operation of the agent.   *Watts's Logick.*
2. A person diseased. It is commonly used of the relation between the sick and the physician.
    You deal with me like a physician, that seeing his *patient* in a pestilent fever, should chide instead of administring help, and bid him be sick no more.   *Sidney.*
    Through ignorance of the disease, through unreasonableness of the time, instead of good he worketh hurt, and out of one evil throweth the *patient* into many miseries.   *Spenser.*
    A physician uses various methods for the recovery of sick persons; and though all of them are disagreeable, his *patients* are never angry.   *Addison.*
3. It is sometimes, but rarely used absolutely for a sick person.
    Nor will the raging fever's fire abate
    With golden canopies or beds of state;
    But the poor *patient* will as soon be found
    On the hard matress or the mother ground.   *Dryden.*

I see
Th' insulting tyrant prancing o'er the field,
His horse's hoofs wet with *patrician* blood!   *Addi.*

PATRI'CIAN. *n. s.* A nobleman.
    Noble *patricians*, patrons of my right;
    Defend the justice of my cause with arms.   *Shak.*
    You'll find Gracchus, from *patrician* grown
    A fencer and the scandal of the town.   *Dryd.*
    Your daughters are all married to wealthy *patricians*.   *Gran.*

PATRIMO'NIAL. *adj.* [*patrimonial*, Fr. from *patrimony*.] Possessed by inheritance.
    The expence of the duke of Ormond's own great patrimonial estate, that came over at that time, is of no consideration in the stock of this kingdom.   *Temp.*
    Their *patrimonial* sloth the Spaniards keep,
    And Philip first taught Philip how to sleep.   *Dryd.*

PA'TRIMONY. *n. s.* [*patrimonium*, Latin; *patrimoine*, Fr.] An estate possessed by inheritance.
    Inclosures they would not forbid, for that had been to forbid the improvement of the *patrimony* of the kingdom.   *Bacon.*
    So might the heir, whose father hath, in play,
    Wasted a thousand pounds of ancient rent;
    By painful earning of one groat a day,
    Hope to restore the *patrimony* spent.   *Davies.*
        In me all
    Posterity stands curs'd! fair *patrimony*
    That I must leave ye, sons.   *Milton's Par. Lost.*
        For his redemption, all my *patrimony*
    I am ready to forego and quit.   *Milton's Agon.*
    Their ships like wasted *patrimonies* shew;
    Where the thin scatt'ring trees admit the light,
    And shun each other's shadows as they grow.
        The shepherd last appears,   *Dryd.*

Sample page from Samuel Johnson's Dictionary, *one of the most famous dictionaries in the English language*

In creating definitions, here are three tips:
1. Make sure the category is familiar.
2. Make sure the category is specific enough to be helpful.
3. Shape the definition to your purpose.

Example

Definition: An Olympic gold medal is an award given to an athlete.

In this definition, A is "An Olympic gold medal," the thing being defined; B, the category being used, is "an award"; C, the differentiating feature, is "given to an athlete," distinguishing this award from others. This definition would be useful to someone who doesn't know what an Olympic gold medal is, but we might think about how it could be improved:

• Make sure the category is familiar. If I'm told that "a swardlarp is a kind of kahoti," I'm not any better off. If I'm told that "a swardlarp is a kind of stew," then the definition is helpful. In the Olympics example, we can probably assume that the audience knows what an award is. But how helpful is that term here? Is the gold medal just any award? The category in this case could be more specific.

• Make sure the category is specific enough to be helpful. Defining a swardlarp as "a kind of stew" is helpful, but "stew" is still a large category. If we said "an Iranian beef stew," then the reader's idea comes into much sharper focus. In the Olympics example, the gold medal is not just "an award." It would be better to say it is "an award given to the best athlete in a particular event in the Olympics," thus differentiating it more effectively.

• Shape the definition to your purpose. If someone wants to know what swardlarp is in order to make it, then an effective definition should include the ingredients. If someone wants to know what to do with it, then saying it is "an Iranian beef stew served only on New Year's Day" would be an effective definition, whereas listing the ingredients wouldn't. Obviously, a category can be made too specific or detailed in the wrong way to be helpful. In the Olympics example, we might say that "a gold medal is an award made of molded gold, weighing fourteen pounds, four inches in diameter." This statement is true, and for certain purposes, it would be an excellent definition. For others, it might be completely useless.

*   *   *

When you are writing an argumentative essay that is based on definition or expanding an argumentative paper by using definition, you're obviously doing more than supplying a dictionary definition. You're *arguing* for a definition. But the strategy for defining is essentially the same. In the example, if you want to argue that the gold medal is a symbol of the competitiveness that blocks cooperation among nations, you will need a category (a symbol of competitiveness) and differentiating characteristics (your explanation of the kind of competitiveness).

It has been said that words mean whatever we choose to make them mean. That, in a nutshell, is the power of definition.

Classification. The act of classification involves grouping related items together on the basis of shared traits. Let's say you were to list all the classes at a particular college or university. That would be quite a list, numbering in the hundreds, perhaps thousands. If someone were to ask you what courses are available at that school, other than reading the entire list, which would take hours, what could you say? Clearly, you'd need to organize the courses into groups. This classification would allow you to deal with the unwieldy complexity of all the individual courses. That's the purpose of classification: to help us make sense of the world by organizing it.

What would your classification of courses look like? The different groupings might look a lot like the various departments on campus, allowing you to say,

"There are English courses available, plus psychology, math, biology, chemistry, physics, music, theater, history, and political science." But such a classification, as natural as it may seem, is not the only way to organize the data. You might divide the courses differently and tell your friend, "We have large lecture, small lecture, discussion, and laboratory courses." Or you might say, "We have courses on the old original campus, courses held on the new east side, and courses at the coliseum complex." The nature of your response depends on the basis of your classification: subject matter, size, place, or whatever.

In expanding an argument by means of classification, you need to watch for a couple of things. First, a common problem is using an inconsistent basis of classification. You don't want to divide courses into large, English, and at the coliseum. Second, try to make the classification complete. If you're classifying by place, what about those courses that take place electronically, via television? They don't fit into the existing categories; therefore, at least one additional category is needed. Third (related to the previous point), it is acceptable for categories to have only one member. However, if you have very many categories like that, the classification may not be very helpful in organizing the data. Likewise, categories with huge numbers of members may not be very revealing.

Do keep in mind that the categories and the bases of classification are constructed by you, the classifier. Some groupings may seem more natural, but categories are made by humans. It may make sense to most people to group biology and chemistry in the same category, but there may be some purpose for which psychology and biology actually make more sense together. Like everything in writing, the way you classify depends on your purpose.

Description. You might believe that an effective description is necessarily one that overwhelms the reader with details, but such is often not the case. An effective description is instead one that serves its intended purpose (to reiterate the point just made above), so the place to begin when you are developing a piece of writing by describing is with this question: Why am I describing this person, place, or thing? Do you want the reader to experience the entity in question, or is the description part of an effort to persuade or inform the reader, or simply for the purpose of expressing yourself?

Example

Let's examine a descriptive passage from Eudora Welty's *One Writer's Beginnings*. Welty has been talking about a trip she and her father made by train, and she talks here about the drinking cup her father carried along:

English Composition

With a thoughtful description, even a brick wall can seem interesting.

segments did it have? Was it scratched? Shiny? What was its shape? Its origin? How large was the carrying ring?) Welty's purpose is not to convey a complete description of the cup, but rather to create a certain impression that is useful to her larger aim.

Later on, Welty tells us that the train trip opened up a dreamworld to her imagination, as she invented what lay beyond the paths, roads, and rivers they passed; and her father "put it all into the frame of regularity, predictability," and "that was his fatherly gift in the course of our journey." Thus, Welty's description of her father's drinking cup contributes to the idea that his presence helped control and channel her imagining. She offers a description of the cup that gives some sense of it as a tangible thing, but we do not need to see it fully. We just need the impression of this cup as one aspect of the father's "regularity, predictability"—he always had this useful cup. We can imagine the rest.

＊ ＊ ＊

Most descriptions in fact are like Welty's: they are evocative, not exhaustive. In order to convey an impression to your readers, you just need to select those details that serve your purpose. In using description to develop a piece of writing, you will probably rely most on the sense of sight. Linguists have observed that languages invariably contain more vocabulary for conveying visual impressions than any other sense. But don't overlook the value of using the other senses in your description: touch, smell, taste, hearing. Welty's passage strikingly mentions "the taste of silver," and the shocking touch of the silver against her teeth is also suggested, along with its smoothness against her lips.

Although a rich vocabulary is helpful in description (and virtually any other writing task), you may notice that Welty's description does not rely on uncommon words. The key to an effective description is careful observation and selection, not a fancy vocabulary. If you do not know the word *azure*, you can nonetheless convey the picture you want: "Her eyes were the color of an unclouded sky." In fact, such comparisons are oftentimes powerfully effective.

> In Daddy's leather grip was his traveler's drinking cup, collapsible; a lid to fit over it had a ring to carry it by; it traveled in a round leather box. This treasure would be brought out at my request, for me to bear to the water cooler at the end of the Pullman car, fill to the brim, and bear back to my seat, to drink water over its smooth lip. The taste of silver could always be relied on to shock your teeth.

Welty's description is detailed: the cup had a lid with a carrying ring; it was collapsible; it was made of silver, and traveled in a round leather box. But there is much we are not told about her father's drinking cup. (What were its dimensions? How many collapsible

Eudora Welty

A modern novelist and short-story writer, Welty is a Southern regionalist in the tradition of William Faulkner and Flannery O'Connor and is known for her insight into the problems and joys of everyday life. She writes with loving, sympathetic humor about the downtrodden, the disillusioned, and the  deformed. Some of the best-known of her works are *The Golden Apples* (1949), *Delta Wedding* (1946), and *The Robber Bridegroom* (1942). She won a Pulitzer Prize in 1972 for *The Optimist's Daughter* and published her memoirs, called *One Writer's Beginnings*, in 1983.

Example

Here is another passage from Welty:

> . . . Sometimes the encroaching walls of mountains woke me by clapping at my ears. The tunnels made the train's passage resound like the "loud" pedal of a piano, a roar that seemed to last as long as a giant's temper tantrum.

The two comparisons in this passage make the

sound of passing through the tunnels memorable: the sound is amplified as if a "loud" piano pedal has been depressed; the sound lasts as long as a giant's temper tantrum. This is wonderful writing.

* * *

Thus, effective description depends on patience and imagination. You need to be patient enough to observe carefully what you are describing (even if the observation is in your mind), and to select those details that serve your purpose. Even a brick, carefully and imaginatively observed, can yield a very rich description, making part of the world vivid and impressive to your readers.

Narration. Like description, narration is a fundamental strategy of development. Whereas description presents the features of an entity, narration exposes the sequence of an action. A description stops time; a narrative moves through time. In other words, a narrative is a story.

We use stories for various purposes, and (as with description) it's crucial for you to consider the purpose your narrative will serve. Are you simply trying to entertain the reader? Are you using an anecdote to support a point? Are you explaining how something happened? Are you narrating the steps one needs to take to do something successfully? Your narrative will grow out of your understanding of your purpose. If, for example, you are attempting to entertain your reader, the most effective way to tell a story may be to begin with you standing in the end zone, holding the ball over your head, even though the story (as you see it) really begins the summer before, when you started

The appreciation of a good story begins at childhood.

lifting weights regularly. Fiction often begins in the middle of things, or at the end, but that is also an appealing and underused technique in nonfiction. But if your purpose is to explain the steps involved in carrying out a task, then you probably want to start at the beginning and go through to the end: conveying information clearly, not engaging the reader's attention and interest, is your top priority in that case.

Even your selection of the events to present should be affected by your purpose. If you are explaining a particular play as an example of how one scores a touchdown in football, then standing in the end zone waving the ball is not an essential event. If you're expressing how it feels to score a touchdown, involving the reader in your experience, then you really should include the event in the end zone. As you develop writing by narration, keep in mind that time can be divided up in various ways: one event may be better seen for some purposes as three separate events, or it may need to be combined with other activities into one larger event. The story of a wedding may involve "taking the vows"; or the event may be simply "the ceremony"; or taking the vows may be discussed as "my vows" and "his vows," or in many other ways.

However you decide to order and organize your narrative, you should keep in mind the following:

• Keep your reader oriented with such time markers as *then, and next, later, first, at the same time*, and so forth. Be explicit about the relationship in time of the various events: what is obvious to you may be fuzzy to someone else.

• Pay attention to your verb tenses. There's no rule against using different tenses in the same paragraph, or even sentences, as far too many students seem to think, but make certain your meaning is clear.

• A good story has conflict—a hero and an antagonist at least. Even though you may not immediately think of your narrative as a story (perhaps you are explaining the process of growing turnips or narrating what you did on your summer vacation), it will often be helpful to conceive it in those terms. By thinking in terms of a story, for instance, you may be better able to decide whether an event should be included. Is it part of the plot? Does it illuminate the hero or the opposing force? You may even be sparked to consider what the opposing force might be in a particular narrative.

• Give some thought to the point of view of your narrative. From what position is the story being told? How does that particular position affect the telling of your narrative?

• Finally, in narrative as in all other things, quotations can be very effective. Almost always, getting some dialogue into a narration can be engaging. Readers like to hear people talking (or even places or things talking, if that seems appropriate).

Compare and contrast. Like other methods of organization, compare and contrast is more than a way of shaping a paper. It is a fundamental strategy of the human brain. It's difficult to imagine how we could understand or know anything in isolation, apart from something else. You know what an apple is because you know it fits into the category *fruit*: it isn't a rock, an animal, or another person, or lots of other things. We compare an apple to other fruits and find that, yes, an apple is one of those. (It is, in fact, very easy to compare apples and oranges, despite what everyone says.) We can identify the object in front of us as an apple, however, because we can also distinguish it from other fruits. Without the ability to compare and contrast, we could not make sense of the world.

Compare and contrast (which can be thought of as one strategy or two) is different from the other fundamental strategies. Description, for instance, allows us to examine closely one item, distinguishing one feature from another. To do that, we need to stop time—we need to take a static view. Of course, nothing in reality is actually static, so we do pay a certain price for the power of describing. Classification groups similar things together, distinguishing them from different things, also stopping time to make such grouping possible. Although these groups may often seem natural, they are always made of words, not things, and so our

Contrary to popular opinion, it is in fact very easy to compare apples with oranges (or with pears or grapes).

classes are always subject to questioning. Narration moves through time, following an activity or process. Again, the steps in any process are an artificial scheme imposed on reality. Comparing looks at how two or more entities are similar, and contrasting examines how two or more entities are different. Compare and contrast takes a static view of what is being compared or contrasted, although one can certainly compare or contrast a sequence of static items. Although it may seem natural to compare or to contrast certain features, it is, again, important to remind yourself that you select what aspects to compare and contrast.

What you select and how you arrange your material depends, as always, on what you're trying to accomplish, but it may be helpful to consider that you have two basic options. Say you're comparing/contrasting a standard pickup truck and a luxury car. You could discuss a feature of the car, then the same feature on the truck. Then take another feature and compare/contrast it. And then another. Or you could discuss all the features of the truck, then all the features of the car.

The advantage of the first strategy is that the reader can see most clearly how the two compare or contrast. The potential problem is that the reader's sense of each item as a whole may be obscured. So, if you choose this structure for compare/contrast, you will want to be sure to remind your reader of the overall picture. The advantage of the second strategy is that the reader does get a clearer picture of one item as a whole, but the weakness is that the reader may not see as clearly how the points compare to each other. So, if you choose this arrangement, you may want to refer back to the first item as you discuss the second, linking the two together, especially if the points of comparison are numerous or complex.

Although some handbooks will tell you to be sure

Structures for compare and contrast

An argument that compares and contrasts two or more items can be written in alternating or sequential patterns. Examples of each follow.

Alternating pattern
#1 is a: The truck performs well in rough terrain.
#2 is b: The luxury sedan is excellent on the highway.
#1 is c: The truck is made in Detroit.
#2 is d: The luxury sedan is made in California.
#1 is e: The truck is tough and moderately comfortable.
#2 is f: The luxury sedan is powerful and extremely comfortable.

Sequential pattern
#1 is a: The truck performs well in rough terrain.
#1 is b: The truck is made in Detroit.
#1 is c: The truck is tough and moderately comfortable.
#2 is d: The luxury sedan is excellent on the highway.
#2 is e: The luxury sedan is made in California.
#2 is f: The luxury sedan is powerful and extremely comfortable.

---

your comparisons and contrasts are balanced, giving roughly equal time to both the first and second, real writers often emphasize one item or the other, using comparison and contrast to make a point (and not as an exercise in proportion). If you'll keep in mind what you want to accomplish, it will usually be clear which pattern will work best.

Cause and effect. Cause and effect is another essential pattern of development. Whenever you attempt to explain how something happened, you're engaging in cause and effect analysis. Thus, cause and effect analysis is related to narrative, because in a sense you're telling a story; but as a structural pattern, cause and effect generally begins at the end of the story and works backward to the cause.

When you use cause and effect patterns to develop a piece of writing, it's a good idea to be cautious about assigning causes. It may seem obvious to you that your sister has tooth decay because she eats a lot of candy. But the causes of events really aren't ever so simple as they may seem. There are people who eat lots of candy and have no tooth decay. So, there must be another cause. Perhaps your sister has tooth decay because she eats lots of candy and doesn't floss and brush as she ought to. Still, there may be people who eat just as much candy, floss and brush just as poorly, and yet do not have the tooth decay your sister has. So perhaps a cause of the effect of your sister's tooth decay is also her personal tendency to have cavities. Perhaps her teeth just don't resist decay as well as some people's.

At this point, you may be wondering about the feasibility of using cause and effect at all. It is, indeed, always tricky. But we have to do it. If the team loses the game, the fans want to know why. If an airplane crashes, everyone wants to know why. If your mate is angry, you'd like to know why. So we do the best we can. The important thing is not to limit your attention to one cause simply because it seems obvious. You also should give some thought to remote causes as well the more obvious and immediate ones. Eating candy and not brushing would seem to be linked rather directly to getting tooth decay. Such nearby causes are often termed *proximate*. Having a genetic makeup that makes one susceptible to cavities is a somewhat more distant cause, contributing to the effect, but not causing it in itself. An even more remote cause might be the evolution of the human diet, which brought refined sugar into our mouths rather late. One could argue that since human beings first ate nuts, fruits, and vegetables, teeth simply haven't yet evolved to deal with candy.

How do you know whether a particular analysis should include more distant causes? By looking to your purpose. Your sister's dentist, explaining why she has so many cavities, probably won't want to talk

about the evolution of human teeth. The dentist's interest is probably in the immediate causes, the ones that your sister can do something about. But let's say the dentist senses that your sister is upset and depressed by the assessment of her teeth. It might be helpful to include in the explanation the more distant cause, reassuring your sister that it's not totally her fault, that other people also have trouble with tooth decay because our teeth really haven't been designed for the foods we eat today. Of course, we should also keep in mind that our understanding of a particular cause could be entirely wrong. It's possible that the candy isn't the problem at all, but rather the culprit is peanut butter, or milk shakes, or something in the water, or even a misdiagnosis in determining that there is decay. In assigning causes and identifying effects, we're always on slippery footing, whether we realize it or not.

In review, here are some tips for cause and effect:
- Expand the number of possible causes as much as you can. Resist simple explanations.
- Distinguish immediate or proximate from more distant causes. Consider which aid your purpose.
- Recognize that in some cases what appears to be a cause isn't a cause at all, but is rather simply something that happened beforehand. Your sister eats lots of candy, she gets tooth decay, but the candy (perhaps) is sugar free. Therefore, the decay is unrelated.

Think clearly and persuasively.

Although scientists have recently been making amazing progress in figuring out how human beings think, we still don't know quite how we do it. But for centuries it has seemed reasonable to think of two kinds of thinking—two different ways of reasoning from what we already know, arriving at something that we didn't know before we started thinking.

Learning a language involves both induction and deduction.

One way of thinking is called *induction*. Here's a simple example. I bite into a green apple, and I observe it's bitter. Later I bite into another green apple, and it too is bitter. A third green apple also proves to be bitter. So I conclude that green apples are bitter and stop biting into them. Science depends on this kind of thinking, beginning with observations, with facts, and drawing some generalizations from these facts.

The other way of thinking is called *deduction*. Here's a simple example of it. I know apples are edible. This thing is an apple. Therefore, this thing is edible. You're probably already familiar with the classic illustration of deduction: All men are mortal. Socrates is a man. Therefore, Socrates is mortal.

As you can see, induction begins with particular observations and moves to a general conclusion. Deduction begins with a generalization, an assumption, and moves to a particular conclusion. Induction and deduction are in a sense opposites. Obviously, we need both kinds of thinking. It makes some sense to say that science grows out of induction, and philosophy depends especially on deduction, but scientists, philosophers, and everyone else certainly use both kinds of thinking all the time. Or, at least, we all seem to think in ways that appear to be deductive and inductive—since we aren't really sure how we think.

The problem with induction. The strength of induction is that it encourages a close observation of reality. Induction tries to begin without preconception and to make some sense of new information. But induction has two weaknesses, making our thinking always tentative. First, the reliability of an induction depends upon the reliability of the observation. Even with my very simple illustration, it's easy to see potential errors. The apples I bite may seem bitter to me, but what if there's something wrong with my taste buds? Then my fact may be wrong. Or what if the apples have been washed in some bitter solution? Or if they've been injected with a substance to make them bitter, perhaps by a seller of red apples?

Second, an induction can also go awry when the conclusion is drawn. How many green apples should one taste before concluding that all green apples are bitter? What if the next apple I would have tasted would have been sweet? When a researcher gives a substance to three patients and nothing happens, can the researcher conclude that the substance is safe? Or should it be given to a hundred? A thousand? Obviously, the probability of a valid induction increases with the size of the sample, but our certainty never reaches 100 percent

How the problem with induction applies to your own writing can be easily stated: Be cautious in your conclusions. Be careful in accepting "facts" as your starting points.

The problem with deduction. The power of deductive reasoning (as with inductive reasoning) is related to its strength. Deductive reasoning allows us to begin with something we know, an assumption, and construct other knowledge. The potential problems in deduction are twofold. First, a deduction is only as valid as its starting point. If we assume something is true, and it isn't, then whatever we base on that statement may not be true. The classic deduction starts from the premise that "All men are mortal," which

Writing, like architecture, requires careful planning and selection of materials.

seems reasonable enough at this point in time. But it is at least thinkable that even mortality might have some loopholes. Perhaps human beings have an immortal soul; perhaps medical science will discover a way to turn off aging and conquer all disease.

The other way that deductive reasoning can go wrong has to do with the rules for joining assertions together. If the rules for deduction are followed, then the conclusion will be just as valid as the starting premise. These rules relate to the syllogism, a three-step sequence of reasoning.

Although it isn't possible here to explain all the rules of deductive (or syllogistic) reasoning, a few comments should help you see how such reasoning works, and how your own common sense can be helpful in spotting errors.

Oftentimes drawing a picture can help you determine the validity of a syllogism:

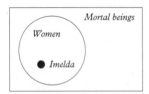

Major premise:
All women are mortal.
Minor premise:
Imelda is a woman.
Conclusion:
Imelda is mortal.

The picture makes clear that Imelda is within the class of mortal things.

Here's another syllogism:

Major premise: All conservatives believe in lowering federal spending.
Minor premise: Richard believes in lowering federal spending.
Conclusion: Richard is a conservative.

Here, the conclusion isn't necessarily true. Even if we accept the major premise, that all conservatives believe in lowering federal spending, it is not necessarily true that Richard is in the class of conservatives. It is possible to believe in lowering federal spending and still be something other than conservative (libertarians, social-ists, anarchists, communists, and others may believe in lower spending).

If a syllogism follows the rules, it's considered to be valid; and if its starting point is accurate, then it's also considered to be sound or true. It's possible, then, to have an argument that is valid but not true, as in the following:

All football players are dumb.
John is a football player.
John is dumb.

There's nothing wrong with the logic here; the problem is that the starting point is inaccurate.

English Composition

Some syllogisms feature an either/or structure.

Either he applied the brakes incorrectly or the
  brakes failed.
He did not apply the brakes incorrectly.
Therefore, the brakes failed.

This syllogism is valid. But you should note that if one alternative is affirmed, the other one is not necessarily false, as in this case:

Either he applied the brakes incorrectly or the
  brakes failed.
He applied the brakes incorrectly.
Therefore, the brakes did not fail.

It is possible that the brakes also failed. The syllogism really doesn't help us to determine.

Rarely will you find a syllogism or a sequence of syllogisms fully articulated in an argument. It's likely that premises will be left unstated. It may therefore be helpful when you're analyzing an argument to fill in the missing premises, allowing you to assess the argument more clearly.

Some logical errors to avoid. There are probably as many ways to violate the rules of logic as there are people on this planet. But some logical errors are so common they're familiar to students of reasoning: they've been perceived as a particular kind of error and have acquired well-known names. Some have been so familiar for so long they have even retained their Latin names. Shown on the next page is a selective sampling of some of the best-known logical errors.

Coherence. Good writing flows. Readers find themselves moving smoothly along as each sentence seems to connect to the preceding sentences. This tightness, this connectedness, is often referred to as coherence, the property of bonding together. There are several strategies that contribute to coherence, linking a sentence to what has gone before and what is coming up. Look for the cohesive features in this excerpt from Martin Luther King, Jr.'s speech, "I Have a Dream" (August 28, 1963, Washington, D.C.):

Example

We can never be satisfied as long as our bodies, heavy with the fatigue of travel, cannot gain lodging in the motels of the highways and the hotels of the cities. We cannot be satisfied as long as the Negro's basic mobility is from a smaller ghetto to a larger one.

We can never be satisfied as long as our children are stripped of their selfhood and robbed of their dignity by signs stating "For whites only." We cannot be satisfied as long as a Negro in Mississippi

Martin Luther King, Jr.

A primary leader of the American civil rights movement, Martin Luther King, Jr., was awarded the Nobel Peace Prize in 1964. Founder and president of the Southern Christian Leadership Conference, King advocated nonviolence in the struggle for racial equality and integration. He was a persuasive orator and a gifted writer. His works include *Stride Toward Freedom* (1963), "Letter from Birmingham Jail" (1963), and *Why We Can't Wait* (1963). King was slain in Memphis, Tennessee, on April 4, 1968.

cannot vote and a Negro in New York believes he has nothing for which to vote. No, we are not satisfied, and we will not be satisfied until justice rolls down like waters and righteousness like a mighty stream.

This speech uses a number of cohesive features:
• Repeated words and phrases, synonyms, antonyms, or other variations of words. Such repetition keeps the reader's attention focused on the subject. In the example above, notice how the repetition of the phrase, "We can never be satisfied" not only underscores the inequalities described, but links each sentence to the next one. Note that the idea of travel and movement in the first paragraph is also repeated in the last line of the last paragraph.
• Pronouns and pointing adjectives. In the example above, *we* and *ourselves* help to create coherence.
• Repeated construction or phrase. In the example above, *and* and *as long as* point out the relationship.

* * *

Of course, using any sort of technique to improve your coherence will be ineffective if your thinking is not coherent. As you're drafting, it is inevitable that ideas will interrupt the progression of your thoughts, taking you down tangential lines of development, leading you to associate the current topic with some other. But in revising, you'll want to look for these distracting or interrupting ideas, and group them together. Coherent writing (usually) doesn't require the reader to make leaps of logic or to fill in narrative omissions. The writing goes step by step, as sentences are linked and related.

Notice how many features contribute to the coherence of the following paragraph, from "The Next New

Logical errors to avoid

hasty generalization. "People from Oregon State University are boring. I went out with a guy from there, and he was really dull."

Generalizing is always risky, of course, but when your sample is a tiny fraction of the whole, then the generalization may well be hasty. Try to keep in mind the possibility or even likelihood of exceptions: your sample may be exceptional; and some members of the group you're characterizing may also be exceptional.

non sequitur. "The basketball team was playing well because the stock market was up."

Literally, *non sequitur* means "doesn't follow." One statement seems to be related to another, but in reality the connection is missing. How does the stock market relate to the basketball team? Unless such a connection is made plausible (perhaps the team consisted of stockbrokers?), the conclusion is a non sequitur, not following logically from the premises. Although non sequiturs are often absurd when analyzed, they can sometimes sound pretty good.

circular argument. "He made an A in the course because he did very well."

A circular argument goes nowhere. It appears that the assertion is supported, but in actuality it is merely repeated in a different way. This error is also called "begging the question." Rather than answering a question ("Why did he make an A?"), the respondent chooses to evade the question.

***ad hominem* argument.** "Her argument regarding the value of supporting the arts is worthless because she is an artist and a liberal Democrat to boot."

Ad hominem means "to the person," and an *ad hominem* argument is directed at the person rather than the argument. This logical fallacy is usually used to try to dismiss or discredit what someone is saying by directing attention to the person saying it. The *ad hominem* argument refers to negative associations, but it would be just as much a fallacy to assume that what someone is saying is valid or intelligent just because we respect the person.

red herring. "We shouldn't punish John for breaking the school windows. He has volunteered a lot of his time for working with the Red Cross, and his girlfriend has just left him."

A *red herring* in an argument is anything that takes attention away from the facts of the case. An *ad hominem* strategy could be seen as a red herring. This fallacy gets its name from the practice in hunting of dragging a herring across the trail of the prey to distract the hunting dogs. The strong scent of the herring would tend to confuse the dogs and lead them astray.

straw man. "I can't support the SAT because it is ruining the lives of some of our finest young people."

A straw man isn't a real person, but a symbol for one; and the *straw man* fallacy refers to the practice of substituting a fake opponent for the real one. In the above example, the speaker suggests that anyone who takes the SAT might ruin his or her life, which is of course false. The complementary fallacy might be to say that anyone who opposes the SAT wants all standards for college admissions done away with. In both cases, the opposing viewpoint is presented in an extreme and implausible way. If the audience mistakes the straw opponent for the real one, then the argument may be persuasive; but the danger is that the audience will perceive the distortion and dismiss the argument altogether. You're better off avoiding the straw man fallacy and representing opposing arguments fairly. Answer the opponent's position rather than distort it.

post hoc, ergo propter hoc. "Don't cut the grass. The last time you cut the grass, the Braves lost the series."

The Latin phrase means roughly "after this, therefore because of it." If one thing happens and then another thing, we are tempted to see some causal relationship. I cut the grass; the Braves lost; maybe the first event affected the second? We would like for everything to have a reason for happening, and for that reason to be perceived by us. But sometimes things happen in sequence even though they're unrelated. So, in cause and effect arguments, watch out for making connections where they don't necessarily exist.

polar thinking. "Either we should have a first-rate physics department, or we should just close down the whole university."

The fallacy of *polar thinking* involves assuming that one thing or an alternative must be true, allowing for only two options. The world, as you know, is rarely so simple, and we usually have more than two possibilities. Whenever a statement takes the form of "either X, or Y," be careful of polar thinking, especially when X and Y represent extremes.

Deal," by Neil Howe and Phillip Longman (*The Atlantic*, April 1992).

Example

Finally, there was the program originally designed to offer all Americans what President Franklin Roosevelt's brain trusters called "a floor of protection" against destitution in old age. But over the course of more than half a century Social Security had evolved into something radically different. By 1991 the system was distributing more than $55 billion a year, or more than a fifth of its benefits, to households with incomes above $50,000. For that much money the government could have provided every American with cradle-to-grave insurance against poverty—including the one American child in twenty who lived in a household reporting a cash income during 1991 of less than $5,000.

*   *   *

How audiences are persuaded. Audiences are persuaded by three factors: their perception of the author, their feelings about the message, and their understand-

Writers, like public speakers, must work to persuade their audience.

ing of the argument's logic. The audience's perception of you as a persuader will be based on many things, including word choice, sentence structure, reasonableness, and anticipation of what the audience already knows and feels. Obviously, poor grammar or obscure wording won't help convince the audience that your ideas are worthy of acceptance. In sum, your relationship to your argument is often important, affecting how the argument itself is received.

You also need to consider how the audience feels about your argument. We sometimes imagine that we live in a world in which arguments are evaluated on the basis of the facts, but in actuality the facts themselves may be perceived differently by different audiences. If you want to be successful as a persuader, you'll want to consider where the audience is starting from emotionally, and how they will respond emotionally to what you're saying.

Further, you will want to consider the logic of your argument, and how that logic will appeal to your audience. What will your audience accept as reasonable evidence? If your evidence is based on scientific studies, for instance, how will your audience respond?

Let's say you're going to argue to the PTA that football should be downplayed and soccer emphasized. Your audience will first want to know who you are, and how you as a person are related to your position. Are you a maker of soccer equipment? Are you some fanatic who's against football? Or are you an experienced soccer player? Are you swept away by emotion, or have you really thought this through? If you explain that you're a parent of children who are choosing

Without a good ending, your essay can go on and on and on.

whether to play soccer or football, and that you're also a former football player, then the audience is likely to be receptive to what you have to say.

You should also consider the audience's emotions. It seems reasonable that many of them are football fans; some have played football. Few have much understanding of soccer. Emotionally, they're unlikely to support soccer. But how could you affect those emotions? You might point out how enthusiastic fans are about soccer worldwide, and how easy it is to understand soccer. Or you might point to the difference in injury rates for soccer players versus football players: *that* should be an effective emotional strategy.

Finally, you'll want to consider what evidence this audience will value. What facts will they most readily accept? What sort of logic will be persuasive for them? What arguments against your position will need to be countered? For instance, in a rural town in Texas, which has been focused for decades on high school football in the fall, facts about the popularity of soccer around the world probably won't carry much weight.

Closers. The ending of an argument is at least as important as any other part. You can engage the reader's attention and pursue an intelligent and convincing thesis, but this success is for nothing if the conclusion still derails all your effort. Imagine a movie that draws you in at first, thrills and fascinates you in the middle, but then ends in a dumb and entirely unconvincing way. In some ways we're even more disappointed than if the whole thing had been lousy.

But what constitutes an effective ending? What should you try to do? Most important, an ending should offer the reader something new. Simply reviewing the points you've already made isn't effective, especially if the essay is relatively brief: it's as if you're saying to the reader, "I really think you're too dumb to remember what I've just said, so I'm going to say it again." This something new in your conclusion can be some logical extension of your argument: for instance, in an essay on the pleasures of visiting Poland, you might suggest that if Poland is now a nice place for a tourist to visit, perhaps we should consider other Eastern European countries as well. Or this something new might be an argument for further study of your topic. Or it might be an application of the point you've made: if the bulk of studies does show that passive smoking is dangerous, then perhaps we should have laws making public smoking illegal. You can move to a

Thinking about closers

- Does the closing add something new? An extension, an application, a recommendation, a connection—some new idea based on the introduction and body?
- Does the closing give the reader a sense of closure? Is it clear that you have finished (and not just quit)?
- Have you avoided claims that are implausible or unwarranted?

larger context, drawing some generalization from your particular point; or you can move to a smaller context, drawing some very specific point from your general discussion.

In any event, don't just review your points in the ending, unless the piece of writing has been lengthy and complex, and unless such a review would be valuable for the average reader. In that case, you're ending with a summary. Generally, you want to press ahead with new ideas based on what has gone before. You do not, of course, want to claim too much in your conclusion or make grandiose applications that do not seem warranted by what has gone before. Be just as reasonable at the end as you have been throughout (we hope).

You probably do not want to say, "In view of such waste in the Social Security system, we ought simply to shut the entire government down." But you might want to say, "In view of such waste in the Social Security system, we ought to reform not only the system but also examine carefully every other governmental activity."

Let's look for a moment at an example, the last two paragraphs from an essay selected for *Best American Essays, 1990*: "Shouting 'Fire,'" by Alan M. Dershowitz. The essay, discussing the First Amendment right of free speech, has argued that the analogy first used by Justice Oliver Wendell Holmes of falsely yelling fire in a crowded theater is an inappropriate analogy.

Holmes had argued that some speech can be prohibited: for instance, yelling "Fire!" in a theater when there is no fire. Dershowitz convincingly gives various reasons for his argument: yelling fire is not a political message; it is a "clang sound," signaling alarm; and the facts surrounding the yelling are not true. Yelling "fire" is not parallel to free political speech. He further supports his argument by giving various examples when the analogy has been invoked, and he debunks those. Clearly, he would have us believe that the law says what it means.

Example

The government does, of course, have some arguably legitimate bases for suppressing speech which bear no relationship to shouting "Fire." It may ban the publication of nuclear-weapon codes, of information about troop movements, and of the identity of undercover agents. It may criminalize extortion threats and conspiratorial agreements. These expressions may lead directly to serious harm, but the mechanisms of causation are very different from that at work when an alarm is sounded. One may also argue—less persuasively, in my view—against protecting certain forms of public

obscenity and defamatory statements. Here, the mechanisms of causation are very different. None of these exceptions to the First Amendment's exhortation that the government "shall make no law . . . abridging the freedom of speech, or of the press" is anything like falsely shouting "Fire!" in a crowded theater; they must all be justified on other grounds.

A comedian once told his audience, during a stand-up routine, about the time he was standing around a fire with a crowd of people and got in trouble for yelling, "Theater, theater!" That, I think, is about as clever and productive use as anyone has ever made of Holmes' flawed analogy.

The closing paragraphs, as you can see, reverse the argument, adding something new. Dershowitz defuses any rebuttal his opponent might give by stating times and places where the government should suppress free speech during times of real danger. Finally, at the end of his serious essay, he changes tone completely and tells us a joke. This funny anecdote seals the argument by pointing to one use of Holmes' analogy that is productive. The others, as Dershowitz has shown, are flawed.

*   *   *

Conveying this sense of closure is also important, although it's difficult to give advice about how to do it. When we are involved in a conversation, we usually have a good sense of when it is over. Occasionally one party will linger on, trying to extend the conversation when there really isn't anything more to say. One key to giving a sense of closure, of ending, is knowing when to quit. When you're finished, stop. We can always think of more things to say, but you want to consider whether you are just repeating yourself or starting off on a tangent.

Preparing the final copy

Revising and polishing. For too many students, *revising* means simply changing a few words, checking the spelling, and looking for typing errors. But for teachers of writing, revising means much more. Revision means "re-seeing," looking anew—rethinking and rewriting.

Thus, the first step in revising is in a sense not a step at all but an attitude: you need to assume that your writing can be improved, and you need to be willing to make changes, even large ones, even trying an entirely different approach. There is in aggressive and effective revising a certain degree of playfulness: you have to be willing to try something else, to play with your text. The worst attitude for revising is one of personal commitment to the way you said it the first time. It's always possible that the first draft is exactly perfect, but experienced writers will tell you that such a possibility rarely comes into being. It doesn't hurt to change your words. View it as a game, a puzzle, an opportunity to get something just right. That's the virtue of writing over speaking, isn't it? We get the chance to take it back and put it another way before the audience has even heard it. And if you don't like the changes, you can always put it back the way it was. Once you've assumed that your work can be changed and improved, here are some things to keep in mind.

Cutting the fat.
Assume, for starters, that your essay can be tighter, leaner. Eliminate from your draft any sentences, phrases, words, even syllables that you don't need. Make every word work, and if a simpler word or phrase will do the same job, choose the shorter, simpler wording. Some specific tips follow.

Sentence subjects. Look at the subject of your sentence. Is it *really* the subject? That is, does the subject of the sentence accurately reflect the focus? Are you saying "The kind of situation involved here is one of hitting between John and Jack"? Or are you putting the real actor and action in the subject and verb positions, as in "John is hitting Jack"? Consider these sentences, adapted from an essay discussing the waste disposal problems we face (by Elizabeth Royte, in *Harper's*, June 1992).

> The situation is one in which still more landfills will be forced to close, following the EPA requirements introduced last September.

Although it is possible that *the situation* is where the writer wants the focus, it seems unlikely. The real subject of the sentence, it seems most likely, is either more landfills or EPA requirements. To decide which one to

use, you'd need to look at the context in which the sentence occurs. Notice how changing the subject changes the sentence:

> More landfills will be forced to close, following the EPA requirements introduced last September.

> EPA requirements introduced last September will force still more landfills to close. [Royte's version]

There are twenty-two words in the first version; fourteen in the second; and eleven in the third, which is cutting the original in half. Imagine if everything you read were half as long as it is, if your physics text were one hundred twenty-five pages instead of two hundred fifty, if your IRS instructions were eight pages instead of sixteen!

Some sentences begin with a subject that is empty:

> There are scarred hillsides of this valley that provide a good vantage point from which to view the nation's garbage wars.

There is just a pointing word, linked by *are* to the rest of the sentence. Sometimes you do want simply to point out a situation or a fact, and beginning with *There are* or *It is* is a good idea. But this sentence seems more effective, not to mention more direct, when the subject position is occupied.

> Scarred hillsides of this valley provide a good vantage point from which to view the nation's garbage.

English Composition

Polishing

Here are some other examples of original sentences and revisions:

Original	*It is largely because of the fact that Grant caused such widespread destruction that many Southerners dislike the North even to the present time.*
Revision	*Grant caused such widespread destruction that many Southerners dislike the North even today.*
Original	*In the event that a hurricane hits Charleston again, the new construction regulations codes will have been applied for the purpose of making buildings stronger.*
Revision	*If a hurricane hits Charleston again, the new building codes to make buildings stronger will have been applied.*

Long phrases. Look for phrases that can be replaced by a word or at least a shorter phrase.

The shift in voter loyalty is due to the fact that the economy grew even worse.

Is there a familiar phrase in this sentence? Yes, of course. It's "due to the fact that." What happens if you try to replace that phrase, then change the subject of the sentence?

The shift in voter loyalty occurred because the economy grew even worse.

Voter loyalty shifted because the economy grew even worse.

Prepositional phrases. Look for any prepositional phrases that can be collapsed or eliminated, especially where you have a string of prepositional phrases.

The imbalance of chemicals in the liver of the patient caused problems for the intern of the evening watch.

If we try to remove some of the prepositional phrases, what happens?

The chemical imbalance in the patient's liver caused problems for the evening-watch intern.

Here we've gone from nineteen words to fourteen, making the sentence a little tighter.

Stilted wording. Watch out for big words and stilted phrasings. One clue to wordiness may be the flowering of words ending in *-ion*. Here's a rather extreme example:

The institution told those directly involved in the educational profession that consultation would be forthcoming.

This sentence means simply:

The administrators told the teachers they would be consulted.

That's fifteen words converted to nine—a reduction of over a third. Plus, the revision just sounds friendlier, more like a person talking.

If you cannot imagine yourself saying what you've written, ask yourself how you would say it. Then write it down and revise that rather than the original written version.

Making your style lively.

Making your
writing lean and direct is helpful. It's also helpful to
make your style livelier, more vigorous, more appealing. How can you do that? Try some of the following—but probably not all at once in every sentence!

Include comparisons. Ask yourself, "What is this
like?" When the U.S. Army was debating whether they
should hire Indian warriors to track and catch Apache
warriors like Geronimo, one officer said, "Using standard methods is like trying to hunt down a deer with a
marching band." The comparison made the case powerfully, and the Indian scouts were hired. In "Travels
in Georgia" (*The New Yorker*, 1975), John McPhee
talks about a turtle that was "run over like a manhole
cover, probably with much the same sound." When a
sheriff puts the turtle out of its misery, McPhee says,
"The gun made an absurdly light sound, like a screen
door shutting." A friend of McPhee's carries the dead
turtle down to the pond "like a heavy suitcase with a
broken strap." These comparisons bring the idea to
life, making us see one thing in terms of another,
enriching our grasp. "Oh, so that's what it sounded
like," we say. (When a comparison uses *like* or *as*, it is
called a *simile*. If it doesn't use *like* or *as*, it is known as
a *metaphor*.)

Replace weak verbs. Use more active, more vivid,
more precise verbs. Instead of saying "He walked
slowly along," you might want to say "He mean-
dered." Instead of "The new recipe is better than the
old one," you might want to say, "The new recipe
grabs your taste buds, while the old one just teased
them." Most teachers and style guides will tell you to
watch out for *to be* or linking verbs—*is, am,* or *was*.
These verbs certainly are useful, and oftentimes they
are fine to use. But when most of your sentences simply say that "X is Y," then it is likely that your prose is
not very vivid or active. So, when you're revising, see if
some of your linking verbs should be converted.

Add details. Perhaps "She went to work" should be
"Mary Catherine crawled out of bed and stumbled
over to her computer, determined to write up the
annual report despite her mind-boggling headache."
One of the most common student shortcomings in

writing classes is saying too little, taking for granted
that the reader can see or understand whatever is clear
to the writer. One effective way to add details is to use
appositives. An *appositive* adds information by renam-
ing a noun: Instead of "Samuel Johnson said many
witty things," you write "Samuel Johnson, the eighteenth-century author, said many witty things." Or
going further, you might say "Samuel Johnson, the
eighteenth-century author, the subject of Boswell's
great biography, said many witty things."

Be specific. Instead of "After a boring day, he went
home," you might want to say "After a lengthy and
lumbering discussion of the toilet paper allotment, an
unnecessary and uneventful meeting with his assistant,
and four hours of staring out his window at the building next door, he went home."

Use one- or two-word sentences. Absolutely. (Just
like that; and also try some parenthetical comments on
what you've just said.) Also try some dashes, semicolons, and colons. Bullet dots are also effective when
you want to list items. These are the sorts of things
magazine writers do to liven up the page. Look closely
at writing that aspires to be popular and try to do what
you see those writers doing.

Choosing the title.

Perhaps the most
important point to make about the title of an argument (or any other sort of writing) is this: Be sure to
have one. All too often, students omit titles for their
essays, or call them "Paper #2" or something equally
unrevealing and unappealing. A title like "Melville's
Moby-Dick" or "Pope's *Dunciad*," for instance, tells
the reader very little. Is the novel itself going to follow?
Will the essay cover every possible aspect of the novel?
You should have a meaningful title because titles are
very powerful. Your own experience as a reader will no
doubt remind you that the title of a piece often determines whether you will read it. There may be of
course a few authors that you will read no matter what
they've written, and some things that you simply have
to read, but for most other things, the title is crucial.
Perhaps students often ignore titles because they know
that in a school setting the reader usually feels compelled to read what they have written, no matter what.
But it is certainly to your benefit even in such compulsory situations if the reader *wants* to read what you've
written.

The title not only can draw readers in, but it also
prepares them for what is to follow. In various issues
of *Esquire*, a magazine consistently noted for excellent
writing, the following titles appear:

"A Nation of Crybabies: What Japan Thinks of Us";
"Rocket Launches, Lust, Croquet, and the Fall of the
West"; and in an annual college life issue, "Inhuman
Architecture, Bad Food, Boredom and Death by Fun

The stakes are higher, but the message is the same: Whether you're a writer or an astronaut, always check for mistakes.

and Games." All these titles indicate that the articles are giving new twists to what may be familiar content. All these titles are slightly descriptive (we know about Japan, the fall of the West, and the sometimes bizarre things that happen on college campuses), but each of these titles grabs our attention, promising new ideas by juxtaposing such different concepts in the titles. The authors have grabbed our attention.

In some contexts, your title should be entirely informational. The third quarter report for your company shouldn't be called "Trouble in Paradise" or "We're in the Money." Instead, "Reorganization Planned" or "Dramatic Increases in Earnings" would be more appropriate.

In your English classes, especially when you are writing argumentative essays (about literature or any other topic), your title should probably be informative and engaging but not cute. For instance, an article by Marshall Brown in *PMLA*, by some accounts the leading journal of literary scholarship, is called "Unheard Melodies: The Force of Form." The first part of the title is an allusion (an implied reference to these lines in Keats's "Ode on a Grecian Urn": "Heard melodies are sweet, but those unheard / Are sweeter"). Brown's use of this line is interesting because *form* is a part of a work that is not heard. It is the arrangement of the parts, not their expression; form is an abstraction. Brown's title is then descriptive and interesting. This

kind of two-part title that Brown uses appears fairly often, especially in academic discourse: one part (usually the first) provides an engaging and suggestive hook; the other part provides more information.

Where can you find your title? Your first resource is the paper itself. Is there perhaps a quotation that has a phrase you can use in your title? Is there a sentence of your own that can be converted into the title? In one way or another, titles are often responses to other works and their titles, so the more widely you read, the more materials you can draw on for your title. But the main thing, of course, is to have one.

Tips on proofreading. It's much better to make marks on your final copy, correcting errors or clearing up obscurities, than to turn in a beautiful paper with errors and obscurities remaining. It would be nice if you could catch those problems before you print out or type up the final version, but most teachers do not mind edited copy—as long as the changes aren't too numerous or too messy. Very few manuscripts sent to publishers are typed perfectly. And if they are, the publishers' editors will very quickly make a mess of them, adding questions, marking the copy for the printer, making suggestions and corrections. Your teacher is certainly going to write on your paper anyway, perhaps making some of the same corrections you might make. So save your teacher this

Proofreaders' marks

Editors use proofreading symbols to edit copy. These symbols are easy to learn and will help you as you edit your own papers. The marks shown here are standard: editors around the world recognize these symbols. The most useful ones are those for deleting, adding, and letting something stand in the original version after it has been changed. You should memorize these symbols and practice using them.

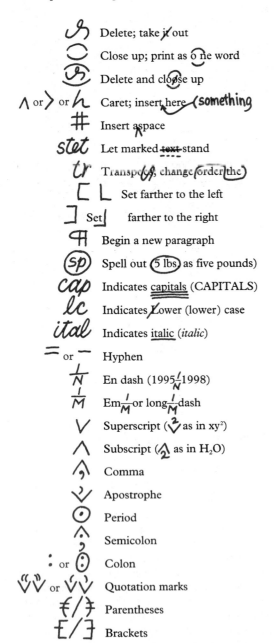

Delete; take it out

Close up; print as one word

Delete and close up

Caret; insert here (something

Insert a space

Let marked text stand

Transpose, change order the

Set farther to the left

Set farther to the right

Begin a new paragraph

Spell out (5 lbs) as five pounds)

Indicates capitals (CAPITALS)

Indicates Lower (lower) case

Indicates italic (italic)

Hyphen

En dash (1995–1998)

Em or long dash

Superscript (^{2} as in xy^2)

Subscript ($_2$ as in H_2O)

Comma

Apostrophe

Period

Semicolon

Colon

Quotation marks

Parentheses

Brackets

time: proofread and edit your final copy, and don't hesitate to make marks on it. You're not in a typing course. (Unless your teacher tells you otherwise.)

One of the difficulties in proofreading, however, once you've decided to do it, is that the paper is so familiar to you that you see what you think it says, not what is really on the page. A cure for this problem is to read the paper backward, proofreading the last sentence first, then the next-to-last sentence, and so forth. That way, it's harder for you to think about what the text is saying, and you're more likely to look at what it says—the spelling, the grammar, the complete thoughts. You can also tell a good bit by reading your paper aloud. This strategy isn't as helpful for finding typing or spelling errors, but it helps you determine if sentences make sense and sound good.

Format and appearance.
Common sense will help you here. You want the paper to make a good impression, so what will accomplish that? It should be easy to read, and what you're saying should be the focus. Make sure you use a clean ribbon. If you're using a dot-matrix printer, be sure to use the letter-quality setting, or at least double-strike or bold. Don't make your reader strain to see what you're saying (after dozens of papers, small difficulties start to seem larger). Make all corrections clearly, with black or blue-black ink. If you're writing by hand, use your best handwriting, and skip lines.

About the paper itself: Don't use the onion-skin kind. It tends to float off the table with the least little breeze. Also, don't use colored paper. Just plain white is strongly preferred. Follow whatever directions your teacher has given you about the format, but be sure to put your name and the teacher's name on every page. Also, a date on the first page is nice (that way, your grandchildren will know when you wrote your masterpiece). It's also helpful to write down information about the course, just in case the paper gets separated from you or your teacher.

Writing about literature

Some special considerations. In writing about anything, it's useful to think about what the "thing" is, but just what is literature? And why is defining literature often so difficult?

There are many different ways to define what literature is, and none of them work entirely satisfactorily. We could say that literature consists of poetry and fiction. But we would be including soap opera scripts, greeting card verse, and all sorts of formulaic pulp fiction. Should we study those kinds of things in literature classes? Some people think so; most people would disagree.

We could of course say that literature means "good" poetry and fiction, but then the category becomes an argument about quality. In one of the *Star Trek* movies, Kirk and Spock refer respectfully to the works of two present-day romance novelists as "the classics," and it is just possible that sometime in the future such works will have become "Literature" and be studied in literature departments. Shakespeare's plays were, after all, popular entertainment.

Even the idea of limiting literature to poetry and fiction is problematic because it leaves out some wonderful essays, biographies, autobiographies, histories, scientific works—all sorts of great works that intelligent people would like to study in a literature class. And what about those in-between works that are partly true, partly fiction? Or works that we thought were true, but turn out to be fiction, or vice versa? Is George Orwell's famous piece "Shooting an Elephant" an autobiographical essay and therefore not suitable for an anthology of literature? Or is it, as has recently been argued, largely a fabrication, a work of fiction, and therefore quite suitable for a literary anthology of short fiction?

The category *literature* is not a natural class, like granite and arthropod are in science studies. It is an artificial construction, human-made. It can refer to anything we agree upon. Thus, the real question to ask is not "What is literature?" but rather "What have people said literature is?" Given this shift in the question, we can say that literature seems to include those works that readers particularly value. Of course, you may particularly value your physics text, but you may not want to study it in an English class. So perhaps we should add to our definition "writing that readers particularly value for reasons beyond the information the work conveys."

If literature does consist of works that human beings believe have enduring value, then it is easy to see why literature often seems challenging: it is the richest, most rewarding, most stimulating writing we have. If a

work is simpleminded, easy to fully comprehend, obvious, then it is unlikely to be valued by readers again and again. It may be literature but not "Literature" of the sort that is carefully studied by generations.

This consideration of defining literature has indirectly raised another issue that also helps explain why literature is often so difficult and yet so important. That issue is the slipperiness of words. If the word *literature* means whatever people say it means, then aren't other words in the same situation? Even what we may think of as natural categories, like granite or arthropod, are ultimately human-made in the sense that human beings use and adapt the language that creates these categories. It seems reasonable to think of all dogs as belonging to a single, natural, biological class. But what about wolves? Are they dogs? What about the offspring of a dog and a wolf? Is it a dog? The point here is that language does not map perfectly onto the world. It is artificial, and it changes as time changes; it even varies from person to person. Literature, along with everything else within language, is therefore open to interpretation. We're always guessing about what someone means. But literature is the most fruitful way we continually learn how to make sense of language, how to improve and enrich our guessing.

Kinds and genres. While it is hard to specifically define literature, convention has given us a number of ways to break down literature into various categories and *genres*, or styles.
Nonfiction vs. fiction. Literature has traditionally been divided into nonfiction and fiction—works that are true and those that aren't. But the two categories often blend together. Some works, for instance, seem to be eyewitness accounts of real events, such as

Daniel Defoe's *Journal of the Plague Year*, but are actually inventions, based on various materials. Historical novels are often very realistic and historically accurate, conveying much of the same information as a history text.

If we ask whether a work is based on reality or not, surely all works are. A work of the most outrageous science fiction may tell us something at least as truthful as a history textbook. Although the distinction between fiction and nonfiction is still useful, the point here is that the way you read a work is not necessarily different for fiction or nonfiction. Both are works of the imagination, and it therefore makes some sense to talk about the symbols, the imagery, the plot, the tone, and many other literary qualities regardless of which category you place a work in.

Poetry vs. prose. Discussions of literature also traditionally distinguish between poetry and prose; but again, explaining the difference between the two is difficult. Certainly the presence or absence of rhyming words cannot be used to differentiate the two: much poetry doesn't rhyme, and prose can include rhyming words. Poetry does (almost always) look different from prose, leaving white space on the page, arranging lines according to the intentions of the poet rather than the conventions of typography.

> But what happens if a piece
> Of Prose
> Is arranged like
> A Poem?
> Does it become poetry?

The definition of poetry is, like that of literature, a perception on the part of the reader. That perception includes the assumption that every word is carefully chosen, and that some conventions (of grammar, spelling, punctuation) may be intentionally violated or suspended.

Readers often assume that poems will require very close attention, but there is no reason that works of some other kind cannot be given the same scrutiny. In poems, the reader may not know who is speaking or what the situation is: poetry often gives the reader a disembodied voice, just words on the page, and the reader has to construct the context of those words. This omission also contributes to the potential difficulty of poetry.

Drama. In drama we usually have not only the words someone is speaking (as in poetry), as well as information about who is speaking and where (as in fiction), but we also get to see an embodiment of the persons speaking—if the drama is staged, at least. Compared to poetry and fiction, drama is much easier to define: Drama is the representation, on some kind of stage, of

a story; or it is the script of such a representation, since a play that has never been performed is still a play.

Ideally, when you're studying a play, you should see it performed. Many plays are available on videocassette, and some of Shakespeare's major plays are available in several versions; check with any major rental outlet. You'll be amazed at how much seeing a play helps your understanding. And if you can't locate a performance on tape, then attempt to "see" a production in your head as you read a play.

Essay. The essay is a very loose and open category for good writing that doesn't seem to fit into the categories of poetry (although an essay may include some poetry), fiction (although an essay may tell an imaginative narrative), or drama (although scenes and characters may be presented).

Some essays are argumentative, presenting facts and

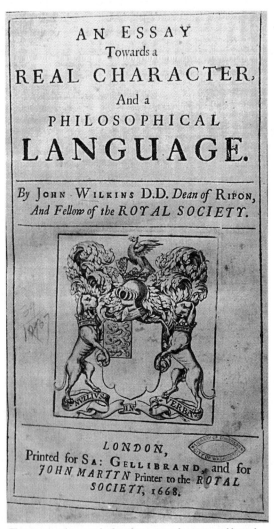

The essay as a form goes back to the seventeenth century and beyond.

attempting to persuade the reader. You'll find such pieces on the op-ed (opinion-editorial) pages of your newspaper. Some essays are more expressive, allowing the writer to present his or her feelings. An essay may describe a scene, or even tell a story. If readers perceive the story is true, then it is an essay, not a short story—although this distinction seems quite arbitrary to many people.

Other works. In recent years, what has been studied in literature classes has been expanded and diversified. The body of works traditionally studied in literature departments has often been called "the canon," and this recent inclusiveness has usually been called "opening up the canon."

Not only have literary works by women and minorities been included and studied at an impressive pace, but also some nonliterary works (by conventional standards) have been studied by rather conventional literary techniques. Advertisements, television shows, films, sporting events, even everyday conversations have been subjected to close readings. Such work has suggested how literary criticism can help us understand ourselves and our world.

Genres. As explained earlier, genre means style, and any work of literature—fiction, nonfiction, poetry, prose, or whatever—can be defined by its style. Some of the most common and enduring genres include comedy, tragedy, satire, and romance.

Few people would argue that human beings need to laugh. Comedy is obviously good for us. Before everything turns out fine in a comedy, there are complications and threatening situations. But for us to laugh, we have to believe that things will eventually turn out well. If the person who slips on the banana peel breaks his hip, then it is not really very funny. If a cartoon coyote chasing a road runner is hit on the head by an anvil and dies, never appearing again in another cartoon, it is not funny. The philosopher Henri Bergson, in a treatise on comedy, refers to this aspect of comedy when he talks about the *anaesthesia* of emotions necessary for humor. Either the threat is not serious, or the disaster looms only for some evil or mean being who we hope will suffer.

Tragedy may seem less healthy and necessary: Why do human beings feel an urge to witness bad things happen to other people? Although many reasons have been offered (when others suffer, we are comforted that we are not suffering, for instance), Aristotle's explanation, put forward many centuries ago, has been the most enduring. According to Aristotle, we are drawn to tragedy because it brings about the release of our fear and pity. Aristotle called this healthy release a *catharsis*. (As a measure of Aristotle's influence, we should note that this word and several others that he defined are still in our vocabulary.) Aristotle's com-

The Castle of Knowledge, Sphere of Destiny, and Wheel of Fortune are Renaissance concepts dealing with the structure of knowledge and the role of destiny in people's lives.

ments on the nature of the tragic hero, who must be good but not perfect, still resonate today. If a bad person meets a bad fate, then where's the tragedy? We are not saddened. If a good person meets a bad fate, then we are puzzled or outraged. Tragedy results when a flaw (a *hamartia* in Aristotle's terms) leads an otherwise good person to disaster. Oftentimes that flaw is *hubris* (again Aristotle's term, still current), or the arrogant pride of self.

Satire is in a sense a blending of comedy and tragedy. Bad things may happen to characters, but we do not care because they deserve it, and because they seem ridiculous—not quite human. The villains in a satire display exaggerated versions of human weaknesses, and the purpose of a satire is to ridicule this weakness. Thus, whereas comedy and tragedy seem to have personal benefits, satire seems to have a social function, shaping morality by ridiculing certain behaviors and values.

If satire is a distortion of life in a grotesque direction, romance is a distortion in the positive direction. Whereas satire ridicules bad qualities, romance celebrates good qualities—courage, faithfulness, cleverness, honesty, kindness. The hero will win out in a romance because the world is good, and because he is the hero.

Elements of literature.

There are a number of terms you'll need to understand in order to write about literature intelligently.

Plot. Plot refers to the ordering of the events in a story. As you probably know, sometimes an author will not present the events to the reader in the same order in which they happened. William Faulkner's "A Rose for Emily" is a famous example of a story that jumps around in time, shaping the reader's response by rearranging the order of what happened. Whenever a story leaps backward in time, that segment is called a *flashback*. If the story begins not at the beginning but in what seems to be the middle of things, it is said to begin *in media res*, which is Latin for "in the middle of things." Sometimes something in the plot seems to look forward to something that happens later; such events are called *foreshadowing*. If, for instance, a character trips on the way to work, such an event may be preparing the reader for a later event when the character clumsily falls off a cruise vessel.

Freytag's pyramid

The progression of the dramatic action of a play has been represented as a pyramid shape since 1863, when Gustav Freytag described the pattern of a typical play in terms of the exposition, rising action (conflict increases), climax, falling action (conflict decreases), and resolution. Freytag's pyramid looks something like this:

Of course, actual plays rarely follow such a neat progression, and the diagram of a particular play's action may look more like this:

Or this:

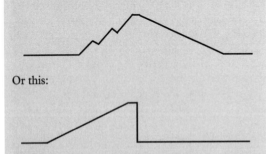

Moreover, many works have a subplot in addition to the main plot, developing parallel to the main plot yet distinct from it. Still, Freytag's pyramid has proved to be a helpful convention for thinking about plot.

Most plots can be tracked along the following four stages:

1. The *exposition* reveals the background information readers need to understand the story. In an artful exposition, this information seems to be a natural part of telling the story.

2. *Conflict* arises when forces of some sort work against, or oppose, each other. Without conflict, there's no story.

3. The *climax* is the moment of most tension in the story, when some decisive action is taken.

4. The *resolution* occurs when the conflict is resolved and the story draws to a close. The French word *dénouement*, which means "untying the knot," is sometimes used for this part of the plot. If this resolution is accomplished by some sort of trick (the hero is hanging off a cliff, for instance, no way to escape, when suddenly a helicopter appears from a rescue ship the reader has not heard of before), then the resolution may be said to be the result of a *deus ex machina*, which is Latin for "god from a machine," referring to the practice in a play of lowering an actor playing the part of a god onto the stage to resolve the action, saving the day. Obviously, a *deus ex machina* resolution is not desirable.

Character. The late-night television host who says, night after night, "Please welcome my good friend so-and-so," will eventually provoke ridicule. We all know that it would be very difficult to know hundreds or even dozens of people well. In presenting characters to readers, authors also must face the impossibility of knowing many characters well. Characters who are complex, who are the object of the author's (and the reader's) attention are usually called *rounded* (following E. M. Forster's term). Such three-dimensional characters may change during the work, and are in such a case called *dynamic*.

Authors handle secondary characters, who are a necessary part of the story but are also necessarily simpler than main characters, in two ways. First, authors may draw on *stock* characters, or familiar types, known for a dominant trait. You're probably familiar with the mad scientist, the blond bombshell, the alcoholic newsman, the loyal servant, the bragging coward, and many other types.

Second, an author may use what is called a *flat* character (also Forster's term), who, like the stock character, is distinguished by a trait or feature. The flat character, however, may be unique; we do not recognize him or her as a type, appearing with minor changes in various stories. We could say that a stock character is a flat character who catches on. Both are usually *static* (as opposed to dynamic), though it is possible for a flat or stock character to change; but if the author puts much effort into explaining that change, then such

characters are probably on the way toward being rounded.

One of the central concerns for someone who is writing about character in literature is *motivation*. Is the action of the main character, or the *protagonist*, sufficiently prepared for and explained? (The agent who opposes the main character is called the *antagonist*—usually another character, but sometimes a force of nature or other entity.) The assumption has generally been that in successful stories, action is motivated, but some modern literature has appeared to question this convention. And after Freud, the possibility of unconscious motivations has made discussing why characters perform an action more interesting and mysterious. The idea of a hero has also been called into question by the emergence in modern literature of the *antihero*, an unremarkable, ordinary, average, or even below-average person.

While these terms will no doubt prove useful, the most important thing to know when you write about character is what the character says and does. Literature provides excellent and invaluable experience in figuring out what people are like by looking at what they do and say. You already know how to do that; use your literary analysis to develop your abilities.

Setting. Setting is primarily where a story or statement takes place. How does the place affect what happens and, more important, our perception of what happens? How is a marriage proposal offered by candlelight in an elegant restaurant different from a marriage proposal offered in a butcher's shop, picking out hamburger? The place may reinforce the action, or contradict it, standing in an ironic relationship; or it

may play some other more complex role. The important thing is for you to note that place often plays an important role and that you should give it some attention. In addition to the physical place, setting also includes the time, the social and political environment—anything that we would consider part of the context of what happens.

Consider for a moment how this passage, the second paragraph from William Faulkner's famous "A Rose for Emily," creates an environment, a mood, a place for the story's events:

It was a big squarish frame house that had once been white, decorated with cupolas and spires and scrolled balconies in the heavily lightsome style of the seventies, set on what had once been our most select street. But garages and cotton gins had encroached and obliterated even the august names of that neighborhood; only Miss Emily's house was left, lifting its stubborn and coquettish decay above the cotton wagons and the gasoline pumps—an eyesore among eyesores. And now Miss Emily had gone to join the representatives of those august names where they lay in the cedar-bemused cemetery among the ranked and anonymous graves of Union and Confederate soldiers who fell at the battle of Jefferson.

What sort of place does this passage create? Among other things, you may see here that the past lingers on in this place. The past is decaying, like the house, or it is dead, like the soldiers, but it is nonetheless still here. The present also seems ugly and industrial, compared to the elegance and beauty of the past. With this setting, Faulkner prepares the reader to see that Emily, like her house, lingers on even though she is really out of place in the present. Like her house, Miss Emily has come to a "stubborn and coquettish decay," becoming "an eyesore among eyesores." Miss Emily, in a number of ways it turns out, is out of place in time; she has trouble with time and its passage. And the setting plays a crucial role in our understanding of her character and the story.

Tone. We all know that the tone of a statement can dramatically affect its meaning. In the sleeting rain, without an umbrella, "My, what a nice day" does not mean what it literally says—most probably. It is just possible that someone really loves such weather; or sells raingear; or has been in jail for several decades. We can always make a better guess about whether someone is serious, and about their other emotions as well, if we can see and hear them—which is why most people prefer face-to-face conversations for really important matters. In literature we cannot, of course, really see or hear who is speaking. But we can pay close attention to what the author tells us about the character and about the setting, and we can make intelligent inferences about tone. Again, literature provides valuable training for life because an ability to discern tone is always useful.

When the tone suggests a tension between what the speaker is saying and what is meant, then the tone is *ironic*. If one character says to another with a smile and a wink, "I really hate you," and then kisses that other character, irony is likely. In addition to such *verbal* irony, where one thing is said and another meant, literary critics also use irony to refer to strange twists of fate: when events are so strange that it seems some force must be orchestrating them (a man named Slim Spud is crushed to death by a potato truck), we refer to cosmic irony or irony of fate.

Point of view. *Point of view* is another term that is used in much the same way in literary criticism as in other contexts. When several people observe the same event, each has a particular angle of vision, or point of view. One person may be able to see something another one misses. One person has more information perhaps than another one, altering his or her understanding of what is being seen. When we talk about point of view in literature, we are usually talking about the angle of vision of the voice telling the story: What can the storyteller see? What does the storyteller know?

Which point of view should I use?

- **First-person narrator**
  An "I" tells the story.
  Major participant: The "I" is a major character.
  Minor participant: The "I" is involved in the story, but not centrally.
- **Observer**
  The "I" simply watches and reports.
- **Naïve narrator**
  The "I" does not understand as much as the reader does about what he or she is telling.
- **Unreliable narrator**
  The "I" does not tell the story accurately or truthfully.
- **Third-person narrator**
  An observer who reports to the reader.
- **Objective**
  The narrator simply reports what happens.
- **Limited omniscient**
  The narrator can enter into the mind of some characters.
- **Omniscient**
  The narrator can reveal what any character is thinking, even knowing what will happen.

Example

Let's look at a little narrative from different points of view:

> She brushed her hair away with a nervous gesture and smiled. "So," she said, "you don't want to do anything about it?" He sat across the marble table with a stone face, neither frowning nor smiling, just waiting. She pulled a brown handgun out of her pocketbook, smoothly, without hurry. His eyebrows lifted, beginning a question. As she raised the gun to her mouth, he sat paralyzed in horror; then she bit into its barrel and began chewing, little flecks of chocolate sticking to her lips.

What is the point of view from which this story is told? It seems to be told by some third party, someone sitting near the table, able to see both characters, who is simply describing what happens and what is said. This sort of narration is called *third-person* point of view; in this case the narrator would be called *third-person objective*. Of course, no perspective can be totally objective. The narrator here decides that the male character (which we assume is human) is "neither frowning nor smiling," which seems to be a pretty safe description, but is still a matter of judgment.

> I brushed away my hair, pretending to be nervous, and smiled. "So," I said, "you don't want to do anything about it?" He sat across the marble table with that stone face, neither frowning nor smiling, just waiting. I pulled a brown handgun out of my pocketbook, smoothly, without hurry. His eyebrows lifted, beginning a question. As I raised the gun to my mouth, the jerk sat there paralyzed in horror; then I bit into its barrel and began chewing, little flecks of chocolate sticking to my lips.

How is this version of the story different? The point of view here is that of one of the participants: an *I* speaks to the reader, revealing what the participant was feeling ("pretending to be nervous"), and her perception (the other character is a "jerk"). This kind of storytelling is referred to as *first-person narration*. The first-person narrator need not be intimately involved in the story:

> I saw the woman on the other side of the room brush her hair away with a nervous gesture and smile. She said something to him, but he just sat there, looking across the marble table with a stone face, neither frowning nor smiling, just waiting.

The first-person narrator could be even further removed from the story:

English Composition

I heard there was a woman sitting somewhere brushing away her hair with a nervous gesture, smiling. She may have said something; I'm not sure.

In the third-person and first-person narratives above, the speakers seem to be characters who have limited awareness of what is going on. It is always possible that what the narrator does know is incorrect. If the narrator just doesn't understand, then he or she may be termed a *naïve* or *innocent* narrator, telling readers things that they will understand more fully than the narrator does. If the narrator is deceptive or insane or for some other reason mistaken, then we have an *unreliable* narrator.

An author may choose a narrator who knows more than any character. An entity who knows everything is said to be *omniscient*. Here's the narrative told by a third-person omniscient narrator:

She brushed her hair away with a nervous gesture; she thought she was only pretending to be nervous, but she really was edgy. She tried to smile, but it looked to him more like a grimace. He thought she was acting strangely, and he wondered if she was about to be ill. "So," she said, "you don't want to do anything about it?" Saying this, she had her head turned down. She meant to be coy. But without his hearing aid turned wide open, which he hated to do in loud and crowded places, he was unable to make out anything beyond "so." He sat there trying not to reveal that he couldn't hear her, hoping she would say something else so he could feign understanding, as the cool marble table grew moist with the sweat from his hands. He had no clue what she was about to do.

This narrator seems to know everything: what the characters intend and what really happens, even down to the table growing moist, which perhaps no character is aware of. Although it seems a bit odd, literary critics also use the term *selected omniscient* or *limited omniscient* to refer to a narrator who knows more than any character but not everything. Such a narrator may see into the mind of one or more characters, but does not know what other characters see, feel, think, hear, or taste. For readers, it seems as if we are watching the scene from the outside but also able to get inside the head of one or more participants at times.

*   *   *

Other elements. Understanding the meaning and proper use of several other elements of literature will help in your overall understanding of the subject and make writing about it that much easier.

Great literature calls forth images that can surpass even the most beautiful photographs.

When a whale appears in a story, it may be just a whale. Or, as in Herman Melville's *Moby-Dick*, it may be a *symbol* for something more. And what does the whale stand for? Many critics have tried to explain what the whale does mean, and this openness is also part of being a symbol. A glass of wine, to take another example, becomes a symbol in the context of Christian worship, but what exactly does that symbol mean? Different things for different people, but it surely stands for more than just a glass of wine. A symbol is an object, then, that takes on a meaning beyond its literal significance.

The word *image* suggests something visualized, something seen; and the *imagery* of a literary work is usually thought of as the visual impressions the work conveys to the reader. Imagery can also include, however, the other senses.

An *allusion* in literature is an indirect reference. If a poem were to say "like the Babe swatting one over center field," the reader would need to know that "the Babe" is a reference to—an allusion to—Babe Ruth, the greatest home run hitter in the history of baseball. Often writers allude to literature. If a sportscaster says, "To pass or not to pass; that is the question," then he or she is alluding to Hamlet's famous "To be or not to be" speech. To know what the sportscaster meant, you would need to know Shakespeare's play, and realize that the sportscaster was placing the play-calling decision alongside Hamlet's momentous consideration of life or death.

Understanding poetry. Do not think you are dumb or slow just because you find poetry hard to read. Even for the most expert and experienced readers, poetry is often difficult to understand. For all students—as you don't need to be told—poetry is often especially frustrating. But poetry represents the most concentrated, thoughtful, inspired writing in our language. A good poem will amply repay your struggles for meaning, in terms of both enjoyment and insight.

Read the poem. The most important advice about making sense of poetry is this: Read a poem at least three or four times if you want to understand it. First, read the poem through to see if there are words or allusions you don't understand, and to see if the *syntax* (the structure of the sentences) makes sense to you. Look up unfamiliar words, of course, and write down their meanings in the margin of the poem; pursue allusions with an encyclopedia or some other resource (including your teacher, librarian, friends, parents, footnotes to the poem).

Next, read the poem again, and this time try to translate it into your own words. Try to state the meaning of each line, even while you recognize that your paraphrase cannot mean the same thing as the poem itself—just as reading a description of a hamburger does not have quite the same taste as eating the hamburger.

Now, read the poem once more, this time assuming there is something wrong with your translation (indeed, you may be certain there's something wrong). Try to explain on paper what the problem might be. How is your paraphrase different? What are the problems with the poem that the paraphrase does not solve? This strategy may help engage you in the poem by giving you some meaning to contrast, something to work against.

Finally, read the poem again. This time, relax and enjoy the experience of moving through it. Copy out (or underline) any words or phrases you find particularly effective. Now you're ready to write about this poem, to quote it, to analyze it, to ask good questions about it, to compare it, whatever.

What should you do if you follow these steps and the poem still makes no sense to you? Move on to another poem, if you can. The more poems you read, the better equipped you'll be to read poems. Succeeding with some poems does in fact require a knowledge of some other poem or poems. But if you can't move on, try to explain why the poem doesn't make sense to you: articulate the problem. This effort may help you understand, or perhaps see how the

English Composition

poem really doesn't make sense. It may be that the poem wasn't supposed to make sense in any direct, simple, logical way.

Let's look at a very famous poem, a Shakespearean sonnet—a poem that is puzzling to many people who read it for the first time. Read it through once or twice slowly—be patient with yourself—and then read the explanation that follows. This explanation will give you some idea of how to proceed in unraveling a poem.

Example
Not Marble, nor the Gilded Monuments

Not marble, nor the gilded monuments
Of princes, shall outlive this powerful rhyme;
But you shall shine more bright in these contents
Than unswept stone, besmear'd with sluttish time.
When wasteful war shall statues overturn,
And broils root out the work of masonry,
Nor Mars his sword nor war's quick fire shall burn
The living record of your memory.
'Gainst death and all-oblivious enmity
Shall you pace forth; your praise shall still find room
Even in the eyes of all posterity
That wear this world out to the ending doom.
    So, till the judgment that yourself arise,
    You live in this, and dwell in lovers' eyes.

Step 1: Definitions

First, we'll want to look up any words that are unfamiliar. For instance (using *Webster's Ninth Collegiate Dictionary*):

Not marble, nor the *gilded* monuments

Gilded—"To overlay with" or "as if with a thin covering of gold." So, a "gilded monument" would be one overlaid with gold. Pretty fancy.

. . . *besmear'd* with *sluttish* time

Besmear'd—Simply a variation of "smeared"; and *sluttish*—the adjective form of "slut," a prostitute or loose woman. So, time is seen as having the characteristics of a prostitute or loose woman. Hmm, I'll have to think about that.

And *broils* root out *the work of masonry*

Broils—There are lots of meanings, but "brawls" seems obviously the right one.
The work of masonry—A mason is someone who works with stone or brick, so the *work of masonry* means "buildings."

Sonnet
XLIII

How do I love thee? Let me count the ways.
I love thee to the depth and breadth and height
My soul can reach, when feeling out of sight
For the ends of Being and ideal Grace.
I love thee to the level of every day's
Most quiet need, by sun and candlelight.
I love thee freely, as men strive for Right;
I love thee purely, as they turn from Praise.
I love thee with the passion put to use
In my old griefs, and with my childhood's faith.
I love thee with a love I seemed to lose
With my lost saints—I love thee with the breath,
Smiles, tears of all my life!—and, if God choose,
I shall but love thee better after death.

Elizabeth Barrett Browning

Nor *Mars* his sword nor war's quick fire shall burn

Mars—the god of war.

'Gainst death and *all-oblivious enmity*

Oblivious—"Lacking memory or lacking knowledge"; therefore, *all-oblivious* means lacking all memory or knowledge.
Enmity—hatred.

That wear this world out to the ending doom.

What is this reference? Does this mean just death? Or is it the end of the world? Also, "the judgment that yourself arise" seems to point to the end of the world. Isn't this an allusion to the second coming of Christ, the final judgment?

Step 2: Summarize the poem

What does the poem say? Let's take the first two lines: "Not marble, nor the gilded monuments / Of princes, shall outlive this powerful rhyme. . . ." Shakespeare is saying that "this powerful rhyme" will outlive both marble and "gilded monuments." What's

Blank verse

(from *Paradise Lost*)

Of man's first disobedience, and the fruit
Of that forbidden tree, whose mortal taste
Brought death into the World, and all our woe,
With loss of Eden, till one greater Man
Restore us, and regain the blissful seat,
Sing, Heavenly Muse, that on the secret top
Of Oreb, or of Sinai, didst inspire
That shepherd who first taught the chosen seed
In the beginning how the heavens and earth
Rose out of Chaos: or, if Sion hill
Delight thee more, and Siloa's brook that flowed
Fast by the oracle of God; I thence
Invoke thy aid to my adventurous song,
That with no middle flight intends to soar
Above the Aonian mount, while it pursues
Things unattempted yet in prose or rhyme.

John Milton

"this powerful rhyme"? What are the possibilities? Some poem or work the speaker is talking about— "this one here," he says. Or the poem we are reading. This rhyme. It does seem a little arrogant for the speaker to refer to his or her own poem as "powerful." We need to read further before deciding for sure what "this powerful rhyme" refers to.

On to the next two lines: "But you shall shine more bright in these contents / than unswept stone, besmear'd with sluttish time." The speaker seems to be assuring the person addressed, the *you*, that "this powerful rhyme" and "these contents" are better than marble, monuments, or stone. The rhyme will outlive the monuments. And the monuments will be "unswept" and "besmear'd." Why is time "sluttish"? Well, time has dealings with everyone: there's no discrimination. "This powerful rhyme," which seems to refer perhaps to this poem we are reading (or perhaps some other poem), won't decay like a monument; it won't get dirty; it won't deal with everyone or anyone.

So, the next sentence: "When wasteful war shall statues overturn, / And broils root out the work of masonry, / Nor Mars his sword nor war's quick fire shall burn / The living record of your memory." The "Nor/nor" construction is strange, but it means (as you may know) simply "neither/nor." This sentence really seems just to repeat what already has been said, but elaborating on what might adversely affect statues and monuments. When war and other fighting destroy statues and buildings, the record of your memory will be unaffected.

The next statement: "'Gainst death and all-oblivious enmity / Shall you pace forth. . . . " Again, the speaker is promising the person addressed a triumph over time: You will pace forth, overcoming death and hatred (since hatred tries to eradicate everything?).

Next: "your praise shall still find room / Even in the eyes of all posterity / That wear this world out to the ending doom." Translation: Your praise will always have a place, even to the end of the world.

Finally: "So, till the judgment that yourself arise, / You live in this, and dwell in lovers' eyes." The first part of this sentence is difficult. What sort of judgment is associated with arising? Until the judgment that you arise? This seems again to be referring, like the previous line, to the end of time, to Judgment Day. It tells the person addressed that this poem will provide an immortality that surpasses that of a statue or building. "You live in this" means you live in this poem, and that seems to be the main point here.

How is this summary different from the poem? What does it say that is missed in the translation? Another way to think about this is to consider what the experience of reading the poem is like and how that experience is different from what the poem says literally. Everyone's experience, of course, will be a bit different (which makes writing about literature interesting). In my own experience, the images that really stand out are of the monuments and statues as being inferior to the poem. The unswept stone, dirty and smeared by time; the marble and gilded statues and monuments; the statues overturned by war—these stick out in my mind as I read the poem; the paraphrase doesn't capture this imagery. I am also struck by how repetitive the poem is. It seems to say the same thing over and over. It says it beautifully, to be sure, but one must wonder why the idea is hammered home.

Finally, as I think about my summary versus the poem, I realize that the person addressed actually has not lived on past the poem. The poem doesn't really deliver what it promises, does it? What is the name of the beloved here? What did he or she look like? Wouldn't a statue have captured the essences of this person better? True, the poem has survived. But the person addressed doesn't seem to live on in any real or specific way. What does that mean?

At this point I do not have an interpretation of the poem, but I am in a good position to invent one. I'm

76   **English Composition**

Heroic couplet

(from *Essay on Man*)

Ask of the learned the way?
The learned men are blind;
This bids to serve, and that to shun mankind;
Some place the bliss in action; some in ease,
Those call it pleasure, and contentment these;
Some sunk to beasts, find pleasure end in pain;
Some swelled to gods, confess even virtue vain;
Or indolent, to each extreme they fall,
To trust in everything, or doubt of all.
Who thus define it, say they more or less
Than this, that happiness is happiness?

Alexander Pope

familiar with the poem; I understand what it says, although I have some questions about what it means—which is, of course, what an interpretation is supposed to provide.

*   *   *

Narrative vs. lyric. *Narrative poetry* tells a story. *Lyric poetry* presents a voice speaking, expressing an emotion, not offering a plot. This distinction is useful because sometimes students may come to a poem expecting a story with a beginning, middle, and end. A lyric poem will frustrate such expectations. Instead of giving the reader a story, a lyric poem requires the reader to create whatever context is needed to make sense of the voice's expression. In a sense, a lyric poem asks the reader to create the narrative, the story, in which someone might speak the words of the poem. And a narrative poem, on the other hand, may ask the reader to respond to a *lyrical* speaker in a particular situation. By understanding what the poem is attempting to do (tell a story, or report the words of a speaker), you will be much better equipped to respond appropriately. The Shakespearean sonnet above is a lyric poem, of course. The reader's task then becomes, in part, to determine what sort of a situation would call forth this expression.

Form. Poems can take a number of different forms; but the most common include sonnet, blank verse,

heroic couplet, epigram, and free verse. The various differences among the forms can be easily understood.

Probably the most distinguished of all forms, the *sonnet* is a fourteen-line poem with a particular rhyme scheme. The Italian sonnet was first popularized by the poet Petrarch in the fourteenth century, and is illustrated by Elizabeth Barrett Browning's famous poem, shown on page 75. The most common form is the Shakespearean, or *English*, sonnet. If we let "A" stand for one rhyming word, "B" for another, "C" another, and so forth, the Shakespearean sonnet just examined would be represented as follows:

A B A B C D C D E F E F G G

As you can see, the first line rhymes with the third line; the second with the fourth; and so on. There are three groups of alternating rhymes, and a final couplet. Often the ideas or structure of a sonnet fall into two parts, with the first part ending after the eighth line or the twelfth line. The shift from the first part to the second is often called *the turn*, and the ideas of the second part may overturn, or balance, or extend, or specify, or apply the ideas of the first part.

Many poems are in *blank verse*, which refers not to the form of the entire poem (as *sonnet* does), but to the shape of an individual line. Blank verse is also called *iambic pentameter*. *Iambic* means the stresses, or beats, of the line go light-heavy, light-heavy, light-heavy, and so on ("I went to see my love," for instance).

Pentameter means that each line has five feet—a *foot* being usually two or three syllables. You should know four kinds of feet: *iambic* (light-heavy), *anapestic* (light-light-heavy), *trochaic* (heavy-light), and *dactylic* (heavy-light-light).

A poem written in the style of a *heroic couplet* (also called the *closed couplet*) features successive pairs of

Epigram

To Doctor Empiric

When men a dangerous disease did 'scape,
Of old, they gave a cock to Esculape;
Let me give two, that doubly am got free;
From my disease's danger, and from thee.

Ben Jonson

The river's tent is broken: the last fingers of leaf
Clutch and sink into the wet bank. The wind
Crosses the brown land, unheard. The nymphs
  are departed.
Sweet Thames, run softly, till I end my song.

T. S. Eliot

iambic pentameter lines that rhyme: *aa bb cc dd ee ff* and so on.

Any brief, witty statement can be called an *epigram*. A very short poem that makes a pointed observation, usually with a striking turn or punch at the end, can also be called an epigram.

Much of modern poetry does not rhyme and does not follow any set form. It is written in what is called *free verse* or *open form*. In this style, the words are arranged spatially on the page according to the poet's intuition or intention. Although Robert Frost observed that "Writing free verse is like playing tennis with the net down," many modern poets seem to have found such a game quite satisfying.

Figures of speech. In discussing poetry, you'll find it helpful to be able to refer to various techniques by name. This section explains some of the most popular figures of speech.

A comparison that does not use the words *like* or *as*, stating that one thing *is* the other thing, is called a *metaphor*. For example: The new director *is* a turnip. It is doubtful that the director really is a turnip. We suspect the language is figurative, not literal, and the sentence is a metaphor, asking us to consider how the director might be *like* a turnip.

A comparison using *like* or *as* is a *simile*. For example: The director is *like* a turnip.

Personification is a popular figure of speech. To personify something is to give human (or personal) attributes to an animal, thing, or idea. For example: Turnips everywhere are offended by the comparison.

An *apostrophe* is a speech spoken to someone or some thing. What makes the speech an apostrophe is that it would not under ordinary circumstances be spoken, and the speaker adopts an elevated tone. One would not, for instance, ordinarily speak to a sparrow, a house, a ghost, or to a person's hair. An apostrophe is the poetic device used to speak to such things. For example: "O thou shiny shafts, caressed by the sun's warm touch, you wave over the director's turniphead."

The figure of speech by which one thing is substituted for another thing is called *metonymy*. The thing substituted is closely associated with the other thing: that's what allows the substitution. When the evening newscaster says, "The White House decided today to give the Iraqi minister another twenty-four hours to decide," the newscaster does not literally mean that the building in which the President lives can think. By "the White House," of course, he means "those who are associated with the President and his authority; those who speak for him or her." For example: The director's office made a statement regarding references to vegetables, especially turnips.

A *synecdoche* is a particular kind of metonymy in which a part of something is used to stand for the whole, or the whole is used to stand for a part (rather than just something associated, as with metonymy). For example: I see the director's hand in this secret sale of turnips.

Hyperbole refers to exaggeration or overstatement. A poet uses hyperbole to create an effect. For example: The director said he had sold enough turnips to fill the Atlantic Ocean.

The opposite of hyperbole, *understatement*, is also called *litotes*. Understatement often has a comical effect. For example: Having thought that radishes and turnips were the same thing, the director admitted that his knowledge of vegetables could possibly be improved.

Other assignments

Expression. While argumentative and critical essays are the types most likely to be assigned in a college class, some teachers may give assignments that ask you to express yourself. For example:

- How do you feel about the increase in tuition?
- What is your reaction to the congressional pay raise vote?
- What do you think of the movie version of *Twelfth Night*?

Sometimes assignments that seem to be asking you to express yourself really mean for you to construct an argument or an analysis. If you're in doubt, by all means do not hesitate to ask your teacher. If the assignment really is an invitation for you to express yourself, then here are a few suggestions that you may find helpful:

- Give yourself plenty of time for preparation, for freewriting. Explore your feelings; allow yourself a chance to see what you think, to develop your response.
- Your feelings need not be coherent or even logical. Most issues of any importance are complex, sparking conflicting emotions.
- One of the most important qualities of an expressive essay is honesty. Strive for an authentic response. If your teacher has assigned an expressive essay, she or he really wants you to express yourself, so don't be afraid to do it.
- Explain the basis of your feelings. Your readers can better understand your self-expression if they understand how you came to your feelings, or if they see some illustrations or examples.

Conveying information. In school, and perhaps even more often at work, you will likely have to do some tasks that ask you to convey information in writing. With such an assignment, your job is to sift through material and determine what your audience needs to know, then package that information in a way that your audience can most effectively grasp.

One obvious consideration is vocabulary. What terms does your audience need to understand? What ideas or concepts need explanation? But thinking of your audience in conveying information requires more than speaking on their level. How you structure the material is crucial. In their scholarly studies of writing structure, professors Linda Flower and John Hayes have made an important distinction between what they call *writer-based* prose versus *reader-based* prose. The simplest way to explain this distinction is with an example.

Imagine that you've been asked by your company to inspect Squishy Tennis Balls, a plant that manufactures tennis balls, and report back to the board of directors. Read the two abbreviated versions of that report below and think about how they differ. Which would you, as a board member, rather read?

Example

Version 1:

    Report on Visit to Squishy Tennis Balls

Tom and I arrived at 8:15 and met the assistant manager, John Roberts, who showed us around the main office. We noticed that every work station had both a computer terminal and a typewriter, but

most of the secretarial staff were using typewriters (approximately ten of sixteen were working at typewriters). Mr. Roberts confirmed that most of the staff were uncomfortable with the computers. We inquired about the details of the computer system, which was installed about two years ago for about one million dollars. It is a very powerful system. We then had coffee in Mr. Roberts's office while we waited for the manager, Robin Shealy, to arrive. After twenty minutes, Mr. Roberts said Mr. Shealy was sure to get there any minute, but he suggested we begin our tour of the plant.

We went from the main office to the loading dock and met Mark Taylor, the foreman. Mr. Taylor was clearly upset by our visit because a truck had arrived to unload some raw materials at the same time that a truck was still being loaded with an outgoing shipment. Mr. Taylor had started loading the shipment because, he said, he had been unaware that the incoming truck's schedule had been changed. He was trying to decide whether he should interrupt loading the outgoing shipment and unload the materials, or finish loading the shipment. Either way, he would be paying truck drivers to sit and wait.

We left the loading dock and went to the finishing room. Mr. Shealy joined us in the finishing room and sent Mr. Roberts back to the main office. Mr. Shealy informed us that Mr. Roberts had told him we would arrive at 9:00. [*The report goes on for six more pages.*]

Version 2:

Report on Visit to Squishy Tennis Balls

In general Tom and I found that the plant is producing a good product, but it is not operating as efficiently as it should. Two problems need to be addressed immediately.

Computer usage: Although the plant was outfitted two years ago with a powerful central computer system, one that is still very nearly state-of-the-art, costing almost one million dollars, the use of this system is minimal. Only the sales department relies on the computer for important tasks. The other departments rely on typewriters, handwritten notes, and verbal communications. Even planning calculations are done by hand. All the departments, but especially Maintenance, Shipping, Finishing, and Preparation, should take advantage of the computer system and the potential for better planning and communication it offers. Transition to computer use will require some training, from secretarial staff to the plant manager. No one seems comfortable with it, but it is a valuable and underused tool. [*The report goes on to a second problem.*]

As you can see, the first version is a story of what happened, in chronological order. There may be situations when such a narrative is what your audience wants, without your ordering of the material. Most of the time, however, such an orientation is *writer-based*. That is, the information and everything about the story are presented in terms that are easiest for the writer.

To write the second version, the author had to produce, in some form, the first version; that is, the author had to keep track of everything that happened. The second version required that the author package the material for the audience, thinking of what they would want. The second version is *reader-based* because it organizes the material for the reader: The board wants to know (the author presumes) what action needs to be taken based on the visit, and the author has accordingly imposed an order on the information. Instead of having to pull out the important information from the stream of what happened, the readers already have the information organized for them because the writer has taken a reader-based stance.

In other words, instead of asking what the information looks like to you, ask yourself how the reader would like to have the information presented, and proceed accordingly.

* * *

Creative writing.
If your teacher asks you to write a poem, a short story, or even a play, don't panic. You can do it. Believe it or not, you might enjoy it.

Just follow the same procedure you'd use for writing anything else. All writing, after all, is creative. Don't sit around waiting for inspiration to strike. Although some writers have endorsed the idea that creative literature comes magically in flashes of insight, these same writers seem to produce multiple drafts with careful rewriting.

Most writers say they don't know what they're going to say until they say it, and even those who plan extensively alter their plans extensively. So, let yourself go: generate lots of material and be prepared to throw away much of it.

You may know from the start what form you're going to use—sonnet, realistic short story, open verse, science fiction—or you may find that the form naturally evolves in the process of writing. In any event, if you possibly can, spend some time reading the sort of thing you want to produce. Then set those works and any other preconceptions aside, and enjoy yourself.

It's difficult to imagine how creative works could be graded other than on effort, so engage yourself in the effort.

Grammar review

Back to basics. In many English classes, students are required to purchase a grammar handbook. The size of these books testifies to the difficulties of mastering something as complex and strange as a language—especially one as diverse and rich as English. Even if a handbook is not required, you will find one helpful as a resource. This section will offer a condensed version of a grammar handbook, allowing you quickly to review the basics and to assess for yourself what you need to work on, using a handbook and other resources discussed below. In a sense, what follows is both an abbreviated handbook and a guide to handbooks.

The sentence. A sentence, the conventional definition tells us, is "a group of words expressing a complete thought." For a thought to be complete, it must have a subject and a verb. One of these can be understood, and so a sentence can be one word: "Come." "Me." In the first, perhaps *you* is understood: "You come." And in the second perhaps *She should give it to* is understood: "She should give it to me." So, when a sentence is only one word, it must exist in a context that implies the missing element, whether subject or verb.

Taken together, a subject and verb constitute a clause. A sentence thus must have at least one clause, but it can have more than one. Clauses that can stand alone as sentences are called *independent* clauses. Clauses that cannot stand alone, that seem incomplete by themselves, are called *dependent* clauses because they are *dependent* on something else to make complete sense.

Example

Governor Filbert offered the bill.

This clause makes sense by itself. "Governor Filbert" is the subject; "offered" is the verb. So this is an independent clause. It is a sentence.

Although Governor Filbert offered the bill.

This clause doesn't make sense by itself. It is a dependent clause. It is not a sentence.

In both clauses above, "the bill" is what is called a direct object, the recipient of the verb's action. It is possible to have an indirect object if the verb describes some kind of "giving" action.

Governor Filbert (subject) offered (verb) local officials (indirect object) the bill (direct object).

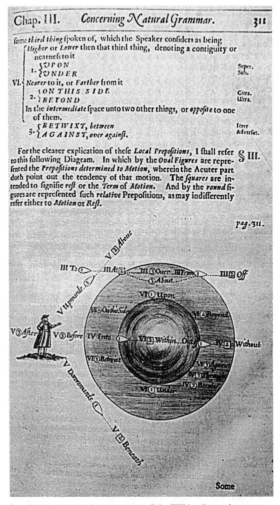

In a famous seventeenth-century essay, John Wilkins discussed grammar.

In simple sentences, the subject comes first. But the subject can appear in various positions, and any number of independent and dependent clauses can appear.

Although no one appreciated the gesture, Governor Filbert offered the bill.

Governor Filbert, even though no one appreciated the gesture, offered the bill, and then he quickly flew to Washington.

No one appreciated the gesture, but Governor Filbert offered the bill anyway, and then he quickly flew to Washington.

*   *   *

Ordinarily, writers put the most important information in the main clauses and supporting material in the dependent clauses. This convention can be violated with comic effect:

Although she is a coward, a thief, and a traitor, she is an excellent typist.

Parts of speech.
Most of us remember, or should remember, the parts of speech from sentence diagramming in grade school. We're not going to ask you to diagram sentences here, but before you can begin to construct a proper sentence, it is important to review the elements that make up a sentence.

Noun. A noun names something—a person, a place, an object, an idea, anything. A proper noun names a specific thing and is capitalized—Shakespeare; Greer, South Carolina; the Milwaukee Brewers.

Verb. Verbs are the engines of sentences. They convey the action. In some cases that action is a state of being, indicated by *to be* or linking verbs (*is, was, are, were, became, remains,* and others).

Pronoun. A pronoun stands for a noun. In "The children went out to play, but they will be back soon," the word *children* is the noun, and *they* is the pronoun, substituting for the noun.

Adjective. An adjective adds information to a noun, *modifying* it, as we usually say. If we add an adjective to "the outfielder," we get "the *agile* outfielder."

Adverb. An adverb modifies a verb, or another adverb, or an adjective.

The cake rose *beautifully*.
(modifying the verb)

The cake rose *very* beautifully.
(modifying the other adverb)

The *beautifully* rising cake was chocolate.
(modifying an adjective)

Preposition. A preposition links a noun or pronoun to a sentence, showing relationship, placing the noun or pronoun in time and space. Words such as *of, around, to,* and *on* are prepositions.

Conjunction. A conjunction joins sentences, clauses, phrases, or even words. *And, hence,* and *also* are all conjunctions. One kind of conjunction, which appears in pairs, is called a *coordinating conjunction* (for instance, *both/and,* or *either/or*).

Pronouns.
There are some common problems with pronouns, and it helps to discuss these problems separately. Once some simple rules are understood, it is easy to use pronouns correctly in speaking and writing.

A working knowledge of grammar is helpful in all types of writing.

Subjective, objective, possessive. Pronouns come in three cases: *subjective, objective,* and *possessive*. For the first-person pronoun, these three cases are *I, me,* and *my* or *mine*.

Subjective: *I* played the Mozart piece last night.

Objective: The Mozart piece was played last night by *me*.

Possessive: *My* version of the Mozart piece was played last night.

The three pronoun cases usually don't cause problems (except with compound subjects, compound objects, and predicate nominatives, which follow).

Compound subjects. Most people would not say "Me have a new house." But a surprising number of people would say "Jane and me have a new house." Whether a sentence has a single subject or a compound subject, the pronoun should be in the *subjective* case: *I, you, he, she, it, we, they, who, whoever*.

Compound objects. Likewise, to most people, "The rocks hit I" sounds wrong. But "The rocks hit Jane and I" apparently sounds fine to many people. So, whenever you have a compound object or subject including a pronoun, eliminate the other subject to see which case to use. If the pronoun is in the object position, receiving the action of the verb, or serving as the object of a preposition, then use the *objective* case: *me, you, him, her, it, us, them, whom, whoever*.

Predicate nominatives. In the following sentence, "Valerie and I" is a predicate nominative: "The leaders of the group are Valerie and I." In sentences with linking verbs, such as *are*, the predicate of the sentence takes the *subjective* case: it is being equated with the subject. Admittedly, this practice does sound a little odd to many people: "The teachers are Laura and she."

82   **English Composition**

And in informal usage, most people accept the use of the objective case of the pronoun after a linking verb: "It is I" (formally correct) and "It is me" (informally accepted).

Than and as. After *than* or *as*, use the pronoun case as if the sentence were completed: "Annette is smarter than I" (*smarter than I am*) "Jane cannot eat as much as he" (*as much as he can eat*).

Appositives. An appositive renames a noun. When a pronoun appears in an appositive, use the same case as the noun being renamed: "The full partners—Jack, Sally, and I—are going to Mexico."

Who and whom. Many Americans never use *whom*, relying instead on *who* exclusively. Other people, aware that *who* and *whom* are troublesome words, assume that whatever sounds right to them must be wrong, and therefore "correct" their speech to the wrong form. For informal usage, *who* is in fact acceptable to most people, but in writing, you want to have the correct form. And unless you perceive it will sound stuffy or stilted, you might as well have the correct form in speech. It really isn't that difficult.

Probably all you need to do is substitute another personal pronoun for *who* or *whom* (or for *whoever* or *whomever*—same rules apply). For instance: Is it "*Who* shall I say is calling?" Or "*Whom* shall I say is calling?"

Since it's easier to deal with statements rather than questions, first turn the question into a statement: "I shall say *who/whom* is calling." If we substitute another personal pronoun, see which of these sounds better: "I shall say her is calling" or "I shall say she is calling."

To almost every native speaker of English, "she is calling" sounds much better. *She* is of course the subjective form, corresponding to *who*, so "Who shall I say is calling?" is right. Here's another example: "Tom was not *who/whom* the new teacher asked. "

In this case, you need to take the sentence apart enough to see what role *who* or *whom* plays. As it turns out, *who* or *whom* is the object of the verb asked: "The new teacher asked *who/whom*." And which of these sounds better—"The new teacher asked her" or "The new teacher asked she"?

Her, the objective case, sounds better; so *whom* is the right choice. Whenever *who* or *whom* appears in a dependent clause, just remove the clause from the sentence and rearrange it to see what role *who* or *whom* plays.

We and us. Again, these two pronouns seem to give most people trouble only in certain situations. In this case, many people have trouble when *we* or *us* is used together with a noun, as in the following sentence: "*We/us* English teachers have to stick together."

The trick to determining which form to use is simply to remove the noun. Decide which sounds better: "We must stick together" or "Us must stick together."

Clearly, to most native speakers, the first version sounds better.

How about this sentence? "The coach really laid it on *we/us* team members." Again, do you prefer "on us" or "on we"? "On us" sounds much better, of course.

Sexist speech. Some writers believe it is defensible to use *he* as an inclusive pronoun, and to use *mankind* as a term that includes both men and women, and to begin letters with *Dear Sir* even though the sex of the person who will receive it is unknown, and many other related usages. It is true that for centuries these have been conventional in our language. Only in the past few decades have their unfairness and narrowmindedness become increasingly evident. If one were to suggest that *she* includes both men and women, the idea would seem absurd. Why should *he* be different? The dean of the dentistry school who wants to thank at graduation "all the supportive wives of our new dentists" is obviously out of touch, since over a third of today's dentistry students are women. Likewise, referring generically to a nurse as *she* makes no sense: today, nurses come in both sexes.

All of us need to become sensitive to the way we use language, because words do convey power. Words reinforce prejudices, sometimes in subtle ways, sometimes blatantly. Here are some tips on avoiding sexist language.

Avoid sexist speech: A scientist can be a he *or a* she.

- Use plural forms. "An engineer must pass *his* certification exam" becomes "Engineers must pass their certification exams."
- Add a pronoun. "An engineer must pass his certification exam" becomes "An engineer must pass his or her certification exam."
- Use another word that is not gendered. For instance, instead of *fireman* use *firefighter*. Instead of *chairman* use *chair*. Instead of *mailman*, use *mail carrier*. Instead of *mankind*, use *humanity*.

Adjectives and adverbs.

Adjectives and adverbs expand our experience of words, adding to nouns and verbs, refining and sharpening what a writer says. In the accompanying sidebar on this page, read the passage from Edgar Allan Poe's classic story "The Tell-Tale Heart." Notice the important role of the adjectives (which modify nouns and pronouns) and the adverbs (which modify verbs, adjectives, and other adverbs). Poe does not overburden this passage with modification, but the adjectives and adverbs he does use make a difference—the difference between a groan and a slight groan, between knowing a sound and knowing it well.

In addition to encouraging you to use adjectives and adverbs, this section covers the most common problems students have with them. If you can distinguish between adjectives and adverbs, you can solve just about any usage problem involving the use of adverbs and adjectives.

Use of adjectives
(from "The Tell-Tale Heart")

Presently I heard a slight groan, and I knew it was the groan of mortal terror. It was not a groan of pain or of grief—oh no!—it was the low stifled sound that arises from the bottom of the soul when overcharged with awe. I knew the sound well. Many a night, just at midnight, when all the world slept, it has welled up from my own bosom, deepening, with its dreadful echo, the terrors that distracted me.

Edgar Allan Poe

Remember that adjectives modify nouns and pronouns, and adverbs modify verbs, adjectives, and other adverbs. Adjectives answer the following questions: Which? How many? What kind? Adverbs answer these questions: How? When? Where? To what extent?

Now, look at these two sentences. Which is right?

I feel bad.

I feel badly.

How can you tell? Does *badly*, the adverb, belong to the verb, modifying the action of feeling? Or does *bad*, the adjective, belong to the subject? Many people say "I feel badly," but that sentence actually means that their ability to sense things physically, to feel, is poor. "I feel bad" is probably what the speaker means to say. The verb *feel* links the subject to the modifier. *Bad* refers to the speaker's condition—what kind of condition he or she is in.

To understand this distinction more clearly, let's consider the difference between the following two sentences:

The quarterback looked cautious.

The quarterback looked cautiously at the linebackers.

In the first version, the word *looked* functions as a linking verb, calling for the adjective *cautious*. In the second version, *looked* is an action verb, calling for the adverb form.

He always dresses formal.

He always dresses formally.

In this case, *formally* modifies *dresses*, so the adverb form, *formally*, is correct.

The pizza tasted bad.

The pizza tasted badly.

Tasted here must be a linking verb. If it is an action verb, then pizza must have the capability to taste, and as an inanimate object, pizza cannot taste. So *bad* is correct.

A final word about adjectives and adverbs. In conversation, *real* is often used for *really*. Be careful in writing, however, to distinguish between the two. It's incorrect to say "We were real happy with our room." Instead, one should say "We were really happy with our room."

Verbs. This section will not try to cover every distinction that can be made about verbs. Instead, it will focus on those kinds that you need to understand in order to make the most of some important advice.

Action vs. state-of-being. Verbs can be divided into action verbs and state-of-being verbs. State-of-being verbs, such as *is*, *was*, *are*, and *were*, are sometimes overused by writers. Try to use your verbs to show the reader some action, which is usually more engaging and revealing than simply linking subject and predicate. Compare:

Willie Mays was a good hitter of high fastballs.

Willie Mays slugged high fastballs.

There are, of course, times when *to be* verbs are exactly what you need. The best advice is simply to notice when you use a state-of-being verb and consider if an action verb would be better.

Transitive vs. intransitive. Action verbs are divided into transitive (those that take objects) and intransitive (those that don't take objects).

President Kennedy believed his assistant's story.
(transitive)

Although many doubted, President Kennedy believed.
(intransitive)

If the subject of a transitive verb is not the agent but rather the recipient of the verb's action, then the verb is said to be *passive*, or in the passive voice. If the subject does perform the action, then the verb is *active*.

Kennedy believed the assistant.
(active, transitive)

The assistant was believed by Kennedy.
(passive, transitive)

Although some students are occasionally told to avoid passive voice, such advice is too simple. You should try to make most of your verbs active, using passive verbs only when you have a reason. Passive verbs are fine—indeed, they're very effective—when you want to emphasize the passivity of the subject. "I was hit by a train" focuses the attention on me as the recipient of the train's action. "A train hit me" shifts the emphasis to the train, and offers a different meaning. Passive verbs are also fine when the agent is unknown or unimportant. In much scientific writing, such use of the passive voice is common. It doesn't matter who held the test tube; it only matters that the chlorine was poured into it. "The test tube was filled with chlorine" focuses our attention differently from "Sam filled the test tube with chlorine."

Tenses. English has three major tenses: *present*, *past*, and *future*. You want to understand these tenses because you want to keep the reader oriented in time,

Over the years, sportswriters have used hundreds of action verbs to describe auto races.

and verb tense is crucial to that orientation. More on this in a moment.

Present tense describes conditions now, which can include timeless events:

My aunt is happy to come.

The newscaster takes the microphone.

A virus mutates under stress.

Events that occur in literary works are usually described in present tense:

Flem Snopes auctions off a diseased horse in the opening scene.

Past tense conveys events that have occurred or conditions that did exist:

My aunt was happy to come.

The virus mutated under stress

Future tense tells about events or conditions to come:

My aunt will be happy to come.

The virus will mutate under stress.

Each of the major tenses has a *perfect* form. Present perfect tense conveys the idea that the events or conditions began in the past and may still continue to the present:

My aunt has been happy to come.

The virus has mutated under stress.

Past perfect tense tells us about a condition or event that occurred in the past and does not extend into the present:

My aunt had been happy to come.

The virus had mutated under stress.

Future perfect tense depicts an event or condition that will occur in the future and then end:

My aunt will have been happy to come.

The virus will have mutated under stress.

Keeping your reader oriented in time does not mean that every verb is in the same tense. It means that position in time remains stable throughout the composition. Consider how this paragraph shifts about in its orientation:

At the news conference, the chief researcher says his resignation was ready. He said the problem is not his fault, however. He thinks the media have been unfair. He wanted everyone to continue to support the center.

It's difficult to tell if the reader is supposed to be situated in the present, looking back at a news conference in the past, or if the reader is supposed to be experiencing the news conference in the present tense.

Subjunctive vs. indicative. If the verb describes a condition that is not true, that is contrary to the facts, then the mood of the verb is said to be *subjunctive*, distinguishing it from the ordinary mood of verbs, which is *indicative*. For instance, if I say "If I *were* king," I am stating a condition that is not true. In the indicative mood, I would say "*was* king"—which is entirely different. Of course, the second is also untrue, but my statement doesn't indicate this condition. You may need to study the accompanying table to learn how the *to be* verbs change from *indicative* to *subjunctive*.

Using the indicative and subjunctive

Indicative			Subjunctive	
		Present tense		
I am	we are		(if) I be	(if) we be
you are	you are		(if) you be	(if) you be
he/she/it is	they are		(if) he/she/it be	(if) they be
		Past tense		
I was	we were		(if) I were	(if) we were
you were	you were		(if) you were	(if) you were
he/she/it was	they were		(if) he/she/it were	(if) they were

Troublesome verbs.

Some verbs are trouble. But the most troublesome are probably *lie* and *lay*, and *sit* and *set*. If no one knew which one of these pairs to use, things would be okay; but there are people who know, and many of them are irritated or shocked by those who don't. So you might as well learn which verb to use, and be one of those people in the know. It's really not that confusing, and there's a certain satisfaction in knowing you're using the right word.

Lie or lay. The easiest way to understand the proper use of these two verbs is to focus on the following two sentences:

I'm going to lie down.

I'm going to lay the book down.

Lie means to recline—to lie down. *Lay* means to place—to lay something down. So *lie* is *intransitive*, not taking an object. *Lay* is *transitive*, taking an object.

This distinction is, I think, easy enough to keep straight. The difficulty lies in the various tenses. Study how the tenses change the verbs. You'll just have to memorize these changes:

I'm going to lie down.
I lay down yesterday.
I have lain down every day.
I have been lying down every day.

I'm going to lay the book down.
I laid the book down yesterday.
I have laid the book down every day.
I have been laying the book down every day.

Sit or set. *Set* means to place. *Sit* means to be seated. Here's how these two verbs change:

I'm going to sit here.
I sat here yesterday.
I have sat here every day.
I have been sitting here every day.

I'm going to set the book here.
I set the book here yesterday.
I have set the book here every day.
I have been setting the book here every day.

To be. Probably the most troublesome agreement problem for most students stems from the way the verb *to be* changes. If the constructions in the accompanying table don't sound natural to you, study them, use them in sentences, recite them until they do.

Agreement. Other agreement problems may arise when writers neglect to add *-s* or *-es* to the verb ending when there's a third-person singular:

I smell good.
You smell good.
He *smells* good.

I hit the ball.
You hit the ball.
She *hits* the ball.

Also, if the subject is compound and joined by *or* or *not*, make the verb agree with the subject closer to it:

Paul or the other Beatles have performed there, but not both.

Neither the brothers nor the father was there.

Finally, watch out for phrases that come between the subject and verb; it's easy to forget what the subject really is and make the verb mistakenly agree with a noun near it. The following sentence demonstrates correct agreement:

The girls, together with their brother, are going to be in town.

Punctuation.

If you think there are firm rules that cover punctuation in every situation, and that for any particular thing you want to say there's only one way to punctuate it, then you are in for a world of frustration and anxiety. We really don't have zillions of punctuation rules governing every contingency. Instead, we have some general guidelines that writers apply as they see fit.

Comma. The essential thing to understand is what a comma does: it signals a pause. It doesn't separate things firmly, saying, "This is different"; instead, the comma says, "What's coming next is related to what you've just read—it's just a different part."

Writer Anne Tyler, quoted in the box on the next page, uses the comma in this example to organize details—here one detail ends, the next begins—but it doesn't isolate them. Each detail is part of the whole picture of the sentence.

Another way to think of it is this: you probably need a comma anywhere you would pause as you read your writing aloud. If you need to indicate a stop, to signal the end of one thought and the beginning of another, you need something stronger than a comma: a connecting word like *and* or *but* added to the comma; or a semicolon; or a colon; or a dash; or a period.

There are a few major conventions that you violate at your peril. Otherwise, there's considerable leeway

Anne Tyler

for your judgment. Here are the most important things to watch out for with a comma.

Don't use only a comma to separate two independent clauses. This error, often called a comma splice, is considered major by virtually every writing teacher. Why? First, let's look at an example of the error:

I have been to see the new dealership, with money in my pocket I felt like a deer on the first day of hunting season.

As experienced readers move through this sentence, they are likely to believe they are reading this sentence:

I have been to see the new dealership, with money in my pocket . . .

The problem is that the sentence goes on past *pocket* until it is obvious that another sentence is coming up with "I felt." At this point, the reader has to drop whatever assumptions have been made and rethink the structure of the sentence. So the reason a comma splice is such a major error is that it often sends misleading signals to readers, confusing them and requiring them go back and correct their understanding.

Avoiding comma splices is easy enough. One method is to add a connecting word:

I have been to see the new dealership, but with money in my pocket I felt like a deer on the first day of hunting season.

A second method is to use another punctuation mark, such as a period, a semicolon, or a dash, to separate the two sentences:

I have been to see the new dealership; with money in my pocket I felt like a deer on the first day of hunting season.

Don't use unnecessary commas. For instance, don't put a comma between the subject and verb of a sentence, as in the following:

The desk Mike made last year, was constructed of virgin mahogany.

This sentence should be written as follows:

The desk Mike made last year was constructed of virgin mahogany.

The following sentence demonstrates a proper use of a comma because there is an interrupting dependent clause:

The desk, which was made in Asheville, was constructed of virgin mahogany.

But the sentence takes on a different meaning without a comma.

The desk which was made in Asheville was constructed of virgin mahogany.

The second sentence distinguishes this desk, made in Asheville, from some other desk, made elsewhere. Compare:

The boy who loves his mother goes to church.

The boy, who loves his mother, goes to church.

The first sentence makes a general statement: the sort of boy who loves his mother goes to church. I can imagine someone saying this to characterize those boys who love their mothers and those who don't. The second statement is specific: a particular boy, who loves his mother, does a particular thing—attends church.

A comma is not needed before a parenthesis. However, it is acceptable to put a comma after a parenthesis if the sentence structure allows it—that is, if a comma would be used if the parentheses were not there. The first sentence below is not correct, but the second sentence uses the comma correctly.

The new dress shop has been doing a booming business, (although Ada refuses to visit it) but it is in a poor location.

The new dress shop has been doing a booming

business (although Ada refuses to visit it), but it is in a poor location.

In other words, a parenthesis is ignored for purposes of punctuation. When a parenthesis ends a sentence, the period goes after the parenthesis; otherwise, the parenthetical material would hang between sentences, not attached to anything:

We went to the game (very bad). Afterward, we had dinner (even worse).

If the parenthetical material is a complete thought and does stand alone, then it can stand apart from other sentences and have its ending punctuation within the parenthesis:

We went to the game. (It was very bad.) Afterward, we had dinner. (It was even worse.)

Semicolon. A semicolon separates, indicating to the reader, "Stop; a new construction begins here; make sense of what you've just read; something else is coming now." Where you can use a period to separate sentences, you can also use a semicolon if the sentences are, in your judgment, too closely related to be separated by a period. With a semicolon, you can tell the reader to see two independent clauses together, while maintaining their distinctness as independent clauses.

John Steinbeck, who wrote the sentence shown in the box on this page, could have used a comma. But the semicolon signals a stronger pause, a stop, increasing the impact of the second sentence. The second sentence isn't a continuation of the first but rather its reversal, so Steinbeck stops the reader to set him or her up for that turn. A period, or a dash, or perhaps even a colon would also have been correct. In this case, as in many others, punctuation is not just a matter of correctness, but a tool of communication.

If the two clauses are complex, perhaps containing internal punctuation, then a semicolon is usually a good idea:

The ancient Egyptians built many stunning monuments; they did not build an impressive legal system respecting human rights, or administering justice openly, or applying the law consistently to all men and women.

Use semicolons to clarify sentences with conjunctive adverbs or transitional phrases. Take a look at these sentences:

You say we have done nothing. The task force has done some study, however.

Use of semicolons

(from "The Chrysanthemums")
A light wind blew up from the southwest so that the farmers were mildly hopeful of a good rain before long; but fog and rain do not go together.

John Steinbeck

These sentences make sense. The word *however* indicates that the second statement contrasts with the earlier statement. Compare them with a second set of sentences:

You say we have done nothing. The task force has done some study, however, it is not finished.

This second set of sentences may mean either of two things: (1) I contradict your statement, because the task force has done some study, and they are not finished yet. They are continuing to do something. (2) I agree that we have done nothing, because even though the task force has done some study, it has not finished. Nothing has been done.

The confusion arises because the reader does not know how *however* fits into the sentence. Does *however* go with "The task force has done some study" or with "it is not finished"? A semicolon would make the meaning clear:

You say we have done nothing. The task force has done some study, however; it is not finished.

You say we have done nothing. The task force has done some study; however, it is not finished.

Therefore, moreover, and other *transitional* words call for a semicolon rather than just a comma:

We want to win the tournament; therefore, we must get some sleep.

Semicolons can also be used to separate items in a series if the items are complex:

Our plumber used his rasp, the destroyer of wood; his hammer, the denter of cabinet finishes; and his flashlight, the seemingly innocent (but deceptively hard-edged) scratcher of laminate finishes.

Colon. Whereas the comma says, "Pause," and the semicolon says, "Stop and separate," the colon says, "Go on, look ahead, here comes something."

The excerpt from the writing of William Faulkner, shown in the box on this page, shows a good use of the colon. What follows a colon illustrates or explains what came before. Most people are aware that a colon can introduce a list. But a colon can really introduce just about anything: a quotation, a sentence, even a word. You can see how a single word can be introduced in this sentence: now.

Also use a colon after the salutation in a formal letter:

Dear Mr. Brown:

(Never use a semicolon after a salutation; but do use a comma if it's an informal, friendly letter.)

Another use for a colon is to separate a title from its subtitle: *Thanks a Hundred: Mastering the Art of Faint Praise.*

Quotation marks. Probably the main problem with quotation marks is knowing where to put them. Put periods and commas inside quotation marks, and put semicolons and colons outside. When there's a quotation within a quotation, use single quotation marks and double quotation marks, like this:

John said, "To quote a famous President, 'I cannot tell a lie.'"

Apostrophe. One job of the apostrophe is to show possession. If the possessing noun is singular, just add an apostrophe and an *s*. If the possessing noun is plural, add only the apostrophe: the horse's stable (singular); the horses' stable (plural). Personal pronouns are an exception: you don't add an apostrophe to show the possessive form of personal pronouns.

Our car is better than yours. Ours is working.

Also, if the singular noun ends in *s*, then you can use only the apostrophe, not adding another *s*, if that sounds correct:

The fans foolishly believed it was Coach Woods' fault.

Finally, apostrophes can be used to show that part of a word or number has been omitted, such as: "I can't bear to write out cannot" or "'57 Chevy."

Use of colons
(from "Barn Burning")

Hit's big as a courthouse, he thought quietly, with a surge of peace and joy whose reason he could not have thought into words, being too young for that: *They are safe from him. People whose lives are a part of this peace and dignity are beyond his touch, he no more to them than a buzzing wasp: capable of stinging for a little moment but that's all.*

William Faulkner

Dashes. Some handbooks will tell you, as one puts it, that "dashes should be used sparingly in college writing." What does *sparingly* mean? Many excellent, widely published writers use dashes freely—they are, after all, extremely versatile, lively, powerful marks of punctuation. So why should you use them sparingly? The advice seems similar to saying that "pitchers should use curve balls sparingly." Of course, if you threw a curve ball on every play, then hitters would get used to it, ruining its effectiveness. And if you used a dash in every sentence, its impact would be dissipated. The key is to use dashes effectively and judiciously. But be aware that some teachers and readers are not comfortable with dashes, and you should find out how your particular reader feels about them.

At the beginning, in the middle, at the end—dashes can be used to insert material into a sentence.

Dashes can be used—at the beginning, in the middle, at the end—to insert material into a sentence.

Dashes can be used to insert material into a sentence—at the beginning, in the middle, at the end.

Any construction that can be put into parentheses can also be put inside dashes. Dashes are often more dramatic, calling attention to the material, whereas parentheses suggest that the information inside is supplementary, or an aside.

Ellipsis points indicate that something has been omitted. You do not need to use an ellipsis if it is obvious you are quoting only part of a text:

William Price Fox told the interviewer that he "didn't like to think very much before writing."

However, when the reader would otherwise be unable to tell that material has been omitted, an ellipsis should be used:

William Price Fox told the interviewer that he "didn't like to think . . . before writing."

Ellipsis points should have a space before the first dot and after the last dot. To show that the end of the sentence has been omitted, just place a period before the ellipsis points. That extra period functions as the period of the sentence.

William Price Fox told the interviewer that he "didn't like to think. . . ."

Brackets have two functions: to insert clarifying material into quotations, making clear that the insertion is not part of the quotation; and to serve as parentheses inside of parentheses.

William Price Fox told the interviewer that he "didn't like to think very much [about his plots] before writing."

We felt very good (the report said, after all, "there was a profit" [page 7]).

Other conventions.

There are several more rules and conventions of writing that are helpful to know. Often college students think they know how to use these elements correctly but are mistaken.

Hyphens. Most teachers and editors prefer that you not divide words at the end of a line, so if you're using a word processing program that automatically hyphenates, turn the hyphenation off. (You should also turn off the feature that lines up—*justifies*—the right-hand margin: although the page may look neater with the right-hand margin justified, funny-looking spaces are often left within the line.)

One time you do need to use a hyphen is with *compound adjectives*. When you use two or more words together as an adjective modifying a noun, hyphenate the words if they come before the noun:

Deion Sanders is a well-known athlete.

As an athlete, Deion Sanders is well known.

End punctuation. You know, I'm sure, that sentences generally end with a period, but where appropriate, you can also choose an exclamation mark or a question mark.

Be reluctant to use exclamation marks: they're the equivalent of shouting, "Hey! Look at me!" Only rarely do you want to yell at someone.

Question marks, most often used at the end of a sentence, can also go in the middle when there is an interrogative element:

Is there anyone alive? was the question running through everyone's mind.

Other marks. There are a number of other punctuation marks that can be used to spice up your writing. As with any good spice, however, do not go overboard. A little goes a long way.

Use *slashes* to indicate options or pairs: "It was a boy-meets-girl/return-of-Godzilla movie." "It was an either/or situation."

Parentheses can be used to add information or commentary (like this). Note that the punctuation comes after the parenthesis, unless the parenthetical material is a complete sentence that is meant to stand alone. (There are sentences like that.) What's inside the parentheses is seen as nonessential. Whereas dashes draw attention to material, parentheses downplay the material, although parenthetical remarks can also be used like whispers or afterthoughts (oh yes), which can oftentimes convey the most interesting information in the sentence.

The feminist movement has affected middle-class values.

The feminist movement has affected the values of the middle class.

A string of modifiers can be used for comic or ironic effect. Many old-time blues songs used this form to good effect. One example to illustrate, written by G. Little and T. Lyman and recorded by Western Swing artist Bob Wills on the Vocalion label: "I've Got Those Wonder-Where-She-Went-and-When-She's-Comin'-Back-Again Blues."

A few *compound nouns* (made by putting two nouns together) are hyphenated: mother-in-law and city-state, for instance. Most compound nouns are either written together or as separate words. You'll just have to check your dictionary and also consider if hyphens would make your meaning clear. There is a big difference between a sold-out house and a sold out-house. As a general rule, the only compound nouns hyphenated are those made up of equally important nouns.

When you use *fractions as adjectives*, hyphenate; but don't hyphenate if the fraction is used as a noun:

We saw a one-third decrease in earnings in the last quarter.

One third of our earnings went down the tube in the last quarter.

Hyphenate numbers from twenty-one to ninety-nine:

One hundred twenty-nine people have won the Florida lottery.

Hyphenate *prefixes* and *suffixes* only to avoid confusion. For instance *re-count*, as in "to re-count the money," needs to be distinguished from *recount*, as in "she wanted to recount the entire story." Otherwise, if the prefix or suffix is clear, do not hyphenate.

Abbreviations. There are a few occasions when abbreviations are acceptable in formal writing, but generally you should avoid them. It's conventional to abbreviate designations before names: Mr. Gern, Mrs. Watermark, Rev. Cloud. But President Reagan or Professor Griffin or most other designations should be spelled out. Many agency names are also commonly abbreviated, often without periods: CIA, YMCA, NCAA, and such. Do spell out the names of cities, states, countries (except of course in addresses); do spell out names of people and companies, unless the abbreviations are the preferred form (IBM and NCR, for example; but Brooks Brothers rather than Brooks Bros.). And spell out measures (quarts instead of qts.).

Abbreviations

Some common Latin abbreviations and their meanings

c.	*circa*	about, as in "c. 1870" (about 1870)
cf.	*confer*	compare, as in "cf. William Shakespeare" (compare to William Shakespeare)
e.g.	*exempli gratia*	for example
etc.	*et cetera*	and so forth (note that "and etc." would mean "and and so forth")
i.e.	*id est*	that is
viz.	*videlicet*	namely

The reason most words are spelled out is quite simple: abbreviations can be unclear. Does *23 pts.* means twenty-three patients or twenty-three payments (or maybe even two three-point plays)?

Some abbreviations for Latin terms are commonly used, and you should know what they mean. But don't use them too much (especially *etc.*). Use English when you can. See the accompanying sidebar for examples of some of the abbreviations you are most likely to see in your college reading.

Numbers. The rules for numbers are numerous. In general, spell out numbers if they can be written with one or two words: eleven, forty-two. Also, spell out a number if it begins the sentence, or rewrite the sentence to avoid beginning with the number. Some exceptions:

• Use numbers for fractions and decimals: 8.7, 1/2.
• Use numbers for hours if *a.m.* and *p.m.* are used, and for dates.
• Use numbers if a sentence has a series of numbers.
• If you have two numbers together, spell out the first: "He kicked two 50-yard field goals."

Italics and underlining. In printed texts, the titles of books and other major works (such as musical compositions, paintings, television shows, newspapers, long poems, ships, and other things) are printed in italics, drawing attention to them as formal names. It's a convention. On your typewriter or printer, it is probably inconvenient to use italics, so most writers use underlining.

You can also underline words for emphasis (yes, for emphasis). And you can underline words or letters being used *as* words or letters: "The word bonkers really appeals to me."

Rules and superstitions

Some superstitions. Most superstitions are founded in fact, although that fact may be lost in antiquity. This is equally true of superstitions about writing. And, like other superstitions, some writing superstitions refuse to die out. Most instructors have favorites that they consider unbreakable. Find out how your instructor feels about any of the following superstitions before your grades are affected. Remember, it is always important to consider your audience, and, in the case of college writing, your instructor is your audience.

Avoid *I*. I can imagine how this "rule" first occurred to some well-intentioned grammarian: Having read essays by adolescents for hours and hours, and having determined that the students seemed to be interested only in themselves, this poor teacher decided to forbid the use of *I* as a way to get the students to talk about something else. Or perhaps, after reading hundreds of sentences that began "I think," a teacher decided "Enough! I know you think it [or rather "One knows you think it"] because you are saying it. In the future, avoid *I*." Still, although one can sympathize with the rule inventors, one can also see that the rule is silly.

The overuse of *I* is what we want to avoid—saying *I* when it is unnecessary. Good writers use *I* all the time. Even scientific papers often use first-person pronouns—usually *we*, since most scientific writing has multiple authors. It often sounds stilted to say "this writer believes," "in the view of this commentator" (which may be good for comic effect). And there's absolutely nothing wrong with saying *I* if you really mean *I*; unless, of course, your teacher forbids it. (In that case, write the way your teacher requests, or get John Trimble's *Writing with Style* and ask your teacher about what Trimble says.)

Avoid *you*. The problem with *you* is that sometimes writers don't really mean "you, the reader." Rather, they mean something more specific but use *you* as a vague substitute for what they really mean. Consider this sentence from an essay about what goes on at a basketball game.

The cheerleaders just want you to yell.

Since some of the writer's readers may have never attended a basketball game, *you* can't really refer to them. The use of *they* as a vague reference is similarly problematic. Just make sure you really mean *you*, and your reader can tell who *they* are.

Don't use contractions. Using contractions makes your writing sound informal, more like conversation than a formal essay. Throughout this chapter I've used contractions for an informal, friendly tone. But in academic writing, you really want to sound more formal; and in many work situations, especially in business letters and legal documents, you probably want to carefully restrict the use of contractions. Andrea Lunsford and Robert Connors, in the instructor's edition of their fine *St. Martin's Handbook*, offer this illuminating observation:

Fred Astaire would have sounded somewhat stiff singing "Is it not romantic?" while Abraham Lincoln would have struck an incongruously chatty tone had he said, "With firmness in the right, as God gives us to see the right, let's strive on to finish what we're in."

Even in formal situations, sometimes a contraction may be right, especially if the alternative sounds stilted or pretentious. When in doubt, however, you should probably err on the side of formality. You just have to consider your audience, your goal, the persona you put forward, the content of your essay. Such decision making is more difficult than simply following an injunction against contractions; but it's also more effective.

Avoid starting a sentence with *and* or *but*. Good writers start sentences with *and* and *but* all the time. There is no valid reason why learning writers shouldn't have access to this effective strategy.

So why is this rule so popular? Perhaps, again,

English Composition 93

because some teachers have been uncomfortable with informality, and such sentence beginnings do sound like a human being talking. Some of the most formal prose in our language, however, includes such beginnings. Sounding like a person talking on paper—if that talking person sounds articulate and intelligent—is not a liability. By no means. Obviously, you don't want to sound chatty or chummy, and you want to be careful not to overuse *but* and *and*. (Indeed, you want to avoid overusing any device.) You want to use a variety of sentence structures and not just string simple sentences together with *and* and *but*.

Given those cautions, begin sentences with *and* or *but* whenever you feel such openings will help your writing flow and enhance the conversational tone.

Don't write a very long or very short paragraph. Another superstition not supported by any extensive examination of what good writers do. Variety in paragraph length is refreshing. Of course, variety for variety's sake is not ideal, and you do want the length of your paragraphs to reflect the ideas they contain. Very

short paragraphs are dramatic, interrupting the flow, standing out, moving a bit faster. Very long paragraphs are useful, obviously, for working through a complex idea, for staying with a line of thought, for extending a meditation. Let your ideas and the effect you're trying to create determine the length of your paragraphs, and not some arbitrary rule.

Begin every paragraph with a topic sentence. In 1974, in the winter issue of *Research in the Teaching of English*, Richard Braddock conducted a study of "The Frequency and Placement of Topic Sentences" by examining how professional writers actually use topic

sentences. Braddock concluded that the usual textbook advice to begin every paragraph with a topic sentence is not supported by the evidence. Braddock found that less than a fifth of those experienced writers' paragraphs contained topic sentences.

What does this finding mean for you? Certainly you want your reader to be able to follow your logic. But there may be advantages to arguing your point in a particular paragraph without stating directly what that point is. Just presenting the evidence may convince a reader in the way that an assertion plus the same evidence would not. Also, paragraphs are often building on a point expressed in an earlier or later paragraph. Essays apparently come in chunks that may range over more than one paragraph.

On the other hand, basing his argument on work in psycholinguistics, Frank D'Angelo (in a 1986 *College English* article entitled "The Topic Sentence Revisited") has asserted that topic sentences do make prose easier to read, allowing readers to process information more efficiently. So, if your goal is simply to convey information, topic sentences may be of more value. If you're conducting an argument, I suggest you think about what you want to say and how you want to affect the reader, and not worry about whether every paragraph has a topic sentence.

Use specific and concrete language. There is nothing inherently good or bad about either general or specific, concrete or abstract language. Some older handbooks and style guides told students to "use specific and concrete language" in an effort, understandably, to get students to avoid vague and imprecise language. But general and abstract terms are essential to writers: without them, we cannot speak in general or abstract terms! A writer may well want to talk about the deployment of Napoleon's small artillery at the battle of Waterloo; but a writer may also want to talk about "war" in general, in the abstract.

What we find in good writing is a mixture of the specific/concrete and the abstract/general. Movement back and forth is effective, from assertion to evidence or vice versa. So, if you want to talk about "the car," that's fine: just include some concrete discussion. And if you want to talk about the windshield-wiper design on your blue Honda Civic, that's fine too: just include some reference to the general big picture.

Never use passive voice. Do use passive voice if you want to emphasize the passivity of the subject: "He was struck by a train while sitting on his front porch." Or if the agent of an action is unknown or unimportant: "The test tube was filled with nitrogen." Otherwise, most instructors prefer active voice unless you have some other reason for using passive.

Never shift verb tenses. What is important is to keep the reader oriented in time. It's when the reader can't tell what the author's point of view is that verb tense becomes important. Even a sentence can have several tenses if the writer's stance is clear.

Confusing stance: She told her mother that he speaks to her when he was dying.

Clear stance: She told her mother that he had spoken to her when he was dying.

Clear stance with multiple tenses: She will tell her parents that you have been the one who sits there.

Rules.

Although there probably are not any rules that always apply, the following rules are pretty solid. Most have been discussed previously in this guide and will just be reviewed here.

Avoid ambiguous or misleading fragments. Sentence fragments are groups of words that are incorrectly used as sentences. Sometimes these fragments take the form of a subordinate (or dependent) clause, which merely modifies another clause and cannot stand on its own. Other times, the fragments lack subjects or verbs that would allow them to stand on their own. A good way to find sentence fragments in your reading is by reading each sentence aloud. If each sentence is not a complete thought, if your reader, hearing only that sentence would go "Huh?," then it is most likely a fragment. Thus: "The boys in the band" is a fragment, and should be changed to something like "We are the boys in the band."

Distinguish correctly between *it's* and *its*. The confusion of the words *it's* and *its* is one of the most common mistakes in student writing. *Its* is a personal pronoun, just like *our* and *their*. It is used in sentences where an object is being talked about, for example: "John just built a birdhouse. Its orange roof can be seen three blocks away." In this sentence, *its* replaces the word *birdhouse* in the second sentence, thus acting as a pronoun. *It's*, on the other hand, is a contraction of the verb phrase *it is*. Contractions are often used in informal writing, less often in formal papers. When using *it's*, be sure you have a verb, not a pronoun: "Have you ever tried to fly a plane? It's fun."

Correctly punctuate the end of a complete thought. You can end a complete thought with a comma only if a connecting word like *and* or *but* and another complete thought follows. You can also end a complete thought with a semicolon if another complete thought follows. You can use a colon followed by a complete thought, a list, a phrase, or a single word. Don't connect complete thoughts with just a comma.

Don't shift tenses unnecessarily. (See the section on "Superstitions," above.) Note the word "unnecessarily." It is perfectly all right to shift tenses when

Unlike the Ten Commandments, most writing rules can occasionally be broken under certain special circumstances.

there is a good reason for it and the meaning of your sentence is clear.

Use an apostrophe for possessives. Most of the time, all you need is an apostrophe and an *s* for possessives. Remember that personal pronouns (hers, his, ours, yours) do not use apostrophes. (For more information, see "Apostrophe" in the earlier section above on punctuation.)

Use commas and semicolons correctly. Try to remember that a comma connects; a semicolon separates. (See "Comma" and "Semicolon.")

Make pronoun references clear. When you use *he*, *she*, or any pronoun, make sure the reader can easily discern the reference. *This* by itself is often obscure to readers; it's a good idea to avoid using *this* alone and just say "this concept," "this actor," or whatever.

Watch out for modifiers that dangle. A dangling modifier can be confusing in a sentence; for example: "Flying low, cows were seen downtown." The phrase "flying low" is not attached to any noun. Obviously it was intended to modify some agent who observed cows downtown by flying low. But because the phrase isn't attached, and is *dangling*, it naturally appears to apply to (or modify) the nearest noun: cows. So it sounds as if the cows were flying low. (Which could be pretty bad!) The problem is easily corrected: just make sure modifiers have the right agent expressed. Usually you'll find dangling modifiers hanging out at the beginning of sentences, and sometimes at the end. Here are a couple more examples so you can get used to spotting the dangling modifier: "Excitedly, the sports car was purchased at a modest price." (Was the sports car excited? This seems highly unlikely.) "Selected for teaching ability, the scholarship of professors actually becomes more important." (The scholarship wasn't selected.)

Make sure sentence elements agree. Subjects and verbs, nouns and pronouns need to agree. Problems with subjects and verbs often arise when these elements are separated; so in proofreading, pay particular attention to complex sentences.

Use the right preposition. Prepositions are often tricky. We say we saw something *on* television but *at* the movies. In English, the right preposition for a particular use is often a matter of convention. If you're uncomfortable with standard English, you'll just have to learn which preposition to use. You'll find the *Oxford Advanced Learner's Dictionary* to be particularly helpful on prepositions.

Use the right word. At some point your teacher will probably write *diction* or just *d* in the margin of a paper. You may have already encountered such a comment. On the one hand, it may mean that the words you choose seem not to fit the level of the paper. See if your diction might be too informal or casual, or perhaps too stuffy. On the other hand, such a comment may mean that the word doesn't mean quite what your teacher thinks you want it to mean. Look it up: a good dictionary will help you distinguish the meaning as well as the usual context of the word, and also help you pick another word.

Place quotation marks correctly. Notice where periods, commas, colons, and semicolons go when used with quotation marks:

"Like this."

"Like this," he said.

"Like this": yes, he said it again with a colon.

He said, "Like this"; she said, "Like this?"

Encouraged by their teachers, children can begin to learn some common-sense writing rules at an early age.

Improving your style

As you write more and more, your style will naturally improve. But expanding your options as a writer, enlarging your vocabulary and the kinds of different sentence structures you can use, usually goes along at the pace of very thick ketchup. Most writers think mainly about what they're saying; the options they have in saying it become secondary. As a result, most of us tend to stay stuck in the same old sentence structures and paragraph patterns. But there are things you can do to dramatically expand your stylistic repertoire, and this section discusses a few.

Imitation. One of the most powerful things you can do to enlarge your options as a writer is imitation, a writing exercise that has been around for hundreds of years. You'll be surprised how quickly and effectively it works. It involves, I will admit, some work; but it is also fun, sort of like solving a crossword puzzle or playing chess. And you will be surprised at the quality of the writing you will produce with this exercise. Here's how to do it.

First, find a passage that is stylistically interesting, one that uses sentence structures and punctuation different from what you characteristically use. You can find such a passage almost anywhere. You could ask your teacher to suggest writers whose style you should emulate, and read them. Anything by Annie Dillard, John McPhee, John Updike, George Will, Alice Walker, Roger Angell, Joan Didion, or Nora Ephron should get you started.

Second, after you've found a passage, write it out. Here's the opening of F. Scott Fitzgerald's well-known piece "The Crack-up":

> Of course all life is a process of breaking down, but the blows that do the dramatic side of the work—the big sudden blows that come, or seem to come, from outside—the ones you remember and blame things on and, in moments of weakness, tell your friends about, don't show their effect at once. There is another sort of blow that comes from within—that you don't feel until it's too late to do anything about it, until you realize with finality that in some regard you will never be as good a man again. The first sort of breakage seems to happen quick—the second kind happens almost without your knowing it but is realized suddenly indeed.

Third, read the passage over until you really understand it—how it develops, how it moves logically. This passage depends on a distinction between two kinds of blows, those from the outside and those from within.

For some people, style comes naturally; the rest of us have to work at it.

Fourth, write your own passage, following the structure of the passage. Your content should be different from the original, and you should use as few of the original's words as possible.

Following is an acceptable imitation. Notice how the sentences of the imitation follow the structure of the original.

> Of course all of teaching is a process of imparting knowledge, but the knowledge that is the most visible—the specific details that are found, or almost always found, in textbooks—the facts you recall and analyze and, in nervous times of testing, put down on paper, don't always last very long. There is another kind of knowledge that comes from people—that you don't notice or consider, until you realize that some knowing comes from interaction. The first kind of knowledge seems to be solid—the second kind seems almost not to exist but is nonetheless enduring indeed.

This is a relatively difficult passage, and you may want to begin by imitating single sentences, and then short passages of two and three sentences.

Here is an easier passage, but one that still can teach a learning writer (as we all are) something about the control of sentences. It comes from P. D. James's *Devices and Desires*.

Imitation is often helpful, but it can be taken to ridiculous extremes, as shown in this gathering of twins.

It was a disagreeable story and, coming as it did after the impact of the portrait, it provoked in Dalgliesh a mixture of depression and foreboding which he tried to shake off as irrational. He was glad to let the subject drop and they drove in silence until he left her at the gate of Martyr's Cottage. To his surprise she held out her hand and gave him, once again, that extraordinary attractive smile.

Here's an imitation of this passage:

It was a happy story and, appearing as it did after the festivity of the dessert, it provoked in Jacob a combination of contentment and joy that he wanted to savor as extraordinary. He was sorry to see the story end and they sat in silence until he asked about the pudding at the edge of the table. To his relief, they passed it down and blessed him, once more, with that marvelous taste.

Copying.

This suggestion may strike you as strange, but it really works. Like imitation, it's been used to teach writing for many centuries. More than one professional writer has revealed using this technique to understand a passage or to loosen up his or her writing. Just find a good passage and copy it.

You do need to write it out by hand. There's something about typing that may encourage you to roll along without paying attention to what you're copying. Don't just copy word by word, but rather study a sentence or phrase, then look away from it and write it out. Then check to see if you've copied it correctly. If not, make the necessary corrections. (Be sure not to include a copied passage in one of your own papers. Plagiarism is definitely frowned upon.)

Copying has been used as an educational tool for centuries.

98   **English Composition**

Quantitative analysis. Understanding your own style in a specific way can be revealing, and comparing your style to that of other writers can also be helpful. For instance, just to take perhaps the most obvious statistic, you could check to see how long your sentences are. Then you might compare your average to that of some other writers. Do your sentences tend to be shorter, or longer, or about the same? Some other things to count and to compare:

• The variation in your sentence length. Just make a chart of the words in every sentence and notice the fluctuation. How does your distribution compare to that of published writers?
• The number of *to be* verbs
• The kinds of sentences: simple, compound, complex
• The number of images or comparisons
• The number of modifying words
• The length of your paragraphs: how many words, how many sentences
• The variation in paragraph length

If you really get into counting and analyzing your prose, you will be interested in Walker Gibson's book *Tough, Sweet, and Stuffy*, which describes in some detail the three kinds of stylistic aberrations that Gibson considers most prevalent in modern writing.

Parallelism. Parallelism can give your prose a pleasing rhythm. It can add force and elegance to your writing, and it's not that hard to create. Here are some tips.

• Nouns in a series should be in the same form. The phrase "dancing, eating, and movies" should be changed to: "dancing, eating, and watching movies."
• Other parts of speech should also be parallel when they appear in a series. For example, "The actor moved behind the screen, around the column, and under the tree."
• Make the items in a list parallel. "The carpenter should follow the usual procedure: dip the furniture in solvent; scrape off the loose paint; sand out any large scratches."
• Parallel clauses are useful in placing ideas side by side for comparison, contrast, or connection. Good examples of this structure can be seen in the famous quotations which are shown in the box below.

Use of parallelism

Samuel Johnson

"There is much in your book that is original and valuable—but what is original is not valuable, and what is valuable is not original."

"The first half of life consists of the capacity to enjoy life without the chance; the last half consists of the chance without the capacity."

Mark Twain

John F. Kennedy

"And so, my fellow Americans, ask not what your country can do for you; ask what you can do for your country."

The research paper

Applying your knowledge. A large part of your academic career will be finding out what other people have learned through research, what other people who have studied and thought extensively have concluded about the world. This is, after all, what happens in most college classrooms. In addition to your regular classroom work, reinforcing and building on what you already know and are learning, you will be expected to read many different authors and theories, synthesizing these ideas, making them your own, and, finally, adding your new thoughts and discoveries to the known body of knowledge. Therefore, you will spend many hours in the college or university library.

Let's say you go into class, the professor assigns a research project or a term paper, you moan and groan and put it off as long as possible. Finally, you have to work on this paper. Your first inclination is to go to the library and find everything you can about the subject. *Stop! Resist the temptation.* Remember what you have learned about the writing process and consider this important fact: the best research papers are those in which the students "own" the work. In other words, your research paper will not be successful if you only report the things you found in other books. You are

trying to learn, but you also are trying to make a contribution with your thoughts and interpretations.

Methods of research. Before you run off to the library, sit down and write everything you know about the subject you are interested in. As with your other writing, you may be surprised to find how much you do already know. Or not. Use one of the techniques mentioned earlier on prewriting. Just answering some self-imposed questions will help you realize what you do and do not know. You may see a pattern or an idea for a possible thesis developing from your freewriting. Whatever happens, you will have a good start on the paper.

When "building" a research paper, the best foundation is an original idea.

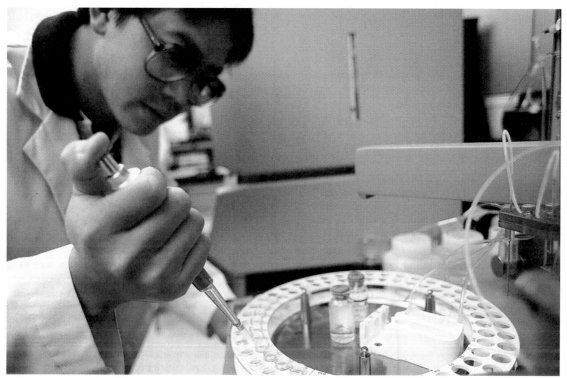

It all begins with research, whether you're performing a scientific experiment or writing a paper.

This paper is in fact most likely just an extension of the kind of writing you have been doing all semester. The only differences may be that this paper will be longer and require documentation to support your argument or your findings. It is critical for you to remember what you know about writing: the first consideration and the overriding questions of audience and purpose must remain in your mind as you go through each step of the research process. If your only audience is the informed professor, remember that she or he is knowledgeable, and do not fill your paper with all the things a professor already knows. If your professor recognizes that all good research needs to be shared with a wider audience, then find out who your audience is and what they know about your subject. Keep them in your mind as you take notes and later write the paper. Picture yourself talking to them, explaining to them, pleading with them.

Primary and secondary sources. The type of sources you need and the documentation you use are also determined by your audience. If they know all about Harry Truman's life, then you would be wasting your time to read and take general notes from his biography. You might, instead, look up a copy of a speech he made. This is what we call a primary source. Primary sources are *firsthand* accounts or the works authors themselves have written. They may include diaries, autobiographies, lectures, interviews, and speeches (all original information). This research gives you a chance to read and interpret for yourself and is another one of the things that makes the research your *own*. In addition to making your information accurate, primary sources can be powerful persuaders because your audience can trust the facts, and they believe you know what you are talking about. Your paper should rely heavily on primary sources.

Secondary sources, as the name indicates, often provide the same information, but it is filtered through another person. For example, you may find a newspaper reporter's account of the speech made by Truman, and that is the secondary source. Of course, you will want to read interpretations and conclusions and comments of other people. Their ideas can support yours or you can refute what others have said.

Observing, experimenting, and interviewing. There are other sources that will add life and interest to your paper. If it is possible, and here you may need to stretch your imagination, think of some type of first-hand knowledge to add to your paper. For instance, you may have a grandparent who remembers going to see Harry Truman on his whistle-stop tour. Interview your grandparent and include that as a source of information. In order for the interview to be most productive, you may want to wait until you have read and studied most of your primary and secondary sources before you conduct the interview. Go to the interview with a list of specific questions. Try to limit the scope of the interview and by all means record the interview.

If it is possible to observe some incident or perform an experiment in conjunction with your research, please do it. You will then be able to add your own findings to the body of existing knowledge with more focus and believable proof. You might, for instance, be working on a paper on the beneficial or detrimental effects of homework. Find some children and follow their daily homework habits. The list of possible sources is endless. If you do decide to include some hands-on research in your paper, you will probably need to discuss your plan with your professor.

Using the library. Before you decide to conduct an interview or an experiment, you probably need to get organized and get to the library. Some of the steps explained here may seem unnecessary, and you may be tempted to bypass them, hoping to speed up the process. Again, resist that temptation. You will save yourself much grief and, possibly, many hours of backtracking if you develop a methodical system and force yourself to stick to it. Eventually, you may change or modify this system to fit your own needs and personality, but for now, try to follow it closely.

It seems obvious to say that you must understand the layout and the rules of your particular library. If this is your first time there, go to the reference librarian and ask for a tour, or at least talk to her or him about the library. Please do not be shy. The reference librarians are there to help. They love the library, are proud of it, and want you to use it. They want you to succeed in college. Make them your friends. Probably, depending on your subject, the first place you will want to look is the card catalogue or the library's on-line computer system.

If you use the *card catalogue*, and you are preparing a paper for English on, say, Eudora Welty, you look up *Welty, Eudora* in the catalogue. You will find many cards. Go through them and read them because often you can save yourself time by eliminating books that are not related to your subject.

If your library stores the card catalogue on an *on-line computer*, be sure to use that. Although you may have to refer to the card catalogue for older materials not yet on computer, most of the holdings of that library will be on the computer. The computer listing will look like the sample shown on the facing page.

The sample indicates that Eudora Welty is still living, which will lead you to appropriate reference books. If you are working on her novels, this is a work

The New York Public Library

English Composition

Sample screen on electronic card catalogue

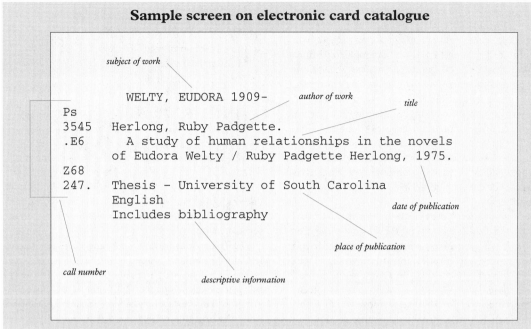

subject of work

WELTY, EUDORA 1909-   author of work

title

```
Ps
3545    Herlong, Ruby Padgette.
.E6       A study of human relationships in the novels
         of Eudora Welty / Ruby Padgette Herlong, 1975.
Z68
247.    Thesis - University of South Carolina
         English
         Includes bibliography
```

date of publication

place of publication

call number

descriptive information

You probably are familiar with the Dewey Decimal System—the way books are catalogued at your local library. But most college and university libraries use the Library of Congress catalogue system, and an example of that system is shown here.

you may want to read; it is, however, a thesis, which means that it is not published by a major company, and it is not likely to be a major, well-known resource. If you can locate major works, cited often by other works, published by university presses or major companies, then the resource is likely to be more valuable.

If you happen to be working on Welty's autobiographical essay, you may want to check the index and table of contents of this thesis; and the bibliography, completed in 1975, may be helpful for your work and lead you to other writings you need. There may be, however, a bibliography devoted to Welty: you'll just have to see. But any list of works about Welty can help keep you from wandering aimlessly around the stacks. Each electronic card catalogue listing will give you at least this much information (it may be a different kind). Just take a few minutes to read through each listing.

The computers in your college library are user friendly: many of them have instructions and on-line help available. Most of them are set up to help you locate a book by searching the following categories: subject, author, title, or key word. The searches of author, title, and subject are fairly well standardized, but the key-word search, allowing you to name at least one word that you think will be in the bibliographic record, may vary. Check with your reference librarian if you have trouble understanding the directions.

The first screen of the computer introduces you to the computer and tells you exactly how to access information (you are safe even if you have never worked on a computer). Just follow the directions. On most computers, you do not need even to worry about capitalization; so you just type in *K* (key word) = *WELTY EUDORA*. Then you will get a list of the holdings your library has by and about Eudora Welty. You probably will need to go one more step to read the individual record, and that just means you have to select one of the books: type in the number and the record will appear. Again, read the entire record.

Pay careful attention to the subject headings, because they are the best clues in determining if you should check this book further. Please note that this entry also tells you that the book is not checked out; if, however, the book had been checked out, then the date the book is due would be listed in the lower right-hand corner.

In addition to the books available in the stacks, the library has a variety of reference books such as *bibliographies* and *indexes* to help you. There is probably at least one room or section of the library set aside for reference. Logically, it should be near the reference librarian's desk. If you are having trouble starting or if the subject is unfamiliar to you, start with an encyclopedia. Usually college students think they are too sophisticated to read them (shades of a report you did in the fifth grade), but encyclopedias are good sources of general information.

If you have some understanding of your subject, you probably need to look first for bibliographies (listings in alphabetical order of books and articles on various subjects) and indexes (usually listings of periodicals, newspapers, and specialized journals) in the general area in which you are working. Sometimes finding the appropriate bibliography can be tricky (another time to check with your new friend, the reference librarian). Often using a key-word search or subject search on the computer will tell you what bibliographic materials and what indexes your library has and where they can be found.

There are general indexes, such as the *Readers' Guide to Periodical Literature* and the *Magazine Index* or *The New York Times Index*, which index articles found in newspapers and popular magazines that might interest the general public. You may want to read some of these, but probably you will want to concentrate on more specialized indexes—those which scholars contribute to—in your field of research.

There are some general, *standard reference books* you need to know. They will be helpful for background information as well as for specific facts and data.

• *The Oxford English Dictionary*, called the OED, is the most complete dictionary in the English language. It has fifteen volumes and traces the history and evolution of a word, giving quotations or examples of usage.

Specialized indexes
These are located in the "Bibliographies and Indexes" section of your library.
  • Humanities Index
  • General Science Index
  • Social Science Index
  • Monthly Catalogues of Government Publications
  • Business Periodicals Index
  • Essay and General Literature Index

• *The World Almanac* has been published yearly since 1868 and gives statistical data on all sorts of subjects. It also gives a chronological list of the events of the previous year.

• *The Times Atlas of the World*, one of the most complete atlases available, comes in five volumes.

• *The Encyclopaedia Britannica* is the most renowned multivolume encyclopedia. Unlike the *World Book*, it is written for college-level audiences. In addition to these standard works, many fields have their own encyclopedias and handbooks, as well as special yearbooks.

• And don't forget Bartlett's *Familiar Quotations*. You might find the perfect introduction or conclusion for your paper there.

How to get the book. Now that you have looked up your topic in many general references and on the computer, finally you can go to the stacks and get a

The reference librarian can be a great help during the research process.

book. Don't forget how important it is to have every number and letter down in the exact order it is printed in the card catalogue or on the computer. It is hard enough to find something in a large library even if you have all the information.

Your library should have a guide posted, showing on which floor your call number is located. When you get to the right floor, a more detailed guide will direct you to the right shelf. If you become confused, just know that you are not alone as you try to get your bearings. Wander in and out of the stacks, and don't be afraid to ask for help; the library staff is on your side.

When you locate the right shelf, you may find that the book is missing. This does not necessarily mean the book is out of the library. First, check the stack of books waiting to be shelved. If you still cannot locate the book, go to the reference desk and ask the librarian to put out a search for the book. Usually a book can be located within a week.

Developing the essay.
All the time you have been searching for material, you have been learning things about your subject. Keep adding to your initial freewriting. It is very important for you to assimilate all the knowledge you accumulate and make it your own. You are doing the work of a scholar, and that begins with a true understanding of the existing research, not just a list.

Reading and taking notes. As you pick and choose among the listings in the library—and you have that luxury because you have prewritten enough to narrow your focus—you should begin to develop your own bibliography. Every time you find a source that may be helpful, fill out a bibliography card giving the author (last name first), the title of the work, the name of the publisher, the place of publication, the date, and the call number of the book. In addition, you should number each of these cards with your own numbering system.

Besides developing a bibliography, you should be taking notes on notecards. Try to limit yourself to writing one fact or idea per card. Make sure you include the page number from which the information came on each notecard. When you finish taking notes, you will be able to shuffle the cards according to topics; and with your own prewriting notes, the paper should quickly form its own structure.

As you read and take notes, remember that you are serving as a filter for the information. Therefore, most of the notes you take should be in your own words. Of course, there will be some quotations that you'll want to include in your paper, and you should be very careful to copy these exactly. For the most part, however, you are trying to digest new and often difficult concepts in order to write about them, and you cannot do this if you simply copy the sources you are reading. You should have the following types of notecards when you complete your research and begin to write.

• Paraphrasings of what you have read
• Direct quotations that are powerful and provocative enough to be included in the paper
• Summary cards for new ideas or concepts
• Personal response cards that help you remember your insights and impressions as you read

Again, each of these cards should be labeled for content and source, including notes as to which are your

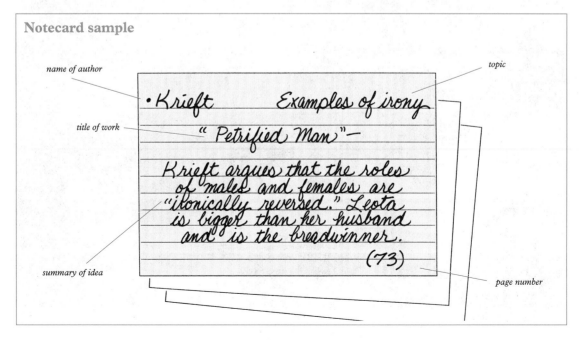

Notecard sample

name of author • Krieft   *topic* Examples of irony

title of work "Petrified Man"—

Krieft argues that the roles of males and females are "ironically reversed." Leota is bigger than her husband and is the breadwinner.

summary of idea

(73) *page number*

own ideas. It may seem silly for you to take the time to write down your thoughts, but the truth is that if you do not write them down as they occur to you, you may lose them. Trust this method, at least for the first time; then, if the process doesn't work for you, you can adjust it to suit your own personality and style.

Discovering your thesis. Whether you realize it or not, as you have gathered information and studied the opinions and facts surrounding your topic, you have been thinking about what you have learned. Now as you read through your notes or continue freewriting, you must develop a *thesis* out of all this.

The thesis, very simply put, is the idea or argument you want to present in your paper. It helps to consider your audience in determining your purpose. The most important thing to remember here is that more than likely you are writing for people who are familiar with your topic; therefore, this paper cannot just present the information that you have learned through research. The paper must have a purpose, a controlling idea, preferably a new interpretation of existing material.

If you have chosen a controversial topic, such as the disposal of nuclear waste in your state, it should be relatively easy to develop a thesis that includes your opinion and then write the paper in support of that opinion. If, however, you are writing for an English or history class on a topic that has been discussed many times, it may be more difficult to create a thesis that shows some originality. You can think about most topics as opportunities to persuade or argue your interpretation of the facts you have uncovered. Good writing almost always involves tension or conflict, and this research paper needs some conflict that it will resolve.

As you write and discover what you know, you may change this thesis, but you need to begin with at least a tentative thesis in your first draft. If you have a thesis, and your notes are labeled according to content, it should be easy for you to see where this paper is going and how to set it up. At this point, most textbooks would suggest you make an outline. If you are comfortable with that, do it. But sometimes it is harder to make the outline than it is to write the paper. Often, as you write, the writing will lead you where you need to go, and you will discover structure as you write. Use your notecards, especially the personal cards, and your

As you do your research, you should be developing a thesis.

freewriting, and begin to write. Think about your reader. All the ideas and information should logically connect to your thesis. Your aim is clear, straightforward prose—no gobbledygook and no pretentious vocabulary.

Avoiding plagiarism. One of the most troublesome areas that beginning researchers encounter is making sure to let the reader know when the ideas or the words in the paper belong to someone else. Although this may seem trivial to you, scholars and teachers take this very seriously. After all, thoughts and new insights are what scholars have to show for their work. If you created something with your own hands, you would not want anyone else to claim it and say she made it. The same is true of researchers. They want to be given credit for their creations. When you take another person's ideas or words and fail to tell the reader, you are stealing, or *plagiarizing*, to use the academic term. You may fail the paper, the course, or even be expelled from college for this offense.

To help you understand what is meant by plagiarism, look at the following examples. First, here is a quotation taken from page 34 of a work by Douglas Kimmel:

A second approach to studying the index of age is a longitudinal study. In this research strategy, a group of subjects is selected, appropriate for the question being studied, and is given a series of questionnaires, tests, or interviews periodically over several years.

This is a general statement of fact that you could find in any dictionary or encyclopedia; if you paraphrase this paragraph, there is no need to cite your source. The paraphrase might read like this:

Researchers choose subjects and give them tests and talk with them at different intervals over many years. This method of research is called a *longitudinal study*.

If, however, you quote from the passage, even just a

part of it, you will have to cite the source. For instance:

A longitudinal study is a research strategy in which "a group of subjects is selected, appropriate for the question being studied, and is given a series for questionnaires, tests, or interviews" at regular intervals over a long period of time (Kimmel 34).

There are cases in which a source must be cited even when there is no direct quotation, as when the source provides you with a new idea. In such cases you must tell your reader where the idea came from, even if you express the idea in your own words. For example, here is a passage from a work by Nancy Sommers, appearing on page 388:

The experienced writers see their revision as a recursive process—a process with significant recurring activities—with different levels of attention and agenda for each cycle. During the first revision cycle their attention is primarily directed towards narrowing the topic and delimiting their ideas. At this point, they are not as concerned as they are later about vocabulary and style.

When I paraphrase these research conclusions, I must give Sommers credit for her work. To do that, I could introduce the idea by saying,

As Nancy Sommers reports, one of the differences between experienced and student writers is the way they approach revision. Experienced writers, Sommers says, understand that revision takes place over time, on many different levels. Usually in the first draft, she argues, these writers are trying to get their ideas down and focused (388).

REMEMBER: Proper documenting of sources is critical to your academic career.

Quoting. As you are writing, there will be times you want to incorporate direct quotations into the body of your paper. Remember your reader. You may understand the quotation and know exactly why you feel it belongs where it does, but your reader has no idea. Don't just insert the quotation without explaining its purpose or introducing it. It needs to flow into the body of the paper just as if you had written it, or it needs to stand out as the authority and be introduced by whistles and bells.

You may edit the quotation slightly to make the verb agree or to avoid an awkward change in tense. But if you change any words, you must put your changes in brackets. If you delete words in the quotation, use ellipsis points—three spaced periods—to indicate the deletion. If the omitted words are at the end of the

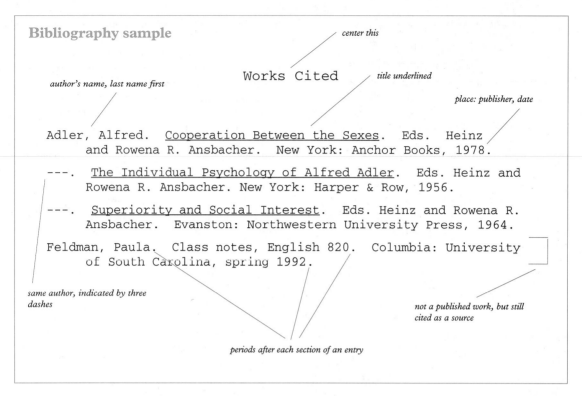

Bibliography sample

center this

Works Cited

title underlined

author's name, last name first

place: publisher, date

Adler, Alfred. <u>Cooperation Between the Sexes</u>. Eds. Heinz
    and Rowena R. Ansbacher. New York: Anchor Books, 1978.

---. <u>The Individual Psychology of Alfred Adler</u>. Eds. Heinz and
    Rowena R. Ansbacher. New York: Harper & Row, 1956.

---. <u>Superiority and Social Interest</u>. Eds. Heinz and Rowena R.
    Ansbacher. Evanston: Northwestern University Press, 1964.

Feldman, Paula. Class notes, English 820. Columbia: University
    of South Carolina, spring 1992.

same author, indicated by three dashes

not a published work, but still cited as a source

periods after each section of an entry

sentence, then use a period and the three points. If the quotation you are using is longer than four lines, do not use quotation marks; instead, indent one inch on each side of the quotation and single-space it. In the next section, you will see how to give credit to authors when you quote their work.

Documentation. Most fields of study have a preferred style of documentation. The rules given here are according to *The MLA Handbook for Writers of Research Papers*, published by the Modern Language Association. Using these guidelines, there are two ways to cite sources:

1. *Parenthetical reference in the text.* This is the easiest form to use. Within parentheses at the proper place in the text, put either the author's last name and the page number or just the page number if the author's name has been cited in the text. It will look like this: "The general's eyes gleamed as he read the penciled words in the lieutenant's note" (Lampman 55). Please note the placement of the quotation marks and the parentheses. There are no punctuation marks in the parentheses, and the period to end the sentence comes outside of the marks. If you mention the author's name in the sentence, only the page number with no other punctuation marks appears in parentheses. The *MLA Handbook* will give you more detailed instructions if you need them.

2. *End notes or footnotes.* These notes have two parts. First, at the place you wish to document, put a raised

number (no punctuation) in the text. Then at the bottom of the page on which the number is located, the footnote will give precise information on the author, work, and date and place of publication. Or your professor may prefer these notes, numbered consecutively throughout, on a separate sheet of paper at the end of the paper. Do not confuse this with the bibliography, or list of works cited, which must be included no matter what type of internal documentation you use.

For the bibliography, using the MLA style manual, list all the works cited in your paper in alphabetical order by author, last name first. The bibliography is normally titled "Works Cited" and is a numbered page of your paper. So if the last page of your text is 9, the Works Cited is page 10.

After the title, skip two lines and begin the first entry all the way to the left. Subsequent lines of the same entry are indented, so the paper looks like reverse indentation. For books, you will want to list the following items, as demonstrated in the example which follows:

1. Author's name, last name first, followed by a period and two spaces
2. Title of the book, underlined, and followed by a period and then two spaces
3. Place of publication, city (or state and city if city is unfamiliar), followed by a colon
4. Publisher's name, followed by a comma and a space

5. Year the book was published, followed by a period

Kimmel, Douglas C. Adulthood and Aging. New York: John Wiley and Sons, 1990.

Citations for magazine and scholarly journals have their own rules:

1. Author's name, last name first, followed by a period and two spaces
2. Title of the article, in quotation marks, followed by a period, close quotes, and two spaces
3. Underlined title of the magazine or the journal
4. Volume number, if applicable
5. Date of publication in parentheses, followed by a colon
6. Page numbers of the complete article, followed by a period. If the page numbers skip around, then include only the first page number and follow it with a plus sign.

Ortez, Alfonso. "Origins." National Geographic (Oct. 1991): 4–13.

As mentioned, there are other styles or formats that are used for documentation. The APA (American Psychological Association) style is used for research in the social sciences. The primary difference for parenthetical citations is the addition of the year and the use of commas (Kimmel, 1990, p. 77). Note, also, the addition of *p.* for page in the APA style.

Following the guidelines in the APA style manual, the Works Cited page becomes a Reference List. Here, the list is arranged alphabetically by author, last name first, followed by a period and a space, and then includes the following information, for books:

1. Date in parentheses, followed by a period and a space
2. Title of book underlined, followed by a space
3. Volume number or edition number, enclosed in parentheses, followed by a space
4. City of publication, followed by a colon and a space
5. Name of the publisher in as short a form as possible

A magazine article has a similar format:

1. Name of the author, last name first, followed by a space
2. Date in parentheses, followed by a period and a space
3. The name of the article, no underlining or quotation marks. Only the first word of the title is capitalized and it is followed by a period.
4. The name of the journal or magazine (capitalize all important words), followed by a comma

5. Volume number, underlined, followed by the page numbers, and a period. Use *p.* or *pp.* when referring to pages in a magazine article or newspaper, but not when you cite a journal.

If you are writing for a science course, you will probably use the *CBE Style Manual: A Guide for Authors, Editors, and Publishers in the Field of Biological Sciences*. The citations are numbered in the appropriate places in the text and refer to a list at the end of the paper with corresponding numbers. The list is called "References" or "Literature Cited."

The most important thing to remember about documentation style is to make sure you use the style that the instructor expects. This means that you'll probably want to purchase a copy of the appropriate manual for your paper.

Revision. Just as with any other paper you write, the research paper needs revision. If you have written on the computer, this will be much easier for you. The difference between experienced writers and student writers is the knowledge and understanding of revision, according to Nancy Sommers. She found from her research that experienced writers revise in levels and see the first draft of a paper as the place to put ideas and discover what you know. Once the ideas are down, the real work begins—the revision. Experienced writers then revise in order to put "shape or form to their arguments" (387), to decide what is effective and should remain, and what needs to be cut or clarified.

As you read your completed first draft (ideally, you should write it and put it aside for a few days), try to become a critical, objective reader instead of the writer: you want to sound like an experienced writer as you become one.

Read the draft aloud several times, checking for consistency and flow, organization of ideas, and, finally, errors in typing or grammar. Ask yourself when you finish the draft if you can summarize your own paper in two sentences. Could you draw the structure? Does one idea lead to another? In other words, are the connections between paragraphs and sentences clear? If you stumble as you read, that is probably a sign that a sentence needs to be reworked.

Every mark of punctuation is important, especially in the Works Cited and the documentation section. Teachers want to make sure you know how to do these two procedures correctly. So take the time to check each documentation and bibliographic entry carefully.

A final word about revision. Most textbooks will tell you to repeat the thesis in the conclusion (you may have been taught that in high school), but in a paper under a hundred pages, any instructor or professor can remember your thesis. You have stated it and defended it throughout the body of the paper. If it is not memorable or understandable by the end of the paper, you had better revise some more. This should not be just an exercise in mechanics; you are adding your special imprint to the body of known knowledge.

Final touches.

Hallelujah! The paper is complete, revised, and ready to be put into final form to be handed in. You have checked and double-checked the spelling, punctuation, and grammar, especially such things as verb and subject agreement and sentence fragments (two things college professors seem to pounce on).

The professor will tell you about the title page or cover sheet for the paper. It should be unnumbered and the title, not underlined or in quotations marks, centered or attractively arranged. Capitalize the first letter of each word of the title, except for conjunctions, articles, or *to* used as an infinitive. Usually in the upper left-hand corner, put your name, the course name, number and section, the professor's name, and the date. The title should be repeated on the first page of the paper, still no quotation marks around it, and you should double-space twice before you begin the text. The first page of the paper is not numbered, but the rest of the paper is numbered consecutively throughout, including final notes and the bibliography. The numbers go in the top right-hand corner and have no punctuation with them. You may place your last name in the right-hand corner before the page number, but you do not use a comma after your name.

There should be a one-inch margin all the way around each page. The paper should be doubled-spaced.

Once the paper is printed or completely typed, read it one last time, checking for errors. You probably cannot make it perfect, but the professor will at least know you are serious about your work.

Congratulations! When you finish your first research paper, you will have made it over an important hurdle in the College Olympics.

Check with your instructor regarding research paper guidelines.

English Composition

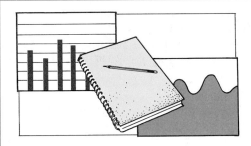

Tests, homework, and projects

Laying the groundwork

In building a house, it's important to begin with a strong foundation. In building a good academic record, that foundation consists of reading, notetaking, and studying.

Reading

Perhaps the most basic building block in mastering an English course or any course is reading. There's nothing quite like a textbook or other printed materials for communicating detailed information in a form that students can tackle in their own style, at their own pace.

When you first open your textbook, before beginning individual reading assignments, take a few minutes to get an overview of the entire text. Begin by scanning the table of contents, then perhaps read the introduction to each section. Flip through the pages to get a feel for number and type of illustrations, tables, and other graphic features. That way, when you begin each chapter you'll have a feel for its format.

Notetaking

The things that are fresh in our memories today are the forgotten details of tomorrow. Whenever you're reading or listening to a lecture or participating in a class discussion, keep your notebook open and handy to jot down key concepts and thoughts, so you can refresh your memory when reviewing later on.

Develop a shorthand of your own for notetaking, so you don't waste time writing out complete sentences and paragraphs. Take notes in outline form, using dashes or "bullets" to highlight brief phrases and key words.

Studying

Don't just read and absorb material mechanically. Make the effort to truly *study*. This means stepping back periodically and trying to see "the big picture," so that individual details can assume their proper place in the overall structure of the course. Remember, the purpose of studying is not to fill your head with facts, but to gain insight into how our world works.

Strategies for success

Much of your success in an English composition course—as well as in other courses—will depend upon your ability to write essays in class. Writing in class may seem to pose an entirely different set of problems from writing assigned to do at home. But really the only difference is time.

When writing an in-class essay, obviously you need to adjust to the impending deadline. But you still need to spend some time inventing, thinking of things to say; you need to think of your audience; and you need to spend some time revising, proofreading, and editing.

This advice may seem unrealistic. If you only have twenty minutes to answer an in-class essay, am I really suggesting you spend time prewriting and rewriting? Yes. Spend two or three minutes thinking and planning; spend fourteen or fifteen minutes writing; and spend two or three minutes reading over what you've written and making necessary changes.

If you start writing immediately, the odds are high that your first few sentences will be the intellectual equivalent of clearing your throat: as you write, you'll be figuring out what you're going to say, what angle you're going to take. Your reader is likely to be disproportionately impressed or depressed by your first few sentences. Although we can assume that teachers ordinarily read their students' papers all the way through, we must realize that in-class essays are likely to be treated differently: teachers are attempting, usually, to see what you know about something, and they are attempting to place your response into some letter-grade category. It may be even more important with in-class essays than with other kinds of writing that you start strongly. A little preparation goes a long way.

Make sure you understand the assignment. Then brainstorm: jot down your ideas using just a word or a phrase; then spend a moment organizing these ideas; then write.

Obviously you'll need to keep track of time, not spending too much time planning, and allowing time at the end for proofreading.

Practice writing under time constraints. This way you'll have a better sense of how much you can say in a given time period. Also, you'll gain some experience pulling your ideas together and expressing them quickly. Like anything else, you improve your ability to write in class with practice. Yet many students practice writing in-class essays only in class, when they're being tested. You wouldn't practice parking only when you're taking your driving test. You wouldn't practice foul shots only when you're playing a game.

By practicing in-class essay writing, you can also be doing yourself another valuable and essential service: namely, anticipating the questions you might be asked. In any given course, you can be sure there are certain important facts and issues your teacher wants you to be able to deal with. From year to year most teachers ask essentially the same questions on essay exams, just wording them differently. If you're thoughtful about what's going on in class, you can probably make a pretty good guess about the kind of questions that may be asked, and you can practice answering these. At the worst, you'll have spent some time thinking about course material, which can't be bad. At best, you'll have practiced working out an answer to a question that may be very close to one you're asked.

If you see you're running out of time, jot down words and phrases that indicate what you would have said given more time. If there are important dates or facts that the question obviously calls for, write those down. Although your teacher may not give you full credit for such shorthand information, you'll almost certainly get partial credit, and many teachers are quite generous if they can see you know the material and just need more time.

Strangely enough, some students feel that if they write poorly, their teacher will assume the illegible things say something intelligent. That's doubtful. More likely, teachers will be irritated by poor handwriting, even if they try not to be.

If your handwriting simply is terrible, I am not suggesting that you painstakingly print out each word. But if you do have lousy handwriting, and there's nothing wrong with your muscular coordination, then strive to improve your penmanship.

Finally, remove from your handwriting any eccentricities: don't dot your i's with a circle or anything other than a dot. Don't make exaggerated curly lines. Don't use a teeny-tiny handwriting; don't scrawl huge letters across the page. Your personality is unique enough without having to express yourself in your handwriting. Express yourself in what you say: that's a much richer medium.

Helpful hints

Essay tests

Unless you're instructed otherwise, skip lines and observe margins. Your paper will be easier to read and it will be easier for you to make legible corrections and changes.

Relax as much as you can. Just do your best. No one can ask for more.

Don't put yourself in a position where you have to cram all night. That's the least effective way to get control of information, and you'll find it more difficult to articulate what you do know. Of course, you know this already.

If, despite your best efforts, you still don't do as well as you would like, don't despair. Find out how you can do better: talk to your teacher; and if your school has a writing center, consider using it. Learning how to write quickly is a valuable skill, and you can do it.

Homework

Successful homework depends on organization. In college you may find yourself with acres of unscheduled time that appears to be free time. If you don't look ahead and schedule that time, you're likely to find yourself in trouble. So be realistic: recognize that a full course load in college is a full-time job. Make your studies your top priority, and you'll do well in school, sticking around long enough to have a good time also.

- Write down all assignments in one notebook.
- Get a calendar and also write the assignments on it as soon as they are announced.
- As assignments are given, make sure you understand them. Ask questions if necessary.
- Set aside a regular time for doing homework.
- Create a comfortable workspace. For most people, silence is important. If you think you are one of those people who work best with music on, make sure you're not really just one of those people who like to have music on.

Projects

Term projects can be among the most stimulating and enjoyable assignments you get in college. The trick is to select a topic which genuinely interests you.

Other suggested topics:
- The use of narrative voice and tone in the works of Ernest Hemingway and William Faulkner
- The rise of the South American novel
- Rap music: Is it poetry?
- The role of magazines in the history of American fiction

English Composition

Usage guide

*This sign looks **as if** it's seen better days.*

*Choosing **between** two files; choosing **among** many.*

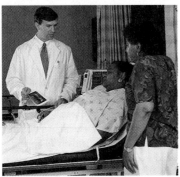

***Disinterested** (but not **uninterested**)*

accept, except. This sentence illustrates the difference in these two words, often confused: "The Congress voted to accept the treaty except for the final provision." Remember, *except* means "an exception."

affect, effect. *Affect* is usually a verb meaning "to influence": "The election affects everyone." *Effect* is usually a noun meaning "the result": "The effects of the election will be profound." Less commonly, *affect* is used by psychologists as a noun to mean "emotional state": "The teenager had a depressed affect." And *effect* is also less commonly used to mean "bring about": "The budget reductions will effect huge unemployment."

ain't. In most contexts, *ain't* ain't acceptable.

all right, alright. Many people use *alright* but *all right* is correct; *alright* isn't. Remember it this way: *alright* mispells "all"; therefore, it's wrong. *All right* spells both words correctly: it's right. All right?

alot, a lot. Use *a lot*, not *alot*. Like *all right*, the two-word version is correct. Some readers feel that *a lot*, even if it is spelled correctly, is very casual, shaky in formal writing. Consider using something else if it will work as well.

among. See *between*.

as. See *like*.

assure, ensure, insure. Use *assure* to talk about making a person certain: "I want to assure you I am ready." Use *ensure* to talk about objects or actions: "I want to ensure the brakes will work." Use *insure* with regard to finances and insurance: "I want to insure my house against falling frozen turkeys."

bad, badly. *Bad* is an adjective, *badly* an adverb: "She sang so badly the audience felt bad." In that sentence, *badly* modifies the verb "sang"; *bad* modifies the noun "audience."

between. The general rule is to use *between* for two persons or things, and use *among* for more than two: "The feud between Jake and the Fatman is over"; "The feud among the networks is over." But you can use *between* for more than two if a close relationship is intended.

bring. See *take*.

can, may. Although the distinction seems a bit fussy to some, *can* refers to an ability: "Can he ski?" asks whether he is able. *May* refers to permission: "May he ski?" requests permission.

cannot. Although *cannot* is preferred, *can not* is also acceptable if special emphasis on "not" is desired.

center on, center around. Many authorities believe *center on* should be used instead of *center around*.

conscious, conscience. *Conscious* means awareness; *conscience* refers to the moral sense.

consensus. There's no need to say "consensus of opinion" or "general consensus" because *consensus* means "the shared opinion." So "consensus of opinion" says literally "the shared opinion of opinion."

continual, continuous. A *continual* process is repeated regularly. A *continuous* process is ongoing, without interruption.

criterion, criteria. *Criterion* is singular: "We judge beauty contestants by only one criterion." *Criteria* is plural and therefore, obviously, shouldn't be used for only one standard: "We judge beauty contestants by many criteria."

data. Though originally a plural noun (the singular is *datum*), the word *data* can be used as either a plural or a singular ("mass") noun. The plural form is most often found in the fields of research and statistics.

different from, different than. Many people feel *different from* sounds better: most usage guides say something like "generally preferred in formal writing." You may find, however, when a long clause follows, that *different than* sounds better.

disinterested, uninterested. You would probably want to be judged by a "disinterested jury," because *disinterested* means they would have no prejudice, no special interests in the case. An "uninterested jury" would be likely not to pay close attention, because *uninterested* means having no interest, being bored.

ensure. See *assure.*

etc. This abbreviation stands for *et cetera*, Latin for "and so forth." Thus, "and etc." literally says "and and so forth." Just put a comma before *etc.*, without an "and": "We want hot dogs, cole slaw, french fries, etc."

farther, further. *Farther* is used with physical distance, *further* with abstract concepts. You travel farther down the road; you try to *further* your career.

first, firstly. *Firstly* appears in British English (along with *secondly*, *thirdly*, and so on). For an American audience, use *first, second, third*, and so on. You may also use numbers in parentheses: (1), (2), and (3).

flammable, inflammable. Though these two words sound and look like opposites, they are in fact synonyms.

good, well. Don't use *good* as a substitute for the adverb *well*: "The team played well" (not "good").

imply, infer. Speakers or authors *imply*; listeners or readers *infer*. To imply something is to hint at it, to suggest it rather than say it directly. To infer is to receive the meaning, to figure it out. The words mean, in other words, very different things: one is passing on, giving; the other is taking in, receiving.

inflammable. See *flammable.*

insure. See *assure.*

irregardless. Although sometimes people say *irregardless* is not a word, obviously it is one: there it is. But it is not a good word, by most people's standards: it means simply "regardless," so why add the useless *ir-*?

its, it's. *It's* means "it is." *Its* is the possessive pronoun. The problem is that possessive forms usually have an apostrophe: Steve's, Mary's, the team's. But note that *hers, yours, ours*, and *theirs* do not take an apostrophe. *Its* works the same way in the possessive, allowing *it's* to stand for the contraction of "it is." You might try thinking of it this way: with *its*, the *s* belongs to the *it*—it is possessive. With *it's*, the apostrophe marks a space where something is missing, namely the *i* in *is*.

lay, lie. The verb *to lie* is used when there is no object: "I will lie on the ground." *To lay* is used when there is an object: "I will lay my books on the ground." (Of course, the issue is muddied by the fact that the past tense of *lie* is *lay*. But that's another story.)

like, as, as if. When trying to decide whether to use *like* or *as*, check to see if a verb follows. If it doesn't, then use *like*, which functions like a preposition: "He wanted a friend like his dad's." If a verb does follow, then use *as*, which can function like a preposition or a conjunction leading to a clause: "He wanted a friend, as every man wants one." Here's an example: "The doctor worked *like* a machine, *as if* she were possessed by some healing spirit."

loan. There is some disagreement about the use of this word as a verb, in place of the word *lend*. Many would say that it is technically correct; however, many others could be found who would disagree strongly. Since one of these latter might be your instructor, it's probably best to use *lend* instead, reserving *loan* for use as a noun.

loose, lose. *Loose* means "not attached." *Lose* means "to come to be without something." For example: "If you keep your keys *loose* you may *lose* one."

may. See *can.*

media. This is a plural noun; its singular is *medium*. It is incorrect to say "The media is . . ." unless you're working in the very specialized world of advertising, in which the singular form is usually considered acceptable.

none. *None* can be either singular or plural, depending on the noun that follows: "None of the park has been renovated"; "none of the children were playing." If there is no noun following, then decide yourself whether you mean *none* of a single thing or *none* of two or more.

only. This word causes trouble if it isn't placed next to what it modifies. Notice the difference in these two sentences:

Professor Grumpy gives C's only to those students he doesn't know.

Professor Grumpy only gives C's to those students he doesn't know.

The first sentence says that only those unknown students will get C's: everyone else will get some other grade. The second sentence says that those unknown students can only get C's: that's the highest grade they'll get.

people, persons. Though it is a rule not strictly followed, the use of *persons* is preferred when a particular number is being specified: "This elevator carries a maximum load of 15 persons."

precede. *Precede* means to come before, but it is often misspelled because it sounds like *proceed*. But the two are spelled differently, as you can see.

principal, principle. A *principle* is a truth, a rule, an idea. This word is always a noun. *Principal* means "the leader," "the chief official," "the money invested or loaned." As an adjective, *principal* means "the chief," "the most significant." If you remember that the school princi*pal* is your "pal," you can keep these two straight.

reason, because. Many writers think it is necessary to use both of these words in the same sentence, but it is redundant. Instead of "The *reason* he left is *because* the food was gone," say "He left *because* the food was gone," or "The *reason* he left is that the food was gone."

shall, will. Today we use *will* in almost every situation, but decades ago a distinction was made: I *shall*, we *shall*, you *will*, they *will*, he/she/it *will*. "I shall" and "we shall" sound very stuffy and fussy to most people, although *shall* can be used for emphasis: "He *shall* come at four o'clock or he's fired."

take, bring. Correct choice depends on the speaker's location. I *take* an object to another location; you *bring* an object to my location.

their, they're, there. Most writers know what they should use when they misuse these words, but it is difficult to keep the mistake from showing up in papers. Remember the correct usage of these words and double-check for them. "*Their* word is not reliable; *they're* going to build the office right *there* on the nature preserve."

therefore. *Therefore* can be used in place of the word *so*:

I passed the final examination; so I will pass the class.

I passed the final examination; therefore I will pass the class.

The two words should not be used together, as this is redundant:

I passed the final examination; so therefore I will pass the class.

uninterested. See *disinterested*.

unique. All the handbooks say that "very unique" makes no sense. Personally, it makes perfect sense to me: a man with purple hands is *unique*; a man with eleven purple hands that flash Morse code is *very unique*, in my opinion. But almost everyone else will think "very unique" is poor usage.

used to, use to. Use *used to*. In speech the final *d* tends not to be heard, but it should be retained: "I *used to* go there every Friday."

who's, whose. *Whose* is possessive; *who's* is the contraction for "who is." For example: "*Who's* going to find out *whose* car was hit?"

would of, would have. Use *would have*. *Would of* is a decayed version, an error based on what "would have" sounds like when some people say it. *Have* should also follow *could, should, might.*

your, you're. *You're* is the contraction for "you are." *Your* is possessive. For example: "*You're* not in *your* right mind."

For further reading

Ede, Lisa. *Work in Progress: A Guide to Writing and Revising.* 3rd ed. New York: St. Martin's, 1995.

Elbow, Peter. *Writing with Power: Techniques for Mastering the Writing Process.* New York: Oxford, 1981.

Hairston, Maxine. *Successful Writing.* New York: Norton, 1992.

Lanham, Richard. *Analyzing Prose.* New York: Scribner's, 1983.

Lynn, Steven. *Texts and Contexts: Writing About Literature with Critical Theories.* 2nd ed. New York: HarperCollins, 1997.

Strunk, William, Jr., and E. B. White. *Elements of Style.* 3rd ed. New York: Macmillan, 1979.

Trimble, John. *Writing with Style.* Englewood Cliffs, N.J.: Prentice-Hall, 1975.

Williams, Joseph. *Style: Ten Lessons in Clarity and Grace.* Glenview, Ill.: Scott, Foresman, 1988.

Calculus

- Functions: Limits and continuity
- Differentiation
- The operation of integration
- In search of an antiderivative
- Applications: Definite integrals
- Infinite sequences and series

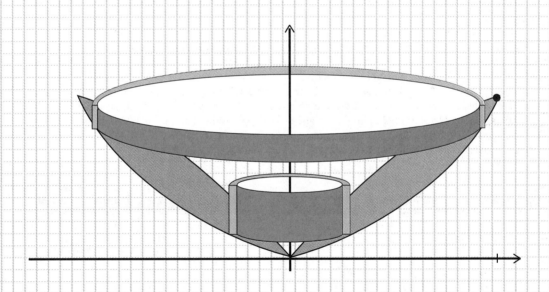

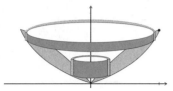

Calculus

It is a well-kept secret that calculus is one of the greatest accomplishments of the human intellect. There are two main branches of study within calculus: differential calculus and integral calculus. Since the times of the ancient Greeks, mathematicians had been laying the foundations for these two branches of study. It wasn't until the seventeenth century that an Englishman, Isaac Newton, and a German, Gottfried Leibniz, discovered independently the connection between these two branches of study. You will share in their great discovery in your study of the fundamental theorem of calculus in the third section of this chapter.

Why are the glories of calculus such a well-kept secret? In many cases, the teaching and learning of calculus puts the main emphasis on "working the problems and getting the right answer." This can smother your opportunity to understand the concepts that underlie the procedures.

Throughout this chapter, we will work many, many problems of the type found in a traditional calculus course. In addition, many exercises are included that will help you to understand the concepts. The problems that are geared toward the understanding of a concept will be much easier to work with a graphics calculator.

Even if your school does not allow a graphics calculator on tests, I would encourage you to buy one for study reasons. The ability to generate graphs quickly and precisely, and to generate tables of values, will not only help you to understand the concepts of calculus, but might also save you some study time. With that in mind, we are including references and exercises that make use of a graphics calculator. However, if you do not own one, you should have no trouble following the text or learning the material.

Functions: Limits and continuity

Before we start to talk about calculus, we need to collect some tools of the trade—the tools of mathematical *functions*. Just as experienced craftspeople are comfortable with the tools of their trade, so should you be comfortable with some of the algebraic and geometric aspects of a mathematical function.

The rest of this section is spent using functions to talk about our first calculus topic: the concept of limits. In fact, we might define calculus as the study of limits, since we will be talking about many different types of limits throughout the following sections.

Functions and graphs. Let's say we define a mathematical function, such as $C(m) = 0.6m + 2$ (read this "C of m is equal to 0.6 times m plus 2").

Why studying calculus pays off Reason #1

Students who plan on doing any decision making in their life, whether it be on the job or at home, will benefit by learning calculus. It can be said that calculus is the study of limits. Any decision maker must not only be aware of the limits of the elements involved in any decision-making process, but also could benefit by having a way to quantify these limits. Additionally, the language and logical structure of the study of limits in calculus could greatly benefit a decision maker.

Functions

Linear

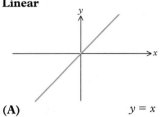

(A) $y = x$

Quadratic

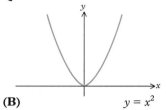

(B) $y = x^2$

Cubic

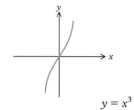

(C) $y = x^3$

Higher-degree polynomial

(D)

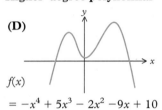

$f(x)$

$= -x^4 + 5x^3 - 2x^2 - 9x + 10$

Rational

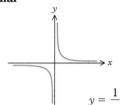

(E) $y = \dfrac{1}{x}$

Radical

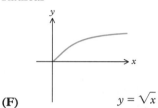

(F) $y = \sqrt{x}$

Exponential

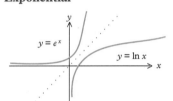

(G)   **Logarithmic**

Absolute value

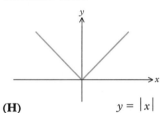

(H) $y = |x|$

Greatest integer

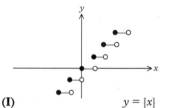

(I) $y = [x]$

Piecewise defined

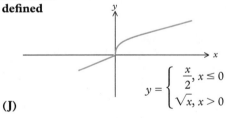

$y = \begin{cases} \dfrac{x}{2}, & x \le 0 \\ \sqrt{x}, & x > 0 \end{cases}$

(J)

Sine and cosecant

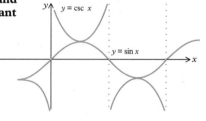

(K)

Cosine and secant

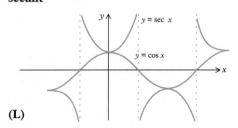

(L)

Tangent and cotangent

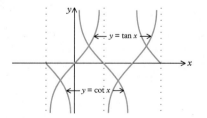

(M)

Typically, we use such a formula to *model* a situation in the physical world. Perhaps $C(m)$ represents the *cost* of a cab ride as a function of the number of *miles* traveled. How much would it cost to go 12 miles? Let $m = 12$ in the formula.

$$C(12) = 0.6(12) + 2 = \$9.20$$

How much would it cost to go 30 miles?

$$C(30) = 0.6(30) + 2 = \$20$$

A powerful visual representation of a function can be obtained by plotting pairs of numbers that relay information about the function, for example, (miles, cost), (12, 9.2), (30, 20).

Now these input and output values may be plotted as *ordered pairs* in a *rectangular coordinate system* (or *xy*-plane); the first number in the pair (called the *abscissa*) would be the input value, and the second number in the pair (called the *ordinate*) would be the output value.

Before you graph this function on your calculator, we should agree on some graphics screen conventions. Most graphics calculators allow you to define what portion of the *xy*-plane you wish to look at with the RANGE key. The portion of the plane we are looking at will be referred to as the *viewing rectangle*. Throughout this article, the notation [*XMIN, XMAX*], *Xscl* and [*YMIN, YMAX*], *Yscl* will be used to indicate a specific viewing rectangle for a function.

Exercise
Graph $y = 0.6x + 2$ on [0, 40], 5 and [0, 25], 5. Use TRACE along the function to find the ordered pairs identified above. You may not be able to get the exact values because of the resolution on the screen. How far can you go for \$14?

NOTE: Answers to exercises can be found beginning on page 596.

The functions illustrated on page 119 should all be familiar to you from your previous math courses. These functions will be used over and over again throughout your study of calculus. You should certainly be familiar with all of them, in the sense that when you see an equation, you should have a general idea of what the graph is going to look like, and vice versa. For example, a parabola could not possibly have an equation like $f(x) = 10x - 11$. (Why not?)

We have been talking about, and looking at, functions without giving a formal mathematical definition:

Definition
A *function* is a formula that assigns to each element in the *domain* a unique element in the *range*.

HINT: This definition should be memorized. It is useful and important.

Important characteristics of the graph of a function

Make a habit of labeling *x*- and *y*-intercepts on all graphs. Also, if a function has asymptotes, these should be drawn as dashed lines and labeled: $x = x_0$ for vertical asymptotes, $y = y_0$ for horizontal asymptotes.

Examine the graph carefully and make a mental note of things like symmetry and smoothness. Is the function one-to-one? What is the domain and range of the function? All of these characteristics will take on new meaning as we study the concepts of calculus.

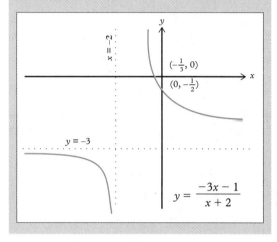

From our cab fare function, is it possible for a 12-mile ride to yield two different costs? The fact that the range (or output) value must be unique for each domain (or input) value is a very important feature of a function. Graphically, this means that the function passes the *vertical line test*; that is, a vertical line drawn anywhere on the graph crosses the function only once.

Exercise
Visually confirm that the vertical line test holds for all the graphs shown on page 119.

It is important that you have a good understanding of the domain and range of a function. Let's explore these concepts algebraically and graphically (see graph opposite).

Refer to graphs A through D on page 119. These are all polynomial functions, which are made up of sums and differences of positive integer powers of x. The domain of *any* polynomial function is all real numbers because you can multiply or add any real number and the output will be a real number. The range of a polynomial varies and is best determined graphically. For example, the range of $y = x^2$ is all nonnegative real numbers. This can be expressed several ways.

$$Domain: x \in \mathbf{R} \text{ or } x \in (-\infty, \infty)$$
$$Range: y \geq 0 \text{ or } y \in [0, \infty)$$

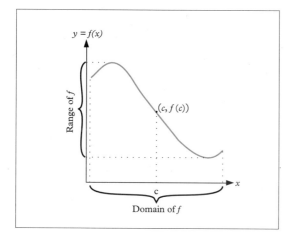

Exercise
Graph $y = 3x^4 - 14x^3 + 24x - 3$ in the viewing rectangle [-4, 6], 1 and [-80, 40], 10. Use TRACE to determine the minimum value in quadrant IV. What is the range of this function?

Now let's consider the rational function

$$y = \frac{1}{x}.$$

Remember, division by 0 is undefined, so

$$Domain: \mathbf{R}, x \neq 0$$
$$Range: \mathbf{R}, y \neq 0.$$

Notice that the line $x = 0$ is a vertical *asymptote*, and the line $y = 0$ is a horizontal *asymptote* on the graph.

Definition
An *asymptote* is a line that the graph of a function gets close to as x gets very large, as in

$$\lim_{x \to \infty} \frac{1}{x} = 0,$$

or very small, as in,

$$\lim_{x \to -\infty} \frac{1}{x} = 0.$$

(These two limits should be memorized.) When considering $\lim_{x \to \infty} \frac{1}{x} = 0$, you could say that as x gets larger, the graph of $y = \frac{1}{x}$ is approaching 0 from above (getting closer to 0 through smaller positive numbers). When considering $\lim_{x \to -\infty} \frac{1}{x} = 0$, you could say that as x gets smaller, the graph of $y = \frac{1}{x}$ is approaching 0 from below (getting closer to 0 through smaller negative numbers).

Consider another example of a rational function

$$f(x) = \frac{2}{x^2 - x - 2}.$$

To determine the domain of a rational function algebraically, set the denominator equal to zero, solve for x, and eliminate those numbers from the domain.

$$x^2 - x - 2 = (x + 1)(x - 2) \Rightarrow x = -1, 2$$

So that, *Domain*: $\mathbf{R}, x \neq -1, 2$. Now the range might be easier to determine graphically.

Exercise
Graph $y = f(x)$ in the viewing rectangle $[-5, 5]$, 1 and $[-3, 3]$, 1. You can see that $y = 0$ is a horizontal asymptote. TRACE to find the maximum value of the lower branch in quadrant IV. Can we agree that
$$Range: f(x) \leq \frac{-8}{9} \cup f(x) > 0?$$

Consider the radical function $g(x) = \sqrt{2x + 3}$. We would like the radicand to be nonnegative, so solve the inequality

$$2x + 3 \geq 0$$
$$x \geq \frac{-3}{2}.$$

Graph $y = g(x)$ in $[-5, 5]$, 1 and $[-3, 3]$, 1.

Can we agree that

$$\text{Domain: } x \geq \frac{-3}{2} \text{ or } x \in \left[\frac{-3}{2}, \infty\right)$$

$$\text{Range: } g(x) \geq 0 \text{ or } g(x) \in [0, \infty)?$$

Exercise
Make a table that has the same number of blocks as "Functions" on page 119. In each block, write the domain and range of the function in the corresponding function from the chart.

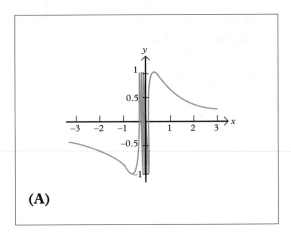

(A)

The functions that model phenomena in the physical world are, most commonly, combinations of the functions found on page 119.

Let $L(x) = x$, $R(x) = \dfrac{1}{x}$, and $S(x) = \sin x$.

Some examples of algebraic combinations are

$$G(x) = L(x) + S(x) = x + \sin x$$

$$M(x) = L(x) \cdot S(x) = x \sin x$$

$$Q(x) = \frac{L(x)}{S(x)} = \frac{x}{\sin x}.$$

(B)

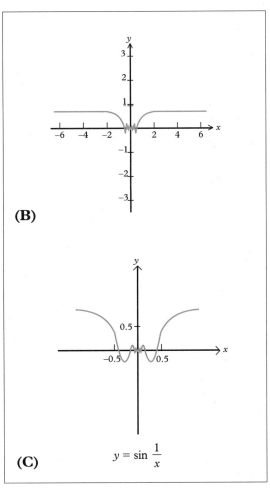

Exercise
Graph $y = G(x)$ in $[-10, 10]$, 1 and $[-10, 10]$, 1. Write a few sentences to describe why the graph looks the way it does. What is the domain and range of $G(x)$? How does that compare to the domain and range of $L(x)$ and $S(x)$? Do the same exercise for $M(x)$ and $Q(x)$.

Now suppose that the outputs of $R(x)$ are the inputs of $S(x)$. Then what we get is a *composition* of functions, written

$$S \circ R = S[R(x)] = \sin \frac{1}{x}.$$

It is virtually impossible to obtain a precise graph of this function in the neighborhood $-1 < x < 1$ because the output values are changing so rapidly (see graph A). Why can we say that $y = 0$ is a horizontal asymptote for very large and very small values of x?

(C) $y = \sin \dfrac{1}{x}$

Graphs B and C show why it may be necessary in some cases to use ZOOM to get a better idea of functional behavior.

Greek alphabet

A	α	alpha	N	ν	nu
B	β	beta	Ξ	ξ	xi
Γ	γ	gamma	O	o	omicron
Δ	δ	delta	Π	π	pi
E	ϵ	epsilon	P	ρ	rho
Z	ζ	zeta	Σ	σ	sigma
H	η	eta	T	τ	tau
Θ	θ	theta	Y	υ	upsilon
I	ι	iota	Φ	ϕ	phi
K	κ	kappa	X	χ	chi
Λ	λ	lambda	Ψ	ψ	psi
M	μ	mu	Ω	ω	omega

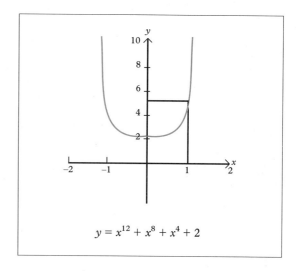

$$y = x^{12} + x^8 + x^4 + 2$$

Limits: An intuitive approach.

When you are a student of mathematics, you must learn a new language. And with the new language come new symbols. Before you read on, familiarize yourself with some of the characters in the Greek alphabet, since many of them will turn up in your study of calculus.

Until now, the equal sign has played a dominant role in your mathematical thinking. Calculus begins with a more subtle type of mathematical thought: the idea of a *limit*, which implies "close to" rather than "equal to." We will now explore the concept of limits.

You may feel that too much time is spent on fairly obvious questions like, "How close is close enough?" Your ability to make sense of and answer such questions, however, will put you in a good position to understand some of the later concepts of calculus.

To introduce the idea of a limit, let's consider the function $f(x) = x^{12} + x^8 + x^4 + 2$ (see graph this page). We see that when $x = 1$, $f(x) = 5$. But what about $f(x)$ when x is close to 1? To explore this question, we will use the notation that will be used in the more formal definition of a limit.

Let's refer to the number in the domain we are trying to get close to as c; in this example, $c = 1$. Now let's say we start 1 unit to the left of c and approach it from the left, always recording the $f(x)$ values as we get closer to c. Then we will start 1 unit to the right of c and approach it from the right, again recording the $f(x)$ values as we get closer to c. We need to know how close we are to c at all times. This distance will be referred to as Δx, read "delta x," which means "change in x."

At any point in this process, we have several quantities to keep track of, which I have organized in the table "Limit values." This table was generated using the program as follows.

Step	Code	Comments
1.	"C"? $\to C$	Prompt for C and store it.
2.	$1 \to D$	$D = \Delta x$.
3.	Lbl 1	Start Looping here.
4.	$C - D \to X$ ◢	Increase X and display it.
5.	$x^{12} + x^8 + x^4 + 2$ ◢	Display $f(X)$.
6.	$D \div 2 \to D$	Decrease Δx.
7.	Goto 1	Repeat.

(This version will generate columns 2 and 3. To get columns 4 and 5, change line 4 to $C + D \to X$.)

Look at the table column "$c - \Delta x$." You can see by reading the successive values that we started at 0 and sneaked up on $c = 1$ from the left. The third column

Limit values

Δx	$c - \Delta x$	$f(c - \Delta x)$	$c + \Delta x$	$f(c + \Delta x)$
1.0	0.0	2.0	2.0	4370.0
0.5	0.5	2.0667	1.5	162.4377
0.25	0.75	2.4482	1.25	24.9538
0.125	0.875	3.1312	1.125	10.2775
0.0625	0.9375	3.8301	1.0625	6.9685
0.03125	0.9688	4.3396	1.0313	5.8568
0.015625	0.9844	4.6484	1.0156	5.4005
0.007813	0.9922	4.8185	1.0078	5.1937
0.003906	0.9961	4.9078	1.0039	5.0953
0.001953	0.9980	4.9535	1.0020	5.0473
0.000977	0.9990	4.9767	1.0010	5.0235
0.000488	0.9995	4.9883	1.0005	5.0117

Calculus 123

indicates that the corresponding function values approached 5; or, starting at $f(0) = 2$, we climbed up a very smooth curve and got very close to $f(1) = 5$.

Now the fourth column shows that we started at $x = 2$ and are sneaking up on $c = 1$ from the right. The corresponding function values in the last column show that we started very high at $f(2) = 4370$, but slid down the curve quickly and got very close to $f(1) = 5$.

In summary, as x approaches $c = 1$, from either direction (columns 2 and 4), $f(x)$ approaches 5 (columns 3 and 5). We say that 5 is the limit, L of $f(x)$ as x approaches c and write

$$\lim_{x \to c} f(x) = L.$$

This would be read "the limit of $f(x)$ as x approaches c is L." Say it aloud.

For the example we just considered,

$$\lim_{x \to 1} x^{12} + x^8 + x^4 + 2 = 5.$$

Read this aloud.

Exercise
1. Graph $f(x) = \dfrac{2}{x - 2}$.

2. Make a copy of the first row and the first column of "Limit values."
3. Replace the function in line 5 of the program above, and complete the table letting $c = 1$.
4. Then describe the behavior of $f(x)$ as x approaches 1.
5. Repeat step 2 and complete the table letting $c = 2$.
6. Now describe the behavior of $f(x)$ as x approaches 2. Does f have a limiting value as x approaches 2?

Definition of a limit.
Some of the techniques of calculus were used to solve problems long before they could be proved with any mathematical certainty. It was only in the late nineteenth century that H. L. Cauchy developed and made rigorous the definition of a limit that is the backbone of calculus.

Here's how it goes:

$$\lim_{x \to c} f(x) = L \text{ if and only if for each } \epsilon > 0,$$

2   1   3   4

there exists $\delta > 0$ such that

6

if $0 < |x - c| < \delta$ then $|f(x) - L| < \epsilon.$

7   5

What does it mean? Read the definition again; then compare the blue numbers to those in graph A opposite.

We use ϵ and δ to answer the question "How close is close enough?" You give me an ϵ, which says how close you want to be to the limit, and I can give you a δ, which says how close you need to be to $x = c$. Let's work a couple of graphical examples.

Consider again

$$\lim_{x \to 1} x^{12} + x^8 + x^4 + 2 = 5.$$

If we let $\epsilon = 0.5$, what would be the corresponding δ?

Exercise
Simultaneously graph the three functions
$y = x^{12} + x^8 + x^4 + 2$; $y = 4.5$; and $y = 5.5$ in the viewing rectangle $[0, 2], 1$ and $[0, 10], 1$. (Notice we are graphing $y = f(x), y = L - \epsilon, y = L + \epsilon$.)

1. ZOOM in so that the graph looks like the figure you see illustrated.
2. Use TRACE to find the intersection point of $y = 4.5$ with the curve. You should get something like $(0.977, 4.5)$.
3. TRACE to find the intersection point of $y = 5.5$ with the curve. You should get something like $(1.019, 5.5)$.
4. Now we will use the x-coordinates to find how far we can stray from $c = 1$, which will give us δ. Since $|0.977 - 1| = 0.023$ and $|1.019 - 1| = 0.019$ (these represent $|x - c|$), we should choose $\delta = 0.023$. Referring to the last line in the definition of a limit, we can say if $|x - 1| < 0.023$, then $|(x^{12} + x^8 + x^4 + 2) - 5| < 0.5$.
5. Try to repeat this activity with $\epsilon = 0.25$. You should find $\delta = 0.011$.

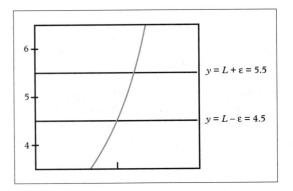

6 —

5 —

4 —

$y = L + \epsilon = 5.5$

$y = L - \epsilon = 4.5$

Calculus

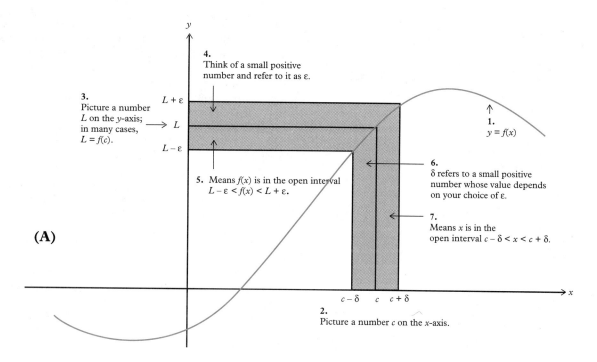

3.
Picture a number
L on the y-axis;
in many cases,
$L = f(c)$.

4.
Think of a small positive
number and refer to it as ε.

1.
$y = f(x)$

5. Means $f(x)$ is in the open interval
$L - \varepsilon < f(x) < L + \varepsilon$.

6.
δ refers to a small positive
number whose value depends
on your choice of ε.

7.
Means x is in the
open interval $c - \delta < x < c + \delta$.

(A)

2.
Picture a number c on the x-axis.

The definition insists that for every ϵ there is a corresponding δ. Can we find a general relationship based on the last two examples? δ is what percent of ϵ?

$$0.023 = 0.5p \Rightarrow p = 0.046$$
$$0.011 = 0.25p \Rightarrow p = 0.044$$

To be safe, we could let $\delta = 0.05\epsilon$.

For simple functions, you can solve algebraically for ϵ in terms of δ.

Example

Use the definition of a limit to show that
$$\lim_{x \to 1} 2x + 1 = 3.$$

We have $c = 1$, $f(x) = 2x + 1$, $L = 3$. Start with the ϵ-inequality and make it look like the δ-inequality
$$\left| (2x + 1) - 3 \right| < \epsilon$$
$$\left| 2x - 2 \right| < \epsilon$$
$$2\left| x - 1 \right| < \epsilon$$
$$\left| x - 1 \right| < \frac{\epsilon}{2}$$

Let $\delta = \dfrac{\epsilon}{2}$ and you can guarantee that if $\left| x - 1 \right| < \delta$, then $\left| (2x + 1) - 3 \right| < \epsilon$.

★   ★   ★

Right- and left-hand limits. The domain of the greatest integer function is all real numbers (see graph B). But does the limit exist everywhere?

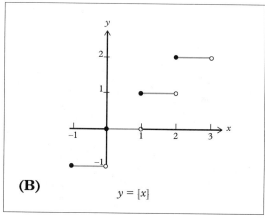

(B) $y = \lfloor x \rfloor$

There is no problem at $x = \dfrac{3}{2}$ since we can see from the graph that
$$\lim_{x \to 3/2} \lfloor x \rfloor = 1.$$

But $\lim_{x \to 1} \lfloor x \rfloor$ causes problems because of the break in the graph.

The output values for $y = \lfloor x \rfloor$ as x approaches 1 from the left-hand side are 0, for example, $\lfloor 0.8 \rfloor = 0$, $\lfloor 0.9 \rfloor = 0$, $\lfloor 0.95 \rfloor = 0$. To describe this situation, we write
$$\lim_{x \to 1^-} \lfloor x \rfloor = 0,$$
which is read, "The limit of the greatest integer function as x approaches 1 from the left is 0."

Calculating limits

Let n be a positive integer, k be a constant, and f and g be functions which have limits at $x = c$. Then the following rules hold:

1. Constant rule

$$\lim_{x \to c} k = k$$

2. Constant multiple

$$\lim_{x \to c} kf(x) = k\lim_{x \to c} f(x)$$

3. Sum rule

$$\lim_{x \to c} [f(x) + g(x)] = \lim_{x \to c} f(x) + \lim_{x \to c} g(x)$$

4. Difference rule

$$\lim_{x \to c} [f(x) - g(x)] = \lim_{x \to c} f(x) - \lim_{x \to c} g(x)$$

5. Product rule

$$\lim_{x \to c} [f(x) \cdot g(x)] = \lim_{x \to c} f(x) \cdot \lim_{x \to c} g(x)$$

6. Quotient rule

$$\lim_{x \to c} \frac{f(x)}{g(x)} = \frac{\lim_{x \to c} f(x)}{\lim_{x \to c} g(x)}, \ if \lim_{x \to c} g(x) \neq 0$$

7. Power rule

$$\lim_{x \to c} [f(x)]^n = \left[\lim_{x \to c} f(x) \right]^n$$

8. nth root rule

$$\lim_{x \to c} \sqrt[n]{f(x)} = \sqrt[n]{\lim_{x \to c} f(x)}, \ if \lim_{x \to c} f(x) > 0$$

for even n

The output values for $y = [x]$ as x approaches 1 from the right-hand side are 1. For example, $[1.1] = 1$, $[1.05] = 1$, $[1.025] = 1$. To describe this situation, we write

$$\lim_{x \to 1^+} [x] = 1,$$

which is read, "The limit of the greatest integer function as x approaches 1 from the right is 1."

What's the connection between one-sided limits and $\lim_{x \to c} f(x)$? The right-hand and left-hand limits don't necessarily have to be equal, which was the case with

$$\lim_{x \to 1^-} [x] \neq \lim_{x \to 1^+} [x].$$

So we say $\lim_{x \to 1} [x]$ does not exist. If the left-hand and right-hand limits are equal, then $\lim_{x \to c} f(x)$ exists and has the same value. For example,

$$\lim_{x \to -1/2^-} [x] = \lim_{x \to -1/2^+} [x] = \lim_{x \to -1/2} [x] = -1.$$

Limit calculations. This section deals primarily with the mechanical aspects of calculating limits. This will give you a great opportunity to brush up on your algebra skills and trigonometry identities. We will work a lot of examples, which will involve using the rules found to the left, in "Calculating limits." To collect your own bag of tricks for calculating limits, keep notes on some 5×7 notecards and save individual problems that require a special technique. Go through these problems over and over again.

The rules summarized here are most frequently used to do operations with limits. They state that the operation of forming the limit is accomplished by addition, subtraction, multiplication, and division (if the limit is not equal to 0) provided that all the limits occurring exist and are finite. Limits at infinity and limits as $x \to \infty$ will be dealt with later.

Rule 1 is simple, yet it surprises some students. It says that no matter what x-value is approached, the limit of a constant is the constant itself. Remember, the graph of a constant is a horizontal line, meaning that no matter what real number is input, you get the same output.

Example

$$\lim_{x \to 0} 5 = 5, \ \lim_{x \to 10} 5 = 5$$

⋆ ⋆ ⋆

Limits of polynomials are easy to deal with because polynomials are smooth, continuous curves whose domain is **R**. Combinations of rules 1, 2, 3, 4, 5, and 7 allow you simply to evaluate the function at $x = c$ to produce the limit.

Example

$$\lim_{x \to 2} 2x - 5 = -1, \ \lim_{x \to 1} 3x^3 - 2x^2 + x - 6 = -4$$

⋆ ⋆ ⋆

What makes calculating some limits a tricky matter is that the function doesn't have to be defined at the point $x = c$. Remember, it's "close to" and not "equal to" that matters with limits.

Example

$$\lim_{x \to 3} \frac{x - 3}{x - 3} = \lim_{x \to 3} 1 = 1$$

⋆ ⋆ ⋆

As we get close to 3 from both sides, $f(x) = 1$.

Example

Use rule 5 and rule 1.

$$\lim_{x \to 1} \frac{x^2 + 4x - 5}{x - 1} = \lim_{x \to 1} \frac{(x + 5)(x - 1)}{(x - 1)}$$

$$= \lim_{x \to 1} (x + 5) \cdot \lim_{x \to 1} 1 = 6 \cdot 1 = 6$$

$\star \quad \star \quad \star$

The graph of this rational function is really just a line, with a hole at $(1, 6)$.

NOTE: This may be hard to see if you graph the function on your calculator since the calculator evaluates the function at evenly spaced x-values in the viewing rectangle, and connects the dots. If the machine doesn't try to evaluate at $x = 1$, it won't know that there's a problem, and draw a continuous line.

Example

Consider $\lim\limits_{x \to -6} \dfrac{x^2 + 2x - 24}{x^2 + 8x + 12}$.

Since the denominator equals 0 when $x = 0$, we need to do some algebra.

$$\lim_{x \to -6} \frac{x^2 + 2x - 24}{x^2 + 8x + 12} = \lim_{x \to -6} \frac{(x + 6)(x - 4)}{(x + 6)(x + 2)}$$

Now we can use rule 5.

$$\lim_{x \to -6} 1 \cdot \lim_{x \to -6} \frac{x - 4}{x + 2} = 1 \cdot \frac{-10}{-4} = \frac{5}{2}.$$

$\star \quad \star \quad \star$

Can we always expect factors to divide out so nicely? Of course not.

Exercise

Find $\lim\limits_{x \to 2} \dfrac{x}{x - 2}$.

Again, $x = c$ yields 0 in the denominator. And we can't factor. Now what? Graph the function in the viewing rectangle [-5, 5], 1 and [-4, 4], 1. As you approach 2 from either side, what happens to $f(x)$?

Write a sentence to explain why $\lim\limits_{x \to 2} \dfrac{x}{x - 2}$ does not exist.

Let's not forget rule 8.

Example

$$\lim_{x \to -2} \sqrt{5x^2 + x} = \sqrt{\lim_{x \to -2} 5x^2 + x}$$

$$= \sqrt{18} = 3\sqrt{2}$$

$\star \quad \star \quad \star$

Limits involving trigonometry functions can be especially challenging. Here is where your graphics calculator will be a great help; a quick look at the graph may confirm or deny a dozen algebraic steps.

Example

We wish to find $\lim\limits_{x \to \pi} \dfrac{\sin^2 x}{1 + \cos x}$.

METHOD 1: Since both the numerator and denominator are equal to 0 at $x = \pi$, we might use a trig identity and some algebra. An identity that relates the sine and the cosine functions is $\sin^2 x + \cos^2 x = 1$.

Now

$$\frac{\sin^2 x}{1 + \cos x} = \frac{1 - \cos^2 x}{1 + \cos x}$$

$$= \frac{(1 - \cos x)(1 + \cos x)}{1 + \cos x}$$

so that $\lim\limits_{x \to \pi} \dfrac{\sin^2 x}{1 + \cos x} = \lim\limits_{x \to \pi} (1 - \cos x)$

$$= 1 - (-1) = 2.$$

METHOD 2: Graph

$$y = \frac{\sin^2 x}{1 + \cos x}$$

in the viewing rectangle $[-2\pi, 2\pi]$, π and $[-1, 2.2]$, 1. ZOOM in on the graph in the area around $x = \pi$ and TRACE to find the y-value at $x \approx 3.14$. The y-value is the limit.

$\star \quad \star \quad \star$

Exercise

Follow the methods used in this example to find

$$\lim_{x \to \pi/2} \frac{\cos^2 x}{1 - \sin x}.$$

Sometimes no amount of algebra and trig identities can help. Geometry and advanced limit theorems are necessary. Instead of these analytical techniques, we can use a graph and a table of values similar to those

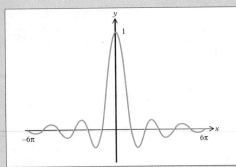

Δx	$\dfrac{\sin(-\Delta x)}{-\Delta x}$	$\dfrac{\sin \Delta x}{\Delta x}$
1.0	.8415	.8415
0.5	.9589	.9589
0.25	.9896	.9896
0.125	.9974	.9974
0.0625	.9993	.9993
0.03125	.9998	.9998
0.015625	1.0000	1.0000
0.007813	1.0000	1.0000

$\dfrac{\sin x}{x}$

The analytical proof that

$$\lim_{x \to 0} \frac{\sin x}{x} = 1$$

is a very complicated endeavor. Let's look at it more intuitively. The graph looks like it goes right through the point $(0, 1)$; actually there is a hole at $(0, 1)$. But remember, with limits, it's close to and not equal to that matters. The table of values indicates that as the input values approach 0 from the left or from the right, the output values approach 1. Also, from rule 7 we have

$$\lim_{x \to 0} \frac{1}{\dfrac{\sin x}{x}} = \lim_{x \to 0} \frac{x}{\sin x} = 1.$$

found on page 123. As an example, we will consider the very famous and useful limit

$$\lim_{x \to 0} \frac{\sin x}{x} = 1.$$

(See the box above.)

Exercise

Use techniques similar to those used for

$$\lim_{x \to 0} \frac{\sin x}{x} = 1$$

to predict the following limits.

1. $\displaystyle\lim_{x \to 0} \frac{\cos 3x - 1}{x^2}$ 2. $\displaystyle\lim_{x \to 1\backslash 2} \frac{\cos \pi x}{2x - 1}$

Now let's see how to use

$$\lim_{x \to 0} \frac{\sin x}{x} = 1$$

to do some traditional limit calculations.

Example

$$\lim_{t \to 0} \frac{\sin 5t}{3t}.$$

★　★　★

We would like to use

$$\lim_{x \to 0} \frac{\sin x}{x} = 1.$$

Since the angle in the numerator of our problem is $5t$, the angle in the denominator must also be $5t$. Then setting $x = 5t$, as $x \to 0$ so does $5t \to 0$. First, get rid of the 3 by factoring out the constant $\frac{1}{3}$ (see rule 2, "Calculating limits"). Then we want to multiply by 5 in the denominator, so we have to multiply the numerator by 5 also.

$$\lim_{t \to 0} \frac{\sin 5t}{3t} = \frac{1}{3} \cdot \lim_{t \to 0} \frac{\sin 5t}{t} = \frac{5}{3} \cdot \lim_{t \to 0} \frac{\sin 5t}{5t}$$

$$= \frac{5}{3} \cdot 1 = \frac{5}{3}.$$

Exercise

See if you can use this procedure to find

$$\lim_{x \to 0} \frac{\sin 2x}{8x} \quad \text{and} \quad \lim_{x \to 0} \frac{\sin 10x}{-x}.$$

We have to do double duty in order to solve the next example.

Example

Find $\lim\limits_{x \to 0} \dfrac{\sin 5x}{\sin 3x}$.

We have found that

$$\lim_{x \to 0} \frac{\sin x}{x} = \lim_{x \to 0} \frac{x}{\sin x} = 1.$$

We need both of these limits to do this problem. Think of our function in the form

$$\frac{\sin 5x}{\sin 3x} = \frac{\sin 5x}{1} \cdot \frac{1}{\sin 3x}.$$

We would like a $5x$ in the denominator for the first fraction, and a $3x$ in the numerator of the second. We will multiply by 1, written three different ways, to get the function in the form we want.

$$\frac{x}{x} \cdot \frac{\sin 5x}{1} \cdot \frac{1}{\sin 3x} = \frac{\sin 5x}{x} \cdot \frac{x}{\sin 3x}$$

$$\frac{3}{3} \cdot \frac{\sin 5x}{x} \cdot \frac{x}{\sin 3x} = \frac{1}{3} \cdot \frac{\sin 5x}{x} \cdot \frac{3x}{\sin 3x}$$

$$\frac{5}{5} \cdot \frac{1}{3} \cdot \frac{\sin 5x}{x} \cdot \frac{3x}{\sin 3x} = \frac{5}{3} \cdot \frac{\sin 5x}{5x} \cdot \frac{3x}{\sin 3x}$$

Now we can use this last statement to take the limit

$$\lim_{x \to 0} \frac{5}{3} \cdot \frac{\sin 5x}{5x} \cdot \frac{3x}{\sin 3x}$$

$$= \left(\lim_{x \to 0} \frac{5}{3}\right) \cdot \left(\lim_{x \to 0} \frac{\sin 5x}{5x}\right) \cdot \left(\lim_{x \to 0} \frac{3x}{\sin 3x}\right)$$

$$= \frac{5}{3} \cdot 1 \cdot 1 = \frac{5}{3}.$$

$\star \quad \star \quad \star$

Remember, you can always use your calculator to graph the function to be sure that the answer makes sense. You can see this illustrated in the graph to the right.

Exercise

Use this procedure to find $\lim\limits_{x \to 0} \dfrac{\sin 2x}{\sin 6x}$.

Summary for rational functions

When considering limits involving rational functions of the form $\lim\limits_{x \to c} \dfrac{f(x)}{g(x)}$, be on the lookout for asymptotic behavior. If $g(c) = 0$, then $x = c$ is a vertical asymptote and

(a) you may get ∞ or $-\infty$ as the limit;

Consider $\lim\limits_{x \to 2} \dfrac{1}{(x - 2)^2}$.

(b) or the limit does not exist.

Consider $\lim\limits_{x \to -3} \dfrac{1}{(x + 3)}$.

(Note that this function has both a right-hand and left-hand limit.)

When considering $\lim\limits_{x \to \pm\infty} \dfrac{f(x)}{g(x)}$, look for horizontal asymptotes. Example:

$$\lim_{x \to -\infty} \frac{5x^2 - 1}{2x^2 + 3x}.$$

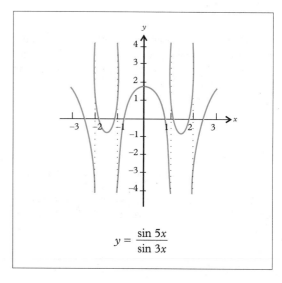

$$y = \frac{\sin 5x}{\sin 3x}$$

Limits involving infinity.
We will start by describing what it means for a function to have a limiting value as x approaches infinity. This is often referred to as the end behavior of a function. Most of the interesting examples of this involve rational functions.

The basic building block for many of these problems is $f(x) = \dfrac{1}{x}$. Try graphing this function in the viewing rectangle $[-10, 10]$, 1 and $[-3, 3]$, 1. Clearly, the graph has a horizontal asymptote at $y = 0$. (You'll remember from page 121 what an asymptote is.)

Example

Find $\lim\limits_{x \to \infty} \dfrac{x^2 - 3x - 4}{x^2 - 1}$.

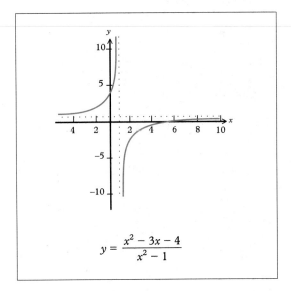

$$y = \frac{x^2 - 3x - 4}{x^2 - 1}$$

METHOD 1: The graph here indicates that the function has a horizontal asymptote at $y = 1$, which means that as x gets larger, the y-values get closer to 1. Using limit notation, we write

$$\lim_{x \to \infty} \frac{x^2 - 3x - 4}{x^2 - 1} = 1.$$

METHOD 2: We can use $\lim\limits_{x \to \infty} \dfrac{1}{x} = 0$ to calculate this limit. The trick is to divide the numerator and denominator of the original expression by the highest power of x.

$$\lim_{x \to \infty} \frac{x^2 - 3x - 4}{x^2 - 1} = \lim_{x \to \infty} \frac{\dfrac{x^2}{x^2} - \dfrac{3x}{x^2} - \dfrac{4}{x^2}}{\dfrac{x^2}{x^2} - \dfrac{1}{x^2}}$$

$$= \lim_{x \to \infty} \frac{1 - \dfrac{3}{x} - \dfrac{4}{x^2}}{1 - \dfrac{1}{x^2}}$$

It looks complicated, but it will soon be simplified because wherever x or x^2 is in the denominator, we can use rule 7 to find

$$\lim_{x \to \infty} \frac{1}{x^2} = \left(\lim_{x \to \infty} \frac{1}{x}\right)^2 = 0^2 = 0.$$

So, the last step becomes

$$\lim_{x \to \infty} \frac{1 - 3 \cdot 0 - 4 \cdot 0}{1 - 0} = 1.$$

> **Exercise**
> Use methods 1 and 2 to find
>
> $$\lim_{x \to \infty} \frac{2x(x - 2)}{x^2 + x - 2}.$$
>
> Graph the function in the viewing rectangle $[-12, 12]$, 1 and $[-5, 5]$, 1.

So far, we have concentrated on the behavior of functions at horizontal asymptotes. Now we will use limits to talk about the behavior of functions near vertical asymptotes.

Again, let's concentrate on rational functions. This would include trig functions, since they are ratios of sides of a right triangle. Recall that the domain of a rational function is all real numbers, except the ones that result in 0 in the denominator.

Let's go back to the functions we have previously worked with in this section; this time, we will be looking for vertical asymptotes.

Make a graph of $f(x) = \dfrac{1}{x}$. Clearly, $\lim\limits_{x \to 0} \dfrac{1}{x}$ does not exist because as we approach 0 from both sides, the y-values go in opposite directions. But what happens when we look at it one side at a time, as we did with the end behavior problems?

Left: When we looked at the left-end behavior of the graph, we found as $x \to -\infty$, $\dfrac{1}{x} \to 0$ from below. Now, as x approaches 0 from the left $(x \to 0^-)$, $\dfrac{1}{x} \to -\infty$, or $\lim\limits_{x \to 0^-} \dfrac{1}{x} = -\infty$.

Right: When we looked at right-end behavior, we found as $x \to \infty$, $\dfrac{1}{x} \to 0$ from above. Now as x approaches 0 from the right $(x \to 0^+)$, $\dfrac{1}{x} \to \infty$. Or,

$$\lim_{x \to 0^+} \frac{1}{x} = \infty$$

Have the tables turned?

Example

Consider $h(x) = \dfrac{2}{(x - 3)^2}$, graphed here.

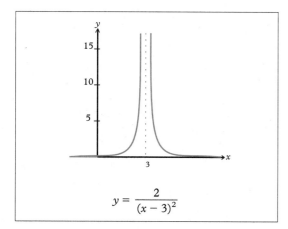

$$y = \frac{2}{(x - 3)^2}$$

As $x \to 3$ from either direction, the y-values grow without bound. So both the left-hand and right-hand limits are positive infinity and we can write

$$\lim_{x \to 3^-} \frac{2}{(x - 3)^2} = \lim_{x \to 3^+} \frac{2}{(x - 3)^2}$$

$$= \lim_{x \to 3} \frac{2}{(x - 3)^2} = \infty.$$

⋆　⋆　⋆

If you are ever in doubt about the limit as $x \to \infty$, graph the function in a viewing rectangle that allows for large x-values—$X[0, 100]$, for example. You may

find the function does not have a limiting value. For example,

$$\lim_{x \to \infty} \frac{x \sin x}{x + \sin x}$$

does not exist since it oscillates forever, as shown in the graph here.

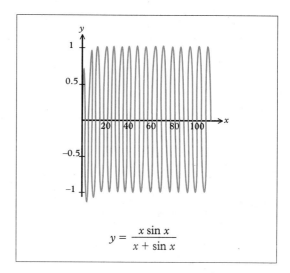

$$y = \frac{x \sin x}{x + \sin x}$$

Continuity of a function. As you sort through all the technicalities of calculating limits, it's hard to keep in mind that functions model real-world phenomena. And in order for us to apply the methods of calculus to them, they must pass certain criteria. The criterion we explore in this section is *continuity*.

Temperature is a continuous function of time. If you plotted the temperature at each moment for several days, you would see a smooth, sine-wave-like graph. If you were to plot the amount of money in your wallet at each moment over several days, you might see a series of horizontal lines, sometimes stepping up, sometimes stepping down. This function would not be continuous.

In exploring the limit of $f(x)$ as $x \to c$, the emphasis was on functional values close to c rather than what happens to the function at $x = c$. But now,

if $\displaystyle\lim_{x \to c} f(x) = f(c)$, then we say the function

f is *continuous* at $x = c$;

if $\displaystyle\lim_{x \to c} f(x) \neq f(c)$, then we say the function

f is *discontinuous* at $x = c$.

Geometrically, the criterion for continuity is to be able to draw the curve without lifting the pencil; there should be no holes or breaks.

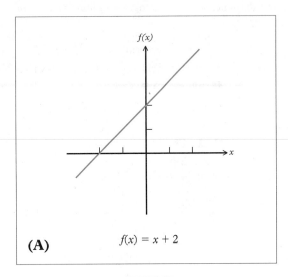

(A) $f(x) = x + 2$

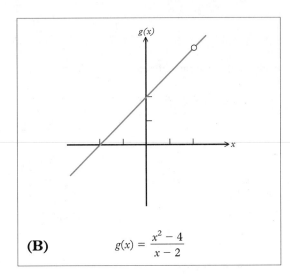

(B) $g(x) = \dfrac{x^2 - 4}{x - 2}$

Example

Consider $f(x) = x + 2$ (see graph A). The domain of this function is **R**. And for any real number c,

$$\lim_{x \to c} x + 2 = c + 2.$$

So we say, $f(x) = x + 2$ is continuous everywhere. NOTE: This is true for all polynomial functions.

★ ★ ★

Example

Consider $f(x) = \dfrac{x^2 - 4}{x - 2}$ (see graph B).

For this function, Domain: **R**, $x \neq 2$. This function is continuous everywhere except at $x = 2$ because even though

$$\lim_{x \to 2} \frac{x^2 - 4}{x - 2} = 4,$$

the value of $f(2)$ is not defined. So we say f is discontinuous at $x = 2$.

★ ★ ★

Trig functions such as $y = \sin x$ and $y = \cos x$ are continuous everywhere. But what about $y = \tan x$? (See graph C.) This function has an infinite number of discontinuities at $x = \ldots \dfrac{-\pi}{2}, \dfrac{\pi}{2}, \dfrac{3\pi}{2}, \ldots$. And to characterize the behavior of tan x in between these ver-

tical asymptotes, we can say tan x is continuous on $\left(\dfrac{-\pi}{2}, \dfrac{\pi}{2} \right)$ $\left(\text{the open interval from } \dfrac{-\pi}{2} \text{ to } \dfrac{\pi}{2} \right)$.

Can we give meaning to continuity on a closed interval? We would need to make special provisions for the endpoints. To do this, consider the function $f(x) = \sqrt{x}$. (You should know what this function looks like, but you might want to graph it on your calculator anyway.) The domain of this function is $x \in [0, \infty)$ or $x \geq 0$. To talk about $\lim_{x \to 0^-} \sqrt{x}$ doesn't make sense, because the function is not even defined to the left of 0. But the function behaves well enough on the right-hand side of 0; we have $\lim_{x \to 0^+} \sqrt{x} = 0$. Since the right-hand limit is equal to the functional value at zero, then we say the function is continuous at the left endpoint, as shown in the table opposite.

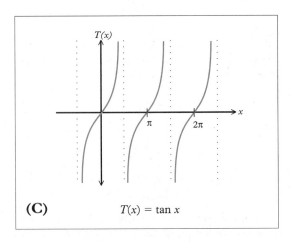

(C) $T(x) = \tan x$

Calculus

A function $y = f(x)$ defined on $[a,b]$ where $a < c < b$ is

continuous at an interior point c if

$$\lim_{x \to c} f(x) = f(c);$$

that is, at $x = c$ both the left-hand and right-hand limit are equal to $f(c)$.

continuous at a left endpoint if

$$\lim_{x \to a^+} f(x) = f(a);$$

that is, the right-hand limit at $x = a$ is $f(a)$.

continuous at a right endpoint if

$$\lim_{x \to b^-} f(x) = f(b);$$

that is, the left-hand limit at $x = b$ is $f(b)$.

Why studying calculus pays off Reason #2

Considering our rapidly changing, technological world, you may be training for a job which does not even exist yet. A solid background in and understanding of calculus will not only broaden your career options, but will put you in a position to be a leader in change and development.

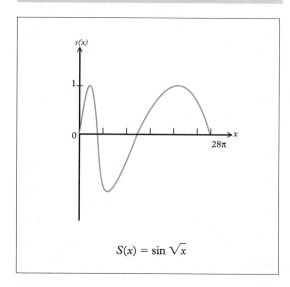

$$S(x) = \sin \sqrt{x}$$

Exercise

Consider the function $S(x) = \sin \sqrt{x}$ on the interval $[0, 28\pi]$ (see graph above). Is the function continuous on the closed interval $[0, 28\pi]$? Write a few sentences to justify your answer.

Example

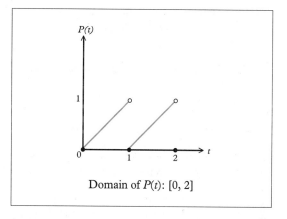

Domain of $P(t)$: $[0, 2]$

Let $D(x)$ be defined by the graph above. The domain of this function is $[0, 2]$, but where is the function continuous and what are the points of discontinuity on this interval? The obvious problem spots are when $x = 1$ and $x = 2$.

$x = 1$:

$$\lim_{x \to 1^-} D(x) = 1 \text{ and } \lim_{x \to 1^+} D(x) = 0.$$

So $\lim_{x \to 1} D(x)$ does not exist, which qualifies $x = 1$ as an interior point of discontinuity.

$x = 2$:

$$\lim_{x \to 2^-} D(x) = 1, \text{ but } f(2) = 0.$$

So since the left-hand limit at the right endpoint is not equal to the functional value there, then there is a discontinuity at the right endpoint. We conclude that $D(x)$ is continuous on $(0, 1)$ and $(1, 2)$ with discontinuities at $x = 1$ and $x = 2$.

Calculus   133

Differentiation

Often in mathematics, everyday words take on new meaning. Commonly, one might say "Chocolate is a delicious derivative of the cocoa plant." But mathematically, the *derivative* of a function of x is a new function that was derived from $f(x)$. This new function, the derivative, yields important information about the original function, $f(x)$. The most important piece of information yielded is the slope of the graph of f. The real-world implications of this characteristic are many. The process of finding the derivative is called *differentiation*.

In this section, we will describe how to find the derivative of a function using limits, we will work with some different techniques for finding derivatives quickly, and we will explore some of the many uses of this new function.

Rate of change of a function. In the previous section, temperature as a function of time was given as an example of a continuous function. During what two hours of the day do you think the temperature rises most rapidly? When does it usually start to cool down each day? What might we look for in the graph of the function to answer these questions? These questions refer to the *rate of change of the function*.

So that you might become more comfortable with quantifying the rate of change, we will look at a detailed example of a familiar rate of change.

Your cousin Elizabeth is having a birthday party which starts at 2 p.m. It is a little before 12 noon and she lives about 84 miles away. So to get there on time your average speed should be

$$speed = \frac{distance}{time} = \frac{84\ miles}{2\ hours} = 42\ mph.$$

But there are many different types of roads between your place and Elizabeth's. Some roads are residential (speed limit, 25 mph), one stretch is a two-lane highway (55 mph), and part of the way is a four-lane divided highway (65 mph). And you need to stop at the mall for a gift.

Your calculus teacher has been talking a lot about rates of change lately, and you realize that speed measures a rate of change: the rate of change of distance with respect to time. Your speedometer is broken, so to keep track of your speed, you take along a piece of graph paper. With time on the horizontal axis and odometer readings on the vertical axis, you can track the rate of change of distance with respect to time.

In the graph, the rates of change indicated by the black line are average speeds over a time interval of 15 or 30 minutes; the black line indicates, for example, that at each moment between 12 noon and 12:15, the car was traveling 32 mph. Not even a Maserati could go from 0 mph to 32 mph in an instant! The blue line is more realistic, since it indicates that the vehicle accelerated (rate of change of speed) and decelerated gradually. In analyzing the black line, you discovered

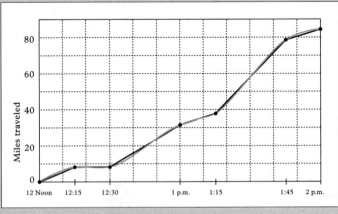

Instantaneous velocity

that the slope of the line was equal to the average speed during that time interval. But if at 12:10 the car hits a tree, it's not the average speed but the speed at the *instant of collision* that determines the amount of damage. The notion of an instant may be useful in everyday life, but how can we make sense of it mathematically? If the lapse of time is pictured as length along a line, then an interval is represented by a line segment, whereas an instant corresponds to a point. So our next task is to give meaning to the slope of a curve at any point on the curve. The slope at any point on the blue line will give us the *instantaneous velocity*, or the speed at any moment in time.

Refer to the blue line of the graph on page 134 and notice that seven points have been plotted along the trip. Use this data to answer the following questions:

1. Determine the average speed during each segment of the trip. How do these numbers relate to the slope of the line segment in the graph?

   (Remember, slope is $\dfrac{change\ in\ y}{change\ in\ x}$.)

2. Describe the trip in terms of the types of roads which would allow such rates. Is it possible that the speed limit was exceeded? If so, does the graph indicate that the driver was stopped and ticketed? When was the stop at the mall?

3. If you connected the first point (at 12 noon) to the last point (at 2 p.m.), and found the rate of change, how does this relate to what we have looked at so far?

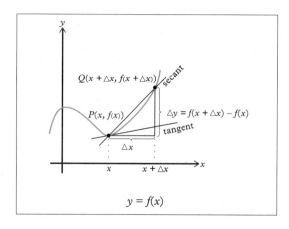

$$y = f(x)$$

Tangent lines and slope.

So far, I have tried to convince you that to determine instantaneous velocity (speed at a particular moment in time) is the same problem as finding the slope of the tangent line to a curve. But do you know the meaning of the phrase "line tangent to a curve"? Before you read on, take a minute to write down your definition of "line tangent to a curve."

Before we look at the definition which works for all cases, let's look at some definitions that don't work.

A tangent line is a line that touches the curve at only one point. This works fine for circles, but doesn't hold up for a more general curve, as in graph A below. *A tangent line is a line that touches the curve, but does not cross it.* Graph B shows a counterexample.

To get the best description of a tangent line, we will use the concept of a limit. Using limits, we will not only be able to describe what a tangent line is, but we will also be able to calculate its slope!

First, let's consider a curve given by the equation $y = f(x)$. Located on the curve is the fixed point P with coordinates $(x, f(x))$. (P is the proposed point of tangency.) Next, locate a point Q close to P on the curve; say Q has coordinates $(x + \Delta x, f(x + \Delta x))$. ($\Delta x$ is how close Q is to P.) Now we can calculate the slope of the secant line PQ.

$$m_{\text{sec}} = \frac{\Delta y}{\Delta x} = \frac{f(x + \Delta x) - f(x)}{\Delta x}$$

But we want the slope of the tangent line. From the graph above, we see that as Q moves closer to P (as Δx gets smaller), the secant line gets closer to the tangent line. So we take the limiting value of the secant slope to be the slope of the tangent line at P.

$$m_{\text{tan}} = \lim_{\Delta x \to 0} m_{\text{sec}} = \lim_{\Delta x \to 0} \frac{f(x + \Delta x) - f(x)}{\Delta x}$$

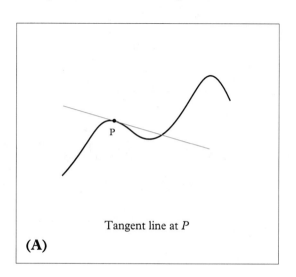

Tangent line at P

(A)

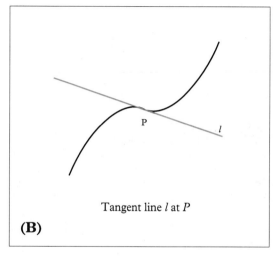

Tangent line l at P

(B)

Example

Find the slope of the tangent line to $y = x^2$ at the points $(-4, 16)$, $(1, 1)$, and $(3, 9)$ and find the equations for these tangent lines.

We will follow the method outlined above. Let P $(x, f(x)) = P(x, x^2)$ and Q is close to P at $Q(x + \Delta x, f(x + \Delta x)) = Q(x + \Delta x, (x + \Delta x)^2)$. Then the slope of the secant line PQ is

$$m_{\text{sec}} = \frac{f(x + \Delta x) - f(x)}{\Delta x} = \frac{(x + \Delta x)^2 - x^2}{\Delta x}$$

$$= \frac{x^2 + 2x(\Delta x) + (\Delta x)^2 - x^2}{\Delta x}$$

$$= \frac{(\Delta x)(2x + \Delta x)}{\Delta x} = 2x + \Delta x$$

so that $m_{\text{tan}} = \lim_{\Delta x \to 0} m_{\text{sec}} = \lim_{\Delta x \to 0} (2x + \Delta x) = 2x$.

The slope of the tangent line

at $(-4, 16)$ is $m = -8$,
at $(1, 1)$ is $m = 2$,
at $(3, 9)$ is $m = 6$.

Using the point-slope form of a line $y - b = m(x - a)$, we can write the equations for these tangent lines:

at $(-4, 16)$: $y - 16 = -8(x + 4) \Rightarrow y = -8x - 16$,
at $(1, 1)$: $y - 1 = 2(x - 1) \Rightarrow y = 2x - 1$,
at $(3, 9)$: $y - 9 = 6(x - 3) \Rightarrow y = 6x - 9$.

★ ★ ★

> ### Exercise
> Graph $y = x^2$ and the three tangent lines in the viewing rectangle $[-7, 7]$, 2 and $[-2, 29]$, 5.

Definition of the derivative.

The primary concept of calculus deals with the rate of change of one variable with respect to another, such as, for example, the rate of change of distance with respect to time, pressure with respect to volume, cost with respect to availability.

In the preceding section, we looked at the rate of change of distance with respect to time over an *interval* of time to give us an *average speed*. And we noticed that the speed was equal to the slope of the line. Then, to give meaning to the idea of determining speed at an instant, we defined the slope of the tangent line at a point as the limiting slope of the secant lines.

$$m_{\text{tan}} = \lim_{\Delta x \to 0} m_{\text{sec}} = \lim_{\Delta x \to 0} \frac{f(x + \Delta x) - f(x)}{\Delta x}$$

The quotient

$$\frac{\Delta y}{\Delta x} = \frac{f(x + \Delta x) - f(x)}{(x + \Delta x) - x} = \frac{f(x + \Delta x) - f(x)}{\Delta x}$$

is the ratio of the *difference* in the y divided by the *difference* in x between the points $(x, f(x))$ and $(x + \Delta x, f(x + \Delta x))$ on the graph of f. Since the quotient is the ratio of differences, it is referred to as the *difference quotient*. And the limit of the difference quotient as $\Delta x \to 0$ has many interpretations in addition to its interpretation as the slope of the tangent line. So, we refer to this limit more generally as the *derivative of f*, and use the notation $f'(x)$ (read "f prime of x").

Definition

The *derivative* of a function f is the function f' whose value at x is the number

$$f'(x) = \lim_{\Delta x \to 0} \frac{f(x + \Delta x) - f(x)}{\Delta x} \qquad (1)$$

provided the limit exists, and is unique.

As noted previously, when you study math, you are studying a language. We have just defined a very important new word, and you should be aware of how to use it properly in speaking the language of calculus.

If the limit in equation 1 exists, then we say that f *has a derivative at x* or f *is differentiable at x*. And if f has a derivative at every point in its domain, we say that f *is differentiable*.

Common notations for the derivative

$f'(x)$	"f prime of x"	Emphasizes that this is a new function generated from f
y'	"y prime"	Short and sweet
$\dfrac{dy}{dx}$	"$dy\ dx$"	Reminds us that the derivative is obtained from the difference quotient
$\dfrac{d}{dx}(f)$	"$d\ dx$ of f"	Emphasizes the idea that taking the derivative is an operation performed on f

Calculus

Using the difference quotient. Before we use the difference quotient to calculate some derivatives, let's modify it a bit to make it easier to work with. In some cases, the difference quotient leads to a lengthy algebraic expression and the Δx's get confused with the x's. To avoid such confusion, we let $\Delta x = h$ so that the difference quotient becomes

$$f'(x) = \lim_{h \to 0} \frac{f(x+h) - f(x)}{h}.$$

In an effort to tie these concepts together, let's do a rather long example.

Example

Let $y = f(t)$ represent the distance traveled by a flying calculus book after t units of time (we'll use t instead of x, since time is the independent variable).

Suppose $f(t) = t^2 + 6t$, where the units for $f(t)$ are feet and the units for t are seconds.
1. Find the distance traveled by the book between $t = 2$ and $t = 10$ seconds.
2. Find the average velocity of the book between $t = 2$ and $t = 10$ seconds ($2 \le t \le 10$).
3. Find the instantaneous velocity at $t = 10$ seconds.

Solution:
1. Distance traveled would be
   $f(10) - f(2) = 160 - 16 = 144$ feet.

2. $V_{avg} = \dfrac{distance}{time} = \dfrac{144 \text{ feet}}{8 \text{ sec}} = 18$ feet per second.

3. First, let's work with the difference quotient, as follows:

$$\frac{f(t+h) - f(t)}{h} = \frac{(t+h)^2 + 6(t+h) - (t^2 + 6t)}{h}$$

$$= \frac{t^2 + 2ht + h^2 + 6t + 6h - t^2 - 6t}{h}$$

$$= \frac{h(2t + 6 + h)}{h}$$

$$= 2t + 6 + h$$

so, $V_{inst} = \lim\limits_{h \to 0} (2t + 6 + h) = 2t + 6.$

At $t = 10$ seconds, $V_{inst} = 2(10) + 6 = 26$ feet per second.

★   ★   ★

We should practice more with the difference quotient in finding derivatives of different types of functions. Let's try a radical function.

Example

Find $f'(x)$ using the definition of the derivative if $f(x) = \sqrt{x+2}$.

To solve, start again with the difference quotient

$$\frac{f(x+h) - f(x)}{h} = \frac{\sqrt{x+h+2} - \sqrt{x+2}}{h}.$$

Our only hope here is to multiply the numerator by its conjugate in the hope that something will happen so that we can cancel that h out of the denominator.

$$= \frac{\sqrt{x+h+2} - \sqrt{x+2}}{h} \left(\frac{\sqrt{x+h+2} + \sqrt{x+2}}{\sqrt{x+h+2} + \sqrt{x+2}} \right)$$

$$= \frac{x+h+2 - (x+2)}{h(\sqrt{x+h+2} + \sqrt{x+2})}$$

$$= \frac{h}{h(\sqrt{x+h+2} + \sqrt{x+2})} \qquad (YAY!)$$

So now $f'(x) = \lim\limits_{h \to 0} \dfrac{1}{\sqrt{x+h+2} + \sqrt{x+2}}$

$$= \frac{1}{2\sqrt{x+2}}.$$

★   ★   ★

Notice that the domain of $f(x)$ is $x \ge -2$, but the domain of $f'(x)$ is $x > -2$. So the derivative does not exist at the endpoint of the graph. But this makes sense because you cannot draw a unique tangent line at an endpoint. Now let's continue the preceding example and find the slope and equation of the tangent line at the point $(0, \sqrt{2})$ on the curve.

Example

Evaluating the derivative at $x = 0$ will give us the slope

$$f'(0) = \frac{1}{2\sqrt{0+2}} = \frac{1}{2\sqrt{2}}.$$

Now, for the equation of the tangent line, we use the point-slope form of a line.

$$y - \sqrt{2} = \frac{1}{2\sqrt{2}}(x - 0) \Rightarrow y = \frac{x}{2\sqrt{2}} + \sqrt{2}$$

★   ★   ★

Exercise
Use the viewing rectangle $[-5, 5]$, 1 and $[-1, 4]$, 1 to graph $f(x) = \sqrt{x + 2}$ along with the tangent line that we just found to verify that it is indeed tangent to the curve at $(0, \sqrt{2})$.

Efficient rules for differentiation.

To use the definition of the derivative to find $f'(x)$, given $f(x) = x^2 - \cos 4\pi x$, would cause a severe brain cramp.

What we need is a short list of efficient rules, interpreted in English, to find the derivative of more complicated functions. A more complete table might list twenty-five rules, but the five below will get you through most problems. Proofs for these rules are found in most calculus textbooks. Throughout this section, we will work many examples so that you will become comfortable using these rules properly.

Rule 1 says that the derivative of a constant is 0. So, if $f(x) = -3$, then $f'(x) = 0$. This seems reasonable if you remember that the graph of the constant function f is a horizontal line, and in this case the tangent line falls right on top. So, since derivatives represent the slope of the tangent line, and the slope of a horizontal line is 0, then the derivative must be 0.

Read rule 2 carefully and then take a look at some applications.

1. If $f(x) = x^4$ then $f'(x) = 4x^3$.

2. If $g(x) = x^{-4}$, then $g'(x) = -4x^{-5}$.

3. If $Q(t) = t^{5/3}$, then $Q'(t) = \dfrac{5}{3}t^{2/3}$.

4. If $R(x) = \sqrt{x} = x^{1/2}$, then
$$R'(x) = \frac{1}{2}x^{-1/2} = \frac{1}{2\sqrt{x}}.$$

NOTE: Rule 2 can be used with rational exponents only. Functions involving irrational exponents, such as $h(x) = x^{\pi}$ or $m(t) = t^{\sqrt{2}}$, require different techniques.

EXTENSION of application 1: Graph $y = x^4$ in the viewing rectangle X $[-4.7, 4.7]$, 1 and Y $[-2, 3]$, 1. Use TRACE to find a point in the neighborhood of $P(-0.7, 0.2401)$. Let's find the equation for the tangent line at that point and then graph it to verify its tangency.

First, use the derivative to find the slope of the tangent line m_{tan} at $P = f'(-0.7) = 4(-0.7)^3 = -1.372$.

Now the equation for the tangent line is $y - 0.2401 = -1.372(x + 0.7)$. Isolate y and graph $y = -1.372x - 0.7203$ along with $y = x^4$ to verify their tangency at $(-0.7, 0.2401)$.

Rules for differentiation (symbolically and in English)

---

1. $\dfrac{d}{dx}(c) = 0$

The derivative of a constant is 0.

2. $\dfrac{d}{dx}(x^n) = nx^{n-1}$

To take the derivative of a power of x, bring the exponent out front, then subtract 1 for the new power of x.

3. $(fg)'(x) = f'(x)\, g(x) + f(x)\, g'(x)$

The derivative of a product is the derivative of the first times the second, plus the derivative of the second times the first.

4. $\left(\dfrac{f}{g}\right)'(x) = \dfrac{f'(x)\, g(x) - f(x)\, g'(x)}{[g(x)]^2}$

The derivative of a quotient is the denominator times the derivative of the numerator, minus the numerator times the derivative of the denominator over the denominator squared.

5. $(f \circ g)'(x) = \dfrac{d}{dx}f(g(x)) = f'(g(x))\, g'(x)$

To differentiate a composite, differentiate f (the outside function) and leave g alone, then multiply by the derivative of g.

To keep the list of rules short, rules that are fairly obvious are not included. For example, the derivative of a sum (or difference) would be the sum (or difference) of the derivatives.

$$\text{If } f(x) = x^6 + x^7 - x^{5/2}, \text{ then}$$
$$f'(x) = 6x^5 + 7x^6 - \frac{5}{2}x^{3/2}.$$

Read rule 3 carefully and take a look at some applications. (These problems are posed differently so that you become familiar with a different notation for the derivative.)

1. If $y = 3x^5$, then $y' = 0(x^5) + 3(5x^4) = 15x^4$.

2. If $y = (7x - 9)(2x^2 + 5x + 2)$, then
$$\begin{aligned} y' &= (7)(2x^2 + 5x + 2) + (7x - 9)(4x + 5) \\ &= 14x^2 + 35x + 14 + 28x^2 + 35x - 36x - 45 \\ &= 42x^2 + 34x - 31. \end{aligned}$$

NOTE: We could have multiplied the original expression to obtain $y = 14x^3 + 17x^2 - 31x - 18$. Find y' for this expression; you should get the same result.

Now an application is given for rule 4, the quotient rule. (Again, these problems are posed differently so that you become familiar with another notation for the derivative.)

1. If $y = \dfrac{5}{x^3}$, then

$$y' = \frac{x^3(0) - 5(3x^2)}{(x^3)^2} = \frac{-15x^2}{x^6} = \frac{-15}{x^4}.$$

And just so we don't lose sight of how these functions are related, verify that the equation for the tangent line to $y = \dfrac{5}{x^3}$ at the point $P(2, 0.625)$ is $y = -0.9375x + 2.5$ (see graph).

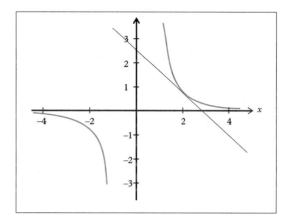

2. If $s(t) = \dfrac{-t^2}{2t^3 + t - 5}$

represents distance with respect to time, then
$$\frac{ds}{dt} = v(t)$$

$$= \frac{(2t^3 + t - 5)(-2t) - (-t^2)(6t^2 + 1)}{(2t^3 + t - 5)^2}$$

$$= \frac{2t^4 - t^2 + 10t}{(2t^3 + t - 5)^3}$$

(Multiply and combine like terms.) The expression ds/dt represents the rate of change of distance with respect to time (velocity).

NOTE: After rule 4 has been applied and you are trying to simplify the derivative, DO NOT multiply out the denominator; all you have to do is multiply and simplify the numerator. Then perhaps you can factor and cancel. This is true in many problems involving the quotient rule.

At this point, you should have a pretty good idea how differentiation goes with polynomials. Next, we

Derivatives of trig functions

$$\frac{d}{dx}(\sin x) = \cos x$$

$$\frac{d}{dx}(\cos x) = -\sin x$$

$$\frac{d}{dx}(\tan x) = \sec^2 x$$

$$\frac{d}{dx}(\cot x) = -\csc^2 x$$

$$\frac{d}{dx}(\sec x) = \sec x \tan x$$

$$\frac{d}{dx}(\csc x) = -\csc x \cot x$$

---

consider differentiating expressions involving trig functions. You should certainly memorize the formulas in "Derivatives of trig functions" above. Consider the following applications.

1. If $g(y) = \sqrt{3} \sin y$, then $\frac{dg}{dy} = \sqrt{3} \cos y$.

2. If $y = (\pi x - x^3)(\tan x)$, then we need the product rule to find that

$$\frac{dy}{dx} = (\pi x - x^3)(\sec^2 x) + (\pi - 3x^2)(\tan x).$$

Recall the algebraic operation of composition:

If $f(x) = \sin x$ and $g(x) = x^2 + 3$,

then $f \circ g = f[g(x)] = f[x^2 + 3] = \sin(x^2 + 3)$.

Now let's use rule 5.

1. $\frac{d}{dx}[\sin(x^2 + 3)] = \cos(x^2 + 3) \cdot (2x)$

$$= 2x \cos(x^2 + 3).$$

2. If $f(x) = \sqrt{x^2 - 5x + 2} = (x^2 - 5x + 2)^{1/2}$, then

$$f'(x) = \frac{1}{2}(x^2 - 5x + 2)^{-1/2}(2x - 5)$$

$$= \frac{2x - 5}{2\sqrt{x^2 - 5x + 2}}.$$

To finish, we'll return to the problem posed at the beginning of this section. If $f(x) = x^2 - \cos 4\pi x$, then $f'(x) = 2x - (-\sin 4\pi x)(4\pi) = 2x + 4\pi \sin 4\pi x$. Next, find the equation for the tangent line at $P(2.22, 5.86)$. (Make sure your calculator is in radians.)

$$f'(2.22) = 2(2.22) + 4\pi \sin 4\pi(2.22) = -2.79$$

So,

$$y - 5.86 = 9.07(x - 2.22) \Rightarrow y = 9.07x - 14.27.$$

Graph this line and $y = x^2 - \cos 4\pi x$ in the viewing rectangle [2, 3], 1 and [0, 10], 2. You should see something like the graph below. TRACE to verify the point of tangency.

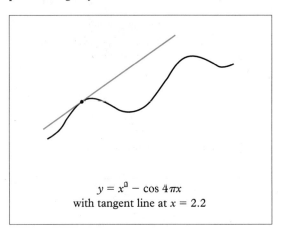

$y = x^2 - \cos 4\pi x$
with tangent line at $x = 2.2$

Exercise
Determine the equation and graph the tangent line at $P(2.3, 6.1)$ on the curve $y = x^2 - \cos 4\pi x$.

Differentiability and continuity. When is a continuous function differentiable? To answer this question, consider the function

$$f(x) = |\sin x| \quad \text{(see the graph below).}$$

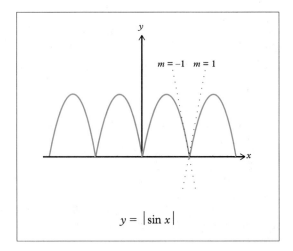

$y = |\sin x|$

Remember that the derivative at a point is the slope of the tangent line. And the way we defined the slope of the tangent line was as the limiting slope of the secant lines. And we insisted that this limit be unique.

Let's try to find the slope of the tangent line to f at the point $P(\pi, 0)$. Before we take the derivative of f, we have to get rid of the absolute value sign. So we must consider two functions.

Left-hand side of P	Right-hand side of P
$f(x) = \sin x$	$f(x) = -\sin x$
$f'(x) = \cos x$	$f'(x) = -\cos x$
$f'(\pi) = \cos \pi = -1$	$f'(\pi) = -\cos \pi = 1$

So we have two different tangent lines at $x = \pi$. Mathematicians don't deal well with ambiguities, so they say the derivative does not exist at $x = \pi$. Are there any other points on this curve where the derivative fails to exist? In general, can you describe what a function might look like at a point where the derivative does not exist?

Special differentiation.

The process of differentiation is used to solve many different types of application problems. The different circumstances are dealt with more easily if you know some special differentiation techniques.

The chain rule. We already considered one version of the chain rule when we found the derivative of a composite function (rule 5 on page 138). Say that we have y as a function of u, and u as a function of x, such that

$$y = 3u^2 \quad (1) \quad \text{and}$$

$$u = 7x^3 - 6x^2 - 9 \quad (2).$$

We can find $\dfrac{dy}{du}$ and $\dfrac{du}{dx}$, but can we find $\dfrac{dy}{dx}$? One way is to form the composition of functions

$$y \circ u = 3(7x^3 - 6x^2 - 9)^2$$

and use rule 5 to get

$$\frac{dy}{dx} = 6(7x^3 - 6x^2 - 9)(21x^2 - 12x).$$

But there is another version of the chain rule which we can use to find $\dfrac{dy}{dx}$ directly from equations 1 and 2.

$$\frac{dy}{dx} = \frac{dy}{du} \cdot \frac{du}{dx} \quad (3)$$

$$= 6u \cdot (21x^2 - 12x)$$

$$= 6(7x^3 - 6x^2 - 9)(21x^2 - 12x)$$

Equation 3 is called the "chain rule" because it deals with a chain of functions. Equation 3 seems to make sense algebraically because the du's on the right-hand side cancel out to leave $\dfrac{dy}{dx}$. Although theoretically that's not the way this formula is proved, at this point in your studies it won't hurt you to think of it that way.

For another example of the chain rule, consider carefully the following example. The cost of produce items at the grocery store is a function of many variables. Let

$$C(v) = -0.5 \sin (2v) - 0.5 \cos v + 1.5$$

represent the cost as a function of availability. And let

$$v(r) = 0.75 \sin r + 0.65 \cos (2r) + 1.5$$

represent availability as a function of the amount of rainfall. And finally, let

$$r(t) = -0.5 \sin (2t) + 0.5 \cos t + 1.5$$

represent the amount of rainfall as a function of time. We would like to calculate the rate of change of the cost as a function of time, $\dfrac{dC}{dt}$. Doing a composition of functions would be a horrendous mess.

Example

Find $\dfrac{dC}{dv}$, $\dfrac{dv}{dr}$, and $\dfrac{dr}{dt}$.

Now we can use the chain rule to find $\dfrac{dC}{dt}$.

$$\frac{dC}{dt} = \frac{dC}{dv} \cdot \frac{dv}{dr} \cdot \frac{dr}{dt}$$

$$= (-\cos 2v + 0.5 \sin v)(0.75 \cos r - 1.3 \sin 2r) \times$$
$$(-\cos 2t - 0.5 \sin t)$$

★ ★ ★

Example

What is the rate of change of cost at time $t = \pi$?
Verify that $r(\pi) = 1$ and $v(1) = 1.86$.
So, the rate of change of cost at $t = \pi$ is given by

$$\frac{dC}{dt} = [-\cos (2 \cdot 1.86) + \sin 1.86] \times$$

$$(0.75 \cos 1 - 1.3 \sin 2)(-\cos 2\pi - 0.5 \sin \pi).$$

$$\frac{dC}{dt} \approx 1.02.$$

★ ★ ★

How about one more example to make sure you understand it?

Example

Find $\dfrac{dy}{dx}$ if $y = \sin(\cos^2 x)$.

This could be fairly tricky if we try to work the problem in its present form. Let's *undo* the composition of functions and use our new chain rule.

Let $y = \sin u$ and $u = (\cos x)^2$.

$$\frac{dy}{dx} = \frac{dy}{du} \cdot \frac{du}{dx}$$

$$= \cos u \cdot 2(\cos x) \cdot (-\sin x)$$

$$= \cos(\cos^2 x) \cdot (-2 \cos x \sin x)$$

★ ★ ★

Notice that we used both versions of the chain rule in solving this problem.

Implicit differentiation. The equation $x^2 + y^2 = 4$ describes a circle centered at the origin with radius 2. The two equations $y = \sqrt{4 - x^2}$ and $y = -\sqrt{4 - x^2}$ describe the same circle. In the second case, y is given as a clearly defined function of x. These two equations can be derived by isolating y in the first equation.

$$x^2 + y^2 = 4 \quad \Rightarrow \quad y^2 = 4 - x^2 \quad \Rightarrow \quad y = \pm\sqrt{4 - x^2}$$
implicit form   *explicit form*

In the first case, it is not readily apparent that y is a function of x, so this is referred to as the *implicit form*.

We know how to find $\dfrac{dy}{dx}$ from the explicit form.

If $y = \sqrt{4 - x^2}$, then

$$\frac{dy}{dx} = \frac{1}{2}(4 - x^2)^{-1/2}(-2x)$$

$$= \frac{-2x}{2\sqrt{4 - x^2}} = \frac{-x}{\sqrt{4 - x^2}}$$

It follows that if $y = -\sqrt{4 - x^2}$, then

$$\frac{dy}{dx} = \frac{x}{\sqrt{4 - x^2}}.$$

Now, can we use the implicit form of the equation to find $\dfrac{dy}{dx}$? Amazingly, we can, and it does make finding the derivative a lot easier. But first, you need to understand the process of *implicit differentiation*. What you need to keep in mind is that y is a function of x.

Here is where the process of implicit differentiation comes from. Let $g(y) = y^n$ and $y = f(x)$. Using the chain rule and the power rule, we get

$$\frac{dg}{dx} = \frac{dg}{dy} \cdot \frac{dy}{dx} = ny^{n-1}\frac{dy}{dx}.$$

Now, to differentiate the equation for the circle, we differentiate each term in the equation with respect to x, keeping in mind that y is a function of x. Here's how it goes:

$$x^2 + y^2 = 4$$

$$\underset{\substack{power \\ rule}}{2x} \quad + \quad \underset{\substack{implicit \\ with\ n = 2}}{2y\frac{dy}{dx}} \quad = \quad \underset{\substack{derivative \\ of\ constant}}{0}$$

Now, use algebra to solve for $\dfrac{dy}{dx}$.

$$2y\frac{dy}{dx} = -2x \Rightarrow \frac{dy}{dx} = \frac{-2x}{2y} = \frac{-x}{y}$$

Let $y = \sqrt{4 - x^2}$, and you see we get the same result for $\dfrac{dy}{dx}$ that we did earlier.

Here's a case that causes a lot of grief for students, but you're lucky because you have this book!

Example

Find $\dfrac{dy}{dx}$ if $xy = 5$.

(It would be easy enough to isolate y here, but of course the problems will get more difficult and you won't always be able to.) You need to be able to deal with this type of expression.) We need to use the product rule.

$$\underset{\substack{derivative \\ of\ first \\ factor}}{1} \quad \cdot \quad \underset{\substack{second \\ factor}}{y} \quad + \quad \underset{\substack{derivative \\ of\ second \\ factor}}{1 \cdot \frac{dy}{dx}} \quad \cdot \quad \underset{\substack{first \\ factor}}{x} \quad = \quad \underset{\substack{derivative \\ of\ constant}}{0}$$

So if you can remember that the derivative of xy is $y + x\dfrac{dy}{dx}$, you will be three steps ahead of your class.

★ ★ ★

Calculus

Simplifying implicit differentiation

Many textbooks (and teachers) overcomplicate the process of implicit differentiation by using too much notation. This is really very simple if you don't mind talking to yourself as you work the problem. Given an implicit equation with x's and y's (with $y = f(x)$), you take the derivative of the x-terms and the y-terms the same way, except when you take the derivative of a y-term, multiply by $\frac{dy}{dx}$.

$$3x^2 + 5y^3 = x + y$$
$$6x + 15y^2\frac{dy}{dx} = 1 + 1 \cdot \frac{dy}{dx}$$

In many equations it would be difficult, or maybe impossible, to isolate y. Then, implicit differentiation is the only way to get the rate of change of one variable with respect to the other.

Example

Given $4x^3 + 11xy^2 - 2y^3 = 0$, find $\frac{dy}{dx}$.

$$12x^2 + 11\left(y^2 + 2y\frac{dy}{dx} \cdot x\right) - 6y^2\frac{dy}{dx} = 0$$

$$12x^2 + 11y^2 + 22xy\frac{dx}{dy} - 6y^2\frac{dy}{dx} = 0$$

$$(22xy - 6y^2)\frac{dy}{dx} = -12x^2 - 11y^2$$

$$\frac{dy}{dx} = \frac{-(12x^2 + 11y^2)}{22xy - 6y^2} = \frac{12x^2 + 11y^2}{6y^2 - 22xy}$$

$\star$ $\quad\star\quad$ $\star$

Example

Given $3y^2 - xy^3 + \cos xy = 4$, find $\frac{dy}{dx}$ at the point $(0, 1)$.

$$6y\frac{dy}{dx} - \left(y^3 + 3y^2\frac{dy}{dx} \cdot x\right) - \sin(xy)\left(y + x\frac{dy}{dx}\right) = 0$$

Rather than isolate $\frac{dy}{dx}$, substitute $x = 0$, $y = 1$.

$$6 \cdot 1\frac{dy}{dx} - \left[(1)^3 + 3 \cdot 1^2\frac{dy}{dx} \cdot 0\right] - \sin(0 \cdot 1) \times$$

$$\left(1 + 0 \cdot \frac{dy}{dx}\right) = 0$$

Higher-order derivatives

1st derivative	$f'(x)$	y'	$\frac{dy}{dx}$
2nd derivative	$f''(x)$	y''	$\frac{d^2y}{dx^2}$
3rd derivative	$f'''(x)$	y'''	$\frac{d^3y}{dx^3}$
4th derivative	$f^{(4)}(x)$	$y^{(4)}$	$\frac{d^4y}{dx^4}$
10th derivative	$f^{(10)}(x)$	$y^{(10)}$	$\frac{d^{10}y}{dx^{10}}$
nth derivative	$f^{(n)}(x)$	$y^{(n)}$	$\frac{d^ny}{dx^n}$

$$6\frac{dy}{dx} - (1 + 0) - 0(1) = 0$$

$$\frac{dy}{dx} = \frac{1}{6}$$

$\star$ $\quad\star\quad$ $\star$

Higher-order derivatives. The operation of differentiation takes a function f and produces a new function f'. If we now differentiate f', we get another function, denoted by f'' (read "f double prime"). This function is called the *second derivative* of f. If we differentiate we get f''' (read "f triple prime"), which is called the *third derivative* of f. How long can this process be continued? As long as you want (or need). Throughout your study of calculus, you will find many uses for these *higher-order derivatives*.

As an example of repeated differentiation, let

$$f(x) = 2x^3 - 5x^2 + 9x - 11.$$

Then

$$f'(x) = 6x^2 - 10x + 9$$
$$f''(x) = 12x - 10$$
$$f'''(x) = 12$$
$$f^{(4)}(x) = 0.$$

Since the derivative of 0 is 0, all the higher-order derivatives of f will be zero. In general, an nth degree polynomial will have n nonzero derivatives. All derivatives of order $n+1$ and greater will be zero. So, if you were asked to find $f^{(10)}(x)$ given

Higher-order derivatives

1st derivative	$f'(x)$	y'	$\dfrac{dy}{dx}$
2nd derivative	$f''(x)$	y''	$\dfrac{d^2y}{dx^2}$
3rd derivative	$f'''(x)$	y'''	$\dfrac{d^3y}{dx^3}$
4th derivative	$f^{(4)}(x)$	$y^{(4)}$	$\dfrac{d^4y}{dx^4}$
10th derivative	$f^{(10)}(x)$	$y^{(10)}$	$\dfrac{d^{10}y}{dx^{10}}$
nth derivative	$f^{(n)}(x)$	$y^{(n)}$	$\dfrac{d^ny}{dx^n}$

$$f(x) = 3x^5 - 4x^3 + 7x^2 - \sqrt{2}x + \pi,$$

you could answer quickly, $f^{(10)}(x) = 0$.

The different notations used for these higher-order derivatives are shown above. When working with repeated differentiation, be on the lookout for substitutions, simplifications, and patterns.

Example

If $y = \sin 3x$, find $\dfrac{d^3y}{dx^3}$, $\dfrac{d^4y}{dx^4}$, and $\dfrac{d^{12}y}{dx^{12}}$.

$$\dfrac{dy}{dx} = 3 \cos 3x$$

$$\dfrac{d^2y}{dx^2} = -3^2 \sin 3x \quad (6) \quad (10) \quad (14)$$

$$\dfrac{d^3y}{dx^3} = -3^3 \cos 3x \quad (7) \quad (11) \quad (15)$$

$$\dfrac{d^4y}{dx^4} = 3^4 \sin 3x \quad (8) \quad (12) \quad (16)$$

$$\dfrac{d^5y}{dx^5} = 3^5 \cos 3x \quad (9) \quad (13) \quad (17)$$

$$\vdots$$

$$\dfrac{d^{12}y}{dx^{12}} = 3^{12} \sin 3x$$

★ ★ ★

In this case, the second, third, fourth, and fifth derivatives keep repeating; the only thing that changes is the power on the 3. Counting through those four deriva-

Patterns of repeated derivatives

Familiarize yourself with the pattern in taking repeated derivatives of

$$f(x) = \frac{1}{x}$$

$$f'(x) = \frac{-1}{x^2}$$

$$f''(x) = \frac{2}{x^3}$$

$$f'''(x) = \frac{-6}{x^4}$$

$$f^{(4)}(x) = \frac{24}{x^5}$$

$$f^{(5)}(x) = \frac{-120}{x^6}$$

tives (the numbers in the columns to the right of the derivatives) will enable us to find the higher order derivatives easily. That's how we found $\dfrac{d^{12}y}{dx^{12}}$. Do you

see that $\dfrac{d^{15}y}{dx^{15}} = -3^{15} \cos 3x$?

Here is an example of a substitution/simplification.

Example

If $x^2 - y^2 = 16$, find $\dfrac{d^2y}{dx^2}$.

$$2x - 2y\frac{dy}{dx} = 0 \Rightarrow \frac{dy}{dx} = \frac{x}{y} \quad \star$$

Now, use the quotient rule and implicit differentiation.

$$\frac{d^2y}{dx^2}$$

$$= \frac{y \cdot 1 - x \cdot \dfrac{dy}{dx}}{y^2} = \frac{y - x \cdot \dfrac{x}{y}}{y^2} \quad (from\star)$$

$$= \frac{y^2 - x^2}{y^3} = \frac{-16}{y^3} \quad \begin{array}{l}(Substitute\ from \\ original\ equation.)\end{array}$$

★ ★ ★

Calculus

Applications of differentiation.

The word *applications* usually hits right near the panic button of most mathematics students, because "applications" means "word problems." Just when you thought you might be getting the hang of finding derivatives, your teacher drops the "applications" bombshell. But you are lucky, because you have this book to cheer you along. Read the sections over and over again until you have extracted all the meaning you can from the examples and descriptions. And most important, DON'T GIVE UP. No one was born knowing how to do calculus; give yourself some time to let the concepts sink in.

Newton's root-finding method. For as long as you have been studying algebra, you have been solving equations. While trying to keep straight the different techniques required to solve different types of equations, have you ever wished for one method that would work on all problems? If so, your prayers will be answered with Newton's method. We will do an example to see how the method works. Suppose we want to find all real roots of the polynomial $f(x) = x^5 - 2x^3 + x^2 - 1$ (see graph below). The equation has three real roots in the interval $[-2, 2]$. Let's first try to find the root between -1 and 0.

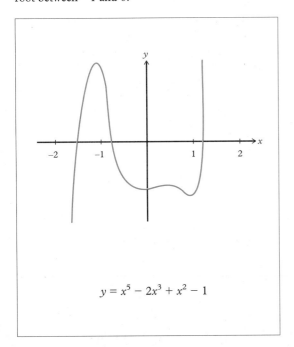

$$y = x^5 - 2x^3 + x^2 - 1$$

Exercise

Using the graph on this page, make a sketch of the tangent line to the curve at $x = -1$ (we'll refer to $x = -1$ as our initial guess, or guess 1). Do you find that the line seems to fall on top of the curve? Now, if we found the x-intercept of the tangent line (a simple matter for a linear equation), we would have something pretty close to the root of the original polynomial. Let's find the equation for that tangent line! We need a point:

at $x = -1, f(-1) = -1 + 2 + 1 - 1$
$$= 1 \Rightarrow P(-1, 1) = (a, b).$$

And we need the slope at $x = -1$:

$$f'(x) = 5x^4 - 6x^2 + 2x \Rightarrow m = f'(-1) = -3.$$

So, from the point-slope form of a line we get

$$y - 1 = -3(x + 1) \Rightarrow y = -3x - 2.$$

Exercise

In the viewing rectangle X $[-1, -0.25]$, 0.25 and Y $[-1, 1]$, 0.25, graph $f(x)$ and the tangent line we just found.

As you can see from this graph, the x-intercept of the tangent line (call it guess 2) comes pretty close to the x-intercept of the curve. Let's use guess 2 to generate another tangent line to see if we can get closer to the root. Since guess 2 is the x-intercept, we can let $y = 0$ in the equation for the tangent line to get

$$0 = -3x - 2 \Rightarrow x = \frac{-2}{3}.$$

Exercise

Use the process already outlined to verify that the tangent line at $x = \frac{-2}{3}$ is $y = -3.0124x$

$- 2.1029$. The x-intercept of this line is $x = -0.6982$ (guess 3).

Notice that $f\left(guess\ 2 = \frac{-2}{3}\right) = -0.0947$ and

$$f(guess\ 3 = -0.698) = 0.0017.$$

What we have is that $x = -0.698$ is the root of the polynomial to two decimal places of accuracy. Finding successive tangent lines would give us greater accuracy. Each time we find where the tangent line intersects the x-axis, we are doing another *iteration* of the same steps. So Newton's method is called an *iterative method*, and we can devise a quick way to find a root on the calculator.

Calculator procedure for Newton's method

1. STORE $f(x)$ in f_1 of the function list.
2. Guess a first approximation to the root of the equation $f(x) = 0$. A graph of $y = f(x)$ will help.
3. STORE $f'(x)$ in f_2 of the function list.
4. Enter (Guess 1) $\rightarrow X$
5. Decide how many decimal places of accuracy you want for the answer. Set your calculator to the number of decimal places *plus 1*.
6. Enter the line $X - f_1 \div f_2 \rightarrow X$, then EXE. This is Guess 2.
7. Keep hitting EXE until the number repeats. Now you have the root!

When we use the formula $y - b = m\ (x - a)$ to get the x-intercept of the tangent line, here's what we get.

$(a, b) = (\text{Guess}, f(\text{Guess}))$

$y = 0$ because we wanted the x-intercept.

$m = f'(\text{Guess})$

$x = \text{New guess}$

So the point-slope form becomes

$0 - f(\text{Guess}) = f'(\text{Guess})[(\text{New guess}) - \text{Guess}]$.

Now, solving this equation for New guess, we get

$$\textit{New guess} = \textit{Guess} - \frac{f(\textit{Guess})}{f'(\textit{Guess})}.$$

Exercise

Follow the procedure for Newton's method to find the other two roots of $f(x) = x^5 - 2x^3 + x^2 - 1$. The table below shows what calculator results should look like.

Exercise

Solve the equation $\frac{x}{2} = \sin x$.

Use Newton's method with $f(x) = \frac{x}{2} - \sin x$ in the viewing rectangle $[-2.2, 2.2]$, 1 and $[-0.5, 0.5]$, 0.1.

The three roots are:

$x = 0$	*by observation*
$x = -1.89549$	*3 iterations with initial guess, −2*
$x = 1.89549$	*symmetry*

Exercise

Solve the same equation trying $x = \frac{\pi}{3}$ as the initial guess. Did you get a MATH ERROR message? That's because $f'\left(\frac{\pi}{3}\right) = 0$. In cases where the initial guess yields a horizontal tangent line, Newton's method will fail since it is based on finding the x-intercept of the tangent line. So just try a different initial guess.

Calculator results

$-2 \rightarrow x$		$1 \rightarrow x$	
	−2.00000		1.00000
$x - f_1 \div f_2 \rightarrow x$		$x - f_1 \div f_2 \rightarrow x$	
	−1.75000		2.00000
	−1.60484		1.68333
	−1.54946		1.46419
	−1.54149		1.34190
	−1.54133		1.30247
	−1.54133		1.29870
			1.29867
			1.29867

Five iterations to converge to the root $x = -1.54133$

Seven iterations to converge to the root $x = 1.29867$

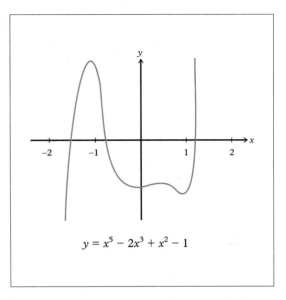

$$y = x^5 - 2x^3 + x^2 - 1$$

Using derivatives to investigate functions and curves. If your teacher asked, "What is a derivative?," you might answer, "It is a function that expresses the rate of change of another function."

Teacher: How does the derivative tell you about rate of change?

Student: With the derivative function, you can find the slope of the tangent line to the original function at any point on the curve. And you said we should use the slope of the tangent line to express the rate of change.

Teacher: Right! Do you think derivatives are good for anything else?

Student: Well, they can be used to approximate the roots of a function and . . . I'm not sure what else. Is there anything else?

Teacher (big smile): Yes. . . .

In the "olden days" (a couple of years ago, before most students had graphics calculators), derivatives were used to sketch curves. For example, if you had to sketch the function $y = x^5 - 2x^3 + x^2 - 1$, you would be able to find the roots since that's what we did in the last section. But, without a graphics calculator or computer, you would have to make a table of values a mile

long to see the curve shown in the graph above. Derivatives can be used to determine all the important characteristics of curves, as shown in the table below. Luckily, we have the calculator to help us with sketching the curve, but we still need to identify with accuracy the characteristics that are listed there.

Exercise
Graph the function $f(x) = x^3 - 6x^2 - 15x + 55$ in the viewing rectangle $[-4, 8]$, 1 and $[-50, 65]$, 10. You can see that there is a local maximum in the second quadrant and a local minimum in the fourth quadrant. Use ZOOM and TRACE to find the coordinates of these points.

You may or may not have found these points exactly, since ZOOM and TRACE depend on the resolution of points on the screen. So, ZOOM and TRACE will yield nice *estimates* but, as calculus students, you can do better than an estimate. And you could not find the inflection points with ZOOM and TRACE.

Important characteristics of the curve $y = f(x)$

Characteristic	Description
x-intercepts	Where f crosses x-axis
Local maximum	Largest y-value in a region
Local minimum	Smallest y-value in a region
Intervals where f is increasing	Graph rises from left to right
Intervals where f is decreasing	Graph falls from left to right
Intervals where f is concave up	Secant line is above the graph
Intervals where f is concave down	Secant line is below the graph
Inflection points	Where f changes from concave up to concave down

The table opposite summarizes the steps needed to accurately describe the characteristics of the curve $y = x^3 - 6x^2 - 15x + 55$. The accompanying graph provides the proof as to why these steps work. *Study the table and the graph carefully.* (That means you should read them over and over again.) At first, the concepts seem very subtle, but once you understand the concepts, they are so obvious that you will know when you understand. Here are some things that should *become* obvious:

- The point A on $f(x)$: If you sketched the tangent line here, it would be horizontal (slope 0). So the graph of $f'(x)$ crosses the x-axis (A').
- On the left-hand side of A, tangent lines to $y = f(x)$ would slant to the right (they have positive slope). So in this interval $y = f'(x)$ is above the x-axis.
- On the right-hand side of A, tangent lines to $y = f(x)$ would slant to the left (they have negative slope). So in this interval, $y = f'(x)$ is below the x-axis. Why does $y = f'(x)$ cross the x-axis at C'?
- If you started drawing tangent lines at the far left side of $y = f(x)$, the slopes would decrease steadily until you reached point B; then the slopes of the tangent lines would start to increase. So at B', $f'(x)$ has a minimum which means $f''(x)$ has a zero.

Now let's use the same steps to accurately describe the curve $y = x^5 - 2x^3 + x^2 - 1$.

1. $f'(x) = 5x^4 - 6x^2 + 2x$, $f''(x) = 20x^3 - 12x + 2$
2. Since there is no simple algebraic solution to $5x^4 + 6x^2 + 2x = 0$, let's use Newton's method. Graphing the function in the viewing rectangle $[-2, 2]$, 1 and $[-2, 2]$ 1, we see there are four roots:

Initial guess	Root	Number of iterations
−1	−1.2345	5
0		By inspection
0.5	0.3785	2
1	0.856	4

3. It is fairly obvious from the graph on page 147 that $x = -1.2345$ leads to a local maximum, but the graph behaves more subtly between −1 and 1. So let's not skip any steps here. (You should have f, f', and f'' in function memory so that they are easy to evaluate.)
   - $f''(-1.2345) = -20.8 < 0$; so since $f(-1.2345) = 1.4195$, then at $A(-1.2345, 1.4195)$ $f(x)$ has a local maximum.
   - $f''(0) = 2 > 0$; so since $f(0) = -1$, then at $B(0, -1)$ $f(x)$ has a local minimum.
   - $f''(0.3785) = -1.4575 < 0$; so since $f(0.3785) = -0.9574$, then at $C(0.3785, -0.9574)$ has a local maximum.

- $f''(0.856) = 4.3 > 0$; so since $f(0.856) = -1.0621$, then at $D(0.856, -1.0621)$ $f(x)$ has a local minimum.
4. Again, there is no simple algebraic solution to the equation $f''(x) = 20x^3 - 12x + 2 = 0$. Enter $f'''(x) = 60x^2 - 12$ into f_3 and alter Newton's formula to $X - f_2 \div f_3 \to X$. Graph $f_2 = f''(x)$ in the viewing rectangle $[-2, 2]$, 1 and $[-2, 2]$, 1, and we see there are three roots:

Initial guess	Root	Number of iterations
−1	−0.8474	3
0	0.1757	3
1	0.6716	5

Let's find the y-values and the inflection points.
$f(-0.8474) = 0.4981$ $E(-0.8474, 0.4981)$
$f(0.1757) = -0.9798$ $F(0.1757, -0.9798)$
$f(0.6716) = -1.0182$ $G(0.6716, -1.0182)$
5. See the graph.

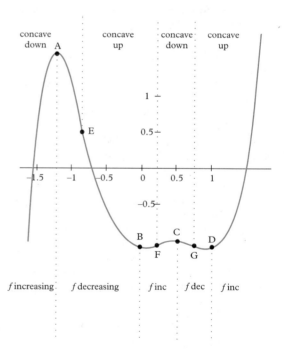

Is that the whole story? Not quite, since there are usually exceptions to rules. As it turns out, it's not necessary that $f''(x) = 0$ at an inflection point. Also, when functions are defined on closed intervals, some maximum and minimum values get a special distinction. (See the box "Local versus absolute extrema" on page 150.)

Using derivatives to investigate functions

General steps for $y = f(x)$

1. Find $f'(x)$ and $f''(x)$

2. Determine when $f'(x) = 0$ and when $f'(x)$ does not exist. These values of x are called the *critical points* of f.

3. Evaluate $f''(x)$ at all critical points.
   If $x = c$ is a critical point, then
   if $f''(c) > 0$ then $x = c$ is a minimum
   if $f''(c) < 0$ then $x = c$ is a maximum

4. Determine where $f''(x) = 0$. These are the *inflection points* of f, where the graph changes from concave up to concave down.

5. Use your calculator to graph f; sketch on paper. Label all critical points; draw vertical lines from these points to indicate intervals where f is increasing and decreasing. Label inflection points; draw vertical lines from these points to indicate where f is concave up and concave down.

Steps if $f(x) = x^3 - 6x^2 - 15x + 55$ (*See graph.*)

$$f'(x) = 3x^2 - 12x - 15 \qquad f''(x) = 6x - 12$$

$$f'(x) = 3(x^2 - 4x - 5) = 0$$
$$(x + 1)(x - 5) = 0 \Rightarrow A' = -1 \; C' = 5$$

$$f''(5) = 18 = C'' > 0 \Rightarrow f(C') = f(5) = -45$$
$$C(5, -45) \text{ is local minimum}$$
$$f''(-1) = -18 = A'' < 0 \Rightarrow f(A') = f(-1) = 63$$
$$A(-1, 63) \text{ is local maximum}$$

$$f''(x) = 6x - 12 = 0 \Rightarrow x = 2 = B''$$
$$f(B'') = f(2) = 9 \Rightarrow B(2, 9) \text{ is inflection point}$$

(*See graph.*)

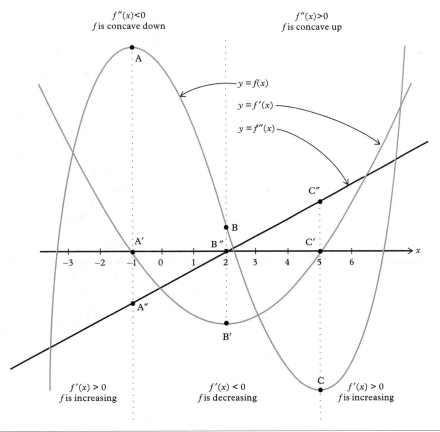

Local versus absolute extrema

A *local maximum* was described as a point with the largest y-value in a region. A curve may have several different local max's with different y-values (points A and C in the graph on page 148).

A *local minimum* was described as a point with the smallest y-value in a region. A curve may have several different local min's with different y-values (points B and D in the graph).

An *absolute maximum* will have the largest y-value in the domain of the function. There may be more than one absolute max, but they will have the same y-value.

An *absolute minimum* will have the smallest y-value in the domain of the function. There may be more than one absolute min, but they will have the same y-value.

Let's explore these ideas with the following problem.

Example

The function $f(x) = \left| 3x^2 - 8 \right|$ is defined on the interval $[-3, 2.5]$ (see the graph below).

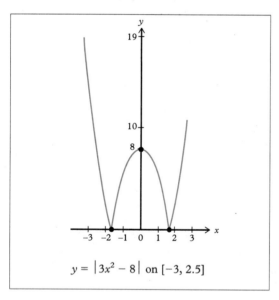

$$y = \left| 3x^2 - 8 \right| \text{ on } [-3, 2.5]$$

To find the roots of this function, we get

$$3x^2 - 8 = 0 \Rightarrow x = \pm\sqrt{\frac{8}{3}} \approx 1.633.$$

Before we find $f'(x)$, we have to get rid of those absolute value signs, so let's recall the definition of absolute value:

$$F(x) = |x| = \begin{cases} x, & \text{if } x \geq 0 \\ -x, & \text{if } x < 0 \end{cases}$$

on $[-3, -1.63] \cup [1.63, 2.5]$	on $(-1.63, 1.63)$
$f(x) = 3x^2 - 8$	$f(x) = -(3x^2 - 8)$
$f'(x) = 6x$	$f'(x) = -6x$

$x = 0$ is not in this interval. $x = 0$ is a critical point.

Also, from the graph we see that $f'(x)$ does not exist at $x = \pm1.633$; these are also critical points.

$$f''(x) = 6 > 0$$

so f is concave up on this interval.

$$f''(x) = -6 < 0$$

so f is concave down on this interval. (Also, since $f''(x)$ is always positive on this interval, then at $(0, 8)$ there must be a local maximum.)

And, we see that at $x = \pm1.633$ there are inflection points.

Now let's evaluate f at its endpoints.

$$f(-3) = 19 \text{ and } f(2.5) = 10.75$$

So, at $x = -3$, $y = 19$ is the absolute maximum of the function, and at $x = -1.633$ and $x = 1.633$, $y = 0$ is the absolute minimum.

> ### Exercise
> Determine local and absolute extrema and any intervals of concavity of the function $f(x) = x^2 - \cos 4\pi x$ on $[2, 3]$.

Related rates of change. In this section we will work on some word problems typical of those found in most calculus books. Related rate problems involve how the rates of change (the derivatives) of two or more variables are dependent upon one another. We will concentrate on rates of change with respect to time.

Before we get into the actual problems, you should review the section on implicit differentiation since that is the technique that is used to solve these problems. And in this section, we will do implicit differentiation with a new twist.

Example

The formula for surface area of a sphere is

$$S = 4\pi r^2.$$

If you were blowing up a balloon, both the radius and the surface area would change during the time you were blowing. So, in effect, both radius and surface area are functions of time in the equation above, and we have introduced a third variable, time.

$$S(t) = 4\pi[r(t)]^2$$

Now let's differentiate with respect to time.

$$\frac{dS}{dt} = 4\pi\left[2[r(t)] \cdot \frac{dr}{dt}\right] \qquad (1)$$

(We used the chain rule on the right-hand side.)

Notice that there are three variables: $\frac{dS}{dt}$, r, and $\frac{dr}{dt}$.

* * *

Let's try one more example like this.

Example

The volume of a right circular cone is given by

$$V = \frac{1}{3}\pi r^2 h$$

where r is the radius of the base and h is the height. If

all three variables were changing with respect to time, what would this relationship look like?

$$V(t) = \frac{1}{3}\pi[r(t)]^2 h(t)$$

When we differentiate with respect to time, we will have to use the product rule and the chain rule on the right-hand side.

$$\frac{dV}{dt} = \frac{1}{3}\pi\left[2r(t) \cdot \frac{dr}{dt} \cdot h(t) + \frac{dh}{dt} \cdot [r(t)]^2\right]$$

Notice there are five variables. Can you list them?

* * *

Example

Suppose that a tumor in a person's body has a spherical shape, and that treatment is causing the radius of the tumor to decrease at a rate of 1 millimeter per month (1). At what rate is the surface area of the tumor decreasing (2) when the radius is 3 millimeters (3)?

from (1): $\dfrac{dr}{dt} = \dfrac{1mm}{mo}$ from (3): $r = 3\ mm$

Procedure for related rate problems

1. State the problem.

2. Use geometric and/or physical conditions to write an equation that relates the variables.

3. Substitute values or relationships that are true at all times.

4. Differentiate both sides of the equation implicitly with respect to time.

5. Substitute the values that are known at the instant of time specified in the problem.

6. Solve the equation for the unknown quantity.

Sand is pouring from a pipe at the rate of 14 cubic feet per second onto a conical pile. If the diameter of the base is always equal to the height, how fast is the height increasing when the pile is 4 feet high?

The volume of a cone is given by $V = \dfrac{1}{3}\pi r^2 h$.

With $r = \dfrac{1}{2}h \Rightarrow V = \dfrac{1}{3}\pi\left[\dfrac{1}{4}h^2\right]h = \dfrac{\pi}{12}h^3$

So $V(t) = \dfrac{\pi}{12}[h(t)]^3$

$$\frac{dV}{dt} = \frac{\pi}{12}\left[3[h(t)]^2 \cdot \frac{dh}{dt}\right]$$

$$\frac{dV}{dt} = \frac{14\ ft^3}{sec}. \text{ So when } h = 4\ ft$$

$$\frac{14\ ft^3}{sec} = \frac{\pi}{12}\left[3(4\ ft)^2 \cdot \frac{dh}{dt}\right]$$

$$\frac{dh}{dt} = \frac{14\ ft^3}{sec}\frac{12}{48\pi ft^2} \approx \frac{1.1\ ft}{sec}$$

So, from equation 1 on page 151, we can then solve for $\dfrac{dS}{dt}$ (2).

$$\frac{dS}{dt} = 8\pi(3\ mm)\frac{1\ mm}{mo} = \frac{75mm^2}{mo}$$

Therefore, when the radius of the tumor is 3 mm, the surface area is decreasing at a rate of 75 mm^2/mo.

If you pay attention to the units, it will provide a nice verification that you have assigned the variables correctly. Using a sphere, for example, we have

length: 1 dimension   radius = 5 ft

area: 2 dimensions   surface area = $4\pi r^2 = 314\ ft^2$

volume: 3 dimensions   volume = $\dfrac{4}{3}\pi r^3 = 523\ ft^3$.

One more example.

Example

Suppose that oil is spreading in a circular pattern from a leak at an offshore rig. If the radius of the oil slick is growing at a rate of 2 feet per minute, at what rate is the area of the oil slick growing when the radius is 700 feet?

The area of the slick would be

$$A = \pi r^2.$$

The area at time t would be

$$A(t) = \pi[r(t)]^2.$$

Differentiating with respect to time, we get

$$\frac{dA}{dt} = 2\pi r(t) \cdot \frac{dr}{dt}.$$

With $r = 700\ ft$ and $\dfrac{dr}{dt} = \dfrac{2\ ft}{min}$, we get

$$\frac{dA}{dt} = 2\pi(700\ ft)(2ft/min) = 8796\ ft^2/min.$$

So that, when the radius is 700 feet, the area is growing at about 8800 ft^2/min.

Introducing L'Hôpital's rule. On pages 126 through 131, we looked at many techniques for evaluating limits. Rational expressions like

$$\lim_{x\to 0}\frac{\sin x}{x} \quad\text{and}\quad \lim_{x\to\infty}\frac{2x}{x^2+1}$$

caused grief because applying the quotient rule for limits leads to $\dfrac{0}{0}$ in the first case, and $\dfrac{\infty}{\infty}$ in the second case. In this section, we will work with a simple rule which will make evaluating limits that involve quotients such as these a breeze.

First, you need to be able to recognize the special forms represented by these limit problems. We say that

$$\lim_{x\to 0}\frac{\sin x}{x}\ \text{has the }\textit{indeterminate form}\ \frac{0}{0}\ \text{at }x=0,\ \text{and}$$

$$\lim_{x\to\infty}\frac{2x}{x^2+1}\ \text{has the }\textit{indeterminate form}\ \frac{\infty}{\infty}\ \text{as }x\to\infty.$$

If a limit problem involves a quotient which leads to either one of these indeterminate forms, then L'Hôpital's (pronounced *lo pee-TAL*) rule can be used.

L'Hôpital's rule

Consider the ratio of functions $\dfrac{f(x)}{g(x)}$. If $\lim\dfrac{f(x)}{g(x)}$
$= \dfrac{0}{0}$ or if $\lim\dfrac{f(x)}{g(x)} = \dfrac{\infty}{\infty}$, then $\lim\dfrac{f(x)}{g(x)} = \lim\dfrac{f'(x)}{g'(x)}$.

Now, let's use this rule to find the limits of the examples at the beginning of this section.

When to use L'Hôpital's rule

L'Hôpital's is a great rule if it's not misused. It can only be used when the limit calculation leads to an indeterminate form. For example,

$$\lim_{x\to 0}\frac{2x}{x^2+1} = \frac{0}{1} = 0$$

so using L'Hôpital's rule is unnecessary and would lead to an incorrect result. Applying the rule would yield

$$\lim_{x\to 0}\frac{2}{2x} = \lim\frac{1}{x}$$

which leads us to believe the limit does not exist.

Example

Since $\lim\limits_{x \to 0} \dfrac{\sin x}{x} = \dfrac{0}{0}$, then we can apply L'Hôpital's rule:

$$\lim_{x \to 0} \frac{\sin x}{x} = \lim_{x \to 0} \frac{\cos x}{1} = \frac{1}{1} = 1.$$

NOTE: We did not use the quotient rule for differentiation, we just divided the derivative of the numerator by the derivative of the denominator. Applying L'Hôpital's rule is a lot easier than applying the quotient rule for differentiation.

★ ★ ★

Example

Since $\lim\limits_{x \to \infty} \dfrac{2x}{x^2 + 1} = \dfrac{\infty}{\infty}$, then we can apply

L'Hôpital's rule:

$$\lim_{x \to \infty} \frac{2x}{x^2 + 1} = \lim_{x \to \infty} \frac{2}{2x} = \lim_{x \to \infty} \frac{1}{x} = 0$$

★ ★ ★

In the next problem, you'll see that L'Hôpital's rule may be applied more than one time in the same problem. As long as the limit expression leads to an indeterminate form, you can keep applying the rule.

Example

Find $\lim\limits_{x \to 0} \dfrac{6x - 2 \sin 3x}{5x^2}$.

We start by letting $x = 0$ in the expression

$$\lim_{x \to 0} \frac{6 \cdot 0 - 2 \sin 0}{5 \cdot 0^2} = \frac{0}{0}.$$

So L'Hôpital's rule applies.

$$\lim_{x \to 0} \frac{6x - 2 \sin 3x}{5x^2} = \lim_{x \to 0} \frac{6 - 6 \cos 3x}{10x}.$$

Evaluating the second expression at $x = 0$ yields $\dfrac{0}{0}$ so apply L'Hôpital's again.

$$\lim_{x \to 0} \frac{6 - 6 \cos 3x}{10x} = \lim_{x \to 0} \frac{0 + 18 \sin 3x}{10} = \frac{0}{10} = 0$$

So, $\lim\limits_{x \to \infty} \dfrac{6x - 2 \sin 3x}{5x^2} = 0$.

★ ★ ★

Exercise

With the process that was used in the last example, you should be able to find that

$$\lim_{x \to 0} \frac{14x - 7 \sin 2x}{6x^3} = \frac{14}{9}.$$

The operation of integration

In the previous section, "Differentiation," we studied what is usually referred to as *differential calculus*. The rate of change, or derivative, of a function is defined by the slope of the tangent line at a point on the graph. Using limiting values of the secant line, the value of the derivative at a point depends only on the values of the function in a small neighborhood around the point.

In this section, we will study some of the more global aspects of a function. In particular, we will solve the problem of finding the area of a region bounded above by $y = f(x)$ and below by the x-axis. To do this requires knowledge about the bounding curve as a whole. The need to solve this area problem brings us to *integral calculus* (*integer* is Latin for "whole"). The bounded area will be approximated more and more closely by summing areas of rectangles. The area of the region is defined as the limiting value of the sums of the rectangles.

So when it comes to derivatives, we're concerned with little bits of the function at a time. With integration, we'll be adding all the little bits to get the whole. As you will discover throughout your study of calculus, there are many applications for the summing process we call integration. But the problem that allows the beauty of the process to shine through is the area problem.

Motivation: An area problem.

For the linear function $f(x) = x$, the problem of finding the area under the line would be a matter of simple geometry. When x is in the interval from 0 to 1, the area under $y = x$ is a right triangle formed by the lines $y = x$, $x = 1$, and the x-axis (A_1 in graph A below).

Using the formula for area of a triangle, we get

$$A_1 = \frac{1}{2}bh = \frac{1}{2}(1)(1) = \frac{1}{2}.$$

When x is in the interval from 1 to 3, the region under the line forms a trapezoid where $y = x$ forms one side, the vertical lines $x = 1$ and $x = 3$ can be considered the bases, and the distance along the x-axis is the height (A_2 in graph A). Using the formula for area of a trapezoid, we get

$$A_2 = \frac{1}{2}(b_1 + b_2)h = \frac{1}{2}(1 + 3)2 = 4.$$

A function of x doesn't have to be very complicated to require more than simple geometry to find the area underneath. What if our problem was to find the area under the graph of $y = x^2$ when $x \in [0, 1]$? (See graph B).

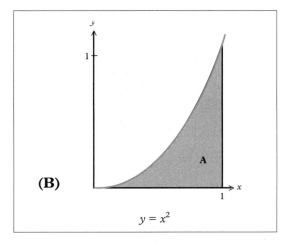

(B)

$y = x^2$

It took the work of many generations of brilliant mathematicians to solve this problem. Luckily for us, we can use their discoveries and our calculators to perform all the operations the process requires.

Let's use A to refer to the region in graph B. In math, a very standard procedure is to take a problem that cannot be solved and relate it to one that *can* be solved. So for our area problem, what we will do first is approximate the area of A using rectangles because we know how to find the area of a rectangle.

We begin by breaking up the interval $[0, 1]$ into four subintervals $[0, 0.25]$, $[0.25, 0.5]$, $[0.5, 0.75]$, $[0.75, 1]$. This breaks A into four subregions A_1, A_2, A_3, and A_4, so that $A = A_1 + A_2 + A_3 + A_4$. We can estimate the area of A by estimating the area of each subregion and adding up the results. We will use rectangles to estimate the areas of the subregions.

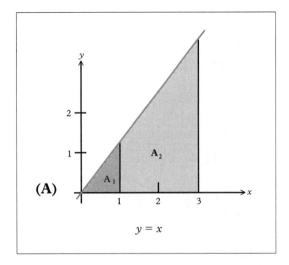

(A)

$y = x$

On each subinterval, we find the minimum value of $f(x) = x^2$ and use this as the height of an *inscribed* rectangle; call these rectangles r_1, r_2, r_3, and r_4. (See graph C.)

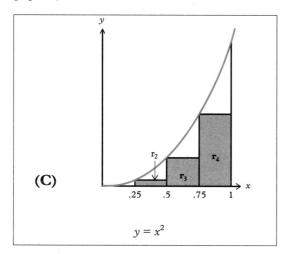

(C)

$y = x^2$

The area of each rectangle would be

$$r = base \times height = (width\ of\ subinterval) \times (f(x) = x^2).$$

Since f is increasing on [0, 1], the left endpoint will always be the minimum value of the function on that subinterval. The width of each rectangle is 0.25 so that

$$r_1 + r_2 + r_3 + r_4 = 0.25(0) + 0.25(0.25)^2$$
$$+ 0.25(0.5)^2 + 0.25(0.75)^2 = 0.21875.$$

Next, on each subinterval, we find the maximum value of $f(x) = x^2$ and use this as the height of a *circumscribed* rectangle, call these rectangles R_1, R_2, R_3, and R_4. (See graph D.)

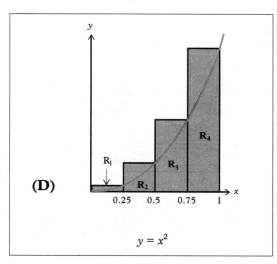

(D)

$y = x^2$

Now the right endpoint of the subinterval is the maximum value, so that

$$R_1 + R_2 + R_3 + R_4 = 0.25(0.25)^2 + 0.25(0.5)^2$$
$$+ 0.25(0.75)^2 + 0.25(1)^2 = 0.46875.$$

It is clear from graphs C and D that the number representing the area of A is somewhere between the area of the sum of the lower rectangles and the area of the sum of the upper rectangles.

$$r_1 + r_2 + r_3 + r_4 < A < R_1 + R_2 + R_3 + R_4$$

If we repeatedly subdivide each subinterval, we will get better and better estimates. But you can see how the notations and computations will quickly get out of hand. The next section will present some compact notations and calculator programs to keep the situation under control.

Upper and lower sums. Let's continue the problem we started in the last section. But before we do, I would like to write the procedure in a compact form that will work for other functions defined on more general intervals.

Again we'll use $f(x) = x^2$, but now I would like to divide the interval [0, 1] into eight subintervals and repeat the process that was developed in the last section. If we let the subintervals be

$$[0 = x_0, x_1], [x_1, x_2], \dots, [x_7, x_8 = 1],$$

then the width of each subinterval would be

$$\frac{(1 - 0)}{8} = 0.125 \text{ so that } x_i = 0.125 \cdot i \text{ where } i = 0,$$

$i = 1, \ldots, i = 8$. For example, $[x_3, x_4] = [(0.125) \cdot 3, (0.125) \cdot 4] = [0.375, 0.5]$. What would $[x_6, x_7]$, $[x_7, x_8]$ be? Does your answer make sense according to the graph below?

On each subinterval, the minimum value of the function is the left endpoint, and we'll use this as the height of rectangle r_i where $i = 1, i = 2, \ldots, i = 8$:

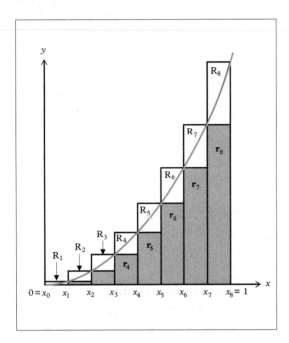

So the area of each rectangle r_i would be

$$r_i = b \times h = 0.125\, f(x_{i-1}) = 0.125(x_{i-1})^2.$$

Adding up the areas of these lower rectangles, we get

$$r_1 + r_2 + \ldots + r_8 = \sum_{i=1}^{8} r_i = \sum_{i=1}^{8} 0.125(x_{i-1})^2,$$

which is called a *lower sum* for $f(x) = x^2$.

Before we do this calculation, let's look at the upper rectangles. On each subinterval, the maximum value of the function is the right endpoint, so we'll use this as the height of the upper rectangle R_i. The area of each R_i would be $R_i = b \times h = 0.125 f(x_i) = 0.125(x_i)^2$ where $i = 1$ to 8. Adding the area of these upper rectangles, we get

$$R_1 + R_2 + \ldots + R_8 = \sum_{i=1}^{8} R_i = \sum_{i=1}^{8} 0.125(x_i)^2,$$

which is called an *upper sum* for $f(x) = x^2$.

Let's make one more observation before we do the calculations. Since the subintervals are adjacent, the right endpoint of the first subinterval is the left endpoint of the second interval, and the right endpoint of the second interval is the left endpoint of the third interval, and so on. The sharing of endpoints coupled with the fact that $y = x^2$ is increasing everywhere on the interval $[0, 1]$ leads us to notice that $r_2 = R_1$, $r_3 = R_2, \ldots, r_8 = R_7$:

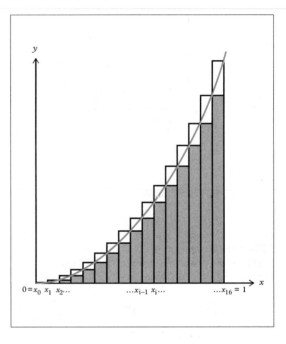

Since $r_1 = 0$, once we find the lower sum we only need to add R_8 to obtain the upper sum! This observation will reduce the amount of calculations.

Here's a simple program to calculate these sums:

Line number	Code	Comments
1	$0 \to S$	Initialize sum.
2	$0 \to X$	Start at left endpoint.
3	$1 \to I$	Interval counter
4	$0.125 \to W$	Width of rectangles
5	Lbl 1	Looping statement
6	$S + WX^2 \to S$	$wx^2 = r_i$
7	$X + W \to X$	Move x to next subinterval.
8	Isz I	Increment counter
9	$I \leq 8 \Rightarrow$ Goto 1	Accumulate sum of 8 lower rectangles.
10	"LOWER SUM": S▶	
11	$S + WX^2 \to S$	Add R_8 to lower sum.
12	"UPPER SUM": S	

(It might be less work to forget the program, and just multiply and add to get these sums, but we are working toward your *understanding* of upper and lower sums.)

You will recall that with four subintervals, we had
$$0.21875 < \text{area of } A < 0.46875$$
From this last program, with 8 subintervals, we have
$$0.27344 < \text{area of } A < 0.39844$$
Notice that the lower sum has increased and the upper sum has decreased, thus we have squeezed a little closer to the area of A. Can you give a geometric explanation as to why this happened?

Let's try to get a little closer to A by subdividing again into 16 subintervals. Now the width of the subinterval will be $\dfrac{1}{16} = 0.0625$, and with some minor editing, we can reuse the last program. Here are the lines to be edited.

Line number	*Code*	*Comments*
4	$0.0625 \to W$	Width of rectangle is $\dfrac{1}{16}$
9	$I \leq 16 \Rightarrow$ Goto 1	Accumulate sum of 16 lower rectangles

Running this program yields

LOWER SUM   0.30273

UPPER SUM   0.36523

Exercise

Edit the SUM program to handle 32 subintervals. Record the results in the table below. Edit the SUM program again to handle 64 subintervals. Record the results in the table below.

n	Lower sums = $\sum_{i=1}^{n} r_i$	Upper sums = $\sum_{i=1}^{n} R_i$	Upper sum minus lower sum
4	0.21875	0.46875	0.25
8	0.27344	0.39844	0.125
16	0.30273	0.36523	0.0625
32	_____	_____	_____
64	_____	_____	_____

1. Give a geometric explanation as to why the lower sums increase and the upper sums decrease.
2. Can you give geometric meaning to the column of values which is upper sum minus lower sum?
3. What would have to happen for us to find the *exact* value of the area of A?

Definition of definite integral.

All right, one more time from the top; and this one's for all the marbles.

Consider the region A bounded on the top by $y = f(x)$, on the bottom by $y = 0$, on the left by $x = a$, and on the right by $x = b$ (see graph). We split $[a, b]$ into n subintervals, such that
$$[a, b] = [x_0, x_1] \cup [x_1, x_2] \cup \ldots \cup [x_{n-1}, x_n]$$

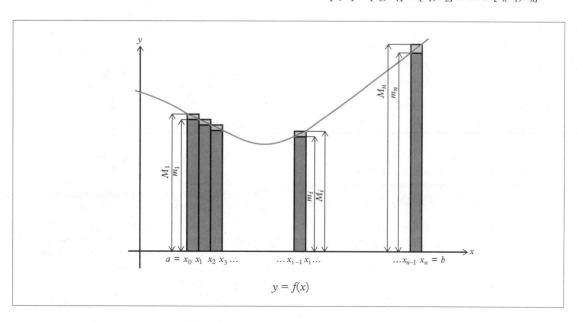

$$y = f(x)$$

So, now we have

$$A = \sum_{i=1}^{n} A_i.$$

We will estimate A by estimating each A_i where $1 \le i \le n$, and adding the results.

Let the width of each subinterval be given by

$$\Delta x = \frac{(b-a)}{n}.$$

We know that if f is a continuous function of x on $[a, b]$, it must have an absolute minimum on each subinterval, and we'll let

$$M_i = maximum\ f\ on\ [x_{i-1}, x_i]$$

$$m_i = minimum\ f\ on\ [x_{i-1}, x_i].$$

Now we're ready to talk about the rectangles.

$$r_i = m_i \cdot \Delta x_i = height \times width$$

$$R_i = M_i \cdot \Delta x_i = height \times width$$

Geometrically, we know that

$$r_i \le A_i \le R_i\ \text{for each}\ i \in [1, n].$$

So this relationship must also hold over the sum.

$$\sum_{i=1}^{n} r_i \le \sum_{i=1}^{n} A_i \le \sum_{i=1}^{n} R_i$$

Recall the tables of upper and lower sums that we generated in the last section. As n gets larger, the difference between the upper and lower sum gets smaller, meaning that we are squeezing in on the number which represents the area of the region. It seems quite reasonable to assume that as n continues to get larger, the difference between the upper and lower sums will continue to get smaller. At what point will this difference be zero? What value for n will give us *the* number which represents the area of the region? It looks as if we need a miracle, and we have one in the notion of a limit.

$$\lim_{n \to \infty} \sum_{i=1}^{n} r_i = area\ of\ A = \lim_{n \to \infty} \sum_{i=1}^{n} R_i \qquad (1)$$

The *unique* number which represents the area of A is called the *definite integral of f on [a, b]* and is denoted by $\int_a^b f(x)\ dx$. This expression is read "the integral from a to b of f of x dx."

Throughout your study of calculus and its application—areas, you will find many circumstances when the definite integral will be used to represent a limit of sums. So if you want a good conceptual understanding, we should take a stab at this from a different direction.

Once you have convinced yourself that equation 1 must be true, then you say, "Well, where did this crazy notation $\int_a^b f(x)\ dx$ come from?" Let me try to help you make some sense of it.

Consider, again, the limits

$$\lim_{n \to \infty} \sum_{i=1}^{n} r_i = \lim_{n \to \infty} \sum_{i=1}^{n} m_i \cdot \Delta x$$

$$\text{and}\ \lim_{n \to \infty} \sum_{i=1}^{n} R_i = \lim_{n \to \infty} \sum_{i=1}^{n} M_i \cdot \Delta x.$$

What happens to Δx as $n \to \infty$? If you said, "$\Delta x \to 0$ as $n \to \infty$," you are absolutely right! And if $\Delta x \to 0$, is there any point in distinguishing between an m_i and M_i? The maximum would equal the minimum, so let's just say $m_i = M_i = f(x_i)$. Now we can write

$$\lim_{n \to \infty} \sum_{i=1}^{n} f(x_i) \cdot \Delta x = \int_a^b f(x)\ dx.$$

The $\int$ is an elongated S, to represent the infinite *sum* of rectangles; $f(x)$ represents the height and dx represents the width. (Recall that as $\Delta x \to 0$, we write Δx as dx.) What we have on the right-hand side is that the sum of the little bits equals the whole area under f on $[a, b]$.

Two fundamental theorems.
In your previous math courses, you may have run across the following theorems.

The fundamental theorem of arithmetic
Every nonnegative integer can be written uniquely as a product of primes.

The fundamental theorem of algebra
Every polynomial of degree 1 or more has at least one complex zero.

Sound familiar? At these earlier levels of study, you were probably concentrating more on "getting the right answer" than on the theory behind the mechanics. As you progress to higher levels of mathematics, the need for you to be able to state theorems will become more important. In other words, your teacher will probably want you to be able to describe how integrals can be used to *define* functions (page 159) and state the theorem that allows you to find the *unique* number represented by $\int_0^\pi \sin x\ dx$. In other words, we would like to be able to evaluate $\int_0^\pi \sin x\ dx$ (page 160) without computing a table of sums of rectangles.

Why does calculus need two fundamental theorems? Well, for one thing, the first one is used to prove the second. Now, don't get too nervous; we won't prove anything here, and what's more, you probably won't have to prove anything until advanced calculus. But you certainly should have a good intuitive notion of what these theorems are all about.

The defining function $F(x) = \int_a^x f(t)\ dt$. Make a list of ordered pairs generated by each of the following functions.

1. $f(x) = \sqrt{x - 5}$. Find $f(x)$ if $x = 0, 10,$ or 21.

2. $f(t) = \sqrt{t - 5}$. Find $f(t)$ if $x = 0, 10,$ or 21.

3. $f(\maltese) = \sqrt{\maltese - 5}$. Find $f(\maltese)$ if $\maltese = 0, 10,$ or 21.

In function 2, for example, the independent variable is t. What is the independent variable in function 3?

For each function, the value of the output depends on the function, or rule itself, and not on the letter chosen to represent the independent variable. In exactly the same way, the value of the definite integral of a function f depends on the function and not on the letter chosen to represent the independent variable. In other words,

$$\int_a^b f(x)\ dx = \int_a^b f(t)\ dt = \int_a^b f(\maltese)\ d\maltese.$$

Since it doesn't matter what letter is used, the variable of integration is called a *dummy variable*.

Now brace yourself to gaze upon what is considered by many to be the most important mathematical discovery in the Western world. To describe this discovery, we begin with a function f that is continuous on a closed interval $[a, b]$. For each x in $[a, b]$ the integral

$$\int_a^x f(t)\ dt$$

is a different number (see the graph below). Consequently, we can define a function of x on $[a, b]$. Let's call it F, so that

$$F(x) = \int_a^x f(t)\ dt.$$

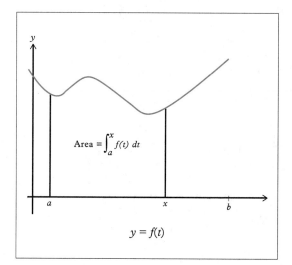

$$\text{Area} = \int_a^x f(t)\ dt$$

$$y = f(t)$$

Let's take an example of an inverse operation from algebra. If

$$f(x) = x^2, \text{ then } f^{-1}(x) = \sqrt{x}\,,$$

or the squaring function and the square root function are inverse operations: they undo each other. The same is true of integration and differentiation: they undo each other.

Here are some things to notice about this expression:
- The independent variable of this function is x; in other words, the value of F depends on the choice of x in the interval $[a, b]$.
- t is a dummy variable. It is the variable of integration and might just as well have been p or q or $\maltese$.

Now, here's the kicker:

$$F'(x) = f(x) \text{ for all } x \text{ in } (a, b).$$

(Remember, we can only differentiate on open intervals.) F is called an *antiderivative* for f on $[a, b]$, and what we have, essentially, is that differentiation is the inverse operation for integration.

The first fundamental theorem of calculus

$$\text{If } F(x) = \int_a^x f(t)\ dt,$$

$$\text{then } F'(x) = \frac{d}{dx}(F(x)) = \frac{d}{dx}\int_a^x f(t)\ dt = f(x).$$

The following example shows you how the theorem works. In the sections to come, we will be exploring numerous techniques for finding antiderivatives.

Example

Find an $F(x)$ for $\int_a^x 2t\ dt$.

We can use $F(x) = x^2$, because if

$$F(x) = x^2 = \int_a^x 2t\ dt$$

then we would have

$$F'(x) = \frac{d}{dx}(x^2) = \frac{d}{dx}\int_a^x 2t\ dt = 2x.$$

$\star \quad \star \quad \star$

The integral evaluation theorem. This theorem is the basic tool for evaluating integrals. (It is also sometimes referred to as the *second fundamental theorem of calculus.*)

The integral evaluation theorem

If f is continuous on $[a, b]$ and if F is an antiderivative of f on $[a, b]$, then

$$\int_a^b f(x)\,dx = F(x)\Big]_a^b = F(b) - F(a).$$

Let's refer to this as the FTC (Fundamental Theorem of Calculus) and put it to work.

Example

Evaluate $\int_0^1 x^2 dx$.

We need to find out what function x^2 is a derivative of. Or, to put it another way, if $f(x) = x^2$, what is $F(x)$ so that $F'(x) = f(x) = x^2$? Here's the rule we need:

If $F'(x) = x^n$, with $n \neq -1$,

then $F(x) = \dfrac{x^{n+1}}{n+1}$.

This rule yields $F(x) = \dfrac{x^3}{3}$ for this example.

So from the FTC we get

$$\int_0^1 x^2\,dx = \frac{x^3}{3}\Big]_0^1 = \frac{1^3}{3} - \frac{0^3}{3} = \frac{1}{3}.$$

This result corresponds to the approximation we got for the area under $y = x^2$ from 0 to 1 using the table of upper and lower sums.

★ ★ ★

The FTC gives us a way to evaluate the area under a curve without using rectangles.

Let's consider an example where $f(x)$ is below the x-axis on the interval $[a, b]$.

$$\int_{-1}^0 x^3\,dx = \frac{x^4}{4}\Big]_{-1}^0 = \frac{0}{4} - \frac{(-1)^4}{4} = -\frac{1}{4}$$

How can we interpret a negative area? (See the graph this page.) On the interval $[-1, 0]$, the height of the rectangles would be represented by a negative number, so the definite integral will be negative.

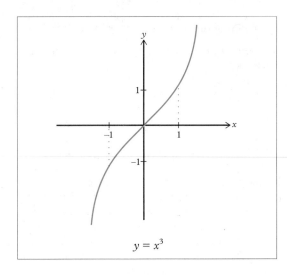

$$y = x^3$$

Exercise

Evaluate $\int_{-1}^1 x^3\,dx$. Give a geometric explanation to interpret your result.

Example

Evaluate $\int_1^3 (3x^3 + 2x - 1)\,dx$.

First, we apply property 3 from "Algebraic properties of definite integrals" opposite.

$$\int_1^3 (3x^2 + 2x - 1)\,dx$$

$$= \int_1^3 3x^3\,dx + \int_1^3 2x\,dx - \int_1^3 1 \cdot dx$$

Applying property 2, we get

$$= 3\int_1^3 x^3\,dx + 2\int_1^3 x\,dx - \int_1^3 1 \cdot dx.$$

(For the third integral, think of 1 as x^0.)

Next, use the FTC and the rule for integrating powers of x.

$$= 3\left[\frac{x^4}{4}\right]_1^3 + 2\left[\frac{x^2}{2}\right]_1^3 - \left[\frac{x^1}{1}\right]_1^3$$

$$= 3\left(\frac{3^4}{4} - \frac{1^4}{4}\right) + 2\left(\frac{3^2}{2} - \frac{1^2}{2}\right) - \left(\frac{3}{1} - \frac{1}{1}\right)$$

$$= 3\left(\frac{80}{4}\right) + 2(4) - 2 = 66$$

★ ★ ★

Now that you see how the properties work, let's work a similar example in a more condensed format.

Example

Evaluate $\int_0^2 (4x^4 - 6x^2 - 7)\, dx$.

$$\int_0^2 (4x^4 - 6x^2 - 7)\, dx = \underbrace{\frac{4x^5}{5} - \frac{6x^3}{3} - \frac{7x^1}{1}}_{F(x)} \Big]_0^2$$

$\underbrace{}_{f(x)}$

(Think of 7 as $7x^0$ to help you integrate. Also, this is a good point to check your work because if you take the derivative of $F(x)$, you should get $f(x)$.)

$$= F(2) - F(0)$$

$$= \left(\frac{4 \cdot 2^5}{5} - 2(2)^3 - 7(2) \right) - (0 - 0 - 0)$$

$$= \frac{128}{5} - 16 - 14 = -4\frac{2}{5}$$

★   ★   ★

Exercise
Graph the function $y = 4x^4 - 6x^2 - 7$ in the viewing rectangle [0, 2], 1 and [−10, 35], 5. Make a sketch and give a geometric explanation as to why

$$\int_0^2 (4x^4 - 6x^2 - 7)\, dx = -4\frac{2}{5}.$$

Algebraic properties of definite integrals

1. Order of limits of integration

$$\int_a^b f(x)\, dx = -\int_b^a f(x)\, dx$$

2. Constant multiples

$$\int_a^b cf(x)\, dx = c\int_a^b f(x)\, dx, \, c \in \mathbf{R}$$

3. Sums and differences

$$\int_a^b (f(x) \pm g(x))\, dx = \int_a^b f(x)\, dx \pm \int_a^b g(x)\, dx$$

So far, we have considered integrating polynomial functions by using the powers. Now let's consider the problem of integrating a function that involves absolute value.

Example

Evaluate $\int_{-1}^4 |x^2 - x - 2|\, dx$.

Applying the definition of absolute value, we see that

$$|x^2 - x - 2| = \begin{cases} x^2 - x - 2 & \text{if } x^2 - x - 2 \geq 0 \\ -(x^2 - x - 2) & \text{if } x^2 - x - 2 < 0 \end{cases}$$

(See graph.)

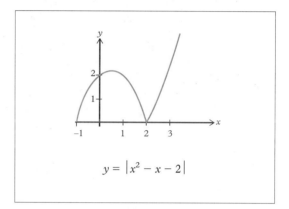

$$y = |x^2 - x - 2|$$

That is,

$$|x^2 - x - 2| = \begin{cases} 2 + x - x^2 & \text{on } [-1, 2] \\ x^2 - x - 2 & \text{on } [2, 4] \end{cases}$$

So we have to evaluate the integral separately on the intervals [−1, 2] and [2, 4] using the corresponding part of the definition of $|x^2 - x - 2|$ on each interval.

$$\int_{-1}^4 |x^2 - x - 2|\, dx$$

$$= \int_{-1}^2 |x^2 - x - 2|\, dx + \int_2^4 |x^2 - x - 2|\, dx$$

$$= \int_{-1}^2 (2 + x - x^2)\, dx + \int_2^4 (x^2 - x - 2)\, dx$$

$$= \left[2x + \frac{x^2}{2} - \frac{x^3}{3} \right]_{-1}^2 + \left[\frac{x^3}{3} - \frac{x^2}{2} - 2x \right]_2^4$$

$$= \left[\left(4 + \frac{4}{2} - \frac{8}{3}\right) - \left(-2 + \frac{1}{2} + \frac{1}{3}\right)\right]$$

$$+ \left[\left(\frac{64}{3} - \frac{16}{2} - 8\right) - \left(\frac{8}{3} - \frac{4}{2} - 4\right)\right]$$

HINT: Don't be afraid to use a calculator here.

$$= 13\frac{1}{6}$$

⋆ ⋆ ⋆

Indefinite integral notation.

The process of differentiation takes us from a function to its derivative. To use the FTC, we need to reverse this procedure. The reverse process, or *antidifferentiation*, is called *integration*. In this section we will not be concerned with finding areas, but rather we will concentrate on using integration to reverse differentiation.

Now consider the following functions and their derivatives:

$$F_1(x) = x^3 \qquad F_1'(x) = 3x^2 = f(x)$$

$$F_2(x) = x^3 + 1 \qquad F_2'(x) = 3x^2 = f(x)$$

$$F_3(x) = x^3 - 2 \qquad F_3'(x) = 3x^2 = f(x)$$

If we were looking for an antiderivative for $f(x) = 3x^2$, which F should we choose? They all have the same derivative, so we choose all of them, and more.

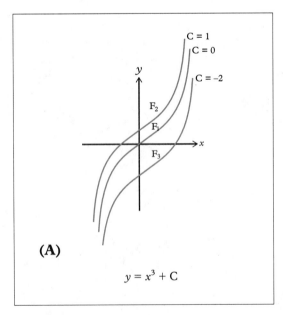

(A)

$$y = x^3 + C$$

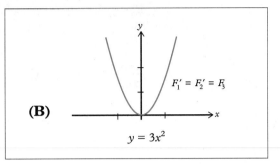

(B)

$$y = 3x^2$$

Exercise
Graph A shows the three functions given as examples earlier, and graph B shows their derivative. How many more functions would have the same derivative? Can you use vertical and/or horizontal shift to describe what the graphs of their antiderivatives would look like compared to the graphs above?

Definition

If the function $f(x)$ is a derivative, then the set of all antiderivatives of f is the *indefinite integral of f*, denoted by

$$\int f(x)\, dx.$$

That is, if $F'(x) = f(x)$, then

$$\int f(x)\, dx = F(x) + C \text{ where } C \in \mathbf{R}.$$

In this definition, notice the following:

- The symbol $\int$ is an integral sign.
- The function f is the integrand.
- x is the variable of integration.
- F is the antiderivative.
- C is the constant of integration.
- There are no limits of integration, so there are no numbers to plug in after finding the antiderivative.

Look at the antiderivative formulas opposite. Now let's see how the definition works.

Example

Find $\int 8\sqrt{x}\, dx$.

We can still use "Algebraic properties of definite integrals" presented in the last section to bring the 8 out front. We will also replace the radical sign with a rational exponent so that we can use the power rule for integration.

Calculus

$$\int 8\sqrt{x}\, dx = 8\int x^{1/2}\, dx$$

$$= 8\left(\frac{x^{3/2}}{\frac{3}{2}}\right) + C$$

$$= \frac{16\, x^{3/2}}{3} + C$$

★ ★ ★

Example

Find $\int\left(4x - \dfrac{5}{x^3}\right) dx.$

In the second term of the integrand, we would like to take the variable out of the denominator so that we can use the power rule for integration.

$$\int\left(4x - \frac{5}{x^3}\right) dx = \int (4x - 5x^{-3})\, dx$$

$$= \frac{4x^2}{2} - \frac{5x^{-2}}{-2} + C$$

$$= 2x^2 + \frac{5}{2x^2} + C$$

★ ★ ★

Example

Find $\int (x + 4\cos x + 2\sin x)\, dx.$

$$\int (x+4\cos x + 2\sin x)\, dx$$

$$= \frac{x^2}{2} + 4\sin x - 2\cos x + C$$

Antiderivatives cannot be found for all functions. To find an antiderivative for something like

$$\int x \sin x\, dx$$

requires some integration wizardry. In the next section, you will collect your own integration wizard's bag of tricks.

★ ★ ★

Antiderivative formulas

$\dfrac{d}{dx}F(x) = f(x)$	$\int f(x)\, dx = F(x) + C$
$\dfrac{d}{dx}(x) = 1$	$\int dx = x + C$
$\dfrac{d}{dx}\left(\dfrac{x^{n+1}}{n+1}\right) = x^n,\, n \neq -1$	$\int x^n\, dx = \dfrac{x^{n+1}}{n+1} + C\, n \neq -1$
$\dfrac{d}{dx}(\sin x) = \cos x$	$\int \cos x\, dx = \sin x + C$
$\dfrac{d}{dx}(-\cos x) = \sin x$	$\int \sin x\, dx = -\cos x + C$

Calculus 163

In search of an antiderivative

Techniques of integration. In the last section, the idea of the integral as a limit of sums was developed. To find the area under a curve, we took the limiting value of the areas of rectangles whose widths were getting infinitely smaller. In the next section, we will use the idea of the limits of sums of geometric shapes other than rectangles to find volumes and surfaces of revolution, and lengths of curves. The types of integrals which are a result of such problems require some manipulation before they can be easily evaluated.

As I promised you, in the following pages you will be transformed into an integration wizard, trained to perform feats of integrating magic from your bag of tricks.

u-Substitution.

This technique will be used more than any other. By using a change of variables, we can transform the integrand into a form which is easier to integrate. What a *u*-substitution accomplishes is that it helps to unsnarl the rule that allows us to find the derivative of a composition of functions (see rule 5, on page 138). Consider the function $F(x) = \sin(x^2 - 5x)$ and its derivative, $F'(x) = (2x - 5) \cos(x^2 - 5x)$. Now the problem will be to recognize $F(x)$ from

$$\int (2x - 5) \cos(x^2 - 5x)\ dx$$

Read the method outlined for *u*-substitution and let's see how it works on this problem.

Example

Evaluate $\int (x - 5)^4\ dx$.

One nasty way to do this problem would be to expand that binomial. And one nice way would be to use a *u*-substitution. Let $u = x - 5$, then $du = dx$.

So, following the steps for *u*-substitution,

$$\int (x - 5)^4\ dx$$

$$= \int u^4\ du \quad = \quad \frac{u^5}{5} + C \quad = \quad \frac{(x-5)^5}{5} + C.$$

   step 1   *step 2*   *step 3*

★   ★   ★

The method for *u*-substitution

To evaluate the integral

$$\int f(g(x))\ g'(x)\ dx,$$

follow these steps:

1. Let $u = g(x)$ and $du = g'(x)\ dx$ and rewrite the integral as

$$\int f(u)\ du.$$

2. Integrate with respect to u.
3. Back substitute. (In the result, put $g(x)$ in for u.)

Wasn't that easy? Let's do a problem now that's a little more difficult.

Example

$$\int (2x - 5) \cos(x^2 - 5x)\ dx$$

Let $u = x^2 - 5x$ and differentiate both sides to get $du = (2x - 5)\ dx$. Now substitute for $x^2 - 5x$ and $(2x - 5)\ dx$ in the integral.

$\int \cos u\ du$ *Now it's easy to integrate.*
$= \sin u + C$
$= \sin(x^2 - 5x) + C$ *Back substitute.*

★   ★   ★

Now take a deep breath and try this one. It's like the first example, but with a new twist.

Example

Evaluate $\int (2x - 5)^4\ dx$.

It looks the same as the earlier problem, so let's assign $u = 2x - 5$ and find $du = 2\ dx$.

But when we look at our original integrand, we don't see that factor of 2 outside the parentheses. Determined to do this problem with a *u*-substitution, we make it work by taking the expression $du = 2\ dx$ and isolating dx to get $\dfrac{du}{2} = dx$.

Calculus

$$\int (2x - 5)^4 \, dx = \int u^4 \, \frac{du}{2}$$

$$= \frac{1}{2} \int u^4 \, du = \frac{1}{2} \left[\frac{u^5}{5} \right] + C$$

$$= \frac{(2x - 5)^5}{10} + C$$

(Take the derivative of the last expression to verify.)

★   ★   ★

We can also use u-substitutions to evaluate definite integrals. But we will need to modify our procedure a bit.

To evaluate the integral

$$\int_{x=a}^{x=b} f(g(x))g'(x) \, dx,$$

follow these steps.

1. Let $u = g(x)$ and $du = g'(x) \, dx$.
2. Evaluate $g(a)$ and $g(b)$ and make these your new limits of integration to obtain

$$\int_{u=g(a)}^{u=g(b)} f(u) \, du.$$

3. Integrate with respect to u, using the FTC.

Example

Find $\displaystyle\int_{-1}^{2} \frac{x^2 \, dx}{(x^3 + 4)^2}$.

Let $u = x^3 + 4$ (use this expression for limits of integration), then

$$du = 3x^2 \, dx \Rightarrow \frac{1}{3} \, du = x^2 \, dx.$$

This should take care of the integrand. Now for the limits of integration.

If $x = 2$, then $u = 2^3 + 4 = 12$.   *upper limit*

If $x = -1$, then $u = (-1)^3 + 4 = 3$.   *lower limit*

So our new integral becomes

$$\int_{3}^{12} \frac{\frac{1}{3}du}{u^2} = \frac{1}{3} \int_{3}^{12} u^{-2} \, du$$

$$= \frac{1}{3} \left[\frac{u^{-1}}{-1} \right]_{3}^{12}$$

$$= \frac{1}{3} \left(\frac{-1}{12} - \frac{-1}{3} \right) = \frac{1}{3} \left(\frac{3}{12} \right) = \frac{1}{12}.$$

★   ★   ★

When an integrand involves a product of trig functions, in many cases a u-substitution works out nicely.

Example

Evaluate $\displaystyle\int_{0}^{\pi} 5 \cos^3 x \sin x \, dx$.

Now, how do you decide what to use for u? If you choose $u = \sin x$, then $du = \cos x \, dx$, but how do you deal with the $\cos^3 x$ in the integrand? You can't; so try letting

$$u = \cos x. \text{ Then } du = -\sin x \, dx.$$
$$\text{So } -du = \sin x \, dx.$$

And for the limits of integration:

If $x = \pi$, then $u = \cos \pi = -1$.
If $x = 0$, then $u \cos 0 = 1$.

So, the new integral is

$$5 \int_{1}^{-1} u^3 \, (-du) = -5 \int_{-1}^{1} u^3 \, du$$

$$= -5 \left[\frac{u^4}{4} \right]_{-1}^{1}$$

$$= -5 \left(\frac{1}{4} - \frac{1}{4} \right) = 0.$$

★   ★   ★

Exercise
Graph the function $y = 5 \cos^3 x \sin x$ in the viewing rectangle $[0, \pi]$, $\pi/4$ and $[-2, 2]$, 1. (Is your calculator in radians?) Does the answer for the definite integral in the last example make sense?

To be honest, when you work a definite integral with a u-substitution, you don't have to change the limits of integration to reflect the transformation of variables. Instead, you can just ignore the limits of integration until you have found the antiderivative. Then BS (back substitute) to put the antiderivative in terms of x, and evaluate with the original limits of integration. The following example will illustrate.

Example

To find

$$\int_1^2 \frac{x\,dx}{(x^2+1)^2},$$

let $u = x^2 + 1$. Then $du = 2x\,dx$.

Now, rewrite the integral in terms of u without the limits of integration.

$$\int \frac{\frac{du}{2}}{u^2} = \frac{1}{2}\int u^{-2}\,du = \frac{1}{2}\left(\frac{1}{-1}u^{-1}\right) = \frac{-1}{2u}$$

Now, BS from your original u assignment ($u = x^2 + 1$) and bring back the limits of integration.

$$\frac{-1}{2(x^2+1)}\Big]_1^2 = \frac{-1}{2(4+1)} - \left(\frac{-1}{2(1+1)}\right)$$

$$= \frac{-1}{10} + \frac{1}{4} = \frac{3}{20}$$

⋆   ⋆   ⋆

Numerical techniques.
There are several reasons for considering numerical techniques to evaluate the definite integral

$$\int_a^b f(x)\,dx.$$

- Implementing these methods on a programmable calculator or computer yields accurate results very quickly. In fact, many calculators have a key for
$$\int dx.$$
- After finding an antiderivative for a complicated integrand, verification with a numerical technique could ease your mind.
- There are many integrals for which an antiderivative does not exist, so a numerical technique is the only way to evaluate.

When we first looked at the problem of finding the area under a curve, rectangles were used to approximate the area. As the number of subintervals increased, the sum of the areas of the rectangles more closely approximated the area under the curve. (See the table of upper and lower sums on page 163). I will refer to the *area under the curve* to keep explanations simple and so that you might keep in mind the geometrical implications of these processes. You should, however, be aware that what we are really doing is approximating $\int_a^b f(x)\,dx;$ the definite integral of f on $[a, b]$. This represents the area between $y = f(x)$ and the x-axis. For example, consider the fact that $\int_0^{2\pi} \sin x\,dx = 0$ (see graph).

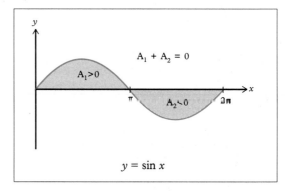

$$y = \sin x$$

From $[0, \pi]$, $f(x) = \sin x > 0$, so $\int_0^x \sin x\,dx > 0$, which represents the area of the region *below* the curve. From $[\pi, 2\pi]$, $f(x) = \sin x < 0$, so $\int_\pi^{2\pi} \sin x\,dx < 0$, which represents the area of the region *above* the curve.

Whenever $\int_a^b f(x)\,dx$ is evaluated using a numerical technique, it usually yields an *approximation*, rather than the exact value. As we saw with rectangles, the accuracy of the approximation is affected most dramatically by increasing the number n of subintervals taken on $[a, b]$. In this section we will consider two different geometric approaches that improve the approximation for any given n. What geometric shapes could improve on what happens with rectangles? Trapezoids and parabolas. For example, if we wanted to approximate

$$\int_0^{\pi/3} (\sin x)^2\,dx$$

to four decimal places of accuracy, it would require about $n = 700$. With trapezoids, we would need only

$n = 44$, and with parabolas, only $n = 5$! So let's shelve the rectangles approach and look at formulas for trapezoidal and parabolic approximations. (Derivations of these formulas are found in most calculus texts. I've tried to concentrate here on how we will *use* them.)

To illustrate these techniques, we shall approximate

$$\int_{-1}^{1} (47x^5 + x^4 - 54x^3 - 5x^2 + 12x + 3)\, dx.$$

To simplify our work, this monster will be referred to as $\int_{-1}^{1} P_5(x)\, dx$ throughout the rest of this example. When considering numerical methods, it's always a good idea to start by looking at a problem which can be solved analytically, which in this case means using the FTC. Then you have a way of checking the results of the numerical method.

Exercise
Find an antiderivative for $P_5(x)$ and store it as f_5 in the function memory list on your calculator. Now, use the FTC to verify that

$$\int_{-1}^{1} P_5(x)\, dx = 3\frac{1}{15} = 3.0\overline{6}.$$

(You can do this with the following steps: $1 \rightarrow X$; Recall f_5; store the result in B; $-1 \rightarrow X$; Recall f_5; store result in A; $B - A = 3.0\overline{6}$.)

The graph below shows $y = P_5(x)$ on $[-1, 1]$ with $n = 8$ subintervals. The line segments joining the

y-coordinates of these subintervals will be used to approximate the curve $y = P_5(x)$. In order to estimate $\int_{-1}^{1} P_5(x)\, dx$, we add the signed areas of the trapezoids made by joining the ends of these segments to the x-axis.

Trapezoidal rule

To approximate $\int_{a}^{b} f(x)\, dx$ with n subintervals, use

$$T = \frac{h}{2}\,(y_0 + 2y_1 + 2y_2 + \cdots + 2y_{n-1} + y_n),$$

where $h = \dfrac{b - a}{n}$.

The error incurred using this method (call it E_T) can be estimated by

$$|E_T| \leq \frac{(b - a)^3}{12n^2} \cdot M$$

where M is an upper bound for $|f''|$ on $[a, b]$.

We will use the calculator program to get this result. (See the box "Trapezoidal approximation" next page.) Before a run of this program, you need to enter the integrand as f_1 in the function list. The program will ask for the left and right endpoints of the interval of integration and how many subintervals you want. The program will allow you to recalculate the trapezoidal sum with a new n value. Press [AC] twice to exit the program.

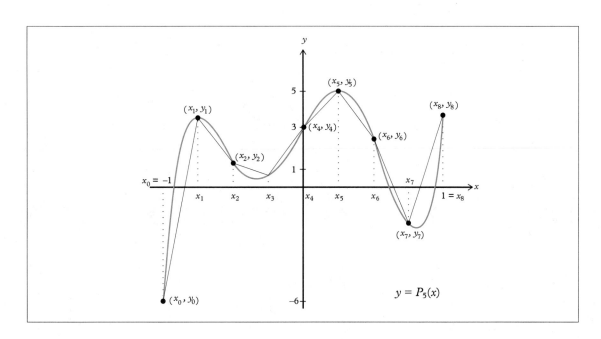

$y = P_5(x)$

Trapezoidal approximation

Code	Comments
"A"? → A: "B"? → B	Lower limit: Upper limit
Lbl 1	Looping statement
"N"? → N	Number of subintervals
$(B - A) \div N \to H$	Length of subinterval
$0 \to K$	Initialize interval counter
$0 \to T$	Sum of trapezoids in T
Lbl 2	Looping statement
$A + KH \to X$	Left endpoint of Kth subinterval
$f_1 + T \to T$	Add $f(x)$ to T.
$X + H \to X$	Right endpoint of Kth subinterval
$f_1 + T \to T$	Add $f(x)$ to T.
Isz K	Increment interval counter
$K < N \Rightarrow$ Goto 2	Repeat until last subinterval.
"TRAP SUM": $\dfrac{HT}{2}$ ◢	Trapezoidal approximation
Goto 1	Repeat with different number of subintervals.

Exercise

Enter $P_5(x)$ as f_1 in your function list. Enter the program for the trapezoidal rule into Prog T. Do a practice run with $A = -1$, $B = 1$, $N = 8$. The result should be "TRAP SUM" 3.00390625. (Doesn't look too bad considering the exact result was 3.06!)

Now let's see how the error estimate works. To use the expression

$$|E_T| \leq \frac{(b-a)^3}{12n^2} \cdot M,$$

we need to find the maximum for the absolute value of the second derivative of $P_5(x)$ on $[-1, 1]$.

Exercise

Find $P_5''(x)$. Verify that $P_5''(x) = 940x^3 + 12x^2 - 324x - 10$. Enter $|P_5''(x)|$ as f_2 in the function list; graph f_2 in the viewing rectangle $[-1, 1]$, 1 and $[0, 85]$, 10. From the graph, we see that the maximum value would occur at the endpoints. We evaluate the function at the endpoints to find $|P_5''(-1)| = 614$ and $|P_5''(1)| = 618$. So then

$$|E_T| \leq \frac{(1 + 1)^3}{12(8)^2} \times 618 = 6.4375.$$

This means the difference between the exact value and the trapezoidal approximation should be less than 6.4375. Let's see.

$$\text{(EXACT)} - \text{(TRAP SUM)}$$
$$3.06 - 3.00390625 = 0.062760,$$

which is definitely less than 6.4375. It usually happens that the actual error is far less than $|E_T|$. The formula for E_T is the worst-case scenario.

Now let's consider a parabolic approximation for $\int_{-1}^{1} P_5(x)\, dx$. The graph here shows $y = P_5(x)$ on $[-1, 1]$ with $n = 8$ subintervals. Three y-coordinates

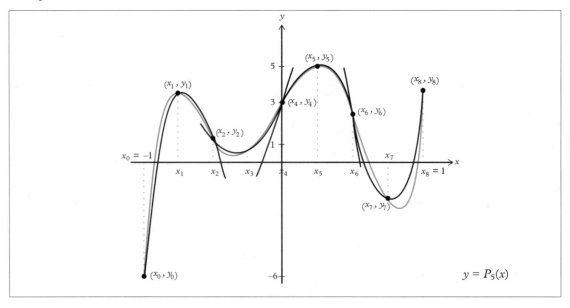

$y = P_5(x)$

are grouped and a parabolic arc is used to approximate short stretches of the curve. Then we add the signed areas underneath the parabolas. This method is usually referred to as Simpson's rule.

Simpson's rule
(parabolic approximation)

To approximate $\int_a^b f(x)\,dx$ with n subintervals (n must be even), use

$$S = \frac{h}{3}(y_0 + 4y_1 + 2y_2$$
$$+\, 4y_3 + \cdots + 2y_{n-2} + 4y_{n-1} + y_n),$$

where $h = \dfrac{(b-a)}{n}$. The error incurred (call it E_S) using this method can be estimated by the following.

$$|E_S| \le \frac{(b-a)^5}{180n^4} \cdot M,$$

where M is an upper bound for $|f^4|$ on $[a, b]$.

Again we will use a calculator program to get this result. But this time we are in luck! The calculator is already programmed to do Simpson's rule.

$$G - \int dx$$
$$[G \leftrightarrow T]$$

will graph the function, shade the area, and give a numerical approximation to the area.

$$\int dx$$
$$[x, \theta, T]$$

will give only a numerical approximation.

Exercise
Set viewing rectangle of $[-1, 1]$, 1 and $[-6, 5]$, 1. You should still have $P_5(x)$ in function memory f_1. Let's try the graphics key.

Shift $\boxed{G \leftrightarrow T}$ Shift 0 $\boxed{F2}$ 1
Shift $\rightarrow -1$ Shift $\rightarrow$ 1
  (Left and right limits of integration)

Shift $\rightarrow$ 3 $\boxed{EXE}$

  (Number of subintervals will be $n = 2^3$.)

Result: $\int dx = 3.1$

NOTE: You should read in detail about numerical integration in the owner's manual for your calculator.

Now let's look at the error estimate. To use the expression

$$|E_S| \le \frac{(b-a)^5}{180n^4} \cdot M,$$

we need to find the maximum for the absolute value of the fourth derivative of $P_5(x)$ on $[-1, 1]$.

Exercise
Find $P_5'''(x)$. Verify that $P_5^4(x) = 5640x + 24$.

Enter the function $|P_5^4(x)|$ as f_4. Graph f_4 in the viewing rectangle $[-0.1, 0.1]$, 1 and $[0, 85]$, 10. From the table below we see that the maximum value would occur at the endpoints. Evaluating at the endpoints, we find

$$|P_5^4(-1)| = 5616 \text{ and } |P_5^4(1)| = 5664.$$
So then

$$|E_S| \le \frac{(1+1)^5}{180(8)^4} \cdot 5664 = 0.24585.$$

This means the difference between the exact value and Simpson's approximation should be less than 0.24585. Let's see:

$$(\text{EXACT}) - (\text{SIMP SUM}) = 3.0\overline{6} - 3.1 = 0.0\overline{3}.$$
So not only does Simpson's rule give a better approximation for the same number of subintervals, but the error estimate is more reasonable.

This table shows approximations for $\int_{-1}^{1} P_5(x)\,dx$ for increasing values of n. What is nice about the built-in Simpson's rule is that it yields a closer approximation for a given n. In addition, it does some internal error checking and will truncate so that the answer you get is accurate to the specified number of digits. For example, for $n = 16$, the answer may have been 3.06690265, but the last five digits were truncated because for $n = 16$, the method can only give three decimal places of accuracy so it only shows you three decimal places.

Comparing results

n	TRAP SUM	Simpson's (built in)
8	3.003906	3.1
16	3.051025	3.067
32	3.062759	3.0667
64	3.065690	3.06667
128	3.066425	3.066667

What is a transcendental function?

At this point in your studies, it would be safe for you to classify a function as algebraic or transcendental. Examples of algebraic functions would be polynomials and radical and rational (fractional) functions. Transcendental functions are everything else. For example, trig functions and their inverses and logarithms and exponentials are transcendental.

Transcendental functions.

Remember, we have been trying to expand the types of expressions that we can integrate. We won't get very far in that endeavor if we don't stop to broaden the types of functions we can differentiate. We will work with derivatives and integrals of the inverse trig functions in addition to the natural logarithm and exponential functions. These types of functions are referred to as *transcendental functions*.

Inverse trigonometry functions. You should recall from the definition of a function that for each x-input there can be only one y-output; graphically this means the function must pass the vertical line test. However, if we wish to find an inverse function, then $y = f(x)$ must also pass the horizontal line test, which means $y = f(x)$ is one-to-one (a particular y-value is produced by only one x). If $y = f(x)$ does not pass the horizontal line test, then $y = f^{-1}(x)$ will not pass the vertical line test, thus f^{-1} would not pass as a function (see the graph below).

This becomes a major issue when looking for inverse trigonometry functions, since by their very nature, the trigonometry functions are cyclic. That means the output values repeat themselves in cycles (the same y is produced by many different x's).

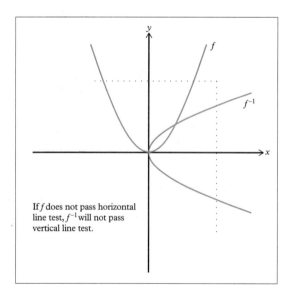

If f does not pass horizontal line test, f^{-1} will not pass vertical line test.

For the sine and cosine, one half-cycle is selected so that all the values in the range are represented.

	Domain	Range
$f(x) = \sin x$	$x \in \left[\dfrac{-\pi}{2}, \dfrac{\pi}{2}\right]$	$y \in [-1, 1]$
$f^{-1}(x) = \sin^{-1} x$	$x \in [-1, 1]$	$y \in \left[\dfrac{-\pi}{2}, \dfrac{\pi}{2}\right]$
$g(x) = \cos x$	$x \in [0, \pi]$	$y \in [-1, 1]$
$g^{-1}(x) = \cos^{-1} x$	$x \in [-1, 1]$	$y \in [0, \pi]$

Remember, since inverse functions are reverse mappings, the domain and range will reverse roles. Graphically, this means the coordinates of inverse functions are reversed (see graphs A and B opposite). Also, composition of inverse functions is a breeze.

$$f \circ f^{-1} = \sin (\sin^{-1} x) = x$$

$$f^{-1} \circ f = \sin^{-1} (\sin x) = x$$

For the tangent, one branch is selected (see graph C).

	Domain	Range
$t(x) = \tan x$	$x \in \left[\dfrac{-\pi}{2}, \dfrac{\pi}{2}\right]$	$y \in \mathrm{R}$
$t^{-1}(x) = \tan^{-1} (x)$	$x \in \mathrm{R}$	$y \in \left[\dfrac{-\pi}{2}, \dfrac{\pi}{2}\right]$

Who goofed?

Since mathematical ideas are most often expressed and developed by way of concise and unambiguous notation, it seems unfortunate that we have been left this legacy of ambiguity around -1 as an exponent.

When -1 is used as an exponent on a variable, it means to reciprocate: $x^{-1} = \dfrac{1}{x}$. However, -1 as an exponent on a function is used to refer to the inverse function. (So in this case, it's really *not* an exponent, it just looks like one.) If $f(x) = \sin x$, then $f^{-1}(x) = \sin^{-1}(x)$, which is the inverse sine function. In other words, $f^{-1} \neq \dfrac{1}{f(x)}$ and $\sin^{-1}$ $\neq \dfrac{1}{\sin x}$. I wish I knew why they didn't use $f^{I}(x)$ instead.

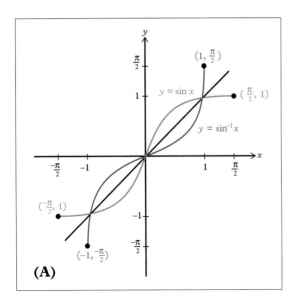

(A)

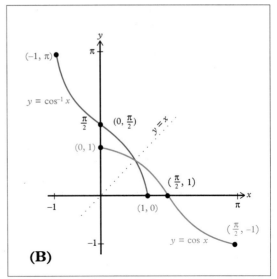

(B)

For the other three trig functions, you need only to remember their reciprocal relationships.

1. $\cot x = \dfrac{1}{\tan x}$ so $\cot^{-1} x = \tan^{-1}\left(\dfrac{1}{x}\right)$.

2. $\sec x = \dfrac{1}{\cos x}$ so $\sec^{-1} x = \cos^{-1}\left(\dfrac{1}{x}\right)$.

3. $\csc x = \dfrac{1}{\sin x}$ so $\csc^{-1} x = \sin^{-1}\left(\dfrac{1}{x}\right)$.

For $\cot^{-1} x$, the domain and range are the same as $\tan^{-1} x$. For $\sec^{-1} x$ and $\csc^{-1} x$, the domain will be the reciprocal of their reciprocal functions.

Since the domain of $\sin^{-1} x$ and $\cos^{-1} x$ is $|x| \le 1$, then the domain of $\csc^{-1} x$ and $\sec^{-1} x$ is $|x| \ge 1$.

Now, let's take a look at derivatives and integrals involving the inverse trig functions. (See table next page.) Depending on the school you attend, you may or may not have to memorize these formulas. At the school where I teach, the students must recognize when and how to use them. To take a derivative, you need to be able to use a formula properly and execute the appropriate algebraic simplification. To integrate, you need to recognize and categorize a particular form of integrand to know how to proceed.

What is most interesting to notice about this table is that there is a relationship between inverse trig functions and rational functions. When you see an integrand that is a rational function, you should think, "That looks like I might be able to use an inverse trig function!" Now we'll put the formulas to work.

Example

Find $\dfrac{dy}{dx}$ if $y = \tan^{-1} x^2$.

Comparing this function to the formula, we have

$u = x^2$ so $\dfrac{du}{dx} = 2x$.

So $\dfrac{dy}{dx} = \dfrac{2x}{1 + (x^2)^2} = \dfrac{2x}{1 + x^4}$.

(Don't you dare cancel out the x. Remember you can't cancel over addition.)

    ★   ★   ★

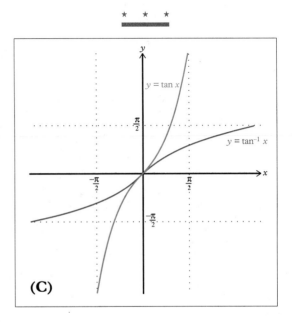

(C)

Inverse trig functions

Derivatives if $u = f(x)$

$$\frac{d}{dx}\sin^{-1} u = \frac{du/dx}{\sqrt{1 - u^2}} \, , \, |u| < 1$$

$$\frac{d}{dx}\cos^{-1} u = \frac{-du/dx}{\sqrt{1 - u^2}} \, , \, |u| < 1$$

$$\frac{d}{dx}\sec^{-1} u = \frac{du/dx}{|u|\sqrt{u^2 - 1}} \, , \, |u| > 1$$

$$\frac{d}{dx}\tan^{-1} u = \frac{du/dx}{1 + u^2}$$

General integrals

$$\int \frac{du}{\sqrt{a^2 - u^2}} = \sin^{-1}\frac{u}{a} + C$$

$$\int \frac{du}{u\sqrt{u^2 - a^2}} = \frac{1}{a}\sec^{-1}\left|\frac{u}{a}\right| + C$$

$$= \frac{1}{a}\cos^{-1}\left|\frac{a}{u}\right| + C$$

$$\int \frac{du}{a^2 + u^2} = \frac{1}{a}\tan^{-1}\frac{u}{a} + C$$

Example

Find $\dfrac{dy}{dx}$ if $y = x^2 \sin^{-1} x$.

We need to use the product rule with the first factor x^2 and the second, $\sin^{-1} x$.

$$\frac{dy}{dx} = 2x \sin^{-1} x + \left(\frac{1}{\sqrt{1 - x^2}}\right)\cdot x^2$$

$$= 2x \sin^{-1} x + \frac{x^2}{\sqrt{1 - x^2}}$$

★   ★   ★

Example

Find $\dfrac{dy}{dx}$ if $y = 3\cos^{-1}\sqrt{5x}$.

That radical sign could cause complications, so let's take this one slowly. From the formula in "Inverse trig functions," we have $u = \sqrt{5x} = (5x)^{1/2}$. So, from the chain rule,

$$\frac{du}{dx} = \frac{1}{2}(5x)^{1/2}(5) = \frac{5}{2\sqrt{5x}}.$$

Now for the big formula:

Multiply by this term to eliminate complex fraction. ↓

$$\frac{dy}{dx} = 3\left[\frac{\frac{-5}{2\sqrt{5x}}}{\sqrt{1 - (\sqrt{5x})^2}}\right]\left(\frac{2\sqrt{5x}}{2\sqrt{5x}}\right)$$

$$= \frac{-15}{2\sqrt{5x}\sqrt{1 - 5x}} = \frac{-15}{2\sqrt{5x}(1 - 5x)} \, . $$

★   ★   ★

Let's try an integral.

Example

Evaluate $\displaystyle\int \frac{x^2}{16 + x^6} \, dx$.

Looking again down the list of integral formulas in "Inverse trig functions," it looks most similar to the last formula. Let's see if we can make it work. By letting $a = 4$ and using the substitution $u = x^3$, $du = 3x^2 \, dx$, we get

$$\int \frac{x^2 \, dx}{4^2 + (x^3)^2} = \frac{1}{3}\int \frac{du}{4^2 + u^2}$$

$$= \frac{1}{3}\cdot\frac{1}{4}\tan^{-1}\frac{u}{4} + C = \frac{1}{12}\tan^{-1}\frac{x^3}{4} + C.$$

★   ★   ★

The natural logarithm e^x. Throughout the ages, mathematical concepts have been pushed forward by humanity's need to quantify the real world. When the Greeks discovered the relationships among the sides of a right triangle, they named them sine, cosine, and so on. Today these functions are used to describe sound waves, electric current, and more. The mathematical functions that describe the relationship between quantities such as population growth and time, heat loss (or gain) of an object over time, and radioactive decay, will be the subject of this section.

The story of these functions begins as we start to look for a name for

$$F(x) = \int_1^x \frac{1}{t}\, dt.$$

Recall the first fundamental theorem of calculus. If f is continuous on $[a, b]$, then we can define F (called the antiderivative of f) by $F(x) = \int_a^x f(t)\, dt$, where $x \in [a, b]$ and $F'(x) = f(x)$. If $f(t) \geq 0$ on $[a, b]$, then $F(x)$ is equal to the area under the graph of f from a to x.

Teacher: Well, maybe we should just call it F?

Student: F is pretty boring and has negative connotations for me. How about a symbol like $\sqrt{\ }$ or sin?

Teacher: Those symbols won't work, because if $F(x) = \sqrt{x}$ or $F(x) = \sin x$, then $F'(x) \neq \frac{1}{x}$ and from the first FTC, if we want

$$F(x) = \int_1^x \frac{1}{t}\, dt,$$

we need $F'(x) = \frac{1}{x}$. We need a new name, because right now we don't have an antiderivative for $1/x$.

Student: All right, let's just call it Ellen.

Teacher: Good choice! Let's see what we can find out about Ellen.

Since $\frac{1}{t} > 0$ on $[1, \infty)$, then Ellen(x) is equal to the area under the graph of $f(t) = \frac{1}{t}$ from 1 to x. Let's try to find some ordered pairs to describe Ellen's graph.

Exercise
Clear the screen on your calculator and enter the following (you should be in mode 1, which is RUN/COMP):

SHIFT $\boxed{\text{G→T}}$ 1 ÷ $\boxed{x,\theta,T}$ SHIFT → 1 SHIFT →

You will then see

Graph $\int 1 \div x, 1$ (Now enter this in function memory f_1)

Keystrokes: SHIFT 0 $\boxed{\text{F1}}$ 1 $\boxed{\text{AC}}$

Set the viewing rectangle $[0, 10]$, 1 and $[-1, 2]$, 1

Recall f_1 to evaluate $\int_1^2 \left(\frac{1}{t}\right) dt$.

Keystrokes: $\boxed{\text{F2}}$ 1 2 $\boxed{\text{EXE}}$

and you should get $\int dx = 0.69315$.

Clear screen, Recall f_1 to find $\int_1^3 dt$, and enter this value in the table below. Complete the table for

x	Ellen (x)
2	0.69315
3	
5	1.60944
8	
1	0
0.5	−0.69315
0.25	

Ellen $(x) = \int_1^x \frac{1}{t}\, dt$. (I know it's confusing to have the integral look like $\int 1 \div x$ on your calculator. But just remember, the variable of integration is a dummy variable. Try to keep in mind that the independent variable x for the function "Ellen" is the upper limit of integration.)

The coordinates from this table have been plotted in the graph below.

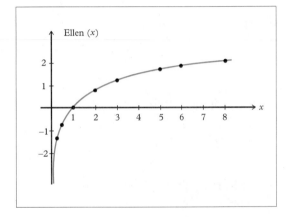

Calculus

173

Teacher: Do you recognize this curve from your previous studies?

Student: It does look familiar; it kind of looks like a logarithm. Could it be?

Teacher: Well, if Ellen is a logarithm, we'll need to know the base. And Ellen should also satisfy some of the properties of logarithms, such as $\log xy = \log x + \log y$ and $\log x^r = r \log x$.

The base of a logarithm is the real number b such that

$$\log_b b = 1.$$

For our function, Ellen, we need to find out: For what real number b do we get $Ellen(b) = \int_1^b \frac{1}{t}\, dt = 1$?

$$\int_1^{2.7} \frac{1}{t}\, dt < \int_1^b \frac{1}{t}\, dt < \int_1^{2.8} \frac{1}{t}\, dt$$

$$0.99325 \le 1 \le 1.0296$$

$$Ellen(2.7) \le Ellen(b) \le Ellen(2.8)$$

As it turns out, the base for Ellen is the irrational number $e \approx 2.71828$. That means Ellen must be the natural logarithm function, $\ln x$! So we have

$$\ln x = \int_1^x \frac{1}{t}\, dt$$

and it follows from the first FTC that

$$\frac{d}{dx} \ln x = \frac{1}{x}.$$

Now we can prove that all the algebraic properties of the logarithm still hold. We will prove one property here: $\ln x^r = r \ln x$, where x is a positive real number and r is a rational number.

We will prove this by differentiating both sides to show that we get the same result.

First, to find $\frac{d}{dx}(\ln x^r)$, we let $u = x^r$ and use the chain rule to differentiate.

$$\frac{d}{dx}(\ln u) = \frac{1}{u} \cdot \frac{du}{dx} = \frac{1}{x^r} \cdot rx^{r-1} = r\left(\frac{1}{x}\right)$$

Next, we differentiate the right-hand side.

$$\frac{d}{dx}(r \ln x) = r\frac{d}{dx}(\ln x) = r\left(\frac{1}{x}\right)$$

We get the same thing, so the property is proved.

Similar techniques can be used to prove the other properties of logarithms.

Now if $f(x) = \ln x$, then $f^{-1}(x) = e^x$ (see graph).

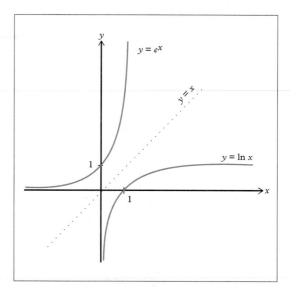

The table below lists the rules for integrating and differentiating the natural logarithm and its inverse function, e^x. Let's work some examples.

Example

Find y' if $y = \ln(x^2 - 5x + 1)$.

We use rule 3.

$$y' = \frac{1}{x^2 - 5x + 1}(2x - 5) = \frac{2x - 5}{x^2 - 5x + 1}$$

$\star \quad \star \quad \star$

Derivatives and integrals

1. $\dfrac{d}{dx} \ln x = \dfrac{1}{x}$ $\qquad \displaystyle\int \dfrac{1}{x}\, dx = \ln |x| + c$

2. $\dfrac{d}{dx} e^x = e^x$ $\qquad \displaystyle\int e^x\, dx = e^x + c$

3.$\star$ $\dfrac{d}{dx} \ln u = \dfrac{1}{u} \dfrac{du}{dx}$ $\qquad$ *To integrate in these*

cases, you would

4.$\star$ $\dfrac{d}{dx} e^u = e^u \cdot \dfrac{du}{dx}$ $\qquad$ *probably have to*

use a u-substitution.

$\star u$ is a function of x.

Find $\dfrac{dy}{dx}$ if $y = \ln(\sin x)$, $\sin x > 0$.

$$\frac{dy}{dx} = \frac{1}{\sin x}(\cos x) = \frac{\cos x}{\sin x} = \cot x$$

★ ★ ★

From this example, we see that

$$\int \cot x \, dx = \ln|\sin x| + C.$$

Find $\int \tan x \, dx$.

Let's try to use what we learned in the last example.

$$\int \tan x \, dx = \int \frac{\sin x}{\cos x} \, dx.$$

Now use a u-substitution.

$$= \int \frac{-1}{u} \, du$$

Let $u = \cos x$.
Then $du = -\sin x \, dx$.

$$= -\ln u + C = -\ln|\cos u| + C$$

★ ★ ★

We have to specify the absolute value when taking the logarithm of a quantity, because the domain of a logarithm includes only positive real numbers, as you recall. We can use a logarithm property to write this in a different form.

$$-\ln|\cos x| = \ln|\cos x|^{-1} = \ln|\sec x|$$

So we have another new integral formula.

$$\int \tan x \, dx = \ln|\sec x| + C$$

Now, let's see what happens when we differentiate and integrate the same exponential function.

Find $f'(x)$ if $f(x) = xe^{x^2}$.

We need to use rule 4 from the table opposite and the product rule.

$$f'(x) = 1 \cdot e^{x^2} + 2x(e^{x^2}) \cdot x = e^{x^2}(1 + 2x^2)$$

★ ★ ★

Find $\int_0^1 xe^{x^2} dx$.

We will now use a u-substitution with $u = x^2$, $du = 2x \, dx$, so

$$\int xe^{x^2} dx = \frac{1}{2} \int e^u \, du$$

$$= \frac{1}{2} e^u = \frac{1}{2} e^{x^2} \Big]_0^1 \quad \text{BS}$$

$$= \frac{1}{2}(e^1 - e^0) = \frac{e-1}{2}.$$

★ ★ ★

Exercise

Use your calculator to approximate $\dfrac{(e-1)}{2}$ to five decimal places. Use the key for $\int dx$ to verify the definite integral from the last example.

Integration by parts.

When you were studying the section on u-substitutions, did you feel as if you were working a jigsaw puzzle? Every piece had to fit correctly and every part had to be accounted for. Well, get ready to take on the granddaddy of all jigsaws. This technique can be a lot of fun if you keep in the spirit and work a lot of problems.

The fairly simple formula should be memorized:

$$\int u \, dv = uv - \int v \, du$$

(The integral of $u \, dv$ equals u times v minus the integral of $v \, du$.) Here is what the formula would look like in the case of a definite integral.

$$\int_a^b u \, dv = uv \Big]_a^b - \int_a^b v \, du$$

When the integral on the left is a product for which you can't find an antiderivative, try this high-powered substitution formula. The hope is that the integral on the right-hand side will be more manageable. Let's work lots of examples.

Example

Find $\int_0^1 xe^{-x}\,dx$.

First, define u and dv. The entire integrand has to be expressed by these two functions. When there is a product of algebraic and transcendental functions, it's usually best to assign the algebraic to u and transcendental to dv.

$$u = x \qquad dv = e^{-x}\,dx$$

Differentiate here *Integrate here*

$$du = dx \qquad v = -e^{-x}$$

Now, $\int_a^b u\,dv = uv\Big]_a^b - \int_a^b v\,du$.

$$= x(-e^{-x})\Big]_0^1 - \int_0^1 -e^{-x}\,dx$$

$$= \left[-xe^{-x} - e^{-x}\right]_0^1$$

$$= (-1e^{-1} - e^{-1}) - (0 - e^0)$$

$$= \frac{-1}{e} - \frac{1}{e} + 1 = 1 - \frac{2}{e}$$

⋆ ⋆ ⋆

Exercise

Approximate $1 - \dfrac{2}{e}$ to 5 decimal places.

Then use Simpson's rule to verify that

$$\int_0^1 xe^{-x}\,dx = 1 - \frac{2}{e}.$$

Working many problems will improve your ability to choose the correct u and dv, but if one choice leads to a nastier integral than you started with, don't be afraid to go back to the beginning to try a different u and dv.

Example

Evaluate $\int x\sqrt{x+1}\,dx$.

I think I would rather differentiate $\sqrt{x+1}$ than integrate it so I let

$$u = (x+1)^{1/2} \qquad \text{and} \qquad dv = x\,dx.$$

Then

$$du = \frac{1}{2\sqrt{x+1}}\,dx \qquad\qquad v = \frac{1}{2}x^2.$$

$$\int x\sqrt{x+1}\,dx = (\sqrt{x+1})\left(\frac{x^2}{2}\right) - \int \frac{\frac{1}{2}x^2}{2}\left(\frac{dx}{\sqrt{x+1}}\right)$$

This integral looks impossible, so let's try a different u and dv assignment.

$$u = x \qquad \text{and} \qquad dv = (x+1)^{1/2}\,dx$$
$$du = dx$$

To integrate dv, try a substitution. Let $w = x + 1$, so $dw = dx$.

$$\int dv = \int w^{1/2}\,dw$$

$$v = \frac{2}{3}w^{3/2} = \frac{2}{3}(x+1)^{3/2} \qquad \text{BS}$$

$$\int u/dv = uv - \int v/du$$

$$\int x\sqrt{x+1}\,dx = x\left(\frac{2}{3}(x+1)^{3/2}\right) - \int \frac{2}{3}(x+1)^{3/2}\,dx$$

$$= \frac{2x(x+1)^{3/2}}{3} - \frac{2}{3}\int (x+1)^{3/2}\,du$$

$$= \frac{2x(x+1)^{3/2}}{3} - \frac{2}{3}\cdot\frac{2}{5}(x+1)^{5/2} + C$$

$$= \frac{2x(x+1)^{3/2}}{3} - \frac{4}{15}(x+1)^{5/2} + C$$

⋆ ⋆ ⋆

Exercise

There are two ways to check this answer. One way is to take the derivative of this last expression and make sure you get the original integrand. The other way is to put limits of integration on the original problem.

Say $\int_0^1 x\sqrt{x+1}\,dx$. Using the key for $\int dx$, what do you get? Now put the antiderivative

$$\frac{2x(x+1)^{3/2}}{3} - \frac{4}{15}(x+1)^{5/2}$$

(drop the C because we're using the FTC) into function memory and evaluate at 1 and 0. Subtract, and you should get the same thing as you did from the key for $\int dx$.

Example

Evaluate $\int (\ln x)^2\, dx$

$$u = (\ln x)^2 \qquad dv = dx$$

$$du = 2 \ln x\, \frac{1}{x}\, dx \qquad v = x$$

$$\int (\ln x)^2\, dx = x\,(\ln x)^2 - \int x \left(2 \ln x \left(\frac{1}{x} \right) \right) dx$$

$$= x\,(\ln x)^2 - 2 \int \ln x\, dx \qquad \textit{Use parts again.}$$

$$u = \ln x \qquad dv = dx$$

$$du = \frac{1}{x}\, dx \qquad v = x$$

$$= x\,(\ln x)^2 - 2 \left[x \ln x - \int x \left(\frac{1}{x}\, dx \right) \right]$$

$$= dx$$

$$= x(\ln x)^2 - 2 \left(x \ln x - \int dx \right)$$

$$= x(\ln x)^2 - 2x(\ln x) + x + C$$

$$= x[(\ln x)^2 - 2 \ln x + 1] + C$$

$$= x(\ln x - 1)^2 + C$$

★ ★ ★

In the last example, you saw that two rounds of integration by parts was necessary in order to find an antiderivative. In some cases, three or more rounds of integration by parts may be necessary. To organize and simplify the work in such a problem, we use a technique called *tabular integration* (see the table below). Use this technique to verify that

$$\int e^{3x}\, (x^2 + 4x - 2)\, dx$$

$$= \frac{1}{3}\, e^{3x}\, (x^2 + 4x - 2) - \frac{1}{9}\, e^{3x}\, (2x + 4)$$

$$+ \frac{2}{27}\, e^{3x} + C$$

$$= \frac{1}{3}\, e^{3x}\, (x^2 + \frac{10x}{3} - \frac{28}{9}) + C$$

Tabular integration

This technique can be used when you have a product of a polynomial and transcendental function.

Evaluate $\int x^3 \cos x\, dx$.

For now, ignore the big arrows and + and − signs.

Start the process with the usual integration-by-parts procedure.

$$u = x^3 \qquad dv = \cos x\, dx$$
$$du = 3x^2 \qquad v = \sin x$$

Now keep differentiating until you get 0.

Keep integrating until you reach the row opposite the 0.

$u =$	x^3	$+$	$dv =$	$\cos x\, dx$
$du =$	$3x^2$	$-$	$v =$	$\sin x$
	$6x$	$+$		$-\cos x$
	6	$-$		$-\sin x$
	0			$\cos x$

Now the arrows go in with alternating + and − signs. Add or subtract the products of the functions connected by the arrows.

$$\int x^3 \cos x\, dx$$

$$= +x^3 \sin x - 3x^2(-\cos x) + 6x(-\sin x) - 6(\cos x)$$

$$= x^3 \sin x + 3x^2 \cos x - 6x \sin x - 6 \cos x + C$$

Trig substitution.

Integrating expressions with radical signs usually takes a certain amount of extra work: a u-substitution or integration by parts. But neither one of these techniques would work on an integral such as:

$$\int \frac{1}{\sqrt{x^2 + 4}}\, dx.$$

The technique presented in this section involves making a trigonometric substitution that will eliminate the radical completely. You need to be very organized and methodical when working this technique, because at first it will be hard to recognize and associate the new trig integral with the original radical integral.

The technique of trig substitutions is based on some of the fundamental trigonometric identities.

$$\sin^2 x + \cos^2 x = 1 \qquad (1)$$

$$\tan^2 x + 1 = \sec^2 x \qquad (2)$$

(Equation 2 can be obtained from equation 1 by dividing through by $\cos^2 x$.)

In the course of using this technique, you may need to integrate $\sin^2 x$ and $\cos^2 x$. To do this, you need to know these trig identities:

$$\sin^2 x = \frac{1}{2}(1 - \cos 2x) \qquad \cos^2 x = \frac{1}{2}(1 + \cos 2x)$$

So that, $\int \cos^2 x\, dx = \dfrac{1}{2}\int (1 + \cos 2x)\, dx$

$$= \frac{1}{2}\left(x + \frac{\sin 2x}{2}\right) + C$$

$$= \frac{x}{2} + \frac{\sin 2x}{4} + C.$$

Similarly, $\int \sin^2 x\, dx = \dfrac{x}{2} + \dfrac{\sin 2x}{4} + C.$

Here are two more integrals you need to know to use the technique of trig substitutions.

$$\int \tan x\, dx = \ln|\sec x| + C$$

$$\int \sec x\, dx = \ln|\sec x + \tan x| + C$$

Now that you have all the necessary background information, study the table below summarizing all the essential parts involved in this method. Again, depending on the school you attend, you may or may not have to have this information memorized.

Let's see how this method of trig substitution works.

Essentials of trig substitution

Expression	Trig substitution	Reference triangle	
Case 1 $\sqrt{a^2 - x^2}$ or $a^2 - x^2$	$x = a\sin\theta$ $a^2 - x^2 = a^2 - a^2\sin^2\theta$ $\quad = a^2(1 - \sin^2\theta)$ $\quad = a^2\cos^2\theta$	$\sin\theta = \dfrac{x}{a}$	$\theta = \sin^{-1}\dfrac{x}{a}$
Case 2 $\sqrt{a^2 + x^2}$ or $a^2 + x^2$	$x = a\tan\theta$ $a^2 + x^2 = a^2 + a^2\tan^2\theta$ $\quad = a^2(1 + \tan^2\theta)$ $\quad = a^2\sec^2\theta$	$\tan\theta = \dfrac{x}{a}$	$\theta = \tan^{-1}\dfrac{x}{a}$
Case 3 $\sqrt{x^2 - a^2}$ or $x^2 - a^2$	$x = a\sec\theta$ $x^2 - a^2 = a^2\sec\theta - a^2$ $\quad = a^2(\sec^2\theta - 1)$ $\quad = a^2\tan^2\theta$	$\sec\theta = \dfrac{x}{a}$	$\theta = \sec^{-1}\dfrac{x}{a}$

Calculus

Example

Find $\displaystyle\int \frac{dx}{\sqrt{x^2+4}}$.

We can use case 2 from the table with $a = 2$. So then the substitution is $x = 2\tan\theta$. Differentiate to get $dx = 2\sec^2\theta\,d\theta$.

$$\int \frac{dx}{\sqrt{x^2+4}} = \int \frac{2\sec^2\theta\,d\theta}{\sqrt{(2\tan\theta)^2+4}}$$

$$= \int \frac{2\sec^2\theta\,d\theta}{\sqrt{4\sec^2\theta}} = \int \frac{2\sec^2\theta\,d\theta}{2\sec\theta}$$

$$= \int 2\sec\theta\,d\theta$$

$$= \ln|\sec\theta + \tan\theta| + C$$

Now, we have to put this back in terms of x. To do this, refer back to the original substitution.

$$x = 2\tan\theta \Rightarrow \frac{x}{2} = \tan\theta$$

Now make a right triangle, label one angle as θ, and remember the definition of the trig functions in terms of opposite, adjacent, and hypotenuse, shown here:

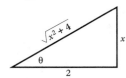

(You can also refer to the reference triangle found in case 2 in the table.)

So we get

$$\ln|\sec\theta + \tan\theta| + C = \ln\left|\frac{\sqrt{4+x^2}}{2} + \frac{x}{2}\right| + C.$$

$\star$ $\star$ $\star$

Example

Evaluate $\displaystyle\int_{-1/3}^{1/3} \sqrt{1-9x^2}\,dx$.

We use case 1 with $a = 1$. So the trig substitution is

$$3x = \sin\theta \Rightarrow x = \frac{1}{3}\sin\theta.$$

Differentiate to get $dx = \dfrac{1}{3}\cos\theta\,d\theta$.

$$\int \sqrt{1-\sin^2\theta}\left(\frac{1}{3}\cos\theta\right)d\theta$$

$$= \frac{1}{3}\int \sqrt{\cos^2\theta}\,(\cos\theta)\,d\theta$$

$$= \frac{1}{3}\int \cos^2\theta\,d\theta$$

$$= \frac{1}{2\cdot 3}\int (1+\cos 2\theta)\,d\theta$$

$$= \frac{1}{6}\left[\theta + \frac{1}{2}\sin 2\theta\right] = \frac{1}{6}\left[\theta + \frac{1}{2}\sin\theta\cos\theta\right]$$

To get this result in terms of x, recall the original substitution was

$$3x = \sin\theta \Rightarrow \sin^{-1}3x = \theta$$

and we can also make our reference triangle:

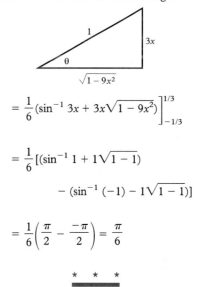

$$= \frac{1}{6}\left(\sin^{-1}3x + 3x\sqrt{1-9x^2}\right)\Big]_{-1/3}^{1/3}$$

$$= \frac{1}{6}\left[(\sin^{-1}1 + 1\sqrt{1-1})\right.$$

$$\left. - (\sin^{-1}(-1) - 1\sqrt{1-1})\right]$$

$$= \frac{1}{6}\left(\frac{\pi}{2} - \frac{-\pi}{2}\right) = \frac{\pi}{6}$$

$\star$ $\star$ $\star$

By using the algebraic technique of completing the square, we can turn a general radical expression into one that has the form which works for a trigonometric substitution.

Example

Evaluate $\displaystyle\int \frac{dt}{\sqrt{t^2-2t-15}}$.

We would like the quadratic expression under the radical in the form $x^2 - a^2$.

$$(t^2-2t-1)-15-1 = (t-1)^2-16$$

so we have $x^2 - a^2$ with $x = t - 1$ and $a = 4$.

$$t - 1 = 4 \sec \theta$$

$$dt = 4 \sec \theta \tan \theta \, d\theta$$

$$\int \frac{dt}{(t-1)^2 - 16} = \int \frac{4 \sec \theta \tan \theta \, d\theta}{\sqrt{16 \sec^2 \theta - 16}}$$

$$= \int \frac{4 \sec \theta \tan \theta \, d\theta}{\sqrt{16 \tan^2 \theta}} = \int \frac{4 \sec \theta \tan \theta \, d\theta}{4 \tan \theta}$$

$$= \int \sec \theta \, d\theta$$

$$= \ln |\sec \theta + \tan \theta| + C$$

The original substitution was $t - 1 = 4 \sec \theta \Rightarrow \dfrac{t-1}{4}$

$= \sec \theta$, so we get the reference triangle found here.

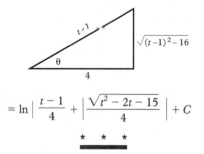

$$= \ln \left| \frac{t-1}{4} + \left| \frac{\sqrt{t^2 - 2t - 15}}{4} \right| \right| + C$$

$\star \quad \star \quad \star$

Partial fraction decomposition.

In this section, we will look at integrating rational algebraic expressions, so get ready to bone up some more on your algebra skills. This method is very important because this form of integrand is difficult to find in a table of integrands.

Compared to some of the other techniques we have looked at in this chapter, this method is fairly easy. And we will use the matrix mode on the calculator to help us with what used to be the most difficult part of this technique, which is solving a system of linear equations.

So that you get a feel for why we have to do what we are going to do in this section, consider the following integration problem.

$$\int \left(\frac{3}{x+1} + \frac{5}{x-3} \right) dx$$

$$= 3 \int \frac{1}{x+1} \, dx + 5 \int \frac{1}{x-3} \, dx \qquad (1)$$

$$= 3 \ln (x + 1) + 5 \ln (x - 3) + C$$

Now, consider this simple algebra problem.

$$\frac{3}{x+1} + \frac{5}{x-3} = \frac{3(x-3) + 5(x+1)}{(x+1)(x-3)}$$

$$= \frac{8x - 4}{x^2 - 2x - 3}$$

What if we had to integrate $\displaystyle\int \frac{8x - 4}{x^2 - 2x - 3} \, dx$? Can we somehow break down this rational expression so that it is in the form we can work with found in equation 1? Yes! Just think about the process of addition of rational expressions in reverse. We would like to *decompose* the expression

$$\frac{8x - 4}{x^2 - 2x - 3}.$$

We start by factoring the denominator and realizing that each factor was generated from a separate term.

1. If the degree of $f(x)$ is greater than or equal to the degree of $g(x)$, use long division.

2. Express $g(x)$ as a product of linear factors $ax + b$ or quadratic factors $ax^2 + bx + c$, so that $g(x)$ is a product of different factors of the form

$$(ax + b)^n \quad \text{or} \quad (ax^2 + bx + c)^n.$$

3. For each $(ax + b)^n$, assign the sum of n partial fractions

$$\frac{A_1}{ax + b} + \frac{A_2}{(ax + b)^2} + \cdots + \frac{A_n}{(ax + b)^n}.$$

Do this for each different linear factor.

4. For each $(ax^2 + bx + c)^n$, assign the sum of n partial fractions

$$\frac{A_1 x + B_1}{ax^2 + bx + c} + \frac{A_2 x + B_2}{(ax^2 + bx + c)^2} + \cdots + \frac{A_n x + B_n}{(ax^2 + bx + c)^n}.$$

Do this for each different quadratic factor.

5. Set the original fraction $\dfrac{f(x)}{g(x)}$ equal to the sum of these partial fractions. Multiply the equation by the least common denominator to clear fractions.

6. Equate coefficients of like powers of x. Form the coefficient matrix and right-hand side matrix and solve using matrix mode on your calculator.

$$\frac{8x - 4}{(x + 1)(x - 3)} = \frac{A}{(x + 1)} + \frac{B}{(x - 3)}$$

Clear denominators. $8x - 4 = A(x - 3) + B(x + 1)$

Distribute. $8x - 4 = Ax - 3A + Bx + B$

Group like terms. $8x - 4 = (A + B)\,x + (B - 3A)$

In order for the left-hand side of the last expression to be equal to the right-hand side, the coefficients of like terms must be equal. This generates the following system of equations.

$$A + B = 8$$
$$-3A + B = -4$$

Here is the associated matrix expression:

$$\begin{bmatrix} 1 & 1 \\ -3 & 1 \end{bmatrix} \begin{bmatrix} A \\ B \end{bmatrix} = \begin{bmatrix} 8 \\ -4 \end{bmatrix}.$$

To solve for A and B, we would find $\begin{bmatrix} 1 & 1 \\ -3 & 1 \end{bmatrix}^{-1}$, so that

$$\begin{bmatrix} A \\ B \end{bmatrix} = \begin{bmatrix} 1 & 1 \\ -3 & 1 \end{bmatrix}^{-1} \begin{bmatrix} 8 \\ -4 \end{bmatrix}$$

The box "Calculator procedure for matrix solution" (opposite) will help to guide you through solving this system with the MATRIX MODE.

Now let's use "Procedure for partial fraction decomposition" (above) to work on some example problems.

Example

Find $\displaystyle\int \frac{6x^2 - 3x + 1}{4x^3 + x^2 + 4x + 1}\, dx$.

Factor the denominator by grouping.

$$(4x^3 + 4x) + (x^2 + 1) = 4x(x^2 + 1) + (x^2 + 1)$$

$$= (4x + 1)(x^2 + 1)$$

So the PFD (partial fraction decomposition) looks like

$$\frac{6x^2 - 3x + 1}{(4x + 1)(x^2 + 1)} = \frac{A}{4x + 1} + \frac{Bx + C}{x^2 + 1}.$$

Multiply through by the LCD.

$$6x^2 - 3x + 1 = A(x^2 + 1) + (Bx + C)(4x + 1)$$

$$= Ax^2 + A + 4Bx^2 + Bx + 4C + C$$

$$= (A + 4B)x^2 + (B + 4C)x + (A + C)$$

Equating coefficients of like terms we get

$$A + 4B = 6$$
$$B + 4C = -3 \Rightarrow \begin{bmatrix} 1 & 4 & 0 \\ 0 & 1 & 4 \\ 1 & 0 & 1 \end{bmatrix} \begin{bmatrix} A \\ B \\ C \end{bmatrix} = \begin{bmatrix} 6 \\ -3 \\ 1 \end{bmatrix}.$$
$$A + C = 1$$

Using the calculator to solve, we get

$$\begin{bmatrix} A \\ B \\ C \end{bmatrix} = \begin{bmatrix} 2 \\ 1 \\ -1 \end{bmatrix}.$$

So $\int \dfrac{6x^2 - 3x + 1}{4x^3 + x^2 + 4x + 1}\, dx = \int \left(\dfrac{2}{4x + 1} + \dfrac{x - 1}{x^2 + 1} \right) dx$

$$= \int \dfrac{2}{4x + 1}\, dx + \int \dfrac{x}{x^2 + 1}\, dx - \int \dfrac{1}{x^2 + 1}\, dx.$$

$$u = 4x + 1 \qquad u = x^2 + 1$$
$$du = 4\, dx \qquad du = 2x\, dx$$

Both of these lead to

$$\dfrac{1}{2} \int \dfrac{du}{u} = \dfrac{1}{2} \ln u.$$

Finally,

$$= \dfrac{1}{2} \ln |4x + 1| + \dfrac{1}{2} \ln |x^2 + 1| - \tan^{-1} x + C.$$

★ ★ ★

Example

Find $\int \dfrac{6x^2 + 17x - 5}{(x - 3)(x + 2)^2}\, dx.$

The PFD looks like

$$\dfrac{6x^2 + 17x - 5}{(9x - 3)(x + 2)^2} = \dfrac{A}{(x - 3)} + \dfrac{B}{(x + 2)} + \dfrac{C}{(x + 2)^2}.$$

Multiply through by the LCD.

$$6x^2 + 17x - 5$$
$$= A(x + 2) + B(x - 3)(x + 2) + C(x - 3)$$

$$= Ax^2 + 4Ax + 4A + Bx^2 - Bx - 6B + Cx - 3C$$

$$= (A + B)x^2 + (4A - B + C)x + (4A - 6B - 3C)$$

Equating coefficients of like terms, we get the following system of equations.

$$A + B = 6$$
$$4A - B + C = 17 \Rightarrow$$
$$4A - 6B - 3C = -5$$

$$\begin{bmatrix} 1 & 1 & 0 \\ 4 & -1 & 1 \\ 4 & -6 & -3 \end{bmatrix} \begin{bmatrix} A \\ B \\ C \end{bmatrix} = \begin{bmatrix} 6 \\ 17 \\ -5 \end{bmatrix}$$

Using the calculator to solve, we get

$$\begin{bmatrix} A \\ B \\ C \end{bmatrix} = \begin{bmatrix} 4 \\ 2 \\ 3 \end{bmatrix}.$$

So $\int \dfrac{6x^2 + 17x - 5}{(x - 3)(x + 2)^2}\, dx$

$$= \int \dfrac{4}{x - 3}\, dx + \int \dfrac{2}{x + 2}\, dx + \int \dfrac{3}{(x + 2)^2}\, dx$$

$$= 4 \ln |x - 3| + 2 \ln |x + 2| - \dfrac{3}{x + 2} + C.$$

★ ★ ★

Improper integrals.
In the definition of $\int_a^b f(x)\, dx$, it was assumed that the interval $[a, b]$ was finite. However, many applications in physics, economics, and probability give meaning to a or b (or both) at infinity. In this section, we will extend the concept of the definite integral to include integrals over infinite intervals. Then we will look at integrals in which the integrand becomes infinite in the interval of integration. These are called *improper integrals*.

Limits of integration at infinity. Let's try to find the area between the curve $y = \dfrac{1}{x^2}$ and the x-axis to the right of $x = 1$. We'll start by finding the area under the curve from $x = 1$ to $x = b$, where b is any number greater than 1 (see graph).

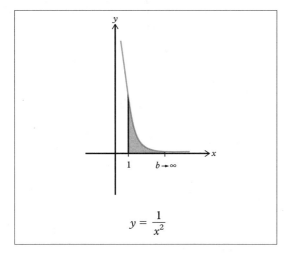

$$y = \frac{1}{x^2}$$

$$A = \int_1^b \frac{1}{x^2}\, dx = -\frac{1}{x}\bigg]_1^b = \frac{-1}{b} - \frac{-1}{1} = 1 - \frac{1}{b}$$

Notice that the larger b is, the closer the area is to 1, since $\lim_{b \to \infty} \frac{1}{b} = 0$. So we can represent the area of the region under $y = \frac{1}{x^2}$ to the right of $x = 1$ using the notation

$$\lim_{b \to \infty} \int_1^b \frac{1}{x^2}\, dx = \lim_{b \to \infty} \left(1 - \frac{1}{b}\right) = 1.$$

This motivates definition of the improper integral:

$$\int_a^\infty f(x)\, dx = \lim_{b \to \infty} \int_a^b f(x)\, dx.$$

If the limit defining the improper integral is a finite number, we say the integral *converges*; if the limit is not a finite number, we say the integral *diverges*.

Example

Evaluate $\int_0^\infty xe^{-x^2}\, dx$.

Use the definition of the improper integral to write

$$\int_0^\infty xe^{-x^2}\, dx = \lim_{b \to \infty} \int_a^b xe^{-x^2}\, dx.$$

We can now evaluate the integral on the right with a u-substitution. Let $u = -x^2$, then $du = \frac{-2x}{dx}$ so $x\, dx = -\frac{du}{2}$.

$$\int_0^\infty xe^{-x^2}\, dx = \lim_{b \to \infty} \int_a^b \frac{-1}{2}\, e^u\, du$$

$$= \lim_{b \to \infty} \frac{-1}{2}\, e^u = \frac{-1}{2} \lim_{b \to \infty} e^{-x^2}\bigg]_0^b$$

$$= \frac{-1}{2} \lim_{b \to \infty} (e^{-b^2} - e^0)$$

$$= \frac{-1}{2} \lim_{b \to \infty} \left(\frac{1}{e^{b^2}} - 1\right)$$

$$= \frac{-1}{2}(0 - 1) = \frac{1}{2}$$

Therefore, $\int_0^\infty xe^{-x^2}\, dx$ converges to $\frac{1}{2}$.

★ ★ ★

Exercise
Check the answer by using your calculator to evaluate the integral $\int_0^{50} xe^{-x^2}\, dx$. Be patient, because the answer takes more than two seconds to come up.

Example

Evaluate $\int_0^\infty \frac{dx}{\sqrt{x}}$.

Use the definition of the improper integral to write

$$\int_0^\infty \frac{dx}{\sqrt{x}} = \lim_{b \to \infty} \int_0^b x^{-1/2}\, dx$$

$$= \lim_{b \to \infty} 2x^{1/2}\bigg]_0^b$$

$$= \lim_{b \to \infty} 2\sqrt{b} - 2\sqrt{0} = \infty.$$

Therefore, $\int_0^\infty \frac{dx}{\sqrt{x}}$ diverges.

★ ★ ★

Now, the definition of another type of improper integral follows.

$$\int_{-\infty}^{b} f(x)\,dx = \lim_{a \to -\infty} \int_{a}^{b} f(x)\,dx$$

Again, if the limit defining the improper integral is a finite number, we say the integral *converges*; if the limit is not a finite number, we say the integral *diverges*.

Example

Determine if

$$\int_{-\infty}^{-2} \frac{1}{x^2 + 4}\,dx$$

converges or diverges.

Let's forget about the limits of integration until we find an antiderivative. This rational integrand looks as if it might be an inverse trig function. Refer to the table on page 172 to see if this form of integrand is there. It looks like the last integrand with $a = 2$.

So

$$\int \frac{dx}{x^2 + 4} = \frac{1}{2}\tan^{-1}\frac{x}{2}.$$

Now let's reintroduce the limits of integration.

$$\int_{-\infty}^{-2} \frac{dx}{x^2 + 4} = \lim_{a \to -\infty} \int_{a}^{-2} \frac{dx}{x^2 + 4}$$

$$= \lim_{a \to -\infty} \left[\frac{1}{2}\tan^{-1}\frac{x}{2} \right]_{a}^{-2}$$

$$= \frac{1}{2}\lim_{a \to -\infty} [\tan^{-1}(-1) - \tan^{-1}(a)]$$

$$= \frac{1}{2}\lim_{a \to -\infty} \left[\frac{-\pi}{4} - \tan^{-1} a \right]$$

$$= \frac{1}{2}\left[\frac{-\pi}{4} - \frac{-\pi}{2} \right] = \frac{\pi}{8}$$

(See the graph above right.)

Therefore, $\int_{-\infty}^{-2} \frac{dx}{x^2 + 4}$ converges to $\frac{\pi}{8}$.

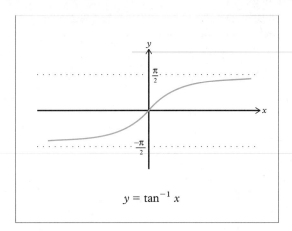

$$y = \tan^{-1} x$$

Discontinuous integrands. The definite integral $\int_{a}^{b} f(x)\,dx$ results in an improper integral if the integrand, $y = f(x)$, has a vertical asymptote at one of the endpoints of $[a, b]$ or if $y = f(x)$ has a vertical asymptote at some number $x = c$ such that $a < c < b$ (that is, c is in the interval of integration).

We will describe how to deal with each case.

If f is continuous on $[a, b)$, but $\lim_{x \to b^-} f(x) = \pm\infty$,

we define $\int_{a}^{b} f(x)\,dx = \lim_{t \to b^-} \int_{a}^{t} f(x)\,dx$

Example

Determine whether

$$\int_{0}^{2} \frac{x}{\sqrt{4 - x^2}}\,dx$$

converges or diverges.

We see from the graph above that

$$f(x) = \frac{x}{\sqrt{4 - x^2}}$$

approaches ∞ as $x \to 2$. From the definition, we have

$$\int_{0}^{2} \frac{x}{\sqrt{4 - x^2}}\,dx = \lim_{t \to 2^-} \int_{0}^{t} \frac{x}{\sqrt{4 - x^2}}\,dx.$$

To integrate, let

$$u = 4 - x^2.$$
$$\text{Then } du = -2x\,dx.$$

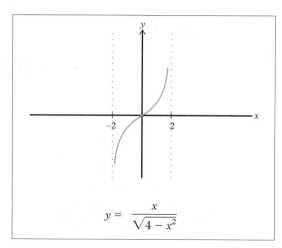

$$y = \frac{x}{\sqrt{4 - x^2}}$$

So, $\int \frac{x \, dx}{\sqrt{4 - x^2}} = \frac{-1}{2} \int u^{-1/2} \, du = -u^{1/2}$

$$= -\sqrt{4 - x^2}.$$

Continuing the limit problem, we have

$$\int_0^2 \frac{x}{\sqrt{4 - x^2}} \, dx = \lim_{t \to 2^-} \left[-\sqrt{4 - x^2} \right]_0^t$$

$$= \lim_{t \to 2^-} \left(-\sqrt{4 - t^2} + \sqrt{4} \right)$$

$$= 0 + 2 = 2.$$

If you're not sure about evaluating the last limit, graph $y = -\sqrt{4 - x^2} + 2$ on your calculator and see what happens to the y-values as x approaches 2 from the left.

We find that

$$\int_0^2 \frac{x}{\sqrt{4 - x^2}} \, dx$$

converges to 2.

★ ★ ★

Next case.

If f is continuous on $(a, b]$, but $\lim f(x) = \pm\infty$, we define $\int_a^b f(x) \, dx = \lim_{t \to a^+} \int_t^b f(x) \, dx$.

Example

Determine whether $\int_0^1 \left(\frac{\ln x}{x} \right) dx$ converges or diverges.

Let's ignore the limits of integration until we find the antiderivative. Use the substitution $u = \ln x$,

$du = \frac{1}{x} \, dx$.

So, to find the antiderivative

$$\int \frac{\ln x}{x} \, dx = \int u \, du = \frac{1}{2} u^2 = \frac{1}{2} (\ln x)^2.$$

Now, we use the definition of the improper integral.

$$\lim_{t \to 0^+} \int_t^1 \frac{\ln x}{x} \, dx = \lim_{t \to 0^+} \left[\frac{1}{2} (\ln x)^2 \right]_t^1$$

$$= \frac{1}{2} \lim_{t \to 0^+} [(\ln 1)^2 - (\ln t)^2]$$

$$= \lim_{t \to 0^+} [0 - (\ln t)^2] = \infty$$

since as $t \to 0^+$, $\ln t \to -\infty$.

Therefore $\int_0^1 \left(\frac{\ln x}{x} \right) dx$ diverges.

★ ★ ★

Now for the last case.

If f has a discontinuity at a number c in (a, b), but is continuous elsewhere on $[a, b]$, then

$$\int_a^b f(x) \, dx = \int_a^c f(x) \, dx + \int_c^b f(x) \, dx.$$

Example

Determine if $\int_{-1}^1 \frac{1}{x^2} \, dx$ converges.

This function has a vertical asymptote at $x = 0$ (see graph below).

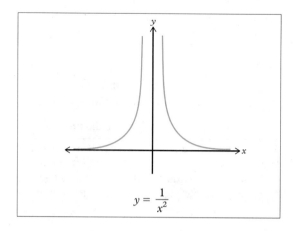

$$y = \frac{1}{x^2}$$

So we use the last definition with $c = 0$ to write

$$\int_{-1}^1 \frac{1}{x^2} \, dx = \int_{-1}^0 \frac{dx}{x^2} + \int_0^1 \frac{dx}{x^2}.$$

Now each of the integrands on the right-hand side is an improper integral with a vertical asymptote at an endpoint. So we write

$$\int_{-1}^{1} \frac{dx}{x^2} = \lim_{t \to 0^-} \int_{-1}^{t} \frac{dx}{x^2} + \lim_{t \to 0^+} \int_{t}^{1} \frac{dx}{x^2}$$

$$= \lim_{t \to 0^-} \left[\frac{-1}{x} \right]_{-1}^{t} + \lim_{t \to 0^+} \left[\frac{-1}{x} \right]_{t}^{1}$$

$$= \lim_{t \to 0^-} \left(\frac{-1}{t} - 1 \right)_1 + \lim_{t \to 0^+} \left(-1 + \frac{1}{t} \right)$$

$$= (\infty - 1) + (-1 + \infty).$$

Therefore, $\int_{-1}^{1} \frac{dx}{x^2}$ diverges.

* * *

Applications: Definite integrals

Now that you have collected an arsenal of integration techniques, let's discuss some uses for evaluating definite integrals.

Remember that the definition of the definite integral was motivated by trying to determine the area of a region in the plane. We defined the definite integral as the limit of sums of rectangles. We now extend the idea of a limit of sums beyond rectangles to determine volumes, lengths, surface areas, and more.

Areas between curves. In this section, we will use the definite integral to find the area of more complicated regions than we worked with before: regions that are bounded on more than one side by a curve.

Let's recall the geometric interpretation of $\int_{a}^{b} f(x)\, dx$.

$$\int_{a}^{b} \qquad f(x) \qquad dx$$

means we want to   *height*   *width of*
add the area of all   *rectangles*
these little rectangles
from x = a to x = b.

As long as $a < b$, dx (or the width of the rectangles) will be a positive number. And, if $f(x) > 0$ on $[a, b]$, then $A = \int_{a}^{b} f(x)\, dx > 0$ and we use the number A to describe the magnitude of the area. It makes sense, intuitively, to describe an area with a positive number.

What if $f(x) < 0$ on $[a, b]$ and $a < b$? Then the "height" of our rectangles will be a negative number and the width will be positive. So $A = \int_{a}^{b} f(x)\, dx < 0$; the magnitude of A will reflect the size of A, but the number will be negative. We take care of this by stipulating that if $f(x) < 0$, then the area between $f(x)$ and the x-axis will be given by $A = -\int_{a}^{b} f(x)\, dx$.

Example
Find the area bounded by the x-axis on top $f(x) = -4 - x^2$ on the bottom, and by $x = -1$ and $x = 2$ on the sides (see graph).

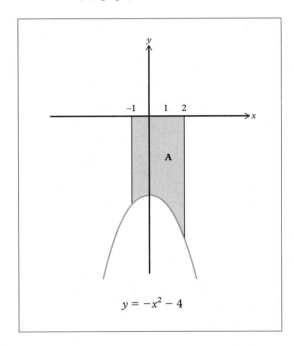

$$y = -x^2 - 4$$

We have

$$A = -\int_{-1}^{2} (-4 - x^2)\, dx = -\left[-4x - \frac{1}{3}x^3 \right]_{-1}^{2}$$

$$= -\left[\left(-8 - \frac{8}{3} \right) - \left(4 + \frac{1}{3} \right) \right] = 15.$$

Not too bad, right?

* * *

Accurate sketch needed

When working these problems, you need a fairly accurate sketch. This problem shows a good reason why that is true. (Since the curves cross, the role of top curve and bottom curve are reversed over the interval of integration.)

Example: Find the area of the region between $y = x$ and $y = x^5$.

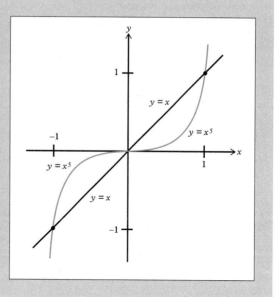

$$\int_{-1}^{0} (x^5 - x)\, dx$$

$$= \left(\frac{1}{6} x^6 - \frac{1}{2} x^2 \right) \Big]_{-1}^{0}$$

$$= (0 - 0) - \left(\frac{1}{6} - \frac{1}{2} \right)$$

$$= \frac{1}{3}$$

$$\int_{0}^{1} (x - x^5)\, dx$$

$$= \left(\frac{1}{2} x^2 - \frac{1}{6} x^6 \right) \Big]_{0}^{1}$$

$$= \left(\frac{1}{2} - \frac{1}{6} \right) - (0 - 0)$$

$$= \frac{1}{3}$$

Now, what if we wanted to find the area *between* two different functions, say $y = f(x)$ and $y = g(x)$ where $f > g$ on $[a, b]$? (See graph below.) We can still use

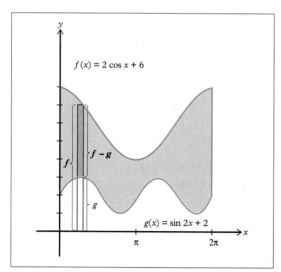

rectangles to find the area, where the width will be given by dx. But, as you can see by the graph, the height of the rectangles will be $f(x) - g(x)$ (top function minus bottom function). So we can still use a definite integral to find the area between $f(x)$ and $g(x)$ on $[a, b]$ with the formula

$$\int_{a}^{b} \underset{height}{[f(x) - g(x)]} \ \underset{width}{dx}.$$

Example

Suppose the equations for the functions in the graph to the left are

$$f(x) = 2 \cos x + 6 \qquad \text{and} \qquad g(x) = \sin 2x + 2.$$
$$\quad top \qquad\qquad\qquad\qquad\qquad\qquad bottom$$

Find the area between the two curves on $[0, 2\pi]$.

$$\int_{0}^{2\pi} [f(x) - g(x)]\, dx$$

$$= \int_{0}^{2\pi} [(2 \cos x + 6) - (\sin 2x + 2)]\, dx$$

$$= \int_{0}^{2\pi} (2 \cos x - \sin 2x + 4)\, dx$$

$$= \left[2 \sin x + \frac{1}{2} \cos 2x + 4x) \right]_{0}^{2\pi}$$

$$= \left(2 \sin 2\pi + \frac{1}{2} \cos 4\pi + 8\pi \right)$$

$$\quad - \left(2 \sin 0 + \frac{1}{2} \cos 0 + 0 \right)$$

$$= \left(0 + \frac{1}{2} + 8\pi \right) - \left(0 + \frac{1}{2} \right)$$

$$= 8\pi$$

$$\star \quad \star \quad \star$$

Again, we will consider finding the area between two functions, $f(x)$ and $g(x)$, but now, what if one or both of these curves falls below the x-axis? As you can see

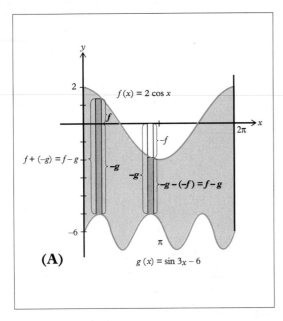

(A) $g(x) = \sin 3x - 6$

by the rectangles that are drawn in graph A, showing $f(x) = 2 \cos x$ and $g(x) = \sin 3x - b$, the height is still given by $f(x) - g(x)$ if

(a) one of the curves falls below the x-axis (for

    example, $\left[0, \dfrac{\pi}{2}\right]$)

(b) or both of the curves fall below the x-axis,

    as on $\left[\dfrac{\pi}{2}, \dfrac{3\pi}{2}\right]$.

What is most important is that $f(x) > g(x)$; that is, f is above g, everywhere on $[a, b]$.

Example

If the equations for the functions in the graph above are given by

$$f(x) = 2 \cos x \quad \text{and} \quad g(x) = \sin 3x - 6,$$
$$\text{top} \qquad\qquad\qquad \text{bottom}$$

you can find the area between the two curves on $[0, 2\pi]$ in the following way.

$$\int_0^{2\pi} [f(x) - g(x)] \, dx = \int_0^{2\pi} [(2 \cos x) - (\sin 3x - 6)] \, dx$$

$$= \left[2 \sin x + \frac{1}{3} \cos 3x + 6x \right]_0^{2\pi}$$

$$= \left(2 \sin 2\pi + \frac{1}{3} \cos 6\pi + 12\pi \right)$$

$$- \left(2 \sin 0 + \frac{1}{3} \cos 0 + 0 \right)$$

$$= \left(0 + \frac{1}{3} + 12\pi \right) - \left(0 + \frac{1}{3} \right)$$

$$= 12\pi$$

★ ★ ★

In some problems, it's handy to reverse the roles of x and y. Instead of finding the area between two functions of x, we can use the same strategies to find the area between two functions of y (see graph B).

In this case, the rectangles will sit sideways and the height of the rectangles will be $f(y) - g(y)$ (or the one on the right minus the one on the left). The width of the rectangles will be dy. The area is computed by integrating along the y-axis, instead of along the x-axis.

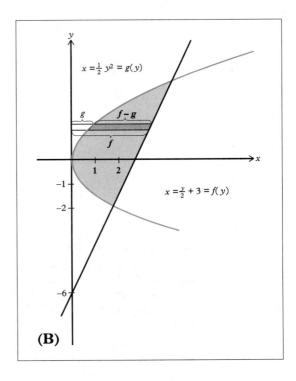

(B)

Example

If the equations for the functions in graph B are given

by $\quad y = 2x - 6 \quad$ and $\quad x = \dfrac{1}{2}y^2,$

$\qquad\qquad\quad$ *right* $\qquad\qquad\qquad$ *left*

find the area between the two curves.

Before we set up the integral, we need to know the limits of integration, so we need to know where the curves intersect. We solve the equations simultaneously with the substitution method.

$$x = \frac{1}{2}y^2 = \frac{1}{2}(2x-6)^2 = 2x^2 - 12x + 18$$

Now we have a quadratic equation in x, so we set it equal to zero.

$$2x^2 - 13x + 18 = 0 \Rightarrow (2x - 9)(x - 2) = 0$$

So, $x = \dfrac{9}{2}$ or $x = 2$. Now, substituting into the linear equation, we get

$$y = 2\left(\frac{9}{2}\right) - 6 = 3 \quad \text{and} \quad y = 2(2) - 6 = -2.$$

So the coordinates of the intersection points are $\left(\dfrac{9}{2}, 3\right)$ and $(2, -2)$. Since we are integrating with respect to y, we use the y-coordinates as our limits of integration.

$$\int_{-2}^{3}\left[\left(\frac{y}{2} + 3\right) - \frac{1}{2}y^2\right] dy = \left[\frac{y^2}{4} + 3y - \frac{y^3}{6}\right]_{-2}^{3}$$

$$= \left(\frac{9}{4} + 9 - \frac{27}{6}\right) - \left(\frac{4}{4} - 6 + \frac{8}{6}\right) = 10\frac{5}{12}$$

★ ★ ★

Volume of a solid of revolution.

Discs. At this point, you should be comfortable with the notion of length as a measurement in one dimension, area as a measurement in two dimensions, and volume as a measurement in three dimensions. Volume formulas for some basic geometric shapes should be familiar to you. Here are a few examples:

Volume of a rectangular solid
$\quad = length \times width \times height$

Volume of a cylinder
$\quad = \pi \times (radius)^2 \times height$

Take a good hard look at this last formula because it is the backbone of the volume formulas that we will be working with shortly.

What is new about the types of volume problems presented in the following sections is the way these shapes are *generated*. In these volume problems, you will not usually be given a three-dimensional solid. Instead, you will be given a function in the xy-plane and be asked to *revolve* this function around either the x- or y-axis, hence generating a three-dimensional solid (thus the description, *solid of revolution*).

Now, for some students, the idea of revolving a curve around a line to generate a solid creates a fairly clear picture in their mind. Others tend to think in words rather than pictures, and will have a more difficult time with these problems. For the visual thinkers, have fun! For the verbal thinkers, here's an opportunity to improve your visual skills; since you're stretching outside your comfort zone, you should congratulate yourself often, and try to have fun with it!

We will develop the formula while considering an example problem.

Example

Find the volume of the solid generated by revolving the curve $f(x) = x\sqrt{\sin x}$ about the x-axis on the interval $[0, \pi]$.

The graph of $f(x) = x\sqrt{\sin x}$ on $[0, \pi]$ is found in graph C. The graph on the next page shows the resulting solid when the curve is revolved around the x-axis. To me, the solid looks like a top sitting sideways. Now, what kind of shapes can be used to build up and approximate the volume?

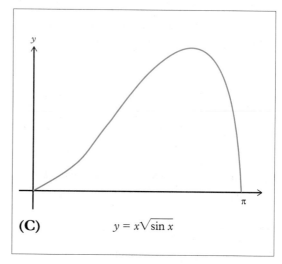

(C) $\qquad\qquad y = x\sqrt{\sin x}$

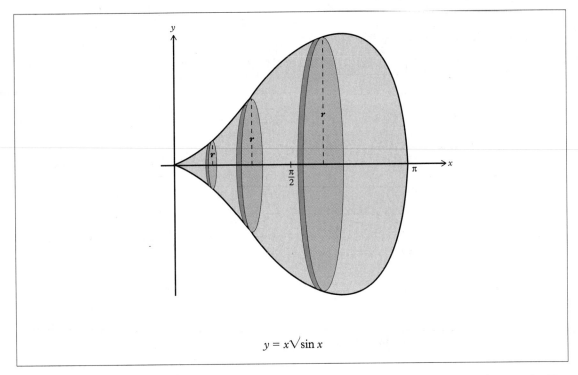

$$y = x\sqrt{\sin x}$$

Recall that when we wanted to approximate the area under $f(x)$ on $[a, b]$, we broke up $[a, b]$ into n subintervals, and used rectangles to approximate the area on each subinterval. So let's start the same way for this volume problem. That is, if we slice $[0, \pi]$ into subintervals, what would the shape look like on each subinterval? (See the graph above) They look like different-sized pancakes to me. Well, we don't have a

geometric formula for the volume of a pancake. But we do have a formula for the volume of a cylinder ($V = \pi r^2 h$). If the height is very small, the cylinder will look like a coin or a pancake.

Now what should we call the radius of these pancakes since there are so many different sizes? As you can see from the graph, the radius depends on the function $f(x) = x\sqrt{\sin x}$. And the height (call it Δx)

Tabular integration

This technique can be used when you have a product of a polynomial and transcendental function.

Evaluate $\int x^3 \cos x \; dx$.

For now, ignore the big arrows and $+$ and $-$ signs.

Start the process with the usual integration-by-parts procedure.

$$u = x^3 \qquad\qquad dv = \cos x \; dx$$
$$du = 3x^2 \qquad\qquad v = \sin x$$

Now keep differentiating until you get 0.

Keep integrating until you reach the row opposite the 0.

$u =$	x^3	$+$	$dv =$	$\cos x \; dx$
$du =$	$3x^2$	$-$	$v =$	$\sin x$
	$6x$	$+$		$-\cos x$
	6	$-$		$-\sin x$
	0			$\cos x$

Now the arrows go in with alternating $+$ and $-$ signs. Add or subtract the products of the functions connected by the arrows.

$$\int x^3 \cos x \; dx$$

$$= +x^3 \sin x - 3x^2(-\cos x) + 6x(-\sin x) - 6(\cos x)$$

$$= x^3 \sin x + 3x^2 \cos x - 6x \sin x - 6 \cos x + C$$

depends on the number, n, of subintervals. So

$$\text{volume of the top} \approx \sum_{i=1}^{n} \pi r^2 h = \sum_{i=1}^{n} \pi [f(x)]^2 \Delta x.$$

The more subintervals there are, the thinner the pancakes become and the closer the sum of our pancakes comes to approximating the volume of the top. The magic of calculus comes in when we let the number of subintervals go to infinity.

$$\lim_{n \to \infty} \sum_{i=1}^{n} \pi [f(x)]^2 \Delta x = \int_a^b \pi [f(x)]^2 dx$$

The definite integral on the right is the one we will use to calculate the volume of the top.

$$V = \int_a^b \pi [f(x)]^2 \, dx = \pi \int_0^{\pi} [x\sqrt{\sin x}]^2 \, dx$$

$$= \pi \int_0^{\pi} x^2 \sin x \, dx$$

Since the integrand is a product of a polynomial (x^2) and a transcendental function $(\sin x)$ then we can use "Tabular integration," described in the table opposite.

$$
\begin{array}{ccc}
x^2 & + & \sin x \\
2x & - & -\cos x \quad \ddagger \\
2 & + & -\sin x \\
0 & & \cos x
\end{array}
$$

$\star$

Keep differentiating until you get 0.
‡*Keep integrating until you reach the 0 row.*

$$V = \pi \int_0^{\pi} x^2 \sin x \, dx$$

$$= \pi \left[-x^2 \cos x + 2x \sin x + 2 \cos x \right]_0^{\pi}$$

$$= \pi \{ [-\pi^2(-1) + 2\pi \cdot 0 + 2(-1)] - (0 + 0 + 2 \cdot 1) \}$$

$$= \pi (\pi^2 - 2 - 2) = \pi^3 - 4\pi$$

So the volume of the top is approximately 18.44 cubic units.

* * *

Your textbook probably refers to this method of calculating volume as the *disc method*. I use pancakes instead of discs, because the idea is the same, but the descriptions are more fun.

Example

Find the volume of the solid of revolution generated by revolving the function

$$f(y) = \frac{5}{\sqrt{y^2 + 1}}$$

around the *y*-axis on the interval [0, 4].

This is another example where the roles of x and y have been reversed. If you have a difficult time sketching the graph as a function of y, start the problem working with something more familiar.

Exercise

Graph the function $f(x) = \dfrac{5}{\sqrt{x^2 + 1}}$ in the viewing rectangle [0, 5], 1 and [0, 6], 1. TRACE to identify the coordinates of the points found in the graph below.

Now reverse the order of these coordinates, and refer to graph A on top of page 192. When the curve is revolved about the *y*-axis, it generates a bell-shaped solid. To find the volume, again we use the formula $V = \pi r^2 h$, but now the radius of the pancake is given by $f(y)$ and the thickness is dy, so we will integrate with respect to y.

$$\int_a^b \pi [f(y)]^2 \, dy = \pi \int_0^4 \left(\frac{5}{\sqrt{y^2 + 1}} \right)^2 dy$$

$$= \pi \int_0^4 \frac{25}{y^2 + 1} \, dy$$

$$= 25\pi \left[\tan^{-1} y \right]_0^4$$

$$= 25\pi (\tan^{-1} 4 - \tan^{-1} 0) \approx 104.1$$

So the volume of the bell is approximately 104.1 cubic units.

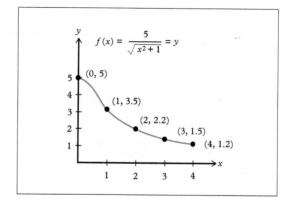

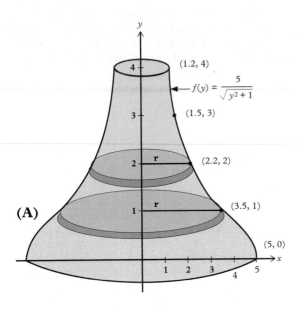

(A)

$f(y) = \dfrac{5}{\sqrt{y^2+1}}$

(1.2, 4)

(1.5, 3)

(2.2, 2)

(3.5, 1)

(5, 0)

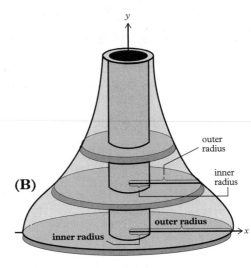

(B)

outer radius

inner radius

outer radius

inner radius

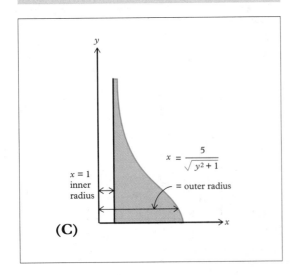

$x = \dfrac{5}{\sqrt{y^2+1}}$

$x = 1$
inner radius

= outer radius

(C)

Volume of a solid of revolution: Discs

1. Given a continuous function on interval $[a, b]$, we have

$$V = \int_a^b \pi (radius)^2 \times thickness.$$

2. If f is a function of x revolved about the x-axis, then this formula becomes

$$V = \int_a^b \pi [f(x)]^2 \, dx.$$

3. If f is a function of y revolved about the y-axis, then this formula becomes

$$V = \int_a^b \pi [f(y)]^2 \, dy.$$

Washers. Now, what if we took our bell from the last problem and drilled a hole in it? (See graph B.) Can we modify our volume formula to find the volume of this newly created solid? (You have to stretch your understanding of a solid since this shape is obviously not solid through and through.)

We will no longer add up the volumes of pancakes to find the volume of this shape. Instead, we will add up the volumes of washers. (Think of the type of washer that might be used to fix a leaky faucet.) So it's like a pancake with a hole in the middle. This leads to the concept of an outer radius and an inner radius. So the volume of the washer would be

$$V = [\pi (outer\ radius)^2 - \pi (inner\ radius)^2] \times thickness.$$

(See graphs B and C.)

Essentially, we find the volume of the solid of revolution of the curve closer to the axis, and subtract this from the volume of the solid of revolution of the curve that is farther from the axis.

The formulas in integral form can be found in the box "Volumes by the washer method." Now let's find the volume of this shape. We will use formula 2 since we have functions of y in this problem.

$$V = \int_0^4 \pi \left[\left(\frac{5}{\sqrt{y^2+1}} \right)^2 - 1^2 \right] dy$$

$$= \pi \int_0^4 \left(\frac{25}{\sqrt{y^2+1}} - 1 \right) dy$$

Volumes by the washer method

$$Volume = \pi\left[\left(\frac{outer}{radius}\right)^2 - \left(\frac{inner}{radius}\right)^2\right] \times thickness$$

1. If the outer and inner radii are both continuous functions of x on $[a, b]$, then the formula becomes

$$V = \int_a^b \pi\left[\left(\frac{outer}{radius}\right)^2 - \left(\frac{inner}{radius}\right)^2\right] dx.$$

2. If the outer and inner radii are both continuous functions of y on $[a, b]$, then the formula becomes

$$V = \int_a^b \pi\left[\left(\frac{outer}{radius}\right)^2 - \left(\frac{inner}{radius}\right)^2\right] dy.$$

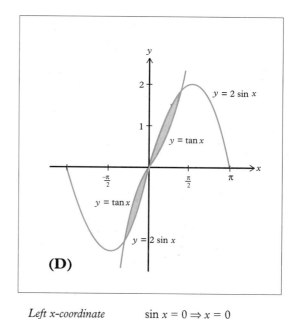

(D)

$$= \pi\left[25 \tan^{-1} y - y\right]_0^4$$

$$= \pi\,(25 \tan^{-1} 4 - 4) - (25 \tan^{-1} 0 - 0)$$

$$= 25\,\pi \tan^{-1} 4 - 4\pi \approx 91.6$$

Left x-coordinate	$\sin x = 0 \Rightarrow x = 0$

$$\left(2 - \frac{1}{\cos x}\right) = 0$$

$$\frac{1}{\cos x} = 2$$

$$1 = 2 \cos x$$

Right x-coordinate $\quad \dfrac{1}{2} = \cos x \Rightarrow x = \dfrac{\pi}{3}$

So the volume of the bell shape with a hole drilled in it is approximately 92 cubic units.

Let's work another example using the washer method.

Example

The region in the first quadrant, bounded by the curves $y = 2 \sin x$ and $y = \tan x$, is revolved about the x-axis to generate a solid. Find the volume of the solid.

We need to determine where the curves (shown in graph D) intersect.

$$2 \sin x = \tan x \Rightarrow 2 \sin x = \frac{\sin x}{\cos x}$$

$$2 \sin x - \frac{\sin x}{\cos x} = 0$$

$$\sin x \left(2 - \frac{1}{\cos x}\right) = 0$$

Set each factor equal to zero to get the x-value of the intersection points.

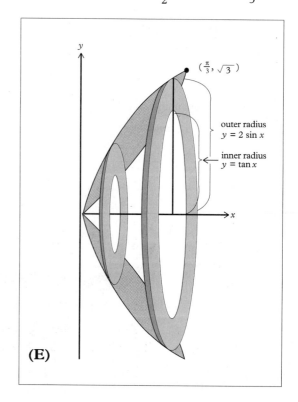

(E)

Since $\tan 0 = 0$ and $\tan \dfrac{\pi}{3} = \sqrt{3}$, the intersection

points are $(0, 0)$ and $\left(\dfrac{\pi}{3}, \sqrt{3} \right)$. But all we really care

about are the x-values since these will be our limits of integration. Since the outer and inner radius are functions of x, we will use formula 1 from page 193.

$$\int_0^{\pi/3} \pi[(2 \sin x)^2 - (\tan x)^2] \, dx$$

$$= \pi \int_0^{\pi/3} (4 \sin^2 x - \tan^2 x) \, dx$$

We need to use some trig identities to integrate the previous expression. Since

$$\sin^2 x = \frac{1}{2}(1 - \cos 2x) \Rightarrow 4 \sin^2 x = 2 - 2 \cos 2x$$

$$\text{and } \tan^2 x = \sec^2 - 1,$$

then $4 \sin^2 x - \tan^2 x = 2 - 2 \cos 2x - \sec^2 + 1$. This last expression will work much better as an integrand. So we get

$$V = \pi \int_0^{\pi/3} (3 - 2 \cos 2x - \sec^2 x) \, dx$$

$$= \pi \left[3x - \sin 2x - \tan x \right]_0^{\pi/3}$$

$$= \pi \left[\left(\pi - \sin \frac{2\pi}{3} - \tan \frac{\pi}{3} \right) - (0 - 0 - 0) \right]$$

$$= \pi \left(\pi - \frac{\sqrt{3}}{2} - \sqrt{3} \right) \approx 1.7075.$$

So the volume of revolution is 1.7075 cubic units.

$$\star \quad \star \quad \star$$

Shells. Let's say the region in the first quadrant bounded by the curves $y = 2 \sin x$ and $y = \tan x$ is revolved about the y-axis to generate a solid. (This is the same region we were working with in the previous example; see graph D on page 193. But now we are interested in revolving the region around the vertical axis. The solid of revolution will have a similar shape, but it won't be exactly the same because the curves which describe the inner and outer radius will reverse roles. So the volume won't be the same either.)

If we try to calculate this volume with washers, we run into a problem. The inner and outer radii are described by functions of x, but the washers are lying flat, so their thickness would be given by dy. Using the formula for washers, we might be tempted to write the integral

$$\int_0^{\sqrt{3}} \pi[(\tan x)^2 - (2 \sin x)^2] \, dy.$$

NOTE: We could also write $1 + 1 = 3$.

The dy indicates that y is the variable of integration. But the integrand is in terms of functions of x. Something is wrong with this picture. Formula 2 on page 193 is the one that relates to washers revolved about the y-axis, and it stipulates that the functions describing the inner and outer radii must be functions of y. Well, can we describe our radius equations as functions of y?

$$y = 2 \sin x$$

$$\frac{y}{2} = \sin x \Rightarrow x = \sin^{-1} \frac{y}{2} \qquad \textit{inner radius}$$

$$y = \tan x \Rightarrow x = \tan^{-1} y \qquad \textit{outer radius}$$

(See the graph below.)

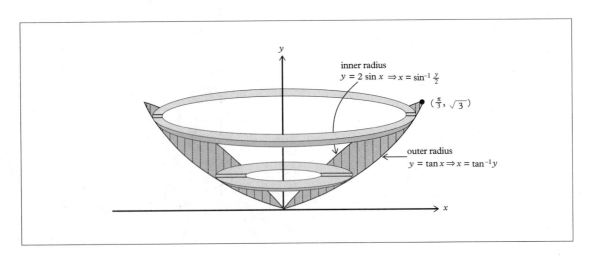

Calculus

Volumes by the shell method (about the y-axis)

If the function or functions that determine the height of the shells are continuous functions of x on $[a, b]$, then

$$Volume = 2\pi \int_a^b x \, (height) \, dx.$$

Now is an appropriate time to apply formula 2.

$$V = \pi \int_0^{\sqrt{3}} [(\tan^{-1} y)^2 - (\sin^{-1} y)^2] \, dy$$

Well, there aren't any tricks to find an antiderivative for the squares of inverse trig functions. So using the key for $\int dx$ (Simpson's rule), we get $V \approx 1.1145$. So our final answer is 1.1145 cubic units, which is not the same as the volume of revolution about the x-axis.

It's not always possible to take a function of x and write it as a function of y ($y = x\sqrt{\sin x}$ is an example). So we should have a technique that allows us to find the volume generated by revolving functions of x about the y-axis. There is such a technique, and it is called the *shell method*. These shells look like cans of different heights with no tops and bottoms (see the graph below). So now, instead of layering pancakes with holes to form the volume, the shells add up like the layers of an onion to form the volume.

Let's apply the formula for "Volumes by the shell method" (above) to the region from the last example revolved about the y-axis.

$$V = 2\pi \int_0^{\pi/3} x(2 \sin x - \tan x) \, dx$$

NOTE: When integrating with respect to x, don't forget to make your interval of integration according to the x-values of the endpoints of the region.

Again, we can't integrate $y = x \tan x$ so we use a numerical method and get $V \approx 1.1145$, which is the same answer we got for this region revolved around the y-axis using washers.

Example

The curve $y = x\sqrt{\sin x}$ is revolved about the y-axis on the interval $[0, \pi]$. Find the volume of revolution (see the graph on page 190).

Shells make sense here, because the height of the shell would be uniquely determined by the curve $y = x\sqrt{\sin x}$. From the "shell method" formula, we get

$$V = 2\pi \int_0^{\pi} x^2 \sqrt{\sin x} \, dx.$$

Numerical integration yields $V \approx 46.1626$.

⋆ ⋆ ⋆

Example

The region between the curves $y = \left(\dfrac{1}{2}\right) e^x$ and $y = 2$

ln x where $x \in [1, 3]$ is revolved about the y-axis. Find the volume of revolution.

We could, if we wanted, express these curves as functions of y. But if we wanted to find this volume with the washer method, the outer and inner radius would have to be uniquely determined throughout the region. This means that horizontal rectangles would have to touch the same curve on the right side for the outer radius, and the other curve on the left side for the inner radius. But as you can see in graph A on page 196, this is not the case. So let's see if we can use the shell method.

In order to use the shell method, we need to be able

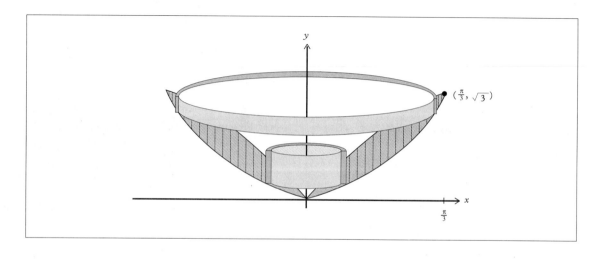

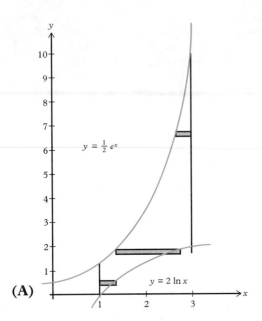

(A)

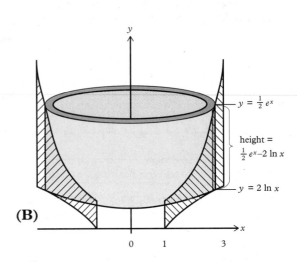

height = $\frac{1}{2}e^x - 2\ln x$

$y = \frac{1}{2}e^x$

$y = 2\ln x$

(B)

to draw vertical rectangles throughout the region so that their height is uniquely determined by the curves. Graph B shows that the height of the rectangles throughout the region would be given by *height* $= \frac{1}{2}e^x - 2\ln x$. So we can use the volume formula found on page 195.

$$V = 2\pi \int_1^3 x\left(\frac{1}{2}e^x - 2\ln x\right)dx$$

$$= \pi \int_1^3 xe^x\,dx - 4\pi \int_1^3 x\ln x\,dx$$

Let's work on these integrals in two separate columns.

$\pi \int_1^3 xe^x\,dx$ $-4\pi \int_3^1 x\ln x\,dx$

		$u = \ln x$	$dv = x\,dx$
x	e^x		
1	e^x	$du = \dfrac{1}{x}\,dx$	$v = \dfrac{1}{2}x^2$
0	e^x		

$$= -4\pi\left[\frac{1}{2}x^2\ln x - \int \frac{1}{2}x\,dx\right]_1^3$$

$= \pi\left[xe^x - e^x\right]_1^3$ $= -4\pi\left[\frac{1}{2}x^2\ln x - \frac{1}{4}x^2\right]_1^3$

$= \pi[(3e^3 - e^3)$ $= -4\pi\left[\left(\frac{9}{2}\ln 3 - \frac{9}{4}\right)\right.$

$\quad - (e - e)]$ $\left.- \left(\frac{1}{2}\ln 1 - \frac{1}{4}\right)\right]$

$= 2\pi e^3$ $= -4\pi\left(\frac{9}{2}\ln 3 - 2\right)$

So, $V = 2\pi e^3 - 4\pi\left(\frac{9}{2}\ln 3 - 2\right) \approx 89.2$

★   ★   ★

Exercise

Graph the function $y = \dfrac{1}{(x-1)(4-x)}$

in the viewing rectangle [0, 5], 1 and [0, 2], 1. Make a sketch. Now draw the vertical lines $x = 1.5$ and $x = 3.5$. This region will be used in the next example.

Example

The region bounded by the curve

$$f(x) = \frac{1}{(x-1)(4-x)}$$

and the lines $x = 1.5$ and $x = 3.5$ is revolved about the y-axis. Find the volume of this solid of revolution.

$$V = 2\pi \int_{1.5}^{3.5} x\left(\frac{1}{(x-1)(4-x)}\right)dx$$

$$= 2\pi \int_{1.5}^{3.5} \frac{x}{(x-1)(4-x)}\,dx$$

196   **Calculus**

To integrate, we need to use a PFD.

$$\frac{x}{(x-1)(4-x)} = \frac{A}{(x-1)} + \frac{B}{(4-x)}$$

$$x = A(4-x) + B(x-1) = 4A - Ax + Bx - B$$
$$= (-A + B)x + (4A - B)$$

$-A + B = 1$
$\underline{4A - B = 0}$
$3A + 0 = 1$

$$A = \frac{1}{3} \qquad\qquad -\frac{1}{3} + B = 1 \Rightarrow B = \frac{4}{3}$$

$$V = 2\pi \int_{1.5}^{3.5} \left[\frac{1}{3(x-1)} \right.$$

$$\left. + \frac{4}{3(4-x)} \right] dx \qquad u = 4 - x$$

$$du = -dx$$

$$= 2\pi \left[\frac{1}{3} \ln(x-1) - \frac{4}{3} \ln(4-x) \right]_{1.5}^{3.5}$$

$$= 2\pi \left[\left(\frac{1}{3} \ln 2.5 - \frac{4}{3} \ln 0.5 \right) \right.$$

$$\left. - \left(\frac{1}{3} \ln 0.5 - \frac{4}{3} \ln 2.5 \right) \right]$$

$$= 2\pi \left[\frac{5}{3} \ln(2.5) - \frac{5}{3} \ln(0.5) \right]$$

$$= \frac{10\pi}{3} \ln \left(\frac{\frac{5}{2}}{\frac{1}{2}} \right) = \frac{10\pi}{3} \ln 5 \approx 16.854$$

The volume is about 16.854 cubic units.

★   ★   ★

Lengths of curves.
In many application problems, it is necessary to know the length of a curve on a continuous interval in its domain. For example, if the path of motion of a particle is known, the distance traveled by the particle from time $t = a$ to $t = b$ can be determined.

You can approximate the length of a curve by taking a ruler and marking off line segments, summing the length of the segments. When you see *summing*, you should think of a definite integral. The definite integral is used to sum the lengths of the line segments as the line segments become infinitely shorter.

Determining arc length

If a function $y = f(x)$ is continuous and differentiable everywhere on the interval $[a, b]$, then the definite integral

$$L = \int_a^b \sqrt{1 + \left(\frac{dy}{dx} \right)^2} \, dx$$

will determine the length of the curve f from a to b.

The box above gives the formula for arc length. To convince ourselves it is valid, we will try it out on a curve for which we have a geometric formula to describe length.

Example
Find the length of the lower half of the unit circle centered at the origin.

The equation for the lower half of the unit circle is

$$y = -\sqrt{1 - x^2} = -(1 - x^2)^{1/2}.$$

$$\frac{dy}{dx} = -\frac{1}{2}(1 - x^2)^{-1/2}(-2x) = \frac{x}{\sqrt{1 - x^2}}$$

$$\left(\frac{dy}{dx} \right)^2 = \left(\frac{x}{\sqrt{1 - x^2}} \right)^2 = \frac{x^2}{\sqrt{1 - x^2}}$$

When you are working these problems, it is a good idea to simplify the expression $\sqrt{1 + \left(\frac{dy}{dx} \right)^2}$ before you plug it into the integral.

$$\sqrt{1 + \left(\frac{dy}{dx} \right)^2} = \sqrt{1 + \frac{x^2}{1 - x^2}}$$

$$= \sqrt{\frac{1}{1 - x^2}} = \frac{1}{\sqrt{1 - x^2}}$$

So, $L = \int_{-1}^{1} \frac{1}{\sqrt{1 - x^2}} \, dx = \sin^{-1} x \Big]_{-1}^{1}$

$$= \sin^{-1} 1 - \sin^{-1}(-1)$$

$$= \frac{\pi}{2} - \left(-\frac{\pi}{2} \right) = \pi$$

Looks good to me!

★   ★   ★

Example

Given $y = \ln x$, find the length of the curve from $x = 1$ to $x = 3$.

$$\frac{dy}{dx} = \frac{1}{x} \rightarrow \left(\frac{dy}{dx}\right)^2 = \frac{1}{x^2}$$

$$L = \int_a^b \sqrt{1 + \left(\frac{dy}{dx}\right)^2}\, dx = \int_1^3 \sqrt{1 + \frac{1}{x^2}}\, dx$$

Our only hope here is to combine terms under the radical to get a form we are more familiar with.

$$\sqrt{1 + \frac{1}{x^2}} = \sqrt{\frac{x^2 + 1}{x^2}} = \frac{\sqrt{x^2 + 1}}{x}$$

So $L = \int_1^3 \dfrac{\sqrt{x^2 + 1}}{x^2}\, dx$ and it looks like we can use a trig substitution. Let $x = \tan\theta$, then $dx = \sec^2\theta\, d\theta$.

$$\int \frac{\sqrt{x^2 + 1}}{x}\, dx$$

$$= \int \frac{\sqrt{\tan^2\theta + 1}}{\tan\theta}\sec^2\theta\, d\theta = \int \frac{\sqrt{\sec^2\theta}}{\tan\theta}\sec^2\theta\, d\theta$$

$$= \int \frac{\sec^3\theta}{\tan\theta}\, d\theta$$

$$= \int \frac{1}{\cos^3\theta}\cdot\frac{\cos\theta}{\sin\theta}\, d\theta = \int \sec^2\theta\csc\theta\, d\theta$$

Now, we need integration by parts.

$$u = \csc\theta \qquad\qquad dv = \sec^2\theta\, d\theta$$

$$du = -\csc\theta\cot\theta\, d\theta \qquad\qquad v = \tan\theta$$

$$\int u\, dv = uv - \int v\, dv$$

$$\int \sec^2\theta\csc\theta\, d\theta$$

$$= \csc\theta\tan\theta - \int \tan\theta\,(\csc\theta\cot\theta)\, d\theta$$

$$= \frac{1}{\sin\theta}\cdot\frac{\sin\theta}{\cos\theta} + \int\left(\frac{\sin\theta}{\cos\theta}\cdot\frac{1}{\sin\theta}\cdot\frac{\cos\theta}{\sin\theta}\right) d\theta$$

$$= \sec\theta + \int \csc\theta\, d\theta$$

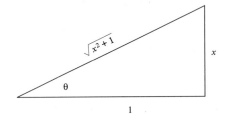

$$= \sec\theta + \ln|\csc\theta - \cot\theta|.$$

So, since originally $x = \tan\theta$ (see figure above) we have the indefinite integral

$$\sqrt{x^2 + 1} + \ln\left|\frac{\sqrt{x^2 + 1}}{x} - \frac{1}{x}\right|.$$

Now don't forget the limits of integration to find

$$I = \left[\sqrt{x^2 + 1} + \ln\left|\frac{\sqrt{x^2 + 1} - 1}{x}\right|\right]_1^3$$

$$= \left(\sqrt{10} + \ln\left|\frac{\sqrt{10} - 1}{3}\right|\right)$$

$$- \left(\sqrt{2} + \ln\left|\frac{\sqrt{2} - 1}{1}\right|\right).$$

You can't do much to simplify, so let's get a numerical approximation to make sure it's a positive number, since we are looking for the arc length.

$$\text{Arc length} \approx 2.302.$$

Exercise

Use the key for $\int dx$ in order to get a numerical approximation for

$$\int_1^3 \frac{\sqrt{x^2 + 1}}{x}\, dx.$$

Ask your teacher why you had to do all that antiderivative stuff.

Calculus

Area of a surface of revolution.

Think for a moment about the types of animals found in arctic regions. Now think about the types of animals found near the equator. In which area would you say there is a larger percentage of large animals?

Larger animals are predominant in arctic regions partly due to the fact that the ratio of surface area to volume is reduced for large animals. This allows them to store body heat more efficiently. Variations on this theme can be found throughout nature.

Objects with different shapes may have the same volume; and depending on the shape, the surface may vary widely.

The box here shows the formula for the surface area of a solid of revolution. Let's take a look at a few example problems.

Example

Find the surface area generated by revolving the region bounded by $y = \sin x$ on $[0, \pi]$ about the x-axis.

From the surface area formula, we have

$$S = 2\pi \int_0^\pi \sin x \sqrt{1 + \cos^2 x}\ dx.$$

This will take some work, but I think we can find an antiderivative if we let

$$u = \cos x \qquad \text{at } x = \pi \qquad u = \cos \pi = -1$$
$$du = -\sin x\ dx. \qquad x = 0 \qquad u = \cos \theta = 1$$

So,

$$S = 2\pi \int_1^{-1} -\sqrt{1 + u^2}\ du = 2\pi \int_{-1}^1 \sqrt{1 + u^2}\ du$$

Let's forget about the limits of integration until we find an antiderivative. How about a trig substitution?

$$u = \tan \theta$$
$$du = \sec^2 \theta\ d\theta$$

So,

$$S = 2\pi \int \sqrt{1 + \tan^2 \theta}\ \sec^2 \theta\ d\theta$$
$$= 2\pi \int \sqrt{\sec^2 \theta}\ \sec^2 \theta\ d\theta$$
$$= 2\pi \int \sec^3 \theta\ d\theta$$

Now, how about parts?

$$u = \sec \theta \qquad\qquad dv = \sec^2 \theta\ d\theta$$
$$du = \sec \theta \tan \theta\ d\theta \qquad v = \tan \theta$$

Surface area formula

If f is continuous and differentiable and nonnegative on $[a, b]$, then the *area* of the surface generated by revolving the graph of f about the x-axis is given by the definite integral

$$S = \int_a^b 2\pi f(x) \sqrt{1 + [f'(x)]^2}\ dx.$$

$$\int \sec^3 \theta\ d\theta = \sec \theta \tan \theta - \int \sec \theta \tan^2 \theta\ d\theta$$
$$= \sec \theta \tan \theta - \int \sec \theta\ (\sec^2 \theta - 1)\ d\theta$$
$$= \sec \theta \tan \theta + \int \sec \theta\ d\theta - \int \sec^3 \theta\ d\theta$$

This last integral is the same as the first integral two lines up, so we do a linear combination.

$$2\int \sec^3 \theta\ d\theta = \sec \theta \tan \theta + \int \sec \theta\ d\theta$$
$$\int \sec^3 \theta\ d\theta = \frac{1}{2}(\sec \theta \tan \theta + \ln|\sec \theta + \tan \theta|)$$

So from

$$S = 2\pi \int \sec^3 \theta\ d\theta$$
$$= \pi \left(\sec \theta \tan \theta + \ln|\sec \theta + \tan \theta|\right)$$

Now, we back substitute and bring back the limits of integration. From $u = \tan \theta$

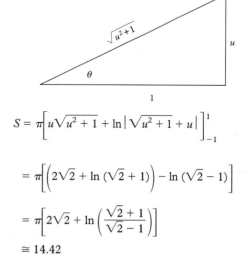

$$S = \pi \left[u\sqrt{u^2 + 1} + \ln|\sqrt{u^2 + 1} + u| \right]_{-1}^1$$

$$= \pi \left[\left(2\sqrt{2} + \ln(\sqrt{2} + 1)\right) - \ln(\sqrt{2} - 1) \right]$$

$$= \pi \left[2\sqrt{2} + \ln\left(\frac{\sqrt{2} + 1}{\sqrt{2} - 1}\right) \right]$$

$$\cong 14.42$$

So, the surface area of this solid of revolution is approximately 14.42 square units.

Infinite sequences and series

We come now to the third major application of the limit. The first was the limit of a function, of which one example was the derivative, defined as the limit of a difference quotient. The second was the limit of a sum of areas of rectangles, which gave us the definite integral. We turn next to sequences and series and another investigation of limits. Very informally, a sequence is a list of expressions with commas between them; a series is a list of expressions with addition (or subtraction) symbols between them. Like derivatives and integrals, sequences and series are rich in applications; many disciplines in science and engineering use the techniques of infinite series.

Sequences.
A sequence is a list of values in a specific order. (Since we will consider only infinite sequences, when you see the word *sequence* you should know that we are referring to an *infinite sequence*.)

$\{1, 2, 3, \ldots\}$, $\{\frac{1}{2}, \frac{1}{3}, \frac{1}{5}, \frac{1}{7}, \ldots\}$, $\{\frac{0}{1}, \frac{1}{2}, \frac{2}{3}, \frac{3}{4}, \ldots\}$, and $\{0, 0.693, 1.099, 1.386, \ldots\}$ are examples of infinite sequences. Because the ordering is done by associating each term with a counting number, here is a more usable definition.

Definition
An *infinite sequence* is a function whose domain is the set of positive integers.

Because the domain is the set of counting numbers, it is conventional to use n as the independent variable.

It can be called the *counter* or *index*. Individual items in the list are called *terms*. When possible, a formula for the function can be given in the usual way. For instance, the third example given above is $a(n) = \frac{n-1}{n}$. The more compact notation a_n is usually used in place of $a(n)$. When we refer to the entire sequence, rather than to a single term, braces are used: the fourth example above is $\{\ln n\}$. Note that the formulas given are normal functions whose domains are real numbers, but here their domains are restricted to positive integers. This will be useful to us.

Exercise
Write out the first several terms of each of the following sequences:

$$\{n^2 + 2\}, \left\{\frac{1}{n(n+1)}\right\}, \{5\}, \left\{1 + \frac{1}{n!}\right\}.$$

(For the last sequence, see definition of *factorial*.)

As with any other function, a sequence can be graphed. Below and bottom right are examples of graphs of sequences. If it can be done clearly, the one-dimensional graphing technique is sometimes used. The behavior of many sequences can be determined by graphing the function (without regard for the restricted domain) and observing any trends.

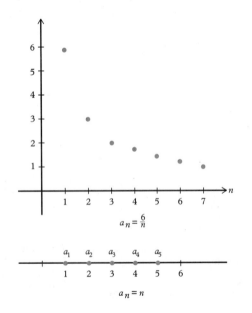

$a_n = \frac{6}{n}$

$a_n = n$

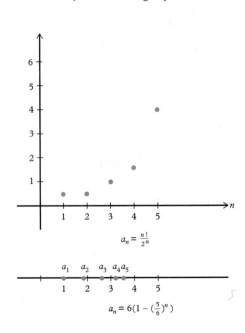

$a_n = \frac{n!}{2^n}$

$a_n = 6\left(1 - \left(\frac{5}{6}\right)^n\right)$

Calculus

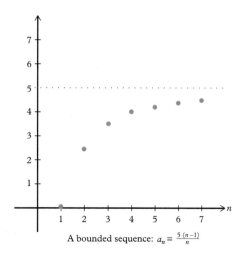

A bounded sequence: $a_n = \frac{5(n-1)}{n}$

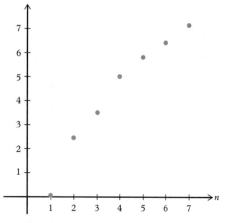

An unbounded sequence: $a_n = k \ln n$ (k constant)

Exercise

Use a graphing calculator to get an idea of the behavior of the sequences:

$$a_n = 1.2^n, \ a_n = 0.98^n, \ a_n = \frac{2^n}{n^2},$$

$$a_n = \sqrt[n]{n}, \ a_n = e^{-n} \sin n.$$

Then answer the questions: Does the sequence increase (or decrease) steadily? Does there seem to be a value beyond which the function does not grow? Do the terms seem to be approaching a particular value? (Uh-oh! I smell a limit coming.)

Definition

The *factorial* is a notation (and an operation) that is frequently encountered in sequences and series. For example, 4! (read "four factorial") is defined as $4 \cdot 3 \cdot 2 \cdot 1 = 24$. Then, $3! = 3 \cdot 2 \cdot 1 = 6$. Because it arises so often in practice, we must define $0! = 1$.

Bounded or unbounded? In the last exercise, the question was asked, "Does there seem to be a value beyond which the function does not grow?" This is the essence of *boundedness*. A sequence $\{a_n\}$ is called *bounded* if there is a number B such that $|a_n| < B$ for every n. For example, the sequence $a_n = \frac{5(n-1)}{n}$

can be seen to be bounded. A graph shows that the rational function approaches $y = 5$ as a horizontal asymptote: $a_n < 5$. The sequence $a_n = 5 \sin^2 n$ (shown in the graph to the left) is clearly bounded, since $|\sin n| \le 1$, so $|\sin^2 n| \le 1$, and $a_n \le 5$.

As examples of sequences that are *unbounded*, consider $a_n = n$ or $a_n = \ln n$. Each of these grows beyond any number you could name.

Exercise

Examine each of the sequences mentioned above in examples, graphs, or exercises to see whether they are bounded or unbounded.

Exercise

Can you construct a sequence that is unbounded and approaches a particular value?

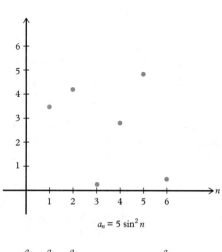

$a_n = 5 \sin^2 n$

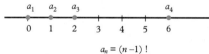

$a_n = (n-1)!$

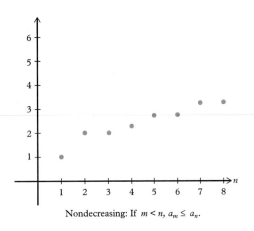

Nondecreasing: If $m < n$, $a_m \leq a_n$.

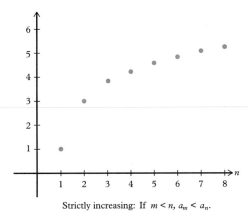

Strictly increasing: If $m < n$, $a_m < a_n$.

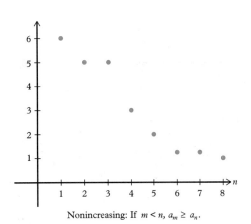

Nonincreasing: If $m < n$, $a_m \geq a_n$.

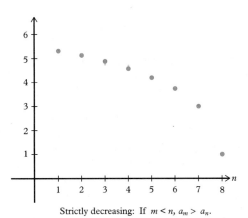

Strictly decreasing: If $m < n$, $a_m > a_n$.

Monotonic sequences

For $m < n$:

$$a_m \leq a_n$$
$\{a_n\}$ is *nondecreasing*

$$a_m < a_n$$
$\{a_n\}$ is *strictly increasing*

$$a_m \geq a_n$$
$\{a_n\}$ is *nonincreasing*

$$a_m > a_n$$
$\{a_n\}$ is *strictly decreasing*

All of these sequences are called *monotone* (or *monotonic*) sequences.

Exercise
Examine each of the sequences mentioned in examples, graphs, or exercises so far to see whether they are monotone or not.

Exercise
Can you construct a sequence that is *not* monotone but approaches a particular value?

Convergence and divergence. We have asked the question, "Does there seem to be a particular value that a sequence approaches?" This is the idea of the *limit* of a sequence. Let us take the sequence whose nth term is $a_n = 1 - \dfrac{1}{n}$ as an example. It is clear that the terms of the sequence are approaching 1, since each term is 1, less some small amount (and getting smaller). If we wanted to ensure that the values of a_n were "sufficiently close" to 1 (say, within 10^{-3}), we could do so. It would only be necessary to look at the terms beyond the thousandth. This is essentially the definition of the limit of a sequence.

Calculus

Definition

A sequence is said to converge to *limit* L if, for any $\epsilon > 0$, there is an N so that if $n > N$, then $|a_n - L| < \epsilon$. A sequence which does not satisfy the definition is said to *diverge*.

Some examples of sequences and their limits (or lack of limits) follow:

- $\{e^{-n}\}$ converges to 0 (another notation—$\{e^{-n}\} \to 0$).
- $\left\{\dfrac{2n-1}{n+1}\right\} \to 2$ (As above, consider the horizontal asymptote.)
- $\{\sin n\}$ does not have a limit (although it is certainly bounded).
- $\{\tan^{-1} n\} \to \dfrac{\pi}{2}$.

It may be that a sequence has a limit L, but never attains the value L. The sequence $\left\{1 - \dfrac{1}{n}\right\}$ is an example of this: $a_n \neq 1$ for any n. On the other hand, a sequence may take on a particular value many times, even infinitely often, and yet not have that value or any value as a limit. For example, if $a_n = (-1)^n$, then the sequence does not have a limit, even though (or, perhaps, because) a_n takes on each of two different values, each infinitely often.

Earlier, an exercise asked you to construct a sequence which was convergent and unbounded. I hope you had trouble doing this. It turns out that boundedness is a necessary condition for convergence. On the other hand, a sequence can be bounded, yet not converge (for example, $\{\sin n\}$).

Finally, we have a useful result: If a sequence is both monotonic *and* bounded, then it has a limit. This theorem does not tell what the limit is, it only guarantees the existence of one. However, this is frequently all that we are able to learn, so this makes the rule a rather powerful one.

Limits of important sequences.

As usual, we must be concerned with the practical application of the definition: Exactly how do we go about computing the limit of a sequence? First, we have some building blocks to work with.

If we are fortunate enough to learn the limits of some important sequences, then there are some theorems we can use to combine what we know into other results:

If $\{a_n\} \to A$ and $\{b_n\} \to B$, then $\{ka_n\} \to kA$, $\{a_n \pm b_n\} \to A \pm B$, $\{a_n \cdot b_n\} \to AB$, and $\left\{\dfrac{a_n}{b_n}\right\} \to \dfrac{A}{B}$ (provided $b_n \neq 0$ and $B \neq 0$).

Some formulas for sequences occur frequently enough that they deserve special mention. The following theorems can be used to compute limits in many common sequence situations.

Some useful sequence formulas

1. $\left\{\dfrac{\ln n}{n}\right\} \to 0$

2. $\{\sqrt[n]{n}\} \to 1$

3. For $x > 0$, $\{x^{1/n}\} \to 1$

4. For $|x| < 1$, $\{x^n\} \to 0$

5. $\left\{\left(1 + \dfrac{x}{n}\right)^n\right\} \to e^x$

6. $\left\{\dfrac{x^n}{n!}\right\} \to 0$ (any x)

The first result is proved by considering the continuous function $\dfrac{\ln x}{x}$ and using L'Hôpital's rule to compute $\lim\limits_{x \to \infty} \dfrac{\ln x}{x}$.

Some of the other rules are derived by using the following sneaky technique. If a limit cannot be computed directly, then we first apply continuous function f, then compute the limit, then apply f^{-1}. Theorems of limits guarantee that the result will be the same.

Consider $x^{1/n}$, using a logarithm for f and an exponential for f^{-1}. $\ln x^{1/n} = \dfrac{\ln x}{n} \to 0$ and $e^0 = 1$.

> **Exercise**
> Compute the limits (if they exist) of the sequences
> $$\{\sqrt[n]{3}\}, \ \{1.2^n\}, \ \{0.98^n\}, \ \left\{\left(1 + \frac{3}{n}\right)^n\right\},$$
> $$\left\{\frac{3^n}{n!}\right\}, \text{ and } \left\{4\sqrt[n]{n} + \frac{\ln n}{n}\right\}.$$

From infinite sequence to infinite series. Let us examine the other topic of this chapter: infinite series. A series is an infinite list of expressions that are added together.

Definition

An *infinite series* is an expression of the form $a_1 + a_2 + a_3 + a_4 + \cdots$, where $\{a_n\}$ is any sequence. Notation:

$$a_1 + a_2 + a_3 + a_4 + \cdots = \sum_{i=1}^{\infty} a_i = \sum a_i$$

The technical difficulty with this kind of expression is that addition is a *binary* operation. It makes perfect sense to add two numbers together. Or, by induction, it is reasonable to add any finite number of terms. But what is meant by adding infinitely many things together? It may seem like a minor point, but it does require something new. And because the process is infinite, the technique we must apply is (surprise!) the limit.

Convergence of an infinite sum. A simple strategy allows us to use our newly gained knowledge of sequences in the investigation of series. We define a sequence $\{S_n\}$ as follows:

$$\begin{aligned}
a_1 &= S_1 \\
a_1 + a_2 &= S_2 \\
a_1 + a_2 + a_3 &= S_3 \\
a_1 + a_2 + a_3 + a_4 &= S_4 \\
&\vdots
\end{aligned}$$

Then if the sequence $\{S_n\}$ converges to a limit L, we say that the series converges to L, or $\sum a_i = L$. If $\{S_n\}$ diverges, we say that the series diverges.

Exercise

Imagine any of the *sequences* in earlier examples turned into *series*. Write out the first few terms of the sequence $\{S_n\}$ as defined above.

Let us consider a particular series:

$$\frac{1}{0!} + \frac{1}{1!} + \frac{1}{2!} + \frac{1}{3!} + \cdots = 1 + 1 + \frac{1}{2} + \frac{1}{6} + \cdots.$$

Here is a nice way to compute the "partial sums", S_n, of the series. In your calculator memory, set $n = 0$ (the counter) and $S = 1$ (S_1, the first partial sum).

Then put the formula for a_n, $\frac{1}{n!}$ into a function memory, say f_1. Now enter the multistatement Isz N: $S + f_1 \to S$. This will increment n and compute and display the next S_n. Repeated execution of this multistatement will generate a list of the partial sums: 1, 2, 2.5, 2.666666667, 2.708333333, 2.716666667, 2.718055556, ... The series converges to e, and we obtain ten digits of accuracy (the limit of the calculator display) after only thirteen terms.

NOTE: The calculator technique just described can be used for *any* series, as long as you are careful about n, S, and the function.

Exercise

Use the calculator technique just described in order to compute the sum of fifteen terms of

$$\sum_{n=1}^{\infty} \frac{1}{n} \quad \text{and} \quad \sum_{n=0}^{\infty} \left(\frac{2}{3}\right)^n.$$

One of the most useful series is the *geometric series*, defined by $a_n = a_1 \cdot r^{n-1}$, where r is fixed. (Its usefulness is primarily due to the fact that, unlike most other series, we can actually compute its limit.) Consider two cases: if $|r| \geq 1$, as in $1 + 2 + 4 + 8 + \ldots$ ($r = 2$), then the series diverges (see the nth term test, below). But if $|r| < 1$, then the series converges, and there is a nice compact formula for the limit,

$$L = \frac{a_1}{1 - r}.$$

$$\sum_{n=1}^{\infty} a_1 r^{n-1} = a_1 + a_1 r + a_1 r^2 + a_1 r^3 + \cdots$$

$|r| < 1$	$|r| \geq 1$
$L = \dfrac{a_1}{1 - r}$	*Series diverges*
$2 + \dfrac{2}{3} + \dfrac{2}{9} + \cdots$	$1 + \dfrac{3}{2} + \dfrac{9}{4} + \dfrac{27}{8} + \cdots$
$\left(a_1 = 2, r = \dfrac{1}{3}\right)$	$\left(a_1 = 1, r = \dfrac{3}{2}\right)$
$L = \dfrac{2}{1 - \dfrac{1}{3}}$	*Series diverges*
$= 3$	

Exercise

Compute the sums of

$$\sum_{n=0}^{\infty} \left(\frac{2}{3}\right)^n, \ \sum_{n=1}^{\infty} (0.2)^n, \ \text{and} \ \sum_{n=0}^{\infty} (1.2)^n.$$

Series with nonnegative terms.

In our initial investigation of infinite series, we will restrict our attention to those which have only non-negative terms. This turns out to be a great simplification. If the a_n are nonnegative, then $\{S_n\}$ is monotonic increasing. It is then only necessary to determine if the sums are bounded in order to know that the series converges.

Test for divergence. One of the simplest tests to be applied to series to determine convergence or divergence is the so-called "nth term test." If a (nonnegative) series is to converge, then $a_n \to 0$. Thus, if the *sequence* a_n either diverges or converges to a number other than 0, then the *series* will diverge. For example,

$$\sum \frac{n}{3n-1} \text{ diverges, because } \frac{n}{3n-1} \to \frac{1}{3} \neq 0.$$

It is very important to note that the converse of this statement is *not* true. For a series to converge, it is necessary that $a_n \to 0$, but it is not sufficient. (See the discussion of the "harmonic series" in the next section, page 206, for an example.)

Test for divergence

If $\lim\limits_{n \to \infty} a_n$ does not exist or is some number other than 0, the series diverges.

If $\lim\limits_{n \to \infty} a_n = 0$, perform further tests for convergence.

The integral test.

Recall that many sequences (and series) can be described by formulas which could be valid over the real numbers; the restriction to the integers is not imposed by the function. This leads us to one of the simplest and most useful tests for convergence of a series.

Suppose we have a function $f(x)$ and a series $\sum a_n$, where $a_n = f(n)$; that is, at the integers, the function takes on the same value as the sequence of terms. Consider the graph of function $f(x)$, partitioned into intervals of width 1 (see below). Then the "upper" and "lower" sums of the areas of triangles are very nearly the series $\sum a_n$. This suggests the theorem: if $a_n = f(n)$, then the series $\sum a_n$ and the improper integral $\int_1^\infty f(x)\ dx$ either both converge or both diverge.

Integral test

If the improper integral $\int_1^\infty f(x)\ dx$ converges, the infinite series $\sum\limits_1^\infty a_n$ converges.

If the improper integral $\int_1^\infty f(x)\ dx$ diverges, the infinite series $\sum\limits_1^\infty a_n$ diverges.

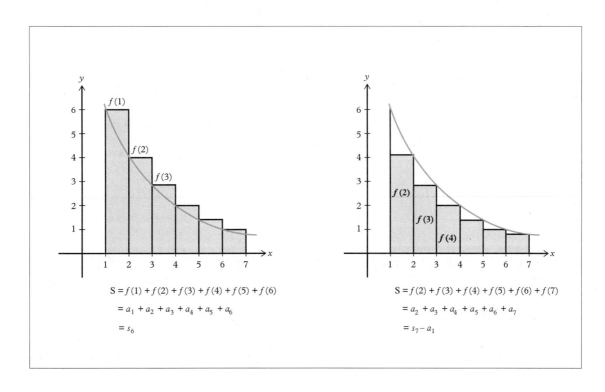

$$S = f(1) + f(2) + f(3) + f(4) + f(5) + f(6)$$
$$= a_1 + a_2 + a_3 + a_4 + a_5 + a_6$$
$$= s_6$$

$$S = f(2) + f(3) + f(4) + f(5) + f(6) + f(7)$$
$$= a_2 + a_3 + a_4 + a_5 + a_6 + a_7$$
$$= s_7 - a_1$$

As an example of the use of the integral test, consider the *harmonic series* $1 + \frac{1}{2} + \frac{1}{3} + \frac{1}{4} + \cdots$. The function $y = \frac{1}{x}$ satisfies the conditions of the test. We have $\int_1^\infty \frac{1}{x}\,dx = \ln x \Big]_1^\infty$, which diverges, because the upper limit "evaluates" to infinity. Then the test shows that the series diverges as well. Note that the nth term of the sequence of terms approaches 0. So the nth term test is satisfied, but the series diverges anyway.

0Exercise

Apply the integral test to

$$\sum_{n=1}^\infty \frac{1}{2n+1}, \quad \sum_{n=1}^\infty \frac{1}{(n+2)^{3/2}}, \quad \text{and} \quad \sum_{n=1}^\infty e^{-5n}.$$

Comparison tests. Another powerful tool for testing the convergence of series is the technique of comparison. Even though these are infinite processes, it may still be possible to arrange a term-by-term comparison of two series and learn something useful from it. If a series $\sum a_n$ is known to diverge, and we know that, for every n, $a_n \le b_n$, then it must also be that the series $\sum b_n$ diverges. On the other hand, if a series $\sum a_n$ is known to converge, and we know that, for every n, $b_n \le a_n$, then it must also be that the series $\sum b_n$ converges. (Remember that for now we are considering only series with nonnegative terms, so the requirement is $0 \le b_n \le a_n$.)

For example, consider the series $\sum_1^\infty \frac{1}{n \cdot 2^n}$. For each n, we have

$$\frac{1}{n \cdot 2^n} \le \frac{1}{2^n},$$

which is a geometric series with $r = \frac{1}{2}$. Because the geometric series converges, the more complicated series must also. Note that the actual limit is not determined by this procedure, only the fact that it exists. In fact, it will rarely be possible to specifically determine a limit; we are usually only able to prove the fact of convergence or divergence.

A more elaborate comparison technique is the limit comparison test, summarized here:

Limit comparison test

If $\lim\limits_{n\to\infty} \dfrac{b_n}{a_n} = 0$ and $\sum a_n$ converges, then $\sum b_n$ converges.

If $\lim\limits_{n\to\infty} \dfrac{b_n}{a_n} = k > 0$, then the series either both converge or both diverge.

If $\lim\limits_{n\to\infty} \dfrac{b_n}{a_n} = \infty$ and $\sum a_n$ diverges, then $\sum b_n$ diverges.

The trick here is to choose a known series, a series that is similar enough to the one under investigation so that the limit of the theorem will be reasonable to compute.

HINT: In rational functions, only the highest powers mean anything.

Let's investigate the convergence of the series

$$\sum \frac{2n-1}{5n^2+2}.$$

We'll use the limit comparison test with $a_n = \frac{1}{n}$. We have

$$\lim_{n\to\infty} \frac{\frac{2n-1}{5n^2+2}}{\frac{1}{n}} = \lim_{n\to\infty} \frac{2n^2-n}{5n^2+2} = \lim_{n\to\infty} \frac{2 - \frac{1}{n}}{5 + \frac{2}{n^2}} = \frac{2}{5}.$$

So, because the harmonic series diverges, the new series must diverge with it.

It may be a good idea to list two other situations.

Other tests

If $\lim\limits_{n\to\infty} \dfrac{b_n}{a_n} = 0$ and $\sum a_n$ diverges, we get no information.

If $\lim\limits_{n\to\infty} \dfrac{b_n}{a_n} = \infty$ and $\sum a_n$ converges, we get no information.

Calculus

Here is another example of the use of the comparison test. We want to determine the convergence of the series

$$1 + \frac{1}{\sqrt{2}} + \frac{1}{\sqrt{3}} + \frac{1}{\sqrt{4}} + \cdots.$$

For each $n > 1$, $\sqrt{n} < n$, and $\frac{1}{\sqrt{n}} > \frac{1}{n}$. Therefore, the series diverges, again by comparison with the harmonic series.

This is an example of a *p-series*:

$$1 + \frac{1}{2^p} + \frac{1}{3^p} + \frac{1}{4^p} + \cdots.$$

(In the example above, $p = \frac{1}{2}$.) We can generalize the above technique: if $p < 1$, then $n^p < n$, $\frac{1}{n^p} > \frac{1}{n}$, and the p-series diverges by comparison with the harmonic series.

Ratio and root tests. The tests of convergence given above will not decide all possible series. Several others exist, but we will conclude this section with just two more: the ratio test and the root test. Both of these have the advantage that the tests are *internal*; only the terms of the series are tested, rather than comparing to some other series.

Ratio test

Given: A series $\sum_{n=1}^{\infty} a_n$, whose terms are all *positive*.

If $\lim_{n \to \infty} \frac{a_{n+1}}{a_n} < 1$, $\sum a_n$ converges.

If $\lim_{n \to \infty} \frac{a_{n+1}}{a_n} > 1$, $\sum a_n$ diverges.

If $\lim_{n \to \infty} \frac{a_{n+1}}{a_n} = 1$, the test gives no information.

As an example, let's apply the ratio test to the series $\sum \frac{n^3}{2^n}$. We have

$$\lim \frac{\frac{(n+1)^3}{2^{n+1}}}{\frac{n^3}{2^n}} = \lim \frac{(n+1)^3}{2n^3}$$

$$= \lim \frac{\left(1 + \frac{1}{n}\right)^3}{2} = \frac{1}{2},$$

so the series converges.

The root test is, in a way, even more internal than the ratio test. In the ratio test, we compare two consecutive terms of the series, while the root test examines each individual term.

Root test

If $\lim_{n \to \infty} \sqrt[n]{a_n} < 1$, $\sum a_n$ converges.

If $\lim_{n \to \infty} \sqrt[n]{a_n} > 1$, $\sum a_n$ diverges.

If $\lim_{n \to \infty} \sqrt[n]{a_n} = 1$, the test gives no information.

Because of the nth root, the root test is very nice to use when an nth power is involved. For example, we investigate $\sum n \left(\frac{2}{3}\right)^n \times$

$$\sqrt[n]{n \left(\frac{2}{3}\right)^n} = \frac{2}{3} \sqrt[n]{n} \to \frac{2}{3},$$

so the series converges.

The ratio test is helpful for expressions involving powers or exponentials. It is also particularly well suited to factorials: Consider $\sum \frac{n!}{2^{n+1}}$.

$$\lim \frac{\frac{(n+1)!}{2^{n+2}}}{\frac{n!}{2^{n+1}}} = \lim \frac{n+1}{2},$$

which diverges, so the series diverges, too.

Alternating series and absolute convergence. We have simplified much of the preceding discussion by assuming that all the terms of our series are nonnegative. We must now look to the situation of series which have some negative terms.

Suppose we have a convergent nonnegative series with limit L, $\sum a_n = L$. If we were to change the signs of *all* of the terms of the series, then it would certainly still be convergent, with limit $-L$. It is clear that if we changed only *some* of the signs of the original series, then the result would still be a convergent series. Unless we changed only a finite number of terms, it would no longer be obvious exactly what the limit must be, although it must be between $-L$ and L.

Now consider the reverse situation. We have a series which contains some positive and some negative terms and we want to investigate its convergence. The above discussion suggests the following test: if we change all the signs of the series to positive (nonnegative) and find that the resulting series is convergent, then our series must be convergent, too. We call this situation *absolute convergence*.

Definition

A series $\sum a_n$ is said to be *absolutely convergent* (and therefore converges) if the series $\sum |a_n|$ converges.

Now, what if we are investigating $\sum a_n$, but $\sum |a_n|$ diverges? It may still be that $\sum a_n$ converges (in which case the series is called *conditionally convergent*), but in general it is difficult to test.

The one straightforward situation left to us is the *alternating series*, in which every other term is positive, every other term is negative. A remarkably simple theorem, thanks to Leibniz, tells us how to test for convergence of an alternating series. If an alternating series passes the nth term test, and if $|a_{n+1}| < |a_n|$ (that is, disregarding the signs, the sequence of terms is decreasing), then the series converges.

A slightly different statement:

Given an alternating series $\sum_{i=1}^{\infty} (-1)^{n-1} a_n$, with the following conditions:

1. All the a_n are positive
2. $\{a_n\}$ is decreasing
3. $\{a_n\} \to 0$,

then the series converges.

As an example of this theorem, I offer you perhaps the most classic case of a conditionally convergent series, the alternating harmonic series

$$1 - \frac{1}{2} + \frac{1}{3} - \frac{1}{4} + \cdots.$$

It clearly satisfies Leibniz's theorem and so converges (to ln 2, as a matter of fact). But the (all positive) harmonic series diverges, and so this is conditionally convergent.

To complete this section, the "nth term test" summarizes the techniques for determining convergence:

---

nth term test

Special case series:

Geometric series	$\sum_{n=1}^{\infty} a_1 r^{n-1}$
p-series	$\sum_{n=1}^{\infty} \frac{1}{n^p}$
Alternating series	$\sum_{n=1}^{\infty} (-1)^{n-1} a_n, \, a_n \to 0$

Comparison test/limit comparison test:

Integral test	If there is an integrable function $f(x)$, where $a_n = f(n)$
Ratio test	Useful for powers, exponentials, rational functions, factorials
Root test	Useful for nth powers

Possible behaviors of a power series

A *power series* is an expression of the form $\sum\limits_{n=0}^{\infty} a_n x^n = a_0 + a_1 x + a_2 x^2 + \cdots$.

The series converges only for $x = 0$ and diverges elsewhere.

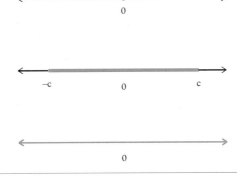

The series converges on the interval from $-c$ to c and diverges elsewhere. The interval may be open, closed, or half open.

The series converges absolutely for all x.

Power series.

For our next topic, we will look at a different kind of infinite series, one whose terms are functions rather than numbers. It is reasonable to expect that if a series of numbers can converge to a particular number, then a series of functions could converge to a function.

We will consider series whose terms are powers of x. There are other types of "function" series, but we will restrict our attention to power series: $\sum\limits_{n=0}^{\infty} a_n x^n$. Note that the series starts at 0, so as to allow for the 0 power, or constant term.

As an example, consider the series

$$\sum_{n=0}^{\infty} x^n = 1 + x + x^2 + x^3 + \cdots.$$

This can be thought of as a geometric series with first term 1 and $r = x$. Thus it converges to the function $\dfrac{1}{1-x}$ as long as $|x| < 1$.

Another example:

$$1 + mx + \frac{m(m-1)}{2!}x^2 + \cdots = \sum_{n=0}^{\infty} \binom{m}{n} x^n.$$

If m is a positive integer, this infinite process terminates with the familiar binomial theorem. Whether m is integral or not, the power series converges to the function $(1 + x)^m$ for any value of x.

The two examples just given illustrate an important point about power series. The first converges for only a limited interval of x-values, while the second is valid

for any x. It turns out that these behaviors are the only possibilities: a series converges only for $|x| < R$ (whether or not the endpoints $x = \pm R$ are included depends on the particular series), or the convergence is everywhere. (It is possible that $R = 0$, so that a series converges only at one point.)

The value c mentioned in the table above is called the *radius of convergence* of the series. As in the first case, c may be 0, or if the convergence is everywhere, we say that the radius of convergence is infinite.

Taylor series.

To motivate the Taylor series, let's consider a particular sequence of polynomials related to a specific function—for instance, the cosine function. The first "polynomial" is the constant, $\cos 0 = 1$. The second, $f_2 = \cos 0 - \sin 0\, x = 1$. The third polynomial is

$$f_3 = \cos 0 - \sin 0\, x - \frac{\cos 0}{2!}x^2 = 1 - \frac{1}{2}x^2.$$

At each stage, the term that is added is

$$\frac{\cos^{(n)} 0}{n!}\, x^n,$$

(where the numerator is the nth derivative, not a power). The rationale for this progression is that each polynomial, f_n, agrees with the cosine, not only in function value, but in the values of $n-1$ derivatives as well. The polynomials so obtained are called *Taylor polynomials*.

The Taylor series is a particular kind of "function" series (very nearly a power series). It is derived from a

Some useful Taylor series expansions

e^x

$$1 + x + \frac{x^2}{2!} + \frac{x^3}{3!} + \cdots = \sum_{n=0}^{\infty} \frac{x^n}{n!}$$

$\sin x$

$$x - \frac{x^3}{3!} + \frac{x^5}{5!} - \cdots = \sum_{n=0}^{\infty} \frac{(-1)^n x^{2n+1}}{(2n+1)!}$$

$\cos x$

$$1 - \frac{x^2}{2!} + \frac{x^4}{4!} - \cdots = \sum_{n=0}^{\infty} \frac{(-1)^n x^{2n}}{(2n)!}$$

$\sinh x$

$$x + \frac{x^3}{3!} + \frac{x^5}{5!} + \cdots = \sum_{n=0}^{\infty} \frac{x^{2n+1}}{(2n+1)!}$$

$\cosh x$

$$1 + \frac{x^2}{2!} + \frac{x^4}{4!} + \cdots = \sum_{n=0}^{\infty} \frac{x^{2n}}{(2n)!}$$

$\tan^{-1} x$

$$x - \frac{x^3}{3} + \frac{x^5}{5} - \cdots = \sum_{n=0}^{\infty} \frac{(-1)^n x^{2n+1}}{(2n+1)}, \; |x| \leq 1$$

$\tanh^{-1} x$

$$x + \frac{x^3}{3} + \frac{x^5}{5} + \cdots = \sum_{n=0}^{\infty} \frac{x^{2n+1}}{(2n+1)}, \; |x| < 1$$

$\ln(1 + x)$

$$x - \frac{x^2}{2} + \frac{x^3}{3} - \cdots = \sum_{n=1}^{\infty} \frac{(-1)^{n-1} x^n}{n}, \; -1 < x \leq 1$$

$\dfrac{1}{1 - x}$

$$1 + x + x^2 + x^3 + \cdots = \sum_{n=0}^{\infty} x^n, \; |x| < 1$$

function $f(x)$, which is required to have derivatives of all orders at a point a. The Taylor series of f at $x = a$ is

$$f(a) + f'(a)(x - a) + \frac{f''(a)}{2!}(x - a)^2 + \cdots$$

$$+ \frac{f^{(n)}(a)}{n!}(x - a)^n + \cdots.$$

This is the extension of the Taylor polynomials to an infinite function series. Continuing the example given above with the cosine, we see that the Taylor series associated with the cosine at $a = 0$ is

$$1 - \frac{x^2}{2!} + \frac{x^4}{4!} - \frac{x^6}{6!} + \cdots.$$

Now, what exactly is the relationship between the Taylor series and the original cosine function? The answer is that the series converges to the function with, in this case, an infinite radius of convergence. In other words, for any x we can write

$$1 - \frac{x^2}{2!} + \frac{x^4}{4!} - \frac{x^6}{6!} + \cdots = \cos x.$$

Operations with Taylor series. One of the beauties of the Taylor series representation of a function is that we can use it in place of the function in many applications. A Taylor series may be differentiated or integrated term by term, just like a polynomial. The result will be another Taylor series with an equal radius of convergence (although it is possible that the endpoints may be lost).

Given a power series $f(x) = \sum_{n=0}^{\infty} a_n x^n$ with radius of convergence c, then the function is differentiable with $f'(x) = \sum_{n=0}^{\infty} n a_n x^{n-1}$ and the power series for f' also has radius of convergence c.

Given a power series $f(x) = \sum_{n=0}^{\infty} a_n x^n$ with radius of convergence c, then the function is integrable with

$$\int f(x) \ dx = \sum_{n=0}^{\infty} \frac{a_n x^{n+1}}{n + 1} + C$$

and the power series for $\int f(x) \ dx$ also has radius of convergence c.

Example

We can compute $\int \left(\frac{\sin x^2}{x} \right) dx$ as a power series.

$$\sin x^2 = x^2 - \frac{x^6}{3!} + \frac{x^{10}}{5!} - \cdots,$$

so $\dfrac{\sin x^2}{x} = x - \dfrac{x^5}{3!} + \dfrac{x^9}{5!} - \cdots$

and $\int \dfrac{\sin x^2}{x} \ dx = \dfrac{x^2}{2} - \dfrac{x^6}{6 \cdot 3!} + \dfrac{x^{10}}{10 \cdot 5!} - \cdots + C.$

$\star \quad \star \quad \star$

Answers to exercises can be found beginning on page 596.

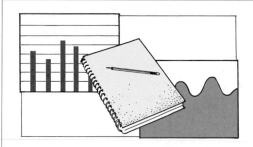

Tests, homework, and projects

Laying the groundwork

Good study skills are more important than a high I.Q. score when it comes to academic success. Good grades in college depend not only on working hard, but also on working smart. The following paragraphs will give you some ideas on how to make the most of your study time for calculus.

Reading

Think of your math textbook as an interactive workbook. You should not read it with a highlighter in your hand, but rather a pencil. Remember, math is not a spectator sport; you learn math by doing it!

It is possible to read a section in a calculus book straight through from beginning to end, but this is not a very practical approach. If you own your text, mark it up with comments and questions. Make detailed notes as you go back and forth between the definitions, examples, graphs, and exercises.

The meaning of a page in a calculus book is only partially given by the text. The rest of the meaning has to be created by you.

Notetaking

Most colleges and universities require a course syllabus to include the date for each class meeting and the topic for that day with corresponding text sections. To make the most of each class meeting, you should have the corresponding text section read in advance. Then, during the presentation, you can be more selective about what needs to be written down.

Since you can't write and listen at the same time, each moment you can save in writing will give you more time to *think* about what is being said. If you have read the section and listened to the presentation and still don't understand, then *ask a question.* You can be quite sure that at least six other students will be thinking, "I am so glad she/he asked that!"

Study your notes and work some exercise problems as soon after the class as possible, ideally sometime that same day. Spending one hour studying soon after class is more beneficial than spending three hours studying two days later. If you wait two or three days to study, you will spend a great deal of time trying to remember and relearn.

Studying

Studying five days a week for two hours at a time is better than studying two days a week for five hours each day. Mathematical concepts take time to sink in, and revisiting the concept over a period of several days is better than saying, "I'm not going to leave this chair until I get this!"

Organize other members of your class to form a study group. Talking about problems, explaining concepts to one another, sharing new approaches and problem-solving strategies are excellent ways to learn calculus. Meeting once or twice a week will not only improve your grade, but make studying and learning a whole lot more enjoyable.

Strategies for success

Tests

Start far enough in advance that you can do a careful and unhurried job of reviewing each section. Set a study schedule, and get a good night's rest before the test.

Try to predict test questions by making your own sample test of a few problems from each section. Have the instructor specify what material will be on the test. The points emphasized in class will most likely be the ones on the test.

On test day, get there on time and try to sit in the front. That way you will be sure to hear directions and can easily read changes written on the board.

Homework

As you work homework problems, keep a set of notecards nearby. On these cards you should write down the problems which you found especially difficult or tricky or impossible. Or you can write more general questions about the concept or process with which you are working.

Then when you meet with your study group or visit your professor during office hours, you will be able to go through your questions in a more orderly fashion.

Your study group can pool all of the tough problems saved on notecards to compile a sample test or final exam.

Glossary

acceleration. Rate of change of velocity with respect to time.

antiderivative. If $F'(x) = f(x)$, then $F(x)$ is called an antiderivative for $f(x)$.

continuity. If a function $f(x)$ is continuous on $[a,b]$, then you may trace the graph of the function on the interval $[a,b]$ without lifting your pencil. (See pages 124–126.)

decreasing. A function is decreasing if the tangent line has negative slope.

definite integral. An integral in which the limits of integration are real numbers. In this case, the *fundamental theorem of calculus* would apply.

derivative. A function which describes the rate of change of another function.

differentiation. The process of taking the derivative.

domain. The set of all possible input values for a function.

function. A rule (or mapping) which assigns to each element in the domain a unique element in the range.

fundamental theorem of calculus. If $F'(x) = f(x)$, then
$$\int_a^b f(x)\, dx = F(b) - F(a).$$

improper integrals. (1) One or both of the limits of integration is at infinity. (2) The integrand is not continuous on the interval of integration.

increasing. A function is increasing if the tangent line has positive slope.

indefinite integral. An integral which has no limits of integration. In general, if $F'(x) = f(x)$, then $\int f(x)\, dx = F(x) + C$.

inflection point. The point at which a function changes from concave up to concave down or vice versa.

integrand. In the expression
$$\int f(x)\, dx$$
the function f is called the integrand.

integration. An operation which is the inverse of differentiation. Integration is an infinite summing operation.

intercept. The point at which a curve crosses the x or y axis.

inverse function. A function which is the reverse mapping of a given function. If the given function is $y = F(x)$, then the inverse function would be denoted $y = f^{-1}(x)$. In this case, $f(x) \times f^{-1}(x) = x$.

local maximum. Largest y-value in a region.

local minimum. Smallest y-value in a region.

Newton's method. An iterative numerical technique which uses the x-intercepts of tangent lines to approximate the roots of a function.

range. The set of all possible output values for a function.

root. The root of a function $f(x)$ is any solution to the equation $f(x) = 0$. The roots of $y = f(x)$ would be where the graph of $f(x)$ crosses the x-axis.

sequence. An infinite list of numbers in a specific order.

series. What results when the elements of a sequence are added.

Simpson's rule. A numerical integration technique which can be used to approximate a definite integral.

transcendental function. Any function which is not an algebraic function.

velocity. Rate of change of distance with respect to time.

For further reading

Barnett, Raymond, and Michael Ziegler. *Applied Calculus with Linear Programming for Business, Economics, Life Sciences, and Social Sciences.* 6th ed. Englewood Cliffs, N.J.: Prentice-Hall, 1995.

Beckmann, Charlene E., and Theodore A. Sundstrom. *Exploring Calculus with a Graphing Calculator.* Reading, Mass.: Addison-Wesley, 1992.

Hoffman, Laurence, and Gerald Bradley. *Calculus for Business, Economics, and the Social and Life Sciences.* 6th ed. New York: McGraw-Hill, 1996.

Hughes-Hallett, Deborah, Andrew Gleason *et al. Calculus.* New York: Wiley and Sons, 1993.

Hunt, Richard A. *Calculus.* 2nd ed. New York: HarperCollins, 1994.

Miller, Robert A. *Bob Miller's Calc I Helper.* New York: McGraw-Hill, 1991.

Salas, S. L., and Einar Hille (revised by Garret J. Etgen). *Calculus: One and Several Variables.* 7th ed. New York: Wiley and Sons, 1995.

Simmons, George. *Calculus Gems, Brief Lives and Memorable Mathematics.* New York: McGraw-Hill, 1992.

Stein, Sherman, and Anthony Barcellos. *Calculus and Analytic Geometry.* 5th ed. New York: McGraw-Hill, 1992.

Stewart, James. *Calculus: Early Transcendentals.* 3rd ed. Pacific Grove, Calif.: Brooks/Cole, 1995.

Thomas, George B., and Ross L. Finney. *Calculus and Analytic Geometry.* 9th ed. Reading, Mass.: Addison-Wesley, 1996.

Answers to exercises can be found beginning on page 596.

Economics

- What is economics?
- Tools of the trade
- The market
- Microeconomics
- Macroeconomics
- Economics every day

Economics

Students often try to avoid or postpone taking economics courses. This is because economics has a reputation for being technical, dry, and mathematical—more theory than fact. Nothing could be further from the truth.

In economics, you will explore how real people make real decisions regarding how to spend their time, their money, and other limited resources. Our aim is to help you see how economics affects *all* of us every day.

In this section, we begin by introducing you to the basic terms and tools of economics. Next, we explore some fundamental economic "laws" as we examine how individual consumers and producers make decisions and interact. This is where you will experiment with the concepts of supply and demand. Last, we broaden our outlook by seeing how individual decisions and actions combine to form a complicated, fascinating whole. We explore national economic issues—such as unemployment and inflation—and then conclude with the motivations and realities of international trade.

What is economics?

The economic problem. Economics is all around you. Whether you are working or not, whether you have investments or not, economics affects you. At its core, economics is about making choices in a world limited by finite resources.

How many times have you heard people say, "There just aren't enough hours in the day" or "Money doesn't grow on trees" or even "I've only got two hands!"? Each of these common sayings illustrates a problem—scarcity. Not enough time, not enough money, not enough hands. How does a person, an organization, or an entire country try to satisfy potentially unlimited wants with very real resource limitations? And what are the trade-offs? That is "the economic problem," and the focus of economic study.

Let's use a real example to examine this problem more closely. In the United States, there has been widespread debate about the desirability of producing more health care for a wider audience. Assuming that is what the country decides to do, how could that goal be accomplished?

> **Why studying economics pays off**
>
> **Reason #1:**
>
> It helps improve your decision-making skills as you explore the opportunity costs of real-life choices.

For one thing, it would mean diverting such resources as people, money, and equipment, into the health-care field *from somewhere else*. In a world of limited resources, providing more of a particular service or good means providing less of other things. But less of what? Schools? Food? Golf courses? All of the above?

In our example, we can make the choices and associated costs even more clear-cut. Consider a case where the U.S. chooses to produce only two items: health care and golf courses. The cost of producing health care can be expressed in terms of the amount of

Economics

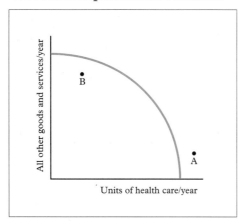

Production possibilities frontier

The line on this graph illustrates all the possible combinations of health care and all other goods and services that a particular society can produce. Points beyond the line (such as point A) are beyond the society's current production capacity; points within it (such as point B) reflect less than perfect efficiency or idle resources.

other products (golf courses) that must be given up. This is called the *opportunity cost* of the choice.

For example, if producing twenty-five new "units" of health care forces us to forgo producing three golf courses, the opportunity cost of our health-care choice is three golf courses. The name aptly reflects the fact that in producing a specific item, we give up the "opportunity" to produce something else.

While the choices in the real world may seem endless, there is a definite limit to what can be produced. The set of all possible combinations of goods and services produced, given the most efficient use of resources, can be illustrated graphically as a *production possibilities frontier*. (See graph above.) Until there is some change in available resources—such as a technology breakthrough or a labor force increase—producing beyond this "frontier" is not possible.

Three basic questions. Because

resources are limited, every economy must deal with three basic questions:

1. *What will be produced?* (Which goods? Which services? How much of each?)
2. *How will it be produced?* (Who will produce the goods and services? Will production be centrally controlled? How will producers choose among the many combinations of inputs available—for example, labor versus technology?)
3. *Who will get what is produced?* (How will goods and services be distributed among individuals in the economy? Will some groups be favored?)

Micro vs. macro. In the process of

studying these basic questions, economics is often divided into two distinct yet interdependent branches: microeconomics and macroeconomics. What differs between them is their perspective and focus, not their underlying subject. Both branches study the same economy.

Microeconomics is like pointing a microscope at the economy; it is a study of specifics. Microeconomics analyzes and predicts the actions of the *individual* within the economy. In this case, "individual" may refer to a particular household, a particular organization, or even a particular industry.

For example, why does one household buy more apparel and less food than another? What affects its current buying patterns? What will change those buying patterns? And on the production side: Why does one firm charge more for its product than a close competitor charges? Why is there a shortage of a particular item? And why is it that some jobs pay better than others?

On the other hand, *macroeconomics* is the study of the "big picture." Rather than analyzing the decisions involving a specific household, firm, or industry, macroeconomics focuses on such overall trends as national output, employment rates, and average consumer prices.

(You may find it helpful to remember the distinctions between the two branches of economics by noting that *micro* means "small" and *macro* means "large" or "on a large scale." This is exactly how the two perspectives differ.)

Micro and macro questions

- **Microeconomics**

  What wage should the ice cream store pay its workers?

  How much corn should the farmer plant?

  Can the high school senior afford to go to college next year?

  Should the mortgage company offer different interest rates on its loans?

- **Macroeconomics**

  Will increased borrowing by the government affect private sector spending?

  How does the Federal Reserve influence the level of national income and prices?

  What are the economic consequences of lowering tax revenues and government spending by equal amounts?

  What effect will there be on interest rates if the government increases its borrowing?

Tools of the trade

The science of economics. Often
people read about various economists who can't agree
on a particular fact or issue. Is unemployment rising or
falling? Is the economy in a recession or a recovery?
What should be done to keep the economy "on track"?
There never seems to be a single answer. As a result,
many conclude that economics must be more art than
science, based more on subjective opinion than on
objective fact.

However, this disagreement and uncertainty is actually the hallmark of all the sciences. The scientific
method employed in other sciences is one of observation and analysis, hypothesis setting, testing, and
reevaluation. In these fields also, scientists question
and disagree, falter and persevere.

So it is that economists observe consumer, producer,
and market behavior, identify factors that may affect
that behavior, and test their theories against reality.
But new facts emerge and theories are always changing. So for every theory, there is often a completely
justifiable, opposite view. Realize, then, that to succeed in economics, one must be able to use economic
tools and interpret data, rather than to simply memorize specific facts or figures.

Within the science of economics, there are two
approaches. When economists attempt to understand,
predict, and explain economic behavior without making judgments about that behavior, it is called *positive
economics*. When they judge those outcomes as good or
bad, and then prescribe actions for improvement, it is
called *normative economics*. Normative economics
places a value on outcomes, positive does not.

Economic models. One important
tool used by economists is the *model*. A model, like
model vehicles or buildings made by children, is

merely a simplified view of some aspect of the real
world. If done properly, a model strips away unnecessary detail.

We use models regularly in our daily lives. A common example is a road map. Not only is the map
smaller than life size (and thus easily transportable), it
also omits a great many real-world details: buildings,
road signs, stoplights. Yet the most important information remains: intersections, street names, mileage
scales. If more information were given, the model
would become too cluttered, confusing, and possibly
unmanageable.

Models, then, are useful precisely because of their
lack of detail. A minimum of carefully selected items is
included so that we can better isolate and understand
their relationships and behavior. Thus, we do not use
models to *observe* the intricacies of the real world, but
rather to help us *understand* and *predict* how the real
world works.

A model can be expressed in a variety of ways: with
diagrams (a two-dimensional graph), words (a descriptive paragraph), or numbers (an equation). Each way
has its own strengths and weaknesses, and each can be
used to support and clarify the others.

Architects and economists make use of models.

Working with graphs. A model frequently used to express relationships in economics is the two-dimensional graph. The two dimensions (vertical and horizontal) allow economists to track how two items relate to each other.

Any two items can be shown on the graph. For example, economists might analyze price versus quantity demanded, cost versus quantity of labor, or cost of production versus quantity of output supplied.

X and y. For convenience, economists use the letter *x* to refer to the item shown along the horizontal axis and *y* to refer to the item on the vertical axis. The letters themselves do not mean anything; they simply refer to positioning on the graph. (You could just as easily use *h* and *v* or *green* and *purple*.)

Sometimes, when values for two variables are plotted on the graph, there is no apparent trend; the graph shows only a random collection of points. What economists typically look for are those instances where variables do relate. This becomes apparent on the graph as points fall into a definite line. The line connecting these points can be straight or curved.

When the line reflecting the values of two variables slopes upward (from left to right), the variables have a *direct* relationship. Their values tend to move in the same direction, increasing or decreasing together.

When the line reflecting the values of two variables slopes downward, those variables have an *inverse* relationship. Their values react in opposite directions.

How to read a graph

Economists often use graphs to provide a visual summary of how two items relate. (*How many* cassette tapes are consumers willing to buy per week at various *prices*? Quantity demanded and price are the two items compared here.) Because each item may have several real-world values, the graph doesn't show just one point, but rather a collection of different quantity/price combinations. The line connecting those points shows the general pattern in quantity demanded at each price.

To read the graph, simply pick a point on the line and read across to find the price at that point, and down to find the quantity. For example, at a price of $13, this graph shows that consumers will want to buy about 75 cassettes.

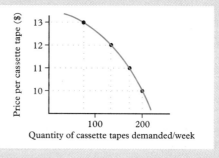

Direct relationship

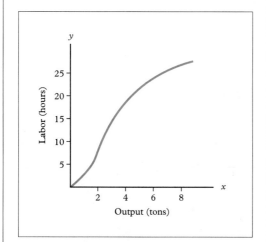

Two variables whose values increase together and decrease together are said to have a direct *relationship. The line representing a direct relationship always slopes upward.*

Inverse relationship

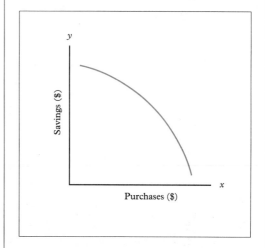

Two variables whose values move in opposite directions (that is, one increases when the other decreases) are said to have an inverse *relationship. The line representing an inverse relationship always slopes downward.*

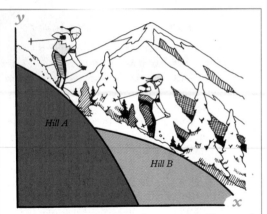

Slope is an important concept in economics. The term is used to describe the steepness of a line, just as we might describe the steepness of a skier's hill. The slope of Hill A is greater (steeper) than the slope of Hill B.

Slope.

The *slope* of a line is a measurement that describes the relationship between the line's two variables. When we know slope, we can determine how much one variable will change, given a one-unit change in the other.

By convention, slope is always expressed as the change in the value of the item on the *y* (vertical) axis compared to the change in the value of the item on the *x* (horizontal) axis. This is sometimes called the *rise over the run*.

The slope of a line is measured by selecting two points along the line. We use a subscript to differentiate between the values of *x* and *y* at those two points, so that point 1's values are called y_1 and x_1, while point 2's values are called y_2 and x_2.

Stated as an equation, then:

$$slope = \frac{y_2 - y_1}{x_2 - x_1}.$$

As an example, refer to the graph that shows the relationship of age and income. At point 1, the values are 20,000 (y_1) and 30 (x_1), respectively. At point 2, the values are 46,000 (y_2) and 60 (x_2). Using the standard slope equation, then,

$$slope = \frac{46,000 - 20,000}{60 - 30} = \frac{26,000}{30} = 867.$$

The value of 867 tells us that a one-year increase in age (*x*) is associated with an increase in income (*y*) of $867. As we will see later, the value of a line's slope can differ at different places on the line, so this example relates only to the portion of the line between 30 and 60 years of age.

It does not matter which point is designated as 1 or 2 when calculating slope. This can be demonstrated by using the points and values from the previous example. If we switch the order of the two points in the equation, we still end up with a slope value of 867.

$$slope = \frac{20,000 - 46,000}{30 - 60} = \frac{-26,000}{-30} = 867.$$

This is true because of the mathematical rule that states that dividing two numbers with the same sign—regardless of whether they are positive or negative—results in a positive number. So whether the slope is calculated as we move up or down the line makes no difference.

One rule to remember: When calculating slope, be sure that the values of *x* and *y* with matching subscripts relate to the same point on the line.

NOTE: Sometimes the equation for slope is stated:

$$slope = \frac{\Delta y}{\Delta x}.$$

The Δ is the Greek letter *delta*, which stands for the *change* in a variable. This is just a shorthand way for restating the standard slope equation.

Here are several facts about slope:

• *The slope of a line showing an inverse relationship is a negative number.* Remember that an inverse relationship is one in which the two variables move in opposite directions. So if *y* increases, by definition *x* will decrease. When appropriate values are inserted into the slope equation, the result is a positive number divided by a negative number. That result is always negative. Moving the opposite direction, so that *y*

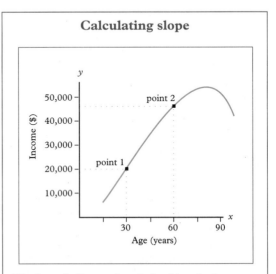

Calculating slope

The slope of a line can be calculated by selecting two points on the line. The slope is equal to the change in the y *(vertical) value, divided by the change in the* x *(horizontal) value. In this graph, the slope of the line between point 1 and point 2 is (46,000-20,000) /(60-30), which is 26,000/30, or 867.*

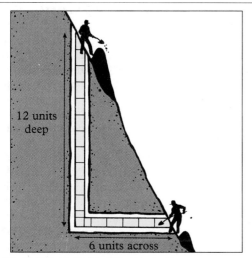

Slope is calculated by comparing the change in a line's vertical value compared to the change in its horizontal value. In this diagram, we compare how deep the top worker must dig compared to how far across the bottom worker must dig before they meet. Thus, the slope of this hill (line) is -12 units/6 units, or -2.

decreases and x increases, also generates a negative slope. That is because the result of dividing two numbers with different signs is always negative.

• *The slope of a line showing a direct relationship is a positive number.* Regardless of whether the x and y values are increasing or decreasing, a direct relationship

ensures they are moving in the same direction. That means the sign of the number representing $y_2 - y_1$ will match the sign of the number representing $x_2 - x_1$ (so both will be positive or both will be negative). The result must be positive because dividing two numbers with the same sign always generates a positive number.

• *The slope of a straight line is constant.* While the values of x and y on a straight line will vary, the steepness will not. This can be tested by selecting random points along any straight line. As an example, refer to the graph "Constant slope."

• *The slope of a completely horizontal straight line is zero.* Why is this so? Because the y value of a horizontal line never changes, the $y_2 - y_1$ value will always be zero. This means that the value of x has no effect on the value of y whatsoever.

• *The slope of a completely vertical line is undefined.* As you might expect, the vertical line is the exact opposite of a horizontal line. Now it is the value of $x_2 - x_1$ that is zero. In mathematics, because it is not possible to divide any number by zero, the result is undefined.

• *The slope of a curved line differs at different places along the line.* Again, by definition, a curved line is one whose slope is constantly changing. Consider a line shaped like a hill. The sides of the hill will be steeper than the top, and the slope values will reflect this (that is, the sides will have larger absolute slope values than the top). Also, as you move from left to right, the upward portion of the line will have a positive slope, while the slope of the downward portion will be negative.

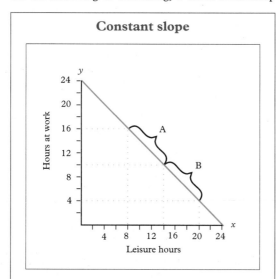

Constant slope

The slope of a straight line is constant anywhere along the line. In this example, note that the slope of section A is (10-16)/(14-8) = -1, while the slope at section B is (4-10)/(20-14), which is also equal to -1.

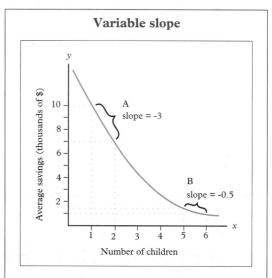

Variable slope

A curved line has a slope that varies. The slope along section A is (10-7)/(1-2) = -3, while section B is (1.5-1)/(5-6), which is -0.5. Note that the steeper section of the line has a larger slope in absolute values.

Working with equations.

As you have seen, equations can be used along with graphs to provide a more complete model of reality.

For example, the slope equation provides a way to assign a precise value to a concept that can be seen visually on the graph. Yes, the slope of this line is steeper than that one, but by how much? The equation provides that answer.

The equations you will probably encounter in introductory economics courses use only the four basic math operations: addition, subtraction, multiplication, and division. At this point, you should not have to be concerned with rules of calculus. This is all just basic math.

Sometimes, however, the equations may look difficult. As was true in the discussion of slope, economists (and mathematicians) often use abbreviations and symbols in their equations. So,

$$slope = \frac{y_2 - y_1}{x_2 - x_1} = \frac{\Delta y}{\Delta x}$$

can intimidate someone who does not know what y_2, y_1, or Δy mean.

In most cases, the jumble of letters and symbols you will encounter is simply a shorthand way for writing something that would otherwise take a line or two of text to describe. It's like a code. Once you know that x_1 always means this, or p usually means that, it's not so intimidating.

At this point, you may wish to review a few basic math rules:

• Unless numbers are grouped by placement (as in the slope equation above) or with parentheses, multiplication and division are performed before addition and subtraction. So, $10 + 4/2 = 10 + 2 = 12$, while $(10 + 4)/2 = 14/2 = 7$.

• When adding numbers with the same sign, add them together, and apply the sign to the sum. So, $-3 + (-2) = -5$.

• When adding numbers with different signs, treat the operation as subtraction, and use the sign of the *larger* (absolute) number for the result. So, $-3 + (+10) = +7$, and $+1 + (-5) = -4$.

• Subtracting a negative number is treated the same as adding a positive. So, $-3 - (-18) = +15$.

• Multiplying or dividing two numbers with the same sign always results in a positive number. Multiplying or dividing two numbers with different signs always results in a negative number.

• The change in the value of an item is found by subtracting the original value from the new value. A percentage change is calculated by dividing the change by the original value of the item. So, if an item rises from 12 to 15, the percentage change is: $(15 - 12)/12 = 3/12 = +0.25$, or 25%.

Economic assumptions.

While economists try to understand and predict economic behavior by looking at how one factor or variable affects another, the real world is often more complicated. That is because there is generally more than one variable affecting behavior. For example, the quantity of ice cream demanded at a particular soda fountain may depend not only on its price, but also on the weather, the flavors available, whether it is a vacation day or school day, and so on.

In formulating their models, economists make an assumption that has been termed *ceteris paribus*, a Latin phrase that means "all else equal." Even though we know that many things can and will change, this assumption allows us to isolate and study the impact of a single factor on another by requiring that all other factors remain unchanged.

Another economic assumption is that individuals behave with *economic rationality*. This term means that economic "players" (such as households, wage earners, businesses, and competitors) understand what gives them satisfaction and, when presented with options, will act in ways that maximize that satisfaction. This assumption relies on individuals' ability to make choices that reflect their preferences, subject to constraints such as financial or time limits.

Common abbreviations

AFC	Average fixed cost
ATC	Average total cost
AVC	Average variable cost
C	Consumption
CPI	Consumer Price Index
D	Demand
G	Government purchases
GDP	Gross domestic product
GNP	Gross national product
I	Investment or income
K	Capital
L	Labor
MC	Marginal cost
MP	Marginal product
MR	Marginal revenue
MRP	Marginal revenue product
MU	Marginal utility
P	Price
Q	Quantity
S	Supply
T	Tax
TC	Total cost
TFC	Total fixed cost
TR	Total revenue
TVC	Total variable cost

The market

No doubt you have all heard the term "market," perhaps in reference to the stock market, the labor market, or to something as close to home as the supermarket.

In economics, *market*—in its broadest sense—refers to the entire environment in which goods and services are produced, bought, and sold. It is not limited to a single location or industry. It may not even be housed in a physical structure; it could be simply a set of methods and rules by which buyers and sellers communicate with one another and exchange their wares.

Circular flow.
A common way to illustrate the key groups within the market and the relationships between them is a *circular flow diagram*.

There are two key groups in the basic circular flow diagram: consumers and producers. As their names imply, *consumers* are the households that use, or consume, final goods and services. *Producers* are the individuals and organizations that create the goods and services and make them available for consumer use. The obvious relationship, then, is one in which goods and services flow from producers to consumers. This is only part of the circle, however.

In one sense, the circle is completed in terms of what consumers give producers in return for their goods and services. Remember, the market is an environment for exchange, and so consumers typically pay a price or fee for the goods and services they receive. (In most markets today, the medium for exchange is money. By contrast, *barter markets* involve a two-way exchange of goods and services.)

Because producers cannot produce goods and services out of thin air, there is also another side to the circular flow of the market. This is the market for production inputs, which include:

- *Labor,* the people who provide producers with needed skill, effort, and expertise;
- *Capital,* the supplies and equipment used by producers to create new goods and services; and
- *Land,* the physical space on which producers locate their stores, offices, and factories, as well as the materials they can extract from that land.

Thus, the other side of the completed circle links consumers and producers in a somewhat less obvious relationship, one in which they trade their traditional roles. In this relationship, producers consume production inputs that are produced by consumers. In other words, consumers go to work for producers, rent or sell land to producers, and invest their savings, making capital available for producer use. In return, producers exchange wages for labor, rent for land, and interest and/or dividends for the capital needed in production.

The circular flow diagram provided here includes

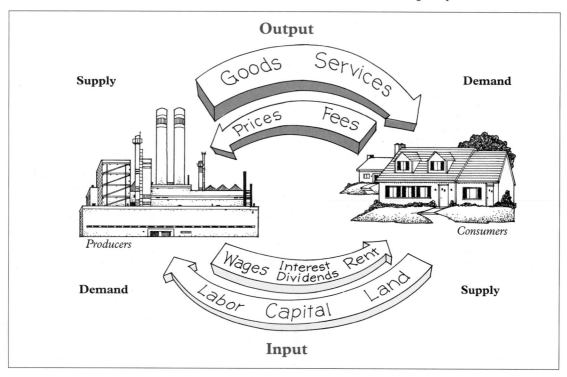

Output

Supply

Goods Services

Prices Fees

Demand

Producers

Consumers

Demand

Wages Interest Dividends Rent

Labor Capital Land

Supply

Input

two circles that reflect this close interdependency of consumers and producers. Goods and services provided are shown along the outer circle, with final outputs on the top half, production inputs on the bottom. Payments for all goods and services are shown within the inner circle.

Types of markets. Every society has to deal with the three basic questions of economics:

1. What to produce?
2. How to produce it?
3. Who will get what is produced?

How each society chooses to answer each of these questions can be very different.

Command economy. At one extreme, a society may choose to make its production and distribution decisions from one central, controlling point—usually a government agency. This type of economy is called a *command economy.*

While the controlling agency establishes production goals, distribution rules, and wage and price limits, it is not the sole producer of the economy's goods and services. A command economy still has individual producers. However, these producers are not free to make production and distribution decisions on their own. On the other hand, even though the central organization makes the majority of market decisions, there is still an element of choice in the system: Consumers can choose not to buy.

Laissez-faire economy. At the other extreme of the market is the *free* or *laissez-faire economy.* The French term *"laissez faire"* literally means "allow them to do." In this type of economy, it is expected that individual producers and consumers, acting in their own best interests, will collectively produce a system that benefits all. No government intervention is required. (The eighteenth-century economist Adam Smith, recognized as one of the fathers of modern-day economics, referred to this tendency toward self-regulation as "the invisible hand.") As with the command economy, there is no perfect example of laissez-faire. Societies that are otherwise laissez-faire still may choose intervention through regulation, taxation, and so on.

Between the two market extremes, then, lies the wide expanse of real-world economies. Each economy is unique, defined by the manner and extent to which it implements the philosophies of one extreme or the other.

Command economy   **Laissez-faire economy**

Real-world economies lie on a continuum between these two extremes.

Market comparison

	Command
Definition	An economy in which a central organization plans and regulates the production and distribution of goods and services
Comments	Opposite extreme from laissez-faire. While a central authority plans output, consumers still determine demand; planners factor actual quantities purchased into future production goals.
	Laissez-faire ("free market")
Definition	An economy in which individuals and firms are free to pursue their own self-interests without intervention by a central organization
Comments	Opposite extreme from command market. Derives from French phrase for "allow them to do." Relies on the market to bring consumers and producers together for exchange; the behavior of the market determines how goods and services will be produced and distributed.
	Mixed
Definition	An economy that incorporates elements of both the command and laissez-faire economies
Comments	All real-world markets are mixed. The U.S.—primarily a free market—still includes substantial government purchases, employment, taxation, redistribution, and regulation.

Microeconomics

Microeconomics deals with *individual* economic decisions and behavior. Why does a particular household make certain buying decisions? How does a particular supplier determine efficient production levels? What is the relationship of supply and demand in a particular industry? In this section, we will explore the actions and motivations for the two prime players in microeconomics: consumers and producers.

Consumers.

While we have stressed that microeconomics deals with individuals, it is important to reemphasize that a single consumer can take many forms and sizes. The student looking for a specific textbook is a consumer, but so too is the college library, placing an order for hundreds of new book titles.

As we focus initially on consumers, we will explore the portion of the circular flow diagram dealing with household purchases of final goods and services. This is the demand side of the goods and services market.

Demand. *Demand* is the relationship between various prices of a product and the amount a consumer would purchase at each price.

Demand is more than just a desire or need for an item. It must reflect not only consumer willingness, but also consumer ability to purchase the full quantity demanded at each price. Demand is determined independently of the quantity supplied by producers. Thus, demand reflects what consumers *would* buy, regardless of real market surpluses or shortages.

We can illustrate the relationship of price and quantity demanded on a two-dimensional graph. By convention, economists plot price on the *y* (vertical) axis and quantity on the *x* (horizontal) axis.

Each combination of price and quantity demanded is shown as a point on the graph. By connecting these points, we create a *demand curve* or *demand schedule*, a line that reflects all the price/quantity combinations demanded for a particular product.

Because consumers usually are willing and able to purchase more of an item at a lower price (and vice versa), demand curves typically slope downward. This inverse relationship between price and quantity is referred to as the *law of demand*.

The economic assumption that "all else [is] equal" is crucial in generating and interpreting demand curves. A single demand curve *only shows the effect of price changes*, nothing else. Moving up and down the curve tells us how the quantity demanded will change based only on price changes. If any other factor varies, an entirely new demand curve is needed.

Economists make this distinction by referring to changes based on price fluctuations as *changes in the quantity demanded*. By contrast, changes due to factors other than item price are called *changes in demand*. The latter changes affect the position of the entire demand schedule.

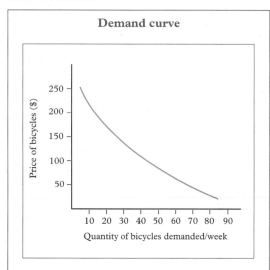

Demand curve

Price of bicycles ($)

250
200
150
100
50

10 20 30 40 50 60 70 80 90
Quantity of bicycles demanded/week

A graph that portrays all of the combinations of quantity demanded and price for a particular good or service is called a demand curve. Because the quantity demanded increases when price decreases, the demand curve has a negative, or downward, slope.

Factors affecting demand. What are some of the factors besides price that affect consumer demand?

As might be expected, a consumer's budget plays a key role in determining demand. Certainly many of us would like to purchase more than we do, but we are constrained by the resources at our disposal.

Consumer resources typically take two different forms: income and wealth. *Income* measures an individual's ongoing stream of earnings by time period (annual wages, quarterly dividends), while *wealth* measures the current stock of net assets (savings and other assets, less all debts) at a particular point in time. Changes in either of these factors will affect demand.

In most cases, the relationship between income or wealth and demand is positive. In other words, when an individual's earnings rise, demand typically increases. Goods and services for which demand rises when earnings rise are called *normal goods*.

This relationship is not always true, however. For

Fluctuations in the stock market and other forms of consumer wealth affect demand.

example, if an item is perceived to have lower status (a mark-down outfit versus a designer dress), demand may actually fall as earnings rise. Goods and services for which demand falls when earnings rise are called

What affects demand?

Factor	Typical effect	Example
Price of item itself	Negative	If the price of an item rises, consumers will typically reduce their quantity demanded, either getting by with less, or possibly purchasing a substitute item.
Consumer income	Positive	A raise in pay gives the consumer the ability to purchase more of a particular item without sacrificing something else. (An exception to this positive effect would be the case where consumers now consider the original item inappropriate to their real or perceived change in means and social status.)
Consumer wealth	Positive	This is similar to income, above. The distinction is that income is a measure of the flow of value into a household (hourly wages, monthly rents, quarterly dividends, profits, and so on), while wealth is a measure of the household's worth at one particular point. As with income, a consumer whose wealth increases can afford to buy more.
Price of complementary items	Negative	If the price of goods or services used along with the item rises (natural gas and gas stoves, staples and staplers), demand for the total "package" will decrease.
Price of substitute items	Positive	If the price of a reasonable substitute rises, consumers may begin to reduce their demand for the higher-priced good/service, choosing the now relatively lower-priced item.
Consumer preferences	Mixed	Consumer choices will vary, both from a society level (such as increased demand for low-cholesterol foods, microwave meals, VCRs) and an individual level.
Consumer expectations	Mixed	Consumer expectations of how income, wealth, prices, and preferences will change also affect current demand. A consumer expecting income to rise steadily will typically purchase more of a particular item than if faced with imminent layoff.

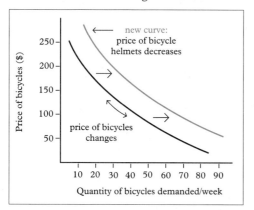

Shift in demand curve vs. movements along the curve

← new curve:
price of bicycle
helmets decreases

price of bicycles
changes

Price of bicycles ($)

250 —
200 —
150 —
100 —
50 —

10 20 30 40 50 60 70 80 90

Quantity of bicycles demanded/week

When a factor affecting demand other than price changes, it often causes a shift in the entire demand curve. This graph shows how a demand curve might move to the right, given that the price of a complementary good (bicycle helmets) decreases. Now, at all the same prices as before, the quantity of bicycles demanded increases.

inferior goods. (In this usage, "inferior" does not imply lower quality.)

Another key factor affecting consumer demand is the price of related goods.

Complementary goods are those used in tandem with the good or service being analyzed. Tape players and cassette tapes, baseballs and baseball bats, hibachis and charcoal: all are examples of complementary goods. Because consumers must consider the cost of the entire "package," a change in the price of a complementary item has a negative (opposite) effect on the demand of the original item.

Substitute goods are items that a consumer might reasonably use instead of the item in question (public transportation versus gasoline; coffee versus tea; Coca-Cola® versus Pepsi®). A change in the price of a substitute item has a positive effect on the demand of the original item. (If gasoline prices rise, the demand for public transportation also rises.)

Other factors that affect demand are consumer tastes and expectations. These factors can have either a positive or negative effect on demand.

In all cases, a change in any factor other than price is reflected as an entirely new demand curve, as shown on the graph above. If higher quantities of products are demanded at each price (if demand increases), the demand curve shifts to the right. Changes that result in lower quantities shift the curve to the left.

Remember: A new demand curve reflects a shift in *demand*. If price is the only factor that changes, no new

curve is necessary. The *quantity demanded* is found by moving along the original curve.

Utility. So far, we have discussed demand only in terms of a single good or service. In reality, a consumer is faced with an entire marketplace of products. How does a consumer make any choice at all? To explain how individuals evaluate the trade-offs among competing products, economists use the term *utility*. Utility describes the amount of satisfaction an individual gains from consuming a product.

Marginal utility is the *extra* satisfaction that an individual gets from consuming *one more unit* of an item. For most goods and services, marginal utility decreases as the number of units increases. For example, while the first ice cream sundae a day may be just the thing for a hungry consumer, chances are the fifth or sixth dish will be much less satisfying. In terms of utility, the individual making this choice receives less utility from the sixth dish than from the first. As a result, the rational consumer will not be willing to pay as much for the sixth dish as for the first.

This idea—that satisfaction from marginal units decreases as more units are consumed—is called the *law of diminishing marginal utility*. It is one of the reasons why demand curves slope downward.

There are a two more things to note about utility:

1. Utility cannot be measured. While economists sometimes use a unit called a *util* to describe utility, this is purely an abstract measure.

2. Economists assume that consumers try to maximize total utility within budget constraints. As a result, choosing between products becomes a process of weighing the expected satisfaction from consuming one product over another. The consumer keeps purchasing more of those goods that provide the greatest utility per extra dollar spent until income is completely exhausted.

Marginal utility

Slope

Definition: On a two-dimensional graph, the change in the value of y compared to the change in the value of x.

Equation: $\dfrac{y_2 - y_1}{x_2 - x_1}$

Comments: On a straight-line demand curve, the slope remains constant. The numerical value of slope is heavily dependent upon the unit of measure of both x and y.

Elasticity

Definition (for price elasticity of demand): The percentage change in the quantity demanded (x) compared to the percentage change in price (y).

Equation: $\dfrac{(q_2 - q_1)/q_1}{(p_2 - p_1)/p_1}$

Comments: On a straight-line demand curve, elasticity varies along the line. Comparison between items with unlike units is possible because changes are expressed in percentages.

Elasticity. *Elasticity* is a way of measuring how sensitive one variable is to changes in another. In economics, one of the most important elasticities is *price elasticity of demand.* This is a measure of how sensitive quantity demanded is to a change in price.

Why is this measure useful? Particularly from the producer perspective, it is important to be able to predict how consumers will react to price changes. For example, given a proposed 10 percent price increase, will quantity demanded decrease by 2 percent? 10 percent? 20 percent? Each of these three responses will have a markedly different effect on the producer's total revenues (revenues will increase, remain unchanged, or decrease, respectively).

An item has a *high price elasticity* if the quantity demanded reacts strongly to small changes in price. In other words, it doesn't take much of a price increase for consumers to substantially reduce their quantity demanded for highly elastic products. High elasticity is associated with goods and services for which there are many reasonable substitutes.

At the opposite end of the spectrum are items whose quantity demanded changes very little, even if the item's price changes dramatically. *Low price elasticity* is often associated with goods and services for which there are no close substitutes. This may be true for a necessity (for example, a life-sustaining drug), but could also be true for an exclusive country club or a one-of-a-kind artwork.

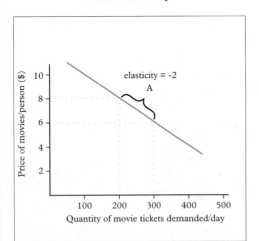

Price elasticity

Price elasticity is a measurement of how responsive quantity demanded is to price. In this example, the elasticity at section A of the demand curve is -2:

$$\frac{(300-200)/200}{(6-8)/8} = \frac{100/200}{-2/8} = -2.$$

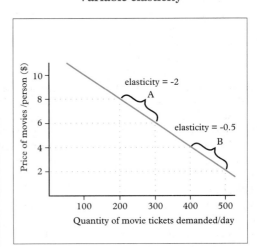

Variable elasticity

Unlike slope, the elasticity of a straight-line demand curve varies along the line. Demand is more elastic at higher prices and less elastic (inelastic) at lower prices. This is reflected in this example, where elasticity at section A is -2, while at section B it is -0.5.

Low price elasticity can also occur for items that account for only a small portion of consumer income. In such instances, consumers may react very little to relatively large price changes because the impact in total dollars is so small.

Price elasticities are calculated by dividing the *percentage change* in the quantity demanded by the *percentage change* in the price. The equation is:

$$price\ elasticity\ of\ demand\ = \frac{(q_2 - q_1)/q_1}{(p_2 - p_1)/p_1}.$$

where q_1 and p_1 refer to the quantity demanded and the original price, and q_2 and p_2 refer to the quantity demanded at the new (or proposed) price.

There are two things to note about calculating elasticities at the outset. First, we always divide the *responding* factor (quantity demanded) by the *causative* factor (price). Second, we look at changes in percentage, not absolute, terms. This allows us to compare and evaluate quantity changes without worrying about unlike units of measure (ounce, pound, dozen, gross and so on).

Referring to the graph "Price elasticity" opposite, we can see that the price elasticity of demand for movie tickets at segment *A* is:

$$price\ elasticity\ = \frac{(300 - 200)/200}{(6 - 8)/8} = \frac{100/200}{-2/8} = -2.$$

Notice that the price elasticity of demand is a negative number. This will always be the case for a typical demand curve, given its downward slope. (Remember, a downward, or negative, slope reflects two variables that change in opposite directions. This means the elasticity ratio will always pair a positive and negative number, resulting in a negative quotient.) Many economics texts drop the negative sign, however, and refer to elasticities only in absolute numbers.

Unlike slope, the elasticity of a straight-line demand

curve is not the same for every point on the line. Refer to the graph "Variable elasticity" opposite. The price elasticity at segment *A* is the same we calculated before: -2. Using the standard equation to calculate elasticity at segment *B*, we get:

$$price\ elasticity\ = \frac{(500 - 400)/400}{(2 - 4)/4} = \frac{100/400}{-1/2} = -0.5.$$

Note that the elasticity at segment *A* is a larger absolute number (2) than at segment *B* (0.5). This means that the demand is more elastic at high prices, and less elastic at low prices, which is true of most goods and services. Another way to say this is that consumer demand is more sensitive to price changes of high-priced goods than low-priced ones.

Where elasticity is less than 1 (as an absolute number), demand is said to be *inelastic*. A price increase here will *raise* a producer's profits because quantity demanded will decrease by a smaller percentage than price increases. The opposite case, where elasticity is greater than one, demonstrates *elastic* demand. In this case, overall profits will decrease as price increases.

As was true in calculating slope, the extremes of elasticity are found in horizontal or vertical demand curves. A horizontal demand curve is *perfectly elastic*: even a tiny increase in price will drive quantity demanded to zero. The vertical demand curve is *perfectly inelastic*: price changes have no effect whatsoever on quantity demanded.

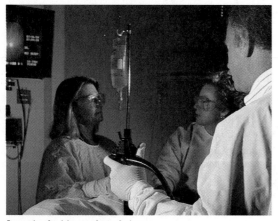

Low price elasticity: no close substitutes

High price elasticity: many substitutes

Producers.

Next we take a look at the other side of the circular flow diagram by observing and analyzing producer behavior. Producers form the supply side of the goods-and-services market.

As was the case with consumers, producers can take many forms and sizes. A producer can be an individual (an author, plumber, dancer, accountant, babysitter, farmer); a small, family-run business; a huge, multimillion-dollar organization; or any other possibility in between.

Likewise, the product can take numerous forms: tangible goods (cars, books, food, housing) or intangible services (information, education, and live performances).

Supply. *Supply* is the relationship between the price of a product and the quantity firms will produce and offer for sale.

We can illustrate the relationship of price and quantity supplied with the same kind of two-dimensional graph used to reflect demand. Again, price is plotted on the y (vertical) axis and quantity on the x (horizontal) axis. All the various price/quantity combinations are shown as points on the graph, and the line that connects these points is called a *supply curve* or *supply schedule*. Note that quantity supplied represents the speed or rate of production, and not a one-time production quota or customer order.

Given the assumption that a firm produces goods and services for profit, it will typically produce more of an item at a higher price than it will at a lower one. This direct relationship between price and quantity supplied is called the *law of supply*. It is reflected in the positive, or upward, slope of supply curves.

A single supply curve *only shows the effect of price changes*, nothing else. As a result, changes in factors other than price result in new supply curves. Economists draw a strong distinction between the two

types of changes by referring to movements along the curve as *changes in quantity supplied*, and shifts in the entire curve as *changes in supply*. As with demand, the term "quantity supplied" refers to one point on the supply curve, while the term "supply" refers to the entire curve.

At some point, the quantity supplied by a producer may no longer rise, even though the price rises. This occurs when producers reach the limit of their current production capabilities. This is a *short-run* condition, however. In the *long run*, producers will try to find a way to increase production to reap the additional profits that higher prices can bring.

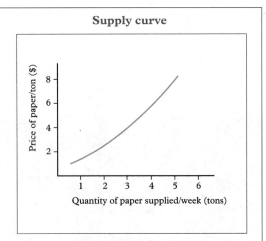

Supply curve

Price of paper/ton ($) (y-axis: 2, 4, 6, 8)
Quantity of paper supplied/week (tons) (x-axis: 1, 2, 3, 4, 5, 6)

A graph that portrays all of the combinations of quantity supplied and price for a particular good or service is called a supply curve. Because producers are willing to supply larger quantities at higher prices, the supply curve has a positive, or upward, slope.

Factors affecting supply. As we saw in examining the issues concerning demand, there are other factors that affect supply besides the selling price of the good or service. One of those factors is the price of *inputs*.

Producers must pay for resources used in producing their output. If the price of these inputs rises, producers react by supplying less. They cut back production because marginal units that had been profitable to produce are no longer profitable after input prices increase.

Another factor affecting supply is technology. If a new advancement in technology allows producers to produce the same quantity of output at a lower cost (or more output at the same cost), producers will increase supply. In the first case, overall costs fall, while in the second case, overall revenues rise. Either way, profits also rise. Some examples of historical technological changes that have increased supply are the printing press, the tractor, factory assembly line processing, and in more recent years, computer microchips, desktop publishing, and video production technology.

The supply of one item can also be affected by the prices of other goods and services. Since resources can be used in different ways to produce different items, producers may allocate more of their resources toward the more profitable item(s).

For example, if the price of corn rises, farmers will dedicate more acreage to corn production and less to other crops such as wheat. This is true even if the price of wheat hasn't changed. In other words, a rise in the price of one product—corn—can reduce the supply of another product—wheat. It can also increase the supply of by-products—corn oil, for example, in this case.

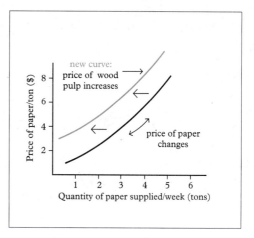

Shift in supply vs. movements along the curve

Price of paper/ton ($) — new curve: price of wood pulp increases; price of paper changes — *Quantity of paper supplied/week (tons)*

When a factor affecting supply other than price changes, it often causes a shift in the entire supply curve. This graph shows how a supply curve might move to the left, given that the price of a production input (wood pulp) increases. Now, at all the same prices as before, the quantity supplied decreases. (Note that a change in the price of the good itself—paper—is reflected by simply moving along the original curve.)

REMEMBER: Changes in factors other than product price represent changes in *supply* that generate new supply curves. An increase in supply shifts the curve to the right, a decrease shifts the curve to the left. By contrast, when the price of a product changes, we move along the original curve to find the new *quantity supplied*.

What affects supply?

Factor	Typical effect	Example
Input costs	Negative	If labor costs rise, producers will reduce the quantity supplied at any given output price to avoid producing some units which were previously profitable but are now unprofitable with higher labor costs.
Technology advance	Positive	If a technological advance (such as "smarter" equipment) reduces the cost of production, firms will produce more at any given output price.
Prices of related items (often alternative outputs)	Negative	If, with the same or similar resources, a producer can shift production to a more profitable output, quantity supplied for the original item will fall.

Labor

Capital

Production inputs. The two main categories of inputs used by producers are *labor* and *capital*. These inputs are key factors in producer decision making because they account for the majority of production costs.

Labor is the workforce needed to produce goods and services. It includes all individuals employed by a producer, regardless of whether they are directly involved in the production process.

Capital includes many types of goods, both tangible and intangible. Equipment, vehicles, furniture, supplies, inventories, factories, and office buildings are all different forms of capital. So too are less obvious "goods," such as copyrights, patents, and even an organization's name recognition (called *goodwill*). Some economists include land as a form of capital.

The simplest economic models focus only on these two inputs: labor and capital. In fact, many textbooks assume that a producer deals only with one type of labor and one type of capital. More sophisticated models include other factors (taxes, maintenance services) that also result in production costs.

One of the questions that we wish to answer with these models is how inputs are related to outputs. For example, if an additional pasta-making machine is purchased by a restaurant, how much additional pasta can be produced? Or what is the impact of hiring an additional cook? The amount of additional output associated with adding *one more unit* of input is called *marginal product*.

In most cases, marginal product initially rises as the firm increases its rate of production. However, as more and more inputs are added, there is a limit to what the fixed production inputs (that is, those that cannot easily be changed in the short term, such as land, office space, or large, costly machinery) can handle. Perhaps there is not enough space or enough

equipment to go around. The result is a decrease in marginal product (although marginal product is still positive). The fact that marginal product declines at some point when variable inputs are being added to fixed inputs is called the *law of diminishing returns*. Note, however, that this does not mean that *total* product is falling. Total product will still increase, but at a slower rate.

Costs. It is important to understand the relationship between a firm's costs and output rate.

Different producers have many different types of inputs and costs. One might rely heavily on a large pool of skilled laborers as employees. Another might get by on a skeletal crew, pulling in contract help only as needed. A third might have large costs of production equipment and inventory stock, while a fourth might need only office equipment and supplies.

Using the simplest model of a firm, all of these costs can be divided into the two main types of inputs: capital and labor. Capital costs are fixed; labor costs are variable.

Fixed costs are those short-run costs that do not change with output rate. Fixed costs are the same, *even if the firm produces nothing at all*. Some examples of fixed costs are rents, leases, taxes, and the cost of keeping property safe, clean, and secure. Note that in the long run, there is no such thing as a fixed cost. This is because, over time, a firm may choose to shut down completely or change its scale of production.

By contrast, *variable costs* are associated with those inputs that change, or *vary*, with output. If more output is needed, more inputs are added. Labor costs are variable costs.

Total cost (TC), then, is the sum of *total fixed cost* (TFC) and *total variable cost* (TVC).

The most important cost in terms of producer decision making is *marginal cost* (MC). Marginal cost is the

Economics

additional cost of producing *one more unit of output.* For example, if it costs $800 to produce 5,000 pamphlets per day, and $820 to produce 5,001, the marginal cost at that level of production is $20.

Firms' costs can be plotted on a two-dimensional graph that relates cost (*y*) with rate of output (*x*). On such a graph, the marginal cost curve starts out with a downward slope, but quickly "bottoms out" and starts to rise. Why is this? (See the graph "AVC and MC" on the next page.)

The point at which marginal cost starts to rise is the *point of diminishing returns.* Recall that diminishing returns set in when the output associated with each additional unit of input starts to drop. So each unit of output takes more input to produce than the previous one did. That is why marginal cost rises.

Marginal cost is not the same as *average cost.* Rather than representing the cost of a unique unit, average cost divides total costs *evenly* among output units. (Average cost = total cost/output.)

Which cost is which?

Abbreviation	Name	Definition	Characteristics
TFC	Total fixed cost	The total of all costs unaffected by quantity of output produced per time period, even if there is no output at all. Fixed costs are often called *overhead.*	The TFC curve is a straight line with a constant dollar value. In the long run, there are no fixed costs. The firm could change its scale of production or stop doing business completely.
TVC	Total variable cost	The total of all costs that vary with the quantity of output produced per time period	TVC always rises with output. The rate of increase in TVC depends upon marginal costs; rising marginal costs result in a steeper slope on the TVC curve.
TC	Total cost	Total fixed cost plus total variable cost: TC = TFC + TVC	TC always rises with output. Unless there are no fixed costs at all, TC is always higher than TVC. The difference between TC and TVC at all outputs is TFC.
AFC	Average fixed cost	Total fixed cost divided by units of output (*q*) produced: AFC = TFC / *q*	Because TFC is a constant, AFC always decreases as quantity of output increases.
AVC	Average variable cost	Total variable cost divided by units of output (*q*) produced: AVC = TVC / *q*	AVC will decrease as long as marginal cost (MC) is below AVC. Once MC exceeds AVC, AVC will rise.
ATC	Average total cost	Total costs divided by units of output (*q*): ATC = TC / *q*; also ATC = AFC + AVC	The difference between ATC and AVC at all outputs is AFC.
MC	Marginal cost	The additional cost associated with producing one more unit of output	MC always intersects AVC and ATC at their minimum points. A profit-maximizing firm will produce at the point where marginal cost equals marginal revenue. The MC curve is the supply curve for a perfectly competitive firm.

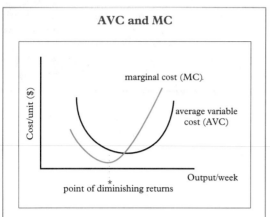

AVC and MC

marginal cost (MC).

average variable cost (AVC)

Cost/unit ($)

Output/week

point of diminishing returns

The line illustrating the marginal cost (MC) for producing a good or service always intersects the average variable cost (AVC) line at the minimum point of AVC. This makes sense. If the marginal cost—the cost of producing one more unit—is below AVC, average cost must continue to fall. If the marginal cost is above AVC, average cost must start to rise. When the two cost figures are equal, it will be where AVC is neither rising nor falling.

The marginal cost curve always intersects the minimum point of the average cost curve. As long as the marginal cost is less than average cost, average cost will fall. Once marginal cost is more than average cost, average cost will rise. (Again, see "AVC and MC.")

In the long run, a firm may alter average costs by using more capital to increase its scale of production. (*Long run* is a time period long enough for a firm to change *all* of the inputs.) If a higher scale results in lower average costs, this is called *economies of scale*. If a higher scale produces higher average costs, this is called *diseconomies of scale*.

Revenues and profits. *Total revenue* is the total dollar amount that a firm receives from selling its product or service, while *profit* is the difference between total revenue and total cost of production.

Total revenue can be calculated very simply by multiplying the price per unit by the quantity of output that the firm produces and sells:

total revenue = p × q.

Like marginal cost, *marginal revenue* is the additional revenue that a firm can generate when it *increases output by one more unit*. In a totally competitive industry (one in which the individual firm cannot influence market price), marginal revenue will be equal to price. (Marginal revenue and price can be unequal for other types of competition. We will discuss competition in more detail later.)

It should be noted that economists make the assumption that firms try to maximize profits. This has proven to be a useful assumption in predicting firm behavior.

For example, if profits do not cover costs, the firm will lose money. We can predict that it will not remain in business in the long run under such conditions. On the other hand, if revenue from added output is greater than the cost of added output, we can predict that the firm may expand production in an effort to expand profits as well.

With all this information about cost, revenue, and profit, how do we predict the level of output at which a firm will produce? The key is the relationship of marginal cost and marginal revenue.

As stated earlier, marginal revenue for a producer in a perfectly competitive industry is the same as price. On a two-dimensional graph comparing dollars (*y*) and units of output (*x*), the marginal revenue curve would be a horizontal straight line, positioned at output price.

We can also overlay the marginal cost curve on the same graph. Recall that marginal cost usually decreases initially, and then increases at the point of diminishing returns.

Unless marginal cost always exceeds marginal revenue, the two curves will intersect at a point on the graph. (See the graph "MC and MR.") The rate of output at this point is the amount that a profit-maximizing firm will produce.

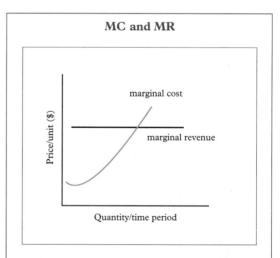

MC and MR

marginal cost

marginal revenue

Price/unit ($)

Quantity/time period

Profit-maximizing firms will produce output at the point where marginal cost (MC) and marginal revenue (MR) are equal. Why? If MC is less than MR, the firm's next unit will generate more revenue than it costs to produce. But if MC is more than MR, the firm will start losing overall profit on marginal units.

Market equilibrium.

Throughout our discussion of microeconomics, we have focused on the factors influencing individual behavior. How does a single consumer select among competing products? How does a single producer determine the optimal scale of production? Now, with a basic understanding of the individual factors, it's time to pull the pieces together and explore how they combine to influence overall behavior in a highly competitive market.

Our first step is the creation of *market demand* and *market supply* curves from the individual demand and supply curves we have used. Each market curve is simply the sum of all the pertinent individual curves for a particular good or service.

Thus, if there is a total of fifty consumers that demand skywriting services, the market demand for skywriting is found by adding together the fifty quantities demanded at each price. Plotted on a graph, the complete set of price and *summed* quantity combinations reflects the market demand curve for skywriting. Market supply is found in the same way: by adding together all of the quantities supplied by each producer at each price.

The next step is to bring consumers and producers together. Although individuals may make decisions independently, it should be obvious that their behavior is closely connected. For example, regardless of quantities demanded, consumers will only be able to buy the amount firms actually produce. Likewise, quantities supplied don't guarantee that consumers will make purchases.

In this step, then, we take the market demand and market supply curves and plot them on a single *x/y* graph. Recall that supply curves slope upward, demand curves downward. The point where the two curves intersect—where quantity demanded and quantity supplied are equal—is called *market equilibrium*. This point reflects *equilibrium price* and *equilibrium*

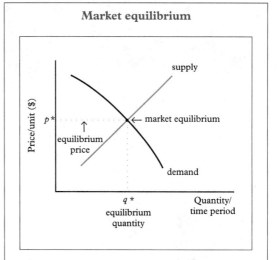

Market equilibrium

When the quantity supplied equals the quantity demanded for a particular good or service, the market for that good or service is said to be in equilibrium. On the graph, the equilibrium quantity and price are shown at the point where the two lines intersect.

quantity. At this point, there are no market forces prompting the price or quantity to change. Equilibrium is a point of natural rest. (See the graph "Market equilibrium.")

Note how at all prices lower than equilibrium, the quantity demanded exceeds quantity supplied. With this excess demand (or shortage), the tendency is for prices to rise as consumers bid against each other to purchase the output in short supply.

Likewise, prices higher than equilibrium reflect points where quantity supplied exceeds quantity demanded. With this *excess supply*, or *surplus*, the tendency is for prices to fall as producers try to rid themselves of excess inventories.

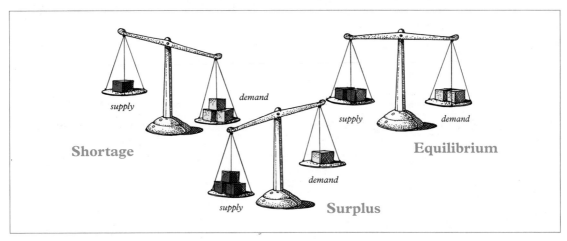

Competition is keen in high-tech industries.

Competition.
Not all product markets are organized the same. They may differ by number of producers (one versus thousands), the individuality of their products (virtually identical versus distinctly different), or the ease in which firms can enter and leave the market (no barriers versus significant start-up costs and/or government regulations). All of these differences will affect market behavior.

Economists have developed several models to explain market differences. The most widely used are the extremes of *perfect competition* and *monopoly*. In addition, several intermediate models fall between these extremes on the competition continuum.

Perfect competition. Perfect competition is a model of market organization where no firm controls or significantly impacts the market. Each firm is small compared to the size of the total market. (Refer to the table "Competition comparison" on the opposite page for examples.)

A perfectly competitive market has several distinguishing characteristics:

• *Suppliers' products are homogeneous.* The product of one supplier is virtually identical to that of another, so consumers can easily substitute one product for another. No producer enjoys the competitive advantage of brand recognition.

• *There are no barriers to entry or exit.* Firms can enter and leave the industry at will. No firm has an advantage that would preclude others from getting into the market (an exclusive patent, for example). Likewise, firms may choose to stop producing the item without penalty.

• *Perfectly competitive firms are price-takers.* Firms are unable to sell output at higher than the market price because consumers will take their business elsewhere. Given that the firm can sell all it wants at market price, there is also no incentive to lower price. Doing so would mean losing potential profits.

Perfect competition

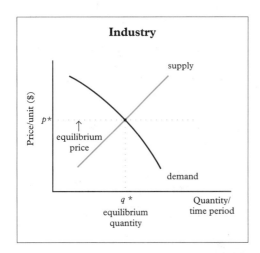

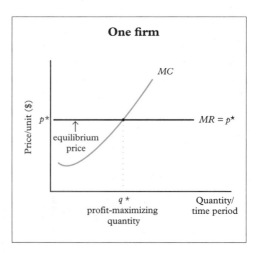

In a perfectly competitive market, each individual firm is a price-taker. It must sell at the market price no matter what its output rate is.

Economics

Monopoly. At the other extreme is the *monopoly*, a model of a market where only one firm (or a group of firms acting together) supplies a good or service. (Again, refer to the table below.)

A monopoly has these characteristics:

• *There are no close product substitutes.* Consumers either buy from the sole supplier or don't buy at all.

• *There are barriers to entry and exit.* One firm has an exclusive location or resource, or the government imposes barriers by protecting a patent or regulating an industry.

• *The monopoly firm can set its own price.* However, monopoly does not guarantee profits. The firm must still be able to produce its product at a cost below the price that consumers are willing to pay.

Intermediate models of competition. Sometimes monopoly and perfect competition models do not adequately explain the behavior in a product market. As a result, a number of intermediate models have been developed.

One of these models is the *oligopoly*. In an oligopoly, there are only a few large firms that dominate the product market. Examples of oligopolies are the automobile, airline, and pharmaceuticals industries. On the competition continuum, an oligopoly is most like a monopoly.

A second intermediate model is that of *monopolistic competition*. In this particular model, many firms compete for the same consumer market, but the products they produce may have slight distinctions between them. Restaurants and publishing houses are examples of producers operating within monopolistic competition. Firms in this model try to establish name and brand recognition, so that at least for their particular product, they can act more as a monopoly (that is, they can exercise more control over the price of their product). However, in monopolistic competition, there are still many close substitutes, so the producer in question can go only so far in raising prices before losing some of its market share. On the competition continuum, monopolistic competition is the most like perfect competition.

One distinguishing feature about many intermediate models is that they involve one firm taking into consideration the action of the other firms. When an automobile manufacturing company such as Honda sets the price for an Accord, it has to worry about Nissan's reaction to that price change and, in turn, General Motors' reaction to that price change, and so on. Thus, the firms in these intermediate models often place great importance on developing pricing and counterstrategies.

Competition comparison

Type	Definition	Characteristics	Examples
Monopoly	A market in which only one firm produces a good or service for which there are no close substitutes	Barriers to entry (natural or government-sponsored). Producer sets price, although still subject to market constraints. Often regulated by government.	Cable TV, public utilities
Oligopoly	A market where a few large firms dominate production	Competing firms typically take into account the actions and reactions of other firms in establishing pricing strategies. Limited market entry.	Automobiles, airlines
Monopolistic competition	A market in which there are many competing firms, but there are also slight distinctions among the products they produce	Many close substitutes. Firms try to induce brand loyalty—and thus, "mini monopolies"—by distinguishing their products from those of their competitors. No barriers to entry or exit.	Casual footwear, restaurants
Perfect competition	A market with many small firms (relative to the total market) whose products are completely interchangeable	Homogeneous, perfect substitutes. No firm can influence price. No barriers to entry or exit.	Farming, pencils

Macroeconomics

Having explored the workings of individual pieces in the economy (such as consumers, producers, specific industries), we can now step back and fit together the pieces of the economic puzzle. Whereas microeconomics was like using a microscope to focus on small segments of the economy, macroeconomics takes the bird's-eye view. Key topics in macroeconomics are overall (national) output, consumption, employment, government fiscal and monetary policies, and international trade.

Before the Great Depression, most economic study was based on the supply-and-demand models of microeconomics. When those models failed to explain such current market behavior as long-term high unemployment, new explanations and models were needed. Much macroeconomic study is rooted in the work of Depression-era economist John Maynard Keynes.

Measuring national output.

Measures of annual output are needed to evaluate and study a nation's economic health. In the United States, the two primary measures are *gross national product* (GNP) and *gross domestic product* (GDP). Both are compiled and published by the government.

While it sounds relatively simple, there are many questions involved in determining national output. Which goods and services are included? What if an intermediate item is used to build a final product—should it be counted twice? What about items sold to foreign consumers?

You will see that national output is measured in dollars. This allows us to combine very different products into one meaningful measure.

Gross national product. Gross national product (GNP) is a measure of the total market value of the output produced by a single country during a given year. There are several types of goods and services that are *not* included in GNP:

Intermediate goods. An intermediate good is one that is produced by one firm, then sold to another to be included as part of a new product. For example, the value of microchips sold to a computer manufacturer to be included in the hardware it produces is not counted separately in GNP. This is because the cost of the *final good* (computer) covers the cost of all intermediate parts (microchips). Otherwise, intermediate goods would be counted twice.

Used goods. Used goods that have not had new goods or services added to them are not included in GNP. The value of used goods was counted when originally produced. For example, the price of an unrestored antique sold today would not be included in this year's GNP. However, any part of the price that reflects restoring the item, or any finder's fee paid to the antiques dealer to locate the item would be included in GNP because it represents the value of new services added.

Government transfer payments. Government payments that are not made in exchange for a current good or service are not included in GNP. Examples of such payments are Social Security, welfare, and veterans' benefits.

GNP and GDP (billions of dollars)

Year	GNP	GDP
1984	3801.5	3777.2
1985	4053.6	4038.7
1986	4277.7	4268.6
1987	4544.5	4539.9
1988	4908.2	4900.4
1989	5266.8	5250.8
1990	5567.8	5546.1
1991	5737.1	5722.9
1992	6025.8	6020.2
1993	6347.8	6343.3
1994	6922.4	6931.4
1995	7237.5	7245.8
1996	7416.1	7421.4

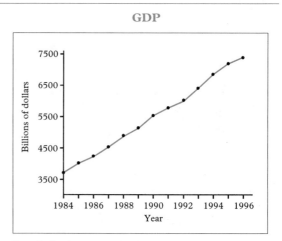

The graph reflects the 1984-1996 statistics from the *Department of Commerce, June 1996, Report.* For updated statistics, please consult more recent reports at your library.

GNP does not include the value of used goods sold.

Goods and services produced within the country by for-eign-owned producers. GNP includes the output of domestically owned producers, regardless of where the actual production plant may be. However, output physically produced in the country but resulting from a foreign-owned producer is not included in GNP. The computations are not always clear-cut, however. For example, the value of domestic labor used to produce a foreign product would be included in GNP; the profits associated with the same product would not.

One way in which GNP is calculated is the *expenditure approach*. This approach adds up all the different types of spending that contribute to the GNP. The expenditure equation for GNP is:

$$GNP = C + I + G + (EX - IM)$$

where C is consumption by domestic households,
I is investment in new capital (equipment, inventories, new buildings),
G is government purchases of goods and services,
EX is exports, and
IM is imports.

Another measure related to GNP is *per capita* GNP. This is simply the value of GNP divided by the country's population.

Gross domestic product. In 1991, the U.S. Department of Commerce switched from GNP to another measure of economic health: *gross domestic product* (GDP). Recall that GNP measures the value of goods and services supplied by a country's residents, regardless of where the goods and services are produced. As a result, profits from a domestic firm's overseas subsidiaries are included in GNP. By contrast, GDP measures the value of only those goods and services produced by labor and property located *within* the nation's borders, regardless of who owns or supplies the resources.

Which do you need: GNP or GDP?

GNP (gross national product)
Historical perspective
In the United States, GNP data has been published since 1941, and continues to be published along with GDP. The switch to GDP as the prime measure of U.S. output occurred relatively recently (December 1991), so historical GDP data may be less accessible.

Per capita use
Some economists argue that because GNP measures output produced by a country's citizens regardless of their location, it can provide a better *per capita* measure than GDP.

Textbook reference
Many economics textbooks and course materials still refer to GNP.

GDP (gross domestic product)
Current emphasis
The U.S. Department of Commerce now emphasizes GDP as the primary measure of national output. GNP figures are still reported, but on a delayed basis.

International comparison
Most other industrialized countries report national output in terms of GDP, so international comparisons will be easier. (Canada adopted GDP as its primary production measure in 1986.)

Policy tool
GDP provides a better guide to domestic production and, arguably, the country's economic health. As such, it may prove more useful in steering economic policy.

Most industrialized countries use GDP rather than GNP to measure economic performance, so the switch to GDP brings U.S. statistics more in line with those of the rest of the world. Yet in most cases, there is not a significant difference between the two economic measures.

For example, the U.S. GNP was only 0.5 percent—1 percent higher than GDP for the entire 1980–1990 decade. In some countries, however, overseas investments account for much larger differences.

Many economists believe that GDP is less likely to be distorted by such factors as volatile oil company profits and wide fluctuations in the value of the U.S. dollar. With its emphasis on domestic production, many economists also consider GDP a better gauge of the country's economic health and, thus, a better tool for evaluating and establishing economic policy.

Measuring price changes. Because

of the diversity of items produced, a country's economic growth is measured in dollars. This allows the combination of goods and services that would otherwise be measured in incompatible units. The use of dollars as an economic measure poses a challenge: how to isolate those changes in GNP (or GDP) that result from changes in the production of goods versus those that result from price fluctuations. Price indexes are the answer.

Consumer Price Index. The most commonly used U.S. price index is the *Consumer Price Index* (CPI), compiled monthly by the Bureau of Labor Statistics. Developed as a means to analyze and adjust ship builders' wages in 1919, the CPI provides the average price change in a representative *market basket* of goods and services purchased monthly by a typical consumer. The CPI crosses all industries.

Each of the goods and services included in the market basket is given a different emphasis, or *weight*, according to the portion of income a typical consumer spends on that item. For example, rather than treating a 50 percent price increase in housing the same as a 50 percent price increase in movie tickets, the CPI gives more weight to the item for which a consumer spends more income. So if consumers tend to spend 30 percent of monthly income on housing, and only 2 percent of income on movie tickets, the price index will give fifteen times more importance (weight) to the housing price increase than to the movie price increase.

The weights assigned to each category of goods and services are updated from consumer surveys conducted every decade. As time elapses from the time the

CPI weights

Because people do not spend the same amount on each type of good or service, the Consumer Price Index is weighted by category. In one recent year, the relative weights were:

Housing	41.5
Transportation	17.0
Food	16.0
Energy	7.4
Medical care	6.7
Apparel and upkeep	6.1
Other	5.3
Total	100.0%

Therefore, a price change in food will have twice the impact of the same price change in energy. This is because the food category has a weight (16.0) over twice as great as that in energy (7.4).

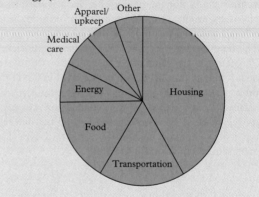

surveys were taken, new goods and services appear, and the weights change.

To construct a price index, a base year or period is chosen, and the price level within that period is given an index number of 100. The index then reflects price changes for the specified bundle of goods *in terms of base-period dollars*. For example, if prices for the bundle of goods in year 1 are 5 percent lower than those in the base period, the CPI for year 1 is 95. Similarly, a 121 CPI translates into a market basket of goods that would have cost $100 in the base year, but now costs $121.

Unless you consume the exact combination and quantity of products included in the market basket, the CPI will not necessarily match the price changes you experience.

The CPI will not accurately reflect individual changes because the CPI is a *fixed-weight* index. This means that the bundle of goods remains constant, even when prices for one item change drastically.

"Market basket" of goods and services

Consumer Price Index (CPI)

Year	All items	Food and beverages	Housing	Apparel and upkeep	Transpor- tation	Medical care	Enter- tainment	Other goods and services	Energy
1985	107.6	105.6	107.7	105.0	106.4	113.5	107.9	114.5	101.6
1986	109.6	109.1	110.9	105.9	102.3	122.0	111.6	121.4	88.2
1987	113.6	113.5	114.2	110.6	105.4	130.1	115.3	128.5	88.6
1988	118.3	118.2	118.5	115.4	108.7	138.6	120.3	137.0	89.3
1989	124.0	124.9	123.0	118.6	114.1	149.3	126.5	147.7	94.3
1990	130.7	132.1	128.5	124.1	120.5	162.8	132.4	159.0	102.1
1991	136.2	136.8	133.6	128.7	123.8	177.0	138.4	171.6	102.5
1992	140.3	138.7	137.5	131.9	126.5	190.1	142.3	183.3	103.0
1993	144.5	141.6	141.2	133.7	130.4	201.4	145.8	192.9	104.2
1994	148.2	144.9	144.8	133.4	134.3	211.0	150.1	198.5	104.6
1995	152.4	148.9	148.5	132.0	139.1	220.5	153.9	206.9	105.2
1996*	155.6	152.0	151.5	132.9	141.8	226.5	158.2	213.0	107.8

Source: *Economic Report of the President* and monthly *CPI Detailed Report*. For updated statistics, please consult more recent reports at your library.
NOTE: Data beginning in 1983 incorporate a rental equivalence measure for homeowners' costs and therefore are not strictly comparable with earlier figures.
*First five months.

Because the CPI does not take into account product substitutions and other fluctuations in consumption patterns, it may overstate price changes.

Besides the CPI, the U.S. government publishes two other price indexes on a regular basis: the Producer Price Index and the GDP deflator.

Producer Price Index. The *Producer Price Index* (PPI) measures the prices paid by producers for intermediate and crude materials, as well as finished goods. Once referred to as the *wholesale price index*, it is based on an entirely different set of goods and services than the CPI.

GDP deflator. The third regularly published government price index is the *GDP deflator*. It is the broadest price index for the U.S. economy.

The GDP deflator is a price index that converts the value of GDP in current dollars to the value of GDP in base-year dollars. This allows economists to distinguish between changes due to true economic growth or decline (including such factors as quantity changes) and those caused by price fluctuations.

GDP measured in the current year's dollars is called *nominal GDP*, while GDP measured in the base year's dollars is called *real GDP*. The GDP deflator is the ratio of nominal GDP to real GDP, multiplied by 100.

In real life, surveys are taken to determine nominal GDP and the GDP deflator. These surveys are then used in the calculation of real GDP:

$$real\ GDP = \frac{nominal\ GDP \times 100}{GDP\ deflator}.$$

It follows, then, that given values for any two of these variables, the third variable can easily be found.

Consumer Price Index

Consumer prices for the specific combination of goods measured by the Consumer Price Index have risen over 40 percent in the past ten years.

So:

$$nominal\ GDP = \frac{real\ GDP \times GDP\ deflator}{100}$$

and

$$GDP\ deflator = \frac{nominal\ GDP \times 100}{real\ GDP}.$$

The GDP deflator differs from the CPI in two key ways. First, the GDP deflator is a price index for *all* goods and services, while the CPI reflects only price changes for consumer goods. Second, the GDP deflator is not a fixed-weight index. It is based on the true combination of goods and services produced, which varies from year to year. Thus, the GDP deflator not only reflects price changes, but also the market reaction to price changes.

NOTE: The GNP deflator serves the same role for GNP as the GDP deflator does for GDP.

Aggregate demand.
A country's demand for all goods and services in the economy is called *aggregate demand*. Aggregate demand equals the national total of all *planned* expenditures made by households (consumption), firms (investment), and government. It is a measure of intended, not actual, spending.

There are many similarities between the demand curves for aggregate versus individual demand. Both demand curves relate measures of price and quantity. Both slope downward. Both must be interpreted carefully to distinguish between movements along the curves versus shifts in the curve.

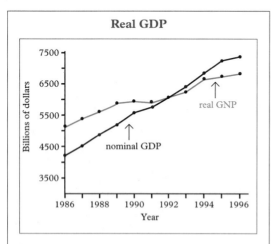

Real GDP

In addition to nominal GDP, this graph now reflects real GDP, which is GDP adjusted to remove the effect of price increases. The base year is 1992.

Source: *Economic Report of the President* and *Department of Commerce, Bureau of Economic Analysis*. For updated statistics, please consult more recent reports at your library.

The money market affects aggregate demand.

But there are very important differences as well. Whereas the graph of an individual demand curve relates price to quantity demanded, the graph for an aggregate demand curve relates an overall price indicator with a measure of planned spending for all goods.

The reasons behind the downward slope of the two demand curves are also quite different. One of the key reasons that *individual* demand curves slope downward is consumers' ability to substitute items. Recall how when the price of one good rises, consumers tend to increase the quantity demanded for substitute items, lowering quantity demanded for the more expensive item.

This is not the case with aggregate demand because the substitutions tend to cancel each other out. While planned spending on some items decreases, planned spending on substitutes increases. Also, because aggregate demand deals with the overall price level, the "all else equal" assumption no longer applies. Many prices rise together. Price changes may include the price of labor, meaning that consumer incomes also rise. In fact, if prices and income rise together, relative prices may remain unchanged.

(Note that because the "all else equal" assumption does not hold with an aggregate demand curve—income cannot be assumed constant—the aggregate demand curve is not the same as a market demand curve. Neither is it the sum of all market curves.)

One reason that aggregate demand curves *do* slope downward is the *real wealth effect*. An increase in the overall price level means that the value of fixed dollar assets (cash, checking accounts, bonds) decreases. This leads to a decrease in planned consumption, one of the components of aggregate demand.

The slope of aggregate demand curves is also tied to the workings of the money market and interest rates.

Economics

As a brief example, consider again what happens when the overall price level rises. First, demand for money rises as more money is needed to consume the same quantity of goods and services as before. Given that the supply of money stays constant, the price of money (reflected in the interest rate) rises to a new equilibrium point. Because borrowing is now more expensive, firms may borrow less, which means less investment spending. And that means less national output.

All of the instances discussed so far—changes in overall price level—are reflected as movements along the aggregate demand curve. As was true with individual demand curves, shifts of the entire curve are also possible.

With aggregate demand curves, shifts are caused by changes in the planned amount of consumption, investment, or government spending. Increases in spending cause the curve to shift to the right, while decreases shift the curve to the left. The federal government often tries to use fiscal and monetary policy to shift the aggregate demand curve for the U.S. economy.

Aggregate supply.
The total of goods and services provided by all firms in the economy is called *aggregate supply*.

Like aggregate demand, there are many similarities between the aggregate and individual supply curves. For example, the aggregate supply curve relates quantity and price, but it does so in terms of total output supplied at each overall price level.

There are also many of the same cautions and differences that apply to aggregate demand. Again, the "all else equal" assumption cannot be applied to the aggregate supply curve because a change in overall price levels affects both input and output prices. In addition, many goods that are outputs to one firm are inputs to another. As a result, the aggregate supply curve is neither a market supply curve nor the sum of market supply curves.

There is a great deal of disagreement by economists as to the shape and behavior of the aggregate supply curve. Most will agree that, at least for part of its range, the slope of the curve is positive.

At lower levels of output, the aggregate supply curve is usually shown with a fairly flat slope. This indicates that, within the given range, real output can be expanded with very little increase in the overall price level. At higher levels of output, the aggregate supply curve gets steeper, eventually becoming vertical. At the vertical point, the economy is producing at full capacity, and no additional output is possible within the short run.

Changes in input costs, such as wages, rents, and energy costs, that are reflected in overall price changes are already built into the shape of the aggregate supply curve. However, when input cost changes lag behind or leap ahead of the overall price level, the aggregate supply curve can shift. If such changes are increases in input costs, the curve shifts to the left (reducing aggregate supply at all levels). Decreases shift the curve to the right (increasing aggregate supply).

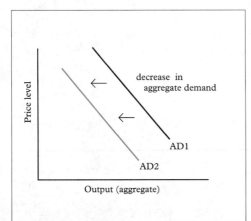

Shift in aggregate demand

Like individual demand curves, the aggregate demand curve can also shift to the left or right. In this example, the decrease in aggregate demand could be caused by such factors as a decrease in government purchases or an increase in net taxes.

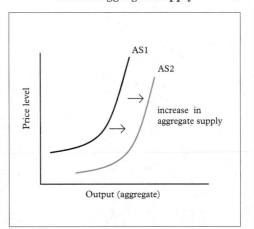

Shift in aggregate supply

Like individual supply curves, the aggregate supply curve can also shift to the left or right. In this example, the increase in aggregate supply could be caused by a decrease in wage rates, land values, or energy costs, or because of technology advancements.

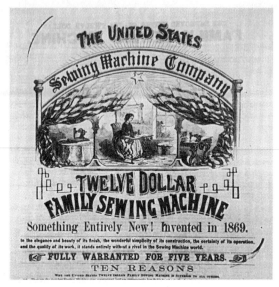

Shifts in the aggregate supply curve are also caused by changes in input quantities. The increase in the labor force caused by higher percentages of working women has shifted the aggregate supply curve to the right. Failure to maintain firms' capital, such as buildings and equipment, shifts the supply curve to the left. Wars or natural disasters that reduce the economy's productive resources also shift the supply curve to the left.

Another factor that can shift the aggregate supply curve is technological change. Productivity improvements increase aggregate supply and shift the supply curve to the right.

Like market supply and demand curves, the aggregate supply and demand curves can be combined on a single graph. The point where the two curves intersect is called *macroeconomic equilibrium*. This point determines the *equilibrium price level* and the *equilibrium national output*.

Inflation. It is difficult to shop for anything today without noticing that prices have risen. But as we have seen in the microeconomics sections on supply and demand, individual prices rise and fall in response to market behavior all the time. That is not inflation. Only when the *overall* price level rises do we have *inflation*. Inflation is one of the chief concerns of the macroeconomist.

Inflation is measured using one or more of the price indexes previously discussed (usually the CPI or the GNP deflator). Recall that a price index takes into account the prices of many goods and services. So inflation occurs when *many* prices are rising at the same time. However, given the mix and weight of each of the goods measured by the index, it is possible for some prices to fall even during a period of inflation.

Although recent history has been dominated by

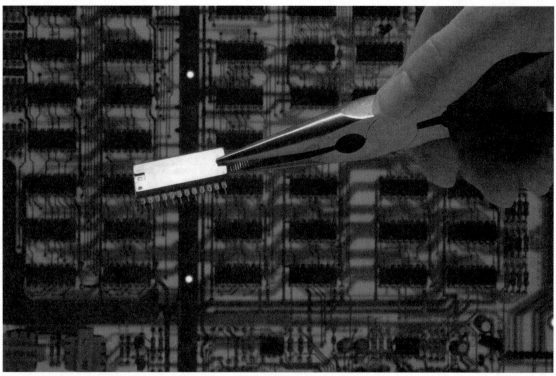

Technological change can shift the aggregate supply curve.

inflation, the overall price level need not always rise. In the 1930s, the CPI both decreased and increased. A decrease in the overall price level is called *deflation*. By contrast, a decrease in the *rate* of inflation is called *disinflation*.

Some economists use the term "inflation" only when referring to a continued increase in the overall price level over a significant time period. Others make this distinction by referring to a steady rise in prices as *sustained inflation* and a brief rise in prices as *one-time inflation*.

Causes of inflation. There are many possible causes of one-time inflation. Most are categorized as a source of either *demand-pull* or *cost-push* inflation.

Inflation caused by an *increase in aggregate demand* is called demand-pull inflation. Increases in aggregate demand can be brought about by increased government spending or measures intended to increase consumer and business spending, such as tax cuts or an increase in the money supply.

Recall that when aggregate demand increases, the aggregate demand curve shifts to the right. If this occurs at a point where the aggregate supply curve is relatively flat, the new macroeconomic equilibrium point will reflect an increase in total output, with only a modest price increase.

This is not the case if the economy is functioning at capacity, where the aggregate supply curve is vertical. If the aggregate demand shift occurs at or near this very steep portion of the aggregate supply curve, the effect will be a price level increase. (See the graph "Demand-pull inflation" below as an example.)

Inflation can also be caused by an *increase in input costs* that is not matched by a comparable increase in demand. This kind of inflation is called cost-push, or supply-side, inflation.

Recall that when input costs increase, the aggregate supply curve shifts to the left. If we assume that no action is taken to increase demand (government does not try to stimulate consumer and/or business spending), the new macroeconomic equilibrium point will reflect a decrease in total output and an increase in the overall price level. This combination—falling output and rising prices—is called *stagflation*. (See the graph "Cost-push inflation" for an example.)

Effects of inflation. Contrary to popular belief, inflation is not necessarily bad. Why is this so? Inflation means higher prices, which in turn reduces the real purchasing power of consumer dollars. (We again use the term "real" to refer to value expressed in some base-period dollars.) But remember that inflation covers all types of prices, including wages, rents, and dividends. These are all various forms of consumer income.

Inflation is undesirable from the consumer perspective when income does not rise *as fast* as the overall price level, resulting in lower real income. But it is also possible for income to rise *faster* than the overall price level. In such a case, inflation actually benefits the consumer.

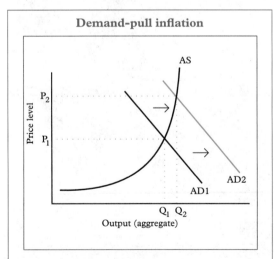

Demand-pull inflation

When the aggregate demand curve shifts right, the equilibrium point will reflect both a higher output and higher price. In this example, the economy is operating at near capacity—a very steep part of the supply curve—so there is a relatively sharp price increase.

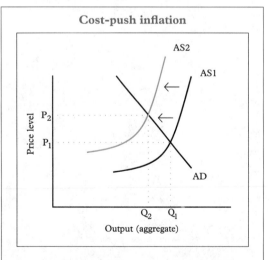

Cost-push inflation

When the aggregate supply curve shifts left, the equilibrium point will reflect a lower output but a higher price. This example shows how an increase in input costs could translate into higher consumer prices.

In general, inflation redistributes real income and wealth among various economic groups. Here are some examples:

Rapid inflation redistributes income from workers to employers. When the price level rises rapidly, wages often lag behind. In the interim, real wages fall, hurting workers and benefiting employers. In the long term, however, wage inflation has generally exceeded price inflation.

Unanticipated inflation and fixed interest rates redistribute income from lenders to borrowers. A common example of the effect of inflation deals with borrowers and lenders. In an inflationary period, the dollars a borrower uses to repay a loan are worth less than those originally borrowed. This fact leads to the common belief that inflation benefits borrowers and hurts lenders.

But this is not necessarily true. At the time the loan is made, the lender tries to take the inflation rate into account. For example, if the lender expects an inflation rate of approximately 5 percent, total interest charged may be 10 percent. This covers the cost of inflation and still provides extra profit to the lender.

The key word, then, is *unanticipated.* If lenders underestimate the degree of inflation and have no mechanism to adjust for higher inflation rates, borrowers will benefit. Real income will be distributed in favor of borrowers. The shift toward borrowing (and away from savings) may also increase aggregate demand, which in turn may lead to even greater inflation.

Inflation redistributes income away from individuals with fixed income. If prices rise and nominal income remains constant, real income falls. Purchasing power falls. However, many individuals, such as Social Security recipients, have income or benefits that are automatically adjusted to keep pace with inflation.

Regardless of who benefits and who suffers, people do not seem to like inflation. It leads to uncertainty and insecurity. And this can negatively affect decisions in every aspect of the economy: household consumption, savings, and labor supply; business investment, hiring, and pricing; and government spending and policy-setting. If expectations turn out to be wrong, the result is a less-than-efficient allocation of economic resources as consumers over- or underspend and businesses over- or underinvest.

Unemployment.
Unemployment statistics are compiled monthly by the Bureau of Labor Statistics, a branch of the U.S. Department of Labor.

Who is included in these monthly estimates of employment? Anyone age sixteen or older who has

Why studying economics
pays off
Reason #3:

It helps you interpret, evaluate, and react to changes in the world around you in such areas as government spending, international trade, and market fluctuations.

The construction industry is subject to seasonal unemployment.

worked at least one hour as a paid employee in the previous month is considered *employed*. So too are individuals age sixteen or older who have worked at least fifteen hours in a family business, paid or not. Individuals on temporary leave are also considered employed.

Individuals who are not employed can fall into one of two categories: *unemployed* or *out of the labor force*. The difference lies in whether the individual is of age, available to work, and actively seeking employment. Those who meet these criteria are unemployed; the rest are out of the workforce. For example, full-time students and homemakers are considered out of the workforce (and therefore not included in unemployment statistics).

The *unemployment rate* is a ratio of those who are unemployed compared to the total *labor force*, not the entire population. To summarize:

total population = labor force + out of labor force
labor force = unemployed + employed
unemployment rate = unemployed / labor force.

There are several difficulties in calculating an accurate unemployment rate. The unemployment rate is overstated to the extent that individuals say they are looking for work, but are not really doing so. At the same time, the unemployment rate is understated to the extent that individuals unable to find work have become discouraged and stopped looking for work altogether. Also, the unemployment rate does not reflect individuals who are *underemployed* (working fewer hours than they are willing and able to), nor the length of time that the average unemployed worker has no job.

It is important to remember that the unemployment rate is an average that crosses all demographic groups, all regions, and all industries. Each subcategory may have an unemployment rate drastically different from the average.

For example, the unemployment rate for individuals age sixteen to nineteen is typically two to three times higher than the overall unemployment rate. (See the table "Unemployment rate" on page 248.)

Causes of unemployment. Economists generally classify unemployment into four categories, based on cause:

1. *Seasonal unemployment* covers those individuals whose jobs require that they work only part of the year. Seasonal unemployment examples include construction work (less activity during bad weather months) and various retail services (stores that focus only on holiday trade).

2. *Frictional unemployment* applies to individuals who are entering the job market for the first time or switching jobs. It is short term (a few weeks), and is considered part of the normal employment process. Generally seen as a positive factor because it reflects freedom of choice in the labor market, frictional unemployment allows time to match a worker's skills to the job, and varies in length due to the availability of information and the mobility of the labor force. The rate of frictional unemployment is never expected to reach zero.

3. *Structural unemployment* is like frictional unemployment in that it also involves matching workers' skills to available jobs. However, structural unemployment is long term, and typically reflects technological changes that make an existing group of workers' skills in a specific industry obsolete. For example, structural unemployment includes individuals whose manufacturing skills are not easy to transfer into newer service industries. Structural unemployment is considered natural in a growing economy.

4. *Cyclical unemployment* is the type of unemployment associated with economic downturns (recessions and depressions). In times of cyclical unemployment, there are many layoffs and few job vacancies across *all* industries.

Unemployment rate (percent)

Year	All workers*	Civilian workers	Males 20 years and over	Females 20 years and over	Males and females 16-19 years	Whites	Blacks and others
1986	6.9	7.0	6.1	6.2	18.3	6.0	13.1
1987	6.1	6.2	5.4	5.4	16.9	5.3	11.6
1988	5.4	5.5	4.8	4.9	15.3	4.7	10.4
1989	5.2	5.3	4.5	4.7	15.0	4.5	10.0
1990	5.4	5.6	5.0	4.9	15.5	4.8	10.1
1991	6.6	6.8	6.4	5.7	18.7	6.1	11.1
1992	7.3	7.5	7.1	6.3	20.1	6.6	12.7
1993	6.7	6.9	6.4	5.9	19.0	6.1	11.7
1994**	N/A	6.1	5.4	5.4	17.6	5.3	10.5
1995	N/A	5.6	4.8	4.9	17.3	4.9	9.6
1996***	N/A	5.6	4.9	4.9	17.3	4.9	9.5

Source: *Economic Report of the President* and *Department of Labor, Bureau of Labor Statistics.* For updated statistics, please consult more recent reports at your library.
*Unemployed as a percent of labor force including resident Armed Forces.   **Data beginning January 1994 are based on the revised Current Population Survey and are not directly comparable with data for earlier periods.   ***First four months.

Economists generally agree that full employment (a zero unemployment rate) is unrealistic. What has developed is the concept of a *natural rate* of unemployment: the rate of unemployment considered normal within a working economy. The natural rate of unemployment can be roughly equated to the sum of the frictional and structural employment rates. The natural rate of unemployment is not a fixed number. It will change whenever there are changes in the size and composition of the workforce, the availability of employment information, and labor mobility.

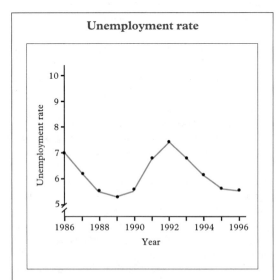

Unemployment rate

This graph reflects 1986-1996 U.S. unemployment statistics in the table above.

Effects of unemployment. Unemployment has a number of negative effects on both society and the individual.

From society's perspective, unemployment means loss of output. Every unemployed individual is someone who is willing and able to work, someone capable of producing output.

When such individuals are unemployed, their output is never produced. What's more, the individual is not the only underutilized resource. So too are the supplies and equipment that now sit idle, producing nothing. In addition, we must take into account the resources that society must divert to provide income for the unemployed.

Unemployment reflects resources that are not contributing to the nation's total output. The lost output is never recovered.

From the individual's perspective, unemployment can be devastating. First, there is the loss of income. Not only are unemployed workers no longer producing, neither are they consuming (or at least not as much). Their unemployment leads to reduced aggregate demand.

Depending on the type and length of unemployment, the individual may also lose valuable job skills. So even when the worker finds a new job, he or she is not as productive as before. The individual loses in terms of income and self-esteem, and society loses in terms of lost productivity.

Economists do not try to quantify the demoralizing effect that unemployment has on workers. However, economists do study the relationship between severe and prolonged unemployment on a host of social problems, including violence, crime, and poverty.

Government fiscal policies.

One of the biggest areas of controversy in macroeconomics deals with the government's role in the economy. Economists who subscribe to Keynesian theories generally believe that government should play a major role by trying to smooth out the fluctuations in the economy. Their opponents claim that government actions are incapable of stabilizing the economy, and that such actions tend to overcompensate and just make matters worse.

Regardless of which view you take, you cannot argue with the fact that government is one of the key players in the economy. So our first step must be to see how government relates to the two players previously defined: consumers and producers. For this we return to the microeconomic circular flow diagram. (See the revised circular flow diagram below.)

We can see that in one sense, government acts very much like a consumer by purchasing goods and services from producers. Government also acts very much like a producer, paying wages and interest to employees and bondholders. These purchases, wages, and interest payments account for most of the expenses in the government budget.

In exchange for the goods and services it provides to the public, government also receives income *from* consumers and producers. These receipts—primarily in the form of taxes (income taxes, property taxes, sales taxes)—account for most of the income in the government budget.

Another factor in the government budget is the sum of *transfer payments* made to individuals who do *not* provide goods or services in exchange. Except for Social Security benefits, most transfer payments, including Aid to Families with Dependent Children and unemployment compensation, are made to redistribute income to people who have little other income. Some economists subtract transfer payments from total tax revenues and use an adjusted income figure called *net taxes*.

How the government controls its budget—how it taxes and spends—is called *fiscal policy*. One word of caution, however. While government can set individual tax rates and control spending decisions, the *total amount* of government income and expenses is *not* set by the government. On the expense side, for example, the total of transfer payments is as much a factor of the country's economic health as it is a government decision. If there is high unemployment, unemployment benefits will rise. Similarly, while government sets tax rates, it does not set income or property values. These are influenced more by the state of economy in terms of wages, employment, and the inflation rate.

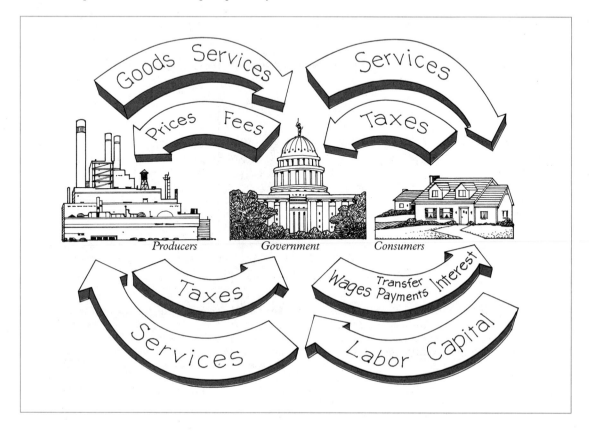

Producers Government Consumers

Expansionary fiscal policy. If the economy is experiencing high unemployment, government may attempt to increase (expand) aggregate demand in one of two ways: increasing government spending or decreasing taxes (or some combination of the two).

In the first case—an increase in government purchases—the actual effect on demand will be much more than the dollar amount of increased government spending. This is because the increase not only translates dollar-for-dollar into higher output, but also generates higher employment and higher incomes. This, in turn, leads to more consumer spending and firm investment. The fact that *multiple* spending increases result from a single increase in planned government expenditure is called the *multiplier effect.*

A decrease in taxes will also result in increased aggregate demand, but not to the same degree as the increase in government spending. This is because the effect on aggregate demand is indirect. While a tax cut increases consumer and firm income, GNP is not affected until that income is spent. Any portion of the tax cut that is saved rather than spent will reduce the overall effect on aggregate demand.

Contractionary fiscal policy. If the economy is experiencing high inflation, government may attempt to decrease (contract) aggregate demand or increase aggregate supply.

As might be expected, a decrease in aggregate demand can be accomplished by taking measures opposite those used to increase it. For example, government may choose to decrease its spending or increase taxes. Once again, the multiplier effect applies, so spending cuts have a greater impact than tax increases.

In the 1970s, a relatively new theory of *supply-side policies* emerged, proposed by economists suggesting that inflation could be curtailed by stimulating production rather than reducing demand. Supply-side policies involve *tax cuts*, not with the aim of increasing aggregate demand but, rather, increasing aggregate supply. The theory is that if consumers and businesses keep a greater percentage of their income, they will be more inclined to work, save, and invest. This will lead to increased aggregate supply, higher employment, and lower inflation.

The federal deficit and federal debt. In any year that government spends more than it receives, the result is a *budget deficit.* Alternately, if government receives more than it spends, the result is a *budget surplus.* Since 1970, the U.S. government has always experienced a budget deficit.

Government must borrow money to finance its deficits. It does this by selling government securities to the public, using the money received to pay off current bills, and promising to repay both principal and interest at some future date. The cumulative amount of money owed by the government at any point is called

Federal deficit and debt

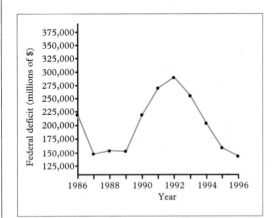

A federal deficit results when the government spends more than it receives in a particular time period. The deficit is not a cumulative figure. This graph shows 1986-1996* federal deficit figures.

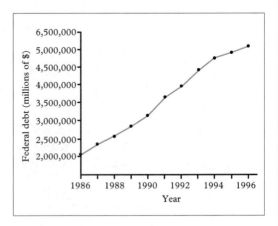

The federal debt is the total amount owed to corporations, banks, foreign lenders, and other government bondholders by the government at any point in time. Large federal deficits have resulted in a sharp rise in the federal debt, as shown in these 1986-1996* statistics.

Source: Graph statistics shown here are from the *Economic Report of the President* and *Department of the Treasury and Office of Management and Budget.* For updated statistics, please consult more recent reports at your library. *1996 data are estimated.

the *federal debt*. Each federal deficit adds to the federal debt.

In 1985, the U.S. Congress passed the Gramm-Rudman-Hollings bill, which required that the federal deficit be reduced by a specified amount annually until a zero deficit was achieved. Any federal budget submitted whose deficit exceeded the target amount would be subject to automatic spending cuts. Portions of the Gramm-Rudman-Hollings bill have subsequently been declared unconstitutional.

Rather than focus on the total value of the federal deficit or federal debt, many economists analyze the *changes* in these variables to measure and evaluate the impact of fiscal policies.

Government monetary policies.

Government can also affect aggregate demand by altering the money supply and interest rates. *Monetary policies* are the tools used by government to do this.

The money supply. To begin to define money, let us first describe the four roles that money serves.

1. *Medium of exchange.* The primary role of money is to enable exchange of goods and services. Therefore, to be considered money, an item must be widely accepted in trade. The alternative to money as a medium of exchange is the *barter* system, where goods and services are exchanged directly for one another.

2. *Unit of account.* Money provides a way to mean- ingfully measure, compare, and add together different types of goods and services.

3. *Store of value.* Money provides a convenient way to hold value for future exchange; it's easier to store than lumber, yogurt, socks, or spaghetti! Because money has a fixed unit value, it is not the best store of value during periods of inflation; in such cases, the real value of money declines. However, during deflationary periods, money increases in real value.

4. *Standard for deferred payment.* Money provides a standard means for identifying the amount of a future payment. For example, if I loan you money today, I can get an I.O.U. for a specific future dollar amount.

Note that money is not the same as income. Neither does money need any intrinsic value. All that is important is that it is a practical (or portable) and acceptable medium of exchange for all parties.

In the United States, there are several different measures of money. The two most common measures are *transactions money* or *M1*, and *broad money* or *M2*.

The main factor for determining what is and isn't money within these different measures is *liquidity*. A liquid asset is one that can be used and accepted *immediately* as a medium of exchange. Currency (both coins and dollar bills) is the most liquid asset of all.

M1 includes currency held outside of banks, as well as checking accounts, traveler's checks, and other checkable deposits. (Checkable deposits are any deposits at a bank or other financial institution on

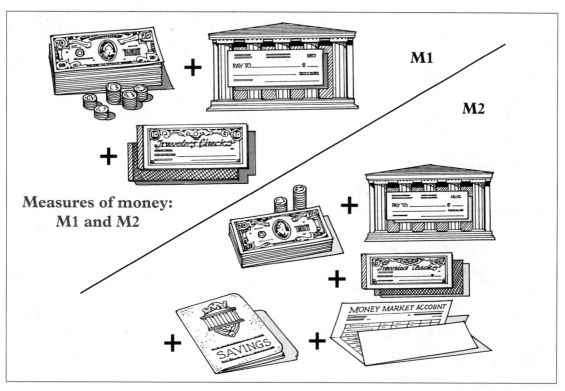

Measures of money:
M1 and M2

M1

M2

which a check can be drawn.) M1 is the most widely used measure of the money supply.

M2 includes everything in M1 *plus* several close substitutes for transactions money: savings accounts and money market accounts. While neither of these two new categories is immediately accepted as a medium of exchange, each is easy to convert into M1.

One reason some economists use M2 instead of M1 is that it is typically a more stable measure than M1. This is because M2 is not affected by transfers between savings accounts and checking accounts or currency.

Interest rates. While M1 or M2 measures the quantity of money, interest rates reflect the opportunity cost of holding currency. The relationship between the quantity demanded of money and the interest rate is inverse. For example, when interest rates rise, there is now more incentive for consumers and firms to save their dollars, removing them from the liquid money supply. Thus, when interest rates rise, the quantity demanded of money still in circulation falls.

The Federal Reserve. In the United States, the money supply is controlled by the *Federal Reserve*. Founded in 1913, the Federal Reserve is the nation's central bank or "banker's bank." It regulates and supervises commercial banks, lends them money, acts as their clearinghouse, and assists banks in serious financial difficulty.

The Federal Reserve system is divided into twelve geographic districts, each served by a Federal Reserve Bank and subsidiary branch offices. All are governed by a seven-person Board of Governors. The chairperson of the board is appointed by the President for four years.

The Federal Reserve controls monetary policy through the *Federal Open Market Committee* (FOMC). This committee sets goals for the money supply, interest rates, and government securities bought and sold. The FOMC includes the Board of Governors, the president of the New York Federal Reserve Bank, and four of the eleven other Federal Reserve Bank presidents. (The latter serve on the FOMC on a rotating basis.)

The Federal Reserve banks are owned by the member banks in their districts; they are not government agencies. Neither is the Federal Reserve the same as the *U.S. Treasury*. The Treasury is a government agency that collects federal taxes and pays federal bills. When the government must borrow money, it is the Treasury that issues government securities. By contrast, the Federal Reserve is only an *agent* of the Treasury that can buy and sell existing securities; it cannot create new ones.

The Federal Reserve Bank has three methods of controlling the money supply: changing reserve requirements, changing the discount rate, and trading government securities on the open market.

Bricks of currency

Federal Reserve districts

District	Headquarters
1	Boston
2	New York
3	Philadelphia
4	Cleveland
5	Richmond
6	Atlanta
7	Chicago
8	St. Louis
9	Minneapolis
10	Kansas City
11	Dallas
12	San Francisco

Changing reserve requirements. All banks are required to hold, with the Federal Reserve, a percentage of the total value of their deposits. (Deposits are what the banks "owe" their customers, such as savings and checking accounts.) This percentage is called the *reserve requirement.*

For example, if the reserve requirement is 10 percent, a bank with reserves of $100,000 is allowed to have up to one million dollars in deposits (10 percent of $1,000,000 is $100,000). Any additional dollars held in reserves are called *excess reserves.* These can be used to cover additional deposits, as long as the 1:10 ratio (in this example) is not violated.

The maximum amount of deposits which can be supported by a given value of reserves can be found with this equation:

$$\text{total deposits} = \frac{\text{total reserves}}{\text{reserve requirement}}.$$

What happens when a bank is able to expand deposits? Banks lend the money out, simply creating a new demand deposit for each new borrower. Because there are now more dollars in circulation than before, the money supply increases.

A reduction in the reserve requirement leads to banks having more dollars in excess reserves. This means they can make more loans, increasing the money supply. *Thus, there is an inverse relationship between reserve requirements and money supply.* When reserve requirements fall, money supply rises. And when reserve requirements rise, money supply falls.

Changing the reserve requirement is very serious, due to its immediate impact upon every bank in the country. As a result, this tool is rarely used to control the money supply.

Changing the discount rate. Another tool the Federal Reserve has for affecting the money supply is the *discount rate*—the interest rate banks pay to borrow money from the Federal Reserve.

Consider what happens to the money supply when a bank borrows. Adding the loan proceeds to its reserves, the bank can now make new loans of its own. For example, if the bank borrows $10,000 from the Federal Reserve and the reserve requirement is 20 percent, up to $50,000 in new deposits are now possible. (Remember, additional deposits can be calculated by dividing the reserve requirement into the reserve value. So, 10,000/0.2 = 50,000.) The money supply increases.

There is an inverse relationship between discount rate and money supply. When the Federal Reserve lowers the discount rate, it expects that banks will borrow more. More borrowing leads to more excess reserves, more new loans, and more money.

Changing the discount rate does not have as direct an impact on the money supply as changing the reserve requirement. Banks don't *have* to borrow just because the Federal Reserve lowers the discount rate. Likewise, raising the discount rate doesn't prevent banks from borrowing. A lot depends on banks' current level of reserves, as well as the interest rates available on investments.

While changes in the discount rate may not have a great effect on money supply, they can provide a signal

Federal Reserve Board, Washington, D. C.

for the direction of future monetary policy. Typically, the Federal Reserve changes the discount rate to keep it consistent with other market interest rates.

Trading in the securities market. The tool most often used by the Federal Reserve to control the money supply is *open market trading* of government securities.

What happens when the Federal Reserve sells securities? First, the individual or organization that buys the security must pay for it, typically by writing a check on some type of bank demand deposit. That reduces the supply of money.

But the effect doesn't stop there. This is because the Federal Reserve deducts the amount of the sale directly from the reserves of the bank where the purchaser maintains a checking account. Assuming the bank had no excess reserves, it must now call in loans (or avoid making new ones) to reduce deposits and bring them in line with the new, lower reserve level. So a sale in securities actually reduces the money supply by a multiple equal to 1 divided by the reserve requirement.

A similar type of process occurs when the Federal Reserve purchases government securities from the public; only this time it's in reverse. The check that the Federal Reserve writes to purchase the security is deposited in the seller's bank account, increasing the money supply. The Federal Reserve adjusts the bank's reserves, so now the bank has excess reserves to cover new loans. So a purchase of securities increases the money supply by a multiple equal to 1 divided by the reserve requirement.

When the Federal Reserve buys government securities from the public, it is actually creating money. (No, it isn't printing new bills; that's the Treasury's job!) The Federal Reserve simply notifies the seller's bank that its reserve account has been increased. The "new" money is instantly available.

There are several reasons why the Federal Reserve uses open market trading as its primary monetary tool. Because the Federal Reserve can decide exactly how much it wants to buy or sell, the effect is very precise and predictable. It is also easy to fine-tune results by switching between purchases and sales, as needed.

International trade. While macroeconomics widened our focus to the economic issues facing an entire nation, one larger perspective is still necessary. That perspective focuses on international trade: how the United States is economically tied to all the nations of the world.

Balance of trade. One measure of the degree of economic interdependency among nations is *balance of trade*. Balance of trade is the value of a country's merchandise exports minus its imports.

Before the 1970s, foreign goods were much less

plentiful in the United States. In those years, the U.S. typically maintained a *trade surplus* by exporting more merchandise than it imported. A trade surplus increases a country's aggregate demand.

Since the 1970s, the United States has consistently imported more than it exports; this is called a *trade deficit*. A trade deficit decreases a country's aggregate demand. The two largest U.S. trading partners are Canada and Japan; the U.S. maintains a trade deficit with both of them. (See the table "Balance of trade" for a summary of recent export and import volume.)

Because countries maintain different monetary systems, some type of currency trade must take place between the time an import or export is produced (and workers are paid in the currency of the producing company) and the item is consumed (and the seller is paid in the currency of the buyer). The *exchange rate* is the price of one nation's currency in terms of another's.

The exchange rate is linked to the balance of trade. When the value of a domestic currency rises in terms of the exchange rate, imports become relatively less expensive, exports relatively more expensive.

As one example, consider an imaginary exchange rate of $1 = 1 Mexican peso. Any import priced at 1 peso costs $1 to the U.S. consumer. If the exchange rate changes to $1 = 2 pesos, that same import (if still priced at 1 peso), now only costs $0.50 in U.S. currency. We can predict that U.S. consumers' demand for Mexican imports will rise.

For the same reason, when the value of a domestic currency falls, imports become relatively more expensive (that is, it takes more domestic currency to buy an item than it did before), while exports become relatively less expensive to foreign consumers.

Absolute and comparative advantage. What is it that causes different countries to trade with one another? The answer has to do with how efficiently each country can produce the items it needs.

A country has an *absolute advantage* when it uses fewer resources to produce an item than another country does. A country has a *comparative advantage* when it produces an item at a lower cost *in terms of other goods*. Comparative advantage does not necessarily go to the most efficient producer.

The difference between absolute and comparative advantage can be explored in a simple two-person, two-product "economy" where each person produces (and consumes) loaves of bread and jars of jelly, but at differing rates.

In one workday, here is the amount of product which each person produces:

Pat:	12 jelly	5 bread
Chris:	4 jelly	3 bread

It is clear that Pat has the absolute advantage producing both goods.

Further, let's assume that Pat produces jelly versus bread at a rate of 2:1 (two jars of jelly takes Pat as long as one loaf of bread), while Chris produces jelly versus bread at a rate of 4:1. Pat has the comparative advantage in baking bread because his opportunity cost is much less; he sacrifices only two jars of jelly instead of four. However, while a jar of jelly costs Pat 1/2 a loaf of bread, it costs Chris only 1/4 loaf. Chris has the comparative advantage producing jelly.

Let's see what happens if these two decide to specialize according to their comparative advantages, and then trade for bread and jelly. If Pat specializes in bread, he can now produce eleven loaves. (Not producing twelve jars of jelly gives him time to bake six new loaves, plus his original five. That makes eleven.) Chris, now specializing in jelly, can produce twelve additional jars (remember the 4:1 ratio), for a grand total of sixteen.

Now they trade: twelve jars of jelly for four loaves of bread. The result?

Pat:	12 jelly	7 bread (11– 4)
Chris:	4 jelly (16-12)	4 bread

Considering what they previously produced on their own, specialization and trading benefit *both* individuals. The total output of bread and jelly increases.

In the same way, when countries specialize in producing the goods for which they have the comparative advantage, world resources are allocated most efficiently. The greatest total output is produced.

Balance of trade (merchandise; billions of $)

Item	1987	1988	1989	1990	1991	1992	1993	1994	1995
Exports	250.2	320.2	362.1	389.3	416.9	440.4	456.8	502.5	568.3
Industrial countries	165.6	207.3	234.2	253.8	261.3	265.1	270.6	295.3	334.7
Other countries except									
Eastern Europe	82.3	109.1	122.2	130.6	150.4	169.5	179.8	201.8	228.2
Eastern Europe	2.3	3.8	5.5	4.3	4.8	5.6	6.2	5.3	5.4
International organizations and unallocated	—	0.1	0.2	0.6	0.4	0.1	0.2	0.1	—
Imports	409.8	447.2	477.4	498.3	491.0	536.5	589.4	668.6	751.3
Industrial countries	259.7	283.2	292.5	299.9	294.3	316.3	347.8	389.8	430.0
Other countries except									
Eastern Europe	148.2	161.8	182.8	196.1	194.9	218.2	238.1	272.9	313.9
Eastern Europe	1.9	2.2	2.1	2.3	1.8	2.0	3.5	5.8	7.5
Balance (excess of exports +)	-159.6	-127.0	-115.2	-109.0	-74.1	-96.1	-132.6	-166.1	-183.0
Industrial countries	-75.9	-58.7	-58.3	-46.1	-33.0	-51.2	-77.2	-94.5	-95.3
Canada	-11.6	-10.3	-8.9	-9.6	-7.1	-9.5	-12.2	-16.2	-20.1
Japan	-56.9	-52.6	-49.7	-42.6	-45.0	-50.5	-60.5	-67.3	-64.6
Western Europe	-27.5	-16.2	-4.0	2.2	14.8	3.1	-9.7	-17.6	-18.4
Australia, New Zealand, and South Africa	2.0	3.2	4.2	3.9	4.4	5.8	5.2	6.6	7.8
Other countries except									
Eastern Europe	-65.8	-52.7	-60.6	-65.6	-44.5	-48.7	-58.3	-71.2	-85.7
Eastern Europe	0.3	1.6	3.5	2.1	3.0	3.7	2.7	-0.5	-2.1
International organizations and unallocated	—	0.1	0.2	0.6	0.4	0.1	0.2	0.1	—

Source: *Economic Report of the President*. For updated statistics, please consult more recent reports at your library.

NOTE: Data are on an international transactions basis and exclude military. The former German Democratic Republic (East Germany) included in Western Europe beginning fourth quarter 1990 and in Eastern Europe prior to that time.

Free trade allows access to output beyond an individual country's internal resource constraints. Free trade can move a country out beyond its own production possibilities frontier. All countries benefit from comparative advantage, although not equally.

It should be noted that comparative advantages are not fixed. They will change as each country's productivity changes.

Protection vs. free trade. In the real world, trade among countries is not totally free. Sometimes, trade barriers are established as a form of *protection* for domestic industries. The two most common trade barriers are tariffs and quotas.

A *tariff* is an import tax. The effect is to raise the price of the imported good so that it is less competitive with domestically produced versions. Tariffs translate directly into higher consumer prices and higher government revenues.

A *quota* is a limit on the number of imports allowed into a country. Because quotas limit supply, they generally lead to higher consumer prices. However, unlike tariffs, quotas produce no government revenues.

There are various reasons why protection measures may be established, including:

To counteract unfair trade practices. While the United States has enacted many laws to regulate economic activity, these laws do not restrict international trade partners. For example, antitrust or minimum wage regulations do not extend beyond U.S. borders. Protection measures reduce the "unfair" advantages gained by such foreign competitors.

To protect infant industries. Protection measures may be instituted temporarily to allow a new domestic industry time to establish itself.

The U.S. steel industry has argued for protection because of its role in national defense.

To protect national security. Even if a foreign producer has the comparative advantage in an industry, it may be better to domestically produce items needed for defense. In case of war, the U.S. would not have to rely on foreign producers for such items.

To protect domestic jobs. This is one of the main arguments for protection against foreign competition. Short-term domestic unemployment can be avoided, although higher consumer prices result. Also, protected industries may never gain comparative advantage, and therefore never reflect the most efficient means of production. Protectionism can invite *retaliation* from foreign trading partners in terms of their own tariffs and quotas. The overall result is a decrease in international trade and higher prices paid by consumers in all affected countries.

Tokyo, Japan

Economics

Economics every day

Just because the textbook is tucked away and all the homework is finished, economics doesn't stop being relevant. That's because economics covers a wide range of topics and concepts relating to everyone, from individual consumers to governments worldwide.

For example, you may be grappling with the decision of whether to go directly to college after high school or to begin full-time work instead. Many economic concepts are involved in this decision.

First, you must consider the financial gains of working full time. If you decide to attend college, you will give up the salary you would have earned at the full-time job. That salary represents an opportunity cost of attending college. On the other hand, if you decide to work full time, you would not receive the education that might be needed for a higher-paying job in the future. Those additional future wages represent an opportunity cost of working full time.

There is more to this decision than opportunity costs, however. Again, economic theories can help. For example, you must also consider the utility you gain from each alternative. If you gain no utility—or satisfaction—from attending college, that fact should also influence your decision.

This is just one example of how economics applies to decision making. There are many other examples, from decisions you face regularly (what brand of toothpaste to buy) to those less frequent but very significant decisions (whether to get married).

You can look around your household to see examples of other economic concepts as well. Take the theory of comparative advantage, where different countries specialize so that, overall, more output is produced. This theory also explains why households don't produce everything they consume. Instead, they specialize in producing one or two goods (through members' occupations) and trading for all other goods.

You may find the same principles apply within your household as well. Does one individual do most of the cooking? Take care of the finances? Maintain the yard? Do the laundry?

Rather than each household member doing a portion of all these tasks, your household may find that resources (that is, time) can be allocated most efficiently if each person "specializes" by doing all of a particular task.

Remember, specialization according to comparative advantage doesn't mean that the person (or group) has an absolute advantage in terms of being the best at the task. It simply means that there will be different opportunity costs associated with each producer, so all

can benefit by dividing tasks according to comparative advantage.

Economics also affects everyone indirectly. For example, all of us are affected by macroeconomic decisions made by the government. If the government raises income taxes (perhaps in an effort to reduce inflation), people's net income will decrease. Or if trade restrictions are imposed, the price of imported goods will increase, affecting our consumption. It is hoped that once you take an economics course and have a better understanding of economics concepts, you will be able to interpret and react to such actions—and all the daily news—in a well-informed way.

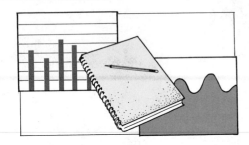

Tests, homework, and projects

Laying the groundwork

One nice thing about economics is that it is all around you. You can't open a newspaper, turn on a television, or even walk down a street without being exposed to situations in which economics plays a role. The key is recognizing and analyzing its effect in all of your reading, notetaking, and studying.

Reading

In just reading the newspaper, you'll find examples of the law of demand, monetary policy, barriers to trade, costs of production, and many other economic concepts. Thinking about which economic concepts are applicable to situations you encounter every day is a major step in being able to apply the appropriate economic tools to the "real world" situations that might be presented on homework problems and exams.

Most economics textbooks are written at an appropriate level for the course. It is very important in an economics class to keep up with the reading on a regular basis.

Notetaking

In taking notes for an economics class, it is important to grasp key ideas rather than every detail. For example, don't try to copy a complex graph that is covered in class if the same graph appears in your textbook. Instead, take notes that help explain the graph, and simply give yourself a page reference for finding it in your textbook.

Perhaps the most important thing to remember is to ask questions if something isn't clear to you. Your notes won't do you any good if you don't really understand what is being discussed.

Studying

In economics classes, there are a few basic concepts that need to be understood, and the bulk of learning economics is knowing how to apply these concepts to economic situations. Memorizing definitions will not be helpful unless you *understand* the definitions as well. You can look over the main headings of this chapter as well as terms in the glossary to get an idea of the basic concepts in economics.

Strategies for success

Most economics professors derive their homework and exam questions from "real world" situations. You can start thinking in economic terms after only a few weeks in an economics class. As you come across various situations, see if you can determine which concepts in your economics class apply.

Tests

To get an idea of what types of questions to expect on homework problems and exams, talk to students who have been in your professor's class before. Many times, professors will make old copies of their exams available to students; ask your professor if this is possible. Also, in large classes, exams are often heavily weighted toward multiple choice questions. In smaller classes, there tend to be more short-answer or essay questions on exams. You can also expect to encounter some basic fill-in and/or definition questions.

Homework

There are some very specific things you can do to get an advantage in tackling homework problems:

- Practice reading graphs whenever you encounter them. Pay attention to what is measured on each axis, and to what the graph itself is showing about the relationship presented.
- Focus on the relationships among various economic concepts: some items can be put on a continuum; others are complete opposites.
- Identify the factors that come into play in various economic decisions, and spend time analyzing how they do so.
- Keep up with the reading assignments in class. Solving homework problems will be easier if you can refer to material you have already read.

Projects

Since economics covers many aspects of everyday life, there are frequent opportunities for the assignment of projects during an economics class. Some projects may be ongoing throughout the term. If there is an opportunity to choose the topic for your project, select one that you find interesting.

Helpful hints

Multiple choice

For multiple choice questions, you will usually be instructed to select the *best* answer among the choices. In some cases, an answer might be partially correct, but only one answer is the best alternative.

You may want to sketch out the different answers to give yourself a visual idea of the various choices. It is also a good idea to eliminate answers as soon as you are sure they are incorrect. Then you can focus on the few choices that remain.

> 1. The demand curve for a perfectly competitive firm is:
> (a) a horizontal line at the equilibrium price of the good
> (b) a vertical line at the equilibrium quantity of the good
> (c) a downward sloping line that intersects the *x*-axis at the equilibrium quantity of the good
> (d) a downward sloping line that intersects the *y*-axis at the equilibrium price of the good

For question 1, use the strategy of making simple sketches for each answer and see which one makes sense.

Sketching answer *a*, you can see that the firm has no influence over price; it is fixed at one point. With answer *b*, the firm can sell only a fixed quantity, but could get any price for it. Answer *c* looks more like a typical demand curve at first, but if it intersects the *x*-axis at the equilibrium quantity of the good, then the price would be zero. The sketch for answer *d* is similar to that for answer *c*, but at the equilibrium price, the firm would sell nothing (quantity=0).
Answer. a

> 2. Which of the following policies by the U.S. Federal Reserve would definitely increase the nation's money supply?
> (a) Selling bonds in the open market and lowering the discount rate
> (b) Buying bonds in the open market and lowering the discount rate
> (c) Selling bonds in the open market and raising the discount rate
> (d) Buying bonds in the open market and raising the discount rate

For question 2, use the strategy of eliminating incorrect answers.

Think about what happens when the Federal Reserve sells bonds on the open market. If you wanted to buy a bond, you'd take money out of your bank account or you'd write a check to buy the bond, which would take money out of the economy and *decrease* the money supply. So answers *a* and *c* can be eliminated.

Next, recall that the discount rate is the rate which the Federal Reserve charges member banks for borrowing. A higher discount rate means that it costs banks more to borrow, and therefore they will have less money available. This would *decrease* the money supply. So, answer *d* can be eliminated.
Answer. b

Fill-in and definition

For fill-in and definition questions, study glossaries, lists of definitions, and tables that are used in class or in your textbook. You're probably better off not memorizing formulas, but rather thinking through the problem intuitively.

Rather than memorizing the words to various definitions, it's often easier to remember an *example* associated with a term. A problem with memorizing definitions is that the items appearing on an exam may not necessarily be the same as those you see in class or in your textbook.

For matching questions, one good approach is to eliminate several answers for each term being defined.

Read questions and answers carefully before responding.

> 1. Fill in the blanks of the following table, which represents GDP figures for a fictitious country.
>
> | Year | Nominal GDP | GDP Deflator | Real GDP |
> | --- | --- | --- | --- |
> | 1990 | 4200 | 96 | ____ |
> | 1992 | 4800 | 100 | ____ |
> | 1994 | 5300 | ____ | 4900 |
> | 1996 | 6000 | ____ | 5000 |
> | 1998 | ____ | 140 | 5110 |
> | 2000 | 7800 | 150 | ____ |
>
> Which year is the base year in this example?____

For question 1, it's important to know the difference between *nominal* and *real*. You can remember this by remembering that real GDP reflects actual output, rather than numbers that are a result of changes in output as well as changes in prices.

Also, if the GDP deflator is greater than one hundred, then real GDP will be lower than nominal GDP. So even if you forget whether to multiply or divide, you can still have an idea of what your answers should look like, even before you do any math.

For example, for 1990, the GDP deflator is less

than 100, so real GDP will be greater than nominal GDP. If you multiply nominal GDP (4200) by the GDP deflator (96) and divide by 100, you get a number less than 4200. So you know that this must not be right, and you divide by 96 and multiply by 100 to get the correct answer. Once you know to divide nominal GDP by the deflator to get real GDP, you can fill in the answers for 1992 and 2000.

Answers.
1990 real GDP = 4375
1992 real GDP = 4800
1994 GDP deflator = 108
1996 GDP deflator = 120
1998 nominal GDP = 7154
2000 real GDP = 5200
Base year is 1992.

2. Match the terms with their definitions.
Terms:
  1. Monopoly
  2. Production possibilities frontier
  3. Inflation
  4. Marginal utility
  5. Gross national product (GNP)
Definitions:
  (a) The total satisfaction gained when an additional unit of a product is consumed
  (b) An increase in the average price level in an economy
  (c) An industry that has only one producer
  (d) An industry that has several firms producing a single identical product
  (e) The quantity of a product that a firm can produce given its capacity
  (f) The additional satisfaction gained from consuming one more unit of a good
  (g) The value of all final goods and services produced by a country in one year
  (h) The various combinations of goods and services that an economy can produce with its available resources

For question 2, you can eliminate several answers for each term even if you don't know exact definitions. For example, *utility* refers to satisfaction gotten by consuming goods; *marginal* means additional. Answer *a* might look right for the definition of marginal utility, but if you read carefully, you'll see that it is not correct, and *f* is a better answer.

To find the definition of monopoly, think of an example of a monopolistic industry. Think about what the characteristics of that type of industry are, and see which definition fits best.

Answers. 1-c; 2-h; 3-b; 4-f; 5-g

Essay

Industries often fight against regulation by the government. When regulation is being considered, the industry to be regulated urges the public to lobby against regulation, saying it will hurt customers. On the other hand, consumer groups often support regulation of certain industries, saying that consumers will be better off if the industry is regulated.

Using cable television as an example, explain the effects of government regulation and indicate whether the effects benefit consumers, the industry, both, or neither.

In answering this essay question, a good strategy is to work from the general to the specific. Talk about regulation in general and its effects on industries and consumers. Then discuss the specific example of the cable television industry and what might happen to prices, quantity demanded, and supply. It is more important to demonstrate your understanding of the concept of regulation rather than the intricacies of cable television.

For essay questions in general, there is almost always the opportunity for partial credit even if you don't answer the question completely, or if your answer isn't all correct. Therefore, it is important to answer as much of a question as you can.

Essay questions are much more difficult to grade than other types of questions. Therefore, unless your class is very small, you probably won't see a lot of essay questions on exams.

Sometimes, essay questions are combined with true/false questions by giving instructions, such as: "Indicate whether the following statements are true or false, and explain why." Even in this type of question, if you get the true/false part wrong, but you have correct statements in your explanation, you could get partial credit. So, once again, answer as much of the question as you can, even if you don't feel you know much about it.

Use essay questions as an opportunity to show what you know about the economic topics covered. Pick out subjects and terms in the question that you know, for example, and write about those. Partial credit may result.

Graphs are common in economics, providing a good basis for essay questions on exams. Therefore, it is a good idea to become very comfortable reading and interpreting graphs.

In answering essay questions, be as neat as possible. Even the most brilliant answer won't count for much if the instructor can barely read it.

Projects

Choose a product that is sold locally, and get information on quantity sold and price charged for that product on a weekly basis throughout the term. See if you can determine the factors that influence demand and quantity demanded for that product. If possible, try to determine elasticity of demand for that product.

Projects in economics classes can be among the most interesting assignments you encounter in any of your classes.

Often, you are able to select a topic. Choose one that you are interested in even if you think other topics might require less work.

Don't wait too long before getting started on a project. Also, if a project is ongoing through a term, be sure to keep up with it. If you need to collect information weekly, or if you need to look something up in the newspaper every day, make sure to do so.

Keep in touch with your instructor throughout the course of a project. Even if regular meetings are not scheduled, check in once in a while to make sure you are on the right track with your project.

Keep the topic of your project as specific as possible. For the project listed above, for example, you might select as the product a large, deep-dish pepperoni pizza at your local pizza parlor.

When you write up the results of your project, be sure to summarize the data that you collected and how you collected it. Carefully explain how you reached your conclusions. Although the content of reports on different topics will vary, most reports should include background information, a section on data collection, a discussion of your findings, and conclusions that you can draw from the project.

Be sure to keep careful and complete records throughout your project. This is useful if you need to verify any of your findings, or if you want to expand your project later.

Other suggested topics

1. Set up an interview with the manager of the local cable television company for your community. Talk to him or her about how rates are determined. If there are other cable TV companies close by, see if their rates are the same for the same services. Talk to some people who subscribe to cable TV and see if they are satisfied with the service and price. Talk to people who do not subscribe to cable TV and ask them why they do not subscribe. Write up what you find, paying attention to factors that influence pricing decisions as well as factors influencing demand for cable TV.

2. Go to a few different banks around your community. Speak with the managers, and ask them how their banks react to monetary policy decisions made by the Federal Reserve.

3. Keep track of your own expenses throughout the term. If possible, keep track of the expenses of some other family members and friends. Compare each person's spending patterns with the composition of the "basket of goods" used to determine the Consumer Price Index. Based on the spending patterns, see how "typical" each person is, given that the CPI is supposed to be representative of spending patterns in general.

4. Track the exchange rate between the United States and any other country for the past thirty years. Based on historical events that took place in both countries, how have these events influenced exchange rates?

5. Look up the budget deficit for the United States over the past fifty years. Is there any noticeable pattern for the deficit in terms of the political party of the President? What other factors influence the budget deficit?

6. Explain what economic factors played a role in the savings-and-loan crisis of the late 1980s and early 1990s.

7. Look up the gross domestic product for a country other than the United States, and draw a graph of its GDP for the past ten years. Compare this graph with a graph of U.S. GDP for the past ten years. Try to determine what factors have influenced each country's GDP over the years in question.

8. Find out and explain how your state or local government budget is determined, and how changes in the budget affect you.

9. Select a product that is subsidized by the government. Explain how the government subsidy has affected supply and equilibrium price for that product.

10. Find a local restaurant that offers regular specials, such as 25-cent soft drinks on Monday evenings. See if you can get information on food sales on a daily basis. Study how the special price affects food sales. Is the product on special a complementary or a substitute good with food? Is there seasonal variation in sales?

11. Interview people on both sides of the debate regarding legalization of a currently illegal drug. Based on your interviews, summarize the economic implications of legalizing the drug. Also discuss social implications, and then suggest a way to resolve the debate. In your conclusions, present an argument on one side of the issue—either for or against legalization.

Glossary

Model

Oligopoly

Revenue

Substitute goods

absolute advantage. The ability to use fewer resources to produce an item.

aggregate demand. A country's demand for all goods and services; equals the total of planned expenditures by firms, households, and government.

aggregate supply. The total of goods and services provided by all of a country's producers.

balance of trade. The value of a country's merchandise exports minus its imports.

budget deficit. The amount by which government spending exceeds receipts in any year.

budget surplus. The amount by which government receipts exceed spending in any year.

capital. Supplies and equipment used by producers to create new goods and services.

ceteris paribus. Latin phrase meaning "all else equal"; the assumption that all factors, other than the one being observed, remain unchanged.

command economy. An economy where all production and distribution decisions are made by a central authority.

comparative advantage. The ability to produce an item at lower cost in terms of other goods or services sacrificed.

complementary goods. Items consumed in conjunction with one another.

Consumer Price Index (CPI). The most commonly used U.S. price index; measures the average price change in a consumer's representative "market basket" of monthly purchases.

deficit. See *budget deficit* or *trade deficit*.

demand. The relationship between the price of a product and amount consumed.

demand curve. A line that reflects all the combinations of price and quantity demanded for a product.

demand schedule. See *demand curve*.

discount rate. The interest rate banks pay to borrow money from the Federal Reserve.

economies of scale. The result when a producer can lower average costs by increasing scale of production; opposite of *diseconomies of scale*.

elasticity. A measure of the sensitivity of one variable to another; *price elasticity of demand* measures how sensitive quantity demanded is to changes in price.

equilibrium. The point at which there are no market forces prompting price or quantity to change.

excess demand. See *shortage*.

excess reserves. Dollars held with the Federal Reserve that exceed required reserves; excess reserves enable banks to expand deposits.

excess supply. See *surplus*.

exchange rate. The price of one nation's currency in terms of another's.

federal debt. The cumulative amount of money owed by the government at any point in time.

Federal Reserve. The central bank of the United States.

fiscal policy. Government program of taxing and spending.

fixed costs. Short-run costs that do not change with output rate.

GDP deflator. A price index that converts GDP in current dollars to base year dollars.

gross domestic product (GDP). Value of output produced annually within a country's borders.

gross national product (GNP). Value of output produced annually by a country's domestically owned producers.

income. An ongoing stream of earnings by time period.

inflation. An increase in the overall price level.

laissez-faire economy. An economy that has minimal or no government intervention; consumer and producer behavior are self-regulated.

macroeconomics. The study of aggregate economic issues, such as trends in national output, employment rates, and overall price levels.

marginal cost. The additional cost of producing one more unit of output.

marginal product. The additional output associated with one more unit of input.

marginal revenue. The additional revenue a firm generates by increasing output by one more unit.

marginal utility. The extra satisfaction an individual gets from consuming one more unit of a good or service.

microeconomics. The study of individual economic decisions and behavior.

model. A simplified view of reality.

monetary policy. Government program for determining money supply and interest rates.

monopolistic competition. A model of a market where many firms compete for the same consumer market, and there are slight distinctions between products.

monopoly. A model of a market where only one firm (or a group of firms acting together) supplies a good or service; there are no close product substitutes.

nominal GDP. GDP measured in the current year's dollars.

oligopoly. A model of a market where a few large firms dominate the product market.

opportunity cost. The cost of an action in terms of what must be given up to pursue that action.

perfect competition. A model of a market where no firm controls or significantly impacts the market; suppliers' products are homogeneous.

production possibilities frontier. A curve on a graph showing all the possible combinations of goods and services that can be produced in an economy.

profit. The difference between revenue and cost.

quantity demanded. The amount of a product that a consumer would buy in a given period at a particular price.

quantity supplied. The amount of a product that a firm would produce in a given period at a particular price.

quota (import). A limit on the number of imports allowed into a country.

real GDP. GDP measured in the base year's dollars.

reserve requirement. A percentage of a bank's total deposits that must be held with the Federal Reserve.

revenue. The dollar amount a firm receives from selling its product or service.

shortage. The condition where quantity demanded exceeds quantity supplied; also called *excess demand.*

slope. A measure of the relationship between the two variables represented by a line on a graph; the change in the variable on the vertical axis when the variable on the horizontal axis changes by one unit.

substitute goods. Items that consumers might reasonably use as alternatives.

supply. The relationship between price of a product and amount produced.

supply curve. A line that reflects all the combinations of price and quantity supplied for a product.

supply schedule. See *supply curve.*

surplus. The condition where quantity supplied exceeds quantity demanded; also called *excess supply.* See also *budget surplus* and *trade surplus.*

tariff. An import tax.

trade deficit. The condition where a country imports more than it exports.

trade surplus. The condition where a country exports more than it imports.

underemployed. Individuals working fewer hours than they are willing and able to.

unemployed. Individuals who are willing and able to work but cannot find jobs.

unemployment rate. The percentage of the labor force that is unemployed.

utility. The satisfaction gained from consuming a product.

variable costs. Costs of production that vary with output rate.

wealth. A measure of the current stock of net assets at a particular point in time.

For further reading

Friedman, Milton and Rose. *Free to Choose: A Personal Statement.* New York: Harcourt, Brace, Jovanovich, 1979.

Gilder, George. *Wealth and Poverty.* New York: Basic Books, Inc., 1981.

Heilbroner, Robert L. *The Worldly Philosophers: The Lives, Times, and Ideas of the Great Economic Thinkers.* New York: Simon and Schuster, 1953.

Kennedy, Charles R., Jr. *Managing the International Business Environment: Cases in Political and Country Risk.* Englewood Cliffs, N.J.: Prentice Hall, 1991.

Krugman, Paul. *The Age of Diminished Expectations: U.S. Economic Policy in the 1990s.* Cambridge, Mass.: The MIT Press, 1992.

North, Douglass C., and Roger LeRoy Miller. *The Economics of Public Issues.* 10th ed. New York: Harper and Row, 1996.

Smith, Adam. *The Money Game.* New York: Vintage Books, 1976.

History of Western Civilization

- The ancient world
- Medieval Europe
- Early modern Europe
- Modern Europe

History of Western Civilization

We study history in order to know who we are. History is like a genealogical tree or a chemical flow chart, showing how we developed, which dreams succeeded and which failed, and how exactly we arrived at the present. To know these things requires study and thought. It can even be fun.

For Americans, the study of Western civilization has special significance. Whether we are Anglo-Americans, African-Americans, Hispanic-Americans, Native Americans, or Asian-Americans, much of our culture is based on the heritage of Western civilization: our legal and governmental system, our educational system, even the way we think, communicate, and compute. The history of Western civilization is therefore more than simply a chronicle of faraway places and long-ago events; for us, it is an important way of learning to understand ourselves.

The ancient world

Mesopotamia. Two parallel rivers, the Tigris and Euphrates, run from near the Black Sea into the Persian Gulf. About 3500 B.C. cities developed in the potentially fertile area between the rivers, in the southern region where the land is hostile but most easily irrigated. This region, now part of modern Iraq, was called Mesopotamia. The Mesopotamians were dominant between 3500 and 2400 B.C. Irrigation and flood control made the area fertile, but the development of this civilization depended on the cooperation of its fiercely independent cities in the maintenance of the flood control canals.

The remains of Mesopotamian cities have been excavated in this century. The buildings were made of clay, the predominant building material in that region, and could wash away with heavy rains. Many of the ruins that have been found are temples. This is not surprising, as priests gave social direction and cohesion to societies in this region.

Mesopotamians were *polytheists*, believing in hun-

Babylonian King Hammurabi, creator of the first law code

dreds of gods. Their major gods were thought to control the unpredictable workings of nature. The deities were generally more feared than loved, hence the

266   **History of Western Civilization**

important role of the priests and temples in Mesopotamian society. Their gods were very human-like (*anthropomorphic*), were disliked, and were jealous of each other's power. The gods of heaven (An) and water (Enki) were most important and often trifled with mortals. Mesopotamians did not believe there was an afterlife. Believing in an afterlife may have required more permanence than could be found in the clay-based Mesopotamian world.

Original Mesopotamian writing took the form of *pictographs* on clay tablets, but after centuries, picture-writing evolved into wedge-shaped marks (*cuneiform*) used to express thoughts and sentiments. Only professional scribes could write these difficult "letters" in Mesopotamian societies.

Between the years 2400 and 1200 B.C., the peoples of Mesopotamia developed mathematics and an astronomical science that also were recorded in cuneiform. For counting, multiplying, and dividing, they used a base-sixty (*sexagesimal*) system. This system was the basis for a naked-eye astronomical science that plotted positions of planets within five-degree margins of error, a margin accounted for by the precession of the equinoxes, which was not known until the seventeenth century.

Egypt. Egypt was divided into two areas: upper Egypt, the river valley to the south; and lower Egypt, the silt-rich delta extending from the coast about fifty

The Great Sphinx

miles inward from the Mediterranean. The Nile, the only source of water in Egypt, originates in central Africa and runs northward to the Mediterranean coast. While the Tigris and Euphrates provided parallel but wild sources for irrigating southern Mesopotamia, the yearly, clocklike flooding of the Nile provided a natural irrigation that made Egypt's desert fertile with the Nile's silt. Since all aspects of life depend on the river, it is not surprising that cities grew up along the Nile. In addition, the Nile's predictability increased the power of the pharaohs, who ruled from Memphis on the Nile, which was the capital of Egypt from about 3100 to 2200 B.C.

Some key events and people: 3000 B.C.–A.D. 500

3000 B.C.
  Earliest civilization in Mesopotamia and Egypt
  Invention of writing
  Beginning of spread of Indo-European peoples
2500
  Mathematical science begins
  Medical science begins
2000
  Babylonian kingdom
  Stonehenge (England)
1500
  Moses and the Hebrew Covenant
1000
  Hebrew kingdoms (1000–600)
800
  Greek city-states founded
  Rome founded
400
  Philip of Macedon
  Alexander the Great
300
  Hellenistic kingdoms
  Punic Wars (Rome against Carthage)

100 B.C.
  Civil wars in Italy
  Julius Caesar's conquest of Gaul
  Overthrow of the Roman Republic
  Augustus and the foundations of the Roman Empire
  Pax Romana (27 B.C.–A.D.180)
  Birth of Christ
A.D. 100
  Tiberius
  Nero
  Trajan
  Hadrian
200
  Attacks on Rome by Germanic tribal confederacies
  Diocletian: Reconstruction of the Roman Empire
300
  Constantine I (the Great)
  Constantinople founded
  Council of Nicaea
400
  Germanic takeover of the Western Roman Empire

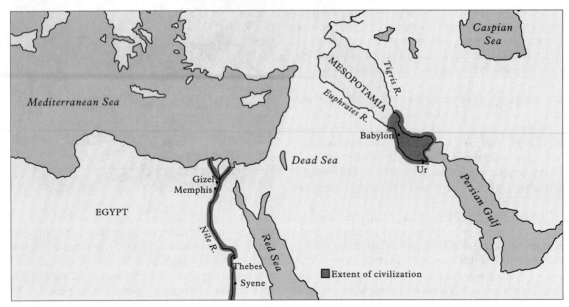

The religious views of Egypt were also primarily the result of the Nile. While the stormy rivers of Mesopotamia fostered belief in capricious gods and no afterlife, the Nile's predictable floods led to belief in eternal life and in generally beneficent gods, at first portrayed as animals and later, as in the case of the Great Sphinx, as half man, half animal. Osiris was the god before whom people were judged and by whom the soul (*ka*) would be sent to eternity in a paradisiacal garden or into the jaws of a crocodile-monster.

The Hebrews and monotheism.

The Mesopotamians, Egyptians, and other ancient peoples such as the Assyrians and Hittites were polytheists. Only the ancient Hebrews, who originally came from Mesopotamia, became monotheists, or believers in one God.

Their sacred books and histories (now called the Old Testament) show that they had refined their concept of monotheism by the time of Moses. They believed their God, Yahweh, had established a special covenant with them, which consisted of the Ten Commandments and the other laws of their religion. They believed that if they obeyed all of these laws, Yahweh would deliver them from their enemies and secure them in their own kingdom.

Although they were a power of considerable importance by the time of King David (c. 1000 B.C.), they eventually lost their position of power to neighboring states. The Hebrews looked forward to a *messiah*, a religious leader and king who would finally deliver them from their enemies and establish their kingdom forever.

Significance. Mesopotamian civilization contributed the idea of law to the Western tradition. The revenge-limiting Code of Hammurabi ("An eye for an eye, a tooth for a tooth") created the idea of comparable value before the law for social equals. This ancient culture also contributed an important astronomical science, whose calculations for the positions of the then-known five planets were as accurate as any for years to come. Finally, the god Marduk, protector god of the city of Babylon, came to be called the creator Ba'al and was the forerunner of Jewish monotheism.

Egyptian mathematics and science were less well developed than their Mesopotamian counterparts. However, the Egyptian idea of the god-king influenced later civilizations, particularly Rome during the imperial period. Egyptian sculpture, painting, and architecture portrayed a stable society and were models throughout the ancient world. Egyptian religion was optimistic and helped create the salvational religions of the Hellenistic world.

Influence of the Hebrews on Western civilization has been substantial, not so much for the breadth of its legacy, as in the case of Mesopotamia and Egypt, but for its depth and impact. The Hebrews' theology and ethics, passed down to us in the form of modern Judaism and Christianity, continue to exert a strong influence on millions of people today.

The Greek world.

The city-state was the basic political unit of Greece. The concept of the city-state originated in Mesopotamia, but Greek city-states were unique. Each circled a protecting hill, was independent in politics and economics, and had its own

The Parthenon, located on the Acropolis in Athens

protecting deity (such as Athena for Athens). The citizens valued their state's independence; they jealously fought each other (as in the Peloponnesian War between Athens and Sparta) and found it difficult to unite against foreign aggression. The city-states, though rivals, felt a oneness, as exhibited by their pan-Hellenic Olympic games.

Athens. Our idea of the balanced life of the Greek city-state is based on that of Athens, largely because Athenians wrote most of Greek history. The apex of Athenian culture was in the fifth century B.C., the age of Pericles. The Athenians, in alliance with Sparta, twice defeated the great kings of the Persian Empire—Darius I and Xerxes I. From these victories developed a lively republican politics and culture. Only free adult males were citizens. They served in the Assembly and were expected to speak effectively if not always charitably to each other. Citizens were chosen by lot to serve as tax collectors, building inspectors, and ship captains. Ten generals were elected to manage the armed forces and the treasury.

Sparta. Sparta was, in a sense, the mirror image of Athens. The Athenians loved democracy and civic discourse and thought the Spartan militaristic life not worth living; Spartans were physically tough and less talkative than Athenians. Landlocked Sparta had an army, while Athens had a navy. Sparta was agricultural, Athens commercial. Social differences were much more pronounced in Sparta than in Athens. The Spartans, like all Greeks, considered non-Greeks to be barbarians.

Culture. Greek plays closely examined the affairs of men and gods. The audience could consider such questions deeply and come to understand the role of fate in their lives, the consequences of choice, and the consequences of injustice by gods and men.

The origins of Greek drama were religious, associated with the cult of Dionysos, the god of fertility, wine, and mirth. Comedy, such as *The Clouds* and *Lysistrata* by Aristophanes, satirized everything from contemporary philosophers to sex. Tragedy, such as the Orestes

Ancient Greece

trilogy by Aeschylus (one of which was *Agamemnon*), the Oedipus cycle by Sophocles (*Oedipus the King*), and the plays associated with the Trojan War by Euripides (*Trojan Women*), dealt with, in the first, family crime and the harshness of human and divine law; in the second, the consequences of exaggerated pride; and, in the third, a radical vision of the harsh and sorrowful consequences of war.

Plays such as these were performed yearly throughout Athens. The playwrights competed with each other, and first place was a valuable prize, such as a year's financial support by the city.

Fifth- and fourth-century B.C. Athens spawned three of the greatest philosophers in the Western tradition: Socrates, Plato, and Aristotle. These three laid the foundations for most of our thinking about the human condition and its relationship to a world beyond.

Socrates lived in the fifth century B.C. Most of what we know of his life and thought comes from the *Dialogues* of his pupil Plato. Socrates opposed the Sophists, who taught that there is no permanence, that all is in flux, and that truth is relative. Socrates believed that the human mind must rid itself of false opinions and search for the truth that the human soul once knew. This truth is to be gained through self-examination and the questioning of others to aid in "remembering" these forgotten truths. Socrates' bold and unusual methods were obnoxious to his fellow Athenians, who enjoyed the easy life of luxury. Sentenced to leave Athens or commit suicide, he chose the latter.

Plato expanded on Socrates' teachings. He argued in his *Dialogues*, whose hero was usually Socrates, that truth can be found in the form of ideas that exist in the real world. Thus, for example, "horse," "mud," "justice," and "good" are pale replications of the ideal Forms of Horse, Mud, Justice, and Good. In the *Symposium*, Plato argues that the soul can, through rigorous contemplation, ascend to a knowledge of these Forms in the real world, and the individual can become a true *philosopher* (lover of wisdom), gaining knowledge of everlasting and absolute truths. Plato founded his Academy in Athens, which was an important intellectual center for nine hundred years. His ideal Forms became attributes of God in the Christian

Venus de Milo

The Discus Thrower

History of Western Civilization

Pericles

During its so-called Golden Age, Athens was ruled by Pericles (c. 494–429 B.C.). This time of great creative achievement, which included the work of playwrights Aristophanes, Euripides, and Sophocles and the philosopher Socrates, was also a time of great political power, principally because of the Athenian navy. However, its achievements as a political power made other Greek states dislike Athens. It was because of this jealousy that Sparta led a league of states against Athens in the Peloponnesian War, which ended after twenty-seven years with the defeat of Athens. If more moderate voices had been able to prevail over Pericles's political goals, the Peloponnesian War might have been avoided, and the Greek *poleis* (city-states) might not have been weakened to become easy prey for their conqueror, Philip of Macedon.

era, and Christianity adopted the Platonic notion of soul.

Aristotle was Plato's pupil. He retained some of Plato's teachings, such as the notion of Forms. Of the two philosophies, Aristotle's was more grounded in the reality of the senses. He worked out strict and systematic rules for logical thinking and for the categories of life forms in this world. He strongly believed that human life is a balance between extremes (for example, courage is the mean between cowardice and foolhardiness) and that soul and body must work harmoniously together. He founded his own school in Athens, the Lyceum, which was the center of Aristotle's Peripatetic philosophy ("peripatetic" because the thinkers would walk in the Lyceum while discussing their ideas). Following the decline of Rome, Aristotle's work was lost, but was preserved by medieval Arab and Jewish scholars to heavily influence European thinkers of later centuries.

Alexander the Great. The Peloponnesian War (431–404 B.C.) pitted Sparta and its allies against Athens and left the populace of the Greek city-states uninterested in civic life. As a result, Philip of Macedonia conquered them. He hoped, in union with the Greeks, to crush the Persian Empire, which had previously threatened the Greek states. But Philip was killed in 336 B.C. His twenty-year-old son, Alexander, succeeded him.

With relatively small forces, Alexander soon conquered the Persian Empire and brought under his control the entire Middle East to the border of India. He tried to unite these lands by designating Greek as the official language, and dreamed of a world empire that fused the cultural traditions of the Middle East and Greece. But only thirteen years after coming to power, he died in 323 B.C. without fulfilling his dreams.

Since Alexander left no heir, his generals divided the empire into three parts, intending to rule it for the Macedonian royal family. The empire remained divided until the Roman conquest of the Middle East. The three generals who carved up the empire were Ptolemy I, who founded the thirty-first dynasty in Egypt, the Ptolemies, who ruled Egypt until Cleopatra; Seleucus I, who founded the Seleucid dynasty in Mesopotamia; and Antigonus I, who founded the Antigonid dynasty in Asia Minor and Macedonia.

Completely independent of the Macedonian royal house, these dynasties still spread Hellenistic culture and encouraged commerce and industry throughout the region, leading to prosperity for upper-class Greeks and Hellenized natives.

During the age of Alexander the Great and his successors (known as the Hellenistic Age), Greek culture spread throughout the eastern Mediterranean and Middle Eastern world; however, this form of Greek culture was marked by traits very different from those of classical Greece. First, the idea of the polis, or Greek city-state, ceased to be valued. No longer was the city-state the center of the citizen's life; no longer did he strive to serve in the various offices of the state. Greeks had become much more inward even before their conquest by Philip of Macedon.

In addition, the Olympian gods seemed no longer to play the role they once had. Athena had not protected Athens in the Peloponnesian War; other gods seemed to have fallen short as well. Thus, increasingly during the Hellenistic Age, the Greek citizen looked toward other religious possibilities and found them in the myriad mystery religions from the Middle East. Philosophy itself became more inward as Middle Platonism and Plotinus' ideas displaced the more worldly ideas of Aristotle and even of Plato.

The city-state was replaced by the large state or the world monarchy. These were state formations first created by the Assyrians and Persians, which later became models for the Roman imperial period, for Charlemagne's empire, and even for Napoleon's empire.

Julius Caesar, Cleopatra, and Mark Antony

In the last century of its existence, the Roman Republic was riddled by a series of civil wars. In one of the key battles, Julius Caesar (c. 100–44 B.C.) defeated the armies of Pompey (106–48 B.C.) at Pharsala and went on to become the sole ruler of Rome.

The last Ptolemy monarch of Egypt, Cleopatra (69–30 B.C.) became romantically involved with Julius Caesar and, following his assassination, with Mark Antony (c. 83–30 B.C.), one of the men who had succeeded Caesar in ruling Rome. Antony was ousted by the Roman Senate soon after, and his forces, along with those of Cleopatra, were defeated by Octavian at the sea battle of Actium in 31 B.C. Following this, Antony and Cleopatra committed suicide, and Octavian went on to rule Rome as the Emperor Augustus.

Significance. Once the Greeks emerged from the age of kings, so ably described in Homer's *Iliad*, they organized themselves into city-states. The Hellenes had a clear sense of *national* identity, as indicated by their participation in the pan-Hellenic Olympic games and their characterization of all non-Greeks as barbarians. They also saw themselves as Athenians, Spartans, Thebans, and Corinthians, as shown by their political division into independent and rival city-states. Greeks—above all, Athenians—delighted in trying to understand human beings' role in the cosmos and on earth. Many of their conclusions have formed the basis for Western thinking about these issues that continues through the twentieth century. Notable examples are belief in the immortality of the soul, the independent reality of ideas, and the importance of harmony between the two.

Ancient Greece can be said to be the birthplace of the human mind. This is not to say that the Egyptians and Mesopotamians were not effective thinkers, for clearly they were. What made the Greeks unique was that, from at least the eighth century B.C. until the Hellenistic Age, they consciously thought about human thinking and about the way people should act in the social and political world, as well as about values such as truth and beauty. As long as we care about these matters, the Greeks are surely our ancestors.

Rome.

The sixth book of Virgil's *Aeneid* states that if the Greeks' forte was thinking, the Romans' was government. This was an accurate assessment, for in all but government, the Romans borrowed from the Greeks.

The Republic. The Roman Republic, which had developed by the fifth century B.C., was a state based on the will of its citizens. Power in the Republic was shared between two consuls, a Senate of aristocrats, and the Twelve Tables, a codified body of law that protected both aristocrats and plebeians. In times of crisis, a dictator elected for six months could override the checks and balances guaranteed by the consular form of government. The Republic used a drafted citizen army, which, by iron discipline, conquered the Italian city-states. The city-states then committed troops to the Roman legions, in exchange for which Rome guaranteed them roads, peace, and prosperity.

After the Romans had conquered the Italian peninsula, they encountered Carthage, which controlled the areas of Sicily, Corsica, North Africa, and Spain. The Romans waged three Punic wars (264–146 B.C.) to dislodge the Carthaginians from Sicily and the western Mediterranean and to become the leading political and trading power in the region. The Roman senator Cato ended each speech in the Senate by saying, "Our rival Carthage must be destroyed." Finally, Rome and its allies defeated the Carthaginian commander Hannibal, conquered Carthage, and leveled the city. Lands formerly possessed by Carthage became the first Roman provinces, and Rome acquired provinces in the eastern Mediterranean as well. These acquisitions brought significant socioeconomic changes. Republican virtues dissipated as Rome became oriented to wealth and luxury. Senators entered into commercial activity and consolidated landholdings into large estates. Small farmers and ex-soldiers settled in cities. The Gracchi brothers (late second century B.C.) tried to reverse the trend toward luxury and urban glut but were assassinated. Decades later, Julius Caesar took up the goals of the Gracchi after illegally returning to Rome from Gaul with his army. He assumed many of the traditional offices of the Republic, but powerful senators banded against him, and in 44 B.C. he was killed. Caesar's fellow consul Mark Antony and heir Octavian took up his cause. They triumphed over the senatorial class but fought with one another. Octavian defeated Mark Antony and assumed imperial powers.

The empire and Christianity. Rome became an empire externally after 250 B.C., when it subdued the Italian peninsula, and internally in 27 B.C., when Octavian ended the Republic and assumed all state powers. Unlike the Republic, the Roman Empire was a state whose power emanated from one man and not from elected representatives.

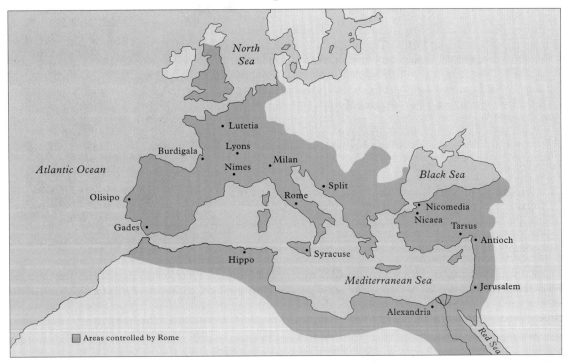

"I am a citizen not of Athens, nor of Greece, but of the world," wrote the Greek writer Plutarch, quoting Socrates. This was the great achievement of Rome between the times of Caesar Augustus and Marcus Aurelius. The emperor could even be Spanish, as were Trajan and Hadrian, for after 212 B.C., all inhabitants of the empire were Roman citizens, all were equal before the law, and all religions were respected. There was peace in this Mediterranean region that had historically known so much strife. In truth, there was a sense of belonging to the human family, fulfilling the dreams of the Hellenistic world that since the time of Alexander had hoped to unite Greek and Asiatic culture. It was into this world that Christianity was born.

Jesus was a Jewish prophet born about 4 B.C. and executed about A.D. 29. Despite his relatively short life on earth, Jesus was accepted as the anticipated messiah by his followers, and this belief is shared today by Christians throughout the world. After his execution, Jesus' followers began preaching the "good news" of salvation beyond the Jewish world to the Greco-Roman world. Christian beliefs, which spread far and wide, have had a major impact on the legal, philosophical, and moral infrastructures of Western civilization.

In the beginning, Christians were persecuted. Many other early followers were martyred. There were several reasons why the new Christian sect met with strong resistance from the Roman authorities. First, the Christians would not worship the emperor. Second,

they would not allow an image of their God to be placed in the Pantheon, the temple in Rome where the Romans kept images of all the gods of the empire. The Christians' fellows in monotheism, the Jews, also refused these two elements of Roman worship. However, the Jews were an ancient national group (the Romans respected tradition) and were not a proselytizing religion. The Christians, on the other hand, sent missionaries throughout the empire from A.D. 44 on. To Roman officials and many devout pagans, the Christians appeared seditious. This was the essential reason for their persecution.

Because Christians were persecuted, their preaching and worship often took place in private homes. The poorer classes especially were drawn to the new religion because of its practice of mutual care and promise of a happier afterlife. Several mystery religions of the period held out similar hopes of a future life, but Christianity was unique in that, first, the believer did not have to belong to an elite class or pass secret initiations; second, unlike even Judaism, women and men were treated equally and could worship together; and third, Jesus was a historical figure, in direct contrast to the gods of the mystery religions.

The acceptance of Christianity in the Roman Empire was aided by the development of a priesthood and a leadership of bishops. This development paralleled the organization of the empire in its provinces and metropolitan areas and drew its strength from that

History of Western Civilization
273

Paul

The original followers of Jesus intended to preach his message only to other Jews. But Paul of Tarsus (c. A.D. 5–67), who had begun as an opponent of the new Christian sect and was himself converted, sought to convert the Gentile (non-Jewish) world. He taught that Jesus was the son of God and that his teachings formed a new law, superseding the Mosaic Law of the Old Testament.

Paul realized that if Christianity was to appeal beyond the Jewish world, the followers of Jesus would have to shed many characteristic Jewish practices. Most important, they would have to relax their rules regarding dietary laws and the rite of circumcision, religious regulations that were repugnant to many Gentiles. Because of these important changes, it could be said that Paul helped create the new religion that spread throughout the Roman world.

organization. By the third century A.D., the Christian religion had made its greatest advances. The age of the able emperors (such as Trajan, Hadrian, and Marcus Aurelius) had passed, and the emperor now was chosen and could be deposed by his army. His safety had become too precarious for him to worry about the Christians. The constant struggle for power in the empire caused the middle and upper classes to look elsewhere for hope and security. By Constantine's reign, about 10 percent of the population had become Christians, crossing all socioeconomic lines.

In A.D. 313, Emperor Constantine issued the Edict of Milan, declaring toleration for Christianity. Theodosius I made Christianity the only legal religion in the empire in A.D. 381, but many Roman aristocrats resisted giving up the old Olympian religion, which they associated with patriotism. The Emperor Julian attempted to restore Olympian worship but failed, putting Christianity solidly in control of the Roman state. The tables were turned; whereas once the pagans had persecuted Christianity, now Roman Christians attacked the temples of the illegal pagan religions and overturned their altars.

When the Romans crossed the Alps into what became known as the transalpine provinces, they encountered very different types of people from those they had met in Greece and the Middle East. Rather than dealing with old and highly developed cultures and civilizations, such as the Greek city-states and Persia, they encountered peoples who were at a stage of development through which the Romans themselves had passed several centuries before—nomadic people who banded together into large tribal organizations and elected chieftains. These people originally had come from what is now northern Germany and Scandinavia. By the third century A.D., they lived close

to the borders of the Roman Empire and were attracted by what the empire had to offer in terms of convenient and sophisticated living. As these "barbarians" increasingly benefited from proximity to the empire in terms of a better life style and acquisition of modern arms, they became ever more dangerous. The empire itself was weakened politically by civil wars fought to appoint new emperors, as well as by disease-related population decline. Unable to turn its attention outward, the empire found itself prey to barbarian looters along its northern border from Spain to Greece.

Because of internal strife and population decline, emperors invited some of the Germanic tribes into the empire and recruited them for the Roman legions. In this way, the Roman army became Germanized up to the highest levels of command. The German soldiers gladly fought their kinsmen from across the borders once they had a stake in preserving the empire and in keeping the education and positions they enjoyed for themselves.

By the fifth century A.D., German tribes along the imperial borders had been pushed inward or aside by tribes from central Asia. The most prominent of these were the nomadic Huns. Under the command of Attila from 434 until his death in 453, the Huns advanced as far as the transalpine provinces but were turned back near Troyes by a Roman army composed of Germans. Soon the Huns were in Italy, where Pope Leo, not the emperor, protected Rome. When Attila died, the threat of the Huns collapsed. Barbarian invasions, however, were only part of the story of Rome's collapse.

Romulus Augustulus, the little emperor-son of a Roman general, died in A.D. 476 after having been in office one year. Having no Roman successor, he was followed in office by Theodoric, an Ostrogothic king.

These two events are often cited as marking the fall of the Roman Empire, but this is not really accurate. Since the death of Emperor Marcus Aurelius in A.D. 180, Rome had been in a process of general decline. Until Marcus Aurelius, the post-Augustan emperors had arranged for successors to be chosen on the basis of merit. Marcus Aurelius, though a philosopher-emperor, chose his incompetent son to follow him. This pattern of rule by generally incompetent, army-chosen emperors continued until 284, when Diocletian, also a former general, became emperor.

Diocletian faced an empire in disarray. Competing army-sponsored candidates for emperor had caused confusion in the state. The economy was in a sad situation, the Italian granaries of the empire were no longer producing as they once had, and the great estates in North Africa and other provinces were also strained to the limit. The new emperor tried to deal with these misfortunes, devaluing the currency, imposing price limits, and even dividing the empire. None of this helped much; some of it caused additional harm. Diocletian also changed the very ideological nature of the empire. All previous emperors had maintained a republican façade, but the traditional republican salute was now changed to a supine sprawl on the ground before the emperor, in imitation of eastern forms of obeisance. This change was an open expression of what Roman citizens had known for years—that the Roman state was nothing more nor less than a dictatorship. Diocletian's successor, Constantine, contin-ued these practices and moved the eastern capital of the empire to the old Greek city of Byzantium, which he renamed Constantinople.

Thus, when Theodoric—a German king, not an imperial general—succeeded the Roman emperor in the west after A.D. 476, the Roman Empire survived in the east for nearly another thousand years as the Byzantine Empire, with Constantinople as its capital.

One could also argue that the empire collapsed because of a failure of nerve. By the fifth century, the Roman aristocracy no longer wanted to expend the energy necessary to maintain the civic virtue or strength of the state. In fact, the new German rulers were a minority; the Romans allowed them to rule and did not seem to have regretted the loss of their unified imperial state. Men of the former upper class, such as Boethius and Cassiodorus, tried to advise the new king, but their tired civilization did not interact well with the crude, energetic culture of the new ruler. Others simply turned away from state affairs toward religion and a concern for the otherworldly. Most seemed to have felt the empire was not worth trying to preserve. This attitude reflected more than just a simple imperial death and Germanic succession. The Romans were happy to keep remnants of their culture, but they were unwilling to preserve the unitary nature of the state. Thus, when Germanic tribes—Visigoths, Vandals, Lombards, Burgundians, and Franks—carved up the formerly unified state, there was no Roman who wanted to prevent it.

Western Christendom, Byzantium, and Islam in A.D. 750

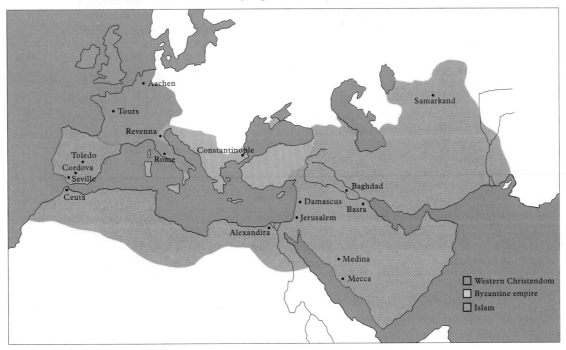

The Eurasian empires.

The Roman Empire split into three areas: the Germanic kingdoms and Eurasian empires; Byzantium in the east; and the Moslem regions of the Middle East and along the southern Mediterranean coast.

Byzantium. Diocletian's and Constantine's half of the Roman Empire did not fall to the Germanic and Asiatic tribes that had filled the vacuum in the western empire during the fifth century. The Byzantine emperor continued to rule areas of the eastern Mediterranean world until 1453. His rule was absolute, as he was head of church and state, a form of government known as *Caesaropapism*.

In the early sixth century, the Emperor Justinian reconquered large areas of Italy from its German rulers. But after Justinian's death in 565, Byzantium lost its Italian possessions when it tried to defend itself against the Persians in the east. Over the next centuries, the Arabs and Ottoman Turks conquered Byzantine territory. In a process that lasted until the tenth century, the Byzantines absorbed the Slavs. The Greek alphabet was adapted by Christian missionaries to Slav language sounds, becoming the Cyrillic alphabet still used in Russia and other Slavic lands. The area ruled by the Byzantine state shrank until the Ottoman Turks conquered Constantinople in 1453, marking the true "fall of the Roman Empire." Constantinople became Istanbul, and Justinian's great church, Hagia Sophia, became a mosque.

Russia. "Rus," or Russians, was the name given to the Viking conquerors of the Slavs who lived between the Black and the Baltic seas. The Scandinavian conquerors and their Slavic subjects developed into an important state, whose capital was Kiev, that traded with and attracted the Byzantines and was heavily influenced by Byzantine culture and religion. In 988, Prince Vladimir of Kiev became a Greek Christian in return for marrying the Byzantine emperor's sister. Thus, by the eleventh century, even this distant land and last so-called barbarian region, Russia, inherited the Greco-Roman and Christian civilization. It came to see itself as "the third Rome."

The rise of Islam. In A.D. 622—the year 1 for the Muslim believer—the merchant Muhammad left Mecca for Medina. There, he began to unite a nomadic people under one book (the Koran), one God (Allah), one prophet (Muhammad), and one language (Arabic). After ten years, Muhammad returned to Mecca and destroyed the idols of the old Arabian religions. In one hundred years, all the Middle East, North Africa, and Spain were united under a new religion, Islam.

"There is one God (Allah) and his prophet is Muhammad." This was the simple tenet of faith that charged Muslims in their quest. Islam was tolerant of Jews and Christians, since Muslims believed that their faith and scripture fulfilled the Old and New Testaments and that their prophet was the last in the line of prophets that ran from Moses to Jesus. Many were converted to the new faith not by the sword but because they were tired or resentful of their domination by Greeks and Christians. Others converted to avoid taxes against nonbelievers.

Soon after Muhammad's death, a number of divisions developed among the Muslims. Some (the Shiites) were loyal to the descendants of Muhammad's son-in-law Ali, while others (the Sunnites) believed the Koran and extra-Koranic traditions were sufficient to define Islam. These two factions struggle to this day. Moreover, the caliph in Spain would not align with the caliph in Baghdad. One God, one prophet, one book, and one language did not preserve political unity.

Heir to Hellenistic world-views, the Judeo-Christian tradition, and Persian architectural opulence, Islam's culture was in many ways far richer than that of its contemporary Western Europe. It preserved and added to the Greek intellectual and medical tradition and contributed to the body of knowledge that Western Europe began to attain only after the eleventh century.

Muhammad

Trained as a caravan trade merchant, Muhammad (c. A.D. 571–632) married well and became a wealthy man. At age 40, he felt himself called by God to be the Arab prophet of true religion. He went on to become the founder of Islam and one of the great figures in world history.

In the Arab world of Muhammad's time, there were numerous competing gods. Muhammad, in contrast, preached a strict monotheism, saying, "There is but one God, and his last prophet is Muhammad." The simplicity of this religion made it easy to understand, and Islam rapidly gained popularity.

Muhammad believed that his teachings, which today can be found in the Koran, the holy book of Islam, completed the teachings of the Old and New Testaments and the revelations of the prophets. During his lifetime, Muhammad converted most of the Arabic peoples and began the conversion of others along the coast of North Africa.

Muhammad's birthplace, Mecca, is today the holiest city of Islam, and the Kaaba, a small building found within the city's Great Mosque, is the religion's most sacred shrine and the goal of Muslim pilgrimage.

Medieval Europe

One of the problems with the way historians divide history into periods (Antiquity, Middle Ages, Renaissance, Modern Age) is that students gain the impression that eras suddenly change, just as acts end and open in a play with the closing and opening of a curtain. But history is not like a play. Some people may have been aware that important events were taking place, but no one woke up after Romulus Augustulus died in 476 or Theodoric came to power in 493 and said, "Antiquity is over; the Middle Ages have begun."

Only after the fact does one know that a new period has begun, and then only after an act of historical interpretation has taken place. In the fourteenth century, the Italian Renaissance scholar Petrarch invented the terms "Middle Ages" and "Dark Ages" to refer to the periods between the fifth and fourteenth centuries. Before Petrarch, no one knew there was a Middle Ages. For example, people did not fully realize that Rome had declined. Evidence from writings and art shows that people still thought of themselves as Romans. They were surrounded by the ruins of Rome, which they saw as belonging to their own age, not to a previous one.

The Middle Ages begin.
Even for the modern historian, the Middle Ages is a complicated era to interpret. It covers that long period of time dur-ing which ways of living slowly changed as an energetic but underdeveloped Germanic culture replaced the Roman culture. Several trends point toward the emergence of the Middle Ages: the development of the church from a primitive to a unified organization; the emergence of a politically and economically strong European society, which followed a stage of disorganization and localism; the expansion of intellectual connections and culture from a purely local level to a European-wide network; and growth and prosperity after the eleventh century that led to the political, economic, and demographic disasters of the fourteenth century. In short, the Middle Ages, far from being the Dark Ages, was a period of active change.

The Pirenne thesis. Belgian historian Henri Pirenne (1862–1935) argued that it wasn't the centuries of Germanic invasions that destroyed the Roman world and led to the subsequent rise of the Frankish empire, but rather the influence of Islam in the seventh and eighth centuries. "Without Islam the Frankish empire would probably never have existed," he once wrote, "and Charlemagne, without Muhammad, would be inconceivable."

Pirenne asserted that cities collapsed as the result of Arab, not Germanic, invasions, as many historians had previously argued. Scanty evidence is at the basis of all assertions about the early Middle Ages, but it can be stated that while Pirenne exaggerated the decline

---

Some key events and people: A.D. 500–1300

A.D. 500
Kingdom of the Franks established by Clovis
Justinian's temporary reconquest of the western
   Mediterranean
Slavs spread through Eastern Europe (550–900)

600
Muhammad and the Koran
Islamic conquest of Middle East and
   Mediterranean world
Rise of Carolingian dynasty

700
Charles Martel drives the Muslims out of France

800
Charlemagne crowned "Roman emperor"
   by Pope Leo III
Breakup of Charlemagne's empire
Invasions of Western Europe by Vikings

900
Emergence of feudal and manorial systems
Monastic reform movements

1000
Revival of trade
Norman Conquest of England
Rise of towns

1100
The Crusades (1096–1204)
Rise of universities
Gothic architecture

1200
Magna Carta
Mongol invasions of Eastern Europe
Growth of banking
Origins of Parliament

---

caused by Islam, he did make subsequent historians realize that the Roman world did not die in the fifth century but lasted until the extreme localism of the eighth century.

Localism. By the late seventh century, the connectedness of the Roman world had given way to its opposite, *localism*. Governmental functions, such as road maintenance, had declined. Cities existed, but travelers between them risked being attacked by wolves or bandits. Many cities were like Arles in southern Gaul: once vibrant and crowded, it had shrunk to about ten thousand souls living in the local coliseum, while cows and goats wandered the streets. Other signs of localism or disconnectedness included the development of local dialects and handwriting, as well as of local economic and political forms called manorialism and feudalism.

Manorialism was an agrarian and economic system by which all foodstuffs and products originated in the manor land. The serfs worked common and private lands. Their production went for their own sustenance and that of the manor lord. This localized production allowed, at best, minimal trade of manorial production from one manor to another; it certainly could not support city populations. Thus, it is not surprising that city populations declined during the early medieval period.

Just as agrarian economy existed only on a small scale, so government could function only on local levels. A king could not rule a kingdom alone, as there were no longer the necessary roads or a literate class to carry out his commands. Localism led to the *feudal* system, whereby a *vassal* swore an oath of loyalty to a feudal lord and would govern at the local level, in return for which the lord would protect him from marauding Vikings and other dangers.

The Carolingian Empire. Since the Merovingian kings of the Franks were inept and powerless, noble families vied to rule as mayors of the palace. Charles Martel, the first Carolingian, became mayor in 714. He defeated the Arabs at Tours in 732, but subsequently angered local churchmen when he granted church lands to his knights, marking the beginning of the feudal system and laying the foundation for a "society of orders," a social grouping system based on those who fight, those who pray, and those who work. Pepin III deposed the Merovingians, and Pope Zacharius crowned him king. In 754, Pepin saved the papacy by defeating the heretical Lombards in Italy and creating the Papal States.

Charlemagne maintained Frankish ties with the papacy and again defeated the Lombards. For his military help, Pope Leo III crowned Charlemagne Emperor of the Romans on December 25, 800. His empire combined Roman unity, though on a much smaller scale, with Christianity and Germanic military power. Each area of the empire retained its own law. Areas were ruled by counts and visiting imperial inspectors (*Missi Dominici*). Charlemagne imitated Rome's imperial culture, including the teaching of the Latin language.

Louis the Pious succeeded Charlemagne in 814. He was unable to pass the empire on to his eldest son and instead, with the Treaty of Verdun in 843, had to follow the Frankish tradition of dividing up the kingdom

Charlemagne

among his three sons. Viking invasions further tore the empire apart, and by 987, the entire area was ruled by new but powerless Frankish kings.

The Holy Roman Empire. Although the Carolingian empire did not last, Charlemagne had recreated the idea of a unitary state sanctioned by the pope. Otto I in Germany followed up by creating the Holy Roman Empire in 962. This "Roman" empire consisted only of Germany and Italy but played a major role in European affairs for the next eight hundred and fifty years. The emperor was chosen by seven great noblemen called *electors*, who always strove to select a relatively weak man so the nobles of Germany could retain their local taxing and war-making powers. In spite of the electors' efforts, there were several emperors who had the strength of personality to be politically dominant within the empire and throughout Europe.

The French and English states. France and England had a symbiotic relationship over the course of the Middle Ages; the English royal house ruled parts of France, and France influenced English culture and politics. All this resulted from the collapse of the Carolingians and their succession by the Capetians in France.

Hugh Capet succeeded the last direct Carolingian heir in 987. He was elected by feudal lords who hoped to establish an elective and powerless monarchy. The success of Hugh and his successors lay in their lack of land and power, and in their ability always to have a male heir. They were no threat to the other lords, and the fact that the Capetians always had male heirs made the nobles forget monarchical election. *Primogeniture*, succession of the eldest son, was thereby established. The Capetians ruled the Île de France, the strip of land running from Paris to Orléans that divided feudal lords from each other and from concerted action. The weakness of the Capetians, whose descendants ruled until 1792, preserved the French monarchy from extinction.

In England, Edward the Confessor became king after the deaths of King Canute's sons in 1042. Canute and his weak sons had had ties with Scandinavia, but Edward had been exiled in Normandy and preferred the Normans. He may have promised Duke William of Normandy the throne. But the powerful noblemen Earl Godwin and his son Harold led a faction of barons against him. Edward also promised Harold the succession.

The two claimants to the English throne, William of Normandy and Harold Godwinson, met at Hastings in 1066, where William defeated Harold's army and Harold was killed. The Normans became masters of England and the Anglo-Saxons a conquered people. England's ties with the Continent were renewed for the first time since the fall of the Roman Empire.

William, duke of Normandy and the conqueror of England, was middle-aged and experienced in administration. He introduced the well-developed and organized feudalism of northern France, reformed the English church, and established a stable monarchy in place of the weak kingship that had existed previously.

With William's conquest, Norman-French replaced Anglo-Saxons as rulers of England. Things became more complex when Henry II of England married Eleanor of Aquitaine in 1152. The French-speaking English king gained five more French provinces. Henry's son Richard I (Lion-heart) went to England only when he needed money; otherwise he was on crusade or in France. Richard's brother John succeeded him. John was defeated by the man who was his feudal lord, the king of France, losing most of his French

Archers of the English army, as shown in the Bayeux Tapestry

Joan of Arc

Called the Maid of Orléans, Joan of Arc (1412?–1431) came from a pious peasant family in the French region of Champagne. Joan claimed that she had conversations with the spirits of St. Michael and other saints, who urged her to go into battle on the side of the Dauphin, rightful heir to the throne of France but prevented from ruling by the English in the Hundred Years' War. Joan's inspirational leadership ultimately proved to be a key factor in France's defeat of England. But Joan was captured by French clerics who were sympathetic to the English, and executed as a witch.

possessions and thus coming to be called John Lackland. John's barons in England (all Norman-French) tried to ensure their new lands and rights in England and so wrested the Magna Carta from John in 1215, which bound the king to England's laws and allowed the barons to make the king obey those laws.

Although the English monarch and barons reached an understanding with the signing of the Magna Carta, the English and French kings could reach no agreement over their counterclaims to French territory. The Hundred Years' War was fought by English and French monarchs between 1337 and 1453, over the former's flimsy claims to the throne of France. The French kings were often inept and the English troops were generally stronger, leading to English victories in the two great battles of Crécy (1346) and Agincourt (1415). However, internal economics and politics undid the English victories on the field. After Agincourt, the English, under Henry V, allied with John of Burgundy, the strongest noble in France. French fortunes faded still more, since Dauphin Charles VII listened only to his flatterers and not to good advice and counsel. Joan of Arc rallied the French, but she was captured by the Burgundians, and the recently crowned king did nothing to save her. The war ended with the English holding only the port of Calais.

During this period, each nation's king advanced the cause of centralized authority. In England, Henry II appointed the *justiciar*, a legal official who guaranteed that royal justice was carried out, rather than the local justice of the great nobles. In France, the late medieval kings such as Philip Augustus began the process of increasing the size of French territories held by the king himself, and they advanced royal justice and authority.

The church. The church also centralized
authority in the Middle Ages. By the eleventh and twelfth centuries, the Roman Catholic Church had become a political and religious power.

The early centuries. The church established its ecclesiastical practices, beliefs, and holy life in the first six centuries after Christ, after which its interests turned outward toward political and lay culture.

At first, the followers of Jesus had only the Jewish sacred books (the Christian Old Testament). The four Gospels and the Letters of Paul were written, with such other texts as the First Letter of Clement and the Gospel of Thomas, by the end of the first century. These latter books, and writings from the second century, were discounted as apocryphal by the mid-fourth century. The remaining Gospels of Matthew, Mark, Luke, and John, the Acts, and Letters of Paul, Peter, and John were declared the canonical, or authoritative, New Testament.

It is not surprising that local congregations followed different liturgies, even after the establishment of scriptural canon. The differences in worship caused major gulfs among the various religious groups. For centuries, the pope worked to achieve agreement in liturgical practice. Finally, sixth-century Pope Gregory the Great succeeded in imposing the Roman liturgy on the entire church, which led to greater uniformity of religious habit and belief.

The early church also dealt with various theological questions and heresies. By the mid-fifth century, the church had a belief structure based on the writings of the church fathers and beliefs (*creeds*) authorized by such councils as that of Nicaea in 325.

Gregory the Great

Pope Gregory I (the Great), who reigned from A.D. 590 to 604, was most responsible for the successful dissemination of Christian rites and doctrines throughout Roman and pagan Europe. He also ensured that all Christians followed the Roman liturgy and gave obeisance to the pope in Rome. For these accomplishments, Gregory, along with St. Augustine, St. Jerome, and St. Ambrose, is considered one of the four "Doctors of the Church," the Christian leaders who played a major role in fashioning the theology and worship of the church.

Those who sought a pure religious life differed widely in their practices. Hermits such as St. Anthony lived in desert caves and fought off the temptations of Satan in their solitude. Symeon the Stylite (389–459) was an extreme example, standing motionless atop a thirty-foot column near Antioch for thirty years.

Such ineffable spirituality could be attained by only a few. A more moderate approach to spiritual life was taken in the sixth century, when St. Benedict founded a monastic order known as the Benedictines. This order became the model for future monastic orders in its call for poverty, chastity, and obedience. It combined the desire to live a life away from the world with duties that guaranteed a more reasonable spirituality than that found among the desert monks.

St. Benedict's spiritual life combined work, study, and prayer interspersed throughout the day. Nothing was done to excess. The body was refurbished by work in the fields, the mind enhanced by study, and both were centered in worship and prayer. Laxity in following the Benedictine Rule led to the formation of new monastic orders throughout the Middle Ages.

The pope and the investiture struggle. The church sought to normalize its dealings with the world as well as within its own institutions. When Charlemagne was crowned emperor of the Romans on Christmas Day, 800, the act itself became a symbol for the investiture struggle that developed two hundred years later. *Investiture* means appointment—in this case, of bishops within a state.

In theory, the pope had the power to appoint bishops of the church, but monarchs sought that power for themselves. In Germany and France, for example, monarchs wanted to appoint bishops as their vassals, since when a bishop died, his feudal estate (*fief*) would revert to the monarch; a nobleman, by contrast, could pass the fief on to his son, thus representing more of a threat to the monarch.

On Christmas Day, 800, Pope Leo III crowned the kneeling Charlemagne. Then Charlemagne kissed the pope's hand. Who then was superior to whom? The same question was raised between ensuing popes and the kings of France and England and debated by both sides as the investiture struggle, between church and state, evolved.

The most famous example of the investiture struggle occurred in the Holy Roman Empire. When Emperor Henry IV tried to appoint the bishops in Germany, Pope Calixtus II excommunicated him. Henry prostrated himself in the snow for three days before the pope's castle at Canossa, and the pope forgave him. Henry promptly reappointed the bishops. Although the pope excommunicated Henry again, it was ineffectual. Historians debate who won.

A subsequent pope, Innocent III, excommunicated and deposed King John of England and allowed him to take back his throne only as a fief from the papacy. Innocent III proclaimed the pope to be the sun and all secular leaders the moon, deriving their power from the pope. This declaration represented the height of the medieval papacy.

Jean de Berry's Book of Hours

Cosmopolitanism.

After 1100, Europe recovered from the localism that had characterized it since the beginning of the Middle Ages. In its place came *cosmopolitanism*, the awareness of connections among lands that are geographically and culturally distant. This trend could be seen in the growth of trade and cities, as well as in the expansion of knowledge that was characteristic of the following centuries.

The commercial revolution. The commercial revolution of the later Middle Ages rested on an agricultural advance of the tenth century: the yoke allowed oxen or horses to be driven more powerfully, resulting in deeper furrows and better soil cultivation; and the three-field method of plowing, allowing one field to lie fallow each year, helped solve erosion problems and guaranteed that the soil would regularly renew itself. As more crops were grown, more people could be fed.

European population increased after the eleventh century, causing the hinterlands to become more populated. Settlers moved beyond the Elbe River in Germany, more cities and abbeys were built in the Low Countries, the Christian Reconquista of Spain advanced, and Crusaders went on crusades.

Surplus food production allowed the expanding population to move into already existing cities as well. The expression "City air makes free" was a favorite late-medieval slogan. A serf could escape from his manor and could, if he lived in a city for a year and a day, become a free man. Those who settled in cities became merchants, artisans, laborers, and craftsmen.

The leading commercial cities were in Flanders and the Low Countries (Bruges and Ghent), and in northern Italy (Genoa, Lucca, Florence). Despite the rise of cities, 90 percent of the European population in the late Middle Ages continued to live rural, manorial lives. In fact, that percentage persisted until the nineteenth century.

Late-medieval cities, especially those in northern Italy, were often under the control of a feudal overlord. In Italy, it was the Holy Roman Emperor. However, as these cities expanded and became more prosperous, they sought to be rid of overlords. In 1176, Genoa and allied cities, in league with bishops whose loyalties lay with the pope, defeated Emperor Frederick I (Barbarossa) at the battle of Legnano. Having overthrown imperial vicars, the cities discarded the propapal bishops. The northern Italian city-states thereby became independent and sovereign.

Medieval walled city in France

Independence did not mean these city-states were centers of harmony. Their early capitalist economies guaranteed that factions would compete fiercely with one another for political power and control of trade.

By the twelfth and thirteenth centuries, a network of trade had developed into a real world-system of commerce. The northern city-states of Italy (Genoa, Lucca, Florence, and Venice) specialized in international trade. They were major producers of woolen products, which they traded in the East as well as in London, Southampton, and Flanders. In addition, they developed "colonies" throughout the eastern Mediterranean, from which they imported spices and various fruits. Italian trade extended all the way across Asia to China and the court of Kublai Khan. The Mongolian rulers of central Asia welcomed such trade. This trans-Asian trade lasted until the mid-fourteenth century, when the Ottoman Turks conquered western Asia and the Middle East and forced the Italians to trade at prohibitive tariffs, sometimes as much as doubling an item's cost.

Italians also traded along routes over the Alps into southern Germany, especially to Augsburg. A vital trading system, called the Hanseatic League, existed in the Scandinavian world. Its trading products were wood and rough woolen products, and its trading posts included Novgorod in Russia, Bergen in Norway, Hamburg in Germany, the Flanders cities, and Southampton. At these latter two trading centers, Hanseatic merchants met Italian merchants and learned more sophisticated trading practices, such as letters of credit and double-entry bookkeeping.

The medieval trading world prospered until the mid-fourteenth century, when a number of events occurred: the English king, Edward III, declared bankruptcy and ruined the great Bardi and Peruzzi banks of Florence; the Ottoman Turks cut off access to China; and the Black Death devastated Europe between 1347 and 1350, killing about 35 percent of the population.

Cluniac and church reform. The tenth century brought with it not only the beginning of economic and demographic recovery but also church reform. This reform began in the duchy of Burgundy at the abbey of Cluny, founded in 910 by the duke of Aquitaine. The Benedictine monasteries had become corrupted by wealth accrued from the land they owned; some abbots lived as well as bishops and kings. Cluny, founded to reform such lapses from the strictness of the Benedictine Rule, placed itself directly under the supervision of the pope so as to prevent local corruption. Sister monasteries were established— over three hundred during a one-hundred-year period. To prevent corruption, these operations were placed under the direction of the abbot in Cluny.

This type of well-conceived reform model inspired other monastic groups, all governed directly by the pope: the Cistercians, founded by St. Bernard of Clairvaux; the Franciscans, begun by St. Francis of Assisi; the Dominicans, founded by St. Dominic. There was a strong rivalry, including theological differences, among these monastic groups. For example, Franciscans accepted the doctrine of the immaculate conception of Mary, while Dominicans opposed it as "the work of the synagogue." Rivalries aside, each of these orders helped reform the church. Reform bred success, which in turn necessitated further reform.

The birth of universities. The first universities were founded in Salerno and Bologna, both in Italy. The former specialized in medicine, the latter in law. The university movement spread northward, first to Montpellier in southern France, then to Paris in the thirteenth century, and thereafter throughout northern Europe.

Universities were established to be independent of local political authorities; often they were chartered by

Abelard and Heloïse

The leading Parisian university teacher of his day, Peter Abelard (1079–1142) fell in love with and married a student named Heloïse. However, in order to teach at the university, he could not be married and so persuaded Heloïse's uncle to permit a secret marriage. The arrangement soon compromised the family's reputation. To save the family's honor, her uncle stole Heloïse away and hired some ruffians to emasculate Abelard. Heloïse entered a convent and Abelard went into a monastery, where he helped pioneer the application of logic to matters of faith.

the church but controlled by professors. Before university buildings were constructed, classes met under trees or in professors' homes. The teaching of students in universities was structured much like the training of workers in guilds, with the professors acting as masters and the students equivalent to apprentices.

Today we are used to having bookstores and all types of learning assistance in universities, but medieval universities were much simpler. Because the printing press had not been invented, books were few and those that existed were handwritten. Thus, if a professor gave a course on the Book of Genesis or Aristotle's *Metaphysics*, he would read the text to his students, and they would write every word on wax tablets. (The terms *lecture* and *lecturer* mean, literally, "a reading" and "a reader.") Later, students would copy their texts onto parchment, since paper did not exist. It was only then that the professor could "profess," or interpret, the text. A course on a major book could consume several months or even years. Because of the scarcity of books, libraries did not have multiple holdings or borrowing privileges as they do today. Therefore, memory was most important to the medieval student.

The curriculum of the universities was based largely on Latin translations of Aristotle and of the Greek and Arabic commentaries on Aristotle's works. Aristotle's writings had been unknown to the Latin west. Most of his works were translated from Arabic in Spain by Jewish scholars and then imported into France and elsewhere. In this way, Aristotle was the preeminent "pagan" authority; medieval university writings constantly refer to him as "the Philosopher," just as they refer to the most important New Testament writer, St. Paul, as "the Apostle." Universities opened up a new world to the Latin west, but it was still a fairly constrained intellectual horizon.

Medieval universities followed a single methodology and employed a common terminology: they were *Aristotelian*—in other words, based on Aristotle. But in spite of common terminology, there was great diversity of opinion within the university world. A comparison of the philosophies of Thomas Aquinas (d. 1274) and Duns Scotus (d. 1308) serves to make this point. Duns Scotus, a Franciscan from Scotland who taught at Paris, was a Nominalist; Scotus believed we cannot know ultimate truth through reason but only through faith. Thomas Aquinas, a Dominican professor from Aquino who taught at Paris and Naples, was a Realist; he believed that faith and human reason together can grasp ultimate religious truths. One of Aquinas's most significant contributions was reconciling the works of Aristotle with religious belief, as in his great work, *Summa Theologiae*.

These two intellectual leaders show us two things. First, there was no one Christian philosopher who dominated the late Middle Ages. There were many different "masters," and they tended to be followed by

Notre Dame Cathedral

Salisbury Cathedral

members of their own orders (such as Aquinas, the Dominicans; Scotus, the Franciscans). Second, the commonality of intellectual vocabulary and methodology meant that scholars everywhere in Europe could read and understand each other, thus overcoming the localism, the lack of intellectual communication, of the earlier Middle Ages.

This cosmopolitanism of intellectual life was paralleled by the international styles of late-medieval art. By the end of the Middle Ages, painters were employing what art historians call "the international Gothic style." In the same way, architects were constructing cruciform churches, consisting of a long *nave* and an *apse* that crossed it in imitation of the cross on which Jesus died. These churches used the same architectural principles: pointed arches and soaring vaults, with exterior flying buttresses that supported the weight of the roof. Finally, there was a common handwriting throughout late-medieval Europe—the Gothic script, another international style that we would still be using if it were not for the Renaissance, which changed handwriting styles as well as styles of painting, building, and learning.

The Crusades. The Crusades were partly the result of the transition of the European mind from the localism that had characterized the earlier period, to the realization that there was another world of other values. Particularly galling to Christians was the fact that the soil where Jesus had trod was now ruled by Islam.

In 1095, Pope Urban II preached the call for the First Crusade. His impassioned sermon ended with the resounding words "God wills it." Those who responded to his call were Europe's warrior class, the nobility, who also were eager to acquire new lands for themselves.

The First Crusade, led by noblemen, was sufficiently successful in the conquest of land that kings and emperors became involved in later crusades. One crusade, for example, was led by King Richard Lion-heart of England and Holy Roman Emperor Frederick Barbarossa (Red Beard). By the end of two hundred years of great crusades, however, nothing had really been gained. Land won, known as the Latin Kingdoms of the East, was eventually lost. Even though Crusaders at one time seized Jerusalem, the ability of Christians to journey to Jerusalem was finally

The Crusades

Crusade	Crusade leader(s)	Destination	Results
First Crusade (1096–1099; "Crusade of the Princes")	Godfrey of Bouillon, duke of Lower Lorraine; Raymond, count of Toulouse; Stephen, count of Blois	Jerusalem	Crusaders massacred inhabitants of Jerusalem, gaining control of the city.
Second Crusade (1147–1149)	Zanghi, governor of Mosul; Louis VII, king of France; Conrad III, emperor of Germany	Damascus	Sultan Saladin established control of Muslim Middle East; Christians lost control of the Middle East, controlling only Antioch, Tripoli, and Tyre by 1189.
Third Crusade (1189–1192)	Frederick I (Barbarossa), emperor of Germany; Richard I ("Lion-heart"), king of England; Philip II, king of France	Port of Acre	Barbarossa drowned; Philip returned to France after the Port of Acre was captured; Richard negotiated with Saladin the right for Christian pilgrims to visit Jerusalem.
Fourth Crusade (1202–1204)	Pope Innocent III	Port of Zara	Crusaders were excommunicated because Zara was a Catholic city; subsequently, Crusaders successfully pursued the succession of the Byzantine throne and established a Latin kingdom of Constantinople that lasted until 1261.
Children's Crusade (1208)	Two contingents of children set off for the Holy Land	Jerusalem	One contingent turned back; the other group was captured and sold into slavery.

Richard Lion-heart

The son of Henry II and Henry's French wife, Eleanor of Aquitaine, Richard I (A.D. 1157–1199) became king of England in 1189. He spent much of his reign in the Holy Land, fighting in the Crusades, where he concluded a truce allowing Christians passage to Jerusalem for a limited time. Richard also waged war in France to protect his family's dynastic possessions from the French king, who wished to take them. He died fighting in France and was buried there, to be succeeded by his brother John. Richard's military achievements made him a central figure in English romance.

battle of Legnano in 1176. Barbarossa's grandson, Frederick II, tried to regain imperial ascendancy over Italy and also over the papacy. He failed, but the story is exciting.

When Frederick II's father died, he left his son to be the designated Holy Roman Emperor and ward of the pope. Under the wardship of Pope Innocent III, Frederick was brought up to be a good son of the church and to obey the pope's wishes. No matter how well trained he was, though, Frederick had inherited the desires of all strong members of the Hohenstaufen family—namely, to centralize his power in Germany, to rule northern Italy, and to be independent of the papacy.

Frederick II became a very independent leader. He inherited southern Italy and Sicily from his mother's side of the family and moved his capital to Sicily where, because of the influence of the Arabs who had once ruled it, he learned to live like a Middle Eastern potentate. He kept a harem and a menagerie, which followed him about as he traveled. He also wrote the book that remains the classic on falconry. Because of all this, he was known as *stupor mundi*, or "wonder of the world."

Frederick conceived the plan of using his army in northern and southern Italy to crush the papacy in a great pincers movement. Had this worked, it would have destroyed the papacy and reduced all of Italy to imperial control; Frederick II, however, died suddenly in 1250 and his plans died with him. The communes were once again independent of the empire. The void in imperial power and the weakness of the papacy, because of its seventy-year captivity in Avignon, France, led to the development of the Italian state system. The Renaissance political world was born.

achieved by treaty and not by war. Another crusade was called the "Children's Crusade," in which preachers led children across Europe toward the Holy Land. Most never returned. They died en route or were taken as slaves.

In retrospect, the Crusades accomplished very little. They appealed to mass hysteria and soured relations between Christians and Muslims.

Italian communes, the empire, and Rome. The northern Italian communes had won their independence from Emperor Frederick Barbarossa at the

Some key events and people: 1300–1700

1300
Travels of Marco Polo to China

1400
Age of despots in Italy: Cosimo de' Medici, Francesco Sforza
New-style armies: cannon and muskets
Fall of Constantinople to Ottoman Turks
Expulsion of Muslims from Spain

1500
Overseas exploration: Christopher Columbus, Vasco da Gama
Establishment of European colonial empires
Rise of national monarchies: Henry VIII, Francis I

Martin Luther and beginning of Protestant Reformation
Charles V, Holy Roman Emperor
Spanish Armada

1600
William Shakespeare
Religious wars (Thirty Years' War)

1650
Peace of Westphalia
Louis XIV
English Revolution
Oliver Cromwell
Mercantilism
Age of absolutism

Early modern Europe

The period including the Renaissance and Reformation and extending into the seventeenth century is often called the *early modern period*. This designation is appropriate from a Europe-wide political and economic perspective. The despotic state that developed in Renaissance Italy emerged as the absolutist state of Western Europe during the seventeenth century. The economic problems of the early Renaissance, caused by bank failures, the Ottoman Turks, and the Black Death, emerged in a different form with sixteenth-century inflation and cyclical fluctuations. These conditions did not stabilize until the eighteenth century.

The meaning of Renaissance.

When did the Renaissance begin? When did it end? Cultural historians ordinarily date the beginning of the Renaissance from the early fourteenth century, with artists such as Giotto, Brunelleschi, and Masaccio, and writers such as Petrarch and Boccaccio. They end it in the late sixteenth century, with artists like Michelangelo and Titian, and writers such as Giordano Bruno, Michel de Montaigne, and John Milton. Renaissance art and writing styles were distinct from those of the late Middle Ages, being more directly and consciously based on Greco-Roman models than previous work had been.

The Renaissance also can be defined in economic terms. The Black Death, or bubonic plague, struck Europe between 1347 and 1350, killing about 35 percent of the European population. The population did not reach preplague levels again until after 1460 and did not exceed them for another hundred years. Bubonic plague continued sporadically into the early seventeenth century. As a result, most of the continent fell into economic decline, hastened by the failures of the Peruzzi and Bardi banks in Florence and the closing of trade routes to Asia by the Ottoman Turks. Evidence abounds showing the results of plague, bank failure, and trade decline: few new city walls were built after 1350; warehouses throughout Europe contained fewer goods; the decline in the Italian wool trade was not made up for by the increase in English woolen output; the richest fifteenth-century family, the Medici, was only about one half as wealthy as the Peruzzi and Bardi families in the fourteenth century. The sixteenth-century price rise, caused by both gold from the New World and climatic changes in Europe, did not ease until 1605. The dates 1347 to 1605 are thus another useful way of defining the Renaissance.

The Italian Renaissance.

One can define the Italian Renaissance, in political terms, as beginning about 1300 and ending in 1494. *Renaissance* in this case means the rebirth of Italian autonomy from control by states beyond the Alps (the Ultramontanes). Beginning in the fourteenth century, the German emperor no longer was a power in Italy, nor was the pope, who at that time was under the control of the French monarchy. After 1350, five major Italian states emerged: the republics of Venice and Florence, the duchy of Milan, the kingdom of Naples, and the Papal States. After 1454, the Sforza family of Milan and the Medici of Florence formed an alliance, causing the other states to band together to avoid being overwhelmed. The Italian Renaissance was a period of shifting alliances of this sort, so that a balance of power was maintained and the independence of each state was preserved.

One can argue that the Italian Renaissance ended in

The Black Death

The Black Death, or bubonic plague, came from fleas carried by infected brown rats. These rats had been on ships that docked in the eastern Mediterranean in 1347. The plague spread westward, reaching Italy in 1348; France, Germany, and England by 1349; and Sweden by 1350. About 35 percent of the European population died as a result.

Many people thought the Black Death was a punishment from God. Others tried to devise ways to protect their communities, including disposing of common sleeping pallets and quarantining plague-infested neighborhoods, towns, and ships. These measures softened its impact, but the disease was not eradicated for years.

1494 when Ludovico Sforza invited the Spanish Hapsburgs into Italy. The Spanish and French royal houses had competing dynastic claims to both Naples and Milan. They fought in Italy until the Hapsburgs were victorious, in 1530. By that time, the Italians had completely lost control of their own affairs, and Italy's political renaissance had ended.

Francesco Petrarch and humanism. Humanism in the Renaissance could be defined as the *studia humanitatis*—study of the humanities—which consisted of grammar, rhetoric, history, poetry, and moral philosophy (ethics). The basis of these studies was always the pagan and Christian authors of Greek and Roman antiquity, such as Cicero, Virgil, and St. Augustine. The humanists were very critical of medieval authors and thinkers, accusing them of bad Latin and confused thinking.

Francesco Petrarch (1304–1374), the foremost humanist of his day, believed he was living in "the age of rebirth" of Greco-Roman culture. He felt that contemporaries could not understand his classical literary values, so he wrote "letters" to ancients such as Cicero and Seneca and to posterity, the only audiences he trusted to understand his values. Petrarch also popularized the *sonnet*, a form of poetry that continues to be much in use.

The belief that a new age was dawning was common to all humanists in the Renaissance. Petrarch's *subjectivism*, the notion that those who came after would be interested in his personal and emotional life, was repeated by many thinkers of the Renaissance, including French thinker Michel de Montaigne, who invented the *essay* to describe his thoughts.

Leonardo da Vinci's Mona Lisa

Machiavelli

Niccolò Machiavelli (1469–1527), the well-known Renaissance humanist, is remembered for his book *Il principe* (*The Prince*). In the book, Machiavelli recommended the same principles for governing tyrannical and republican states: that is, that the government must exhibit *virtù*, or force and strength, in doing whatever is required to maintain its power. This advice has come down to us over the years in the phrase "the ends justify the means." Machiavelli wrote *The Prince* hoping he would be hired by the ruling Medici family; ironically, in spite of the attention the book has received over the years, the Medici chose to ignore the book and Machiavelli.

Civic humanism. Civic humanism was a form of Renaissance humanism that originated in Florence between 1385 and 1425, during the period when the Florentine republic was threatened by the military advances of Gian Galeazzo Visconti, the tyrant of Milan. Coluccio Salutati and Leonardo Bruni, the humanist chancellors of Florence between 1375 and 1425, were the leading practitioners of this school of thought, which extolled the republican form of government, liberty over tyranny, family values, and hard work. Important documents of civic humanism include Salutati's republican letters to Florentine allies in Italy, and Bruni's book *On the Family*, which became the basis of bourgeois-capitalist family values in ensuing centuries.

The civic humanists educated a generation of Florentine upper-class men in their values and in this way were responsible for the defense of Florentine liberty against the Milanese. Civic humanism was also associated with republicanism, as these values formed the basis of republican traditions that developed elsewhere in Renaissance Italy, as well as in England and its North American colonies.

The spread of humanism in Italy. The *studia humanitatis* was influential throughout Italy, both in the republican and princely states, perhaps because the literature of Rome and Greece was written in republican settings (Roman and Athenian republics) as well as imperial ones (Roman Empire, Hellenistic Age).

In 1434, the banker Cosimo de' Medici returned to Florence from exile. From then until the fall of the

Medici regime in 1494, the Medici family ruled Florence under the façade of a republic. During this sixty-year period, civic humanism was no longer in vogue; rather, a different kind of humanism, *courtly humanism*, flourished. This humanism valued transcendental ideas, which could be construed as a psychological antidote to the despotism of the period. Elsewhere in Italy (in Baldassare Castiglione's *Book of the Courtier*, for example), humanist values were oriented to shaping the perfect courtier who served his prince, carried himself with dignity, and looked good in court.

The Renaissance idea that is most well known today is that of the dignity of human beings. It is important to note that not all Renaissance thinkers asserted human dignity; some humanists wrote of the misery of the human condition. However, the Renaissance argument for the individual's essential dignity is the most optimistic position ever expressed up to that point in history. It was based on the idea of the Florentine philosopher Marsilio Ficino that the human being is the center of God's creation, that he shares the qualities of *soul* with God and the angels above, and *matter* with animals and plants below. Giovanni Pico della Mirandola, another Florentine, adopted a position that drew from all the ancient philosophies and not just from Platonism, as Ficino did. In his *Oration on the Dignity of Man*, Pico maintained that since humans were created with no fixed nature, they could be like the angels and God himself, or like the meanest brute

or vegetable. Human dignity, he said, lies in man's ability to adapt whatever nature he chooses.

Protestant reformers, such as Martin Luther and John Calvin, and humanists, such as Michel de Montaigne, made strong counterarguments. Many Protestants argued that man completely lost his dignity with Adam's sin and was, as a result, a mere seedbed of evil. Montaigne argued that humans are inferior even to animals and that they cannot attain certain knowledge or truth. These views on man's nature would be modified again in the scientific revolution of the seventeenth century, when it was argued that man could know with certitude the laws of nature.

Humanism and art. Humanism was the most pervasive intellectual current of the Renaissance. As such, it had an impact on Platonic and Aristotelian philosophy, on universities, and on music, theology, and art.

Artists in the Middle Ages often painted classical Greco-Roman subjects, such as Dido and Aeneas from Virgil's *Aeneid*. Virgil's story tells about the journey of the Trojan prince Aeneas to Italy, where, according to

Detail, Sistine Chapel ceiling, by Michaelangelo

myth, his landing was the basis for the settlement of Rome. Before reaching Italy, Aeneas supposedly landed in Carthage, where he fell in love with its queen, Dido. Medieval representations of their encounter show them dressed in medieval clothing and playing chess, neither of which was accurate for the Greco-Roman period. Only after humanist scholars had discovered, edited, and published ancient Greco-Roman texts could such a scene be shown more accurately. The impact of humanist scholarship on Renaissance painting was that the context and form of ancient stories such as this could be restored to accuracy.

Another example of humanist influence on Renaissance art was the way in which Neoplatonic humanism influenced architecture. The medieval church's cruciform shape emphasized the death of Jesus on the cross and, according to the Christian religion, the consequent redemption of mankind. The Renaissance church, in contrast, was domed, with light coming through a hole at the top of the dome, and the entire space was constructed according to mathematical measures of the average person. Thus, when worshipers walked into a Renaissance church, they entered a building based on human proportion and representing God as a mathematical, geometric Creator. Both aspects clearly show how the humanist-Platonic ideas of Ficino influenced Renaissance church architecture.

The humanist emphasis on human beings can also be seen in Michelangelo's *David*. This product of the restored Florentine republic, and therefore of civic humanism, shows an interest in the accurate portrayal of the human body, which was characteristic of Renaissance humanism and art.

The northern Renaissance.

Humanism in the despotic courts of Italy abandoned civic republicanism for the ideal of the *courtier*, or house scholar. This concept of humanism moved north to England, France, Germany, Spain, and Eastern Europe in the late fifteenth and early sixteenth centuries, lagging behind Italy by about a hundred years.

The spread of humanism to the north. Northern European scholars who journeyed to Italy were very much impressed by humanism. They returned home and helped foster humanist education in their own countries. The French scholar Jacques Lefèvre d'Etaples was influenced by the humanist study of Aristotle in Italy. John Colet, dean of St. Paul's in London, was similarly affected. The Dutch scholar Desiderius Erasmus was influenced in Italy, as well as in London by John Colet. Others were struck by the Platonic Academy of Florence, which was founded by Marsilio Ficino with grants from Cosimo de' Medici.

Desiderius Erasmus, *by Metsys Quentin*

Still others brought Italian ideas and treasures back to French Valois and Hispano-Germanic Hapsburg lands after the Italian wars began in 1494.

Many adherents of northern humanism were influenced by the combination of northern mystical traditions and Italian Platonist or Aristotelian humanism. Lefèvre d'Etaples, for example, combined Aristotelian studies with studies of the Old Testament Psalms and the Pauline Epistles. John Colet hoped that "good studies," as the *studia humanitatis* were often called, would combine with New Testament studies to help reform the church and its members. Others, such as Guillaume Budé in France, founded "trilingual colleges," rivaling the universities, at which classical Latin and Greek as well as Old Testament Hebrew were taught.

Northern humanists were critical of the *scholastics*, who focused on religious dogma and the teachings of the medieval scholars. The humanists denounced the scholastics' sloppy Latin and writing, claiming their prose was neither precise nor eloquent, and criticized their theology as eccentric.

Desiderius Erasmus (d. 1536) was one of the most famous humanists of northern Europe. He began his career as a monk, but left the monastery because it lacked good wine and would not allow him to read the pagan classical writers. After leaving the monastery, Erasmus wrote *Adages*, a document that ultimately became the standard by which sixteenth- and seventeenth-century schoolboys were taught good Latin. Toward the end of the fifteenth century, he became inspired to study the fathers of the early church, especially St. Jerome, as well as the earliest manuscripts he could find of the Greek New Testament. Erasmus made major contributions to a better understanding of the church fathers and of the New Testament.

Europe on the eve of the Reformation. Humanist scholarship on the eve of the Reformation had established a list of complaints against the church. Humanists like Lefèvre d'Etaples and Erasmus had made major criticisms, not only of "Old Learning," but of the mechanistic religious practices of the day: salvation hinging on numbers of indulgences acquired, on pilgrimages, and on fasting. Erasmus criticized the ignorance and folly of the monks, whose religious lives were often less than spiritual, chaste, and impoverished. In spite of these latter criticisms, the first Protestant, Martin Luther (1483–1546), broke with the church based on issues of theology and not of immoral behavior.

Reform and counter-reform.

The Protestant Reformation took place between 1517 and 1564; the Counter-Reformation of the Roman Catholic Church took place between 1543 and 1565. Many of the differences between the two, in theology and psychology, can be traced to the differences between these two eras.

Goals of the reformers. Humanists of the pre-Reform, such as Erasmus, criticized the Old Learning and the lackadaisical ways of the monks and clergy. Martin Luther's concept of reform originated in a theological dispute with the church.

Luther the monk obeyed church rules but did not feel that he could be saved. Yet all around him, people performed rather mechanical religious practices that were supposed to assure them of salvation. One day Luther saw the monk Tetzel selling indulgences, the proceeds of which supported him and went to Rome to help build St. Peter's basilica. "As soon as the coin goes into the box, a soul flies out of purgatory and into heaven," Tetzel said. Luther was outraged; he wrote the *Ninety-five Theses*, which argued that people are not saved by good works, but by faith given by the grace of God, as was "clearly" taught in Holy Scripture, according to Luther.

Thus was born the doctrine of salvation accepted by the classical reformers of the sixteenth century, including Luther, John Calvin (1509–1564), and others. These so-called *right-wing* reformers believed in the three "alones": salvation comes through grace alone, faith alone, and the Bible alone, and not through the teachings of the Roman Church, its popes, councils,

Martin Luther

An Augustinian monk, Martin Luther (1483–1546) was critical of the church's teaching that salvation was gained by faith and good works. In his *Ninety-five Theses*, Luther argued that salvation, as discussed in the writings of Paul, was simply a matter of God's grace. He broadened his criticism of the church to include advocacy of German control over local churches, and later he translated the New Testament into German so that worshipers could read the scriptures for themselves. His doctrines spread, and Luther is today remembered as the leader of the Protestant Reformation.

or theologians. Implicit in this concept was the belief that no matter how many good deeds you perform, you can never do enough to win salvation through merit, since human beings are inherently evil. God must "impute righteousness" to humans; that is, he must pretend they are good enough to be saved. This belief also meant that there was no real difference between the saved and the damned. The saved, or *elect*, really deserved to be damned, and the damned justly deserved their punishment. These reformers also agreed that election was by God's predestination, consisting of decrees that God had made in advance for each person, and had nothing to do with an individual's conduct in life.

Although the mainstream Reformation churches (Lutheran, Zwinglian, Calvinist) held these views in common, they differed on other matters. All reformers had reduced the number of sacraments to two (baptism and the Eucharist, or communion), believing the remaining Roman Catholic sacraments were unscriptural. However, they had major differences over the nature of the Eucharist. Martin Luther abandoned the Catholic belief in *transubstantiation*, which held that the bread and wine on the altar are changed miraculously by the priest into the real body and blood of Jesus. Since Luther denied the priesthood, saying that all Christians are priests, he felt that this kind of miraculous change was not possible. Instead, Luther believed in what he called *consubstantiation*—that Jesus is always present in the sacramental bread and wine. Huldreich Zwingli (1484–1531) could not accept this view, since he conceived of the Eucharist as only a commemorative meal of the faithful. Calvin also believed in its commemorative nature, maintaining that Jesus was spiritually, not physically, present in the bread and wine.

The *left wing* of the Reformation, the *Anabaptists* (rebaptisers), believed in baptism of adults on the basis of their personal faith, and so infants were

Thomas More   *John Calvin*

excluded. They also believed that the church included only the saved—those who had chosen Jesus and believed in good works—not both the saved and the damned. They held that the Bible must be taken literally, and therefore members could not swear oaths of citizenship, testify in law courts, or bear arms. The Anabaptists were pacifists, as Erasmus had been. Their biblical literalism often resulted in common ownership of possessions and wives. Some stressed mystical experiences and direct contact with God. The only thing the Catholics, Zwinglians, Lutherans, and Calvinists could agree on was the necessity of eliminating the Anabaptists.

Protestants also spoke of a purified or "reformed" religion. However, they could not agree among themselves on what this meant—for example, how simple their liturgy should be and how unlike Rome's. "The seamless robe of Christ," as Erasmus had called the church, had fragmented into many parts, each of which considered itself the true church.

Goals of the Counter-Reformation. There was considerable confusion in Europe as to which religion one's local church belonged. Local priests and ministers were often not sufficiently trained to know the difference between Protestant and Roman Catholic, and their parishioners certainly could not recognize the subtle turn of phrase that distinguished a Catholic from a Lutheran priest or a Zwinglian from a Lutheran. This confusion was resolved by the settlement of the religious wars, which contributed the phrase "his region, his religion."

John Calvin wrote *Institutes of the Christian Religion* between 1536 and 1559, in which he attempted to define once and for all the doctrines that a classical reformer should believe. The Roman Catholic Church sought to achieve the same goal at the three meetings of the *Council of Trent* (1545–1547, 1551–1552, and 1562–1563).

At the Council of Trent, the pope achieved primacy over the Catholic Church. National churches (French, German, Italian) did not vote as entities but as individual church congregations, which gave an advantage to the Italian (usually propapal) prelates, who outnumbered all others. The doctrinal decrees that emerged from the Council of Trent were the mirror image of Protestant doctrines, so that by the end of the Council it was perfectly clear who was a Protestant and who was a Roman Catholic. There was no longer any room for negotiation or compromise between the two religious camps, and it would remain that way until the middle of the twentieth century.

The Council of Trent also set about reforming church abuses, many of which were centuries old: ecclesiastical offices being sold, bishops not residing in their dioceses, clergy living with women (a practice outlawed in the eleventh century). Some of these reforms had been urged by humanists such as Erasmus and Lefèvre d'Etaples. However, other reforms recommended by Erasmus, such as the abandonment of pilgrimages and the establishment of a more interior faith, were ignored by the mid-century Catholic Counter-Reformation. The goal of the reformers at Trent was to cleanse the church of faults that Protestants could criticize, not to redefine spirituality. In the process, the theology of Thomas Aquinas was given great authority, which it still enjoys today. Rather than just "the Dominican philosopher," as he had been thought of in the late Middle Ages, Aquinas became "the Catholic theologian"—philosophical spokesman for the entire Roman Catholic Church.

Whereas the reformers simplified Christian liturgy, the church at the time of the Council created a liturgy and art to capture the eye and ear and to inculcate certain Roman Catholic values. The music of the church, both sung and played (written by composers such as Palestrina and Giovanni Gabrieli), was the opposite of the simple music of the Protestant service (such as Luther's hymn "A Mighty Fortress Is Our God" and the Calvinists' and Anabaptists' psalm singing). The church's visual art showed St. Peter walking on water and healing the sick (expressing the papal primacy that the Protestants had denied); emphasized the new feast of Corpus Christi (countering the Protestants' denial of transubstantiation); and praised the mystical visions of the saints (such as the ecstasy of St. Teresa) to stress the rewards of good works.

Baroque architecture demonstrated the church's desire to impress and psychologically move the public. Grand churches, such as the Church of Jesus in Rome, featured flamboyant façades and paintings gilded with gold. This architecture, along with baroque art and literature, reflected the sense of triumph over Protestant enemies that characterized the post-Trentine Catholic Church and papacy.

The elaborate baroque creations of the Roman Catholic Church exhibited a faith very different from the simplicity of Protestant worship. The latter was expressed, for example, in plain wooden Eucharist cups and in the unadorned and sometimes white-washed churches of the followers of Calvin and Zwingli. Protestant art and architecture were expressions of the inward faith of believers and their direct relationship with God, which were at the heart of the Protestant movement.

Another goal of the Counter-Reformation was to regain souls lost to the Reformation. To this end, the *Inquisition* was approved and the *index of forbidden books* was created. Another method was through the creation of new orders such as the Society of Jesus, or *Jesuits*, founded by the Spanish soldier-mystic Ignatius of Loyola. This order was directly under the control of the pope, and its adherents were known in the sixteenth and seventeenth centuries as the "apes of the pope." Their task was to debate Protestant theologians and to gain the ear of European princes so that the Catholic Church would benefit. Although the Jesuits were a very learned order, they earned a reputation for subterfuge because of their role as papal advisers to the Catholic princes of Europe.

The Counter-Reformation church also tried to regain the souls it had lost in Europe through conversions in the New World. Such conversions were gained more by battle and capture than by reasoned argument.

St. Ignatius of Loyola

Sixteenth-century politics.

In this era, politics could be separated into two periods that divide in the year 1559, with the Treaty of Cateau-Cambrésis. The first period was marked by dynastic and balance-of-power politics; the second by ideological politics caused by the Reformation.

Dynastic politics: 1494–1559. In 1494, Ludovico Sforza, duke of Milan, invited the French under the Valois king, Charles VIII, into Italy. Since the Valois family had dynastic claims on the kingdom of Naples, Sforza thought that control of the French could result in his becoming the leader of Italy. The next Valois, Louis XII, had dynastic claims to the duchy of Milan and invaded Italy in 1499, ending Sforza's rule and Italian independence.

Holy Roman Emperor Charles V, a Hapsburg, inherited dynastic claims to Milan and Naples. This drew him into Italy to fight the French over these rival claims. The Hapsburgs and French fought until they went bankrupt, during the reigns of Philip II of Spain (Hapsburg) and Henry II (Valois), who in 1559 made peace at Cateau-Cambrésis. The Hapsburgs had proven victorious, but not before the French had played clever balance-of-power politics by allying with the Ottoman sultan and German Protestants.

In summary, during the era of dynastic politics, war and political relations were governed by the need to advance the royal families' interests and increase their holdings.

Conflicting ideologies: 1559–1598. After 1559, politics significantly changed in Europe. Monarchs became more involved with ideological struggles within their own realms, and their alliances with other countries tended to be based on religion, not on purely dynastic needs. In 1559, Henry II of France was accidentally killed in the Place des Vosges and was succeeded by his weak young son, Francis II, who had just married the Queen of Scotland, Mary Stuart, a Catholic. It was at this time that the greatest complications arose in France concerning the French Calvinists, called *Huguenots*, and their noble leaders. Francis II died, and Mary returned to Scotland, where she was ousted by the local Calvinists. She sought the help of her cousin, Elizabeth I, who "protected" Mary by placing her under house arrest. It seemed that Mary had a claim to replace Elizabeth as queen and had been linked to Catholic plots against her cousin.

Henry II had three young sons, all of whom were aided in regency by their clever mother, Catherine de' Medici. She tried to protect the throne for them against the Protestant and Catholic claims of the competing French noble families, the Bourbons and the Guises. In 1572, following St. Bartholomew's Eve, she and her son Charles IX perpetrated the massacre of Huguenots in Paris and throughout France. Sixteen years later, Philip II of Spain wanted to put down the Calvinist rebels in Holland, replace Elizabeth with Mary in England, and establish the Catholic Guise family on the throne in France. The Spanish Armada sailed in 1588 in an attempt to quash the Dutch Protestant revolt against Spanish rule, to depose Elizabeth, and to replace the French Valois monarchs with the Guise claimant. Elizabeth had Mary beheaded, and the Armada was defeated by the English. The Dutch gained their independence. James I, Mary's son, succeeded in England; the Calvinist-turned-Catholic Henry IV ascended the throne in France; and Philip II used his belief in Roman Catholic orthodoxy to stimulate Spain's political cohesion. Spain was closed to outside ideas, and Hapsburg intermarriage eventually produced mentally deficient monarchs.

In summary, during the period following 1559, balance-of-power politics gave way to religious and ideological conflicts, often within and across state borders, the goal being destruction of one side by the other.

European religions in 1600

□ Mostly Protestant   □ Mostly Catholic

New developments.

The early modern period saw four developments that changed the world. These increased the power of the state and at the same time decreased confusion caused by local magnates. In addition, the technologies caused the exploitation of others and the exchange of foods and diseases.

Capitalism. It has been argued that capitalism is a product of Protestantism. However, the capitalist means of production were already established in fifteenth-century Italy and sixteenth-century England, when, because of the depressed economy, great merchants such as the Medici diversified their activities.

Such merchants owned raw materials, such as wool and silk, and sold the finished products on the international markets. Their agents followed the creation of the goods all the way through the production process. Most important, in almost every step of that process the entrepreneur owned the means of production (looms, fulling machines) and hired the workers. Craft traditions diminished as the status of master craftsman became hereditary and as apprentices less frequently moved up in the production process; instead, a *cottage industry* system was used. In this way, a working class, or *proletariat*, began to develop.

Exploration. During the fifteenth and sixteenth centuries, explorers sought gold, spices, and individual wealth. Spanish explorers in the New World required natives to convert to Catholicism or be killed. Indeed, Spanish notaries read very formal documents to the natives, outlining the history of Christianity and the papacy. Of course, the natives understood little or none of this, but when they saw their people being slaughtered, they realized they had little choice. The converts continued to practice their old beliefs, often incorporating the new religion into the old.

The most famous explorer of the era was Christopher Columbus. Some historians have painted the bleakest picture of the Columbian encounter, emphasizing exploitation, slavery, and the spread of disease; they argue that the Spaniards easily beat the Aztecs because the latter had no immunities to the measles or smallpox which the Spaniards introduced. Others have portrayed the event in a more positive way, stressing Columbus's role in the opening of the Western Hemisphere. Whatever our opinion of Columbus, there is no doubt that he changed the world for all time.

Printing. Early printers such as Johann Gutenburg, Johann Fust, and Peter Schöffer tried to imitate manuscript production as closely as possible. Thus, early printed books continued to use the abbreviations, scripts, and decorations of manuscripts, so much so that in documents of the era, sometimes it is difficult to tell which part is printed and which is written by hand.

Censorship

Printers such as Johann Gutenberg, whose printing press is shown here, brought the printed word to a much wider audience. Along with printing, however, came the growth of censorship. The case of Martin Luther shows why people in authority felt that censorship was necessary.

Luther, an obscure German monk in Saxony, demanded church reforms in his *Ninety-five Theses* (1517). In earlier times, he would have nailed his handwritten document to the door of the cathedral, a university debate would have ensued, and the matter would have been taken care of locally. But by having his document printed and distributed, Luther caused an uproar that reverberated throughout Europe and down through the ages.

Similar situations, though less famous, occurred with other dissidents during the sixteenth century, until both Catholic and Protestant leaders felt it necessary to expunge the cancer of heresy from their lands. Toward that end, monarchs and church leaders established censorship mechanisms. Kings, for example, granted printing "licenses," so that printers who produced unauthorized works would lose their right to publish, and their fonts would be destroyed. The church also used elaborate forms of censorship, perhaps the most dramatic being the Inquisition, during which heretics could be imprisoned or turned over to the secular authorities for execution.

Printing was truly revolutionary. Previously, the accuracy of each manuscript depended on the linguistic skill of the copyist, as well as on such factors as eyesight, fatigue, and quality of light. Accordingly, many mistakes crept into the work. The advantage of the printed book was not only that five hundred or a thousand copies could be made at a time, but that they would be relatively error free, so that a reader in Rome and a reader in Cracow could discuss the same text in their letters.

The result was a great advance in scholarship. In the early fifteenth century, for example, Bohemian religious reformer Jan Hus was declared a heretic and executed. Without the aid of printing, his ideas did not spark a religious revolution. Between 1517 and 1524, however, thousands of copies of Luther's works were published, and he became known all over Europe. Printing thus helped transform heresy into Reformation.

Warfare. The technology of war also underwent a revolution in the early modern period. Inventions were refined that had come from China but up to that time had not yet been fully developed.

During the Middle Ages, warfare had been conducted by knights in armor riding on horseback, and a code of chivalry had developed around this practice. *The Song of Roland*, for example, depicts noble warriors on one side actually selecting noble warriors on the other side with whom to do battle. However, the practice was rendered ineffective by the English in

Fifteenth-century French castle

Why studying history pays off
Reason #2:

The study of history pays off because it introduces us to other ways of thinking and acting, and in so doing, teaches us more about ourselves.

1346 at the battle of Crécy and again in 1415 at Agincourt, when the French cavalry was attacked not by other noblemen but by peasant longbow men who shot from a great distance.

In 1326, warfare was changed forever by the introduction of gunpowder. Using it, cannons could put massive holes in castle walls, making it no longer necessary to lay siege to a castle for weeks or months. Gunpowder in rifles also allowed noblemen to be shot down by peasants, who now made up the bulk of the army.

The very tactics of war changed. Fortifications were armed with cannonry. With the demise of chivalry, kings rather than noblemen controlled larger armies of commoners and enforced the royal will; nobles became mere generals in the royal armies. Pikemen and musketeers operating in military formations called *phalanxes* replaced cavalry as the "sinews" of armies. Warfare strategies developed that placed pikemen at the perimeter of phalanxes and squares; when cavalry attacked, the horsemen would meet a prickly mass of *pikes*, or wooden shafts with pointed steel heads. Then the pikemen would give way to the musketeers firing from the center of the formation. The dehorsed nobility were easy targets even for the inaccurate early guns. It was in this way that in 1525 at the Battle of Pavia the ranks of French knighthood were decimated and the French king, Francis I, was captured.

Equally profound changes occurred as a result of the use of cannons. The most striking example was the capture of Constantinople in 1453. The Byzantine capital had been considered impregnable, having a formidable wall on its landward side and a navy that used a combination of "Greek fire" (flames scattered on the water, burning attacking ships) and deadly crossbows. However, when the Ottoman Turks attacked with huge cannons made by Hungarian craftsmen, the city's walls were breached, and the Byzantine ships were no match for Ottoman ships that had superior cannon firepower.

People at the time were not oblivious to these changes in the style of warfare. Noblemen found it loathsome that mere peasants with bullets could vanquish them more easily than could valiant foes on horseback. The "poetry" of war was no more.

Modern Europe

The modern period began with the new science of the Enlightenment, which seemed to suggest an unalterable line of progress for humanity. These hopes have been dampened by the consequences of modern state formation and war, which have cast doubt on the future of the West. Even the hopeful nationalist movements of the nineteenth century only hid sectional animosities that still exist today.

The Age of Science.
The Middle Ages, Renaissance, and Reformation have been called the Age of Faith; modern European history can be called the Age of Science.

It began with the *scientific revolution*, which refers to that period between Nicholas Copernicus and Sir Isaac Newton, when a new science was constructed, based on a new way of thinking (humanism), a new instrument (the telescope), and a new mathematics (calculus). It is a mistake, though, to think that science did not exist before the scientific revolution. In fact, the Babylonians and Greeks had an astronomical science that was very accurate, even though they used only naked-eye observation.

New science and cosmology. People in the Hellenistic world and the Middle Ages had an earth-centered cosmology, believing the sun and all the planets circled the earth, which stood motionless at the center of the universe. Copernicus's new cosmology represented a radical departure, depicting a cosmos in which the earth and all the planets circled the sun. Based on naked-eye observation, the former view seems more reasonable, but the new science taught that observation does not always lead to correct conclusions; to know nature's truth, one must understand mathematics and imagine space as geometric.

In 1543, Copernicus, a Polish cleric in the Roman Catholic Church, published *On the Revolution of the Heavenly Spheres*, in which he described his *heliocentric*, or sun-centered, thesis. Copernicus had journeyed to Italy and perhaps had been inspired by humanist Platonistic beliefs that the sun, as God's representative, ought to be at the center of the universe.

Galileo Galilei became a Copernican around 1597. In 1609, using a crude telescope he had assembled, Galileo observed the mountainous surface of the moon and discovered the five satellites of Jupiter, which he

Some key events and people: 1700–2000

1700
Rise of Prussia
Rise of Russia: Peter the Great
Jean Jacques Rousseau

1750
Industrial Revolution
American Revolution
U.S. Constitution
French Revolution

1800
Napoleon I and empire of the French
Congress of Vienna
Spread of political and economic liberalism

1850
Growth of nationalism
French Second Empire: Napoleon III
German unification and empire: Otto von Bismarck
The new imperialism
Triple Alliance

1900
British Empire at full extent

Triple Entente
World War I
Russian Revolution
Rise of fascism and Nazism
The Great Depression (1930–1940)
Franklin D. Roosevelt and the New Deal
World War II and the Holocaust
Atomic bomb
United Nations

1950
The Cold War (U.S. and U.S.S.R.)
Indochina War (Vietnam)
European Economic Community (Common Market)

1970
U.S.–China renewal of relations: Richard Nixon

1980
Cold War renewal: nuclear arms race
Mikhail Gorbachev and revolution in Eastern Europe

1990
End of Cold War
German reunification

Newtonianism

It is important to remember that Isaac Newton (1642–1727), though considered by many to be the greatest scientist of all time, was nonetheless a man of his time and not ours. This becomes apparent when we realize that Newton studied alchemy, a field (discredited today) in which practitioners sought to change base metals into gold or silver. In fact, it was from what Newton thought he found in his alchemical studies that he derived his law of gravity. Later scientists divorced Newton's alchemy from his physics and created what we know as modern Newtonianism.

named the Medicean planets. An excellent experimenter and observer, he correctly formulated the rate of acceleration for falling bodies. In 1632, he published the *Dialogue on the Two Great World Systems*, which resulted in the forced recanting of his Copernicanism before the Inquisition in Rome in 1633. He lived the rest of his life under house arrest, but his *On the Two New Sciences* was published in Holland in 1638.

Two other great scientists during this time were Johannes Kepler and René Descartes. Kepler discovered that the planets do not revolve about the sun in circles but in elliptical orbits. Descartes's *Cartesianism* was the dominant cosmology before Newton. It posited a universe full of matter in the form of atoms; the motion of atoms in vortices explained all motion. Descartes also invented analytic geometry.

Vitalism and *alchemy* were based on the beliefs that objects in the universe are alive and that occultists can transmute one living thing into another. These seemingly unscientific views, popular during the Renaissance, played a part in the pioneering discoveries of another great scientist, Isaac Newton.

Newton discovered the law of gravity: that any body in the universe is attracted to any other, no matter

where, by the product of their masses and inversely by the square of their distances. Unlike Descartes, who believed the universe to be full of matter, Newton believed that the universe is empty of matter. He also believed that the universe is governed by laws of nature that permeate empty space.

Since the universe is largely empty, Newton realized something was necessary to act as a glue—to hold it together and prevent its parts, such as the moon, from flying off into space. The moon circles the earth, Newton posited, because the force of gravity pulls it toward the earth. Newton called that pulling an "active force"—that is, a force by which God makes the universe run. Such forces seemed to show that God was active in the universe in a way that Descartes's theories did not allow.

The Enlightenment. By the middle of the eighteenth century, the view of many people was that the universe was like a giant clock, made by a great clockmaker who seldom needs to intervene in its working. In this view, God had become a kind of "do-nothing deity" at the outskirts of the universe.

Voltaire, an important Enlightenment thinker, believed that God exists but exerts no individual providence. Thus, to cite a story he wrote, if Lesbia's pet sparrow is sick, one should not pray for its recovery. If according to natural law it will recover, there is no need to pray. If according to nature's course it will not, prayer will only insult God.

Anti-Christianism strongly marked the *Encyclopédie*, which was published in the mid-eighteenth century. Besides offering useful instruction in manual crafts, this book took the usual Enlightenment jabs at religious "enthusiasm." For example, an article on Noah's Ark contains cross references not only to *Bible* but to *Superstition*.

Jean Jacques Rousseau opposed many of the most cherished values of the Enlightenment. He became the enemy of reason when he wrote *The Social Contract*, *Émile*, and *The Discourse on the Origins of Social Inequality*. Unlike most enlightened thinkers, Rousseau praised the state of nature rather than civilization, finding in the latter the source of all inequality and unhappiness. He is read today as a father of both fascism and democracy.

The Age of Revolutions. James I of England and VI of Scotland ascended the throne of Great Britain after the death of Queen Elizabeth I in 1603. Thus began the era of monarchical absolutism. The Stuart kings of England and the Bourbon kings of France claimed kingship by divine right. However, the English Revolution of 1641, led by Oliver Cromwell, thwarted this pretension when the reigning king, Charles I, was deposed and executed by act of Parliament, and Cromwell became Protector of the Commonwealth.

Voltaire

Louis XIV

Charles II and James II (again Stuarts) succeeded Cromwell. Their claim to divine right kingship and their preference for Roman Catholicism were overturned by the so-called Glorious Revolution of 1688, when William and Mary succeeded after James II fled.

In France, Louis XIV was the most grand of the Bourbon absolute monarchs. His grandson, Louis XV, succeeded him at a time of economic turmoil in France. This turmoil, combined with social unrest, culminated in revolution.

The French Revolution began in 1788 when Louis XVI called the Assembly of Nobles, attempting to exact taxes. The Assembly demanded that the Estates-General be called. The three "estates" were representatives of the nobility, clergy, and workers—the eighteenth-century heirs of the "society of orders" that had begun in the Carolingian period. In 1789, the third estate (the commons) declared itself the National Convention, or "the people." They stormed the Bastille and marched on Versailles, the immense and ornate palace built by Louis XIV to display royal majesty to the French nobility. In the face of these events, Louis XVI acceded to the third estate's demands: that he recognize his status as a constitutional, not a divine right, monarch; that all people

The execution of Louis Capet

When Louis XVI (1754–1793), king of France,

tried to flee the country during the course of the French Revolution, he and the queen, Marie Antoinette, were caught and brought back to Paris as prisoners. Louis was brought before the National Assembly not as king, but as a mere man, referred to as Citizen Capet. Louis Capet was condemned as an enemy of the Republic and executed. The French monarchy was dead.

have equal rights (a cause for which Americans had recently fought in their own revolution); and acceptance of the tricolor flag to replace the monarchical flag.

Louis tried to flee France, but he and the queen, Marie Antoinette, were recognized and brought back to Paris. Louis was guillotined in January 1793; his wife was executed later. Their son died in prison.

The revolution had entered its radical stage, the Reign of Terror. Many nobles who had not fled France and were friends of the moderate revolution were guillotined. The Terror was followed by a conservative reaction, the Directory, and in 1800 by a Consulate of three men. The First Consul was a successful Corsican general, Napoleon Bonaparte (1769–1821), who became emperor of the French in 1804. He reigned until his abdication in 1814. Exiled to the island of Elba, Napoleon returned but was defeated one hundred days later, on June 18, 1815, at the battle of Waterloo. The monarchy was restored to power until the Revolution of 1848.

Significance of the era. The Age of Revolutions established the modern concepts that all people are equal; that they should live under constitutional government, which assures their liberties; and that advancement in society should be the result of merit and not of heritage or blood.

Machines and *isms*.
The social fragmentation that had begun with the Renaissance and Reformation culminated during the eighteenth and nineteenth centuries in a series of political, economic, and artistic revolutions and *ism*s.

The Industrial Revolution. The Industrial Revolution of the eighteenth and nineteenth centuries is probably of even greater significance than the French Revolution or the Age of Revolutions. Two of the most important consequences were the increase in velocity of trade and the possibilities presented by the building of railroads.

Before the Industrial Revolution, velocity of trade depended on the quality of sail and the speed and persistence of wind, if the carrier was a ship; or the strength of animals and quality of roads, if the carrier went overland. The development of the steam engine changed all that. On the sea, steamships were not hostage to the weather. On land, railroads could go great distances; they were called "iron horses" and their tracks "iron roads." The resulting acceleration in velocity of trade was not the result of harder work or better trained merchants, but simply from the use of machines. Machines created geometric increases in trade, whereas harder work and better training created only arithmetic increases.

Steamboats and railroads opened up artistic as well

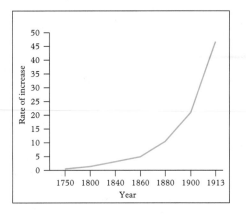

Volume of trade 1800–1913

This graph shows the effects of European industrialization and colonization on trade volume.

as economic possibilities. Painters who lived in Paris, for example, had been restricted to city scenes. Now trains allowed them to leave the city and depict subjects as new as the railroads they traveled on, such as the bridge at Argenteuil and the village of Arles in the south of France. The painter Paul Gauguin (1848–1903) even left Europe to paint native women on the Pacific island of Tahiti.

It is an undeniable fact that machines, railroads, and factories fouled cities. But cities also benefited through the building of the city sewer and rail systems.

Standardization of urban society. For the men and women who migrated from country farms to city factories, time completely changed. The pace of rural life in the nineteenth century was much slower than that of urban life. On the farm, time was measured by the sun and by the season, by the procreative seasons of the animals and the milking needs of the cows. In a city factory, workers were governed by the clock; they had to rise at a certain hour, go to work at a precise time, eat lunch on schedule, and stay on the job until the final bell.

There were social differences as well. In the country, men and women worked side by side, or at least on the same farm. In the city, women usually stayed at home, and that home was often some distance from the factory, not just next door as in the country village. Tramways and underground rail systems were needed to get from one part of the city to the other.

One overriding fact of city life was its standardization. City workers wore the same work clothes and used the same tools, provided for them at the job. They received the same type of paper wages at the same time each week, which tended to funnel them into the same types of after-work recreation. They

lived in similar homes, decorated from the same catalogues. Over time, such similarities or standardization led to alienation and loss of a sense of uniqueness, which in turn has caused many historically urban problems.

Reactions against capitalism. The Industrial Revolution increased the volume of trade but created the alienation and hardships of the factory. Soon, criticism of capitalist society developed.

Workers' lives in the nineteenth century were hard. They usually lived in miserable conditions, with little or no hope for improvement. It was this misery that spawned nineteenth-century *utopian socialism*. The term utopian was created to contrast this idealized vision with the proportedly more scientifically based writings of Karl Marx (1818–1883) and Friedrich Engels (1820 1895). Utopian communities were formed, such as the one at New Harmony, Indiana.

Marx's doctrine, in contrast, was characterized as *scientific socialism* because it was not based on what society should be, but on historical investigations of what society had been, with particular reference to the structures of work and changing modes of production. At the time, it was thought that Marx's system might predict future historical events and social forms.

Marx was originally a follower of the German philosopher Georg Wilhelm Friedrich Hegel (1770–1831). Hegel's complicated idealist philosophy was based on a *dialectic*, whereby thesis is answered by antithesis, leading in turn to synthesis. Karl Marx's

Karl Marx

reinterpretation of Hegel's ideas posited that feudal society was the thesis; bourgeois or capitalist society was the antithesis; and the predicted proletarian, classless society was the synthesis. The joining of the Hegelian dialectic with historical trends, two phases of which had culminated by the middle of the nineteenth century, seemed to lend validity to Marx's ideas, called *dialectical materialism*.

Many midcentury socialists were impressed by Marx's theories. When his ideas were further advanced by others—Engels in the nineteenth century and Vladimir Lenin (1870–1924) in the twentieth—they appeared even more formidable and convincing. By the late nineteenth century, Marx's historical philosophy had been adopted by the International, the socialist body whose professed goal was the perfection of human beings and society. Until the time of Stalin, this organization believed a revolution was coming that would cross all national boundaries.

Related in spirit to revolutionary movements, *romanticism* began in the late eighteenth century and continued through the mid-to-late nineteenth century. This movement affected painting, music, and poetry. Displaying the primal instincts and imagination of human beings, it was appropriate for an age of revolutions and railroads, an age of power.

The foremost romantic painter of the period was Eugène Delacroix (1798–1863). His earlier work depicted such exotic subjects as Middle Eastern and Oriental potentates and harems. Later he depicted political scenes in such works as *Liberty Leading the People*, which shows the working class attempting to seize power from the aristocracy and bourgeoisie in the Revolution of 1830. The people failed, but their dream was immortalized in Delacroix's painting, driven as it is by passion and romantic fervor.

The romantic movement culminated during the latter part of the nineteenth century with the musical dramas of German composer Richard Wagner (1813–1883). Wagner, intent upon uniting the force of drama with that of music, used musical phrases or *leitmotifs* throughout his operas to reference previous characters, stories, even other operas. Wagner's early opera, called *Rienzi, Tribune of the People*, is about a fourteenth-century hero whose goal was to free Florence and make it a true republic. Clearly, this opera picked up on romantic and revolutionary themes of the period. His four-opera masterpiece, *Der Ring des Niebelungen*, pitted a superman hero, Siegfried, against conniving gods who had lost their ability to rule, in an attempt to possess the gold of the Rhine River. In the end, all are dead, and the stolen gold has returned to nature at the bottom of the Rhine. Nature, Germanic gods, supermen: these were some of the themes of late romanticism.

Unification movements.
Three great European states were unified in the mid-to-late nineteenth century: Germany, France, and Italy. Germany is a model for state formation. France is an example of cultural unification. Italy shows the difficulties faced by all states caught up in the process of state formation and cultural unification.

Germany. Germany as a cultural entity had existed since the sixteenth century, but German-speaking lands were divided into kingdoms and principalities that seemed to defy unification. At the opening of the nineteenth century, the king of Prussia dominated the rulers of the northern German principalities, while the king of Austria exerted a strong influence over Bavaria and the other southern German states. Following the fall of Napoleon in 1815, the separation of these two groups was made more pronounced by the fact that the northern states, through a customs union called the *Zollverein*, formed an economic federation to which the southern states did not belong. A single state did not yet exist, but a combination of strong rulers and dramatic events in the middle of the century was about to change that.

The Prussian ruler in the mid-nineteenth century, Kaiser Wilhelm (William) I, was a very powerful and ambitious monarch. He chose an equally strong prime

Richard Wagner

Richard Wagner (1813–1883) was a man in whom dwelt both the best and the worst of nineteenth-century German romanticism. His towering achievement was to combine musical and theatrical elements into a form which he called *music-drama*, as exemplified in *Der Ring des Nibelungen*, created during the period 1853–1874. This tetralogy was made up of *Das Rheingold*, *Die Walküre*, *Siegfried*, and *Götterdämmerung*. Other operas include *Rienzi*, *The Flying Dutchman*, *Tannhäuser*, and *Lohengrin*.

Late in his life, Wagner moved to Bayreuth, Bavaria, where he built a theater designed for his monumental music-dramas. His works are still performed there today.

Like many Europeans of the era, Wagner was anti-Semitic. These beliefs, combined with the inspirational quality of his music, made him a favorite composer of Adolph Hitler over a half century later. Wagnerian themes were often played at Nazi rallies and events.

The events of World War II have made Richard Wagner a somewhat controversial composer today. Yet even among his detractors, few would deny his musical genius.

minister, Count Otto von Bismarck. Their conservative policies strengthened the economic union of the north and thwarted the liberal parliament, or *Reichstag*, which had hoped to govern Prussia. Bismarck, following the example of France's Emperor Napoleon III, undercut the German parliament, appealing directly to the people by granting liberal domestic social policies while strengthening the autocratic powers of the king and prime minister. Hoping to unify the German people by rallying them behind a common cause, Bismarck and Wilhelm I declared and won a war against Austria in the 1860s, breaking Austria's hold over the southern German states and assuring Prussian domination of German affairs. A new German empire resulted, of which Austria was not a part.

To further cement the emerging empire, the Prussian leaders went to war against the France of Napoleon III, defeating it at the Battle of Sedan in 1870. Germany's victory allowed Wilhelm to proclaim the Second Reich in the Hall of Mirrors at Versailles in France and to annex Alsace and Lorraine, regions that included both German- and French-speaking citizens. This Franco-Prussian War (1869–1870) set the stage for many of the events that would unfold a half century later. For example, France's desire to avenge

defeat and reclaim lost territories was one of the causes of World War I; and years later, in World War II, recovering these same territories for Germany would become a Nazi goal.

France. France had been a monarchy for centuries. Then it became a republic, an empire, a monarchy, a republic, an empire, and finally, in the nineteenth century, a republic again. By this time there was a state to rule, but was there a national identity? Did people consider themselves "French"?

The Third Republic, established in 1870 after the fall of Napoleon III, realized that its most important task was to create a united people. The three tools for achieving this task were education, the railroad, and the army.

France was replete with public and Roman Catholic schools at the time of the founding of the Third Republic. One of the important acts of the Republic was to found a ministry of education, which created a very precise national curriculum that every child in the nation had to take. The school system acted like a filter: only the best students attended the finest schools in the system, while all others were consigned to lesser schools or technical schools. This regimentation in education helped bring unity to the state.

By the late nineteenth century, there were railroads

Delacriox's Liberty Leading the People

History of Western Civilization

throughout France. Trains were important for carrying food from the country to Paris, then back to the country. In addition, railroads had an effect on schools. Paris-trained teachers were sent by rail to even the most far-flung areas of France, guaranteeing that the centralized educational system could be implemented.

Universal military service was required in the Third Republic, which also promoted a unified France. Whether in barracks, on the train, or in drill formation, men who spoke different dialects had to learn to understand each other and get along. The common language became Parisian French, so that thereafter, people might speak their own dialects at home or in their villages, but when they traveled, they would speak like Parisians. Because of education, railroads, and the army, a national identity was created that went beyond the purely political. The slogan "From peasants to Frenchmen" expressed the ideal that was the great achievement of the Third Republic.

Italy. Because Italy had been divided historically, the state lacked even the most rudimentary borders. But between 1840 and 1870, the movement known as the *Risorgimento* united Italy. It was inspired by Giuseppe Mazzini (1805–1872), who convinced the people that they should be both united and free from tyranny.

Independence, however, could only be achieved with military and political cunning. Victor Emmanuel II (1820–1878), king of Sardinia, realized there was a movement toward independence and that he could lead it. Fortunately, he had a capable prime minister, Count Camillo di Cavour, who was familiar with the intricacies of Italian and European politics. Whereas Mazzini had been utopian about the future Italian state, Cavour recognized that his own liberalism had to be balanced with authoritarianism.

A third architect of Italian independence and unity was Giuseppe Garibaldi (1807–1882), leader of his guerrilla "red shirts" and, briefly, dictator of the Kingdom of the Two Sicilies. By 1860, all Italy except for the Papal States was united under the king of Sardinia. With the help of Garibaldi, Rome was conquered, and the kingdom of Italy was fully united.

The unification of Italy under the house of Savoy did not mean that Italy identified itself as one state. Whereas France had provincial dialects or languages, Italy had city and village dialects and languages. In addition to this problem, in 1871 almost 69 percent of the population was illiterate. This figure disguised regional differences: more southern than northern Italians were illiterate. The process of creating a unified state would therefore be more difficult in the south than in the north.

One way to begin the process was through schools and the army, as had been the case in France. An incentive for army conscripts to learn to read was to make it a requirement of service, to be completed before discharge. But since there was no literature to read in many of the local dialects, there was no incentive for veterans to continue the practice. The problem was compounded by the fact that well into the twentieth century, the Italian educational system was much inferior to that of France, and it lacked the French meritocratic spirit. As a result of these and other factors, Italian unity is still a problem today.

Developmentalism. Charles Darwin (1809–1882) sailed to the Pacific on his ship, the *Beagle*, and returned to England with a scientific revolution. Underlying all his writings was the concept of *developmentalism*—that is, the belief that things progress or develop from simple to more complex.

Developmentalism was a major notion coursing through nineteenth-century thought. It is present, for instance, in Marx's and Hegel's theories, since dialectics presupposes a progression from a primordial and less perfected state to a future perfection. For that matter, Enlightenment scholars as far back as the eighteenth century had looked forward to a time when human beings and society would be perfect.

In 1899, Sigmund Freud (1856–1939) published *On the Interpretation of Dreams*. This was Freud's first explanation of his new science of dreams. He, too, was a product of nineteenth-century developmentalism. Freud argued that adults are the product of childhood experiences, and that the repression of unacceptable

Social Darwinism

In the late nineteenth century, many Europeans, taking their cue from Charles Darwin's "survival of the fittest" theories, pointed to their own wealth and power as proof of cultural superiority over the peoples of Africa, Asia, and South America. This came to be known as Social Darwinism. Because Europeans understood their meetings with non-Europeans in terms of this misapplication of Darwin's theories, they believed they had a duty to "civilize" and force their own customs on the rest of the world. This duty, referred to as "the white man's burden," was often used to justify the desire to increase trade and expand power.

Sigmund Freud

childlike behaviors causes neuroses in later life. In Freud's psychoanalytic treatment, patients undergo a therapy in which they recount experiences of their youth, as well as dreams whose meaning is associated with real life experiences.

Freud's theory held that there are three parts to human nature: *ego* (the self), *superego* (the self expressed with the constraints of society imposed on it), and *id* (the inner self that seeks expression but is thwarted by the superego). Whereas Jean Jacques Rousseau had believed that humans in their natural state are good and are destroyed by civilization, Freud believed that civilization is good, because the superego it creates is necessary to repress the irrational and subconscious wishes of the human id. This civilized superego, however, is also the cause of human neuroses, which must be treated by the psychoanalyst. Freud's was the first major voice in modern times to speak against the perfectibility of man by positing an irrational side to man's nature.

European imperialism. The map of
the world in 1914 shows the results of British, French, German, and American imperialism. The Great Powers, seeking markets and raw resources for their industries, colonized much of the world. Even lesser powers such as Holland and Belgium were involved in imperialist ventures. Examples of colonization include the French in Indochina, the Americans in the Philippines, the Dutch in Burma, and the Belgians in the Congo.

Imperialism did not always begin as a government-sponsored venture. The British trading companies were first in Africa and India, followed in the middle-to-late nineteenth century by the home government of England. Thus, India became part of the British Raj, or empire. By the late nineteenth century, the governments of these European states began to clash as they divided up the vast territories of Africa. In 1898, the British and French met at Fashoda, and war between them was narrowly avoided. War was also barely avoided during the two Morocco crises of 1905 and 1911.

During the process of empire formation, all the great powers were emboldened by their conviction that they were superior to the peoples they were conquering. It was their duty, they believed, to bring civilization and Christianity to the peoples of Africa, India, and Southeast Asia. Never had religious zeal, monetary gain, and geopolitics been so completely and happily united as in the late nineteenth and early twentieth centuries. Whether it was Henry Stanley (1841–1904) and David Livingstone (1813–1873) meeting in central Africa, or Cecil Rhodes (1853–1902) running diamond mines in what is now Zimbabwe, the Europeans were certain of their mission.

World War I. Then, with a shocking suddenness, civilization came apart. A political assassination in the Balkans was the spark that drew all the great powers into a war. The sides were aligned according to the so-called Secret Accords prior to the war, with Britain, France, Italy, Russia, and (after 1917) the United States on one side; and the German, Austro-Hungarian, and Ottoman empires on the other. Soldiers from the far-flung colonies of these states also were called to arms, making it truly a world war.

Both sides had thought that the war would be short.

American cemetery in France, World War I

Instead, the fighting settled down to four years of trench warfare: soldiers would surge forth, a ferocious battle would ensue (as at Marne and Verdun), thousands would be killed or gassed, but only a few feet of territory would be won or lost before new trenches were dug. About 1,400,000 French, 1,800,000 Germans, and 1,700,000 Russians lay dead in the fields of Europe. Because the United States didn't enter the war until 1917, fewer Americans were killed. Worldwide, a total of eight million people lost their lives. It was "the war to end all wars," said President Woodrow Wilson (1856–1924), but others disagreed. The veneer of civilization had been stripped away.

Late in the war, Vladimir Lenin's Bolsheviks in Russia settled with the German empire: With the abdication of the German kaiser, the Weimar Republic was created in its place. Its government met with the Allied victors at the Versailles peace conference. At the conference, Wilson sought a League of Nations, open treaties so that the great powers would never again fall into war, and self-determination for all peoples. Premier Georges Clemenceau (1841–1929) of France prevailed in his demands that Germany pay reparations for World War I and the Franco-Prussian War. In time, Germans came to blame the Versailles Treaty's tough terms on the Weimar Republic. Adolf Hitler took advantage of these feelings and gained power in 1933, preparing Germany for what in many ways would be the continuation of World War I.

Depression and dreams. World War
I was followed by worldwide economic depression, the failure of the League of Nations, and the subsequent establishment of Marxist-Leninism in Russia and fascism in Italy. Many people hoped that the new communist and fascist leaders could help build a better world.

Money. The Great Depression hit the United States in 1929; but in the decade prior to that, there was economic depression in Europe. Germany was particularly hard hit by monetary inflation, in which basketsful of Deutsch marks were required to purchase the barest necessities of life. In such a situation, who or what was to be blamed? The Versailles Treaty? The Weimar Republic? Many Germans concluded that the blame should be placed squarely on the Jews. Adolf Hitler (1889–1945) used and focused these ideas.

Parades and trains. Hitler and Italy's Benito Mussolini (1883–1945) were not simply purveyors of hate. They could also claim accomplishments: in Germany, the Volkswagen and superhighways, or *autobahns*; and in Italy, on-time trains and the eradication of malaria from Roman marshes. As both countries readied themselves for conflict, more people were put to work in factories producing war materiel. And there were the parades. Hitler's great celebrations of the Aryan warriors at Nuremberg could stir people to frenzies of patriotism. In Italy, people were asked to put fascist symbols and candles on their windowsills

The Holocaust

When Adolf Hitler became dictator of Germany in 1933, he instituted a crackdown on the Jewish population. Hitler and the Nazis made it impossible for Jews to remain in the professions, businesses, or universities of Germany. In 1942, the Nazi elite gathered in Potsdam to put the finishing touches on a plan called the "final solution." This plan foresaw the killing of all Jews in lands controlled by Germany, as well as all handicapped and retarded people and all Gypsies. In death camps such as Auschwitz and Buchenwald, victims were led off to gas chambers or killed and then thrown into common ditches for graves. Six million Jews and about two million others died in this manner.

economic difficulties in the 1920s and 1930s. Some historians have argued that the Weimar Republic itself wanted Germany to regain its territory lost with the Versailles Treaty and that, once in power, Hitler simply adopted those same goals. Moreover, it seems clear that Hitler's policy of *Anschluss*, the regaining of German-speaking territories, was pursued in order to make Germany the most powerful central European state.

Whatever the interpretation of Hitler's goals, once he became chancellor of Germany in 1933, he installed a totalitarian regime that took a terrible toll in human life before its fall in 1945. As in Mussolini's Italy, emphasis was placed on devotion to the state. Jews, Gypsies, and other minority groups that did not fit Hitler's patriotic mold lost employment and, in some cases, their lives. In 1942, the Nazis made final plans for the ultimate destruction of Jews and all other non-Aryans in Europe.

during parades, but many did not take these activities very seriously. There was more bluff to Mussolini than to Hitler: Mussolini had difficulty seizing Ethiopia; Hitler marched into Vienna. Once Hitler overran Poland in 1939, Mussolini immediately joined Hitler, against his own earlier warnings that Italy could not be prepared for war before 1942.

Totalitarianism and the "reign of evil." What went wrong? Why did Germany's so-called liberal democracy fail? Certainly Germany was plagued by

World War II. After having made a nonaggression treaty with Josef Stalin (1879–1953), complete with an agreement about the division of Poland between Germany and the Soviet Union, Hitler invaded Poland on September 1, 1939. On September 3, Great Britain and France declared war on Germany, and nine months later, in June 1940, Germany invaded and conquered France. The British were driven off the

The "Big Three" at Yalta: Winston Churchill, Franklin D. Roosevelt, and Josef Stalin

European mainland at Dunkirk, leaving Germany and Italy to rule most of the continent. Then suddenly, in spite of the nonaggression treaty, Hitler turned east and attacked the Soviet Union. This act engaged Germany in a war on Russian soil that cost twenty million lives and dealt a severe blow to Hitler's plans.

One could argue that World War II actually began in the Pacific in September 1937, when Japan attacked Manchuria. In so doing, Japan's militaristic cabinet was trying to assure Japan of economic hegemony in the region. Its goals, however, conflicted with those of the United States, which also had ambitions to be a major Pacific power. Japan allied with Germany and Italy, forming the Axis powers.

The United States declared war on Japan and the other Axis powers, Germany and Italy, after Japan attacked Pearl Harbor on December 7, 1941. Fighting lasted for another three and a half years. In May 1945, Nazi Germany surrendered. Japan followed suit in August after atomic bombs were dropped on the cities of Hiroshima and Nagasaki.

World War II changed the configuration of Europe for years to come. The nature of the resulting alliances meant that the conquered states and freed territories had to be divided up almost as spoils among the victors. The democracies of Eastern Europe did not emerge free after the war, and Germany and its capital Berlin were divided up among the four great powers.

Many of these decisions were made at Yalta and then at Potsdam just after President Roosevelt's death and the end of the war. Stalin exacted what he wanted:

satellite states in Eastern Europe to serve as a buffer for the vanquished Germany. The Soviets did not want Germany ever to be able to attack their heartland again. Stalin had been an ally of the United States during the war, but once the war ended, his goals—and alliances—changed.

Statism and the clash of titans. The twentieth century has seen statism, along with national leaders who have represented the best and worst aspirations of their people. *Statism* is the belief that the state is superior to individual or group interests within the state. It asserts that work for the state is the most important activity of the citizenry, thus treating the state almost as a mystical entity. These views have led to the search for a leader who is unlike other citizens in his abilities.

In Italy, this view was embodied in the figure of Benito Mussolini. The Italian leader appeared in uniform, as did Hitler, and was called *il Duce*, the leader. He liked to be portrayed as a horseman and swimmer in order to suggest a man of superior physical abilities. It was a popular stance; even American President

Europe after World War II

Nuclear-bomb test after World War II, at Bikini atoll

Franklin D. Roosevelt refused to be shown in a swim suit, which would show his crippled legs.

The myth of the great man was also carried on by Josef Stalin in the Soviet Union. Concerned about always being perceived as correct, Stalin frequently ordered the Soviet encyclopedia to be rewritten and republished to correct or hide mistakes he had made.

From order to chaos. When historians discuss the post-1945 world, they are dealing with nearly contemporary events. Not enough time has elapsed to allow the historian to make firm interpretations, but some broader trends can be observed.

European history since 1945 can be divided into two categories: a period of order, the Cold War, during which a struggle between the two superpowers simpli-fied the way one saw the world; and since 1990, the end of the Cold War, a period whose unfolding may be fraught with new dangers because of the collapse of old structures and the emergence of new and unknown states.

Order. The period between 1945 and 1990 is normally called the Cold War. Order during that period was established and maintained by the United States and the Soviet Union, with each superpower flexing its muscles from time to time, as in the Cuban missile and Berlin Wall crises. Americans worried that the Soviet Union sought world domination through the influencing of smaller states such as Vietnam. Signs of disorder—Yugoslavia's break with the Soviets; China's disagreements with Moscow; Gaullist France's break with NATO—left the West somewhat baffled. What would real disorder do?

A peculiarity about the Cold War period is that often the same agencies that threatened war also preserved peace. The most notable forces of this type were NATO, the Warsaw Pact, and the nuclear arms industries of the two superpowers. The promise of mutual disaster seemed to constrain the urge for a first strike. Other agencies were created expressly to maintain the peace, most notably the United Nations and the European Economic Community. Although fault can be found with such organizations, they do at least offer a forum for communication and compromise.

The conclusion of World War II brought with it renewed independence efforts throughout Africa, India, and Indochina. These struggles for independence ultimately destroyed the European empires that

Mikhail Gorbachev

Interpreting history from close range is a difficult business, but it seems clear even from our present vantage point that Mikhail Gorbachev, the last Soviet president, will be remembered as one of the key figures of the twentieth century. In a period of only six years, he engineered the breakup of the Soviet Union and Soviet bloc, set the resulting governments on the road toward becoming capitalist democracies, and significantly advanced the process of world disarmament.

Perhaps just as important, he dreamed of a new openness and freedom in Soviet society and started the process of making those dreams a reality, although the ensuing collapse of the Soviet state and the discrediting of communism remained beyond his vision.

Gorbachev (b. 1931) did not set out to accomplish all these things; rather, his remarkable flexibility and vision enabled him to make dramatic policy changes in the midst of tumultuous events. At the beginning of his time in office, for example, he did not anticipate having to eliminate the ruling Communist Party. As events unfolded and the forces of democracy and freedom were unleashed, however, he realized he would have to do away with the Communist Party as the sole political party in the country, then as a political party altogether.

Finally, events and forces, rather than Gorbachev, began to run the Soviet state. In his last year in power, he tried to remake the Soviet state along democratic lines, creating capitalist forces and yet trying to retain some of the values of pre-Leninist socialism. Ultimately his efforts failed, and the Union of Soviet Socialist Republics disintegrated. Gorbachev resigned as president of the Soviet Union on December 25, 1991.

had developed in the eighteenth and nineteenth centuries. In 1948, British rule ended in India, leaving the subcontinent divided between Pakistan and India, Muslims and Hindus. The year 1948 also brought an end to the British mandate in Palestine. The creation of Israel, a national homeland for the Jews, divided the Middle East between the Arabs and the Jews. Since that time, terrible animosities and war have characterized both areas.

The French empire in Africa and Asia also ended in the years following World War II. Since Britain and France did not have the economy to maintain a military presence in the world, that role fell to the United States, notably in the Middle East and Vietnam.

Chaos. The Soviet Union collapsed in 1989, the result of economic failure and Communist Party corruption, and the Soviets' eastern European satellites regained their autonomy. The German Democratic Republic (East Germany) united with the Federal Republic of Germany (West Germany), and the Berlin Wall, constructed in 1961, was torn down. The union of the two Germanies has caused severe economic and social problems.

The Soviet Union was replaced by the Commonwealth of Independent States, a coalition of economically fragile republics. Russia, the largest of the republics, suffers from monumental problems as it attempts to introduce a market economy and to quell uprisings such as that in Chechnya. In addition, some elements in Russian and other eastern European states desire to restore communist economics and perhaps even Soviet-style rule. The economic reforms of President Boris Yeltsin have been hard on Russian citizens. Nonetheless, Yeltsin was reelected in 1996, although his poor health has raised questions about his ability to rule. Rivals are already jockeying for succession.

Ethnic hatred has devastated the former Yugoslavia. The western European states, NATO, and the United States finally dealt with the Yugoslav mayhem and "ethnic cleansing." The United States brought the warring Croatian, Serbian, and Muslim-Bosnian leaders together and negotiated the Dayton Accord. According to this treaty, the peace was to be maintained for a year by NATO-American forces, but recent elections indicate that ethnic hatred and not democratic ideals continues to dominate the region.

While a fragile plan is now in place for dealing with the chaos in Yugoslavia, problems threaten the future of the sixteen-member European Union (EU) itself. According to the Maastricht Treaty (1993), the European states must cut their state deficits from five percent of GNP to three percent; this action will enable them to adopt the new European currency, the "Euro," by the year 2002. In response, the French government proposed draconian reforms to cut its deficit, but unrest over the economy and high unemployment occurred in late 1995 and led the government to try to expel Muslims from the country, leaving in question France's ability to comply with the treaty. The long-range success of the European Union has also been put into question by the dispute between Britain and the continental states over the so-called mad cow disease, which led the Europeans to demand that a recalcitrant Britain kill a large portion of its cattle herds.

In the Middle East, a hopeful sign had been the agreements reached between the Palestinian Liberation Organization (PLO) and Israel, establishing Palestinian autonomy in Jericho and the Gaza strip, as well as the recent peace treaty between Israel and Jordan. However, progress toward peace has been threatened by domestic events in Israel, namely the assassination of Prime Minister Itzhak Rabin in 1995 and the election victory of the politically and religiously conservative Likud majority in 1996, led by Prime Minister Benjamin Netanyahu. Hardly had the Likud government been in power for 100 days when serious fighting broke out between Israeli forces and Arabs, an event that has thrown the peace process into disarray. Problems also occurred on the Middle East's perimeter as Saddam Hussein attacked Kurds opposing his regime in northern Iraq. American missiles responded, but Saddam Hussein seemed to have gained what he wanted: damage to his Kurdish enemies and the quashing of a C.I.A. plot to overthrow him.

Conclusion. The twentieth century has been the first era in which the achievements of science and technology have made possible the creation of a more comfortable life and a better world. The century has also been arguably the bloodiest in human history. Only time and the efforts of all nations will determine which trend will predominate.

Israeli soldiers train in the West Bank town of Hebron.

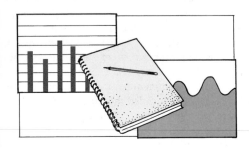

Tests, homework, and projects

Laying the groundwork

Success in a Western civilization course results from careful reading, notetaking, and studying. It requires passing various kinds of exams and sometimes doing research projects.

Reading

When you first open your textbook, take a few minutes to get an overview of the entire text. Begin by scanning the table of contents, then perhaps read the introduction to each section.

Reading and studying should be done without extraneous noise and interference, such as television or music. If you own the book, underline important ideas and terms. Ask yourself: What is the main idea here? What is the author's point of view? What does the author want me to remember as being of importance in this section?

Notetaking

You should take careful notes on your readings and on class lectures and discussions. Keeping a journal also may be helpful. Notetaking organizes your understanding of the professor's lecture as well as of the textbook's content.

When taking notes, try to jot down key concepts and ideas rather than random words and phrases. Notes should be organized, reviewed after class or reading, and redrafted in order that they make accurate sense.

Studying

Studying should not be done haphazardly; it takes deliberate preparation and strength of purpose. Most educators recommend two to three hours outside of class for every hour in class. But perhaps even more important than the *amount* of time spent studying is the *quality* of time. Set aside well-defined blocks of time for reading and notetaking. Break up these blocks with fresh air and exercise. Study periods that are too short lead to a lack of coherent understanding, while overly long study periods can lead to a point of diminishing returns.

Strategies for success

Success depends on the quality of study and on the student's willingness to make the effort. Positive mental attitudes are very important in studying and succeeding in any class. *Never assume that you are going to do badly.* If you have been attending class, keeping up with your reading, asking questions when things are unclear to you, and taking notes, you should be able to succeed in a Western civilization course.

Tests

Find out in advance what types of questions will be asked on an exam: multiple choice, fill-in, or essay. Then tailor your study accordingly. While studying, be sure to take regular breaks for fresh air or to stretch your legs. If possible, try not to "cram" for tests. Begin studying for an exam two or three evenings before the test and devote at least two hours of study each evening.

Homework

In addition to more traditional assignments, homework also consists of reading and redrafting your lecture or reading notes while the material is fresh in your mind, usually on the same day. Notes on reading should be in the form of brief summaries and statements of key concepts and chronologies. Keep in mind that history is a story; try to capture the flow and theme of that story in your notes. Keep up with reading and homework assignments, as failure to keep up can often have a snowballing effect that is difficult to overcome.

Projects

Projects can be helpful to understanding Western civilization. In history classes, these projects usually take the form of papers, although they can also consist of skits, art, or interviews of people involved in historical events (called *oral histories*). Above all, if you have a choice, select a project topic that interests you.

Helpful hints

Multiple choice

> Which of the following monarchs was proclaimed "Empress of India" during the last half of the nineteeth century? (a) Queen Victoria (b) Catherine the Great (c) Queen Elizabeth II (d) Eugénie

In any multiple choice question, first eliminate the answers that are obviously wrong. In this case, it would be those monarchs who did not live in the nineteenth century: Catherine the Great (eighteenth-century czarina of Russia) and Queen Elizabeth II (twentieth-century queen of England). This leaves Queen Victoria and Eugénie. If you do not know the correct choice between these two, you can make an educated guess and eliminate Eugénie on the basis of her French name, since India was a British colony. This leaves Eugénie's contemporary (and the correct answer), Queen Victoria.

This sample question is a good illustration of how, by eliminating options that are inappropriate, you can sometimes answer a multiple choice question correctly even if you couldn't have volunteered the information on your own. The criteria for elimination will differ from question to question, but the process is similar.

Answer: a

Fill-in

> _____ was the founder of the Society of Jesus, an order that slowed the spread of Protestantism and returned many to Catholicism.

On the face of it, this fill-in question appears to be harder than a multiple choice question, since you cannot proceed by the process of elimination. On the other hand, the term "Society of Jesus" might call to mind "Jesuit," and that might in turn lead to your remembering the order's founder, St. Ignatius. Or, looking at the rest of the question, you might recall the fervancy and combativism of the Counter-Reformation, and this might remind you of one of its most ardent leaders, Ignatius of Loyola.

In other words, for fill-in questions, be alert to context; it may jostle your memory. Study every word, because each may contain hidden clues and hints. It should be added, however, that if you have not engaged in careful reading and studying, the context may be of little help.

Answer: St. Ignatius of Loyola

Essay

> What was the impact of the Norman Conquest of England on the history of England and France? Were the consequences all beneficial to France?

Writing a good essay involves gathering and organizing evidence, then stating conclusions.

In this question, some of the pieces of evidence are: the imposition of a well-organized feudal system in England, thus avoiding many of the confused feudal loyalties that existed in Europe; the creation of an English monarchy that controlled vast areas in France, thus making the powerful English king a vassal of the French king; the claims of the English king on the French throne and the resulting One Hundred Years' War that almost destroyed the French monarchy.

Show how well you can construct a case with the evidence you present. When you've thought through the various points of your argument, fit the pieces together in a well-organized essay: Write a strong introduction giving your view or interpretation; present the evidence supporting your argument; and then summarize your findings.

Projects

> Review the history of British colonialism in West Africa, and discuss its objectives.

A term project usually requires outside reading and research, taking notes, and then writing an essay to show your understanding of the topic. For this particular topic, you'd be dealing with the history and purposes of British trading companies' outposts along the Niger River. Projects can and sometimes should be handled in less traditional ways. This project could be done as a dramatic skit with several students working together to write a short play about the Royal Niger Company.

Other suggested topics
- Compare and contrast the goals of the Reformers and Counter-Reformers.
- Discuss the achievements of ancient Mesopotamian civilization, comparing them with the achievements of the Greeks.
- Present a debate between Karl Marx and an English factory owner.
- Explore the consequences of the Versailles Treaty of 1919. To what degree were they beneficial to the Allies? To what degree not?

Glossary

Mont St. Michel

Fief

Parliament

ancien régime. Literally, "old regime," the society of nobility, kings, and clergy in pre-Revolutionary France.

Anglo-Saxons. Germanic tribes who settled in and ruled England until the Norman Conquest in 1066.

aristocrats. A class of society whose "noble" status is based on birth.

Bolsheviks. Vladimir Lenin's revolutionary party, which overthrew the more moderate Menshevik revolutionaries.

bourgeois; bourgeoisie. In capitalist society, a person who is a member of the middle class; the middle class.

Caesari. Term from the name of Julius Caesar, which referred to the rulers of the subdivided Roman Empire, below the level of the *Augusti*.

Carolingians. Kings of the Franks, such as Charles Martel, Pepin I, II, and III, and Charlemagne.

Carthage. Phoenician colony on the Mediterranean coast of North Africa and then a major naval and commercial city-state. Defeated by Rome in the three Punic wars.

Cluny. Reformed monastery in France that sparked church reform in the eleventh century.

Crusades. Wars conducted by Christians against Muslims between the eleventh and fourteenth centuries.

deism. Eighteenth-century "rational" religion, whose members believed the world operated according to universal law and had been created by a God who did not intervene in the clocklike workings of the universe.

dictator. Originally an ancient Roman magistrate appointed to deal with a temporary crisis or emergency; today, an autocratic ruler.

divine-right kingship. Theory that kings receive their power directly from God.

double-entry bookkeeping. Italian accounting method from the late Middle Ages that allowed merchants to keep a careful accounting of their monies and transactions.

Enlightenment. The period roughly covering the eighteenth century, characterized by scientific and intellectual advancement and a growing belief in human ability to manage their affairs rationally.

Estates-General. In France, the assembly of three "estates," or legislative groupings, normally called when the king wanted to raise taxes. These consisted of clergy (first estate), nobles (second estate), and everyone else (third estate).

fascism. Dictatorial system of government in which the citizen is subservient to the state. Hitler, Mussolini, and Franco were fascists.

feudalism. Political and social system dating from the late ninth century A.D., in which workers were bound to the lord of the manor in a local agricultural economy.

fief. Area a nobleman contracts to rule and protect; a feudal estate.

Gaul. Province of the Roman Empire roughly equivalent to today's France.

Glorious Revolution. The 1688 bloodless revolution whereby James II left England and was replaced by William and Mary.

Gothic. Medieval architectural style notable for its high towers and pointed arches.

Hapsburgs. Ruling family of Austria from 1282 to 1919, as well as rulers of the Holy Roman Empire, Spain, the Low Countries, and others.

History of Western Civilization

Hellenistic world. Areas around the Mediterranean Sea that were influenced by Greek culture after the conquests of Alexander the Great.

heresy. Religious teachings considered false by a religious community.

Huns. Mongolian tribe that after A.D. 370 pressured Germanic tribes, the Visigoths and Ostrogoths, to overrun the Roman Empire.

indulgences. Release from time in Purgatory, first given by popes to Crusaders who died in battle, then later given or sold to pilgrims.

Justinian (483-565). Byzantine emperor.

knight. A mounted warrior who served a feudal lord or nobleman.

levée en masse. General draft of all males into the French army.

liege-lord. Nobleman to whom a vassal swears fealty.

liturgy. Ceremony of religious worship.

mayors of the palace. Officials in the Merovingian period who had the political power that the kings had formerly exercised.

meritocracy. Social system based on individual ability.

Merovingians. Frankish kings in the seventh and eighth centuries.

messiah. The anticipated king and deliverer of the Jews.

monotheism. The belief in a single God.

Mont St. Michel. Medieval monastery off the coast of northern France.

orthodoxy. Teachings considered true by a religious community.

Ostrogoths. Germanic tribe, already settled in the Roman Empire, whose King Theodoric became the ruler of Italy in 493.

Pantheon. Roman temple that housed images of all the empire's gods.

Parliament. The first and most long-lasting of all democratic, deliberative bodies.

pharaoh. Title used by ancient Egyptians for their king.

philosophes. Enlightenment thinkers of the eighteenth century such as Voltaire and Diderot.

pictographs. Symbols based on pictorial representations, such as a circle for the sun.

plebeians. The common people of Rome.

polis. The Greek city-state.

primogeniture. Inheritance by the first-born son.

proletariat. The working class, as defined by Karl Marx.

putting-out system. System in which early rural capitalists, who had been distributing textile work to female employees operating in their homes, replaced those workers with people who worked in factories and who did not own their own tools.

rabbi. A person authorized to interpret Jewish law.

Reconquista. The Christian reconquest of Spain from the Muslims.

relics. Holy objects said to have been touched by Jesus and the saints.

Risorgimento. Nineteenth-century movement that led to the unification of Italy under the house of Savoy.

scholasticism. Late-medieval Aristotelian academic training.

sexagesimal system. Base-sixty mathematical system.

society of orders. Tripartite society based on "those who pray (clerics), those who fight (nobility), and those who work (commoners)." Originating in the eighth century, it finally was overthrown in 1789 with the French Revolution.

three-field method of plowing. Tenth-century method of field rotation that allowed greater food production.

vassal. In the feudal system, one who swears fealty to a nobleman.

Vikings. Fierce barbarian Norsemen who invaded Europe and the British Isles from the ninth to the eleventh centuries.

vitalism. Theory of nature according to which occult, living forces rather than abstract, mechanical causes are the basis of motion in the universe.

For further reading

Bainton, Roland. *The Reformation of the Sixteenth Century.* Boston: Beacon, 1961.

Chiera, Edward. *They Wrote on Clay.* Chicago: University of Chicago Press, 1938.

Finley, M. *The Ancient Greeks.* New York: Oxford University Press, 1963.

Gay, Peter. *The Enlightenment: An Interpretation.* Vol. 1., *The Rise of Modern Paganism.* New York: Vintage, 1966.

Gilbert, Felix, ed. *The Norton History of Modern Europe.* New York: W. W. Norton, 1971.

Glenny, Misha. *The Rebirth of History: Eastern Europe in the Age of Democracy.* New York: Penguin, 1990.

Kennedy, Paul. *The Rise and Fall of the Great Powers: Economic Change and Military Conflict from 1500 to 2000.* New York: Vintage, 1989.

Lopez, Robert. *The Birth of Europe.* New York/Philadelphia: Evans/Lippincott, 1972.

McNeil, William H. *The Pursuit of Power: Technology, Armed Force, and Society Since A.D. 1000.* Chicago: University of Chicago Press, 1982.

Sale, Kirkpatrick. *The Conquest of Paradise: Christopher Columbus and the Columbian Legacy.* New York: Plume, 1990.

Business Administration

- Business fundamentals
- Business formation
- Management
- Managing people
- Managing production
- Marketing
- Management tools
- Finance
- The business environment

Business Administration

Businesses come in countless varieties. They range from a single person working out of the home a few hours a week to a multinational firm with hundreds of thousands of employees based in dozens of countries. Despite differences in size and scope, all businesses share common challenges. Each must decide what form to take and how to raise funds. The firm must have goals, and plans to achieve those goals. Workers need to be hired and compensated—even in the case of a one-person operation. The product must be produced and brought to the market. An account of the firm's transactions must be maintained. The business operates in an environment governed by laws and regulations.

This chapter describes these common challenges and the opportunities that go along with them. It also looks at the tools that businesses use to meet their challenges head on.

Business fundamentals

Businesses are the backbone of the world's economies. They transform a society's resources into goods and services that fulfill the demands of that society. These resources are the *factors of production* and include land, labor, and capital. In today's economy, information is also considered a factor of production. *Entrepreneurs* are the driving forces who bring these resources together and set businesses in motion.

What is business? Businesses are made up of people, whether one or hundreds of thousands, who work in an organized way to earn a profit. They earn profit by producing and selling goods and services that are of value to society. Businesses provide employment to the individual members of society. In addition, they buy the goods and services of other businesses. Competition among businesses encourages new ideas, which in turn improve the quality of life for society. Over time, the American economy has shifted from primarily agricultural to primarily manufacturing. In recent years, service industries have grown significantly.

Profit. The amount of money that remains after a business's expenses are deducted from its income is *profit*. Profit increases the value of a firm. It can be reinvested in the firm in order to generate even greater profits in future years, or it can be returned to the firm's owners, providing them with a return on their investment in the firm. Even not-for-profit businesses have an interest in surplus income; they are able to use their surplus to increase the services they provide or to build reserves that provide long-term security.

The owner of a small business provides a service by selling goods to the local community.

Goods and services. A business generates income by selling products. These products can be categorized as either goods or services. *Goods* are tangible products; they include such items as bicycles, steel, apples, houses, and sweaters. *Services* are intangible products; examples include legal advice, haircuts, airplane travel, electrical repair, entertainment, and medical care. The retail industry is a service industry. While a retailer sells goods, its central purpose is to provide a service to the customer—bringing the customer and the product together at the same location.

Entrepreneurs. A business gets its start when someone gathers factors of production together to produce goods or services. That person, the *entrepreneur*, assumes the risk for failure. The entrepreneur also has the most to gain if the business is successful.

Entrepreneurs have vision. They see opportunities and seize them. Through the years, they have provided many of the technological innovations that have so dramatically changed our lives. All companies, no matter how large, ultimately trace their roots back to entrepreneurs who took chances. For example, General Motors was a merging of several individual automobile companies, each founded by entrepreneurs such as Ransom Olds (of the Oldsmobile).

Social responsibility. Businesspeople

do not operate in a vacuum. The decisions they make and the way they conduct business affect the local community, consumers, and the environment, as well as employees and investors. Some argue that the only responsibility of business is to make a profit legally. Being socially responsible is a long-term investment, which can often hurt short-term profit.

Business and the community. Businesses have an immediate impact on their local community. They provide jobs. In turn, the salaries paid to local workers have a ripple effect in that community—workers spend their salaries buying goods and services from local businesses. A decision to close a plant can devastate a community. A decision to build a plant can provide the benefits of jobs and taxes, but can also generate growth that strains public services and the way of life in a community.

Business and the consumer. One hundred years ago, the rule of thumb was *caveat emptor*: Let the buyer beware. But much has changed. Today, businesses have an obligation to provide products that consumers can use safely; that obligation includes providing consumers with accurate claims about the benefits of the product. Nevertheless, when a product fails or poses a danger to the consumer, businesses are faced with decisions about how far to go—and what costs to incur—to protect the consumer.

Business and the environment. Businesses use the earth's natural resources to produce their goods and services. They also generate pollution, often releasing chemicals and waste into the air, water, and ground. Who pays clean-up costs when accidents such as oil spills occur is subject to much debate.

Society's concern with environmental issues has led businesses to pay more attention to their own impact on the environment. In recent years, many firms have changed the way they package their products, switching to recycled and recyclable materials and reducing overall costs.

Social responsibility takes many forms. Plant closings undermine the local economy.

Business formation

Many businesses are started by people who cannot find the right opportunities in other companies. People starting their own firm must decide what business form to use and whether to go with a new venture or a franchise.

Legal forms of business.

The three most common forms of business organization are: sole proprietorship, partnership, and corporation. Each has its own set of advantages and disadvantages.

Sole proprietorships. A *sole proprietorship* is a business with one owner, though it may have many employees. Examples include farmers, dry cleaners, florists, landscapers, and tutors. While some fields (lawyer, electrician) require licensing, sole proprietorships are generally easy to open. They involve relatively little capital or paperwork, and they have personal tax advantages. Owners work for themselves and have control, freedom, and privacy.

However, sole proprietors face several challenges. Their profit potential and financial resources are often limited. With the control and freedom come long hours, broad responsibility, and inability to protect their personal assets.

Partnerships. A *partnership* is a business with two or more owners who share a legal association. Partnerships vary considerably; they can be two people running a catering business, or an accounting firm with hundreds of partners. *General partners* share full responsibility and liability with other partners. *Limited partners* are usually less involved in management and are liable only for their own investment in the firm.

Partnerships are easy to form, providing tax advantages, increased borrowing power, and continuity. But partners are responsible for the firm's debts. Disagreements can be hard to resolve. Withdrawing an investment from a partnership can also be difficult.

Partnerships are often formed by professionals such as accountants, doctors, architects, and attorneys.

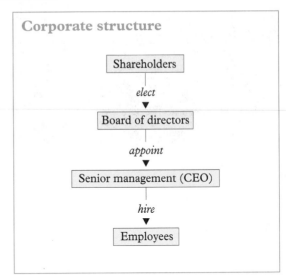

Corporate structure

Shareholders

elect
▼

Board of directors

appoint
▼

Senior management (CEO)

hire
▼

Employees

Corporations. A *corporation* is a legal entity chartered by a state. It has many of the legal rights of a person but is owned by its shareholders.

The life span of a corporation is unlimited. It can borrow money, own property, and sue or be sued. The corporation's liability is limited to corporate

Types of corporations
- **Public corporation.** Shares traded in open market (General Electric)
- **Private corporation.** Shares privately held, not traded in open market (Hallmark)
- **S corporation.** Fewer than thirty-five shareholders, not traded publicly (many small businesses)
- **Parent corporation.** Has controlling interest in another corporation (Time-Warner)
- **Subsidiary.** Corporation owned or controlled by another (HBO)
- **Holding company.** Owns other companies, stays out of active role, often found in banking and utilities (Southern Company)
- **Quasi-public corporation.** Has governmental approval for limited monopoly (Pacific Bell)
- **Nonprofit corporation.** Services, education, arts are central rather than profits (American Red Cross)
- **Joint venture.** Separate firm owned by other firms for specific project (New United Motor Manufacturing, Inc.)
- **Cooperative.** Nonprofit, owned by members, provides marketing and other support (Land O' Lakes)

assets, protecting the personal assets of the shareholders.

Corporations require extensive paperwork and are relatively expensive to form. Activities are restricted by the corporate charter. Income is taxed at a higher rate than in sole proprietorships and partnerships, and it is taxed a second time when distributed as dividends. Financial reports of public corporations are available to anyone, although many private and S corporations keep their reports confidential.

Corporations are owned by *shareholders* who purchase stock in the corporations. Shareholders can be individuals or such institutions as pension funds, banks, and colleges. Each share of common stock entitles the owner to one vote in decisions made by the corporation, such as electing the *board of directors*. The board of directors sets corporate policy, hires senior management, and approves major decisions (such as the distribution of dividends).

The *chief executive officer*, or CEO, is appointed by the board to run the corporation. The CEO recommends policy for board approval and oversees the implementation of that policy. The *employees*, who ultimately report to the CEO, carry out the day-to-day operations of the business.

Public corporations, familiar to most people, are traded on the open market, and anyone can own stock. *Private* and *S corporations* are not traded publicly. *Parent corporations* own a controlling interest in other corporations, which are called *subsidiaries*. Other types include *holding companies*, whose primary business is holding a controlling interest in other companies; and *quasi-public corporations*, whose mode of operation is essentially public but whose ownership is private.

Mergers and acquisitions. Companies can grow through mergers and acquisitions. A *merger* occurs when two companies bring their resources together to

A diversified company

Procter & Gamble operates in the following industries:

- **Household products** such as laundry and cleaning products
- **Personal care products** including deodorants, cosmetics, and hair products
- **Food and beverage products** including shortening and oil, snacks, and peanut butter
- **Pulp products** such as cellulose pulp and chemicals

form a new company. An *acquisition* is similar to a merger, except that one company purchases the other. Both businesses remain intact, but often with some change in personnel. The acquired business is now accountable to the parent business.

Similarly, a business may sell an acquired company. This sale, called a *divestiture*, may occur because the parent company needs cash, the acquisition is not profitable, or the acquisition no longer fits with the purchaser's line of business.

When a company buys other companies not directly related to its business, it is said to have *diversified*, and the resulting company is called a *conglomerate*. An example is General Electric's purchase of RCA, which brought it control of the National Broadcasting Company (NBC).

Some acquisitions are not friendly, but are *hostile takeovers*. In a hostile takeover, the business does not want to lose its independence and be controlled by a parent company. A business's board of directors and management attempt to block the acquisition, although they are not always successful.

Advantages and disadvantages of ownership

Sole proprietorship	Partnership	Corporation
Easy to form	Easy to form	Harder to form
Limited opportunity to borrow	Better opportunity to borrow	Best opportunity to borrow
Unlimited liability for owner	Unlimited liability for general partners	Owner's liability limited to investment in corporation
Personal tax advantage	Personal tax advantage	Higher taxes
Management responsibility all on owner	Management responsibility shared by partners	Managers hired to represent owners
Limited lifespan	Ongoing lifespan	Unlimited lifespan
Operations are private	Operations private within partners	Public disclosure required regarding operations

Small business. Well over 95 percent of all businesses in the United States have fewer than one hundred employees and can be termed *small business*. They make a vital contribution to the economy and are responsible for much of the nation's economic growth. In the last two decades, the number of people who have started up their own companies has grown dramatically.

What is a small business? Definitions of small business vary. The U.S. Department of Commerce defines a small business by the number of employees (fewer than 500). The Small Business Administration (SBA) has a more complex definition based on sales, which also takes into account the nature of the business. A service company must have relatively small sales revenue in order to be a "small business," but a wholesaler can have a much larger sales revenue and still be considered "small." Perhaps the most important criteria are that a small business is independently owned and is not dominant in its industry.

Advantages and disadvantages. The men and women who head small businesses report that the greatest advantage of running their own company is the opportunity to work for themselves. Small businesses provide opportunities for independence and convenient work situations. An increasing number of businesses are conducted out of the home or in the local community, enabling owners to spend more time with their families and less time commuting. Small businesses encourage creativity and innovation. Relations between small business owners and their employees tend to be close, as do the relations with customers and clients.

However, running a small business often means long hours and financial insecurity. When problems arise, there is no one to whom owners can "pass the buck." When the economy is weak, the small business has fewer resources to act as a reserve. Owners have the added responsibility of their employees' security.

Types of small businesses. Some businesses are started with the intent that they will stay relatively small. That is, the owner wants to develop a family business, not to grow into a large corporation. Many of these types of businesses are found in your own neighborhood: dry cleaners, restaurants, and small grocery stores, for example.

Other people start businesses with the intent that they will grow large. Many examples exist in the computer industry, such as Apple Computers and NeXT (both started by Steven Jobs) and Yahoo (started by two college students). While the owners of these companies might have been surprised by how quickly the companies grew, they always intended for the companies to become big. Risks in developing these *high-risk ventures* are much greater than for businesses that will remain small and nondominant in their industries. The individuals who start high-growth ventures are called *entrepreneurs*, and they generally are individuals who are comfortable taking risks.

Small Business Administration (SBA). The SBA is a government agency that supports small businesses through loan and advisory programs. *Direct loans* are available to businesses rejected by two banks; they are targeted to selected veterans and disabled owners. *Guaranteed loans* help small businesses get bank loans by guaranteeing repayment. Other SBA loan programs are aimed at women and minorities who want to start businesses. Also, *SBICs*—small business investment corporations—provide loans of funds raised from individual investors. *Small business development centers* are found on college campuses, providing community support. *SCORE* (Service Corps of Retired Executives) and *ACE* (Active Corps of Executives) provide advice from retired executives who volunteer their time to small businesses.

Small businesses are often able to meet individual needs within their community. Here, a print shop prepares manuals for a local customer.

Small business resources

For information about programs and services, try your local SBA office, or contact:

Small Business Administration
409 3rd Street, S.W.
Washington, D.C. 20416
(800) 827-5722

The SBA also has a home page on the World Wide Web. Its address is:

http://www.sba.gov

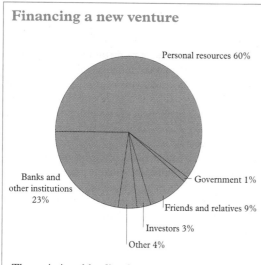

Financing a new venture

Personal resources 60%

Banks and other institutions 23%

Government 1%

Friends and relatives 9%

Investors 3%

Other 4%

The majority of funding for new ventures comes from the entrepreneur's personal resources; the least amount comes from government investment.

New ventures.

People who run their own businesses can buy an existing company, get a franchise, or start a new venture from scratch. Of the three, starting from scratch can be both the riskiest and the most rewarding.

Starting a new business. In one sense, starting a new company requires only five elements: an idea, a plan, start-up money, motivation, and follow-through. A little good luck never hurts. But without the idea, the other elements do not matter.

Small business owners usually start with a field they know well. The idea is formed by talking to potential customers, competitors, and other small business owners. The business itself is formed by talking to professionals: accountants, bankers, and lawyers. In addition to developing a new product, many businesses are started to serve a new set of customers, or to improve an existing product or service.

The business plan. After the idea comes the business plan. The plan is a required tool for raising funds; equally important is its use to the entrepreneur. The plan is a road map. It starts the owner on the trip and helps to focus on the destination. It suggests the path to follow, how long it will take to get there, potential adjustments en route, and alternative ways to reach the goal in case of obstacles. A good plan has several components, including the following:

The *summary* provides an overview of the entire plan. Descriptions of the *company*, the *industry*, and the *product* come next. The plan reviews the *target market* along with *marketing strategies* needed for success. The plan needs to describe *product development*

and the company's *operations*: How will the goods or services be produced? Investors will want to know about the company's *management team* and *organization*. The plan then needs to address *schedules* and *budgets* for sales, cash flows, and development. *Risks* should also be addressed.

Entrepreneurs. Many of us talk about the things we should do or would like to do. Entrepreneurs go beyond talking; they commit themselves, gather resources, and take action. Rather than be defeated by obstacles, they are risk takers who overcome them. They are not afraid of hard work and long hours.

Frequently, entrepreneurs have been frustrated in careers with larger corporations; many have had their advancement blocked. Starting a new business lets them use all their talents and creativity.

Achieving success. Not everyone who is a good entrepreneur is a good manager; the skills are different. Being a successful entrepreneur often means knowing when to let someone else run the day-to-day operations of the company.

Sometimes success can get in the way of success! Too much business can drain the company's financial and human resources, leading to burnout, angry customers, and lost business. Pacing development and being prepared for growth are vital to success.

Are you an entrepreneur?

- Do you like being in charge?
- Are you flexible?
- How have you handled obstacles in the past?
- How is your health and energy?
- Are you willing to work long hours?
- Do you consider yourself a risk taker?
- Do you take responsibility?
- Do you think of yourself as organized?
- Are you comfortable making decisions?
- Can you handle stress and time pressures?
- In what shape are your personal finances?
- Do you listen well?
- Can you motivate others?
- Do you like doing many things at once?

Franchising. For many people, franchising provides an alternative to starting a new venture. A franchise is a license: the company selling the license (*franchiser*) lets the buyer (*franchisee*) use the company's trademark and products, and operate in a specified territory. The franchisee pays an initial fee and an ongoing percentage of sales or profit. The initial fee can range from a thousand to over a million dollars.

For example, a franchisee who opens a fast-food restaurant might pay an initial fee of $350,000, which guarantees no one else will open up that restaurant in the community. Each month the franchiser is also paid 10 to 20 percent of all sales.

Advantages of franchising. Franchising has several advantages. Franchisees get name recognition that brings in customers right away. They get considerable help developing the business plan and operating the business. Risk is low; the franchisee builds on the success of other franchises. Economies of scale reduce equipment costs. The franchisee benefits from the franchiser's quality control, and sometimes financial support.

The franchiser benefits by being able to expand operations without incurring debt. Successful franchises provide a steady cash stream from the monthly fees that are paid to the franchiser.

Disadvantages of franchising. Franchising also has disadvantages: start-up costs are often more than the cost of starting a business from scratch. The monthly franchise fee can be a dramatic drain on profits. The franchisee must conform to the rules of the franchiser, often right down to uniforms, colors, and product line, thus reducing creativity. Furthermore, while most established franchises are reliable, there is the potential for fraud—franchisers who take the money but do not offer support in return. For the franchiser, one of the risks is that a poorly run franchise will hurt its image and reputation.

Management

Managers coordinate the resources available to them, including people and capital, in order to achieve the company's goals. The decisions that managers make and implement in order to achieve these goals are at the heart of management.

The role of management. Whether in a Fortune 500 corporation, a small bookstore, or a group of volunteers planning a fundraising dinner, the fundamental role of management is to establish goals, determine how to achieve those goals, and then see that the necessary work is carried out.

Goals are set based on the wants and needs of the customer for the product or service provided. The job of management is to stay in touch with the customers, to ensure that the business is responding to changes in the customers' wants or desires, and to see that the business is doing so in an efficient manner.

Levels of management. As companies grow, they develop a managerial pyramid with three levels. The upper level is *top management*, which establishes goals and sets policy. The next level, *middle management*, develops the plans and oversees the activities of the lowest level, *supervisory* or *first-line management*, which supervises the remaining workers in their day-to-day tasks.

Top management includes the CEO and executive vice presidents. Middle management includes plant managers and directors of departments. First-line management includes supervisors and foremen.

Managers ensure that individual efforts are coordinated and directed toward company goals, as in this 1940 albacore packing plant in Portland, Oregon.

Managerial skills. Most successful managers demonstrate strength in three distinct areas: interpersonal, technical, and conceptual skills.

Managers need strong *interpersonal* skills. They need to motivate and evaluate workers, resolve conflicts, manage time, listen, and communicate.

The president of a computer company does not need to be able to design computers but should have enough *technical* knowledge to understand industry trends. Each level of manager down the pyramid needs additional technical expertise.

Conceptual skills are also important: drawing connections, seeing the big picture, and understanding how change in one area affects other areas.

Communication skills. All managers, regardless of level, must develop strong communication skills to be effective. They must be able to receive and transmit information. The better they are at doing this, the smoother their company's operations will be.

Oral communications include not only the ability to speak clearly and appropriately for the audience, but the ability to listen and understand others.

Written communications must be tailored to different audiences. An industry report for a boss is quite different from an evaluation of a subordinate. Other types of written communication include internal memos, letters to customers and suppliers, and policy statements.

The management process. Early in this century, Henri Fayol, a French management theorist, identified five functions of management: planning, organizing, commanding, coordinating, and controlling. Today these functions usually are condensed into four: planning, organizing, leading, and controlling.

All managers, regardless of their level, engage in all four functions. The purpose of these four functions is to ensure that the business is (*a*) serving its customers' needs and (*b*) working efficiently. These ideas are often expressed as "doing the right things" and "doing things right."

Planning. Though every project requires a plan, in this section we will confine ourselves to the basic steps of planning for the organization as a whole. First, the organization establishes its *purpose* (What needs does the organization serve?) and *mission* (How will it go about accomplishing this?). For example, Hershey's purpose may be to meet customers' desires for sweet snack food, and its mission is to manufacture candy.

Establishing goals and objectives are the next two steps. *Goals* are broad targets (to increase market share by 10 percent over three years), while *objectives* are specifically defined, shorter-term targets (to increase sales by 10 percent a year; to introduce two product improvements next year).

To meet goals and objectives, a company must develop strategies and tactics. *Strategies* are long-range plans describing actions taken over several years. For example, to increase market share, the company may expand its product line or invest in research and development to improve products. *Tactics* are short-range plans; they describe actions for the coming year. For

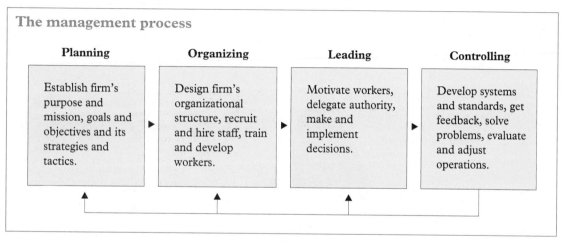

The management process

Planning	Organizing	Leading	Controlling
Establish firm's purpose and mission, goals and objectives and its strategies and tactics.	Design firm's organizational structure, recruit and hire staff, train and develop workers.	Motivate workers, delegate authority, make and implement decisions.	Develop systems and standards, get feedback, solve problems, evaluate and adjust operations.

example, in the first year, the firm may build market share by increasing product recognition through mail-out samples. It may try to learn more about what customers want by conducting a series of group interviews (called focus groups), and then direct its research and development efforts based on what the customers say. Additional steps would be taken in subsequent years.

Management by objectives (MBO) is a technique that involves workers at all levels in the planning process. Workers are aware of the firm's long-range objectives and define their own performance targets in terms of those objectives. Individual goals, broad participation, and ongoing evaluation are central to MBO. While MBO can be motivational, it is also time consuming. Its key steps are:

1. Top management sets and communicates long-range objectives;
2. Middle management meets with other managers and staff to set measurable goals and action plans;
3. Managers meet frequently with participants to measure progress; and

4. All participants meet to measure progress toward long-range objectives.

To be successful in the long run, a company must understand how one set of decisions affects other decisions, and how the company, industry, and marketplace are changing. Understanding these relations is central to *strategic planning*.

For example, a company may have as its objective a sales increase of 10 percent a year in order to support its goal of increasing market share. But what if production capacity is reached in two years? Will the company need a new plant? When should it make that commitment? How will it raise the capital? How will the expense affect profits? These questions are strategic issues that must be addressed immediately, not two years later when the production limit is reached.

Organizing. Once a plan takes form, the manager must consider how best to organize the company's resources. Central to this step are *staffing* the firm and developing the *organizational structure*.

The choices made in this step will vary based on the kind of company involved. Decisions need to be made about such issues as the organizational level of departments or work groups, how communication will flow, and how employees will be grouped into work units.

Usually, top management makes these decisions for the departments or divisions at the executive level, letting lower levels of management make decisions further down the organization.

Leading. An important part of a manager's responsibility is getting workers to do their jobs so that goals and objectives can be achieved. Leading (also called *directing*) calls on a variety of skills.

Managers must establish a *leadership style* that defines how they execute authority and delegate responsibility. They must learn tools for *motivating* workers. Also, they must master *decision making*.

Leadership style reveals much about a manager. The best leaders serve as role models. They inspire their workers to give optimum performance, and they make sure that workers have the tools necessary to succeed.

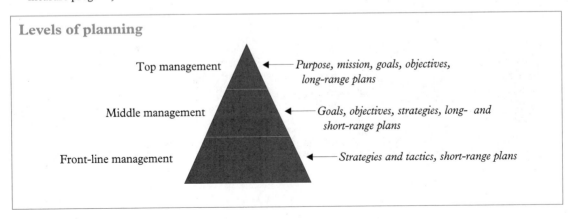

Levels of planning

Top management ← *Purpose, mission, goals, objectives, long-range plans*

Middle management ← *Goals, objectives, strategies, long- and short-range plans*

Front-line management ← *Strategies and tactics, short-range plans*

The most common types of leadership style are autocratic, democratic, and laissez-faire. *Autocratic* leaders make their own decisions without consulting employees. *Democratic* leaders involve their employees in decision making. *Laissez-faire* leaders let employees make decisions, although the leader may act as a consultant. Leader support is usually not available.

Ultimately, the most effective managers vary their style based on the situation. When quick decisions are needed, the autocratic style can be the most effective. In other situations, employee participation is extremely important to gain new insights or to garner support of employees.

While most managers could simply order employees to do their jobs, the most effective leaders find ways to motivate workers to do their best willingly. Motivated workers are generally more focused, more productive, and more creative. The best managers know this and develop self-motivation in their employees.

Managers make numerous decisions: whether to introduce a new product, sell a division, fire one employee, or promote another. The decision-making process has several clear steps. First, the problem must be defined. Alternative solutions must then be identified and evaluated, leading to a choice. The choice is implemented; the outcome of that decision is monitored to see if further adjustments are needed.

Controlling. The control function provides a way to evaluate the company's performance on an ongoing basis, making adjustments to stay on track with desired goals and objectives. It enables managers to reshape goals and objectives, strategies and tactics, in response to change inside and outside the company.

An important part of the control function is setting *standards* in all areas of the business. Sales representatives may have a monthly sales quota. Production may have both quantity and quality standards. Managers may have standards regarding how much employee turnover is acceptable. Budgets provide standards for both revenues and expenses.

Standards are useful only if performance is measured and adjustments are made. *Feedback* provides the con-

nection between standards and adjustments. First, a feedback system, such as a daily sales report, is used to gather data. Then the data are evaluated against standards to indicate where adjustments are needed.

Organizational structure.

Most firms consist of several components ordered in some kind of formal structure. This formal organization defines jobs and reporting relationships. Its purpose is to encourage productivity and communication.

Organization chart. An organization chart, such as the sample shown on the next page, is a diagram providing a roadmap to the formal organization. It shows how workers are grouped and how departments are arranged in a hierarchy. The organization chart indicates direct reporting relationships. The solid lines on the sample chart represent the organization's *chain of command*. These chains reflect the lines of authority; that is, who has the power to direct others lower in the chain or must answer to others higher in the chain. Dotted lines indicate advisory roles.

Instead of having workers perform all the steps needed to complete a project, a *division of labor* can be used to organize the work into specialized tasks. The sample chart does not show the division of labor, as "employees" are all grouped together at the bottom. But, for example, one group cuts wood into pieces, a second assembles those pieces into a chair, a third stains the chairs, and so on. *Specialization* increases productivity and reduces setup and training costs. On the other hand, it can significantly increase boredom and job dissatisfaction.

Larger organizations must organize employees into manageable work groups or *departments*. Grouping by *function*, as shown in the sample chart, organizes employees by activity: sales employees, warehouse employees, and so on. Some companies organize by *geography*, based on where employees are located. Other ways to departmentalize include by *product* (soap, detergent), by *customer* (commercial, government), or by *production process* (assembly, painting).

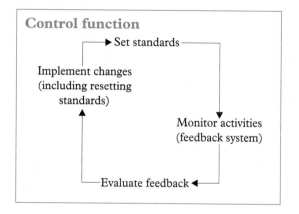

Control function

Set standards →

Implement changes
(including resetting
standards)

Monitor activities
(feedback system)

Evaluate feedback ◄

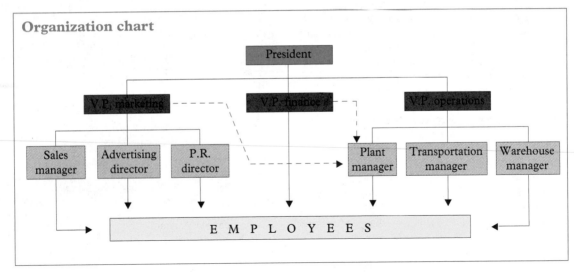

Organization chart

- President
  - V.P. marketing
    - Sales manager
    - Advertising director
    - P.R. director
  - V.P. finance
  - V.P. operations
    - Plant manager
    - Transportation manager
    - Warehouse manager
- EMPLOYEES

Delegation. When managers assign tasks to their employees in a process that is called *delegation*, they assign responsibility, authority, and accountability. *Responsibility* is the obligation to complete an assignment once accepted. *Authority* is the power to see that work is carried out. *Accountability* refers to accepting credit or blame for a task's success or failure. A source of frustration for many workers is being responsible and accountable for a task, but not having the authority needed to complete it successfully.

In many organizations, power is held closely by top management, often working out of a central location. Managers limit both the authority and the responsibility that they delegate. Decisions are often passed through several levels of management. Most small businesses are *centralized*; as they grow larger, power is delegated more frequently. The United States military services are examples of centralized organizations.

The more that top managers delegate responsibility and authority to middle and front-line management, the more *decentralized* the business is. Such firms, which are also called *flat* organizations (versus *tall*, centralized organizations), have relatively few levels of management. As a result, managers must delegate more decision making to their employees.

In centralized firms, managers are likely to have few workers reporting directly to them; in decentralized firms, that number rises. Companies with many workers reporting to each manager have a wide *span of management*; that is, decision making will be more widely spread through the firm. However, there are limits to how many workers managers can effectively direct. The span often depends on how skilled the workers are.

Technology. Improvements in technology have changed the way many managers interact with their employees. The ability to communicate rapidly by fax and computer allows managers more easily to supervise employees who work out of different locations. For example, a work group may be made up of employees located across the country, but they can easily share ideas, files, reports, and other information as if they were in the same office.

Types of organizations. *Simple structures* have the most direct chain of command, with power concentrated at the top. *Functional organizations* group workers by task, creating training efficiencies but muddying lines of authority. *Professional organizations*, which group employees by both the function performed and the type of customer served, provide very specialized services. *Divisional organizations* create parallel structures, based on product output. *Matrix organizations* combine functional and *project management* approaches: workers are grouped by function but are assigned temporarily to project teams.

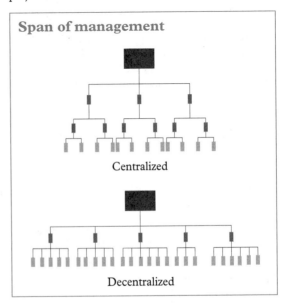

Span of management

Centralized

Decentralized

Managing people

Employees are a business's most valuable resource. The best machinery and the most money will not go far without the skills and efforts of the firm's employees. Without people, nothing happens.

Human resource management.

Traditionally, the overseeing of a firm's workers was called personnel management. Today, employees are seen as more than just people who perform tasks; they are *resources* requiring careful attention and development—thus the more contemporary term *human resource management* (HRM).

Planning. In competitive times, good workers are hard to find. Job vacancies and weak employees can prove costly to a company. Planning is the part of HRM that projects positions that will open, forecasts the supply of available workers, and facilitates decisions about hiring or outplacing. Regardless of whether a firm is growing or shrinking, decisions must be made about which people to hire or to place out. *Job analysis* looks at tasks to be performed and skills needed; this leads to *job descriptions* detailing the responsibilities, reporting relations, and work environment of specific positions. *Job specifications* list experience, skills, and other background that ideal candidates for any specific job will have.

Staffing. Once a firm has identified positions to be filled and prepared descriptions and specifications, workers must be hired. Staffing is the part of HRM that involves recruiting, selecting, and hiring workers—in short, ensuring the best match between job requirements and employee skills.

Recruiting is the process of finding qualified candi-

dates. *Internal recruiting* is the effort to find candidates within the firm; *external recruiting* is the effort to find candidates outside the firm. Methods include sending recruiters to locations such as college campuses and work fairs. Other means include advertisements, employment agencies, and referrals. Also, many firms will try to recruit employees from competitors.

Once a pool of candidates is gathered, the process of *selecting* the best ones begins. Tools for screening out unacceptable candidates include application forms, résumés, interviews, tests, and references. A *résumé* provides an account of education and employment. Tests must be job related; they might check typing speed or compare personality traits with others who are successful in similar jobs. The final hiring decision could be made by the immediate supervisor or by the work group as a whole (in team-oriented companies).

Staffing does not end once the best candidate is selected. The candidate must then be *hired*. A job offer is made, detailing the position, salary, benefits, and other conditions of employment. An employer should have backup offers ready as needed.

Job description and specifications

Editorial assistant

Duties (Job description)
- Find and coordinate manuscript reviewers
- Summarize incoming reviews and surveys
- Maintain files and computer data base
- Handle correspondence, payments, and phone
- Coordinate schedules for manuscript and supplements
- Proofread front matter, cover, and marketing copy

Qualifications (Job specifications)
- 1 year preferred in clerical, secretarial position
- 60 wpm typing, computer experience required
- Evidence of excellent organizational skills

The job interview provides a valuable opportunity for both the employer and the prospective employee to explore the potential for a beneficial relationship.

Having well-trained employees is critical to a company's success.

Training and development. All employees require training. This is true for employees who have just been hired by the company and those who have changed jobs from within. Trained workers are more productive and independent than others. Development programs build the skills of workers, preparing them for greater responsibilities. The costs of training and development are offset by productivity, loyalty, and lower turnover.

New employees need to learn about the company. *Orientation* programs educate them about the firm, provide background information, and describe the firm's chain of command. They explain benefits, including vacation, insurance, and pension programs, as well as company standards, from dress codes to codes of ethics to grievance procedures.

Employees develop job skills both on and away from the job. *On-the-job training* involves supervisors or experienced peers. Sometimes special assignments are used. *Off-the-job training* can take place in a classroom setting. Many employees receive training on new computer systems or software in a classroom setting; sales representatives may learn selling techniques; project managers may learn budgeting.

Training focuses on technical skills needed to perform a job; *management development* focuses on interpersonal and conceptual skills. Topics vary and include interviewing skills, negotiating strategies, conflict resolution, delegation and decision making, financial analysis, and strategic planning.

Evaluating. Effective managers must observe and evaluate the job performance of their subordinates. Many managers involve the employee's peers, subordinates, and even customers in the evaluation (called a *360-degree appraisal*). Performed properly, evaluation helps employees understand what they are doing well and how to develop for the next job. Performed poor-

ly, evaluation can be demoralizing and result in lower performance. Thus, training the evaluators to assess employees properly is very important.

Once employees understand what is expected of them, their work performance should be periodically appraised. *Appraisals* measure the extent to which job expectations are met. Ways to build on strengths or correct weaknesses are discussed. Employees should be active participants, not passive recipients. Effective appraisals lead naturally to goal setting.

Promotions reward top employees, build employee morale, and lower costs of filling positions. A danger of promotion comes when good employees are advanced beyond their skills, interests, or preparation. The results are unpleasant for the company and the employee.

Employees may leave a company voluntarily, by resigning to go to another position or by retiring and leaving the workforce. *Involuntary separations* include temporary layoffs, permanent reductions-in-force, or firing due to inadequate performance. In cases of involuntary separation, the company will do best if the least effective employees are separated. Documentation of poor performance is always necessary.

Compensating. Except in volunteer firms, employees do not work for free. Employee compensation includes wages or salary, benefits, and intangible rewards. The

Types of separation
- **Resignation.** Voluntary, permanent. Employee initiates.
- **Retirement.** Usually voluntary, permanent, after set age or years of service. Employee receives long-term benefits, such as a pension.
- **Layoffs.** Involuntary, temporary. Due to weak business conditions; workers rehired if and when conditions improve.
- **Reduction-in-force (RIF).** Involuntary, permanent layoff. Due to business conditions, not worker performance.
- **Termination.** Involuntary, permanent. Known as firing; tied to individual's unsatisfactory performance.

human resources department is responsible for ensuring that employees are compensated in proportion to the value of their services and that compensation is distributed fairly across the company.

Wages and salary are the core of any compensation program. *Wages* are paid based on hours worked or productivity. *Salary* is based on the performance of a job rather than on hours. Other forms of compensation include *commissions* (based on revenue generated) and *bonuses* (based on the employee measurably exceeding performance).

Benefits provide additional compensation. By law, the company must pay Social Security, unemployment, and disability benefits. Health benefits are currently a major topic of debate. Pension plans and insurance policies are also part of the package, as are vacation, sick leave, holidays, and tuition refund programs. Parental leave and daycare are increasingly important components.

Companies offer *intangible* benefits as well. Many offer flex-time, allowing workers to set hours within a reasonable range. Others offer parking or transportation. Relaxed dress codes, independence on the job, and open and informal communication provide workers with additional rewards.

Motivation.
Money was once thought to be the only way to motivate workers. The *piecework system*, in which workers were paid a higher rate if they exceeded established quotas, was based on this theory. Current thought is that supporting self-motivation is more important than offering external motivators.

Hawthorne studies. Over sixty years ago, studies at Western Electric's Hawthorne plant provided insight into worker productivity. Changes in lighting, temperature, and pay had little effect; the informal organiza-

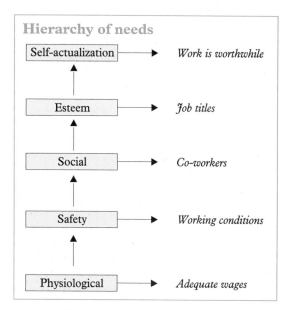

Hierarchy of needs

- Self-actualization → *Work is worthwhile*
- Esteem → *Job titles*
- Social → *Co-workers*
- Safety → *Working conditions*
- Physiological → *Adequate wages*

tion and social pressure were greater factors. Most important, productivity rose when workers perceived that the company was paying attention to them and cared about them.

Maslow's hierarchy of needs. In 1943, Abraham Maslow's theory of motivation identified five levels of human need, each of which must be satisfied before moving up the hierarchy. The lowest-level needs are physiological: food and shelter; adequate wages meet these needs. Next are safety needs, met by factors like insurance and job security. Social (co-workers) and esteem (promotion) needs follow, then self-actualization, or the need to grow.

Intrinsic and extrinsic factors. Motivation can be influenced by factors that are intrinsic to the job itself, such as responsibility, recognition, challenge, achievement, and fulfillment, or by external factors such as company policies, compensation, working conditions, supervision, and social interaction. Research suggests that intrinsic factors have more lasting positive effects on motivation than external factors.

Theory X and Theory Y. In 1960, American sociologist Douglas McGregor proposed two theories regarding motivation. In Theory X, managers assume that employees (a) dislike work, (b) must be coerced, and (c) have little ambition, wanting direction and security. Theory X managers tend to be authoritarian, motivating by fear or loss of rewards. Theory Y is more optimistic and assumes that (a) workers enjoy working, (b) they can commit to goals, (c) rewards can affect commitment, (d) workers sometimes seek responsibility, (e) workers can be creative problem-solvers, and (f) employee potential is not fully realized in most traditional firms. Theory Y managers tend to motivate by challenge, growth, and self-direction.

Sample benefits

- **FICA** (*Federal Insurance Contribution Act*). The company matches the employees' contributions to Social Security and Medicare.
- **State contributions.** Unemployment, disability, and workers' compensation are paid by the company.
- **Retirement.** A variety of programs are offered to provide workers with steady income or lump sum at retirement.
- **Health insurance.** A wide range of health insurance options can include maternity leave, dental care, and family benefits.
- **Holidays.** Most companies provide five to twelve paid holidays.
- **Vacation.** Most companies provide two weeks or more paid time off.

Theory Z. Theory Z companies treat employees as family; workers at all levels are involved in shaping and working toward company goals. The group process is used to set directions and solve problems. Decision making is shared, and workers at all levels take responsibility for the achievement of goals.

Labor-management relations.

In all organizations, employees and management have an interdependent relationship that can lead to conflict. Both are concerned with the firm's overall success and viability. Yet labor's priorities are with wages, hours, and working conditions, while management's priorities are with costs, productivity, and bottom line profitability.

History of unions. Worker dissatisfaction and safety hazards during the Industrial Revolution resulted in *unions*, organizations of employees that protect the interests of their members. Early unions represented

---

Major labor legislation

- **Norris–LaGuardia Act of 1932.** Supported union membership as a legal right of employees; restricted court injunctions against strikes, picketing, union-membership drives, and other lawful activities.
- **National Labor Relations Act of 1935 (Wagner Act).** Provided workers with the right to organize, bargain, and strike; forbade discrimination involving union members; set procedures for employees to decide on union certification; established the National Labor Relations Board (NLRB). The NLRB oversees all elections regarding union representation and investigates complaints.
- **Labor-Management Relations Act of 1947 (Taft–Hartley Act).** Amended the Wagner Act; forbade unfair union practices; barred harassment of nonunion workers; forbade closed shop; regulated collective bargaining; allowed federal injunctions to protect national interest; numerous other provisions.
- **Landrum–Griffin Act of 1959.** Amended the Wagner Act; regulated illegal union practices; required unions to publish financial reports; forbade secondary boycotts; numerous other provisions.
- **Civil Service Reform Act of 1978.** Gave federal employees the right to organize; defined unfair labor practices in the management of federal agencies; established general areas subject to collective bargaining; prohibited strikes in the federal sector.

Organizing a union

- **Organizing campaign**
  Select target group (plant or location)
  Measure the interest
  Present information to employees on *nonwork* time
  Distribute authorization cards
  After 30 percent of employees have signed cards, request election
- **Certification election**
  Ask NLRB to supervise election
  Up to forty-five days of campaigning
  Hold election
  Simple majority makes union the bargaining agent
  If union loses, new election must wait one year

---

craftsmen such as shoemakers. Local craft unions formed national organizations like the United Cigarmakers. In 1869, the *Knights of Labor* was formed; it eventually had 700,000 members. But violence, like the Haymarket Riot in Chicago, led to its decline and dissolution.

The *American Federation of Labor* (AFL) took over the leadership. It focused on wages, work conditions, and hours, using collective bargaining, supporting strikes when necessary. The *Congress of Industrial Organizations* (CIO) represented unskilled industrial workers, previously overlooked. The AFL and CIO merged in 1955. Unions once represented over 30 percent of workers; today, fewer than 15 percent.

Labor legislation. Early unions such as the Knights of Labor focused on social and moral as well as worker issues; the AFL, only on work concerns. Not until the Great Depression and Franklin Roosevelt's presidency did unions receive governmental backing. Over time, the rights of unions to organize and strike have been recognized. The rights of management and nonunion labor have also been addressed. Other issues of concern to all workers have received legislative attention; these include the work week, minimum wage, and child labor. Contemporary issues include job security, parental and family leave, health insurance, and pension protection.

Organizing a union. National unions represent workers in selected industries or crafts. *Locals* are smaller groups; all national unions are made of many locals. The *shop steward* is elected by local members to act as a go-between with management.

In an *organizing campaign*, employees request the union as their bargaining agent by signing *authorization cards*. When 30 percent or more have signed cards, the union can request an election. The National Labor Relations Board (NLRB) then supervises a

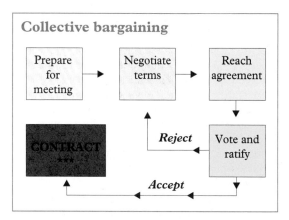

Collective bargaining

Prepare for meeting → Negotiate terms → Reach agreement

CONTRACT

Reject

Vote and ratify

Accept

Sample grievance procedure

1. Employee brings complaint to shop steward.
2. Shop steward and employee meet with the employee's supervisor.
3. The grievance and response are prepared in writing.
4. If grievance is not resolved, it goes to a member of union's grievance committee and company's industrial relations department.
5. If grievance is still not resolved, it goes to full grievance committee and senior executives.
6. If still not resolved, it goes to arbitration.

certification election, held within forty-five days. The election is determined by simple majority. A decertification election can be held to remove the union as bargaining agent. A full year must pass between elections, whether for certification or decertification.

Collective bargaining. A union's primary role is to negotiate a work contract with management. *Collective bargaining* is the process of reaching this agreement. Both sides select committees, which are required by law to negotiate in good faith. Unions want such concessions from management as higher wages and improved safety. Management wants cooperation from the unions in return.

Once terms are reached, the contract goes to members for *ratification*, a vote to approve or reject. If talks stall, *mediation* can bring a neutral third party to help reach compromise. In *arbitration*, both sides agree to let a neutral third party resolve disagreements and make a binding decision. Common issues in negotiations include union rights, compensation, job security, work rules, safety, health, and grievance procedures.

Weapons of negotiation. If negotiations break down entirely, both sides have tactics they can use to try to influence or coerce the other side.

Best known of labor's weapons is the *strike*, which is a work stoppage. Employees *picket* the firm, marching with signs and leaflets that encourage others to support their work stoppage. A strike can be costly to employees and the union; labor assumes the strike will be even more costly to management, leading to resolution of the dispute. Other tactics include *slowdowns* (workers report but work at a slower pace) and *boycotts* (the union and supporters avoid doing business with the firm). Sometimes unions also mount publicity campaigns.

Management has tactics, too. *Strikebreakers* can replace striking workers; workloads can be reassigned to managers. A *lockout* occurs when management refuses entrance to workers, pressuring the union to accept the most recent proposal. The company can also seek an *injunction*, which is a court order that requires striking employees to return to work.

Managing production

At the heart of any business are the goods and services it produces. Companies gather together resources and transform them into something the marketplace desires. *Production* is the process of giving form to these resources. How resources are organized to support production is the subject of *operations management*.

Producing goods. Because they are tangible products, goods can be held in inventory. Many goods can be produced in a way that does not immediately depend on the demand of the customer for a product. Production managers are concerned with the best way to transform resources into goods, the steps that should be used to accomplish that transformation, and productivity.

Production processes. A company that produces goods takes a combination of inputs, converts them in one of several ways, and delivers a combination of outputs. The inputs may be basic raw materials such as water, coal, or wheat, or they may be materials that have already been processed in some way, like steel or flour.

The outputs of one company may be the inputs of another. For example, the fabric that is the output produced by Company A from a combination of cotton fibers and dyes becomes the input for Company B, which produces dresses as its output. Another firm, Company C, may take metals and plastics as inputs and transform them into zippers and snaps as its output; these also become an input for Company B.

Production processes can be categorized by the way a company transforms inputs into outputs. Some processes transform raw material inputs *chemically*: Iron ore is transformed into steel; wood is transformed into the pulp used to make paper. A second process, *fabrication*, changes the form and shape of the input: Plate glass is cut into windowpanes; leather is cut into the pieces that will become shoes. A third process, *assembly*, combines various inputs into a final product. For example, the leather pieces that were fabricated in an earlier process are combined with rubber, nails, glue, and thread to become a pair of shoes. Petroleum is chemically transformed into plastic which is fabricated into the shapes that are assembled into children's toys.

Another way to categorize production processes is by the way resources are used to produce outputs. *Analytic processes* take a resource and break it down into parts that are either finished products or can be used as inputs elsewhere. *Synthetic processes*, on the other hand, combine resources into a finished product.

Analytic processes do not depend on high technology. Native Americans applied these processes to trees: bark was stretched for canoes, wood was used for cooking and other purposes. The chemical transformation of iron into steel was noted above; that transformation is also a synthetic one, combining other minerals with the iron. Similarly, a synthetic process is used to combine flour, yeast, and other ingredients into baked bread.

Production processes can be categorized by the way products *flow* through the manufacturing facility. Products such as soap, soda, and chemicals do not change. They are manufactured by a *continuous process*; the same goods are produced daily. The same set of inputs are introduced into the process, the manufacturing process does not change, and the output is the same.

Some products are produced in long, but not continuous, production runs. A publisher, for example, may produce large quantities of a best-seller, and then stop the publishing process to change over to another book. In this type of *intermittent process,* the production process remains the same, but surface features are changed to produce a different product.

Types of production. Goods can be produced by a wide range of steps that involve differing levels of human and machine involvement. These steps also differ in terms of the number of finished goods that are completed at a given time. The type of production affects the cost, the consistency, and the customization of the product.

An *assembly line* is used for *mass production*, in which a product moves through a line of workers to have a specific process completed. In making dolls, for example, one worker might attach the arms, a second the legs, and a third the head. Subsequently, the doll would be dressed, the face painted, and the hair attached. Mass production is used to create large numbers of identical products, whereas *batch production*, using a similar process, results in a smaller "batch" of products. Each batch can be customized to a consumer's request.

Over time, human labor has been replaced by machine labor in many cases; people operate the machinery rather than work on the product. The production of many food and household goods is *automated*: machines measure the components of household cleaner, mix them, and pour measured amounts of the cleaner into bottles that are placed by other machines. The bottles are moved automatically so that caps and labels can be added by still other machines, then packed for shipment.

The age of computers has expanded the ability of machines considerably so that they can now perform many mechanical functions—for example, welding, painting, and assembling—that before only humans could do. Computerized programs direct *robots* to perform tasks repeatedly with complete precision. Unlike humans, robots do not tire or get bored by repetitive work; they are also more consistent.

Computer technology has had a profound impact on production. *Computer-aided design* (CAD) enables engineers and product designers to develop products using computer graphics. Computers help with specifications; three-dimensional programs and simulations reduce the need for prototypes. *Computer-aided manufacturing* (CAM) uses computers to plan, schedule, and monitor much of production. *Computer-integrated manufacturing* (CIM) links many manufacturing activities through a central computer, usually including both CAD and CAM systems.

Productivity. When Henry Ford introduced the assembly line to build his Model T automobile, he substantially reduced the time needed to build the

Automation

chassis. The number of cars produced rose dramatically relative to the amount of labor; Ford was able to pass these savings to the customers; sales rose significantly. *Productivity* measures the efficiency with which a company's resources are used to create its products. Efficiency has increased dramatically through automation, but the costs of automating and computerizing production must be justified by an accompanying increase in productivity.

Producing services. Unlike goods, services cannot be inventoried, as they are produced and consumed simultaneously. Services must be available

Sample service industries

- **Retailing**
  Grocery store
  Book store
- **Transportation**
  Overnight mail delivery
  Passenger ferry
- **Finance**
  Bank
  Stockbroker
- **Professional services**
  Architect
  Teacher
- **Personal services**
  Beautician
  Tailor

at the right time; for example, empty seats on an airline flight are lost sales.

Service industries. Most economic growth in the United States during recent years has come from the service sector. Among the major service industries are retailing and wholesaling, transportation, utilities, finance, insurance, entertainment, education, and professional and personal services. Some, like the passenger airline industry, are *capital intensive*; others, like accounting services, are *labor intensive*.

Service operations. As with goods, there are a variety of processes used to produce (or perform) services. In the production of goods, the firm takes inputs, converts them, and produces outputs that are sold to customers. In the production of services, the customers themselves, or their possessions, are part of the conversion process. The customer may be a sick patient who needs to be restored to health, a traveler who needs to go to another place, or a hungry diner who needs to be fed. The customer may have a lawn to mow, a letter to mail, or a pet to groom. In all these cases, customers specify the service required and interact directly with the service provider. The nature of this interaction helps determine the production process.

In many ways, the *transformation processes* for services are almost as varied as the services themselves. The *mediating* process is seen especially in the retail and food industries. A department store assembles a variety of goods that the customer may select. A restaurant provides the customer the opportunity to choose a meal. The *transportation* process moves goods and people from one location to another. A third process transforms *information*, not only in data processing and word processing, but also in many professional fields. An accountant transforms raw data into useful financial information; an architect transforms ideas and information into a blueprint for a building.

Service flow. Because production and consumption of services occur at the same time, service industries are typically characterized by intermittent flow. The customer is treated individually, with a different "package" of services offered to each. There are some exceptions to this rule, however. Large educational institutions offer a set of uniform service packages, as do specialized hospitals.

Some services can be thought of as continuous, and are offered whether customers ask for them or not. Buses and airplanes, for example, travel on predetermined schedules, whether passengers ride them or not. Large medical centers have a nearly continuous flow of patients who move from department to department (for example, from X ray to laboratory testing) much as material on an assembly line is moved about. Customers frequently think of large service organizations as impersonal, but they are quite efficient.

Types of operations. Most services are labor intensive, not capital intensive. Despite this, and despite the need in most cases to provide individualized service to each customer, the production of services frequently involves a high use of mechanization, automation, and computerization.

Many services, while providing personal attention, are *mechanized* to varying degrees. Dry cleaners use machinery to press shirts and dresses; they do not hand-iron most clothing. Car washes, with exceptions such as the efforts of high school students raising funds, provide mechanized washing and waxing. Many catalogue stores use conveyor belts to transport goods from the warehouse to the check-out line.

More sophisticated machinery has *automated* the delivery of services, altering even further the role of employees. Landscapers set up automatic sprinkling systems to water lawns at set times. Rental-car clients enter a destination into a machine that provides them with directions. Bank customers can deposit and withdraw funds without ever seeing a bank teller.

Computers play an important role in many service industries. Customers buy tickets for plays in London from a New York ticket broker who orders via a computer. Stockbrokers rely on computers to buy and sell securities. Computers play a central role in modern medicine, from monitoring vital signs to assisting with surgical procedures.

Operations. Transformation processes are but

Mechanization helps many companies improve their personal service to customers.

one part of an operations system that changes inputs into finished products. Other key elements include selecting production facilities, designing the specific process, scheduling the order of operations, ordering the input materials, managing the inventory of finished goods, and ensuring quality.

Facility planning for goods. Once a company knows what goods it will produce, steps are taken to ensure availability of facilities. Especially when levels of production are changing, existing facilities must be evaluated for long-term viability. Location and layout are important factors.

Many factors shape the decision of where to *locate* a production facility. These include cost, availability, and accessibility of land, utilities, and labor; union strength; access to suppliers and markets; quality of life; and government and community support.

How equipment, supplies, work areas, and storage are arranged is the *plant layout*. Some plants use a *process layout*. For example, a process layout for furniture has cutting in one area, lathing in another, drilling in a third, and so on. Assembly lines use a *product layout*, taking a product from start to finish. The *fixed-position layout* places the product (such as a house to be built) in a stationary location; workers come to the product.

Planning and scheduling goods. Without inputs, no production takes place. *Purchasing* ensures that inputs are available when they are needed. Purchasing managers work with more than prices; they balance costs with quality, accessibility, and availability of materials. Ordered too soon, materials tie up the firm's capital; ordered too late, they hold up production.

Routing determines the work flow and the sequence of steps that take place in production. For example, before chairs can be assembled, the legs must be shaped and drilled. *Scheduling* takes this sequence and determines time needed for each step, which steps can be performed simultaneously, and when steps have to start in order to be completed for subsequent steps.

Goods vs. services

- **Goods**
  Tangible products
  Can be inventoried
  Little contact between production and customer
  Transformation processes:
      Chemical
      Fabrication
      Assembly
  High percentage of continuous flow
  Output can be specified exactly

- **Services**
  Intangible products
  Cannot be inventoried
  High contact between production and customer
  Transformation processes:
      Mediation
      Transportation
      Information
  High percentage of intermittent flow
  Output is specified somewhat vaguely

The fixed-position layout is used for large products such as the space shuttle and airplanes.

Graphs and charts often give a useful overview of the sequence and overlap of production steps. *Gantt charts*, developed in the early 1900s by Henry Gantt, are bar charts that provide this picture. One side indicates the total time period for producing the goods or services. Against that are the individual steps, listed by department, that must be completed. Each bar indicates when a specific step is undertaken.

While Gantt charts are useful for simpler production processes, more sophisticated methods are needed for complex production such as home construction. Assume steps 1 and 2 can be undertaken simultaneously. Both are started on Monday; step 1 requires one day to complete, step 2 two days. Both must be complete to start step 3. If all goes well, or even if step 1 takes an extra day, step 3 begins on Wednesday. But if step 2 takes an extra day, then step 3 is delayed. The sequence of events that shapes the overall schedule is the critical path; *critical path method* (CPM) is the technique used to determine this path. *Program evaluation and review technique* (PERT) charts are similar but rely on statistical probabilities.

After all the planning, routing, and scheduling have been completed, there is still no product available. Production must somehow be set in motion. *Dispatching* is the process of setting and keeping the process in motion by issuing work orders to make individual steps operational. The dispatcher gives the go-ahead, sending out paperwork to the appropriate department heads to begin work.

In order for production to begin and continue smoothly, parts, materials, and equipment must be in the right place at the right time. For companies that provide customized work, in which the combination of parts and materials is always shifting, the challenge to keep components on hand is especially challenging. The process of determining what materials are needed, and when, and ensuring their availability is called *material requirements planning* (MRP). Many companies use computerized MRP systems. MRP systems coordinate materials and activities not only within production, but also with human resources, marketing, engineering, and finance departments.

One way to ensure that inputs are available is to have excess inventory—or to have the full quantity ready in inventory at the start of production. While this avoids the cost of interrupting production, it drives up other costs. Inventory requires storage and ties up capital that could be used more productively.

Gantt chart

	Step 1	Step 2	Step 3	Step 4	Step 5
Department	A	B	C	D	E
Week 1	▌	▌			
Week 2		▌	▌		
Week 3				▌	
Week 4					▌

As a result, many organizations are implementing *just-in-time* (JIT) inventory for both inputs and outputs. With just-in-time inventory, new materials arrive at the production facility just at the time they are needed. In Japan, just-in-time inventory works so well that many automakers receive hourly delivery from their suppliers, with materials arriving just at the moment they are needed. Such hourly scheduling is not usually possible in the U.S. due to the distances between suppliers and customers. Yet many U.S. manufacturers have reduced inventory significantly, down to just that which is needed for a day or week of production.

In addition, many companies no longer carry an inventory of finished goods "just in case" a customer has an order. Many companies produce goods just-in-time. That is, production begins only when a customer's order is received; the item is made to meet the customer's requirements. This system requires a flexible manufacturing system.

Facility planning for services. Decisions about facilities are as important for service companies as for manufacturing companies. Location decisions are crucial, because the customer must come to the business for most services. *Location*, *layout*, and *attractiveness* are important to grocery store shoppers or a doctor's patients.

For many service companies, the decision about where to locate is the most important one it may ever make. Factors such as cost, labor, utilities, access to suppliers, and government and community support are important, just as they are for manufacturing plants. For service businesses, however, convenience for the customers is crucial to success. Fast-food restaurants owe much of their success to sound decisions about location; the same is true for hotels, gas stations, and convenience stores. Firms that have relatively low interaction with customers may be more concerned with cost and availability of labor; this is

An attractive environment promotes customer satisfaction.

true for telemarketing and direct-mail companies.

As with location, the layout of a service company's facilities is strongly influenced by the amount of interaction with the customer. Bank customers want easy access to tellers and automatic money machines; they want privacy when meeting with bank officers about loans; they don't want to be troubled with the rest of the bank's operations. A typical bank's layout reflects these preferences.

A theme park has several challenges in planning its layout. Restrooms are placed in convenient locations; food stands are often positioned near the beginning of the lines for rides. These lines are generally laid out to minimize frustration and provide a sense of constant movement. Often, the route away from a ride leads directly through a gift shop.

Planning and scheduling of services. The fact that services cannot be inventoried underlies their planning and scheduling. An auto repair shop, for example, must schedule repairs carefully to minimize the time that it has the customer's car. Poor scheduling may cause the customer to choose another repair shop.

Manufacturing companies use inventory to maintain even production runs. *Low-contact* service companies can often maintain even production levels, but *high-contact* companies cannot. For example, one morning fifty customers bring their clothes to a dry cleaner. They place their order, but the service itself takes place later; as long as clothes are ready one week later, customers are not concerned when the actual cleaning takes place. Bank customers, in contrast, expect full services at the time of their visit.

High-contact companies need to monitor waiting lines, or *queues*. If fifty bank customers arrive over a two-hour period, a few tellers will be able to provide service. If they all arrive together, the queue will be extremely long. The bank will need more tellers, but only for a brief period. In order to minimize lines and excessive employee costs, service companies need to project when their customers will demand services.

Two ways that service companies try to control the timing of their customers' demand are appointment scheduling and fixed scheduling. *Appointment scheduling* is often seen in professional and personal services: patients make appointments to see doctors, lawyers, counselors, and beauticians. Transportation and entertainment companies use *fixed schedules*: an airline tells the customer when its service is available; cinemas provide fixed schedules to show motion pictures.

The biggest difference between *routing* goods and services is that the customer is often part of the service route. For example, patients enter a doctor's reception area, where forms are completed. They are weighed and brought to a private room where blood pressure and temperature are checked. Routine tests are run next; patients follow a route through examination, blood tests, X rays, and other tests before returning to dress, exiting through reception where bills are paid. The sequence is neither random nor based solely on the exam itself. It is also designed so that patients do not arrive for X rays simultaneously, and privacy is maximized. Furthermore, while patients are proceeding through the sequence, others are starting, increasing the number who can be seen.

Quality management. Quality is important for both goods and services. Defective products must be recalled at a cost to the manufacturer, and consumers may switch to other products.

Quality management is generally viewed as a statistical process, when in fact it should be a company-wide operational concern. Moving beyond the percentage of products that are merely acceptable, *quality assurance* goes back to basics. Efforts are made to improve production processes and find defects where they are introduced—at the design and purchasing stages. Design improvements, such as rounding the edges of toys, improve overall quality and customer satisfaction. Purchasing quality materials reduces the opportunity for production problems.

Statistical quality control ensures that the production process is harnessed. If a process is designed to meet a particular standard, such as filling bottles with 16 ounces of soda, there will be variation in the actual amount of soda in the bottle. Statistical control determines an acceptable upper and lower limit for the variation (such as 15.9 to 16.1 ounces); the process is then monitored to make sure standards are met. If an operation is out of control, something about the production process has gone awry and must be brought back in control.

Total Quality Management, or TQM, is a total, system-wide effort at producing high-quality goods or

services. A TQM system starts with getting to know the company's customers well so that the company can provide exactly what the customer wants.

A TQM system requires that employees who produce the product or service be viewed as human resources, not merely as workers. These employees best understand the customer or process. In TQM, they are encouraged to contribute ideas for process changes; the company is willing to experiment with some of their new ideas. TQM systems rely on teams, rather than individuals, to do the work of the company.

A TQM system also requires the company to attend to its own production systems. If, for example, a fast-food restaurant sets a goal of serving customers within two minutes, then it should measure the time required to serve each customer. Without measurement, employees will not know if they are reaching their goal. Companies using TQM try to quantify as many goals regarding quality as possible, then measure how well goals were attained. Employees are fully involved in specifying both goals and the measurement process.

Marketing

According to the American Marketing Association, marketing is "the process of planning and executing the conception, pricing, distribution, and promotion of ideas, goods, and services to create exchanges that satisfy individual and organizational objectives."

The components of this extremely important process are commonly known as the *four Ps*: product, price, place, and promotion. Thus, marketing is far more than advertising. The very nature of the product, decisions about what to charge, and the process of getting the product to the potential buyer are all part of marketing.

Fundamentals. Transactions occur when buyers and sellers *exchange* something of value. Buyers will not exchange money for a product unless the product has *utility*: it satisfies some need. Form utility, which marketing shares with production, refers to product characteristics such as size, function, and shape. Place utility ensures that products are located where purchasers expect to buy them, just as time utility ensures products are available when customers want them. Possession utility is value of ownership.

Market. A *market* is a group of people or organizations that has the demand for a product and the ability to purchase it. The consumer market consists of individuals who buy products for personal use, not for resale. The industrial market consists of organizations that purchase products for resale or to help them conduct business.

Market research. Most successful marketing strategies rely on *market research*. Information thus gathered can support product development and can identify a price range customers are willing to pay, where they are likely to purchase products, and what kind of message will most likely reach them. Evaluation after products are introduced leads to adjustments and improvements that can dramatically improve sales and customer satisfaction.

Market researchers use a variety of techniques to gather information. These include surveys by telephone and mail, interviews, and direct observation. This information is used at all stages of product development. Companies continue to conduct research as long as a product or a service is on the market. Researchers also analyze the marketing strategies of their competitors, as well as demographic and census information.

Understanding why consumers act the way they do leads to greater success in the marketplace. Economic factors influence buying behavior: consumers worried about job security often delay major purchases. *Demographic factors*—age, gender, race, religion, and others—influence buying choices. Psychological factors are important: How do consumers feel about themselves? What makes them happy? Consumer behavior helps shape many marketing decisions: Where will golf clubs and tuxedos sell best? Who would be a good product spokesperson? What price can or will the market pay before it switches to another product?

Industrial markets

- **Producer market**
  Fast-food restaurants purchase potatoes
  Printers purchase computer equipment and training
- **Institutional market**
  Universities purchase maintenance services
  Churches purchase hymnals
  Hospitals purchase accounting services
- **Governmental market**
  Federal agency purchases engines for helicopters
  State agency purchases forms for statewide testing
  Local agency purchases food for homeless shelter
- **Reseller market**
  Grocery store purchases milk for resale to consumer
  Wholesaler purchases candy for resale to drug stores

Telemarketing is just one way companies gather information about their products.

Marketing mix. As we have seen, four major components of marketing provide the tools used to satisfy the market's needs: *product, price, place,* and *promotion.* The interplay of these four components is the *marketing mix.* For example, the finest shoes, promoted for comfort and quality, and priced at the high end, can be very successful at selected places, but not at the local discount store. The mix for each product must be evaluated carefully. Market research is essential in determining the appropriate marketing mix.

The perfect marketing mix does not guarantee success; other elements come into play, enabling the company to devise a complete *marketing strategy.* Without demand, the product will fail. The company must understand both the *target market* and the *competitive environment.* It must focus efforts to match products with customers. A marketing strategy must also have a clear sense of scheduling: A new line of Christmas ornaments should not be introduced on December 31. Strategic marketing fits marketing plans into long-term corporate plans. It identifies investment, production, and human resource needs, and analyzes product cash flows.

Market segmentation. Even though products like soap can be sold to all markets, there are subgroups, or *segments,* that want different features. One segment wants tough deodorant soap, another soft facial soap, a third gentle soap for infants. Understanding market segments helps firms target their marketing efforts. *Demographic factors* determine many segments: denture adhesives are marketed to older consumers. *Geographic factors* shape marketing efforts: snow shovels will sell more in Minnesota than in Arizona. *Psychographics* look at customers' opinions, attitudes, activities, and life styles: Young families who live in rural areas and enjoy hiking and camping will buy different cars than single, urban professionals who date frequently and like spending time at the beach.

Product and pricing. *Products* are goods

and services that customers buy to satisfy their demands. *Price* is the amount a company charges customers for a product. Product and price are the first two *P*s of the marketing mix.

Products. Some companies are built around one product; other companies sell one or more groups of products. Each of these groups is a *product line*. For example, a company specializing in consumer goods may have a product line of soaps, another of detergents, and a third of furniture polishes and waxes. Companies try to distinguish their products: color, taste, and image are ways firms encourage *product differentiation*.

Brands identify products, distinguishing them from others. A *brand name* is the spoken part, such as Pepsi. A *brand mark* is a symbol, such as the McDonald's golden arches. A *trademark* is a legally protected brand; only the owner may use its name or symbol. Firms try to build *brand loyalty* among customers, from *brand recognition* through *brand preference* to *brand insistence*, the point where buyers will not accept substitute products. Brands can be truly international and multicultural. They uniquely identify a product in countries around the world. Many international companies invest a great deal of money developing brand recognition and brand loyalty, hoping to build brand insistence throughout the world.

The container and wrapping that hold a product are its *package*. How a product is sent to the market influences its package; so does the way it is displayed. Packages help draw customers' attention; they communicate information, either through labeling or other means (package colors can indicate flavor or scent). The *label* provides information about the product's contents, features, or use. Government regulations require that labels provide accurate information.

A company's *product mix* is the particular combination of products it sells to the marketplace. For diversified companies, the mix is the total of all available product lines.

Product mix can be measured for depth and width. A company may only have one product line—for example, ice cream—but offer many variations; its mix is narrow but deep. Another company may have many diverse product lines; its mix is wide.

Product development. Most new products are only introduced after significant investment in their development. They have several stages of development, a life cycle of their own. If a company is to succeed in the long term, it must know where its various products are in their life cycles. At different points, products require different strategies to continue to satisfy customer needs.

Most products go through a four-stage *product life cycle*: introduction, growth, maturity, and decline. In the *introductory stage*, the product is unknown to the market. Investments are made to develop the product and promote it, building customer awareness and demand. In the *growth stage*, sales are rapidly increasing as the market becomes aware of the product. While this stage usually brings profits, promotional expenses are still quite high. The *maturity stage* is the most profitable stage: sales are level or only slightly dropping; costs are relatively low. The *decline stage* sees declining sales and profits. The firm decides whether it can revive or extend the product; otherwise it will drop the product when it is no longer profitable.

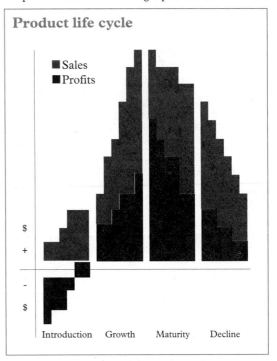

Product life cycle

■ Sales
■ Profits

\$
+
-
\$

Introduction   Growth   Maturity   Decline

Most new product development goes through six steps.

1. Ideas are generated, often suggested by unmet customer desires.
2. Ideas are screened based on practicality.
3. A business analysis is prepared, looking at projected sales, costs, problems, and cash flows.
4. The product is developed.
5. The product is test marketed and usually refined based on consumer reactions.
6. If the product has generated sufficient interest in the market for it to be profitable, then it is commercialized.

Pricing. What customers are willing to pay is important in determining a product's price. Company objectives also shape the decision, as do competitors' prices and production costs. Wholesalers and retailers, who set the final price, also influence the company's price decision.

A firm may have several *pricing objectives* when it sets price. If profits are the main goal, it will estimate sales at each price and find the most profitable level. A firm that wants to build sales may sacrifice short-term profits and set a low price. A firm struggling to survive may price extremely low to generate cash flow and cover fixed costs. Image is a factor; low prices at specialty boutiques may send mixed messages to wealthy customers. Ethical concerns are also a factor when pricing products (such as drugs) that can literally mean life or death for the customer.

A firm has several methods it can use to determine price. *Competitive pricing* tracks prices set by compet-

ing firms and responds; the airline industry often uses competitive pricing. *Mark-up pricing* calculates the cost of making the product and adds a profit margin. The cost includes *fixed costs* (which are incurred regardless of the level of production, like the cost of machinery) and *variable costs* (which increase as production increases, like the costs of raw material inputs and labor). If cost is twenty dollars and mark-up is 20 percent, the price is $20 + (.2 × $20) = $24.

Price skimming sets high prices when products are introduced, lowering them as demand rises. *Penetration pricing* sets low prices in order to build up market share, then raises them when demand rises. Existing products can be priced below, above, or at market price (the average price that consumers pay). Products at the market price emphasize features and personal selling. Products priced below the market promote value, while products priced above the market promote quality and image.

Pricing decisions reflect how firms think consumers react to price. *Psychological pricing* creates an illusion of lower prices: $299 seems lower than $300. *Threshold pricing* assumes limits to what consumers will pay; rather than exceed the limit, firms reduce quantity or some other feature. *Price lining* establishes levels of pricing: A firm may sell socks at $2, $5, and $9 per pair; consumers pick their own level. *Multiple unit pricing* encourages consumers to buy more than one of a product. *Prestige pricing* projects a high-quality image.

Break-even analysis

Break-even analysis calculates how many units need to be sold in order to cover all fixed and variable costs. Each unit sold above the break-even point contributes profit. The formula for calculating break-even is:

break-even = fixed cost ÷ (selling price - variable cost)

Suppose a publisher has fixed costs of $2,000 and variable costs of $20 per book. How many books must the company sell to break even if it sells the book for $30?

$$break\text{-}even = \$2,000/(\$30 - \$20) = \$2,000/\$10$$
$$= 200 \ books$$

Here are break-even points at other prices:

Price	Formula	Break-even point
$25	2,000/(25-20)	400 books
$28	2,000/(28-20)	250 books
$32.50	2,000/(32.50-20)	160 books

Psychological pricing is designed to make products appear to cost less than they really do.

Distribution. The third *P* of the marketing mix, *place*, focuses on where products are sold, what distribution methods are used, where products are inventoried while waiting to be sold, and how products are transported to the customer.

Channels. Some companies sell directly to the customer. Others use different means. *Distribution channels* describe the different routes products travel to get from the producer to the customer. Consumer and industrial channels are not quite the same: wholesalers and retailers play a greater role for consumer products.

In addition to traveling directly from the producer to the customer, consumer goods can go from producer to retailer to consumer, producer to wholesaler to retailer to consumer, or producer to agent to wholesaler to retailer to consumer. Industrial goods may also go through agents or wholesalers on the way to the user.

Retailers, wholesalers, and agents are *middlemen* or *intermediaries*. While each intermediary in a channel adds cost, overall they lower costs. Especially for convenience goods, they effectively cut labor and transportation costs for producers; imagine if a candy manufacturer needed its own staff to sell and distribute the candy to every retail outlet it used.

The number of sales outlets that a product has in an area shapes its *market coverage*. *Intensive distribution* aims for as many outlets as possible; while *selective distribution* limits the number of outlets. *Exclusive distribution* restricts outlets; one outlet is allowed to carry the product in a specified area.

The manufacturer and channel can be part of the same company; this relation creates a *vertical marketing system* (VMS). One example is an oil company that has its own service stations.

Wholesalers. Wholesalers do not distribute products directly to the public; they sell to other firms that will resell the product. Wholesalers are especially important to firms that have goods sold through thousands of outlets. Many wholesalers carry products from a variety of producers.

Wholesalers help outlets through advertising assistance, promotional displays, market and product information, and credit assistance. They provide producers with a sales force and market information. They maintain their own inventory, enabling producers to lower carrying costs. By extending credit to outlets, wholesalers lower the manufacturers' credit risks.

Most wholesalers are *merchant wholesalers*. They take legal title to products, store them in warehouses, and have a sales force. *Agents* do not take title; they sell products in specified territories. Agents are paid on commission, a percentage of sales. *Brokers* focus on a particular commodity such as real estate or insurance. They bring buyers and sellers together; sellers pay them commissions when sales go through. *Branch offices* and *sales offices* can be owned by the manufacturer and provide most wholesaler services.

Retailers. Retailers sell products to the end user. In recent years, many have become increasingly specialized, while others have diversified the products they offer.

Department, specialty, chain, and discount stores vary in products, quality, service, and price. In catalogue showrooms, buyers choose products they pick up from an adjoining warehouse; in warehouse stores, they shop in the warehouse. Higher prices, but more open hours, are typical at convenience stores. Supermarkets sell food and household supplies; hypermarkets combine supermarkets and discount stores under one roof.

Many products are sold door-to-door (books, magazines), through neighborhood parties (cosmetics), or through vending machines (candy). Mail-order companies use catalogues to generate sales, while telemarketing relies on the phone. Sales through television networks (such as QVC) and paid programs devoted to one product (*infomercials*) have risen dramatically in recent years. The computer is also a key channel, with many retailers using home pages on the World Wide Web to generate sales through the Internet.

Physical distribution. Successful sales depend on many factors. Products need to be available when customers want them, and then be physically delivered to the customer (or the channel). Demand must be monitored so that production knows how much to provide, and revenues must be collected.

Good *inventory control* reduces carrying costs while ensuring products are available when needed. *Order*

Intermediaries

Producers

Buyers

Intermediary
(middleman)

A distribution center in action

processing covers the steps of arranging to ship products, bill customers, collect revenues, and grant credit. Products waiting to be shipped are held in private or public warehouses. *Distribution centers* are fast-paced warehouses used often by large retailers. Manufacturers deliver large shipments which are then divided among trucks taking a combination of products to individual outlets. *Materials handling* looks at ways to limit handling and to package products so as to reduce breakage during shipment.

The biggest cost of distribution is transportation. *Ground transportation*, notably railroads and trucks, is the most common form. Railroads move large volumes across long distances at low cost. Unlike railroads, trucks can bring products directly to the customer. Trains often carry loaded truck trailers which are then attached directly to vans to continue distribution, reducing handling. *Air transportation* is speedier but more expensive; weight and size are limiting factors. *Ships* are less expensive but slow. They are often used for moving products such as oil and grains, especially internationally. *Telecommunications*, such as faxes, voice mail, and electronic mail, transport information.

Promotion.

The techniques a company uses to generate customer sales make up *promotion*, the fourth *P* of the marketing mix. Promotion has three major goals: informing customers about the products, influencing a customer's decision, and reminding the customer of product features and availability.

Promotional mix. Just as the marketing mix has four elements, there are four elements that make up the promotional mix. These elements are advertising, personal selling, sales promotion, and publicity (including public relations). The mix for any given product will vary throughout its life cycle.

Advertising delivers a paid message through the mass media to an audience; the message is attributed to its sponsor. *Personal selling* provides interaction directly between a seller and a buyer. *Sales promotion* influences buyers through coupons and other activities. *Publicity* is news about the firm, delivered through the media; *public relations* is company-influenced publicity.

Promotion generates sales by communicating information about products: availability, improvements, features, and uses. Promotion creates images that distinguish products from competitors' offerings. It influences the timing of sales, maximizing sales of seasonal products during certain months or smoothing out demand for other products over a period of time, like hotel rooms.

Push strategies encourage wholesalers and retailers to push the product; personal selling and discounts are among the tools firms use. *Pull strategies* are aimed at the end user and create demand; tools include coupons, advertising, and contests.

Advertising. While advertising can be expensive, it often provides the lowest cost per person for reaching customers. Advertising can go after a broad market, as with a billboard, or it can address a narrowly defined audience, as with a mailing to subscribers of a statewide journal.

Product advertising promotes specific products. Some product advertising tries to create an immediate response; other types compare products or simply remind buyers about the product. *Institutional advertising* promotes the firm rather than a specific product. The firm hopes that the image created by the ad will help all of its products. *Advocacy advertising* tries to influence public opinion and attitudes, as when insurance companies try to influence rates within a state. *Primary demand advertising* promotes a generic product rather than a specific brand; for example, ads promoting milk benefit all dairy farmers. Advertising can be either national or local.

Developing an *ad plan* starts with knowing a product's target market and understanding which features will best appeal to that market. Next, a budget is determined, and decisions about the medium and message are made. Deciding on medium and message at the end of the process rather than at the beginning leads to more effective advertising.

The ad plan
- Target the market.
- Clarify the purpose of the ad.
- Identify selling features.
- Establish the budget.
- Determine the best media to use.
- Create the message.
- Distribute the message.
- Evaluate the effectiveness.

Media channels

	Newspaper	Magazine	TV	Radio	Direct mail	Billboard
High cost		✔	✔		✔	
Low cost	✔			✔		✔
Wide audience	✔		✔			✔
Targeted audience		✔		✔	✔	
Print	✔	✔			✔	✔
Color		✔	✔		✔	✔
Sound			✔	✔		
Motion			✔			
Message stays with receiver		✔			✔	

Newspapers are inexpensive media channels that reach a wide audience. *Magazines* can target an audience and have strong visual images, but are more expensive. *Television* reaches great numbers with sound and image, but is costly and disappears quickly. *Radio* does not have visuals, but is less expensive than television and can be more effectively targeted. Other channels include direct mail, Internet sites on the computer, billboards, directories, and displays.

Personal selling. Personal selling is the most widely used form of promotion and the most expensive. It is also the most flexible, as sales representatives can adapt a message to their customers' needs. Personal selling is often used with higher-priced items for which features and competition are major issues.

Retail sales involve selling products to end users. In addition to in-store sales, door-to-door sales and telemarketing are common types of retail selling. *In-store demonstrators* help retailers sell products to end users. *Business and industrial sales* can target firms that use the product, or wholesalers and retailers. *Government sales* often involve formal bidding.

The numerous styles and approaches to personal selling, depending on time frame and product, share several features. Sales representatives establish rapport with the buyer, present the product, respond to concerns, and close the sale. Some approaches emphasize getting buyers to describe their needs before presenting the product.

Sales promotion. In many ways, the most creative segment of the promotion mix is sales promotion. Coupons, contests, displays, incentives, free samples, exhibits, and factory tours are just a few of the techniques a company uses to persuade end users and intermediaries to purchase the product.

Several types of sales promotion are aimed at consumers. *Coupons* provide buyers with a savings at the time they purchase a product. *Point-of-purchase displays* are special displays set at the retail outlet, often at the cash register. *Incentives* include free samples and premiums (gifts that come with buying the product). *Rebates* offer customers a refund if they purchase products.

Other types of sales promotion are aimed at intermediaries. One of the most common is the *trade allowance* in which the producer offers a special discount to the intermediary; even though the savings are passed on to the consumer, the profit margin is a higher percent. *Trade shows* offer producers opportunities to exhibit current and new products to buyers.

Publicity and public relations. Publicity can be negative or positive; the company has little control. Product defects or accidents will appear in the news, as will product breakthroughs and successes. Companies create positive publicity through public relations. A local firm may sponsor a softball team; the players wear jerseys with the company's name. Many large companies sponsor charity events, support public television, or donate supplies to schools. All of these are examples of public relations.

The selling process

Find prospects → Determine interest → Establish rapport → Present product → Close sale → Follow up sale

Present product → Handle objections → Close sale

Management tools

Land, labor, and capital are considered the traditional factors of production. Today, with the advent of computers, information is a fourth factor. Firms that successfully manage and interpret information increase their competitiveness. The challenge is having access to good information at the right time to support the decision-making process.

MIS and computers. Most companies today do not suffer from a lack of data; most have too much data and need a structure for organizing and applying it. That structure is a *management information system* (MIS). While computers increase the power of an MIS, they are not a requirement; students who keep notecards for a paper create an MIS.

The relevance of information depends on timing. To evaluate day-to-day performance, for example, sales managers need to know a salesperson's name, territory, daily sales, and previous sales; for an annual review, different information is necessary, such as yearly sales and the salesperson's salary. A well-run MIS enables employees to work with information relevant to their particular needs at any given time.

Just as the production department creates finished products, an MIS creates information, with *raw data* as the input. Data come in a variety of forms. *Internal data* come from the firm's own records, such as sales and financial reports, while *external data* come from numerous sources outside the firm. *Primary data* are based on original research; *secondary data* summarize already existing primary and secondary data.

Even data produced within the firm must be *collected* and stored. In most cases, the data needed can be read from another data base. In other cases, they can be taken from records. Data coming into the company from outside can take many forms (industry reports, letters from customers, government reports) and must be organized in a way that is consistent with the firm's MIS.

Function of MIS

- **Collect data**
  Facts, statistics, projects, possibilities, ideas
- **Organize and store data**
  Data banks and data bases, computer files, index cards, lists
- **Create information**
  Organize data, alphabetically, chronologically, or by size; select relevant data for a given situation
- **Present information**
  Reports, charts, tables, graphs, summaries

Computers profoundly affect the way companies operate, allowing greater control and analysis of financial, production, sales, and personnel performance; firms can expand globally in ways that were never before possible. But computers also bring problems to be overcome.

Mainframe computers process enormous amounts of data; hundreds of users throughout a company may access them. *Minicomputers* are often used by midsized firms to handle such applications as payroll. *Microcomputers* (personal computers or PCs) are smaller desktop and lapsize computers used by millions of workers for day-to-day operations. They can link with each other and larger computers by *networking*.

Word processing turned computers into very powerful typewriters. This capability led to *desktop publishing*, which enables users to publish their own top-quality material. *Spreadsheets* are electronic ledgers that allow users to ask "what if?" and get fast answers. *Financial analysis packages* enable users to handle financial and statistical information, and *data-base management* allows information to be stored, organized, and accessed through data-base files.

On the negative side, computers can disrupt daily routines, generating unnecessary data and leading to information overload. While computers enable analysts to simulate many potential situations, they create standardized ways to interact with customers, not responding to individual situations (such as bill collection notices sent to subscribers who have died). The health impact of computers on users is not yet known.

Statistics. Statistics summarize facts in a numerical form that allows the user to interpret their meaning easily. Statistics are a daily part of our lives—for example, a team's win-loss percentage, grade point averages, consumer satisfaction ratings, mortgage interest rates, and inflation rates.

Averages. *Averages* are used to summarize data by finding numbers that represent observations. Such *measures of central tendency* describe central points in a group of data, such as average sales by a sales force, average income of consumers, or average cost of raw materials.

Averages do provide a useful summary of a set of measures, but can at times be misleading. When observations are widely dispersed, a measure of central tendency does not represent the set very well. In these cases, the measure will provide more information if it is accompanied by some measure of dispersion—for example, the range (highest observation minus lowest observation).

Calculating an index

To calculate an index, choose a base year and compare it with data from other years. Suppose, for example, a market basket of goods cost $325 in the base year and $364 in the current year:

$$\frac{current\ year\ market\ basket}{base\ year\ market\ basket} = \frac{364}{325} = 1.12$$

The most common averages, *means*, are found by adding all the items in a group, then dividing that sum by the number of items. Suppose Al, Ben, and Carl earn $21,000, Deb $25,000, Earl and Fay $32,000, and Grace $37,000. The sum of salaries is $189,000; divide that by 7 (the number of items) to find a mean salary of $27,000.

The *median* organizes items from low to high, then identifies the midpoint: half the items will be higher, half lower. In the example, $25,000 is the median. The *mode* identifies the most frequently occurring number in a group. In the example, $21,000 occurs more than any other salary; it is the mode. If no item occurs more than once, there is no mode.

Index numbers. Does bread cost more today than it did ten years ago? In absolute terms, the answer is yes. But after accounting for inflation and other factors, the bread today may be less expensive. Index numbers are percentages that compare costs or prices in one time period with those of another. For example, they can help a company compare sales in one year with sales from previous years.

Economists who want to track inflation and forecast economic changes often cite the *Consumer Price Index* (CPI). The CPI determines the cost of a sample of goods and services that typical consumers would purchase (called a market basket); it then measures the costs of those same goods and services in other years, comparing changes relative to the base year.

The Dow Jones Industrial Average (the Dow) tracks the stock prices of thirty stocks, providing a measure of overall stock performance over time. Numerous other indices are used by investors to track securities performance, including the Standard & Poor's 500 Index (S & P 500) and the NASDAQ (National Association of Securities Dealers Automated Quotations) Index.

Time-series analysis. Retailers who look only at December sales will be shocked when Christmas season sales do not hold up throughout the year. *Time-series analysis* provides a way to look at data, focusing on patterns, cycles, and long-term trends to support the decision-making process.

Some patterns repeat themselves on a yearly basis.

Seasonal variations are predictable. For example, tie sales will increase around Father's Day, iced tea and lemonade mix will sell more in summer than in winter, retailers will need temporary employees during the Christmas season, and a supply of temporary employees will be readily available during summer months.

Other patterns take place in cycles that last many years. This *cyclical variation* often ties in to such national economic patterns as inflation, employment levels, housing starts, and business failures. Demand for engineers and teachers is cyclical.

Other trends are long term, based on industry changes. Such *secular trends* include the long-term growth of compact disk players with the related decline of the market for record albums. Changes in one product can have long-term impact on others.

Correlation analysis. Firms often study relationships between two variables in their business. *Correlation analysis* provides tools for such a study.

Some variables move together, such as sales of hot dogs and hot dog buns. This kind of relationship demonstrates a *positive correlation*. By contrast, a *negative correlation* occurs when two variables move in opposite directions, such as the price of a product and the number of units sold.

Reporting information. Statistical information is most useful to decision-makers when data is summarized and condensed. Raw data should be available if the decision-maker requests it, but a report should illustrate the big picture quickly, clearly, and accurately. Business reports often begin with a brief synopsis of the problem to be studied and the methods used. Also important are the conclusion, which directly addresses the problem, and recommendations, which build from the conclusions.

Process chart

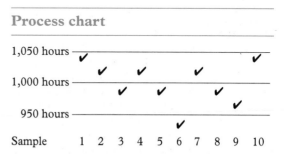

Process charts track the mean of a small sample of products from a production process. In the statistical quality control process here, small samples of light bulbs (5-10) are tested to see how long they burn (the overall mean is 1,000 hours). If the mean from a small sample is too far away from the overall average, then the manufacturing process must be investigated for problems. Here, the mean of sample 6 falls outside the acceptable range.

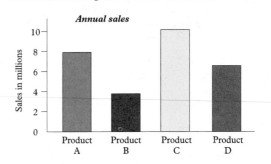
Graphs. Statistical information can be presented visually by using graphs. *Line graphs* are especially effective for showing the change in one variable relative to another variable (usually time). For example, line graphs might show how the country's population has grown from year to year.

Bar charts are useful for comparing several variables against a common variable. While a line graph might show how sales of one news magazine have changed from year to year, a bar chart might compare the sales of several news magazines for the same time period. A separate bar would represent each different magazine.

Pictographs are very much like bar charts, but instead of bars, they use symbols and pictures to summarize data. The bars and symbols can be arranged either vertically or horizontally in bar charts and pictographs.

Pie charts compare parts of a whole. The chart is a circle divided into sections, similar to a pie cut into slices. The entire circle represents 100 percent; each section represents a percentage of the whole. If a company has five products, a pie chart can show the portion of total sales that each product generates.

Tables. Graphs are useful for giving a visual representation of data, rather than precise numbers. But when precise figures are needed, tables can be far more helpful. They usually combine word descriptions and exact numerical data, all presented in a format that uses columns and rows of information.

Accounting. While a management information system provides a way to organize and manage a firm's operational information, an *accounting system* focuses on the firm's financial information. Accounting is a vital part of management's control function. Through an accounting system, information about the firm's business transactions is collected, classified, recorded, totaled, reported, and analyzed. *Bookkeeping* is an important part of accounting; it maintains the records of transactions that are then used to measure performance. A successful accounting system can help managers identify trouble spots and opportunities.

Use of financial information. Accounting information is helpful to both external and internal users. Certain information is required by agencies at different levels of government; some use it to determine the company's taxes, while others use it as part of the regulatory process.

Stockholders use the information to help them evaluate investments and risks. Both lenders (banks) and suppliers need it to measure the risk of extending credit to the company. Internally, managers use financial information for such purposes as measuring sales, controlling costs, pricing products, monitoring inventory levels, financing new investments, managing cash flow, projecting labor needs, and determining stockholder dividends.

Accountants. *Public accountants* are not employees of the firms they serve; they work for accounting firms or for themselves. They prepare financial statements and evaluate financial reports. *Certified public accountants* (CPAs) are licensed by states once they have met education and experience requirements; they also must pass a rigorous exam sponsored by the American Institute of Certified Public Accountants (AICPA). Laws often require a CPA, rather than a public accountant, to evaluate financial statements. *Private accountants* are employees of the firms they serve. They develop the accounting system, oversee bookkeeping, and prepare financial statements.

Financial vs. management accounting. *Financial accounting* focuses on statements used by banks, lenders, investors, suppliers, and the government. Standards for external reports have developed over time, including rulings from the Financial Accounting Standards Board (FASB) and *generally accepted accounting principles* (GAAP). *Management accounting* focuses on reports that help decision making, supporting both the internal control function and the budgeting process. Because these reports are not for public use, firms have much flexibility in determining their format.

The accounting cycle. Central to all accounting is the premise that what a company has of value (assets) equals what it owes. In turn, the accounting cycle has five steps. Transactions are classified, using source documents. They are then entered in a general journal in chronological order. Next, each transaction is posted to a general ledger, based on the type of account (rent, salary). At the end of the time period, a trial balance is prepared. Last, if totals balance, financial statements are prepared.

Most bookkeeping systems use a *double-entry* system in which each entry is matched by a corresponding entry. For example, if a firm borrows $1,000 from a bank, the asset *cash* increases $1,000 as does the liability *bank loan*. If $500 is used to buy machinery, the

The accounting equation

The accounting equation underlies all acounting systems. The equation usually appears in one of two forms:

$$assets = liabilities + owners'\ equity$$

$$assets - liabilities = owners'\ equity$$

asset *cash* decreases $500 and the asset *machinery* increases, keeping the accounting equation in balance.

Financial statements. The three most important financial statements are the *balance sheet*, the *income statement*, and the *statement of cash flows*. The balance sheet is a detailed picture of the accounting equation at a moment in time. The income statement compares revenues and expenses over a time period. The statement of cash flows summarizes how cash is generated and how it is used.

Balance sheet. The balance sheet details assets, liabilities, and owners' equity at a given time. Many financial ratios, described below, that are used to analyze performance and financial stability are based on the balance sheet. On the balance sheet, total assets must equal the sum of liabilities and owners' equity.

What the company has of value, its *assets*, can be classified as current, fixed, and intangible. *Current assets* are those assets expected to be converted to cash within a year. They include cash, marketable securities (company investments that can be sold quickly), accounts receivable (due from customers), inventory, and prepaid expenses. *Fixed assets* are assets such as land, buildings, equipment, and machinery that the firm maintains over the long term. *Intangibles* are not physical assets but have value: trademarks, patents, and copyrights are expected to produce future revenue; a company's goodwill—its reputation—encourages customers to buy products and protects the firm against bad publicity.

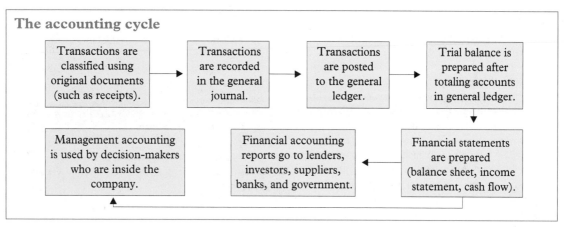

The accounting cycle

Transactions are classified using original documents (such as receipts). → Transactions are recorded in the general journal. → Transactions are posted to the general ledger. → Trial balance is prepared after totaling accounts in general ledger. ↓

Management accounting is used by decision-makers who are inside the company. ← Financial accounting reports go to lenders, investors, suppliers, banks, and government. ← Financial statements are prepared (balance sheet, income statement, cash flow).

Sample balance sheet

I-812 Bakery, Inc.
Balance sheet, December 31, 199x

Assets			Liabilities and owners' equity		
Current assets			**Current liabilities**		
Cash	$14,520		Accounts payable	$10,740	
Marketable securities	6,300		Notes payable	6,380	
Accounts receivable (net)	11,810		Salaries payable	7,915	
Notes receivable	5,930		Taxes payable	6,483	
Merchandise inventory	12,800		*Total current liabilities*		$31,518
Prepaid expenses	3,250		**Long-term liabilities**		
Total current assets		$54,610	Note payable at 10.5%	22,340	
Fixed assets			*Total long-term liabilities*		22,340
Delivery equipment (net)	$22,050		*Total liabilities*		53,858
Bakery equipment (net)	7,280		**Owners' equity**		
Total fixed assets		$29,330	Common stock	$24,000	
Intangible assets			Retained earnings	13,582	
Trademark and goodwill	7,500		*Total owners' equity*		$37,582
Total intangible assets		$ 7,500	TOTAL LIABILITIES AND		
TOTAL ASSETS		$91,440	OWNERS' EQUITY		$91,440

The amount a company owes consists of *liabilities* (the firm's debts) and *owners' equity* (the shareholders' portion). *Current liabilities* must be paid within a year. They include accounts payable (due to suppliers), notes receivable (promises to pay back money plus interest within a certain time), and accrued expenses (expenses not yet paid, though undertaken, such as salary or taxes for a previous time period). *Long-term liabilities* are due over a period longer than a year. They include mortgage payable and other debts. Usually the amount of a mortgage that is payable within the coming year is listed as a current liability. Similarly, interest owed for the coming year is listed as a current liability.

If a company sold the assets needed to pay all liabilities, the remaining value, owners' equity, would belong to its investors. *Capital stock* (paid-in capital) is the value of the stock when first sold. *Retained earnings* reflect the cumulative net profit (or loss) for a company after taxes and dividends.

Income statements. While the balance sheet describes a moment in time, the income statement looks at the firm over time. It compares incoming revenue with outgoing expenses to determine the firm's profit. Taxes, dividends, and *depreciation* (the decline in value of the firm's assets due to aging) are included. The income statement is a record of the firm's operating activities over a year, which may be compared to the record of any previous year. A critical factor that shapes the income statement is whether the company is operating on a cash or accrual basis. With a cash basis, revenues and expenses are reported only when

money is exchanged. With an accrual system, revenues and expenses are reported when transactions occur, even if money is not exchanged until later.

Money generated by sales is the major part of any company's *revenues*. *Gross sales* refers to the total of all

Sample income statement

I-812 Bakery, Inc.
Income statement
For the year ended December 31, 199x

Revenues		
Gross sales	$223,670	
Less: Returns	9,230	
Net sales		$214,440
Cost of goods sold		
Beginning inventory	$ 11,060	
Purchases for the year	128,437	
Cost of goods available	139,497	
Less: Ending inventory	12,800	
Cost of goods sold		126,697
Gross profit		$ 87,743
Operating expenses		
Selling expenses	$41,930	
General expenses	32,750	
Total operating expenses		$ 74,680
Net operating income		$ 13,063
Less: Net income expense		1,440
Net income before taxes		$ 11,623
Income taxes		2,345
NET INCOME		$ 9,278

receipts from purchases of the firm's goods or services. However, many companies do offer discounts. Additionally, some products will be returned and refunds paid. Both discounts and refunds reduce gross sales; what remains are *net sales*.

A firm's expenses are its costs of doing business. These include costs of goods and services that are sold and the costs of operating the company. *Operating costs* consist of selling and general expenses. *Selling expenses* include salaries for sales representatives, advertising and promotion, depreciation of any sales equipment, and those overhead costs such as rent and insurance that can be directly tied to the selling process. *General expenses* include salaries for general managers and support staff, office rent, depreciation of office equipment, fees for professional services such as accountants and lawyers, and other overhead costs.

An important part of the income statement for a manufacturer is the cost of the raw material, labor, and plant for products it sells. For a retailer, the focus is the cost of goods it purchases for resale. In both cases, the firm starts with beginning inventory (this matches the balance sheet from the start of the time period). Production or purchasing costs are added (this sum is the cost of all the goods that were available for sale during the time period). Ending inventory is subtracted (this figure should match the balance sheet for the end of the time period). The difference is the *cost of goods* that were actually sold.

The difference between revenues and the cost of goods sold is called the *gross profit*. Once operating expenses are subtracted from gross profit, the remainder is *net operating income*, also called *earnings before interest and taxes* (EBIT). Interest expenses are then calculated, leading to income before taxes. After taxes are withheld, the remaining profit is referred to as *net income* or *net loss*. Stock dividends are paid from net income; the remaining amount is added to retained earnings.

Statement of cash flows. Another useful financial report is the statement of cash flows. This report looks at sources and uses of cash. The statement of cash flows helps explain changes in the amount of cash a company has available to pay the expenses. The statement identifies how cash was used in three major areas—operations, investments, and financing—and helps to measure the firm's ability to cover its current liabilities.

Analyzing financial statements. After financial reports are completed, analysts evaluate the firm in many ways. *Liquidity ratios* look at how easily the firm can meet its obligations. *Debt ratios* evaluate the firm's long-term liabilities. *Activity ratios* look at how well the company is using its assets to carry out its mission. *Profitability ratios* measure the company's overall profits relative to other components. These ratios and others help to evaluate the firm's success in the short term, over time, and relative to competitors.

Financial ratios

- **Liquidity**
  Working capital: current assets - current liabilities = working capital
  $54,610 - $31,518 = $23,092
  Current ratio: current assets/current liabilities = current ratio
  $54,610/$31,518 = 1.73
  Quick (acid test) ratio: quick assets/current liabilities = quick ratio
  $38,560/$31,518 = 1.22

- **Debt**
  Debt-to-equity ratio: total liabilities/owner's equity = debt-to-equity ratio
  $53,858/$37,582 = 1.43
  Debt-to-assets ratio: total liabilities/total assets = debt-to-assets ratio
  $53,858/$91,440 = 0.59

- **Activity**
  Inventory turnover: cost of goods sold/[(beginning inventory + ending inventory)/2] = turnover
  $126,697/[($11,060 + $12,800)/2] = $126,697/$11,930 = 10.62

- **Profitability**
  Net profit margin: net income after taxes/net sales = net profit margin
  $9,278/$214,440 = 4.33%
  Return on equity: net income after taxes/owners' equity = return on equity
  $9,278/$37,582 = 24.69%
  Earnings per share: net income after taxes/number of common stock shares outstanding
  $9,278/4,000 = $2.32 per share

Finance

In the long run, companies need to be profitable. As important, however, is the need to manage the flow of cash. A profitable firm that cannot pay its bills will be out of business long before an unprofitable one that pays bills on time.

Money and banking.

Early societies did not require money. Members traded goods and services in a system called *bartering*. As the use of money increased, banking developed to manage and regulate its flow.

Money. In order to purchase goods and services, the buyer must provide something of comparable value to the seller. In complex societies, money serves that purpose—it is the *medium of exchange*. Most of us are familiar with paper, gold, silver, and other metals as money, but other societies have used a wide range of items.

Money must be portable so that people can carry it to exchange with sellers. It must be durable; it should not easily crumble or break. Money should be divisible to give the widest possible range of values. It should also be stable; people should have confidence that its value in the future will be somewhat comparable to its present value. Finally, money should inspire confidence for its authenticity; it should not be something that can be easily copied.

Money enables buyers to exchange something of value for products. In this regard, money stores value, providing a way to accumulate resources. A person could barter a gallon of milk for a basket of apples. But by using money, the person can decide the next day to purchase a half basket of oranges instead of the apples. Thus, money helps measure value. In this simple example, money provides the gallon of milk, the basket of apples, and the half-basket of oranges with equal value.

Money takes many forms in our society. *Currency* includes coins and paper money as well as personal and traveler's checks, bank and cashier checks, and money orders. *Demand deposits* are held by banks and are available on demand by the owner. *Time deposits* are not immediately available on demand. In exchange for this restriction, such deposits earn greater amounts of interest for the owner. Time deposits include certificates of deposit (CDs) and money-market certificates. *Plastic money* (credit cards) is not really money; rather it is a form of credit or loan from the provider. However, it serves one of the main functions of money by being a medium of exchange.

Banking. Banks and a variety of other financial institutions help regulate the monetary system. Banks developed to store funds for traveling merchants and provided documents enabling the merchants to conduct their business. This basic service still survives today.

Commercial banks take demand and time deposits, make loans, provide checking services to customers, and provide other financial services. If the interest they earn on loans exceeds the interest they pay on deposits plus operating expenses, then they make a profit. The bulk of the service offered by *savings and loan associations* (S&Ls) was once home mortgages, but they have diversified into other services, including investment counseling. *Credit unions* are owned by their depositors, with services limited to owners. Most are affiliated with companies or unions.

Not all financial institutions accept demand deposits. *Finance companies* provide short-term loans to individuals and businesses. *Pension funds* invest in securities, mortgages, and other areas, creating retirement income for depositers. *Insurance companies* use premiums for long-term loans and investments.

As competition has intensified, banks have offered increasing services. They provide checking accounts with varying interest, based on balances and restrictions. Many banks assist customers with estate, financial, and retirement planning. They make loans for homes, cars, vacations, and other uses; many issue credit cards. Some manage funds left in trust. Most banks now offer various electronic services, including automatic deposit of wages, cash withdrawals, and transfers between accounts.

In order to regulate the national banking system, Congress created the *Federal Reserve System*—the Fed—in 1913. Each of the twelve regional banks that make up the Fed is owned by member banks in that region. Federally chartered national banks must be members; other banks can join if they wish and if they meet requirements. Among its many functions, the Fed lends money to the government and to other banks, and regulates the supply of money. Members are required to maintain a reserve (a percentage of the bank's deposits) with the Fed at a level set by the Fed. The interest rate the Fed charges its members is the *discount rate*, which in turn affects the *prime rate* that banks charge to their best borrowers.

Credit. An important function of financial institutions is to issue credit to customers, both individuals and firms. Credit enables the borrower to purchase a product now, with the pledge to repay later. While interest is usually charged in exchange for credit, sometimes it is not. For example, a furniture company may let customers take furniture home one day and pay for it over time, paying only the price of the furniture, without further charges. Other institutions charge varying rates of interest.

Many companies establish a *line of credit* with a bank: as long as sufficient funds are available with the bank, the company may borrow a preset level of funds without having to apply for a loan each time. The loan is then repaid, usually within a year.

Financial institutions consider a number of factors in determining whether to issue credit. These factors help the lender determine the loan's riskiness and how likely the borrower is to repay. *Collateral* is an asset (property, stocks) the borrower pledges as security for the loan; if the borrower does not repay the loan, the collateral can be sold to pay the debt. *Capital* refers to the net worth or assets of the borrower. *Character* involves general trustworthiness and track record for repaying loans. *Capacity* measures the ability to repay the loan based on sources of income and other obligations. *Conditions* are risks in the general environment that may affect the loan—for example, if a recession could affect the borrower's ability to pay.

Financial management. Firms need loans for a variety of reasons, including balancing their expenses against cyclical revenues or paying for investments. While excessive borrowing is a sign of trouble, certain levels of borrowing are reflective of a healthy company that is expanding.

Leverage. The financial goals of a firm are simple enough: to increase the wealth of the owners. In order to do so, the company must invest in its future. Sometimes this means borrowing money to make money, a process called *leverage*. For this process to be successful, the earnings that are generated by the investment must exceed the cost of the funds borrowed for investment. Imagine a small company with equity of $5,000 and annual earnings of 12 percent, or $600. If the company had $20,000, it could earn $2,400. An opportunity arises to borrow $15,000 at 8 percent interest. The firm borrows the money, earns $2,400, and pays $1,200 interest, for a net profit of $1,200. Leveraging has enabled the company to double its earnings from $600 to $1,200.

Sources of funds. Funds are available from both internal and external sources. Sales revenues are the primary source for most companies. A firm can sell unneeded assets as well or use retained earnings for investment. Financial institutions provide sources of funds through lines of credit, commercial loans, and promissory notes. The company can also sell additional stocks or bonds to raise funds.

Uses of funds. Funds are used for day-to-day operations, including rent, utilities, payroll, production, and advertising. Companies make long-term investments in equipment and plant. While eventually profitable, these investments represent a cash drain in the short run. Because of their cash requirements, such investments are usually not funded from revenues, but from special financing.

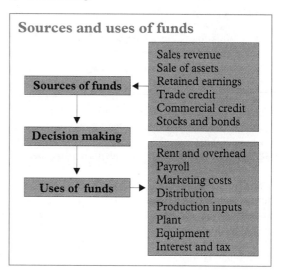

Sources and uses of funds

Sources of funds ← Sales revenue / Sale of assets / Retained earnings / Trade credit / Commercial credit / Stocks and bonds

Decision making

Uses of funds → Rent and overhead / Payroll / Marketing costs / Distribution / Production inputs / Plant / Equipment / Interest and tax

Planning for funds. A primary responsibility of a financial manager is to develop a *financial plan*, ensuring that funds are allocated to match the firm's priorities, are available when needed, and are used efficiently. Budgets are developed to identify sources and uses of funds. Budgets are developed over a time horizon; a firm with high expenses in spring and high revenues in fall may be profitable at year's end, but it will need financing through the summer. Outside sources of funding need to be identified, evaluated, and contacted to ensure the availability of funds. Finally, the flow of funds must be continually monitored relative to expectations.

Short-term financing. Sometimes a company needs outside financing to balance cash flows. *Short-term financing* provides such funding; the company expects to repay the loan within a year. A company that has seasonal sales but year-round production may need short-term financing during the months before its highest sales.

Rather than bringing funds into the firm, *trade credit* delays the outgoing flow. Firms obtain production inputs or resale products but do not pay upon delivery; they may have thirty days or more to pay. A retailer may be able to sell goods before it has to pay the supplier for them, ensuring the needed cash flow. Suppliers often offer purchasers discounts for early payment. For example, an invoice that reads "2/15, net 45" offers a 2 percent discount if the bill is paid within 15 days; otherwise full payment is due within 45 days.

Companies often seek secured or unsecured loans from banks and other lenders. To get a secured loan, a company pledges assets such as accounts receivable and inventory as collateral; if the company fails to repay the loan, the collateral becomes the lender's property. Unsecured loans do not require collateral but carry higher interest rates. A line of credit is the lender's agreement to provide a predetermined sum at any time, if funds are available. A revolving line of credit is similar, but it guarantees availability of funds.

To obtain short-term funds, large companies often issue commercial paper—a short-term note at an agreed-upon rate, secured by the firm's reputation. For example, a company needs to borrow funds for a week. It issues a $500,000 offering; the lender pays $499,000 and receives $500,000 one week later. The $1,000 the lender earns is equivalent to a 10.4 percent annual interest rate.

Long-term financing. Firms often need to borrow funds for periods longer than one year, to invest in acquisitions, plant, equipment, or product development. Such investments are profitable in the long run but may not provide incoming revenue for several years.

Commercial banks provide many long-term loans,

> ## Financing strategy
>
> Whether to raise long-term financing by debt or equity is a strategic decision. If the stock price is low, new stock may not be desirable; the lower the price, the more shares the company has to issue. If interest rates are high, then interest payments on bonds can be a steady cash drain on the company. These are just two of the many considerations the company takes into account.

as do insurance companies and pension funds. Long-term loans are riskier than short-term loans; thus interest rates tend to be higher. Mortgages are among the most common form of long-term secured loans. Instead of purchasing equipment or property, a company may make a long-term arrangement to lease the asset, making regular payments in exchange for using the asset. Both the borrower and lender gain tax advantages; for lenders, such loans are less risky since they still own the asset.

Firms that need to borrow large sums of money may issue *bonds*, which are sold to many investors rather than to a single source. Firms that issue bonds pay a preset level of interest in exchange for borrowing the funds. At the end of the bonds' time period, which may range from three years to thirty, the company buys the bonds back at their face value, or denomination. Like loans, bonds can be secured or unsecured. Investors who purchase bonds may sell them to others through the securities market. This activity affects neither the amount of interest the firm must pay nor the amount it pays to repurchase the bonds when they mature.

The sources of long-term financing described thus far involve expending funds for interest or repayment. *Equity* financing provides funds that do not require repayment, such as when companies issue new shares of stock or use retained earnings for investment. In the latter case, the company does so instead of paying dividends; if the investment is profitable, it raises the stock's value, providing a return that is often better than dividends.

Working capital. Central to the success of any financial plan is sound management of working capital. (Recall that: working capital = current assets - current liabilities.) Because a firm must pay current liabilities immediately, *working capital* is those assets it could still put to immediate use. Companies without enough working capital must raise more to stay in business. Companies with too much working capital are not successfully managing their assets. Such companies should seek out long-term investments or pay investors more dividends.

invest funds in a variety of markets, such as real estate, precious metals, or art. Securities, among the most popular, include stocks, bonds, and other documented forms of ownership or debt.

Markets. Securities can be obtained through primary and secondary markets. In the *primary market*, companies raise funds by selling securities to investors, often through investment banking firms. Once the securities are sold, the *secondary market* takes over, enabling investors to trade securities by selling and purchasing them from other investors.

Stocks. Investors who buy a company's stock are buying part of that company and thus become owners of the firm. Firms decide how many shares of stock to authorize; they usually issue a portion of those shares and hold the rest for subsequent use. Firms often decide to pay a portion of their profits, *dividends*, to their stockholders.

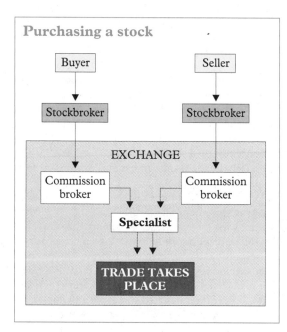

Major securities legislation

- **Securities Act of 1933.** Required corporations issuing new securities to fully disclose key financial information; required publication of prospectus.
- **Securities Exchange Act of 1934.** The all-encompassing act that established the Securities and Exchange Commission (SEC) to develop and enforce regulations overseeing the New York and American Stock Exchanges; SEC also given responsibility to regulate trading and license brokers.
- **Maloney Act of 1938.** Amended Securities Exchange Act of 1934; set up the National Association of Securities Dealers (NASD), regulating the over-the-counter market.
- **Investment Company Act of 1940.** Expanded the SEC's jurisdiction to include mutual funds; protects the public against unfair practices by investment firms.
- **Federal Securities Act of 1964.** Amended Securities Exchange Act of 1934; expanded the SEC's jurisdiction to include many over-the-counter stocks.
- **Securities Investor Protection Act of 1970.** Set up the Securities Investor Protection Corporation to insure investors for up to $500,000 of securities or $100,000 cash in cases of fraud or the brokerage failing.

The most popular way to raise equity funds is through *common stock*. Common stock shareholders elect the board of directors, approve changes in by-laws, and authorize mergers and acquisitions. The value of common stock for successful firms can rise dramatically, adding to the investor's return. Common stock shareholders are the last to receive dividends from company profits; should the company face bankruptcy, their claim is lower than any other.

A second type of stock combines features of common stock and bonds (see below). Like bonds, *pre-*

52-Week High Low	Stock - Div	Yld %	P/E Ratio	Sales 100s	High	Low	Last	Chg.	52-Wee High L
		— A —							18½
									54½
15⅝ 10⅝	AAR .48	4.3	18	63	11¼	11	11¼	+ ⅛	68¾
11⅜ 10⅝	ACMIn .96	8.5		542	11¼	.11⅛	11¼	....	8⅞
10⅜ 9	ACMOp .80	8.2		188	9⅞	9¾	9¾	....	10⅜
11⅞ 10	ACMSc .96	8.5		698	11¼	11⅛	11¼	....	12½
9¾ 8¼	ACMSp .80	8.4		1087	9½	9⅜	9½	....	7⅜
10⅝ 8¼	ACMMI 1.08	10.4		609	10½	10⅜	10⅜	− ⅛	27¾
12⅞ 9⅞	ACMMM .99	9.8		146	10¼	10⅛	10⅛	....	31⅜
2½ 1	ADT wt			254	1½	1	1⅛	+ ⅛	5⅜
9½ 5	ADT			530	6¾	6⅝	6¾	....	33⅛
34 23¾	AFLAC .44	1.4	15·	1404	30⅜	30	30⅜	....	11¼

A stock listing indicates the past year's price range, the stock name, dividend and yield information, price-earnings ratio, and previous day's activity and price range.

Purchasing a stock

Buyer → Stockbroker

Seller → Stockbroker

EXCHANGE

Commission broker ← → Commission broker

→ **Specialist** ←

TRADE TAKES PLACE

Types of bonds

- **Debentures.** Unsecured bonds, no assets pledged. Firm in default if it fails to pay interest.
- **Subordinated debentures.** Unsecured bonds, riskier than debentures. Bondholders have lower claim to assets if company defaults; higher interest rate.
- **Secured bonds.** Backed by fixed assets. If firm defaults, bondholder has claims.
- **Serial bonds.** Mature at different dates. Firm does not have to redeem all at once.
- **Term bonds.** Mature at the same date. Company redeems all at once.
- **Sinking-fund bonds.** Firm pays regularly into fund to redeem bonds at maturity, increasing security of bond.
- **Convertible bonds.** Converts to stock if bondholder chooses; conversion price is part of the issue.
- **Callable bonds.** Issuing firm may redeem before maturity for a premium.
- **Zero-coupon bonds.** Does not pay ongoing interest. Sold at a discount, redeemed at full value (U.S. savings bonds, for example).

HOW TO READ BOND TABLES

Yield is current yield. **cv**—Convertible. **ct**—Certificates. **dc**—Deep discount. **f**—Dealt in flat. **m**—Matured bonds, negotiability impaired by maturity. **na**—No accrual. **r**—Registered. **rp**—Reduced principal amount. **st**—Stamped. **wd**—When distributed. **ww**—With warrants. **x**—Ex interest. **xw**—Without warrants. **zr**—Zero coupon. **vj**—In bankruptcy or receivership or being reorganized under the Bankruptcy Act, or securities assumed by such companies.

Bond	Crnt. Yield	Close	Chg.
NYSE CORPORATION BONDS			
AForP 5s30	8.6	58⅛	−⅞
AMR 9s16	9.0	100⅛	+½
AMR zr06		43⅜	−⅛
Advsl 9s08	cv	88	....
AetnLf 8⅛07	7.9	102⅜	....
AirbF 6¾01	cv	89	....
AlskAr 6⅞14	cv	80	−2
AlskAr zr06		35¼	+¼
AlbnyInt 5s02	cv	81	....
AlldC zr96		84½	+½
AlldC zr2000		56⅜	−1⅝
AlldC zr95		86⅜	+⅛
AlldC zr99		62¾	+⅝
AlldC zr05		35	−⅞
AlldC zr09		24⅜	....
AlegCp 6½14	cv	87	+½
AldSig 9⅞97	9.5	104	....
Allwst 7¼14	cv	90	....
ABrnd 9⅛16	8.7	105¼	−¾
ACyan 8⅜06	8.2	102	....
AmStor 01	cv	109½	−¾
ATT 4⅜cld		100⅛	....

Bond	Crnt. Yield	Close	Chg.
Chryslr 12s15	11.9	101¼	−1
Chryslr 9.6s94	9.2	104⅛	−⅛
Chryslr 10.95s17	11.0	100	−⅜
Chryslr 10.4s99	10.3	101	−½
CitiPP 12½96	cv	102⅛	....
Citicp 5¾00	cv	100	+2½
Citicp 8.45s07	8.4	100⅛	−⅞
Citicp 8⅛07	8.2	99⅛	−¼
Citicp 6.5s98f	6.6	99	....
Citicp 6½04f	6.6	97¾	−½
ClrkOil 9½04	9.6	99	−⅛
Clml zrD92		98⁷⁄₁₆	−1
Clml zrD93		91⅞	+1⅛
Clml zrD98		58⅜	+1
ClevEl 9¼09	8.9	104	−⅞
ClevEl 8⅜11	8.4	100¼	−⅞
ClevEl 8⅜12	8.4	100	−⅜
Coastl 11¼96	10.8	103¾	−¼
Coastl 11⅛98	10.3	108½	....
vjColG 9s94f		103	+1⅜
vjColuG 7½97Jf		99⅛	....
vjColuG 7½97Of		98¾	−¼
vjColuG 7½98f		97⅞	−¼
vjColuG 9⅞99f		105⅜	−⅜
vjColuG 10⅛95f		105⅞	−1¾

Bond	Crnt. Yield
GrowGp 12½94	12.
Grumn 10½11	10.
GlfUSA 12½04	16.
HallB 10.20s05	10.
Hallwd na 13½09	
Hlltrst 10¾02	10.
vjHills 11s02f	cv
HmGrp 14⅞99	14.
HomeDp 4½97	cv
HudFd 8s06	cv
HudFd 14s08	cv
Huffy 7¼14	cv
ICN 12⅞98	13.
IllBel 7⅝06	7.
IllPw 7⅝03	7.
IllPw 8¼07	8.
IllPw 9⅜16	9.
Inco 7¾16	8.
IndBel 8⅛11	7.
IndBel 8⅛17	7.
IndBel 8s14	7.
InldStl 7.9s07	8.
Intlgc 11.99s96	17.
IBM 7⅞cld	c
IBM 9s98	8.
IBM 8⅜19	8.
IPap dc5⅛12	7.
IntTch 9⅜96	10
Intnr 11s95	10
Jckpt 8¾14	c
Jamswy 8s05	c
vjJonsL 16¾94f	
vjJoneL 6¾94f	
vjJoneL 8s98f	
vjJoneL 9¾96f	
Kmart 8⅜17	8
KaufBd zr04	
KerrMc 7¼12	
viKoger 9¼03f	
Kolmrg 8¾09	
Kraft 6⅞96	
Kroger 9s99	

A typical bond listing in a newspaper

from company profits; should the company face bankruptcy, their claim is lower than any other.

A second type of stock combines features of common stock and bonds (see box above). Like bonds, *preferred stock* provides fixed payments; however, the payments are dividends paid from profits and therefore can be cut. Dividends on preferred stock must be paid before any common stock dividends. If the firm is liquidated, preferred shareholders have a higher claim than common shareholders.

Bonds. Investors provide loans to firms by buying *bonds* in exchange for interest and repayment. Once a bond is available in the secondary market, prices fluctuate based on how the interest rate compares with other options and how secure the bond is.

Government securities. Debt issued by federal, state, and local governments usually offers lower interest rates than corporate bonds, but is more secure. Interest earned from most *local municipal bonds* is exempt from most taxes, unlike interest from corporate bonds. *Treasury bills* are short-term debt issued by the U.S. government, while *treasury notes* are medium-term securities; long-term bonds are also available. Small investors often favor *U.S. savings bonds,* which are available in smaller denominations than other offerings. Securities are also available from government agencies such as the Federal National Mortgage Association ("Fannie Mae").

Other investments. The *commodities* market enables investors to speculate about the price and availability of raw materials such as corn, wheat, and petroleum. *Spot trading* deals with immediately available inputs; the even riskier *futures market* deals with commodities available at a future date.

Mutual funds enable investors to buy many stocks at once, by pooling resources into a fund that buys a portfolio of securities. Funds have different goals; some might focus on high dividends, others on riskier securities. *Money-market funds* are similar but invest solely in short-term securities. *Load funds* charge sales commissions to investors; *no-load funds* do not.

Exchanges. Most securities are bought and sold through stock exchanges. Over fifteen hundred of the largest corporations list their stocks through the *New York Stock Exchange* (NYSE). To be listed on the NYSE, a company must meet several criteria, including annual earnings of $2.5 million. The next largest exchange, the *American Stock Exchange* (AMEX), lists about eight hundred smaller and medium-sized corporations. There are also regional exchanges. The *over-the-counter* (OTC) market deals with thousands of stocks not listed elsewhere. OTC dealers use a computerized system, *NASDAQ,* to automate trading.

Buying and selling securities. Trading securities in the secondary market involves bringing a buyer and seller together. A buyer places an order with a *stockbroker*, an expert registered to trade securities. A *round lot* is an order for a hundred shares (or a multiple); an *odd lot* is less than a hundred shares. A *market order* authorizes the sale at the going price; a *limit order* sets a price range. The broker places the order with a *commission broker*, who goes to a specified location on the exchange floor where a specialist oversees trading for that stock. A similar process takes place simultaneously for sellers. When the buyer and seller agree in price, the transaction occurs.

Regulation. Government agencies regulate securities trading in order to protect the public. Many regulations help ensure that investors have access to accurate and timely information. Regulations are also designed to prohibit *insider trading* (the use of nonpublic information by investors to make large profits).

Risk and insurance. All companies face

risk. Sometimes products fail and accidents occur. Companies must anticipate the likelihood and extent of loss or injury. Insurance helps the company cover its costs when losses occur.

Risk. *Pure risk* is beyond a company's control. It also involves either a loss or no loss. A tornado represents pure risk; either it hits a factory or not. If it does, there is loss; if it does not, there is no loss. Unlike pure risk, *speculative risk* involves the possibility of gain as well as loss. Investors risk funds for the opportunity to increase their wealth. Firms invest in new products, hoping to make profits.

Insurance. Using the *law of large numbers*, an insurance firm anticipates the amount of loss that will occur to a large group, but not to individual members of the group. It collects premiums from all members in order to cover costs for those members who suffer loss. Meanwhile, it has the full use of those funds to invest for profit.

Insurance companies will cover risks that they can

Managing risk

- **Risk avoidance.** The firm avoids the possibility of loss. For example, by not operating in an unstable country, it avoids the risk of war in that country.
- **Risk financing.** The firm assumes the loss directly, rather than buying insurance. For example, a firm repairs damage to cars used by its sales force, rather than buying insurance.
- **Risk transfer.** The firm purchases insurance from an outside provider. In doing so, it transfers risk to the insurer.
- **Risk reduction.** The firm reduces the likelihood of loss, without avoiding it. For example, a firm hires security guards to protect factories at night; it increases the amount of safety equipment employees must wear; it provides yearly physical examinations and health facilities to employees.

---

anticipate. Most pure risk falls into this category. While the insurer may not know which firm will be damaged by a fire, it can look at historical records to determine how many fires occur and how much damage they cause. Insurers who provide company health benefits can anticipate the number of illnesses that will occur during a given time.

Other risks cannot be anticipated or measured, such as declining sales because of change in consumer taste. Losses that occur as a result of political decisions, such as changes in tariffs, cannot be anticipated either; they are generally considered uninsurable. The same holds for losses that occur from war or even long-term weather patterns, such as droughts.

Both public and private sources offer insurance. For example, the government provides benefits to workers who lose their jobs; it collects premiums from employers to cover these costs. It also provides workers' compensation to cover losses from job injuries. Private insurers include *stock companies*, which are owned by shareholders and pay dividends, and *mutual companies*, which are owned by policyholders. Usually, mutual companies use profits to reduce insurance premiums for their policyholders.

Property insurance covers losses due to fires, natural disasters, theft, or other sources that damage or destroy a firm's property. *Liability insurance* covers losses that occur to others (or their property) as a result of actions by the firm or product failure. Insurance is also available to cover revenues a business loses as a result of temporary interruptions or the death of key employees. Still other insurance covers a firm's employees, providing them with various forms of health, disability, life, and retirement insurance.

Types of insurance

- **Property**
  Fire
  Disaster
  Burglary, theft
- **Liability**
  Workers' compensation
  Product liability
  Professional liability (malpractice)
  Public liability
- **Loss-of-income**
  Business interruption
  Loss of services
- **Employees**
  Health
  Life
  Disability

The business environment

Federal, state, and local governments play vital roles in shaping the business environment. In addition to its roles as regulator and tax collector, government is also a key consumer and sponsor for business.

Role of government.
While business and government often seem at odds with one another, their relationship is strongly interdependent. Government is the nation's largest consumer of goods and services. The success of a government at any level is measured by the economic success and prosperity of business. In turn, government provides incentives, tax credits, investments, and policies that nurture, sustain, and protect individual companies and industries. Other government policies also shape the business environment; for example, investment in education influences the quality of the workforce.

In addition to paying *corporate income tax*, businesses are responsible for withholding *personal income tax* from their employees' wages. The levels of each, determined by government, influence the funds available for investment. Businesses also pay *property tax* on land and buildings, usually at higher rates than for individuals. *Sales taxes*, which can be both state and locally imposed on goods and services sold, can affect consumer purchasing. *Excise taxes* on specific products can help pay for programs (gasoline taxes fund highways) or influence behavior (liquor taxes discourage drinking). *Tariffs* and *customs duties* on goods brought into this country help protect domestic industries from imports.

A wide variety of government agencies and policies have been established to regulate business. Many of these aim to encourage competition, protect businesses from monopolies and trusts, and promote the orderly conduct of commerce. Numerous regulations and agencies are designed to protect against pollution, health hazards, and fraud.

Because government actions so strongly affect the business environment, firms work hard to influence governmental decisions. *Lobbyists* represent individual firms as well as *trade associations*, groups made up of many firms within an industry. *Political action committees* (PACs), which represent businesses and other interest groups, provide contributions to candidates' election campaigns, hoping to elect lawmakers sympathetic to their concerns.

Additional legislation regulates the way that a business interacts with its employees. Equal Employment Opportunity laws, for example, impose fair treatment standards on companies with respect to the hiring and promoting of employees. The Americans with Disabilities Act is a recent piece of legislation passed to protect the disabled from discrimination in the workplace.

Business law.
Business practices are governed by a wide variety of laws enforced at all levels of government. While laws restrict actions that businesses can take, they also protect businesses from the actions of others. Most important, laws and the legal system provide a means of resolving conflicts within the society. *Public law* addresses the relationship between society (government) and an individual or a firm. *Private law* addresses the relationship between two or more individuals, between individuals and business, or between two or more businesses. While businesses often protest that they are subject to an overabundance of regulations and restrictions, they are not guaranteed rights under the U.S. Constitution and Bill of Rights; individuals are. What at times might seem like overvigilance by the government is often an attempt to balance the rights of individuals against the greater economic power of businesses.

Categories of law. *Statutory law* is based on legislation passed at the federal, state, and local level. *Common law* is unwritten. It is based on tradition and precedents established by court decisions. Such precedents often are the basis for legislation that moves the policy from common law to statutory law. *Regulatory law*, also called administrative law, consists of the policies, rules, and regulations established by government agencies to enforce statutory law.

Antitrust legislation

- **The Sherman Antitrust Act of 1890.** Prohibited monopolies and efforts to restrain trade.
- **The Clayton Act of 1914.** Strengthened Sherman Antitrust Act; prohibited tying contracts that forced buyers to take unwanted goods along with desired goods; also prohibited price discrimination and interlocking boards of directors.
- **Federal Trade Commission Act of 1914.** Created the Federal Trade Commission (FTC) to regulate competition and protect against unfair methods.
- **Robinson–Patman Act of 1936.** Amended Clayton Act; protected small buyers against unfair practices used to give special pricing, promotional, and other support to large buyers.
- **Celler–Kefauver Act of 1950.** Amended Clayton Act; prohibited mergers with direct competitors or purchase of their assets.

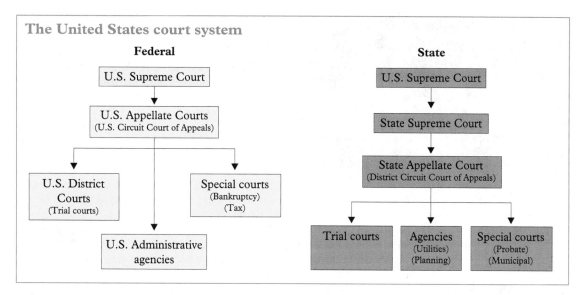

The United States court system

Federal

- U.S. Supreme Court
  - ↓
- U.S. Appellate Courts
  (U.S. Circuit Court of Appeals)
  - ↓
- U.S. District Courts (Trial courts)
- Special courts (Bankruptcy) (Tax)
- U.S. Administrative agencies

State

- U.S. Supreme Court
  - ↓
- State Supreme Court
  - ↓
- State Appellate Court
  (District Circuit Court of Appeals)
  - ↓
- Trial courts
- Agencies (Utilities) (Planning)
- Special courts (Probate) (Municipal)

Court system. The judicial system operates at the federal, state, and local levels. The U.S. Constitution shapes the *federal court system*, with the U.S. Supreme Court as the highest court in the nation. Issues addressed by federal courts include those related to the Constitution, bankruptcy, patents and copyrights, and federal tax policies. State and local courts address issues such as family, criminal, probate, and traffic law. Appellate courts provide the means to appeal court decisions at a higher level.

Contract law. A contract is an agreement between two or more parties. To be enforceable by law, the contract must meet several criteria: agreement, real consent, competence, consideration, legal purpose, and proper form. Business contracts cover such broad areas as union and employee relations, acquisitions, and credit.

Fundamental to all contracts is the *agreement* that takes place between the parties. One party must make a serious, clear, and specific offer to which the other party must agree.

A contract is not enforceable unless there is *real consent* between the two parties. The contract cannot be based on fraudulent claims (selling a new car that has in fact been used), honest mistakes (arithmetic errors), or duress (one of the parties has been pressured or threatened to sign the contract).

If either party signing the contract is not *competent*, the contract is not enforceable. Contracts might be restricted by the age of the party. The mental or physical state of the party can determine competence, including such temporary factors as intoxication or long-term factors such as Alzheimer's disease.

A contract requires an exchange; both parties must give and receive something of value, called *consideration*. The exchange does not have to be money, goods,

or services, or even of equal value, but there must be an exchange.

If a contract is not for a *legal purpose*, then it is not enforceable. For example, a contract regarding the exchange of counterfeit art, when both parties are aware of the counterfeit, is not enforceable, nor are contracts related to the manufacture, distribution, or sale of illegal narcotics.

For a contract to be enforceable, it must be in *proper form*. In many cases, the contract must be in written form; examples include home or land purchases or the exchange of over $500 worth of goods.

In most cases, if one of the parties fails to fulfill the terms of the contract, then a *breach of contract* may be claimed by the other party. The contract is the basis for judicial enforcement of the terms.

Tort law. Unlike a crime, which is a violation of an existing law, a tort does not violate a law (nor does it violate a contract). But it is an act that results in an injury to another party or property. The injured party can bring a suit through the judicial system to receive compensation for the injury.

An *intentional tort* is a deliberate action. Deliberately spreading a false written statement about someone is libel, and an intentional tort. Being aware of a product defect and willfully choosing not to correct that defect is an intentional tort, if that defect subsequently leads to injury to another party.

Negligence, while not based on a deliberate action, can often lead to the same injury as an intentional tort. It is based on the failure to use reasonable care to prevent injury to others.

Product liability assigns responsibility to a firm for an injury that its product causes to another party. *Strict product liability* holds the producer responsible, even without an intentional tort or negligence.

Trademarks can be held indefinitely, and the owner has full legal rights to their use.

Property law. Property is any tangible or intangible object that can be owned. Property law focuses on rights of ownership and on the transfer of property from one party to another. *Real property* consists of land and whatever is attached to it permanently (such as trees). *Personal property*—tangible or intangible—is all remaining property.

A *deed* is a legal document that is required for the permanent transfer of real property from one party to another. It lists both the previous and new owners and a description of the property. A *lease* is used for the temporary transfer of property from one party to another; it lists time period and cost of the transfer.

The *title* to personal property, legal ownership, is transferred when one party takes possession of it from another. When an intermediary is used, possession is more complicated. For *FOB (free on board) point of origin*, the buyer takes possession when the property leaves the supplier. For *FOB destination basis*, the transfer occurs when the property is delivered to the buyer. The time of transfer is less precise with *COD* (cash on delivery) purchases.

Three key types of intangible property are patents, copyrights, and trademarks. *Patents*, which protect ownership rights of processes, products, and other inventions, are granted by the government for seventeen years. *Copyrights* protect intellectual works such as songs and plays; they grant the owner exclusive rights to use the work for fifty years beyond the creator's life. *Trademarks* protect rights to names and symbols, such as the Pillsbury Doughboy, and can be owned forever so long as the owner renews the rights every twenty years.

Agency law. In many aspects of business, one person, an *agent*, will act on behalf of another, the *principal*. Often associated with entertainment and sports, agents can also include attorneys who negotiate contracts for others, sales representatives who promote a company's products, technicians who repair products, or almost any representative. Because the principal can be held responsible for an agent's actions, it is extremely important to have contracts that articulate what actions an agent may or may not undertake for the principal.

Bankruptcy law. Individuals and companies unable to pay their debts may undertake bankruptcy proceedings, which ensures funds are distributed fairly among creditors. *Voluntary bankruptcy* is initiated by debtors; *involuntary bankruptcy* by creditors. Three major methods are known by their chapter in the Bankruptcy Reform Act of 1978. *Chapter 7* involves liquidation, selling all assets to repay as much debt as possible. *Chapter 11* lets a firm reorganize operations, under close supervision. *Chapter 13* is for individuals, focusing on plans to repay debts over time.

Commercial law. Much of the nation's business takes place across state borders, yet each state can write its own laws regulating business. In order to ease the ability of businesses to conduct interstate commerce, a set of standard laws has been developed to provide uniformity. These standards, the *Uniform Commercial Code* (UCC), have been adopted by all states except Louisiana. The UCC includes contracts and warranties, protecting both buyers and sellers. For example, if buyers do not hold up their end of a contract, the sellers can cancel the contract, withhold the product, or sue for payment.

Business ethics.
Not all business practices are governed by laws. Many practices are shaped by the ethical and moral standards that an individual business applies to its decision making.

Many believe that firms are obliged to provide customers with products that can be used safely; that those customers have a right to be informed about product use and contents and to be warned of any possible hazards; and that customers with complaints are entitled to be heard by the company.

Business ethics also focus on the rights of a firm's investors, who must have accurate and timely information about the firm to help guide their investment decisions. They are also entitled to have the firm's assets and earnings managed in their interest, not for the personal gain of employees.

Many laws have been enacted to protect firms from practices that restrict competition. Ethical considerations frequently conflict with the desire to know a competitor's business. There is a fine line between obtaining public information and using questionable practices to gain an advantage.

The relationship between a company and its employees is under continual scrutiny. Areas of ethical consideration include discrimination in hiring and promotion practices, sexual harassment, management of pension programs, job security, and the broad area of occupational health and safety.

One way companies encourage ethical behavior is by distributing to all workers a *code of ethics* that describes expected behavior. Managers who act ethically become role models for employees. Supporting those employees who report unethical or illegal action can reinforce company standards.

International business.

The desire for trade with other societies and nations has been a driving force throughout human history. In today's world, not only is trade international, but businesses themselves are international.

Some nations specialize in certain goods because of their *absolute advantage* over others: Chile can grow bananas; Canada cannot. Nations also specialize because of their *comparative advantage:* Taiwan can produce many goods more efficiently and less expensively than many other nations.

Imports and exports. *Imports* are products brought into a country after being purchased from another. *Exports* are products sold and shipped to another country. Chile exports bananas to the United States; the United States imports bananas from Chile. A country's *balance of trade* measures the difference between its total imports and exports. If imports exceed exports, and more money goes out to purchase products than comes in, a *trade deficit* exists. If exports exceed imports, and more money comes in than goes out, the country has a *trade surplus*.

Levels of involvement. A firm can choose several ways to become active internationally. It can *license* products to another firm, allowing the licensing firm to act internationally. It can export products directly for sale in another country. *Franchising* allows for international expansion. Many firms develop *joint ventures* with firms in other countries, sharing costs and gaining a partner based in the host nation. Firms might also invest directly in another country, for example, by building plants there. *International firms* may operate throughout the world but will generally have headquarters in one nation. *Multinational firms* have headquarters throughout the world, with no specific tie to any one nation.

Trade regulations. Nations regulate commerce to manage their balance of trade and to support their own companies and workers. Methods include tariffs, quotas, embargos, subsidies, and restrictions. Many international organizations help groups of countries reach agreement about trade relations. The trend in trade agreements is to reduce restrictions on international trade.

Tariffs are taxes a government charges on imports. *Revenue tariffs* generate funds for the government. *Protective tariffs* shelter a domestic industry from foreign competition; the tariff raises the cost consumers pay for the import, increasing the competitiveness of the domestic product. Protective tariffs are still used in many instances, but reliance on tariffs to protect domestic markets has declined in recent years.

Quotas limit the number of products that can be imported. *Embargos* are used to completely ban the import or export of a product. Import embargos can be politically motivated or designed to protect industries or public health. Export embargos protect a nation's secrets and competitiveness.

Through *subsidies*, nations provide direct financial support to an industry; thus, the industry's cost is sufficiently low that, even with tariffs, the product will be extremely competitive in the international arena. *Restrictive standards* place many requirements on products before they can be imported, putting foreign companies at a disadvantage.

Two major trade organizations are the *General Agreement on Tariffs and Trade* (GATT) and the *North American Free Trade Association* (NAFTA). GATT has influenced international trade for all member nations. NAFTA has reduced restrictions on trade among North American nations (notably the U.S., Canada, and Mexico). Both organizations attempt to reduce trade restrictions and encourage international business.

Engaging in international business involves a knowledge not just of business, but of history, politics, and culture as well. Businesses are likely to continue to increase their international efforts. Thus, those who enter business educated in international studies will often have an advantage over others.

International strategies

Whether to expand internationally and how to expand are both strategic decisions. Expanding beyond domestic markets raises revenue potential, but brings many challenges that can drain managerial and financial resources. Choosing how to expand is as fundamental a decision as a company's original decision about its basic legal form of business.

World trade organizations

- International Monetary Fund (IMF)
- World Bank
- European Union (EU)
- Latin American Integration Association (LAIA)
- North American Free Trade Association (NAFTA)
- Organization of Petroleum Exporting Countries (OPEC)
- General Agreement on Tariffs and Trade (GATT)

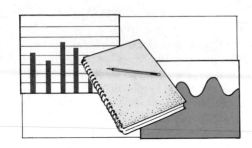

Tests, homework, and projects

Laying the groundwork

In building a house, it's important to begin with a strong foundation. In building a good academic record, that foundation consists of reading, notetaking, and studying.

Reading

Perhaps the most basic building block in mastering a course in business administration is reading. There's nothing quite like a textbook or other printed materials for communicating detailed information in a form that students can tackle in their own style, at their own pace.

When you first open your textbook, before beginning any of the individual reading assignments, take a few minutes to get an overview of the entire text. Begin by scanning the table of contents, then perhaps read the introduction to each section. If there are tables and charts, look them over and get a feel for the types of data you'll be dealing with. That way, when you begin each assignment, you'll have some idea of terms, concepts, and most important, context.

Notetaking

The things that are fresh in our memories today are the forgotten details of tomorrow. Whenever you're reading or listening to a lecture or participating in a class discussion, keep your notebook handy to jot down key concepts and thoughts so you can refresh your memory when reviewing later on.

Develop a shorthand of your own for notetaking so you don't waste time writing out complete sentences and paragraphs. Take notes in outline form, using dashes or "bullets" to highlight brief phrases and key words.

Studying

Don't just read and absorb material mechanically. Make the effort to really *study*. This means stepping back periodically and trying to see the "big picture," so that individual details can assume their proper place in the overall structure of the course. Remember, the purpose of studying business administration is not to fill your head with facts, but to gain insight into how our world works.

Strategies for success

There are students who know a subject and yet perform poorly on assignments; conversely, there are students who don't know the subject and always manage to do well on assignments. The point is that, in addition to a mastery of subject matter, there are strategies for tackling assignments that can help you improve your performance and even your grades.

Tests

In business classes, you'll ordinarily run across three different types of test questions: multiple choice, fill-in, and essay.

For multiple choice questions, usually one or more of the choices is obviously wrong; eliminate those, and instead of a one-in-four chance at a correct answer, you'll have improved your odds to one-in-three, or even one-in-two.

It's hard to guess for most fill-in questions, since these often involve definitions. Perhaps the best strategy is to be sure to study definitions ahead of time—for example, with flash cards.

There are two keys to answering essay questions: express yourself in a neat, organized way; and go for partial credit when you don't know the full answer.

Homework

Don't think of class time as the primary learning zone. Class is a time for exploring or interpreting, but the nuts and bolts of the course are the concepts you'll be reading about outside of class. Commit yourself to a regular schedule of study and homework. Be sure all your written homework assignments are done promptly and neatly.

Projects

If approached in the proper way, a term paper or project can be—dare we say it?—fun. This is your chance to take some facet of business that's caught your eye and really delve into it. Perhaps the most important thing you can do to succeed in a term project is to make an extra effort at the outset to come up with an interesting topic. If you're excited about it, your paper will be better. If you're bored writing the paper, how do you think your professor will feel reading it?

Helpful Hints

Multiple choice

> 1. The accounting function of a business supports which types of decisions?
>   a. Operational
>   b. Marketing
>   c. Financial
>   d. All of the above

The "obvious" answer is that financial indicators should support financial decisions (*c*). However, it is important to remember that the financial position of a business should influence all the aspects of the company.
Answer: d

> 2. The first requirement for someone who is thinking about starting a new business is
>   a. a lot of money
>   b. a location for the business
>   c. a good idea
>   d. all of the above

As you read this question, you will note that option *d* can be eliminated immediately—all three aspects cannot come *first*. You will also recall that businesses thrive on new ideas and innovation; if the idea isn't good, then money and a good location will not make the business successful.
Answer: c

Fill-in

> The three general categories of important managerial skills are
>   1. _____
>   2. _____
>   3. _____

Think about the areas that are important to running a successful business: information, people, and operations. The skills required must be tied to those three areas. In terms of information, one must be able to synthesize, integrate, and extrapolate—these are all *conceptual* skills. Skills in interacting with people are termed *interpersonal* skills. Skills in managing the operation of the business itself are *technical* skills, which completes the three general categories.
Answer: Conceptual, interpersonal, technical

Essay

> Develop a plan for a business that you might like to own someday.

In writing a business plan, you must remember the components that a bank or other lending institution will look for. The plan must also help you, the owner, to run the business. Thus, you will need to indicate the *type of business*, the *industry*, and the *product or service* offered. You must also indicate the *marketing strategies* that will allow you to reach your *target market*. Describe the company's *operations* (how the work will be done), and the company's *organization and management* (who will be responsible for the work). *Budgets* must be developed so that potential lenders will be assured their investment is relatively secure. Each of these components should be considered in a business plan. A *summary* at the beginning of the plan will help guide the reader and will show that the writer truly understands the business plan.

Projects

> Determine the preparations you will need to make for the business career of your choice.

This project requires you to focus on a particular area of business you think would provide you with long-term job satisfaction. It will be most helpful to interview one or more people who have set out on your planned career path, finding out about educational background and work experiences, and to gather anecdotal information. You need to find out about both skill requirements and personality traits to discover whether this particular job or career "fits" you. Then you need to decide what classes, college or vocational programs, and work or volunteer experiences will be most beneficial to you in order to be successful in your chosen career.

Whatever your career choice, and however completely you carry out all the above steps, be sure to put the best face on your project by printing it out neatly on a typewriter or computer, placing a summary sheet or table of contents on the first page, and placing the paper in a good-looking report folder.
Other suggested topics
- Select a small business in your community and do a complete profile of the organization.
- Prepare an oral report to stockholders, assuming you are the CEO of a poorly performing business.

Glossary

Asset

Benefit

Partnership

Sole proprietorship

acquisition. One company purchased and controlled by another company.

assembly-line production. A method of mass production in which large numbers of identical outputs are produced.

asset. An item of value, either tangible or intangible, that a company owns.

automation. Mechanization of the production process so that people operate machines rather than actually make the product.

balance sheet. Presentation of a firm's assets, liabilities, and owners' equity at a specific point in time.

batch production. A production process in which small numbers of products are completed to fit a customer's specification.

benefit. Nonsalary tangible compensation offered to an employee, such as paid vacation days or health insurance.

bonds. As a form of raising long-term capital, bonds are sold to investors and repurchased after a period of years; interest is paid to the bondholder.

certification election. An election supervised by the National Labor Relations Board to designate a specific union as the employees' bargaining agent.

certified public accountant (CPA). An accountant licensed by a state to prepare and evaluate a company's financial statements for public use.

chain of command. The line of direct-reporting relationships from the top of the organization.

collective bargaining. Negotiating a contract between a union and management.

compensation. The total package of rewards, including salary, benefits, and intangibles, that an employee receives from working for a company.

Consumer Price Index (CPI). Cost of a standard set of goods and services, adjusted for inflation; a standard of comparison for economic conditions over time.

corporation. A legal entity owned by shareholders with the right to do business in a state; a corporation has many legal rights and it is responsible for its own debts (the shareholders are not).

critical path method (CPM). A technique used to identify and monitor the critical steps in a project.

decentralization. The degree to which decision making is distributed to all levels of the organization.

double-entry bookkeeping. A bookkeeping system in which each entry is matched by a corresponding entry in another category.

Federal Reserve System ("the Fed"). A system set up by Congress to regulate the national banking system.

financial accounting. Preparation of financial statements that will be used by parties outside of the organization.

fixed costs. The costs a company incurs in producing a product or service, regardless of how much of the product or service is produced.

franchise. A license to sell a particular, trademarked product or service in a specified area.

Gantt chart. Chart that provides a visual indication of the degree to which a project is progressing on schedule.

income statement. A financial statement that compares incoming revenue with outgoing payments to determine the profit a business has made.

insider trading. Investors using nonpublic information about securities for personal gain.

job description. A listing of the major tasks included in a job.

job specification. The set of skills required to perform a job.

just-in-time (JIT) inventory. An inventory system designed so that materials or finished goods arrive just as they are needed.

liability. Debt that a company owes.

line of credit. A preset amount of money a company can borrow from a bank without applying for a loan.

management accounting. Preparation of documents indicating financial positions that will be used by parties inside of the organization.

management information system (MIS). A structure for collecting, organizing, maintaining, and accessing information; often (although not necessarily) computerized.

market segment. An identifiable subgroup within a market that desires specific product or service characteristics.

material requirements planning (MRP). A system, often computerized, by which the amount of material required and the date of the requirement are determined.

merger. Two companies joining their resources together to form a new company.

organizational chart. A diagram indicating the formal structure of an organization.

partnership. A legal association between two or more owners of a single business; partners are responsible for the firm's debts.

productivity. The amount of output (product or service) relative to the amount of input used.

product life cycle. A four-stage cycle of market response to a product or service, including introduction, growth, maturity, and decline.

Program Evaluation and Review Technique (PERT). A technique used to monitor a project using probabilities to determine the likelihood of meeting deadlines.

public relations. The methods other than advertising that a company uses to influence public opinion about the company and its products or services.

shareholders. Owners of a corporation; each share of corporate stock entitles the owner to one vote.

Small Business Administration (SBA). An agency of the U.S. government set up to promote and support small business.

sole proprietorship. A form of business in which one owner is legally responsible for the business and all of its debt.

span of management. The number of people who report directly to a manager.

specialization. Narrowing the focus of an employee's job; the result of the division of labor.

statement of cash flows. A report that details the sources and uses of cash for a business.

stock. Ownership of a corporation; sold in units called "shares."

strategy. A long-term plan describing actions undertaken over several years to accomplish an organization's mission.

tactics. A short-range plan describing specific actions for the next year to carry out organizational strategy.

Total Quality Management (TQM). A company-wide system of ensuring high-quality goods or services; the system is focused simultaneously on customers, process, and employees.

union. An association of nonmanagement employees designed to protect the interests of the workers.

variable costs. The costs related to producing a product or service that are directly dependent on the quantity of a product or service produced.

For further reading

Blanchard, K., J. P. Carlos, and A. Randolph. *Empowerment Takes More than a Minute.* San Francisco: Berett-Koehler Publishers, 1996.

Drucker, P. F. *Managing in a Time of Great Change.* New York: Dutton-Truman Talley, 1995.

Dunfee, Thomas W., and Frank F. Gibson. *Modern Business Law.* New York: McGraw-Hill, 1996.

Farrell, P. B. *Investor's Guide to the Net.* New York: John Wiley & Sons, 1996.

Goldratt, E., and J. Cox. *The Goal.* Great Barrington, Mass.: North River Press, 1992.

Kotler, Philip, and Gary Armstrong. *Principles of Marketing.* 7th ed. Englewood Cliffs, N.J.: Prentice Hall, 1996.

Rachman, D. A., M. H. Mescon *et al. Business Today.* 8th ed. New York: McGraw-Hill, 1996.

Robbins, Stephen P. *Organizational Behavior.* 7th ed. Englewood Cliffs, N.J.: Prentice Hall, 1993.

Sease, D., and J. Prestbo. *Barron's Guide to Making Investment Decisions.* Hauppauge, N.Y.: Barron's, 1994.

Thurow, L. *Head to Head.* New York: Warner Books, 1993.

Warren, Carl S., and Philip E. Fess. *Accounting Principles.* 18th ed. Cincinnati, Ohio: South-Western, 1997.

Weston, J. Fred, and Eugene F. Brigham. *Essentials of Managerial Finance.* 11th ed. Orlando: Harcourt Brace, 1996.

Natural Sciences

- Science, Measurement, and Math
- Biology
- Chemistry
- Geology
- Physics

Science, Measurement, and Math

Measurement in science

The natural sciences are largely experimental and deal with things that can be measured, such as length, mass, volume, density, and pressure. These measurements are then used in calculations to obtain other related quantities. Because measurement is such an important and integral part of the sciences, scientists have established certain conventions for both the units of measurement and the way the resulting numbers are handled.

Units of measurement

Measured quantities require a number and a reference label, called the *unit of measure*. These units tell what is being measured and the type of measuring system used. For example, length might be measured in feet, meters, inches, or centimeters. For many years, the units used in science were generally metric units, which were developed in France in the eighteenth century. In 1960, the General Conference of Weights and Measures created a revised metric system called the

International System of Units (abbreviated SI units). In this system, there are seven base units—those for mass, length, time, temperature, electric current, luminous intensity, and amount of a substance. The units for a number of other quantities can be derived from these basic units. For example, volume can be derived from the base unit of length, and density can be derived from length and mass. Because the SI units are based on powers of ten, different prefixes can be used to represent multiples of the basic units. The most common prefixes should be memorized.

Converting units

Units can be multiplied, divided, and canceled like algebraic quantities. However, quantities can be manipulated only if they have the same dimensions. A technique known as dimensional analysis is used to keep track of units when calculations are carried out. Dimensional analysis can be used whenever two quantities are directly proportional to each other. For example, suppose it is necessary to find the length of

SI base units and derived units

Base units			Common derived units		
Quantity	*Unit name*	*Symbol*	*Quantity*	*Unit name*	*Symbol*
Length	meter	m	Area	square meter	m^2
Mass	kilogram	kg	Volume	cubic meter	m^3
Time	second	s	Density	kilograms per cubic meter	kg/m^3
Temperature	kelvin	K			
			Force	newton	N or $kg \cdot m/s^2$
Electric current	ampere	A			
			Pressure	pascal	Pa or N/m^2
Luminous intensity	candela	cd			
			Energy	joule	J or $N \cdot m$
Amount of a substance	mole	mol	Power	watt	W or $N \cdot m/s$

an object in meters, but the measurement of the object is given in feet. By using the conversion factor of 1 foot = 0.3048 meters, which is equivalent to 1, it is possible to convert the measurement into meters. The following four steps show how to solve a problem using dimensional analysis:

1. Begin by writing the given quantity. Then identify the unit of the wanted quantity. For example, convert 2 feet into meters.
2. Determine the conversion factor needed to change the given quantity to the wanted quantity: 1 meter = 3.281 feet.
3. Write the set-up for the problem, multiplying or dividing the given quantity by the conversion factors. Be sure to write all units, and then cancel to be sure that the answer is expressed in the correct units: 2 feet (1 meter/3.281 feet).
4. Multiply and/or divide to get the numerical value of the answer: 2 feet = 0.6096 meters.

Scientific notation

In science, people often deal with numbers that are either extremely large or extremely small. These numbers are cumbersome to handle, and it is easy to make mistakes when using them in computations. Therefore, scientists have developed a system for handling these numbers known as scientific notation (or exponential notation, because it involves the use of exponents). In this system, numbers are written in the form: $N \times 10^n$, where N is a number between 1 and 10 and n is an exponent that is either a positive or negative exponent.

To change an ordinary number to scientific notation, count the number of places the decimal point must be moved so it will appear immediately to the right of the first nonzero digit. This number is n. If the decimal point is moved to the left, then n is positive. If the decimal point is moved to the right, then n is negative. For example, to write the number 568.762 in scientific notation, the decimal point needs to be moved two places to the left. Thus, $n = 2$, and the number is written: 5.68762×10^2.

To add or subtract using scientific notation, each number must be rewritten with the same exponent n. Then the N parts of the numbers may be added or subtracted. To multiply numbers in scientific notation, first multiply the N parts of the numbers. Then add the exponents together. To divide, first divide the N parts of the numbers, then subtract the exponents.

Significant figures

No physical measurement is exact. Every measurement has some uncertainty associated with it. The amount of uncertainty depends on various factors such as the quality of the measuring device, the skill of the experimenter, and the number of measurements performed. For this reason, it is important to know how reliable a measurement is. One way to do this is to use *significant figures*, which are the meaningful digits in a measured or calculated quantity.

In general, it is fairly easy to determine how many significant figures are present in a number by following these rules:

- Any digit that is not zero is significant. Therefore, 745 cm has three significant figures, 3.245 has four significant figures, and 1.2 has two.
- Zeros between nonzero digits are significant. For example, 103 contains three significant figures, as does 2.05.
- Zeros to the left of the first nonzero digit are not significant. So, 0.05 contains only one significant digit, and 0.00034 contains only two significant figures.
- If a number is greater than 1, then all zeros to the right of the decimal point count as significant figures. If a number is less than 1, then only the zeros at the end of the number and the zeros between nonzero digits are significant. Thus, 2.0 and 0.020 both have two significant figures, while 0.1020 has four significant figures.

Sometimes when measured quantities are manipulated, the answer contains some figures that are not significant. When this happens, the results must be rounded off.

In addition and subtraction, the number of significant figures to the right of the decimal point in the final answer is determined by the lowest number of significant figures to the right of the decimal point in any of the original numbers. In multiplication and division, the number of significant figures in the final answer is the smallest number of significant figures in the original numbers.

Common prefixes for SI units

Prefix	Multiple	Symbol
giga	10^9	G
mega	10^6	M
kilo	10^3	k
deci	10^{-1}	d
centi	10^{-2}	c
milli	10^{-3}	m
micro	10^{-6}	μ

Biology

There are as many as forty million species of living organisms on earth today, ranging from single-celled bacteria to complex multicellular mammals, such as human beings. However, all of these share certain characteristics. They take in and process materials from their surroundings, they grow and reproduce, they respond to their environment, and over long periods of time, they adapt to the environment. Biologists study these living organisms, the relationships between them, and the interaction of living organisms with the world around them. Biology also includes the ongoing process of asking and answering questions about the structure and function of living organisms.

Molecules of life

All organisms and the world around them are composed of chemical substances. Of the over 104 chemical elements in the world, just four of them—carbon, hydrogen, oxygen, and nitrogen—together constitute over 99 percent of the living matter of all organisms. The basis of these elements are atoms.

Atoms and molecules. *Atoms* are the building blocks of all matter, and consist of three types of subatomic particles: *protons* and *neutrons*, which are tightly bound in the atom's *nucleus*, and *electrons*, which surround the nucleus. Protons and neutrons have the same mass, but protons have a positive electric charge, while neutrons have a neutral electric charge. Electrons have very little mass and a negative electric charge that is equal to but opposite of that of a proton.

When two or more atoms are linked together by chemical bonds, they form a *molecule*. Molecules have specific sizes and shapes that give them specific properties. Some molecules are formed when two atoms share a pair of electrons, a process known as *covalent bonding*. Most biological molecules are formed by covalent bonding.

Some combinations of atoms play a very important role in chemical reactions. These groups of atoms, known as *functional groups*, bond easily to the element carbon and give the molecules distinctive chemical properties. The six important functional groups are the hydroxyl group (OH), the carbonyl group (CO and COOH), the carboxyl group (COOH), the amino group (NH_2), the phosphate group (PO_4^{-2}), and the sulfhydryl group (SH).

Macromolecules. The large molecules found in all living organisms are called *macromolecules*. They are composed of individual molecules called *monomers* that are assembled into long chains called *polymers*. There are four major groups of biological compounds: carbohydrates, proteins, lipids, and nucleic acids.

Carbohydrates. *Carbohydrates*, which include the simple sugars (monosaccharides), double sugars (disaccharides), and polymers of simple sugars (polysaccharides), are the major source of energy for most organisms. Monosaccharides, the simplest carbohydrates, are used directly for fuel, converted to other types of organic molecules, or form the building blocks for the other polymers. Disaccharides consist of two

Water: The key to life

Water is the primary ingredient for life: all familiar organisms are made mostly of water and live in a world where water dominates the climate and many other features of the environment. Unicellular creatures and most cells of multicellular organisms are surrounded by water; in fact, cells contain from about 75 to 95 percent water.

The water molecule is deceptively simple. It consists of two hydrogen atoms joined to an oxygen atom by covalent bonds. The unequal sharing of electrons between the oxygen and hydrogen molecules, coupled with the lopsided shape of the molecule, results in a *polar molecule*—a molecule whose poles have opposite charges. This structure makes water an extremely good solvent, and gives it other characteristics that make water essential to life.

monosaccharide monomers connected by a bond. Polysaccharides may consist of thousands of monomers. These carbohydrates are often used for storage and structure. Starch in plants and glycogen in animals are both forms of storage polysaccharides.

Proteins. *Proteins* are composed of chains of monomers called *amino acids*. There are twenty different types of amino acids found in nature. The amino acids are linked together in long chains by bonds between the amino group of one amino acid and the carboxyl group of another. The sequence of amino acids in a protein is known as its *primary structure*. Short amino acid chains are called *oligopeptides*; long chains are called *polypeptides*. The number and type of amino acids in each chain determines the type of protein that is formed.

The diverse functions of proteins include regulation of chemical reactions, defense of the animal body against microorganisms, and support and protection.

Lipids. *Lipids* are substances such as fats, oils, and waxes. The characteristic structure of lipids is quite different from those of the other macromolecules. Most lipids are *hydrophobic*; that is, insoluble in water. Thus, a mixture of water and lipids will form two separate layers.

Three important groups of lipids are the triglyc-

erides, phospholipids, and steroids. Triglycerides are found in the wax, fat, and oils of plants and animals; phospholipids are found in nerve tissue and cell membranes; and steroids are found in hormones and cholesterol. As a group, lipids are used for fuel, energy storage, membrane building, and as chemical messengers.

Nucleic acids. *Nucleic acids* are important to the storage, transmission, and interpretation of hereditary information. They also regulate the formation of proteins. There are two major classes of nucleic acids: DNA (deoxyribonucleic acid) and RNA (ribonucleic acid). Both are composed of *nucleotides*, which consist of a phosphate group, a sugar (either deoxyribose or ribose), and a nitrogen-containing base—adenine (A), guanine (G), cytosine (C), thymine (T), or uracil (U). Adenine and guanine are called *purines*; the other nitrogen-containing bases are known as *pyrimidines*.

Chemical reactions.
All life requires energy, and the primary source of energy is the sun. However, most living organisms cannot use the energy of sunlight directly. Instead, they must store light energy from the sun as potential energy in the chemical bonds of molecules. When the bonds in which energy is stored are broken in chemical reactions, the energy is released for use by cells.

Energy and chemical reactions. In living cells, energy is stored primarily in molecules of ATP (adenosine triphosphate). ATP consists of an adenosine group with three phosphate groups bonded to it. The molecule is formed when ADP (adenosine diphosphate) joins with an inorganic phosphate molecule.

Energy is required to form ATP. The main source of this energy is glucose. Certain organisms, such as plants, can use light energy to convert molecules into glucose. These organisms are called *autotrophs*. Other

Major types of macromolecules

Type	Examples
Carbohydrates	Sugar, starch, cellulose
Lipids	Fats, waxes, cholesterol
Proteins	Collagen, hemoglobin, myosin, enzymes
Nucleic acids	DNA, RNA

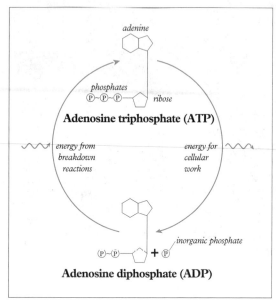

phosphates
Ⓟ–Ⓟ–Ⓟ

adenine

ribose

Adenosine triphosphate (ATP)

energy from
breakdown
reactions

energy for
cellular
work

inorganic phosphate

Ⓟ–Ⓟ + Ⓟ

Adenosine diphosphate (ADP)

The ATP cycle

organisms, known as *heterotrophs*, cannot use light energy. Instead, they digest or break down the large organic molecules formed by other cells into the sim-

pler glucose molecules. When the cell converts food, the energy released in the process is used to bond ADP and inorganic phosphate molecules, producing ATP. Later, when the cell requires energy, the bond between one or more of the phosphate bonds is broken, releasing energy. During the process, ADP and a free phosphate are regenerated.

Enzymes and chemical reactions. Energy that is needed to start a chemical reaction is called *activation energy*. The larger the activation energy the harder it is to start a reaction. *Catalysts* are substances that speed up a chemical reaction by lowering the activation energy without being used up or changed in the process.

Enzymes are proteins that function as biological catalysts. They enable the reactions that support life to proceed quickly at the temperatures found in living cells. Each enzyme acts on a chemical substance known as a *substrate*. The enzyme has a uniquely shaped *active site*, which is an area that interacts specifically with the substrate. The substrate binds to the active site of an enzyme as a key fits into a lock. After the enzyme and substrate bind, they form an *enzyme-substrate complex*, which undergoes a change in shape. This change stretches the bonds of the substrate, which in turn lowers the activation energy.

The cell

A *cell* is the basic component of living things and the smallest unit that is capable of performing all of the functions we associate with life. Living cells can be divided into two classes: *prokaryotic cells*, such as those of bacteria and blue-green algae, which lack true nuclei and membrane-bound organelles; and *eukaryotic cells*, which have a nucleus and generally contain a large number of membrane-enclosed organelles.

Cell organization. Although it is difficult to generalize about the size and shapes of cells, most cells have certain common features. All are surrounded by a *cell membrane* that separates the cell from its surroundings. This membrane encloses the *cytoplasm*, which in many cells contains a variety of *organelles* that function as tiny organs. Cells also contain all of the information they need to reproduce more cells, which, in many cases, is organized within a structure called the *nucleus*.

Cell membranes. The outer membrane of the cell is very thin and composed of a double layer of lipids and protein molecules. The primary function of the membrane is to act as a selective barrier, limiting what can move into and out of a cell.

Substances move across the membranes by a number

of different processes. One important process is *diffusion*. In diffusion, substances move along a *concentration gradient* from an area of high concentration to an area of low concentration. *Facilitated diffusion* occurs when substances pass through the cell membrane with the help of special transport proteins. If substances move through the cell membrane against the concentration gradient, the movement is called *active transport* because it requires a carrier molecule and a source of energy to drive the process.

The movement of water across the cell membrane involves a special type of diffusion called *osmosis*. Water moves along a concentration gradient from areas of more concentration to areas of less concentration. The force produced by this movement is called *osmotic pressure*, and it plays an important role in many biological systems.

In addition to the cell membrane, plant cells have a rigid *cell wall*, which lies outside the membrane. This wall is mainly composed of cellulose and provides additional support to the cell structure. It also plays a small role in controlling the passage of material into and out of the cell.

Internal cell membranes. The cytoplasm of eukaryotic cells contains various organelles made largely of

Components of cells and their functions

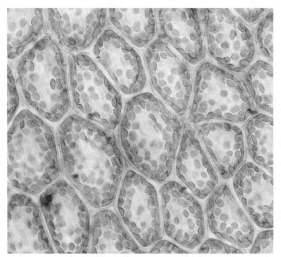

Plant cell

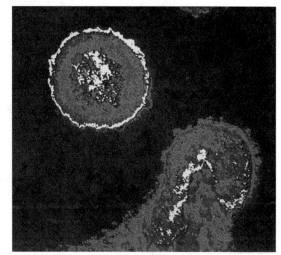

Animal cell

Structure	Location	Function	Present in Plants	Animals
Cell wall	Surrounding cell membrane	Support, protection, cell shape	yes	no
Centrioles	Within cytoplasm	Auxiliary to cell division	no	yes
Chloroplasts	Within cytoplasm	Site of photosynthesis, food storage	yes	no
Chromosomes	Within nucleus	Carry ultimate control of cell activities	yes	yes
Cilia, flagella	Surface of cell	Locomotion, feeding	some	yes
Endoplasmic reticulum (ER)	Throughout cytoplasm	Transport of materials, connection between cell parts, attachment surfaces	often	often
Golgi complex	Within cytoplasm	Site of secretion synthesis	yes	yes
Vacuoles	Within cytoplasm	Transport, storage, processing centers	yes	some
Lysosomes	Within cytoplasm	Store enzymes, ingest and destroy foreign materials	some	often
Mitochondria	Within cytoplasm	Site of respiration	yes	yes
Nuclear membrane	Surrounding nucleus	Traffic control into and out of nucleus	yes	yes
Nucleolus	Within nucleus	Site of ribosome synthesis	yes	yes
Plasma membrane	Surrounding cell	Traffic control into and out of cell, cell shape	yes	yes
Ribosomes	Within cytoplasm	Site of protein synthesis	yes	yes

membranes. The most extensive portion of intercellular membrane is called the *endoplasmic reticulum* (ER) and comes in two varieties: rough and smooth. Rough ER has many ribosomes attached to its surface. It helps replenish the cell membrane and manufactures proteins. Smooth ER lacks ribosomes and can synthesize steroids, store calcium in muscle cells, and detoxify poisons in liver cells. In addition, smooth ER helps transfer proteins to distant locations.

Other internal cell membranes include the Golgi apparatus, lysosomes, vacuoles, and vesicles. The *Golgi apparatus* is a flattened stack of membrane sacs that packages and modifies proteins for delivery outside the cell. *Lysosomes* contain powerful digestive enzymes which the cell uses for digesting food and recycling monomers from cell macromolecules. Lysosomes are not found in plants. *Vacuoles* are simple organelles composed of a single membrane that encloses food, waste, or water. Large vacuoles are found in many plant cells, while smaller food vacuoles and contractile vacuoles (which help with cell movement) occur in some of the protists. Membranes of a eukaryotic cell are interrelated and may change from one form to another.

Other organelles. The cytoplasm also contains organelles that are responsible for protein synthesis, for energy production and photosynthesis, and for movement.

The small units essential to protein synthesis are *ribosomes*. These organelles are composed of proteins and RNA. Ribosomes can either be free in the cytoplasm or attached to other organelles, such as the endoplasmic reticulum.

Mitochondria and *chloroplasts* are complex organelles which are involved in the processes of energy transformation. Mitochondria provide most of the ATP needed by eukaryotic cells in a process which is known as *cellular respiration*. Chloroplasts are found in plant cells, and carry out photosynthesis, converting the energy of the sunlight into chemical energy. Both mitochondria and chloroplasts contain their own DNA and are not produced by the cell but instead reproduce themselves.

The *cytoskeleton* is an integrated network of fibers in the cytoplasm of eukaryotic cells. It is constructed from microtubules, microfilaments, and other fibers, and dictates cell circulation pathways, anchors organelles, and gives the cell support, shape, and the ability to move.

The nucleus. The distinctive feature of a eukaryotic cell is its *nucleus*, which contains the cell's genetic material in the form of long, thin threads of DNA. These strands, known as *chromatin*, condense during cell division to form a number of bodies called *chromosomes*. Another body in the nucleus, known as the *nucleolus*, is responsible for the production of ribosomes and functions in the process of protein synthesis. The nucleus is bound by a *nuclear envelope*, which is a double membrane that maintains the structure of the nucleus and allows the nucleus to interact with the cytoplasm.

Reproduction. The ability to reproduce is one of the principle characteristics of living organisms. When cells reproduce, they do so by a process known as *cell division*. Cell division perpetuates life by generating new single-celled organisms and by producing and repairing new multiple-cell organisms.

Cell division in prokaryotes. Prokaryotic cells divide by a simple process known as *binary fission,* which means "to split in two." In this process, the cell duplicates the single chromosome in the cell and then splits in two. The division occurs when the plasma membrane is pinched between the two new chromosomes. This pinching process eventually divides the cell into two new organisms, each with its own chromosome.

Cell division in eukaryotes. Eukaryotic cells divide by a more complicated process known as *mitosis.* Mitosis consists of four stages—prophase, metaphase, anaphase, and telophase. Between division, cells are in *interphase,* during which new organelles are produced and DNA is replicated.

During *prophase* in animal cells, two structures in the center of the cell, known as *centrioles,* duplicate and migrate to opposite sides of the nucleus. They are associated with the formation of a structure of fine filaments known as the *spindle.* The nuclear envelope slowly disintegrates and chromosomes begin to appear. These chromosomes consist of two identical strands called *chromatids,* which are joined at a region called the *centromere.*

In the next stage, *metaphase,* the chromosomes line up along the center, or equator, of the cell to form a *metaphase plate.* Then, during *anaphase,* the centromeres of each chromosome divide in half. The sister chromatids separate and move toward opposite poles of the cell. Finally, during *telophase,* the chromosomes reach the opposite poles and uncoil. New nuclear membranes form around each set of chromosomes and the cell divides into two daughter cells. The actual

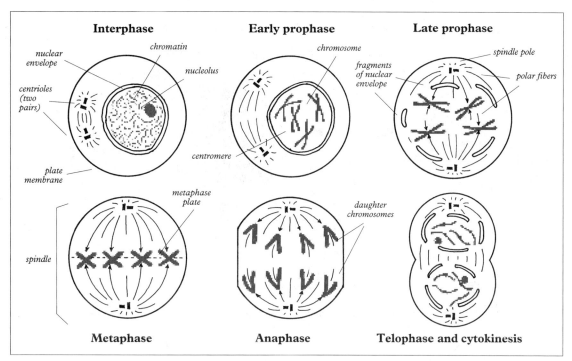

Top row labels:

Interphase — nuclear envelope, chromatin, nucleolus, centrioles (two pairs), plate membrane

Early prophase — chromosome, centromere

Late prophase — fragments of nuclear envelope, spindle pole, polar fibers

Bottom row labels:

Metaphase — spindle, metaphase plate

Anaphase — daughter chromosomes

Telophase and cytokinesis

Mitosis

division of the cytoplasm is called *cytokinesis*. In animal cells, the cytoplasm divides by constricting between the two nuclei until the cell is pinched in two. In cells with rigid cell walls, such as plant cells, a series of bubblelike vesicles gradually fuse to form a cell plate that divides the cytoplasm.

Metabolic pathways.

Metabolism is the various chemical and physical activities that go on within the cell and make life possible. Aided by enzymes, metabolism proceeds through a series of cyclical steps known as *metabolic pathways*. *Anabolic pathways* build up large molecules from smaller ones and require energy input. *Catabolic pathways* break down large molecules and release energy.

Some of the most important pathways are those catabolic pathways that extract energy from food material. The most prevalent and efficient of these is *cellular respiration*, in which oxygen and organic fuel, such as sugar, are combined to produce energy. Some other ways of creating energy include fermentation and photosynthesis.

Cellular respiration. Cellular respiration occurs in the mitochondria of all eukaryotic cells. This complex process involves converting the primary source of energy—glucose—into water and carbon dioxide, releasing energy in the process. Major processes involved in the production of energy from glucose include glycolysis, the citric acid cycle, and electron transport. Glycolysis is an *anaerobic* process; that is, it occurs in the absence of oxygen. The citric acid cycle and electron transport are *aerobic* processes—they require the presence of oxygen.

Glycolysis is a series of reactions in which a molecule of glucose is converted to two molecules of a carbon compound known as pyruvic acid. The first steps in this series actually use up energy—they require two molecules of ATP in order to convert glucose to a sugar phosphate. The remaining steps produce energy by bonding the phosphate groups to ADP, creating four molecules of ATP and pyruvic acid. All organisms carry out glycolysis.

After glycolysis, most of the energy that was stored in the glucose molecule is still present in pyruvic acid. When oxygen is present, cellular respiration can continue to break down the acid via the *citric acid cycle* (also known as the *Krebs cycle*). This process mainly takes place in the mitochondrion of the cell. Although one step of the citric acid cycle does produce ATP, most of the ATP formed by respiration occurs in the electron transport system. The electrons move into the inner portion of the mitochondrion and pass through the *electron transport chain*. As the electrons move through the chain, they create an "electrical pump" that powers the formation of ATP. The electrons are ultimately paired with oxygen to form water. At the end of one cycle of respiration, thirty-six molecules of ATP have been formed for each original molecule of glucose.

Photosynthesis. Photosynthesis and respiration can

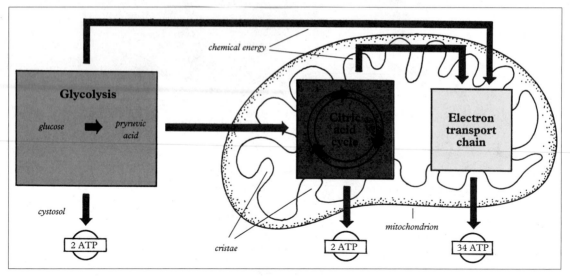

Overview of cellular respiration

be considered complementary processes. During *photosynthesis*, carbon dioxide and water combine to produce molecules of glucose and oxygen. This process, occurring in plants and some bacteria, takes place in specialized organelles called chloroplasts and requires pigment molecules, such as chlorophyll. Organisms that perform photosynthesis are capable of sustaining themselves without ingesting organic molecules.

Photosynthesis can be divided into light-dependent reactions and light-independent reactions. During the light-dependent reactions, red and blue violet rays are absorbed by chlorophyll and used to break water molecules into two parts: oxygen and hydrogen. The electrons of the hydrogen are ultimately stored in the bonds of ATP and NADPH. This energy can now be used to drive the light-independent reactions, or dark reactions, which combine carbon dioxide with other molecules to form glucose and other carbohydrates.

Genetics

Genetics is the study of inheritance—how biological characteristics are passed from one generation to the next. Geneticists look at two characteristics of an organism: its *genotype* (that is, the overall genetic make-up of the organism) and its *phenotype* (the appearance of the organism). Genotypes are revealed through breeding experiments, while phenotypes can be observed through close examination.

Mendel, genes, and alleles. Though the science of genetics has made tremendous advances since the 1960s, the foundation of current knowledge began in the late 1800s, with the work of an Augustinian monk named Gregor Mendel. Much of what we know about basic genetics is the result of experiments on common garden peas that Mendel published in 1866. Mendel studied how traits are inherited. He identified seven easily recognizable traits, which he called "unit characters," each of which occurred in two alternative forms. He then proceeded to breed the plants for those traits. After years of exper-

imentation, Mendel proved that hereditary traits are transmitted by pairs of "unit characters," now called *genes*, which reshuffle, segregate, and redistribute, rather than blend, in offspring. Mendel's work demonstrated the concept of dominance and the laws of segregation and independent assortment.

Dominance. Mendel observed that when organisms with two contrasting traits, such as wrinkled and non-wrinkled, were crossed, one trait appeared in the next generation while the other remained hidden. The expressed trait is called the *dominant* trait, while the hidden trait is the *recessive* trait.

Segregation. The first generation of plants Mendel worked with were *true-breeding*; that is, when a plant was self-fertilized, it would always display the same characteristics. When two true-breeding plants with different characteristics were cross-fertilized, a *hybrid* plant would form—a plant with mixed characteristics. In the first generation of hybrids, only dominant traits appear. But in the second generation, one-fourth of the plants would display a recessive trait. Mendel explained this by showing there are alternate forms of genes, known as *alleles*, and that for each characteristic an organism has two alleles, one from each parent. These allele pairs separate (segregate) from each other during the production of gametes, and then recombine during fertilization. An organism that has a pair of identical alleles for a characteristic is said to be *homozygous* for that trait. Organisms that have two different alleles for a trait are said to be *heterozygous* for that trait.

Independent assortment. Mendel believed that each trait is inherited independently of others and remains unaltered throughout all generations. Scientists now know that not all genes separate from each other in a random fashion. The reason for this is that the genes are located on chromosomes and that each chromosome contains many genes—a condition known as gene linkage. Because the chromosomes, not the genes, separate during cell division, genes on the same section of a given chromosome may be transferred as a group.

Chromosome mapping. Today a concerted effort is being made to map human chromosomes. The identification and localization of genes on chromosomes will have a significant impact upon the new field known as *cytogenetics*.

Meiosis.
In species that reproduce sexually, the sorting out and recombining of chromosomes are responsible for most of the genetic variations that arise in each generation. This is accomplished by a type of cell division known as *meiosis*.

Many of the steps of meiosis closely resemble corresponding steps in mitosis. Meiosis, like mitosis, is preceded by the replication of chromosomes. However, this single replication is followed by two consecutive cell divisions, called meiosis I and meiosis II. These divisions result in four daughter cells (rather than the two formed by mitosis), each with only half as many chromosomes as the parent. When the male and female gametes come together during fertilization, each contributes chromosomes to form the full complement of chromosomes in the zygote. The two divisions of meiosis are illustrated below.

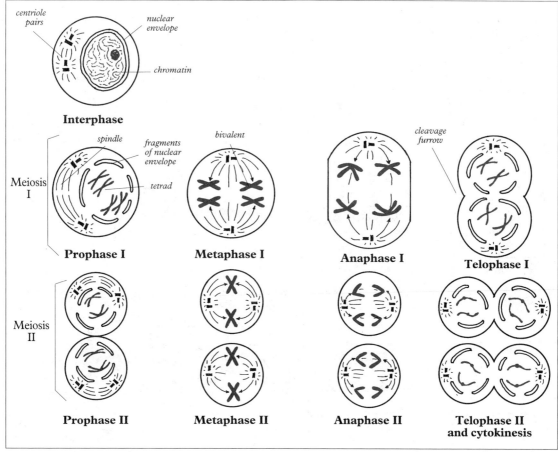

Meiosis

DNA and protein synthesis.

James Watson and Francis Crick discovered the structure of DNA. The molecule is shaped like a double helix. It consists of two long chains of nucleotides turned around each other in the shape of a double spiral. The chains are held together by hydrogen bonding between their nitrogenous bases, and the bases are arranged so that adenine is always paired with thymine and guanine is paired with cytosine. This structure helps explain how DNA is able to reproduce itself and how it carries genetic information.

Replication. DNA can make more of itself in a process called *replication*. During the replication process, the double-stranded helix begins to unwind, forming a structure that resembles a Y-shaped fork. The strands at the fork separate and each strand picks up complementary nucleotides, forming two complete strands of DNA.

Protein synthesis. The DNA molecule carries coded instructions for controlling all functions of the cell. At the present time, scientists know most about how DNA forms the proteins that direct the activity and appearance of the cell, a process known as *protein synthesis*. There are two principle processes in protein synthesis: transcription and translation.

Transcription is the formation of a messenger RNA (mRNA) molecule with a base sequence complementary to that of one strand of DNA. Unlike DNA, most RNA are single-stranded chains in which uracil replaces thymine in the complementary pairing.

In *translation*, the information transcribed into mRNA is used to make a specific polypeptide from a collection of amino acids. Translation is a multistep process. First, the mRNA moves from the nucleus into the cytoplasm, where it attaches itself to several ribosomes. Specific transfer RNA (tRNA) molecules then carry amino acids to the ribosomes. Each mRNA has sequences of three nitrogenous bases, known as *codons*. Some codons supply start and stop signals, while others are coded for a particular amino acid. The tRNA molecules attach themselves to complementary sets of three bases along the mRNA strand. When the amino acids are in position, a peptide bond is formed and the protein chain grows, one amino acid at a time.

Genetic engineering. In a relatively new field called *genetic engineering,* DNA is removed from one organism and incorporated into the genome of another. Cells are therefore "taught" to do things that they previously could not do. For example, some bacteria are now able to synthesize human insulin. The question lingers as to whether the benefits of genetic engineering will outweigh the potential dangers.

DNA fingerprinting. This is a field of active investigation. The specificity of DNA sequences allows the establishment of individual genetic profiles. This type of "fingerprinting" is being used as evidence in courts. Tests have become so specific that DNA from a single cell is sufficient to establish an individual's profile.

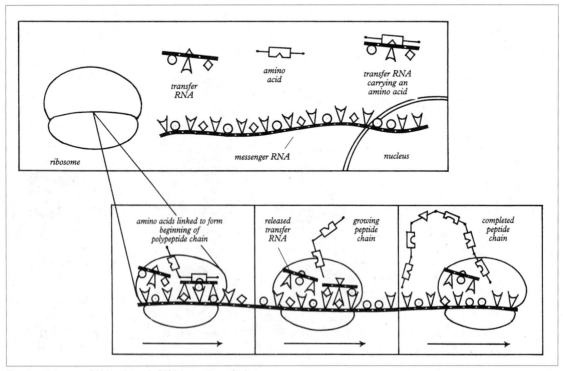

Function of messenger RNA and transfer RNA in protein synthesis process

Biological classification

To study the vast array of organisms that populate the natural world, and exchange information about them, biologists have developed a system based on the work of an eighteenth century Swedish botanist, Carolus Linnaeus (Carl von Linné). In this system of classification, living things are organized into a hierarchical system of seven groups. These groupings are based not only on obvious traits such as fur, wings, or number of legs, but also on molecular characteristics. They also reflect the developmental relationships of the organisms.

The broadest categories are called *kingdoms*. Currently there are five recognized kingdoms: Monera, Protista, Fungi, Plantae, and Animalia. Each of these kingdoms is then subdivided into smaller groups—phyla (or divisions), then classes, orders, families, genera, and finally species. If a living thing is discovered for which no current classification exists, a new category can be created.

Kingdom Monera. This kingdom consists of the modern prokaryotes, which are the bacteria and blue-green algae. These single-celled organisms lack a nucleus and complex organelles, but they are extraordinarily diverse. Bacteria are the most abundant life form on earth.

Kingdom Protista. The kingdom Protista consists of single-celled eukaryotic organisms. The organisms contain a distinct nucleus as well as other cell organelles. Protista includes the animal-like protozoans, such as the amoeba, some funguslike organisms, and plantlike organisms such as the single-celled algae.

Kingdom Fungi. Fungi are heterotrophic organisms that cannot produce their own food. Instead, they obtain food by absorbing material from other organisms. This kingdom contains over 100,000 species, including the slime molds, the water molds, mildews, yeasts, mushrooms, toadstools, and penicillium molds.

Kingdom Plantae. This kingdom consists of multicellular organisms that produce nutrients by means of photosynthesis. Plants have cellulose in their cell walls and store carbohydrates as starch.

Kingdom Animalia. Animals are multicellular eukaryotes that do not produce their own food. Instead, they obtain it by ingestion. Animal cells lack cell walls and store carbohydrates as glycogen. Members of this kingdom basically fall into two large groups: *invertebrates*, animals without backbones; and *vertebrates*, animals with backbones. The vertebrates are a subphylum that includes classes of fish, reptiles,

Kingdom Fungi (shelf fungus on tree)

Kingdom Animalia (grasshopper)

amphibians, birds, and mammals. Amphibians, reptiles, and fish are cold-blooded—as the temperature of the environment changes, their body temperature changes. Birds and mammals are warm-blooded—their temperature remains the same regardless of the environment. Among the members of the mammal class are dogs, cats, rats, porpoises, and humans.

Kingdom Monera (nitrogen-fixing bacteria nodules on pea root)

Kingdom Plantae (apple blossom)

Kingdom Protista (amoeba)

Comparison of the five kingdoms

Cell type	Obtains food by	Mobility	Reproduction	Examples
Monera Single-celled, prokaryotic	Absorption, photosynthesis, chemosynthesis	Some nonmobile, some mobile	All can reproduce asexually, sexual reproduction sometimes occurs	Bacteria, blue-green algae
Protista Single-celled, multicelled, or eukaryotic	Absorption, photosynthesis, or ingestion	Some nonmobile, some mobile	All can reproduce asexually, some forms reproduce sexually as well	Protozoans, such as amoebae
Fungi Mycelia or single-celled eukaryotic	Absorption	All nonmobile	Asexually and sexually	Yeasts, molds, puffballs, mushrooms
Plantae Multicelled, eukaryotic	Photosynthesis	Mostly nonmobile	Asexually and sexually	Flowering plants, mosses
Animalia Multicelled eukaryotic	Ingestion	Most mobile	Sexually	Sponges, insects, mammals, fish

Biology

Plant systems

The term *plant* is often used to refer to all members of the kingdom Plantae, as well as to all algae. When classifying plants, botanists use the term *division* rather than *phylum* to designate the major groups. There are several different divisions, which are distinguished by the plants' reproductive structures and the organization of their vascular tissue.

Algae, the simplest plants, often lack specialized organs. *Bryophytes*, which were the first type of plants to become adapted to life on land, have a waxy coating, which helps deter water loss, and hairlike fibers called *rhizoids*, which anchor the plant to the soil. However, unlike higher-level plants, bryophytes lack vascular tissue. *Tracheophytes*, or vascular plants, are the most advanced plants. These plants contain specialized conducting, or vascular, tissue which enables them to move water efficiently over long distances. There are two main types of tracheophytes: *gymnosperms* (cone-bearing plants) and *angiosperms* (flower-bearing plants). The angiosperms are further subdivided into two groups—*monocotyledons* (or monocots), which contain only one seed leaf, and *dicotyledons* (dicots), which contain two seed leaves.

Plant structure and function.

The angiosperms, which are the most abundant of the land plants, contain roots, stems, and leaves. The *roots* anchor the plant to the ground and channel water and minerals from the soil into the plant's body. The *stem* supports the plant and contains conducting tissue that carries water and nutrients from the roots to the leaves. The *leaves* are the principal organs of photosynthesis.

The root system. There are two types of root systems: fibrous roots and taproots. *Fibrous roots* have many slender main roots of equal size with numerous branch roots that are smaller in size. These roots form a dense network near the surface of the soil and hold the soil together. *Taproots* are single main roots that grow almost straight down. Smaller branch roots grow off the main root.

In both types of root systems, the surface of a root is covered with fine, threadlike structures called *root hairs* that make direct contact with the soil and absorb water and minerals. The root hairs are part of an outer covering known as the *epidermis*. Beneath the epidermis are several different layers of cells—the cortex, the endodermis, and the pericycle. The pericycle contains two types of vascular tissue: *xylem*, which conducts water and minerals from the roots up to the other parts of the plant, and *phloem*, which circulates nutrients throughout the plant.

The stem system. Like roots, stems contain both xylem and phloem, which conduct water and nutrients throughout the plant. In monocots, these tissues are embedded throughout the tissue of the stem, which is known as *ground tissue*. In dicots, the vascular tissues may be arranged in bundles or in annular rings. Ground tissue in dicots that is located within the ring of vascular tissue is known as *pith*, while the ground tissue outside the ring is referred to as *cortex*. The whole stem is surrounded by a layer of cells with thick cell walls and waxy coatings that help protect the stem and give it support.

The leaf system. Leaves consist of two parts: a stalk or *petiole*, and the blade. The petiole attaches the blade to the stem of the plant. The outer cells of the blade, called the *epidermis*, are often covered by a protective coating. Openings called *stomata* in the epidermis allow carbon dioxide for photosynthesis to enter the leaf and restrict the loss of water.

The mesophyll cells that make up the ground material of leaves contain the chloroplasts responsible for photosynthesis. In a typical leaf, the upper layer of mesophyll contains tightly packed cells known as *palisade cells*. Below these cells is the spongy mesophyll, which is less densely packed.

The xylem and phloem in the leaf are arranged in vascular bundles that form the leaf veins. In monocots, the veins tend to be parallel; in dicots, they tend to be branched.

Monocots vs. dicots

	Monocots	**Dicots**
Embryos	One cotyledon	Two cotyledons
Leaf veins	Veins usually parallel	Veins usually branched
Stems	Vascular bundles scattered throughout stem	Vascular bundles arranged in ring
Roots	Fibrous root system	Taproots usually present
Flowers	Floral parts in multiples of three	Floral parts in multiples of four or five

Nutrition. Although plants can make all of their own organic compounds through photosynthesis, they must obtain inorganic raw materials to do so. For a plant to grow and reproduce, it requires sources of water, carbon dioxide, nitrogen, and a variety of minerals. Roots absorb water and minerals from the soil, while carbon dioxide, the source of carbon for photosynthesis, diffuses into leaves from the surrounding air. Once the plant has obtained these inorganic nutrients, photosynthesis and other metabolic pathways convert them into carbohydrates, proteins, and other organic compounds.

Of all the minerals that the plant takes from the soil, nitrogen is one of the most important because it is used to make proteins. Although the atmosphere is rich in nitrogen, plants require the assistance of bacteria living in the soil to supply them with the form of nitrogen they need. Such bacteria possess an enzyme that converts atmospheric nitrogen into ammonia by means of a process called *nitrogen fixation*. The ammonia is then converted into nitrates which are absorbed by the plants.

Some plants are involved in symbiotic relationships to increase their ability to obtain the necessary nutrients. The roots of legumes, alders, and some tropical grasses, for example, have nodular swellings that house nitrogen-fixing bacteria. Other plants supplement their nitrogen intake by capturing small animals such as insects in specially modified leaves. This type of plant is called an *insectivorous plant*. Common insectivorous plants include the Venus's-flytrap and the pitcher plant.

Reproduction. Plants can reproduce both asexually and sexually. *Asexual* or *vegetative reproduction* is rapid and efficient, giving rise to *clones* of genetically identical individuals. Genetic diversity within a population of asexually reproducing plants arises from mutation. *Sexual reproduction* provides for genetic diversity through recombination, random distribution, and the slower process of mutation.

Asexual reproduction. The easiest way for plants to reproduce is asexually. There are several different types of asexual reproduction. Some of these methods occur naturally, while others have been developed by farmers and scientists.

In the process of *fragmentation,* parts of a root, stem, or leaf can produce an entirely new plant that is genetically identical to the parent. Some plants reproduce asexually by sending off *runners* above or just below the soil. The ends of these runners establish roots and produce new plants. *Rhizomes* are underground stems that can give rise to new shoots. *Bulbs* are actually large buds that store food and then later give rise to plants. Many other plants produce *corms*, which are modified stems that function very much like bulbs.

In horticulture and agriculture, plants are propagated using *grafting* and *tissue culturing*. Grafting allows

Types of vegetative reproduction

Runners
Strawberries and some grasses produce runners, which are horizontal stems that form roots at intervals and which establish independent daughter plants.

Rhizomes
Ginger reproduces by way of rhizomes, which are underground stems that can give off new shoots.

Bulbs
Lilies and onions form bulbs, which are large buds that function in food storage and can later give rise to new plants.

Corms
Crocuses, gladioli, and other like plants produce corms, which are modified stems that function very much like bulbs.

Fragmentation
During fragmentation, a parent plant is separated into parts that reform into whole plants.

Plant with runners (strawberry)

Plant with bulbs (tulip)

scientists to combine the best characteristics of two plants, while tissue cultures allow scientists to grow new plants from the pith of mature plants. Plants are also propagated through *cuttings*.

Sexual reproduction. In angiosperms, sexual reproduction occurs in the flowers. Most flowers are composed of four parts: the sepals, the petals, the stamen, and the pistil. The *sepals* are leaflike structures that enclose the flower in the bud stage. All of the sepals together form the *calyx*, the outer covering of the flower. The *petals* of the flower are often colored to attract insects and other animal pollinators. The *stamen* is the male portion of the flower—it consists of a long filament that terminates in an expanded sac known as the *anther*. *Pollen* grains, which produce sperm nuclei, are produced in the anther. The *pistil* is the female portion of the flower. It consists of one or more *carpels*, which are fused, leaflike structures each containing an *ovary* in which eggs are produced. The top of the pistil tapers to form a filament known as the *style*, which terminates in a sticky structure called the *stigma*.

The transfer of pollen from the anther to the stigma is called *pollination*. Pollen is moved from anther to stigma by wind, water, and insects or other small animals. When pollen moves from the anther of one flower to the stigma of another flower, *cross-pollination* takes place. When a stigma receives pollen from the anther of the same flower, *self-pollination* occurs.

The process of *fertilization* begins when a pollen grain sticks to a stigma. The protective coat on the grain ruptures, and a tube, called the *pollen tube*, grows from the pollen grain through the stigma to an opening in an *ovule*, which has developed in the ovary. There are two nuclei in a pollen grain. One disintegrates during the formation of the pollen tube; the other divides by

mitosis to form two sperm. The sperm nuclei move down the pollen tube and enter the ovule. One sperm nucleus fuses with the egg to form a zygote. The other fuses with the *endosperm mother cell* and develops into the endosperm tissue that supplies food for the embryo.

Following fertilization, the wall of the ovule develops into a protective seed coat, the zygote develops into an embryo, the ovary develops into fruit, and the endosperm mother cell produces the endosperm. The cells of the embryo divide by mitosis, and the embryo grows and begins to form the vascular tissue and seed leaves (cotyledons). As the embryo matures, the plant fills the cotyledons and endosperm with proteins, carbohydrates, and lipids. When embryonic development is complete, water is removed until the moisture content of the seed is less than 10 percent of its mass. The seed coat hardens and the seed enters a period of dormancy. The *fruit*, or ripened ovary of the plant, protects the enclosed seeds and aids in the dispersal of the seeds over long distances.

The final seed consists of an embryo plant, a food reservoir, and an outer protective coating. During *germination*, the embryo plant is reactivated and sprouts. Three factors are important in the germination process: water, oxygen, and temperature. The seed begins germinating by absorbing large amounts of water. As the water content increases, the seed swells and begins metabolism. The swelling causes the seed coat to break, while the increase in metabolism creates a demand for oxygen. Because the enzymes involved in metabolism are sensitive to temperature, the seed must be at the appropriate temperature before it will germinate.

After the seed coating breaks, the primary root penetrates the soil and begins absorbing water and nutrients. The plant begins sending roots downward and a shoot upward. The production of new cells occurs only in tissue called *meristem*. Meristematic cells are unspecialized and divide to generate new cells near the growing points of the plant. *Apical meristems*, located at the tips of roots and in the buds of shoots, supply cells for the plant to grow in length. *Ground meristems* give rise to the ground tissue system. Unlike animals, some plants continue to grow larger as long as they live, a condition known as *indeterminate growth*.

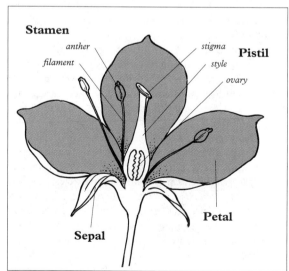

Parts of a flower

Animal systems

Every animal has some means of carrying out each of its life functions: obtaining food and extracting nutrients from it, exchanging gases with its surroundings, transporting and circulating materials within its body, controlling water balance and getting rid of wastes, and reproducing. Complex organisms usually have specialized organs for each of the major functions. Many animals also have specialized cells for warding off infections, specialized skeletal tissue for support, and special contractile tissue called muscle.

Animal structure and function.

Cells in the body of multicellular organisms are differentiated into specialized cells, each of which has a particular role within the body. These specialized cells are arranged in groups called *tissues*, which work together to perform a certain function. Tissues are further grouped into organs, and organs into systems.

Tissues. Four basic types of tissue are found in humans and many other animals: epithelial tissue, muscle tissue, connective tissue, and nervous tissue. *Epithelial tissue* acts as a lining on both the outside and inside of the body. *Muscle tissue* is modified for the purpose of contracting, which in turn supplies the force for movement. *Connective tissue* is composed of both cells and noncellular material. This group of tissue includes bones and fat tissue, as well as tissue that connects one type of tissue or organ to another. *Nervous tissue* conducts information from one part of the body to another.

Organs and organ systems. In complex organisms, groups of tissues combine to form *organs*. An organ is a group of tissues that work together to perform a special function for the benefit of the organism. *Organ systems* are groups of organs that function as a unit to perform a particular job. Twelve major organ systems in the human body are shown in the series of diagrams on pages 384–385.

Homeostasis. For the body's tissue and organ cells to survive, all the cells must function as a unit to ensure that the vital processes take place at the right time and in the proper order. However, the environment in the cell is constantly changing, so the cell must make appropriate adjustments to maintain a balanced state. To do this, organisms must have a means of monitoring and regulating the activity of the cells. The regulatory process is called *homeostasis*. Homeostatic mechanisms respond to changes in the local environment by bringing about appropriate changes in the cells that are affected.

Nutrition and digestion. Organisms

require food for two reasons: first, to generate energy to power all the different chemical processes that support life; second, to supply the materials necessary for growth, maintenance, and repair. If adequate energy is not supplied, the body uses existing tissues, such as muscle, as a source of energy. The result of a chronic lack of nourishment is damage to the body tissues and ultimately death.

Most animals cannot produce all of the materials they need for proper health. Those molecules that an animal cannot synthesize must be supplied in the diet. Like other animals, humans require nutrients from six different sources to maintain proper health. These include water, carbohydrates, proteins, fats, vitamins, and minerals.

Obtaining food. Organisms have evolved many different ways of obtaining and processing the food they need. Some organisms, called *herbivores*, eat only plants. Others, the *carnivores*, eat only other animals. And still others, known as *omnivores*, eat both plants and animals.

The mechanisms by which animals obtain their food also vary. Most animals are *holotrophs*, eating other organisms whole or by the piece. Many aquatic animals are *filter feeders*, sifting small food particles from the water. *Deposit feeders*, such as earthworms, eat their way through partially decayed organic matter, salvaging bits and pieces as they go. *Fluid feeders*, such as mosquitoes, suck fluids from a living host.

Digestion. Regardless of what it eats or how it feeds, an animal must digest its food. *Digestion* is the process of breaking food down into molecules small enough for

Deposit feeder (earthworm)

Biology

the body to absorb. The simplest animals have digestive sacs called *gastrovascular cavities*, with single openings. Food enters into the opening and enzymes break down the particles. More complex animals have digestive tracts, or *alimentary canals*, which move food through a one-way tube with specialized regions for digestion and absorption. The basic pathways lead from the mouth, pharynx, and esophagus to a crop, gizzard, or stomach, and then through the intestines to the anus. In mammals, there is a four-layered wall from the esophagus to the large intestine. The smooth muscle layer of the wall propels food along the tract and regulates its passage. Enzymes in the stomach and intestine convert complex foods into simple substances. These substances are absorbed through the intestinal wall into the blood and lymph systems.

Circulation and respiration. In all
but the simplest animals, special systems are required to transport materials such as nutrients, wastes, and gases from one area to another. These systems are known, respectively, as the circulatory and respiratory systems.

Circulation. *Circulatory systems* carry nutrients from the digestive tract to each of the body's cells. In a similar fashion, the circulatory system picks up waste from the cells and carries it to a site specialized for elimination.

Some circulatory systems are open systems. In an open system, the heart pumps blood through spaces that surround the organs. Chemical exchange between the interstitial fluid and the blood occurs as the blood oozes through the spaces. In a closed circulatory system, the blood is confined to the blood vessels. The blood performs its exchange with the cells of the body via the walls of tiny blood vessels called *capillaries*. Humans and other vertebrates have a closed circulatory system called the *cardiovascular system*. This system consists of the heart, blood vessels, and blood. There are two types of blood vessels—*arteries*, which carry blood away from the heart, and *veins*, which carry blood back to the heart.

Respiration. Animals require a continuous supply of oxygen for cellular respiration, and they must expel carbon dioxide, the waste product of this process.

Multicellular organisms have developed different types of *respiratory systems* that both supply oxygen and remove carbon dioxide wastes. In aquatic animals, gills carry on the process of gas exchange. Some invertebrates, such as insects, use a system of tubes called *trachea* to carry oxygen directly to the cells that need it. Larger animals have internal lungs. These saclike structures are connected to the rest of the body by way of the circulatory system. Mammalian lungs are enclosed in a double-walled sac whose layers adhere to one another and follow the movements of the chest cavity during breathing. Air is inhaled through the mouth and nose, and passes from the nasal chamber into the pharynx, larynx, trachea, bronchi, and bronchioles, and then finally into the air sacs in the lungs, where gas exchange occurs.

Excretion and regulation. When
cells metabolize, they produce waste products. These products are toxic in large quantities and must be removed for the organism to remain alive. At the same time, the amount of water and many inorganic ions must be maintained at proper levels. Excretory systems perform these important functions.

Excretion. The specific details of excretory systems vary from group to group of animals; some systems are open at both ends, others only at one. Liquid enters some systems by osmosis, others by being filtered directly into a tube, and yet others by being filtered through a membrane. Vertebrates, including humans, have complex, paired organs called *kidneys* that not only remove waste but also maintain a proper balance of water and salts. The bladder and ureters are also part of the system.

In all cases, animals excrete some type of nitrogen-containing waste in one of three ways: as ammonia, as uric acid, or as urea. Most aquatic animals excrete ammonia, a highly toxic but very water-soluble molecule that easily passes across the body surface or gill into the surrounding water. Land animals, however, would lose too much water if they constantly excreted wastes. Thus, in land animals, ammonia is converted into other forms. The liver of some vertebrates, including mammals, converts ammonia into the less toxic urea, which is transported to the kidneys and then excreted. Birds, insects, and some reptiles convert ammonia into uric acid, which is excreted as a pastelike substance.

Water regulation. Organisms must maintain a water and salt balance. Thus, as water and salt are excreted, an equal amount of the substances needs to enter the body. The way an organism's body regulates water and salt intake depends on how well it tolerates a wide range of salt concentration and how much it can vary its internal salinity.

Human organ systems

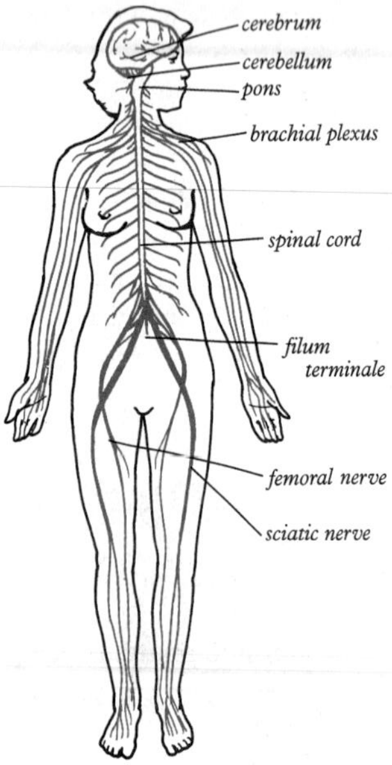

Nervous system

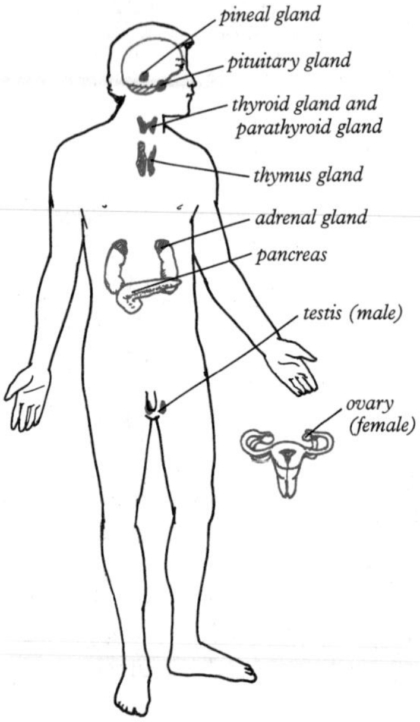

- cerebrum
- cerebellum
- pons
- brachial plexus
- spinal cord
- filum terminale
- femoral nerve
- sciatic nerve

Endocrine system

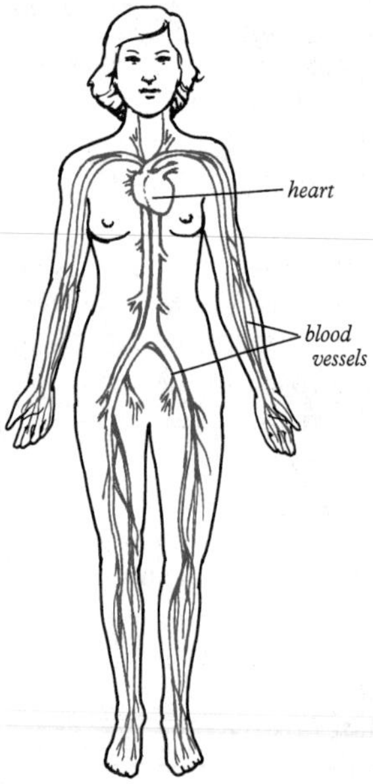

- pineal gland
- pituitary gland
- thyroid gland and parathyroid gland
- thymus gland
- adrenal gland
- pancreas
- testis (male)
- ovary (female)

Circulatory system

- heart
- blood vessels

Digestive system

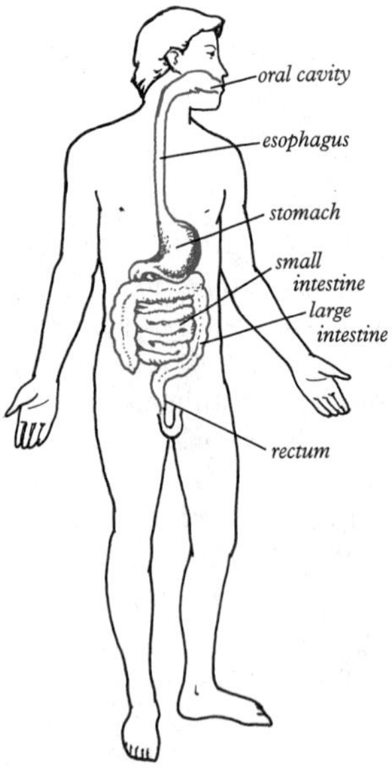

- oral cavity
- esophagus
- stomach
- small intestine
- large intestine
- rectum

Urinary system

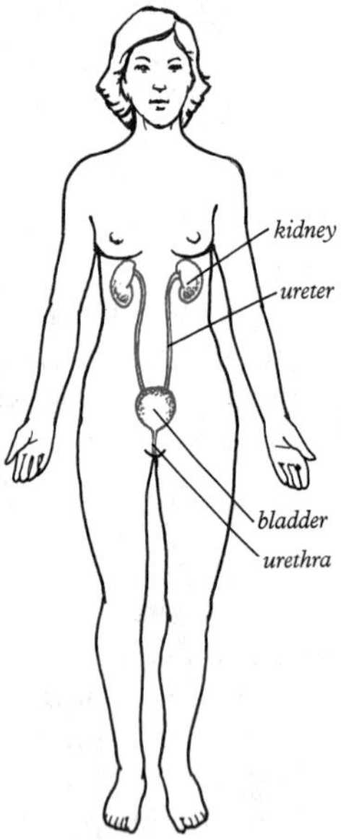

- kidney
- ureter
- bladder
- urethra

Reproductive system

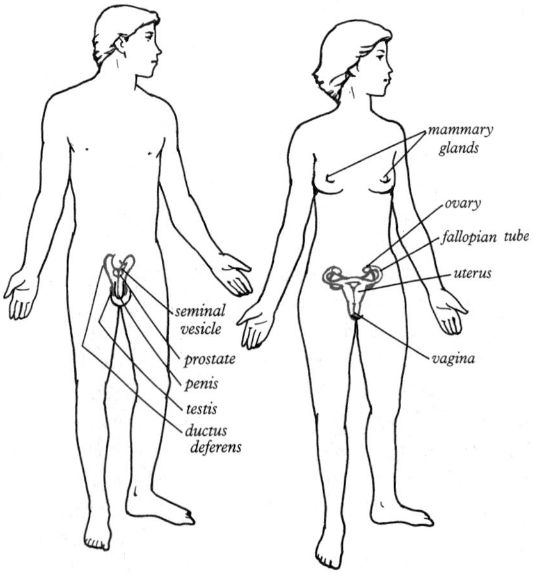

- seminal vesicle
- prostate
- penis
- testis
- ductus deferens
- mammary glands
- ovary
- fallopian tube
- uterus
- vagina

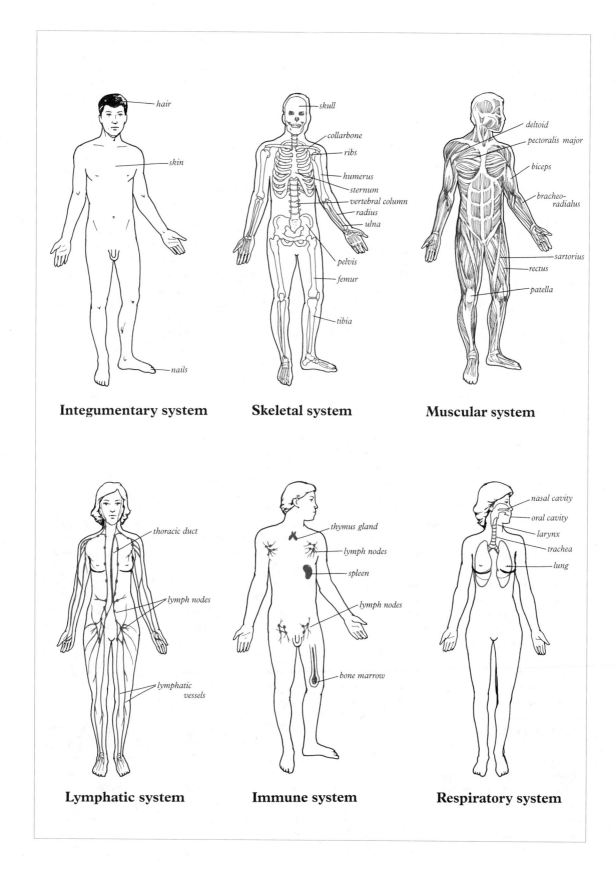

Integumentary system

Skeletal system

Muscular system

Lymphatic system

Immune system

Respiratory system

Chemical coordination. To coordinate the body's activities, it is necessary for the cells to communicate with each other. Two major organ systems are involved in the process of cellular communication: the nervous system and the endocrine system. The nervous system generally handles responses that must take place very quickly, while longer-term responses are generally handled by the endocrine system by way of chemical messengers which are known as hormones.

Nervous systems. An animal's ability to respond to its environment depends on its ability to detect and process incoming signals. Even in simple animals, complex responses are integrated by a special coordinating system that receives, processes, and transmits information. This system, which is called the *nervous system*, makes use of a combination of electrical and chemical messages to select appropriate responses to stimuli.

The nervous system is composed of nerve cells, or *neurons*, and support cells called *glial cells*. There are several types of neurons. *Sensory neurons* respond to changes in the environment and transmit that information to the spinal cord and brain. *Motor neurons* carry information from the brain and spinal cord to the muscles, glands, and other organs that are controlled by the nervous system.

The neuron itself is composed of a cell body, finely branched *dendrites* that carry information toward the cell body, and an *axon* that carries the information away from the cell body. Neurons connect with other neurons and with the organs by way of specialized regions called *synapses*. Signals are relayed from the axon of one neuron to the dendrites of another at the synapse.

Endocrine systems. The endocrine system consists of ductless glands that produce chemical messengers called *hormones*. Hormones are released by the cells of the glands into the bloodstream, where they travel to target cells elsewhere in the organism. The endocrine system usually responds more slowly than the nervous system; thus hormone levels can build up over time to control slow changes such as sexual development, growth, or metamorphosis.

The effect a hormone has on its target cells is determined by the type of *receptor* in that cell. Steroid hormones, such as the male and female sex hormones, act by combining with receptors that are usually located in the nucleus of the cell. This combination activates certain genes and allows for the production of proteins that alter the activity of the cell. Other hormones, such as protein hormones, combine with receptors on the cell's surface. When this happens, the hormone activates an enzyme in the membrane that activates yet another molecule.

Reproduction. Single-celled organisms, such as bacteria, reproduce quickly by a simple form of cell division. Asexual organisms clone themselves as they reproduce. More complex organisms reproduce by means of sexual reproduction. Although sexual reproduction may seem less efficient than asexual reproduction, it is the primary source of genetic diversity in most species.

In sexually reproducing animals, both males and females produce mature sexual reproductive cells called *gametes*. Each gamete is a *haploid* cell; that is, it contains only one set of chromosomes. The tiny gametes of male animals are called *sperm* or *spermatozoa*. The larger female gametes are called *eggs* or *ova*. Sperm and eggs are produced in *gonads*; female gonads are called *ovaries*, and male gonads are the *testes*. The gonads are referred to as the *primary sex organs*. The *accessory sex organs*, which are found in all animals except the simplest, include a variety of ducts, glands, and other structures. In vertebrates, these organs include the oviduct, uterus, and cloaca or vagina in females, and the vas deferens, urethra, and cloaca or penis in males. Together the primary and accessory sex organs constitute the *reproductive system*. The primary function of the reproductive system is the production of sex cells.

When a sperm cell and egg join, *fertilization* occurs. Fertilization of the egg by a sperm occurs either within the body of the female or externally, depending upon the species. In *external fertilization*, gametes meet only after they have been released from the parents' bodies. External fertilization is common among aquatic organisms. With *internal fertilization*, which occurs in humans as well as in many other species, eggs are retained within the female, where they are fertilized by the sperm that have made their way through fluid-filled tubes.

During fertilization, the nuclei of the egg and sperm combine to form a single nucleus with a complete set of chromosomes, half from the egg and half from the sperm. In addition, fertilization activates the egg, initiating a chain of metabolic reaction within the egg that triggers the onset of embryonic development. In humans, the newly formed zygote then travels down an oviduct toward the uterus, where it begins to divide. About seven days after fertilization, the zygote develops into an embryo.

The development of the embryo entails three important processes: cell division, differentiation, and morphogenesis. Cell division occurs through a succession of miotic division. Differentiation occurs in order to form the specialized cells that then are ordered into the tissues and organs of the animal. And the third process, *morphogenesis*, is the development of an animal's shape and organization.

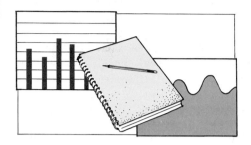

Tests, homework, and lab reports

Laying the groundwork

Students of the natural sciences should recognize that one of the main objectives of biology is to understand the relationship between structure and function. Analyzing a biological structure may give you clues about what it does and how it works. Conversely, knowing the function of a structure may provide insight into its construction. When reading the assigned material, try to focus on these goals. List the key points in each section using your own words. Keep track of vocabulary by writing down each word and then, without looking at the text, writing down its meaning. Use mnemonics when necessary. In class, ask questions while taking notes. When studying for tests, remember "cramming" just increases anxiety. Instead, schedule short study sessions to break up information into small units.

Strategies for success

Homework, lab work, field work, and tests are used to assess your basic knowledge and challenge you to apply this information in new ways. Most exams in biology consist of essay questions and multiple choice questions. Other questions may involve classification and identification. Plan ahead for tests by scheduling enough time for studying; come to the test well rested. Be sure to bring a calculator in case some questions involve mathematical calculations.

Helpful hints

Discussion

Why do large multicellular organisms need a circulatory system?

Notice this question is really testing two ideas: your knowledge of the structure as well as the function of the circulatory system. By reviewing the function of the system, you have a good shot at finding the answer.

Answer. In large, multicellular organisms, not every cell is in a position to exchange gases with the air, nutrients with the digestive area, or wastes with the outside. A circulatory system provides this.

Multiple choice

Ribosomes can be found in the (a) cytoplasm (b) Golgi complex (c) microbodies (d) all of the above.

A rule of thumb for this kind of question: If at least two options are correct, you should choose "all of the above," but if you think one item is incorrect, eliminate "all of the above" and the incorrect term to narrow down your choices.

Answer. a

Tests

Compare and contrast the processes of mitosis and meiosis.

Successful test answers highlight the major ideas or themes in an organized format. When working on essay questions, you can improve your flow of ideas by outlining your key points and then listing some transition words to tie them together. Your professor is also looking for your basic understanding of the subject matter in your use of technical vocabulary. Think ahead, and make a list of key terms you want to incorporate before you start writing. Given the choice, try answering multiple choice questions first; they may help you recall terms.

Lab reports

Using a microscope, examine a prepared slide of an onion-root tip undergoing mitosis.

Lab work allows you to apply theoretical knowledge, learn the techniques for using equipment, and practice data collection and recording. Before starting a lab, try to understand the procedure of the experiment and the theory underlying it. Once in the lab, carefully record in a notebook the question you are trying to answer, the procedure and equipment you are using, your observations during the experiment, your calculations, and your conclusions. The exact format you use for your records will depend on your instructor.

Glossary

Arthropod

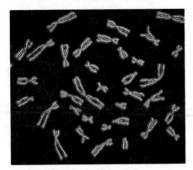

Chromosomes

Vascular plant

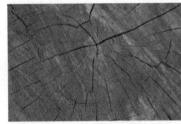

Xylem

active site. The region on the surface of an enzyme where the substrate binds.

alleles. Alternative forms of a gene.

amino acids. Organic molecules that possess both carboxyl and amino groups. The basis of proteins.

angiosperms. Flowering plants, which form seeds inside a fruit.

arthropod. Any member of the phylum Arthropoda with jointed legs and a segmented body, such as insects, crustaceans, and arachnids.

asexual reproduction. A type of reproduction involving only one parent, which produces genetically identical offspring.

atom. The smallest unit of a chemical element.

ATP. Adenosine triphosphate. A universal energy storage compound. When its bonds are broken, energy is released.

autotrophs. Organisms capable of obtaining food molecules without eating other organisms.

binary fission. The kind of cell division found in prokaryotes, in which dividing daughter cells each receive a copy of the single parental chromosome.

carnivore. A heterotrophic animal that eats meat.

cell membrane. The membrane that surrounds the cell.

cell nucleus. The part of the cell that contains chromosomes.

cellular respiration. The most prevalent and efficient pathway for the production of ATP.

cell wall. A relatively rigid structure that encloses cells of plants, fungi, many protists, and most bacteria.

chlorophyll. Various green pigments located within chloroplasts.

chloroplasts. An organelle which is found only in plants containing the enzymes and pigments of photosynthesis.

chromosomes. Long, threadlike associations of genes consisting of DNA and protein, which are found in the nucleus of all eukaryotic cells.

citric acid cycle. A set of chemical reactions in cellular respiration. Also called Krebs cycle.

codon. A three-nucleotide sequence in messenger RNA that directs the placement of an amino acid.

cotyledons. The one (monocots) or two (dicots) seed leaves of an angiosperm embryo.

cytokinesis. The division of the cytoplasm immediately after mitosis.

cytoplasm. The contents of the cell, excluding the nucleus.

dicot. Flowering plants in which the embryo produces two cotyledons.

diffusion. The spontaneous tendency of a substance to move from a more concentrated area to a less concentrated area.

DNA. Deoxyribonucleic acid. The fundamental hereditary material of all living organisms.

dominant trait. A trait that is fully expressed in the phenotype.

endoplasmic reticulum (ER). A system of membranes which is found in the cytoplasm of eukaryotes.

endosperm. A special seed tissue found only in angiosperms.

enzymes. A class of proteins that serve as catalysts.

epidermis. In plants and animals, the outermost cell layers.

eukaryotes. Organisms whose cells contain their genetic material inside a nucleus.

fertilization. The union of gametes to form a zygote.

fruit. The ripened ovary of a flower.

functional groups. Specific configurations of atoms that are usually involved in reactions.

Biology

gametes. The mature sexual reproductive cell: the egg or the sperm.

genes. A unit of hereditary information located on the chromosomes.

genotype. The genetic makeup of an organism.

glycolysis. The enzymatic breakdown of glucose to pyruvic acid.

gonad. An organ that produces sex cells in animals: either an ovary or testis.

gymnosperm. A plant whose seeds do not develop within an ovary.

herbivore. A heterotrophic animal that eats plants.

heterotrophs. Organisms that obtain food molecules by eating other organisms.

heterozygous. Having two different alleles for a given trait.

homeostasis. The maintenance of a steady state by means of feedback responses.

hormones. One of many types of circulating chemical signals found in multicellular organisms.

invertebrates. Animals without backbones.

lipids. Fats, oils, waxes, and steroids.

macromolecule. A giant molecule of living matter formed by the joining of smaller molecules.

meiosis. A two-stage cell division found only in sexually reproducing organisms.

meristem. Plant tissue made up of actively dividing cells.

metabolic pathways. A series of cyclical steps that either build up large molecules from smaller ones or break down large molecules.

metabolism. The sum total of the chemical reactions that occur in an organism.

mitosis. A form of cell division occurring in eukaryotes.

molecule. A particle made up of two or more atoms.

monocots. Flowering plants in which the embryo produces one cotyledon.

monomers. Small molecules that serve as the building blocks of a polymer.

neuron. A nerve cell.

nitrogen fixation. Conversion of nitrogen gas to ammonia, which makes nitrogen available to living things.

nucleic acids. Long-chain polymers of deoxyribose or ribose and phosphate groups.

omnivore. A heterotrophic animal that consumes both meat and plant material.

organ. Body part composed of different tissues integrated to perform a distinct function.

organelles. Organized structures that are found in eukaryotic cells, such as ribosomes, mitochondria, cilia, and vacuoles.

organ systems. Systems of organs that work together to perform specific functions.

osmosis. The movement of water across a selectively permeable membrane.

ovary. Any female organ, in plants or animals, that produces an egg.

phenotype. The expressed traits of an organism.

phloem. In vascular plants, the food-conducting tissue.

photosynthesis. Metabolic process, carried out by green plants, by which light is trapped and the energy is then used to synthesize compounds.

pistil. The female structure of a flower.

pollen. The fertilizing element of seed plants.

pollination. Process of transferring pollen from the anther to the stigma of a flower.

polymer. A large molecule consisting of many smaller molecules.

prokaryotes. Organisms whose genetic material is not contained within a nucleus.

protein. One of the most fundamental building substances of living organisms.

recessive trait. A trait that is hidden in the phenotype.

RNA. Ribonucleic acid. A single-strand nucleic acid involved in protein synthesis.

sexual reproduction. A type of reproduction in which two parents produce offspring that have unique inherited combinations of genes.

stamen. The male structure of a flower.

stigma. The part of the pistil that is receptive to pollen.

substrate. The substance on which an enzyme works.

synapse. The narrow gap between the axon of one neuron and the dendrite or cell body of another.

tissue. A group of cells with common structure and function.

transcription. The synthesis of RNA.

translation. The synthesis of a protein.

vascular plants. Plants with vascular tissue.

vertebrates. Animals which have backbones.

xylem. In vascular plants, the woody tissue that conducts water and minerals.

For further reading

Bishop, J. E., and M. Waldholz. *Genome.* New York: Simon & Schuster, 1990.

Gould, S. J. *Ever Since Darwin: Reflections in Natural History.* New York: Norton, 1977.

Lackie, J. M., and J. A. T. Dow. *The Dictionary of Cell Biology.* New York: Academic Press, 1995.

Starr, Cecie. *Biology: Concepts and Applications.* Belmont, Calif.: Wadsworth Publishing Co., 1996.

Thomas, Lewis. *The Lives of a Cell.* New York: Bantam, 1980.

Watson, J. D. *The Double Helix.* New York: Atheneum, 1968.

Chemistry

The word *chemist* conjures up images of a mad scientist working with bubbling concoctions in test tubes. Actually, *chemistry* is the study of the materials that make up the universe, and the changes that these materials undergo. It is an active, growing field that helps explain such diverse concepts as the rusting of nails, the colors of paints, the burning of a match, the melting of tar, the aging of a person, the cooking of food, and the causes of air pollution.

   Like the other sciences, chemistry is both qualitative and quantitative. In its qualitative role, chemistry explains how and why chemical changes occur. Quantitatively, chemistry measures how much of a substance is used or produced in a chemical reaction and how quickly a change will occur. This chapter will examine some of the key ideas behind both the qualitative and quantitative aspects of the field.

Basic concepts

Chemistry deals with the composition, structure, and properties of substances, the transformations of these substances, and the energy changes that accompany these transformations. An understanding of how things change is closely tied to an understanding of the nature and composition of matter—the physical material of the universe.

Matter. *Matter* is any material that occupies space and takes up mass. Matter exists in three physical *states*: gas, liquid, and solid. A *gas* has no fixed volume or shape—it takes the volume and shape of its container. A *liquid* has a definite volume but no specific shape. A *solid* has both a fixed volume and a fixed shape.
Classification of matter. There are several other ways in which matter can be classified. If a sample of matter consists of only one kind of matter, the sample is a *pure substance*. When the sample consists of two or more kinds of matter, the sample is a *mixture*. If a mixture has a uniform appearance and composition throughout, it is *homogeneous*; if not, the mixture is *heterogeneous*. There are also two kinds of pure substances: *elements*, which are made of only one type of atom; and *compounds*, which consist of two or more elements that are combined in a definite ratio.

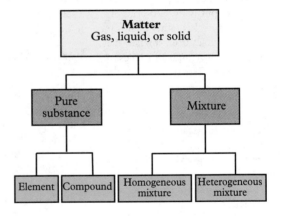

Properties and changes of matter. Each substance has a unique set of *properties*, or characteristics, that distinguishes it from other substances. *Physical properties*, such as color and density, can be measured without changing the basic identity of the substance. *Chemical properties* describe the way a substance may change to form other substances.

When matter undergoes a change, the change may be either a *physical change*, in which a substance changes in its physical appearance but not its basic identity, or a *chemical change*, in which one substance is converted to another. During a chemical change, the total mass of the original substance always equals the total mass of the new substance. This principle, called the *law of conservation of mass*, is often stated as follows: In a chemical change, mass is conserved; it is neither created nor destroyed.

Energy.
When physical or chemical changes occur, *energy*—the ability to do work or to transfer heat—is either absorbed or released. Changes in which energy is absorbed are called *endothermic changes*. Changes in which energy is released are known as *exothermic changes*.

Energy appears in a variety of forms—light, sound, heat, mechanical energy, electrical energy, and chemical energy. One form of energy can be converted to another form, but energy itself can be neither created nor destroyed. This principle is called the *law of conservation of energy*.

Two general classifications of energy are potential energy and kinetic energy. *Potential energy* is the energy of an object due to its position. *Kinetic energy* is the energy of an object due to its motion. The difference between these two forms of energy can be illustrated using a book and a table. If the book is raised off the floor onto the table, its potential energy increases with respect to the floor. If the book is pushed off the table, its potential energy is converted into kinetic energy as it falls. In both cases, energy is conserved.

Atoms.
An *atom* is the smallest particle of an element that can exhibit the properties of that element. Atoms consist of subatomic particles—electrons, protons, and neutrons. *Protons* and *neutrons* have approximately the same mass and constitute the *nucleus* of the atom. *Electrons* have almost no mass and move around the outside of the nucleus. The subatomic particles also carry electrical charges: the proton has a single positive charge, the electron has a single negative charge, and the neutron is electrically neutral.

Atomic number, mass number, and isotopes. All atoms of a given element have the same number of protons. This number is called the *atomic number* and is abbreviated by the letter Z. The *mass number* of an atom, abbreviated by the letter A, is equal to the number of protons and neutrons in the nucleus. The total number of neutrons equals A minus Z. Sometimes the number of neutrons in atoms of the same element may vary. Consequently, these atoms may have different masses. Atoms of the same element that differ in mass are known as *isotopes*.

The isotope of an element is identified by its *nuclear symbol*, which shows the symbol for an element and the mass number of the element. For example, carbon has a few important isotopes. The most common one has a mass number of 12 and another isotope has mass number 13. They are written ^{12}C (or carbon 12) and ^{13}C (carbon 13).

Molecules and ions. Atoms can combine to form *molecules*. Both atoms and molecules can gain or lose electrons, resulting in electrically charged particles called *ions*. The loss of electrons forms positively charged particles called *cations*; the gain of electrons forms negatively charged particles called *anions*.

The simplest type of molecule is called a *diatomic* molecule and contains two atoms—either two of the same type or two different types. Seven elements exist as diatomic molecules—hydrogen, oxygen, nitrogen, fluorine, chlorine, bromine, and iodine. Molecules that have more than two atoms are called *polyatomic* molecules.

Subatomic particles

Particle	Symbol	Charge	Mass	Location	Discovered
Electron	e^-	-1	0.00055 amu	Outside nucleus	1897 J. J. Thomson
Proton	p or p^+	+1	1.0073 amu	Inside nucleus	1919 E. Rutherford
Neutron	n or n^0	0	1.0087 amu	Inside nucleus	1932 Sir J. Chadwick

Atomic structure

The modern theory of atomic structure was developed from studies of light. When electrons strike the atoms of a gas, the atoms emit *electromagnetic waves*, such as light, X rays, and radio waves. These emissions can be observed as discrete lines (called *line spectra*) using a device known as a *spectrometer*. Each atom produces its own unique spectrum.

The Bohr model.
In 1913, Danish physicist Niels Bohr created a model of the hydrogen atom that explained the observed line spectra of hydrogen. Bohr based his model on the assumption that the energy possessed by an electron was *quantized*: at any instant an electron may have one of several possible energy values, but at no time may it have an energy that falls in between those values. Bohr proposed that electrons move around the nucleus in circular paths, called *orbits*, and that these orbits are restricted to certain radii and energy levels. Each allowed orbit was assigned an integer *n*, known as the *principle quantum number*. Higher quantum numbers were associated with higher orbital energies.

Bohr stated that the electron of hydrogen was normally in the lowest energy level, known as the *ground state*. By absorbing energy, the electron could be raised to an unstable *excited state*. When the electron dropped back to its ground state, it emitted energy that appeared as a line in the atom's line spectrum.

The quantum model.
Although Bohr's model successfully explained the observation of line spectra, later experiments showed that his concept of well-defined orbits could not be true. In 1924, Louis de Broglie suggested that matter in motion has properties normally associated with waves. In 1926, Erwin Schrödinger took this concept a step further and developed the *Schrödinger equation*, which describes the motions and energies of particles. From this equation,

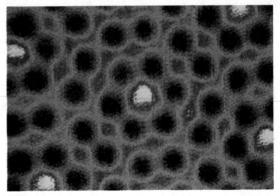

Silicon atoms

the *quantum-mechanical model* of the atom was developed. This model describes electron behavior in terms of wave mechanics.

Principal energy levels and sublevels. The fixed energy levels in the quantum-mechanical model are called *principal energy levels*. Each energy level is identified by a principal quantum number, *n*. Within each principal level are one or more *sublevels* designated by the letters *s, p, d,* and *f*. The total number of sublevels within a given principal energy level is equal to the principal quantum number. A sublevel is identified by both the principal energy level number and the sublevel letter, for example, 1*s*, 2*s*, 2*p*, 3*s*, and so on.

Orbitals. Instead of orbits, the quantum-mechanical model proposed *orbitals*—regions in space around the nucleus where there is a high probability of finding the electron. The *s* sublevel has one orbital, the *p* sublevel has three orbitals, the *d* sublevel has five, and the *f* sublevel has seven.

The size and energy of an orbital is described by its principal quantum number. A collection of orbitals having the same principal quantum number is called an *electron shell*.

Sublevels and orbitals

Energy level	Number of sublevels	Sublevel designations	Orbitals per sublevel
n = 1	1	1s	1
n = 2	2	2s 2p	1 3
n = 3	3	3s 3p 3d	1 3 5
n = 4	4	4s 4p 4d 4f	1 3 5 7

Chemistry

Electron configurations. The *electron configuration* of an atom describes the distribution of electrons among the atom's orbitals. Electrons occupy the orbitals in order of increasing energy. All orbitals that are equal in energy are filled with electrons before the next level of energy begins to fill up.

The *Pauli exclusion principle* places a limit of two on the number of electrons that may occupy a single orbital. In addition, these two electrons must have opposite spins. *Spin* is the property of an electron that makes it behave as though it were a tiny magnet. There are two forms of spin: up spin ($\uparrow$) and down spin ($\downarrow$).

The electrons in the electron shell with the largest principal quantum number are called the outer shell, or *valence shell,* electrons. These valence shell electrons take part in chemical bonding. Most bonded atoms tend to share a total of eight valence electrons. This observation is called the *octet rule.*

The periodic table.
A nineteenth-century chemist named Dmitri Mendeleev arranged the elements in a chart in order of increasing atomic weight. In 1869, Mendeleev's first *periodic table* showed that elements with similar properties were found at regular intervals in his chart. Mendeleev left several blanks in the table to account for undiscovered elements. He also thought that a few elements were out of order due to inaccurate atomic weights. Years later, Henry Moseley showed that when elements are arranged according to increasing atomic number, Mendeleev's order is shown to be correct.

The modern periodic table. Today, elements are arranged in order of increasing atomic number so that elements with similar physical and chemical properties occur at regular intervals. Each element occupies a separate square in the table and is represented by its symbol, its atomic number, and its atomic weight.

Elements that have similar chemical properties and the same number of valence electrons are placed in vertical columns which are referred to as *groups* or *families.* The groups are usually numbered across the top of the table as shown on the following page. An international organization has recently suggested labeling the eighteen columns 1 through 18. Some groups have been given names. Groups 1A and 2A are known as the *alkali metals* and the *alkaline-earth metals,* respectively. The elements of group 7A are the *halogens,* and the elements in group 8A are the *noble gases.*

The horizontal rows of the table are called *rows* or *periods.* The periods correspond to the sequential filling of the electron shells. Each row terminates with an element that has a complete valence shell.

Electron configurations of some elements

Element	Total electrons	Orbital diagram 1s	2s	2p			3s	Electron configuration
H (hydrogen)	1	$\uparrow$						$1s^1$
He (helium)	2	$\uparrow\downarrow$						$1s^2$
Li (lithium)	3	$\uparrow\downarrow$	$\uparrow$					$1s^2 2s^1$
Be (beryllium)	4	$\uparrow\downarrow$	$\uparrow\downarrow$					$1s^2 2s^2$
B (boron)	5	$\uparrow\downarrow$	$\uparrow\downarrow$	$\uparrow$				$1s^2 2s^2 2p^1$
N (nitrogen)	7	$\uparrow\downarrow$	$\uparrow\downarrow$	$\uparrow$	$\uparrow$	$\uparrow$		$1s^2 2s^2 2p^3$
0 (oxygen)	8	$\uparrow\downarrow$	$\uparrow\downarrow$	$\uparrow\downarrow$	$\uparrow$	$\uparrow$		$1s^2 2s^2 2p^4$
Ne (neon)	10	$\uparrow\downarrow$	$\uparrow\downarrow$	$\uparrow\downarrow$	$\uparrow\downarrow$	$\uparrow\downarrow$		$1s^2 2s^2 2p^6$
Na (sodium)	11	$\uparrow\downarrow$	$\uparrow\downarrow$	$\uparrow\downarrow$	$\uparrow\downarrow$	$\uparrow\downarrow$	$\uparrow$	$1s^2 2s^2 2p^6 3s^1$

The periodic table

1A																	8A
1 **H** 1.008	2A											3A	4A	5A	6A	7A	**2** **He** 4.003
3 **Li** 6.941	**4** **Be** 9.012											**5** **B** 10.81	**6** **C** 12.01	**7** **N** 14.01	**8** **O** 16.00	**9** **F** 19.00	**10** **Ne** 20.18
11 **Na** 22.99	**12** **Mg** 24.31	3B	4B	5B	6B	7B	8B			1B	2B	**13** **Al** 26.98	**14** **Si** 28.09	**15** **P** 30.97	**16** **S** 32.07	**17** **Cl** 35.45	**18** **Ar** 39.95
19 **K** 39.10	**20** **Ca** 40.08	**21** **Sc** 44.96	**22** **Ti** 47.88	**23** **V** 50.94	**24** **Cr** 52.00	**25** **Mn** 54.94	**26** **Fe** 55.85	**27** **Co** 58.93	**28** **Ni** 58.69	**29** **Cu** 63.55	**30** **Zn** 65.39	**31** **Ga** 69.72	**32** **Ge** 72.59	**33** **As** 74.92	**34** **Se** 78.96	**35** **Br** 79.90	**36** **Kr** 83.80
37 **Rb** 85.47	**38** **Sr** 87.62	**39** **Y** 88.91	**40** **Zr** 91.22	**41** **Nb** 92.91	**42** **Mo** 95.94	**43** **Tc** (98)	**44** **Ru** 101.1	**45** **Rh** 102.9	**46** **Pd** 106.4	**47** **Ag** 107.9	**48** **Cd** 112.4	**49** **In** 114.8	**50** **Sn** 118.7	**51** **Sb** 121.8	**52** **Te** 127.6	**53** **I** 126.9	**54** **Xe** 131.3
55 **Cs** 132.9	**56** **Ba** 137.3	**57** ***La** 138.9	**72** **Hf** 178.5	**73** **Ta** 180.9	**74** **W** 183.9	**75** **Re** 186.2	**76** **Os** 190.2	**77** **Ir** 192.2	**78** **Pt** 195.1	**79** **Au** 197.0	**80** **Hg** 200.6	**81** **Tl** 204.4	**82** **Pb** 207.2	**83** **Bi** 209.0	**84** **Po** (210)	**85** **At** (210)	**86** **Rn** (222)
87 **Fr** (223)	**88** **Ra** (226)	**89** **†Ac** (227)	**104** (261)	**105** (262)	**106** (263)	**107** (262)	**108** (265)	**109** (266)									

Atomic number — 1
Chemical symbol — **H**
Atomic mass — 1.008

*Lanthanide series	**58** **Ce** 140.1	**59** **Pr** 140.9	**60** **Nd** 144.2	**61** **Pm** (147)	**62** **Sm** 150.4	**63** **Eu** 152.0	**64** **Gd** 157.3	**65** **Tb** 158.9	**66** **Dy** 162.5	**67** **Ho** 164.9	**68** **Er** 167.3	**69** **Tm** 168.9	**70** **Yb** 173.0	**71** **Lu** 175.0
†Actinide series	**90** **Th** 232.0	**91** **Pa** (231)	**92** **U** 238.0	**93** **Np** (237)	**94** **Pu** (242)	**95** **Am** (243)	**96** **Cm** (247)	**97** **Bk** (247)	**98** **Cf** (251)	**99** **Es** (254)	**100** **Fm** (257)	**101** **Md** (258)	**102** **No** (259)	**103** **Lr** (260)

Entries with atomic mass in parentheses are approximate values for mass. The official names and symbols for the elements 104 through 109 have not yet been agreed to.

There are three distinct regions of the periodic table: Groups 1A through 8A, taken together, comprise the *representative elements.* Groups 3B to 2B comprise the *transition metals.* The elements in the two 14-member rows that are placed below the main portion of the table are the *inner transition metals.* The inner transition metals of the first row are called the *lanthanides,* and those of the second row are called the *actinides.*

Metals, nonmetals, and metalloids. Elements can also be divided into metals, nonmetals, and semimetals, also known as *metalloids.* Generally, metallic character increases from top to bottom of the periodic table and decreases from left to right.

Chemically, an element is known as a *metal* if it can lose one or more electrons and become a positively charged ion. Metals comprise roughly 70 percent of the known elements and are situated on the left side of the table. Groups 1A and 2A are often called *active metals* because they are chemically more reactive than most other metals. For the most part, metals have a metallic luster, exhibit good electrical and thermal conduc-tivity, and can be flattened or drawn into wire as solids.

Nonmetals—elements that do not lose electrons—are located in the upper-right corner of the periodic table. These elements vary greatly in appearance and are generally poor conductors of heat and electricity.

Between the metals and the nonmetals are the *semimetals,* which have properties characteristic of both metals and nonmetals.

Trends in atomic properties. Many atomic properties are periodic—the properties of elements are basically repeated through each family. For example, the size of an atom varies for each element. However, within each group, the atomic radius tends to increase going from top to bottom; and within each period, the atomic radius tends to decrease moving from left to right. Other trends include such things as reactivity, metallic character, and ionization energy.

Knowing the types of periodic relationships that exist between families or periods allows scientists to predict the properties of new elements that have not yet been discovered.

Chemical bonding

Atoms with incomplete valence shells will interact with certain other atoms in such a way that each partner completes its valence shell. Atoms do this by either sharing or completely transferring valence electrons. These interactions usually result in atoms staying close together, held by attractions called *chemical bonds*. The tendency of atoms to gain, lose, or share their valence electrons can often be viewed as attempts to follow the octet rule discussed earlier.

Types of bonds.

The type of chemical bond formed depends on differences in *electronegativity*—the ability of an atom to attract electrons—between the atoms of the molecule. The two strongest kinds of bonds are ionic bonds and covalent bonds.

Ionic bonds. An *ionic bond* forms when two atoms differ so much in electronegativity that one or more electrons are actually transferred from one atom to the other. The recipient atom becomes negatively charged; the donor atom becomes positively charged. In this way, recipient atoms and donor atoms complete their valence shells yet stay mutually attracted to each other because of their opposite charges.

In *ionic compounds*—a compound made up of ions—the sum of the positive charges must equal the sum of the negative charges. Thus, the total charge of cations is exactly balanced by the total charge of the anions.

Covalent bonds. A *covalent bond* forms when two atoms share a pair of electrons. The sharing of one pair of electrons produces a *single bond*, the sharing of two or three pairs of electrons produces *double bonds* and *triple bonds*, respectively. *Lewis diagrams* are often used to show the bonding arrangement between the atoms.

The strength of a covalent bond is measured by its *bond energy*. The strengths of covalent bonds increase with the number of electron pairs shared between two atoms. In single bonds, the bond strengths are generally higher between atoms of smaller size.

If both atoms are equally electronegative, a *nonpolar covalent bond* is formed. If one atom is somewhat more electronegative, a *polar covalent bond* results. In polar covalent bonds, the electron pair is pulled closer to one atomic nucleus than to the other. This atom becomes partially negative and the other becomes partially positive.

Molecular geometry.

The overall shape of a molecule, its *molecular geometry,* is determined by the bond angles in the molecule. A *bond angle* is the angle between any two bonds formed by the same atom. The size of a molecule is determined by its *bond lengths,* the distances between the nuclei of bonded

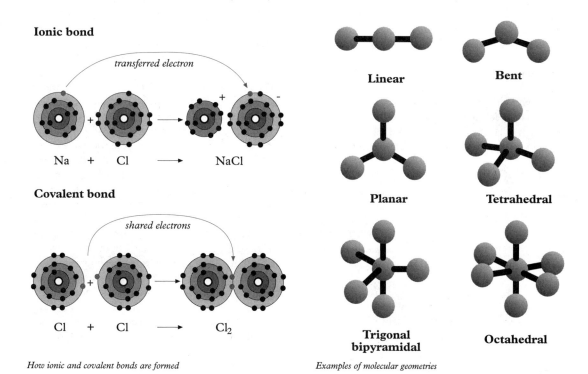

Ionic bond

transferred electron

Na + Cl ⟶ NaCl

Covalent bond

shared electrons

Cl + Cl ⟶ Cl_2

How ionic and covalent bonds are formed

Linear

Bent

Planar

Tetrahedral

Trigonal bipyramidal

Octahedral

Examples of molecular geometries

Drawing Lewis diagrams

Lewis diagrams are used to represent covalent bonds in molecules. Usually each electron pair shared between atoms is shown as a line, and the unshared electron pairs are shown as dots. When drawing Lewis diagrams it is a good idea to follow a regular procedure. Each step will be illustrated by drawing the diagram for nitric acid (HNO_3).

1. *Draw a tentative diagram for the molecule. A hydrogen atom always forms a bond at the end position. If the molecule has two or more oxygen atoms and a nonmetal atom, the oxygen atoms usually are placed around the central nonmetal atom.*

$$O \quad N \quad O \quad H$$
$$O$$

2. *Count the total number of valence electrons in the molecule or ion.* If necessary, adjust the number of electrons for charge: add one for each negative charge and subtract one for each positive charge.

In HNO_3, there is 1 valence electron from hydrogen, 5 from nitrogen, and 6 from each oxygen: $1 + 5 + (3 \times 6) = 24$. There are no ions, so it is not necessary to adjust for charge.

3. *Draw a single bond between each atom. Then distribute the remaining electrons around each symbol until each atom is surrounded by eight electrons.* Remember that each single bond counts as two electrons for each element.

$$:\ddot{O}\!-\!N\!-\!\ddot{O}\!-\!H$$
$$|$$
$$:\ddot{O}:$$

4. *If there are not enough electrons to give the central atom an octet, use one or more of the unshared pairs of electrons to form double or triple bonds.*

$$\ddot{O}\!=\!N\!-\!\ddot{O}\!-\!H$$
$$|$$
$$:\ddot{O}:$$

atoms. Together, the shape and size of a molecule play an important role in determining the physical and chemical properties of a substance.

The number of different ways that bonds can be arranged in space is rather limited. For example, a molecule consisting of two atoms can be arranged only in a linear fashion. A molecule of three atoms can be a linear molecule or a bent molecule.

The shape of a molecule helps determine the distribution of charge in the molecule. A *polar molecule*, or *dipole*, is a molecule in which there is an unsymmetrical distribution of electrical charge, even though the molecule as a whole is electrically neutral. One region of a

dipole has a negative charge (the negative pole) while another region has a positive charge (the positive pole). A *nonpolar molecule* has a symmetrical charge distribution. Molecules that have no polar covalent bonds are nonpolar. Molecules that have polar covalent bonds may still be nonpolar molecules if the polar covalent bonds are perfectly symmetrical (for example, CO_2).

Intermolecular forces.
The forces that act between molecules or between molecules and ions are called *intermolecular forces*. Generally these forces are much weaker than bonding forces. Three important intermolecular forces—dipole forces, hydrogen bonds, and dispersion forces—are forms of electrostatic attraction. *Dipole forces* occur when the positive region of one polar molecule is attracted to the negative region of another polar molecule. *Hydrogen bonds* are another form of dipole force. These bonds form when the partially positive hydrogen atom of a polar covalent bond in one molecule is attracted to the partially negative atom of a polar covalent bond in another molecule. This type of bonding generally occurs between molecules in which a hydrogen atom is bonded to an atom of nitrogen, oxygen, or fluorine. *Dispersion forces*, or *London forces*, are attractive forces between nonpolar molecules that have been distorted, or polarized, to create temporary dipoles. Even the simplest molecules have some dispersion attraction.

Dipole forces

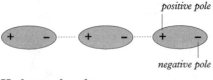

positive pole

negative pole

Hydrogen bonds

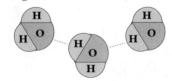

Two types of intermolecular forces

Chemical arithmetic

Much of chemistry deals with how substances interact with each other. Often it is necessary to investigate the quantitative relationships between substances undergoing chemical changes. The study of these quantitative relationships is known as *stoichiometry*. In a sense, stoichiometry is chemical arithmetic—it involves manipulating measurements, formulas, and equations.

Formulas and equations.

Chemists have developed standard methods of describing chemical reactions. These methods, which include formulas and equations, help chemists describe molecules and compounds and how they interact.

Chemical formulas. A chemical formula expresses the composition of a compound using the symbols of the elements involved. Subscripts are used to show the number of atoms of each element in the compound. If only one atom of an element is present, the number is not shown as a subscript.

Two important types of chemical formulas are molecular formulas and empirical formulas. *Molecular formulas* show the exact number and type of atoms combined in each molecule of a compound. For example, N_2H_4 is the molecular formula for the compound hydrazine, a type of rocket fuel. The formula states that in each molecule of hydrazine there are two nitrogen atoms (N_2) and four hydrogen atoms (H_4). *Empirical formulas* show the simplest ratios of the atoms combined in a molecule. The empirical formula of hydrazine is NH_2. Although the ratio of nitrogen to hydrogen is 1:2 in both the molecular formula and the empirical formula, only the molecular formula shows the actual number of N atoms and H atoms present in a hydrazine molecule.

Chemical equations. Chemical reactions can be represented in a concise way using *chemical equations*. For example, when molecular hydrogen (H_2) burns, it reacts with molecular oxygen (O_2) to form water (H_2O). The chemical equation for this reaction is:

$$2H_2 + O_2 \rightarrow 2H_2O.$$

The plus sign in this equation means "reacts with" and the arrow means "produces." The chemical formulas to the left of the arrow represent the starting substances, called *reactants*, while the formulas to the right of the arrow show the substances produced, the *products*. The numbers in front of the formulas are called *coefficients* and indicate how many units of the substances are used and produced in the reaction.

Naming inorganic compounds

Currently there are about ten million known chemical substances. Naming them all would be a difficult task at best if each had a special name independent of all the others. Instead, a set of rules has been developed that allow chemical substances to be named in an informative and systematic way. The following are some of the rules used to name inorganic compounds.

Binary covalent compound (2 elements). Name of the first element, followed by the name of the second element, which includes a prefix indicating the number of atoms and ends in *ide*—carbon *di*ox*ide*.

Monoatomic cation (1 positive ion). Name of the element, followed by the word *ion*—sodium *ion*. If the element can form more than one positive ion, the positive charge of the ion is indicated by a roman numeral in parentheses following the name of the element—iron *(II)* ion.

Monoatomic anion (1 negative ion). Drop the ending of the element name and add the ending *ide*—chlor*ide*.

Oxyanions (anion containing oxygen). Depends on the relative numbers of oxygen atoms in the anion. If the element forms only two oxyanions, the oxyanion that contains more oxygen ends in *ate*, and the name of the one with less oxygen ends in *ite*—1 nitrogen and 2 oxygens is nitr*ite* ion while 1 nitrogen and 3 oxygens is nitr*ate* ion. If three or four oxyanions are formed, the oxyanion with less oxygen than the *ite* oxyanion has the prefix *hypo* attached to the name of the *ite* oxyanion—*hypo*chlorite has less oxygen than chlorite. The oxyanion with more oxygen than the *ate* oxyanion has the prefix *per* attached to the name of the *ate* oxyanion—*per*chlorate has more oxygen than chlorate.

Ionic compounds (2 ions). Name of the cation followed by name of the anion—lithium bromide.

Binary acids (H and anion). Add the prefix *hydro* and change the ending of the nonmetal element to *ic*—*hydro*chlor*ic* acid or *hydro*sulfur*ic* acid.

Oxyacids (H and oxyanion). Names usually derived from corresponding oxyanion. If the oxyanion has an *ate* ending, the corresponding acid is given an *ic* ending. If the oxyanion ends in *ite*, then the corresponding acid name ends in *ous*. Prefixes in the name of the oxyanion are kept in the name of the oxyacid—if oxyanion = chlorate, then oxyacid = chlor*ic* acid; if oxyanion = hypochlorite, then oxyacid = *hypo*chlor*ous* acid.

However, a coefficient of 1 is usually not written.

When writing chemical equations, chemists also often indicate the physical states of the reactant and products by using the abbreviations *g, l, s,* and *aq* in parentheses to denote gas, liquid, solid, and the aqueous (water) environment, respectively. So the equation for the creation of water might look like this:

$$2H_2(g) + O_2(g) \rightarrow 2H_2O(l).$$

Because atoms are neither created or destroyed in a reaction, an equation must have an equal number of atoms of each element on each side of the arrow. This creates a *balanced equation.* When balancing equations, be sure to keep the following in mind:

- Formulas of substances must be written correctly.
- The number of atoms of each type of element must be the same on both sides of the equation.
- Only coefficients in front of substances may be changed to change the number of atoms on the reactant or product side. Subscripts in chemical formulas must not be changed.
- The sum of charges of ions on the left side of the arrow must be the same as the sum of charges of ions on the right side.

Types of measurements. Chemists do
not ordinarily work with single molecules or atoms, but rather with trillions upon trillions of them. Therefore, instead of trying to count individual atoms or molecules, chemists usually determine the number of atoms or molecules indirectly from their masses.

Atomic, formula, and molecular weights. The mass of a single atom is much too small to be measured on a balance. So instead, chemists use a method of ratios to calculate relative atomic weights based on the mass of an atom of carbon 12, the most abundant isotope of carbon. The *atomic weight* of an element is defined as the average mass of the atoms of an element compared to an atom of carbon 12, which is defined as exactly 12 *atomic mass units*. The *formula weight* of a substance is the sum of the atomic weights of each atom in its chemical formula. If the chemical formula of a substance is its molecular formula, then the formula weight is often called the *molecular weight.*

Moles. To facilitate the counting and weighing of large samples, chemists have created a quantity called the mole. A *mole* of any type of substance equals the number of carbon 12 (^{12}C) atoms in exactly 12 grams of ^{12}C. In 12 grams of ^{12}C, there are 6.022×10^{23} atoms. This number is known as *Avogadro's number.* Thus, one mole of any substance contains Avogadro's number of atoms, molecules, or ions. For example, a mole of water contains 6.022×10^{23} molecules of water. In addition, one mole of a substance has a mass in grams that is numerically equal to its formula weight in atomic mass units. The term *molar mass* is used to describe the mass in grams of one mole of a substance.

Chemical reactions. Although tens of
millions of chemical reactions can occur, many of these can be classified into six general types of reactions: combination reactions, decomposition reactions, combustion reactions, single replacement reactions, precipitation reactions, and neutralization reactions. Understanding the characteristics of each helps chemists predict what type of reaction will occur when different reactants are combined.

Types of reactions

Reaction type	Reactants	Products
Combination $A + X \rightarrow AX$	Element or compound + element or compound	One compound
Decomposition $AX \rightarrow A + X$	One compound	Element or compound + element or compound
Combustion $A + O_2 \rightarrow AO$	Element or compound + oxygen	Oxides
Single replacement $A + BX \rightarrow AX + B$	Element + acid or ionic compound	Element + ionic compound
Precipitation (double replacement) $AX + BY \rightarrow AY + BX$	Solution + solution	Precipitate of ionic compound + acid or ionic compound
Neutralization (double replacement) $HX + MOH \rightarrow HOH + MX$	Acid (H^+) + base (OH^-)	Ionic compound (salt) + water (H_2O)

In a *combination reaction*, two or more substances combine to form a single product. A *decomposition reaction* is the opposite of a combination reaction—one reactant breaks down into two or more substances. *Combustion reactions* almost always contain molecular oxygen as a reactant, and produce a flame. The products of complete combustion are carbon dioxide (CO_2) and water.

Single replacement reactions are a type of *oxidation-reduction reactions* (see page 403). In these reactions, an atom or ion in a compound is replaced by an atom or an ion of another element. In a *precipitation reaction*, the reactants are solutions and the products include a solid, known as a *precipitate*, that separates from the solution. *Neutralization reactions* involve *acids* (compounds whose solution contains hydrogen ions, or H^+) and *bases* (compounds whose solutions contain hydroxide ions, or OH^-). The products of neutralization reactions include water and a salt. Both precipitation reactions and neutralization reactions are types of *double-displacement reactions*.

Energy and reactions.

As mentioned earlier, nearly all chemical changes involve an energy transfer, usually in the form of heat. This heat flow is referred to as the *heat of reaction* or the *enthalpy of reaction*. *Enthalpy*, designated by the letter H, may be thought of as the amount of heat possessed by the chemical involved in a reaction at a given temperature and pressure.

The absolute enthalpy of a substance cannot be measured directly. Instead, chemists measure the change in enthalpy, ΔH, which is the heat change during a reaction. This change in enthalpy can be calculated using the formula

$$\Delta H = \Sigma H_{final} - \Sigma H_{initial}$$

where ΣH_{final} is the sum of the final enthalpies and $\Sigma H_{initial}$ is the sum of the initial enthalpies. In *exothermic reactions*, the products of the reaction have a smaller heat content than the reactants, so ΔH is a negative quantity. In *endothermic reactions*, the products of the reaction have a greater heat content than the reactants, so ΔH is a positive quantity.

States of matter

The physical properties of a substance often depend on the state of the substance. The difference between the three states is how densely the molecules of the substance are packed. In a solid, the molecules are packed tightly together so there is little freedom of movement. In a liquid, the packing of the molecules is looser—the molecules can move past one another but not totally break loose, thus liquids flow. In a gas, the molecules can move essentially independent of one another.

Gases.

Gases have certain characteristics that are identifiable:
- they have low density;
- they can be compressed—that is, a fixed quantity of gas may be made to occupy a smaller volume by applying pressure;
- they expand to fill the containers uniformly;
- and confined gases exert constant pressure on the walls of their containers uniformly in all directions.

The properties of gases are often given at a condition called *standard temperature and pressure* (STP). These conditions are 1 atm (760 mm Hg) of pressure at 0°C (273 K). The molar volume of a gas at STP is 22.4 L/mol.

Kinetic theory of gases. Scientists have devised a theory, known as the *kinetic theory of gases*, to try to account for the properties of gases. According to this theory, gas molecules are in constant motion. They collide with each other and with the walls of the container. The molecules of gas are spaced widely apart, which causes the strength of interparticle attractions to be very weak in most gases. A gas that conforms

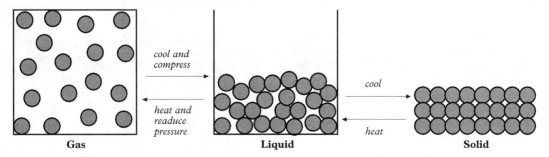

cool and compress

heat and readuce pressure

cool

heat

Gas   **Liquid**   **Solid**

The three states of matter

perfectly to this model of gas behavior is known as an *ideal gas*.

The gas laws. Experiments with a large number of gases reveal that the state, or condition, of many gaseous substances can be defined using four variables: temperature (T), pressure (P), volume (V), and the quantity of gas measured in moles (n). The relationships between these variables are described by several different equations, or laws. *Boyle's law* states that for a fixed quantity of gas maintained at constant temperature, the volume of the gas is inversely proportional to the pressure. *Charles's law* states that for a fixed quantity of gas at constant pressure, the volume of the gas is directly proportional to its temperature. *Avogadro's law* states that at constant temperature and pressure, the volume of the gas is directly proportional to the moles of gas.

The three laws have been combined together in one equation, known as *the ideal gas law*:

$$PV = nRT.$$

The constant R is known as the *gas constant*. The standard value for R is 0.0821 L·atm/mol·K. The ideal gas equation can be used to find any one variable when given the other three.

Gas mixtures. Gases may be mixed together by adding one gas to another gas already occupying a rigid container of fixed volume. The *partial pressure* of one component of the mixture is the pressure that the component would exert if it were present alone at the same volume and temperature. According to *Dalton's law of partial pressure*, the total pressure exerted by a mixture of gases is the sum of the partial pressures of the gases in the mixture.

Liquids.

The intermolecular forces in a liquid are stronger than those of a gas. This increased strength means that the molecules in a liquid are packed more tightly, so that liquids have a larger density and are less compressible than gases. Several other properties of liquids that are also directly related to the strength of the intermolecular attractions include surface tension and viscosity. At the surface of a liquid, the intermolecular forces pull the surface molecules into a sort of tight "skin" over the liquid or around a drop. The *surface tension* of a liquid is the amount of energy needed to stretch or increase the surface "skin." Liquids with

strong intermolecular attractions have higher surface tension than liquids with weak intermolecular forces. Within a liquid, the liquid molecules are free to move past one another. This freedom to move is what allows liquids to flow. *Viscosity* may be thought of as an internal resistance to flow. Liquids that have strong intermolecular forces are generally more viscous than liquids with weak intermolecular forces.

Solids.

The solid state is the most ordered state: the particles of a solid are generally fixed in a definite position and maintain a definite shape. A solid whose particles are arranged in a geometric pattern that repeats itself, such as salt (NaCl), is called a *crystalline solid*. Each particle occupies a fixed position in the crystal. Although the particle can vibrate, it cannot move past its neighbors. In an *amorphous solid*, such as glass or rubber, the particles lack a well-defined arrangement.

The structure and properties of crystalline solids are determined by the kinds of forces that hold the particles together. Crystals can be classified as one of four types: ionic, covalent, molecular, or metallic. *Ionic crystals* are held together by electrostatic attraction. *Covalent crystals* are held together by covalent bonds. *Molecular crystals* are held together by intermolecular forces, while *metallic crystals* are held together by *metallic bonds*—electrostatic attractions between positive metal ions and electrons.

Changes of state.

Any substance may exist in more than one state of matter. The change of matter from one state of matter to another is called a *phase change*. Conversions of a solid to a liquid (*melting*), a liquid to a gas (*vaporization*), or a solid to a gas (*sublimation*) are all *endothermic processes*. The reverse processes—conversion of a liquid to a solid (*freezing*), a gas to a liquid (*condensation*), or a gas to a solid (*deposition*)—are all *exothermic*.

There is a continuous transfer of particles from one

Vitamin A crystal

phase to another, and the state of a substance at any given time depends on temperature and pressure. The temperatures and pressures at which the various phases of a substance can exist can be summarized in a *phase diagram*. Although the phase diagram for each substance is different, they all contain the same type of information. Each region in the diagram represents a pure phase—that is, a phase in which the substance is entirely a gas, liquid, or solid. The boundaries between the regions show the temperatures and pressures at which the substances are in equilibrium between two states. The point where all three boundaries intersect is known as the *triple point*. Phase diagrams are used to anticipate transitions in phase brought about by changes in temperature and pressure.

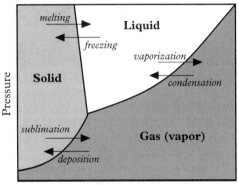

General shape for a phase diagram of a system

Solutions

Solutions are found throughout nature: air is a solution, the oceans are solutions, even rain is a solution. A *solution* is a homogeneous mixture of two or more substances, which may be gases, liquids, or solids. When solids or gases are dissolved in liquids, the solid or gas is said to be the *solute* and the liquid is the *solvent*. Generally, the solute is the substance present in a relatively small amount, and the solvent is the medium in which the solute is dissolved.

Solutions contain differing amounts of solutes and solvents. A *concentrated* solution has a relatively large quantity of solute per unit amount of solution; a *dilute* solution has a relatively small quantity of solute per unit amount of solution. In addition, the *solubility*—the measure of how much solute dissolves in a given amount of solvent at a given temperature—of the solution varies.

Forming solutions. A solution is formed when one substance disperses uniformly throughout another substance. This process involves three distinct steps: the separation of solute molecules, the separation of solvent particles, and finally the mixing of solvent and solute molecules so that the solute particles occupy positions that are normally taken by solvent molecules.

The ease with which a solute particle may replace a solvent molecule depends on the relative strengths of the interactive forces between the solute and solute, the solute and solvent, and the solvent and solvent. If the solute-solvent attraction is stronger than the solvent-solvent attraction, then the solute will dissolve readily. If the solute-solvent forces are weaker than the other forces, then only a relatively small amount of the solute will dissolve.

Temperature and pressure also have an effect on solubility. Generally, the solubility of most solids increases as the temperature increases. On the other hand, the solubility of most gases decreases at higher temperatures. Pressure mainly affects the solubility of gases; as pressure decreases, solubility decreases.

Concentration units. Quantitative study of a solution requires knowing the solution's *concentration*—the amount of solute present in a given amount of solution. Chemists use several different concentration units. The choice of concentration unit is generally based on the kind of measurement made of the solution.

Percent by weight is the percentage of mass of a component of a solute in a given mass of the solution.

$$\% \ by \ weight \ of \ solute = \frac{grams \ solute}{grams \ solution} \times 100$$

The *mole fraction* (X) is the ratio of the number of moles of a component to the total number of moles of all the components.

$$X = \frac{moles \ component}{moles \ all \ components}$$

Molarity (M) is the number of moles of solute in a liter of solution.

$$M = \frac{moles \ solute}{liters \ solution}$$

The *molality* (m) of a solution is the number of moles of solute in a kilogram of solvent.

$$m = \frac{moles \ solute}{kilograms \ solvent}$$

Acids and bases

Acids and bases are characterized by their opposite effects in certain physical and chemical properties and their ability to neutralize each other in a chemical reaction.

Definitions and properties. Over the years, scientists have tried to explain the fact that all acids and bases show certain characteristic properties. Two important theories that explain these properties are the Arrhenius theory and the Brønsted–Lowry theory.

The Arrhenius theory. In 1884, the chemist Svante Arrhenius observed that all substances classified as acids contain hydrogen ions, H^+, and that all substances known as bases contain the hydroxide ion, OH^-. An *Arrhenius acid* was thus identified as a substance whose water solution contains a high concentration of hydrogen ions, and an *Arrhenius base* was identified as a substance whose water solution contains a high concentration of hydroxide ions.

The Brønsted–Lowry theory. In 1923, Johannes Brønsted and Thomas Lowry independently announced that an acid-base reaction is a proton-transfer reaction in which a proton (a hydrogen ion) is transferred from the acid to the base. According to this theory, a *Brønsted acid* can be defined as a proton donor, and a *Brønsted base* is a proton acceptor. The general equation for a Brønsted–Lowry reaction is:

$$B + HA \rightarrow HB^+ + A^-,$$

where B is the base proton receiver and HA is the acid proton donor. Notice that if this reaction were reversed, then A^- would be the base and HB^+ would be the acid. Combinations such as the acid HA and the base A^- that result from an acid losing a proton or a base gaining one are called *conjugate acid-base pairs*.

Strengths of acids and bases. According to the Brønsted–Lowry theory, *acid strength* is a measure of the tendency of an acid to lose protons. A *strong acid* donates protons easily, while a *weak acid* clings to its protons. A *strong base* has a strong attraction for protons; a *weak base* has a weak attraction for protons. In addition, the strengths of conjugate acid-base pairs are related: the stronger the acid, the weaker its conjugate base; the weaker the acid, the stronger its conjugate base.

Equilibrium constants and pH.
Water spontaneously ionizes into H^+ and OH^- ions. The product of the concentrations of these ions is called the *equilibrium constant* for the ionization of water and given the symbol K_w. At 25°C,

$$K_w = [H^+][OH^-] = 1.0 \times 10^{-14}.$$

In this formula, the $[H^+]$ and $[OH^-]$ are the concentrations of the hydrogen ion and the hydroxide ion, respectively.

Theoretically, the concentrations of H^+ and OH^- are equal in pure water. If the concentrations are equal, the water or aqueous solution is said to be *neutral*. If $[H^+]$ is greater than $[OH^-]$, the solution is *acidic*; if $[H^+]$ is less than $[OH^-]$, the solution is *basic*.

For convenience, the hydrogen-ion concentration of a solution is commonly expressed in terms of *pH*, which is equal to the negative logarithm of the hydrogen ion concentration: $pH = -\log[H^+]$. Most solutions have a pH range of 0 to 14. Solutions with pH less than 7 are acidic; those with pH greater than 7 are basic, and those with pH equal to 7 are neutral.

Common acids and their conjugate bases

Acid		Base	
Hydrochloric acid	(HCl)	Chloride ion	(Cl^-)
Nitric acid	(HNO_3)	Nitrate ion	(NO_3^-)
Hydrocyanic acid	(HCN)	Cyanide ion	(CN^-)
Perchloric acid	($HClO_4$)	Perchlorate ion	(ClO_4^-)
Sulfuric acid	(H_2SO_4)	Hydrogen sulfate ion	(HSO_4^-)

Oxidation and reduction

When metallic and nonmetallic elements join together to form ionic compounds, the overall reactions can be considered as two separate steps—the loss of an electron by the metal, and the gain of an electron by the nonmetal. Each of these reactions is called a *half-reaction*. The half-reaction that involves loss of electrons is called an *oxidation reaction*. The half-reaction that involves gain of electrons is called a *reduction reaction*. When the two half-reactions are combined, the result is an *oxidation-reduction reaction*, or *redox reaction*.

In a redox reaction, the substance that loses electrons is *oxidized*, while the substance that gains electrons is *reduced*. Oxidation and reduction always occur together. The total number of electrons lost by the reducing agent must equal the number of electrons gained by the oxidizing agent. For example, during the formation of MgO, there are two half-reactions: Mg loses two electrons to become Mg^{2+} and O gains two electrons to become O^{2-}. In this case, Mg is oxidized and is the reducing agent because it loses two electrons; O is reduced and is the oxidizing agent because it accepts two electrons.

Oxidation numbers.

In some redox reactions, it is very easy to determine which substance has gained electrons and which has lost electrons. But many redox reactions are not so readily analyzed. For this reason, chemists have created a form of "electron bookkeeping" to keep track of electrons in chemical reactions. This "bookkeeping" is accomplished by using *oxidation numbers*, which are numbers assigned to each element in a compound, ion, or elemental species based on the following rules:

- The oxidation number of any uncombined element is 0.
- The oxidation number of a monoatomic ion is the same as the charge on the ion.
- The oxidation number of combined oxygen is -2, except in peroxide (-1), and superoxides (-1/2).
- The oxidation number of combined hydrogen is +1, except in hydrides (-1).
- The oxidation number of combined fluorine is -1.
- In any molecular or ionic species, the sum of the oxidation numbers of all atoms in the formula unit is equal to the charge on the species.

When using oxidation numbers, oxidation is an increase in oxidation number, and reduction is a decrease in oxidation number.

Balancing redox reactions.

There are two main ways to balance redox reactions: the oxidation-number method, and the half-reaction method.

Oxidation-number method. This method of balancing redox reactions is based on identifying and following changes in oxidation numbers. The procedure involves the following steps:

1. Write the overall unbalanced equation.
2. Assign oxidation numbers to the atoms in each element on both sides of the equation and determine which elements have been oxidized and which have been reduced.
3. Assign coefficients to make the total gain in oxidation numbers for the substances being oxidized equal to the total decrease in oxidation numbers for the substances being reduced.
4. Balance the remaining atoms by inspection. For reactions in acidic solution, add H^+ or H_2O or both to the equation as needed. For reactions in basic solutions, add OH^- or H_2O or both to the equation as needed.

Half-reaction method. In this method, the overall equation is divided into two reactions—one for oxidation and one for reduction. The equations for the two half-reactions are balanced separately and then added to give the overall balanced equation. The steps for this method are as follows:

1. Write the overall unbalanced equation, then divide the overall reaction into two equations, one for oxidation and the other for reduction.
2. Balance the atoms in each half-reaction that undergo oxidation or reduction, then balance the elements other than H and O.
3. Balance the O atoms by adding H_2O and balance the H atoms by adding H^+. If the reaction is in a basic solution, then also add an OH^- ion for every H^+ ion. If H^+ and OH^- appear on the same side, combine the ion to form H_2O.
4. Balance charge on each side of the equation by adding e^- to the side with the greater positive charge. If necessary, equalize the number of electrons by multiplying one or both half-reactions by the appropriate coefficients.
5. Add the two half-reactions together and balance the final equation by inspection.

Reactions and equilibrium

It is not only important to be able to predict whether or not a reaction will take place; it is also important to calculate how fast a reaction occurs and how far the reaction will go before it is finished.

Reaction rates.
The area of chemistry concerned with the speeds, or rates, at which a chemical reaction occurs is called *chemical kinetics*. According to the *kinetic theory of chemical reactions*, reactions occur as a result of collisions between molecules. Not all collisions result in reactions—a reaction occurs only when molecules collide with enough energy to break the bonds and initiate the reaction. The minimum energy required for a reaction is called the *activation energy*.

When a reaction occurs, the *rate* of the reaction describes how the concentration of reactant or product changes over time. The rate of a reaction can be calculated using the ratio of the change in concentration of a reactant or product to the time interval required for the observed concentration change.

Factors affecting rates.
There are three factors that can influence the rate of a reaction: temperature, catalysts, and concentration.
Temperature. Chemical reactions are faster at higher temperatures. This is primarily because an increase in temperature increases the number of particles with sufficient kinetic energy to overcome the activation energy barrier.
Catalysts. A *catalyst* is a substance that increases the rate of a chemical reaction by lowering the activation energy for the reaction. Catalysts exist in several different forms—some are mixed in with the reacting chemicals, while others seem to provide a surface upon which the reaction may occur. Regardless of its form, a catalyst is not permanently affected by the reaction.

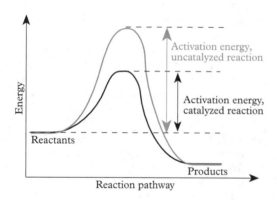

A catalyst lowers the activation energy for a reaction.

Concentration. The initial concentration of the reactants can also influence reaction rate. Generally, it can be stated that the higher the concentration, the faster the reaction.

Chemical equilibrium.
Few chemical reactions proceed in only one direction. Instead, most are *reversible*. At the start of a reversible reaction, the reaction proceeds toward the formation of products. Then, as soon as some product molecules are formed, the formation of reactant molecules from product molecules begins to take place. When the rates of the forward and reverse reactions are equal, a state of *chemical equilibrium* exists. In a system at equilibrium, the concentrations of reactants and products no longer change with time. The relative concentrations of reactants and products at equilibrium can be expressed in terms of a quantity called the *equilibrium constant* (K).

Factors affecting equilibrium.
Chemical equilibrium represents a balance between forward and reverse reactions. In most cases, this balance is quite delicate and can be easily disturbed by change. A rule, known as *Le Châtelier's principle*, makes it possible to predict the direction in which an equilibrium will shift if some change causes the forward and reverse reactions to become unequal.
Concentration changes. If a system is at equilibrium, an increase in the concentration of a reactant or product will shift the reaction in the direction that uses more of that substance, so that equilibrium is reestablished. A decrease in the concentration of a reactant or product will shift the reaction in the direction that forms more of that substance.
Pressure and volume changes. Changes in pressure and volume ordinarily do not affect the concentrations of liquids and solids. However, a change in pressure or volume will affect a system that includes one or more gases. In general, an increased pressure (or decreased volume) will shift the reaction in the direction that decreases the total number of gas molecules, and a decreased pressure (or increased volume) will shift the reaction in the direction that increases the total number of gas molecules.
Temperature changes. A change in temperature not only changes both forward and reverse reaction rates, but also changes the value of the equilibrium constant. In general, when heat is added to an equilibrium system, the reaction shifts in the direction that absorbs heat; when heat is removed from an equilibrium system, the reaction shifts in the direction that gives off heat.

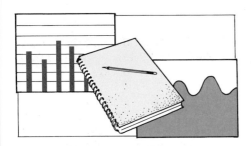

Chemistry

Tests, homework, and lab reports

Laying the groundwork

Students of a natural science such as chemistry must understand the basic concepts and principles before attempting to solve assigned problems. Read assigned material carefully before attending the lecture on that material, and jot down points that are not clear to you. Focus on key concepts and skills, particularly the skills stressed in the homework exercises. Keep in mind that several readings of the text may be necessary—few people are able to absorb the full meaning of scientific material after one reading. It is also important to keep up with your studying day to day. In chemistry, new material builds on the old. It is important not to fall behind. Lectures and laboratory work should supplement the text and clarify some of the more difficult material. Ask questions whenever necessary. Your understanding of the material will be enhanced through a combination of effective study habits, discussions with other students and instructors, and your ability to solve the assigned problems.

Strategies for success

Learning chemistry involves learning several key skills: using a basic chemical vocabulary, writing routine chemical formulas and names, writing and balancing chemical equations, solving chemical problems, and visualizing what happens during chemical reactions on the atomic or molecular level. Memorizing the periodic table is the first step in learning these skills. It is also important to recognize how to apply your knowledge. Make use of the examples and exercises in your text using the following routine:

1. Study the examples carefully. Identify both the steps taken in the examples and why those steps were taken. Try working through each example as you read.
2. Identify the knowns and unknowns in each exercise problem. Then select the most appropriate method for solving the problem. Write out each step in the solution.
3. Check your work. Examine the reasonableness of the solution and the process you used.

Helpful hints

Tests

> Potassium iodide is the additive in "iodized" table salt. Calculate the molarity of a solution prepared by dissolving 3.59 g of potassium iodide in water and diluting to 50.0 mL.

On tests, your professor is usually more concerned with how you approach a problem than the actual answer to a problem. Therefore, it is important to use the same problem-solving strategy during a test as you use on homework problems. Be sure to clearly show all your work—you will often get points for setting up a problem correctly, even if your final answer is wrong. Don't spend time before the test trying to learn all the equations. Instead focus on how the concepts are related. Remember that some questions are qualitative, and require essay answers. These problems usually include words such as *describe*, *suggest*, or *explain*. Quantitative questions require calculations, and include words such as *calculate*, *find*, and *how many*.

Lab reports

> Treat the amine, aniline, with acetic anhydride to form the amide, acetanilide.

Lab work allows you to apply theoretical knowledge, learn the techniques for using equipment, and practice data collection and recording. Before starting a lab, try to understand the procedure of the experiment and the theory underlying it. Also review all lab safety techniques that may apply to the experiment. This is extremely important! Once in the lab, carefully record in a notebook the question you are trying to answer, the procedure and equipment you are using, your observations during the experiment, your calculations, and your conclusions. It is important to make sure that you record exactly what you do during a lab and the observations you made. The exact format you use for your records will depend on your instructor.

Glossary

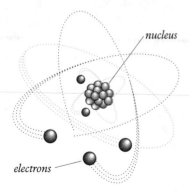

nucleus

electrons

Bohr model

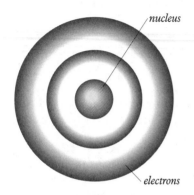

nucleus

electrons

Electron-cloud model

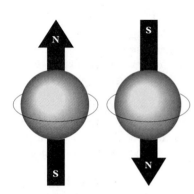

Electron spin

absolute dating. A system of determining how long ago a geologic event occurred.

absolute zero. The temperature where kinetic energy theoretically becomes zero; zero on the Kelvin temperature scale, which is equivalent to -273.15°C.

acid. A substance that yields hydrogen atoms in aqueous solution (Arrhenius definition); a substance that donates protons in a chemical reaction (Brønsted–Lowry definition).

activation energy. The energy barrier that must be overcome to start a chemical reaction.

anion. An ion with a net negative charge.

atom. The smallest particle of an element that can combine with atoms of other elements to form chemical compounds.

atomic mass unit (amu). A unit of mass that is exactly 1/12 of the mass of an atom of carbon 12.

atomic number. The number of protons in an atom of an element.

atomic weight. The average mass of the atoms of an element expressed in atomic mass units.

Avogadro's number. The number of units in 1 mole (6.02×10^{23}).

base. A substance that yields hydroxide ions in aqueous solution (Arrhenius definition); a substance that accepts protons in a chemical reaction (Brønsted–Lowry definition).

catalyst. A substance that increases the rate of a chemical reaction by lowering activation energy.

cation. An ion with a net positive charge.

chemical bond. A general term that sometimes includes all of the electrostatic attractions among atoms, molecules, and ions, but more often refers to covalent and ionic bonds.

chemical equilibrium. A chemical state in which no net change can be observed.

compound. A pure substance that can be broken down into two or more other pure substances by a chemical change.

conjugate acid-base pair. A Brønsted–Lowry acid and the base derived from it when it loses a proton; or a Brønsted–Lowry base and the acid developed from it when it accepts a proton.

covalent bond. The chemical bond between two atoms that share a pair of electrons.

crystalline solid. A solid in which the ions and/or molecules are arranged in a definite geometric pattern.

dipole forces. Forces between polar molecules.

dispersion forces. Weak electrical attractions between molecules, that can be temporarily produced by the shifting of electrons within molecules.

electron. A subatomic particle carrying a unit negative charge found outside the nucleus of an atom.

electron configuration. The orbital arrangement of electrons in ions or atoms.

element. A pure substance that cannot be decomposed into other pure substances by ordinary chemical means.

empirical formula. A formula that shows the types of elements present and the ratios of the different kinds of atoms.

enthalpy. The heat content of a chemical system.

excited state. The state of an atom in which one or more electrons have absorbed energy to raise them to energy levels above ground state.

formula weight. The weight in amu of one formula unit of a substance.

ground state. The state of an atom in which all electrons occupy the lowest possible energy levels.

heat of reaction. Change of enthalpy in a chemical reaction.

ideal gas. A hypothetical gas that behaves according to the ideal gas model over all ranges of temperature and pressure.

ideal gas law. The equation $PV = nRT$ that relates quantitatively the pressure, volume, quantity, and temperature of an ideal gas.

intermolecular forces. Forces that exist among molecules.

ion. A charged particle formed when a neutral atom or group of atoms gain or lose one or more electrons.

ionic bond. The chemical bond arising from the attraction forces between oppositely charged ions in an ionic compound.

ionic compound. A compound in which ions are held by ionic bonds.

isotope. Two or more atoms of the same element that have different atomic masses because of different numbers of neutrons.

Lewis diagram. A diagram representing the valence electrons and covalent bonds in an atomic or molecular species.

line spectra. The spectral lines that appear when light emitted from a sample is analyzed in a spectroscope.

matter. That which occupies space and has mass.

metal. A substance which possesses metallic properties; an element that loses electrons to form monatomic cations.

mixture. A sample of matter containing two or more pure substances.

mole. The quantity of any species that contains the same number of units as the number of atoms in exactly 12 grams of carbon 12.

molecular formula. A formula showing exact numbers of atoms of each element in a molecule.

molecular geometry. A description of the shape of a molecule.

molecular weight. The number that expresses the average mass of the molecules of a compound compared to the mass of an atom of carbon 12 at a value of exactly 12.

molecule. The smallest unit particle of a pure substance that can exist independently and possess the identity of the substance.

neutron. An electrically neutral subatomic particle found in the nucleus of the atom.

nonmetal. Elements that are usually poor conductors of electricity.

nonpolar molecule. A molecule having a symmetrical distribution of electric charge.

nucleus. The extremely dense central portion of the atom that contains the neutrons and protons.

octet rule. The general rule that atoms tend to form bonds until they are surrounded by eight valence electrons.

orbit. The circular or elliptical path supposedly followed by an electron around the atomic nucleus.

orbital. The mathematically described region within an atom in which there is a high probability that an electron will be found.

oxidation. A chemical reaction with oxygen; a chemical change in which the oxidation number of an element is increased.

oxidation number. A number assigned to each element in a compound, ion, or elemental species by an established set of rules.

pH. A way of expressing hydrogen-ion concentration; the negative of the logarithm of the hydrogen-ion concentration.

polar molecule. A molecule having an unsymmetrical distribution of electric charge.

precipitate. A solid that forms when two solutions are mixed.

principal energy levels. The main energy levels within the electron arrangement in an atom.

products. The substances created by a chemical reaction.

proton. A subatomic particle carrying a unit positive charge found in the nucleus of the atom.

pure substance. A sample consisting of only one kind of matter, either compound or element.

reactants. The original substances used in a chemical reaction.

redox reaction. A reaction that involves a transfer of electrons.

reduction. A chemical change in which the oxidation number of an element is reduced; the gain of electrons in a redox reaction.

solubility. The quantity of solute that will dissolve in a given quantity of solvent.

solute. The substance dissolved in the solvent.

solution. A homogeneous mixture of two or more substances.

solvent. The medium in which the solute is dissolved.

states of matter. The states in which matter can exist—gases, liquids, or solids.

stoichiometry. The quantitative relationships between substances involved in a chemical reaction.

valence electrons. The outer electrons of an atom, which are involved in chemical bonding.

For further reading

Brown, T. L., H. E. LeMay, and B. E. Bursten. *Chemistry: The Central Science.* 6th ed. Englewood Cliffs, N.J.: Prentice-Hall, 1994.

Daintith, J., ed. *Dictionary of Chemistry.* New York: Warner Books, 1986.

Hoffmann, Roald. *The Same and Not the Same.* New York: Columbia University Press, 1995.

Snyder, C. H. *The Extraordinary Chemistry of Ordinary Things.* 2nd ed. New York: Wiley and Sons, 1995.

Geology

Although the earth seems stable and permanent, it is constantly changing—molten rock within the earth churns and spews out onto the surface. Huge land masses collide and crumple. Wind and water carve deep canyons and destroy mountains. *Geology* is the study of the earth, its composition, the processes by which it was formed, and the forces (both external and internal) that continue to change it. *Earth science* encompasses geology as well as oceanography, meteorology, and other like sciences. Astronomy and cosmology, for example, promote an understanding of the earth's position in the universe. Applying biology and geography helps scientists understand the relationship between the planet and the organisms that inhabit it.

The earth's structure

The physical environment of the earth is divided into three major parts: the solid earth, which consists of several layers known as the crust, the mantle, and the core; the liquid *hydrosphere*, which includes the oceans, rivers, lakes, and glaciers; and the gaseous *atmosphere*, which incorporates the layer of gases that surrounds the earth.

The outermost layer of the earth, the *crust*, is a 10- to 40-km-thick layer of rock and soil that covers the earth like a skin. There are two forms of crust: *continental crust* and *oceanic crust*. Beneath the crust is the *mantle*, which is about 2,900 km thick. The boundary separating the crust and mantle is called the *Moho*. At the center of the earth is the *core*, which consists of two parts: the *outer core*, a 2,270-km-thick layer of molten iron and nickel; and the solid *inner core*, which is 1,216 km thick. The crust and the upper mantle, to a depth of about a hundred kilometers beneath the surface, form the *lithosphere*, a rigid shell of rock. This shell rests on the *asthenosphere*, a relatively fluid, partially molten layer of the upper mantle, also about a hundred kilometers deep.

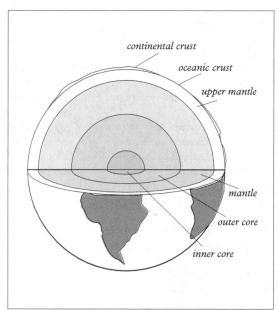

Cross section of the earth

Rocks and minerals.

Scattered throughout the earth's crust are inorganic crystalline solids, known as *minerals*. Minerals contain elements such as oxygen, aluminum, iron, and magnesium. Minerals are identified by various physical properties, including crystal shape, color, streak (color in powdered form), luster (light-reflecting property), hardness ("scratchability"), and cleavage (tendency to split along certain planes). *Rock* consists of one or more minerals. There are three major classes of rock: igneous, sedimentary, and metamorphic. The way a rock is formed determines the class to which the rock belongs.

Igneous rock. *Igneous rock* is formed when *magma* (molten material from deep in the earth's crust) cools and solidifies—a process known as *crystallization*. This process takes place either beneath the earth's surface or, more often, on the surface as a result of volcanic eruption. Igneous rock that formed at the surface is known as *volcanic* or *extrusive*; igneous rock that cooled underground is called *plutonic* or *intrusive*.

Igneous rock is classified by both its composition and texture. The texture depends mainly on the rate at which the magma cooled. At great depths, magma may take millions of years to cool. At the surface, it crystallizes quickly. A slow rate of cooling results in a larger crystalline structure, hence a coarse texture. Granite, a common igneous rock, is formed as a result of slow cooling beneath the earth's surface. A fast cooling rate tends to produce finely textured rock with small crystals. A rapid cooling rate at the earth's surface may produce glassy igneous rock (obsidian, for example) in which crystals have not adequately formed.

Sedimentary rock. Unlike other types of rock, *sedimentary rock* always forms at the earth's surface. Exposed rock tends to break down into smaller particles through weathering. The solid particles, or *sediment*, are carried away by wind, water, and ice, and deposited in valleys, seas, lakes, and elsewhere. As sediment accumulates, it is compressed by its own weight and cemented by various minerals to form sedimentary rock. Sedimentary rock also forms when solid particles dissolve in water (usually sea water) that eventually evaporates and leaves a chemical precipitate behind. Sedimentary rock is classified both by mineral composition and by particle size. Shale, limestone, sandstone, and coal are all sedimentary rocks.

Metamorphic rock. When existing igneous or sedimentary rock is exposed to extreme heat or pressure, the mineral composition or texture of the rock may be altered. This process, known as *metamorphism*, takes place deep in the earth's crust. The resulting *metamorphic rock* can be distinguished from the original rock type by composition and texture. For example, marble—a metamorphic rock—looks quite different from its original form, which is limestone. There are several types of metamorphism. *Regional metamorphism* occurs when rock is compressed beneath developing mountains; the extreme pressure changes the texture of the rock. *Contact metamorphism* occurs when a rock is altered by heat from nearby magma. Metamorphism also may occur through contact with chemically active gases or liquids from nearby magma. In that case, the chemical composition of such metamorphic rock may be altered.

Stratigraphy

Layers of sedimentary rock, or strata, provide evidence of the changes that have taken place over time on the earth's surface. The study of strata for such purposes is called *stratigraphy*. Specific types of sedimentary rock offer clues about the environment that existed at the time the rock was forming. They may reveal, for example, that the region had a dry or humid climate, that the sediment settled in a fast-moving streambed or a still and shallow lake, or that the region supported abundant plantlife. Geologic changes such as uplifting and faulting of the crust also are recorded in the strata. Fossils, or the remains of organisms left or imprinted in settling sediment, are of special significance in paleontology because they leave a record of life on earth.

Landforms.

Landforms are the physical features of the earth's surface. Continents and ocean basins form the most fundamental types of landform. The continents contain mountain ranges, valleys, and plateaus, while ocean basins contain ridges, trenches, and plains. Each of these also contains smaller-scale features.

Most landforms are the result of tectonic forces in the earth's crust and superficial processes such as erosion and deposition. Landforms created by the flow of water are known as *fluvial* landforms; valleys, flood plains, deltas, and alluvial fans (which occur at the mouths of canyons) are the most common fluvial landforms. Landforms shaped by the wind (sand dunes, for example) are called *aeolian* landforms.

Oceans.

About 71 percent of the earth's surface is covered by the water of the oceans and seas. The average depth of this water is 3.8 kilometers—nearly five times greater than the average elevation (above sea level) of the continents.

Ocean basins can be divided into three main topographic regions: continental margins, ocean basin floors, and mid-ocean ridges. The *continental margin,* the portion of the ocean floor that is adjacent to the continents, may be further divided into several regions as it slopes from the continental crust to the oceanic crust: the *continental shelf,* which dips gently from the shoreline; the *continental slope,* which drops dramatically from the continental shelf to the deep ocean floor; the *continental rise,* which is the gently sloping surface at the base of the continental slope; and the *abyssal plain,* a level area of the ocean floor at the base

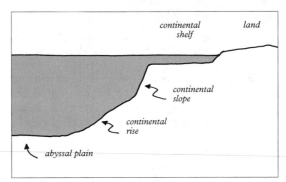

The continental margin

of the continental rise. The *ocean floor* offers diverse geological features, including mountain ranges (called *mid-ocean ridges*), valleys and canyons, deep-ocean trenches, and underwater volcanoes (called *seamounts*).

The topographic regions of the ocean basins have been shaped by a number of forces. Powerful underwater streams, called *turbidity currents,* carve huge V-shaped clefts into the continental slope. Some of the material eroding from these canyons cuts channels into the continental rise. Tectonic forces form the immense mountain ranges and underwater volcanoes.

Nearly all elements found on earth are found in ocean water. Two processes contribute to the presence of these elements: the weathering of rocks on the continents, and the emission of gases from the earth's interior during volcanic eruptions. Some elements (in particular chlorine, bromine, sulfur, and boron) are present in greater quantities in ocean water than in the earth's crust; this fact is evidence that volcanic eruptions contributed to the development of oceans.

Plate tectonics

The theory of plate tectonics developed in the 1960s, after ocean research yielded evidence of *seafloor spreading* (the formation of new crust along specific zones in the ocean floor). The theory of plate tectonics provides an explanation for this phenomenon, and also incorporates the earlier idea of *continental drift,* which describes the global movement of land masses.

Continental drift.

The concept of continental drift was first proposed in 1912 by Alfred Wegener, a German meteorologist. Wegener proposed that all of the continents had at one time been joined together to form a "supercontinent," which he referred to as *Pangaea.* This supercontinent was surrounded by one ocean, now considered to be the ancestral ocean of the Pacific. Wegener also proposed that forces beneath the earth's surface, and in conjunction with

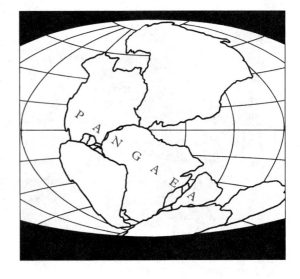

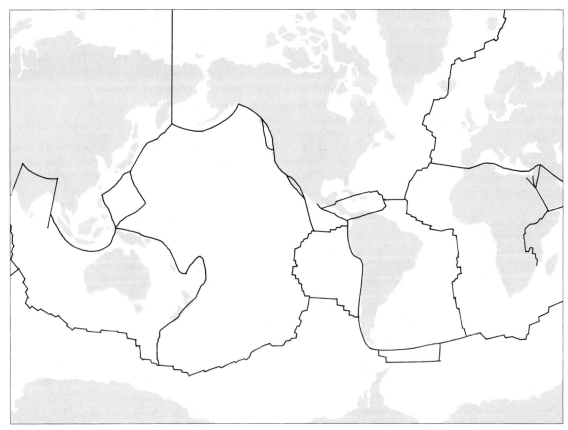

The lithospheric plates

the earth's rotational movement, caused the continents to break apart, at first creating two separate oceans—the Atlantic and the Indian.

Long before Wegener, scientists noticed that the shapes of the continents (especially the west coast of Africa and the east coast of South America) seemed to match like pieces in a puzzle. (Modern oceanographic studies reveal that the continents could indeed fit together like puzzle pieces, with little overlapping and few gaps.) In fact, not only do the continents match in shape, but they match in geologic structure. However, it was not until the 1960s that Wegener's ideas were generally accepted.

Seafloor spreading.

Seafloor spreading is the process by which new crust is formed between diverging crustal plates on the ocean floor. In 1960, Harry H. Hess, an American geologist, first proposed this process. His hypothesis provided an explanation for earlier oceanographic research that revealed a surprisingly thin layer of sediment on top of the mainly young volcanic ocean floor. Previously, most geologists believed that the ocean floor consisted of continental sediment washed into the ocean; they expected to find older rock at the bottom of the ocean.

Geologists now accept that the continents contain older crust, and that crust is continually renewed and consumed on the ocean floor between crustal plates.

Along the ocean floor is a network of mid-ocean ridges. These ridges mark the boundaries where new crust is continuously forming. Magma rises in small valleys in the crust (called *rifts*) along the crests of mid-ocean ridges. The magma cools in the ocean water and hardens, adding new crust. The rate of spreading is from one to ten centimeters per year (at least ten kilometers per million years).

Plates and plate boundaries.

According to the theory of plate tectonics, the outer layer of the earth is composed of approximately ten major *lithospheric plates* and about twenty minor ones. The rigid lithospheric plates rest, or "float," on the surface of the partially molten (sometimes called "plastic") asthenosphere. Each plate moves as a unit, independently of surrounding plates. The *plate boundaries*, zones along which two or more plates meet, are a focus of activity, where mountain building, earthquakes, and volcanoes often occur. The location of the plates and their boundaries slowly shifts over geologic time. It is uncertain exactly how plate movement occurs; one explanation suggests that a system of thermal convection currents in the upper mantle creates the force that generates plate movement.

Plate boundaries are classified according to the type of movement that occurs there. When geologists describe plate motion, they refer to the movement of plates relative to each other, not in terms of absolute motion. There are three types of possible movements: the two adjacent plates either move away from each other, move toward each other, or slide sideways along each other's edges. As movement occurs at one boundary, this movement must be compensated for along another boundary. For example, if two plates move toward each other, consuming crust, there is likely to be spreading and the creation of new crust along their opposite edges.

Diverging plates. When two plates move away from each other, they create a spreading center, or *divergent boundary*. This type of boundary, usually located along an ocean ridge, is associated with seafloor spreading. Activity at diverging plates eventually produces new crust on the ocean floor.

The Atlantic Ocean formed as a result of diverging plates. As two plates began to spread apart, magma rose from beneath the lithosphere, breaking through and adding to the existing crust. As spreading continued, a shallow sea formed in the valley, which then became broader and deeper. A mid-ocean ridge, now called the Mid-Atlantic Ridge, formed along the rift site. This ridge is part of an interconnected underwater mountain chain that runs about 64,000 kilometers around and through all of the ocean basins.

Converging plates. When two plates collide, the boundary is referred to as a *convergent boundary*. At these boundaries, the edge of one plate usually is forced underneath the edge of the adjacent plate—a process which is referred to as *subduction*. Regions where subduction occurs are known as *subduction zones*. During the process of subduction, crust is destroyed.

Convergent boundaries can bring together regions of ocean crust and continental crust, two ocean crusts, or two continental crusts. When converging plates bring ocean crust and continental crust together, the heavier ocean crust generally slips down into the asthenosphere, creating a deep-ocean trench. As the subducting edge of the plate descends into the hot asthenosphere, it melts, rises as magma, and forms volcanoes. This type of collision occurred at the boundary between the Nazca plate and the South American plate; the Nazca plate subducted beneath the South American plate, pushing up the Andes. A similar result occurs when converging plates bring together two regions of ocean crust. The Mariana Islands, for example, formed when the Pacific plate subducted beneath the Philippine plate. When two continental crustal plates collide, however, neither plate subducts. Rather, the crust is forced upward and deformed, creating a mountain range, as happened when India collided with Asia and formed the Himalayas.

Transform boundaries. The movement of plates sliding sideways past each other neither creates new crust (as does plate divergence) nor loses existing crust

Geomagnetism

The earth's magnetic field is thought to be caused by an electric current generated by fluid metals in the outer core. The field radiates from the north and south magnetic poles, which are near (but not aligned with) the geographic poles of the earth's rotational axis. The study of *paleomagnetism*, how the earth's magnetic field has changed through time, provides additional evidence for the theory of plate tectonics. Geologists have discovered that rocks, whether created today or millions of years ago, retain their original magnetic alignment, even though their geographic location today may not match their original geographic position and magnetic "signature." Data from seafloor exploration show that the polarity of the earth's magnetic field has reversed many times throughout geologic time, and these reversals are recorded in the rocks as seafloor spreading occurs.

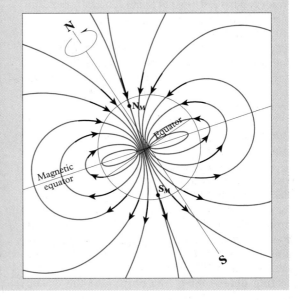

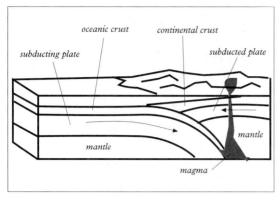

Subduction zones

(as does plate convergence). Rather, this movement creates breaks in the crust, called *transform faults*. The meeting of the North American plate and the Pacific plate along the coast of California is one example of this type of boundary; the Pacific plate moves in a northwest direction relative to the North American plate, creating the San Andreas fault.

Plate movement.
About 230 million years ago, Pangaea began to break apart into two subcontinents—Laurasia in the northern hemisphere and Gondwanaland in the southern hemisphere. The two subcontinents were joined at Gibraltar, with the newly forming Atlantic Ocean to the west and the Tethys Sea to the east.

A rift in Gondwanaland formed a Y-shaped fracture, causing India to break off and move north toward Asia, and separating South America–Africa from Australia–Antarctica. By 135 million years ago, Africa and South America were starting to split apart to form the South Atlantic. The plates continued to move and split apart. As of 45 million years ago, North America and Eurasia separated, Africa separated from Eurasia, and Madagascar separated from Africa. In addition, India collided with Asia, Australia broke from Antarctica and drifted northward, and South America and North America (which had split completely from Europe) drifted toward each other and eventually were bridged.

As the plates continue to move, the Pacific Ocean grows smaller, the Atlantic and Indian oceans grow larger, and the positions of land masses continue to change in relation to one another. A narrow sliver of land west of the San Andreas fault in California will continue for millions of years to drift northward toward Alaska. As the Arabian peninsula moves north to join Asia, and Africa drifts northwest toward Europe, the Red Sea will continue to widen. Eventually, East African rift valleys will split from the continent of Africa, and Australia will drift northward and bump into Asia.

Geologic processes

Over millions of years, mountains have crumbled and been created, valleys have broadened into huge plains, and deep chasms have opened. Most of the forces and processes that have created these changes are so slow and gentle they are barely noticeable. Others, such as volcanoes and earthquakes, are quite abrupt. Large-scale forces that deform the earth's crust are called *tectonic forces*.

Different processes affect the earth's surface in different ways. On one hand, erosion and weathering cause an overall lowering and wearing down of landforms on the earth's surface. Tectonic activity, on the other hand, works in opposition, lifting the crust upward. These opposing but balanced destructive and creative forces are constantly in the process of changing the landscape.

Volcanoes.
A *volcano* is a type of mountain that forms as a result of tectonic activity. Unlike other mountains, volcanoes encompass pipelines that release matter from the earth's interior. Because of this, volcanoes allow scientists to observe processes that occur

> **Why studying geology pays off**
>
> **Reason #1**
>
> Understanding the processes that shape the earth help scientists predict future changes.

many kilometers below the earth's surface. A volcano is actually an accumulation of matter that has spewed from an opening in the crust, collecting and building up around the opening. The opening often is located at the volcano's peak; this large depression is called a *crater*. Lava can also erupt from fissures along the flank of a volcano.

There are about five hundred active volcanoes on earth, and the most powerful eruptions take place where plates collide. The Pacific Rim is often called the "ring of fire" because of the many active volcanoes around the Pacific plate. Volcanic eruptions also occur where crustal plates are separating.

Eruptions. A volcanic eruption occurs when magma rises through a vent leading from a magma chamber deep within the earth's crust. The main products of an erupting volcano are *lava* (molten rock), gases (steam, carbon dioxide, nitrogen, sulfur dioxide, and other gases), and *pyroclastic* material. Pyroclastic fragments include pumice, rock, cinders, and ash propelled into the air by superheated volcanic gases and ejected by the force of the eruption.

The chemical composition of magma as well as the quantity and content of gases determine how violent a volcanic eruption will be. Molten rhyolite contains a high percentage of silica, which gives it a higher viscosity and results in violent eruptions. Rhyolitic magma also contains a large quantity of dissolved gases and fluids. Molten basalt contains less silica, is thinner, and has less dissolved gases, resulting in gentler eruptions. Magma composition affects not only the violence of the eruption but also the shape and size of volcano that forms.

Types of volcanoes. There are three main types of volcanoes: cinder cones, shield volcanoes, and composite volcanoes. A *cinder cone* is formed by the piling up of pyroclastic cinders ejected from a single vent. Cinder cones, such as Parícutin, in Mexico, are small, with steep slopes. They often develop at the base of larger volcanoes or in clusters.

A *shield volcano* is a very large, broad, gently sloping structure formed by the build-up of successive lava

flows. Eruptions from shield volcanoes are relatively gentle because they release fluid basaltic magma. Slopes of shield volcanoes seldom exceed 8 degrees. Consequently, they take up substantial surface area and are the largest type of volcano. The Hawaiian Islands developed from shield volcanoes.

A *composite volcano* (or stratovolcano) has a classic cone shape made of alternating layers of lava and pyroclastic material. Side vents can feed small volcanoes that develop at the base. Composite volcanoes, such as Vesuvius and Mount St. Helens, can erupt violently and unpredictably. Sometimes, as a volcanic eruption progresses, the magma chamber empties and the volcano collapses in on itself, creating a large depression known as a *caldera*.

Mountain building. The process of
mountain building is called *orogenesis*. Mountains are formed through volcanic activity, by the convergence of crustal plates, and through movement along *faults*— breaks in the earth's crust where movement occurs. Individual mountains are often formed by volcanic activity; great mountain ranges are formed through the

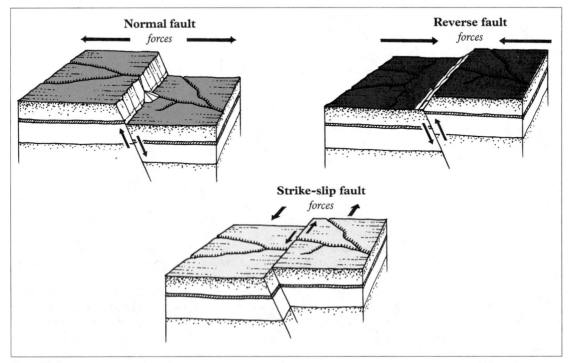

Types of faults

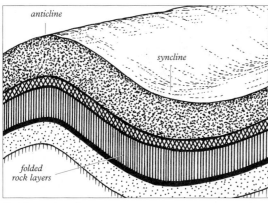

Anticlines and synclines

uplifting and deformation of continental crust driven by tectonic forces.

Crustal deformation. The motion along faults can subject rocks to stresses greater than the strength of the rocks. When this happens, the rocks begin to deform. Rocks can behave plastically by *folding* under pressure, or they can fracture by breaking or *faulting*. Both faulting and folding are associated with mountain building.

There are three main types of faults: normal, reverse, and strike-slip. Along a *normal fault*, the upper block of crust is displaced downward along the dip of the fault plane; movement along this fault is extensional and broadens the area of crust. Along a *reverse fault*, the block of crust above the fault is displaced upward; movement along this fault shortens the crustal area. Movement along a *strike-slip fault* is lateral rather than vertical. This last type of fault is also called a transform fault. When geologists describe fault motion, they refer to the direction that one fault block moves relative to the other. In reality, both blocks or only one may move.

When crust is compressed horizontally, it can bend, forming a series of *folds*. When this happens, the crust grows shorter and thicker. Rocks folded in a concave-down manner are called *anticlines*; folds that are concave-up are called *synclines*. Rocks do not necessarily deform and fold symmetrically; folds can be tilted (plunging), overturned, or asymmetrical.

Types of mountains. Mountains are classified by the main processes that cause their outstanding features. *Upwarped mountains* are created when a region is lifted without breaking the crust, sometimes forming an arch. The Black Hills of South Dakota are an example of upwarped mountains. *Fault block mountains* form when blocks of crust are tilted upward along normal faults. The Sierra Nevada of California is an example of a fault block mountain range. All major mountain chains are *folded mountains*, characterized by folds of sedimentary rock, caused by horizontal pressure.

Earthquakes. An *earthquake* is a vibration in the earth's crust, caused by a sudden release of energy. Earthquakes occur most often along plate boundaries, but they also have been known to occur along all types of faults.

When an earthquake occurs, energy is released in the form of shock waves, or *seismic waves*, in all directions from its point of origin, called the *focus*, located deep inside the crust. (The *epicenter* is the point directly above the focus on the earth's surface.)

Earthquakes generate three kinds of seismic waves: P-waves (short for "primary waves"), S-waves (short for "secondary waves"), and surface waves. Each of these three types of waves behaves in a unique way. *P-waves* are like springs that are compressed and released; they cause particles of matter to vibrate back and forth along the direction of travel. *S-waves*, on the other hand, cause particles of matter to vibrate side to side, perpendicular to the direction of travel. *Surface waves* travel only along the ground, causing vertical and horizontal vibrations. P-waves travel somewhat faster than S-waves and arrive at any particular location first.

P-waves and S-waves travel outward from the focus, continuing through the crust and mantle but changing velocity at the Moho. S-waves cannot travel through liquids, thus they cannot penetrate the molten outer core. However, P-waves can travel through liquids. The P-waves are refracted, or bent, at the boundary between the mantle and core, changing direction and velocity but maintaining a path through the core. P-waves will travel all the way through to the other side of the planet. It is from this evidence that geologists know about the internal structure of the earth.

The energy released during an earthquake is related to the magnitude of the quake. A simple scientific instrument called a *seismograph* records the vibrations. Scientists then analyze and interpret the reading, cal-

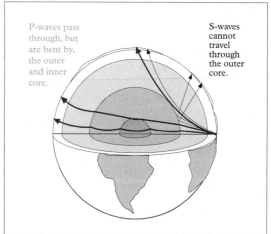

P-waves pass through, but are bent by, the outer and inner core.

S-waves cannot travel through the outer core.

P-waves and S-waves

culating the magnitude. A well-known measure of magnitude is the *Richter scale*—a logarithmic scale for calculating the amount of ground motion. On this scale, a tenfold increase in the amplitude of the wave corresponds to an increase of one on the magnitude scale. In addition, each unit of magnitude increase is equal to roughly a thirtyfold increase in the energy released. Therefore, an earthquake of 5.0, for example, is ten times greater than an earthquake of 4.0, but it will release 31.5 times more energy. A 3.0 quake is scarcely noticeable; 6.0 is considered a moderate quake; 7.5 is a large quake and can cause a great deal of destruction.

Most earthquakes occur without people noticing. About thirty thousand earthquakes occur each year globally that can be detected by seismographs; only a small percentage of these is serious enough to cause damage. Some factors that affect total damage are the location of the epicenter in reference to urban areas, the density and type of underlying rock and soil, the general terrain, and the materials and methods used to construct buildings.

Glaciation.
A *glacier* is a thick, mobile ice mass. Glaciers form only in areas where falling snow accumulates faster than it melts and evaporates. As the snow compacts under its own weight, the snow crystals are transformed into ice crystals. Today, glaciers cover about 10 percent of the earth's land area. However, in the past, ice sheets were three times more extensive, covering vast areas with ice thousands of meters thick. A significant amount of the earth's water is stored in glacial ice.

There are two main types of glaciers: *continental glaciers* are enormous ice masses that cover large land areas and flow in more than one direction; *alpine glaciers* form in high mountain valleys and are shaped like rivers, flowing downward from 2.5 centimeters to 15 meters daily. Like running water, glaciers are in constant motion. As glaciers flow, small stones embedded in the ice gouge the underlying rock, causing striations in the rock. The landforms that are created by glacial flow depend on the type of glacier. In general, alpine glaciers cause more erosion than continental glaciers.

Climate changes cause glaciers to retreat (melt) and advance (increase in size). This shifting should not be confused with glacial flow; a glacier is always moving. Advancing and retreating glaciers leave deposits that remain long after the glacier has moved or melted. These deposits become evidence of past glaciation.

Erosion.
Weathering, mass wasting, and erosion are external processes that alter the earth's surface. *Weathering* is the decomposition of rocks and minerals

Erosion

due to chemical and physical changes. Weathering is caused by water, wind, climate or temperature extremes, forces exerted by organisms (people, animals, tree roots, and so on), or similar factors. *Mass wasting* is the downward shifting of rock and soil due to gravity; rockslides and mudflows are examples of mass wasting. *Erosion* is the shifting of rock particles by wind or moving water, such as streams, tides, or glaciers. The rate at which these external processes take place depends to some extent on climate: a warm, humid climate promotes these processes. The rate of weathering also depends on the composition of the rock: hard rock (such as granite) or chemically stable minerals (such as quartz) will weather more slowly than some softer sedimentary rocks.

Water runoff contributes greatly to erosion, shaping the earth's surface. Particles dissolved in the water, as well as larger particles carried along by the water, dig into the underlying slope and carve out valleys and canyons. Some of the dissolved particles, or *sediment*, are deposited at deltas where the stream or river empties into a lake or ocean. Most sediment eventually collects along the shallow continental slopes and ocean floor. The shape of landforms and their surroundings often reveals the processes by which they were formed. Streams create V-shaped valleys. Alpine glaciers, on the other hand, scoop out U-shaped valleys.

Soil erosion is the transport of topsoil by moving water or wind. Soil, which consists of water, air, mineral matter, and organic matter (microorganisms and decayed plant and animal material), forms continuously as a by-product of weathering. Soil that contains a high percentage of organic matter is better able to support growing plants, which in turn protect soil from erosion. However, in most locations around the earth where topsoil is valued, erosion takes place at a faster rate than soil formation. Agricultural practices and other human activity can also affect the rate of soil erosion. For example, clear-cutting areas tends to increase soil erosion.

Geologic time

Geologists divide the earth's history into four *eras*—Precambrian, Paleozoic, Mesozoic, and Cenozoic. Eras are subdivided into *periods*, which are further subdivided into *epoch*s. "Geologic time scale," found on page 419, charts these blocks of time and notes special features.

The earth's history. Scientists have theorized that the universe was formed through an explosion of matter and energy packed into a single nucleus, or "cosmic egg." The initial explosion, referred to as the "big bang," released subatomic particles that fused to form chemical elements, which eventually composed the stars and other bodies of the universe. Matter thrown outward from the nucleus began to travel through space in ever-expanding swirls of dust and gases, called *nebulae*. The solar system is believed to have developed from such a nebula. The gravitational attraction between the traveling particles caused the nebula to contract. At the same time, the contraction caused the particles to become heated. Over time, the mass of interstellar gases and dust at the center of the nebula became sufficiently heated to cause a hydrogen fusion reaction. This reaction is the source of the sun's energy. It also stabilized the sun's mass. As the sun developed, cooled gases from the dispersed nebula crystallized into solid matter and accumulated to form the planets, the asteroids, and so on. Most astronomers believe that the solid planets formed relatively quickly.

The earth. Geologists are uncertain how the separate layers of the solid earth, distinguished by density, were

formed. The layers may have formed simultaneously from an even mixture of elements. Radioactive decay of elements may then have caused the planet's interior to melt; heavy elements such as iron and nickel, which melt at lower temperatures, would have sunk to the earth's center to form the core, while lighter elements (such as silicon and aluminum) would have been forced away from the core and toward the surface.

Gases trapped in rock deep inside the earth were brought to the surface through volcanic activity. These gases, which included water vapor, carbon dioxide, hydrogen, nitrogen, ammonia, methane, and chlorine, almost certainly were the beginnings of earth's atmosphere and ocean. Today, though, the atmosphere consists mainly of nitrogen and oxygen. As life developed on the planet, organic changes contributed to the altering of the atmosphere.

Life forms. All organisms on earth are made up of complex compounds of hydrogen, carbon, nitrogen, and oxygen—elements that existed in the primordial ocean and atmosphere. The first living things may have developed when energy from the sun transformed molecules of simple compounds of these elements into complex compounds.

The first evidence of life is found in fossil remains of primitive blue-green algae (capable of photosynthesis) and bacteria. The earliest animals were primitive marine invertebrates—worms, sponges, and jellyfish.

All early forms of life thrived only in the ocean, protected from ultraviolet rays, which destroy living cells. Eventually the oxygen released by marine plants began to accumulate in the atmosphere, altering the ratio of oxygen to carbon dioxide and leading to the development of the ozone layer in the upper atmosphere, which further protects living cells from ultraviolet radiation. Over time, the atmosphere became conducive to plant life on land. Subsequently, the first land creatures appeared.

The survival of various life forms on earth is closely tied to changes in climate. Ice ages, for example, favored large mammals, which were better adapted to life in cold climates. Plate tectonics also may have played a role in the development of species. Long-lived species surviving from Pangaea may be found on all continents today. Some species that developed on land masses isolated from the rest of the world are likely to be unique to those regions, such as the marsupials in Australia.

Tracing the past.
Rocks and fossils provide clues to the earth's past. The age of a rockbed can be determined by identifiable fossils embedded within it. The position of the rockbed in the strata identifies its relative age; this is known as *relative dating*. Relative dating does not necessarily tell how long ago something took place—only that the event followed one event and preceded another. Modern methods based on radioactivity make possible *absolute dating*—a method of closely determining how long ago a geological event occurred.

Fossils. If an organism dies and is buried in sediment before its remains decompose or are consumed by scavengers, the remains themselves may be preserved, or *fossilized*. Dung, stomach contents, and other animal remains can become fossilized, too. Fossils can also preserve the footprints of animals moving over sediment or the body impressions made by burrowing animals.

Organic material may be preserved whole and unchanged (for example, encased in ice or amber). Remains may also be changed chemically by the minerals in the surrounding sediment. Fossils indicate not only the life forms that existed during periods of time, but also the climate and environmental conditions that supported those life forms.

Correlation of strata. Sedimentary deposits are formed as successive layers (strata), one on top of the next. Naturally, the layers toward the top are younger than the layers beneath. This simple principle is known as the *law of superposition* and is the basis for

relative dating. The sequence predicts the relative age of the layers. Each layer can be correlated with a period of geologic time.

Due to gravity, layers of sediment originally form in horizontal layers. Crustal movement from earthquakes or mountain building, as well as other geologic processes, can later disturb this pattern. Mountain building deforms the layers, causing them to bend and curve and fold over; erosion flattens the mounded layers, eventually leaving the mounds crestless. Earthquakes cause breaks and misalignment of the layers. By observing the position of breaks or deformities in relation to the layers, a geologist can identify the order in which the events and processes took place, reconstructing the geologic history of a region.

The successive layers of strata provide a continuous record of geological events. Layers of rock are said to be *conformable* when they are found to have been deposited essentially without interruption. Sudden breaks in this otherwise continuous record indicate a missing part—often an eroded area. This break, called an *unconformity*, usually represents a long interval of time. There are occasions when the time missing from the geologic record can be longer than that which is preserved.

Radiometric dating. Absolute dating of rocks is based on known decay rates of various naturally radioactive isotopes. Different isotopes of an element have different numbers of neutrons in their nuclei. Atoms of radioactive isotopes have unstable nuclei that decay over time to produce a different element. Uranium 238 is one such isotope. Over time, it decays to become lead 206, a stable isotope.

For example, suppose a rock sample contained an equal amount of uranium 238 and lead 206. It takes 4.5 billion years for half of the nuclei in this particular parent isotope to decay to its stable daughter product. (The unit for rate of decay is a half-life.) If the ratio of parent to daughter is equal—that is, 1:1—the rock can be judged to be 4.5 billion years old. If the ratio were 2:1, only half of a half-life would have passed, and the rock would be dated at 2.25 billion years old.

Five radioactive isotopes are commonly used in radiometric dating. Each one has a different half-life. Potassium 40, which decays to argon 40, has a half-life of 1.3 billion years. Because it is commonly found in volcanic rock, it has been important in determining the age of ocean floors. Carbon 14, or radiocarbon, with a half-life of 5,730 years, is used for dating only very young specimens that contain some organic matter. The three other isotopes—rubidium 87, uranium 235, and uranium 238—are used to date rocks that are millions of years old. The half-lives of these isotopes are 47 billion years, 713 million years, and 4.5 billion years, respectively.

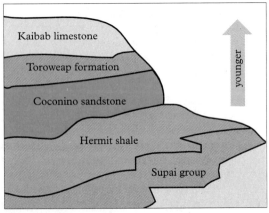

Strata in the Grand Canyon

Geologic time scale

Era	Period	Epoch	Millions of years ago (approximate)	Key geologic events during the interval of time
Cenozoic	Quaternary	Holocene		Glaciers make major retreat. Deserts become more extensive.
		---- 0.01		
		Pleistocene		Glaciers are widespread.
			2	
	Tertiary	Pliocene		Isthmus between North and South America created.
		---- 5		
		Miocene		Himalayas, Alps, and Andes greatly increase in height.
		---- 24		
		Oligocene		African and European plates collide. Rift in Africa forms Red Sea.
		---- 37		
		Eocene		Volcanoes begin to build Rockies.
		---- 58		
		Paleocene		Greenland splits from North America and North Atlantic begins to open.
			66	
Mesozoic	Cretaceous			Gondwanaland starts to break up. North Atlantic widens and South Atlantic starts to form.
			144	
	Jurassic			North America and Africa split and North Atlantic begins to form. Pangaea begins to break apart.
			208	
	Triassic			Rift begins to form between North America and Africa.
			245	
Paleozoic	Permian			Oceans cool. End of Appalachian mountain building. Pangaea assembled.
			286	
	Carboniferous			Coal formation begins. Urals begin to form.
			360	
	Devonian			Continents drift northward into more humid climates.
			408	
	Silurian			Salt deposits are extensive, as continents enter drier subtropics.
			438	
	Ordovician			Pangaea begins to form. Appalachians begin to form.
			505	
	Cambrian			Most land masses are located in Southern Hemisphere.
			570	
Precambrian	Proterozoic			Most Proterozoic rocks have been metamorphosed.
			2,500	
	Archaean (Earth forms)		4,500	Permanent crust develops.

Earth resources

Everything we use or manufacture comes from the earth. Humans have always been dependent on raw resources from the earth, and modern life and technology have made us even more resource-dependent. The goal now is to balance a growing need for resources with the need to preserve or care for them. The task becomes increasingly more difficult with expanding populations.

Mineral resources are the minerals used commercially. These resources include materials such as ores, building stones, road aggregates, abrasives, ceramics, metals, and precious metals. The necessary rocks and minerals are mined all over the world. Unfortunately, mining can cause mass wasting and accelerates erosion. In addition, the use of some minerals can be even more destructive than their removal. The use of ores in nuclear industries, for example, has the potential for gross, long-term destruction. Thus, as the need for mineral resources grows, the need to locate additional supplies grows, and becomes more challenging.

Humans depend on running water not only for sustaining life, but also for energy, travel, and irrigation. Yet the source of most water—groundwater—is being abused by industrialization and modern agriculture. Sediment, which is the leading cause of water pollution in the United States, is a by-product of timber cutting, agriculture, ranching, mining, and construction. In some areas, the abundance of sediment threatens the groundwater supply, while in other areas, pollution and contamination decrease the amount of usable supply.

Energy resources are classified either as renewable or nonrenewable. *Renewable resources* are those that eventually can be replenished. Wind, moving water, and the sun's radiation are the most important renewable resources. Wood, a common energy resource in much of the world, is considered renewable because it can be replenished fairly quickly (within the lifetime of populations using it); in many regions, though, demand has outweighed replenishable supply. *Nonrenewable resources* are those that cannot be replenished easily, of which the most commonly used are fossil fuels (coal and oil). Coal is the fossilized remains of plants that lived more than 300 million years ago and still contain carbon. Oil and natural gas developed from microscopic marine organisms buried beneath accumulating sediment many millions of years ago. Heat and compression transformed the organisms into hydrogen-carbon compounds (hydrocarbons). Eventually the gas and liquid percolated up through porous rock, becoming trapped in folds of hard, impenetrable rock. Reserves of fossil fuels are rapidly

being depleted. Of greater concern is the environmental impact of their use. The burning of fossil fuels changes the composition of the atmosphere, which can possibly change the global climate.

As the world's population grows, and the need for natural resources increases, earth scientists and geologists, as well as chemists, physicists, and biologists, continue to search for new ways in which to care for these important resources within the social, political, and economic structures that play a role in influencing the environment.

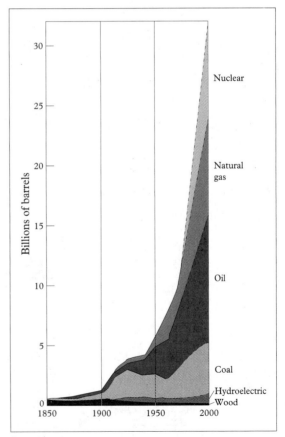

Increasing energy use

420 **Geology**

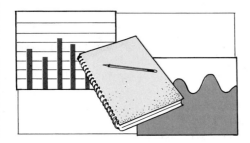

Geology
Tests, homework, and lab reports

Laying the groundwork

Students of geology and earth science should recognize the course objectives of the class. Generally these include two points: distinguishing between geologic processes and the products of those processes, and identifying the ways in which various systems involved in geologic processes are interrelated. When reading material, try to focus on these goals. List the key points in each section using your own words. Keep track of vocabulary by writing down each word. Then, without looking at the text, write down its meaning. Use mnemonic techniques when necessary. In class, ask questions while taking notes.

Strategies for success

Homework, lab work, field work, and tests are used to assess your basic knowledge and challenge you to apply this information in new ways. Most exams in earth science and geology consist of essay questions. Other questions may involve classification and identification. When studying for tests, remember "cramming" just increases anxiety. Instead, schedule short study sessions to break up information into more easily remembered units. Plan ahead for tests by scheduling enough time for studying; come to the test well rested. Be sure to bring a calculator in case some questions involve mathematical calculations.

Helpful hints
Vocabulary

> How are faults, foci, and epicenters related?

Notice this question is really testing two ideas: your knowledge of vocabulary and your understanding of a geologic process—earthquakes. By recognizing the connecting idea among the three terms, you have a good shot at finding the answer, even if you don't know the exact definition of each word.
Answer. A focus is the zone where an earthquake occurs, the epicenter is the spot on the earth's surface directly above the focus, and a fault is the break in the rock mass along which the movement occurs.

Fill-in

> When magma cools and crystallizes, _____ rocks are formed.

Your notetaking strategy—listing important points—will help you remember details for fill-in questions. One of your lists would include the different types of rocks and how they form.
Answer. Igneous

Field work

> During the field trip, collect at least three rock specimens and identify them.

Successful field work requires careful gathering and analysis of data, and tests the practical application of knowledge.
Before a trip, you should be familiar with your tools and the rules of the area. Obtain any permits for collecting specimens if necessary. The most important strategy in field work is conscientious notetaking. Label each specimen adequately. Indicate where and when it was collected, as well as why. Also provide notes about the surrounding structures and formations, and any additional information known about the sample.

Lab reports

> Use the equipment provided to simulate the effects of runoff on a hillside.

Lab work allows you to apply theoretical knowledge, learn the techniques for using equipment, and practice data collection and recording. Before starting a lab, try to understand the procedure of the experiment and the theory underlying it. Once in the lab, carefully record in a notebook the question you are trying to answer, the procedure and equipment you are using, your observations during the experiment, your calculations, and your conclusions.

Glossary

Glacier

Paleontology

Relative dating

Weathering

absolute dating. A system of determining how long ago a geologic event occurred.

abyssal plain. Very level area of the deep-ocean floor, usually lying at the foot of the continental rise.

alluvial fan. A fan-shaped deposit of sediment formed when a stream's slope is abruptly reduced.

alpine glacier. A glacier confined to a mountain valley, which in most instances had previously been a stream valley.

anticline. A concave-down fold in the earth's crust.

asthenosphere. A portion of the mantle located below the lithosphere. The asthenosphere is a fluid (or plastic) layer on which the lithospheric plates "float."

atmosphere. A layer of gases that surrounds the planet.

caldera. A huge depression at the peak of a volcano caused when the volcano collapses. Occasionally, very large craters are called calderas.

cleavage. The tendency of a mineral to break along planes of weak bonding.

conformable. Layers of rock deposited without interruption.

continental drift theory. A theory that originally proposed that the continents move about on a layer of fluid. It has essentially been replaced by the plate tectonics theory.

continental glacier. An enormous ice mass that covers a large land area and flows in more than one direction.

continental margin. The portion of the ocean floor adjacent to the continents.

continental rise. The gently sloping surface at the base of the continental slope.

continental shelf. The gently sloping submerged portion of the continental margin extending from the shoreline to the continental slope.

continental slope. The steep gradient that leads to the deep-ocean floor and marks the seaward edge of the continental shelf.

core. The innermost layer of the earth, believed to consist of iron and nickel.

crust. The very thin outermost layer of the earth.

deep-ocean trench. A long, narrow depression in the ocean floor.

delta. An accumulation of sediment formed where a stream enters a lake or ocean.

epicenter. The point on the earth's surface directly above an earthquake's focus (point of origin).

erosion. The incorporation and transportation of material by agents such as water, wind, or ice.

fault. A break in a rock mass along which movement has occurred.

fissure. Any crack along the earth's crust occurring as a result of seismic activity.

fossil. The preserved remains of organisms, or traces of those organisms, from the geologic past.

glacier. A thick mass of ice originating on land from the compaction and recrystallization of snow.

hydrosphere. All of the water contained on earth.

igneous rock. A rock formed by the crystallization of molten magma.

intrusive rock. Igneous rock that formed below the earth's surface.

isotope. A variety of a chemical element that has a different mass number as its related element.

lithification. The process of converting sediments to solid rock.

lithosphere. The rigid outer layer of the earth, consisting of the crust and the upper mantle.

magma. Molten rock beneath the earth's crust.

     Geology

mantle. A thick layer of molten and solid rock that lies between the crust and the core.

mass wasting. The downslope movement of rock, regolith, and soil under the direct influence of gravity.

metamorphic rock. Rocks formed by the alteration of pre-existing rock deep within the earth by heat, pressure, and/or chemically active fluids.

metamorphism. The changes in mineral composition and texture of a rock subjected to high temperature and pressure within the earth.

mid-ocean ridge. A mountain range on the ocean floor along which seafloor spreading has occurred over time.

mineral. A naturally occurring, inorganic crystalline material.

Moho. Common abbreviated term for Mohorovicic discontinuity, the boundary between the earth's crust and mantle.

orogenesis. The process of mountain building.

paleomagnetism. The magnetic alignment in rocks that has been preserved over geologic time.

paleontology. The study of ancient life forms through fossils.

Pangaea. The name for the supercontinent that began to break apart as a result of tectonic forces about 200 million years ago, forming the subcontinents Gondwanaland and Laurasia.

plate. One of numerous rigid sections of the lithosphere that move as a unit over the material of the asthenosphere.

plate tectonics. The theory proposing that the earth's outer shell consists of individual plates, which interact in various ways.

radiometric dating. A system for determining the age of rocks and minerals based on the presence of radioactive isotopes.

relative dating. Determining the chronological order of geologic events based on strata.

Richter scale. A scale of earthquake magnitude based on the motion of a seismograph.

rock cycle. The sequence of geologic processes through which earth materials pass and are transformed.

seamount. An underwater volcano that develops on the ocean floor.

sediment. Particles created by the weathering and erosion of rock, by precipitation in water, or from the secretions of organisms.

sedimentary rock. Rock formed from the weathered products of preexisting rock that have been transported, deposited, and lithified.

seismograph. A simple instrument that measures ground motion and is used to determine the magnitude of earthquakes.

strata. Accumulated layers of sedimentary rock.

striations. Usually glacial striations. As a glacier moves, the many stones embedded in the ice scrape the underlying rock deeply.

subduction zone. An area where two lithospheric plates are moving toward each other, with one plate slipping beneath, or subducting under, the other. Where separate plates of ocean crust and continental crust meet, the ocean crust subducts beneath the continental crust.

superposition, law of. A principle of geologic chronology stating that any given rockbed in the strata is younger than the underlying beds.

syncline. A concave-up fold in the earth's crust.

tectonic. Of or related to forces in the earth's crust.

turbidity current. A downslope movement of dense, sediment-laden water created when sand and mud on the continental shelf are dislodged and thrown into suspension.

unconformity. An area in the strata that represents a break in the rock record, often caused by erosion.

uniformitarianism. Doctrine formulated by eighteenth-century Scottish scientist, James Hutton, that states that the geologic processes currently shaping the earth's surface are the same processes that have shaped it since ancient times.

vent. An opening through which gases and magma escape, usually through a volcano's peak.

water cycle. The stages through which water passes, from water vapor to liquid or solid precipitation, accumulating on land, and then returning to the atmosphere as water vapor through evaporation or transpiration.

weathering. The disintegration and decomposition of rock which takes place at or near the surface of the earth.

For further reading

Bates, D. E. B., and J. F. Kirkaldy. *Field Geology in Color.* New York: Arco, 1976.

Eicher, Don L., A. Lee McAlester, and Marcia L. Rottman. *The History of the Earth's Crust.* New York: Prentice Hall, 1984.

Ernst, W. G. *The Dynamic Planet.* New York: Columbia University Press, 1990.

Hamblin, W. Kenneth, and Eric H. Christiansen. *Earth's Dynamic Systems.* Englewood Cliffs, N.J.: Prentice-Hall, 1995.

Muller, Robert A., and Theodore M. Oberlander. *Physical Geography Today: A Portrait of a Planet.* 3rd ed. New York: Random House, 1984.

Thompson, Graham R., Jonathan Turk, and Harold L. Levin. *Earth: Past and Present, An Environmental Approach.* Orlando, Fla.: Harcourt, Brace and Co., 1995.

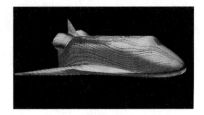

Physics

Physics is the oldest and most basic of all the sciences: it is the study of how and why the different parts of the universe interact. Classical physics, which was developed prior to 1900, includes the theories, laws, and principles that explain such seemingly diverse phenomena as motion, gravity, heat, electricity, and magnetism. A new era in physics, referred to as modern physics, began near the end of the nineteenth century. It developed mainly because of the discovery that many physical phenomena could not be explained by classical physics. The developments of modern physics have led to the creation of semiconductors, advanced medical devices, planetary exploration, modern communication equipment, and views of the atomic world.

Mechanics

Everything moves—even objects that seem to be resting on the ground. Thus, understanding the motion of objects is an important part of describing the physical world. *Mechanics* is the study of motion and the forces that both produce it and determine the way an object moves. Physicists often categorize motion as either *linear* (in a straight line) or *rotational*.

Linear motion. To describe how an object moves, it is necessary to know three things: first, the *displacement* of the object—where the object starts and where it stops; second, the *velocity* of the object—the rate and direction in which it's traveling; and third, the *acceleration* of the object—the time rate of change of the velocity.

Speed versus velocity. *Speed* is the rate at which something moves—it is measured by dividing the total distance traveled by the time taken to travel that distance. Velocity is similar to speed, but with one important difference—it not only includes the rate at which something moves, but also gives the direction of motion. Thus, velocity is the rate at which the position of an object changes, and is represented by a *vector* (see the box on vectors). Speed is the magnitude of the velocity vector.

> ### Why studying physics pays off
> ### Reason #1:
> Understanding motion and forces helped scientists send rockets and humans into space.

Acceleration. If the velocity of an object changes either in magnitude or in direction while an object is moving, the object is said to be *accelerating*. Acceleration is defined as the time rate of change of the velocity, that is, the change in velocity divided by the time it takes for the change to occur. Like velocity, acceleration is a vector.

Most motion is accelerated motion—it does not occur at a constant velocity. Physicists look at several different types of acceleration. *Constant acceleration*—acceleration that does not change over time—may occur when an object is starting or stopping its motion. *Instantaneous acceleration* is the acceleration of an object at one instant in time. This is not the same as constant acceleration, since the acceleration may change from instant to instant.

Newton's laws.

Although displacement, velocity, and acceleration allow someone to calculate *how* an object moves, they do not describe *why* the object moves. In the late 1600s, Sir Isaac Newton explored the causes of motion and developed several laws that are still applicable today. These laws, known as *Newton's laws of motion* and *Newton's law of gravitation*, describe why things move. All contain two important concepts that are fundamental to physics: *mass*, the amount of matter in an object; and *force*, any "push" or "pull" that causes an object to move or accelerate.

Newton's first law of motion. This law, often called the *law of inertia*, states that a body (object) continues in its state of rest, or of uniform motion in a straight line, unless it is acted upon by an outside force. Thus, an object at rest remains at rest unless some force starts it moving. Furthermore, a moving object keeps moving in a straight line unless some force makes it slow down, speed up, or change direction.

This law may seem to contradict everyday experience—if a book is pushed along a table top, the book stops moving when it is no longer pushed. And a car seems to move around a curve without outside forces acting on it. But, in fact, outside forces are acting on both objects. A frictional force is exerted on the sliding book by the table top, in a direction opposite to the book's motion. This force prevents the book from continuing its motion. This same type of frictional force is needed to swerve a car from its natural straight-line path so it can round a curve. If the road were extremely slippery, so that there was no friction, the car would continue straight ahead. In addition, another force is required to hold a moving object in a circular path.

Stop-motion photograph of a bullet

Newton's second law of motion. Newton's second law helps predict what will happen when outside forces act on an object. It states that when external forces act on an object, the acceleration is inversely proportional to the mass of the object and directly proportional to the sum of the forces. This law, which is written in symbols as

$$\sum \mathbf{F} = m \frac{\Delta v}{\Delta t} = ma,$$

basically says that when a body is acted upon by a constant net force, it will move with constant acceleration.

Vectors and scalars

What is the difference between a vector and a scalar? A *vector* is a physical quantity that has direction, while a *scalar* is a quantity with no direction. Thus, quantities such as displacement, velocity, and acceleration are vectors, while quantities such as time, temperature, volume, work, and energy are scalars.

Vectors are usually represented with an arrow—the direction of the arrow indicates the direction of the vector, and the length of the arrow is the magnitude of the vector.

Vectors can be added and subtracted, but they do not obey the same rules of mathematics as scalars. Instead, two vectors can be added by drawing the tail of one vector (**B**) from the head of the other (**A**). Then, draw a vector from the tail of **A** to the head of **B**. This new vector is the resultant vector (**C**), and it equals the sum of **A** + **B**. The negative of a vector is the vector with the head and tail reversed. Thus, subtracting two vectors can be done by finding the sum of **A** + (-**B**).

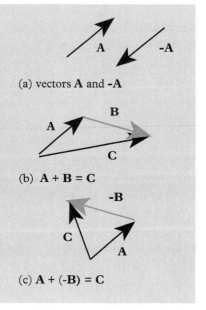

(a) vectors **A** and -**A**

(b) **A** + **B** = **C**

(c) **A** + (-**B**) = **C**

The acceleration increases as the force increases, and decreases as mass increases.

Notice that the equation for force contains the quantity of mass times velocity. This quantity is known as *momentum*. Momentum can be thought of as a measurement of the tendency of a body to remain in motion or the resistance of a body to being stopped. The *law of conservation of momentum* states that in any interaction of bodies, if the net force on the body or bodies is zero, the total momentum of the bodies does not change.

Newton's third law of motion. Newton's third law states that if two bodies interact, the force exerted on body 1 by body 2 is equal to and opposite the force exerted on body 2 by body 1. This is sometimes restated as "For every action, there is an equal and opposite reaction." This law is important because it shows that forces always occur in pairs. For example, if someone hits a wall, the wall, in turn, exerts an equal force against the person's hand.

Newton's law of gravitation. Newton discovered the law of gravitation while he was studying the motion of the planets around the sun. This law states that any two bodies in the universe attract each other with a force that is directly proportional to the masses of the objects and inversely proportional to the square of the distance between the objects, or

$$F = G\frac{m_1 m_2}{r^2}$$

where F is the force of attraction, m_1 and m_2 are the masses of the objects, r is the distance between their centers, and G is a constant which is known as the *gravitational constant*.

The gravitational force of attraction exerted by the earth on an object is called the *weight* of the object. It is given by the equation $W = mg$, where g equals Gm_{earth}/r^2. Unlike mass, weight is dependent on the distance between the object and the center of the earth, so it varies slightly with location.

Rotational motion.
When an object, such as a wheel, rotates about its axis, different parts of the object have different velocities and accelerations at any given time. However, even though this motion—called *rotational motion*—is more complex than linear motion, the rotation of an object can be described by rotational analogs of displacement, velocity, and acceleration. In addition, Newton's laws apply to rotation as well as linear motion.

Some key equations of motion

Linear motion

Displacement	Δx
Velocity	$v = \dfrac{\Delta x}{\Delta t}$
Acceleration	$a = \dfrac{\Delta v}{\Delta t}$
Constant acceleration	$v^2 = v_0^2 + 2a(x - x_0)$
	$v = v_0 + at$
	$x = x_0 + v_0 t + \dfrac{1}{2}at^2$
Mass	m
Momentum	$\mathbf{p} = m\mathbf{v}$
Force	$\mathbf{F}$
Power	$P = Fv$
Newton's 2nd law	$\sum \mathbf{F} = \dfrac{\Delta \mathbf{p}}{\Delta t} = ma$

Rotational motion

Angular displacement	$\Delta \theta$
Angular velocity	$\omega = \dfrac{\Delta \theta}{\Delta t}$
Acceleration	$\alpha = \dfrac{\Delta \omega}{\Delta t}$
Constant angular acceleration	$\omega^2 = \omega_0^2 + 2\alpha(\theta - \theta_0)$
	$\omega = \omega_0 + \alpha t$
	$\theta = \theta_0 + \omega_0 t \dfrac{1}{2}\omega t^2$
Moment of inertia	I
Angular momentum	$L = I\omega$
Torque	τ
Power	$P = \tau \omega$
Newton's 2nd law	$\sum \tau = \dfrac{\Delta L}{\Delta t} = I\alpha$

Angular velocity and acceleration. A point on a rotating object moves in a circular arc. As it moves, the radius of the circle sweeps out an angle. The *angular displacement* is the change in angle as the point moves. Like velocity, the *angular velocity* is simply the rate of change of the displacement; in this particular case, the change in angular displacement over a given time period. Similarly, angular acceleration is the rate of change of the angular velocity.

Moment of inertia. Just as mass is a measure of the resistance of a body to changes in its linear motion, *moment of inertia* is a measure of the resistance of a body to changes in its rotational motion. The moment of inertia of an object depends on the way in which the mass of the object is distributed relative to the axis of rotation of the object.

Thus, a cylinder that rotates about a perpendicular line through its center has a different moment of inertia from a cylinder that rotates about a perpendicular line through one end.

Torque. Unless all the forces applied to an object are acting on a single point, the object will tend to rotate. The measure of the ability of a force to produce rotation is called *torque*. The torque of any force is equal to the magnitude of the force multiplied by the distance between the pivot point and the point where the force is applied.

Together torque, moment of inertia, and angular acceleration provide the rotational analog of Newton's second law, where the sum of all the torques acting on an object is equal to the moment of inertia of the object times the angular acceleration: $\sum \tau = I\alpha$. This equation relates the rotational motion of a body to the torques acting on it, just as the linear version of Newton's second law relates the linear motion of a body to the forces acting on it.

Work and energy.
When the acceleration of an object is not constant, it is difficult to predict the speed or position of an object using Newton's laws. However, physicists have developed a way to determine the speed and position of an object without having to know the details of its motion. To do this, they use the concepts of work and energy.

In science, work is given a precise definition that differs from everyday usage. *Work* is done only when a force moves an object over a distance and there is a component of the force along the line of motion. Thus, work is done when someone lifts a weight, but not when the same person simply holds the weight above the ground. The time rate at which work is done is called *power*. Power is the amount of work done per unit of time.

Energy is the capacity to do work, and is measured by the amount of work performed. There are many types of energy, including electrical, heat, mechanical, chemical, and nuclear.

According to the *law of conservation of energy*, the total energy in the universe is a constant quantity, thus it can be neither created nor destroyed, only converted from one form to another. *Mechanical energy* includes two forms of energy: *kinetic energy*, which is the energy associated with the motion of a body; and *potential energy*, which is the energy associated with the of position of a body. The *work-energy* theorem states that the work which is done on an object undergoing displacement equals the change in kinetic energy of the object, or

$$W = KE_f - KE_i = \frac{1}{2}mv_f^2 - \frac{1}{2}mv_i^2$$

In addition, the work done on a object falling to the ground is the change in potential energy.

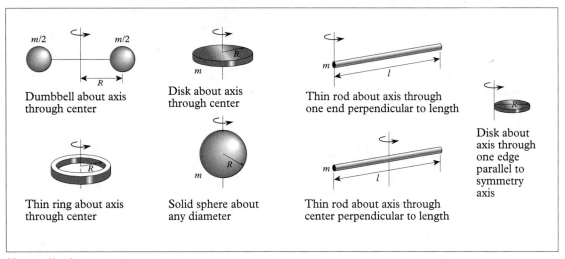

Moments of inertia

Dumbbell about axis through center

Disk about axis through center

Thin rod about axis through one end perpendicular to length

Disk about axis through one edge parallel to symmetry axis

Thin ring about axis through center

Solid sphere about any diameter

Thin rod about axis through center perpendicular to length

Thermodynamics

Thermodynamics is the study of temperature, heat, and energy exchange. Although the science of thermodynamics is concerned with the study of heat flow from a *macroscopic* viewpoint, thermal phenomena can also be understood on a molecular scale. In fact, the thermal behavior of a substance—how it reacts when heated—is closely related to the structure of the substance. Gases react differently from liquids, which react differently from solids.

Temperature. *Temperature* is the degree of
hotness or coldness of an object. Although people perceive temperature through touch, our senses are often misleading. For example, if someone takes a metal ice tray and a package of frozen food out of a freezer, the ice tray will feel colder even though both are at the same temperature. Thus, scientists have created *thermometers* for establishing the relative hotness or coldness of bodies.

Thermometers work because of a situation known as thermal equilibrium. When two objects are in *thermal contact* with each other, they exchange energy. Eventually they reach a point when the amount of heat leaving each body is equal to the amount of heat entering the body. At that point, the objects are in a state of *thermal equilibrium*, and have the same temperature. Thus, when a thermometer is placed in a glass of hot liquid, the temperature of the liquid decreases while the temperature of the thermometer increases until the two are in thermal equilibrium.

Heat and internal energy. The energy
that is exchanged from one object to another because of a difference in temperature is called *heat*. Heat flows from a hotter substance to a cooler substance, regardless of the amount of each substance. In most cases, when heat energy is added to a substance, the temperature of the substance rises. *Heat capacity* of any substance is the amount of heat energy needed to raise the temperature of a set amount of substance by one Celsius degree. There are some situations where the flow of heat does not result in a change in temperature. Instead, the physical characteristics of the substance change from one form to another. This is called a *phase change*, and includes changes such as melting and boiling.

Unlike heat, which is an energy transfer that takes place because of temperature, the *internal energy* of a substance is the energy the substance has because of its temperature.

The first law. The *first law of thermodynamics*
extends the principle of conservation of energy to include not only the forms of mechanical energy but also energy associated with heat. To understand the relationships between mechanical energy and heat transfer, it is necessary to understand the concept of a thermodynamic system. A *thermodynamic system* is an object, or collection of objects, that can exchange energy with its surroundings. This energy is exchanged by means of both heat and work.

The first law of thermodynamics states that the change in the internal energy of a system is equal to

---

Kinetic theory of gases

Although many everyday thermometers contain mercury, gas thermometers (those that contain gas) show more clearly what happens to molecules when they are heated or cooled—either the pressure changes while the volume remains constant, or the volume changes while the pressure remains constant. Scientists have created a model, called the kinetic theory of gases, to show why this happens. This model includes three assumptions: (1) A gas consists of a very large number of molecules, with great empty spaces between them; (2) the molecules are moving at random in all directions; and (3) the molecules interact with each other only through collisions so that kinetic energy is conserved.

Based on these assumptions, a gas in a container exerts pressure because of the kinetic energy of its moving molecules. When the molecules strike the sides of the container, they push on it, creating pressure. Both the speed of the molecules and the distance the molecules must travel between collisions affect the amount of pressure the gas exerts. The faster a molecule is moving, the more often it will hit any given wall, and the greater the pressure. And the closer a molecule is to a wall, the more likely it is to hit the wall, so again, the pressure is greater. If volume is increased, then every molecule has to travel farther before colliding with the wall, so pressure is decreased. And if the temperature of the gas is lowered, movement of the molecules slows down, once again decreasing the pressure. In fact, if all the kinetic energy could be taken away by stopping the molecules completely, they would cease to exert any pressure. Scientists have found that to stop all motion, a gas needs to be cooled to -273° C (O K). This point is called *absolute zero*.

---

the heat added to the system plus the work done on the system. In practice, the first law says that an increase in one form of energy must be accompanied by a decrease in some other form of energy. Thus, the internal energy of a body may be increased either by adding heat to it, which decreases the amount of work done by the body, or by doing work on the body, which decreases the amount of heat.

The second law.
Although the first law of thermodynamics states that energy is conserved, some forms of energy are more useful than others. The *second law of thermodynamics* establishes which types of energy conversions can take place. It also helps establish the sequence, or order, in which the conversions naturally take place. For example, although it is possible to convert mechanical work completely into heat or into the internal energy of a system with no other changes, in practice it is impossible to remove heat or internal energy from a system and convert it completely into work without changing the surroundings. This fact is known as the *Kelvin-Planck statement* of the second law of thermodynamics, and can be applied to engines. Another statement of the second law, known as the *Clausius statement*, says that it is impossible to construct a machine that transfers heat from a colder body to a hotter body with perfect efficiency—some amount of energy is lost.

Some equations of thermodynamics

Temperature scales

Fahrenheit to Celsius	$T_F = \dfrac{9}{5} T_C + 32$
Celsius to Fahrenheit	$T_C = \dfrac{5}{9}\left(T_F - 32\right)$
Celsius to Kelvin	$T = T_C + 273.15$
Heat capacity	$Q = Cm\Delta t$
Ideal gas law	$PV = nRT$ $R = 8.314\,\text{J/mol}\cdot\text{K}$
Work done by a gas	$W = F\Delta x = P\Delta U$
The 1st law	$\Delta U = Q - W$
Kinetic energy of an ideal gas	$KE = \dfrac{3}{2} RT$
Internal energy of an ideal gas	$U = \dfrac{3}{2}\mu RT$
Entropy	$\Delta S = \dfrac{\Delta Q_{\text{rev}}}{T}$

Vibrations and waves

Although many people associate waves with the water at an ocean beach, sound, light, radio, television, and even earthquakes are also waves. A *wave* is any disturbance from an equilibrium condition that travels, or *propagates*, over time from one region to another. Although waves seem to "move" along straight or circular lines, matter is not transported when waves move. Instead, *wave motion* is the transport of energy and momentum from one point in space to another. The movement normally associated with waves is closely related to the phenomena of vibration. As the energy of a wave travels through a medium such as air or water, the molecules of the medium oscillate back and forth, or up and down. As the wave energy is transferred from one particle to the next, each particle in turn oscillates. When the particles' oscillations are perpendicular to the line of wave motion, the wave is called a *transverse wave*. When the oscillations are parallel to the wave motion, then the wave is a *longitudinal wave*.

Vibrations also produce waves. If a rock is dropped into a pond, the force of the rock causes the particles of the water to vibrate, creating a *wave pulse*. If the source of vibration has a continuous motion, then it creates a *wave train*—a succession of waves. If each particle in a wave train has a regular, repeated oscillation, then the wave is a *periodic wave*. The most common and important type of periodic wave is called a *harmonic wave*. This type of wave can be represented as a sine curve.

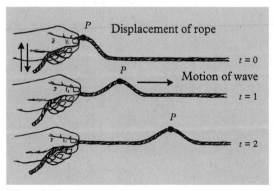

Wave pulse along a rope

Wave characteristics.

Although the variety of wave phenomena observed in nature is immense, there are several features common to all types of waves. These include amplitude, wavelength, period, frequency, and velocity.

The *amplitude* (*A*) of a wave is the maximum displacement of a particle as it oscillates from the equilibrium position. The *wavelength* (λ) is the distance between one peak, or *crest*, of a wave and the next. The *period* (*T*) is the time it takes a particle to complete one full cycle of oscillation. *Frequency* (*f*) is the reciprocal of period: the frequency of a wave is the number of full cycles each second, and is written $f = 1/T$. Waves propagate at specific velocities that depend on the properties of the medium being disturbed. Since a wave travels one wavelength in the time of one period, the speed (*v*) of a wave can be found using the formula

$$v = \frac{\lambda}{T} = f\lambda$$

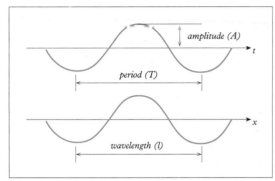

Characteristics of a wave over time and distance

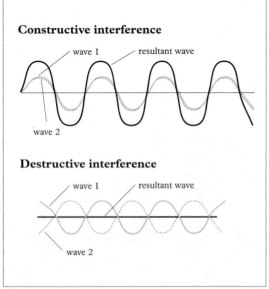

Interference

Interference.

An important aspect of waves is the combined effect of two or more waves traveling in the same medium. When two waves meet, the wave forms are combined to create a new wave form. This change is known as *interference*. The *principle of superposition* states that the net wave disturbance at a given time and space is the sum of all the wave disturbances at that particular time and place. In other words, waves add together. The shape of the resultant wave depends on the types of interference between the two waves. *Constructive interference* occurs when two crests or two troughs come together, forming a crest or trough of increased amplitude. *Destructive interference* occurs when a trough and a crest come together, resulting in a point of minimum disturbance. For harmonic waves, maximum constructive interference occurs at points that are in phase with each other, and maximum destructive interference occurs at points that have equal amplitude and are exactly 180 degrees out of phase.

Sound waves and music

Sound waves, which are also called compressional waves, are produced by a series of compressions and expansions of the media through which they are traveling. This is similar to the type of compression and expansion that occurs when a spring is stretched or compressed. The amplitude of a sound wave diminishes quickly as the wave travels. This occurs because the wave is spreading out in three-dimensional space instead of traveling in a single line along a one-dimensional medium.

What someone hears depends a great deal on the amplitude and frequency of the sound wave. The amplitude of the sound wave affects how loud or soft a sound is. Loud sounds are high-amplitude waves, while soft sounds are low-amplitude waves. A musical *tone* is heard only if the vibration of the source, and therefore of the sound waves coming from it, have a definite frequency. Irregular vibrations create *noise*. The *pitch* of a sound (its degree of highness or lowness on the musical scale) is determined by the frequency of the wave. The higher the frequency, the higher the pitch. Combinations of musical notes sound harmonious when their frequencies are in simple whole number ratios.

Different instruments have different sounds because they produce many frequencies simultaneously. The lowest frequency, which is called the *fundamental*, specifies the pitch. The remaining frequencies are known as the *overtones* of the note. Some instruments, such as a flute, have few overtones, while others, such as violins, have many.

Electricity and magnetism

Electricity is so much a part of everyday life, it is hard to imagine being without it. In fact, electricity and magnetism play a central role in the operation of many common devices—lights, refrigerators, computers, phones, and so on. Until the early nineteenth century, electricity and magnetism were thought to be separate and distinct phenomena. But the experiments of such nineteenth century scientists as Hans Oersted, Michael Faraday, and Joseph Henry showed that electricity and magnetism are intimately related, so much so that one can produce the other.

Electric fields and forces. *Electricity*

is a form of energy based on electrons that can produce light, heat, magnetism, and so on. An *electric charge* is the amount of electricity that can be given off by an object. There are two forms of electric charge: positive (protons) and negative (electrons). Opposite charges attract; negative charges repel.

Electricity consists of charges that are either at rest or moving. Charges at rest are called *static electricity*. Charges in motion are called *electric current*. When charges can flow easily through an object, the object is known as a *conductor*. Objects through which charges flow poorly, or not at all, are known as *insulators*.

Electric fields. A charged object creates a force that surrounds the object in all directions. The area around an object in which this force exists is called an *electric field*. It is convenient to represent an electric field by drawing *lines of force* (also called *field lines*) to indicate the direction of the field at any point. If the field is surrounding a positive charge, then the field lines diverge outward in all directions from the charge. If the field is surrounding a negative charge, the field lines converge inward toward the charge. In both cases, the further the distance from the charge, the weaker the electric field, and the further apart the field lines.

Coulomb's law. If two charges are placed near each other, then a force is exerted by one charge on the other. The force is repulsive if the charges are the same, and attractive if the charges are opposite. *Coulomb's law* states that the force is directly proportional to the product of the charges and inversely proportional to the square of the distance between the two charges, or

$$F = k\frac{q_1 q_2}{r^2}$$

where k is a constant (known as *Coulomb's constant*). Coulomb's law is helpful in determining the amount of charge an object has. If an object with a known charge—called a *test charge*—is brought to a given distance from an object with an unknown charge, then the unknown charge can be measured by determining the force of one object on the other.

Potential energy and electric potential. *Electric potential energy* bears some similarities to mechanical potential energy—the work needed to move a charged object against an electric field increases the electric potential energy of the charge. The *potential difference* is the change in potential energy divided by the amount of charge; that is, the work per unit charge necessary to move the charge at constant speed between two points. Potential difference is not the same as potential energy—it is proportional to it.

Capacitors and capacitance. A *capacitor* is a device for storing electric charge. It consists of two conductors that carry equal and opposite charges. The capacitor is intially charged by transferring charges from a lower potential conductor to a higher potential conductor. The ability of a capacitor to take on more charge is measured by its electrical *capacitance*, which is the ratio of the magnitude of charge on either conductor to the potential difference between the conductors: $C = q/v$, where v is the potential difference and q is the charge.

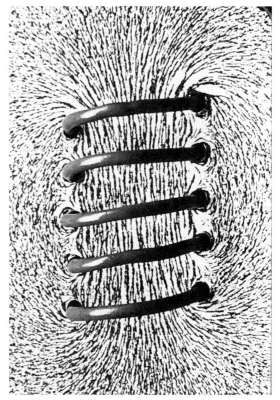

Electric field

Current and resistance.

Electric current flows through wire conductors much as water flows through pipes. The strength (or flow) of the electric current is measured by the amount of charge that passes a given point per unit time; that is, the change in charge over time. The directions of the flow can be either negative or positive—convention has set the direction of positive flow as the direction from high potential to low potential. To have a steady current in a conductor, it is necessary to provide a supply of electrical energy. A device that supplies electrical energy is called a *source of electromotive force* (emf). Batteries and generators are two common sources of emf.

For most conducting materials, the current in a wire is proportional to the potential difference between the ends of the wire. This is known as *Ohm's law*, and is written $I = V/R$, where R is a constant called the *resistance*. Resistance of a wire to current is similar to the resistance of pipe to water flow—it is the opposition of the wire to the flow of current. The resistance of a conducting wire depends on the length of the wire, its cross-sectional area, the type of material, and the temperature. A *resistor* is a conductor that is made to have a particular resistance.

When current flows through a conducting wire, the current transfers energy from one part of the wire to another. The rate of this energy transfer is the *power*—the potential difference times the current.

Magnets and magnetic fields.

A magnet is a solid that has the property to attract metal. Regardless of how small the magnet is, if left to swing freely, one end of a magnet will always swing toward the north, while the other end will always swing toward the south. The two ends are called the north and south poles of the magnet, respectively. Like magnet poles repel; opposite poles attract. Although in theory, a magnet with only one pole could exist, at this point none have been found—all magnets have two poles, and the force of attraction between two poles is directly proportional to the product of their pole strengths and inversely proportional to the square of the distance between them.

A permanent magnet will exert a force from a distance away. The space around a magnet in which the magnetic force is felt is called the *magnetic field*. As with an electric field, the force lines of a magnetic field radiate out from the magnet—diverging from the north pole and converging on the south pole.

Electromagnetism.

Danish physicist Hans Oersted (1777–1851) discovered that a wire carrying an electric current produced a magnetic field in a circular pattern around the wire. Later, French physicist André Ampère (1775–1836) found that if a wire carrying a current was wound in a coil, like a spring, the magnet effect was greatly increased. These coiled

Some key equations in electricity and magnetism

Coulomb's law

$$F = k \frac{q_1 q_2}{r^2}$$

Electric field

$$\mathbf{E} = \frac{\mathbf{F}}{q_0}$$

Potential difference

$$\Delta V = \frac{\Delta U}{q}$$

Potential of a point charge

$$V = \frac{kq}{r}$$

Capacitance

$$C = \frac{q}{v}$$

Capacitance of capacitors
in series

$$\frac{1}{C_s} = \frac{1}{C_1} + \frac{1}{C_2} + \frac{1}{C_3} + \ldots$$

in parallel

$$C_p = C_1 + C_2 + C_3 + \ldots$$

Electric current

$$I = \frac{\Delta q}{\Delta t}$$

Ohm's law

$$I = \frac{V}{R}$$

Resistance

$$R = \frac{V}{I}$$

Resistance of resistors
in series

$$R_s = R_1 + R_2 + R_3 + \ldots$$

in parallel

$$\frac{1}{R_p} = \frac{1}{R_1} + \frac{1}{R_2} + \frac{1}{R_3} + \ldots$$

Magnetic field for straight wire carrying current

$$B = \frac{\mu_0 I}{2\pi d}$$

Force of an object in a magnetic field

$$F = qvB \sin\theta$$

Faraday's law

$$emf = -\frac{N \Delta \phi_m}{\Delta t}$$

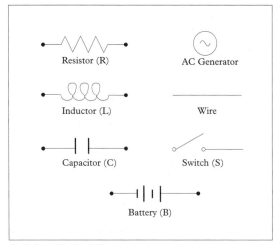

Symbols used in circuit diagrams

wires are called *solenoids*. Scientists also found that electric current could be produced by magnetism. Michael Faraday discovered that when one pole of a magnet was moved quickly toward a coil of wire, a current was induced. The strength of the current is related to the strength of the magnet, the speed of the motion, and the number of turns in the wire. The direction of the induced current is always such that its magnetic field opposes the operation that causes it.

Circuits. Current will only flow in a complete circuit that includes a source of emf and a complete conducting path. Charge moves in a circuit from a point of high potential to one of low potential. In addition, any current that flows into a point in the circuit must also flow out; thus, current in a circuit is conserved. When the path of a circuit is complete so that electricity is free to flow, the circuit is called a *closed* circuit. If the path is interrupted at any point, the circuit is called an *open* or *broken circuit*.

Circuits may consist of combinations of devices such as resistors, capacitors, inductors, and switches. When a number of circuit elements are connected to provide a single conducting path, they are said to be in *series*. If the elements are set up to provide several paths, they are said to be in *parallel*.

Light and wave optics

The nature and properties of light have been a subject of great speculation since ancient times. The Greeks believed that light consisted of tiny particles, which they called corpuscles, that were emitted by a light source. Later scientists, such as Christiaan Huygens (1629–1695), explained many of the properties of light by proposing that light was wave-like in character. Today, scientists view light as having a dual nature— sometimes it behaves like a particle, and at other times it behaves like a wave.

Light and electromagnetic waves.

Light is a type of *electromagnetic wave*—a transverse wave that involves the propagation of electric and magnetic fields through space. Other electromagnetic waves include radio waves, X rays, gamma rays, and microwaves. The large range, or *spectrum*, of electromagnetic waves is known as the *electromagnetic spectrum*.

Electromagnetic waves are produced by the oscillation of electric charges. The frequency of the oscillation

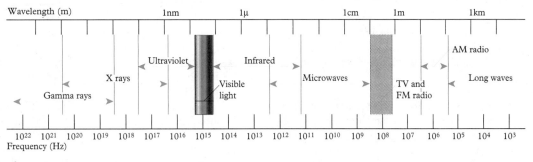

Electromagnetic spectrum

determines the frequency—and therefore the wavelength—of the waves. The various types of electromagnetic waves differ only in wavelength and frequency. All travel at the same speed in a vacuum, which is 3×10^8 m/s, otherwise known as the *speed of light*. The relationship among wavelength, frequency, and speed of light is $f = c/\lambda$, where c is the speed of light.

The human eye is sensitive to electromagnetic radiation of wavelengths from about 400 to 700 nm, the range called *visible light*. The shortest wavelengths in the visible spectrum correspond to blue or violet light and the longest to red light, with all the colors of the rainbow in between. Electromagnetic waves with wavelengths shorter than those of visible light include ultraviolet radiation, X rays, and gamma rays. Electromagnetic waves with wavelengths longer than those of visible light include infrared radiation, microwaves, radio waves, and television waves.

Because the wavelengths of visible light are in such a narrow range, waves of light can often be approximated by a straight line, called a *ray*. This approximation is useful when studying the behavior of light when it strikes a boundary.

Reflection and refraction.

When a light ray strikes a boundary between two different media, some or all of the ray bounces back away from the boundary. This phenomenon is known as *reflection*. The angle between the incident ray and the normal (a line perpendicular to the boundary) is called the *angle of incidence*. The angle between the reflected ray and the normal is the *angle of reflection*. The angle of incidence equals the angle of reflection. This result is known as the *law of reflection*.

When a light ray strikes a boundary separating two different media, part of the light ray may enter the second medium. When this happens, the change in direction of light rays as they pass from one medium to another is called *refraction*. The ray that enters the second medium is called the *refracted ray*, and the angle between the refracted ray and the normal is the *angle of refraction*. The angle of refraction depends on the ratio of the speeds of the waves in the two media as well as on the angle of incidence. The speed of light in a medium, such as glass or air, is characterized by the *index of refraction (n)*, which is equal to the ratio of the speed of light in a vacuum to the speed of light in the medium. The angle of refraction is given by *Snell's law*: $n_1 \sin \theta_1 = n_2 \sin \theta_2$.

Interference and diffraction.

The phenomenon of interference of light waves from two sources was first demonstrated by the English scientist Thomas Young in 1801. Young discovered that when *monochromatic light*—light of a single wavelength—was

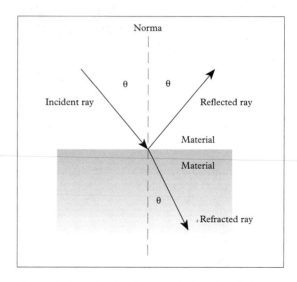

directed through closely spaced pinholes, light and dark bands (called *fringes*) were produced on a screen behind the holes. Bright fringes of light are the result of constructive interference of light waves, and occur when waves from both slits arrive at the screen in phase. Dark fringes are the result of destructive interference, and occur when waves from both slits arrive at the screen out of phase.

When light waves pass through a small opening, or *aperture*, such as a pinhole, an interference pattern rather than a sharp spot of light is observed. This shows that light spreads in various directions beyond the aperture into regions where a shadow would be if light traveled in straight lines. This bending of waves when they pass through an aperture or near the edge of an obstacle is called *diffraction*. When a diffraction pattern is observed far away from the obstacle or opening, it is called a *Fraunhofer diffraction pattern*. When it is observed close to the obstacle or opening, it is called a *Fresnel diffraction pattern*. The fact that light can be diffracted is one evidence that it behaves like a wave.

When light from two point sources that are close together passes through an aperture, the diffraction patterns of the sources may overlap. If the overlap is too great, the two sources cannot be distinguished, or *resolved*, as two separate sources. *Rayleigh's criterion*, which is a limiting condition of resolution, says that two images formed by an aperture are just distinguishable if the central maximum of the diffraction pattern for one image falls on the first minimum of the other image.

A *diffraction grating* has a large number of closely spaced slits. It is used to measure the wavelength of light emitted by a source. When diffraction grating diffracts a beam of light, the colors of the spectrum are produced.

Modern physics

At the end of the nineteenth century, many scientists believed that they had learned most of what there was to know about physics. However, Max Planck and Albert Einstein soon formulated new theories about the interactions of objects, inspiring the birth of modern physics.

Relativity. Most everyday experiences and observations deal with objects that move at speeds less than the speed of light. Newton's laws and other early ideas on space and time were formulated to describe the motion of such objects. However, although these laws worked well for objects at normal speeds, they failed when applied to objects that moved extremely fast. In 1905, Albert Einstein published his special theory of relativity, which described the motions of objects that moved at nearly the speed of light.

The special theory of relativity deals with the way that events appear to different observers, each of whom is moving at a different velocity. Each observer is associated with a *reference frame*, a coordinate system that moves along with the observer. These reference frames are inertial, which means they are not accelerating and not subject to external gravitational influences.

According to Einstein's theory, if two systems are moving uniformly in relation to each other, then it is impossible to determine anything about their motion except that it is relative. Einstein also showed that a moving object appears shortened in the direction of the motion to an observer at rest, a clock in motion appears to run slower than a stationary clock to an observer at rest, and mass increases with velocity.

Einstein based his theory on the following several assumptions: First, the measured value of the speed of light in a vacuum is always the same no matter how fast the observer or light source is moving. Second, the maximum velocity possible in the universe is that of light. And third, absolute speed cannot be measured, only speed relative to some other object.

Quantum physics. Although many problems were resolved by the introduction of the theory of relativity, other problems remained. One such problem was the unsuccessful attempt to describe the behavior of matter on the atomic scale using classical physics. Between 1900 and 1930, a new approach to explaining the behavior of atoms, molecules, and nuclei emerged. This approach, known as *quantum mechanics*, is based on Max Planck's *quantum theory*. While studying a type of energy transmission known as *black-body radiation*, Planck realized that his results

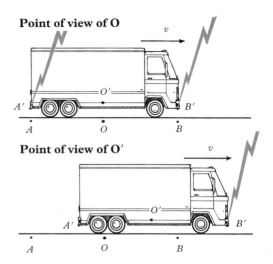

Point of view of O

Point of view of O'

Because an observer's measurements between two events depend on the motion of the observer's reference frame, an observer at O sees the lightning strike both ends of the truck at the same time, while someone at O' sees the right-hand flash first.

could only be explained if energy were produced in individual bundles, or packets, called *quanta*. A *quantum* of energy is emitted as visible light called a *photon*. The amount of energy in each quantum is not the same; instead, it is proportional to the frequency of radiation. When the energy of a photon is divided by its frequency, the resulting quantity is a constant which is known as *Planck's constant* (h) such that $h = E/f$.

Scientists also noticed that when light is incident on certain metallic surfaces, electrons are ejected from the

Some key equations in modern physics

Energy-mass relationship	$E = mc^2$
Mass increase with motion	$m = \dfrac{m_0}{\sqrt{1 - \dfrac{v^2}{c^2}}}$
Planck's constant	$h = 6.63 \times 10^{-34}\,\text{J} \cdot \text{s}$
de Broglie wavelength	$\lambda = \dfrac{h}{p}$
Heisenberg uncertainty principle	$\Delta x \Delta p_x \geq h$ $\Delta E \Delta t \geq h$

surface. This process is known as the *photoelectric effect*. Einstein provided a successful explanation of this effect by extending Planck's quantum theory to the electromagnetic field.

Application of Planck's and Einstein's findings led to the development of *quantum mechanics*. Quantum mechanics explains the process through which atoms emit and absorb photons. Quantum mechanics includes several important principles, one of which is the *Heisenberg uncertainty principle*. This principle states that it is impossible to determine both the exact position and momentum of a particle simultaneously, since the act of making the measurements disturbs the particle and introduces an error into the measurement.

Atomic and nuclear physics.

The concepts of quantum physics are extremely useful in explaining the structure of the atom and its constituent parts (electrons, protons, and neutrons). An electron has different amounts of energy when it is in different orbits around the nucleus. From an energy viewpoint, an electron is said to be in different energy levels when it is in different orbits. The electrons in an atom normally occupy the lowest energy levels available. However, an electron can be boosted to higher levels by various means. When it returns to its stable level, it emits a photon. The energy of the photon is exactly equal to the difference in the energy levels in the atom.

Nuclear physicists are interested in the nucleus of the atom. When the nuclei of certain atoms disintegrate, energy is released along with particles, including alpha particles, beta particles, and gamma rays. This type of disintegration is known as *radioactivity*. The radioactivity of a substance decreases with time and the rate of decrease is different for each element, usually expressed as the *half-life*—that is, the time it takes for half the atoms to decompose.

Particle physics.

Although scientists once believed that the nucleus of an atom only contained three particles, it is now known that a number of subatomic particles exists. Particle physics examines these particles and the forces underlying their interactions:

gravity, electric forces, strong forces, and weak forces.

Particles can be classified into two broad groups, depending on the interactions they experience. *Hadrons* are particles that interact through the strong force; these are further subdivided into *mesons* and *baryons*. *Leptons* are groups of particles that participate in weak interactions.

Applications.

Advances in modern physics have changed the world in which we live.

In medicine, X-rays are used to investigate bones and organs without invading the body. Fetuses can be "viewed" using ultrasound waves. Radioactive particles are used to trace the movement of blood inside veins, arteries, and organs, thus enabling doctors to detect circulatory problems. Certain artificially produced radioactive isotopes are being used to provide gamma rays that can destroy tumors (cancer cells).

In other fields, carbon dating methods have allowed physicists to determine the age of materials such as bones and wood. Self-sustaining chain reactions of radioactive elements can produce heat to propel large ships or turn turbines to generate electricity. Perhaps the most pervasive changes have been caused by advances in electronics, giving us countless household conveniences and communication devices such as the radio, television, digital sound systems, and the ever-present computer.

Some nuclear particles

Particles	Symbol	Charge	Mass (MeV/c2)
Photon	γ	0	0
Neutrino	ν	0	0
Electron	e^-	-1	0.511
Positron	e^+	+1	0.511
Muon	μ	-1	105.7
Proton	p	+1	939.3
Neutron	n	0	939.6

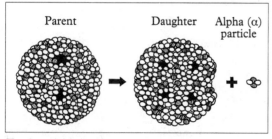

Parent   Daughter   Alpha (α) particle

The release of alpha particles during radioactive decay

Physics

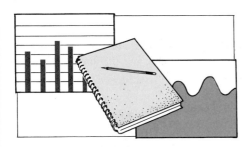

Physics
Tests, homework, and lab reports

Laying the groundwork

Students of a natural science such as physics must understand the basic concepts and principles before attempting to solve assigned problems. Read assigned material carefully before attending the lecture on that material, and jot down points that are not clear to you. In addition, you should reduce memorization to a minimum. Remember that in physics many equations are derived from a few key equations.

Learn how to use the key equations rather than memorize all the equations you see. Lectures and laboratory work should supplement the text and clarify some of the more difficult material. Ask questions whenever necessary. Your understanding of the material will be enhanced through a combination of effective study habits, discussions with other students and instructors, and your ability to solve the assigned problems.

Strategies for success

Problem solving is your key to success in physics. Most courses require the student to learn the skills of problem solving, and tests are largely composed of problems that test such skills. One way to increase accuracy, enhance understanding of concepts, and eliminate lack of direction is to adopt a problem-solving strategy.

In physics, five basic steps to solving problems are commonly used.

1. Draw a suitable diagram with appropriate labels and coordinate axes if needed.
2. Reread the question to identify the basic physical principle involved and list the knowns and unknowns.
3. Select a basic relationship or derive an equation that can be used to find the unknown; solve the equation for the unknown symbolically.
4. Substitute the given values along with the appropriate units into the equation.
5. Obtain the numerical value for the unknown.

Check to make sure the answer is reasonable, that the units match, and that the signs are meaningful.

Helpful hints

Tests

> A traffic light weighing $100 \, n$ hangs from a cable tied to two other cables fastened to a support. The upper cables make angles of 37° and 53° with the horizontal. Find the tension in the three cables.

On tests, your professor is usually more concerned with how you approach a problem than the actual answer to a problem. Therefore, it is important to use the same problem-solving strategy during a test as you use on homework problems. Be sure to clearly show all your work—you will often get points for setting up a problem correctly, even if your final answer is wrong. Don't spend time before the test trying to learn all the equations. Instead, focus on how the concepts are related. For open-book or open-note tests, highlight or tab key equations before the exam, then use the marked equations to derive the equations you need. Don't forget to spend your time efficiently: answer easy questions first, and save time for difficult questions.

Lab reports

> Approximate free fall by rolling a ball down an inclined channel and make measurements to show that acceleration is constant.

Lab work allows you to apply theoretical knowledge, learn the techniques for using equipment, and practice data collection and recording. Before starting a lab, try to understand the procedure of the experiment and the theory underlying it. Then, once in the lab, carefully record in a notebook the question you are trying to answer, the procedure and equipment you are using, your observations during the experiment, your calculations, and your conclusions. It is very important to make sure that you record exactly what you did during a lab and the observations you made.

Glossary

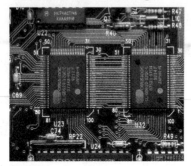

Electricity

Energy

Heat

Refraction

acceleration. Time rate of change of velocity—a vector quantity.

alternating current (AC). The type of current that results from the continued turning of an electromagnet in a fixed magnetic field. The flow of charge alternates direction.

amplitude. The distance between the position of rest and the highest position (crest) of a wave or vibration.

angular displacement. The amount of rotation of a body about an axis.

angular velocity. The time rate of change of angular displacement.

capacitance. Rating, stated in ohms, of the ability of a conductor to store and receive electrical charge.

capacitor. A device for receiving and storing electrical charge.

circuit. A complete path through which electric current flows.

conductor. A material that allows electric charge to pass freely.

conservation of energy. The principle that the total amount of energy in the universe does not vary, although energy can be changed from one form into another.

conservation of momentum. The principle that the total momentum of any system remains constant in the absence of outside forces.

crest. The high part, or peak, of a wave.

diffraction. The bending of waves when they pass near the edge of an obstacle or through a small opening.

direct current (DC). The type of current in which charge flows continually in one direction.

displacement. The change in position of an object in space; the difference between the initial position of an object and a later position.

electric current. An electric charge in motion; the flow of electricity.

electric field. Space in the vicinity of charged objects in which a force due to the charge exists.

electricity. A form of energy that can produce light, heat, magnetism, and chemical changes. Electricity is regarded as consisting of oppositely charged particles—electrons and protons.

electromagnetic induction. Production of an electric current by means of a magnet.

electromagnetic spectrum. The entire range of the different types of electromagnetic waves.

electromagnetic waves. A wave of energy generated by a varying electric and magnetic field when an electric charge oscillates or is accelerated.

electromotive force. The force resulting from differences of potential that causes an electric current.

energy. The capacity to do work or to produce change.

equilibrium. Point when the resultant force acting on an object is zero.

force. Something that causes a body to move or accelerate; a vector quantity.

frequency. Number of vibrations per given unit time of a wave form.

gravitation. The attraction of one body for another.

gravity. The natural force that causes objects to move or tend to move toward the center of the earth, moon, or planet.

heat. A form of energy that consists of motion of the molecules of a substance, capable of being transmitted from one body to another.

heat capacity. The ratio of the quantity of heat applied to a system or body to the change in temperature which the heat induces.

incidence, angle of. The angle that a ray or wave makes with a line perpendicular to a boundary between two media.

inertia. A tendency of all objects and matter to stay still if still, or if moving, to go on moving unless acted on by some outside force.

insulator. A nonconductor; material that impedes the passage of electric charge.

interference. The reciprocal action of waves by which they reinforce or diminish one another.

internal energy. The total kinetic and potential energy associated with the motions and relative positions of the molecules of an object.

kinetic energy. The energy a body has because of its motion.

linear motion. Motion in a straight line.

longitudinal wave. Wave in which individual particles of a medium move back and forth in the same direction as the wave moves.

magnetic field. The space around a magnet in which a magnetic force is felt.

mass. Amount of matter an object or substance contains.

mechanics. The branch of physics dealing with the action of forces on objects at rest or in motion.

moment of inertia. A measure of the resistance of a body to angular acceleration.

momentum. A measure of the motion of a body equal to the mass times the velocity.

Newton's laws of motion. (1) A body continues in a state of rest or in a uniform straight-line motion unless acted upon by an outside force. (2) The change in motion of a body is proportional to the force applied. (3) For every action, there is an equal and opposite reaction.

normal. A line perpendicular to the boundary or surface of a material.

period. The time required for one complete cycle in a vibration or wave.

potential difference. Difference in electrical charge between two points; voltage.

potential energy. The energy of a body due to its position.

power. The rate at which work is done.

reflection. The turning back of a ray of light or wave when striking a surface.

reflection, angle of. The angle that a ray or wave makes with a line perpendicular to a reflecting surface.

refraction. Change in the direction of rays going through a boundary when coming in at an angle to the normal.

refraction, angle of. The angle that a ray or wave makes with a line perpendicular to a surface separating two media.

refraction, index of. The ratio of light's speed in a vacuum to its speed in a given material.

resistance. The capacity of an object or material to impede electric current.

resistor. A device used to control an electric current because of its resistance.

solenoid. A current-carrying coil surrounding a movable iron core.

speed. The rate at which something moves.

static electricity. An electric charge resting on an object.

temperature. The degree of hotness or coldness of an object or an environment.

thermodynamics. The branch of

physics that deals with the relations between heat and other forms of energy.

thermodynamics, laws of. (1) When work is transferred into heat or vice versa, the amount of work is always equivalent to the amount of heat. (2) It is impossible by any continuous self-sustaining process for heat to be transferred from a colder body to a hotter body.

torque. The ability of a force to produce rotation.

transverse wave. A wave in which individual particles of the medium move at right angles to the direction of the wave's propagation.

trough. The lowest point of a wave.

velocity. The rate at which a body moves in a given direction—a vector quantity.

wave. Any disturbance traveling through a medium by which energy is transferred from one particle to another without causing any permanent displacement of the medium itself.

wavelength. The distance between one peak of a wave and the next corresponding peak.

wave pulse. A single wave sent out along a path from a vibrating body.

wave train. A group of waves sent out at successive intervals along the same path from a vibrating body.

weight. The force with which a body is attracted to the earth or some other field of gravitation.

work. Transfer of energy to an object by the application of force.

For further reading

Brancazio, P. J. *Sport Science*. New York: Simon & Schuster, 1984.

Coletta, Vincent. *College Physics*. New York: Mosby, 1995.

Glashow, Sheldon. *The Charm of Physics*. New York: Simon & Schuster, 1991.

Jewell, John W., Jr. *Physics Begins With an M: Mystery, Magic, and Myth*. Boston: Allyn & Bacon, 1994.

Jones, Edwin, and Richard Childers. *Contemporary College Physics*. Reading, Mass.: Addison-Wesley, 1993.

Social Sciences

- Psychology
- Sociology
- Political Science
- Cultural Anthropology

Psychology

Why do human beings behave the way they do? Throughout human history, people have tried to answer that question. Those answers were the subject matter of literary works, philosophic debates, and medical prognoses. But one hundred and fifty years ago, the answers grew more precise when psychology, the scientific study of behavior, was born.

Today there is a great diversity of interests within the field of psychology, placing psychologists in clinical, laboratory, educational, and business settings. The field continues to evolve because new information is always generating new questions about human and animal behavior. Though the activities and interests are varied, all subfields of psychology are concerned with the prediction and control of behavior.

Foundations

The science of psychology has grown out of many different disciplines. Two of the driving forces in the early development of psychology were philosophy (study of wisdom) and anatomy/physiology (study of the structure and functions of the human body).

Philosophers. In their attempts to explain the mysteries of human behavior, philosophers relied on pure reason. Aristotle astutely guessed that mental disorders were linked to body ailments, but he also speculated that thinking took place in the heart. In the 1600s, René Descartes reasoned that the mind and body were separate entities connected by a single gland. John Locke proposed that the mind was a blank slate ("tabula rasa") at birth. Obviously, more than logic was needed to explain the complexities of thought and behavior.

Nevertheless, the philosophers were first to pose the two questions about human nature that are central to the science of psychology. The *nativism* of Descartes asked how much of who we are is based on what we are born with. The *empiricism* of Locke asked how much of who we are is due to the manner in which we are raised.

Wilhelm Wundt   *Sigmund Freud*

Physiologists. In the 1800s, physiologists brought scientific method to the study of behavior. Based on systematic observation, measurement, and testing, their studies could be replicated and shared. E. H. Weber and Gustav Fechner examined perception differences among subjects. Hermann von Helmholtz focused on perception and the physiology of sensation. Paul Broca's discovery of the brain's speech area opened more windows into the perceptual systems of the brain.

Major movements. In the late nineteenth century, a school of psychological thought called *structuralism* developed from the ideas of Wilhelm Wundt. Wundt used scientific method to study the various elements of consciousness. Structuralists broke down the concept of consciousness into basic components such as feelings and perceptions, which could then be analyzed. Participants were trained in introspection, a technique that called for them to monitor and report on their own sensations. *Functionalism*, which was established in 1890 by William James, argued that structuralism didn't acknowledge the fluid state of the mind. By studying the "stream of consciousness," James hoped to be able to determine the function of human consciousness.

Behaviorism studied only those behaviors that were observable, in an attempt to determine the relationship between events in the environment (stimuli) and behaviors (responses). The work of John Watson, Ivan Pavlov, and B. F. Skinner illustrated how environment shapes behavior.

Gestalt psychology used the study of perception to demonstrate that the whole of anything, especially a human being, may have qualities that don't exist in any of its individual parts. Gestaltists such as Max Wertheimer believed that humans are always striving for completeness and that the whole is more meaningful than the sum of its parts.

Psychoanalytic psychology looked beneath awareness

to examine unconscious elements that shape personality, emotional reactions, and behaviors. Sigmund Freud developed a method called psychoanalysis, in which subjects, by talking to an analyst, bring unconscious, primitive drives to conscious awareness. *Humanism* emphasized human beings' powerful drive toward growth. Carl Rogers argued that behavior isn't governed by the environment or the unconscious, but rather by a self-concept that is in harmony or conflict with a person's life experience.

In the last thirty years, two new interdisciplinary movements have arisen in psychology. *Cognitive science* is the study of thinking and decision making. *Neuroscience* seeks to understand behavior through the study of the brain and neural mechanisms.

In 1892 G. Stanley Hall helped to establish the American Psychological Association. Today more than 60,000 psychologists with a wide variety of beliefs and backgrounds belong to this organization.

Major movements

Movement	Contributors	Theory
Structuralism (1878)	W. Wundt G. S. Hall	Analysis of conscious experiences
Functionalism (1890)	W. James	Study of the purpose and function of consciousness
Psychoanalysis (1909)	S. Freud C. G. Jung	Study of personality and disorders through the exploration of the unconscious
Behaviorism (1913)	I. Pavlov B. F. Skinner	Study of observable behavior as it is caused by the environment
Gestalt (1920)	M. Wertheimer	Study of whole being rather than analysis of the parts
Humanism (1951)	C. Rogers A. Maslow	Study of self-concept and self-regard in human beings
Cognitive science (1965)	N. Chomsky H. Simon	Study of higher mental processes
Neuroscience (1970)	D. O. Hebb R. Sperry	Study of behavior through the study of the brain and neural mechanisms

The human organism

There are over one billion nerve cells (*neurons*) in the human body. These receive, integrate, and transmit messages along the *central nervous system* (the brain and spinal cord) and the *peripheral nervous system* (nerves and structures outside the brain and spinal cord).

Through recent developments in psychopharmacology and brain tissue transplants, psychologists believe that cures for diseases such as Alzheimer's and Parkinson's are on the horizon.

The nervous system.

Neurons, which are densely interconnected, receive information from the environment or from other neurons through their branchlike *dendrites*. The signal, or nerve impulse, is then transmitted along the neuron's *axon* to terminal buttons at the end of the axon. The buttons release chemicals called *neurotransmitters*, which allow the signal to leap across the gap (*synapse*) to a dendrite of the next neuron. When information is received, many types of neurons must communicate with each other in order to coordinate a response.

The brain organizes all the incoming messages and sends responses through the spinal cord, a long, thin extension of the brain that runs down past the waist. From the spinal cord, messages travel to the rest of the body through the peripheral nervous system, which contains the *somatic system* (sense receptors and voluntary muscles) and the *autonomic system* (functions such as heartbeat and breathing). Messages are transmitted to the muscles through cells called *motor neurons*.

The brain is divided into three areas called the hindbrain, midbrain, and forebrain. The *hindbrain* begins where the spinal cord attaches to the brain stem. It

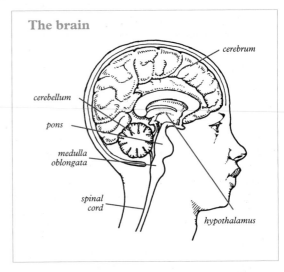

The brain

- cerebrum
- cerebellum
- pons
- medulla oblongata
- spinal cord
- hypothalamus

contains the structures (the medulla, pons, and cerebellum) that handle automatic functions of the body. The *midbrain*, located between the hindbrain and the forebrain, helps to process sensory information and control movements. The *forebrain* contains several small structures responsible for many complex brain activities: the *thalamus* (integrates and relays sensory information), the *hypothalamus* (regulates biological drives), and a group of structures called the *limbic system* (involved with emotion and memory). The forebrain is also part of the largest portion of the brain, the *cerebrum*, which controls complex processes such as thought, learning, and awareness. The cerebrum is divided into two halves, which are called the right and left hemispheres.

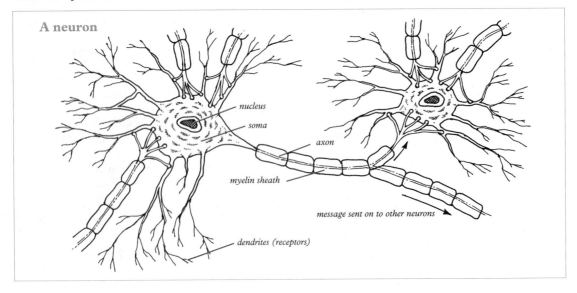

A neuron

- nucleus
- soma
- axon
- myelin sheath
- message sent on to other neurons
- dendrites (receptors)

The endocrine system.

Another system that controls behavior and body function is the *endocrine system*, a network of glands and their chemical secretions (*hormones*) that uses the bloodstream to travel throughout the body. The endocrine system controls body functions such as sleep, sexual behavior, digestion, metabolism, and physical development. The communication begins at the base of the forebrain with the hypothalamus. The hypothalamus sends messages to the *pituitary gland*, which then secretes hormones into the bloodstream, affecting glands throughout the entire body. Complex processes such as sexual development, in which many body parts develop at the same time, use the pituitary gland to coordinate body functions.

The perceptual systems.

The perceptual systems use seven senses to relay external data to the brain.

The *visual system* (sight) is the most complex perceptual system, not only because it is the primary sense in humans, but also because elements in the visual field are always changing. The eye must process light and dark, movement, depth, color, pattern, and form. The eye's *lens* focuses light, while the *pupil* controls the amount of light landing on the neural tissue (*retina*) at the back of the eye. *Receptor cells* in the retina are specialized to receive different kinds of data. The complex visual input is organized only after the information arrives at the back of the brain in the visual cortex.

The *auditory system* (hearing) perceives sound waves, which are similar to water ripples created when a stone enters a pond. If the distance between the waves is long, the sound is perceived as a low note; if the waves are close together, the note is high. A tall wave is perceived as a loud sound and a low wave as a quiet sound. Sound waves are converted into neural signals within the inner ear, then transmitted to the thalamus and auditory cortex.

The *olfactory system* (smell) uses the nose and the olfactory bulb at the base of the brain to translate chemical stimuli in the air or mouth into a perception of smell. In the *gustatory system* (taste), *taste buds* on the tongue relay information about flavor to the thalamus. The *tactile system* (touch) has sensors all over the body that receive data about the external world (hard/soft, hot/cold, pain), which are transmitted to the *somatosensory cortex*. The *kinesthetic sense* transmits information about body position. The *vestibular system* monitors body location in space and responds to gravity.

Consciousness.

During waking hours there are varying levels of consciousness. When a person learns something new, attention is focused on the task at hand, excluding other stimuli; once learned, the task can be done automatically, even while a person is engaged in another activity. During sleep, levels of consciousness also vary. *Electroencephalograms* (EEGs) demonstrate five stages of sleep. *REM* (or rapid eye movement) sleep is the dreaming stage, when brain activity resembles wakefulness and the eyes move rapidly under the eyelids. People cycle through all five stages several times in the night, with longer and longer REM periods.

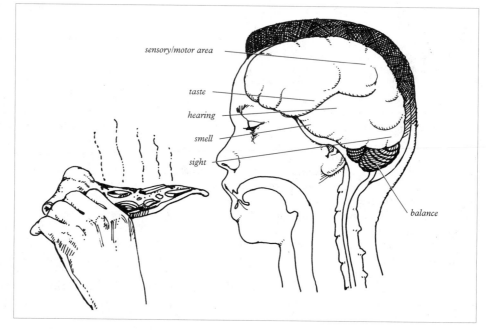

Many sense receptors are stimulated at the same time during the simple act of eating.

sensory/motor area

taste

hearing

smell

sight

balance

Development

Every human being is unique, having been created and molded through a combination of genetics and life experiences. But as different as people are from each other, everyone passes the same developmental milestones.

The beginning.
Human development begins at the moment of conception and progresses rapidly during the nine months of gestation. Throughout that period, the developing fetus is vulnerable to damage from the mother's illnesses, poor nutrition, or drug and alcohol use.

In the germinal stage (the first two weeks of gestation), the fertilized egg, or *zygote*, implants itself in the uterine wall. In the *embryonic stage* (the third week through the second month), all the major structures of the body are developing. During the *fetal stage* (the third month through birth), movements can be felt by the mother as bones and muscles develop and are used by the growing fetus.

Infancy and childhood.
Every child develops at a different pace. Temperament and intelligence, like hair and eye color, seem to be based on genetics and may be established at birth.

Soon after the baby is born, bonds between parents and baby are formed which are vital for the baby's emotional development. From birth to the age of two, the baby uses movement to develop musculature. Learning that it is safe to separate from the parents, the child spends the next few years refining motor skills and taking on challenges associated with language and first friendships. From ages six to twelve, the child's cognitive, intellectual, emotional, and moral growth reach past the self-focused, concrete thinking of early childhood to a more abstract, empathic view of the world.

Jean Piaget proposed in 1929 that the thought processes of children progress through four stages: the *sensorimotor period*, in which children gradually recognize that objects are permanent; the *preoperational stage*, marked by egocentrism, centration, and irreversibility; the *concrete operations period*, when children begin using conservation and classification skills; and the *formal operations period*, during which children learn to think logically and in the abstract.

In 1963, the American psychoanalyst Erik Erikson divided human development into psychosocial stages. Believing that personality continues to evolve throughout a person's life, he proposed that personality is shaped by how people deal with psychological crises. In childhood, Erikson's stages are:

Adolescence is a time of learning, experimenting, and growing.

1. *Trust vs. mistrust (birth to age 1)*. If the infant's needs are adequately met, the child will develop personality traits that exhibit optimism and trust.

2. *Autonomy vs. doubt (ages 2-3)*. In this stage, the toddler takes some responsibility for personal care and the parents set limits on behaviors. If parent-child conflicts are successfully resolved, the child will develop self-sufficiency and a sense of adequacy.

3. *Initiative vs. guilt (ages 4-6)*. The child develops purpose and self-confidence by successfully interacting within the family.

4. *Industry vs. inferiority (ages 6-puberty)*. In this stage, the child begins to function outside the family in school and neighborhood environments and develops competence in cognitive, physical, and social skills.

Adolescence.
During adolescence, young people experience dramatic growth and change in their bodies as secondary sexual characteristics begin to emerge. Social relationships broaden to include interest in members of the opposite sex.

The many physical, cognitive, and social changes during this time create confusion and turbulence, and so young people seek stability by working out a self-concept that addresses the questions *Who am I?* and *What do I want to do?* During this stage of development, adolescents may experiment with different kinds of values, experiences, friendships, and modes of self-expression. Young peers help each other test these emerging values and identities, and establish their roles. Power struggles between parents and children are a normal part of the separation process as young people prepare for life on their own.

Adulthood.

The end of adolescence does not mean that developmental stages come to an end. Though some personality traits remain stable, the personality itself continues to evolve throughout adult life. As in the case of children, however, the rates of development differ from person to person.

Research on adult development supports the theory that adulthood can also be divided into stages—predictable periods of stability at some points, and of crisis and self-examination at others. For the young adult, there are questions about embarking upon vocation, marriage, and family life. The transition to middle adulthood is marked by reflection as one's life goals are examined and reworked. The resulting instability is usually followed by calm. Professional productivity and problem-solving abilities remain stable well into late adulthood. Though the speed of cognitive processing declines with age, judgment tends to improve.

Erik Erikson, as was mentioned previously, developed one of the most widely accepted models of adult development. This model describes three crises that must be resolved: intimacy versus isolation; generativity versus self-absorption; and integrity versus despair.

Contemporary American psychologist Daniel Levinson focused on transitional crises as adults enter their thirties, forties, and fifties—crises that are frequently based on an increasing awareness of mortality. Often during these transitional times, life goals are reevaluated.

> ### Why studying psychology pays off
> ### Reason #2:
>
> When you study the roots of behavior and techniques of self-control, you will be able to make better choices about your actions. You will be able to act, instead of react.

Stages of human development

Erikson's stages	Piaget's stages	Stage/age	Growth	Language	Cognition	Personality	Social
Trust vs. mistrust	Sensorimotor	0-2 years	Lifts head at 1 month, can run by 1 year	From babbling to 1-word sentences (holophrases)	Object permanence by 2 years	Temperament can be seen early on	Bonding, stranger/separation anxiety
Autonomy vs. doubt Initiative vs. guilt	Preoperational	2-6 years	Improving gross motor control, fine motor emerging	From 3-word sentences to well-developed syntax	Centration; irreversibility	Separation from parents	First friendship
Industry vs. inferiority	Concrete operations	6-12 years	Girls developing more quickly than boys	Language play (puns, metaphors)	Conservation; long-term memory improves; decentration; reversibility	Role taking, empathy	Same-sex friends
Identity vs. role confusion	Formal operations	12-20 years	Boys gain in height and weight; secondary sex characteristics developing	Finer handling of language, syntax	Abstract, reflective thinking	Identity exploration	Interaction with opposite sex

Late adulthood. As human beings mature into late adulthood (sixty-five years and older), they need to adjust to many physical and life-style changes. Retirement from the workplace can bring an increase in life satisfaction because more time is finally available for the pursuit of personal interests. Some older adults start post-retirement careers in new fields or in areas related to their previous career, such as consulting or teaching. Though the life-style and health of the older adult will affect productivity, the creative and intellectual performance of the adult can remain stable well into the adult's seventies. Marital satisfaction often increases in late adulthood, and older parents enjoy their role as grandparents.

There is a gradual decline of cognitive speed, memory, and problem solving, but the rate of decline differs among adults just as growth rates differ among children. Only 5 percent of adults over sixty-five experience the abnormal deterioration in mental faculties known as senility. Changes in vision and hearing can be compensated for with the use of glasses, cataract surgery, and hearing aids. Many older adults are staying healthier longer with low-impact exercise.

Moral development. Though the morality of an issue is often debated for years within political, philosophic, and religious institutions, parents pass on their own feelings about right and wrong to children as young as one year old, and those feelings continue to evolve throughout subsequent stages of life.

American psychologist Lawrence Kohlberg pioneered an influential model of moral development by presenting difficult moral dilemmas to children, adolescents, and adults. He asked what the subject would do if faced with a particular dilemma and why, and he described the "why" as moral reasoning. In his studies, Kohlberg discovered six stages as the child matured toward adulthood. These six stages, in three levels, are shown in the table below.

As Piaget first proposed, moral development seems tied to cognitive development. But feminist psychologist Carol Gilligan theorized that an additional factor is present for females in their moral decision making, and that is the factor of self-sacrifice. For both males and females, however, the relationship between moral reasoning and moral behavior appears to be strong.

Kohlberg's levels of moral development

Level 1 Preconventional morality		Level 2 Conventional morality		Level 3 Postconventional morality	
Stage 1 Actions guided by fear of punishment	*Stage 2* Actions guided by desire for reward	*Stage 3* Actions guided by desire for approval of others	*Stage 4* Actions guided by law and order mentality	*Stage 5* Actions guided by flexible social contract	*Stage 6* Actions guided by internal principles and conscience

A woman steals milk for her baby because she has no money. Should she have done that?

"She might go to jail."	"Her baby would be around when she got out of jail."	"People would understand."	"It's her duty as a mom."	"Her baby has the right to be fed."	"Life is more important than law."

Learning and cognition

A renewed interest in *cognition*—the mental processes involved in acquiring knowledge—has yielded valuable information in the areas of intelligence testing, memory, language, and problem solving.

Intelligence and mental abilities.

In the late nineteenth century, Sir Francis Galton hypothesized that intelligence was passed down genetically in families. To find an objective measure for intelligence, Galton tested sensory acuity in his subjects on the assumption that bright minds would exhibit more of this quality than would average minds. He invented the testing term *correlation*. In France, Alfred Binet was commissioned in 1904 to design the first intelligence test to help identify and predict which children would need special help. The mental age of the child was compared with the subject's chronological age, and discrepancies were interpreted as indicating retardation or giftedness. At Stanford University in 1916, Lewis Terman incorporated a new scoring system called the *intelligence quotient*, or I.Q., in his revision of the Binet intelligence test, and this system helped to compare children of different ages. In 1939, David Weschler at Bellevue Hospital in New York developed an adult intelligence test (WAIS) and two children's tests (WISC and WPPSI), which added nonverbal components and subtests to the intelligence test.

Today, there are many *psychological tests* that measure the individual differences among people in the categories of mental ability and personality. Test results can aid in determining the intellectual potential, vocational interests, and personality traits of children and adults. Results from psychological tests, however, must be interpreted with caution, because the measurements represent only a portion of a person's overall abilities and character. With this in mind, researchers try to make sure that tests are *standardized* (administered and scored uniformly), *reliable* (yielding the same results when repeated), and *valid* (able to measure what the test is designed to measure). But human behavior isn't always consistent, and so results must be interpreted carefully.

Aptitude tests measure the ability to learn, and *achievement tests* measure present knowledge. High school students may elect to take the SAT I and II, ACT, and driving exams. Proficiency testing is required to receive a high school diploma in many states.

Among theorists, there is a continuing debate as to whether nature (heredity) or nurture (environment) can influence intelligence. American psychologist Arthur Jensen interpreted the differences in I.Q. scores

Identical twins

among ethnic groups as reflecting genetic differences. His controversial position has since been brought into question by adoption studies, in which I.Q. scores went up when children were moved from deprived households to enriched households. These studies seem to indicate that I.Q. can indeed be shaped by environment. In addition, there has been renewed interest recently in the cultural bias that may exist in I.Q. testing. Studies comparing twins who were reared separately are also being used to assess hereditary and environmental influences on intelligence. Researchers agree, however, that *Down's syndrome* and some other forms of mental retardation are caused by genetic abnormalities.

Memory.

The first step in creating memory is attention. Once attended to or selected, the information is converted into a memory code that is either *structural* (related to something physical), *phonemic* (related to pronunciation), or *semantic* (related to meaning). These types of memory code provide progressively deeper levels of processing and slower rates of forgetting. The most effective memory code links the information to a visual image.

Once the information is encoded, it goes into the memory for storage. There are three types of memory storage: *sensory memory* keeps the memory lingering for a few seconds, as if the item were still present; *short-term memory* can store approximately seven unrehearsed items for thirty seconds; *long-term memory* is parceled into subdivisions, where memories are stored indefinitely.

Information can be retrieved from memory storage through searches, either by associated ideas or context clues. Forgetting can be caused by faulty encoding,

Skinner box

interference, or motivated forgetting, as in the case of a traumatic memory. Some psychologists believe memories are never forgotten. They believe that through hypnosis or therapy, these long-forgotten memories can be recalled. Therapists believe that by bringing these memories into consciousness, people can better understand their unconscious motives and fears, and thereby make changes in their lives.

Learning. During his study of dogs' digestive processes in 1903, Ivan Pavlov observed that his dogs were salivating when they heard the preliminary clicking sound of the meat-powder dispenser. He decided to pair a neutral stimulus that did not elicit salivation (the sound of a bell) with a stimulus that did elicit sali-

vation (meat powder). After repeated pairings, the dogs salivated at the sound of the bell. Pavlov labeled that reaction a *conditioned response*, and his technique came to be known as *classical conditioning*. Pavlov postulated that people make similar learned associations.

In the 1930s, B. F. Skinner proposed that behaviors are voluntary but can be controlled by the manipulation of consequences that result from those behaviors. Known as *operant conditioning*, this type of learned association was illustrated with rats in a specialized apparatus, called the *Skinner box*. Skinner showed that favorable consequences—*reinforcers*—strengthened the subject's tendency to make a response. More complicated forms of conditioning were also studied by Skinner, using punishments as well as reinforcers. He investigated schedules for delivering reinforcers and developed new techniques for shaping and extinguishing chosen behaviors.

In 1973, American psychologist Albert Bandura expanded conditioning theories to include people who learn by observation. *Observational learning* occurs when one person observes and picks up behaviors from another person, called a *model*. According to the theory of observational learning, viewing television violence may be linked to aggressive behavior. Cognitive theories of learning, however, give more weight to thought processes. For example, studies with lab rats have shown that rats can actively filter out certain kinds of stimuli.

Classical conditioning

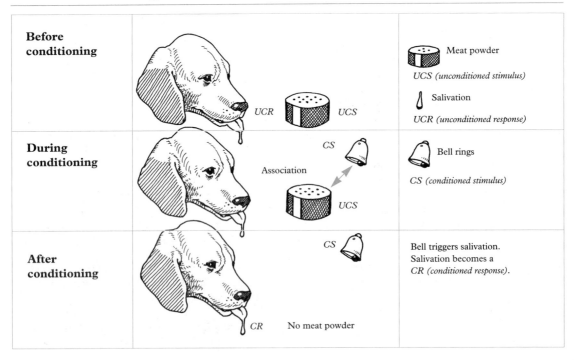

         Psychology

Washoe and son

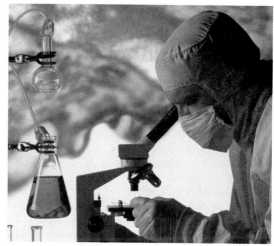

Problem solving

Cognitive processes.

The complex processes of thought and language set human beings apart from all other animals. Only the human brain can sort, manipulate, and recombine symbols to generate new thoughts and concepts. Just how thoughts evolve into the symbols called language is still a topic of debate among theorists.

Language. The first sounds made by babies are the same, across all cultural boundaries. By six months, however, babbling noises narrow down to the sounds found in the family's native language. Babies start imitating *phonemes*, the basic sound units of language. Later, toddlers begin to understand *morphemes*, which are the basic units of meaning, and try to combine them into first words. The first stage in this process is to use *holophrases* (one-word sentences), such as "Cookie" to mean "I want a cookie." Next, toddlers speak in *telegraphic sentences*, in which nonessential words are left out. Finally, through imitation, toddlers learn *syntax*, or rules of word order. Later, when an understanding of *semantics*, or meaning, is developed, the child might become adept at puns and other word play.

Language may not be uniquely human. A chimpanzee named Washoe was taught to use American Sign Language. (Sign language was used because chimps lack the vocal apparatus to produce human speech.) Trained in the same way as a deaf child, Washoe developed a sign vocabulary of over 160 words and learned to combine them into her own simple sentences. However, the debate remains over whether she and chimps in similiar studies were generating original sentences or just imitating and repeating gestures that would produce reinforcers, as in operant conditioning.

Language contains symbols that humans employ to form concepts. But the relationship between thought and language is complex. Children may use a word correctly but still have no conceptual understanding of its meaning; for example, *dog* may mean only their dog rather than the more general concept of dog, which includes common characteristics of all dogs. And conversely, people can think and solve problems without language, as toddlers prove.

Problem solving and creativity. Each person forms concepts, decisions, and solutions in a different way. The decisions made during problem solving follow one of two methods: *algorithms* or *heuristics*. The *algorithm method* accomplishes an end in a step-by-step procedure. Since this method is time consuming, algorithms are often more efficiently used by computers than by humans. The *heuristic method* selectively seeks solutions in a way that often amounts to trial and error. This method is often faster, but it may lead to less accurate solutions.

Why are some people more creative in problem solving and forming new concepts? Much of it has to do with whether a person is skilled in *divergent thinking* (generating many possible solutions) or *convergent thinking* (narrowing down solutions). Divergent thinking is more likely to result in creative answers, as in the process of brainstorming, while convergent thinking is more likely to aid in the process of decision making once the options are laid out.

Since intelligence tests measure convergent thinking skills, which are not central to the creative process, it is difficult to find a correlation between intelligence and creativity. But there is a high correlation between certain personality traits and creativity. Creative people tend to be independent thinkers with a high tolerance for ambiguity and complexity.

In the field of *artificial intelligence*, psychologists and computer scientists are attempting to create computers that can "think" as humans do.

Personality and disorders

As Gestaltists would agree, human beings are more than complex neural transmissions, reflexes, drives, and thoughts. All of us have unique traits and responses to life that define our personalities. Theories differ regarding how personality develops and functions, and why it malfunctions. There are three major schools of thought, and therapies for behavior disorders are based on one of the three.

Personality. The *psychodynamic view* of personality, developed by Sigmund Freud, posits that personality is made up of the *id* (primitive drives), the *superego* (moral conscience), and the *ego* (which seeks a balance between the two). Behavior is the result of interaction among the three. Disorders stem from unresolved conflicts and unconscious fixations from childhood. The *behavioral view* of B. F. Skinner focuses on a person's history of reinforced responses. In this view, maladaptive behavior is simply faulty learning. The *humanistic view* of Carl Rogers looks at the self-concept that evolves during the various stages of development. Rogers believed disorders may result when self-concept does not fit with life experience, and that unconditional love fosters a self-concept that will mesh well with real life.

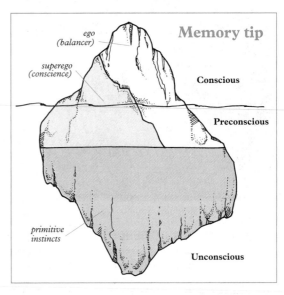

ego (balancer)
superego (conscience)
primitive instincts

Memory tip

Conscious

Preconscious

Unconscious

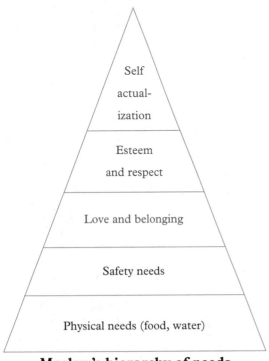

Self actual-ization

Esteem and respect

Love and belonging

Safety needs

Physical needs (food, water)

Maslow's hierarchy of needs
Basic needs / Growth needs

Psychologists study *motivation* to better understand the underlying biological and social drives in human beings. Biological needs motivate the kinds of behavior that will satisfy bodily needs such as thirst, hunger, and pain avoidance. Social needs for belonging, respect, and achievement motivate other behaviors. Biological and social needs often mesh, as in the need to parent. In an attempt to understand human motivation, Abraham Maslow suggested a *hierarchy-of-needs model* that integrated biological and social needs. He proposed that *basic needs* must be met before human beings can focus on *growth needs* and the fulfillment of their human potential.

Emotion is another area of study that has yielded information about behavior. The *James–Lange theory* proposes that emotions are created through body arousal to a stimulus. The *Cannon–Bard theory* suggests simultaneous brain activity and physiological arousal. *Schachter's two-factor theory* combines aspects of both theories by adding interpretation to the perception process: People look at external cues in determining what label to give the particular type of body arousal they are experiencing. Contemporary psychologist and author Albert Ellis believes we can alter our appraisal of stressful events and thus prevent certain emotional reactions from taking place.

Abnormal behavior and therapies.
Three criteria are used to decide if a behavior is abnormal: the presence of *personal distress*; *deviance* from the cultural norms; and *maladaptive behavior* that interferes with daily functioning.

Psychology

The *Diagnostic and Statistical Manual of Mental Disorders (DSM)* subdivides psychological disorders into small groups with common symptoms, removing the general terms of neurosis and psychosis. The *DSM-III-R* (most recent revision) has classified over two hundred types of psychological disorders. Controversy exists over the type and number of disorders that have been added over the years to the *DSM*. Nevertheless, assessment has come a long way from the days when mental disorders were blamed on supernatural forces and the mentally ill were locked up in asylums, where they were far away from help and hope.

Abnormal behavior can take many forms. Most people with psychological disorders are in touch with reality, even though their coping behaviors are based on avoidance. *Anxiety disorders* are characterized by feelings of excessive fear and apprehension. When people suffer *somatoform disorders*, they complain of physical problems, though the basis of the problems is in fact psychological. Amnesia and multiple personalities are features of *dissociative disorders*. *Personality disorders* are marked by some traits which are extreme or inflexible enough to impair various types of social and occupational functioning.

Unlike the above problems, *schizophrenic disorders* exhibit a loss of touch with reality, including irrational thought, maladaptive functioning, and distorted perception (hallucinations). Genetic, neurochemical, and structural factors have been linked to schizophrenia. Neurochemical abnormalities also occur in *mood disorders*, which are marked by emotional disturbances that affect functioning.

Psychological disorders, whatever their type, are assessed through neurological exams, clinical observations, and a variety of psychological tests. The MMPI and other self-report inventories are designed to measure various aspects of personality, including attitudes and traits known by the respondent, as well as unconscious drives.

Therapy for psychological disorders may involve client insight, behavior conditioning, or therapeutic drugs in various treatment approaches. Many therapists today use an eclectic combination of therapies that meet the complex, individual needs of the client. *Insight therapies* help clients better understand themselves through their verbal interactions with the therapist. In *psychoanalysis*, unconscious motivations and repressed memories are brought to conscious awareness through free association and dream interpretation. In *client-centered therapies*, clients are given unconditional positive support as they restructure their self-concept through value clarification and self-acceptance. *Cognitive therapies*, using a rational-emotive approach, help clients recognize and change their own self-defeating thoughts, behaviors, and beliefs.

Some behavior therapies use systematic desensitization, which pairs relaxation with the phobic stimulus. Others reinforce desired behaviors with tokens in a so-called *token economy*. In *aversion therapy*, the unwanted behavior is paired with an unpleasant stimulus to help eliminate the response. Shaping and modeling appropriate behaviors can facilitate the development of social skills.

Biomedical therapies use therapeutic drugs successfully to treat a variety of psychological disorders. But the side effects of drug treatments must be weighed against their proven benefits. Less often, in the treatment of severe mood disorders, *electroconvulsive therapy* is used.

Therapy styles

Type	Major contributors	Therapy style
Biomedical	J. Delay A. Deniker	Let me listen to your heart. Any problems with your medication?
Psychoanalytic	S. Freud C. G. Jung	What do you think of when I say "mother"? What do you think water means in that dream?
Behavior	B. F. Skinner J. Wolpe	You will get a shock every time you pick up that cigarette. Every time you go an hour without smoking, give yourself a treat.
Cognitive	A. Ellis	What's the payoff for hanging on to that negative thought? What thought can you substitute for it?
Humanistic/ client-centered	C. Rogers A. Maslow	I hear what you're saying. You sound angry. Am I getting that right?

The social animal

Since human beings live and work in groups, many aspects of personality and behavior are influenced by others. *Social psychology* studies how thoughts and behaviors are shaped in interpersonal relationships and within social contexts.

Social behavior.
People use social schemata, such as *stereotypes*, in grouping others, so that they will know what to expect during social interactions. But stereotyping can alter a person's perception of the differences that exist within a group. Blanket judgments about groups are called *attitudes*. Negative attitudes, like prejudice, carry a predisposition to behave in a certain way toward a person from a group. Attitudes can sometimes be changed through observational learning that disproves such blanket judgments.

Attraction is strongest among people who live or work near each other. Similarities in attitude, attractiveness, and reciprocity of behavior can also attract people to each other. The study of human love has provided information about various styles of loving. Some studies suggest that the quality of attachment between infant and caretaker is related to the style of love that the caretaker adopts (trusting and intimate, anxious and jealous) in intimate relationships.

Aggressive behavior, whether displayed physically or verbally, is sometimes used to achieve a goal or to hurt another. Researchers believe that while temperament and genetics influence aggressive behavior, aggression can also be learned from role models in the home and on television.

Why studying psychology pays off
Reason #3:

By understanding how other people see the world, you will develop more empathy and patience interacting with others, and your communications skills will be enhanced.

Altruistic behavior may also be influenced by genetics and role models. Helpful behavior is often seen in people with higher levels of moral development.

Roles are behaviors that are expected of people in particular functions and social stratifications. The changes in gender and occupational roles in the last twenty years have caused changes in many social settings.

Groups.
Human beings have a strong need to belong to groups. By definition, a group consists of two or more people who are interdependent. These ties are so compelling that membership in a group can often result in individual behavior changes.

People tend to conform to group opinion because they fear rejection by group members. If a member chooses not to conform to group norms and values, the group often will shun that person. This process serves to educate group members about rules of the group.

Studies of crowd behavior show that bystander apathy occurs when a group of people observe each other not assisting in an emergency situation. Crowd behavior is often analyzed after events such as riots, panics, or tramplings that have occurred in stadiums and auditoriums.

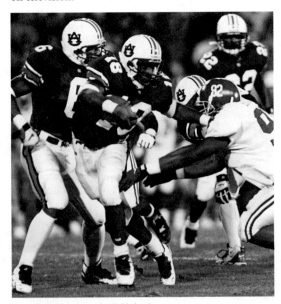

Competition is a form of social behavior.

Children learn about intimacy and love from their parents.

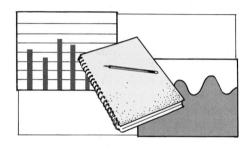

Tests, homework, and projects

Laying the groundwork

Students of a social science like psychology must understand many differing theoretical perspectives, and success in class depends on getting the most out of reading, notetaking, and taking tests. When reading assigned material, try not to get bogged down with supportive facts. First, scan the chapter and note the headings and subheadings. Then, list the key points in each section using your own words. In class, ask questions while you are taking notes. This helps you remember information because it is then reorganized in a way you can understand. When studying for tests, remember "cramming" just increases anxiety. Instead, schedule short study sessions to break up information into more easily remembered units.

Strategies for success

Homework, class projects, and tests are used to assess your basic knowledge and challenge you to apply this information in new ways. Professors assign reading homework to help you prepare for the next day's lecture. You will take better notes if you are already familiar with the material. A speed-reading course may help you cut down on reading time and increase your comprehension. Class projects are opportunities for exploration. Choose a subject that interests you. Break down the project into a series of short-term goals that you can accomplish throughout the term. Plan ahead for taking tests by scheduling enough time to study; come to the test well rested. During the test, answer easy questions first, and save time for difficult questions.

Helpful hints

Multiple choice

> Psychology is the scientific study of (a) behavior (b) perception (c) information processing (d) all of the above.

A rule of thumb for this kind of question: If at least two options are correct, you should choose "all of the above"; but if you think one item is incorrect, eliminate "all of the above" and the incorrect item to narrow down your choices. Listing key points while taking notes will help you to answer this type of question.

Answer. d

> Illustrate the differences between insight and behavior therapies in dealing with a water phobia.

Essay

Successful essays highlight the major ideas or points of a perspective in an organized format. You can improve your flow of ideas even under the time pressure of an exam by outlining your key points and listing some transition words to tie them together before you actually start the essay. Your professor is also looking for a basic understanding of the subject matter in your use of the technical vocabulary of the subject. Think ahead, and before you start writing, make a list of key terms you want to incorporate in your essay.

Project

> Use divergent thinking to generate some solutions for drug abuse in our communities.

Projects help you test and evaluate theoretical perspectives. This is a typical in-class project. Semester projects usually require advance preparation, reading journal articles, or recording your observations. The format for the presentation of your project may be a lecture, research paper, or even a tape recording or slide show.

Other suggested topics
- How your emotions impact the effectiveness of communication
- What your dreams reveal about your unconscious motivations
- How to work out a change in behavior
- An inventory of successful coping mechanisms for people under stress
- The play themes of children

Glossary

Emotion

Intimacy

Learning

achievement tests. Standardized (group) tests which are designed to evaluate skill mastery in academic subjects.

anxiety disorders. A group of psychological disorders marked by excessive fear.

aptitude tests. Standardized (group) tests designed to evaluate talent and ability for learning.

association. The processes that connect a stimulus to a response.

attention. Focus on a narrow area of stimuli.

auditory system. Organs responsible for the sense of hearing.

autonomic system. Nerves that connect to the blood vessels, heart, glands, and smooth muscles to perform involuntary body functions.

aversion therapy. A type of behavior therapy used to change responses to a stimulus. An unpleasant stimulus is paired with the stimulus that elicits maladaptive behaviors such as smoking or gambling.

axon. Nerve fiber that transmits signals from a neuron to another neuron or to a muscle.

behaviorism. Theoretical approach that proposes psychology should study only observable behavior.

behavior therapies. Treatment that applies the principles of learning to change maladaptive behaviors.

biomedical therapies. Treatment that uses physiological interventions to reduce symptoms of psychological disorders.

centration. Focus on one aspect or feature of a problem.

cerebellum. The structure within the hindbrain that helps coordinate balance and movement.

cerebrum. The part of the brain that contains the forebrain and midbrain.

client-centered therapy. Therapy in which the client explores feelings and thoughts in an atmosphere of unconditional acceptance and concern.

cognition. The mental events which are involved in information processing.

conditioning. The learned association between a stimulus and a response.

consciousness. Internal and external awareness in a person.

convergent thinking. The process of narrowing down alternatives to a single solution.

creativity. Generating ideas that are original, useful, and new.

development. A sequence of changes in people as they grow from conception to death.

dissociative disorders. A group of psychological disorders marked by loss of contact with portions of memory or awareness.

divergent thinking. Expanding the number of alternatives to generate many useful solutions.

dream. Visual images during sleep state.

drive. An inner urge motivating behavior to reduce tension.

ego. The part of the personality responsible for balancing the impulses of the id and the restraints of the superego.

elicit. To evoke or bring forth; responses are brought forth in classical conditioning.

emotion. An experience that occurs with body arousal and behavior.

encoding. Storing information in the memory by use of a meaningful pattern.

extinction. Process by which a learned association is undone.

Gestalt psychology. Theoretical approach to perception that examines the whole picture rather than the individual parts.

gustatory system. Organs responsible for the sense of taste.

hallucinations. Sensory perceptions that occur in the absence of external stimuli.

heuristic. Strategy used in problem solving.

hormones. Chemical substances secreted by the endocrine glands.

humanism. Theoretical approach that emphasizes the free will and personal-growth needs of people.

hypothesis. A statement about the relationship between two or more variables that has to be tested to be proved.

id. The instinctive part of the personality.

information processing. Refers to the input, transfer, and storage of information in the brain.

insight therapies. Psychotherapy approach promoting beneficial changes in behavior and personality through verbal interactions between therapist and client.

intelligence. The ability to learn and to solve problems.

intimacy. Sharing and closeness in a relationship.

language. The set of symbols and rules used for communicating.

learning. A change in behavior due to experience.

limbic system. Structures involved in the control of emotion, motivation, and memory.

mental retardation. A condition marked by subnormal mental ability.

motivation. Something directing behavior toward the fulfillment of a need.

nerves. Bundles of axons in the peripheral nervous system.

neuron. A nervous system cell which receives and transmits information.

neurotransmitter. Chemical that transmits information between neurons.

olfactory system. Organs responsible for the sense of smell.

operant conditioning. Form of learning in which voluntary responses are controlled by their consequences.

parallel play. Side-by-side play among young children, with little interaction.

perception. The process of selecting, organizing, and interpreting sensory input.

personality. The unique set of behavioral traits in a person.

phobia. Irrational fears associated with particular events or objects.

phoneme. The smallest unit of speech.

pituitary gland. An endocrine gland that releases a variety of hormones to stimulate other endocrine glands in the body.

punishment. An event following a response that weakens or suppresses the response in the future.

rational-emotive therapy. Therapy in which the client is able to reduce unwanted behaviors by altering thought patterns.

reinforcement. An event following a response that strengthens the response in the future.

response. A behavior that is associated with a stimulus event.

schizophrenic disorders. A group of psychological disorders marked by thought disturbances affecting perception and emotional responses.

self-concept. One's beliefs about oneself.

self-esteem. One's sense of personal adequacy and value.

somatic system. Nerves that connect to the sensory receptors and voluntary skeletal muscles to perform voluntary body functions.

standardization. Uniform testing procedures in administrating and scoring tests.

stimulus. Perceived input from the environment.

synapse. Junction where message is transmitted from one neuron to the next.

tactile system. Organs responsible for the sense of touch.

theory. A set of ideas used to explain a set of observations.

unconditioned response. A response to a stimulus that has not been previously conditioned.

unconditioned stimulus. A stimulus that evokes a response without previous conditioning.

vestibular system. Organs that respond to gravity and relay information about body location in space.

For further reading

Carlson, N. R. *Foundations of Physiological Psychology*. Boston: Allyn & Bacon, 1995.

Freud, S. *The Basic Writings of Sigmund Freud*. Translated by A. A. Brill. New York: Random House, 1938.

Haberlandt, K. *Cognitive Psychology*. Boston: Allyn & Bacon, 1994.

Hock, R. R. *Forty Studies That Changed Psychology*. New York: Prentice Hall, 1992.

Hunt, M. *The Story of Psychology*. New York: Doubleday, 1993.

Lefrancois, G. R. *The Lifespan*. 5th ed. Belmont, Calif.: Wadsworth, 1996.

Maslow, A. H. *Toward a Psychology of Being*. Princeton, N.J.: Van Nostrand, 1968.

Piaget, J. *Origins of Intelligence in Children*. Madison, Conn.: International Universities Press, 1952.

Rogers, C. R. *Client Centered Therapy: Its Current Practice, Implications, and Theory*. Boston: Houghton Mifflin, 1951.

Skinner, B. F. *Beyond Freedom and Dignity*. New York: Knopf, 1971.

Stevens, S. S. *Handbook of Experimental Psychology*. New York: John Wiley & Sons, 1951.

Zimbardo, P. G. *Psychology and Life*. New York: HarperCollins, 1992.

Sociology

Healthy human beings don't live in isolation. The diverse welfare and survival needs of human beings are met by various groups. As children grow up in these social environments, they learn about the resources and skills needed to influence their society as adults. But they may not be aware that, along the way, culture has been shaping their attitudes and behavior, too. Sociology examines this complex relationship between the individual and society.

Though sociologists use scientific methods to study human interaction, they still run the risk of observing behavior through the filters of their own personal experience and attitudes. To avoid this, sociologists use what is called the *sociological imagination*, first advocated by C. Wright Mills. Mills proposed that individuals observe their own society from a detached point of view to obtain a fresh, creative look at daily life.

The sociological perspective

Sociologists examine many layers of social reality. First, they look at the rules and patterns that underlie social behavior, then they consider the social implications of individual behavior. Rather than attributing individual behavior to human nature, sociologists examine how social conditions shape individual as well as collective behavior.

Microsociology.
This level of analysis focuses on the small group and the social interaction that takes place among people. Microsociologists study the thoughts, feelings, and motives behind social behavior. They also examine nonverbal forms of communication, such as personal space and body language, and forms of interaction, such as cooperation and competition. How well children learn these unspoken rules of social interaction can affect their ability to interact with others throughout their lives.

During the nineteenth century, determinists such as Charles Darwin and Cesare Lombroso suggested

Why studying sociology pays off
Reason #1:

You will learn about the dynamics of groups and then see your interactions with other people objectively (from a distance) instead of subjectively (from only your viewpoint).

behavior was a product of unchangeable conditions. Some social theorists, such as Jeremy Bentham and Cesare Beccaria, disagreed, believing instead that all human behavior was based on rational choice. Today, underlying all microsociological studies is the assumption of free will and rational choice. Using qualitative research methods such as face-to-face interviews and direct observation, microsociologists have determined that individuals choose to accept or reject the values, norms, and structures of their society.

Macrosociology.

Providing a broader focus, this level of analysis examines large-scale social phenomena such as social change, stratification and inequality, population, and crime trends, as well as the impact of social structures on individuals, groups, and institutions.

One type of macrosociology, *structural-functionalism,* views society as an orderly system of social structures, each of which contributes to the overall functioning of the society. This perspective diminishes the role of free will in social behavior. Structural-functionalists see people as products of the social structures and societal forces exerted on them.

Other macrosociologists, known as *conflict theorists,* have a different view of social life. They believe conflict and change, rather than stability, are key features of society. Contemporary sociologists find both theoretical approaches useful.

Research methods.

Because social behavior takes many forms, different research methods have been developed to gather information. It is difficult for sociologists to study social phenomena that aren't directly observable—attitudes such as prejudice, and concepts such as social class; however, sociologists formulate an operational definition that translates concepts into measurable social variables. For example, the variable "social class" can be measured by individual and household income.

In beginning their work, researchers first review the literature to determine what has been learned about the topic of interest. Then they formulate a problem and develop a hypothesis that can be tested. The third step is to design a valid and reliable study. This step is necessary before researchers can proceed with data collection.

The *survey* is the most frequently used method of data collection in sociological research. In designing a survey, researchers must first specify the population of interest (such as students, voters, nurses) and then select a representative sample of the population. A variety of survey formats, such as mailed surveys and

Elements of a survey

- Questionnaire (survey instrument)
- The selection of a "sample" of individuals whose characteristics reflect the larger group from which they are chosen (a random sample)
- Various formats: Mailed questionnaire, telephone survey, face-to-face survey
- Measurement criteria: Questionnaire items that are both *valid* (accurate) and *reliable* (consistent) measures of the behavior or attitude

face-to-face interviews, is used to collect data from respondents.

A second research method, *direct observation,* allows sociologists either to remain detached from the people they observe, or to participate in the ongoing activity under observation. The latter strategy, called participant observation, is subject to potential bias, since researchers may become too involved and thus be unable to objectively analyze and interpret what they see.

Experiments provide a third method for the collection of data. This particular research strategy, which involves the introduction of an experimental stimulus, is most often used for establishing cause and effect relationships.

Unobtrusive measures use existing data such as documents to reconstruct or interpret social actions or attitudes. Such measures are termed unobtrusive because these data are collected after the behavior has occurred, and thus they have no effect on the behavior being studied.

When conducting research using human subjects, social scientists must consider the possible ethical implications of their inquiry. For instance, it is unethical to expose subjects to physical and psychological harm or to violate assurances of confidentiality. Subjects must also be informed about the nature of the research, and voluntary consent from the participants must be obtained.

Free will vs. determinism

Jeremy Bentham Cesare Beccaria	Contemporary social theorists	Charles Darwin Cesare Lombroso
Free will	**"Soft determinism"**	**Determinism**
Human behavior is completely random (no predictability).	Assumes individual choice but recognizes the existence of behavioral patterns	Rigid, predictable patterns; no individual choice

Schools of thought

There are three major theoretical perspectives through which sociologists interpret events and understand society: *functional theory, conflict theory,* and *interactionist theory.*

These varying perspectives help sociologists understand the multiple layers of social reality. The sociological imagination, advocated by C. Wright Mills, helps sociologists discern these layers by observing and studying with a detached viewpoint the impact of social forces on individual behavior. This awareness frees observers from their own personal and cultural biases and reveals how settings, cultural histories, and personal experiences produce certain social behaviors, patterns, or trends.

Origins. The Industrial Revolution of the nineteenth century brought such social upheaval that many European social philosophers were compelled to find solutions. First they had to understand the new social problems, and early sociologists developed many theories and methods.

Because the scientific method was successful in explaining the workings of the physical world, Auguste Comte advocated the scientific study of society and social behavior. He proposed that a scientific knowledge of society would help steer society in a healthy, orderly direction. Emile Durkheim developed the first systematic application of the scientific method to sociology. He also introduced the concept of the *social fact*—a reality, external to human beings, that shapes behavior. Max Weber believed that sociologists must go beyond observations and put themselves in their subjects' places to better understand the subjective meaning people attach to their own behavior. Karl Marx advocated that all social life is built on the conflict which is inherent in the economic system of the society.

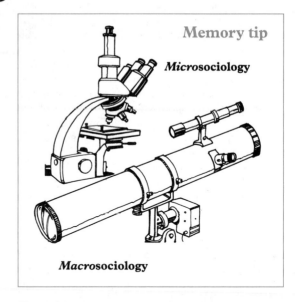

Memory tip

Microsociology

Macrosociology

The Chicago school. European methods and theories appeared in the United States in the early twentieth century, but American sociologists chose to deal with social questions and problems in different ways. Using the city of Chicago as a field laboratory, sociologists Robert Park and his colleagues at the University of Chicago began a tradition known as the Chicago school, which studied social problems and adaptations by focusing on individual communities as social systems. G. H. Mead began a new line of thought within the Chicago school called *symbolic interaction*. Mead's theories focused on how people perceive their roles in the social system, adapt to situations, and use symbols—language, gestures, and signs—to communicate. Later trends in sociology made greater use of statistics in order to maintain a value-neutral view of social phenomena.

Major theories

Theoretical perspective	Level of analysis	Focus
Functional theory	Macro	Examines social structures in terms of their consequences for society. Institutions and practices that persist are functional for society; they are essential features of social systems.
Conflict theory	Macro	Social arrangements are a product of group conflict and competition for wealth, status, and power.
Interactionist theory	Micro	Examines face-to-face interaction between individuals and the basis for social interaction.

Emile Durkheim

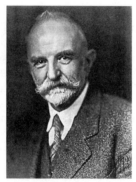

G. H. Mead

Functional theory.

The functionalist orientation assumes that society is a vast system of interrelated parts and behavior patterns, each of which serves a function in maintaining stability in society. In their approach to understanding social phenomena, functional theorists examine how social phenomena such as values, groups, and stratification are structured to keep the society integrated.

Robert Merton examined the manifest (stated) and latent (unintended) functions of social institutions. For example, elementary schools fulfill their manifest function of passing on knowledge, but they also serve as a type of child care for young children. This latter function is not planned or intended, but it exists and serves a definite function for working mothers. Functionalists also study dysfunctional elements and behavior patterns that may disrupt or destabilize a society.

Conflict theory.

Conflict theorists view society in terms of the conflict and tension that exist among competing groups. Instead of seeing how the elements of social structure work together to create stability, conflict theorists propose that certain institutional arrangements perpetuate the privileges of some groups while at the same time keeping other groups subservient.

Based on Karl Marx's views that social classes clash in pursuit of their own self-interest, the conflict approach views relationships in society as experiencing ongoing tension. Conflict theorists use their interpretation of this tension to examine issues of equality and opportunity within society. A conflict among people can arise from differences other than economic inequalities. People are divided by differences of opinion on a wide variety of hotly debated issues. Groups that are able to mobilize resources may be able to legislate their position and then reinforce their power and influence.

Interactionist theory.

Proponents of the interactionist theory focus on the meaningful ways in which people interpret and respond to the world and each other. This approach argues that people aren't shaped by uncontrollable and massive societal forces, but rather that people create the society in which they live by their day-to-day actions. Interactionists focus on the micro level—by studying thoughts, feelings, and motives, as well as nonverbal forms of communication—to better understand how people interpret the behavior of others during social interaction.

G. H. Mead, a symbolic interactionist, has studied how people are able to communicate with one another through the development of shared meanings. Through social interaction, children develop an ability to understand the perspectives of others. Although our ability to define social situations is not perfect, we are still able to interpret certain gestures, statements, and actions—and understand what they mean and how we should react to them. Mead suggested that only by taking the role of others can we understand the thoughts, feelings, and motivations which give meaning to behavior.

Milestones

Theorists

Auguste Comte (1798–1857)	Karl Marx (1818–1883)	Emile Durkheim (1858–1917)	Max Weber (1864–1920)	Robert Park (1864–1944)

Questions asked

How can society and human behavior be studied scientifically?	How is social and economic inequality created and perpetuated?	What is the basis of social order?	How do people attach subjective meaning to their actions?	How can cultural differences among people be resolved in order to achieve social control and order?

Components of social life

The social life of a group or society is made up of several interlocking parts. Members of a society are exposed to these components through the process of socialization that takes place throughout their lifetime. Culture, social structures, socialization, and social controls vary so much among cultures that each of these components can be examined separately. Sociologists are also keenly interested in how these components work together.

Elements of culture.

People of diverse personalities and life styles can still feel a sense of belonging in a group when they are connected by a common *culture*. The culture of a society contains the common symbols, language, beliefs, values, and behaviors that people learn throughout their lives and are expected to uphold as members of a culture.

Symbols and language. Culture is composed of the symbols that represent the complex ideas behind the political, economic, and socialization systems of the society. Symbols may be material, like a wedding ring, a flag, a house with a white picket fence, or a Cadillac; or nonmaterial ideas, such as democracy or patriotism. Language is a complex set of symbols that members of a group use to communicate with each other either verbally or in writing. Recorded language helps people understand their past and shape their future.

Nonverbal forms of communication are also part of the language of the culture. For example, the size of personal space, facial expressions, and tones of voice all vary significantly in meaning across cultures.

Cultural norms. The conduct and thoughts of people, despite differences in individual self-concept and personality, reflect the *cultural norms* of a society. Norms are made up of four types of expectations. *Values* are the deeply held beliefs of the society. *Folkways* are cultural habits, like pumpkin carving and eating hot dogs at a baseball game. *Mores* are customs labeled right and wrong in the society, which are incorporated into the legal, religious, and education systems of the society. *Laws*, the fourth type of cultural norm, are formalized mores that are enforced with threat of punishment.

Subcultures and countercultures. Members of a *subculture* may accept the dominant culture's norms, but may also share additional norms and values peculiar to their particular subculture, as in the case of ethnic, religious, and class subcultures. Members of *countercultures,* on the other hand, while living within the dominant culture, reject many of its cultural norms. They may develop distinctive styles of dress and language that separate them from the dominant culture.

Members of a counterculture can try to instigate social change and attempt to reform the dominant culture, as did the "hippie" movement of the 1960s; or, like the Gypsies of Great Britain, they may try to hold on to their own traditions and values, which may be in conflict with those of the dominant culture.

Ethnocentrism. Most people believe that the norms and values of their cultural system are superior to those of other cultures. This attitude, called *ethnocentrism,* can promote unity and pride in the group, but more often it leads to intolerance and conflict. Ethnocentrism can appear in social structures as small as a subculture or as large as a nation. Conflicts can be exhibited in individual behavior, such as discrimination against those who are different, or in political behavior, as with international conflicts.

Cultural relativism. This perspective, the opposite of ethnocentrism, recognizes that different cultures and societies have different values from one another, and no one culture is superior or inferior to another. From this perspective, sociologists try to understand the behavior of people belonging to other cultures by focusing on what that behavior means to those people. The behaviors are judged by the standards of the culture in which they occur, not by standards of the sociologist's culture.

Multicultural neighborhood

Elements of social structure.

Though societies vary significantly in the values and traditions their members uphold, all societies contain similar features. Individuals are socialized by the groups and institutions of their society to perform certain roles that will help the society function and survive.

Status and role. An individual's *status* is the social position he or she occupies within a group. At birth, people acquire a set of ascribed statuses, such as race and gender; beyond that, they earn or choose several achieved statuses.

People expect certain behaviors from individuals who occupy particular social statuses. These behaviors, or *roles,* are learned through socialization in family, school, and community settings. Throughout life, one may perform many roles at the same time, depending on the nature of the relationship with others. Role strain occurs when expectations are ambiguous or draining in their demands. Role conflict occurs when expectations between roles are contradictory.

Primary and secondary groups. In a *primary group,* such as the family, members ordinarily feel mutual trust, cooperation, and affection for one another and are valued for who they are. *Secondary groups* are formed to get something done, and members are valued for their talents. However, because members often share similar values and attitudes, companionship is also experienced in secondary group associations.

Institutions. *Social institutions* are systems of behavior patterns and beliefs that help the society survive and flourish. They are structured around common norms, values, and cultural symbols, and perform specific functions to meet the needs of their members. In complex societies, institutions are interrelated to varying degrees.

A primary group, such as the family, was even more important as an agent of socialization when people were more isolated.

Socialization.

Throughout their lives, members of a society are constantly being socialized and resocialized to learn the norms that guide social interaction. The primary influences on social behavior come from key agents of socialization, such as families, schools, peer groups, and the mass media. But all along the way, people make choices concerning what values are important to them and what behavior they will engage in. Intense debate was sparked in the early part of the twentieth century over the roles that heredity and environment play in human development.

Nature and nurture. Social scientists have wondered if criminals are biologically different from law-abiding citizens, or whether involvement in crime is simply a matter of personal choice. Are I.Q. differences between the classes the result of genetics, cultural deprivation, or biased test questions? There are no firm answers to these questions, and today sociologists acknowledge an interaction among all factors.

Agents of socialization. The *family* is the first agent of socialization in the life of an individual. Within the family, people acquire their first sense of self, develop strong attachments to others, play their first roles, and learn how to have their needs satisfied within a system of rules and values. Socialization between parent and child is reciprocal as children help resocialize their parents in new patterns of dress, custom, and thought.

Schools share the responsibility with parents to teach children the cultural values and norms of the society. Children are introduced to new authority figures with whom they must cooperate and whom they should respect. Schools also teach skills that are necessary to live and work as members of society, including effective communication, clear thinking, and the ability to interact with others in a variety of situations. Conformity tends to be more strongly enforced in the school setting than in the family.

The *peer group* becomes a more important influence as children grow older. Within a peer group, young people develop independence from the family and often use the opportunity to experiment with different roles. Peer groups are useful in the transition from adolescence to young adulthood.

In the last fifty years, the *mass media* have grown into powerful agents of socialization. The influence of television in particular has disturbed many researchers and parents because of the negative role models and portrayals of violence that children are routinely exposed to. But television can also provide a unifying effect by educating people about other cultures and life styles.

Socialization through life. In adulthood, socialization continues during the many transitions people experience. Adults assume multiple roles, such as employee, parent, spouse, civic leader, or volunteer,

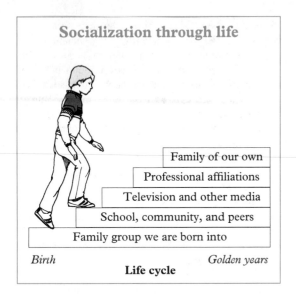

Socialization through life

Family of our own
Professional affiliations
Television and other media
School, community, and peers
Family group we are born into

Birth   *Golden years*

Life cycle

and they must learn the new rules and expectations that accompany each role. During transitions, adults discard some roles and take on others.

Deviance and social control. A

behavior is defined as *deviant* when it violates societal expectations and rules of behavior. But that definition varies by the time, place, and situation in which a behavior occurs. For example, murder is a deviant and illegal behavior across all cultures, but a shooting by a police officer is defined and treated differently from a shooting by a criminal. Sometimes a behavior that vio-

lates the law is really an act of conformity to a deviant subculture's norms.

Illegal behaviors are not necessarily deviant behaviors, and vice versa. Some illegal behaviors, such as exceeding the speed limit, are not considered deviant because many people speed, while some forms of deviance, such as odd forms of dress, are not illegal but may receive public reactions that suggest a norm of appearance has been violated.

Sociologists study deviance at different levels. Microsociologists look at why individuals and groups choose to deviate from societal norms. Macrosociologists look at rates of deviance and the larger societal influences that contribute to deviant behavior. Many theories have been developed to explain crime and deviance.

Individuals learn what behaviors are acceptable and unacceptable through the process of socialization. If the information is internalized, the individual will routinely conform. However, even law-abiding people may occasionally violate the law. Informal social controls such as ridicule, laughter, or ostracism can also regulate behavior and promote conformity.

Formal social control is achieved through formal intervention. An example of this is the criminal justice system, which uses legal mechanisms to enforce conformity. A system of deterrents and punishments, called *sanctions*, also encourages conformity within a society. Thus, it is expected that people will realize that the costs associated with crime, such as imprisonment, exceed what is gained illegally.

Theories of crime and deviance

Theoretical perspective	Focus
Structural strain	People commit criminal and deviant acts because they lack the legitimate means to attain economic goals. The cultural emphasis on economic "success" reinforces the importance of reaching these goals using any means available.
Learning theories	Criminal and deviant behaviors are learned in a variety of ways, such as face-to-face interaction and exposure to mass media.
Social control theory	People refrain from violating the law because they possess strong social bonds to family, school, and other groups and institutions. A weak social bond may lead to deviant or criminal behavior.
Labeling theory	People develop a pattern of law breaking in response to public labeling and stigmatization. These individuals may develop a deviant self-concept as well as be viewed by others as deviant or criminal.
Conflict theory	Crime is a function of class conflict. The law reflects the interests of the ruling class, which determines what behaviors become criminalized and what laws are rigorously enforced.

Social and economic inequality

As unique as human beings are in personality and behavior, people also have common values, backgrounds, life styles, and levels of income. Such groupings, organized around these shared socioeconomic variables, are known as *social classes*.

Social stratification.
In every society, social classes are identified and ranked by the amount of desirable resources each class possesses. These desirable resources vary across cultures and are not equally shared by all the members of a society. Sociologists define social class in the United States primarily by education, income, and occupation. A person's opportunities are strongly influenced by his or her social class. In this country, it is possible to change social class, but an individual born into poverty begins at a distinct disadvantage and must overcome significant social and economic obstacles to get ahead.

Functions. Functional theorists believe that rewards such as income, status, and power are allocated to the most skilled and diligent worker. They see the stratification and competition for desirable positions as functions of a healthy society.

Conflict. Conflict theorists believe that the wealthy or elite classes possess most of the power and use their advantage to exploit the poor and reinforce the status quo. They believe that opportunities should be available to all members of a society, rather than just a privileged few. There are two versions of the conflict theory, one from Marx and the other from Weber.

Karl Marx used economic criteria to define stratification. He believed that two classes exist, each determined by its relationship to the means of production within the society. According to Marx, class conflicts are inevitable, because the owners (the *bourgeoisie*) control the social institutions and desirable resources at the expense of the workers (the *proletariat*).

Max Weber felt that Marx's definition of stratification was too limited. He expanded the definition using a multidimensional approach that identified three elements: wealth, power, and prestige. Weber believed that if a person is high in one area and lower in any of the other areas, *status inconsistency* occurs.

Social mobility. Social mobility refers to the movement people can make from one social class to another. Horizontal mobility occurs when a person makes a lateral change within his or her social class. Vertical mobility refers to a move up or down the social ladder in terms of wealth, occupation, and/or status. Intergenerational upward mobility occurs when children move up from the social class they were born into.

Gender.
In the socialization process, men and women learn the behaviors and roles that are associated with their gender. Home, school, and the media give men and women different messages so that each will seek different and sometimes unequal roles in society.

Some functionalists see traditional male-dominant sex roles as essential to family stability, but conflict theorists believe that traditional sex roles make families no more functional than those families where power is more equitably shared between the sexes. Conflict theorists believe that gender inequality in occupational status, income, and power exists because men benefit from it.

In recent decades, women have challenged gender inequalities and have formed influential women's movements that have helped bring about legal changes and created greater awareness of the impact of gender on opportunities.

Age.
Stratification by age also exists in every society. High status is usually given to the members who are most useful and powerful. Throughout history, children have been powerless and have often been mistreated or neglected. Today, however, parents in many of the industrialized nations see beyond the child's

Often, only low-paying jobs are available to older workers.

The homeless are often isolated in today's society.

immediate position and offer children many opportunities to grow up healthy, happy, and productive.

The status and prestige accorded the elderly have varied throughout history and across cultures. In some cultures, the elderly are highly valued for their experience and wisdom. In other cultures, the elderly are viewed as an economic and social burden. This is especially true in more industrialized nations where the life span is becoming longer. Discrimination and prejudice directed toward the elderly are sometimes referred to as *ageism*.

One of the manifestations of the high degree of economic inequality in the United States is the presence of a large and growing class of homeless people. A great deal of publicity has surrounded this social issue and various policies have been suggested to address this problem, such as affordable housing and increased minimum wage. Although the size of the homeless population in the U.S. is disputed, it is undoubtedly the result of complex social and economic factors.

Besides their economic disadvantages, these people are often treated as social outcasts. Individuals who encounter the homeless may rely on stereotypic images of the lazy, mentally ill, or untrustworthy person in an effort to understand the plight of these people.

This tendency to blame the victim helps people distinguish "us" from "them." However, it prevents people from gaining an understanding of the social and economic conditions that have led to the proliferation of homelessness.

Race and ethnicity.
Most people think of race as the physical differences among groups of people. Sociologists, however, have a different view. Using socially visible distinctions among groups, sociologists have defined two perspectives to explain racial and ethnic inequality.

The first is the functionalist perspective. In this view, inequality results from ethnocentrism and cultural differences. Ethnocentrism, of course, can be valuable when it promotes pride and solidarity among members of a particular racial or ethnic group. But often its consequences include prejudice and conflict, which can enable one group to gain unfair advantages over others.

The second perspective, based on the notion of conflict, views racial and ethnic inequality as resulting from economic conflicts as groups compete for limited resources. As seen in this perspective, an unequal balance of power allows one group to gain unfair advantages over others through exploitation.

This perceived inequity can lead to intergroup conflict, prejudicial attitudes, and acts of violence. Feelings of injustice coupled with residential segregation can foster racial and ethnic tensions that sometimes result in acts of individual and collective violence.

Sociologists consider race to include more than physical differences.

Social institutions

Social institutions are relatively permanent, organized systems of social relationships that meet the needs of a society. Systems such as family, education, and religion perform multiple functions in the socialization process and embody the values and traditions of the society.

Family. The family is the fundamental social institution in every society. Ideally, one learns identity, value systems, and social skills within the family.

Functions. Traditionally, the economic function of the family was the production of household goods and services for the family members. In industrialized nations, that responsibility has been transferred out of the home to employers and manufacturers. Often, the responsibility for children's religious and educational training has also shifted from the family to social institutions such as the church and the educational system. Families confer on their members a status position based on the family's place in the social structure. Families also reflect and reinforce the values of their social class in their personal values, recreational choices, and expectations. An essential function of the family is to provide emotional support for its members.

Conflict. One important source of family conflict is economic strain. Other sources are sex role confusion, communication problems, and parenting styles. Within the home, children learn appropriate ways to deal with conflict, which will assist them in coping with conflict outside the family. Often, however, unresolved conflicts in the home can lead to divorce and changes in the family structure.

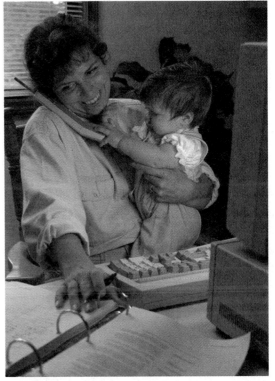

Working mother

Changes. Because social institutions are interrelated to some extent, changes in one institutional setting can produce changes in other settings. Twenty years ago in the United States, for example, a change in ideology

---

Functions of social institutions

The family
- The family as a social institution is responsible for replacing members of society through reproduction.
- The family fulfills a socialization function whereby individuals learn societal values and norms.
- The family is responsible for providing for the physical needs of its members, such as food and shelter.

Education
- Educational institutions prepare individuals for the labor force by providing knowledge and technical skills.
- Educational institutions determine an individual's capacity to learn and place these individuals into academic and vocational programs compatible with their aptitude.
- A "hidden" function of educational institutions is to promote in young children certain behavioral expectations such as obedience to teachers and parents, sharing, and a general sense of responsibility.

Religion
- Religion creates group unity and solidarity among members of a community of faith.
- Religion promotes social control of behavior; a "moral conscience" is acquired through religious socialization.
- Religion facilitates social adaptation among groups of people who are faced with social and cultural change in their lives (for example, immigrants adapting to a new culture).

created more job opportunities for women. When women began entering the work force, many chose to delay marriage and childbearing until their careers were established. Over time, since the childbearing years were shortened, this shift produced a decline in the birth rate. As a result there has been a noticeable change in the age structure of our society.

Economic circumstance or divorce influences some women to enter the job market. Increases in divorce have meant increases in one-parent families and "blended" or step-families. Many of the one-parent families headed by women are living at or near the poverty line.

Education.
The educational systems of a society transmit knowledge from one generation to the next. The functionalist perspective identifies manifest (obvious) functions and latent (hidden, unintended) functions of the educational system. Conflict theorists believe that education maintains social stratification by passing on economic, sexual, and racial inequalities to the next generation.

Functions. One of the manifest functions of education is to provide technical training to the members of the society. Technologically advanced cultures need workers who can use the modern tools of the society. Members must also be able to solve problems and communicate effectively.

Another manifest function is to identify student strengths and motivate students to achieve their potential. Education acts as an agent of mobility, because what is learned or not learned at school can affect social status. However, when the credentials that students earn become more important than knowledge, status competition can occur.

A latent function of education is the transmission of culture, supporting the dominant beliefs of the society. As an important agent of socialization, schools help build consensus and solidarity by presenting positive aspects of the society to the students. In higher education, a more balanced view of the society is usually presented. Other latent functions include building peer relationships and acculturating immigrants.

Conflict. Conflict theorists observe that inequality in a society is passed on in the educational system through unequal funding of schools, differing teacher expectations, and hidden curricula that teach different values to different social classes.

Educational attainment can be used to predict occupation, income, and status. The incomes of people with college degrees are higher than incomes of those without college degrees, although sex and race differences still exist. Generally, a college education improves social skills, enhances interest in learning, and leads to greater tolerance and respect for others.

Religion.
Religion, perhaps more than any other institution, is immensely important to societies and their individual members across cultures. Sociologists do not analyze religious beliefs or make value judgments concerning religious preferences; rather, they look at the unique ways in which religion meets human needs and which no other social institution can fulfill.

Functions. An important function of religion across cultures is the consecration of important events during the course of a lifetime. The religion of a society interprets and provides meaning for events such as birth, coming of age, marriage, and death. Emile Durkheim used the term *sacred* to describe the aspects of a culture that inspire awe and deep respect; and he defined religion as the system of beliefs and behaviors involving the sacred.

Another function of religion is to communicate values. In the United States, where freedom of religion is a constitutional right, the interaction of political and religious values continues in public debate over government policy.

Religion also acts to provide group solidarity, help immigrants make social adaptations into a new culture, and teach the social values and norms of the larger society.

Conflict. Religious conflicts sometimes involve class or ethnic struggles supported by strong religious convictions. Throughout history, some of the most violent confrontations have involved people divided by religious differences.

Changes. The *secularization* of society refers to a trend in which people rely more on scientific explanations about life events and human behavior than on religious interpretations of these events. This is often true in more industrialized nations.

However, the United States is in the midst of a religious revival because many people believe that though science explains physical life, only religion has been able to interpret the true meaning of human existence and social relationships.

Social change

The social structures, patterns, and relationships of a society change over time. Sociologists examine the sources of change and ask the following questions: Does all social change represent progress? Is social change random or systematic?

The source of some change is internal, as in the case of technological advancements. For example, the widespread use of computers is causing ripple effects in business, education, and personal lifestyle. Other internal sources of change within a society include ideologies, population shifts, structures of inequality, and governmental reforms.

Some changes are caused by external forces, as in the case of *cultural diffusion*, where the cultural symbols or products of a powerful society move into weaker or developing societies. A good example of this phenomenon is the great popularity of American products in the countries of the former Soviet Union.

Cultural lag occurs when some aspects of a society are changing at a faster rate than others. For example, technological breakthroughs are being used in societies before social ethics and norms have been created to govern their use.

Population.
Demography is the scientific study of human populations. Demographers can determine and project information about growth, composition, and age structure of groups by studying patterns of fertility, mortality, and migration.

In most industrialized countries, the birth rate is balanced with the death rate, so populations grow slowly. In less-developed countries, the birth rate is extremely high. The world's population is now estimated at nearly six billion, with one billion added every ten years. In the United States, the lower birth rate and recent

medical advancements are leading to an increase in the number of older people.

The aging of the American population has important implications for society in terms of social roles, economics, and health care. An aging population will require more health care and support services and may bring about changes in institutional practices, such as the age for retirement.

A central issue created by world population demographics is food supply and distribution. Other concerns about limited energy supplies exist, as well as the consequences of vast energy use, such as the greenhouse effect and pollution.

Future trends. Technological advancement is a key influence on social change in the United States because it speeds up the pace of change and affects many important social structures, such as medical institutions.

A crisis is emerging in health care related to the proliferation of medical technology on one hand and the unequal access to health care on the other. Health care costs are soaring, and the number of Americans without health coverage is increasing.

Population issues directly affect the health of a society. As the median age of Americans rises, more demands on the health care system will be made. New illnesses, such as those caused by the HIV virus and drug-resistant strains of bacteria, make advanced medical research and new technologies necessary for the health of the society.

Functionalists believe that the sick role and the healing role contribute to social order. From this view, medical care is beneficial to society by maintaining health or reducing illness. Conflict theorists, however, believe that medical care is actually serving the medical and corporate community. They believe that the health of a population can be better maintained by improving the quality of people's lives and the environments in which they live.

Social movements.
Social change can occur through social movements, which are conscious efforts to bring about or prevent change in a society. These movements are well-organized, purposeful efforts that can endure for years and build large memberships. Because social movements seek different degrees of change, they are divided into four types.

Expressive movements effect changes (secular or religious) in people without altering the structure of society. Examples of these movements include the "New Age" movement and the Moonies of the 1970s. *Resistance* movements try to stop or reverse trends that

Resident population by age

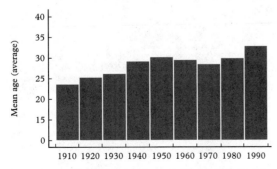

Source: U.S. Bureau of the Census, *Statistical Abstract of the U.S.: 1991* (111th edition). For updated statistics, please consult more recent reports at your library.

threaten to change the existing system, as exemplified by the American Nazi Party, which has tried to stop racial integration.

Reform movements, such as the women's and civil rights movements, use legal methods to change a part of society. They support the existing social system, but want to improve upon it. Each reform movement focuses on a single issue. *Revolutionary* movements seek total change of an existing social system. They resort to illegal or violent means to overthrow the existing government in order to replace it with a new government.

Collective behavior. *Collective behavior* is spontaneous group behavior that is engaged in by large numbers of people responding to a common stimulus. Riots, panics, fads, rumors, and mass hysteria are all examples of collective behavior. Some sociologists argue that while people appear to give up their individuality during collective behavior, they are in fact only conforming to the norms emerging from the situation in which the crowd finds itself. During the Los Angeles riots of 1992, for example, some normally law-abiding citizens joined the collective illegal behavior.

Sociologists believe that precipitating factors may spark a collective behavior such as looting and violence. One of the precipitating factors in the Los Angeles riots may have been the social strain of economic inequality in the area. Generalized beliefs can also lead to a collective behavior, such as the residents' perception of injustice.

Collective behavior is a social phenomenon that is difficult to study scientifically because it is so unpredictable and unstructured. The rarest and least structured form of collective behavior is a *panic. Crowds* are more subject to social norms, and members can be persuaded to work toward a common goal. *Fashions* and fads go through stages. *Rumors* have more structure and even a division of labor as some people are the messengers, the skeptics, or the audience. *Social movements* are purposeful forms of collective behavior.

Well-organized social movements can bring about lasting changes.

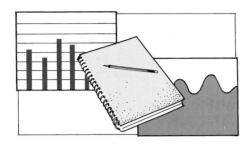

Tests, homework, and projects

Laying the groundwork

Students of a social science like sociology must understand many differing theoretical perspectives; success in class depends on getting the most out of reading, notetaking, and taking tests. When reading assigned material, try not to get bogged down with supportive facts. First, scan the chapter and note the headings and subheadings. Then, list the key points in each section using your own words. In class, ask questions while you are taking notes. This helps you remember information because it is then reorganized in a way you can understand. When studying for tests, remember "cramming" just increases anxiety. Instead, schedule short study sessions to break up information into more easily remembered units. Try to study in an area free from distractions.

Strategies for success

Homework, class projects, and tests are used to assess your basic knowledge and challenge you to apply this information in new ways. Professors assign reading homework to help you prepare for the next day's lecture. You will take better notes if you are already familiar with the material. A speed-reading course may help you cut down on reading time and increase comprehension. Class projects are opportunities for exploration. Choose a subject that interests you. Break down the project into a series of short-term goals that you can accomplish throughout the term. Plan ahead for taking tests by scheduling enough time to study; come to the test well rested. During the test, answer easy questions first, and save time for difficult questions.

Helpful hints

Multiple choice

The study of social stratification reveals that (a) one's occupation always reflects one's ability. (b) the greatest rewards are given only to those with the most demanding jobs. (c) occupational prestige generally results from social power.

When you see qualifiers like "always," and "only," the assertion is usually incorrect because it is making a generalization. Moderate qualifiers like "generally" and "often" signal a more probable answer.

Answer. c

Essay

Describe the sociological implications of the rising median age in the United States.

This kind of essay is asking you to apply theoretical knowledge to a social problem. While you are answering questions in other sections of the test, write down the major ideas and the related vocabulary that you may see listed in other questions. When you get to the essay, you will have half of your work already finished.

Fill-in

An important agent of socialization for preschool children is _____.

Sometimes fill-ins have more than one possible answer. Be sure to read the statement carefully to look for words that will narrow down your choices.

Answer. Family or school.

Project

Determine gender-role attitudes according to age and gender.

This is a typical class project, which requires that you design a survey and convert the collected information (data) into a table that will make the information easier to understand. You may be asked to determine an attitude on a topic of your interest. This is a good opportunity for exploration.

Other suggested topics
• Study the strain experienced by working mothers.
• Interview for the attitude differences between grandparents and grandchildren.
• Survey to determine the heroes of children today.

Glossary

Alienation

Family

Peer group

Religion

achieved status. The status acquired by an individual's actions.

agents of socialization. Social institutions that help individuals learn the attitudes, values, and norms of the society.

alienation. A condition in which an individual feels powerless, isolated, and detached from society.

anomie. A social condition in which social control of behavior is ineffective.

anticipatory socialization. The process that teaches a person how to assume a future role.

ascribed status. A status conferred at birth.

assimilation. The process by which minority members conform to the dominant group's culture.

authority. Legitimate power.

beliefs. Subjective, unverifiable ideas.

bureaucracy. A form of social organization characterized by formal rules and procedures, specialization of tasks, and hierarchy of authority.

class consciousness. An awareness of one's standing in society; identification with a particular social class.

closed system. A social system with little or no opportunity for mobility.

collective behavior. Unstructured behavior of people in crowds instigated by particular events or stimuli.

conflict perspective. An approach that focuses on understanding social behavior in terms of conflict between competing groups.

control group. Subjects not exposed to the independent variable in an experiment.

correlation. A measure of the strength of the association between two variables.

counterculture. A subculture whose norms and values sharply contradict the norms and values of the larger society.

crime. Acts that violate laws, serious enough to result in social condemnation and punishment.

culture. Symbols, ideas, and objects associated with life in a particular social system and handed down from one generation to another.

demography. A study of human populations.

dependent variable. A characteristic that is considered to be the effect of another variable in an experiment.

deviance. Behavior that violates societal or group norms.

discrimination. Prejudicial attitude that results in the unfair treatment of particular individuals and groups.

ethnic group. A group of people with a common language, national origin, or religion.

ethnocentrism. A belief that one's own culture is superior to others.

extended family. A family composed of more than two generations of relatives.

family. People related by blood, marriage, or adoption.

folkways. Weakly sanctioned norms governing daily behavior.

functional perspective. An approach that focuses on how the parts of a society contribute to the maintenance of the whole society.

gender. Social status assigned to males and females.

gender role. A set of behaviors that apply separately to males and females.

group. Two or more people who interact in patterned ways.

hypothesis. A tentative statement to explain how various social facts are related to one another.

Sociology

independent variable. A variable that produces change in another variable.

institution. A relatively stable set of roles and relationships designed to accomplish goals.

interactionist perspective. An approach that focuses on everyday social exchanges.

life chances. The presence or absence of opportunities for living a "good" life in society based on one's social position.

macrosociology. A level of analysis that focuses on large-scale social phenomena.

microsociology. A level of analysis that focuses on small-group social relationships.

minority group. A category of people with a different identity and less power than the dominant group in society.

mobility. Movement from one social class to another.

mores. Strongly sanctioned norms that are regarded as necessary to the welfare of the society.

norms. Standards of appropriate behavior.

nuclear family. A group consisting of parents and their children.

occupational prestige. Status attached to particular jobs.

open system. A social system with opportunities for social mobility.

participant observation. A strategy in field research that involves the researcher in the ongoing activity under observation.

peer group. A group of people who interact with one another, are about the same age, and influence each other's norms and values.

positivism. The belief that scientific methods can be applied to the study of social life.

prejudice. Attitude about a category of people based on real or imagined characteristics.

primary group. A social group characterized by long-term intimate associations.

qualitative research. A research orientation that emphasizes the interpretive description of social behavior.

quantitative research. A research orientation that involves numerical analysis of data to describe population characteristics and test hypotheses.

reference group. A group used by individuals to define desirable or undesirable behavior.

religion. A set of symbols, ideas, and behaviors that focus on the meaning of life and the nature of the universe.

research design. A set of procedures that guide scientific inquiry.

role. Behaviors associated with a particular status.

secondary group. A social group whose members come together to accomplish particular goals.

secularization. A process in which nonreligious forces influence society.

social class. A group of people with similar income, education, and prestige levels.

social control. A variety of formal and informal processes that are intended to produce conformity.

socialization. A process that teaches individuals the norms, roles, and values of a society.

social movement. An organized group effort aimed at changing or preserving aspects of a social system.

social stratification. A system in which people are ranked according to their relative wealth, status, and power.

social structure. Patterned ways people interact with each other.

society. People living in the same territory who participate in a common culture.

socioeconomic status (SES). A measure of social class that ranks individuals according to their income, occupation, and educational attainment.

status. Socially defined positions in society.

stereotype. Generalizations about members of a group that ignore individual differences.

subculture. A group of people within a society who subscribe to the basic values and norms of the larger culture, but who also hold certain norms and values that make them culturally distinct.

survey research. A frequently used method of data collection in sociology that involves asking people questions about their attitudes and behavior.

symbols. Language, gestures, and material objects used for human communication.

theory. A set of underlying principles which serves to explain the relationship among various observed phenomena.

values. Ideas about what is good and desirable (as well as undesirable) in a society.

variable. A characteristic that varies among individuals or groups.

For further reading

Babbie, Earl R. *The Practice of Social Research.* 6th ed. Belmont, Calif.: Wadsworth, 1992.

Berger, Peter L. *Invitation to Sociology: A Humanistic Perspective.* New York: Doubleday, 1963.

Charon, Joel M. *Ten Questions: A Sociological Perspective.* 2nd ed. Belmont, Calif.: Wadsworth, 1995.

Coser, Lewis A. *Masters of Sociological Thought.* New York: Harcourt, Brace, Jovanovich, 1977.

Mills, C. Wright. *The Sociological Imagination.* London: Oxford University Press, 1959.

Political Science

The politics of a country define the social and economic life of its citizens. Therefore, to better understand a nation of people, political scientists study its government. They apply scientific principles in their study of the ideologies, laws, organization, and methods of government to determine what government does as well as what it should do as defined by its ideology.

In this chapter, the study of political science is broken down into three subjects: political theory (doctrines, theories, and ideologies that drive political systems), American government (structure and functions of the many components of the American political system), and international relations (an analysis of the ways nations interact with one another).

Political theory

Governments make decisions for a society through a process called *politics*. Though the form and purpose of governments may vary, at the center of every kind of political system is *power*—government's capacity to get someone to do something willingly or because it can use force. Without power, the decisions of government would not be binding. Political scientists are keenly interested in the ways power is used in determining who gets what, when, and how.

The nature of politics. Three types of decisions government officials make using the political process deal with allocation and distribution of public goods and services; conflict resolution; and deciding what they will provide to achieve what is believed to be a "good society."

As resources are always scarce, governments must decide how public resources are to be allocated in order to provide public goods and services for a society (education, roads, and national defense, for example). Governments also get involved in resolving conflicts that inevitably arise between individuals and groups

that want access to the scarce resources. The definition of the "good society" tends to change over time, as the needs of the society change.

Sources of power. Power can be based on one's office, whether elected or appointed. For example, the office of the President confers an amount of power on anyone who occupies it; the power is inherent in the office. This form of power is known as *legal/rational authority*.

Charismatic individuals obtain power through personal characteristics such as oratorical skills, warrior prowess, or an ability to inspire. Gandhi and Martin Luther King, Jr., used their charisma in a positive way to inspire the people they led. But charisma can also be the basis of destructive power, as was seen in Adolf Hitler and the Ayatollah Khomeini.

Power may be used legitimately with the consent of the people or it can be abused. In democracies, power is *legitimate* when it is exercised in a manner that is consistent with public expectations. In nondemocratic societies, the old dictum "might makes right" sums up the legitimacy of the power in control.

Authority. In theory, the *state*—the set of formal institutions designed to service human needs within a geographic area—holds a monopoly of public power, but the extent of power held can vary from one state to another. *Sovereignty* refers to the supreme source of states' authority to make or change laws. It may be vested in a king, an elite group, or in citizenry (popular sovereignty). In democratic societies such as the United States, power and sovereignty reside in the people, who then delegate it to office holders. There are also clear limits on power in democratic societies. The limits may be written into a *constitution* or they may be limited by laws, long-standing attitudes, and customs.

In nondemocratic societies, such as China, power is often unlimited and concentrated in the hands of a small group (*oligarchy*) or one person (*autocracy*). Both oligarchies and autocrats are referred to as authoritarian or dictatorial leaders. Today, most nondemocratic countries are dictatorships of the left (toward communism and party dominance) or of the right (toward fascism and a dictatorship).

Totalitarian states try to exercise total control over the lives of their people, making ample institutionalized use of propaganda and refined techniques of terror. They often dictate a command economy, rather than a market economy in which economic decisions are influenced by the needs and wants of the citizenry. Very few totalitarian states exist today. Recent examples are Castro's Cuba, the People's Republic of China, and Saddam Hussein's Iraq.

Political values.

Political behavior is based on political values. Contemporary political scientists ask the same questions as most ancient Greek philosophers: What is the good society? How are public resources distributed? How should public resources be

distributed? What is the proper relationship between state authority and individual freedom? Each answer reflects a political value.

The philosophers. Plato (427–347 B.C.), regarded as the father of Western political philosophy, based his political values on insight. Aristotle, regarded as the father of Western political science, based his values on observable fact. These two philosophers, as well as politicians from ancient Rome, contributed to long-lasting political values such as equality, and the natural rights and value of the individual.

Absolutism. Another political idea that later developed into a doctrine in the sixteenth and seventeenth centuries was the *divine right* of kings, providing divine approval for the leader's actions on behalf of the new "state" system called the *monarchy*. The monarchy was sovereign, the supreme authority during the sixteenth century.

In the Middle Ages, the state was less important than the church. But after the Reformation, the writings of Niccolò Machiavelli (1469-1527) contributed to the notion of the separation of church and state power. The *might-makes-right* doctrine had some popularity in the sixteenth century. This doctrine allowed government to claim authority as long as it had the power to enforce its claim. Accordingly, authority was based on the ruler's capacity to use physical force.

Types of authority

Traditional   Charismatic   Legal / rational

Contract theories. Various political philosophers, such as Thomas Hobbes (1588–1679) and Jean Jacques Rousseau (1712–1778), developed contract theories as a challenge to the absolutism that was defended by the divine right of kings and might-makes-right doctrines. These theories sought to explain the origins of the state and government, and they described the obligations and responsibilities of both the government and the governed. According to the theories, a political body was first created through a compact or contract, then the government was founded and empowered through a second contract or constitution.

Thomas Hobbes believed that the most stable government form required very strong political leadership. Because he was so concerned with political stability, he advocated an authoritarian relationship between the rulers and the ruled. He viewed human beings as so destructive in nature that only a strong, centralized power could keep humanity's natural urges in check.

The democratic implication of modern contract theories emerged during the Age of Enlightenment, largely through the advocacy of John Locke, Jean Jacques Rousseau, and others. John Locke (1632–1704) believed that sovereignty resides in the people, not the state. Locke believed that people are capable of making rational decisions in their own self-interest. He believed government was indispensable for settling disputes and performing other activities that individuals could not handle easily on their own, and therefore, citizens should enter into a social contract with the government. The government breaks the contract whenever it trespasses on a citizen's natural rights, which include rights to life, liberty, and private property.

Jean Jacques Rousseau expanded on Locke's ideas by insisting that no government is legitimate unless all men (all classes) give their consent to it; all men are created equal, having equal right to participate in the

making of law. There must also be initial agreement when establishing a government.

Karl Marx explained mankind's social and political relationships in terms of material needs and the state of tension and conflict that naturally occurs between the owners of production and the workers. Marx viewed those who controlled the means of production as politically dominant.

Modern political scientists, such as Robert Dahl, Gabriel Almond, and Harry Eckstein, study and compare authority structures and political influence to help determine what shapes modern political behavior.

Political ideologies.
Ideologies are systems of belief that move people to action while helping them feel secure that they are doing the right thing. These systems are reflected in the political, economic, and social arrangements in any society. Ideologies can unite many individuals of different personalities, interests, and social strata. An ideology can justify an existing social system or propose a future order, but it always ascribes an ethical basis to the way political power is used in the society. In the view of many thinkers on the subject, a common but unfortunate use of ideology is to facilitate manipulation of the masses by political leaders.

Anarchism. Anarchists propose an equal distribution of power to every citizen, each having the right to legislate for him or herself and to maintain private owner-

---

Continuum of ideologies

Left	Center	Right
Anarchism **Communism** **Socialism**	**Progressive liberalism** **Conservative liberalism**	**Fascism**
Advocates radical or revolutionary change that gives all power to the masses and individuals, and gets rid of the state.	Advocates moderate approaches to solving social and economic problems. Seeks to balance individual rights, popular participation, and government authority.	Advocates reactionary, corporative programs that restrict individual rights; and gives all power to a ruling group or state (collective strength).

---

ship of material goods. Because anarchists see the state as a tool to dominate and exploit others, they advocate no state control. Some propose that anarchy can only happen after a violent overthrow of the state.

Communism. Communists argue that private ownership leads to inequality because unequal ownership implies unequal power. Therefore economic equality is a prerequisite for political equality in this ideology. Communism prescribes a society where land, capital, and the means of production are collectively owned, and power is exercised by the masses. Built on the theories of Karl Marx, and modified by V. I. Lenin, communist ideology was used to attack capitalism through doctrines of class conflict, historical inevitability, and economic determinism. Modern communism never reached its pure communist state. Political scientists believe it was betrayed by its own leadership, resulting in inequality of ownership and power between Communist party members and the people. Stalinist communism is an example of a leftist dictatorship. The collapse of the communist political system in the USSR was precipitated by government corruption, an inability of the economy to meet the needs of the people, and the people's unwillingness to sacrifice for an abstract idea.

Socialism. Socialists advocate government and group ownership of the means of production and the distribution of goods for the welfare of the individual members. It replaces competition with cooperation. Authoritarian socialist systems are run by a ruling elite who believe they know what is in the best interest of the people. In socialist democracies, the people elect representatives who decide on policies for regulating the economy and promoting general welfare.

Liberalism and conservatism. American democracy is a system of government based on the ideologies of liberalism and conservatism. Liberalism is considered slightly "left" and conservativism is slightly

Who should govern?

	Justifications	*Critiques*
The few		
Aristocracy	Rule by the better class of society will elevate the community to the highest level of achievement.	The interests of the many are systematically sacrificed to the interests of the few.
Authoritarianism	A prince is necessary to organize and protect people, as well as create good laws and institutions.	The prince is a self-interested despot exercising power for power's sake.
Monarchy	Sanctioned by the church, it is the monarch's "divine right" to rule. But the monarch has obligations to respect the rights of the people.	Fails to meet popular demands for political participation and can be despotic.
Totalitarianism (communism and fascism)	Both communism and fascism seek absolute domination of all aspects of life to realize a perfect society, based on "scientific" theories of race or class.	Complete loss of individual liberty results in states that use absolute and arbitrary power, state terror, and genocide to dominate society.
The many		
Liberal democracy	Individual liberty is balanced with community needs through limited, representative government.	The elitist representative government is favored.
Participatory democracy	Ordinary people have an equal say in deciding issues that affect their lives.	Ordinary people are not competent enough to make complex political decisions.
Socialism	Distributive justice through public ownership of the means of production provides equal access to basic necessities like education, health care, shelter, food, and transportation.	There is loss of individual control, liberty, and initiative.

"right." The American democratic system can be viewed as trying to find the balance between individual freedom and government authority.

Whereas socialism places primary emphasis on the value and welfare of the group, liberalism's key concept, called *individualism*, places its emphasis on the worth and well-being of the individual. Individualism argues for less government to assure that each person can reach his or her highest potential. The belief is that where there is less law, there is more freedom. Paradoxically, liberalism favors more government regulations in promoting general welfare. Liberalism also assumes that human nature is rational and that people can make moral judgments and decisions for their lives. Because it assumes that social truths are relative, a liberal democracy is also more tolerant of differences of opinion.

Conservatives believe that reason serves as an aid in making decisions, but reason is not trusted to be infallible. Conservative democracies are reluctant to initiate changes and rely more on what has worked in the past. They believe there are general limits on what government can and should do to promote the general welfare.

In democracies, all people are said to possess inalienable rights to freedom and equality before the law, but they are expected to cooperate in creating a healthy society. Democracies advocate equal access to opportunities. Other crucial freedoms in a democracy are based on civil rights and liberties such as freedom of speech, press, religion, assembly, and petition. Decision-making processes in a democracy are based on majority rule with allowances for protection of minority rights.

Totalitarianism. Our experiences with fascism and communism leave little doubt that both are totalitarian

Berliners celebrate the opening of the East-West German border.

states, with fascism on the right end of the ideological continuum and communism on the left. Fascism advocates private ownership of land and capital, but all economic and social activity is controlled by the state. Communism declares that the people own everything (we now know they had very little), and the communist party leadership is to decide who gets what and when. Fascism and communism are both committed to the total control of a country's social, economic, and political life, and to the total subjugation of the individual's interests to those of the state (under fascism) or the party (under communism).

Who should rule? The nature of a particular government can be understood by an examination of its ideology because ideologies are the driving forces that justify the form and role of government. Governments can also be examined by their power structure, set up in one of three ways: self-rule, rule of the few, or rule of the many. Ideologies rationalize the system, then justify it.

Political change.
Societies are always changing in their economic, political, and social characteristics. Political stability requires adaptability, as paradoxical as that may seem. Developments in science and technology can create new problems and questions, such as those concerning health care and the environment, thus making society more complex. Economic changes can also require some political adaptation.

Interest groups mobilize to solve a society's problems and put pressure on political institutions to adapt to the new complexity and capture resources controlled by government. When governments are slow to adapt to the new complexity, instability can be expected. Civil disturbances, riots, and even revolutions can result from the failure of a political system to adapt. A revolution is a process of political change influenced by a mass social movement. The members of the movement are prepared to use violence to seize power and initiate reform. Modern examples include revolutions in Cuba (1959) and Iran (1979).

Theories. Two traditional theories of social and political adaptation are the unilinear and circular theories of change.

During the nineteenth century, it was assumed by *unilinear* theorists that change was a one-line progression of stages through which all societies must pass. *Circular* theorists believe that there is an inevitable rise and fall in all civilizations.

In recent years, a third theory has gained popularity. This new theory, called the *multilinear* theory of change, acknowledges that not only does change occur in several ways, it may even progress in divergent directions.

American government

The distinguishing feature of the American political system is the extent to which the Founding Fathers avoided the concentration of political power. Acknowledging the frailties of human nature, they carefully diffused political power by separating executive, judicial, and legislative powers, assigning overlapping responsibilities to the different branches (*checks and balances*), and giving the courts the power to overrule the executive and legislative branches.

The Constitution.

Constitutions embody the rights of citizens and depict the nature of the state's authority and power. In effect since 1789, the United States Constitution is the most successful written constitution in history. Its authors built a flexible document that has remained an effective government tool requiring only twenty-seven amendments in over two hundred years. The first ten amendments, referred to as the *Bill of Rights*, were added in 1791.

The writers divided up power between the central and state governments through *federalism*, a system in which the central government and state governments share powers. *National supremacy* established that federal laws are superior to state laws and that the Constitution is enforceable as law. The authors separated government powers into three branches—executive, legislative, and judicial—in a system called the *separation of powers*. Through checks and balances, each branch shares power with the others, making them interdependent. For example, the practice of judicial review allows the courts to declare executive and legislative actions unconstitutional. The President nominates individuals to serve on the Supreme Court, but the U.S. Senate must approve those nominees.

Congress.

The Founding Fathers expected the U.S. Congress to be the supreme branch of the three branches of government. The Congress is a *bicameral* (two-house) legislative body; the upper chamber is the *Senate* and the lower chamber is the *House of Representatives*. Each chamber has exclusive powers; for example, the Senate has power to ratify foreign treaties, and the House has power to originate all legislation requiring money.

Each state has two senators, but its number of representatives is determined by its size. Senators serve for six years and are elected by voters statewide. Representatives serve for two years and are elected by voters in one of 435 congressional districts.

Three activities seem to dominate the agenda of Congress: *casework* (constituent service), *pork barrel legislation* (expenditures of public money for local projects), and *public lawmaking*. In addition, members of Congress have an enormous number of requests to help their constituents with personal problems or needs whose satisfaction often is the key to reelection.

Each house must approve a bill before it becomes law. This process often leads to lengthy debate and compromise. Once a bill is approved, the President must sign it for it to become law. If the President vetoes a bill, it can be overridden by a two-thirds majority in each house.

Federalism

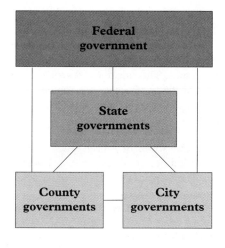

Functions of federal government
(broad national issues)
Regulating interstate trade
Defense

Functions of state, county, and city governments
(local matters)
Education
Safety
Welfare

Shared functions
(overlapping)
Education
Health
Raising revenues (taxes)
Welfare

The presidency.
The President is widely viewed as the symbol of the nation. As required by the Constitution, the President wears many hats: commander in chief over the military; chief executive over the entire bureaucracy; chief diplomat and ceremonial head, entertaining leaders of other countries; as well as head of state, representing the nation on somber occasions of state. Over time, the President has become party chief as well as chief legislator.

The President is required to cooperate with Congress, since Congress controls the funds and enacts laws needed to maintain the military and fulfill domestic goals. But one of the most important presidential powers is the power to persuade, which the President uses to win public and congressional support for his initiatives and appointments. The President's success in persuasion is largely dependent on his or her personality and leadership style.

Presidential power is limited by the system of checks and balances, including the Senate's power to approve nominees and the House's "power of the purse." The Supreme Court interprets the constitutional limits of the President's office. By forcing the three branches of government to work together, the Founding Fathers promoted a natural tension among them that urges them to be sensitive to the imperatives of cooperation and compromise.

The U.S. Congress in session

The bureaucracy.
The federal bureacracy is made up of fourteen cabinet-level departments. Each of these is headed by a cabinet secretary. There are also hundreds of independent agencies, authorities, bureaus, and government corporations. For years the number of civilian employees in the bureaucracy has been approximately three million.

The bureaucracy has three tasks. In its legislative capacity, it provides detailed regulations and rules for loosely defined acts of Congress. In its executive capacity, it implements laws, rules, and regulations. In its judicial capacity, it resolves conflicts arising from its rules and regulations.

Government corporations, like the Tennessee Valley Authority and the Panama Canal Corporation, are given greater independence from Congress than cabinet-level departments. In crucial areas of the economy, such as energy, communications, business trade practices, and commerce, there are independent regulatory commissions, which are charged with promoting competition, the well-being, and the health of the industry itself.

The President is the chief administrator, but the bureaucratic administrators are also mindful of the fact that Congress has important legislative and investigatory powers. They are also aware that it controls the "purse."

The judiciary.
The United States has a dual court system. There are fifty state court systems and one federal court system, which is headed by the Supreme Court. The federal court system is the more important of the two because the Supreme Court has said that the Constitution is superior to state laws and constitutions.

Federal judges are appointed for life. The Supreme Court has the power of *judicial review*, which is the authority to rule a legislative or executive act unconstitutional. The Supreme Court is also responsible for *interpreting* the Constitution. This power fulfills two important functions: it resolves disputes which are immediately before it, and it develops the law which is consistent with the direction of the country's needs or desires.

Political parties.

Political parties, unlike the President, Congress, and Supreme Court, are not mentioned in the Constitution. But the political party has been and continues to be an important institution for articulating and representing citizens' concerns.

The United States has had a *two-party system* through most of its history. Though there are other parties, only two have been viable at any one time. The dominant parties today are the Democrats and the Republicans. Political parties function to stimulate voter interest, develop programs for governmental consideration, recruit candidates, campaign, and govern. Their importance has been undermined in recent years by television, which allows candidates to address the electorate directly; by the emergence of single-issue interest groups, whose commitment to an issue is more important than allegiance to a party; and by the loosening of restrictions on campaign finance, reducing the importance of party campaign workers.

The major political parties are not rigidly ideological; rather, their positions shift because they are devoted to capturing public office. By contrast, minor parties such as the Socialist Labor party and the Libertarians are more likely to be strongly ideological, seeing their mission as the education of the American public. In articulating and representing citizens' concerns, political parties serve as a counterweight to the powerful structure of organized interest groups.

Interest groups.

There are tens of thousands of interest groups in the United States. Though all are interested in influencing governmental officials and public opinion, some are more influential than others.

Interest groups are often thought of as cohesive groups of individuals with shared values and goals; in reality, some are and some are not. These powerful groups offer a diversity of incentives for membership.

One of the largest interest groups in the United States today is the American Association of Retired People (AARP). Its membership is said to exceed 30 million. These people count on the AARP to protect their Social Security benefits, cost of living allowances, and health care benefits. The National Association for the Advancement of Colored People (NAACP) and the National Rifle Association (NRA) are other examples of powerful interest groups that have helped enact change in public policy.

Interest groups *lobby* public officials (try to persuade legislators to support a certain course of action). Their most effective tactic is providing accurate information, which ensures their credibility. They also contribute cash to candidates, incumbents, and challengers. Indeed, in recent years the influence of interest groups has greatly increased, because corporations and unions now can contribute money directly to candidates through *political action committees (PACs)*.

Some federal agencies

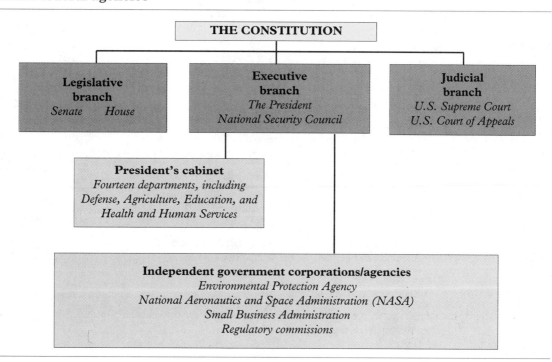

Political Science

The 1996 Republican national convention

Civil rights and liberties.

At the heart of the democratic process is the protection of the basic freedoms and rights of the citizens. *Civil liberties* refer to those freedoms identified in the first ten amendments to the Constitution, known as the Bill of Rights. The scope of civil liberties has been expanded over the past two hundred years. Civil liberties protect citizens from arbitrary interference of government officials and serve as a restraint on government rather than on individuals.

Civil rights are not civil liberties. Civil rights deal with participatory rights, such as the right to vote, and to equal treatment in the workplace, in housing, and in job opportunities. They ensure that citizens cannot be discriminated against because of a personal characteristic, such as race, sex, origin, age, or disability. One key civil right—the right to vote—was extended through the passage of the fifteenth (vote extended to males of all races and colors), the nineteenth (vote extended to women), and the twenty-sixth (vote extended to eighteen-year-olds) amendments.

In the form of statutes (public and private laws), civil rights are positive acts of government that protect citizens against arbitrary or discriminatory treatment by government or individuals. Although they are particularly important to racial minorities, women, and persons with disabilities, they are important features in any society that believes in the dignity and worth of the individual.

The Supreme Court must make decisions when two contending civil rights are competing with one another for authority—for example, when trying to balance the rights of the individual against the interests of society. Changes in the membership of the Supreme Court are significant because the Court defines the civil rights and liberties of citizens and can choose to overturn earlier decisions.

Significant amendments

Freedom of expression

First amendment: freedom of religion, speech, press, assembly, and petition
- May result in innovative and useful solutions to political and social problems
- Criticisms can lead to reform
- Censorship leads society toward totalitarianism
- Maximizes freedom of expression but does not protect people from illegal acts

Rights of the criminally accused

Fourth amendment: security from unreasonable searches and seizures
- Warrants necessary before most seizures

Fifth amendment: protects against self-incrimination
- Defendants can't be forced to testify against themselves
- Accused can't be tried for the same offense twice

Sixth amendment: right to counsel
- Right to a speedy and public trial

Eighth amendment: protects those accused of a crime from cruel and unusual punishment
- Prohibits excessive bail

International relations

The study of international relations is an attempt to describe and understand the ways in which nation states (a country's people united under a single government) interact with each other. Today, nation states are the main actors in the arena of international politics. The proliferation of new states from the former Soviet Union and the nationalist demands elsewhere promise a larger number of states and many short-term uncertainties in the world community.

Conflict. States are constantly trying to position themselves to attain or maintain status, power, and security in the world community. Tensions among nations require diplomatic handling.

When a treaty is broken by one of the parties, there is the possibility that military force may be used to enforce the terms of the treaty. The claim to lands and resources often precipitates conflict. In 1990, Iraq objected to Kuwait's tapping into Iraqi oil fields and subsequently invaded Kuwait.

Sometimes, conflicts also result from nationalist movements, such as those in Bosnia-Herzegovina and earlier conflicts in Slovenia and Croatia as they asserted their independence in 1991 from the central Yugoslav government, which was controlled by Serbia. Religious or racial differences are another source of conflict, such as the conflicts between Catholics and Protestants in Northern Ireland, the Hausa and Ibo tribes in Nigeria, Muslim and Hindu groups in India, and the Greeks and Turks on Cyprus. Thus, conflicts can stem from many conditions. There is also no single means for their resolution.

The use of military force is one means of resolving disputes, as was illustrated by the United States in its Desert Storm operation in Kuwait and Iraq in 1991. In terms of dollars and, more importantly, human lives, aggression is the most costly strategy of political actions. There are international laws that govern warfare and distinguish legal war from the use of force.

Underground activities such as sabotage, guerilla warfare, and terrorism are a form of violent force. Subversion and espionage are nonviolent tactics of underground activity. Nonviolent force can also take the form of boycotts and blockages, as illustrated by U.S. policy toward Cuba in the late twentieth century.

Diplomacy is an important means for peacefully resolving disputes. It usually means that all parties in the dispute give some and gain some as concessions are negotiated. Aggression and violence in the international community can also be avoided through alliances.

Alliances. Alliances are agreements between two or more states to come to each other's aid, usually from the threat of military attack. Traditionally, nations achieved their interests largely through the development and promotion of military strength. States would form alliances to ensure a "balance of power," so that no one state was able to coerce others.

Military alliances continued to be the dominant pattern after World War II. That war ended in a division between East and West, communism and democracy—with the Soviet Union leading the Eastern bloc nations and the United States leading the Western nations.

The *North Atlantic Treaty Organization* (NATO) was formed to defend Western nations from Soviet aggression. The United States also initiated the *Southeast Asia Treaty Organization* (SEATO) to protect its allies in Asia. The Soviet Union responded with the *Warsaw Pact* in central Europe. The emergence of independence movements in many undeveloped states—so-called *Third World* nations—added a further dimension to the formerly bipolar picture, prompting some observers to envision a multipolar world.

However, with the disintegration of the Soviet Union and the independence of its former satellite countries in central Europe, this entire system of alliances is changing rapidly. Today, cooperation among nations is likely to be based on economic as well as military factors.

In 1988, Canada and the United States agreed to an open trade border between the two nations. This was extended to include Mexico when, in December 1993, President Bill Clinton signed into law the *North American Free-Trade Agreement* (NAFTA), establishing a free-trade zone among these North American countries. This agreement reflects a new emphasis on economic cooperation among states. The *European Economic Community* (EEC) is a parallel development in Europe.

International relations today are increasingly influenced by a country's economic system, and by the realization that all are now part of a global economy.

From technological inventions—nuclear power, missiles, satellite communications, and modern means of transportation—came a different world order, one in which communities are ever more interdependent. The hazards to our environment and the geometric increase in the world's population, for example, are problems shared by all.

Interdependence.
It is becoming increasingly clear that nations of the world are affected by each other's behavior, an interdependence that went unrecognized or was ignored before World War I. Today, a new perspective is being realized—that of nations as members of a global society, a community of nations.

The most notable beginning of these cooperative arrangements was the *League of Nations*, established in the aftermath of World War I. The League did not last long. The *United Nations (U.N.)* was established after World War II as an organization that represented a peaceful alternative to inter-nation tension and armed conflict. Today the role of the U.N. in resolving international conflict is not limited to disputes between countries, such as its intervention in the dispute between Kuwait and Iraq. The U.N. also has helped mediate disputes within a country, notably in its efforts to establish and maintain peace between Muslims and Christians in Bosnia-Herzegovina. Clearly the U.N. has become an increasingly important institution in the community of nation states.

Treaties.
Treaties are the glue that holds alliances together. These formal agreements set down in explicit terms the mutual duties, rights, and obligations of each party. Agreements can be *bilateral* (two parties) or *multilateral* (more than two parties). In the United States, treaties must be ratified by a two-thirds vote of the Senate. Presidents have attempted to avoid this by increased use of executive agreements with foreign heads of state that do not need the consent of the Senate. When presidents need strong public and congressional support, however, they choose to depend on treaties over executive agreements.

In the United States, treaties take precedence over the state constitutions and law, and very few are voted down by the Senate. But many treaties are killed by the inaction of the Senate. Two very important treaties were voted down—one providing for U.S. membership in the League of Nations, and another for membership in the first World Court.

Some treaties expire after a specific length of time, by mutual understanding, or after a condition has been met. For example, in 1976 President Jimmy Carter had committed himself to returning the Panama Canal to the government of Panama. The U.S. Senate ratified the Panama Canal Treaty in 1978, which stipulated that the government of Panama was to gain control of the canal in 1998.

Whatever the specific conditions of a treaty, it is certain that these agreements help stabilize relationships and provide predictability among nations and alliances.

United Nations General Assembly in session

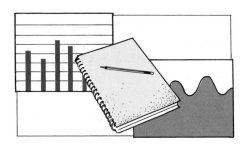

Political Science

Tests, homework, and projects

Laying the groundwork

Students of a social science like political science must understand many differing theoretical perspectives; success in class depends on getting the most out of reading, notetaking, and taking tests. When reading assigned material, try not to get bogged down with supportive facts. First, scan the chapter and note the headings and subheadings. Then list the key points in each section using your own words. In class, ask questions while you are taking notes. This helps you remember information because it is then reorganized in a way you can understand. When studying for tests, remember "cramming" just increases anxiety. Instead, schedule short study sessions to break up information into smaller units.

Strategies for success

Homework, class projects, and tests are used to assess your basic knowledge and challenge you to apply this information in new ways. Professors assign reading homework to help you prepare for the next day's lecture. You will take better notes if you are already familiar with the material. A speed-reading course may help cut down on reading time and increase comprehension. Class projects are opportunities for exploration. Choose a subject that interests you. Break down the project into a series of short-term goals that you can accomplish throughout the term. Plan ahead for taking tests by scheduling enough time to study. During the test, answer easy questions first, and save time for difficult questions.

Helpful hints

Multiple choice

Which of the following principles is a basis of democracy? (a) limited government (b) public ownership of the means of production (c) might makes right

As you read a multiple choice question, anticipate the answer. But even if you see the answer among the options, read all the possible answers. Discard any ideas that are obviously wrong to narrow down your choices.

Answer. a

Fill-in

According to the _____ approach in the study of international relations, nations cooperate with each other because they share common problems, needs, and objectives.

Sometimes fill-ins have more than one possible answer. Scan questions in other sections of the test for clues to your fill-in. You may see the approaches listed elsewhere.

Answer. Moralist or idealist

Essay

Discuss why citizens of a nation generally obey laws.

Read the essay at the beginning of the exam so you have time to plan as you go over the other test questions. You may see some key terms and clues in the other questions. As major ideas and subject vocabulary occur to you, write them down. Then when you get to the essay, you will have half your essay already written.

Project

Conduct a public opinion poll on a topic of your interest and present your findings to the class.

Projects are an opportunity for exploration. Choose topics that interest you and let you apply some theoretical perspectives. The format for your presentation may be a lecture, research paper, tape-recorded survey results, or slide show.

Other suggested topics
• Observe your city government in action.
• Make changes in your neighborhood or community.

Glossary

Conflict resolution

Freedom

Nation

Power

absolutism. Political system where government power is not subject to restraints or limitation (such as checks and balances).

anarchy. Society without a state, government, or ruler, theoretically based on voluntary cooperation.

authoritarianism. Theory in which ruler's power cannot be challenged. Independent organizations (such as social or religious) are tolerated if they do not threaten the ruler's privileges.

authority. Obedience based on voluntary consent; legitimate power.

behavioralism. A methodology modeled after the "scientific method" of the natural sciences that studies political behavior as it is, rather than as how it ought to be.

bill. A draft of legislation presented to a legislature for enactment or to an executive for approval.

citizen. A recognized member of a state, who owes allegiance to that state and is entitled to full rights, duties, privileges, and protection under the law.

city-state. Small, autonomous country consisting of an urban area and surrounding territory.

communism. According to Marxist theory, the final stage of social development, where capitalism is overthrown and a classless society is established. Goods are distributed from each according to ability, to each according to need.

confederation. An organization of states in which states are sovereign and supreme. Central government has only the powers that subnation governments have given it.

conflict resolution. A function of government: to keep peace by mediating and resolving private disagreements or disputes.

conservatism. A preference for the status quo; a mistrust of rapid change; belief in the wisdom of one's own culture and traditions built up slowly over time.

constitutionalism. Limited governmental power.

corporatism. A political society based upon group unity and cooperation, rather than individualism and competition.

democracy. Rule of, by, and for the people, based upon direct and equal participation in public decisions and majority rule.

despot. Any authoritarian or absolute ruler; also, an abusive or oppressive leader, a tyrant.

dialectical materialism. Marx's theory of human progress, based on class conflict; human history is thought to be driven by material forces, rather than ideas.

dialectics. A theory of change, based upon the collision of opposites, and the resulting emergence of something new; thesis × antithesis = synthesis.

electoral process. Means by which candidates seek political office, to be selected by popular vote.

fascism. Governmental system in which nation and community are placed above the individual and are ruled by a strong, dictatorial government.

federalism. A division of sovereign power between a central government and several constituent units (such as our fifty states).

formalism. Political analysis of how government is supposed to work, rather than how it works in practice.

franchise. The right to vote.

freedom. The right to participate in political decisions: town meetings, jury service, voting.

ideology. A systematic, integrated, and comprehensive set of political beliefs.

Political Science

institutions. Organized offices and structures of government, such as legislatures, courts, military, and police.

interest group. Organized, cooperative association of individuals, sharing a common political, social, religious, or economic agenda.

justice. (1) Fairness: if the means are fair, the end is just; (2) goodness: reaching a desired end by any means necessary.

legitimacy. A government, institution, or leader viewed as lawful; voluntary obedience to a command because it conforms to recognized and accepted rules and standards.

liberalism. Governmental system based upon pluralism, tolerance, and individual liberty under a limited representative government.

liberty. The right to be left alone; the power to do as one pleases; to be free of government or other controls.

monarchy. Undivided, sovereign power vested in a single person. Usually based on an inherited right to rule.

nation. A people with strong feelings of common identity, based on shared values and beliefs, which distinguishes them from all others.

participatory democracy. A political society in which all citizens have an equal voice in making political decisions. Decisions are by majority rule.

political equality. The measure of trust citizens place in government, institutions, and officials.

political party. An organization formed primarily to promote and elect certain persons to public office, and to enact a plan of political action.

politics. (1) Who gets what, when and how; (2) the authoritative allocation of values or goods; (3) the art or science of government; (4) decisions made through public discussion, not based on economic concerns of survival or scarcity.

power. The ability to compel a person or persons to act in a way they would not otherwise have behaved. Power can be exercised either through threat of force or by voluntary compliance.

radical. To favor abrupt and extreme methods of changing, preserving, or restoring a political system.

republic. A state with a popularly elected, representative government, whose chief of state is not a monarch. Officials are selected through regular elections, with open contestation for offices. Government is responsible to the electorate, and must govern according to law.

republicanism. (1) Theory based on elected, representative, responsible, and limited government; (2) theory based on a preference for direct public involvement in government decisions.

revolution. A drastic, fundamental, and violent change in the established political order. The violent overthrow of a government by the governed, and its replacement with a new form of government.

social contract. (1) A covenant among free and equal citizens, reciting mutual promises that establish the rules of civil society; (2) a covenant between a ruler and the ruled, establishing the rights and obligations of both.

socialism. A state in which the government, on behalf of the people, owns and operates the means of production. In Marxism, socialism is the transition state between capitalism and communism, governed by (or on behalf of) the working classes. According to Lenin, justice under socialism means from each according to abilities, to each according to work.

sovereign. The supreme or ultimate authority in a political society.

sovereignty. Autonomous, independent authority; freedom from external control.

state. A political society which has a defined territory that distinguishes one society from all the rest; a minimal level of ordered social sophistication and hierarchy.

totalitarianism. A governmental theory involving the complete domination of all aspects of society—by an absolute leader. All aspects of life are completely controlled by the state and subject to the will of the leader, without restriction.

unitary government. Undivided sovereignty in a single, central government.

For further reading

Almond, Gabriel, and Sydney Verba. *The Civic Culture.* Princeton, N. J.: Princeton University Press, 1963.

Gordon, George J., and Michael E. Milakovich. *Public Administration in America.* 5th ed. New York: St. Martin's Press, 1995.

Graham, Hugh Davis. *The Civil Rights Era: Origins and Developments of National Policy, 1960-1972.* New York: Oxford University Press, 1990.

Lederach, John Paul. *Preparing for Peace: Conflict Transformation Across Cultures.* Syracuse, N.Y.: Syracuse University Press, 1995.

Page, Benjamin I. *Who Gets What from Government.* Berkeley: University of California Press, 1983.

Welch, Susan, and John Gruhl, Michael Steinman, John Comer, and Susan M. Rigdon. *American Government.* 6th ed. Minneapolis, Minn.: West Publishing Company, 1996.

Cultural Anthropology

Anthropology is the youngest of the social sciences and, in many ways, the most ambitious. Its goal is to understand the human condition, both biologically and culturally, as it developed in the past and as it exists now: where humans came from; what they were like in the past; how they became what they are; and what they are like today. It is divided into four major subfields, or subdisciplines: *physical anthropology* (also called human biology—the study of human origins, evolution, and contemporary human variation); *archaeology* (the study of past cultures and extinct ways of life); *anthropological linguistics* (how cultures map their different worlds using language); and *cultural anthropology* (the comparative study of present human lifeways). Due to their richness and complexity, these are usually divided into several introductory courses at most universities; in this text, we shall cover cultural anthropology.

The concept of culture

Culture, for anthropologists, includes the learned and shared behaviors and the rules for those behaviors that define what it means to be human. A culture, or one culture, would be a particular subset of that whole. For example, when we speak of "American culture," we are speaking of how the American people think, act, believe, and behave. In some ways, American culture may be similar to other cultures; in some ways, it may be different. Cultures often contain *subcultures*, which share most of their characteristics yet differ in some significant ways. It is the study of the similarities and differences among cultures, as well as the reasons for their occurrence, that forms the core of cultural anthropology.

Another way to think about culture is that it is basically what makes "us" appear different from "them." It is a primary cognitive and diagnostic device of the human species, by which people can be grouped into similar and dissimilar sets, which then come to act, regarding each other, as groups rather than as individuals. Culture, in a sense, defines society. A society, then, is those people who share a common culture.

Malinowski's theory. Bronislaw Malinowski, one of the founders of modern anthropology, reminded us that humans are, after all, animals. Like all animals, we have a variety of biological needs (such as subsistence and reproduction) that must effectively be met if we as a species are to survive. Other animals meet these needs almost exclusively by innate, instinctive, programmed mechanisms not subject to their modification or control. Human beings, on the other hand, use almost entirely learned behaviors for this, behaviors that they can then change if need be.

For Malinowski, this set of ideas and activities that we use to meet our biological needs is our culture. We have invented, made, tried, tested, accepted and continued, or rejected and forgotten many ways to do the various things we need to do. In this way, we can and do change our culture.

Different groups in varying circumstances may develop different sets of cultural mechanisms. Cultural diversity is both useful and necessary. Not everyone is the same; not everyone lives in the same "world."

Culture as adaptation. Culture is the means by which humans adapt to their environment. If the environment changes, other animals must adapt through the long process of natural selection, migration, or else die out; but humans can invent warmer clothing or irrigation or trade to import foods, allowing them to stay where they are with minimized loss or biological change. Through our culture, we can even keep people alive and well in outer space or the depths of the oceans. No other animal has the ability to live in so many different environments. Our culture has made us the most adaptable animal of all.

Components of culture. Human subsistence needs are met by our *technology* (or economy). Reproduction is controlled by our system of *kinship and marriage*. We need protection from predators (and, increasingly, from ourselves), which we obtain through our *politics and law*. Humans, as an intelligent species, need to explain things; *religion* is often the way we do so. To do all this together, we need the most sophisticated communications system possible, so we have *language*. And we need to be able to balance our lives through *expressive culture* such as art, music, and dance.

Basic tenets. There is a complex interrelationship among all of these components, such that a change in any one of them may affect not only other things within its own domain, but all of the other components as well. For example, if there is a recession (fall in economic product), not only will people be laid off and withdraw their savings (reducing loans banks can make, another economic effect), but there will also be demands for change in the political system (to find new leaders); in family life (people will delay getting married and having children); in religion (people may question their old religion or pray harder to make it work better); in art (moods, themes, and productivity); and so forth. The components of culture can really be understood only as parts of a larger whole, not as separate entities. This means that any attempt to change any single aspect of a culture should be very carefully evaluated for its potential effects in other areas of people's lives.

Some anthropologists have suggested that since every culture has its own set of characteristics, each in tune with its own circumstances and meeting its own needs, each culture must be judged solely on its own terms. This doctrine of *cultural relativism* has been hotly debated for many years. Does it mean that each culture can do whatever it wants, without regard for anything we might call universal human rights? Today, most anthropologists would probably answer no: understanding how and why a culture works in its own terms does not necessarily mean approving of what it does. On the other hand, our standards do not necessarily have any greater validity just because they are ours.

The question of how to define a universally applicable, culture-free set of basic human rights will undoubtedly be with us for some time.

Major schools of anthropological thought

School	Major contributor	Theory
Evolutionism	L. H. Morgan (1818–1881)	Cultures move through a fixed order of stages.
Historicism	F. Boas (1858–1942)	Each culture must be viewed in the field with an understanding of its unique history.
Functionalism	B. Malinowski (1884–1942) A. R. Radcliffe-Brown (1881–1955)	Each culture is made up of interrelated parts which normally balance each other.
Structuralism	C. Lévi-Strauss (b. 1908)	Cultural behaviors and beliefs are organized in binary pairs by the mind.
Cultural ecology	J. H. Steward (1902–1972)	Culture is the adaptive mechanism used to interact with an environment.
Culture and personality	M. Mead (1901–1978) R. Benedict (1887–1948)	Each culture determines its personality types through the socialization of children.
Symbolism	M. Douglas (b. 1921)	Cultural meaning is expressed symbolically through language and other codes.
Interpretivism	C. Geertz (b. 1926)	Cultures are to be interpreted like texts, using the insider's point of view.
Postmodernism	M. M. Fischer (b. 1946)	Ethnographies show multiple interpretations of each culture.

Research

As part of the social sciences, anthropology bridges the gulf between science and the humanities. As a science, anthropology does more than just collect facts, although this documentation of human diversity is itself important. It also generates hypotheses about the reasons these facts occur as they do and tests those hypotheses to build theories to explain things. As part of the humanities, anthropology attempts to describe and interpret the social realities of the peoples it studies, taking into account the intricacies of conducting cross-cultural research.

The goals, objectives, and research methods of anthropologists vary considerably, as do the products of their research. Some cultural descriptions (called *ethnographies*) read like technical reports; others read like works of literature. In both approaches, however, the accurate and systematic gathering of information is crucial.

The fieldwork revolution. The
infant study of anthropology, begun in the nineteenth century by aristocratic European travelers, was soon changed, largely through the efforts of one man, Bronislaw Malinowski. He left his home in Poland to study anthropology in England with the greatest of the Victorian anthropologists, but he found their work unsatisfying. He decided that the problem was with their data: it was all secondhand, of dubious reliability, and most likely inaccurately translated.

Malinowski set about to correct this problem by obtaining on his own the data needed for research, rather than relying on the accounts of tax collectors, missionaries, conquering colonels, and the like, as the others had done. As fate would have it, he got stuck on a small island off the coast of New Guinea during most of World War I and thus had the opportunity to learn as much about the life of its people as he was able. He established the anthropological tradition of *fieldwork*—going to the people, living with them, learning their language, and obtaining his data first hand. His resulting studies of the Trobriand Islanders, such as *Argonauts of the Western Pacific*, have become world-famous for their detail and analysis.

In the years since, many researchers followed Malinowski's example and went to live with the people they wished to study. One of the principle challenges they faced in doing fieldwork was to avoid reaffirming their own predispositions, especially those that were racist, colonialist, and *ethnocentric* (meaning centered on their own cultural values). This is a continuing challenge that every generation of anthropologists must take up anew.

Participatory methods. The heart of
anthropological methodology is *participant observation*. This means that the researcher attempts to become integrated into the situation being studied and become a participant, essentially "learning by doing" rather than remaining an outsider.

Anthropologists build canoes or igloos, go on fishing and hunting expeditions, plant yams or rice, cry at funerals, laugh at jokes, and eat or starve (depending on the circumstances) until they get sick. However, this is not the same as "going native": The researcher must retain enough objectivity to be able to analyze what is going on and remember that he or she is not a true native, but an outsider, after all.

Nonetheless, the process of sharing experience with the people being studied gives the researcher personal insight into the physical and psychological dynamics involved in being a member of that culture. A good participant observer learns how to be accepted and allowed close enough to key people and events to learn what is worthwhile.

Good participant observation is hard work. One must be skilled at taking notes, recording music, photographing people and events, listening to what is being said, and asking questions in an unobtrusive way. When it comes time to say goodbye, informants are no longer strangers or numbers on cards but brothers and sisters and friends.

Other methods. Anthropologists use other
methods to put the data from participant observation into a larger, more useful context. Anthropologists interview both *key informants* (people who know specific things, such as ritual leaders) as well as random selections of individuals. These interviews are conducted in the native language, if possible, to avoid any distortion from translation during or following the interview process.

Life histories are collected, especially from older or key informants, who are asked to talk about their lives, constructing verbal autobiographies. With the permission of the subject, all these are tape-recorded or videotaped, often to be transcribed or edited later.

Demographic data are obtained through standard census procedures, though there may be special problems in cultural census-taking because of taboos, such as mentioning dead or absent persons. *Maps* are a critical part of the anthropological record, showing where people live and where important places are located. *Videotaping* is now a common technique used in fieldwork, to make an audiovisual document of the culture.

Production and distribution

Anthropologists have found that the economic component of culture—how people produce and distribute their various goods and services—is one of the most basic, and it is therefore the one with which most analyses begin.

The concept of economy.
Economists define the economy as the production, distribution, and consumption of goods and services. Most Western economics is done in aggregates of millions or billions, because our economies are so huge. Some anthropologists (called *substantivists*) believe that the smaller economies they study have rules different from our own. They feel it is not appropriate to study them using the same analytical tools used for our own because the abstract forces and arrangements of our economy have no meaning in such small, face-to-face units. Likewise, the personal types of relationships that characterize these small-scale cultures are largely irrelevant to our economy, since we largely buy and sell things from or to people we do not know. In other words, the economy of these smaller cultures is more personalized. As economic anthropologist Karl Polanyi (1886-1964) phrased it, their economy is *embedded* in their social relations. It cannot be analyzed separately. Although many anthropologists today continue to use Western (or *formal*) economic models, they do so with sensitivity to this issue and with substantial attention to the differences presented by each non-Western case.

Subsistence systems.
Four major types of subsistence systems, which developed sequentially over time and under different social and environmental conditions, are used by different cultures.

Foraging, which means some combination of hunting, gathering, fishing, and scavenging, was the first human subsistence system to appear. It is the simplest in its technology, employs the smallest number of people, and has largely disappeared today. Except for some fishermen, such as the Kwakiutl of British Columbia, most foragers are highly mobile, since they have to follow the game or cycle of wild plant maturation from one area to another. As a result, they usually live in relatively small groups, like the San of southern Africa, and have very little in the way of personal belongings.

Pastoralism

Foraging

Industrial agriculture

Nonindustrialized agriculture

Horticulture developed out of intensified hunting and gathering as people gradually began caring for particularly useful wild plants and animals and as groups grew larger and more complex. Horticulture means the growing of plant food using only simple tools and possibly raising some animals as well. Most horticulturalists, such as the Tiv of Nigeria, live in fixed areas and have a greater population density and a more rigid sense of property rights than foragers, whom they usually displace due to their superior numbers. A transitional form, *incipient agriculture*, involves the use of larger metal tools, such as plows, and the use of oxen or other draft animals.

Pastoralism means exclusively raising animals (camels, cows, goats, sheep) or herding semidomesticated animals (such as reindeer). Farmers have pushed pastoralists out of almost all areas suitable for farming. Pastoralists like the Tuareg of North Africa or the Lapps of Scandinavia are usually highly mobile, moving with their herds to seasonal pastures. They have slightly greater material wealth than foragers, since they can carry things on their animals. Pastoralists often trade with farmers for things they cannot produce themselves.

Industrial agriculture involves the use of machinery, large-scale irrigation, or artificial fertilizer in crop production and is typically practiced in very large, very complex societies such as ours. Our agricultural productivity is extremely high compared to that involving only human or animal power, but it is not really more efficient when the costs of fossil fuels and of the machines, electricity, fertilizer, and other resources involved are included. So, although one U.S. farmer can feed ninety-seven nonfarming Americans, a lot of those Americans are helping him do it.

Patterns of distribution.
There are three patterns of distribution that cultures use to connect producers and consumers. They, like the subsistence systems to which they are closely connected, also developed, in order, from simple to complex: *reciprocity* (most foragers), *redistribution* (most horticulturalists), and *market exchange* (most agriculturalists).

Types of distribution

Reciprocity

Generalized

1. A shares with B and C

A ⟶ B
↘
C

2. B shares with A and C

A ⟵ B
↘
C

3. C shares with A and B

A ↖   ↗ B
C

Balanced

1. A shares with B

A ⟶ B

C shares with D

C ⟶ D

2. B shares with A

A ⟵ B

D shares with C

C ⟵ D

Redistribution

1. King or government

A   B   C

Producers keep some of their own products for themselves

2. King keeps some products for self

Redistributes products

A   B   C

Reciprocity can take three forms: generalized, balanced, and negative. In *generalized reciprocity*, people share what they have with the group, without expecting any formal thank-you or direct return. No formal accounting is kept. This reinforces group solidarity. Foragers such as the !Kung San of Namibia distribute food on this basis. In *balanced reciprocity*, each person gives to another of equal status and expects an equal return. This reinforces their bonds as equals. We usually do this in our culture when we exchange birthday and Christmas presents. *Negative reciprocity* involves taking without giving, as in a situation of conquest, or taking more than is given, as in a situation of caste tithes or tributes, and serves to reinforce the superiority of those who can take more than they have to give.

In *redistribution*, producers are required to give a certain portion of their product, whatever it may be, to a central authority or their representatives who, in turn, keep some for their own needs and some for future or emergency use and then redistribute the rest among the producers, so that each producer obtains some of all the products available. This allows for a wider variety of products to be circulated among a larger number of participants than does reciprocity. It also builds and reinforces differences in wealth, knowledge, status, and power between those who control the system (those at the apex) and those who are on the periphery.

Redistribution is associated with class stratification and hereditary wealth and leadership, as in the ancient kingdom of Hawaii. We continue to use redistribution for our centralized social and administrative needs, through the payment of taxes and the provision of government benefits in return, but we do not organize our

Visualize Malinowski's scientific theory of culture as people living in a giant bubble within a hostile environment. Culture is the protective bubble that helps them survive. It provides mechanisms for such activities as subsistence, reproduction, protection, and communication to meet the biological needs of the group.

whole economy in this fashion. The severe problems in the allocation of resources and products that China and the former Soviet bloc countries had are evidence of the unsuitability of redistribution for the huge numbers of peoples, products, and decisions involved in today's large-scale industrialized economies.

Market exchange is the mechanism of distribution used by most large and generally industrialized economies such as ours today. It involves the negotiation of trade among unrelated parties, largely according to the principle of *comparative advantage* (each should benefit), so that the system as a whole benefits from their transaction by improving the distribution of resources and minimizing inefficiency.

Economic systems often retain elements of earlier forms, which serve important economic functions not as well met by the new. In Hawaii, for example, although the economy was officially redistributive and controlled by the king, reciprocal exchanges of food, labor, and products continued to be important among interrelated lineages, in accordance with their ancient social status. In our own market economy, our redistributive system of taxation shows the importance of economic control by the state. At the same time, our personal gift-exchanges and charity manifest ancient ties of kinship, friendship, and commonweal which we still consider valuable.

Market exchange

Kinship and gender

Throughout most of human existence, the basis of most human groupings has been the recognition of different categories of persons such as men, women, kin, and non-kin. Particularly in non-Western, nonindustrialized cultures, where voluntary organizations, large-scale political allegiances, and universal religious affiliation are absent, gender, marriage, family, and kinship systems are the central organizing parameters of life for many people even today. As a result, for many anthropologists, gender and kinship are the central focus of cultural anthropology.

All societies define men and women in ways that blend their biological identities as males and females with cultural expectations about how they will live. These *gender roles*, the tasks and activities expected of males and females, include many aspects of social life: kinds of work *(division of labor)*, reproductive duties, use of language, even styles of clothing and body adornment.

It is the link of reproduction that ties gender roles to kinship systems. A woman's roles in society may, for example, be influenced by the ways kinship is calculated. The behavior expected of her by her husband, her brother, and her son will vary depending on how kin groups are structured. If, for example, her son and her brother are classified as belonging to different kin groups, through her relationships with them she may exert influence in each group. Participation in both groups may be expected of her. The ways in which societies define the rights and privileges of individuals as members of kin groups also has a strong impact on what is considered acceptable behavior for men and women in the culture.

Most societies differentiate between the types of social power, prestige, and access to resources which are available to men and women; this is known as *gender stratification*. In general, where the division of labor separates women's and men's activities sharply, there will be a high level of gender stratification. By contrast, where women and men share tasks or engage in activities that are equally valued, gender stratification usually decreases.

Modern anthropologists Sherry Ortner and Michelle Rosaldo have suggested that gender stratification parallels the distinction between those activities which are associated with "nature" and those which are associated with "culture" and that there is a differentiation between the ways that domestic tasks and public activities are valued. The ways in which these symbolic value differences influence gender and kinship systems across cultures are being explored by anthropologists today.

Marriage and family. Defining marriage and family across cultures has proved to be a challenging task, since there is no one type of marriage or form of family that all cultures utilize. The nuclear family as we know it—mother, father, and children—is a cultural generality but not a universal. The one-on-one form of marriage *(monogamy)* that is most widely practiced in American society also is not universal; various kinds of *polygamy*, such as *polygyny* (marriage of one man with two or more women) and *polyandry* (marriage of one woman with two or more men) occur around the world. Some versions of same-sex marriage have been documented as well in societies as widespread as the Ibo of Nigeria and the Yuma of the southwest United States. What is clear is that all societies have rules about who may marry whom and that each culture's rules are designed to protect the *incest taboo*, the purpose of which is to prevent marriage and reproduction between close relatives. Most societies also have rules of *exogamy*, which encourage individuals to marry outside of their group, or of *endogamy*, which promote marriage within one's own group.

Marriage rules and consequences. Marriage rules have important cultural functions: they define the categories of persons who may intermarry; they allocate human resources for work and reproduction; they bond existing families and social groups through the grown children; and they blend variations in tradition, maintaining some uniformity for the group as a whole. Most important, by setting standards for preferred age at marriage and number of spouses, they act as one of the few available controls on birthrate, to balance population and resources.

Basic building blocks. In most cultures, people's most important social ties are to their family in some form, though not all cultures see and value their family ties the same as we do. In some cultures, fathers and children are closer than mothers and children; in others, fathers are rather marginal figures. In all cultures, people's social ties change as they pass through different stages in their lives. But the ties with which they began life—mother, child, father—usually remain in some form the strongest they ever have. As people mature, they must shift their focus from their *family of orientation* (in which they grew from childhood under their parents' orientation) to that of their *family of procreation* (which they form on their own, with their own spouse and children). Thus, according to this model, people are always members of a family—if not one they have started, then the one they started in. So families, broadly defined and in their various forms, are the building blocks of all larger social structures.

Postmarital residence rules. Many cultures have rules that regulate where newly married couples can live. These rules act to perpetuate some of the control that old family ties held. For example, in cultures where inheritance of land, power, or other important things is from father to son, and where the authority of the father over his sons is high, *patrilocal residence* rules will require a newly married son and his wife to live with or near his father. Thus, the important father-son tie is not broken by the son's marriage and is maintained until the son succeeds his father at the latter's death. Similarly, where mother-daughter ties are most important, *matrilocal residence* will require a newly married daughter and her husband to live with or near her mother. In cultures like ours, where the independence of young adults is stressed, *neolocal residence* allows the newly married couple to reside wherever they wish, illustrating that their ties to each other are to be stronger than the ties to either set of parents.

Lineages and kindreds. In many cultures, families are organized together on the basis of descent.

The most common type of *unilineal* (single-sex-line) descent group is the *patrilineage*. In this type, people are members of their father's group, so women cannot transmit membership to their children, who belong to their own father's group. These groups are usually patrilocal, and females can be very subordinate as a result. At the same time, women in patrilineal societies may be able to exert powerful influence in two groups at the same time, so there is considerable cultural variation on this point.

In the *matrilineage,* people are members of their mother's group, but boys cannot transmit membership. These groups are usually matrilocal and accord females a higher status. They usually occur when men are often away on business, or in certain horticultural situations where female contributions to subsistence are pronounced. Lineages are sometimes organized into *clans* along the same principles but using a mythical common ancestor to unite them.

There are also many *nonunilineal* cultures, including our own, which consider the ties to each parent to be equally important. Ours is called *bilateral,* which means "two-sided," since we are supposed to treat our mother's side of the family the same as our father's. Our group of kin is called a *kindred.* Each person's kindred disintegrates when he or she dies. *Lineages,* on the other hand, are ancestor-focused and continue into the future as long as the family has sons or daughters to propagate its line.

Most bilateral cultures are neolocal. While unilineal descent is often found with farming cultures (where children inherit the family farm), nonunilineal descent is more often found in foraging and industrialized cultures, where people cannot be tied down to one group or to one place forever. When the subsistence system changes, kinship rules will usually change to accommodate it, though this is not automatic.

Marriage rules and consequences

Marriage type	Rules	Consequences
Agamy △/O	Nobody can marry	Society dies out except by adoption (for example, Shakers)
Monogamy △═O	Only one spouse at a time	Maintains demographic balance
Polygyny O═△═O	One man may have two or more wives simultaneously.	Increases population growth
Polyandry △═O═△	One woman may have two or more husbands simultaneously.	Lowers population growth
Serial monogamy △═O═△ △═O═△	A person may have more than one spouse as long as the previous marriage is dissolved by death or divorce.	Increases population growth slightly

KEY: △ Male; O Female; □ Sex not specified; ═ Marital tie; | Parent/child tie; — Blood tie; ⊏⊐ Siblings; ✕ Termination of relationship or death

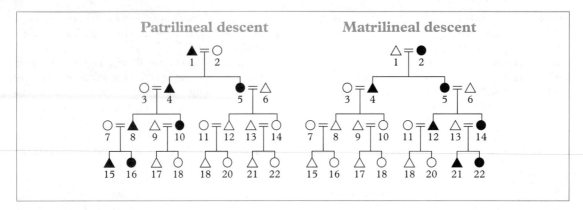

Patrilineal descent **Matrilineal descent**

Kinship terminology.

Different kinship systems require different kin terms. Along with most bilateral cultures, we have what is called an *Eskimo* system, in which, for example, we use the same term ("aunt") for both mother's sister and father's sister, even though they are differently related biologically, because we are supposed to treat each side equally. In cultures with "generational" or *Hawaiian* terminology, age or generation is most important, so, again for example, all female kin of my mother's generation are called "mother," whether they are actually my mother or not. In *Iroquois* systems, siblings of the same sex are supposed to be called and treated the same, but distinguished from nonsibling relatives of the same sex and generation, so my mother's sister is called "mother," but my father's sister is called something else.

Class, caste, and association.

Societies with complex subsistence bases cannot be organized solely on the basis of kinship. Those who can profit from this complexity (by trading, for example) eventually become wealthier than others, and a new focus of social identity, the *class*, is formed. Classes comprise people who identify with each other on the basis of common incomes, life styles, education, or whatever is important to them. If these differences are passed from generation to generation, *castes* are formed. Also, many types of voluntary *associations* (from bowling clubs to political parties) appear as cultures become more complex, again bringing together those of common interest or goals. Kinship becomes increasingly less important as societies become more complex.

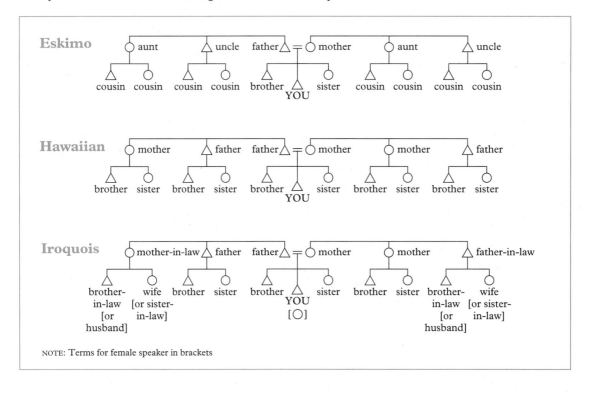

NOTE: Terms for female speaker in brackets

Cultural Anthropology

Political systems and law

All societies, large or small, have to maintain a minimum of peace, order, and harmony. All cultures have standards, rules, and sanctions, written or unwritten. All cultures have to organize themselves, make decisions, and carry them out. All have politics and laws.

Political systems.

The least complex form of political organization is known as the *band*. These are almost always small groups of highly mobile foragers. Bands have little material wealth, so there is normally no dominant class to monopolize power. Band-level politics is usually egalitarian, democratic, and participatory. Everybody gets to vote. Band leaders are called *headmen*; they are selected on the basis of experience, charisma, and skill, have no formal powers, and lead by example. If people do not like their leadership, they may join another band.

Tribes are more complex socially and politically than bands. They are usually sedentary and horticultural, have a greater population divided into several villages, and have a greater investment in fixed property, often the source of many disputes. However, tribes are still largely egalitarian, and differences of wealth are not extreme. As in bands, tribal leadership is based on skill, charisma, and experience, and is not hereditary, as it is in most chiefdoms.

Chiefdoms are even more complex than tribes in their internal differentiation. No longer are all people equal. There is social and economic stratification (sometimes including slavery), an incipient ruling class or nobility, and occupational and craft specialization. All of this is based on incipient agriculture—a form transitional between horticulture and industrialized farming—with a complex division of labor and high productivity. Redistribution is a common practice in chiefdoms.

States are the most complex of all political systems and the latest to appear. They intensify the trends seen in chiefdoms, such as complex and productive economic systems, hierarchical social organization, higher population density (and larger territories), hierarchical and bureaucratic administration, and the centralization of decision making and control. Warfare is common: states are the first political entities to maintain standing armies. The modern-day state has the power to enforce its decisions by force and to control its population in ways no previous political system ever did. Early states generally developed together with institutional religion, mutually legitimizing and strengthening each other. Later states have tended to be more secular, since religious support for their power is no longer necessary.

Law and order.

Bands and most tribal cultures have no police force, no judges, no juries, no jails. Law and order is a function of the society in general and not of specialists, as in our case. In the Inuit (Eskimo) band, for example, song duels were held in which two parties sang songs of insult and evidence against their opponent until the audience was won by one side or the other. Many Native American tribes of Northern California had a standardized system of fines of rare shells or red woodpecker scalps. A person would think twice before committing a crime, knowing how hard it would be to pay the fine off. Larger horticultural tribes and most pastoral peoples have specialists designated to adjudicate disputes. In the case of the Nuer of Africa, this person wore a special leopard-skin cloak as a mark of respect. But he was not a "chief." In true chiefdoms, the chief is usually also the judge, although he might be advised by a council of elders. Very large chiefdoms were subdivided into districts governed by subchiefs, who usually had judicial authority in their region. States are usually so large and complex that special judicial and police officers must be appointed as full-time specialists to preserve law and order.

Traditional ruler, Nigeria

Religious systems

Regardless of their particular details, all religions are concerned with providing an understanding of self, existence, and the otherwise unexplainable. They give meaning to many people's lives. Religion is one of the most important components of cultures everywhere.

Structure of the spirit world.

Most Western cultures distinguish between those things we can perceive with the senses (the *natural* world) and those we cannot (the *supernatural*), and posit a causal relationship between the two: the supernatural caused (or created) the natural and may still affect it; the natural, through proper behaviors (such as prayer or ritual), may be able to modify those effects. It is important for us to understand, whatever our own personal beliefs, that not all cultures believe the same way. As anthropologists, we must try to understand the religions of others on their own terms, not our own.

Many cultures believe the spiritual and natural are one and the same. (Even some Christian religions are bitterly opposed over whether Jesus was man or God or some combination thereof.)

Many other cultures see the spiritual and natural worlds as separate, but envision different form, structure, or components from ours. They may see a multitude of spirits or gods (*polytheism*), rather than one (*monotheism*)—or three, as some Christians believe. They may see a ranked hierarchy in the spirit world, or a series of equal, independent spirits, which have little to do with each other. Many also believe in a formless type of supernatural power termed *mana* in Polynesian societies and *nyama* in Mande cultures of West Africa. Anthropologists have found a strong correlation between the structure of the spirit world and the structure of society in most cultures. Band and tribal (egalitarian) cultures usually have diffuse belief systems; class-structured societies (chiefdoms) are usually polytheistic; and highly structured societies (states) are most liable to be monotheistic. Of course, there are some overlaps and exceptions.

Belief and ritual behavior. The

structure of ritual in most cultures is also related to their social organization. Bands and most tribes, where social organization is not very complex, have *individualistic* rituals. Each person is responsible for finding his or her own way to religious experience, such as in the vision quest of many Native North American cultures. Their part-time specialists in religion and curing, called *shamans*, work mainly with individuals on their personal problems or needs. Larger, more complex

societies, with more people to share the same concerns, usually have *communal* rituals, held by trained but not full-time specialists. These serve as much to reinforce the people's sense of community as to resolve the specific problem being addressed. *Ecclesiastical* rituals (in complex chiefdoms and states) are performed by highly specialized, full-time personnel on behalf of the community, which is composed of a largely passive audience. Their beliefs and ceremonies are now beyond the average layperson.

Rites of passage. Almost all cultures have

rituals that mark transitions from one status or stage of life to another, called *rites of passage*. In our culture, for example, we have such things as baptisms, bar mitzvahs, confirmations, fraternity initiation ceremonies, graduations, weddings, and funerals. These rituals are generally structurally similar everywhere. First, they take individuals out of their existing status. They may be carried away, for example (perhaps screaming amid the cries of their mothers). Second, they are taught or prepared for their new status. This may involve hunger, exhaustion, or fear, which helps remake them into their new state. Lastly, they are returned to society in their new form. Often, for this, they are given a new name, clothing, body decoration, residence, or other markers of their new existence, so that all around will know they are new people. Some rites of passage involve religion (as our baptisms or church weddings, for example) while others may be purely secular.

Cultures vary as to which of life's natural changes (birth, puberty, death) they wish to commemorate with rites of passage, and even more in which cultural ones (such as confirmation, initiations, or graduations) are worthy of this. This, of course, tells us much about what else is important in their culture.

Burial, a universal right of passage

Ritual systems.

Rituals are designed to produce a sense of accomplishment and security in their participants. Both Emile Durkheim, the founder of modern sociology, and Sigmund Freud, the founder of modern psychoanalysis, pointed out the *symbolic value* of ritual systems. Each part of a ritual has a meaning to the participants, speaks to some concern they have, accomplishes something for them as they perform the ceremony, at the same time as it supposedly influences the gods, makes it rain, or drives away the enemy. As in any other part of culture, the words, colors, shapes, social groupings, or dance patterns used in ritual have meanings that transcend their immediate purpose. Through their repetition in other contexts, they unite that particular event with all similar events and with all other events involving similar symbolism, both before and after. Nowhere is this as apparent as in religious ritual, where the culture's most important symbols must be integrated into a meaningful whole. Ritual is thus one of the key points for the anthropological investigation of any culture, since so much of the culture will be exposed there. This also explains why, when people convert to a new religion, the world does not seem to make sense to them for a while, and much of the rest of their old culture disappears. The symbols do not really fit together anymore.

Cherokee shaman mask

Myth and symbol.

Although they may vary considerably in form and in content, all cultures have myths. Some are religious, others appear secular, though even these are usually related to the underlying principles of that culture's religion.

Myths explain how things came to be what they are, or how things happened in the past. They often use analogy, metaphor, and partly human, partly imaginary characters to impart messages of basic importance about the values, morals, and guiding principles at the heart of that culture. In addition, the structure of the plot itself, and the relationship among the characters involved, is often symbolic of the structure of the social and physical world in which the people live or lived.

People have other things to do with their time than memorize worthless stories, so, particularly in nonliterate cultures, the set of myths that they do remember and pass on from generation to generation can provide anthropologists with important insights into their symbolic meanings. This mythology is often one of the most valuable records of a culture's history, values, and perception of self. Together with religion, it is also often swept away in the face of new learning, new heroes, and new ways. Then the people have to create new myths.

Totemism.

Totems are objects that symbolize a person's membership in a particular group, clan, lineage, club, brigade. They show that person's place in society to those who know the system. These meanings are not obvious to outsiders, since they are highly symbolic. For many people, but not all, their totem is indeed a mythological figure (it need not always be an animal) and figuratively their ancestor. For this reason, early accounts of totemism indicated such people really believed they were descended from beavers, ravens, or whatever their totem was. Some people consider their totem sacred and will not eat it; others do not have this belief.

Totems are found in many cultures, not just non-Western ones. We have totems, too. Many organizations such as political parties, sports teams, military units, and gangs have mascots and/or emblems on their flags and equipment. These symbolize certain shared values, mark their territory, and show their identity as a group against the world, but do not necessarily have a mythical meaning.

Mascots and emblems can be potent symbols, however, as anyone who insults one may find out. Their use or misuse by others, such as the Native American logos of some American sports teams, may be deeply offensive to those who feel that this represents a fundamental misappropriation of the symbols of their identity.

Social communication

Communication is not a uniquely human skill. Other animals and many plants can communicate with their own kind and some even can communicate with other species. However, this is very limited, usually biologically programmed, and inflexible. Humans, the most social of all organisms, have the most sophisticated communication.

Language. Verbal language is the most complex, flexible, and productive of all forms of communication. It requires the most intricate brain, the most precise motor control, and the most adaptable body parts. The complexity of human cultures and that of our languages developed together.

Structure of language. All languages are made up of discrete units of sound and meaning that are combinable in different ways. The study of all of the sounds used in languages and produced by the vocal tract (vocal cords, tongue, teeth, lips, palate) is called *phonetics*. Each language uses a distinctive subset of sounds that it strings together into words. The linkage between these strings of sounds and the meaning they convey is both *arbitrary* and *conventional*: there is no particular reason why a small, four-footed, domesticated feline should be called *cat* in English, *neko* in Japanese, and *jakuma* in Bamana (a language of West Africa). These combinations of sounds are understood to designate that animal in each language because speakers of those languages have learned the convention that links the word to the meaning.

Every language has certain sounds that may occur together and others that may not; the patterns formed by these co-occuring sounds are the subject of study for *phonology*. For example, in English, the combination of sounds /str/ may occur at the beginning of a word (for example, *strike, strip*), but the combination /stl/ may not. Words are composed of distinctive units also: the word *walked* is comprised of the verb *walk* and the past-tense marker *ed*; the study of the combination of units of meaning into words is called *morphology*. The further combination of words into sentences follows rules of word order, called *syntax*, particular to each language, which also affect the meaning or *semantics*: "The dog bit that man" is vastly different from "That man bit the dog."

Language and culture. Every culture has an associated language or languages, which often include subsets of language used by specialized groups in the society. In American cultures, Standard English is considered to be the common language, but there are dialects that communicate cultural information such as geographical or ethnic origins, educational level, and even professional

occupation. Many people exhibit gender differences in their language as well, sometimes based on the division of labor and sometimes on ideas about appropriate masculine and feminine ways of speaking. For example, women tend to know and use more color terms than men; men know and use more names of tools. The types of cultural information transmitted through language and the content of the messages can change from one generation to the next. The study of the cultural content of language is called *anthropological linguistics*.

Art. Art, music, and dance are important not only because they make life more pleasing, but because of how they do this. Anthropologists do not ascribe these things to creativity, genius, or pleasure in a pure sense. Those motives are common to humanity. What interests anthropologists is how in each culture these universal motives obtain their specific expression, so that each culture comes to have its own style.

It is not too difficult to see that art, music, and dance express themes that are important to a culture, utilizing environmental motifs and portraying characters that have some relevance to the history and life styles of a particular people. They use colors and media that can be obtained from the resources available. Totem poles from the western Canadian coast, for example, are beautiful, carved portrayals of the mythological figures of clan ancestry and oral history. Made from the huge cedar trees of the area, the totem poles were originally painted with indigenous dyes and represent both tribal art and history.

But art, music, and dance are much more than this. Not all of the members of these tribes had totem poles, although all of them had ancestral histories. The totem poles were placed in front of the houses or at the grave sites of important people or kin groups who could afford to have them made and who had a family history worth the effort. Their dances and their music all showed not the exploits of the past, but the social status of the present. That is why, if you have a real Renoir, you hang it where your friends can see it; it is beautiful, but it also says who you are.

Cultural change

Culture is not a static thing. Our culture is not the same now as it was a thousand, two hundred, or even one hundred years ago. All cultures change, but we want to know why they change at different rates and in particular directions. For this, cultural anthropology draws a lot on archaeology, and vice versa: archaeology reveals the record of human cultural change in the past, and cultural anthropology provides models of cultural process to help explain it. We would also like to be able to predict the future.

Mechanisms.
Diffusion is borrowing or learning from one's neighbors. Its rate varies depending on how close they are geographically, how friendly they are, how often they are in contact; the desirability or importance of the change involved; and the ability of the receiving culture to utilize or incorporate it.

Innovation or *invention* can occur independently within a culture. Many inventions have no immediate utility or generate no immediate interest. Most inventions are actually the result of cumulative smaller developments, and are evolutionary rather than revolutionary. In the same way, most knowledge is cumulative and builds upon what has already been discovered.

Ecological accommodation is an important aspect of cultural change. All cultures must take account of changes in their environment, even when they are caused by human actions to begin with (like the greenhouse effect).

Lastly, there is forced change. The usual term for this is *acculturation*. Through war, forcible religious conversion, or drastic economic necessity, one culture may be forced to please or to acquire characteristics from another. These changes are often of great magnitude. Slaves brought to the New World, for example, had to drastically change almost all aspects of their culture against their will.

Results.
Due to their interaction and the common effects of necessity and sharing in a largely similar environment, cultures tend to develop into regional clusters. These are called *culture areas*. An example would be the native Great Plains in North America, where tribes of different languages and backgrounds came to share a common reliance on the horse and the buffalo. Many other aspects of their cultures, such as warfare or gender roles, also converged.

Some parts of culture seem to change more rapidly than others. Economics, for example, changes faster than family structure. Secular cultures seem to change more quickly than theocratic ones, religion usually being a conservative force.

The future of our culture.
Current trends suggest some of the ways American culture might be different a hundred years from now.

Even with continued technological growth, larger portions of our population may be employed in service industries. Environmental and economic issues are likely to further imbalance our food production. The U.S. may therefore import even more of the goods and food that it used to produce. Capital may be increasingly concentrated and investment even more subsidized by foreigners.

The American family may become even more flexible than it is now. Kindreds could have less meaning and families could be more isolated than ever before. This may bring the family together; it may not. Class differences could accentuate and social conflict grow.

The growing diversity of interests in America might well lead to a more European style of politics, with many parties and a parliamentary system.

Religion, art, and language would have to become more diversified to accommodate these new directions. American culture in the year 2100 could seem chaotic and almost unrecognizable to a person from our times.

Acculturation

Applied anthropology

Increasingly, anthropologists have become concerned with the application of their knowledge for good or ill. They want to use their knowledge and skills in ways that are of practical benefit, rather than purely academic. Many anthropologists are now employed as *applied anthropologists*, doing just this.

Contract anthropology.
Government and nongovernmental organizations (such as the United Nations) have always been the largest nonacademic employers of anthropologists. During much of this century, many colonial powers, including the United States, turned to anthropologists to help them understand what was going on in the areas they controlled. In American Micronesia, British Africa, and Danish Greenland, for example, much valuable research was done and many valuable *ethnographies* (accounts of native cultures) were written under governmental sponsorship. How much this actually smoothed the path of the government is hard to say, but as a result many populations became distrustful of anthropologists and remain so today.

Today, anthropology still functions as an interface between governments and people. Anthropologists work for school districts, health agencies, the park service, USAID, EPA, and the Congress. However, they are careful to make it clear beforehand whom they are working for and what their goals are, so no one feels misled. Often anthropologists will reject projects that they find harmful to the people to be studied or when it is not clear how their results are to be used.

More recently, given the success that anthropology has had in dealing with social problems, and given the increasing internationalization and differentiation of the American economy, private businesses (such as Xerox, IBM, and Martin Marietta) have begun to employ anthropologists in a variety of applied settings. Some do an ethnography of the company, to find out what really makes it tick. Others teach management how to function effectively in foreign situations, such as when doing business abroad. Anthropologists study and recommend solutions to problems of racial or ethnic incompatibilities, analyze worker/client interactions, and translate company materials into culturally understandable form for workers and clients, among other things.

Action anthropology.
Most anthropologists care deeply about the welfare of those they get to know through their research. They are often compelled to speak out and organize support on their subjects' behalf when they see events such as war or famine, or developments such as hydroelectric systems, mining, or agribusiness projects overtaking or harming them. Cultural Survival, in Cambridge, Massachusetts, is one of the organizations dedicated to action anthropology.

Advocate anthropology.
Many cultures now hire their own anthropologists to help them deal with the outside world, recognizing that they understand both sides better than anybody else. The Zuni tribe of New Mexico, the Northern Cheyenne of Wyoming, and many other native peoples employ anthropologists as consultants or full-time employees in areas such as litigation research, social programs, tourism management, and archaeological research. In land disputes, they often testify about archaeology and history, for example, trying to prove the land was native territory.

Ethics and responsibilities.
Any discipline involved with people needs to have a clear code of conduct. The 1970 "Principles of Professional Responsibility" of the American Anthropological Association states that "It is a prime responsibility of anthropologists to . . . damage neither those whom they study nor . . . their scholarly community. Where these conditions cannot be met, the anthropologist would be well-advised not to pursue that particular piece of research. . . .

"An anthropologist's paramount responsibility is to those he studies. [He] must do everything within his power to protect their physical, social, and psychological welfare and to honor their dignity and privacy."

Anthropologists can be asked to testify in court.

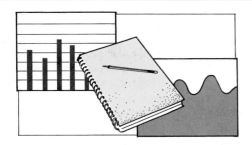

Cultural Anthropology
Tests, homework, and projects

Laying the groundwork

Students of a social science such as cultural anthropology must understand many differing theoretical perspectives; success in class depends on getting the most out of reading, notetaking, and studying for tests. By being conscientious about these background activities, you'll lay a firm foundation and be able to perform better on class assignments in which you are graded.

When reading assigned material, try not to get bogged down with supportive facts. First, scan the chapter and note the headings and subheadings. Then list the key points in each section using your own words.

In class, don't be afraid to ask questions while you are taking notes. This helps you remember information because it is then reorganized in a way you can understand.

When studying for tests, remember "cramming" just increases anxiety. Instead, schedule short study sessions to break up information into more easily remembered units.

Strategies for success

Homework, class projects, and tests are used to assess your basic knowledge and challenge you to apply this information in new ways.

Professors assign reading homework to help you prepare for the next day's lecture. You will take better notes if you are already familiar with the material. In this regard, you may want to consider taking a speed-reading course. Such a course can often prove very helpful and may help cut down on reading time and increase comprehension.

Class projects are opportunities for exploration. Choose a subject that interests you. Break down the project into a series of short-term goals that you can accomplish throughout the term.

Plan ahead for taking tests by scheduling enough time to study; come to the test well rested. During the test, spend your time efficiently: answer easy questions first, and save time later for more difficult questions.

Helpful hints
Multiple choice

When we say people are ethnocentric, we mean they are (a) making judgments based on their own culture (b) senile (c) from another culture.

First eliminate answers that are obviously wrong, then if you still have difficulty making your choice, try breaking apart the word to see if you can figure out its meaning.

Answer. a (*ethnos*, culture; *centros*, center)

Essay

In what ways would your life be different if you were a member of a band-level society?

Read the essay at the beginning of the exam so you have time to plan as you go over the other test questions. Questions like this one ask you to compare and contrast your knowledge of a subject with your own experience. List similarities and differences before you begin, and think of effective transition words to use. When writing, use appropriate technical jargon to show subject area knowledge.

Project

Interview a grandparent (or an older friend or neighbor), and describe his or her way of life as a child. Present your findings to the class.

This is a typical class project, involving a study of comparative cultures. Formulate questions based on the categories that cultural anthropologists study, such as economics, kinship, religion. Your final project can be formatted like a compare/contrast essay (then and now) and enhanced with photographs that the respondent may share with you.

Other suggested topics
• Interview a friend or neighbor from another culture about his or her traditions and values.
• Find out about cultural diversity in your area.

Glossary

Adaptation

Culture

Household

Reciprocity

acculturation. Forced cultural change.

action anthropologist. Takes action on behalf of those studied.

adaptation. Adjustment to the environment.

advocate anthropologist. Hired by a culture as an interface with the outside world.

agriculture. Mechanized food production.

applied anthropology. Deals with practical problems and issues.

avunculocal. Newly married couple establishes residence with or near groom's mother's brother.

balanced reciprocity. The exchange of goods and services on an equal basis.

band. A seminomadic, kinship-based foraging group.

big man. The leader in a tribal society.

bilateral. Relatives on both sides of a family treated equally; equal inheritance from each side.

caste. An inherited, unchangeable social class.

chief. The hereditary leader of an intermediate-level political unit, with considerable power.

chiefdom. Socially stratified political unit with several villages, based on redistribution.

clan. A group of lineages whose members believe they are all descended from a common ancestor.

class. Group of people who share certain social and economic characteristics.

contract anthropologist. Works for government, firm, or non-governmental organization to resolve cultural problems.

cultural relativism. The principle that behaviors must be understood within their cultural context.

culture. The way of life of a group of people; their beliefs, feelings, rules, and behavior.

culture area. Area of basic cultural and geographical similarity or homogeneity.

descent. Kinship relationship between parents and their children over generations.

diffusion. The transfer of cultural traits (such as customs) from one culture to another by borrowing or imitation.

distribution. The allocation of a society's resources among its members.

emic analysis. The description of a culture from the viewpoint of an "insider."

enculturation. The learning of one's own culture, as for a child.

ethnocentric. Judging other cultures by one's own.

ethnography. A descriptive study of a particular culture.

ethnology. The comparative study of cultures and the search for general cultural principles.

etic analysis. A description of a culture from the viewpoint of an "outsider."

extended family/household. Married couple (and their children) live with one set of their parents.

family of orientation. Family into which one is born.

family of procreation. New family one establishes as an adult.

fieldwork. Obtaining firsthand data where people live and work.

foraging. A subsistence system based on hunting, fishing, and collecting plant foods.

formalism. View that there are general or formal models which can be used to analyze any economy.

generalized reciprocity. Sharing with one's group as a whole.

head man. The leader in a band-level society.

horticulture. A subsistence system that uses only simple hand tools to cultivate crops.

Cultural Anthropology

household. A group of people who share a common residence.

informants. People "inside" a culture who provide information to anthropologists.

joint family/household. Siblings and their spouses and children who live together.

key informants. People who occupy specific positions or control special bodies of knowledge.

kindred. A kinship group in a bilateral descent system.

kinesics. Nonverbal communication through posture, gesture, and body movement.

kinship group. People related by ties of descent and/or marriage.

limbic communication. Involuntarily shows basic physiological or psychological conditions, such as screaming in fear, blushing in embarrassment.

lineage. A kinship group linked by descent from a common ancestor.

mana. Pervasive, nonspiritual supernatural power.

market exchange. Complex distribution system; most values set by supply and demand.

marriage. A rite of passage that unites two people as spouses.

matrilineal descent. Descent which is defined only through the mother.

matrilocal residence. Newly married couple sets up residence with or near bride's family.

moiety. One of the two halves into which some societies are divided.

monogamy. Having only one spouse at a time.

monotheism. Belief in a single god.

myths. Accounts of the origins of things, such as the universe, human beings, and social order.

natolocal. Both spouses of a newly married couple remain with their own parents until they have children.

negative reciprocity. One individual or group attempts to get more than it gives.

neolocal residence. Newly married couple sets up residence apart from either spouse's family.

participant observation. Research technique involving participation in the events being studied.

pastoralism. A subsistence system based on animal husbandry.

patrilineal descent. Descent defined only through the father.

patrilocal residence. Newly married couple sets up residence with or near groom's family.

phratry. Group of clans believed by members to be related by kinship.

polyandrous marriage. A woman may have more than one husband simultaneously.

polygynous marriage. A man may have more than one wife simultaneously.

proxemics. Communication through spatial position.

reciprocity. The exchange of goods and services on the basis of sharing.

redistribution. Resources are pooled, then distributed by central authority.

rites of passage. Rituals that mark changes in social status or the life cycle.

ritual. Behavior through which human beings interact with or try to influence the supernatural.

sacred. Having to do with the supernatural.

serial monogamy. Individuals may have more than one spouse during their lifetime but only one at a time.

shaman. A religious practitioner believed to heal with the aid of the supernatural.

speech. Ordered verbal symbols used to transmit meaning among humans.

state. A centralized, bureaucratic, stratified polity.

subsistence. How people obtain food and other necessities from their environment.

taboo. A rule forbidding certain behavior that is thought to bring harm.

totem. An object (usually an animal species) symbolic of group membership.

tribe. A semisedentary, kinship-based horticulture or pastoral political group.

unilineal descent. Descent traced through a single sex of parent (fathers for patrilineality, mothers for matrilineality).

For further reading

Collier, Jane F., and Sylvia Junko Yaganisako, eds. *Gender and Kinship: Essays Toward a Unified Analysis.* Stanford: Stanford University Press, 1987.

Harris, Marvin. *Cows, Pigs, Wars, and Witches: The Riddles of Culture.* New York: Random House, 1974/Vintage, 1989.

Kottak, Conrad Phillip. *Cultural Anthropology.* 6th ed. New York: McGraw-Hill, 1994.

McGee, R. Jon, and Richard L. Warms, eds. *Anthropological Theory.* Mountain View, Calif.: Mayfield Publishing Company, 1996.

Rosaldo, Michelle Zimbalist, and Louise Lamphere, eds. *Women, Culture, and Society.* Stanford: Stanford University Press, 1974.

Spradley, James P., and David W. McCurdy, eds. *Conformity & Conflict: Readings in Cultural Anthropology.* 7th ed. Glenview, Ill.: Scott, Foresman/Little, Brown, 1990.

Van Willigen, John, ed. *Anthropology in Use.* Boulder, Col.: Westview Press, 1991.

Winthrop, Robert H. *Dictionary of Concepts in Cultural Anthropology.* New York: Greenwood Press, 1991.

Study Skills

- Developing study habits
- Time management
- Successful strategies
- Electronic skills
- Campus services
- College subjects
- Reading for enrichment

Study Skills

Most colleges recommend you get a good physical examination before going to school. This exam assesses your well-being and identifies problem areas. If concerns exist, the doctor prescribes a program to fit your needs. This program cannot prevent all problems, but it can help protect you and minimize problems that come your way.

Colleges apply a similar approach to your academic well-being, with methods such as orientation programs, placement testing, questionnaires, career exploration, and pre-advising. Through use of these tools, you and the college personnel committed to your success—counselors, faculty, advisers—can design a college program that will fit your personal needs.

No matter what preparations you make for college, however, your success or failure will probably come down to two things: study skills and study habits. The first is the ability to learn, and the second is the self-discipline and will. Those all-important topics are the subject of this chapter.

Developing study habits

Transition from high school.

Graduating from high school and entering college is an important and exciting transition. With it come many changes—big, small, and often unexpected. With so much emphasis on college selection and the admission process, as well as special senior year activities, you may not have many opportunities to discuss with your parents, teachers, counselors, and friends the changes taking place in your life.

For many students, this will be their first time away from the family for any extended period. But a great number of other students—nearly a third of the college population—will continue to live at home, commuting to school. Will life change for these students as well? Most definitely.

Students who commute will find that, although they don't have dormitory or apartment life to contend with, living at home while attending college will present special challenges. There may be fewer rules and less structure than before, necessitating increased self-discipline and motivation. Perhaps the rules will remain the same, and students will need to prove their increased maturity and responsibility.

Of course, once commuting students arrive on campus, they will also be facing the same life changes confronted by every student: separating from close friends; in some cases, juggling work and school; handling money; taking responsibility for choosing courses; and, ultimately, selecting a profession and life style.

Other changes are more subtle. The level of independence in college is greater than you might expect, while the amount of structure is far less. Students are often surprised to discover how important family and school structure have been to prior success. Some may be surprised by class size, large or small, competitiveness, or by the standards for social success. The level of freedom in one's social life can be unnerving. Whatever the changes, if you anticipate and plan for them, you'll be able to take the steps necessary to reap the many rewards of the college years.

Self-assessment. The saying "An ounce of prevention is worth a pound of cure" applies to academics as well as to medicine. The key to prevention is a personal plan based on honest self-assessment. You cannot prepare for every change. However, identifying factors such as your goals, motivation, behavior, attitudes, past performance, and specific study skills helps you prevent or minimize roadblocks. Honestly assessing these factors is as important to your academic well-being as a physical examination is to your health.

Goals. Having specific goals increases the likelihood of academic success. Identify reasons you want to go to college or to a specific school. Take time to think seriously about your plans. Ask yourself tough questions: "Do I really want to go to college? Why did I choose the school I did? Are my career plans realistic given my abilities and interests? Can I change my mind later?" If you are uncertain about your reasons, speak to someone who will listen and help you set goals.

Learning style. All students have a style in which they learn best. That style is made up of many factors, including academic strengths and weaknesses, visual and auditory skills, stamina, cultural background, and personality. For example, if your cultural background does not encourage assertiveness in a classroom setting, you may prefer lecture classes. Conversely, if you enjoy classroom discussion, you may feel more comfortable in small classes. Talk with faculty and counselors about your concerns. Learning style won't necessarily limit your choice of colleges, teachers, courses, or careers. However, understanding it will help you adapt to opportunities and obstacles that await you.

Behaviors. Successful behaviors include attending class regularly, sitting close to the instructor, being organized and on time, meeting with advisers, studying daily, and setting and maintaining priorities that match your goals. Unsuccessful behaviors include procrastination, disorganization, and tardiness. Some students underestimate the extent to which, during high school, external controls imposed by parents and

Self-assessment (Part 1)

Assessing your goals, learning style, motivation, behavior, and past performance will contribute greatly to your future success. Read each statement. Select the number that best applies to you and place it in the space provided. There are no right or wrong answers. The goal is to assess yourself honestly so you can prepare for a successful college career.

5–Strongly agree   4–Agree   3–Somewhat agree/neutral   2–Disagree   1–Strongly disagree

1. _____ I have definite reasons for going to college.
2. _____ I have decided on a field of study and/or a career.
3. _____ I plan and complete my work without procrastinating.
4. _____ I have no problem concentrating.
5. _____ My social life does not affect my studies.
6. _____ I work well under pressure.
7. _____ I rarely worry about performing well.
8. _____ I seek help when needed.
9. _____ I learn well in a variety of situations.
10. _____ I am flexible and adjust to new people and situations.
11. _____ I enjoy studying.
12. _____ I am a self-starter and remain motivated.
13. _____ I expect to adapt well to my college living arrangements.
14. _____ My family, personal, and financial pressures are minimal.
15. _____ I perform well regardless of the course structure, content, or teacher.

school supported their successful behaviors. Greater flexibility and freedom in college may cause some students to falter; others will thrive. In assessing yourself, ask to what extent your success has been related to internal and external controls.

Motivation. Some students are self-motivated; others are motivated by external factors. For example, some study because they love to learn, others because they need good grades to get the job they want. Discover what motivates you to learn. Are you self-motivated? To what extent are you motivated by rewards? If rewards are not forthcoming, are you able to sustain your efforts? These questions have no right or wrong answers, but by answering them you may gain insight into your strengths so that you can plan for the challenges ahead.

Attitudes. Your attitudes—feelings, emotions, opinions, values—influence your success, especially during times of change or stress. Some people have more self-confidence than others. Some accept responsibility; others look elsewhere for blame. Some people are optimists; others expect the worst. Attitudes shape your choices and behaviors. Understanding them will keep them from being obstacles to your success.

Past performance. Your high school academic performance is an important part of self-assessment. Grades provide one way to measure performance, but not the only way. Consider the difficulty of your courses and the effort you exerted. Were your study skills efficient? Did you have weaknesses such as slow reading speed or problems in specific subjects? If you received good grades with minimal effort, how would you have done with tougher courses or a heavier work load?

Placement tests. Many colleges and universities give placement tests to incoming freshmen. While these tests do not affect admission, they do help place students at the appropriate academic level in basic course areas such as English and math. If you take placement tests, consider the results carefully. Do they reinforce your own view of your skills? Do they provide you with new insights? Use this information to plan for success.

As you begin your college career, careful self-assessment will help maximize all that is good about change and minimize that which is stressful, making it easier for you to stay on the course you've charted for yourself.

Roadblocks to success.
You may be aware of obstacles you are likely to face based on past performance, current circumstances, or careful self-assessment. You may also run into unexpected obstacles. Some roadblocks can be avoided with minor fine tuning; others involve major modification. The best place to start is by recognizing a problem when you see one.

Overcommitment. A common roadblock students face is overcommitment, particularly in their first year of college. While taking on too many responsibilities and activities is an obvious way to overcommit, there are subtler ways as well. Some students enroll in too many courses, challenging their self-discipline and study skills. Sometimes the course combination is the problem—too many courses in difficult or uninteresting areas. Making friends, joining organizations, and dating involve commitment, too. The best way to avoid overcommitment is to establish clear priorities and strive for balance.

Procrastination. The cost of procrastination is high. When you put off until tomorrow what you could have done today, time is wasted, anxiety and stress increase, even self-esteem is affected. Procrastination is sometimes perceived as laziness, but that's not necessarily the case. Hardworking people can and do procrastinate. For students, this roadblock is most potent when they are tired, pressured, preoccupied, or coping with change.

To break the habit of procrastination, assess past and present behavior to determine when you procrastinate. Establish long-term and short-term priorities.

Self-assessment (Part 2)

Continue your self-assessment with the instructions from Part 1.

1. _____ I was a good student in high school.
2. _____ My study skills are equally strong for all subjects.
3. _____ I manage my time well and can establish a schedule.
4. _____ I have a good memory.
5. _____ My reading speed and comprehension are satisfactory.
6. _____ I perform well on all types of exams.
7. _____ I enjoy writing and have good writing skills.
8. _____ I know how to use a computer.
9. _____ I scored as well as I expected on college entrance exams.
10. _____ I expect to do equally well in English and math placement exams.

Study Skills

Then develop a realistic schedule that you can strictly follow and that reflects your priorities. Use "to do" lists on a daily or weekly basis so that you have a concrete way to measure your progress.

Environment. Think about the various environments in your life: where you study, eat, and sleep, or where you work, travel, and socialize. These environments can support you or present significant roadblocks. For example, students who live at home may expect but not find greater freedom than before. Commuting to school may complicate study schedules. Students who live on campus may have to adjust to roommates, a different geographical climate, dining halls, and greater freedom. Coping with such changes and challenges can get in the way of achieving success.

Try to anticipate the changes you'll encounter in your environment as you begin college. Identify those that cause you concern. Talk to your family ahead of time about your hopes, concerns, and expected adjustments. Familiarize yourself with campus resources in advance so that you can better handle surprises if and when they occur.

Health and stress. Maintaining your health and minimizing stress are important to success in college. Yet college students can easily let health and stress become twin roadblocks. Preventing these problems involves a combination of common sense and planning. Among the most important pieces of advice: eat balanced meals; get ample sleep; exercise regularly; avoid over-

scheduling; plan time for studying, relaxation, and recreation. If you're sick, seek medical treatment—don't put it off. If you have a known health problem, inform the appropriate college personnel in advance. Learn to distinguish between stress that motivates you and stress that wears you down due to overcommitment or lack of planning.

Physical handicaps and learning disabilities. While there is no doubt that physical handicaps and learning disabilities can produce significant challenges for college students, these challenges do not have to result in major roadblocks to success. Colleges are required by law to provide access and reasonable accommodation; many are committed to providing services beyond what is required. Students who face special challenges should assess their needs, then evaluate colleges for their ability to address those concerns; otherwise, the process of selecting a college is the same as for other students.

Family, teachers, counselors, and others can help students evaluate available resources. Students should

Social commitments can distract students from their academic schedules.

contact the admissions and disabled student services offices before applying, to ensure that the college can address specific needs. Directly addressing these challenges early will help the student achieve success.

Social skills. Adjusting to campus life is an individual matter. No exact profile describes who will face obstacles and who will not. For example, while introverted and shy students may find it difficult to meet people, gregarious students may let their social life affect their studies. Assessing your social skills can help you understand the possible obstacles you may face. For example, do you tend to get homesick? Are you bold or modest? Are you easily influenced, or do you know your own mind? Do you usually follow or lead? Are you self-confident, or worried about the opinions of others? Answer these and similar questions; ask friends if they agree with your answers.

Evaluate college choices to ensure a match with your social skills in such areas as living arrangements, school and class size, social organizations, and campus activities. College requires adjustment. Feeling uncomfortable at times or occasionally socializing when you should study are a natural part of adjusting. As with other roadblocks, strive for balance and don't be afraid to ask for help.

Losing focus. If you "can't see the forest for the trees" or tend to "make a mountain out of a molehill," then you may be prone to lose focus. This roadblock can sneak up on students unexpectedly and in different ways. Examples include students who put equal study effort into each subject every night; students who are used to straight *A*'s in high school and become discouraged when their college grades aren't perfect; students struggling to choose a major who then question their reasons for going to college; students who are not selected for a fraternity or sorority and feel as if the world is coming to an end.

Losing focus is a serious roadblock. The causes are varied; so are the solutions. Recognizable signs include

A cluttered room can interfere with successful studying.

stress, lack of concentration, anxiety, and procrastination. The solution often involves stepping back to look at the big picture, then making a reality check and readjusting attitudes and habits. Counselors and advisers can help you regain focus.

Be your own master. The best way to ensure success is to be your own master. Assuming responsibility for reaching your goals will get you at least halfway to where you want to go. The rest of the road is paved with careful planning and preparation.

Tools for success.
To succeed, you need the right tools. You can determine which these are by combining common sense, ideas from other college students, and information acquired through freshmen orientation and campus services. The proper tools are not necessarily expensive. You may already have such basics as a dictionary, a thesaurus, and a calculator. Obtain enough supplies to get started, and add the rest once you learn more about your classes. Buy textbooks early; supplies can run out. You should have a computer, if at all possible, preferably one with a CD-ROM drive and a modem, giving you access to the Internet. Computers are increasingly important for students in all disciplines. Graphing calculators are used frequently in math, science, engineering, and business courses. Remember too the tools needed for the physical aspects of studying—desk, chair, lamp. Determine what you have, what will be provided, and what you will need. Organizing these tools for success will give you a head start when the term begins.

Campus resources. Colleges provide a variety of services designed to promote success and enhance enjoyment of campus life. Many schools have preenrollment and early registration programs. Academic, career, and personal counseling centers provide a wide range of assistance. Academic support services include tutoring and learning labs, as well as specialized services for students with physical and learning disabilities. Libraries are perhaps the most important and widely

Study Skills

used service. These may be affiliated with learning resource centers, which provide tutoring, audiovisual equipment, and computers. Campus bookstores sell many items besides books and supplies. The financial aid office offers help with scholarships, loans, grants, and student employment. Campuses also provide cultural, social, athletic, leadership, and recreational activities.

Getting off to a good start. In addition to acquiring the necessary tools and becoming familiar with campus resources, it's important to get off to a good start. Take advantage of orientation and early registration programs. These will help you make friends and schedule the classes you want when you want them. Review the catalogue; learn college policies, including the grading system. Study course descriptions for your classes. Check the term calendar, noting holidays and campus events.

Work out transportation and parking in advance, and learn your way around campus. Carry a campus map with you. Make schedule adjustments early. When classes begin, sit close to the front of the room. Remember that attendance is important. Think of campus resources as "an ounce of prevention" rather than "a pound of cure." Do not be afraid to ask for help. Inquire about study groups or partners—a great technique for making friends and developing strong, routine study practices. If you need basic computer skills, consider taking a high school or summer school class prior to starting college or a workshop during your first term.

Look at a proper balance of study and relaxation as essential to your well-being and success. Use campus

Campus resources

- **Admissions.** Enrolling in college; general information about programs; orientation
- **Advising.** Course selection
- **Bookstore.** Texts, student supplies, and all-purpose store
- **Counseling.** Career exploration and job placement; personal, social, academic, or adjustment problems
- **Disabled and disadvantaged student services.** Provides assistance to students with physical handicaps or learning problems
- **Financial aid office.** Scholarships, loans, grants, and work-study opportunities
- **Learning resource center.** Learning labs with audio and visual support, tutors, computers, or other resources
- **Library.** Books, periodicals, newspapers, journals, government documents, recordings, films, and other services
- **Registrar.** Registration services; academic records and transcripts
- **Testing.** Placement; skills and career assessment
- **Tutoring.** Provides low-cost or free tutoring to students in need of additional academic help

resources devoted to helping you achieve this balance. If you are well-prepared and willing to seek help from qualified college staff when you need it, then you will have made an excellent start toward mastering college life.

Time management

Think about the various sayings you have heard on the subject of time or time management:

You have to take time to save time.

A stitch in time saves nine.

Work expands to fill the time you have.

Early to bed, early to rise makes a man healthy, wealthy, and wise.

If the worst possible thing can go wrong at the worst possible moment, it will.

Time is money.

Procrastination is the thief of time.

Never put off until tomorrow what you can do today.

Make haste slowly.

These are only a few examples. People have been concerned with time—saving it, scheduling it, budgeting it—since the beginning of (you guessed it) time.

Time is an important factor for college students. In fact, college students cite time management as one of the major causes of stress and anxiety. Managing time skillfully, if not the most important, is certainly one of the most important factors in a successful college career.

The purpose of time management should never be to control or schedule every sleeping and waking moment. Life is filled with unexpected, spontaneous events. The key reason for successfully managing time is to free you to handle or enjoy the unexpected and spontaneous moments when they arise.

Important factors. Managing time is in many ways similar to managing money: you work to meet short- and long-term obligations and to save for special or unexpected future events. Managing time requires a plan based on clearly identified goals, responsibilities, and needs. Once these are established, there are very specific ways college students can manage time in order to fulfill them. A good place to start is learning to understand what must be scheduled and what the various scheduling options are.

Scheduling classes. Colleges publish a schedule of classes for each term. Unquestionably, the schedule of classes is the most important tool you will have for planning and building your individual schedule. Unlike the college catalogue, which includes descriptions of all courses offered, the schedule of classes tells you whether a course is offered during a specific term, how many sections are offered, and the days, time, and location of each section. Knowing the location of each class helps ensure that you build in enough time to get from one class to another.

Some schedules also list course instructors. This may not seem important in building your schedule.

However, scheduling classes with instructors whose teaching style matches your learning style may become a major factor later on in helping you manage your time. The schedule of classes usually includes a term calendar and final exam schedule, enabling you to mark in advance some of the key dates on your individual calendar.

When planning your schedule, consider the following:

1. *The type of schedule best suited for you.* Are you an early riser who likes to get going in the morning, or a late riser whose top form is in the afternoon? Do you prefer to schedule two or three days for all your classes, with the other days free for study, or do you need the discipline of classes every day? Would you rather have time between classes to immediately review what was taught and to prepare for the upcoming class, or do you prefer a tighter, more fast-moving schedule?

2. *Required courses and limited offerings.* A specific course you want or need may be offered only at a time you would not normally choose; your personal scheduling style may have to bend in such cases.

3. *Scheduling other required activities.* Nonacademic commitments and priorities, such as working, eating, family responsibilities, team practices, and rehearsals, may be an important scheduling factor.

4. *Registering early.* You are most likely to develop the best schedule by registering at the earliest date. Check with your adviser about registration options.

Time demands. An important factor in effectively managing your time is understanding the commitments required by college courses. As a general rule, each college credit equates to a certain number of hours per week in class. For example, a three-credit course usually meets three hours per week. Students taking courses with fifteen credit hours can expect to be in class fifteen hours per week.

In addition, for each hour students spend in the classroom, they should expect to spend an additional two to three hours per week outside the classroom either studying or preparing for class. For example, if you take a history class with three credit hours, you should expect to spend three hours per week in class and an additional six to nine hours per week studying. Thus, your total time commitment to this one class would be approximately nine to twelve hours per week.

This time commitment explains why students who take twelve or more credits during a term are considered full-time students: the number of hours they should spend, both inside and outside of class, equals or exceeds a full-time work week. A student taking four courses, each with three credit hours, may be in class twelve hours per week and spend an additional twenty-four to thirty-six hours studying and preparing. This represents thirty-six to forty-eight hours per week for four courses—and it is not uncommon for some students to take five courses, with an even higher demand on their time.

The time formula is a general rule; specific circumstances may alter it somewhat. For example, factors such as course content, format, and assignments may make a course more or less difficult for a particular student; these factors will affect the number of hours required for each course. Individual study skills, including reading and typing speed, also can influence the time commitment needed for each class. Some courses require a lot of reading, while others emphasize projects, writing, or laboratory time. If you have a low reading speed, for example, you will want to make sure that the schedule for any one term does not include too many courses with exceptionally high reading requirements.

Other factors influence the amount of time a course requires. Students who have strong word processing skills may need less time to complete writing assignments than other students. Learning problems or disabilities may also be a factor. Undertaking an honest self-assessment, as described earlier, will help you to anticipate the demands that your courses will make on your time.

College and the rest of your life. Time is a precious commodity. When scheduling time, many people, including college students, short-change themselves or create added stress. They forget that there is more to life than work and study.

Many people, for example, forget to factor in enough time for such basic activities such as sleeping, eating, health, hygiene, exercise, and commuting. They forget the discretionary activities that are so important to the quality and enjoyment of life. People also tend to forget about events that cannot be planned for or predicted, but that can be better managed if everything else is under control.

None of us, for instance, can plan when we will get the flu. However, the likelihood of getting it may be greater without proper rest and nutrition. Cutting corners on sleep, meals, and exercise can increase the chances of getting ill, which is a far more costly schedule breaker than that extra hour of sleep or those extra laps you swam. Sometimes people get sick despite the best efforts to stay healthy. The effects of being ill and

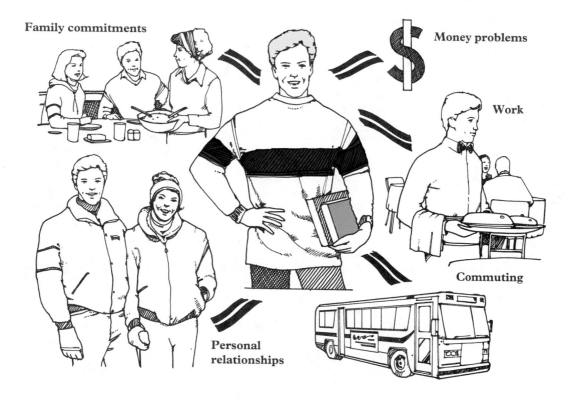

Family commitments

Money problems

Work

Commuting

Personal relationships

missing class will be far greater for students who have let their schedule slide and are already behind on their work.

In short, your college experience will be far more fulfilling if you are in control of your time, enabling you to sidestep pitfalls and take advantage of opportunities to the greatest extent possible.

The balancing act. Managing time is a balancing act. You balance the things you must do with those you want to do, factoring in such realities as class hours, exam and assignment schedules, and commuting time. Careful planning, motivation, and self-discipline will be your strongest allies, along with the ability to make the necessary adjustments along the way.

Maintaining a schedule means bypassing some things you would prefer to do. Yet the rewards outweigh the sacrifices: you reduce stress and anxiety, while gaining control of your studies. Your ability to maintain a schedule can follow you throughout life, increasing your ability to seize opportunities as they arise.

Building your schedule. By applying
several basic principles, you should be able to build a realistic schedule that can be followed and maintained. These principles include finding an appropriate format, developing a master schedule, and distinguishing between fixed and discretionary activities.

Chart your schedule. A schedule must be planned to be followed. It must be displayed in a form that enables you to visualize your weekly activities at a glance. Perhaps the best format is one that lists days with time divided into half-hour intervals. Such a format can be used when you set about to build your master schedule.

The schedule should fit on a single page or card and be placed in readily available locations such as in your notebook and on your desk. Charting your schedule in this manner enables you, on any given day, to determine at a glance when you are in class, when you plan to study, when you are due at rehearsal or practice, and so on. The schedule can lift the burden of remembering what you have to do and when you have to do it. Furthermore, the schedule can help you to maintain better self-discipline.

Master schedule. At the start of each term, you should develop a master schedule, reflecting adjust-

ments that each term demands. Even if certain activities, such as work hours, do not vary from term to term, it is unlikely you will always be able to schedule classes at the exact same hours each term. Therefore, whether in major or minor ways, your master schedule will change each term.

A master schedule provides a written record of a typical week. Consisting of a one-page visual display that can be easily reviewed at a glance, a master schedule works best when charted as described above. It comprises two major types of activities: fixed and discretionary.

Fixed activities are those that cannot or should not be changed. They include classes, sleep, work, exercise, hygiene, regularly scheduled study hours, and meals. Some fixed activities must be scheduled at one particular time. For example, if a required seminar is only offered on Wednesdays at 4:30, then there is no choice about where to place it on the master schedule. Another course, which is also required, may be offered at several times. It still must appear on your master schedule, but you might have some flexibility about where to place it.

Discretionary activities may vary from week to week. These include recreation, study breaks, social interests, and hobbies. Discretionary activities are very important, and time should be allotted for them. Because they are discretionary, however, you can vary them from term to term, depending on the fixed activities in your schedule.

For example, if a discretionary activity such as intramural soccer takes place only on Wednesday afternoons, it may have to be canceled during the term of the required seminar listed above. The conflict may disappear the following term, at which time you can resume intramural soccer.

In preparing your schedule, try for one week to keep track of all of your activities, big and small; also note the length of time involved for each. You may be surprised. A realistic schedule considers everything you must do, should do, and want to do. Your plan should include the little things that take time, not just major activities. It should include time allotted for reward and renewal, both of which energize you and help you avoid procrastination. Ironically, scheduling time to do absolutely nothing may actually help you become more efficient!

With this information in hand, you are ready to build your master schedule. Using a format such as the one shown on the next page, fill in your fixed activities. Note which ones may have some flexibility. Now build in discretionary activities. These should be added in sensible ways and should reflect your individual makeup. For example, some students concentrate better when they exercise vigorously before studying;

others are too tired after a workout and have difficulty focusing on studies. Some prefer to leave their discretionary time more flexible than others, allowing for more spontaneity.

Taking time to plan your time helps you accomplish all you need to do and want to do. Students who plan and follow a master schedule are usually the most successful at achieving what they hope to accomplish in college.

Other types of schedules. Besides preparing a master schedule for the term, you may want to set up weekly schedules and even daily schedules. To do these properly, you'll need information about important academic and personal dates.

Most teachers announce long-term assignments and major test dates in advance; these may be indicated on the course syllabus. You will want to merge information from each syllabus onto your master schedule.

In addition to important academic dates, you may have information about personal dates, such as an upcoming wedding or family reunion. Taking all key dates into account will help you to be prepared and pace your work. For example, you will know that the due date for a term paper falls on the same day as a major test; you may have to complete the paper ahead of its due date in order to leave adequate time for test preparation. Knowing your conflicts will enable you to discuss them in advance with instructors, many of whom will be receptive to working them out with you.

Understanding the big picture is very important. Working from your master schedule and course syllabi, you may want to write out a goals schedule on a weekly basis. On this schedule, you would list key goals for the week, such as selecting a topic for one paper, researching the topic for another, preparing for a major test, and so on.

Master schedule

	MONDAY	TUESDAY	WEDNESDAY	THURSDAY	FRIDAY	SATURDAY	SUNDAY
7:00 AM	Swim	Breakfast			Breakfast		
8:00	Breakfast	/////	Breakfast	Swim			
9:00	Business 101		Business 101	Breakfast	Business 101	Breakfast	Breakfast
10:00	Precalc	Psych	Precalc	Psych	Precalc		
11:00		↓		↓	/////	Job	
12:00 PM	Lunch	Lunch	Lunch	Lunch	Lunch		
1:00	Accounting	English	Accounting	English	Precalc	↓	Lunch
2:00	↓	↓	↓	↓	Study Group ↓	↓	/////
3:00	/////	Tutoring	/////	/////	/////	Lunch	/////
4:00	/////	Student Govt.	Job	/////	Student Govt.		/////
5:00	Dinner	/////	↓	Dinner			
6:00	Job	Dinner	↓	/////			Dinner
7:00	↓	/////	Dinner	/////	Dinner		/////
8:00	↓					Dinner	/////
9:00		/////	/////				
10:00	/////		/////				
11:00	Bed	Bed	Bed	Bed			Bed
12:00 AM						Bed	
	/////	Study Time					

Daily schedule

	TUESDAY, OCT. 1
7:00 AM	Breakfast
8:00	Review PSYCH chapter
9:00	Buy Birthday card, read newspaper.
10:00	PSYCHOLOGY (lecture on memory)
11:00	↓
12:00 PM	Lunch (meet Tom + Fran)
1:00	ENGLISH (MOBY DICK)
2:00	↓
3:00	TUTORING (ACCOUNTING CHAP. 3)
4:00	Student govt. (Octoberfest planning)
5:00	Study - read PSYCH chapter
6:00	Dinner
7:00	Study - PRECALC homework
8:00	Relax
9:00	Study - BUS 101 homework
10:00	Catch-up - leftover homework, etc.
11:00	Bed
	↓

Understanding the day-to-day picture is equally important. Some teachers give daily assignments not listed on the syllabus, including reading, written exercises, and computer assignments. Others may give pop quizzes requiring different levels of preparation. You may find a particular course or topic especially hard, requiring special preparation. A teacher may require you to see a guest speaker or documentary, an activity that may occur during preset study times.

Thus, you should also have daily plans. How will you use the time you set aside for study on your master schedule? Daily plans let you schedule the preparation that you must complete that day, the projects that arise suddenly, and the steps you must complete for long-term assignments. Daily plans help you complete the goals you have established on your weekly schedule, which in turn helps you stay on track for the entire term.

Managing your time.

Scheduling time is one thing; sticking to the schedule is quite another. Even students with self-discipline and the best of intentions need to know when an established schedule is not working and when adjustments must be made. Because time management is so important to students, most campuses offer a variety of services that help students develop this skill.

Many students dislike schedules, finding them restrictive. Such students often point out that they did not use a written master schedule in high school. In making this point, however, they forget the key differences between high school and college, including how parents, teachers, and other school personnel help keep students on track. Successful students find that having and maintaining a schedule enables them to be in control, to enjoy discretionary time, and to achieve goals. Rather than restricting students, schedules can free them from unnecessary stress, anxiety, poor health habits, and overload.

Maintain focus. Effective time management depends on your ability to maintain focus. No matter what classes you take, or how much time you allot for studying, if you have trouble concentrating, find yourself daydreaming, or feel overly anxious or stressed, you will find it almost impossible to use your time effectively.

Maintaining focus involves many factors. First, it involves maintaining a clear idea of why you are going to college and what you hope to accomplish. At minimum, this means that you have determined college is the best place to be and that you want to obtain a degree or specific skills you can learn at college.

In your first few terms of college, it's possible that you may not select a major, or that you may change majors. This is normal, and during these early terms you may be required to take general education courses that support all programs of study. Take advantage of this time, and explore different avenues of study. Don't worry about losing focus in this process, since delving into a variety of courses can add to, rather than detract from, your sense of focus. Also, campus services exist to help students select and change majors.

Other factors interfere with students' ability to maintain focus. Homesickness and personal, family, and financial problems are frequently cited factors. Heavy course loads, course difficulty, and overcommitment may also be factors. Poor study or reading skills contribute as well. Some students find that their study environment interferes with the ability to concentrate. Still others respond to peer pressure and use a schedule or study environment that works for others, but not for them. Teaching style and class format can also make it difficult to focus. Even students who do not have these problems may find that, despite the best scheduling, their assignments are all due at one time, which creates conflicts greater than they can handle.

When you find yourself losing focus, don't be afraid to act. Try visiting the counseling center, arranging for tutoring, adjusting your schedule, getting more sleep, exploring the possibility of financial aid or campus work, taking specialized study skills courses, or even dropping a particular class.

Study Skills

Be efficient. Efficient use of time is a must for college students. In addition to developing and maintaining your schedule, efficient time management means using time wisely.

When you go to class, arrive prepared. Adjust your schedule to meet daily and weekly circumstances. For example, if you have an English test the next day but nothing due in history, devote more of your study time to English.

Avoid changes that switch a portion of your time designated for fixed activities to discretionary activities. For example, if you are caught up in all subjects, use your designated study time to work on a long-range project or to get ahead in your reading. Under such circumstances, you may be able to reward yourself for being ahead on your work by ending your study session a little early. Using time to get ahead enables you to prepare for the unexpected, whether it be the flu, free concert tickets, or a visit from an out-of-town friend.

Equally important, use effective work and study habits. If a particular study technique works for you, do not abandon it lightly; if it is not working, however, be willing to try a different approach. If your skills are weak, take steps to improve them. Use techniques that compensate for weak skills. For example, if you need to improve your notetaking skills, arrange to copy a classmate's notes to supplement your own. Unburden your memory by using calendars, lists, and mnemonic devices.

Plan a study environment that enhances your ability to concentrate. Make sure the environment is organized, and maintain adequate supplies. Equally impor-

tant, organize your living space in a manner that enables you to relax when not studying. In your living space, personal comfort is the primary consideration.

Many campuses enable students to register well in advance of a term by phone, mail, or in person. Take advantage of such opportunities to secure desired classes and the best possible schedule.

Finally, when it comes to studying, seize the day. If you get a sudden urge to study or work on a project, go for it, even if the urge comes during discretionary time. However, do not replace designated study or recreational times on a regular basis.

Fine-tune your schedule. All schedules require fine-tuning for one reason or another. You may need to adjust your master schedule if you find you need more time to study a particular subject, or if you find it helpful to build in review time right before or after a particular class.

Transportation may be a factor, especially for students who commute. Rearranging a schedule might be easier, for example, than finding a new commuting partner. Even factors such as changing the location of a class, particularly on large campuses, can require adjustment of the master schedule.

Daily or weekly fine-tuning is sometimes required. One particular assignment may be more challenging

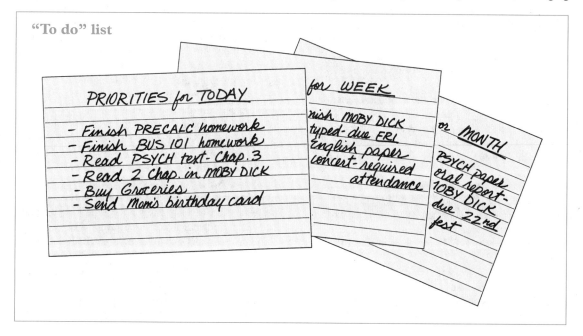

"To do" list

PRIORITIES for TODAY

- Finish PRECALC homework
- Finish BUS 101 homework
- Read PSYCH text - Chap. 3
- Read 2 chap. in MOBY DICK
- Buy Groceries
- Send Mom's birthday card

for WEEK

nish MOBY DICK
typed - due FRI
English paper
concert - required
attendance

or MONTH

PSYCH paper
oral report -
MOBY DICK
due 22nd
fest

In scheduling, you may want to allow time for socializing before and after group project meetings.

than earlier ones, requiring additional time to complete it. An unexpected event can occur—an illness, a fire drill, a delay while waiting for computers or laboratory equipment, an appointment that runs longer

Steps to time management

1. Establish commitments and priorities.
2. Write your fixed commitments in your master schedule.
3. Fit your top goals in your master schedule, as well as any remaining commitments.
4. Make room for sleep, meals, transportation, studying, and breaks in your schedule.
5. Schedule lower-level priorities and goals, as time permits.
6. Schedule leisure time into your schedule.
7. Evaluate your schedule. Do you have time for unplanned events, such as illness, flat tires, extra assignments?
8. Adjust your schedule. Remember to expect the unexpected.
9. Create weekly plans from your master schedule and adjust as needed.
10. Set daily goals and evaluate on an ongoing basis.

than planned. All these may require that your schedule be adjusted. Group projects often can throw schedules off, since your group partners may need to meet at times that are inconvenient for you, and since group meetings often involve socializing before or after.

Fine-tuning a schedule is normal. In fact, fine-tuning is essential if a master schedule is to be effective over the long run. However, students who find themselves making major adjustments week after week, or abandoning their master schedule altogether, either need to revise their master schedule, change their habits, or reestablish their priorities.

Reward yourself. Work hard. But don't forget to reward yourself for managing your schedule, completing assignments, and staying on track. The maxim "All work and no play makes Jack a dull boy" is quite applicable. Academic success requires hard work, like any other job. But like people in the working world, students need to have their energy and enthusiasm renewed periodically; otherwise, burnout may occur.

The discretionary activities in your schedule provide a form of reward for sticking to the rest of your schedule. Campuses provide a wide variety of student activities and cultural events. These are available not only for their recreational value, but also because they promote another form of student growth. Other rewards might include anything from watching a favorite television show or reading a book for enjoyment, to going out on a date, playing a game of pickup basketball, or going home for the weekend.

Needless to say, don't overdo it. You shouldn't suspend studying for two days as a reward for passing a quiz. However, taking an evening off after completing a major project or series of exams, especially if no other tests or assignments are pressing, is an appropriate reward.

Students should use discretionary time for motivation, renewal, and reward. It is often far easier to study if, following the study period, you plan to do something relaxing or enjoyable. Staying on schedule for a long-term project may be easier if early completion means going home for a special occasion or joining a friend for a day of skiing. Perhaps most important, using rewards as a motivator to stay on schedule with all other activities makes "free time" truly free. No one wants to engage in what should be an enjoyable activity while feeling guilty, anxious, or depressed because of responsibilities that have not been met.

Building in short- and long-term rewards is as important to effective study strategies as any other factor. Rewards provide a goal. They motivate you to

Why studying pays off

Reason #4:

Staying on schedule frees up your time for other school, work, and leisure activities.

avoid procrastination and stick with the task at hand. They re-energize you.

You may find that, on a regular basis, you are too far behind to take advantage of scheduled recreational time; or you may find that you're not allowing yourself to participate in such activities even though you're keeping up with assignments. If you find yourself in either of these situations, speak with an adviser or counselor who can help you assess possible reasons as well as solutions.

Ultimately, you are in college to work and to achieve certain goals. These goals do not preclude you from enjoying yourself and rewarding yourself for hard work and success. In fact, even when things have not gone as planned, despite lots of hard work, it's important to relax. Taking such time allows you to assess what went wrong and to move forward toward your goals.

Staying on schedule frees up time for leisure activities.

Successful strategies

Honest self-assessment enables you to understand those aspects of your personality that add to or detract from your success in college. Thoughtful scheduling and active time management contribute to an environment for success. Still, to do well in college, there's no getting around the fact that you need practical study skills. By building these skills, you will be more effective in class and more in charge of your daily life. Stress and anxiety from academic pressures will be reduced, motivation will increase, and outside influences will not be as disruptive. Because your time will be used more efficiently, you will be in a better position to achieve your goals.

Specific skills. Academic success is built on many study techniques. Some, such as listening, notetaking, oral communication, and test-taking skills, are applied most often in the classroom. Other techniques are applied away from the classroom—whether in the library, in learning labs, or at home—such as making the best use of your textbook, combining speed and comprehension in your reading, building your word power, writing clearly, and completing homework assignments. These days, electronic skills are helpful both in and out of class. Similarly, developing memory skills supports all other study skills.

These study areas interact with each other. As you develop your word power and reading ability, your class participation will improve. Strong listening skills prepare you for reading and homework assignments; these in turn, along with improvements in your writing, add to your test scores. Building on your strengths enables you to tackle study areas in which you feel less secure.

Listening and notetaking. While

such resources as textbooks, computers, laboratories, and videos provide an enormous pool of information for students, the classroom experience distinguishes college from other learning environments, especially self-study. Your instructors have spent many years mastering their areas of specialty. The information and perspectives they share are the core of your academic experience. In courses where class participation is encouraged or required, the experiences and perspectives of your classmates also provide you with a tremendous resource. Yet these valuable resources will go to waste without strong listening and notetaking skills. The two go hand in hand.

Listening requires active participation. Think, for example, of the times you have listened to the radio. There are occasions when the radio provides nothing more than background; you are aware the music is

there, but you are not paying close attention. This is not truly listening. On other occasions, you might be paying close attention to the lyrics of a new song you like; when that song is played, you concentrate on every word the performer is singing. This is not just listening; it is active listening.

Some of the same principles apply when you are listening to your instructor. To get the most from a lecture, be prepared to listen actively. Focus on what the instructor says. Block out distractions, whether a noise from the hallway or a whispered conversation between other students in class. Anticipate what the instructor will say next. Focus on key words and the way the instructor presents a lecture. Which words are emphasized? Which ideas are written on the chalkboard or presented on an overhead transparency?

Be prepared when you come to class. Follow the syllabus handed out at the start of the term. For example, if the next topic in your business class is advertising and promotion, read the relevant text material ahead of time. This will help you follow your instructors' lectures in class and focus on areas of emphasis.

Listening carefully also helps you to identify the parts of a lecture that may not be clear to you. In such cases you will be better able to ask thoughtful questions, whether during or after class. Similarly, you may make connections with other material covered, which could enable you to contribute to a class discussion.

Taking notes

Your notes will be "dynamite" if you remember these **T**op **N**otetaking **T**ips (TNT).

1. Assess your notetaking skills.
2. Prepare for class.
3. Play to win by attending class.
4. Look and listen in class.
5. Date and title your notes.
6. Copy graphs and charts.
7. Abbreviate where possible.
8. Write legibly.
9. Ask questions to clarify your notes.
10. Leave space to add more notes later.
11. Tailor your notes to *your* needs.

Study Skills

Careful listening and notetaking greatly increase the value of classroom lectures.

Taking good notes in class is an important part of active listening. Unless you have mastered shorthand, you are unlikely to be able to write down everything that is said. Being prepared for class means anticipating important ideas ahead of time. When taking notes, start with clean paper, enough to get you through class. Leave wide margins so that you can fill in missing pieces later. Write on only one side of the page, leaving the back for follow-up. Also, it is easier to read notes if there is no writing visible from the other side of the page.

Pay special attention when the instructor writes ideas and concepts on the board or overhead projector. But don't get so caught up in writing every word that you stop listening to the instructor's comments. Develop an abbreviation system for each class. For example, you can save a lot of time when taking notes about the American Revolution by letting *GW* stand for George Washington. Other abbreviations can be used across all classes: *w/* and *w/o* can mean *with* and *without*, and so forth. Be sure you have a key to your abbreviation system. For example, *lng* may clearly stand for *learning* when you write it in September; by December, when you're studying for finals, it may be a complete mystery.

Not only should you know how to decode your notes; you should also take time after class, or later that day, to go back through them. Fill in missing concepts that you were not able to write down in class. Add ideas that connect various parts of the lecture. Write out your abbreviations. Especially if your handwriting is not very legible, or if you were particularly hurried during class, make sure your notes are clear. The most thorough notes are useless to you if you cannot read them.

Finally, if your system of taking notes is not working for you, try another system. Talk to your classmates to see what system they use. Speak with a counselor for further ideas. In your search, however, make sure to look for a system that works for you. Even if your notes are illegible to someone else, they're just fine so long as *you* can read them.

Textbooks. Some students dismiss their textbooks as an unnecessary expense. Unfortunately for these students, they miss the meaningful contribution that a good text can make toward their education. Far too often, they fail to take full advantage of their texts. Understanding how to work with your textbooks is an important study skill that can increase your likelihood of success.

Many students, when they are asked to read a chapter of their text, just open the chapter to the first page, read it once, and then close the book. But as with listening and notetaking, working with a text requires active participation. Simply turning pages is not enough.

Start by learning the role of the text in your class. Are chapters assigned as a preview of class sessions, or as a follow-up review to a lecture? Are students expected to participate in class based on material in the text? Does the textbook duplicate a lecture, or does it provide background or contrast? Classes that depend on exercises from the text, such as math

Highlighting important passages, phrases, and words reinforces learning and helps with test preparation.

courses, usually follow the text fairly closely. History courses may use supplemental readings that describe people, places, and events. Government texts are often chosen because the authors have a different point of view from the instructor, who may want to expose students to many perspectives.

When first opening a text, take note of how the book is organized. Look at the table of contents for overall topic coverage. Compare the contents to your course syllabus. Does the course follow the same order as the text? What topics are emphasized or skipped? Read the preface to see what the author says about the text, its structure, philosophy, special features, and supplementary materials available from the publisher.

Look through the text's features. Headings and subheadings within a chapter provide a built-in outline of the material; learning objectives help readers set goals. Key words and ideas may be set in boldface, italic, or a second color. The text may use boxes and charts for emphasis. Margin notes—comments on the sides of pages—summarize information, add further comment, and provide background.

Check to see what material is at the end of sections, chapters, and the entire book. Many texts provide exercises and other summary and review material. All texts will have an index. Other back-of-book materials include suggested readings, glossaries, tables and charts, answers to selected exercises, and appendices that review material from earlier classes. Many texts have supplements available through the bookstore or the library. These include study guides, lab manuals, videotapes, audiotapes, and computerized tutorials.

Be rested and focused when you read. Avoid outside distractions. Preview material by scanning it first, getting a sense of the topics to be covered and the special features. If you own the book, use a marker to highlight important passages. Write a star, check, or other mark in the margin next to especially important passages. Write question marks next to material that is not clear. However, try not to highlight too much material; otherwise, nothing will stand out.

Take notes during or after your reading, much the way you take class notes. You might try notecards, marking an important piece of information on one side, with examples, support material, and page references on the other. You may prefer to outline the material, tying the key concepts together on one page rather than on individual notecards. Compare your text notes with your classroom notes. Determine if they fit together, if your questions have been answered, if other questions remain, and if any contradictions appear that need to be resolved. The notes you take will be important to you later when studying for tests and other assignments.

Many texts, especially at the introductory level, incorporate learning systems to help build your study skills. One of the most popular is *SQ3R*, which stands for Survey, Question, Read, Recite, and Review. Many other systems exist; you can learn about them through academic counselors.

In SQ3R, begin by *surveying* the material to be read, looking through it for a sense of what will be covered. Then ask *questions* that you expect to be addressed in the material. Many of these questions will be tied to the headings and subsections. Next, *read* the material. See if your questions are answered. After you read the material, determine how well you can *recite* key information without looking at the text. This is often a good time to take notes, to reinforce your learning. Last, *review* the material. Check to see if the notes you took were accurate. Look for material you omitted or areas in which you misunderstood the text.

Systems such as SQ3R are powerful learning tools. You may want to consider using one of them whether or not they are presented in your text.

Reading and word power.
No study skill is more important to your success than reading. Reading is more than a collection of skills such as vocabulary, comprehension, and speed; it is an active process, requiring constant thought and evaluation on the part of the reader. How you approach reading depends on the type of material and your purpose for reading it. For example, reading an article to determine its use in a research paper is quite different from

reading it once the research is underway. The first time you skim an article, you are looking for key words and concepts; the second time, you are reading far more intently.

College students face a reading load that is greater than any they have seen in high school. Skills that worked in high school, therefore, are not always sufficient. Recognizing this problem, many colleges test incoming students, placing them in reading skills classes if needed. For many students, these developmental reading classes can become a turning point in their academic lives.

Word power increases reading power. If you do not understand the words you read, overall comprehension will be limited. Developing vocabulary improves reading skills and carries over into listening, speaking, and writing skills.

Build word power actively. Read as often as you can. Work from a list of books recommended for college-bound students. Such lists include classic works chosen not only because of important themes, but also because of their richness in vocabulary. Even if these lists don't work for you, *keep reading.* The more you read, the stronger your word power will become, whether you are reading classics, mysteries, magazines, newspapers, or romance novels.

Keep a good dictionary nearby; have one in your room and, if possible, carry one. Make use of the glossaries in your texts. Look up new words that you encounter. If you hear an unfamiliar term in conversation or in class, jot it down and look it up later. If the word does not appear in your dictionary, use an unabridged dictionary from the library. If the new word is from a particular discipline, such as medicine or law, see if the library has specialized dictionaries. You may want to maintain a word bank on notecards alphabetically or by subject. If you know that your vocabulary skills are weak, you may want to attend a specialized course.

Understand your purpose for reading, and choose the appropriate technique. You may want to scan a chapter to get an overall sense of its content. If you need a specific piece of information or a particular topic, you may skim the reading until you find a key word, then read the material closely. Other times, you will read in a focused, detailed manner.

Prepare to read. Ask yourself how the reading relates to the text or the lecture. Is there anything from the syllabus, lecture, or class notes that indicates what you should look for? Are there specific questions to answer? Are you expected to summarize what you have read?

Recognize key words and phrases. Some (*significantly, most important*) indicate key ideas. Others (*first, finally*) are clues to chronological order of events. Still others illustrate a point (*for example, such as*). Some compare or contrast (*similarly, conversely*), show cause and effect (*because, as a result, therefore*), or summarize (*in conclusion, to summarize*).

Recognize main ideas and important information. In addition to the outline provided by the headings, note the author's style. See where topic sentences are placed, how supporting ideas are organized, and whether the author summarizes main ideas.

Learn to read and use graphics. Pictures, tables, maps, charts, and graphs are an important part of many texts. Learn to interpret them; ask for help if needed.

The best method for improving reading speed is to improve comprehension. Skilled readers vary their speed based on purpose. If speed is your only reading concern, look into specific techniques, and perhaps special seminars. Read frequently: the more you read, the stronger your skills will be.

If you know that reading is a problem area for you, take action. Assess your skills honestly. Do not despair if you need improvement; most campuses offer services to help students.

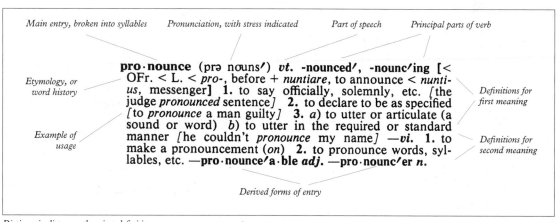

Dictionaries list more than just definitions.

Reading tips

- Word power increases reading power.
- Have a dictionary and glossary nearby.
- Recognize and use key words.
- Maintain your own word bank for each course.
- Identify the purpose for your reading.
- Choose the appropriate reading method for your assignment.
- Select a text study technique that fits your needs; use it faithfully.
- Stay ahead of your reading assignments.
- Learn to read visual aids (charts, tables).
- Read actively—*think* about what you are reading.
- Create a picture of what you've read.
- If reading is a problem for you, get help.

Finally, enhance your ability to concentrate. Stay ahead of assignments, avoiding pressures and anxieties that can cause loss of concentration. Select a good reading environment. Set goals and monitor your progress. Take scheduled breaks. Successful reading combines a clear purpose, variety of techniques, highlighting, and active concentration.

Oral communications. Few areas cause students as much discomfort as oral communications. Speaking in class—whether asking a question, offering an opinion, or delivering a prepared speech—can strike fear into the hearts of even the best students. Oral communication is public; students share knowledge, or lack thereof, with others. When oral communication is required, many students avoid classes they might enjoy. Even if not required, students who lack confidence and skills do not maximize their enjoyment or the benefit of the class.

Oral communication skills are important in many ways. Class participation involves asking questions, responding when called upon, and participating in a classroom exchange. Some teachers grade students for participation. Seminars usually require participation. Well-framed questions and comments demonstrate your interest in the class. Actively participating can help you clarify information and ideas.

Oral assignments include speeches, debates, group presentations, interviews, readings, and skits. Few students complete college without oral assignments. Such skills are vital to most career fields; many majors require a public speaking class. Students face many situations where they must gather information or seek assistance: asking questions in class, meeting with instructors, speaking with librarians, contacting other students, and participating in study groups. Success in gathering information often depends on effective oral communication skills. These skills are also important in sharing information and ideas.

Students who are uncomfortable speaking publicly often confuse quantity with quality. Yet one well-thought-out statement is more valuable than lengthy, unfocused speeches. Whether you are shy or bold, consider the following reminders.

1. To motivate yourself, keep in mind that most careers involve effective oral communications.

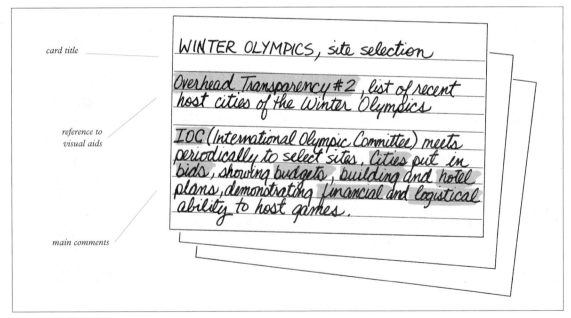

card title

reference to visual aids

main comments

WINTER OLYMPICS, site selection

Overhead Transparency #2, list of recent host cities of the Winter Olympics

IOC (International Olympic Committee) meets periodically to select sites. Cities put in bids, showing budgets, building and hotel plans, demonstrating financial and logistical ability to host games.

Sample notecard for oral presentation

2. Try to build effective listening skills. By listening carefully to others, you can prevent embarrassing situations, trigger an important thought, or strengthen a point you are trying to make.

3. Attend class and be prepared, especially for classes that require participation.

4. Seek help building your skills. Discuss concerns positively with your instructor, acknowledging the value of participation. Prepare questions or comments prior to class.

5. Avoid dominating class discussions. Too much participation is as counterproductive as too little.

Once you're actually assigned an oral presentation or speech, be sure to plan and organize in advance. Understand the purpose and range of the speech, including time limitations. Establish your purpose and a desired audience reaction.

Speeches have three major portions. The *introduction* sets the tone and captures an audience's attention. Use the *main body* of the speech to prove your point. Use key words, transitions, and visual aids. Examples are effective if focused. The *summary* is as important as the introduction. End with a clear statement summing up your point.

Practice your speech. Tape yourself, rehearse in front of a mirror or, even better, in front of someone who will offer feedback. Use visuals when possible; practice with them. Get familiar with the location where you will give the speech. When possible, give your speech early; this limits nervousness. Make eye contact with the audience.

You'll want to prepare notes and visual aids in advance. Notes should be well organized, clear, and easy to use. Some students like spiral-bound notecards; others prefer using cards of different colors to distinguish different parts of the speech. Number or highlight key points, words, and phrases. This helps emphasize important ideas and assists you in finding your place in the notes. Use a system that is comfortable for you. Visual aids are also helpful, providing a way to summarize key points and maintain your audience's interest. If you need specific equipment, such as an overhead projector, request it beforehand. Keep in mind, however, that visuals should never distract from the speaker.

Writing assignments. Throughout college you will have numerous writing assignments requiring different writing styles. For some assignments, you will present and analyze a series of facts and theories. On research papers, for example, much time will be spent finding and organizing the data you gather; the writing style used to present the data should be direct and logical. A report is somewhat shorter; it usually requires you to undertake a basic

amount of research, though not as much as a research paper requires. The style for a summary should be even more direct; you are often reading another piece of writing, then reporting major ideas in brief. For many essays, you will analyze a single topic. Your ability to compare and contrast or to show cause and effect will be especially helpful.

Other assignments call on you to express observations and experiences. Your writing in these cases will depend more on word choice, pace, and rhythm. For descriptive writing, you will use more modifiers than in research papers and summaries. Vivid, concrete words will go far to relay your observations to the reader. Narratives tell stories and often include speech and characters. Descriptive passages are more slowly paced; action paragraphs move swiftly, with short, snappy sentences.

Poetry includes restricted and free forms. Some poetry forms have preset meter and rhyming patterns. Other forms allow you to choose patterns as you please; rhyming is not required, nor are specific patterns of emphasis.

For more detailed information about writing assignments, see the chapter in this Handbook titled *English Composition*.

Common writing assignments

Summary. A brief account of a reading assignment or some other observation. Direct style, few modifiers, little or no research.

Essay. Brief analysis of a topic, often taking a point of view and showing different sides of an argument. Comparing and contrasting as well as cause and effect are important.

Research paper. A full presentation of a topic, backed up by extensive research with footnotes and bibliography.

Description. Goal is to convey a picture, observations and impressions. Writing style especially important, along with use of modifiers.

Poetry. Can be restricted or free form. Word choice and images especially important. More restricted forms may rely on rhyme and emphasis patterns.

Homework. College homework is quite different from high school homework. Assignments, whether reading, labs, or exercises, are usually not checked or collected on a daily basis. Some are laid out in the course syllabus, explained early in the term, then discussed infrequently except for major assignments and exams. The responsibility for following up and completing the assignment is left to the student.

Thus, self-discipline is very important. Students can be lulled by a false sense of security. Since they do not "get caught" on a daily basis if homework is not completed, they often let themselves fall behind. The price is paid at exam time or when major projects are due.

Potential problems can be headed off by following a few guidelines. Start with a manageable course load. Match your courses with your study skills. Be prepared before each term. Register early. Balance your schedule with relatively easy and hard courses; also balance required courses that may be of less interest with high-interest courses. Get your syllabus and books as early as possible, so you can become familiar with them before classes begin.

Be prepared before each class. If you have assigned reading, complete it before the lecture, not after. Completing assignments before class improves your ability to participate in class discussion.

As you manage your master schedule, distinguish between the time demands of assignments, dividing them into categories of *daily* (math exercises, reading), *short term* (quizzes, essays), and *long term* (exams, term papers). If you do not monitor your progress on long-term assignments, you will find yourself trying to complete them at the last minute. Quality will be diminished, as will your ability to keep up with daily assignments.

Never put off until tomorrow what can be done today. If you wait until the last minute to begin work on a term project, you may find that library resources you need are already checked out and that, as a result, the time required to complete the project has increased tremendously.

Some courses require you to study in an especially consistent manner. Course content in classes such as math, accounting, and science is built upon topics taught earlier in the course. If you fall behind, it will be difficult to catch up.

Expect the unexpected. Most teachers are forthcoming about exam and assignment schedules, but some like the element of surprise in the form of pop quizzes or assignments. Other unexpected events, such as illness and personal problems, can affect your ability to keep up with homework. The more aggressive you are in tackling it to start with, getting ahead when possible, the less affected you will be by life's little surprises.

Most instructors reward honest effort. Seek your teacher's assistance when you honestly need help with an assignment. Sometimes you may find you need an extension for a project; if you have been diligent, have consistently communicated with the teacher, and have presented an honest case for the extension, most teachers will be flexible. But you must earn that flexibility. Furthermore, never take advantage of it; be certain to turn in a good product on the revised schedule.

More information about homework assignments for specific courses is presented at the end of each chapter of this Handbook in the sections called *Tests, homework, and projects.*

Memory. Memory is often cited as a reason for outstanding achievement or as an excuse for unsatisfactory performance. Both imply that remembering is passive, something over which we have no control, and this is simply not the case. The best memory can be overburdened; weak memory skills can be improved with the right techniques.

There are two types of memory: short-term and long-term. The ability to move information from one to the other is critical to learning. Most memory loss takes place immediately before the transfer, owing to distractions such as anxiety, noise, and interruptions. In contrast, memory loss can be minimized by such factors as interest, attentiveness, and purposefulness.

It's usually easier to remember something if it has a relationship or *association* with other things. For this reason, it's easier to remember a list of names than a list of nonsense words; it's easier yet to recall a list of people you know. When organizing items to be remembered, therefore, divide them into manageable portions and group them by relationship. In a list of names, for example, the list might be organized into subgroups of family, classmates, co-workers, neighbors, and so on.

Use associations to boost your memory power. Create acronyms (words formed by the initial letters of a group of words), rhymes, and sentences in which the first letter of each word stands for a term that must be remembered. For example, many math students learn the sentence "Please excuse my dear Aunt Sally." The first letter of each word, P-E-M-D-A-S, remind students of the order of operations in math: parentheses, exponents, multiplication and division, addition and subtraction.

Decide to remember; then do what it takes. Be attentive. Avoid distractions. Work to understand the material. Identify your purpose for remembering. Review lecture notes as soon after class as possible. Relate notes to your text, supplementary reading, or other course material.

Review often, especially for courses in which memory is a major factor. The more often you are exposed to what you must remember, the more likely you are to remember it. Involve yourself actively when studying. Write things down; say them aloud. Quiz yourself. Help others or work with a study partner. Visualize often, using pictures, charts, diagrams, and graphs to summarize course material.

Organize your material, distinguishing the most critical information from that of lesser importance. Set priorities by outlining your reading, organizing information by topic, and cross-referencing lecture and text notes.

Be kind to your memory; avoid overburdening it. It's not necessary to remember everything. Use notes, left in places where you will see them, to remember meetings or tasks to complete. Be certain you know what material will be on a quiz; then you can limit your review to that material. Alter a regular habit to jolt your memory—for example, wearing your watch on the opposite wrist. When you have struggled to remember something, put it in a "safe" place as soon as possible. For example, as soon as you begin a math examination, write the difficult-to-remember formula on the top margin for reference; do not wait until halfway through the exam, when the information is called for.

Taking tests.
Perhaps no element of college creates as much anxiety for students as tests. Many students view tests—whether pop quizzes, midterms, or final exams—as the dramatic moment when all their failings will be exposed for the world to see. Yet there is much that students can do to gain control of the process and improve their test-taking skills.

First and foremost is to change the attitude toward tests. Instead of viewing exams as a means of finding out what they don't know, students should consider tests an opportunity to show what they *do* know.

The role of time management is central to preparing for tests. If you have maintained the schedule you established at the beginning of the term, then much of your test preparation will already be complete. You will have attended classes, listened to classroom lectures, taken notes, and completed your homework assignments and reading. Rather than trying to learn material for the first time, you will be concentrating on reviewing information you have already learned.

Another key step in preparing for tests is to establish priorities. Start by learning the range of topics and course material the test will cover. Check, for example, whether the final exam will cover the entire term or only those topics discussed since the previous exam.

Next, find out what form the test will take. Studying for an objective exam is different from studying for an essay exam. An objective exam focuses primarily on facts; it will generally include some combination of multiple choice, true–false, fill-in, and matching, as well as some short-answer questions. In contrast, an essay exam tends to deal with broader themes. There is less emphasis on individual facts, and there is more emphasis on the ability to recall information, analyze and discuss topics, and make connections between them.

Many exams combine objective and essay portions. In an American history class, for example, the objective portion may ask students to match presidents with their accomplishments, fill in the names of presidents and other historical figures, and answer multiple-choice questions about the causes and outcomes of conflicts. The essay portion may then ask students to discuss the impact of an historical event on the nation's development or how governmental and societal actions have affected various population groups. Generally speaking, the more objective the test, the more important it is to focus on specifics.

Use your text and lecture notes as study tools. Key portions of the text, often shown in boldface, italics, or boxes, will tend to stand out for purposes of reviewing, as will the sections you have highlighted on first reading. The same thing is true of sections you've highlighted in your notes, as well as sections you marked in the margin.

Studying in a group can be an effective way of preparing for a test. Group members can take turns quizzing each other about facts and themes. Different members will tend to emphasize different topics, perhaps filling in gaps for others. At the same time, the group might collectively agree on certain topics that stand out relative to others.

For essay exams, focus on broad themes. One helpful technique is to play the role of the instructor and try to predict what questions will be asked on the exam. Think of an essay question the instructor might ask; then anticipate what your answer would be. Sometimes this technique pays off in surprising ways, such as when an instructor gives students an opportunity to make up their own exam questions.

Some tests are made up of all multiple-choice questions, much like college entrance exams. Rather than writing in an exam booklet, you may be asked to mark answers in pencil on a form that will be read by a machine. When taking tests of this type, it is important to follow directions carefully. Make sure that you are marking the space you want on the answer sheet. If you skip a question, planning to return to it later, make sure you also skip a line on the form.

As you prepare for exams, try to monitor your health. Because tests tend to create anxiety, sleep patterns can be disrupted, nutrition ignored, and exercise forgotten. This is especially true toward the end of the term, when papers are due, finals are taking place, and fatigue from all the hard work is starting to catch up.

During this period, make a special effort to schedule study times and avoid distractions. Assess the number of hours needed to prepare for each exam, keeping in mind that different courses require different amounts of time. Also, make sure to schedule time for sleep. The value of an extra hour of studying is frequently lost when it comes at the expense of being well-rested for the exam.

Occasionally, despite your best efforts throughout the term, you will find yourself having to "cram" for a test. Recognize cramming for what it is: too much information in too few hours. Realizing that you can't study everything, decide what you can master in the time available and cut your losses on the rest. If you then find yourself with spare time, expand your range of material. By following this procedure, you can walk into the exam confident about your control over the most important information from the course.

As you prepare for tests, be active. Rewriting your notes reinforces learning more effectively than just reading your notes. Creating flashcards gives you a way to check your memory; ironically, the act of creating flashcards will be useful even if you never actually use the cards. Sometimes exams from previous terms are available through the library or the teacher. If so, obtain copies. Reading them may help you rank the topics to study; actually taking them will give you a chance to simulate the test.

Be organized the night before; the last thing you need is to arrive at the test and realize your pencil is broken or your calculator batteries are dead. Regarding supplies, assume that what can go wrong will go wrong. Expect the pen to run dry or the pencil point to break, and have backup.

For essay exams, you may be able to bring a text, a dictionary, or an outline with you; know in advance if this is the case. Some instructors will allow you to bring equations and notes. In such cases, their concern is not that you have memorized a specific equation, but that you can successfully use it to solve a problem. If such an opportunity is allowed, seize it.

At the test, find a comfortable seat with good lighting and few distractions. Have a watch with you so that you can monitor time. Answer the easy questions first; do not spend excessive time on difficult questions if they interfere with others, as you can come back to them later. For essays, take a few moments early on to organize your thoughts and outline a plan of attack. In the long run, organizing your essay can save you time. It also prevents the problem of getting most of the way through an essay and realizing you left out an important piece of information.

Read directions carefully. Be sure you answer the question being asked. In quantitative subjects such as math and economics, show your work. Sometimes the logic of your answer is correct, but an arithmetic error has led to an incorrect answer. Many teachers give partial credit for following the correct steps.

Finally, keep tests in perspective. They measure your mastery of a topic on a particular day with a particular set of questions. They are not a judgment of you as an individual.

ABCs of studying

Ask. Ask your instructor what material will be covered, or what type of test will be given (such as essay, fill-in, multiple choice).

Book. Review your textbook and student guide. Did you highlight your reading?

Class notes. Review your class notes. Recopy them if needed to emphasize key points.

Dry run. Think about what will be asked. Write down some of the questions you think will be included and possible answers.

Exams. Find out if exams from previous semesters are available at the library or department office.

Flashcards. Try making flashcards with key information on each card. This is especially useful for objective exams.

Groups. Find a study group or partner to work with.

Help. Well before the test, identify what your problem areas are; then get help from the instructor or a tutor.

Electronic skills

Calculator, CD-ROM, and computer skills, including those in word processing, data-base, and spreadsheet programs, can be tremendous timesavers and are often required. For example, students who arrive at college trained in word processing have an advantage over other students on many assignments, especially when writing papers. Today, word processing plays as important a role as typing did in years gone by. Having your own computer is helpful. However, having skills using computers is essential.

Computer literacy.
Most colleges will provide special services to help you learn how to work with computers. However, if at all possible, learn before you arrive at college. If you are not already comfortable working with computers, consider taking a course through your high school or through special training available in your community.

Word Processing. Most students today use a computer to prepare their writing assignments. Word processing programs enable you to make changes easily. Some of the changes are as simple as correcting spelling or weak grammar. In other cases, you may decide to move an entire passage to another section of your paper. With word processing, you can make these changes in a matter of seconds.

Computers can help you find out quickly whether the first draft of a paper is too long or too short; you can then make any necessary adjustments for length. In many cases, you may want to insert a table, graph, or chart into your paper. For example, you can enter data from a survey into a spreadsheet program, then create a bar graph through your computer, and insert the graph into the middle of your table.

Keep in mind some key tips when you use your computer for writing papers. Save your file frequently. Many students have learned this lesson the hard way: they write several pages without saving, only to have a power surge or some other interruption completely erase their work. Make backup copies, especially of

longer works. These copies can help protect you should your computer develop some kind of problem. If you are writing a paper with many different drafts, save each draft under a different name. You may find that some material you wrote for the first draft, then did not use in the second draft, can be handy after all. If you have saved each draft separately, then you can copy this material from the first draft and use it later. If you save each draft over the previous one, then the old material is lost.

Most word processing programs enable you to have the computer check for spelling. You can also find programs that check grammar. While these are useful as a first pass, do not rely on them for overall accuracy. For example, the spell-check programs cannot distinguish between insects found in the desert and insects found in the dessert!

Data bases. Many students' first experience with data bases will be in dealing with the library's electronic card catalogue. Data bases are also very important in statistics and social science classes, as well as a variety of other studies. Suppose you are conducting a survey about people's attitudes toward a political issue, such as whether to fund a particular government program. You would ask each participant the same set of questions. Some questions would be about the specific issue, whereas other questions might be about the participant's background, such as gender, age, income, or geographical background.

You could then enter the information you gather into a data base you have created. Each survey would be a record. Each item within the survey would be a field, such as the age of the participants. The computer organizes this information. Now you can look at the complete response for each participant (record) or you can look at the responses of all the participants for an individual question such as age (field).

At first you might find that the participants are split evenly about whether to fund the program. Data bases let you dig deeper. For instance, you might find that the vast majority of male participants favor funding the program, whereas the majority of female participants oppose funding. Data-base programs make this kind of analysis easy to handle.

Data-base programs also have important uses outside of the classroom. For example, when you are looking for a job, you can easily keep records about the companies in which you are interested and your various contacts with them. You can also use the data base program to generate mailing lists and labels that will save time.

Spreadsheets. Electronic spreadsheets are finding their way into many courses, such as accounting and physics, where they enable users to work with financial and budgeting information and equations.

You may be familiar with spreadsheets already. Many are used in the home to help with personal budgeting and record keeping. Spreadsheets enable you to enter in a variety of formulas and data, then make quick changes. For example, suppose you are trying to set up a small business. You can enter information about how many units you think you will sell each month for twelve months. Then you can use a formula to project sales for the second year, say an increase of 10 percent over the previous year. You can then enter information about the selling price of the unit and a formula to calculate total sales (the number of units times the price).

But that's just scratching the surface of a spreadsheet. Now suppose you want to see what will happen if you lower the price by 10 percent and increase the number of units sold by 5 percent. Instead of having to start all over again, you can enter these changes into your original formulas and, in a matter of moments, you will have new totals.

In this regard, spreadsheets are extremely important tools for helping you ask the question "What if?" For example, what if we raise the price; what if we increase the costs; what if we change the level of sales?

Research on the computer. The ways in which students gather information for research papers has changed a lot in the past several years. Most libraries now have computers with programs that help you search for materials available at the library, including magazine and newspaper articles. You can even do research at your own computer.

The Internet and the World Wide Web bring the entire world of information to your fingertips. Millions of people and companies around the world have set up home pages and sites that have individual addresses. When you travel to that address through your computer, you can then look at the information available at that site.

Companies that provide you with access to the Internet also provide you with access to browsers and search engines like Yahoo and Lycos. These browsers help you find your way through the Internet by searching for specific information. For example, suppose you are writing a report about a particular author. You could begin your research by entering the author's name with one of the browsers. Within moments, you will have a list of sites across the Internet where you can get information about the author. Some of the sites might provide biographical information; others might provide summaries or analysis of the author's works. You might even find a location where people from around the world discuss their own views of the author.

In turn, when you go to one of the sites, you might find links to other sites with related information. If you click on one of these links, you will move through the Internet to that new site. For example, in going to a site about Shakespeare, you might find a link to a home page that tells you about Stratford-upon-Avon, where Shakespeare lived.

In some cases, these sites can provide you with up-to-the-minute data that will be handy in your report. This ability to find information is especially important when you need a lot of current statistics for your research paper.

CD-ROM. Knowing how to use computers also opens up a wide range of resources that would not otherwise be available to you. For example, a lot of study tools such as encyclopedias and other reference materials are now available in CD-ROM format. CD-ROMs link text with photographs, art, maps, charts, and other visual images as well as sound. They also link material, saving you time going from one source to another.

For instance, you might start by reading about Pennsylvania, click onto an article about the town of Gettysburg, click into another article about the Civil War battle at Gettysburg, then into a map of the battle, into a biography of Robert E. Lee (including calling up a portrait of Lee), move onto a broader article about the Confederacy, back into an article about music of the time, and listen to a recording of Civil War songs. From there, you might move into other music, back to the Confederacy or the Civil War, on to various composers, or anyplace else you want. All from one CD!

As we've noted already, hooking into the Internet increases your resources far, far beyond what any CD-ROM can offer. The advantage of CD-ROMs is that they are focused; you can often find material you want more quickly. The advantage of the Internet is the wealth of information available to you; however, you need to learn to find your way around it.

Computer tips. The following guidelines are important to helping you work with computers.

1. If you own a computer, be sure to use surge protectors. These help protect you against changes in the level of power. Try to avoid using your computer during electrical storms.

2. Maintain and store backup disks. Have formatted disks ready. Save your work frequently; never turn off your computer until you save your work.

3. For all equipment, contact campus security for advice on the best way to prevent tampering and burglary. Students living in apartment complexes should purchase a renter's insurance policy.

4. Take advantage of high school, college, and library courses to learn basic skills as early as possible. Familiarize yourself with the manuals that accompany equipment and programs. Many software programs have built-in tutorials that help you learn their use.

5. If you do not have your own equipment, locate campus equipment available for student use. Plan early for assignments that require campus computers, as there may be a waiting list or time limit.

6. Welcome computers as a fact of life. Master them as useful tools in the world of learning.

Calculator skills.
In preparing for college, plan to purchase a calculator. Find out in advance what kind you need. Many have graphing ability; they may even allow you to enter computer programs into them. Some can be connected to printers or even to your computer.

Calculators vary in the way they are designed. Some calculators are particularly useful for business students; these have special buttons and programs that let you perform applications commonly used in business, for example, finding the future value of an item you purchase today. Other calculators are designed for engineering and science uses; still others are especially useful in mathematics or statistics.

Be aware of the mathematical capability of any calculator you need. Some are algebra-based, while others can perform calculus-based operations. Graphing calculators are often required for math classes and, increasingly, for science, engineering, and business classes.

Keep in mind the following guidelines for calculator use:

1. Keep new batteries on hand. Do not wait until they run out to decide to purchase new ones.
2. Always check batteries before exams.
3. Be aware whether your calculator clears its memory when you change the batteries.
4. Check with your professors before a test about which calculators will be allowed.
5. Be prepared to clear your calculator's memory prior to taking tests.

Campus services

You and your college share a common goal: your success. Campuses offer many services designed to help you fulfill your academic goals. These services can help you over the rough spots and help you reach your full potential. As a result, when you arrive on campus it's important for you to identify campus services as soon as possible, to know their locations, and to understand how and when to use them.

Library.
Library services vary from campus to campus. Some colleges have more than one library. Universities often have undergraduate and graduate libraries as well as specialty libraries. Libraries may be organized in a traditional manner familiar to most students, or as part of a larger learning resource center that also houses computer and audiovisual labs and tutoring centers.

Soon after arriving on campus, arrange to visit the library or learning center. Many schools include library tours as part of orientation. Libraries also offer programs to familiarize students with resources, equipment, policies, and other important information. Be certain to locate the main information, circulation, and reference desks, the periodical and reference sections, the stacks, and the various types of equipment and study stations available to you.

If you need to use library resources but are not sure where to start, the *main information desk* is a good place to begin. A librarian or assistant on duty can point you in the right direction. The *circulation desk* is where you check out materials to take with you. Professors often assign reading in addition to the required text; these materials are usually available at the circulation desk, where they can be checked out for a brief time and returned for other students to use. The circulation desk can also provide help with the use of card catalogues and electronic data bases, or with finding materials in the *stacks*, where books are stored. Some stacks are open; students can enter them

directly to look for specific titles. Other stacks are closed; a circulation assistant must retrieve the desired book.

Many encyclopedias, indexes, almanacs, digests, and other sources of information cannot be checked out and must be used in the library. Most of these are available in a reference room. The *reference desk* is the place to go for help with these materials. Reference librarians can also help you find supporting material when you are preparing a research paper.

Libraries keep records of the materials they have available. Some maintain *card catalogues*, others rely on electronic *data bases*, and many combine the two. Together, they list the books available at the library; each book can be located by author, title, or subject.

Resources at the library

- **Card catalogue.** Maintains listing of all books in the library; increasingly computerized.
- **Circulation desk.** Where you check out books and other resources; get help finding books in stacks; borrow reserve materials.
- **Main desk.** Information center for the library.
- **Periodical section.** Magazines, newspapers, and journals; *Reader's Guide to Periodical Literature* is an important reference.
- **Reference section.** Encyclopedias, atlases, yearbooks, indexes, and a wide variety of reference books; reference materials cannot be checked out of the library.
- **Stacks.** Shelves where books are stored; can be open or closed to borrowers.
- **Other resources.** Audiovisual facilities, photocopiers, film and recordings, interlibrary loans, computers, vertical file with articles and clippings, government documents, microfiche and microfilm, and study areas.

Study Skills

Electronic data bases make it easy to locate periodicals and magazines, enabling students to find specific articles. Also, electronic data bases can provide information beyond what is immediately available at the library. Many libraries have reciprocal arrangements with other libraries to lend, borrow, or share information, thereby increasing resources available to students.

In addition to finding out where information is stored, learn about available *equipment*. Learn to use microfiche and microfilm machines, photocopiers, and various audiovisual devices that can help supplement reading assignments. Find *study areas* that fit your style, whether large rooms with long desks or quiet cubicles that minimize outside distractions. The library is an invaluable resource. Knowing how to use it will help you get the most out of your study time.

Tutoring.

Many schools report a surprising fact: it is their best students who make the most use of campus tutoring services. Already motivated to do well, these students know that "an ounce of prevention is worth a pound of cure," taking advantage of tutoring services before problems arise.

Tutoring services vary from campus to campus. Some schools offer individual and group tutoring; others offer only one or the other. Tutoring services may be available free of charge, at a fixed rate, or on a sliding scale. Some colleges have specially funded programs that provide tutoring to targeted student groups. Schools may have peer, faculty, volunteer, or professional tutors. Scheduling varies, too. Tutoring may be available by appointment or on a drop-in basis. A math lab tutor, for example, might help whichever students happen to come in on a particular day.

Tutoring may be available through a centralized service such as the learning center, or it may be decentralized, offered through individual departments. Many students use tutoring in a preventive manner, signing up for assistance in advance of need. Other students use tutoring to help them develop self-discipline and avoid procrastination. Since tutoring is frequently available on a first-come, first-serve basis, it's important to request or reserve time in advance.

Learning labs.

Many colleges have learning labs; math, English, foreign language, and computer labs are the most common. For example, students who are studying foreign languages often use labs to listen to audiotapes that help them practice speaking and understanding the language. Students studying computer science are frequently given assignments to write computer programs, requiring them to spend time on a computer in the lab.

The time students spend in labs is by no means limited to required assignments. Labs usually have open hours when students can drop in to work on assignments, practice, or receive assistance from faculty, lab assistants, or peer tutors. For example, a math student

may watch a videotape on a difficult topic; an English student might complete practice worksheets in order to strengthen punctuation skills. Depending on the subject area and the college's resources, labs are equipped with anything from additional texts and printed practice materials to audio- and videotapes, computers, software, and interactive videodisks. If you are enrolled in classes in which access to labs is available, make a point of identifying open hours and fitting them into your schedule as part of your study plan.

Writing center.

In many schools, writing assignments used to be reserved for English, history, and selected social science courses. In recent years, colleges have mounted a concerted effort to improve their students' writing skills in all subject areas. Writing centers have been established on many campuses to provide students with valuable assistance for tackling written coursework.

Writing centers provide assistance in a range of areas. They can help students improve the mechanics of writing, including grammar, punctuation, and sentence structure. They can give pointers in preparing essays and research papers, from the basics of selecting a topic, developing an outline, planning research, taking research notes, and organizing overall structure, to the finishing touches of revising, developing style, editing a final product, and producing a bibliography.

Frequently students have assignments with which they are uncomfortable or unfamiliar. Writing centers can be a student's ally. For example, students who are not comfortable writing poetry can get advice about how to tackle a poetry assignment. Other students may be required to prepare written assignments for courses not commonly associated with writing, such as math.

Writing centers are usually located in easily accessible places, such as the library or learning center. Like labs, they have posted hours, which may include times set aside for specific courses or types of assignments. Writing centers are generally staffed by lab assistants and faculty. You'll want to make a special note of the schedule of those individuals who have been very helpful to you. This is especially important when working on long-term assignments, since having the same person work with you over time will be beneficial.

As with labs, determine the writing center's location, hours, and specific services as soon as possible when you begin the term. Review your course outlines or syllabi to identify written assignments and due dates. Include the writing center in your study plans.

Counseling and advising.

Most students either have not settled on a major when they enter college, or they will change majors during their college career. If you anticipate that this might be the case for you, then academic advising can help you select courses with the broadest application to a variety of majors, until a major area of study is selected. Career counseling can help you identify the types of careers that might be of interest to you and the majors that will build a good foundation for pursuing those areas.

The importance of receiving good academic advising cannot be overstated. Academic advising ensures that you enroll in courses needed for your major or as a prerequisite to other courses you will take. It helps ensure that you complete your academic objectives and requirements on time. When you enter college, you will be assigned to an academic adviser. Whether required or not, schedule appointments with your adviser to prepare your schedule each term, select or change your major, and monitor your progress toward graduation.

Colleges recognize problems that interfere with students' abilities to succeed academically. These problems may be in skill areas, such as time management or organization, or they may involve personal concerns such as homesickness, loneliness, stress, anxiety, or problems with drugs or alcohol. Trained counselors are available to assist and maintain confidentiality. Even if you never have such a need, you are likely to know a student who does. Familiarity with counseling services can help you to help someone else.

Large schools often have separate counseling and advising centers. At some schools, students initially work through counseling and advising centers and then are assigned to faculty advisers affiliated with the students' major field of study. Academic advising may be offered by advisers, counselors, or faculty. Many schools have career centers that provide information through computerized career exploration programs, employment data bases, and other resources. Career testing and counseling are often available from trained personnel.

Special services.

Campuses across the nation are becoming increasingly accessible to students with disabilities. Much credit can be given to legislation requiring postsecondary schools to increase access for disabled students; in fact, many schools have far exceeded the letter of the law. Many campuses also provide services for economically and educationally disadvantaged students.

The range of services varies from campus to campus. Services include liaison services that assist students in gaining access to campus resources. Many schools make available special tutoring, counseling, transportation, workshops, and equipment. For example, they might help blind students by arranging for Braille or audiotaped editions of textbooks. Many schools offer, as part of their orientation program, special workshops for disadvantaged students in order to help them make some of the adjustments required to succeed.

Services are often provided through counseling or learning resource centers; some schools have separate offices that coordinate services. Student eligibility, especially for disadvantaged students, varies as well. It is often based on requirements mandated by funding sources. For example, some programs are funded to promote and support the success of minority students, regardless of their income or educational background. Other programs may be funded to assist economically or educationally disadvantaged minorities.

Faculty assistance.
There is no better source of information regarding a course than the faculty member who teaches it. Almost all faculty have office hours; large universities also have graduate assistants available to help students. Establish a relationship with your instructors early in the term. Attend class; let them know you are interested and motivated. Make the best possible use of their time and yours by being prepared with specific questions.

Meet with faculty in preparation for exams and assignments or to receive help with difficult course material. Try whenever possible to bring your work with you. For example, if you have difficulty with a set of exercises, try to solve it first and then show the

Most college campuses offer numerous accommodations for disabled students.

instructor your efforts. If you are having trouble with a research paper, start by sharing with the instructor the ideas you have had and the obstacles you have encountered. The instructor will be able to provide you with more focused help and perhaps identify where you got off track. In the meantime, you will have demonstrated an honest effort to tackle the coursework.

Faculty, like the rest of us, expend extra time and effort for those who make every effort to help themselves. These advisers can derive as much satisfaction from your success as you do. In addition, they may write your first job reference, recommend you for scholarships or special programs, or help you in other significant ways.

Using college resources

Problem	Resource
Health and stress	
I feel like I have the flu.	Campus infirmary
I'm completely stressed out.	Counseling
I'm tired and sluggish.	Nutritionist, infirmary, or athletic center
Academics	
I don't know what courses to take.	Advising, career center
I need extra help in math.	Learning labs, tutoring center, faculty office
I missed class.	Faculty office
I can't get my paper started.	Writing center
Goals	
Can I get into this class?	Registrar, adviser
What major should I choose?	Advising, counseling
Daily life	
I don't get along with my roommate.	Housing, resident life
There has to be more to college than books.	Music and art center, dean of students, athletic center, student government
I have dyslexia.	Disabled student services, counseling
I can't afford tuition.	Financial aid office

College subjects

Courses required in your first few terms may be preset by your college to meet its general education requirements, established to ensure that students have been exposed to a variety of disciplines. After completing these requirements, the majority of your courses will be in your major. Study and homework requirements tend to vary by subject area.

English.

Many students are required to take two terms of English: one focusing on writing skills and the other on literature. In writing courses, students may be asked to write essays or short papers every week. A course may be organized around rhetorical modes, such as cause and effect, comparing and contrasting, or argument and persuasion. It may also center around themes, such as inner feelings or social issues.

Literature courses require much reading time and may also include several papers. In contrast to writing courses, little classtime attention is given to grammar, punctuation, and sentence mechanics; students who need additional help in these areas should go to a campus writing center or seek remedial assistance.

Humanities.

The humanities are areas of study that focus on human thought and imagination, such as history, philosophy, and religion; and art, music, and theater. History views the activities of individuals and societies over time; courses are likely to include term papers, as well as tests with a high percentage of essay questions. Philosophy and religion courses are dominated by reading and written analysis, in which the ability to understand and choose words selectively is important.

Art and music history courses may combine reading assignments with time spent evaluating creative works. Term papers may be required, and tests often consist of essay and objective questions. Studio art and music performance courses involve hands-on time: students create original artwork and musical compositions or spend time refining their skills, whether these involve practicing piano or mixing paints. Likewise, theater courses focus on studying dramatic works and on stage production and performance. In addition to these courses, many colleges offer general survey courses that present the arts from an historical perspective.

Sample majors and related coursework

Business administration
(four-year program)

Principles of accounting
Introduction to marketing
Computer systems
Management theory
Organizational behavior
Human resource management
Production and operations management
Financial management
International business
Business policy
Business calculus
General psychology
Public speaking

Government
(four-year program)

Introduction to political science
American government
Comparative government
State and local government
Principles of economics
The presidency
Congress and the legislative process
The U.S. Constitution

Media broadcasting
Introductory sociology
Public speaking

Nursing
(two-year program, leading to licensing exam)

Human development across the life span
Anatomy and physiology
General psychology
College algebra or mathematics for nursing
Introductory sociology
Microbiology
Clinical nursing courses

Teaching
(four-year program, elementary education)

Methods and materials of education
General or developmental psychology
Children's literature
Geography
Math for elementary education
Reading
American or world history
Technology in the classroom
Introduction to the exceptional child
Student teaching

Study Skills

Social sciences. The study of individuals and society is central to the social sciences. Pyschology focuses on individual behavior; sociology studies group and societal behavior. Social psychology examines the relationship between the individual and society. Anthropology concentrates on the physical and cultural development of human beings. Political science focuses on systems of government as well as public policy. Economics examines systems of money and national or global economies. Criminology looks at legal systems and crime. Human development is an interdisciplinary field combining the study of psychology with anatomy and physiology.

Most courses in these disciplines have a steady amount of reading. While standard texts are common, especially at the introductory level, many courses rely on readings from primary or original sources. Tests often combine objective and essay formats. Higher-level courses in psychology, sociology, and criminology often have quantitative elements. Courses in research methods and statistics are offered, in which students learn to conduct field research and laboratory studies.

Students in higher-level courses also work with large computerized data bases; thus, computer skills can be important. Many students who plan to attend law school major in the social sciences, as do many who are planning to pursue careers in government or human services.

Natural sciences. While the social sciences focus on individuals and society, the natural sciences examine the natural and physical world. Biology is the study of living things, whether human, animal, or plant. Chemistry analyzes the elements making up the natural and physical world. Physics examines the laws of nature and physical forces, such as gravity and electromagnetism. Geology is the study of the earth and its formations. Astronomy explores the universe and outer space, while oceanography studies the marine world. Agriculture and forestry are also often included within the natural sciences. Connecting most of these and emerging as its own field of study is environmental science, which looks at the ecological relationships of our planet.

In natural science courses, especially in physics, quantitative skills are important. Many science courses have a laboratory component, requiring students to spend additional time outside the classroom conducting experiments.

Most colleges require students to take a laboratory science course to fulfill general education requirements. Oftentimes, science courses involve a great deal of memorization, as well as vocabulary that may be unfamiliar.

Math and engineering. Most college students are required to study mathematics in some form. Courses in algebra, trigonometry, geometry, and calculus provide skills students may need in virtually all other disciplines. Perhaps more than any other discipline, math requires students to keep up with assignments, since concepts and skills taught in one session are dependent on material learned in earlier sessions. Students can expect homework for every class, mostly in the form of computational exercises and word problems. Calculator skills are needed in most courses; computer skills increasingly so.

Engineering applies mathematical and scientific theories to the real world. Chemical engineering focuses on chemistry, electrical engineering on electromagnetism, and mechanical engineering on machines. Civil engineering concentrates on infrastructure: construction, water resources and management, soils and steel, sanitation, and the environment. Other engineering branches include architecture and urban planning, computer engineering, industrial engineering, and material science and metallurgy. Quantitative and computer skills are central to all engineering courses. Students usually will need a calculus background. Communication skills are most important in areas such as civil and industrial engineering and architecture, which involve regular interaction with the public.

Foreign languages. Many colleges require students to demonstrate proficiency in a foreign language. The most commonly studied languages are French and Spanish; others include German, Russian, and Italian, as well as Japanese, Chinese, Arabic, Hebrew, and Portuguese.

Students who major in a language frequently have the opportunity to spend a term or a full year (usually junior year) studying abroad, for college credit, at a university where the language they are studying is the native language.

Like math, the study of a language builds on skills learned in previous classes. Class participation is usually part of the grading process. Nowhere are listening skills more important. Languages combine speaking, listening, reading, and writing skills. Students can expect to spend time in language labs listening to and practicing with audiotapes.

Computer sciences. Computer science courses may focus on the hardware and technology of computers, or on software and computer languages. Hardware is the machinery; software the programs that transform data input into useful information.

The study of computer languages helps students with writing or repairing programs. The study of hardware crosses into the area of computer engineering. Software studies teach students to use commercially available programs. Management information systems (MIS), often taught as part of business administration courses, focus on the application of computers in the business world.

Computer science students spend a lot of time working directly with computers. Like math, computer science requires students to keep up with assignments and to balance theory and applications.

Career courses. Many areas of study prepare students for careers. In business administration, students learn skills in management, marketing, human resources, production and operations, and finance; quantitative skills are important. Students who plan to teach take a variety of education courses; course requirements are often established to satisfy state teaching requirements. In a similar way, nursing programs are based on requirements set by state and national accreditation organizations; nurses are certified at various levels, depending on their program of study.

Many other career courses are available at the college level—especially at two-year colleges, whose curricula often take into account the job needs of the community; in fact, many two-year college programs are supported by local business. Areas of study include automotive repair, computers, construction, office systems, bookkeeping, carpentry, criminal justice, dental hygienics, electronics, fashion merchandising, retailing, and small business management.

Books on study skills

Brownstein, Samuel C., Mitchel Weiner, and Sharon Weiner Green. *A Pocket Guide to Vocabulary.* Hauppauge, N.Y.: Barron's, 1991.

Daniels, David, and Barbara Daniels. *English Grammar.* New York: HarperCollins, 1991.

Estell, Doug, Michele L. Satchwell, and Patricia S. Wright. *Reading Lists for College-Bound Students.* New York: Arco, 1994.

Frank, Stanley D. *Remember Everything You Read.* New York: Times Books, 1990.

Fry, Ronald W., *et al. How to Study Program.* Audiocassette. New York: Penguin Highbridge Audio, 1997.

Fry, Ronald W. *Improve Your Memory.* Franklin Lakes, N.J.: Career Press, 1996.

Jensen, Eric. *Student Success Secrets.* Hauppauge, N.Y.: Barron's, 1989.

Langan, John. *Reading and Study Skills, Form A.* 6th ed. New York: McGraw-Hill, 1997.

Langan, John. *Sentence Skills: A Workbook for Writers, Form A.* 6th ed. New York: McGraw-Hill, 1997.

Mathsoft Studyworks! Cambridge, Mass.: Mathsoft, 1996.

McEwan, Elaine K. *The Dog Ate It: Conquering Homework Hassles.* Wheaton, Ill.: Harold Shaw, 1997.

Meriwether, Nell N. *12 Easy Steps to Successful Research Papers.* Lincolnwood, Ill.: NTC Publishing Group, 1997.

Schaffzin, Nicholas Reid. *Reading Smart.* New York: Princeton Review, 1994.

Strunk, William, Jr., and E.B. White. *The Elements of Style.* 3rd ed. Boston: Allyn & Bacon, 1979.

Reading for enrichment

Many high schools and colleges provide lists of suggested books for students to read in preparation for college. Below is a sampling of some of those books, mostly fiction. For many authors, you should feel comfortable substituting another work they wrote. See your English teacher, counselor, or librarian for additional suggestions, including nonfiction.

Agee, James. *A Death in the Family*
Angelou, Maya. *I Know Why the Caged Bird Sings*
Anouilh, Jean. *Becket*
Austen, Jane. *Pride and Prejudice*
Bradbury, Ray. *The Martian Chronicles*
Brontë, Charlotte. *Jane Eyre*
Brontë, Emily. *Wuthering Heights*
Buck, Pearl. *The Good Earth*
Bulfinch, Thomas. *The Age of Fables*
Bunyan, John. *Pilgrim's Progress*
Camus, Albert. *The Stranger*
Carroll, Lewis. *Alice's Adventures in Wonderland*
Cather, Willa. *My Antonia*
Chaucer, Geoffrey. *The Canterbury Tales*
Conrad, Joseph. *Lord Jim*
Cooper, James Fenimore. *The Last of the Mohicans*
Crane, Stephen. *The Red Badge of Courage*
Defoe, Daniel. *Robinson Crusoe*
Dickens, Charles. *A Tale of Two Cities*;
  David Copperfield
Dostoyevsky, Fyodor. *The Brothers Karamazov*
Doyle, Sir Arthur Conan. *The Hound of the Baskervilles*
Dumas, Alexandre. *The Count of Monte Cristo*
Du Maurier, Daphne. *Rebecca*
Eliot, George. *Silas Marner*; *Middlemarch*
Ellison, Ralph. *Invisible Man*
Euripides. *Medea*
Faulkner, William. *As I Lay Dying*
Fielding, Henry. *Tom Jones*
Fitzgerald, F. Scott. *The Great Gatsby*
Flaubert, Gustave. *Madame Bovary*
Franklin, Benjamin. *The Autobiography of Benjamin Franklin*
Garland, Hamlin. *Main-Travelled Roads*
Golding, William. *Lord of the Flies*
Haley, Alex. *Roots*
Hamilton, Edith. *Mythology*
Hardy, Thomas. *The Mayor of Casterbridge*
Harte, Bret. "The Luck of Roaring Camp"
Hawthorne, Nathaniel. *The Scarlet Letter*
Hemingway, Ernest. *The Sun Also Rises*;
  The Old Man and the Sea
Hersey, John. *Hiroshima*
Heyerdahl, Thor. *Kon-Tiki*

Homer. *The Iliad*; *The Odyssey*
Hugo, Victor. *Les Misérables*
Huxley, Aldous. *Brave New World*
Ibsen, Henrik. *A Doll's House*
Irving, Washington. *The Sketch Book*
Kesey, Ken. *One Flew over the Cuckoo's Nest*
Kipling, Rudyard. *Kim*
Lee, Harper. *To Kill a Mockingbird*
Lewis, Sinclair. *Babbitt*
London, Jack. *The Call of the Wild*
Malamud, Bernard. *The Natural*
Melville, Herman. *Moby-Dick*
Miller, Arthur. *The Crucible*
Norris, Frank. *McTeague*
O'Hara, John. *Appointment in Samarra*
O'Neill, Eugene. *Long Day's Journey into Night*
Orwell, George. *Animal Farm*
Poe, Edgar Allan. *Tales* ("Cask of Amontillado")
Remarque, Erich Maria. *All Quiet on the Western Front*
Salinger, J. D. *The Catcher in the Rye*
Scott, Sir Walter. *Ivanhoe*
Shakespeare, William. *Macbeth*;
  A Midsummer's Night Dream
Shaw, George Bernard. *Pygmalion*
Solzhenitsyn, Aleksandr. *One Day in the Life of Ivan Denisovich*
Sophocles. *Oedipus the King*
Steinbeck, John. *The Pearl*; *The Grapes of Wrath*
Stevenson, Robert Louis. *Kidnapped*
Stoker, Bram. *Dracula*
Stowe, Harriet Beecher. *Uncle Tom's Cabin*
Swift, Jonathan. *Gulliver's Travels*
Thoreau, Henry David. *Walden*
Tolkein, J. R. R. *The Hobbit*; *Lord of the Rings*
Twain, Mark. *The Adventures of Huckleberry Finn*
Verne, Jules. *Journey to the Center of the Earth*
Vonnegut, Kurt. *Cat's Cradle*
Wells, H. G. *The Time Machine*
Wharton, Edith. *The Age of Innocence*
Whitman, Walt. *Leaves of Grass*
Williams, Tennessee. *The Glass Menagerie*
Wright, Richard. *Native Son*

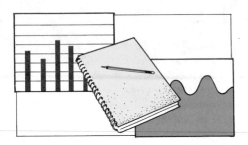

Test-taking strategies

Multiple choice

To answer a multiple choice question, select the response that best answers the question or completes the statement.

> Which of the following cities hosted the 1992 Summer Olympics? (a) Atlanta (b) Barcelona (c) Seoul (d) Sydney

If you are unsure of the answer, eliminate answers you know are incorrect. This will improve the likelihood of choosing the correct answer. For example, if you know Atlanta is the site of the 1996 games and Sydney is the site of the 2000 games, then your choice is between Barcelona and Seoul.

Answer. b

> In the 1996 Summer Olympics, Michael Johnson
> (a) was the fastest American in the men's marathon.
> (b) did not earn a medal in the decathlon.
> (c) competed in the long jump.
> (d) was among the top three finishers in the decathlon.

Sometimes answers contradict each other in such a way that one of them must be true. If you see this pattern, then you can eliminate other answers. In this example, if an athlete was among the top three finishers in the decathlon (d), then he earned a medal. If he was not among the top three finishers in the decathlon (b), then he did not earn a medal in the decathlon. Either (b) or (d) must be true. Thus, both of the answers (a) and (c) can be automatically eliminated.

Suppose you confuse Michael Johnson with Carl Lewis, who won the gold medal in the long jump. Whether or not Johnson competed in the long jump or some other track and field event, it would still be true that he did not earn a medal in the decathlon. By finding contradictory answers, you can narrow your choice.

Answer. b

Matching

You will see two columns in a matching question. Find pairs of responses, one from each column, that answer the question.

> Match each of the following cities with the year the Winter Olympics took place there.
> 1. ___ Lake Placid   (a) 1988
> 2. ___ Calgary   (b) 1994
> 3. ___ Squaw Mountain   (c) 1980
> 4. ___ Lillehammer   (d) 1960

First, check to see if there is a one-to-one correspondence between the two columns. Sometimes the right-hand column will have more choices than are needed.

Look over both columns and answer the easiest items first. You do not need to go in order down the columns. For example, suppose you do not remember when either the Lake Placid or Squaw Mountain Olympics took place. However, you know in an instant that the Lillehammer Olympics were held in 1994. You can match (4) from the left column with (b) from the right. Suppose among your Olympic memories were Dan Jansen's first dramatic losses in speedskating, that they were in Calgary, and you remember about how old you were when they happened. You then realize that the Calgary Olympics were around 1988, so you match response (2) with (a).

Now you are left with Squaw Valley and Lake Placid on the left as well as 1960 and 1980 on the right. While you do not remember either, you are fairly confident that the Lake Placid games were held more recently than the Squaw Valley games and can thus match (1) with (c) and (3) with (d). If you had not first eliminated 1988 and 1994 from the right column, the question would have been far more difficult.

Answer. 1-c, 2-a, 3-d, 4-b

True-false

To answer a true-false question, identify whether the statement is true or false. Then, in most cases, mark the blank next to the statement with either *T* or *F*.

Study Skills

___ Los Angeles has twice hosted the Winter Olympics.

Look for a trick in the wording. For example, Los Angeles has twice hosted the Olympics, but these were the Summer Olympics. Read the entire statement carefully. In other cases, look for qualifiers such as *usually*, *sometimes*, and *occasionally*, as well as absolute qualifiers like *never*, *always*, and *all*. Statements with absolute qualifiers are frequently false, while statements with less rigid qualifiers are frequently true.

Answer. False

Fill-in

To answer a fill-in question, write in the word or phrase that makes the statement true.

The United States did not participate in the 1980 Summer Olympics, which were held in the city of
_____.

If more than one answer comes to mind, write your choices lightly in pencil. Then you can move on to other questions and come back later, having already narrowed your choices. Watch for other clues. If the word *an* precedes the blank, then the word begins with a vowel. (Do not assume that the answer begins with a consonant if the word preceding it is *a*.) In this example, realize that you need to enter a city, not a country.

For example, write down cities that have hosted Summer Olympics. You remember Atlanta, Barcelona, Los Angeles, Munich, Moscow, and Montreal. If you can think of no others, then your answer will come from this group.

You may then eliminate Atlanta and Los Angeles (the United States was host) and Barcelona (too recent). You then remember a twenty-fifth anniversary report about terrorism that marred the Munich Olympics. Now you are down to Moscow and Montreal. It is possible neither is correct, but those are the only ones left on your list. Of these two possible answers, which is the more likely for the United States to have boycotted?

Answer. Moscow

Short answer

Answers to short-answer questions range from a phrase or list to a couple of sentences or brief paragraph. Check with the instructor or the directions if full sentences are needed.

Briefly explain why the International Olympic Committee decided to alternate the Winter and Summer Olympics beginning with Barcelona in 1992.

Look at key words. The question asks you to *explain*; your answer should be in sentences. Another version of the same question might ask you to *list* reasons; in that case, a listing of phrases would be appropriate. Read carefully to determine what is being asked. This question asks for *reasons why* the Olympics will alternate. Short-answer questions are usually very focused, looking for specific information with relatively little interpretation.

Answer. These will vary. Reasons might include the increasing broadcast revenues by spacing out the games; spreading out over time the demands on staff; and the desire to promote the Olympic spirit every other year rather than every four years.

Essay

Answers to essay questions are usually complete paragraphs or longer. In addition to providing factual information, students evaluate or interpret the information.

There was controversy regarding the decision to alternate the Winter and Summer Olympics every two years. Some opponents believed the problems that led to this decision could be solved by creating permanent Summer and Winter Olympic sites. Explain the controversy regarding this decision and discuss your views.

Read the question carefully and note key words, such as *discuss*, *compare*, and *summarize*. Before writing, quickly outline or list the key points you want to make in the essay. In this essay, you are being asked to compare two points of view and then reach your own conclusion. The short-answer example above asks only for information about why the games should be alternated. This essay question also asks for reasons why the games should *not* be alternated. Make sure your essay discusses both sides. After presenting both sets of arguments, reach your own conclusion. You do not need to agree with either side, but can present another viewpoint altogether.

Answer. Reasons in favor of alternating are given in the previous section. Reasons against alternating might include the break with tradition and the dilution of the Olympic movement by having the games held so often.

College Entrance Exams

- Entrance exam basics
- Registering for tests
- Test structure
- Scores
- Taking the test
- Sample test questions

College
Entrance
Exams

College entrance exams are one factor among many that can influence where students go to college. Not all colleges use entrance exams as part of the admissions process. For those that do, entrance exams are one way to measure a student's potential for success.

Not only colleges use the exams for admissions decisions. Students and counselors frequently use scores to help them determine colleges and universities to which students can realistically apply. While relatively weak scores may discourage students from applying to certain schools, strong scores often encourage students to expand their range.

Test scores are not the be-all and end-all for getting into college. How they are used varies from one college to the next. While the thought of spending several weekend hours taking tests is daunting to many, proper preparation can enhance the experience and help you achieve your goals.

Entrance exam basics

Major exams. Many colleges require students to submit entrance exam scores as part of the application process. Those that do will specify that students take either the SAT I: Reasoning Test (Scholastic Aptitude Test) or the ACT (American College Test). Some schools, though not all, have a preference. Both tests are taken primarily by high school juniors and seniors. From year to year, the various tests are updated. Occasionally these changes are fairly dramatic—for example, incorporating the use of calculators. Be sure you work with current information about the tests.

The PSAT/NMSQT, a preliminary version of the SAT I, is administered primarily to juniors. Some schools administer it to sophomores as practice. It enables students to prepare for the SAT I and helps students select colleges where they will apply. This test also serves as the NMSQT (National Merit Scholarship Qualifying Test), enabling juniors to compete for the National Merit Scholarship Program,

Major acronyms used	
ACT	American College Test
AP	Advanced Placement
ATP	Admissions Testing Program
CEEB	College Entrance Exam Board
ETS	Educational Testing Service
NMSQT	National Merit Scholarship Qualifying Test
PSAT	Preliminary Scholastic Aptitude Test
SAT	Scholastic Aptitude Test
SAT I	SAT Reasoning Test
SAT II	SAT Subject Test
SDQ	Student Descriptive Questionnaire
TOEFL	Test of English as a Foreign Language
TSE	Test of Spoken English
TWE	Test of Written English

which annually awards about 6,500 scholarships.

Some schools require the SAT II: Subject Tests as part of the application process. These tests, previously known as the Achievement Tests, cover specific subject areas. Foreign students may have to take the TOEFL (Test of English as a Foreign Language) as well as the TWE (Test of Written English) as part of the college admissions process.

How exams are used. College entrance exams do not measure a student's I.Q. (intelligence quotient). Nor do they measure motivation, creativity, personality, or achievement. Their goal is to test basic skills, along with students' abilities to reason and apply their skills to new material.

Colleges use tests in several ways. Those colleges that require entrance exams as part of the admissions process use them as one measure of ability to succeed and a way to compare students from different schools. Test scores are important, but by no means the sole factor; high school records, recommendations, class rank, personal accomplishments, and the student's application are important factors.

Entrance exams double as placement exams at many colleges. For example, verbal SAT I scores are used by some colleges to determine freshmen English placement. Test scores on the language SAT II Subject Tests help to place freshmen in foreign language courses.

Many students take Advanced Placement (AP) courses during high school, followed by Advanced Placement tests. While not entrance exams, these tests may enhance admission standing and scholarship opportunities, as well as enable students to earn college credit. For example, the AP test for calculus may exempt students from taking a term or two of calculus, enabling them to start further along in the curriculum. Some colleges provide special sections for AP students; these sections tend to be faster-paced than other sections of the same course.

Exam schedules. Most entrance exams are offered several times during each academic year. For example, the SAT I is generally offered in October, November, December, January, March, May, and June; the SAT II tests are on many of the same dates as the SAT I; and the ACT, in October, December, February, April, and June. The PSAT/NMSQT is offered less frequently (on one of two dates in October), the TOEFL/TWE more frequently.

Entrance exams have registration deadlines, which generally fall about one month prior to the test date; tests are not offered everywhere on each date. Furthermore, not all tests are offered on every date. For example, some SAT II subject tests are offered only once or twice each year.

Test sites. Many locations are used to administer entrance exams. High schools and colleges are the most frequently used test sites. Your own high school may or may not be a test site. You may need to travel a substantial distance from home to get to the test site; if this is the case, you will need to make travel arrangements in advance.

Not all test sites are used every time. The test site closest to you may administer a test three of the times it is offered, but not the other times. Checking to see

College entrance exams are frequently given on college campuses.

the date a test is offered is not sufficient. You must also check that it is offered in your state and at a test site that is within your reach.

You must register as early as possible to ensure that you will be assigned the site of your choice. The registration packet you receive will provide additional information.

Should you take an exam?

If you are thinking of applying to a college that requires entrance exams, then clearly you need to take them. Even if you are not quite sure if or where you will apply to college, you should still consider taking entrance exams. You always have the opportunity to retest and take steps to improve your scores. Some colleges count scores less than others. However, a good performance can shore up a weakness in your academic record. Simply taking the test can place your name on college mailing lists.

The PSAT, with its fairly low fee, helps you determine the level of preparation you will need for the SAT I. Taking it may provide you with perspective on other exams.

Which exam should you take?

Colleges indicate in admissions materials if either the SAT I or ACT is required. Many let you choose. If this is the case, obtain the bulletins for each and compare the tests. See if you are more at ease with one than the other. Some colleges also require SAT II: Subject Tests. You may or may not be able to choose the subject areas. If you can choose, select subjects in which you excel.

Which test is for you?
- Have you spoken to your school counselor yet?
- What tests, if any, are required by the colleges where you plan to apply?
- Does the college to which you are applying give you a choice?
- Does your high school offer special testing programs?
- Have you taken an entrance exam before?
- In which areas, if any, does the college you're applying to require specific subject tests?

When should you take exams?

In a sense, you have been preparing for entrance exams throughout your school career. Your day-to-day studies help you strengthen your basic skills. Taking entrance exams in your junior year enables you to assess your performance and allows time to take measures to improve your scores. By waiting until your senior year, you may increase the pressure on yourself to perform well.

Students who are thinking about attending college benefit from taking the PSAT/NMSQT in the fall of their junior year. As noted, it provides both practice and the chance to qualify for scholarship and placement on college mailing lists. Often, these students then take the SAT I or ACT in the spring of their junior year, providing time to retake the tests as needed early in their senior year. Ideally, SAT II: Subject Tests and AP exams are taken as closely as possible to the time the specific subject was studied.

Comparison of SAT I and ACT

SAT I
- The SAT I is the most commonly required college entrance exam in the country.
- The SAT I has two major sections: verbal and mathematics.
- The SAT I is offered seven times a year: October, November, December, January, March, May, and June.
- The SAT I is administered by Educational Testing Service.
- Scores for each major section are reported on a scale of 200 to 800. Combined scores range from 400 to 1600.

  For more information, contact:
  College Board SAT Program
  P.O. Box 6200
  Princeton, NJ 08541-6200
  609-771-7600
  http://www.collegeboard.org

ACT
- The ACT is most commonly required by midwestern colleges.
- The ACT has four major sections: English, mathematics, reading, and science reasoning.
- The ACT is offered five times a year: October, December, February, April, and June.
- The ACT is administered by American College Testing Program.
- Scores are reported on a scale of 1 to 36. Sub-scores are on a scale of 1 to 18.

  For more information, contact:
  ACT Registration
  P.O. Box 414
  Iowa City, Iowa 52243
  319-337-1270

Registering for tests

How to register.
During your sophomore or junior year, talk with your counselor about which tests to take, when to take them, and how to register. Your counselor should have the forms and information that you will need. You can also write to the appropriate testing company to request registration information. In the case of the SAT I, you need two booklets: *SAT Program Registration Bulletin*, which provides registration information and forms for both SAT I and SAT II, and *Taking the SAT I Reasoning Test*, which provides background about the SAT I itself, tips for taking the test, sample questions, and an explanation of the scoring system. A similar booklet about taking the SAT II is also available. Corresponding information is available for the ACT.

Select your test date and center. Be sure to file forms by the deadline and pay the appropriate fees. Most tests have a date for late registration; the fee is higher. You may also be able to register on a standby basis on the day of the test, though the fee will be still higher, with no assurance of space—going standby is strongly discouraged. After registering, you will receive from the testing company confirmation as well as an admission ticket, which you will need to get into the test. If you do not receive this packet, or if you lose the ticket, call the testing company.

Registration forms.
Follow directions carefully when you complete exam registration forms. The forms are processed by machine; you will need to use a No. 2 pencil to complete them.

The forms ask for routine information such as your name, address, phone number, Social Security number, date of birth, and grade level. You enter codes that represent the high school you attend and the center where you want to take the test. Obtain your school code from your counselor. The test center

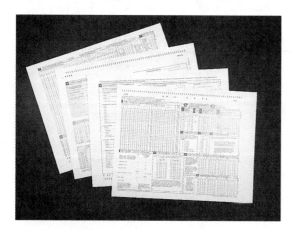

code, as well as codes for scholarships and colleges where you would like to have scores sent, are in the registration bulletin. The fee covers the cost of sending scores to several schools; you can send them to more locations at additional cost. You may be able to list a first and second choice for the test center. Register early.

The registration form for the SAT I and SAT II includes the Student Descriptive Questionnaire (SDQ), which you complete once, not each time you register. The SDQ is a voluntary form; it asks questions about your courses, grades, activities, goals, and interests. By completing this questionnaire, you can share information with colleges and your counselor; colleges often use this information to recruit students. You may update the information on the SDQ whenever you want, for example, if you have finished courses you have taken since first completing the form.

Use the same name on all forms. Be consistent in the way you write your name—for example, middle name versus initial; full name versus nickname; and the use of suffixes such as *Jr.* or *III*. In general, use your full name. Also, be precise when you fill out codes. For example, on the SAT form, if you write "1841" for the college code, your scores will be sent to the University of Notre Dame in Indiana. If you write "1851" instead, the scores will go to the University of Illinois in Chicago. Similarly, be sure to find the exact schools you want. For example, on the SAT form, Colby Community College in Kansas is 6129, Colby College in Maine is 3280, and Colby-Sawyer College in New Hampshire is 3281.

Registration fees.
A set fee is charged each time you take an entrance exam; the fee can be paid by check or money order (credit card for phone or electronic registration). Late fees are charged if you do not register on time. Other fees may need to be paid for additional services. Some of these charges are for sending scores to additional colleges or sending them after you have taken the test.

You may have an option to receive a scoring sheet for your test or to have your test scored by hand rather than machine. You may also be able to select other services, such as informational books or guides that carry additional costs. If you cannot afford the test fee, speak with your counselor; you may be eligible for a fee-waiver card.

Special circumstances. Sometimes

students have circumstances that require special accommodations. For example, most entrance exams are offered on Saturdays. However, some students have religious practices that prevent them from taking the test on Saturday; they may request a Sunday test date, provided they have supporting documentation from their cleric (such as a minister or rabbi).

Students who are hearing impaired may not be at a disadvantage with the test itself, but rather with the preliminary directions. Arrangements can be made to have a signer available at the test site to interpret the directions.

Students with visual impairments may be able to arrange to take the test with large type, Braille, or cassette; they may also be allowed to have a reader with them or to have the use of a magnifying glass. Furthermore, they may be able to take their test at their own school rather than one of the regularly scheduled test centers. Selected practice materials are available to accommodate visually impaired students.

Students with learning disabilities may not need a special form of the test, but rather additional time to accommodate their need. This too can be arranged under specific circumstances.

Other needs are temporary and students can usually

Reasons for test accommodations
- Visual impairment
- Hearing impairment
- Physical disability
- Learning disability
- English as a second language
- Religious convictions
- Illness
- Injury
- Death in family
- Inability to get to test site
- Weather conditions
- Score cancellation

arrange to take the test at another time. Weather conditions, illness or injury, or a death in the family may prevent a student from taking the test when originally planned. If possible, students should try to reschedule their test for a later date when the test is normally offered. However, if they are running into a time problem in which delaying the test could result in a missed application deadline, they should speak with their counselor to seek help.

These accommodations are not available for all tests, nor are they available at all times. Read the test bulletin to learn more about them. If you find that you need a special accomodation, first speak with your counselor to determine what arrangements can be made.

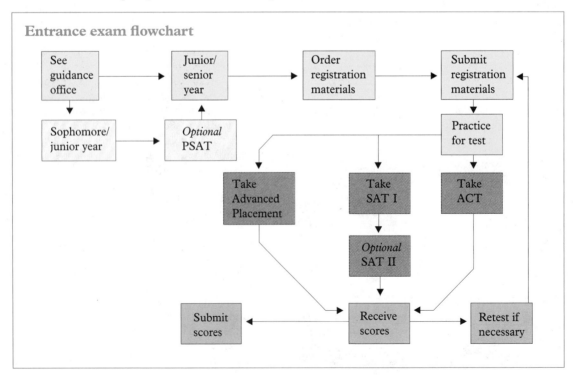

Entrance exam flowchart

See guidance office → Junior/senior year → Order registration materials → Submit registration materials

Sophomore/junior year → *Optional* PSAT → Junior/senior year

Submit registration materials → Practice for test

Take Advanced Placement

Take SAT I → *Optional* SAT II

Take ACT

Submit scores ← Receive scores ← Retest if necessary

Test structure

SAT I: Reasoning Test.
Tests change over time. The following information is based on the latest information available at time of publication.

The SAT I has seven parts. Two thirty-minute parts and one fifteen-minute part make up the verbal section. All questions in these parts are multiple choice. Similarly, two thirty-minute parts and one fifteen-minute part make up the math section. Most, but not all, questions in this section are multiple choice. Some are more open-ended, requiring you to develop your own answers and use the answer sheet grids to fill in your answer.

The seventh part might be either a verbal or math part. Its scores do not count toward your total score. Instead, its purpose is either to validate prior exam questions or to experiment with questions to be used for future exams. Because the order of these seven parts varies from test to test, you will not know which section is the experimental part.

PSAT/NMSQT.
This test is similar to the SAT I, but instead of seven sections it consists of four: two verbal and two math. You will be given thirty minutes to complete each section. The verbal portion has fifty-eight multiple choice questions; the math portion has fifty questions.

American College Test (ACT).
The ACT differs in format from the SAT I and is somewhat more content oriented. The test has four sections, including reading, English, mathematics, and science reasoning.

The reading section includes passages from arts and literature as well as from social studies and science. Students have thirty-five minutes to answer forty questions. The English section tests grammar, writing, and rhetorical skills. Students have forty-five minutes to answer seventy-five questions. (The SAT I includes reading comprehension as part of the verbal section.) The mathematics section has sixty questions and a sixty-minute time frame. The fourth section, on the topic of science reasoning, consists of forty questions and a thirty-five-minute time frame.

SAT II: Subject Tests.
Numerous Subject Tests are available. The number of multiple choice questions varies from subject to subject. For example, the literature test has about sixty questions, the physics test seventy-five questions, and the Spanish test eighty-five questions.

The writing test, which replaced the English composition test, combines forty minutes of multiple choice questions with a twenty-minute essay. The mathematics tests are offered at two different levels. The test for Math II (Level IIC) requires the use of a calculator. Several foreign language tests—French, German, Spanish, Japanese, and Chinese—include listening components.

Structure of SAT I and ACT

SAT I

Verbal section
- Analogies
- Sentence completion
- Critical reading questions
  (may include pairs of
  related passages)

Math section
- Standard multiple choice questions
  Arithmetic, algebra, and geometry
  Logic and symbols
  Probability and counting
- Quantitative comparison
- Student produced response questions
- Calculators permitted

Additional section (verbal or math)

ACT

English
- Usage and mechanics
- Rhetorical skills

Mathematics
- Pre-algebra and elementary algebra
- Intermediate algebra and coordinate geometry
- Plane geometry and trigonometry

Reading
- Arts and literature
- Social studies and sciences

Science Reasoning
- Data representation
- Research summaries
- Conflicting viewpoints

Scores

How tests are scored. The way that entrance exams are scored and reported varies. For the SAT I, the first step in scoring determines a raw score based on the number of correct answers within a section minus a fraction of the incorrect answers. This fraction varies from one-fourth to one-third. The total raw scores for the verbal and math sections are rounded to whole numbers, then converted to scores ranging from 200 to 800. Scores are reported in multiples of ten (500, 510, 520, and so on).

NOTE: On the SAT I, students are penalized for incorrect answers. Therefore, random guessing may result in lower scores than skipping questions.

Your combined score is the sum of your verbal and math scores. For example, a verbal score of 600 and a math score of 540 produce a combined score of 1140. At the same time, a verbal score of 550 and a math score of 590 also produce a combined score of 1140. Colleges may seek students with certain combined scores. They may also set minimal cutoffs for verbal and math scores.

Like the SAT I, the PSAT converts raw scores to a scale, but this scale is 20 to 80. Students receive a *selection index*, which is calculated by adding the verbal score twice and the math score once. The National Merit Scholarship Corporation uses this index to screen participants in the scholarship program.

The ACT converts raw scores to overall scores, on a scale of 1 to 36. Students receive scores for each of the four major sections and a composite score for the whole test. They also receive subscores, on a range of 1 to 18, for different parts of tests. There are seven subscores including two within the English test (one subscore for usage and mechanics, and another for rhetorical skills). Within the mathematics test, students receive three subscores (one for pre-algebra and elementary algebra, one for intermediate algebra and coordinate geometry, and one for plane geometry and trigonometry). The reading test has two subscores (one for arts and literature and the other for social studies and sciences). Unlike the SAT I, *the ACT does not penalize for incorrect answers.*

The information packets from the testing companies explain the scoring process in more detail.

Who receives scores. Students receive their scores approximately six weeks after taking their entrance exams. The information they receive includes not only their scores but information about how their scores compare nationally to other students. Scores are also sent to the high school, provided the high school code is listed on the registration forms.

Students can designate colleges and scholarship pro-

grams where scores should be sent. Unless they cancel such requests, the scores are sent at about the same time they are sent to students. In addition, students can request that scores be sent to additional locations, subsequent to taking the test.

Sending scores. Test scores should be sent to all colleges where you plan to apply and which require or recommend that you take a particular test. You may also want to send scores to colleges where you are thinking of applying. For example, when you take the SAT I, your fees include sending your scores to four colleges or scholarship programs. If you are only sure of two, but are strongly considering other colleges, then go ahead and send your scores to two more—you've already paid to have scores sent to four locations.

Plan to send your scores at the time that you take the test, at least to the number of locations covered by your fee. If possible, choose these locations at the time that you register. When you receive your admission ticket, you will also receive a cancellation form that will let you add, drop, or substitute names of colleges right up to the day of the exam.

Test scores are cumulative. Suppose you take the SAT I three times. If you report scores to a particular college the third time you take the SAT I, your scores from the first two times will also be reported.

Canceling scores. Frequently students complete a test sensing they did poorly on it. They have an option when leaving the test center to cancel scores altogether. If you choose this option the day of the test, ask the test supervisor for a form to complete. You generally will have a few days more after the test to cancel scores; check the information packet for more details.

When you cancel scores, you are canceling the entire test, not just one section. Your scores will not be reported anywhere; it will be as if you never took the test. Because you will not receive your scores, you will not know how you did. Therefore, unless you are absolutely sure that you did poorly on the test, and are confident that you would do significantly better on another date, you should not cancel your scores.

Taking the test

Preparing for the test. Many books, guides, software programs, and courses have been developed around entrance exam preparation. Separate from the registration process and decisions about which tests to take and where to send scores, test preparation has three major components: preparing for test content, preparing for the test day itself, and developing test-taking strategies for test format, time factors, and scoring rules.

Should you prepare? No preparation substitutes for being a conscientious student. Still, there are steps you can take based on the specific test to enhance your performance. These range from improving your general knowledge and basic skills to building your vocabulary and studying specific subject areas.

Preparation schedule. As soon as possible, become familiar with the demands of a test. Fully understand what the test encompasses in the way of content, format, time constraints, scoring rules, and your own level of self-confidence. Take a practice test. Based on the results, establish how much preparation you need and build a schedule. Incorporate other commitments in your plans. If you decide to take a coaching course, find out its duration.

Cramming for these exams is not a productive technique. What will be asked is not as predictable as a course exam. Longer-term strategies are far more effective. For example, if vocabulary is your weakness, develop a long-term plan to improve it, instead of trying to cram a list of words two weeks before the test.

Learning vs. reviewing. Before you prepare for the content portion of tests, assess whether you need to learn material, review material, or simply focus on test strategies. Each of these requires a different type of preparation. Learning is the most time-intensive. You are studying material for the first time or studying material you've had difficulty mastering. For example, memorizing the Pythagorean theorem is of little value if you have not learned to apply it. Reviewing involves reinforcing information you have already learned.

Good software programs are available to help you prepare for entrance exams.

Developing test-taking strategies ensures that the test format does not interfere with your ability to demonstrate your knowledge and skills.

Ways to prepare. There are several ways to prepare for exams. At minimum, obtain the sample materials that are free of charge from the testing companies. Assess your test-taking skills. Are you self-motivated? Are you confident when approaching tests? How well do you manage your time when taking tests? Know the format of the test that you are taking; be familiar with the types of questions to be asked and the types of directions.

Preparation beyond this minimal level basically involves more practice. Take the practice tests that are available from the testing companies. Diagnose your weaker areas and focus on them. For the first time you take an exam, purchase a preparation book or software program. Speak to your counselor for suggestions about which book to purchase. Each has a different viewpoint. Find one to match your style. When you practice the tests, focus in the beginning on accuracy and understanding test content and directions, rather than watching the clock. Practice again, focusing on the timed aspect of the test and strategies that help you improve speed. Then take a third test, combining accuracy with speed. Evaluate your accuracy, speed, and general strategies.

Try to recreate test conditions as closely as possible. Take the test, calculate your results, and determine whether more structured measures are necessary, such as a course or tutoring.

Additional resources. Numerous study books, some with software disks, can be found at most bookstores. Some focus solely on practice questions and lots of them. Others provide a trade-off: you may get fewer questions, but more explanation of answers. Books vary on how much emphasis they give to strategies and the kind of strategies they recommend. For example, some tell you to guess on an SAT question, even if you have no idea of the answer. Others tell you to guess only if you can eliminate at least one of the answers. Settle on one method and stay with it.

Perhaps the biggest challenge students face when they take the test is the time factor. Any resource you purchase should provide timed tests.

Software packages are available; they can help break up the monotony of test preparation. However, paper and pencil is the best way to practice, since it most closely replicates exam conditions.

Many students enroll in special preparation or coaching courses. These can be helpful in many ways, especially in helping you to develop test-taking strategies. But do not expect them to substitute for your studies in terms of developing your content knowledge and basic skills.

Evaluate courses before investing time and money.

Entrance exam guidebooks

Bobrow, Jerry, *et al. Cliffs American College Testing Preparation Guide*. 5th ed. Lincoln, Neb.: Cliffs Notes, Inc., 1996.

Brownstein, Samuel C., Mitchel Weiner, and Sharon Weiner Green. *How to Prepare for SAT I, Books and Disks*. Hauppauge, N.Y.: Barron's Educational Series, Inc., 1996.

Brownstein, Samuel C., Mitchel Weiner, and Sharon Weiner Green. *Pass Key to the PSAT/NMSQT*. 3rd ed. Hauppauge, N.Y.: Barron's Educational Series, Inc., 1995.

Carris, Joan, with Michael R. Crystal. *SAT Success*. Princeton, N.J.: Peterson's, 1997.

Deptula, Edward J. *Preparation for the SAT and PSAT, with Study Planning Software*. New York: Arco, 1997.

Ehrenhaft, George, *et al. ACT Computer Study Program*. Hauppauge, N.Y.: Barron's Educational Series, Inc., 1995.

Look Inside the SAT I. Video. New York: The College Board, 1994.

Martinson, Thomas H. *SAT Supercourse*. 2nd ed. New York: Arco, 1994.

Martinson, Thomas H., and Juliana Frizzone. *SAT II Subject Tests Supercourse*. 2nd ed. New York: Arco, 1994.

One on One with the SAT. Software. New York: The College Board, 1995.

Real SATs. New York: The College Board, 1995.

Robinson, Adam, and John Katzman. *The Princeton Review: Cracking the SAT and PSAT*. New York: Villard Books, 1996.

Weber, Karl. *Complete Preparation for SAT I*. 2nd ed. Orlando: Harcourt, Brace, 1995.

Ask students who have attended about their experience and success. Compare course offerings and fees with what is available for free from the testing companies and your high school. The advantage of courses is that they provide structure. For this reason, if you have performed poorly on an entrance exam, courses are often a good way to reverse poor performance.

Test-taking strategies. One group of basic strategies applies to marking answer sheets. In an entrance exam, you answer multiple choice questions by filling in an oval or a box with a No. 2 pencil. A machine reads the answer sheet. Each marking should be dark and match the question you intend to answer. Mismarking answer sheets is a common and serious test error. Working in blocks of questions helps you

In this section solve each problem, using any available space on the page for scratchwork. Then decide which is the best of the choices given and fill in the corresponding oval on the answer sheet.

The following information is for your reference in solving some of the problems.

Circle of radius r: Area $= \pi r^2$; Circumference $= 2\pi r$
The number of degrees of arc in a circle is 360.
The measure in degrees of a straight angle is 180.

Definition of symbols:
$=$ is equal to	$\leq$ is less than or equal to
$\neq$ is unequal to	$\geq$ is greater than or equal to
$<$ is less than	$\parallel$ is parallel to
$>$ is greater than	$\perp$ is perpendicular to

Triangle: The sum of the measures in degrees of the angles of a triangle is 180.
If $\angle CDA$ is a right angle, then

(1) area of $\triangle ABC = \dfrac{AB \times CD}{2}$

(2) $AC^2 = AD^2 + DC^2$

Note: Figures that accompany problems in this test are intended to provide information useful in solving the problems. They are drawn as accurately as possible EXCEPT when it is stated in a specific problem that its figure is not drawn to scale. All figures lie in a plane unless otherwise indicated. All numbers used are real numbers.

You can save valuable time on the test day if you have already read and understood the directions for the test. Directions are standard for each part.

ensure that your answer matches the question. If you skip a question, be sure you also skip the corresponding space on the answer sheet. Do not make stray marks on the page. Periodically stop to double-check that the question you are answering corresponds to your place on the answer sheet.

A common error occurs when the number of possible answers differs from the number of corresponding spaces on the answer sheet. For example, the answer sheet may list five answers (A, B, C, D, E), but the question may only provide four choices (A, B, C, D). If you select the last answer, you may intend to mark choice (D), but in fact mark choice (E). Avoid this error. Also, erase any incorrect marks *completely*.

Except for reading comprehension sections, questions are ordered easiest to most difficult. Complete the easy questions first. Your score is not based on the number of easy versus hard questions you answer. Rather, it is based on the total number you answer correctly. If a question is taking too much time, skip it and come back to it later. Do not get bogged down.

You can write in your exam book. Use that space effectively, especially for mathematical questions. If you have started a question and then decide to move on and return if time permits, what you write in the book might save you time when you return to the question.

Practice time management. At the start of each section, have a sense of the number of questions versus the amount of time. The ratio will change from section to section. A watch is a must.

Never waste valuable test time learning directions that you could know in advance. Use sample materials to study directions ahead of time. Read each question carefully; be sure you are clear about what is being

Strategy checklist

- Take the PSAT for practice. You may also qualify for a National Merit Scholarship or for other scholarships.
- Work with practice tests. Recreate test conditions as closely as possible.
- Increase your reading to build vocabulary.
- Learn the directions; know them before taking the test.
- Practice accuracy and speed.
- Organize your materials the night before.
- Get plenty of sleep the night before the test.
- Find a comfortable seat with good lighting.
- Follow the test supervisor's instructions carefully.
- Bring a watch with you; monitor your time.
- Answer easy questions first.
- Do not take too much time with any one question.
- Read the question carefully; answer what is asked.
- Mark the answer corresponding to the question.
- Eliminate wrong answers before guessing.
- Leave no questions unanswered on the ACT; there is no penalty for wrong answers.
- Do not mark answer (E) for questions with four choices.

Don't look ahead

Never look ahead in your test booklet. It's against the rules and you could be penalized. If you finish a section early, review that section and your answer sheet. If you still have time, then simply relax while waiting for the next section.

Should you guess?

SAT I and II

In both tests, one point is added to your raw score for a correct answer and one-fourth of a point is subtracted for an incorrect answer if the question has five choices. One-third of a point is subtracted for an incorrect answer if the question has four choices. (Your raw score is then converted to the test score.)

ACT

The ACT has no penalty for guessing.

General strategy

There is disagreement about the issue of whether you should guess on the SAT I or II if you cannot eliminate any of the choices. However, most experts will tell you that you should guess if you can eliminate at least one of the choices. Since the ACT has no penalty, you should provide an answer for every question.

Do not guess randomly, even on the ACT. Always try to eliminate as many choices as you can before guessing; this will dramatically improve your chances of answering correctly. Focus on questions you know. Save guessing for the end.

asked. Identify key words that point you in the right direction.

If you know an answer immediately, and you are sure of it, mark it and move on. Sometimes it is easier to substitute an answer into the question rather than solve for it. For example, if the question states "150% of some number is 375," it may be faster for you to multiply answers by 150 percent to find which leads to a product of 375, than to set up the equation that solves the question.

When you are not sure of an answer, see if you can eliminate wrong answers. Doing so improves the likelihood of guessing correctly. Cross out wrong answers in the test book (not the answer sheet). Then if you skip a question and return to it later, you can pick up from where you left off. If you plan to change an answer which you have already marked, be sure that your reasoning is logical; often your initial hunches are correct.

If you possibly can, try to leave time at the end to recheck your work. This may be even more valuable than trying to answer one more hard question. You do not have to answer all the questions to do well. For example, in the SAT I, if you answer sixty of the verbal questions correctly, and do not answer the other questions, your verbal score will be 600, which is considered an excellent score.

Exam day.

A key testing strategy is preparing for the test day itself. Prior to the test, make a list of required materials. Gather these materials in advance.

Arrange transportation in advance. If you are not familiar with the location of the test center, try to visit it prior to test day to ensure you have proper directions and have allotted adequate travel time. If you are taking public transportation, remember that weekend and weekday schedules may differ.

Do not cram the night before the test. Try to relax and get to bed early. If you do review the night before, you will probably do best to focus on test directions and strategies.

What to bring. You will need your admission ticket and identification to enter the test. The identification will vary by test; you may be required to bring a photo I.D., a school letter of identification, or a notarized statement with a photo. The information packet lists exactly what you will need. Also bring with you the test bulletin, information packet, directions to the test center, and a map. If you arrive early, you will then be able to review sample test questions, if you choose.

Bring at least two sharpened No. 2 pencils; you will use them to fill out the answer sheet. The pencils should have good erasers. Try out your erasers in advance to make sure they do not leave smudges, which could interfere with a machine's ability to read your answer sheet correctly. A small pencil sharpener and a separate eraser are optional items.

A watch is an absolute necessity. Do not count on the test room to have an accurate clock. Avoid watches that beep, as these are not allowed. Calculators are allowed in some, though not all, tests. Always check in advance that the calculator you plan to bring is on the approved list.

Dress comfortably, preferably in layers that you can adjust to room temperature. Food and drink are not allowed in the test room; you may want to have gum or hard candy. Have change for phone calls after the test is over. Determine in advance if you need change for a parking meter.

Finally, check your registration packet to learn what you cannot bring. For example, dictionaries, rulers, and portable radios or cassette players are not allowed into the test room.

Gathering these materials in advance will leave you more relaxed the morning of the test.

Arriving at the test site. Plan to arrive early, though not so early that you become anxious. Find a seat that has good lighting and few distractions. Factor room temperature into seat selection. If the test room is near a busy street, you might avoid a seat near the window. But if the room is overly warm or stuffy, you might sit near the window to get more air.

Find a comfortable seat, because you will be sitting for several hours with few breaks. Comfort is extremely important. Take advantage of breaks to stand up and stretch. Shift your position to stay alert and comfortable. There are numerous ways you can stretch your muscles even while sitting.

Follow the supervisor's directions carefully. Avoid talking with others or letting your eyes wander. Any suspicion of cheating, whether or not warranted, could cause you to be dismissed from the test, or result in cancellation of your scores.

You are not allowed to go back to sections you completed earlier. Nor are you allowed to look at upcoming sections. If you are caught doing either, you could find yourself being dismissed from the test. If you have extra time at the end of a section, review your work or take advantage of the time to relax in your seat.

Any markings you make in your test book are not factored into the test. For example, in math, there is no partial credit for setting up an equation. All that gets scored is the answer sheet itself.

After the test. At the end of the test you will turn in your answer sheet and test booklet. You are not allowed to take the booklet out of the room with you.

You know ahead of time when the test will be done. The only differences in schedule are how long it takes the supervisor to distribute and collect materials and how long it takes to give directions.

You should receive your test scores about six weeks following the exam. You may feel pressure to talk about your performance, both immediately after the test or when scores are mailed. Only do so if you feel comfortable. But do not be pressured into talking about it if you do not want to. At the same time, do not pressure others into talking about their experience. Once the test is over, take time to relax!

What to pack

- Test admission ticket
- Driver's license or other photo I.D.
- School identification
- Other identification, as needed
- Test bulletin
- Test registration information
- Directions to test site
- Map

- Two or three sharpened No. 2 pencils
- Good eraser
- Pencil sharpener
- Watch
- Calculator, if test permits

- Comfortable layered clothing
- Change for phone calls and vending machines
- Gum or hard candy, if desired
- Medicine, if needed (such as inhaler for asthma)
- Reading glasses, if needed

After the test is over, only talk about your answers if you feel comfortable doing so.

Sample test questions

SAT I: Reasoning Test.

As previously noted, the SAT I, as of publication date, consists of verbal and math sections (including one research section). The verbal sections cover analogies, sentence completions, and critical reading questions. The math section covers standard computational questions, as well as those involving quantitative comparisons. The sections may appear in any order. Omitting a question does not affect the SAT score. However, incorrect answers do lower the score. Questions are sequenced from easy to difficult, except for critical reading.

The changing SAT. The SAT went through significant changes in the 1993-94 year. As of spring 1994, the SAT I: Reasoning Test was introduced. The Test of Standard Written English (TSWE) was phased out, as were antonyms in the verbal section. Instead, more emphasis is now being placed on critical reading, with more reading passages, including pairs of readings that students are asked to compare and contrast. Now there are fewer questions and more time. In the math section, problem solving is being emphasized. Calculators will be permitted. In addition, several questions now require students to enter their own answers rather than select from a group of existing choices. Also in 1993-94, SAT II: Subject Tests replaced the Achievement Tests.

Verbal section. The combined verbal section consists of seventy-eight questions presented in one fifteen-minute and two thirty-minute parts. These include nineteen analogies, nineteen sentence completions, and forty questions evaluating critical reading skills. No specific knowledge of other fields is needed, even for reading passages, but well-read students have a vocabulary and comprehension advantage.

Analogies are words or phrases that have a relationship similar to other words or phrases. In the context of the SAT I, a pair of words will be given that bear a certain relationship to each other. This pair will be followed by five more pairs of words. The student must select the pair that has a relationship similar to (analogous to) the original pair.

When working with analogies, it is often helpful to develop a sentence that states the relationship between the original pair of words. Then see if another pair can be substituted into the sentence. The sentence should be as specific as possible, using as precise a meaning as possible for each word. Keep in mind that the relationship is between the first word and the second word within the pair, not between a word from one pair and a word from the second pair.

Words often have more than one meaning, and all must be considered. For example, the word *fast* can suggest many things, including a description of speed or the act of going without food. If you were to see the word pair *fast : food*, you would need to determine which meaning was intended.

Fast has many meanings and can be any of several parts of speech. Other words are clearly nouns or verbs or other parts of speech. With analogies, parts of speech are as important as meanings and relationships. The correct answer will likely be a pair of words that not only have a similar relationship, but also represent the same parts of speech.

Sentence completions are questions that provide a statement with one or two blank spaces. The answers are words or sets of words that fit into the blanks. The questions check not only a student's understanding of the words, but also the ability to place the words correctly into a sentence, given the content and structure of the sentence.

If a sentence has two blanks, then the words must be substituted in the order they appear, the first word in the first blank, the second word in the second blank. Even if one of the words makes sense, do not assume it is the correct answer; *both* words must fit.

Sometimes one choice fits, but another fits even better. Try all answers before choosing one. Be sure the entire sentence makes sense. Watch for transitional words and phrases like *despite*, *even though*, and *however*. They signal that one part of the sentence is in contrast to another.

Critical reading questions provide you with passages to read and then several questions to answer based on the passage. Sometimes two passages will be given and the questions will draw on both. The passages range from 400 to about 850 words in length.

All the information you need to answer questions is contained within the passage. You will not need additional, outside information. Passages are generally drawn from existing materials. They may be narratives or arguments, or cover fields such as physical science, biological science, social studies, or humanities.

Read the entire passage. Make sure the question you answer is the one that is asked. Sometimes wrong answers are true statements, but they do not answer the question. Similarly, a correct answer may include a false statement; the question could be about what the author says, even if the author says something wrong. Key words will help you find correct answers.

Try to answer an entire block of questions at one time so that you do not have to reread the passage later. Read all answers. Some may be partly true, but one will be best. If a passage is especially difficult, skip it and return to it later.

College Entrance Exams

Mathematical section. The combined mathematical section consists of sixty questions presented in one fifteen-minute and two thirty-minute parts. Of these sixty questions, thirty-five are standard multiple choice questions that cover topics from arithmetic, algebra, and geometry, as well as logic, symbols and operations, and probability and counting. Another fifteen questions are quantitative comparisons. The remaining questions require students to produce their own answers rather than choose one from a selection already provided in the test.

Use the test booklet itself for scratch paper, rather than performing calculations in your head. Seeing the calculation on paper helps reinforce that an answer is correct. Having the calculations on paper also helps in the latter part of the test, when questions that were tried and skipped are retried. Remember too that you may now use a calculator; check in advance to determine which kinds you may bring with you.

Most concepts needed for the mathematical portion are reviewed in the SAT I information packet. They include odd and even numbers, integers, and prime numbers; percents, including those over 100 and less than 1; averages, including weighted averages; distance/rate/time problems; squares of integers and properties of signed numbers; and factoring. Key geometric concepts include parallel lines; relationships of angles; the Pythagorean Theorem and the relationship of sides of a triangle; formulas for area and perimeter of rectangles, triangles, and circles; and volume of rectangular solids.

Questions now also cover topics such as slope, median, and mode. Just as the verbal section has increased its emphasis on reasoning skills, so too has the mathematical section.

Directions for the mathematical section include a guide to symbols and key concepts, including area of a circle; the degree measure of circles, straight angles, and triangles; the area of a right triangle; and the Pythagorean Theorem. The figures that are included in questions are not always drawn to scale.

Most of the time, numerical answers will list values either from smallest to greatest or from greatest to smallest. In either case, answer (C) will generally be the middle value. Sometimes plugging a number into a problem is a faster way to approach a question than setting up an equation, solving it, and then finding an answer that matches. When using this approach, start with answer (C) if the numbers are arranged in order. Then if (C) is too high, work next with the two smaller values; if (C) is too low, work with the two greater values.

When preparing for the mathematical section, practice estimation skills. They can often help save time on the test, especially when answers are not close together. For example, suppose a question is to find 48% of

794. Note that 48% rounds to 50% while 794 rounds to 800. It is much faster to calculate 50% of 800, which equals 400. The answer should be fairly close to 400, and lower than 400, since the original numbers are lower than 50% and 800. Thus, answers over 400 can be quickly eliminated, as can answers that are much smaller than 400. If the choice of answers is 165.42, 360.64, 381.12, 404, and 536.84, then all but 360.64 and 381.12 can be eliminated fairly quickly.

Quantitative comparisons list two quantities, one in column A and one in column B. You must determine if either of the two quantities has a greater value, if the two are of equal value, or if there is insufficient information to compare the quantities.

Unlike other questions on the SAT I, quantitative comparisons have only four possible answers. While (E) is not considered wrong, it is treated as an omission. If you choose to use a guessing strategy toward the end of a test, realize that marking in (E) will have no impact on your score.

For many comparisons, you will have to calculate both quantities in order to answer the question. On other comparisons, though, other skills can help you out. Suppose the question compares $\sqrt{5} + 1$ with $\sqrt{6} + 1$. By subtracting 1 from both sides, you realize that you are comparing $\sqrt{5}$ and $\sqrt{6}$. Even at this point, you may forget how to compare them. However, you can compare $\sqrt{4}$ and $\sqrt{9}$, which equal 2 and 3 respectively. In making this comparison, you remind yourself that the square root of the larger number is greater than the square root of the smaller number, and with assurance choose the answer that $\sqrt{6} + 1$ is the greater quantity.

Your preparation should include practicing shortcuts that will help you narrow your choices. When you take the test, see if one answer jumps out at you as being correct; then see if you can quickly demonstrate to yourself that the choice is correct. If so, mark it and move on. As in the verbal section, if a question is difficult, but you are able to eliminate some answers, cross them out in the test booklet and move on. When you return to the question later, you will not have to start at the beginning.

The student-produced response questions do not provide answers. You must develop your own answer and enter it on a grid. Read the advance materials to learn how to enter answers to these questions.

Use figures effectively. Drawing your own often helps you when solving a geometry problem or a word problem. When using figures from the test booklet, realize that they are often not drawn to scale. This is especially important when you are measuring angles. Do not assume, for example, that because an angle is drawn as an acute angle (less than 90°), its measure is in fact acute; the real answer could be 90° or more.

SAT I verbal examples

In each part, the directions and the question marked with an asterisk (*) are from Educational Testing Service, which develops and administers the SAT I.

Analogies. Each question below consists of a related pair of words or phrases, followed by five pairs of words or phrases labeled (A) through (E). Select the lettered pair that best expresses a relationship similar to that expressed in the original pair.

1. DOG : PUPPY :: (A) poodle : terrier (B) horse : lamb (C) rooster : hen (D) cat : kitten (E) fawn : deer

The relationship is that the second word is the name given to a young version of the first. The words can be used in the sentence "A young *dog* is called a *puppy*." Poodle and terrier are types of dogs, but they do not bear an age relationship to each other. A horse is a mature animal and a lamb is a young animal; that choice may be tempting. But a lamb is a young sheep, not a horse. The relationship between rooster and hen is gender, not age. The relationship between fawn and deer is age, but the younger animal is listed first. The relationship between cat and kitten is also age. The statement "A young *cat* is called a *kitten*" is true; the relationship between this pair of words most parallels the original pair. (D) is correct.

*2. SHIELD : PROTECTION :: (A) car : insurance (B) gun : trigger (C) cane : support (D) helmet : head (E) bandage : infection

The relationship in the original pair is that a *shield* provides *protection*. Answers (D) and (E) may be tempting: a helmet protects the head and a bandage protects against infection. But *protects* is not the key word in the relationship, *provides* is. A cane provides support, the same relationship as exists between shield and protection. (C) is correct.

3. NOTES : MELODY :: (A) bricks : fireplace (B) stadium : baseball (C) chef : pastry (D) oven : bread (E) hose : fire fighter

When notes are assembled in a particular order, they form a melody. Answer (C) may be tempting because a chef makes pastry. But the chef assembles ingredients such as flour and sugar to form the pastry; the chef is not part of the final product. (A) is correct.

4. TENSION : ARGUMENT :: (A) war : peace (B) symphony : coda (C) story : conclusion (D) thunder : lightning (E) recklessness : accident

Choices (B) and (C) might be considered similar in that a coda comes at the end of a symphony and a conclusion comes at the end of a story, much like an argument can come toward the end of tension. However, more precisely, if tension is not brought under control, it results in an argument. Similarly, if recklessness is not brought under control, it results in an accident. This comparison is more precise; (E) is correct.

Sentence completions. Each sentence below has one or two blanks, each blank indicating that something has been omitted. Beneath the sentence are five words or sets of words labeled (A) through (E). Choose the word or set of words that, when inserted in the sentence, best fits the meaning of the sentence as a whole.

1. Even though she is not a football fan, Rita said she would go to the _____ with the others.
   (A) museum (B) restaurant (C) game (D) movies (E) store

The phrase *even though* suggests that Rita will do something she would not normally do. From the sentence, Rita does not like football. Unless (A), (D), and (E) were referring to a special exhibit on football, a movie with a football theme, or a store that sells football memorabilia, these choices do not make sense. (B) might make sense in that Rita might join others at a restaurant before or after football. However, football is most associated with *game*; Rita would go to the game with the others, even though she is not a fan of football. (C) is correct.

*2. To protest the _____ conditions on the trains, the members of the commuters' organization refused to surrender tickets to the conductors and thereby ensured that attention would be given to their legitimate _____.
   (A) intolerable..demands (B) uneventful.. participation (C) immaculate..complaints (D) unspeakable..satisfaction (E) unequaled.. victory

Choices (B) and (C) are not correct; commuters would not be likely to protest uneventful or immaculate conditions. (E) is also not correct; if they had already achieved their victory, then they would not be protesting to get attention. The first part of (A) and (D) both could work; commuters would protest either intolerable or unspeakable conditions. However, their protest would be aimed at getting them satisfaction, not at paying attention to satisfaction they already have. (D) is therefore not correct, but (A) is.

College Entrance Exams

3. Mr. Rodriguez recommended that all his American history students read the _____ book about the Battle of Antietam that describes the conflict in _____ detail.
(A) brief..painstaking (B) dull..exciting
(C) tedious..snappy (D) comprehensive.. considerable (E) tragic..humorous

The adjective that describes *detail* must support the adjective that describes *book*. For example, in answer (A), if the book is brief, then it would not have painstaking detail, which would add length. *Painstaking* does not support *brief*. The correct answer is (D).

Critical reading. The passages below are followed by questions based on their content; questions following a pair of related passages may also be based on the relationship between the paired passages. Answer the questions on the basis of what is <u>stated</u> or <u>implied</u> in the passages and in any introductory materials that may be provided.

NOTE: The actual passages may be longer than the examples provided.

It is a perennial puzzle why women apparently wrote hardly a word of the extraordinary literature of the Elizabethan time, when it seemed every man was capable of producing a song or a sonnet. I looked for the answer in Professor Trevelyan's *History of England*, where I read that "the daughter who refused to marry the gentleman of her parents' choice was liable to be locked up or beaten without any shock being inflicted on public opinion." Yet even so, Professor Trevelyan later concludes, "Shakespeare's women do not seem wanting in personality and character." Indeed, if women had no existence save in the fiction written by men, one would imagine them people of utmost importance, heroic and mean, splendid and sordid. But these are women in fiction. In fact, as Professor Trevelyan points out, real women were liable to be locked up.

A very strange composite female emerges when one reads the historians first, the poets afterward. In imaginative creations she is of the highest importance; in the historical record, she seems completely insignificant. She pervades poetry from cover to cover; she is all but absent from history. What one must do is to think poetically and prosaically at one and the same moment—imagine that she is the embodiment of all sorts of idealized virtues, and that she is Mrs. Martin, middle-aged, dressed in blue, wearing a black hat and brown shoes.

*1. The primary focus of the passage is on
(A) major literary heroines as viewed by men.
(B) Professor Trevelyan's historical analysis of England.
(C) the hard life endured by female poets in Shakespeare's time.
(D) the differences between Elizabethan women as presented in history and in fiction.
(E) the disparity between the respect accorded to female writers and that accorded to male writers.

There is no indication that the author or Professor Trevelyan are male; (A) refers to the *view* of literary heroines, the passage to the *creation* of literary heroines. Trevelyan's work is introduced to *support* a point; it is not the primary focus (B). Choices (C) and (E) imply that the lives or reputations of female writers were central to the article. But the author establishes that there are few female writers and does not focus on them. Throughout, the author notes that women in fiction were presented as important and idealized, while women of history seemed far less significant. The correct answer is (D).

2. Who is Mrs. Martin?
(A) A Shakespearean character
(B) A representative of a poet's ideal woman
(C) A representative of an historical woman
(D) The author of *History of England*
(E) The author of the passage

In the second paragraph, the author compares women of poetry and women of history. Choices (A), (D), and (E) are incorrect because there are no references to specific Shakespearean characters or to the gender of the author or Professor Trevelyan. According to the passage, women of fiction are "people of utmost importance . . . splendid and sordid," while women of history appeared to be "completely insignificant." Mrs. Martin is described as an ordinary person, not an idealized person. (C) is correct.

In Passage 1, the author presents his view of the early years of the silent film industry. In Passage 2, the author draws on her experience as a mime to generalize about her art. (A mime is a performer who, without speaking, entertains through gesture, facial expression, and movement.)

Passage 1
Talk to those people who first saw films when they were silent, and they will tell you the experience was magic. The silent film had extraordinary powers to draw members of an audience into the story, and an equally potent capacity to make their imaginations work. It required the

audience to become engaged—to supply voices and sound effects. The audience was the final, creative contributor to the process of making a film.

The finest films of the silent era depended on two elements that we can seldom provide today—a large and receptive audience and a well-orchestrated score. For the audience, the fusion of picture and live music added up to more than the sum of the respective parts.

The one word that sums up the attitude of the silent filmmakers is *enthusiasm*, conveyed most strongly before formulas took shape and when there was more room for experimentation. This enthusiastic uncertainty often resulted in such accidental discoveries as new camera or editing techniques. Some films experimented with players; the 1915 film *Regeneration*, for example, by using real gangsters and streetwalkers, provided startling local color. Other films, particularly those of Thomas Ince, provided tragic endings as often as films by other companies supplied happy ones.

Unfortunately, the vast majority of silent films survive today in inferior prints that no longer reflect the care that the original technicians put into them. The modern versions of silent films may appear jerky and flickery, but the vast picture palaces did not attract four to six thousand people a night by giving them eyestrain. A silent film depends on its visuals; as soon as you degrade those, you lose elements that go far beyond the image on the surface. The acting in silents was often very subtle, very restrained, despite legends to the contrary.

Passage 2
Mime opens up a new world to the beholder, but it does so insidiously, not by purposely injecting points of interest in the manner of a tour guide. Audiences are not unlike visitors to a foreign land who discover that the modes, manners, and thought of its inhabitants are not meaningless oddities, but are sensible in context.

I remember once when an audience seemed perplexed at what I was doing. At first, I tried to gain a more immediate response by using slight exaggerations. I soon realized that these actions had nothing to do with the audience's understanding of the character. What I had believed to be a failure of the audience to respond in the manner I expected was, in fact, only their concentration on what I was doing; they were enjoying a gradual awakening—a slow transfer-

ence of their understanding from their own time and place to one that appeared so unexpectedly before their eyes. This was evidenced by their growing response to succeeding numbers.

Mime is an elusive art, as its expression is entirely dependent on the ability of the performer to imagine a character and to re-create that character for each performance. As a mime, I am a physical medium, the instrument upon which the figures of my imagination play their dance of life. The individuals in my audience also have responsibilities—they must be alert collaborators. They cannot sit back, mindlessly complacent, and wait to have their emotions titillated by mesmeric musical sounds or visual rhythms or acrobatic feats, or by words that tell them what to think. Mime is an art that, paradoxically, appeals both to those who respond instinctively to entertainment and to those whose appreciation is more analytical and complex. Between these extremes lie those audiences conditioned to resist any collaboration with what is played before them; and these the mime must seduce despite themselves. There is only one way to attack those reluctant minds—take them unaware! They will be delighted at an unexpected pleasure.

*1. Both passages are primarily concerned with the subject of
(A) shocking special effects
(B) varied dramatic styles
(C) visual elements in dramatic performances
(D) audience resistance to theatrical performances
(E) nostalgia for earlier forms of entertainment

Notice that this question asks about both passages. Answers that apply somewhat to one passage but not the other, such as (E), are not correct. Answer (A) is also not correct; certainly *shocking* special effects is not relevant to the second passage.

At a surface level, one passage is about silent film, the other about mime. At the heart of both, their connection, is the importance of the visual element. Both forms are without music or spoken dialogue. Both passages touch upon dramatic effects (B), but as a side issue. The first passage does not discuss audience resistance (D), but if anything, audience support. Because it describes a subject that is central to both, (C) is correct.

*2. What additional information would reduce the apparent similarity between these two art forms?
(A) Silent film audiences were also accustomed to vaudeville and theatrical presentations.

(B) Silent film could show newsworthy events as well as dramatic entertainment.

(C) Dialogue in the form of captions was integrated into silent films.

(D) Theaters running silent films gave many musicians steady jobs.

(E) Individual characters created for silent films became famous in their own right.

Answers (A) and (D) do not address the art forms themselves, but rather side issues such as the audience's experiences. (B) does not point to a difference; mime artists are also capable of showing newsworthy events. (E) implies, incorrectly, that a mime artist cannot create a memorable character. Answer (C), however, points to a clear distinction. Neither form has spoken dialogue (a similarity); however, silent film can have written dialogue. Thus, by reducing a similarity between silent film and mime, (C) is correct.

SAT I mathematical examples

Standard multiple choice. In this section, solve each problem using any available space on the page for scratchwork. Then decide which is the best of the choices given and fill in the corresponding oval on the answer sheet.

NOTE: The directions will include a guide to key formulas and symbols; also, many questions include figures.

1. If $6x + 8y = 12$, then $3x + 4y =$
   (A) 3/4 (B) 4/3 (C) 6 (D) 14 (E) 24

First, note the relationship between $6x + 8y$ and $3x + 4y$. Factoring $6x + 8y$ leads to $2(3x + 4y)$. Also $12 = 2(6)$. Thus $2(3x + 4y) = 2(6)$. Divide both sides by 2 to find that $3x + 4y = 6$. (C) is correct.

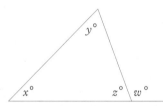

*2. In the figure above, $x + y = 110$. What is the value of $w + x + y + z$?
   (A) 220 (B) 235 (C) 250 (D) 290 (E) It cannot be determined from the information given.

In the directions, you will be reminded that the sum of the measures of the three angles of a triangle is 180 and that the measure of a straight angle is 180. The three angles of this triangle are x, y, and z; thus $x + y + z = 180$. We are told that $x + y = 110$, therefore, $110 + z = 180$ and $z = 180 - 110 = 70$. Also, z and w form a straight angle: $z + w = 180$. Substitute 70 for z and solve $70 + w = 180$ or $w = 180 - 70 = 110$. Now you have all the pieces. Substitute 110 for w, 110 for $x + y$, and 70 for z to find that $w + x + y + z = 110 + 110 + 70 = 290$. (D) is correct.

3. If $3a = 4b = 6c$, what is $8a + 8c$ in terms of b?
   (A) 10b (B) 12b (C) 14b (D) 16b (E) 18b

Estimating can help you eliminate some answers. If $3a = 4b$, then $6a = 8b$. Thus, $6a + 6c = 8b + 4b = 12b$. This is too little, so both (A) and (B) can be cut from the choices. Note that $3a = 6c = 2(3c)$; in turn, $8a = 2(8c) = 16c$. Thus, $8a + 8c = 16c + 8c = 24c$. Now the problem has become to state $24c$ in terms of b. Note that $24c = 4(6c)$; since $4b = 6c$, we have $24c = 4(6c) = 4(4b) = 16b$. Thus, (D) is correct. There are several other ways to solve this problem.

Quantitative comparison. The next two problems consist of two quantities, one in column A and one in column B. You are to compare the two quantities and on the answer sheet fill in oval

(A) if the quantity in column A is greater;
(B) if the quantity in column B is greater;
(C) if the two quantities are equal;
(D) if the relationship cannot be determined from the information given.

	Column A	Column B
1.	$(374 + 62)^2$	$(374 - 62)^2$

You could take the time to add within the parenthesis and square the sum, but that would take considerable time. Instead note that $(374 + 62)$ and $(374 - 62)$ are both positive and that $(374 + 62)$ is greater than $(374 - 62)$. If two positive numbers are squared, the square of the larger number will be greater than the square of the smaller number. Thus, the quantity in column A is greater and (A) is correct.

*2.	$x + x$	$x - x$

At first glance, it is tempting to say that the quantity in column A is greater. But you would be falling into a trap. First, simplify both expressions. Note that $x + x = 2x$ while $x - x = 0$. Is $2x$ always greater than 0? Not if x is zero, in which case $2x = 0$, or if x is a negative number, in which case $2x$ is negative. Therefore, unless you know the exact value of x or at least know if x is positive, negative, or zero, there is not enough information and (D) is correct.

ACT. The ACT tests somewhat different skills than the SAT I. Unlike the SAT I, the ACT English section includes material covering usage and mechanics. The mathematics section relies more on geometry and trigonometry skills. The section on science reasoning does not have a counterpart in the SAT I.

Another key difference is that there is no penalty for a wrong answer on the ACT, while there is a fractional deduction on the SAT I. Thus, while you might hesitate to answer an SAT I question if you cannot eliminate any choices, you should always answer an ACT question, since doing so can never hurt your score.

English. In the English section of the ACT, seventy-five questions are presented to test skills in punctuation, grammar, and sentence structure (which make up the subsection on usage and mechanics) and on strategy, organization, and style (which make up the subsection on rhetorical skills).

You will read a passage consisting of several paragraphs. Several words and phrases in each passage will be underlined. The usage and mechanics section asks about the specific underlined portions. Four choices are given. Three of the choices suggest changes to be made; the other choice is to accept the passage as is with no change. While you will not be expected to identify specific rules of grammar and punctuation, you will be expected to apply them.

The rhetorical skills section asks about broader issues. These issues might include whether quotation marks have been used effectively throughout the passage, how the paragraphs could be better ordered to provide a more logical structure, who the intended audience is, and how the author could make an individual point stronger.

Mathematics. The sixty math questions cover topics from pre-algebra, elementary and intermediate algebra, coordinate and plane geometry, and trigonometry. Use the ACT information packets and any guidebooks to identify individual topics that will be covered, such as fractions, inequalities, literal expressions, percent, conics, and problem solving. Then take practice tests to build skills and identify areas of weakness. When you see which questions are difficult for you, talk with your counselor or math teacher about them. Identify specific topics that you need to review. You may even borrow texts from earlier courses in order to review specific topics and solve related exercises.

Wrong answers are provided for a reason. They reflect common errors made when solving a problem. For example, if the question asks the value of $4 + 6 \div 2$, the correct answer is 7 (divide before you add, so $(4 + [6 \div 2] = 4 + 3 = 7)$; however, 5 is likely to be given, in case students add $4 + 6$ before dividing by 2. An answer cannot just appear correct; solve the problem to ensure you have selected the correct answer.

Reading. The reading section of the ACT includes four passages, each followed by ten questions. The passages cover different types of reading that college students are likely to encounter, and are drawn from four broad areas: fiction, humanities, social sciences, and natural sciences. Questions might ask about the broad themes of a passage, specific factual content, implied arguments and perspectives that are not directly stated, meanings of words and phrases, and style. There are forty questions to complete in thirty-five minutes. This is less than one minute per question; therefore balance a close, careful reading with the need to keep pace.

For each passage, first read the questions that will be asked; this helps focus your reading. Do not take the time at this point to read the answers. Next, read the passage. Underline key phrases and ideas that pertain to the questions. Then go back to the questions and answer each. Often it is helpful to eliminate wrong answers as a way to close in on the correct one; be sure that you read all possible answers.

Science reasoning. The science reasoning section of the ACT is perhaps what distinguishes it most from the SAT I. While you are not asked to show specific knowledge of biology, chemistry, earth science, and physics, you do need to demonstrate knowledge and understanding of the scientific process.

This section presents several passages, followed by questions about the passages, which fall into three broad categories: data representation, research summaries, and conflicting viewpoints. In the first category, information is presented in tables and graphs. Questions center around understanding and interpreting the data and drawing conclusions.

In the second area, descriptions of related experiments are presented. Questions involve comparing and contrasting the experiments and summarizing the information presented. These questions complement the data representation section, since not all experiments and data can be presented easily in tables and graphs.

In the third area, general questions are asked, such as *Is there life on other planets?* Two different scientific perspectives about the question follow. Students are asked about various assumptions in each perspective, as well as conclusions that can be drawn. Some questions are about the argument itself, evaluating the evidence needed to justify the different conclusions that the authors reach, and whether the assumptions that have been made are valid.

As with the reading section, it is often helpful to read the questions first. Next, read the passages or evaluate the data, keeping the questions in mind. Then answer the questions. By reading the questions first, you can focus on the most important infomation.

College Entrance Exams

ACT examples

The following questions and directions are similar to those that appear on the ACT.

English. In the following passage, words and phrases are underlined and numbered. Below the passage, choices are listed for each underlined part. Select the choice that best expresses the ideas, uses standard written English, or is consistent with the style or mood of the entire passage. Select NO CHANGE if you think the original version is the best.

Next, you are presented with a question about a section of the passage as a whole. For this question, select the best choice.

Businesses use the <u>Earth's</u> natural resources
                          1
to produce their goods and services. They also generate pollution, often releasing chemicals and waste into the air, water, and ground. Who pays clean-up costs when accidents such as oil spills occur is subject <u>to much debate?</u>
                                    2

Society's concern with environmental issues has led businesses to pay more attention to their impact on the environment. In recent years, many firms have changed the way they package their products, switching to recycled and recyclable materials and reducing overall costs. ⬚3⬚

1. (A) NO CHANGE
   (B) Earths'
   (C) earth's
   (D) earths'

This question covers rules of capitalization and punctuation. Note that the word *the* precedes *Earth's*; therefore, the name of the planet is not being used, so *earth* is not capitalized. Furthermore, *earth* is singular, not plural; thus, the apostrophe should precede the letter *s*. (C) is the answer.

2. (A) NO CHANGE
   (B) too much debate.
   (C) to too much debate?
   (D) to much debate.

This sentence begins as if it is a question, but it is a statement. Therefore (A) and (C) are incorrect. A topic can be *subject to much debate* or it can be *subject to too much debate*, but it can not be *subject too much debate*. (B) is incorrect; (D) is the answer.

3. If the author wanted to expand the information

about how businesses are paying more attention to their impact on the environment, what addition would be most relevant to the passage?

(A) A list of companies that are changing their packaging.
(B) A brief description of the way communities are struggling to deal with landfill shortages due to excessive packaging.
(C) A description of how one music publisher has reduced the amount of packaging for its compact disks.
(D) A bibliography of books about the environment.

(B) and (D) are not directly relevant; they deal with environmental issues but not with the changes businesses are making. (A) is too general, whereas (C) provides a specific example. (C) is the answer.

Mathematics. Solve each of the following problems. Choose the correct answer from the available choices.

1. What is the value of b if $5a^2b = -135$ and $a = -3$?
   (A) -9
   (B) -3
   (C) 3
   (D) 9

First substitute -3 for a. Thus $5(-3)^2b = -135$. This leads to $5 \cdot 9 \cdot b = -135$ and $45b = -135$. Divide -135 by 45 to find that (B) is the correct answer. Follow the order of operations (parentheses, exponents, multiplication and division, addition and subtraction) and take care with negative signs.

2. If the area of a circle is 16π, what is the diameter?
   (A) ±4
   (B) 4
   (C) 8
   (D) 16

$A = \pi r^2$ is the area of a circle where r is the radius. Thus, $16\pi = \pi r^2$, leading to $16 = r^2$. While both 4^2 and $(-4)^2$ equal 16, a radius is a physical length and must be positive. Thus, $r = 4$. Now go back to the question; it asks for the diameter, not the radius. The diameter is twice the radius, or 8. (C) is the answer.

3. Cal scored 84, 96, and 88 on his first three tests. If he wants to end the term with an average of 91, what score must he receive on the remaining test?
   (A) 86
   (B) 91
   (C) 93
   (D) 96

Set up an equation for averages. The average score is the sum of his scores divided by the number of scores. Let s represent the fourth test score. The sum of the scores is $84 + 96 + 88 + s$. The number of scores is 4, the number of tests. Thus, $91 = (84 + 96 + 88 + s) \div 4$. Multiply both sides by 4; $4 \times 91 = 84 + 96 + 88 + s$ or $364 = 268 + s$. Subtract 268 from both sides to find that $96 = s$. Thus, (D) is the answer.

Reading. Read this passage. Then choose the best answer to each of the questions that follows the passage. You may reread the passage as often as you think is necessary.

Worker dissatisfaction and increased safety hazards were a byproduct of the Industrial Revolution. Unions, organizations of employees that protect the interests of their members, formed as a result. Early unions represented craftsmen such as shoemakers. Local craft unions formed national organizations like the United Cigarmakers. In 1869, the Knights of Labor was formed; it eventually had 700,000 members. But violence, like the Haymarket Riot in Chicago, led to its decline and dissolution.

The American Federation of Labor (AFL) took over the leadership. It focused on wages, work conditions, and hours, using collective bargaining, supporting strikes when necessary. The Congress of Industrial Organizations (CIO) represented unskilled industrial workers, previously overlooked. Unions once represented over 30 percent of workers, today fewer than 15 percent.

1. What can the reader conclude from this passage about the Knights of Labor?
   (A) It was first organized before the Industrial Revolution.
   (B) The United Cigarmakers were part of the Knights of Labor.
   (C) The Knights of Labor disbanded.
   (D) It represented both skilled and unskilled workers.

The last sentence of the first paragraph states that violence led to the Knights of Labor's *decline* and *dissolution*. Thus, it was dissolved, or disbanded. (C) is the answer.

2. According to the passage, one of the focal points for the AFL was
   (A) company profitability.
   (B) how much workers earned.
   (C) job security.
   (D) productivity.

The second sentence of the second paragraph states that the AFL *focused on wages, work conditions, and hours*. None of these relate directly to profitability and productivity. Work conditions may or may not include job security, but wages clearly refer to what workers earn. Therefore, (B) is the answer.

Science reasoning. Read this passage. Then choose the best answer to each of the questions that follows the passage. You may reread the passage as often as you think is necessary.

A study was conducted to investigate the power provided by the flow of electric current through a wire. The following table summarizes the results.

Experiment	Current (amps)	Battery (volts)	Power
1	1	9	9
2	2	9	18
3	2	6	12
4	0.5	6	3
5	4	6	24
6	1	12	12
7	4	12	48
8	2	12	24

1. According to this table, how much current is needed for a 12-volt battery to deliver 24 units of power?
   (A) 0.5 amps
   (B) 2 amps
   (C) 4 amps
   (D) Cannot be determined

Find the experiment that uses 12 volts to produce 24 units of power. Look at experiment 8, in which 2 amps are required. (B) is the answer.

2. If you were studying the relationship between battery and power, which experiment would be a control for experiment 5?
   (A) Experiment 2
   (B) Experiment 3
   (C) Experiment 6
   (D) Experiment 7

Note that 4 amps are used in experiment 5, producing 24 units of power with a 6-volt battery. In only one other experiment are 4 amps used, allowing you to study how a change in the battery affects power: experiment 7. (D) is the answer.

SAT II: Subject Tests. As of publication, these Subject Tests are offered: two in English (writing and literature), eleven in foreign languages (Chinese with listening, French with and without listening, German with and without listening, Modern Hebrew, Italian, Japanese with listening, Latin, and Spanish with and without listening), two in history and social studies (American history/social studies and world history), two in mathematics (Level I and Level IIC with calculator), and three in sciences (biology, chemistry, and physics).

You can take the Subject Tests the same day as the SAT I, or you can take them separately. Admission requirements or personal choice determine which you take. The tests assess content knowledge in specific disciplines. They provide a means of comparing students in subject areas, thus getting past texts, grades, and teaching styles.

The information packet provides details regarding content coverage for each of the tests. For example, the American history and social studies test asks varying numbers of questions on political history, economic history, social history, intellectual and cultural history, and foreign policy. Furthermore, the questions are categorized by historic period: one-fifth of the questions covers pre-Columbian history to 1789, another two-fifths cover from 1790 to 1898, while the remainder covers 1899 to the present.

Similarly, the biology test can be broken down by topics and skills. The topics include cellular and molecular biology, ecology, classical genetics, organismal structure and function, and evolution and diversity, while the skills include knowledge of fundamental concepts, application, and interpretation.

Not all tests are offered every time. For example, the Modern Hebrew test is offered only in June. Check when individual tests are offered. Also be aware of the requirements for admission; some colleges require the tests be taken at certain times.

Other than the essay component of the writing test, the questions are multiple choice. However, in addition to figures, students may encounter maps, posters, drawings, tables, and other visual information during the test.

In addition, not all of the questions are straightforward multiple choice. Some are multiple-multiple choice: the question is followed by a set of answers in which none, some, or all may be correct. A second set of answers follows that lists various combinations of the first group as being correct.

One of the math tests allows the use of calculators. It is possible that, over time, other tests covering quantitative topics will allow them as well. Not all calculators are allowed; it is important to confirm which calculators may be used in a given test. The registration materials provide information about the types of calculators that may be used as well as those that are not permitted.

Other tests have distinctive features. Know these features and directions in advance. For example, one type of question in the chemistry test provides an assertion and a reason: something happens *because of* something else. The first part of the question asks you whether the assertion (statement I) is true or false. The second part asks you whether the reason (statement II) is true or false. The third part then asks whether statement II correctly explains statement I. (For example, 2 + 2 = 4 because Paris is the capital of France; both the assertion 2 + 2 = 4 and the reason *Paris is the capital of France* are true, but the reason is not a correct explanation of the assertion.)

Another type of question that appears in both chemistry and physics is similar to a matching question; it lists a group of five choices—for example, properties in physical science. The group is followed by questions asking which of the choices has a particular characteristic. The group of choices may be a group of graphs or other figures.

The foreign language listening tests offer a unique challenge. Students listen to something being said and then answer a question related to what they hear. They might only hear the passage once or twice, and from that must answer the question. The spoken words will not appear in print anywhere; students will not be able to return to the question in the usual way, as they can in other tests.

In the coming years, the Subject Tests, previously known as the Achievement Tests, will continue to undergo changes. The writing test will take on more prominence and be offered more frequently. The essay component will be evaluated by two independent graders. Ongoing changes will be made in order to reflect changes in content and teaching methods. You should be sure when preparing for the Subject Tests that you work from the most current information available.

TOEFL. The Test of English as a Foreign Language (TOEFL) contains three major sections: listening; structure and written expression; and reading comprehension.

The listening section has three parts. In one, students hear brief conversations and then answer questions. In another, they hear longer conversations; in the third part, they hear several talks. The section on structure and written expression includes sentence completions and other questions in which students identify words or phrases that need correction. The reading comprehension section provides passages, then asks questions about the passages.

SAT II: Subject Test examples

These questions, representative of the Subject Tests, are from Educational Testing Service, which administers the SAT I and the SAT II.

Writing. If there is an error, select the one underlined part that must be changed in order to make the sentence correct. The sentence may be correct.

1. It is startling <u>to realize</u> that in this rich country

      A

thousands of people live out <u>their life</u> <u>without ever</u>

                B   C

<u>having</u> <u>enough to eat</u>. <u>No error</u>

   D   E

(A) to realize

(B) their life

(C) without ever having

(D) enough to eat

(E) No error

Their is a plural pronoun, but it is followed by the singular noun *life*. These are not in agreement. The part should read *their lives*. (B) is the answer.

The composition test asks questions about tenses, agreement, and parallelism; logical expression of ideas; diction and clarity; and conventions of writing such as idioms, fragments, and double negatives.

Literature. This test provides several passages from both American and English literature; the selections are divided fairly evenly across three time periods: Renaissance and seventeenth century; eighteenth and nineteenth centuries; and twentieth century. They are also divided evenly between poetry and prose, occasionally from other sources. Students read a passage and then answer questions about it, often drawing on the language of critical analysis.

American history and social studies. The question below is followed by five suggested answers. Select the one that is best.

1. All of the following statements about the Puritans in seventeenth-century New England are true EXCEPT:

(A) They were a highly religious people who believed in predestination.

(B) They were tolerant of other religions and encouraged religious diversity.

(C) They preferred to be governed by local rather than by distant government authorities.

(D) They were primarily farmers, although some of them enjoyed considerable commercial success.

(E) They used slaves primarily as household servants rather than as farm laborers.

Note that the structure of this question is different from others. Four of the choices provide correct information. The correct answer states something that is *not* true. The question relies on specific, not general, knowledge. Still, there are clues that can help. For example, the question is set in seventeenth-century New England. The Industrial Revolution had not yet occurred, so most societies were still farming societies; (D) is not likely to be the correct answer. While highly religious people can be tolerant of other religions, answers (A) and (B) seem to be somewhat in contrast to each other. One of them is likely to be correct. The Puritans were *not* tolerant of other religions; the information in (B) is incorrect, making it an exception and therefore the correct answer.

World history. About 45 percent of this test covers European history and culture; the remainder covers other parts of the globe. Some questions are factual, others are interpretive and analytical. Many questions include visual materials.

Each question is followed by five suggested answers or completions. Select the one that is best.

1. How did the Norman Conquest most affect the development of the English language?

(A) Words lost inflectional endings.

(B) Syntax changed.

(C) Many Latin words were borrowed.

(D) Many French words were borrowed.

(E) Many Norse words were borrowed.

While this question is interpretive, it helps to understand the reference to the Norman Conquest. It is the invasion of England by William of Normandy, leading to the Battle of Hastings in 1066, which established the British monarchy that has continued to this day. While the Normans' roots were originally Scandinavian (Northmen or Norsemen), they had settled in France; the invasion was from French Normandy. The Latin impact would have been a thousand years earlier when the Romans invaded Britain. (D) is correct.

2. "The princes act therefore as ministers of God and as His lieutenants on earth. It is by His ministers that He exercises His sway. . . . For such a reason the royal throne is not the throne of man, but of God Himself. . ."

   The author of this passage is justifying which of the following political doctrines?

(A) Caesaropapism

(B) Popular sovereignty

(C) Christian democracy

College Entrance Exams

(D) Divine right of kings
(E) Theocracy

Even if you are not sure of the distinctions between these doctrines, there are clues that can help you answer this question. In the passage, God is central, the people are not mentioned. Therefore, both (B) and (C) can seemingly be eliminated; the passage seems to run counter to *popular* and *democracy*. The royal throne suggests a king and the passage refers to the relation between God and royalty. (D) emerges as the answer.

Mathematics. For each of the following problems, decide which is the *best* of the choices given.

1. The positive difference between the mean and the median of the numbers 27, 27, 29, 32, and 35 is
   (A) 0 (B) 1 (C) 2 (D) 3 (E) 8

This is a Level I question. Answering it depends on understanding *mean* and *median*, which are both ways to calculate an average. Again, specific content knowledge is necessary. The mean is found by adding the numbers, then dividing by the amount of numbers (5). Thus, the mean is $(27 + 27 + 29 + 32 + 35)/5 = 150/5 = 30$. The median is the number such that half the numbers have greater value and half have lesser value. There are five numbers arranged in ascending order. The median is 29: two numbers are lower than 29 and two numbers are higher. Now compare the mean 30 and the median 29. The positive difference (or the absolute value difference) is 1 and (B) is the answer.

2. If $f(x) = x^2 - x^3$, then $f(-1) =$
   (A) 2 (B) 1 (C) 0 (D) -1 (E) -2

This Level II question uses function notation. Substitute (-1) for x, then solve. Here, $f(-1) = (-1)^2 - (-1)^3 = 1 - (-1) = 2$. (A) is the answer.

Biology. The following question is followed by five suggested answers. Select the one that is best.

1. True statements about the development of the frog and mouse embryos include which of the following?
   I. Both the frog and the mouse embryos develop in an aqueous environment.
   II. Both the frog and the mouse embryos depend on a large supply of yolk to sustain the developing embryo.
   III. Both the frog and the mouse embryos develop a 4-chambered heart.
   (A) I only (B) III only (C) I and II only
   (D) II and III only (E) I, II, and III

After reading the question, read answers I, II, and III. Determine which are true. Then look for the combination in answers (A) through (E). Sometimes you can find the answer by elimination. Suppose you know II and III are false, but you don't know if I is true or false. Because II is false, you eliminate answers (C), (D), and (E). Because III is false, you eliminate (B), (D), and (E). Therefore only (A) is left; it is the answer.

Physics. Over a third of the physics test covers mechanics; other major portions cover electricity and magnetism, as well as waves. Still other questions cover heat, kinetic theory, thermodynamics, modern physics, and miscellaneous skills such as laboratory and measurement. Students should have an algebra and trigonometry background. Metric units are used.

The set of lettered choices below refers to the numbered questions immediately following it. Select the one lettered choice that best answers each question. A choice may be used either once, more than once, or not at all.

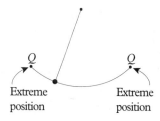

Extreme position   Extreme position

A small sphere attached to the end of a string swings as a simple pendulum. The sphere moves along the arc shown above. Consider the following properties of the sphere.
   (A) Acceleration
   (B) Kinetic energy
   (C) Mass
   (D) Potential energy
   (E) Velocity

1. Which property remains constant throughout the motion of the sphere?
2. Which property goes to zero and changes direction at each extreme position Q?

Questions 1 and 2 both work with the same figure, situation, and choice of answers. Answers can be used more than once; do not assume you can eliminate an answer. For question 1, the sphere itself is constant as it moves back and forth. Answers (A), (B), (D), and (E) relate to the movement, while (C) relates to the sphere. (C) is the answer to question 1. A key phrase in question 2 is *changes direction*. Velocity has speed and direction. (E) is the answer to question 2.

Thinking About College

- Preparing for college
- College basics
- Selecting a college
- Getting into college
- College costs
- Financial aid
- Living arrangements

Thinking About College

Whether you realize it or not, from the time you enter high school, you are setting a course for yourself that opens or closes doors of opportunity. As a high school student, you may receive much advice from parents, teachers, counselors, friends, and others. You also have your own ideas regarding the present and the future. How you respond to these influences will shape your plans, hopes, and dreams, at least for the immediate future.

During these high school years, students assume a greater responsibility for their own future than ever before. Some students realize this only in hindsight; others use this realization to prepare in ways that open doors of opportunity.

If you are thinking about college as a way to prepare for the future, you need information and lots of it. This chapter provides you with basic information to help you prepare for college as well as to acquaint you with additional resources. Knowing the facts is the best preparation of all.

Preparing for college

Education beyond high school is no longer a luxury chosen only for love of learning or a choice related only to future career plans. For an increasing number of careers, it is a basic necessity. As a result, a growing number of high school students are including college in their future plans.

However, a lack of information or preparation can result in incorrect assumptions or decisions. For example, many students rule out possibilities based on finances; they have not explored the many forms of financial aid and scholarship. Finances should never limit a student's initial exploration of colleges; without all the facts, however, they could.

There are no guarantees in college admission. For example, many schools have more qualified applicants than they can accept. Yet you can control most of the factors colleges value and place high on their list of admissions criteria. These factors include grades, course selection, work, extracurricular activities, life experiences, and standardized test scores.

The importance of class rank

Colleges concerned with class rank can look at a student's rank, relative to the entire class, in one of three ways:

1. Specific rank (such as first in the class)
2. Specific percentile
3. Broad percentile (such as the top fifth or the top half)

A student who graduates fortieth in a class of three hundred students can be ranked in the following ways:

1. A specific rank of 40th
2. A specific percentile of 13th percentile (The specific percentile can be found by dividing 300 by 40.)
3. A broad percentile of top fifth

Grades.

High school grades are an important factor in college admissions. They reflect your knowledge, work ethic, and motivation, and provide a way to compare you with others. They are the basis of *class rank*, a selection factor for many colleges.

Overall grade point average (GPA) is not all that counts. Some colleges recalculate GPA excluding physical education or certain electives. Some focus most on core courses like English, math, science, and history. Some look especially at courses related to the major you intend to pursue. Most look at grades as an indicator of future achievement.

A high GPA broadens the number of colleges you will be eligible to attend; many colleges favor students whose GPA satisfies certain levels. A high GPA also increases possibilities for financial assistance, especially scholarships and grants.

Courses.

In addition to grades, the courses you have taken are an important factor in college admissions. Like your grades, your coursework indicates much about your knowledge, self-discipline, motivation, and willingness to take on challenges. Courses also provide a basis of comparison between you and other students applying to the same college.

Admissions personnel often know a lot about your school and the difficulty level of its various courses. This helps account for those cases in which a student with a lower GPA but more challenging courses is admitted rather than a student with a higher GPA but less challenging courses. Colleges also review course selection in relation to a student's intended major.

The importance of courses does not suggest that students should get in over their heads academically. However, students should be willing to accept reasonable challenges; those who do will usually be rewarded in the college admissions process. Students gain other practical rewards as well. For example, students who take Advanced Placement courses and the AP test might earn college credits. Other course selections may result in some form of advanced standing or a waiver of placement tests at selected colleges. For some colleges, the completion of either very specific courses or a certain number of courses in a specific area, such as foreign language, is a requirement for admission. Working closely with your guidance counselor and carefully researching the requirements of colleges that interest you will help you select appropriate courses during high school.

Employment.

Colleges recognize that students work for a variety of reasons, and not always by choice. They also recognize that students who work are often unable to participate in the extracurricular activities that many colleges look for in their search for well-rounded students.

Students can turn work into an admissions asset. Maintaining good grades in challenging courses while participating in extracurricular activities *and* working speaks for itself. But in many cases, accomplishing all of this is not pragmatic; for example, work schedules often conflict with activities such as athletics.

If you plan to go to college and work, either by choice or necessity, you must first set clear priorities. Your first priority should be to earn good grades in the most challenging courses you can manage. Explain this priority to your employer from the start; try to establish a schedule each of you can handle. Many employers will be very supportive; if not, consider finding another job. Whenever possible, find a job related to your academic, career, or other interests. For example, if you are interested in journalism, you might get a job selling advertising for the community newspaper. Note such relationships, without exaggerating them, on your college applications and during

High school student working at a hospital

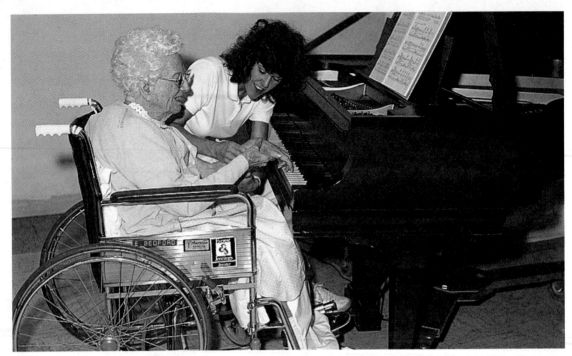

Community activities can enhance college opportunities.

any interviews you have. Also point out any promotions or increased responsibilities you have earned. Establish a relationship with your employer that can lead to an excellent recommendation. If your work has prevented you from participating in other activities, explain in positive terms your reasons for working, whatever they are, when you apply to college.

Extracurricular activities. Activities

in which students participate outside of the classroom are *extracurricular activities*. They include athletics and cheerleading, student government, plays, the school newspaper, service organizations, and clubs like the debate team, Future Teachers, and foreign language clubs, among others. Extracurricular activities enrich your life and enhance your enjoyment of school. The extent to which they influence admissions decisions varies from college to college; selective colleges are more likely to factor them in.

Students often question why such activities are important to admissions decisions. One reason is that they provide another way to compare applicants. More important, colleges often seek well-rounded students with a variety of interests. Colleges also look for clues as to how students will fit into the campus environment and bring diversity or individuality to a campus. Extracurricular activities can indicate motivation, leadership, and commitment. The variety of activities may not be as important as the sustained commitment to specific ones. Colleges need individuals willing to give

as well as receive; they look for patterns that will reflect well on them after graduation.

Not all extracurricular activities are school-based. Colleges value involvement in community, youth, religious, and political organizations. Volunteer service in the community is viewed positively, as is the pursuit of talents such as art or music. Involvement in extracurricular activities can help balance or overtake a weakness in your academic profile, enabling a college to give you the benefit of the doubt. You cannot replace good grades and challenging courses; however, participation in extracurricular activities can help smooth over rough spots in your application.

Life experiences. Many students have

unique personal experiences that are important factors in college admissions. The list of such experiences is diverse; each college will view them differently. Examples include travel and living overseas; skills in multiple languages; special recognitions, honors or awards; unique educational opportunities; publications; and amateur or professional careers. Other experiences that may be important for college admissions officers to know about include special challenges, such as serious illness or the loss of a family member.

Special people or events that have influenced you or shaped your values, beliefs, or ideas in a significant way may also be important to communicate. Special challenges may emphasize the significance of an outstanding record or explain, as opposed to excuse, certain problems or weaknesses in your record. For example, a childhood ailment, from which you no longer suffer, may have slowed you down academically in elementary school. Your high school record would indicate your performance in high school only, not the efforts that it may have taken to get caught up with your classmates after combatting this problem.

Perhaps more than any other factor that influences college admissions, life experiences emphasize what makes a student unique. Colleges that require essays frequently use topics related to life experience in order to weigh this factor fully. Students should not exaggerate their experiences. But if experiences are relevant to an application, they should be brought forward so that colleges can include them in the admissions decision.

Entrance exams. Entrance exam scores are a key factor for many colleges. For these colleges, test scores help fill in a student's profile. For example, students who have a secure B average in challenging courses and a strong commitment to extracurricular activities benefit from strong test scores. However, unusually low scores might point to weaknesses not immediately apparent on the high school record. Such scores may lead the college to examine factors such as course selection more closely.

Some schools, realizing that test scores are not always valid indicators of future performance, rely on other aspects of a student's record, particularly grades and coursework. (The chapter "College Entrance Exams" explains these issues in greater detail.)

College basics

One of the first steps you should take in thinking about college is to understand some basics about the structure of colleges as well as their differences.

Types of colleges. Throughout this chapter, the word *college* is used to mean four-year colleges, universities, and two-year colleges. A *college* usually refers to a school of higher learning that offers four-year undergraduate degree programs. A *university* is made up of one or more colleges as well as numerous graduate degree programs. For example, Harvard University combines two undergraduate colleges, Harvard and Radcliffe, with several graduate schools including law, medical, business, divinity, and government. Two-year colleges are usually referred to as *community colleges* or *junior colleges*. They offer two-year transfer and career programs; their course offerings are influenced by the needs of the local community as well as their states' four-year colleges.

Colleges can be categorized as *public* or *private*. Public colleges are supported by government, usually at the state level, while private colleges are funded primarily from other sources. Given the funding support they receive, public colleges tend to be less expensive to attend than private colleges; furthermore, a student residing in the state that supports the college usually pays less than an out-of-state student. For example, at the University of Iowa and at Iowa State University, students who are from out of state pay over $2,000 more per year in tuition than do Iowa residents.

Colleges differ in their setting. Some, like Wayne State University in Detroit and Miami-Dade Community College, are urban colleges located right in the city. Others, like Williams College in Massachusetts and Oberlin College in Ohio, have rural campuses located in small towns. Still others have suburban campuses set in large towns and small cities; many community colleges fit this description, as do colleges like the University of Michigan and Stanford University.

Colleges vary considerably by size. Many have enrollments of well below five hundred students. For example, Sterling College in Vermont enrolls fewer than a hundred full-time students. Others have tens of thousands of students at a single campus, for example, the Columbus campus of Ohio State University, with over thirty thousand full-time students and thousands more part-time students.

Many colleges have multiple campuses or are part of an interlocking network of colleges. For example, there are numerous campuses of the University of Texas. The oldest and largest one is in Austin, with other campuses in Arlington, Dallas, El Paso, and San Antonio, among others; each of these enrolls thousands of students.

Virtually all combinations of size and setting exist throughout the United States. For example, Montana

State University is a large university with over eight thousand full-time students, but a rural setting. Agnes Scott College is a small college with about six hundred full- and part-time students, located a few miles from downtown Atlanta. The varying combinations apply to two-year colleges as well as four-year colleges.

Some states have a state college system with campuses ranging from selected flagship institutions to other four-year universities and colleges as well as numerous community colleges. There are certain standard rules and regulations governing these campuses, though admission and transfer requirements may vary. Programs offered on one campus may or may not be offered on another campus within the system. Community college programs are designed to feed into the four-year colleges. California, New York, and Maryland are examples of states with such a network.

There are various organizations that *accredit* colleges, ensuring that the colleges meet selected standards determined by the accrediting board. When selecting colleges, be sure that those you choose meet state requirements and are fully accredited.

Types of degrees and majors.

At most colleges, students are awarded a *degree* after completing a four-year program of study. The most common undergraduate degrees are B.A. (bachelor of arts) and B.S. (bachelor of science) degrees. At community colleges, students who earn a degree complete a two-year program of study leading to an associate degree. The length of time needed to earn a degree varies, based on how many courses a student takes each term; the four-year and two-year time frames assume students attend full time.

Choosing a major field of study is one of the most important decisions students make. There are certain course combinations all students must take regardless of major, often referred to as *distribution* or *general education requirements*. Students also must take numerous courses directly related to their major. Within specific majors, students might specialize further. For example, depending on the course offerings at a particular college, students might major in biology, botany (a field within biology), or plant genetics (a field within botany).

Not all colleges offer all fields of study. Nor is the quality of each field uniform within a college. For example, two colleges may offer the same courses, but one might be much stronger in biology and economics, while the other is stronger in sociology and physics. Sometimes a college's strengths are influenced by the surrounding community. For example, many colleges in Washington, D.C., tend to have strong political science, international studies, and pre-law programs. Students interested in film or broadcasting should include New York City and Los Angeles in their search for a college. Large colleges in the midwest have strong agriculture programs; colleges in coastal settings are more likely to have strong marine biology programs.

Affiliations.

Many colleges have special affiliations. Some of these are religious. Examples include Villanova University (Roman Catholic), West Virginia Wesleyan College (United Methodist), and Brigham Young University (Morman). Some colleges, including Grambling State University and Spelman College, are traditionally African-American.

Although most colleges today are coeducational (both male and female students), some accept only men (such as Morehouse College) or only women (such as Randolph-Macon Woman's College).

Many colleges specialize in particular fields. These fields include the military (United States Air Force Academy and Maine Maritime Academy), seminary (University of the South and Talmudic College of Florida), teaching (Northern State University and Shippensburg State College), business (Babson College), engineering (Stevens Institute of Technology and Colorado School of Mines), health (Albany College of Pharmacy and Deaconess College of Nursing), arts (San Francisco Conservatory of Music and Rhode Island School of Design), and agriculture and technology (SUNY A&T at Cobleskill and Wentworth Institute of Technology). Some colleges meet special needs—for example, Gallaudet College, which is for the hearing impaired.

Also, hundreds of colleges offer Reserve Officers' Training Corps (ROTC) programs in affiliation with the U.S. Air Force, Army, and Navy.

Sample college affiliations

Religious
 Catholic University of America
 Yeshiva University
 Brigham Young University
Military
 U.S. Air Force Academy
 The Citadel
ROTC
 University of Maryland
Women's
 Wellesley College
 Spelman College
Minority
 Grambling State University
Hearing impaired
 Gallaudet University

Selecting a college

You may have a friend who is going to a specific college for all the right reasons. The chances are good that this friend will have a successful collegiate career. You too can be successful if your choices are your own and also made for the right reasons. The keys to selecting a college are careful self-assessment and information gathering. While pragmatic considerations will influence your *final* selection, an important part of selecting a college is determining which of your goals and dreams are most important to you and balancing them with the realistic considerations that apply to you.

For example, many students rule out expensive colleges without ever exploring financial aid and scholarship opportunities. This could result in paying more to go to a school assumed to be less costly. Students should first explore if a desired college can help meet their goals and if they can get in; *then* they should explore ways to cover the costs. Learning as much as possible—about yourself, the schools you would like to attend, financial aid, and other factors—will help you select the best college for you.

Self-assessment. Begin by asking some
basic questions.
- Do I want to continue my education after I graduate from high school?
- Is going to college the form of education I want, and why?

Other opportunities to continue your education may better match your goals, including trade schools, apprenticeship programs, and the military.

College is, however, the choice for a growing number of students. The fact that a college education is required for many careers is not the only reason students cite for attending. Many valid reasons are linked to academic success and careful decision making. You may find your reasons for going are that you do not know what else to do or that your family and friends expect you to go. If so, you must clarify your goals and concerns further before continuing the selection process. If all you clarify is that your reasons remain uncertain, you will still gain important information that will help you choose a specific college.

Next, ask questions that help you honestly assess your academic record.
- What are my grade point average and class rank?
- What types and levels of courses have I taken?
- What are my entrance exam scores?
- What special achievements and extracurricular activities have I had?
- What recommendations can I expect to receive?

Self-assessment checklist
- Do I want to go to college?
- Do I have the right academic background?
- Did I take entrance exams? What were my scores?
- What major or career am I interested in?
- How far from home should I go?
- What size college would I like?
- What are my financial resources?
- What range of schools should I apply to?
- Who can help me select a college?

The next phase explores the type of college you want to attend and the environment in which you will be most comfortable.
- Do I know what career I want or the subject areas I would like to study?
- What size school do I prefer?
- Will I be most comfortable at a college, university, or community college?
- What factors are important to me about the college's location (distance from home, climate, and setting)?
- How important to me are a school's affiliations (military, ethnic)?
- What kind of campus environment do I want (religious organizations, student activities, housing)?

- Do I hope to be active in specific ways or have special opportunities (athletics, student government, theater, exchange programs)?
- Do I have special needs that must be taken into consideration (health, disability)?
- How much pressure and competition will I feel comfortable with?
- Is it important for me to know others who go there?

The purpose of self-assessment is not to limit your choices. Rather, it ensures that you are focused and productive as you prepare to move through the next phase of the college selection process. After you have completed your self-assessment, talk with your family and counselor to gain additional perspective.

Developing your criteria. The information you gather through self-assessment helps you establish specific criteria, which you will use to select the best colleges for you. Developing these criteria involves identifying important college characteristics based upon your self-assessment; it also involves establishing priorities. Few colleges will match all the criteria you develop. Some, however, will have certain features that will make you willing to forego some of the criteria.

If you plan to apply to selective colleges, then the time, effort, and cost realistically required will help narrow your list of schools to a manageable level. If you are fortunate enough to be admitted to more than one of the colleges you have selected, you will still have many decisions to make. These decisions are far easier if you are clear about criteria and priorities from the start. College admissions is *not* just about a college choosing you; it is also about you making a careful and wise choice about a college.

As you identify important characteristics based upon your self-assessment, be clear why the information is important and how it ties in to the selection process. For example, if the distance a college is from home is an important criterion, ask why. If you want to be

One of the best ways to evaluate a college is to visit the campus and speak with students.

College criteria

- Location
- Size
- Selectivity
- Entrance exam requirements
- Setting (urban, suburban, rural)
- Climate (cold weather, humid)
- Religion (affiliation, diversity)
- Programs (majors available, strength)
- Type of college (2-year, 4-year)
- Living arrangements (dorms, commuter)
- Exchange programs (international, domestic)
- Cost
- Financial aid availability
- Military ties
- Special services (writing center, labs)
- Disabled student services
- Campus security

within a hundred miles of home because of commitments to help your family, then your choice of schools is quickly narrowed. You still want to ask if other factors could move you beyond the hundred-mile radius. For example, if your ideal college was located two hundred and fifty miles away, but offered substantial scholarship support and was easily accessible by affordable transportation, would you consider it? If not, then your criterion of the hundred-mile radius defines your choice.

Your academic record in high school is important for several reasons. It enables you realistically to assess the selectivity of colleges to which you can expect to be admitted. Within the range of selectivity, your academic record enables you to evaluate priorities that colleges have. For example, if you have excellent grades in challenging courses and activities that show commitment and leadership, but you also have weak entrance exam scores, look for colleges that discount or minimize scores, focusing instead on the total picture you present. Your academic record also helps you assess the degree of pressure, challenge, and stress you are willing to take on compared to what is required of you at one college versus another.

There are no right and wrong criteria or priorities. What matters is that the criteria and priorities you develop match *your* needs, goals, and abilities. For example, if one of your priorities is to go to as prestigious a college as possible, be sure that the ones you select and apply to also meet other needs that are important to you. In the long run, you are far better off being satisfied and successful at a somewhat less prestigious college than being unhappy or dropping out of a more prestigious school, even if you are accepted to both.

Sources of information.
Numerous sources of information about college are available, many for little or no cost to students. Most libraries and bookstores have sections devoted to college information. These include books, computer software, and CD-ROM resources that provide summary information regarding colleges across the nation. They also include specialized resources regarding topics such as financial aid, colleges for students with learning disabilities, the admission and application process, specific majors, and application essays.

A good initial source is one of the major guidebooks that provide information about thousands of individual colleges, usually organized alphabetically by state. Use these books to locate colleges near where you live, travel, or vacation; then visit some of these colleges. Whether or not you would consider going to them is immaterial. Visiting enables you to explore different campus environments, comparing factors such as size, location, geography, living arrangements, and campus resources. As you get closer to the final selection process, you can make arrangements to visit the specific schools that interest you.

Many of these guides can be purchased in CD-ROM format so that you can search for colleges on your computer. Some of the guides are also available through computer services such as America Online and CompuServe.

Attend the *college fairs* and other gatherings that are hosted by high schools, school districts, colleges, and organizations. Such events provide an opportunity to collect information about specific colleges and to speak with representatives who can place your name on mailing lists, provide information about campus tours, and answer a full range of questions you may have. Fairs and symposia often include workshops

Where to look
- Print materials (library, bookstore)
- College fairs and representatives
- Campus tours and college visits
- Alumni representatives
- College viewbooks and catalogues
- Videotapes
- Computerized data bases
- Online services
- College home pages on the Internet
- School counselors, teachers, and librarians
- Writing to colleges
- Family and friends

about important topics such as financial aid, the application process, and college life. College fairs are not all-inclusive; not all colleges are represented. You may learn about previously unfamiliar colleges, but do not limit yourself to selecting among only those colleges represented at the fairs you attend.

Most colleges distribute *viewbooks*, which provide overviews of courses, faculty, the campus, student life, and special programs. Viewbooks often provide enough information to help students determine if they are interested in learning still more about the college. Harder to obtain, *college catalogues* provide detailed information about graduation requirements, majors, individual courses, faculty, student services, and special programs, along with much additional information that is useful to the applicant.

Many colleges produce promotional videotapes. Short of an actual visit to the campus, these tapes provide the best information about the campus environment itself. Computerized data bases help students select colleges. Multimedia programs are becoming

College guidebooks
Allen, Joseph. *10 Minute Guide to Choosing a College*. New York: Alpha Books/Arco, 1996.

Barron's Educational Series. *Profiles of American Colleges*. 21st ed. Hauppauge, N.Y.: Barron's, 1997.

Cass-Liepmann, Julia. *Cass & Birnbaum's Guide to American Colleges*. 17th ed. New York: HarperCollins, 1997.

Cassidy, David J. *The Scholarship Book*. 5th ed. Englewood Cliffs, N.J.: Prentice Hall, 1996.

Custard, Edward T. *The Complete Book of Colleges, 1997, Princeton Review Series*. New York: Villard Books, 1997.

Fiske, Edward B., and Kathleen Blease. *The Fiske Guide to Colleges 1997*. New York: Times Books, 1997.

Greenfeld, Barbara C., and Robert A. Weinstein. *The Kids' College Almanac: A First Look at College*. Matawan, N.J.: Gerson Publishing, 1996.

McGinty, Sarah Myers. *Writing Your College Application Essay*. New York: The College Board, 1992.

Peterson's. *Internships 1996*. 16th ed. Princeton: N.J.: Peterson's, 1995.

Paul, William Henry, and Bill Paul. *Getting In: Inside the College Admissions Process*. Reading, Mass.: Addison-Wesley, 1996.

Pope, Loren. *Colleges That Change Lives*. New York: Penguin, 1996.

Wexler, Debra L. *College Check Mate: Innovative Tuition Plans That Make You a Winner*. Alexandria, Va.: Octameron Associates, 1996.

Wolff, Michael. *Netcollege 1997*. New York: Wolff New Media, 1996.

increasingly popular. Students identify important criteria; then the program searches its data base to find colleges that match the criteria, often providing additional information, including visual images.

Colleges are now accessible through the computer. Most colleges have *home pages* on the World Wide Web. Sometimes students can get the addresses of these home pages from one of the comprehensive guides or from a representative at a college fair. But most often, students can find the home page directly through the computer. After entering the Internet, students can enter the name of an individual college in one of the programs like Yahoo or Lycos that browses the Internet, acting like a huge electronic index. Students can then connect directly to the home page or type in the address at a later date.

Home pages often provide the same kinds of information that viewbooks and catalogues offer. They often include photographs of the campus. Some offer even more information—for example, the opportunity to read the campus newspaper, find out about campus events, or read profiles of individual professors or departments. The home pages usually enable students to use electronic mail (*e-mail*) to send requests for additional information directly to the colleges. In some cases, students can even send their application to college through the computer.

As useful as print, computer, and other media resources are, the most important resources are people, starting with your guidance counselor and teachers. Along the way, talk with family and friends about their own college experiences; talk with alumni or others familiar with colleges or careers in which you are interested. If a college interests you, contact its admissions office to see if there are any alumni who live near you and would be available to talk with you. The more information you gather, the more likely you are to find the college that is best for you.

Organizing your information.

As your data base of information grows, keeping it organized becomes very important. During your search, you will be gathering two types of information. One is general information that applies to all colleges. You might pick up various articles about topics such as financial aid, entrance exams, or housing. Organize this information in a general file—or several based on the topics and type of information you gather.

The second type of information is specific to individual colleges. As you narrow your list, you will want to keep a file on each college. Be certain you have relevant application materials and deadlines. Photocopy all application forms. File these materials with care along with other information.

Build a data base, on cards or computer. Start with

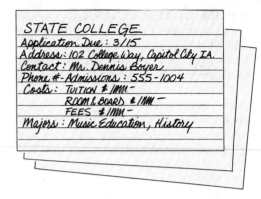

the criteria you have developed, as well as general information such as address, phone number, tuition, contact person, and due date for the application. Then as you learn more about the college, update your records.

Narrowing your list.

As your information base grows, you will be able to start narrowing your list. Part of this process is evaluating where you are likely to be accepted. Categorize colleges based on whether you know you will get in, whether you have a good to excellent likelihood of getting in, or whether you have a possibility of getting in. Decide how many colleges you want to apply to from each category.

Start comparing within each category. Go back to the criteria and priorities you established earlier, making adjustments for any changes in your thinking. At this time, you might start factoring in cost, including one or two colleges that you could afford and at least one or two colleges that are most desirable regardless of cost.

After eliminating various choices, determine what additional information you need about the remaining colleges. Use that information to narrow your list down to the colleges to which you will apply.

Range of schools

- **The sure thing.** Apply to at least one school where you are sure to be admitted, either a school with open admissions or a school that has admissions criteria that you fully meet or exceed.
- **The perfect fit.** Apply to a few schools whose profile of a typical student matches yours. Your grade point average, test scores, course selections, and activities should be similar to the profile. You may not get in, due to space limitations, but you think your chances are pretty good.
- **Room to grow.** Consider applying to a couple of schools that have strong appeal for you through the selection process and where you come close to meeting most of the criteria and strongly meet or exceed a couple of others. You may not get in, but the opportunity is too good not to take a chance.

Getting into college

The time you spend in school, particularly high school, lays the foundation on which your admission to college is based. But other factors, such as the steps you take to select a college, also affect your admission to the college of your choice. The application process is the final step leading to admission. The significance of this final phase should not be underestimated. How you approach it can dramatically affect whether or not you get into the school of your choice.

Understanding admissions. To negotiate the admissions process effectively, you must first understand it. Start by becoming familiar with *selectivity*. A college's degree of selectivity influences the complexity of its admissions process. *Open enrollment* colleges accept almost all applicants, usually year-round. To be admitted, you complete an application form used to enter you in the school's data base and to provide important information for course placement. Application fees are minimal or nonexistent. High school transcripts are often not required, nor are entrance exams. Most community colleges have open admissions policies. Be aware that specific programs and courses within an open admissions college, like allied health, mathematics, or honors programs, may be more restricted.

Other colleges have different admissions standards ranging from selective to highly competitive. Many state colleges and universities use a formula to determine who is admitted. The formula might involve a minimum GPA and level for entrance exam scores; more information may be required of students applying for honors programs or other special opportunities. Students are not compared to each other, but rather against an objective standard determined by the formula. Usually, an appeals process exists.

Competitive colleges may have higher admissions standards in terms of grades, class rank, course selection, exam scores, and activities. The application process itself includes more tasks—for example, essays, interviews, and recommendations. Some highly selective colleges look at students as a whole, rather than set strict standards for each criterion. Regardless of selectivity, every college builds flexibility into its admissions process, allowing for individual circumstances and diversity within a reasonable range. The selection criteria are usually listed in college guides, often in order of importance.

Be aware of a college's timetable for admissions. Even colleges that accept students year-round have deadlines for certain programs. Colleges with *rolling admissions* evaluate students, accepting, rejecting, and notifying them on a rolling basis, as applications are received. They may have a final deadline. For such colleges, apply as early as you can since the class may fill before the final deadline.

Most colleges have priority and closing dates for admissions. While all students will be notified at the same time, students who apply by the priority date often have an advantage over those who apply later.

The most competitive colleges usually start by screening out applicants who do not meet minimum requirements. The remaining applicants are reviewed and compared, sometimes by committee. Most competitive colleges accept more students than they intend to enroll, assuming that some will elect to attend elsewhere. Some students may be put on a waiting list; they will be accepted if space becomes available.

Many colleges offer early decision plans. *Early decision* is aimed at students who are sure they want to attend a particular college. The process enables them to apply and be notified early; however, various guidelines may restrict students' opportunities to apply elsewhere. Students interested in early decision must complete their entrance exams in their junior year and apply in the fall of their senior year.

Early admission enables exceptional students to attend college during their senior year of high school. Some colleges provide the option for students to apply for admission at a later date than fall of the freshman

Admissions terminology

Open admissions. Anyone can enroll.

Selective admissions. Those who meet preset criteria (such as grade point average) can enroll.

Competitive admissions. More students apply than can be admitted. Students are in competition with each other for admission. There are different degrees of competitiveness based on the number of students who apply versus the number of spaces.

Rolling admissions. Students are accepted as they apply. The longer a student waits to apply, the fewer spaces will remain.

Waiting list. The student has not been rejected, but must wait to see if space opens up. Admission depends on how many students who have been accepted choose to go to that college.

Qualified admissions. At many large universities, a student may be accepted to the university for a year, but must then be accepted by the end of a preset time into a specific program.

year. For example, Colby College has a February Freshman plan—students can apply for admission for the second semester of the freshman year.

Realize that, in the admissions process, there are factors you can control and factors you cannot. To a great extent you can control grades, course selection, and extracurricular activities. You can turn work into an advantage. You can develop relationships with teachers and counselors that will result in good recommendations. Though it is more difficult to control entrance exam scores, you can take steps to maximize your scores. You can select colleges wisely and well. With care and attention, you can organize your approach to the application process, improving your chances.

Yet there are factors you certainly cannot control. You cannot change the past, such as poor performance during a school year, though you can show improved performance. You cannot create certain advantages that might give another applicant preference, such as geography or alumni connections. Colleges place different emphases on candidates from year to year to gain a particular diversity; your qualifications could serve you well one year, but not another. Also, you have little control over your family's financial position and its impact on your ability to obtain financial aid. The key to successfully applying to college is focusing your energies on those factors that you can control.

Forms, forms, forms. When you apply
to college, you can expect to see numerous forms. These forms include entrance exam and Advanced Placement forms, score reports, application forms, and financial aid forms. Just within the application form, you must manage numerous components including

Paperwork for college admissions
- Secondary school report form
- Entrance exam application
- Request for information and application
- Application form
- Application essays
- Recommendations (usually 2 to 3 per college)
- Transcripts
- Financial aid forms
- Thank you notes

the application itself, recommendations, essays, secondary school reports, and financial aid requests. As noted below, the financial aid forms include several components.

In the case of application forms, you must manage a set for each college to which you apply. Forms have different time frames and different deadlines. Colleges set different due dates. You have direct control over the completion of the basic applications and essays. You are dependent on others to complete forms such as recommendations and the secondary school report. However, it is up to you to give people sufficient time to complete these forms. It is your responsibility to maintain a schedule that enables you and others to submit all components on time.

Plan to create a grid that shows all the forms you must submit and the dates they are due. Follow the schedule carefully. Be aware of fees that are associated with forms. Make copies of any forms (although you cannot make copies of confidential forms that others have filled out). Keep the copies in a safe place. Set up a filing system similar to the one you established to select a college; use it to help you manage the application process.

BY	COLLEGE 1	COLLEGE 2	COLLEGE 3	COLLEGE 4
JAN 1	(SAT)	(SAT)	see campus (ACT)	
JAN 15	see campus	Recommendations	Recommendations	receive info
FEB 1	Recommendations	Complete Form	complete Form	visit campus
FEB 15	Complete Form	Transcripts	Transcripts	Audit class
MAR 1	Transcripts	—	nancial Aid form	
MAR 15	—	Financial Aid form	e campus	Application
APR 1	Financial Aid form	see campus	from college	Transcripts
APR 15	—	hear from college		
MAY 1	hear from college		ly date	
MAY 15	reply date	reply date		hear from college

Thinking About College

Applying to college.

The two key steps in applying to college are deciding where to apply and completing application forms in a way that makes the best case for your acceptance. Assuming that you have assessed yourself and set priorities wisely, you have probably selected a realistic set of colleges. Now that you have sold yourself *on* these colleges, the time has come to sell yourself *to* the colleges. You will do your best to convince college personnel that your qualifications and enthusiasm for their college should justify your admission.

Where to apply. There is no magic number of colleges to which you should apply. If you plan to attend a community college or specific state college and know you will be admitted, you may have no need to apply elsewhere. But if you apply to colleges with competitive admissions, you do not have the same guarantee; you should therefore consider a range of colleges. One or two colleges in this range should be "safety schools," where you are fairly certain of being admitted because of the admissions policy or because you well exceed admissions criteria; safety schools should be affordable even if you do not qualify for aid.

The range can also include "stretch schools," which are somewhat more selective than you think you qualify for, but which are not unrealistic. The remaining colleges should be those that meet your criteria and where your profile matches the expected criteria. If

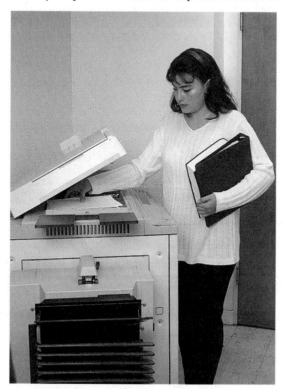

Students should photocopy completed forms before mailing them.

Don't let your financial resources limit where you apply. If you have the grades, scores, and background to get into a college that strongly appeals to you, go ahead and apply, regardless of cost. Then do what you can to put together the financial aid package needed to attend.

you are dependent on financial aid, you should consider applying to slightly more colleges. However, do not apply with reckless abandon. Be clear about your reasons for applying to a particular college, and be clear about where you would be willing to go if admitted. Choose wisely and choose well.

The application form. Application materials vary somewhat from one college to another, not only in design, but also based upon selectiveness. Open enrollment colleges usually have relatively simple applications that primarily request demographic information (such as address and date of birth) and other information for reporting purposes (such as ethnic background). Some information may be used for placement purposes.

Applications for competitive colleges have four components. Like the open enrollment application, the first part asks for demographic information. You must also provide other background information, such as work experience and extracurricular activities. The second component consists of essays; you will often have forms for completing them. Before completing the final version, you should prepare them in draft. Then type your responses on the original copy whenever possible.

The next component consists of forms for your high school to complete; they are sometimes called the *secondary report form*. These forms are usually completed by the guidance office—particularly the registrar, if

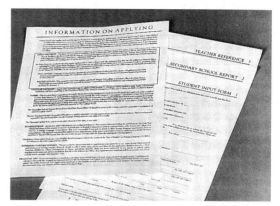

The application package may have many forms to complete.

Good relationships with teachers can lead to letters of recommendation.

your high school has one. The final component consists of teacher recommendation forms. In addition, students may submit financial aid forms with their applications, depending on the school to which they are applying.

The application often makes a first and lasting impression. Allow yourself time to do a good job; do not be caught rushing at the last minute. Follow directions precisely. Submit a neat, legible, complete, organized, and error-free document before the priority date. These are essential not only for making a good initial impression, but also to the actual decision making regarding your application. In most cases, an application fee must be submitted with an application; these vary from college to college. Fee waivers based on need may be available.

Be sure to photocopy your application forms and all accompanying materials once they are complete. File them carefully. You should receive notification from the college that your application has been received. If you do not receive notification, contact the admissions office to confirm that it has arrived.

Recommendations. Some competitive colleges, particularly private colleges, require one or more recommendations. Depending on the college, you will be requested to submit recommendations from teachers, counselors, clergy, alumni, or members of the community. Some colleges may be very specific, for example, requesting that at least one recommendation be from a teacher in a certain subject area.

Recommendation forms vary. Some colleges simply ask for a letter. Others have forms with checklists, a specific list of questions, or a specific question on which the recommendation may be based. Some colleges supply forms with space for a narrative recommendation and a space on the bottom where teachers or counselors must select one overall rating from among several choices. Many colleges realize the problems posed by requesting multiple recommendations from individuals; some will accept photocopies. However, do not assume photocopies are acceptable; confirm that they are before using them.

Select individuals who know you well and will write the best possible recommendation for you. They must also meet the qualifications set forth by the college. Ask the individuals if they would be willing to write on your behalf. Give them all the information they need, including appropriate forms and specific directions. Provide them with an envelope for the recommendation. Include an addressed, stamped envelope if they are to mail the recommendation. Do not overreact if someone declines your request; it may be no reflection on you. Always write a note of thanks to those who write in your behalf. Finally, maintain a record of those you asked to provide recommendations, including all deadlines and destinations. As the due date nears, politely ask about the status of the recommendation, thanking the individual again.

The essay. Most often, essays are required by competitive colleges; some require multiple essays. More than any other element of your application, essays provide admissions personnel with a glimpse of you as an individual, what makes you different compared to others. This explains why essay topics often are designed to provide insight into the way you think and feel, rather than your more impersonal qualities. They are also designed so that a broad range of applicants can respond to the questions, providing a basis of comparison while showing individuality.

While essays provide information about your writing skills and abilities, this is not their primary purpose. Many colleges value essays even more highly than interviews for many reasons. Students can be very nervous during interviews; factors such as time and distance also limit interviews. Essays can reflect effort and thought processes more effectively.

For many, essays can be a challenging aspect of the college admissions process. First, each college might require a different topic. Some simply require a personal statement, with no more specific guidance. Second, colleges are not always explicit about what they are looking for. Third, limitations such as length or topic can in some cases complicate the student's ability to respond.

Colleges usually want depth, not breadth. Approach the essay determined to communicate who you really are, not the person you think the college wants you to be. What you write should be consistent with other elements of your application. Stick to the topic; do not use the essay to communicate additional information about yourself unless the question provides this opening specifically. A unique approach is often rewarded, if it is not forced.

If you concentrate on answering questions in a way that truly reflects your attitudes and feelings about the topic, admissions personnel will gain insight about you as an individual. They will also gain insight into your commitment to that institution, evidenced by the time and attention you take to tailor your responses to their questions, rather than writing them in a generic way that can be used repeatedly in other essays.

Allow ample time to think and write. Do not procrastinate! Writer's block can be overcome simply by starting, even if your first attempts bear no resemblance to your finished product. When given the opportunity, write something about which you feel strongly and about which you have a definite point of view. Allow others to review your essay for grammar, punctuation, and typographical errors. Do not let others change your ideas or your writing style. Many ideas, opinions, attitudes, styles, and approaches will be tolerated, but grammatical errors and sloppiness are not acceptable. Always type your response. Photocopy it and add it to your file—things do get lost in the mail and even in admissions offices.

Interviews. Many colleges, particularly public colleges, do not require interviews as part of the admissions process. Other colleges do require interviews, while at still other colleges, interviews are optional and provided at the student's request.

Once you have selected a college, review the admissions materials or check with the admissions office to determine the college's policy on interviews. Even if they are only optional, plan to arrange one. Find out about each college's interview process: how to schedule them, who will conduct them, where they will take place. Determine the purpose of an interview. Some are used to evaluate you, while others simply provide you with a chance to learn more about the college.

Evaluative interviews are used in much the same way as essays. They help the college obtain insight into your individual qualities. Do not look at them as pass or fail situations. Colleges look for a variety of qualities and characteristics, including intellectual qualities, the ability to articulate ideas, and self-confidence. They are also trying to balance their search for students who fit a particular profile with their effort to bring a diversity of personalities, backgrounds, viewpoints, and other qualities to campus.

Special situations. Some students have special situations that factor into the admissions process. Some have physical or learning disabilities and are unsure

Interview tips
- Confirm the time and place of the interview in advance.
- Be on time.
- Dress appropriately.
- Use good posture.
- Maintain good eye contact.
- Speak clearly and confidently.
- Be ready with questions to ask.
- Communicate your interest.
- Thank the interviewer.
- Send a follow-up note.

about the implications of informing admissions personnel. Others have personal, family, or health problems that interfered with academic achievement. Still others may have financial circumstances that limit their ability to pay application fees. As a general rule, you benefit by providing information relevant to your application; doing so enlightens admissions personnel about your record.

Disabled students are not obligated to inform colleges about their disability. However, they need to determine if the college has programs, services, the student-teacher ratio, and optimal accomodations to contribute to their success and also to their fullest participation and enjoyment of campus life. Colleges cannot reject otherwise qualified students based on their disability; it is against the law.

Other ways to apply. Many colleges now allow students to send their application by computer. A few companies provide services, helping students obtain application forms, formatting the information, and even sending in the completed information. Some colleges allow students to use a standard form called the Common Application. Students may need to supplement this form with specific information requested by individual colleges.

Being accepted. The admissions process is
not over upon acceptance. If you are attending a selective admissions college or a specific program, such as nursing, at an open enrollment college, you must take steps to secure your enrollment.

NOTE: Your admission is not final until you have successfully completed your senior year of high school; this is especially true in the case of selective colleges.

Being notified. When and how you are notified varies. Open enrollment colleges generally admit students as they apply. Acceptance letters formalize what students already know. Colleges with rolling admissions notify students throughout the year, depending on the date when they applied.

Other selective colleges have specific dates for notifying students. Notification regarding admission is received by mail. The most common notification dates are in March and April.

While it is acceptable to contact colleges before priority or closing dates for application in order to ensure that materials have arrived, you should not contact colleges before the notification date regarding the outcome of your application.

You may be placed on a college's waiting list. If you are on the waiting list at one of your top choices, you can take steps that may enhance your chances of being admitted. Write to the director of admissions to reassert your special interest and desire to attend. Consider asking your counselor to contact the college

Choose what's right for you

The advice of others and financial realities are important. But in the end, the choice of where to attend is yours. Choose a college that will serve *your* academic, social, and extracurricular needs, one that will challenge but not overwhelm you.

on your behalf. Also, contact one or two appropriate individuals who know you well and would be willing to write a letter of recommendation on your behalf. They should be different people from those who wrote the recommendations submitted with your application.

If your application to a college is rejected, do not read too much into this decision. Similar colleges have diverse needs that vary from year to year. Do not compare your outcome to a friend's, no matter how similar your profiles may be.

Making a decision. Sometimes there is no decision to be made—you have been accepted to the college of your dreams, or at least the one that makes the most sense for you to attend, and you have adequate financing. Often, the decision is not that easy. You may be accepted to more than one college and do not have a clear top choice. You may receive a better financial package from a college that is lower down on your list of choices. Other factors may complicate your choice. Your family may move unexpectedly to a different region of the country, placing you farther away than expected from a particular college. You may get into a special program in a college in which you were not otherwise interested.

Before making your final decision, you should visit the colleges that have accepted you. Visiting them is especially important if you are uncertain about your decision or if you have never visited the college before. Either attend a general visitation program or arrange an individual appointment. Talk with students on campus; carefully judge your comfort level. Recognize that in addition to your academic life, a large portion of your social life will take place at the college for several years.

When to reply. Whatever your options, you will almost certainly need to make your decision prior to May 1, the national Candidates Reply Date. Almost all colleges agree to abide by this date. Its purpose is to ensure that students will not be required to respond to an offer of admission until they have heard from all the colleges to which they applied and that the students will have time to make a final decision.

Selective colleges will require you to secure your acceptance with a deposit. If you are hoping to be admitted to a college where you have been placed on the waiting list, you will probably need to submit a

Thinking About College

nonrefundable deposit for your second choice school while waiting to hear from your first choice. Students who have been placed on waiting lists are generally not notified about the final outcome until well after the Candidates Reply Date.

If you have been accepted prior to being informed about the financial aid package, if any, that you will receive, ask for more time to respond. Never be afraid to ask for reconsideration of the aid package you have been awarded, particularly if it is a factor in whether or not you can attend a particular college.

College etiquette. If you have been accepted at a college to which you applied, but which you do not plan to attend, you have an obligation to notify it as soon as possible. Although you may have chosen not to attend, other students may be anxiously awaiting word of their acceptance to that college.

There will be other forms that the college you plan to attend will require you to complete. Do so in a timely fashion. In addition to completing these forms, you should write a note of thanks to any col-

---

Acceptance is conditional

Remember, once you've been accepted to a college:
1. You must notify the college by the deadline date to secure your place.
2. Make the required financial deposits: securing your spot depends on it. Financial aid students should contact the college if specific instructions are not provided.
3. Successfully complete your senior year. Colleges can and do withdraw acceptance.

---

lege staff who have helped you along the way. The same is true regarding anyone who has written a letter of recommendation, provided you with general advice, or helped in some other way. Teachers, counselors, and others who have been helpful throughout the process will appreciate learning about your final decision as well as being thanked for their efforts on your behalf.

College costs

College costs should not interfere with the process of exploring opportunities and deciding where to apply. However, costs ultimately are a critical factor in making the final decision about where to attend. In order to plan effectively and make a sound decision about where to attend, you should understand the full range of costs associated with college and also be aware of the different ways to finance your education.

Tuition and fees. When people think about the cost of college, tuition is often the first thing that comes to mind. Tuition is the money that students are charged and pay for instruction. Colleges where virtually all students attend full time generally have a flat rate for tuition for each term. This tuition is charged regardless of how many credit hours the full-time student takes during each term. However, at many other colleges, tuition is calculated on a per credit hour basis. Most of these colleges have a cap on tuition for full-time students. For example, a college might charge $200 per credit hour; students might pay per credit hour cost, up to fifteen credit hours. If they enroll in more than fifteen credit hours, they do not pay additional tuition. In this example, a full-time student would not pay more than $3,000 tuition for each term.

Tuition covers only a portion of a student's costs. Fees also make up a portion of college costs. Many colleges charge all students a fee each term that sup-

In addition to tuition, laboratory and studio fees are often charged.

ports student government, activities, clubs, access to athletic facilities, as well as other services such as tutoring. This type of fee may be a flat charge or a percentage of tuition. Instruction, lab, and studio fees are charged for specific courses such as science, studio arts, or performing arts where special equipment and supplies are needed. Fees might also be charged for other courses such as foreign language and specialized physical education courses, like scuba diving.

The costs of tuition and fees vary widely. Private colleges are generally more expensive than their public college counterparts. Publicly funded colleges usually charge residents of their state less than nonresidents. Community colleges tend to be the least expensive because they are strongly supported by local and state funds. Other factors affect tuition, including inflation and costs specific to the college itself. For example, some colleges maintain a low student-to-faculty ratio and may raise tuition to maintain that ratio. As an example of the range of tuition, in the late 1990s, annual tuition and fees were about $21,000 at Wesleyan University in Connecticut, about $4,800 at the University of Connecticut (for residents), and about $1,700 at a public community college (for Connecticut residents).

Room and board.

The cost of housing and meals is referred to as *room and board*. Many colleges offer on-campus housing; they may even require freshmen to live on campus. In the late 1990s, annual room and board ranged from a little over $3,000 to over $6,000. Virtually all colleges have dining facilities. Those colleges with on-campus housing usually have dining halls with package deals that cover all meals, rather than a charge for each meal. For students who live off campus, this room and board charge is a good starting estimate for the expense of living off campus and paying for food. Whether or not students live on campus, housing costs must be planned for.

Other expenses.

In addition to tuition and fees, the cost of books and supplies is significant, regardless of where you go to school. Expect to have at least one required text for each course. Some courses may require that you buy several books. Text prices have risen dramatically in past years for a variety of reasons. Supplementary materials that help both students and instructors, such as test banks, student videotapes, and tutorial software, are becoming increasingly popular. The cost of books for a semester surprises many students and their parents, especially since they are used to having their high school texts "loaned" to them each year.

In addition to books, students must buy supplies. Some are general: pencils, pens, paper, and so forth. Some are specific to certain subjects: graph paper for math, paint brushes for art, lab supplies for biology. Others are long-term investments—for example, a dictionary, a thesaurus, a calculator (the type of calculator varies according to the classes you will take), and, if possible, a computer and printer.

Other costs relate to living expenses. These include basics such as clothing and laundry. You should budget for entertainment and recreation—for example, movies, dating, concerts, and ski trips. There are some expenses that high school students may not think about but college students must, especially when first living away from home. These include toiletries, postage, phone calls, and magazines or newspapers.

Also budget transportation costs. If you have your own car, you will have gas, insurance, and maintenance costs, as well as campus parking fees. If you commute, you will have car or public transportation costs for traveling between home and campus. Even if living on campus without a car of your own, you must budget for local travel and transportation for school breaks or vacations. Transportation costs must also be factored into the final decision of where you will go to college.

Preparing for college costs.

Fewer and fewer students and their families can afford to pay for college outright, especially at the more expensive colleges. The finances needed to pay for college often come from numerous sources.

A key starting point is savings and investments. Ideally, a college fund should be set up at an early age. Even if the student chooses not to attend college, the fund can pay for other career training. Students who work during high school should set aside some of their earnings for a college fund. Though it is best to begin saving early, any savings that you can set aside will prove helpful.

Wages earned from working are an important source. Many students work during college and vacations. One option, especially when money is tight, is to

Part-time and summer jobs provide opportunities to save for college.

Thinking About College

stretch the first half of college over time, while working, then attend full time for the last half. Many students attend a community college for two years, then transfer to a four-year college to finish their education.

Scholarships, loans, and work-study programs are a key source of funding; options are discussed in "Financial aid." Loan programs, whether offered through government, colleges, banks, or other sources, provide different payment plans. These include installment plans in which each payment is the same, with the loan paid over time. One popular plan provides low payments in the first years, and increased payments as students' post-college income rises. Other tuition management plans are available. Some colleges provide early payment and other creative plans. Funds are also available from local businesses, organizations, and other sponsors.

Students who borrow money for college should try to restrict borrowing to tuition, fees, and room and board, while paying for all other expenses, including books and supplies, as they occur. Try to explore your financial options as early as possible. Consult your guidance counselor, admissions or financial aid officer, the family's financial advisor, and the many available guidebooks for further information.

Tuition & fees	$ //////–
- Lab fees	
- Course fees	
Room & board	$ //////–
Books & supplies	$ //////–
Transportation	$ //////–
Personal expenses	$ //////–
- Clothing	
- Recreation	
- Phone	
- Memberships	
- Extracurricular	
TOTAL COSTS (one year)	$ //////–

Financial aid

The majority of college students depend on some sort of financial assistance to supplement funds that come from personal savings, investments, income, and family support. *Financial aid* refers to the support that is available through colleges, government, private foundations, and other sources.

The guidelines for determining who gets how much support are continually changing. One reason is that much of the funding comes from government support and is therefore subject to political shifts and changes in legislative programs and administrative regulations. Furthermore, the amount of private funding depends on the combination of the amount of private money donated to financial aid programs, as well as the income generated by the investment of existing financial aid endowments. Because these fluctuate from year to year, the amount of private money which is available to provide financial support varies. In turn, guidelines that determine how to distribute funds vary as well.

Calculating need. The single most important factor in determining how much financial aid a student receives is how much the student needs. While some support is completely independent of need, the

vast majority is provided to students who could not afford to attend college without further support.

In the simplest sense, *need* is the difference between the resources that students have available to pay for college, and the actual costs of college. The goal of financial aid is to make up as much of the difference as possible.

The resources that students are considered to have available to pay for college consist of several components. Personal savings and investments, such as stocks and bonds, are two key elements. A student's summer earnings are another element. Earnings do not reflect what students already have put aside; rather they project what students will be able to contribute in the future.

The contributions that parents, other family members, and friends make are also considered. Parents may have built a college fund for the student over the years. Other family members and close friends may give monetary gifts to help pay for college. Like personal savings and investments, these reflect resources available at the time need is calculated.

A family's ability to contribute further is a very important factor. This particular element is likely to be redefined on an ongoing basis. In the past, not only

Need-based financial aid includes consideration of the family's financial resources.

has the income of the parents been included, but also assets such as equity in the family home. However, as a result of changes introduced for 1993, the determination of a family's ability to contribute differs from previous years, especially with regard to home equity.

The student may have still other resources available in the form of awards, honorariums, and local scholarships as well as support from sources such as the National Merit Scholarship. For example, a local church might award a graduating senior a stipend to help pay for textbooks; a civic organization might make a small contribution toward college to a student who has been active in community affairs; a local business might provide grants to any of its employees' children who plan to attend college.

The total resources indicate the *expected family contribution* (EFC) to the student's education. The EFC is based on a formula used by Congress. Even though the formula may not accurately reflect the real ability of a family to contribute, it is applied to all families in the same way. The EFC is compared to the projected costs of attending an individual college. The remainder is the amount a student needs to supply, through either a financial aid package or other sources of income.

Personal savings	$ 1,000 —
Personal investments	$ 1,000 —
Employment earnings	$ 1,000 —
Parents' contribution	$ 1,000 —
Gifts from family & friends	$ 100 —
Awards & honorariums,	
local scholarships	$ 1,000 —
Other	$ 100 —
TOTAL RESOURCES	$ 1,000 —
Total College Costs	$ 1,000 —
less - Total resources	1,000 —
NEED	$ 1,000 —

Financial aid packages. Once a student's need is established, the student works with the financial aid officer to develop a *financial aid package*. This package may combine scholarships, loans, and work-study programs. Being accepted by a college does not guarantee a package that will cover the difference between a student's resources and college costs. Some packages rely more heavily on loans and work-study programs than students are comfortable assuming. Furthermore, students who have been admitted to more than one college may be offered a different package from each school. These differences represent one more element students must weigh when choosing where to attend.

Types of financial aid.

The three major types of financial aid are scholarships (or grants), loans, and work-study. *Scholarships* and *grants* are essentially gifts. Students are not obligated to repay the financial support provided by such gifts. *Loans* provide temporary financial support. Students are expected to repay the funds over time. The interest rate is usually lower than what is available through banks and finance companies. Also, interest is often not charged until after students graduate. *Work-study* provides campus jobs to help students earn funds they need to cover their expenses. Financial aid is usually based on need, merit, or affiliation.

In addition to financial aid for students, there are programs that are directed at parents, enabling them to provide greater assistance to their children.

Need-based aid. Much financial aid is limited to students who demonstrate need. Such aid ensures that students who would otherwise not be able to afford college have access to the necessary funds.

Federal and state governments provide a large portion of need-based aid. For example, federal aid includes Pell Grants and Supplemental Educational Opportunity Grants, which are not repaid, and Stafford Loans and Perkins Loans, which are repaid over time.

Need-based aid can come from a variety of other sources. Many colleges have their own scholarship and loan programs, which have been funded by alumni, businesses, and foundations. Many private foundations provide funding based primarily on need, though students may have to meet other criteria, such as geography, intended major, or academic achievement.

Most work-study support is directed at students who demonstrate need. Campus jobs are provided to supplement other funding; students may work in the dining hall, campus mailroom, library, or other campus locations. Having worked for the funding, students do not repay what they have earned from work-study.

Sample financial aid programs

Need-based programs (most common form of aid, based on student's financial need)
- Pell Grant
- Supplemental Educational Opportunity Grants
- Stafford Loans and Perkins Loans
- State scholarships
- Federal work-study

Merit-based programs (based on academic, artistic, athletic, and leadership ability)
- National Merit Scholarships
- Rotary Club
- McGraw-Hill Foundation

Affiliation-based programs (may or may not be need/merit-based; primary factor is some sort of affiliation)
- ROTC
- Military service options (U.S. Naval Academy)
- United Negro College Fund
- American Medical Association

Financial management programs (programs for extended payment of tuition and other costs)
- Monthly installment plans
- Tuition guarantee/lock-in plans
- Family plans

Other means
- Employee fringe benefits
- Cooperative education
- National Service Plan

Merit-based aid. Other sources of financial aid are given to students who have demonstrated success or strong potential in academic and other areas. For example, the National Merit scholarships are awarded through a competitive program to about seven thousand students annually. Of these, two thousand students receive "National" scholarships of $2,000 each, while about eleven hundred more students receive scholarships from corporate sponsors and about thirty-nine hundred more receive scholarships sponsored by colleges.

Some academic scholarships are given to students with proven success across the board; grade point average and class rank are influential factors. Other academic scholarships are specific to selected disciplines. Students with demonstrated skills in math will be eligible for certain scholarships; students with strong English skills or strong science skills will be eligible for yet others. Some of the academic support is available through associations of people and companies with an interest in specific subject areas. Also, some college aid is controlled to some extent by departments or individual scholarship donors. Thus, a

College officials can help you develop a financial aid package.

chemistry department may have funds available to support a student planning to major in chemistry.

Not all merit-based aid is related directly to academic performance. Athletic scholarships are given, generally at a specific college, to students who will participate in sports at that college. Although such aid is not based on academic performance, strong efforts have been made in recent years to ensure that all athletes receiving scholarships meet academic standards determined both by the college and by national governing boards overseeing college athletics.

Other merit-based aid is available for students with proven ability in the arts. For example, some students receive aid to study piano performance, others to develop as dancers, and still others to refine their skills as sculptors and painters.

Leadership, too, is a factor considered in merit-based aid. Civic organizations, such as the Rotary Club and others, provide aid to students who have demonstrated leadership, either within the school or the community. For example, a student who is president of student government or who also helps organize a community program to collect toys for the homeless is a strong candidate for aid based on leadership.

Not all merit-based aid is in the form of scholarship. Loans and work-study are also provided. For example, a work-study student with a strong science background and an intention to major in physics may have an opportunity to be a research assistant to a physics professor. The student has to work a selected number of hours, much like other students receiving work-study aid. However, based on academic merit, the work is more likely to be directly related to and contribute to the student's academic development.

Affiliation-based aid. Much aid is available to students who meet various other criteria. Sometimes the criteria are based on race, religion, or gender. The United Negro College Fund, for example, provides financial support to African-American students. Aid based on religion might be available both through national organizations or through local churches and synagogues. Many aid programs are specifically for either men or women; in fact, the Miss America Pageant, while considered outdated by some, is the nation's single largest provider of scholarship support to women.

Some aid is based on geography. A college in one state may have a specific program set up by an alumnus to provide support to students from a second state. A separate program, not affiliated with any college, may be restricted to students from a particular city, regardless of where they choose to attend.

The intended program of study may qualify students for further aid. For example, students who plan a military career may receive aid through the ROTC program or free education at a military academy. Other aid may be available for students training to become teachers, nurses, accountants, or other professionals, or those planning to study in a particular subject area, regardless of specific career goals. Again, such aid may be specific to a college, set up by an alumnus, or it may be available through national programs or other sources. Often these kinds of gifts and loans are based on career goals and academic achievement.

In addition to broadly established criteria for aid, there are thousands of aid programs available with narrowly defined criteria. Many are established through the colleges and through private foundations. Others are sponsored by corporations, sometimes for their employees' children, or by clubs, fraternal and civic organizations, and individuals. Sometimes the criteria are highly unusual. For example, it is possible (though unlikely) that some organization or individual has a grant available for a left-handed violinist who is a quiltmaker and also plans to major in criminology!

Dependents of deceased or disabled veterans, POWs, and MIAs, as well as active-duty military personnel are eligible for various gifts and loans.

Financial management programs. Financial aid is not only about finding the resources needed to pay for college; it is also about finding alternative ways to pay the college or to repay the source of loans.

Many colleges provide various payment plans so that large payments are not due all at once. Some offer installment plans, others offer extended payment plans. Family plans offer reduced tuition for the children of alumni or when multiple family members enroll at the same college. Some payment programs do not charge interest while the student is attending college; they may even provide a grace period of about six months following graduation before charging interest or requiring payments. Some also hold off on required payments for an additional length of time if the student continues on to graduate school. Different colleges are experimenting with different programs.

Thinking About College

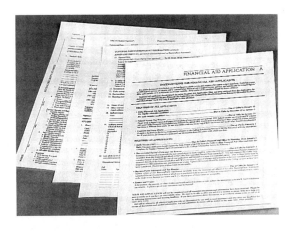

Some states have unique investment plans and tuition rate guarantee programs. Other state savings programs include tax-free savings plans. Some states have reciprocal in-state arrangements.

Various loan forgiveness programs exist for specific jobs. For example, students who teach in inner cities may have some of their debt reduced.

Lenders, or agencies such as the Student Loan Marketing Association (SLMA) who service loans, often offer a variety of payment plans to students or parents who undertake large loans. For example, sometimes different interest rates are offered based on how many months will be given for the borrower to repay the loan.

Cooperative education. A popular way to finance college is to participate in a cooperative education program, or co-op, which enables students to work while attending college. Participating companies often let students work half time or alternate between being a full-time student and a full-time employee.

Federal financial aid. The federal government is a major source of financial aid for college students. Federal funds include grants, loans, and work-study. All programs are not necessarily available at all schools. You must apply for federal financial aid on a yearly basis.

Pell grants, provided directly by the government, do not need to be repaid; recipients must demonstrate need. The annual amount of the grant can exceed $2,000. Another federal grant program is the Supplemental Educational Opportunity Grant (SEOG), aimed at students with exceptional financial need. Unlike Pell grants, SEOGs are administered by colleges.

Stafford Loans provide long-term, low-interest loans which can be repaid over a period of up to ten years. They are made by financial institutions and insured by federal and state agencies. Students can borrow increasing amounts each year. They do not have to make payments until several months after the time of graduation. Perkins Loans are administered by colleges. They are set at even lower interest rates than Stafford Loans.

Students who participate in the Federal Work-Study (FWS) program receive federal support for working a limited number of hours on or off campus, usually with public or private nonprofit organizations.

The Parent Loan for Undergraduate Students (PLUS) provides loans to parents. Interest rates are higher than those on student loans. Payments can be deferred while the student is in college, though interest will accumulate. Another program, Supplemental Loans for Students (SLS) is aimed at students who are considered independent.

For more information, obtain a copy of *The Student Guide*, published by the U.S. Department of Education. You can also call (800) 4-FED AID (800-433-3243).

Applying for financial aid. Most
aid is coordinated through a college's financial aid office. To receive aid, you must provide information that enables colleges to evaluate your need and qualifications. Unless you are considered independent, your parents will also need to provide colleges with substantial information.

Getting the needed information. Many guidebooks about financial aid, often by those companies that administer entrance exams or publish admissions guides, can be found in libraries and stores. Free information is available as well from the federal government, especially regarding federal financial aid.

Other sources include your guidance counselor and reference librarian. College fairs and symposia often include financial aid workshops. Software programs are available to help you search for financial aid. Also, there are companies that specialize in matching students to scholarships and grants. Financial aid officers at local public colleges are an additional good source of information.

Forms, forms, forms. Generally you apply for financial aid at the same time you apply for admission; you do not wait until you have been accepted to begin the financial aid process. Many colleges have a specific form in which students provide general information about their resources and project their need based on the college's expected costs. Most colleges require a form that details the family's income and financial status. The most commonly used form is the Free Application for Federal Student Aid (FAFSA). Colleges may specify other forms; however, they may not require fee-based forms for students applying for federal financial aid. (A fee-based form, PROFILE, is sometimes required when applying for nonfederal financial aid.) Many colleges allow you to apply for financial aid electronically.

When you complete FAFSA, you will need access to income tax returns for both you and your parents (or stepparents). Several weeks after filing FAFSA, you will receive a Student Aid Report (SAR) which summarizes the information, your expected family contribution (EFC), and your eligibility for Pell Grants.

Organizing your information. The process of applying for financial aid to just one college requires that you manage information and forms carefully. When you expand the process from one college to several, it becomes even more complicated. Start by building a master schedule to track due dates. You may want to keep a separate schedule for financial aid or integrate it with the schedule you develop for admissions. Keep copies of all forms and where you send them; have your parents keep copies of their forms as well.

Receiving and bargaining. About the same time you are admitted to a college, you will be notified about the amount and type of aid that you will be offered. You do not have to accept an offer of admission until you know how much aid the college will provide as well as the likelihood of receiving the aid for more than one year. You can also ask for additional time to accept, if necessary. If you are not offered sufficient aid, contact the financial aid officer; you may be able to bargain for more. This is especially true if you are accepted at more than one college. Keep in mind that what you receive from the college is an offer, not necessarily the final word.

Responsibility of aid

Some forms of financial aid may involve long-term commitments, such as loan repayment and service obligations. These are excellent ways of financing your college education. However, in accepting such aid, be sure that you and your family understand the nature of these commitments and agree to the obligations that come with them.

Obligations of aid. Receiving aid carries with it responsibility on the student's part. First is the responsibility and legal obligation to repay loans. Those who do not repay loans make it more difficult for others to receive these benefits. When taking on loans, assess how much you think you can realistically assume. You do not want to assume a level of debt that will unreasonably burden you for years to come.

You are under no obligation to repay grants and scholarships. There may be certain obligations attached, such as maintaining a particular grade point average, participating in athletics, or majoring in an agreed-upon subject area. But many would say that those who receive such gifts should make contributions to scholarship funds when they can, ensuring that students who follow will benefit as they did.

Should you apply? Many students, especially in middle to upper income levels, falsely assume that their financial resources are too high to qualify for aid. Furthermore, many who can afford less expensive colleges fail to apply to more expensive colleges for this reason. However, these students should not limit their possibilities. If they are qualified to enroll, then they should apply for admission. The worst case is that they will not receive aid and will not be able to attend that particular college. However, not applying guarantees that they will not attend. Financial aid should open doors of opportunity, not close them.

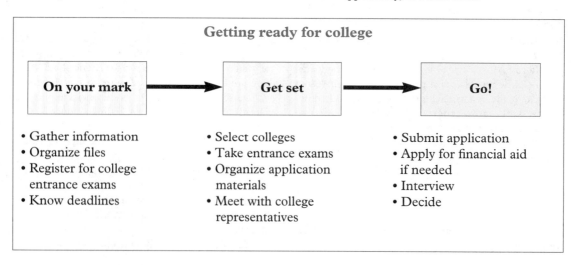

Getting ready for college

On your mark	Get set	Go!
• Gather information • Organize files • Register for college entrance exams • Know deadlines	• Select colleges • Take entrance exams • Organize application materials • Meet with college representatives	• Submit application • Apply for financial aid if needed • Interview • Decide

Thinking About College

Living arrangements

Living arrangements are one of the most important criteria in choosing a college. For many reasons, some students are not able or do not wish to leave home; their search is restricted to colleges within commuting distance, whether by car or public transportation. For others, part of the attraction of college is the opportunity to make the first break from home without the responsibility of living completely independently. Some colleges require first-year students to live on campus to ensure that students are fully integrated and acclimated to campus life. Conversely, other colleges cannot guarantee on-campus housing for students. For students who go away, college living arrangements provide an opportunity to make an important transition in their lives.

Housing options
- **Dormitories**
  Single-gender
  Co-ed by floor
  Co-ed within floor
  International dorms
  Honors dorms
  Smoke-free dorms
  Alcohol-free dorms
- **Fraternities and sororities**
- **College apartments**
- **Off-campus houses and rooms**
- **Living at home**

Types of housing.
Dormitories, operated by the college, are the most common form of on-campus housing. Most students share rooms with one to three other students; several rooms share bathroom facilities. Some dormitories house only men or only women. Many are coeducational, some separating men and women by floors within a dormitory, and others by rooms within a floor. Some campuses have international dormitories, housing students from many countries. Dormitories may be designated for students with common interests. An increasing number of dormitories are smoke-free or alcohol-free.

Colleges will usually select roommates for freshmen based on questionnaires that ask about interests, hobbies, and habits. Upperclassmen generally choose their own roommates.

Many larger colleges operate college apartments, either on or off campus. Each unit is self-contained,

with private bathroom and kitchen. Fraternities and sororities often provide housing to their male and female members respectively.

Students may also rent off campus houses or rooms. This is an option used by upperclassmen or students attending campuses short on dormitory space.

Deciding where to live.
As a general rule, it is best for first-year students who go away to college to live on campus to ensure the best adjustment to college life. Even for students living at home, life changes in important ways. Students and their parents need to discuss these changes and the need for greater privacy and independence.

Students who live off campus have additional challenges. They must consider transportation to and from campus, meals, bills, and household chores, in addition to their academic responsibilities. Despite these added tasks, many upperclassmen find that living off campus provides them with more control over their study environment. A comfortable environment, regardless of where you live, is absolutely essential— not only to your academic success, but also to your overall adjustment to college.

Whether you are living on or off campus, or at home, you are likely to have roommates who may be friends, siblings, or new acquaintances. Sharing living space with others is filled with rewards as well as challenges. If your living arrangement should prove unsatisfactory, speak with a member of the dormitory staff or someone in the housing office, which is often affiliated with the dean of students office.

All colleges are required by law to provide information regarding campus security. Students should acquire this information before making a final decision about where to attend and where to live.

Calculus Answers

NOTE: Exercises are numbered by page, with the first exercise shown as **A,** the second exercise shown as **B,** and so on. When exercises have more than one part, these parts are numbered **(1), (2), (3),** and so on, unless otherwise noted.

120A $m = 20$ miles

120B Mental exercise. No written answer.

121A Minimum value in quadrant IV is approximately -71.16.
Range: $y \geq -71.16$ or
$\qquad y \in [-71.16, \infty)$.

121B Maximum value in quadrant IV occurs at $x = 0.5$. Yes, we can agree.

122A
(A) Dom: $\mathbb{R}$, Range: $\mathbb{R}$
(B) Dom: $\mathbb{R}$, Range: $y \geq 0$
(C) Dom: $\mathbb{R}$, Range: $\mathbb{R}$
(D) Dom: $\mathbb{R}$, Range: varies
(E) Dom: $\mathbb{R}$, $x \neq 0$, Range: $\mathbb{R}$, $y \neq 0$
(F) Dom: $x \geq 0$, Range: $y \geq 0$
(G) Exponential Dom: $\mathbb{R}$, Range: $y > 0$,
    Logarithmic Dom: $x > 0$, Range: $\mathbb{R}$
(H) Dom: $\mathbb{R}$, Range: $y \geq 0$
(I) Dom: $\mathbb{R}$, Range: $\mathbb{R}$
(J) Dom: $\mathbb{R}$, Range: $\mathbb{R}$
(K) sin Dom: $\mathbb{R}$, Range: $|y| \leq 1$, csc Dom: $\mathbb{R}$,
    $x \neq n\pi$, Range: $|y| \geq 1$
(L) cos Dom: $\mathbb{R}$, Range: $|y| \leq 1$, sec Dom: $\mathbb{R}$,
    $x \neq \dfrac{(2n + 1)\,\pi}{2}$, Range: $|y| \geq 1$
(M) tan Dom: $\mathbb{R}$, $x \neq \dfrac{(2n + 1)\,\pi}{2}$
    Range: $\mathbb{R}$, cot Dom: $\mathbb{R}$, $x \neq n\pi$, Range: $\mathbb{R}$

122B

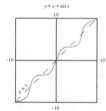

(1) See graph.
(2) The line $y = x$ becomes the axis of oscillation of the sine wave.
(3) Both the domain and range of the function cover all real numbers.
(4) Since range of $y = \sin x$ is $[-1, 1]$ and range of $y = x$ is $(-\infty, \infty)$, then range of their sum would be $(-\infty, \infty)$.

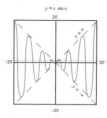

(5) See graph. The amplitude of the sine wave increases as x increases.

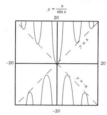

(6) See graph. The function $\dfrac{x}{\sin x}$ looks like a cosecant wave with the tips of the branches moving away from the x-axis along the lines $y = \pm x$.

124A

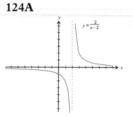

(1) See graph.

(2–3) Limit values
For $c = 1$

Δx	$c - \Delta x$	$f(c - \Delta x)$	$c + \Delta x$	$f(c + \Delta x)$
1.0	0	-1	2	undefined
0.5	0.5	-1.3333	1.5	-4.0
0.25	0.75	-1.60	1.25	-2.6667
0.125	0.8750	-1.7778	1.1250	-2.2857
0.0625	0.9375	-1.8824	1.0625	-2.1333
0.03125	0.9688	-1.9394	1.0313	-2.0645
0.015625	0.9844	-1.9692	1.0156	-2.0317
0.007813	0.9922	-1.9845	1.0078	-2.0157
0.003906	0.9961	-1.9922	1.0039	-2.0078
0.001953	0.9980	-1.9961	1.0020	-2.0039
0.000977	0.9990	-1.9980	1.0010	-2.0020
0.000488	0.9995	-1.9990	1.0005	-2.0010

(4) In column 2, we see domain values approaching 1 from the left-hand side, and in column 3 the corresponding range values are approaching -2. In column 4, we see domain values approaching 1 from the right-hand side, and in column 5 the corresponding range values are approaching -2. Therefore, since approaching 1 from either direction in the domain results in range values approaching -2, we say the limit as x approaches 1 is equal to -2.

(5) For $c = 2$

Δx	$c - \Delta x$	$f(c - \Delta x)$	$c + \Delta x$	$f(c + \Delta x)$
1.0	1.000	-2	3	2
0.5	1.5000	-4	2.5	4
0.25	1.75	-8	2.25	8
0.125	1.875	-16	2.125	16
0.0625	1.9375	-32	2.0625	32
0.03125	1.9688	-64	2.0313	64
0.015625	1.9844	-128	2.0156	128
0.007813	1.9922	-256	2.0078	256
0.003906	1.9961	-512	2.0039	512
0.001953	1.998	-1024	2.002	1024
0.000977	1.999	-2048	2.001	2048
0.000488	1.9995	-4096	2.0005	4096

(6) In column 2, we see the domain values approaching 2 from the left-hand side, and in column 3 we see the corresponding range values decreasing without bound. In column 4, we see the domain values approaching 2 from the right-hand side, and in column 5 we see the corresponding range values increasing without bound. Therefore, since domain values approaching 2 from either side result in range values shooting off in opposite directions, we say the limit as x approaches 2 does not exist.

124B (1–4) Answers contained within exercise.

(5.1) $y = L + \epsilon = 5.25$
$y = L - \epsilon = 4.75$
(5.2) The intersection point $y = 4.75$ with the curve is approximately $(.989, 4.75)$.
(5.3) The intersection point of $y = 5.25$ with the curve is approximately $(1.01, 5.25)$.
(5.4) Now use the x-coordinate to see how far we can stray from $c = 1$, which will give us δ. Since $|.989 - 1| = .011$ and $|1.01 - 1| = .01$ we choose the larger for $\delta = .011$.

127A $f(x)$ approaches $+\infty$ as x approaches 2 from

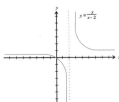

the right, and $f(x)$ approaches $-\infty$ as x approaches 2 from the left. The limit does not exist because $f(x)$ approaches different values as x approaches 2 from either side.

127B
Method 1:

$$\frac{\cos^2 x}{1 - \sin x} = \frac{1 - \sin^2 x}{1 - \sin x}$$

$$= \frac{(1 - \sin x)(1 + \sin x)}{1 - \sin x}$$

So, $\displaystyle\lim_{x \to \pi/2} \frac{\cos^2 x}{1 - \sin x} = \lim_{x \to \pi/2} (1 + \sin x) = 1 + 1 = 2$

Method 2:

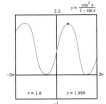

As x gets close to $\dfrac{\pi}{2} \approx 1.57$, y gets close to 2.

128A (1) -4.5 **(2)** $-\dfrac{\pi}{2}$

128B (1) $\dfrac{1}{4}$ **(2)** -10

129A $\dfrac{1}{3}$

130A 2

131A (1) 4 **(2)** $\dfrac{5}{2}$ **(3)** $-\infty$ **(4)** $+\infty$

131B (1) 0 **(2)** -3 **(3)** $-\infty$ **(4)** $+\infty$

133A $\sin \sqrt{x}$ is continuous on $[0, 28\pi]$ since it is well defined at each point in the interval.

135A
(1)

12:00 – 12:15	32 m.p.h
12:15 – 12:30	0
12:30 – 1:00	48 m.p.h.
1:00 – 1:15	24 m.p.h
1:15 – 1:45	80 m.p.h.
1:45 – 2:00	24 m.p.h.

(2) It is possible that the speed limit was exceeded, but the driver was not stopped owing to the fact that the distance continues to increase after the stop at the mall between 12:15 and 12:30.
(3) The average velocity over the entire interval.

136A

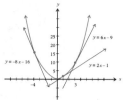

138A

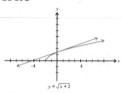

$y = \sqrt{x+2}$

139A

(1) $10x^9$ **(2)** $\dfrac{9}{5}x^{4/5}$ **(3)** $\dfrac{1}{3}x^{-2/3}$

139B $y' = 60x^3 + 18x^2 - 10x - 7$
Tangent line at $(0, -2)$ is $y = -7x - 2$.

140A Tangent line $y = -2.786x + 12.509$

145A Observation and verification exercise. No answer necessary.

145B Observation and verification exercise. No answer necessary.

145C Observation and verification exercise. No answer necessary.

146A The three roots of this function are -1.5413, $-.6975$, and 1.2987.

146B Calculator exercise. Results given.

146C Calculator exercise. Results given.

147A

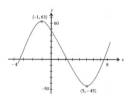

Coordinates are $(-1, 63)$ and $(5, -45)$.

150A Local max at $(2.2795, 6.1282)$.
Absolute max at $(2.7866, 8.6612)$.
Local min at $(2.4679, 5.1708)$.
Local min at $(2.9610, 7.8852)$.
The function is concave down on $x \in (2.126, 2.374) \cup (2.626, 2.874)$ and concave up on $x \in (2, 2.126) \cup (2.374, 2.626) \cup (2.874, 3)$.

153A Answer given.

157A For $n = 32$ lower $= .31787$, upper $= .34912$ and upper $-$ lower $= .03125$. For $n = 64$ lower $= .32556$, upper $= .34119$ and upper $-$ lower $= .01563$.
(1) As n gets larger, the lower rectangles fit under the curve better leaving less space unaccounted for. Also, as n gets larger, the heights of the upper rectangles move down closer to the curve.
(2) As the upper sum decreases and lower sum increases, the difference will decrease.
(3) $n \to \infty$

160A $\displaystyle\int_{-1}^{1} x^3\, dx = 0.$

Explanation: The region in quadrant III has a negative area, while the region in quadrant I has a positive area. Since this is an odd function the areas are symmetric and cancel each other.

161A

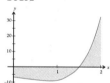

The negative area below the x-axis is larger than the positive area above.

162A
(1) Infinitely many
(2) All graphs would be vertical shifts of F_1, F_2, or F_3.

165A

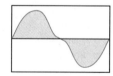

Total area is zero.

167A Verification exercise. Answer given.

168A Calculator exercise. Answer given.

168B Calculator exercise. Answer given.

169A Calculator exercise. Answer given.

169B Calculator exercise. Answer given.

173A
(1) For $x = 3$ Ellen$(x) = 1.09861$
(2) For $x = 8$ Ellen$(x) = 2.0794$
(3) For $x = 0.25$ Ellen$(x) = -1.3863$

175A 0.85914

176A 0.26424

176B 0.64379

177A Verification exercise. Answer given.

183A Verification exercise. Answer given in previous example.

191A Verification exercise. Answers given in the graph on page 191.

196A

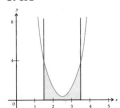

198A 2.30199

200A
(1) $\{n^2 + 2\} = \{3, 6, 11, 18, \ldots\}$

(2) $\left\{\dfrac{1}{n(n + 1)}\right\} = \left\{\dfrac{1}{2}, \dfrac{1}{6}, \dfrac{1}{12}, \ldots\right\}$

(3) $\{5\} = \{5, 5, 5, 5, \ldots\}$

(4) $\left\{1 + \dfrac{1}{n!}\right\} = \left\{2, \dfrac{3}{2}, \dfrac{7}{6}, \dfrac{25}{24}, \ldots\right\}$

201A
(1)

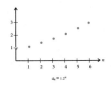

The sequence increases steadily.

(2)

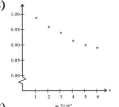

The values decrease and will approach zero.

(3)

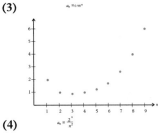

After $n = 3$, the values increase without bound.

(4)

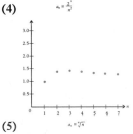

After $n = 3$, the values seem to decrease and approach 1.

(5)

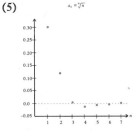

Output values approach zero.

201B Observation exercise. No answer required.

201C No

202A All cases are demonstrated. Answers contained within the definition.

202B An example is $1 + (-.5)^n$. There are many others.

203A (1) 1 (2) Limit does not exist. (3) 0
(4) e^3 (5) 0 (6) 4

204A Optional exercise. Answer contained within the definition.

204B (1) 3.31823 (2) 2.99315

204C (1) 3 (2) $\dfrac{1}{4}$ (3) Diverges

206A (1) Diverges (2) Converges (3) Converges

207A (1) Converges (2) Converges (3) Diverges

207B $p > 1$

Index

How to use the index.
The index to the *Student Handbook, College and University Edition,* is arranged alphabetically according to a letter-by-letter system. All entries are in precise alphabetical order, except for articles, prepositions, and conjunctions.

> **Marshall Islands**
> **Marshall, John**
> **Marshall Plan**
> **Mars (planet)**

Names beginning with Mac or Mc are also arranged in strict alphabetical order. The abbreviation St. is indexed as if it were spelled out as Saint.

Most main entries are indexed under the main element of the name, such as Sinai, Mount (not Mount Sinai); Marathon, Battle of (not Battle of Marathon); Verdun, Treaty of (not Treaty of Verdun). Handy cross-references are provided when a listing may be ambiguous or confusing.

Few abbreviations are used in the index, and those that are used are so standard as to eliminate the need for an abbreviations list.

Titles of literary works are italicized. Also italicized are works that appear in "Usage guide," beginning on page 113.

What Happened When

STAFF

Executive Editor	Raymond V. Hand, Jr.
Contributing Editors	Fon W. Boardman, Jr.
	David H. Scott
Copy Editor	Felice Levy
Indexer	Cynthia Crippen
Computer Keyboarder	Antje Munroe
Researchers	Sally Bunch
	Ellen Sackelman
Proofreaders	Barbara Bergeron
	Bernie Borok
	Rina Cascone
	Bitite Vinklers
	Brenda Woodward

What Happened When

A Chronology of Life and Events in America

Gorton Carruth

Abridged edition of *The Encyclopedia of American Facts & Dates*

HarperPerennial
A Division of HarperCollins*Publishers*

ISBN 0-06-273250-1

Library of Congress has catalogued the previous edition as follows:

Carruth, Gorton.
  What happened when.

  Abridgment of: The encyclopedia of American facts & dates / Gorton Carruth. 10th ed. 1997.
  Includes index.
  1. United States—History—Chronology. I. Carruth, Gorton. Encyclopedia of American facts & dates. II. Title.
E174.5.C32   1989   973′.02′02   88-45550
ISBN 0-06-096318-2

93   93   94   95   97   10   9   8   7   6   5   4   3   2   1

To Gisèle Carruth

Preface

What Happened When is a chronologically arranged encyclopedia of the most important events in American history, from 986 A.D., when Europeans first sighted North America, to the presidential elections of 1997. It contains the essential information students and general readers need in order to understand our country's past. And its unique arrangement makes it an indispensable desk reference book.

Its coverage of subjects is exceptionally broad. A partial listing would include:

Architecture
Art
Books and publishing
Business
Crime
Disasters
Discovery, exploration, settlement
Economics
Education
Fashions
Foreign affairs
Inventions
Politics and government
Religion
Science
Sports
Suffrage
Technology
Television
Theater

Treaties
Vital statistics
Wars and battles
Women

The entries are arranged in convenient time periods, for example, one-year or five-year periods, making it easy to find the entries for contemporaneous events. Within each of these time periods the entries are placed under four broadly conceived topic heads:

I. Civil Rights
   Exploration and Settlement
   Government
   Statistics
   Wars

II. Architecture
    Arts and Music
    Popular Entertainment
    Publishing
    Theater

III. Business and Industry
     Education
     Philosophy and Religion
     Science

IV. Fashion
    Folkways
    Holidays
    Social Issues and Crime
    Sports

Entries concerning civil rights, say, or sports are thus placed together, which speeds the location of events of the same kind.

A brief but detailed introduction under each topic head provides an overview of what was then happening in the country in that subject area, for example, a political campaign or in sports.

With the addition of an exceptionally complete index *What Happened When* becomes the most accessible and comprehensive of inexpensive desk encyclopedias on American life and events.

The parent volume for *What Happened When* is *The Encyclopedia of American Facts and Dates,* now in its tenth edition and a standard reference in its field. In the preface to *American Facts and Dates* are acknowledgments that should be repeated here:

> Acknowledgment should be made to those single-volume American date and reference books that have been especially valuable: *The Reader's Encyclopedia* edited by William Rose Benét (Harper & Row); *Documents of American History* by Henry Steele Commager (Prentice-Hall); *The Columbia Encyclopedia* (Columbia University Press); *Information Please Almanac* (Hough-
> ton Mifflin); *Famous First Facts* by Joseph Nathan Kane (H. W. Wilson); *A Short Chronology of American History, 1492–1950* by Irving S. and Nell M. Kull (Greenwood); *The Encyclopedia of Sports* by Frank Menke (A. S. Barnes); *Encyclopedia of American History* edited by Richard B. Morris (Harper & Row); *The World Almanac* (K-III Reference Corporation). Acknowledgment should especially go to *The New York Times* for much of the recent detail. Thanks should go to the many readers who have made corrections and suggestions for improvement. Warm thanks must be extended to librarians across the country who have adopted *American Facts and Dates* as a standard reference, but the staff of the Mount Pleasant Public Library in Pleasantville, N.Y., must be singled out for special thanks for their cheerful assistance given in every stage of our research.

In addition, I am especially grateful for the contributions made by Fon W. Boardman, Jr., who has written extensively in American history and who has helped immeasurably to make *What Happened When* a more accurate, useful book.

Gorton Carruth
1997

I. **Civil Rights**
Exploration and Settlement
Government
Statistics
Wars

The first Europeans to see the North American continent were Norsemen, led by the navigator Bjarni Herjulfson, who, in 986, while seeking Eric the Red's settlement on the coast of Greenland, was blown off course and sighted an unidentified land mass. In 1000 Leif Ericson, a son of Eric the Red, explored the coast of North America and established a settlement he called Vinland. In the 1960s evidence of such a settlement was unearthed at L'Anse aux Meadows, Newfoundland. Between 1004 and 1008 Leif's brothers, Thorvald and Thorstein, carried out further exploration of the North American coast and may well have seen what is now New England. Thorfinn Karlsefni, a trader from Iceland, visited the coast of North America between 1010 and 1013. The last Norse voyage to the New World took place in 1014–1015 when, according to the Greenland Saga, Eric's daughter, Freydis, sailed with Thorfinn Karlsefni.

1492 Oct 12: The expedition of **Christopher Columbus** sighted what was probably present-day Watling Island, in the Bahamas. That day they went ashore and claimed the island for the king and queen of Spain. Columbus explored the northeastern coast of Cuba and northern coast of Hispaniola, then set sail for Spain on Jan. 16, 1493. On his second expedition (1493–1496) he discovered Jamaica, and on his third (1498–1500) he made further discoveries, including the island of Trinidad. During his fourth and final expedition (1502–1504) Columbus discovered Martinique and explored the coasts of present-day Honduras, Nicaragua, Costa Rica, and Panama.

1513 Apr 2: Juan Ponce de León discovered Florida, claiming it for the king of Spain.

1526 Summer: The **first European settlement** in what is now the U.S., San Miguel de Guadalupe, was established by Lucas Vazquez de Ayllón, who led some 500 or 600 settlers from Hispaniola to the coast of South Carolina. The site of the settlement was thought to have been just north of the mouth of the Peedee R. Many of the settlers died of fever. After Ayllón succumbed on Oct. 18, the approximately 150 surviving settlers returned to Hispaniola.

1539 May 30: Fernando de Soto landed in Florida and began the consolidation of Spain's dominion over the peninsula.

1541 May 8: The **first Europeans to reach the Mississippi R.** were members of the de Soto expedition. De Soto died the next year and was buried in the river.

1542: The **first Europeans to reach the Pacific coast** of what is now the U.S. were members of the expedition of Juan Rodriquez Cabrillo, who was sent on an exploratory voyage by Spanish administrators in Mexico. Cabrillo landed near what is now Ballast Point, San Diego, Calif., then continued his explorations and discovered Santa Catalina Island, San Pedro Bay, the Santa Barbara Channel, and other West Coast landmarks.

1562 Apr 30: The **first French colonizers** in what was to become the U.S., Huguenots led by Jean Ribaut, established Port Royal on Parris Island, off the coast of present-day South Carolina. In early 1564, when supplies failed to arrive from France, the colony was abandoned.

1565 Sep 8: The **first permanent white colony** in what is now the U.S. was founded at St. Augustine, Fla., by the Spanish under Pedro Menéndez de Avilés, a naval officer.

1565 Sep 20: Fort Caroline was destroyed by the Spanish under Menéndez, who massacred most of its inhabitants. He renamed it San Mateo and in the next two years built a string of forts to Tampa Bay while looking for a water passage across Florida.

1579 June 17: The expedition of **Sir Francis Drake** anchored in a harbor just north of present-day San Francisco Bay in California, during Drake's celebrated circumnavigation of the globe. Drake named the land Nova Albion and claimed it for England. The members of the expedition spent a month repairing their ship. Then on July 26 Drake sailed from California, continuing north and then west across the Pacific Ocean.

1585 Aug: The **Roanoke Island colony,** sponsored by Sir Walter Raleigh, was established on Roanoke Island, off the northeast coast of what is now North Carolina, under the leadership of Sir Richard Grenville and Sir Ralph Lane. The settlers fared badly and returned to England in June of 1586. In 1587 Raleigh sent out another group, under John White, consisting of 117 men, women, and children. White returned to England for supplies but was unable to get back to Roanoke until Aug. 17, 1590. He found all the colonists gone; the only clue to their fate was the word *CROATOAN* carved on a tree. The meaning of this remains unexplained and no trace was ever found of the settlers.

II. Architecture
Arts and Music
Popular Entertainment
Publishing
Theater

Almost as soon as the early explorers of America returned to Europe, they wrote accounts of their adventures. These accounts expressed great enthusiasm and, like later accounts, might be classed as promotional material. The first eyewitness report in English of what today is part of the U.S. was written in 1588 by Thomas Hariot, who took part in the Roanoke Island adventure sponsored by Sir Walter Raleigh. Hariot's account was entitled *A Brief and True Report of the New Found Land of Virginia.* It depicted America as a paradise where a little work would yield great prosperity. In the following year appeared *The Principal Navigations, Voyages, Traffics, and Discoveries of the English Nation* by Richard Hakluyt. Not an explorer himself but a collector of the reports of others, Hakluyt later enlarged his book and included the adventures of Sir Francis Drake, Sir Humphrey Gilbert, Sir Martin Frobisher, and others. In the early seventeenth century, further works were written by such explorers as John Smith and Samuel de Champlain. Mapmakers also went to work almost as soon as the New World was found, although their maps were very inexact by today's standards and reflected the prevailing belief or hope that America was but a minor obstacle in the way of ships seeking the riches of the Far East. One such map was prepared by Sebastian Cabot in 1544 and another by Gerardus Mercator in 1569.

1507: The term *America* was first used for the New World in Martin Waldseemüller's short geography book *Cosmographiae Introductio.* Wrote Waldseemüller, "But now that these parts have been more extensively examined, and another fourth part has been discovered by Americus Vespuccius . . . I do not see why anyone should by right object to name it America . . . after its discoverer, Americus, a man of sagacious mind, since both Europe and Asia took their names from women." Waldseemüller mistakenly attributed discovery of the New World to Amerigo Vespucci.

1584: Richard Hakluyt wrote *A Discourse Concerning Western Planting,* at the request of Sir Walter Raleigh, for Queen Elizabeth I of England. This work urged that the queen promote English settlement in America and offered a complete plan for such a program. Hakluyt said such settlement would help promote religion, supply goods for England, employ men who would otherwise be idle, increase revenues, provide overseas bases for use in the event of war with Spain, and be useful in the search for a Northwest Passage to the Orient. Hakluyt wrote enthusiastically that "this Realm shall have by that meane Shippes of great burden and of great strengthe" for defense. Further, he wrote, colonial trade would "breed more skilfull, connynge and stowte pilotts and maryners than any other belonging to this land: For it is the long voyaiges . . . that harden seamen and open unto them the secrets of navigation." The queen apparently read the *Discourse* but did not act on it. It was not published until almost three centuries later, when it was issued by the Maine Historical Society. As for Hakluyt, an ordained clergyman of the Church of England, he never saw America. Although he had intended to go to Jamestown, Va., in 1607 as rector, he was not physically able to make the trip. He died and was buried in Westminster Abbey in 1616.

1598 Apr 30: The **first theatrical performance** given in North America was acted on the Rio Grande near present-day El Paso, Tex. The play was a Spanish *comedia* dealing with an expedition of soldiers. On July 10 the same group produced *Moros y los Cristianos* (Moors and Christians), an anonymous play.

III. Business and Industry
Education
Philosophy and Religion
Science

When John Cabot discovered Newfoundland in 1497, he also discovered one of the world's great fishing areas. He enjoyed the codfish his crew found and he saw nets on shore, but not their Indian owners. England, however, was slow to develop this economic and trade resource. The French and Portuguese were the first to exploit it. They took fish home for trading purposes and also traded fish, which they cured on shore, with the Indians for furs. By 1577, according to Richard Hakluyt, there were 150 French fishing craft, 100 Spanish, and 50 Portuguese, but only 15 English vessels fishing in Newfoundland. English fishing, however, became dominant in the next century. Despite the competition of the European nations in other areas, this fertile fishing ground provided a peaceful international exchange.

1112: The **first bishop of America** was appointed. He was Eric Gnupsson, named by Pope Paschal II. His see included Greenland and Vinland.

1540: The **first recorded baptism** in what is now the U.S. was performed by priests accompanying the Fernando de Soto expedition. They baptized an Indian guide, Peter, in the waters of the Acmulgee R., near present-day Macon, Ga.

1550-1600: Discovery of **new agricultural products** during the Spanish explorations of the New World proved a great benefit to European economic development. Spanish expeditions brought back to the Old World such things as potatoes, tomatoes, quinine extracted from the bark of the cinchona tree, cocoa, tapioca from the cassava root, and tobacco. In return settlers brought to the Americas such things as barley, oats, rye, sugar cane, cattle, pigs, poultry, rabbits, and horses, which later found a natural home on the plains.

1565 Sep 8: The **first Catholic parish** in what is now the U.S., the parish of St. Augustine, Fla., was founded by Fr. Don Martin Francisco Lopez de Mendozo Grajales, chaplain of the Spanish expeditionary forces.

1566: The **first Jesuit missionaries** in what was to become the U.S., three Jesuits sponsored by Pedro Menéndez de Avilés, arrived in Spanish Florida, followed by a second group two years later. The first missions were established at Guale, in present-day Georgia, and Orista and Santa Elena, in present-day South Carolina. The Jesuits were forced out of Florida by the Indians within a few years.

1579: The **first Protestant service** in the New World, and the first religious service in English held there, was conducted in California. Participants were members of the crew of Adm. Francis Drake's expedition. Having sailed around South America, the expedition put into a bay at the 38th parallel where, according to the ship's log, "the admiral ordered divine service to be performed at his tent."

1587: The **first Indian convert** to Protestant Christianity was Manteo, who was baptized into the Church of England by members of Sir Walter Raleigh's expedition to Roanoke. Manteo was later named Lord of Roanoke by Raleigh.

IV. Fashion
Folkways
Holidays
Social Issues and Crime
Sports

At the beginning of European colonization, there were some 600 tribes of North American Indians, speaking some 500 different dialects. They were chiefly hunters and gatherers, but some tribes had developed agriculture, and bartered or used wampum to exchange goods. There was a good deal of warfare between tribes and most Indians prided themselves on their courage in battle. But the Indians' chief weapon, the bow and arrow, was no match for European firearms, and against Old World diseases such as smallpox they had no defense. As soon as European settlement began in the early sixteenth century, the fragile structure of North American Indian society began to crumble.

1007: The **first white child** born in North America was Snorro, the son of Thorfinn and Gudrid Karlsefni, members of Leif Ericson's expedition to Vinland. Later Snorro became an important member of the Norse community in Iceland.

1540: The **horse was first introduced** on a large scale into what is now the U.S. by Francisco Coronado, the Spanish explorer, who traveled through Kansas with 260 horses, most escaping to the Midwest, Mexico, and Canada. These animals eventually mingled with large French Norman horses brought to Canada by

French settlers, producing the wild horses later found in North America.

1565: Smoking of tobacco was introduced to England by John Hawkins. Hawkins was primarily a slave trader, carrying Africans to the West Indies. Most of his dealings were with the Spanish in the West Indies, but during his second trip to the region (1564–1566) he visited the small French colony in Florida and learned to smoke tobacco from the colonists, who had learned from the Indians. Hawkins returned to England with a shipload of tobacco. He described the Indian use of the plant this way: "The Floridians when they travell have a kinde of herbe dried, who with a cane and an earthen cap in the end, with fire, and dried herbs put together, doe sucke thorow the cane the smoke thereof, which smoke satisfieth their hunger, and therwith they live foure or five days without meat or drinke, and this all the Frenchmen used for this purpose."

1585: The first eyewitness picture of **American Indians at play,** a drawing by John White, showed Indians participating in lacrosse, archery, and foot racing, and pitching balls at a target on top of a high tree.

1587 Aug 18: The **first English child** born in North America was Virginia Dare. Her parents were Ananias and Ellinor Dare, members of Sir Walter Raleigh's colony at Roanoke Island, in present-day North Carolina. Ellinor Dare was the daughter of Gov. John White, who had led a company of 150 householders to establish a colony on the island.

1600–1609

I. **Civil Rights**
  Exploration and Settlement
  Government
  Statistics
  Wars

From the beginning a chief purpose of voyages to the New World was to find a trade route to the Far East. When it became clear that there was a large land mass between Europe and the East, the search for a sea route became a search for the Northwest Passage, a way around the northern part of North America. Sir Martin Frobisher in 1576–1578 was the first European to search for such a route. John Davis made a similar attempt in 1585–1587. When Henry Hudson sailed up the Hudson R. in 1609 he hoped he had

found the route, and in 1610 when he discovered Hudson Bay he was on a similar mission. In 1616 William Baffin discovered Baffin Bay, which many years later was to provide a key to the actual route, long after the Northwest Passage had lost any commercial appeal.

1602 May 15: The **first Englishman** to land in what is now New England was Capt. Bartholomew Gosnold, who anchored at what is now New Bedford, Mass. He had sailed on Mar. 26 from Falmouth, England, on the *Concord,* touched at the Maine coast, and explored the New England coastline. He named Cape Cod, Martha's Vineyard, and other landmarks.

1604: The **first northern French colony** was established by Pierre du Guast, Sieur de Monts, at Neutral Island in the St. Croix R. in southeastern Maine. His patent had been granted by the French king.

1606: Colonial charters were granted to the Virginia Company of London and the Virginia Company of Plymouth by the English Crown. The grants extended from Cape Fear, N.C., to the St. Croix R. on the border between what are now Maine and New Brunswick, Canada. The London Company was permitted to establish settlements in a tract between 34 and 41 degrees north latitude. The Plymouth Company was granted an equal tract between 38 and 45 degrees north latitude. The overlapping area was a neutral zone where both companies could establish settlements.

1607 May 13: The **first permanent English colony** in North America, Jamestown, Va., was founded by more than 100 colonists on the left bank of the "River of Powhatan" (James R.). Dispatched by the London Company, the colonists had sailed aboard the *Sarah Constant, Goodspeed,* and *Discovery.*

1607 Dec: Capt. **John Smith** and two companions were captured by Indians while in search of provisions. His companions were killed, but he was spared, Smith reported, by the intercession of Pocahontas, Chief Powhatan's daughter.

1607 Dec: Probably the **first act of rebellion** in the American colonies, a conspiracy against the Council of Jamestown, was uncovered in Virginia. George Kendall, its leader, was shot for mutiny.

II. **Architecture**
  Arts and Music
  Popular Entertainment
  Publishing
  Theater

The key factor determining the design of the first colonial structures was the availability of building materials. In New England, the settlers tried to copy the architecture of their homelands, using wood, which was in abundance. In the South, brick soon displaced wood as the favorite building material. In the Southwest, the Spaniards adapted Indian materials and methods for their buildings. Such a structure, the oldest surviving non-Indian building in the U.S., was the governor's palace in Santa Fe, N. Mex., built in 1609 by Don Pedro de Peralta. The building of forts, usually of logs, for defense against Indian attacks, became a necessity. The Jamestown colonists began such work less than a month after they landed in 1607. In August of that year, a Plymouth Company expedition to Maine erected a fort that encompassed other structures.

1606 Nov 14: One of the **earliest theatrical performances** in North America, the French masque *Le Théâtre de Neptune en la Nouvelle-France* (Neptune's Theater in New France), took place at Port Royal, Acadia (Nova Scotia).

1608: What is considered the **first American book,** *A True Relation of Such Occurrences and Accidents of Noate as Hath Hapned in Virginia Since the First Planting of that Collony* by Capt. John Smith, was printed in London. The book strangely omitted the famous tale of Pocahontas. It was not until 1624, with the publication of his book *The Generall Historie of Virginia, New-England, and the Summer Isles,* that Smith included a reference to the famous romance.

1609: The last work of **Richard Hakluyt,** *Virginia Richly Valued,* was published. It was based upon a Portuguese work, *Relacam,* which was written by a voyager who claimed to have been with Fernando de Soto on the expedition through Florida, Georgia, Alabama, Arkansas, and Louisiana. One of three extant histories of this voyage, *Virginia Richly Valued* has been attributed to the original authorship of de Soto.

III. Business and Industry
Education
Philosophy and Religion
Science

In the early days of the English colonies, trade was a one-way street. The colonists badly needed supplies from the homeland. The colony at Jamestown, Va., for example, was not self-sufficient for many years. On June 22, 1607, Capt. Christopher Newport left Jamestown with a cargo for England. Unfortunately, the cargo was fool's gold, but it was an indication of the economic motives of those who sponsored outposts in the New World. In Dec. 1608 Newport sailed

with a more practical cargo: pitch, tar, soap, ashes, and glass. There is evidence that sassafras was shipped from Cape Cod earlier, but this Jamestown cargo was the first instance of American manufactures being exported.

1603: A **monopoly of the fur trade,** granted for a ten-year period to Pierre du Guast, Sieur de Monts, by the king of France, reflected the importance the French placed on the trade. The English and Dutch were far behind in developing a fur trade with the Indians. Monts was associated with Pierre Chauvin, Sieur de Tonnetuit, a naval officer and trader; and with Samuel de Champlain, who in 1608 founded Quebec and the following year discovered the lake that now bears his name, in what is now New York State. They established trading posts in eastern Canada, working their way south to the Penobscot R. in what is now Maine. Monts' monopoly of the fur trade was rescinded in 1607, then restored for a year in 1608. He withdrew from the trade about 1612. Even with a monopoly, it was difficult to prevent others from engaging in fur trading. Eventually the English and Dutch became strong competitors in the fur trade.

IV. Fashion
Folkways
Holidays
Social Issues and Crime
Sports

Settlers as well as explorers were beginning to come to the English territories on the Atlantic coast. Unfortunately, some of the earliest pioneers, as at Jamestown, Va., were adventurers interested more in making a quick fortune from the alleged riches of the New World than in engaging in agriculture or forestry. In later years, though, a greater diversity of settlers arrived and brought with them a variety of skills. They ranged from wealthy Englishmen, who wanted to carve out large estates, to servants. Merchants saw the opportunity for trade as populations grew. Groups seeking religious freedom were also prominent, bringing with them a tradition of hard work and a willingness to start life anew.

1600: The **Indian population** of what was to become the U.S. was about 1,000,000 when European exploration began. Because the pattern of settlement here differed from that of the Spanish penetration of Central and South America, the change in customs of the Indians was, at first, comparatively slow. Pioneer groups of European colonists were small. They entered regions with sparser populations and more fluid cultures than the larger and more stable Indian communities of Central America, the Andes, and the Caribbean islands. Contact was sometimes mutually beneficial, but there was no fusion of European and Indian cultures as occurred in South America. In retrospect, the first decade of the seventeenth century was the twilight of aboriginal Indian life.

1608: John Smith had two Indians teach him how to raise **Indian corn.** Faced with starvation the colonists accepted this new grain, although opposition to it existed everywhere. In French Louisiana, the women, accustomed to fancier European fare, staged a petticoat rebellion against daily consumption of corn. The governor reported that the women " . . . inveigh bitterly against His Grace, the Bishop of Quebec, who, they say has enticed them away from home under the pretext of sending them to enjoy the milk and honey of the land of promise."

1609: In what was probably the **first marriage** in the American colonies, Anne Burrows and John Laydon were wed in Virginia.

1610–1619

I. Civil Rights
Exploration and Settlement
Government
Statistics
Wars

The colonies, as soon as they were established, had to have leadership and a system of government. The proprietors of the companies that were granted colonizing rights appointed their own colonial governors. The Virginia Company, on Feb. 28, 1610, named Thomas West De La Warr, Lord Delaware, the first lord governor and captain general of the Virginia colony. On May 23, 1611, he was succeeded by Sir Thomas Dale, whose new law code amounted almost to martial law. Within a few years, however, the colonists had more voice in government, and the New England colonies, although theocratic, were not under comparably absolute rule.

The estimated European **population** in the colonies was 210.

1612: The **foundation of New York City** was laid when the Dutch sent two ships, *Tiger* and *Fortune*, to trade with the Indians on the Hudson R. Huts were built on Manhattan Island (approximately where 45 Broad-

way now stands) to house trade goods. One year later, a permanent trading post was established. The next year a fort was erected on the tip of the island.

1614: The **first important Dutch settlement** in the New World, preceding New Amsterdam, was Fort Nassau, a stockaded post at Castle Island, near present-day Albany, N.Y. Established by Dutch fur traders, it was abandoned in 1617 and a new fort was built on the shore of the Hudson R. Fort Orange, near Albany, was established in 1624 by the Walloons. The region was later dominated by the patroonship of Rensselaerswyck.

1619 July 30: The **first legislative assembly** in America, the House of Burgesses, convened at Old Church, Jamestown, Va. All legislation needed the approval of the London Company.

1619 Aug: The **first slaves** arrived in Virginia when a Dutch ship carried 20 blacks to Jamestown, Va., for sale.

II. Architecture
Arts and Music
Popular Entertainment
Publishing
Theater

An important figure in early colonial literature was John Smith, the explorer and adventurer who wrote seven books about the New World. Among these were *A Map of Virginia* (1612), probably his best-known work; *A Description of New England* (1616); and *New England's Trials* (1620). These works contributed to further exploration and settlement and offer excellent views of early colonization. Smith's autobiography, *The True Travels, Adventures, and Observations of Captaine John Smith,* was published in 1630, the year before his death.

1610: An **early report of Virginia** was contained in *A True Reportory of the Wrack and Redemption of Sir Thomas Gates, Knight, upon and from the Islands of the Bermudas, his coming to Virginia and the Estate of that Colony then and after the Government of the Lord La Ware,* a firsthand account of New World settlement by William Strachey. First published in 1625, the manuscript has been offered as one of the sources that might have suggested *The Tempest* to William Shakespeare.

1612: An early **detailed study of Virginia** was provided in *A Map of Virginia* by Capt. John Smith. The book, describing Virginia's land, its commodities, people, government, and religion, was published in Oxford, England.

III. Business and Industry
Education
Philosophy and Religion
Science

Early explorers were astonished to see Indians smoking tobacco, a plant unknown in Europe. Tobacco leaves were soon taken to Europe, where smoking became a rage. For a time it was believed that the fumes had miraculous curative powers. As a result of its popularity, tobacco became an economic asset in America, especially in Virginia, where a young planter, John Rolfe, planted the first successful crop in 1612. By 1619 tobacco was the leading export of Virginia, and it was later used as a basis for currency. Unfortunately, tobacco production came to require a large number of slaves, and the crop quickly depleted the soil.

1611: The **first Presbyterian congregation** in America was established at Jamestown, Va., by the Rev. Alexander Whitaker, a volunteer from the Puritan community at Cambridge, England. He is best known as the clergyman who instructed Pocahontas in Christianity and baptized her.

1613: Pocahontas, daughter of Powhatan, head of a confederacy of Algonquian tribes in Virginia, was baptized, perhaps the first Indian convert in the colony. Taken hostage to compel the release of colonists held by her father's tribe, she came into contact with the Rev. Alexander Whitaker, was converted, baptized, and given the Christian name of Rebecca. On Apr. 14, 1614, she married the young planter John Rolfe. On a trip to England, her old friend, Capt. John Smith, introduced her to the royal court.

1616: A **smallpox epidemic** among Indians relieved future New England colonies of the threat of major hostilities with the Indians. The tribes from the Penobscot R. in Maine to Narragansett Bay in Rhode Island were virtually destroyed.

IV. Fashion
Folkways
Holidays
Social Issues and Crime
Sports

Colonists from Europe brought with them their customs with regard to recreation. As early as May of 1611, the men of Jamestown, Va., played a game of bowls in the street, the first such event on record. At Christmas in 1625, a Virginian recorded that "the extreame winde, rayne, froste and snow caused us to keepe Christmas among the savages where we were never more merry, nor fed on more plenty of good

Oysters, Fish, Flesh, Wilde fowl and good bread, nor never had better fires in England." In 1619, however, Virginia prohibited gaming at dice or cards. A few years later the Pilgrim and Puritan fathers of New England frowned on almost all frivolity.

1617: Women started to arrive in Virginia. Unlike the Puritans in the North, Virginia settlers came over "not as men, but more as soldiers sent out to occupy an enemy's country." The arrival of women insured the growth and development of permanent communities.

1618: In a move to **compel church attendance,** Gov. Samuel Argall of Virginia decreed that all who failed to attend church service would be imprisoned in the guardhouse, "lying neck and heels in the Corps of Gard ye night following and be a slave ye week following." Sunday dancing, fiddling, card playing, hunting, and fishing were also forbidden.

1620–1629

I. Civil Rights
Exploration and Settlement
Government
Statistics
Wars

In 1629 the Dutch West India Company introduced the patroon system to New Netherland. To encourage emigration, the company on June 7 proclaimed a Charter of Freedoms and Exemptions, by which large tracts of land were granted to those who could establish settlements of 50 persons within four years. In return, the landholder, or patroon, received what amounted to feudal rights and authority. By 1630 five such patroonships had been established, but only three were ever colonized: Pavonia, which included what is now Staten Island, N.Y.; Swaanendael on Delaware Bay; and Rensselaerswyck on the upper Hudson R. Of these, only Rensselaerswyck was successful.

The estimated colonial **population** was 2499.

1620 Nov 21: The **Mayflower Compact,** the first social contract for a New England colony, was drafted and signed by 41 adult males in Provincetown Harbor, Mass. The Pilgrims did not settle there, but went on after a time to Plymouth.

1620 Dec 26: The **Pilgrims reached Plymouth,** Mass., aboard the *Mayflower* after setting out from England on Sept. 16. The company consisted of 41 men and their families.

1621: A peace treaty and defensive alliance between the Wampanoag Indians and the Pilgrims was concluded at Strawberry Hill, Plymouth, Mass. Arranged by Squanto, an English-speaking Indian, it was one of the earliest recorded treaties between Europeans and Indians in North America. Squanto had been kidnaped and sold as a slave in Spain. He escaped to England, where he learned English, and lived in Newfoundland for a time before returning to Massachusetts in 1619.

1622 Mar 22: The **first Indian massacre,** led by Powhatan's brother, almost wiped out the settlements outside Jamestown, Va., which was itself heavily fortified.

1622 Aug 10: The province of **Maine** was granted to John Mason and Ferdinando Gorges. It included the land between the Merrimack and Kennebec rivers.

1624 May: The Dutch colony of **New Netherland,** which at this time consisted of the Hudson River Valley north to Fort Orange, was established when Cornelis J. Mey reached what is now New York Bay with 30 families. Mey was the first governor of New Netherland.

1624 Dec 21: The **first Swedish colony** in America was authorized by a charter granted to the South Company of Sweden. No colony was established until 1638, after organization of the New Sweden Company (1637).

1625 Spring: The Dutch settlement of **New Amsterdam** was constructed at the tip of Manhattan, or Manhattes, Island. The settlement was under the direction of Willem Verhulst, who succeeded Cornelis Mey as governor of New Netherland. On May 4, 1626, Peter Minuit arrived with a new group of settlers and succeeded Verhulst, with the title director general of New Netherland.

1626: Manhattan Island was sold by the Indians for goods valued at 60 guilders, later calculated as the legendary sum of $24. The purchase was made by Peter Minuit.

1629 June 27: The first settlers of **Massachusetts Bay Colony** entered Salem Harbor. Led by John Winthrop, they were 900 strong, and arrived in five ships.

II. Architecture
Arts and Music
Popular Entertainment
Publishing
Theater

One of the great stories of American literature concerns Myles Standish, military leader of Plymouth colony. According to tradition, in 1621 Standish, whose wife Rose had just died, asked John Alden, a young Pilgrim rising in importance, to court Priscilla Mullens on his behalf. When Alden did so, the maiden said to Alden, "Prithee, John, why do you not speak for yourself?" John did so, they were married, and Standish forgave Alden. This tale, although historically unfounded, was enshrined in American tradition by Henry Wadsworth Longfellow's poem "The Courtship of Miles Standish" (1858).

1620: The **first public library** in the English colonies was established at a college planned for Henrico, Virginia. The library received bequests of books from English estates; but the college was never developed, and the collection of books was soon broken up.

1622: The journal of William Bradford and Edward Winslow, long known as ***Mourt's Relation*** and containing the first detailed and accurate account of the landing of the Pilgrims at Plymouth, was published. Printed anonymously in England as *A Relation or Journall of the Beginning and Proceedings of the English Plantation Setled at Plimoth in New England,* it included a preface bearing the signature G. Mourt, possibly that of George Morton, who served as an agent for the colony.

1624: ***The Generall Historie of Virginia, New England, and the Summer Isles*** by John Smith was published in England. The book consisted of accounts of his observations in the New World. Besides helping to found Virginia, he had mapped the coastal area of New England around Cape Cod in 1614. This exciting report, which included the first complete account of Smith's rescue by Pocahontas, was in part promotional literature designed to encourage immigration.

III. Business and Industry
Education
Philosophy and Religion
Science

A major factor in the establishment of the English colonies was the search for religious freedom. Much of the seventeenth century was a period of religious dissent in the British Isles against the established Church of England. The best known of the dissenters were the Pilgrims, who were Separatists, and the more numerous Puritans, who established the Massachusetts Bay Colony. Their church, the Congregational Church, became established in New England and was supported by taxes. Maryland was founded as a Roman Catholic sanctuary, and later the persecuted Quakers found a haven in Pennsylvania. Baptists, Presbyterians, and, later, Methodists added to the denominational mix of English colonists in America. Virginia was settled largely by Anglicans.

1620: A **Congregational Church** was founded in Plymouth, Mass., by 102 Pilgrim Separatists under William Brewster, William Bradford, and Edward Winslow, all of whom were part of the Scrooby-Leiden congregation in Holland. In England, Congregationalists were known as Independents. Ralph Smith, the first successful pastor of the church, arrived later.

1624 Mar: The **first cattle** brought to New England were three heifers and one bull imported from Devon, England, by Edward Winslow, later governor of Plymouth colony.

1628: The **Reformed Protestant Dutch Church** was established in New Amsterdam under the leadership of the Rev. Jonas Michaelius. Before this date Dutch settlers had held informal meetings of worship. The Rev. Michaelius also established the first school in New Netherland. The Reformed Church was the established church of the colony until the English conquest in 1664. Four churches in New York City—Fort Washington Collegiate Church, Middle Collegiate Church, Marble Collegiate Church, and West End Collegiate Church—now collectively known as the Collegiate Reformed Dutch Church, grew out of this early church.

1629 July 10: The **first non-Separatist Congregational Church** in America was established in Salem, Mass. The church was founded by Francis Higginson and Samuel Skelton, two ministers newly arrived from England.

IV. Fashion
Folkways
Holidays
Social Issues and Crime
Sports

An important albeit lowly position in the colonial social structure, between free men and slaves, was that of the indentured servant. Indentured servants, in return for passage to America, agreed to work for a period of time, usually five years, in return for little more than their keep. Many came of their own free will, but the English government also sent over hundreds of hardened criminals on such terms. Often, after the servants' terms of service had expired, they were granted plots of land. Others became tenant farmers, as in Virginia, where by 1619 their farms extended for 20 miles along the James R.

1621 Dec: The **earliest American harvest festival** was celebrated by the Pilgrims at Plymouth, Mass.

1621 Dec 25: Game playing on Christmas Day by newcomers to Plymouth colony was halted by Gov. William Bradford. The governor, scandalized at the settlers' playing of such games as "pitching the barr" and "stoole-ball," confiscated the equipment needed to play the games.

1623: Seafood was the main source of nutrition for women and children arriving in New England this year to join their Pilgrim husbands and fathers. The settlers were feasted with "a lobster or a piece of fish without bread or anything else but a cup of spring water." Many lobsters weighed 25 lbs. and were so abundant that the smallest child could catch them.

1625: The **first child** born in New Amsterdam was in the family of Jan Joris Rapaelje, marking the beginning of family life in the Dutch settlement.

1627: 1500 kidnaped children arrived in Virginia. They came from Europe and some became great successes. A six-year-old, kidnaped by a sailor and sold in America, married his master's daughter, inherited his fortune, and bought the sailor, by then a prisoner.

1628 May 1: The celebration of **May Day** at Mare Mount, Thomas Morton's settlement at what is now Quincy, Mass., was colorfully although bitterly described by Gov. Bradford: "They allso set up a May-Pole, drinking and dancing aboute it many days together, inviting the Indean women, for their consorts, dancing and frisking together, (like so many faries or furies rather) and worse practices. As they had anew revived and celebrated the feasts of the Roman Goddes Flora, or the beastly practieses of the Madd Bacchinalians."

1630–1639

I. Civil Rights
Exploration and Settlement
Government
Statistics
Wars

The first of the many wars between whites and Indians was fought in 1637 between the Pequots and New England settlers. The Pequots were a warlike tribe centered along the Thames R. in southeastern Connecticut. By 1630, under their chief, Sassacus, they had pushed west to the Connecticut R. There they had numerous quarrels with colonists, culminating in the murder by the Pequots of a trader, John Oldham, on July 20, 1636. On Aug. 24 Gov. John Endicott of Massachusetts Bay Colony organized a military force to punish the Indians, and on May 26, 1637, the first battle of the Pequot War took place when the New Englanders, under John Mason and John Underhill, attacked the Pequot stronghold near present-day New Haven, Conn. The Indian forts were burned and about 500 men, women, and children were killed. The survivors fled in small groups. One group, led by Sassacus, was caught near present-day Fairfield, Conn., on July 28, and nearly all were killed or captured. The captives were made slaves by the colonists or were sold in the West Indies. Sassacus and the few who escaped with him were put to death by Mohawk Indians. The few remaining Pequots were scattered among other southern New England tribes.

The estimated colonial **population** was 5700.

1630: Rensselaerswyck, the only successful Dutch patroonship, was founded by Kiliaen Van Rensselaer, a director of the Dutch West India Company. The patroonship, comprising present-day Albany and Rensselaer counties, extended 24 miles on both sides of the Hudson R., and its inhabitants numbered several thousand tenants. It was never seen by Van Rensselaer, who managed the entire enterprise from his home in Old Amsterdam.

1630: A settlement at Trimountain, also known as Shawmut, an Indian name meaning living fountain, was established by John Winthrop. The settlement was an extension of the colony at Salem, Mass., which was under the governorship of John Endicott. On Sept. 17 the settlement was named Boston.

1630 Sep 30: The **first criminal executed** in the American colonies, John Billington, was hanged for murder. A member of the original Pilgrim band, he had waylaid and shot a man with whom he had quarreled.

1632 June 20: A charter for the settlement of **Maryland** was granted to Cecilius Calvert, second Lord Baltimore. Under his proprietorship, the Roman Catholic settlement of St. Marys was established. Leonard Calvert, his brother, was the first governor of Maryland.

1636 June: Rhode Island was founded by Roger Williams, who established Providence with a small group of colonists from Massachusetts Bay. It was the first English colony in America to grant complete religious tolerance.

1638 Mar: The **first Swedish settlers** in America landed at Fort Christiana, Del., after crossing in Dutch ships under Peter Minuit. They established the first Lutheran congregation in America, led by Rev. Reorus Rorkillus. In 1643 Swedish colonists from

Delaware, under John Printz, settled at Upland, now Chester, Pa.

1639 Jan 14: The **first constitution** in the colonies, the Fundamental Orders, composed by Roger Ludlow, was adopted by representatives from Hartford, Windsor, and Wethersfield in Connecticut. The resulting instrument, with some changes, remained in force until 1818.

II. Architecture
Arts and Music
Popular Entertainment
Publishing
Theater

The history of American publishing dates from 1638, when the first printing press in the colonies arrived in Cambridge, Mass. It was the property of the Rev. Jose Glover, who died on the voyage from England. He had brought it with him under contract with Stephen Daye. In Cambridge, Glover's widow and Matthew Daye, Stephen's son, helped set up the press. In 1639 the press produced the first English document printed in America, "Oath of a Free-Man." This broadsheet read in part: "I doe solemnly bind myself in the sight of God, that when I shal be called to give my voyce touching any such matter of this State, in which Freemen are to deal, I will give my vote and suffrage as I shal judge in mine own conscience may best conduce and tend to the publike weal of the body, without respect of persons, or favour of any man." An almanac soon followed this broadsheet and in the course of the next decade more than 20 items were printed.

1630: *History of Plimmoth Plantation* by William Bradford, the first account of the settlement of Plymouth colony, was begun. Bradford was the second governor of Plymouth colony. His book took more than 20 years to complete and was first published in full in 1856. Devout, sincere, and learned, Bradford wrote feelingly of the *Mayflower* crossing and of the pioneer life of the early settlers. His authenticity earned him the title "father of American history."

1630 May 29: *The History of New England,* a chronicle of events from 1630 to 1649, was begun by John Winthrop, first governor of Massachusetts Bay Colony. The journal was the inspiration for many of Henry Wadsworth Longfellow's *New England Tragedies.* It was published in a two-volume edition in 1790. When an additional manuscript was found some time later, the whole work finally appeared as *The History of New England,* published in 1825–1826.

Winthrop touched upon all major aspects of life. His work is a vast compendium of what the early colonists felt and thought and traces the evolution of their ideas and ideals. It remains an unparalleled primary source for the history of the period.

1634: The **first Roman Catholic** church built by English colonists was raised at St. Marys City, Md. Excavations have revealed its foundation, but nothing else is known about its appearance.

1636: The **oldest extant house** of the English-speaking colonies, the Adam Thoroughgood House, was built near Norfolk, Va. Its design typified that of the small, southern colonial brick farmhouse of the seventeenth century.

1637: The *New English Canaan,* a book by Thomas Morton describing New England life and satirizing the Plymouth Pilgrims, was published in Amsterdam. Morton founded the colony at Mare Mount, where Maypole dances and other so-called debauched customs stirred the wrath of Puritan leaders. Morton was the square peg in the round hole of New England Puritanism. He spent his life traveling back and forth across the Atlantic, spending enough time in various colonies to outrage the local authorities and be shipped back to England and prison. Before he published his book, he was engaged by the English as an informer against the Massachusetts Bay Colony. The book served partly as revenge for the treatment he had received from the Puritans and partly as justification for his own activities. Nathaniel Hawthorne wrote about Morton in "The Maypole of Merry-Mount."

1638: Construction of **Old College** was begun at Harvard College in Cambridge, Mass. The most ambitious building of its time in the U.S., it housed the entire student body, library, lecture halls, etc.

1638: The **American log cabin,** originally a Finnish building, was introduced to the New World by the Swedish settlers of Delaware. Unlike other colonists, they brought over their own timber. The colonists also introduced the steam bath.

1638: The **first almanac** in the English colonies, *An Almanak for the Year of Our Lord, 1639, Calculated for New England* by William Pierce, was published at Cambridge, Mass., by Stephen Daye. Pierce, a shipmaster, used the almanac as a broadside to attract new settlers for the colonies and passengers for his ship.

1639: Hezekiah Usher, who became the **first American bookseller and publisher,** settled in Cambridge, Mass. He later (1657) imported presses and type from England to print John Eliot's *Indian Bible* (1661–1663).

III. Business and Industry
Education
Philosophy and Religion
Science

Education was an early concern of the colonists, in large part because it was believed necessary, especially in New England, that everyone be able to read the Bible. Also, many of the early settlers had some education—there were, in fact, about 130 university alumni in New England by 1640. The first schoolmaster was a Dutchman, Adam Roelantsen, who arrived in New Amsterdam in 1633 and set up the first school in America. It was an adjunct of the Dutch Reformed Church. That same year the first secondary school in America, the Boston Latin School, was established with a classical curriculum derived from English schools. By 1720 five public schools were maintained in Boston and were so well regarded that they enrolled students from as far away as the West Indies. Boston Latin School, the oldest public school in the U.S., is still in existence.

1630 Summer: Boston's first church was founded. It had been formed under a covenant adopted by John Winthrop, Thomas Dudley, Isaac Johnson, and the pastor, John Wilson, in Charlestown before these men and their followers crossed the Charles R. and founded the settlement that became Boston. It was a Puritan but non-Separatist Congregational church.

1631 Feb 5: Roger Williams, the great early American dissenter and the founder of the American Baptist Church, arrived at Boston from England. He became pastor of the Separatist church at Plymouth in 1632.

1631 Nov 3: The Rev. **John Eliot,** who became the first Protestant minister in America to dedicate himself to the religious conversion of Indians, arrived at Boston from England. Settling as a teacher at Roxbury, now part of Boston, he began preaching to the Indians in 1646 and came to be called the apostle of the Indians.

1634 Mar 25: The **Roman Catholic Church** gained a permanent foothold in America when the *Dove* and the *Ark* arrived in Maryland with colonists carefully selected by Cecilius Calvert, second Lord Baltimore, proprietor of Maryland and a Roman Catholic. The colony was led by Leonard Calvert, Lord Baltimore's brother.

1636 Oct 28: Harvard College was founded by an act of the General Court of Massachusetts that allowed £400 for the establishment of a school. Its entrance requirements were: "When any scholar is able to understand Tully or such like classical author extempore, and make and speak true Latin in verse and prose . . . and decline perfectly the paradigms of nouns and verbs in the Greek tongue, let him then and not before, be capable of admission into the college." The Rev. Henry Dunster was Harvard's first president.

1637 Nov 7: Anne Hutchinson was banished from Massachusetts Bay Colony. Charged with heresy for preaching that faith alone was sufficient for salvation, a belief that contradicted Puritan orthodoxy, she was condemned by an ecclesiastical synod at Newtown, Mass., and fled to Rhode Island.

1638: The **first Baptist church** in America was established at Providence by Roger Williams, who became its first pastor but remained in the church for only a few months.

1639 May 20: The **first school maintained by community taxes** was established by the Council of Dorchester, Mass. Only certain property owners were taxed, and no general tax rates were established.

IV. Fashion
Folkways
Holidays
Social Issues and Crime
Sports

The tavern, a favorite European institution, began to thrive in America about this time. Drinking was looked on with tolerance in some circles, deplored and opposed in others. The first tavern in Boston was opened by Samuel Cole on Mar. 4, 1634. Taverns became important social institutions and at the time of the American Revolution were meeting places for patriotic groups. Nevertheless, they were frowned on by the authorities. In 1637 Gov. Willem Kieft of New Amsterdam lamented that one-quarter of all the buildings there were occupied by "grog-shops or houses where nothing is to be got but tobacco and beer." On Sept. 4, 1639, the General Court of Massachusetts enacted a law against drinking toasts, saying that, "The common custom of drinking to one another is a mere useless ceremony, and draweth on the abominable practice of drinking healths." It proved impossible to suppress such a time-honored custom, and the law was repealed in 1645.

1631 Feb 22: The **first public thanksgiving**, a fast day, was celebrated in Massachusetts Bay Colony, though many private celebrations had been recorded before this.

1634: A **sumptuary law** was passed by the Massachusetts General Court prohibiting the purchase of

woolen, linen, or silk clothes with silver, gold, silk, or thread lace on them. Slashed clothing was limited to one slash in each sleeve and in the back.

1638: Dutch justice was prompt and harsh during the early days of Manhattan. Guysbert Van Regersland was sentenced to throw himself from the sail-yard of a yacht three times and receive three lashes from each sailor for "drawing his knife upon a person."

1639: New England laws governing the **clothing of men** reflected the gay attire of the day: men were censured for wearing "immoderate great breeches," broad shoulder-bands, capes, and double ruffles. Silk roses were worn as adornment on shoes.

1639: A woman of Plymouth convicted of **adultery** was sentenced to "be whipt at a cart tayle" and to "weare a badge upon her left sleeue during her aboad" in the community. If found in public without the badge, she was to be "burned in the face with a hott iron." Generally the letters AD made up the badge.

1640–1649

I. Civil Rights
Exploration and Settlement
Government
Statistics
Wars

The first federation of American colonies was formed on May 19, 1643, when representatives of Connecticut, Massachusetts Bay, New Haven, and Plymouth colonies met in Boston and organized the United Colonies of New England. The federation was to provide a "firm and perpetual league of friendship and amity, for offense and defense, mutual advice and succor upon all just occasions." John Winthrop of Massachusetts Bay Colony was the first president. Two commissioners from each colony administered the federation, which could not interfere in internal affairs but could resolve boundary disputes among themselves and with the Dutch, who were attempting to encroach on territory claimed by New Englanders. The federation was also intended to provide support against the Indians when necessary. Provision was made for the return of runaway indentured servants, and a fund for the conversion of Indians to Christianity was administered. In 1653 Massachusetts Bay Colony, with the largest population and therefore liable for more soldiers and money than the others, refused to join a proposed war against the Dutch. The federation gradually declined but revived in 1675 on the occasion of King Philip's War. It was dissolved in 1684.

The estimated colonial **population** was 27,947.

c1640: The **first woman barrister** in America was Margaret Brent, colonial attorney for Cecilius Calvert, Lord Proprietor of Maryland.

1641 Dec: The **Body of Liberties,** a legal code framed by the General Court of Massachusetts, contained strong hints of the growing spirit of colonial independence. Five years later, in 1646, the court had occasion to reply to criticism of its provisions: "Our allegiance binds us not to the laws of England any longer than while we live in England."

1643: Development of the coastal towns of **Boston, Salem, Dorchester, and Charleston** in Massachusetts Bay colony dwarfed the Plymouth settlement. There were an estimated 20,000 inhabitants in the London Company's Bay Colony.

1643 Mar: **Roger Williams** left Providence for England to obtain a formal charter. In this way Rhode Island secured a legal position from which to fight against pressure from hostile New England colonies.

1647 May 29-31: The **Rhode Island General Assembly** convened at Portsmouth, drawing from the towns of Providence, Portsmouth, Newport, and Warwick. This body drafted a remarkably liberal constitution which, among other things, called for separation between church and state.

II. Architecture
Arts and Music
Popular Entertainment
Publishing
Theater

As mid-century approached, houses and commercial buildings in the colonies became larger, more imposing, and more like those of Europe than, for example, the first homes of Boston, which had been one-story structures covered with thatch and put up at random. By 1636 the Dutch West India Company had built in New Amsterdam five large stone structures for use as shops, although most houses there were built of wood. William Coddington, who founded Newport, R.I., in 1639, two years later built a large townhouse of the type that had a central chimney and two or four rooms on a floor, rather than the older pioneer style house of one room with the fireplace at one end. The City Tavern, the first inn built in New Amster-

dam, in 1641, was a four-story stone house, an excellent example of the Dutch colonial style. In 1654 it became the Stadthuys, or Town-House. The first of the great Virginia mansions was erected in 1642 by Gov. William Berkeley about three miles north of Jamestown. Called Greenspring, it was L-shaped, with a brick main wing nearly 100 feet long.

1640: The **first book printed** in America, *The Whole Booke of Psalmes Faithfully Translated into English Metre,* was published in Cambridge, Mass. More commonly called the *Bay Psalm Book,* it contained new versions of all the psalms. Early editions had no music, but included explicit instructions on which tunes should be used for each psalm. Translations and tunes were crude, jog-trot ballads, easier to sing but much less interesting than older versions in Henry Ainsworth's or Thomas Sternhold and John Hopkins' psalters.

1643: The **first American word book,** *A Key into the Language of America, or an help to the language of the natives of that part of America called New England,* by Roger Williams, founder of Providence, R.I., was published in London. Williams compiled his Indian language dictionary aboard ship during a journey to Southampton, England.

1647: The **earliest painting** of New York, by an unknown artist, also provided the first representation of a striped flag. The flag's four stripes symbolized the confederacy of four colonies: Plymouth, New Haven, Connecticut, and Massachusetts.

III. Business and Industry
Education
Philosophy and Religion
Science

It was many years before manufacturing was of much importance in the colonies compared with agriculture, forestry, and fishing, but by this period stirrings of the entrepreneurial spirit could be seen. In 1642 Joseph Jencks, a skilled English ironmaker, was induced to come to America to help develop the iron and brass works at Lynn, Mass. Jencks obtained a Massachusetts patent for a scythe-grinding machine in 1646, the first American patent for machinery. In 1643, what was probably the first American textile factory, a small woolen and fulling mill, was established at Rowley, Mass. The next year the first successful ironworks in what is now the U.S. was founded on the Saugus R. near Lynn, Mass. Its founders were called the Company of Undertakers of Ironworks. They were headed by John Winthrop, a colonial governor who in 1663 became the first resident of the American colonies to become a member of the Royal Society.

1641 Oct: The **first patent** in the colonies was awarded to Samuel Winslow of Massachusetts for a process of manufacturing salt, the term of the patent to extend ten years.

1646 Nov 4: A severe **heresy law** enacted in Massachusetts made death the punishment for any person who persisted in denying that the Holy Scriptures were the word of God "or not to be attended to by illuminated Christians."

1647: The **first important public education law** in America was passed in Massachusetts, providing that every community of 50 homeowners maintain free elementary education and that communities of more than 100 households provide secondary school education as well.

1647 May 26: Roman Catholic priests were forbidden to enter territory under Puritan jurisdiction, according to a law passed in Massachusetts. Any person suspected who could not clear himself was to be banished. For a second offense death was the penalty.

1647 Nov 11: The **first American compulsory school law** was passed in Massachusetts. It provided for the appointment of a teacher in every community of more than 50 families and for the establishment of a grammar school in every community of more than 100 families.

1648: The **first person executed for witchcraft** in America was Margaret Jones of Charlestown, Mass. Gov. John Winthrop wrote "that she was found to have such a malignant touch, as many persons, (men, women and children), whom she stroked or touched with any affection or displeasure, etc., were taken with deafness . . . or other violent pains or sickness . . . Her behaviour at the trial was very intemperate, lying notoriously, and railing upon the jury and witnesses, etc., and in the like distemper she died."

1648 Oct18: The **first labor organization** in America was authorized by the Massachusetts Bay Colony. "The shoomakers of Boston" were permitted to meet whenever they wanted to choose officers and clerks.

1649 Apr 21: The **Toleration Act** was pushed through the Maryland Assembly by Lord Baltimore, Roman Catholic Proprietor of Maryland. Though the colony was a haven for Roman Catholics, Lord Baltimore had from the beginning encouraged Protestant immigration. As Protestant groups became more numerous, religious disturbances became frequent and bitter. The rise of Oliver Cromwell in England in 1642 intensified anti-Catholic feeling among the Puritans in Maryland and other colonies. Increased pressure from England for the suppression of Catholicism in the colonies led Baltimore to sponsor the Act of Toleration as a means of averting a serious test of authority.

IV. Fashion
Folkways
Holidays
Social Issues and Crime
Sports

As towns grew and more houses were crowded together, the danger of fire led to development of the volunteer firefighting system. In Massachusetts, laws of 1638 and 1646 forbade smoking "out of dorcs." This move was inspired not so much by Puritan mores as because "fires have beene often occasioned by taking tobacco." Boston in 1649 required that between nine in the evening and half past four in the morning all fires be covered or put out. In 1648 in New Amsterdam, Gov. Peter Stuyvesant forbade construction of chimneys of "wood or plaister in any house," since defective chimneys caused most fires. He appointed four firemasters to inspect chimneys and to collect three guilders for any chimney found "neglected and foul." The fines were to be used to buy hooks, ladders, and leather buckets for a firefighting organization called The Prowlers, a group of eight men who patrolled the streets at night.

1640: The **high-backed settle** appeared in American households. Designed to rest in front of fireplaces, it was fitted with a high back and arms to ward off drafts, with seats extremely narrow and left unupholstered.

1644: The **first Thanksgiving Day** celebrated in New Amsterdam commemorated the safe return of Dutch soldiers from the battle with Connecticut Indians near Stamford.

1647: An unusual blue law forbidding **social smoking** was enacted in Connecticut. Tobacco could be used once a day, at meals or elsewhere, "and then not in company with any other." Tobacco could only be used in one's own house. Behind this law lay the belief that smoking in a group paved the way to dissipation.

1647: Marriages by agreement were declared illegal in Rhode Island. Cases of common law marriage were frequent in the colonies, especially among the Quakers. In one case a New England woman, after living with her "husband" for 20 years, petitioned for separation and her property. The court stigmatized her as a fornicator, fined both £20, and ordered them "not to lead soe scandalose life."

1650–1659

I. Civil Rights
Exploration and Settlement
Government
Statistics
Wars

Of all the Indians the English colonists encountered in the colonies, none were more powerful or better organized than the Iroquois. The five tribes—Mohawk, Oneida, Onondaga, Cayuga, and Seneca—were concentrated in New York in that order between the Hudson R. and the Genesee R. to the west. Their league, possibly organized as early as 1570, numbered no more than 25,000 persons by about 1650 but it dominated others in all directions. Their particular enemies were the Hurons to the north, who with their French allies dominated the fur trade. In 1649 the Iroquois won a resounding victory over the Hurons; in 1651 they nearly wiped out the Neutral Nation along the northern shore of Lake Erie; and in 1656 they defeated and dispersed the Eries. They continued to increase their power and became allies of the English after the Dutch lost New Netherland. As a result, the Iroquois were a serious problem for the patriot forces during the American Revolution.

The estimated colonial **population** was 51,700.

1652: Exportation of **African slaves** to New Netherland was approved by the Dutch government. In the colony strict laws prevented mistreatment of slaves. Whipping was forbidden unless the owner received permission from the authorities.

1652: New Amsterdam was granted self-government by the Dutch authorities in the Netherlands. Peter Stuyvesant, since his arrival in the town in 1647 as governor of New Netherland, had ruled as an autocrat. A board of advisers he appointed was dismissed by him in 1651 when they complained of his rule to the homeland. By Feb. 2, 1653, Stuyvesant had no choice but to proclaim New Amsterdam a self-governing municipality, but he reserved the right to enact laws and ordinances.

1652 May 31: Maine was part of the Massachusetts Bay colony, according to a ruling by the Massachusetts General Court. Despite an appeal to the English Parliament, Maine was unable to resist and so was annexed.

1652 June 10: The **first mint** in America was established in Boston in defiance of English colonial law, with John Hull as its first master. It issued the famous Pine Tree Shilling, designed by Hull, a silversmith.

1653: Settlement of **North Carolina** by Virginia colonists began. They migrated through the Nansemond Valley and settled north of Albemarle Sound between the Chowan R. and the sea. The move was endorsed by the Virginia Assembly, which wanted a buffer settlement as protection for Virginia's southern frontier.

1655: New Netherland took **control of New Sweden,** the Swedish colony on the Delaware R., after years of pressure on the colony by Peter Stuyvesant. Much later, in 1683, the Swedes and Finns along the Delaware R. gladly became English citizens when William Penn founded Pennsylvania.

1656 Sep 22: The **first all-woman jury** in the colonies was empaneled by the General Provincial Court in session at Patuxent, Md., to hear evidence against Judith Catchpole. The defendant, accused of murdering her child, claimed she had never even been pregnant. After hearing her evidence, the jury acquitted her.

II. Architecture
Arts and Music
Popular Entertainment
Publishing
Theater

The Puritan settlers of New England were quick to defend their actions and their beliefs, and many felt that the substantial criticism of them being voiced in England during this time required answering. One of the stalwart defenders was Edward Johnson, who first emigrated to Boston in 1630. In 1653 he published in London *The Wonder-Working Providence of Sions Saviour in New England,* a history of Puritan settlement from 1628 to 1652. Johnson pictured the Puritan settlers as soldiers of Christ waging war against the wilderness and unbelievers.

1650: Anne Bradstreet became New England's first published poet when a volume of her verse, *The Tenth Muse Lately Sprung Up in America,* was published in London. Bradstreet was the wife of Simon Bradstreet, who later served as governor of Massachusetts colony from 1679 to 1686 and again from 1689 to 1692. The manuscript for her book had been taken to London by a brother-in-law who so admired her work that he arranged to have it published without her knowledge. Her poetry showed the influence of Edmund Spenser, Francis Quarles, Sir Philip Sydney, and others. The longer poems dealt with a variety of subjects, such as the four seasons and the four ages of man. Her shorter poems dealt with her New

England experiences. Among the latter were "The Flesh and the Spirit," "On the Burning of Her House," "On My Son's Returning Out of England," and "The Author to Her Book." Cotton Mather and other eminent New England figures praised her poetry. A second edition of her poetry, *Several Poems*, was published posthumously in Boston in 1678.

1653: The **first Indian book** was a *Catechism* translated into a dialect of the Algonquian language by John Eliot, missionary to the Indians. Eliot later translated the complete Bible into Algonquian, the first Bible printed (1661, 1663) in the colonies.

III. Business and Industry
Education
Philosophy and Religion
Science

Although many of the early settlers came to America to secure religious freedom, they were not always willing to extend this freedom to others. When the first Quakers, Mary Fisher and Ann Austin, arrived in Boston from Barbados on July 1, 1656, they were imprisoned and mistreated, then expelled by Massachusetts authorities. On Oct. 2 Connecticut enacted a law to fine and banish Quakers. Massachusetts legislation enacted on Oct. 14 decreed that 40-shilling fines be levied against anyone sheltering Quakers and prescribed various physical mutilations for those who returned to the colony after having been banished. The commissioners of the United Colonies of New England expressed their support for such legislation. The first five Quakers to land in New Amsterdam, on June 1, 1657, were imprisoned for eight days before they were allowed to leave for Rhode Island. On May 29, 1658, the Massachusetts General Court passed a law forbidding the holding of Quaker meetings. The first two Quakers hanged on Boston Common, on Oct. 27, 1659, for violating the law against returning to Massachusetts after they had been banished, were William Robinson and Marmaduke Stevenson. Except in Rhode Island, Quakers were persecuted in all the colonies in this period. It was not until the founding of Pennsylvania in 1682 that the Quakers had a haven in the New World.

1654: Production of wool became an important New England industry, partly because many early settlers had been in the wool business in England.

1654: A commission for the **first fire engine** in America was awarded by the Boston selectmen to Joseph Jencks, an ironmonger from Lynn, Mass. The machine, set on wheels, spurted water from a cistern filled by a bucket brigade.

1654: Probably the **first toll bridge** in what became the U.S. was authorized by the General Court of Massachusetts, which licensed Richard Thurley to build and maintain a toll bridge over the Newbury R. at Rowley. The court fixed the toll at two shillings for horses, cows, and oxen; one-half shilling for hogs, sheep, and goats. Humans crossed free.

1654 July 8: The **first Jew** to settle in North America, Jacob Barsimson, arrived on Manhattan Island, first of 24 Jewish immigrants that year. In September three Jews fleeing the Spanish Inquisition in Brazil arrived in New Amsterdam, and more followed. Their right to stay was upheld by the Dutch West India Company against the wishes of Gov. Peter Stuyvesant. They founded Congregation Shearith Israel, with Saul Brown as first rabbi.

1655: Illiteracy among women was about 50%, as shown by an examination of legal documents that required signatures of women in Massachusetts. More than half were obliged to sign with a cross. In New Netherland the rate was 60% and in Virginia 75%.

1656: The **Copernican system,** the conception of the solar system that has the sun rather than Earth at its center, was formally accepted by Harvard College only 23 years after Galileo Galilei had been forced by the Roman Catholic Inquisition to repudiate it.

1658: Perhaps the **first hospital** in what is now the U.S. was set up in New Amsterdam by a Dr. Varravanger, surgeon of the Dutch West India Company. It consisted of a clean house with plenty of firewood and a fire, and was supervised by a matron.

IV. Fashion
Folkways
Holidays
Social Issues and Crime
Sports

Furniture manufacture in the colonies began about this time. Production was hampered for some time by a shortage of carpenters and cabinetmakers. Since the early houses were small, there was not a great deal of space for furniture, and a cramped effect was not unusual. Chests and cupboards provided storage space. An alcove bed was common. Sometimes the parlor, the best room in the house, also seved as the parents' bedroom. The so-called Turkish carpet was placed on table tops, not on the floor. The first known American cabinetmaker, an example of whose work is still extant, worked during this period. He was Nicholas Disbrowe, active in the Connecticut Valley. This area, then the frontier, became the site of a flourishing furniture industry.

1653: An interesting example of **New England snobbery** was demonstrated by the arrest of two women in Newbury, Mass., for adorning themselves with silk hoods and scarves. They were released when they presented proof that both their husbands had net worths of £200.

1656: A Capt. **Kemble** of Boston was made to sit for two hours in the stocks for his "lewd and unseemly behavior" in kissing his wife "publicquely" on Sunday. He had just returned from a three-year sea voyage.

1656: To ensure that **Sunday** would be a day of rest, the burgomasters of New Netherland passed a law forbidding drinking, sowing, mowing, building, sawing, smithing, bleaching, hunting, fishing, dancing, cardplaying, tick-tacking, bowling, jaunting in a boat or carriage, etc.

1657: The first reference to **golf** in America was a complaint issued by the sheriff of Fort Orange, now Albany, N.Y., against three men for playing kolven on Sunday. Kolven is believed to have been an early form of golf.

1658: A colonial writer took note of the **fortunes of women** in America: "They no sooner arrive than they are besieged with offers of matrimony, husbands being ready soon for those whom nature had apparently marked out and predestined for lives of single blessedness." Many servants, innocent country girls kidnaped in England and sent penniless to America, married well and attained distinction.

1659 Sep 30: The first mention of **tennis** in America appeared in a proclamation issued by Gov. Peter Stuyvesant of New Netherland forbidding tennis playing, among other things, on certain days.

1660–1669

I. Civil Rights
Exploration and Settlement
Government
Statistics
Wars

Some seeds of the American Revolution were sown at this time by the Navigation Acts of the English Parliament, aimed at the rising power of the Dutch merchant fleet. A law passed in 1651 required that most products be shipped to England in English-owned vessels. The First Navigation Act, of 1660, listed colonial articles that could be supplied only to England. Other Navigation Acts followed in 1662, 1663, 1670, and 1673. The 1663 law required that all foreign goods be shipped to the colonies through English ports. Colonists benefited from the laws to the extent that they were given a monopoly on the shipment of some products to England and preferential tariff treatment in some instances. Colonial businessmen nevertheless resented the restrictions imposed upon them.

The estimated colonial **population** was 84,800.

1660 Dec 1: The **First Navigation Act,** passed by the English Parliament to govern colonial trade, stated that all goods carried to and from England must be transported by British ships manned chiefly by British sailors. It further provided that certain articles, which included sugar, tobacco, cotton, wool, ginger, and dyestuffs, were to be exported to England only.

1662 May 3: A **legal charter for Connecticut** was secured through the efforts of Gov. John Winthrop, Jr. The charter united the colonies of New Haven and Connecticut, neither of which was protected by royal charter. New Haven, however, opposed merger with Connecticut.

1664: A **slavery act** in Maryland provided for lifelong servitude for black slaves. The law was designed to prevent slaves who had converted to Christianity from claiming freedom on the basis of English court decisions holding that infidel slaves must be freed once they had been baptized as Christians and had taken legal residence in the country. Similar acts were passed in Virginia, North Carolina, New York, South Carolina, and New Jersey. Such action was not taken in Georgia, Pennsylvania, or Delaware.

1664 June 24: Proprietorship of **New Jersey,** land between the Hudson and Delaware rivers, was granted by James, Duke of York, to Lord John Berkeley and Sir George Carteret. The new grant was named New Jersey for Carteret, who had been governor of the Isle of Jersey.

1664 Sep 7: Gov. **Peter Stuyvesant surrendered New Netherland** to an English naval force led by Col. Richard Nicolls. Not a shot was fired. Thus ended Dutch power in the New World. Dutch holdings were reorganized into the English colonies of New York and New Jersey. New Amsterdam was renamed New York, and Fort Orange was renamed Albany.

1665 Feb 28: The **Duke's Laws,** sponsored by the English proprietor of New York, James, Duke of York, provided for official recognition of all Protestant sects within the colony. Specific mention was made of the Reformed Protestant Dutch Church, the only church recognized by name. This unusual toleration of the Dutch Church by English authorities contrasted sharply with the restrictive policies of the Dutch West India Company before its loss of the colony to the British in 1664. Up to 1664 the Reformed Protestant Dutch Church was the only legal church in the colony. Despite this restriction, a great many unauthorized religious groups established footholds in the Dutch colony. This religious diversity inherited by the English proprietor in 1664 made the policy of toleration a practical necessity.

1667 July 21: New Netherland was ceded to England by the Dutch by the Peace of Breda, which ended the Second Anglo-Dutch War (1664–1667).

II. Architecture
Arts and Music
Popular Entertainment
Publishing
Theater

Puritans resorted to poetry as well as prose to defend and extend their beliefs. The poetry was always stronger on the theological side than on the poetic. Most famous of such seventeenth-century poet-preachers was Michael Wigglesworth, a clergyman in Malden, Mass. In 1662 his volume *The Day of Doom,* accurately labeled in its subtitle *A Poetical Description of the Great and Last Judgement,* was published. Eighteen hundred copies were sold the first year. It was estimated that one of every twenty persons in New England and one in every forty-five in all the colonies bought a copy. Wigglesworth continued his poetic efforts with *Meat Out of the Eater* (1670), a long poem presenting the Christian view of suffering and the benefits to be derived from it.

1661: The **first Bible printed in America,** the New Testament translated by John Eliot into the Algonquian language and financed by the Corporation for Propagating the Gospel in New England, was published. Of this remarkable work, Cotton Mather wrote: "Behold, ye Americans, the greatest honor that ever you were partakers of! This is the only Bible that ever was printed in all America from the very foundation of the world." Eliot's translation into Algonquian of the Old Testament was published in 1663.

1665 Aug 27: The **first play performed in the North American colonies,** *Ye Bare and Ye Cubb* by Philip Alexander Bruce, was presented at Acomac, Va. Three local residents were fined for acting in this play. Most colonies had laws forbidding public performances. What is strange is that this incident occurred in Virginia, where no such legislation existed.

1669: The first comprehensive **history of New England** was published in Boston, Mass.: *New England's Memoriall, or a Brief Relation of the Most Memorable and Remarkable Passages of the Providence of God, Manifested to the Planters of New England in America; With Special Reference to the First Colony Therefore, Called New Plymouth* by Nathaniel Morton, secretary of Plymouth colony.

III. Business and Industry
Education
Philosophy and Religion
Science

An early political document stressing religious toleration in America was *Fundamental Constitutions,* drawn up for the governance of the Carolinas in 1669. It was the work of the English philosopher John Locke, who prepared it for his friend Anthony Ashley Cooper, later first earl of Shaftesbury, one of the proprietors of Carolina. The document combined liberal principles and an aristocratic social system while stressing religious tolerance. Although it never became law, it exercised a profound influence on colonial religion, particularly in the Carolinas. *Fundamental Constitutions* provided that "Noe person whatever shall disturb, molest or persecute another for his speculative opinions in Religion or his way of worship." Official recognition and support could be granted only to the Church of England, but it was specified that any seven adherents of a religious faith could establish a church under any name they desired, with the provisos that they accept the existence of God and declare that the parishioners of the church would worship Him.

1660: The **first Indian church** in New England was founded by John Eliot at Natick, Mass., on the Charles R. He had established Natick as a native village for "praying Indians" in 1657.

1661: The **first annual meeting of American Quakers** was held in Rhode Island.

1661 Mar 24: The **last Quaker executed** in Boston was William Leddra, who suffered the death penalty for returning from banishment.

1661 Sep: Persecution of Quakers in Massachusetts was halted by Gov. John Endicott on orders from Charles II, a personal friend of William Penn.

1662 Mar: Adoption of the **Half-Way Covenant** by a general synod of Massachusetts churches led to a schism in New England Congregationalism. The covenant permitted parents who had been baptized in the church, but who no longer professed their faith, to have their children baptized. The Half-Way Covenant was symptomatic of the decline of power of the New England founders and the emergence of a more liberal second generation.

1669: The **first Sunday school** of record was established at Plymouth, Mass.

IV. Fashion
Folkways
Holidays
Social Issues and Crime
Sports

Seventeenth-century colonists enjoyed a variety of sports and games. Since horses were a part of everyday life, it was not surprising that, in 1664, horse racing became the first organized sport in the colonies. Before then the governor of Virginia and his friends had raced their horses on a short stretch of road after church services, thereby developing the fast "quarter horse." The Dutch in New Amsterdam enjoyed the cruel sport of "riding the goose" until it was banned in 1658. In Boston, in spite of the Puritan atmosphere, football was played on the streets. Gambling and card playing also were popular there until laws were passed to forbid them. At Newport, R.I., from 1640 to 1690, men amused themselves by bowling on the green.

1660: The **first divorce case** in Delaware involved a Finnish couple. It was said that the "wife receives daily a severe drubbing and is expelled from the house like a dog." The husband was an adulterer, and the divorce was granted. New England at this time showed the most liberality in granting divorces. New Netherland and the rest of the Middle Atlantic colonies made divorce almost impossible except in cases of proved or confessed adultery.

1660: To promote **stable marriages,** a Connecticut law ordered all married men to live with their wives. Any man who was separated from his wife for more than three years was ordered out of the colony.

1660: A **sumptuary law** passed in Virginia forbade settlers from importing "silke stuffe in garments or in peeces except for whoods and scarfs, nor silver or gold lace, nor bone lace of silk or threads, nor ribbands wrought with gold or silver in them." But with the Restoration in England in 1660, periwigs came into fashion on both sides of the Atlantic. Authorities in New England made repeated efforts to prevent their use.

1660 May: The celebration of **Christmas** was forbidden by a law of Massachusetts, with a fine of five shillings levied on violators.

1664: Marriage by a justice of the peace instead of a clergyman was made lawful in New York by the Duke's Laws, actually a continuation of a Dutch law of 1590. The law has never been altered.

1664: The **first organized sport** in America, horse racing, began when New York's first governor, Richard Nicolls, established the Newmarket Course at Hempstead Plains, Long Island, instituted rules of racing, and offered prizes to winners. His purpose was to improve the breed of horses in the colonies.

1670–1679

I. Civil Rights
Exploration and Settlement
Government
Statistics
Wars

While the English colonists were settling along the Atlantic coast and river valleys, the French, from their bases in Canada, were using the St. Lawrence R. and the Great Lakes to explore and claim western North America. At Sault Sainte Marie in 1671, Daumont de St. Lusson claimed the entire interior for France. In 1673 the explorer Louis Joliet and the missionary Jacques Marquette reached the upper Mississippi R. and traveled down it as far as Arkansas. Marquette established a mission at what is now Chicago on Dec. 4, 1674. Another expedition began in late 1678 under the leadership of Robert Cavelier, Sieur de La Salle, and Father Louis Hennepin. They passed Niagara Falls, and later Hennepin was the first European to write a description of it. The party explored the upper Mississippi River Valley. On Apr. 9, 1682, La Salle reached the mouth of the Mississippi, where he claimed control of the whole valley for France and named it Louisiana after King Louis XIV of France.

The estimated colonial **population** was 114,500.

1670 Apr: Charleston, S.C., was founded. English colonists under Joseph West settled at Port Royal Sound, then moved northward to the Ashley R. at Albemarle Sound for fear of Spaniards. There they established Charles Town, later known as Old Charles Town. In 1680, this settlement was moved once again to the juncture of the Ashley and Cooper rivers, the present site of the city.

1671: The first of the great **Hudson Valley manors** was established at Fordham by the English colony of New York. Others followed: Fox Hall (Kingston), 1672; Rensselaerswyck, 1685; Livingston, 1686; Pelham, 1687; Philipsborough, 1693; Morrisania, 1697; Cortlandt, 1697; and Scarsdale, 1701.

1671: A new **slavery act** in Maryland extended the scope of the slavery law passed in 1664 by declaring that conversion or baptism of slaves before or after their importation did not entitle them to freedom. The act was passed on behalf of slave owners who hesitated to import slaves for fear of losing their investments through prior or subsequent conversion and, also, to encourage slave owners to convert their slaves to Christianity.

1673: The **first native-born governor** of an American colony, Josiah Winslow of Plymouth, was elected governor of Plymouth colony. His term extended until his death in 1680. Winslow also succeeded Myles Standish as commander in chief of the Plymouth military defense.

1673 Aug 8: The **surrender of New York** was demanded by a Dutch force of 23 ships and 1600 men anchored near Sandy Hook. They held possession of the colony until Feb. 9, 1674, when the English regained control.

1674 Dec 4: The **first dwelling** in what is now Chicago was built by Father Jacques Marquette as a mission.

1675-1676: Pressures on the **Indian population** of New England resulted in King Philip's War. The tribes most affected by early colonial expansion were the Wampanoags, originally from the Atlantic coast, now forced back to east of Narragansett Bay; the Narragansetts, whose territory between Narragansett Bay and the Thames R. was menaced by a land company that claimed it held a mortgage to the areas; the Mohegans, between the Connecticut and Thames rivers; the Podunks, directly to the north; and the Nipmucks, who ranged over the northern parts of the Thames and Pawtucket rivers. A coalition of these tribes, known as the Five Nations, was headed by King Philip, Indian name Metacomet, chief of the Wampanoags.

1675 June 24: **King Philip's War** (1675–1676) began with a massacre of colonists at Swansee, Plymouth, by a band of Indians. The war was started by King Philip after three of his people were executed by the English for murdering an Indian in English employ.

1676 Feb 10: **Lancaster, Mass., was attacked** by Indians led by King Philip. The settlement was destroyed by fire after all the men were killed and the women and children taken prisoners.

1676 Aug 12: **King Philip's War** (1675–1676) ended when the Wampanoag leader was surprised and shot by an Indian in the service of Capt. Benjamin Church. The conflict had grown to include the Wampanoag, Nipmuck, Narragansett, Mohegan, and Podunk tribes and ended with their virtual destruction, opening southern New England to unimpeded colonial expansion.

1676 Sep 19: Jamestown, Va., was burned in **Bacon's Rebellion,** an uprising led by Nathaniel Bacon. The rebellion was prompted by Virginia Gov. William Berkeley's repeated refusal to organize necessary defensive measures against marauding Indians. Among the buildings destroyed was the Episcopal Church in Jamestown, the first Protestant church in America. The ruins of the church tower are still standing on the site of the community.

1678: The **first vessel** to penetrate Lake Ontario, the *Griffin,* carried a French expedition led by Robert Cavelier, Sieur de La Salle, from Fort Frontenac (later Kingston) to the present site of Fort Niagara.

1679: A **Boston fire,** the worst in the colonies in the seventeenth century, destroyed 150 houses in Boston. Thereafter, frame houses were abandoned by city ordinance, and all houses were constructed of "stone or bricke, & covered with slate or tyle."

II. Architecture
Arts and Music
Popular Entertainment
Publishing
Theater

A colonial tradition in architecture was that a house should be designed and built to last, and to grow as the family that owned it grew. This was reflected in the history of the House of the Seven Gables in Salem, Mass. Originally known as the Turner House, its first two rooms were built in 1670. Successive additions greatly expanded the structure, and it eventually came to have eight gables. Nathaniel Hawthorne was thought to have modeled the house in his novel *The House of the Seven Gables* (1851) after this structure, which he had visited in his youth.

1676: An example of **early American satire** was the ballad *A Looking-Glass for the Times; or, The former spirit of New England revived in this generation* by Peter Folger, grandfather of Benjamin Franklin. In strong, manly doggerel, he lashed into the Christians of New England for their behavior toward Quakers, Baptists, and others.

1677: A **classic historical book,** *Narrative of the Trouble with the Indians in New England* by William Hubbard, was published. The book reflected the colonials' hostility to red men, who were described as "treacherous villians," "children of the Devil," "the dross of mankind," and "dregs and lees of the earth."

1679: A colonial **best seller,** *A Guide to Heaven* by Samuel Hardy, was published in Boston. A book of Puritan rules and practices of piety, it was less fiery than Bishop Lewis Bayly's *The Practice of Piety.*

III. Business and Industry
Education
Philosophy and Religion
Science

By 1675 more than 600 ships and 4000 New England men were engaged in fishing. From early times, fishing had been important to the colonies not just for food for the settlers but for commerce. When the Pilgrims sailed for America in 1620, they intended their colony to be in part a fishing settlement. In the 1630s the Puritans entered the field. The Rev. Hugh Peter organized fisheries at Marblehead, Mass., and discovered a market for dried codfish. Fishing for cod became so important in the Massachusetts Bay Colony that a wooden image of a cod was installed in the capitol in Boston. Salted fish was in demand in Catholic Europe and in the West Indies. New England fishermen divided their catch into three classes. The largest and fattest, the most difficult to cure, were consumed at home. Somewhat smaller fish were cured and exported to Europe. The smallest fish were sold, usually traded for molasses, in the West Indies as food for slaves.

1673 Jan 1: The first regular **mounted mail service** was inaugurated between New York and Boston. A postman rode without a change of horse from New York to Hartford, through woods and over streams, keeping a lookout for runaway servants and soldiers. The road was little more than a trail but it would soon become the Boston Post Road, the first important highway in the colonies. A post road was so called because men or horses were posted at intervals along the route. They would take packages or messages and carry them to the next post. In this way goods and information were relayed with relative speed. Nonetheless, it still took three weeks to get the mail from Boston to New York City.

1674: Increase Mather was appointed a fellow at Harvard College, beginning a distinguished career in education. Although he once refused the presidency of Harvard, Mather was named acting president in 1685. The following year he took charge, with the title of rector, and held that post until 1701. Mather promoted the study of scientific subjects while maintaining the college's Congregationalist ties. In 1675 his eldest son, Cotton Mather, was admitted to Harvard at the age of 12. He was the youngest person ever admitted to the school. Cotton Mather, the son and grandson of Puritan clergymen, even at this early age believed himself destined to follow in their footsteps and become the preeminent religious and political leader of Massachusetts. Perhaps it was young Mather's sense of destiny that led his fellow students to consider him something of a prig.

1677: The first charter guaranteeing **separation of church and state** in the American colonies was framed by William Penn at the Quaker colony of West Jersey.

IV. Fashion
Folkways
Holidays
Social Issues and Crime
Sports

From the beginning, dress styles had varied from colony to colony, in large part because of national origin, class, or religion. New Englanders tended to be plain of dress, although not as austere as they were later depicted, while many Virginians copied the fashions of upper-class English men and women. By the later seventeenth century, colonial life had improved to where fashion became substantially more elegant and luxurious. This gave rise, particularly in New England, to sumptuary laws intended by colonial authorities to control excesses in dress, hairstyle, and the like.

1670: The **coffee house** appeared in America when a license was given by Boston authorities to a woman to sell coffee and chocolate.

1674: A rule against **horse racing** on public thoroughfares in Plymouth colony stated that "whatsoever person ran a race with any horse in any street or common road should forfeit five shillings or sit in the stocks for one hour."

1675: New York City, which had always had a mixed population, began to take on a really cosmopolitan air. The combination of religious toleration and commercial activity encouraged an influx of Englishmen, Jews, Africans, Indians, Madagascan pirates, and French Huguenots.

1675: Laws upbraiding **current fashions** were enacted by the Massachusetts General Court. Indian attacks were blamed on the sins of the people, among which was "the manifest pride openly appearing amongst us in that long hair, like women's hair, is worn by some men, either their own or others' hair made into periwigs."

1675: In a case involving **sumptuary laws** in Connecticut, 38 women were brought before a magistrate for wearing clothes not befitting their social position. One young girl was accused of "wearing silk in a flaunting manner, in an offensive way and garb not only before but when she stood presented." This year 30 young men were arrested for wearing silk and sporting long hair.

1678: Tobacco consumption of the Dutch inhabitants of New York was substantial. An English chaplain reported that "the Dutch are obstinate and incessant smokers, whose diet . . . being sallets and brawn and very often picked buttermilk, require the use of that herb to keep their phlegm from coagulating and curdling."

1680–1689

I. Civil Rights
Exploration and Settlement
Government
Statistics
Wars

The flight of King James II of England to France, and his succession on the English throne by William of Orange and his wife Mary on Feb. 13, 1689, marked the climax of the Glorious Revolution, by which the English Parliament asserted its authority over the king and ensured the succession of a Protestant to the throne. The abdication of James II, a Catholic and an autocratic ruler, had almost immediate repercussions in the colonies. In 1689 the unpopular governor of Virginia, Lord Howard, was removed; Gov. Edmund Andros surrendered in Boston; the counties of New York, Queens, and Westchester in New York ousted the royal government and set up their own rule; Rhode Island and Connecticut reestablished governments under their old charters; and a Protestant Association overthrew the old government in Maryland.

The estimated colonial **population** was 155,600.

1680 Sep: New Hampshire was separated from Massachusetts by royal commission.

1681 Mar 4: What is now roughly the state of **Pennsylvania was granted to William Penn,** a member of the Society of Friends (Quakers) by King Charles II of England. The grant was apparently made to offset a debt of £16,000 the king owed to Penn's father, Sir William Penn.

1682: A site for the city of **Philadelphia** was laid out by Thomas Holme, one of four commissioners who had been sent to Pennsylvania by William Penn to prepare settlers for the new government. Penn, who was in the colony at the time, helped in planning the city.

1682: The **first European settlement in Texas** was made by Spaniards at Yselta, on the site of present-day El Paso. The settlers were refugees from New

Mexico who had been driven out after the Pueblo revolt of 1680. Several missions were established in this area but they did not flourish because the Comanche, Apache, and other Indian tribes were unfriendly.

1682 May 5: William Penn's *Frame of Government* was put into effect. An unusually liberal document, it provided for a governor, council, and assembly to be elected by freeholders. The council had legislative, judicial, and administrative powers. At first, the assembly could not initiate legislation, but this was altered in 1696.

1682 Aug 24: Delaware was awarded to William Penn by James, Duke of York, who had no legal title to the land. This made Penn's control over Delaware tenuous, particularly since it conflicted with other claims. The issue was finally resolved by the Charter of 1701, which gave Delaware autonomy.

1683 Oct 6: The **first German settlers** in America, Mennonites from Krefeld, Germany, arrived at Philadelphia. They settled Germantown, near Philadelphia, at the bidding of William Penn. Their leader, Francis Daniel Pastorius, was considered by many the most learned man in America at the time.

1684 June 21: The **Massachusetts Bay Colony charter was revoked** by King Charles II of England, acting through the Court of Chancery. Massachusetts had violated its charter by discriminating against the Church of England, setting religious rather than property qualifications for suffrage, and establishing an illegal mint. The revocation had been prompted by Edward Randolph, who had been appointed surveyor of customs and collector in 1678. He sent two unfavorable reports to England in 1682, then returned to England the next year to help prosecute Massachusetts for its charter violations. Revocation of the charter led to dissolution of the New England Confederation.

1687: The **Charter Oak incident** occurred as the result of the high-handed actions of Sir Edmund Andros, the English colonial governor. In 1685 King James II of England decided to consolidate the New England colonies into the Dominion of New England and named Andros governor. The dominion came to include New York and East and West Jersey. Andros dissolved colonial assemblies and infringed on other rights and customs. He also demanded that the colonial charters be turned over to him. According to legend, when he met with Connecticut officials in Hartford to demand their charter, the candles in the room were suddenly blown out and the royal charter, which had been granted Connecticut in 1662, disappeared. It was then hidden by Capt. Joseph Wadsworth in a hollow in a white oak tree, which became known as the Charter Oak. The tree was said to be 1000 years old and it stood until 1856.

II. Architecture
Arts and Music
Popular Entertainment
Publishing
Theater

A leading figure in colonial literature during this time was William Penn, one of the more unusual personalities among those who founded English colonies in America. The son of an English admiral, he became a Quaker in 1666, when he was 22. Two years later he was imprisoned for writing a religious tract. While in the Tower of London he composed another. Although a liberal in government and deeply religious, he was also politically adept at the royal court. During this period he founded Pennsylvania and wrote both in praise of the colony and in defense of his Quaker beliefs.

1681: An **early description of Pennsylvania** was provided in *Some Account of the Province of Pennsylvania* by William Penn. Like numerous other accounts of the colonies, this was intended to induce emigration from England by indicating ways in which one could earn a living in the New World.

1681: The **Old Ship Meeting House** was erected at Hingham, Mass., by the Puritans, who never referred to a house of worship as a church. This meeting house has been in continuous service since its completion, and it is the last remaining example of the four-square meeting house, a native American contribution to church construction. The meeting house was intentionally denied a cross or spire. Instead a functional tower held a bell and supported a practical weather vane.

1682: A famous **account of Indian life,** *The Sovereignty & Goodness of God, Together With the Faithfulness of His Promises Displayed; Being a Narrative of the Captivity and Restoration of Mrs. Mary Rowlandson* by Mary Rowlandson, was published. It was the first example of an American literary genre, the Indian captivity narrative. It reflected the hostile attitude of colonists to the American Indian. The book went through more than 30 editions.

1682: The **Newport Parish Church,** the most complete and authentic of extant seventeenth- century Virginia churches, was built at Smithfield, Isle of Wight County. Also called the Old Brick Church, it is a remarkable example of Tudor Gothic (late medieval) architecture transferred to America.

III. Business and Industry
Education
Philosophy and Religion
Science

By the late seventeenth century, the African slave trade was a large-scale business enterprise. Largely in the hands of the Dutch until the 1660s, it was continued by the English, with New Englanders especially active after the Royal Africa Trade Company lost its monopoly in 1696. In the trade, a ship sailed from New England with rum and other goods for the Slave Coast. The slaves were then carried, under the most miserable conditions, to the West Indies or to the colonial South, where they were exchanged for sugar, molasses, and tobacco for the North. During this period Virginia planters relied more on white indentured servants from Europe than on slaves from Africa. There were 6000 indentured servants in Virginia in 1681, compared with 2000 slaves. Some indentured servants came voluntarily, signing papers for five or more years, at the end of which time they would receive some clothing and perhaps a parcel of land. They often then became tenant farmers. Criminals, vagrants, and debtors were sent involuntarily to the New World, usually for a term of service of seven years; they were known as "His Majesty's Seven Year Passengers." Others, children and adults, were victims of kidnaping. They were sold to shipmasters who in turn sold them into servitude in America. Many servants caused trouble in the colonies. As a result, the end of the seventeenth century saw a steady growth in the slave trade.

1680: A major **scientific achievement** of colonial America was the calculation of the orbit of a comet of 1680 by Thomas Brattle, an early Boston mathematician. He sent word of his discovery to the royal astronomer at Greenwich, England, who checked Brattle's observation. Brattle's calculation supported Isaac Newton's theory of cometary orbits, and Newton acknowledged Brattle's work. Nonetheless, a curious mix-up by the Royal Society left Brattle's contribution to science unrewarded. In 1714, a year after he died, the society elected his brother, William, to membership. William Brattle declined the honor.

1686: The **importance of water transportation** to early colonial commerce was remarked on by a Frenchman traveling in Virginia, who noted: "None of the plantation houses, even the most remote, is more than 100 or 150 feet from a 'crik' and the people are thus enabled not only to pay visits in their canoes, but to do all their freight carrying by the same means." Until the coming of the railroads in the nineteenth century, most American commerce, particularly transportation of heavy goods, was conducted by water transportation.

1689: The **first public school** in America with such practical subjects as science and inventions, the William Penn Charter School, was founded in Philadelphia. The school charged tuition only for students who could afford it.

IV. Fashion
Folkways
Holidays
Social Issues and Crime
Sports

A new element was added to colonial society when in France the Edict of Nantes was revoked in 1685 by King Louis XIV. The edict had protected the Huguenots, French Protestants, from persecution, and its revocation led to a wave of Huguenot emigration to the New World. Thrifty and industrious middle-class merchants and artisans, they settled in New York, Massachusetts, Rhode Island, Virginia, and South Carolina, and established such illustrious family names as Jay, Revere, DeLancey, Faneuil, Bowdoin, and Maury. In New York they founded and named New Rochelle in 1688. The Huguenots were especially important in South Carolina, where 500 of them took up 50,000 acres along the Santee R. They were prominent in Charleston life, and in their cultivation of rice in the lowlands they did much to increase the use of slaves in the colony.

1681: The appearance of the **first dancing master** in Boston provoked an outburst from the authorities. He was cited as "a person of very insolent & ill fame that Raues & scoffes at Religion." He soon was driven out. Dancing was a constant source of complaint among the ministers. Shortly after ouster of the first dancing master, Increase Mather thundered forth his condemnation in the tract *An Arrow against Profane and Promiscuous Dancing, Drawn out of the Quiver of the Scriptures.*

1682: The **first Freemason** to settle in America, John Skene, arrived in Burlington, N.J. He belonged to the lodge in Aberdeen, Scotland, and came to the colonies through arrangements made by the Earl of Perth, chief proprietor of New Jersey and an outstanding Freemason.

1685: For **performing marriages in Boston,** a Huguenot minister was haled before a New England court. A growing tendency to make marriage an ecclesiastical function was strongly suppressed. Marriage was regarded as a civil contract and the courts were determined to enforce this.

1687 June 28: William Phipps, the **first knighted native American,** was dubbed by King James II of England in ceremonies at Windsor Castle. He was so honored for having found a treasure ship off the coast of Hispaniola. Later he returned to Massachusetts and became governor of the colony.

1690–1699

I. Civil Rights
Exploration and Settlement
Government
Statistics
Wars

King William's War (1689–1697) was the first of what came to be known in America as the French and Indian Wars. In fact, the French and Indian Wars were a series of colonial wars between Great Britain and France that lasted three-quarters of a century. Hostilities in King William's War began in 1690, when in the course of a few months Schenectady, N.Y., was burned by the French and Indians, and colonial English forces launched attacks on Port Royal (now Annapolis Royal), Nova Scotia, and on Quebec. Despite further raids by the French and Indians, the war ended in a stalemate. The Treaty of Ryswick, by which were ended the war and its European counterpart, the War of the Grand Alliance, restored all colonial possessions to their prewar status.

The estimated colonial **population** was 213,500.

1690 Feb 3: The **first paper money** was issued. It was used by Massachusetts to pay soldiers who had served the campaign in Quebec.

1690 Feb 8: In **King William's War** (1689–1697) French and Indian forces from Montreal attacked and burned Schenectady, N.Y.

1690 May 11: Port Royal (now Annapolis Royal), Nova Scotia, was captured by the English under Sir William Phips. French forces recaptured it in 1691.

1690 Oct 7: The city of **Quebec was attacked** by English forces in the first major military operation of King William's War. They were repulsed by the French under Louis de Buade, comte de Palluau et de Frontenac.

1691: A **charter** uniting the colonies of Plymouth and Massachusetts Bay provided "liberty of conscience to all Christians, except Papists."

1691: Albemarle was renamed **North Carolina** and put under the governorship of a deputy answerable to the Crown.

1692 Apr: A patent to found a **post office** in the English colonies was issued to the Englishman Thomas Neale. It was first put into effect in Virginia. Andrew Hamilton, Neale's colonial deputy, later did much to organize widespread postal service.

1696: The **importation of slaves** by Quakers was forbidden at the yearly meeting of American Quakers, with expulsion from membership the penalty for violators.

1697: An epidemic of **smallpox** ravaged Charleston, S.C. After running its course for over a year, it diminished, only to be followed in Aug. 1699 by yellow fever, which killed 150 people in six days. Infections were generally brought from the West Indies.

1697 Sep 3: **King William's War** (1689–1697) was ended by the Treaty of Ryswick. From the standpoint of the American colonies, the war was completely pointless. Both French and English forces won a number of engagements and managed to occupy part of each other's territory. However, the treaty restored all possessions to their prewar status.

II. Architecture
Arts and Music
Popular Entertainment
Publishing
Theater

Printing and publishing, although hampered by government restrictions, had become more or less common in the larger cities by the end of the seventeenth century. John Foster had established Boston's first press in 1674, and by 1700 presses in Boston were producing more print than those in any English city except London. The first press in Philadelphia had been set up in 1685 by William Bradford, who that year issued an almanac, *Kalendarium Pennsilvaniense or America's Messenger.* Bradford, however, had trouble with the city council in 1693 and moved to New York City. In Philadelphia, Regnier Jansen established another press in 1698. In New York, Bradford began issuing almanacs in 1694, and in 1696 he published *Le Trésor des Consolations Divine et Humaine* [Treasury of Comforts Divine and Human]. Almanacs became popular in the eighteenth century. The most famous, *Poor Richard's Almanack,* was first issued by Benjamin Franklin in 1732.

1690: The famous **Wayside Inn** of Henry Wadsworth Longfellow's *Tales of a Wayside Inn* (1886) was built in Sudbury, Mass. It was called the Red Horse Tavern, and was characterized by a raftered ceiling and a bar in the form of a cage. It was damaged by fire in 1955 but was restored.

1690: The *New England Primer,* a standard colonial elementary textbook, made its first appearance. It combined the teaching of the alphabet and Puritan theology in moral couplets, as "In Adam's fall-We sinned all."

1690 Sep 25: The **first newspaper** in the colonies appeared in Boston. It was Benjamin Harris's *Publick Occurrences.* It expired four days later because Harris had presumed to publish without official permission.

1695: The cornerstone was laid for the first building at the **College of William and Mary in Virginia,** based on plans said to have been drawn in London by Christopher Wren. The building, an excellent example of early Georgian style in its purest, Virginian form, was completed in 1702.

1698: The **Old Swedes Church** in Wilmington, Del., said to be the oldest Protestant church in continuous use in America, was erected by Swedish Lutherans. It is now a Protestant Episcopal church.

III. Business and Industry
Education
Philosophy and Religion
Science

The history of New England's great religious leaders was magnified and epitomized in the prolific yet contradictory career of Cotton Mather, last and greatest of the Puritan divines. Pictured as a central figure in the Salem witch hunts because he helped bring on the witchcraft trials there in 1692, he later had second thoughts on witchcraft. He was smug and stern but was also a leader in the revolt against the autocratic rule of Gov. Edmund Andros in Massachusetts. Mather did much to promote education and was deeply interested in science. He wrote more than 440 works and collected a library of 4000 books. He was a man of his time in whom all traits good and bad were greatly magnified.

1690: The **first paper mill** in America was set up by German settlers in Pennsylvania. The paper was handmade from linen rags pounded into pulp. The first American watermark was the word "company" formed in paper made by William Rittenhouse.

1690: The American **whaling industry** first began large-scale operations out of Nantucket, Mass.

1692: The **first divinity degree** conferred in the American colonies was given to Increase Mather, sixth president of Harvard College. Mather received a Doctor of Divinity degree from Harvard under a new charter just granted by William and Mary, the English sovereigns.

1692 Mar: The **Salem witch hunt** was unleashed when some children, called upon to explain their odd behavior, claimed that three old women had bewitched them. The women were tried, convicted, and condemned on the testimony of the children. Although Gov. William Phips halted the trials in Oct. 1692, by Jan. 1693 twenty persons condemned for witchcraft had been executed and two had died in prison.

1693 Feb 8: A charter founding the **College of William and Mary in Virginia** was signed. A grant was given to James Blair to "furnish Virginia with a seminary of ministers, to educate the youth in piety, letters and good manners and to propagate Christianity among the Indians."

1697: Official repentance for the **Salem witch trials** was highlighted by a day of prayer for forgiveness by the Massachusetts Court. Samuel Sewall, one of the Salem judges, publicly confessed his feeling of guilt from his pew in the South Church.

1697 Oct: A severe enactment against **blasphemers and atheists** was passed in Massachusetts. Anyone denying the divine nature of the Bible could be imprisoned for six months, confined to the pillory, whipped, bored through the tongue with a hot iron, or forced to sit on the gallows with a rope around his neck.

IV. Fashion
Folkways
Holidays
Social Issues and Crime
Sports

As towns and cities grew, the problem of street cleaning arose. Throwing rubbish of all kinds into the street was an old English custom. The tidy Dutch in New Amsterdam were the first to do something about the problem when they forbade in 1657 the throwing of "any rubbish, filth, oyster shells, dead animal or anything like it" into the street. Boston first took action in 1662 when Thomas Willsheer was hired as a scavenger to get rid of "all Carrion & matters of Offenciue natuer." Beginning in 1684 four scavengers were at work. Street cleaning was introduced in New York in 1695 when a Mr. Vanderspiegle was hired at £30 a year. By 1710 the city was employing public cartmen to remove trash placed before houses.

1691: The **ducking stool,** a form of punishment for scolds, was ordered built on the wharf in front of City Hall, New York. Although this form of punishment

by plunging into water was not used frequently in New York City, it was common in the South.

1693: The **Huguenots** of South Carolina, considered foreigners, were threatened with the loss of their estates upon death. Discrimination against the French was marked throughout the century in South Carolina, probably because of envy of their refinement, education, and superior economic ability.

1699 Spring: Capt. **William Kidd,** the notorious pirate, paid a visit to an old friend in Narrangansett, R.I., and left some treasure. Thus began the myth of Capt. Kidd's buried treasure, which has sent thousands digging up beaches for trinkets and pieces of eight. Legend says that Kidd murdered a helper and buried him with the treasure chest as a means or warding off searchers.

1699 June: A **card game** was suppressed by Judge Samuel Sewall of Boston. A few days later he found a pack of cards strewn over his lawn, as if to mock his efforts. Gambling was rampant in all the colonies despite numerous laws against it. Even lotteries came under ban in New England by an order promulgated in 1719.

1700–1704

I. Civil Rights
Exploration and Settlement
Government
Statistics
Wars

Queen Anne's War (1702–1713), the second of the French and Indian Wars, began May 4, 1702. In Europe it was known as the War of the Spanish Succession. The Grand Alliance (England, the League of Augsburg, Denmark, Portugal, and the Netherlands) declared war on France and Spain to prevent union of the French and Spanish thrones following the death of King Charles II of Spain. In North America British and French colonial forces, with their Indian allies, raided and attempted to capture a number of border settlements. New England colonists successfully attacked the French settlements of Minas and Beaubassin in Nova Scotia in July 1704, while the French destroyed Deerfield, Mass., in February and took the English colony of Bonavista on Newfoundland in August. The most notable colonial success was the British capture of Port Royal, Nova Scotia, on Oct. 16, 1710, following unsuccessful assaults in 1704 and 1707; however, a British naval attack on Quebec in 1711 failed. In the South, Carolina forces captured the town of St. Augustine, Fla., in Sept. 1702, although the fort there held out. Another force wiped out all but one of fourteen missions in northwestern Florida in 1704.

c1700: The **population** of the colonies was sparsely scattered over the large area. Below the Delaware R. an isolated farm was the usual settlement, save for Charleston, which had about 250 families. Philadelphia had approximately 700 houses, New York about 5000 inhabitants, Newport less than 2000, and Boston, the largest city, about 7000. There were approximately 275,000 inhabitants in the colonies.

1701: The capture of Capt. **William Kidd** marked the passing of the pirate era from colonial trade. William Kidd, at one time a wealthy New York landowner who had served as a privateer for the Crown against the French, was tried and hanged in London on May 23. He left many legends of buried treasure in his wake.

1701 July 24: A settlement at **Detroit** was established by Antoine de la Mothe Cadillac. The area of Michigan was early known to trappers, priests, and traders from French Canada. The Jesuits, led by Isaac Jogues, founded a mission at Sault Ste. Marie in 1641. There, in 1668, Jacques Marquette established the first permanent settlement in Michigan. When the French government lost interest in outposts in the West, Cadillac went to France with a proposal that would save the fur trade from the English. He was granted the land by the narrows of the river connecting Lake Huron with Lake Erie. There he set up a large colony he called Fort Pontchartrain. The name Detroit comes from the French words for the narrows (*détroit*), where the fort was located.

II. Architecture
Arts and Music
Popular Entertainment
Publishing
Theater

Journalism was one of the trades that followed the colonists to America. The first successful newspaper in the English colonies appeared on Apr. 24, 1704. This was the Boston *News-Letter*, founded by John Campbell, the Boston postmaster. It published until 1776. Although its early circulation was only about 300, the paper was passed from person to person and was available in coffee houses and taverns. It carried advertising, including notices placed by dancing and music teachers. Other early newspapers were the

Boston *Gazette* (1719), Philadelphia *American Mercury* (1719), *New England Courant* (Boston, 1721), New York *Gazette* (1725), Maryland *Gazette* (Annapolis, 1727), and *Pennsylvania Gazette* (Philadelphia, 1728).

1700: Perhaps the **first denunciation of slavery** in the colonies was *The Selling of Joseph* by Samuel Sewall, which put forth antislavery arguments. Typical of his time, Sewall relied mainly on biblical citations.

1702: *Magnalis Christi Americana; or the Ecclesiastical History of New England,* the *magnum opus* of Cotton Mather, was published. Mather wanted to bring people back to the early spirit of Puritanism at a time when feeling against the clergy ran high because of witch burnings.

1704: The earliest known example of a **Dutch gambrel roof** in America was built on the Ackerman house in Hackensack, N.J. This roof type became common throughout New York and northern New Jersey in the eighteenth century.

1704 Oct: A **classic travel book**, *Private Journal*, was begun by Sarah Kemble Knight; she made entries until Mar. 1705. A schoolmistress (young Benjamin Franklin attended her school in Boston), she took a trip alone to New York and reported on her experiences. She also commented on the character and mores of the Yankee inhabitants she encountered. Her book was not published until 1825.

III. Business and Industry
Education
Philosophy and Religion
Science

The Church of England made great efforts in the eighteenth century to propagate its cause in the English colonies. The Society for the Propagation of the Gospel in Foreign Parts was granted a charter in 1701 by King William III of England. This charter was granted at the instigation of the Rev. Thomas Bray of London, who had been chosen in 1696 to establish the Anglican Church in Maryland. Bray recruited missionaries and sent out more than 30 parish libraries. Between 1702 and 1783 the society maintained 54 missionaries in South Carolina, 33 in North Carolina, 84 in New England, 47 in Pennsylvania, 58 in New York, 44 in New Jersey, 13 in Georgia, 5 in Maryland, and 2 in Virginia. In all, 202 central missions were maintained and the society spent £227,454 in this period. Although the Anglican Church made some gains as a result of this effort, the various other Protestant sects and denominations—Presbyterian, Congregationalist, Quaker, and Baptist—held their ground, as did the small Roman Catholic community. American

Anglicans fought the establishment of an episcopate because the selection would be imposed from England. Southern laymen especially insisted on the right to choose their own clergymen. During the American Revolution the Patriot leadership was dominated by such southern Anglicans as George Washington and such northern Congregationalists as John Adams. The Loyalists for the most part were Anglicans.

1700 June 17: Massachusetts enacted a law requiring **Roman Catholic priests** to leave the colony within three months. If any priest remained, he was to be considered an "incendiary and disturber of the public peace and safety and an enemy to the true Christian religion." If found guilty, he could be imprisoned for life or executed.

1701 Oct 16: Yale was founded as Collegiate School in Killingworth, Conn., by Congregationalists dissatisfied with the growing liberalism at Harvard. The school was named after Elihu Yale, son of one of the founders of New Haven, who had gained great riches in India as governor for the East India Company. The school was moved in 1745 to New Haven, Conn., where it became Yale College. Yale became a university in 1887. Its first degrees were awarded in 1716.

IV. Fashion
Folkways
Holidays
Social Issues and Crime
Sports

The Bowery, about three miles north of New York City, was a popular recreation center. The well-known traveler Sarah Kemble Knight visited the Bowery in 1704 and found that visitors did not "spare for any diversion the place offered, and sociable to a degree." John Clap, a tavern keeper there, offered "any Gentlemen Travellers that are strangers to the City . . . good Entertainment, for themselves and Horses." Knight reached the Bowery by sleigh and on one occasion noted that she met "50 or 60 sleys."

c1700: The American **slat-back chair** made its first appearance simultaneously in New England, Pennsylvania, and New York. In the nineteenth century Shakers produced quantities of this type of chair, popular for general home use. An early type used a rope seat. This design should not be confused with the splat-back chair, which showed the influence of Dutch craftsmanship and design and was a product of this period.

1704: New York **women's fashions** were described by a contemporary traveler and diarist: "The English go very fasheonable in their dress. The Dutch, especially the middling sort, differ from our women, in their habitt go loose, were French muches which are like a Capp and a head band in one, leaving their ears bare, which are sett out with Jewells of a large size and many in number. And their fingers hoop't with Rings, some with large stones in them of many Coullers as were their pendants in their ears, which You should see very old women wear as well as Young."

1704 Sep 28: Separation of couples by a minister was legalized by a statute passed in Maryland. A minister could separate a man and woman if he disapproved of the woman. If the man did not obey, he was haled into court and, if convicted, fined or whipped until blood began to flow.

1705–1709

I. Civil Rights
Exploration and Settlement
Government
Statistics
Wars

In the early nineteenth century the prevailing political and economic theory held that colonies existed for the benefit of the mother country and that the colonies should produce only raw materials, accepting in return manufactured goods from the homeland. An English law of 1705, for example, expanded the list of goods that the American colonies could export to English ports only. Among these were rice, molasses, and naval stores—pitch, rosin, tar, hemp, masts, yards, and bowsprits. At this time there was little organized political opposition to the rule of Crown and Parliament. As long as home nation and colonies prospered, the political situation remained manageable.

1705: A Virginia **slavery act** decreed that all imported servants were to remain in lifelong servitude. Excepted were those who had been Christians in their native country or who had been free in a Christian country. This law limited slavery to blacks and confined almost all imported blacks to slavery. An interesting exception was inserted for "Turks and Moors in amity with her majesty."

1706: An important American **customhouse** was built at Yorktown, Va. Yorktown had been appointed the port of entry for New York, Philadelphia, and other northern cities, though many merchants disregarded the law. Yorktown was the site of Virginia's "tea party" in 1774, when Richard Ambler, collector of revenue, led a boarding party to the *Virginia* and tossed its tea cargo overboard. The customhouse was restored in 1928.

1709 Sep 3: The first major influx of **Swiss and German immigrants** came to the Carolinas. They had been encouraged by a grant of 13,500 acres by the proprietors to two sponsors representing German refugees from the Palatinate and Swiss emigrants from Berne.

II. Architecture
Arts and Music
Popular Entertainment
Publishing
Theater

Accounts of persons who had been held captive by Indians provided popular reading matter in colonial times. One of the best examples of the genre, and a best seller in the early eighteenth century, was *The Redeemed Captive, Returning to Zion* (1707) by John Williams, Congregational minister of Deerfield, Mass. Williams and his family were captured by the Indians in 1704 during the raid on Deerfield in Queen Anne's War. His book, written at the urging of Cotton Mather, recounted the cruelties he witnessed and suffered during two years of captivity; it also detailed attempts by Jesuits to convert him to Catholicism. William's narrative and an earlier account, *The Sovereignty of God, Together with the Faithfulness of His Promises Displayed; Being a Narrative of the Captivity and Restauration of Mrs. Mary Rowlandson* (1682) by Mary Rowlandson, were models for a number of books about Indian captivity published during the eighteenth and early nineteenth century.

1706: Work was begun on the **Governor's Palace** at Williamsburg, Va., the finest residence of its time in the colonies. It was not formally completed until 1720. The Governor's Palace was occupied by royal governors until the Revolutionary War, and thereafter by the state governors, Patrick Henry and Thomas Jefferson, until the capital was moved to Richmond in 1780.

1708: A **popular satirical poem** by one Ebenezer Cook was *The Sot-Weed Factor; or, A Voyage to Maryland,—a satire in which is described the laws, government, courts, and constitution of the country, and also the buildings, feasts, frolics, entertainments, and drunken humors of the inhabitants in that part of America.* Little is known about the author.

III. Business and Industry
Education
Philosophy and Religion
Science

The various Protestant denominations were active in establishing themselves in the English colonies in the early eighteenth century. The first Anglican parish in Connecticut was established in 1706 at Stratford through the efforts of Caleb Heathcote. He was a wealthy merchant and public official who in 1701 had been granted the manor of Scarsdale in Westchester County, N.Y., the last manor to be granted in the colonies. In Mar. 1706 the first presbytery was established in Philadelphia, Pa., through the efforts of the Rev. Francis Makemie. Born in Ireland, Makemie first came to America in 1683 and began organizing Presbyterian churches. In 1707 he was arrested in New York, charged with preaching without a license. Although he was acquitted, he incurred heavy costs. About this time the Baptists in Philadelphia organized their first church, which had quarters in a brew house. In 1707 the first meeting of a Baptist association was held in Philadelphia, with five churches represented. Connecticut Congregational churches, meeting at Saybrook, Conn., adopted the Saybrook Platform in 1708, which moved toward a church system like that of the Presbyterians rather than the more democratic Massachusetts Congregationalists. In Charleston, S.C., both the Baptists and the Quakers organized churches as early as 1699, but the largest religious groups there were the Huguenots and the Anglicans.

1706: What was perhaps the **first lithotomy** (surgical removal of stones from the bladder) in New England gave prominence to Zabdiel Boylston, the Boston surgeon who performed it. Following this, he performed many successful operations; in 1718 he removed a cancerous breast from a woman.

1709: The **first private home for mental illness** in America was established by the Quakers of Philadelphia, Pa. In 1751 it became a part of Pennsylvania Hospital.

IV. Fashion
Folkways
Holidays
Social Issues and Crime
Sports

With the introduction of paper money in the colonies, counterfeiting was not long in appearing. In 1705 Thomas Odell of Boston counterfeited the £4 notes of Massachusetts and tried to pass them in Pennsylvania. He was arrested and sentenced in Boston to a fine of £300 and a year in prison. James Mar, a New York engraver, applied his skill to counterfeit bills. He was sentenced to be hanged, but was granted clemency by the governor, who could not refuse a tearful petition from "Most of the Gentlewomen of the City." In Philadelphia in 1720 Edward and Martha Hunt were implicated in counterfeiting and sentenced to death and life imprisonment respectively.

1705: Intermarriage between a white person and a black was declared illegal in Massachusetts. Any minister performing such a marriage was fined £50. This prohibition remained in force until 1843, when the law was repealed.

1706: A **closed season on deer hunting** was established on Long Island, where continual hunting had almost eliminated this popular game.

1708: A **closed season,** Apr. 1 to July 31, was established on turkeys, heath hens, partridges, and quail in Kings, Queens, and Suffolk counties in New York.

1710–1714

I. Civil Rights
Exploration and Settlement
Government
Statistics
Wars

Settlers from European lands other than the British Isles began to come to the English colonies in large numbers. On Sept. 3, 1700, the proprietors of Carolina granted a tract of 13,500 acres to agents representing Swiss and German Palatinate emigrants. Besides wanting to better themselves economically, many of the emigrants sought religious freedom. New Bern, the second town in North Carolina, was settled in 1710 by some 650 Swiss and German colonists under the leadership of Baron Christopher de Graffenried and John Dawson. The same year 3000 Germans from the Palatinate settled near Livingston Manor, N.Y., intending to produce naval stores. They were brought to America by Robert Hunter, commissioned governor of New York and the Jerseys in 1709. The settlement was not successful and in 1713, under the leadership of Conrad Weiser, the settlers moved first to the Schoharie Valley and then to the Mohawk Valley. Eventually many of them moved to Berks and Bucks counties in Pennsylvania.

The estimated colonial **population** was 357,500.

1711 Sep 22: The **Tuscarora Indian War** (1711–1713) began with a massacre of settlers on the Chowan and Roanoke rivers in northeastern North Carolina. The settlement at New Bern was abandoned. White encroachment, which included the enslaving of Indian children, led to the war.

1712 May 9: The **Territory of the Carolinas** was provided with two governors, one for the north and one for the south. Though theoretically a single province, the settlements were far apart, and so each section was accorded its own governor. From 1691 to 1712 a single governor usually resided in Charleston.

1713 Mar 23: The **Tuscarora War** ended with the capture of the Indian stronghold at Fort Nohucke, S.C. The Indians fled northward and were admitted into the League of the Iroquois as a sixth nation.

1713 Apr 11: Queen Anne's War (1702–1713) was ended by the Treaty of Utrecht, which brought the War of the Spanish Succession to a close in Europe. By the treaty France ceded the Hudson Bay territory, Newfoundland, and Nova Scotia to Great Britain. France also agreed to a British protectorate over the Iroquois Indians. France kept Cape Breton Island and the islands of the St. Lawrence.

II. Architecture
Arts and Music
Popular Entertainment
Publishing
Theater

Bookselling in the colonies began before the turn of the century and so was flourishing by this time. Around 1698 Regnier Jansen, a printer in Philadelphia, was selling books. By 1714 Andrew Bradford's Philadelphia store, the Bible and Crown, was filling orders from as far away as Barbados. In 1718 John Copson sold books along with other merchandise, a common practice. William Bradford, who set up in New York as a printer in 1694, also ran a bookshop, as did Thomas Adams, a stationer, after 1698. Boston, however, led the way in the book business, with about 30 stores there by 1711. In 1724 the Boston booksellers formed an association to fix prices and otherwise regulate the trade. Boston supplied books to all the other colonies, but its trade was especially brisk in New England.

1713: King's Chapel, the Anglican church in Boston, acquired an organ in a bequest from Thomas Brattle. Few organs were to be found in colonial churches, since Puritan practice prohibited instrumental music in religious services and most congregations of other denominations could not afford to import instruments from England.

III. Business and Industry
Education
Philosophy and Religion
Science

Deism, a rationalistic theology holding that the course of the universe demonstrates the existence of God, so no formal exercise of religion is necessary, made considerable headway in the colonies. Published in 1711, *Characteristicks of Men, Manners, Opinions, Times* by Anthony Ashley Cooper, third earl of Shaftesbury, had much influence in America. Shaftesbury postulated an innate moral sense that did not require religious incentives to reveal itself. Many of his admirers in America seized upon this idea as the basis of deistic thought. Deism was strongest in the large towns, especially in Philadelphia, where men such as Benjamin Franklin became believers. In New England even Cotton Mather, of the leading family of Puritan divines, flirted with the idea of "Nature and Nature's God" by 1715. The painter Robert Fcke led a group in Newport, R.I., that read and discussed deistic works. Later in the century men as prominent as Thomas Jefferson were deists.

1710: Trinity School was established in New York City under the auspices of the Society for the Propagation of the Gospel. The founding of Trinity School represented a victory of private and parochial school adherents over supporters of free public schools.

1712: The **first sperm whale** captured by an American was taken by Christopher Hussey, of Nantucket, Mass. The event radically changed the character of the Nantucket whaling business. Whalers previously had plied close to shore, seeking right whales. Thereafter they hunted in deep waters on longer voyages. In 1715 Nantucket had a fleet of six sloops engaged in sperm whaling.

1713: The **first American schooner** was built by Capt. Andrew Robinson in Gloucester, Mass.

1714: Support for **scientific observation** over dogma was demonstrated by the famous Puritan theologian Cotton Mather, who accepted the Copernican theory of the universe as against the Ptolemaic. His sermon of acceptance was unfavorably received by the eminent Puritan moralist Judge Samuel Sewall, who considered the subject too controversial.

IV. Fashion
Folkways
Holidays
Social Issues and Crime
Sports

By 1710 the favorite nonalcoholic beverage of the colonists was probably chocolate. This drink resulted from the discovery of the cacao tree and its seed by Spanish explorers in Mexico. They took it to Europe, where it spread to England and then back to the North American colonies. Coffee was introduced into North America about 1668, and the first coffee house was opened in October 1676 in Boston by John Sparry. It soon became the place where businessmen gathered to exchange news. Tea was first brought to Europe by the Dutch East India Company in the early seventeenth century. It was carried by settlers to America almost as soon as colonization began. Coffee did not take first place over tea and chocolate until the time of the Boston Tea Party (1773), when it became a patriotic duty not to drink English tea because of the tax on it and the monopoly on its trade. However, the popularity of tea actually increased in the first half of the eighteenth century because of widespread smuggling, which provided a plentiful and inexpensive supply. Among alcoholic beverages, rum was a favorite in New England and beer in the middle colonies. Madeira took first place in wines followed by canary, claret, burgundy, port, brandy, and champagne.

c1710: In contrast to the sober dress of the Quakers, **colonial fashions** were often extravagant. High heels, stiff stays, and large curled wigs were worn by both men and women. Men's coat skirts were stiffened with buckram, and sleeve cuffs often reached the elbows. The invention of the hoop in England in 1711 governed dress styles in America for many years. Originally these hoops were flat, projecting only at the sides. Over them were worn layers of skirts, and a sacque, or overdress, was hung on top. Women's hairstyles were characterized by the "tower," or "commode." From the top of this tower "lappets," or lace pendants, hung down alongside the face.

1712: The **first fines for speeding** were levied against reckless carters in Philadelphia.

1715–1719

I. Civil Rights
Exploration and Settlement
Government
Statistics
Wars

Another of the many conflicts between whites and Indians that were to go on until the late nineteenth century occurred at this time. The Yamassee Indians, encouraged by the Spanish, massacred several hundred Carolina settlers in Apr. 1715. In Jan. 1716 the South Carolina settlers, aided by Cherokee Indians, defeated the Yamassee northwest of Port Royal, at the southern tip of what is now South Carolina. The conflict was a result of the desire of Carolina settlers moving into Yamassee territory to take up large areas of coastal land for raising cattle. This southward movement also brought the English colonists into areas claimed by the Spanish.

1718: New Orleans was founded by French settlers from Canada and France. The Canadians generally brought their wives and families with them. French officers, however, usually younger sons of nobility, refused to marry below their rank, inspiring the plea of one of the early governors to France: "Send me wives for my Canadians; they are running in the woods after Indian girls."

II. Architecture
Arts and Music
Popular Entertainment
Publishing
Theater

When the colonists left England for new homes in America, they brought their music with them and in the eighteenth century were practicing and enjoying music in a variety of ways. In 1715 appeared the *Introduction to the Singing of Psalm-Tunes* by Rev. John Tufts. This was the first American instruction manual, and no copy of it is known to exist. In New York in 1720 gentlemen might gather at someone's home "to hear some good Musick, and to take a Tiff of fresh Lime Punch." The first public "Concert of Musick on Sundry Instruments" took place on Feb. 18, 1729, in Boston. The first piece of music criticism in America was perhaps an *article in the Philadelphia Mercury* in 1729. And in 1732 a school of "Vocal Musick" was opened at Newport, R.I., by a Mr. Beal, who had previously taught singing at Yale.

1716: The **first theater** in the colonies was built in Williamsburg, Va., by William Levingston.

1719: *Divine and Moral Songs for the Use of Children,* a juvenile best seller by Isaac Watts, was published. The book was popular for at least 150 years, with more than 240 editions being published in England and America.

1719: Fraunces Tavern, the earliest residential building remaining in Manhattan, was built at Pearl and Broad streets in New York. Originally built as a residence for Stephen De Lancey, it was purchased for a tavern by Samuel Fraunces in 1762. It became famous for its Long Room, where George Washington delivered his Farewell Address to his officers in 1783.

III. Business and Industry
Education
Philosophy and Religion
Science

The growth of shipping and commercial trade was encouraged in 1717 when colonial merchants were allowed to send ships to the French West Indies. The chief item of this lucrative trade was molasses, from which New England distilleries produced rum, a profitable staple of colonial trade. The Treaty of Utrecht (1713) provided for trading concessions with the Spanish colonies. Commercial fishing was also booming and shipbuilding began to be important in the economy. An early shipbuilder was Capt. Andrew Robinson of Gloucester, Mass., who in 1713 built a schooner of his own design. From Charleston, S.C., much trade was carried on, not only with the West Indies but also with Dutch settlements in South America. In 1718 £150,000 worth of goods, mostly woolens from England, came into Charleston. New York, Newport, and Philadelphia were also growing as shipping and trading centers, but Boston was the leading commercial center of the colonies in the early eighteenth century.

1716: Probably the **first lighthouse** in the colonies was put up by Massachusetts Colony on Little Brewster Island to guard Boston Harbor.

1719: Potato cultivation in the colonies began with the settlement of Londonderry, N.H., by Scottish-Irish immigrants.

IV. Fashion
Folkways
Holidays
Social Issues and Crime
Sports

Piracy, although declining, still existed on a fairly large scale and was not entirely frowned upon. This reflected the narrow difference between privateering, a wartime act in which a shipowner could legitimately attempt to capture merchant ships owned by his country's enemy, and piracy, which was much the same act in time of peace. Nevertheless, steps were taken to end piracy. The English Parliament in 1700 had ordered establishment of special courts in the colonies to try those accused of piracy. In 1718 Gov. Alexander Spotswood of Virginia offered a reward for capture of Blackbeard, the most notorious pirate of the time, whose real name was Edward Teach. He had been both a privateer and a pirate. Even though protected by the governor of North Carolina, who shared some of his booty, Blackbeard was caught and hanged. Also in 1718 another pirate, Stede Bonnet, was captured by an expedition from Carolina, and he too was hanged.

1719: Perhaps the **first street light** in America, a single lantern, was presented to the town of Boston by Eliakim Hutchinson. Boston's selectmen ordered that the town be "well fixed with Lights on all or Stormy Nights."

1719 Mar: New Jersey enacted its most important **marriage statute.** It provided that no person under 21 years of age could be married without the consent of a parent or guardian. It was the result of many instances of young people being enticed into clandestine marriages.

1720–1724

I. Civil Rights
Exploration and Settlement
Government
Statistics
Wars

In the eighteenth century northern New England was claimed both by the English and the French, and both established forts and settlements in the disputed area. The English in 1724 built Fort Dummer, named for William Dummer, lieutenant governor and acting governor of Massachusetts. It was near the site of present-day Brattleboro, Vt., named for William Brattle, who with Dummer had purchased the tract of land on which the fort stood. Brattleboro was the first permanent European settlement in Vermont. A French stronghold at this time was the Abnaki Indian village of Norridgewock on the Kennebec R. in Maine. The leader there was a French Jesuit missionary, Father Sébastien Rasle. Father Rasle escaped a British raid in 1721, leaving behind a dictionary of the Abnaki language he had been preparing. The raiders took it away, and it was not published until 1833. In 1724 the British again raided Norridgewock, captured it, and killed Father Rasle, gun in hand. These and similar events of the period became known as Dummer's or Lovewell's War (1721–1725). The Lovewell in question was John Lovewell, a Massachusetts

Indian fighter who was killed in a skirmish with Pigwacket Indians at Fryeburg, Maine, on May 8, 1725.

c1720: A period of **French expansion and entrenchment** in the Mississippi Valley began. The French erected forts in 1720 and 1726 at the mouths of the Kaskaskia and Illinois rivers, and made peace with the Indians in the South. Fort Toulouse was erected among the Creeks on the Alabama R. In the North powerful Fort Louisbourg on Cape Breton Island, constructed in 1720, guarded the entrance to the St. Lawrence R. Farther south the French established fortifications at Crown Point on Lake Champlain in 1731. Fort Miami, constructed in 1704, protected the northern approach to the Mississippi Valley. Fort Ouiataon on the Wabash R. was built about 1719, and Fort Vincennes on the lower Wabash R. about 1724.

1720: The estimated colonial **population** was 474,388. City populations were: Boston, 12,000; Philadelphia, 10,000; New York, 7000; Charleston, 3500; and Newport, 3800. All urban dwellers at this time were only 8% of the total population.

1722: The **League of Six Nations,** an Iroquois confederation that included the Tuscarora tribe, concluded in Albany, N.Y., a treaty with Gov. Alexander Spotswood of Virginia. The Indians agreed not to cross the Potomac R. or Blue Ridge Mts. The Iroquois league always remained friendly to the English and hostile to the French, mainly because the latter often aided Indian tribes who were enemies of the Iroquois. Thus the League of Six Nations was an effective and necessary guard for the English colonies' western borders during this period of French expansion in the Mississippi R. Valley.

II. Architecture
Arts and Music
Popular Entertainment
Publishing
Theater

Georgian architecture came into fashion in England and the English colonies at about this time. The style, named in honor of the three kings of England who reigned during the period, marked a return to classical forms. It was greatly influenced by the designs of the sixteenth-century Italian architect Andrea Palladio and the seventeenth-century English architect Inigo Jones. In Apr. 1723 the cornerstone was laid for Christ Church, known as Old North Church, in Boston. Designed by William Price, who had studied Christopher Wren's London churches, it was the first Georgian church in New England. Today it is the oldest church in Boston. From its steeple in 1775 were hung lanterns that started Paul Revere on his ride by horseback to Lexington and Concord to warn of the approach of British troops. In Philadelphia James Porteus designed a new Christ Church, completed in 1731 and the most ornate example of the Georgian style in America. A new state house for the Pennsylvania Assembly, completed in 1735, was the largest and most elaborately formal structure in the colonies. Perhaps the most distinguished private residence of the type was Westover, built about 1734 for William Byrd, II, on the James R. in Virginia. Another practitioner of the Georgian style was the Newport, R.I., architect Peter Harrison, sometimes called the first American architect. Among his works were Newport's Touro Synagogue and the Redwood Library.

1722: **The Alamo,** to become famous as the site of a great battle of the war for Texan independence in 1836, was constructed at about this time as a Franciscan mission.

1723: Perhaps the **first house with running water** in America was John Headly's in Newport, R.I. It was equipped in this year with a pipe "underground from the Spring."

III. Business and Industry
Education
Philosophy and Religion
Science

A major step forward in preventive medicine was introduced to the colonies. The first smallpox inoculations in America were given on June 26, 1721, in Boston by Dr. Zabdiel Boylston. He had been urged to do so by Cotton Mather, the influential Puritan clergyman. Even though an epidemic was raging in Boston at the time, many persons objected fiercely on religious grounds. The homes of both Mather and Boylston were stoned by mobs. Dr. Boylston first inoculated his son, Thomas, and two black slaves. In all he inoculated 240 persons, of whom all but six survived. During the epidemic there were 5889 cases of smallpox in Boston, and 844 persons died. It is said that Dr. Boylston's slave, Onesimus, had previously told him of similar inoculations administered in Africa. Smallpox epidemics were a constant menace in colonial times. In Charleston, S.C., in 1698 an epidemic raged unchecked for about ten months. During another Boston epidemic, in 1702, it was ordered that bodies be buried without elaborate funerals so as to prevent the spread of infection. There were serious outbreaks in New York and Philadelphia in 1731–1732. In New York it was estimated that 6% of the population died of smallpox at the time.

1721: **A Jesuit college,** founded at Kaskaskia, in what is now Illinois, was one of the first institutions of higher learning in the Middle West. It had an especially distinguished library containing many volumes of eighteenth-century French philosophers.

1723: The **first permanent school for Indians** in the colonies was established at Bafferton Hall, built at the College of William and Mary in Williamsburg, Va. The school was maintained by funds left for the purpose by Robert Boyle, the English scientist.

1723: The **first recorded commercial corporation** in America, a Connecticut trading company, was organized. Up to this time, land companies, universities, and philanthropic enterprises were the only forms of corporate enterprise. Colonial restrictions on the distribution of currency and restrictions from England on local trade and industry served to inhibit the formation of corporations in the modern sense.

IV. Fashion
Folkways
Holidays
Social Issues and Crime
Sports

An increase in crime was noted in the colonies. The cause was attributed to the growth of cities, increasing wealth, and the changes brought on by the colonial wars, the first of which began in 1689. From then on, Boston, New York, Philadelphia, and Charleston, S.C., had night watches most of the time. By 1709, for example, Charleston had an armed watch of ten men who patrolled the town nightly. In New York in 1711 one John Riemer reported the theft of 25 gallons of cider, beer, and Madeira from his house. There was a great deal of theft in Boston in 1720, and it was blamed on the fact that there was much wealth there. Also at that time some people felt that Bostonians were "inclined to Riots and Tumults." Death was the usual penalty for theft, and in Philadelphia in Mar. 1720 William Smith and Hannah Travis, the latter known as Dancing Hannah, were convicted of theft and received death sentences. By 1723 the Boston police force consisted of 12 men who were instructed "to walke Silently and Slowly, now and then to Stand Still and Listen in order to make discovery. And no smoaking to be on their walking rounds."

1721 May: After a succession of **blue laws** limiting travel on Sunday, Connecticut passed a law providing that people could not go from their homes unless to attend worship or perform some indispensable task.

1722 Apr 30: The game of **billiards** was mentioned in the *New England Courant,* which reported that a public house in Charlestown, Mass., had set up tables for customers who wished "to Recreate themselves with a Game of Billiards."

1725–1729

I. Civil Rights
Exploration and Settlement
Government
Statistics
Wars

The French and English began to compete for control of the area west of the Allegheny Mts., especially in the Ohio R. Valley. The French, who claimed the region and had done the most to explore it, were alarmed by the number of English colonists beginning to cross the mountains. In 1729 they sent Chaussegros de Léry to fortify the river down to the Miami R. in Ohio. Earlier, in 1724, the French had built Fort Vincennes on the lower Wabash R. The British government had done little to oppose the French, even though the English colonies claimed their land grants extended westward to include the Ohio Valley. King George I had been petitioned by the Lords of Trade in 1721 to "fortify the passes in the back of Virginia" to interrupt French communications, but nothing was done. Meanwhile, the French built another fort in 1726 on the Mississippi R. at the mouth of the Illinois R., and, to protect their routes to the Ohio country from Quebec, had that same year erected Fort Niagara on the Niagara R. at its junction with Lake Ontario.

1725: The **slave population** in the American colonies reached 75,000.

1725 Feb 20: The first known instance of **scalping by Europeans** occurred in a fight between Indians and a party led by Capt. John Lovewell at Wakefield, N.H. Ten Indian scalps were taken. A bounty of £100 per scalp was paid to the victors in Boston.

1726: A **riot in Philadelphia** by the city's poorer residents broke out in the heart of town. The rioters tore down the pillory and stocks and set them on fire before the governor of Pennsylvania put down the uprising. Similar outbursts continued to crop up in the city: in 1729 crowds broke into the mayor's gardens and destroyed his plants; in 1738 a riot ensued when the administration limited fishing on the Schuylkill R.

1729 June: The **Carolina grant was purchased** by the English Crown from its proprietors for £17,500. Carolina was divided into two royal provinces, North Carolina and South Carolina, in 1730. Even after independence there were disputes as to the exact boundary between the two states. These were not resolved until 1815.

II. Architecture
Arts and Music
Popular Entertainment
Publishing
Theater

Printing and publishing in the colonies began to thrive during this period, and one of the leading figures in the field was William Bradford. Born in England, he became in 1685 the first printer in Philadelphia. In 1690 he was one of the founders of the first paper mill in the colonies. In 1693 he moved to New York, where, in the course of 50 years, he issued some 400 items, including the first American *Book of Common Prayer* (1710); the first printed American play, *Androboros* (1714) by Gov. Robert Hunter of New York; and many almanacs and pamphlets. In 1725 he established the first newspaper in the colony, the *New York Gazette* (1725–1744). The paper was royalist in its politics, as Bradford was the official government printer. Andrew Bradford, William Bradford, and other Bradford descendants also became printers.

1725: The *Astronomical Diary and Almanack* by Nathaniel Ames, a Massachusetts physician, was published. Extremely popular, it may have been used by Benjamin Franklin in preparing his own almanac. Typical of its entries were:

> Dec 7–10 Ladies take heed,
>   Lay down your fans,
>   And handle well
>   Your warming pans.
> Dec 15–18 This cold, uncomfortable weather
>   Makes Jack and Gill lie close
>   together.

1725: The **Union Oyster House,** a famed Boston restaurant, was built as a private residence. It became a public eating place in 1826.

1729: The **Old South Meeting House** was built in Boston by Joshua Blanchard, a master mason who later built Faneuil Hall in Boston. The meeting house has been a museum since 1876.

1729 Oct: The *Pennsylvania Gazette* was bought by Benjamin Franklin. Under the title *Universal Instructor in All Arts and Sciences and Pennsylvania Gazette*, it was founded by Samuel Keimer in 1728. At that time it had a subscription list of 90. Under Franklin it became in time the leading newspaper between New York and Charleston. He managed the *Gazette* until 1766, and it was continued until 1815 by David Hall, Franklin's partner from 1748, and by Hall's descendants. The claim of the popular magazine *The Saturday Evening Post* that it was a continuation of the Gazette *is a* myth. The *Post* was founded in 1821, six years after the *Gazette* had expired, by men with no connection with the *Gazette*.

III. Business and Industry
Education
Philosophy and Religion
Science

Although few in number, Jewish immigrants were strong contributors to the religious life of America. The first permanent Hebrew congregation in the colonies was formed in 1729 in New York City; the next year the members constructed a synagogue on Mill St. that was described as a "solid, neat, stone Temple." The congregation later added the first school for Jewish children. Around this time Jewish communities were also developing in Charleston, S.C., Newport, R.I., and Philadelphia, Pa., and by the time of the American Revolution, there were between 2000 and 3000 Jews in the colonies, mostly merchants and traders. An act of Parliament in 1740 allowed Jews to be naturalized, and in the colonies they found more political and religious freedom than anywhere else in the world.

1725: The **U.S. Reformed Church** was established by John Philip Boehm at Falkner Swamp, Pa.

1729: The **third Anglican parish** in Boston was established in Trinity Church. The new parish reflected the rapid expansion of Anglicanism in New England.

1729 Mar 15: The **first Catholic nun** to be professed in the colonies was Sister St. Stanislaus Hachard, who celebrated the Ceremony of Profession at the Ursuline Convent in New Orleans, La.

IV. Fashion
Folkways
Holidays
Social Issues and Crime
Sports

Voluntary associations formed for a variety of purposes became a feature of colonial life. One of the prime movers was Benjamin Franklin of Philadelphia, who in 1727 organized a group of artisans and tradesmen into the Leather Apron Club, later called the Junto. The club held meetings in taverns to discuss morals, politics, literature, and science, and to exchange books. The idea for a subscription library grew out of this last function, and on July 1, 1731, the Library Company was formed with 24 members. It imported its first books from England the next year. The club registered formal opposition to slavery and what it considered other inhumane practices. Out of the Junto grew the American Philosophical Society, founded in 1743.

1725: Queen Anne–style furniture, characterized by double curves, broken pediments, and curved legs in furniture of walnut, became fashionable in the colonies five years after its greatest popularity passed in England and some 11 years after the death of Queen Anne of England. This period marked the first appearance of the cabriole, or curved, style for table and chair legs; and the first appearance of the American Windsor chair, in Philadelphia. Windsor chairs were generally painted green, brown, or red, but rarely white.

1728: Boston Common was enclosed in order to preserve its grass from carts and horses. Soon it became the custom after tea for gentlemen and ladies to stroll about the green before going to their homes.

1728: The arrival in Louisiana of **casket girls,** so called because they received a dress in a casket as a gift for their immigration, introduced a new element into Louisiana society. Since these girls were not inmates of penal institutions, as were many of their predecessors, it became and has remained an honor to be descended from a casket girl.

1728: Importation of rum in the colonies for this year amounted to 2,124,500 gal., or £25,000 of liquor. Drinking was extremely heavy. This printed doggerel gave one reason why people did not drink:

> There's but one Reason I can Think
> Why People ever cease to drink,
> Sobriety the Cause is not,
> Nor Fear of being deam'd a Sot,
> But if Liquor can't be got.

1730–1734

I. Civil Rights
Exploration and Settlement
Government
Statistics
Wars

Georgia, the last of the 13 original colonies to be founded, came into being under somewhat different circumstances than the others. On June 9, 1732, a royal charter was granted by King George II of England to James Edward Oglethorpe, an English general and philanthropist. Originally this region had been part of the grant of the Carolinas; it also was claimed by Spain. One of the purposes of founding Georgia, therefore, was to protect the other southern colonies from Spanish intrusion. Oglethorpe saw the colony as a refuge for English debtors. The first colonists, led by Oglethorpe, arrived on Feb. 12, 1733, and founded Savannah, the first settlement in Georgia. Forts were built and the friendship of the Creek Indians was secured. Slavery was originally prohibited, but members of Georgia's ruling class felt this would hinder them economically. In 1752 the colony was turned over to the Crown and thereafter became profitable, but by then it had already achieved its major objective, the blocking of Spanish northern expansion.

The estimated colonial **population** was 654,950.

1730: The **most populous area** of colonial America was New England, with 275,000 Europeans. By 1760 this number rose to 425,000, and at the close of the Revolution to 800,000.

1733: An **epidemic of influenza,** the first outbreak in North America, swept New York City and Philadelphia.

1733 May 17: The **Molasses Act** was passed, placing high duties on rum and molasses imported from the French and Spanish West Indies. Admission of American merchants into the rum trade of the French West Indies (1713) caused a boom in sugar on those islands. Planters on the English islands lost out as New England ships put into French and Dutch ports to load up with cheap sugar. The English planters petitioned Parliament and forced passage of the Molasses Act, which levied prohibitive duties on sugar and molasses brought to the colonies from other than British possessions.

II. Architecture
Arts and Music
Popular Entertainment
Publishing
Theater

Growth of American music was stimulated in colonial times by immigrant European musicians, many of whom were talented and creative composers as well as accomplished performers. Often the musicians were obliged to travel from place to place seeking work as church organists, teachers, or the like. Such a musician was Carl Theodorus Pachelbel, an organist and composer and son of Johann Pachelbel, who had been a noted influence on his younger contemporary Johann Sebastian Bach. Carl Theodorus Pachelbel emigrated from Germany to Boston in 1733. There he taught children to play the harpsichord and the spinet. He soon moved on to Newport, R.I., where he became organist at Trinity Church. In Jan. 1736 he gave a concert of vocal and instrumental music at Todd's Tavern in New York City, "the Harpsichord Part Perform'd by himself. The Songs, Violins, and German Flute by private hands." Enough people paid four shillings apiece to attend to allow another performance to be given in March. Later Pachelbel moved to Charleston, S.C., where he died on Sept. 14, 1750.

1730: The **Old State House** in Philadelphia, known as Independence Hall, was designed by Andrew Hamilton. Completed in 1753 and rebuilt in 1828, it is an excellent example of Georgian public architectural style.

1732 May: The *Philadelphische Zeitung* [Philadelphia Newspaper], the first foreign-language newspaper in the English colonies, was founded by Benjamin Franklin in Philadelphia, Pa.

1732 Dec 19: *Poor Richard's Almanack* was first published by Benjamin Franklin at Philadelphia, Pa. In continuous publication for 25 years, Franklin's *Almanack* sold on average more than 10,000 copies yearly and thus was one of the most popular writings of colonial America.

1734 Oct: In a landmark case involving **freedom of the press,** John Peter Zenger, founder and publisher of the New York *Weekly Journal,* was arrested for libel. Zenger had founded the *Weekly Journal* on Nov. 5, 1733, and had used its pages to oppose the administration and policies of Gov. William Cosby of New York. In 1735 he was acquitted after a defense by Andrew Hamilton that was later cited in many cases involving freedom of the press. The Sons of Liberty, an organization founded to aid Zenger's defense, later became the Tammany Society of New York. The *Weekly Journal* was published until 1751.

III. Business and Industry
Education
Philosophy and Religion
Science

The prominent part religion played in the settlement and development of the English colonies was emphasized by the revival movement known as the Great Awakening, which began in New England in 1734, triggered by the preaching at a revival in Northampton, Mass., of Jonathan Edwards, the theologian and philosopher. Edwards emphasized man's sinful nature and the torments of eternal damnation. His fame spread widely and he received many invitations to preach. His influence was strong among young people. Many converts were made, amid public scenes of great emotion. In the middle colonies, William Tennent, a Presbyterian clergyman, led the movement. The Great Awakening reached all the colonies with the 1739–1741 visit to America of George Whitefield, the Methodist evangelist who preached from New England to Georgia. In the South Samuel Davies carried the message to the Presbyterians of Virginia. The movement reached the Baptists of North Carolina in the 1760s, but by that time it had already died out in New England. The Great Awakening resulted in bitter doctrinal disputes in New England between two groups known as the New Lights and the Old Lights. The latter opposed revivalism as extravagant and impermanent. The Old Lights were led by Charles Chauncy, a Boston clergyman who became the leader of the theological liberals. His beliefs developed into Universalism, or Unitarianism. The theology of the New Lights was more conservative and developed into a somewhat modified Calvinism.

1731: The **Library Company of Philadelphia,** the first circulating library in the New World, was founded by Benjamin Franklin. The extent to which libraries were to grow and flourish in the U.S. is indicated by the fact that by 1984 there were 8796 public libraries, with an additional 6260 branches, in the U.S.

1732: The **first stage coach line** was established between Burlington and Amboy, N.J. Connections could be made from Amboy to New York City and from Burlington to Philadelphia by boat.

1732 Feb 26: The **only Roman Catholic Church** built and maintained in the colonies until the Revolutionary War held its first mass in Philadelphia.

c1733: Pennsylvania Dutch kilns produced perhaps the finest pottery in America. The earliest specimen

dates from this period—a barber basin inscribed "Putz und Balwir mich heibsh und fein das ich gefal der liebste mein [Clean and shave me nicely and fine so that I'll please my loved one]." Later Pennsylvania Dutch sgraffito, pottery in which a design is etched through the surface coating to show the layer beneath, and slipware bore short verses like the following:

In the dish on the table
Merry he who yet is single
Sad is he who is engaged.

If loving were unhealthy
Surely the doctor would avoid it
And if it would hurt the wives
Surely they would not allow it.

IV. Fashion
Folkways
Holidays
Social Issues and Crime
Sports

By 1730 summer resorts were being patronized by the well-to-do. A Dr. Thomas Bond encouraged his patients to picnic and take the waters at Spring Garden on the outskirts of Philadelphia. Near Bristol, Pa., was the so-called Bath spring, which also became a popular summer resort. The most popular and fashionable resort was Newport, R.I., whose climate attracted patrons from the Carolinas and the West Indies who came ostensibly for reasons of health. Newport's offerings included excursions to New Shoreham and Prudence Island. There were races on the beach by Narragansett pacers, and the winners were awarded silver tankards. Tea parties, dances, and lavish dinners added to the atmosphere of pleasure and sophistication. Newport's popularity contributed to its growth as a cultural and trade center as well. In 1730 a Philosophical Society was established, out of which the Redwood Library was formed 20 years later. Within a few years Newport became an important port in the "triangular trade," whereby rum was traded for slaves in Africa and the slaves were exchanged for sugar and molasses in the West Indies.

c1730: A great craze for **white stockings** for men and women set in, replacing varicolored hose of the seventeenth century. The stockings were made of thread, silk, cotton, or worsted, and were supported by ornate garters. Often the name of the wearer was woven into the garter with a "posy." White hose were worn until the end of the century.

1732: The **oldest sporting organization** and first fishing club in North America was formed as the Schuylkill Fishing Company in Philadelphia. It is now known as the Fish House Club, its membership limited to 30, its function limited to annual meetings at the Andalusia, Pa., headquarters.

1735–1739

I. Civil Rights
Exploration and Settlement
Government
Statistics
Wars

The War of Jenkins' Ear (1739–1742), which began in Europe on Oct. 19, 1739, and a year later merged into the War of the Austrian Succession, had its repercussions in the southern colonies. England went to war with Spain over the mistreatment of English seamen whom the Spaniards accused of smuggling. The war took its name from Robert Jenkins, captain of the ship *Rebecca,* who claimed Spanish coast guards had cut off his ear in 1731. He exhibited the ear in the House of Commons and so aroused public opinion that the government of the British Prime Minister Robert Walpole reluctantly declared war on Oct. 23, 1739. Basically, the war was one of commercial rivalry between England and Spain. By the Treaty of Utrecht (1713), which ended Queen Anne's War, Britain was to be allowed to participate in slave traffic with the Spanish colonies. A special Spanish fleet, however, interfered with this activity and the Spanish also objected to the English logwooders operating on the coast of Honduras. The other cause of the war was the continued dispute over the boundary of Spanish Florida in relation to Georgia. As soon as war was declared, Gov. James Edward Oglethorpe called on the citizens of Georgia and South Carolina to join in an invasion of Florida. The Spanish retaliated by attempting to invade those colonies by sea.

1738: Lewis Morris was named the first governor of New Jersey colony. Since 1702 New York and New Jersey had shared the same governor, although New Jersey had become autonomous for all practical purposes. Morris, who had been born in New York to a wealthy and prominent family, served as governor of New Jersey until his death in 1746.

1739: Three **slave uprisings** broke out in South Carolina this year. The incidents have been attributed to the preaching of the Spanish missionaries who allegedly created in the slaves a false expectation of deliverance. On Sept. 9 a band of slaves from Charleston set out for St. Augustine, Fla., and freedom, slaying all Europeans they met on the way. They were themselves surrounded and massacred. Twenty-one Europeans and 44 blacks perished. At Stone River a slave named Cato led another insurrection. The third uprising was in St. John's Parish in Berkeley County.

II. Architecture
Arts and Music
Popular Entertainment
Publishing
Theater

Many colonists were deeply concerned with religion, and hymn singing was of major importance. This led to the publication of hymnals. When John Wesley, the founder of Methodism, visited America in 1737 he had published at Charleston, S.C., *A Collection of Psalms and Hymns.* Some of the selections were adaptations from the German Moravian *Gesangbuch.* Wesley had met Gov. James Edward Oglethorpe of Georgia in 1735, when Oglethorpe was in England. Oglethorpe invited Wesley and his brother Charles, then students at Oxford and members of an Oxford group known variously as the Holy Club, Bible Moths, and Methodists, to come to Georgia. They arrived in Georgia Feb. 5, 1736. Notwithstanding Oglethorpe's invitation, the visit was marked by difficulties. In Savannah John was charged with inserting into the Anglican church service unauthorized psalms and hymns. Charles Wesley is said to have produced about 5000 hymns in his lifetime, many of which became popular in America, including "Hark! The Herald Angels Sing." Another prolific and popular hymn writer was Isaac Watts, an English clergyman. The first American edition of his *Hymns and Spiritual Songs,* which appeared in England in 1707, was published in America in 1739, although his hymns had been sung there before that. Watts wrote "O God, Our Help in Ages Past," among several hundred hymns that reflected a stern Calvinism with touches of sympathy and tenderness.

1735 Feb 8: The **first opera** produced in the colonies was performed at the Courtroom, in Charleston, S.C. It was *Flora; or The Hob in the Well* by Colley Cibber.

c1737: The **oldest extant house** in the U.S. Midwest was built by an unknown French colonist at Cahokia, Ill. The house later became the Cahokia County Courthouse. The structure was of poteaux-sur-sole style construction, characterized by upright posts driven into the earth and chinked with clay, with a double-pitched, hipped roof, and a surrounding balcony.

III. Business and Industry
Education
Philosophy and Religion
Science

Science and scientists were flourishing in the colonies. The first chair in mathematics and natural philosophy was endowed at Harvard in 1727, and its first incumbent was Isaac Greenwood, who gave a course in fluxions (calculus). He retired in 1737, his lectures having done much to stimulate interest in science. Greenwood was succeeded by John Winthrop, IV, who is sometimes called the father of seismology because of his studies of earthquakes. In 1746 he gave the first laboratory demonstration of magnetism and electricity. In 1766 Winthrop was elected a fellow of the Royal Society and in 1773 Harvard conferred on him an L.L.D. degree, the first ever awarded in America. The Rev. Jared Eliot of Connecticut, the first American experimenter in physiological botany, was interested in making agriculture more scientific and worked on the fructification of maize before 1739. He also developed a process for smelting iron from black magnetic sand. Ezra Stiles, a theologian as well as a scientist, calculated the true position of the sun and moon, using the work of Sir Isaac Newton. As president of Yale from 1778 to 1795, he liberalized the curriculum, bringing in the thought of the enlightenment of the eighteenth century.

1736 Feb 5: The history of **Methodism** in America began with the arrival in Georgia of John Wesley, at the invitation of Gov. James Edward Oglethorpe. When Wesley came to America his career had not yet reached the spectacular proportions later brought on by his achievements as a public preacher. Six years earlier the name Methodists had been applied to his group of religious ascetics, but Methodism as a religious movement was still in the future. His stay in America was notable for his romance with Sophia Hopkey, who wooed but did not win him. When Sophia married another, Wesley barred her from his congregation and her new husband retaliated with the threat of a lawsuit. Wesley then decided to return to England.

1737: The **first copper coinage** minted in the colonies was produced by John Higley at his furnace on Hopmeadow Brook, Simsbury, Conn. Known to numismatists today as "Higley pennies," the coins were stamped "I am good copper" and "Value me as you will."

1739: Caspar Wistar, the glass designer and manufacturer, set up his glassworks at Allowaystown, N.J., on tracts of land ideal for production of window and bottle glass. The factory went into operation July 30, 1740, and was staffed by Belgian glassblowers specially drafted from Europe. Wistar's enterprise was responsible for the most distinctive type of early American glass, South Jersey glass, known for its wide, bulbous forms, often with superimposed winding thicknesses on the bottom. Wistar's glassworks was one of the first successful co-ops in America.

IV. Fashion
Folkways
Holidays
Social Issues and Crime
Sports

Because of the religious atmosphere and growing colonial affluence, funerals became more elaborate and expensive. It was customary to give away mourning rings or gloves at funerals. At the funeral of Gov. Jonathan Belcher of Massachusetts in 1741, his widow gave away 1000 pairs of gloves. Clergymen and doctors accumulated hundreds of such items over their careers. In 1721 the General Court of Massachusetts passed laws against "extraordinary expenditures for funerals" to protect those who could not afford "gloves, scarfs and scutcheons," but when Andrew Faneuil was buried in 1738 more than 1100 persons accompanied his funeral cortege, which was described as "generous and expensive." Newport, R.I., also witnessed elaborate funerals, that of Rosewell Lavine in 1716 costing £55. One livery stable in Boston kept black horses for hire for funerals, while a "Mr. C.H." offered to supply engraved sets of ready-to-use obituaries, "With Void Spaces for the Name, Age, Distinction, and Profession, or such Particular and Eminent Qualities as do not properly fall under the Notice of General Description."

c1735: The **status of women** changed with the increase of wealth in the colonies. More women left their husbands when they found living together incompatible; newspaper items told of runaway wives and elopements.

1735 Jan: The often tense **relations between Europeans and blacks** in New York was demonstrated when John van Zandt, a Dutch burgher of New York, horsewhipped his slave to death for having been picked up at night by a watch. The coroner's jury judged the "Correction given by the Master was not the Cause of his Death, but it was by the Visitation of

God." One reason for such tension was that the slave population was about one-fifth that of the entire colony. Blacks were lynched and burned for theft, rape, etc.

1737 Mar 17: The first celebration of **St. Patrick's Day** outside the confines of the Roman Catholic Church was held in Boston by the Charitable Irish Society, which had been founded that year. The Friendly Sons of St. Patrick in New York City followed suit in 1784. An oddity of the New York society was its joint sponsorship by Irish Roman Catholics and Presbyterians, with the first president of the organization being a Presbyterian.

1738: A Masonic warrant for the **first Masonic lodge** was issued by the Grand Lodge of Massachusetts to Abraham Savage. A similar authority was granted to Richard Gridley in 1756 for a military expedition against Crown Point, N.Y., during the French and Indian War (1754–1763).

1740–1744

I. Civil Rights
Exploration and Settlement
Government
Statistics
Wars

King George's War (1744–1748), the third of the French and Indian wars, was known as the War of the Austrian Succession in Europe, where it began in 1740. The war included most of the European nations in a complicated series of alliances. It began after the death of Charles VI, the Holy Roman Emperor and ruler of the Hapsburg lands. The Archduchess Maria Theresa succeeded her father but there were counterclaimants. Fighting began when King Frederick II of Prussia invaded Austrian-held Silesia. In America and elsewhere in the world, France and England fought for colonial power and possessions. The French unsuccessfully attacked Port Royal, Nova Scotia, in 1744, the year in which fighting broke out in America.

The estimated colonial **population** was 889,000.

1740 Jan: The **War of Jenkins' Ear** (1739–1742) continued with an invasion of Florida led by Gov. Oglethorpe of Georgia. He was protected on the west from the French by friendly Indians. He captured forts San Francisco de Pupo and Picolata on the San Juan

R. From May to July he besieged St. Augustine, but broke off the attack when his rear guard was threatened by the Spanish.

1741: A group of **German Moravians** moved from Georgia, where their colony had been unsuccessful, to Pennsylvania. They joined others of their faith in the establishment of Bethlehem on the Lehigh R. Count Nikolaus Ludwig Zinzendorf, their leader, arrived from Europe this year, bringing with him a band of new immigrants. Zinzendorf returned to Europe in 1743.

1742 June 9: In the **Battle of Bloody Marsh** on St. Simons Island, one of the Sea Islands off the southeast coast of Georgia, the Spanish attacked Fort Frederica, which had been constructed by Gov. Oglethorpe in 1736 to protect the colony. The Spanish were repulsed in a bloody battle that was a decisive engagement of the War of Jenkins' Ear.

1744: An **Indian treaty** signed with the Iroquois League at Lancaster, Pa., ceded to England the territory of the Ohio R. Valley north of the Ohio R.

II. Architecture
Arts and Music
Popular Entertainment
Publishing
Theater

Before the American Revolution, about 15 magazines began publication in the colonies, but they had an average life of only ten months. The first of these, published by Andrew Bradford, was the *American Magazine; or, A Monthly View of the Political State of the British Colonies.* Bradford's magazine began in Philadelphia in Jan. 1741 but published only three monthly issues. Bradford by three days had beaten Benjamin Franklin, who started his *General Magazine and Historical Chronicle* also in Philadelphia and also in January. Franklin's magazine lasted for six issues. In Boston in 1743, Gamaliel Rogers and John Fowle began the *Boston Weekly Museum,* which died that same year. More successful was the *American Magazine and Historical Chronicle,* which began publication in Boston in 1743. It was edited by Jeremy Gridley and published for more than three years. Gridley was a lawyer, and while the magazine was devoted largely to politics, he also wrote about literary and cultural subjects.

1741: The **first symphony orchestra** in America was organized by Moravian settlers in Bethlehem, Pa. By 1748 it had 14 pieces: two first violins, two second violins, two violas, one cello, one double bass, two flutes, two trumpets, and two French horns.

1742: The **Carpenters' Company** was established by the master carpenters of Philadelphia, who sought to establish an architectural library and teach themselves the elements of design and craftsmanship. In 1770 they built Carpenters' Hall, which became the meeting place of the first Continental Congress in 1775.

1742 Sep 24: Faneuil Hall in Boston was opened to the public. A Georgian structure designed by the painter John Smibert, it was enlarged in 1805 according to plans by Charles Bulfinch that retained the original Georgian style. The famous weather vane on its cupola is a giant grasshopper of beaten copper.

III. Business and Industry
Education
Philosophy and Religion
Science

The first American scientific association, the American Philosophical Society, was founded in Philadelphia in 1743 as an outgrowth of the Junto, a club Benjamin Franklin and a group of friends had begun in 1727. The society was formed "for the promotion of useful knowledge among the British planters in America." Its first president was a lawyer named Thomas Hopkinson, and Franklin was the first secretary. In 1769 it merged with the American Society for Promoting Useful Knowledge, and Franklin was elected the first president of the combined organization. He held the post until his death in 1790. He was succeeded by David Rittenhouse, an astronomer and instrument maker, who was succeeded by Thomas Jefferson. In 1769 the society began publication of its *Transactions*. The original inspiration for the society was the Royal Society of England. The society continues to exist with a membership of distinguished persons in intellectual and scientific fields. It has a large library especially rich in materials dealing with the American Revolution and the history of science in America.

1741: The **Great Awakening,** a religious revival movement in New England, reached an oratorical peak with the famous sermon delivered by Jonathan Edwards at Endfield, Mass. Entitled "Sinners in the Hands of an Angry God," Edwards's sermon proclaimed man's "abominable" sinfulness in the eyes of God.

1741: The **first true porcelain** manufactured in the colonies was produced by Andrew Duché, a craftsman of Huguenot descent who had founded a pottery in Savannah, Ga., in 1730. Lack of financial backing hampered pottery manufacture, but Duché prospered by exporting his clay to England. In 1764 the

Bristol Journal acknowledged that the first porcelain made in an English-speaking country came from North America.

1742: The **Moravian Seminary for Women** was founded at Bethlehem, Pa. Men were first admitted in 1746, and in 1807 a full college curriculum was adopted. The institution is now known as Moravian College.

1742: The so-called **Franklin stove,** a variation on an open firebox of German design, was invented by Benjamin Franklin.

IV. Fashion
Folkways
Holidays
Social Issues and Crime
Sports

The growing problem of crime and racism in the increasingly populous cities, and a decline in social and economic stability, was reflected in the so-called Negro Conspiracy of 1741 in New York City. A number of robberies in February were attributed to the customers of John Hughson's dram shop, which was frequented by blacks. Hughson had a bad reputation and it was suspected that he was a fence for stolen goods. In March Fort George burned and the fire was thought to have some connection with the robberies. Many people panicked for fear of crimes by blacks, and their fears were fed by sensational tales of a conspiracy, described by one Mary Burton, a European servant. Hundreds of people fled to the Bowery and Harlem, and then outside the city proper, for fear of a black uprising. The militia was called out and many blacks were jailed and given summary judicial treatment. Two slaves, Quack and Cuffee, were burned at the stake, and Hughson and his wife were hanged. Before the frenzy subsided, 13 blacks had been burned alive, eight hanged, and 71 transported out of the colony. The claim of a conspiracy had no basis. Even Daniel Horsemanden, the prosecutor, admitted later that there had been no plot.

1741: The prevalence of **alcohol abuse** in the colonies was demonstrated in the death of a child about five years old after consuming a great quantity of rum. Drunkenness was the most prevalent vice of colonial settlers. Each colony had stringent laws meant to suppress excess drinking. Boston even went so far as to post the names of drunkards. A contemporary quatrain sounded this note:

> This town would quickly be reclaimed,
> If drams no more had vent,
> And all the sorts that could be named,
> To *Strombolo* were sent.

1745–1749

I. Civil Rights
Exploration and Settlement
Government
Statistics
Wars

The Treaty of Aix-la-Chapelle was signed on Oct. 18, 1748, ending the War of the Austrian Succession, known in America as King George's War (1744–1748). For the most part it restored the status quo in the New World, returning Fort Louisbourg, on Cape Breton Island in Canada, to France. The New Englanders, whose forces had fought brilliantly to capture heavily defended Louisbourg, were outraged. As a result, the English Crown agreed to bear the cost of the expedition. Great Britain's privilege of transporting slaves to Spanish America was renewed, but the treaty turned out to be merely a truce before the last and greatest of the French and Indian Wars.

1745: In **King George's War** (1744–1748), French and Indian forces began the year with raids on English fortifications in Maine.

1745 June 16: Fort Louisbourg, a powerful French stronghold on Cape Breton Island in Nova Scotia, was captured by New Englanders under William Pepperell and an English fleet under Sir Peter Warren.

1745 Nov 28-29: Saratoga, N.Y., was attacked and burned by French and Indian forces after the English had succeeded in persuading the Iroquois league to enter the war against the French.

II. Architecture
Arts and Music
Popular Entertainment
Publishing
Theater

In the mid-eighteenth century portrait painting flourished. The best colonial painter of this period was Robert Feke. He probably studied in Europe at one time, but he developed a personal style of painting. Feke practiced in New York City, Philadelphia, Newport, and Boston, painting excellent portraits of leading citizens. Perhaps his best, in terms of characterization, was a portrait of the Rev. Thomas Hiscox done in 1745. Feke's portraits were noted for their charm and for the elegance of the costumes worn by his subjects. Examples of his work include a portrait of Mrs. Barlow Trecothick done in Boston; and *Unknown Lady,* now in the Brooklyn Museum, noted for its almost cubist depiction of the subject's bell-shaped skirt and funnel-shaped torso. Feke's work was influenced by John Smibert, the first painter of skill in New England. Feke disappeared at sea in 1750.

1745: Selections from the writings of Charles de Secondat, Baron de la Brède et de **Montesquieu,** were first published in American periodicals. The selections were from *Lettres Persanes* (*Persian Letters,* 1721). These were followed several years later by excerpts from *L'Esprit des Lois* (*Spirit of the Laws,* 1748) in the Boston *Gazette.* This book had a profound effect on the evolution of American political theory and the formulation, some 40 years later, of the U.S. Constitution.

1749 Aug 22: Colonial **opposition to acting** was demonstrated when an early troupe of English actors, Murray and Kean's, performed Joseph Addison's *Cato* (1713) in a Philadelphia warehouse. Protests by the city council forced them to leave for New York.

III. Business and Industry
Education
Philosophy and Religion
Science

Seven colleges—Harvard, the College of William and Mary, Yale, Princeton, Columbia, Brown, and Rutgers—were established before the Revolution. Typical of them was Princeton, chartered Oct. 22, 1746, as the College of New Jersey and opened in 1747 in Elizabethtown, N.J. Its first president was Jonathan Dickinson, who taught the first classes in his home. He was a leading preacher of the Great Awakening and founded the college to train leaders for the revival movement. Its first degrees were conferred in 1748. In 1756 the college moved to Princeton, N.J., where its name was changed. In the years following its founding, Princeton became a stronghold of conservative doctrine in the bitter theological conflicts within the Presbyterian Church. Princeton's second president was Aaron Burr, whose son, also named Aaron Burr, was to kill Alexander Hamilton in a duel. During the Revolution both sides occupied the school buildings, which were heavily damaged. As time passed, the original purpose of training clergymen disappeared and the university devoted itself to higher education.

1745: The growth of **literacy** in early America was spurred by the founding of 22 newspapers between 1713 and 1745.

1747: The **New York Bar Association,** the first legal society in America, was organized by lawyers of New York City to defend themselves against attacks by Lt. Gov. Cadwallader Colden. In 1765 the group spearheaded colonial resistance to the Stamp Act.

IV. Fashion
Folkways
Holidays
Social Issues and Crime
Sports

Coffee houses began to gain popularity about this time, as the populations of cities grew. New York had two coffee houses in 1744. A coffee house was opened in Charleston, S.C., by William Monat in 1743, but lost business to Charles Shepheard, whose British Coffee House grew in popularity after its owner became deputy postmaster. Three coffee houses were available to Philadelphians before 1750, two of them named the Widow Robert's and the Widow Jones's. The former was the most popular, providing newspapers and magazines, tea, coffee, and chocolate, and the "constant Attendance" of the proprietor until the Widow Roberts died in 1754. Boston had the Crown and the North End. Jacob Hassey, described as "a comicall old whimsical fellow," kept a coffee house at Newport, R.I. Prior to the opening of coffee houses, taverns fulfilled some of the same purposes, but many taverns became notorious for their patrons' heavy drinking and lawlessness. As a result, coffee houses became centers where businessmen met and where notices of ship sailings, sales, and other matters were posted.

c1745: Whist became very popular in the colonies, having been brought over from England, where it was the rage. The game afforded men the opportunity to keep company with women. Ladies often played for money, as evidenced in accounts of Thomas Jefferson and George Washington concerning their wives' expenses.

1749: The **consumption of cider** in New York rivaled that of beer. A Swedish visitor to the colonies noted the abundance of apple orchards and number of cider presses in New York. In winter cider was used extensively; in summer it was mixed with water, sweetened, and spiced with nutmeg.

1749: The **eating habits** of the Dutch in New York were carefully recorded by a foreign traveler: "Their Breakfast is tea, commonly without milk. . . . They never put sugar into the cup but put a small bit of it into their mouths while they drink. Along with tea they eat bread and butter with slices of hung beef. . . . They breakfast generally about seven. Their din-

ner is buttermilk and bread. . . . They sometimes make use of buttermilk instead of fresh milk to boil a thin kind of porridge with, which tastes very sour but not disagreeable in hot weather. To each dinner they have a great salad prepared with abundance of vinegar and little or no oil [probably koolslaa—modern coleslaw]. Their supper is generally bread and butter, or milk and bread."

1750–1754

I. Civil Rights
Exploration and Settlement
Government
Statistics
Wars

The first attempt to unite the English colonies was made at the Albany Congress, which was called in Albany, N.Y., in 1754 to negotiate a treaty with the Iroquois Indians in the event of further war with the French. Represented at the Albany Congress were the four New England colonies and New York, Pennsylvania, and Maryland. Benjamin Franklin took the occasion to present his "Plan of the Union" of the colonies, which the delegates approved on July 19, 1754. The plan included amendments proposed by Thomas Hutchinson of Massachusetts and would have united all the American English colonies, except Georgia and Nova Scotia, under a president general who would be named by the British government and paid by it. The various colonial assemblies would elect a grand council that would have legislative power, subject to the president general and the English Crown. However, the plan was rejected by the colonies and by the Crown. England proposed a looser union with a commander in chief and a commissioner for Indian affairs, but nothing came of the idea.

The estimated colonial **population** was 1,207,000.

1753 Oct 31: George Washington was sent by Gov. Robert Dinwiddie of Virginia to demand French withdrawal from the Ohio territory. Dinwiddie had been impressed by Washington's achievement as surveyor and fieldsman, and picked him for the commission although he was only 21. As adjutant general of the Northern Division, Washington set out from Williamsburg, Va. With Christopher Gist as his guide, he made observations of French fortifications and estimations about needed English fortifications. During the expedition he kept a journal, which Dinwiddie later obtained and had printed. It indicted French intentions for the territory and attributed to a French officer the indiscreet admission that " . . . it was their absolute Design to take possession of the Ohio, and by G— they would do it."

1754 Apr 17: The **French continued to advance** on the Ohio River Valley with the occupation of the junction of the Allegheny and Monongahela rivers on the site of present-day Pittsburgh, Pa. There they built Fort Duquesne. The move anticipated similar intentions by an English force led by George Washington and dispatched by Gov. Dinwiddie.

1754 May 28: The **first skirmish of the French and Indian War** (1754–1763), the last and most significant of the French and Indian Wars, occurred when a small force under George Washington engaged and defeated a reconnaissance party of French and Indians near Fort Duquesne. Unable to proceed against the superior French forces in the fort, Washington erected Fort Necessity at nearby Great Meadows.

1754 July 4: George Washington surrendered **Fort Necessity** when attacked by a large French contingent from Fort Duquesne. This defeat left the French in possession of the Ohio River Valley.

II. Architecture
Arts and Music
Popular Entertainment
Publishing
Theater

The fortunes of American theater rose considerably when Lewis Hallam brought his theatrical troupe to America in 1752. The company's first performance was *The Merchant of Venice* in Williamsburg, Va. Moving to New York City in 1753, Hallam built a new theater on Nassau St. that was well patronized by upper-class New Yorkers. In April the company moved on to Philadelphia, where it gave 30 performances at Plumstead's Theater, which had been renovated for them. The performance of *The Fair Penitent* was received "with universal applause." After touring the South, Hallam went to Jamaica in the West Indies, where he died in 1756. The company was said to have had a repertoire of over 40 plays. Hallam's widow married David Douglass. With him she formed the American Company, which came to New York in 1759. The opening bill at Cruger's Wharf was *Jane Shore*, which played to "great applause, to a most crowded audience." Hallam's son, Lewis, Jr., was a member of this troupe and a noted performer of comedy. In 1767 he appeared in Thomas Godfrey's *Prince of Parthia*, the first American drama to be produced professionally.

1750: Parlange, one of the finest plantation houses of the bayou country in Louisiana and a classic example of French colonial architecture, was built at New Roads, Pointe Coupée Parish, La., by Marquis Vincent de Ternant, whose descendants still own it.

1752: The **Georg Muller House,** the best surviving example of Pennsylvania Dutch architecture, was built at Milbach, Pa. Its layout was based on designs common in the Rhine Valley.

1754: What was perhaps the **first American political cartoon** was published by Benjamin Franklin in his *Pennsylvania Gazette*. The cartoon showed a snake cut into eight parts, the head representing New England and the other seven parts representing the remaining colonies. The caption was "Join or Die." The cartoon was prompted by rumors of an impending war with the French.

III. Business and Industry
Education
Philosophy and Religion
Science

Medical care in the colonies was somewhat primitive and unorganized in the early eighteenth century. During this period both the quality and availability of medical treatment improved as medical education increased and general hospitals made their first appearance. In 1734 William Bull of South Carolina received a medical degree in Europe, the first of 40 or so colonial physicians to be educated abroad. Forerunners of hospitals were the pesthouses, such as those established in Boston (1717), Philadelphia (1742), Charleston, S.C. (before 1752), and New York City (1757). The first general hospital was organized in Philadelphia by Dr. Thomas Bond; it opened its doors Feb. 6, 1752, as the Pennsylvania Hospital. Admission was on a paying or charity basis for persons who were mentally or physically ill, except for incurables and those having infectious diseases.

1750: The **Great Awakening,** the New England religious revival sparked by Jonathan Edwards, came to an end when Edwards was compelled to resign from his pulpit at Northampton, Mass., by liberal members of his congregation. The liberals opposed his emphasis on the sinful nature of mankind.

1751: The **first sugar cane** grown in America was introduced into Louisiana by Catholic missionaries from San Domingo on the island of Hispaniola. It was used to make taffia, a kind of rum.

1752 Jan 31: The **first American-born nun** in the Roman Catholic Church was Sister St. Martha Turpin, who celebrated the Ceremony for the Profession at the Ursuline Convent, in New Orleans, La.

1752 June: Benjamin Franklin conducted his celebrated experiment with kite and key to prove lightning a manifestation of electricity. A kite with a projecting wire was flown during a thunderstorm, and an electrical charge was conducted to the key through light twine. The experiment was conducted in a pasture near what is now the corner of Fourth and Vine streets in Philadelphia, Pa.

1753: The **first steam engine** in the colonies was brought to North Arlington, N.J., by John Schuyler to pump water from his copper mine. The machine came from England and was assembled in America by Joshua Hornblower.

1754: The **first clock made entirely in America** was constructed by Benjamin Banneker, a 30-year-old black who had never seen a clock before. It continued to run accurately, striking all hours regularly, for 20 years.

IV. Fashion
Folkways
Holidays
Social Issues and Crime
Sports

By the mid-eighteenth century social customs and forms of entertainment were somewhat relaxed compared with earlier periods. At the same time, many forms of entertainment and recreation were those to be expected of small towns and farming areas—hunting, fishing, folk dancing, and corn husking bees, for example. One observer noted that at one of the husking bees the "neighboring Swains . . . cannot carry in the husks without a Rhum bottle." There was widespread observance of the custom that any young man who found a red ear of corn could kiss any girl he chose. It was recorded that one young woman, Sarah Tuttle, charged with having enjoyed the occasion too much, was brought before a magistrate who denounced her as a "Bould Virgin."

1752: The inscription for the **Liberty Bell,** the biblical sentence "Proclaim liberty throughout all the land unto all the inhabitants thereof," was chosen by the Pennsylvania Provincial Assembly. The bell was cast in England and delivered to the colony in this year. While being tested in Philadelphia, it suffered its first crack.

1754: Curious **Valentine customs** were recorded by a colonial girl: "Last Friday was St. Valentine's Day, and the night before I got five bay leaves and pinned four on the corners of my pillow and the fifth to the middle; and then if I dreamt of my sweetheart, Betty

said we should be married before the year was out. But to make it more sure I boiled an egg hard and took out the yolk and filled it with salt; and when I went to bed ate it shell and all, without speaking or drinking after it. We also wrote our lovers' names on bits of paper, and rolled them up in clay and put them into water; and the first that rose up was to be our Valentine. Would you think it? Mr. Blossom was my man. I lay abed and shut my eyes all the morning, till he came to our house, for I would not have seen another man before him for all the world." It was about this time, in the middle of the century, that the history of American valentines began. A certain simplicity was apparent in the style of the sketches and verses of early valentines, though they often displayed some talent. So-called valentine writers, guides to the composition of valentines containing sample verses, were imported from England from 1723 on, and many senders were willing merely to copy their verses from these.

1755–1759

I. Civil Rights
Exploration and Settlement
Government
Statistics
Wars

The Seven Years' War (1756–1763), the European counterpart to the French and Indian War (1754–1763), began officially between France and England on May 15, 1756, when the latter made a formal declaration of war. Actually, fighting had been going on in America for two years. The war involved all the major European powers and was worldwide in scope, but to the colonists it was a struggle against the French for control of North America. The war did not go well for England until the elder William Pitt came to power in 1756. He concentrated on fighting the French and sent badly needed troop reinforcements to North America.

1755 July 9: In the **French and Indian War** (1754–1763), British Gen. Edward Braddock was mortally wounded when he and his force of British troops and colonial militia were caught in a French and Indian ambush. Braddock had just crossed the Monongahela R. on his way to attack Fort Duquesne, on the site of what is now Pittsburgh, Pa. Braddock died

July 13, and George Washington assumed command of the retreating army.

1755 Nov 30: The **first refugees** from the French and Indian War, some 900 Acadian French deported by British authorities from Nova Scotia, arrived in Maryland. Years later Henry Wadsworth Longfellow used this exile as the background for his poem *Evangeline* (1847).

1756 Aug 14: Fort Oswego in north central New York was captured by the French under Gen. Joseph de Montcalm de Saint-Véran. Gen. Montcalm rendered the fort useless for military purposes and returned to Montreal.

1757 Aug 9: Fort William Henry, at the southern tip of Lake George in northeastern New York, capitulated to the French commanded by Gen. Montcalm. Many of the British soldiers in the garrison were killed by the Indian allies of the French on the next day.

1758 July 8: A British and colonial assault on **Ticonderoga,** at the northern end of Lake George in New York, was beaten back by the French under Gen. Montcalm. Nearly 2000 of the attacking force of 17,000 were killed or wounded.

1758 July 26: The French at the **fortress of Louisbourg,** Nova Scotia, surrendered to the British under Adm. Edward Boscawen and Gen. Jeffrey Amherst after a 48-day siege. Almost 6000 prisoners were captured and the fortress was razed.

1758 Nov 25: British forces drove the French from **Fort Duquesne,** which the British renamed Pittsburgh.

1759 July 26: Ticonderoga was abandoned by the French as Gen. Amherst threatened a siege. The French commander, the Chevalier de Bourlamaque, withdrew to Crown Point, N.Y.

1759 Sep 13: The French were defeated on the **Plains of Abraham** at Quebec. Both Gen. Montcalm and the British commander Gen. James Wolfe were killed. The city of Quebec was surrendered to the British Sept. 18.

II. Architecture
Arts and Music
Popular Entertainment
Publishing
Theater

Colonial America was developing its own intellectual class, whose members were noted for their wide-ranging interests and varied talents. None of them was more versatile than Francis Hopkinson, a musician and poet, accomplished harpsichordist, and leader of musical pursuits in Philadelphia. In 1759 Hopkinson wrote what was probably the first secular song written by a native American, "My Days Have Been So Wonderous Free." The song, based on the poem by Thomas Parnell, was not published until the twentieth century. Hopkinson went on to become a signer of the Declaration of Independence, wrote the celebrated Revolutionary poem "The Battle of the Kegs" (1778), and, as a member of the Continental Navy Board (1776–1778), may have designed the American flag. His book *Seven songs, for the Harpsichord or Forte-Piano* (1788) was the first book of music published by an American composer.

1755: According to legend, the words of the song "**Yankee Doodle**" were written by Dr. Richard Shuckburg, a British army surgeon, as a satire on the ragged American troops. More likely the song was of folk origin among the British soldiers. Adopted as a favorite marching tune by American troops, "Yankee Doodle" quickly lost its satirical aspect. In 1781, during the American Revolution, the song was played at the British surrender at Yorktown, Va.

1757: Mount Vernon, a cottage of one and one-half stories acquired by George Washington, was remodeled for the first time. It was enlarged and remodeled at least three more times in the next 30 years, probably in accordance with Washington's own designs. The result was a structure not as well designed as other Virginia mansions but, aside from its historical associations, interesting for its record of architectural growth.

III. Business and Industry
Education
Philosophy and Religion
Science

The opening in 1756 of a through stage route linking Philadelphia and New York City marked another step forward in the development of colonial transportation. As the first colonial settlements grew into towns and then into cities, the need for roads and reliable means of transportation also grew. By 1717 there was a continuous road along the East Coast connecting all the colonies. Other roads went into the interior, but many were rough. The first stage line between Boston and Newport, R.I., began to operate in 1736. Beginning in 1744, part of the heavily traveled route between New York and Philadelphia was served by twice-weekly stages between New Brunswick and Trenton, N.J. Perhaps the most heavily traveled road was the Great Philadelphia Wagon Road, which ran west to Lancaster and then to York. The 1756 Philadelphia-New York stage used Jersey Wagons, wagons without spring suspensions, which operated in relays. Faster passenger service was offered in

1766 by the Flying Machine, a box wagon that ran from Camden, N.J., to what is now Jersey City, N.J. The 90-mile trip took two days and passengers had to use a ferry at each end.

1755 June 16: The **first nonsectarian college** in America, the University of Pennsylvania, was chartered as the College, Academy, and Charitable School in Philadelphia through the efforts of Benjamin Franklin. Its first degrees were awarded in 1757.

IV. Fashion
Folkways
Holidays
Social Issues and Crime
Sports

As soon as streets were laid out in colonial cities, citizens and city councils alike pointed to the necessity and desirability of paving them. Paving not only made streets drier and smoother, but also contributed to public health by providing drainage. After 1700, Boston, New York City, and Newport, R.I., began to pave streets. Later, between 1743 and 1760, paving became more common and colonial streets were probably in better shape than those in England. In 1757 over 16,000 yards of roadway on Boston Neck were paved at a cost of £3000. A lottery in Newport in 1752 provided funds for paving more streets. Philadelphia also used a lottery to pay the cost of paving.

1756 July 26: Bosom bottles were advertised in the *Boston Evening Post.* They were small, beribboned glasses worn on stiff dresses of the period, filled with water, and containing flowers that served much the same function as corsages do today.

1757: Street lights appeared in Philadelphia on a small scale. Whale oil lamps, specially designed by Benjamin Franklin, were installed on a few streets. The year before, Franklin had introduced a bill to the Pennsylvania Assembly for street illumination.

1760–1764

I. Civil Rights
Exploration and Settlement
Government
Statistics
Wars

The Treaty of Paris, signed by Great Britain, France, and Spain on Feb. 10, 1763, ended the Seven Years'

War and its American counterpart, the French and Indian War (1754–1763). By terms of the treaty, France ceded Canada and all its territory east of the Mississippi R. to England, and Spain yielded Florida to England. France retained the islands of St. Pierre and Miquelon in the Gulf of St. Lawrence. Worldwide, France was humbled and the treaty marked the start of the colonial and maritime supremacy of Great Britain. Britain's success was costly, however, and Parliament's attempt to cover its debts, and to pay for a continuing military presence in America, by direct taxation of the colonists soon caused strained relations between mother country and colonies.

The estimated colonial **population** was 1,610,000.

1760 Aug 7: In the **French and Indian War** (1754–1763), Fort Loudon, Tenn., capitulated to the Cherokee Indians. Capt. Demere surrendered under condition that his troops be allowed to retreat unimpeded. On Aug. 10 the garrison was massacred by Indians while retreating to Fort Prince George in South Carolina.

1760 Sep 8: The **French surrendered Montreal** to Gen. Jeffrey Amherst. After the defeat of this last French stronghold, Canada was split into three parts: Quebec, Montreal, and Three Rivers.

1760 Nov 29: Detroit was surrendered to Maj. Robert Rogers by the French Commander Belêtre.

1763 May 7: Pontiac's Rebellion, named for the Ottawa Indian chief who led the uprising, began when Pontiac led an attack on the fort at Detroit. The raid failed and the Indians began a siege. News of the attack sparked similar raids throughout the region until all but three forts—Detroit, Pitt, and Niagara—had fallen. British forces rushed to their relief. With no French aid materializing, Pontiac in October secured a truce and withdrew to the west. A final peace agreement in 1766 marked the end of the rebellion.

II. Architecture
Arts and Music
Popular Entertainment
Publishing
Theater

The growth of the colonies brought with it a strong interest in cultural activities. In the mid-eighteenth century musical concerts were flourishing in the colonial centers, and musical societies, music dealers, and instrument makers all benefited. As in other matters, Boston, New York City, Philadelphia, and

Charleston, S.C., led the way, with Charleston seeming to have a special affinity for music. The first music society in America, the St. Cecilia Society, was founded there in 1762. In Europe, Charleston was considered the chief cultural center of the colonies, and many artists, actors, and musicians chose to settle there when they emigrated to America. Other cities could boast of cultural achievements as well. In Boston a group of gentlemen sponsored a concert in Faneuil Hall as early as 1744, and in 1754 the first concert hall in Boston was opened by Gilbert Deblois. Philadelphia boasted four organ makers who produced spinets and virginals as well as organs.

1764: The *Connecticut Courant* began publishing as a weekly newspaper in Hartford, Conn. Renamed the *Hartford Daily Courant,* it became a daily in 1837, changing to its present name, the *Hartford Courant,* in 1887. It became the oldest continuously published newspaper in the U.S. The *Courant* was a patriotic journal during the Revolution and after independence supported the Federalist Party.

III. Business and Industry
Education
Philosophy and Religion
Science

The most useful contribution to transportation produced in the colonies was the Conestoga Wagon. Although it existed in primitive form by about 1725, it came into its own after 1760, by which time craftsmen of Lancaster, Pa., living along the Conestoga Creek, had converted the wagon into an enormous conveyance using six horses and carrying up to eight tons of goods. The bottom was curved to help keep the load in place whether going uphill or down. The top was a huge white cover, first made of homespun hempen and later of canvas. It rose out and up at each end, giving a poke bonnet effect. The driver rode on the left wheelhorse or on a lazyboard that could be pulled out from the side of the wagon. By so doing, he could see oncoming traffic. This arrangement is thought to be the origin of the custom of driving on the right-hand side of the road. The Conestoga Wagon was vital to the settlement of the Allegheny region. Thousands of these wagons carried farm produce to the cities and hauled to the west the goods needed by pioneer settlers. The prairie schooner, which made up the wagon trains that later took settlers to Mississippi regions, was a light version of the Conestoga Wagon.

c1760: The **first bifocal lenses** were invented by Benjamin Franklin. Twenty years later Franklin wrote to a friend that he had become tired of carrying two pairs of spectacles and had ordered a pair made with two kinds of lenses cut in the same circle of glass.

1763: A pioneer attempt at **steam navigation** was made by Henry Williams. Inspired by the work of James Watt in England, Williams built the first steam-powered boat and tested it on the Conestoga Creek in Lancaster, Pa. Although the tests were a failure, they helped encourage Robert Fulton and his experiments.

IV. Fashion
Folkways
Holidays
Social Issues and Crime
Sports

Student life at colonial colleges was reflected in the experience of Thomas Jefferson, who entered the College of William and Mary at Williamsburg, Va., on Mar. 25, 1760, when not quite 17. About this time the students complained about the food. The faculty told the housekeeper, Isabella Cocke, that both salt and fresh meat must be served at dinner, puddings and pies provided on Sunday and two weekdays, and supper must be the same at all tables, even if made up of scraps. Jefferson described the buildings as "rude, mis-shapen piles, which, but that they have roofs, would be taken for brick-kilns." The College of William and Mary was the second oldest college in the colonies, opened in 1694, and its main building was already 60 years old.

1761 June 10: The influence of **Puritan morality** on colonial society was demonstrated in the production of a play presented at Newport, R.I., by the Douglass Company: *Moral Dialogues in 5 parts, Depicting the Evil Effects of Jealousy and other Bad Passions, and Proving that Happines can only Spring from the Pursuit of Virtue.* The play was actually Shakespeare's *Othello.* The advertisement for the performance read: "... Commencement at 7, conclusion at half past 10, in order that every spectator may go home at a sober hour and reflect upon what he has seen before he retires to rest." This description failed to disarm Puritan critics of theater. After a few performances by the company in Newport and Providence, the Rhode Island Assembly enacted legislation barring theatrical performances in the colony, with a penalty of £100 for each actor.

1765–1769

I. Civil Rights
Exploration and Settlement
Government
Statistics
Wars

The Stamp Act, passed by Parliament on Mar. 22, 1765, raised the subject that was to be a major cause of the American Revolution, taxation without representation. The act levied a tax on all newspapers, legal documents, pamphlets, almanacs, playing cards, and dice by requiring that they bear a stamp. The receipts from the tax were to be used to pay for defense of the colonies. The tax was to take effect on Nov. 1, but even before then American opposition was intense. Merchants refused to buy English goods, stamp agents were threatened with harm if they did not resign, and in some places the official stamps were destroyed. As a result the tax was repealed on Mar. 18, 1766, but not before delegates from nine of the thirteen colonies attended the Stamp Act Congress in Oct. 1765. The congress issued a series of resolutions stating the reasons for colonial opposition to the tax. The same day the tax was repealed, Parliament passed the Declaratory Act, asserting that the British government had the right to make any laws it wished concerning the American colonies.

1765 May 29: Patrick Henry attacked the Stamp Act in the Virginia House of Burgesses, declaring that only colonial legislatures could impose taxes on their respective colonies. Shouts of "Treason!" interrupted Henry's speech, to which he replied: "If this be treason, make the most of it."

1765 Oct 7-25: The **Stamp Act Congress** met at City Hall, New York City, in answer to a circular from the Massachusetts House of Representatives. Twenty-eight delegates from nine colonies attended to organize a united resistance to the Stamp Act. On Oct. 19 the congress adopted the Declaration of Rights and Grievances, a series of resolutions protesting taxes imposed by the act, and resolved not to import any goods that required payment of duty. This led to the Petition of London Merchants in 1766, which urged repeal of the act and stressed the injury to English trade caused by the colonial policy of nonimportation.

1766 Mar 17: The **Stamp Act was repealed** by Parliament. The repeal was approved the next day by King George III and became effective on May 1.

1767 June 29: The **Townshend Revenue Act** was passed by Parliament. It required that colonists pay an import duty on tea, glass, painter's colors, oil, lead, and paper. The £40,000 that the act was expected to yield was to pay salaries of royal governors and judges in the colonies. In Feb. 1768 the Massachusetts House of Representatives sent a letter to other colonial legislatures calling upon them to join with it in action against the duties. The British ordered the letter repudiated and threatened to dissolve any assembly in sympathy with Massachusetts. In Virginia the burgesses responded with a declaration that they had the exclusive right of taxation in the colony. While protesting loyalty to the king, they entered into an agreement not to import goods on which Parliament raised revenues and, after a certain date, to stop buying a long list of embargoed items.

II. Architecture
Arts and Music
Popular Entertainment
Publishing
Theater

The American school of painting, still in its infancy during this period, was diminished by the death in 1765 of Joseph Badger, whose use of realism in portraiture was a significant move away from traditional European techniques. Badger's works owed nothing to the more refined and technically superior British school of portraiture. Badger was a glazier and house painter who became Boston's favorite artist. His work had charm, but a stiff, archaic style. His best work portrayed children, such as Jeremiah Belknap. He also did portraits of Revolutionary era notables such as Jonathan Edwards and John Adams. Many thought his plain style was more suited to the young, raw, and vigorous colonials than to studied portraits of English nobles. His work reflected the general tendency in all the colonial arts during this period to establish independent styles and techniques.

1766 Oct: The **first permanent theater** in the colonies, the Southwark Theater, was erected on South St. in Philadelphia by David Douglass, owner and manager of the American Company of Comedians. Douglass also built New York City's first permanent theater, the John Street Theater, in 1767.

1767 Apr 24: Probably the **first professionally performed American play**, *The Prince of Parthia* by Thomas Godfrey, opened at the Southwark Theater in Philadelphia.

1768: A commemorative bowl molded in silver by **Paul Revere** was presented to each of 92 legislators in the Massachusetts House of Representatives who resisted royal authority by protesting to King George III about restrictive trade measures.

1769: Whitehall, an impressive late Georgian mansion, was built in Anne Arundel County, Md. It was equipped with the only known interior water closet in colonial America.

III. Business and Industry
Education
Philosophy and Religion
Science

The last of the large Protestant denominations to establish itself in America was the Methodist Church. In England it did not formally separate from the Church of England until late in the century. In 1766 Philip Embury, originally from Ireland, formed the John Street church in New York City and preached there. About the same time Robert Strawbridge started a congregation in Maryland, and in Virginia the Rev. Devereux Jarratt, an Anglican, acted as chaplain to the Methodists. Francis Asbury came from England in 1771 and made many converts to Methodism. The first annual Methodist conference in America was held in 1773. In 1784, with authority from John Wesley, the founder of Methodism, Thomas Coke formally organized the Methodist Episcopal Church in America.

1765: The **first chocolate** manufactured in North America was produced at Dorchester Lower Mills on the Neponset R. in Massachusetts by John Harmon. In 1780 the plant came into the possession of Dr. James Baker, who had sponsored Harmon. From Baker's business evolved the world-famous Walter Baker & Co., Ltd., chocolate manufacturers.

1765 May 3: The **first medical school** in the colonies, the medical department of the College of Philadelphia, was organized by Drs. John Morgan and William Shippen, Jr. The school later became the University of Pennsylvania School of Medicine.

1767: The **first planetarium** in America was built by David Rittenhouse of Philadelphia. Rittenhouse, a noted clockmaker, plotted the orbits of Venus and Mercury in 1769.

1768 Oct 30: The **first Methodist Church** in America was dedicated. It was the Wesley Chapel on John St. in New York City. The church was rebuilt in 1817 and again in 1840.

1769: A famous American **glassmaking plant** opened at Manheim, Pa., by Henry William Stiegel, whose name became identified with a type of American glassware that reflected a German tradition.

1769: Anthracite coal was used in a forge for the first time in Wilkes-Barre, Pa. It had been discovered as early as 1762 by Connecticut pioneers in Pennsylvania. It was little used until the beginning of the nineteenth century.

IV. Fashion
Folkways
Holidays
Social Issues and Crime
Sports

This period, following the last of the French and Indian Wars, saw the opening of vast new tracts for westward expansion and the rise of the western frontiersman as an American folk hero. The most celebrated folk hero was Daniel Boone who, after hunting and exploring his way through the Cumberland Gap, saw Kentucky for the first time on June 7, 1769. Boone spent two years exploring the region, then in 1773 made an unsuccessful attempt to settle Kentucky. In 1775, with a company of 30 men, he blazed the Wilderness Road and founded Boonesborough, Ky. The next year he joined the Patriot cause in the American Revolution as a captain in the Virginia militia. In 1778 he was captured by the Shawnee Indians but managed to escape and alert Boonesborough to an impending Indian raid. Boone's land titles in Kentucky were overturned in the courts on technicalities, and he eventually moved to Missouri, where he continued his pioneer existence until his death in 1820. Boone's adventures became widely known after publication in 1784 of *Discovery, Settlement, and Present State of Kentucky* by John Filson, which contained material purporting to be autobiographical.

1765: Education for women in colonial America emphasized practical learning, as illustrated by the advertisement of a Philadelphia teacher who promised to teach young ladies to spell and print with propriety. He advised them not to be discouraged in their pursuit of knowledge by their age or fear of not obtaining a husband, since he had given "the finishing stroke" to several New York ladies who married shortly afterward.

1766: Some **popular games** in New York City were suggested by James Rivington's advertisement that he imported "battledores, shuttlecocks, cricket balls, pellets, racquets for tennis and fives, and backgammon tables."

1770–1774

I. Civil Rights
Exploration and Settlement
Government
Statistics
Wars

The first clashes of the coming revolution occurred during this period, among them the Boston Massacre in 1770 and the Boston Tea Party in 1773. This period also saw the rise of organized political resistance to parliamentary and royal excesses in the form of the first Continental Congress, which met from Sept. 5 to Oct. 26, 1774, in Philadelphia. There were 55 delegates representing all the colonies except Georgia. Peyton Randolph of Virginia was elected president and Charles Thompson of Pennsylvania secretary. The most important action, taken on Oct. 20, was the formation of the Continental Association, which forbade the importation and use of English products and proposed that colonial exports be prohibited. The delegates also adopted a number of resolutions opposing the Intolerable Acts, the Quebec Act, the maintenance of British troops in towns in peacetime, and the dissolution of colonial assemblies. The rights of the colonists, including rights to "life, liberty, and property," were also expressed. The congress voted to assemble again on May 10, 1775.

The estimated colonial **population** was 2,205,000.

1770 Mar 5: In what came to be called the **Boston Massacre,** five colonists were killed when British troops fired on a mob of men and boys who had been taunting them and throwing stones. Capt. Thomas Preston, commander of the British contingent, and six of his men were charged with murder. They were defended in court by John Adams and Josiah Quincy. All were acquitted but two soldiers who were found guilty of manslaughter.

1770 Apr 12: The **Townshend Acts** were repealed through the efforts of Lord Frederick North. Realizing that the colonies were being pushed too far, Parliament was persuaded to withdraw all Townshend duties except that on tea. The colonies responded by lifting their embargo on goods shipped from England, thus improving relations between England and America. The tax on tea remained, as did the colonial embargo on tea.

1773 Apr 27: The **Tea Act** was passed by Parliament. The act was designed to save the East Indian Company from bankruptcy by remitting all British duties on tea while retaining the tax on tea exported to America. This enabled the company to cut its price and undersell colonial competition. The company's resulting monopoly all but destroyed American tea merchants.

1773 Dec 16: In the celebrated **Boston Tea Party,** a group of men dressed as Indians boarded three British ships in Boston harbor and threw their cargoes of tea, 342 chests worth £18,000, into the water. The action was the climax of growing colonial opposition to the Tea Act.

1774 Mar 31: The first of the **Intolerable Acts,** also known as the Coercive Acts, was passed by Parliament. The Coercive Acts were punitive measures against Massachusetts for the Boston Tea Party. This act closed the port of Boston until payment was made for the destroyed tea. The three subsequent acts were the Massachusetts Government Act (May 20), which forbade public meetings unless sanctioned by the governor; the Administration of Justice Act (May 20), under which any British officials accused of capital offenses were to be transferred from Massachusetts to England or to another colony for trial; and the Quartering Act (June 2), which required Massachusetts residents to house and feed British troops.

1774 June 22: The **Quebec Act** was passed by Parliament. It established a permanent government in Quebec and extended its boundaries south to the Ohio R. to include land contested by several American colonies. For this, it was considered by the colonists to be one of the Intolerable Acts.

1774 Dec 14: The **first military encounter of the American Revolution** occurred. On the report (the news was carried by Paul Revere) that the British intended to station a garrison at Portsmouth, N.H., Maj. John Sullivan led a band of militia to Fort William and Mary, broke into its arsenal, and carried off a store of arms and ammunition. Neither side suffered casualties.

II. Architecture
Arts and Music
Popular Entertainment
Publishing
Theater

The rising prestige of American artists in the world was reflected in the career of John Singleton Copley, who was at the peak of his powers at this time, and was soon to become one of America's earliest expatriate artists. A Bostonian and a successful portrait painter by the time he was 20, Copley moved to England about 1775 and remained there for the rest of his life. In England he enjoyed great popularity, and completed a number of his best historical paintings, such as *The Death of Lord Chatham* (c1780), which won him election to the Royal Academy, and the *Siege of Gibraltar* (1790). He also painted portraits of the royal family and the famous *Family Picture* of his wife and children. Nevertheless, Copley's reputation rests primarily on the portraits he painted in America, including those of many of the leading citizens of New England.

1770: The first house at **Monticello** was built by Thomas Jefferson from his own designs. Its plan showed his great interest in pure classicism and in the temple forms of Greek and Roman architecture, especially as evidenced by large porticoes. Monticello later was completely rebuilt and enlarged, but still in keeping with classical forms. Plans for Monticello absorbed Jefferson's attention from his early manhood. Its foundations were dug in 1769, the year of his first election to the House of Burgesses. Monticello stands to this day.

1774 Oct 20: American theater was suspended after an order of the Continental Congress that the colonies "discountenance and discourage all horse racing and all kinds of gaming, cock fighting, exhibitions of shows, plays and other expensive diversions and entertainments."

III. Business and Industry
Education
Philosophy and Religion
Science

The curious history of the American Shaker movement began during this period. The Shakers, officially the United Society of Believers in Christ's Second Coming, had been established in England for a number of years when Ann Lee, known as Mother Ann, arrived in New York State on Aug. 6, 1774, following a vision that told her to travel to America. In 1776 she and eight followers—six men and two women—settled at Watervliet, near Albany. Members of the movement became known as Shakers because of the trembling movements their bodies made when they were in a state of religious fervor. Mother Ann's tour of New England in 1781 aroused animosity because her followers claimed she embodied the second coming of Christ. The Shaker faith centered upon public confession of sins and preparation for the second coming, and Mother Ann added strictures against sexual intercourse and marriage (which ultimately doomed the sect), war, the bearing of arms, and oath-taking. After her death in 1785, her followers composed a life story that made much of the persecutions she encountered in England and America

and the supposedly miraculous manner of her deliverance from them. By 1825, eighteen Shaker communities had been founded in eight states, as far west as Indiana, but by 1860 the movement had begun to decline. Today the movement is known especially for its furniture and handcrafts, which were famous for their simplicity and high quality of workmanship.

1770: The **first mental hospital** in the colonies, the Public Hospital for Persons of Insane and Disordered Minds, was opened at Williamsburg, Va. It later became the Eastern Lunatic Asylum, and still later the Eastern State Hospital.

1773 Jan 12: The **first museum** officially established in the American colonies was founded at Charleston, S.C. In 1915 it was incorporated as the Charleston Museum.

1773 July 14: The first annual **conference of American Methodists** convened at St. George's Church, Philadelphia, Pa.

IV. Fashion
Folkways
Holidays
Social Issues and Crime
Sports

The first large-scale street lighting projects began during this period, although street lighting had begun in the major colonial cities in the 1750s. Philadelphia had installed some 320 oil lamps by 1767, and in Charleston, S.C., in 1762 one Joseph Wilson contributed £300 for street lamps and three months of maintenance. The need for street lighting as an aid to citizens engaged in evening commerce or cultural activities and also as a deterrent to steadily rising urban crime, had been growing throughout the mid-eighteenth century. In 1770 Charleston began a program of street lighting at public expense, and in 1771 Philadelphia purchased a large number of new lamps. It also levied a £20 fine for breaking a lamp. Boston street lighting came comparatively late, but on Mar. 2, 1774, its streets were illuminated by 310 lamps, tended by one Edward Smith with the assistance of seven lamplighters. The lamps were kept lighted in the evenings from Oct. 1 to May 1.

1773: In a comment on **women's fashions**, a Virginia diarist sadly noted the arrival of a batch of women's stays (corsets): "[They] are produced upwards so high that we can have scarce any view at all of the Ladies' Snowy Bosoms; and on the contrary, they are extended downwards so low that whenever ladies who wear them, either young or old, have occasion to walk, the motion necessary for Walking, must, I think, cause a disagreeable Friction of some part of the body against the lower edge of the Stays which is hard and unyielding." Stays were worn by old and young alike. Even ten-year-old girls were forced to girdle their bodies.

1773 Mar: The rioting and wild festivities that marked **New Year's Day** in New York were somewhat curbed by the colonial legislature, which outlawed the discharge of firearms and explosives. New Year's Day had been the most important holiday in the colony during Dutch rule, when it was the traditional day to visit and exchange gifts. When the English took over the colony in 1664, they adopted Dutch customs completely and added a turkey shoot to the day's festivities.

1775–1779

I. Civil Rights
Exploration and Settlement
Government
Statistics
Wars

This period saw the beginning of the American Revolution (1775–1783). Of the numerous events that occurred, none was more momentous than the drafting and adoption of the Declaration of Independence at the Second Continental Congress, which convened in Philadelphia in May 1775. On June 6, 1776, Richard Henry Lee of Virginia introduced a resolution that "these united colonies are, and of right ought to be, free and independent states." On June 11 John Adams, Benjamin Franklin, Thomas Jefferson, Robert R. Livingston, and Roger Sherman were appointed to draft a declaration. Jefferson prepared the first draft; then improvements by Adams and Franklin were incorporated. Lee's resolution of independence was adopted on July 2 by a vote of 12 to 0, New York abstaining. The actual Declaration was approved July 4, after the congress made some further changes. It was not until Aug. 2, however, that a formal parchment copy was ready for signing. Eventually 61 patriots affixed their signatures. The importance of the document lay in its declaration that each person has certain unalienable rights, and that governments derive their powers from the consent of the governed. In an age of kings who were thought to rule by divine right, this was truly a revolutionary philosophy. The Declaration of Independence, combined with the ultimate success of the American Revolution, was destined to usher in a new political age.

1775 Mar 23: Patrick Henry, addressing the second Virginia convention in Richmond, Va., delivered his immortal speech against arbitrary British rule, closing with "Give me liberty or give me death."

1775 Apr 19: The opening volleys of the American Revolution were exchanged at the Battle of **Lexington** in Massachusetts. Capt. John Parker, commanding some 70 Minutemen, engaged a British column marching on Concord, Mass., to seize military stores there. The brief fight at Lexington left eight Minutemen dead and ten wounded. The British then marched to Concord, destroyed some colonial supplies, and fought another engagement before beginning a long and costly retreat under colonial fire back to Boston. By day's end, the British had suffered about 273 casualties, the Americans 93.

1775 May 10: Fort Ticonderoga, N.Y., was taken by American forces under the command of Col. Ethan Allen.

1775 June 15: The Second Continental Congress chose **George Washington** commander in chief of the Continental Army. He declined to accept pay for his services, but in 1783, after eight years of war, submitted records of his expenses totaling £24,700.

1775 June 17: The Battle of **Bunker Hill** was actually fought on Breed's Hill. British forces under Gen. Howe assaulted the Continental positions three times before the Americans, under Col. William Prescott, ran out of gunpowder and were forced to retreat. The British then occupied Bunker Hill after another skirmish.

1775 Sep 25: Col. **Ethan Allen** was captured while attacking Montreal. He was taken to England and held prisoner until the end of the war.

1775 Oct 13: A **naval force was established** by the Continental Congress when it authorized construction of two warships, increasing the number to four on Oct. 30. The Continental Navy was formally established on Nov. 28 and rules for its regulation approved.

1775 Nov 10: Two battalions of **Continental Marines** were organized by the Continental Congress as a component of its naval force. The U.S. Marine Corps was not formally established until July 11, 1789.

1775 Nov 29: In an important **naval victory,** the American cruiser *Lee* captured the British brig *Nancy*, which was laden with guns and ammunition destined for Quebec. *Nancy* was renamed *Congress* and played a key role in forcing the British evacuation of Boston in Mar. 1776.

1775 Dec 22: Esek Hopkins was appointed the **first commander in chief of the Continental Navy.** His rank was to correspond with Gen. Washington's. His first fleet consisted of the *Alfred, Columbus, Andrea Doria,* and *Cabot,* to which four more converted merchant ships were soon added. On Jan. 2, 1777, Hopkins was formally dismissed because he failed to follow orders from the Continental Congress.

1776 Mar 17: The **British evacuated Boston** after American forces seized and fortified Dorchester Heights on Mar. 4. Gen. Howe sailed for Halifax, Nova Scotia, to await reinforcements.

1776 Apr 12: North Carolina became the **first colony to propose independence** formally when the North Carolina Provincial Congress instructed its delegates to the Continental Congress to vote for independence.

1776 Aug 2: The **Declaration of Independence was signed** by the members of the Continental Congress. Though it had been approved on July 4, the draft document had been signed only by John Hancock and Charles Thomson, the president and secretary. The names of the signers were withheld from the public for more than six months because, if independence were not achieved, their treasonable act might result in their deaths.

1776 Aug 27: In the Battle of **Long Island,** N.Y., American forces commanded by Gen. Israel Putnam and Gen. John Sullivan were defeated by the British under Gen. Sir William Howe and Gen. Sir Henry Clinton. Howe took Gen. Sullivan prisoner. On Aug. 30 the Americans evacuated Long Island and crossed to Manhattan.

1776 Sep 6: The **first submarine attack,** by David Bushnell's submersible craft *Turtle,* was initiated unsuccessfully against Adm. Richard Howe's flagship *Eagle* in New York Bay off Manhattan Island. A second attempt to sink British shipping later in September also failed.

1776 Sep 15: The **Continental Army evacuated New York City,** which was then occupied by the British under Howe.

1776 Sep 22: Capt. **Nathan Hale** of Connecticut was executed by the British in New York City for spying. Before he was hanged he said, "I only regret that I have but one life to lose for my country."

1776 Dec 19: The first number of ***The Crisis*** by Thomas Paine, a series of pamphlets written to bolster the morale of the Continental Army, was issued. It was immortalized by its famous first sentence, "These are the times that try men's souls."

1776 Dec 26: In the Battle of **Trenton,** N.J., Gen. Washington captured nearly 1000 mercenary Hessian troops in an early morning surprise raid.

1777 Jan 3: The Battle of **Princeton,** N.J., was fought and won by the Continental Army. Gen. Washington again attacked in the early morning, as he had at Trenton the previous week.

1777 July: The **Vermont state constitution,** drafted this month, made Vermont the first state to abolish slavery and adopt universal male suffrage without regard to property. It was followed to a lesser degree by other New England states, which with Vermont were destined to become strongholds of abolitionism in the 1850s. Vermont had declared itself an independent state on Jan. 16, 1777.

1777 Aug 16: Americans under Gen. John Stark defeated the British at **Bennington,** Vt., killing about 200 and capturing 600. The British detachment commanded by Lt. Col. Friedrich Baum had been sent by Gen. Burgoyne in search of provisions.

1777 Sep 11: In the Battle of **Brandywine,** Pa., the Continental Army under Gen. Washington was defeated by British forces under Gen. Howe, who continued to advance on Philadelphia.

1777 Sep 19: In the first Battle of **Bemis Heights,** also known as the Battle of Freeman's Farm, the British under Gen. Burgoyne gained some ground from the Americans under Gen. Horatio Gates but lost 500 men. Almost 300 Americans were killed.

1777 Sep 19: The **Continental Congress fled Philadelphia,** which was threatened by British forces.

1777 Sep 26: Philadelphia was occupied by British forces under Gen. Howe.

1777 Oct 4: At **Germantown,** near Philadelphia, Gen. Washington attacked the British but was repulsed by Gen. Howe. The Americans lost about 600 men in this battle.

1777 Oct 7: In the second Battle of **Bemis Heights,** near Saratoga, N.Y., the Americans routed a force of some 1500 British. Benedict Arnold was wounded while attempting to force an entrance into the Hessian camp, and British Gen. Simon Fraser was killed.

1777 Oct 17: At **Saratoga** Gen. Burgoyne, surrounded by a superior force, capitulated to Gen. Horatio Gates, surrendering 5642 British and German troops.

1777 Nov 15: The **Articles of Confederation** were adopted by the Continental Congress at York, Pa. They were ratified in 1781.

1777 Dec 17: Gen. Washington retired with his troops to **Valley Forge,** Pa., for the winter.

1778 Feb 6: A **Treaty of Alliance with France** was signed. It was in part commercial and in part political and military. France recognized U.S. independence, which was for the Americans the goal of the treaty. It was the first and only treaty of alliance made by the U.S. until the North Atlantic Treaty Organization pact of 1949.

1778 June 18: The **British evacuated Philadelphia,** fearing blockade by French ships.

1778 June 28: In the Battle of **Monmouth**, N.J., American forces under Gen. Washington defeated the British under Gen. Clinton after initial reversals.

1779 July 15: The fort at **Stony Point**, N.Y., was seized by American forces under Gen. Anthony Wayne. More than 600 British were killed or taken prisoner.

1779 Sep 3-Oct 28: An unsuccessful **siege of Savannah**, Ga., which had been captured by the British in late 1778, was conducted by a French fleet under Adm. d'Estaing supported by American forces on land. On Oct. 9 Count Casimir Pulaski, a Polish officer in American service, was mortally wounded in a disastrous assault on the city.

1779 Sep 23: John Paul Jones, commanding the *Bonhomme Richard,* defeated and captured the *Serapis,* a British man-of-war commanded by Capt. Richard Pearson. It was during this engagement that Jones, when asked if he had struck his colors (surrendered), replied "I have not yet begun to fight." After three hours of brutal fighting, Pearson surrendered to Jones. The Americans transferred to the *Serapis* from their own ship, which sank a day later.

II. Architecture
Arts and Music
Popular Entertainment
Publishing
Theater

The American Revolution provided fresh material for the new nation's poets. Philip Freneau, who was later to earn the title "poet of the American Revolution," wrote a number of satirical poems, among them "General Gage's Soliloquy" (1775) and "General Gage's Confession" (1775), before leaving America in 1776 for the Caribbean. Returning in 1778, he was captured by the British and released. He then turned his poetic talents to the revolutionary cause. Francis Hopkinson, in his ballad "The Battle of the Kegs" (1778), satirized the British reaction during an actual incident, a mine attack launched by David Bushnell on the British fleet in Philadelphia in Jan. 1778. The poem enraged the British and delighted the Patriots, and was the most popular poem of its day. Later poets found the American Revolution a rich source of material. Henry Wadsworth Longfellow immortalized Paul Revere's 1775 ride to alert the Minutemen at Lexington and Concord in his classic American poem "Paul Revere's Ride" (1861).

1776 Jan 10: *Common Sense* by Thomas Paine was published. The pamphlet, which contained the first demand for complete independence for the American colonies, sold 100,000 copies in less than three months. No other book in the U.S. has had such a quick or large sale relative to population. The pamphlet was highly influential in swinging the tide of popular opinion toward a clean break with the mother country.

1776 July 6: The **Declaration of Independence was published** for the first time in the *Pennsylvania Evening Post* under the title "A Declaration by the Representatives of the United States of America, in General Congress assembled." The *Post* was sold for "only two coppers" and was published every Tuesday, Thursday, and Saturday evening. A four-page paper, it devoted its entire front page and the first column of its second page to the Declaration.

1777: The first American edition of the **Bible** in English was published. It consisted of the New Testament alone. The first complete Bible in English published in America appeared in 1782.

III. Business and Industry
Education
Philosophy and Religion
Science

Despite the outbreak of war, new religious groups continued to find the colonies an excellent place in which to grow. Among them was the Universalist Church of America, founded by John Murray, a convert from Methodism who came to America from England in 1770. He traveled and preached for four years in New Jersey, New York, and New England before settling in Gloucester, Mass. In 1775 George Washington named him chaplain to the Rhode Island troops. In 1779 Murray became pastor of the Gloucester First Church, the first Universalist church in the U.S. The Universalist movement spread and in 1790 a convention was held in Philadelphia that drew up a profession of faith and a congregational organization. Murray's Universalism was basically Calvinistic. Later, under Hosea Ballou, pastor for may years of the Second Universalist Society in Boston, the Calvinist strains of Universalism began to diminish.

1775 Feb 22: The **first joint stock manufacturing company** in America, the American Manufactory of Woolens, Linens, and Cottons, was established to promote the production and distribution of textile products. Shares sold on a subscription basis at £10 apiece.

1775 Mar 10: Daniel Boone began blazing the **Wilderness Road,** from Fort Chiswell in the Shenandoah Valley of Virginia, southwest then west through the Cumberland Gap into Kentucky and to the Ohio R., where Boone established a fort and terminal station he named Boonesborough. Although the Wilderness Road was for many years the main route for western traffic, it was not improved for wagon traffic until 1795.

1776 Dec 5: The **Phi Beta Kappa** fraternity was founded at the College of William and Mary as a social fraternity of five students. It was the first social fraternity at an American college. In 1831 Phi Beta Kappa became an honorary fraternity for students of academic distinction.

IV. Fashion
Folkways
Holidays
Social Issues and Crime
Sports

The somewhat obscure and uncertain history of the American flag began during this period. In Oct. 1775, when Congress created the first naval force, it also set down rules for creation of a flag. The result, variously called Congress Colors, the Grand Union Flag, or the First Navy Ensign, was a flag of 13 alternating red and white stripes, with a field of blue bearing the crosses of St. George and St. Andrew. This flag is believed to be the one raised by Lt. John Paul Jones aboard Commodore Esek Hopkins's flagship *Alfred* on the Delaware R. at Philadelphia on Dec. 3, 1775. The first land raising of the Grand Union Flag occurred at Prospect Hill in Somerville, Mass., on Jan. 1, 1776, during the American siege of Boston. On June 14, 1777, Congress adopted what became known as the Stars and Stripes, a flag of 13 red and white stripes with a blue field bearing 13 stars, one for each state. The tradition that Betsy Ross designed the flag has been almost completely discredited. It has been suggested that Francis Hopkinson, a member of the Continental Navy Board from 1776 to 1778, was the father of the Stars and Stripes.

1775: James Adair wrote a description of a **lacrosse** game played by Cherokee Indians in Florida. They used a deerskin ball stuffed hard with deer's hair and bats two feet long with deerskin thongs. The game usually was played for high stakes between two large groups, equal in number, and the ball was kept in the air for long periods of time. The Indians were evidently very good at the game.

1775 June 17: The memorable words **"Don't fire until you see the whites of their eyes"** were uttered, according to tradition, by Col. William Prescott at the Battle of Bunker Hill. The injunction, by no means completely original, was also ascribed to Gen. Israel Putnam.

1775 Dec 3: Raising of the **first official American flag** took place aboard the *Alfred,* the flagship of Commodore Esek Hopkins, on the Delaware R. Because the Navy was governed by Congress the flag was called Congress Colors, and was later variously known as the Grand Union Flag and First Navy Ensign. This standard remained the colonial flag until superseded by the Stars and Stripes on June 14, 1777.

1777 June 14: Congress authorized the **Stars and Stripes,** a flag consisting of 13 stripes alternating red and white, and 13 white stars on a field of blue "representing the new constellation." June 14 has since been observed as Flag Day, although the resolution did not go into effect until Sept. 3, 1777.

1780–1784

I. Civil Rights
Exploration and Settlement
Government
Statistics
Wars

By 1780 the Continental Army had suffered its worst privations, its greatest defeats, and its darkest hours. It would continue to lose battles but, by this time turned into a well-trained fighting force by European officers and aided by allied French forces, it endured and marched to ultimate victory at Yorktown, Va., in Aug. 1781. The military phase of the conflict ended at Yorktown, but the diplomatic struggle continued. Preliminary articles of peace were secured on Nov. 30, 1782, after long and difficult negotiations. The Treaty of Paris, by which the war was officially ended and independence formally acknowledged by Great Britain, was not signed until Sept. 3, 1783.

1780: The estimated colonial **population** was 2,781,000.

1780 Mar 1: Pennsylvania became the **first state to abolish slavery** (Vermont had not yet joined the Union). The law provided that no child born after the date of its passage would be a slave.

1780 Aug 16: In the Battle of **Camden,** S.C., American forces uder Gen. Horatio Gates were defeated by the British under Gen. Charles Cornwallis. Baron Johann de Kalb, a Prussian officer who was commissioned a general in the Continental Army, was mortally wounded in the battle.

1780 Oct 2: Maj. **John André,** adjutant general to British Gen. Sir Henry Clinton, was hanged as a spy at Tappan, N.Y. André had been apprehended on Sept. 23 by three militiamen as he returned from a secret meeting with Gen. Benedict Arnold, who, as commander of West Point, had agreed to surrender the key American fort on the Hudson R. to the British. The plot uncovered, Arnold fled to safety in New York City.

1780 Oct 7: British and Tory forces were defeated at **King's Mountain,** S.C., by Americans under Col. William Campbell, Col. Isaac Shelby, and Col. Benjamin Cleveland. The British commander, Maj. Patrick Ferguson, and 150 others were killed. Nearly 800 prisoners were taken.

1781 Mar 1: The **Articles of Confederation** were ratified by Maryland, the last state to do so.

1781 Mar 15: In the Battle of **Guilford Court House,** N.C., Gen. Cornwallis defeated an American force led by Gen. Nathanael Greene, but heavy losses were suffered by both the British and Americans.

1781 Aug 1: Yorktown, Va., was occupied by the British under Gen. Cornwallis, who sought supplies and reinforcements from Gen. Clinton in New York City.

1781 Sep 9: At **Eutaw Springs,** S.C., the American forces under Gen. Nathanael Greene were forced to withdraw after an assault upon the British under Col. Alexander Stewart.

1781 Oct 19: Gen. **Cornwallis surrendered at Yorktown.** The capitulation, which yielded about 8000 British prisoners, virtually brought the war to an end.

1782: An **emancipation law** was enacted by the Virginia legislature under urging by Thomas Jefferson. The bill made it lawful for any man "by last will and testament or other instrument in writing sealed and witnessed, to emancipate and set free his slaves."

1782: The **Great Seal of the United States** was adopted. It was first used on Sept. 16, 1782, on a document granting Gen. Washington authority to consult with the British about prisoner exchanges. On Sept. 15, 1789, Congress declared that the Great Seal was to be the official seal of the U.S. and that it was to be kept in custody of the secretary of state. Since then six dies of the seal have been officially cut and used.

1783: Slavery was made illegal in Massachusetts by a judicial interpretation of the state constitution of 1780, in which text stating that all men were "born free and equal" was construed as legal nullification of slavery. This year also saw the slave trade outlawed in Maryland.

1783 Sep 3: The **Treaty of Paris** was signed by representatives of the U. S. and Great Britain, thus ending the American Revolution. American independence was recognized by the British and the boundaries of the new republic agreed upon: the Great Lakes and Florida to the north and south, and the Mississippi R. to the west. Benjamin Franklin, John Jay, and John Adams were the American agents during the peace negotiations in Paris.

1784: Slavery was abolished in Connecticut and Rhode Island.

II. Architecture
Arts and Music
Popular Entertainment
Publishing
Theater

During the American Revolution and the early uncertain days of independence, American intellectual life continued its steady development. The American Academy of Arts and Sciences, the second oldest learned society in the U.S., was founded in Boston on May 4, 1780. The academy, like others of the period, was largely local but kept in touch with other groups. It joined, for example, in an unsuccessful attempt to have the duty on foreign books repealed. The academy began publishing *Memoirs* in 1785 and *Proceedings* in 1846. The moving spirit in starting the academy was James Bowdoin, a leading political figure in Massachusetts who, like many other public figures of the time, was interested in arts and sciences. He was the academy's first president. Bowdoin College in Maine was named for him.

1782: *M'Fingal* by John Trumbull was published in its complete form. The first two of its four sections had been published in 1775. A lively debate on revolutionary matters, it was for a time considered one of the greatest of the American poems.

1782: *Letters from an American Farmer* by J. Hector St. John de Crèvecoeur, an extremely popular book on early American life around the time of the American Revolution, was published. The author, whose real name was Michel Guillaume Jean de Crèvecoeur, was a Frenchman who settled in New York, where he collected his famous impressions of the New World. The *Letters* reflected the "noble savage" views of the eighteenth century. The book was reprinted five times in English and appeared in three French editions and two German translations. Crèvecoeur traveled extensively in America, became a naturalized citizen, and was an experienced woodsman and farmer. *Letters from an American Farmer* contains 12 letters reflecting in warm and vivid detail his knowledge of farm life, animals, and the geography of the colonies. He believed in the simple life espoused by Jean Jacques Rousseau and popularized the idea of the Physiocrats that the goodness of man was traced from his connection with the soil. Crèvecoeur in his writings idealized the new man who was to come from the American experiment.

1783: *The American Speller* by Noah Webster was published. It was the first part of Webster's *A Grammatical Institute of the English Language*, which included a grammar (1784) and a reader (1785). As a separate work, Webster's *Speller* supplanted for a time the *New England Primer* as the principal text for the early grades of public school. It included stories, aphorisms, and maxims on ethical behavior.

1783 May 30: The **first daily newspaper** in the U.S., the *Pennsylvania Evening Post* published by Benjamin Towne, began publication in Philadelphia, Pa.

III. Business and Industry
Education
Philosophy and Religion
Science

By the late eighteenth century medical scientists in Europe and America were questioning older practices and theories. In the U.S. Benjamin Rush was the foremost medical scientist of his time, and he typified the new attitude. He was the author of the earliest important work on mental disorders, *Medical Inquiries and Observations upon the Diseases of the Mind* (1812). Another of Rush's studies, *An Inquiry into the Effects of Spiritous Liquors on the Human Body and Mind* (1784), provided scientific support for the temperance movement. Rush, a signer of the Declaration of Independence, became the first professor of chemistry in America in 1769, at the College of Philadelphia and, at the University of Pennsylvania after 1792 he developed the best medical school in the U.S. Unfortunately, in spite of his pioneering investigations of the relationship of bodily and mental illnesses, Rush also remained a strong advocate of bloodletting and purging and so delayed discontinuance of these practices.

1781 Dec 31: The **Bank of North America** was established by Congress. Under the Articles of Confederation, Congress could not tax, so the Bank of North America was founded with a capitalization of $400,000 to supply the federal government with money.

1783: The **first Protestant Episcopal bishop** in America, Dr. Samuel Seabury, was elected by ten of his fellow ministers at Woodbury, Conn.

1784: A major **depression** crippled the U.S. economy, prompting the states to institute separate measures to aid recovery. The hardships suffered during this depression, which did not end until 1788, led to Shays' Rebellion in 1787.

1784: A lucrative new **trade route** was opened to American merchantmen when the *Empress of China* sailed from Sandy Hook, N.J., around Cape Horn with a cargo of ginseng root for which the Chinese were willing to pay enormous prices. The voyage lasted a year and was very profitable. The trade route enabled American commerce to recover from the crippling British blockade during the American Revolution. By 1789, eighteen American merchantmen were plying their way to the harbor of Canton. Salem, Mass., had become the main American port for the China trade.

1784 Nov 18: Samuel Seabury, the first American Protestant Episcopal bishop, was consecrated by the Scottish bishops in Aberdeen and Moray in contravention of the wishes of the Archbishop of Canterbury.

1784 Dec 24: The **Methodist Church** was organized in America at a conference in Baltimore, Md., even though in England the Methodists did not formally separate from the Church of England until 1791. John Wesley, the founder of Methodism, had sent the Rev. Thomas Coke to America this year as superintendent of the Methodist societies. Francis Asbury was to be associate superintendent. Asbury, however, dominated the conference, was elected superintendent, and then assumed the title of bishop. Although in ill health all his life, Asbury traveled on horseback more than 5000 miles a year to supervise and expand the Methodist Church.

IV. Fashion
Folkways
Holidays
Social Issues and Crime
Sports

American cabinetmakers and furniture designers were becoming the equal of any in artistic ability. Chief among them were William Savery, John Goddard, Jonathan Gostelow, and, beginning in the 1790s, Duncan Phyfe. Savery is believed to have lived in Philadelphia from about 1740 and was noted for his original interpretation of eighteenth-century English designs, especially the Queen Anne style. John Goddard was a member of a Newport, R.I., Quaker family of cabinetmakers. His pieces, especially his secretaries, were known for their stateliness. Goddard developed a characteristic block front design that divided the front of his pieces into three equal sections. Examples of Goddard's work are quite scarce. Gostelow worked in Philadelphia and showed originality at a time when many Americans were following English designs. His work had graceful but substantial lines rather than elaboration or ornamentation. In 1788 Gostelow was elected chairman of the Gentlemen Cabinet and Chair Makers of Philadelphia, and in 1789 he made and presented an elaborate font to Christ Church. Phyfe emigrated from

Scotland and about 1792 set up shop in New York. He was noted for his use of mahogany and held to high standards of workmanship. His early designs boasted excellent proportions and graceful curves. Later he adopted the Empire style. His final designs were heavily ornamented. He was so much copied that a Duncan Phyfe style came into being.

1783: The **pace of public transportation** in the U.S. was painfully slow. It took Thomas Jefferson five days to travel from Philadelphia to Baltimore.

1783: By this time some **100,000 Loyalists had fled the U.S.** Also known as Tories, they had suffered various penalties for their loyalty to the Crown, including confiscation of property, removal from public office, and punitive taxation. Probably no more than 10% of the colonials were Tories, who were generally well-to-do, engaged in commerce or the professions, or public officials. Many fled to Canada, some to England. Some returned after the war. Many, however, had remained behind. After the conflict many were able to recover at least some of their confiscated property.

1783 May 13: The **Society of Cincinnati** was founded by veteran officers of the American Revolution. Its membership was restricted to the eldest male descendants of Revolutionary soldiers. George Washington was its first president-general and Gen. Alexander Hamilton its second.

1785–1789

I. Civil Rights
Exploration and Settlement
Government
Statistics
Wars

In the nation's early years, it became clear that the Articles of Confederation, which had gone into effect in 1781, were inadequate for the effective government of the United States. On May 25, 1787, the Constitutional Convention convened in Philadelphia. Eventually, all the newly independent states except Rhode Island sent delegates to the session that at first was expected merely to amend the Articles of Confederation. As it turned out, the delegates wrote a new charter, the Constitution of the U.S. Many problems were solved after long debate, such as the question of fair representation for large and small states. This issue resulted in a compromise whereby in the Senate all states would be equally represented but in the House of Representatives representation would be based on population. George Washington was president of the convention and other leading delegates included Benjamin Franklin, James Madison, Gouverneur Morris, Roger Sherman, and Edmund Randolph. Final agreement was reached on Sept. 17 and the document was submitted to the states for ratification. This process reached a conclusion on June 21, 1788, by which time nine states had ratified, the number necessary to put the Constitution into effect. The debate had been long and aroused great passion along with much opposition. Eventually, the other four original states also ratified.

1785: Slavery was made illegal in New York.

1785 July 6: A new **coinage system,** based on the Spanish milled dollar, was proposed in Congress by Thomas Jefferson. He proposed a gold piece with a value of ten dollars, a dollar in silver, a tenth of a dollar in silver, and a hundredth of a dollar in copper. This proposal was adopted by Congress, and on Aug. 8, 1786, a full plan of coinage was enacted.

1786: Slavery was outlawed in New Jersey.

1787 Jan 25: Shays' Rebellion, a farmers' uprising named for its leader Daniel Shays, reached its climax when Shays led 1100 men in an attempt to seize the arsenal in Springfield, Mass. State militia commanded by Gen. William Shepherd routed the insurgents. The uprising had been caused by the harsh economic conditions faced by Massachusetts farmers, who sought reforms and the issuance of paper money.

1787 July 13: The **Northwest Ordinance,** enacted by Congress under the Articles of Confederation, established the Northwest Territory, the region bounded by the Great Lakes on the north, the Ohio R. on the south, and the Mississippi R. on the west. The ordinance established a government for the territory, provided that it could form no fewer than three nor more than five states, set up the procedure by which statehood was to be achieved, and barred slavery in the territory.

1787 Dec 7: Delaware became the first state to ratify the Constitution.

1787 Dec 12: Pennsylvania ratified the Constitution and became the second state of the Union.

1787 Dec 18: New Jersey ratified the Constitution and became the third state of the Union.

1788 Jan 2: Georgia ratified the Constitution and became the fourth state of the Union.

1788 Jan 9: Connecticut ratified the Constitution and became the fifth state of the Union.

1788 Feb 6: Massachusetts ratified the Constitution and became the sixth state of the Union.

1788 Apr 28: Maryland ratified the Constitution and became the seventh state of the Union.

1788 May 23: South Carolina ratified the Constitution and became the eighth state of the Union.

1788 June 21: New Hampshire ratified the Constitution and became the ninth state of the Union. With this ratification the Constitution became effective, though not declared in effect until Mar. 4, 1789.

1788 June 25: Virginia ratified the Constitution and became the tenth state of the Union.

1788 July 26: New York ratified the Constitution and became the 11th state of the Union. For a time North Carolina and Rhode Island refused to ratify, but the introduction of a bill of rights and the threat of economic sanctions eventually induced them to join.

1788 Sep 30-1790 Aug 31: In the **first congressional elections** under the Constitution the federalists gained a 17–9 Senate majority over the antifederalists. In the House the federalists took a 38–26 majority. Senators were chosen by state legislatures until 1913, when the Seventeenth Amendment provided for their popular election. Members of the House were elected by popular vote, but some states held statewide elections and others held elections by district. Also, some states held elections in odd-numbered years, a practice that faded out in the late nineteenth century.

1789: The **Federalist Party** was formed by those who had supported ratification of the Constitution. Considered pro-English, they enjoyed considerable success until 1800, when Thomas Jefferson, a Democratic-Republican, defeated John Adams for the presidency. Eventually the party lost its supporters and ceased to exist about 1820. Alexander Hamilton was one of the party's founders and foremost leaders.

1789 Mar 4: The **first session of the U.S. Congress** convened, but only 9 of 22 senators and 13 of 59 representatives appeared. The House had its first quorum on Apr. 1, the Senate on Apr. 5. On Apr. 6 the first Congress was formally organized.

1789 Apr 30: George Washington, Federalist of Virginia, was inaugurated president of the United States.

1789 July 27: The U.S. **State Department** was established by Congress. Thomas Jefferson became the first secretary of state in Feb. 1790.

1789 Aug 7: The U.S. **War Department** was established. Pres. Washington selected Henry Knox to be the first secretary of war. At this time the regular army numbered 840 men who supervised public lands and guarded the Indian frontier.

1789 Sep 2: The U.S. **Treasury Department** was established by Congress. Alexander Hamilton became the first secretary of the treasury.

1789 Sep 26: Congress confirmed John Jay's appointment as the **first chief justice of the U.S. Supreme Court.** He was appointed by Pres. Washington and served for six years.

1789 Sep 26: Samuel Osgood was appointed the **first postmaster general** of the U.S. by Pres. Washington. Osgood resigned in Aug. 1791 because of the government's removal from New York City to Philadelphia.

1789 Sep 26: Edmund J. Randolph was appointed **attorney general** of the U.S. by Pres. Washington. In 1794 he succeeded Thomas Jefferson as secretary of state.

1789 Nov 21: North Carolina ratified the Constitution and became the 12th state of the Union.

II. Architecture
Arts and Music
Popular Entertainment
Publishing
Theater

The leading publishing event of the period was the serial publication, beginning Oct. 27, 1787, of *The Federalist*, probably the greatest American work on political theory. This series of essays, an outgrowth of the debate over adoption of the Constitution, began with the intent of persuading New York State and others to ratify the new document. The last essay was published on Apr. 4, 1788. The series of 85 essays was initiated by Alexander Hamilton of New York, who wrote at least 51 of the papers. James Madison of Virginia wrote 14 and John Jay of New York wrote five. The authorship of the other 15 is debatable as between Hamilton and Madison. The essays were widely read as they appeared in newspapers, but actually had little effect on the debate over ratification. They did, however, make clear the basic problems of republican government and defended federalism as a means of creating a strong state while perserving individuals from tyranny. The essays appeared in book form in two volumes published between March and May of 1788.

1786: The **first extended theatrical engagements** in America were seen this year. Lewis Hallam, Jr.'s, American Company, performing in New York City, gave seven performances of Richard Brinsley Sheridan's *The School for Scandal* (1777) and 18 of John O'Keefe's *The Poor Soldier.* This year also saw the first U.S. performance of *Hamlet,* in New York City at the John Street Theater by Hallam's company with the Irish actor John Henry.

1787 Apr 16: *The Contrast* by Royall Tyler, the first American comedy to be performed on a regular stage by a company of professional actors, opened at the John Street Theater in New York City. It became an immediate success. The first stage Yankee in American history appeared as the hero in this pro-democratic play, which ridiculed aristocratic values while extolling the rustic virtues of the hero.

1788: A volume of *Miscellaneous Works* by Philip Freneau was published. This book, combined with Freneau's collected *Poems* (1786), marked Freneau's emergence as a major American poet. Some memorable poems appeared in these volumes, for example, "To the Hurricane" and "The Indian Burying Ground." "The Wild Honey Suckle" was considered Freneau's finest poem.

1789: What has been called the **first American novel,** *The Power of Sympathy; or The Triumph of Nature* by William Hill Brown, was published. The book was written "to expose the dangerous Consequences of Seduction and to set forth the advantages of female Education."

1789: The **Virginia Capitol** was built at Richmond from plans by Thomas Jefferson. It was generally considered the first building of the Classic Revival style in the U.S.

1789 Mar 2: **A law prohibiting theatrical performances** was repealed in Pennsylvania. A more permissive attitude toward theater was seen in all the states.

III. Business and Industry
Education
Philosophy and Religion
Science

Unitarianism took root in the U.S. during this period. Although the foundations of Unitarianism—the belief that God exists in only one being rather than in the trinity of Father, Son, and Holy Spirit—originated in the sixteenth century, it was 1785 before the doctrine came to the U.S. The Unitarian movement in America originated from a change in the Episcopalian liturgy at King's Chapel in Boston. The clergyman responsible was James Freeman, a Harvard graduate. In 1796 Joseph Priestley, the English scientist, established a Unitarian church in Philadelphia. Separate congregations gradually formed themselves into a denomination, adopting the name Unitarian about 1815. Unitarianism grew out of the liberal wing of Congregationalism and was strongest in New England.

1785: **Regular stage routes** linking New York City, Boston, Albany, and Philadelphia were initiated. The trip from Boston to New York took six days with coaches traveling from 3 A.M. until 10 P.M.

1785: The **first American turnpike,** known as the Little River Turnpike, was authorized by the state of Virginia.

1785: The charter of the **Bank of North America** was revoked by the Pennsylvania legislature. The bank's enemies charged it with causing the economic depression that had begun in 1784. When things did not get better, supporters of the bank claimed that trade was bad because the bank's charter had been lost. In 1787 Democratic-Republicans won control of the state legislature and rechartered the bank. It was the first bank owned and operated by and for merchants. It acquired capital and influence so quickly that it became a center of political rivalry and ambition.

1786: The **first steamboat in America,** built by John Fitch, sailed on the Delaware R. On Aug. 22, 1787, Fitch ran his second and improved boat on the Delaware R. It used a system of upright paddles at the sides of the boat and attained a speed of three mph.

1786: The first recorded **strike** in the U.S. was called by the printers of Philadelphia, Pa. They were successful in obtaining a wage of $6 a week.

1787: The **first cotton factory** in New England was established at Beverly, Mass., under the management of John Cabot and Joshua Fisher.

1787: In a move to promote **manufacturing,** the Pennsylvania Society for the Encouragement of Manufactures and Useful Acts was organized. It supported a protective tariff, inventions, and research. Its Committee on Manufactures, chosen by subscribers to a manufacturing fund, agreed to promote cotton manufacturing and ordered two English carding and spinning machines. By the end of 1788, its factory put out 10,000 yards of cotton and linen. New York City, Boston, and Baltimore established similar societies in the same year, and were soon followed by other cities.

1789 July 4: The **first tariff bill** enacted by Congress set up protective duties on more than 30 different commodities.

IV. Fashion
Folkways
Holidays
Social Issues and Crime
Sports

The widely practiced custom of bundling, prevalent in colonial days in New England and Pennsylvania especially, was dying out. The cold of northern winters, which had been a major contributor to the custom's popularity, was now alleviated by better heating and sturdier houses. To bundle, engaged or courting couples got into bed together, but with most or all of their clothes on. The couple was sometimes separated by a board and some girls tied their ankles together. Although bundling implied no improper relationship, it became the target of reformers and was abandoned by the early nineteenth century, although there were reports of bundling in the backwoods of western Pennsylvania in the 1840s.

c1785: The style of **men's clothing** during this period was reflected in a description by a printer of Boston: "He wore a pea-green coat, white vest, nankeen small clothes, white silk stockings, and pumps fastened with silver buckles which covered at least half the foot from instep to toe. His small clothes were tied at the knees with ribbon of the same colour in double bows, the ends reaching down to the ancles. His hair in front was loaded with pomatum, frizzled or craped and powdered. Behind, his natural hair was augmented by the addition of a large queue called vulgarly a false tail, which, enrolled in some yards of black ribbon, hung half-way down his back."

1788 May: A celebrated gray stallion, **Messenger,** believed to be the original sire of a fine breed of trotting horses, arrived from England. His line was so successful that upon his death he was buried with military honors on Jan. 8, 1808.

1789: The beginning of a **social courtesy** that was soon to spread elsewhere was seen in the following announcement at a performance in the Park Theater, New York City: "The offensive practice to Ladies, and dangerous to the House, of smoking segars during the performance, it is hoped, every gentlemen will consent to an absolute prohibition of."

1789 May 7: The **first inaugural ball,** to honor Pres. Washington, was held at the Assembly Rooms, New York City.

1789 May 12: The **Society of Tammany** held its first meeting in New York. Its name was derived from an ancient and wise chief of the Delaware Indians, Tammany, and the society was essentially anti-Federalist in character. Its chief founder and first grand sachem was William Mooney.

1789 Nov 26: Thanksgiving Day was celebrated for the first time as a national holiday. Pres. Washington, at the request of Congress, had proclaimed it a day of thanksgiving for the Constitution. Anti-Federalists protested that his proclamation violated states' rights.

1790–1794

I. Civil Rights
Exploration and Settlement
Government
Statistics
Wars

Probably the most important political event of this period was adoption of the Bill of Rights, the first ten amendments to the U.S. Constitution. Some had opposed adoption of the Constitution because of its lack of guarantees of such rights as freedom of worship, freedom of speech, freedom of the press, and freedom of assembly. Supporters of the Constitution had promised that if ratified, it would be amended in these respects. Accordingly, on Sept. 25, 1789, Congress voted to submit the amendments to the states. They became part of the Constitution on Dec. 15, 1791, when Virginia ratified them, thereby completing the required number of state ratifications for passage into law.

1790-1791: In **congressional elections** the Federalists took a 16–13 Senate majority over the Republicans. In the House the Federalists led 37–33.

1790 Mar 1: The **first U.S. Census** was authorized by Congress. It was completed on Aug. 1. The population was placed at 3,929,625 including 697,624 slaves and 59,557 free blacks. The most populous state was Virginia, with 747,610 people, and the largest city was Philadelphia, with a population of 42,444. The center of U.S. population was about equally divided between New England and the Middle Atlantic States, and the South. Massachusetts was the only state to report no slaves.

1790 Apr 10: The **first circumnavigation of the globe by an American vessel** was accomplished when Capt. Robert Gray docked the *Columbia* in Boston harbor. On a voyage for a group of Boston merchants, Gray had sailed from Boston in Sept. 1787 with a cargo of goods to be traded for furs with Indians of the Pacific Northwest. Gray then carried a valuable cargo of sea otter skins to Canton, China, and sailed on around the world, a voyage of almost 42,000 miles. His trip opened up trade between New England and the Pacific Northwest, which brought great wealth to New England merchants. The trip also helped establish U.S. claims to the Oregon Territory. On May 11, 1792, during a second voyage, Gray became the first white man to enter the Columbia R.

1790 Apr 17: Benjamin Franklin died in Philadelphia at 84. Lord Jeffrey, editor of the *Edinburgh Review,* wrote of him: "In one point of view the name of Franklin must be considered as standing higher than any of the others which illustrated the Eighteenth Century. Distinguished as a statesman he was equally great as a philosopher, thus united in himself a rare degree of excellence in both these pursuits, to excel in either of which is deemed the highest praise." Franklin's funeral and burial in Christ Church Yard drew 20,000 spectators, the largest gathering in the U.S. to that time.

1790 May 29: Rhode Island ratified the Constitution and became the 13th state of the Union.

1790 May 31: The **first U.S. copyright act** was signed by Pres. George Washington. The new law protected plays, maps, and books. The term of protection was for 14 years, with the right of renewal for another 14 years. The work's title page had to be deposited in the clerk's office of the local U.S. district court. Passage of the law was credited largely to the efforts of Noah Webster. Until the eighteenth century copyright had remained, on the whole, a matter of common law, and protection ebbed and flowed with the tides of political fortune. But in 1710 Parliament passed the Statute of Anne, which provided protection for up to 28 years. It became standard in the colonies as well as in England. After the American Revolution, however, the various states were lax about establishing copyright prerogatives. When Webster was ready to publish his *American Spelling Book,* he soon discovered that he would have no say in the disposition of his work. He began a tour of the states to campaign for new legislation. His campaign for a uniform copyright law coincided with the Federalists' desire for a strong central government, and the measure was passed.

1791 Mar 3: The **first internal revenue law** was passed by Congress. Fourteen revenue districts were created and a tax of 20 to 30 cents a gallon put on distilled spirits. The legislatures of North Carolina, Virginia, and Maryland passed resolutions of disapproval shortly thereafter.

1791 Mar 4: Vermont joined the Union, becoming the 14th state. It had ratified the Constitution in January.

1792-1793: In **congressional elections** the Federalists held a 17–13 Senate majority over the Republicans. In the House the Republicans took a 57–48 majority over the Federalists.

1792: The **Republican Party,** also known as the Demo-cratic-Republican or Antifederalist Party, was formed. This party later became the Democratic Party. It was formed to oppose the Federalists, who were considered pro-English and against a republi-can form of government. Thomas Jefferson, who was sympathetic toward the French Revolution, became party leader. The Republicans enjoyed overwhelm-ing popularity until 1820.

1792 Apr 2: Congress passed the **Coinage Act,** estab-lishing the first U.S. Mint, to be constructed in Phila-delphia, Pa. The act provided for a decimal system of coinage and a standard of bimetallism, with silver and gold as legal tender at a ratio of 15 to 1 by weight. David Rittenhouse, the astronomer and instrument maker who had succeeded Benjamin Franklin as president of the American Philosophical Society in 1791, was named first director of the mint.

1792 June 1: Kentucky became the 15th state. It previ-ously had been part of Virginia territory.

1792 Dec 5: George Washington was reelected presi-dent of the United States. John Adams was elected vice president. The electoral vote was Washington, 132; Adams, Federalist of Massachusetts, 77; George Clinton, Antifederalist of New York, 50.

1794-1795: In **congressional elections** the Federalists gained two Senate seats for a 19–13 majority. In the House they gained six seats for a 54–52 majority.

1794 July-Nov: The **Whiskey Rebellion** broke out in western Pennsylvania among farmers opposed to a federal excise tax on liquor passed in 1791. On Aug. 7 Pres. Washington issued a proclamation ordering the insurgents to go home and calling out a militia force of several thousand from four states. He issued another proclamation on Sept. 24 and ordered the militia to suppress the uprising. For a time Washing-ton led this force in person. By mid-November the trouble was over. Two men were convicted of treason but Washington pardoned them.

1794 Nov 19: The **Jay Treaty** was concluded between Great Britain and the U.S. It was widely denounced in America because it continued to allow the British the right to search U.S. ships and impress American seamen on the grounds that they were actually of British birth and citizenship.

**II. Architecture
Arts and Music
Popular Entertainment
Publishing
Theater**

Scientists traveled widely in the U.S. because there was much to study that was new and because there were unique flora and fauna. Invariably, such men wrote about their journeys. While these men wrote as scientists, their writings can also be categorized as travel books. The travelers gloried in the beauty and magnitude of American scenery and often were imbued with the spirit of the Romantic movement. Such a naturalist-author was William Bartram, son of John Bartram, who had earlier recorded his trips to Lake Ontario and Florida. William wrote *Travels Through North and South Carolina, Georgia, East and West Florida, the Cherokee Country, the Extensive Territories of the Muscogulges, or Creek Confederacy, and the Country of the Chactaws* (1791). In the book Bartram revealed a vision of "natural man." His enthusiastic descriptions of scenery influenced such writers as William Wordsworth and Samuel Taylor Coleridge, the latter terming the book one of "high merit."

1790: Printing began on ***Dobson's Encyclopaedia,*** a magnificent American edition in 18 volumes of the *Encyclopaedia Britannica.* Special types were prepared for the task, and a great number of engravings of fine workmanship were made on Pennsylvania paper. Printing required seven years, the cost of the venture being covered by subscription. When completed, the encyclopedia was hailed as the greatest achievement of the press in America up to that time.

1791 Mar: The first part of ***The Rights of Man*** by Thomas Paine was published in England. An incendiary document, it attacked monarchy, supported the French Revolution, and argued forcibly in favor of democracy, republican government, and personal freedom and rights. The British government considered the work seditious and charged Paine with treason. He fled to France in 1792, was tried in absentia, and was banished from Great Britain.

1792: The cornerstone of the **Capitol** was laid in Washington, D.C. The building was completed about 1830, though it was in use before then. It was designed by William Thornton following lines of English country mansions in the Palladian mode.

1792: Work on the **White House** in Washington, D.C., was begun, following plans by James Hoban. The building was a sumptuous example of post-colonial architecture, modeled after the palace of the Duke of Leinster in Ireland. Burned by the British in 1814, it was rebuilt in 1818 and restored in 1951.

1793: ***American Poems, Selected and Original,*** an anthology of poems selected by Elihu Hubbard Smith, was published at Litchfield, Conn. The anthology was devoted largely to the group of writers who became known as the Hartford Wits or Connecticut Wits, including John Trumbull, Joel Barlow, Timothy Dwight, and Lemuel Hopkins, all of whom were friends of Smith.

1793: **New York City's first daily newspaper** and the second daily in the country, the *American Minerva,* was founded by Noah Webster. He edited the paper for ten years, during which time it was strongly Federalist and anti-French. In 1797 the name was changed to the *Commercial Advertiser.* In 1905 the *Advertiser* in turn was combined with the New York *Globe,* which in turn was absorbed by the New York *Sun* in 1923.

1794: The **Boston Theater** was opened under the management of Charles Stuart Powell after repeal of the law of 1750 prohibiting plays in Boston.

1794: The first part of ***The Age of Reason*** by Thomas Paine was published in Paris. This deistic work was written with frequently faulty logic but unmistakable fervor and conviction. The book had a profound effect and was especially popular with common people, who resented religious as well as political tyranny. On Dec. 27, 1793, after completing the first part of the book, Paine was thrown into prison for his opposition to the Reign of Terror then raging in revolutionary France. He completed the rest of his book under the shadow of the guillotine, and it was published on his release in 1795.

III. Business and Industry
Education
Philosophy and Religion
Science

Although the U.S. was primarily an agricultural nation, some manufacturing had begun. There were those who thought that with independence the new nation should encourage manufacturing as a way of avoiding dependence on other nations. Chief among these persons was Alexander Hamilton, first secretary of the treasury, who submitted his *Report on the Subject of Manufactures* in 1791. The report favored tariffs and government bounties and said such policies would create employment, attract immigrants, and stimulate investment. Hamilton, however, received little support. Merchant and shipping interests had more to gain from free trade, and the expanding cotton regions of the South did not want tariffs that would increase their costs.

1790 July 31: The **U.S. Patent Office** was opened. It has been said that a dozen men from Connecticut were waiting at the door, a colorful way of noting that traditionally more inventors from Connecticut have registered patents than from any other state. However, the first U.S. patent was issued to Samuel Hopkins of Vermont for a new method of making pearlash and potash.

1790 Aug 4: Interest-bearing **government bonds** were authorized by Congress. The 6% bonds were sold to pay off the federal debt.

1790 Aug 15: The **first Roman Catholic bishop** in the U.S., Father John Carroll, was consecrated at Lulworth Castle, England. He was selected by Pope Pius VI, who also chose Baltimore as the first episcopal see in America. Bishop Carroll held his first synod on Nov. 7, 1791.

1790 Dec 21: The **cotton mill** of Almy, Brown, and Slater began operation in Pawtucket, R.I., using British industrial methods. Samuel Slater had come to America with a thorough understanding of the new machinery invented in Britain by Richard Arkwright, Samuel Crompton, and James Hargreaves. His factory was manned by children between four and ten years of age. Slater was the first American industrialist to break down the production process into simple parts, enabling child labor to outproduce skilled artisans.

1791 Dec 12: The **Bank of the U.S.** opened its main branch in Philadelphia and additional branches in the main urban centers of America. The bank served the federal government as its fiscal representative.

1792: The first important **wooden truss bridge**, invented to suit American needs, was completed by Col. Ewel Hale at Bellows Falls, Vt. Wood was plentiful in the area but rafts and barges would have been impeded by a bridge built on piles or with rows of arches. Hale's bridge consisted of two spans of 175 ft. each resting on an island.

1792 May 17: The **New York Stock Exchange** was organized at the Merchants Coffee House, New York City.

1793 May 25: The **first Roman Catholic priest ordained** in the U.S., Father Stephen Theodore Badin, was ordained in Baltimore, Md. He was a refugee from the French Revolution. After his ordination he served in Kentucky where he dedicated the first Catholic chapel in Lexington in 1800.

1793 Oct 28: Eli Whitney of Mulberry Grove, Ga., filed an application for a patent on the cotton gin. The patent was granted on Mar. 14, 1794. Cotton production mounted spectacularly after Whitney's invention, rising from 138,000 lbs. exported in 1800. Whitney, however, received very little in return for his invention. His machine's operating principle was stolen or duplicated by others in spite of his patent, and powerful interests opposed his fight for royalties. In 1812 Congress refused to renew his patent.

1794: The first independent **Methodist Church for blacks** was established in Philadelphia by Richard Allen, a former slave. In 1816 Allen became the first bishop of the African Methodist Episcopal Church when 16 black congregations united to form the new denomination.

1794: The first major **turnpike** in America was completed between Philadelphia and Lancaster, Pa. The large profits that could be realized by sponsoring such a company led to the construction of many such roads throughout America, often in areas where they were not necessary. Lancaster Turnpike, 62 mi. long, was the first macadam road in the U.S.

1794: One of the earliest American **canals** was built to circumnavigate South Hadley's falls on the Connecticut R. in Massachusetts. Its lift operated by means of inclined planes and cables powered by the current. At about the same time construction of the Middlesex Canal from Boston to the Merrimack R. was begun. Its first section opened in 1804. The Middlesex Canal was 27 miles long, and it cost about $3.50 for a standard barge to go its length. The sizes of the barges were fixed by regulations. The barges were pulled by horses.

IV. Fashion
   Folkways
   Holidays
   Social Issues and Crime
   Sports

During and after the American Revolution patriotic societies sprang up in several cities. Among them were the Tammany societies founded in New York City, Philadelphia, and other cities. The societies were named for the Delaware Indian chief Tammany, who was said to have welcomed William Penn to Pennsylvania. The Tammany Society, or Columbian Order of New York City, was formed in 1786 and incorporated in 1789. The first Columbus Day was celebrated on Oct. 12, 1792, under the auspices of this society. The New York Tammany was the only such society to have a long life, and it became the most powerful political organization in the city in the nineteenth century. Its headquarters, Tammany Hall, became a symbol of graft, corruption, and machine politics in the 1860s and 1870s. The organization maintained substantial political influence well into the twentieth century.

1790: New York City, the state's capital, had a population of 30,000 and five markets. Gov. George Clinton moved into Government House to save the $750 per year rent he was paying for his own house.

1790: The phrase *not worth a continental* expressed a common attitude toward the continental currency issued by Congress at the end of the American Revolution. Paper money valued at $200,000,000 shrank rapidly in purchasing power until it took $40 in paper to buy one silver dollar.

1790: The **Pennsylvania system** of prison management, based on the concept of absolute solitary confinement, was introduced at the Walnut St. Prison in Philadelphia. It was supposed to promote moral regeneration by means of enforced meditation. The philosophy of the Pennsylvania system was opposed to that of the later Auburn system, which was initiated by the state penitentiary in Auburn, N.Y., in 1816, and which permitted congregation of prisoners during the day. At night, however, Auburn prisoners slept in separate cells. In general, the Auburn system came to prevail in the U.S.

1790 Dec 6: Philadelphia became the nation's capital when Congress opened its legislative session there. On July 10, 1790, the House of Representatives had approved, by a vote of 32 to 29, the move from New York City to Philadelphia as part of a deal to establish a permanent capital. Congress had authorized George Washington to select a site for a new capital on the Potomac R. Philadelphia remained the nation's capital until 1800, when Washington, D.C., became the permanent seat of government. In 1799 Philadelphia had ceased to be the capital of Pennsylvania when the state government moved to Lancaster.

1792: The first edition of ***The Farmer's Almanac*** was published. Edited by Robert Bailey Thomas, a native of Grafton, Mass., it contained much information about New England life and manners along with valuable data on weather and other practical matters. Its homespun flavor and its depiction of New England ways captivated readers and turned the almanac into an American institution. Thomas, until his death in 1746, edited *The Farmer's Almanac,* later retitled *The Old Farmer's Almanac* to differentiate it from its numerous imitators.

1792 June 1: Statehood Day in Kentucky was instituted to commemorate admission of the Blue Grass State to the Union on this date.

1792 Oct 12: The first celebration of **Columbus Day** in America was held in New York City under the auspices of the Society of St. Tammany. St. Tammany had been chosen as the patron saint in a spirit of ridicule since he had been an Indian savant. The ridicule was directed at such societies as those of St. George, St. Andrew, and St. David.

1794: Powdering of men's hair went out of fashion after more than 100 years. However, men's hair was still worn in a queue tied with a black ribbon.

1795–1799

I. Civil Rights
Exploration and Settlement
Government
Statistics
Wars

What came to be known as the XYZ Affair marked a new low in Franco-American relations at the end of the eighteenth century. A three-man commission, consisting of Elbridge Gerry, John Marshall, and Charles Cotesworth Pinckney, was sent to France in 1797 by Pres. John Adams to negotiate a treaty of commerce and amity. The French foreign minister, Charles Maurice de Talleyrand, refused to deal with them directly and instead on Oct. 18 sent three agents who later were designated X, Y, and Z in the reports of the American delegation. The French agents suggested that the U.S. make a loan to France and also offer a bribe of about $250,000 to Talleyrand. The Americans refused, with Pinckney replying, "No, no, not a sixpence." On Apr. 3, 1798, Pres. Adams submitted the XYZ correspondence to Congress, and the disclosure aroused great resentment in the U.S. against France.

1795 Jan 29: The **Naturalization Act** was passed. It required a residence period of five years and renunciation of allegiances and titles of nobility as prerequisites to citizenship.

1796-1797: In **congressional elections** the Federalists gained one Senate seat for a 20–12 majority over the Republicans. In the House the Federalists gained four seats for a 58–48 majority.

1796 June 1: Tennessee became the 16th state of the Union.

1796 Sep 17: What has come to be known as **Washington's Farewell Address** was delivered by Pres. Washington before Congress. One of the outstanding American political documents, the address warned against America's involvement in foreign disputes and thus paved the way for the isolationist policy of the nineteenth century.

1796 Dec: John Adams was elected president of the United States. Adams was the last Federalist candidate to gain the presidency. The electoral vote was Adams, 71; Thomas Jefferson, Democratic-Republican of Virginia, 68; Aaron Burr, Democratic-Republican of New York, 30; and Thomas Pinckney, Federalist of South Carolina, 59. Jefferson, the candidate with the second highest electoral vote, became vice president.

1798-1799: In congressional elections the Federalists lost one Senate seat but held a 19–13 majority over the Republicans. In the House they gained six seats for a 64–42 majority.

1798: The **first secretary of the Navy** was appointed by Pres. Adams. He was Benjamin Stoddert, and he found himself with a weak navy in a time of trouble with France. Within two years he acquired 50 ships and planned a marine corps, naval hospital, and dock yards.

1798 Jan 8: The **Eleventh Amendment** to the Constitution was adopted. It stipulated that federal courts shall not have jurisdiction over litigation between individuals from one state against individuals from another state.

1798 June 18: The first of four acts known collectively as the **Alien and Sedition Acts,** amending the Naturalization Act of 1795, was adopted. The act required of prospective citizens a residence period of 14 years and a declaration of intention for five years.

1798 June 25: The **Alien Act,** second of the Alien and Sedition Acts, was passed, granting the president power for two years to deport any alien he deemed dangerous to the country's safety.

1798 July 6: The **Alien Enemies Act,** third of the Alien and Sedition Acts, was passed. It provided for the apprehension and deportation of male aliens who were subjects or citizens of a hostile country.

1798 July 14: The **Sedition Act,** fourth and last of the Alien and Sedition Acts, was passed. It provided for arrest and imprisonment of any person who attempted to impede the lawful processes of government, foment insurrection, or write, publish, or utter any false or malicious statement about the president, Congress, or government of the U.S. The Alien and Sedition Acts reflected the panic of the Federalist Party in the face of the XYZ Affair, the general conflict with France, and the growing strength of the Democratic-Republican Party. Intended to curb domestic opposition, the acts caused confusion and injustice and brought the Federalist Party ultimately into contempt, political defeat, and dissolution.

II. Architecture
Arts and Music
Popular Entertainment
Publishing
Theater

After American independence was won, more and more periodicals began to be published, with over 70 appearing before 1800. Most of them did not last long. Among the periodicals were *Columbian Magazine* (1786–1792), *Massachusetts Magazine* (1786–1796), *New York Magazine* (1790–1797), and *Monthly Magazine and American Review.* The last one was established in New York in April of 1799 by Charles Brockden Brown, the nation's first professional novelist. In 1801 it became a quarterly under the title *American Review and Literary Journal;* it published until the end of 1802. Brown also edited the *Literary Magazine and American Register* from its founding in Philadelphia in 1803 until 1807, when it too failed. Most magazines of the time carried a mix of educational, literary, and scientific material.

1796: Gilbert Stuart completed his portrait *George Washington,* probably the most famous portrait of the first president. It also came to be known as the Athenaeum head. Stuart made numerous tries before this successful result. Nothing but the head of Washington can be seen, his character being derived from his facial features alone. This likeness is the accepted one and has become familiar to millions. The portrait was placed in the Boston Athenaeum, and later on permanent loan to the Boston Museum of Fine Arts.

1799: The ***Baltimore American,*** the first newspaper outside Washington, D.C., to give verbatim reports of Congressional debates, began publication. The paper published for 130 years.

III. Business and Industry
Education
Philosophy and Religion
Science

Both in the U.S. and abroad, the day of the general scientists, who took many fields of inquiry as their province, was coming to an end. Professional, or at least more specialized, scientists were taking over. An outstanding example of the generalists who had contributed so much to eighteenth-century progress was Samuel Latham Mitchill. His accomplishments and interests revealed the scope of his life's work. Mitchill established the first medical journal, *Medical Repository,* in 1797; was professor of natural history at Columbia College from 1798 to 1801; published the first good description of the geology of eastern New York State in 1798; was professor of the College of Physicians and Surgeons in New York City from 1807 to 1826; and served in the New York State Assembly and the House of Representatives and the U.S. Senate. In addition, he introduced into American science the chemical nomenclature of Antoine Lavoisier, founder of modern chemistry, and by 1814 was the foremost zoologist as a result of his work on the fish of New York.

1796: The first experiments with **gas illumination** were conducted in Philadelphia, Pa.

1796: The first important **suspension bridge** in the U.S. was built between Uniontown and Greensborough, Pa., over Jacob's Creek. The bridge, no longer standing, was based on a principle of suspension developed mainly by James Finley of Fayette County, Pa.

1797: The first U.S. **clock patent** was awarded to Eli Terry for his newly devised method of employing wooden works in his clocks. Terry's clocks were sold rather cheaply—$18 to $70—and sales were brisk. Terry became the first manufacturer to use water power to cut parts.

1797 June 26: The first U.S. **plow patent** was issued to Charles Newbold of New Jersey. After expending his entire fortune in developing a practical plow of cast iron, Newbold was unable to sell it to farmers because of their fear of harmful effects of iron on soil. Thomas Jefferson had made the first studies of plows in America and designed a moldboard plow according to the distinctive requirements of American soil, but he never applied for a patent.

1798: The revolutionary concept of manufacturing **interchangeable parts** was incorporated by Eli Whitney in production of firearms for the U.S. government.

1798 Dec 14: A patent for a **screw threading machine** was awarded to David Wilkinson of Rhode Island. In Aug. 1848, Congress awarded Wilkinson $10,000 for his invention.

IV. Fashion
Folkways
Holidays
Social Issues and Crime
Sports

Americans—at least those who could afford to—dined well and heartily on holiday occasions, as the menus of some presidential Christmas dinners indicated. A Christmas menu from Mount Vernon showed that George and Martha Washington served 34 different dishes and wines on one holiday, beginning with onion soup and ending with port and Madeira. Five different meat dishes were available. In the White House John and Abigail Adams called one of their holiday repasts "A Most Sinful Feast."

Among the 29 dishes was "Skillet Cranberries for a Slack Oven."

1796: A social trend away from **capital punishment** was reflected in reforms in the criminal code of Virginia, which reduced the number of crimes for which capital punishment was decreed.

1796: **Travel** between the cities of America frequently presented challenges and dangers to tradesmen and vacationers. Harried travelers on the Philadelphia–Baltimore roads complained of chasms six to ten feet deep along the way. They were lucky when their vehicles did not overturn. It sometimes took a stagecoach five days to make a trip.

1797: A new **water supply** for Philadelphia, Pa., drawing from the Schuylkill R., went into operation. There were three underground tunnels for distributing water in the city, and these were supplied from a tower in the center of the city. This was the first attempt in the U.S. to construct a centralized water distribution system.

1798 June 18: **"Millions for defense, but not one cent for tribute"** entered American political history at a banquet at O'Eller's Tavern in Philadelphia, Pa., in honor of John Marshall, one of the three presidential envoys to French Foreign Minister Charles Maurice de Talleyrand-Périgord. Honored by the Federalists for refusing a bribe by one of Talleyrand's agents, Marshall listened to 16 toasts in honor of his part in the XYZ Affair. The 13th toast, proposed by Rep. Robert Goodloe Harper, Federalist of South Carolina, contained the well-known phrase. Although the statement was correctly attributed to Harper in Philadelphia's *American Daily Advertiser* on June 20, the expression came to be identified with Charles Cotesworth Pinckney, another of the American envoys to whom the bribe request had been directed. Pinckney, shortly before his death, denied ever having made the statement, but because the expression seemed more apt as a diplomatic reply than as a toast, the legend persisted that Pinckney had spoken these words to the French agent.

1799 Dec 26: **"First in war, first in peace, first in the hearts of his countrymen,"** forever associated with George Washington, was first said as part of Henry Lee's funeral oration before Congress, after Washington's death on Dec. 14. Lee, known as "Light Horse Harry" Lee, had served under Washington in the Revolution and become his close friend. He was the father of Robert E. Lee. On the same day as Lee's eulogy, the House of Representatives passed a resolution incorporating Lee's words almost verbatim: "First in war, first in peace, first in the hearts of his fellow citizens."

1800

I. Civil Rights
Exploration and Settlement
Government
Statistics
Wars

This year's contest for the presidency revealed a sharp political division between the Federalist Party and the Republican, or Democratic-Republican, Party (forerunner of the Democratic Party). The Federalists, advocates of a strong central government and representing the well-to-do business class, chose as their candidate Pres. John Adams. The Republicans, the party of limited government and the agricultural interests, selected Thomas Jefferson of Virginia. The Constitution provided for each elector in the electoral college to vote for two candidates. The candidate with the most votes would become president and the one with the second highest total, vice president. The Republican electors cast 73 votes for Jefferson and the same number for Aaron Burr, the Republican candidate for vice president. The Federalist electors cast 65 votes for Adams; 64 for Charles Cotesworth Pinckney, their candidate for the vice presidency; and one for John Jay. The tie between Burr and Jefferson for the presidency meant the election would have to be decided in early 1801 by the House of Representatives. The problems caused by this election contributed to the passage, and ratification in 1804, of the Twelfth Amendment to the Constitution.

The second U.S. **Census** recorded a population of 5,308,483, including 896,849 slaves. The total number represented a ten-year increase of 1,379,269; the number of slaves increased by 199,168. The center of U.S. population was 18 miles southwest of Baltimore, a westward shift from 1790 reflecting the expansion of the frontier.

1800-1801: In **congressional elections** the Republicans gained six Senate seats to take an 18–13 majority over the Federalists. In the House they gained 27 seats to take a 69–36 majority.

May 7: The **Northwest Territory was divided** by a law enacted by Congress into two territories, Ohio and Indiana, the latter out of the western portion, including Illinois, Wisconsin, Indiana, and parts of Michigan and Minnesota. The provisions of the Treaty of Paris (1783), which ended the Revolutionary War, had defined the borders of the U.S. Among other concessions, Great Britain agreed to a line through the Great Lakes that placed in U.S. control the territory called the Old Northwest, between the Ohio and Mississippi rivers. States that had previously laid claim to parts of the region had ceded their territories in anticipation of the Northwest Ordinance of 1787.

June: The new city of **Washington** in the District of Columbia became the U.S. capital, succeeding Philadelphia. This occurred when government departments began to move into their new buildings on land ceded to the federal government by Maryland and Virginia. The radial design of the city was created by the French architect Pierre Charles L'Enfant. Construction began in 1791 but was delayed following L'Enfant's dismissal in 1792. The first Congress to sit in Washington convened on Nov. 17, 1800. The first president to live in the Executive Mansion, John Adams, moved in, also in November. The first president to be inaugurated there, Thomas Jefferson, was sworn into office March 4, 1801. The U.S. was probably the first modern nation to design a city exclusively as a capital.

Oct 1: The territory of **Louisiana,** the entire region of the Missouri-Mississippi river valleys, was ceded by Spain to France in the secret treaty of San Ildefonso, in effect giving back territory awarded Spain by France in the Treaty of Fontainebleau in 1762. This territory was acquired by the U.S. in 1803 through the Louisiana Purchase.

II. Architecture
Arts and Music
Popular Entertainment
Publishing
Theater

Almost as soon as George Washington died in 1799, writers began to depict him as a hero of almost mythical proportions. Chief contributor to this legend was Mason Locke Weems, an Episcopal clergyman usually referred to as Parson Weems, who is supposed to have had Washington as a parishioner in Virginia. In 1800 the first edition of his best-known work appeared, *The Life and Memorable Actions of George Washington.* There were nine editions of the book by 1809. It was in the fifth edition, issued in 1806, that Weems first included the story of Washington and the cherry tree. In all, the biography went through 86 printings between 1800 and 1927. Weems's practice was to fictionalize biographies to increase their sales. For more than 30 years he was primarily a book peddler, selling his own books as well as those of other authors. He worked for Mathew Carey, the leading publisher and bookseller of Philadelphia. Weems wrote biographies of Francis Marion, Benjamin Franklin, and William Penn. He also composed moral tracts such as *The Drunkard's Looking Glass* (1812) and *Hymen's Recruiting Sergeant* (c1799).

The number of **libraries** in the U.S. was about 50, with holdings of some 80,000 volumes. Most of these libraries required membership or payment of a fee for access to their books. By 1825, however, the nation's four largest cities could claim a total of 50 libraries, including some 1,500,000 volumes. Between 1800 and 1830 about 50,000 pamphlets, books, and magazine titles were issued in the U.S. Most of the books sold no more than 1000 copies, a respectable number considering the population of the country.

III. Business and Industry
Education
Philosophy and Religion
Science

The need to improve transportation facilities sparked a boom in canal building in the early nineteenth century. In South Carolina the Santee Canal, the first true canal in the U.S., was constructed between 1792 and 1800 to connect the Santee and Cooper rivers. This canal was 22 miles long, with ten locks that raised and lowered boats 103 feet. Its construction was directed by Christian Senf, a Swedish engineer imported for the job. He employed 110 men and women, mostly black slaves, to do the hard work. The canal cost $1,000,000 but ultimately failed because of inadequate supply of water. In New York State the Western Inland Lock Navigation Company had started a canal at the same time. This was only one mile long, with five locks. It was constructed to make navigation possible around the rapids of the Little Falls Gorge, on the Mohawk R.

The **Library of Congress** was established by the federal government. Housed at first in the Capitol, it was moved in 1897 to its own building, the largest and most costly library building in the world.

The first shoemaker in America to make **shoes designed specifically for the right and left feet** was William Young of Philadelphia.

The **Church of the United Brethren in Christ** was organized. Philip William Otterbein and Martin Boehm were elected bishops. The movement to form the church had originated among Mennonites in Lancaster County, Pa., in 1766 and spread among the German settlers of Pennsylvania, Maryland, and Virginia through the evangelistic labors of Otterbein and Boehm.

Sep: Cayuga Bridge, an engineering marvel of its time, was completed. It crossed the northern end of Cayuga Lake and the Montezuma Swamp in west central New York. The bridge, one and one-eighth of a mile long, was built of wood and was wide enough for wagons to pass abreast. Stages of the Genesee Turnpike used it, as did American troops in the War of 1812 on their way to the Niagara frontier. The bridge cost $150,000. It was financed by a loan from the Manhattan Company of New York City, which was founded in 1799 by Aaron Burr. Ostensibly established as a water supply company, the Manhattan Company had a charter broad enough so that it could function as a bank.

IV. Fashion
Folkways
Holidays
Social Issues and Crime
Sports

The remarkable career of Johnny Appleseed began about 1800. Born John Chapman in Massachusetts about 1775, he moved to Pennsylvania, where he sold or gave away saplings and apple seeds to settlers moving west. Chapman then moved on to Ohio, sowing and giving away apple seeds en route. For more than 40 years he traveled throughout Ohio, Indiana, and western Pennsylvania. He pruned trees he had previously planted and helped pioneers care for the orchards grown from his seeds. His work bore fruit, literally, over an area of perhaps 100,000 sq. mi. Chapman was ragged in dress and eccentric in his ways. He was also an itinerant preacher, expounding his faith in the Church of the New Jerusalem, the religious organization that grew out of the teachings of Emanuel Swedenborg, the Swedish mystic whose teachings had been introduced to the U.S. in 1784 and whose empathy with the natural world apparently appealed to Chapman. During the War of 1812 Chapman traveled 30 miles to bring troops to Mansfield, Ohio, to forestall a raid by Indian allies of the British. Chapman also introduced and encouraged the raising of many useful medicinal herbs. He died near Fort Wayne, Ind., in 1847.

Four-tined forks came into common use in American homes at about this time. Two- and three-tined forks had been customary.

The **Sheraton and Directoire styles** in furniture, both reflecting a continued classical influence and a return to simpler design, appealed strongly to public taste. The New York City workshop of Duncan Phyfe turned out many superb examples.

1801

I. Civil Rights
Exploration and Settlement
Government
Statistics
Wars

As a result of the tie vote between Thomas Jefferson and Aaron Burr in the electoral college in the 1800 presidential election, the process of presidential selection went to the House of Representatives, where each state would have one vote. Burr publicly professed support for Jefferson, his fellow Republican, but did nothing to take himself out of the race, even though the Republicans intended that Burr become vice president. Many Federalists favored Burr for president, but Alexander Hamilton, the leading Federalist, detested Burr and worked behind the scenes on Jefferson's behalf, despite his disagreement with Jefferson's policies. Beginning Feb. 11, the House took 35 ballots without breaking the deadlock. On the 36th ballot, on Feb. 17, barely two weeks before a new president was to be inaugurated, Jefferson received a majority vote when certain Federalists gave up their support of Burr. Burr was elected vice president.

Jan 20: John Marshall was appointed chief justice of the U.S. Supreme Court. He became one of the greatest judges in U.S. history, establishing the Supreme Court as final authority in determining state and federal powers.

Mar 4: Thomas Jefferson, third president of the United States, became the first president to be inaugurated in Washington, D.C. He held the office for eight years, and was the first of the Republican (later Democratic) Party elected to the presidency.

II. Architecture
Arts and Music
Popular Entertainment
Publishing
Theater

With the new century and the establishment of political parties came newspapers and journals that strongly supported one side or another. Among the leading editors of such publications was Joseph Dennie, who first edited the *Farmer's Weekly Museum* in Walpole, N.H. The publication became influential because of the "Lay Preacher" essays Dennie wrote for

it. Later, in Philadelphia, he edited *The Port Folio* from 1801 to 1809. An avid Federalist, Dennie made such strong verbal attacks on Thomas Jefferson that he was tried in 1805 for seditious libel but was acquitted. He did, however, publish literary articles of quality, including works of Thomas Moore, Leigh Hunt, and Thomas Campbell. Dennie was a founder of the Tuesday Club of Philadelphia, which supported both the magazine and the Federalist cause.

The **New York** *Evening Post,* a newspaper that enlisted some of the foremost editorial writers of the nineteenth century, was established. Under the editorship of William Cullen Bryant from 1826–1878, it was Free-soil and supported Abraham Lincoln. In the 1880s Carl Schurz and Edwin Lawrence Godkin steered the paper in its attack on local corruption. After passing through many hands, it became the New York *Post* in Mar. 1934.

III. Business and Industry
Education
Philosophy and Religion
Science

A religious revival began to sweep the West in this period. It started with the preaching of James McGready, a Presbyterian minister who began preaching in Logan County, Ky., in 1797. Encampments at which he preached formed the beginnings of the camp meeting, a gathering that for many typified evangelical Protestantism on the frontier. Such meetings generally featured hell-fire sermons preached at congregations gathered in open fields or groves of trees.

Oct 19: The **first Philadelphia aqueduct** was opened, providing a new supply of fresh water for the growing city.

IV. Fashion
Folkways
Holidays
Social Issues and Crime
Sports

Pioneer farmers in the backwoods had no opportunity to go to concerts or plays, but they created their own recreation, geared to their circumstances and their way of life. They met their neighbors at log-rollings, barbecues, and religious camp meetings. Some of them drank too much of the raw whiskey produced on the frontier, or gambled on horses or at cards. Since good marksmanship was a necessity, competition arose out of men's pride in their skill. There were competitive squirrel hunts and shooting at targets for such prizes as a turkey or a barrel of whiskey. Dances such as Virginia reels and country jigs were popular; they gave the women some much-needed social life.

Mar 4: The expression *entangling alliances* was coined by Thomas Jefferson and used in his first inaugural address: "Peace, commerce, and honest friendship with all nations—entangling alliances with none." These words have been commonly attributed to George Washington; although Washington supported the idea expressed, there is no record of his having used this phraseology.

1802

I. Civil Rights
Exploration and Settlement
Government
Statistics
Wars

In April the U.S. learned that Napoleon I of France in 1800 had secured through a secret agreement the return of the Louisiana territory from Spain. This was alarming news because the mouth of the Mississippi R. was now in the hands of an aggressive power, and Americans west of the Allegheny Mts. depended on free passage and use of the port of New Orleans to transfer their products to oceangoing ships. Pres. Thomas Jefferson ordered Robert R. Livingston, U.S. minister to France, to buy land on the lower Mississippi for use as a port, or to secure a guarantee of free navigation. In October Spanish officials, still in New Orleans, refused to allow Americans to use the port. This serious disruption of American commerce led Jefferson in the next year to begin negotiations for purchase of Louisiana.

1802-1803: In **congressional elections** the Republicans gained seven Senate seats for a 25–9 majority over the Federalists. In the House they gained 33 seats to the Federalists' gain of three, for a 102–39 majority.

Mar 16: The **U.S. Military Academy** at West Point, N.Y., was established by Congress. The academy opened officially on July 4.

Apr 30: Pres. Jefferson signed the **Enabling Act,** establishing procedures under which a territory organized by the provisions of the Ordinance of 1787 could become a state. The law authorized the people of Ohio Territory to hold a convention and frame a constitution. Subsequently, in 1803, Ohio became the 17th state of the Union and the first created out of the Northwest Territory. This precedent was later followed by other parts of the territory.

II. Architecture
Arts and Music
Popular Entertainment
Publishing
Theater

In the nineteenth century almost all American artists studied abroad and many of them became expatriates, chiefly in England and Italy. The first of these was Benjamin West, one of the best historical painters. West settled in London in 1763, becoming prominent as historical painter to King George III and president of the Royal Academy. He trained or advised a number of younger American painters. Among his paintings were *Saul and the Witch of Endor* and *The Death of Wolfe.* His paintings treating American subjects included *William Penn's Treaty with the Indians* (1772) and *Franklin Drawing Electricity from the Sky* (c1805). He completed an enormous canvas of *Christ Healing the Sick* in 1816, intended as a gift for the Pennsylvania Hospital in Philadelphia. It created such a sensation in London that he was offered 3000 guineas for it, so he painted a duplicate to send to America. The picture was so large that a special gallery had to be built to house it.

The **American Academy of Arts** was established in New York City. Shares of stock in the organization were sold as if the academy were a business corporation, reflecting the domination of the upper class in American culture.

III. Business and Industry
Education
Philosophy and Religion
Science

American scientists, often self-taught, showed a bent for practical matters rather than research in theoretical problems. A good example was Nathaniel Bowditch. After having learned algebra at age 14, Bowditch made five sea voyages between 1795 and 1803, during which he perfected his knowledge of mathematics and navigation. As a result he corrected some 8000 errors in J. Hamilton Moore's *The Practical Navigator,* a standard work. Bowditch devised a practical method of computing longitude with a sextant, by measuring the angular distances between certain fixed stars and the moon. A new edition of Moore's work appeared under Bowditch's name in 1802 as

The New Practical American Navigator. Nine more editions appeared in his lifetime, and in 1867 the rights were acquired by the U.S. Hydrographic Office, which has published it since. Bowditch also found time to translate four volumes of Pierre Simon, Marquis de Laplace's *Mécanique Celeste,* and to be president of the Essex Fire and Marine Insurance Co.

The **first brass mill,** built by Abel Porter & Co. and operated by horsepower, began operation in Waterbury, Conn., which became the leading brass manufacturing center in America.

IV. Fashion
Folkways
Holidays
Social Issues and Crime
Sports

By the early nineteenth century the division between North and South on the question of slavery was becoming clear-cut. By 1802 all states north of the Mason-Dixon line, except for New Jersey, had passed antislavery laws or measures for gradual emancipation. In Congress a bill to make the Fugitive Slave Law of 1793 more stringent was defeated by a narrow margin. In the South there was fear of slave insurrections, which were reported in six North Carolina counties and nine Virginia counties in 1802.

The **first hotel** in the U.S., the Union Hotel in Saratoga Springs, N.Y., was built by Gideon Putnam. What distinguished the Union as a hotel was its emphasis on lodging and services rather than food and drink.

1803

I. Civil Rights
Exploration and Settlement
Government
Statistics
Wars

A landmark decision was handed down by the Supreme Court this year in the case of *Marbury* v. *Madison.* In Mar. 1801, in the last hours of John Adams's presidency, William Marbury was awarded a commission as justice of the peace of the District of Columbia. The new president, Thomas Jefferson, instructed his secretary of state, James Madison, not to deliver the commission. Marbury and three other men in the same situation sued Madison. The Court's decision, written by Chief Justice John Marshall and issued on Feb. 24, held that the law under which the suit was brought was null and void because it contravened the Constitution. This was the first decision of the Supreme Court to declare an act of Congress unconstitutional, thereby establishing the doctrine of judicial review and expanding the power of the judiciary.

Feb 19: Ohio became the 17th state. Although slavery had been outlawed in the Northwest Territory by the Northwest Ordinance in 1787, Ohio was the first state in which slavery was forbidden by law from the beginning of statehood. Vermont had outlawed slavery with the adoption of its constitution in July 1777, some six months after its declaration of independence as a republic.

Apr 30: The **Louisiana Purchase,** the first territorial acquisition made by the U.S., added to the country some 828,000 sq. mi. of land between the Mississippi R. and the Rocky Mts. It was bought from France for 80,000,000 francs (about $15,000,000). The price included 20,000,000 francs for assumption by the U.S. of claims against France by U.S. citizens. The Louisiana Purchase increased U.S. national territory about 140%. The territory later formed Missouri, Nebraska, Iowa, Arkansas, North and South Dakota, most of Louisiana, Kansas, Minnesota, Montana, Wyoming, and parts of Colorado and Oklahoma.

II. Architecture
Arts and Music
Popular Entertainment
Publishing
Theater

A versatile American of the early national period was William Wirt of Virginia. A lawyer, politician, and essayist, he served as U.S. attorney general for 12 years. His most popular literary work was *Letters of a British Spy,* purporting to be written by a member of the British Parliament during a visit to the southern U.S. Wirt's essays, attempting to mimic the style of Joseph Addison, first appeared anonymously in a Richmond, Va., newspaper. They followed the example of eighteenth-century commentators who posed as foreign observers of the customs of a strange society. Published in book form in 1803, the essays became very popular and went through 12 editions. The essays dealt with southern customs, education, politics, and history. In 1817 Wirt published *Life and Character of Patrick Henry,* the first book to appear under his own name. In it he recreated many of Henry's speeches.

Feb 4: William Dunlap, often called America's first professional playwright, adapted the French melodrama *La Voix de Nature* by L.C. Caigniez, and produced it in New York City. Melodrama, newly developed abroad, notably in France, involved virtuous and villainous stock characters, with the virtuous always triumphant. *The Voice of Nature* was the first melodrama to reach the American stage.

III. Business and Industry
Education
Philosophy and Religion
Science

Among the religious groups that attempted to fund utopias in the U.S. were the Rappites, so-called after their leader George Rapp, who emigrated from Germany in 1803. In 1805 he and his followers founded Harmony, Pa., where they developed a prosperous industrial and agricultural community. In 1814 and 1815 they moved to Indiana and founded another Harmony. There they also prospered but in 1825 sold their property to Robert Owen, the English manufacturer and social reformer. Moving back to Pennsylvania, the Rappites established Economy (now Ambridge), northwest of Pittsburgh. The Harmony Society was an austere group who practiced celibacy. The group weakened after Rapp's death and faded as its members grew old. It ceased to exist in 1906.

The **first tax-supported public library** was founded in Salisbury, Conn. It was launched by a gift from Caleb Bingham, a Boston publisher, and was continued by grants of town moneys.

IV. Fashion
Folkways
Holidays
Social Issues and Crime
Sports

The British Passenger Act of 1803 appeared to be a humanitarian measure, but its practical effect was to cut down dramatically on the number of immigrants coming to the U.S. Ships from Londonderry and Belfast, Ireland, had been carrying 400 to 500 emigrants on each voyage, but the new law required that 43 sq. ft. of space be allowed for each passenger, so they soon could transport only a few score. As a result, fares increased so after 1803 only about 1000 emigrants a year left Ireland for the U.S. Between 1810 and 1812 these ships were preyed upon by British naval vessels, which impressed hundreds of young men into service. The falling off of immigration to the U.S. during the early years of independence gave more time for earlier settlers to become assimilated before the next influx.

John Randolph of Roanoke, an aristocratic Virginia congressman, set tongues wagging in Philadelphia with an announcement that he had fathered an illegitimate child.

1804

I. Civil Rights
Exploration and Settlement
Government
Statistics
Wars

Pres. Thomas Jefferson's scientific curiosity, and his concern for the economic and political security of the western U.S., were reflected in his sponsorship of the Lewis and Clark Expedition of 1804–1806. The expedition was headed by Merriwether Lewis, Jefferson's private secretary, and William Clark, an Army officer. The expedition was to explore the Northwest from the Mississippi R. to the Pacific Ocean, find the best travel route, and establish U.S. claims to the Oregon Territory. The expedition, including about 30 persons, left St. Louis, Mo., on May 14, 1804, and traveled up the Missouri R., spending the winter in North Dakota. In July 1805, the group found the headwaters of the Missouri and learned there was no easy route to the Pacific. They were also the first Americans to cross the Continental Divide. Traveling down the Columbia R., the expedition reached the Pacific on Nov. 8, 1805, and wintered there. On Sept. 23, 1806, the expedition arrived back at St. Louis, bringing with it great quantities of information on vegetation, animals, Indians, and the geography of the region. As Theodore Roosevelt wrote later, the expedition "opened the door into the heart of the Far West."

1804-1805: In **congressional elections** the Republicans gained two Senate seats for a 27–7 majority over the Federalists. In the House they gained 14 seats for a 116–25 majority.

July 11: Alexander Hamilton was fatally wounded in a pistol duel with Aaron Burr. Hamilton had fought Burr's run for the presidency in 1800, and for the governorship of New York in 1804, when Hamilton and others suspected that Burr intended to attach New York to the disgruntled New England states in a plan to disunite from the Union and form a northern confederacy. Burr challenged Hamilton, who deliberately misfired before Burr fired with intent to kill.

Sep 25: The **Twelfth Amendment** to the U.S. Constitution was ratified, providing in part that voters shall "name in their ballots the person voted for as President and in distinct ballots the person voted for as vice president." In the election of this year, electors for the first time voted separately for president and vice president. Previously the candidate having the second largest number of votes in the electoral college became vice president.

Dec 5: Thomas Jefferson was reelected president of the United States. George Clinton, first governor of New York and like Jefferson a Democratic-Republican, was elected vice president. The electoral vote was Jefferson, 162; Charles C. Pinckney, Federalist of South Carolina, 14. This was the first election with separate ballots for president and vice president.

II. Architecture
   Arts and Music
   Popular Entertainment
   Publishing
   Theater

Like other American artists before and after them, Washington Allston and John Vanderlyn found Europe more congenial for exercising their talents than the U.S. Beginning in 1801, Allston studied in England under Benjamin West, then spent four years in Rome. The period from 1810 to 1818, spent in England, was Allston's most productive. He was an early and important artist of the Romantic school, as exemplified in such works as *The Deluge* (1804) and *The Rising of a Thunderstorm at Sea* (1804). His work lost its vitality when he returned to the U.S. and was marked by such failures as *Belshazzar's Feast,* over which he labored for 26 years. John Vanderlyn was the first American painter to study in Paris instead of London or Rome. He spent the years from 1796 to 1815 in the French capital and in Rome. His early work featured nudes painted so realistically that they shocked viewers. Vanderlyn was primarily a historical painter, and such works as *Marius Amid the Ruins at Carthage* won him a high reputation but did not sell. He also did excellent portraits but worked so slowly that few people had the patience to pose for him.

The first volume of **Life of George Washington** by John Marshall was published. The fifth and final volume appeared in 1807. Although the work reflected Marshall's Federalist bias and lacked literary style, it was considered the most impressive and authoritative biography of the first president to appear in the 50 years following Washington's death. Shorter biographies of Washington were written by Aaron Bancroft (1807) and David Ramsay (1807).

III. Business and Industry
   Education
   Philosophy and Religion
   Science

Even as late as the eighteenth century, religious and political persecution was spurring men of above ordinary talent to immigrate to the U.S. Such a man was Joseph Priestley, theologian and scientist. His greatest scientific achievement was the discovery of oxygen, although he did not realize the importance of his work. His strongly expressed Unitarian views and his support of the French Revolution made him many enemies. A mob wrecked his house and destroyed his scientific apparatus in 1791, prompting him to leave England for the U.S. in 1794. Among his friends and correspondents was Thomas Jefferson. Priestley settled at Northumberland, Pa., and spent the last years of his life writing and continuing his scientific studies. He died at Northumberland on Feb. 6, 1804.

What was perhaps the **first automobile** was built by Oliver Evans, an American inventor, who was commissioned by the Philadelphia Board of Health to build a steam engine for dredging the Schuylkill R. and cleaning the city docks. His five-hp engine propelled a scow 12 ft. wide and 30 ft. long. The scow weighed 15½ tons and was driven 1½ miles from its construction shed, down Center St., much to the amusement of Philadelphians. Evans offered to bet an onlooker $3000 that he could build a steam-driven vehicle that would go faster than any horse in the world. The scow's drive belt was shifted from its rollers to paddlewheels and it went steaming down the river against the wind, leaving all sailboats behind. Despite this demonstration, the public was not much impressed with the principle of steam locomotion.

IV. Fashion
   Folkways
   Holidays
   Social Issues and Crime
   Sports

One result of Napoleon's establishment of the French Empire in Europe in 1804 was the development of the

Empire style in furniture and house furnishings. The style was not long in reaching the U.S. and dominated until after Napoleon's fall in 1815. By contrast with late eighteenth-century styles, which favored the classical manner of straight lines and minimal carving, Empire furniture was heavier and more massive. There were combinations of marble and brass, and ormolu and wood. Animal forms, such as claw feet and eagle heads, were used together with elaborate decorative carvings. Heavy textiles were used in upholstery. Larger and more imposing interiors were needed to set off the monumental furniture so couches were modeled after Roman beds and bookcases with facades like temples appeared. Although most American pieces were not as lush as the French originals, the furniture suggested wealth and power in the Napoleonic manner but did not provide a relaxed setting for social life.

The **Coonskin Library** was founded in Marietta, Ohio. This unique institution came into being when settlers along the Ohio R. bartered coonskins for books from Boston merchants.

1805

I. Civil Rights
Exploration and Settlement
Government
Statistics
Wars

U.S. merchant shipping, as it grew in volume, was increasingly preyed upon by pirates of the states of the Barbary Coast of North Africa, who had attacked the shipping of European nations for many years. These states were Tripolitania, Tunisia, Algeria, and Morocco. The Tripolitan War (1801–1805), the first of a number of conflicts, began when the American government refused to pay tribute to the rulers of these states in return for a guarantee of protection. After sporadic fighting, John Rodgers, a naval officer, negotiated a peace treaty, which was signed June 4, 1805. Tripoli renounced all rights to collect tribute or halt U.S. shipping. The U.S. agreed to pay $60,000 to ransom the crew of the warship *Philadelphia,* which had been captured after having drifted aground. The treaty was the most favorable any nation had negotiated with the pirate states, but it did not put an end

to piracy. Another decade was to pass before the threat was entirely ended.

Apr 27: In the **Tripolitan War,** the U.S. achieved its major victory when William Eaton, a special U.S. naval agent, led a small force of Marines and Arab mercenaries in capturing the Tripolitan port city of Derna. Eaton's force, a squad of U.S. Marines under Lt. Preston N. O'Bannon and about 100 Arab mercenaries, had marched 500 miles from Egypt to Derna and were assisted by a coordinated bombardment of Derna by U.S. naval vessels. Eaton's ultimate mission, approved by Pres. Thomas Jefferson, was to replace the ruling pasha of Tripoli with the rightful ruler. However, the coming of peace in early June aborted the plan. The phrase "to the shores of Tripoli" in the official song of the U.S. Marine Corps refers to the Derna campaign, which was the first engagement of U.S. land forces in North Africa. The campaign marked the first time that the U.S. flag was raised over an Old World fort.

II. Architecture
Arts and Music
Popular Entertainment
Publishing
Theater

In the early years of independence the U.S. was still dependent on Europe, especially England, for architects and architectural styles. Benjamin Henry Latrobe, who came to the U.S. from England in 1796, is considered the first professional architect in the U.S. Pres. Thomas Jefferson appointed him surveyor of public buildings in 1803. Latrobe introduced classical Greek designs and styles, which contributed greatly to the Classical revival. His 1799 design for the Bank of Pennsylvania in Philadelphia was modeled after a Greek Ionic temple. Latrobe also designed the Roman Catholic Cathedral in Baltimore. Built between 1805 and 1815, it was the first cathedral in the U.S. and represented the best monumental architecture of the period. In 1800 Latrobe designed Sedgeley, a residence near Philadelphia, said to be the first executed example of the Gothic revival in the U.S. After the British burned the Capitol in Washington, D.C., in 1814, Latrobe took charge of its rebuilding.

The **Pennsylvania Academy of Fine Arts** was founded by Charles Willson Peale. It is the oldest extant art institution in the U.S. The New York Academy was founded in 1801 but survived only four years.

III. Business and Industry
Education
Philosophy and Religion
Science

A book of theological thought published this year marked a change in the course of belief within the Universalist Church. The book was *A Treatise on the Atonement* by Hosea Ballou, who for about 34 years was pastor of the Second Universalist Society in Boston. After about 1796 Ballou was the most influential voice in the denomination and turned it away from its Calvinistic tendencies. Ballou emphasized "Christ's subordination to the Father," giving Universalism a position much the same as that of Unitarianism. His basic viewpoint was that of anti-Trinitarianism, with God the universal father and Jesus Christ, His son, the spiritual authority and leader in uniting man with God. Ballou affirmed the freedom of man's will, with the sacrifice of Christ an example of the perfection man can attain by turning away from sin. The Winchester Profession, stating the doctrinal position of the church, had been adopted in 1803.

A **labor dispute** was taken into court for the first time by a struck employer. The result was conviction of leaders of the Philadelphia Society of Cordwainers, workers in cordovan leather, for criminal conspiracy for the purpose of increasing their wages. The conviction was secured under English common-law doctrine.

IV. Fashion
Folkways
Holidays
Social Issues and Crime
Sports

Not all commentators praised the morals and manners of the young U.S. Among those who emphasized the excesses of a raw democracy was Scottish-born Hugh Henry Brackenridge, author and jurist. The influence of satirists such as Miguel de Cervantes and Jonathan Swift was evident in his novel, *Modern Chivalry*, published between 1792 and 1815 in four volumes, a revision, and a final edition. In it he wrote: "In the American republic, we retain yet a great deal of the spirit of monarchy. . . . The first lesson I would give to a son of mine would be to have nothing to do with public business, but as a duty to his country. . . . beware of flatterers, whose object is not to serve them, but themselves. The demagogue in a democracy, and the courtier in a monarchy, are identical."

Sacajawea, a Shoshone Indian woman, gained a place in American folklore by her activities this year. The wife of the Lewis and Clark expedition's official interpreter, Toussaint Charbonneau, she joined the expedition in what is now South Dakota, and accompanied the party to the Pacific and part of the way back east. Her presence with the explorers helped convince the Indians they met en route that the newcomers were not members of a war party. Her knowledge of edible wild plants was a great help to the expedition. In February she gave birth to a baby boy. The midwife was Meriwether Lewis.

1806

I. Civil Rights
Exploration and Settlement
Government
Statistics
Wars

One of the most puzzling incidents of the early nineteenth century involved Aaron Burr, the brilliant but erratic political figure. Shortly after he fatally wounded Alexander Hamilton in a duel in 1804, Burr journeyed to New Orleans and entered into a conspiracy with U.S. Gen. James Wilkinson, although it is not clear what they conspired about. Wilkinson was actually in the pay of Spain at the time. Speculation was that Burr intended either to establish an independent nation in the Southwest or to seize territory for the same purpose in Spanish America. Burr secured financing from Harman Blennerhassett, of Blennerhassett Island in the Ohio R. near present-day Parkersburg, W. Va. He set out from there in the fall of 1806 with about 60 well-armed men and headed downstream. The expedition aroused suspicion and Wilkinson, seeking to save his own skin, turned against Burr. He spread stories of Burr's intentions and sent dispatches to the government in Washington accusing Burr of treason. Burr was arrested and charged with treason, but he was acquitted in 1807.

1806–1807: In **congressional elections** the Republicans gained one Senate seat for a 28–6 majority over the Federalists. In the House they gained two seats for a 118–24 majority.

July 15: Zebulon Pike began his exploration of what is now the southwestern U.S. He traveled up the Missouri R., through Kansas and southern Nebraska to New Mexico, through the Rio Grande Valley and on to Mexico City. On Nov. 15 Pike first saw the famous mountain named for him, Pike's Peak, in what is now Colorado.

II. Architecture
Arts and Music
Popular Entertainment
Publishing
Theater

More and larger book publishing firms began to emerge as the nation grew. The most important publisher before the turn of the century was Isaiah Thomas of Worcester, Mass., whose firm published everything from magazines to reference books to almanacs. Thomas wrote a valuable *History of Printing in America* (1810). Another publisher was Matthew Carey of Philadelphia, who also labored for a protective tariff system. His son, Henry Charles Carey, became the head of Carey, Lea, and Carey, whose authors included Washington Irving. Henry Carey, like his father, was deeply interested in economics and the protective tariff.

Noah Webster's *Compendious Dictionary of the English Language* represented a retreat from Webster's earlier attempts to Americanize the English language. Although many supporters of a purely American language continued to agitate for linguistic change, Webster's dictionary compromised with the British mother tongue, and its standards became the accepted practice in the U.S. The dictionary was the culmination of a series of works by Webster, beginning in 1783 with *The Grammatical Institute of the English Language* and including readers, spellers, and grammars with enormous circulation in America.

III. Business and Industry
Education
Philosophy and Religion
Science

Many trails long used by the Indians became roads for pioneer settlers. Such a trail was the Natchez Trace, which ran from present-day Nashville, Tenn., southwest to Natchez, Miss. By 1806 it was much used by traders, causing Congress to pass legislation for construction of a better road over its route. In the War of 1812 Andrew Jackson marched troops on the Natchez Trace as he moved on New Orleans to oppose the British.

The **first industry-wide strike** in the U.S. resulted when 200 journeymen shoemakers in New York City, suspecting that struck employers were having their work done in other establishments, obtained a nationwide strike order from the Journeyman Cordwainers' Society of Baltimore. Leaders of the strike were indicted for criminal conspiracy in their attempt to secure higher wages.

IV. Fashion
Folkways
Holidays
Social Issues and Crime
Sports

Dueling was dying out but had not yet disappeared. One of its most active practitioners was a future president of the U.S., Andrew Jackson. In 1803 he became embroiled in a dispute with Gov. John Sevier of Tennessee who was said to have insulted Jackson's wife. A duel was arranged, but the confrontation was averted because of confusion at the scene. In 1806 a duel resulted from a bet on a horse race and yet another insult to Jackson's wife, this time by a lawyer, Charles Dickinson. When Jackson and Dickinson met on May 30, both men fired and Jackson suffered a broken rib. His shot felled Dickinson, who bled to death.

The first picture of a soccer-type **football game** in America showed president Timothy Dwight watching Yale students kicking a ball. According to Yale tradition, the game of football had been played there for 45 years. The modern American game of football, however, did not begin to develop until about 1869.

1807

I. Civil Rights
Exploration and Settlement
Government
Statistics
Wars

An early incident presaging the War of 1812 was the *Chesapeake-Leopard* affair of June 22, 1807. The U.S. warship *Chesapeake* was stopped by the British frigate *Leopard* off Norfolk, Va. The British commander insisted that the Chesapeake had four British deserters on board. When James Barron, commanding the *Chesapeake,* refused to surrender the men, the British ship opened fire, killing three Americans and wounding 18. The four alleged deserters were forcibly removed. In spite of Pres. Thomas Jefferson's protest, the British government on Oct. 17 announced it would continue its policy of impressing seamen on American ships who were thought to be British. As for Barron, he was court-martialed and suspended from active duty for five years, during which time he served in the French navy. In 1820 Barron killed Stephen Decatur in a duel sparked by Decatur's opposition to Barron's reinstatement.

Mar 2: The **African slave trade** was prohibited after Jan. 1, 1808, by an act of Congress, which outlawed importation of slaves into any place within the jurisdiction of the U.S.

Sep 1: Aaron Burr was acquitted of treason by a circuit court in Richmond, Va., on the grounds that he was not present when an overt act was committed. Pres. Thomas Jefferson, having been warned of Burr's activities with respect to annexation of Spanish territory, had issued a warning on Nov. 27, 1806, to all citizens forbidding any expedition against Spanish territory. Burr had been arrested in Alabama on Feb. 19 and indicted on June 24 on charges of treason.

II. Architecture
Arts and Music
Popular Entertainment
Publishing
Theater

The nation's new sense of political independence was reflected in the lives and works of its writers, who felt that American letters should also be independent of the Old World. Leaders in this movement were the Connecticut Wits, also known as the Hartford Wits because they were centered in that Connecticut city. This informal group began as one devoted to modernizing the Yale College curriculum. The members soon, however, entered the political arena. They shared the views of the conservative Federalists and collaborated on satirical verse attacking the liberal position. Among the group's members were Joel Barlow, John Trumbull, Timothy Dwight, Theodore Dwight, and Lemuel Hopkins. The group's political and literary importance was greatest in the late 1700s but continued to be an influence into the early 1800s.

Jan 24: The first number of *Salmagundi,* a series of whimsical, mildly satirical, and very popular essays written by William and Washington Irving and James Kirke Paulding, was published. Following the informal style of London essayists of the previous century, these pieces afforded delightful glimpses of New York's social, cultural, and political life in the early 1800s. They also marked the beginning of what came to be called the Knickerbocker movement in

American literature. Many imitations followed at once. Paulding and the Irvings were men of affluent background and similar literary taste. At this point in their lives they were little concerned with the major issues of the day. *Salmagundi,* therefore, remains charming embroidery rather than basic fabric in the development of American literature. But the essays are a lasting memorial to the old days of New York City and its Hudson R. Valley suburbs, and they established the tradition of metropolitan wit that continues unbroken to our day.

III. Business and Industry
Education
Philosophy and Religion
Science

In the late eighteenth and early nineteenth centuries, American physicians and surgeons made significant contributions to medical science. Samuel Bard wrote a manual on midwifery and a forward-looking report on medical education. Nathan Smith helped found Yale's medical school and wrote a treatise on typhus fever. Philip Syng Physick performed many operations for cataracts and improved methods for treating fractures. Ephraim McDowell, who practiced in Kentucky, performed the first ovariotomy on record in 1808.

Aug 11: Robert Fulton's steamboat *Clermont* made its first run to Albany from New York in 32 hours, traveling at about 5 mph. The initial trial of the *Clermont* had taken place the previous spring when it crossed the Hudson R. from New York to New Jersey. Also in 1807 Pres. Jefferson corresponded with Fulton about the torpedoes Fulton was proposing as the chief defense of harbors. But Jefferson could not see gambling the safety of the nation on the success of a single weapon. Fulton had also proposed the development of submarines. Jefferson noted how effective torpedoes launched from submarines would be, and encouraged Fulton in his research and experiments.

IV. Fashion
Folkways
Holidays
Social Issues and Crime
Sports

Most Americans had plenty to eat, but few enjoyed a balanced diet. Farmers grew their own food and shot wild game. In the cities the lack of refrigeration and even of canning until about 1820 meant that much salt pork and other preserved items were staples. Fresh fruits and vegetables were not available for much of the year. Foreign visitors were impressed by the amount of greasy food consumed by Americans and the speed at which it was eaten. A visiting French count reported that he was nearly made ill by a breakfast that included fish, steak, ham, sausage, salt beef, and hot breads. "The whole day passes in heaping indigestions on one another," he complained.

Feb 27: Henry Wadsworth Longfellow, one of America's most popular and revered poets, was born in Portland, Me. His birthday came to be celebrated for many years in public schools throughout the nation. One of the earliest records of such a celebration appeared in the biennial report of the superintendent of schools in West Virginia in 1905. The Historical Society of Cambridge, Mass., celebrated the centenary of Longfellow's birth in 1907 with addresses by William Dean Howells, Charles W. Eliot, Charles Eliot Norton, and Thomas Wentworth Higginson.

1808

I. Civil Rights
Exploration and Settlement
Government
Statistics
Wars

The war between Great Britain and Napoleonic France in the early nineteenth century caused great damage to America's economy and led to government action to solve the problem. On Dec. 22, 1807, an Embargo Act became law. In effect the act banned all trade with foreign countries in an attempt to show England and France, who were trying to keep U.S. ships from reaching each other's ports, the importance of U.S. products and markets. Another Embargo Act was passed on Jan. 9, 1808, and still a third on Mar. 12. None of the acts had the desired effect. Trade to and from Canada was difficult to stop, and neither Britain nor France suffered. The chief result was damage to shipping and commercial interests of the North, especially New England.

1808-1809: In **congressional elections** the Republicans maintained their 28–6 Senate majority over the Federalists. In the House they lost 24 seats but kept a majority, 94–48.

Dec 7: James Madison was elected president of the United States. George Clinton, Republican of New York, was elected vice president. The electoral vote was Madison, Democratic-Republican of Virginia, 122; Charles Cotesworth Pinckney, Federalist of South Carolina, 47; George Clinton, 6. In the vice presidential race the electoral vote was Clinton, 113; Rufus King, Federalist of New York, 47.

II. Architecture
Arts and Music
Popular Entertainment
Publishing
Theater

Pocahontas (real name, Matoaka), daughter of the Indian chief Powhatan, became a favorite subject of American writers as a result of John Smith's tale of her intercession to save his life. The first book to treat Pocahontas as a literary figure was a novel, *The First Settlers of Virginia* (1805) by John Davis. The first play to use an American Indian as its subject was *The Indian Princess; or, La Belle Sauvage* by James N. Barker; it was first staged in Philadelphia on Apr. 6, 1808. The play was interspersed with songs and told the story of Pocahontas in a romantic vein. Another play, *Pocahontas* appeared in 1830; it was the work of George Washington Parke Custis, grandson of Martha Washington. Another drama with the same title, by Robert Dale Owen, the social reformer, appeared in 1837. Seba Smith, the humorist and journalist, wrote a verse romance, *Powhatan* (1841).

III. Business and Industry
Education
Philosophy and Religion
Science

One of America's first and most successful entrepreneurs was German-born John Jacob Astor, who came to the U.S. in 1784. On Apr. 6, 1808, he received a charter for the American Fur Company, planning to compete in the far Northwest with the long established Canadian firms. In 1811 a subsidiary company established Fort Astoria (now Astoria, Oreg.) on the Columbia R. estuary, the first permanent U.S. settlement on the Pacific coast. By the 1820s Astor held a virtual monopoly on fur trading in the U.S. West. Manuel Lisa, William Clark, Pierre Chouteau, and others operating out of St. Louis, Mo., formed the Missouri Fur Company on July 16, 1808, to compete but in 1821 Astor formed an alliance with them. Astor retired in 1834 and at his death on Mar. 29, 1848, was the wealthiest man in the U.S.

The first volume of **American Ornithology** by Alexander Wilson, a major contribution to American scientific scholarship, was published. Wilson's study ran to nine volumes and was completed in 1814. A pioneer work, it also appealed to laymen because of its attractive illustrations and frequent analogies to human nature.

IV. Fashion
Folkways
Holidays
Social Issues and Crime
Sports

Horses and horse racing continued to fascinate a large part of the population. The thoroughbred stallion Diomed was imported from England in 1798 and put out to stud. Diomed sired Sir Archie, sold to Gen. William R. Davie, a veteran of the American Revolution, for the unheard of sum of $5000. There was widespread mourning when Diomed died in 1808 in Virginia. The most important horse of the period was Justin Morgan, foaled in 1792 and the sire of the breed that became known by his name. The horse was named for its owner, a schoolteacher who brought him to Vermont, where there still is a Morgan horse farm near Middlebury. The Morgan horse is small, has great endurance, and can do almost anything but hunt or run well in long races.

Oct 30: Benjamin Ireson, skipper of the schooner *Betty*, brought his vessel into Marblehead, Mass., where he was accused unjustly of sailing away from another skipper's sinking ship because he feared losing his own vessel. The women of Marblehead tarred and feathered him and ran him out of town in a cart. This story was related years later by John Greenleaf Whittier in his ballad "Skipper Ireson's Ride" (1857).

1809

I. Civil Rights
Exploration and Settlement
Government
Statistics
Wars

Great Britain's attempts to restrict U.S. shipping during Britain's war with France continued to cause dissension in the U.S. The ineffective Embargo Act of 1807 was repealed on Mar. 1, 1809, largely through the efforts of Sen. Timothy Pickering of Massachusetts. Pickering was an ardent Federalist who typified the bitter opposition of New England to the law that had almost destroyed its shipping. The Non-Intercourse Act was passed the same day, permitting trade with all nations except England and France. Trade with the belligerents would be resumed when they agreed to respect the rights of the U.S. On Apr. 19 Pres. James Madison issued a proclamation allowing trade with England; the British minister to the U.S. had stated that British orders against U.S. shipping would be withdrawn on June 10. Unfortunately, the minister did not have the authority to make this promise, and on Aug. 9 Pres. Madison reinstated the Non-Intercourse Act.

Mar 1: The **Non-Intercourse Act** was signed by Pres. Thomas Jefferson in retaliation for English and French interference with American commerce. The act closed ports of the U.S. to France and England and outlawed their imports. It was repealed when the loss in customs revenue became excessive.

II. Architecture
Arts and Music
Popular Entertainment
Publishing
Theater

The Wyoming Valley Massacre of 1778, a relatively minor event in the course of the American Revolution, was remembered because of a later poem about it. On July 3, 1778, a force of Loyalists and Indians commanded by John Butler of Connecticut attacked a settlement in the Wyoming Valley of northeastern Pennsylvania. The Americans were promised safe conduct, but when they surrendered on July 4, the Indians killed the settlers and looted and burned their homes. In 1809 Thomas Campbell, a Scottish poet, wrote *Gertrude of Wyoming*, a long narrative poem that described horrible events that had never occurred. It also told the sad story of two fictional lovers whose future happiness was doomed by the massacre. The poem was one of the earliest works by a European writer based on an American historical incident.

A *History of New York* by Washington Irving, the first American humorous masterpiece, was published. It was also the first American work to impress European critics and readers. Written under the pseudonym Diedrich Knickerbocker, a comic scholar "a little queer in his ways," Irving's book was a tongue-in-cheek history of Dutch New Amsterdam. It became a best seller. Although it has been said that the descendants of the original Dutch settlers were put out by the treatment Irving gave their ancestors, the Dutch patroons were but one target among many. Irving had as good a time with Thomas Jefferson, Republicans, Yankees, Swedes, European literature, and historians who wrote the sort of books that did please the descendants of the Dutch. He also possessed the redeeming quality of being able to laugh at himself.

III. Business and Industry
Education
Philosophy and Religion
Science

Among those who contributed to the growing knowledge about the U.S. and to the achievements of American scientists was William Maclure, a well-to-do Scottish merchant who became a U.S. citizen in 1796. His *Observations on the Geology of the United States* (1809) included the first geological map of the U.S. In preparing a revised edition (1817), Maclure crossed the Allegheny Mts. dozens of times. He also introduced to the U.S. the educational theories of Johann Heinrich Pestalozzi, the Swiss educational reformer. Pestalozzi emphasized individual development and the study of nature.

The **Boston Crown Glass Company** was incorporated. The company had been in business since 1792, when it made the first successful window glass in the U.S. Its glass was said to be superior to any imported product. The charter of incorporation suspended company taxes and freed employees from military service.

IV. Fashion
Folkways
Holidays
Social Issues and Crime
Sports

One of the most impressive American Indian leaders was Tecumseh, chief of the Shawnees. Alarmed by the steady westward movement of settlers, Tecumseh on July 2, 1809, began a campaign to unite in a defensive confederacy the Indian tribes of the Old Northwest, the South, and the eastern Mississippi R. Valley. Americans had by treaty already acquired 30,000,000 acres of land in the region. Tecumseh was aided by his brother, Tenskwatawa, called the Shawnee

Prophet. In spite of Tecumseh's efforts, on Sept. 30 William Henry Harrison, governor of the Indiana Territory, signed a treaty at Fort Wayne by which the Indian tribes ceded three more tracts of land along the Wabash R. Tecumseh's continuing efforts to halt further encroachment on Indian lands alarmed the settlers, who urged military action against him. The dream of an Indian confederacy died for good with the battle of Tippecanoe in Nov. 1811.

Oct 31: A **missing persons advertisement** was placed by one George Hicks of Brooklyn in the New York *Post*. Hicks offered a $25 reward for the return of a "Negro woman named Charity and her female child . . . 25 years of age, five feet high, of a yellowish complexion . . . has lost the use of one of her fingers, occasioned by a fellon . . . took with her several suits of clothes."

1810

I. Civil Rights
Exploration and Settlement
Government
Statistics
Wars

The western and northern boundaries of the area known as West Florida were long in dispute between the U.S. and Spain, England, or France—all three controlled it at various times. The U.S. claimed some of the area as part of the Louisiana Purchase of 1803. In dispute was the land between the Mississippi R. on the west and the Perdido R. on the east. In 1810 American settlers in the region rebelled against Spanish control. On Sept. 26 they captured the fort at Baton Rouge and proclaimed a republic. On Oct. 27 Pres. James Madison proclaimed U.S. annexation of West Florida and declared it part of Orleans Territory.

The third U.S. **Census** recorded a population of 7,239,881, an increase of 1,931,398 over 1800. Black population rose by 481,361 to 1,378,110. Of this total, 186,746 were free citizens, a group omitted in the 1800 census. The center of population moved to a point 40 mi. northwest of Washington, D.C.

1810-1811: In **congressional elections** the Republicans gained two Senate seats for a 30–6 majority over the Federalists. In the House they gained 14 seats for a 108–36 majority.

II. Architecture
Arts and Music
Popular Entertainment
Publishing
Theater

Interest and support for musical enterprises continued to grow. The first regular orchestra in the U.S. was formed about this time in Boston by Gottlieb Graupner, a German-born musician who came to the U.S. in 1795. For nearly 25 years Graupner played a leading role in the musical life of Boston, especially as the founder of the Handel and Haydn Society. The semiprofessional Philharmonic Orchestra he founded played a significant role in the development of Boston's cultural life. The orchestra gave its last performance on Nov. 24, 1824, at the Pantheon, on Boylston Square.

A **theater season** was launched in Lexington, Ky., the first time west of the Appalachians. From then on, road companies mostly offering contemporary melodramas and farces brought stage presentations to the smaller cities of the U.S. until the high costs of production and travel in the mid-twentieth century made the business unprofitable.

III. Business and Industry
Education
Philosophy and Religion
Science

Because of the vast expanse of the U.S., the development of new means of transportation was inevitable. Cornelius Vanderbilt was one of the first of the new developers. He began his career in 1810, operating a small boat as a ferry between Staten Island and Manhattan, New York. By age 40 he was worth a small fortune as a result of his major share in shipping interests around New York harbor and on the Hudson R. During the gold rush of the mid-nineteenth century, he operated a shipping line to the West Coast by way of Nicaragua, where he put together a combined land and water route across Central America. Turning his attention to railroads after the Civil War, Vanderbilt built or secured control of the lines that became the New York Central Railroad between New York and Chicago. Some of his methods, like those of his competitors, were ethically questionable, but at his death in 1877 Vanderbilt was said to be worth $100,000,000.

The **Newburyport Bridge** over the Merrimack R. in Massachusetts, the most famous suspension bridge in nineteenth-century America, was erected by John Templeman, holder of several patents on suspension bridge improvements. The bridge had a span of 224 ft. In 1909 it was rebuilt, with its original structure carefully preserved.

Growth of higher education in the U.S. was reflected in the establishment of seven new colleges during the decade beginning in 1810. The new schools brought to 37 the number of institutions of higher learning in the nation.

July 12: The **Journeymen Cordwainers** trial began in New York City. Members of this trade union were accused of conspiring to raise their wages by calling a strike. They were found guilty and fined $1.00 each plus costs because "Even to do a thing which is lawful in itself, by conspiracy, is unlawful." This decision followed the precedent established in the 1806 trial of bootmakers in Philadelphia. In 1842 the Supreme Court of Massachusetts reversed the trend by stating that the legal definition of *conspiracy* excluded union actions.

IV. Fashion
Folkways
Holidays
Social Issues and Crime
Sports

Although cricket had a long headstart over baseball, it quickly lost out in popularity once baseball was introduced later in the century. A form of cricket was played in Virginia as early as 1709, and a match was played in New York City in 1751. Boston's first cricket club was organized in 1809, and the sport spread west with English settlers. There were reports of cricket being played in Kentucky in 1818 and in Illinois a year later. Chicago in 1840 had three teams. But Philadelphia was the center of cricket in the U.S., and its factory workers of English origin played weekly matches.

Dec 10: The first unofficial **heavyweight champion** of the U.S., Tom Molineaux, a freed slave from Virginia, was beaten in the 40th round by Tom Cribb, the English champion, in a boxing match at Copthall Common, London.

1811

I. Civil Rights
Exploration and Settlement
Government
Statistics
Wars

Two incidents involving warships were portents of the coming war between the U.S. and Great Britain. On May 1, off Sandy Hook, N.Y., the 38-gun British frigate *Guerrière* stopped the American brig *Spitfire* and seized an American-born seaman. On May 6 the 44-gun American frigate *President* was ordered to the area to protect U.S. shipping; en route it came upon a ship thought to be the *Guerrière*. Actually it was a British 20-gun corvette, *Little Belt*. The *President* attacked the *Little Belt* on May 16, disabling it, killing nine, and wounding 23 of the crew. The U.S. government told the British minister in Washington on Nov. 1 that it would reach an agreement about the incident if Great Britain would rescind orders that restricted American commercial shipping. The British refused to negotiate.

Feb 11: Trade with Britain was prohibited by Pres. Madison, the third time in four years that such action was taken. Madison hoped to effect repeal of the Orders in Council by which Britain placed restrictions on neutral commerce.

Apr 12: Colonists sent by **John Jacob Astor** on the *Tonquin* to operate a Pacific coast fur-trading center of the newly formed Pacific Fur Company arrived at the mouth of the Columbia R. via Cape Horn. Under the leadership of a Capt. Thorn, they disembarked at Cape Disappointment, Wash., but soon moved a few miles upstream and founded Astoria in what is now Oregon. This was the first permanent American colony in the Pacific Northwest.

II. Architecture
Arts and Music
Popular Entertainment
Publishing
Theater

An unusual case of plagiarism involved one of the most popular American novels of the early nineteenth century. Isaac Mitchell, a newspaper editor, serialized in 1811 in his Poughkeepsie, N.Y., *Political Barometer*, a novel he had written, *The Asylum; or, Alonzo and Melissa.* In the same year there appeared

Alonzo and Melissa; or, The Unfeeling Father, signed by Daniel Jackson, a teacher at the Plattsburgh, N.Y., Academy. Mitchell died before he could sue for damages, but authorship later was restored to him. The novel, a Gothic romance, featured ghosts, separated lovers, haunted castles, and a happy ending for the young couple. It sold well for some 40 years.

James Fenimore Cooper left the U.S. Navy to marry Susan De Lancey and settle down in Mamaroneck, N.Y., as a gentleman farmer. Cooper did not begin his career in letters for another nine years. In 1814 Cooper moved to Cooperstown, N.Y., then to Scarsdale, N.Y., in 1817. There, it is said, he claimed he could write a better book than the novel he was then reading, and his wife challenged him to do so. Thus began the career of one of the most popular novelists in American literary history.

III. Business and Industry
Education
Philosophy and Religion
Science

The first large-scale highway construction project of the federal government began this year. The project was the National Road, the first part of which was known as the Cumberland Road because it connected Cumberland, Md., already linked to Baltimore, with Wheeling, in present-day West Virginia. The Cumberland Road was completed in 1818. Originally the National Road was to run to the Mississippi R., but after it reached Vandalia, Ill., in 1830 construction stopped. Until it lost its importance, first to canals and then to railroads, the National Road was the main route west for settlers and a vital commercial artery for farm products moving to eastern cities.

The **first steamboat** to sail down the Mississippi R. was owned by a Mr. & Mrs. Roosevelt. After several interruptions, including an earthquake at New Madrid, Mo., and the birth of a baby to Mrs. Roosevelt, the boat reached New Orleans on Jan. 12, 1812, where it caused a sensation. The boat then commenced regular runs between New Orleans and Natchez, charging $18 for the downstream trip and $25 for the upstream trip.

IV. Fashion
Folkways
Holidays
Social Issues and Crime
Sports

Even as the nation grew in size, its social fabric was being enriched by the introduction of new national groups. In 1811 Russians were exploring and claiming areas of the Far West that eventually became U.S. territory. On Feb. 2 Russians landed at Bodega Bay, north of San Francisco, and established Fort Ross, a fur-trading post. Russians had been the first Europeans to reach Alaska, in 1741, under the leadership of Vitus Bering, a Dane in Russian employ. They established the first settlement in Alaska in 1784 on Kodiak Island, and further strengthened their claim to the region with the founding of the Russian-American Company in 1799.

Jan: A **slave insurrection** took place in Louisiana when some 400 slaves rose up, killed the son of a plantation owner, and marched on New Orleans. Armed soldiers and planters put down the uprising, and some 75 of the slaves were killed. The uprising was an indication of the frail foundation on which the southern economy and social fabric were based. Fear of further bloody uprisings was to play an important role in the nation's political and social history leading up to the Civil War.

1812

I. Civil Rights
Exploration and Settlement
Government
Statistics
Wars

The War of 1812 began on June 18, when Pres. James Madison officially proclaimed the U.S. to be at war with Great Britain. Congress had voted for war on June 4 and June 8. The war, which caused great harm to the U.S. economy, came after a long period of troubled relations between the two countries, caused mainly by Britain's conflict with Napoleonic France. The British seized American ships, impressed seamen from them, some of whom were U.S. citizens, and attempted to keep U.S. ships from reaching French ports. The war was also the result of the influence of the so-called War Hawks in Congress, Henry Clay and other westerners who wanted to acquire more land by conquering Canada. Ironically, on June 23 Great Britain, not yet aware of the declaration of war, suspended the orders that had hampered U.S. shipping.

1812-1813: In **congressional elections** the Republicans lost three Senate seats but still led the Federalists

27–9. In the House the Federalists gained 32 seats to the Republicans' four, but the latter maintained a majority, 112–68.

Apr 30: Louisiana was admitted to the Union, the 18th state. Formerly known as Orleans Territory, it was made up mainly of land from the Louisiana Purchase of 1803, but also included the part of West Florida annexed in 1810 west of the Pearl R.

May 14: Annexation by a congressional act added the **West Florida territory** to the territory of Mississippi and to the nation.

Aug 16: Brig. Gen. **William Hull surrendered Detroit** to British forces under Gen. Isaac Brock, making no attempt to defend the city though the attacking force was smaller than his own. Hull was court-martialed two years later for yielding without resistance.

Oct 13: Gen. **Stephen Van Rensselaer** was defeated in the battle of Queenstown Heights, Canada, on the Niagara frontier by the British and Indians. About 1000 U.S. troops were killed or wounded. British Gen. Isaac Brock, captor of Detroit, was killed during the engagement.

Dec 2: James Madison was reelected president of the United States, defeating De Witt Clinton of New York, who had been endorsed by the Federalists and by Democratic-Republicans opposed to the war. Elbridge Gerry, Democratic-Republican of Massachusetts, was elected vice president. The presidential electoral vote was Madison, 128; Clinton, 89. The vice presidential electoral vote was Gerry, 131; Charles Jared Ingersoll, Federalist of Pennsylvania, 86.

Dec 29: The U.S. frigate *Constitution* destroyed the British frigate *Java* in a fight off the coast of Brazil. *Old Ironsides* was under the command of Commodore William Bainbridge.

II. Architecture
Arts and Music
Popular Entertainment
Publishing
Theater

Thomas Sully was an Anglo-American who became the leading portrait painter of his day. Born in England, Sully came to the U.S. as a child and later lived and worked in both countries. He was influenced by Benjamin West and Sir Thomas Lawrence, and his portraits were in the Romantic style, urbane and elegant. They included likenesses of Queen Victoria, Fanny Kemble, Andrew Jackson, and Samuel Coates. The Coates portrait shows the subject standing by his desk, quill pen in hand, a cosmopolitan gentleman. Sully also did historical paintings, his best known being *Washington's Passage of the Delaware*. He produced some 2000 portraits in all as well as miniatures.

Apr 13: *Marmion* by James N. Barker, a highly successful dramatization of the poem by Sir Walter Scott, opened in New York City. With the U.S. at war with Great Britain, the anti-English sentiments expressed by Scott's characters held great appeal for New York audiences. Yet the producer listed the play as written by an Englishman, Thomas Morton, to cater to the esteem Americans placed on British culture.

III. Business and Industry
Education
Philosophy and Religion
Science

American religious groups, which in colonial days had been the object of missionary efforts from England and other countries, in the early nineteenth century began to proselytize abroad. The American Board of Commissioners for Foreign Missions was formed in 1810. The Baptists established a group to support missions in 1814, the Methodists in 1819, the Episcopalians in 1820, and the Presbyterians in 1837, although work by the Presbyterians had begun much earlier. Adoniram Judson, a leader of the missionary movement that had spawned the American Board, went to India in 1812. In 1813 he traveled to Burma, where he remained for 30 years and where he translated the Bible into Burmese. By 1848 there were 283 American missionaries in the Orient.

The **Academy of Natural Sciences of Philadelphia** was founded, dedicated to the advancement of the natural sciences. It was immediately popular and generously supported. Within two years the original membership of seven doubled, 33 correspondents were making contributions, and a program of lectures on plants and insects was scheduled. The public was admitted in 1828, two years after the museum had been expanded by the addition of another building. Among today's more than 140,000 volumes, those presented by the original donors maintain a place of honor.

IV. Fashion
Folkways
Holidays
Social Issues and Crime
Sports

The first use of *Uncle Sam* to personify the federal government occurred during the War of 1812. It seems to have been used derisively at first by those opposed to the war and stemmed probably from the "U.S." stamped on uniforms and government wagons. Some attribute the origin of the term to Samuel Wilson of Troy, N.Y. His nickname was Uncle Sam and he was an inspector of Army supplies. The "U.S." stamped on supplies was referred to by workmen as Uncle Sam. The first recorded use of the term in print was in the Troy *Post* of Sept. 3, 1813, and the first appearance in a book was in *Adventures of Uncle Sam* (1816) by an author who used the name Frederick Augustus Fidfaddy, Esq.

Gerrymandering entered the national vocabulary as a term indicating political abuse. The Massachusetts legislature had passed a bill that would facilitate the rigging of contests for senatorial offices by a systematic reapportionment of the electoral districts within the state. In 1812 the senatorial districts corresponded to the areas of the counties. When the Republicans gained control of the legislature, they cited a provision of the state constitution that invested the legislature with the power of determining electoral districts. Elbridge Gerry, the governor, signed the bill into a law. The districts followed no regular lines. One district resembled a salamander or, in the words of a Federalist, a *Gerrymander.*

1813

I. Civil Rights
Exploration and Settlement
Government
Statistics
Wars

An Indian uprising in the South brought on the Creek Indian War (1813–1814). Creeks who lived mainly in Alabama and Georgia were alarmed by encroachments on their lands and were convinced by Tecumseh, the Shawnee chief, to unite with many other tribes against the settlers. The leader of the Creeks was William Weatherford, also known as Red Eagle. On Aug. 30, 1813, he led an attack on Fort Mims, a temporary stockade near the confluence of the Tombigbee and Alabama rivers. Although Weatherford attempted to restrain his warriors, they massacred some 500 whites. The U.S. retaliated on Nov. 3 when Gen. John Coffee attacked and destroyed the Indian village Talladega, in Alabama, killing more than 500 warriors. In Jan. 1814, however, Tennessee militiamen were defeated in three minor engagements. The war did not end until the Battle of Horsehoe Bend in Mar. 1814.

Apr 27: British forces surrendered **York, Canada,** now Toronto, to Americans commanded by Brig. Gen. Zebulon M. Pike, who was killed in the battle.

June 1: Capt. **James Lawrence** cried "Don't give up the ship" to his crew as he lay mortally wounded aboard the *Chesapeake,* which was subsequently defeated and captured by the British frigate *Shannon* in an engagement off the Massachusetts coast.

Sep 10: The **Battle of Lake Erie** was a significant American naval victory. An improvised American fleet commanded by Oliver Hazard Perry decisively defeated the British after a bloody engagement. During the battle Perry's flagship *Lawrence* was crippled and he had to continue the fight from another ship. He returned to the *Lawrence* to accept the British surrender, then sent to Gen. William Henry Harrison, commander in the west, the victory dispatch containing the words "We have met the enemy, and they are ours." The Americans gained control of Lake Erie, and the British were obliged to withdraw from Detroit, further strengthening the U.S. position in the Great Lakes.

II. Architecture
Arts and Music
Popular Entertainment
Publishing
Theater

The most successful woman author of the late eighteenth and early nineteenth centuries was Susanna Rowson, who had come to America from England in 1793. In England she had published in 1791 the sentimental and didactic novel *Charlotte Temple: A Tale of Truth.* It was issued in America in 1794, described as "designed . . . for the perusal of the young and thoughtful of the fair sex." By 1933 it had gone through 161 editions in the U.S. Mrs. Rowson was also an actress and author of comedies and comic operas. Although she left the stage in 1797 and opened a girls' boarding school near Boston, Mrs. Rowson continued to write, her work including the novel *Sarah; or, The Exemplary Wife* (1813).

Sep 4: The **first religious weekly** in America, *Religious Remembrancer,* founded in Philadelphia by John W. Scott, began publication. Through successive mergers the magazine grew, and eventually became the *Christian Observer.*

III. Business and Industry
Education
Philosophy and Religion
Science

In 1813 Jethro Wood, a farmer in New York State, invented a cast-iron plow that he patented the following year. This was the 19th patent for a plow issued in the U.S. Charles Newbold had patented the first cast-iron plow in 1797. In 1819 Wood patented an improved plow that had replaceable iron parts and a curved plate, the moldboard. The modern moldboard derives from Wood's moldboard. Wood's design remains little changed today, but John Deere's substitution of steel for cast iron two decades later proved more effective in turning the heavy, sticky soil of the prairies.

Feb 26: **Robert R. Livingston,** one of the leading figures in the development of steam transportation, died. Livingston had financed Robert Fulton's first successful steamboat, the *Clermont,* which had sailed up the Hudson R. in 1807. As a result of Fulton's early support, Livingston had secured a monopoly on steamboat shipping in New York waters. Livingston was a man of many achievements. He had been a member of the committee that drafted the Declaration of Independence in 1776. As the first chancellor of the State of New York, he had administered the presidential oath of office to George Washington in 1789, and in 1801, as U.S. minister to France, conducted the negotiations that led to the Louisiana Purchase.

IV. Fashion
Folkways
Holidays
Social Issues and Crime
Sports

The gambling game of craps, derived from the English and French game of hazard, began to be played in the U.S. at about this time. At least as early as the sixteenth century, the throw of 1–1 with dice was called crabs, and the word *craps* stems from this term. According to one legend, blacks around New Orleans, La., began playing hazard about 1800, when the game was already sometimes called crabs or craps. Rules were so modified that craps became a separate game. Another explanation is that a rich playboy of New Orleans, Bernard Xavier Philippe de Marigny de Mandeville, introduced craps to America. He is said to have lost most of his money shooting craps. In any event, New Orleans seems to have been the starting point for the game of craps.

The celebrated "witch" **Moll Pitcher** died in Lynn, Mass. Her fame had spread throughout the region. Hundreds went to her for prophecy, love potions, and knowledge of lost things. She is reputed to have presided at conventions of witches at Lynn. Every time she visited a community, she entered its folklore. Years later she became the subject of the long poem *Moll Pitcher* (1832) by John Greenleaf Whittier.

1814

I. Civil Rights
Exploration and Settlement
Government
Statistics
Wars

The Treaty of Ghent, ending the War of 1812, was signed on Dec. 24 by representatives of the U.S. and Great Britain. The Senate ratified the treaty in Feb. 1815. The American negotiators were John Quincy Adams, James A. Bayard, Henry Clay, Jonathan Russell, and Albert Gallatin. By terms of the treaty, all conquered territory was to be returned by both sides, and a commission was to settle the boundary between the U.S. and Canada from the St. Croix R. west to Lake of the Woods. The British did not achieve their aim to set up an Indian buffer state in the Northwest. The emotional issues that helped cause the war—impressment of American seamen and the rights of neutral commerce—were not mentioned.

1814-1815: In **congressional elections** the Republicans lost two Senate seats but led the Federalists 25–11. In the House they gained five seats for a 117–65 majority.

Mar 29: The **Creek War** (1813–1814) ended as Gen. Andrew Jackson defeated the Creeks under Chief Weatherford at the decisive battle of Horseshoe Bend, Ala., where nearly 900 of 1000 Indians were killed. The Creeks had fought with British troops against the Americans in the War of 1812.

Aug 24: Washington, D.C., was captured by British troops under Gen. Robert Ross. The Capitol, White House, and other government buildings were set afire in retaliation for the earlier burning of Canadian government buildings in York, Toronto, by U.S. troops.

Sep 11: At the **Battle of Lake Champlain** a newly built U.S. fleet under Master-Commandant Thomas Macdonough annihilated a British squadron. This forced British Gen. Sir George Prevost and his army to abandon their siege of the U.S. fort at Plattsburgh and to retreat to Canada on foot.

II. Architecture
Arts and Music
Popular Entertainment
Publishing
Theater

The words to "The Star Spangled Banner" were written during the War of 1812 by Francis Scott Key, a lawyer, on the night of Sept. 13–14, 1814, during the unsuccessful bombardment of an American fort by British warships. Key was on his way to the British fleet to try to secure release of an American citizen held by the British. He was detained by the British during their attempt to capture Fort McHenry, near Baltimore. Key was inspired by the sight of the American flag still flying and wrote the words that were set to the music of "Anacreon in Heaven," anthem of the Anacreontic Societies of England, which were clubs of amateur musicians. Key's song was first printed as a handbill; on Sept. 20 it appeared in the Baltimore *Patriot.* Although long considered the national anthem of the U.S., "The Star Spangled Banner" did not officially gain that status until 1931.

A report on the **Lewis and Clark Expedition** (1803–1806), based on the papers of Meriwether Lewis and made available by William Clark, was published by editors Nicholas Biddle and Paul Allen. The report, *History of the Expedition under the Command of Captains Lewis and Clark,* carried a preface by Thomas Jefferson in which the career of Lewis was related in succinct but memorable detail. In 1806 Jefferson himself had given advance notice of the findings of the expedition in his *Message from the President of the United States, Communicating Discoveries Made by Captains Lewis and Clark.* Lewis had intended to arrange publication of the material himself. But immediately after the expedition and retirement from the Army, Jefferson appointed Lewis governor of the Louisiana Territory. Lewis was so busy with the affairs of his office that he found no time to finish his revision before his mysterious death in an inn in Tennessee in 1809. Clark contributed to this edition of the journals, but final discretion was left to his editors. The complete papers remained unpublished until 1903.

III. Business and Industry
Education
Philosophy and Religion
Science

Important improvements in education in the early nineteenth century, especially education of women, were the result of the efforts of Emma Willard. In 1807, when only 20, she took charge of the Female Academy at Middlebury, Vt. She opened a school of her own in 1814. There she taught subjects not otherwise available to women. An appeal to the New York State legislature in 1818 to support her plan for improving the education of women induced Gov. De Witt Clinton to invite Mrs. Willard to move to New York. She accepted, and opened a school at Waterford in 1819. In 1821 she moved to Troy and established the Troy Female Academy. Mrs. Willard wrote textbooks and a volume of poems (1831), which included the popular "Rocked in the Cradle of the Deep."

Francis Cabot Lowell built the first U.S. plant designed to manufacture cloth from raw cotton by power machinery. A Boston importer, Lowell had observed power machinery in British textile plants and had violated British laws by smuggling secretly drawn sketches of that machinery out of the country. With the financial backing of his brother-in-law, Patrick Tracy Jackson, and the mechanical skill of machinist Paul Moody, Lowell secured a charter for the Boston Manufacturing Company, with a capitalization of $300,000. The machinery used in the Waltham factory and all subsequent equipment of the company came to be known as Lowell-Moody machinery and soon was quite different from the English models upon which they had been based. The city of Lowell, Mass., was named after Lowell.

IV. Fashion
Folkways
Holidays
Social Issues and Crime
Sports

A ubiquitous institution of the period was the country store. Most communities were too small to support a variety of retail stores, each specializing in a particular line of goods. The result was the country store, carrying virtually everything—food, clothing, farm equipment, housewares, and more. The Great Western Store, opened by Jedediah Barber at Homer, N.Y., in the central part of the state in 1813, was typical. Starting in one medium-sized room, Barber

expanded his establishment to three stories, attic, and cellar. Like other storekeepers of the time, Barber did much of his business in barter, with customers exchanging products they had made or grown for store goods. Storekeepers often became leading citizens of their communities, sometimes adding real estate and banking to their business enterprises.

The **cost of education at Harvard** was about $300 a year. John Thornton Kirkland became president in 1810 and continued the innovations that had established the liberal bent of the college. He made it possible for poor students to meet fees by offering a number of jobs in which they could earn some money. He also supervised grants and scholarships, as well as an annual subsidy of $2500 that Massachusetts donated to encourage gifted but needy students. In Kirkland's time Harvard had the reputation of being a poor man's school, because he did so much to make it easy for indigent students to attend. Yet the tradition of gentility was already apparent, since the aim of the college was to create the same kind of gentlemen who were described in prospectuses of Cambridge and Oxford. Students attended classes five days a week from 6 A.M. to 4 P.M., with an hour free between the morning and afternoon sessions. Campus social life was encouraged by Kirkland. He contributed to the beginnings of some of the most famous clubs, including Hasty Pudding, Porcellian, Hermetic Society, and Speaking Club. There were extracurricular pleasures in parties and dances, and the college was just far enough from Boston to provide the attractions of both city and country life.

1815

I. Civil Rights
Exploration and Settlement
Government
Statistics
Wars

The greatest battle of the War of 1812 and its finest American victory came on Jan. 8, 1815, two weeks after the war had been ended officially by the Treaty of Ghent. The Battle of New Orleans was fought on the British side by 7500 veterans under the command of Gen. Sir Edward Pakenham. The U.S. force, under the command of Gen. Andrew Jackson, comprised about 4500 troops, many of them expert marksmen from Kentucky and Tennessee armed with exceedingly accurate long rifles. The U.S. troops were strongly entrenched when on the morning of Jan. 8 the British, in close ranks, made two assaults on their lines. In half an hour the British were driven back, Pakenham was killed, and 2036 of his men were killed or wounded. U.S. forces suffered 8 killed and 13 wounded. Although the battle had no bearing on the outcome of the war, it was a stimulus to U.S. pride, which had suffered from several embarrassing defeats during the conflict. The battle made a military hero of Gen. Jackson, whose political career was advanced.

Mar 3: War against Algeria was declared by Congress. The dey of Algiers had molested U.S. ships and insisted on payment of tribute.

June 17: Commodore **Stephen Decatur** captured the Algerian frigate *Mashouda.* Hammida, the renowned Algerian admiral, was killed during this engagement.

June 19: Capt. **Decatur**'s squadron captured *Estido,* an Algerian brig, off Cape Palos in southeastern Spain.

June 30: The **war against Algeria** and the Barbary Coast pirates ended when a peace treaty was signed with the dey of Algiers. It was followed by similar treaties with Tunis on July 26 and Tripoli on Aug. 5. The treaties, exacted by Commodore Stephen Decatur, required the pirates to cease their hostile acts, free all American prisoners, and compensate the U.S. for vessels seized.

II. Architecture
Arts and Music
Popular Entertainment
Publishing
Theater

America's first professional journalist, Philip Freneau, was also the "poet of the American Revolution." In 1775, at the beginning of the war, he wrote eight satirical poems, such as "General Gage's Confession." During the war he was captured by the British on a voyage from the West Indies and in 1781 wrote of the brutal treatment he had received in "The British Prison Ship." Freneau's anti-British sentiments were also expressed during the War of 1812 in such poems as "On British Commercial Depredations." Freneau edited various newspapers, such as the *National Gazette* in Philadelphia from 1791 to 1793. As an editor he was a vigorous Jeffersonian, often in-

volved in editorial quarrels. Beyond his political and patriotic activities, Freneau was the earliest American lyrical poet of importance, writing such poems as "The Wild Honeysuckle" and "Eutaw Springs." An edition of his *Collected Poems* was published in 1815.

The *North American Review,* for a century the most influential review in the U.S., was founded by William Tudor, Edward T. Channing, and Richard Henry Dana, Sr. It soon became a major influence among educated readers. The review published articles by leading American writers, who wrote in professional and scholarly fashion.

III. Business and Industry
Education
Philosophy and Religion
Science

One of the most important economic activities in the U.S. from the late eighteenth century to the middle of the nineteenth century was whaling. In 1791 American whalers for the first time rounded Cape Horn to hunt whales in the South Pacific. New Bedford, Mass., became the greatest whaling port in the world. Although set back by the War of 1812, whalers prospered more than ever after the virtual disappearance of British whaling ships. U.S. ships sailed throughout the Pacific Ocean, often on hunts of three years or more. Shortly before the Civil War, the whaling industry declined because the demand for sperm oil lessened with the coming of the petroleum industry. In addition, the number of whales had been reduced by overhunting.

The **Conestoga wagon** proved to be the most efficient mode of transportation for long treks from the East into the prairie regions. The "prairie schooner" was often bedecked with lively colors, its team of four-to-six horses festooned with bells. It carried a load of several tons and sometimes was built to a length of 60 ft.

IV. Fashion
Folkways
Holidays
Social Issues and Crime
Sports

With the end of the Napoleonic wars in Europe, immigration to the U.S. increased to new levels. Between 1815 and 1860, 5,000,000 persons came to the U.S. Over half of the immigrants came from the British Isles, mostly from Ireland. The next largest contingent arrived from Germany, 1,500,000, not counting German-speaking French citizens from Alsace and Lorraine. More than half the German immigrants settled in the upper Mississippi and Ohio river valleys.

Jean Lafitte, the pirate, became an American folk hero because of his actions at the Battle of New Orleans. Since 1810 Lafitte had been operating off the Baratarian coast, south of New Orleans, as a privateer, preying on Spanish commerce for several Latin American nations. In Sept. 1814, a few days after a U.S. naval force raided his base at Barataria, Lafitte was offered a commission by the Royal Navy. Instead of accepting, Lafitte offered to help Andrew Jackson in return for a U.S. pardon for his piratical offenses. Lafitte and his men acquitted themselves admirably in the Battle of New Orleans, but in 1817 he moved his crew to the site of present-day Galveston, Tex., where they resumed a life of piracy.

1816

I. Civil Rights
Exploration and Settlement
Government
Statistics
Wars

The presidential election of 1816 resulted in continuation of the so-called Virginia dynasty of presidents that had begun with Thomas Jefferson's election in 1800. The Democratic-Republican candidate was James Monroe of Virginia, who had been wounded in the American Revolution, and had served as diplomat, senator, and secretary of state. The Federalists by now scarcely existed as a national political party. They nominated Rufus King, who had been a delegate to the Constitutional Convention and one of New York's first senators. He carried only Massachusetts, Connecticut, and Delaware. The election was yet one more indication of the moribund condition of the Federalist Party. From this election on, it became ever weaker and ceased to exist in the 1820s.

1816-1817: In **congressional elections** the Republicans gained nine Senate seats for a 34–10 majority over the Federalists. In the House they gained 24 seats for a 141–42 majority.

Dec 4: James Monroe was elected president of the United States. Daniel D. Tompkins was elected vice president. Monroe, secretary of state under Pres. James Madison, gained the presidency in a landslide victory over his Federalist opponent, Rufus King of New York. The presidential electoral vote was Madison, 183; King, 34; and four abstentions.

Dec 11: Indiana was admitted into the Union as the 19th state. Five years earlier, at the Tippecanoe R., it had been the scene of a decisive encounter between the confederated Indians under Tecumseh and U.S. forces under Gen. William Henry Harrison. After that encounter the Indians had made one last major raid, in 1812, then chose to sell out to the settlers and move beyond the Mississippi R. In June 1816 a constitution for the new state was drafted in the Indiana state capital at Corydon. In 1825 the state capital was moved to Indianapolis.

II. Architecture
Arts and Music
Popular Entertainment
Publishing
Theater

It was believed in some quarters and hoped in others that one result of securing independence from England would be development of an American language. Differences in spelling and vocabulary increased, but the American language has never achieved true independence from the mother tongue.

Aug: "The Culprit Fay," a poem of more than 600 lines, was written in three days by Joseph Rodman Drake. Drake died of tuberculosis in 1820, and his poem was not published until 1835, in the volume *The Culprit Fay and Other Poems.* On his deathbed Drake had ordered his wife to destroy the manuscripts of what he described as his "trifles in rhyme." Fortunately, she did not do so. "The Culprit Fay," set against the background of the Hudson R. Valley, is considered an important milestone in the development of American literature.

III. Business and Industry
Education
Philosophy and Religion
Science

Black religious groups began to break away from largely white Protestant denominations to form their own churches. In 1796 black members of the Methodist Episcopal Church in New York City formed the

African Methodist Episcopal Zion Church, which in 1821 was organized as a national group. The African Methodist Episcopal Church was founded in 1816 by Richard Allen, a clergyman who had been born a slave. He was pastor of a group that broke away from the Methodist Church in Philadelphia. On Apr. 11 he became the first bishop of the new denomination.

The **American Bible Society** was founded in New York City. The purpose of the organization was to increase circulation of the Bible. Through the society translations of the Bible in over 1000 tongues have been printed and distributed around the world. The society emphasizes distribution of the Bible to the poor. It was incorporated in 1841 and in cooperation with the British and Foreign Bible Society has developed into an organization of worldwide influence with a large membership and many auxiliaries.

June: Baltimore, Md., became the first city in the U.S. to launch a **gas company**. The Gas Light Company of Baltimore was organized to provide coal gas for lighting the city's streets.

Dec 13: The **first savings bank** in the U.S. was organized in Boston as The Provident Institution for Savings.

IV. Fashion
Folkways
Holidays
Social Issues and Crime
Sports

Transportation of blacks from the U.S. to Africa was often proposed as a partial solution for the slavery question. The first important step along these lines was taken at a meeting in Washington, D.C., in Dec. 1816 and Jan. 1817, when the American Colonization Society was formed. The principal founder was Robert Finley, a clergyman. Freeing many black slaves created a new problem: freedmen did not enjoy equal status with whites. In 1821 land was secured in Africa that later became the independent nation of Liberia, but by 1860 only about 11,000 blacks had been transported there. Abolitionists opposed resettlement, claiming it merely made slavery stronger in the South by removing free blacks. At the same time, many blacks born in the U.S. showed little enthusiasm for resettlement in Africa.

"Our country, right or wrong" was included in a toast offered by Stephen Decatur at a Virginia dinner commemorating his success against the pirates of the Barbary Coast. Called on to propose a toast he said: "Our Country! In her intercourse with foreign governments may she always be in the right; but our country, right or wrong."

1817

I. Civil Rights
Exploration and Settlement
Government
Statistics
Wars

The first step in a process of mutual disarmament along the U.S.-Canadian border was taken this year in the Rush-Bagot Convention, signed on Apr. 28–29. The agreement was contained in an exchange of notes in Washington, D.C., between Richard Rush, acting secretary of state, and Charles Bagot, the British minister to the U.S. By its terms, each nation would have no more than four warships on the Great Lakes and Lake Champlain, and none would exceed 100 tons. The Senate unanimously approved the agreement on Apr. 16, 1818. The agreement set a precedent for solving Anglo-American disagreements by negotiation, although it was not until the Treaty of Washington of 1871 that complete mutual disarmament obtained along the U.S.-Canadian border.

Nov 20: The **First Seminole War** (1817–1818) began when settlers attacked Florida Indians and the Indians retaliated by raiding isolated Georgia homesteads. Americans believed Spain had incited the Seminoles against the white settlers.

Dec 10: Mississippi was admitted into the Union, the 20th state.

II. Architecture
Arts and Music
Popular Entertainment
Publishing
Theater

More than any other painter, John Trumbull provided future generations with a record of the Revolutionary era. After studying under Benjamin West in London, he began copying his teacher's grand style in historical paintings. An early and moving example was *The Death of General Montgomery at Quebec.* In 1816 Trumbull secured a commission from Congress to decorate the Capitol, and the best known result was *Signing of the Declaration of Independence* (1818). Others were *Surrender of Burgoyne at Saratoga, Surrender of Cornwallis at Yorktown,* and *Resignation of Washington.* In 1831 he founded Trumbull Gallery at Yale and placed much of his work in it.

Sep: The poem **"Thanatopsis"** by William Cullen Bryant won for American poetry its first attention and respect from British critics. Printed in the *North American Review,* the poem's appearance was "much as if a classic temple had been exorcised from the wilderness by the strains of a new Amphion." Its quiet reflections on death and nature created an entire school of American poets.

III. Business and Industry
Education
Philosophy and Religion
Science

The distribution by religious groups of Christian literature not only spread religion but also contributed significantly to education. The Connecticut Tract Society was formed in 1807. In 1814 it joined with half a dozen similar groups to form a national organization, the American Tract Society. After 1817 the society supplied much religious literature, which was distributed widely by circuit riders. In many homes these were the only books, and from them children learned to read and spell. Peter Cartwright, a Methodist circuit rider for nearly 50 years, wondered whether he "had done the most good by preaching or by distributing religious books." He felt "it was part and parcel of a Methodist preacher's most sacred duty to circulate good books." Cartwright sometimes handed out a thousand dollars worth of books a year, a large amount at that time.

July 4: Construction of the **Erie Canal** was begun under Gov. De Witt Clinton of New York, elected in spring of 1817. The canal was to affect the development of New York, both city and state, bringing Great Lakes trade to the Atlantic Ocean.

IV. Fashion
Folkways
Holidays
Social Issues and Crime
Sports

Fashions in clothing changed considerably in the early nineteenth century. Under the influence of the romantic movement and the French Revolution, women's fashions became simpler. Light dresses, low-cut and sleeveless, replaced the elaborate billowing gowns of the old aristocracy. Hair was cut shorter, not piled high. About 1815 fashion began moving back to the era of stiff corsets, leg-of-mutton sleeves, and full skirts that developed into the hoop skirt. Men's fashions also changed. Knee-length pantaloons, with buckles, silk stockings, and low-cut shoes, as well as the wig, were on their way out by 1800. Pres. James Monroe was the last chief executive to dress this way, and an 1823 painting of him and his cabinet shows Monroe the only person so clothed. Long trousers came in, reflecting the French Revolution, whose supporters came from the middle and lower classes and dressed this way to contrast with the nobility. The style seemed appropriate for democratic America.

Cup plates became the rage at about this time. They were miniature plates with a center cavity about the diameter of a cup bottom used as a dainty but practical perch for cups while a drinker sipped from his saucer. Cup plates were decorated with lavish attention to detail, came in a great variety of patterns, and fairly chronicled the taste of the period. They were introduced first as chinaware. The development of the glass industry, especially of the glass press, made them even more plentiful and, considering their use, necessary. Cup plates lasted as long as it was considered polite to drink from a saucer but went out of vogue before the Civil War.

1818

I. Civil Rights
Exploration and Settlement
Government
Statistics
Wars

The First Seminole War (1817–1818) began in earnest this year with a U.S. invasion of East Florida to punish hostile Seminole Indians, whose territory had become a refuge for runaway slaves. American troops on July 27, 1816, had destroyed the Seminole stronghold of Fort Apalachicola, on the river of that name. On Dec. 27, 1817, Gen. Andrew Jackson took command, with orders to pursue the Indians across the Florida boundary. Jackson marched his troops into Florida and captured St. Marks on Apr. 7, 1818, and Pensacola on May 24. In the course of his campaign, Jackson seized two British traders, Alexander Arbuthnot and Robert Ambrister. He accused them of aiding the enemy and had the former hanged and the latter shot. There was a great outcry in England and considerable criticism in Washington. Nevertheless, popular opinion approved the campaign, which brought East Florida under American control and resulted in its cession to the U.S. by Spain in 1819.

1818-1819: In **congressional elections** the Republicans gained one Senate seat for a 35–7 majority over the Federalists. In the House they gained 15 seats for a 156–27 majority.

Oct 20: A **diplomatic convention** signed between Britain and the U.S. gave fishing rights to American seamen off parts of Newfoundland and the coast of Labrador. The U.S. renounced such activity within three miles of any other British territory. The boundary between Canada and the U.S. between Lake of the Woods and the crest of the Rocky Mts. was fixed at the 49th parallel. No boundary was decided upon farther west, and Oregon was declared open territory for ten years.

Dec 3: Illinois was admitted into the Union, the 21st state.

II. Architecture
Arts and Music
Popular Entertainment
Publishing
Theater

An unusual example of an American playwright of the early years of independence who won acclaim, although not riches, on both sides of the Atlantic was John Howard Payne (1791–1852). Showing a precocious interest in the drama, he published the *Thespian Mirror* in New York City when he was only 14. It so impressed the literary and theater world that he was encouraged to write. He proceeded to write a melodrama, *Julia; or, The Wanderer* in 1806. His early fame waned, and it was not until 1818, in England, that he regained recognition. Success stemmed from the production by Edmund Kean, the noted British actor, of Payne's *Brutus; or, The Fall of Tarquin,* which opened on Dec. 3. This romantic tragedy, in blank verse, was equally successful in New York in 1819. It was performed for many years. By 1832, after other successes and writing the poem "Home, Sweet Home," which was put to music, Payne was honored but died in debt while working on further literary and dramatic works.

Jan 1: The **White House,** as the restored Executive Mansion in Washington, D.C., was now called because of its gleaming new coat of white paint, was opened for a general reception. Burned out by the British in 1814, the building was ready for occupancy in the fall of 1817, but lacked proper furnishings.

III. Business and Industry
Education
Philosophy and Religion
Science

Americans in the early nineteenth century continued to show interest in science. One of the foremost scientists was Benjamin Silliman, who in 1802 became the first professor of chemistry and natural history at Yale. In 1813 he began an illustrated lecture course in geology and mineralogy and in 1818 was one of the founders of the Yale Medical School. Also in 1818 he became one of the founders of the *American Journal of Science and Arts,* the first important scientific journal in the U.S., which he edited for nearly 28 years.

Jan: Transatlantic ship crossings on a regular monthly basis were initiated between U.S. and British ports when the *James Monroe* sailed from New York City and the *Courier* from Liverpool, England. Four ships formed the Black Ball Line.

IV. Fashion
Folkways
Holidays
Social Issues and Crime
Sports

Bowling had been introduced to America by the Dutch in the seventeenth century, when the game became a ten-pin rather than nine-pin game. By mid-nineteenth century there was a boom in the building of indoor alleys. Gambling began to invade the sport, and in 1841 bowling was banned in Connecticut for this reason. Still it remained a regular amusement at the fashionable Saratoga, N.Y., spa. In literature, the game of ninepins plays an important part in Washington Irving's "Rip Van Winkle," probably his most popular story, issued serially in *The Sketch Book* (1819–1820).

Apr 4: A **U.S. flag with 13 stripes** was settled on by Congress. On admission of each new state to the Union, another star would be added to the flag, the number and pattern of stripes remaining the same.

1819

I. Civil Rights
Exploration and Settlement
Government
Statistics
Wars

The Supreme Court, under the leadership of Chief Justice John Marshall, continued to set precedents increasing the power of the judiciary and the national government. In the case of *McCullock v. Maryland* in 1819, Marshall found an opportunity to assert the power of the federal government over the states. Maryland had levied a tax on a branch of the Bank of the United States. Marshall argued that if the government had the right to coin money, which the Constitution gave it, it had the implied right to establish a bank. Thus, the government was supreme in that sphere and a state could not tax an instrument of the central government. This argument is generally agreed to be Marshall's most brilliant opinion on constitutional law, but it was not universally accepted at the time.

Feb 22: The **Florida Purchase Treaty** was signed by Spain and the U.S. In a triumph of diplomacy by Sec. of State John Quincy Adams, Spain ceded the remainder of its old province of Florida at no cost beyond that of U.S. assumption of up to $5,000,000 of the claims of U.S. citizens against Spain. Adams also obtained for the U.S. a transcontinental southern boundary that legitimized U.S. interests on the northern side of the line to the Pacific.

Dec 14: Alabama was admitted into the Union, the 22nd state.

II. Architecture
Arts and Music
Popular Entertainment
Publishing
Theater

One of the earliest satirical writers on public affairs in the U.S. was Joseph Rodman Drake, a poet of New York. A series of satirical poems called "The Croaker Papers" appeared anonymously in the New York *Evening Post* and *National Advertiser* this year. Of the 35 poems, Drake wrote 14 and collaborated on eight with his friend Fitz-Greene Halleck. Drake also wrote "The Culprit Fay," a serious poem, and "The American Flag," a patriotic poem that was declaimed on

many occasions for years after. Drake died of consumption on Sept. 21, 1820, at 25. Halleck's poem "On the Death of Joseph Rodman Drake" is considered one of the finest elegies in American literature.

Washington Irving's *Sketch Book* became an immediate best seller and still ranks among the most popular American books of all time. With this book Irving established himself as a beloved literary genius.

III. Business and Industry
Education
Philosophy and Religion
Science

In the Dartmouth College case the Supreme Court, under Chief Justice John Marshall, continued to uphold the power of the federal government. In 1816 New Hampshire, without the consent of Dartmouth College, amended the college charter, which in legal terms was a contract. The college brought suit, with Daniel Webster as counsel. Marshall wrote the court's opinion, holding that New Hampshire acted unconstitutionally, violating the Constitution's prohibition against any state passing laws "impairing the Obligation of Contracts." The decision became a major instrument for protection of property rights against state abridgment.

What was probably the **first food canning business** was begun in New York City when Ezra Daggett and Thomas Kensett started canning fish as a commercial enterprise. In 1825 Kensett obtained a patent, the first, for tin-plated cans. In Boston William Underwood opened a successful canning plant in 1820.

William Ellery Channing delivered his famous sermon, "Unitarian Christianity," in Baltimore. In it he outlined the Unitarian view and provided liberals with a platform. The sermon heightened tensions among Protestant factions and led to formation of the American Unitarian Association.

IV. Fashion
Folkways
Holidays
Social Issues and Crime
Sports

The eastern U.S. was slowly becoming urbanized, but the frontier, moving ever westward, was still the place for the vigorous outdoor activities associated with newly settled rural areas. Marksmanship was highly prized and involved such sports as squirrel shooting by four-man teams. On one occasion, a team shot 152 squirrels by nightfall and the other, 141. A brutal sport was the rough-and-tumble fight. There were no rules and the two contestants were free to bite off ears or gouge out eyes until a fighter gave up or was knocked unconscious.

Apr 26: The **Independent Order of Odd Fellows** made its first appearance in the U.S. with the organization of Washington Lodge No. 1 in Baltimore, Md., by Thomas Wildey, who had arrived from England in 1818. On Feb. 1, 1820, the new lodge was chartered by Duke of York Lodge, Preston, England.

1820

I. Civil Rights
Exploration and Settlement
Government
Statistics
Wars

The first serious clash between slavery and antislavery interests, in 1819 and 1820, strained relations between the North and the South and hinted at worse trouble to come. At the end of 1818 the Union consisted of 11 free and 11 slave states. The North, however, was rapidly outdistancing the South in population and held a growing numerical advantage in the House of Representatives. Southern leaders felt strongly, therefore, that the number of free and slave states should remain balanced so that the South would be equal to the North in the Senate. Ready for statehood were Maine, certain to be a free state, and Missouri, part of the Louisiana Purchase and likely to be a slave state. After much political maneuvering, Congress passed on Mar. 3, 1820, a bill that became known as the Missouri Compromise. By its terms Maine was to be admitted as a free state and Missouri as a slave state, but slavery was to be forever prohibited in the rest of the Louisiana Purchase north of the line of latitude 36°30′, which was the southern boundary of Missouri.

The fourth U.S. **Census** recorded a population of 9,638,453. The center of population was placed 16 miles east of Moorefield, W. Va.

1820-1821: In **congressional elections** the Republicans gained nine Senate seats for a 44–4 majority over the Federalists. In the House they gained two seats for a 158–25 majority.

Mar 15: Maine was admitted into the Union, the 23rd state.

Dec 6: James Monroe was reelected president of the United States. Daniel D. Tompkins was reelected vice president. The electoral vote was Monroe, 231; John Quincy Adams, a Federalist and Monroe's secretary of state, 1.

II. Architecture
Arts and Music
Popular Entertainment
Publishing
Theater

The Knickerbocker Group was a school of writers with similar literary tastes who were associated with New York City. The name was a tribute to Washington Irving's *Knickerbocker's History of New York* (1809); those who followed Irving tried to carry on his spirit and style. Among the Knickerbockers were William Cullen Bryant, James Kirke Paulding, Joseph Rodman Drake, Lydia Maria Child, and Fitz-Greene Halleck. In 1819 Halleck's long poem *Fanny* was published. In it, in imitation of the style of Lord Byron, he satirized in rollicking fashion life in New York—finance, society, women, etc. Halleck also found time to be personal secretary to the entrepreneur John Jacob Astor.

A great **literary theme** of the 1820s was the romantic treatment of the Indian. Works in this vein included *Frontier Maid, or the Fall of Wyoming* (1819); *Yamoyden* (1820) by Eastburn and Sands; *Logan, an Indian Tale* (1821) by Samuel Webber; *The Land of Powhatten* (1821) by a Virginian; and *Ontwa, Son of the Forest* (1822) by Henry Whiting.

III. Business and Industry
Education
Philosophy and Religion
Science

Americans were beginning to take an interest in the history and culture of the Indians. The foremost pioneer in this field was Henry Rowe Schoolcraft, a self-taught ethnologist and geologist. This year Schoolcraft accompanied an expedition to the upper Mississippi R. and Lake Superior region, and two years later he was appointed Indian agent for the tribes in that area. This enabled Schoolcraft to carry on his research into Indian history and culture and resulted in voluminous writings. These included a six-volume history published between 1851 and 1857. Schoolcraft married the daughter of an Ojibwa woman and a fur trader. Henry Wadsworth Longfellow used Schoolcraft's writings as source material for his narrative poem *The Song of Hiawatha* (1855).

The **number of college graduates** in the U.S. was estimated by James Fenimore Cooper to be 8000, in a population of 10,000,000.

The evolution of **interchangeable machine parts** was stepped up by Thomas Blanchard's invention of a special lathe to finish off wooden stocks of firearms. Stocks could be cut out in rapid order and used with standardized metal parts of guns. Success with his lathe encouraged Blanchard to apply his invention to more general industrial uses.

IV. Fashion
   Folkways
   Holidays
   Social Issues and Crime
   Sports

The frontier attracted rugged types who liked to boast of their toughness, since the West was a region where physical strength was often a necessity. The phrase *half horse, half alligator,* first recorded in 1809 by Washington Irving, was an appellation such persons liked to use in referring to themselves. Mark Twain later wrote of a rough-and-tumble fighter who introduced himself in this way: "the original iron-jawed, brass-mounted, copper-bellied corpse-maker from the wilds of Arkansaw," concluding with "cast your eye on me, gentlemen, and lay low and hold your breath, for I'm 'bout to turn myself loose."

During this decade the **first soccerlike games** appeared in American colleges. A large round ball was kicked toward a goal. The game served as a form of hazing, especially at Yale and Harvard. Sophomores and freshmen were supposed to kick the ball, but sophomores generally kicked freshmen instead. The games were banned during the 1830s because of the large number of injuries sustained by students.

1821

I. Civil Rights
   Exploration and Settlement
   Government
   Statistics
   Wars

As part of the westward movement, American traders probed the Southwest, which put them in contact with Spanish regions. Traffic over what was to become the Santa Fe Trail began on Sept. 1, 1821, when William Becknell led a party from Independence, Mo., headed for Santa Fe, N. Mex. Spanish authorities had forbidden trading with Americans, but such trade was welcome after Mexico won its independence in Nov. 1821. The trip of about 780 miles was made yearly by caravans comprising as many as 100 wagons, the trip taking 40 to 60 days. The caravans carried textiles and hardware to Santa Fe, where the traders usually remained for four or five weeks before returning to Missouri.

Aug 10: Missouri was admitted into the Union, the 24th state.

Dec: The **first American settlement in Texas,** San Felipe de Austin, was established by Stephen Austin.

II. Architecture
   Arts and Music
   Popular Entertainment
   Publishing
   Theater

Music was made more available to amateurs and students by the publication of songbooks and by the introduction into schools of music education. A pioneer in this field was Lowell Mason, a banker and church organist in Savannah, Ga. In 1821 he helped compile the *Boston Handel and Haydn Society's Collection of Church Music.* Its success was one reason why Mason gave up banking and turned to music, becoming the musical director of three Boston churches. He was a founder of the Boston Academy of Music in 1832. Mason also found time to compose 1210 hymns, including "Nearer, My God, to Thee."

The Spy by James Fenimore Cooper, a romance of the American Revolution, was published and quickly went through three printings in its first year.

III. Business and Industry
   Education
   Philosophy and Religion
   Science

The need for more and better roads to transport people and goods also meant that more and better bridges were needed. Ithiel Town, an architect, contributed to the cause by patenting in 1820 a form of truss bridge with a diamond pattern of closely spaced diagonals. This was simple to construct and required no special materials. In 1821 he wrote an article that considered the problem of rigid iron bridges. It was to take 15 years before such structures were built in the U.S.

May 31: The **first Catholic cathedral** in the U.S., the Cathedral of the Assumption of the Blessed Virgin Mary, Baltimore, Md., was dedicated by Archbishop Maréchal. The cornerstone had been laid in 1806.

IV. Fashion
Folkways
Holidays
Social Issues and Crime
Sports

The most serious attempt to find a home outside the U.S. for freed black slaves was the establishment in 1821 of the colony of Liberia in western Africa. With government and private funds, the American Colonization Society purchased the area from local tribal chiefs. Settlement began in 1822, when the first of about 15,000 persons arrived in Liberia. The colony had many difficulties, and its survival in the early years was due mainly to the efforts of Jehudi Ashmun, who was sent there by the society and who built up the colony in spite of epidemics and native attacks. The colony was declared independent in 1847. Immigration of American blacks ended for the most part after the Civil War.

During the next decade and a half **coffee** came into general use in America. But temperance movements directed heavy campaigns against it, and in some quarters it was considered an aphrodisiac.

1822

I. Civil Rights
Exploration and Settlement
Government
Statistics
Wars

Fear of slave insurrections was common in the South in the early nineteenth century. While there were few actual instances of trouble, a serious uprising took place in Charleston, S.C., this year. It was led by a free black, Denmark Vesey, who had purchased his freedom in 1800. Over the years Vesey had organized a plot to seize control of Charleston, but word leaked out in June. Militia and federal troops were called out, many slaves were arrested, and Vesey and 34 others were executed. Some estimates put the number of slaves involved as high as 9000.

1822-1823: In **congressional elections** the Republicans kept their 44–4 Senate majority over the Federalists. In the House they gained 29 seats to the Federalists' gain of one, for a 187–26 majority.

II. Architecture
Arts and Music
Popular Entertainment
Publishing
Theater

Men with a variety of talents aided progress in literature, religion, and education in the first quarter of the nineteenth century. One of these was Timothy Dwight of New England, a leader of the Connecticut Wits, clergyman, and educator. His long poem *Greenfield Hill* (1794) was an attempt to convince Europeans that America provided suitable material for poetry. His *Travels in New England and New York* (four volumes, 1821–1822) is an indispensable source for the life of the period. An orthodox Congregational minister, Dwight was sometimes called the "Protestant pope of New England." He was president of Yale from 1795 to 1817 and did much to modernize its curriculum.

The Pilot by James Fenimore Cooper was published and became a best seller. Cooper's fourth novel, and the first with a maritime setting and theme, was a product of Cooper's determination to outdo Sir Walter Scott in the production of a sea novel. The unnamed hero, known only as the Pilot, represents John Paul Jones, the foremost U.S. naval figure of the time. The novel's action takes place during the American Revolution. Cooper's novel was long popular.

III. Business and Industry
Education
Philosophy and Religion
Science

Agitation by manufacturing interests for a protective tariff system, which had begun with Alexander Hamilton in the late eighteenth century, continued as industry grew. The chief proponent was Mathew Carey of Philadelphia. One of the most important publishers and booksellers of his day, Carey was also a self-taught economist who wrote and spoke in favor of what was beginning to be called the American system: tariffs and internal improvements at the federal government's expense. Carey's *Essays on Political Economy* was published in 1822. His frequent addresses before the Philadelphia Society for the Promotion of National Industry reflected the rise of protectionist sentiment.

The first patent for making **false teeth** was awarded to C.M. Graham.

IV. Fashion
Folkways
Holidays
Social Issues and Crime
Sports

Exploration of the western U.S. was aided by fur trappers and those who organized the fur trade. One such man was William Henry Ashley, whose 1822 expedition built a post at the confluence of the Yellowstone and Missouri rivers. Ashley's innovation in the fur trade was to initiate an annual rendezvous at which time the trappers gathered to sell their furs and purchase supplies. The trappers, who had had no taste of civilization for a year, sometimes spent on drinking and gambling everything they had earned for the year's work.

The primitive U.S. form of **football** was prohibited at Yale College by Pres. Timothy Dwight, who ordered any violations to be reported and violators to be penalized by a fine not to exceed half a dollar.

1823

I. Civil Rights
Exploration and Settlement
Government
Statistics
Wars

Many Americans, especially in the South, were beginning to cast eyes at Texas as an area for agricultural expansion. Long part of the Spanish Empire, Texas had become part of the independent nation of Mexico in 1821. Spain had made a grant of land and in 1820 given Moses Austin permission to bring in 300 settlers. The Mexican government having confirmed the grant, Moses's son Stephen took up the work of his late father and brought in settlers in Dec. 1821. Mexico further encouraged American settlement in 1823 with an offer of cheap land. More Americans came, and half a dozen settlements had been established within a decade.

Dec 2: What came to be called the **Monroe Doctrine** was enunciated by Pres. James Monroe. His annual message to Congress expounded a foreign policy based on two principles. First, any attempt by Europeans to colonize the Americas or interfere in the internal affairs of the Western Hemisphere would be viewed with displeasure by the U.S. Secondly, the U.S. would remain aloof from European quarrels. In essence, this was the foreign policy advocated by John Quincy Adams, Monroe's secretary of state.

II. Architecture
Arts and Music
Popular Entertainment
Publishing
Theater

The portrayal of blacks on the stage posed problems in a nation in which most blacks were slaves. The first acting group of blacks, the African Company, began giving performances in New York City in 1821. Both Shakespearean drama and lighter plays were produced. In 1823 Edwin Forrest, who was to become a national idol and one of the great tragedians of the century, appeared in blackface as Ruban in a farce by Sol Smith, *Tailor in Distress*. No white actress would black her face, so a black woman was engaged to play opposite Forrest.

May 8: "Home Sweet Home" by John Howard Payne, the most popular song yet written by an American, was sung for the first time at Covent Garden in London. It was an aria sung by the homesick heroine in a play by Payne with music composed by Sir Henry Bishop.

III. Business and Industry
Education
Philosophy and Religion
Science

The banking system of the U.S. centered on the second Bank of the United States, chartered in 1816 by the federal government. Its headquarters was in Philadelphia and it had 25 branches around the land. It prospered under the presidency of Langdon Cheves, a legislator from South Carolina who assumed the post in 1819, and even more under Nicholas Biddle, who took over in 1823. Biddle was a financier, editor, and diplomat. State-chartered banks were growing in numbers. The leading private banker was Stephen Girard, a French-born financier who had helped the government finance the War of 1812.

Charles J. Ingersoll offered a major defense of American culture against the criticism of British intellectuals in an address before the American Philosophical Society. In his *Discourse Concerning the Influence of America on the Mind,* he accepted the challenge of British critics by comparing American culture with European, suggesting that the average intellect in America far surpassed the corresponding intellect in Europe. He suggested that America's great contribution to world civilization had been self-government.

IV. Fashion
Folkways
Holidays
Social Issues and Crime
Sports

In an era when entertainment in the home had to be supplied by family and guests, music with humorous or sentimental words that could be sung to well-known melodies, was popular. Among such songs were "Believe Me if All Those Endearing Young Charms" (1808); "'Tis the Last Rose of Summer" (1813); "The Minstrel's Return from the War" (1827); and "Zip Coon" (c1834), later known as "Turkey in the Straw."

May: The **first major horse race** in the U.S. was between American Eclipse from the North and the challenger Sir Henry from the South for a purse of $20,000. About 100,000 spectators jammed the Union Course on Long Island to see American Eclipse take two out of three heats, doing the four-miles in 7:49 and 8:24. Victory of the northern horse spread gloom in the South.

1824

I. Civil Rights
Exploration and Settlement
Government
Statistics
Wars

Russia and the U.S. settled a territorial dispute involving regions in the far Northwest. On Sept. 4, 1821, Czar Alexander I asserted a claim on all of the Pacific coast north of the 51st parallel, bisecting the Oregon Territory claimed jointly by the U.S. and Great Britain. On July 17, 1823, Secretary of State

John Quincy Adams notified Russia that this claim was unacceptable under the principles set forth by Pres. James Monroe the following December. On Apr. 17, 1824, Russia and the U.S. signed a treaty by which Russia agreed to 54°40' as the southern limit of its claim. The treaty also removed a ban Russia had tried to impose on commercial fishing off the coast of the land it claimed.

1824-1825: In **congressional elections** the traditional parties broke down. The Federalist party disappeared as a national force and the Republican party split into Administration supporters, who backed John Quincy Adams, and Jacksonians, who supported Andrew Jackson. In the Senate the Administration faction led the Jacksonians 26–20. In the House they took a 105–97 majority.

Aug: The **first nominating convention** was held at Utica, N.Y. For the first time, electors of nominees for office were chosen by popular vote. Nominations for president and for state offices had previously been made in caucus, but this method was replaced by the convention. The Utica convention nominated candidates for the offices of governor and lieutenant governor of New York.

Dec 1: In the **1824 presidential election** no candidate received an electoral majority. John Quincy Adams of Massachusetts received 84 votes; Andrew Jackson of Tennessee, 99; Secretary of State William H. Crawford, who had suffered a stroke and was effectively out of the running, 41; Henry Clay, 37. John C. Calhoun of South Carolina was elected vice president. On Feb. 9, 1825, John Quincy Adams was chosen as president by the House of Representatives.

II. Architecture
Arts and Music
Popular Entertainment
Publishing
Theater

Of the many accounts of Indian captivity, none was more popular than *A Narrative of the Life of Mrs. Mary Jemison* by James E. Seaver, published in 1824. Mary Jemison was captured by a French and Indian war party in western Pennsylvania in 1758, when she was 15. She was married twice, once to a Delaware and once to a Seneca, and had eight children. Becoming known as the "White Woman of the Genesee," Mrs. Jemison refused to leave the Senecas. In 1817 New York State confirmed her possession of a tract of land on the Genesee R. that had first been given to her in 1797.

The **Meeting House** at Deerfield, Mass., was built

from plans by Isaac Damon, the most popular country architect of New England in the early nineteenth century. The building is considered a very good example of his somewhat monumental style.

III. Business and Industry
Education
Philosophy and Religion
Science

A new institution with religious and secular functions was the Sunday school. Originating in England, Sunday schools were first established to educate children who worked in mines and factories. Under church sponsorship, the schools soon came to offer religious instruction. The Methodist leader, Francis Asbury, established the first Sunday school in the U.S. in 1786 in Hanover County, Va. On May 25, 1824, representatives of a number of denominations from several states founded the American Sunday School Union to coordinate activities of these schools. Publication of *Sunday School Magazine* began in 1824, and over the years an enormous amount of literature was issued to serve the widespread institution.

The first recorded **strike involving female employees** in the U.S. occurred in Pawtucket, R.I. Male and female weavers struck against a proposed decrease in wages and an increase in hours. Prior to this time, organized labor had met with little success in or out of court in improving working conditions. By 1820, however, textile mill workers had been organized into a union numbering some 100,000. This growth in union strength was one of the factors that contributed to the strike in Pawtucket.

IV. Fashion
Folkways
Holidays
Social Issues and Crime
Sports

Memories of the American Revolution were revived when the Marquis de Lafayette, who had come from France in 1777 to fight on the Patriot side, arrived in the U.S. on Aug. 14, 1824. He was 67 years old when he returned. In October of 1824, Gen. Lafayette met Pres. James Monroe, the last U.S. president to have fought in the Revolution. On his tour of the U.S., which lasted until Sept. 1825, Lafayette was welcomed with enthusiasm, his natural charm and easy self-confidence winning over men and women alike.

The **first written American Indian language,** Cherokee, was finished by Sequoyah, the son of a white trader and a Cherokee Indian woman. Sequoyah, who also used the name George Guess, devised a syllabary of 85 characters to represent the spoken sounds of the Cherokee language. He demonstrated the alphabet's utility in a dramatic way. He had his young daughter transcribe speeches at a tribal council in his absence. Then he entered the council chamber and read the speeches aloud from his daughter's transcription. In the years following, Sequoyah taught thousands of Cherokee Indians to read and write. He also translated parts of the Bible into the new language, and in 1828 began publication of a weekly newspaper.

1825

I. Civil Rights
Exploration and Settlement
Government
Statistics
Wars

The first secular Utopian society in the U.S. was established on Jan. 3 by Robert Owen, a social reformer who had made a fortune as a cotton manufacturer in Great Britain. He took over Harmony, Ind., from the followers of George Rapp and set up New Harmony, a community that was to have complete equality of property and opportunity. About 1000 settlers were attracted to the 20,000 acres of New Harmony, including educators, scientists, and writers. However, dissension arose and there was lack of direction among those who were supposed to cooperate. Owen left in 1827. In 1828 the community ceased to exist as a Utopian enterprise.

Feb 9: John Quincy Adams was elected president of the United States by the House of Representatives, into which the election had been thrown by the failure of any of the four candidates to win a majority in the electoral college. In the four-way race of Adams, Andrew Jackson, Henry Clay, and William Crawford, Jackson had received more electoral votes than Adams, but no majority. Clay assisted the Adams cause in the House.

Feb 12: The Creek Indian treaty was signed. Tribal leaders agreed to turn over all their lands in Georgia to the government and promised to migrate west by Sept. 1, 1826. The treaty was rejected by most Creeks.

II. Architecture
Arts and Music
Popular Entertainment
Publishing
Theater

Henry Wadsworth Longfellow, one of the first American poets destined to be read and honored in the U.S. and Europe, began to see his poems appear in print. His first poem to be published was "The Battle of Lovell's Pond," on Nov. 17, 1820, in the Portland, Maine, *Gazette*. In 1825, the year he was graduated from Bowdoin College, a number of Longfellow's early poems were published in the *United States Literary Gazette*. They included "Autumnal Nightfall," "Woods in Winter," "The Angler's Song," and "Hymn of the Moravian Nuns." Longfellow soon left for Europe to prepare for a teaching position at Bowdoin, to which he returned in 1829.

June 17: Word of the oratorical brilliance of **Daniel Webster** spread after his celebrated "Bunker Hill Oration" at the laying of the cornerstone for the Bunker Hill Monument in Boston. His other early speeches included "The Dartmouth College Case" (1818) and "The Landing of the Pilgrims" (1820), matched perhaps only by Webster's "Reply to Hayne" in the U.S. Senate in 1830.

III. Business and Industry
Education
Philosophy and Religion
Science

The era of canal building was gathering momentum. On Oct. 26, 1825, the most important and successful of all American canals, the Erie, was officially opened. The Erie Canal stretched for more than 350 miles between Lake Erie and the Hudson R. at Albany and thus connected the Great Lakes with the Atlantic Ocean at New York City by way of the Hudson R. The father of the Erie Canal was Gov. De Witt Clinton of New York, whose enthusiasm had gotten the project under way. Construction had begun on July 4, 1817, and on Oct. 22, 1819, the first boat to travel on the canal went from Rome to Utica. The canal cost $7,000,000, which was returned many times over by the traffic it attracted. The Erie Canal became the most important passenger and freight route from the East to the Midwest and made New York the Empire State.

Mechanical pressing of glass, the first technical innovation in glassmaking since ancient times, was introduced into American factories. The change enabled production of intricately designed glassware.

Famous glassworks established this year by Deming Jarves at Sandwich, Mass., were noted for their large-scale production of pressed glass.

IV. Fashion
Folkways
Holidays
Social Issues and Crime
Sports

Controversy over women's place in society was stimulated by Frances Wright, who had moved from England to the U.S. in 1824. An earlier visit (1818–1820) had resulted in her volume *Views of Society and Manners in America* (1821), which praised the country enthusiastically. Now, however, she was lecturing from public platforms, addressing workmen's groups and openly discussing such forbidden subjects as equal rights, birth control, and abolition. One newspaper editor denounced her as a "bold blasphemer and voluptuous preacher of licentiousness."

"**Devil tales,**" involving pacts with the Devil, were a popular form of short story. Washington Irving contributed to the vogue by his legendary tale "Tom and the Devil," in his *Tales of a Traveler*, published this year. Tom and his wife strike a bargain with Old Nick when he promises them the treasure of Captain Kidd.

1826

I. Civil Rights
Exploration and Settlement
Government
Statistics
Wars

Trappers, explorers, adventurers, and scientists were beginning to unlock the secrets of the immense expanse of the American West, much of it still unknown to settlers. One of the most daring yet practical of these men was Jedediah Strong Smith. Already a veteran of various expeditions, Smith set out on Aug. 22, 1826, with a small band of men from Great Salt Lake, Utah. They crossed the Colorado R. and the Mojave Desert before arriving at the San Gabriel Mission on Nov. 27. On leaving California, Smith and two of his men became the first men other than Indians to cross the Sierra Nevada and the Great Salt

Desert from west to east. In 1831, while traveling along the Santa Fe Trail, Smith was killed by Comanches. Smith's most important contributions were his mapping and establishment of trails in the areas he explored.

1826-1827: In **congressional elections** the Jacksonians gained eight Senate seats for a 28–20 majority over the Administration faction. In the House they gained 22 seats for a 119–94 majority.

Jan 24: The Creek Indians signed the **Treaty of Washington** with the federal government. It nullified a previous treaty and ceded less territory to the government. It also granted the Indians the right to stay on their lands until Jan. 1, 1827.

II. Architecture
Arts and Music
Popular Entertainment
Publishing
Theater

American actors were competing with their British counterparts, who long had dominated the stage. The most notable rivalry was between the American Edwin Forrest and William Charles Macready of Great Britain. Forrest became a great tragedian, first playing Othello in 1826. He was very popular but some thought he displayed his powerful voice too often. Macready made his first visit to the U.S. in 1826, making his debut Oct. 2 at the Park Theater in New York in the play *Virginius* by James Sheridan Knowles. He, too, was a great tragedian. Forrest played Macbeth in England in 1845 but met with hostility from those who preferred Macready. Their rivalry was to have fatal consequences in 1849.

James Fenimore Cooper's ***The Last of the Mohicans*** began its phenomenal publishing record. The most popular of Cooper's novels, selling over 2,000,000 copies, it was also a best seller across the Atlantic. The Leatherstocking Tales, of which *The Last of the Mohicans* is the second novel of five, are still popular in the U.S. and Europe, especially France.

III. Business and Industry
Education
Philosophy and Religion
Science

Legal scholarship flourished in the U.S. as the American legal system began to separate from British tradition and establish its own foundations and precedents. America's first great legal scholar was James Kent, who in 1794 became the first professor of law

at Columbia and later became chief justice of New York State courts. Kent modified English chancery practice to conform to American institutions and virtually created equity jurisdiction in the U.S. Out of his opinions and lectures came his *Commentaries on American Law* (4 volumes, 1826–1830). The section on constitutional law was Federalist in approach. The *Commentaries* were an immediate success. Kent updated them five times since. Kent's influence on the legal profession and the teaching of law in the U.S. was second only to that of John Marshall. Kent's classic work has been compared with that of William Blackstone, the English jurist who wrote a similar four-volume work (1765–1769).

IV. Fashion
Folkways
Holidays
Social Issues and Crime
Sports

Combining entertainment with education, the lyceum movement became a familiar part of American life. A lyceum was an organization that provided a platform for speakers on a great variety of subjects. The first lyceum was organized in 1826 in Millbury, Mass., by Josiah Holbrook, a teacher whose Agricultural Seminary had failed in 1825. Within two years he helped establish more than 100 lyceums. The National American Lyceum was formed in 1831, and by 1834 some 3000 lyceums were in operation, offering information on the arts, science, history, and public affairs. Many so-called reformers took advantage of this platform to promote their notions, but leading figures of the day, such as Daniel Webster and Ralph Waldo Emerson, also were happy to appear on lyceum platforms.

June 30: **"Independence now and Independence forever!"** was penned by John Adams in response to a request for a toast to be offered in his name on July Fourth. The entire toast by Adams read: "It is my living sentiment, and by the blessing of God it shall be my dying sentiment—Independence now and Independence forever!"

1827

I. Civil Rights
Exploration and Settlement
Government
Statistics
Wars

Oregon Country, the region north of the California border and extending to Alaska, was still claimed by both the U.S. and Great Britain. On Aug. 6, 1827, the two nations signed a treaty extending an 1818 agreement to continue joint occupation of the territory. American and British fur-trading companies were in competition in the region, with the English Hudson's Bay Company having the better of it. At the same time, Americans were exploring the area, and in 1829 Hall J. Kelley of Boston founded the Amcrican Society for Encouraging the Settlement of the Oregon Territory.

Nov 15: The **Creeks** ceded their remaining territory in the Southeast to the U.S. The area included all their lands in Georgia.

II. Architecture
Arts and Music
Popular Entertainment
Publishing
Theater

The birds of North America, abundant and colorful, attracted scientists and nature lovers alike. It remained for an artist and ornithologist, John James Audubon, to give them recognition by painting some 500 of the birds in all their splendor. Later paintings may be more scientific, but none has ever matched Audubon's in popular appeal. *The Birds of America* was published in elephant folio size in parts between 1827 and 1838 in London. An accompanying text, *Ornithological Biography,* was issued in five volumes between 1831 and 1839. In the text Audubon had the help of William MacGillivray, who supplied scientific information. Earlier, in the course of observing birds, Audubon had made the first American bird-banding experiments.

The first book of poems by **Edgar Allan Poe,** *Tamerlane and Other Poems,* was printed in Boston. Little attention was paid the slim volume. In 1829 a second volume, *Al Aaraaf, Tamerlane and Minor Poems,* also went unnoticed.

Feb 7: Ballet was introduced to the U.S. by Mme. Francisquy Hutin, famed French danseuse, with *The Deserter,* staged at the Bowery Theater, New York City. Mme. Hutin's light and scanty attire so shocked the public that every woman in the lower tier of boxes immediately left the theater.

III. Business and Industry
Education
Philosophy and Religion
Science

As the U.S. economy began to shift from agriculture to manufacturing, causing a relative decline in commerce and shipping, economists who favored manufacturing began finding arguments for protecting and encouraging it. Among these was a German-born economist, Friedrich List, who emigrated to the U.S. in 1820 and returned to Germany in 1832. List wrote *Outlines of American Political Economy* (1827), arguing that a nation's true wealth stemmed from its productive industrial forces rather than from commercial transactions. Such a view was especially popular in New England, where the shift to light and heavy manufacturing was most pronounced. Thus, New England favored high tariffs on imported goods to protect the young American industries.

Encyclopedia Americana was begun by the German refugee political philosopher, Francis Lieber. Organized along Germanic principles of research and scholarship, the 13-volume work began to appear in 1829. It made a significant contribution to American culture.

IV. Fashion
Folkways
Holidays
Social Issues and Crime
Sports

During the first half of the nineteenth century, the American diet and eating habits amazed English visitors. Frances Trollope noted: "They eat with the greatest possible rapidity and in total silence." Harriet Martineau reported a breakfast that consisted of "cornbread, buns, buckwheat cakes, broiled chicken, bacon, eggs, rich hominy, fish, fresh and pickled, and beef-steak." And Charles Dickens was repelled by "those dyspeptic ladies and gentlemen who eat un-heard-of quantities of hot corn bread (almost as good for the digestion as a kneaded pincushion), for break-fast and supper."

July 23: The **first swimming school** in the U.S. opened in Boston, Mass. Swimming was taught by placing a belt "around the bodies, under the arms, attached to a rope and pole, by which the head and body are kept in the proper position in the water, while the pupil is learning the use of his limbs." The school was at-tended by many notables, including John James Audubon and John Quincy Adams. Adams is reputed to have done some diving from the 6-foot board when he was 61 years old.

1828

I. Civil Rights
Exploration and Settlement
Government
Statistics
Wars

Growing discord between North and South over the tariff came to the fore this year when, on May 19, Pres. John Quincy Adams signed into law what be-came known as the Tariff of Abominations. Political maneuvering between supporters of Pres. Adams and those of Andrew Jackson caused much bitterness. The Jacksonians had hoped to discredit Adams by making the bill so objectionable that it would be de-feated. Southerners, led by Vice Pres. John C. Cal-houn, felt the law discriminated against the agricul-tural South, which relied on imports from abroad, and favored the North and West. With strong New England support, the bill passed both houses of Con-gress.

The **Democratic Party** was formed. Essentially it was an extension of the Democratic-Republican (Jef-fersonian) Party (formed May 13, 1792), and was backed by southern agrarians and northern urban workers. It advocated Jeffersonian principles of per-sonal liberty and attacked special privilege. Andrew Jackson became the new party's first nominee for president.

The **National Republican Party** was formed dur-ing Pres. John Quincy Adams's term of office (1824–

1828). Ill feeling between Adams and Jackson was polarizing U.S. politics. The National Republican Party of Adams advocated a nationalistic program including a national bank, protective tariffs, feder-ally sponsored internal improvements, and a conser-vative land-sale policy. This package, called the American System, was put together by Henry Clay, an ally of Adams, to appeal to the North and West. After loss of the election to Jackson, the coalition of National Republicans, Whigs, and splinter groups fell apart, and the Whig Party emerged as the party of opposition to the Jacksonian Democrats.

1828-1829: In **congressional elections** the Democrats gained a 26–22 Senate majority over the National Republicans. In the House they took a 139–74 major-ity.

Dec 3: Andrew Jackson was elected seventh presi-dent of the United States. Jackson, a senator from Tennessee until his nomination, received 647,231 popular votes and 178 electoral votes against 509,097 popular votes and 83 electoral votes for John Quincy Adams, candidate of the National Republican Party. John C. Calhoun was reelected vice president, receiv-ing 171 electoral votes. The election was swung by Martin Van Buren of New York on the understanding that he would continue to exercise power in the state through the spoils system.

II. Architecture
Arts and Music
Popular Entertainment
Publishing
Theater

Women were beginning to enter journalism, and the most prominent woman journalist was Sarah Jose-pha Hale. In 1828 in Boston she became editor of a new journal, *Ladies' Magazine.* She moved to Phila-delphia in 1837, becoming editor of *Godey's Lady's Book* and holding that post for 40 years. In 1846 Mrs. Hale began using the pages of the magazine to agitate for a national Thanksgiving Day, and by 1858 all but six states celebrated thanksgiving on the last Thurs-day in November. Mrs. Hale had great influence on fashions and manners and regularly urged higher education for women. Her volume *Poems for Our Children* (1830) contained "Mary Had a Little Lamb."

The monumental ***American Dictionary of the English Language*** by Noah Webster was published, a labor of more than 20 years. Webster spent much time in England gathering material for his work and completed it while living in Cambridge, England.

III. Business and Industry
Education
Philosophy and Religion
Science

For practical purposes, the age of the railroad in the U.S. began on July 4, 1828, when ground-breaking ceremonies for the Baltimore and Ohio Railroad, led by Charles Carroll, the last surviving signer of the Declaration of Independence, were held in Baltimore, Md. The first section of the B&O, as it came to be known, opened in May 1830 between Baltimore and Ellicott's Mills, Md. The first source of power was the horse, but on August 30 the line was converted to steampower. The B&O kept laying rails westward and reached St. Louis, Mo., in 1857.

A **strike of factory workers,** the first recorded, occurred in a textile plant in Paterson, N.J. The strike was doubly significant because it led to the first recorded summoning of the militia to end labor violence. The workers' agitation for a ten-hour day ended in failure.

IV. Fashion
Folkways
Holidays
Social Issues and Crime
Sports

Performances by white entertainers in blackface, destined to develop into the popular minstrel shows of the 1840s and 1850s, probably got their start in 1828. In that year Thomas Dartmouth Rice gave a solo performance in blackface, dancing and singing "Jim Crow." Rice is said to have taken the tune from an elderly black who worked near the Louisville Theater, in Louisville, Ky. When Rice went to England in 1836, "Jim Crow" became an international hit song and the term Jim Crow became a synonym for blacks. Rice became known as "the father of American minstrelsy."

America's **first archery club** was formed by a group of famous artists. The United Bowmen of Philadelphia was formally organized by Franklin Peale, Titian Ramsey Peale, Samuel P. Griffith, Jr., Thomas Sully, and others. The initiation fee was $5.00 and dues 50 cents a month. Members wore Lincoln green frock coats with gold trim and broad straw hats decorated with three black ostrich plumes. It held annual tournaments and awarded silver trophies until it disbanded in 1859. It was the forerunner of the National Archery Association, founded in 1879. The National Field Archery Association was founded in 1939.

1829

I. Civil Rights
Exploration and Settlement
Government
Statistics
Wars

Inauguration of Andrew Jackson as seventh president was a turning point in the history of the executive office. Jackson was a self-made man, in contrast with his six predecessors, four of them upper-class Virginians and two affluent New Englanders. Jackson was also the first president nominated by the Democratic Party, which had evolved from the old Jeffersonian Democratic-Republican Party. The events of his inauguration symbolized the new Jacksonian era. After the ceremony thousands of his followers accompanied him back to the White House where, uninvited, they took over the reception, standing on chairs and crowding so that people were trampled and china and glassware broken. Tubs of punch were set out on the White House lawn to lure some of the crowd before a disaster occurred. The new president himself had to be eased out a rear door for protection against his surging admirers. Jacksonians felt that the true democracy of America had triumphed.

The **Workingmen's Party** began to appear in Philadelphia and New York and spread quickly into northern industrial cities. Really an association of like-minded labor assemblies, the Workingmen's Party, including in its ranks several liberal newspaper editors, called for universal suffrage, abolition of imprisonment for debts, a nonmonopolistic banking system, and compulsory, tax-supported schools. Jacksonians exploited the party for political purposes. Though the party did not last long, its members and platform found their way ultimately into the Democratic Party.

II. Architecture
Arts and Music
Popular Entertainment
Publishing
Theater

Sculptors were never as numerous as painters in nineteenth-century America, but the making of statues was becoming a profession. Horatio Greenough was America's first professional sculptor. He is best known for his colossal statue of George Washington, but he did other notable work, such as *The Rescue* (1846) for the Capitol in Washington, D.C., depicting a settler saving his wife and children from attacking Indians. He also created *The Chanting Cherubs* (1829) for the novelist James Fenimore Cooper, but the nude cherubs shocked public taste. Greenough is remembered as well for his writings on architecture, in which he advocated that form follow function.

Scrimshaw, the art of making pictures on or carving the teeth or jaw of a sperm whale, flourished during this period. Busks for corsets, chessmen, vases, cutlery, etc. were carved as were historical scenes. The hobby filled long, lonely hours on whaling cruises.

III. Business and Industry
Education
Philosophy and Religion
Science

A landmark in American education and publishing was the work of a German-born political philosopher, Francis Lieber, who came to the U.S. in 1827. Between 1829 and 1833 he edited the 13-volume *Encyclopedia Americana,* the first such reference work published in the U.S. Important to the work was the fact that Lieber persuaded specialists in various fields to write for the general public. As a professor at the University of South Carolina (1835–1836), he wrote the first works in political science by an American scholar not in public life. Among his other activities was popularization of physical education, which he saw as contributing to the well-being of a cultivated mind. During the Civil War he wrote *Instructions for the Government of Armies of the United States in the Field* (1863).

Oct 17: The **Chesapeake and Delaware Canal** was formally opened. Linking the Delaware R. and Chesapeake Bay, the canal was 14 miles long and cost some $2,250,000, which was shared by the U.S. government, Delaware, Maryland, and Pennsylvania, and various private citizens.

IV. Fashion
Folkways
Holidays
Social Issues and Crime
Sports

Americans have always liked tales of men of outsized stature and achievement, and Mike Fink was an early favorite. Born at Fort Pitt, Pa., before the American Revolution, Fink was an Indian scout but most of his fame came from his exploits as a keel-boatman on the Ohio and Mississippi rivers. The first account of his adventures appeared in print in 1829 in *The Western Souvenir,* in an article by Morgan Neville. The account told of Fink's marksmanship, physical prowess, and tall tales. There are about 11 versions of his death, but he probably was shot dead somewhere near the mouth of the Yellowstone R. while trapping and exploring up the Missouri R. in 1822. Bernard DeVoto described this legendary figure as one in which "Casanova, together with Paul Bunyan, merges with Thor."

Oct 16: The **Tremont Hotel** in Boston, the first luxurious hotel in the New World, opened with a dollar-a-plate dinner attended by such notables as Daniel Webster and Edward Everett. The 170-room hotel offered many first-time-ever luxuries and conveniences: private bedrooms with door locks, soap and a pitcher of water in each room, indoor toilets (eight water closets), menus in the dining room, room clerks, and bellboys, called rotunda men. Architects of luxury hotels in the next few decades generally used the Tremont as their model.

1830

I. Civil Rights
Exploration and Settlement
Government
Statistics
Wars

The constitutionality of internal improvements (roads and canals) carried out by the federal government continued to be debated and to cause political divisions. On May 27, 1830, Pres. Andrew Jackson vetoed the Maysville Road bill, which would have provided government financial support for a 60-mile road construction project entirely in Kentucky. On May 31 Jackson approved a bill to provide funds for the Cumberland Road because it involved more than one state. Jackson believed in internal improvements in principle but felt a constitutional amendment was necessary. His stand helped him politically. The South's belief in states' rights was supported by his veto, which was also aimed at Henry Clay and the National Republicans.

The U.S. **Census** recorded a population of 12,866,020. The center of population was placed 19 miles west-southwest of Moorefield, W. Va.

1830-1831: In **congressional elections** the Democrats and National Republicans each lost a Senate seat to minor parties, but the Democrats held a majority of 25–21. In the House they gained two seats for a 141–58 majority, with 14 seats going to minor parties.

Jan 19-27: The **Webster-Hayne debates** took place. They began when Sen. Samuel A. Foot of Connecticut offered a resolution to restrain sale of public lands in the West. Sen. Thomas Hart Benton of Missouri replied by declaring that eastern interests were trying to check the prosperity of the West. He was supported by Sen. Robert Y. Hayne of South Carolina, who defended states' rights. Hayne stated that "the very life of our system is the independence of the states, and that there is no evil more to be deprecated than the consolidation of this government." Sen. Daniel Webster of Massachusetts replied by criticizing the tendency of some senators "to habitually speak of the union in terms of indifference, or even of disparagement." The debate evolved into a discussion of the powers of the Constitution and the nature of the Union. In his speech of Jan. 26–27, Webster declared that the states were sovereign only in that area where their power is not qualified by the Constitution, and that the Constitution and the government were sovereign over the people.

Sep: The **Anti-Masonic Party,** the first major third party in the history of U.S. politics, held its first national convention in Philadelphia. Its candidate was William Wirt of Maryland. It would draw votes from Henry Clay in the 1832 elections and win several House seats in New England.

II. Architecture
Arts and Music
Popular Entertainment
Publishing
Theater

Inspired by the Romantic movement while studying in Europe, a group of American painters, beginning about 1825 and lasting for half a century, formed what came to be called the Hudson River school. They took interest in the natural beauty of the U.S. and concentrated on painting the Hudson River Valley, Catskill Mts., White Mts., and Niagara Falls. Best known of the school were Thomas Doughty, Asher B. Durand, Thomas Cole, John Frederick Kensett, and George Innes.

Plays about Indians flooded the American stage in the decades before the Civil War. Among the more successful were the anonymous *Indian Wife* (1830), *Pontiac, or the Siege of Detroit* by General Alexander Macomb, and *Metamora, or The Last of the Wampanoags* by John A. Stone. Approximately 50 plays about Indians appeared between 1825 and 1860.

Sep 16: Oliver Wendell Holmes wrote the poem "Old Ironsides" for the Boston *Daily Advertiser.* Stirred by the notice that the frigate *Constitution* was to be dismantled, he composed his impassioned poem, which became so popular that the order for destruction of the ship was rescinded.

III. Business and Industry
Education
Philosophy and Religion
Science

The Church of Jesus Christ of Latter-Day Saints, known as the Mormon Church, was founded on Apr. 6, 1830, by Joseph Smith at Fayette, N.Y., with 30 members. Smith in 1827 said he had unearthed golden tablets near Palmyra, N.Y., the writing on which he translated and published in 1829 as *Book of Mormon.* These writings of the prophet Mormon were an early history of America from about 600 B.C. to about A.D. 420, showing that colonization of America had been carried out by a lost tribe of Israel. Mormon also revealed God's special message for America. This made Mormonism a distinctly American religion at a time when nationalistic feeling was strong. Smith set up the headquarters of his church in Kirtland, Ohio, in 1831.

Canal mileage in America totaled 1277 as against 73 miles of railroads. By 1840 there were 3326 miles of canals and 2818 miles of railroads. By 1850 there were 3698 miles of canals and 9021 miles of railroads. In 1830 New York was first in canals, with 546 miles, while Pennsylvania had virtually all railroads, 70 out of 73 miles. In 1840 Pennsylvania seized first place with 954 miles of canals, keeping its lead in rail mileage with 576 miles. In 1850 Pennsylvania retained its lead in canal mileage with 954 miles, yielding rail leadership to New York with its 1361 miles.

Alexander Campbell and his followers, often called Campbellites, formed the Disciples of Christ. The denomination rejected all creeds and confessions and urged restoration of New Testament beliefs, practices, and polity. Undivided on the issue of slavery, the Disciples grew rapidly in number and influence throughout the last half of the nineteenth century.

IV. Fashion
Folkways
Holidays
Social Issues and Crime
Sports

Fads and reforms in diet attracted reformers and dieters alike. The most successful experimenter was Sylvester Graham, a clergyman and temperance lecturer of the period who believed proper diet would prevent alcoholism. He developed Graham bread, or Graham crackers, the name still linked to his product. Made of coarsely ground whole wheat flour, Graham's bread preserved vitamins, although nothing was known about vitamins at the time. His name also became attached to health clubs and boardinghouses. Graham advocated bathing at least three times a week, daily exercise, open bedroom windows in winter, and cheerful dispositions at meals. The well-known newspaper editor Horace Greeley at one time lived on a diet of beans, potatoes, boiled rice, milk, and Graham bread. In 1850 the American Vegetarian Society was founded.

Jan 27: "Liberty and Union, now and forever, one and inseparable!" was included in a speech delivered by Sen. Daniel Webster of Massachusetts in debate with Sen. Robert Y. Hayne of South Carolina. Webster held that the Union was stronger than the separate states, and that its acts could not be nullified by them.

Sep 18: A celebrated **race between horse and steam** was won by the horse over the Tom Thumb, the first locomotive built in America. During the race the locomotive pulled 40 passengers over a nine-mile course from Riley's Tavern to Baltimore, Md. Mechanical failure, ever the plague of railroads, caused Tom Thumb's poor showing. The engine sprang a leak in the boiler and failed to finish the course.

1831

I. Civil Rights
Exploration and Settlement
Government
Statistics
Wars

A bloody slave insurrection, long feared by many southerners, began on Aug. 21 in Southampton County, Va. It was led by Nat Turner, a black who believed he had been chosen to lead his people out of slavery. With about 70 followers, Turner first killed his master, Joseph Travis, and his family. Within 24 hours, 60 or 70 whites had been murdered. Militia and federal troops who were called out killed about 100 blacks. Turner was captured on Oct. 30 and, after confessing to the uprising, was hanged on Nov. 11. The shaken South retaliated by passing more stringent laws relating to slaves. Southerners blamed abolitionists for inciting the slaves.

Mar 4: John Quincy Adams returned to Congress, the first former president to do so. He represented the Plymouth, Mass., district in the House of Representatives for eight terms.

June 27: Black Hawk, leader of the Sauk Indians, and Gen. Edmund P. Gaines, commanding U.S. troops, reached an agreement under which the Sauks would move out of the Rock R. area of Illinois and across the Mississippi R. into Iowa. Once there, the Sauks nearly starved and in the spring of 1832 returned to their old corn fields in Illinois.

Dec 12: The **first nominating convention** of a major party was held by the National Republican Party. It nominated Henry Clay for President.

II. Architecture
Arts and Music
Popular Entertainment
Publishing
Theater

The early nineteenth century was a period of strong patriotic feeling on the part of Americans. Independence had been confirmed by the War of 1812, and the growing population was spreading over a vast continent. One result of this fervor was the writing of patriotic verse and song. The most notable song, after "The Star Spangled Banner," was "America," which was first sung in public on July 4, 1831, at a service in the Park Street Church, Boston. The words had been written by the Rev. Samuel Francis Smith, a Baptist clergyman, earlier in the year. The words of this American hymn were sung to the tune of "God Save the King," and it is said that Smith did not know it was the British anthem.

Jan 1: The first issue of ***The Liberator***, edited and published by William Lloyd Garrison in Boston, was issued. Probably the leading abolitionist journal, *The Liberator* was published until 1865.

III. Business and Industry
Education
Philosophy and Religion
Science

American inventors, less hampered by tradition than their European counterparts, and faced with a labor shortage and an almost limitless expanse of arable land, were early encouraged to invent labor-saving devices for farmers. Chief among the inventors was Cyrus H. McCormick, who demonstrated his reaper in 1831 and patented it in 1834. A similar machine was invented independently by Obed Hussey, who first announced his invention in 1834. McCormick in 1847 built a factory in Chicago to produce his own reaper and by 1850 had established a nationwide business. In 1851 he introduced the reaper in England and later on the Continent. During the Civil War McCormick's reaper helped make it possible to feed Union armies.

Aug: The **Adventist movement** in American Protestantism was born when William Miller, a Baptist, began public preaching. His theme was the imminence of Christ's return to earth, based on his interpretation of passages from Daniel and Revelation. Miller predicted that the "cleansing by fire" would begin at some point between March 21, 1843, and March 21, 1844.

IV. Fashion
Folkways
Holidays
Social Issues and Crime
Sports

In the first half of the nineteenth century the diet and health of Americans were improved by the introduction of canning and refrigeration. Canned foods began to be produced commercially in 1820 by William Underwood in Boston and Thomas Kensett in New York. Canning became more efficient after introduction of the tin can, first patented in the U.S. in 1825. By the 1840s canning was being done on a large scale. By this time, too, improvements in the cutting and storing of ice made ice cheaper, so refrigeration came into common use.

Aug 10: The term *Old Glory,* denoting the U.S. flag, was first used by William Driver, of Salem, Mass., captain of the *Charles Daggett.* Presented with a large American flag, Driver raised it to the masthead and proclaimed: "I name thee Old Glory." By the end of the 1850s, the term was in widespread use.

1832

I. Civil Rights
Exploration and Settlement
Government
Statistics
Wars

The issue of states' rights had come to the fore as a result of the tariff bill of 1828, known to its enemies in the South as the Tariff of Abominations. This year, for the first time, a state threatened both nullification and secession. On Nov. 24, 1832, a South Carolina convention passed an ordinance declaring null and void both the 1828 tariff and one enacted in 1832, reducing somewhat the tariff duties to which the South objected. The ordinance stated further that the state would secede if the federal government used force. Pres. Andrew Jackson reacted strongly to this declaration on Dec. 10 with a proclamation to South Carolina asserting supremacy of federal law and calling nullification an act of rebellion.

1832-1833: In **congressional elections** the Democrats and National Republicans fell into a 20–20 Senate tie, with eight seats held by minor parties. In the House the Democrats had a 147–53 majority over the Anti-Masonic Party, with 60 seats held by minor parties.

Apr 6: The **Black Hawk War** began soon after the Sauk Indians, led by Black Hawk, faring poorly in Iowa where the government had moved them, recrossed the Mississippi R. and moved back to their former corn fields to plant a new crop. As tensions mounted, panicky settlers killed two Indians seeking a parley and bearing a white flag. Black Hawk, enraged, began killing white settlers.

May 21: The **Democratic Party,** formerly known as "Republican Delegates from the Several States" and called both Republican and Democratic-Republican, formally adopted its present name at its convention in Baltimore, Md. The convention nominated Pres. Andrew Jackson for a second term and nominated Martin Van Buren of New York for vice president.

Aug 2: Sauk followers of **Black Hawk** were massacred at the mouth of the Bad Axe R. in Wisconsin by Illinois militia led by Gen. Henry Atkinson. Old men, women, and children were all killed without regard for pleas of mercy or white flags.

Aug 27: Black Hawk, deserted by his Winnebago allies, surrendered, thus ending the Black Hawk War.

Dec 5: Andrew Jackson was reelected president of the United States by 687,502 popular votes and 219 electoral votes, against 530,189 popular votes and 49 electoral votes for Henry Clay. Martin Van Buren was elected vice president.

II. Architecture
Arts and Music
Popular Entertainment
Publishing
Theater

As in the past, many of the most popular figures on the American stage during this period were English actors and actresses, some of whom remained in the U.S. and made careers there. The most popular of them all was Fanny Kemble, who made her debut with her father Charles at the Park Theater, New York City, in 1832. Two years later Miss Kemble married Pierce Butler, whose family owned a large plantation in Georgia. The marriage was a failure, largely because she could not stand life on a slave-operated estate. She wrote *Journal of a Residence on a Georgia Plantation in 1838–39,* which was published in 1863. She hoped it would turn British opinion against the South.

The collected *Poems* of **William Cullen Bryant** were published and hailed by the *North American Review* as "the best volume of American verse that has appeared." Among the 89 poems were such favorites as "O Fairest of the Rural Maids," "The Death of the Flowers," "June," "A Forest Hymn," "Hymn to Death," "A Meditation on Rhode Island," and "To a Fringed Gentian."

III. Business and Industry
Education
Philosophy and Religion
Science

The need for faster ships to connect the East and West coasts of the U.S. by way of Cape Horn, and to carry on the lucrative trade with China, resulted in the development of the clipper ship, the fastest merchant sailing vessel ever built. The clippers were characterized by great length in proportion to beam and an enormous area of sail. The first true clipper, the *Ann McKim,* was built in Baltimore in 1832. Donald McKay of Boston became the foremost builder, completing such famous clippers as *Flying Cloud* and *Lightning.* In 1854 *Flying Cloud* set a record for the Boston to San Francisco route of 89 days, 8 hours. The clipper as a type ruled the seas until the development of steam-powered vessels.

The **Ohio and Erie Canal** connected Cleveland to the Ohio R. at Portsmouth. Construction of the canal took seven years, with malaria and a shortage of funds crippling the year-round labor of some 2000 workers. The canal, opened in 1833, gave Ohio farmers an outlet to the Mississippi R. and to the markets of the South.

Nov 26: The **first streetcar in the world** was put into operation by the New York & Harlem Railroad in New York City. Built by John Stephenson, it was named *John Mason* and was a horse-drawn car that ran on lower Fourth Ave.

IV. Fashion
Folkways
Holidays
Social Issues and Crime
Sports

A unique link with the birth of the nation was broken this year when Charles Carroll, the last surviving signer of the Declaration of Independence, died on Nov. 14, at 95. He had inherited a large estate from his father near Frederick, Md., known as Carrollton Manor. Carroll was one of a delegation that tried unsuccessfully in 1776 to get support from Canada for the Revolutionary cause. Later he was a U.S. senator from Maryland (1789–1792). Said to be the wealthiest man in America in his time, Carroll was a pioneer in promoting transportation projects and was chairman in 1828, of the first board of directors of the Baltimore and Ohio Railroad.

Oranges and lemons entered the American diet with the arrival of the first large shipment, direct from Sicily. Previously they had been a delicacy for the rich. Oranges and lemons have both been traced to Asia. It was not until the conquests and migrations of the Arabs that the fruit became of major agricultural consequence. The Arabs planted lemon trees in Spain during their occupation. Christopher Columbus was credited with planting the first orange tree in the New World. Trees were distributed by the Spaniards throughout the regions they explored and settled. Neither the orange nor the lemon became of commercial importance in the U.S. until years later.

Apr 1: Robert the Hermit, of Massachusetts, one of the most colorful and famous hermits in American history, died in his hermitage at Seekonk, Mass. Robert was a bonded slave, born of an African mother and probably an Anglo-Saxon father, in Princeton, N.J. He obtained his freedom, was swindled out of it and shipped to a foreign slave market, escaped to America, was parted from his first wife by force, rejected by his second wife after a long voyage at sea, and otherwise buffeted about before withdrawing from the society of men.

1833

I. Civil Rights
Exploration and Settlement
Government
Statistics
Wars

That the abolition movement was gaining strength was demonstrated this year when the first national abolitionist organization, the American Anti-Slavery Society, was formed in Philadelphia on Dec. 4. Its first president was Arthur Tappan, who like his brother Lewis was a wealthy New York City businessman. Both were active in the antislavery cause for many years. Also prominent in the movement was William Lloyd Garrison, the fiery editor of *The Liberator,* who with his followers seized control of the society in 1840 because he did not think it was radical enough. The society saw slavery as a moral evil and called for immediate abolition. In 1835 it began a propaganda campaign that flooded the slave states with abolitionist literature.

Mar 2: In the continuing **controversy over nullification,** Pres. Andrew Jackson signed two bills. The first was Henry Clay's compromise Tariff of 1833, which was intended to ease the trouble between the federal government and South Carolina. The second was called the Force Act; it authorized the president to enforce collection of tariffs by use of the Army and Navy if necessary.

Mar 15: The South Carolina **Ordinance of Nullification** was revoked by a state convention. However, on Mar. 18 the convention passed an ordinance nullifying the Force Act.

II. Architecture
Arts and Music
Popular Entertainment
Publishing
Theater

The day of newspaper sensationalism dawned with the establishment of the New York *Sun* on Sept. 3.

Founded by 23-year-old Benjamin H. Day, its first issue consisted of four pages, which Day wrote and set in type himself. The paper sold for one penny while all other New York papers sold for 6 cents. Day was the first publisher in the city to use newsboys and by 1835 he claimed that the 19,360 circulation of the *Sun* was the largest in the world.

Nathaniel Currier moved his lithography business from Philadelphia, Pa., to New York City, going into business with J.H. Bufford. In 1850 Currier went into business with James Merritt Ives, and by 1857 all of the prints issued by the company bore the Currier & Ives imprint. The lithographs, inexpensive and enormously popular, gave an eloquent pictorial account of sights and events of nineteenth-century America.

Jan 17: William Rush, the first native American sculptor, died at 76. Working in wood and clay, Rush in his work reflected the neoclassical influence. His work included busts of many notables, American and European; carved wooden female figureheads for ships; the personifications of Tragedy and Comedy seen at the Actor's Home outside Philadelphia; and also the *Spirit of the Schuylkill,* in Fairmount Park in Philadelphia.

III. Business and Industry
Education
Philosophy and Religion
Science

An invention that contributed as much to the history and folklore of the American West as it did to the firearms industry was the Colt revolver, invented by Samuel Colt in 1833 and patented on Feb. 25, 1836. Colt began producing the weapon at the Patent Arms Company in Paterson, N.J. As the first firearm that could be used effectively by a man on horseback, this six-shooter soon became associated with the frontier and the Great Plains. In time the name Colt became almost synonymous with the term revolver. Colt's business failed, but it was revived by an order from the government for 100 revolvers in 1847 for use in the Mexican War. Colt established a new company and plant in Hartford, Conn.

A **tax-supported public library** was established in Peterborough, N.H., under the leadership of the Rev. Abiel Abbot. The library charged a small membership fee. It is considered the oldest public library in the U.S. except for the Library of Congress, established in 1800 by an act of Congress.

IV. Fashion
Folkways
Holidays
Social Issues and Crime
Sports

The frontier and the westward movement produced a number of semilegendary folk heroes. None of these figures has ever surpassed Davy Crockett in popularity or scope and number of alleged exploits. Crockett began as a frontiersman and Indian fighter, but by 1833 he was serving his third term as a congressman from Tennessee. As a legislator, he made the most of his backwoods humor, style of dress, racy language, and naive but often shrewd comments on public affairs. More sophisticated politicians used Crockett, who opposed Pres. Andrew Jackson's policies, to lure Democratic backwoodsmen to the Whig Party. One of their ploys was to prepare books and attribute them to Crockett, who may have had a hand in some of them. *Sketches and Eccentricities of Col. David Crockett* appeared in 1833. He died in 1836 as one of the defenders of the Alamo in San Antonio, Tex. That year there appeared posthumously *Col. Crockett's Exploits and Adventures in Texas.*

The promotion of **fly-fishing** highlighted the angler's year. Jerome Van Crowninshield Smith's *Fishes of Massachusetts* reported that the angler "enjoys the sport and exults in its success, according as it requires an exertion of his skill. . . . There are not only individuals of whom we speak, but others who availing themselves of all the information to be acquired from books and experience, are fully aware that fly-fishing is the perfection of angling."

1834

I. Civil Rights
Exploration and Settlement
Government
Statistics
Wars

A new national political party coalesced this year out of several groups whose common cause was opposition to Pres. Andrew Jackson and his policies. In 1834 this coalition formally adopted the name Whig, after the English political party that opposed excessive royal prerogatives. Its leaders were Henry Clay of Kentucky, John C. Calhoun of South Carolina, and Daniel Webster of Massachusetts. The party brought together those who favored the so-called American system of protective tariffs combined with internal improvements, states' rights groups, those opposed to Jackson's Bank of the United States policy, southern planters, and northern industrialists. In 1836 the party absorbed the remnants of the Anti-Masonic Party. Although in general it represented the conservative political view, the party lacked leadership and disappeared after it failed dismally in the 1852 presidential election.

1834-1835: In **congressional elections** the Democrats took a 27–25 Senate majority over the Whigs. In the House they lost two seats but held a majority of 145–98 over the Whigs.

June 24: Roger Brooke Taney, serving as secretary of the treasury on a recess appointment from Pres. Jackson, was rejected by the Senate when his name was sent up for confirmation. Again in 1835 Taney was rejected when nominated to be an associate justice of the Supreme Court, but in 1836 he was nominated and confirmed as chief justice.

II. Architecture
Arts and Music
Popular Entertainment
Publishing
Theater

American historians of the middle years of the nineteenth century were not as objective in their treatment of the nation's history as most of those who came later. The last great subjective historian was George Bancroft, whose ten-volume *History of the United States* appeared between 1834 and 1874. Bancroft was professionally trained as a historian, but he was nationalistic and rhetorical, using the story of the U.S. to express commonly held beliefs in democracy, manifest destiny, and the virtues of Anglo-American Protestantism. Bancroft also held public office and as secretary of the navy in 1845–1846 he established the U.S. Naval Academy at Annapolis, Md.

The song **"Zip Coon"** was performed in New York City by Bob Farrell. It would soon become known as "Turkey in the Straw" and gain popularity in minstrel shows. It originated as a folk song about 1815 in the frontier states of the Southwest.

III. Business and Industry
Education
Philosophy and Religion
Science

Growing interest in science brought with it advocates and followers of pseudo-sciences. One was phrenology, which began in Germany and was now being popularized in the U.S. by Orson Fowler. Phrenology claimed that from the shape of the human skull one could determine character traits and mental abilities. Furthermore, phrenology taught that man could alter his personality and develop the brain by training. The lectures and writings of Fowler, self-appointed professor of phrenology, became very popular, and even so eminent a person as Horace Mann, the educator, said it helped him in his work.

A true prototype of the modern **electric motor** was constructed by Thomas Davenport, a Vermont blacksmith. Davenport recognized the versatility of Joseph Henry's electromagnet and saw that it could be adapted for use in an electric power machine. He connected four electromagnets to a battery and set them up on a wheel that rotated rapidly when current was turned on. This is the basic design of the standard electric motor of today. Davenport received a patent in 1837, but could not create a market for his device before his death in 1851.

Cyrus McCormick patented an early model of his famous reaper. Although 20 patents for reapers in the U.S. preceded his, McCormick's persistent experimentation and technical improvements soon made his product preeminent in its field. He did not put his reaper on the market until certain defects had been eliminated. He sold his first two reapers in 1841; produced 4000 in 1856; and 23,000 in 1857. McCormick's reapers revolutionized American agriculture.

IV. Fashion
Folkways
Holidays
Social Issues and Crime
Sports

From about 1825 to the outbreak of the Civil War in 1861, there was a strong atmosphere of reform in the U.S. Most noticeable was the antislavery movement, but it was only one of many causes for which people organized, labored, and contributed money. Dedicated people worked for women's rights, prison reform, educational reform, religious liberalism, social welfare, and other causes. One group called itself the

Society to Improve the Condition of the Sailors. This urge to reform had several sources: the religious revival that began in the 1820s; the rational spirit of the Enlightenment with its idea of the possibility of progress, and the spirit of romanticism, which was related to the older notion that the New World was a second Eden where people could start over.

The legend of **Davy Crockett** was augmented by publication of his supposed autobiography, *A Narrative of the Life of David Crockett.* He was featured as a great bear hunter and congressman. Interspersed were tall tales. Anti-Jacksonians, of whom Crockett was one, expected to profit politically from promotion of Crockett's image. Political opponents meanwhile characterized him as "fresh from the backwoods, half-horse, half-alligator, a little touched with the snapping-turtle."

Americans began to eat **tomatoes** at about this time, but not until 1900 would they become popular. Despite the fact that tomatoes had been introduced into Europe from Mexico as ornamental plants c1550, and were soon afterward eaten in Italy, they were popularly regarded in the U.S. as poisonous and in France as an aphrodisiac.

1835

I. Civil Rights
Exploration and Settlement
Government
Statistics
Wars

The federal government was committed to a policy of removing all eastern Indians to reservations west of the Mississippi R. To that end a treaty had been signed in 1832 with the Seminole Indians of Florida. When the time came in 1835 to begin the move, many Seminoles refused to go. Resistance was led by the Indian chief Osceola, whose father was not an Indian. In November the Second Seminole War (1835–1842) erupted. Federal troops were sent to Florida but had little success against the Indians, whose raiding parties struck quickly and then vanished. Osceola was taken prisoner in 1837 while negotiating under a flag of truce; he died in prison on Jan. 30, 1838. The American forces did not overcome Seminole resistance until 1842. The cost to the U.S. was 1500 dead and $20,000,000.

Jan: **Daniel Webster** of Massachusetts was nominated for president by the Whigs of the Massachusetts legislature. With other Whig candidates in the field and the Anti-Jacksonians divided, Webster won only his home state.

Jan: Sen. **Hugh L. White** of Tennessee was nominated for president by independent anti-Jacksonian Democrats in the legislatures of Tennessee and Alabama. John Tyler was his running mate. White won the electoral votes of Tennessee and Alabama in the 1836 election.

Jan 30: Pres. **Andrew Jackson** was attacked in the first attempt on the life of a U.S. president. Richard Lawrence fired twice while Jackson was attending the funeral of Rep. Warren Ransom Davis of South Carolina, but both shots misfired. Lawrence was later declared insane.

May 20: The **Democratic National Convention nominated Martin Van Buren** of New York for the presidency. Richard M. Johnson of Kentucky was nominated for the vice presidency.

Dec 16: The **Anti-Masonic Party nominated William Henry Harrison** of Ohio for the presidency and Francis Granger of New York for the vice presidency.

II. Architecture
Arts and Music
Popular Entertainment
Publishing
Theater

Compared with that of Europe, the history of the U.S. did not go back very far, but already it was being recorded professionally. Scholars began to edit papers and documents of the first heroes of the nation. Among these historians was Jared Sparks who, at Harvard in 1839, became the first professor of American history in the U.S. Sparks did much to find and publish previously unprinted manuscripts, but he bowdlerized them to enhance the reputations of his subjects. His largest work was *The Writings of George Washington* (12 volumes, 1834–1837). The initial volume was a biography of the first president.

The **New York *Herald*,** a penny daily, was begun by James Gordon Bennett. It soon became pro-Tammany and proslavery. In 1869 it astounded everyone by sending Stanley to Africa to find Livingstone. In 1924 it was merged with the New York *Tribune* to form the *Herald Tribune.*

III. Business and Industry
Education
Philosophy and Religion
Science

Almost since its discovery, America had been popular with European intellectuals, who visited here because of its novelty. Now the U.S. began to attract visitors who wanted to study the world's preeminent experiment in democracy. Perhaps the most thoughtful of these visitors was Alexis de Tocqueville, a French liberal who visited the U.S. in 1831–1832. In 1835 his classic volume *De la Démocratie en Amérique* was published in Belgium. It was issued in the U.S. in an English-language edition, *Democracy in America,* in 1838. Tocqueville had been favorably impressed with the U.S. and its attempt to have both liberty and equality. His book, objective for the most part, was the earliest important analysis of the American system of government.

A model **telegraph** was constructed by Samuel F. B. Morse and demonstrated for a few friends. Morse's model was severely limited and inefficient because he was unfamiliar with advances made in electromagnetism by his contemporaries. It had about the same applicability as a telephone with a range of 40 feet. In the next two years he applied the results of more recent research, improved his equipment, and extended the range of his system to ten miles. He received a patent in 1840.

Nov 23: A machine to manufacture **horseshoes** was patented by Henry Burden of Troy, N.Y., a Scottish immigrant. The machine could produce 60 horseshoes a minute. In the Civil War most of the shoes for Union cavalry came from Burden's plant in Troy.

IV. Fashion
Folkways
Holidays
Social Issues and Crime
Sports

Although the nation was still basically one of farms and small towns, a trend toward urbanization was becoming apparent. Between 1820 and 1850 the combined population of New York City, Philadelphia, Baltimore, and Boston nearly tripled. In 1830 farmers outnumbered city dwellers by about 10.5 to 1; by 1840 the ratio was only 5.5 to 1. The population of towns of 8000 or more nearly doubled between 1830 and 1850. Urbanization brought with it such problems as slums, poor sanitation, and crime. In 1835 *The People's Magazine* blamed the growth of cities for a new type of young man, characterized as unhealthy, badly postured, pale, and nervous.

A well publicized **ten-mile foot race** at Union Course, L.I., was watched by nearly 30,000 spectators. The offer of $1000 to any man who could run ten miles in less than an hour drew nine contestants. Henry Stannard of Killingsworth, Conn., won. He covered the first mile in 5:36, the last mile in 5:54, and the entire course in 59:44. At the conclusion of the race, amid great jubilation, Stannard leaped on a horse and triumphantly retraced his winning course.

1836

I. Civil Rights
Exploration and Settlement
Government
Statistics
Wars

The presidential election campaign of 1836 pitted Democratic Vice Pres. Martin Van Buren against a field of three Whig candidates. They were William Henry Harrison, who also ran on the Anti-Masonic ticket; Daniel Webster, representing the North; and Hugh L. White, whose support came from the South and Southwest. The Whig Party hoped the vote would be split enough to throw the election into the House of Representatives, where they had a chance of prevailing. Issues played little part in the campaign. Those who approved of Pres. Andrew Jackson's policies of the past eight years were for Van Buren; those who were anti-Jackson backed a Whig candidate.

1836-1837: In **congressional elections** the Democrats gained four Senate seats for a 30–18 majority over the Whigs, with four seats going to minor parties. In the House they lost 37 seats for a nominal majority of 108–107, with 24 seats going to minor parties.

Mar 2: Texas declared itself an independent republic. Two weeks later it wrote a constitution and organized a government. The new republic sent commissioners George Childress and Robert Hamilton to Washington, D.C., where their authority was not accepted because the U.S. was unwilling to recognize the Republic of Texas.

Mar 6: The Alamo, a fortified mission at San Antonio, Tex., where fewer than 200 Texans were garrisoned, was captured by the Mexican leader Gen. Antonio López de Santa Anna, who had led 3000 troops across the Rio Grande. Every Texan except a mother, a child, and a servant was killed.

Apr 21: At the **Battle of San Jacinto,** the Texas army under Gen. Sam Houston defeated the Mexican army under Santa Anna. This battle ended the war, and Texas earned its independence from Mexico.

June 15: Arkansas was admitted into the Union, the 25th state.

Oct 22: Sam Houston was sworn in as the first president of the Republic of Texas. He later became a U.S. senator from Texas.

Dec 7: Martin Van Buren was elected president of the United States. The electoral vote was Van Buren, 170; William Henry Harrison, Anti-Masonic candidate, 73; Sen. Hugh L. White of Tennessee, anti-Jacksonian Democrat, 26; Daniel Webster, Massachusetts Whig candidate, 14; and Willie P. Mangum of North Carolina, 11. The popular vote was Van Buren, 761,549; Harrison, 549,567; White, 145,396; Webster, 41,287. None of the four vice presidential candidates received a majority of the electoral votes. The Senate, for the first and only time, had to choose, naming Richard M. Johnson of Kentucky to the office.

II. Architecture
Arts and Music
Popular Entertainment
Publishing
Theater

This year proved a turning point in American intellectual life. Ralph Waldo Emerson's first book, *Nature,* in which he stated his fundamental philosophy, was published anonymously. Emerson had visited Europe in 1832 and 1833, where he met Thomas Carlyle, William Wordsworth, and Samuel Taylor Coleridge. Through them he was introduced to transcendental thought, derived from Immanuel Kant and German idealism. In *Nature* he set forth the principles of American Transcendentalism, which was to become the most influential school of philosophy of the nineteenth century. Transcendentalism also owed much to the Romantic movement. Emerson expressed a deeply felt love for the natural world in *Nature* and went on to combine this with a belief in the spiritual nature of reality and the importance of self-reliance.

Building of the **Washington Monument** in Washington, D.C., was begun from plans by Robert Mills. The monument was outstanding for its freedom from ornamentation in a period when taste ran toward the decorative.

Maria Monk's scandalous narrative, *Awful Disclosures of Maria Monk, as Exhibited in a Narrative of*

Her Suffering During a Residence of Five Years as a Novice, and Two Years as a Black Nun, in the Hotel Dieu Nunnery at Montreal, was published. The book, today known to be a hoax, quickly sold hundreds of thousands of copies. The period was one of considerable anti-Catholic feeling.

III. Business and Industry
Education
Philosophy and Religion
Science

Politics, religion, and education all shaped American thought and action. In the field of education, nothing was more influential than the *Eclectic Readers,* compiled by William Holmes McGuffey, a clergyman and teacher. His first and second readers appeared in 1836, the third and fourth in 1837, the fifth in 1844, and the sixth in 1857. They became almost universally used in the public schools of America and were often revised. After nearly two generations of use, they had sold 122,000,000 copies. The readers taught literary and moral lessons, and included selected writings of the best English-language authors.

The **Transcendental Club,** with Ralph Waldo Emerson, A. Bronson Alcott, George Ripley, Henry Hedges, Orestes Brownson, Theodore Parker, Margaret Fuller, William Ellery Channing, Nathaniel Hawthorne, Elizabeth Peabody, Henry David Thoreau, James Freeman Clark, and others as participants, began as a casual discussion group. The group convened frequently, but the note of informality was never lost. The club had no officers, office, or schedule, and membership waxed and waned. One outcome of the Transcendental Club was the beginning, in 1840, of the Transcendental organ, *The Dial.*

IV. Fashion
Folkways
Holidays
Social Issues and Crime
Sports

In the 1830s circuses developed into tent shows when acrobatic troupes merged with menageries and equestrian shows. By this time, 30 shows were traveling around the country and one, the Zoological Institute, boasted 47 carriages and wagons, over 100 horses, 14 musicians, and 60 performers. An integral part of the entertainment was a parade heralding the arrival of the circus in a town. Floating theaters in the form of showboats on the Mississippi and Ohio rivers in particular added to the entertainment. The first showboat was built in Pittsburgh, Pa., in 1831.

The political slogan **Tippecanoe and Tyler too** caught the public fancy during this year's presidential campaign. Troops under William Henry Harrison, the Whig candidate, had engaged the Indians at Tippecanoe and beaten them off with heavy losses. Harrison thus became identified with the place. John Tyler, a former Democratic senator from Virginia, was his running mate.

Remember the Alamo was the stirring battle cry of Texans at San Jacinto, where the army of Gen. Antonio López de Santa Anna was routed and revenge taken for the massacre of the previous year. The Alamo, a fort in San Antonio, had been besieged for ten days. After being taken, its defenders were slaughtered. Among the dead were Davy Crockett and James Bowie.

So-called **cold water societies** were introduced by the Rev. Thomas P. Hunt, who enlisted children, mainly through Sunday schools, in a temperance crusade. Each child was issued a pledge card and sent out to gather signatures of those who agreed to abstain from drink.

Nov 12: The telling phrase **the almighty dollar** was coined by Washington Irving in his story "The Creole Village," which appeared in *The Knickerbocker Magazine* on this date. The full phrase was "The Almighty Dollar, that great object of universal devotion throughout the land."

1837

I. Civil Rights
Exploration and Settlement
Government
Statistics
Wars

A severe financial panic struck the U.S. in 1837. It was triggered on May 10, when New York banks stopped making payments in specie, but the causes were more deep-seated. Pres. Andrew Jackson's administration had created too much credit. The result was inflation and speculation in western lands. The Specie Circular drained gold and silver to the West. During the year 618 banks failed. A depression followed, bringing widespread unemployment. The panic did not end until 1843.

Jan 26: Michigan was admitted into the Union as the 26th state.

Mar 3: The **Republic of Texas** was recognized by Pres. Andrew Jackson and approved by Congress.

Nov 7: Elijah P. Lovejoy was killed by proslavery rioters at Alton, Ill. His antislavery printing press had previously been smashed several times but was replaced by the Ohio Anti-Slavery Society. Lovejoy became known as the martyr abolitionist.

Dec 29: The *Caroline* Affair (1837–1842) began when, on the U.S. shore of the Niagara R. near Buffalo, Canadian authorities seized and burned the American vessel *Caroline*. The ship was leased to run supplies to Navy Island for support of Canadian revolutionaries led by William Lyon MacKenzie. In the fracas an American was killed by a Canadian militiaman. Ultimately the Canadian was acquitted.

II. Architecture
Arts and Music
Popular Entertainment
Publishing
Theater

While authors such as Nathaniel Hawthorne and Ralph Waldo Emerson were writing novels and essays that are still read and honored, other authors were publishing books of less than permanent quality. A good example of popular taste in historical fiction was a trilogy by William Ware, a Unitarian clergyman. The first part of the trilogy, *Zenobia*, appeared in 1837; the second, *Aurelian*, in 1838; and the final volume, *Julian*, in 1841. These epistolary novels dealt with the political and social struggles of Christians against the Roman Empire.

Twice-Told Tales by Nathaniel Hawthorne, the author's second book and first collection of tales, was published. Digging deep into chronicles and histories of colonial New England and adding symbolic overtones, Hawthorne achieved some of the finest moral allegory ever written.

Thomas Cole produced a masterpiece of the Hudson River school of landscape artists, *In the Catskills*. A resident of the region, Cole as usual romanticized the rural setting. In a clearing surrounded by trees, two figures rest by a winding stream that loses itself in the foliage of the background. In the rear the mountains rise gently.

Aug 31: Ralph Waldo Emerson delivered his celebrated *American Scholar* address before the Phi Beta Kappa Society at Harvard. Oliver Wendell Holmes called it "our intellectual Declaration of Independence." Although many previous writers and speakers had dealt with the same theme, Emerson raised the subject to the level of philosophy.

III. Business and Industry
Education
Philosophy and Religion
Science

The U.S. was beginning to develop its own economists. These new economists approached their subject from the point of view of American optimism, in contrast to the pessimism of English economists. Chief among the Americans was Henry C. Carey of Philadelphia, who had gained substantial business experience by running efficiently the large bookstore he inherited from his father. In general, Carey believed in laissez-faire capitalism but favored a protective tariff for American industries. In his three-volume work *Principles of Political Economy* (1837–1840), his economic nationalism was apparent.

John Deere produced his first plow incorporating a steel blade at his blacksmith shop in Grand Detour, Ill. While visiting a sawmill he noticed a smooth-surfaced saw blade and thought that, shaped into a plow blade, it might easily cut furrows in the moist and sticky midwestern soil without clogging. His experiments proved successful and he soon moved to Moline, Ill., where he began to manufacture steel plows. Deere plows, known as singing plows, contributed greatly to the expansion of farming in the Midwest and West.

Sep: Samuel F.B. Morse filed for a patent on his telegraph. It was not granted until 1844.

Dec 29: A portable **combined thresher and fanning mill** earned a patent for the inventors, Hiram Avery and John Avery Pitts of Winthrop, Me. Eventually Hiram moved to Chicago where he manufactured Chicago-Pitts brand threshers, which were widely used throughout the grain belt for more than half a century.

IV. Fashion
Folkways
Holidays
Social Issues and Crime
Sports

Americans liked showmanship, natural wonders, freaks, and all kinds of believe-it-or-not items. One man in the mid-nineteenth century gave them all this and more. He was Phineas T. Barnum, who began his career this year by exhibiting an old black woman, Joyce Heth. He claimed she was 161 years old and had been George Washington's nurse. She was actually about 80. A crowd of some 10,000 flocked to see her at Niblo's Garden in New York City. In 1842 Barnum opened his American Museum in New York City. There at various times he was to exhibit the original Siamese twins, Chang and Eng, and the Fiji Mermaid, half monkey and half fish. The most popular attraction, though, was Tom Thumb, a dwarf who stood only 40 inches tall. Exhibited in the U.S. and abroad, Thumb was seen by 20,000,000 people.

About this time **Amos Lawrence** became a well-known model of the virtuous merchant by his practicing of moral hygiene. Lawrence gave up tea and coffee in 1832, fish, meat, and gravies in 1835, and butter in 1836. Lawrence conducted regular family prayers, conscientiously observed the Sabbath, and contributed to many worthy charities. In the midst of his piety, Lawrence prospered as a landlord and businessman to such an extent that his example was cited as evidence of the rewards of good living. Lawrence died on Dec. 31, 1852. His sons collected his papers, published as *Extracts from the Diary and Correspondence of the Late Amos Lawrence* (1855).

1838

I. Civil Rights
Exploration and Settlement
Government
Statistics
Wars

The Underground Railroad was a loosely organized apparatus operated by northern abolitionists to bring slaves from the South and set them free. More than 3000 persons were involved in the effort. The name apparently was first used in 1831. The best known leaders were Levi Coffin, who is said to have assisted 3000 slaves, and Harriet Tubman, an escaped slave. Slaves were passed along from one safe station to another until they reached a free state. Some went on to Canada. By the time of the Civil War, the Underground Railroad may have assisted as many as 50,000 slaves to escape bondage, although after the passage of the Fugitive Slave Law of 1850 the number decreased to 500 to 1000 a year.

1838-1839: In **congressional elections** the Democrats lost two Senate seats but still led the Whigs 28–22. In the House the Democrats picked up 16 seats and the Whigs gained 11, for a Democratic majority of 124–118.

Jan 26: The **first prohibition law** in the U.S. was passed in Tennessee, making it a misdemeanor to sell alcoholic beverages in taverns and stores. Later in the year a political storm erupted in Massachusetts over a law prohibiting the sale of alcoholic beverages in amounts of less than 15 gallons, except for "medicinal or mechanical purposes."

May 18: Charles Wickes was placed by Congress in command of a naval exploring and surveying expedition of the South Seas. On Aug. 18 his fleet of six ships left Hampton Roads, Va., to explore hundreds of islands of the Pacific; a large sector of Antarctica, later named Wickes Land; and the American Northwest coastline. The expedition returned in July 1842. Wickes's five-volume report was published in 1844.

June 12: A new **Iowa Territory,** including the two Dakotas and much of Minnesota in addition to Iowa, was formed with its separation from Wisconsin Territory.

Dec: Cherokee Indians remaining in Georgia and southeastern Tennessee, 14,000 in all, were forcibly removed from their lands by 7000 U.S. soldiers and herded into Oklahoma. The phrase *Trail of Tears* refers to this final tragic act in the enforcement of the fraudulent treaty of New Echota in 1835. Four thousand Cherokees died en route; perhaps 1000 escaped. In the end 7,000,000 acres of Cherokee land had been seized by whites.

II. Architecture
Arts and Music
Popular Entertainment
Publishing
Theater

Although the North seemed to supply most of the nation's authors, the South was not without its contributors to the literary world. A worthy example was John Pendleton Kennedy, a lawyer and politician as well as author. His *Swallow Barn* (1832) was a series of sketches about Virginia, written in the manner of Washington Irving. Kennedy wrote two novels, *Horse-Shoe Robinson* (1832) and *Rob of the Bowl* (1838). Although its subject matter was melodramatic, the latter novel was a realistic tale of Maryland in 1681. It concerned an attempt by Protestants to overthrow Lord Baltimore, a Catholic.

John Greenleaf Whittier joined the list of authors of books supporting abolition with the publication of his *Ballads and Anti-Slavery Poems.* Noteworthy among the pieces were "To William Lloyd Garrison," "The Hunters of Men," "The Slave Ships," "Stanzas for the Time," "Toussaint L'Ouverture," "Hymn," the extremely popular "Stanzas," and "The Moral Warfare."

III. Business and Industry
Education
Philosophy and Religion
Science

The Mormon Church was going through a difficult period. On Jan. 12, 1838, Joseph Smith, the founder, and his followers left Kirtland, Ohio, partly as a result of the panic of 1837. They moved to Independence, Mo., where they met with hostility, partly because of their beliefs and partly because of their communal economic organization and efficiency. Moving back east in 1839, the Mormons founded Nauvoo, Ill. By 1844 Nauvoo had a population of 15,000 and was the most prosperous city in Illinois. Again, however, the Mormons were distrusted for their religious beliefs and disliked for their economic competition.

Apr 23: The **first transatlantic steamship service** began with the arrival in New York harbor of the steamer *Great Western* after less than 16 days at sea. The previous day the *Sirius* had arrived from England. Both ships were British steam-sail packets. For the next generation Great Britain led the world in transatlantic steamer service. Scheduled service was not established until 1840.

IV. Fashion
Folkways
Holidays
Social Issues and Crime
Sports

Comparatively brief as American history was, Americans were exceedingly proud of it and were beginning to give a mythological flavor to the Revolutionary War period and its heroes. Foremost among these, of course, was George Washington. In 1832, on the 100th anniversary of Washington's birth, Daniel Webster had declaimed: "His age and his country are equally full of wonders; and of both he is the chief." An attempt in Congress at this time to have the remains of the first president removed from their Mount Vernon, Va., tomb and reburied in the capital city caused bitter debate. Southerners refused to have such a precious possession moved even a few miles north.

The term *Trail of Tears* referred to the route taken by the Cherokee Indians on their removal from Georgia to new lands in Oklahoma. The Indians were forced into prison camps by troops under Gen. Winfield Scott. The first migration began in October. Conservative estimates placed the Indian death toll at 10% of the population. The removal had been legalized by the Treaty of New Echota in 1835.

1839

I. Civil Rights
Exploration and Settlement
Government
Statistics
Wars

An unusual incident involving a mutiny on a slave ship added to the tension between North and South. A Spanish ship, the *Amistad,* sailed from Havana, Cuba, in June 1839 with 54 black slaves aboard. An uprising by the slaves on July 1, in which two men were killed, gave them control of the ship and they attempted to sail to Africa. However, the vessel was captured by a U.S. Navy ship off Long Island. Slave interests, led by Sec. of State John Forsyth, attempted to turn the slaves over to Spain. Abolitionists brought suit to prevent this, and the case reached the Supreme Court, which in Mar. 9, 1841, found that the slaves had been illegally kidnaped and set them free. Former Pres. John Quincy Adams defended the blacks.

Feb 12: The **Aroostock War** began with the seizure of Rufus McIntire, a U.S. land agent sent to the Aroostock region between New Brunswick, Canada, and Maine, to expel Canadian lumberjacks who had entered the disputed area. The boundary question had been an Anglo-American issue since 1783 and had never been satisfactorily settled. After McIntire's arrest, Maine and New Brunswick called out their militias, and the Nova Scotia legislature appropriated war funds. Congress authorized a conscription of 50,000 men and voted $10,000,000 toward the prosecution of this action. Calmer voices prevailed: Gen. Winfield Scott arranged a truce, and both parties agreed to refer the dispute to a boundary commission. The issue was settled in 1842 by the Webster-Ashburton Treaty.

Nov 13: The **Liberty Party,** an antislavery party, held its first national convention at Warsaw, N.Y. It nominated James G. Birney of New York for president. Birney, a former Kentuckian and slaveholder, wielded strong political influence in western New York and the Ohio R. Valley. Francis J. Lemoyne was nominated for vice president.

Dec 4-7: The **Whig National Convention nominated William Henry Harrison** for the presidency. John Tyler of Virginia was nominated for the vice presidency.

II. Architecture
Arts and Music
Popular Entertainment
Publishing
Theater

In architecture the Gothic Revival, beginning in the late 1830s, competed with the earlier Classic Revival. Copying the tall towers and pointed arches of the Middle Ages, the Gothic style was used primarily for churches, schools, and libraries, but was adapted to country houses also. The first important architect of the Gothic Revival was Richard Upjohn, who in 1839 was given the task of rebuilding Trinity Church in New York City. His design was soon copied by other churches. James Renwick was also a leading architect of the style. He planned beautiful Grace Church in New York City (1843–1846), and was then chosen in 1853 to be the architect for St. Patrick's Cathedral, also in New York City. This was the most ambitious structure of the Gothic Revival. In the field of country houses and landscape gardening, Andrew Jackson Downing was the leading figure. His book, *Treatise on the Theory and Practice of Landscape Gardening Adapted to North America*, appeared in 1841. It at once became the standard work in its field, going through ten editions.

An Englishman, **Alexander Forbes**, wrote *California*, the first book in English about the territory. A businessman, Forbes stopped off at Yerba Buena (San Francisco) on a voyage to the Pacific and saw the possibilities of the new land. He urged the British government to take over the territory before Russian or American settlers pushed into it. To make the territory more accessible, he suggested cutting a canal across the Isthmus of Panama.

III. Business and Industry
Education
Philosophy and Religion
Science

Increased attention was now being paid to education: in requiring school attendance, in providing free public schools, and in teacher education. The leader in the field was Horace Mann of Massachusetts. It was through his efforts that in 1839 the first state-supported school to educate teachers was established in the U.S., in Massachusetts. As secretary of the state board of education there, Mann instituted longer school terms, insisted on better schoolhouses, and secured higher pay for teachers. His successful upgrading of education influenced states throughout the nation.

Vulcanized rubber was first made by Charles Goodyear, after many failed experiments. This was the first successful attempt to make rubber nonsticky and solid at high temperatures. Rubber had interested inventors for years but none had succeeded in creating a product that did not melt easily when subjected to heat. Goodyear made his first tests with rubber while in jail for debt in 1834. His ultimate success was the result of an accident—he dropped a mixture of sulfur and rubber on top of a hot stove, thereby discovering a process he called vulcanization. Goodyear secured patents for his process and made arrangements for royalties, but he became entangled in lawsuits. At the time of his death in 1860, he was $200,000 in debt.

The importance of **wheat** as a cash crop was increasing steadily. In 1839 production amounted to 84,823,000 bushels. Ten years later the number had climbed to 100,485,000 bushels. By the 1840s large areas of Iowa and Nebraska were being used to grow wheat. Canals and railroads were used to transport the bulky crop, and by 1840 there were 4354 grist mills in the U.S. to grind the wheat into flour. Large mills were located in Baltimore, Buffalo, and Rochester.

IV. Fashion
Folkways
Holidays
Social Issues and Crime
Sports

Even though a commission reported in 1908 that Gen. Abner Doubleday, veteran of the Mexican and Civil wars, had invented baseball in 1839 at Cooperstown, N.Y., hardly anyone credits this story any more. Too many other similar games, such as rounders, played mostly by children, antedated 1839. In addition, the game lacked many phases of its development until later in the century, when it became the American national sport. The first organized baseball team of which much is known was the Knickerbocker Base Ball Club in New York, organized in 1842. Three years later the club found a permanent home at the Elysian Fields in Hoboken, N.J., and adopted a set of rules.

The **first woman horse thief** of record in the U.S., Josephine Amelia Perkins achieved notoriety by a confession that was published with the following description of herself: "A young woman, who, in early life was deservedly esteemed for her exemplary behavior, yet for three years last past (friendless and unprotected) has been unhappily addicted to a criminal propensity, more singular and surprising in its nature (for one of her sex) than can be found on record; in the commission of which, she has been four times detected, twice pardoned on account of her sex, once for reasons of supposed insanity, and the fourth and last time, convicted and sentenced to two years imprisonment in Madison County jail, Kentucky. Annexed is a well-written Address to Parents and Children." Miss Perkins was born in Devonshire, England, in 1818. She stole her first horse from her father to make an elopement journey of 117 miles. Through a series of misadventures, she landed in America without any money and with only the clothes on her back. Her career in horse stealing soon began.

1840

I. Civil Rights
Exploration and Settlement
Government
Statistics
Wars

The presidential election campaign of 1840 was something new in American life, engaging as it did in the use of slogans, parades, campaign hats, and mudslinging. The Democrats renominated Pres. Martin Van Buren, but could not agree on a vice presidential candidate. The Whigs nominated William Henry Harrison of Ohio and, for vice president, John Tyler of Virginia. The Democrats ran on a platform that emphasized strict construction of the Constitution. They opposed congressional interference with slavery, a national bank, and internal improvements paid for by the federal government. The Whigs, on the other hand, based their campaign on personalities. They pictured Van Buren as luxury-loving and aristocratic. Most of all, they made use of a remark of a Democratic newspaper, the Baltimore *Republican,* "that upon condition of his receiving a pension of

$2000 and a barrel of cider, Gen. Harrison would no doubt consent to withdraw his pretensions, and spend his days in a log cabin on the banks of the Ohio." The Whigs used this statement to run a "Log Cabin and Hard Cider" campaign. They presented the hero of the Battle of Tippecanoe as a simple man of the people, although he came from an aristocratic Virginia family. The Whig campaign song was "Tippecanoe and Tyler Too," with a refrain, "Van, Van is a used up man." Their placards portrayed Harrison at the door of a log cabin, welcoming visitors to his humble home.

The U.S. **Census** recorded a population of 17,069,453. The center of population was placed 16 miles south of Clarksburg, W. Va.

1840-1841: In **congressional elections** the Whigs gained six Senate seats for a 28–22 majority over the Democrats, with two seats held by minor parties. In the House the Whigs gained 15 seats for a 133–102 majority, with six seats going to minor parties.

Jan 19: The **U.S. expedition** to the South Seas led by Capt. Charles Wilkes laid claim to a portion of the continent of Antarctica for the U.S.

May 5: The **Democratic National Convention nominated Pres. Martin Van Buren** for a second term. The convention was unable to agree on a vice presidential candidate.

Dec 2: William Henry Harrison was elected president of the United States. John Tyler of Virginia was elected vice president in a Whig landslide. The electoral vote was Harrison, 234; Martin Van Buren, incumbent Democrat, 60. The popular vote was Harrison, 1,275,017; Van Buren, 1,128,702; James G. Birney, Liberty Party candidate, 7059.

II. Architecture
Arts and Music
Popular Entertainment
Publishing
Theater

Magazines with high standards and espousing particular points of view were established in this period. The most notable was *The Dial,* first published in July 1840 and lasting only until April 1844. It was the voice of the transcendentalists and was edited by Margaret Fuller. It published articles by Ralph Waldo Emerson, Henry David Thoreau, Theodore Parker, and others. *The Living Age* was founded in 1844 by Eliakim Littel and edited by him until his death in 1870. It was a general magazine of fiction, poetry, and comment. *Brownson's Quarterly Review* was also first published in 1844, by Orestes Brownson; it reflected Brownson's conversion to Catholicism. *The Southern Literary Messenger* was founded in Richmond, Va., in 1834, while the year before James Hall had brought out the *Illinois Monthly Magazine,* the first literary magazine west of the Ohio R.

Two Years Before the Mast by Richard Henry Dana, Jr., an American classic dealing with the nineteenth-century maritime industry, was published. The book drew on the author's experience as a sailor to the West Coast and back (1834–1836). A sensitive man, Dana was revolted by the cruelty, especially the flogging, aboard ship, and later was instrumental in having the practice outlawed. His realistic approach to writing about life at sea set the standard for later writers.

Tales of the Grotesque and Arabesque, the first collection of short stories by Edgar Allan Poe, was published in Philadelphia in Dec. 1839 but bore the date 1840 on its title page. The two-volume collection included such classic tales of the macabre as "MS. Found in a Bottle," "The Fall of the House of Usher," and "William Wilson." Although Poe was gaining a substantial literary reputation, he failed to find a wide readership or any financial security from his writing. He spent his entire career in virtual penury.

III. Business and Industry
Education
Philosophy and Religion
Science

Dentistry was about to become a separate profession and the U.S. took the lead. The first dental school in the world, the Baltimore College of Dental Surgery, was founded this year in Baltimore, Md. It later became part of the University of Maryland. Chapin Aaron Harris, a pioneer in the field, was the founder. The previous year he had established the *American Journal of Dental Science* and in 1840 helped organize the American Society of Dental Surgeons.

Photography of the moon was accomplished for the first time by John William Draper, a physicist and astronomer at New York University. Draper's photograph of the moon was not impressive by later standards, but it foreshadowed America's pioneering role in astronomical photography. Draper also had the distinction of being the first photographer to capture an image showing a human subject with eyes open.

Mar 31: A ten-hour workday was established by executive order for all federal employees engaged on public works. It had long been a goal of U.S. labor.

IV. Fashion
Folkways
Holidays
Social Issues and Crime
Sports

An indication of the social issues confronting Americans during this period was the burgeoning of societies and associations formed to improve health, labor conditions, moral values, education, and other social conditions. The Washington Temperance Society, formed this year by a small group, held a series of meetings in which alcoholics discussed their problems with one another. Within three years the society claimed that 500,000 intemperate drinkers and 100,000 confirmed alcoholics had reformed under its auspices. As early as 1834 the North Carolina Temperance Society had 50 branches with 4700 members. A temperance novel, *My Mother's Gold Ring,* by Lucius Manlius Sargent, was published in 1833 and sold 113,000 copies. What had begun as a movement for temperance in drinking alcoholic beverages turned into a moral crusade for total abstinence, led primarily by Protestant clergymen. Many employers backed the drive on the grounds that nondrinking workers would be more efficient. Among laymen, Neal Dow of Maine was the foremost champion of temperance. He made his first temperance speech when he was 24 and in 1838 was instrumental in the founding of the Maine Temperance Union.

The expression *O.K.* came into popular use this year. The first recorded use of the term was in the Boston *Morning Post* of Mar. 23, 1839, as the initials of the jocularly misspelled phrase *oll korrect.* It came into use in Boston and New York City, then in the presidential election of 1840 was used also to mean *Old Kinderhook,* a reference to Martin Van Buren, whose birthplace and home were in Kinderhook, N.Y.

1841

I. Civil Rights
Exploration and Settlement
Government
Statistics
Wars

For the first time a vice president succeeded to the presidency because of the death of an incumbent.

William Henry Harrison, 68, who caught cold at his inauguration on Mar. 4, died of pneumonia on Apr. 4. Harrison was succeeded by Vice Pres. John Tyler who, although he had run on the Whig ticket, was not a Whig at heart. He had previously supported the Democrat, Pres. Andrew Jackson, in 1828 and 1832, and had major political disagreements with the northern, conservative wing of the Whig Party. His administration was characterized by bickering and frustration, as Henry Clay and Daniel Webster tried to control Tyler and shape the Whig Party to their own interests.

Oct 27: What came to be called the **Creole incident** began when the U.S. brig *Creole* sailed from Hampton Roads, Va. At sea its cargo of slaves mutinied and took over the vessel, then made for the Bahamas, where the mutineers were arrested and the crew allowed to go free. Sec. of State Daniel Webster, arguing that the slaves were on an American vessel and therefore subject to U.S. law, led the attempt to recover the slaves. Rep. Joshua Giddings, Whig of Ohio, introduced a series of resolutions (Mar. 21–22, 1842) against federal sanction of slavery, and particularly against the coastal slave trade, and was censured (Mar. 23, 1842). He resigned from Congress but was returned the next month by his constituents in a special election.

II. Architecture
Arts and Music
Popular Entertainment
Publishing
Theater

A new literary genre, the detective story, was created in the U.S. this year. It was introduced by Edgar Allan Poe with "The Murders in the Rue Morgue." The story appeared in the April issue of *Graham's Lady's and Gentleman's Magazine,* of which Poe was editor. Poe followed this with "The Mystery of Marie Rogêt" in 1842–1843 and "The Purloined Letter" in 1845. The forerunner of the modern fictional detective appeared in these stories in the person of C. Auguste Dupin, an amateur who demonstrated his ability to find and analyze clues that baffled the police. Thus Poe introduced the puzzling crime, the eccentric detective, his loyal but unperceptive companion, the dull-witted policeman, the surprise solution, and the rational explanation. These works of Poe were popular, but it was later in the century that detective stories by foreign authors such as Wilkie Collins and Arthur Conan Doyle brought wide readership of the genre. Nevertheless, Poe brought this distinct form of fiction to a level matched by only a few later writers.

Essays (first series) by Ralph Waldo Emerson appeared. His second series of *Essays* was published in 1844. Initially both books had only a small sale, but with the advent of the "cheap libraries" of the 1870s and 1890s the *Essays* reached best-seller status. Transcendentalism found its best expression in these essays.

The Deerslayer by James Fenimore Cooper, the last of the frontier novels known as the Leather-Stocking Tales, was published. Leatherstocking, also called Natty Bumppo and Hawkeye, was shown in his youth, skillful in the hunt, resourceful, tough, and sinewy. Above all he was virtuous, sincere, and unspoiled by civilization. When asked about his church, he replied: "I am in church now; I eat in church, drink in church, sleep in church. The 'arth is the temple of the Lord. . . ."

Henry Wadsworth Longfellow gained wide readership with the publication of his *Ballads and Other Poems,* in which he displayed a spirited narrative technique. Poems such as "The Skeleton in Armor" and "The Wreck of the Hesperus" have become part of the American folk heritage. In seven years the Longfellow collection went through ten printings.

III. Business and Industry
Education
Philosophy and Religion
Science

Nativism, chiefly an anti-Catholic movement, increased as the number of Catholic immigrants grew. By 1841 it began to involve education. At this time there were about 200 parochial schools in the country. In New York, on Oct. 29, Bishop John Joseph Hughes urged state support for such schools and encouraged Catholics to use their votes to achieve this purpose. His efforts led to the establishment of an independent Catholic school system, and aroused anger and fear among many American Protestants. Agitation over government support for parochial schools contributed to the founding of the Native American Party, which consisted of Protestants who saw a conspiracy on the part of the growing Catholic population and especially its clergy. Riots resulted, including an attack on Bishop Hughes's home in 1842.

The **Brook Farm Association** was created by members of the Transcendental Club to apply their theories in an experimental cooperative community on a farm nine miles from Boston. A stock company was formed, with George Ripley as its prime organizer and first manager. On April 1 he and his wife and some 20 others began seeking a life balanced between manual labor and intellectual pursuits. Emerson was a party to discussions but never committed himself. Hawthorne and two other transcendentalists lived at Brook Farm for a period. The experiment ended after a serious fire in 1847, with the problems of combining plain living and high ideals unresolved.

IV. Fashion
Folkways
Holidays
Social Issues and Crime
Sports

Foreign visitors continued to arrive in the U.S., look about them, return home, and publish their impressions. Perhaps the most indefatigable of all, both as to miles traveled and words written, was James Buckingham, a British lecturer and a member of Parliament. He made a four-year tour of the U.S., from 1837 to 1840. In 1841 appeared his *America: Historical, Statistical, and Descriptive,* in two volumes. In the following year he published four more volumes, two devoted to the eastern and western states and two to the slave states. His encyclopedic approach yielded a more or less impartial guide. In one observation he found upstate New York frugal and staid, but New York City speculative and extravagant.

The current vogue in **ladies' dresses,** *Godey's Lady's Book* commented, was for tight sleeves. Further, it predicted that the style would last and "again exhibit the beautiful contour of a lady's arm." Yet bare limbs were not proper. Ladies who attended summer resorts were warned against "brocade breakfast dresses" with sleeves and neckline so short that they caused brothers to blush "through the tediousness of three courses and dessert."

1842

I. Civil Rights
Exploration and Settlement
Government
Statistics
Wars

A turning point in U.S.-British relations came with the signing on Aug. 9, 1842, of the Webster-Ashburton Treaty, which settled several matters between the two nations. The treaty took its name from Sec. of State Daniel Webster and Lord Ashburton, the British envoy in Washington. It adjusted the Maine-New Brunswick boundary, which had been the cause of the Aroostock War of 1838–1839. The U.S. received most of the territory in dispute as well as navigational rights on the St. John R. The treaty also settled the question of the U.S.-Canada boundary between Lake Superior and Lake of the Woods. As a result, the U.S. gained territory that included the rich Mesabi iron deposits discovered later. The two nations also agreed to cooperate in suppressing the slave trade. In a separate action Ashburton apologized for the *Caroline* affair, which involved the seizure in 1837 of that American-owned small steamer on the Niagara R.

The **first expedition of John Frémont** began this year. Frémont was placed at the head of a party sent to explore the route to Oregon beyond the Mississippi R. as far as the South Pass of the Continental Divide in Wyoming. Frémont had previously traced the headwaters of the Des Moines R. in 1841.

1842-1843: In **congressional elections** the Democrats gained three Senate seats but the Whigs kept a majority, 28–25, with one seat going to a minor party. In the House the Democrats picked up 40 seats for a 142–79 lead, with one seat going to a minor party.

June 25: A **congressional reapportionment act** was passed. It provided that all congressmen were to be elected by districts equal in number to each state's quota of representatives.

II. Architecture
Arts and Music
Popular Entertainment
Publishing
Theater

Growing interest in classical music was indicated by the number of musical organizations founded in the mid-nineteenth century. Foremost among them was the New York Philharmonic Society, established on Apr. 2, 1842. The orchestra was led by a German-trained musician from Connecticut, Ureli Corelli Hill. It gave its first performance on Dec. 7. Only Hill and the librarian received salaries, while the 60-odd orchestra members, mostly Germans, shared in the modest ticket receipts. The Chicago Philharmonic Society was formed in 1850 but lasted only four years. The first important chamber music group was the Mendelssohn Quintette Club of Boston, founded in 1849.

Cheap publishing made its first appearance in the U.S. Because of low postal rates for newspapers and improvements in printing, novels were published in a newspaper format and sold for as little as 6 ¼ cents. This forced regular publishers to produce cheap paperbacks. The newspaper extras lasted only four or five years, having been killed off by the handier paperbacks.

III. Business and Industry
Education
Philosophy and Religion
Science

Of the nineteenth-century advances in medical science, none was more welcome to patients than the development of anesthetics. The properties of chloroform had been discovered in 1831, but it was not used as an anesthetic until 1847 in Great Britain. In the meantime, on Mar. 30, 1842, Dr. Crawford W. Long of Jefferson, Ga., used ethyl ether while removing a tumor from the neck of a patient. For several years thereafter he continued to use ether. He even administered it to his wife during childbirth. Long, however, did not make his work public until 1849, after others had demonstrated the value of anesthetics. Dr. William T. G. Morton demonstrated the beneficial effects of ether in Boston on Oct. 16, 1846, before members of the medical profession.

The **legality of labor unions** was established by the Massachusetts Supreme Court in the case of *Commonwealth v. Hunt.* This included the right of workers to strike in order to obtain a closed shop, higher wages, shorter working hours, and better working conditions. It was held further that individual members of unions could not be indicted collectively for the illegal actions of other union members. This decision was significant in its reversal of traditional judicial hostility to labor organizations.

Mar 3: Child labor legislation was advanced when Gov. John Davis of Massachusetts signed a law to regulate the workday of children under 12 years of age. Such children were limited to a ten-hour day. But the law applied only to "manufacturing establishments" and was not easily enforceable. Similar laws were passed in other states, particularly in New England and the Middle Atlantic states, but it was not until after the Civil War that enforcement of minimum age and maximum hour provisions began to affect child employment practices.

IV. Fashion
Folkways
Holidays
Social Issues and Crime
Sports

At this time horse racing was the most popular spectator sport. It was also popular with those who liked to wager on sporting events. The Union Course, on Long Island, N.Y., held a series of intersectional races that drew large crowds. On May 20, 1842, the entry from the South, Fashion, and the entry from the North, Boston, raced for a purse of $20,000. Although Boston was the outstanding horse of the period, it lost to Fashion, which ran the four-mile course in a record 7:32. In 1845 Fashion raced Peytona, from Alabama, on the same course; the latter won. This time it was estimated that 50,000 people tried to reach the track, tying up traffic to the extent that some fans never arrived.

In **women's fashions,** the pelerine, a type of cape or mantle, was very popular, as were watered silk and velvet cardinals (short cloaks) and scarves. However, it was not considered good taste to wear a cardinal with a dress of the same color.

1843

I. Civil Rights
Exploration and Settlement
Government
Statistics
Wars

The U.S. was concerned over the interest shown in the Hawaiian Islands by France and Great Britain. In 1842 the U.S. recognized the islands' independence and Pres. John Tyler said the U.S. would be "dissatisfied" if any nation took possession of them. To affirm its interest, the U.S. signed a trade treaty with Hawaii in 1843 and sent a diplomatic agent, George Brown, to represent American interests. Earlier in the year the commander of a British frigate had made an abortive attempt to obtain cession to Great Britain from King Kamehameha III.

May 29: The second and most fruitful **Frémont expedition,** under John C. Frémont, left Kansas City. The journey yielded an accurate survey of the emigrant route to Oregon. The return journey allowed members of the expedition to correct many misconceptions about the geography of California. Frémont discovered the nature of the Great Basin, and probably first used that term to describe the independent system of lakes and rivers divided from the ocean by the mountains. Frémont made a great contribution to geographical knowledge. He arrived back in St. Louis on Aug. 7, 1844.

June: The **American Republican Party** was formed at New York City largely through the efforts of the Native American Association, an anti-Catholic, anti-immigrant organization. In 1845, this party evolved into the Native American Party, which called for sweeping changes in immigration laws. Having no position on the Mexican War, it failed. Revived in 1853, it collapsed again in division over the slavery issue.

Aug 31: The abolitionist **Liberty Party nominated James G. Birney** of Kentucky for the presidency and Thomas Morris of Ohio for the vice presidency.

II. Architecture
Arts and Music
Popular Entertainment
Publishing
Theater

American humor continued to favor the regional, folksy approach of the naive but shrewd storyteller. Two such storytellers were Seba Smith and William Tappan Thompson. The latter was the editor of the Savannah, Ga., *Morning News.* His humorous accounts of Georgia characters, which had first appeared in his paper, were collected in 1843 in *Major Jones's Courtship.* The sketches were written as letters to the editor, and the supposed author, Major Jones, appeared to be a semiliterate Georgia planter. The pieces were filled with descriptions of everyday events, weddings, military service, and the like, all in dialect. Thompson's book went through 20 printings. He published four more books in a similar vein. Seba Smith founded the Portland, Me., *Courier* and published in it letters from the fictional "Major Jack Downing," a Down East Yankee whose forte was political commentary. Smith, through his alter ego, was thus the first of a line of homespun political philosophers to delight American readers. Smith collected Downing's writings in book form first in 1833.

The Conquest of Mexico, an American historical and literary classic by William Hickling Prescott, was published. It was a monumental work for which he had to import a small reference library. Concerned always with style, Prescott had a passion for fact, making his work authoritative as well as compelling. In 1847 he added *The Conquest of Peru* to his history of Spanish America. Both books have sold hundreds of thousands of copies.

III. Business and Industry
Education
Philosophy and Religion
Science

The era of nineteenth-century Utopian communities came to a climax with the establishment this year of the North American Phalanx at Red Bank, N.J. Its founder was Albert Brisbane, a disciple of the social philosophy of Charles Fourier of France, who proposed organizing people into economic units called phalanxes. About 1200 formed the Red Bank group, which built a three-story phalanstery and a gristmill. The land was fertile and the group's members, mostly people of culture and refinement, developed a successful truck gardening operation. The members ate their meals together but each family had separate quarters. After the mill burned down in 1854, the association was dissolved, having enjoyed a longer life until then than any other community of its type.

The **Harvard Astronomical Observatory** acquired by private subscription the largest telescope available. In March a comet had appeared in daytime and aroused such interest that a subscription for fitting out the observatory with the latest astronomical equipment had been proposed. The purchase of the telescope indicated that lectures and public addresses by scientists were having the intended effect: establishing American astronomy. Harvard Observatory was begun through the initiative of William Cranch Bond, who had made observations for some years at his home and then moved to Dana House in 1839. A main branch of the Harvard Observatory is still maintained at Cambridge, Mass.

IV. Fashion
Folkways
Holidays
Social Issues and Crime
Sports

Rowing and sailing were popular sports. They were mainly enjoyed by the well-to-do and hence had high social status. Rowing was introduced at Harvard this year by a student, William Weeks, who bought and outfitted a shell. Yale took up the sport the next year. On Aug. 3, 1852, the Harvard crew defeated the Yale crew on Lake Winnepesaukee, N.H., in the first intercollegiate sports event of any kind. In the 1830s and 1840s in New York City, the Castle Garden Amateur Boat Club Association was restricted to "young men of the highest respectability, who were determined to combine with pleasure the utmost propriety of conduct."

July 12: Joseph Smith, leader of the Mormon Church, announced that a divine revelation had sanctioned the practice of polygamy. This announcement caused bitter feeling both within Mormon ranks and between Mormons and non-Mormons around Nauvoo, Ill., where Smith's followers were settled at this time.

1844

I. Civil Rights
Exploration and Settlement
Government
Statistics
Wars

The presidential election campaign of 1844 saw some unusual happenings in American politics. Pres. John Tyler wanted a term in his own right, and a Democratic faction nominated him in 1844. It was clear, however, that he stood no chance, and he withdrew on Aug. 20, becoming the first president who did not stand for a second term. At the Democratic National Convention, former Pres. Martin Van Buren tried to secure the nomination but could not muster enough support, largely because of his opposition to the annexation of Texas. The Democrats nominated the first so-called dark horse in U.S. history, James K. Polk of Tennessee. The Whigs unanimously nominated Henry Clay of Kentucky for the presidency. There was a third party this year, the Liberty Party, which in 1843 had nominated James G. Birney of Kentucky on an antislavery platform. The Democratic platform was nationalistic, calling for annexation of Texas and control of the entire Oregon Territory, then shared with England. The Whig platform was more general, making no reference to Texas or to the question of a national bank.

1844-1845: In **congressional elections** the Democrats gained six seats for a 31–25 majority over the Whigs. In the House the Democrats gained one seat for a 143–77 majority, with six seats going to minor parties.

May 1: The **Whig National Convention nominated Henry Clay** of Kentucky for the presidency. Theodore Frelinghuysen of New Jersey was nominated for the vice presidency.

May 27-29: The **Democratic National Convention nominated James K. Polk** of Tennessee for the presi-dency on the ninth ballot. Polk won the nomination after all other candidates withdrew. Former Pres. Martin Van Buren was unable to secure the nomination largely because of his opposition to the annexation of Texas. George M. Dallas of Pennsylvania was nominated for the vice presidency. This was the first convention at which a dark horse candidate won, and also the first to be reported by telegraph.

June 8: The **Texas Annexation Treaty** failed to win the necessary two-thirds vote for passage in the Senate.

Dec 4: James K. Polk was elected president of the United States by a popular vote of 1,337,243 against 1,299,068 for Henry Clay, the Whig candidate, and 62,300 for James B. Birney, the Liberty candidate. Birney's strong showing in New York cost Clay the state's electoral votes and the election. The electoral vote was Polk, 170; Clay, 105.

II. Architecture
Arts and Music
Popular Entertainment
Publishing
Theater

Fictional tales of the violence, real or imagined, of the western frontier were popular. One of the most successful authors of such works was Charles W. Webber, who served in the Texas Rangers, studied at Princeton Divinity School, and died on an expedition to Nicaragua. Among his novels were *Jack Long; or, The Shot in the Eye* (1844) and *Old Hicks* (1848). Emerson Bennett wrote 50 novels of adventure and intrigue, most of them with western settings. *Prairie Flower* and *Leni-Leoti*, both published in 1849, sold about 100,000 copies each.

The second series of *Essays* by Ralph Waldo Emerson was published. Among the essays included were "Experience," "Gifts," "New England Reformers," "The Poet," "Character," "Politics," "Nature," and "Manners." It proved more popular than Emerson's first series of *Essays* (1841), but it has not enjoyed equal literary reputation.

The Dial suspended publication. Founded in 1840, the publication was never popular and its 16 issues did not, from circulation reports, indicate that it ever would be. Yet it was of crucial importance in the history of New England transcendentalism and has had an influence on American life and letters that is belied by its short life. *The Dial* remains a primary source for an understanding of the views of the transcendentalists. As first editor, Margaret Fuller drew on an outstanding list of contributors, among them Ralph Waldo Emerson and Henry David Thoreau.

III. Business and Industry
Education
Philosophy and Religion
Science

American inventors tended to concentrate on the development of practical and marketable devices. Such a man was Charles Goodyear, who on June 15, 1844, received a patent for vulcanizing rubber. In 1839 Goodyear, while trying to find a way of making rubber useful at high temperatures, accidentally dropped some rubber that had been mixed with sulfur on a hot stove, and the vulcanization process was discovered. Poor and in debt, Goodyear sold his patent for far less than it was worth. He died in poverty.

May 24: The **first telegraph message,** "What hath God wrought," was sent from the U.S. Supreme Court room in Washington, D.C., to Alfred Vail in Baltimore, Md., by Samuel F. B. Morse, the inventor of the telegraph. The federal government appropriated the money for the line.

June 27: The founder of Mormonism, **Joseph Smith,** and his brother, Hiram Smith, were murdered by a mob in Carthage, Ill.

Sep 19: The **Marquette iron range** in the Upper Peninsula of Michigan near Lake Superior was discovered accidentally by a group of government surveyors headed by William A. Burt. Burt observed that his compass was deviating 87 degrees from normal. Upon investigating the soil, he found evidence of large deposits of iron ore.

IV. Fashion
Folkways
Holidays
Social Issues and Crime
Sports

Foot racing was a popular sport, largely because it offered a fine opportunity for betting. The runners of the time were professionals and were called pedestrians. In 1835 in New York City a $1000 purse was offered to anyone who could run a ten-mile course in less than an hour. An enormous and unruly crowd turned out to see one of the nine starters finish in just under an hour. In 1844 at Hoboken, N.J., a similar race was run in which John Gildersleeve of New York triumphed out over several British entrants. Gildersleeve finished in 57:01.5 and won $1000. A crowd estimated at 25,000 watched the race and was again unruly.

The catchy phrase *Fifty-four Forty or Fight* was adopted as a campaign slogan by forces supporting James K. Polk, the expansionist Democrat, for the presidency. It applied to the Oregon controversy between Great Britain and the U.S. Many Americans felt that the country should press U.S. claims to the 54°40'th parallel. Settlement was finally made on the 49th parallel, with everything north becoming part of Canada and everything south part of the U.S. Northwest.

The **first private bath** in an American hotel was introduced at the New York Hotel. The first bridal suite in an American hotel was introduced at the Irving House in New York City.

The **first female mannequin** ever exhibited in America was employed by Paulina Wright in her public lectures on the physiology of women before female audiences.

June 26: Pres. **John Tyler was married** to Miss Julia Gardiner at the Church of the Ascension in New York City. Tyler was the first president to marry during his term of office.

July 29: The **New York Yacht Club** was founded on board the schooner *Gimcrack* docked off the Battery. John C. Stevens was elected its commodore. It is the oldest surviving yacht club in the U.S.

1845

I. Civil Rights
Exploration and Settlement
Government
Statistics
Wars

The annexation of Texas finally became a reality after long political bickering. Antislavery forces were opposed to annexation because Texas was certain to become a slave state. Others wanted to act lest Great Britain or France develop a relationship with the Republic of Texas, whose independence Mexico refused to recognize. In Apr. 1844 Pres. John Tyler submitted to the Senate a treaty of annexation, but the Senate rejected it in June. In December Tyler offered a joint resolution to cover annexation. This required only a majority vote by both houses of Congress instead of the two-thirds vote needed to ratify a treaty. Action on the resolution was completed on Feb. 28, 1845, when the House accepted it in revised form. On June 23 the congress of Texas accepted annexation.

Jan 23: A uniform election day for presidential elections was established by an act of Congress. States had previously set their own election days. The act named the first Tuesday after the first Monday in November as Election Day. The first national election fell on Nov. 4.

Mar 3: Florida was admitted to the Union, becoming the 27th state.

Spring: John C. Frémont left on his third expedition, this time directly to California, with 60 armed men. Ostensibly their mission was to survey the central Rockies and the Great Salt Lake region. However, war with Mexico was in the air. In 1846 Frémont supported and may have instigated the Bear Flag Revolt, in which American settlers in the San Francisco Bay area seized the town of Sonoma. The settlers raised a flag with the figure of a bear on it and proclaimed the Republic of California.

June 15: U.S. protection of Texas was assured if it agreed to annexation. Tangible evidence was given to the Texans when Gen. Zachary Taylor was ordered to defend a line "on or near the Rio Grande."

Dec 29: Texas was admitted to the Union, the 28th state.

II. Architecture
Arts and Music
Popular Entertainment
Publishing
Theater

Writings about the western frontier now included works by authors who saw the process of pioneering in realistic terms. One such author was Caroline Kirkland, an early settler of Pinckney, Mich. Her first book was *A New Home—Who'll Follow?* (1839). In it she described many aspects of frontier life, from log houses to land booms, as well as social life, politics, and teaching methods, etc. Later Mrs. Kirkland wrote *Forest Life* (1842) and *Western Clearings* (1845), which were more sentimental and self-conscious than her first and more humorous book had been.

June: *Tales* by Edgar A. Poe was published in New York City by Wiley & Putnam, which also issued Poe's *The Raven and Other Poems* in October. The former contained 12 stories, including "The Gold-Bug," "The Fall of the House of Usher," "A Descent into the Maelstrom," and "The Murders in the Rue Morgue." The latter included all of Poe's best poems to date. Despite growing recognition and the publication of these volumes, his eighth and ninth books, Poe was in such dire need of money that his magazine, *Broadway Journal,* failed in December, ending a remarkably productive two years.

III. Business and Industry
Education
Philosophy and Religion
Science

There were as yet few leaders or writers who took up labor's cause, and those who did generally cloaked their efforts under the broad heading of social reform. There were also few attempts to form labor unions. Unusual for his time was George Henry Evans, who had retired in 1836. He emerged again in 1844, reestablishing his former paper, the *Workingman's Advocate*. In 1845 he formed the National Reform Association. At the heart of Evans's reform was his proposal to have the government give every workingman a free homestead of 160 acres. His strategy was to get candidates for public office to support this idea if they wanted the votes of labor.

Dr. **William Keil** founded the communal settlement of Bethel in Shelby County, Mo. He led 500 German immigrants with Anabaptist backgrounds and Utopian ideas into this haven. There he established his Church of the Living God, a successful enterprise. Keil held autocratic power. His subjects seldom received any money for their efforts, but all their needs were satisfied—food, clothing, shelter, education for their children, and other benefits.

Oct 10: The U.S. Naval Academy opened at Annapolis, Md. It combined at one site a group of schools previously located in the port cities of New York, Boston, Philadelphia, and Norfolk. Its first graduation exercises were held on June 10, 1854.

IV. Fashion
Folkways
Holidays
Social Issues and Crime
Sports

The exuberant, nationalistic, even jingoistic, spirit of the times was perfectly exemplified in the phrase *manifest destiny,* which first appeared this year in connection with the annexation of Texas. In the July issue of the *United States Magazine and Democratic Review,* John L. O'Sullivan, its editor, wrote of "our manifest destiny to overspread the continent allotted by Providence for the free development of our yearly multiplying millions." The phrase soon gained wide usage in connection with the dispute over the Oregon Territory, even by those who wanted to annex Cuba.

The popularity of **lectures** among American audiences was reflected in the career of John Bartholomew Gough, an English-born reformed alcoholic who made a handsome living giving lectures on his victory over drink. Every lecture ended with the taking of pledges of abstinence. At his peak Gough was paid $175 per lecture, many times the fee of the average temperance speaker. Before his death Gough estimated he had given 9600 temperance lectures to 9,000,000 people. In 1843 he traveled 6840 miles to make 383 addresses.

Baseball took a giant step toward the modern game when Alexander J. Cartwright, a New York City fireman, drew up a set of rules and organized the first baseball club, The Knickerbockers. Other clubs were formed and adopted Cartwright's rules. Cartwright fixed four as the number of bases, not two, three, or five; set them 90 feet apart; stood the batter in a box at home plate, not at some distance from it; made the bases flat; and ruled out "plugging" a baserunner with a thrown ball to put him out.

1846

I. **Civil Rights**
   Exploration and Settlement
   Government
   Statistics
   Wars

With the annexation of Texas in early 1845, war with Mexico became all but inevitable. Pres. James K. Polk hoped to settle matters peacefully but was determined to have his way by war if necessary. In Nov. 1845 he sent John Slidell to Mexico with an offer of $5,000,000 for the purchase of New Mexico and $25,000,000 for California. The offer was refused. On May 9, 1846, word reached Washington, D.C., that American troops had been attacked by Mexican forces on Apr. 24. Polk asked Congress for, and was granted, a declaration of war. Congress authorized the president to call for 50,000 volunteers and appropriated $10,000,000. Congress and the nation, however, were far from united on the idea of waging war. Southerners favored war as likely to extend slave territory, while northerners opposed the war for the same reason.

1846-1847: In **congressional elections** the Democrats increased their Senate majority to 36–21, with one seat going to a minor party. In the House the Whigs gained 38 seats to take a 115–108 majority, with four seats going to minor parties.

Jan: Pres. **James K. Polk** ordered U.S. troops into the region in southern Texas disputed with Mexico, between the roughly parallel Nueces and Rio Grande rivers. The commanding general was Zachary Taylor.

Feb 10: The **Mormon migration** westward from Nauvoo, Ill., began. It was organized and led by Brigham Young after the murder of Joseph Smith, founder of Mormonism.

Apr 30-May 1: The **Mexican army** crossed the Rio Grande and on May 3 placed Fort Texas under siege.

May 4: Capital punishment was abolished for the first time in the U.S. by the Michigan legislature, effective Jan. 1, 1847. Treason against the state remained a capital crime.

May 8: The **Battle of Palo Alto,** the first important engagement of the Mexican War, was fought, with the Mexicans on the losing side.

May 9: In the **Battle of Resaca de la Palma,** U.S. forces under Gen. Taylor forced the Mexican army back across the Rio Grande.

May 13: A **declaration of war** against Mexico was passed several days after hostilities commenced. War measures were passed over Whig opposition, which increased as the war progressed.

May 18: U.S. forces crossed the Rio Grande, led by Gen. Zachary Taylor. The Americans occupied Matamoros.

June 14: The **Bear Flag Revolt** began with the proclamation by a group of California settlers of the Republic of California. The name came from their standard, which included the name of the republic, a grizzly bear, and a star on a field of white. On Aug. 17 Robert F. Stockton, a naval officer commanding U.S. forces on the Pacific coast, issued a proclamation declaring the annexation of California by the U.S., and establishing himself as governor.

June 15: The **Oregon Treaty** with Great Britain was signed. It established the 49th parallel as the boundary between the U.S. and the British Northwest territory. Idaho, Oregon, Washington, and part of Montana became undisputed U.S. territory. This was a compromise from the campaign slogan of Polk in 1844: "Fifty-four Forty or Fight." Canada was granted navigation rights to part of the Columbia R. south of the 49th parallel.

Sep 25: Monterrey, Mexico, was captured by U.S. forces under Gen. Zachary Taylor after a four-day engagement that made "Old Rough and Ready" Taylor, a Whig, into a national hero. His relations with Pres. Polk, a Democrat, cooled subsequently.

Dec 28: Iowa was admitted into the Union, becoming the 29th state.

II. Architecture
Arts and Music
Popular Entertainment
Publishing
Theater

The talented author whose career becomes disjointed and whose works lapse into obscurity, only to be revived and hailed by a later generation, is not unique in literary history. No one fitted this situation better than Herman Melville, in 1846 deemed one of America's most promising new writers. In his lifetime Melville worked as a bank clerk, farmer, teacher, and sailor; he spent 19 of his later years working as customs inspector in New York City. His career seemed more than ensured when his first novel, *Typee,* was published in 1846. This romance of the South Seas, based on his own experiences, was followed by several more well received novels. His greatest work, *Moby-Dick* (1851), was misunderstood by readers and critics alike, and Melville began a long, heartbreaking slide into literary oblivion. His greatness was not fully appreciated until well into the twentieth century.

Margaret Fuller published her critical essays as *Papers on Literature and Art.* Up to and even past her time, Fuller was the most formidable American female intellectual. She was known in her own time for her support of the rights of women, her intellect, her knowledge of German, and her understanding of philosophy. From 1840–1842 she edited *The Dial,* and she was considered the best American critic up to 1850, but her writings had a limited and select audience. Hawthorne used her in conceiving his character Zenobia in *The Blithedale Romance.*

III. Business and Industry
Education
Philosophy and Religion
Science

One of the most important events in the scientific world at this time was the establishment by Congress this year of the Smithsonian Institution in Washington, D.C. In 1829 James Smithson, an illegitimate son of the Duke of Northumberland, left about $550,000 in his will to establish such an institution. Congress, however, did not resolve exactly how to use the money for 17 years, finally determining that it should be "for the increase and diffusion of knowledge among men." The Smithsonian over the years has grown into a complex of museums and other facilities serving professionals and nonprofessionals alike. It supports many scientific endeavors.

The **Eastern Exchange Hotel,** the first public building heated by steam, opened in Boston.

The **first rotary printing press** was devised and produced by Richard M. Hoe. It was capable of turning out 8000 newspapers an hour. The press was first installed in 1847 by Philadelphia's *Public Ledger.*

Sep 10: The **first sewing machine** in the U.S. with an eye-pointed needle was patented by Elias Howe, called the father of the modern sewing machine.

Oct 16: Anesthesia was given its first public demonstration before doctors by William T. G. Morton, a Boston dentist. Morton administered sulfuric ether during an operation performed by John Collins Warren at the Massachusetts General Hospital. A neck tumor was removed. Earlier, on Sept. 30, Morton had painlessly removed an ulcerated tooth from a patient anesthetized by ether.

IV. Fashion
Folkways
Holidays
Social Issues and Crime
Sports

The lecture circuit was popular with Americans, who found lyceum speakers entertaining and sometimes inspiring. The lecture hall became a center for promotion of social movements, including the rising agitation for prohibition laws. At this time there emerged a new voice for temperance, John Bartholomew Gough, an Englishman and reformed alcoholic. He lectured for 40 years, and thousands of people signed the teetotaler's pledge after hearing his story of the evils of drink. Gough advocated that a prohibition amendment be added to the Constitution.

The **exodus of the Mormons** from Nauvoo, Ill., after open hostilities with their Illinois neighbors came on the heels of a hard winter of preparation. The Mormons had turned their homes into workshops and equipped 12,000 wagons to carry their families and belongings. Beginning in February, small groups began to leave Nauvoo. They crossed the Mississippi R. by flatboat. Later in the month the river froze and some groups were able to cross on the ice. By the end of the month, 2000 men, women, and children were in Iowa and ready to move on. The sprawling caravan was broken into companies of 50 wagons. The leading parties advanced slowly, setting up resting spots along the route where tired people and cattle could recover from the ravages of ice, snow, and rain. By the middle of May 16,000 Mormons had crossed the Mississippi. The stragglers left Nauvoo by September. Through the fall and following winter, from fear of winter and Indians on the plain ahead, the main body of the wagon train was bogged down in the bottomlands of the Missouri R., near Council Bluffs, Iowa.

June 19: The **first recorded baseball game** in history resembling the modern sport was played at Elysian Field, Hoboken, N.J., between the New York Club and the Knickerbockers. The New York Club won 23–1. Davis, their pitcher, was fined six cents for swearing at the umpire. Alexander J. Cartwright, founder of the Knickerbockers, had written the rules under which the game was played.

1847

I. Civil Rights
Exploration and Settlement
Government
Statistics
Wars

One of the most horrifying incidents in the history of the westward movement occurred in early 1847 in the Sierra Nevada range of California. The previous December a pioneer group of 87 persons, headed by two brothers, Jacob and George Donner, had attempted to take a shortcut through the Wasatch Mountains, only to find themselves trapped by snow when they reached the Sierra Nevada. A party of eight men, five women, and two Indian guides set out for help. While they were gone, the rest of the party realized that no one would survive unless they practiced cannibalism on those who died. When relief reached the stranded party on Feb. 19, there were only 45 survivors.

Jan 16: The **Oregon Bill,** providing for territorial government of that area, passed the House. It excluded slavery under the restrictions of the Northwest Ordinance. The bill was tabled in the Senate.

Feb 22-23: At the **Battle of Buena Vista,** U.S. forces under Gen. Zachary Taylor defeated the Mexicans under Gen. Antonio López de Santa Anna.

Mar 9: U.S. forces under Gen. Winfield Scott landed near **Vera Cruz,** Mexico. Some 10,000 troops landed just south of the city, site of the most powerful fortress in the Western Hemisphere, in what was the first large-scale amphibious operation in U.S. history. Scott began a siege of Vera Cruz on Mar. 22. The fortress fell on Mar. 27 and was occupied two days later. On Apr. 8 Scott moved toward Mexico City.

Sep 14: Gen. **Winfield Scott entered Mexico City.** A battalion of U.S. Marines made its presence felt at the "halls of Montezuma."

II. Architecture
Arts and Music
Popular Entertainment
Publishing
Theater

The death in New York City on Nov. 2 of Nathaniel Bannister, a prolific southern playwright who ended his days in poverty, was a reminder of the period's love of historical and melodramatic plays. Bannister's work also reflected the vogue for foreign settings, as in *Gaulantus* (1837), *England's Iron Days* (1837), and *Gentleman of Lyons* (1838). His most popular play, *Putnam,* however, which had been produced at the Bowery Theater in New York City in 1844, had a Revolutionary War setting.

An idyllic tale in verse, ***Evangeline*** by Henry Wadsworth Longfellow, was published. Based on an account told to the poet by Nathaniel Hawthorne, the narrative concerns the fate of two lovers in French Acadie (Nova Scotia) who are separated when the French are expelled from Nova Scotia. It is a tale of virginal love that maintains itself through disappointments and frustrations.

Sep 11: "**Susanna,**" by Stephen Foster, was performed for the first time at a concert in the Eagle Saloon, Pittsburgh, Pa. It became Foster's first widespread success, being taken up by minstrel troupes and carried to the West Coast by the forty-niners.

III. Business and Industry
Education
Philosophy and Religion
Science

Liberal Protestant clergymen were stirring controversy by their espousal of a less harsh view of humanity than that offered by Calvinism. The early intellectual leader of this group was Horace Bushnell, a Congregational clergyman who emphasized the divine in humanity and in nature. His views were expressed in *Christian Nurture* (1847) and *God in Christ* (1849). *Nature and the Supernatural* (1858) attacked transcendentalism. Bushnell was accused of heresy for his views on the Trinity but was never brought to trial.

May 1: The **Smithsonian Institution** was formally dedicated in Washington, D.C. Joseph Henry, a Princeton physicist, was named its first secretary.

July 1: The **first official U.S. postage stamps** were issued by the Post Office Department in five-cent and ten-cent denominations. This action had been authorized by Congress on Mar. 3. The new stamps were also the first adhesive postage stamps in the U.S.

July 24: Brigham Young, with a party of 143, reached the valley of Great Salt Lake. The flight of Joseph Smith from Missouri to Illinois had ended with a quarrel among the factions of the Mormon Church, the imprisonment of Smith by order of the Illinois governor, and his assassination by a mob that stormed the jail at Carthage and shot him and his brother to death. Brigham Young had been chosen to succeed Smith as leader of the Mormons. Hostility toward the Mormons continued and violence increased. Young was compelled to lead the Mormons' western trek, which was one of the great migrations of the American West. When Salt Lake City was established, Young returned to lead the rest of the eastern Mormons from Council Bluffs, Iowa, to their permanent home in Utah.

IV. Fashion
Folkways
Holidays
Social Issues and Crime
Sports

Light entertainment in the 1840s consisted of burlesque and *tableaux vivants*. Burlesque usually took the form of musical satire. Even William Shakespeare was burlesqued, as in *Much Ado about the Merchant of Venice*. Most daring were *tableaux vivants* in which scantily clad men and women posed in such classical scenes as "Venus Rising from the Sea" and "Psyche Going to the Bath."

The **legal status of women** was slightly improved in Vermont by passage of a state law that guaranteed to the wife full ownership of real estate held by her at the time of her marriage or gained by gift or bequest afterward. The husband's consent was still necessary, however, if the wife wished to transfer ownership of the property.

Flogging boys and girls as an educational practice was attacked by Lyman Cobb in *The Evil Tendencies of Corporal Punishment as a Means of Moral Discipline in Families and Schools*. Cobb listed some 60 arguments against the practice. An advanced educator, Cobb even announced that he did not want his pupils to suffer over tedious reading. His views were widely held by those opposing the old-fashioned "school of the rod."

Oct: Maria Mitchell, a Nantucket, Mass., librarian and astronomical observer, discovered a new comet. For this she received a gold medal from the astronomy-minded King of Denmark and election into the American Academy of Arts and Sciences, the first woman so honored. When Vassar College opened in 1865 she was named to the staff as the first woman professor of astronomy in the U.S.

1848

I. Civil Rights
Exploration and Settlement
Government
Statistics
Wars

The Treaty of Guadalupe Hidalgo, signed by the U.S. and Mexico on Feb. 2, 1848, formally ended the Mexican War (1846–1848). By its terms Mexico recognized Texas as part of the U.S. and ceded to the U.S. over 500,000 square miles of territory, including all of the future states of California, Nevada, and Utah, almost all of New Mexico and Arizona, and parts of Colorado and Wyoming. In return the U.S. agreed to pay Mexico $15,000,000 and to assume the claims of U.S. citizens against Mexico, amounting to $3,250,000. The U.S. became an enormous continental republic, but the acquisition of the new territory aggravated the dispute between slavery and antislavery forces. The war resulted in 1721 dead and 4102 wounded. In addition, some 11,155 Americans died of disease as a result of the war. The total cost of the war was estimated at $97,500,000.

1848-1849: In **congressional elections** the Democrats lost one Senate seat for a 35–25 majority over the Whigs, with one seat held by a minor party. In the House they gained four seats for a 112–109 majority, with nine seats held by minor parties.

May 22-26: The **Democratic National Convention nominated Lewis Cass** of Michigan for the presidency and William O. Butler of Kentucky for the vice presidency.

May 29: Wisconsin was admitted to the Union, becoming the 30th state.

June 7-9: The **Whig National Convention nominated Gen. Zachary Taylor** of Louisiana for the presidency and Millard Fillmore of New York for the vice presidency.

July 19-20: A women's convention at Seneca Falls, N.Y., called by Lucretia Mott and Elizabeth Cady Stanton, discussed women's rights. Susan B. Anthony joined the convention, where such subjects as voting, property rights, and divorce were debated. Similar conventions were held annually until the Civil War.

July 27: The **Clayton Compromise,** named for Sen. John M. Clayton, National Republican of Delaware, was passed by the Senate. It excluded slavery from Oregon, prohibited legislation regarding slavery by the new territories of California and New Mexico, and authorized the appeal of territorial slave cases to the Supreme Court. The House tabled the bill the next day.

Nov 7: **Zachary Taylor was elected president** of the United States. Millard Fillmore was elected vice president. The electoral vote was Taylor, 163, Lewis Cass, Democratic candidate, 127. The popular vote was Taylor, 1,360,101; Cass, 1,220,544; Martin Van Buren, Free-Soil and Barnburners candidate, 291,263.

II. Architecture
Arts and Music
Popular Entertainment
Publishing
Theater

New developments in cast-iron production combined during this period with innovative architectural concepts to produce a new kind of structure, both as to materials and design. Pioneer architect James Bogardus built in 1848 and 1849 the first cast-iron building, a five-story structure located in New York City at Centre and Duane streets. It consisted of cast iron instead of masonry, except that the floor beams may have been timber. The facade consisted of cast-iron columns similar to the stone columns of the Classical style, interspersed with windows. The style remained popular for the rest of the century. Foundries such as Badger's Iron Works in New York City began to turn out prefabricated parts for columns and capitals.

James Russell Lowell had a banner year with the publication of three major poetic works. *The Biglow Papers* (first series) consisted of nine poems that humorously voiced opposition to the war with Mexico and the annexation of Texas. The Yankee dialect of Ezekiel and Hosea Biglow immediately caught popular fancy. *A Fable for Critics*, in the tradition of Pope's *Dunciad* and Byron's *Vision of Judgment*, dealt with contemporary writers and critics. Lowell also published *Poems: Second Series* and *The Vision of Sir Launfal.*

III. Business and Industry
Education
Philosophy and Religion
Science

The only successful industrial Utopian community was established in 1848 in Oneida, N.Y. It was founded by John Humphrey Noyes and his followers. In 1839 Noyes had established a so-called Perfectionist community at Putney, Vt. His system of polygamous marriage so outraged his neighbors that the group was forced to flee. They moved to Oneida where they established the Oneida Community. There the group held all property in common and children were raised in a communal nursery. The community prospered, at first by manufacturing a trap for small animals and later by producing silverware. In 1879, however, opposition again arose to the community's style of living and Noyes went to Canada, where he remained for the rest of his life. In 1881 the group, having abandoned Noyes's theories, was reorganized as a business corporation.

The **Associated Press** (AP) was organized by a group of New York City journalists. The AP was a result of the impatience of Moses Beach, publisher of the New York *Sun,* with established news lines. He experimented with ways of getting the news faster, including use of carrier pigeons. Reports from the Mexican War came in so slowly that Beach finally set up his own express service. The arrangement was successful enough to convince other New York publishers to carry the expense of a private news-gathering service, which became the Associated Press.

June 27: **Air conditioning** for a theater was offered by the Broadway Theater in New York City, perhaps for the first time. The theater issued this notice in its bill: "The public is respectfully informed that an Extensive Apparatus for the Perfect Ventilation of the Entire Building is now in operation. The Steam Power by which it is impelled, being capable of conveying to the Audience part alone, 3000 Feet of Cool Air per minute, thus rendering the Establishment during the hottest and most crowded nights in all respects comfortable. The machinery patented by Mr. J. E. Coffee."

Sep: The **American Association for the Advancement of Science** was founded. The charter of the association expressed a determination to "advance science in the New World" in every possible way. The association developed as a joint endeavor of American and Canadian scientists.

Nov 1: The **first medical school for women** opened with an enrollment of twelve. It was founded and further developed by Samuel Gregory, a pioneer in medical education for women. Known as the Boston Female Medical School, it was merged in 1874 with the Boston University School of Medicine to form one of the first coed medical schools in the world.

IV. Fashion
Folkways
Holidays
Social Issues and Crime
Sports

The first significant sign that women were becoming an organized force in American society was seen in 1848. A group of women called a convention to be held in Seneca Falls, N.Y., on July 19. There they formulated a "Declaration of Sentiments," which cleverly paraphrased the Declaration of Independence, addressing "man" rather than King George III of England. The document called for women's "immediate admission to all the rights and privileges which belong to them as citizens of the United States." The organizers of the convention were Lucretia Mott and Elizabeth Cady Stanton; they led the movement for many years. Mrs. Mott was one of the earliest women lecturers for temperance, the rights of labor, and abolition. Mrs. Stanton was particularly interested in securing the right to vote. When she married Henry B. Stanton in 1840, she refused to have the word "obey" used in the ceremony.

New York State granted **property rights for women** equal to those of men. This was a significant improvement in women's legal status, but New York's example was not copied elsewhere. Similar women's property rights laws had been passed in Mississippi (1839) and Maine (1844).

John B. Curtis of Bangor, Maine, manufactured the first chewing gum commercially sold in the U.S. Curtis later traveled as a drummer throughout western territories and is reputed to be the first commercial traveler for an eastern firm in the West.

Jan 24: Discovery of gold on the estate of John Sutter made California and broke Sutter. From the day he settled in Nueva Helvetia, at the junction of the American and Sacramento rivers, Sutter prospered. Then gold was found by James W. Marshall, who was building a sawmill for Sutter. The workers on the estate left to look for gold. Every kind of adventurer squatted on Sutter's land. In four years he was ruined. For the rest of his life, Sutter petitioned the state and the federal government for aid. He died on June 18, 1880, at age 77, while the bill he sought was being argued in the House of Representatives. The boom provided a wealth of material for writers. Mark Twain, Joaquin Miller, Bret Harte, Ambrose Bierce, George Horatio Derby, Charles Warren Stoddard, and Edward Rowland Sill were all in the ranks of those who found inspiration in the volatile new atmosphere. There were few voices in the whole country to caution against the excesses of the gold rush. However, the Mormon Church in Salt Lake City, having heard reports of gold in California, cautioned its children to hoard up other riches: "The true use of gold is for paving streets. . . . When the Saints shall have preached the gospel . . . and built up cities enough, the Lord will open up the way for a supply of gold to the perfect satisfaction of his children. . . . Let them not be over-anxious, for the treasures of the earth are in the Lord's storehouses."

1849

I. Civil Rights
Exploration and Settlement
Government
Statistics
Wars

News of the discovery of gold in California in Jan. 1848 was slow in reaching the East. Word of it first appeared in the New York *Herald* on Aug. 19, but no great excitement was created until Pres. James K. Polk expressed enthusiasm about it in his message to Congress on Dec. 5. The rush began by land across the continent and by sea and land via the Isthmus of Panama. The first shipload of prospectors arrived in San Francisco via Cape Horn on Feb. 28. About 80,000 people made their way to California in 1849—55,000 overland and 25,000 by sea. About 5000 who started out overland never made it because Asiatic cholera swept their ranks. By the end of 1849, gold worth $10,000,000 had been mined.

Mar 3: The **U.S. Department of the Interior** was created by Congress as an administrative catchall for the General Land Office, the Bureau of Indian Affairs, the Pension Office, the Patent Office, and the Bureau of the Census. Its prime purpose for many decades seemed to be to locate resources in the West for exploitation by white settlers. Not until the end of the century would the department regard the protection of natural resources as a part of its responsibility.

Mar 3: Minnesota Territory was established by Congress. Slavery within the territory was prohibited.

Sep 1: A **California convention** called by the territorial governor, Gen. Bennett Riley, met in Monterey. The convention created a state government without waiting for congressional action. On Oct. 20 the delegates adopted a constitution. On Nov. 13 the constitution was ratified by California voters, and a governor and legislative representatives were chosen. Slavery was prohibited.

II. Architecture
Arts and Music
Popular Entertainment
Publishing
Theater

Civil disobedience, which had been practiced by many patriots before the Revolution and was to be used as a means of protest again late in the twentieth century, in 1849 found its most eloquent spokesman in Henry David Thoreau. A transcendentalist and observer of nature and of man, he opposed the Mexican War. In protest, Thoreau refused to pay his poll tax. He was jailed just overnight because, to his distress, a friend paid the tax for him. As a result of the experience, Thoreau wrote the essay "Civil Disobedience," in which he stated: "There will never be a really free and enlightened State until the State comes to recognize the individual as a higher and independent power, from which all its own power and authority are derived. . . ."

May 10: The **Astor Place riot,** a notorious theater riot, erupted outside the Astor Place Opera House in New York City, where the celebrated British actor William Charles Macready was performing. Angry crowds reacted against dress requirements for admission to the theater and against Macready's scornful public utterances on the vulgarity of American life. Macready's rival, the American actor Edwin Forrest, who had asserted the cause of the masses both in his stage roles and in his public statements, fueled the indignation of common citizens. On May 8 Macready's performance of *Macbeth* was stopped by Forrest's followers. Two days later, a mob led by E. Z. C. Judson, later to gain fame as Ned Buntline, used clubs, paving stones, and brickbats to shatter the windows of the theater during Macready's performance. Troops were summoned and when order could not be restored by their presence, they were ordered to fire, killing 22 and wounding 56.

III. Business and Industry
Education
Philosophy and Religion
Science

Spiritualism began to attract believers, who held that the human personality continues to exist after death and can communicate through a medium with the living. In 1848 two adolescent sisters of Wayne County, N.Y., claimed they heard rappings on floors and walls and that these spelled out messages from the spirit world. Margaret Fox was the central figure in this new cult, along with her sister Katherine. Margaret later admitted it was all a fraud and that the sounds were made by cracking toe knuckles. Nevertheless, there were many believers. In the next decade séances became common and there were at least six spiritualist publications.

Elizabeth Blackwell became the first woman in the U.S. to receive a medical degree and the first female doctor of medicine of modern times. After some hospital experience in Paris and London, she and her sister in 1853 founded the New York Infirmary and College for Women, the first hospital run entirely by women.

IV. Fashion
Folkways
Holidays
Social Issues and Crime
Sports

Prize fighting was illegal but popular. Condemned for its brutality by many, the sport had many ardent followers. When Tom Hyer, the unofficial American champion, fought Yankee Sullivan this year, the participants and spectators were chased by militia and had to flee Peel Island, Md., the site of the match, to woods on the Western Shore. A few years later, when John C. Morrissey claimed the title vacated by Hyer, the site again had to be changed at the last minute. Bare fist boxing was brutal and there were few rules. In one bout that lasted three hours, one fighter, after being knocked down 81 times, dropped dead. A history of boxing in America was published this year. It was *The American Fistiana;* the book recorded the most important bouts of the previous four decades.

Jan: Amelia Bloomer, the temperance and woman's suffrage advocate, began publication of *Lily.* The first issue printed 200 copies, but by 1853 Bloomer was issuing 4000 copies twice monthly. The articles dealt with contemporary education, marriage laws, woman's suffrage, etc. Bloomer began to have a major influence on American society.

1850

I. **Civil Rights**
   Exploration and Settlement
   Government
   Statistics
   Wars

The territory acquired from Mexico in the Mexican War, particularly California, caused the reopening of the question of free or slave status for new states. After acrimonious debate, Congress passed five bills on the subject between Sept. 9 and Sept. 20. As signed by Pres. Millard Fillmore, they constituted what became known as the Compromise of 1850 and once more postponed a showdown on slavery. The compromise was the result of eight resolutions that had been introduced in the Senate on Jan. 29 by Henry Clay of Kentucky. The five final bills dealt with all the pressing questions, and for the most part reaction was favorable, but extremists in the North and South were displeased.

The seventh U.S. **Census** fixed the population of the 31 states of the Union at 23,191,876. The center of population was located 23 miles southeast of Parkersburg, W. Va.

The **number of immigrants** entering America in 1850 totaled 369,980. The figures reflected the Irish famine of the late 1840s, and social and political unrest in northwest Europe.

1850-1851: In **congressional elections** the Whigs lost one Senate seat, resulting in a Democratic majority of 35–24 with three seats going to minor parties. In the House the Democrats gained 28 seats for a 140–88 majority with five seats going to minor parties.

Mar 7: Daniel Webster supported Sen. Henry Clay's compromise in a famous speech to the Senate in which he espoused the provisions of the Fugitive Slave Bill. John Greenleaf Whittier had Webster in mind when he wrote in his poem "Ichabod":

> All else is gone; from those great eyes
> The soul has fled;
> When faith is lost, when honor dies
> The man is dead.

Apr 19: The **Clayton-Bulwer Treaty** was signed. The U.S. and Great Britain agreed to the neutrality of a canal to be built across Central America. Both governments were to act as joint protectors of the terri-tory, and neither was to establish any military post on, or assume control over, any part of Central America.

May 25: New Mexico, impatient for statehood, formed its own state government. A convention set the boundaries of the state, banned slavery, and applied for statehood.

July 8: The **overland gold rush** to California through Fort Laramie, Wyo., involved 42,300 emigrants and 9720 wagons between Jan. 1 and July 8. Over 90% of the population of California was male. Nine years later men still outnumbered women six to one.

July 9: Pres. **Zachary Taylor died** of cholera at the age of 55. Vice Pres. Millard Fillmore was sworn in as the 13th president of the United States on July 10.

Sep 9: California was admitted to the Union as a free state, giving free states a majority in the Senate. This was one of the bargains of the Compromise of 1850 and a concession to the North. California was the 31st state admitted to the Union.

Sep 9: The **Texas and New Mexico Act** was passed by Congress. The act established the Texas boundaries, authorized payment to Texas of $10,000,000 for relinquishing its claims to territories beyond the new state lines, and established the boundaries of New Mexico Territory. As a concession to the South, New Mexico would be a free or a slave state according to its constitution upon admission to the Union. This option was part of the Compromise of 1850.

Sep 9: The **Utah Act** established the territorial boundaries of Utah. It was to be a free or slave state according to the constitution it adopted on admission to the Union. Part of the Compromise of 1850, this option was a concession to the South.

Sep 18: The **Fugitive Slave Bill** was passed by Congress. Known as the second Fugitive Slave Law (a first, enacted on Feb. 1, 1793, was largely circumvented in the North), this legislation required return of escaped slaves to their owners. Fugitives were not permitted a jury trial and could not testify in their own behalf. The commissioners earned $10 if their decision favored the claimant but only $5 if it favored the fugitive. This law was part of the Compromise of 1850 and a concession to the South.

Sep 20: Slave trade was abolished in the District of Columbia. This was a concession to the North in the Compromise of 1850.

Oct 23-24: The **first national women's rights convention,** held in Worcester, Mass., was attended by delegates from nine states. The first women's convention in history had been held in Seneca Falls, N.Y., in 1848.

II. Architecture
Arts and Music
Popular Entertainment
Publishing
Theater

The extremes to which the public would go in its adulation of popular entertainers, especially when urged on by clever promotion, was nowhere better shown than in connection with the American tour of Jenny Lind, called the "Swedish Nightingale." Miss Lind was brought to the U.S. in 1850 by master showman and promoter Phineas T. Barnum. On her arrival 30,000 people surrounded her New York City hotel, hoping to see the coloratura soprano. Tickets for her Sept. 11 debut at Castle Garden Theater were auctioned at $225. Boston topped that with a $625 bid when she sang there. Miss Lind gave 95 concerts around the country from 1850 to 1852, for which she received $17,675. Barnum made a fortune.

The Scarlet Letter, a classic American novel by Nathaniel Hawthorne, was a best seller from the beginning. Four thousand copies were sold in the first ten days; the second printing immediately sold out. Its daring subject matter accounted in part for its immediate success.

Representative Men by Ralph Waldo Emerson was published. It was a collection of lectures he had given on Plato, Swedenborg, Montaigne, Shakespeare, Napoleon, Goethe and others. Emerson set forth his view of the roles played by great men. He believed that man was not the victim of his environment but had creative powers within him to change things and live his own life.

Washington Crossing the Delaware was painted in Düsseldorf, Germany, by Emanuel Leutze, an American historical and portrait painter residing abroad. Gen. Washington stands in a theatrical, unseamanlike pose in the boat; the Delaware R. is really the Rhine R. as seen from the artist's window. But in this and other U.S. historical subjects, such as *Westward the Course of Empire,* the gigantic mural on the wall of the west staircase of the House of Representatives, Leutze communicated the fortitude and courage of American national heroes and contributed significantly, if not realistically, to people's conceptions of American history.

Sep 27: The great American actor **Edwin Booth** made his New York City debut at age 16 as Wilford in the play *The Iron Chest* at the National Theater. His acting debut had been at the Boston Museum on Sept. 10, 1849, when he played the role of Tressel in Colley Cibber's version of *Richard III.* His first major role also came at the National Theater, when he took over the role of Richard III in 1851 after his father, Junius Brutus Booth, became ill.

III. Business and Industry
Education
Philosophy and Religion
Science

The textile industry was the first U.S. manufacturing group to develop on a sizable scale. More than two-thirds of all cotton manufacturing was carried out in New England, where by 1850 there were 564 plants, capitalized at more than $58,000,000 and employing 61,893 operators. The South, by contrast, had only 166 plants, capitalized at $7,250,000 and employing 10,043 workers. The New England textile industry employed many female workers, most of them young girls.

A **cholera epidemic** swept through the Middle West after passing through the South the previous year. From New Orleans it fanned through the U.S. and was checked in successive advances only by cold weather.

The **house sparrow,** also known as the English sparrow, was imported from England by Nicholas Pike. The first flock of eight pairs died. In 1851 a new flock of sparrows was imported and released at Brooklyn, N.Y. They flourished and soon spread across the country.

A new **speed record for sailing ships,** 13 days from Boston Light to the Equator, was set by the *Stag Hound,* a clipper designed by Donald McKay, premier U.S. shipbuilder.

July 8: The **Mormon colony** on Beaver Island in Lake Michigan near the Straits of Mackinac crowned as its king James Jesse Strang, who founded the colony in 1847. In 1856 Strang was assassinated by disaffected followers. An expedition of mainlanders then broke up the colony, and some 2500 Mormons left Michigan.

IV. Fashion
Folkways
Holidays
Social Issues and Crime
Sports

Some advocates of women's rights attracted attention by means of odd dress. Amelia Bloomer, who edited *Lily,* a women's rights and temperance magazine, began wearing in public a skirt over full trousers, much like Turkish trousers. As a result, the fashion became known as the *bloomer costume*, although it had been designed in the mid-1840s by Elizabeth Smith Miller. With the pantaloon, called *bloomers*, Mrs. Bloomer wore an ordinary vest over her blouse. Because the outfit evoked derision, she abandoned it, but not before bloomers gathered higher on the leg were found suitable for women's gymnastics.

The memorable quote "**I would rather be right than be president**" was uttered by Henry Clay in the Senate during his impassioned plea for the compromises proposed by him to settle the dispute between slave and free factions. Bitter because of his failure to achieve the presidency, he threw off his famous remark when taunted by his colleagues.

A reflection of the rise of a new class, **the homeless,** was seen in the 18,456 persons sheltered in 8141 cellars in New York City. By 1856 tenements had been built to house some of these unfortunates.

The **federal policy toward Indians** at this time was summed up in the dictum that it was "cheaper to feed the Indians for a year than fight them for a day."

July 25: Gold in Oregon was discovered on the Rogue R., providing new prospecting territory for the forty-niners of California's gold rush.

1851

I. Civil Rights
Exploration and Settlement
Government
Statistics
Wars

The new, harsher Fugitive Slave Law of 1850 aroused immediate anger in the North. In turn, landowners and legislators in the South became upset because northern states refused to help enforce the act. The law provided for federal commissioners who could order warrants for arrest of fugitive slaves; it also provided heavy penalties for interfering with enforcement. Anyone aiding a fugitive slave could be fined and jailed. In reaction, a number of free states enacted "personal liberty laws," intended to make it difficult for a slave owner to repossess his property. The actual number of runaway slaves was small, estimated in 1850 at about 1000 out of 3,000,000 slaves. Most of the runaways were ultimately captured.

Feb 15: Shadrach, a **fugitive slave,** was rescued from forcible return to his master by a mob in Boston. Attempts to put the Fugitive Slave Act of 1850 into effect caused much bitterness in the North and increased abolitionist sentiment. Many states (Vermont, 1850; Connecticut, 1854; Rhode Island, 1854; Massachusetts, 1855; Michigan, 1855; Maine, 1855 and 1857; Kansas, 1858; and Wisconsin, 1858) passed personal liberty laws, in large part designed to circumvent the federal fugitive slave law. These state laws aroused much controversy and contributed greatly to the split between North and South that led to the Civil War. South Carolina later cited these laws as one of the grievances justifying its secession from the Union. Other outstanding rescues or attempted rescues included that of James Hamlet in New York City (1850), Thomas Simms in Boston (1851), "Jerry" M'Henry in Syracuse, N.Y. (1851), and Anthony Burns in Boston (1854).

Dec 24: A fire at the Library of Congress in Washington, D.C., destroyed two-thirds of its collection.

II. Architecture
Arts and Music
Popular Entertainment
Publishing
Theater

Americans in several fields were beginning to acquire reputations in Europe. In sculpture, the first was Hiram Powers, who had gone to Italy to study classical art in 1837. There in 1843 he produced his marble *Greek Slave* which, when exhibited in London in 1851 at the Crystal Palace, became the most celebrated statue of its time. The nude, a Greek maiden in chains, symbolized Greece's subjection to Turkey. The statue's nudity shocked many, but critics, including many clergymen, ultimately recognized the sculptor's moral purpose and the symbolism of the stark nudity. Several copies of the statue were made. Powers became wealthy and famous as a result of the busts he sculpted, but his fame did not last. Marble busts went out of fashion after his death.

The New York Daily Times was begun as a Whig paper under the editorship of Henry Jarvis Raymond. Its name was changed to *The New York Times* in 1857. During the Civil War it strongly supported Lincoln and his policies, while after the war it fought the Tweed Ring and Tammany in New York City. In 1896 it was purchased by Adolph S. Ochs. In 1935 control passed to Ochs's son-in-law, Arthur Hays Sulzberger.

The House of the Seven Gables by Nathaniel Hawthorne was published. The story centered on a curse laid on a house in Salem at the time of the witch trials (1692).

Moby-Dick, Herman Melville's powerful novel of the sea, was published and little understood. Ostensibly the story of a whaling captain's obsessive search for a white whale, it deals with man's conflict with evil in the universe. Not until 70 years later was the novel widely accepted as a masterpiece.

Francis Parkman began his multivolume account of the colonial French in America and their struggles with the British. The first volume was *The Conspiracy of Pontiac,* which ultimately proved to be the last of the series chronologically. Parkman combined a historian's temperament for painstaking scholarship with a love for the wilderness and respect for the Indians.

Stephen Foster composed "Old Folks at Home." Noting the prejudice against "Ethiopian songs" and wanting to preserve his name for more genteel compositions, Foster sold the first performance rights to Edwin P. Christy, the famous minstrel, and allowed Christy's name to appear on the published music as composer.

III. Business and Industry
Education
Philosophy and Religion
Science

The Young Men's Christian Association, founded in England in 1844, came to North America in 1851 with the organization of chapters in Boston, Mass., and Montreal, Canada. Other U.S. cities soon formed similar groups. The first convention of the North American association was held in Buffalo, N.Y., in 1854. In 1858 chapters for students were formed at the universities of Michigan and Virginia. The organization emphasized the improvement of the spiritual and moral well-being of young men. It also sponsored social and athletic activities.

Aug 12: A patent for a **practical sewing machine** was granted to Isaac Merrit Singer, who quickly organized I. M. Singer & Company. The unique feature of Singer's machine was its continuous stitching action. Elias Howe, whose machine was then the most popular, initiated a royalty suit against Singer for producing a machine similar to Howe's. Singer lost and was forced to make a settlement of $15,000; his machine in the meantime had achieved a leading position. It was improved in the next decade by additional patented devices.

IV. Fashion
Folkways
Holidays
Social Issues and Crime
Sports

The first important U.S. victory in international sports came on Aug. 22, 1851, when the 170-ton schooner-rigged yacht *America* defeated 14 British vessels in a race around the Isle of Wight for the Hundred Guinea Cup. *America* was built for $30,000 by a syndicate headed by Commodore John C. Stevens, a wealthy Hoboken, N.J., financier and yachtsman who also served as captain. The trophy won became known as the *America's Cup* and has been in competition ever since. The cup was successfully defended by U.S. boats until 1984, when Australia became the first foreign country to win the event.

"Go West, young man, go West" originated as the title of an editorial by John B. L. Soule, editor of the Terre Haute *Express.* Horace Greeley, editor of the New York *Tribune* who had been deeply impressed with the West on his travels, reprinted the piece with full credit to Soule. Later, in a letter to a friend, Greeley repeated the advice, adding "and grow up with the country." The quote has since been attributed to Greeley because of his prominence in national affairs.

June 3: The **first baseball uniforms** were worn by the New York Knickerbockers. The outfits consisted of straw hats, white shirts, and blue full-length trousers.

1852

I. Civil Rights
Exploration and Settlement
Government
Statistics
Wars

Disagreement over the Compromise of 1850 was not the only matter dividing the nation. The North was becoming more industrial, but the South remained tied to its slave-operated agricultural system. There were now 16 free and 15 slave states, causing the South to be outnumbered in the Senate as well as in the House, where the North had 144 seats to 90 for slave states. With improvement of transportation, the East and West were becoming more closely integrated by mutual economic interests. The West's interests were reflected particularly in the demand for laws to make it easier to acquire public land. Thus a prosperous and growing nation approached another presidential election with some disunity.

1852-1853: In **congressional elections** the Democrats gained three Senate seats for a 38–22 majority over the Whigs, with two seats going to minor parties. In the House they gained 19 seats for a 159–71 majority, with four seats going to minor parties.

June 1-6: The **Democratic National Convention nominated Franklin Pierce** of New Hampshire for the presidency and William R. King of Alabama for the vice presidency. The convention adopted a platform that favored the Compromise of 1850 as a solution to the slavery question.

June 16-21: The **Whig National Convention** nominated Gen. Winfield Scott of New Jersey for the presidency and William A. Graham of North Carolina for the vice presidency. The candidates were committed to strict enforcement of the Compromise of 1850.

Aug 11: The **Free-Soil National Convention** nominated John P. Hale of New Hampshire for the presidency and George W. Julian of Indiana for the vice presidency.

Nov 2: Franklin Pierce was elected president of the United States. William R. King was elected vice president. The electoral vote was Pierce, 254; Winfield Scott, Whig candidate, 42. The popular vote was Pierce, 1,601,474; Scott, 1,386,578; John P. Hale, Free-Soil candidate, 156,149.

II. Architecture
Arts and Music
Popular Entertainment
Publishing
Theater

The most important book of the 1850s, not for literary quality but for impact on the growing controversy over slavery, was *Uncle Tom's Cabin, or Life Among the Lowly* by Harriet Beecher Stowe. Her book appeared in 1852 and within a year 300,000 copies had been sold. For the first time blacks were treated as individuals, not stereotypes. The South denounced the book but in the North it was taken to be a true picture of the horrors of slavery. The novel may have hastened the final break between North and South. George L. Aiken, actor and playwright, dramatized *Uncle Tom's Cabin* and performed in it. It was first performed at Troy, N.Y., on Sept. 27, 1852, where it ran for 100 nights.

Stephen Foster composed "Massa's in de Cold Ground" and in 1853 "My Old Kentucky Home." In the latter, he dropped black dialect for standard English, thus ensuring widespread popularity for the song.

III. Business and Industry
Education
Philosophy and Religion
Science

The trend toward taller and taller buildings could only continue if two conditions were satisfied. Iron and steel to support such structures had to be readily available, and a practical way to get up and down had to be devised. Elisha Graves Otis, a Vermont-born inventor, solved the latter problem in 1852 when, while supervising construction of an industrial plant in Yonkers, N.Y., he developed a device to keep hoisting machinery from falling even if the lift chain or rope broke. From this start he developed a safe passenger elevator. The first of its kind was installed in E. V. Haughwout's store at 488 Broadway, New York City, on Mar. 23, 1857.

A **school attendance law** was enacted by Massachusetts. It required all children between the ages of 8 and 14 to attend school at least 12 weeks a year, 6 of them to be consecutive.

May 9: The **first U.S. Roman Catholic Church Council** was held at the Cathedral in Baltimore, Md.

Oct: St. Ann's Church for deaf mutes was founded in New York City by the Rev. Thomas Gallaudet. Its first service was held in the chapel at the University of the City of New York. In 1859 the church moved to a building on West 18th St.

IV. Fashion
Folkways
Holidays
Social Issues and Crime
Sports

About this time a Norwegian musician with a love for America and independence initiated a grandiose settlement scheme in western Pennsylvania. Ole Broneman Bull of Norway was a violinist who toured Europe and the U.S. giving concerts to raise money for his project. In 1852 he bought 125,000 acres, which he called Oleana and which was to be a colony for his countrymen, "consecrated to freedom, baptized in independence, and protected by the mighty flag of the Union." The plan failed and Bull lost a great deal of money.

Godey's Lady's Book began featuring paragraphs with the heading "Employment of Women." The items told of the most recent entries of women into the world of business and industry. *Godey's* itself was staffed largely by women in both editorial and press rooms.

The trend toward **women teachers** in public schools was reflected in the following figures. In Boston, 6000 of 8000 teachers were women; in Brooklyn, 103 of 120 teachers were women; and in Philadelphia, 699 of 781 teachers were women.

Jan 28: The famous sentence "**Eternal vigilance is the price of Liberty**" was uttered by abolitionist Wendell Phillips in an address before the Massachusetts Anti-Slavery Society. Phillips' words are thought to have been based on the statement "The condition upon which God hath given liberty to man is eternal vigilance . . . ," made in a speech by the Irish politician John Philpot Curran on July 10, 1790.

Apr 6: The word *telegram* was first used in the Albany *Evening Journal.* It read in part: "A friend desires us to give notice that he will ask leave . . . to introduce a new word. . . . It is 'telegram,' instead of 'telegraphic dispatch' or 'telegraphic communication.' " The British refused to accept this piece of Yankee slang until 1857, when the London *Times* used the word in a heading over an official British dispatch.

Aug 3: The **first intercollegiate rowing race** was conducted by Harvard and Yale, whose crews rowed a two-mile course on Lake Winnepesaukee, N.H. Harvard won by four lengths.

1853

I. Civil Rights
Exploration and Settlement
Government
Statistics
Wars

The U.S. became the first western nation to establish relations with Japan since the country was closed to foreigners in 1683. On July 8, 1853, Commodore Matthew Calbraith Perry sailed into Yedo (now Tokyo) Bay with a squadron of four vessels. For a time Japanese officials would have nothing to do with Perry, but on July 14 he was able to deliver the documents he carried from Pres. Millard Fillmore to two royal princes at the village of Kurihama. Perry then sailed away to give the Japanese time to consider the idea of external relations. He returned to Yedo the following March and on Mar. 31, 1854, signed a treaty that opened Japan to trade with the West.

Yellow fever took the lives of over 5000 persons in New Orleans, La., from 1853 to 1855. A few cases were reported in the spring, but epidemic proportions were not reached until mid-summer. Two hundred deaths were recorded in the week ending July 16. Vicksburg, Miss., lost one-sixth of its population in the epidemic.

The **Native American, or Know-Nothing, Party** was formed. Its adherents viewed with alarm the steadily growing number of immigrants. The party hoped to exclude anyone not native-born from holding federal, state, or municipal office, and urged the repeal of naturalization laws. "Know Nothing" became the party's unofficial name because its followers' typical reponse to questions regarding policy was, "I don't know." The reply was not from ignorance but secrecy.

Mar 2: The **Territory of Washington** was formed after separation from the Oregon Territory.

Dec 30: The **Gadsden Purchase,** negotiated by James Gadsden, U.S. minister to Mexico, was signed. By its terms the U.S. acquired 29,644 sq. mi. of territory, comprising the southernmost portions of present-day Arizona and New Mexico, for $15,000,000 (later reduced to $10,000,000). The purchase established the final boundaries of the contiguous United States. The treaty, amended with consent of the Mexican government, was ratified on June 30, 1854. The territory had been sought for a route for the Southern Pacific Railroad.

II. Architecture
Arts and Music
Popular Entertainment
Publishing
Theater

The distinctive culture and humor of the old Southwest, along the Gulf of Mexico, were colorfully recorded by Joseph Glover Baldwin in *The Flush Times of Alabama and Mississippi,* which was published this year. The 26 sketches included a mixture of comic anecdotes and biographies of notable lawyers and judges of the 1830s and 1840s. The book was both realistic and satirical and typified the humorous exaggeration of the time as practiced by the region's best orators, gamblers, and tellers of tall tales.

The **Crystal Palace** was built in New York City to house the 1853 exhibition. Constructed of cast iron and glass, it had the largest dome yet erected in the U.S. It was hailed for integrating engineering and decoration in a new national architectural style.

Feb: The women's suffrage magazine *Una,* published by Paulina Wright Davis and edited by Caroline H. Dall, issued its first number in Washington, D.C.

III. Business and Industry
Education
Philosophy and Religion
Science

The iron rails of the railroads were weaving a network of lines around the nation at an ever greater rate. In 1850 there were about 9000 miles of track, by 1860 more than 30,000. The Pennsylvania Railroad connected Philadelphia and Pittsburgh in 1852. The New York Central came into being in 1853, combining seven short lines between Albany and Buffalo, N.Y., into one. On Jan. 12, 1853, the Baltimore & Ohio Railroad began rail service to Wheeling, W. Va., from Baltimore. Rail service between New York and Chicago was available, although not in one continuous line. In 1856 the Illinois Central became the longest railroad in the world, with 700 miles of main line track. The Illinois Central was also the first railroad to which the federal government granted large tracts of public land as a subsidy; it was given 3,736,000 acres.

The **first terra cotta** in the U.S. was produced by James Renwick, professor of natural philosophy and experimental chemistry at Columbia University in New York City. Renwick, the father of the architect of the same name, proposed its use as paving material.

May: Gail Borden applied for a patent on his process for making evaporated milk in a vacuum. The Patent Office doubted its patentability until Borden reargued his application, after which the patent was issued, on Aug. 19, 1856. Production began in 1858. Originally conceived as a boon for immigrant and tenement-dwelling children who needed a source of safe, nutritious milk, evaporated milk skyrocketed in sales during the Civil War because of Army purchases.

IV. Fashion
Folkways
Holidays
Social Issues and Crime
Sports

Popular entertainment was taking new forms, and larger theaters were built to serve growing audiences. The Hippodrome, in New York City, which opened in 1853, could seat 4600 people. It offered chariot races as well as acrobats and clowns. Other entertainment included Swiss bell ringers and a steam calliope drawn by 40 horses.

The **Crystal Palace Exhibition of the Industry of All Nations** was held in New York City to demonstrate American inventions and industrial progress. Called a world's fair, it was inspired by the London Exhibition of 1851. The building that housed the exhibition was impressive enough to be referred to as Aladdin's palace.

Waitresses, now beginning to appear, were commented on by Amelia Bloomer, American feminist: "Stopping over night at the Delavan House in Albany, we were very agreeably surprised on entering the dining-room for supper to see about a dozen young women in attendance on the tables. This was something new. When we visited the house last winter the waiters were all men, as is usual in such places. Now not a man was to be seen in that capacity; but in place of their heavy tread, and awkward motions, was woman's light footfall and easy, graceful movements. In a conversation with the proprietor we learned that the change was made in May . . . entirely satisfactory . . . the only objectors being a few women . . . preferring black men."

The celebrated New York-Brooklyn **baseball rivalry** began when an all-New York team defeated an all-Brooklyn team in a best-of-three series, two games to one.

Oct 12: The **heavyweight boxing championship** was decided on a technicality. John C. Morrissey, claiming the title vacated by Tom Hyer, was losing to challenger Yankee Sullivan. But between rounds Sullivan left the ring to slug a few Morrissey supporters who had heckled him. He failed to get back into the ring to answer the bell for the next round, and the referee awarded the decision to Morrissey.

1854

I. Civil Rights
Exploration and Settlement
Government
Statistics
Wars

The signing of the Kansas-Nebraska Act on May 30 by Pres. Franklin Pierce brought civil war a step nearer. The bill, sponsored by Sen. Stephen A. Douglas, Democrat of Illinois, created two new territories and provided what Douglas called "popular sovereignty," also called "squatter sovereignty." This meant that those who settled in each territory would have the right to decide whether the territory, when admitted as a state, would be free or slave. In the North some people were infuriated because the law had the effect of repealing the Missouri Compromise of 1820, which said that there would never be slavery north of the southern boundary of Missouri, except for Missouri itself. Douglas was harmed politically by his sponsorship of the bill.

1854-1855: In **congressional elections** the fledgling Republican party gained 15 Senate seats but trailed the Democrats 40–15, with five seats held by minor parties. In the House the Republicans took a 108–83 majority, with 43 seats held by minor parties.

June 2: Fugitive slave Anthony Burns was the central figure in the most dramatic event of the year. Burns escaped by boat from Richmond, Va. On May 24 he had been arrested by federal officials in Boston on a trumped-up charge of theft. Abolition and women's suffrage groups were holding conventions in the city. When on June 2 Burns was taken from a jail to Long Wharf to begin his return trip to Richmond, the streets had to be guarded by thousands of troops and policemen. Buildings were draped in black, and church bells tolled. In a few months Burns was sold to a friendly master who in turn sold him to people in Boston interested in setting him free. It cost the U.S. government at least $100,000 to return this one fugitive slave to the South.

June 5: The **Canadian Reciprocity Treaty** opened the U.S. market to Canadian agricultural products, timber, and fish. In return American fishermen received new rights in Canadian waters and freedom of operation on the Great Lakes and the St. Lawrence R.

July 6: The **Republican Party was formed** in Jackson, Mich., and nominated the first Republican state ticket for the November elections. A preliminary meeting had been held at Ripon, Wis., on Feb. 28 by 50 disaffected Whigs, Free-Soilers, and northern Democrats, and the name "Republican" proposed. The Jackson meeting also attracted individuals from other splinter groups. The common bond was antislavery, more specifically anger over the Kansas-Nebraska Act.

II. Architecture
Arts and Music
Popular Entertainment
Publishing
Theater

Opera was thriving, as witnessed by a new and opulent opera house, the Academy of Music, which opened this year on 14th St. at Irving Place in New York City. It replaced the Astor Place Opera House, built in 1847. The new structure, which cost $335,000, opened on Oct. 2 with a performance of Vincenzo Bellini's *Norma.* The cast included two well-known artists of the day, Giulia Grisi and Giuseppe Mario, and was conducted by Luigi Arditi.

Walden, an American classic and the most famous work of Henry David Thoreau, was published. It was a series of 18 essays based on the two years Thoreau spent close to nature. The book stresses simplicity and holds that happiness is not to be had by pursuit of wealth. Descriptions of plants, birds, and animals are interspersed with reflections on life.

Novelist **Mary Jane Holmes** began her highly successful publishing career with *Tempest and Sunshine; or, Life in Kentucky.* By 1905 Mrs. Holmes had written 39 novels, many appearing originally in paperback, and had sold over 2,000,000 copies. In the decade or two after the Civil War, she was probably the most popular U.S. novelist. Her hallmark was highly sensitive heroines and noble heroes going through a series of stereotyped situations supported by a simplistic moral code.

The melodramatic *Ten Nights in a Barroom and What I Saw There* by Timothy S. Arthur was published. *Ten Nights* was second in sales to Harriet Beecher Stowe's *Uncle Tom's Cabin.* This favorite of the temperance forces was dramatized successfully by W. W. Pratt in 1858.

The **first fireproof building** in the U.S. was constructed for Harper & Brothers for its publishing headquarters in New York City. It was built with wrought-iron beams set in masonry walls.

III. Business and Industry
Education
Philosophy and Religion
Science

The era of public libraries was beginning, and this year it received an important impetus with the opening of the Astor Library in New York City. The library was made possible by a bequest of $400,000 from John Jacob Astor, the wealthiest man in the U.S. at his death in 1848. The library was chartered in 1849 and opened its own building on Lafayette Place as a reference library in 1854. Astor had little formal education but maintained a lifelong interest in literature and science. Fitz-Greene Halleck and Washington Irving, two of America's leading authors, are said to have been instrumental in persuading Astor to make the bequest.

The **Boston Public Library** was opened to the public. The library had been founded two years earlier. The library is credited with having inaugurated the practice of having popular books kept in large enough supply to fill the demands of many readers while keeping a regular complement of books of more limited circulation. This policy permitted development of the libraries of manuscripts and rare books for which Boston Public Library is famous. The original building was replaced in 1895 with a new structure designed by Charles McKim. It is a masterpiece of the new Italian Renaissance style.

May 6: Transatlantic cable communication became possible when a company headed by Cyrus W. Field was granted a charter and a 50-year monopoly. Not until 1866 was a permanently successful cable laid.

IV. Fashion
Folkways
Holidays
Social Issues and Crime
Sports

Paris set the style in women's dress and the Empress Eugenie of France set the Paris style. This was the dawn of the era of the hoop skirt, which ballooned out from a woman's waist. Around 1870 the bustle, a horsehair pad or wire cage worn in back under a woman's skirt, became the fashion. With it went very long, elaborate dresses with puffed upper sleeves. For men, the long cutaway coat of the 1850s went out of fashion, but black suits and white shirts were still in style.

The trotting horse **Flora Temple** broke all records by running the mile at Kalamazoo, Mich., in 2:19½—the first time a horse had run a mile faster than 2:20. The news, flashed immediately throughout the nation by telegraph, made Flora Temple a national celebrity.

Growing interest in **baseball** in New York City was evidenced by the establishment of many clubs, including: the Eagle and the Empire of New York City and the Excelsior of Brooklyn. By 1855 Morrisania had the Union Club and Brooklyn had added the Atlantic and the Eckford.

Oct 31: In an article on **women postal workers** the *Nebraska Palladium* reported that "the number of females at present holding the office of Post Master is 128." An interesting aspect of this story was the report that women postmasters received the same pay as men. No other occupation could make that claim.

1855

I. Civil Rights
Exploration and Settlement
Government
Statistics
Wars

This period showed a great increase in immigration to America from Europe, both for economic and political reasons. The growth was reflected in the fact that this year the New York State Immigration Commission leased Castle Garden, at the tip of Manhattan Island, as a reception center. During the 1850s a total of 2,314,000 people arrived in the U.S. Almost all came from Germany, Ireland, England, Scotland, and Wales. Immigrants for the most part settled in the northeastern part of the country. The Irish tended to remain in the large cities, but many Germans moved west to farmland.

Feb 10: U.S. **citizenship laws** were amended to provide that all children born abroad of U.S. parents be granted U.S. citizenship.

Mar 30: Kansas's first territorial election chose legislators amid armed violence. Some 5000 so-called Border Ruffians invaded territory from western Missouri and forced the election of a proslavery legislature. The number of votes cast far exceeded the number of eligible voters. To prevent widespread bloodshed, Andrew H. Reeder, appointed territorial governor by Pres. Pierce, reluctantly allowed the fraudulent election to stand.

June 5: The **American Party** was chosen as the new name for the Native American Party, commonly called the Know-Nothing Party, during its national meeting at Philadelphia. Control had been won by southern and proslavery forces, resulting in the disaffection of northern members, most of whom turned to the Republicans. The party virtually ceased to exist after the 1856 presidential election.

Sep 5: Antislavery settlers in Kansas, at a convention held in Big Springs, repudiated the fraudulently elected territorial legislature. Arms were sent to the settlers from northern states and an army was formed, called the Free State forces. The abolitionist firebrand, John Brown, arrived in Kansas and became a leader of these forces.

Oct 23: The **Topeka Constitution** drawn up by Kansas Free State forces set up a governor and a legislature. Kansas now had two governments. The Topeka Constitution outlawed slavery.

II. Architecture
Arts and Music
Popular Entertainment
Publishing
Theater

American composers were still few in number. Two who became pioneer composers of opera in the U.S. were William H. Fry and George F. Bristow. Fry wrote the first American opera, *Leonora,* in 1845, but it was not successful. Bristow's *Rip Van Winkle,* the second American opera, opened at Niblo's Garden in New York City on Sept. 27, 1855, and ran for four weeks. Richard Storrs, contemporary critic, announced, "A new American opera has succeeded in New York!" Fry and Bristow tried to encourage compositions by American composers.

Leaves of Grass by Walt Whitman, one of the most famous books of poetry of all time, was published at the author's expense. The first edition, containing only 12 poems, fared badly in the marketplace, but it did receive helpful praise from Ralph Waldo Emerson, ending with "I greet you at the beginning of a great career." A second edition, with 33 poems added, appeared in 1856; in 1860 a third, greatly enlarged and rearranged edition appeared. After the Civil War, revised and enlarged editions were published periodically; the final, ninth edition, under the author's direction, is dated 1892. In the 1940s a book club distributed 250,000 copies to its members. *Leaves of Grass* today is in many reprint series.

The Song of Hiawatha by Henry Wadsworth Longfellow was published. The poem was a broad collection of Indian legends tied together by a fictional character. Its publication marked the peak of Longfellow's fame. Using the meter of the Finnish epic *Kalevala,* Longfellow obtained musical effects by his repeated use of euphonious names for Indian persons and places. The poem epitomized the glorification of the American literary concept of the noble savage.

III. Business and Industry
Education
Philosophy and Religion
Science

Bridge building continued, and structures were getting longer and stronger. The most expert designer and builder of bridges was John Augustus Roebling. Roebling came to the U.S. from his native Germany in 1831 and became a citizen in 1837. He was a pioneer in suspension bridge construction, completing the Allegheny Suspension Bridge at Pittsburgh in 1845 and the Niagara Suspension Bridge in 1855. In the latter bridge Roebling made the first full-scale use of a wire cable of his own design; the cable was made up of parallel wires that were wire-bound. Previous cables had consisted of twisted wire. Roebling first developed this wire cable, or wire rope, in 1841.

The **first lighthouse** on the Pacific coast was built on Point Loma, San Diego, Calif.

The **Panama Railroad,** owned and built by a U.S. company, was completed across the Isthmus of Panama.

IV. Fashion
Folkways
Holidays
Social Issues and Crime
Sports

Few blacks achieved any prominence or became well-known to the general public in the age of slavery. An exception was Frederick Douglass. Born a slave in Maryland, he escaped and made his way to Massachusetts in 1838. A speech delivered by Douglass at an antislavery meeting so impressed his hearers that the American Anti-Slavery Society engaged him as one of its lecturers. In 1847 Douglass founded an abolitionist newspaper, the *North Star.* During the Civil War he persuaded Pres. Abraham Lincoln to use blacks as soldiers. In 1889 he became U.S. ambassador to Haiti.

Mrs. **Sarah Josepha Hale** launched a campaign in the columns of *Godey's* against the use of the word "female" in reference to women in public life. Elimination of the term became one of the objectives of feminism in America.

The phrase *cotton is king* came into prominence. It was taken from the title of a book, *Cotton is King, or the Economical Relations of Slavery,* by David Christy, which was published this year. At this time export of cotton amounted to one-half of all U.S. exports. Its value was more than $100,000,000 annually.

The practice of **selective law enforcement** was exemplified this year in instructions issued to New York City police by Mayor Fernando Wood concerning prohibition. A statewide prohibition law had gone into effect on July 4. Mayor Wood's instructions read in part: "Whether liquors exhibited in your presence . . . are intoxicating liquors . . . you must judge with great circumspection, and be careful to avoid seizing any thus exempt. An error in this regard may lay you liable to severe personal responsibility. . . . Keeping liquor with intent to sell or give away, is not an offense fully within the scope of the eye. . . . You can not see the violation . . . for an intent can not be seen. . . . These violations . . . do not . . . compel you to arrest or seize without complaints." This situation of selective law enforcement was disposed of by the judiciary when it declared the New York State statute unconstitutional in Mar. 1856. Twelve states and two territories had prohibition by the end of 1855, but drinking was an established American habit. Even the cop on the beat liked his beer.

1856

I. Civil Rights
Exploration and Settlement
Government
Statistics
Wars

The presidential election campaign of 1856 saw two new parties fielding candidates for the presidency. One was the American Party, the Know-Nothings, which had reached its peak in 1854 and was disintegrating over the slavery issue. The other was the Republican Party, whose strength lay in the North and West and among antislavery forces. The main issue of the campaign was the fight between slavery and antislavery forces for control of Kansas Territory. Although the Democrats won the presidency, the combined popular vote for the American, Republican, and Whig candidates was more than that for the Democratic winner, James Buchanan.

1856-1857: In **congressional elections** the Democrats lost four Senate seats but kept a majority, 36–20, over the Republicans, with eight seats going to minor parties. In the House the Democrats took a 118–92 majority, with 26 seats going to minor parties.

Feb 22: The **Republican Party** held its first national meeting at Pittsburgh, Pa. Delegates met to plan a national presidential nominating convention to be held in June.

Feb 22: The **national convention of the American, or Know-Nothing, Party** met at Philadelphia and nominated former Pres. Millard Fillmore for president and Andrew J. Donelson of Tennessee for vice president.

June 2: An **antislavery section of the Know-Nothing Party** met in New York City and nominated John C. Frémont of California for president and W. F. Johnston of Pennsylvania for vice president.

June 2-5: The **Democratic National Convention nominated James Buchanan** of Pennsylvania for president and John C. Breckinridge of Kentucky for vice president.

June 17-19: The **Republican National Convention nominated John C. Frémont** of California for president and William L. Dayton of New Jersey for vice president.

Aug 1: Bleeding Kansas, as the territory was known at this time, was without any settled government. Raids between the two factions continued, with an estimated 200 killed and $2,000,000 in property lost between Nov. 1855 and Dec. 1856. The House refused to seat either proslavery or Free State territorial delegates from Kansas.

Sep 17: The **Whig National Convention nominated** Millard Fillmore for the presidency and Andrew J. Donelson for the vice presidency. Fillmore and Donelson were also the candidates of the Know-Nothing Party.

Nov 4: James Buchanan was elected president of the United States. John C. Breckinridge was elected vice president. The electoral vote was Buchanan, 174; John C. Frémont, Republican, 114. The popular vote was Buchanan, 1,838,169; Frémont, 1,335,264; Millard Fillmore, Whig and American (Know-Nothing) Party candidate, 874,534. The election marked the end of the Whig Party as a national force.

II. Architecture
Arts and Music
Popular Entertainment
Publishing
Theater

Until this time American historians had mostly confined their writings to American and related British subjects. John Lothrop Motley went further afield and devoted his life's work to a study of the Netherlands. *The Rise of the Dutch Republic* appeared in 1856 in three volumes; it was followed by six more volumes in later years. Motley, writing with great enthusiasm for his subject, attempted to show how Protestantism in northern Europe had brought freedom there. Warmly partisan toward William of Orange, he created a dramatic narrative of the Dutch struggle against Spanish oppression. He drew analogies with the struggles of the U.S. and George Washington. The work sold over 30,000 copies in England and the U.S. in its first year.

"The Barefoot Boy" by John Greenleaf Whittier, one of America's most endearing poems, was included in his *The Panorama and Other Poems*, published this year. Turning here from his concerns about slavery, Whittier called up memories of his own boyhood and created a small masterpiece of local color.

Mar 1: George F. **Bristow**'s *Second Symphony in D Minor* was performed by the New York Philharmonic Society. This was one of the few orchestral works by a native-born composer that it presented during the mid-nineteenth century.

Aug 18: A **copyright law** was passed by Congress, giving the author of a play "along with the sole right to print and publish the said composition, the sole right also to act, perform, or represent the same."

III. Business and Industry
Education
Philosophy and Religion
Science

Along with the growing railroad system, the telegraph was vital to the transportation and communication network that was uniting the nation from coast to coast. Ezra Cornell, a financier who had supported the experiments of Samuel F. B. Morse that led to the invention of the telegraph, set out in 1855 to organize a national telegraph system. Given the name Western Union Telegraph Company on Apr. 1, 1856, Cornell's company by 1866 became a national system controlling some 75,000 miles of telegraph lines. The telegraph was essential to the railroads because it was the only way a message could be sent ahead of trains to give operational orders.

The **first kindergarten** in the U.S. was opened in Watertown, Wis., under the guidance of Mrs. Carl Schurz, wife of the prominent German refugee and leading Republican figure in the Lincoln-Hayes administration. It was a German-language school. Mrs. Schurz was an ardent disciple of Friedrich Froebel, the progressive educator in Thuringia whose theories, including those on the kindergarten, had great influence on American education.

A patent for a **milk-condensing process** was awarded to Gail Borden. Manufacture began in 1858. In 1851 Borden had won the Great Council Medal at the London Exposition for his development of a one-pound meat biscuit containing the nutritional qualities of five pounds of meat and ten ounces of flour. Borden was the first American food producer to win such an honor.

IV. Fashion
Folkways
Holidays
Social Issues and Crime
Sports

Gambling continued to be a favorite pastime of Americans. It was estimated that in the 1850s there were 2000 professional gamblers working the riverboats. Faro, monte, and chuck-a-luck were the favorite games. There was also three-card monte to help innocents lose their money even faster. The gamblers were easily recognized by their elegant, if gaudy, clothing, which featured a broadcloth coat and a ruffled white shirt.

By 1856 **baseball** was already considered a national pastime, as evidenced by the following passage from the sporting paper *Spirit of the Times:* "With the fall of the leaf and the diminution of the daylight, many of the out-of-door sports and pastimes come to a close for the season. The manly and exhilarating pastimes of Base Ball, Cricket, Foot Ball, and Racket are not playable.... We feel a degree of old Knickerbocker pride at the continued prevalence of Base Ball as the National game in the region of the Manhattanese."

1857

I. Civil Rights
Exploration and Settlement
Government
Statistics
Wars

A Supreme Court decision handed down on Mar. 6 in the case of *Dred Scott v. Sandford* was a setback for antislavery forces and further aggravated the growing ill feeling between North and South. Dred Scott was a slave whose owner had taken him from Missouri to Illinois, a free state, in 1834. Scott later returned to Missouri and in 1846 sued for his liberty on the grounds that his stay in free territory ended his slavery. The Court ruled, however, that Scott could not sue because slaves were not citizens. Going beyond the specific case, the Court also said that Congress had no power to prohibit slavery in territories and therefore the Missouri Compromise of 1820, already repealed by the Kansas-Nebraska Act, was unconstitutional.

Jan 15: The **State Disunion Convention,** favoring peaceful separation of North and South, met at Worcester, Mass. The most fiery speech was delivered by William Lloyd Garrison, who declared, "No union with slaveholders."

May 1: A **literacy test** as a requirement for voting was adopted as an amendment to the Massachusetts state constitution.

Sep 11: The **Mountain Meadows Massacre** resulted in the death of 120 emigrants headed for California. They were killed in Utah by Indians incited by the Mormon fanatic John D. Lee. Lee's justification was that he was retaliating against Pres. Buchanan's order removing Brigham Young as governor of Utah.

Oct 5: **Kansas** elected a free-state legislature under Gov. Robert J. Walker. The elections were held under supervision, and thousands of fraudulent proslavery votes were rejected.

II. Architecture
Arts and Music
Popular Entertainment
Publishing
Theater

Books and articles attacking and defending slavery began to appear in increasing numbers. This year *Cannibals All! or, Slaves Without Masters* by George Fitzhugh, a lawyer and editor of the Richmond, Va., *Examiner,* challenged the idea that freedom was inherently better than slavery. Fitzhugh compared the northern wage system unfavorably with the slave system, arguing that factory workers were "slaves without masters" who had no guarantee of care in illness or old age. Another southerner, Hinton Rowan Helper of North Carolina, also published a book in 1857, *The Impending Crisis of the South,* which was at the same time antislavery and antiblack. He argued that slavery retarded the South and that white farmers who had no slaves suffered from competition with large plantations operated by slaves. Helper's book enraged the South. In 1860 the Republicans distributed 100,000 copies in a condensed version to aid Abraham Lincoln's presidential campaign.

Dec 8: *The Poor of New York* by Dion Boucicault, the Irish actor-playwright, opened in New York City during the panic of 1857, an event that was incorporated into the play. Boucicault wrote or adapted over 100 plays, among them *London Assurance,* produced in London Mar. 4, 1841, before he emigrated to the U.S.; *The Octoroon* (1859), dealing with the love of a white

man for a black girl; and *Rip Van Winkle* (1865), in which the famous actor Joseph Jefferson played with so much success. Boucicault is credited with inaugurating the "road system." The revision of the copyright law that guaranteed a dramatist the sole right to "act, perform, or represent" his play was the result of his efforts.

III. Business and Industry
Education
Philosophy and Religion
Science

Awarding on June 23 of a patent for a process for the economical production of steel marked an important advance in a basic industry. The patent was awarded to William Kelly, whose process involved the oxidation of impurities in iron by blowing air through molten iron. He had first developed the process in 1851. Independently, Henry Bessemer had perfected the technique in England in 1856. Their rival claims were settled in 1866. The first Bessemer converter was built at Troy, N.Y., in 1864. Kelly's process was used in a converter at Wyandotte, Mich., the same year. Steel at once began to replace iron for railroad tracks, with 259,699 tons of steel rail produced in 1875.

Mar 3: A **U.S. subsidy of overseas cable** was voted by Congress, paying the company formed by Cyrus W. Field $70,000. The project was also supported by England and private resources on both sides of the Atlantic. The laying of cable from Ireland to Newfoundland began this year, but the cable broke some several hundred miles out from Valentia, Ireland. It was decided to use two ships, beginning from the midpoint between Newfoundland and Ireland and traveling in opposite directions. After three more failures, a copper wire 1950 miles long was laid between Trinity Bay and Valentia, the ships both arriving at their destinations on Aug. 5, 1858. Queen Victoria of England sent the first message on Aug. 16, 1858, to Pres. Buchanan. The feat was considered a glorious achievement until the cable broke two weeks later, perhaps from faulty insulation. After financial reverses and the interruption of the Civil War, Field succeeded in laying the cable in 1866, using the largest steamship of the time, *Great Eastern.*

Aug 24: A **financial panic** was precipitated by the failure of the New York City branch of the Ohio Life Insurance Company. Some 4932 businesses failed this year. By 1859 another 8000 had failed. The bankruptcies were primarily the result of overspeculation in railway securities and real estate.

IV. Fashion
   Folkways
   Holidays
   Social Issues and Crime
   Sports

One of the first large and well-planned city parks, and one that set an example, began to be laid out this year. It was Central Park in Manhattan, New York City, comprising 840 acres acquired in 1856. Frederick Law Olmsted and Calvert Vaux won a competition for designing it in 1857; Olmsted was appointed the park's chief architect in 1858. He and Vaux laid out a park that embodied the naturalistic and romantic ideas of the time. Olmsted spent most of his life designing parks and park systems in such cities as Brooklyn, Chicago, Buffalo, and Boston.

Charity balls were originated in New York City. The balls enabled society to dispense with its charitable obligations while displaying its wealth. The first annual charity ball was given at the Academy of Music.

The **New Orleans Mardi Gras** for the first time offered a pageant of decorative floats organized and paid for by societies called Krewes. The first society, Comus, began functioning this year as a patron and promoter of the festivities.

The **America's Cup,** won in England by the U.S. schooner-yacht *America,* was presented to the New York Yacht Club by members who owned *America:* J.C. Stevens, Edwin A. Stevens, Hamilton Wilkes, J. Beekman Finley, and George L. Schuyler. The gift stipulated that the cup be used perpetually as a trophy in international challenge yacht races.

Oct 6: The **American Chess Association** was organized at the first American Chess Congress, held in New York City. There Paul C. Morphy, a 20-year-old chess wizard from New Orleans, La., won the American championship. Morphy toured Europe in 1858 and 1859, defeating all the masters who would meet him. Although he played only sporadically thereafter, he was recognized as the first American international chess master.

1858

I. Civil Rights
   Exploration and Settlement
   Government
   Statistics
   Wars

A landmark series of political debates took place this year between Aug. 21 and Oct. 15, when Sen. Stephen A. Douglas of Illinois and Abraham Lincoln, little known Republican of Illinois, held a series of seven debates in towns across Illinois, competing for a seat in the Senate. Their points of view showed clearly the growing gap between North and South. Lincoln opposed slavery. The nation, he said, would have to decide on the issue—either the whole country should accept slavery or eliminate it. Douglas did not defend slavery, but he did uphold the right of the people in a given territory to decide the issue for themselves. The Democratic majority in the Illinois legislature elected Douglas to the Senate seat, but Lincoln's efforts brought him into the national spotlight.

1858-1859: In **congressional elections** the Republican Party made a strong showing. In the Senate the Democrats took a majority of 38–26 over the Republicans, with two seats held by minor parties. In the House the Republicans took a 113–101 majority over the Democrats, with 23 seats going to minor parties. Abraham Lincoln, Republican candidate for senator from Illinois, was defeated by his Democratic rival Stephen A. Douglas.

Mar 23: The Senate voted to accept Kansas into the Union under the **Lecompton Constitution** after the constitution had been rejected by Kansas. The House, however, voted to resubmit the constitution to a popular vote.

May 11: Minnesota was admitted as a state, the 32nd to join the Union.

Aug 2: The **Lecompton Constitution** was submitted by the federal government to the people of Kansas for popular vote for the third time. It was rejected and the territory became nonslaveholding. Kansas did not enter the Union until 1861.

II. Architecture
Arts and Music
Popular Entertainment
Publishing
Theater

Changing critical standards in historiography were exemplified in the work of John Gorham Palfrey, a Unitarian clergyman of Boston and a former editor of the *North American Review.* He was the author of *History of New England,* which appeared in five volumes between 1858 and 1890. At the time the work was considered impartial and was praised for bringing colonial and English events together in its chronology. Later critics, however, considered the volumes biased in favor of New England, especially Massachusetts, and the clergy.

"The Courtship of Miles Standish" by Henry Wadsworth Longfellow, a verse account of a bit of Puritan history of the domestic kind, was published. Miles Standish, John Alden, and Priscilla became living traditions to millions through this work. In London 10,000 copies were sold on the day of its appearance. Longfellow's popularity among his contemporaries is revealed by the fact that over 300,000 of his books had been sold by 1857.

III. Business and Industry
Education
Philosophy and Religion
Science

Japan was further opened to American commerce in 1858, following Commodore Matthew C. Perry's original treaty of 1854. In 1855 the U.S. sent Townsend Harris, a New York merchant, to Japan as its first diplomatic representative. Harris came to exercise considerable influence with the Japanese government because of his sound advice. He signed agreements on June 18, 1857, and July 29, 1858, that opened more ports to U.S. commerce and gave Americans residence rights.

Philadelphia's first horsecar went into operation. As in New York City, where regular passenger runs began in 1852, the horsecar soon replaced the older omnibus. The horsecar effected a minor revolution in city planning, for the tracks it ran on were permanent and inflexible. Boston adopted a horsecar line in 1852, Chicago in 1859.

Aug 16: The **first cable message** was sent across the Atlantic Ocean from Queen Victoria of England to Pres. James Buchanan.

Oct 9: The stage inaugurating the **first overland mail service** connecting the West and East coasts reached St. Louis from San Francisco after a trip of 23 days 4 hrs. At St. Louis the mail was transferred to a train for the remainder of the journey to the East.

IV. Fashion
Folkways
Holidays
Social Issues and Crime
Sports

Another gold rush captured the nation's attention when gold was discovered in Colorado in the Pike's Peak area in 1857 and at Cherry Creek, Denver, in 1858. About 100,000 gold seekers headed west, but about half never made it to the gold regions. Within two years Denver was enough of a city to have a theater, circulating library, and debating club. The town of El Dorado, near present-day Colorado Springs, was founded by miners as Fountain Creek in 1859. The rallying cry of the fortune hunters in this period was "Pike's Peak or bust."

Birth control came to the fore with H. C. Wright's popular *The Unwelcomed Child; or the Crime of an Undesigned and Undesired Maternity.* It indicated a growing frankness about sexual matters in American society.

Apr 12: The **first U.S. billiard championship** was held at Fireman's Hall, Detroit, Mich. Michael J. Phelan defeated John Seereiter in a match lasting nine and a half hours. It was witnessed by a "genteel" audience that included a few ladies.

June 16: **"A house divided against itself cannot stand"** was included by Abraham Lincoln in his speech of acceptance of the Republican nomination for the U.S. Senate. "I believe," he went on, "this government cannot endure permanently half slave and half free."

July 20: The **first admission charge to a baseball game** (50 cents) was levied for the contest between Brooklyn and the New York All Stars at Fashion Race Course in Long Island. About 1500 spectators saw New York defeat Brooklyn 22–18.

1859

I. Civil Rights
Exploration and Settlement
Government
Statistics
Wars

A court case stemming from opposition to the Fugitive Slave Law of 1850 found a northern free state arguing for states' rights, usually the preserve of the South. In 1854 the Wisconsin Supreme Court freed Sherman M. Booth, an abolitionist editor who had been convicted in federal court of violating the Fugitive Slave Law, on the grounds that the law was unconstitutional. In *Abelman v. Booth* (Abelman was a U.S. marshall), the Supreme Court on Mar. 7, 1859, denied the right of a state to interfere in a federal case, and upheld the constitutionality of the law. The Wisconsin legislature then adopted a resolution defending state sovereignty.

The **Comstock Lode,** the richest known U.S. silver deposit, was discovered in western Nevada. It was the first major U.S. silver strike.

Feb 14: Oregon was admitted to the Union, the 33rd state.

July 5: The **Kansas constitutional convention** convened at Wyandotte, Kans. The chief issue was whether the state should be free or slave. On Oct. 4 an antislavery constitution was ratified by a vote of 10,421 to 5530.

Oct 16: The federal arsenal at **Harpers Ferry** (now in W. Va.) was seized by John Brown and 21 followers. Brown wanted to establish an abolitionist republic in the Appalachians and to fight slavery with fugitive slaves and abolitionist whites. On Dec. 2 he was hanged at Charlestown, Va., for murder, conspiracy, and treason against Virginia. In the South he was thought of as a murderer and traitor who deserved the gallows, but in the North his gibbet was described as "the cross of a martyr." In Concord, Mass., Henry David Thoreau wrote of Brown: "When a government puts forth its strength . . . to kill the liberators of the slave, what a merely brute . . . force it is seen to be." Lincoln was philosophical and brooded over the fates of historical zealots who had taken it upon themselves to end oppression. Longfellow sounded a prophetic note: "This will be a great day in our history, the date of a new revolution. . . . As I write, they are leading old John Brown to execution. . . . This is sowing the wind to reap the whirlwind, which will soon come."

II. Architecture
Arts and Music
Popular Entertainment
Publishing
Theater

Most of the opera singers heard in America were European-born and trained, and it was rare for an American-trained singer to reach the top ranks in Europe. The first to accomplish this was Adelina Patti, a coloratura soprano born of Italian parents in Madrid, Spain. She made her operatic debut in New York City on Nov. 24, 1859, in the title role of *Lucia di Lammermoor.* For years after that she sang in such cities as London, Paris, and Milan, returning to the U.S. in 1881. Patti was the most popular and highest paid singer of her time. It became a custom for audiences to demand that she sing "Home, Sweet Home" as one of her encores.

"**Dixie,**" first known as "I Wish I Was in Dixie's Land," was composed by Dan Emmett as a "walk-around" for Bryant's Minstrels. The song was later claimed by both sides during the Civil War, but eventually became associated almost completely with the Confederacy. Emmett was a northerner from Ohio.

Sep 5: Probably the **first novel by a black** to appear in the U.S., *Our Nig; or Sketches from the Life of a Free Black* by Harriet E. Wilson, was issued in Boston. It had been privately printed for the author, about whom little is known, by the Boston printing firm of George C. Rand and Avery. Autobiographical in nature, the novel was intended by Mrs. Wilson to raise funds to care for her son, who died in 1860. Despite its significance, the novel remained virtually unrecognized until its rediscovery and republication in 1983.

III. Business and Industry
Education
Philosophy and Religion
Science

A turning point in the economic history of the U.S. came this year when on Aug. 27 the first producing oil well began to flow at the rate of 20 barrels a day. The well had been drilled to a depth of 60 feet by Edwin L. Drake, near Titusville, Pa. An oil rush, reminiscent of the California gold rush, began almost at once. Boom towns grew up overnight and within three years of Drake's discovery 128,000,000 gallons had been produced. Oil became an important export product and kerosene displaced whale oil and candles as a source of illumination.

The **first hotel passenger elevator** in the U.S. was installed in the Fifth Avenue Hotel, New York City. Many patrons continued to climb the stairs.

July: **Electric home lighting** was given its first successful demonstration by Prof. Moses G. Farmer in the parlor of his home at Salem, Mass. Current, supplied by a voltaic battery, was conducted to two lamps on a mantelpiece. Strips of platinum provided the illuminating medium. This device produced the best artificial light then known but was much more expensive than gaslight.

Sep 1: George M. Pullman's first sleeping car made its first run. It was a converted coach. In 1863 he built the *Pioneer,* the first modern sleeping coach with a folding upper berth and extensible seat cushions to form a lower berth. In 1868 he introduced a dining car, in 1875 a chair car.

IV. Fashion
  Folkways
  Holidays
  Social Issues and Crime
  Sports

Even though prizefighting was still bare-knuckled and brutal, it fascinated people of all classes. This was shown by the interest aroused when John C. Heenan sailed for England in 1859 to meet the British champion, Tom Sayers. Heenan had justly claimed the American heavyweight title on the retirement of John C. Morrissey. On Oct. 20, 1858, Morrissey had been awarded a decision over Heenan on a technicality. When Heenan and Sayers met on Apr. 17, 1860, they fought for 42 rounds in a bout that lasted 2 hrs. and 20 min. Heenan battered Sayers but the police broke up the illegal match. The crowd invaded the ring, and the bout was declared a draw. Even so, *The Spirit of the Times,* in an extra edition of 100,000 copies, hailed Heenan as the world champion.

June 30: Niagara Falls was crossed by a tightrope walker, Charles Blondin. In five minutes the sensational Frenchman, watched by 25,000 spectators, passed across a cable 1100 feet long and 160 feet above the seething water. In later performances Blondin made the same crossing blindfolded, pushing a wheelbarrow (July 4); carrying a man on his back (Aug. 19); and walking on stilts (Sept. 14, 1860). At age 72, in 1888, Blondin was still thrilling crowds in the U.S. and abroad with his high-wire skills.

July 1: In the **first intercollegiate baseball game** in history, Amherst defeated Williams, 66–32.

July 26: In the **first intercollegiate regatta,** Harvard defeated Yale and Brown at Lake Quinsigamond, Worcester, Mass. The race was in six-oared shells, at three miles. A similar regatta planned for the previous year was cancelled when the Yale stroke, George E. Dunham, drowned.

1860

I. Civil Rights
  Exploration and Settlement
  Government
  Statistics
  Wars

Even before the presidential election campaign of 1860 began, it was clear that slavery would be the only issue. The first result of this situation was a complete split in the Democratic Party between its northern and southern supporters. The Republican Party, drawing its strength from the North and West, was united in its antislavery stand and represented the largest part of the nation. There was also an attempt at a coalition of factions to hold the Union together at any cost. There were now 33 states, 18 of them free and 15 slave. This situation, combined with the split in the Democratic Party, made a Republican victory inevitable. Abraham Lincoln carried all the free states, except for a split in New Jersey. He won a clear majority in the electoral college but not in the popular vote.

The U.S. **Census** recorded a population of 31,443,321. The center of population was located 20 miles southeast of Chillicothe, Ohio. There were 448,070 free blacks and 3,953,760 slaves in the country.

1860-1861: In **congressional elections** the Republicans took control of both houses of Congress. As southern states seceded, the 37th Congress had the following representation: Senate, 31 Republicans, 10 Democrats, 8 other parties; House, 105 Republicans, 43 Democrats, 30 others.

Feb 27: Abraham Lincoln delivered his memorable address at Cooper Union, New York City. He set forth the issues on which the new Republican Party would appeal to voters and his no-compromise position on slavery. This projected Lincoln into the lead for the Republican presidential nomination.

Apr 23: The **national convention of the Democratic Party** met at Charleston, S.C. On Apr. 30 delegates from the South walked out over platform disputes. The remainder, led by Stephen A. Douglas, supported constitutional decisions and congressional noninterference on the issue of slavery in the territories. The convention adjourned on May 3 without making any nominations.

May 9: The national convention of the **Constitutional Union Party** nominated John Bell of Tennessee for the presidency and Edward Everett of Massachusetts for the vice presidency. The party was composed of remnants of the Whig and American parties.

May 16-18: The **Republican National Convention nominated Abraham Lincoln** of Illinois for the presidency and Hannibal Hamlin of Maine for the vice presidency.

June 18-23: Reconvening in Baltimore, Md., the **Democratic Party nominated Stephen A. Douglas** of Illinois for the presidency and Herschel V. Johnson of Georgia for the vice presidency.

June 28: The **southern Democrats nominated John C. Breckinridge** of Kentucky for the presidency and Joseph Lane of Oregon for the vice presidency. Their platform supported slavery in the territories.

Nov 6: Abraham Lincoln was elected president of the United States in a Republican victory over the divided Democrats. Hannibal Hamlin was elected vice president. The electoral vote was Lincoln, 180; John C. Breckinridge, southern Democrat, 72; John Bell, Constitutional Union candidate, 39; Stephen A. Douglas, Democrat, 12. The popular vote was Lincoln, 1,866,252; Douglas, 1,375,157; Breckinridge, 849,781; Bell, 589,581.

Dec 20: South Carolina seceded from the Union, the first state to do so. Its action was taken as a consequence of Lincoln's election.

II. Architecture
Arts and Music
Popular Entertainment
Publishing
Theater

Poets of the period often devoted their talents to the controversy over slavery and the events of the Civil War. The leading voice of the South was Henry Timrod of South Carolina, who was to become known as the poet laureate of the Confederacy. Timrod's collection of *Poems* was published this year, but it was not until 1873 that his poetry dealing with the war appeared. Most notable was "Ode Sung at the Occasion of Decorating the Graves of the Confederate Dead," written in 1867, the year of his early death.

Dime novels made their first appearance under the aegis of the publisher Erastus Beadle. The first dime novel was *Malaeska; The Indian Wife of the White Hunter* by Mrs. Anna Sophia Stephens; it sold more than 300,000 copies in its first year. Another dime novel, *Seth Jones; or, the Captives of the Frontier* by Edward S. Ellis, also published this year, sold some 450,000 copies in less than a year. By 1865 Beadle's dime novel series had sold over 4,000,000 copies. The novels featured such larger-than-life characters as Deadwood Dick, Calamity Jane, and Kit Carson. Published in orange jackets, the books were read extensively by soldiers in camp. In 1870 a second series, Beadle's Pocket Novels, was begun. Literary fare in these novels consisted of tales of the West, Indians, hunters, pioneers, and the gunmen. In general, the morality of the books was unobjectionable if simplistic, for the villain and the hero were obvious from the opening pages, and evil was always punished.

"**Old Black Joe,**" the last of Stephen Foster's "plantation songs," was published. Foster, suffering from alcoholism and financial problems, moved to New York City and began to write sentimental potboilers—as many as 46 songs in one year. He died in Bellevue Hospital, New York City, on Jan. 13, 1864.

The Conduct of Life by Ralph Waldo Emerson was published. For several years Emerson had lectured on the subject popularly and effectively. At the peak of his powers, he was now clearly an astute social commentator as well as moral philosopher. Among the book's topics were the discoveries of science, evolution, uses of wealth, importance of culture, faith, art, and a reevaluation of the position of the transcendentalists.

III. Business and Industry
Education
Philosophy and Religion
Science

Education of children at a very early age was a European innovation that now came to America. The first English-language kindergarten in the U.S. was opened in Boston this year by Elizabeth Palmer Peabody, a member of the New England intellectual elite. (A German-language kindergarten had been established in Watertown, Wis., in 1856.) Miss Peabody was interested in social reform and education and had been associated with A. Bronson Alcott and his experimental Temple School. In her kindergarten she followed the precepts of Friedrich Froebel, the German educator and founder of the kindergarten system. Miss Peabody was a member of the Transcendental Club, and her home was the setting of the notable conversation classes of Margaret Fuller, another of the transcendentalists.

A **U.S. Department of Education survey** showed a total of 321 high schools in the country; more than half were in Massachusetts, New York, and Ohio.

Feb 22: The **most significant strike of the period** began in Lynn, Mass. Shoemakers there struck for higher wages and union recognition. The strike, which followed the introduction of new machinery in the shoe industry, soon spread to include 25 towns and 20,000 shoemakers. The workers protested because youngsters were being brought in to work the new machines, cutting the salary of skilled men to $3.00 a week. The Mechanics' Association, formed in 1859 at Lynn, organized the strike. On Apr. 10 the manufacturers agreed to a 10% wage increase. Some 1000 workers went back to their jobs. The effort to win general union recognition was largely frustrated.

Apr 3: The first relay of the **Pony Express** mail service left St. Joseph, Mo., and arrived in Sacramento, Calif., on Apr. 13. The cost of mailing a letter was at first $5.00 a half-ounce, later reduced to $1.00. The Pony Express was discontinued in Oct. 1861, when the transcontinental telegraph began service.

May 10: The **Morrill Tariff Bill** was passed by the House of Representatives, opening the era of protectionism. The tariff became law in Mar. 1861. It became the regulator of imports and was superseded only by the McKinley Bill, passed by the 51st Congress in 1890.

June 23: The **Government Printing Office** was established by an act of Congress. Later the government bought an existing commercial press in Washington, D.C. Today, the Government Printing Office is the largest printing establishment in the world, with the plant valued at over $20,000,000.

IV. Fashion
Folkways
Holidays
Social Issues and Crime
Sports

The game of croquet was introduced to America from England. It was soon popular but did not reach the height of its popularity until after the Civil War. Croquet was the first outdoor athletic activity in which women participated. Even more important, it could be played by men and women together. Consequently, it became as much a social as an athletic activity and afforded fine opportunity for courting. In the 1870s the vogue for croquet was so great that sets with candle sockets for night playing were introduced.

Prices for shaves, haircuts, and curling were raised at Tony Delight's in Chicago, one of the famous tonsorial enterprises in America. Shaves went up from 5 cents to 6 cents, haircuts from 10 cents to 12 cents, and curling from 15 or 20 cents to 25 cents. Shampoos were priced at 25 cents.

The term *seventh-inning stretch* became common at baseball games. It referred to the custom of spectators standing up and stretching just before the home team came to bat in the seventh inning. The custom served two functions, one practical and one superstitious. Spectators relieved cramped muscles and brought good luck to their team as well, since the number seven was seen as lucky.

The **popular attitude toward strikes** was reflected in the reaction of the U.S. press this year to the Massachusetts shoemakers' strike, which was looked upon as a virtual revolution. "Rebellion among the workers in New England" and "Revolution at the North" were among the warnings that greeted newspaper readers over their morning coffee. Some of the newspapers were shocked by the part played by women workers in the strike and bewailed the effects of the feminist movement. Churches generally supported the strikers, while the New England manufacturers threatened the German and Irish immigrants, who formed the bulk of the strikers, with legislative retaliation that would take away their voting privileges.

1861

I. Civil Rights
Exploration and Settlement
Government
Statistics
Wars

The Civil War (1861–1865) began in the early morning hours of Apr. 12 when Confederate forces at Charleston, S.C., opened fire on the federal garrison at Fort Sumter in Charleston harbor. The action was the culmination of months of effort by Confederate officials to force federal troops out of Charleston harbor. They had been successful elsewhere in occupying federal arsenals and forts and in removing federal garrisons. Pres. Abraham Lincoln tried to deal firmly with South Carolina authorities without provoking violence, but the attempt failed. When the federal garrison at Fort Sumter surrendered on Apr. 13, the citizens of Charleston were filled with joy. Little did they realize that they had witnessed the beginning of four years of vicious warfare.

Jan 9: *Star of the West,* an unarmed federal supply ship, was fired on by the South Carolina state battery at Charleston harbor; the command to fire was given by Francis Wilkinson Pickens, governor of the state. The ship had been sent under orders from Pres. James Buchanan to supply and reinforce the federal garrison at Fort Sumter in Charleston harbor.

Jan 9: Mississippi became the second state to secede from the Union.

Jan 10: A **Florida convention** voted for secession from the Union. "United States" was changed to "Confederate States" in their constitution.

Jan 11: Alabama seceded from the Union.

Jan 19: Georgia seceded from the Union.

Jan 26: Louisiana seceded from the Union.

Jan 29: Kansas was admitted to the Union, the 34th state. It entered as a free state.

Feb 4: The **Confederate States of America was formed** at Montgomery, Ala. Jefferson Davis of Mississippi was elected president, Alexander H. Stephens of Georgia vice president. Both were chosen on Feb. 9.

Feb 9: The **Confederate Provisional Congress** asserted that all laws under the U.S. Constitution that were not inconsistent with the constitution of the Confederate states would be recognized.

Feb 13: The action that led to the awarding of the **first U.S. Medal of Honor** took place at Apache Pass, Ariz., where Col. Bernard John Dowling Irwin led his troops to victory over hostile Chiricahua Apache Indians. The medal was not given to Irwin until Jan. 24, 1894.

Feb 18: Jefferson Davis was inaugurated president of the Confederacy. The Confederate capital was established in Montgomery, Ala., where Davis lived at 626 Washington St., in a building known as the White House of the Confederacy. The capital was later moved to Richmond, Va.

Feb 23: Texas seceded from the Union, following a state convention's recommendation of Feb. 1. It was the seventh state to secede.

Mar 2: A congressional act establishing the **territories of Nevada and Dakota** was signed by Pres. James Buchanan. Nevada Territory was formed from Utah Territory, Dakota Territory from Nebraska Territory.

Mar 4: An official **Confederate flag,** "Stars and Bars," was adopted by a Confederate convention at Montgomery, Ala. The flag had seven stars and three stripes, and was raised over the Confederate capitol at Montgomery. Later, after the similarity between Union and Confederate flags created confusion at the Battle of Bull Run, the Confederate army adopted a battle flag consisting of a red field and the blue cross of St. Andrew, with 13 stars.

Mar 4: Abraham Lincoln was inaugurated president of the United States. A Republican, he was elected to two terms but was assassinated early in his second term. Hannibal Hamlin was inaugurated vice president.

Mar 11: The **Confederate constitution** was adopted unanimously by the Confederate congress in session at Montgomery, Ala. It declared the sovereignty of states and forbade passage of any law prohibiting slavery.

Apr 11: At **Fort Sumter,** surrender of the federal garrison was demanded by South Carolina authorities. Maj. Robert Anderson refused to surrender, but added that he would soon be forced to do so if supplies were not forthcoming.

Apr 12: The **Civil War began** at 4:30 A.M. when Confederate shore batteries under command of Gen. P. G. T. Beauregard opened fire on Fort Sumter. The federal garrison, out of supplies, surrendered on Apr. 13 and evacuated the fort the following day.

Apr 17: A **Virginia convention voted for secession** from the Union as a result of Lincoln's call for troops. The proposal was put before the people of Virginia on May 23 and passed. Virginia was the eighth state to secede.

Apr 19: A **blockade** of Confederate ports was ordered by Pres. Lincoln. The blockade would ultimately weaken the Confederacy by disrupting the importation of war supplies.

Apr 19-20: Norfolk Navy Yard was destroyed and evacuated by Union forces. Among the ships scuttled was the steam frigate *Merrimack*, which was burned to the waterline.

May 6: Arkansas seceded from the Union, the ninth state to join the Confederacy.

May 20: North Carolina seceded from the Union.

May 21: Richmond, Va., was made capital of the Confederate States of America. Virginia at this time was the most populous of the southern states.

June 8: Tennessee seceded from the Union.

July 21: At the first Battle of **Bull Run,** near Manassas, Va., Union forces under Gen. Irvin McDowell were defeated by the Confederates. McDowell delayed the attack for two days, allowing Confederate Gen. Beauregard to call on reinforcements from the Shenandoah Valley. Their arrival late in the day gave the Confederates a numerical advantage. It was in this battle that Confederate Gen. Thomas J. Jackson was nicknamed "Stonewall" for his firm stand at a crucial moment.

Sep 13: The **first naval engagement** of the Civil War took place at Pensacola, Fla. Lt. John Henry Russell sailed the frigate *Colorado* past shore batteries at night and, as day broke, with a force of 100 sailors and Marines, went for the southern privateer *Judah* in the shipyard. After hand-to-hand fighting, the contingent burned the vessel to the waterline and left with few losses. Pres. Lincoln thanked Russell personally, and the Navy Department honored him.

Nov 7: Union forces captured Port Royal Island on the South Carolina coast. A Navy fleet under Samuel F. Du Pont bombarded the protecting forts, Beauregard and Walker, which were then overrun by Army troops under Lt. Col. Thomas W. Sherman. The victory was important to the North, for it now had a base on the flank of the South. From this base its South Atlantic Blockading Squadron under Du Pont proceeded to capture or render inoperative nearly all the South's Atlantic ports below North Carolina.

II. Architecture
Arts and Music
Popular Entertainment
Publishing
Theater

East Lynne, a phenomenally successful novel and dramatization by Mrs. Henry Wood, an English author, was published in the U.S. this year. The tear jerker sold at least 1,000,000 copies, but its greatest success came as a stage play. The drama packed theaters for most of the rest of the century. *East Lynne* later became a synonym for the crudest of melodramas.

Aug 15: Civil War events became theatrical material. Charles Gayler's *Bull Run* was presented in New York City less than a month after the battle itself. Other plays dealing with the war were *Capture of Fort Donelson* (1862) by Henry Seymour; *How to Avoid Drafting* (1862), anonymous; *A Supper in Dixie* (1865) by William C. Reynolds; *The Guerrillas* (1862) by James D. McCabe, Jr.; and *Grant's Campaign* (1865) by John Poole.

III. Business and Industry
Education
Philosophy and Religion
Science

An important step in the development of the nation's communication system came on Oct. 24, 1861, when Pres. Abraham Lincoln in Washington, D.C., received the first transcontinental telegraph message, from Sacramento, Calif. The lines of the Overland and the Pacific telegraph companies had been linked at Fort Bridger, Utah. A side effect of the completion of the transcontinental line was the almost immediate demise of the far more romantic Pony Express, which had begun operating in Apr. 1860 between St. Joseph, Mo., and Sacramento.

Apr 20: Thaddeus Sobieski Coulincourt Lowe, inventor and balloonist, made a record balloon voyage from Cincinnati, Ohio, to near the coast of South Carolina—900 miles in 9 hrs.—to demonstrate the value of balloons for observation by the military. He was briefly held as a Union spy. On Oct. 1 Pres. Lincoln made him chief of the Army's aeronautic section.

Aug 5: Congress adopted an **income tax law** as a war finance measure. Income was defined broadly as "derived from any source whatever." The rates were 3% on incomes from $600 to $10,000 and 5% for incomes above $10,000.

Oct 4: Construction of the *Monitor* was authorized by the U.S. Navy. This steam-powered, propeller-driven, armored, and rotary-turreted warship was designed and made by John Ericsson. It was launched at Greenpoint, L. I., on Jan. 30, 1862, less than 100 days after its keel was laid. Naval warfare was changed irrevocably by its design.

IV. Fashion
Folkways
Holidays
Social Issues and Crime
Sports

A change in American society's attitude toward light entertainment came in 1861 when Antonio "Tony" Pastor, a singer and dancer, opened his first theater at 444 Broadway in New York City. The variety theater had had a reputation for vulgarity, but Pastor's performers and acts were suitable for the whole family. He attracted women patrons by offering door prizes such as kitchenware and dress patterns. Pastor eventually became known as the father of American vaudeville. He introduced performers who were to become famous, such as Lillian Russell (born this year). His style of entertainment was soon copied in other cities.

Mar 4: In Abraham Lincoln's **first inaugural address** the new president began with a sentiment that has become an integral part of the literature and history of America: "This country, with its institutions, belongs to the people who inhabit it. Whenever they shall have grown weary of the existing government, they can exercise their constitutional right of amending it, or their revolutionary right to dismember or overthrow it." He concluded: "We are not enemies, but friends. We must not be enemies. . . . The mystic chords of memory . . . will yet swell the chorus of the Union, when again touched, as they surely will be, by the better angels of our nature."

1862

I. Civil Rights
Exploration and Settlement
Government
Statistics
Wars

An important milestone in settling the West was the signing of the Homestead Act on May 20 by Pres. Abraham Lincoln. This law gave 160 acres of public land to any person who was head of a household and 21 years of age or older, provided that the person settled on the land for five years and then paid a nominal fee. If settlers wished to acquire title earlier, they could do so after six months by paying $1.25 an acre. The law was a boon to the approximately 2,000,000 people who ultimately found new homes under it, but it was not the major contributor to the overall settlement of the West. Far greater acreage was available from other sources, particularly the railroads, which received enormous grants of good land as subsidies.

1862-1863: In **congressional elections,** the Republicans kept control of both houses of Congress with a 39–12 majority in the Senate and 103–80 majority in the House.

Feb 8: Union forces captured Roanoke Island, N.C. Gen. Henry A. Wise and his Confederate garrison of 2675 men were taken prisoner.

Mar 6-7: The Battle of **Pea Ridge,** Ark., was fought. A Confederate army of 16,000 under Gen. Earl Van Dorn attacked a Union army of 10,500 under Brig. Gen. Samuel Ryan Curtis, whose last reserves prevented a Union disaster on the second day. Among the heavy losses on both sides were two Confederate generals, Benjamin McCulloch and James McQueen McIntosh.

Mar 8: The **Confederate ironclad** *Virginia* destroyed two Union frigates at Hampton Roads, Va., sinking the *Cumberland* and setting the *Congress* on fire. The *Virginia* had been built from the raised hull of the Union ship *Merrimack*, which had been burned to the waterline when Union forces evacuated Norfolk Navy Yard in Apr. 1861.

Mar 9: In the **first battle between ironclad warships,** the Confederate ship *Virginia* and Union ironclad *Monitor* fought to a draw at Hampton Roads, Va., whereupon the *Virginia* retired, leaving the Union blockade intact. The crew of the *Monitor*, following

naval regulations, had been using only half charges in its two 12-inch guns.

Apr 6-7: The Battle of **Shiloh** was fought near Pittsburg Landing, Tenn. The Union army of Tennessee was commanded by Gen. Ulysses S. Grant, the Confederate army of Mississippi by Gen. Albert S. Johnston. Over 100,000 men were engaged, the largest number yet in the Western Hemisphere. Johnston was close to a brilliant victory on the first day, but it cost him his life. Grant, with timely reinforcements on the second day, turned the tide against Gen. P. G. T. Beauregard. Losses were severe on both sides, sobering Washington and Richmond and the public perception of the struggle.

May 1: Capt. David G. Farragut and Union forces took **possession of New Orleans** after running past Forts Jackson and St. Philip on the Mississippi R. at night and then defeating a small Confederate flotilla. Farragut was promoted to rear admiral in July.

May 11: The Confederate ironclad *Virginia* was destroyed by its crew on the evacuation of Norfolk, Va.

June 1: Gen. **Robert E. Lee** was appointed commander of the Confederate Army of Northern Virginia.

July: The **first black troops** were organized by Maj. Gen. David Hunter in the Union's First Carolina Regiment. Many of the soldiers were former slaves.

July 1: The **Seven Days Campaign** ended with the indecisive Battle of Malvern Hill (Va.). Gen. Lee had started the campaign with an attack on McClellan's Union army at Mechanicsville, Va., on June 26. The Confederates gradually pushed the timid McClellan back to the safety of his base on the James River. McClellan's Peninsular Campaign had failed and his army was withdrawn. Casualties for the week stood at Union, 15,849; Confederate, 20,141.

July 12: Congress authorized the **Medal of Honor** for noncommissioned Army officers and privates who exhibited supreme gallantry in action. This highest U.S. military decoration had been authorized for men of the Navy in 1861. In 1863 the award was extended to include commissioned officers.

Aug 9: In the Battle of **Cedar Mountain,** Va., near the Rappahannock R. northwest of Richmond, Confederate troops under Gen. Stonewall Jackson, planning a move northward in advance of Gen. Lee's larger forces, defeated two brigades of Union forces led by Gen. John Pope and Gen. N.P. Banks. Badly outnumbered, the Union army suffered 2381 killed or wounded, the Confederates, 1276.

Aug 29-30: At the second Battle of **Bull Run,** the maneuvers of Gen. Stonewall Jackson and his teamwork with Gen. Lee were too much for the 45,000 Union troops under Gen. John Pope, who broke and retreated to Washington, D.C. Union losses were 1724 killed, 8372 wounded, 5958 missing. Confederate losses stood at 1481 killed, 7627 wounded, 89 missing.

Sep 15: The Union arsenal at **Harpers Ferry, W. Va.,** was captured by Gen. Stonewall Jackson. A tremendous quantity of materiel was seized, and 12,500 men were captured. Harpers Ferry was abandoned and the captured troops set free by the Confederates on Sept. 20 and reoccupied by the North on the 22nd.

Sep 17: At the Battle of **Antietam** Creek near Sharpsburg in western Maryland, Gen. Lee's first invasion of the North was halted by Union troops under Gen. McClellan. This was the bloodiest one-day battle of the Civil War. Each side lost over 2000 killed and 9000 wounded.

Sep 22: A preliminary **Emancipation Proclamation** was issued by Pres. Lincoln. It was announced that on Jan. 1, 1863, slaves within all areas still in rebellion would be declared free forever.

Dec 13: The Battle of **Fredericksburg, Va.,** was a grave defeat for the North under Gen. Burnside. Gen. Lee's men killed or wounded 12,653 Union soldiers. Confederate casualties were 5300.

Dec 31: The Union ironclad *Monitor* sank in a gale off Cape Hatteras, N.C.

II. Architecture
Arts and Music
Popular Entertainment
Publishing
Theater

Typical of the style of humor favored by Americans of the period was that of Charles Farrar Browne, who wrote under the name of Artemus Ward. His writings began as newspaper columns in 1857, and in 1861 some of them were collected in *Artemus Ward, His Book.* Browne's column recounted the fictional adventures of Ward, a traveling carnival man. Ward's humor was based on naive sounding but shrewd comments on current events, with a great many misspellings that were considered amusing. Ward was an early influence on another writer, Samuel Langhorne Clemens, who began writing for the Virginia City, Nev., *Territorial Enterprise* this year. Clemens adopted the pseudonym Mark Twain in 1863.

An early romantic **western novel** set in the Rockies, *John Brent* by Theodore Winthrop, was published. The author, a Connecticut gentleman of leisure, had been killed in a Civil War skirmish in June 1861. That year saw the posthumous publication of Winthrop's novel *Cecil Dreeme,* about a young woman masquerading as a male artist in Washington Square, New York City. Another novel, *Edwin Bro-*

thertoft (1862), and two travel books followed *John Brent.* Winthrop's popularity lasted for a generation.

III. Business and Industry
Education
Philosophy and Religion
Science

What eventually proved to be a cornerstone of higher education, especially in its practical aspects, was the Morrill Act, signed July 2 by Pres. Abraham Lincoln. The law took its name from Rep. Justin Smith Morrill, Republican of Vermont, who had first introduced the bill in 1857. The law granted to each loyal state 30,000 acres of land for each senator and representative serving in Congress. The schools to be established on the land were to emphasize agriculture, home economics, engineering, and mechanical arts. These land-grant colleges still exist in most states.

John D. Rockefeller, 23 years old, invested in an oil refining business $4000 he had accumulated through a partnership in a produce commission house, Clark & Rockefeller. Five years later he was the major owner of Rockefeller, Andrews, and Flagler, the progenitor of Standard Oil Company of Ohio, incorporated in 1870.

Aerial reconnaissance for Union forces was carried out by American balloonist Thaddeus Lowe, who photographed Confederate ground emplacements around Richmond, Va., at an altitude of 1000 ft. This was the earliest use of cameras to provide panoramic shots of military positions.

Congress established the **Department of Agriculture** "to acquire and diffuse useful information." In its first years its annual budget was about $50,000. Previously agriculture had been handled by the Patent Office, since many patents pertained to farm machinery.

Nov 4: The **Gatling gun,** designed by Richard Jordan Gatling, was given a patent. Its chief feature, six barrels revolving around a central axis, permitted high rates of fire. It was not employed by Union forces until the siege of Petersburg, Va., in 1864–1865.

IV. Fashion
Folkways
Holidays
Social Issues and Crime
Sports

Strong emotions aroused by the war were reflected in the use of such epithets as *Copperhead.* The term was applied to northern Democrats who opposed the war and the Republican administration. The Copperheads were particularly strong in Ohio, Indiana, and Illinois. The name came from the Copperheads' custom of cutting the head of the goddess of liberty from copper pennies to wear in lapels; it also referred to the venomous snake. Some Republicans used the term to condemn the entire Democratic party as disloyal to the Union. The term probably first appeared in print in the Cincinnati *Gazette* on July 30, 1862.

Dec 29: Walt Whitman wrote from Washington, D.C., to tell his mother about his brother George, whom he had visited in camp. He had a hard time locating his brother's outfit, and his pocket had been picked while he was changing trains in Philadelphia. But he found George safe and promoted to captain of the 51st New York Volunteers, at Falmont, Va., near Fredericksburg. George Whitman was sharing a tent with a Capt. Francis, and Walt lived with them: "There were five of us altogether, to eat, sleep, write, etc., in a space twelve feet square. George is about building a place, half hut and half tent, for himself. Every captain has a tent, in which he lives, transacts company business . . . has a cook (or a man of all work) and in the same tent mess and sleep his lieutenants, and perhaps the first sergeant. They have a kind of fireplace—and the cook's fire is outside on the open ground. . . ."

1863

I. Civil Rights
Exploration and Settlement
Government
Statistics
Wars

On Jan. 1, 1863, Pres. Abraham Lincoln issued his Emancipation Proclamation, which in spite of its title neither freed all the slaves nor satisfied the abolitionists. The proclamation applied only to slaves in territory under control of the Confederacy. It did not apply to areas occupied by Union forces or to the four slave states that had not seceded (Delaware, Kentucky, Maryland, and Missouri). In effect, it freed the slaves where Lincoln could not enforce the proclamation, and left slavery intact where the slaves could have been freed. Lincoln had no intention of driving the loyal slave states into the Confederate camp. The proclamation enraged many southerners, who saw it as an attempt to spark a slave insurrection.

Free delivery of mail in cities was initiated by Congress. Rural free delivery (RFD) did not begin until 1896.

Feb 24: The **Territory of Arizona** was formed from the Territory of New Mexico. Its first capital was established at Fort Whipple in 1864.

Mar 3: The **Territory of Idaho** was carved from four existing territories: Washington, Utah, Dakota, and Nebraska. It included the later states of Montana and Wyoming.

Mar 3: A **conscription act,** first in the nation's history, was passed by Congress. It called for registration of all male citizens between 20 and 45 years of age and aliens in the same age bracket who had declared their intention of becoming citizens. Conscripts could be exempted from military service by payment of $300 or by providing a substitute.

May 1-4: At the Battle of **Chancellorsville,** 50 miles southwest of Washington, D.C., Gen. Robert E. Lee won his greatest victory over huge Union forces under Gen. Joseph Hooker. In the North, 17,275 were killed or wounded; in the South, 12,821. Gen. Stonewall Jackson, one of the wounded, died a few days later.

June 20: West Virginia was admitted to the Union, the 35th state.

July 1-3: At the Battle of **Gettysburg,** Gen. Lee made a desperate bid to smash through Union forces and approach Washington, D.C., from the west. Gen. George G. Meade met him accidentally at Gettysburg, Pa. Lee's assaults on federal positions brought heavy losses to both sides. On July 3, when the famous charge of Gen. George E. Pickett's division failed, with one unit leaving 3393 out of 4800 men dead or wounded on the field, the battle was lost to the South. On July 4 both sides were exhausted. On July 5 Lee's army retreated across the Potomac R., never to return to northern territory. The South suffered 30,000 killed, wounded, or missing; the North, 23,000.

July 4: At the Battle of **Vicksburg** a Confederate army under Gen. John C. Pemberton surrendered to Gen. Ulysses S. Grant after a campaign that had begun on Mar. 29. The South lost 8000 killed and wounded; and more than 29,000 surrendered. Union casualties were 8910. This loss of manpower and control of the Mississippi R., atop the loss at Gettysburg, doomed the Confederacy.

July 13-16: Antidraft riots broke out in New York City, and nearly 1000 persons were killed or wounded before federal troops restored order.

Sep 19-20: At the Battle of **Chickamauga,** Tenn., Union forces under Gen. William S. Rosecrans were defeated by troops under Gen. Braxton Bragg. Both sides, evenly matched, saw over a quarter of their men killed or wounded. Union forces retreated to Chattanooga, Tenn.

Nov 23-25: At the Battle of **Chattanooga, Tenn.,** Union reinforcements under Gen. Grant systematically captured Confederate positions around the city. The siege was broken and Confederate forces under Gen. Bragg fled to Dalton, Ga. Tennessee was no longer a battleground.

II. Architecture
Arts and Music
Popular Entertainment
Publishing
Theater

The Civil War continued to influence American literature. This year marked the appearance of a short novel that was destined to become a classic. *The Man Without a Country* by Edward Everett Hale, clergyman and author, first appeared anonymously in *Atlantic Monthly* in December. The story was inspired by a remark that had been made by Clement L. Vallandigham, leader of the northern antiwar Copperheads, in which he implied he did not care to live in a country that had Abraham Lincoln as president. In the story, Philip Nolan, charged with treason, declares that he never wants to hear of the U.S. again. He is sentenced to spend the rest of his life at sea, with all news of the U.S. withheld from him.

The first part of *Tales of a Wayside Inn,* stories in verse by Henry Wadsworth Longfellow, was published, demonstrating Longfellow's narrative skill. Using the convention of Chaucer and Boccaccio, he and six congenial acquaintances gather at an inn in Sudbury, Mass., and tell tales, including such favorites as "Paul Revere's Ride," "The Saga of King Olaf," "The Legend of Rabbi Ben Levi," and "The Birds of Killingworth."

Nov 19: The **Gettysburg Address** was delivered on the bloodstained battlefield at Gettysburg, Pa., by Pres. Abraham Lincoln, at ceremonies dedicating a national cemetery. The three brief paragraphs are marked by orderly thought, lucid expression, and a noble sense of the tragedy of the conflict.

III. Business and Industry
Education
Philosophy and Religion
Science

The Civil War increased the pace at which labor unions were organized. The war raised economic and social questions concerning free versus slave labor.

At the same time, the increase in the cost of living caused by the war brought agitation for higher wages. As a result, at least ten national unions were organized between 1863 and 1866. Among them was the first of the railroad brotherhoods, the Brotherhood of Locomotive Engineers, formed this year as the Brotherhood of the Footboard. Conductors organized in 1868, trainmen in 1873, and firemen in 1883.

Butterick paper clothes patterns began when Ebenezer Butterick, a tailor and shirtmaker of Sterling, Mass., received a patent. The first patterns were cut from stiff paper and limited to children's wear, but were immediately successful. By 1864 Butterick had an office at 192 Broadway, New York City, and was making his patterns of tissue paper. In 1871 he sold 6,000,000 patterns.

Mar 3: The **National Academy of Sciences** was founded in Washington, D.C., as a private nonprofit organization to promote science and investigate scientific problems for the government. Today it has about 1250 members.

Apr 14: A **continuous-roll printing press** was patented by William Bullock, who put a press of this type into operation in his Pittsburgh, Pa., printing plant. He turned to manufacture of the press as soon as the Civil War ended. This was the first printing press capable of printing on both sides of a sheet.

IV. Fashion
Folkways
Holidays
Social Issues and Crime
Sports

A new sport became available to Americans this year with the introduction of roller skating by James L. Plimpton. Plimpton invented the four-wheel skate, which worked on rubber pads, thus permitting skaters to change direction by shifting their weight to one side or the other without lifting the wheels of the skate off the ground. Roller skating became fashionable in New York City and soon spread to other cities. In Newport, R.I., the Roller Skating Association leased the Atlantic House and turned its dining hall and plaza into a skating rink. In Chicago, the Casino could accommodate 3000 spectators and 1000 skaters. In San Francisco, a rink advertised 5000 pairs of skates available for rent.

The first attempt at **base-stealing** in baseball history was made by Eddie Cuthbert of Philadelphia, Pa., when his team, the Keystones, played against the Brooklyn Atlantics.

Oct 3: Thanksgiving Day was proclaimed a national holiday by Pres. Lincoln, to be observed on the last Thursday in November. In 1939 Pres. Franklin D. Roosevelt moved Thanksgiving Day one week back to stimulate Christmas shopping. In 1941 Congress adopted a joint resolution confirming the fourth Thursday, not the last Thursday, as Thanksgiving Day.

1864

I. Civil Rights
Exploration and Settlement
Government
Statistics
Wars

A presidential election while the Civil War was being fought posed special problems. In the North there was considerable dissatisfaction with the progress being made in defeating the Confederacy, so Pres. Abraham Lincoln did not think his chances of reelection were good. The Democrats were split between those who supported the war and those who wanted peace at almost any price. The Democratic nominee was Gen. George B. McClellan, commander of the Union Army, who had let several opportunities for victory slip away. The Democratic platform called for peace through reunification of the states but did not say how this was to be done. Fortunately for Lincoln and the Republicans, several important military victories were won in time to influence the outcome.

1864-1865: In **congressional elections** the Republicans increased their majorities to 42–10 in the Senate and 149–42 in the House.

Feb 7: A **Union expedition to Florida** to return the state to Union allegiance entered Jacksonville under command of Gen. Truman Seymour.

Feb 20: At the Battle of **Olustee,** Fla., near Jacksonville, Union forces under Gen. Seymour were badly defeated by Confederate troops under Gen. Joseph Finegan. The Union lost some 2000 killed or wounded. The effort to set up a loyal state government was severely hampered in what was the largest land engagement in Florida.

Apr 17: The **exchange of prisoners of war** was discontinued by Gen. Grant. He stated that the practice served to prolong the conflict.

May 5-6: The Battle of the **Wilderness** ended indecisively as the armies of Robert E. Lee and Ulysses S. Grant wrought mutual destruction near Chancellorsville, Va. Because of thick forest growth, most of the fighting was done at close hand. Despite heavy Union losses, Grant's progress southward was only briefly halted.

May 11: James Ewell Brown "Jeb" Stuart, Confederate general and cavalry leader, was mortally wounded at Yellow Tavern, Va., where an inadequate Confederate force was attempting to block Gen. Philip H. Sheridan. Sheridan, with Gen. Grant's approval, was making his first independent cavalry action.

May 12: The heaviest action of the Battle of **Spotsylvania** began at dawn, when Gen. Winfield Scott Hancock, with 20,000 men, attacked a Confederate salient. Creating a gap, Hancock's men captured some 4000 men and 20 guns.

May 26: The **Territory of Montana** was formed by Congress from the Territory of Idaho.

June 3: At the Battle of **Cold Harbor,** Gen. Lee won his last victory over Union forces, numbering 108,000 against his 59,000. On this day federal troops lost 7000 men against 1500 for the Confederate troops. In an eight-minute period more men fell in an assault on entrenched Confederate troops than in any other like period of time. Between May 7 and June 3, federal losses were 50,000 men, Confederate 32,000. The North could replace its losses fully, but the South could not.

June 7: The **Republican National Convention nominated Pres. Lincoln** for a second term. Andrew Johnson of Tennessee was nominated for the vice presidency.

June 15-18: At the Battle of **Petersburg,** Va., Union forces were unable to take the strategic city in the face of brilliant strategy by Gen. Lee. Gen. Grant began a siege that continued until Apr. 1865.

June 19: The Confederate cruiser *Alabama* was sunk by the U.S.S. *Kearsarge* off Cherbourg, France, while trying to escape into the Atlantic. Fifteen thousand Frenchmen watched the battle from shoreline cliffs. In two years of roaming the Atlantic, the *Alabama* had destroyed or captured 69 vessels.

Aug 5-23: At the Battle of **Mobile Bay,** Ala., David G. Farragut commanded a fleet of fourteen wooden ships and four ironclads. Running through a minefield and past Confederate forts Gaines, Morgan, and Powell, Farragut's fleet defeated a Confederate flotilla, including the Confederate ironclad *Tennessee,* and took one of the South's last major ports. The city of Mobile was taken in 1865.

Aug 29: The **Democratic National Convention nominated Gen. George B. McClellan** for the presidency and George H. Pendleton of Ohio for the vice presidency. The party platform attacked Pres. Lincoln's prosecution of the war, calling his program a failure.

Sep 1: Atlanta, Ga., was evacuated by Confederate forces under Gen. John B. Hood. The next day the city was occupied by Union forces under Gen. William Tecumseh Sherman.

Oct 31: Nevada was admitted to the Union, the 36th state.

Nov 8: Abraham Lincoln was reelected president of the United States. Andrew Johnson of Tennessee was elected vice president. The electoral vote was Lincoln, 212; Gen. George B. McClellan, Democratic candidate, 21. The popular vote was Lincoln, 2,216,067; McClellan, 1,808,725.

Nov 16: Gen. **Sherman's march to the sea** with 62,000 men began. Leaving Atlanta, Ga., in flames and sweeping across a 60-mile front with little serious opposition, his army destroyed everything useful to the Confederates and ravaged the countryside. The South was cut in two. Gen. William J. Hardee and his remaining Confederate forces evacuated Savannah, Ga., on Dec. 21. Sherman occupied the city that day.

II. Architecture
Arts and Music
Popular Entertainment
Publishing
Theater

The Civil War created a large demand for statues of leading figures in the conflict. A sculptor who provided many such works was John Quincy Adams Ward. In 1861 Ward set up his studio in New York City. This year he completed what was perhaps his finest work, *Indian Hunter,* for New York City's Central Park. He completed this after a long trip among Indians in the West and Northwest. Ward later did other statues for Central Park and for several cities, including statues of Gen. William T. Sherman and Gen. George H. Thomas, as well as *Private of the Seventh Regiment.*

The Nasby Papers by Petroleum Vesuvius Nasby, pseudonym of the Ohio journalist David Ross Locke, was published. It was a collection of Locke's satiric "letters" to a newspaper by Nasby, an illiterate country preacher supposedly supporting the South but in effect caricaturing its positions. Pres. Abraham Lincoln enjoyed the Nasby letters, often reading them to his Cabinet and visitors.

III. Business and Industry
Education
Philosophy and Religion
Science

Efforts to educate the deaf, almost entirely the work of the Gallaudet family during the nineteenth century, were rewarded in 1864 when Congress authorized the granting of degrees by the new college division of the Columbia Institution for the Deaf, Dumb, and Blind, in Washington, D.C. The school was renamed Gallaudet College in 1894. Early in the century Thomas Hopkins Gallaudet had pioneered in the field. His eldest son, Thomas Gallaudet, was a clergyman who devoted almost all his time to missionary work among the deaf; he founded St. Ann's Church for Deaf-Mutes in New York City. The youngest son, Edward Miner Gallaudet, had opened the Washington school about 1857. It remains the only liberal arts college in the world for the deaf.

Feb 17: The **first successful submarine attack** was made by the Confederate vessel *Hunley,* which sank the federal sloop *Housatonic* while it was blockading Charleston, S.C. In 1863 the Confederate submarine *David* had damaged the federal ship *Ironsides.* Both the *Hunley* and the *David* were lost in these engagements.

June 30: A new **Internal Revenue Act** was passed by Congress. It increased taxes on many items, including tobacco, and introduced a second income tax. The tax rate was 5% on incomes between $600 and $10,000 and 10% on incomes over $10,000.

IV. Fashion
Folkways
Holidays
Social Issues and Crime
Sports

In the early days of baseball there was a rule against paying players. However, by 1864 the rule had been stretched or broken a number of times. At least as early as 1860 the Brooklyn Excelsiors reputedly paid Jim Creighton (under the table, of course), although Albert J. "Al" Reach is often cited as the first professional baseball player. He accepted money in 1864 to leave the Brooklyn Eckfords for the Philadelphia Athletics. Reach later became a prominent manufacturer of sporting goods.

The motto **"In God We Trust"** appeared on a coin for the first time, on the 1864 two-cent piece.

A **new political expression** was coined by Pres. Lincoln in his campaign of 1864 when he observed, " . . . it was not best to swap horses while crossing the stream, and . . . I am not so poor a horse that they might not make a botch of it in trying to swap."

The **first curve ball** by a baseball pitcher was thrown by William A. "Candy" Cummings of the Brooklyn Stars. He was pitching against the Brooklyn Atlantics. Skeptics thought it was an optical illusion.

May 11: "**I propose to fight it out on this line if it takes all summer**" was said by Gen. Ulysses S. Grant during the Spotsylvania campaign, reflecting the Union general's determination to take Richmond, Va., and win the war, despite the heavy losses he would suffer.

Aug 5: Adm. David G. Farragut exclaimed, "**Damn the torpedoes! Full speed ahead**" when the lead ship of his flotilla, the *Tecumseh*, struck a mine, then called a torpedo, and sank at the entrance to Mobile Bay. The federal fleet ran the minefield and the forts at the entrance and captured the small Confederate flotilla in the harbor.

1865

I. Civil Rights
Exploration and Settlement
Government
Statistics
Wars

The Civil War was scarcely over before Pres. Abraham Lincoln was assassinated, the first president to be killed. The assassin struck as Lincoln watched a comedy, *Our American Cousin*, at Ford's Theater in Washington, D.C., on the evening of Apr. 14. He died at 7:22 A.M. the next day. The assassin, John Wilkes Booth, an actor and Confederate sympathizer, escaped from Washington but broke his leg jumping from the president's box to the stage. He was cornered in a barn near Bowling Green, Va., on Apr. 26 and shot to death. Of the nine persons charged with the conspiracy, four were hanged and four were jailed. Dr. Samuel A. Mudd, the physician who, not recognizing Booth, set his broken leg, was sentenced to life imprisonment but was pardoned in 1869.

Jan 15: Fort Fisher, N.C., fell to Union forces under a joint sea and land assault. Some 2000 soldiers were captured, including Maj. Gen. William H.C. Whiting, mortally wounded. This engagement gave the federals control of Cape Fear R. Wilmington, the last Confederate port, was now closed.

Feb 17: Columbia, S.C., was set afire while being entered by federal troops under Gen. William Tecumseh Sherman. Bales of cotton were put to the torch, perhaps by Confederates to prevent their falling into federal hands. Strong winds scattered the burning cotton across most of the city.

Mar 2: Gen. Lee asked Gen. Grant for a conference to iron out differences between North and South. Pres. Lincoln rejected the proposal, demanding the surrender of the Confederates before such negotiations could take place.

Mar 3: The **Freedmen's Bureau was created by Congress** to help the destitute but free blacks of the South. In 1866 Congress greatly extended the bureau's power, over Pres. Andrew Johnson's veto. The first bureau commissioner was Union Gen. Oliver O. Howard, who later founded Howard University in Washington, D.C.

Mar 4: Pres. **Lincoln was inaugurated** for his second term. Sen. Andrew Johnson, Republican of Tennessee, succeeded Hannibal Hamlin as vice president.

Mar 25: At the Union siege of **Petersburg,** Va., Gen. Lee made a desperate attempt to break through the Union line at its weakest point, Ft. Stedman, east of the city. Despite initial success the Confederates were beaten back. Losses on both sides were heavy.

Apr 2: The **evacuation of Richmond** was urged by Gen. Lee, who informed Confederate Pres. Davis that he himself must withdraw from Petersburg, Va. Davis left the city that night with his cabinet, retreating to Danville. The now small Confederate army began evacuation of Petersburg.

Apr 3: Union forces occupied Petersburg, Va., one day after the Confederate evacuation. Lee's forces moved south but were blocked by Union units.

Apr 9: At **Appomattox** Court House, Va., Gen. Lee surrendered to Gen. Grant. The Civil War was virtually ended.

Apr 14: Pres. **Lincoln was shot** by John Wilkes Booth at Ford's Theater in Washington, D.C. He died the following morning.

Apr 15: Vice Pres. **Andrew Johnson was sworn in** as 17th president of the United States. He completed Lincoln's term.

Apr 26: Gen. **Joseph E. Johnston surrendered** the Confederate Army of Tennessee to Gen. Sherman near Durham Station, N.C.

Apr 26: John Wilkes Booth was hunted down by military police in a barn near Fort Royal, Va. The barn was set afire, and Booth was mortally wounded, possibly by his own hand.

May 10: Jefferson Davis was captured at Irwinville, Ga., by a contingent of Gen. James H. Wilson's cavalry, led by Lt. Col. Benjamin Pritchard.

May 29: Pres. Johnson issued a **proclamation of amnesty,** specifying classes of persons who must make application for pardon. A second proclamation looked toward establishment of a loyal government in North Carolina, with the state to determine the voting rules.

Aug 14: Mississippi overturned its secession ordinance of 1861 at a state convention that also abolished slavery in the state.

Nov 9: North Carolina overturned its secession ordinance, prohibited slavery, and elected representatives to the U.S. Congress. The state was readmitted to the Union in 1868.

Dec 2: Adoption of the **Thirteenth Amendment,** prohibiting slavery, became a certainty when Alabama became the 27th state to ratify it, raising state ratifications to the necessary two-thirds. The declaration of ratification was issued on Dec. 18.

II. Architecture
Arts and Music
Popular Entertainment
Publishing
Theater

The end of the Civil War was marked by an outpouring of war-related writings: poetry commemorating the dead, accounts of wartime experiences, and reflections on its causes and consequences. One of the first and best of the war poems was James Russell Lowell's "Ode Recited at the Commemoration to the Living and Dead Soldiers of Harvard University," read on July 21, 1865. It was first privately printed and did not attract much attention until it appeared in the Sept. 1865 *Atlantic Monthly*. Lowell, who had lost three nephews in the war, portrayed Abraham Lincoln as the symbol of the courageous warrior. During the war Lowell had written two series of verses, *The Biglow Papers*, for the *Atlantic*. These were published in book form in 1867. They strongly supported the Union and criticized England for its unfriendly attitude toward the North.

The popular children's story *Hans Brinker; or The Silver Skates* by Mary Mapes Dodge, begun as a serial, quickly became a best seller.

Josh Billings, His Sayings by Henry Wheeler Shaw, rural apostle of horse sense, was published with the assistance of Charles Farrar Browne (Artemus Ward). Shaw's aphorisms, in the semiliterate vernacular, delighted the public and earned him the title of "Aesop and Ben Franklin condensed and abridged." Typical of his aphorisms is the following: "The muel iz haf hoss and haf Jackass, and then kums tu a full stop, natur diskovering her mistake."

Walt Whitman's *Drum-Taps* drew on the poet's experience as a nurse in Washington, D.C., during the Civil War. Later incorporated into Whitman's ever-expanding *Leaves of Grass*, this volume included such favorites as "Pioneers! O Pioneers!" and "Beat! Beat! Drums." A supplement published after Lincoln's death contained "O Captain! My Captain!" and "When Lilacs Last in the Dooryard Bloom'd."

Winslow Homer's *Prisoners from the Front* presented a series of paintings depicting the plight of men at the front during the Civil War. Homer, now 25, had been engaged by *Harper's Weekly* as a special correspondent and artist.

Nov 18: Mark Twain (Samuel Langhorne Clemens) was catapulted to fame when his version of a California tall tale, "Jim Smiley and His Jumping Frog," was printed in the New York *Saturday Press*. It was quickly reprinted by major newspapers across the country. It is now known under the title "The Celebrated Jumping Frog of Calaveras County."

III. Business and Industry
Education
Philosophy and Religion
Science

Women were slowly being accepted in the professions and the sciences. Among them was Maria Mitchell, an astronomer. She discovered a comet in 1847. In 1865 she became the first woman professor of astronomy in the U.S., being appointed to a chair at Vassar College. Mitchell was noted especially for her studies of satellites, nebulas, and sunspots. She was the first woman to be elected to the American Academy of Arts and Sciences. Her reputation in the U.S. and abroad was a significant reflection of the rising reputation of Vassar.

Free delivery of mail was provided in all cities with populations of 50,000 or more.

Louis Agassiz began a 19-month expedition with his wife and six assistants to study the natural history of Brazil and add to his collection of specimens. Agassiz, who had become a naturalized American citizen, began his career at the University of Munich where, at 21, he published *The Fishes of Brazil* (1829), the most important work yet published in ichthyology. The study was based on a collection brought back to Germany by an expedition to Brazil in 1821. Agassiz always cherished the ambition to see the natural life of Brazil firsthand. The trip was financed primarily by Nathaniel Thayer of Boston, but other people, organizations, and government officials in the U.S. and Brazil also lent support. *A Journey to Brazil*, by Mrs.

Agassiz, published in 1868, recounted the day-to-day experiences of the expedition.

IV. Fashion
Folkways
Holidays
Social Issues and Crime
Sports

Beards were fashionable at this time. Scarcely a picture exists of a Civil War general on either side who did not sport one. All presidents from Ulysses S. Grant (elected in 1868) to Chester A. Arthur had beards. Pres. Grover Cleveland (elected in 1884) broke the custom, although he had a large, drooping mustache. Men's clothing continued to be plain and conservative. Collars, cravats, and waistcoats were worn regardless of the weather, although some men were beginning to wear white linen or seersucker suits in summer.

Clara Barton was placed in charge of a government-sponsored search for missing soldiers of the Civil War. During the war, as a personal enterprise, she had obtained and distributed hospital supplies for Union troops. Her distribution agency often delivered supplies right at the front.

The popular **Stetson hat** had its origin this year when John Batterson Stetson opened a one-man hat factory in Philadelphia, Pa. Stetson, the son of a hatmaker, had previously attempted to establish himself in the business, but ill health had forced him to travel to Illinois, Missouri, and Colorado. During his travels he had noticed the style of hat favored by westerners and, after a slow start in Philadelphia, he began to design new hats based on the western styles. His business began to expand rapidly. By 1906 he employed 3500 workers and was selling 2,000,000 hats a year. The Stetson hat had a broad brim and its crown was tall enough to sport ten ornamental braids, known as galloons. It was the mispronunciation of the word *galloon* that gave the world the term *ten-gallon hat.*

Mar 4: Pres. **Lincoln's second inaugural address** brought tears to the eyes of many in the audience. It was a silent audience, befitting an occasion made even more solemn by Lincoln's words. The war was not over, but there was room for hope, if not certainty. Lincoln began by saying that the occasion did not call for an extended address, such as the one delivered at his first inaugural. The audience was as familiar as he with the progress of the war. Lincoln asked his listeners to relive with him the forebodings of four years before, when both sides were rushing toward war, though "neither party expected the magnitude or duration which it has already attained. Nei-

ther anticipated that the cause of the conflict might cease before the conflict itself should cease. Each looked for an easier triumph and a result less fundamental and astonishing. Both read the same Bible and pray to the same God. Each invokes His aid against the other. It may seem strange that any man should dare to ask a just God's assistance in wringing bread from the sweat of other men's faces; but let us judge not, that we be not judged." He expressed the common hope that the war would soon end, and bade his hearers to continue what they had begun: "With malice toward none, with charity for all, with firmness in the right, as God gives us to see the right, let us strive on to finish the work we are in, to bind up the nation's wounds, to care for him who shall have borne the battle, and for his widow and orphans; to do all which may achieve and cherish a just and lasting peace among ourselves and with all nations." The address was not followed by any demonstration, either public or personal, to indicate to Lincoln whether it had been effective. He felt himself that it was among the best he had ever delivered, and he expressed this sentiment in a letter to Thurlow Weed, thanking Weed for a few words of congratulation.

May 5: The **first railroad train robbery** took place at dawn at North Bend, Ohio, when an Ohio & Mississippi Railroad train was derailed by a gang. Male passengers were robbed and the express car looted.

Dec 24: The **Ku Klux Klan** had its beginning in the law office of Thomas M. Jones in Pulaski, Tenn. The name evolved from Greek *kyklos* (circle), suggested by John B. Kennedy. It was broken up into the more euphonious Ku Klux by James R. Crowe, who added Klan as a reflection of the predominantly Scotch-Irish population of the area.

1866

I. Civil Rights
Exploration and Settlement
Government
Statistics
Wars

Reconstruction, the process of dealing with the former Confederate states and the millions of freed black slaves, was to occupy the government and the nation for the next decade. Pres. Andrew Johnson proposed fairly lenient treatment of the secessionists but showed no interest in securing civil rights for blacks. Opposing him was a group of radical Republicans who wanted the South severely punished. The congressional election in the fall gave the radicals an overwhelming victory that paved the way for harsh treatment of the South.

A **cholera** epidemic decimated many U.S. cities. About 200 a day died in St. Louis, Mo., during the height of the epidemic.

1866-1867: In **congressional elections** the Republicans held a Senate majority of 42–11, the Democrats gaining one seat. In the House the Republican majority was 143–49.

Feb 19: The **New Freedmen's Bureau bill** was passed by Congress. The law authorized military trials for those accused of depriving newly freed blacks of their civil rights. Pres. Andrew Johnson vetoed the bill on the grounds that it violated the Fifth Amendment, and that the legislation affected 11 southern states not represented in Congress. The veto served to widen the rift between Congress and the president. Legislators retaliated by overriding the veto on July 16.

Apr 2: The **state of insurrection** was declared over by presidential proclamation in Georgia, South Carolina, Virginia, North Carolina, Tennessee, Alabama, Mississippi, Louisiana, Arkansas, and Florida. On Aug. 2 the president announced that the insurrection was at an end in Texas, and that civil authority existed in the U.S.

Apr 9: A **Civil Rights Act** was passed over Pres. Johnson's veto. It granted citizenship to all persons born in the U.S., except Indians. It declared that all citizens had the same civil rights and provided for the punishment of persons who prevented free exercise of these rights. The Fourteenth Amendment was proposed when the constitutionality of the first section of this act was questioned.

II. Architecture
Arts and Music
Popular Entertainment
Publishing
Theater

Southern writers of the war and postwar period tended to idealize both the recent and the colonial past, perhaps to compensate for loss of the struggle for secession. One such writer was John Esten Cooke, a Virginian who had served as a captain in the Confederate army. This year Cooke began a series of wartime romances with the publication of *Surry of Eagle's Nest.* The series continued with *Hilt to Hilt* (1869), *Mohun* (1869), and *Hammer and Rapier*

(1871). Cooke's writing showed sentimentality, but he achieved his aim: to entertain. Cooke also wrote *Life of Stonewall Jackson* (1863) and *Life of General Robert E. Lee* (1871).

Among the **books published** this year was *Snow-Bound,* the most famous poem by John Greenleaf Whittier. Drawing on his memories of youth and home life in rural New England, Whittier painted an inviting picture of a homestead buried in snow. The poem described the blazing hearth, the family members, the sparkling snowbanks, the schoolmaster, etc. Other books published this year included *Surry of Eagle's Nest* by John Esten Cooke, which harked back to the chivalry of antebellum Virginia and evoked vivid pictures of southern leaders and Civil War battles; and *Venetian Life* by William Dean Howells, who served as U.S. consul to Venice throughout the Civil War and described his impressions of the city, its life and literature.

III. Business and Industry
Education
Philosophy and Religion
Science

The steadily growing movement to promote animal welfare scored a major victory this year with the founding on Apr. 10 of the American Society for the Prevention of Cruelty to Animals. It was patterned after the Royal Society for the Prevention of Cruelty to Animals in England, which had been founded in 1824. The founder and first president of the ASPCA was the philanthropist Henry Bergh. Its purpose was to shelter homeless animals, help enforce game laws, and guide farmers in caring for livestock.

Apr 1: **Western Union,** with capital of about $40,000,000, absorbed the U.S. Telegraph Company, with $6,000,000 worth of shares. This was on the tenth anniversary of the day that Western Union was named. The absorption of U.S. Telegraph made Western Union the first complete monopoly serving all parts of the country with uniform rates.

July 27: Final laying of the **Atlantic cable** between Great Britain and the U.S. was completed when the steamship *Great Eastern* reached the U.S. The final cable-laying voyage of the *Great Eastern* took two weeks, July 13 to July 27. The previous year the steamship had attempted to complete the laying of the cable, only to have it break in mid-ocean. Success came after 12 years of effort. Cyrus Field chartered his company on May 6, 1854, with Peter Cooper, Moses Taylor, Marshall Roberts, and Chandler White on the board of directors. Six hundred men worked on the first line, which had to be cut at sea because of a gale. Seven more efforts were needed before the cable was completed. A cable laid in 1858 was able to carry a message, but was probably badly insulated, and went out after three weeks of operation.

IV. Fashion
Folkways
Holidays
Social Issues and Crime
Sports

A lighter and more daring form of entertainment heralded the coming of what was to be known as burlesque. The first long-running musical show on Broadway, combining melodrama and ballet in a lavish production, was *The Black Crook,* which opened on Sept. 12 at Niblo's Garden and ran for 474 performances. Some considered it immoral because of its 50 lightly clad dancing girls. Even more daring was *British Blondes,* imported from England two years later. It played around the country for 20 years.

The expression "**Forty acres and a mule**" gained currency during the Reconstruction period. Many freed blacks had their hopes built up by the promise that Congress would divide southern estates and distribute acreage to each freed slave. The expression came to characterize vain expectations foisted on blacks by Reconstructionists.

1867

I. Civil Rights
Exploration and Settlement
Government
Statistics
Wars

Purchase of Alaska, 586,400 sq. mi. of almost unknown land in the far northwest of North America, added an unusual chapter to the story of the expansion of the U.S. On Mar. 30, 1867, Sec. of State William Henry Seward concluded negotiations with Russia whereby the U.S. agreed to pay $7,200,000, about two cents an acre, for the territory. The Senate ratified the purchase on Apr. 9, and ownership was transferred on Oct. 18. Alaska was known to be rich in furs and fish, but otherwise it seemed useless. It was many years before the natural riches of Alaska were appreciated and Americans began to settle it as a new frontier.

Jan 8: Suffrage was given to blacks in Washington, D.C., by a bill passed over Pres. Andrew Johnson's veto.

Mar 1: Nebraska was admitted as a state, the 37th to join the Union.

Mar 2: The **first Reconstruction Act** was passed by Congress over Pres. Johnson's veto. The bill imposed martial law on the southern states, which were split into five districts, and provided for the restoration of civil government as soon as the states were restored into the Union and passed the Fourteenth Amendment.

Mar 2: The **Tenure of Office Act** was passed. In substance, it denied power to the president to remove officials who had been appointed by and with the consent of the Senate. This act was ruled unconstitutional by the Court of Claims in 1926 in the case of *Myers v. U.S.*

Mar 23: The **second Reconstruction Act** was passed over Pres. Johnson's veto. It provided for the registration of all qualified voters, who were subsequently to decide on readmittance to the Union.

July 19: The **third Reconstruction Act** was passed over Pres. Johnson's veto. The bill was essentially a restatement of the two previous acts except for the added provision that the Fifteenth Amendment must be ratified before the southern states could be admitted to the Union.

II. Architecture
Arts and Music
Popular Entertainment
Publishing
Theater

In keeping with the spirit of the times were the novels of Horatio Alger, Jr. The mid-nineteenth century was an age when many proclaimed the virtues of the self-made man. Alger's books gave the formula for success. His first of the Ragged Dick series appeared in 1867. Like all those to come, it preached hard work and resistance to temptation as the road to wealth and renown. In most of the books, though, the young hero first gets a break by catching the eye of a well-to-do patron, perhaps by rescuing his pretty daughter from a runaway horse. Alger followed with the Luck and Pluck series (1869) and Tattered Tom tales (1871). These stories found a ready market in the steady wave of boys moving from farms or small towns to the cities to seek work. More than 20,000,000 copies of Alger's novels were sold.

Dec 2: Charles Dickens gave his first reading in a theater in New York City. This was his second visit to the U.S. Before the box office opened, people were standing in two lines, almost a mile long, waiting for tickets. Scalpers were asking $20 for a ticket. Thirty-one different editions of Dickens's collected works were published in 1867.

III. Business and Industry
Education
Philosophy and Religion
Science

The first organization of American farmers was founded in 1867 when Oliver H. Kelley, a Minnesota farmer and an employee of the Bureau of Agriculture in Washington, D.C., established the National Grange of the Patrons of Husbandry. The Grange movement had a slow start, but it greatly expanded as a result of the panic of 1873 and reached a membership peak of 858,000 in 1875. The Grange began as a social and educational organization but soon became involved in politics. Its main targets were the railroads and the owners of grain storage elevators who, the Grange claimed, charged exorbitant prices for their services. As a result of pressure from the Grange, some midwestern states passed laws to limit such rates.

The **eight-hour day,** a main goal of labor unions, was enacted in Illinois, New York, and Missouri, but it was not enforced.

A major **contribution to education** in the postwar South was made by George Peabody with a fund of $3,500,000. The Peabody fund hastened construction of town and city schools and provided for the training of teachers.

Cigarettes began to appear in America. Cigarette production had formerly been confined to Europe. Production in America did not provide a major source of revenue until the 1880s.

The **first elevated railroad** in America began operation in New York City. Built by the West Side Elevated Railroad Company, its single track ran from Battery Place through Greenwich St. and 9th Ave. to 30th St.

IV. Fashion
Folkways
Holidays
Social Issues and Crime
Sports

Life in the mining towns of the far West was boisterous and extravagant. The height of fun and games was achieved in Virginia City, Nev., site of the fabulous Comstock Lode, in the period from 1860 to 1880. The town had more than 100 saloons, five legitimate theaters, six variety houses, and other establishments such as dance halls. The single most popular performer was Adah Isaacs Menken, known for performing while clad only in a flimsy gown.

The phrase **Seward's folly** was coined to characterize the purchase of Alaska from Russia. The purchase was negotiated by Sec. of State William Henry Seward. Alaska was also ridiculed as *Seward's icebox.*

"Now is the time for all good men to come to the aid of the party," a slogan created by Charles Weller, a court reporter, was used to test the efficiency of the first practical typewriter, invented by his friend, Christopher Sholes.

June 19: The **first annual Belmont Stakes** was won by Ruthless, with a time of 3:05. The jockey was J. Gilpatrick. The race was held at Jerome Park, N.Y., from 1867 to 1889; at Morris Park, N.Y., from 1890 to 1905; and at Belmont Park, N.Y., from 1906 to the present. In the beginning the distance was $1\frac{5}{8}$ miles, but it has been changed from time to time. The Belmont Stakes is the oldest of the three classic American races.

1868

I. Civil Rights
Exploration and Settlement
Government
Statistics
Wars

For the first time in the nation's history a president was impeached. Pres. Andrew Johnson was accused by Congress of having violated the Tenure of Office Act of 1867, which forbade the president to discharge any federal officeholder appointed "by and with the consent of the Senate." Johnson tested the act by removing Sec. of War Edwin M. Stanton on Feb. 21. The impeachment was brought largely because the radical Republicans bitterly opposed Johnson's plans for Reconstruction. Johnson's firing of Stanton gave them the opportunity they had been seeking. On Feb. 24 the House of Representatives voted to impeach. The trial, conducted by the Senate, began on Mar. 13. On May 16 and again on May 26 the Senate voted on the charges brought against Pres. Johnson. Both times the vote was 35 for conviction and 19 for acquittal. Because a two-thirds vote was needed to convict, Johnson was judged not guilty. The radicals then dropped the matter.

Susan B. Anthony founded the suffragette newspaper *The Revolution*. It adopted the motto "The true Republic—men, their rights and nothing more; women, their rights and nothing less."

The **Ku Klux Klan** formulated its revised constitution, which declared that the organization was to be guided by chivalry, humanity, mercy, and patriotism. The southern states were to be its empire, with the grand wizard as supreme leader and its body of officers designated as "ghouls." In reality, the order was formed to intimidate blacks and carpetbaggers and to regain white supremacy in the South.

1868-1869: In **congressional elections** the Republicans kept majorities in both houses: 56–11 in the Senate and 149–63 in the House.

Mar 11: The **fourth Reconstruction Act** was passed. Under its provisions a majority of the votes actually cast would decide the adoption or rejection of a state constitution (the second Reconstruction Act required a majority of the registered voters). The measure was taken to counter the intimidation of black voters by the Ku Klux Klan and disenfranchised whites.

May 20-21: The **Republican National Convention** nominated Gen. Ulysses S. Grant for the presidency and Schuyler Colfax of Indiana for the vice presidency. At the same meeting, the convention adopted the name National Republican Party.

June 25: Congress passed a law providing an **eight-hour day** for laborers and workmen employed by the government. The concept of the eight-hour day was still something of a novelty, although ineffectual eight-hour laws had already been passed in a few states.

June 25: Congressional representation was granted to North Carolina, South Carolina, Louisiana, Georgia, Alabama, and Florida by an omnibus bill passed over Pres. Johnson's veto.

July 4-9: The **Democratic National Convention** nominated Horatio Seymour of New York for the presidency and Francis P. Blair, Jr., of Missouri for the vice presidency.

July 28: The **Fourteenth Amendment,** which granted citizenship to all those born or naturalized in the U.S., notably slaves freed by the Civil War, was adopted. It also validated debts incurred during the Civil War but denied federal or state responsibility for any debts incurred in aid of conspiracy or insurrection against the U.S.

Oct 21: A severe **earthquake** rocked San Francisco, Calif., causing about $3,000,000 in property damage.

Nov 3: Ulysses S. Grant was elected president of the United States, defeating Horatio Seymour. Schuyler Colfax was elected vice president. Grant's popular majority was a scant 306,000 out of 5,715,000 votes, although his margin in the electoral college count was 214 to 80. The black vote, which totaled over 700,000, decided the election for Grant.

Dec 25: Unqualified **amnesty** was granted by presidential proclamation to all who participated in the "insurrection or rebellion" against the U.S.

II. Architecture
Arts and Music
Popular Entertainment
Publishing
Theater

The literary genre known as juvenile or children's literature received new vitality this year with publication of *Little Women* by Louisa May Alcott, daughter of A. Bronson Alcott. Up to this time, many of the books intended for children moralized to the extent that they did not entertain their readers. Miss Alcott's book, based on her own family experiences, was more realistic and less sentimental than most. The book became the most popular girls' story in American literature and has sold more than 2,000,000 copies. It earned its author about $200,000 by the time she died. Miss Alcott also wrote *Little Men* (1871), *Jo's Boys* (1886), and other books. Her writings brought financial security to her family, the head of which was well-intentioned but improvident. Miss Alcott greatly influenced the trend of juvenile literature by avoiding didacticism and by using characters drawn from life.

Hiram Powers completed his celebrated sculpture *Clytie*. Powers, who had settled in Florence, Italy, in 1837, was then enjoying great popularity, largely on the strength of such works as his statue of *Daniel Webster* (1859) in front of the Boston State House, as well as works in marble of other famous Americans, including John C. Calhoun, Andrew Jackson, and George Washington.

III. Business and Industry
Education
Philosophy and Religion
Science

As important as rail transportation had become, it still remained potentially dangerous for both passengers and freight. This year George Westinghouse solved a major problem with the invention of the air brake. This allowed equal and simultaneous braking, through one control, of each car in a train, and also provided for automatic braking if cars should accidentally uncouple or brake lines become disabled.

Westinghouse's system was first put to use on a train this year. It made possible the safe braking of both long trains and high-speed trains, paving the way for a revolution in rail travel.

The **open-hearth process** in the American steel industry was introduced from England by Abram S. Hewitt in Trenton, N.J. The process expanded steel production by making more ore available through the extraction of sulfur and phosphorus.

Jan 16: A patent for a **refrigerator car** was granted to William Davis, a fish dealer in Detroit, Mich. Davis, wanting to increase his area of sales, had worked for many years to develop his "ice box on wheels." He used his new invention for the transportation of fish and fruit. He also designed the first railroad refrigerated car, which was built in 1869.

June 23: Two patents for the **typewriter** were granted to Christopher Sholes, Samuel Soulé, and Carlos Glidden. For five years afterward, Sholes worked to complete his machine but did not succeed. In 1871 he received an additional patent for improvements he had made to his original invention. Two years later he sold his rights to the Remington Arms Company for $12,000. Remington mechanics quickly converted Sholes's crude machine into a marketable product. The Remington Company had an improved model by 1873. Sholes carried on with ideas for improvements and took out another patent in 1875, but finally turned all of his work over to Remington, which marketed the machine as the Remington typewriter.

IV. Fashion
Folkways
Holidays
Social Issues and Crime
Sports

Ice skating, which had begun a rise in popularity around the 1850s, had become a major winter pastime. Steel skates had first been made in the 1850s. They had straps and clamps to fasten them to shoes. In the 1860s Jackson Haines, an American, invented figure skating. By 1868 ice skating was so widespread that a skating congress was held in Pittsburgh to set regulations and encourage the sport. In a single winter some 200,000 skaters used the lakes in New York City's Central Park. In Boston daily excursion trains carried a thousand or more skaters to Jamaica Pond. One reason for the sport's popularity was that both sexes could participate, making skating a social as well as athletic occasion.

The new sport of **velocipeding** (cycling) attained great vogue in America three years after it had been perfected in Paris. Schools for all ages and both sexes were set up throughout the large cities. Newspapers reported on the vogue. The fact that women could participate added greatly to its rapid spread.

The **Benevolent Protective Order of Elks** was formed in New York City.

May 30: Decoration Day was celebrated nationally for the first time. The day was chosen by John A. Logan, national commander of the Grand Army of the Republic, for decoration of Civil War graves. Previously, local communities had held decoration days at various times.

Nov 11: The first indoor **amateur track and field meet** was held by the New York Athletic Club. The club, which had been organized Sept. 8, later held outdoor meets, established rules for the conduct of meets, and built the first cinder track. It continues to this day to promote track and field and other sports.

1869

I. Civil Rights
Exploration and Settlement
Government
Statistics
Wars

This year, Ulysses S. Grant was inaugurated 18th president of the United States. After a checkered career in and out of the Army, Grant began to rise in public esteem through his military exploits in the Civil War. Until 1862 it had seemed as though no Union commander was competent to win the war. By war's end Grant had become, after Abraham Lincoln, the leading figure in the Union war effort. Although Grant had had nothing to do with politics, the Republicans in 1868 were glad to nominate him, a certain winner, for the presidency. As it turned out, while Grant was honest and well-intentioned, he had almost none of the abilities required in a president and was fated to be the victim of dishonest friends and associates.

Arabella Mansfield was admitted to the Iowa bar as the **first woman lawyer** in the U.S. and the first woman lawyer in America since Mistress Margaret Brent, attorney for Cecilius Calvert, lord proprietor of Maryland in the 1640s.

Feb 6: The first caricature of **Uncle Sam** with chin whiskers appeared in *Harper's Weekly*. The figure had been used without whiskers by cartoonists for several years and had evolved from the Revolutionary caricature of Brother Jonathan. After 1869 Uncle Sam became a stock device of political cartoonists.

Apr 10: The **Fifteenth Amendment** was ratified by Georgia, Mississippi, Texas, and Virginia, and these states were then readmitted into the Union. This amendment states that suffrage shall not be denied or abridged because of race, color, or previous condition of servitude.

May 15: The **National Woman Suffrage Association** was formed. Elizabeth Cady Stanton was chosen as first president and held the post until 1890. The other chief founder of the association was Susan B. Anthony.

Sep 1: The **Prohibition Party** was organized during the National Prohibition Convention in Chicago. The convention was called by the National Temperance Convention in Cleveland.

Dec 10: The **first women's suffrage** in the U.S. was granted by Wyoming Territory.

II. Architecture
Arts and Music
Popular Entertainment
Publishing
Theater

Musical performances were becoming widely available, although many of those providing music for American audiences were born abroad. One of the most able and energetic among them was Theodore Thomas, who came from Germany in 1845 and organized his own orchestra in 1862. Every year from 1869 to 1878 he toured the U.S. with the orchestra, introducing to Americans major works by Franz Liszt, Richard Wagner, Johannes Brahms, and others.

Among **books published** this year was *Innocents Abroad* by Mark Twain, a collection of articles written by Twain during a tour of Europe and the Near East. The extremely popular and humorous book poked fun at Old World institutions and distorted historical facts. Also published this year was *Oldtown Folks* by Harriet Beecher Stowe. The series of sketches, which demonstrated admirable use of local color, was based on Mrs. Stowe's memories of Litchfield, Conn., and those of her husband. Her description of New England life contributed to the later success of Sarah Orne Jewett and Mary Wilkins Freeman.

III. Business and Industry
Education
Philosophy and Religion
Science

Higher education was undergoing changes in the U.S., particularly at Harvard College in Cambridge, Mass., where Charles W. Eliot was inaugurated president on Mar. 10. Eliot was the first non-clergyman to hold the post and was an administrator rather than a teacher. He changed Harvard from a small undergraduate college into a modern university. Eliot introduced the elective system, organized graduate schools, insisted on written exams, and relaxed student discipline. He greatly influenced higher education throughout the country.

Henry J. Heinz and L. C. Noble established a food-packing company at Sharpsburg, Pa. Its first product was grated horseradish. Heinz eventually had widespread commercial success.

Jan 23: The **first state bureau of labor** in the U.S. was organized in Massachusetts.

May 10: The **first transcontinental railroad** in the U.S. was completed at Promontory Point, Utah, with the linkup of the Central Pacific Railroad from the west and the Union Pacific Railroad from the east.

Sep 24: Black Friday, a day of financial panic on Wall Street caused by the manipulation of Jay Gould and James Fisk, ruined thousands of gold speculators. In an attempt to corner the gold market, Gould and Fisk tried to keep Pres. Grant from selling government gold, and assured the public that they had been successful. However, Grant ordered the sale of $4,000,000 in gold, forcing the price down.

IV. Fashion
Folkways
Holidays
Social Issues and Crime
Sports

Although boxing would not become a major American sport until the 1880s, when John L. Sullivan popularized it, an important bare knuckle boxing match was fought this year between Tom Allen, an English boxer who had moved to the U.S., and Mike McCoole, an American who claimed the U.S. title. Allen challenged McCoole and the two squared off in St. Louis on June 15. McCoole won the fight on a ninth-round foul and claimed the American championship. The following year Allen lost a bid for the international bare knuckle championship. Allen and McCoole met again in 1873 for a bout near St. Louis. Allen beat

McCoole, this time in seven rounds. McCoole quit the ring. Allen claimed the world championship but was whipped soundly in 1876 by the English fighter Joe Goss in a 27-round bout in Kentucky.

Mar 15: The **first professional baseball team** was the Cincinnati Red Stockings. The team announced regular payments to players and began a successful eight-month tour of the East and Middle West.

Nov 6: The **first intercollegiate football game** was played at New Brunswick, N.J. Rutgers beat Princeton 6–4 in a game more like soccer than football. There were 25 men on each team, and no running with the ball was allowed.

1870

I. Civil Rights
Exploration and Settlement
Government
Statistics
Wars

A short chapter in the history of American expansion ended this year in a personal defeat for Pres. Ulysses S. Grant. A group of land speculators interested Pres. Grant in a scheme to annex the Dominican Republic, which had gained independence from Spain in 1865. Ignoring the State Department and normal diplomatic procedure, Grant sent his private secretary, Orville E. Babcock, to negotiate a treaty of annexation. This treaty was submitted to the Senate on Jan. 10, and although Grant did his best to force its acceptance, the Senate rejected it on June 30.

The ninth U.S. **Census** recorded a population of 39,818,449. America's center of population was located 48 miles east by north of Cincinnati, Ohio.

1870-1871: In **congressional elections** the Democrats gained six seats in the Senate, but the Republicans still enjoyed a 52–17 majority, with five seats going to minor parties. In the House the Republicans lost 31 seats but still led 134–104, with five seats going to minor parties.

Jan 15: The first political cartoon to use the **donkey** as a symbol for the Democratic Party appeared in *Harper's Weekly*. The cartoon, by Thomas Nast, was called "A Live Jackass Kicking a Dead Lion."

Feb 25: The **first black in Congress**, Sen. Hiram R. Revels, Republican of Mississippi, took his seat. The first black member of the House was Joseph H. Rainey, Republican of South Carolina, who also entered Congress this year.

Mar 30: The **Fifteenth Amendment was adopted.** It stipulated that no state shall deprive any citizen of the right to vote because of race, color, or previous condition of servitude.

June 22: Congress passed an act to create the **Department of Justice** under direction of the attorney general. The department today supervises all government police, the FBI, and the Bureau of Prisons.

Dec: The first **impeachment** of a state governor in the U.S. was conducted against Gov. William Woods Holden, the highly unpopular "scalawag" governor of North Carolina. He was replaced by Gov. Tod R. Caldwell.

II. Architecture
Arts and Music
Popular Entertainment
Publishing
Theater

John La Farge, a talented author and artist, was a pioneer in the art of stained glass. His celebrated work *Battle Window*, in Memorial Hall at Harvard University, was installed in 1870. In 1876 he did the mural decorations for Trinity Church in Boston. La Farge also executed stained glass windows for churches in Buffalo, N.Y., and Worcester, Mass., and for the chapel of Columbia University in New York City. What is referred to as American glass is an outgrowth of his experimentation.

Among the **books published** this year was *The Story of a Bad Boy*, a favorite boys' book by Thomas Bailey Aldrich. Semiautobiographical, the book provided a fresh account of boyhood, eschewing the moralizing that characterized most juvenile fiction. Other books published this year included the *Rubáiyát* of Omar Khayyám, translated by Edward Fitzgerald, and *The Luck of Roaring Camp and Other Sketches* by Bret Harte, which catapulted the author to international fame.

Feb 14: **Frontier drama** burst on the stage with the popular *Kit the Arkansas Traveler* by Thomas Blades DeWalden. It was followed by *Horizon* (1871) by Augustin Daly, *Davy Crockett* (1872) by Frank Murdock, *The Gilded Age* (1874) by Mark Twain and Charles Dudley Warner, *The Two Men from Sandy Bar* (1876) by Bret Harte, and *The Danites in the Sierras* (1877) by Joaquin Miller.

III. Business and Industry
Education
Philosophy and Religion
Science

Formation of the Standard Oil Company this year marked the start of what was to become the biggest influence by far in the growing oil industry, and the first industrial combination to exercise a virtual monopoly. The moving spirit in the company was John D. Rockefeller, who had begun his career as a bookkeeper in Cleveland, Ohio, center of the oil refining industry at this time. Rockefeller and his partners, including his brother William, started with two refineries in Cleveland and a sales agency in New York City. From this modest beginning, Rockefeller set out to control not only the refining of oil but also its transportation from the oil fields and marketing of the finished product.

The **Great Atlantic and Pacific Tea Company** was organized "for the purpose of importing and distributing pure and reliable teas and coffees and subjecting the purchaser to but one profit from the foreign factor." The company grew into the largest single chain of grocery stores in the U.S. in terms of volume of business. The company's early advertising stressed that the chain could provide bargains by eliminating middlemen from grocery sales.

The **refrigerated railroad car** emerged in the 1870s as an important factor in the development of certain industries. Pioneer development of the refrigerated car is credited to Gustavus Franklin Swift, who in the 1870s began to ship dressed beef from Chicago to the East, the first time this was done successfully. He employed a railroad car in which fresh air was forced over ice and then circulated through the storage compartments. George Henry Hammond also pioneered at about this time in the use of refrigerated cars, shipping meat from Omaha, Nebr., and from Hammond, Ind.

The **growth of unions** in America was reflected in a total membership of 300,000.

Jan 2: Construction of the **Brooklyn Bridge** began. It was to span the East R. from Park Row, Manhattan, to Sands and Washington streets in Brooklyn.

Feb 9: The **U.S. Weather Bureau** was established by Congress. Originally part of the Signal Corps, it became part of the Department of Agriculture on July 1, 1891. On June 30, 1940, it was transferred to the Commerce Department.

IV. Fashion
Folkways
Holidays
Social Issues and Crime
Sports

The sporting year was marked by an important event in international yachting. For the first time since the U.S. won the America's Cup from England in 1851, a British yacht issued a challenge to win it back. Accordingly, on Aug. 8 in New York Bay, the *Cambria* sailed against 23 American boats of the New York Yacht Club. The winner was *Magic*, owned by Franklin Osgood. *Cambria* came in tenth. The bay was dotted with ships of all descriptions, and an estimated 100,000 people lined the shores to see the spectacle.

The craze for **roller skating** spread throughout the U.S. as it did throughout the world. By 1863 four rollers had been added to "parlor skates" and a young skater, William H. Fuller, developed the art of figure skating, which he displayed on a tour around the world.

The **first boardwalk** in America was completed at Atlantic City, N.J.

Yale and Harvard met in a **crew race** on a circular course at Worcester, Mass. Yale came in first but was disqualified for having run into the Harvard team.

Aug 16: Fred Goldsmith demonstrated that the **curve ball** was not an optical illusion. Before a large crowd at the Capitoline Grounds, Brooklyn, N.Y., Goldsmith set up three poles in a straight line and hurled a ball that went to the right of the first pole, to the left of the second, and to the right of the third.

1871

I. Civil Rights
Exploration and Settlement
Government
Statistics
Wars

One of the great disasters in American history occurred between Oct. 8 and Oct. 11, when Chicago was burned nearly to the ground. According to legend, the fire began when a cow belonging to a Mrs. O'Leary kicked over a lantern. In fact, the fire started in the barn of a laborer named Patrick O'Leary, who lived on DeKoven Street on the West Side. Before the fire was out, about 17,500 buildings had been destroyed over an area of 2124 acres, with damage estimated at about $200,000,000. Some 250 people were killed and about 98,500 left homeless. It was a tribute to the spirit of the city and the times that rebuilding began at once and recovery took a surprisingly short time. Lost to fire was the original draft of Pres. Abraham Lincoln's Emancipation Proclamation, destroyed when the Chicago Historical Society building burned.

Feb 28: A **federal election law** was passed, providing for federal supervision of elections in any city having more than 20,000 inhabitants. The measure was taken primarily to protect black voters in the South.

Mar 3: The **Indian Appropriation Act** was passed. It made all Indians national wards and nullified all Indian treaties.

Mar 4: Pres. Ulysses S. Grant established the **first civil service commission,** headed by George William Curtis of New York City. The unwillingness of Congress to make additional appropriations rendered the commission ineffective.

May 8: The **Treaty of Washington** was signed between the U.S. and Great Britain at Washington, D.C. It provided for arbitration for the *Alabama* claims by an international tribunal to meet at Geneva. These claims were for damages to U.S. shipping during the Civil War by the raider *Alabama* and other Confederate vessels built or armed by the British. The treaty also renewed Canadian-American fishing arrangements in the North Atlantic.

II. Architecture
Arts and Music
Popular Entertainment
Publishing
Theater

America had never lacked for nature writers and in the later nineteenth century the best was John Burroughs, who followed in the footsteps of Ralph Waldo Emerson and Henry David Thoreau. His first work, *Wake-Robin,* was published this year. The book was poetic in manner, as was *Birds and Poets* (1877). *Wake-Robin* was an invitation to ornithology and imparted the author's enthusiasm for bird watching. Burroughs' later writings paid more attention to scientific observation, although in his final years he believed that the salvation of society depended more on teachers, prophets, poets, and mystics than on science.

Among **books published** this year was the best seller *The Hoosier Schoolmaster* by Edward Eggleston. A classic of regional literature, Eggleston's novel sold some 500,000 copies, a circulation never reached by Eggleston's *The Circuit Rider* (1874) or *Roxy* (1878), considered better novels. Also published this year were *Their Wedding Journey,* the first novel of William Dean Howells, a combination of travelogue and novel of manners tracing the honeymoon journey of the Marches (who appear in later novels) to Niagara, Montreal, and Quebec; and *Passage to India,* a collection of poems by Walt Whitman that reflected a broadening of the poet's scope and subject matter. In the 72 poems, Whitman's artistic powers embraced peoples of all lands.

Probably the **best-known painting** by an American, popularly known as *Whistler's Mother,* was exhibited by James McNeill Whistler at the Pennsylvania Academy of Fine Arts. It was entitled *Arrangement in Grey and Black.* Whistler remarked relative to the title that no one would have an interest in the identity of the sitter. Actually millions since have identified the canvas with their feelings for their own mothers.

III. Business and Industry
Education
Philosophy and Religion
Science

As communication and transportation improved, and as the U.S. came to be more concerned with events on other continents, an interest in religions other than Christianity was aroused. The outstanding scholar in this field was James Freeman Clarke, a Unitarian clergyman and liberal reformer. His *Ten Great Religions* (2 volumes, 1871–1883) was an important work in comparative religion. It went through 21 editions by 1886.

May 1: The **Legal Tender Act** was declared constitutional by a Supreme Court decision in the case of *Knox v. Lee.* Passed in 1862, when national credit was ebbing, the Legal Tender Act had authorized issuance of $450,000,000 in treasury notes, making them legal tender for all private debts and public dues except import duties and interest on public debt. A second act was passed in 1863. The Supreme Court, reduced to seven members, declared the Legal Tender Acts unconstitutional on Feb. 7, 1870, in the case of *Hepburn v. Griswold,* on the grounds that they exceeded any delegated or implied powers of Congress, violated the spirit of the Constitution, and deprived creditors of property without due process of law. Pres. Ulysses S. Grant made nominations to the empty Supreme Court posts on the same day the decision was handed down; four days later the Supreme Court voted to reargue the issues. The decision of May 1, 1871, found the power to issue legal tender implied in the power to coin money and wage war. It also declared that the Constitution forbade the states, but not Congress, from impairing contracts. Whether Pres. Grant actually packed the Court is still argued among historians.

IV. Fashion
   Folkways
   Holidays
   Social Issues and Crime
   Sports

An American type still popular in song, story, and movies is the cowboy of the western cattle country. He flourished from the late 1860s to the late 1880s, when cattle were driven long distances to market. The cowboy's heyday was brief; it was ended by the spread of railroad lines and by the fencing in of ranges and farms. The cowboy's life was not glamorous. It meant hard work, danger, and low pay. After a drive he would frequently spend all his pay in the saloons of such cow towns as Abilene, Kans. Between 1867 and 1871 cowboys drove 1,460,000 cattle into Abilene, the first of the famous western railheads.

Mar 17: The **first professional baseball asssociation,** the National Association of Professional Baseball Players, was organized. It replaced the amateur National Association.

1872

I. Civil Rights
   Exploration and Settlement
   Government
   Statistics
   Wars

The presidential election campaign of 1872 was a strange one. As a result of the scandals in Pres. Ulysses S. Grant's administration, and because Grant sided with the radical Republicans in Reconstruction policies, many Republicans, liberals, and reformers split off to nominate their own candidate, Horace Greeley, editor of the New York *Tribune.* Greeley had been a leading figure in the antislavery movement and a key figure in the election of Abraham Lincoln. He was a champion of universal suffrage and other radical causes. He was also viewed by many as a champion of fads, a visionary. Even though the Democrats also nominated Greeley, Grant won the election handily. Greeley died less than a month after the election.

Susan B. Anthony tested the Fourteenth Amendment by leading a group of women to cast ballots in the presidential election. She was arrested, found guilty, and fined $100. She refused to pay the fine and never did. Her reward came 14 years after her death when in 1920 the Nineteenth Amendment, guaranteeing women's suffrage, was adopted.

1872-1873: In **congressional elections** the Republicans lost two Senate seats, for a 49–19 majority, with five seats held by minor parties. In the House, which had gained 50 seats since 1870, the Republicans made spectacular gains, leading 194–92, with 14 seats going to minor parties.

Feb 22: The **Prohibition Party** held its first national nominating convention in Columbus, Ohio. James Black of Pennsylvania was nominated for the presidency and the Rev. John Russell of Michigan for the vice presidency.

May 1: The first national convention of the **Liberal Republican Party nominated Horace Greeley** for the presidency and Gov. Benjamin Gratz Brown of Missouri for the vice presidency. The same slate was nominated by the Democratic convention on July 9.

June 5-6: The **Republican National Convention nominated Pres. Grant** for reelection. Sen. Henry Wilson of Massachusetts was nominated for the vice presidency. This was the first major party convention in which black delegates participated. Speeches were delivered from the rostrum by three black delegates, William E. Gray of Arkansas, B.B. Elliott of South Carolina, and John Roy Lynch of Mississippi.

July 9: The **Democratic National Convention nominated Horace Greeley,** editor of the New York *Tribune,* for the presidency and Gov. Benjamin Gratz Brown of Missouri for the vice presidency.

Nov 5: Ulysses S. Grant was reelected president of the United States, defeating Horace Greeley by an electoral vote of 286 to 66. Pres. Grant received a popular vote of 3,597,132 against 2,384,124 for Greeley.

II. Architecture
    Arts and Music
    Popular Entertainment
    Publishing
    Theater

Of the scores of magazines first published this year, two were especially notable. The first was *Publishers' Weekly,* originally issued with the title *The Publishers' and Stationers' Weekly Trade Circular.* Founded in New York City by Frederick Leypoldt, the first issue was dated Jan. 18, 1872. The second magazine of note was *Popular Science Monthly,* published by D. Appleton & Company and edited by Edward L. Youmans. Its first issue, which appeared in May 1872, carried the first part of *The Study of Sociology* by the British philosopher Herbert Spencer, and the first part of *Natural History of Man* by the French anthropologist Armand de Quatrefages. The magazine scored an immediate success, reflecting the growing American interest in science.

Among **books published** this year was *Roughing It* by Mark Twain, a "record of several years of variegated vagabondizing" in the West. A boisterous and exciting book, it described the rough-and-tumble life of the Nevada miners, stagecoach days on the Overland Trail, Western tall tales, hilarious optimism, and desperadoes and pioneers. Twain also included chapters on his stay in Hawaii. Other books published this year included *The Poet of the Breakfast Table* by Oliver Wendell Holmes; and *Barriers Burned Away* by Edward Payson Roe, a best-selling novel based on the Chicago fire of 1871.

III. Business and Industry
    Education
    Philosophy and Religion
    Science

A new era in retail merchandising began in 1872 with the establishment of Montgomery Ward & Company in Chicago. Its founder was Aaron Montgomery Ward, a clerk and traveling salesman who thought he could sell goods directly to people in rural areas by mail. He began with a one-sheet leaflet that offered bargains to Granges. Ward's business expanded and was copied by others.

The **Jehovah's Witnesses** was organized by Charles Taze Russell, a lay member of the Presbyterian Church. First called Russellites, International Bible Students, and Millennial Darwinists, Russell's fundamental followers officially became Jehovah's Witnesses in 1931. In 1939 the sect was incorporated in New York as the Watch Tower Bible and Tract Society.

The **Burbank potato** had its origin this year when Luther Burbank found an Early Rose potato plant that had produced a seed ball, a rare event for that type of potato. Burbank had bought a 17-acre plot in Lunenburg, Mass., in 1871 and had taken up market gardening as a livelihood. He collected the seeds and planted them the following year. Of the 23 seeds, only two produced plants worth investigating. In 1874 Burbank grew both varieties, then picked the more promising one. In Oct. 1875 Burbank sold this potato variety to James J.H. Gregory of Marblehead, Mass., for $150 and moved to California to continue his horticultural research. Gregory named the new variety the Burbank and made a fortune.

IV. Fashion
    Folkways
    Holidays
    Social Issues and Crime
    Sports

The nation was in its Gilded Age, and those who were reaping fortunes from enterprises honest or dishonest were eager to display their new wealth. Society in New York City came to be based almost entirely on wealth. A self-appointed leader of this glittering society was Ward McAllister, who had married a millionaire's daughter. In 1872 he chose a group of men from prominent New York families who were to lead society as "patriarchs." McAllister also groomed Mrs. William Astor to become the grande dame of New York high society.

Yellowstone National Park Reserve was established for the enjoyment of the public. It was designated the first Federal Forest Reserve by Congress in 1891. John Colter, a member of the Lewis and Clark expedition, is credited with reaching the region in 1806. His report on his adventures and the things he saw set the pattern for the fantastic stories about Yellowstone that were to circulate for years to come. The government finally sent exploratory parties to the area in 1859 and 1870. The reports on these expeditions were widely read and became the grounds for the act of Congress that established Yellowstone as a public park. Yellowstone is the oldest and biggest of the national parks. The area was originally marked off as 3348 sq. mi. In subsequent years, the boundaries of Yellowstone were substantially increased, and the Shoshone National Forest, a timber and land reserve, was added.

Nov 7: The brigantine *Mary Celeste,* commanded by Capt. Benjamin S. Briggs, sailed from New York harbor bound for Genoa, Italy, carrying some 1700 barrels of alcohol. On Dec. 4 the British brigantine *Dei Gratia* found the *Mary Celeste* between the Azores and Portugal, her sails slightly damaged, several feet of water in her hold, and completely abandoned. The cargo was intact, the ship was in good order, and there was plenty of food and water aboard, but the lifeboat was gone. The mystery of the disappearance of Capt. Briggs, his wife and daughter, and the eight crewmen aboard has never been solved, and the story of the *Mary Celeste*'s voyage has become a classic of sea lore.

1873

I. Civil Rights
Exploration and Settlement
Government
Statistics
Wars

After a period of unprecedented prosperity, fueled originally by the economic demands of the Civil War, the nation plunged into a depression. The panic of 1873 was triggered by the failure on Sept. 18 of the leading brokerage firm, Jay Cooke & Company, which had been financing construction of the Northern Pacific Railroad. The actual causes lay deeper: overspeculation in land and securities, issuance of too much paper money, and increasing inflation. Over 5000 businesses failed this year and another 5000 or so failed before recovery was complete about six years later.

Mar 3: An act prohibiting the **mailing of obscene literature** was passed by Congress. The bill was promoted by Anthony Comstock, secretary of the Society for the Suppression of Vice. Comstock, formerly a dry-goods store clerk, joined the YMCA and began to agitate for a New York vice society. He drew his inspiration from a London society that for 75 years had been engaged in ferreting out and bringing to trial moral offenders.

Oct 31: The U.S. steamer *Virginius* was captured by the Spanish gunboat *Tornado* while transporting supplies to Cuban revolutionary forces. Eight U.S. citizens from the steamer were subsequently executed in Cuba by Spanish authorities.

Nov 19: William Marcy "Boss" Tweed was convicted on 204 charges of fraud. He was sentenced to 12 years in prison and fined $12,550.

II. Architecture
Arts and Music
Popular Entertainment
Publishing
Theater

The founding of *St. Nicholas* magazine and the appointment of Mary Mapes Dodge as its editor marked 1873 as a notable year for children's literature. Mrs. Dodge edited the magazine and contributed to it until her death in 1905. In the process she had more influence on literature for young people than any other contemporary person or publication. Among the many contributors to *St. Nicholas* were Louisa May Alcott, Rudyard Kipling, Howard Pyle, Robert Louis Stevenson, Frank Stockton, and Mark Twain.

Among **books published** this year was the classic science fiction adventure story *Twenty Thousand Leagues Under the Sea* by Jules Verne, a French writer. Another Verne novel, *Around the World in Eighty Days,* topped the 1,000,000 mark in sales. Other books published this year included *Marjorie Daw* by Thomas Bailey Aldrich, a collection whose title story achieved both critical and popular success; *The Mystery of Metropolisville* by Edward Eggleston, a novel that included a preface by the author declaring that he considered the novel a proper vehicle for contributing to the history of civilization in America; and *Mrs. Skaggs's Husbands and Other Stories* by Bret Harte, which included some of the author's best writing of this period, notably the story "The Head of Sandy Bar."

III. Business and Industry
Education
Philosophy and Religion
Science

The first important railroad tunnel in the U.S., and the longest until 1927, was completed on Nov. 27. This was the Hoosac Tunnel, through the Hoosac Range in northwestern Massachusetts. Work on the tunnel had begun in 1851. The new explosive nitroglycerin had its first practical use in the U.S. in construction of the tunnel. So did the compressed air drill, which earlier had been used in the Mont Cenis Tunnel in the Swiss Alps, the only tunnel in the world longer than the Hoosac at that time. The Hoosac Tunnel was 4.75 miles long. It was traveled by trains of the Boston and Maine Railroad from New England to

New York City. It was 20 feet high and 24 feet wide, and required 20,000,000 bricks for archwork support. It cost $20,000,000 to build and took the lives of nearly 200 workmen.

The **Union of American Hebrew Congregations,** the first national grouping of Jewish congregations, was organized. Two years later this group founded Hebrew Union College in Cincinnati, Ohio, the oldest rabbinical seminary in the U.S. A conference in Cleveland in 1855 had resulted in a breach between the eastern and the western rabbis; their division was not bridged until 1879. The Union of American Hebrew Congregations, therefore, consisted of congregations from the South and the West only.

Free mail delivery was provided in all cities with a population of at least 20,000.

May 1: The **first penny postcards** in the U.S. were issued.

IV. Fashion
Folkways
Holidays
Social Issues and Crime
Sports

By 1873 the American bison, also called the buffalo, was almost extinct, even though at the start of the nineteenth century estimates placed the North American bison population as high as 60,000,000. Bison were essential to the way of life of the Indians of the Great Plains, who depended on them for food, clothing, and shelter. The symbiotic relationship of the Indians and the bison threatened neither group. However, with the coming of the railroad, professional buffalo hunters, and the settlement of the West, the situation changed. Bison were slaughtered far beyond any need for food or hides. Although in 1865 about 10,000,000 bison still roamed the plains, by 1890 only 1000 or so were left.

Memorial Day became a legal holiday in New York, the first state to recognize it. Rhode Island followed suit in 1874; Vermont in 1876; New Hampshire in 1877; and Wisconsin in 1879.

May 27: The first annual **Preakness Stakes** was won by Survivor, with a time of 2:43. The jockey was G. Barbee. The race was run at Pimlico, Md. The Preakness Stakes is one of the three classic races in American racing. It is grouped with the Kentucky Derby and the Belmont Stakes in importance. A horse that has won all three has earned the Triple Crown of American racing. The Preakness Stakes has been run over varying distances.

Aug 18: Mt. Whitney, the second highest mountain in the U.S., was scaled by an American team for the first time. The climbers were John Lucas, Charles D. Begole, and A. H. Johnson.

1874

I. Civil Rights
Exploration and Settlement
Government
Statistics
Wars

Growing out of the hardships caused by the panic of 1873, a convention in Indianapolis, Ind., formed the Greenback Party on Nov. 25, 1876. Its supporters were mostly farmers from the West and the South who wanted to inflate the currency so as to relieve themselves of the burden of debt they had incurred in times of high prices. Originally, the Greenback Party hoped to gain control of the Democratic Party, but it could not do so. It fielded its own candidates until 1884, when the party did so badly that it disbanded. In 1878, with the assistance of labor organizations, the Greenback-Labor Party elected 14 representatives to Congress. At the 1874 convention the party nominated Peter Cooper, New York industrialist and philanthropist, as its candidate for the presidency in 1876.

The **Woman's Christian Temperance Union,** called the WCTU, was established at Cleveland, Ohio. It stemmed from the women's crusade against liquor traffic in midwestern states. Mrs. Annie Wittenmyer was elected first president.

1874-1875: In **congressional elections** the Democrats picked up ten seats in the Senate but still lagged behind the Republicans 45–29, with two seats going to minor parties. In the House the Democrats took a 169–109 majority, with 14 seats going to minor parties.

June 20: Territorial government in the **District of Columbia** was abolished and replaced by a commission.

Nov 7: The first cartoon featuring an **elephant** to symbolize the Republican Party appeared in *Harper's Weekly.* Entitled "Third Term Panic," the cartoon by Thomas Nast showed Republican concern that Pres. Grant would be elected for a third term on the Democratic ticket.

II. Architecture
Arts and Music
Popular Entertainment
Publishing
Theater

The American theater prospered in the late nineteenth century and became completely professional, counting among its ranks numerous stars and a number of energetic and able producers. Among comediennes no one was better or more successful than Ada Rehan, who first appeared on the stage in 1863 at the age of 13. She was for many years the leading lady of Augustin Daly's company, popular both in America and England. Her most famous part was Katherine in *The Taming of the Shrew.*

Among **books published** this year was *The Gilded Age* by Mark Twain and Charles Dudley Warner, a novel that epitomized the corruption of post-Civil War America. In the character of Colonel Sellers the authors represented "the grandfather of all American boosters . . . with his dreams of an immediate future gilding a present of poverty-stricken, whiskey-soaked, rough-and-tumble frontier." Other books published this year included the first American edition of *Lorna Doone* by Richard Doddridge Blackmore; *The Circuit Rider,* a major novel by Edward Eggleston, with a pioneer preacher as its main character whose pulpit was the saddle of his horse and whose flock was the citizenry of communities without churches; *The Hanging of the Crane,* an ambitious long poem by Henry Wadsworth Longfellow, not generally classed among his best works; and *The Old Regime in Canada* by Francis Parkman, a volume in his cycle of histories about the struggles of the English and the French for dominion over North America.

III. Business and Industry
Education
Philosophy and Religion
Science

An invention that revolutionized life on the Great Plains had its first practical use in 1874. The invention was barbed wire, the work of Joseph F. Glidden of Illinois. Until 1874, considering the lack of timber on the Great Plains, there had been no economical way to fence the land. Cattle roamed where they would. Now the range was fenced in. Cowboys had to become ranchers and farmers had to protect their crops from marauding cattle. At first there were battles between ranchers and farmers, but eventually barbed wire won. In 1874 only 10,000 lbs. of it were produced, but in 1880 the output was 80,500,000 lbs.

The **Chautauqua movement** was founded by Lewis Miller, an Ohio industrialist, and John H. Vincent, a Methodist clergyman, as an annual summer meeting for the training of Sunday school teachers. The movement derived its name from the site of its meetings on the shores of Lake Chautauqua, N.Y. The meetings gradually expanded their educational scope and the size of the student body.

IV. Fashion
Folkways
Holidays
Social Issues and Crime
Sports

A new sport, lawn tennis, appeared in the U.S. this year. Invented in England, the game came to the U.S. by way of Bermuda, where a New Yorker, Mary Ewing Outerbridge, was introduced to the game. She returned home with a net, balls, and rackets, and had the first lawn tennis court in the U.S. laid out on Staten Island. Another court soon was laid out in Nahant, Mass., and the game spread around the country. Tennis was such a genteel game that women could play despite their long skirts, since they were not expected to run about.

Rugby football was first introduced to an American campus in a match between Harvard and McGill University of Canada. Canadian rules for the game greatly interested sports-minded Americans and were instrumental in the development of modern football.

The **first public zoo** in the U.S., the Philadelphia Zoological Gardens of Philadelphia, Pa., was opened.

Aug 21: Henry Ward Beecher was sued for $100,000 by Theodore Tilton, accusing the famous preacher of committing adultery with Tilton's wife. The trial attracted national publicity and controversy, especially since the jury handed down a split decision, 9–3, in favor of Beecher. A special investigating committee made up of members of his congregation, the Plymouth Congregational Church, Brooklyn, N.Y., had previously exonerated Beecher after interviewing 36 people, including Tilton.

1875

I. Civil Rights
Exploration and Settlement
Government
Statistics
Wars

One of the worst scandals of the administration of Pres. Ulysses S. Grant surfaced this year with revelations involving what was called the Whiskey Ring. A group of distillers, chiefly in St. Louis, Mo., and corrupt Treasury Department officials had conspired to defraud the government of millions of dollars in taxes on liquor. Two hundred thirty-eight persons were indicted on May 10. Later in the year Grant's private secretary, Orville E. Babcock, was also indicted. Grant intervened to make sure Babcock was not convicted. Babcock retired shortly after his acquittal.

Jan 30: The **Hawaiian Reciprocity Treaty** was signed. It provided that no Hawaiian territory be turned over to any third power.

Mar 1: A **Civil Rights Act** was passed guaranteeing blacks equal rights in public places. The law also prohibited exclusion of blacks from jury duty.

Dec 4: **William Marcy "Boss" Tweed** escaped from prison at Ludlow St., New York City, and fled to Cuba.

II. Architecture
Arts and Music
Popular Entertainment
Publishing
Theater

The growing place of music in cultural life was indicated by the appointment in 1875 of John Knowles Paine to a professorship of music at Harvard, the first such post at any American university. Paine was a composer and organist, but his importance in American music lay in his educational efforts. Many of his pupils became notable composers.

A **masterpiece of realism** in the style of Jean Léon Gérôme and Léon Joseph Florentin Bonnat was Thomas Eakins' *Gross Clinic.* The objectivity with which Eakins approached the subject corresponded to the scientific objectivity of the doctor who is the subject.

An **inspired sculpture** of Abraham Lincoln was the famous *Emancipation* in Lincoln Park, Washington, D.C., by Thomas Ball. A replica was set up in Boston in 1877. Lincoln was shown with his hand lifted over a kneeling slave.

III. Business and Industry
Education
Philosophy and Religion
Science

Dwight L. Moody, a new, forceful personality in evangelical Christianity, began his life's work this year with revival meetings in the East. Moody was to play a major role in the religious life of the country to the end of the nineteenth century. He preached a simple biblical message, concentrating on the salvation of individual souls at a time when many clergymen were turning to social reform. Moody founded the Northfield School for Girls (1879) and the Mt. Hermon School for Boys (1881) in his native town of Northfield, Mass., and the Moody Institute (1889) in Chicago.

Luther Burbank set up a plant nursery in Santa Rosa, Calif., in which he developed new strains of berries, fruits, vegetables, grains, and grasses.

Henry Bergh became the first president of the new **Society for the Prevention of Cruelty to Children.** In 1866 Bergh had incorporated the Society for the Prevention of Cruelty to Animals after a long and lonely crusade. The Society for the Prevention of Cruelty to Children was organized with the help of Elbridge T. Gerry, and quickly became the more prominent society, though Bergh remained more intimately asssociated with efforts to eliminate cruelty to animals.

The **Christian Science** movement received a powerful impetus with publication of *Science and Health* by Mary Baker Eddy.

Mar 15: The **first American cardinal,** Archbishop John McCloskey of New York City, was invested at St. Patrick's Cathedral.

IV. Fashion
Folkways
Holidays
Social Issues and Crime
Sports

The traveling circus was evolving into "the greatest show on earth," aided by that master of showmanship, Phineas T. Barnum, who had organized such a show in 1871. His tent covered the largest area of any in the world and he introduced the three-ring circus. In 1881 Barnum merged his circus with that of James A. Bailey to form an even bigger enterprise. Barnum's greatest single coup came in 1882 when he purchased Jumbo, the world's largest elephant, from the Royal Zoological Gardens of London.

Football uniforms were first worn at a match between Harvard and Tufts.

The **baseball glove** was introduced by Charles G. Waite, first baseman for a Boston team. The glove was unpadded.

May 17: The **first Kentucky Derby** was run at Churchill Downs, Ky. The winner was Aristides, with a time of 2:37¼. The jockey was Oliver Lewis.

1876

I. Civil Rights
Exploration and Settlement
Government
Statistics
Wars

For the first time since the Civil War, the Democratic Party was optimistic about its chances of winning a presidential election. The Grant administration was riddled with scandals, and the depression that had begun in 1873 had not completely disappeared. The Republicans were in disarray. Pres. Ulysses S. Grant would have liked a third term, but had strong opposition within the party. Rep. James G. Blaine, Republican of Maine, was favored by one faction but he too was touched by scandal. He lost the nomination but in July took a seat in the Senate. In the campaign the Democrats blamed the Republicans for the nation's ills, while the Republicans "waved the bloody shirt," still taking credit for having saved the Union during the Civil War. Neither party discussed the long-standing argument between so-called hard money businessmen and soft money proponents, mostly farmers.

1876-1877: In **congressional elections** the Republicans lost ground in the Senate but held a 39–36 majority, with one seat going to a minor party. In the House the Democrats held a 153–140 majority.

May 17: The **Prohibition Party** held its second national convention in Cleveland, Ohio. Green Clay Smith of Kentucky was nominated for president and Gideon T. Stewart of Ohio for vice president.

May 18: The **Greenback Party** held its first national convention at Indianapolis, Ind. The convention named Peter Cooper of New York for president and Samuel F. Perry of Ohio for vice president.

June 14-16: The **Republican National Convention nominated Rutherford B. Hayes** of Ohio for president. His running mate was William A. Wheeler of New York.

June 25: At the Battle of **Little Big Horn** in Montana, Gen. George A. Custer and all of the 265 men of the Seventh Cavalry were slaughtered by Sitting Bull's Sioux Indians.

June 27-29: The **Democratic National Convention nominated Samuel J. Tilden** of New York for president and Thomas A. Hendricks of Indiana for vice president.

Aug 1: Colorado was admitted to the Union, the 38th state.

Nov 7: The **presidential election** gave Samuel J. Tilden, the Democratic candidate, a popular vote plurality of 250,000, but Republicans refused to concede on the grounds that returns from Florida, Louisiana, South Carolina, and Oregon were in dispute. Hayes needed the electoral votes of those states to win. On Dec. 6 two different sets of electoral returns were reported from the four states. The electoral vote ultimately was to be determined by a special 15-member electoral commission.

Nov 23: William Marcy "Boss" Tweed, after his capture in Spain, was delivered to authorities in New York City to serve his prison sentence.

II. Architecture
Arts and Music
Popular Entertainment
Publishing
Theater

An unusual book published this year was not intended for personal reading but to help organizations of all kinds conduct their meetings with standard rules. The book was *Pocket Manual of Rules of Order for Deliberative Assemblies;* the author was Henry M. Robert, an Army engineer. The small volume was at once popular, as many groups recognized it as a means of ensuring order and fairness in business meetings. It was revised in 1915 and 1943 and has continued to be the standard work, known to millions as *Robert's Rules of Order.*

Among **books published** this year was *Clarel: A Poem and Pilgrimage in the Holy Land* by Herman Melville. Published in two volumes, the work was based on Melville's trip to the Holy Land in 1857. Its publication did nothing to enhance the reputation of the author, then working as a customs inspector in New York City. Other books published this year included *Helen's Babies* by John Habberton, a humorous novel that was enormously popular; *Roderick Hudson,* a novel by Henry James; *Among My Books: Second Series* by James Russell Lowell; *The One Fair Woman,* a novel by Joaquin Miller, the "poet of the Sierras"; *The Adventures of Tom Sawyer* by Mark Twain, an American classic that became his most popular book but was barred from libraries in Brooklyn, N.Y., Denver, Colo., and elsewhere as being unfit for young readers; and *My Winter on the Nile* by Charles Dudley Warner, a book of travel sketches based on the author's 1875 trip to Africa and the Middle East.

The gigantic **statue of *Daniel Webster*** now standing in Central Park, the work of Thomas Ball, was unveiled. Fourteen feet in height, the statue was cast in Munich. Popularity of the work brought Ball orders for statues of Josiah Quincy and Charles Sumner.

III. Business and Industry
Education
Philosophy and Religion
Science

Before the twentieth century most American scientists worked with practical objectives in mind. One of the few who devoted himself to what may be called pure research was Josiah Willard Gibbs, at Yale University. His work later had practical applications in industry. Gibbs's most important contribution was his theory of thermodynamics, the basis for modern physical chemistry and chemical engineering. His most important publication was "On the Equilibrium of Heterogeneous Substances," which appeared this year in *Transactions of the Connecticut Academy of Arts and Sciences.* The second half of this classic paper was published in 1878. Gibbs also contributed to statistical mechanics, vector analysis, crystallography, and electromagnetic theory.

The **first photograph of the solar spectrum** was taken by John William Draper, a physicist and astronomer at New York University. Draper was credited in 1840 with the first photograph of the moon.

A **mimeograph** device was invented by Thomas A. Edison in his laboratory at Menlo Park, N.J. The machine employed a stencil for making impressions. The impressions were inserted into a set frame and ink was applied. It was probably the first practical duplicating machine.

The **New York Society for Ethical Culture** was established by Dr. Felix Adler. In the same year Adler founded the first free kindergarten in New York City in connection with his Ethical Culture School.

Central Park was completed along the design of its planners, Frederick Law Olmsted and Calvert Vaux, as a growing part of New York City. It was to be expanded as the city expanded.

Mar 7: The first U.S. patent for the **telephone** was awarded to Alexander Graham Bell.

IV. Fashion
Folkways
Holidays
Social Issues and Crime
Sports

The nation celebrated its 100th birthday with a world's fair, the Centennial Exposition, held appropriately in Philadelphia, where the Declaration of Independence was written and proclaimed in 1776. The exposition covered 450 acres. Each state had its own building and 50 foreign nations sent exhibits. Between May and November, almost 10,000,000 people visited the fairgrounds. The most popular attraction proved to be Machinery Hall, with its vast displays of inventions heralding the latest technology.

Polo was brought to the U.S. by James Gordon Bennett, publisher of the New York *Herald.* The sport was launched at Dickel's Riding Academy, New York City.

In track, the **100-yard race** was run for the first time in ten seconds, by Horace H. Lee of Pennsylvania.

The **tenderloin section of New York City** (24th to 40th streets between 5th and 7th avenues) was so named by Police Captain A. S. Williams, who is reported to have said, on being transferred to the West 30th St. precinct: "I've been having chuck steak ever since I've been on the force, and now I'm going to have a bit of tenderloin." The expression was taken up by the press and soon was applied to the vice-laden sections of any city.

Jan 1: The **Philadelphia Mummers' parade** was organized in its present form in celebration of the American centennial. The parade was sponsored mainly by the Silver Crown New Year's Association. The Mummers' parade dates back to early colonial times. It combines the boisterous Swedish custom of celebrating the New Year with the English tradition of the Mummers' play, in which St. George slays the dragon. The city of Philadelphia did not officially recognize the parade until 1901, when 42 fraternal organizations received permits to stage a parade for which prizes would be awarded for costumes, music, and comic antics.

Apr 2: In the **first official National League baseball game,** Boston beat Philadelphia 6–5, with Jim O'Rourke getting the first hit.

May 23: The **first no-hitter** in National League history was pitched by Joe Borden of Boston. Borden lost his effectiveness soon after and ended the season as the club's groundskeeper.

June 6: The **Imperial Council of the Ancient Arabic Order of Nobles of the Mystic Shrine** for the U.S., a Masonic order, was organized by Dr. Walter Fleming, assisted by Charles T. McClenachan.

Aug 11-12: The **America's Cup** was successfully defended by the yacht *Madeleine,* which won two straight races from the Canadian challenger *Countess of Dufferin.*

Nov: The **first cooking school** in the U.S., the New York Cooking School, was begun by Juliet Corson at St. Mark's Place in New York City. Corson was interested in teaching wives and daughters of workingmen how to buy and prepare good food. In Aug. 1877 she paid for the publication of 50,000 pamphlets entitled *Fifteen-Cent Dinners for Working-Men's Families.* She wrote other books and pamphlets on the subject in later years.

Nov 23: **Rules for football** were discussed at the invitation of Princeton, by delegates from Yale, Harvard, Rutgers, Columbia, and Princeton meeting at Massasoit House, Springfield, Mass. Princeton had recently adopted Harvard's rules, which in turn were chiefly based on the rules of the British Rugby Union, and these were adopted by all colleges represented at the meeting. The Intercollegiate Football Association grew out of the meeting.

1877

I. Civil Rights
Exploration and Settlement
Government
Statistics
Wars

The nation had never before faced a dispute over the results of a presidential election but it did this year. A candidate needed 185 electoral votes to win and Samuel J. Tilden, the Democratic candidate, clearly had 184. In dispute were the 19 electoral votes of three states still under carpetbag rule—Florida, Louisiana, and South Carolina—plus one vote in Oregon. In Congress both parties agreed on Jan. 29 to establish an electoral commission to decide the issue. The commission, with five members from each house of Congress and five members from the Supreme Court, was made up of eight Republicans and seven Democrats. All the commission's decisions were to fall along party lines. On Mar. 2 Congress accepted the commission's decision, which awarded all the disputed votes to the Republican candidate, Rutherford B. Hayes, who thus received 185 electoral votes to Tilden's 184. The Republicans were accused of offering southern Democrats economic favors for their region if they supported Hayes's claim. In any event, the new president showed a conciliatory attitude toward the South: the last federal troops were withdrawn and there was no further effort to protect the rights of blacks. Reconstruction was over.

Apr 24: **Carpetbag rule** ended in Louisiana, the last southern state to regain control of its internal government. Withdrawal of federal troops here and in South Carolina was a part of the bargain between Republicans and southern Democrats for quiet acceptance of the decision of the electoral commission.

June-Oct: Nez Percé Indians went to war with the U.S. in Idaho. The war ended when federal troops captured Chief Joseph and evacuated the Indians to a reservation.

June 15: The **first black was graduated** from the U.S. Military Academy at West Point, Henry O. Flipper.

II. Architecture
Arts and Music
Popular Entertainment
Publishing
Theater

Two actors destined to appear together many times and to be among the most popular and successful of their era made their debuts this year on opposite coasts. In Philadelphia, Otis Skinner appeared at the Museum Theater, and in San Francisco the Polish actress Helena Modjeska played the lead role in *Adrienne Lecouvreur.* The two would ultimately tour the U.S. together. Skinner became best known for his role in *Kismet* (1911). Madame Modjeska in 1883 played the role of Nora in *A Doll's House* in Louisville, Ky., the first American production of a play by Henrik Ibsen.

Among **books published** this year was *Deephaven* by Sarah Orne Jewett, one of America's finest novelists in the use of local color. The author's first major work, *Deephaven* contained sketches of a New England town that resembled her own South Berwick, Maine. Other books published this year included *Birds and Poets* by John Burroughs, marking the author as a worthy successor to Henry David Thoreau; *The American* by Henry James, continuing the author's exploration of contrasts and conflicts of American life in Europe; and *Poems* by Sidney Lanier, a volume which would be enlarged and reissued in 1884.

The **cakewalk** became a popular feature of minstrel shows following the success of a number called "Walking for Dat Cake" by the New York musical comedy team of Harrigan and Hart. The cakewalk now was an imitation of antebellum plantation cakewalks, set to syncopated tunes taken from black sources and later developed into ragtime.

May 1: The most popular **"cheap library,"** George Munro's *Seaside Library*, made its first appearance. Munro made a fortune publishing a novel a day, offering works by Charles Dickens, Sir Walter Scott, Charlotte and Emily Brontë, and many other foreign authors without paying any royalty.

III. Business and Industry
Education
Philosophy and Religion
Science

Strikes on a national scale, accompanied by violence, occurred this year for the first time in American history. The labor trouble began on July 17 when Baltimore & Ohio Railroad workers struck. The line had cut wages 10% even though it was paying large dividends to its stockholders. Violence broke out first in Martinsburg, W. Va., where federal troops were used to restore order. On July 20 nine strikers were killed in Baltimore when state militia fired on a crowd. On July 21 strikers in Pittsburgh rioted, destroying some 2000 freight cars. Police aided by cavalry troops attacked a gathering in Chicago on July 26, causing more bloodshed. The strikes spread to other railroads and to many other industries. In the end, most rail workers gained little or nothing, but coal miners won a 10% wage increase. Although the strikes were not especially successful, they did bring more unity to labor and generally promoted the growth of labor unions, which had suffered during the recent depression.

The detection of two **satellites of Mars** by Asaph Hall made a major contribution to astronomy. This discovery, made at the Naval Observatory in Washington, D.C., was ranked as the most significant since the discovery of Neptune in 1846.

Dec 6: Thomas A. Edison completed his **phonograph.** He filed for a patent for the device on Dec. 15. The first full description of the phonograph appeared in *Scientific American* (Dec. 22), at whose New York offices Edison demonstrated its operation.

IV. Fashion
Folkways
Holidays
Social Issues and Crime
Sports

Flag Day was observed for the first time this year, on June 14, to mark the centennial of the adoption of the stars and stripes design by the Continental Congress. It is not a legal holiday, but is observed by presidential proclamation. The question of who designed the flag has never been resolved. Possibly it was Francis Hopkinson, who was chairman of the Navy board of the Congress, where the design originated.

The first annual **Westminster Kennel Club dog show** was held at Gilmore's Garden in New York City; it was sponsored by the Westminster Kennel Club. Setters of English, Irish, and Gordon types, pointers, spaniels, mastiffs, St. Bernards, terriers, and poodles were well represented.

1878

I. Civil Rights
Exploration and Settlement
Government
Statistics
Wars

Epidemics struck the nation fairly often during this period, when causes and cures were not known. Especially rampant this year was yellow fever, which swept through the South. New Orleans was hardest hit, and as people fled the disease there they spread it elsewhere. Louisiana, Alabama, Mississippi, and Tennessee were most affected, but the epidemic reached as far north as Cincinnati, Ohio. There were 24,000 cases in New Orleans and 4000 fatalities. The national toll was 14,000. Cigars and whiskey were recommended by some as remedies. In Memphis, Anna "Madame Annie" Cook, who operated the Mansion House brothel, discharged her prostitutes to provide hospital quarters. She died in September of yellow fever contracted while caring for patients. The epidemic broke out again in 1879.

1878-1879: In **congressional elections** the Democrats gained control of both houses of Congress for the first time since 1858. The Democratic majorities were 42–33 in the Senate, with one seat going to a minor party; 149–130 in the House, with 14 minor party seats.

Jan 10: A **women's suffrage amendment** was introduced by Sen. Aaron A. Sargent of California in the exact words of its final form when adopted after World War I. Defeated in the Senate 16–34, the amendment would be reintroduced in each succeeding Congress.

Jan 14: The **Supreme Court** declared unconstitutional any state law requiring a railroad to provide equal accommodations for all passengers regardless of race or color.

June 11: The **District of Columbia** was given a new government by Congress. The three commissioners, two residents and one U.S. Army engineer, were empowered to recommend governing legislation to Congress. Residents would have no direct voice in either local or national government. The president made appointments to the commission on June 23.

II. Architecture
Arts and Music
Popular Entertainment
Publishing
Theater

This was a landmark year for newspaper publishing in the U.S., although it was not perceived as such at the time. On Dec. 9 Joseph Pulitzer, who had been involved in politics and publishing for a number of years, bought the St. Louis *Dispatch*, a bankrupt evening newspaper, for $2500. Pulitzer calculated that after the purchase he had enough operating capital to keep going for 17 weeks. Almost immediately he merged his paper with John A. Dillon's St. Louis *Post*, and within a year the new paper, the St. Louis *Post-Dispatch*, had doubled in circulation and was making money. From this point Pulitzer turned his interest away from politics and toward journalism. His influence would eventually change the newspaper business around the world.

Among **books published** this year was *The Leavenworth Case* by Anna Katharine Green, the first in a score or more of best-selling mystery novels. Other books published this year included *Roxy* by Edward Eggleston, a novel set in nineteenth-century Indiana; *The Europeans* by Henry James, which reversed the usual plot in the author's novels by introducing European characters into an American setting; *Through the Dark Continent* by Henry M. Stanley, the explorer; and *History of American Literature, 1607–1765* by Moses Coit Tyler, a pioneering study of early American literature.

III. Business and Industry
Education
Philosophy and Religion
Science

Law had been a widely practiced profession in the U.S. from the start. It was taught as early as 1779 by George Wythe in Virginia, and in 1784 by Tapping Reeve in Connecticut. There was not, however, a national organization for the legal profession until Aug. 21, 1878, when the American Bar Association was formed at Saratoga, N.Y., at a meeting called by the Connecticut Bar Association. James O. Broadhead was chosen the first president.

Jan 1: The **Knights of Labor** was established as a national organization at its first general assembly. This was the first labor union to attempt to organize all workers into a single union. Its growth was rapid after the election in 1879 of Terence Vincent Powderly as its grand master workman.

Jan 28: The first commercial **telephone exchange** opened at New Haven, Conn. It provided eight lines and served 21 telephones.

Oct 15: The **first electric light company** was formed. It was the Edison Electric Light Company, located at 65 Fifth Ave., New York City.

IV. Fashion
Folkways
Holidays
Social Issues and Crime
Sports

The bicycle first attracted attention when exhibited at Philadelphia's Centennial Exposition in 1876. It was first manufactured in the U.S. in 1878. These bicycles had front wheels about five feet in diameter, but the rear wheels were no more than a third this size. Such a machine was difficult and dangerous to ride. Nevertheless, bicycling became a fad. It became a popular sport after the safety bike, basically like the modern bicycle, was introduced in 1887. By 1882 there were about 20,000 cyclists in the country; the League of American Wheelmen was formed in 1880. Cycling clubs held parades and competitive meets. Women could not ride the high-wheeled bikes but the tricycle was available to them.

Oct 27: A celebrated **robbery** of $3,000,000 from the Manhattan Savings Institution in New York City was credited to a gang leader called George L. "Western" Leslie. Although two of his accomplices were convicted of the robbery, Leslie was not brought to trial because of lack of evidence. New York's chief of police attributed four-fifths of the bank holdups in the U.S. to Leslie, whose career was terminated by his murder in 1884.

1879

I. Civil Rights
Exploration and Settlement
Government
Statistics
Wars

Opposition to Chinese immigration, growing stronger in California in particular, came to a head with passage by Congress of a bill to restrict such immigration. Pres. Rutherford B. Hayes vetoed the bill on May 11 on the grounds that it violated the Burlingame Treaty of 1868, which established free immigration between the two countries. On May 7 California adopted a new constitution that forbade employment of Chinese laborers. Between 1850 and 1882 about 300,000 Chinese came to the U.S., almost all remaining on the Pacific coast. Chinese laborers had first been brought in large numbers in the 1860s to work on construction of the transcontinental railroad. The feeling against them at this time was economic rather than racial, since they worked for less than American workers.

Jan 1: Specie payment was resumed by the U.S. government for the first time since it was suspended in 1861. Lack of specie payment had kept the currency in an unsettled state, partly contributing to the panic of 1873. Its approaching resumption caused much apprehension that the government could not provide enough coin to meet the expected demand. Mints had been kept open after hours to produce additional coinage, and there was surprise when little currency was presented by the public for redemption. This showed the extent to which public confidence in government fiscal policies had been restored since the Civil War. Payment of specie has been maintained ever since.

Feb 15: Women attorneys won the right to argue cases before the U.S. Supreme Court by an act of Congress.

II. Architecture
Arts and Music
Popular Entertainment
Publishing
Theater

The history of one of the world's great entertainment palaces began this year when Madison Square Garden opened to the public in New York City. The first Garden was not elaborate, just a converted railroad structure at 26th St. In 1890 it was replaced by an elegant structure designed by the firm of McKim, Mead, and White; it featured a tower modeled after the Giralda in Seville, Spain. The second Garden was designed not for the average sports fan but for the wealthy and cultured citizens of New York and such events as the annual horse show of the Equestrian Society. This building was torn down and in 1925 replaced by a third Garden, on Eighth Ave. and 50th St. It was in turn replaced by the fourth and present Madison Square Garden, 31st to 33rd streets between Seventh and Eighth avenues.

Among **books published** this year was *Daisy Miller* by Henry James. It became the most popular of the author's early novels, perhaps because of an endearing young American heroine pitted against the complexities of Continental society. Other books published this year included *Old Creole Days* by George Washington Cable, the author's first collection of short stories, many of which first had appeared in *Scribner's Monthly; Progress and Poverty* by Henry George, a landmark work in economics concentrating on land and its value and advocating a "single tax" on land to replace all other forms of taxation; *A Lady of Aroostook* by William Dean Howells, the author's fourth novel; and *Rudder Grange* by Frank R. Stockton, a whimsically humorous novel that was so popular it inspired a sequel, *The Rudder Grangers Abroad* (1891).

III. Business and Industry
Education
Philosophy and Religion
Science

A venture in retailing that began in 1879 set the stage for development of nationwide chains of stores in various merchandising fields. This year, Frank W. Woolworth, having had a five-cent store fail in Utica, N.Y., opened a five-and-ten-cent store in Lancaster,

Pa. It was a success and by the 1890s Woolworth operated 28 stores. By 1911 the F. W. Woolworth Company owned over 1000 such outlets. Chain stores aroused the antagonism of local merchants, but the public approved, as their steadily increasing patronage showed.

The first public **electrical street lighting** system in the U.S. was installed in Cleveland, Ohio, by Charles F. Brush. Wabash, Ind., was the first city to be completely lighted by electricity (Mar. 31, 1880). Brush used arc lights for illumination rather than incandescent lamps.

The **Church of Christ, Scientist** was organized by Mary Baker Eddy, founder of Christian Science. Mrs. Eddy, who resided in Lynn, Mass., was the author of *Science and Health with Key to the Scriptures*, published in 1875.

Oct 21: The first practical **incandescent electric lamp** was perfected by Thomas A. Edison in his laboratories at Menlo Park, N.J. He found that a carbonized filament of cotton would last for about 40 hrs.

IV. **Fashion**
   Folkways
   Holidays
   Social Issues and Crime
   Sports

Two popular forms of recreation during this period were fox hunting and coaching. Clubs of wealthy persons on Long Island, in the suburbs of Philadelphia, and in New England, Virginia, and Maryland took up fox hunting in the English style. One newspaper described the last hunt of the season at Newport, R.I., this way: "All Newport mustered at the meet, the road to Southwick's Grove being literally chock-full of vehicles of every sort, shape, size, and description." Coaching was also imported from England and such resorts as Tuxedo, N.Y., and Lenox, Mass., found roads jammed with expensive dog-carts, buckboards, landaus, and phaetons. In New York City there was an annual coaching parade during which such rigs as four-in-hands and tally-hos coursed down Fifth Ave. The elite of society rode atop these magnificent vehicles, the men in striped waistcoats and silk top hats, the ladies with parasols held over enormous picture hats.

The **National Archery Association** was founded at Crawfordsville, Ind., signalizing the beginning of modern archery in the U.S. The first target archery tournament was held at Chicago this same year, with Will Thompson the first champion.

1880

I. **Civil Rights**
   Exploration and Settlement
   Government
   Statistics
   Wars

The field for the presidential nominations of 1880 was wide open, Pres. Rutherford B. Hayes having announced he would not seek a second term. For the first time since the Civil War, the Republicans could not claim they alone saved the Union: the Democratic nominee, Gen. Winfield Scott Hancock, had fought in both the Mexican and Civil wars. The tariff was the only major issue and Hancock was inept at discussing it. The candidates for the most part stayed home, and for the first time interested supporters came in large numbers to visit them at their homes. James A. Garfield especially received gifts and poems composed for the occasion, watching silently as supporters trampled his flowers and shrubs.

The U.S. **Census** recorded a population of 50,155,783. The center of population was located at eight miles west by south of Cincinnati, Ohio (in western Kentucky). New York became the first state with a population above 5,000,000.

Mar 1: Excluding blacks from jury duty was held unconstitutional by the Supreme Court. The decision was based on section five of the Fourteenth Amendment. It advised jury commissioners that they were forbidden to carry out their offices in such a way as to discriminate on racial grounds in the selection of jurors.

June 2-8: The **Republican National Convention nominated James A. Garfield** of Ohio for the presidency. Chester A. Arthur of New York was named as his running mate. During the convention's meetings Sen. Blanche Kelso Bruce of Mississippi was made temporary chairman of the convention, becoming the first black to preside over a major party convention.

June 22-24: The **Democratic National Convention nominated Winfield S. Hancock** of Pennsylvania for the presidency and William H. English of Indiana for the vice presidency.

Nov 2: James A. Garfield was elected president of the United States. Chester A. Arthur was elected vice president. The electoral vote was Garfield, 214; Winfield S. Hancock, Democratic candidate, 155. The popular vote was Garfield, 4,449,053; Hancock, 4,442,035; James B. Weaver, Greenback-Labor candidate, 308,578; Neal Dow, Prohibition candidate, 10,305. In congressional elections the Republicans fell into a 37–37 tie with the Democrats in the Senate, with one seat going to a minor party. In the House the Republicans took a 147–135 majority, with 11 seats going to minor parties.

Nov 17: The **Chinese Exclusion Treaty** was signed with China at Peking. It gave the U.S. the right to "regulate, limit, or suspend" but not to exclude completely the entry of Chinese nationals.

II. Architecture
Arts and Music
Popular Entertainment
Publishing
Theater

The riches accumulated by the new millionaires of the Gilded Age provided them with the opportunity to become art collectors. This was also the period when public art museums began to appear, led by the Metropolitan Museum of Art in New York City. Formed in 1870, it opened its doors ten years later on its present site in Central Park, facing Fifth Ave. It was destined to become the most comprehensive art museum in the U.S. and one of the great museums of the world. Its early sponsors were from families of wealth and social position who tended to look down on the new rich. However, the latter were not ignored for long; their financial support was vital to the growth of such institutions as the Metropolitan. The new rich, in turn, were eager to secure the favorable publicity that came through substantial gifts to the arts.

Among **books published** this year was *Ben-Hur* by Lew Wallace, a highly successful historical romance about early Christians in the Roman Empire. It has not been out of print since and has twice been made into Hollywood movie extravaganzas. Other books published this year included *Democracy* by Henry Adams, a novel set in Washington, D.C.; *Ultima Thule* by Henry Wadsworth Longfellow, the venerable poet's next to last collection; *Bricks Without Straw* by Albion W. Tourgee, a novel of life in postwar North Carolina; and *A Tramp Abroad* by Mark Twain, another delightful travel narrative, based on a walking tour of Germany, Switzerland, and Italy.

III. Business and Industry
Education
Philosophy and Religion
Science

The Salvation Army, one of the most energetic and successful evangelical and philanthropic organizations in the world, made its debut in the U.S. this year. The Salvation Army had been founded in England in 1865 by William Booth and his wife Catherine. In 1880 Commissioner George Railton and seven women members arrived in the U.S. to found a branch in Pennsylvania. In 1904 Evangeline Booth, daughter of the founder, took charge of the U.S. branch. From its early days the street bands of the Army have been familiar and popular. The organization has from the beginning treated its women workers the same as its men.

Illiteracy in America was estimated at 17% of the population, a decrease of 3% over the previous decade.

A **successful roll film** for cameras was patented by George Eastman of Rochester, N.Y. In 1885 he placed on the market his first commercial film, cut into strips and sealed in a box camera that was returned to the factory for removal and developing. The introduction of daylight loading film came in 1891, and the first pocket Kodak in 1895.

House paint was manufactured for the first time from standard formulas. The Sherwin-Williams Company of Cleveland, Ohio, began producing an all-purpose paint for wood from an unvarying formula. This production method was later applied to stains, varnish stains, varnishes, and enamels.

Jan 27: A patent for an **incandescent lamp** was received by Thomas A. Edison. The filament was made with a carbonized cotton thread. The first public demonstrations of the lamp had been held on Dec. 31, 1879, at Edison's laboratories at Menlo Park, N.J. The first commercial installation of these lamps was made in the steamship *Columbia* of the Oregon Railroad and Navigation Company.

IV. Fashion
Folkways
Holidays
Social Issues and Crime
Sports

Wrestling was more popular than boxing as an American combat sport, especially on the frontier and in mining towns, until well into the nineteenth century.

Abraham Lincoln in his younger days had been a skilled wrestler. In 1880 the leading wrestler in the U.S. was William Muldoon, who won the heavyweight title this year. Muldoon wrestled in the U.S. and in England and toured America with John L. Sullivan, the boxing champion. Muldoon once had an eight-hour match with Clarence Whistler; the bout ended in a draw. Muldoon also organized the Police Athletic Association and invented the medicine ball.

The **world heavyweight bare knuckle boxing championship** was won by Paddy Ryan this year. Ryan beat the defender, Joe Goss of England, in an 87-round bout near Colliers Station, W. Va.

Orange Blossom, a pseudonym for Joseph M. Mulholland of Washington, Pa., became famous as the byline for implausible stories printed as serious news items. Mulholland's most spectacular hoax was his account of a flaming meteor that supposedly landed in western Pennsylvania, setting fire to a huge area. In later years his stories came to be printed as short works of the imagination, not to be taken literally.

1881

I. Civil Rights
Exploration and Settlement
Government
Statistics
Wars

For the third time in U.S. history, a vice president succeeded to the highest office after death of the incumbent. Chester A. Arthur of New York came to the presidency on the death of Pres. James A. Garfield. Arthur had a poor reputation, a result of his association with Sen. Roscoe Conkling of New York, who had made the most of the spoils system. Arthur was also considered too fond of high living. Nevertheless, his administration brought no scandal to the office and, to the surprise of many, supported badly needed civil service reform. Arthur also supported the rebuilding of the U.S. Navy, which had languished since the Civil War.

Jan 24: The **federal income tax law of 1862** was declared constitutional by the Supreme Court in the case of *Springer v. United States.* Counsel for Springer argued that the tax was a direct tax, forbidden by Article 1, sections 2 and 9 of the Constitution. The Supreme Court ruled that there were only two kinds of direct tax—real property tax and poll tax—and the income tax was neither of these.

July 2: Pres. **Garfield was shot** in a Washington, D.C., railroad station by Charles J. Guiteau, a disgruntled and perhaps insane office seeker. Garfield survived for 80 days after he was shot, being treated in Washington and Elberon, N.J., where the Garfield family was summering at the seashore. The doctors' reports provided no guidance on the president's ability to fulfill his duties. Vice Pres. Chester A. Arthur served as acting president. Garfield died Sept. 19, 1881, without ever leaving his bed. He was buried in Cleveland, Ohio. Guiteau was hanged in Washington on June 30, 1882.

Sep 20: Chester A. Arthur was inaugurated president of the United States, succeeding to the presidency on the death of Pres. Garfield. The 21st president and a Republican, he served three years and five months.

II. Architecture
Arts and Music
Popular Entertainment
Publishing
Theater

Literary magazines and their editors exercised great influence in this era. Among the best was Richard Watson Gilder, who this year became editor of *The Century Illustrated Monthly,* the successor to the celebrated literary journal *Scribner's Monthly.* He continued as editor until his death in 1909. In its first years *The Century* specialized in the memoirs of Civil War generals. The magazine published the works of such leading authors as William Dean Howells, Josh Billings, F. Marion Crawford, and Joel Chandler Harris. Gilder also wrote 16 volumes of poetry. His sister, Jeannette, assisted him at editing and wrote for newspapers what was probably the first American literary gossip column.

Among **books published** this year was *A Century of Dishonor* by Helen Hunt Jackson. Previously a writer of popular but minor fiction, poems, and prose sketches, and now living in the West, Mrs. Jackson provided an eye-opening account of the U.S. government's ruthless treatment of Indians. Among other books of this year were *Uncle Remus: His Songs and His Sayings* by Joel Chandler Harris, full of authentic black folklore in dialect; *Dr. Breen's Practice,* a novel about a society woman as a physician by William Dean Howells; and two novels by Henry James, *Portrait of a Lady,* the masterpiece of his early novels, and *Washington Square,* a story unusual for James about Americans in their home environment.

America's most talented woman painter, **Mary**

Cassatt, an expatriate, for the third year in a row exhibited her work in Paris beside the works of other Impressionists. Cassatt, owing much to Edgar Degas and Gustave Courbet, abhorred conventional art and espoused naturalism. Her renderings of mothers and children in intimate scenes, her etchings and color prints soon won her an international reputation.

John Singer Sargent in his *Vernon Lee* and *Portrait of a Lady* foreshadowed the brilliant success of *Madame X* (1884) and the stream of portraits of the great and near great that followed. His work was marked by an air of aloof elegance, seemingly spontaneous poses, and technically brilliant use of light colors to reveal shapes.

III. Business and Industry
Education
Philosophy and Religion
Science

Founding of an American branch of the Red Cross on May 21, 1881, inspired by the establishment of the International Red Cross in Europe in 1863, was largely the work of one woman, Clara Barton. Miss Barton, a teacher, volunteered to nurse wounded Union soldiers during the Civil War; in 1864 she was put in charge of all hospitals of the Union Army of the James. She became known to the soldiers as "the angel of the battlefield." At the request of Pres. Abraham Lincoln, she headed a search for missing Union soldiers after the war. The American National Red Cross received a federal charter in 1900 and is the only organization with such a charter. Miss Barton headed the Red Cross until 1904.

The **first central electric power plant** in the world was constructed on Pearl St., New York City, under the direction of Thomas Edison. Operations began with one generator. Edison had solved the problem of designing a system for the efficient distribution of power from a central generating system.

IV. Fashion
Folkways
Holidays
Social Issues and Crime
Sports

There were many organizations for Americans to join at this time. Some were patriotic, some religious, some social. Others, such as volunteer fire companies, combined civic service with sociability. Some carried extravagant names, such as the Ancient Arabic Order of Nobles of the Mystic Shrine, or Daughters of Isis. Some went in for gaudy uniforms and much ceremony and ritual. Patriotic groups were especially popular in the late nineteenth century. The Sons of the American Revolution, the Daughters of the American Revolution, and the Colonial Dames of America were all founded between 1875 and 1894. Largest of all was the Grand Army of the Republic, made up of veterans of the Union Army, which reached a peak membership of 400,000 in 1890.

The home of **William Kissam Vanderbilt,** at the corner of Fifth Ave. and 52nd St., was completed at a cost of $3,000,000. It marked the beginning of the great and often monumental edifices erected by American millionaires in imitation of the chateaus and palaces of Europe.

Nov 9-10: The **America's Cup** was successfully defended by the yacht *Mischief,* which won two straight races from the Canadian challenger *Atlanta.*

1882

I. Civil Rights
Exploration and Settlement
Government
Statistics
Wars

The first federal law restricting immigration was passed by Congress on Aug. 3. It set a head tax of 50 cents on each immigrant and excluded convicts, the insane, and persons likely to become public charges. The law was the result of agitation by states controlling the main ports of entry. They had attempted to regulate immigration with state laws and to set a tax in order to support needy newcomers. The Supreme Court declared such laws unconstitutional in 1876 on the grounds that they attempted to regulate foreign commerce, a right reserved to Congress. In the decade from 1881 to 1890, over 5,000,000 immigrants arrived in the U.S.

Mar 16: The **Geneva Convention** of 1864 for the care of wounded war personnel, accepted by most European nations, was ratified by the U.S. Senate. Clara Barton, founder of the American branch of the Red Cross in 1881, did much to promote public sentiment in favor of ratification.

Mar 31: A **pension for widows of presidents** was voted by Congress. Mrs. Polk, Mrs. Tyler, and Mrs. Garfield were each voted $5000 a year. This initiated the custom of voting pensions to widows of presidents.

May 6: The first **Exclusion Act** barred further Chinese immigration for ten years. The act was regularly renewed by Congress and was still on the books in 1920.

Nov 7: In **congressional elections** the Democrats gained 50 seats in the House to take a 197–118 majority, with ten seats going to minor parties. In the Senate the Republicans gained one seat to take a 38–36 majority over the Democrats, with two seats going to minor parties.

II. Architecture
Arts and Music
Popular Entertainment
Publishing
Theater

English actors and actresses continued to be popular in the U.S., although in some cases not entirely for their abilities on stage. Such a figure was Lillie Langtry, who married into London society and became the first society woman to go on the stage. Having made her debut in London in Dec. 1881, she made her first visit to the U.S. this year. On Nov. 6 she appeared as Rosalind in Shakespeare's *As You Like It* at the Fifth Avenue Theatre in New York City. Although not a great actress, Langtry was welcomed wherever she appeared in the U.S., as much for her beauty and her scandalous reputation as for her acting.

Among **books published** this year was the realistic novel by William Dean Howells, *A Modern Instance.* In it Howells traced the history of a marriage that led to divorce and the disintegration of character. Other books published included *John Randolph* by Henry Adams, a biography that reflected the author's sustained interest in the Founding Fathers of the U.S.; *Mr. Isaacs,* the first of many romantic novels by Francis Marion Crawford, based on the adventures of a gem dealer the author had met in India; *L'Abbé Constantin,* by a French dramatist and novelist, Ludovic Halévy, which delighted American readers in translation with its likable village priest and his problems, including two American women who had acquired a home in his idyllic parish; *The Prince and the Pauper* by Mark Twain, set in the reign of England's King Edward VI; and *Anne* by Constance Fenimore Woolson, the first of her five novels dealing realistically with life in northern Michigan.

"The Lady or the Tiger?" by Frank R. Stockton was published in *Century Magazine.* Sensationally popular at the time, this short story has since appeared in nearly every American anthology of fiction.

III. Business and Industry
Education
Philosophy and Religion
Science

A development in 1882 in the way large businesses were organized had economic repercussions for many years. John D. Rockefeller of the Standard Oil Company sought a means of legally controlling under one management companies owned in several states. A lawyer, Samuel C. T. Dodd, hit on the idea of the trust. Stockholders set up a board of trustees to whom were turned over the stocks of about 40 companies. The stockholders received trust certificates, which gave the trustees, Rockefeller and his close associates, the right to operate the companies as they saw fit. The Standard Oil trust, organized on Jan. 2, 1882, was capitalized at $70,000,000. Rockefeller himself owned about a third of all the trust certificates. The trust idea was soon copied in such fields as sugar and tobacco processing. The result was monopolistic control of a number of industries, leading eventually to political action to restore competition.

Prof. **Granville Stanley Hall** of The Johns Hopkins University, Baltimore, Md., was appointed to a special lectureship in psychology and given $1000 to establish a psychological laboratory. William James at Harvard University had previously organized a laboratory for work in "psycho-physics," but Johns Hopkins soon took over leadership.

The nation's **first hydroelectric plant** was built at Appleton, Wis., where the first electric streetcar went into service in 1886.

Feb 2: The **Knights of Columbus,** the first fraternal benefit society of Catholic men, was founded in New Haven, Conn., by the Rev. Michael Joseph McGivney. The society was chartered on March 29, 1882.

IV. Fashion
Folkways
Holidays
Social Issues and Crime
Sports

Americans have a tendency to make folk heroes of outlaws; one of the first of these heroes was Jesse James. Born on Sept. 5, 1847, in Missouri, Jesse Woodson James fought for the Confederacy in Quantrill's Raiders. In 1866 he and his brother, Frank, became leaders of a Midwest gang that first held up banks, then turned to train robbery. A reward offered by the governor of Missouri tempted a member of the gang, Robert Ford, to shoot and kill Jesse on Apr. 3,

1882. After Jesse's death Frank James surrendered, was acquitted of the charges against him, and lived out his life on a Missouri farm. Much has been written about the James gang, including a song, "The Ballad of Jesse James."

Handball was an unknown sport in the U.S. until Phil Casey, one of Ireland's finest handball players, this year came to live in Brooklyn, N.Y. Casey soon built a court and opened a school. He introduced the sport in the U.S. with the help of fellow immigrants from the British Isles.

The phrase **"the public be damned"** was offered by William H. Vanderbilt in answer to a question by Clarence Dresser, a reporter for the Chicago *Daily News*. When asked whether Vanderbilt, owner of the New York Central Railroad, was running the railroad for the public or the stockholders, Vanderbilt tossed off his remark, which was to become a symbol of the arrogance of the railroad barons.

The **U.S. Intercollegiate Lacrosse Association** was founded. The original members were Harvard, Princeton, and Columbia; Yale and New York University were admitted in the following year.

Feb 7: The **world heavyweight bare knuckle boxing championship** was won by John L. Sullivan, who defeated Paddy Ryan in a nine-round bout in Mississippi City, Miss. This year Sullivan toured the country, giving boxing exhibitions under Marquis of Queensberry rules, and offering $500 to any person who could last four rounds with him. His efforts gave boxing new respectability and wider popularity.

June 24: The only major league **baseball umpire expelled for dishonesty,** Richard Higham left the National League.

Sep 25: The **first major league double header** was played between the Providence and Worcester teams.

1883

I. Civil Rights
Exploration and Settlement
Government
Statistics
Wars

Shocked by the suggestion that the assassination of Pres. James A. Garfield in 1881 by a disappointed office seeker was an indirect result of the spoils system, Congress on Jan. 16 passed the Pendleton Act, which was signed into law by Pres. Chester A. Arthur. The law established a three-man Civil Service Commission and specified rules for filling federal government positions by a merit system, including competitive examinations. At the start, only about 14,000 of 100,000 positions were covered by the act, but by 1900 about 106,000 of 250,000 were covered. The worst evils of political patronage were ended, but the question of whether the act improved the efficiency of government, as reformers declared it would, remained unanswered.

Oct 15: The **Civil Rights Act of 1875,** which forbade racial discrimination or separation in public accommodations, was vitiated by a narrow Supreme Court decision. The Court held that only state-imposed discrimination was forbidden, not that by individuals or corporations.

Nov 18: A system of **standard time** was adopted by the railroads of the U.S. and Canada to eliminate problems in printed schedules caused by the unsystematic setting of local times. In 1884, at an international conference in Washington, D.C., a worldwide system of standard time was adopted. The prime meridian was assigned to the meridian passing through the British Royal Observatory at Greenwich, England.

II. Architecture
Arts and Music
Popular Entertainment
Publishing
Theater

A marvel of design and engineering that captured the imagination of the public was officially opened on May 24. This was the Brooklyn Bridge, spanning the East R. between Brooklyn and New York City. John A. Roebling, a pioneer in suspension bridge design, planned the bridge. Shortly after work began in 1869, Roebling was injured when a barge crushed his foot against a pier. Tetanus set in and he died on July 22, 1869. His son, Washington A. Roebling, took over. In 1872 he too was felled, by nitrogen narcosis, or the bends, the result of too much time spent in the underground caissons built to sink the massive foundations of the bridge towers. From 1872 on, he directed construction from an apartment overlooking the bridge site. The bridge has a span of 1595 feet. The striking towers at either end are 272 feet high, with foundations 78 feet below water level. A great civic celebration, attended by Pres. Chester A. Arthur and Gov. Grover Cleveland, marked opening day.

Among **books published** this year was the semiautobiographical *Life on the Mississippi* by Mark Twain. Although soon recognized as a classic account of the difficult art of piloting steamboats on the Mississippi R., and written with the verve of Twain at his peak, the book was not a best seller until it was issued in a paperback edition in the 1940s. Other books published included *The Story of a Country Town* by Edgar Watson Howe, published privately after rejection by many commercial publishers. It was a frequently republished pioneering work of naturalistic fiction set in a midwestern community. *The Old Swimmin' Hole and 'Leven More Poems* by James Whitcomb Riley contained some of Riley's most famous verse depicting rustic life in Indiana. It was written in Hoosier dialect and reached a wide audience.

The **highest masonry building** in the U.S., the Monadnock Building, was erected in Chicago. All 16 stories rest entirely on masonry walls, which are five feet thick at the base.

III. Business and Industry
Education
Philosophy and Religion
Science

Two American scholars were the leading sociologists of the time, but differed completely on the meaning of the theory of evolution, which was much discussed by intellectuals. They were Lester Frank Ward and William Graham Sumner. Ward, whose *Dynamic Sociology* was published this year, believed that the human mind, when properly used, could take an active part in the process of human evolution. He did not believe that evolution is an inevitable and uncontrollable process. Ward further developed his ideas in *Psychic Factors in Civilization* (1893) and *Pure Sociology* (1903). Sumner, on the other hand, believed that the fittest survived and deserved to survive, and that the fittest were those who lived by hard work and individualism. His views were expressed in *What Social Classes Owe to Each Other* (1883).

Experiments leading to development of the **fountain pen** were begun by Lewis E. Waterman. The first to apply the principle of capillary action, Waterman obtained patents and produced a practical pen in 1884, thus founding the Ideal Pen Company in New York City. By 1887 his business had expanded vastly and a new L. E. Waterman Company was incorporated.

Mar 24: The **first telephone service** between New York and Chicago was initiated.

Sep 21: The first direct **telegraph service to Brazil** from the U.S. was established.

IV. Fashion
Folkways
Holidays
Social Issues and Crime
Sports

The far West fascinated Americans in the late nineteenth century, as it has continued to do ever since. A taste of that region was brought east and to Europe with some authenticity by William Frederick "Buffalo Bill" Cody. A Pony Express rider, buffalo hunter, and Army scout, he organized "Buffalo Bill's Wild West Show" in 1883. The show may have given its first performance at North Platte, Neb., on July 4. Buffalo Bill toured with the show for years, both in the U.S. and abroad. It was a smash hit in England. Queen Victoria enjoyed watching stage coaches being held up and Indian attacks repulsed, all to the accompaniment of heavy gunfire.

June 2: The **first baseball game played under electric lights** took place in Fort Wayne, Ind. Fort Wayne beat Quincy 19–11 in seven innings.

June 16: The **first Ladies' Day baseball game** was staged by the New York Giants. On Ladies' Day, both escorted and unescorted ladies were admitted to the park free.

Oct 22: The **first annual New York Horse Show** opened at Gilmore's Gardens, New York City. It was organized by the National Horse Show Association of America. Represented were 165 exhibitors and 299 horses; many workhorses, including fire-engine horses, police mounts, and draught horses, were shown. The show was immediately popular and became an annual event. After 1913 the character of the show altered; working breeds were no longer allowed, and entries were limited to show horses, gaited horses, and the like.

1884

I. Civil Rights
Exploration and Settlement
Government
Statistics
Wars

The presidential election campaign of 1884 was fought mainly with attacks on the reputations of the rival candidates. The Republican candidate, James G. Blaine, on the basis of letters he had written, was accused of having profited from the Crédit Mobilier scandal involving the building of the Union Pacific Railroad. His opponents sang: "Blaine, Blaine, James G. Blaine, the continental liar from the state of Maine." The Democratic candidate, Grover Cleveland, was accused of having fathered an illegitimate child, which in his forthright manner he admitted. The turning point of the election was a remark made on Oct. 9 by the Rev. Samuel D. Burchard in New York, in the presence of Blaine, that the Democrats were the party of "Rum, Romanism, and Rebellion." Blaine did not disavow the remark, and the Irish-American Roman Catholics of New York were outraged. Cleveland carried the state by 1149 votes and thereby won the presidency.

The **National Equal Rights Party** was formed by a group of suffragists who nominated Mrs. Belva A. Lockwood of Washington, D.C., for president. Mrs. Lockwood, a lawyer and the first woman admitted to practice before the Supreme Court, was renominated in 1888. She was the first woman candidate for the presidency.

June 3-6: The **Republican National Convention** nominated James G. Blaine of Maine for the presidency on the first ballot. Gen. John A. Logan of Illinois was nominated for the vice presidency.

July 8-11: The **Democratic National Convention nominated Gov. Grover Cleveland** of New York for the presidency and Thomas A. Hendricks of Indiana for the vice presidency.

July 23: The **Prohibition Party National Convention** nominated John P. St. John of Kansas for the presidency and William Daniel of Maryland for the vice presidency.

Aug 5: The cornerstone of the pedestal of the **Statue of Liberty** was laid at Bedloe's Island (now Liberty Island) in New York harbor. The pedestal, which holds the statue by the French sculptor Frédéric Auguste Bartholdi, is 151 feet high.

Nov 4: Grover Cleveland was elected president of the United States. Thomas A. Hendricks was elected vice president. The electoral vote was Cleveland, 219; James G. Blaine, Republican of Maine, 182. The popular vote was Cleveland, 4,911,017; Blaine, 4,848,334; Benjamin F. Butler, Greenback Party candidate, 175,370; John P. St. John, Prohibition candidate, 150,369. In congressional elections the Republicans gained five seats in the Senate to gain a 43–34 majority. In the House the Republicans gained 22 seats but the Democrats held a 183–140 majority. Robert M. La Follette, Republican of Wisconsin, was elected to his first term in the House of Representatives.

II. Architecture
Arts and Music
Popular Entertainment
Publishing
Theater

Although newspaper chains had not yet come into existence, there was a market for news and feature material gathered by a news organization and made available for a fee to newspapers all over the country. The first such syndicate was founded on Nov. 8 by Samuel Sidney McClure, who had come to America from Ireland as a boy. In 1893 he founded *McClure's Magazine,* which became a great success under his editorship. The magazine was especially noted for the articles it published in the early twentieth century by such leading muckrakers as Ida Tarbell and Lincoln Steffens.

Among **books published** this year was *Huckleberry Finn* by Mark Twain. A world classic, this picaresque novel of Huck's adventures with his black friend Jim drew on the author's experiences on the Mississippi R. The river also served as a backdrop for a variety of rivermen, actors, and rascals, authentic vernacular speech, tall tales, and folklore. Also published this year were *A Roman Singer* and *To Leeward,* novels with an Italian setting by Francis Marion Crawford; *Excursions of an Evolutionist* and *The Destiny of Man in the Light of His Origin* by John Fiske, the best-known defender of Darwinism in the U.S.; the romantic novel *Ramona* by Helen Hunt Jackson, which reached millions of readers with its impassioned plea for justice for American Indians; *A Country Doctor,* another minor but solid novel by Sarah Orne Jewett; *In the Tennessee Mountains* by Mary Noailles Murfree, using the pseudonym Charles Egbert Craddock, the first collection of short stories with realistic settings and genuine Cumberland Mts. dialect; and *Montcalm and Wolfe,* the sixth and next-to-last of Francis Parkman's volumes in his mammoth history of French and English relations in North America.

John Singer Sargent, the brilliant American painter living abroad, exhibited *Mme. Gautreau,* his portrait of a lady in a decolleté black dress. The painting caused a sensation. Critics accustomed to stodgy, rather unrealistic portraits charged Sargent with eroticism and provocativeness. Sargent withdrew the portrait to his studio, where as *Madame X* it remained until 1915. It was one of his masterpieces.

III. Business and Industry
Education
Philosophy and Religion
Science

The formation of national and local learned societies accelerated. At least 79 were organized in the 1870s and 121 in the 1880s. The American Historical Association, founded at Saratoga, N.Y., in 1884, was among the most important of these societies; it began publishing the *American Historical Review* in 1895. There were also more specialized groups, such as the American Society for Church History (1897) and the American Irish Historical Association (1897).

The **Linotype** automatic typesetting machine, which could form an entire line of type as one piece of metal, was patented by Ottmar Mergenthaler. Mergenthaler received patents for improvements in 1885. The first Linotype machines were put into operation by the New York *Tribune* on July 3, 1886. Mergenthaler's typesetter revolutionized the publishing industry.

IV. Fashion
Folkways
Holidays
Social Issues and Crime
Sports

One method of showing off newly acquired wealth in the Gilded Age was to build an elaborate and costly mansion. This went on chiefly in New York City, Chicago, and San Francisco, and at such summer resorts as Newport, R.I. At Fifth Ave. and 91st St. in New York City, Andrew Carnegie, the steel magnate, erected a mansion with gold plumbing fixtures. In Chicago the Potter Palmers, society leaders, constructed a castlelike home with a tower 80 feet high. On Nob Hill in San Francisco, James C. Flood, whose wealth came from mining, built a 42-room house that was surrounded by a block-long bronze fence. It took the full-time services of a man to keep it polished.

The derisive term *mugwump* had wide currency during this election year. It was applied to those Republicans, reformist or liberal, who bolted the party to vote for the Democratic nominee, Grover Cleveland. The word derives from an Algonquian word meaning "big chief." Its first prominent use was by Charles Dana, editor of the New York *Sun,* with the implication that Republican bolters thought themselves above party affiliations. The term is now applied to bolters of any party.

The Knights of Labor, at their convention, desig-

nated that **Labor Day** be celebrated annually on the first Monday in September. Previously, the holiday had been celebrated sporadically. In 1887 several states established the first Monday in September as Labor Day; others followed suit shortly. Not until 1894 did Congress declare Labor Day a legal holiday for federal employees.

The **first black major league baseball player** was Moses Fleetwood Walker, who played for Toledo in the American Association.

June 5: Gen. **William Tecumseh Sherman,** a hero of the Civil War, declined the offer of the Republican presidential nomination with these words to the Republican convention: "I will not accept if nominated and will not serve if elected." Sherman was without political experience or inclination.

1885

I. Civil Rights
Exploration and Settlement
Government
Statistics
Wars

Under pressure from the Knights of Labor and other workers' groups, Congress on Feb. 26 passed the Contract Labor Law, or Foran Act, to further restrict immigration. The Knights had charged that American employers were signing up foreign workers with the promise of paying their passage to the U.S. and then were bringing them in for use as strikebreakers. Actually, most strikebreakers were hired from private labor agencies in large cities. The new law, virtually outlawing alien contract labor, did not, however, apply to skilled laborers needed by new industries or to certain other groups, such as actors and servants.

Feb 25: Fencing of public lands in the West was prohibited by an act of Congress. On Aug. 17 Pres. Grover Cleveland reinforced the act with orders to remove all illegal enclosures. Five years before, Carl Schurz, secretary of the treasury, had conducted an investigation into public land abuses. Since then, pressure mounted steadily to prevent railroad and cattle interests from exploiting the weak postwar management of western lands. By fencing in all water sources, special interests were concentrating great holdings. They reacted to the strictures of 1885 by forcing William A. J. Sparks, in 1887, from his presidential appointment as land commissioner. Agitation for reform persisted and eventually won out.

Mar 3: Special delivery service was inaugurated by the U.S. Post Office Dept.

II. Architecture
Arts and Music
Popular Entertainment
Publishing
Theater

Ragtime, the earliest form of jazz, began its rise to popularity with the arrival this year in St. Louis, Mo., of Scott Joplin. Joplin was born in Texarkana, Tex., in 1868, the son of a former slave. A self-taught musician, he was only 17 when he arrived in St. Louis. He began playing the piano in honky-tonks along Chestnut and Market streets. In ragtime the melody is syncopated on the piano with the right hand while the left keeps a regular beat in march style. In the late 1890s Joplin turned to composing. Among his best known works are "Maple Leaf Rag" and "The Entertainer," the latter supplying the background music for the 1973 movie *The Sting.* Joplin also composed a ragtime opera, *Treemonisha.*

Among **books published** this year, *The Rise of Silas Lapham* by William Dean Howells showed Howells at the peak of his form in depicting a self-made man and his family transplanted into Boston society. Also published were Ulysses S. Grant's unassuming *Personal Memoirs* in two volumes, a work that became a best seller and saved his heirs from penury; and the first major work by the Harvard philosopher and teacher Josiah Royce, *The Spirit of Modern Philosophy.*

The **Marshall Field Building,** designed by Henry Hobson Richardson, was completed, marking the beginning of a new era in commercial architecture. One of the Boston architect's masterpieces, it reflected Richardson's grasp of the realities of commercial problems and his talent for achieving, despite functional requirements, a logical, even exuberant, effect. His influence on Louis Sullivan and later Chicago architects is clear.

Feb 21: The **Washington Monument** was dedicated in the nation's capital, 37 years after the cornerstone was laid, four and a half years after construction began. Total cost was a bit less than $1,200,000. The monument is 555 feet 5 and one-eighth inches high. Ascent and descent can be made by elevator or by negotiating 898 steps. The monument was opened to the public on Oct. 9, 1888.

III. Business and Industry
Education
Philosophy and Religion
Science

One of the most dreaded diseases of the time was tuberculosis, for which there was no specific remedy. Edward Livingston Trudeau, a New York physician, contracted the disease while taking care of his tubercular brother and went to live in the Adirondack Mts. in New York State. There, spending much time in the open air, he regained his health. He believed the cold dry air of the mountains and his way of life, which included much rest, were the cause of his cure. As a result, he opened the Adirondack Cottage Sanatorium in 1885 at Saranac Lake, N.Y. This first institution of its kind in the U.S. was initially a one-room cottage with simple furnishings and facilities. The sanatorium functioned until 1954, when it closed for lack of patients, modern methods of diagnosis and treatment having by then reduced deaths from tuberculosis in the U.S. by 95%.

Furnaces for **garbage disposal** began to be introduced in many cities, particularly in the landlocked Middle West, as a health measure. It had been discovered that swine fed with garbage from the cities contracted trichinosis, which could be transmitted to consumers of the infected meat.

IV. Fashion
Folkways
Holidays
Social Issues and Crime
Sports

A world's fair in the U.S., the New Orleans Exposition, attracted international attention when it opened on Jan. 24, 1885. It was the largest yet held in the U.S., being a third again larger than the Centennial Exposition in Philadelphia in 1876. Many nations, including England, France, China, Japan, Austria, and all the nations of South America, had exhibits. The U.S. was represented by exhibits from each department of the federal government and from the Smithsonian Institution, which had a display of "almost every survival of prehistoric times." Americans took special pride in what one observer termed "the unrivaled collection of American products and resources."

The **fashion in clothing** was described thus in *Harper's Bazaar:* "'Moyen âge' is the term used to describe the new fashion in the spring of 1885. Scarfs, handkerchiefs, wide ribbons and fabrics are emblazoned to imitate medieval banners. Vieux rouge (old red) is showing two tones while the new blue is called vieille blouse usée, the color of workmen's shirts. Much beige and cream color and bright gold is being shown. Flowers and scarfs are replacing feathers on hats. Combinations of two materials with long drapery and plain lawn skirts are being used in both suits and dresses."

Sep 14-16: The **America's Cup** was successfully defended by the U.S. yacht *Puritan,* which won two straight races from the British challenger *Genesta.*

Dec 20: A **weightlifting feat** of incredible proportions was accomplished by William B. Curtis, who was reported to have lifted 3239 lbs. "with harness."

1886

I. Civil Rights
Exploration and Settlement
Government
Statistics
Wars

The nation was stirred by an incident on May 4 in Chicago's Haymarket Square. A labor rally there, which included speeches by anarchists, was breaking up when a large force of police arrived. A bomb exploded among them, killing seven officers and wounding about 60. The anarchists were blamed and the police arrested eight leaders of what came to be known as the Haymarket Riot. Their trial began on June 19. Although no evidence was ever presented to identify any of the accused as the bomb thrower, all eight were convicted on Aug. 20. Seven were sentenced to death, one to jail. Of the condemned, four were hanged on Nov. 11, one committed suicide in jail, and two had their sentences changed to life imprisonment. Seven years later, on June 26, 1893, Gov. John Peter Altgeld of Illinois pardoned the three still in jail. For this act he was denounced by some as little better than an anarchist himself.

Jan 19: A **Presidential Succession Act** was passed by Congress. It provided that in the event of removal, death, resignation, or inability of the president and vice president, the heads of the executive departments, in the order of the creation of their offices, would succeed to the presidency. A new order of succession was adopted in 1947, and it was superseded by the Twenty-fifth Amendment to the Constitution in 1967.

Sep 4: Geronimo, the inveterate Apache raider along the Mexican border, surrendered to Gen. Nelson A. Miles in Arizona. All the Chiricahua Apaches were then resettled in Florida as war prisoners. They were relocated to Fort Sill, Okla., in 1894.

Oct 28: The **Statue of Liberty** was unveiled and dedicated by Pres. Grover Cleveland in a ceremony on Bedloe's Island. The 225-ton, 152-ft. tall copper statue was presented to the U.S. by France in commemoration of 100 years of American independence.

Nov 2: In **congressional elections** the Republicans lost four seats in the Senate but held a 39–37 majority over the Democrats. In the House the Democrats lost 14 seats but held a 169–152 majority, with four seats going to minor parties.

II. Architecture
Arts and Music
Popular Entertainment
Publishing
Theater

Not surprisingly, the Civil War became a source of material for playwrights. The first important drama using this subject opened in Brooklyn, N.Y., on Feb. 22. It was *Held by the Enemy* by William Gillette, the actor and dramatist. Its plot concerned two soldiers in love with the same woman in an occupied southern city. In 1895 Gillette again used a Civil War setting, this time in a spy episode in *Secret Service.* Gillette's most popular play, however, was *Sherlock Holmes* (1899), in which Gillette was to act the title role until a few years before his death in 1937.

Among **books published** this year was an immensely popular story for children, *Little Lord Fauntleroy* by Frances Hodgson Burnett. The little gentleman-hero has long since lost any appeal for youngsters, but the illustrations by Reginald Bathurst Birch set a durable fashion for children's clothing, and 40 years later Mary Pickford played Fauntleroy in one of her box office successes. Also published were *The Midge* by Henry Cuyler Bunner, a graceful novelette by the poet-editor of *Puck; Indian Summer,* a romantic novel set in Florence, *Tuscan Cities,* a travel book, and *The Garroters,* a farcical play, all by William Dean Howells; *Princess Casamassima,* a novel by Henry James in which he uncovered the social ferment underlying the surface placidity of upper-class life in London; and *Hugh Wynne* by Silas Weir Mitchell, a noted Philadelphia physician and neurologist, partly a historical romance, partly a novel of psychology, first appearing as a serial in *Century Magazine.*

III. Business and Industry
Education
Philosophy and Religion
Science

A significant step in the growth of the labor movement was taken on Dec. 8 in Columbus, Ohio, when the American Federation of Labor (AFL) was organized by about 25 labor groups representing 150,000 members. The new union grew out of the Federation of Organized Trades and Labor Unions, formed in 1881. The first president of the AFL was Samuel Gompers, president of the Cigarmakers Union, who held the office except for one year until his death in 1924. The AFL was craft-oriented and favored skilled labor. Under Gompers' leadership, it had nothing to do with politics or socialistic programs, but put its efforts into securing higher wages, shorter working hours, and better working conditions. By 1890 the AFL had 225,000 members; by 1900 its membership was 550,000.

A cheap process for extracting **aluminum** from its ore was invented by Charles Martin Hall. His electrolytic method caused the price of aluminum to drop from $5.00 a lb. in 1888 to 18 cents in 1914.

The **Whiskey Trust** was formed on the model of the Standard Oil Trust. It included 80 distilleries, of which all but 12 were closed down; profits were distributed pro rata.

IV. Fashion
Folkways
Holidays
Social Issues and Crime
Sports

What a person will do to achieve instant notoriety was demonstrated on July 23 when Steve Brodie, a bookmaker, allegedly jumped off the Brooklyn Bridge into the East R., a drop of about 140 feet. Some said that a dummy was dropped while Brodie hid under a pier, waiting to appear at the proper moment. In any event, Brodie opened a profitable saloon on the strength of the feat. Brodie later took to the stage and repeated his act by jumping from a "bridge" in the melodrama *Mad Money*, first performed at Niblo's Garden in New York City on Feb. 22, 1891.

The **first international polo match** was held between England and the U.S. at Newport, R.I.; it was a gala occasion. Both teams were colorfully dressed in satin and full-length leather boots. The grounds were lined with members of the social set of New England and New York. The visiting team, more practiced, swept the match 10–4 and 14–2.

Jan 1: The **first Tournament of Roses** was held in Pasadena, Calif., staged by the Valley Hunt Club, which had been founded by Charles Frederick Holder, a distinguished naturalist. Mr. Holder suggested that the members of the Valley Hunt Club decorate their carriages with the natural flowers of California on New Year's Day and that after a parade of these carriages a program of athletic events be devised to round out the day. Holder's floral motif has remained a feature of the tournament to this day.

Sep 9-11: The **America's Cup** was successfully defended by the U.S. yacht *Mayflower*, which won two straight races from the British challenger *Galatea*.

1887

I. Civil Rights
Exploration and Settlement
Government
Statistics
Wars

Growing agitation by farmers and others over the abuses of railroads in setting rates and in other matters resulted in the establishment of the first regulatory commission in U.S. history. This was the Interstate Commerce Commission, set up by the Interstate Commerce Act of 1887, which became law on Feb. 4. The law stated that interstate railroads must charge reasonable, not discriminatory, rates, and prohibited them from engaging in pooling operations. Drawbacks and rebates, both forms of rate reduction for preferred customers, were outlawed, and charging more for a short haul than a long haul was forbidden. In part, the law was an outgrowth of the Wabash case of 1886, in which the Supreme Court ruled that a state could not regulate an interstate railway that went through its territory. The railroads soon found ways to evade the act, and the Supreme Court reversed decisions of the commission.

Free delivery of mail was provided in all communities with a population of 10,000 or more.

Feb 3: The **Electoral Count Act** was created by Congress to avoid disputed national elections. It made each state responsible for its own electoral returns and forced Congress to accept the results except in the case of irregularity.

Mar 2: Pres. Grover Cleveland signed the **Hatch Act,** which called for establishment of an agricultural research and experiment station in each state with a land-grant college. The act also authorized annual appropriations to each state on the establishment of such a station.

II. Architecture
   ### Arts and Music
   ### Popular Entertainment
   ### Publishing
   ### Theater

The variety of American stage offerings in the late nineteenth century could be seen in a listing of plays that opened in New York City in 1887. Rapidly becoming a favorite was the young Edward Hugh Sothern, who played in a popular comedy, *The Highest Bidder,* which opened at the Lyceum Theater on May 3. *The Still Alarm,* which opened at the 14th Street Theater on Aug. 30, featured Harry Lacey playing a fireman. *A Hole in the Ground,* with William Mack, opened at the same theater on Sept. 12. David Belasco and Henry C. De Mille scored a resounding success with their first collaboration, *The Wife,* which opened at the Lyceum Theater on Nov. 1. That same night Ada Rehan, already popular, starred in *The Railroad of Love* at Daly's Theater, with Mrs. George H. Gilbert and John Drew in the cast. This year Rehan also gave her New York debut performance as Kate in Shakespeare's *The Taming of the Shrew.*

Augustus Saint-Gaudens completed his famous standing statue of Abraham Lincoln for Lincoln Park, Chicago. Lincoln, with slightly bowed head, stands before a chair from which he has seemingly just risen.

III. Business and Industry
   ### Education
   ### Philosophy and Religion
   ### Science

Copying the lead of the Standard Oil trust in 1882, other industries rushed to establish trusts to secure monopolies and eliminate competition. In the decade beginning in 1887, 86 combinations of companies were made. Another 149 combinations were formed by 1900. This year saw formation of the Sugar Trust (American Sugar Refineries Company), the Whiskey Trust (Distillers' and Cattle Feeders' Trust), the Lead Trust, and the Cotton-Oil Trust, as well as monopolies in the wallpaper, shoelace, and oatmeal industries. When trusts were formed, some plants in the industry were closed to restrict supplies and raise prices, thus putting people out of work. In the case of the Sugar Trust, 11 out of 18 refineries were immediately shut down.

The interest of **Theodore Roosevelt** in the protection of big game and wildlife became manifest in his appeal for the formation of the Boone and Crockett Club, named for two of his heroes. Since 1883, Roosevelt had been buying Dakota ranchlands. He gave up these investments in 1887, but contact with the open spaces had stimulated his interest in nature. In 1888 he set down his western experiences in the book *Ranch Life and the Hunting Trail.*

IV. Fashion
   ### Folkways
   ### Holidays
   ### Social Issues and Crime
   ### Sports

Trade, manufacturing, transportation, and technology were greatly increasing the nation's wealth, yet there seemed to be a growing gap between the poorest and the richest Americans. For the poor, clothing tended to be drab and dark, as did furniture. Men went to work in overalls. Among women of all levels, clothing was mainly heavy and dark, except for the young and those in society who could spend freely. Gentlemen in society wore full dress suits to social affairs. The growing middle class enjoyed the good things of life to an increasing extent, living in comfortable homes. The average middle-class home was crowded with weighty furniture, thick draperies, and innumerable knickknacks.

The **first true golf club** in the U.S. was probably the Foxbury Golf Club, founded in Foxbury, Pa., as a result of John Mickle Fox's trip to Scotland, where he learned the game. The club is still in existence. There were golf clubs calling themselves such in Savannah, Ga., and Charleston, S.C., as far back as 1795 and 1796, but there is no record that their members ever played golf.

Mar 2: The **American Trotting Association** was organized at Detroit, Mich.

Sep 17-30: The **America's Cup** was successfully defended by the U.S. yacht *Volunteer,* which won two straight races from the British challenger *Thistle.*

1888

I. Civil Rights
Exploration and Settlement
Government
Statistics
Wars

The main issue in the presidential election campaign of 1888 was whether the tariff should be reduced; Democrats said yes, Republicans no. Pres. Grover Cleveland, the Democratic candidate, did not campaign, feeling it was beneath the dignity of the office of president. Benjamin Harrison, the Republican candidate, brought the front porch campaign to its peak. Republican groups were told when to visit Harrison's home, and the candidate was well prepared for each, including the Republican White Hat Club of Ohio. In all, he addressed about 300,000 people without leaving home. Late in the campaign, on Oct. 26, the British minister to the U.S. was tricked into writing a letter saying it would be best for England if Cleveland were reelected. Sensing there was still some latent dislike of the mother country, the Republicans turned this against Cleveland even though he had sent the hapless diplomat home.

The **secret ballot** was first used in the U.S. in local elections in Louisville, Ky. Adopted in Australia as early as 1858, the secret ballot came to be referred to in America as "kangaroo voting." Henry George, proponent of the single land tax, was among the earliest American public figures urging adoption of the secret ballot. In 1950 South Carolina became the last state to adopt the secret ballot.

Mar 12: A 36-hour **blizzard,** which struck the region around New York City, cost 400 lives and destroyed millions of dollars of property. The city was virtually isolated from the world when the heavy snows halted transportation and disrupted communications. Messages to Boston had to be relayed via England.

June 5: The **Democratic National Convention nominated Pres. Grover Cleveland** for a second term. Allen G. Thurman of Ohio was nominated for the vice presidency.

June 25: The **Republican National Convention nominated Benjamin Harrison** of Indiana for the presidency and Levi P. Morton of New York for the vice presidency.

July 29: A **yellow fever epidemic** broke out in Jacksonville, Fla., and persisted until Dec. 7. Over 4500 cases were reported, and more than 400 persons died. Similar epidemics struck throughout the South during this period.

Nov 6: Benjamin Harrison was elected president of the United States. Levi P. Morton was elected vice president. The electoral vote was Harrison, 233; Pres. Grover Cleveland, the Democratic candidate, 168. The popular vote was Harrison, 5,444,337; Cleveland, 5,540,050; Clinton B. Fisk, Prohibition candidate, 250,125; Alson J. Streeter, Union Labor candidate, 146,897; Robert H. Cowdrey, United Labor candidate, 2808. In congressional elections the Republicans kept their 39–37 majority in the Senate and gained 14 seats in the House to take a 166–159 majority.

II. Architecture
Arts and Music
Popular Entertainment
Publishing
Theater

A new generation of musicians was emerging; they were to dominate American music until the time of World War I. These composers, whose works and writings reflected particularly the influence of Johannes Brahms, became known as the New England Academicians or Boston Classicists. Among them was Arthur William Foote, the only important American composer of the period educated entirely in the U.S. His choral work *The Wreck of the Hesperus* was enthusiastically received in Boston this year. He composed an overture, *In the Mountains,* in 1887 and *Suite for Strings* in 1889.

Among **books published** this year was *Looking Backward, 2000–1887,* a Utopian fantasy by Edward Bellamy, a little-known journalist and novelist. Bellamy hit on the right medium for expressing his concern with social problems in an industrialized society. The book sold 1,000,000 copies in a few years, and Bellamy clubs devoted to the nationalization of industry and redistribution of wealth sprang up everywhere. Also published this year were *The American Commonwealth,* a classic that ranks with Alexis de Tocqueville's *Democracy in America* as a sympathetic but penetrating analysis, by James Bryce, British historian, frequent visitor to the U.S., and later ambassador to the U.S. (1907–1913); *Acres of Diamonds* by Russell Conwell, an inspirational classic first delivered as a lecture in 1861 but polished through use on the Chautauqua circuit (over 6000 times); *The Critical Period of American History, 1783–1789* by John Fiske, who was now turning from evolution to history; *The History of the Inquisition in the Middle Ages* by Henry C. Lea, probably the best historical work to date by an American historian in a field other than U.S. history; *Political Essays,* the last published work of James Russell Lowell; and the first volumes in *The Library of American Literature,* edited by the poet, stockbroker, and critic Edmund Clarence Stedman.

May: "**Casey at the Bat,**" by Ernest Thayer, was given its first public recitation by the popular actor DeWolf Hopper, at Wallack's Theater, New York City.

III. Business and Industry
Education
Philosophy and Religion
Science

Scientists and inventors were beginning to put electricity to practical use. Among the leaders in this field was Nikola Tesla, who was born in Austria-Hungary in 1857 and came to the U.S. in 1884. In 1888 he invented the alternating current motor, one of his most important contributions. Other inventions included an arc lighting system (1886), an alternating current transmission system (1888), and high-frequency current generators (1890). Tesla also worked on a system for transmitting power without wires. In his later years he was occupied with telephony and telegraphy.

George Eastman introduced the **Kodak,** a square box camera using roll film. Kodak camera No. 1 was at first marketed already loaded; the photographer mailed the Kodak to the factory, which returned prints and the reloaded camera. Photography became a practical hobby overnight, and sales skyrocketed.

June 13: A **Department of Labor** without Cabinet status was established by an act of Congress. In 1903 it was reduced to the status of a bureau in the Dept. of Commerce and Labor. On Mar. 4, 1913, Congress created a Department of Labor headed by a Cabinet member.

July 27: The **first electric automobile,** designed by Philip W. Pratt, was demonstrated in Boston. It was a tricycle driven by storage batteries, and was built by the Fred W. Kimball Company of Boston.

IV. Fashion
Folkways
Holidays
Social Issues and Crime
Sports

Although it was not the first golf club established in the U.S., St. Andrews Club in Yonkers, N.Y., founded this year, clearly marked the point at which the game became firmly rooted in the U.S. Clubs were soon set up in Boston, New York, and Philadelphia. By 1892 the game was moving westward, soon reaching the Pacific coast. In 1893 a course for women only was opened in Morristown, N.J., and by 1894 there were 100 courses in the country. At this time golf was a game for the well-to-do, and the players, who wore rather odd costumes, including scarlet coats, were often objects of ridicule.

The political slogan "**As Maine goes, so goes the nation**" was adopted by the Republican Party after the election of Benjamin Harrison. State elections in Maine for decades to come were held weeks before national elections, so they were used as gauges for predicting the results in the national balloting. Maine remained staunchly Republican until the era of Franklin D. Roosevelt.

Jan 21: The **Amateur Athletic Union** of the U.S. (AAU) was formed, winning control over amateur athletics from unscrupulous promoters. The AAU's ideal was to preserve "sport for sport's sake." It came to supervise and conduct programs and competitions in about 20 sports and to represent the U.S. in international amateur sports federations. Its influence has been reduced since World War II by the takeover of collegiate sports by the National Collegiate Athletic Association (NCAA) and by the increasing professionalization of many sports.

June 9: The 22nd annual **Belmont Stakes** was won by Sir Dixon, with a time of 2:40¼. The jockey was Jimmy McLaughlin, who picked up his sixth Belmont Stakes win. McLaughlin was the only jockey in Belmont history to twice win the race three times in a row (1882–1884, 1886–1888).

1889

I. Civil Rights
Exploration and Settlement
Government
Statistics
Wars

A controversy involving the U.S., Great Britain, and Germany over the Samoan Islands in the Pacific

Ocean threatened to break out into armed conflict. In 1889 warships of the three nations converged in the region, reflecting the three powers' interest in the civil war being fought on the islands. A showdown among the naval vessels in the harbor of Apia was averted only when a fierce storm destroyed all the warships except one English vessel. On Apr. 29 a conference opened in Berlin and on June 14 the three nations agreed on a treaty that provided for a three-power protectorate to guarantee Samoan independence.

Feb 11: The **Department of Agriculture** was raised to Cabinet status by Congress. Pres. Grover Cleveland appointed Norman J. Colman as its first secretary. He served less than three weeks before being replaced by Jeremiah M. Rusk, appointed by incoming Pres. Benjamin Harrison.

Apr 22: At noon the great **Oklahoma land rush** began. The federal government, pressured by cattlemen, opened for settlement 1,900,000 acres in central Oklahoma bought from the Creek and Scminole tribes. Thousands of settlers raced in after a pistol shot signaled the opening. Many Oklahomans had already made illegal entry to stake claims to the best land. In fact, by 10 A.M. of the opening day, Guthrie, the designated central city for the new territory, had swelled with settlers seeking plots in the new territorial capital.

May 31: The disastrous **Johnstown flood** killed 2295 persons when the dam above Johnstown, Pa., broke after heavy rains had swelled the Conemaugh R. The flood destroyed four valley towns before drowning Johnstown in 30 feet of water. Every Johnstown survivor lost a relative or friend in this calamity.

Nov 2: North and South Dakota were admitted into the Union, the 39th and 40th states.

Nov 8: Montana was admitted into the Union, the 41st state.

Nov 11: Washington was admitted into the Union, the 42nd state.

II. Architecture
Arts and Music
Popular Entertainment
Publishing
Theater

A new approach to women's magazines was introduced this year by Edward W. Bok, who took over editorship of the *Ladies' Home Journal.* Hitherto such periodicals had offered only light entertainment and household hints. By publishing serious articles on civic affairs, waging crusades against social ills, and printing the writings of leading authors such as Mark Twain and Rudyard Kipling, Bok demonstrated that women's interests were wider than had been assumed. By the time Bok retired in 1919, the *Journal's* circulation had increased from 440,000 to 2,000,000.

Among **books published** this year was *A Connecticut Yankee in King Arthur's Court* by Mark Twain, in which the author further explored the ironies of human nature and existence by setting a Yankee industrialist in the not-so-romantic days of chivalry. Also published were the first two volumes of *The History of the United States* by Henry Adams, for many years the best account of the administration of Thomas Jefferson; *Sant'Ilario,* one of Francis Marion Crawford's better romantic novels of life in Italian society, part of his trilogy begun in *Saracinesca* and concluded in *Dr. Orsino* (1892); *A Little Book of Western Verse* by Eugene Field, which brought the Chicago columnist-poet a wider following; *Chita: A Memory of Last Island* by Lafcadio Hearn, the first novel by an atypical American author on an atypical theme, the destruction of an island and the hazards faced by a lost child; *Annie Kilburn* by William Dean Howells, a novel in which Howells took up the cause of labor; and the first two volumes of *The Winning of the West* by Theodore Roosevelt.

III. Business and Industry
Education
Philosophy and Religion
Science

Liberal thinkers within American Protestantism reacted to the problems caused by rapid industrialization with a movement that came to be known as the Social Gospel, or Christian Socialism. These leaders believed that Christian churches should do more than strive for personal salvation. They worked to abolish child labor, secure better working conditions for women, and gain a living wage for all workers. They believed that the growing concentration of wealth was inimical to the teachings of Christ. The early leader of the Social Gospel movement was the Rev. Washington Gladden, who wrote *Burning Questions* (1890). Somewhat later, the Rev. Walter Rauschenbusch became an important figure. Among economists, Richard T. Ely took a forceful part. Others active in the Society of Christian Socialists, which held a meeting in Boston this year, were

Josiah Strong, David Jayne Hill, and E. Benjamin Andrews.

Hull House, a settlement house that would become famous, was established in a slum neighborhood in Chicago by Jane Addams. Like other settlement houses of this period, Hull House was patterned after Toynbee Hall in London.

The **first movie film** was developed by Thomas A. Edison on a base devised by George Eastman.

The **Singer Manufacturing Company** of Elizabethport, N.J., produced and marketed the first electric sewing machine known in the U.S.

IV. Fashion
Folkways
Holidays
Social Issues and Crime
Sports

As methods of transportation improved, there was a temptation to see how far one could go in the shortest time. Nellie Bly (Elizabeth Cochrane Seaman), a reporter for Joseph Pulitzer's New York *World,* set out on Nov. 14 to better the record of 80 days around the world set by Jules Verne's fictional hero Phileas Fogg. Using trains, boats, bullock carts, and her own energy, Nellie made it back to New York City on Jan. 25, 1890, with a time of 72 days, 6 hrs., 10 min., 58 sec. She was much acclaimed, especially by the *World.* She recounted her trip in *Nellie Bly's Book: Around the World in Seventy-Two Days* (1890). The year it was published, someone named George Train went around the world in 67 days, 12 hrs., 3 min., but no one paid him much attention. This was not Nellie Bly's first headline-grabbing exploit. Earlier she had had herself committed to a facility for the mentally ill on Blackwell's Island, New York City, and in 1887 recounted her adventures in *Ten Days in a Mad House.*

Walter Camp listed in *Collier's Weekly* the first **All-American football team,** selecting 11 college football players as best in the nation at their positions. The selection was made by Caspar Whitney, who chose the All-American teams through 1896. The selections appeared in articles in *Collier's* annually until Camp's death in 1925, when Grantland Rice took over the task. Today selections are made by various polls of sportswriters and coaches.

July 8: Bare knuckle boxing had its last and most memorable bout when John L. Sullivan knocked out Jake Kilrain in the 75th round for the U.S. heavyweight championship at Richburg, Miss. Sullivan then claimed the world's championship, for Kilrain had fought a draw with the champion of England,

Jem Smith. After this bout boxing with gloves under Marquis of Queensberry rules was introduced.

1890

I. Civil Rights
Exploration and Settlement
Government
Statistics
Wars

Mounting pressure for federal restraint of monopolistic industrial trusts resulted in the passage on July 2 of the Sherman Antitrust Act, named for Sen. John Sherman, Republican of Ohio. The law stated: "Every contract, combination in the form of trust or otherwise, or conspiracy, in restraint of trade or commerce among the several States, or with foreign nations, is hereby declared illegal." In practice, the lack of definition of such words as trust weakened the law. Also, it was not clear whether the law applied to labor unions. The act did not accomplish as much as its advocates hoped because of the way federal courts interpreted it and because, for the first ten years at least, no vigorous attempt was made to enforce it.

The **Census** recorded a population of 62,947,714. The center of population was placed at 20 mi. east of Columbus, Ind.

Feb 10: Some 11,000,000 acres of **Sioux Indian territory,** ceded to the U.S. in 1889, were opened for general settlement.

Apr 14: The **Pan-American Union** was created by a resolution of the Pan-American conference held in Washington, D.C., between Oct. 2, 1889, and Apr. 21, 1890.

May 2: The **Oklahoma Territory,** the last territory in the contiguous United States, was created by an act of Congress. It was established by redefining Indian territory and creating an area for settlers within Indian lands.

July 3: Idaho was admitted to the Union, the 43rd state.

July 10: Wyoming was admitted to the Union, the 44th state. As a territory it had given women the vote in 1869. It was the first territory and the first state to do so.

Oct 1: The **Weather Bureau** was created in the Dept. of Agriculture by an act of Congress. Weather information had previously come from the Army Signal Corps.

Nov 4: In **congressional elections** the Republicans gained eight seats in the Senate to lead the Democrats 47–39, with two seats going to minor parties. In the House a Democratic landslide gave Democrats a 235–88 majority, with nine seats going to minor parties.

Dec 15: Sitting Bull, chief of the Sioux Indians, was killed in a skirmish with U.S. soldiers along the Grand R. in South Dakota.

II. Architecture
Arts and Music
Popular Entertainment
Publishing
Theater

Toward the end of the nineteenth century, light and comic operas became popular. The two leading composers were Victor Herbert and Reginald De Koven. The latter wrote 19 comic operas, of which the most popular by far was *Robin Hood,* first produced in Chicago this year on June 9. It contained his two most popular songs, "Brown October Ale" and "Oh, Promise Me." De Koven also wrote two grand operas, *Canterbury Pilgrims* (1917) and *Rip Van Winkle* (1920).

Among **books published** this year was *Poems,* a selection of poems among many by Emily Dickinson that were found after her death by her sister. It received mixed reviews because her poetry, often unrhymed and subtle, struck an unfamiliar note. Her place in U.S. poetry gradually became secure, and her popularity and reputation skyrocketed after World War II. Also published this year were *A Hazard of New Fortunes,* a long, complex novel by William Dean Howells, in which a cast of 15 major characters and many minor figures scramble for success in New York City; *The Influence of Sea Power upon History,* by Navy Capt. Alfred Thayer Mahan, a classic analysis of sea power; *Abraham Lincoln: A History* in ten volumes by John Nicolay and John M. Hay, wartime secretaries to the president which became a standard biography; and *Black Beauty,* by Anna Sewell, an English book for children issued in the U.S. under the aegis of the American Humane Society.

Louis H. Sullivan's Wainwright Building was erected in St. Louis. The Chicago architect has been called the father of modern architecture and the inventor of the skyscraper. The Wainwright Building was one of his best works. Also this year, Sullivan's Chicago Auditorium was completed. It was for many years the greatest structure of its type anywhere.

May 30: The cornerstone of the **Washington Memorial Arch,** in marble, was laid. The arch was originally built of wood. This masterpiece by architect Stanford White stands at the foot of Fifth Ave. in New York City.

III. Business and Industry
Education
Philosophy and Religion
Science

As the century neared its end, the U.S. developed a school of philosophy of its own—pragmatism. The term had been used in a magazine article as early as 1878 by Charles Sanders Peirce. Pragmatism taught that truth was to be found not in theoretical speculation, but in the practical outcome of ideas. It judged ideas and actions by their consequences, if any. This truly American philosophy was developed by William James, who became the most influential thinker of his time. He earned an international reputation and brought the concept of pragmatism to a wide audience. James's *Principles of Psychology,* published this year, became a classic. The book was thoroughly empirical and made a laboratory science of psychology.

The growth of **child labor** in the South was reflected in the fact that some 23,000 children were now employed in the factories of the 13 southern states. Adoption by industry of the traditional agricultural family system of employment was mainly responsible for the high number of children employed.

Illiteracy in America was estimated at 13.3% of the population, a decrease of 3.7% in a decade.

The establishment of **Sequoia and Yosemite national parks** by the federal government assisted the cause of conservation in the U.S. by protecting native species of animal and plant life from hunters and timber interests.

Formation of the **American Tobacco Company,** after a price war among cigarette companies, created a monopoly organized by James Buchanan Duke. Duke later created similar monopolies for plug tobacco and snuff. Ultimately he established the Duke Endowment, principally for the benefit of Trinity College in Durham, N.C., in 1924 renamed Duke University.

Pyramiding of wealth in the U.S. led to estimates that 1% of the people possessed more wealth than the rest of the people combined.

Jan 23: The **fastest railroad time** for an American train was claimed for the Atchison, Topeka & Santa

Fe Railroad, which carried reporter Nellie Bly from La Junta, Colo., to Chicago at an average speed of 78.1 mph.

Oct 6: The sanctioning of **polygamy** was discontinued by the Mormon Church. Thereafter most cases in conflict with federal law concerned men who had married polygamously before 1890.

IV. Fashion
Folkways
Holidays
Social Issues and Crime
Sports

The existence of urban slums was well known by many, but it was not until the publication this year of *How the Other Half Lives* by Jacob A. Riis, a Danish-born New York City journalist, that the reality of the miserable lives led by thousands in the slums was brought home to the general public. The book triggered efforts to alleviate these conditions by improving labor conditions and instituting building codes. In his book Riis cited facts and figures and told of his experiences in the slums. Battling alone at first, Riis gained many supporters and found a powerful ally in Theodore Roosevelt. He also made enemies of landlords and politicians who were profiting from the slums.

Smoking by men at social functions became more acceptable during this decade, but the social taboo against women smoking in the company of men remained strong.

The **two-step** came into vogue. This lively dance step probably owed much to John Philip Sousa's fast "Washington Post March." In any case, the two-step replaced several older dances, such as the galop, quadrille, lancers, reel, polka, and Portland fancy.

Aug 6: The **first electrocution** took place at Auburn Prison, Auburn, N.Y. The executed prisoner was William Kemmler of Buffalo, who had been convicted of the hatchet murder of Matilde "Tillie" Ziegler, his common-law wife, on Mar. 28, 1889. The execution was botched. George Westinghouse, Jr., reported: "It has been a brutal affair. They could have done better with an axe."

Nov 29: The **first Army-Navy football game** was played at West Point, N.Y. The score was Navy 24, Army 0. The contest became an annual event between the two service academies (except for 1909, 1917–1918, and 1928–1929).

1891

I. Civil Rights
Exploration and Settlement
Government
Statistics
Wars

The tide of immigration continued to flow strongly. To help deal with it, the position of superintendent of immigration was created on Mar. 3. In this one year, 560,319 immigrants arrived at American ports, and during the 1890s the total was 3,687,000. Until the 1880s, most of the immigrants had come from western and northern Europe. However, in the 1880s such immigration decreased and the numbers arriving from southern and eastern Europe and the Middle East swelled greatly. These new immigrants were less equipped to fit into American life, and almost all had to start at the bottom of the economic ladder.

Mar 3: U.S. **Circuit Courts of Appeal** were created by an act of Congress. This relieved the Supreme Court of some of its appellate jurisdiction.

Mar 4: Congress passed the **International Copyright Act,** which gave British, French, Belgian, and Swiss authors copyright protection in the U.S. American publishers had previously pirated works by foreign authors, depriving them of their royalties and injuring American authors, whose books had to be priced higher than those of foreign authors because of the inclusion of royalties in the price. Copyright protection was later extended to include most other countries of the world.

May 19: The **People's, or Populist, Party** was launched in Cincinnati, Ohio. Farmers in the West and South were in desperate economic plight, and backers of the new party, thinking eastern bankers were hoarding gold, advocated free coinage of silver. High railroad rates also were hurting farmers, so they advocated government ownership of railroads. Free silverites captured the Democratic Party in 1896, but lost the election by 600,000 votes.

Sep 22: Nine hundred thousand acres of **Indian land** in Oklahoma were opened for general settlement by a presidential proclamation. The land had been ceded to the U.S. by Sauk, Fox, and Potawatomi Indians.

II. Architecture
Arts and Music
Popular Entertainment
Publishing
Theater

One of the greatest careers of the American stage, extending over more than 40 years, came to an end on Apr. 4 at the Brooklyn, N.Y., Academy of Music when Edwin Booth appeared for the last time in *Hamlet.* Booth had always been popular and his restrained style of acting departed from the more emotional style of many others, but his career had been checkered, marked by bankruptcy and then by scandal when his brother, John Wilkes Booth, assassinated Pres. Abraham Lincoln. Among Booth's most notable achievements were the 100-night run of *Hamlet* in 1864 in New York City; the building of Booth's Theater in New York in 1869, where Booth presented the works of William Shakespeare; and the bequest of his New York home to the Players' Club, which he founded in 1888 and served as first president.

Among **books published** this year was *Tales of Soldiers and Civilians* by the San Francisco journalist Ambrose Bierce, a writer fascinated by the supernatural, the mysterious, the terrifying, and the intensely emotional. His *Tales,* based on his Civil War experiences, was later reissued under the title *In the Midst of Life.* It included the oft-anthologized "An Occurrence at Owl Creek Bridge" and "A Horseman in the Sky" and established his reputation in the East. Other books published were *Poems, Second Edition,* by Emily Dickinson; *The American Revolution* by the skillful popularizer of U.S. history, John Fiske; *A New England Nun and Other Stories* by Mary Wilkins Freeman, offering expert portrayals of Massachusetts farm folk undergoing deformation of character or spirit in an era that was leaving them behind; *Main-Traveled Roads,* stark short stories and sketches against a background of dreary midwestern farm life, by Hamlin Garland; *Colonel Carter of Cartersville,* a novelette about a gentleman of the old South down on his luck, which made Francis Hopkinson Smith a popular author; and a final collection of poems and prose by the aging Walt Whitman, *Goodbye, My Fancy.*

Nov 9: The **longest consecutive theatrical run** to date was begun with the opening of *A Trip to Chinatown,* a farce about San Francisco by Charles H. Hoyt. It ran 650 performances, closing on Aug. 17, 1893, and held the record until 1918. Hoyt had already satirized

spiritualism, the plumbing industry, railroad operations, and politics.

III. Business and Industry
Education
Philosophy and Religion
Science

As the nation grew, it became increasingly industrialized. Industrial and agricultural production was rising, and imports and exports rose steadily as well. Agricultural products still represented the largest part of exports, but in the 1890s they declined from 74.5% of the total to 61% by 1900. During the decade, manufactured goods' share of exports rose from 17.87% to 31.65%. The value of imports increased from $789,310,404 in 1890 to $849,941,184 in 1900.

Henry O. Havemeyer created the **American Sugar Refining Company** under a New Jersey charter, after having his Sugar Refineries Company in New York broken up by the state's antitrust laws. Thus reorganized and without legal impediment, American Sugar went on to control half the sugar consumed in the U.S. by the time of Havemeyer's death in 1907.

Aug 24: **A patent for a motion picture camera,** the first in its field in the U.S., was filed by Thomas A. Edison.

Oct 16: The **first correspondence school** in the U.S. was opened by Thomas Jefferson Foster, editor of the Shenandoah *Herald.* Now known as the International Correspondence School, Scranton, Pa., it was begun to teach mining methods to workers to increase safety in coal mines.

Dec 29: An early patent for **wireless telegraphy** was issued to Thomas Edison for a "means of transmitting signals electrically . . . without the use of wires." The patent was the result of experiments conducted in 1885. On Nov. 15, 1883, Edison had received a patent for his two-element vacuum lamp, the forerunner of the vacuum tube rectifier.

IV. Fashion
Folkways
Holidays
Social Issues and Crime
Sports

A unique event in sports history occurred this year when James Naismith, a physical education instructor at what is now Springfield College, Springfield, Mass., invented the game of basketball. No other sport is known to owe its origin to one person. Basketball is the only popular American game that does not have English origins. Naismith was seeking to create a game that could be played indoors in winter and allow fast action and competition but not be as rough as football, which was gaining a reputation for violence. The first basketball game employed a soccer ball and two peach baskets. The rules Naismith devised have not been changed basically in nearly 100 years.

Oct 18: The **first International six-day bicycle race** in the U.S. was run in Madison Square Garden, New York City. Riders used high-wheelers and worked alone, pumping until exhausted, then resting and starting again for 142 hours. The first winner was "Plugger Bill" Martin. The record under one-man rules was established in 1898 by Charlie Miller at Madison Square Garden, who rode 2093.4 miles. Most of his competitors ended up in hospitals, suffering from exhaustion.

1892

I. Civil Rights
Exploration and Settlement
Government
Statistics
Wars

As the 1892 presidential election approached, there was dissatisfaction among voters with both the Democratic and the Republican parties. Many thought the tariff rates too high, the farmers complained of low prices for their products, and there was a feeling that the government favored bankers and industrialists at the expense of the common man. The only party to show much concern about these issues, the People's Party, usually referred to as the Populists, was organized this year. The Populists campaigned vigorously for such proposals as public ownership of the railroads, an eight-hour day for labor, and a currency system controlled by the federal government, not the banks. In the election, the Populists became the first third party since 1860 to win electoral college votes, carrying Kansas, Colorado, Idaho, and Nevada.

Jan 1: Ellis Island in upper New York Bay became the receiving station for immigrants. On Nov. 12, 1954, it was closed after 62 years and the processing of 20 million immigrants. It is now part of the Statue of Liberty National Monument.

June 7-11: The **Republican National Convention nominated Pres. Benjamin Harrison** for reelection and Whitelaw Reid of New York for the vice presidency.

June 21-23: The **Democratic National Convention nominated Grover Cleveland** of New York for the presidency and Adlai Ewing Stevenson of Illinois for the vice presidency.

Oct 15: The **Crow Indian reservation** in Montana was opened to settlers by presidential proclamation. The territory covered 1,800,000 acres.

Nov 8: Grover Cleveland was elected president of the United States. Adlai E. Stevenson was elected vice president. The electoral vote was Cleveland, 277; Pres. Benjamin Harrison, Republican incumbent, 145; James B. Weaver, Populist candidate, 22. The popular vote was Cleveland, 5,554,414; Harrison, 5,190,802; Weaver, 1,027,329; John Bidwell, Prohibition candidate, 271,058; Simon Wing, Socialist Labor candidate, 21,164. In congressional elections the Democrats gained five seats in the Senate for a 44–38 majority, with three seats going to minor parties. In the House the Democrats lost ground but kept a 218–127 majority, with 11 seats going to minor parties.

II. Architecture
Arts and Music
Popular Entertainment
Publishing
Theater

The cornerstone for what was intended to be the largest church in America, the Protestant Episcopal Cathedral of St. John the Divine, was laid on St. John's Day, Dec. 27. It was located on 11.5 acres of land in upper Manhattan, New York City. In a competition, the architectural firm of George Lewis Heins and Christopher Grant La Farge had won the award with plans for a structure in the Romanesque style. It was to be 601 ft. long, 146 ft. wide at the nave, and 320 ft. wide at the transept. Construction proceeded in fits and starts because of the great amount of money needed. In 1911 the trustees decided to change the partly built cathedral to the Gothic style, which would make it the largest Gothic cathedral in the world. Plans originally submitted by the architect Ralph Adams Cram were adopted. Today the cathedral is still incomplete, although work is once more in progress.

Among **books published** this year was the final edition of *Leaves of Grass* by Walt Whitman. Also published were *The West from a Car Window* by Richard Harding Davis, editor of *Harper's Weekly,* which collected reports on his extensive travels in the U.S.; *The Adventures of Sherlock Holmes,* the first collection of the short stories by Arthur Conan Doyle about literature's most famous detective; *The Quality of Mercy,* a novel by William Dean Howells in which he again probes the relationship between the economic order and the crimes of individuals; *Barrack-Room Ballads* by Rudyard Kipling, demonstrating the English poet's heroic view of his nation's imperialism; *The Old South* by Thomas Nelson Page, offering vivid if sentimental essays and sketches about plantation life; *Green Fields and Running Brooks,* another collection of Hoosier poems by James Whitcomb Riley; and *The History of David Grieve* by Mrs. Humphry Ward, a novel promoting the social application of Christianity.

Jack "Papa" Laine formed the Reliance Brass Band in New Orleans. A white musician, Laine was one of the first to imitate black styles of hot music. His later organization, Jack Laine's Ragtime Band, was probably the first white Dixieland jazz band.

"After the Ball Is Over," a perennial favorite song in the U.S., was composed by Charles K. Harris, one of the most successful songwriters of the 1890s and early 1900s. "After the Ball" became a tremendous hit during the Columbian Exposition of 1893 in Chicago.

The first home designed by **Frank Lloyd Wright,** it is widely believed, was Charnley House, built in Chicago. Wright made the plans while still working for the firm of Adler & Sullivan.

III. Business and Industry
Education
Philosophy and Religion
Science

The growing conflict between capital and labor resulted this year in violent conflict in the Homestead Strike. On July 1, when a contract between the Amalgamated Association of Iron and Steel Workers and the Carnegie Steel Company expired, the company cut wages and refused to recognize the union. The workers struck on June 26. On July 6 the company brought in 300 Pinkerton guards to protect the Homestead plant, near Pittsburgh, Pa. A pitched battle resulted. The Pinkertons were turned away with three dead and many wounded; ten strikers were killed. The company hired strikebreakers and at its request the governor of Pennsylvania, Robert E. Pattison, sent in the state militia on July 12. The militia protected the strikebreakers hired by Carnegie. The strike ended on Nov. 20 with the workers admitting

defeat. The union was destroyed and many of the men never got their jobs back.

The **fundamentalist-modernist controversy** was heated up by the heresy trial of Charles A. Briggs, professor of the Old Testament at Union Theological Seminary, New York City. Prof. Briggs, on his elevation to a distinguished chair at the seminary, delivered a paper taking a liberal approach on the authority of the Bible. Many orthodox Presbyterian ministers, sensing a threat in Briggs's modernist biblical views, persuaded the General Assembly of the Presbyterian Church, which held veto power over the seminary's appointments, to exercise its veto. The New York Presbytery then tried Briggs for heresy; he was acquitted. The prosecution appealed the decision to the assembly, which condemned Briggs and suspended him from the ministry. The case aroused partisan feelings among Presbyterian ministers across the country, and several defenders of Briggs were suspended, notably Prof. H. P. Smith of Lane Theological Seminary in Cincinnati, Ohio. At the end, the seminary broke off its Presbyterian relationship, became nondenominational, and kept its distinguished scholar.

The **First Church of Christ, Scientist** was founded in Boston, Mass., by Mary Baker Eddy and a small group of followers.

The **boll weevil,** a beetle of Mexican or Central American origin, was first seen in Texas; from there the pest spread widely, causing severe damage to U.S. cotton crops.

Nikola Tesla developed the first motor that could effectively utilize alternating current for power.

Sep: The **first successful gas-powered automobile** made in the U.S. was built by Charles and Frank Duryea, bicycle designers and toolmakers, at Chicopee, Mass. Afraid of ridicule if they tested the vehicle publicly, the builders tested it indoors. A more powerful model was given a successful trial run at Springfield, Mass., in 1893.

IV. Fashion
Folkways
Holidays
Social Issues and Crime
Sports

One of the most intriguing murder cases in U.S. history began on Aug. 4 when Andrew J. Borden and his second wife, Abby, were murdered with blows from an ax in their Fall River, Mass., home. Mr. Borden's 32-year-old unmarried daughter, Lisbeth A. Borden, was accused of the crime, although she denied it. Miss Borden did not testify at her trial. She was acquitted and the case was never solved, although it gave the world a still well-known jingle:

> Lizzie Borden took an ax,
> Gave her mother 40 whacks.
> When she saw what she had done,
> She gave her father 41.

Lizzie Borden spent the rest of her life as a virtual recluse and died in her Fall River home on June 1, 1927, at 68.

The phrase *the 400* with reference to society's elite achieved an almost instant place in American idiom after it was used by New York City's social arbiter, Ward McAllister. Asked to shorten a long list of persons to be invited to a ball in the Astor ballroom, which would hold only 400, McAllister commented that there were "only 400 persons in New York society." Social commentators and society gossips quickly gave the remark wide circulation. Those with social pretensions who were left off the list were outraged.

George W. G. Ferris designed the **Ferris wheel.** He built the first one in 1893 for the Columbia Exposition. Forty passengers could be carried 250 feet high in its 36 cars.

Sep 7: James J. Corbett won the **world heavyweight boxing championship** by knocking out John L. Sullivan in the 21st round. The bout, held at New Orleans, La., has been considered the first heavyweight title bout fought with gloves under Marquis of Queensberry rules, including three-minute rounds.

Oct 5: The notorious **Dalton gang** of robbers was virtually wiped out at Coffeyville, Kans., while attempting to rob a bank.

Oct 20-23: The **World's Columbian Exposition** was opened with magnificent dedication ceremonies at Chicago. Vice Pres. Levi Morton gave the opening address. John Philip Sousa, who resigned from the Marine Corps this year to organize his own band, conducted. The exhibition was the result of public demand for fitting commemoration of the discovery of America. On Apr. 25, 1890, Congress had passed an act that authorized an "exhibition of the arts, industries, manufactures, and products of the soil, mine and sea." Pres. Benjamin Harrison had recommended that a sum of "not less than $10 millions" be allotted to the fair. Total expenditures have been estimated as over $22,000,000. The fair was set out on an area of 644 acres, with the exposition itself covering 150 acres. There were 50 acres of concessions and 55 acres of state, transportation, electric, arts, and liberal arts buildings. It officially opened May 1, 1893.

1893

I. Civil Rights
Exploration and Settlement
Government
Statistics
Wars

A bitter political battle was fought over repeal of the Sherman Silver Purchase Act of 1890, which required that the U.S. treasury buy at market value 4,500,000 ounces of silver a month. When, by Apr. 15, 1893, the gold reserve in the treasury fell below the $100,000,000 level because silver had been overvalued in relation to gold, Pres. Grover Cleveland and others blamed the Sherman Act for creating too much money. Cleveland called a special session of Congress for Aug. 7, but it was Oct. 30 before both houses of Congress, after much debate, voted repeal. Cleveland was thus able to keep the U.S. on the gold standard, but he alienated members of the Democratic Party who wanted easy credit.

Jan 17: A **revolution in Hawaii** deposed Queen Liliuokalani with at least the foreknowledge of the U.S. minister to Hawaii, John L. Stevens. A provisional government headed by Sanford B. Dole was protected by 300 U.S. Marines from the cruiser *Boston.* The provisional government requested the U.S. to annex the islands. The queen later protested her ouster to Pres. Grover Cleveland.

Apr 3: The **first U.S. ambassador to the Court of St. James** was named: Thomas Francis Bayard, secretary of state in Pres. Cleveland's first administration. Up to this time the highest U.S. diplomatic title had been minister.

July 17: Commissioner James H. Blount's **report on the Hawaiian revolution,** delivered to Sec. of State Walter Q. Gresham, accused Minister Stevens of active participation in all phases of the Hawaiian uprising. Stevens's supporters countercharged Blount with compiling a lopsided report based on a small sampling of Hawaiian opinion and of failing to question Stevens himself. Not until 1898 was Hawaii annexed as a territory.

Aug 24: A devastating **cyclone** ripped through Savannah, Ga., and Charleston, S.C., killing some 1000 persons and causing terrible damage.

Sep 16: The **Cherokee Strip,** between Kansas and Oklahoma, was opened for land rush settlement. More than 100,000 persons rushed into an area of

6,000,000 acres that had been purchased from the Cherokee Indians in 1891.

Sep 17: **Yellow fever** cases reached epidemic proportions in Brunswick, Ga.

Nov 7: **Women's suffrage** was adopted in Colorado.

II. Architecture
Arts and Music
Popular Entertainment
Publishing
Theater

American playwrights were relying more and more on domestic themes, characters, and settings for their plays, and were writing more realistic, if still melodramatic, plays. One such author, and also a leading actor, was James A. Herne, whose play *Shore Acres*, depicting life in New England, became a hit in 1893. The play deals with tensions in a family in a quietly realistic way. The play ran for 113 performances in Boston, beginning in Feb. 1893, and then became a success in New York City, opening on Dec. 25 at Daly's Theater.

Among **books published** this year was *Maggie: A Girl of the Streets*, by a 21-year-old newspaper reporter, Stephen Crane. Unable to find a publisher for a realistic novel about a prostitute, Crane published privately; no one paid attention to it until the success of his *Red Badge of Courage* in 1895. The significance of *Maggie* became clearer as grimly naturalistic portrayals of the seedy side of American life became increasingly the material of American writers. Also published this year were *Can Such Things Be?* by Ambrose Bierce, hair-raising tales of the supernatural; *The Cliff Dwellers*, a novel about the relationships of people working in a Chicago skyscraper, by Henry Blake Fuller; *Nights with Uncle Remus*, another of the popular collections of tales by Joel Chandler Harris; *The World of Chance* by William Dean Howells, expressing a stark view of life and society; *The Heavenly Twins* by Sarah Grand (pen name of Mrs. Frances Elizabeth M'Fall, an English women's rights activist), a best seller treating hitherto taboo subjects fictionally; and *The Strange Case of Dr. Jekyll and Mr. Hyde* by Robert Louis Stevenson, six years after its appearance in England.

The world premiere of **Antonín Dvořák's** *New World Symphony* was given in New York City. Dvořák, who had been in the U.S. only a year, produced the most American composition of the nineteenth century. Though no theme of the symphony is specifically drawn from folk music, many are close to the spirit of plantation songs and Indian melodies.

The first completely independent architectural commission of **Frank Lloyd Wright,** the Winslow residence in Chicago, was built this year.

Oct 23: *In Old Kentucky* by Charles T. Dazey opened in New York City, a melodrama so popular that it ran for 27 consecutive seasons either in New York City or on the road. The play makes use of fights, murder, horse racing, and conflict between mountaineers and plainsmen.

III. Business and Industry
Education
Philosophy and Religion
Science

A worldwide financial panic and economic depression began in the spring of 1893. Sensing weakness in the American economy, foreign investors began withdrawing their capital. Railroads began to go into bankruptcy, the steel industry declined, and the banking system was strained to the limit. On May 5 and June 27 stocks fell sharply on the New York Stock Exchange. On June 26 the value of the U.S. silver dollar had fallen from 67 cents to less than 60 cents in gold. A panic in New York City was averted on June 29 by a loan of $6,000,000 by clearinghouse banks. Pres. Cleveland directed the treasury to sell government bonds to New York City banks for gold; four issues of such bonds totaled $293,000,000. Nevertheless, by December about 600 banks had failed and by June 1894 no fewer than 194 railroads had gone bankrupt. Unemployment climbed, and by the winter of 1893–1894 there were about 2,500,000 persons out of work. Democrats blamed the high tariff and excess government spending by Republicans. Gold standard advocates blamed the depression on agitation for more and cheaper money. The populists blamed everything on the gold standard and a shortage of currency. The economy gradually improved, but it was 1897 before it could be said that good times had returned.

Frederick Jackson Turner made his famous contribution to American historiography with "The Significance of the Frontier in American History," an address delivered before the American Historical Association. Turner argued that the ever-expanding frontier of the U.S. provided the key to understanding the differences between Europeans and Americans.

A **zipper,** or slide fastener, was patented by Whitcomb L. Judson. It consisted of a series of hooks and eyes that fastened with a slider. An improved zipper with the meshed tooth type of slide familiar today was patented in 1913 by Gideon Sundbach.

Jan 4: Violators of the **Anti-polygamy Act** of 1882 were granted amnesty in a pronouncement by Pres. Grover Cleveland, with the stipulation that they observe the law henceforward. The pronouncement applied chiefly to elderly Mormons.

Dec 24: Henry Ford completed construction of his first successful gasoline engine. His first motor car was assembled in 1896. It made a successful run on June 4 powered by a two-cylinder, four-cycle gasoline motor.

IV. Fashion
Folkways
Holidays
Social Issues and Crime
Sports

The World's Columbian Exposition, on the shores of Lake Michigan in Chicago, was officially opened to the public on May 1 to mark the 400th anniversary of the discovery of America by Christopher Columbus. The exposition had been authorized by Congress in 1890 and formally dedicated on Oct. 12, 1892. The exposition's 150 buildings of Greek, Romanesque, and Renaissance styles of architecture became known as the White City; the buildings exhibited the talents of the foremost American architects and sculptors. Seven thousand workmen were employed in construction of the exposition. Popularly known as the Chicago World's Fair, the exposition covered 600 acres, brought exhibits from 72 countries, and by the time it closed on Oct. 30 attracted more than 27,000,000 visitors. The architecture and the landscaping had a powerful effect on the nation and was largely responsible for the so-called City Beautiful movement, which sought to make American cities more attractive and livable through the planning of buildings and parks.

The **rise of bicycling** as a means of transportation and recreation in the U.S. was indicated by the increase of bicycles in use from some 20,000 in 1882 to over 1,000,000 in 1893.

The first recorded **intercollegiate relay race** was run at Philadelphia between teams representing the University of Pennsylvania and Princeton University. In 1895 Penn initiated its Penn Relay Carnival with a series of mile relay races. Today the Penn Relay is considered the foremost annual track and field meet in the world. Relay races are an American contribution to an ancient sport.

June 14: Flag Day was first officially observed by the city of Philadelphia by order of the mayor, who ordered that the flag be displayed over every public building in the city. The mayor's order was pursuant to a resolution of the Colonial Dames of the State, whose president, Mrs. Elizabeth Duane Gillespie, was directly descended from Benjamin Franklin.

Oct 7-13: The **America's Cup** was successfully defended by the U.S. yacht *Vigilant,* which won three straight races from the British challenger *Valkyrie.*

1894

I. Civil Rights
Exploration and Settlement
Government
Statistics
Wars

A new form of protest over economic conditions appeared this year when Coxey's Army, a band of unemployed workers, began a march on Washington, D.C. Jacob S. Coxey was an Ohio businessman and social reformer who gathered together some hundred unemployed followers. Headed by a six-piece band, the group set out for the capital on Mar. 25 from Massilon, Ohio. Coxey expected to gather a large throng on the way to call attention to the plight of the unemployed and to demand government action, such as a large-scale road building program. The men were well received along the way but on Apr. 30, when they arrived in Washington, the army numbered only about 400 men. The next day Coxey and two others were arrested for trespassing on the Capitol lawn when they tried to present petitions to Congress. The army disbanded. Similar armies set out from other starting points, even from the West Coast, but of these, only 17 out of some 1200 persons reached Washington.

Jan 8: A **fire** at the site of the Chicago World's Columbian Exposition destroyed virtually all the buildings, with property damages estimated at $2,000,000.

Mar 17: A **Chinese Exclusion Treaty,** by which China agreed to exclusion of Chinese laborers from the U.S., was signed. The Senate ratified the treaty on Aug. 13.

June 21: The **Democratic Silver Convention** was held in Omaha, Neb.; 1000 delegates attended. William Jennings Bryan led the convention to the adoption of a free-coinage plank on a silver-to-gold ratio of 16 to 1.

Aug 8: The **Hawaiian Republic** was officially recognized by the U.S. government. On May 31 the U.S. had recognized that Hawaii should have its own government and that interference from any foreign power would be considered unfriendly to the U.S. On July 4 the Republic of Hawaii had been proclaimed and a progressive constitution adopted.

Aug 27: The **first graduated income tax law** was passed by a predominantly Democratic Congress after acrimonious debate. It was denounced by Sen. John Sherman (Ohio) as "socialism, communism, devilism." The law was declared unconstitutional in the next year by the Supreme Court. It was part of the Wilson-Gorman Tariff Act, which became law without the signature of Pres. Cleveland.

Nov 6: In **congressional elections** the Republicans regained control of both houses of Congress, taking a 43–39 majority in the Senate, with six seats going to minor parties, and taking a 244–105 majority in the House, with seven seats going to minor parties. William Jennings Bryan of Nebraska, defeated in his bid for a Senate seat, became editor in chief of the Omaha *World-Herald*. He became an enormously popular speaker on the national lecture circuit.

II. Architecture
Arts and Music
Popular Entertainment
Publishing
Theater

Few American women became professional painters at this time, but one who did so was Mary Cassatt, who spent most of her life in France. There she took part in the impressionist movement and became a friend of Edgar Degas and Edouard Manet. She was the only American invited by the impressionists to exhibit with them. Motherhood was one of her favorite subjects; she did several versions of *Mother and Child*. In 1893 she painted a mural, *Modern Women*, for the women's building at the Chicago World's Fair. In 1894 her painting *La Toilette* was exhibited in Paris.

Among **books published** this year was *Coin's Financial School* by William Hope Harvey, a free silver advocate. The book, on economics, was of little merit but sold 300,000 copies within a year. Also published this year were *A Kentucky Cardinal* by James Lane Allen, a novel about an amiable, nature-loving recluse in love with a girl of quite different interests; *Songs From Vagabondia* by Bliss Carman and Richard Hovey, the first of three refreshing poetic collaborations; *Glimpses of Japan* by Lafcadio Hearn, the best study to date of Japanese culture; *The Prisoner of Zenda* by Anthony Hope, a historical romance that became a classic; *A Traveler from Altruria* by William

Dean Howells, a Utopian novel; *The Jungle Book* by Rudyard Kipling, a children's classic; *Wealth Against Commonwealth*, a study of the Standard Oil Company by Henry Demarest Lloyd, one of the first of the muckraking journalists; *Beautiful Joe* by Margaret Marshall Saunders, a dog story that eventually sold some 1,000,000 copies; and *The Tragedy of Pudd'nhead Wilson*, a generally underestimated novel by Mark Twain.

"The Sidewalks of New York" was written and composed by Charles Lawler, a buck-and-wing dancer in out-of-the-way music halls. The song was popular in the 1890s, but it became even more popular when Gov. Alfred E. Smith used it in his campaign for the Democratic presidential nomination in 1924.

III. Business and Industry
Education
Philosophy and Religion
Science

The Gilded Age might well have been called the Age of the Railroad. Railroad building and operation was the single largest economic enterprise by far. On the New York Stock Exchange in 1898, 60% of the stocks listed were those of railroads. The pace of track-laying was never surpassed: in 1880 the mileage was 93,261; in 1890, 167,191; in 1900, 198,964. By 1900 the railroads employed 1,018,000 persons and were valued at a little more than $10,000,000,000. One reason for the affluence of the lines was the generous way in which states and the federal government gave them public land as subsidies for building: nearly 50,000,000 acres from the states and about 130,000,000 acres from federal grants, most of it west of the Mississippi R.

The **American Federation of Labor** (AFL), under the leadership of Samuel Gompers, voted against adopting socialist reform programs. Gompers believed that U.S. labor should work with capitalism, not against it, and that the AFL's proper concerns were shorter hours, higher wages, and better working conditions. Gompers' victory set U.S. labor on a nonideological course quite different from that of labor in European countries.

Apr 20: A **strike by 136,000 coal miners** for higher wages began at Columbus, Ohio. This year, like the previous one, would be marked by widespread labor unrest.

May 11: The bitter **Pullman strike** began at the Pullman railroad car plant in south Chicago. The depression had induced the company to cut wages sharply without reducing the rents of the workers in company-owned housing. Considerable violence, pillaging, and burning of railroad cars ensued; mobs of nonworkers joined in.

June 26: A **general railway strike** followed the boycotting of the servicing of Pullman cars by the American Railway Union (ARU), an industrial union headed by Eugene V. Debs. Earlier this year Debs had led a successful strike against the Great Northern Railway. The ARU boycott tied up railroads across the nation.

Aug 3: The **Pullman strike** was declared over by the American Railway Union. Labor had been dealt a blow by being brought under the Sherman Antitrust Act and by the introduction of the court injunction as a weapon against it. The ARU specifically had been crushed. No further attempt to create an industrial union was made until the Depression of the 1930s. Only the AFL and the railroad brotherhoods survived. The AFL had 1,675,000 members by 1904.

Sep 4: A **garment workers' strike** was launched by some 12,000 tailors in New York City. They were protesting sweatshop conditions and the piecework system of payment.

IV. Fashion
   Folkways
   Holidays
   Social Issues and Crime
   Sports

Golf was becoming popular in the U.S. but was still largely pursued by the well-to-do at private country clubs. The United States Golf Association (USGA) was formed on Dec. 22 at a meeting of five golf clubs from Long Island, N.Y., Mount Hope, N.Y., Brookline, Mass., Newport, R.I., and Chicago. The association was to standardize rules, conduct national championship tournaments, and stimulate interest in the game. The USGA held its first amateur and open golf tournaments in 1895 at Newport. The new association did much to organize golf and establish consistent rules and guidelines, but it took another 20 years for golf to catch on with the American public.

The **highest batting average** for a season ever compiled by a major league baseball player was Hugh Duffy's .438. He was a member of the Boston Nationals.

June 16: The **squeeze play** was first employed in baseball by George Case and Dutch Carter, players on the Yale team, in a game against Princeton. The squeeze play is a batting maneuver in which, with a runner at third base and with less than two out, the batter bunts the ball slowly to the infield, enabling the runner on third to come home safely. It was introduced in the major leagues in 1904 by Clark Griffith, manager of the New York Highlanders in the American League.

Two types of squeeze play are now in use. One is called the delayed squeeze; in it the runner on third base does not run until the ball has been bunted. The other, more dramatic, type is called the suicide squeeze, in which the runner on third base breaks toward home plate as the pitcher begins his delivery.

June 28: Labor Day was made a legal holiday by a congressional resolution.

1895

I. Civil Rights
   Exploration and Settlement
   Government
   Statistics
   Wars

A boundary dispute between Great Britain and Venezuela drew England and the U.S. to the verge of war this year. The boundary between Venezuela and British Guiana had been in dispute for 80 years. Tension grew when gold was discovered and Venezuelan troops entered the disputed area. Great Britain refused to submit the quarrel to arbitration, which caused a belligerent reaction by Pres. Grover Cleveland's administration. Sec. of State Richard Olney, on July 20, as much as told Great Britain that the U.S. ruled the Western Hemisphere. This statement irritated Latin Americans and Canadians as well as the British. On Nov. 26 the British prime minister, Robert A. T. Gascoyne-Cecil, Lord Salisbury, replied that the dispute did not concern the U.S., but the U.S. would not yield, citing the Monroe Doctrine. On Dec. 21 Pres. Cleveland asked Congress to establish a commission to settle the dispute and Congress did so. Great Britain, faced with pressing problems elsewhere in the world, wanted no more trouble and on Feb. 27, 1897, agreed to arbitration. On Oct. 3, 1899, a boundary was agreed on which largely upheld England's claim. In the aftermath, many Americans were appalled at how close to war the two English-speaking nations had come, especially since Great Britain was far stronger militarily than the U.S.

Feb 24: The **revolt of Cuba against Spain** broke out. On June 12 Pres. Cleveland called on U.S. citizens to avoid giving aid to the insurgents. A partial cause of the rebellion was the panic of 1893, which caused a severe depression in the Cuban sugar industry. Repressive measures taken by the Spanish aroused American sympathy, which was inflamed to a war pitch by the yellow journalism of William Randolph Hearst's New York *Journal* and Joseph Pulitzer's New York *World*.

Nov 5: Women's suffrage was provided for in the constitution of Utah. The constitution came into effect Jan. 4, 1896, the day Utah entered the Union. It was the second state to give women the vote.

II. Architecture
Arts and Music
Popular Entertainment
Publishing
Theater

The influence of William Morris, the English poet, craftsman, social reformer, and above all a devotee of the Middle Ages, was reflected in the career of the writer and editor Elbert Hubbard. Born in Illinois in 1856, Hubbard abandoned a career in business and turned to writing. This year he established the Roycroft Press at East Aurora, N.Y., and attempted with little success to imitate Morris's Kelmscott Press. He began publishing the monthly magazine *The Philistine*, noted for its inspirational writings and platitudes, contributed mainly by Hubbard. He started another magazine, *The Fra*, in 1908, the title coming from the sobriquet Hubbard had bestowed on himself. Hubbard was best remembered for the essay "A Message to Garcia" (1899), an enormously successful inspirational piece based on an incident in the Spanish-American War. It so appealed to employers that they distributed copies freely to their employees. By 1940 the total circulation of the article was estimated at 40,000,000.

Among **books published** this year was *The Red Badge of Courage*, a realistic Civil War novel by Stephen Crane. It was a remarkable performance: the author was 23 and without any war experience. The novel put American fiction on a firm path toward naturalism. Also published this year were *A House Boat on the Styx* by John Kendrick Bangs, a novel in a humorous vein drawing together various historical figures; *With the Procession* by Henry Blake Fuller, a novel of social strivings in Chicago; *Rose of Dutcher's Coolly*, a novel by Hamlin Garland about a girl's revolt against the bleak life on a Dakota farm; a second *Jungle Book* by Rudyard Kipling; *Amos Judd* by John Mitchell, founder of the original *Life* magazine, a novel about a young Indian rajah brought to the U.S. to save his life; and *The Jucklins* by Opie Read, a best-selling novel by the former editor of *The Arkansas Traveler*.

July 4: "America the Beautiful" by Katherine Lee Bates, a Wellesley College professor, was published in the *Congregationalist*, a church publication. The poem was revised in 1904 and put in final form in 1911.

III. Business and Industry
Education
Philosophy and Religion
Science

Advances in science and technology in the late nineteenth century included great progress in the field of astronomy, particularly in the construction of observatories. As early as 1874–1875, the Lick Observatory on Mt. Hamilton, Calif., was established through gifts from James Lick. The Lowell Observatory was founded in Flagstaff, Ariz., in 1894 by the astronomer Percival Lowell, who caught popular attention with his belief that intelligent life might exist on Mars. The Yerkes Observatory, on the shores of Lake Geneva, Wis., was founded in 1892 with money from Charles T. Yerkes, the financier and urban transportation system magnate. The Yerkes Observatory's 40-inch refracting telescope, then the largest of its type in the world, was completed in 1897.

June 11: The first U.S. patent for a **gasoline-driven automobile** by a U.S. inventor was issued to Charles E. Duryea. On June 26 of the previous year, the Patent Office had granted a patent for a motor car developed in Germany by Karl Benz.

IV. Fashion
Folkways
Holidays
Social Issues and Crime
Sports

The work of Charles Dana Gibson began to have a major influence on Americans' perceptions of themselves. Gibson's idealized depiction of the perfect American woman, who came to be known as the Gibson Girl, soon swept the country. She was slim, small-waisted, and had a pompadour hairstyle. She also had a cool, aloof beauty. The young man she was depicted with was created by Gibson somewhat in his own image. This ideal male was clean-shaven and had much to do with the disappearance of the hitherto popular mustache. He also had a strong jaw and broad shoulders, thus not needing padding in his jackets. Gibson's pair were frequently depicted in settings that made sharp and amusing comments on the social scene. Gibson's work appeared in many magazines and books, notably the works of Richard Harding Davis.

Women's skirts were shortened for bicycling wear. They were shortened an inch or two from the ankle, and the hems were weighted with lead.

Aug 31: The **first professional football game** was played in Latrobe, Pa., when Latrobe's team of profit-sharing players met the Jeannette, Pa., team. Latrobe hired a substitute quarterback, John Brallier, for $10 in expense money, making him the game's first professional player.

Sep 7-12: The **America's Cup** was successfully defended by the U.S. yacht *Defender*, which won three straight races from the British challenger *Valkyrie II.*

Oct 4: The **first U.S. Open golf tournament,** held at Newport Golf Club in Newport, R.I., under the auspices of the U.S. Golf Association, was won by Horace Rawlins. Rawlins, 19, had come from England earlier in the year to work at the Newport club.

Nov 28: The **first gasoline-powered automobile race** in the U.S., the Chicago to Evanston Thanksgiving Day Race, was won by the brothers Charles E. and J. Frank Duryea.

1896

I. Civil Rights
Exploration and Settlement
Government
Statistics
Wars

The presidential election of 1896 was decided after one of the hardest fought campaigns in U.S. history. The division between the Republicans and the Democrats was clear. Republicans were for hard money, a high tariff to protect American industry, and other conservative policies. The Democrats were now in the hands of the populists. The free coinage of silver was their primary campaign issue. This appealed to the farmers and miners of the South and West. The Republicans waged a front-porch campaign for William McKinley, spending about $7,000,000, mostly on mailings that reached 5,000,000 families a week. The Democrats, with only about $300,000 to spend, sent their candidate, William Jennings Bryan, on an 18,000-mile campaign trip, during which he made 600 speeches. But Bryan could not attract the votes of the urban workers, despite his personal attractiveness and oratorical power.

Jan 4: Utah was admitted into the Union, the 45th state.

May 18: The so-called **Jim Crow Car Law** of Louisiana was declared constitutional by the Supreme Court in *Plessy v. Ferguson,* which advanced the separate but equal doctrine. The court held that segregation was legal if equal facilities were offered to both races. The U.S. Supreme Court reversed this doctrine in civil rights decisions on May 17, 1954; May 31, 1955; and Nov. 7, 1955. Chief Justice Earl Warren said in the first of these decisions that the separate but equal doctrine had no place in the field of public education, and maintained that separate facilities were inherently unequal.

June 18: The **Republican National Convention nominated William McKinley** of Ohio for the presidency and Garret A. Hobart of New Jersey for the vice presidency.

July 11: The **Democratic National Convention nominated William Jennings Bryan** of Nebraska, a dark horse, for the presidency. Bryan's famous "cross of gold" speech united the silverite wing of the party and took the convention by storm. The platform advocated "free and unlimited coinage of both silver and gold at the present legal ratio of sixteen to one." Arthur Sewall of Maine was nominated for the vice presidency.

Oct 1: Rural free postal delivery was established.

Nov 3: William McKinley was elected president of the United States. Garret A. Hobart was elected vice president. The electoral vote was McKinley, 271: William Jennings Bryan, Democratic candidate, 176. The popular vote was McKinley, 7,104,779; Bryan, 6,502,925; John M. Palmer, National Democratic candidate, 133,148; Joshua Levering, Prohibition candidate, 132,007; Charles H. Matchett, Socialist Labor candidate, 38,274. In congressional elections the Republicans gained four seats in the Senate to lead 47–34, seven seats going to minor parties. In the House the Republicans lost 40 seats but still held a 204–113 majority, 40 seats going to minor parties.

II. Architecture
Arts and Music
Popular Entertainment
Publishing
Theater

A new form of American humor, art, and journalism came into being this year with the appearance of "The Yellow Kid," by Richard F. Outcault, in the New York *World.* It was soon to become the comic strip. A single-panel drawing, which appeared each week, showed the adventures of a boy in a long, yellow, sacklike garment; Outcault soon began to add words. This marked the first time a cartoon caption had appeared inside the frame of a picture. Circulation of the *World* boomed. In 1897 Rudolph Dirks introduced "The Katzenjammer Kids" and was the first to make use of a sequence of panels to tell a story. Another pioneer was Frederick Burr Opper with "Happy Hooligan" (1899). The first comic strip to appear six days a week made its appearance in 1907 in the San Francisco *Chronicle*. It was Harry C. "Bud" Fisher's "A. Mutt," a forerunner of "Mutt and Jeff."

Among **books published** this year was the immensely popular *Quo Vadis?* by the Polish novelist Henryk Sienkiewicz. This vivid, powerful tale of Roman life under Nero and of early Christians has been dramatized, filmed, and translated into all major languages. Also published were *Joan of Arc*, the last major work of Mark Twain, presenting a somewhat idealized Joan set against the malign forces arrayed against her; *Poems, Third Series* by Emily Dickinson, bringing to light more of the hundreds of her poems found by Lavinia Dickinson, Emily's sister; *The Damnation of Theron Ware* by Harold Frederic, a realistic novel about a hypocritical small-town Methodist minister; *The Country of the Pointed Firs*, the masterpiece of the mistress of the local-color novel, Sarah Orne Jewett; *The Seats of the Mighty*, a historical novel by Sir Gilbert Parker about the capture of Quebec; the first story about the fabulous fictional character Frank Merriwell, the creation of Gilbert Patten under the pseudonym Burt L. Standish; *The Torrent and the Night Before*, poems by Edwin Arlington Robinson, noteworthy only because it was the first publication of this important American poet; the fourth and final volume of *The Winning of the West* by Theodore Roosevelt; *The Sense of Beauty* by George Santayana, his first major philosophical work and a classic study of aesthetics; *In His Steps* by Charles M. Sheldon, an all-time best seller about a Kansas minister following the example of Jesus, translated into 25 or more languages; and another religious classic, *The Story of the Other Wise Man* by Henry Van Dyke, still in print.

Apr 23: The **first moving pictures** on a public screen were shown at Koster and Bial's Music Hall in New York City. The program included films of two blonde girls performing the umbrella dance, a view of the surf breaking on a beach, a comic boxing exhibition, a bit of comic allegory entitled "The Monroe Doctrine," and a performance of the skirt dance. *The New York Times* review the following day described the exhibition as "all wonderfully real and singularly exhilarating."

III. Business and Industry
Education
Philosophy and Religion
Science

Pulpit-thumping Christian evangelism was thriving as the twentieth century neared. In these years the most popular practitioner was William Ashley "Billy" Sunday. A professional baseball player from 1883 to 1900, Sunday had also worked for the YMCA in Chicago from 1891 until he turned evangelist in 1896. On Apr. 15, 1903, he was ordained a Presbyterian minister. Sunday was agile on the platform and colloquial in his speech. He preached the kind of Bible fundamentalism that many wanted to hear and promoted prohibition. It is said that by the time of his death in 1935 he had preached to more people than any other Christian.

Seven-eighths of the **wealth of the U.S.** was controlled by one-eighth of the people.

June 4: Assembly of the **first Ford automobile** was completed at 2 A.M. in a brick workshed in Detroit, Mich., by Henry Ford and his associates. The road test of the car was delayed an hour or so because genius had overlooked one detail: the car was wider than the shed door. The men had to use an ax to knock bricks out of the framework.

Aug 12: Gold was discovered on the Klondike R. about three miles from Dawson in the Yukon Territory of northwest Canada. This sparked the second great gold rush in U.S. history, the Klondike stampede of 1897–1898. News of the strike reached the U.S. in June of 1897, and within a month thousands were on their way by a variety of difficult routes. In 1898 there were about 25,000 people in the Klondike area. Total gold production there from 1885 to 1929 exceeded $175,000,000.

IV. Fashion
Folkways
Holidays
Social Issues and Crime
Sports

Newspapers, in search of greater circulation and more advertising, were becoming less political and more concerned with everyday interests of average people. They began to publish material to entertain as well as inform the reader. Among the innovations was the advice to the lovelorn column, which made its debut in 1896 in the New Orleans *Picayune*. Its author was Elizabeth Meriwether Gilmer, who used the pen name Dorothy Dix. Her column was later syndicated, and collections of her advice on various topics appeared in book form into the 1930s.

Apr 6: The **first modern Olympic Games** began in Athens, Greece. The games were dominated by a small team of Americans who arrived just as athletes for the first events were being called. The U.S. team, out of condition from the long ocean trip, with no time to limber up, won nine of the 12 events. James B. Connolly, who won the first event—the hop, step, and jump—was the first Olympic champion to be crowned in 15 centuries. Revival of the games was brought about by the efforts of a young French baron, Pierre de Coubertin of Paris. His plan to hold international contests every four years has been carried out for the most part.

July 7: The sentence "**You shall not crucify mankind upon a cross of gold**" marked William Jennings Bryan's stirring speech at the Democratic National Convention. The reference was to the insistence by the gold faction, which opposed free coinage of silver, on gold alone as the basis for U.S. currency.

July 18: The **U.S. Open golf tournament** was won by James Foulis.

1897

I. Civil Rights
   Exploration and Settlement
   Government
   Statistics
   Wars

The tariff continued to be a controversial issue, but after the presidential election of 1896 the Republican Party was free to have its way. Pres. William McKinley called a special session of Congress, and on July 7 the lawmakers passed the Dingley Tariff Bill, named for its sponsor, Rep. Nelson Dingley, Republican of Maine. This law, which remained in effect until 1909, put tariffs at the highest level ever, raising them an average of 57%. It reimposed the duty on woolen goods and set the rate at 91%. The new tariff rates were much higher than was necessary because many American industries no longer needed protection against foreign goods.

Jan 12: The **National Monetary Conference** met at Indianapolis, Ind., and endorsed the existing gold standard. A commission appointed later in the year offered Congress a plan for the monetary system.

With the free silver issue finally settled, the U.S. entered a decade of prosperity.

Mar 4: William McKinley was inaugurated president of the United States, the 25th. A Republican, he was elected to two terms but was assassinated before completing his second term.

II. Architecture
   Arts and Music
   Popular Entertainment
   Publishing
   Theater

Popular songs were being turned out by the hundreds. Many of them had a nostalgic air and expressed a yearning for rural life. Quite a few were humorous and, of course, many were about love. Among the most successful composers of the period was Paul Dresser, real name Dreiser, whose brother Theodore was to become one of America's greatest novelists. Dresser is remembered for "On the Banks of the Wabash, Far Away" (1897), on which his brother helped with the lyrics, and "My Gal Sal" (1905). Another popular songwriter of the day was Harry Von Tilzer, who is said to have composed more than 3000 songs, including "Wait Till the Sun Shines, Nelly" (1906).

Among **books published** this year was *Soldiers of Fortune* by Richard Harding Davis, a novel that became a best seller. Davis was a newspaperman, war correspondent, and author. His work found a large audience from the early 1890s to his death in 1916; however, his novels and many stories did not stand the test of time and, except for a few, are largely forgotten. Other books published this year included *The Spoils of Poynton* and *What Maisie Knew* by Henry James; *Captains Courageous* by Rudyard Kipling, a novel of the sea that became a classic; *Hugh Wynne, Free Quaker* by S. Weir Mitchell, a novel of the American Revolution considered by some to be Mitchell's masterpiece; *The Children of the Night* by Edwin Arlington Robinson, the author's second collection of poems, which included "Richard Cory" and other well-known poems; and *The Literary History of the American Revolution* by Moses Coit Taylor.

III. Business and Industry
   Education
   Philosophy and Religion
   Science

As the population of cities grew and their geographical boundaries expanded, transportation of large numbers of people became a serious problem. Elevated railroads had already been built, but they were noisy and dirty. Municipalities now turned to underground railways, or subways, as a solution. An experimental underground railway had been built in New York City more than 30 years before, yet New York City officials were still working out plans to finance subway construction. The first practical and successful subway line in the U.S. was the Tremont St. subway in Boston, which opened in 1897 and was completed the next year. It ran for only 1.8 miles and the cars were ordinary trolley cars. Later the Boston subway was extended to 22 miles.

July 2: A **coal miners' strike** shut down mines in Pennsylvania, Ohio, and West Virginia and put 75,000 men out of work. On Sept. 10 more than 20 miners were killed at Hazelton and Latimer, Pa., when deputy sheriffs opened fire on them. One day later the strike was settled. The miners won an eight-hour work day, semimonthly pay, abolition of company stores, and biennial conferences.

IV. Fashion
Folkways
Holidays
Social Issues and Crime
Sports

Conspicuous consumption in the Gilded Age exceeded anything ever seen before in the U.S. The most lavish party of all was that given in 1897 by the Bradley Martins of New York City. The ballroom of the Waldorf-Astoria Hotel was turned into a replica of the Palace of Versailles. Mrs. Martin attended dressed as Mary Queen of Scots, wearing a necklace that had once belonged to Marie Antoinette. The ball was held just as the nation was emerging from its worst depression ever, and thus produced a wave of criticism in the press. So much disapproval descended on the Martins that they fled to England and stayed there.

The **first Frontier Day** was conceived and celebrated by citizens of Cheyenne, Wyo., at the town's fair grounds. The celebration has since become a five-day Wild West Show, held annually at Frontier Park.

Mar 17: The **world heavyweight boxing championship** was won by Bob Fitzsimmons, who defeated James J. "Gentleman Jim" Corbett in a 14-round bout at Carson City, Nev. This was the first boxing match photographed by a motion picture camera.

Apr 19: The **first Boston Marathon** was won by John J. McDermott of New York City, with a time of 2 hrs., 55 min., 10 sec.

Sep 17: The **U.S. Open golf tournament** was won by Joe Lloyd of England.

1898

I. Civil Rights
Exploration and Settlement
Government
Statistics
Wars

Victory in the Spanish-American War made the U.S. a nation with global interests. In one brief clash of arms the U.S. acquired Guam, Puerto Rico, and the Philippine Islands from Spain. In addition, Cuba was granted independence, with Spain assuming its national debt. Many Americans were appalled by the new U.S. foreign policy, which they equated with imperialism. Andrew Carnegie, the steel magnate and philanthropist, offered to buy the Philippines for $20,000,000 and give the country its freedom. Many other Americans, however, talked of manifest destiny and the duty of the U.S. to spread its form of civilization far and wide.

Feb 15: The U.S. **battleship *Maine*** exploded in Havana harbor; two officers and 258 crew members were killed. U.S. sympathies were already strongly with Cuba in its revolt against Spanish tyranny, and the *Maine* disaster made U.S. intervention inevitable. The cause of the explosion and the people responsible for it were never determined.

Apr 19: Congress adopted a **joint resolution on Cuba,** which stated that the U.S. had no plans for Cuban annexation, demanded Spain's withdrawal, and authorized the president to use military force. Spain immediately severed diplomatic relations.

Apr 22: A **blockade of Cuban ports** was ordered by Pres. McKinley. Rear Adm. William T. Sampson sailed from Key West, Fla., with a sizable fleet.

Apr 22: The Spanish ship ***Buena Ventura*** was captured by the U.S. gunboat *Nashville,* the first prize of the Spanish-American War.

Apr 24: The **Spanish-American War** officially began when Spain declared war on the U.S. The following day Congress passed a declaration of war, effective Apr. 21.

May 1: At the Battle of **Manila Bay,** the six-ship Asiatic squadron of Commodore George Dewey decisively defeated a larger but outgunned and underprepared Spanish fleet. The U.S. flotilla emerged virtually unscathed, with only eight wounded. The Spanish fleet was destroyed, with heavy casualties. The action cleared the way for U.S. occupation of Manila in August.

May 25: The **first troop expedition to Manila** set sail from San Francisco with some 2500 men.

June 11: About 600 **U.S. Marines landed at Guantánamo,** Cuba. They engaged Spanish forces the next day.

June 12-14: U.S. forces embarked from Key West, Fla. Some 17,000 troops under Gen. William R. Shafter sailed to undertake capture of Santiago de Cuba, the chief Spanish naval base in Cuba.

June 15: At **Guantánamo,** U.S. Marines repulsed a Spanish assault.

June 15: Annexation of Hawaii was approved in a joint resolution adopted by the House of Representatives, and by the Senate on June 17. It was signed by Pres. McKinley on July 7.

June 21: Guam, one of the Mariana Islands in the western Pacific, surrendered to Capt. Henry Glass on the U.S.S. *Charleston.* The Spanish commander on the island obviously had not heard of the outbreak of the war, for on the previous day when Capt. Glass fired on the island a message was sent to the *Charleston* with an apology for not having returned the salute—there was no ammunition on the island.

June 24: At the Battle of **Las Guasimas,** U.S. troops won the first major land battle of the war with Spain. The division of cavalry volunteers led by the aggressive Maj. Gen. Joseph Wheeler, with Col. Leonard Wood now a regimental commander and Col. Theodore Roosevelt leading the Rough Riders, performed well.

July 1-2: El Caney and San Juan Heights, Spanish outposts to Santiago de Cuba, were stormed and taken over stubborn resistance by U.S. troops. There were heavy casualties on both sides. The Rough Riders participated in the attack.

July 3: The **Spanish fleet at Cuba,** under Adm. Pascual Cervera y Topete, was destroyed by U.S. ships in an attempt to break out of Santiago. The Spanish lost 323 dead, 151 wounded. The U.S. lost one man. The war was virtually over.

July 8: Isla Grande, in Subic Bay near Manila, was occupied by forces under Adm. George Dewey. The German gunboat *Irene,* which had attempted to hamper American operations, was forced to withdraw.

July 17: Santiago de Cuba was surrendered along with 24,000 Spanish troops by Gen. José Toral to U.S. Gen. William R. Shafter.

July 25: Puerto Rico was invaded by U.S. forces led by Maj. Gen. Nelson D. Miles. The landing was made at Guanica, on the southern coast. Resistance was minimal.

July 26: Spain sought peace terms through the French ambassador in Washington, D.C.

July 28: Ponce, Puerto Rico's second largest city, surrendered to Gen. Miles.

Aug 1: Casualties from disease were exceedingly high during the conflict in Cuba. At this time there were some 4200 sick U.S. personnel in Cuba, most suffering from yellow fever or typhoid. Fewer than 400 troops were killed in battle or died of wounds in Cuba. Fully 90% of U.S. casualties were caused by disease.

Aug 7: The **Rough Riders left Cuba,** along with other units, for Montauk Point, Long Island, to escape epidemics in Cuba.

Aug 9: At **Coamo,** Puerto Rico, U.S. forces under Brig. Gen. Oswald H. Ernst defeated a Spanish force.

Aug 12: Hostilities between Spain and the U.S. were halted by a protocol in which Spain agreed to give Cuba its independence and to cede Puerto Rico and Guam to the U.S. Spain agreed to negotiate the status of the Philippines in a postwar conference.

Nov 8: In **congressional elections** the Republicans continued to gain strength in the Senate and lose strength in the House, taking a 53–26 lead in the Senate, with eight seats going to minor parties, and holding a majority of 185–163 in the House, with nine seats held by minor parties. In New York State, Theodore Roosevelt was elected governor on the Republican ticket. The Republicans had chosen him partly because of his war service and partly to overcome the taint of corruption left by the previous administration.

Dec 10: The **treaty ending the Spanish-American War** was signed in Paris.

II. Architecture
Arts and Music
Popular Entertainment
Publishing
Theater

Sentimentality seemed to hold sway in the field of song, resulting in the composition of some musical pieces that were at least as popular for their words as for their music. An outstanding example, "The Rosary" by Ethelbert Nevin with lyrics by Robert Cameron Rogers, was published this year. It was the most popular song in the U.S. for a quarter of a century. Nevin was a pianist and composer who wrote other similar music, such as "Narcissus" (1891), and who set to music such poems as Eugene Field's "Little Boy Blue."

Among **books published** this year was *David Harum* by Edward Noyes Westcott, a Syracuse lawyer. The novel had been rejected by six publishers before being accepted by D. Appleton & Company. It was published shortly after Westcott's death from tuberculosis on Mar. 31. The story, centering on a shrewd, humorous, and lovable small-town banker, sold 400,000 copies by Feb. 1, 1901, and 1,000,000 in 35 years. It was dramatized in 1900 and twice made into a movie, the second time with Will Rogers in the title role. Other books published this year included *The Open Boat and Other Stories* by Stephen Crane; *Mr. Dooley in Peace and War* by Peter Finley Dunne; *The Turn of the Screw* by Henry James, a masterpiece of horror by a master of English prose; *Prisoners of Hope* by Mary Johnston, a novel of colonial Virginia; *When Knighthood Was in Flower* by Charles Major, a historical romance that became a best seller; *The Adventures of Francois* by S. Weir Mitchell, a picaresque novel of the French Revolution; and *Songs from the Ghetto* by Morris Rosenfeld, an immigrant from Russian Poland, translation by Leo Wiener.

III. Business and Industry
Education
Philosophy and Religion
Science

As the end of the century neared, American industry was becoming the most productive in the world. Steel production had passed that of Great Britain in 1865; by 1900 it was 10,000,000 tons a year, and the U.S. was turning out more than Great Britain and Germany combined. Cotton textile mills were built in the South as well as the North, and by 1900 the two regions were using 3,500,000 bales of cotton a year. Meat packing was becoming an assembly line process, and large firms in the Midwest were leading the way. The Niagara Falls power plant had ushered in the era of hydroelectric power in 1894, and steam turbines and electric motors were beginning to change the face of American industry.

Nome, Alaska, was founded as the result of a gold strike on the Seward Peninsula, for which it was the port. Nome was named for a misspelling of a nearby cape on a map. The cape was referred to as "no name."

June 1: The **Erdman Arbitration Act,** sponsored by Rep. Jacob Erdman, Democrat of Pennsylvania, was passed. It authorized governmental mediation between interstate carriers and their employees. It forbade interstate carriers to discriminate against or blacklist union laborers. But on Jan. 27, 1908, the Supreme Court held the provision against discrimination unconstitutional according to the Fifth Amendment. On July 15, 1914, Congress replaced the Erdman Act by the Newlands Act, which set up a mediation board.

IV. Fashion
Folkways
Holidays
Social Issues and Crime
Sports

A great deal of entertainment for the general public was being provided by amusement parks, usually located on the outskirts of cities and often built by traction companies to create traffic for their trolley car lines. Whole families could enjoy parks such as Palisades Amusement Park in New Jersey, just across the Hudson R. from New York City, which opened in 1897. Among the many attractions at these parks were roller coasters, merry-go-rounds, shoot the chutes, dance halls, bathing beaches, and, of course, food and drink.

The impassioned slogan **"Remember the Maine"** became the war cry of Americans urging war with Spain. The battleship *Maine* had been destroyed by an explosion while docked at Havana. The American public was led to believe that it had been blown up by agents of Spain. This feeling supported American resentment against Spanish oppression of Cuban nationalism.

June 18: The **U.S. Open golf tournament** was won by Fred Herd.

1899

I. Civil Rights
Exploration and Settlement
Government
Statistics
Wars

The first international discussion of the problems of armaments and warfare was held from May 18 to July 29 at The Hague, the Netherlands. Delegates from the U.S. and 25 other nations met at the invitation of Czar Nicholas II of Russia. The conference considered disarmament, limitations on methods of warfare, and establishment of a forum for arbitrating international disputes. Nothing was accomplished in disarmament and little in issues concerning warfare, except for conventions having to do with neutral shipping and the protection of noncombatants. The conference did establish the Permanent Court of International Arbitration, although arbitration was not compulsory and the U.S. specified reservations with regard to disputes that involved application of the Monroe Doctrine.

Feb 4: Philippine guerrillas under **Emilio Aguinaldo** fired on American forces at Manila, starting skirmishes lasting several days. Before the insurgents were driven out and scattered, 57 Americans were killed and 215 wounded. Some 500 Filipinos were killed, 1000 wounded, and 500 made prisoners. This was the beginning of a rebellion against U.S. rule that lasted until Mar. 23, 1901, when Aguinaldo was captured by Gen. Frederick Funston at Palawan, Luzon.

Feb 10: The **peace treaty** with Spain was signed by Pres. William McKinley. It had been ratified by Congress on Jan. 9. By its terms the U.S. acquired Puerto Rico and Guam, and Spain relinquished its claim to Cuba. The U.S. paid Spain $20,000,000 for specific Spanish holdings in the Philippines, but many interpreted the payment as purchase of the Philippines from Spain.

II. Architecture
   Arts and Music
   Popular Entertainment
   Publishing
   Theater

The last few years of the nineteenth century saw publication of a number of popular songs that were to endure. Among them were "A Bird in a Gilded Cage" (1899) by Harry Von Tilzer, "My Wild Irish Rose" (1899) by Chauncey Olcott, and "The Stars and Stripes Forever" (1897) by John Philip Sousa. The first named was not widely popular at first, but in later years it came to be identified closely with the 1890s. For every song that found a permanent place in U.S. musical history, there were many that did not make it to the new century, such as "Gold Will Buy Most Anything but a True Girl's Heart" (1898), and "She Was Happy Till She Met You" (1899), both by Monroe H. Rosenfeld.

Among **books published** this year was *The Theory of the Leisure Class* by Thorstein Veblen, professor of political economy at the University of Chicago. Though little read except among students of economics, this outspoken assault on the moneyed class made Veblen famous in his field. Also published this year were *Fables in Slang* by George Ade, who eventually found in the follies and foibles of his fellow Americans enough material for 12 books; *Richard Carvel* by Winston Churchill, a Revolutionary War romance, the first important novel by a writer capable of probing beneath historical events to underlying forces and ideals; *The School and Society* by John Dewey, a work that revolutionized American educa-

tional theory and practice; *Janice Meredith* by Paul Leicester Ford, a historical novel widely read, perhaps because the heroine and members of her family were involved in many of the major events of the Revolutionary War; *The Man with the Hoe and Other Poems* by Edwin Markham; *McTeague,* by Frank Norris, a novel about unromantic lower-class people in San Francisco, written in a naturalistic manner; and *The Gentleman from Indiana* by Booth Tarkington, his first novel, about a crusading country editor.

Jan 15: "**The Man with the Hoe,**" a poem by Edwin Markham, a California schoolteacher, was published in the San Francisco *Examiner.* The poem was a social protest; it pictured a farmer brutalized by forces he could not control or understand. Within a week it had been reprinted by newspapers across the country. Antitrust forces called it "the cry of the Zeitgeist [cultural climate of the era]." It was the most popular poem in the U.S. by far.

III. Business and Industry
   Education
   Philosophy and Religion
   Science

Propagation of the Christian faith was not left to the clergy or the churches, especially among evangelical Protestants. One group that came to play a unique role in this endeavor was the Christian Commercial Men's Association of America, formed by a group of traveling salesmen meeting in Boscobel, Wis., on July 1. The organization became better known as the Gideons International, and best known for its chief work, placing Bibles in hotel rooms. The first Gideon Bible was placed in the Superior Hotel, Iron Mountain, Mont., in Nov. 1908.

Feb 14: Congress authorized **voting machines** for federal elections if desired by the individual states.

IV. Fashion
   Folkways
   Holidays
   Social Issues and Crime
   Sports

More attention was being paid to providing parks and playgrounds in America's cities. By this time Manhattan Island, the heart of New York City, had 1140 acres of parks, but most of it was accounted for by Central Park; there was little parkland in crowded areas. An exception was Mulberry Park, opened in 1896, which consisted of only three acres but offered a little green space in one of the worst slum areas. Kansas City, Mo., in 1893 began planning a system of

16 miles of boulevards to connect 2000 acres of parkland. Boston began to organize a park system in the 1890s. By 1898 some 14 cities in the East had children's playgrounds, many of them in schoolyards.

June 9: The **world heavyweight boxing championship** was won by James J. Jeffries, who knocked out Bob Fitzsimmons in the 11th round of a bout at Coney Island, N.Y.

Sep 15: The **U.S. Open golf tournament** was won by Willie Smith.

Oct 16-20: The **America's Cup** was successfully defended by the U.S. yacht *Columbia*, which won three straight races from the British challenger *Shamrock I.*

1900

I. Civil Rights
Exploration and Settlement
Government
Statistics
Wars

Bitter antagonism against all foreigners in China broke into open warfare this year when a nationalist group, the Boxers, occupied Peking on June 20 and besieged members of the diplomatic corps, their families, and others in the British legation. The Boxers wanted to rid China of all foreigners. After a siege of nearly two months, troops from the U.S., Great Britain, France, Russia, Germany, and Japan reached Peking on Aug. 14 and put down the Boxer Rebellion. Under pressure from the U.S., the other powers agreed not to partition China further. On Sept. 7, 1901, China and eleven other nations signed the Boxer Protocol, by which China agreed to pay $333,000,000 in indemnity. The U.S. received $24,500,000, but in 1908 this amount was reduced and the money was used to educate Chinese students in the U.S.

The **Census** recorded a population of 75,994,575. The center of population was placed at six miles southeast of Columbus, Ind.

Mar 14: The currency act, which established a **gold standard** for all U.S. currency, was passed by Congress. The act was made possible by increased gold production in South Africa and the Klondike fields. It put an end to the free silver controversy, although William Jennings Bryan and other advocates of the free coinage of silver continued to agitate for ten years more.

Apr 30: An act establishing the **Territory of Hawaii** was passed by Congress. It went into effect on June 14. On that date Pres. McKinley appointed Sanford B. Dole the first governor of Hawaii. Dole had been born in Honolulu of American missionary parents.

June 19-21: The **Republican National Convention nominated Pres. McKinley** for reelection. Gov. Theodore Roosevelt of New York was nominated for the vice presidency, but he felt he was being sidetracked from the center of political activity. Roosevelt nonetheless conducted one of the most vigorous campaigns on record, visiting 24 states, traveling 21,000 miles, and delivering some 700 speeches. McKinley conducted a front-porch campaign, never stirring from his home.

June 21: Amnesty was granted to the Filipino insurgents by a proclamation issued by Gen. Arthur MacArthur, military governor of the Philippines.

July 5: The **Democratic National Convention nominated William Jennings Bryan** of Nebraska for the presidency and Adlai E. Stevenson of Illinois for the vice presidency.

Sep 8: A **hurricane** killed 6000 persons at Galveston, Tex. Winds up to 120 mph drove Gulf waters over land. Afterward looters were found with ringed fingers they had cut off the hands of the dead. Property damage amounted to $20,000,000.

Nov 6: William McKinley was reelected president of the United States. Gov. Theodore Roosevelt, Republican of New York, was elected vice president. The electoral vote was McKinley, 292; William Jennings Bryan of Nebraska, candidate on the Democratic and Populist tickets, 155. The popular vote was McKinley, 7,219,530; Bryan, 6,358,071; John G. Woolley of Illinois, Prohibition candidate, 209,166; Eugene V. Debs of Indiana, Social Democratic candidate, 94,768; and Wharton Barker of Pennsylvania, middle-of-the-road Populist, 50,232. In congressional elections both major parties gained Senate seats from the minor parties, the Republicans taking a 55–31 majority, with four seats held by minor parties. In the House the Republicans led 197–151, with nine seats held by minor parties.

II. Architecture
Arts and Music
Popular Entertainment
Publishing
Theater

The U.S. had produced painters of talent and accomplishment in the fields of portraiture, historical paint-

225

ing, and landscape studies. No American painter of standing, however, fell into quite the same class in this period as did Albert Pinkham Ryder. Mostly self-taught, Ryder many times used as his subject the sea or moonlight. His work evokes a feeling of loneliness and mysterious force of nature. Of some 160 paintings, perhaps his best known is *Toilers of the Sea* (1900), which includes a dark sail and a wan moon giving off an aura of ghostliness. Ryder also did paintings with such titles as *Death on a Pale Horse* and *Temple of the Mind.*

Among **books published** this year was *Sister Carrie,* a first novel by Theodore Dreiser. An unflinchingly naturalistic novel, it examined in economic and moral terms the rise of a young woman from rural obscurity to success on the New York stage. Steeped in tragedy, the story was published only after Dreiser made extensive cuts. The book was issued, then recalled, by the publisher. The book's failure sent Dreiser into a deep depression. Reissued in 1912, the book was eventually recognized as an American classic. In 1981 it was republished with Dreiser's deleted text restored. Other books published this year included *Eben Holden, A Tale of the North Country* by Irving Bacheller, which sold 300,000 copies within six months; *The Wonderful Wizard of Oz* by L. Frank Baum; *Whilomville Stories* by Stephen Crane, a posthumous collection; *Literary Friends and Acquaintances* by William Dean Howells, a collection of the author's essays; *To Have and to Hold* by Mary Johnston, the author's best-known romance; *The Son of the Wolf* by Jack London, a first collection of stories; and *Alice of Old Vincennes* by Maurice Thompson, a historical novel set in Indiana in the late eighteenth century.

III. Business and Industry
Education
Philosophy and Religion
Science

The new century brought with it the automobile as a practical means of transportation. In 1900 there were only 8000 autos registered in the entire country and only about ten miles of paved roads for them to travel on. Only 4000 autos were produced in 1900, but ten years later 187,000 rolled out of the factories. The appearance of cars was changing, too. New autos looked less like horseless carriages and more like powered vehicles. The Automobile Club of America held its first meeting on Oct. 16, 1900; it sponsored the first automobile show, in Madison Square Garden, New York City, from Nov. 3–10. Nevertheless, the auto was viewed with displeasure by some. One

editor wrote, "It is well named the devil-wagon." At the turn of the century there were still about 18,000,000 horses and mules providing transportation and power, and 10,000,000 bicycles for pleasure and work.

Rural free delivery served 185,000 customers. By 1924 this number would rise to 6,500,000.

A survey of **Protestant religious sects** in the U.S. at the end of the nineteenth century showed reformed and evangelical denominations in the vast majority: 6,000,000 Methodists; 5,000,000 Baptists; 1,500,000 Lutherans; 1,500,000 Presbyterians; 350,000 Mormons; and 80,000 Christian Scientists.

Illiteracy in the U.S. reached a new low of 10.7% of the population, a decline of 2.6% from 1890 and a decline of 9.3% from 1870.

The **International Ladies' Garment Workers Union** was established at a time when the average work week in the trade was 70 hours. Jacob A. Riis reported that women sewing at home for the clothing industry were earning 30 cents a day at best.

Telephone service in the U.S. had grown to 1,335,911 telephones in use.

Mar 5: The **Hall of Fame** was founded in New York City for the purpose of commemorating great Americans. It still exists today. New members are voted on every five years by a committee of 100 men and women from all the states. To be elected a nominee must have been dead at least 25 years, have been a citizen of the United States, and have the approval of three-fifths of the committee. Any citizen may make a nomination. A bust of a person elected is placed in the open air colonnade at the former campus in The Bronx of New York University.

IV. Fashion
Folkways
Holidays
Social Issues and Crime
Sports

The growth of tennis around the world received a tremendous impetus in 1900 when Dwight F. Davis, a player of championship caliber, offered a cup for international contests between male players of the U.S. and Great Britain. The first five-match event was played in Boston, Mass. The U.S. won three matches, one match was not finished, and the last match was not played. The annual competition was soon opened to teams of other nations. Within a few years Australia and France presented teams that gave the U.S. and Britain strong competition.

Only 12,572 dozen pairs of **silk stockings** were sold

in the U.S. this year, a ratio of one pair for every 2000 Americans. By comparison, 18,088,841 pairs were sold in 1921, one pair for every six persons.

Photography as a pastime received a tremendous boost when the Eastman Kodak Company introduced the Brownie Box Camera. The camera cost only $1.00 and a six-shot roll of film cost 10 to 15 cents, depending on the type of film the photographer chose. At these prices, virtually everyone who wanted to take pictures could afford to do so. The result was that photography made a grand leap out of the studio and into the real world. Brownie cameras were manufactured until the mid-1960s, when they were superseded by the equally popular Instamatic cameras.

Jan 29: The **American League** was formed in Chicago, Ill. The new baseball league demanded recognition as a major league, but was refused by the National League until 1903 when the National, American, and minor leagues joined forces and set up a ruling body known as the National Commission.

Apr 30: At 3:52 A.M. railroad engineer John Luther "Casey" Jones died at the throttle slowing down the *Cannon Ball* express train from Memphis, Tenn., to Canton, Miss., as it slammed into the rear of a stopped train. Although Jones was speeding to make up lost time, his final action saved his passengers' lives and he became a folk hero.

May 20-Oct 28: At the **Olympic Games** in Paris, France, the U.S. finished with 20 gold medals. France was first with 29 gold medals.

Oct 5: The **U.S. Open golf tournament** was won by Harry Vardon of England.

1901

I. Civil Rights
Exploration and Settlement
Government
Statistics
Wars

For the third time in the nation's history a president was assassinated. On Sept. 6 Pres. William McKinley visited the Pan-American Exposition in Buffalo, N.Y. While greeting visitors he was shot twice in the abdomen by a young anarchist, Leon Czolgosz, who was carrying a concealed pistol in a handkerchief. For a few days McKinley seemed to be recovering, but he

took a turn for the worse and died on Sept. 14 at 2:15 A.M. McKinley, 58, was succeeded by Vice Pres. Theodore Roosevelt, who became the 26th president of the United States. Roosevelt took the presidential oath in the same house in Buffalo where the body of McKinley awaited transportation to Canton, Ohio, for burial. Roosevelt was not quite 43 years old and so was the youngest person to hold the office of president. Conservative Republicans, who had been happy with McKinley, were appalled. As governor of New York, Roosevelt had shown liberal tendencies. He had gained the vice presidential nomination in 1900 partly because Republican leaders sought to keep him in a harmless post.

The **Socialist Party** was organized by the merger of the Social Democratic Party under Eugene V. Debs with the reformist section of the Socialist Labor Party under Morris Hillquit.

Mar 4: Pres. **William McKinley was inaugurated** for his second term. Theodore Roosevelt was sworn in as vice president.

Apr 19: The **rebellion in the Philippines was ended** by proclamation. It had been the most unpopular war ever fought by the U.S., mainly because many Americans believed that the Philippines should have been given its independence.

Nov 18: The **Hay-Pauncefote Treaty** was signed, abrogating the Clayton-Bulwer Treaty of 1850. By its terms the British consented to U.S. control of an isthmian canal linking the Atlantic and Pacific oceans. The Senate ratified the treaty on Dec. 16.

II. Architecture
Arts and Music
Popular Entertainment
Publishing
Theater

For a number of years journalists had been documenting the corruption of the railroads and trusts. This year Frank Norris turned his skills as a novelist to a campaign against the excesses of big business. Concerned about the social and economic evils he saw, Norris planned a trilogy of novels, his *Epic of the Wheat*. The first volume, *The Octopus*, was published in 1901. It dealt with the struggle of farmers in the San Joaquin Valley of California against the power of the Southern Pacific Railroad. In *The Pit* (1903) Norris told the story of speculation on the Chicago wheat exchange and the damage it brought to individuals and society. Norris died on Oct. 25, 1902, at 32. *The Wolf*, which was to have concluded the trilogy, was never written. Norris viewed social and economic factors and nature itself as the determining elements in molding human lives.

Among **books published** this year were *D'ri and I* by Irving Bacheller, a novel set during the War of 1812; *Cardigan* by Robert W. Chambers, a novel of the American Revolution; *Graustark* by George Barr McCutcheon, a best-selling romance about a mythical Balkan kingdom; *Mrs. Wiggs of the Cabbage Patch* by Alice Hegan Rice; and *Springtime and Harvest* by Upton Sinclair, the author's first novel, which later was retitled *King Midas*.

III. Business and Industry
Education
Philosophy and Religion
Science

The extent to which the economy of the country had grown was made clear when the first billion-dollar corporation was formed this year. The United States Steel Corporation, formally organized on Mar. 3, was capitalized at $1,402,846,000. The actual value of the tangible property of the corporation was estimated at $682,000,000, indicating that a good deal of the capitalization was for good will. The enterprise netted the organizers, including the financier J. Pierpont Morgan, large sums. The corporation was formed primarily from the Carnegie Steel Company, but it brought in other mills as well. The new firm manufactured 60% of all iron and steel produced in the U.S. Andrew Carnegie received 5% bonds with a par value of $225,639,000 for his company and spent the next 20 years distributing his wealth in benefactions amounting to $350,000,000.

A report on **yellow fever** read by the Yellow Fever Commission to the Pan-American Medical Congress at Havana, Cuba, described experiments proving for the first time that the disease was transmitted by a mosquito *(Stegomyia calopus)*. Such a theory had been held for 20 years by Dr. Carlos Finlay of Havana, but he had been unable to offer proof and had been ridiculed by the medical profession. The Yellow Fever Commission, sent by the U.S. government to Cuba after the Spanish-American War, included Walter Reed, Aristides Agramonte, Jesse W. Lazear, and James Carroll. Doctors Lazear and Carroll both died from the effects of yellow fever contracted during the experiments.

Jan 10: The first great **oil strike in Texas** launched a fabulous era in the Southwest. The Spindletop claim near Beaumont, Tex., owned by Anthony F. Lucas, blew in on this date to open the door for the international petroleum industry.

IV. Fashion
Folkways
Holidays
Social Issues and Crime
Sports

Men who were to become legends of baseball were coming to the fore in the early years of the century. Among them was Connie Mack (Cornelius Alexander McGillicuddy), who began as a catcher for Washington (NL) in 1886, then played for Buffalo in the Players League in 1890 before joining Pittsburgh, where he ended his career as player-manager (1894–1896) with a .247 career batting average. In 1901 he was named manager of the Philadelphia Athletics (AL) and eventually became owner of the team. Under his long management the Athletics won nine league championships and five World Series. Mack was elected to the Baseball Hall of Fame in 1937. He did not fully retire until 1954, when the team was sold and moved to Kansas City, Mo.

June 15: The **U.S. Open golf tournament** was won by Willie Anderson.

Sep 2: "**Speak softly and carry a big stick**" was credited to Theodore Roosevelt a few weeks after becoming president. The saying, emphasizing the need for a strong foreign policy, caught the fancy of the entire nation and "the big stick" proved a favorite prop of political cartoonists.

Sep 28-Oct 4: The **America's Cup** was successfully defended by the U.S. yacht *Columbia,* which won three straight races from the British challenger *Shamrock II.*

1902

I. Civil Rights
Exploration and Settlement
Government
Statistics
Wars

Interest in conservation of natural resources was growing, and the nation found a strong advocate in Pres. Theodore Roosevelt. During his term of office Roosevelt added almost 150,000,000 acres of land to the government reserve. On July 17, 1902, Congress passed the Newlands Reclamation Act, named for its sponsor, Francis G. Newlands, Democratic congressman from Nevada. By its terms the government would build irrigation dams in 16 western states and use the proceeds from the sale of public lands for further projects. The law also set up the U.S. Bureau of Reclamation in the Department of the Interior.

Jan 24: A treaty with Denmark for the purchase of the **Virgin Islands** (Danish West Indies) was signed. The U.S. Senate approved the treaty, but the Danish Rigsdag rejected it. In 1917, after a Danish plebiscite (Dec. 14, 1916) favored the sale, the islands of St. Croix, St. Thomas, and St. John were finally purchased for $25,000,000.

May 20: Cuban independence was achieved, four years after the end of the Spanish-American War. The U.S. flag was lowered from government buildings in Cuba and replaced with the new Cuban flag.

June 28: The **Isthmian Canal Act** was passed by Congress. It authorized financing and building of a canal across the Isthmus of Panama, and also authorized an alternative route across Nicaragua in the event the president could not obtain a concession from the Panama Canal Company of France (which he eventually did for $40,000,000) and negotiate a proper treaty with Colombia. Treaty difficulties were obviated by the successful rebellion and separation of Panama from Colombia in Nov. 1903. The new republic immediately granted a ten-mile-wide strip of land for the canal.

July 1: The **Philippine Government Act** was passed by Congress. It declared the Philippine Islands an unorganized territory and all inhabitants territorial citizens. It authorized a commission, appointed by the president, to govern the territory. On July 4 Pres. Theodore Roosevelt issued an order establishing civil government and granting amnesty to all political prisoners.

Nov 4: In **congressional elections** both major parties made gains in the Senate from minor party or vacant seats, but the Republicans maintained their majority over the Democrats, 57–33. In the House of Representatives the total number of seats rose from 357 to 386, and the Republicans kept their majority over the Democrats, 208–178.

II. Architecture
Arts and Music
Popular Entertainment
Publishing
Theater

Plays dealing with strong characters, both virtuous and otherwise, were successful at this time. Foremost among American playwrights was Clyde Fitch, au-

thor of more than 30 popular plays. His play *The Stubbornness of Geraldine*, a study of fidelity, opened in New York City on Nov. 3, 1902. He also produced this year *The Girl With the Green Eyes*. The play dealt with the psychological aspects of jealousy; it was his best work. *The Climbers* (1901) and *The City* (1909) dealt seriously with New York City's financial and political life. Fitch also wrote such popular farces as *Captain Jinks of the Horse Marines* (1901).

Among **books published** this year was *The Virginian* by Owen Wister, a story of life in Wyoming that became one of the most celebrated western novels of all time. Wister dedicated the book to his friend Pres. Theodore Roosevelt. *The Virginian* was reprinted 14 times in eight months, and in two years had sold some 300,000 copies. Other books published this year included *The Captain of the Gray-Horse Troop* by Hamlin Garland, a novel chronicling the exploitation of the Sioux by white men; *The Mississippi Bubble* by Emerson Hough, a historical novel; *The Wings of the Dove* by Henry James, a novel; *The Story of My Life*, the autobiography of Helen Keller; *A Daughter of the Snows* by Jack London, the author's first novel, and *The Cruise of the Dazzler*, for children, also by London; *Brewster's Millions* by George Barr McCutcheon, a novel that sold in the millions and was the basis for at least six motion pictures; *Dorothy Vernon of Haddon Hall*, a novel by Charles Major; and *The Blazed Trail* by Stewart Edward White, a novel.

III. Business and Industry
Education
Philosophy and Religion
Science

As American business enterprises grew, debate increased as to whether large and powerful corporations were good for the nation. Experience so far indicated that industrial giants cared little for anything except profit and that only government regulation could restrain their actions. Into this argument came the International Harvester Company, incorporated in New Jersey on Aug. 12, 1902, with a capital of $120,000,000. The combination of interests represented by the concern produced 85% of all farm machinery in the U.S. However, Harvester conducted its business in such a moderate manner that there was little complaint. Both capitalists and consumers were beginning to recognize that, given the extent of the nation and its economy, bigness was here to stay.

Feb: Discovery of the **hookworm** was announced by Dr. Charles Wardell Stiles. He declared that the so-called poor whites in the South were neither lazy nor innately slovenly, but were suffering on a wide scale from the debilitating effects of the parasite. An anti-hookworm campaign began throughout the South, supported by the Rockefeller Foundation.

IV. Fashion
Folkways
Holidays
Social Issues and Crime
Sports

The early years of twentieth-century professional baseball saw the founding of the American League in 1900 out of the Western Association, the new league's first season in 1901, and the start of an annual championship series with the National League in 1903. This expansion created more heroes of the diamond. One of the most admired and successful managers of this period was John J. McGraw, nicknamed "Little Napoleon," who left as manager for Baltimore (AL) midway through the 1902 season to become manager of the New York Giants (NL). McGraw held that position for 31 years, during which the Giants won ten National League championships, four in succession, and three World Series. McGraw was elected to the Baseball Hall of Fame in 1937.

Jan 1: The **first Tournament of Roses Association football game,** and the first post-season football game, was held at Pasadena, Calif. Michigan defeated Stanford 49–0. The event came to be known as the Rose Bowl game in 1923.

Apr 19: The sixth **Boston Marathon** was won by Samuel A. Mellor of Yonkers, N.Y., with a time of 2 hrs., 43 min., 12 sec.

Oct 11: The **U.S. Open golf tournament** was won by Lawrence Auchterlonie.

1903

I. Civil Rights
Exploration and Settlement
Government
Statistics
Wars

By 1903 it became clear that legislation on the books could not keep railroads from engaging in business practices that gave certain shippers a decided advantage. As a result, on Feb. 19 the Elkins Act, named for Sen. Stephen B. Elkins, Republican of West Virginia, was passed by Congress. This law made it illegal for railroads to give rebates on their published freight rates. Finding that this did not solve the problem, Congress on June 29, 1906, passed the Hepburn Act, named for William P. Hepburn, Republican congressman from Ohio. That law empowered the Interstate Commerce Commission to regulate the rates charged by railroads, pipelines, and terminals.

Jan 22: The **Hay-Herrán Treaty,** granting a 99-year lease and U.S. sovereignty over a canal zone in Panama, was signed with Colombia. The U.S. Senate ratified it on Mar. 17, but on Aug. 12 the Colombian Senate rejected it.

Nov 3: **A revolt in Panama** against Colombian rule broke out one day after Pres. Roosevelt ordered U.S. naval forces to the area. The U.S. presence kept Colombian forces from halting the rebellion, which was engineered in part by officers of the Panama Canal Company and by Panamanian groups, all with the tacit approval of the Roosevelt administration. On Nov. 6 the U.S. recognized the Republic of Panama, three days after it had been proclaimed.

Nov 18: The **Hay-Bunau-Varilla Treaty** was negotiated. It gave the U.S. full control of a ten-mile-wide canal zone in Panama in return for $10,000,000 in gold plus a yearly payment of $250,000.

II. Architecture
Arts and Music
Popular Entertainment
Publishing
Theater

Realism was becoming an influence in adult American fiction, but it was not noticeable in children's literature. Sentimentalism and a happy ending were what sold, as witnessed by the popular books of Kate Douglas Wiggin. *The Birds' Christmas Carol* (1887) was the story of the life and death of an ethereal child. Wiggin's most successful book, *Rebecca of Sunnybrook Farm,* was published this year and sold more than 1,000,000 copies. This children's classic was about a girl's experiences on her widowed mother's farm. Another Wiggin classic was *Mother Carey's Chickens* (1911), about a warm-hearted widow who had a great many children.

Among **books published** this year was *The Ambassadors* by Henry James, a novel about Americans in Paris that showed the author at the peak of his literary powers. Other books published this year included *The Land of Little Rain* by Mary Austin, a collection of sketches; *The Bar Sinister* by Richard Harding Davis, a novel; *The Little Shepherd of Kingdom Come* by John Fox, Jr., a novel; *The Call of the Wild* by Jack London, a study of the forces of nature and civilization in the framework of a classic dog story, and *The People of the Abyss,* also by London, a study of the slums of London's East End; *Canterbury Pilgrims* by Percy MacKaye, a drama in blank verse that set Chaucer's characters in poetic adventures; *The Pit* by Frank Norris, the second volume of the author's *Epic of the Wheat* trilogy; and *The Testimony of the Suns* by George Sterling, a book of poetry.

The **first male motion picture star** made his debut in *The Great Train Robbery,* a landmark film considered the first motion picture with a plot. The actor, Max Aaronson, also used the names Max Anderson, G. M. Anderson, and Bronco Billy.

Mar: The vogue for what came to be called the **Nantucket limerick** hit U.S. newspapers, inspiring many variations and sequels. The original went:

> There once was a man from Nantucket
> Who kept all his cash in a bucket;
> But his daughter, named Nan,
> Ran away with a man,
> And as for the bucket, Nantucket.

III. Business and Industry
Education
Philosophy and Religion
Science

A historic moment in technology and transportation arrived on Dec. 17, when Orville Wright made the first powered flight in a heavier-than-air machine. As early as 1898 Orville and Wilbur Wright, owners of a bicycle repair shop and factory in Dayton, Ohio, had been working on the problem of flight. Years of experimentation had led to their development of a working glider. Meanwhile, refinements of internal combustion engines gave them the power plant they needed to keep the glider aloft. On Dec. 17, 1903, on the beach at Kitty Hawk, N.C., Orville Wright flew the 750-lb. craft, which was powered by a 12-hp gasoline engine, for 12 seconds, traveling about 120 feet. Four flights were made that day, with Wilbur setting the record of 59 seconds in the air traveling 852 feet. The aviation age had arrived.

The **University of Puerto Rico** at Rio Pedras, P.R., was chartered. Its first classes had been held in 1900, when the institution was a normal school.

A **heavier-than-air flying machine,** built by Samuel P. Langley, was tested from a houseboat on the Potomac R. On takeoff, its wing hit a houseboat stanchion and the machine crashed. Langley was subjected to much public ridicule for his efforts. In 1914 the machine was reconditioned and flown. It was a 14-ft. model and flew without a pilot. There are those who maintain that Langley achieved powered flight before the Wright brothers.

Mar 21: In a **victory for organized labor,** the report of the Anthracite Coal Strike Commission, appointed by Pres. Roosevelt to investigate conditions in the mining industry, established that "no person shall be refused employment, or in any way discriminated against, on account of membership or non-membership in any labor organization."

July 4: The **first Pacific communications cable** was opened. Pres. Roosevelt sent a message around the world and back to him in 12 minutes.

IV. Fashion
Folkways
Holidays
Social Issues and Crime
Sports

This year was born an American sports institution, the World Series. For the first time, the champions of the National and American leagues met for a postseason playoff, which ran from Oct. 1 to Oct. 13; it was a best-of-nine series. The Pittsburgh Pirates, the National League champs, took three of the first four games from the Boston Red Sox, originally called the Red Stockings. On Oct. 7 the American League champs rebounded with an 11–2 romp over the Pirates, then won the next three games to take the series five games to three and prove to the world that the American League had arrived. Boston's win no doubt ruffled a few feathers in the National camp. In 1904, when Boston again took the American League pennant, John J. McGraw, manager of the champion New York Giants, already involved in a running feud with Ban Johnson, president of the American League, refused to allow a post-season playoff. The bitterness between the two leagues was only temporary. In 1905 the World Series resumed and has been played every year since.

June 27: The **U.S. Open golf tournament** was won by Willie Anderson.

Aug 8: The U.S. lost the **Davis Cup** international tennis challenge round to Great Britain, four matches to one.

Aug 22-Sep 2: The **America's Cup** was successfully defended by the U.S. yacht *Reliance,* which won three straight races from the British challenger *Shamrock III.*

1904

I. Civil Rights
Exploration and Settlement
Government
Statistics
Wars

By 1904 Pres. Theodore Roosevelt had achieved great popularity as well as control of the Republican Party. His nomination for a term in his own right was certain and his conservative Democratic opponent, Alton B. Parker, conducted a dull campaign. Roosevelt, although representing the conservative party in American politics, was the hero of the progressives. The progressives of this period inherited some of the goals of the populists of a few years earlier, but the populists represented chiefly southern and western farm interests. The progressives were urban-oriented, and concerned primarily with problems of industrial monopoly, corruption in government, assimilation of new immigrants, and the relief of poverty.

Jan 4: In a ruling on the **status of territorial citizens,** the Supreme Court ruled that citizens of Puerto Rico were not aliens and could not be refused admission to the continental limits of the U.S. However, they were not classified as U.S. citizens.

May 5: The **Socialist National Convention nominated Eugene V. Debs** of Indiana for the presidency and Benjamin Hanford of New York for the vice presidency.

June 21-23: The **Republican National Convention nominated Pres. Roosevelt** for the presidency and Charles W. Fairbanks of Indiana for the vice presidency.

July 6-9: The **Democratic National Convention nominated Alton B. Parker** of New York for the presidency and Henry G. Davis of West Virginia for the vice presidency.

Nov 8: Theodore Roosevelt was reelected president of the United States. Charles W. Fairbanks was elected vice president. The electoral vote was Roosevelt, 336; Alton B. Parker, Democratic candidate, 140. The popular vote was Roosevelt, 7,628,834; Parker, 5,884,401; Eugene V. Debs, Socialist candidate, 402,460; Dr. Silas C. Swallow, Prohibition Party, 259,257; Thomas E. Watson, People's Party, 114,753. The Republicans carried Missouri for the first time since the Civil War in what was the biggest election victory since 1872. They maintained a 57–33 majority over the Democrats in the Senate and picked up 43 seats in the House for a 250–136 majority.

II. Architecture
Arts and Music
Popular Entertainment
Publishing
Theater

This was the era of the muckrakers, journalists and authors who investigated and wrote about corruption in government and business. One of the leading muckrakers was Lincoln Steffens, a magazine editor who collected his articles on corruption in municipal government in *The Shame of the Cities* (1904). Steffens held that such corruption stemmed from alliances between businessmen and politicians who were able to enrich each other at the expense of the taxpayer.

Among **books published** this year was *The Golden Bowl* by Henry James. Other books published this year included *The Crossing* by Winston Churchill, a novel set in Kentucky during the American Revolution; *The Deliverance* by Ellen Glasgow, a novel; *Cabbages and Kings* by O. Henry, the author's first collection of short stories; *The Sea Wolf* by Jack London, a study of human nature and the concept of the superman as embodied in the character of a brutal ship's captain; *Freckles* by Gene Stratton-Porter, a novel; and *The History of the Standard Oil Company* by Ida M. Tarbell, a muckraking classic.

The **American Academy of Arts and Letters** was founded by the National Institute of Arts and Letters. Membership was limited to 50, to be chosen from among the members of the institute.

III. Business and Industry
Education
Philosophy and Religion
Science

The first section of the New York City subway system, which was to become the largest in the country, was opened on Oct. 27, 1904. Work on the line had begun in 1900. It ran from the Brooklyn Bridge north to 145th St. and Broadway in Manhattan. Construction of this first part of the subway system was supervised by Alexander Ector Orr. Some of the present system runs on elevated tracks, but there are 134 miles of tunnels, some driven through rock. The first tunnel under the East R. was driven between 1903 and 1906 and put into service in 1908.

The **diesel engine** was shown for the first time in the U.S. at the St. Louis Exposition. The engine was based on the plans of the German inventor Rudolf Diesel.

Mar 14: The **Northern Securities Company** was ordered dissolved by the Supreme Court in a landmark case reflecting the federal government's relation to big business. Theodore Roosevelt's reputation as a trust-buster rested largely on the prosecution of this case and the angry comments he drew from J. P. Morgan, who controlled the railroad holding company.

Oct 19: The **American Tobacco Company** was formed by a merger of its two subsidiaries, the Consolidated and the American & Continental tobacco companies.

Nov 2: **Evangeline Booth** was appointed commander of the Salvation Army of the U.S.

IV. Fashion
   Folkways
   Holidays
   Social Issues and Crime
   Sports

As soon as automobiles were invented and manufactured, men began racing them against time and against one another. Automobile racing as an organized sport began on Oct. 8, 1904, with the Vanderbilt Cup race, sponsored by William K. Vanderbilt. Vanderbilt was an early auto fancier. It was said he had garages that would hold 100 cars and that he hired 20 mechanics to service them. The race, on Long Island, was as much a social as a sporting event, with about 25,000 spectators on hand. The winner was George Heath, driving a 90-hp French Panhard. He defeated 17 other starters by completing ten laps around a 28.4-mi. course in 5 hrs., 26 min., 45 sec.

The **World Series** was called off this year by John McGraw, manager of the New York Giants, the National League champions. Incensed by the abuse Ban Johnson, president of the American League, had heaped on him when he switched from the Baltimore Americans in 1903, McGraw got even by refusing to let the Giants meet Boston, the American League leaders, for the post-season series. It took the persuasion of owners, managers, players and fans to smooth the incident over. By that time it was too late for the games to be played.

May 5: The **first perfect baseball game,** in which the pitcher did not allow any opposing player to reach first base, was pitched by Denton T. "Cy" Young of the Boston Americans (AL), who led his team to a 3–0 victory over Philadelphia.

May 14: The first **Olympic Games** to be held in the U.S. opened as part of the St. Louis Exposition in St. Louis, Mo. The U.S. won 21 events and the unofficial

team championship in the third Olympiad of the modern era.

July 9: The **U.S. Open golf tournament** was won by Willie Anderson.

1905

I. Civil Rights
Exploration and Settlement
Government
Statistics
Wars

Pres. Theodore Roosevelt gained international prominence by arranging a peace conference between Russia and Japan; the nations had been at war since Feb. 10, 1904. Although Japan had fared better in the military and naval engagements of the Russo-Japanese War, neither side was in a position to go on fighting much longer. In a note to the two powers on June 8, Roosevelt urged an end to hostilities and suggested a conference. The peace conference met at Portsmouth, N.H., on Aug. 9, and the belligerents signed the Treaty of Portsmouth on Sept. 5. The U.S. sought to keep a balance of power in the Far East between the two nations and also to preserve the Open Door Policy in China. However, by the terms of the treaty, Japan came out ahead and was on its way to becoming a world power. Japan's paramount interest in Korea was recognized and it was given the South Manchurian Railway and the Southern Liaotung Peninsula. Roosevelt was able to keep Japan from securing more than half of Sakhalin Island. For his efforts Roosevelt was awarded the Nobel Peace Prize in 1906.

Jan 21: A **protocol with the Dominican Republic** was signed, giving the U.S. complete charge of its customs and international debt, with the purpose of satisfying European creditors of Santo Domingo. The U.S. was also to guarantee the territorial integrity of the republic. Though the U.S. Senate refused to ratify the protocol, Pres. Theodore Roosevelt made a temporary arrangement with the republic, incorporating the key elements of the protocol. The action was a reflection of the so-called Roosevelt Corollary to the Monroe Doctrine, which Roosevelt stated on Dec. 6, 1904. Roosevelt held that "in flagrant cases of wrongdoing or impotence" of nations in the Western Hemisphere, the U.S. might be obliged to undertake "the exercise of an international police power."

II. Architecture
Arts and Music
Popular Entertainment
Publishing
Theater

Higher education joined hands with theater this year when George Pierce Baker established his 47 Workshop at Harvard. He taught playwriting techniques and provided a laboratory for experimental stage productions. Among those whom Baker taught were Eugene O'Neill, Philip Barry, Sidney Howard, and S. N. Behrman. Baker taught at Harvard until 1925, when he went to Yale to continue his work there.

Among **books published** this year was *The House of Mirth* by Edith Wharton, a novel analyzing with great subtlety a group of wealthy, artificial, and oversophisticated people, and their tragic influence over the life of a young woman. Other books published this year included *Isidro* by Mary Austin, the author's first novel; *The Clansman* by Thomas Dixon, Jr., a novel about the Ku Klux Klan that was the basis for D. W. Griffith's landmark motion picture *The Birth of a Nation; The Game* by Jack London, a novel about prizefighting; *The House of a Thousand Candles* by Meredith Nicholson, a novel; and *Sandy* by Alice Hegan Rice, a novel.

III. Business and Industry
Education
Philosophy and Religion
Science

Life insurance had joined the ranks of big business, the three largest firms having combined assets of $1,250,000,000 by 1904. The major firms also had arrangements with certain banks by which the insurance company purchased large blocks of securities placed on the market by the banks. The funds for these lucrative transactions came from the thousands who paid insurance premiums. Reports of a scandal surfaced and an investigating commission was appointed by New York State in 1905. Headed by Charles Evans Hughes, it held 57 public hearings from Sept. 6 to Dec. 30 and uncovered numerous excesses. The probe disclosed, for example, that Charles Hazen Hyde, son of the founder of the Equitable Life Assurance Society, earned $100,000 a year, although still in his twenties. Hyde once charged to company expenses a $12,000 dinner for the French ambassador. The investigation resulted in reform legislation. It also brought Hughes into public life. He went on to become governor of New York, Repub-

lican candidate for president, and in 1930 chief justice of the U.S. Supreme Court.

The number of **automobiles** registered in the U.S. rose to 77,988, compared with 300 a decade earlier, but the automobile was still considered a useless toy by most people.

Feb 20: State compulsory vaccination laws were ruled constitutional by the U.S. Supreme Court in the case of *Jacobson v. Massachusetts.*

Apr 17: State laws limiting working hours were ruled unconstitutional by the U.S. Supreme Court.

July 7: The **Industrial Workers of the World** (IWW) was established in Chicago as a reaction against the more conservative American Federation of Labor. Its members came to be known as Wobblies.

IV. Fashion
Folkways
Holidays
Social Issues and Crime
Sports

Greyhounds had been chasing hares for several thousand years, but it was not until 1905 that an American developed the idea of racing the dogs around a circular track in pursuit of an artificial hare. Owen Patrick Smith of Hot Springs, S. Dak., decided to promote tourism through such races. There had been public opposition to the slaughter of live hares, so Smith substituted a stuffed rabbit skin attached to a motorcycle, thus launching the greyhound racing industry.

The **world heavyweight boxing championship** was won by Marvin Hart, who knocked out Jack Root in 12 rounds in the final bout of an elimination tourney. He filled the title vacated by James J. Jeffries' retirement this year.

Football rules were revised this season by the Rules Committee of Football as a result of Pres. Theodore Roosevelt's threat to abolish football after he had seen a newspaper picture of a badly mangled player. The changes included legalization of the forward pass and elimination of certain dangerous scrimmage plays.

At the **Wimbledon** tennis championships in England, May G. Sutton won the women's singles championship, becoming the first foreigner to win the women's singles and the first U.S. player to win any Wimbledon singles title.

Sep 22: The **U.S. Open golf tournament** was won by Willie Anderson.

Oct 9-14: The second annual **World Series** was won by the New York Giants (NL), defeating the Philadelphia Athletics (AL) four games to one.

1906

I. Civil Rights
Exploration and Settlement
Government
Statistics
Wars

The worst natural disaster in U.S. history occurred on the morning of Apr. 18, 1906, when a devastating earthquake struck San Francisco, Calif. Most of the damage came not from the shock but from the fire that followed. Flames swept the city for three days. By the time the fire was brought under control, 490 blocks had been leveled, 25,000 buildings had been destroyed, 225,000 people had been made homeless, and 452 had been killed. Damage was estimated to be at least $350,000,000. The nation rallied to the aid of the stricken city, whose residents began at once to rebuild. Banks offered to lend money and stores reordered stock.

The **first American Nobel Prize winner** was Pres. Theodore Roosevelt, who was awarded the Nobel Peace Prize this year for his role in mediating an end to the Russo-Japanese War (1904–1905).

June 30: The **Pure Food and Drug Act** was passed. It prohibited the sale of adulterated foods and drugs and demanded an honest statement of contents on labels. Dr. Harvey W. Wiley was mainly responsible for pointing up the necessity for this act. On the same day a Meat Inspection Act was passed by Congress. It was the result of the Reynolds and Neill report of June 4, which revealed shockingly unclean conditions in meat-packing plants. The Meat Inspection Act required sanitary conditions and federal inspection for all plants in interstate commerce.

Aug 23: A **request for U.S. intervention** in Cuba was issued by Tomás Estrada Palma, the first president of Cuba, to quell a revolt arising from election disputes. Pres. Roosevelt held off but finally sent troops, who took over the Cuban government for 13 days in October.

Sep 22: Race riots in Atlanta, Ga., left 21 persons dead, including 18 blacks, and many more injured in one of the worst race riots in U.S. history. The city was placed under martial law.

Sep 29: The **Platt Amendment,** authorizing U.S. intervention in Cuba, was invoked and the U.S. assumed military control of the country. Sec. of War William Howard Taft was provisional governor.

Nov 6: In **congressional elections** the Republicans gained four Senate seats for a 61–31 majority. In the House the Republicans lost 28 seats but maintained a 222–164 majority.

II. Architecture
Arts and Music
Popular Entertainment
Publishing
Theater

The reading public's fascination with an American West more imaginary than real seemed insatiable. One man who did his best to feed this craving was Zane Grey, whose more than 60 books sold over 13,000,000 copies before he died in 1939. His first western novel, published in 1906, was *The Spirit of the Border.* His most popular novel was *Riders of the Purple Sage* (1912). Grey was quite authentic as to geography and topography, but his plots and characters were melodramatic and sometimes simplistic. Strong and brave heroes, nasty villains, and pretty, innocent heroines were his stock in trade. Many of his novels were made into movies.

Among **books published** this year was *The Jungle* by Upton Sinclair, a novel exposing the sordid aspects of the Chicago meat-packing industry, particularly the hardships imposed on its workers and the practice of selling questionable or tainted meat. The book came to the attention of Pres. Theodore Roosevelt, who summoned Sinclair for further information. Roosevelt then pushed for passage of the Pure Food and Drug Act of 1906. Other books published this year included *The Spoilers* by Rex Beach, a novel of Alaska based on actual events and the author's experiences in the territory; *Coniston* by Winston Churchill, a novel about boss rule in a state legislature; *The Awakening of Helena Ritchie* by Margaret Deland, a novel; *The Wheel of Life* by Ellen Glasgow, a novel; *The Four Million* by O. Henry, his second collection of stories; *White Fang* by Jack London, a sequel to *The Call of the Wild,* and *Before Adam,* a novel also by London; and *What Is Man?* by Mark Twain, a bitter essay in the form of a Platonic dialogue, published privately.

Ferdinand "Jelly Roll" Morton, the celebrated New Orleans ragtime piano player, wrote "The King Porter Stomp." Morton gave the St. Louis ragtime style of Scott Joplin a heavy beat. Among his many other ragtime compositions were "The Pearls," "Kansas City Stomps," "Chicago Breakdown," "Black Bottom Stomp," "Buddy Carter's Rag," and "The Perfect Rag."

III. Business and Industry
Education
Philosophy and Religion
Science

An event rare in U.S. religious history occurred this year when the Rev. Algernon Sidney Crapsey, rector of St. Andrew's Protestant Episcopal Church in Rochester, N.Y., was tried for heresy before an ecclesiastical court. His church was known for its social work, but it was charged that under the influence of the writings of Karl Marx and Ernest Renan, Crapsey had made heretical remarks about the divinity of Christ. The trial began on Apr. 18 at Batavia, N.Y., with detachments of lawyers, secular and clerical, representing both sides. The trial was fully reported by newspapers throughout the U.S. and England. Crapsey was convicted on Dec. 5 and expelled from the ministry.

Apr 7: Announcement was made of a successful **transatlantic wireless transmission** from a 40,000-watt transmitter at Manhattan Beach, New York City, to Lee De Forest at a receiving station in Ireland. This year De Forest invented the triode tube, the cornerstone for the development of modern wireless communication.

Dec 24: The first known **radio broadcast of voice and music** was made by Reginald A. Fessenden, a private radio experimenter, at Branch Rock, Mass. Fessenden had demonstrated his system at Branch Rock on Dec. 11. Also this year he established two-way wireless communication with Scotland.

IV. Fashion
Folkways
Holidays
Social Issues and Crime
Sports

The most talked about murder of the first decade of the twentieth century was the killing of Stanford White, the prominent architect. On the evening of June 25, 1906, White was at the roof garden of New York City's Madison Square Garden, which he had designed, when he was shot and killed by Harry K. Thaw. The wealthy playboy claimed that White had been having an affair with his wife, Evelyn Nesbit Thaw, a former chorus girl. Thaw's trial fascinated the country. After one hung jury, Thaw was found "not guilty because insane" in 1908. In 1913 Thaw escaped from the mental hospital where he was being held but was found in Canada and brought back. In

1915, at still another trial, he was declared sane and released.

Devil's Tower, Wyo., was designated the **first national monument** by Pres. Theodore Roosevelt. Devil's Tower, a natural rock formation 1000 ft. in diameter at its base and about 275 ft. in diameter at its top, is 865 ft. high.

Feb 23: The **world heavyweight boxing championship** was won by Tommy Burns, who defeated Marvin Hart in 20 rounds at Los Angeles, Calif. James J. Jeffries, who retired in 1905 because he could find no worthy adversary, refereed the fight.

Mar 17: The term *muckraker,* taken from a passage in John Bunyan's *Pilgrim's Progress,* was first used in its modern meaning by Pres. Theodore Roosevelt in an address to the Gridiron Club, Washington, D.C. Muckrakers were authors of "literature of exposure," who in the early 1900s helped stimulate reform by exposing unpleasant sides of American life. The best-known muckrakers included Lincoln Steffens, Ida M. Tarbell, Ray Stannard Baker, and David Graham Phillips. A prime example of the influence of muckraking literature can be seen in Upton Sinclair's *The Jungle,* which helped passage of the Meat Packing Act of 1906.

Apr 22-May 2: Olympic Games were held in Athens, Greece, but they were not accepted as official by the International Olympic Committee. The U.S. won 12 gold medals, behind France with 15.

June 29: The **U.S. Open golf tournament** was won by Alex Smith.

Oct 9-14: The third annual **World Series** was won by the Chicago White Sox (AL), who defeated the Chicago Cubs (NL) four games to two.

1907

I. Civil Rights
Exploration and Settlement
Government
Statistics
Wars

Pres. Theodore Roosevelt was especially interested in the preparedness and political value of the U.S. Navy. Now that a powerful Navy existed, he proposed to show it to the world, partly to deter Japan from further adventurism in the Pacific. On Dec. 16, 1907, a squadron of 16 battleships, known as the Great White Fleet because of the ships' appearance, steamed out of Hampton Roads, Va., under Rear Adm. Robley D. Evans. Instead of causing alarm as some had feared, the fleet was enthusiastically received in many ports of call, including those in Japan, Australia, New Zealand, and Gibraltar. The fleet arrived back at Hampton Roads on Feb. 22, 1909, having convinced the world that the U.S. was a major naval power.

Feb 20: The **Immigration Act of 1907** was signed by Pres. Theodore Roosevelt. It included a provision empowering the president to restrict immigration by Japanese laborers.

Mar 14: Japanese laborers were excluded from immigrating to the continental U.S. by presidential order.

Mar 21: U.S. Marines landed in **Honduras** to protect life and property during a period of political disturbance.

Nov 16: Oklahoma was admitted to the Union, the 46th state.

II. Architecture
Arts and Music
Popular Entertainment
Publishing
Theater

The Broadway theater always offered a variety of productions, some dramatic, some humorous, and some appealing as much to the eye as to the ear or the mind. One of the most successful producers of visually lavish entertainment was Florenz Ziegfeld, who offered his first *Ziegfeld Follies* this year. Ziegfeld put on this annual revue for 24 years, featuring "the most beautiful girls in the world" together with comedians and singers. Among the stars he presented were Anna Held, Fanny Brice, Eddie Cantor, and W. C. Fields. Ziegfeld also staged such hits as *Rio Rita* and *Show Boat.*

Among **books published** this year was *Three Weeks,* a romantic novel by the English author Elinor Glyn that was suppressed in Boston because of its description of an illicit affair. It sold 50,000 copies in three weeks and eventually sold in the hundreds of thousands. Other books published this year included *The Trimmed Lamp* and *Heart of the West,* two more collections by O. Henry; *Songs of a Sourdough* by Robert W. Service, which included the celebrated ballad "The Shooting of Dan McGrew" and which

was reissued as *The Spell of the Yukon; Christian Science* by Mark Twain; and *The Fruit of the Tree* by Edith Wharton, a novel.

The Education of Henry Adams, a masterpiece of autobiography by the noted historian and author, was privately printed and distributed to Adams's friends. Adams revealed that his education had not prepared him for modern living and expressed skepticism and loss of faith. The work was published posthumously in 1918 and was awarded the Nobel Prize for Biography in 1919.

The first public showing of a **color motion picture with sound** was held in Cleveland, Ohio. The Chromophone process was used in the film, which consisted of footage of grand opera, a bull-fight with naturalistic sound effects, and a political speech accompanied by derisive sounds.

The **Robey House,** one of Frank Lloyd Wright's earliest designs, was built in Chicago. The structure showed the broad low roofs and horizontal lines that were the hallmark of Wright's prairie houses.

III. Business and Industry
Education
Philosophy and Religion
Science

Once more overspeculation and a flawed and unregulated banking and credit structure caused a financial panic that turned into a brief depression. A large drop in the stock market on Mar. 13 presaged trouble. On Oct. 21 a run on the Knickerbocker Trust Company in New York City caused panic elsewhere. The bank was forced to close its doors. The government called on J. Pierpont Morgan, the nation's leading financier, for help. By the force of his personality, Morgan secured the cooperation of his fellow bankers, who combined their resources to import $100,000,000 in gold from Europe to restore confidence and end what came to be known as the panic of 1907. One result of the panic was passage of the Aldrich-Vreeland Act on May 30, 1908. It levied a tax of up to 10% on notes based on securities other than federal bonds. It also established a commission to investigate the currency and banking system.

The **Nobel Prize in Physics** was awarded to Prof. Albert Abraham Michelson, head of the Physics Department at the University of Chicago. Michelson was honored particularly for his studies of the speed of light, carried out with apparatus designed and built by himself.

Sep 12: The *Lusitania,* the largest steamship in the world, arrived in New York harbor on its maiden voyage. The liner set a new speed record of 5 days, 54 min. between Queenstown (now Cobh), Ireland, and New York.

IV. Fashion
Folkways
Holidays
Social Issues and Crime
Sports

One of the best-remembered infield combinations in the game of baseball is the trio of Joe Tinker, Johnny Evers, and Frank Chance, who played shortstop, second base, and first base, respectively, for the Chicago Cubs (NL). These three turned the double play into an art form. Chance had become manager of the Cubs in 1905. In 1907 the team finished first and went on to dominate the Detroit Tigers in the World Series. Evers and Tinker made six errors in the series, but the trio combined to steal eight bases and kept Detroit from scoring effectively. Franklin Pierce Adams later recalled them in a piece called "Baseball's Sad Lexicon":

Ruthlessly pricking our gonfalon bubble,
Making a Giant hit into a double,
Words that are weighty with nothing but trouble:
"Tinker to Evers to Chance."

At the **Wimbledon** tennis championships, May G. Sutton won the women's singles title.

May: An early **Mother's Day** observance was held in Grafton, W. Va., through the efforts of Miss Anna M. Jarvis, who arranged a special church service marking the second anniversary of her mother's death in 1905. She requested that those attending the service wear white carnations, which she supplied. The first formal observances of Mother's Day were held in Grafton and in Philadelphia, Pa., on May 10, 1908. The custom spread rapidly until, by 1911, every state in the Union was participating in Mother's Day exercises held on the second Sunday in May.

June 21: The **U.S. Open golf tournament** was won by Alex Ross.

Oct 8-12: The fourth annual **World Series** was won by the Chicago Cubs (NL), who swept the Detroit Tigers (AL) in four games after the first game ended in a tie.

Dec 2: The **world heavyweight boxing championship** was successfully defended by Tommy Burns, who knocked out Gunner Moir in ten rounds at London, England.

1908

I. Civil Rights
Exploration and Settlement
Government
Statistics
Wars

There was little doubt that Pres. Theodore Roosevelt, if he chose to run again in 1908, would be reelected. However, he had said in 1904 he would not seek a third term, although he had been elected in his own right only once. Instead he handpicked the Republican nominee, William Howard Taft, who had been a lawyer, judge, U.S. solicitor general (1890–1892), governor of the Philippines (1901–1904), and secretary of war (1904–1908). The campaign was a dull one, the Democratic candidate, William Jennings Bryan, having lost most of the glamor he showed when first nominated for the presidency 12 years before.

Feb 18: An agreement on the **restriction of Japanese immigration** was reached through a note sent to the American ambassador to Japan acknowledging Pres. Theodore Roosevelt's order of Mar. 14, 1907. The Japanese government agreed not to issue any more passports to Japanese laborers for immigration to the U.S.

May 10-17: The **Socialist Party National Convention** nominated Eugene V. Debs of Indiana for the presidency and Benjamin Hanford of New York for the vice presidency.

June 16-20: The **Republican National Convention nominated William Howard Taft** of Ohio for the presidency and James S. Sherman of New York for the vice presidency. When Chairman Henry Cabot Lodge spoke in praise of Pres. Theodore Roosevelt, who had chosen not to seek renomination, the delegates began a demonstration that lasted 45 minutes, breaking all previous records for both major parties.

July 7-10: The **Democratic National Convention nominated William J. Bryan** of Nebraska for the presidency and John W. Kern of Indiana for the vice presidency.

Nov 3: William Howard Taft was elected president of the United States. James S. Sherman was elected vice president. The electoral vote was Taft, 321; William Jennings Bryan, Democrat of Nebraska, 162. The popular vote was Taft, 7,679,006; Bryan, 6,409,106; Eugene V. Debs, Socialist candidate, 420,820; Eugene W. Chafin, Prohibition candidate, 252,683; Thomas

L. Hisgen, Independence Party, 83,562; Thomas E. Watson, Populist, 28,131; August Gillhaus, Socialist Labor Party, 13,825. In congressional elections the Republicans held a 61–32 majority, the Democrats gaining one seat. In the House, which added five new seats, the Republicans lost three seats but maintained a majority, 219–172.

II. Architecture
Arts and Music
Popular Entertainment
Publishing
Theater

A new generation of American painters was arriving on the art scene. The work of these painters was realistic and showed concern with the contemporary world. In 1908 they became known as The Eight when they organized an exhibition of their work in February at the Macbeth Gallery in New York City. The eight artists were Arthur B. Davies, Maurice Prendergast, Ernest Lawson, Robert Henri, George Luks, William J. Glackens, John Sloan, and Everett Shinn. Henri was their leader. Their painting represented a turning away from the pretty but insipid pictures of the older, academic school of painting. Some of their works, depicting the seamier side of modern, urban life, won them the title of the Ash Can school from their detractors. Frank Jewett Mather of *The Nation* wrote that there "was more green, yellow and red sickness about their position than positive talent." Nevertheless, they brought to art a new vitality and proved that everyday scenes showing ordinary people could be worthwhile subjects for the painter, even when the subject was a city backyard, a crowded business street, or lonely city people at night.

Among **books published** this year was *The Trail of the Lonesome Pine* by John Fox, Jr., a novel set in the Cumberland Mts. of Kentucky. The author used his own experiences and knowledge of the region and its people in the novel, which became a best seller. Other books published this year included *The Barrier* by Rex Beach, a novel of adventure; *Mr. Crewe's Career* by Winston Churchill, a novel dealing with control of a state government by a railroad; *Friendship Village* by Zona Gale, stories of midwestern life; *The Iron Heel* by Jack London, a novel that predicted the rise of fascism; *The Circular Staircase* by Mary Roberts Rinehart, the mystery novel that launched her career; and *The Metropolis* by Upton Sinclair, a novel.

There were between 8000 and 10,000 **nickelodeons,** or movie theaters, in the U.S., drawing an estimated 200,000 customers a day. The first such thea-

ter had been launched in 1905 in Pittsburgh, Pa., by John P. Harris and Harry Davis.

Julia Ward Howe, author of the poem "The Battle Hymn of the Republic," became the first woman member of the American Academy of Arts and Letters. This year William Dean Howells was made president of the academy.

III. Business and Industry
Education
Philosophy and Religion
Science

The age of the skyscraper was dawning. In Chicago architects and engineers had pioneered in new technology and materials, especially the steel skeleton that made such structures possible. But it was in New York City that the first real skyscrapers were erected. The first New York City skyscraper was the Flatiron Building, constructed between 1902 and 1904. Its name came from the triangular plot on which it was built, at the intersection of Fifth Ave. and Broadway. Its 22 stories rose 180 ft. high. In 1908 the Singer Building set a new record, its 47 stories rising to a height of 612 ft. It held the title of the world's tallest building for less than a year, however, being eclipsed by the Metropolitan Life tower of 50 stories and 700 ft. The Woolworth Building, completed in 1913, set still another record with its 55 stories and height of 760 ft. Although exceeded in height many times since, this distinguished Gothic-ornamented tower remains the proudest symbol of the age of early skyscrapers.

Feb 3: In an **antitrust decision** in the case of *Loewe v. Lawlor,* the so-called Danbury hatters case, the Supreme Court ruled that the antitrust law applied to labor combinations as well as to capital combinations and declared union boycotting illegal.

June 12: A new **transatlantic speed record** was set by the liner *Lusitania,* which traveled from Queenstown (now Cobh), Ireland, to New York, a trip of 2780 miles, in 4 days, 15 hrs.

Sep 17: Orville Wright crashed in his airplane at Fort Myer, Va., when a propeller blade broke and the plane fell 150 ft. to the ground, injuring Wright seriously and killing his passenger, Lt. Thomas W. Selfridge of the U.S. Signal Corps. Selfridge was the first person killed in an airplane accident. Orville and Wilbur Wright, still using their original machine, though with improvements, had made thousands of flights, had remained in the air as long as 38 min., and had flown distances up to 24 mi., but their work was still unknown in the U.S. to all but a few hundred observers. This year Wilbur Wright went to Europe to make tests for the French. Vast crowds watched his flights.

On Sept. 21 he set a new flight endurance record over Le Mans, France—1 hr., 31 min., 25 sec. in a flight of 61 miles.

Oct 1: The celebrated **Model T Ford** was introduced. It originally cost $850 but by 1926 the price, because of efficient manufacturing, had dropped to $310 for a machine that included a self-starter and other improvements.

IV. Fashion
Folkways
Holidays
Social Issues and Crime
Sports

The sporting event of the year turned out to be an around-the-world auto race, from New York City to Paris, France, by way of Alaska and Siberia. It was sponsored by *The New York Times* and *Le Matin.* The race began on Feb. 12, when six autos and their crews, French, German, Italian, and U.S., left New York City at 11 A.M. and traveled north toward Albany, N.Y. The cars drove west, across the U.S., Russia, and eastern Europe, experiencing breakdowns and encountering muddy roads, snow, ice, timber wolves, and gasoline shortages. The two lead cars were the huge German Protos driven by Lt. Hans Koeppen and the U.S. Thomas Flyer with George Schuster at the wheel. The German team was penalized 30 days for shipping their car by rail to Seattle, Wash., so, despite the fact the Germans arrived in Paris on July 26 and the Americans on July 30, the U.S. team was declared the winner. The only other entrant to finish, the Italian Zust, arrived two weeks later. When the U.S. team returned, New York City turned out in great numbers to greet them. Pres. Theodore Roosevelt received them at the White House on Aug. 20.

Apr 27-Oct 31: At the **Summer Olympics** in London, England, the U.S. won the unofficial team championship by taking 15 of 28 events, with 23 gold medals. The team was honored in New York City on Aug. 29 on its return from the games.

Aug 28: The **U.S. Open golf tournament** was won by Fred McLeod.

Sep 23: Perhaps the **greatest dispute in baseball** was a call made in what was supposed to be the decisive game, at the Polo Grounds, N.Y., of the Chicago Cubs-New York Giants National League pennant race. In the bottom of the ninth inning with two men out and the score tied at 1–1, New York was at bat with two men on. The batter hit safely to center field, scoring the winning run. The Chicago players claimed, however, that when Fred Merkle, the man on first, saw the winning run score, he started to walk toward the clubhouse without advancing to second base, invalidating the play. Johnny Evers, the Chicago second baseman, tried to get the ball and tag Merkle out, but the fans streamed onto the field and bedlam reigned. Days later Harry C. Pulliam, head of the National Commission of Organized Baseball, decided to call the game a tie. The teams were forced to play a post-season playoff game, which the Cubs took 4–2. Fans invented the terms "boner" and "bonehead" to apply to Merkle's play.

Oct 10-14: The fifth annual **World Series** was won by the Chicago Cubs (NL), who beat the Detroit Tigers (AL) four games to one.

Dec 26: The **world heavyweight boxing championship** was won by Jack Johnson, who defeated Tommy Burns in 14 rounds at Sydney, Australia.

1909

I. Civil Rights
Exploration and Settlement
Government
Statistics
Wars

The tariff remained a controversial issue. The new president, William Howard Taft, had said he would call a special session of Congress to lower rates. When Congress finished with the matter, however, the Payne-Aldrich Tariff Act, signed by Taft on Aug. 5, included some reductions but on the whole made few changes. Sen. Nelson Aldrich, Republican of Rhode Island, advocated a high tariff and led the fight to keep rates high. In September, Taft defended the bill in a speech at Winona, Minn., thus alienating liberals and progressives who had thought he would follow in the footsteps of their hero, Theodore Roosevelt.

The **National Association for the Advancement of Colored People** was founded, principally by liberal whites under the leadership of Oswald Garrison Villard, grandson of William Lloyd Garrison, to promote the rights and welfare of black Americans.

Apr 6: Robert Edwin Peary reached the North Pole. With his servant Matt Henson, who was black, and four Eskimos, Peary made a final dash from an advance base and reached latitude 90 degrees north for the first time in recorded history.

July 12: A resolution for a **Sixteenth Amendment** to the U.S. Constitution was passed by the Senate and submitted to the states for ratification. The amendment authorized Congress to impose income taxes.

Sep 1: Dr. **Frederick Cook,** of Brooklyn, N.Y., claimed to have reached the North Pole on Apr. 21, 1908, beating Robert E. Peary in the feat by nearly a year. The claim sparked a bitter debate, which continued even after Congress and the scientific community at large recognized Peary's claim.

II. Architecture
Arts and Music
Popular Entertainment
Publishing
Theater

The blues as a recognized musical form had been around for some time, but 1909 was a landmark year in the history of the blues. This year W. C. Handy, the composer and bandleader, wrote "Mr. Crump" as a campaign song for Edward H. Crump, the Democratic boss of Memphis, Tenn. In 1912 it was published as "Memphis Blues" and became a hit, the first composition ever to be published as a blues song.

Among **books published** this year was *Martin Eden* by Jack London. It was an autobiographical novel about a strong and intelligent laborer and seaman who educates himself, strives for wealth and fame as a writer and, once he succeeds, finds life devoid of meaning and commits suicide on a voyage to the South Seas. Other books published this year included *The Silver Horde* by Rex Beach, a novel; *Roads of Destiny* and *Options,* two collections of stories by O. Henry; *54-40 or Fight!* by Emerson Hough, a historical novel about the conflict over the border between Canada and the Oregon Territory; *A Girl of the Limberlost* by Gene Stratton-Porter, a novel; *Three Lives* by Gertrude Stein, stories; and *A Certain Rich Man* by William Allen White, a novel.

The first notable **animated motion picture** shown in the U.S., *Gertie the Dinosaur,* utilized 10,000 drawings by Winsor McCay, a cartoonist for the New York *American.*

III. Business and Industry
Education
Philosophy and Religion
Science

Although commercial production of celluloid, the first important synthetic plastic, had been achieved in 1872 by John W. Hyatt, it was in the early twentieth century that development of synthetics progressed significantly. In 1902 Arthur D. Little patented rayon (cellulose ester). In 1909 Leo H. Baekeland, Belgian-born inventor, announced his development of Bakelite, a synthetic thermosetting resin. It had many uses, and soon a large number of commercial products were being made in whole or in part of Bakelite. Because of its extremely high electrical resistance, it was used to make insulators and other components for the electrical, and later the radio, industry. Another feature of Bakelite was that it could be molded to any shape. It offered virtually limitless opportunities for manufacturers.

Henry Ford produced 19,051 **Model T Fords.** He led the auto industry in production and sales by building only one model, the "universal" car, which "customers could have in any color as long as it was black."

July 27: Orville Wright made a new **flight duration record,** remaining in the air 1 hr., 1 min., 40 sec. and carrying a passenger in addition to Wright.

IV. Fashion
Folkways
Holidays
Social Issues and Crime
Sports

Former Pres. Theodore Roosevelt left for a hunting trip in Africa on Mar. 23, 1909, partly to let Pres. William Howard Taft have the limelight and partly because of his restless, energetic nature. Roosevelt received $50,000 from *Scribner's Magazine* for his account of the trip. When he returned in Feb. 1910 he brought back numerous animal trophies, which were given to the American Museum of Natural History in New York City. On June 18, 1910, he was off again on a trip to Europe. He reviewed troops with Kaiser Wilhelm of Germany and lectured at the Sorbonne in Paris and at Oxford University in England.

New standards of **fashion and beauty** were adopted as the automobile gained importance in American life. The suntanned, even red-faced Outdoor Girl replaced the soft, pale Gibson Girl when women took up automobile driving. "Automobile wrinkles" were soothed by application of freshly cut cucumbers. A new field was opened for fashion designers: special clothes for motoring, including a long veil to keep a lady's hat in place.

June 25: The **U.S. Open golf tournament** was won by George Sargent.

Oct 8-16: The sixth annual **World Series** was won by the Pittsburgh Pirates (NL), who defeated the Detroit Tigers (AL) four games to three.

1910

I. Civil Rights
Exploration and Settlement
Government
Statistics
Wars

The Mann-Elkins Act was passed by Congress on June 18. Named for Sen. Stephen B. Elkins, Republican of West Virginia, and Rep. James R. Mann, Republican of Illinois, the law increased the authority of the Interstate Commerce Commission in enforcing its rulings on rates. The new law also extended the ICC's jurisdiction to cover telegraph, telephone, and cable companies and authorized the commission to suspend railroad rate increases pending investigation and court decisions. A Commerce Court was set up to hear appeals of the commission's rulings.

The U.S. **Census** recorded a population of 91,972,266. The center of population was at Bloomington, Ind.

Prohibition had been adopted by the following states: Maine (1858), Kansas (1880), North Dakota (1889), Georgia (1907), Oklahoma (1907), Mississippi (1908), North Carolina (1908), Tennessee (1909).

The last five years had seen the worst period for **mine disasters** in U.S. history. From 1906 through 1910 there were 84 coal mine disasters that killed 2494 miners. Most of the accidents were explosions. The worst year was 1907 with a total of 919 fatalities; Dec. 1907 alone saw 702 fatalities.

Mar 26: An amendment to the **Immigration Act of 1907** was passed. It forbade entrance to the U.S. of criminals, paupers, anarchists, and persons carrying disease.

June 25: The **Mann Act,** popularly called the "white slave traffic act," was passed by Congress. The act prohibited interstate or international transport of women for "immoral purposes." It grew out of public agitation over "white slavery," particularly the importation of European girls to work in American brothels.

Nov 8: In **congressional elections** the Democrats took control of Congress for the first time since 1894. In the Senate the Republicans held a 51–41 majority, but combination with insurgent Republicans opposed to the policies of the Taft administration gave the Democrats control. In the House the Democrats took a 228–162 majority. The only minor party representative in the House was Victor L. Berger of Milwaukee, Wis., the first Socialist ever sent to Congress. In state elections, Franklin Delano Roosevelt was elected to the New York legislature. Oregon adopted a presidential preferential primary, and Washington State adopted woman suffrage.

II. Architecture
Arts and Music
Popular Entertainment
Publishing
Theater

Songs about unrequited love remained popular with Americans. A songwriter who made a fortune from such songs was Carrie Jacobs Bond, a self-taught musician who wrote both the words and music for some 175 songs. In 1910 she brought out one of her most popular, "A Perfect Day." Other hits included "Just a-Wearyin' for You" and "I Love You Truly"; the latter has been sung at innumerable weddings since its composition.

Among **books published** this year was *The Spirit of Romance* by Ezra Pound, the first book of essays by the leading figure in the new imagist movement in American poetry. Pound's subjects included the barrenness of American culture and the need for absolute criteria in evaluating art. Other books published this year included *Molly Make-Believe* by Eleanor Abbott, a book for children; *The Rosary* by Florence Barclay, a novel that sold some 500,000 copies in three years; *A Modern Chronicle* by Winston Churchill, a novel; *Whirligigs* and *Strictly Business,* collections of stories by O. Henry, who died this year; *My Mark Twain: Reminiscences and Criticisms* by William Dean Howells; *The Finer Grain* by Henry James, stories; *Burning Daylight* by Jack London, a novel, and *Lost Face,* also by London, a collection of stories including "To Build a Fire"; *The Town Down the River* by Edwin Arlington Robinson, a collection of poems including the classic "Miniver Cheevy"; and *The Bungalow Book* by Henry L. Wilson, which went through five editions and was immensely popular.

The first exhibition of the **Younger American Artists** took place with the opening of Alfred Stieglitz's "291." This show, at the Stieglitz Photo-Secession Gallery at 291 Fifth Ave. in New York City, offered works by Max Weber, John Marin, Abraham Walkowitz, William Zorach, Gaston Lachaise, Bernard Karfiol, Joseph Stella, and others.

III. Business and Industry
Education
Philosophy and Religion
Science

This year thousands of people became convinced that the end of the world was at hand. The cause of this prognosis was the passage of Halley's Comet, named for the English astronomer Edmund Halley, who had observed the comet's passage in 1682 and determined that it was the subject of similar observations made in 1531 and 1607. Enough people were frightened by stories of impending catastrophe that comet pills, supposed to protect from the comet's dire effects, went on sale. Miners refused to work on May 18, when the earth was due to pass through the fiery tail of the comet; they did not want to die underground. Many workers stayed home to spend their last day with their families. Farm families hid in cyclone cellars. Others took shelter in caves. In Milwaukee, Wis., two men were said to have committed suicide. Mark Twain, who said he had come in with Halley's Comet and expected to go out with it, was not disappointed. He died on Apr. 21, at 74. Halley's Comet returned in 1985–1986, but did not make much of a show, since its path was much farther from the earth. In 1910, by contrast, the comet's tail could be seen across much of the night sky.

The **farm population** continued its steady decline. There were 32,077,000 farm inhabitants this year, 30,529,000 in 1930, and 25,058,000 in 1950.

Illiteracy in the U.S. reached a new low of 7.7% of the population, a decline of 3% from 1900 and 12.3% from 1870.

A **grade-school education** had been acquired by less than half the population over 25 years of age. Only about 4% of the population held college degrees.

Nov 14: The **first naval aircraft launching** from the deck of a U.S. warship was accomplished by Eugene Ely, who took off from the cruiser *Birmingham* at Hampton Roads, Va.

IV. Fashion
Folkways
Holidays
Social Issues and Crime
Sports

The most successful and popular organization for American boys was chartered on Feb. 6, 1910. It was the Boy Scouts of America. The incorporator was William D. Boyce, a Chicago publisher who took the idea from the English Boy Scout movement, founded in 1908 by Sir Robert Baden-Powell. Daniel Carter Beard, the illustrator and naturalist, had earlier founded the Sons of Daniel Boone, and Ernest Thompson Seton, author and artist, had organized the Woodcraft Indians. Both organizations had much the same purpose as the Boy Scouts.

This year's **national college football championship** was won by Harvard, with a record of eight wins, no losses, one tie.

Mar 16: A new **land speed record** of 133 mph was set by Barney Oldfield, who ran a timed mile in a Benz auto at Daytona Beach, Fla.

Mar 17: The **Camp Fire Girls** was organized by Dr. and Mrs. Luther Halsey Gulick, Mr. and Mrs. Ernest Thompson Seton, and others. It was incorporated in 1912. After 20 years there were more than 200,000 members in the U.S.

June 18: The **U.S. Open golf tournament** was won by Alex Smith.

June 19: Father's Day was celebrated for the first time in Spokane, Wash. Initiated by Mrs. John B. Dodd, it was backed by the Ministerial Association and the YMCA. Today it is celebrated on the third Sunday of June.

July 4: The **world heavyweight boxing championship** was successfully defended by Jack Johnson, who outclassed former champ Jim Jeffries in 15 rounds. After the match, Johnson's mother is reported to have said, "He said he'd *bring home the bacon,* and the honey boy has gone and done it." No earlier citation is known for this expression.

Oct 17-23: The seventh annual **World Series** was won by the Philadelphia Athletics (AL), who defeated the Chicago Cubs (NL) four games to one.

1911

I. Civil Rights
Exploration and Settlement
Government
Statistics
Wars

A tragic industrial disaster occurred on Mar. 25, 1911, when the Triangle Waist Company, a sweatshop in New York City, caught fire. About 850 employees were trapped in the building, which was full of inflammable materials used in making shirtwaists.

The fire began only minutes before the Saturday workday was to end and lasted but half an hour. The building was considered fireproof but had only one fire escape, and its exit doors were blocked. Some 146 persons were killed, most of them young women. The proprietors were tried but acquitted. However, the fire led to revision of the local building code and labor laws. The tragedy also added impetus to the organizational work of the International Ladies Garment Workers Union, which had been formed in 1900.

Jan 21: The **National Progressive Republican League** was formed in Washington, D.C., by Sen. Robert M. La Follette of Wisconsin. Sen. Jonathan Bourne of Oregon was elected president. The organization's chief aims were enactment of progressive legislation and promotion of popular government. It called for direct primaries, direct election of delegates to national conventions, and amendments to state constitutions providing for initiative, referendum, and recall.

Aug 22: Arizona statehood was vetoed by Pres. William Howard Taft on the grounds that its constitution permitted the recall of judges, which Taft considered a threat to the independence of the judiciary. After removing this provision, Arizona was admitted to the Union in 1912, after which it reinstated the provision.

II. Architecture
Arts and Music
Popular Entertainment
Publishing
Theater

The American appetite for fiction about the West, with rugged heroes and pure heroines, seemed insatiable. An author who catered to this appetite successfully was Harold Bell Wright, whose most popular novel, *The Winning of Barbara Worth*, was published this year; it eventually sold some 1,500,000 copies. Wright's stories were set in the Southwest. They were a careful mix of love story, adventure story, and moral instruction. Wright knew his craft and his readers. He turned out enormously popular novels for nearly 40 years. Other successful Wright books included *The Shepherd of the Hills* (1907), *The Calling of Dan Matthews* (1909), and *When a Man's a Man* (1916).

Among **books published** this year was the novel *Jennie Gerhardt* by Theodore Dreiser, which sold well enough to warrant republication in 1912 of Dreiser's first novel, *Sister Carrie* (1900). Other books published this year included *The Devil's Dictionary* by Ambrose Bierce, which originally appeared as *The Cynic's Word Book* (1906); *The Iron Woman* by Margaret Deland, a sequel to her novel *The Awakening of Barbara Richie* (1906); *Dawn O'Hara* by Edna Ferber, the author's first novel; *The Miller of Old Church* by Ellen Glasgow, a novel; *Sixes and Sevens* by O. Henry, a posthumous collection; *The Outcry* by Henry James, a novel; *South Sea Tales* by Jack London; and *Mother* by Kathleen Norris, the author's first novel, a best seller.

"Alexander's Ragtime Band" was composed by Irving Berlin. Although not strictly a ragtime tune, it was the first song to popularize ragtime outside the limited area of the Mississippi Delta.

III. Business and Industry
Education
Philosophy and Religion
Science

Before he left office, Pres. Theodore Roosevelt had ordered the Justice Department to act against the Standard Oil Company of New Jersey under the Sherman Antitrust Act of 1890, but it took more than four years for the case to reach the Supreme Court. Standard Oil controlled about 85% of the domestic oil industry at this time. On May 15, 1911, the Court ordered Standard Oil dissolved because it violated the antitrust law. In so doing, it added to the law by ruling that trusts were unlawful if they engaged in "unreasonable" restraint of trade.

Sep 17-Nov 5: The **first cross-country flight** was made by Calbraith P. Rodgers, who flew a Burgess-Wright biplane from Sheepshead Bay, N.Y., to Pasadena, Calif., in 82 hrs., 4 min. of flying time.

Nov 10: The **Carnegie Corporation** of New York was established by Andrew Carnegie with an initial endowment of $125,000,000. It was the first of the great foundations for scholarly and charitable endeavors. Other funds Carnegie established included the Carnegie Institute of Pittsburgh (1896), $24,000,000; the Carnegie Institute of Washington (1902), $22,000,000; the Carnegie Foundation for the Advancement of Teaching (1905), $15,000,000; and the Carnegie Endowment for International Peace (1910), $10,000,000.

IV. Fashion
Folkways
Holidays
Social Issues and Crime
Sports

Baseball continued to produce heroes for American sports fans. The best all-around player of the era was

Tyrus Raymond "Ty" Cobb, who joined the Detroit Tigers in 1905 and played for 24 years in the American League. In his first year in the majors he batted .240. After that his batting average was never below .320. When he retired he held an incredible list of records, including a career batting average of .367, a record 2244 runs, 892 stolen bases, and 12 league batting championships. He was perhaps the most spectacular player the game has ever produced. In 1936 he became the first player elected to the Baseball Hall of Fame. His career total of 4191 hits stood as a record until 1985, when Pete Rose surpassed him.

May 30: The **first annual Indianapolis 500** auto race was won by Ray Harroun, completing the 500-mile course in 6 hrs., 42 min., 8 sec., with an average speed of 74.59 mph.

June 24: The **U.S. Open golf tournament** was won by John J. McDermott in a playoff round.

Oct 14-26: The eighth annual **World Series** was won by the Philadelphia Athletics (AL), who beat the New York Giants (NL) four games to two.

1912

I. **Civil Rights**
Exploration and Settlement
Government
Statistics
Wars

The 1912 presidential election began as a three-way race but soon became a contest between former Pres. Theodore Roosevelt, the Progressive Party candidate, and Woodrow Wilson, the Democrat. Pres. William Howard Taft, the Republican candidate, fell far behind. The mood of the country called for reform, and Roosevelt and Wilson differed only on the best way to achieve it. Roosevelt talked of the Square Deal and the New Nationalism; Wilson spoke of the New Freedom. Roosevelt would deal with industrial monopoly by regulating it; Wilson called for breaking up big business to restore competition. When Wilson won in November, he was only the second Democrat to be elected to the presidency since the Civil War.

Jan 6: New Mexico was admitted to the Union, the 47th state.

Jan 22: U.S. troops began **occupation of Tientsin** for the protection of American interests in the Chinese Revolution, which had begun in Oct. 1911.

Feb 14: Arizona was admitted to the Union, the 48th state.

Apr 14-15: The British liner *Titanic* struck an iceberg off the coast of Newfoundland and sank on its maiden voyage, killing about 1500 persons, including many U.S. and British notables. An investigation showed that the ship had insufficient lifeboats and that safety procedures had not been followed. The company was blamed for poor equipment and for ordering the ship to speed through dangerous waters.

June 5: U.S. **Marines landed in Cuba** to protect American interests there.

June 18-22: The **Republican National Convention** nominated **Pres. William Howard Taft** for a second term, but only after bitter political maneuvering against the progressive elements favoring Theodore Roosevelt. James S. Sherman was renominated for the vice presidency. Taft forces won parliamentary control of the convention through the election of their candidate for convention chairman, Elihu Root, and through the seating of their delegates in disputed delegations. After Taft's nomination on June 22, Roosevelt announced the formation of the Progressive Party, under his own leadership.

June 25-July 2: The **Democratic National Convention** nominated **Woodrow Wilson** of New Jersey for the presidency and Thomas R. Marshall of Indiana for the vice presidency.

Aug 5: The **Progressive (Bull Moose) Party** nominated **Theodore Roosevelt** for the presidency and Hiram Johnson of California for the vice presidency. The party platform called for women's suffrage, direct primaries, and other progressive measures.

Oct 14: Theodore Roosevelt was shot from a distance of six feet by John Schrank of New York. The incident occurred in a Milwaukee, Wis., hotel during Roosevelt's campaign tour. The bullet struck a bulky manuscript and entered Roosevelt's chest. Despite the wound, Roosevelt insisted on delivering his speech before he was taken to a hospital.

Nov 5: Woodrow Wilson was elected president of the United States in a landslide Democratic victory. Thomas R. Marshall was elected vice president. The electoral vote was Wilson, 435; Theodore Roosevelt, Progressive Party, 88; William Howard Taft, Republican, 8. The popular vote was Wilson, 6,293,454; Roosevelt, 4,119,538; Taft, 3,484,980; Eugene V. Debs, Socialist candidate, 900,672; Eugene W. Chafin, Prohibition candidate, 206,275. In congressional elections the Democrats took a 51–44 majority in the Senate, with one minor party seat, and a 291–127 majority in the House, with 17 seats going to minor parties.

II. Architecture
Arts and Music
Popular Entertainment
Publishing
Theater

The writing, or at least the publishing, of poetry in a modern style seemed to lag behind fiction. However, poetry received a decided stimulus in 1912 with the founding of *Poetry: A Magazine of Verse* in Chicago. The founder was Harriet Monroe, a poet. The magazine had a lasting influence on American poetry under her editorship, which continued until her death in 1936. *Poetry* published the work of such poets as Carl Sandburg, Amy Lowell, Ezra Pound, Hilda Doolittle, T. S. Eliot, Vachel Lindsay, and Hart Crane. Many new poets first came to public attention in its pages.

Among **books published** this year was *The Financier* by Theodore Dreiser, the first novel of a trilogy about Frank Cowperwood, a predatory businessman modeled after Charles T. Yerkes, the financier and transportation magnate. Dreiser continued the Cowperwood trilogy with *The Titan* (1914) and the posthumous volume *The Stoic* (1947). Other books published this year included *A Woman of Genius* by Mary Austin, a novel; *The Squirrel Cage* by Dorothy Canfield, a novel of domestic life; *Alexander's Bridge* by Willa Cather, the author's first novel; *Riders of the Purple Sage* by Zane Grey, the author's most popular novel; *The Autobiography of an Ex-Colored Man* by James Weldon Johnson, a novel; *Smoke Bellew* by Jack London, a novel; and the three-volume *Mark Twain, A Biography* by Albert Bigelow Paine.

III. Business and Industry
Education
Philosophy and Religion
Science

A strike of textile workers at Lawrence, Mass., in 1912 brought prominence in the East to the Industrial Workers of the World (IWW), a radical labor union that had hitherto been active chiefly in the West among miners, migratory farm workers, and lumbermen. The strike began on Jan. 12 over a reduction in wages. It lasted two months and there was

considerable violence. The workers ultimately prevailed, and the strike established the IWW as a force to be reckoned with in the textile industry. The IWW's best-known leader was William D. "Big Bill" Haywood, an advocate of mass action, and violence if necessary, to achieve better conditions for workers.

May 1: A new **ship safety regulation** was issued by federal inspectors following the sinking of the *Titanic* in April. Steamships were ordered to carry enough lifeboats to hold all passengers.

June 19: A new **labor law** was passed by Congress. It extended the eight-hour working day to all workers under federal contract.

IV. Fashion
Folkways
Holidays
Social Issues and Crime
Sports

Americans had a new athletic hero to cheer in 1912, James Francis "Jim" Thorpe, perhaps the best all-around athlete in history. An American Indian, Thorpe attended Carlisle Indian School in Pennsylvania. There he participated in several sports and, under the tutelage of Glenn "Pop" Warner, led the small school to football triumphs over such powers as Harvard. At the Olympic Games in Stockholm in 1912, he won both the pentathlon and the decathlon, but his medals were taken from him the next year when it was discoverd that he had played semiprofessional baseball in 1909. On Jan. 18, 1983, 30 years after his death, his medals were restored to his daughter. In 1950 Thorpe had been voted by sportswriters "the greatest football player and male athlete of the first half of the twentieth century."

The spreading fad for **ragtime music** led at about this time to a series of so-called animal dances. The dances were execrated in press and pulpit. Among them were the fox trot, horse trot, crab step, kangaroo dip, camel walk, fish walk, chicken scratch, lame duck, snake, grizzly bear, turkey trot, and bunny hug.

May 5-July 22: At the **Olympic Games** in Stockholm, Sweden, the U.S. won 23 gold medals and took first place in the unofficial team championships.

Aug 2: The **U.S. Open golf tournament** was won by John J. McDermott.

Oct 8-16: The ninth annual **World Series** was won by the Boston Red Sox (AL), who beat the New York Giants (NL) four games to three in an eight-game series. The second game, played at Boston on Oct. 9, was a tie; it had been called in the 11th inning on account of darkness.

1913

I. Civil Rights
Exploration and Settlement
Government
Statistics
Wars

For many years tariff revenue had been the largest single source of government income. The adoption on Feb. 25, 1913, of the Sixteenth Amendment to the Constitution, permitting the levying of income tax on individuals and businesses without apportionment on the basis of the population of states, was soon to affect the importance of tariff revenues. The change did not come at once, however, for the first income tax law specified graduated rates of 1 to 6% of income.

Mar 1: The **Webb-Kenyon Interstate Liquor Act** was passed over Pres. Taft's veto. It stated that no liquor could be shipped into states where its sale was illegal. This was the first nationwide victory of the Anti-Saloon league.

Mar 21-26: What was called the **Dayton flood** raged in the Miami River Valley of Ohio, killing more than 400 people. Property damage was estimated at $100,000,000. An additional 200 or more persons were killed by floods along the Indiana R. and elsewhere in the West and South. In 1925 five dams were completed across the upper Miami R. and its tributaries at a cost of $32,000,000. These dams provided significantly increased protection against floods.

May 19: The **Webb Alien Land-Holding Bill** was signed by Gov. Hiram W. Johnson of California in the face of objections by Pres. Wilson and Japan. It excluded Japanese from ownership of land in California.

May 31: The **Seventeenth Amendment** to the U.S. Constitution went into effect. It provided for popular election of U.S. senators. Previously, senators had been chosen by their state legislatures. Thus, the amendment reduced the power and status of state governments and increased popular control of the federal legislature.

II. Architecture
Arts and Music
Popular Entertainment
Publishing
Theater

The single most important event to date in the American art world was held at the 69th Regiment Armory at Lexington Ave. and 26th St. in New York City, beginning Feb. 17. It was the International Exhibition of Modern Art, known to this day as the Armory Show. Organized originally to show works of younger U.S. artists, it came to include European artists as well. There were about 1600 paintings and sculptures in all. The show drew large crowds and horrified conservative critics. Ridicule was showered on Marcel Duchamp's cubist painting *Nude Descending a Staircase*, which one commentator called an "explosion in a shingle factory." In reviewing the show, Theodore Roosevelt was sympathetic but wrote that there was "apt to be a lunatic fringe among the votaries of any forward movement." The exhibition did much to change the direction of American painting.

Among **books published** this year was *O Pioneers!* by Willa Cather, the author's second novel and her first set in the Nebraska of her youth. The story dealt with Alexandra Bergsen, a second-generation Swedish-American who, through courage, diligence, and sacrifice, triumphed over the barren land. Other books published this year included *The Inside of the Cup* by Winston Churchill, a novel that became a best seller; *The Enjoyment of Poetry* by Max Eastman, which went through six editions by 1920; *Virginia* by Ellen Glasgow, a study of the life and values of a southern woman; *Rolling Stones* by O. Henry; *A Small Boy and Others* by Henry James, autobiographical writings; *General William Booth Enters into Heaven and Other Poems* by Vachel Lindsay; *The Valley of the Moon* by Jack London, a novel, and *John Barleycorn*, also by London, an autobiographical account of his struggles against alcohol; and *Pollyanna* by Eleanor Hodgman Porter, a juvenile novel that eventually sold more than 1,000,000 copies and inspired the term *Pollyanna*, meaning an irrepressibly optimistic person.

The **Woolworth Building**, tallest in the world, was built in New York City. It measured 792 feet and was considered a wonder by New Yorkers when it was first built.

III. Business and Industry
Education
Philosophy and Religion
Science

For many years the nation had needed a central banking system to bring stability to currency and credit markets. Bankers wanted a system they could control. Agrarian interests and others wanted a system controlled by the federal government that would provide easy credit. Pres. Woodrow Wilson pledged to reform the banking system and on Dec. 23, 1913, the Owen-Glass Act became law. It set up the Federal Reserve System. The act established a central Federal Reserve Board and a dozen regional banks. All national banks were required to join the system. State banks could do so if they wished. The system could issue currency and control credit by raising or lowering the discount rate it charged member banks. The general aim was to increase economic stability and make it impossible for speculators to upset the economy of the nation.

May 14: John D. Rockefeller donated $100,000,000 to the **Rockefeller Foundation,** chartered by the New York State legislature. His contribution was thought to be the largest single philanthropic act in history.

Summer: Henry Ford set up his **first automobile assembly line** for production of the inexpensive Model T. Ford introduced a revolutionary high wage for his workers of $5 a day. Between 1909 and 1924, the price of the Model T dropped from $950 to $290. Ford engineers had adapted the meat packers' conveyor belt system, and soon 1000 Fords a day were turned out.

Oct 10: The **waterway across the Isthmus of Panama** was completed when the Gamboa Dike was blown up. Pres. Woodrow Wilson set off the explosion by pressing an electric button at the White House.

IV. Fashion
Folkways
Holidays
Social Issues and Crime
Sports

This period is often looked back on as the golden age of professional baseball. The sport was truly national, with no competition as yet from professional football or basketball. Fans were as enthusiastic about their favorite teams. Millions of people attended National and American League games, and minor league teams were gaining in popularity as well. One of the top minor leagues was the United States League. In 1914 it was reorganized into the Federal League. It had good financial backing and started pulling top players from both the National and American leagues. Despite its claim to major league status, it lasted only through 1915.

July 25-28: The **Davis Cup** international tennis challenge round was won for the first time since 1902 by the U.S., beating the British team three matches to two.

Oct 7-11: The tenth annual **World Series** was won by the Philadelphia Athletics (AL), who beat the New York Giants (NL) four games to one.

Nov 1: The **first Army-Notre Dame football game** was a memorable one. The Notre Dame team was almost unknown in Eastern football circles, so its victory over Army, 35 to 13, stunned the losers. While legend tends to focus on the passing combination of Gus Dorais and Knute Rockne, the team from South Bend, Ind., was in fact bigger than Army and was favored to win. Its All-American fullback is said to have torn "the Army line to shreds." Notre Dame demonstrated that forward passes could be devastating.

1914

I. Civil Rights
Exploration and Settlement
Government
Statistics
Wars

In August the fragile peace that had prevailed in Europe was broken. European armies that had been preparing for the conflict for years mobilized, and guns began firing. The U.S. was completely unprepared for war, and Pres. Woodrow Wilson intended to keep the country out of the conflict. He viewed the U.S. as the nation that would bring the warring parties to the conference table and help fashion a lasting peace. The U.S. had only a small standing army, and much of it was tied down by the continuing dispute with Mexico. Its air arm was virtually nonexistent—a curious fact for the nation that had pioneered powered flight. Even the U.S. Navy was no match for either the British or German navies. Stories of German atrocities in Belgium hurt the Central Powers in U.S. public opinion, but the British blockade of Europe and subsequent seizure of neutral shipping hurt public perception of the Allies. Almost all Americans wanted the U.S. to stay out of the war.

Apr 9: In an incident at **Tampico,** Mexico, several U.S. Marines from the ship *Dolphin,* coming ashore for supplies, were arrested and detained for an hour and a half by Mexican authorities. Their release was followed by an apology from the Mexican commander at Tampico and an expression of regret by Pres. Victoriano Huerta, but the U.S. commander, Adm. Henry T. Mayo, demanded a special salute to the U.S. flag by the Mexican troops. On Apr. 11 Pres. Huerta refused the demanded salute and on Apr. 14 Pres. Wilson ordered the U.S. fleet to Tampico Bay.

Apr 16: A second **Coxey's Army** was organized at Massillon, Ohio, to march on Washington, D.C. Made up of unemployed workers, it was headed by Jacob S. Coxey, who had organized the first march in 1894.

Apr 21: At **Vera Cruz,** Mexico, U.S. forces seized the customhouse and Marines occupied the city. The detachment was sent to exact an apology from Pres. Huerta for the arrest of several U.S. Marines early this month. U.S. losses were 4 dead, 20 wounded.

Apr 22: Diplomatic relations with the U.S. were severed by Mexico.

Nov 3: In **congressional elections** the Democrats gained five Senate seats for a 56–40 majority. In the House they lost 61 seats but kept a 230–196 majority, with nine seats held by minor parties.

Nov 23: U.S. forces in **Vera Cruz,** Mexico, were withdrawn.

II. Architecture
Arts and Music
Popular Entertainment
Publishing
Theater

Most poets were content to write their poetry and see it published in magazines or books. One who was just as much interested in reciting his poetry in public as in writing it was Vachel Lindsay, who began his career by going on tours during which he exchanged his verses for food and lodging. It was not until publication this year of *The Congo and Other Poems* that he was recognized as a leading voice of the so-called new poetry movement. Lindsay's work is full of strong rhythms, sometimes pounding in their effect. He emphasized gestures and chant when he appeared in public, as he did regularly. *The Chinese Nightingale and Other Poems* (1917) probably saw his talent at its peak.

Among **books published** this year was *Tarzan of the Apes* by Edgar Rice Burroughs, an action-filled story of a man raised by apes in Africa. Burroughs' tale appealed to millions of readers and made the author famous and wealthy. Other books published this year included *North of Boston* by Robert Frost, a first collection of poems that included the classic "Mending Wall" and "The Death of the Hired Man"; *The Poet* by Meredith Nicholson, a biography in fictional form of Nicholson's fellow Hoosier writer James Whitcomb Riley; *Insurgent Mexico* by John Reed, who had been sent to cover the Mexican Revolution by *Metropolitan Magazine; Penrod* by Booth Tarkington, an enormously popular novel about the adventures of a 12-year-old midwestern youth that led to two sequels, *Penrod and Sam* (1916) and *Penrod Jashber* (1929); and *The Eyes of the World* by Harold Bell Wright, which became a best seller.

III. Business and Industry
Education
Philosophy and Religion
Science

One of the greatest construction projects of all time, and one of strategic importance to the U.S. in terms of national defense and foreign commerce, was marked by completion and official opening of the Panama Canal on Aug. 15, 1914. To build the canal, about 240,000,000 cubic yards of earth were moved and $366,650,000 spent. The first passage through the whole length of the canal was made on Jan. 7, 1914, by a small boat, *Alexander la Valley.* On Aug. 15 the *Ancon,* carrying a full load of government officials, sailed from the Atlantic to the Pacific Ocean, a distance of just over 40 miles. In its first year of operation, 1108 ships passed through the canal.

The **death rate** in the Panama Canal Zone had dropped to six per 1000 against 14.1 per 1000 in the U.S. When work on the canal began in 1904, the area was dangerous to human health. The fight against yellow fever and malaria had been won by Gen. William Gorgas, whose campaign to eradicate mosquitoes had been pushed through in spite of official opposition.

The 1914 **Nobel Prize in Chemistry** was awarded to Theodore William Richards, the first American to receive the prize in that category. Richards was honored for his work in determining the exact atomic weights of a number of elements, in some cases correcting erroneous measurements. His investigation of the atomic weights of oxygen and hydrogen led ultimately to discovery of deuterium, commonly known as heavy hydrogen, a key component in atomic research.

Apr 10: Successful **heart surgery** on an animal was announced by Dr. Alexis Carrel. He said the operation was performed while he suspended blood circulation for several minutes.

May 18: The **Panama Canal** was opened to barge service.

IV. Fashion
Folkways
Holidays
Social Issues and Crime
Sports

American society's restless favorite son, former Pres. Theodore Roosevelt, set off on an exploring expedition in Brazil in Oct. 1913; he returned in May 1914. In the jungle he explored a 400-mile-long river that had been called Rio da Duvida [River of Doubt] and which was renamed Rio Roosevelt in his honor by the Brazilian government. Roosevelt wrote a book about his journey, *Through the Brazilian Wilderness* (1914).

America's favorite **dances** were changing. The colorful and elaborate cotillion, once the most fashionable dance of society, took second place about this time to the waltz and two-step.

May 7: A resolution establishing **Mother's Day,** to be celebrated on the second Sunday in May, was passed by Congress. On May 9 Pres. Wilson issued a proclamation calling on the public to display the U.S. flag on that day as an expression "of our love and reverence for the mothers of our country."

Aug 15: In the **Davis Cup** international tennis challenge round the U.S. was defeated by Australia three matches to two.

Oct 9-13: The 11th annual **World Series** was won by the Boston Braves (NL), who swept the Philadelphia Athletics (AL) in four straight games.

1915

I. Civil Rights
Exploration and Settlement
Government
Statistics
Wars

A major step in strengthening the country's coastal maritime services, with regard to lifesaving and prevention of smuggling, was taken on Jan. 28, 1915, when Congress established the U.S. Coast Guard. It combined the Revenue Cutter Service, which had been established in 1790, with the more recent Life Saving Service. The Coast Guard was placed under the authority of the Treasury Department, except in times of war. It absorbed the Lighthouse Service in 1939 and the Bureau of Marine Inspection and Navigation in 1942.

May 7: The British steamship *Lusitania,* queen of the Cunard fleet, was sunk without warning off Ireland by a German submarine. Of 1924 persons aboard, 1198 were drowned, including 63 infants. The number of Americans drowned was 114. American indignation over the sinking contributed to the U.S. entry into World War I against Germany in 1917.

July 29: U.S. Marines landed in Haiti one day after the assassination of Haitian president Vilbrun Guillaume Sam.

Aug 5: A **Latin-American conference** to debate ways to end the political disorder in Mexico opened in Washington, D.C. It was attended by representatives from Argentina, Brazil, Bolivia, Chile, Guatemala, Uruguay, and the U.S.

Sep 16: Haiti became a U.S. protectorate under the terms of a ten-year treaty. The Senate approved the treaty on Feb. 28, 1916.

II. Architecture
Arts and Music
Popular Entertainment
Publishing
Theater

Booker T. Washington, the most important black American of the late nineteenth and early twentieth centuries, died Nov. 14, 1915. Washington was born into slavery in 1856, the son of a mulatto mother and a white father. Securing an education by his own efforts, Washington, at age 25, was selected to organize what became Tuskegee Institute, a school he turned into a leading educational institution for blacks. Washington was a controversial figure after 1895 when he made a speech in which he said blacks should not attempt to achieve social and political equality until they had secured economic equality. This pleased many whites and resulted in financial support for Tuskegee, but other black leaders denounced his approach. Washington's autobiography, *Up From Slavery* (1901), is a classic.

Among **books published** this year was *Spoon River Anthology* by Edgar Lee Masters, a Chicago lawyer who had had a number of collections published but without much success. This collection of poems, written as epitaphs for people buried in a midwestern cemetery, made Masters a national literary figure.

Other books published this year included *America's Coming-of-Age* by Van Wyck Brooks, nonfiction; *The Rivet in Grandfather's Neck* by James Branch Cabell, a novel; *The Song of the Lark,* a novel by Willa Cather; *Verse,* a posthumous collection by Adelaide Crapsey; *The Genius* by Theodore Dreiser, a novel; *Bib Ballads* by Ring Lardner, the author's first book, a minor collection of verse; *Dreams and Dust* by Don Marquis, poetry; *The Song of Hugh Glass* by John G. Neihardt, a long poem that was the first part of Neihardt's five-part *A Cycle of the West* (1949); and *The Harbor* by Ernest Poole, a proletarian novel centering on New York harbor.

Margaret Sanger was arrested on obscenity charges in connection with her book *Family Limitation,* a pioneer work on birth control. Taken to court by the New York Society for the Suppression of Vice, she was found guilty of circulating a work "contrary not only to the law of the state, but to the law of God." She was subsequently jailed.

Feb 8: *The Birth of a Nation,* D. W. Griffith's landmark motion picture, opened at Clune's Auditorium in Los Angeles, Calif. The most spectacular film made up to that time, it aroused bitter protests from liberals for its sympathetic treatment of the Ku Klux Klan during Reconstruction. Black leaders objected to its lurid racism. The film was based on the novel *The Clansman* (1905) by Thomas Dixon.

III. Business and Industry
Education
Philosophy and Religion
Science

Although Thomas A. Edison had built his first phonograph in 1877, it was not until the early years of the twentieth century that it became a practical machine. In 1903 an American company issued recordings of opera stars singing to piano accompaniment. About ten years later, orchestral recordings were attempted for the first time. The Victor Talking Machine Company brought out a phonograph in 1915 under the name Victrola; the name soon was applied to all phonographs. By 1919 Americans were spending more on phonographs and recordings than on musical instruments, books and periodicals, or sporting goods.

The **taxicab** made its appearance on the American scene when automobile owners found that many people were willing to pay for a short ride. The price was a nickel, or *jitney,* and the term soon was applied to the cars themselves. Drivers were known as *hackers* or *hackies* in the East, *cabbies* in the Midwest. Intercity bus lines sprang from regular jitney service.

Jan 25: The **first transcontinental telephone call** was made by the same men who had made the original telephone call in 1876. Alexander Graham Bell, speaking from New York City, said to Dr. Thomas A. Watson in San Francisco, "Mr. Watson, come here, I want you."

Dec 10: In a landmark for **Ford auto production,** the millionth Model T rolled off Ford's Detroit, Mich., assembly line.

IV. Fashion
Folkways
Holidays
Social Issues and Crime
Sports

On Aug. 17 Leo M. Frank, 29, was lynched for the Apr. 26, 1913, murder of Mary Phagan, 14, at the National Pencil Company Factory in Atlanta, Ga. Frank had been superintendent of the factory and was charged with the murder after the girl's body was found there. In a sensational trial, Frank was convicted, largely on testimony by Jim Conley, the factory janitor. After futile appeals by Frank's attorneys, up to the Supreme Court, Gov. John M. Slayton commuted Frank's sentence to life imprisonment. An enraged mob took him from a jail in Marietta, Ga., and hanged him. Outside the South it was widely believed that Frank, a Jew, was a victim of hatred and bigotry. In 1982 Alonzo Mann, who had worked as Frank's office boy, revealed to the newspaper *The Tennessean* that on the day of the murder he had seen Jim Conley carrying the body of Mary Phagan to the factory basement, and that Conley had threatened him to keep quiet about the matter. In 1986 Frank's conviction was overturned, more than 70 years after his death.

The quip "**What this country really needs is a good five-cent cigar**" originated with Indiana-born Thomas R. Marshall, vice president under Pres. Woodrow Wilson. During one of the tedious debates in the Senate he came out with the observation.

Ty Cobb set a major league record for bases stolen in one season, 96. The record stood until 1962 when Maury Wills stole 104 bases. In 1974 Lou Brock shattered the record again with 118 steals. During his career, Cobb set more records than any other player in the history of baseball.

A new **record for the mile run** was set in Cambridge, Mass., by Norman Taber, who completed the distance in 4:12.6, nearly two seconds under the old record.

Feb 23: An **easy divorce** bill, requiring only six months' residence, was signed into law in Nevada.

Apr 5: The **world heavyweight boxing championship** was won by Jess Willard, who defeated Jack Johnson in a 23-round bout in Havana, Cuba. It was not clear whether a blow by Willard or the blazing sun caused Johnson's descent to the canvas, described as a slow sinking.

June 18: The **U.S. Open golf tournament** was won by Jerome D. Travers.

Oct 8-13: The 12th annual **World Series** was won by the Boston Red Sox (AL), who beat the Philadelphia Phillies (NL) four games to one.

Oct 9: A new **auto speed record** of 102.6 mph was set by Gil Anderson, who won the celebrated Astor Cup at Sheepshead Bay, N.Y.

Dec 4: The **Peace Ship,** chartered by Henry Ford to carry a peace expedition to Europe, left the U.S. on a historic but futile mission. Ford's slogan "Out of the trenches and back to their homes by Christmas," became a rallying cry for the American pacifist movement. Ford's attempt to find a diplomatic end to the world conflict soon collapsed.

1916

I. Civil Rights
Exploration and Settlement
Government
Statistics
Wars

The presidential election campaign of 1916 was carried on in the shadow of World War I, then ravaging Europe and threatening to embroil the U.S. Pres. Woodrow Wilson, the Democratic candidate, made good use of the slogan "He kept us out of war," although he knew it was unlikely the country could remain neutral much longer. The Republican candidate, Charles Evans Hughes, might have won had he not snubbed Gov. Hiram Johnson of California when he visited that state. Johnson lost his enthusiasm for Hughes, and Hughes lost California.

Prohibition was voted in by Michigan, Montana, Nebraska, South Dakota, and Utah, making it law in 24 states. It now affected about 32,500,000 citizens.

Mar 9: The Mexican revolutionary and bandit **Francisco "Pancho" Villa** led a band of 1500 guerrillas across the border and attacked Columbus, N. Mex., killing 17 Americans. U.S. troops pursued the Mexicans, killing 50 on U.S. soil and 70 more in Mexico.

Brig. Gen. John J. Pershing was ordered to Mexico to capture Villa.

June 3: The **National Defense Act** was passed. It increased the standing Army to 175,000 and the National Guard to 450,000.

June 7-10: The **Republican National Convention nominated Charles Evans Hughes** of New York for the presidency and Charles Warren Fairbanks of Indiana for the vice presidency.

June 14-16: The **Democratic National Convention renominated Pres. Wilson** for the presidency and Vice Pres. Thomas R. Marshall for the vice presidency.

June 17: U.S. forces crossed into Mexico and an ultimatum was issued by the Mexican consul at Brownsville, Tex. It asserted that U.S. forces would be attacked unless withdrawn.

June 20: A note to Mexico by Sec. of State Robert Lansing asserted that troops would not be withdrawn from Mexico until order was restored on the border.

June 21: U.S. troops were attacked at Carrizal, Mexico. The Americans lost 17 killed or wounded; 38 Mexicans were killed, including the Mexican commander.

July 22: A **bombing in San Francisco** during a Preparedness Day parade killed 10 persons and wounded 40. In 1917 labor leader Tom Mooney was sentenced to hang and Warren K. Billings was sentenced to life imprisonment for the deed. Pres. Wilson commuted Mooney's sentence to life imprisonment in 1918, but because of confessions of perjured testimony at the trial the case was an international cause célèbre for many years. On Jan. 7, 1939, Mooney was pardoned by Gov. Culbert L. Olson of California. Billings was released later in the year.

Aug 4: A treaty for the purchase of the **Danish West Indies** (Virgin Islands) for $25,000,000 was signed by the U.S. and Denmark. It was ratified on Jan. 17, 1917.

Nov 7: Woodrow Wilson was reelected president of the United States. Thomas R. Marshall was reelected vice president. The election was so close that the outcome was uncertain for three days, when it became clear that Wilson had carried California, but by fewer than 4000 votes. The electoral vote was Wilson, 277; Charles Evans Hughes, Republican candidate, 254. The popular vote was Wilson, 9,128,837; Hughes, 8,536,380. In congressional elections the Democrats lost three seats in the Senate but maintained a 53–42 majority, with one seat going to a minor party. In the House the Democrats again narrowed their majority over the Republicans, 216–210, with six seats held by minor parties.

II. Architecture
Arts and Music
Popular Entertainment
Publishing
Theater

The nation's growing interest in the ballet was indicated by both the number of visiting foreign dancers and the development of American dance groups. Anna Pavlova, the Russian ballerina, had made her American debut in 1910. In 1916 Serge Diaghilev brought the Ballet Russe from Paris to New York City's Metropolitan Opera House for a January-to-May season. The noted Russian dancer Vaslav Nijinsky made his debut in New York on Apr. 12. Among American dancers, Ruth St. Denis and Ted Shawn were becoming well known.

Among **books published** this year was *Chicago Poems* by Carl Sandburg, a volume that heralded the arrival of a major new poetic voice and reflected the rise of the American Midwest as a force in American literature. Sandburg's book included the poems "Chicago" and "I Am the People, the Mob." Other books published this year included *The Certain Hour* by James Branch Cabell, short stories; *The Rising Tide* by Margaret Deland, a novel dealing with women's suffrage; *Life and Gabriella* by Ellen Glasgow, a novel; *A Heap o' Livin'* by Edgar Guest, verse; *The Man Against the Sky* by Edwin Arlington Robinson, poetry; *Seventeen* by Booth Tarkington, a novel; *The Mysterious Stranger*, a posthumous tale by Mark Twain; *Xingu and Other Stories* by Edith Wharton; and *When a Man's a Man* by Harold Bell Wright, a novel.

III. Business and Industry
Education
Philosophy and Religion
Science

The automobile was seen everywhere, and the automobile industry was soon to become the largest single manufacturing section of the economy. In 1916 auto and truck production passed the 1,000,000 mark for the first time; the value of this production was nearly $1,000,000,000. The average price of a new car was just over $600, but Henry Ford's Model T, of which 577,036 were produced this year, was selling for only $360, down from the $850 price of just eight years earlier. It was estimated that there were about 3,500,000 cars on the nation's roads.

The theory of **progressive education** was formulated by John Dewey in his *Democracy and Education*. According to Dewey, intelligence should be seen as an instrument for changing one's environment and should be trained accordingly. He held that subject matter should be adjusted to the child, not child to the subject matter, and that there should be no distinction between cultural and vocational training.

The **submachine gun** was invented by Brig. Gen. John Taliaferro Thompson. The weapon came to be known as the Tommy gun.

Jan 24: The **federal income tax** was ruled constitutional by the U.S. Supreme Court in the case of *Brushaber v. Union Pacific Railroad Co.*

Jan 28: Louis D. Brandeis was appointed to the Supreme Court by Pres. Woodrow Wilson. The appointment was confirmed on June 1. Brandeis was the first Jew to become a justice of the Supreme Court.

Aug 25: The **National Park Service** was established as part of the Interior Department.

Sep 3: The **Adamson Eight-Hour Act** was signed by Pres. Wilson. The act made an eight-hour day standard for most railroad workers. The bill had been hurriedly passed by both houses of Congress to stave off a nationwide railroad strike called for Sept. 4. The strike was averted, but the president was severely critized and accused of wooing labor during an election year.

Oct 16: The **first birth control clinic** was opened by Margaret Sanger, Fania Mindell, and Ethel Burne at 46 Amboy St., Brooklyn, N.Y.

IV. Fashion
Folkways
Holidays
Social Issues and Crime
Sports

Among the baseball heroes of the early twentieth century was Grover Cleveland Alexander, a right-handed pitcher who between 1911 and 1930 played for the Philadelphia Phillies (NL), Chicago Cubs (NL), and St. Louis Cardinals (NL). In the 1916 season he set an unsurpassed record by pitching 15 shutouts for the Phillies. In all, Alexander recorded 90 shutouts during his career. He is exceeded in this respect only by Walter Johnson, who had 113 shutouts during his years with the Washington Senators (AL), from 1907 to 1927. Johnson also compiled a record 3503 strikeouts in his 27-year career.

Jan 1: In the second **Tournament of Roses Association football game** (the first had been played in 1902), and the first annual game, Washington State defeated Brown 14–0. This game marked the beginning of the annual football contest that in 1923 came to be called the Rose Bowl game.

June 15: Boy Scouts of America was incorporated by a bill signed by Pres. Woodrow Wilson.

June 30: The **U.S. Open golf tournament** was won by Charles Evans, Jr. The competition was suspended until 1919 because of U.S. entry into World War I in 1917.

Sep 30: The **longest baseball winning streak** on record was stopped at 26 games when the New York Giants (NL) were beaten 8–3 by the Boston Braves in the second game of a double header.

Oct 7-12: The 13th annual **World Series** was won by the Boston Red Sox (AL), defeating the Brooklyn Dodgers (NL) four games to one.

1917

I. Civil Rights
Exploration and Settlement
Government
Statistics
Wars

Pres. Woodrow Wilson had tried hard to keep the U.S. out of World War I, although his sympathies were with the Allied cause. Through the course of the war public opinion had shifted to the Allies' favor, but many still hoped to avoid U.S. involvement. By early 1917, however, it was clear that the U.S. would be unable to stay on the sidelines much longer. Wilson called a special session of Congress and on Apr. 2 delivered his war message. The Senate voted for war, 82–6, on Apr. 4 and the House followed on Apr. 6, 373–50. Wilson signed the war resolution the same day.

Jan 31: A note announcing the German renewal of **submarine warfare** against neutral and belligerent ships, effective Feb. 1, was delivered to the State Department by Count Johann-Heinrich von Bernstorff, the German ambassador.

Feb 3: Diplomatic relations with Germany were severed. On the same day the U.S. liner *Housatonic* was sunk by a German submarine after a one-hour warning.

Feb 24: The **Zimmermann note,** a coded message from German foreign minister Alfred Zimmermann to the German ambassador to Mexico, was given to Walter Hines Page, U.S. ambassador to Great Britain, by the British, who had decoded it. The note suggested that in the event of U.S. entry into the war against Germany, Germany would propose an alliance with Mexico. The contents of the note were made public on Mar. 1.

Mar 2: The **Jones Act** was passed, making Puerto Rico a U.S. territory and its inhabitants U.S. citizens.

Apr 2: The **first woman in the House of Representatives,** Rep. Jeannette Rankin, Republican of Montana, was seated.

Apr 24: The **Liberty Loan Act,** a war finance measure, authorized Sec. of the Treasury William G. McAdoo to issue for public subscription $2,000,000,000 worth of $3\frac{1}{2}$% convertible gold bonds.

May 18: The **Selective Service Act** was passed, authorizing federal conscription for the armed forces. The act required registration of all males from 21 to 30 years of age.

June 26: The **first U.S. troops in Europe** arrived at St.-Nazaire, France, under command of Maj. Gen. William L. Sibert.

Nov 3: The **first engagement** involving U.S. forces in Europe occurred near the Rhine-Marne Canal in France. German forces attacked American infantrymen training in front-line trenches. American losses: three dead, five wounded, twelve captured or missing.

Nov 6: Women's suffrage was made law in New York State by constitutional amendment.

Dec 18: The **Eighteenth Amendment** to the U.S. Constitution, outlawing manufacture, sale, or transportation of alcoholic liquors, was passed by Congress and submitted to the states for ratification. It was ratified on Jan. 29, 1919.

II. Architecture
Arts and Music
Popular Entertainment
Publishing
Theater

Middle West farm life in the last half of the nineteenth century was a subject that interested authors and readers. Hamlin Garland, who knew farm labor first-hand, had for a number of years been producing realistic books on the subject. In 1917 his autobiography, *A Son of the Middle Border,* was published. In *Main-Travelled Roads* (1891) he fictionalized the hardships of farm life. Garland's influence on the development of realism helped prepare the way for a new wave of writers.

Among **books published** this year was *The Cream of the Jest* by James Branch Cabell, a novel about a jaded writer who escapes to a dream world called

Storisende, has a number of adventures, and returns to the real world happier for the experience. Other books published this year included *The Innocents* and *The Job: An American Novel* by Sinclair Lewis, both novels; *Jerry of the Islands*, a posthumous novel by Jack London, who died in 1916; *Tendencies in Modern American Poetry* by Amy Lowell; *Parnassus on Wheels* by Christopher Morley, a novel; *Susan Lenox: Her Fall and Rise*, a posthumous novel by David Graham Phillips, considered his best work; *Merlin* by Edwin Arlington Robinson, the first volume of a poetic trilogy dealing with the Arthurian legends that concluded with *Lancelot* (1920) and *Tristram* (1927); and *King Coal* by Upton Sinclair, a novel about coal mining in Colorado.

June 4: The **first Pulitzer prizes** were awarded in the following categories: biography, *Julia Ward Howe* by Laura E. Richards and Maude H. Elliott assisted by Florence H. Hall; history, *With Americans of Past and Present Days* by Jean Jules Jusserand, the French ambassador to the U.S. The prizes also included awards in journalism.

III. Business and Industry
Education
Philosophy and Religion
Science

On Oct. 13 in New York City Mayor John P. Mitchell dedicated the Catskill Aqueduct at ceremonies in Central Park. The aqueduct, a remarkable work of engineering and construction, pointed up the need of cities for reliable sources of water. It had been under construction for 12 years and had cost $177,000,000. It was 92 miles long and at Storm King Mt. it passed under the Hudson R. at a depth of 1114 feet. Much of the aqueduct had to be cut through solid rock.

There were 4,842,139 **motor vehicles** registered in the U.S., 435,000 of them trucks. In all the other nations of the world it was estimated there were only 719,246 motor vehicles. This year alone, 1,795,840 passenger cars and 181,348 commercial vehicles were made in the U.S., and there were 25,500 garages and 13,500 repair shops to service them. The average price of a new car was $720.

Mar 19: An **eight-hour day** for railroad workers was accepted by railroad managers in cooperation with the defense program, thus removing the threat of a railroad tie-up. Labor also gained by keeping the same pay scale.

Sep 5: Federal **raids on IWW headquarters** in 24 cities were prompted by the labor organization's antiwar activities. Federal agents seized documents and books and made ten arrests, including William D. "Big Bill" Haywood, a leader of the organization.

IV. Fashion
Folkways
Holidays
Social Issues and Crime
Sports

Most professional baseball players of the era learned the game on sandlots or in school, but few played the game at college before entering the ranks of the pros. One of the game's top players during this period was Edward T. "Eddie" Collins, a Columbia College graduate of 1907. Beginning in 1906, Collins played for 25 years in the American League with the Philadelphia Athletics and the Chicago White Sox, becoming one of the best second basemen the game has known. His lifetime total of 3311 hits placed him eighth on the all-time list. Collins was four times the American League's base-stealing champion, in 1917 stealing 51 bases. In 1910 he stole 81 bases, his career high.

Apr 2: The memorable sentence "**The world must be made safe for democracy**" appeared in a speech by Pres. Woodrow Wilson before Congress, requesting a declaration of war against Germany.

May 2: The **first double no-hit nine-inning baseball game** in the major leagues was played in Chicago. Jim Vaughn of the Chicago Cubs (NL) and Fred Toney of Cincinnati both pitched the full game without allowing a hit. The Reds scored in the tenth inning to win 1–0.

June 23: A **perfect baseball game,** no hits and no walks, was pitched by Ernie Shore of the Boston Red Sox (AL) in a 4–0 win over the Washington Senators.

Oct 6-15: The 14th annual **World Series** was won by the Chicago White Sox (AL), who defeated the New York Giants (NL) four games to two.

1918

I. Civil Rights
Exploration and Settlement
Government
Statistics
Wars

World War I ended on the 11th hour of the 11th day of November this year. At the designated moment, the entire western front opened up with gunfire as war-worn troops sought to fire the last shot. Then silence fell. In the U.S. and elsewhere enormous crowds poured into the streets for a noisy celebration. In New York City 150 tons of paper and ticker tape had to be cleaned off the streets after the festivities. Although the U.S. did not enter the war until nearly three years after the conflict began, the country had mobilized 4,743,829 men and women. Of these, 2,084,000 reached France. U.S. intervention was the deciding factor after years of heavy casualties brought England, France, and Germany to virtual exhaustion. U.S. casualties were 53,513 battle deaths; 63,195 other deaths, mostly from disease; 204,002 wounded. The cost was $21,850,000,000, not counting loans to allies.

Jan 8: Pres. Woodrow Wilson listed his **14 points** for a just and lasting peace in an address to Congress stating the "war aims and peace terms of the United States." It was translated and distributed to German soldiers and civilians throughout middle Europe by the Office of Public Information.

Apr 14: The **first American air ace** was Lt. Douglas Campbell, who shot down his fifth German aircraft.

May 16: The **Sedition Act** was passed. It provided heavy penalties for those who hindered the war effort by making false statements, obstructing enlistment, or speaking against production of war materials, the American form of government, the Constitution, the flag, etc. It was signed by Pres. Wilson on May 21.

June 4: At **Château-Thierry,** the U.S. Second Division halted German forces advancing toward Paris.

June 6-25: In the Battle of **Belleau Wood,** in France, the U.S. Second Division and Fourth Marine Brigade halted the Germans and recaptured the area after bitter fighting. American deaths: 285 officers and 7585 enlisted men.

July 15: In the Second Battle of the **Marne,** German forces attacked east and west of Reims but made no substantial gains. Some 85,000 U.S. troops fought in the battle.

July 18-Aug 6: The **Aisne-Marne offensive** was launched by more than 250,000 Americans in conjunction with French units to counter the German attack of July 15. The offensive forced the Germans out of the Soissons-Reims salient and gave the Allies the initiative.

Aug 8: At **Amiens** Allied forces began a prolonged offensive against the German salient at the Somme R.

Sep 12-13: At **St. Mihiel,** U.S. forces cut off and reduced the German salient, taking about 15,000 prisoners.

Sep 26-Nov 11: The Battle of the **Meuse-Argonne,** involving 1,200,000 U.S. troops, had as its objective the cutting of the German supply line, the Sedan-Mézières railroad. American forces cut the railway in early November. The armistice of Nov. 11 brought the American advance to a halt.

Nov 3: An **armistice with Austria-Hungary,** effective Nov. 4, was signed.

Nov 5: In **congressional elections** the Republicans gained control of both houses, taking a 49–47 lead in the Senate, and a House majority of 240–190, with three seats going to minor parties.

Nov 9: Kaiser Wilhelm II of Germany abdicated. Two days later the armistice went into effect and the war was ended.

Nov 21: The **Wartime Prohibition Act,** effective from June 30, 1919, until demobilization, was signed by Pres. Wilson. It banned manufacture or sale of liquor except for export.

II. Architecture
Arts and Music
Popular Entertainment
Publishing
Theater

Despite the many new plays being written and produced every year, interest in the works of great playwrights remained high. In fact, a number of actors and actresses spent all or most of their careers acting Shakespearean roles. A leading actor was Walter Hampden, an American who acted in England before making his New York City debut in 1907. In Shakespeare's plays he acted the roles of Caliban, Oberon, Romeo, Macbeth, Othello, Shylock, and Hamlet. His appearance as Hamlet in 1918 was hailed as the best American interpretation of the role since Edwin Booth. In 1925 Hampden took over the Colonial Theater in New York and renamed it for himself.

Among **books published** this year was *The Education of Henry Adams,* a posthumous volume, privately printed in 1907 that Adams had written to complement his *Mont-Saint-Michel and Chartres* (1913). The work decried the multiplicity of modern society, symbolized by the electric dynamo, and the failure of modern education to prepare Adams for a happy and useful life. Other books published this year included *My Antonia* by Willa Cather, a masterly novel of prairie life; *Cornhuskers* by Carl Sandburg, a collection of poetry; and *The Magnificent Ambersons* by Booth Tarkington, a study of three generations of a family in Indianapolis from 1873 to 1916, years in which Indianapolis grew from a town to a city.

Aug 26: *Lightnin'* by Winchell Smith and Frank Bacon opened on Broadway at The Gaiety Theatre. It was destined to have one of the longest runs, 1291 performances, in U.S. stage history.

III. Business and Industry
Education
Philosophy and Religion
Science

The U.S. war effort required mobilization and control of the nation's economic life. The War Industries Board, established on July 28, 1917, was reorganized on Mar. 4, 1918, with Bernard Baruch, a financier, as its head. Food and fuel were rationed, taxes were increased, and millions of dollars worth of Liberty bonds were sold. The railroads were taken over by the government by a presidential proclamation on Dec. 26, 1917, an arrangement formalized by the Railroad Control Act of Mar. 21, 1918. Industries such as steel had already been stimulated by the war because of large purchases by the Allies. Between 1914 and 1917 the production of steel ingots and castings nearly doubled. During the 19 months the U.S. was at war, 875 seagoing vessels were built.

A **compulsory school attendance law** was passed in Mississippi, the last state to do so.

In 1918 there were 1,000,000 more **women employed** than in 1915. On Sept. 30 Pres. Woodrow Wilson told the Senate that women's suffrage was a "vitally necessary war measure." But the Senate lacked the strength to pass any legislation on the matter.

May 13: The **first airmail stamps** were issued by the Post Office Department, in denominations of 6 cents, 16 cents, and 24 cents.

May 15: The **first airmail service** was inaugurated with regular flights between New York City and Washington, D.C.

July 26: The **sugar ration** was reduced to two pounds a person a month by edict of the U.S. Food Board.

Oct: A devastating **influenza epidemic** reached its height. The disease had first appeared in early September in Boston, New York, and Philadelphia. By mid-October the death rate in these cities had risen over 700%. Doctors were baffled. The epidemic spread to 46 states and ultimately killed between 400,000 and 500,000 persons, far more than the number of Americans killed in the war. Many war plants shut down, telephone service was cut in half, and the draft was suspended in several cities. Panic spread rapidly. Newspapers were filled with outlandish theories of the epidemic's cause and long lists of the

dead. The epidemic disappeared in 1919, but it left many afflicted with Bright's disease, cardiac diseases and tuberculosis.

IV. Fashion
Folkways
Holidays
Social Issues and Crime
Sports

The war prompted an innovation in time-keeping this year. On Mar. 31 Pres. Woodrow Wilson signed a law providing for Daylight Savings Time, by which clocks were to be set ahead one hour so that more daylight was available. Daylight savings was disliked by some, especially farmers, and the law was repealed in 1919. It was not reestablished nationwide until World War II.

Sep 5-11: The 15th annual **World Series** was won by the Boston Red Sox (AL), who beat the Chicago Cubs (NL) four games to two. Each player on the winning team received $1102.51, the all-time low payment to World Series winners.

1919

I. Civil Rights
Exploration and Settlement
Government
Statistics
Wars

With the war won, the Allies prepared to make the peace official. At the peace conference convened at Versailles, France, the American delegation was headed by Pres. Woodrow Wilson. His idealism contrasted with the attitudes of England and France, who wanted to punish Germany. When the Treaty of Versailles was signed on June 28, the war was officially ended. Germany was forced to admit guilt for the war and was stripped of Alsace-Lorraine, the Saar Basin, and its overseas colonies. Germany was also to pay reparations, later fixed at $56,000,000,000, and was required to disarm. Wilson got his wish to establish a League of Nations.

Jan 18: The **peace conference** opened in Paris. For Pres. Woodrow Wilson it was the beginning of a fight to preserve the principles of the 14 points on which he believed a lasting peace should be established. He failed to have many of his most important points included because of the demands of other victorious Allies.

Jan 29: The **Eighteenth Amendment** to the Constitution, prohibiting transportation and sale of alcoholic beverages, was ratified. It was the first amendment to have a time limit on ratification, seven years, and the only one that was subsequently repealed.

Feb 14: The draft of the **League of Nations covenant** was presented by Pres. Wilson to the Paris Peace Conference. Wilson embarked from Brest on Feb. 15 for the U.S. Later he returned to Europe, remaining at the peace conference until it ended on June 28 and returning to New York City on July 8.

July 10: The **Treaty of Versailles** and League of Nations covenant were sent by Pres. Wilson to the Senate for ratification. Wilson declared that acceptance of the treaty would ensure future peace.

Aug 31: The **Communist Labor Party** of America was founded at Chicago, Ill. The party adopted the platform of the Third International, including a badge featuring the hammer and sickle encircled by strands of wheat. The party motto was "Workers of the world unite!"

Sep 26: Pres. **Wilson suffered a stroke** while traveling to Wichita, Kans. His national tour was halted and he was taken back to Washington, D.C.

Oct 28: The **Volstead Act,** or National Prohibition Act, was passed by Congress over Pres. Wilson's veto of the previous day. The act defined as intoxicating liquor any beverage containing at least one-half of 1% alcohol and provided for enforcement of the provisions of the Eighteenth Amendment.

Nov 19: The **Treaty of Versailles** failed to achieve ratification in the Senate by a vote of 55–39.

II. Architecture
Arts and Music
Popular Entertainment
Publishing
Theater

A younger generation of composers was now presenting works that differed from the romantic style. Among them was Charles T. Griffes, whose *The White Peacock* (1915–1916), originally a piano piece, was presented in 1919 in a version orchestrated for ballet at the Rivoli Theater in New York City. It was received with considerable enthusiasm. Griffes composed a major work for orchestra, *The Pleasure Dome of Kubla Khan*, in 1920. That year he died at the age of 35.

Among **books published** this year was *Jurgen, A Comedy of Justice* by James Branch Cabell, an excursion through the world of fantasy, allegory, and escape. A reworking of the story of Faust set in the mythical kingdom of Poictesme, the novel was suppressed because of the erotic adventures of its protagonist. The book became extremely popular and made Cabell's reputation. Other books published this year included *Winesburg, Ohio* by Sherwood Anderson, a series of connected stories hailed by critics and readers, and Anderson's most successful book; *Java Head* by Joseph Hergesheimer, a novel of East and West, and *Linda Condon*, also by Hergesheimer and also a novel; *On the Makaloa Mat* by Jack London, a posthumous collection of stories; *The American Language* by H. L. Mencken, the author's major scholarly work, which he subsequently augmented; and *Ten Days That Shook the World* by John Reed, a firsthand account of the Russian Revolution, later issued with an introduction by Lenin.

June 2: Pulitzer prizes were awarded for the following: fiction, *The Magnificent Ambersons* by Booth Tarkington; biography, *The Education of Henry Adams* by Henry Adams; poetry, *Old Road to Paradise* by Margaret Widdemer and *Cornhuskers* by Carl Sandburg.

III. Business and Industry
Education
Philosophy and Religion
Science

Charismatic religious leaders continued to attract followers in large numbers. The latest was Father Divine (George Baker), a black evangelist whose nonsectarian and interracial movement got its start in Harlem, in New York City, during this period. In 1919 his establishment at Sayville, L.I., attracted attention. Divine set up "heavens" for his "angels," mostly women, where he preached fundamentalist religion and stressed the value of economic and social equality and cooperation. Many of his followers believed he was God. During the years of the Great Depression, Father Divine's heavens provided food and shelter for many people.

Sep 9: A police strike in Boston began when the policemen's union called its members off the job. Some 1117 out of 1544 patrolmen walked off their jobs. Many merchants locked up their shops, but looting occurred on a wide scale. New police were hired and the strike was put down. Gov. Calvin Coolidge told AFL president Samuel Gompers: "There is no right to strike against the public safety by anybody, anywhere, any time," a sentence that became well known.

IV. Fashion
   Folkways
   Holidays
   Social Issues and Crime
   Sports

Jack Dempsey, new and popular king of boxing, who was to set records in coming years, won the world heavyweight boxing championship on July 4. He scored a technical knockout against the defending champion, Jess Willard, after the third round of a bout at Toledo, Ohio. Dempsey fought four championship bouts and one non-title fight as champion, each of which grossed over $1,000,000, an enormous sum in those days. Dempsey was known as the Manassa Mauler (he was born in Manassa, Colo.) and earned more money than any previous boxer in history. In his fights he was ever on the attack, punching savagely. The crowds loved him for it.

May 10: The 45th annual **Kentucky Derby** was won by Sir Barton, ridden by Johnny Loftus, with a time of 2·09⁴/₅. Sir Barton, ridden by Loftus, went on to win the Preakness and Belmont Stakes, thereby becoming the first horse to win racing's Triple Crown.

May 14: The 44th annual **Preakness Stakes** was won by Sir Barton, with a time of 1:53. The jockey was Johnny Loftus.

June 11: The **U.S. Open golf tournament** was won by Walter Hagen.

June 11: The 51st annual **Belmont Stakes** was won by Sir Barton, with a time of 2:17²/₅. The jockey was Johnny Loftus.

Sep 20: The **PGA golf tournament** was won by Jim Barnes.

Oct 1-9: The 16th annual **World Series** was won by the Cincinnati Reds (NL), who defeated the Chicago White Sox (AL) five games to three in a best-of-nine series, which the major leagues adopted from 1919 through 1921.

1920

I. Civil Rights
   Exploration and Settlement
   Government
   Statistics
   Wars

The presidential election of 1920 was in part a referendum on whether the U.S. should join the League of Nations. The Democratic nominee, James M. Cox, pledged to do his best to take America into the league. The Republican platform straddled the issue; candidate Warren G. Harding did not seem to feel strongly either way. Harding's election was an indicator that the American people wanted to forget the war. They rejected Woodrow Wilson's idealism and returned to everyday pursuits. This was the first presidential election in which women could vote, and they apparently voted the same way as the men—overwhelmingly Republican.

The U.S. **Census** recorded a population of 105,710,620. The center of population was placed at eight miles south-southeast of Spencer, Owen County, Ind. For the first time a decline was recorded in rural population to less than 50% of the total. The number of farm residents had dwindled to less than 30%.

Apr 15: In what came to be called the **Sacco and Vanzetti** case, Frank Parmenter and Alexander Berardelli, paymaster and guard for a shoe factory in South Braintree, Mass., were shot and killed. The payroll they were carrying was seized by the murderers. Three weeks later Nicola Sacco and Bartolomeo Vanzetti, workmen of Brockton, Mass., were arrested and charged with the crime.

May 8-14: The **Socialist Party National Convention nominated Eugene V. Debs** of Indiana for the presidency, for the fifth time, and Seymour Stedman of Ohio for the vice presidency. Debs was serving a ten-year prison sentence.

June 8-12: The **Republican National Convention nominated Warren G. Harding** of Ohio for the presidency and Gov. Calvin Coolidge of Massachusetts for the vice presidency. The nomination was decided on the tenth ballot.

June 28-July 5: The **Democratic National Convention nominated Gov. James M. Cox** of Ohio for the presidency and Franklin D. Roosevelt of New York for the vice presidency. Other chief candidates for the hotly contested presidential nomination had been A. Mitchell Palmer, attorney general in Pres. Woodrow Wilson's Cabinet, and former Sec. of the Treasury William G. McAdoo.

July 13-16: The **Farmer Labor Party National Convention** nominated Parley P. Christensen of Utah for the presidency and Max S. Hayes of Ohio for the vice presidency.

Nov 2: Warren G. Harding was elected president of the United States. Calvin Coolidge was elected vice president. The electoral vote was Harding, 404; James M. Cox, Democratic candidate, 127. The popular vote was Harding, 16,152,200; Cox, 9,147,353; Eugene V. Debs, Socialist candidate, 919,799; Aaron S. Watkins, Prohibition candidate, 189,408; W. W. Cox, Socialist Labor candidate, 31,175; Parley P. Christensen, Farmer Labor candidate, 26,541. The Republicans increased their majorities in both houses, leading 59–37 in the Senate and 301–131, with one minor party seat and two vacancies, in the House.

Nov 20: The **Nobel Peace Prize** was awarded to Pres. Woodrow Wilson in recognition of his efforts to promote world peace through the League of Nations.

II. Architecture
Arts and Music
Popular Entertainment
Publishing
Theater

What was to become a new industry and a new system of public entertainment and communication got its start on Nov. 2, 1920, when radio station KDKA in Pittsburgh, Pa., broadcast the results of the presidential election. There were few listeners, but for the first time radio broadcasting had become a service for the general public. By 1922 there were about 500 stations, but conditions were chaotic because all employed the same wavelength. Sec. of Commerce Herbert Hoover called a conference for Feb. 27, 1922; there, a system for allocating wavelengths was agreed on. In 1921 Americans were to spend about $10,000,000 on radio sets and parts.

Among **books published** this year was *Main Street* by Sinclair Lewis, a novel about life in a midwestern town that caused a sensation across the country and established Lewis as a leading literary figure. The novel, a bitter indictment of the drabness, hypocrisy, stupidity, and pride of the residents of Gopher Prairie, Minn., became an American classic. Other books published this year included *The Ordeal of Mark Twain* by Van Wyck Brooks, a controversial study of the great author; *This Side of Paradise* by F. Scott Fitzgerald, the author's first novel and a smashing success; *Miss Lulu Bett* by Zona Gale, a novel of rural life in the Middle West; *A Few Figs from Thistles,* a collection of poetry by Edna St. Vincent Millay; *The Great Impersonation* by E. Phillips Oppenheim, an adventure story that sold more than 1,000,000 copies; *Smoke and Steel* by Carl Sandburg, poetry; and *The Age of Innocence* by Edith Wharton, a novel of New York City society in the 1870s.

June 2: **Pulitzer prizes** were awarded for the following: biography, *The Life of John Marshall* by Albert J. Beveridge; history, *The War with Mexico* by Justin H. Smith; drama, *Beyond the Horizon* by Eugene O'Neill.

III. Business and Industry
Education
Philosophy and Religion
Science

A new era in transportation and communication was opened this year when the first New York to California mail plane left New York City on Sept. 7, arriving in San Francisco on Sept. 11. At first airmail service was difficult and risky. The planes were barely more than canvas and wood held together with wire, and instrumentation was virtually nonexistent. A plane's range was small, which meant the pilots had to hop from field to field to get across the country. Flying in bad weather was extremely dangerous. Nonetheless, many pilots who had learned to fly during World War I found the air service to their liking. Aircraft technology grew steadily through the 1920s and 1930s, and airmail service, like air transportation itself, became a fact of life.

Illiteracy in the U.S. reached a new low of 6% of the population, a decline of 1.7% from 1910 and a decline of 14% from 1870.

The average **life expectancy** in the U.S., as determined by the Bureau of Public Health, was 54.09 years; in 1901 it had been 49.24 years.

The **first measurement of a star** was accomplished by Albert A. Michelson, who calculated a stellar diameter with the aid of the interferometer he had invented in 1880. He demonstrated that the diameter of Alpha Orionis was 260,000,000 miles.

The **automobile** had become part of American life. By 1923 about 15,000,000 cars were registered. One out of every four families in the U.S. bought or sold an automobile each year. There were 1,000,000 fewer cars than telephones and only 7,000,000 fewer cars than dwelling places.

IV. Fashion
Folkways
Holidays
Social Issues and Crime
Sports

Whatever might happen in other sports, finance, or politics, American fans found it hard to believe scandal could ever touch baseball. Yet on Sept. 28, 1920, eight members of the Chicago White Sox (AL) were indicted on charges of having taken bribes to throw the World Series with the Cincinnati Reds the previous fall. Sportswriters soon referred to the team as the Black Sox, a name that stuck. On Aug. 2, 1921, after a few hours of deliberation, a jury acquitted the players. While spectators cheered, the jurors carried the players around on their shoulders. There was considerable doubt as to the justice of the verdict, and the players were banned from organized baseball.

The term *smoke-filled room* came into use to describe machine politics after the Republican National Convention in June. When the convention became hopelessly deadlocked over a presidential candidate, Ohio politican Harry M. Daugherty told the press: "The convention will be dead-locked, and after the other candidates have gone their limit, some twelve or fifteen men, worn out and bleary-eyed for lack of sleep, will sit down about two o'clock in the morning around a table in a smoke-filled room in some hotel and decide the nomination. When that time comes, Harding will be selected."

Apr 20-Sep 12: At the **Olympic Games** in Antwerp, Belgium, the U.S. won the unofficial team championship, winning nine gold medals. Finland was the second-place team.

July 3: At the **Wimbledon** tennis championships in England, William T. Tilden won the men's singles title.

July 9-16: The **Davis Cup** international tennis challenge round was won, for the first time since 1913, by the U.S., which swept Australia in five straight matches.

Aug 13: The **U.S. Open golf tournament** was won by Ted Ray of England.

Aug 21: The **PGA golf tournament** was won by J. Fowler Hutchison.

Oct 5-12: The 17th annual **World Series** was won by the Cleveland Indians (AL), who beat the Brooklyn Dodgers (NL) five games to two.

1921

limiting future construction. The conferees agreed on a 5-5-3 ratio for capital ships for the U.S., Great Britain, and Japan. In all, nine treaties were signed on Feb. 6, 1922, including one that restricted use of submarines in warfare and outlawed poison gas, and another in which the U.S., Great Britain, France, and Japan agreed to respect each other's rights over Pacific possessions. Eventually the work of this conference was destroyed by the events leading to World War II, but it did slow down the international arms race for a time.

Jan 13: A **report on urbanization** by the Census Bureau showed that 51% of Americans lived in cities and towns of more than 2500.

May 19: The **first generally restrictive immigration act** in the U.S. was signed by Pres. Harding. The act, effective June 3, initiated a quota system that restricted immigration in any given year to 3% of the number of each nationality reported in the Census of 1910. The total number of immigrants allowed to enter in any given year was set at 357,000.

June 10: The **Bureau of the Budget** and the office of Comptroller General of the U.S. were established by Congress as part of the Treasury Department. The first comptroller general was John Raymond McCarl, who took office on July 1.

July 2: The **state of war** between the U.S. and Germany was declared at an end by a joint resolution of Congress. The resolution also claimed all rights, reparations, or indemnities awarded to the U.S. under the Treaty of Versailles.

Aug: A reemergence in the South of the **Ku Klux Klan** was marked by lawlessness. Whippings, brandings, tarrings, and destruction of property were directed against blacks and whites, although no direct motive could be found for some of the violence.

Aug 25: A **peace treaty with Germany** was signed in Berlin. It stipulated that none of the provisions of the joint resolution of Congress of July 2, 1921, or of the Versailles Treaty would be vitiated by this treaty.

I. Civil Rights
Exploration and Settlement
Government
Statistics
Wars

The 1920s witnessed several attempts to reduce armaments and lessen the danger of another war. The U.S. invited the major naval powers to the Washington Conference for Limitation of Armament, which opened in Washington, D.C., on Nov. 12, 1921. The U.S. proposed scrapping warships already built and

II. Architecture
Arts and Music
Popular Entertainment
Publishing
Theater

The 1920s saw the rise to national prominence of one of the great American humorists and political commentators, William Penn Adair "Will" Rogers, an authentic cowboy, with Indian ancestry, from Oklahoma. Rogers got his start on the stage as a rope twirler. Soon he was commenting wryly on public events. His perceptive remarks took him to fame in the movies and on the stage, especially in the *Ziegfeld Follies,* in which he first appeared in 1915. His newspaper column was syndicated nationally. The growth of radio as an entertainment medium in the late 1920s and early 1930s brought him an immense audience. Typical of his remarks were such gems as, "The U.S. has never lost a war or won a conference," "Everything is funny as long as it happens to somebody else," and "I tell you folks, all politics is applesauce."

Among **books published** this year, the runaway best seller was *The Sheik* by Edith W. Hull, the adventures of a beautiful girl carried off into the desert by an Arab chief. The novel inspired a motion picture of the same name, starring Rudolph Valentino, and a host of imitative books, including the parody *The Shriek* by Charles Somerville. Other books published this year included *The Brimming Cup* by Dorothy Canfield, a novel; *Three Soldiers* by John Dos Passos, a novel dealing with the aftermath of World War I; *A Daughter of the Middle Border* by Hamlin Garland, autobiography; *The Old Soak* by Don Marquis, the journalist and poet; *Collected Poems* by Edwin Arlington Robinson; *Alice Adams* by Booth Tarkington, a novel; and *Nets to Catch the Wind* by Elinor Wylie, poetry.

This year's **popular songs** included "Blue Moon," "If You Would Care for Me," "Look for the Silver Lining," "Kitten on the Keys," "I Never Knew," and "Down in Chinatown."

Oct 5: The **first radio coverage of the World Series** was carried by a wireless station set up at the Electrical Show at the 71st Regiment Armory in New York City, and by station WJZ in Newark, N.J. Both stations carried play-by-play bulletins. The first actual play-by-play coverage began in 1922.

Nov 11: The **Unknown Soldier** of World War I was buried at Arlington National Cemetery after lying in state at the Capitol rotunda in Washington, D.C.

III. Business and Industry
Education
Philosophy and Religion
Science

The war period had brought boom times to American industry and American workers. With the wartime demand for all kinds of goods ended, the nation experienced a depression by the middle of 1921. Fortunately, recovery began as early as the spring of 1922.

In its initial stages, the depression brought wage reductions, such as a 22.5% pay cut imposed by the New York Central Railroad on 43,000 workers, and a 15% cut suffered by clothing workers. Sec. of Commerce Herbert Hoover called a national conference on unemployment. It opened on Sept. 21 and recommended a cut in prices instead of wages so that demand would be stimulated. It was also proposed that a program of public works be started to provide jobs.

The **death rate** in the U.S. was 1163.9 per 100,000 population. In 1900 it had been 1755.

Apr 30: Ford Motor Company assets were reported to be $345,140,557. Henry Ford announced that a temporary crisis had ended. Six months previously, Ford had had 175,000 finished surplus automobiles. Ford then closed his plants and forced the surplus on unwilling dealers. An upsurge of buying saved the day.

June 25: Samuel Gompers was chosen president of the American Federation of Labor for the 40th time. He polled more than twice as many votes (25,022) as John L. Lewis (12,324), his opponent in the election.

July 21: The possibilities of **concentrated bombing** were shown by an Army test directed by Gen. William "Billy" Mitchell in which the former German battleship *Ostfriesland* was sunk by aircraft. The test was held off Hampton Roads, Va. Many believed that the demonstration vindicated Gen. Mitchell's belief in the superiority of air power over sea power.

IV. Fashion
Folkways
Holidays
Social Issues and Crime
Sports

The Volstead Act, the national prohibition law, was a year old on Jan. 16, but prohibition had not become the law of the land. In fact it fostered the rise of crime in the U.S. and thereby greatly changed America's social fabric. By 1921 bootleggers were doing a good business, although some of the liquor they supplied was of poor quality, even dangerous. Some people made their own, called bathtub gin or homebrew, but others depended on liquor smuggled over the Canadian border. Offshore lay ships loaded with alcoholic beverages, which small speedy boats brought ashore in darkness, defying the Coast Guard. Between 1920 and 1930 some 500,000 people were arrested for violating the Volstead Act.

June 29: At the **Wimbledon** tennis championships, Elizabeth Ryan won the women's singles title. William T. Tilden won the men's title on July 2.

July 2: The **world heavyweight boxing championship** was defended by Jack Dempsey, who knocked out Georges Carpentier in the fourth round. This was the first fight with a $1,000,000 gate.

July 22: The **U.S. Open golf tournament** was won by James M. Barnes.

Aug 3: In the **Black Sox scandal,** Judge Kenesaw Mountain Landis, the baseball commissioner, ruled that the Chicago White Sox players charged with throwing the 1919 World Series would not be allowed to play again despite their acquittal in 1920.

Sep 3: The **Davis Cup** international tennis challenge round was won by the U.S., defeating the Japanese team in five straight matches.

Sep 8: The **first Miss America** title was won by Margaret Gorman of Washington, D.C., at the end of a two-day pageant and festival at Atlantic City, N.J.

Sep 28: The **PGA golf tournament** was won by Gene Sarazen.

Oct 5-13: The 18th annual **World Series** was won by the New York Giants (NL), who beat the New York Yankees (AL) five games to three.

Nov 5: Armistice Day, Nov. 11, was proclaimed a legal holiday by Pres. Warren G. Harding.

1922

I. Civil Rights
Exploration and Settlement
Government
Statistics
Wars

A vexing problem of international relations in the postwar world was that of war debts. During World War I and after, U.S. loans to its allies and to newly formed nations totaled $10,350,479,074. Great Britain, France, and Italy were the largest borrowers. In turn, such countries as Great Britain and France were creditors of other nations. The European allies expected to pay their debts with the reparations assessed against Germany by the Treaty of Versailles. Britain had proposed canceling out debts but Pres. Woodrow Wilson had refused. On Feb. 9, 1922, Con-

gress established a Foreign Debt Commission to settle the problem. In the final arrangement, debtor nations accepted obligations of about $11,500,000,000, payable to the U.S. over 62 years at an average interest rate of 2.135%. When Germany became unable to pay reparations, debts owed the U.S. were scaled down in 1925 and 1926.

Feb 27: The **Nineteenth Amendment** to the Constitution, providing for women's suffrage, was declared constitutional by a unanimous decision of the Supreme Court.

Apr 15: In the first formal action of the investigation that uncovered the **Teapot Dome** scandal, Sen. John B. Kendrick of Wyoming introduced a resolution that called on Sec. of the Interior Albert B. Fall to explain why the Teapot Dome oil lands in Wyoming, which had been set aside by the Senate for use of the Navy, were being leased secretly to the Mammoth Oil Company, controlled by Harry F. Sinclair. Sen. Kendrick's information had come to him from one of his constituents, a small businessman in Wyoming.

Oct 3: The **first woman U.S. senator,** Mrs. W. H. Felton, 87, of Cartersville, Ga., was appointed by Gov. Thomas W. Hardwick of Georgia to the seat vacated by the death of Sen. Thomas E. Watson. Voters chose a successor to Felton in November.

Nov 7: In **congressional elections,** the Republicans suffered substantial losses but maintained majorities in both houses. In the Senate they led the Democrats 51–43, with two seats going to minor parties. In the House the Republicans lost 76 seats but still led 225–205, with five seats going to minor parties.

II. Architecture
Arts and Music
Popular Entertainment
Publishing
Theater

Jazz, a unique American contribution to music, hit a new peak of popularity and respectability in the 1920s. The period came to be known as the *jazz age.* One of the musicians who made jazz so popular was Louis "Satchmo" Armstrong, who in 1922 joined King Oliver's Creole Jazz Band in Chicago as a cornetist. The melodic development of jazz owed a great deal to Armstrong, and he made solo renditions an important part of band performances. Later Armstrong organized several big bands, appeared on Broadway, and made successful foreign tours.

Among **books published** this year was *The Enormous Room* by E. E. Cummings, the poet and artist.

Cummings' only novel, it was based on the author's imprisonment by French authorities during World War I for some indiscreet remarks he made in letters home while serving on the front as an ambulance driver. Other books published this year included *One of Ours* by Willa Cather, a novel; *The Waste Land* by the expatriate poet T. S. Eliot, a remarkable poem echoing the disillusionment caused by war and modern life; *Tales of the Jazz Age* by F. Scott Fitzgerald, and *The Beautiful and Damned,* also by Fitzgerald, a novel; *The Covered Wagon* by Emerson Hough, a novel; *Babbitt* by Sinclair Lewis, a novel about a stereotypical midwestern businessman; *Vandemark's Folly* by Herbert Quick, a novel set in Iowa in the mid-nineteenth century, the first of a trilogy that included *The Hawkeye* (1923) and *The Invisible Woman* (1924); *Rootabaga Stories* by Carl Sandburg, a collection of stories for children; and *Merton of the Movies* by Harry Leon Wilson, a novel.

May 21: Pulitzer prizes were awarded for the following: fiction, *Alice Adams* by Booth Tarkington; biography, *A Daughter oj the Middle Border* by Hamlin Garland; history, *The Founding of New England* by James Truslow Adams; poetry, *Collected Poems* by Edwin Arlington Robinson; drama, *Anna Christie* by Eugene O'Neill.

May 30: The **Lincoln Memorial** was dedicated in Washington, D.C.

III. Business and Industry
Education
Philosophy and Religion
Science

The year was marked by technical and commercial progress in radio broadcasting, an enterprise that was soon to foster a major industry and profoundly influence American society. On Aug. 28 the first commercial was broadcast over WEAF in New York City, which had begun operation on Aug. 16. The sponsor was the Queensborough Corporation, a real estate firm, that bought ten minutes of air time to extol Hawthorne Court, a group of apartment buildings in Jackson Heights, Queens. This year also saw one of the earliest long-distance relays; it used a telephone hookup to broadcast in New York a football game between the University of Chicago and Princeton University. On Oct. 4 the first radio play-by-play coverage of the World Series, reported directly from the Polo Grounds in New York City by Grantland Rice, was carried by radio station WJZ in Newark, N.J. Radio stations WGY in Schenectady, N.Y., and WBZ in Springfield, Mass., also carried World Series coverage.

The first successful use of the **Technicolor** film process was made by Herbert T. Kalmus. The process was not to become widely used for motion pictures until almost 20 years later.

Feb 21: The **aerial explosion** of the lighter-than-air ship *Roma,* after hitting high tension wires at Hampton Roads Army Airbase, Va., killed 34 of its 45-man crew. The airship had been purchased from the Italian government.

June 14: The **first president to be heard over radio** was Pres. Warren G. Harding, whose dedication of the Francis Scott Key Memorial in Baltimore was broadcast. The first official government message was not broadcast until Dec. 6, 1923.

Nov 15: Dr. **Alexis Carrel** of the Rockefeller Institute announced his discovery of leukocytes, or white corpuscles, agents in the blood that prevent the spread of infection.

IV. Fashion
Folkways
Holidays
Social Issues and Crime
Sports

The 1920s had more than their share of sensational murder cases, or perhaps it seemed that way because of the extravagant manner in which the press reported them. Typical was the Hall-Mills case, which began on Sept. 16 with the discovery, side by side under a crab apple tree in New Brunswick, N.J., of the bodies of the Rev. Edward Wheeler Hall and his choir leader, Mrs. Eleanor R. Mills. No one was indicted until four years later, when agitation by a New York City tabloid got the case reopened. The dead man's widow, two brothers, and a cousin were indicted for the murders. In the first 11 days of the trial, newsmen sent out some 5,000,000 words of copy. Billy Sunday, the evangelist, was also there to help report. In the end, all the defendants were acquitted and the case was never solved.

June 14: The **PGA golf tournament** was won by Charles Hoffner.

July 15: The **U.S. Open golf tournament** was won by Gene Sarazen.

Aug 31-Sep 5: The **Davis Cup** international tennis challenge round was won for the third straight year by the U.S., defeating Australia four matches to one.

Oct 4-8: The 19th annual **World Series** was won by the New York Giants (NL), who took four of five games from the New York Yankees (AL). The second game of the series (Oct. 5) had ended in a 3–3 tie after ten innings, when the game was called on account of darkness.

1923

I. Civil Rights
Exploration and Settlement
Government
Statistics
Wars

For the first time since Zachary Taylor's death in 1850, a president of the United States died in office of natural causes. Pres. Warren G. Harding was in poor health by early 1923. His reputation was in decline because friends he had appointed to federal office had proven corrupt or incompetent. Scandals were about to break all around him. To get away from the unpleasantness, Harding began a tour on June 20 of the West and Alaska. He took ill on the return journey and died in a San Francisco hotel on Aug. 2, at the age of 58. Harding died of an embolism while recovering from an attack of ptomaine poisoning and pneumonia, but there were rumors of foul play at the time. At 2:43 A.M. on Aug. 3, Vice Pres. Calvin Coolidge was sworn in as president by his father, a notary public, in the family home in Plymouth, Vt. Harding was buried at Marion, Ohio, on Aug. 10.

May 4: A bill repealing the **New York State Prohibition enforcement act** was passed by the state assembly. Despite Pres. Harding's warning that federal authorities would have to take over the enforcement of Prohibition in states that did not do the job themselves, Gov. Alfred E. Smith signed the repeal bill. This was thought by many to have been the beginning of the end of Prohibition.

Sep 15: Oklahoma was placed under martial law by Gov. John Calloway Walton because of terrorist activities of the Ku Klux Klan, which had become a powerful force in Midwest politics. This year several newspapers began exposing the Klan and its secret activities.

II. Architecture
Arts and Music
Popular Entertainment
Publishing
Theater

After jazz was brought north to Chicago by black musicians from New Orleans and other southern cities, white performers took up the style in greater numbers and became important contributors to it. Among them was Leon Bismarck "Bix" Beiderbecke, who was first influenced by recordings of the Original Dixieland Band. It did not take him long to win a reputation as a cornetist, and in 1923 he organized the Wolverine Orchestra in Chicago. Beiderbecke was also a pianist and a composer, one of his works being "In a Mist." A lonely, driven man, he died in 1931 at age 28.

Among **books published** this year was a slim volume entitled *Three Stories & Ten Poems* by Ernest Hemingway, a young expatriate living in France, where the book was published. Two of the stories were republished in Hemingway's *In Our Time* (1925). Other books published this year included *A Lost Lady* by Willa Cather, a novel; *Tulips and Chimneys* by E. E. Cummings, the author's first volume of poetry; *Streets of Night* by John Dos Passos, a novel; *New Hampshire: A Poem with Notes and Grace Notes* by Robert Frost; *Collected Poems* by Vachel Lindsay; *Harmonium* by Wallace Stevens, poetry; and *Cane* by Jean Toomer, a collection of poetry, stories, and a play focusing on the black experience in the U.S.

May 13: Pulitzer prizes were awarded for the following: fiction, *One of Ours* by Willa Cather; biography, *The Life and Letters of Walter H. Page* by Burton J. Hendrick; history, *The Supreme Court in United States History* by Charles Warren; poetry, *The Ballad of the Harp-Weaver, A Few Figs from Thistles,* and *Eight Sonnets,* all by Edna St. Vincent Millay; drama, *Icebound* by Owen Davis.

III. Business and Industry
Education
Philosophy and Religion
Science

Inventors and scientists had been working for years at laying the technical groundwork for radio, talking pictures, and television. Lee De Forest, who came to be called "the father of radio" as early as 1906, had developed the triode vacuum tube, which made long-distance telephone and radio communications a possibility. On Mar. 13, 1923, in New York City, De Forest demonstrated a sound motion picture process called Phonofilm. The film he showed included a performance by an orchestra. De Forest held more than 300 patents, yet his career was not an easy one. Like many other inventors during this period, De Forest struggled to secure capital for research and was at times forced into court to protect his patent and licensing rights.

Auto production continued to climb. More autos were built this year than had been produced in the first 15 years of the twentieth century. About 15,000,000 passenger cars were in use in the U.S. New

York, New Jersey, Pennsylvania, and Maryland combined had more autos than all the rest of the world outside the U.S.

The DuPont Corporation began the production of **cellophane** through the purchase of American rights to the Swiss patent of Jacques F. Brandenberger. Swiss factories had been producing cellophane, cellulose film, since 1912.

Jan: William Jennings Bryan stirred up controversy over evolution in addressing a group of ministers in St. Paul, Minn. The theory of evolution, he said, is a "program of infidelity masquerading under the name of science." The debate was taken up by newspapers, which gave the names *fundamentalist* and *modernist* to the two sides.

Oct 6: A new average **air speed record** of 243.76 mph was set by Lt. Al Williams, flying a Curtiss racer at the Pulitzer Trophy contest in St. Louis, Mo.

Nov 6: A patent for the **first electric shaver** was issued to Col. Jacob Schick. Schick received several additional patents and in 1931 established his own company, the Schick Dry Shaver Company, Inc., Stamford, Conn.

IV. Fashion
Folkways
Holidays
Social Issues and Crime
Sports

Thanks to the rugged personality and heroic achievements of Jack Dempsey as heavyweight boxing champion, the sport was more popular than ever and had attained a degree of respectability. On the night of Sept. 14, Dempsey met challenger Luis Angel Firpo, called the Wild Bull of the Pampas. The fight, held at the Polo Grounds in New York City, was one of the most exciting ever seen. Firpo was knocked out in the second round after 3 min., 57 sec. fighting time, but not before there had been 11 knockdowns, including one on a first-round punch by Firpo that knocked Dempsey out of the ring. Sportswriters into whose laps he fell shoved the champion back into the ring in time to save him from losing his crown.

July 15: The **U.S. Open golf tournament** was won by Robert T. "Bobby" Jones, an amateur who beat Robert Cruickshank by two strokes in a playoff round.

Aug 18: The **U.S. Lawn Tennis Association singles championships** were won by Helen Wills in the women's division and William T. Tilden in the men's division (Sept. 15).

Aug 30-Sep 1: The **Davis Cup** international tennis challenge round was won for the fourth year in a row by the U.S., defeating Australia four matches to one.

Sep 29: The **PGA golf tournament** was won by Gene Sarazen, who beat Walter Hagen by one stroke.

Oct 10-15: The 20th annual **World Series** was won by the New York Yankees (AL), defeating the New York Giants (NL) four games to two.

1924

I. Civil Rights
Exploration and Settlement
Government
Statistics
Wars

Republican victory in the presidential election was anticipated. The Democrats had torn themselves apart in a struggle for the nomination. Gov. Alfred E. Smith of New York represented the East and the big cities, and William G. McAdoo of Tennessee, the southern and western parts of the country. The eventual nominee was John W. Davis, an able man but almost unknown to the voters. The Republicans, on the other hand, could point with pride to Calvin Coolidge and a record of prosperity. The Democrats tried to make much of the scandals of the Harding administration but failed to stir the electorate. In fact, despite a strong third party in the field, only about half of those eligible to vote did so.

June 12: The **Republican National Convention nominated Pres. Coolidge** for reelection and Charles G. Dawes of Illinois for the vice presidency.

June 19: The **Farmer-Labor Progressive Party National Convention** nominated Duncan MacDonald of Illinois for the presidency and William Bouck of Washington for the vice presidency. On July 10 the candidates stepped down and William Z. Foster and Benjamin Gitlow became the nominees.

June 30: In the **Teapot Dome** oil leasing scandal, a federal grand jury indicted Albert B. Fall, former secretary of the interior; Harry Sinclair, president of Mammoth Oil Company; Edward L. Doheny, president of Pan-American Oil and Transport Company; and Edward L. Doheny, Jr., on charges of bribery and conspiracy to defraud the United States. Sinclair was accused of bribing Fall to secure a lease for the Teapot Dome reserve in Wyoming. The Dohenys were charged with giving a $100,000 bribe to Fall in return for leases on the Elk Hills naval reserve in California.

July 4: The **Conference for Progressive Political Action nominated Sen. Robert M. La Follette,** Republican of Wisconsin, for the presidency and (July 18) Sen. Burton K. Wheeler of Montana for the vice presidency.

July 9: The **Democratic National Convention nominated John W. Davis** of West Virginia for the presidency on the 103rd ballot. Charles W. Bryan of Nebraska, brother of William Jennings Bryan, was nominated for the vice presidency.

July 10: The **Workers' Party National Convention** nominated William Z. Foster of Illinois for the presidency and Benjamin Gitlow of New York for the vice presidency.

Nov 4: Calvin Coolidge was reelected president of the United States. Charles G. Dawes was elected vice president. The electoral vote was Coolidge, 382; John W. Davis, Democratic candidate, 136; Robert M. La Follette, Progressive candidate, 13. The popular vote was Coolidge, 15,725,016; Davis, 8,385,503; La Follette, 4,822,856; Herman P. Faris, Prohibition candidate, 57,520; Frank T. Johns, Socialist Labor candidate, 36,429; and William Z. Foster, Farmer-Labor Progressive and Workers' Party candidate, 36,386. In congressional elections the Republicans picked up five seats in the Senate for a 56–39 majority, with one seat going to a minor party. In the House the Republicans picked up 22 seats for a 247–183 majority, with four seats going to minor parties.

II. Architecture
Arts and Music
Popular Entertainment
Publishing
Theater

Light operas were a very popular form of theatrical entertainment in the 1920s. They were upbeat and romantic for the most part, and this went well with the generally content American public. No composer of such works was more popular than Rudolf Friml, who was born in Prague in 1881 and settled in New York City in 1906. Friml wrote the music for some 33 light operas, most of which now are long forgotten. One of his most popular works was *Rose Marie,* with libretto by Otto Harbach and Oscar Hammerstein II and music by Friml and Herbert Stothart. It opened at the Imperial Theatre in New York on Sept. 2 and ran for 557 performances. *Rose Marie* contained two of Friml's best remembered songs, "Indian Love Call" and "Rose Marie." Two other well-known Friml operettas were *The Firefly* (1912) and *The Vagabond King* (1925).

Among **books published** this year was *Billy Budd,*

Foretopman by Herman Melville, a work of beauty and force that the author completed shortly before his death in 1891. The manuscript was found in a tin box among the Melville family possessions. The novel's publication was an important event in the growing movement to recognize Melville as a literary giant. Other books published this year included *The Marble Faun* by William Faulkner, poetry; *Tamar and Other Poems* by Robinson Jeffers; *How to Write Short Stories* by Ring Lardner, a collection that brought him recognition as a perceptive and accomplished writer; and the *Autobiography* of Mark Twain.

May 11: Pulitzer prizes were awarded for the following: fiction, *The Able McLaughlins* by Margaret Wilson; biography, *From Immigrant to Inventor* by Michael I. Pupin; history, *The American Revolution—A Constitutional Interpretation* by Charles Howard McIlwain; poetry, *New Hampshire: A Poem with Notes and Grace Notes* by Robert Frost; drama, *Hell-Bent fer Heaven* by Hatcher Hughes.

III. Business and Industry
Education
Philosophy and Religion
Science

By early 1923 Germany, in default in reparations payments called for by the Treaty of Versailles, was undergoing extreme monetary inflation. It was clear that economic instability in Europe was a danger to U.S. economic growth. On Dec. 15, 1923, Pres. Calvin Coolidge had appointed Charles G. Dawes, a banker and government official, to head a commission to study the problem. On Apr. 9, 1924, the commission proposed what came to be known as the Dawes Plan, a program to reorganize German debt payments and stabilize its currency. The plan substantially reduced Germany's reparations, which had been set at the enormous sum of 132,000,000,000 marks. Payments would be graduated from 1,000,000,000 gold marks in the first year to 2,500,000,000 in the fifth. The plan was agreed to at an international conference that began in London on July 16, and that went into effect on Sept. 1. The economic crisis was alleviated for a time.

Ford auto prices hit their lowest point after a series of price cuts: $290 without a self-starter. The price for the Model T had been $950 back in 1909.

Jan 1: The number of **radios** in U.S. homes was over 2,500,000. In 1920 there had been no more than 5000 receivers in the U.S., most of them in the hands of experimenters and technicians.

June 2: The struggle against **child labor** took the form of a proposed amendment to the Constitution. But by 1950 only 26 of the necessary 36 states had ratified the amendment.

June 15: The **Ford Motor Company** announced manufacture of its 10,000,000th automobile. Ford had taken seven years to make the first million cars, but only 132 working days to make the tenth million.

IV. Fashion
Folkways
Holidays
Social Issues and Crime
Sports

Americans' general enthusiasm for sports made college football a natural for prime interest, professional football being in its infancy in the early 1920s. Among players of the time, the best known was Harold "Red" Grange of the University of Illinois, dubbed the Galloping Ghost of the Gridiron, who scored 31 touchdowns in his college career. The best-known team was Notre Dame, known as the Fighting Irish even though many of the team's players had no Irish connection. This year Notre Dame won all nine of its games and took the national college football championship. The team's success was due in large part to its coach, Knute Rockne, who did much to revolutionize the game by stressing the use of the forward pass and by drilling his players to near perfection.

Jan 25-Feb 4: The **first Winter Olympics** was held at Chamonix, France. The U.S. finished fourth in the unofficial team standings, behind Norway, Finland, and Great Britain, and won one gold medal.

May 4-July 27: At the **Summer Olympics** in Paris, France, the U.S. took first place in unofficial team standings for the eighth consecutive time and won 45 gold medals.

May 12: The **PGA golf tournament** was won by Walter Hagen.

June 6: The **U.S. Open golf tournament** was won by Cyril Walker, who beat Bobby Jones by three strokes.

July 21: Nathan Leopold and Richard Loeb were sentenced to life imprisonment for the kidnaping and murder of Bobby Franks in one of the strangest and most publicized crime cases of the twentieth century. The two well-educated young men had decided on a random killing, apparently to see what the experience would be like. Loeb was killed by a fellow inmate on Jan. 28, 1936, after 12 years in prison. Leopold was ultimately released on parole on Mar. 13, 1958. He died on Aug. 29, 1971, at age 66.

Aug 16: The **U.S. Lawn Tennis Association singles championships** were won by Helen Wills in the women's division and William T. Tilden in the men's division (Sept. 2).

Sep 11-13: The **Davis Cup** international tennis challenge round was won for the fourth year running by the U.S., defeating Australia in five straight matches.

Oct 4-10: The 21st annual **World Series** was won by the Washington Senators (AL), defeating the New York Giants (NL) four games to three.

1925

I. Civil Rights
Exploration and Settlement
Government
Statistics
Wars

The rapid development of aviation technology and the use of the airplane in World War I combat led to a controversy over the future of military air power. Gen. William "Billy" Mitchell, who had served during the war in the Army's air service, was convinced that air power would dominate future warfare. He set out to prove it and, in tests from 1921 to 1923, had land-based bombers attack and sink obsolete warships off the Virginia coast. In 1923 he predicted that bombers would make battleships useless, an opinion that was resented by Navy admirals. On Sept. 5 and 9, 1925, he charged government officials and military commanders with "incompetency, criminal negligence, and almost treasonable administration of national defense." As a result Mitchell was brought before a court-martial on Oct. 28, charged with "conduct prejudicial to good order and military discipline, insubordination, and utterances contemptuous of the War and Navy departments." On Dec. 17 he was found guilty and suspended without pay from rank, command, and duty for five years. Mitchell resigned from the service on Jan 29, 1926, and died in 1936.

Jan 5: The **first woman governor** in U.S. history, Mrs. William B. Ross, was inaugurated governor of Wyoming.

Aug 8: The **Ku Klux Klan** held a massive political demonstration in Washington, D.C. Some 40,000 white-robed klansmen and klanswomen marched down Pennsylvania Ave. in a massive parade that reflected the Klan's resurgence in strength during the 1920s. They did not wear their hoods, which were prohibited by a local ordinance against wearing masks. Many of the marchers were seen to raise their arms in a manner much like the fascist salute. It was probably the largest Klan parade on record, although there had been larger gatherings of Klan members.

II. Architecture
Arts and Music
Popular Entertainment
Publishing
Theater

The early 1920s saw first publication of several magazines that were unlike any published before. They were in keeping with the faster pace of life in the postwar world. *Reader's Digest,* with its condensed articles for quick reading, was founded in 1921. *Time,* a news magazine with a jazzy, know-it-all-style began publication in 1923. And on Feb. 21, 1925, a new type of magazine appeared with the founding of *The New Yorker,* edited by Harold Ross. It was said to be for the "caviar sophisticates" and "not for the old lady in Dubuque." It set new styles in fiction and humor, and featured cartoons that spoke for themselves or carried only one-line captions. Its reviews of books, plays, and films set high standards. The first issue was 32 pages and sold for 15 cents.

Among **books published** this year was *An American Tragedy* by Theodore Dreiser, a novel based on an actual murder in upstate New York in 1906. Dreiser explored the influence of money on human actions as well as the importance of heredity in this story. Other books published included *Manhattan Transfer* by John Dos Passos, a novel that presented in kaleidoscopic fashion a fictional cross-section of New York City; *The Great Gatsby* by F. Scott Fitzgerald, the classic novel of the Jazz Age; *Porgy* by Du Bose Heyward, a novel that was the basis for his successful 1927 play *Porgy and Bess,* written with his wife Dorothy, and George Gershwin's 1935 opera *Porgy and Bess; Roan Stallion, Tamar, and Other Poems* by Robinson Jeffers; *Arrowsmith* by Sinclair Lewis, a novel about an idealistic medical researcher and the forces at work in the world of scientific research; *The Song of the Indian Wars* by John G. Neihardt, the third installment of the poet's *Cycle of the West;* and *A Draft of XVI Cantos* by Ezra Pound, the first part of a continuing work remarkable for its scholarship, poetic versatility and, for most readers, its obscurity.

Apr 26: Pulitzer prizes were awarded for the following: fiction, *So Big* by Edna Ferber; biography, *Barrett Wendell and His Letters* by M. A. DeWolfe Howe; history, *A History of the American Frontier* by Frederic L. Paxson; poetry, *The Man Who Died Twice* by Edwin Arlington Robinson; drama, *They Knew What They Wanted* by Sidney Howard.

III. Business and Industry
Education
Philosophy and Religion
Science

Labor unions did not benefit from the prosperity of the 1920s. In 1921 the American Federation of Labor had almost 4,000,000 members, but by 1929 it was down to 2,961,096. The recession of 1921–1922 hurt, and employers' associations offered strong opposition to organized labor. In addition, there were unfavorable court decisions, such as the 1923 Supreme Court ruling declaring unconstitutional a minimum wage law in the District of Columbia. The decision challenged the legality of similar laws in several states.

Of the many **automobile manufacturing companies** that were founded before 1905, only 15 were still in existence: Apperson (1901); Buick (1903); Cadillac (1902); Ford (1903); Franklin (1900); Haynes (1896); Locomobile (1899); Maxwell (1904); Olds (1897); Overland (1902); Packard (1902); Peerless (1900); Pierce-Arrow (1901); Stearns (1900); and Studebaker (1898). More than 1000 had failed.

A **National Spelling Bee** was initiated by the Louisville, Ky., *Courier Journal.* In 1939, the annual event came under sponsorship of the Scripps-Howard newspapers.

Jan 24: A **total solar eclipse** was seen in New York City for the first time in three centuries.

July 10-21: The celebrated **Scopes monkey trial** was held in Dayton, Tenn. John T. Scopes had been arrested on May 5 for teaching the theory of evolution to his students in violation of state law. Scopes was defended by Clarence Darrow and Dudley Field Malone. William Jennings Bryan was one of the prosecuting attorneys. Darrow questioned Bryan on his fundamentalist beliefs during the trial (July 20). The trial was thought to have been too severe a strain on Bryan, who died on July 26. Scopes was convicted and fined $100.

Sep 3: In an **airship disaster,** the U.S. Army dirigible *Shenandoah* was wrecked in a storm near Ava, Ohio, killing 14 persons. In spite of this and similar disasters, advocates of lighter-than-air machines continued to espouse their craft.

Oct: The **Florida land boom** reached a peak about this time. Speculation in Florida properties was said to surpass any other business stampede in U.S. history.

Oct 16: Evolutionary theory was prohibited by the Texas State Text Book Board in any of its school textbooks.

IV. Fashion
Folkways
Holidays
Social Issues and Crime
Sports

The tempos of popular dances increased along with the pace of life in the Jazz Age. Sweeping the country in the early 1920s was the Charleston, an energetic dance that called for outward heel kicks and an up and down movement achieved by bending the knees to the syncopated rhythm of jazz. The dance had been performed in Charleston, S.C., as early as 1903, but its performance in the 1923 Broadway musical *Runnin' Wild* made the Charleston a hit elsewhere. The Charleston went well with short skirts and short hair. One writer claimed that in this period some 30,000,000 Americans danced frequently.

June 5: The **U.S. Open golf tournament** was won by Willie Macfarlane, who beat Robert T. "Bobby" Jones by one stroke in the second round of a playoff.

Aug 24: The **U.S. Lawn Tennis Association singles championships** were won by Helen Wills, for the third time running, in the women's division and William T. Tilden, for the sixth time in a row, in the men's division (Sept. 19).

Sep 12: The **Davis Cup** international tennis challenge round was won for the sixth straight time by the U.S., defeating France in five straight matches.

Sep 26: The **PGA golf tournament** was won by Walter Hagen.

Oct 7-15: The 22nd annual **World Series** was won by the Pittsburgh Pirates (NL), who beat the Washington Senators (AL) four games to three.

1926

I. Civil Rights
Exploration and Settlement
Government
Statistics
Wars

The question of whether the U.S. should join the Permanent Court of International Justice, which had been established in 1919 as part of the League of Nations, continued to be controversial. On Jan. 27, 1926, the Senate approved membership by a 76–17 vote, but it attached five reservations. Four were acceptable to the members of the World Court but one, relating to advisory opinions, was not. On Dec. 9, 1929, Pres. Herbert Hoover authorized the signing of a protocol of adherence that contained provisions agreed to by both the court and the U.S., but when this was submitted to the Senate, action on it was blocked. Pres. Franklin D. Roosevelt made another attempt, on Jan. 16, 1935, but the Senate rejected membership by a vote of 52–35.

May 10: U.S. **Marines landed in Nicaragua** following an uprising (May 2) led by Gen. Augusto César Sandino against Emiliano Chamorro, who had seized power in Oct. 1925. The force, under Rear Adm. Julian L. Latimer, was withdrawn on June 5.

Sep 18: A disastrous **hurricane** swept Florida and the Gulf states, killing 372 people and injuring more than 6000. Some 5000 homes were destroyed by the storm, leaving almost 18,000 families homeless. Property damage was estimated at more than $80,000,000.

Nov 2: In **congressional elections** the Democrats made gains in both houses. In the Senate the Republicans led 49–46, with one seat going to a minor party. In the House the Republicans' majority was reduced to 237–195, with three seats going to minor parties.

Dec 10: The **Nobel Peace Prize** for 1925 was awarded jointly to Vice Pres. Charles G. Dawes, for his work on the Dawes Plan of 1924 for reconstruction of German finances, and to Sir Austen Chamberlain of England, for his years of work to promote peace in Europe.

II. Architecture
Arts and Music
Popular Entertainment
Publishing
Theater

About the turn of the century traditional music had begun to give way to a wave of highly original and experimental works by such composers as Charles Ives, Igor Stravinsky, and Edgard Varèse. One of the exponents of a dissonant, neoclassic style was the composer Virgil Thomson. His *Sonata da chiesa* [Church Sonata] for E flat clarinet, C trumpet, viola, F horn, and trombone, completed this year, was in this vein. Its second movement incorporated a tango, which aroused considerable comment. Later Thomson changed his style. His works included several operas, the ballet *Filling Station* (1937), and music for the film *River* (1937). He also served as music critic of the New York *Herald Tribune* from 1940 to 1954.

Among **books published** this year was *Abraham Lincoln, The Prairie Years* by Carl Sandburg, the first two volumes of the poet's landmark six-volume biography of Lincoln. Other books published this year included *The Mauve Decade* by Thomas Beer, a study of American life in the 1890s; *The Story of Philosophy* by Will Durant; *Soldiers' Pay* by William Faulkner, the author's first novel; *The Sun Also Rises* by Ernest Hemingway, a novel of postwar disillusion that has become an American classic; *The Weary Blues* by Langston Hughes, poetry; and *Topper* by Thorne Smith, a novel about a timid soul, Cosmo Topper, and two zany ghosts who befriend him.

Ferdinand "Jelly Roll" Morton began a series of recordings made with his Red Hot Peppers in Chicago. The records, some of the most important in the history of jazz, included "Black Bottom Stomp," "Smoke House Blues," "Original Jelly Roll Blues," and "Doctor Jazz." The band consisted of George Mitchell, Omer Simeon, Kid Ory, Johnny St. Cyr, John Lindsay, and Andrew Hilaire.

May 3: Pulitzer prizes were awarded for the following: fiction, *Arrowsmith* by Sinclair Lewis; biography, *The Life of Sir William Osler* by Harvey Cushing; history, *The History of the United States* by Edward Channing; poetry, *What's O'Clock* by Amy Lowell; drama, *Craig's Wife* by George Kelly.

May 5: Sinclair Lewis declined the Pulitzer Prize award for his novel *Arrowsmith,* declaring that prizes tend to make writers "safe, polite, obedient and sterile." Lewis urged all novelists to refuse such awards if they wished to remain free.

III. Business and Industry
Education
Philosophy and Religion
Science

Evangelists offering various approaches to salvation continued to attract followers. A leading figure in the movement was Aimee Semple McPherson, who had founded the International Church of the Foursquare Gospel and in 1923 had opened the Angelus Temple in Los Angeles, Calif. She was successful in attracting a following in California. Then, on May 18, 1926, she disappeared while at the beach. Her followers believed she had drowned. About a month later Sister Aimee, as she liked to be called, turned up in Mexico, claiming she had been kidnaped. Investigation revealed she had run off with a former operator of her radio station. The affair caused a sensation. McPherson was tried for fraud and acquitted, but her days of glory were coming to an end.

The **40-hour work week** was introduced by Henry Ford to boost the ailing automobile industry. American industrial leaders were shocked, but the proposition was warmly received by the AFL as a means of checking overproduction and limiting unemployment.

Feb 9: Teaching of the **theory of evolution** was prohibited in the public schools of Atlanta, Ga., by a decision handed down by the Board of Education.

Mar 7: The first successful **transatlantic radiotelephone conversation** was held between New York City and London at a demonstration by the American Telephone and Telegraph Company, The Radio Corporation of America, and the British General Post Office.

May 9: The **first successful flight over the North Pole** was made by Rear Adm. Richard E. Byrd and Floyd Bennett.

IV. Fashion
Folkways
Holidays
Social Issues and Crime
Sports

A new kind of heavyweight boxing champion was crowned in 1926. James Joseph "Gene" Tunney, born in New York City, reflected a more refined background than that of most professional fighters. A man of intellect as well as action, he liked the company of college professors. On Sept. 23 Tunney beat the champion, Jack Dempsey, on points in a ten-round bout in Philadelphia. The fight attracted a crowd of 118,736 and generated record receipts of $1,895,723. The next year, on Sept. 22, the two met in a rematch in Chicago and again Tunney won the decision. That fight was controversial because of a so-called long count in the seventh round, when Tunney was knocked down but the referee refused to start the count until Dempsey went to a neutral corner. The rematch attracted an even larger crowd, about 145,000 people, and set another record for gate receipts, $2,658,660. Tunney, a better boxer but far less colorful figure than the dethroned champion, retired undefeated in 1928.

July 10: The **U.S. Open golf tournament** was won by Robert T. "Bobby" Jones.

Aug 6: The **first woman to swim the English Channel** was Gertrude Ederle of New York City, 19, who accomplished the feat in 14 hrs., 31 min.

Sep 11: The **Davis Cup** international tennis challenge round was won for the seventh time in a row by the U.S., defeating France four matches to one.

Sep 25: The **PGA golf tournament** was won by Walter Hagen.

Oct 2-10: The 23rd annual **World Series** was won by the St. Louis Cardinals (NL), who defeated the New York Yankees (AL) four games to three.

1927

I. Civil Rights
Exploration and Settlement
Government
Statistics
Wars

On May 20, 1927, Charles A. Lindbergh, a 25-year-old aviator, took off from Roosevelt Field, Long Island, in the monoplane *Spirit of St. Louis,* and headed for Paris, 3600 miles away. The world held its breath as infrequent reports of his progress were heard. At last, 33½ hours after he took off, Lindbergh landed at Orly, completing the first nonstop solo flight from New York to Paris. He was welcomed by a crowd estimated at 100,000. Lindbergh, tall, lanky, shy, and soft spoken, was modest about his feat, but the world considered him a hero. Pres. Calvin Coolidge sent a Navy cruiser to bring him home. Lindbergh's ticker-tape parade up Broadway in New York City was watched by an estimated 4,000,000 people.

Aug 2: Pres. **Calvin Coolidge declined renomination,** announcing "I do not choose to run for president in 1928." It had been generally assumed that he would seek reelection.

Aug 23: Nicola Sacco and Bartolomeo Vanzetti were executed in Massachusetts despite agitation in support of them. Many thought the two were innocent of the 1920 killing of a factory guard and were being railroaded for their radical beliefs.

Oct 10: The lease of the **Teapot Dome** oil reserve lands in Wyoming to the Mammoth Oil Company by former interior secretary Albert B. Fall was ruled by the Supreme Court to have been fraudulently negotiated and therefore invalid.

Dec 17: In a **submarine disaster,** the entire crew of 40 of the U.S. submarine *S-4* died after the craft, at-tempting to surface off Provincetown, Mass., collided with the Coast Guard destroyer *Paulding* and sank. Divers said they heard tappings on the inside of the submarine and pleas for food and water for three days but were helpless to free the trapped men. On Jan. 4 the first bodies were removed.

II. Architecture
Arts and Music
Popular Entertainment
Publishing
Theater

This year the monument at Mount Rushmore, S.D., was dedicated, a colossal 500-foot sculpture carved on the side of the mountain by Gutzon Borglum. Visible for 60 miles were the busts of George Washington, Thomas Jefferson, Abraham Lincoln, and Theodore Roosevelt. Borglum died in 1941, and his work was completed by his son, Lincoln. In 1916 Borglum had begun a similar work on Stone Mt., Ga., as a Confederate memorial, but he ended his association with the project in the mid-1920s because of disagreement with the sponsors.

Among **books published** this year was *The Bridge of San Luis Rey* by Thornton Wilder, a novel exploring the nature of destiny and divine providence in connection with the deaths of five persons in a bridge collapse. Other books published this year included *Blue Voyage* by Conrad Aiken, the author's first novel; *Death Comes for the Archbishop* by Willa Cather, a novel of the Southwest during the age of Spanish exploration and settlement; *Copper Sun* and *The Ballad of the Brown Girl*, both volumes by the poet Countee Cullen; *Elmer Gantry* by Sinclair Lewis, a novel; *archy and mehitabel* by Don Marquis, adventures in free verse of archy the cockroach and his friend mehitabel, a cat; *Giants in the Earth* by Ole Rölvaag, a novel of the Norwegian settlement of Dakota Territory in the nineteenth century; and *Oil!* by Upton Sinclair, a novel based in part on the Teapot Dome oil leasing scandal.

May 2: Pulitzer prizes were awarded for the following: fiction, *Early Autumn* by Louis Bromfield; biography, *Whitman* by Emory Holloway; history, *Pinckney's Treaty* by Samuel Flagg Bemis; poetry, *Fiddler's Farewell* by Leonora Speyer; drama, *In Abraham's Bosom* by Paul Green.

Oct 6: The **first talking motion picture** using the sound-on-film process was released. The film was *The Jazz Singer,* starring Al Jolson.

III. Business and Industry
Education
Philosophy and Religion
Science

This was a period of tremendous growth for the radio industry. As stations of all types proliferated and available output power climbed, it became clear that a supervisory body was needed. On Feb. 23, 1927, the Radio Control Act was signed by Pres. Calvin Coolidge. It authorized establishment of a five-man Federal Radio Commission, each commissioner to supervise one of the five zones into which the country was divided. The commission was authorized to classify types of stations, assign frequency bands for each type, and issue rules and regulations to prevent interference between stations. It also was given power to rule on operating changes requested by radio stations. The Federal Radio Commission was temporary. Its authority reverted to the secretary of commerce after one year, after which the commission became an appellate body, ruling on appeals of decisions made by the secretary of commerce. Nonetheless, it brought some order to radio. In 1934 it was superseded by the Federal Communications Commission (FCC).

Jan 7: Commercial **transatlantic telephone service** was opened between New York City and London. Walter S. Gifford, president of the American Telephone and Telegraph Company, officially inaugurated the line by saying, "Hello, London."

Spring: The **15,000,000th Model T Ford** rolled off the assembly line. Shortly after this the Model T was discontinued and the Model A was introduced. Retooling took six months and cost $200,000,000, not counting losses attributable to nonproduction.

Apr 7: The first successful demonstration of **television** took place in New York City. Walter S. Gifford, president of the American Telephone and Telegraph Company, in New York City spoke with and saw Sec. of Commerce Herbert Hoover, who was in his office in Washington, D.C.

July 29: An electric respirator, later called the **iron lung,** was installed at Bellevue Hospital, New York City. Devised by two physicians, Philips Drinker and Louis A. Shaw of Harvard University, the new device was useful in overcoming many kinds of respiratory failure.

Nov 10: The **Nobel Prize in Physics** was awarded jointly to Arthur Holly Compton of the University of Chicago for his discovery of the Compton effect, observed in collisions of x-rays and gamma rays and their variation in wavelength; and to Charles Thomson Rees Wilson of Scotland for his development of the vapor condensation method for tracking the paths of electrically charged particles.

Nov 13: The **Holland Tunnel,** the first underwater motor vehicle tunnel in the U.S., was opened to commercial traffic. The tunnel, linking Manhattan with New Jersey, had two tubes, each large enough to accommodate two lanes of traffic.

IV. Fashion
Folkways
Holidays
Social Issues and Crime
Sports

In the 1920s baseball changed from a pitcher's game, characterized by relatively few runs scored and even fewer home runs, to a slugger's game. The leading hitter was George Herman "Babe" Ruth, who had begun his major league career in 1914 as a pitcher for the Boston Red Sox (AL). Ruth joined the New York Yankees (AL) in 1920 and hit 54 home runs that season, a new record. The next year his total was 59; in 1927 he knocked out a record 60, hitting the last one on Sept. 30. The record-setting blow came on a pitch by Tom Zachary, of the Washington Senators. Ruth's record stood until 1961 when another Yankee, Roger Maris, hit 61 home runs. (In Ruth's day the season consisted of 154 games; in Maris's time, 162.) When the Babe's career ended in 1935 he had hit 714 homers, a record surpassed only by Hank Aaron, of the Milwaukee (and later Atlanta) Braves (NL), who reached a total of 755 in 1976.

Walter Johnson, pitcher for the Washington Senators (AL), ended the last season of his 20-year career by setting two major league career records. Johnson had pitched a total of 113 shutouts and struck out 3503 batters.

June 16: The **U.S. Open golf tournament** was won by Tommy Armour.

July 2: At the **Wimbledon** tennis championships, Helen Wills won the women's singles title. Other titles won by U.S. players were men's doubles, Francis T. Hunter and William T. Tilden (July 4); women's doubles, Helen Wills and Elizabeth Ryan (July 5); mixed doubles, Francis T. Hunter and Elizabeth Ryan (July 5).

Aug 30: The **U.S. Lawn Tennis Association singles championship** were won by Helen Wills in the women's division and Rene Lacoste of France in the men's division (Sept. 17).

Sep 10: The **Davis Cup** international tennis challenge round was won by France, which defeated the defending U.S. team three matches to two. The U.S. would not regain the cup until 1937.

Oct 5-8: The 24th annual **World Series** was won by the New York Yankees (AL), who swept the Pittsburgh Pirates (NL) in four straight games.

Nov 5: The **PGA golf tournament** was won by Walter Hagen, for an unprecedented fourth time in a row.

1928

I. Civil Rights
Exploration and Settlement
Government
Statistics
Wars

The presidential election campaign of 1928 was marked by a clash of personalities and positions. The Republican candidate, Herbert Hoover, was known as a manager who got things done. His Democratic opponent, Gov. Alfred E. Smith of New York, was a Catholic who favored repeal of the Eighteenth Amendment. In addition, he was perceived as a big-city politician, although he was a liberal reformer. Radio played an important part in a campaign for the first time, and Smith's harsh voice did not go over well. The attack on his Catholicism was vicious, and the election brought out nearly two-thirds of the registered voters. For the first time since the Civil War, the Republicans carried some of the southern states.

Apr 13-18: The **Socialist Party National Convention** nominated **Norman Thomas** of New York for the presidency and James H. Maurer of Pennsylvania for the vice presidency.

June 12-15: The **Republican National Convention** nominated **Herbert Hoover** of California for the presidency and Charles Curtis of Kansas for the vice presidency.

June 26-29: The **Democratic National Convention** nominated **Gov. Alfred E. Smith** of New York for the presidency and Sen. Joseph T. Robinson of Arkansas for the vice presidency.

Aug 27: The **Kellogg-Briand Peace Pact** was subscribed to by 15 nations at Paris, France. The pact called for outlawing war and settling international controversies by arbitration. The pact was eventually signed by 62 nations.

Nov 6: Herbert Hoover was elected president of the United States in a landslide Republican victory.

Charles Curtis was elected vice president. The electoral vote was Hoover, 444; Alfred E. Smith, Democratic candidate, 87. The popular vote was Hoover, 21, 392,190; Smith, 15,016,443; Norman Thomas, Socialist candidate, 267,835; William Z. Foster, Workers' Party candidate, 48,228; Verne L. Reynolds, Socialist Labor candidate, 21,181; William F. Varney, Prohibition candidate, 20,106; Frank E. Webb, Farmer Labor candidate, 6391. In congressional elections the Republicans increased their majorities in both houses, leading in the Senate 56–39, with one seat going to a minor party, and controlling the House 267–167, with one seat held by a minor party.

II. Architecture
Arts and Music
Popular Entertainment
Publishing
Theater

American poets have frequently used U.S. history as material for their works. The most prominent such writer in the 1920s was Stephen Vincent Benét, whose *John Brown's Body* was published this year. It was a long narrative poem about the abolitionist hero, evoking the period of strained North-South relations before the Civil War. Benét introduced an even larger project in poetic history with the publication of *Western Star* in 1943. It was the first part of an epic poem that was to trace the westward migration across the continent. *Western Star* depicted the settling of Jamestown and Plymouth colonies. Benét's death in 1943 put an end to the work.

Among **books published** this year was *Scarlet Sister Mary* by Julia Peterkin, a realistic and sympathetic chronicling of the life of a black woman on a South Carolina plantation. The novel was awarded the Pulitzer Prize in 1929 and was dramatized the following year. Other books published this year were *West-Running Brook* by Robert Frost, a collection of poetry; *The Man Who Knew Coolidge* by Sinclair Lewis, a novel; *Buck in the Snow*, a collection of poems by Edna St. Vincent Millay; *Good Morning, America* by Carl Sandburg, poetry; and *Boston* by Upton Sinclair, a novel.

Walt Disney introduced his most famous animated character, Mickey Mouse, in the cartoon *Plane Crazy*, the first cartoon released by Walt Disney Productions. It was followed by *Galloping Gaucho* and *Steamboat Willie*, the latter introducing sound to animated film.

May 7: Pulitzer prizes were awarded for the following: fiction, *The Bridge of San Luis Rey* by Thornton Wilder; biography, *The American Orchestra and*

Theodore Thomas by Charles Edward Russell; history, *Main Currents in American Thought* by Vernon L. Parrington; poetry, *Tristram* by Edwin Arlington Robinson; drama, *Strange Interlude* by Eugene O'Neill.

May 11: The **first program of scheduled television broadcasts** was inaugurated by station WGY in Schenectady, N.Y.

III. Business and Industry
Education
Philosophy and Religion
Science

Anthropology was advancing, now concerning itself to a greater degree with the implications of its findings for modern life. No one contributed more to this process than Franz Boas, who became Columbia University's first professor of anthropology in 1899 and held the post for 37 years. The most influential American anthropologist of his time, he taught and inspired generations of younger scientists. Boas was concerned with refuting the idea that race and culture could be correlated. He attacked the idea of a master race in works such as *Anthropology and Modern Life* (1928).

May 25: The **first woman to fly across the Atlantic,** Amelia Earhart, took off from Boston with two passengers in her airplane *Friendship.*

July 30: The **first color motion pictures** in the U.S. were exhibited by George Eastman at Rochester, N.Y. The scenes ran the gamut of colorful subjects, including goldfish, peacocks, scarlet-beaked doves, butterflies, flowers, Fifth Avenue fashion models, and pretty girls in pretty dresses. Maj. Gen. James Harbord, president of RCA, and E. F. A. Alexanderson, a pioneer in television, on the strength of the showing predicted the application of color to television.

IV. Fashion
Folkways
Holidays
Social Issues and Crime
Sports

No sport expanded more in the 1920s than golf. Some of this growth was related to the social status of the game rather than to its fun or healthful properties. Along with the growth of suburbia came a proliferation of golf courses and country clubs. This made the game expensive, adding club membership fees to the considerable cost of clubs, balls, and baggy plus-fours, but every rising young executive felt it was the thing to do. By the late 1920s there were more than 5000 courses, and golfers were spending about $200,000,000 a year on the sport.

Feb 11-19: At the second **Winter Olympics** in St. Moritz, Switzerland, the U.S. finished second in team standings and won two gold medals.

June 24: The **U.S. Open golf tournament** was won by Johnny Farrell, who beat Robert T. "Bobby" Jones by one stroke in a 36-hole playoff.

July 7: At the **Wimbledon** tennis championships, Helen Wills won the women's singles title for the second year in a row. The mixed doubles title was won by Elizabeth Ryan teamed with P. D. B. Spence of South Africa.

July 26: The **world heavyweight boxing championship** was successfully defended by Gene Tunney, who scored a 12th-round knockout over Tom Heeney in a bout in New Zealand. Shortly after, Tunney announced his retirement.

July 29-Aug 12: At the **Summer Olympics** in Amsterdam, Holland, the U.S. took first place in team standings and won 24 gold medals. U.S. athletes set 17 new Olympic records, 7 world records.

Aug 27: The **U.S. Lawn Tennis Association singles championships** were won by Helen Wills in the women's division and Henri Cochet of France in the men's division (Sept. 17).

Oct 4-9: The 25th annual **World Series** was won by the New York Yankees (AL), who swept the St. Louis Cardinals (NL) in four straight games.

Oct 6: The **PGA golf tournament** was won by Leo Diegel.

1929

I. Civil Rights
Exploration and Settlement
Government
Statistics
Wars

As the 1920s neared an end, many were convinced the prosperous times that had begun in 1922 would go on forever, but beneath the surface there were signs of trouble. Several aspects of the economy had begun to decline in 1927. The appearance of growth was, in fact, being produced by wild speculation in the stock market. On Sept. 3, 1929, stock prices reached their highest levels ever, but a slow decline began. On Oct. 24 an abrupt decline began. Leading bankers tried without success to stem the tide. On

Oct. 29, Black Tuesday, a record 16,410,030 shares were traded as huge blocks of stock were dumped for whatever they would bring. By Dec. 1 stocks on the New York Stock Exchange had dropped in value by $26,000,000,000. The day after the crash, Pres. Herbert Hoover said, "The fundamental business of the country . . . is on a sound and prosperous basis." In actuality the Great Depression of the 1930s had begun.

Jan 15: The **Kellogg-Briand Peace Pact** was passed by the Senate 85–1, Sen. John J. Blaine of Wisconsin casting the only negative vote.

Sep: National **income statistics** showed that at about this time, some 60% of U.S. citizens had annual incomes of less than $2000, which was estimated as the bare minimum to supply a family with the basic necessities of life.

Oct 7: In the continuing **Teapot Dome** oil leasing scandal, the trial of former Secretary of the Interior Albert B. Fall began in the Supreme Court of the District of Columbia. He was accused of accepting a $100,000 bribe from Edward L. Doheny in return for a lease on the Elk Hills, Calif., naval oil reserve. On Oct. 25 the court declared him guilty as charged. Fall was sentenced to one year in prison and fined $100,000.

II. Architecture
Arts and Music
Popular Entertainment
Publishing
Theater

American painters were taking up the abstract style. A painter who adapted the principles of abstract art to her own distinctive style was Georgia O'Keeffe, whose *Black Flowers and Blue Larkspur* was painted in 1929. Her depictions of flowers, of which she did many, used a close-up technique. O'Keeffe lived in New Mexico for many years, until her death in 1986. Her paintings, done in an almost bleak style, captured the vastness and forbidding beauty of the Southwest in brilliant representations of bleached bones, barren hills, and desert blossoms. Her later work was more abstract than that of her early years.

Among **books published** this year was *Sartoris* by William Faulkner, the author's first novel about the fictional Yoknapatawpha County and its people, including the Sartoris, Benbow, and Snopes families. Yoknapatawpha County was modeled after Lafayette County in Mississippi, Faulkner's home. Other books published this year included *Selected Poems* by Conrad Aiken; *Red Harvest* and *The Dain Curse* by Dashiell Hammett, both detective novels; *A Farewell to Arms* by Ernest Hemingway, a novel combining a love story with a realistic depiction of war; *Dear Judas and Other Poems* by Robinson Jeffers; *Laughing Boy* by Oliver La Farge, a novel depicting Navajo Indian life; *Round Up*, a collection of stories by Ring Lardner; *Dodsworth* by Sinclair Lewis, a novel chronicling the collapse of a midwestern auto manufacturer's marriage during a trip to Europe; *Cup of Gold* by John Steinbeck, the author's first novel; and *Look Homeward, Angel* by Thomas Wolfe, a novel introducing Wolfe's celebrated alter ego, Eugene Gant, a sensitive and gifted young man whose quest for adventure closely mirrored the author's own.

May 12: Pulitzer prizes were awarded for the following: fiction, *Scarlet Sister Mary* by Julia Peterkin; biography, *Life and Letters of Walter H. Page* by Burton J. Hendrick; history, *The Organization and Administration of the Union Army, 1861–1865* by Fred Albert Shannon; poetry, *John Brown's Body* by Stephen Vincent Benét; drama, *Street Scene* by Elmer L. Rice.

May 16: The **first Academy Awards** were presented by the Academy of Motion Picture Arts and Sciences. Among the winners were best picture of 1927–28, *Wings;* best actor, Emil Jannings; best actress, Janet Gaynor.

III. Business and Industry
Education
Philosophy and Religion
Science

Sociologists were beginning to apply accepted anthropological principles and methods to their examinations of contemporary communities. A pioneer study in this field, *Middletown: A Study in American Culture* by Robert S. and Helen M. Lynd, sociologists of Columbia University, was published this year. "Middletown" actually was the city of Muncie, Ind. The Lynds' study covered such areas as education, leisure, religion, government, and community affairs. A basic finding was that the people of Middletown learned and accepted "new ways of behaving toward material things more rapidly than new habits addressed to persons and non-material institutions."

Apr 15: The **Birth Control Clinical Research Center** established in New York City by Margaret Sanger was raided by New York police. They were acting on a complaint by the Daughters of the American Revolution. Three nurses and two doctors were arrested and thousands of records were confiscated. The case caused an uproar as physicians and private citizens indicated their support of the clinic. In May the case was thrown out of court as an infringement of a physician's right to practice medicine.

Sep: The Standard Statistics index of **common stock prices** reached an average of 216. Its climb was as follows: 100 during 1926; 114 by June 1927; 148 by June 1928; 191 by June 1929. This increase represented the biggest bull market the U.S. had ever known.

Sep 24: The **first blind airplane flight,** in which the pilot used only instruments to guide the plane, was completed by Lt. James H. Doolittle at Mitchell Field, N.Y. Doolittle had received pilot training during World War I, then studied at the University of California and MIT. During this period, Doolittle was one of the leading figures in the development of flight. In 1930 he resigned from the Army Air Corps and went to work for Shell Oil Company as head of its aviation department.

Nov 29: The **first flight over the South Pole** was completed by Lt. Commander Richard E. Byrd. The flight, from a base at Little America over the Pole and back, with a stop at an advance fueling station, lasted 19 hours. The flight was made with a Ford trimotor airplane. Byrd had started from Little America on Nov. 28 with Bernt Balchen, pilot; Harold June, radio operator; and Capt. Ashley C. McKinley, photographer and aerial surveyor. The flight to the pole and back to Little America took about 18 hours. At one point, to gain enough altitude, Byrd jettisoned a month and a half's worth of food to lighten the plane.

IV. Fashion
Folkways
Holidays
Social Issues and Crime
Sports

Criminal gangs that battled to control the illegal liquor business were widespread in Chicago, where Al "Scarface" Capone was soon to emerge as the top gangster. Between 1920 and 1927, about 250 persons were murdered in gang warfare. The climax to this almost open warfare came on Feb. 14, 1929. Five members of one gang, some of them dressed as policemen, walked into a garage on Chicago's North Side, where seven members of the rival George "Bugs" Moran gang were about to begin the day's illegal activities. They lined the seven up against a wall and mowed them down with submachine guns. The mass murder became known as the St. Valentine's Day Massacre and it was suspected that Capone was behind the killings.

The **world heavyweight boxing championship** was up for grabs this year. Max Schmeling of Germany became a contender after successful fights against Johnny Risko (Feb. 1) and Paulino Uzcudun

(June 27). Jack Sharkey defeated William L. "Young" Stribling in a ten-round bout (Feb. 27). Schmeling and Sharkey met each other in a championship fight in 1930.

June 30: The **U.S. Open golf tournament** was won by Robert T. "Bobby" Jones, who beat Al Espinosa by 23 strokes in a playoff.

July 5: At the **Wimbledon** tennis championships in England, the women's singles title was won for the third straight year by Helen Wills. On July 6 the men's doubles was won by Wilmer Allison and John Van Ryn, and the mixed doubles was won by Helen Wills and Francis T. Hunter.

Aug 24: The **U.S. Lawn Tennis Association** singles **championships** were won by Helen Wills, for the sixth time, in the women's division and William T. Tilden, for the seventh time, in the men's division (Sept. 14).

Oct 8-14: The 26th annual **World Series** was won by the Philadelphia Athletics (AL), who beat the Chicago Cubs (NL) four games to one.

Dec 7: The **PGA golf tournament** was won for the second year in a row by Leo Diegel.

1930

I. Civil Rights
Exploration and Settlement
Government
Statistics
Wars

Early in 1930 Pres. Herbert Hoover called a special session of Congress to take up tariff revision, which he had promised in his presidential campaign the previous fall. Hoover primarily wanted to have tariff rates raised on agricultural products. By the time Congress finished its work, however, it sent Hoover the Smoot-Hawley Act, a bill that included some of the highest rates in history on manufactured products. In all, duties on 890 articles were raised to high levels. Hoover signed the act into law on June 17 despite the fact that on May 4 a petition signed by 1028 economists had been sent to Washington urging defeat of the proposed legislation. Within two years, 25 nations retaliated by raising duties on U.S. goods. The economic nationalism triggered by this legislation has been blamed for deepening the worldwide depression.

The U.S. **Census** recorded a population of 122,775,046. The center of population was located three miles northeast of Linton, Green County, Ind.

Mar 13: In the **Teapot Dome** oil leasing scandal, the trial of Edward L. Doheny, charged with bribing Albert B. Fall to obtain a lease for the Elk Hills naval oil reserve, began at the Supreme Court of the District of Columbia. Doheny was acquitted on Mar. 22.

May 26: In a decision affecting enforcement of **Prohibition,** the U.S. Supreme Court ruled that purchase of intoxicating liquor was not a violation of the Constitution.

Sep 9: Immigration of foreign laborers was virtually prohibited by an order issued by the State Department, a reflection of grave concern over U.S. unemployment.

Nov 4: In **congressional elections** the Republicans lost eight seats in the Senate for a nominal 48–47 majority, with one seat going to a minor party. In the House the Democrats took a 220–214 lead, with one seat going to a minor party.

II. Architecture
Arts and Music
Popular Entertainment
Publishing
Theater

This year was notable for a number of events that brought serious music to radio listeners. On Mar. 16, in the first opera broadcast directly from a stage in Europe (Dresden, Germany), station WEAF in New York City carried part of a performance of Beethoven's *Fidelio*. The program was relayed to New York via shortwave transmission. On Apr. 17 the National Broadcasting Company produced the premiere of Charles Sanford Skilton's one-act Indian opera, *The Sun Bride*. And on Oct. 5 the Columbia Broadcasting System began live Sunday broadcasts of the New York Philharmonic Symphony Orchestra. Arturo Toscanini was its conductor. Seven years later the NBC Symphony Orchestra was formed with Toscanini as conductor.

Among **books published** this year was *I'll Take My Stand: Humanism and America*, an anthology of the writings of a number of southern authors, including John Crowe Ransom, Allen Tate, and Robert Penn Warren. Other books published this year included *The Bridge*, Hart Crane's most memorable work; *The 42nd Parallel* by John Dos Passos, the first novel in the author's *U.S.A.* trilogy; *As I Lay Dying* by William Faulkner, a novel; *Cimarron* by Edna Ferber, a novel; *Collected Poems* by Robert Frost; *The Maltese Falcon*

by Dashiell Hammett, the classic detective novel; and *Arundel* by Kenneth Roberts, a historical novel.

The painting ***American Gothic*** was completed by Grant Wood. Wood had applied the techniques of Flemish and German primitives in the work, which he intended as a satire. The result came to be one of the best known American paintings.

May 12: Pulitzer prizes were awarded for the following: fiction, *Laughing Boy* by Oliver La Farge; biography, *The Raven* by Marquis James; history, *The War of Independence* by Claude H. Van Tyne; poetry, *Selected Poems* by Conrad Aiken; drama, *The Green Pastures* by Marc Connelly.

Nov 5: The **Nobel Prize in Literature** was awarded to Sinclair Lewis, particularly in recognition of his novel *Babbitt*. Lewis was the first American to win the prize in literature.

III. Business and Industry
Education
Philosophy and Religion
Science

The Institute for Advanced Study was chartered this year and opened its doors three years later in Princeton, N.J. Its establishment was made possible by gifts from Louis Bamberger and his sister, Mrs. Felix Fuld. The institute's first director was Abraham Flexner, a prominent educator; among its first members was Albert Einstein. The institute was formed as a center for graduate studies. It has no classes and does not confer degrees. As the institute developed, it became known particularly as a research center in mathematics and the natural sciences.

Illiteracy in America reached a new low of 4.3% of the population, a decline of 1.7% from 1920 and a decline of 15.7% from 1870.

According to an **automobile survey,** one of every 4.9 Americans owned an automobile.

Mar 13: Identification of the planet Pluto was made from a photograph taken on Jan. 21 at Lowell Observatory in Flagstaff, Ariz. The discovery boosted the prestige of mathematical astronomers, who had predicted existence of the planet.

Aug 11: The **American Lutheran Church** was formed at Toledo, Ohio, by the merger of the Lutheran Synod of Buffalo, the Evangelical Lutheran Synod of Iowa, and the Evangelical Lutheran Joint Synod of Ohio. On Oct. 31 the church, at an organizational convention, completed the merger of seven synods in the U.S. and Canada.

Oct 30: The **Nobel Prize in Physiology or Medicine** was awarded to Dr. Karl Landsteiner of the Rockefeller Institute for his discovery of human blood groups.

Landsteiner was the first American citizen to win the prize for medicine.

Dec 11: The **Bank of the United States** in New York City, with 60 local branches and 400,000 depositors, closed. More than 1300 banks throughout the country had been closed down by the deepening economic crisis.

IV. Fashion
Folkways
Holidays
Social Issues and Crime
Sports

Golf's first nationally known figure and perhaps the best golfer who ever played, Robert Tyre "Bobby" Jones, Jr., announced his retirement on Nov. 17, after a year in which he set records never achieved by any other player. On Sept. 27 he became the only player ever to make the grand slam in golf by winning the 1930 U.S. Amateur golf tournament after winning the U.S. Open, the British Open, and the British Amateur tournaments. Jones had played serious golf for only eight years, spending much of his time studying law, literature, and engineering. But of the 27 major championship tournaments he entered, he won 13. In retirement he made instructional films and, with Clifford Roberts, founded the Augusta National Golf Club in Georgia and organized the Masters Tournament, one of the major U.S. golf tournaments.

Apr 19: The **Boston Marathon** was won for the seventh time by Clarence H. DeMar of Melrose, Mass., with a time of 2 hrs., 34 min., 48.2 sec.

May 9: The 55th annual **Preakness Stakes** was won by Gallant Fox, with a time of 2:00$^3/_5$. The jockey was Earl Sande.

May 17: The 56th annual **Kentucky Derby** was won by Gallant Fox, with a time of 2:07$^3/_5$. The jockey was Earl Sande, who scored his third Derby victory.

May 30: The 18th annual **Indianapolis 500** auto race was won by Billy Arnold, who completed the course in 4 hrs., 58 min., 39.72 sec., with an average speed of 100.44 mph.

June 7: The 62nd annual **Belmont Stakes** was won by Gallant Fox. The jockey was Earl Sande. This was the second time that a horse had won the Triple Crown. The winning time was 2:31$^3/_5$.

June 12: The **world heavyweight boxing championship** was won by Max Schmeling of Germany. Schmeling was awarded the victory over Jack Sharkey, who fouled him in the fourth round of the bout in New York City.

July 4: At the **Wimbledon** tennis championships, the women's singles title was won by Helen Wills, now called Helen Wills Moody, her married name. Other titles taken by Americans were men's singles, William T. Tilden (July 5); women's doubles, Helen Wills Moody and Elizabeth Ryan (July 5); men's doubles, Wilmer Allison and John Van Ryn (July 7).

July 12: The **U.S. Open golf tournament** was won by Robert T. "Bobby" Jones.

Sep 13: The **PGA golf tournament** was won by Tommy Armour.

Sep 13-17: The **America's Cup** was successfully defended by the yacht *Enterprise*, which defeated the British challenger *Shamrock V* in four straight races.

Oct 1-8: The 27th annual **World Series** was won by the Philadelphia Athletics (AL), who defeated the St. Louis Cardinals (NL) four games to two.

1931

I. Civil Rights
Exploration and Settlement
Government
Statistics
Wars

Breakdown in enforcement of the Prohibition laws appeared to be affecting law enforcement in general. As a result, in May of 1929 Pres. Herbert Hoover had appointed a National Commission on Law Observance and Law Enforcement. He named George W. Wickersham, a former U.S. attorney general, as its head. The body came to be known as the Wickersham Commission. It issued its report on Jan. 19, 1931, noting that enforcement of antiliquor laws was hindered by the great profits to be earned in illegal traffic and by the apathy, even hostility, of the general public. The commission believed enforcement should be left to the federal government. It recommended revisions but not repeal of the Eighteenth Amendment. Pres. Hoover, in submitting the report to Congress on Jan. 20, said he also did not favor repeal. The report did not result in any effective action.

Sep: A **bank panic** spread across the nation. In September 305 banks closed; in October 522 shut down. Fear that the U.S. would go off the gold standard led to hoarding of the metal throughout the country.

Dec 10: The **Nobel Peace Prize** was awarded jointly to Nicholas Murray Butler, president of Columbia University, and to Jane Addams of Chicago. Butler had been the first major figure to support the Kellogg-Briand Peace Pact of 1928, and Addams had been the first international president of the Women's International League for Peace and Freedom. She was honorary president at the time of the award.

II. Architecture
Arts and Music
Popular Entertainment
Publishing
Theater

Widespread disillusionment with politics, prompted in large part by the seeming inability of the federal government to end the Depression, was reflected in this year's hit musical comedy, *Of Thee I Sing*, with music by George Gershwin, lyrics by Ira Gershwin, and book by George S. Kaufman and Morrie Ryskind. It was a sharp but good-natured satire on presidential politics. The show opened at the Music Box Theatre in New York City on Dec. 26 and ran for 441 performances. When the show won the Pulitzer Prize for drama the next year, it was the first musical ever to be so honored. The title song was a hit too. A sequel, *Let 'Em Eat Cake* (1933), was less successful, having only 90 Broadway performances.

Among **books published** this year was *The Good Earth* by Pearl S. Buck, the author's first novel. For two years this best seller was at the top of the sales list in bookstores. Other books published this year included *Shadows on the Rock* by Willa Cather, a beautifully written novel set in seventeenth-century Quebec; *ViVa* by E. E. Cummings, poetry; *Newspaper Days* by Theodore Dreiser, autobiography; *Sanctuary* by William Faulkner, a novel; *American Beauty* by Edna Ferber, a novel; *The Glass Key* by Dashiell Hammett; the *Autobiography* of Lincoln Steffens; *The Forge* by T. S. Stribling, the first novel of a trilogy dealing with the fictional Vaiden family of Alabama; *The Long Christmas Dinner* by Thornton Wilder, a collection of one-act plays; and *Axel's Castle* by Edmund Wilson, a collection of essays on symbolism and symbolist writers.

Mar 3: An act making **"The Star-Spangled Banner"** the national anthem was signed by Pres. Herbert Hoover. Francis Scott Key wrote the words in 1814 during the bombardment of Fort McHenry in the War of 1812.

May 4: Pulitzer prizes were awarded for the following: fiction, *Years of Grace* by Margaret Ayers Barnes; biography, *Charles W. Eliot* by Henry James; history, *The Coming of the War: 1914* by Bernadotte E. Schmitt; poetry, *Collected Poems* by Robert Frost; drama, *Alison's House* by Susan Glaspell.

III. Business and Industry
Education
Philosophy and Religion
Science

Research in physics in the U.S. and Europe was leading to discoveries that in a few years would be applied in production of the atomic bomb. A leader in the U.S. was Harold C. Urey, a professor of physics at Columbia University. This year Urey announced that he and his associates had discovered an isotope of hydrogen with an atomic weight of two instead of one. This was heavy hydrogen, or deuterium. Molecules of water containing deuterium atoms instead of hydrogen atoms came to be known as heavy water. This was a key component in atomic fission experiments. Urey later served as director (1942–1945) of the Manhattan Project, which developed the world's first atomic bombs.

Jan 7: Unemployment was estimated at between 4,000,000 and 5,000,000 by Col. Arthur Woods, head of the President's Emergency Committee for Unemployment Relief.

May 1: The **Empire State Building,** the world's tallest building, was dedicated and opened to the public in New York City.

June 23: A **flight around the world** was begun by Wiley Post and Harold Gatty, who took off from Roosevelt Field, Long Island, N.Y., in their plane *Winnie May*. They landed back at Roosevelt Field 8 days, 15 hrs., 51 min. later.

Oct 5: The **first nonstop flight across the Pacific** Ocean was completed by Hugh Herndon and Clyde Pangborn, who flew from Sabishiro, Japan, to Wenatchee, Wash., a distance of 4860 mi., in 41 hrs., 13 min.

Oct 24: The **George Washington Bridge,** linking Manhattan with New Jersey across the Hudson R., was officially opened. Gov. Franklin D. Roosevelt of New York and Gov. Morgan F. Larson of New Jersey took part in the ceremonies. The Port Authority of New York had completed the bridge eight months ahead of schedule and under budget. The bridge, one of the most beautiful and best known in the world, was opened to traffic the next day.

IV. Fashion
Folkways
Holidays
Social Issues and Crime
Sports

The American gangster was a prominent personality in the 1920s and 1930s. Foremost was Alphonse "Al"

Capone, also known as "Scarface." He ruled the Chicago underworld in the 1920s with unprecedented lawlessness and brutality. It was estimated that in 1927 alone he took in $105,000,000. Finally, in 1931, Capone was indicted for income tax evasion. He was convicted on Oct. 17 and sentenced to 11 years in prison. He was released in 1939, mortally ill from syphilis. In the East, Jack "Legs" Diamond attracted the most attention because of the unusual scrapes he got into and the number of times he was wounded, but not killed, by gunfire. On Dec. 18, 1931, he was shot to death in an Albany, N.Y., boardinghouse shortly after being acquitted of kidnaping.

July 3-4: At the **Wimbledon** tennis championships, the men's singles title was won by Sidney B. Wood, Jr., 20, the youngest winner in the history of the event. The men's doubles title was won by George Lott, Jr., and John Van Ryn, and the mixed doubles was won by George Lott, Jr., and Mrs. L. A. Harper.

July 6: The **U.S. Open golf tournament** was won by Billy Burke, who beat George Von Elm by one stroke after two 36-hole playoffs.

Aug 20: The **U.S. Lawn Tennis Association singles championships** were won by Mrs. Helen Wills Moody in the women's division and H. Ellsworth Vines, Jr., in the men's division (Sept. 12).

Sep 19: The **PGA golf tournament** was won by Tom Creavy.

Oct 1-10: The 28th annual **World Series** was won by the St. Louis Cardinals (NL), who beat the Philadelphia Athletics (AL) four games to three.

1932

I. Civil Rights
Exploration and Settlement
Government
Statistics
Wars

It was a trying year for the nation. Pres. Herbert Hoover tried desperately to stem the Great Depression by granting generous credit to industry and ordering a stern check on government spending. Not only did he reduce his personal salary by 20%, but he also persuaded Vice Pres. Charles Curtis and nine members of the Cabinet to accept similar cuts. Public works programs were planned to alleviate staggering

unemployment. Hoover's plans, however, were never realized, for the voters insisted on a change of administration, electing Franklin D. Roosevelt to the presidency in a Democratic landslide.

The number of **unemployed** in the U.S. reached 13,000,000. National wages were 60% less than in 1929, dividends 56.6% less. Total business loss during the year was placed at $5,000,000,000 to $6,000,000,000. Two and a half years after the Oct. 1929 stock market crash, U.S. industry as a whole was operating at less than half its maximum 1929 volume.

Jan 22: The **Reconstruction Finance Corporation** was established with $2,000,000,000 at its disposal to lend to failing banks, farm mortgage associations, building and loan societies, railroads, and insurance companies.

Mar 1: In the **Lindbergh kidnaping,** one of the most highly publicized crimes of the twentieth century, Charles A. Lindbergh, Jr., an infant of 20 months, was kidnaped from his parents' home at Hopewell, N.J. The body of the child was found on May 12, after payment of a $50,000 ransom. Outraged public opinion made kidnaping a federal crime carrying the death penalty.

May 29: The so-called **Bonus Army,** a group of some 1000 former servicemen seeking cash payments for their veterans' bonus certificates, arrived in Washington, D.C. In June other groups of veterans arrived from every section of the country, swelling the army to about 17,000. Camped in the open or in unused buildings near the Capitol, they vowed to stay until Congress authorized immediate cash in full for their certificates. A bill authorizing payment passed the House on June 15, but was killed in the Senate on June 17. The government provided money for veterans to return to their homes, but about 2000 refused the offer and did not move. Finally, on July 28, federal troops under Gen. Douglas MacArthur drove them out.

June 14-16: The **Republican National Convention** renominated Pres. Hoover for the presidency on the first ballot. Charles Curtis was renominated for the vice presidency.

June 27-July 2: The **Democratic National Convention** nominated Franklin D. Roosevelt for the presidency, ending a deadlock produced by opposing factions supporting Roosevelt, John Nance Garner of Texas, and Alfred E. Smith of New York. The deadlock was broken and Roosevelt nominated on July 1, when Garner was persuaded to give his delegates to Roosevelt in return for the vice presidential nomination. Roosevelt broke precedent by flying to Chicago to accept the nomination. In his speech, he called for a "new deal for the American people."

Nov 8: Franklin D. Roosevelt was elected president of the United States in a Democratic landslide. John Nance Garner was elected vice president. Roosevelt carried all but seven states, with 472 electoral votes to 59 for Herbert Hoover. The popular vote was Roosevelt, 22,821,857; Hoover, 15,761,841; Norman Thomas, Socialist, 881,951; William Z. Foster, Communist, 102,785; Verne L. Reynolds, Socialist Labor, 33,276; William D. Upshaw, Prohibition, 81,869; Jacob S. Coxey, Farmer Labor, 7309. In congressional elections the Democrats gained 13 Senate seats for a 60–35 majority, with one seat held by a minor party. In the House the Democrats gained 90 seats for a 310–117 majority, with five seats going to minor parties.

II. Architecture
Arts and Music
Popular Entertainment
Publishing
Theater

This year 15,279 books were published or reprinted in the U.S. Of these, 1996 were novels. The novelists' main preoccupation this year seemed to be with the problems of the South. Despite the publication of several outstanding works, not much of literary value was offered to the public. In fact, a virtual paralysis had settled over the arts. Opera houses in Chicago and Philadelphia gave no performances. A number of new orchestral works were ventured, but none with serious claim to stature. Painters looking for inspiration found it in the formalized primitivism of the Mexican artist Diego Rivera and his compatriots. Architects, deprived of the opportunity to build, chose to quarrel over the so-called International school of design. The theater enjoyed only one real hit—Philip Barry's *The Animal Kingdom.*

Among **books published** this year was *Tobacco Road* by Erskine Caldwell. This novel, dealing with the family of Jeeter Lester, a poor Georgia sharecropper, was the basis for an enormously successful dramatization in 1933 by Jack Kirkland; it has since become an American classic. Other books published this year included *Beyond Desire* by Sherwood Anderson, a novel set in the South; *1919* by John Dos Passos, the second novel in his trilogy *U.S.A.; Light in August* by William Faulkner; and *The Store* by T. S.

Stribling, the second novel of a trilogy set in the South.

E. Y. "Yip" Harburg wrote one of the most popular songs of the year, "Brother, Can You Spare a Dime."

May 2: Pulitzer prizes were awarded for the following: fiction, *The Good Earth* by Pearl S. Buck; biography, *Theodore Roosevelt* by Henry F. Pringle; history, *My Experiences in the World War* by John J. Pershing; poetry, *The Flowering Stone* by George Dillon; drama, *Of Thee I Sing* by George S. Kaufman, Morrie Ryskind, and Ira Gershwin. This was the first time a musical received the drama award.

III. Business and Industry
Education
Philosophy and Religion
Science

Poor demand for goods, uncertain manufacturing conditions, and a wobbly stock market combined to make this one of the most unfavorable business years in modern history. Labor, however, hailed its most important victory to date—passage of the Federal Anti-Injunction Law, or Norris-LaGuardia Act. The battle for the five-day work week was also being won, as Pres. Herbert Hoover made it standard for most government employees. With unemployment hovering at about 11,000,000, labor could make little headway in its demands for compulsory unemployment insurance. In science, progress was made in the study of cosmic rays; in the discovery of the neutron by James Chadwick; in the enunciation of the uncertainty principle; and in laboratory production of gamma rays. In addition, an isotope of hydrogen was produced and vitamin C was isolated and identified. Automation was fast becoming a specialty of its own with the construction of large and versatile computing machines.

May 20: Amelia Earhart became the first woman to cross the Atlantic in a solo flight when she landed near Londonderry, Ireland, 2026½ miles from Harbor Grace, Newfoundland, her starting point. The flight took 13 hrs., 30 min.

Nov 10: The **Nobel Prize in Chemistry** was awarded to Irving Langmuir "for his discoveries and investigations in surface chemistry." Langmuir conducted his prize-winning research on surface actions of glass, water, and metals. His discoveries led to improvements in incandescent lighting, reduction of light glare from glass surfaces, and cloud seeding to induce rainfall.

IV. Fashion
Folkways
Holidays
Social Issues and Crime
Sports

The movement to repeal Prohibition received a boost when the redoubtable "dry" John D. Rockefeller spoke out for the repeal of the Volstead Act. Both presidential candidates asked for its erasure from the law books. With such powerful forces against it, Prohibition was doomed. In baseball Jimmy Foxx threatened to eclipse Babe Ruth's home run record of 60, falling short by two runs. Tennis had a dazzling new name—16-year-old Frankie Parker, who mowed down veteran opposition wherever he played. The greatest blot on the nation's conscience was its fantastic crime wave. The citizens of Chicago this year shelled out some $145,000,000 to racketeers.

Feb 4-13: At the 1932 **Winter Olympics** in Lake Placid, N.Y., the third such games in history and the first held in the U.S., the U.S. team won ten gold medals and the unofficial team championship.

June 21: The world **heavyweight boxing championship** was won by Jack Sharkey, who took a 15-round decision over Max Schmeling of Germany in New York City, thus returning the title to the U.S.

June 25: The **U.S. Open golf tournament** was won by Gene Sarazen.

July 1: At the **Wimbledon** tennis championships, Helen Wills Moody won the women's singles title. H. Ellsworth Vines, Jr., won the men's singles on July 2.

July 2: The term *New Deal* was introduced by Franklin D. Roosevelt in his speech accepting the Democratic nomination for the presidency. Before the assembled delegates in Chicago, Roosevelt said: "I pledge you, I pledge myself, to a new deal for the American people. Let us all here assembled constitute ourselves prophets of a new order of competence and courage. This is more than a political campaign; it is a call to arms."

July 30-Aug 14: At the 1932 **Summer Olympics** in Los Angeles, Calif., the U.S. won 16 gold medals and the unofficial team championship.

Aug 21: The **U.S. Lawn Tennis Association singles championships** were won by Helen Hull Jacobs in the women's division and H. Ellsworth Vines, Jr., in the men's division (Sept. 3).

Sep 4: The **PGA golf tournament** was won by Olin Dutra.

Sep 28-Oct 2: The 29th annual **World Series** was won by the New York Yankees (AL), who swept the Chicago Cubs (NL) in four games.

1933

I. Civil Rights
Exploration and Settlement
Government
Statistics
Wars

The change of administration deepened the economic crisis. The low point was reached by inauguration day, with the nation gripped by a bank panic. To meet the situation, the administration demanded and was given unprecedented powers. These led to wide changes in the monetary system and to creation of an array of federal agencies to regulate private industry and find jobs for millions on government-sponsored projects. While this program, known as the New Deal, restored some confidence, its more radical measures came under conservative attack. Its critics, however, failed to win popular support. In world affairs, America's Good Neighbor policy fostered an era of Pan-American political and economic cooperation. The gravity of domestic problems distracted attention from international affairs: the rise of Adolf Hitler in Germany, warfare in the Far East, and disintegration of the League of Nations.

Feb 6: The **Twentieth Amendment** to the U.S. Constitution was adopted. It abolished the so-called lameduck session of Congress and changed the presidential inauguration date from Mar. 4 to Jan. 20. It also specified that the vice president-elect would succeed to the presidency if the president-elect died before inauguration.

Mar 1: Bank holidays were declared in six states, effectively preventing runs on bank assets by worried depositors. By Mar. 4 bank panics reached their greatest intensity. At 4:30 A.M. that day, Gov. Herbert H. Lehman of New York declared a state bank holiday; Gov. Henry Horner of Illinois immediately followed suit.

Mar 4: Franklin D. Roosevelt was inaugurated president of the United States. In his inaugural address, Pres. Roosevelt included the memorable sentence: "The only thing we have to fear is fear itself." The address outlined an aggressive policy to deal with the economic emergency.

Mar 4: Frances Perkins, the first woman to hold a Cabinet post, was appointed secretary of labor by Pres. Franklin D. Roosevelt.

Mar 12: The **first fireside chat,** a radio address to the entire nation, was delivered by Pres. Roosevelt on this Sunday evening. His subject was the reopening of the banks during the following week.

Mar 13: Banks began reopening across the country. Before the end of the month over 75% of all banks were operating again.

Mar 31: The **Civilian Conservation Corps** (CCC) was initiated by the Reforestation Unemployment Act to create jobs through a national reforestation program.

May 12: The **Agricultural Adjustment Act** (AAA) restricted production of certain crops, to be determined by farmers, and paid them bounties for uncultivated acreage. The bounties were to be paid from the revenue obtained from a processing tax. The Supreme Court ruled the AAA unconstitutional in 1936.

May 18: The **Tennessee Valley Act** was passed, establishing the Tennessee Valley Authority (TVA). Its purpose was to control Tennessee R. floods, institute a reforestation program on marginal lands in the Tennessee R. Valley, and provide rural electrification.

June 16: The **National Industrial Recovery Act** (NIRA) was created. It established the National Recovery Administration (NRA) and the Public Works Administration (PWA). Gen. Hugh Johnson was named administrator of the NRA, and Harold L. Ickes was named head of the PWA.

June 16: The **Banking Act of 1933** was passed by Congress, establishing the Federal Bank Deposit Insurance Corporation.

Nov 8: The **Civil Works Administration** was set up with an initial appropriation of $400,000,000. Its first director was Harry L. Hopkins. The plan was intended to provide work for about 4,000,000 unemployed and to put two-thirds of the families then receiving relief on a self-sustaining basis.

Dec 5: The **Twenty-first Amendment was adopted** when it was ratified by Utah, the 36th state to do so. Prohibition in the U.S. was thereby repealed.

II. Architecture
   Arts and Music
   Popular Entertainment
   Publishing
   Theater

Theater had a lackluster year despite offerings by established playwrights and stars. The most notable exception was Eugene O'Neill's *Ah, Wilderness!* Opera houses and symphonic societies curtailed their seasons. Painters and sculptors were helped by com-

missions from the Civil Works Administration. At one time, the government employed as many as 2500 artists and 1000 architects, most of whom worked at supplying murals for public buildings. The two most popular films of the year were *Little Women*, starring Katherine Hepburn, and *She Done Him Wrong*, featuring Mae West.

Among **books published** this year was *Anthony Adverse* by Hervey Allen, a long, sprawling novel set in the Napoleonic era. Despite criticism concerning Allen's historical accuracy, readers made the book a best-seller. Other books published this year included *Death in the Woods*, a collection of stories by Sherwood Anderson; *Winner Take Nothing* by Ernest Hemingway, also a collection of stories; *Give Your Heart to the Hawks, and Other Poems* by Robinson Jeffers; *Principles of Harmonic Analysis* by Walter Piston, one of the most influential textbooks on the methods of modern composition; *Rabble in Arms* by Kenneth Roberts, a historical novel; and *The Autobiography of Alice B. Toklas* by Gertrude Stein, which sold surprisingly well.

A significant **obscenity ruling** was handed down in New York City concerning Erskine Caldwell's novel *God's Little Acre*. City Magistrate Benjamin Greenspan exonerated the book of the charge of obscenity made by the New York Society for the Prevention of Vice. The decision was based on three criteria: consideration of the book as a whole rather than a few isolated sections, the aptness of coarse language when spoken by coarse characters, and reactions of a cross-section of citizens on reading the work.

May 4: Pulitzer prizes were awarded for the following: fiction, *The Store* by T. S. Stribling; drama, *Both Your Houses* by Maxwell Anderson; history, *The Significance of Sections in American History* by Frederick J. Turner; biography, *Grover Cleveland* by Allan Nevins; poetry, *Conquistador* by Archibald MacLeish.

Dec 6: In a major ruling on **censorship,** the ban on *Ulysses* by James Joyce was lifted by Federal Judge John M. Woolsey, who wrote in part: "[It is] a sincere and honest book. . . . I do not detect anywhere the leer of a sensualist."

III. Business and Industry
   Education
   Philosophy and Religion
   Science

Encouraged by sympathetic legislation, especially creation of the National Labor Relations Board

(NLRB), organized labor became more militant in making its demands—particularly its right to organize. The American Federation of Labor boasted 4,000,000 members in 29,669 local bodies, and counted as allies the workers enrolled in the railroad brotherhoods. Scientists, meanwhile, confirmed the discovery in 1932 of the positron (positive electron). Television pioneers were jubilantly hailing a new communication medium and pointed with pride to a cathode-ray screen already on the market. American education presented a more somber picture. Two thousand rural schools failed to open in the fall. More than 1500 commercial schools and colleges were forced to suspend activities. Some 200,000 certified teachers were unemployed, and it was estimated that 2,280,000 children were not attending school.

Average **life expectancy** was 59 years, a gain of ten years since the turn of the century.

The first report of the **National Survey of School Finance,** authorized by Congress in 1931, was delivered. The report stated that one-third of America's schoolchildren were receiving an inadequate education.

Feb 25: The **first U.S. aircraft carrier** specifically designed for the purpose, the U.S.S. *Ranger,* was christened at Newport News, Va., by Mrs. Herbert Hoover. The U.S. had other carriers, but they were ships that had been converted for use as carriers.

Oct 20: The **Nobel Prize in Physiology or Medicine** was awarded to Thomas Hunt Morgan "for his discoveries concerning the function of the chromosome in the transmission of heredity." Morgan performed his most significant experiments as head of the California Institute of Technology in Pasadena, Calif.

IV. Fashion
Folkways
Holidays
Social Issues and Crime
Sports

The Depression damped most professional sporting activities. The exception was horseracing, which boomed as never before. State legislatures, recognizing the revenue produced by betting at tracks, compromised their moral positions by encouraging the sport. Maryland this year earned some $66,000,000 from racing revenues alone. League-leading baseball clubs played before packed parks, but the losing teams could not fill their stands. College football contests enjoyed a 13% rise in attendance over the previ-

ous season—a popularity that extended to the professional game as well.

May 27-Nov 2: The **Century of Progress Exposition** was held in Chicago, Ill., in honor of the centennial of the founding of Chicago.

June 10: The **U.S. Open golf tournament** was won by Johnny Goodman.

June 21: The **world heavyweight boxing championship** was won by the Italian giant, Primo Carnera, who knocked out Jack Sharkey at Long Island City Bowl.

July 6: In the **first all-star baseball game,** the American League defeated the National League by a score of 4–2. The game was held at Comiskey Park in Chicago before 49,200 fans.

July 8: The **Wimbledon** women's singles championship was won by Mrs. Helen Wills Moody.

Aug 13: The **PGA golf tournament** was won by Gene Sarazen.

Aug 26: The **U.S. Lawn Tennis Association singles championships** were won by Helen Hull Jacobs in the women's division and Frederick J. Perry of Great Britain in the men's division (Sept. 10).

Oct 3-7: The 30th annual **World Series** was won by the New York Giants (NL), defeating the Washington Senators (AL) four games to one.

Dec 17: In the **first National Football League (NFL) championship playoff,** the Chicago Bears defeated the New York Giants 23–21 to become NFL champions of 1933. This year the NFL was divided into Eastern and Western divisions, the leaders of the divisions meeting in a playoff game to determine the league winner. Previously the league championship went to the team with the highest winning percentage.

1934

I. Civil Rights
Exploration and Settlement
Government
Statistics
Wars

Federal agencies continued to control many phases of American life, but there was no controlling the weather. Plagued by record cold snaps in February and searing heat in July, farmers watched their crops wither in the most destructive drought the Midwest had ever seen. Rising agricultural prices afforded temporary relief for them, but not for city dwellers. Internal affairs were complicated by congressional and local elections. Republican orators had only one real issue—the dubious constitutionality of some of the more radical New Deal provisions. According to opponents of the New Deal, federal boondoggles had reached outrageous proportions and were seriously crippling the nation's financial resources, as witnessed by 33 new government agencies, 24,303 new employees, and an increase in the national debt of nearly 20%. Few voters responded, for conditions were slowly improving; only 58 banks had failed in 1934—901 had been the annual average since 1921.

Mar 24: The **Tydings-McDuffie Act,** granting independence to the Philippines, was passed by Congress. The Philippine legislature approved it on May 1. Complete independence would not be proclaimed until July 4, 1946.

June 6: The **Securities Exchange Act** was signed by Pres. Roosevelt. It provided for creation of the Securities and Exchange Commission. It also provided for licensing stock exchanges and declared certain speculative practices illegal.

June 28: The **Federal Farm Bankruptcy Act,** also known as the Frazier-Lemke Act, was signed by Pres. Roosevelt. It established a moratorium on farm mortgage foreclosures.

June 28: The **National Housing Act** was passed by Congress. It established the Federal Housing Administration to help home owners finance repairs and enlargements and to spur private building through federal mortgages.

July 22: **John Dillinger,** public enemy number one, was shot in Chicago, Ill., by FBI agents.

Nov 6: In **congressional elections** the Democrats gained nine Senate seats for a 69–25 majority, with two seats held by minor parties. In the House the Democrats gained nine seats for a 310–117 majority, with five seats going to minor parties.

II. Architecture
Arts and Music
Popular Entertainment
Publishing
Theater

Although the Depression was far from over, an upbeat mood in America was evidenced by a revitalization in publishing. Government-sponsored art projects encouraged the talented and were responsible for some 15,000 works of art being produced. Holly-

wood introduced to America a new child star, Shirley Temple.

Among **books published** this year was *Tender Is the Night* by F. Scott Fitzgerald, a novel exploring the lives of Dick Diver, a psychiatrist, and his schizophrenic wife Nicole. Now considered a masterpiece, the novel was published at a time when Fitzgerald's prestige as a writer was slipping and his own life was beginning to disintegrate. Other books published this year included *Doctor Martino and Other Stories* by William Faulkner; *The Thin Man* by Dashiell Hammett; and *Goodbye, Mr. Chips* by James Hilton.

May 7: Pulitzer prizes were awarded for the following: fiction, *Lamb in His Bosom* by Caroline Miller; biography, *John Hay* by Tyler Bennett; history, *The People's Choice* by Herbert Agar; poetry, *Collected Verse* by Robert Hillyer; drama, *Men in White* by Sidney Kingsley.

III. Business and Industry
Education
Philosophy and Religion
Science

There was hope that the Depression was coming to an end. Unemployment had dropped by more than 4,000,000. Organized labor, which had claimed 58.3% of the national income in 1929, now earned 62.5%. Business failures dropped sharply. The purchasing power of industrial workers went up by 25%. The American Federation of Labor claimed 2,000,000 new members. The near-disastrous plight of the nation's schools was eased as capital outlay for education grew more generous. Scientists induced artificial radioactivity for the first time, extended the periodic table, tapped the sun's energy with two experimental solar motors, and predicted that man would soon harness atomic energy.

Jan 7: The Rev. Dr. William Ashley Sunday, better known as **Billy Sunday,** began an intensive two-week revival campaign in New York City at the Calvary Baptist Church. Dr. Sunday, 70, had not visited New York City for this purpose since 1917. At that time, he had evangelized for ten weeks in Washington Heights. People looked on Billy Sunday as the last of the old-fashioned revivalists.

May 23: What became known worldwide as **nylon** was first produced by Dr. Wallace H. Carothers, a research chemist in the Du Pont laboratories. Carothers succeeded in spinning a synthetic fiber that met exhaustive tests of durability. He called his invention polymer 66.

July 16: The **first general strike** in U.S. history took place in San Francisco, Calif., as an expression of support for the striking 12,000 members of the International Longshoremen's Association.

Oct 25: The **Nobel Prize in Physiology or Medicine** was awarded jointly to George R. Minot, William P. Murphy, and George H. Whipple for their discovery of liver therapy to combat anemia. They were the fourth, fifth, and sixth Americans to receive the Nobel Prize in this field.

Nov 15: The **Nobel Prize in Chemistry** was awarded to Harold Clayton Urey for his discovery in Dec. 1931 of deuterium, or heavy hydrogen, an isotope of hydrogen. Deuterium and its oxide, commonly known as heavy water, were used in fission experiments to slow neutrons so they would split atomic nuclei on impact, a major advance in atomic physics.

IV. Fashion
Folkways
Holidays
Social Issues and Crime
Sports

Although Prohibition had been repealed nationally, the dry forces stubbornly refused to concede defeat, renewing their campaign on the local level. However, they were powerless to stop the revival of the huge liquor industry. Distillers this year produced 35,000,000 barrels of beer and 42,000,000 gallons of hard liquor. For the sports fan, the two most imposing figures in the country were Dizzy and Daffy Dean, brothers who rolled up 45 victories between them in pitching the St. Louis Cardinals into a world championship and the first million-dollar World Series gate.

June 9: The **U.S. Open golf tournament** was won by Olin Dutra, beating Gene Sarazen by one stroke.

June 14: The **world heavyweight boxing championship** was won by Max Baer, who scored a technical knockout over Primo Carnera in the 11th round of a fight held before a crowd of 48,495 in New York City.

July 29: The **PGA golf tournament** was won by Paul Runyan.

Aug 19: The **U.S. Lawn Tennis Association singles championships** were won by Helen Hull Jacobs in the women's division and Frederick J. Perry of Great Britain in the men's division (Sept. 12).

Sep 17-25: The **America's Cup** was successfully defended by the U.S. yacht *Rainbow*, which defeated the British challenger *Endeavour* four races to two.

Oct 3-9: The 31st annual **World Series** was won by the St. Louis Cardinals (NL), defeating the Detroit Tigers (AL) four games to three.

Dec 9: The **NFL championship** was won by the New York Giants, defeating the Chicago Bears 30–13.

1935

I. Civil Rights
Exploration and Settlement
Government
Statistics
Wars

The economic gains registered in 1934 seemed to produce a heady effect on the nation this year. Labor and capital squared off for a no-holds-barred brawl. The New Deal suffered a stunning setback when the Supreme Court declared the National Industrial Recovery Act unconstitutional. This provided anti-administration forces with effective ammunition to use against the New Deal, accusing it of being un-American, Bolshevistic, communistic, and socialistic. Rebellions minor and major destroyed Democratic unity in Congress and made it difficult for Pres. Franklin D. Roosevelt to maintain control of his own supporters. In short, the nation was feuding.

Jan 29: U.S. membership in the **World Court** was killed when the Senate refused by a vote of 52–36 to ratify participation in the court. The vote fell seven short of achieving the necessary two-thirds majority.

May 6: The **Works Progress Administration** (WPA) was instituted under the authority of the Emergency Relief Appropriation Act, which passed on Apr. 8.

May 11: The **Rural Electrification Administration** was established by executive order to build power lines and finance electricity production in areas not served by private distributors.

May 27: The **National Industrial Recovery Act was declared unconstitutional** by the Supreme Court. The decision invalidated the National Recovery Administration (NRA) and implied that any government attempt to legislate prices, wages, working conditions, etc., would be unconstitutional. This followed from the Court's strict interpretation of interstate commerce.

Aug 14: The **Social Security Act** was signed by Pres. Roosevelt. It established a Social Security Board to supervise payment of old-age benefits, such payments to be determined by the amount of money earned by recipients before their 65th birthdays.

Sep 8: Huey Long was assassinated. A powerful demagogue in Louisiana and national politics, he was shot to death in the corridor of the state capitol in Baton Rouge, La., by Dr. Carl Austin Weiss, Jr.

II. Architecture
Arts and Music
Popular Entertainment
Publishing
Theater

Conflicting social forces at work were reflected in the new, so-called proletarian novel, which found a receptive audience, and in the establishment of a left-wing book club. The trend even extended to the most conservative of all arts, the theater. Clifford Odets electrified audiences with his glorification of the little man. Imaginative artists discovered American primitivism through a surprising interest in African art. The Federal Music Project sponsored thousands of free concerts and employed some 18,000 musicians. Film makers produced a raft of epics, such as *Mutiny on the Bounty* and *A Tale of Two Cities,* as well as one of the finest films of all time, *The Informer.* The death of Will Rogers in an airplane crash with Wiley Post on Aug. 16 near Point Barrow, Alaska, was widely mourned.

Among **books published** this year was *Of Time and the River* by Thomas Wolfe, the author's second novel about Eugene Gant. Here the young southerner comes in contact with the cosmopolitan world of New York City. Other books published this year included *Judgment Day* by James T. Farrell, the second novel of his trilogy about young Studs Lonigan; *The Last Puritan* by George Santayana, the philosopher's only novel; and *Tortilla Flat* by John Steinbeck, a novel lovingly recounting the lives of the *paisanos* of Monterey, Calif., and the first of Steinbeck's books to become a commercial success.

May 6: **Pulitzer prizes** were awarded for the following: fiction, *Now in November* by Josephine Winslow Johnson; drama, *The Old Maid* by Zoë Akins; history, *The Colonial Period of American History* by Charles McLean Andres; biography, *R. E. Lee* by Douglas S. Freeman; poetry, *Bright Ambush* by Audrey Wurdemann.

III. Business and Industry
Education
Philosophy and Religion
Science

Organized labor was furious over the Supreme Court's adverse decision on the NRA, and over management's attitude toward what labor considered to be workers' basic rights. However, labor found itself in the midst of a major civil war on the issue of craft unions vs. industrial unions. The chief opponents were John L. Lewis of the newly organized Committee for Industrial Organization and William Green, head of the American Federation of Labor. Crisis level was reached when Lewis resigned from the parent group and took his followers with him. Widespread unrest disturbed members of the Daughters of the American Revolution and the American Legion, who pressed state legislatures to pass laws requiring loyalty oaths for teachers. In all, 19 states put such measures on their books.

An epidemic of **infantile paralysis,** or poliomyelitis, sparked renewed interest in combatting the disease. The drive was led by Pres. Roosevelt, who had been stricken with the disease, also known as polio, in 1921.

June 10: **Alcoholics Anonymous** was organized in New York City.

Nov 9: The **Committee for Industrial Organization** was established by John L. Lewis from a dissenting faction within the American Federation of Labor. In 1938 its leaders were expelled from the older organization and reorganized their group as the Congress of Industrial Organizations.

IV. Fashion
Folkways
Holidays
Social Issues and Crime
Sports

Troubled times drew fresh blood into Prohibition ranks, and soon many counties were dry again. The highly charged emotional level of the people was reflected in an upsurge of lynchings in the South and intense interest in the trial of Bruno Richard Hauptmann, charged with the kidnaping and murder of the infant son of Charles and Anne Morrow Lindbergh.

May 4: The 61st annual **Kentucky Derby** was won by Omaha, with a time of 2:05. The jockey was Willis Saunders.

May 11: The 60th annual **Preakness Stakes** was won by Omaha, with a time of 1:58^2/5. The jockey was Willis Saunders.

May 24: The **first night baseball game** in the major leagues was played between the Cincinnati Reds (NL) and the Philadelphia Phillies (NL) before more than 20,000 fans at Crosley Field, Cincinnati, Ohio. The Reds beat the Phillies 2–1.

June 8: The 67th annual **Belmont Stakes** was won by Omaha, with a time of 2:30^3/5. The jockey was Willis Saunders. This was the third time that a horse had won the Triple Crown.

June 8: The **U.S. Open golf tournament** was won by Sam Parks, Jr.

June 13: The **world heavyweight boxing championship** was won by James J. Braddock over Max Baer on points in 15 rounds.

July 6: At the **Wimbledon** tennis championships the women's singles title was won by Helen Wills Moody. This was her seventh victory.

Sep 11: The **U.S. Lawn Tennis Association singles championships** were won by Helen Hull Jacobs, for the fourth consecutive time, in the women's division and Wilmer L. Allison in the men's division (Sept. 12).

Oct 2-7: The 32nd annual **World Series** was won by the Detroit Tigers (AL), defeating the Chicago Cubs (NL) four games to two.

Oct 23: The **PGA golf tournament** was won by Johnny Revolta.

Dec 15: The **NFL championship** was won by the Detroit Lions, defeating the New York Giants 26–7.

1936

I. Civil Rights
Exploration and Settlement
Government
Statistics
Wars

Despite criticism of New Deal policies by its opponents, the administration received a vote of confidence in the national elections. Pres. Franklin D. Roosevelt carried all but two states, in the largest presidential vote cast to date. Democratic ranks closed and party leaders hailed the advent of good times. However, bad times continued for farmers as another scorching drought created a vast dust bowl and sent thousands westward in search of fertile land. Critics of the New Deal stressed the fact that since its election in 1932 the Roosevelt government had swelled the national debt by $12,000,000,000. Countering these statistics was the fact that at the same time the national income had risen by $30,000,000,000. In international affairs, Germany reoccupied the Rhineland, which had been taken from it after World War I; Italy annexed Ethiopia, which it had invaded the year before, thus crippling

the League of Nations as an international peacekeeper; and civil war broke out in Spain.

Mar 2: The **Soil Conservation and Domestic Allotment Act** was signed by Pres. Roosevelt. It replaced the Agricultural Adjustment Act, which had been invalidated Jan. 6 by the U.S. Supreme Court. The new measure provided benefit payments to farmers who practiced soil conservation in a cooperative program to replace soil-depleting crops with soil-conserving crops.

June 9-12: The **Republican National Convention** nominated Gov. **Alfred M. Landon** of Kansas for the presidency and Col. Frank Knox of Illinois for the vice presidency. The Republicans were supported during their campaign by some conservative Democrats, among them Alfred E. Smith.

June 23-27: The **Democratic National Convention** renominated Pres. **Roosevelt** by acclamation for the presidency. It chose John Nance Garner for the vice presidency. In general the platform took its stand on the administration's record. The American Labor Party endorsed Roosevelt's candidacy.

Nov 3: Franklin D. Roosevelt was reelected president of the United States in a Democratic landslide that carried every state except Maine and Vermont. John Nance Garner was elected vice president. Congress became more than three-quarters Democratic in both houses. The electoral vote was Roosevelt, 523; Gov. Alfred M. Landon of Kansas, 8. The popular vote was Roosevelt, 27,751,612; Landon, 16,687,913; William Lemke, Union Party, 891,858; Norman Thomas, Socialist, 187,342; Earl Browder, Communist, 80,181; Dr. D. Leigh Colvin, Prohibition candidate, 37,609; John W. Aiken, Socialist Labor Party, 12,729. The campaign was bitter. About 80% of the press opposed Roosevelt. In congressional elections the Democrats gained seven Senate seats, for a 76–16 majority, with four seats going to minor parties. In the House their majority was 331–89, with 13 seats going to minor parties.

II. Architecture
Arts and Music
Popular Entertainment
Publishing
Theater

The theater enjoyed one of the most distinguished seasons in years and was heartened by the founding of the Federal Theater Project under the Works Progress Administration (WPA). As the Depression eased, more concerts meant more new works performed and more musicians employed. Over 5000 artists in

44 states were employed by the Federal Art Project of the WPA. They painted between 600 and 700 murals for government buildings and a great number of works in oil and watercolor. The demand so far outstripped the supply that some artists were turning out a finished work each week. Movies enjoyed their most prosperous year since the Depression, even though four out of five films were called financial failures by their producers. The industry turned out some 500 feature films. Technicolor had been developed, but few ventured to use the innovation.

Among **books published** this year was *Gone With the Wind* by Margaret Mitchell, a blockbuster novel of Georgia in the Civil War that won a Pulitzer Prize in 1937 and was the basis for the classic 1939 motion picture. The novel sold 1,000,000 copies in six months. Other books published this year included *A Further Range* by Robert Frost, which included the poem "Two Tramps in Mud Time"; and *The Big Money* by John Dos Passos, the third novel of his *U.S.A.* trilogy, which included *The 42nd Parallel* (1930) and *1919* (1932). The trilogy was collected in 1938.

May 4: Pulitzer prizes were awarded for the following: fiction, *Honey in the Horn* by Harold L. Davis; drama, *Idiot's Delight* by Robert E. Sherwood; history, *The Constitutional History of the U.S.* by Andrew C. McLaughlin; biography, *The Thought and Character of William James* by Ralph Barton Perry; poetry, *Strange Holiness* by Robert P. Tristram Coffin.

Nov 12: The **Nobel Prize for Literature** was awarded to Eugene O'Neill, the foremost American dramatist.

III. Business and Industry
Education
Philosophy and Religion
Science

The nation's commerce was much improved over the previous year. Farm prices were up, metals were up, and automobile production increased 20%. However, 8,000,000 still were unemployed. Labor warfare continued and unions discovered a new weapon in the sit-down strike. Education looked considerably brighter as fewer schools cried out for federal assistance. Teachers were granted slight increases in salaries; enrollment in lower grades dropped because of the falling birth rate; and 35,000 illiterates were taught to read and write by Civilian Conservation Corps instructors. Educators hailed widespread interest in adult classes.

The age of the **trailer** reached full swing. It was estimated that there were 160,000 trailers on the road. Observers on Jan. 1, 1937, counted an average of 25 trailers an hour crossing the state line into Florida. Some statisticians, like Roger Babson, predicted that soon half the population of the country would be living in trailers.

May 9: The first scheduled **transatlantic dirigible flight** was completed when the *Hindenburg* landed at Lakehurst, N.J. Built by the German Zeppelin Transport Company, the craft was 830 ft. long, 135 ft. in diameter, and propelled by four 1050 hp Daimler Benz Diesel engines. It had a range of 8000 mi.

Nov 12: The **Nobel Prize in Physics** was awarded jointly to Carl David Anderson of the California Institute of Technology for his discovery in 1932 of the positron, and to Victor Francis Hess of Austria for his discovery of cosmic radiation. The discoveries opened new areas of nuclear physics for scientists to explore. Anderson's research confirmed theories about the structure of matter.

IV. Fashion
Folkways
Holidays
Social Issues and Crime
Sports

More Americans attended athletic events this year than ever before. Football gate receipts were up 15% and there was a great increase in the popularity of basketball when it was included in the roster of Olympic Games for the first time.

Feb 5-16: At the **Winter Olympics** in Germany, the U.S. won two gold medals and placed fifth in the unofficial team scoring after Norway, Germany, Sweden, and Finland.

June 6: The **U.S. Open golf tournament** was won by Tony Manero, who shot a world's record 282 for a 72-hole title tournament.

July 4: At the **Wimbledon** tennis championships in England, the women's singles title was won by Helen Hull Jacobs.

Aug 5-16: At the **Summer Olympics** in Berlin, Germany, the U.S. won 20 gold medals and placed second in the unofficial team scoring behind Germany. The star of the games was the U.S. athlete Jesse Owens, who won four gold medals.

Sep 30-Oct 6: The 33rd annual **World Series** was won by the New York Yankees (AL), defeating the New York Giants (NL) four games to two.

Nov 22: The **PGA golf tournament** was won by Denny Shute.

Dec 13: The **NFL championship** was won by the Green Bay Packers, defeating the Boston Redskins 21 to 6.

1937

I. Civil Rights
Exploration and Settlement
Government
Statistics
Wars

The New Deal entered a period of transition in which its measures lost much of their emotional impact. As administration forces tried to press on, voices were increasingly raised against the program. Economic and political disputes rippled across the nation, aggravated to a degree by world events: civil war in Spain, German rearmament, and Japan's undeclared war on China. The worst of the Depression seemed over, but other dangers threatened.

Jan 20: Pres. **Franklin D. Roosevelt was inaugurated** for his second term. This was the first time the presidential inauguration was held on this date, as required by the Twentieth Amendment. Subsequent inauguration ceremonies have been held on this date, except in 1957 and 1985 when Jan. 20 fell on a Sunday and the ceremonies were conducted on Jan. 21.

Feb 5: In a move to alter composition of the **Supreme Court,** Pres. Franklin D. Roosevelt, after informing congressional leaders at a special Cabinet meeting in the morning, sent a message to Congress at noon recommending revision of statutes governing the federal judiciary. Although the recommendations were intended ostensibly to provide more efficient and younger judges in all federal courts, Roosevelt was charged with attempting to pack the Supreme Court, which in the past had invalidated important parts of the New Deal legislative program.

May 6: The dirigible *Hindenburg* was destroyed by fire as it approached its mooring mast at Lakehurst, N.J. It was thought that a spark caused while mooring set off the hydrogen contained within the giant airship. The *Hindenburg* burst into flames and fell to earth in a few horrifying seconds. The disaster marked the virtual end of lighter-than-air transport.

July 22: The **Supreme Court Bill,** by which Pres. Roosevelt sought to modify the federal judiciary, specifically the Supreme Court, was voted back into committee by Congress, effectively killing the bill. In the meantime, Justice Willis Van Devanter had resigned from the Supreme Court, allowing Pres. Roosevelt to appoint a liberal justice, Hugo L. Black,

on Aug. 12 and swing the Court's balance in favor of the New Deal.

Sep 2: The **National Housing Act,** also called the Wagner-Steagall Act, was signed by Pres. Roosevelt. It created the U.S. Housing Authority for the purpose of administering loans to small communities and states for rural and urban construction.

Dec 12: The U.S. gunboat *Panay* was sunk in Chinese waters by Japanese air force planes, killing two and sparking a crisis in U.S.-Japanese relations. On Dec. 14 the U.S. demanded an apology and reparations. The Japanese complied immediately but continued to wage war in China.

II. Architecture
Arts and Music
Popular Entertainment
Publishing
Theater

Uncertainty in the nation's economic and political situation carried over to its creative life, resulting in a general sense of apathy. Federal support of the arts served merely to keep its practitioners alive and working. Architects debated the merits of functional design and drew much of their inspiration from builders abroad.

Among **books published** this year was *The Late George Apley* by John P. Marquand, a novel told in the form of a memoir recounting the stagnation of Boston's aristocracy. The story traced the history of several generations and showed the impact of new immigration on the old, settled society of Boston. Also published this year was the novelette *Of Mice and Men* by John Steinbeck that became a perennial favorite. It was the basis for a successful play and motion picture.

May 3: **Pulitzer prizes** were awarded for the following: fiction, *Gone With the Wind* by Margaret Mitchell; biography, *Hamilton Fish* by Allan Nevins; history, *The Flowering of New England* by Van Wyck Brooks; poetry, *A Further Range* by Robert Frost; drama, *You Can't Take It with You* by Moss Hart and George S. Kaufman.

III. Business and Industry
Education
Philosophy and Religion
Science

Labor placed the administration in the awkward position of having to choose sides between warring factions. However, despite internal difficulties, significant successes were won by unions in their effort to organize companies and industries that never before had recognized them. In medicine, the National Cancer Institute was founded, and Dr. E. C. Rosenow of the Mayo Clinic announced progress in the search for a serum against infantile paralysis, or polio. Experiments were based on the recent discovery that polio was caused by a transformed streptococcus.

In a wave of **industrial unrest** during the winter of 1936–1937, more than 500,000 workers quit their jobs. Many engaged in illegal sit-down strikes.

Mar 29: A **minimum wage law for women** was upheld by the U.S. Supreme Court in the decision of *West Coast Hotel v. Parrish*. The judgment reversed two previous rulings.

Apr 12: The **National Labor Relations Act** of 1935 was upheld by the U.S. Supreme Court.

May 6: The **first coast-to-coast radio program** was conducted by Herbert Morrison, reporting the *Hindenburg* disaster.

May 12: In the **first worldwide radio broadcast** received in the U.S., listeners heard the coronation of King George VI of England.

May 27: The **Golden Gate Bridge** in San Francisco, Calif., was dedicated.

Aug: The first signs of a **new recession** became apparent in a selling wave on the stock markets. The retreat became sharper after Labor Day, and many stocks fell rapidly. On Oct. 19 the New York market was near demoralization, with total transactions of 7,290,000 shares—the largest since 1933.

Nov 11: The **Nobel Prize in Physics** was awarded jointly to Clinton Joseph Davisson of Bell Telephone Laboratories in New York City and Sir George Paget Thomson of Great Britain, for their independent "discovery of the interference phenomenon in crystals irradiated by electrons."

IV. Fashion
Folkways
Holidays
Social Issues and Crime
Sports

An event affecting the American people was the Spanish Civil War. While the U.S. government took no official position in the conflict, a considerable portion of the public offered highly emotional support to the Loyalist, antifascist side. American volunteers by the hundreds went to Spain, where they joined Loyalist armies.

May 8: The 63rd annual **Kentucky Derby** was won by War Admiral, with a time of 2:03 1/5. The jockey was Charles Kurtsinger.

May 15: The 62nd annual **Preakness Stakes** was won by War Admiral, with a time of 1:58 2/5. The jockey was Charles Kurtsinger.

May 30: The **PGA golf tournament** was won by Denny Shute.

June 5: The 69th annual **Belmont Stakes** was won by War Admiral, with a time of 2:28 3/5. The jockey was Charles Kurtsinger. War Admiral thus became the fourth horse to win the Triple Crown.

June 12: The **U.S. Open golf tournament** was won by Ralph Guldahl.

June 22: The **world heavyweight boxing championship** was won by Joe Louis, who knocked out James J. Braddock in the eighth round at Chicago.

July 2: At the **Wimbledon** tennis championship in England, the men's singles championship was won by J. Donald Budge.

July 7: The fifth annual **baseball All-Star Game** was won by the American League, which defeated the National League 8–3 and picked up its fourth victory in the event.

July 27: The **Davis Cup** tennis tournament was won by the U.S., defeating Great Britain four matches to one.

July 31-Aug 5: The **America's Cup** was successfully defended by the yacht *Ranger*, which won four straight races from the British challenger *Endeavour II*.

Oct 6-10: The 34th annual **World Series** was won by the New York Yankees (AL), defeating the New York Giants (NL) four games to one.

Dec 12: The **NFL championship** was won by the Washington Redskins, defeating the Chicago Bears 28 to 21.

1938

I. Civil Rights
Exploration and Settlement
Government
Statistics
Wars

A return of economic adversity led to increased government spending. This eased the situation a little, but led to further disillusionment with the New Deal. Congressional elections saw a sudden increase in the number of Republican winners. However, the center of government activity and concern was swinging toward foreign affairs. German occupation and annexation (Apr. 10) of Austria, and the crisis in September sparked by German demands on Czechoslovakia, culminating in the Munich Pact (Sept. 29), showed the democratic nations to be paralyzed in the face of German aggression. For the first time, isolationism vs. limited intervention became an active national issue. There was widespread nervousness about the possibility of war, but few believed it likely.

Feb 16: The second **Agricultural Adjustment Act** was signed by Pres. Roosevelt. It maintained the soil conservation program; provided acreage allotments, parity payments, marketing quotas, and commodity loans to farmers; and authorized crop insurance corporations and the "ever-normal granary" proposals of Sec. of Agriculture Henry A. Wallace.

May 26: The **House Committee to Investigate Un-American Activities** (HUAC) was formed. It was also known as the Dies Committee after its chairman, Rep. Martin Dies, Democrat of Texas.

June 25: The **Wage and Hours Act** was signed by Pres. Roosevelt. It raised the minimum wage for workers engaged in interstate commerce from 25 cents to 40 cents an hour. Hours were limited to 44 per week in the first year of the law's enaction, dropping to 40 after the third year. Congress declared that it possessed the power in this act to ban interstate shipment of products made by unlawful exploitation of child labor.

July 17: Douglas G. **"Wrong-way" Corrigan,** unable to obtain a flight exit permit to Europe, took off from New York and landed in Dublin, Ireland, claiming he had headed for California. Despite his illegal action, he became a national celebrity for a time.

Sep 26: Pres. Roosevelt sent **private memorandums** to Britain, France, Germany, and Czechoslovakia. He recommended arbitration of the Sudetenland crisis, brought on by German demands in the Sudetenland, then part of Czechoslovakia. This set the stage for the Munich Pact (Sept. 29), which in effect surrendered the Sudetenland to Germany along with all Czechoslovakian fortresses on the frontier with Germany. British Prime Minister Neville Chamberlain, key figure in negotiations with Adolf Hitler, returned to England and announced he had secured "peace in our time."

Nov 8: In **congressional elections** the Democrats lost seven Senate seats but kept a 69–23 majority, with four seats going to minor parties. In the House Democrats lost 70 seats, for a 261–164 majority, with four seats going to minor parties.

II. Architecture
Arts and Music
Popular Entertainment
Publishing
Theater

It was an active year for performing and creative arts, although little of distinction was produced. Authors rediscovered the past and flooded the market with historical novels. The organization of two world fairs, scheduled for the following year at New York City and San Francisco, sent architects to their drawing boards and artists to their easels. Commissions were made subject to competition, so the level of work done was somewhat more imaginative than it had recently been. Movie attendance dropped some 40%. The top money maker of the year was Walt Disney's *Snow White and the Seven Dwarfs,* which made Disney famous around the world and became a film classic.

Among **books published** this year was *Our Town,* a play by Thornton Wilder that was also produced and awarded a Pulitzer Prize in 1938. A thoughtful fantasy set on a bare stage, the play examined the lives and relationships of the residents of a small New England village. A central character was the "stage manager," who served as narrator. Other books published this year included *The King Was in His Counting House* by James Branch Cabell, a novel; *The Unvanquished* by William Faulkner; the *Selected Poems* of John Gould Fletcher; *The Fifth Column* by Ernest Hemingway, a play dealing with the Spanish Civil War whose title came to mean a body of agents working secretly within a country to overthrow it; *The Selected Poetry of Robinson Jeffers; The Prodigal Parents* by Sinclair Lewis; *Land of the Free,* poetry by Archibald MacLeish; *Black Is My Truelove's Hair* by Elizabeth Madox Roberts, a novel; and *Uncle Tom's Children* by Richard Wright, a collection of stories that heralded Wright's arrival as a writer.

Estimates showed that the ***Music Appreciation Hour,*** a program conducted by Walter Damrosch over a national radio network, was heard by 7,000,000 schoolchildren each week.

May 2: Pulitzer prizes were awarded for the following: fiction, *The Late George Apley* by John P. Marquand; biography, *Pedlar's Progress* by Odell Shepard and *Andrew Jackson* by Marquis James; history, *The Road to Reunion, 1865–1900* by Paul Herman Buck; poetry, *Cold Morning Sky* by Marya Zaturenska; drama, *Our Town* by Thornton Wilder.

Oct 30: Orson Welles staged his radio play *War of the Worlds,* based on the novel by H. G. Wells. The program caused widespread panic when listeners took as true the realistically performed news reports of an invasion from Mars. The experience demonstrated the power of the new medium to influence large numbers of people.

Nov 10: The **Nobel Prize for Literature** was awarded to Pearl S. Buck, author of the novel *The Good Earth.*

III. Business and Industry
Education
Philosophy and Religion
Science

Because of government support, business conditions at year's end were healthier than at the start. Labor forces won two rousing victories—passage of the maximum hour and minimum wage bill and a long-sought measure that prohibited child labor in interstate industries. Isolated sit-down strikes still plagued industry, but public opinion seemed to swing against these tactics, so unions stopped them entirely. Technological advances were steady: James Slayter and John H. Thomas of Newark, Ohio, perfected methods to manufacture fiberglass. In addition, scientists made further advances in atomic physics.

Patents were issued for **nylon,** the pioneer synthetic fabric. Commercial production began immediately. Du Pont manufactured toothbrushes with nylon bristles, the first nylon product to reach the market.

Howard Hughes won the International Harmon Trophy for his flight around the world in the record time of three days, 19 hrs., 14 min.

Mar: The stock market **recession** reached its lowest point. Most of the leading stocks had fallen 50 points or more since the preceding August. The Federal Reserve Board's Adjusted Index of Industrial Production fell to 76.

May 27: The continuing **recession** prompted passage of the Revenue Bill of 1938 by Congress, on grounds that tax concessions were needed to stimulate business. The bill reduced taxes on corporations and was supported by Republican and Democratic opponents of the New Deal.

June 23: Civilian air transportation in the U.S. came under federal control with passage of the Civil Aeronautics Act, which established the Civil Aeronautics Authority as an independent agency of the federal government. The agency regulated the licensing of civil pilots, use of airways, introduction of new equipment, and rules of flight.

Nov: An early **radar** system, developed by the U.S. Army Signal Corps in 1936 and demonstrated before

the secretary of war in 1937, was subjected to exhaustive tests by the Coast Artillery.

Nov 14-18: The **Congress of Industrial Organizations** (CIO) was established by the delegates to the annual convention of the Committee for Industrial Organization, held at Pittsburgh, Pa. John L. Lewis was unanimously elected president.

Dec 13: The number of Americans receiving **federal relief** had dropped to 2,122,960, compared with 3,184,000 the previous year, according to a report issued by the Works Progress Administration.

IV. Fashion
Folkways
Holidays
Social Issues and Crime
Sports

It was a good year for sports. The number of active golfers was up, winter sports showed phenomenal growth in popularity, and both football and baseball were thriving. In football some 1,100,000 fans flocked to see professional games in 1938. Major league baseball drew about 10,000,000 to the stadiums in a year when many longtime records were broken. The New York Yankees (AL) became the first team to win the World Series three times running (in 1939, the first to win the series four times in a row). Yankee star Lou Gehrig set eight new major league records, including most consecutive games (2122), most consecutive years with 150 or more games (12), and most home runs with bases filled (23).

The number of **automobile-related deaths** for the year was put at more than 32,000 by the National Safety Council. About one-third of the fatalities involved pedestrians. Almost 9000 deaths resulted from collisions between motor vehicles.

June 11: The **U.S. Open golf tournament** was won by Ralph Guldahl.

July 1: At the **Wimbledon** tennis championships in England, the men's singles title was won by J. Donald Budge. The next day Helen Wills Moody won the women's singles.

July 16: The **PGA golf tournament** was won by Paul Runyan.

Sep 5: In the **Davis Cup** international tennis matches, the U.S. defeated Australia three matches to two in the challenge round.

Oct 5-9: The 35th annual **World Series** was won by the New York Yankees (AL), defeating the Chicago Cubs (NL) in four straight games.

Nov 2: The projected **visit of the king and queen of England** to Canada and the U.S. prompted a letter from Pres. Roosevelt to King George VI. In the letter

Roosevelt expressed his pleasure at the forthcoming visit, made suggestions for possible routes and schedules, and added some advice about what the American people would expect of their royal guests. He cautioned the king that the "essential democracy" of the royal couple would be the thing most likely to appeal to Americans. In particular, he urged the homely touch of a visit with the Roosevelts at Hyde Park, N.Y. He outlined stopovers in Washington, D.C., New York City, and Chicago, as well as at Hyde Park, but he did not think that it would be wise for the king and queen to drive through the "narrow, crowded" streets of New York City or Chicago.

Dec 11: The **NFL championship** was won by the New York Giants, defeating the Green Bay Packers 23 to 17.

1939

I. Civil Rights
Exploration and Settlement
Government
Statistics
Wars

Prosperity seemed just around the corner. Unfortunately, this was largely due to the tremendous volume of orders for military supplies that flooded the nation's factories. The administration could now concentrate for the first time on the problems engendered by approaching war in Europe. Germany completed the dismemberment of Czechoslovakia, and Adolf Hitler turned his attention to Poland. The signing in August of a nonaggression pact between Russia and Germany cleared the path to war between Germany and the other European powers. The principal question for the U.S. was how it would be able to stay out of the conflict.

June 8: King George VI and Queen Elizabeth of Great Britain arrived in Washington, D.C., on their visit to the U.S. (June 7–12). They were the first British sovereigns to visit the U.S.

Sep 1: Germany invaded Poland without declaration of war. On Aug. 24 Pres. Roosevelt had cabled Germany, Poland, and Italy, urging arbitration, conciliation, or negotiation to avoid war.

Sep 3: Great Britain and France declared war on Germany. On the same day Belgium declared its neutrality and Pres. Roosevelt, in a fireside chat, declared the U.S. to be neutral.

Sep 3: Thirty Americans died when the British passenger ship *Athenia* was sunk by a submarine. The following day, Sec. of State Cordell Hull advised U.S. citizens to travel to Europe only under "imperative necessity."

Oct 18: All **U.S. ports and waters were closed** to belligerent submarines by presidential order.

Nov 4: The **Neutrality Act of 1939** was passed by Congress. It repealed the prohibition of arms exports in the Neutrality Act of 1937 and authorized the "cash and carry" sale of arms to belligerent powers.

II. Architecture
Arts and Music
Popular Entertainment
Publishing
Theater

U.S. novelists were taking a long, fond look back on America's past. Historical novels had never been so plentiful. The theater mourned the passing of the Federal Theater Project but rejoiced in a sudden rebirth of interest in the legitimate stage. A shortage of New York City playhouses was felt for the first time in many years. Painters seemed to be exploring two areas: depiction of the regional American scene, which stressed people in relation to their land or locale; and the use of art as a vehicle for political statement or social satire. Film producers faced the bleak prospect of the loss of a lucrative European market. Nonetheless, this was the year of *Gone with the Wind*, one of the most expensive and most successful motion pictures of all time.

Among **books published** this year was *The Grapes of Wrath* by John Steinbeck, a powerful novel dealing with an Oklahoma farm family who lose their farm to the bank and are forced to travel to California to seek work as migrant laborers. Described as a proletarian novel, the book examined in moving detail the plight of the Okies, and by extension the plight of all people caught up in tragic circumstances not of their own making. The novel won a Pulitzer Prize in 1940 and was the basis for an outstanding motion picture. Also published this year were *Adventure of a Young Man* by John Dos Passos, the first novel of a trilogy entitled *District of Columbia*; *The Wild Palms* by William Faulkner, a novel; *Captain Horatio Hornblower* by C. S. Forester; *Collected Poems* by Robert Frost; *Pale Horse, Pale Rider* by Katherine Anne Porter, stories; *Abraham Lincoln: The War Years* (four volumes) by Carl Sandburg; and *Collected Poems* by Mark Van Doren.

May 1: Pulitzer prizes were awarded for the following: fiction, *The Yearling* by Marjorie Kinnan Rawlings; biography, *Benjamin Franklin* by Carl Van Doren; history, *A History of American Magazines* by Frank Luther Mott; poetry, *Selected Poems* by John Gould Fletcher; drama, *Abe Lincoln in Illinois* by Robert E. Sherwood.

III. Business and Industry
Education
Philosophy and Religion
Science

Business underwent a gradual decline from 1938 levels, followed by gradual recovery and then a spectacular upsurge in the fall, attributable to the outbreak of war in Europe. The biggest event of the year, however, received scant press attention. Scientists announced that they had succeeded in splitting uranium, thorium, and protactinium atoms by bombarding them with neutrons.

Discovery of the **Rh factor** in human blood by Dr. Philip Levine and Dr. Rufus Stetson of New York led to a clearer understanding of pregnancy and blood transfusion complications. The Rh factor is a component of red blood cells. Those with the factor are classified as Rh+, and those lacking it are Rh−. Transfusion of one type of blood into a person with the other type can cause a serious immune reaction. In pregnancies, women with Rh− blood bearing Rh+ fetuses can develop an immune reaction to the baby's blood, leading to difficulties in subsequent pregnancies.

Frequency modulation, a new method of radio transmission and reception, was developed by Edwin H. Armstrong. Armstrong had devised the regenerative receiver during World War I. The latter type of radio became the standard for amplitude modulation, or AM, broadcast applications. However, AM broadcasting was susceptible to static, and in the 1930s and 1940s Armstrong worked to perfect FM transmission and reception, which was not affected by static emissions. He received virtually no support from public opinion, the radio industry, or the FCC. On Jan. 31, 1954, Armstrong, suffering from poor health, plagued by lawsuits, and lacking financial resources, committed suicide.

May 10: The **Methodist Church was reunited** after 109 years of division. The conflict within the church had been marked by two major crises. In 1830 the Methodist Protestant Church had separated from the Methodist Episcopal Church over the question of episcopal authority and had established a separate branch in which lay members were given a voice in church government. The Methodist Episcopal Church, South, had separated from the Methodist

Episcopal Church in 1844, ostensibly over an administrative dispute, but probably over the slavery question. A Declaration of Union issued on this date unified some 8,000,000 American Methodists.

June 28: The first regular **transatlantic passenger air service** began when *Dixie Clipper*, a Pan American Airways airliner, left Port Washington, Long Island, with 22 passengers aboard. The flight reached Lisbon, Portugal, 23 hrs., 52 min. later.

Nov 9: The **Nobel Prize in Physics** was awarded to Ernest Orlando Lawrence of the University of California for his development of the cyclotron and for subsequent discoveries in the field of radioactivity, specifically the study of artificially radioactive elements. Lawrence's invention of the cyclotron provided nuclear scientists with an invaluable instrument with which to produce the subatomic particles required for study of nuclear reactions.

IV. Fashion
Folkways
Holidays
Social Issues and Crime
Sports

World fairs in New York City and San Francisco opened, and millions flocked to the expositions to glimpse wonders of the future. Observers noted the unreality of the enthusiasm, in face of the impending war in Europe. However, Americans paid little notice to the prophets of doom, instead lining up to take "death-defying" rides on the roller coaster and the parachute jump.

The **latest fashions** were advertised in the Sears Roebuck catalog, which offered dresses "inspired by Schiapparelli." In the following year, Sears would announce that "the traditional lapse between the acceptance of new fashions . . . in metropolitan centers and on farms apparently no longer exists."

Mar 27: The **NCAA basketball championship** was won by the University of Oregon, which defeated Ohio State 46–33.

June 12: The **U.S. Open golf tournament** was won by Byron Nelson.

July 7-8: At the **Wimbledon** tennis championships in England, Robert L. Riggs won the men's singles title and Alice Marble won the women's singles. Riggs and Elwood T. Cooke took the men's doubles, Marble and Sarah Palfrey Fabyan the women's doubles.

July 17: The **PGA golf tournament** was won by Henry Picard.

Oct 4-8: The 36th annual **World Series** was won by the New York Yankees (AL), sweeping the Cincinnati Reds (NL) in four games.

Dec 10: The **NFL championship** was won by the Green Bay Packers, defeating the New York Giants 27 to 0.

1940

I. Civil Rights
Exploration and Settlement
Government
Statistics
Wars

With the outbreak of war in Europe in Sept. 1939, the key political question facing the U.S. became how to stay out of the conflict and still help the forces of democracy. Realizing that America was facing a crisis, Pres. Franklin D. Roosevelt decided to run for an unprecedented third term. His rival was a political newcomer, Wendell L. Willkie, whose plainspoken manner made him a powerful contender. Roosevelt won, largely because people felt it was better not to change administrations in dangerous times. This year Germany would invade Norway, overrun Denmark, Luxembourg, Belgium, and the Netherlands, and defeat France. In August Adolf Hitler launched the Battle of Britain, a brutal air assault intended to destroy the Royal Air Force and enable invasion of England.

The **U.S. population** was 131,669,275, according to Census Bureau figures. The center of population was two miles southeast by east of Carlisle, Sullivan County, Ind.

June 24-28: The **Republican National Convention** nominated Wendell L. Willkie of Indiana for the presidency and Charles L. McNary of Oregon for the vice presidency.

June 28: The **Alien Registration Act,** also known as the Smith Act, was passed by Congress. It was signed into law on the next day by Pres. Roosevelt. It required registration and fingerprinting of aliens and made it unlawful to belong to any organization advocating overthrow of the U.S. government. Subsequent registration showed approximately 5,000,000 aliens living in the U.S.

July 15-19: The **Democratic National Convention** nominated Franklin D. Roosevelt for the presidency on the first ballot. Henry A. Wallace of Iowa was nominated for the vice presidency.

Sep 3: The **U.S. gave 50 outdated destroyers** to Great Britain in exchange for 99-year leases on naval and air bases in Newfoundland and the West Indies.

Sep 16: The **Selective Service Act** was passed by Congress. The law, the first U.S. peacetime draft, provided for 900,000 selectees to be taken each year. All men between the ages of 20 and 36 were required to register. Length of military service was one year, but this was extended to 18 months in Aug. 1941.

Nov 5: Franklin D. Roosevelt was reelected president of the United States. Henry A. Wallace was elected vice president. The electoral vote was Roosevelt, 449, Wendell L. Willkie, Republican of Indiana, 82. The popular vote was Roosevelt, 27,244,160; Willkie, 22,305,198; Norman Thomas, Socialist candidate, 100,264; Roger W. Babson, Prohibition candidate, 57,812; Earl Browder, Communist, 48,579; John W. Aiken, Socialist Labor candidate, 14,861. In congressional elections the Democrats lost three Senate seats but kept a 66–28 majority, with two seats going to minor parties. In the House the Democrats gained seven seats for a 268–162 lead, with five seats going to minor parties.

II. Architecture
Arts and Music
Popular Entertainment
Publishing
Theater

Book production was up, with 11,328 titles published, and war novels led in popularity. The New York stage labored through an uninspired season, relying principally on foreign imports. On Broadway, the biggest musical hits of the season were *Du Barry Was a Lady* by Cole Porter and *Louisiana Purchase* by Irving Berlin. Musicologists noted a trend away from ultramodernism—the 12-tone system, for instance—which had intrigued composers. The art world showed the influence of European refugee painters, who were forced by war into American exile. Their work centered on the individual rather than on aesthetics. This tendency was seen in architecture as well, where outstanding work was done on buildings designed for shelter, care of the sick, social services, and recreation.

Among **books published** this year was *Native Son* by Richard Wright, a powerful novel considered by many to be Wright's masterpiece. It told the story of Bigger Thomas, a young black drawn into crime and ultimately to execution as a murderer. The novel was adapted for Broadway by Wright and Paul Green in 1941 and had a successful run. Other books published this year included *The Hamlet* by William Faulkner, the first novel of a trilogy about the Snopes family; *For Whom the Bell Tolls* by Ernest Hemingway, set in Spain during that country's civil war; and *You Can't*

Go Home Again by Thomas Wolfe, who had died in 1938. Critics found this novel of Wolfe's quieter and better organized than his earlier works.

May 6: Pulitzer prizes were awarded for the following: fiction, *The Grapes of Wrath* by John Steinbeck; biography, *Woodrow Wilson, Life and Letters, Vols. VII and VIII* by Ray Stannard Baker; history, *Abraham Lincoln: The War Years* by Carl Sandburg; poetry, *Collected Poems* by Mark Van Doren; drama, *The Time of Your Life* by William Saroyan.

III. Business and Industry
Education
Philosophy and Religion
Science

Unemployment dropped dramatically because of the military conscription of many industrial workers as well as increased orders, resulting in increased hiring. Labor suffered setbacks in its right to organize and in efforts for better hours and wages. By and large, this was expected and accepted, as the labor force agreed that sacrifice was necessary to maintain America's pledge to support its allies. The next step toward development of the atomic bomb was taken when scientists determined that a chain reaction was possible and would soon become a reality.

The **first antibiotic** developed in the U.S., actinomycin, was produced by Dr. Selman Waksman of Rutgers University, a pioneer in antibiotics. However, it was found too poisonous for humans.

The average **life expectancy** was 64 years. This represented a major increase from 49 years in 1900.

Illiteracy in the U.S. reached a new low of 4.2% of the population, a decline of 0.1% from 1930, and a 15.8% drop from 1870.

Radios could be found in 30,000,000 homes, according to a survey.

Apr 20: An **electron microscope** was first publicly tested at the Radio Corporation of America laboratory in Camden, N.J. The instrument, about 10 ft. high and weighing 700 lbs., magnified by as much as 100,000 diameters. It had been developed by Dr. Ladislaus Marton and coworkers under the supervision of Dr. Vladimir Kasma Zworykin.

May 15: The first successful **helicopter flight** in the U.S. was completed by the VS-300, an experimental helicopter manufactured by the Vought-Sikorsky Corporation.

Oct 24: The **40-hour work week,** part of the Fair Labor Standards Act of 1938, went into effect.

Nov 7: A **suspension bridge collapse** over the Narrows at Tacoma, Wash., was caused by wind vibration. The bridge tumbled 190 feet into Puget Sound.

IV. Fashion
Folkways
Holidays
Social Issues and Crime
Sports

The coming of war to Europe threatened a complete halt in international sports competition. The 1940 Olympic Games were not held, and Olympic competition would not resume until 1948. Also suspended were the Davis Cup and Wimbledon tennis championships. Joe Louis did, however, defend the world heavyweight boxing championship in two bouts (Feb. 9 and June 20) against Arturo Godoy of Chile. In baseball the New York Yankees ended up in third place in the American League, losing a chance to become the first team to win five consecutive World Series.

Cornelius Warmerdam became the first person to pole-vault 15 ft. Two years later he set a new record when he vaulted 15 ft. 7¾ in. He retired from competition in 1943 after having vaulted 15 ft. or more 43 times.

Mar 30: The **NCAA basketball championship** was won by Indiana University, defeating the University of Kansas 60–42.

June 9: The **U.S. Open golf tournament** was won by W. Lawson Little.

Sep 2: The **PGA golf tournament** was won by Byron Nelson.

Oct 2-8: The 37th annual **World Series** was won by the Cincinnati Reds (NL), defeating the Detroit Tigers (AL) four games to three.

Dec 8: The **NFL championship** was won by the Chicago Bears, who defeated the Washington Redskins by the incredible score of 73 to 0.

1941

I. Civil Rights
Exploration and Settlement
Government
Statistics
Wars

Two events overshadowed all others this year. On June 22 Germany invaded the U.S.S.R. After several weeks of spectacular German success it seemed that Russia would fall before year's end. On December 7 Japanese forces launched a surprise attack on the

U.S. base at Pearl Harbor, Hawaii. Almost instantly the American nation attained a unity it had not known since the dark days of 1933. No longer were Americans to debate the fact that the U.S. was a neutral power and yet had spent $13,000,000,000 on lend-lease appropriations—all of it for war materiel earmarked for use against Germany and Italy—and had created some 35 separate agencies and offices that in effect were war bureaus. The U.S. was in the war at last.

Jan 20: Pres. **Franklin D. Roosevelt was inaugurated** for an unprecedented third term. Henry A. Wallace was inaugurated vice president.

Feb 3: The **Federal Wage and Hour Law** was upheld unanimously by the U.S. Supreme Court. The law prohibited employment of children under 16 in mining and manufacturing and children under 18 in any dangerous occupation. The main provision of the law, however, was its regulation of minimum wages and maximum hours for industries engaged in interstate commerce.

Mar 11: The **Lend-Lease Bill** was signed by Pres. Franklin D. Roosevelt. It furnished a system by which the U.S. could lend goods and munitions to democratic countries in return for services and goods.

July 25: An **embargo** on shipments of scrap iron and gasoline to Japan was ordered by Pres. Roosevelt. The order also froze Japanese assets in the U.S.

Aug 9-12: The **Atlantic Charter** was formulated by Pres. Roosevelt and Prime Minister Winston Churchill at a secret meeting off Newfoundland. It contained eight articles of agreement and defined the aims of the two governments during and after the war.

Aug 18: A **Selective Service Act Extension** was signed by Pres. Roosevelt. It extended the period of military service to not more than 30 months in time of peace and removed the 900,000-man limit on selectees.

Oct 17: The U.S. destroyer *Kearny* was torpedoed and damaged by a German submarine off the coast of Iceland.

Oct 30: The U.S. destroyer *Reuben James* was torpedoed and sunk off the coast of Iceland by a German submarine during the night of Oct. 30–31. Some 100 lives were lost. It was the first American warship to be sunk in the war.

Dec 7: The **Japanese attacked Pearl Harbor,** Hawaii. The American battleships *Arizona, California, Oklahoma,* and *Utah* (an old target battleship) were sunk; the battleship *West Virginia* settled in shallow water and the *Nevada* ran aground. Damaged battleships were the *Pennsylvania, Maryland,* and *Tennessee.* Destroyers *Cassin, Downes,* and *Shaw,* and the minelayer *Oglala,* were sunk or badly damaged. In all, about 19 ships were sunk or damaged. About 3000 Americans lost their lives. The Japanese lost 28 planes and three midget submarines. Japanese forces also attacked Guam, Wake Island, the Philippines, and other strategic points in the Pacific at the same time Pearl Harbor was attacked.

Dec 8: A **declaration of war** against Japan was passed by Congress. The sole dissenting vote was cast by Rep. Jeannette Rankin, Republican of Montana. She had also cast the sole dissenting vote against entering World War I.

Dec 10: The **Japanese invaded** Luzon in the Philippines, where Gen. Douglas MacArthur commanded the defending U.S. and Philippine forces.

Dec 11: Germany and Italy declared war against the U.S., and Congress adopted a resolution recognizing a state of war.

Dec 22: Wake Island fell to the Japanese after a heroic 15-day stand by 400 U.S. Marines.

II. Architecture
Arts and Music
Popular Entertainment
Publishing
Theater

Of all the art forms, theater alone seemed concerned with the fact that the U.S. was at war. A number of propaganda plays were written by new as well as established writers. Unfortunately, many playwrights looked on the stage as a soapbox, and quality suffered. There were, however, the surprising flowering of a truly American painting style and a new musical awareness. New York City was no longer the sole arbiter of these arts; symphonic societies, ballet companies, opera houses, and museums mushroomed across the nation, sometimes presenting works of uncertain quality but always of unflagging enthusiasm despite wartime conditions.

Among **books published** this year was *Berlin Diary* by William L. Shirer, a study of Adolf Hitler and Nazi Germany that became a best seller. Other books published this year included *Random Harvest* by James Hilton; *H. M. Pulham, Esq.,* a novel by John P. Marquand; *The White Cliffs of Dover* by Alice Duer Miller, a book of verse celebrating the British people in wartime; and *My Friend Flicka* by Mary O'Hara, the story of a boy in Wyoming and his horse Flicka.

Mar 8: Sherwood Anderson, the writer, died at 64 of peritonitis in Cristobal, Canal Zone. He had achieved fame in 1919 with the publication of *Winesburg, Ohio,* a critically and popularly acclaimed collection of short stories.

May 5: Pulitzer prizes were awarded for the following: biography, *Jonathan Edwards* by Ola Elizabeth Winslow; history, *The Atlantic Migration, 1607–1860* by Marcus Lee Hansen; poetry, *Sunderland Capture* by Leonard Bacon; drama, *There Shall Be No Night* by Robert E. Sherwood.

III. Business and Industry
Education
Philosophy and Religion
Science

The nation's industry tooled up for full-scale war production. Realizing that wartime is usually a time of inflation, the government prepared to curb prices and limit consumption. Numerous bureaus were established to develop and direct America's vast economic potential. For the most part, the civilian population took controls in their stride, convinced that they were part of the price of winning the war. Anticipating a wage freeze, labor attempted to win boosts before it was too late. There were some 4000 strikes this year, twice as many as in 1940. Scientists turned their attention to increasing the U.S. arsenal of weapons. Federal educators prepared to meet the shortage of adequately trained personnel.

British pioneers in **penicillin** development, Sir Howard Florey and Dr. N. G. Heatley, flew to the U.S. to argue the necessity of large-scale production of the life-saving substance. American drug companies responded to their appeal, and penicillin in time became a household word.

Jan 3: A **shipbuilding program** of 200 merchant vessels was called for by the federal government.

Apr 11: The **Ford Motor Company** signed its first contract with a labor union. It settled a strike that began Apr. 2, when the CIO called out 85,000 workers at Ford's River Rouge plant. Ford closed the plant after rioting had injured 150.

Apr 11: The **Office of Price Administration and Civilian Supply** (OPACS, but better known as OPA) was established with limited powers to recommend price control measures. Its first head was Leon Henderson.

Apr 16: A **steel price freeze** at the levels of the first quarter of the year was announced by the OPA in its first official act. Industry cooperated.

Apr 17: A **cut in auto production** of 20% beginning Aug. 1 was agreed to by the auto industry.

May 1: U.S. Defense Savings Bonds and Stamps went on sale.

July 24: A **no-strike agreement** for the duration of the national emergency was signed by AFL building trade unions and the OPM.

Aug 3: A **gasoline curfew** was begun at midnight in 17 eastern states. The curfew closed filling stations from 7 P.M. to 7 A.M.

Dec 27: Rubber rationing was announced by the OPA. The measure decreased civilian consumption by 80%. Tire rationing was the first rationing regulation.

IV. Fashion
Folkways
Holidays
Social Issues and Crime
Sports

Remember Pearl Harbor became the war cry of the man in the street, who used it more as a grim reminder than as an outburst of patriotism. Women's fashions, reflecting the general restraint, kept to subdued colors and inconspicuous lines. Prior to the Pearl Harbor attack, the greatest fashion furor of the year came when an embargo on Japanese silk was announced. It caused a panic in the hosiery business and sent thousands into shops to snatch up every available silk stocking. In golf the top money winner was Ben Hogan, with $18,358. In boxing, Joe Louis defended the world heavyweight title five times. When war came Louis entered the military, and title competition was suspended. This year Americans mourned the death of Lou Gehrig, longtime first baseman for the New York Yankees (AL), who died in New York on June 2 at age 37.

Jan 6: The term *Four Freedoms* was introduced by Pres. Franklin D. Roosevelt in his annual speech before Congress. These freedoms, which he envisaged as the cornerstone of a new world, were freedom of speech and expression, freedom of worship, freedom from fear, and freedom from want.

Mar 29: The **NCAA basketball championship** was won by Wisconsin, which defeated Washington State 39–34.

May 3: The 67th annual **Kentucky Derby** was won by Whirlaway, with a time of 2:01²/₅, a new Derby record. The jockey was Eddie Arcaro, who had won the event in 1938.

May 10: The 66th annual **Preakness Stakes** was won by Whirlaway, with a time of 1:58⁴/₅. The jockey was Eddie Arcaro.

May 20: Pres. Roosevelt announced **Thanksgiving** would be moved forward again, to the last Thursday of November, after a two-year experiment during which the holiday was celebrated on the next-to-last Thursday in November. Roosevelt had originally moved the holiday to stimulate business activity.

June 7: The **U.S. Open golf tournament** was won by Craig Wood. This was the last time the U.S. Open would be played until 1946.

June 7: The 73rd annual **Belmont Stakes** was won by Whirlaway, with a time of 2:31. The jockey was Eddie Arcaro. Whirlaway thus became the fifth horse to win racing's Triple Crown.

July 13: The **PGA golf tournament** was won by Vic Ghezzi.

July 17: Yankee center fielder **Joe DiMaggio's hitting streak** was ended by pitchers Al Smith and Jim Bagby, Jr., of the Cleveland Indians. DiMaggio had hit safely in 56 consecutive games, from May 15 through July 16, a major league record.

Sep 23: A six-ton **monument marking a time capsule** from the New York World's Fair of 1939–1940 was unveiled in Flushing Meadow, Queens, N.Y., the site of the fair. The capsule contained artifacts and information about twentieth-century culture and was to be opened in the year 6939.

Oct 1-6: The 38th annual **World Series** was won by the New York Yankees (AL), defeating the Brooklyn Dodgers (NL) four games to one.

Dec 7: The wartime phrase *praise the Lord and pass the ammunition* was uttered by Howell M. Forgy, chaplain on the U.S. cruiser *New Orleans*, under attack at Pearl Harbor, Hawaii. While sweating sailors kept up a continuing antiaircraft barrage, he kept their spirits up with this phrase.

Dec 21: The **NFL championship** was won by the Chicago Bears, who defeated the New York Giants 37 to 9.

1942

I. Civil Rights
Exploration and Settlement
Government
Statistics
Wars

American military pride was subjected to rude shocks early this year as U.S. forces were forced from island after island in the Pacific. The chief defeat was the fall of the Bataan peninsula on Luzon in the Philippines, followed a month later by the fall of the island fortress of Corregidor in Manila Bay. Only days later, in early May, American fortunes changed when a U.S. fleet defeated the Japanese in the Battle of the Coral Sea, and again in June when U.S. torpedo bombers routed a second enemy naval task force in the Battle of Midway. At home, thousands of civilians over draft age flocked to Washington, D.C., to man the offices created to handle the mammoth war program.

Jan 2: In the Philippines, **Manila fell** to the Japanese, forcing U.S. and Philippine forces under Gen. Douglas MacArthur to withdraw to the Bataan peninsula.

Feb 10: The French liner *Normandie* burned and capsized at its pier in New York harbor. The world's fastest liner, it was being fitted out for service as a military transport when the fire broke out. The cause of the fire was never discovered, but sabotage was ruled out.

Feb 27-Mar 1: The **Battle of the Java Sea** was a major U.S. naval defeat. The Japanese inflicted heavy losses on the U.S. fleet commanded by Adm. Thomas C. Hart.

Mar 17: Gen. **MacArthur left Bataan** by presidential order when defense of the peninsula became hopeless. He withdrew to Australia and soon was named commander in chief of the Southwest Pacific Command.

Apr 9: **Bataan fell** to the Japanese after a heroic defense by a greatly outnumbered force. Gen. Jonathan M. Wainwright, with about 3500 soldiers and nurses, withdrew to Corregidor.

Apr 10: The **Bataan Death March** began at dawn. American and Philippine prisoners taken at Bataan were forced to march 85 miles in six days with but one meal of rice during the period. By the end of the march, which was punctuated with atrocities, more than 5200 Americans and many more Filipinos had lost their lives.

Apr 18: An **air raid on Tokyo** was conducted by carrier-launched bombers under command of Maj. Gen. James H. Doolittle. This was the first American offensive blow in the Pacific and did much to boost American morale. It also caused consternation in Japan.

May 4-8: In the **Battle of the Coral Sea,** U.S. naval air forces inflicted heavy losses on the Japanese fleet. This battle was the first ever fought in which neither fleet came within sight of the other. All the fighting was carried on by planes. The U.S. lost the carrier *Lexington*, the destroyer *Sims*, and a tanker. Seven Japanese warships, including one carrier, were sunk.

May 6: **Corregidor fell** to the Japanese. Gen. Wainwright surrendered the fortress to Japanese troops under Gen. Tomoyuki Yamashita.

June 4-6: In the **Battle of Midway** the U.S. gained an important victory over the Japanese. Americans repulsed an attempt to seize the island, sinking 17

Japanese ships, including four aircraft carriers. Japan lost 275 planes and 4800 men. The U.S. lost over 300 men and two ships.

June 28: The **first U.S. ground assault** on the Japanese in the South Pacific was executed when a contingent of commandos assaulted Salamaua, New Guinea, at night.

Aug 7: U.S. Marines landed on **Guadalcanal,** in the Solomon Islands, opening the first major U.S. amphibious operation in the Pacific. The struggle to force the Japanese off the island involved some of the bloodiest fighting of the war. The fighting continued until Feb. 1943.

Aug 18: Carlson's Raiders, a special guerrilla unit led by Lt. Col. Evans Fordyce Carlson, landed on Makin Island, at the northern end of the Gilbert Islands, with orders to destroy the radio station on the island. In 40 hours every Japanese member of a force of 350 was killed, 1000 gallons of gasoline were set aflame, and the island was rendered militarily useless.

Sep 15: The U.S. carrier *Wasp* was sunk off Guadalcanal.

Nov 3: In **congressional elections** the Democrats lost eight Senate seats but kept a majority of 58–37, with one seat held by a minor party. In the House they lost 50 seats but held a 218–208 majority, with four seats going to minor parties.

Nov 7: In **North Africa,** U.S. forces began landing with support of British naval and air units. Lt. Gen. Dwight Eisenhower commanded the 50 vessels and 400,000 troops employed in the operations.

Nov 12-15: In a **naval engagement off Guadalcanal,** the U.S. scored a major victory, inflicting heavy losses on a Japanese task force and preventing Japanese reinforcements from reaching the island.

II. Architecture
Arts and Music
Popular Entertainment
Publishing
Theater

Far from destroying the performing arts, World War II gave them an impetus they had not enjoyed for years. Producers scrambled for available playhouses, selling tickets at high prices and counting their profits. Entertainment-hungry civilians and servicemen were given escapist fare, in most cases unclad ladies of the chorus dancing to a loud pit orchestra. Hundreds of serious artists and musicians were absorbed into the armed forces. Architects responded to the demand for fast, prefabricated housing. This year Americans also mourned the loss of some artistic

greats: John Barrymore, youngest member of the celebrated family of actors, May 29, at 60; Carole Lombard, actress and wife of Clark Gable, in a plane crash while returning home from a War Bond drive, Jan. 16, at 32; and Grant Wood, known best for *American Gothic* (1930), his portrait of a dour farm couple, Feb. 12, at 50.

Among **books published** this year was *The Moon Is Down* by John Steinbeck, a novel about the military occupation of a small town and the effect of that occupation on both conqueror and conquered. The book was published simultaneously with its dramatization on the New York City stage, an experiment that proved successful. Other books published this year included *The Just and the Unjust* by James Gould Cozzens, a novel about American lawyers; *The Robe* by Lloyd C. Douglas; *Go Down, Moses* by William Faulkner, a collection of stories that included Faulkner's novelette "The Bear"; and *See Here, Private Hargrove* by Marion Hargrove, an immensely popular chronicle of the soldier's life.

May 4: Pulitzer prizes were awarded for the following: fiction, *In This Our Life* by Ellen Glasgow; biography, *Crusader in Crinoline* by Forrest Wilson; history, *Reveille in Washington* by Margaret Leech; poetry, *The Dust Which Is God* by William Rose Benét.

III. Business and Industry
Education
Philosophy and Religion
Science

Anti-inflation measures, such as rent ceilings and wage and price freezes, were put into effect as the nation settled down to the grim business of war. The AFL and CIO voluntarily agreed not to strike for the duration of the war and to submit all labor disputes to a federal mediation board. The War Manpower Commission held virtually dictatorial power over all essential workers and was empowered, if the emergency warranted, to mobilize every adult in the country. Hard hit were colleges and universities, whose enrollments dropped off sharply. Adult education classes, however, increased in number and helped keep the schoolrooms at least partially filled.

Henry J. Kaiser, the industrialist, headed the Liberty Ship program, which incorporated techniques of prefabrication and mass production to speed ship production. By June of this year his four West Coast shipyards had been assigned one-third of the U.S. shipbuilding program. His yard in Vancouver built and launched a 10,500-ton liberty ship in a record four days.

Jan 30: The **Price Control Bill** was signed by Pres. Franklin D. Roosevelt, officially giving the Office of Price Administration the power to set all prices except those for farm products.

Feb 9: War time became effective throughout the nation. Clocks were set ahead one hour, as in daylight savings time, and were kept one hour ahead of standard time throughout the year.

Mar 17: A **no-strike agreement** was announced by William Green of the AFL and Philip Murray of the CIO.

Apr 28: Rents were stabilized by the OPA. The ruling affected 86,000,000 people housed in 301 areas.

May 5: Sugar rationing began.

May 15: Gasoline rationing began in 17 eastern states. The limit set was three gallons a week for nonessential driving. On July 22 a coupon system of rationing was initiated.

June 13: The **Office of War Information** was established by Pres. Roosevelt to control dissemination of official news and propaganda. Elmer Davis, the newspaperman and radio commentator, was named as OWI head.

June 22: The **first V-mail** was sent overseas, from New York City to London. V-mail involved the transfer of letters written on prescribed forms to microfilm, which was sent overseas. There the letters were printed on photographic paper and delivered.

Oct 1: The first American **jet airplane,** the XP-59, was tested at Muroc Army Base, Calif., by Robert Stanley, chief pilot for Bell Aircraft Corporation.

Nov 29: Coffee rationing began.

Dec 1: Nationwide **gasoline rationing** went into effect.

Dec 2: The first sustained **nuclear reaction** was demonstrated in Chicago, Ill., before scientists at the University of Chicago, in a project known as the Argonne Project.

IV. Fashion
    Folkways
    Holidays
    Social Issues and Crime
    Sports

American society underwent enormous changes. Millions of young men went off to combat, women took up new posts in war industries and military support units, and rationing was introduced to control consumption and preserve resources for war production. In contrast to these changes, trends in fashion continued to emphasize simplicity and economy of design. Crime rates across the nation jumped; officials claimed that youths were having one last fling

before entering the Army. In golf the top money winner again was Ben Hogan with $13,143.

Jan 9: The world **heavyweight boxing championship** was successfully defended, for the 20th time, by Joe Louis, who knocked out Buddy Baer in the first round.

Mar 28: The **NCAA basketball championship** was won by Stanford, which defeated Dartmouth 53–38.

May 31: The **PGA golf tournament** was won by Sam Snead.

Sep 30-Oct5: The 39th annual **World Series** was won by the St. Louis Cardinals (NL), defeating the New York Yankees (AL) four games to one.

Dec 13: The **NFL championship** was won by the Washington Redskins, who defeated the Chicago Bears 14 to 6.

Dec 21: Nevada divorces were ruled valid in all states by the U.S. Supreme Court.

1943

I. Civil Rights
    Exploration and Settlement
    Government
    Statistics
    Wars

An uncertain year dawned for U.S. military forces. The nation was engaged in a seesaw battle in North Africa and an agonizing struggle in the Pacific. U.S. forces advanced against the Japanese in New Guinea, the Solomons, and the Gilbert Islands, and new names were added to the American battle lexicon—Bougainville, Lae, Tarawa. In the European theater, American troops in North Africa swept across the Mediterranean to Sicily, then to the Italian mainland itself. To the north U.S. bombers wrought destruction in Europe and helped blast Nazi invasion ports in France.

A **polio epidemic** struck the U.S., killing 1151 and crippling thousands more.

Jan 14: The **Casablanca conference** opened in Morocco. It was attended by Pres. Franklin D. Roosevelt and other Allied officials. The Allies planned their military strategy for 1943 and agreed to demand unconditional surrender from the Axis nations.

Feb 20: At the **Kasserine Pass,** Tunisia, U.S. forces were driven back by Gen. Irwin Rommel's Afrika

Korps using the 62-ton Mark VI tank. On Feb. 25 U.S. forces recaptured the pass.

Mar 2-4: In the **Battle of the Bismarck Sea,** a major U.S. victory in the Pacific, an entire Japanese convoy of 22 ships was sunk by American bombers. More than 50 Japanese planes were shot down.

May 7: Bizerte, Tunisia, was captured by American troops. The British took Tunis.

May 12: The **North African campaign** ended. Gen. Jurgen von Arnim, commander of Axis forces after Rommel's recall to Europe, was captured in the Cape Bon peninsula along with other Axis officers.

May 30: Attu in the Aleutian Islands was retaken by U.S. forces after intense fighting.

July 10: Sicily was invaded by Allied forces, including Gen. George S. Patton's Seventh Army, British Field Marshal Bernard Law Montgomery's Eighth Army, and French and Canadian troops.

July 19: Rome was bombed by some 500 Allied planes. The highly strategic city, containing a network of railroads and freight yards, had been spared for four years by the Allies because of its religious significance.

Aug 11-24: The **Quebec conference** was held in Canada to work out the Pacific campaign. Some Chinese representatives were present during the conference. There was some difficulty in arriving at an accord with the Russians over future European operations and postwar problems. Pres. Roosevelt and British Prime Minister Winston Churchill met privately on Aug. 17.

Aug 15: Kiska in the Aleutians was retaken by American and Canadian units. When the troops landed, the Japanese were gone.

Aug 17: Sicily was conquered by Allied forces 37 days after it was invaded. The Axis powers had lost 167,000 men in the campaign, the Allies 25,000.

Aug 28: New Georgia in the Solomon Islands was secured by U.S. forces.

Sep 3: Invasion of Italy was commenced by Allied forces crossing the Strait of Messina.

Sep 8: Italy surrendered unconditionally to the Allied powers. German troops there fought on.

Sep 9: The **Allies landed at Salerno,** Italy. Upward of 700 American, British, Dutch, French, and Polish ships took part in the operation. The U.S. Fifth Army, under command of Gen. Mark Clark, participated in the landing.

Oct 13: Italy declared war on Germany. The new Italian government was headed by Pietro Badoglio. Mussolini, who had been placed under arrest, had been rescued (Sept. 12) by German commandos led by Col.

Otto Skorzeny. Mussolini formed a new fascist government in northern Italy.

Oct 19: The **Moscow conference** opened. Representatives of Great Britain, the U.S., the U.S.S.R., and the Chinese agreed to collaborate on surrender terms for the enemy. The powers recognized the need for an international organization to prevent future wars.

Nov 1: U.S. forces landed on **Bougainville** Island in the Solomons.

Nov 2: A U.S. **air raid on Rabaul,** New Britain, proved a major defeat for the Japanese. Gen. Douglas MacArthur, suspecting an attack would be launched from Rabaul on Empress Augusta Bay, off the west coast of Bougainville, had ordered the mission. Nearly every ship in Rabaul's harbor was hit or sunk, about 94,000 tons of shipping.

Nov 20: U.S. forces landed on **Tarawa and Makin** in the Gilbert Islands. On Nov. 22 landings were made on Abemama. Occupation of the Gilbert Islands was completed on Nov. 23.

Nov 22: At a **conference in Cairo,** Egypt, Pres. Roosevelt, Prime Minster Churchill, and Generalissimo Chiang Kai-shek planned military strategy against Japan and declared that Japan, when defeated, would be stripped of all Pacific territories seized since 1914.

Nov 28-Dec 1: At the **Teheran conference** in Iran, Pres. Roosevelt, Prime Minister Churchill, and Premier Joseph Stalin met to map strategy for the coming Allied invasion of western Europe.

Dec 17: A bill repealing the **Chinese Exclusion Acts** and setting an annual immigration quota of 105 Chinese was signed by Pres. Roosevelt. On the next day, in Chicago, Edward Bing Kan filed an application for citizenship. On Jan. 18, 1944, he became the first Chinese to be naturalized under the new law.

Dec 24: Gen. **Dwight D. Eisenhower** was named Supreme Commander of Allied forces for the invasion of Europe.

II. Architecture
Arts and Music
Popular Entertainment
Publishing
Theater

Roy Harris, Aaron Copland, and William Schuman all produced fresh, inventive works for the concert stage this year. Led by such painters as Thomas Hart Benton, American regionalism was rediscovered once again. Some artists painted with almost exotic lushness, others with defiant realism. Refugee artists, including Piet Mondrian, Marc Chagall, Fernand Léger, and Yves Tanguy, flourished in the U.S., producing such striking works as Chagall's *The Juggler* and Mondrian's *Broadway Boogie-Woogie.* In theater, Richard Rodgers and Oscar Hammerstein, II, elevated the musical comedy with their remarkable production of *Oklahoma!* The year was good for the motion picture industry as well. Top box office attractions were Betty Grable, Bob Hope, Abbott and Costello, Bing Crosby, and Gary Cooper. Notables who died included Lorenz Hart, the lyricist who collaborated with Richard Rodgers, Nov. 22, at 47; and Sergei Rachmaninoff, the Russian-born composer who had made his home in the U.S. after World War I, Mar. 28, at 70.

Among **books published** this year was *A Tree Grows in Brooklyn* by Betty Smith, a novel about a young girl and her family living in a Brooklyn slum. Also published this year were *The Human Comedy* by William Saroyan; *Thirty Seconds Over Tokyo* by Capt. Ted W. Lawson; *Here Is Your War* by Ernie Pyle; *God Is My Co-Pilot* by Col. Robert L. Scott, Jr.; *Guadalcanal Diary* by Richard Tregaskis; and *One World* by Wendell Willkie, an optimistic work that sold more than a million copies within two months of publication.

May 3: **Pulitzer prizes** were awarded for the following: fiction, *Dragon's Teeth* by Upton Sinclair; biography, *Admiral of the Ocean Sea* by Samuel Eliot Morison; history, *Paul Revere and the World He Lived In* by Esther Forbes; poetry, *A Witness Tree* by Robert Frost; drama, *The Skin of Our Teeth* by Thornton Wilder. *Secular Cantata No. 2, A Free Song* by William Schuman won the first Pulitzer prize for a musical composition.

May 5: A **postal-zone numbering system** was inaugurated in 178 cities. Postmaster General Frank C. Walker expected the use of numbers to speed up mail deliveries.

III. Business and Industry
Education
Philosophy and Religion
Science

The CIO and AFL generally kept to their no-strike pledges, making this a quiet year on the labor front. The United Mine Workers, however, stood in defiance of the War Labor Board, claiming that working conditions and wages were unacceptable. A 48-hour minimum work week was proclaimed by Pres. Roosevelt for all essential war industries in labor-scarce areas. Colleges and universities were promised relief in a plan to send thousands of men to school to be trained as officers for the Army and Navy. In October the Swedish government announced that for the fourth year Nobel Prizes would not be awarded. However, in 1944 retroactive prizes were awarded for 1943. George Washington Carver, the scientist and educator known best for his studies on uses of the peanut, died on Jan. 5, at age 78.

Large-scale production of **penicillin** in the U.S. was made possible by the discovery of a mold on a cantaloupe in a fruit market in Peoria, Ill. This mold was found to yield ten times as much penicillin as the original mold obtained by Sir Alexander Fleming of England.

In **salvage drives** this year, 255,513 tons of tin cans, 43,919 tons of fat, 6,000,000 tons of wastepaper, and more than 26,000,000 tons of iron and steel scrap were collected for use in essential industries.

Jan 18: The **American Medical Association** (AMA) was found by the U.S. Supreme Court to have violated antitrust laws by preventing activities of cooperative health groups. The action had been initiated on Dec. 20, 1938.

Feb 7: Shoe rationing began, limiting civilians to three pairs a year.

Feb 9: A **minimum 48-hour work week** in war plants was ordered by Pres. Franklin D. Roosevelt.

Mar 1: Rationing of canned goods began.

Mar 29: Rationing of meat, fat, and cheese began.

Apr 17: Essential workers were frozen, that is, prohibited from leaving their jobs, by order of the War Manpower Commission. The order affected some 27,000,000 workers.

May 22: Radar detection devices, according to an article in *Collier's* magazine, were being used by Allied and Axis armed services. The U.S. War and Navy departments disputed the British claim to have discovered the principle of radar.

June 14: In a challenge of the **compulsory flag salute** brought by Jehovah's Witnesses, the Supreme Court ruled that under the Bill of Rights, schoolchildren could not be compelled to salute the flag if the ceremony conflicted with their religion.

June 20: Race riots hit Detroit, Mich. The influx of some 300,000 whites and blacks to war plants in the area contributed to the outbreak of violence. In two days, 35 people were killed, and more than 500, mostly blacks, were wounded. Police arrested 300 whites. Race riots also broke out this summer in Mobile (May 25), Los Angeles (June 4), Beaumont, Tex. (June 19), and Harlem, New York City (Aug. 1).

IV. Fashion
Folkways
Holidays
Social Issues and Crime
Sports

Conversation everywhere concerned war news; emergence of a new form of music called jive, a danceable form of jazz; and a steady stream of baseball players drafted into the military. Their departure made for a duller game, but the fans remained loyal. This year Judge Kenesaw Mountain Landis, baseball's first commissioner, was elected to the Baseball Hall of Fame. As in several years past, the standard male garb of America's hepcats was the zoot suit. It consisted of a long, one-button jacket for men, with broad, padded shoulders and peaked lapels, high-waisted trousers that ballooned at the knees and gripped the ankles, a wide silk tie worn against a colored or striped shirt, a knee-length key chain, and a broad-brimmed hat. Jitterbug was the most popular dance of the year, and variations on its basic routine, called the Lindy hop, proliferated. In a nine-page article, *Life* magazine hailed the Lindy hop as "the true national folk dance of America."

Women's fashions were emancipated from the Paris tradition when American designers produced clothing of fabrics available despite wartime shortages. Two silhouettes were featured: a slim, straight, clinging line, caught at the waist by a belt; and a more bulky figure created by wool box coats and suits.

A new **pitching record** for the twentieth century was set by the New York Giants relief pitcher Ace Adams, who pitched in 70 games, only one of them a complete game for him.

Mar 30: The **NCAA basketball championship** was won by the University of Wyoming, which defeated Georgetown 56 to 43.

May 1: The 69th annual **Kentucky Derby** was won by Count Fleet, with a time of 2:04. The jockey was Johnny Longden.

May 8: The 68th annual **Preakness Stakes** was won by Count Fleet, with a time of 1:57²/₅. The jockey was Johnny Longden.

June 5: The 75th annual **Belmont Stakes** was won by Count Fleet, with a time of 2:28¹/₅. The jockey was Johnny Longden. Count Fleet thus became the sixth horse to win racing's Triple Crown.

Oct 5-11: The 40th annual **World Series** was won by the New York Yankees (AL), defeating the St. Louis Cardinals (NL) four games to one.

Dec 26: The **NFL championship** was won by the Chicago Bears, who defeated the Washington Redskins 41 to 21.

1944

I. Civil Rights
Exploration and Settlement
Government
Statistics
Wars

In the European theater Russian forces made spectacular but costly progress against the Germans. In May Italy fell and on June 6 Allied forces landed in Normandy. In August American armored units began to move rapidly across France. By year's end Allied forces were poised on Germany's eastern and western borders, preparing for the final assault. Similar successes in the Pacific theater led many to hope for victory within the year despite repeated warnings by responsible leaders that the Axis war potential was still formidable. In mid-June the Germans introduced a new weapon, the V-1 pilotless bomb; they launched it against London and other British cities. In September they followed it with the V-2, a supersonic rocket causing great destruction.

Jan 22: Allied troops landed at **Anzio,** Italy, in a move to outflank the German defensive positions on the Gustav line across central Italy. British and American troops were unable to advance and the German line held.

Feb 2: Roi Island in the Marshall Islands was taken by the Fourth Marine Division and positions were secured on Namur and Kwajalein. For the first time Allied troops set foot on prewar Japanese territory.

Mar 6: Berlin was bombed by 800 U.S. Flying Fortresses. Some 2000 tons of bombs were dropped on the German capital.

Apr 22: Netherlands New Guinea was invaded by U.S. forces.

May 18: Cassino, the key point on the Germans' Gustav line in Italy, was evacuated after two months of bitter resistance.

June 4: Allied forces entered Rome on this day, Trinity Sunday. Out of respect for the religious holiday, the American Fifth and British Eighth armies did not occupy the city until the next morning.

June 6: The **Normandy invasion** began on this date, designated D-Day. Code named Operation Overlord, the invasion included landings on five beachheads in Normandy, France. The operation, under command of Gen. Dwight D. Eisenhower, involved more than 4000 ships, some 3000 planes, and Allied troops eventually numbering more than 4,000,000.

June 16: Bombing of Japan began with a raid on the island of Kyushu by U.S. Superfortresses.

June 26-28: The **Republican National Convention nominated Thomas E. Dewey,** governor of New York, for the presidency and Gov. John W. Bricker of Ohio for the vice presidency.

July 6: A **circus tent fire** at an afternoon performance in Hartford, Conn., destroyed the main tent of Ringling Brothers and Barnum & Bailey Circus. The blazing canvas fell on fleeing spectators. In the scramble 167 persons were killed and more than 175 were injured.

July 10: Saipan fell to U.S. forces after 25 days of hard fighting. Upward of 25,000 Japanese soldiers were killed. Some 2359 Americans died and more than 11,000 were wounded.

July 18: St. Lô, a key position in the German line in Normandy, fell to the U.S. First Army.

July 19-21: The **Democratic National Convention nominated Pres. Roosevelt** for his fourth term. Sen. Harry S Truman of Missouri was nominated for the vice presidency.

July 25: A **breakout at St. Lô** by the U.S. First Army under Gen. Omar Bradley led to collapse of the German line in northwestern France.

Aug 8: Brittany fell to the rapid Allied advance south from Normandy. U.S. forces launched a powerful drive eastward toward Paris.

Aug 9: Guam fell to U.S. forces after 20 days of bloody fighting. The conquest cost the Americans 1214 dead and nearly 6000 wounded. Some 17,000 Japanese were killed and almost 500 prisoners were taken.

Aug 15: Southern France was invaded by the U.S. Seventh Army under Lt. Gen. Alexander M. Patch.

Aug 21: The **Dumbarton Oaks conference** opened at Washington, D.C. It was attended by delegates from the U.S., Great Britain, China, and the U.S.S.R. The conference agreed on "proposals for establishment of a general international organization," laying the groundwork for establishment of the United Nations.

Aug 25: Paris was liberated. The German commander Gen. Dietrich von Choltitz surrendered to French Gen. Jacques-Philippe Leclerc.

Sep 12: In the **first American engagement on German soil,** the U.S. First Army pushed five miles into west central Germany. For the first time the Allies fought where the local population was hostile.

Sep 17-27: An unsuccessful **airborne invasion of Holland,** code named Operation Market-Garden, was staged by combined British and American forces. Airborne units were dropped behind German lines to seize five bridges across the Rhine R., including the key bridge at Arnhem. The units met unexpected resistance and suffered heavy casualties. Relief forces were unable to link up with airborne troops, who were forced to evacuate.

Oct 20: Americans landed at **Leyte,** Philippine Islands, fulfilling Gen. Douglas MacArthur's promise to return. It was during the Leyte campaign that the kamikaze, or suicide plane, was first used.

Oct 23-26: In the **Battle of Leyte Gulf** the Japanese fleet, which had been unable to halt U.S. invasion of the Philippines, suffered heavy losses. It was the largest naval battle of the war.

Nov 7: Franklin D. Roosevelt was reelected president of the United States, the only person ever to win a fourth term. Harry S Truman was elected vice president. The electoral vote was Roosevelt, 432; Gov. Thomas E. Dewey, Republican, 99. The popular vote was Roosevelt, 25,602,504, Dewey 22,006,285. In congressional elections the Democrats lost two Senate seats but held a 56–38 majority. In the House they gained 24 seats for a 242–190 lead, with two seats held by minor parties.

Dec 15: The new rank **general of the Army** was conferred by Congress on Henry "Hap" Arnold, Dwight D. Eisenhower, Douglas MacArthur, and George C. Marshall. Popularly known as five-star generals, the new appointees wore insignia of rank consisting of five stars joined in a circle.

Dec 16: The **Battle of the Bulge,** last major German offensive of the war, began as German forces broke through Allied defenses in the Ardennes. Led by Gen. Karl von Runstedt, the drive was intended to seize Antwerp and split the Allies in the west. Bad weather hampered Allied air and supply operations. U.S. forces at Bastogne, a strategic point, were surrounded but did not surrender. American resistance stiffened after the massacre of American prisoners at Malmédy (Dec. 17). On Dec. 23 Allied air operations resumed when bad weather lifted. German armored columns halted for lack of fuel and were destroyed. By Dec. 27 a U.S. relief column reached Bastogne. By mid-January 1945 all ground taken in the offensive had been recaptured.

II. Architecture
Arts and Music
Popular Entertainment
Publishing
Theater

The arts enjoyed a boom year. Paper shortages forced publishers to experiment with soft-cover books, and the success of the experiment was overwhelming. Painters who had not been drafted profited when a plentiful supply of money created new buyers who could not shop in the European market. Broadway producers found eager audiences for practically everything they presented. The sellers' market did not improve the quality of the offerings. Architects were still learning a new trade—that of the efficiency builder, since the criterion for a contract was speed of construction. All their new ideas were confined to paper to await the end of the war. The movies enjoyed their greatest year in box office history, grossing close to $2,000,000,000 as the European market began to open in liberated areas. Such established stars as Bing Crosby and Gary Cooper took advantage of the tax laws by producing their own films. Top box office draws were Crosby, Cooper, Bob Hope, Betty Grable, and Spencer Tracy. The nation mourned the deaths of Charles Dana Gibson, the artist and illustrator who created the Gibson Girl, Dec. 23, at age 77; and Maj. Glenn Miller, director of the U.S. Air Force Band and, before the war, one of the most talented musicians and big band leaders. Miller was reported missing on a flight from Paris to London on Dec. 24.

Among **books published** this year was *Forever Amber* by Kathleen Winsor, a historical novel laced with sex. Set in England during the Restoration, the novel sold more than 1,000,000 copies in a year. Other books published this year included *Yankee from Olympus* by Catherine Drinker Bowen, a biography of Justice Oliver Wendell Holmes; *The World of Washington Irving* by Van Wyck Brooks; *A Bell for Adano*, a novel by John Hersey; *The Major Phase* by F. O. Matthiessen; *Brave Men* by Ernie Pyle; *Strange Fruit* by Lillian Smith, a novel whose central characters, a black woman and a white man, were torn between their love for each other and the strictures of southern society; and *Immortal Wife* by Irving Stone, a fictionalized biography of Jessie Frémont.

May 1: Pulitzer prizes were awarded for the following: fiction, *Journey in the Dark* by Martin Flavin; history, *The Growth of American Thought* by Merle Curti; biography, *The American Leonardo: The Life of Samuel F. B. Morse* by Carlton Mabee; poetry, *Western Star* by Stephen Vincent Benét. A special award was given to *Oklahoma!* by Richard Rodgers and Oscar Hammerstein, II.

Oct 1: The **Declaration of Independence** and other historic documents sent away from Washington, D.C., for safekeeping in Dec. 1941 were put on display again at the Library of Congress.

Nov 11: An agreement on **record royalties** ended a two-year battle between recording companies and the American Federation of Musicians. Two major recording companies signed a contract agreeing to pay the union a fee on each record manufactured.

III. Business and Industry
Education
Philosophy and Religion
Science

Industry had done such a remarkable job in producing war materiel that the government was able to relax many of its priority regulations. Manufacturers took advantage of the move by looking forward to a consumer economy. Labor controls remained in full effect, however, as did the many curbs against inflation. Despite these checks, living costs rose by nearly one-third, engendering unrest in union ranks. Institutions of higher education mourned the virtual end of the ASTP (Army Specialized Training Program). Some 110,000 of the 145,000 young men who had been enrolled in the nation's colleges were removed and sent to active service. Notables who died this year included Aimee Semple McPherson, the Canadian-born evangelist, fundamentalist preacher, and faith healer, Sept. 27, at age 54.

Penicillin, medical wonder of the year, was shown to be effective against wounds and a wide variety of infectious diseases. Further uses were also found for the sulfa drugs. In one of the more important medical feats of the war, the armed forces used the insecticide DDT to control and wipe out typhus, transmitted by body lice among troops and civilians.

In **salvage drives** this year, nearly 7,000,000 tons of wastepaper, 84,807 tons of fat, 18,500,000 tons of iron and steel scrap, 185,676 tons of tin cans, and 544,739 tons of rags were collected.

Apr 26: The **Montgomery Ward plant was seized** by the Army. Troops entered the Chicago plant after company chairman Sewell Avery refused to extend the firm's contract with the CIO as ordered by the WLB. Labor trouble continued, and on Dec. 28 troops again seized the plant and other company properties.

May 3: Meat rationing was ended, except for steak and choice cuts of beef, by order of the OPA.

May 8: The **first eye bank** was established by New York Hospital, New York City, in conjunction with 19 other New York hospitals. The eye bank was used to store human corneas, which could be used to restore sight in certain kinds of blindness.

May 20: The **Communist Party voted to disband** at a convention held in New York City. Its leaders formed a non-party group, the Communist Political Association.

Aug 14: Production of consumer goods such as vacuum cleaners, electric ranges, and cooking utensils was resumed under order of the WPB. The order was provisional and could be revoked depending on war needs.

Oct 26: The **Nobel Prize in Physiology or Medicine** was awarded to Joseph Erlanger of the Washington University Medical School in St. Louis and to Herbert Spencer Glasser of the Rockefeller Institute in New York for their research on the functions of single nerve fibers and their discovery that various types of nerve fibers conducted impulses at various speeds. At the same time the Nobel Prize in Physiology or Medicine for 1943 was awarded jointly to Edward A. Doisy of the St. Louis University School of Medicine and to Henrik Dam, the Danish biochemist. Dam was credited with discovering vitamin K, and Doisy with isolating vitamin K from alfalfa and determining its chemical nature.

Nov 10: The **Nobel Prize in Physics** was awarded to I. I. Rabi of Columbia University for his studies of the magnetic properties of atomic nuclei. At the same time the Nobel Prize in physics for 1943 was awarded to Otto Stern of Carnegie Institute of Technology in Pittsburgh, Pa. A German born physicist who came to America in 1933, Stern was honored for his contributions to the development of the molecular beam method for studying the magnetic attributes of atomic nuclei, and for his discovery of the magnetic movement of the proton.

IV. Fashion
   Folkways
   Holidays
   Social Issues and Crime
   Sports

Fashions swung toward bare midriffs, slim skirts, and large hats. Victories in both military theaters raised civilian morale and led to hopes the war would soon end. In boxing, a dispute over the lightweight championship arose in March when Bob Montgomery outpointed Beau Jack in 15 rounds at Madison Square Garden in New York City. Five days later his title, recognized by the New York State Athletic Commission, came into dispute when Juan Zurita defeated Sammy Angott in Hollywood and the National Boxing Association recognized Zurita as the lightweight champion. In golf the top money winner was Byron Nelson, with $37,967. Notables who died this year included Kenesaw Mountain Landis, commissioner of organized baseball for nearly 24 years, Nov. 25, at age 78.

Cartoonists **Bill Mauldin and George Baker** gave armed services newspapers their most popular features. In "Up Front with Mauldin," a pair of long-suffering GIs, Willie and Joe, endured combat stoically ("Just gimme th' aspirin. I already got a Purple Heart"). Baker created the "Sad Sack," an unlucky, confused, unkempt but well-meaning GI forever in trouble. In postwar years, Baker's "Sad Sack" became a regular feature of comic sections, and Mauldin took naturally to political cartooning.

Mar 28: The **NCAA basketball championship** was won by Utah, which defeated Dartmouth 42 to 40.

May 1: Ninety-year-old **Jacob S. Coxey,** standing on the steps of the Capitol in Washington, D.C., delivered the speech he was prevented from making 50 years before when he led Coxey's Army, a body of unemployed workers demanding a program of federal work projects.

Aug 20: The **PGA golf tournament** was won by Robert Hamilton, a relatively unknown pro from Indiana who beat Byron Nelson by one stroke in an upset victory.

Oct 4-9: The 41st **World Series** was won by the St. Louis Cardinals (NL), defeating the St. Louis Browns (AL) four games to two.

Dec 17: The **NFL championship** was won by the Green Bay Packers, who defeated the New York Giants 14 to 7.

1945

I. Civil Rights
   Exploration and Settlement
   Government
   Statistics
   Wars

It was a monumental year—the end of an era and the beginning of a new one. Germany and Japan were forced to accept unconditional surrender. Atomic bombs were dropped on two Japanese cities—a fact that changed the complexion of future wars and of the world in general. A new instrument of peace—the United Nations—was launched at San Francisco. The presidency of the United States changed hands as Franklin D. Roosevelt died in office. Another notable who died this year was Gen. George S. Patton, of injuries sustained in an auto accident on Dec. 9. Patton died in Heidelberg, Germany, Dec. 21, at age 60.

Jan 9: A landing on Luzon in the Philippines was made by the U.S. Sixth Army. In the operation, a task force of 850 ships sailed into Lingayen Gulf, 100 miles north of Manila.

Feb 4-11: The **Yalta conference,** a top-secret meeting in the Ukraine attended by Roosevelt, Winston Churchill, and Joseph Stalin, dealt with the postwar reorganization of Europe. Its communiqué, issued Feb. 12, called for a United Nations Conference on Apr. 25 to prepare a charter for a new peacekeeping organization.

Feb 7: Gen. **Douglas MacArthur returned to Manila** more than three years after he was forced out of the city by the Japanese.

Feb 23: On **Iwo Jima** the American flag was raised on Mt. Suribachi by Lt. Harold C. Shrier.

Mar 7: The **Remagen Bridge** over the Rhine R. was crossed by the U.S. First Army. Not since the days of Napoleon had an invading army crossed the Rhine.

Mar 16: Iwo Jima fell to the U.S. Marines after 36 days of bitter and bloody fighting. More than 4000 Marines were killed, 15,000 wounded. The Japanese lost more than 20,000 men.

Apr 1: Okinawa was invaded by U.S. forces.

Apr 12: Pres. **Franklin D. Roosevelt died** in Warm Springs, Ga., on the 83rd day of his fourth term; he was 63. He was succeeded by Harry S Truman.

Apr 24: The **United Nations conference** opened at San Francisco with delegates from 50 nations attending. The UN charter was signed June 26.

May 8: On this day, known as **V-E Day,** for victory in Europe, the instrument of unconditional surrender was ratified in Berlin, ending the European phase of World War II.

June 21: Japanese forces on **Okinawa** surrendered after two and a half months of deadly struggle. More than 100,000 Japanese soldiers were killed. American deaths ran to almost 13,000, with nearly 40,000 wounded.

July 5: The **Philippine Islands were declared liberated** by Gen. Douglas MacArthur. In ten months of fighting since the first American landings at Leyte, more than 400,000 Japanese soldiers had been killed and upward of 12,000 Americans had lost their lives.

July 16: The **first atomic bomb** was detonated near Alamogordo, N. Mex., at 5:30 A.M.

July 28: In a bizarre **airplane crash,** a B-25 bomber flew into the Empire State Building in New York City. It became lodged between the 78th and 79th floors, killing 13 persons. The accident occurred on a foggy Saturday morning.

July 28: The **United Nations Charter** was ratified by the U.S. Senate by a vote of 89 to 2.

Aug 6: Hiroshima, Japan, was destroyed by the first atomic bomb to be used in war.

Aug 9: Nagasaki, Japan, was destroyed by the second atomic bomb to be used in war.

Aug 15: V-J Day, for victory over Japan, marked the end of the Pacific phase of World War II.

Sep 2: The formal **document of surrender** was signed aboard the U.S.S. *Missouri* in Tokyo Bay.

Nov 12: The **Nobel Peace Prize** was awarded to former secretary of state Cordell Hull for his contributions to the establishment of the United Nations. At the same time the 1944 prize was awarded to the International Red Cross. These were the first awards made since 1938.

II. Architecture
   ## Arts and Music
   ## Popular Entertainment
   ## Publishing
   ## Theater

Book publishing had a boom year, with the paperback trade continuing to create hundreds of thousands of book buyers. Hollywood, hungry for plots, was willing to pay as much as $250,000 for rights to a good story. With such prizes before them, writers tailored their techniques to fit the requirements of the screen. The result, by and large, was undistinguished. By war's end, the Hollywood Victory Committee had arranged for 55,619 personal appearances of movie stars at bond rallies and military camps. The motion picture industry kept up a high level of production, even though the major companies were under fire by government lawyers who charged them with conspiring to form illegal trusts. Americans mourned the passing of Robert Benchley, the humorist, Nov. 21, at age 56; and Ernie Pyle, the celebrated war correspondent, who was killed on Iwo Jima on Apr. 18, at age 44.

Among **books published** this year was *Black Boy* by Richard Wright, the grim story of the author's childhood. Other books published this year included *A Masque of Reason* by Robert Frost; *Cass Timberlane* by Sinclair Lewis; *The Age of Jackson* by Arthur M. Schlesinger, Jr., a fascinating account of the life and times of Andrew Jackson; and *Captain from Castile* by Samuel Shellabarger, a historical novel.

May 7: Pulitzer prizes were awarded for the following: fiction, *A Bell for Adano,* by John Hersey; history, *Unfinished Business* by Stephen Bonsal; biography, *George Bancroft: Brahmin Rebel* by Russel Blaine Nye; poetry, *V-Letter and Other Poems* by Karl Shapiro; drama, *Harvey* by Mary Coyle Chase; music, *Appalachian Spring* by Aaron Copland.

III. Business and Industry
Education
Philosophy and Religion
Science

Aside from the war victory, the biggest news of the year was the use of atomic energy. Scientists questioned the moral and ethical value of their contribution to victory in the war. At first, the public refused to share the alarm of the physicists, believing that the people who had created this new force would soon tell the world how to control it. Unfortunately, this did not come to pass.

Vitamin research in the U.S. continued with the discovery of folic acid, a component of the large vitamin B family and a necessary element for cell growth. Folic acid was found effective in the treatment of pernicious anemia, but later analyses revealed adverse affects on the nervous system.

Jan 15: A **nationwide dimout** was ordered to conserve diminishing fuel supplies.

Apr 30: Sugar rations were cut by 25% as reserves neared rock bottom.

May 8: The **nationwide dimout** was lifted.

July 1: The **New York State Commission Against Discrimination,** the first such agency in the U.S., was established. The commission was authorized to take steps to prevent "discrimination in employment because of race, creed, color, or national origin."

July 27: The **Communist Party** was reestablished by the Communist Political Association, which voted to disband itself.

Aug 14: All **manpower controls** were lifted by the War Manpower Commission.

Aug 18: Moving to **restore the civilian economy,** Pres. Truman ordered full restoration of civilian consumer production and collective bargaining, and a return of free markets.

Oct 30: Shoe rationing ended.

Nov 23: Meat and butter rationing ended.

Dec 20: Tire rationing ended.

IV. Fashion
Folkways
Holidays
Social Issues and Crime
Sports

It was a year of changes in sports. A new baseball commissioner was selected and both the Yankees and the Dodgers were sold to new owners. The annual baseball All-Star Game was canceled because of wartime transportation restrictions. In boxing a newcomer named Rocky Graziano scored five knockouts at Madison Square Garden. In golf the top money winner was Byron Nelson, with $63,335.66. American fashion designers stressed delicacy and prettiness in their designs. Crime statistics recorded a startling upward swing, which experts interpreted as symptomatic of postwar uncertainty.

The phrase *Kilroy was here* appeared almost overnight throughout the world, at least wherever American GIs set foot. Kilroy represented a kind of abstract conglomerate of all GIs. The phrase was scribbled by U.S. Army gagsters on streets, billboards, latrines, walls, and all other available surfaces.

Mar 29: The **NCAA basketball championship** was won by Oklahoma A&M, which defeated DePaul 52–44.

Apr 24: Sen. **Albert B. "Happy" Chandler,** Democrat of Kentucky, was named baseball commissioner, filling the post vacated by the death of Kenesaw Mountain Landis in 1944.

July 15: The **PGA golf tournament** was won by Byron Nelson.

Oct 3-10: The 42nd annual **World Series** was won by the Detroit Tigers (AL), defeating the Chicago Cubs (NL) four games to three.

Dec 16: The **NFL championship** was won by the Cleveland Rams, who defeated the Washington Redskins 15 to 14.

1946

I. Civil Rights
Exploration and Settlement
Government
Statistics
Wars

Spiraling inflation, acute shortage of housing, and bitter labor disputes were facing Americans. In addition there were rumblings of what came to be known as the Cold War, and poverty-stricken Europe was looking to the U.S. for aid. It quickly became apparent that the U.S. would not be returning to a state of political isolation. Soviet expansionism became a new threat to world security, although some disagreed that Russia had territorial designs on the West. The administration took the view that complete isolation was a luxury Americans could not afford, primarily because of the existence of the atomic bomb, so the U.S. assumed the role of peacemaker in a world still in disorder.

July 1: Atomic bomb tests were held at Bikini Atoll in the Pacific. A Nagasaki-type bomb was dropped from 30,000 feet. It destroyed five ships, heavily damaged nine, and did varying amounts of damage to 45 others.

July 4: Philippine independence was proclaimed by Pres. Harry S Truman. He was keeping a promise made by the U.S. on acquiring the islands in 1898.

Aug 1: The McMahan Act, creating the **Atomic Energy Commission,** was signed by Pres. Truman. The commission was to be composed of a five-man control board without military representation but with military liaison. The act allowed the Army and Navy to manufacture atomic weapons and prohibited the distribution of fissionable materials or information on atomic energy.

Nov 5: In **congressional elections** the Republicans gained 13 Senate seats to take a 51–45 majority, and picked up 55 House seats for a 245–188 majority, with one seat held by a minor party.

Nov 14: The **Nobel Peace Prize** was awarded jointly to John Raleigh Mott and Emily Greene Balch. Mott, a Methodist layman and a leader in international church activities, headed the YMCA's relief activities for prisoners of war during World War I. Balch was a founder, in 1915, of the Women's International League for Peace and Freedom at The Hague, Netherlands.

Dec 14: The **UN accepted a gift** of $8,500,000 from John D. Rockefeller, Jr., for purchase of property along New York City's East R. for permanent UN headquarters.

II. Architecture
   Arts and Music
   Popular Entertainment
   Publishing
   Theater

Literary critics looked for a spate of fine books this year, calling up as their precedent the year immediately following World War I. Unfortunately, they were disappointed and had to be content with noting a new development in fictional technique—a modified stream of consciousness in which a highly sensitive story was told by a perceptive observer. Responding to high building costs, architects designed houses with small rooms and compensated by using more glass. U.S. painters exhibited in London and succeeded in shocking rather than boring viewers. Theatergoers were treated to one of the most extensive revival seasons in memory. The quality of motion pictures was up, as foreign producers made a strong bid for American markets, offering colorful spectacles and realistic dramas. Repeal of the federal excess profits tax and higher admission prices produced a record in box office receipts.

Among **books published** this year was *Memoirs of Hecate County* by Edmund Wilson, stories that caused a furor because of the author's treatment of sex. It raised a censorship issue reminiscent of the one inspired by James Branch Cabell's 1919 novel *Jurgen.* Lawsuits against Wilson and his publishers led eventually to withdrawal of the book for a time. Other books published this year included *Do I Wake or Sleep?* by Isobel Bolton, a novel written in the stream-of-consciousness style; *This Side of Innocence,* a novel by Taylor Caldwell; *Mr. Roberts* by Thomas Heggen; *B.F.'s Daughter* by John P. Marquand, a novel; *The Fields* by Conrad Richter, the second novel in a trilogy about a pioneer family that began with *The Trees* (1940); *The Hucksters* by Frederic Wakeman, a bitter novel about the advertising industry; *All the King's Men* by Robert Penn Warren, a novel about a southern political boss with parallels to the life of Huey Long; and *Delta Wedding,* a novel by Eudora Welty.

The first test of a new **Massachusetts obscene literature statute** was applied to Kathleen Winsor's 1945 best seller *Forever Amber.* The book was cleared in Suffolk County Superior Court and the decision upheld in the Massachusetts Supreme Court with the observation of Judge Frank J. Donahue that the book was more of a "soporific . . . than an aphrodisiac."

The **ranch style house** caught the architectural fancy of the public this year. Soon the countryside mushroomed with low-slung, one-story and split-level homes.

May 6: Pulitzer prizes were awarded for the following: biography, *Son of the Wilderness* by Linnie Marsh Wolfe; history, *The Age of Jackson* by Arthur M. Schlesinger, Jr.; drama, *State of the Union* by Russel Crouse and Howard Lindsay.

III. Business and Industry
   Education
   Philosophy and Religion
   Science

It was a year of confusion and warfare between management and labor. Held down by years of wage controls, practically all the powerful labor unions struck for higher pay. Industry insisted that labor's demands were exorbitant, but could not afford walkouts at a time when consumer buying was at an unparalleled high. The country had a supply of ready money, saved from the days when nothing could be bought, and a new carefree desire to spend it. The changeover from war production to consumer goods took time, and tempers grew short when orders were not met immediately. The government, meanwhile, tried to convince people that the emergency was not yet over, that ruinous inflation still threatened, and that the shift to peacetime habits should be made cautiously.

Strikes this year involved some 4,600,000 workers, at a cost of 116,000,000 man-hours.

Feb 15: ENIAC, the electronic numerical integrator and computer, was dedicated at the Moore School of Electrical Engineering in Philadelphia, Pa. The first electronic digital computer, it had been developed by Dr. John W. Mauchly and J. Presper Eckert, Jr. It contained 18,000 vacuum tubes, occupied a 30 foot by 60 foot room, and weighed some 30 tons. The computer took 150,000 watts of power to run, had more than 500,000 soldered connections, and had taken 200,000 man-hours to build. Despite the fact that continual replacement of defective tubes was required to keep the machine running, ENIAC heralded a new age for science, engineering, industry, and mathematics.

July 7: Mother Frances Xavier Cabrini was canonized in ceremonies presided over by Pope Pius XII. She was the first American to be canonized. Mother Cabrini was the founder of the Missionary Sisters of the Sacred Heart of Jesus. Her principal shrine is at Mother Cabrini High School in New York City; her feast day is Dec. 22.

Oct 31: The **Nobel Prize in Physiology or Medicine** was awarded to Hermann Joseph Muller of Indiana University for his discovery of the production of mutations by x-ray irradiation. Muller obtained his first evidence of such mutations while at the University of Texas in 1926. His discoveries contributed greatly to genetics and radiology.

Nov 9: Wage and price controls were ended except for rent, sugar, and rice.

Nov 14: The **Nobel Prize in Physics** was awarded to Percy Williams Bridgman of Harvard University for his contributions to high-pressure physics. Bridgman developed an apparatus for production of very high pressures and made numerous discoveries in the study of high pressures.

Nov 14: The **Nobel Prize in Chemistry** was awarded jointly to James B. Sumner of Cornell University, for his work in the crystallization of enzymes, and to John Northrop and Wendell M. Stanley of the Rockefeller Institute, for their preparation of enzymes and virus proteins in pure form. They were the fourth, fifth, and sixth Americans to receive the Nobel Prize in Chemistry.

IV. Fashion
Folkways
Holidays
Social Issues and Crime
Sports

Baseball stars returning from service improved the game and afforded fans a breathtaking pennant race, with a playoff necessary in the National League. In golf the top money winner was Ben Hogan, with $42,556.36. In keeping with peacetime optimism and to retain leadership in the fashion world now that styles again were coming from Paris, U.S. designers showed lighthearted feminine collections. Chief topics of conversation included rising prices, the shortage of housing, the menace of Russian communism, and the atomic bomb.

Mar 23: The **NCAA basketball championship** was won by Oklahoma A&M, which defeated California 52 to 35.

May 4: The 72nd annual **Kentucky Derby** was won by Assault, with a time of 2:06³/₅. The jockey was Warren Mehrtens.

May 11: The 71st annual **Preakness Stakes** was won by Assault, with a time of 2:01²/₅. The jockey was Warren Mehrtens.

June 1: The 78th annual **Belmont Stakes** was won by Assault, with a time of 2:30⁴/₅. The jockey was Warren Mehrtens. Assault became the seventh horse to win racing's Triple Crown.

June 16: The **U.S. Open golf tournament** was won by Lloyd Mangrum, who defeated Byron Nelson and Vic Ghezzi by one stroke.

July 6: At the **Wimbledon** tennis championships in England, Pauline Betz won the women's singles title. Louise Brough and Margaret Osborne won the women's doubles, and Tom Brown and Jack Kramer won the men's doubles.

Aug 25: The **PGA golf tournament** was won by Ben Hogan.

Sep 8: The **U.S. Lawn Tennis Association singles championships** were won by Jack Kramer in the men's division and Pauline Betz in the women's division.

Oct 6-15: The 43rd annual **World Series** was won by the St. Louis Cardinals (NL), defeating the Boston Red Sox (AL) four games to three. On Oct. 3 the Cardinals had won the first National League playoff, beating the Brooklyn Dodgers in two games straight.

Dec 15: The **NFL championship** was won by the Chicago Bears, who defeated the New York Giants 24 to 14.

Dec 26: In the **Davis Cup** international tennis matches, the U.S. defeated Australia 5–0, regaining the trophy lost to Australia in 1939.

1947

I. Civil Rights
Exploration and Settlement
Government
Statistics
Wars

Economic equilibrium was the administration's chief concern. A restless population complained of constantly rising prices of food, clothing, rent, and other necessities of life. Manufacturers blamed rising costs on industry-wide wage boosts. Housing conditions everywhere became so tight that Pres. Harry S Truman called the shortage "the foremost of the many problems facing the nation." The most dramatic successes of the year were scored in foreign policy. The European Recovery program, or Marshall Plan, earned the gratitude of western European nations but the abuse of Iron Curtain countries. The intensity of the Cold War was stepped up as an executive order banned all members or sympathizers of the Communist Party from holding office in the executive branch of the U.S. government.

Apr 16-18: A **ship explosion** in Texas City, Tex., killed some 500 persons. The city itself was virtually annihilated by the blast. The nitrate-laden French freighter *Grandcamp* had caught fire early on the morning of Apr. 16. Fireman thought they had gotten the blaze under control until the ship exploded. Fire then swept the Monsanto Chemical Co. plant, and further explosions were set off in the ensuing conflagration. Also destroyed were a number of oil storage tanks. On Apr. 17 the freighter *High Flyer* exploded. The blasts and fires left the waterfront section of the city in complete devastation. Eyewitnesses said the scene was worse than anything they had seen in Europe during World War II.

May 22: The **Greek-Turkish Aid Bill** was signed by Pres. Truman. The bill authorized some $400,000,000 in aid to Greece and Turkey on their request. This authorization was subject to withdrawal on the disapproval of the interested countries, the U.N. Security Council or General Assembly, or the president if he deemed the aid to have been either improperly used or unnecessary. When Pres. Truman requested the legislation on Mar. 12 he said: "I believe that it must be the policy of the United States to support free peoples who are resisting attempted subjugation by armed minorities or by outside pressures." This political stance came to be known as the Truman Doctrine.

June 5: The **Marshall Plan** for reconstruction of Europe was proposed at Harvard University by Sec. of State George C. Marshall. He stated that careful study of European needs, on which U.S. aid should be based, was essential before progress could be made in the economic rehabilitation of Europe.

June 14: Peace treaties between the U.S. and Italy, Rumania, Bulgaria, and Hungary were ratified by the U.S. Senate and signed by Pres. Truman.

July 18: The **Presidential Succession Act** was signed by Pres. Truman. The act designated the Speaker of the House and then the president of the Senate pro tempore next in succession after the vice president.

Dec 27: A record-breaking **snowstorm** struck the Northeast, dumping a record 25.8 in. of snow on New York City and causing nearly 80 deaths in the North Atlantic states. Stalled trains stranded commuters. Marooned suburbanites crowded downtown hotels.

II. Architecture
Arts and Music
Popular Entertainment
Publishing
Theater

Two noticeable trends in American publishing were a reawakening interest in U.S. history and a turn toward philosophic introspection. The latter may have been prompted by increased concern with the fate of the human race now that it had discovered the power to destroy itself. Exhibitions of paintings featured non-objective and expressionistic works and leaned less on realism and surrealism. Composers took heart as orchestral societies encouraged production of new works. Despite a continuing boom on Broadway, producers found it difficult to find backers for their plays, with production costs twice what they had been five years earlier. Reluctant to risk so much on new scripts, producers resorted to revivals. Architects produced little that was new, since three-fourths of the building in the country was in the hands of large-scale developers. The biggest news in the movie industry was the investigation of alleged communist subversion. Senate committees claimed that ten screenwriters were communists or sympathizers and should not be allowed to work on films. A 20% federal amusement tax helped drive some customers away from movies to the new medium of television.

Among **books published** this year was *Under the Volcano*, a novel by the English-born writer Malcolm Lowry. The novel recounted the last day in the life of Geoffrey Firmin, an alcoholic British ex-consul in Mexico. The novel met with moderate success and critical acclaim, but eventually was recognized as a masterpiece. Other books published this year included *The Times of Melville and Whitman* by Van Wyck Brooks; *Butterfly* by James M. Cain, a novel; *Inside U.S.A.* by John Gunther; *The Big Sky* by A. B. Guthrie, a novel; *Gentleman's Agreement* by Laura Z. Hobson, a novel exploring anti-Semitism that became a best seller and was adapted for motion pictures; *Kingsblood Royal*, a novel by Sinclair Lewis; *Tales of the South Pacific* by James Michener; *The Harder They Fall*, a novel about boxing by Budd Schulberg; *I, the Jury* by Mickey Spillane; *The Wayward Bus* by John Steinbeck; and *Aurora Dawn* by Herman Wouk, the author's first novel.

Jan 28: A copy of the **Bay Psalm Book** was bought for $151,000 at an auction of the Parke-Bernet Galleries in New York City. This was the highest price paid to date for a book.

Apr 7: The first annual **Antoinette Perry, or Tony, Awards,** for outstanding contributions to the American theater during the 1946–1947 season, were presented. Among those honored were José Ferrer for his performance in *Cyrano de Bergerac;* Fredric March for *Years Ago;* Ingrid Bergman for *Joan of Lorraine;* Helen Hayes for *Happy Birthday;* and Patricia Neal for *Another Part of the Forest.* The awards were named after Antoinette Perry, who died in 1946. She served as director of the wartime board of the American Theater Wing.

May 5: Pulitzer prizes were awarded for the following: fiction, *All the King's Men* by Robert Penn Warren; biography, *The Autobiography of William Allen White;* history, *Scientists Against Time* by James Phinney Baxter, III; poetry, *Lord Weary's Castle* by Robert Lowell.

III. Business and Industry
Education
Philosophy and Religion
Science

Many of labor's hard-won gains were erased this year by passage of the widely debated Taft-Hartley Bill.

While many citizens applauded the law's effective curb on alleged union excesses, labor leaders pledged an all-out effort to repeal the legislation, particularly the provision outlawing closed-shop contracts. Despite this setback, organized labor grew more powerful as a continuing business boom sent more and more workers into its ranks. American education was concerned with five major areas: improving the economic lot of teachers; meeting the challenge of increased enrollment; taking advantage of federal aid for schools while keeping schools free of government control; settling the growing controversy over the role of religion in education; and implementing a growing interest in international educational cooperation.

Enrollment of veterans in American colleges, spurred by the Servicemen's Readjustment Act of 1944, known as the G.I. Bill of Rights, reached its peak. Over 1,000,000 former servicemen were among some 2,500,000 students attending college classes.

Magazine circulation figures climbed. Thirty-eight magazines reported circulations of more than 1,000,000. In 1900 no U.S. magazine had a circulation of more than 500,000.

June 17: The **first globe-circling passenger airline** was inaugurated by Pan American Airways, Inc. A round-the-world fare was $1700. The new service began when the clipper *America*, a Lockheed Constellation, took off from La Guardia Airport en route to Gander, Newfoundland, the first stop on a 22,170-mile trip around the world. The plane was scheduled to return to New York on June 30.

June 23: The controversial **Taft-Hartley Act** was passed over Pres. Harry S Truman's veto. The act reduced or eliminated many labor union advantages provided for in the National Labor Relations Act of 1935, including the unconditional closed shop, the check-off system, which enabled unions to collect dues from all employed members; the unconditional right to strike at any time; and immunity from employer lawsuits over breaches of contract and strike damage. New obligations for labor unions included publication of financial statements and a mandatory affidavit of all union leaders attesting to nonmembership in the Communist Party.

Oct 14: The **first supersonic aircraft,** the Bell X-1 research airplane, was piloted faster than the speed of sound for the first time by Capt. Charles E. Yeager, USAF, during a test at Muroc Air Force Base, Calif.

Oct 23: The **Nobel Prize in Physiology or Medicine** was awarded jointly to Carl F. Cori and his wife Gerty T. Cori of Washington University in St. Louis for "the discovery of how glycogen is catalytically converted," and to Dr. Bernardo A. Houssay of Buenos Aires, Argentina, for his studies of the hormone produced by the pituitary gland. The Coris were the third husband and wife team to be awarded a Nobel Prize in the field of scientific research. Born in Czechoslovakia, they came to the U.S. in 1922.

IV. Fashion
Folkways
Holidays
Social Issues and Crime
Sports

Baseball took a historic step forward as Jackie Robinson signed with the Brooklyn Dodgers, of the National League, becoming the first black to play in the major leagues. Later in the year other black athletes played in the American League for the first time. In boxing, Joe Louis resumed his defense of the world heavyweight title, winning (Dec. 5) a split decision over "Jersey Joe" Walcott. In golf, the top money winner was Jimmy Demaret, $27,936.83. In women's fashion, the topic of conversation was the so-called New Look, inspired by the Paris designer Christian Dior, who screened women's legs with a long skirt, pinched in their waists, and flattened their bosoms.

Mar 25: The **NCAA basketball championship** was won by Holy Cross, which defeated Oklahoma 58–47.

June 15: The **U.S. Open golf tournament** was won by Lew Worsham, who beat Sam Snead by one stroke on the last green in an 18-hole playoff.

June 24: The **PGA golf tournament** was won by Jim Ferrier.

July 4-5: At the **Wimbledon** tennis championships in England, Jack Kramer won the men's singles title and Margaret Osborne won the women's singles. Kramer teamed with Robert Falkenburg to win the men's doubles, Doris Hart and Patricia Canning Todd won the women's doubles, and Louise Brough teamed with John E. Bromwich of Australia to win the mixed doubles.

Sep 30-Oct 6: The 44th annual **World Series** was won by the New York Yankees (AL), defeating the Brooklyn Dodgers (NL) four games to three.

Dec 28: The **NFL championship** was won by the Chicago Cardinals, who defeated the Philadelphia Eagles 28 to 21.

Dec 30: In the **Davis Cup** international tennis challenge round, the U.S. defeated Australia four matches to one.

1948

I. Civil Rights
Exploration and Settlement
Government
Statistics
Wars

The administration and the lawmakers fought all year. Pres. Harry S Truman called the 80th Congress the "worst in our history." One of the chief areas of disagreement was over the supposed presence of communists in governmental positions. The House Committee on Un-American Activities wrote alarming reports, which the president largely ignored, calling one finding a "red herring." The president maintained that the FBI together with the Justice Department was more than equal to the task of cleaning house. Some 2,000,000 federal employees were investigated; as a direct result, 526 resigned and 98 were dismissed. In foreign affairs, the European Recovery Program continued with military aid to Greece, Turkey, and China. The most dramatic development of the year was the Soviet blockade of Berlin, which the U.S. broke by maintaining an airlift to resupply the beleaguered city.

Mar 30: The **Rent Control Bill,** which extended controls until Mar. 31, 1949, was signed by Pres. Truman. The bill also designated an Emergency Court of Appeals to decide on decontrols or increases recommended by local boards but rejected by the federal housing expediter.

Apr 3: The **Foreign Assistance Act** of 1948 was signed by Pres. Truman. The act provided $5,300,000,000 for a one-year European Recovery Program, known popularly as the Marshall Plan. The act also provided $275,000,000 for military aid to Greece and Turkey, $463,000,000 for economic and military aid to China, and $60,000,000 for a UN Fund for Children.

June 24: The **Selective Service Act** was signed by Pres. Truman. It provided for the registration of all men between 18 and 25 and the draft of enough men to constitute an Army of 837,000, a Navy and Marine Corps of 666,882, and an Air Force of 502,000.

June 25: The **Displaced Persons Bill** was signed by Pres. Truman. It admitted 205,000 European displaced persons, including 3000 nonquota orphans.

July 15: The **Democratic National Convention** nominated **Pres. Truman** for reelection, and Sen. Alben W. Barkley of Kentucky for the vice presidency.

July 17: The **States Rights Democrats** nominated Gov. Strom Thurmond of South Carolina for the presidency and Gov. Fielding L. Wright of Mississippi for the vice presidency. The political group, also known as the Dixiecrats, were members of the Democratic Party who had walked out of the national convention in opposition to the party's strong civil rights platform.

July 20: Twelve American **Communist Party leaders were indicted** and charged with advocating overthrow of the U.S. government.

Nov 2: **Harry S Truman was reelected president** of the United States in a major political upset. Alben W. Barkley was elected vice president. Political analysts and polls had predicted that Truman's Republican opponent, Gov. Thomas E. Dewey of New York, would win. The electoral vote was Truman 304, Dewey 189. The popular vote was Truman 24,104,836; Dewey 21,969,500; Strom Thurmond, States Rights Democrat, 1,169,312; Henry A. Wallace, Progressive, 1,157,172; Norman M. Thomas, Socialist, 132,138; and Claude A. Watson, Prohibition Party, 103,343. In congressional elections the Democrats gained nine Senate seats for a 54–42 majority. In the House they gained 75 seats for a 263–171 lead, with one seat going to a minor party.

Dec 15: **Alger Hiss,** a former State Department official, was indicted by a federal grand jury on two counts of perjury. Hiss, who had worked in the State Department in 1937 and 1938, denied giving official documents to Whittaker Chambers, a self-proclaimed courier for a communist spy group. He also denied ever meeting Chambers after Jan. 1, 1937.

II. Architecture
Arts and Music
Popular Entertainment
Publishing
Theater

World War II was one of the leading subjects of this year's books, and first novels dealing with the war by Norman Mailer and Irwin Shaw were among the year's best. The newest communication medium, television, was cursed in many quarters as the eventual destroyer of American reading, theater, and movies. Actually, TV broadcasts of concerts and operas led to creation of music festivals and commissions for new composers, while movie studios suffered a 25% drop in employment, in part due to stiff European competition.

Among **books published** this year was *Raintree County* by Ross Lockridge, a first novel that achieved both critical and popular success. It was to be the author's only book. He died on March 6 at the age of 33, an apparent suicide. Other books published this year included the best-selling religious novel *The Big Fisherman* by Lloyd C. Douglas; *Crusade in Europe* by Dwight D. Eisenhower; *The Naked and the Dead* by Norman Mailer, the author's first novel and one of the best fictional works about World War II; and *The Young Lions* by Irwin Shaw, another first novel, also about World War II and a critical and popular success.

The first **Supreme Court hearing on a state obscenity law** related to a specific book concerned Edmund Wilson's *Memoirs of Hecate County* and its suppression in New York State. The Court was deadlocked on the question and thus upheld the lower court conviction of the publisher.

May 3: **Pulitzer prizes** were awarded to the following: fiction, *Tales of the South Pacific* by James Michener; biography, *Forgotten First Citizen: John Bigelow* by Margaret Clapp; history, *Across the Wide Missouri* by Bernard De Voto; poetry, *Age of Anxiety* by W. H. Auden; drama, *A Streetcar Named Desire* by Tennessee Williams.

Nov 4: The **Nobel Prize for Literature** was awarded to T. S. Eliot. Born in St. Louis in 1888, Eliot moved to England and in 1927 became a British subject. Among his works of poetry were *The Waste Land* (1922), and *Ash Wednesday* (1930).

III. Business and Industry
Education
Philosophy and Religion
Science

Bolstered by increased defense expenditures and a costly foreign-aid program, American industry enjoyed a peak year. Relations between labor and management were particularly mellow. General Motors granted an automatic cost-of-living increase to some 265,000 hourly workers. Strikes were fewer and less violent. However, education had a number of new problems to consider, including sharply rising enrollments; inadequate facilities; the failure of teachers to gain better economic status, mainly because rising prices offset salary increases; a shortage of teachers; a decline in enrollment of veterans at colleges and universities; and an ever-swelling tide of foreign students on exchange scholarships.

Conquest of **pernicious anemia** was completed with the discovery of vitamin B-12, the substance in liver extracts responsible for earlier cures. Vitamin B-12 was found to have phenomenal efficiency. A daily dosage equivalent to one hundredth of a grain of salt was sufficient to cure a victim of pernicious anemia, and the same quantity taken twice a week maintained the cured person in good health.

The **Polaroid Land Camera,** patented by Edwin H. Land in 1947, went on sale. The first camera to carry its own darkroom, it processed prints in one minute. It was an instant hit with professional photographers, who saw the value in obtaining instant prints of subjects. The Polaroid gave them greater flexibility in experimenting with lighting and settings for their subjects.

Mar 5: A new **U.S. rocketry record** was set by the Navy. A speed of 3000 mph and an altitude of 78 miles were achieved during tests at White Sands, N. Mex.

Mar 8: Religious education in public schools was declared a violation of the First Amendment by the U.S. Supreme Court.

June 3: The **world's largest reflector telescope** was dedicated. It was the 200-inch Hale telescope at Palomar Mountain Observatory, maintained by the California Institute of Technology.

Nov 20: A new **balloon altitude record** was claimed by the U.S. Army Signal Corps. It was 140,000 feet (26½ miles).

IV. Fashion
Folkways
Holidays
Social Issues and Crime
Sports

The major leagues provided baseball fans with the first post-season playoff in the history of the American League when the Cleveland Indians ended the year with the same won-and-lost record as the Boston Red Sox. This year the Baseball Hall of Fame elected two new members: Herbert J. Pennock, the pitcher, and Harold "Pie" Traynor, longtime third baseman for the Pittsburgh Pirates. Plaques honoring the two were unveiled at Cooperstown, N.Y., in the 1949 annual ceremonies. In golf the top money winners were Ben Hogan, $36,812, and Mildred "Babe" Didrikson Zaharias, $3400. Meanwhile, the nation's crime rate remained steady. Racketeers concentrated on large-scale gambling operations, some of which had the tacit approval of local authorities. In fashion, the so-called New Look, in vogue last year, was rejected. Women now wanted the more natural lines of the body to show. Notables who died included George Herman "Babe" Ruth, the Sultan of Swat, Aug. 16, at 53.

Jan 30-Feb 8: At the **Winter Olympics** in St. Moritz, Switzerland, the U.S. won three gold medals and finished third in unofficial team standings, behind Sweden and Switzerland.

Mar 13: The **NCAA basketball tournament** was won by Kentucky, which defeated Indiana State 82 to 70.

May 1: The 74th annual **Kentucky Derby** was won by Citation, with a time of 2:05²/₅. The jockey was Eddie Arcaro.

May 15: The 73rd annual **Preakness Stakes** was won by Citation, with a time of 2:02³/₅. The jockey was Eddie Arcaro.

May 25: The **PGA golf tournament** was won by Ben Hogan.

June 12: The 80th annual **Belmont Stakes** was won by Citation, with a time of 2:28¹/₅. Citation thus became the eighth horse in history to win the Triple Crown of racing. The jockey was Eddie Arcaro, who chalked up his second Triple Crown victory.

June 12: The **U.S. Open golf tournament** was won by Ben Hogan, with a tournament record-breaking score of 276, five strokes lower than the previous tournament record.

June 25: The **world heavyweight boxing championship** was successfully defended by Joe Louis, who defeated "Jersey Joe" Walcott in an 11-round bout.

July 2: At the **Wimbledon** tennis championships in England, Robert Falkenburg won the men's singles title. The next day Louise Brough won the women's singles, then teamed with Margaret Osborne du Pont to win the women's doubles, and with John Bromwich of Australia to win the mixed doubles.

July 29-Aug 14: At the **Summer Olympics** in London, England, the U.S. won 33 gold medals and the unofficial team championship.

Sep 6: In the **Davis Cup** international tennis challenge round, the U.S. won its fifth straight match from Australia, sweeping the round 5–0 and retaining the trophy.

Oct 6-11: The 45th annual **World Series** was won by the Cleveland Indians (AL), defeating the Boston Braves (NL) four games to two. The Indians had won the American League pennant by beating the Boston Red Sox 8 to 3 in a single-game playoff, the first time a playoff was needed in the league.

Oct 24: The term *Cold War* to characterize East-West relations after World War II was given national prominence after a speech by Bernard M. Baruch before the Senate War Investigating Committee. "Although the war is over," said Baruch, "we are in the midst of a cold war which is getting warmer."

Dec 19: The **NFL championship** was won by the Philadelphia Eagles, who defeated the Chicago Cardinals 7 to 0.

1949

I. Civil Rights
Exploration and Settlement
Government
Statistics
Wars

In his message to Congress this year, Pres. Harry S Truman presented a program of domestic legislation that he called the Fair Deal. It included repeal of the Taft-Hartley law, reenactment of the Wagner Act, a law calling for a minimum wage of 75 cents an hour, generous farm price supports, expansion of Social Security, federal aid to local school systems, low-rent public housing, slum clearance, and broad civil rights proposals. In foreign affairs, the Senate ratified the North Atlantic Treaty Alliance and pledged over $1,250,000,000 to finance a military assistance program. Worry over communists at home continued as the U.S.S.R. disclosed that it too had atomic weapons, and eleven Communist Party leaders in New York City were found guilty of advocating overthrow of the government.

Feb 7: The **Hoover Commission on Organization of the Executive Branch of the Government** issued the first part of its report, recommending streamlining of the executive branch. On Feb. 17 the commission suggested that the Post Office Department be placed beyond politics and run on a business basis. On Mar. 21 it suggested creation of a new Cabinet post, secretary of a department of national welfare and education. In its final report, on Apr. 1, the commission characterized many government enterprises as corrupt and inefficient.

Apr 4: The **North Atlantic Treaty Organization** (NATO) was formed when the North Atlantic Treaty was signed in Washington, D.C., by representatives of Belgium, Canada, Denmark, France, Great Britain, Italy, Iceland, Luxembourg, The Netherlands, Norway, Portugal, and the U.S.

May 18: The first U.S. civilian **high commissioner of Germany** was appointed. He was John J. McCloy, president of the International Bank for Reconstruction and Development.

May 31: The perjury trial of **Alger Hiss** opened in New York City. Hiss had been indicted on Dec. 15, 1948, on two counts of perjury relating to his testimony to a federal grand jury on alleged espionage activities while a State Department official. Whittaker Chambers, a confessed courier for a communist spy ring, testified that Hiss had passed him official documents. Hiss denied giving Chambers any documents while at the State Department in 1937 and 1938, and denied seeing Chambers after Jan. 1, 1937. On July 8 the jury reported a deadlock and was dismissed. A new trial opened on Nov. 17.

June 29: The last **U.S. forces in Korea** were withdrawn. They had been occupying the southern portion of the peninsula since the end of World War II. Only a military mission remained.

Aug 31: The **Grand Army of the Republic,** veterans of the Civil War, held its 83rd and last encampment. It was attended by six of the 16 surviving veterans at Indianapolis, Ind.

Oct 14: Eleven American communist leaders were convicted of conspiring to advocate the overthrow of the government after a long, bitter trial marked by personal attacks on the presiding federal judge, Harold Medina. All were sentenced on Oct. 21 by Judge Medina to fines of $10,000. Ten were sentenced to five years imprisonment, one to three years. Originally, 12 leaders had been indicted but the case against William Z. Foster had been separated from the others because of Foster's ill health.

Oct 24: The permanent **UN headquarters** in New York City were dedicated.

II. Architecture
Arts and Music
Popular Entertainment
Publishing
Theater

The year in publishing was marked by an increasing popularity of books on religion, studies of world affairs, and books that discussed the plight of black Americans. Architects rejoiced in slightly decreased building costs, which enabled them to plan more luxury residences. The trend toward decentralization of cities afforded new opportunities to design factories, laboratories, and offices in rural areas. The League of New York Theaters instituted an investigation into the ills of the theater. Its findings recommended fairer policies toward the public in the matter of ticket distribution, pooling of production techniques, more careful advertising and promotion, and the training of theater staffs. The motion picture industry regained its momentum and enjoyed a healthy financial year.

Among **books published** this year was *The Man With the Golden Arm* by Nelson Algren, the powerful story of Frankie Machine, a Chicago poker dealer whose heroin addiction keeps him from escaping the slums and ultimately leads him to suicide. Other books published this year included *The Brave Bulls* by Tom Lea, the author's first novel; *The Waters of Siloe* by Thomas Merton, a history of the Trappist Order; *A Rage to Live* by John O'Hara, a novel; *The Greatest Story Ever Told* by Fulton Oursler; *A Guide to Confident Living* by Norman Vincent Peale; and *Peace of Soul* by Fulton J. Sheen.

Feb 19: The **first Bollingen Prize** for poetry was awarded to Ezra Pound for his 1948 collection The *Pisan Cantos*. The award sparked bitter controversy because Pound had been charged with treason for making pro-fascist broadcasts in Italy during World War II.

May 2: **Pulitzer prizes** were awarded for the following: fiction, *Guard of Honor* by James Gould Cozzens; biography, *Roosevelt and Hopkins* by Robert E. Sherwood; history, *The Disruption of American Democracy* by Roy Franklin Nichols; poetry, *Terror and Decorum* by Peter Viereck; drama, *Death of a Salesman* by Arthur Miller.

III. Business and Industry
Education
Philosophy and Religion
Science

A record national debt of $250,000,000,000 was offset by rising national income, estimated at $222,000,000,000. Agricultural productivity was at an all-time high. Economists noted a slight decline during the first half of the year, but pointed out that such a sag was inevitable after the inflation of 1948. Total salaries and wages reached new highs; the automotive industry sent some 6,000,000 cars and trucks off assembly lines—a new record. Unemployment increased by 1,500,000. Labor pressed for the fourth round of wage increases since the end of the war. The most significant development for labor was growing involvement in national politics. Candidates for elective office took great care to draw up platforms designed to attract the labor vote.

Feb 25: A **flight altitude record** was set when an American guided missile, the WAC-Corporal, was launched at White Sands, N. Mex., and reached an altitude of 250 miles. It was the highest altitude ever achieved by a manmade projectile.

Mar 2: The **first nonstop round-the-world flight** was completed by the U.S. Air Force Superfortress *Lucky Lady II*, which touched down at Carswell Air Force Base, Tex. The airplane had been refueled in the air four times.

Apr 20: The discovery of **cortisone** was announced. The hormone promised to bring relief to sufferers of

rheumatoid arthritis, the most painful type of arthritis.

Oct 26: A **minimum wage bill** was signed by Pres. Truman, raising the minimum wage in certain industries engaged in interstate commerce from 40 cents to 75 cents an hour.

Nov 3: The **Nobel Prize for Chemistry** was awarded to William Francis Giauque for his work in chemical thermodynamics, specifically his studies of substances at very low temperatures. Giauque, born in Canada, was professor of chemistry at the University of Canada.

IV. Fashion
Folkways
Holidays
Social Issues and Crime
Sports

The two major league baseball leagues staged breathtaking shows for their fans as both pennants were clinched on the last day of the season. In golf the top money winners were Sam Snead, $31,593.83, and Mildred "Babe" Didrikson Zaharias, $4650. In boxing, Joe Louis officially retired in March. On June 22 Ezzard Charles defeated "Jersey Joe" Walcott in a 15-round decision and became the new world heavyweight champion. For a change, American men cheered Parisian fashion designers as they decreed daring decolletage for evening wear and bikini bathing suits for the beach.

Mar 26: The **NCAA basketball championship** was won by Kentucky, which defeated Oklahoma State 46 to 36.

May 31: The **PGA golf tournament** was won by Sam Snead.

June 11: The **U.S. Open golf tournament** was won by Cary Middlecoff.

July 1-2: At the **Wimbledon** tennis championships in England, Ted Schroeder won the men's singles title and Louise Brough won the women's singles. Louise Brough and Margaret Osborne du Pont won the women's doubles, and Frank Parker and Richard Gonzales won the men's doubles.

Aug 28: In the **Davis Cup** international tennis challenge round, the U.S. won the final two matches from Australia to take the round 4 to 1 and retain the trophy.

Oct 5-9: The 46th annual **World Series** was won by the New York Yankees (AL), defeating the Brooklyn Dodgers (NL) four games to one.

Dec 18: The **NFL championship** was won by the Philadelphia Eagles, who defeated the Los Angeles Rams 14 to 0.

1950

I. Civil Rights
Exploration and Settlement
Government
Statistics
Wars

The nation was concerned with inflation, the threat of communism, and a foreign policy that never seemed to bring lasting peace. Profound pessimism gripped the country when in June North Korean troops crossed the 38th parallel and invaded South Korea. The action was given over to the United Nations to handle; the organization sent an international police force with orders to end the hostilities. Since no other nation could afford to enter the area in force, the U.S. embarked on a costly, unpopular war. Hatred of communist influences within the country mounted as FBI director J. Edgar Hoover announced that there were 55,000 party members and 500,000 sympathizers active within the U.S. The Senate appointed a special investigating committee to probe charges of communist activity in the State Department that had been leveled by Sen. Joseph McCarthy, Republican of Wisconsin.

The U.S. **Census** reported a population of 150,697,361. The center of the population was placed at eight miles north-northwest of Olney, Richland County, Ill.

Jan 21: Alger Hiss was convicted on two counts of perjury. The jury at this, his second trial on the perjury indictments, found Hiss guilty of lying to a federal grand jury. The jury was investigating allegations of espionage made by Whittaker Chambers, an avowed courier for a communist spy group. On Jan. 25 Hiss was sentenced to two concurrent five-year prison terms.

Jan 31: Development of the **hydrogen bomb** was authorized by Pres. Truman.

June 25: The **Korean War** (1950–1953) began when North Korean forces launched an invasion across the 38th parallel into South Korea. The UN ordered an immediate cease-fire and withdrawal of invading forces.

June 27: U.S. forces were ordered to Korea by Pres. Truman to help South Korea repel the North Korean invasion. The president received the approval of Congress for his action, and the UN Security Council adopted a U.S. resolution for armed intervention.

June 30: A naval blockade of the Korean coast and the use of U.S. ground forces were authorized by Pres. Truman.

July 1: The **first U.S. ground forces** landed in Korea.

July 8: Gen. **Douglas MacArthur** was named commander of UN forces in Korea.

Aug 4: The **U.S. Army** called up 62,000 enlisted reservists for 21 months of active duty.

Sep 8: Emergency powers over the entire national economy were granted to Pres. Truman under the Defense Production Act.

Sep 15: U.S. forces landed at **Inchon,** on the west coast of Korea just south of the 38th parallel, and began a drive inland. The operation was intended to relieve South Korean and UN forces hemmed in at Pusan on the southeastern end of the Korean peninsula, and to recapture Seoul, which had fallen to North Korean forces on June 28.

Sep 22: The **Nobel Peace Prize** was awarded to Dr. Ralph J. Bunche, director of the UN Trusteeship Division, for his work as UN mediator between Israel and the Arab states from Sept. 1948 to Apr. 1949. Dr. Bunche was the first black to win the award.

Sep 26: Seoul, capital of South Korea, was recaptured by U.S. troops.

Sep 29: South Korean troops reached the 38th parallel.

Oct 7: U.S. forces invaded North Korea across the 38th parallel.

Nov 6: Chinese Communist troops were reported in action along with North Korean forces by Gen. Douglas MacArthur.

Nov 7: In **congressional elections** the Democrats lost five Senate seats but retained a 49–47 majority. In the House they lost 29 seats but kept a majority of 234–199, with one seat going to a minor party.

Nov 20: U.S. troops reached the Yalu R. on the Manchurian border.

Nov 29: U.S. forces retreated under heavy attack from Chinese Communist units.

Dec 16: A state of national emergency was declared by Pres. Truman. Charles E. Wilson was appointed director of defense mobilization.

II. Architecture
Arts and Music
Popular Entertainment
Publishing
Theater

The confusion and uncertainty of the times produced some curious results. The book *Dianetics* by L. Ron

Hubbard, a science fiction writer, promulgated a new field of mental health. Architects expended their talents on shopping centers, supermarkets, motels, and outdoor movies, in response to a mass movement to suburbia. That chronic invalid, the theater, reported bad times. Production costs were so high that only smash hits could afford to pay their backers. Yet, with characteristic perversity, the Broadway stage produced some of its most interesting work in recent years. Particularly noteworthy was a renaissance of poetic drama, as witnessed by production of plays of T. S. Eliot, Christopher Fry, and Robinson Jeffers, all of which met with public acclaim.

Among **books published** this year was *World Enough and Time* by Robert Penn Warren, a novel based on an 1825 murder case known as the Kentucky tragedy. Other books published this year included *The Wall* by John Hersey, a story of the last days of the Warsaw ghetto under Nazi attack during World War II; *The Cardinal* by Henry Morton Robinson, the story of the rise of a Catholic priest; and *The Disenchanted* by Budd Schulberg, a biting novel of the struggle for success in Hollywood.

The **United Nations Secretariat,** designed by an international board of architects under the direction of Wallace K. Harrison, was built in New York City. It was a 39-story building with narrow end walls of white marble and wide elevations of green-tinted glass.

Mar 27: The **Bollingen Prize** for poetry was awarded to Wallace Stevens.

May 1: **Pulitzer prizes** were awarded for the following: fiction, *The Way West* by A. B. Guthrie; biography, *John Quincy Adams and the Foundations of American Foreign Policy* by Samuel Flagg Bemis; history, *Art and Life in America* by Oliver W. Larkin; poetry, *Annie Allen* by Gwendolyn Brooks; drama, *South Pacific* by Richard Rodgers, Oscar Hammerstein, II, and Joshua Logan.

Oct 11: A license to begin **color television broadcasting** was issued by the FCC to the Columbia Broadcasting System, effective Nov. 20. This touched off an industry-wide controversy. RCA charged that CBS's device was not the best. On Nov. 15 a temporary restraining order was issued by the Chicago Federal District Court.

Nov 10: The **Nobel Prize in Literature** for 1949 was awarded to William Faulkner at the 1950 awards ceremony in Oslo, Norway. The prize had not been awarded in 1949 because none of the candidates had won a majority of votes.

III. Business and Industry
Education
Philosophy and Religion
Science

A continuing upward trend in prices led organized labor to press for higher wages and improved working conditions. The Korean War cut the number of unemployed down to 1,900,000. The average weekly earning in industry was up to $60.53, an all-time high. Having pledged the defeat of Sen. Robert A. Taft of Ohio, labor entered into the state election campaign. But this, labor's first major attempt to function as a political force, ended in dismal failure when Taft was returned to office by an overwhelming majority. Growing financial difficulties faced colleges and universities. Public schools were beset by the charge that communists had filtered into school systems and by the issue of desegregation in classrooms. Religious leaders reported a rise in church membership. The Roman Catholic Church announced a 2% gain, Protestant churches a 2.9% gain.

The phenomenal popularity of **antihistamines** for the treatment of the common cold was reflected in sales amounting to $100,000,000 despite warnings by medical authorities.

Illiteracy in the U.S. reached a new low of 3.2% of the population, a decline of 1% from 1940 and 16.8% from 1870.

Jan 24: A **minimum wage** of 75 cents an hour went into effect under an amendment to the Fair Labor Standards Act. From 1950 to 1981 the federal minimum wage was increased 13 times, to $3.35 an hour. In 1967 the first minimum wage for farm workers, $1.00 an hour, went into effect.

Mar 13: The **largest corporate income** ever reported was announced by General Motors. Net earnings in 1949 were $656,434,232.

Mar 17: Discovery of a **new element, californium,** was announced by the University of California, Berkeley. This element, the heaviest yet known, was discovered in experiments with the cyclotron, which also yielded another element, berkelium. They were numbered 98 and 97 respectively.

Mar 23: **Wages** were up 130% from 1939 according to a U.S. Labor Department report. However, buying power increased only 35%.

May 25: The **longest vehicular tunnel** in the U.S., the Brooklyn-Battery Tunnel in New York City, was opened to traffic. Still the longest tunnel for automotive use, it has been surpassed in length by the 3.6-mile Bay Area Rapid Transit (BART) tubes under San Francisco Bay.

Oct 26: The **Nobel Prize in Physiology or Medicine** was awarded jointly to Philip Showalter Hench of the Mayo Clinic; Edward Calvin Kendall, head of the Department of Biochemistry, Mayo Foundation, University of Minnesota; and Tadeus Reichstein of the University of Basel, Switzerland, for their research into the nature of suprarenal cortex hormones and the use of cortisone.

IV. Fashion
Folkways
Holidays
Social Issues and Crime
Sports

In boxing, Ezzard Charles successfully defended the world heavyweight title against Freddie Beshore (Aug. 15), Joe Louis (Sept. 27), and Nick Barone (Dec. 5). In golf the top money winners were Sam Snead, $35,758.83, and Mildred "Babe" Didrikson Zaharias, $14,800. In fashion, designers acted with more modesty as the bikini bathing suit lost its popularity and dresses became more wearable and natural. The biggest single fashion note was the reappearance of stoles for use during the day as well as at night. The younger set wore their hair short and dressed in dungarees and ballet shoes. This latter fad may have been prompted by an outburst of activity in the dance world. American dance companies won over European audiences, and dancers from abroad toured the U.S., enjoying packed houses wherever they played.

Feb 8: Man o' War was named the greatest horse of the first half of the century by an Associated Press poll. Known as a horse that excelled as sprinter and distance runner, he ran as a two-year-old and a three-year-old, winning 20 out of 21 starts and breaking five track records.

Mar 28: The **NCAA basketball championship** was won by CCNY, defeating Bradley University 71 to 68.

Apr 8-23: The **first NBA (National Basketball Association) basketball championship** was won by the Minneapolis Lakers, who beat the Syracuse Nationals four games to two.

June 10: The **U.S. Open golf tournament** ended regular play with a three-way tie among Ben Hogan, Lloyd Mangrum, and George Fazio. On June 11 Hogan, in a spectacular comeback after an auto accident in 1949, won an 18-hole playoff round, beating Mangrum by four strokes and Fazio by six strokes.

June 27: The **PGA golf tournament** was won by Chandler Harper.

July 7: At the **Wimbledon** tennis championships in England, the men's singles title was won by V. Ed-

ward "Budge" Patty. The next day Louise Brough won the women's singles. Louise Brough and Margaret Osborne du Pont won the women's doubles and Brough teamed with Eric Strugess of South Africa to win the mixed doubles.

Sep 26: In the **Davis Cup** international tennis challenge round, the Australian team won its third straight match from the U.S., thereby ensuring victory. The Australians went on to win the round 4 to 1.

Oct 4-7: The 47th annual **World Series** was won by the New York Yankees (AL), defeating the Philadelphia Phillies (NL) in four straight games.

Dec 24: The **NFL championship** was won by the Cleveland Browns, who defeated the Los Angeles Rams 30 to 28.

1951

I. Civil Rights
Exploration and Settlement
Government
Statistics
Wars

The world hovered close to the brink of a third world war. Chinese Communist troops had unofficially entered the Korean campaign, operating from bases above the Yalu R. Gen. Douglas MacArthur advocated attacks on strategic positions within Chinese territory, a move that would be tantamount to declaring war on China, which had a military alliance with the U.S.S.R. American casualties had reached 100,000 and tempers at home were getting short. With this crisis before them, government leaders framed a foreign policy emphasizing preparation for war. A huge increase in taxes was asked, universal military training was urged, and a ring of bases around the U.S.S.R. was suggested. General war was averted when the administration stood with the UN on the decision not to attack Chinese bases.

Jan 1: Chinese Communist troops in Korea broke through the defense perimeter around Seoul and took Inchon and Kimpo airfield. Seoul was abandoned three days later.

Feb 26: The **Twenty-second Amendment** to the U.S. Constitution was adopted. It stipulated that no person may be elected to the presidency for more than two terms. A vice president succeeding to the presidency and serving more than half the term of his predecessor would be eligible for only one more term.

Mar 14: Seoul was recaptured by U.S. forces. This was the second time the South Korean capital was recaptured by UN forces. The reoccupation of Seoul marked a strategic and psychological victory over the enemy forces, whose lines had been broken and who were steadily being forced north, back over the 38th parallel and into North Korea.

Mar 21: U.S. armed forces numbered 2,900,000 according to Defense Sec. George C. Marshall. This was double the strength of U.S. armed forces at the outbreak of the Korean War (1950–1953).

Apr 4: SHAPE (Supreme Headquarters, Allied Powers in Europe) was established in Paris. Gen. Dwight D. Eisenhower assumed command.

Apr 11: Gen. **Douglas MacArthur was relieved** of all commands by Pres. Harry S Truman. His posts as supreme commander, Allied powers; commander in chief, UN command; commander in chief, Far East; and commanding general, U.S. Army, Far East were all filled by Lt. Gen. Matthew Ridgway.

Apr 19: Gen. **Douglas MacArthur** addressed a joint session of Congress, defending his Korean policies and beliefs and declaring his military career to be at its end. Recalling words of a ballad, "Old soldiers never die, they just fade away," MacArthur stated: "I now close my military career and just fade away, an old soldier who tried to do his duty as God gave him the light to see that duty."

June 23: A **cease-fire in Korea** was proposed by Jacob Malik, Soviet delegate to the UN, who called for withdrawal of troops from the 38th parallel. On June 30 Gen. Matthew Ridgway sent North Korea a proposal to negotiate a cease-fire agreement. Kim Il Sung, the North Korean commander, and Gen. Peng Teh-huai, the Chinese commander, agreed the next day to meet UN representatives to discuss cease-fire proposals.

July 10: The **first Korean truce talks** were held between UN and Korean representatives at Kaesong, on the 38th parallel in North Korea.

July 11-25: The costliest **flood** to date in U.S. history occurred when the Missouri R. and its tributaries flooded more than 1,000,000 acres of farmland in Kansas, Oklahoma, Missouri, and Illinois. Kansas City suffered particularly severe damage on July 14. Property loss was estimated at more than $1,000,000,000.

Sep 8: A **peace treaty with Japan** was signed in San Francisco by delegates of 48 nations. The U.S.S.R., Poland, and Czechoslovakia did not sign.

Oct 10: The **Mutual Security Act of 1951** was signed by Pres. Truman. It authorized $7,483,400,000 in U.S. foreign economic, military, and technical aid, and established a Mutual Security Agency. W. Averell Harriman was named head of the agency on the following day.

Oct 24: The **state of war with Germany** was declared officially ended by Pres. Truman.

II. Architecture
Arts and Music
Popular Entertainment
Publishing
Theater

Some 11,000 book titles were published this year. The phenomenal sale of paperback books led many publishers to launch a series of these editions. Architects were forced to concentrate on industrial and defense work, although some work was accomplished in the design of school buildings. Painters continued to work in abstractions, and American regionalism all but vanished from contemporary exhibitions. After a brief season of experimentation, the theater returned to the tried-and-true musical.

Among **books published** this year was *Requiem for a Nun* by William Faulkner, a novel written partly in the form of a play. The novel continued the story of Temple Drake, central character in Faulkner's 1931 novel *Sanctuary*. Other books published this year included *The Morning Watch* by James Agee, the author's first novel; *The Grass Harp* by Truman Capote, a novel; *The Sea Around Us* by Rachel Carson; *Mr. Lincoln's Army* by Bruce Catton; *Barbary Shore* by Norman Mailer, a novel; *Lie Down in Darkness*, a first novel by William Styron; and *The Caine Mutiny* by Herman Wouk, a novel.

Jan 22: The **Bollingen Prize** for poetry was awarded to John Crowe Ransom for his contributions to American poetry.

May 7: Pulitzer prizes were awarded for the following: fiction, *The Town* by Conrad Richter; biography, *John C. Calhoun: American Portrait* by Margaret Louise Coit; history, *The Old Northwest, Pioneer Period 1815–1840, Volumes I-II* by R. Carlyle Buley; poetry, *Complete Poems* by Carl Sandburg.

III. Business and Industry
Education
Philosophy and Religion
Science

Employment of women in American industry reached its highest point in history, even higher than during World War II. Wages were up, but so were prices; total employment figures were robust.

Alarmed over the growing inflation, the administration tried to institute a program of production controls. Two hundred thousand consumer items were placed under price controls, but attempts to freeze all prices and wages failed. Sen. Estes Kefauver of Tennessee, chairman of a Senate committee on organized crime in interstate commerce, opened hearings to television cameras. For weeks the nation watched as underworld figures testified—or refused to do so—before the committee. In education, universities and colleges saw a sharp drop in enrollment.

May 15: The **American Telephone and Telegraph Company** reported that it was the first corporation to have more than 1,000,000 stockholders.

June 14: UNIVAC, an electronic digital computer designed by Dr. John W. Mauchly and J. Presper Eckert, Jr., and the first such computer built for commercial purposes, was dedicated and demonstrated in Philadelphia, Pa. Mauchly and Eckert had developed ENIAC, the world's first electronic digital computer, in the 1940s, then set up their own company to develop computers for business and industry. They ran into financial difficulties, and their operation was ultimately taken over by Remington Rand.

June 25: The **first commercial color TV broadcast** was presented by the Columbia Broadcasting System, which had spent $5,000,000 over 11 years to develop the required new technology. The four-hour program was carried by stations in New York City, Baltimore, Boston, Philadelphia, and Washington, D.C. Unfortunately, no color TV sets were owned by the public. CBS itself had only 30 or 40 color receivers, and most of these were used for technical or monitoring purposes. It would be months before the first color sets would become available for purchase.

July 11: Released time for **religious studies** for schoolchildren in New York State was upheld by the New York State Court of Appeals. It was upheld again by the U.S. Supreme Court on Apr. 28, 1952.

Oct 18: The **Nobel Prize in Physiology or Medicine** was awarded to Dr. Max Theiler of the International Health Division of the Rockefeller Institute for development of vaccine 17-D to combat yellow fever.

Nov 10: The first transcontinental **direct dial telephone service** was inaugurated when Englewood, N.J., mayor M. Leslie Denning called Alameda, Calif., mayor Frank P. Osborn. The call marked the beginning of a test program involving some 10,000 customers of the New Jersey Bell system.

Nov 15: The **Nobel Prize in Chemistry** was awarded jointly to Dr. Edwin M. McMillan and Dr. Glenn T. Seaborg of the University of California for their research in transuranic elements. They were the eighth and ninth Americans to win the Nobel Prize in Chemistry.

Dec 20: The **first atomic-powered generator** began producing electricity at the U.S. Reactor Testing Station in Idaho.

IV. Fashion
Folkways
Holidays
Social Issues and Crime
Sports

The baseball season gave fans the ultimate home run thrill. The Brooklyn Dodgers and New York Giants battled their way to a tie for the National League pennant. Each team had won one of the playoff games. Brooklyn led in the third and deciding contest 4 to 1, going into the ninth inning. New York managed one run and then two men got on base. Finally, at the last moment, Bobby Thomson, the Giants' third baseman, slammed a home run off a pitch of Ralph Branca that decided the game and the season. In golf the top money winners were Lloyd Mangrum, $26,088.83, and Mildred "Babe" Didrikson Zaharias (for the fourth year in a row), $15,087.

Feb 3: The **largest purse** to date in horse racing, $144,323, was won by Great Circle in the Santa Anita Maturity at Santa Anita Park, Arcadia, Calif. The jockey was Willie Shoemaker.

Mar 27: The **NCAA basketball championship** was won by Kentucky, which defeated Kansas State 68 to 58.

Apr 7-21: The **NBA basketball championship** was won by the Rochester Royals, who beat the New York Knickerbockers 79 to 75.

June 16: The **U.S. Open golf tournament** was won for the second year in a row by Ben Hogan.

July 3: The **PGA golf tournament** was won by Sam Snead. It was his third PGA victory.

July 6-7: At the **Wimbledon** tennis championships in England, Dick Savitt won the men's singles title and Doris Hart won the women's singles. Hart and Shirley Fry won the women's singles.

July 14: The **first horse to win $1,000,000** was Citation, who brought his total earnings to $1,085,760 by winning the Hollywood Gold Cup at Inglewood, Calif. The bay horse had run out of the money only once in 45 starts during a four-year career.

July 18: The **world heavyweight boxing championship** was won by "Jersey Joe" Walcott, who knocked out Ezzard Charles in the seventh round at Pittsburgh, Pa. At 37 Walcott was the oldest person to gain the title.

Oct 4-10: The 48th annual **World Series** was won by the New York Yankees (AL), who defeated the New

York Giants (NL) four games to two. The Giants had won the National League pennant by beating the Brooklyn Dodgers two games to one in a spectacular ninth inning recovery in the third game of the league playoff.

Dec 23: The **NFL championship** was won by the Los Angeles Rams, who defeated the Cleveland Browns 24 to 17.

1952

I. **Civil Rights**
   Exploration and Settlement
   Government
   Statistics
   Wars

Early in the year British Prime Minister Winston Churchill visited the U.S. to reestablish close ties between Great Britain and the U.S. and to formulate unified policy on problems facing the West. The leading problem was the spreading danger of communist domination. U.S. policy was to arm western Europe and make it too costly for the U.S.S.R. to start a war. Opponents of this U.S.-British alliance included former Pres. Herbert Hoover, who claimed the U.S. was carrying Europe at disastrous expense. A far better plan, he maintained, was to retire to the Western Hemisphere and build a "bastion of liberty." Although 1952 was an election year, this issue was never a serious part of the campaign since the two major candidates, Adlai E. Stevenson and Dwight D. Eisenhower, supported the NATO alliance. While both Stevenson and Eisenhower enjoyed enormous popularity, the Democrats suffered from charges of corruption in the administration of Pres. Harry S Truman. Eisenhower's eventual victory was interpreted by many as a rebuke to the Truman administration. In spite of truce negotiations in Korea, some ground and air action continued; it intensified in October when truce talks were temporarily postponed.

Mar 8: Charges of **germ warfare** were formally lodged against the U.S. by Chinese Foreign Minister Chou En-lai. The charges, reported by Radio Peking, were supported by the Soviet representative to the UN, Jacob A. Malik. An offer by the International Red Cross to investigate was rejected by Malik, and on Mar. 28 the UN ruled Malik's charges out of order.

Mar 20: The **Japanese Peace Treaty** was ratified by the U.S. Senate by a vote of 66 to 10.

June 25: The **McCarran-Walter Bill** to revise and limit immigration was vetoed by Pres. Truman as un-American and discriminatory. The following day the House of Representatives overrode the veto 278–113. The Senate took similar action on June 27 by a vote of 57–26. The law abolished racial restrictions on immigration and retained a quota system based on the national origins count of 1920.

July 11: The **Republican National Convention nominated Gen. Dwight D. Eisenhower** for the presidency. Sen. Richard M. Nixon of California was nominated for the vice presidency.

July 16: A **G.I. Bill of Rights** was signed by Pres. Truman. It offered Korean veterans with 90 days of service as of June 27, 1950, rights and benefits similar to those granted to veterans of World War II.

July 26: The **Democratic National Convention nominated Gov. Adlai E. Stevenson** of Illinois for the presidency and Sen. John J. Sparkman of Alabama for the vice presidency.

Oct 24: Gen. **Eisenhower vowed to go to Korea** to seek an early and honorable conclusion to the conflict there if elected to the presidency. Eisenhower spoke in Detroit, Mich., on the last stop of his whistle-stop campaign tour.

Nov 4: Dwight D. Eisenhower was elected president of the United States. Sen. Richard M. Nixon of California was elected vice president. The electoral vote was Eisenhower, 442, Gov. Adlai E. Stevenson, Democrat, 89. The popular vote was Eisenhower, 33,938,285; Stevenson, 27,312,217; Vincent Hallinan, Progressive, 140,138; Stuart Hamblen, Prohibition, 72,881; Darlington Hoopes, Socialist, 20,189. In congressional elections the Republicans gained one Senate seat for a 48–47 majority, with one seat going to a minor party. In the House they gained 22 seats, for a 221–211 majority, one seat going to a minor party.

Nov 29: President-elect **Eisenhower flew to Korea,** fulfilling his campaign promise, and inspected the UN forces there. On a three-day tour, he visited front-line positions. The tour was kept secret until he had returned from the zone of danger.

II. **Architecture**
   Arts and Music
   Popular Entertainment
   Publishing
   Theater

A building boom spurred architects to design with distinction, using new types of construction, notably employing prestressed concrete. The year saw much travel by musical organizations both in the U.S. and abroad. The Boston Symphony made its first European tour. George Gershwin's *Porgy and Bess* played to enthusiastic houses in Berlin, Vienna, and London. The most noticeable trend was a growing acceptance of so-called modern works. Igor Stravinsky, for instance, was slowly achieving full acceptance as a composer. In painting, a movement away from abstractionism toward representationalism was noted. This year's Broadway offerings were so lackluster that George Jean Nathan refused to issue his annual volume reviewing the season.

Among **books published** this year was *Invisible Man* by Ralph Ellison, a powerful novel about the struggle of a young black to find a sense of personal worth as a human being. The novel followed the young man as he moved from southern town to university to Harlem, from innocence to bitter pessimism. Other books published this year included *The Old Man and the Sea* by Ernest Hemingway, a short novel relating the symbolic tale of an old Caribbean fisherman struggling to catch a giant marlin; *Collected Poems 1917–1952* by Archibald MacLeish; and *East of Eden* by John Steinbeck, the author's longest novel, a panoramic story of a California family from the late nineteenth century through World War I.

Jan 11: The **Bollingen Prize** for poetry was awarded to Marianne Moore for her 1951 volume *Collected Poems*.

May 5: Pulitzer prizes were awarded for the following: fiction, *The Caine Mutiny* by Herman Wouk; biography, *Charles Evans Hughes* by Merlo J. Pusey; history, *The Uprooted* by Oscar Handlin; poetry, *Collected Poems* by Marianne Moore; drama, *The Shrike* by Joseph Kramm.

III. Business and Industry
Education
Philosophy and Religion
Science

Inflation was now a reality. Employment had reached a record high of 62,500,000. Prices continued to zoom. The U.S. Treasury recorded a deficit of $4,000,000,000. A major development on the labor front was the three-way struggle involving the steel industry, the Steelworkers of America (C.I.O.), and the U.S. president. When the union prepared to walk out for wage hikes, Pres. Truman seized the mills on the grounds that steel was vital to U.S. defense. Management retaliated by securing an injunction against the seizure; a federal district court then pronounced the president's action unconstitutional, a ruling upheld by the Supreme Court. This sent steelworkers out on what developed into a 54-day strike. Pres. Truman asked Congress for legislation permitting seizure of vital industries, but the Senate advised him to use the provisions of the Taft-Hartley law. Instead, he called both sides to the White House, where they settled the dispute in a conference.

Mar 2: Those considered **subversives could be barred from teaching** in public schools, according to a U.S. Supreme Court decision.

Apr 8: The nation's **steel mills were seized** by presidential order to prevent a shutdown by strikers. The next day three major steel companies instituted legal action in federal court, Washington, D.C., to contest the seizure. They were denied a temporary restraining order.

Apr 29: The **seizure of steel mills** was declared unconstitutional by U.S. District Judge David A. Pine. Steelworkers immediately went on strike.

May 2: The **steel strike was ended** by the steelworkers' union at presidential request.

June 2: Presidential **seizure of steel mills** was declared unconstitutional by the U.S. Supreme Court. Pres. Truman ordered the plants returned to their owners, and the steelworkers resumed their strike.

June 30: American stockholders numbered some 6,500,000. Of these, 76% earned less than $10,000 a year after taxes, according to a report made by the Brookings Institute.

July 7: A new **transatlantic speed record** for ships was set by the S.S. *United States* on its first round trip with an eastward crossing of 3 days, 10 hrs., 40 min. On July 14 it set a westward crossing record of 3 days, 12 hrs., 12 min.

July 24: The **steel strike was settled** when management and labor reached a compromise agreement at a White House conference called by Pres. Truman.

Oct 23: The **Nobel Prize in Physiology or Medicine** was awarded to Dr. Selman A. Waksman of Rutgers University for his discovery, with others, of streptomycin.

Nov 6: The **Nobel Prize in Physics** was awarded jointly to Dr. Edward Mills Purcell of Harvard University and to Dr. Felix Bloch of Stanford University for their work in the measurement of magnetic fields in atomic nuclei. They were the eighth and ninth Americans to receive the award in this field.

Nov 25: George Meany of New York was appointed president of the AFL to fill the unexpired term of William Green, who died on Nov. 21.

Dec 4: Walter P. Reuther, president of the United Auto Workers, was chosen to head the CIO.

IV. Fashion
    Folkways
    Holidays
    Social Issues and Crime
    Sports

This was a year of flying saucers, panty raids, and prison riots. Unidentified flying objects, frequently described as luminous disks or saucers, were reported flashing across night skies all over the nation. The Air Force even published photographs of the phenomena. There was widespread conjecture that these objects were manned by emissaries from outer space. While the nation watched the night skies, college boys across the country seemed intent on besieging sorority houses and girls' dormitories demanding as ransom articles of feminine underclothing, which were freely bestowed. Disturbances of a more serious nature plagued prison officials. Inmates pressing for more liberal treatment took guards as hostages while they bargained with prison authorities. These riots led to a review of state and federal prison systems.

Feb 15-25: At the **Winter Olympics** in Oslo, Norway, the U.S. won four gold medals and finished second in unofficial team standings .

Mar 26: The **NCAA basketball championship** was won by Kansas, which defeated St. John's 80 to 63.

Apr 12-15: The **NBA basketball championship** was won by the Minneapolis Lakers, who beat the New York Knickerbockers four games to three.

June 14: The **U.S. Open golf tournament** was won by Julius Boros, who beat Ed Oliver by four strokes and Ben Hogan, the defending champion, by five.

June 25: The **PGA golf tournament** was won by Jim Turnesa.

July 5: At the **Wimbledon** tennis championships in England, Maureen Connolly won the women's singles title. Doris Hart and Shirley Fry won the women's doubles.

July 19-Aug 3: At the **Summer Olympics** in Helsinki, Finland, the U.S. won 40 gold medals and finished first in the unofficial team standings.

Sep 23: The **world heavyweight boxing championship** was won by Rocky Marciano, who knocked out "Jersey Joe" Walcott in the 13th round of a bout in Philadelphia. It was Marciano's 43rd straight win as a professional boxer, with no losses.

Oct 1-7: The 49th annual **World Series** was won by the New York Yankees (AL), defeating the Brooklyn Dodgers (NL) four games to three.

Dec 28: The **NFL championship** was won by the Detroit Lions, who defeated the Cleveland Browns 17 to 7.

1953

I. Civil Rights
    Exploration and Settlement
    Government
    Statistics
    Wars

The nation watched with interest as a Republican administration took over the reins of government for the first time in 24 years. Pres. Dwight D. Eisenhower had uncertain control of Congress, the Republicans ruling there by the grace of conservative southern Democrats. The president made immediate attempts to improve his position with the legislative branch by announcing he favored a close presidential-congressional partnership. The new chief executive had four major areas of foreign policy to deal with: countering Russian expansion all over the globe; bolstering European allies by economic and military aid; fostering European unity; and forcing an equitable armistice in Korea. The most explosive internal problem was Sen. Joseph R. McCarthy, Republican of Wisconsin, charging Soviet espionage activities in the U.S. The administration's most outstanding success was a peace agreement in Korea. Pres. Eisenhower announced the agreement to a relieved country but warned, "We have won an armistice on a single battleground, not peace in the world."

In the **Korean War** (1950–1953), U.S. armed forces casualties totaled 137,051; of this number, 25,604 were killed; 103,492 were wounded; and 7955 were reported missing.

Jan 2: A report on the actions of Sen. **Joseph R. McCarthy** of Wisconsin issued by a Senate privileges and elections subcommittee stated that some of McCarthy's political activities had been "motivated by self-interest." McCarthy was known for his headline-grabbing charges of communist infiltration in various organizations.

Jan 21: Thirteen communist leaders were convicted by a federal jury in New York City of conspiring to advocate overthrow of the U.S. government.

Apr 1: The **Department of Health, Education and Welfare** (HEW) was created by joint congressional action. On Apr. 11 Mrs. Oveta Culp Hobby of Texas was sworn in as the department's first head.

Apr 24: Record **taxes** of $68,500,000,000 were collected in 1952 according to the U.S. Bureau of Internal Revenue.

Apr 25: A **record for filibustering** was set in the U.S. Senate by Sen. Wayne Morse, Independent of Oregon, who held the floor for 22 hrs., 26 min. opposing a bill that would return offshore oil reserves to the individual states. His marathon failed to sway the Senate, which passed the measure on May 5 by a vote of 56–35.

June 18: The worst **air accident** to date occurred near Tokyo, Japan, when a U.S. Air Force Globemaster crashed, killing 129 persons.

June 19: Julius and Ethel Rosenberg were executed at Sing Sing Prison in Ossining, N.Y. They were the first civilians to be executed in the U.S. for espionage. The couple had been convicted on Apr. 5, 1951, of passing secret information about the atom bomb to the U.S.S.R. Their deaths were the subject of protests around the world.

July 27: A **Korean armistice** was signed at Panmunjom by UN, North Korean, and Chinese delegates.

Aug 1: A broader **Social Security Act** was proposed by Pres. Eisenhower, who recommended provisions to include another 10,500,000 persons under the law. The proposed legislation was passed on Sept. 1, 1954.

Aug 7: The **Refugee Relief Act** of 1953 was signed by Pres. Eisenhower. It admitted 214,000 more refugees than permitted under existing immigration quotas.

II. Architecture
Arts and Music
Popular Entertainment
Publishing
Theater

There was a bountiful supply of good books this year, but few really distinguished ones. Of particular interest was the publication of a large number of books, mostly novels, by highly competent black writers. Architects looked forward to boom times with commercial construction up 43.2%. Important music festivals in the U.S. and abroad attracted many composers. American painting reverted to the abstract form, but it also discovered the primitivism of Grandma Moses, who received worldwide recognition. Despite Broadway's usual complaints of rising production costs and shortages of houses and scripts, the season showed a marked improvement. Filmgoers were treated to several innovations, including stereophonic sound; 3-D, intended to give the illusion of three dimensions; and several wide-screen processes. The most popular type of film was the science fiction thriller.

Among **books published** this year was *The Adventures of Augie March* by Saul Bellow, a novel offering a panoramic view of middle-class Chicago in the 1920s and 1930s. Other books published this year included *Go Tell It on the Mountain* by James Baldwin, the author's first novel; *Simple Takes a Wife* by Langston Hughes; *The Bridges at Toko-ri* by James Michener; *The Light in the Forest* by Conrad Richter; *Always The Young Strangers* by Carl Sandburg, an account of the poet's youth; *Battle Cry* by Leon Uris; and *The Outsider* by Richard Wright.

Jan 10: The **Bollingen Prize** for poetry was awarded jointly to Archibald MacLeish for his 1952 volume *Collected Poems, 1917–1952,* and to William Carlos Williams for his entire body of work.

May 4: Pulitzer prizes were awarded for the following: fiction, *The Old Man and the Sea* by Ernest Hemingway; biography, *Edmund Pendleton, 1721–1803* by David J. Mays; history, *The Era of Good Feeling* by George Dangerfield; poetry, *Collected Poems, 1917–1952* by Archibald MacLeish; drama, *Picnic* by William Inge.

III. Business and Industry
Education
Philosophy and Religion
Science

Americans numbered nearly 161,000,000. The country continued to enjoy unprecedented prosperity, even though the 1953 dollar was worth about 52 cents compared with its 1935–1939 equivalent. Greatly increased personal income more than made up the difference for much of the population. This year saw the end of wage and salary controls. Labor continued its fight for abolition of the Taft-Hartley law. A broad economic program was announced by the administration. It included revision of the tax laws—including modification or elimination of the excess profits tax to benefit corporations—and double taxation of dividends; shifting of the national debt to long-term bonds; and providing for a sliding scale interest rate based on demand. This last provision was designed as a check to inflationary borrowing.

The Ford Foundation established **The Fund for the Republic** and gave it $15,000,000 "to help fight restriction on freedom of thought, inquiry and expression."

Mar 30: Jet-propelled guided missiles were under production according to the U.S. Navy.

May 25: The **first atomic artillery shell** was fired at a military testing range in Nevada.

Oct 22: The **Nobel Prize for Physiology or Medicine** was awarded jointly to Dr. Fritz Albert Lipmann of Harvard University Medical School for his discovery of co-enzyme A and its function in metabolic processes; and to Dr. Hans Adolf Krebs of Sheffield University in England for his discovery of the citric acid cycle, known as the Krebs cycle.

Dec 16: A new **airplane speed record** was achieved by U.S. Air Force Major Charles E. Yeager, who flew a Bell X-1A rocket powered plane more than 1600 mph.

IV. Fashion
   Folkways
   Holidays
   Social Issues and Crime
   Sports

The year's biggest fashion news was a designers' invasion into the field of men's clothes. Bermuda shorts were promoted for the hot summer months. For the ladies, a mood of sleek elegance was decreed. Skirts were shorter, and so were hair styles. The Italian haircut became the vogue. It called for a carefully casual female crew cut that gave the wearer a gamin-like, windblown look. This year Rocky Marciano defended his world heavyweight title in bouts against "Jersey Joe" Walcott (May 15) and Roland LaStarza (Sept. 24). In golf the top money winners were Lew Worsham, $34,002, and Louise Suggs, $19,816. Fans mourned the death of one of the greatest athletes of all time, Jim Thorpe, Mar. 28, at age 64.

Mar 18: The **NCAA basketball championship** was won by Indiana, defeating Kansas 69–68.

Mar 18: The move of the **Boston Braves** baseball franchise to Milwaukee, Wis., was approved by the National League. This year Milwaukee led both leagues in attendance.

Apr 4-10: The **NBA basketball championship** was won by the Minneapolis Lakers, who defeated the New York Knickerbockers four games to one.

June 13: The **U.S. Open golf tournament** was won by Ben Hogan, who beat Sam Snead by six strokes to become the third person in history to win the tournament four times.

July 3: At the **Wimbledon** tennis championships in England, Victor Seixas won the men's singles title. The next day Maureen Connolly won the women's singles. Doris Hart and Shirley Fry won the women's doubles, and Hart and Seixas won the mixed doubles.

July 7: The **PGA golf tournament** was won by Walter Burkemo.

Sep 16: The shift of the **St. Louis Browns** baseball franchise to Baltimore, Md., was approved by the American League. The Browns would play the 1954 season as the Baltimore Orioles.

Sep 30-Oct 5: The 50th annual **World Series** was won by the New York Yankees (AL), defeating the Brooklyn Dodgers (NL) four games to two. This was the first time a team had won five consecutive World Series.

Dec 27: The **NFL championship** was won by the Detroit Lions, who defeated the Cleveland Browns 17 to 16.

1954

I. Civil Rights
   Exploration and Settlement
   Government
   Statistics
   Wars

Pres. Dwight D. Eisenhower declared that his foreign policy would be dedicated to regaining the initiative in the world fight against communism and to winning the confidence of U.S. allies. With regard to defense, the president advocated intensive research on atomic weapons and an integrated transcontinental transportation system for civil as well as military travel. It included development of the St. Lawrence Seaway to open the central states to seagoing traffic via the Great Lakes. He advocated greater discretion in loyalty investigations, but promised decisive action in all cases of espionage or sabotage. He also revealed that some 2200 government employees had been dropped under the administration's new security system. Later in the year, the president asked Congress to enact legislation to enable the Atomic Energy Commission to share certain atomic secrets with U.S. allies and to pave the way for industrial development of the atom. The U.S. took part in the London conference (Sept. 28-Oct. 3) and the Paris conference (Oct. 20–23) in which it was agreed that U.S. and British forces would remain in Europe to help keep the peace. The West German Federal Republic (West Germany) was admitted to NATO on Oct. 23. But the major international event was the French defeat at Dien Bien Phu on May 7, causing withdrawal of French forces from Vietnam and the partition of the country into northern and southern states, with elections for reunification to be held in July 1956.

Mar 1: Five congressmen were shot on the floor of the House of Representatives by Puerto Rican nationalists. All recovered from their wounds.

Mar 8: A **mutual defense agreement** was signed by Japan and the U.S. It provided for gradual and partial rearming of Japan.

Mar 10: The **first atomic power plant** was planned for the Duquesne Power Co., Pittsburgh, Pa., by the Atomic Energy Commission. Pres. Eisenhower, using a special remote hookup, broke ground for it from Denver, Colo., on Sept. 6.

Apr 8: Construction of an **early warning radar net** stretching 3000 miles across the Canadian far north was announced by the U.S. and Canada.

Apr 23-June 17: The **Army-McCarthy hearings** were conducted by the Senate Permanent Subcommittee on Investigations. The hearings were held to investigate charges by its chairman, Sen. Joseph R. McCarthy, Republican of Wisconsin, that Sec. of the Army Robert T. Stevens and Army counsel John G. Adams were hampering the committee's attempts to uncover communists in the military. Stevens and Adams countercharged that McCarthy and his staff had tried to get preferential treatment for one of its former staff members, Pvt. G. David Schine. The hearings, given broad television and newspaper coverage, did much to end the anticommunist witch hunt led by McCarthy.

May 17: Racial **segregation in public schools** was declared unconstitutional by the U.S. Supreme Court. The Court handed down a single ruling on four state cases, including *Brown v. Board of Education* of Topeka, Kans., and another involving the District of Columbia. The rulings outlawed the practice of "separate but equal" facilities in public school systems.

May 24: Communist Party membership was declared to be sufficient grounds for deportation of aliens in a U.S. Supreme Court decision that upheld the constitutionality of the Internal Security Act of 1950.

July 30: A **resolution of censure** against Sen. Joseph R. McCarthy for conduct unbecoming a senator was introduced in the Senate by Sen. Ralph E. Flanders, Republican of Vermont. A Senate select committee subsequently voted to censure McCarthy on two counts of the resolution.

Sep 1: Hurricane Carol struck Long Island, N.Y., and New England, killing 68. Property losses were estimated at $500,000,000.

Sep 3: The **Espionage and Sabotage Act** of 1954 was signed by Pres. Eisenhower. The death penalty was authorized for peacetime sabotage and the statute of limitations for these crimes was removed.

Sep 30: The **first atomic-powered submarine,** the U.S.S. *Nautilus,* was commissioned at Groton, Conn.

Oct 15: Hurricane Hazel, the most violent hurricane of the year, killed 99 persons in the U.S. and 249 in Canada. Combined U.S. and Canadian property losses were put at $100,000,000.

Nov 2: In **congressional elections** the Democrats gained one Senate seat for a 48–47 majority, with one seat going to a minor party. In the House they gained 21 seats, for a 232–203 majority.

Dec 2: Sen. **McCarthy was condemned** in a vote of a special session of the U.S. Senate for his conduct in Senate committees.

Dec 11: The **largest warship** ever built, the 59,650-ton aircraft carrier U.S.S. *Forestal,* was launched at Newport News, Va.

Dec 27: A new **land speed record** of 632 mph was announced by the Air Force. The speed was achieved by an experimental rocket-powered sled.

II. Architecture
Arts and Music
Popular Entertainment
Publishing
Theater

Books on the Cold War, U.S. foreign policy, government loyalty programs, subversion, and the A-bomb filled rental libraries and bookstore. Novelists favored an exploration of the psychopathic mentality, but said little new or surprising. A major development for poets was an ever-increasing list of awards and prizes open to them; they responded by writing more and better verse. The building boom of 1953 showed no signs of letup; in fact, July set a record with $3,135,000,000 in new construction. All areas of musical endeavor reported great demand. Established symphonic societies and popular musical festivals continued to give composers commissions. Four works by Igor Stravinsky were introduced this year: *Septet* for violin, cello, viola, clarinet, horn, bassoon, and piano; *Three Songs from William Shakespeare; In Memoriam: Dylan Thomas;* and *Four Russian Peasant Songs.* Filmgoers were treated to a rash of spectacular historical epics and westerns. Some 7448 movie houses had CinemaScope facilities.

Among **books published** this year was *A Fable* by William Faulkner, a retelling of the crucifixion and resurrection of Jesus set against the background of World War I. Other books published this year included *No Time for Sergeants* by Mac Hyman, a delightful tale of an innocent Georgia youth drafted into the Air Force; *The Bird's Nest* by Shirley Jackson, a novel about a girl with four personalities; *The Bad Seed* by William March, a novel depicting a young girl as the incarnation of evil; *Sweet Thursday* by John Steinbeck, a sequel to his novel *Cannery Row* (1945); *The Collected Poems of Wallace Stevens;* and *The Ponder Heart,* a novel by Eudora Welty.

Some 29,000,000 households had **television** sets.

This represented about 60% of American households. Television had not been marketed seriously until about 1947.

Jan 10: The **Bollingen Prize** for poetry was awarded to W.H. Auden.

May 3: Pulitzer prizes were awarded for the following: biography, *The Spirit of St. Louis* by Charles A. Lindbergh; history, *A Stillness at Appomattox* by Bruce Catton; poetry, *The Waking: Poems 1933–1953* by Theodore Roethke; drama, *The Teahouse of the August Moon* by John Patrick.

Oct 28: The **Nobel Prize for Literature** was awarded to Ernest Hemingway "for his powerful style-forming mastery of the art of modern narration." Among Hemingway's works were *The Sun Also Rises* (1926), *A Farewell to Arms* (1929), and *For Whom the Bell Tolls* (1940).

III. Business and Industry
Education
Philosophy and Religion
Science

A business recession coupled with rising unemployment worried some Americans, but administration spokesmen told the nation that some fallback from unprecedented economic highs was desirable. The downward trend was reversed about the middle of the year. By September personal income had exceeded the August figure by $2,000,000,000. Unemployment, though, totaled 2,893,000, about twice the figure reported for 1953. The AFL and CIO agreed to merge, and AFL president George Meany predicted that the merger would take place in 1955. Huge crop surpluses resulted in stringent curbs by the Agriculture Department. Sec. of Agriculture Ezra Benson was given authority to barter surplus crops on the world market in exchange for strategic goods. Schools were suffering from overcrowding and, with the Supreme Court decision on May 14 outlawing segregation in public schools, there was confusion in the ranks of school administrators.

Feb 2: Detonation of the **first hydrogen bomb** was officially reported by Pres. Eisenhower. It had taken place at Eniwetok Atoll in the Pacific in 1952.

Feb 23: Antipolio inoculation of schoolchildren was begun in Pittsburgh, Pa., by Dr. Jonas E. Salk, developer of the serum.

Mar 24: A **hydrogen bomb** explosion in the Marshall Islands on Mar. 1 exceeded all estimates of its power, according to a statement made by Pres. Eisenhower.

May 13: The **St. Lawrence Seaway Bill,** authorizing construction of a joint U.S. and Canadian artificial waterway connecting the Great Lakes and the Atlantic Ocean, was signed by Pres. Eisenhower. On June 9 he named Sec. of Defense Charles E. Wilson director of the St. Lawrence Seaway Development Corporation.

Oct 13: The **first supersonic bomber,** the B-58, was ordered into production by the Air Force.

Oct 21: The **Nobel Prize for Physiology or Medicine** was awarded to John F. Enders of the Harvard School of Medicine, Thomas H. Weller of the Harvard School of Public Health, and Frederick C. Robins of Western Reserve Medical School for their work in the cultivation of the polio virus.

Nov 3: The **Nobel Prize in Chemistry** was awarded to Linus Pauling of the California Institute of Technology for his study of the forces holding together protein and other molecules.

Dec 31: New York Stock Exchange prices were the highest quoted since 1929. The volume of shares traded during 1954 (573,374,622) was the highest since 1933.

IV. Fashion
Folkways
Holidays
Social Issues and Crime
Sports

The continuing antics of Sen. Joseph R. McCarthy was a topic of conversation along with rising juvenile crime and delinquency. Families discussed discipline and examined outside influences. Lurid comic books and violence-spattered pulp magazines came under attack from parents' groups and, in some cases, legislators. Fashion designers introduced a softer silhouette that deemphasized the bust and showed a longer torso. In boxing, Rocky Marciano defended his world heavyweight title twice (June 17, Sept. 17) in bouts with Ezzard Charles. In golf, the top money winners were Bob Toski, $65,891.24, and Patty Berg, $16,011. Studies showed that the average American's favorite meal was fruit cup, vegetable soup, steak and potatoes, peas, rolls with butter, and pie à la mode. Some 90% of adult Americans drank three to four cups of coffee a day; 64% drank beer, wine, or liquor; and 45% smoked one pack of cigarettes a day. About 60% of the male population and 30% of the female population smoked.

Mar 20: The **NCAA basketball championship** was won by La Salle, defeating Bradley 92 to 76.

Mar 31-Apr 12: The **NBA basketball championship** was won by the Minneapolis Lakers, who defeated the Syracuse Nationals four games to one.

June 19: The **U.S. Open golf tournament** was won by Ed Furgol.

July 3: At the **Wimbledon** tennis championships in England, Maureen Connolly won the women's singles title, Louise Brough and Margaret Osborne du Pont the women's doubles, and Victor Seixas and Doris Hart the mixed doubles.

July 27: The **PGA golf tournament** was won by Chick Harbert.

Sep 29-Oct 2: The 51st annual **World Series** was won by the New York Giants (NL), defeating the Cleveland Indians (AL) in four straight games.

Nov 8: The shift of the **Philadelphia Athletics** baseball franchise to Kansas City, Mo., was approved by the American League.

Dec 26: The **NFL championship** was won by the Cleveland Browns, who defeated the Detroit Lions 56–10.

Dec 28: The **Davis Cup** international tennis challenge round was won by the U.S., which defeated Australia three matches to two.

1955

I. Civil Rights
Exploration and Settlement
Government
Statistics
Wars

The marked easing of the Cold War brought about by what was called the Geneva spirit was engendered by Pres. Dwight D. Eisenhower's proposal to the U.S.S.R. for exchange of military blueprints and mutual aerial inspection. Nations that had been suspicious of U.S. foreign policy began to trust the U.S. a little more. At home, Americans enjoyed a new prosperity. They remodeled their cities in an unprecedented building boom, bought more expensive cars, planned dream homes, and flocked to buy home appliances, especially color TV sets. The Far East, however, was still a sorely troubled area, particularly in Indochina following the French defeat at Dien Bien Phu in May 1954.

Jan 14: The U.S. **Senate investigation of communism** was approved for continuation in a Senate vote of 84–0.

Jan 19: The **first filmed presidential press conference** took place. Both TV and motion picture newsreel photographers covered the event.

Jan 28: Defense of **Formosa and the Pescadores Islands** was pledged by the Senate by a vote of 85–3. On the following day the Chinese demanded that the U.N. order U.S. withdrawal from the entire Formosan area.

Feb 26: Some 4000 **atomic bombs** had been stockpiled by the U.S., and 1000 by the U.S.S.R., according to an unofficial estimate of Prof. Cecil F. Powell, the British scientist and winner of a Nobel Prize in Physics.

Mar 16: The **use of atomic weapons** in case of war was upheld in a statement made by Pres. Eisenhower.

July 18: The **Geneva conference,** attended by heads of state of the U.S., Great Britain, U.S.S.R., and France, opened at Geneva, Switzerland.

Aug 2: Funding for 45,000 new **public housing** units was approved by the House of Representatives, 187–168. The units were to be built by July 31, 1956.

Sep 8: A treaty establishing **SEATO,** the Southeast Asia Treaty Organization, was signed in Manila, the Philippines, by the U.S., Australia, France, Great Britain, New Zealand, Pakistan, the Phillipines, and Thailand. The mutual defense pact, the Southeast Asia Collective Defense Treaty, was ratified by the Senate on Feb. 1, 1955 and went into effect on Feb. 19. SEATO was formally ended on Feb. 20, 1976.

Nov 25: Racial segregation in interstate trains and buses was banned by the Interstate Commerce Commission.

II. Architecture
Arts and Music
Popular Entertainment
Publishing
Theater

A noteworthy trend in the year's publishing was the number of nonfiction books, especially those on child behavior. Architects hailed the continuing high level of construction, and church building reached its highest rate in history. New materials such as aluminum and plastics were being used in construction. The New York Philharmonic and Philadelphia orchestras embarked on extensive European tours. The Symphony of the Air headed east and played in Japanese concert halls. Highlights of the year in music included premieres of *Symphony No. Six* by Darius Milhaud (Boston, Oct. 7) and *Symphony No. Five* by Walter Piston (Boston, Nov. 25). A showing of contemporary American and European painters at the Museum of Modern Art, New York City, revealed that for the first time U.S. artists were surpassing their European peers in imaginative style and technique. The show featured Willem de Kooning, Jackson Pollock, Robert Motherwell, and Adolph Gottlieb.

Among **books published** this year was *Andersonville* by MacKinlay Kantor, a powerful Civil War novel about the notorious Confederate prison. Other books published this year included *The Day Lincoln Was Shot* by Jim Bishop; *A Good Man Is Hard to Find, and Other Stories* by Flannery O'Connor; *Band of Angels* by Robert Penn Warren, a novel set in the Civil War; *The Man in the Gray Flannel Suit* by Sloan Wilson; and *Marjorie Morningstar* by Herman Wouk, a novel.

Jan 9: The **Bollingen Prize** for poetry was awarded jointly to Louise Bogan for her *Collected Poems, 1922–1953* and Leonie Adams for her volume *Poems, A Selection,* both published in 1954.

May 2: Pulitzer prizes were awarded to the following: fiction, *A Fable* by William Faulkner; biography, *The Taft Story* by William S. White; history, *Great River, the Rio Grande in North American History* by Paul Horgan; poetry, *The Collected Poems of Wallace Stevens;* drama, *Cat on a Hot Tin Roof* by Tennessee Williams.

III. Business and Industry
Education
Philosophy and Religion
Science

The economy enjoyed a year of nearly full employment and peak production. Net business income was up 33% over the previous year. Labor stated new objectives, chief of which was attainment of a guaranteed annual wage. The organized labor force in the U.S. totaled 15,000,000 after the AFL and the CIO merged to become the American Federation of Labor and Congress of Industrial Organizations (AFL-CIO). The major concern of labor leaders was the increasing use of automation in industrial plants. Walter P. Reuther, vice president of the newly merged labor group, predicted a second industrial revolution as a result of automation. Farm income was down 5½% from 1954. Educators reported a shortage of 250,000 classrooms and 141,300 teachers.

Jan 8: Thorazine and reserpine, two new drugs, showed some success in the treatment of mental patients, according to the New York State Department of Mental Hygiene.

Feb 9: The **AFL-CIO merger** agreement was made public.

Apr 12: A successful **antipolio vaccine** was announced by Dr. Jonas E. Salk. Tests carried out in 44 states indicated its effectiveness against poliomyelitis.

May 23: The ordination of **women ministers** was approved by the General Assembly of the Presbyterian Church.

May 31: Racial segregation in U.S. public schools was banned by the U.S. Supreme Court.

Sep 12: A study of **foundations** by the American Foundations Information Service listed 7300 charitable, welfare, and research foundations in the U.S. Over 4000 had assets above $4,700,000.

Sep 26: The **New York Stock Exchange** recorded its heaviest single day dollar loss in history, $14,000,000,000. In all, 7,720,000 shares were traded, the highest volume since July 21, 1933. This sharp break in prices occurred two days after an announcement that Pres. Eisenhower had suffered a heart attack in Denver, Colo.

Oct 7: The aircraft carrier U.S.S. *Saratoga,* the world's most powerful warship, was launched at the Brooklyn (N.Y.) Navy Yard.

Oct 18: The **antiproton,** a new atomic subparticle, was discovered at the University of California.

Nov 2: The **Nobel Prize in Chemistry** was awarded to Dr. Vincent du Vigneaud of Cornell University Medical College for his work on two hormones important in childbirth and in regulation of vital organs.

Nov 2: The **Nobel Prize in Physics** was awarded jointly to Dr. Willis E. Lamb of Stanford University and to Dr. Polykarp Kusch of Columbia University for their work on atomic measurements.

Dec 5: The **AFL and CIO formally merged.** The new organization, the American Federation of Labor and Congress of Industrial Organizations (AFL-CIO), was headed by George Meany, former president of the AFL.

Dec 27: Traffic fatalities over the Christmas weekend numbered 609, a new record.

IV. Fashion
Folkways
Holidays
Social Issues and Crime
Sports

Davy Crockett and rock 'n' roll highlighted the year 1955. Originally, the Davy Crockett fad was started by a Technicolor movie produced in Hollywood by Walt Disney. Publicity agents then parlayed the legend of the frontiersman who died at the Alamo into a national fad—millions of Davy Crockett coonskin hats were manufactured and distributed, and fur dealers in New York City enjoyed one of the most prosperous years ever. Equally contagious was the mania for rock 'n' roll music, which many attacked as immoral, allegedly because of its monotonous, primitive beat. It was a gala year in Flatbush. The faithful rejoiced as the Brooklyn Dodgers won their first baseball championship, doubly welcome since they beat the mighty New York Yankees. In boxing, Rocky Marciano successfully defended the world heavyweight title in bouts with Don Cockell of Great Britain (May 16) and Archie Moore (Sept. 21). In golf the top money winners were Julius Boros, $65,121, and Patty Berg, $16,492. Fashion designers combined sophisticated sex appeal with fresh youthfulness, and favored a semifitted sheath of oriental design and color.

More than 1,000,000,000 **comic books** were sold annually, according to a report issued by the University of California, at an estimated cost of $100,000,000, four times the book budget of all U.S. public libraries combined. New York State passed a law banning the sale of lurid crime and horror comic books to persons under 18 years of age. Violations were punishable by a year in prison and/or a $500 fine.

Mar 19: The **NCAA basketball championship** was won by San Francisco, defeating La Salle 77 to 63.

Mar 21-Apr 10: The **NBA basketball championship** was won by the Syracuse Nationals, who beat the Fort Wayne Pistons four games to three.

June 19: The **U.S. Open golf tournament** was won by Jack Fleck, who beat Ben Hogan by three strokes in a playoff round.

July 1-2: At the **Wimbledon** tennis championships in England, Tony Trabert won the men's singles title and Louise Brough won the women's singles. Victor Seixas and Doris Hart won the mixed doubles.

July 26: The **PGA golf tournament** was won by Doug Ford.

Sep 28-Oct 4: The 52nd annual **World Series** was won by the Brooklyn Dodgers (NL), who defeated the New York Yankees (AL) four games to three.

Dec 26: The **NFL championship** was won by the Cleveland Browns, who defeated the Los Angeles Rams 38 to 14.

1956

I. Civil Rights
Exploration and Settlement
Government
Statistics
Wars

Tension with the U.S.S.R. still dominated the American scene. John Foster Dulles summed up the Cold War in his "brink of war" statement: "The ability to get to the verge without getting into the war is the necessary art." At home, there was bitter rivalry between the armed services, heightened in May by Army charges that the Air Force was not doing its job. Americans again found a conflict between the North and South. Southern states either ignored or rebelled against the Supreme Court ruling against segregation in the public schools. In Montgomery, Ala., blacks boycotted buses, and on November 13 the Supreme Court ruled that segregation on buses and streetcars was unconstitutional. Among those who died this year was Albert Woolson, the last surviving veteran of the Union Army, Aug. 2, at age 109.

Jan 9: In what was interpreted as a vote for **segregation,** Virginia amended a state prohibition against the use of public funds for private schools. The amendment helped support private education in a state where public schools had been shut down because of the 1954 Supreme Court ruling against segregation in public schools.

Feb 15: To enforce **school desegregation** in New Orleans, La., a federal court banned all Louisiana laws opposing the Supreme Court ruling against segregation in public schools.

Mar 27: The communist *Daily Worker* was seized by Internal Revenue Service agents for nonpayment of income taxes. The newspaper's New York, Chicago, and Detroit offices were returned on Apr. 3 after *Daily Worker* officers posted $4500 against their tax bill.

Apr 8: Six Marine recruits drowned while on a disciplinary march at Parris Island, S.C. Platoon Sgt. Matthew C. McKeon was convicted on Aug. 3 of drinking on duty and negligent homicide. He was reduced in rank to private and served a three-month prison sentence.

June 30: In the worst **commercial air disaster** to date, 128 persons were killed when two airliners crashed into the Grand Canyon. The accident involved a Trans-World Airlines Super-Constellation and a United Air Lines DC-7, which were thought to have collided in midair.

Aug 13-17: The **Democratic National Convention nominated Adlai E. Stevenson** of Illinois for the presidency on the first ballot. Sen. Estes Kefauver of Tennessee was nominated for the vice presidency.

Aug 20-24: The **Republican National Convention nominated Pres. Dwight D. Eisenhower** for a second term. Vice Pres. Richard M. Nixon was renominated as Eisenhower's running mate.

Aug 24: The **first transcontinental helicopter flight** was completed by an Army H-21 helicopter, which flew nonstop from San Diego, Calif., to Washington, D.C., in 37 hrs. With a crew of five, it flew 2610 miles.

Nov 6: Dwight D. Eisenhower was reelected president of the United States in a landslide. Eisenhower was the first Republican president to win reelection since William McKinley in 1900. Although Eisenhower carried 41 states, the Democrats retained control of both houses of Congress. The electoral vote was Eisenhower, 457; Adlai E. Stevenson, Democrat of Illinois, 74. The popular vote was Eisenhower, 35,387,015; Stevenson, 25,875,408. In congressional elections the Democrats gained one Senate seat for a 49–47 majority. In the House they gained one seat for a 233–200 majority.

II. Architecture
Arts and Music
Popular Entertainment
Publishing
Theater

The year in publishing was marked by a growing market for books from abroad, perhaps a reflection of Americans' growing interest in world affairs. In architecture, the volume of construction, particularly of industrial and commercial buildings, continued to increase. The outspoken elder statesman of architecture, Frank Lloyd Wright, completed work on the Price Tower in Bartlesville, Okla., and began construction of the Guggenheim Museum in New York City. Contemporary American paintings by such artists as Jackson Pollock were characterized by a distinct abstractionism; in fact, abstractionism had become conventional. On Aug. 11 the art world mourned the death of Pollock, age 44, in an automobile accident.

Among **books published** this year was *The Last Hurrah* by Edwin O'Connor, a novel about an Irish-American politician in his final political campaign. Critics noted the similarities between the fictional politician Frank Skeffington and the Boston mayor, James M. Curley. The novel was a best seller. Other books published this year included *Seize the Day* by Saul Bellow, a collection including the title novella, a play, and several stories; *A Single Pebble* by John Hersey, a novel; *Peyton Place* by Grace Metalious, a racy novel about the residents of a New Hampshire town that became the best seller of the year; and *The Letters of Thomas Wolfe*, edited by Elizabeth Nowell, which revealed how close the author's novels were to his actual life.

Jan 8: The **Bollingen Prize** for poetry was awarded to Conrad Aiken for his 1955 volume *A Letter From Li Po, and Other Poems.*

May 7: Pulitzer prizes were awarded for the following: fiction, *Andersonville* by MacKinlay Kantor; biography, *Benjamin Henry Latrobe* by Talbot F. Hamlin; history, *The Age of Reform* by Richard Hofstadter; poetry, *North and South—A Cold Spring* by Elizabeth Bishop; drama, *The Diary of Anne Frank* by Frances Goodrich and Albert Hackett.

III. Business and Industry
Education
Philosophy and Religion
Science

About 2,000,000 workers received pay increases during the first half of the year, while rising business investments and earnings were benefiting all of labor. The new federal hourly wage minimum of $1.00 an hour was expected to help approximately 2,000,000 workers. In addition, despite widespread drought and crop restrictions, American farmers produced a new all-time high in food and fiber output. Although there were no great discoveries in physics or astronomy during 1956, scientists were active in planning for the International Geophysical Year, to take place in 1957–1958.

Feb 6: Three days of **campus violence** at the University of Alabama were climaxed by the suspension of Autherine Lucy, the first black student to be enrolled there. On Mar. 1 she was permanently expelled for her accusations against the school in a legal suit handled by the National Association for the Advancement of Colored People.

Mar 20: A major **strike** at Westinghouse Electric Corporation, the longest walkout in more than 20 years, was settled after 156 days when the union accepted contract terms proposed by the company.

May 2: Racial **segregation in Methodist churches** was ordered abolished by the General Conference of the Methodist Church in Minneapolis, Minn.

June 11: In Chicago, reports on **polio** were presented to the American Medical Association by Dr. Jonas E. Salk and Surgeon Gen. Leonard A. Scheele. They stated that the crippling disease would be eliminated as a threat within three years through use of the Salk vaccine.

Aug 1: The **Salk antipolio vaccine** was put on the open market by manufacturers. It was sold through normal distribution channels.

Sep 24: The world's **first transatlantic telephone cable system** began operating. The twin cables, 2250 miles long, stretched from Clarenville, Newfoundland, to Oban, Scotland. The cable, which cost $42,000,000, had three times the capacity of radio telephone circuits between Europe and the U.S.

Oct 19: The **Nobel Prize in Physiology or Medicine** was awarded jointly to Dr. Dickinson W. Richardson and Dr. Andre F. Cournand of Columbia University, and to Dr. Werner Forssmann of West Germany, for their work in cardiology and their contributions to the treatment of heart disease.

Nov 1: The **Nobel Prize in Physics** was awarded jointly to William Shockley, Walter H. Brattain, and John Bardeen, all of Bell Telephone Laboratories, for their discovery of the transistor effect in semiconductors and the development of the transistor.

IV. Fashion
Folkways
Holidays
Social Issues and Crime
Sports

American society was being changed by political, social, and technological forces of great magnitude. One result of these pressures was a new spirit of youthful rebelliousness, as evidenced by the rise of a Tennessee rock-'n'-roll singer, Elvis Presley, who skyrocketed to fame despite objections from parents all over the U.S. A cult also grew up around the late James Dean, a promising young actor who had been killed in an automobile accident in 1955. Dean epitomized the American loner, daring to oppose a society that would not or could not understand him. In the more conventional world of boxing, Rocky Marciano retired as the undefeated world heavyweight champion. In golf, the year's top money winners were Ted Kroll, $72,835, and Marlene Bauer Hagge, $20,235.

Jan 20: Following an investigation of **tipping** conducted by the Internal Revenue Service, Hans Paul, headwaiter at the Waldorf-Astoria Hotel in New York City, was indicted on charges of not reporting tips averaging $500,000 to $1,000,000 a year. Paul was fined $7500 and sentenced to four months' imprisonment on Apr. 25.

Jan 26-Feb 5: At the **Winter Olympics** in Cortina d'Ampezzo, Italy, the U.S. won two gold medals. Hayes Alan Jenkins and Tenley Albright took top honors in singles figure skating competitions.

Mar 23: The **NCAA basketball championship** was won by San Francisco, defeating Iowa 83 to 71.

Mar 31-Apr 7: The **NBA basketball championship** was won by the Philadelphia Warriors, who defeated the Fort Wayne Pistons four games to one.

Apr 19: Actress **Grace Kelly,** 26, was married in Monte Carlo to Prince Rainier III of Monaco, 32, in one of the most publicized marriages of the decade. Prince Rainier was a member of the Grimaldi dynasty, founded in 1017.

June 16: The **U.S. Open golf tournament** was won by Cary Middlecoff, who beat Ben Hogan and Julius Boros by one stroke.

July 7: At the **Wimbledon** tennis championships in England, Shirley Fry won the women's singles title. Althea Gibson teamed with Angela Buxton of Great Britain to win the women's doubles, and Shirley Fry and Victor Seixas won the mixed doubles.

July 16: The **Ringling Brothers and Barnum and Bailey Circus** performed its last show under canvas. Rising costs for a tented show had forced the move to performances in permanent structures.

July 25: The **PGA golf tournament** was won by Jack Burke.

Oct 3-10: The 53rd annual **World Series** was won by the New York Yankees (AL), defeating the Brooklyn Dodgers (NL) four games to three. On Oct. 8 Don Larsen, the Yankee right-hander, pitched the first no-hit, no-run game in World Series history, beating Brooklyn 2 to 0.

Nov 22-Dec 8: At the **Summer Olympics** in Melbourne, Australia, the U.S. won 32 gold medals and finished second in unofficial team standings, behind the U.S.S.R.

Nov 30: The **world heavyweight boxing championship** was won by Floyd Patterson, who knocked out Archie Moore in the fifth round in Chicago to win the title vacated by Rocky Marciano on Apr. 27. Patterson, 21, was the youngest fighter to win the championship.

Dec 30: The **NFL championship** was won by the New York Giants, who defeated the Chicago Bears 47 to 7.

1957

I. Civil Rights
Exploration and Settlement
Government
Statistics
Wars

On Oct. 4 the Soviet Union launched the first Earth satellite, Sputnik I. Americans were stunned by the Soviets' technological progress, and politicians, scientists, and educators called for a major U.S. initiative to regain superiority in missiles development and space technology. Thus 1957 was another year of world tension. Pres. Dwight D. Eisenhower presented the Eisenhower Doctrine; its aim was to resist communist aggression in the Middle East. Despite the race against the U.S.S.R. in outer space, the president continued to release uranium-235 for peaceful purposes; by the end of the year a total of 100,000 kilograms of U-235 had been made available for research and energy. The Air Force, which celebrated its golden anniversary (dating from the founding of the Army Air Corps—the Air Force was officially established in 1947), became the largest enterprise in the U.S.; its total assets for the year were over $70,000,000,000. Notables who died included Sen. Joseph R. McCarthy, Republican of Wisconsin, whose widely publicized charges of communist subversion in government earned him Senate censure and condemnation, on May 2, at age 48.

Jan 5: The **Eisenhower Doctrine** was proposed by Pres. Eisenhower before a joint session of Congress. The plan offered protection to any Middle East nation seeking aid against communist aggression. Eisenhower requested authority to use U.S. forces to oppose communist or communist-backed attempts to overthrow any government in the region. He stated he would send such forces only under three conditions: first, only if requested by a Mideast nation under attack; second, only with hour-by-hour communication with Congress; third, only in accord with U.S. treaty obligations and the UN Charter.

Feb 8: The **European Atomic Energy Community** was pledged full U.S. support for establishment of an atomic energy industry in Europe within ten years.

Feb 9-12: The U.S. **Communist Party** held a convention in New York City during which its members adopted a new party constitution. One of the new rules in the constitution specified that party members could be expelled for subversion of the U.S. government. FBI chief J. Edgar Hoover stated that the new rules were merely an attempt by the party to gain acceptance by U.S. citizens.

Mar 30: The United States' second **atomic submarine,** the *Seawolf,* was commissioned. On May 16, *Skate,* the third atomic submarine and the first designed for assembly-line production, was launched at Groton, Conn.

July 16: A new **transcontinental speed record** (Long Beach, Calif., to Brooklyn, N.Y.) was set by Maj. John H. Glenn, Jr., USN, in a Navy F8U-1P jet. The time was 3 hrs., 23 min., 8.4 sec.

Aug 30: A new **filibuster record** was set by Sen. Strom Thurmond, Democrat of South Carolina, who held the floor arguing against civil rights legislation for 24 hrs., 27 min.

Sep 19: The **first underground atomic explosion** was set off at proving grounds near Las Vegas, Nev.

Sep 24: Racial violence in **Little Rock,** Ark., prompted Pres. Eisenhower to send a force of some 1000 U.S. Army paratroopers to enforce the desegregation of Central High School. The president said that violence had caused the removal of nine black students in the newly integrated school. The students entered the guarded school on Sept. 25.

Oct 8: Jack Soble, a confessed Soviet spy, was sentenced in New York to a seven-year imprisonment for espionage. Soble had pleaded guilty to obtaining national defense secrets with the knowledge that they would go to the U.S.S.R. His wife Myra Soble, and another member of the conspiracy, Jacob Albam, previously had been sentenced to seven years in jail, but their sentences were reduced to four and five years, respectively. Other charges against him were dropped, including one that carried the death penalty.

II. Architecture
Arts and Music
Popular Entertainment
Publishing
Theater

Architects continued to explore the use of new construction materials. A highlight of the year was the completion of the Seagram Building in New York City, the first such structure to be sheathed in bronze. Also in 1957 extraordinary prices were being paid for painting and sculpture. The Edward G. Robinson collection was sold for well over $3,000,000, and one painting in the Georges Lurcy collection, Renoir's *La Serre,* brought $200,000. Americans mourned the passing of Humphrey Bogart, actor, Jan. 14, at 57; James Francis "Jimmy" Dorsey, bandleader, June 12, at 53; Oliver Hardy, of the team of Laurel and Hardy, Aug. 7, at 55; Frederick Law Olmsted, landscape architect, Dec. 25, at 87; and Laura Ingalls Wilder, author of the popular "Little House" books, Feb. 10, at 90.

Among **books published** this year was *By Love Possessed* by James Gould Cozzens, the major novel of the year. Not all critics praised the book but it stayed on the top of the best-seller list. The novel depicted two days in the life of a middle-aged lawyer. Other books published this year included *A Death in the Family* by James Agee, the author's only full-length novel, dealing with a boy's reaction to his father's death; *The Wapshot Chronicle* by John Cheever, a novel; *The Town* by William Faulkner, part of the author's Yoknapatawpha County saga; *Simple Stakes a Claim* by Langston Hughes; and *On the Road* by Jack Kerouac, a semiautobiographical novel of the Beat generation in which the author explored the use of jazz, sex, and drugs by young people.

Jan 13: The **Bollingen Prize** for poetry was awarded to Allen Tate.

Feb 25: In a **censorship ruling,** the Supreme Court ruled unanimously against the conviction of a Detroit, Mich., bookseller for selling John Howard Griffin's book *The Devil Rides Outside.* The ruling voided the section of Michigan penal law banning the sale of books that might corrupt youth. Justice Felix Frankfurter said the law would reduce adults in Michigan to reading only what might be deemed fit for children.

May 6: Pulitzer prizes were awarded for the following: biography, *Profiles in Courage* by John F. Kennedy; history, *Russia Leaves the War* by George F. Kennan; poetry, *Things of This World* by Richard Wilbur; drama, *Long Day's Journey into Night* by Eugene O'Neill. A special award was made to Kenneth Roberts for his historical novels.

III. Business and Industry
Education
Philosophy and Religion
Science

In September wages for factory workers averaged $2.08 an hour, $82.99 a week. Employment remained high during most of the year, but in autumn began to decline. Farm production exceeded the crop yield record set in 1956, and farm prices continued the advance begun in 1956. In religion, leaders of various faiths played important parts in the fight to implement the Supreme Court's decision to bar racial segregation in public schools. Official bodies of several southern church groups requested peaceful compliance with the decision, and the Vatican approved the move by the archbishop of New Orleans to desegregate church schools. But at the end of the year, desegregation in the schools was still a major issue. Americans mourned the death of Adm. Richard E. Byrd on Mar. 11 at age 68. He had led five expeditions to Antarctica and was the first person to fly over the North and South Poles.

In a **survey** of 60,000 high school juniors and seniors, Dr. Ernest V. Hollis of the U.S. Office of Education discovered that 51% of students with an IQ of 133 or higher would not attend college because of the expense or because of a lack of goals.

Jan 21: The first **nationally televised videotaped TV broadcast** was carried by the National Broadcasting Co. The program was a recording of the presidential inauguration ceremonies in Washington, D.C. The first use of videotape in TV had occurred on Nov. 30, 1956, when taped broadcasts of *Douglas Edwards and the News* began running in the western U.S. The first national show to be videotaped was *Truth or Consequences,* beginning on Jan. 22, 1957.

May 2: Teamsters Union president **Dave Beck was indicted** by a federal grand jury in Seattle, Wash., on charges that he had evaded payment of $56,000 in income taxes in 1950. Further investigation revealed that Beck had used union funds for himself and his family.

June 13: The *Mayflower II* landed at Plymouth, Mass., 54 days after setting out from Plymouth, England, to duplicate the voyage of the Pilgrims.

July 1: The **International Geophysical Year** (July 1, 1957-Dec. 31, 1958) launched its first major scientific project, the firing of a rocket on San Nicolas Island, Calif., by the Naval Research Laboratory. The goal was to study the effects of the sun's radiation on communications. Scientists of 67 nations participated in the International Geophysical Year, a coordinated study of Earth, its atmosphere and oceans, and the sun.

July 12: A link between **cigarette smoking and lung cancer** had been established by scientific research, Surgeon General Leroy E. Burney reported. Burney stated that the studies showed a "direct relationship between the incidence of lung cancer and the amount smoked."

Aug 19-20: A new **balloon ascent record** was set when Maj. David G. Simons, USAF, went up 101,486 feet supported by a plastic balloon. The record also marked man's longest stay on the edge of space.

Sep 18: James R. Hoffa, international vice president of the Teamsters Union, was charged by the Ethical Practices Committee of the AFL-CIO with fostering criminals in the Teamsters Union. The AFL-CIO advised the union to expel Hoffa or leave the AFL-CIO. On Dec. 6 the Teamsters Union was expelled.

Oct 16: The **first American objects launched into space** were two aluminum pellets lofted by the U.S. Air Force.

Oct 31: The **Nobel Prize in Physics** was awarded jointly to Dr. Tsung Dao Lee of Columbia University and Dr. Chen Ning Yang of the Institute for Advanced Study at Princeton for their studies of the behavior of subatomic particles.

Nov 1: The **world's longest suspension bridge,** the Mackinac Straits Bridge between Michigan's upper and lower peninsulas, was opened for traffic. The bridge cost an estimated $100,000,000.

Dec 12: A new **jet speed record** was set by Maj. Adrian E. Drew, USAF, in his F-101 Voodoo. Drew's speed, over a course above the Mojave Desert, Calif., was 1207.6 mph.

IV. Fashion
Folkways
Holidays
Social Issues and Crime
Sports

The sack was the most discussed fashion since the New Look. The sack's silhouette was an unfitted drape, and men were heard to comment: "It looks like a flour sack." The most highly praised man of the year in boxing was Carmen Basilio, who outpointed Sugar Ray Robinson in a savage fight for the middleweight championship. But by 1958 Robinson had defeated Basilio again. Floyd Patterson defended the world heavyweight title against Tommy "Hurricane" Jackson (July 29). In golf the top money winners were Dick Mayer $65,835, and Patty Berg, $16,272. Baseball was marked by the departure of the New York Giants for San Francisco and the Brooklyn Dodgers for Los Angeles, leaving the pennant-winning Yankees with sole dominion over New York baseball.

A new **baseball attendance record** for the National League was set by the Milwaukee Braves, who drew 2,215,404 fans to home games this year.

Mar 23: The **NCAA basketball championship** was won by North Carolina, which beat Kansas 54 to 53 in three overtime periods.

Mar 30-Apr 3: The **NBA basketball championship** was won by the Boston Celtics, defeating the St. Louis Hawks four games to three.

June 15: The **U.S. Open golf tournament** was won by Dick Mayer, who beat defending champion Cary Middlecoff by seven strokes in a playoff round.

July 6: At the **Wimbledon** tennis championships in England, Althea Gibson won the women's singles title. She then teamed with her opponent, Darlene Hard, to win the women's doubles. Gardnar Mulloy and V. Edward "Budge" Patty won the men's doubles. Hard teamed with Mervyn Rose of Australia to win the mixed doubles.

July 19: The **first U.S. runner to break the four-minute mile** was Don Bowden, who ran the mile in 3:58.7 at Stockton, Calif.

July 21: The **PGA golf tournament** was won by Lionel Hebert.

Oct 2-10: The 54th annual **World Series** was won by the Milwaukee Braves (NL), defeating the New York Yankees (AL) four games to three.

Oct 25: Umberto "Albert" Anastasia, an underworld figure, was slain by two gunmen as he sat in a barbershop. The gangster had been nicknamed "Lord High Executioner" of a crime syndicate known as Murder, Inc.

Dec 29: The **NFL championship** was won by the Detroit Lions, who defeated the Cleveland Browns 59 to 14.

1958

I. Civil Rights
Exploration and Settlement
Government
Statistics
Wars

The political scene was heated during the congressional election campaign by Republican charges that Democrats were guilty of radicalism. Former Pres. Harry S Truman countered with the claim that Pres. Dwight D. Eisenhower had surrendered in Korea. Informal polls showed that the Republicans were losing ground because of continued world tension, including that engendered by America's rush to beat the U.S.S.R. into space, but they continued the fight until election day. When the smoke cleared, the Democrats had scored the biggest gains in more than 20 years.

Mar 4: The verdict against Brig. Gen. **William "Billy" Mitchell,** the pioneer in military air power charged with bringing discredit to the Army more than 37 years earlier, was upheld by Sec. of the Air Force James H. Douglas. Douglas added that Mitchell's faith in air power had been vindicated.

Apr 18: Treason charges against **Ezra Pound,** accused of making broadcasts for the fascists in Italy during World War II, were dropped in federal court in Washington, D.C. The poet had been confined at St. Elizabeths Hospital, a mental institution, since 1946. A key figure in securing Pound's release was his fellow poet Robert Frost. On July 1 Pound sailed with his wife for Italy.

May 1: Four antinuclear protesters were seized on their ship, *Golden Rule,* by the Coast Guard when they attempted to leave Honolulu for Eniwetok, the atomic testing area.

May 16: A new **world jet speed record** was set by Capt. Walter Irwin, USAF, who flew a single-jet F-104A Starfighter over Edwards Air Force Base, Calif., for an average speed of 1404.19 mph.

June 17: Sherman Adams, assistant to the president, denied before a House investigating committee that he had interceded with federal agencies on behalf of industrialist Bernard Goldfine. The president backed Adams on June 18, saying he was a man of integrity.

July 7: The **Alaska statehood bill** was signed by Pres. Eisenhower, making Alaska the 49th state on ratification by the voters of the territory in August. A formal declaration of statehood was planned for 1959.

Aug 5: The world's **first undersea crossing of the North Pole** was made by the U.S. atomic submarine *Nautilus*. The ship submerged near Point Barrow, Alaska, Aug. 1 and sailed under the 50-foot-thick ice cap for 96 hours before surfacing.

Sep 22: A new **underwater endurance record** was set by the atomic-powered submarine U.S.S. *Skate*. During a transpolar voyage it ran for 31 days under polar ice without surfacing.

Sep 22: Sherman Adams, assistant to the president, resigned under pressure from fellow Republicans who felt he was endangering GOP chances in the coming elections. In a nationwide radio-TV broadcast, Adams insisted he had done no wrong in accepting gifts from Boston industrialist Bernard Goldfine.

Oct 6: A new **underwater endurance record** was set by the atomic-powered submarine U.S.S. *Seawolf,* which surfaced after 60 days.

Nov 4: Congressional elections marked the greatest Democratic gains since the New Deal. The Democrats gained 13 Senate seats to take a 62–34 majority. In the House they won 47 new seats to take control 282–153. In state elections the Democrats made a net gain of five governorships to control 34 state houses against the Republicans' 14.

II. Architecture
Arts and Music
Popular Entertainment
Publishing
Theater

Book publishing had another year of growth in number of new titles and total number of books sold. At the beginning of 1958, some 45,592,000 households had television sets. TV was offering strong competition to the film industry, which produced fewer movies and showed a slight decline in attendance. Music experienced a few changes. Under the direction of a young, dynamic Leonard Bernstein, the New York Philharmonic Orchestra began to play more works by contemporary American composers. Painters were still fighting the battle of abstractionism versus representation, but abstractionism was the winner in most American exhibits. Among notables who died was Mike Todd, 49, the film producer, whose private plane crashed near Grants, N. Mex., Mar. 22.

Among **books published** this year was *Home From the Hill* by William Humphrey, a first novel that became a best seller. It told the story of a Texas family, concentrating on a boy who tried to emulate his father, a man obsessed with hunting and women. Other books published this year included *95 Poems* by E. E. Cummings; *The Ginger Man,* a novel by the expatriate American writer J. P. Donleavy; *The Affluent Society* by John Kenneth Galbraith; *J. B.* by Archibald MacLeish, a verse drama based on the biblical story of Job; and *Lolita* by Vladimir Nabokov, a novel about a middle-aged man and his love affair with a twelve-year-old girl. The book caused a sensation among readers and critics alike.

Jan 6: The **Bollingen Prize** for poetry was awarded to E.E. Cummings.

Jan 13: The Communist newspaper ***Daily Worker*** **suspended daily publication** because of declining revenue. Its final edition before becoming a weekly declared, "We'll Be Back."

Apr 11: Texas pianist **Van Cliburn,** 23, won the Tchaikovsky International Piano and Violin Festival held in Moscow. His playing of the *Third Piano Concerto* by Sergei Rachmaninoff filled the auditorium of the Tschaikovsky Conservatory with a frenzy of applause.

May 5: Pulitzer prizes were awarded for the following: fiction, *A Death in the Family* by James Agee; biography, *George Washington* by Douglas Southall Freeman; history, *Banks and Politics in America— from the Revolution to the Civil War* by Bray Hammond; poetry, *Promises: Poems 1954–1956* by Robert Penn Warren; drama, *Look Homeward, Angel* by Ketti Frings.

III. Business and Industry
Education
Philosophy and Religion
Science

A serious recession affected the entire country. In February the jobless represented 7.7% of the total labor force; by March the total number of unemployed had jumped to 5,198,000. After antirecession legislation, the situation began to improve by early fall. School desegregation was still a major issue. State authorities in Little Rock, Ark., closed the public schools and reopened them as private institutions that would not admit blacks. A new cry was heard for better educational standards as critics of American schools claimed that standards were lower than ever before.

The **Van Allen belt,** a zone of radiation around Earth about 600 miles in space, was detected by U.S. satellites and named after James A. Van Allen, who led development of the satellite experiments. Radiation was shown to be 1000 times more intense than expected.

Jan 31: The **first U.S. Earth satellite,** Explorer I, was launched at 10:48 P.M. from Cape Canaveral, Fla. It was bullet-shaped, 80 in. long, 6 in. in diameter with the last stage attached, and weighed 30.8 lbs.

Mar 8: William Faulkner, the Nobel Prize-winning novelist, said at Princeton University that parents and educators were endangering U.S. education by not facing up to important realities and that schools were turning into "baby-sitting organizations."

Mar 17: Vanguard 1, a 3¼-lb. satellite, the second U.S. space vehicle, was launched after more than three months of highly publicized delays. The 6.4-in. aluminum sphere, the smallest satellite launched so far, went into a wider orbit than any other manmade satellite.

Apr 26: The **highest Vatican post held by an American** pro-prefect of the Vatican's Sacred Congregation for the Propagation of the Faith was given to Samuel Cardinal Stritch, archbishop of Chicago. On Apr. 28 a blood clot forced amputation of his right arm; on May 27 he died after a stroke.

Apr 28: Speaking on the **danger of nuclear fallout,** the Nobel-Prize-winning scientist Dr. Linus Pauling said that radioactive carbon-14 already left in the air by detonated atomic bombs would cause 5,000,000 genetically defective births and millions of cancer and leukemia cases in the next 300 generations.

June 27: A new **transatlantic speed record** from New York to London was set by Col. Harry Burrell, USAF, flying an Air Force KC-135. The new time was 5 hrs., 27 min., 42.8 sec., for an average of 630.2 mph.

Sep 30: The Supreme Court ruling against **racial segregation** in public schools was defied by Gov. Orval E. Faubus of Arkansas, who closed four high schools in Little Rock. On Sept. 17 the Little Rock Private School Corp. was chartered in a move to reopen the city's schools on a segregated basis as private but state-financed institutions.

Oct 11: In a **lunar exploration** mission, a Pioneer rocket was launched in an attempt to circle the moon. The mission failed on Oct. 12, but the vehicle obtained a record maximum altitude of 79,193 miles—30 times the altitude of any previous manmade object.

Oct 30: The **Nobel Prize in Physiology or Medicine** was awarded jointly to Joshua Lederberg of the University of Wisconsin for his studies of the genetic organization of bacteria; and to George W. Beadle of the California Institute of Technology and Edward L. Tatum of the Rockefeller Institute for their discovery that genes control specific chemical processes.

IV. Fashion
Folkways
Holidays
Social Issues and Crime
Sports

The year in international sports competition was highlighted by U.S. defense of the America's Cup and by American capture of the grand prize of tennis, the Davis Cup, which the U.S. had lost to Australia in 1955. Althea Gibson announced she would quit tennis for a year to launch a career as a popular singer. In boxing, middleweight champion Sugar Ray Robinson disproved the theory that former champions cannot make a comeback when he regained his crown for the fifth time, and heavyweight champion Floyd Patterson defended his title in a bout (Aug. 18) with Roy Harris. In golf the top money winners were Arnold Palmer, $42,407, and Beverly Hanson, $12,629.

Mar 22: The **NCAA basketball championship** was won by Kentucky, which defeated Seattle 84 to 72.

Mar 25: The **world middleweight boxing championship** was regained for an unprecedented fifth time by Sugar Ray Robinson, who outpointed Carmen Basilio in 15 rounds at Chicago.

Mar 29-Apr 12: The **NBA basketball championship** was won by the St. Louis Hawks, who defeated the Boston Celtics four games to two.

June 14: The **U.S. Open golf tournament** was won by Tommy Bolt.

June 28: A new **world swimming record** for the 100-meter butterfly was set by Nancy Ramey of Seattle, Wash., who won the event with a time of 1:09⅗ during a meet in Los Angeles, Calif.

July 5: At the **Wimbledon** tennis championships in England, Althea Gibson won the women's singles title. She then teamed with Maria Bueno of Brazil to win the women's doubles.

July 20: The **PGA golf tournament** was won by Dow Finsterwald.

Aug 6: A new **world 400-meter hurdles record,** 49.2 sec., was set by Glenn Davis of Columbus, Ohio, during a meet in Budapest, Hungary.

Sep 20-27: The **America's Cup** was defended by the U.S. 12-meter sloop *Columbia,* which defeated the British challenger *Sceptre* in four straight races.

Oct 1-9: The 55th annual **World Series** was won by the New York Yankees (AL), defeating the Milwaukee Braves (NL) four games to three. Yogi Berra, the Yankees catcher, marked his tenth World Series, tying records set by Babe Ruth and Joe DiMaggio.

Dec 28: The **NFL championship** was won by the Baltimore Colts, who defeated the New York Giants 23 to 17.

Dec 31: The U.S. regained the **Davis Cup** when Alejandro "Alex" Olmedo defeated an Australian, Ashley Cooper, in singles competition for the third American match victory. The U.S. went on to win the international challenge round three matches to two.

1959

I. Civil Rights
Exploration and Settlement
Government
Statistics
Wars

The year was highlighted by a visit of Vice Pres. Richard M. Nixon to the U.S.S.R. in July and August, and by a visit of Soviet Premier Nikita S. Khrushchev to the U.S. in September. Nixon's well-publicized tour increased his chances of gaining the Republican presidential nomination in 1960. His major competitor was Gov. Nelson A. Rockfeller of New York. For the Democrats, however, no fewer than eight possible candidates were making their opening moves. Americans mourned the deaths of William J. "Wild Bill" Donovan, director of the Office of Strategic Services in World War II, Feb. 8, at 76; John Foster Dulles, secretary of state under Pres. Dwight D. Eisenhower, May 24, at 71; William F. "Bull" Halsey, Jr., one of the most colorful naval commanders in the Pacific during World War II, Aug. 16, at 76; and George C. Marshall, secretary of state under Pres. Harry S Truman and originator of the Marshall Plan for reconstruction of Europe after World War II, Oct. 16, at 78.

Jan 3: Alaska was proclaimed the 49th state by Pres. Eisenhower.

Mar 18: The **Hawaii statehood bill** was signed by Pres. Eisenhower. Statehood was conditional on a later vote for statehood by Hawaii's electorate.

Mar 30: Double jeopardy was upheld in two U.S. Supreme Court decisions stating that a person could be tried for the same offense in both federal and state courts.

Apr 7: Prohibition in Oklahoma was repealed after 51 years, leaving Mississippi the only dry state in the Union.

May 22: The **first black general** in U.S. history, Brig. Gen. Benjamin O. Davis, Jr., USAF, was promoted to the rank of major general.

June 8: Investigations of communist subversion conducted by Congress and by individual states were ruled constitutional by the U.S. Supreme Court in two 5–4 decisions.

July 7: An **omnibus housing bill** was vetoed by Pres. Eisenhower, who termed it excessive, defective, inflationary, and an obstacle to constructive progress toward better housing for Americans.

July 23: Vice Pres. **Richard M. Nixon arrived in Moscow,** beginning a two-week tour of the U.S.S.R. and Poland. The next day he held a highly publicized kitchen debate, a discussion with Soviet Premier Nikita S. Khrushchev while standing before a kitchen exhibit in the U.S. exhibition in Moscow. After the impromptu, so-called kitchen debate, Nixon formally opened the exhibition.

July 29: The **accidental death rate** for 1958 was declared by the National Safety Council to be the lowest since 1954, 52.5 persons in 100,000. Total deaths were 91,000, of which 37,000 were auto accident deaths, raising the all-time U.S. death toll in auto accidents to 1,265,000.

Aug 21: Hawaii was admitted to the Union as the 50th state, by a proclamation signed by Pres. Eisenhower. Hawaiians had voted by an overwhelming majority on June 27 for statehood in a special referendum. The president also issued the order for a new flag of 50 stars arranged in staggered rows: five 6-star rows and four 5-star rows, the flag to become official July 4, 1960.

Sep 7: In a move to ensure **voting rights** for blacks, the U.S. Civil Rights Commission requested Pres. Eisenhower to appoint federal registrars to supervise voting in areas where local officials had prevented blacks from voting.

Sep 15-27: Soviet Premier **Khrushchev visited the U.S.** Arriving at Andrews Air Force Base, where he was welcomed by Pres. Eisenhower, the premier stated he was visiting the U.S. with "open heart and good intentions." On Sept. 18 he addressed the UN, calling for total nuclear disarmament within four years, and on Sept. 25 he began a series of negotiations with Pres. Eisenhower at Camp David. On Khrushchev's departure for Moscow on Sept. 27, it was revealed that he and Pres. Eisenhower had reached understandings designed to relieve world tensions, including the withdrawal of a proposal Khrushchev had made in Nov. 1958 for major changes in the status of Berlin.

Nov 16: A **defense budget request** for 1961, totaling some $41,000,000,000, was presented by Pres. Eisenhower. It was also decided that there would be no immediate reduction in U.S. troops overseas.

Dec 7: Travel restrictions imposed by the federal government were upheld by the Supreme Court, which refused to consider lower court decisions banning American travel to China.

II. Architecture
Arts and Music
Popular Entertainment
Publishing
Theater

One of the year's cultural high points was the extensive foreign tour of Leonard Bernstein and the New York Philharmonic Orchestra. Commencing in Athens (Aug. 5) and concluding in London (Oct. 10), the tour included a series of 18 concerts in the U.S.S.R. The Soviet Union was the scene of another notable artistic event when *Welcome Home,* a painting by Jack Levine that had been sharply criticized by Pres. Eisenhower, proved popular with the Russians. Notables who died this year included Ethel Barrymore, the celebrated actress, June 18, at 79; Ernest Bloch, composer, July 15, at 78; Raymond Chandler, author, Mar. 26, at 70; Lou Costello, comedian, Mar. 3, at 50; Cecil B. DeMille, motion picture producer, Jan. 21, at 77; Edgar Guest, poet, Aug. 5, at 77; Billie Holiday, one of the greatest jazz vocalists of all time, July 17, at 44; and Frank Lloyd Wright, celebrated architect and pioneer of modern design, Apr. 9, at 89.

Among **books published** this year was *Advise and Consent* by Allen Drury, a novel dealing with a Senate confirmation hearing for a highly controversial nomination for secretary of state. Other books published this year included *Henderson the Rain King* by Saul Bellow, a novel; *Breakfast at Tiffany's* by Truman Capote, a short novel; *The Mansion* by William Faulkner, the author's last Snopes family novel; *The War Lover* by John Hersey, an antiwar novel; *History of the United States Naval Operations in World War II* by Samuel Eliot Morison; *Goodbye, Columbus* by Philip Roth, which included the title novella and five short stories; and *Poorhouse Fair* by John Updike, a collection of associated stories.

Jan 5: In a case involving **protection of journalists' sources,** Marie Torre of the New York *Herald Tribune* began a ten-day jail sentence for contempt of court for refusing to reveal a source used in one of her columns.

Jan 11: The **Bollingen Prize** for poetry was awarded to Theodore Roethke for his 1958 volume *Words for the Wind.*

May 4: Pulitzer prizes were awarded for the following: fiction, *The Travels of Jamie McPheeters* by Robert Lewis Taylor; history, *The Republican Era: 1869–1901* by Leonard D. White with Jean Schneider, who shared the prize with White's estate; biography, *Woodrow Wilson* by Arthur Walworth; poetry, *Selected Poems, 1928–1958* by Stanley Kunitz; drama, *J.B.* by Archibald MacLeish.

June 11: *Lady Chatterley's Lover,* by D. H. Lawrence, was banned from the mails by Postmaster General Arthur E. Summerfield, who said, "Any literary merit the book may have is far outweighed by the pornographic and smutty passages and words, so that the book, taken as a whole, is an obscene and filthy work."

June 15: An **equal time ruling** issued by the FCC earlier in the year was reaffirmed by the commission. It required radio and television stations to give equal time to opposing political candidates in debate and news broadcasts.

Sep 14: A bill lifting FCC **equal time** requirements for radio and television news broadcasts was signed by Pres. Eisenhower.

III. Business and Industry
Education
Philosophy and Religion
Science

After a two-week delay at the request of Pres. Dwight D. Eisenhower, the United Steelworkers of America began a nationwide walkout on July 15. Negotiations proceeded slowly. On the order of Pres. Eisenhower, an 80-day Taft-Hartley injunction was issued on Oct. 21 and, after a court fight ending in the Supreme Court, was executed on Nov. 7, halting the 116-day steel strike, the longest in U.S. history. The U.S. scored a spectacular success when it launched an Atlas missile designed to function as a satellite. This was the fifth and largest Earth satellite successfully launched by the U.S. Besides much information-collecting instrumentation, the missile contained a recording of Pres. Eisenhower's voice, which was automatically broadcast. The message was subsequently received and recorded by U.S. radio stations and distributed throughout the world.

Jan 19: Discriminatory school laws in Virginia, designed to prevent school integration by automatically closing schools receiving final federal court orders to integrate, were ruled invalid by the Virginia Supreme Court. On Feb. 2 schools in Arlington and Norfolk were desegregated with no serious disorders occurring.

Feb 17: Vanguard 2, a 21.5-lb. satellite designed to function as the first weather station in space, achieved orbit after being launched from Cape Canaveral, Fla., by the U.S. Navy.

Feb 28: Discoverer 1, the first satellite in the Discoverer military research satellite program, was launched successfully from Vandenberg Air Force Base, Calif.

Apr 5: The U.S. Naval Research Laboratory reported an increase in **atmospheric radioactivity** of 300% in the eastern United States following nuclear tests by the U.S.S.R. in Sept.-Oct. 1958.

Apr 9: The **first seven U.S. astronauts** were picked from the ranks of military test pilots by NASA. After a vigorous training and testing program, one would be selected to ride a Project Mercury space capsule into Earth orbit in 1961.

Apr 13: Discoverer 2, a military research satellite, was successfully launched from Vandenberg Air Force Base, Calif.

May 28: Two **monkeys were launched into space** by the U.S. Army from Cape Canaveral, Fla. They were recovered unhurt from the Caribbean area after a 300-mile-high space flight.

June 3: By **bouncing radio signals off the moon,** a message recorded by Pres. Eisenhower was transmitted from Westford, Mass., to Canadian Prime Minister John George Diefenbaker in Prince Albert, Saskatchewan.

June 15: It was announced by the New York Stock Exchange that **stock in public U.S. corporations** was owned by 12,490,000 persons as of early 1959.

June 18: The **Arkansas school law** used by Gov. Orval Faubus to close public schools in Little Rock and maintain de facto segregation was ruled unconstitutional by a three-judge federal court.

July 15: A nationwide **steel strike** was begun by the United Steelworkers against 28 steel companies after a breakdown of negotiations.

July 21: The **first U.S. nuclear merchant ship** was christened *Savannah* by Mrs. Dwight D. Eisenhower at Camden, N.J.

Aug 4: Teamster president **James R. Hoffa** and two of his chief aides were denounced for union abuses in a special U.S. Senate committee report.

Aug 7: Explorer 6, a 142-lb. satellite called the paddle wheel satellite because of its four vanes of solar cells, was placed in orbit from Cape Canaveral, Fla. It was the first satellite to be handled by NASA from initiation to orbit.

Aug 12: High schools in Little Rock, Ark., were reopened, integrating two previously all-white schools. About 200 to 250 segregationists demonstrated near Central High School, but policemen held them back with fire hoses and clubs.

Aug 13: Discoverer 5 was launched successfully into polar orbit from Vandenberg Air Force Base, Calif. This followed unsuccessful launchings of Discoverer 3 (June 3) and Discoverer 4 (June 25).

Aug 19: Discoverer 6 was launched into polar orbit from Vandenberg Air Force Base, Calif.

Sep 7: The National Council of Churches announced that **church membership** as of 1958 had increased to 109,557,741. This was a gain of 5% since 1957 and indicated that 64% of the population were church members.

Sep 11: A bill was passed by Congress authorizing **food stamps** in a program to distribute surplus food to impoverished Americans.

Sep 18: Vanguard 3, the 12th successful U.S. satellite, was launched from Cape Canaveral, Fla.

Sep 22: The **International Longshoremen's Association** was readmitted on two-year probation to the AFL-CIO. The ILA had been expelled from the labor organization because of corruption and crime, conditions that AFL-CIO president George Meany said were much improved.

Oct 1: In a **longshoremen's strike,** some 70,000 members of the International Longshoremen's Association walked off the job in Atlantic and Gulf Coast ports. Pres. Eisenhower invoked the Taft-Hartley Act on Oct. 6 by appointing a board of inquiry. An injunction on Oct. 8 halted the strike.

Oct 10: Initiation of the **first passenger service circling the globe** was announced by Pan American World Airways.

Oct 15: The **Nobel Prize in Physiology or Medicine** was awarded to Severo Ochoa of NYU College of Medicine and Arthur Kornberg of Stanford University Medical School for their joint work on the chemistry of heredity.

Oct 26: The **Nobel Prize in Physics** was awarded jointly to Emilio Segre and Owen Chamberlain of the University of California at Berkeley for their discovery of the antiproton.

Nov 7: Striking steelworkers were ordered back to work by the U.S. Supreme Court, which upheld a Taft-Hartley injunction against the strike.

Dec 30: The U.S.S. *George Washington,* the first nuclear submarine capable of carrying and launching missiles, was commissioned at Groton, Conn.

IV. Fashion
Folkways
Holidays
Social Issues and Crime
Sports

U.S. fans suffered a major blow when Floyd Patterson lost the world's heavyweight boxing title to Ingemar Johansson in the third round of a Yankee Stadium bout. Archie Moore retained the light heavyweight title by knocking out challenger Yvon Durelle of Canada, also in the third round. In baseball, the Los Angeles Dodgers, in their second season on the West Coast, gave California its first championship by winning the 1959 World Series. In golf, the top money winners were Art Wall, $53,142, and Betsy Rawls, $26,774.

Feb 14-15: A two-day **narcotics sweep** in New York City smashed a major heroin ring. Recovering an estimated 28.5 lbs. of heroin valued at $3,600,000, and $50,000 in cash, agents arrested 27 importers and distributors.

Mar 21: The **NCAA basketball championship** was won by California, defeating West Virginia 71 to 70.

Apr 4-9: The **NBA basketball championship** was won by the Boston Celtics, who defeated the Minneapolis Lakers in a four-game sweep.

May 20: Some 4978 **Japanese-Americans** who had renounced their U.S. citizenship during World War II and later applied for restitution were restored to citizenship by the Dept. of Justice.

May 25: A Louisiana ban on **boxing matches between blacks and whites** was declared unconstitutional by the U.S. Supreme Court.

June 13: The **U.S. Open golf tournament** was won by Billy Casper.

Aug 2: The **PGA golf tournament** was won by Bob Rosburg.

Aug 28-31: In the **Davis Cup** international tennis challenge round, Australia beat the defending U.S. team three matches to two.

Oct 18: The 56th annual **World Series** was won by the Los Angeles Dodgers (NL), defeating the Chicago White Sox four games to two. The Dodgers had won the National League pennant by sweeping two games from the Milwaukee Braves in a league playoff.

Nov 5: The newly formed **American Football League** announced that eight professional teams would begin play in 1965.

Nov 9: Consumers were warned against buying **cranberries** grown in Washington and Oregon. Arthur S. Flemming, secretary of Health, Education, and Welfare, announced that a weed killer causing cancer in rats had contaminated cranberries grown in Washington and Oregon during the 1958–1959 season.

Dec 19: The **last Civil War veteran,** Walter Williams, died in Houston, Tex., at the age of 117.

Dec 27: The **NFL championship** was won by the Baltimore Colts, defeating the New York Giants 31 to 16.

1960

I. Civil Rights
Exploration and Settlement
Government
Statistics
Wars

Relations with the U.S.S.R., which improved in 1959 after Vice Pres. Richard Nixon's trip to Moscow and Premier Nikita Khrushchev's tour of the U.S., deteriorated sharply after a U.S. U-2 reconnaissance plane was shot down inside the U.S.S.R. on May 1. The incident gave Khrushchev a propaganda advantage and led to cancellation of a planned Paris summit meeting. The U-2 incident and a later one concerning an American RB-47 airplane, together with U.S. involvement in Laos, the Congo, Germany, Cuba, and Japan, caused a sharp increase in the American public's concern with loss of national prestige. This concern may have played a decisive role in John F. Kennedy's successful bid for the presidency in the November elections after one of the most colorful campaigns and one of the closest votes in U.S. political history.

Jan 18: A controversial **mutual security treaty** was signed by the Japanese and U.S. governments. Among other pledges, the treaty stated that both the U.S. and Japan would "maintain and develop . . . their capacities to resist armed attacks."

Feb 23: Sen. Stuart Symington, Democrat of Missouri, declared in the Senate that the "American people are being misled" about the **missile gap** between the U.S. and the U.S.S.R. Pres. Eisenhower vehemently denied the charge.

Feb 24: The **U.S. population** had reached 179,245,000 by Jan. 1, 1960, according to a Census Bureau estimate.

Feb 29: A filibuster against **civil rights legislation** was begun by 18 southern senators.

Apr 8: A **civil rights bill** was passed by the Senate 71–18. Though it was the first civil rights legislation to survive a southern filibuster, Sen. Joseph S. Clark,

Democrat of Pennsylvania, an advocate of civil rights, said his side had "suffered a crushing defeat," calling the bill "only a pale ghost of our hopes."

May 5: The **downing of a U.S. plane** over the U.S.S.R. on May 1 was announced by Premier Nikita S. Khrushchev, who called the captured pilot, Francis Gary Powers, a spy and vowed he would be put on trial. On May 7 the U.S. admitted that the unarmed U-2 plane had been on a spy mission.

May 9: The U.S. announced discontinuance of **U-2 flights** similar to the one intercepted by the U.S.S.R.

May 16: The **Paris summit conference** was canceled by Soviet Premier Khrushchev, who cited the U-2 incident as his reason. Khrushchev also canceled an invitation to Pres. Eisenhower to visit the U.S.S.R.

June 16: Pres. Eisenhower's **Japanese visit** was canceled in view of riots in Japan against the mutual security treaty between Japan and the U.S.

June 26: On return from his **Far East goodwill tour,** Pres. Eisenhower defended his foreign policies and proclaimed his tour a success despite cancellation of a visit to Japan.

July 4: The **50-star U.S. flag,** reflecting the admission of Hawaii to the Union in 1959, became official.

July 11: The U.S.S.R. announced that a **U.S. plane had been shot down** by a Soviet fighter on July 1. The U.S.S.R. alleged that the RB-47 reconnaissance bomber had been in Soviet air space over Arctic waters and accused the U.S. of continuing the espionage program revealed by the downing of a U-2 over Russia earlier in the year.

July 13: The **Democratic National Convention nominated Sen. Kennedy** of Massachusetts for the presidency. Kennedy was the second Roman Catholic in the party's history to be nominated for that office.

July 25: The **Republican National Convention nominated Vice Pres. Nixon** for the presidency. Nixon was virtually unchallenged for the nomination, although Sen. Barry Goldwater of Arizona received ten votes after his name had been put into nomination against his wishes.

Aug 19: Francis Gary Powers, pilot of the U-2 spy plane shot down in the U.S.S.R., was sentenced by the Soviets to ten years of "deprivation of freedom."

Sep 12: Sen. Kennedy stated that as president his **actions would be dictated solely by the public welfare** rather than by the Roman Catholic hierarchy, in a speech in Houston, Tex. Kennedy stated he would resign "if the time should ever come . . . when my office would require me to either violate my conscience or violate the national interest."

Sep 26: The first of a series of **television debates** between Vice Pres. Nixon and Sen. Kennedy took place in Chicago, Ill.

Oct 10-12: Former Pres. **Harry S Truman** was reported to be campaigning vigorously for Sen. Kennedy in the presidential campaign. It was reported that Truman said Vice Pres. Nixon "never told the truth in his life"; told a San Antonio audience that if it voted for Nixon, "You ought to go to hell"; and responded to a demand for an apology for his San Antonio remark by saying, "Tell 'em to go to hell."

Nov 8: John Fitzgerald Kennedy was elected president of the United States. Sen. Kennedy, Democrat of Massachusetts, was the second-youngest man ever to win the nation's highest office. Sen. Lyndon Baines Johnson, Democrat, was elected vice president. The electoral vote was Kennedy, 303; Nixon, 219; and Sen. Harry F. Byrd, 15. Kennedy won 49.7% and Nixon 49.6% of the popular vote, making the election one of the closest in U.S. history. In congressional elections the Democrats took a 65–35 majority in the Senate. In the House they lost 20 seats but kept a majority of 263–174.

Dec 16: The **worst air disaster** to date occurred when a United Air Lines DC-8 jet and a Trans-World Airlines Lockheed Super-Constellation collided in fog over New York harbor. The death toll was 132.

II. Architecture
   Arts and Music
   Popular Entertainment
   Publishing
   Theater

The opera year was highlighted by the performance in San Diego of *Die Frau ohne Schatten* by Richard Strauss, a gigantic musical drama replete with strange people and flying fish. The music season was tragically marked by the deaths of renowned musicians: Ernst von Dohnanyi, Feb. 9, at 82; Dimitri Mitropoulos, Nov. 2, at 64; Jussi Bjoerling, Sept. 9, at 49; and Leonard Warren, Mar. 4, at 48. The country also mourned the deaths of Franklin Pierce Adams, newspaper columnist, Mar. 23, at 78; H.L. Davis, winner of a Pulitzer Prize for his 1935 novel *Honey in the Horn,* Oct. 31, at 64; Oscar Hammerstein, II, lyricist and theatrical producer, Aug. 23, at 65; John P. Marquand, novelist and short story writer, July 16, at 66; and Richard Wright, who chronicled the black experience in America in *Native Son* (1940) and *Black Boy* (1945), Nov. 28, at 52.

Among **books published** this year was *To Kill a Mockingbird,* Harper Lee's first novel, which won a Pulitzer Prize in 1961. The novel, set in the South, concerned two children whose father, a lawyer, defended a black man charged with the rape of a white woman. Other books published this year included

Grant Moves South by Bruce Catton, which dealt with the 1861–1863 campaign of Gen. U.S. Grant during the Civil War; *The Liberal House* by John Kenneth Galbraith, essays on the improvement of the U.S. economic situation; *The Child Buyer,* a novel by John Hersey; *Tristessa,* a novel by Jack Kerouac; *No High Ground* by Fletcher Knebel and Charles W. Bailey, an account of the development of the atomic bomb and the consequences of its use at Hiroshima; *Ourselves to Know,* a novel by John O'Hara; *Thrones* by Ezra Pound, the latest installment of his poetic work *Cantos; The Uncertain Trumpet* by Gen. Maxwell D. Taylor, which described U.S. military competence as dangerously diminished; *Apologies to the Iroquois* by Edmund Wilson, which dealt with the history and social spirit of the Iroquois; and *Marilyn Monroe* by Maurice Zolotow, a biographical study.

Jan 10: The **Bollingen Prize** for poetry was awarded to Delmore Schwartz for his 1959 collection *Summer Knowledge.*

Jan 25: Payola, money illegally offered or accepted by disc jockeys for broadcasting phonograph records, would bring a $500 fine and one-year prison term in a law proposed by Donald H. McGannon, chairman of the National Association of Broadcasters' TV code review board. The proposal followed extensive investigations into payola practices in the broadcasting industry.

Feb 11: Jack Paar, protesting **NBC censorship** of one of his jokes the night before, walked off his late-night television show. Later, at a meeting with network officials, Paar agreed to return to the program Mar. 7.

Mar 25: *Lady Chatterley's Lover* by D.H. Lawrence was ruled not obscene, and therefore mailable, by the U.S. Circuit Court of Appeals in New York. Chief Judge Charles E. Clark, alluding to Postmaster General Arthur E. Summerfield, asked, "Should a mature and sophisticated reading public be kept in blinders because a government official thinks reading certain works of power and literary value is not good for him?"

Apr 29: In a **payola investigation,** Dick Clark, one of the nation's best paid and most influential disc jockeys, denied involvement in illegal payments. Clark stated before the Special House Subcommittee on Legislative Oversight, "I believe in my heart that I have never taken payola."

May 2: Pulitzer prizes were awarded for the following: fiction, *Advise and Consent* by Allen Drury; biography, *John Paul Jones* by Samuel Eliot Morison; history, *In the Days of McKinley* by Margaret Leech; poetry, *Heart's Needle* by W.D. Snodgrass; drama,

Fiorello! by George Abbott, Jerome Weidman, Sheldon Harnick, and Jerry Bock.

May 19: In the **payola scandal,** Alan Freed, radio disc jockey, television personality, and originator of the term "rock 'n' roll," was arrested on charges of commercial bribery. Seven other persons accused of payola were also arrested.

Oct 17: Charles Van Doren, former star contestant on the TV quiz show *21,* and 13 others were arrested on charges of perjury. They had stated before a grand jury that the quiz shows involved in a recent scandal had not provided contestants with questions and answers before the shows were broadcast.

Nov 17: Anti-integration riots in New Orleans were the worst since initiation of school integration there. Almost 200 people were arrested.

III. Business and Industry
Education
Philosophy and Religion
Science

The U.S. demonstrated considerable technical progress by launching 17 space satellites and probes. The most spectacular of the objects sent into space were Tiros 1, which took 22,952 pictures of Earth's cloud cover; Discoverer 13, whose capsule was the first orbited object ever returned to Earth; and Discoverer 14, whose capsule was later retrieved in midair. Other aspects of national life, however, were showing less progress. A dangerous outflow of gold prompted the government to curtail spending abroad by military personnel, and there was a high rate of unemployment. The government continued its fight for southern school integration, but some public schools remained closed and were marred by mob violence and vandalism, such as that which erupted in November during attempts to integrate schools in New Orleans.

Jan 2: The **age of the solar system** was estimated by Dr. John H. Reynolds of the University of California (Berkeley) to be 4,950,000,000 years. His estimate was based on study of a meteorite found 41 years previously near Richardton, N.D.

Jan 4: The **longest steel strike** in the nation's history was settled when the steel companies and the United Steel Workers agreed on a wage increase. The strike had begun on July 15, 1959.

Jan 7: A new **ocean diving record** was established when Lt. Donald Walsh, USN, and Jacques Piccard descended 24,000 ft. in the bathyscaphe *Trieste.* The world record dive was made in the Pacific Marianas Trench, 60 miles from Guam. The dive was surpassed on Jan. 23 when the *Trieste* made a dive of 35,800 ft. to the bottom of the Marianas Trench.

Jan 9: Some methods and instances of **birth control** were approved by the bishops and other leaders of the Protestant Episcopal Church. The approbation was limited to countries in which the population increase threatened the general welfare.

Mar 11: Pioneer 5, the third spacecraft to be orbited around the sun, was launched by the U.S. from Cape Canaveral. The other two were Pioneer 4 (U.S.) and Lunik 1 (U.S.S.R.).

Mar 22: Dr. J.R. Heller, director of the National Cancer Institute, reported that **cancer** of the stomach was declining and cancer of the lung increasing.

Apr 1: The **first weather satellite,** Tiros 1, was orbited by the U.S. It sent thousands of photographs of cloud cover back to Earth.

Apr 9: School integration had reached only 6% of southern schools, it was reported by *Southern School News,* in spite of the 1954 Supreme Court decision against segregation.

Apr 14: A **Polaris missile** was fired from under water off San Clemente Island, Calif., for the first time.

Apr 27: Sit-ins by blacks in the South were again endorsed by the National Council of the Protestant Episcopal Church.

Apr 28: Marital sex relations without procreative intentions were declared not to be sinful by leaders of the 100th General Assembly of the Southern Presbyterian Church.

May 10: The **first undersea voyage around the world** was completed by the nuclear submarine U.S.S. *Triton,* the largest known submarine.

May 12: Lockheed Aircraft announced that the **Electra crashes** in Sept. 1959 and Mar. 1960 were caused by a structural deficiency. The cost of correcting the fault was estimated at $25,000,000.

May 15: Taxes reached 25% of earnings, according to a Tax Foundation report that lumped together federal, state, and local taxes.

May 20: The U.S. set a **world missile record** when an Atlas intercontinental ballistic missile flew 9000 miles, from Cape Canaveral, Fla., to beyond the tip of Africa.

May 24: Designed to act as an **early warning system** against surprise missile attacks, Midas 2, a 5000-lb. satellite, was launched from Cape Canaveral, Fla.

May 31: The Joint Commission on Mental Illness and Health reported that **mental illness** afflicted 25% of all Americans at one time or another in their lives to the extent that they required professional help.

June 6: For middle-aged men, **coronary death rates** "were found to be from 50% to 150% higher among heavy cigarette smokers" than among nonsmokers, according to the American Heart Association.

July 20: The first successful launching of **Polaris missiles** from a submerged craft was accomplished by the nuclear submarine U.S.S. *George Washington.* The missiles flew 1150 miles.

Aug 3: The first phone conversation in which **voices were bounced off the moon** was accomplished by U.S. scientists.

Aug 4: A **world air speed record** of 2196 mph was set by the X-15 experimental U.S. rocket plane. The plane was piloted by Joseph A. Walker, a civilian test pilot.

Aug 11: The **first payload recovered from orbit** was lifted from the Pacific Ocean by a U.S. helicopter. The capsule was placed in orbit by Discoverer 13 on Aug. 10.

Aug 19: A **spacecraft was snagged in midair** by the U.S. Air Force. The 300-lb. space capsule was ejected from Discoverer 14 at an altitude of 10,000 ft. and retrieved at 8500 ft.

Nov 3: The **Nobel Prize in Chemistry** was awarded to Prof. Willard Frank Libby of the University of California for discovering a method of radioactive carbon dating.

Nov 3: The **Nobel Prize in Physics** was awarded to Prof. Donald A. Glaser of the University of California for his development of the bubble chamber, a device that makes visible the paths of subatomic particles.

IV. Fashion
Folkways
Holidays
Social Issues and Crime
Sports

Floyd Patterson, using an eclectic boxing style, defeated Ingemar Johansson to become the first man in history to regain the heavyweight championship of the world. Another outstanding fighter, 40-year-old Sugar Ray Robinson, lost the world middleweight title to Paul Pender. Boxing was under fire, and a congressional investigation tried to determine the nature and extent of underworld influence in the sport. Congress also investigated the practice of payola in the recording and broadcasting industries.

Jan 2: The **U.S. chess championship** was successfully defended by Brooklyn's 16-year-old chess wonder, Bobby Fischer, in a tournament in New York City.

Jan 12: The **first 15,000-point NBA player,** Dolph Schayes of the Syracuse professional basketball team, reached a 15,013-point total for his career. Schayes was famed for his rebounding ability.

Jan 24: In a **Chicago police scandal,** Richard Morrison, an ex-convict awaiting trial for burglary, named eight Chicago policemen as confederates. In the ensuing investigation, 17 policemen were suspended on suspicion of robbery, bribery, and burglary.

Feb 18-28: At the **Winter Olympics** in Squaw Valley, Calif., the unofficial team championship was won by the U.S.S.R. Sweden was second and the U.S. was third.

Feb 23: Demolition of **Ebbets Field,** home park of the Brooklyn Dodgers (now the Los Angeles Dodgers), was begun. An apartment project was planned for the site.

Mar 7: In **racial violence,** Felton Turner, a black 27-year-old resident of Houston, Tex., was beaten with a tire iron and suspended upside down in an oak tree. The initials KKK were carved on his chest. Turner had been abducted by four masked youths, who said their actions were related to the sit-down strikes of Texas Southern University black students.

Mar 19: The **NCAA basketball championship** was won by Ohio State, which defeated California 75 to 55.

Mar 25: Wilt Chamberlain retired from professional basketball. Though he decried the rough tactics by opponents on the court, Chamberlain admitted that racial difficulties he encountered as a black had influenced his decision. Chamberlain relented later in the year and signed another pro basketball contract.

Mar 27-Apr 9: The **NBA basketball championship** was won by the Boston Celtics, who beat the St. Louis Hawks four games to three.

May 2: Caryl Chessman, convicted of kidnaping, rape, and robbery in Jan. 1948, was executed in the gas chamber at San Quentin Prison, Calif., after a 12-year battle for his life.

June 18: The **U.S. Open golf tournament** was won by Arnold Palmer, who beat Jack Nicklaus by two strokes.

June 20: The **world heavyweight boxing championship** was won by Floyd Patterson, who defeated Ingemar Johansson in a fifth-round knockout. Patterson thus became the first fighter in boxing history to regain the heavyweight championship.

July 24: The **PGA golf tournament** was won by Jay Hebert, beating Jim Ferrier by one stroke.

Aug 12: In a case of **racial discrimination,** a Troy, Mich., cemetery rejected the body of Winnebago Indian George V. Nash because he was not white. Nash, a World War I veteran, was buried in Pontiac, Mich., after his family refused to permit burial in Arlington National Cemetery.

Aug 25-Sep 11: At the **Summer Olympics** in Rome, Italy, the U.S. won 34 gold medals and took second place in team standings, behind the U.S.S.R.

Oct 3: In a **narcotics raid,** U.S. agents confiscated $3,500,000 worth of heroin (110 lbs.) and arrested four people, among them the Guatemalan ambassador to Belgium, Mauricio Rosal.

Oct 5-13: The 57th **World Series** was won by the Pittsburgh Pirates (NL), defeating the New York Yankees (AL) four games to three.

Oct 18: Casey Stengel, manager of the New York Yankee baseball team since 1949, was fired. Although the official announcement stated that Stengel had reached retirement age, he attributed dismissal to a controversy with the club owners.

Dec 26: The **NFL championship** was won by the Philadelphia Eagles, who defeated the Green Bay Packers 17 to 13.

1961

I. Civil Rights
Exploration and Settlement
Government
Statistics
Wars

John F. Kennedy was inaugurated president of the U.S. in a year that provided many explosive and dangerous situations. He was met with civil war in Laos and the Congo and continued Russian threats in Berlin. Rising tensions in Berlin culminated in the sealing off of East Berlin by East German and Soviet guards on Aug. 13, and the construction of a concrete and barbed wire barrier that came to be called the Berlin Wall. In September the Soviets resumed atmospheric nuclear testing. In the domestic arena, the president was confronted with several difficult problems. How to eliminate unemployment continued to be a major concern. Congress refused to provide substantial aid to U.S. education and passed an impotent civil rights bill. Notables who died included Whittaker Chambers, accuser of Alger Hiss, July 9, at 60; William Z. Foster, chairman of the American Communist Party from 1945 to 1957, Sept. 1, at 80; Learned Hand, distinguished jurist, Aug. 18, at 89; Sam Rayburn, longtime Speaker of the House, Nov. 16, at 79; Walter Bedell Smith, chief of staff to Gen. Eisenhower during World War II, Aug. 9, at 75; and Sumner Welles, diplomat, Sept. 24, at 68.

Jan 3: The **U.S. broke diplomatic relations with Cuba** after a series of mutually hostile actions, the last being Cuba's demand that the U.S. reduce its Havana embassy staff to 11 members.

Jan 20: John F. Kennedy was inaugurated president of the United States. A Democrat and the 35th president, Kennedy was assassinated on Nov. 22, 1963.

Mar 13: Elizabeth Gurley Flynn, 70, was named to succeed Eugene Dennis as national chairman of the U.S. Communist Party. She was the first woman to fill the office.

Apr 17: In what came to be called the **Bay of Pigs invasion,** some 1500 anti-Castro Cuban exiles landed at the Bay of Cochinos in Cuba. Organized by the U.S.-based National Revolutionary Council and trained by the CIA, the force enjoyed initial success but collapsed within a few days because of inadequate supplies, lack of air support, and overwhelming opposing forces. On Apr. 24 Pres. Kennedy stated he accepted full responsibility for failure of the invasion.

May 27: A bill establishing the **Alliance for Progress** was signed by Pres. Kennedy. The bill provided $600,000,000 in special aid to Latin America.

June 3-4: At the **Vienna summit meeting,** Pres. Kennedy and Premier Nikita S. Khrushchev discussed problems of mutual interest to the U.S. and the U.S.S.R., particularly nuclear disarmament and troubles in Laos and in Berlin.

July 24: A U.S. **passenger jet was hijacked.** An armed passenger forced the pilot of an Eastern Airlines Electra en route to Tampa from Miami to divert to Havana. Cuba later entrusted the plane to the UN Security Council to discourage what it alleged to be "imminent military aggression" by the U.S.

Aug 2: U.S. support for the Republic of China and its membership in the UN was reaffirmed in a joint communiqué issued following meetings between Pres. Kennedy and Premier Ch'en Ch'eng of the Republic of China. The statement reiterated U.S. opposition to UN membership for the People's Republic of China.

Sep 5: A **hijacking bill** making air piracy a crime punishable by death or imprisonment was signed by Pres. Kennedy.

Oct 6: Speaking on **civil defense,** Pres. Kennedy advised families to build or buy a shelter against atomic fallout. He said that the U.S. civil defense program should provide such protection for every American.

Nov 8: A **plane crash** killed 74 U.S. Army recruits flying in a chartered Imperial Airlines Constellation over an area near Richmond, Va. It was later revealed that the airline had been penalized twice for infractions of CAA regulations.

II. Architecture
Arts and Music
Popular Entertainment
Publishing
Theater

Tropic of Cancer by Henry Miller, originally published in France in 1934, became available in the U.S. after many years of prohibition on grounds of obscenity. Imported and reprinted by the same company that was responsible for U.S. publication of *Lady Chatterley's Lover, Tropic of Cancer* encountered considerably less legal difficulty than the D. H. Lawrence novel. The U.S. literary scene was saddened by the death of Ernest Hemingway; he was said to have shot himself while cleaning a shotgun. Joan Sutherland made an impressive U.S. debut at the Metropolitan Opera. She displayed a capacity for combining agility, color, subtlety, and volume of sound. Equally impressive was a New York City recital series by pianist Arthur Rubinstein, who enchanted U.S. music lovers. Playing ten Carnegie Hall recitals within 40 days, Rubinstein, at 72, announced joyfully that he had decided not to make the series his "final touch." Notables who died this year included Gary Cooper, actor, May 13, at 60; Hilda Doolittle, poet, Sept. 27, at 75; Dashiell Hammett, detective writer, Jan. 10, at 66; Moss Hart, playwright, Dec. 20, at 57; George S. Kaufman, playwright and producer, June 2, at 71; Chico Marx, Oct. 11, at 70; Grandma Moses, painter, Dec. 13, at 101; Eero Saarinen, architect, Sept. 1, at 51; and James Thurber, writer and cartoonist, Nov. 2, at 66.

Among **books published** this year was *Webster's Third New International Dictionary.* The massive new unabridged dictionary received a mixed response. Many linguists objected to its refusal to set standards of English and felt that too much valuable old material had been omitted. Other books published this year included *The Coming Fury* by Bruce Catton, the first volume of a trilogy to be called *Centennial History of the Civil War; Midcentury* by John Dos Passos, a novel; *Kaddish and Other Poems* by Allen Ginsberg; *Catch-22* by Joseph Heller, an antiwar novel that became a best seller; *Spirit Lake* by MacKinlay Kantor, a novel about frontier life in Iowa in the 1850s; *Franny and Zooey* by J. D. Salinger, stories; *Sinclair Lewis: an American Life* by Mark Schorer; *The Winter of Our Discontent* by John Steinbeck, a novel; and *The Agony and the Ecstasy* by Irving Stone, a novel based on the life of Michelangelo.

Jan 8: The **Bollingen Prize** for poetry was awarded to Yvor Winters for his 1960 volume of *Collected Poems.*

Jan 23: In a **film censorship** ruling, the U.S. Supreme Court upheld a Chicago, Ill., ordinance forbidding the showing of any motion picture without permission of the city censors.

May 1: Pulitzer prizes were awarded for the following: fiction, *To Kill a Mockingbird* by Harper Lee; biography, *Charles Sumner and the Coming of the Civil War* by David Donald; history, *Between War and Peace: The Potsdam Conference* by Herbert Feis; poetry, *Times Three: Selected Verse from Three Decades* by Phyllis McGinley; drama, *All the Way Home* by Tad Mosel.

May 9: Calling **television a "vast wasteland,"** Newton N. Minow, chairman of the FCC, in a vehement criticism of TV programming, said, "It is not enough to cater to the nation's whims—you must also serve the nation's needs."

Nov 15: A **record art price** of $2,300,000 was paid by the New York Metropolitan Museum of Art for Rembrandt's *Aristotle Contemplating the Bust of Homer.* The painting was formerly in the collection of the late Alfred W. Erickson and his wife.

III. Business and Industry
Education
Philosophy and Religion
Science

This was a year for adventure in space. Two Americans and two Russians invaded a frontier of the future. Though the U.S. was unable to equal the impressive Soviet feat of putting men into orbit, it succeeded in propelling two men to the threshold of space and then recovering them safely. The U.S. also launched an impressive series of Earth satellites and space probes, mostly designed to transmit data back to Earth. Progress of a different sort was made in civil rights in educational facilities. Court after court voided—but some upheld—various state laws designed to prevent school integration. Even though some civil rights battles were won, integration was slow and marked by sporadic violence, such as that encountered during the so-called freedom rides. Education as a whole became more of a national concern as it became increasingly evident that educational facilities were inadequate and growing more so and that the quality of instruction was poor in many parts of the country. Among the notables who died this year was Lee De Forest, whose invention of the audion tube in 1906 ushered in the age of radio, June 30, at 87.

Jan 28: Plans for establishing the **Peace Corps,** a project advocated by Pres. John F. Kennedy, were made public by the U.S. State Department.

Jan 31: In a **Project Mercury** suborbital test flight, the U.S. shot a 37½-lb. chimpanzee into space and recovered him successfully. The capsule containing the animal traveled 5000 mph to a height of 155 miles.

Feb 9: Earth is a "slightly irregular ellipsoid," according to photographic data received from Vanguard 1 and 2.

Feb 18: Discoverer 21 was launched into orbit by a Thor-Agena-B rocket. An unusual feature of the shot was a control mechanism that enabled the rocket engine to be restarted while in orbit.

Feb 22-23: Birth control as a means of family limitation was endorsed by the National Council of Churches at a meeting in Syracuse, N.Y.

Feb 23: The most costly **airline strike** in aviation history ended. The six-day strike had completely shut down Trans World, Eastern, Flying Tiger, American, and National airlines and had hampered operations of several others.

Apr 27: Explorer 11, a 95-lb. research satellite, was launched into orbit by a Juno 2 rocket. Carrying a "lensless telescope," the satellite was intended to determine the nature of interstellar matter.

May 4: A new **balloon altitude record** was set by two Navy scientists who ascended to 113,500 ft. aboard the balloon *Stratolab High No. 5.* One of the balloonists drowned after he fell from the sling of the helicopter that had picked him up.

May 5: A bill setting the federal **minimum wage** at $1.25 an hour and expanding coverage to include 3,624,000 workers not covered previously was signed by Pres. Kennedy.

May 5: The **first American in space** was Navy Commander Alan Bartlett Shepard, Jr., who made a successful suborbital flight aboard the Project Mercury capsule *Freedom Seven.*

June 16: Discoverer 25 was launched. Its capsule was ejected and recovered on June 18. The satellite carried samples of various minerals to determine how they would be affected by space conditions.

June 29: Three satellites were launched simultaneously by a Thor-Able-Star rocket. These satellites, Transit 4-A, Greb 3, and Injun, constituted the first triple launching in history.

July 7: James R. Hoffa was reelected president of the International Brotherhood of Teamsters by an overwhelming vote. The election was held at the Teamsters' convention in Miami Beach, Fla.

July 21: The **second American in space** was Capt. Virgil I. "Gus" Grissom, USAF, who ascended to an altitude of 118 miles in a suborbital flight aboard the Project Mercury capsule *Liberty Bell Seven.*

Sep 8: In a report on **smoking and heart disease** in the *Journal of the American Medical Association,* it was held that there was statistical evidence connecting the two.

Oct 19: The **Nobel Prize for Physiology or Medicine** was awarded to Dr. Georg von Bekesy of Harvard University for his studies of the inner ear.

Nov 2: The **Nobel Prize for Chemistry** was awarded to Melvin Calvin of the University of California at Berkeley for determining the sequence of chemical reactions involved when a plant assimilates carbon dioxide.

Nov 2: The **Nobel Prize in Physics** was awarded jointly to Robert Hofstadter of Stanford University for his work on the atomic nucleus and to Rudolf L. Mössbauer of West Germany for developing a method of using radiation from excited nuclei to measure time.

IV. Fashion
Folkways
Holidays
Social Issues and Crime
Sports

In boxing Floyd Patterson again defeated Ingemar Johansson in a close but quick fight in Miami Beach, Fla. Patterson withstood the power of the Swedish champion's savage right hand and scored a knockout, the second in a row for the American heavyweight. In golf, the top money winners were Gary Player, $64,540, and Mickey Wright, $22,236. In baseball, the National League announced that it would add two new franchises in 1962, the Houston Astros and the New York Mets. Americans mourned the death of Tyrus Raymond "Ty" Cobb, considered by many the greatest baseball player of all time, July 17, at 74.

Jan 2: The **AFL championship** for 1960 was won by the Houston Oilers, who defeated the Los Angeles Chargers 24 to 16.

Mar 13: The **world heavyweight boxing championship** was successfully defended by Floyd Patterson, who knocked out Ingemar Johansson in the sixth round in Miami Beach, Fla.

Mar 25: The **NCAA basketball championship** was won by Cincinnati, defeating the defending champions, Ohio State, 70 to 65.

Apr 2-11: The **NBA basketball championship** was won by the Boston Celtics, who defeated the St. Louis Hawks four games to one.

May 14: Two groups of **freedom riders,** people who traveled by private car and public transportation to sites in the South to protest racial segregation, were attacked by white citizens of Anniston and Birmingham, Ala., while on a journey from Washington, D.C., to New Orleans.

June 9: In a **college basketball bribery** scandal, four former players were indicted in New York City in connection with a point-shaving plot, in which players would deliberately control the score of a game as instructed by gamblers. Two gamblers, Aaron Wagman and Joseph Hacken, were named as co-conspirators. Both had been indicted earlier on related charges in the grand jury probe that began on Apr. 4. As the summer progressed, further revelations and indictments showed the practice of point-shaving to be widespread.

June 17: The **U.S. Open golf tournament** was won by Gene Littler.

July 8: At the **Wimbledon** tennis championships in England the women's doubles title was won by Karen Hantze and Billie Jean Moffitt.

July 30: The **PGA golf tournament** was won by Jerry Barber, who beat Don January by one stroke in a playoff round.

Oct 1: Yankee slugger **Roger Maris** hit his 61st homer, setting a new season record. He did it in a season of 162 games. Babe Ruth had hit 60 home runs in a 154-game season.

Oct 4-9: The 58th annual **World Series** was won by the New York Yankees (AL), beating the Cincinnati Reds (NL) four games to one.

Dec 4: The **world heavyweight boxing championship** was successfully defended by Floyd Patterson, who knocked out Tom McNeeley in the fourth round of a bout in Toronto, Canada.

Dec 24: The **AFL championship** was won by the Houston Oilers, who defeated the San Diego Chargers 10 to 3.

Dec 31: The **NFL championship** was won by the Green Bay Packers, who defeated the New York Giants 37 to 0.

1962

I. Civil Rights
Exploration and Settlement
Government
Statistics
Wars

In international affairs, Pres. John F. Kennedy appeared stronger and more sure. He visited Mexico and the Bahamas in an effort to strengthen alliances. Communist violation of a cease-fire in Laos in May led Kennedy to order U.S. troops into Thailand until guarantees of Laotian sovereignty could be secured. Chinese invasion of India in September prompted increased U.S. aid to India. The key event of the year came in October, when Pres. Kennedy, on national TV, revealed that Soviet nuclear missiles and jet bombers were located in Cuba and ordered a blockade of Cuba until the weapons were removed. The world appeared to stand on the brink of nuclear war until Premier Khrushchev agreed to withdraw the weapons. At home, the president was less successful. Congress continued to defeat or alter proposed legislation. The nation mourned the death of Eleanor Roosevelt, widow of Pres. Franklin D. Roosevelt and a key figure in the early years of the United Nations, Nov. 7, at 78.

Jan 15: U.S. tanks were withdrawn from the Berlin Wall in an effort to improve relations with the U.S.S.R. Two days later 12 Soviet tanks that had stationed near the wall since Oct. 1961 were removed.

Jan 29: The **nuclear test ban conference** of the U.S., U.S.S.R., and Great Britain in Geneva adjourned after 353 sessions in three years. The talks were deadlocked over a monitoring system for international control.

Feb 3: A trade ban with Cuba, effective Feb. 7 and including almost all products, was ordered by Pres. Kennedy.

Feb 8: Creation of the **Military Assistance Command** (MAC), a new U.S. military command in South Vietnam, was announced by the Defense Department.

Feb 10: U-2 pilot **Francis Gary Powers** was released in Berlin by Soviet authorities in exchange for Soviet spy Rudolf Abel. Frederic L. Pryor, an American student, was released by the Soviets at the same time.

Feb 26: Segregation laws in transportation facilities, both interstate and intrastate, were ruled unconstitutional by the U.S. Supreme Court. The Court ordered a federal court in Mississippi to act against state segregation laws in terminals.

Mar 19: The **Communist Party was sued** in New York by the Justice Department, which also sued four of its officials—Elizabeth Gurley Flynn, Gus Hall, Benjamin J. Davis, and Philip Bart—in an effort to collect $500,000 in income taxes and interest for 1951.

Apr 3: Full **racial integration in military reserve units,** exclusive of the National Guard, was ordered by the Defense Department.

Apr 8: Cuba announced that 1179 **Bay of Pigs prisoners** had been convicted of treason and sentenced to 30 years in prison. Officials offered to free all prisoners on payment of a $62,000,000 ransom. Six days later, 60 sick and wounded prisoners were returned to the U.S. on a promise to pay the ransom.

Apr 25: The **U.S. resumed nuclear testing** in the atmosphere after a three-year moratorium, with the explosion of a device near Christmas Island. The U.S.S.R. had broken the U.S.-Soviet moratorium the preceding September.

May 12: Some 1800 U.S. **Marines were sent to Thailand** with other naval, air, and land forces for defense against possible attack by communist forces from Laos. By May 29, more than 5000 U.S. military personnel were in Thailand.

June 16: Two U.S. Army officers were killed in an ambush by guerrillas north of Saigon, South Vietnam.

July 27: The last **Marines in Thailand** were withdrawn.

Aug 15: For the first time in history, the **national debt** exceeded $300,000,000,000.

Aug 27: At the **Geneva disarmament conference,** the U.S. and Great Britain proposed adoption of a total nuclear test ban open to international inspection. They also proposed an alternative plan that would reduce nuclear tests without international inspection. The U.S.S.R. rejected both proposals.

Aug 27: The **Twenty-fourth Amendment** to the Constitution, barring the poll tax as a requirement for voting in federal elections, was approved by Congress.

Oct 22: The **Cuban missile crisis** was the subject of a television address by Pres. Kennedy. He said that the U.S.S.R., contrary to its assurances, had been building missile and bomber bases in Cuba. Kennedy authorized a blockade of Cuba effective Oct. 24, to halt shipment of offensive weapons to Cuba. The day after Kennedy's address, the Council of the Organization of American States voted unanimously to authorize the use of armed force to prevent shipment of offensive weapons to Cuba.

Oct 25: Aerial photos of offensive missile bases in Cuba were displayed to the UN by Ambassador Adlai Stevenson. The next day the U.S. Navy boarded and searched a Soviet-chartered freighter en route to Havana.

Oct 27: Premier **Khrushchev offered to remove the Cuban missile bases** under UN supervision, demanding that the U.S. take corresponding action in Turkey. A U-2 reconnaissance plane was shot down over Cuba.

Oct 28: Withdrawal of Soviet missiles, under UN inspection, and a halt to construction of bases in Cuba, was agreed to by Premier Khrushchev. Pres. Kennedy agreed to lift the trade and weapons ban when the UN had acted, and pledged that the U.S. would not invade Cuba.

Oct 29: The U.S. **blockade of Cuba** was suspended for the duration of a trip by acting UN Secretary-General U Thant for a conference with Cuban Prime Minister Fidel Castro. No agreement was reached after UN inspection.

Nov 2: The **missile bases in Cuba were being dismantled,** Pres. Kennedy reported to the nation, adding that "progress is now being made toward restoration of peace in the Caribbean."

Nov 6: In **congressional elections** the Democrats gained two Senate seats for a 67–33 majority. In the House they lost five seats for a 258–177 majority.

Nov 7: Billie Sol Estes, a Texas financier whose business manipulations involving the Department of Agriculture had created a political scandal, was sentenced to eight years in prison after conviction on a charge of swindling a Texas farmer. He still faced numerous other state and federal indictments.

Nov 20: Lifting of the **naval blockade of Cuba** was announced by Pres. Kennedy, following assurances by Premier Khrushchev that all Soviet jet bombers in Cuba would be removed within 30 days.

Nov 20: An **executive order prohibiting racial discrimination in housing** built or purchased with federal funds was signed by Pres. Kennedy.

Dec 23: The **Cuban government began releasing prisoners** captured in the Bay of Pigs invasion under an agreement with a U.S. committee of private citizens by which Cuba would get more than $50,000,000 in food and medical supplies.

II. Architecture
Arts and Music
Popular Entertainment
Publishing
Theater

In art, the interest of the general public and collectors focused on so-called pop art, the depiction and sometimes the actual display of the most banal objects of American life: canned foods, electric appliances, comic strips, and the like. An international art scandal broke when Canadian authorities questioned the authenticity of many of the paintings from Walter P. Chrysler's famous collection, then on tour in Canada. Formation of Citizens for Decent Literature kept the question of censorship in the news; two particular targets of this watchdog group were *The Car-*

petbaggers by Harold Robbins and *The Tropic of Capricorn* by Henry Miller. In architecture, one of the year's most interesting structures was the 600-foot Space Needle, at the Century 21 Exposition in Seattle, Wash. Notables who died this year included Sylvia Beach, proprietor of the celebrated bookstore Shakespeare & Co. in Paris, about Oct. 5, at 75; William Beebe, naturalist, author, and explorer, June 4, at 84; E. E. Cummings, poet, Sept. 3, at 67; William Faulkner, winner of the 1949 Nobel Prize for Literature, July 6, at 64; Robinson Jeffers, poet, Jan 20, at 75; Franz Josef Kline, expressionist painter, May 13, at 51; Ernie Kovacs, television writer, performer, and producer, Jan. 13, at 42; Fritz Kreisler, violinist, Jan. 29, at 86; Marilyn Monroe, who died in her Los Angeles home of an apparent overdose of sleeping pills, Aug. 5, at 36; and Bruno Walter, conductor, Feb. 17, at 85.

Among **books published** this year was *Ship of Fools* by Katherine Anne Porter, a long-awaited novel 20 years in the writing. It was an account of a voyage from Mexico to Germany of a German ship in 1931, on the eve of Adolf Hitler's rise to power. Other books published this year included *Another Country* by James Baldwin, a novel; *Fail-Safe* by Eugene Burdick and Harvey Wheeler, a novel about the accidental launching of a nuclear strike against the U.S.S.R.; *Silent Spring* by Rachel Carson, a well-documented indictment of the indiscriminate use of pesticides and other chemicals; *In the Clearing,* a collection of poems by Robert Frost; *The Thin Red Line* by James Jones, a novel dealing with the invasion of Guadalcanal in World War II; *Seven Days in May* by Fletcher Knebel and Charles W. Bailey, II, a novel dealing with the military overthrow of the U.S. government; *Six Crises* by Richard M. Nixon; *A Simple Honorable Man* by Conrad Richter, a novel; and *Travels With Charley: In Search of America* by John Steinbeck.

WNYC-TV, the nation's first **municipally owned television station,** began operation in New York City. The city also received its first publicly supported educational television station, WNDT, this year.

Jan 7: The **Bollingen Prize** for poetry was awarded jointly to John Hall Wheelock for his 1961 volume *The Gardener,* and to Richard Eberhart for poetic excellence over a 30-year period.

May 7: Pulitzer prizes were awarded for the following: fiction, *The Edge of Sadness* by Edwin O'Connor; history, *The Triumphant Empire: Thunder-Clouds Gather in the West* by Lawrence Gibson; nonfiction, *The Making of the President, 1960* by Theodore H. White; poetry, *Poems* by Alan Dugan; drama, *How to*

Succeed in Business Without Really Trying by Frank Loesser and Abe Burrows.

May 31-June 3: The **first International Jazz Festival,** presented in Washington, D.C., by the President's Committee of the People-to-People Program, proved a disappointment. There was unanimous praise for the Duke Ellington orchestra and the old-style jazz of the Eureka Brass Band of New Orleans, but the classical-jazz hybrid composition called "Third Stream," by Ellington, Gunther Schuller, and André Hodeir, was received coolly.

Sep 23: Philharmonic Hall, the first building to be completed in New York City's **Lincoln Center for the Performing Arts,** opened with a gala concert. Live television coverage was supplied as Leonard Bernstein conducted the New York Philharmonic before an audience of dignitaries, musicians, and patrons of the arts. The hall's acoustics were to prove disappointing. For a long time afterward, engineers made adjustments in the ceiling baffles and other sound-enhancing devices.

Oct 23: A **postal error** involving a U.S. commemorative stamp issued on this date to honor the late secretary general of the UN, Dag Hammarskjold, was reported in early November by several stamp collectors, who had obtained stamps with one color printed incorrectly. Postmaster General J. Edward Day subsequently caused an uproar when he ordered 10,000,000 of the errors printed to prevent speculation in the rarities. A suit against Day by a New Jersey collector was withdrawn after the Post Office Department authenticated his 50-stamp pane as a "discovery" item.

Oct 25: The **Nobel Prize for Literature** was won by John Steinbeck, whose works included *Tortilla Flat* (1935), *Of Mice and Men* (1937), *The Grapes of Wrath* (1939), *The Moon Is Down* (1942), *Cannery Row* (1945), and *East of Eden* (1952). The award cited his "realistic and imaginative writing . . . distinguished by a . . . social perception." He was the sixth American, the seventh American-born, author to win a Nobel Prize for Literature.

III. Business and Industry
Education
Philosophy and Religion
Science

This year's space achievements included the launching of Telstar, a communications satellite, and the orbiting of three astronauts on perfect missions. Experimentation with nuclear submarines and with thermonuclear detonations added to U.S. technological development. In the South, segregation in university education was broken, but only after mob violence and several deaths. Official nondenominational prayers in public schools were ruled unconstitutional by the Supreme Court. Congress took no steps to provide funds for the improvement of educational facilities for the nation's youth. In industry, an effort by steel industry management to raise prices was stopped by Pres. John F. Kennedy. The AFL-CIO announced a drive to establish a national 35-hour work week.

Jan 12: A **railroad merger** of two of the nation's largest systems, the Pennsylvania and the New York Central railroads, was approved by the companies' boards of directors.

Jan 26: Ranger 3, a lunar probe designed to transmit close-up television pictures of the moon before landing scientific instruments on its surface, was launched from Cape Canaveral, Fla. Two days later, because of excessive velocity, it passed the moon and went into orbit around the sun.

Feb 14: Plans for an **underwater telephone cable** costing $84,000,000 and running between Hawaii and Japan, via Midway, Wake, and Guam islands, was announced by the American Telephone & Telegraph Company.

Feb 20: The **first American to orbit Earth,** Lt. Col. John Glenn, circled the globe three times aboard a Mercury capsule *Friendship 7* before splashdown. It was launched from Cape Canaveral, Fla.

Mar 1: In the **biggest antitrust case** in U.S. history, E. I. du Pont de Nemours & Company was ordered by a federal district court to divest itself of 63,000,000 shares of General Motors stock.

Mar 4: The Atomic Energy Commission announced that the **first atomic power plant in Antarctica** was in operation at McMurdo Sound.

Mar 8: A two-year **cultural agreement** was signed with the U.S.S.R. to expand cultural, scientific, technical, and educational exchanges.

Mar 16: Titan 2, the most powerful U.S. ICBM, on its maiden flight, covered more than 5000 miles from Cape Canaveral, Fla., to a spot near Ascension Island in the south Atlantic.

Mar 27: Segregation in all Roman Catholic schools in the New Orleans, La., diocese was ordered ended by Archbishop Joseph Francis Rummel.

Apr 19: Skybolt, the first U.S. airborne ballistic missile, was launched from a B-52 bomber at Cape Canaveral, Fla. Its second stage failed to fire and the missile fell short of its target.

Apr 26: The **first international satellite,** Ariel, bearing six British experiments and propelled aloft by a U.S.

Delta rocket, was launched from Cape Canaveral, Fla. It was intended to study the ionosphere.

Apr 26: Ranger 4 crashed into the far side of the moon 64 hours after being launched from Cape Canaveral, Fla. Fifty-five hours into the flight, its radio system went dead.

May 6: In the **first submarine-launched nuclear detonation,** a Polaris missile armed with a nuclear warhead and launched from the nuclear submarine *Ethan Allen* was successfully exploded near Christmas Island. It was also the first U.S. test of a nuclear warhead carried by a long-range missile.

May 24: The **second American in orbit,** astronaut M. Scott Carpenter, circled Earth three times aboard the Mercury capsule *Aurora 7*, which was launched by an Atlas rocket from Cape Canaveral, Fla.

May 25: A nationwide campaign for a **35-hour work week** was announced by George Meany, president of the AFL-CIO.

May 28: In the **largest stock loss since Oct. 29, 1929,** shares on the New York exchange lost $20,800,000,000 in value. The stock market quickly recovered.

June 25: A New York State law permitting recitation of an **official prayer** in public schools was ruled unconstitutional by the Supreme Court.

July 9: A **thermonuclear explosion** equivalent to 1,400,000 tons of TNT was set off by the U.S. 250 miles above Johnston Island in the Pacific. The blast caused a substantial radiation increase in the Van Allen belt, disrupting communications and satellite operations.

July 10: Telstar, the experimental communications satellite developed and owned by American Telephone & Telegraph and Bell Telephone Laboratories, was placed in orbit from Cape Canaveral, Fla. It later relayed live TV pictures from Andover, Maine, to France and Great Britain.

Aug 22: The *Savannah*, the world's first nuclear-powered ship, completed its maiden voyage from Yorktown, Va., to Savannah, Ga.

Aug 22: Pres. Kennedy announced that a **submarine rendezvous** beneath the North Pole had been effected by two U.S. nuclear submarines.

Aug 27: Mariner 2 was launched successfully from Cape Canaveral, Fla., on a projected 15-week trajectory toward the planet Venus.

Sep 20: The application by **James H. Meredith,** a black, for admission to the University of Mississippi was denied by Mississippi Gov. Ross R. Barnett in defiance of a federal court order.

Sep 28: Gov. **Ross R. Barnett** of Mississippi was found guilty of civil contempt by a U.S. court of appeals. He was ordered to cease interference with desegregation at the University of Mississippi or face arrest and a fine of $10,000 for each day of further interference.

Sep 30: James H. Meredith was escorted onto the University of Mississippi campus by U.S. marshals. Two men were killed in the ensuing mob violence, which was quelled with the aid of 3000 federal soldiers. The next day Meredith was enrolled and began to attend classes amid continuing disruption by protesters.

Oct 3: The **third American in orbit,** astronaut Walter N. Schirra, completed five and three-quarter orbits aboard the Mercury capsule *Sigma 7* before splashing down near Midway Island in the Pacific within four miles of the recovery carrier U.S.S. *Kearsarge.*

Oct 18: The **Nobel Prize for Physiology or Medicine** was awarded jointly to Dr. James D. Watson of Harvard University, Dr. Maurice H. F. Wilkins of King's College in London, and Dr. Francis H. C. Crick of Cambridge, England, for their discovery of the molecular structure of deoxyribonucleic acid (DNA), the physical basis of heredity.

Dec 8: The **first black bishop** to serve a predominantly white diocese of the Protestant Episcopal Church in the U.S., the Right Rev. John Melville Burgess, was consecrated as suffragan bishop of Massachusetts.

Dec 13: Relay 1, an intercontinental communications satellite, was put in orbit. Two days later transmission was turned off for an indefinite period because of a power failure.

Dec 14: Mariner 2, on its 109th day of flight, transmitted information about Venus for 42 minutes.

Dec 21: Mississippi Gov. **Ross R. Barnett** and Lt. Gov. Paul B. Johnson were charged with criminal contempt of court in the U.S. Fifth Circuit Court of Appeals in New Orleans for their actions in September violating court orders for admission of James H. Meredith to the University of Mississippi.

IV. Fashion
Folkways
Holidays
Social Issues and Crime
Sports

In boxing Floyd Patterson lost his heavyweight crown to Sonny Liston in less than three minutes. In November 20-year-old Cassius Clay knocked out Archie Moore and moved closer to a title match against Liston. In baseball two new teams, the Houston Colt .45's and the New York Mets, joined the National League roster. The New York Yankees won their 20th World Series. In golf the leading money winners were Arnold Palmer, $81,448, and Mickey Wright,

$21,641. A new dance craze, the twist, was born in a New York City nightclub, The Peppermint Lounge. In women's fashions wigs became popular, and boots became a fashion accessory. The romance between Elizabeth Taylor and Richard Burton on the set for the motion picture *Cleopatra* in Rome was in and out of the headlines all year. Notables who died in 1962 included Edward Britt "Ted" Husing, sports announcer, Aug. 10, at 50; Charles "Lucky" Luciano, gangster, Jan. 26, at 65; Clem McCarthy, sports announcer, June 4, at 79; and Benny "Kid" Paret, a welterweight fighter who died of injuries sustained in a bout with Emile Griffith, Apr. 3, at 24.

A **UPI survey** showed that in the 24 states with legalized betting at race tracks, 33,881,860 fans bet a total of $2,679,461,505. Attendance was up 1.28% over 1961, and betting was up 5.57%. Mrs. Richard C. du Pont's Kelso was named horse of the year for the third straight year. Kelso earned $254,585 to boost lifetime earnings of the horse to $1,011,940. Kelso became the fifth horse in racing history to top the $1,000,000 mark.

Jan: The use of **nudity in advertising** became a national controversy after Christina Paolozzi, a 22-year-old model, appeared in the nude in a full-page color ad in *Harper's Bazaar*. The photograph was the work of fashion photographer Richard Avedon.

Feb 2: The **first person to vault 16 feet** was a Marine Corps corporal, John Uelses, at the Millrose Games in Madison Square Garden in New York City. Using a springy fiberglass pole, he cleared 16 ft. ¼ in. On the following night, in Boston, he raised the mark to 16 ft. ¾ in.

Feb 10: Jim Beatty, the **first American to break the four-minute mile indoors,** was clocked at 3:58.9 in Los Angeles, a new indoor record. On June 8, also in Los Angeles, he set a new world record of 8:29.8 for two miles. Beatty won the James E. Sullivan Memorial Trophy as the outstanding amateur athlete of 1962.

Mar 2: The **first basketball player to score 100 points** in a game was Wilt Chamberlain, star of the Philadelphia Warriors, who made 36 goals and 28 foul shots in a game against the N.Y. Knicks.

Mar 24: The **NCAA basketball championship** was won by Cincinnati, which defeated Ohio State 71 to 59.

Apr 3: Eddie Arcaro, considered by many the greatest American jockey in modern turf history, retired from racing. During his 31-year career he had ridden 4779 winners and had brought home purses totaling $30,039,543.

Apr 7-18: The **NBA basketball championship** was won by the Boston Celtics, defeating the Los Angeles Lakers four games to three.

Apr 21: The **Century 21 Exposition,** the world's fair at Seattle, Wash., was opened by remote control from Palm Beach, Fla., by Pres. Kennedy, who activated the carillon in the 600-foot Space Needle tower.

June 17: The **U.S. Open golf tournament** was won by Jack Nicklaus, who beat Arnold Palmer by three strokes in a playoff.

July 7: At the **Wimbledon** tennis championships in England, Karen Hantze Susman won the women's singles title. Susman teamed with Billie Jean Moffitt to win the women's doubles, and Margaret Osborne du Pont teamed with Neale Fraser of Australia to win the mixed doubles.

July 22: The **PGA golf tournament** was won by Gary Player of South Africa, who became the first nonresident of the U.S. to win the championship.

Aug 14: In a **mail truck robbery** in Plymouth, Mass., thieves took a record cash haul of $1,551,277.

Sep 8: The **richest purse in thoroughbred racing history,** $357,250, was offered in the Arlington-Washington Futurity, a race for two-year-olds. The winner's share, $142,250, went to Candy Spots.

Sep 15-25: The **America's Cup** was successfully defended by the U.S. 12-meter yacht *Weatherly*, which defeated the Australian challenger *Gretel* four races to one. It was the closest competition in years and the first time since 1934 that the U.S. entry failed to sweep the first four races.

Sep 25: The **world heavyweight boxing championship** was won by Sonny Liston, who knocked out the defending champion Floyd Patterson in two minutes and six seconds of the first round.

Sep 27: The **New York Mets,** a new National League baseball team, finished their first season, under former Yankee manager Casey Stengel. The Mets lost 120 of the 160 games they played. However, the fans loved them; nearly 1,000,000 came to the Polo Grounds to witness the heroic ineptitude of the players and the antics of their manager.

Oct 4-16: The 59th annual **World Series** was won by the New York Yankees (AL), defeating the San Francisco Giants (NL) four games to three. The Giants had won the National League pennant by beating the Los Angeles Dodgers two games to one in a league playoff.

Dec 23: The **AFL championship** was won by the Dallas Texans, who defeated the Houston Oilers 20 to 17. The game went to two extra quarters and was decided by a field goal by Tommy Brooker.

Dec 30: The **NFL championship** was won for the second year running by the Green Bay Packers, who defeated the N.Y. Giants 16 to 7.

1963

I. Civil Rights
  Exploration and Settlement
  Government
  Statistics
  Wars

The death of Pres. John F. Kennedy on Nov. 22 shocked the nation and the world. The 34th person elected president of the United States, Kennedy was the fourth to die by an assassin's bullet. The respect he had evoked throughout the world was attested to by the presence at his funeral of representatives of 92 nations, among them Charles de Gaulle of France, Anastas I. Mikoyan of the U.S.S.R., and Prince Philip of Great Britain. Although Kennedy did not live to see the passage of his civil rights bill, his program of medical care for the aged, or his tax-reduction bill, Congress did approve his proposal for aid to the mentally retarded. This year also saw a $3,600,000,000 appropriation for foreign aid, a reduction of $300,000,000 from the previous year. The signing of a limited nuclear test-ban treaty in October was counterbalanced by continuing conflict with Cuba and with the U.S.S.R. The U.S. became more heavily involved in the war in Vietnam. On Nov. 1 the government of Pres. Ngo Dinh Diem of South Vietnam was overthrown by South Vietnamese armed forces, and Diem was assassinated. On Nov. 7 the U.S. recognized the provisional government of Nguyen Ngoc Tho, Diem's vice president. Notables who died this year included W. E. B. Du Bois, a prominent black writer and educator, Aug. 27, at age 95; and Medgar W. Evers, civil rights leader, assassinated on June 12, at age 37.

Jan 17: The largest **federal budget** to date, totaling $98,800,000,000 with a projected deficit of $11,900,000,000, was sent to Congress by Pres. Kennedy.

Feb 8: Underground nuclear testing was resumed by the U.S. A suspension of tests had been ordered on Jan. 20 during the U.S.-U.S.S.R. test ban talks.

Feb 21: Medicare, a medical-hospital insurance plan financed through Social Security, was submitted to Congress by Pres. Kennedy.

Mar 13: Two **Soviet reconnaissance planes flew over Alaska.** On Mar. 16 the U.S. protested what was termed the "first clearly established incident of a Soviet overflight of the U.S."

Mar 18: The Supreme Court held that **free counsel for all indigents** facing serious criminal charges must be supplied by the states.

Apr 10: The nuclear-powered submarine *Thresher* **sank in the Atlantic** with 129 men on board during a test dive. A Navy board of inquiry concluded that a system failure probably created progressive flooding and that the interference with electrical circuits caused loss of power.

June 12: Medgar Evers was assassinated by a sniper, who shot the civil rights leader in the back outside the Evers home in Jackson, Miss. The crime sparked numerous demonstrations, and Pres. Kennedy and many other leaders condemned the killing. After a funeral in Jackson, Evers was buried in Arlington National Cemetery.

June 23: Pres. Kennedy, beginning a **ten-day tour of Europe,** arrived in West Germany. On June 26, speaking to a crowd of more than 1,000,000 in West Berlin, Kennedy stated he was proud to say "Ich bin ein Berliner" [I am a Berliner].

July 8: Virtually all **financial transactions with Cuba were banned** by the U.S. in another move toward economic isolation of that country.

July 12: A modified form of **martial law** was declared in Cambridge, Md., after National Guard troops were sent into the city for the second time in a month to control racial violence.

July 25: A **limited nuclear test-ban treaty,** prohibiting testing in the atmosphere, in space, and under water, was initialed in Moscow by the U.S., Great Britain, and the U.S.S.R.

Aug 28: A **Freedom March** on Washington, D.C., brought an estimated 200,000 participants, who listened to speeches by ten civil rights leaders, among them Dr. Martin Luther King. Dr. King told the group, "I have a dream," describing a U.S. free of divisiveness, hatred, and injustice.

Aug 30: The **hot line** went into operation. It was an emergency communications link between Washington, D.C., and Moscow, intended to reduce the risk of accidental war.

Sep 15: A **church bombing** in Birmingham, Ala., left four young black girls dead. The attack on the 16th Street Baptist Church sparked further violence in the city, leaving two more dead and 19 injured.

Oct 7: Robert G. "Bobby" Baker resigned as secretary to the Senate majority after being charged with using his position for personal financial gain.

Oct 7: The **limited nuclear test-ban treaty was signed** by Pres. Kennedy. It went into effect Oct. 10.

Oct 10-12: A **U.S. military convoy to Berlin** was blocked by Soviet troops in a dispute over troop counting procedures. The U.S. lodged strong formal protests, and the convoy was allowed to proceed.

Oct 16: Two **U.S. military satellites** were secretly launched from Cape Canaveral, Fla., for the detection of any violation of the treaty banning nuclear tests in space.

Nov 4: A **U.S. military convoy was blocked** by Soviet troops at the western border of Berlin. The U.S. protested and after 41 hours the convoy was allowed to proceed.

Nov 12: Travel restrictions on diplomats were imposed by the State Department, which barred diplomats of Bulgaria, Czechoslovakia, Hungary, Poland, and Rumania from 355 U.S. counties, about 11% of the continental U.S., for "reasons of national security."

Nov 22: Pres. **John F. Kennedy was assassinated** while riding in a motorcade in Dallas, Tex. He was pronounced dead at 1 P.M. Gov. John B. Connally of Texas, accompanying Kennedy, was severely wounded. Vice Pres. Lyndon Baines Johnson was sworn in as the 36th president of the United States at 2:39 P.M. at Love Air Field in Dallas. That same afternoon, Lee Harvey Oswald, a suspect in the assassination, was captured by Dallas police.

Nov 24: Lee Harvey Oswald was shot and killed by a man named Jack Ruby while in the custody of Dallas police. The nation saw the murder on television. Ruby was apprehended immediately.

Nov 25: John F. Kennedy was buried at Arlington National Cemetery following a mass at St. Matthew's Roman Catholic Cathedral.

Nov 29: What came to be called the **Warren Commission** was established by Pres. Johnson. The special commission, headed by Chief Justice Earl Warren, was appointed to investigate the assassination of John F. Kennedy and related events.

II. Architecture
Arts and Music
Popular Entertainment
Publishing
Theater

The best plays on Broadway were revivals, such as Eugene O'Neill's *Strange Interlude;* British imports, such as John Osborne's *Luther;* and translations, such as Bertolt Brecht's *Mother Courage and Her Children.* New buildings at Harvard and Yale made most of the architectural news. Le Corbusier, the great Swiss-French master, designed the Visual Arts Center at Harvard, his first building in the U.S. At Yale two new college buildings, the first since the 1930s, were completed. Eero Saarinen and Associates

were the designers. Also new at Yale were the Beinecke Rare Book and Manuscript Library and Paul Rudolph's Art and Architecture Building, a six-story structure that incorporated 36 different floor and ceiling levels. The Ford Foundation made history when it allocated $7,700,000 for development of ballet in the U.S. William Schuman, president of Lincoln Center for the Performing Arts in New York City, announced that $300,000 would be spent on improving acoustics in the center's Philharmonic Hall. Notables who died this year included Van Wyck Brooks, critic and biographer, May 2, at 77; Robert Frost, poet and four-time winner of the Pulitzer Prize, Jan. 29, at 88; Paul Hindemith, composer, Dec. 28, at 68; Oliver La Farge, author and anthropologist, Aug. 2, at 83; Elsa Maxwell, the celebrated New York City hostess, Nov. 1, at 80; Adolphe Menjou, actor, Oct. 29, at 73; Clifford Odets, playwright, Aug. 14, at 57; Zasu Pitts, film comedienne, June 7, at 63; Theodore Roethke, poet, Aug. 1, at 55; William Carlos Williams, poet and physician, Mar. 4, at 79; and Edgar Mantillon "Monty" Woolley, the actor who gained fame in *The Man Who Came to Dinner,* May 6, at 74.

Among **books published** this year was *Terrible Swift Sword* by Bruce Catton, the second volume in Catton's trilogy *Centennial History of the Civil War.* The book covered the period from just after the first Battle of Bull Run in June 1861 through Lincoln's Emancipation Proclamation. Other books published this year included *Eichmann in Jerusalem: A Report on the Banality of Evil* by Hannah Arendt; *The Civil War: A Narrative, Fredericksburg to Meridian* by Shelby Foote, the second volume of a history of the war; *Idiots First* by Bernard Malamud, stories; *The Group* by Mary McCarthy, a novel; *The Sand Pebbles* by Richard McKenna, a novel; *The American Way of Death* by Jessica Mitford, a scathing study of American funeral customs; *The Two Ocean War* by Samuel Eliot Morison; *Raise High the Roof Beam, Carpenters* and *Seymour: An Introduction* by J. D. Salinger, two stories in one volume; and *Cat's Cradle* by Kurt Vonnegut, Jr., a novel.

The painting *Her Room* by **Andrew Wyeth** was bought by the William A. Farnsworth Library and Art Museum in Rockland, Maine, for $65,000. It was the highest price ever paid by a museum for the work of a living American artist.

The **Bollingen Prize** for poetry was awarded to Robert Frost, whose final volume, *In the Clearing,* was published in 1962.

Happenings, the name given to ultra avant-garde theatrical events, were performed in various places, except in theaters, in many cities. A series of abstract events generally of an absurd or comic nature, a happening combined mime, painting, music, and modern dance.

Jan 8-Mar 4: The ***Mona Lisa*** by Leonardo da Vinci was exhibited in New York City and Washington, D.C., on loan from the Louvre. Nearly 1,000,000 people waited on line to see the painting. Another Louvre masterpiece, James McNeill Whistler's *Portrait of My Mother,* was shown in Atlanta, Ga., in February as a memorial tribute to a group of Georgia art lovers killed in a plane crash near Paris in 1962.

Mar-June: The first large-scale exhibition of **pop art** was held at the Guggenheim Museum in New York City. The show moved on to other American cities later in the year, bemusing critics and public alike with its representational paintings of such prosaic subjects as soup cans and comic strips. Prominent in the three-year-old pop-art movement were Andy Warhol, Jasper Johns, Robert Rauschenberg, and Roy Lichtenstein.

May 6: **Pulitzer prizes** were awarded to the following: fiction, *The Reivers* by William Faulkner; biography, *Henry James, Vol. II: The Conquest of London, 1870–1881* and *Henry James, Vol. III: The Middle Years, 1881–1895* by Leon Edel; history, *Washington, Village and Capital, 1800–1878* by Constance McLaughlin Green; general nonfiction, *The Guns of August* by Barbara Tuchman; poetry, *Pictures from Brueghel* by William Carlos Williams. A furor was caused when it was announced that there would be no drama award. The advisory board for drama had recommended Edward Albee's *Who's Afraid of Virginia Woolf?* When their recommendation was not announced, both John Mason Brown and John Gassner resigned.

Oct 16: The **New York** *Mirror* ceased publication. Although the Hearst newspaper's circulation was the second largest among U.S. dailies, the paper fell victim to an economic squeeze, partly the result of the 114-day New York City newspaper strike (from Dec. 8, 1962 to Mar. 31, 1963), and partly the result of decreasing advertising income. The *Mirror's* assets were sold to the rival *Daily News.*

III. Business and Industry
Education
Philosophy and Religion
Science

Progress toward civil rights was made when South Carolina and Alabama opened their colleges to blacks. The federal government appropriated nearly $2,000,000,000 for construction and improvement of U.S. college facilities and for student loans. The building and construction trades union of the AFL-CIO adopted a program to eliminate racial discrimi-

nation. In July demonstrations in New York City supporting increased hiring of minority workers at construction sites led to more than 700 arrests. During the year, the nation's unemployment rate rose. George Meany, president of the AFL-CIO, condemned automation as a "curse to society." A threatened national railroad strike resulted in a congressional act requiring arbitration, the first time arbitration was imposed in peacetime. Federal legislation required that women receive pay equal to that of men for similar work. The nation's farmers, in a referendum called for by the Food and Agriculture Act of 1962, overwhelmingly voted down a government program to decrease wheat production and to support the price of wheat. Traffic deaths reached an all-time high of 40,804.

Jan 3: **Relay 1,** a communications satellite launched Dec. 13, 1962, but silent since Dec. 15 owing to malfunction, was reactivated by radio signals from the ground. It began transmission between North and South America and Europe.

Jan 28: School desegregation in South Carolina, the last state to end segregation in its schools, was achieved when a student named Harvey B. Gantt was enrolled in Clemson College, Clemson, S.C.

Feb 14: Syncom 1, an experimental forerunner of a series of communications satellites, was launched from Cape Canaveral, Fla. Although a near synchronous orbit was achieved, radio contact with Earth was lost the same day.

Mar 17: Elizabeth Ann Seton was beatified by Pope John XXIII. She was the first native-born American to be so honored. She was declared a saint by Pope Paul VI in 1974 and canonized on Sept. 14, 1975.

Apr 5: J. Robert Oppenheimer, the U.S. physicist declared a security risk in 1954, was named winner of the Atomic Energy Commission's 1963 Fermi Award.

Apr 12: The Rev. **Martin Luther King, Jr., was arrested** in Birmingham, Ala., during a desegregation drive that had begun on Apr. 2.

Apr 18: Successful **human nerve transplants** were reported by Dr. James B. Campbell of the New York University Medical Center.

May 7: Telstar 2, the second communications satellite, was launched from Cape Canaveral, Fla. It began relaying color and black-and-white television signals between the U.S. and Europe.

May 9: A secret **military satellite** was launched by the Air Force from Point Arguello, Calif. It released some 400,000,000 tiny copper hairs into a polar orbit, providing a cloud of reflective material for relaying radio signals from coast to coast within the U.S.

May 15-16: The **fourth American in orbit,** Maj. L. Gordon Cooper, Jr., completed 22 orbits around Earth aboard the Mercury capsule *Faith 7,* in the final flight of Project Mercury.

June 4: A **Federal Reserve bill** changing the backing of $1.00 and $2.00 bills from silver to gold was signed by Pres. Kennedy.

June 8: A **drive against cigarette smoking** was opened by the American Heart Association, the first voluntary public agency to do so.

June 10: A bill requiring **equal pay for equal work,** regardless of sex, was signed by Pres. Kennedy.

June 11: The **University of Alabama was desegregated.** Gov. George C. Wallace, who had literally stood in the way of desegregation, stepped aside when confronted by federalized National Guard troops. Two black students were enrolled.

July 26: Syncom 2 was successfully launched and on Aug. 15 placed over Brazil in a geostationary Earth orbit. It transmitted telephone and Teletype messages between the U.S. and Nigeria.

Sep 7: Krebiozen, a so-called miracle drug, was declared by the Food and Drug Administration to be creatine, a common amino acid, and ineffective against tumors.

Sep 10: Public **school desegration** in Huntsville, Ala., was effected after Pres. Kennedy federalized the Alabama National Guard, forcing Gov. Wallace to end his attempt to block school integration.

Oct 10: The deferred 1962 **Nobel Peace Prize** was awarded to Dr. Linus C. Pauling of the California Institute of Technology. The award committee did not specify Pauling's achievements, but his efforts to secure a ban on nuclear testing were well known.

Nov 5: The **Nobel Prize in Physics** was awarded jointly to Eugene P. Wigner of Princeton, Maria G. Mayer of the University of California, and Hans Jensen of the University of Heidelberg, Germany, for their studies of atomic structure.

Dec 4: In a major change in the **Roman Catholic mass,** the use of English in the U.S. in place of Latin for parts of the mass and for the sacraments was approved by the Roman Catholic Ecumenical Council.

IV. Fashion
Folkways
Holidays
Social Issues and Crime
Sports

The sports world lost two of its most popular competitors in the retirements of baseball slugger Stan Musial and basketball back-court artist Bob Cousy. The strike zone in major-league baseball was enlarged at the beginning of the season. To compensate for the bigger target, perhaps, National League um-

pires began applying the rule that a pitcher must wait one second between windup and delivery. Rigorous enforcement of the one-second rule evoked such outrage from fans and players that the Rules Committee dropped it within a month. Golf's leading money winners were Arnold Palmer, $128,230, and Mickey Wright, $31,269. Rogers Hornsby, the great slugger whose .424 batting average for 1924 has never been equaled, died on Jan. 5, at 66. Davey Moore, world featherweight boxing champion, fell into a coma shortly after losing his title on Mar. 21 in a bout with Ultiminio "Sugar" Ramos. Moore died on Mar. 25, at age 29.

Mar 20: Hope Cooke, a recent graduate of Sarah Lawrence College, married Crown Prince Palden Thondup Namgyal of Sikkim in a Buddhist ceremony in Gangtok. On Dec. 2 the prince succeeded to the throne as maharajah on the death of his father, Sir Tashi Namgyal.

Mar 23: The **NCAA basketball championship** was won by Loyola, Ill., which defeated the University of Cincinnati 60 to 58.

Apr 24: The Boston Celtics' brilliant guard **Bob Cousy,** 34, retired from competition after leading the team to its fifth straight NBA championship. The Celtics had downed the Los Angeles Lakers four games to two (Apr. 14–24).

June 23: The **U.S. Open golf tournament** was won by Julius Boros, who beat Arnold Palmer and Jacky Cupit in a playoff.

July 6: At the **Wimbledon** tennis championships in England, Chuck McKinley won the men's singles championship.

July 21: The **PGA golf tournament** was won by Jack Nicklaus.

July 22: The **world heavyweight boxing championship** was successfully defended by Sonny Liston, who knocked out Floyd Patterson 2 min., 10 sec. into the first round.

Aug 5: Craig Breedlove set an unofficial **world auto speed record** of 407.45 mph on the Bonneville Salt Flats in Utah, driving a sleek three-ton, three-wheeled, jet-powered auto. The U.S. Auto Club established a new class for its records: "Jet-Powered Vehicles."

Aug 24: Don Schollander of Santa Clara, Calif., became the first person to break the two-minute mark for the 200-meter freestyle swim. At Osaka, Japan, he won the event with the time of 1:58.4.

Aug 24: John Pennel became the **first person to pole vault 17 feet,** reaching 17 ft. 3/4 in. at a meet in Miami, Fla.

Sep 27: Joseph M. Valachi, hoodlum turned informer, identified the alleged chiefs of organized crime in the

U.S. in televised testimony before the Senate Permanent Investigations Subcommittee.

Sep 29: Stan "The Man" Musial played his last game for the St. Louis Cardinals, retiring at 42 to take an executive position with the club. In his 22 years in baseball, all with the Cards, the great hitter set or tied 17 major league and 30 National League records.

Oct 2-6: The 60th annual **World Series** was won by the Los Angeles Dodgers (NL), who swept the New York Yankees (AL) in four games. Dodgers pitcher Sandy Koufax set a new series record by striking out 15 players in the opening game.

Dec 26-29: The U.S. regained the **Davis Cup,** which it had lost in 1959, by beating the Australian tennis team three matches to two.

Dec 31: The **NFL championship** was won by the Chicago Bears, who defeated the New York Giants 14 to 0.

1964

I. Civil Rights
Exploration and Settlement
Government
Statistics
Wars

Campaigning on the promise of achieving the Great Society, Pres. Lyndon Baines Johnson was elected to the presidency by a record-breaking vote. For the first time since 1920, the conservative wing had dominated the Republican campaign, alienating moderates and liberals. At the same time, the Democratic Party lost five southern states because of Pres. Johnson's success in putting through a civil rights bill in July. He was equally successful with the other primary legislative aim of his administration, the anti-poverty bill. His economy-in-government drive was reflected in his first budget, which contained a $1,100,000,000 cut in defense spending. Johnson asked for $3,400,000,000 for foreign aid, the smallest amount requested in 16 years. In domestic affairs, the year was marked by racial violence in many U.S. cities, including New York, Philadelphia, and St. Augustine, Fla. In the summer a coalition of civil rights groups mounted a voter registration and education drive in Mississippi; this sparked acts of violence. Foreign relations reflected continuing tension with Cuba and in Berlin. Deterioration of the situation in Southeast Asia resulted in greater U.S. military and economic assistance to South Vietnam. In the Congo, a number of American citizens were taken hostage, along with many Europeans. Two Americans were killed after U.S. aircraft dropped Belgian troops into the area, but most of the hostages were freed. The U.S. and U.S.S.R. made efforts to reduce threat of nuclear war by reducing stockpiles of materials for nuclear weapons. Steps were taken toward international cooperation in developing peaceful uses of atomic energy and sharing technological advances. Notables who died this year included Elizabeth Gurley Flynn, the American communist leader, Sept. 5, at 74; Herbert Clark Hoover, 31st president of the United States, Oct. 20, at 90; Douglas MacArthur, Apr. 5, at 84; and Alvin C. York, whose bravery during World War I earned him some 50 medals, including the Medal of Honor, Sept. 2, at 76.

Jan 23: The **Twenty-fourth Amendment** to the U.S. Constitution, abolishing the poll tax, was ratified by South Dakota, the 38th state to do so. The amendment was declared part of the Constitution on Feb. 4.

Mar 10: A **U.S. reconnaissance plane was shot down** by Soviet air defense forces after it accidentally crossed into East German airspace. It was the second such incident in six weeks. Following U.S. protests, the plane's three crewmen were released.

Mar 14: Jack Ruby was convicted by a Dallas, Tex., jury of the murder of Lee Harvey Oswald, the accused assassin of Pres. John F. Kennedy. Ruby was sentenced to death.

Mar 27: A major **earthquake in Alaska,** centered in Anchorage, killed 117 people and caused enormous damage. The next day Pres. Johnson declared Alaska a major disaster area.

May 18: In a ruling on **citizenship rights,** the Supreme Court declared unconstitutional a federal statute depriving naturalized citizens of U.S. citizenship if they return to the land of their birth for three years.

May 19: The State Department announced the **U.S. embassy in Moscow had been bugged.** A network of more than 40 microphones had been found embedded in the embassy's walls.

June 9: George Gessner was convicted of spying. The 28-year-old Army deserter and defector was found guilty of having passed U.S. nuclear secrets to the U.S.S.R. He was sentenced to life imprisonment, the first conviction under the 1946 Atomic Energy Act.

June 22: The provisions of the **Internal Security Act of 1950** denying U.S. passports to communists were ruled unconstitutional by the Supreme Court.

July 2: The **Civil Rights Act of 1964** was signed by Pres. Johnson in a televised ceremony a few hours after the House approved Senate amendments by a vote of 289 to 126.

July 8: The Senate Rules Committee reported that it had found **Robert G. "Bobby" Baker,** former secretary to the Democratic Senate majority, guilty of "many gross improprieties" while employed by the Senate; however, it did not accuse him of any specific violation of law.

July 15: The **Republican National Convention nominated Sen. Barry Goldwater** for the presidency. The next day Rep. William E. Miller of New York was nominated for the vice presidency.

July 18: A **race riot** broke out in Harlem, New York City, after an off-duty policeman shot a black youth who allegedly attacked him with a knife.

July 22: The section of the **Civil Rights Act of 1964** barring racial discrimination in public accommodations was upheld by a federal court in Atlanta, Ga. The court ordered a restaurant and motel in Atlanta to admit blacks.

July 24: An international **satellite communications agreement** was initialed by representatives of 18 nations in Washington, D.C. The agreement specified international management and ownership of the global communications satellite system being developed in the U.S.

Aug 2: In what came to be called the **Gulf of Tonkin incident,** three North Vietnamese PT boats attacked the U.S. destroyer *Maddox* in the Gulf of Tonkin in international waters, but were fought off by fighter planes from the U.S. carrier *Ticonderoga.* Three days later U.S. planes bombed North Vietnamese installations and naval craft.

Aug 4: Three young **civil rights workers were found murdered** and buried in an earthen dam on a farm outside Philadelphia, Miss. The three, James Chaney, 21, of Meridian, Miss., and Andrew Goodman, 20, and Michael Schwerner, 24, both of New York City, had disappeared on June 21 after being held for six hours by Neshoba County police on charges of speeding. Their burned station wagon was found June 23, prompting Pres. Johnson to order an FBI search for the three men.

Aug 7: The **Gulf of Tonkin Resolution,** a joint resolution approving U.S. action in Southeast Asia, was passed by Congress. A resolution passed on Aug. 1 had granted authority to the president to use all necessary measures to repel armed attack and to help any SEATO nation asking assistance in defense of its freedom.

Aug 26: The **Democratic National Convention nominated Pres. Johnson** for the presidency. Sen. Hubert M. Humphrey of Minnesota was nominated for the vice presidency.

Aug 30: The **Economic Opportunity Act of 1964** was signed by Pres. Johnson. The bill authorized $947,500,000 for youth programs, community action antipoverty measures in rural areas, small business loans, and job training, including a Job Corps for youth.

Aug 31: The **most populous state** as of July 1, 1964, was California, the Census Bureau reported. New York dropped to second place.

Sep 3: A bill establishing a permanent **national wilderness** system comprising 9,200,000 acres was passed by Congress and signed by Pres. Johnson.

Sep 27: The **Warren Commission report** on the assassination of John F. Kennedy was released with the finding that there was no conspiracy, either domestic or international, in the assassination, and that Lee Harvey Oswald alone was responsible for it. The report found also that Jack Ruby, convicted murderer of Oswald, had had no prior contact with Oswald.

Nov 3: **Lyndon Baines Johnson was elected president** of the United States. Sen. Hubert Horatio Humphrey was elected vice president. The electoral vote was Johnson, 486; Sen. Barry M. Goldwater, Republican, 52. The popular vote was Johnson, 43,126,506; Goldwater, 27,176,799. In congressional elections the Democrats gained one Senate seat for a 68–32 majority, and 37 House seats for a 295–140 majority.

Dec 4: The **FBI arrested 21 Mississippians** on charges of conspiracy to violate the civil rights of the three civil rights workers found murdered on Aug. 4. On Dec. 10 the charges against 19 of the men were dropped in Meridian, Miss. Charges against the other two were dropped at the federal government's request.

Dec 5: The **Medal of Honor** was presented to Capt. Roger H. C. Donlon, U.S. Army, for heroism in South Vietnam. He was the first person to receive the medal since the Korean War.

II. Architecture
Arts and Music
Popular Entertainment
Publishing
Theater

Great interest was aroused by the purchase of the G. & C. Merriam Co. by Encyclopaedia Britannica, Inc. The Warren Commission's report on the assassination of Pres. John F. Kennedy was published by the U.S. Printing Office and by five commercial publishers. Bantam Books, with the help of *The New York Times,* prepared a paperback edition that was available to the public 80 hours after the report was released. In the year that followed Kennedy's death, more than 50 books about him were published, some quick productions to catch the popular market, many moving tributes to the dead president. A new force in the theater world was The Repertory Theater of Lincoln Center, which had its first season in an off-Broadway theater while construction continued on its permanent home, the Vivian Beaumont Theater. The Robert Joffrey Ballet fell on hard times when the Harkness Foundation withdrew its subsidy and then took Joffrey's sets, scores, and ballets for the new Harkness Ballet. In November the Ford Foundation made a grant to keep the Joffrey Ballet going. Notables who died this year included Gracie Allen, the zany comedian, Aug. 27, at 58; Marc Blitzstein, composer, Jan. 22, at 58; Eddie Cantor, singer and comedian, Oct. 10, at 72; Rachel Carson, biologist and author, Apr. 14, at 56; Ben Hecht, playwright, Apr. 18, at 70; Alan Ladd, actor, Jan. 29, at 50; Peter Lorre, actor, Mar. 23, at 59; Arthur "Harpo" Marx, Sept. 28, at 70; Flannery O'Connor, the author, Aug. 3, at 39; and Cole Porter, songwriter, Oct. 15, at 71.

Among **books published** this year was the posthumous volume *A Moveable Feast* by Ernest Hemingway, a collection of sketches about Paris and its artistic colony during the years 1921–1926. Other books published this year included *The Rector of Justin* by Louis Auchincloss, a novel; *Herzog,* by Saul Bellow, the author's sixth novel; *Little Big Man* by Thomas Berger, a novel of the old West; *77 Dream Songs* by John Berryman, poems; *The Wapshot Scandal* by John Cheever, a novel; *Why We Can't Wait* by Rev. Martin Luther King, Jr., a forceful treatment of the civil rights movement; *Candy,* a sex farce by Terry Southern and Mason Hoffenberg; and *Julian* by Gore Vidal, a novel about the Roman emperor Julian the Apostate.

Feb 7: The **Beatles** arrived at Kennedy Airport in New York at the start of their first U.S. musical tour. After appearing on the *Ed Sullivan Show* on television, they gave their first concert on Feb. 12 at Carnegie Hall. Their second U.S. tour, a 33-day sweep beginning Aug. 19 in San Francisco, was a phenomenal success. Also successful were the group's album *Meet the Beatles,* which became an overnight best seller, and their movie *A Hard Day's Night,* which was released just before their second tour.

Apr 24: The **New York City Ballet,** under George Balanchine, opened its first season in its new house, the New York State Theater at Lincoln Center for the Performing Arts. A new ballet, *A Midsummer Night's Dream,* was performed in celebration of the 400th anniversary of William Shakespeare's birth. This was also the opening night of the new theater, which had been designed by Philip Johnson. In a modern interpretation of traditional theatrical elegance, the interior was red and gold and studded with giant faceted lamps that resembled jewels.

May 4: Pulitzer prizes were awarded for the following: biography, *John Keats* by Walter Jackson Bate; history, *Puritan Village: The Formation of a New England Town* by Sumner Chilton Powell; general nonfiction, *Anti-Intellectualism in American Life* by Richard Hofstadter; poetry, *At the End of the Open Road* by Louis Simpson.

Oct 1: An **equal time ruling** was issued by the FCC. It stated that any radio or television station carrying a presidential press conference in full must grant equal time to other presidential candidates.

III. Business and Industry
Education
Philosophy and Religion
Science

The first close-up pictures of the moon's surface were obtained by the U.S. At the same time, the U.S. successfully launched a spacecraft designed to fly by and photograph the surface of Mars. The first cooperative U.S.-U.S.S.R. space program—Echo 2, a communications satellite—was established. Also in this year, racial violence in both the North and South marked the nation's continuing efforts to assure equality in education for all. Harlem, Brooklyn, Rochester, northern New Jersey, Jacksonville, Fla., Chicago, and Philadelphia were scenes of violent rioting. Schools were boycotted in New York City, Cleveland, Cincinnati, Cambridge, Md., Boston, and Chicago to protest de facto segregation. Federal aid to universities was increased and extended. Notables who died this year included Leo Szilard, the atomic physicist who with Enrico Fermi produced the first nuclear chain reaction in 1942, May 30, at 66; and Norbert Wiener, the mathematician who was called the "father of automation," Mar. 18, at 69.

Jan 11: The **surgeon general's report on cigarette smoking** was released. A commission headed by U.S. Surgeon General Luther Terry found that the use of cigarettes "contributes substantially to mortality from certain specific diseases and to the overall death rate."

Jan 25: Echo 2, the first U.S.-U.S.S.R. cooperative space program, was launched from Vandenberg Air

Force Base, Calif. It sent messages around the world by reflecting radio signals from one point on Earth to another.

Jan 29: A **new weight-into-orbit record** was set by the fifth Saturn rocket test in preparation for the manned Apollo program. A 20,000-lb. payload was boosted into orbit by the rocket from Cape Kennedy, Fla.

Mar 4: James R. Hoffa, president of the International Brotherhood of Teamsters, was found guilty of tampering with a federal jury in 1962 by a Chattanooga, Tenn., federal jury. He was sentenced to eight years in prison and fined $10,000.

Apr 8: An unmanned **Gemini spacecraft was successfully launched** into orbit from Cape Kennedy, Fla.

May 25: The **closing of schools to avoid desegregation** was ruled unconstitutional by the Supreme Court. The Court ruled that the schools of Prince Edward County, Va., which had been closed in 1959, must be reopened and desegregated.

June 14: An **agreement to end racial discrimination** in the steel industry was announced by the United Steelworkers of American and 11 steel companies.

June 24: Health warnings on cigarette packages would be required starting in 1965, the Federal Trade Commission announced.

July 26: James R. Hoffa, president of the International Brotherhood of Teamsters, was convicted of fraud and conspiracy in the handling of his union's pension fund by a federal jury in Chicago. He was sentenced to five years in prison and fined $10,000.

July 31: The U.S. lunar probe **Ranger 7** crashed into the moon after sending back to Earth 4316 photographs of the lunar surface taken within a 1300-mile range.

Aug 14: Elementary school desegregation in Mississippi began without incident at previously white elementary schools in Biloxi, Miss. This marked the first desegregation of schools below the college level in that state.

Aug 19: Syncom 3, a communications satellite, was successfully launched from Cape Kennedy, Fla. In October it transmitted live broadcasts of the 1964 Olympic Games from Tokyo to California.

Aug 28: Nimbus 1, an advanced meteorological satellite, was launched from Vandenberg Air Force Base, Calif. Although it failed to achieve its intended circular orbit, it sent back exceptionally clear close-up pictures of Earth's nighttime cloud cover.

Oct 14: The **Nobel Peace Prize** was awarded to the Rev. Martin Luther King., Jr., civil rights leader of Atlanta, Ga. He donated the award, valued at $54,600, to the civil rights movement.

Oct 15: The **Nobel Prize for Physiology or Medicine** was awarded jointly to Dr. Conrad E. Block of Harvard University and Feodor Lynen, a German professor, for their work on the relationship between heart disease and cholesterol.

Oct 29: The **Nobel Prize in Physics** was awarded jointly to Charles H. Townes of the Massachusetts Institute of Technology and to Nikolai Basov and Aleksandr Prokhorov of the U.S.S.R. for their work in quantum electronics.

Nov 21: The **Verrazano-Narrows Bridge** between Brooklyn and Staten Island, N.Y., was formally opened. At 6690 feet, it was the world's longest suspension bridge.

Nov 28: Mariner 4 was launched from Cape Kennedy, Fla., to transmit close-up TV pictures of Mars on its projected flyby within 8600 miles of that planet in July 1965.

IV. Fashion
Folkways
Holidays
Social Issues and Crime
Sports

At the New York World's Fair, the General Motors Futurama proved to be the most popular attraction. Ranking just behind GM in attendance was the Vatican Pavilion, its chief attraction being Michelangelo's *Pietà*. While this was the largest, most lavish, and in many ways the best fair of all time, attendance lagged behind fair president Robert Moses' predictions, and many exhibitors began to feel an economic pinch. Worst hit were the extravagant shows in the Lake Amusement Area that had been so popular at the 1939–1940 fair. Most of these shows closed before the end of the fair's first season. In baseball the St. Louis Cardinals beat the New York Yankees in the World Series; the following day Cardinal manager Johnny Keane resigned. Yankee manager Yogi Berra was moved to another position in the club, then quit to become player-coach of the New York Mets. Meanwhile, Keane was named manager of the Yankees. In boxing Cassius Clay gained the heavyweight title from Sonny Liston and enthralled many with his declarations of his own beauty, ability, and greatness. This year he also declared that he was a Black Muslim and changed his name to Muhammad Ali. In golf the top money winners were Jack Nicklaus, $113,284, and, for the fourth year in a row, Mickey Wright, $29,800.

Popular **rock 'n' roll dances** of the younger set had

animal names: the Dog, the Monkey, the Chicken; but the favorites were the Watusi and the Frug. In these dances the partners gyrated, squirmed, jerked, and waved their arms—at a distance from one another, of course. The swinging set crowded into discothèques, where the music was supplied by records. The "in" places were Shepheard's and Trude Heller's in New York City and Whiskey à Go-Go in Los Angeles. Dancers were often abetted by scantily clad go-go girls, who performed in relays on raised platforms or in cages.

Jan 5: The 1963 **AFL championship** was won by the San Diego Chargers, who defeated the Boston Patriots 51 to 10.

Jan 29-Feb 9: At the **Winter Olympics** in Innsbruck, Austria, the U.S. finished eighth in the unofficial team standings, taking one gold, two silver, and three bronze medals.

Feb 25: The **world heavyweight boxing championship** was won by Muhammad Ali, in a bout at Miami Beach, when Sonny Liston could not answer the bell for the seventh round because of an injury to his left arm. Ali announced he would give Liston a rematch, but the World Boxing Association (WBA), claiming it had a rule forbidding return bouts, declared the heavyweight title vacant and made plans for an elimination tournament. When their contender Cleveland Williams was shot by Texas highway police, the WBA postponed its plans until 1965. The Ali-Liston bout, scheduled for Nov. 16 in Boston, was called off 70 hours before the bell, after Ali went to the hospital for a hernia operation.

Mar 21: The **NCAA basketball championship** was won by UCLA, which defeated Duke University 98 to 83. The victory climaxed a perfect season for UCLA, which won all 30 of its games, the first major team to have an undefeated season since 1957.

Apr 18-26: The **NBA basketball championship** was won, for the sixth time in a row, by the Boston Celtics, who defeated the San Francisco Warriors four games to one.

Apr 22: Opening-day ceremonies of the **New York World's Fair** of 1964–1965 were marred by threats of a massive traffic tie-up by members of the Congress of Racial Equality (CORE), who planned to have their cars run out of gas on all major arteries leading to the fair. The so-called stall-in, intended to dramatize CORE's demand for city action against racial discrimination, did not materialize, but it was probably a major factor along with bad weather in cutting attendance from an expected 250,000 to 92,646. Pres. Lyndon B. Johnson's dedication speech was interrupted by demonstrators' chants. When the fair closed its first season on Oct. 18, it was apparent that it was in dire financial straits. Low attendance was blamed on fear of racial violence, high prices, and characterization of the fair as a cultural desert.

May 31: In the **longest baseball game** to date, the San Francisco Giants beat the New York Mets 8–6 after 7 hrs., 23 min. of the second game of a double header. The end came in the 23rd inning, matching the fourth longest game in innings played.

June 20: The **U.S. Open golf tournament** was won by Ken Venturi, who beat Tommy Jacobs by two strokes.

June 21: A **perfect baseball game,** the first in a regular season since 1922, was pitched by Jim Bunning of the Philadelphia Phillies, who led his team to a 6–0 victory over the New York Mets at Shea Stadium in New York City.

July 19: The **PGA golf tournament** was won by Bobby Nichols, who beat both Arnold Palmer and Jack Nicklaus by three strokes.

Sep 12: In the **New Hampshire Sweepstakes,** the first legal sweepstakes in U.S. horse racing history, six persons won the first prize of $100,000 at Rockingham Park in Salem, N.H.

Sep 15-21: The **America's Cup,** yachting's oldest trophy, was successfully defended by the U.S racer *Constellation,* which easily outdistanced the British challenger *Sovereign* in four races off Newport, R.I.

Sep 25-28: For the first time in the history of **Davis Cup** tennis competition, the international challenge round was played on clay courts. The play took place in Cleveland, Ohio, where Roy Emerson and Fred Stolle led a strong Australian team to beat the U.S. defenders three matches to two.

Oct 7-15: The 61st annual **World Series** was won by the St. Louis Cardinals (NL), defeating the New York Yankees (AL) four games to three. Cardinal pitcher Bob Gibson struck out 31 batters in three games, a Series record. Mickey Mantle of the Yankees hit his 16th Series homer, breaking the record held by Babe Ruth.

Oct 10-24: At the **Summer Olympics** in Tokyo, Japan, the U.S. won the unofficial team championship with 36 gold medals.

Dec 26: The **AFL championship** was won by the Buffalo Bills, who defeated the San Diego Chargers 20 to 7.

Dec 27: The **NFL championship** was won by the Cleveland Browns, who swept the Baltimore Colts 27 to 0.

1965

I. Civil Rights
Exploration and Settlement
Government
Statistics
Wars

U.S. participation in the war in Vietnam was protested by many in demonstrations across the nation. Before year's end, U.S. losses in Vietnam since Jan. 1961 exceeded 1300 dead and 6100 wounded. The use of helicopters for medical evacuation helped keep the fatality rate below 2% of those wounded. Pres. Lyndon B. Johnson's administration obtained passage of most of its programs. Total appropriations were a record high for peacetime: $119,300,000,000, of which $46,900,000,000 went for defense. At the same time, Pres. Johnson's request for foreign aid was the smallest in the history of the program—$3,380,000,000, of which $3,200,000,000 was granted. The Medicare program was passed, as were antipoverty and voting rights bills and increased aid to education. Although turned down on his requests for repeal of Section 14-b of the Taft-Hartley Act, state right-to-work laws, and self-government for the District of Columbia, Pres. Johnson was given a $1,100,000,000 appropriation for development in Appalachia. In addition, excise taxes were cut, a new immigration law was passed to replace the 41-year-old national-origins quota system, and a new Cabinet-level Department of Housing and Urban Development was established. The nation's rate of population growth, 1.21%, was the slowest since 1945. Notables who died this year included Frances Perkins, secretary of labor from 1933 to 1945, May 14, at 83; Adlai E. Stevenson, unsuccessful Democratic candidate for the presidency in 1952 and 1956, July 14, at 65; and Henry A. Wallace, vice president of the United States from 1941 to 1945, Nov. 18 at 77.

Jan 28: Pres. Johnson asked Congress to propose **constitutional amendments** that would cover presidential disability; provide for filling a vice presidential vacancy; and reform the electoral college system so that voters could not be overridden by electors.

Feb 16: A plot to dynamite the Statue of Liberty, the Liberty Bell, and the Washington Monument was foiled. Four persons were arrested, including the self-styled leader of the Black Liberation Front and a woman member of a Quebec separatist party.

Feb 21: Malcolm X was assassinated by rival Black Muslims while addressing a gathering at the Audubon Ballroom in Washington Heights, New York City. Born Malcolm Little, the 39-year-old leader founded the extremist Black Nationalist movement after breaking with the Black Muslims in 1964. In recent months he had been moving toward a less violently anti-white stance. Two days after his death, Black Muslim headquarters in San Francisco and New York City were burned.

Mar 8: Ruling on **conscientious objectors,** the Supreme Court held unanimously that a person holding a sincere belief in a Supreme Being, even though differing from the beliefs held by accepted religions, may be exempted from military combat training and service.

Mar 8-9: The **first U.S. combat forces in Vietnam,** more than 3500 Marines, landed in South Vietnam to guard the U.S. Air Force base at Danang. They joined 23,500 other Americans serving as advisers in South Vietnam.

Mar 11: The Rev. **James Reeb died** from a beating he received in Selma, Ala., on Mar. 9. A Unitarian minister from Boston, Reeb had been working in a civil rights drive. Three whites were subsequently indicted for the murder, but they were found not guilty on Dec. 10.

Mar 15: Sweeping voting rights legislation was requested by Pres. Johnson in a nationally televised address to a joint session of Congress. Later Johnson submitted a voting rights bill to Congress. One provision of the bill would empower the attorney general to assign federal registration examiners in the six states requiring literacy or other voter-qualification tests.

Mar 21: A five-day **civil rights march from Selma to Montgomery,** Ala., was begun by some 3200 marchers led by Dr. Martin Luther King, Jr. At the end of the march, some 25,000 demonstrators gathered in front of the state capitol in Montgomery.

Mar 25: Viola Gregg Liuzzo, a civil rights worker from Detroit, Mich., was shot and killed in Selma, Ala. On Dec. 3 Collie LeRoy Wilkins and two other Ku Klux Klansmen were convicted of conspiracy charges in the murder. They were sentenced to ten years' imprisonment.

June 7: An 1879 **Connecticut law banning the use of contraceptives** by anyone, including married couples, was ruled unconstitutional by the U.S. Supreme Court.

June 7: The 1962 conviction of **Billie Sol Estes** on swindling charges was overturned by the Supreme Court on the grounds that televising criminal trials was a violation of the due process clause of the Fourteenth Amendment, and that the presence of TV cameras might affect jurors, witnesses, and judges.

June 17: In the **first mass bombing raid** in the Vietnam War, Guam-based B-52s bombed a Vietcong concentration 30 miles north of Saigon. It was the first combat use of the heavy jet bombers since they were placed in operation in 1952.

June 30: In its final **report on the investigation of Robert G. "Bobby" Baker,** former secretary to the Senate Democratic majority, the Senate Rules Committee recommended that the Senate consider indicting Baker for violation of conflict-of-interest laws. It also recommended new Senate rules for control of outside business activities of Senate employees. Republican members of the committee termed the majority report a whitewash and filed a minority report criticizing the conduct of the investigation.

July 28: Pres. Johnson announced that **U.S. troop levels in South Vietnam** would be increased from 75,000 to 125,000, and the draft would be doubled from 17,000 to 35,000 a month.

Aug 11-16: Riots in Watts, a black section of Los Angeles, Calif., left 35 dead and hundreds injured. The riots, which caused about $200,000,000 in damage, were sparked when a white policeman stopped a black driver suspected of being drunk.

Aug 16: Total **U.S. casualties in Vietnam** since Jan. 1, 1961, were 561 killed, 3024 wounded, 44 missing in action, and 269 dead of noncombat causes.

Sep 24: Agreement in principle on a new **Panama Canal treaty,** to supersede the 1903 pact giving the U.S. sole control over the Panama Canal, was announced by Pres. Johnson. The new treaty would provide for joint administration of the canal.

Oct 4: Pope Paul VI visited New York City to address the UN General Assembly on world peace. During the visit he celebrated a papal mass in Yankee Stadium and attended the New York World's Fair.

Oct 15-16: Nationwide antiwar demonstrations were held, followed by a series of rallies and petitions supporting U.S. policy. Several persons burned their draft cards publicly; one person was arrested three days later under a law effective Aug. 31 that made destruction of a draft card a crime.

Nov 9-10: A massive **Northeast power blackout** struck an 80,000-square-mile area comprising New York, most of New England, parts of New Jersey, Pennsylvania, and Ontario and Quebec, Canada. The blackout, lasting as long as 13 hours in some areas, was initiated by the malfunction of an automatic relay device at a generating plant near Niagara Falls.

Nov 20: U.S. casualties in Vietnam after a week-long battle in the Iadrang Valley were placed at 240 dead, 470 wounded, and six missing, exceeding the Korean War weekly average of 209 killed.

Nov 27: An **anti-Vietnam War demonstration in Washington, D.C.,** was conducted by some 15,000 to 25,000 protesters from 140 groups.

Dec 4: Two airliners collided in midair over Danbury, Conn. Four persons of the 112 passengers aboard the planes were killed.

II. Architecture
Arts and Music
Popular Entertainment
Publishing
Theater

The most sensational theatrical offering of the year was Peter Weiss's *The Persecution and Assassination of Marat as Performed by the Inmates of the Asylum of Charenton Under the Direction of the Marquis de Sade,* a production of the Royal Shakespeare Company directed by Peter Brook, which opened Dec. 27. The playwright's cynical view of the French Revolution was conveyed by actors manifesting a wide variety of psychoses. The Repertory Theater of Lincoln Center occupied its new home, the Vivian Beaumont Theater. The most significant development in art this year was the appearance of op (optical) art, abstract painting that commanded viewers' attention by the dazzling interaction of colors and/or optical illusion. The most important op art show, "The Responsive Eye," opened at the Museum of Modern Art in New York City; it was seen subsequently in St. Louis, Seattle, Pasadena, and Baltimore. Notables who died this year included Thornton W. Burgess, author of the Peter Rabbit stories, June 5, at 91; Nat "King" Cole, born Nathaniel Adams Coles, singer, Feb. 15, at 45; T.S. Eliot, the poet, Jan. 4, at 76; Lorraine Hansberry, playwright, Jan. 12, at 34; Judy Holliday, actress, June 7, at 42; Shirley Jackson, writer, Aug. 8, at 45; Stan Laurel, born Arthur Stanley Jefferson, comedian, Feb. 23, at 74; David O. Selznick, motion picture producer, June 22, at 63; and Edgard Varèse, the French-born composer regarded as the father of electronic music, Nov. 6, at 90.

Among **books published** this year were two biographies of John F. Kennedy that became the nonfiction standouts of 1965. *Kennedy* by Theodore Sorensen was an intimate account of Kennedy's career from 1953. *A Thousand Days* by Arthur M. Schlesinger, Jr., dealt with Kennedy's tenure as president. Other books published this year included *Going to Meet the Man* by James Baldwin, short stories; *Manchild in the Promised Land* by Claude Brown; *Never Call Retreat* by Bruce Catton, the third volume in the Civil War trilogy *Centennial History of the Civil War; Country Without Maps* by Jean Garrigue, a collection of poems; *Up the Down Staircase* by Bel Kaufman; *The Autobiography of Malcolm X; The Oxford History of the American People* by Samuel Eliot Morison; and *Everything That Rises Must Converge* by Flannery O'Connor, stories.

Jan 10: The **Bollingen Prize** for poetry was awarded to Horace Gregory for his 1964 volume *Collected Poems.* Beginning this year the cash award was increased to $5000 and the prize was to be awarded every other year.

May 3: Pulitzer prizes were awarded for the following: fiction, *The Keepers of the House* by Shirley Ann Grau; biography, *Henry Adams* by Ernest Samuels; history, *The Greenback Era* by Irwin Unger; poetry, *77 Dream Songs* by John Berryman; drama, *The Subject Was Roses* by Frank D. Gilroy.

June 14: A **Festival of the Arts and Humanities** at the White House was attended by some 400 artists, who were welcomed by Pres. Johnson. The 13-hour event included exhibitions of paintings, sculpture, and photography; prose and poetry readings; music recitals; and a ballet. Robert Lowell, the poet, refused an invitation because of his distrust of U.S. foreign policy.

Sep 30: The Federal Aid to the Arts Act, establishing the **National Foundation on the Arts and the Humanities,** was signed by Pres. Johnson. The act appropriated $63,000,000 to finance the first three years of the program.

Oct 28: Eero Saarinen's steel **Gateway Arch** in St. Louis, Mo., the year's most awesome architectural project, was topped out. The 630-ft. parabolic arch commemorated the Louisiana Purchase and the city's role in westward expansion. It was part of the 40-block Jefferson National Expansion Memorial along the city's riverfront. The Spanish Pavilion from the New York World's Fair was to be reconstructed near the arch.

III. Business and Industry
Education
Philosophy and Religion
Science

The first U.S. walk in space and the successful rendezvous of two Gemini capsules 185 miles above Earth assisted NASA in its preparations for a manned trip to the moon. Photographs of the surface of Mars showed no trace of the famous canals and provided evidence that the planet had little atmosphere. Commercial communication using an Earth satellite was realized with the aid of Early Bird. The most spectacular comet since Comet Halley in 1910 was spotted by two Japanese amateur astronomers; it was named Comet Ikeya-Seki. The U.S. gross national product rose from $628,000,000,000 to $672,000,000,000, exceeding by $14,000,000,000 the predictions of the president's economic advisers. In December it was announced that the unemployment rate had fallen to 4.2%, an eight-year low. Notables who died this year included the religious leader Father Divine, real name believed to be George Baker, Sept. 10, at about 83; H. V. Kaltenborn, radio commentator, June 14, at 86; Edward R. Murrow, radio and television journalist, Apr. 27, at 57; and Paul Tillich, theologian, Oct. 22, at 79.

Feb 3: In a **cheating scandal** at the U.S. Air Force Academy, 105 cadets resigned for cheating on examinations. Four more resigned later, when the cadet wing honor board found they had had knowledge of the cheating but had not reported it.

Feb 16: Pegasus 1, a micrometeoroid detection station with 96-foot wings as sensors, was put into orbit.

Feb 17: Ranger 8, a moon probe, was successfully launched. It sent back 7137 photos of the moon's surface before crashing into the Sea of Tranquillity on Feb. 20.

Mar 21: Ranger 9 was launched. It transmitted 5814 photos of the moon's surface before crashing into Alphonsus crater on Mar. 24. It was the last moon probe of the Ranger series.

Mar 23: Gemini 3, the first manned Gemini flight, was successfully launched from Cape Kennedy, Fla. The craft, nicknamed "Molly Brown," was put through delicate maneuvers by its pilots, Maj. Virgil Grissom and Lt. Commander John Young, during its three-orbit flight. It was retrieved by the carrier *Intrepid* in the Atlantic Ocean.

Apr 6: Early Bird, the world's first commercial communications satellite, was launched and placed in orbit 22,300 miles above Earth. Owned by ComSat, Early Bird transmitted phone calls, TV, Teletype, and other communications.

Apr 16: The **Saturn S-1C rocket,** to be the first stage for the Apollo lunar flight and the largest U.S. booster ever produced, was successfully fired at Cape Kennedy, Fla.

May 24: A federal law authorizing **postal interception of communist propaganda** was declared unconstitutional by the Supreme Court. The law, empowering the postmaster general to hold foreign mail deemed to be communist propaganda and to make the addressee submit a written request for it, was ruled to violate the First Amendment.

June 3: Gemini 4, manned by Maj. James McDivitt and Maj. Edward White, was successfully launched from Cape Kennedy, Fla. During the four-day, 62-orbit mission White completed the first U.S. space walk; it lasted some 20 minutes while White, 135 miles above North America, was attached to the craft by a lifeline.

June 18: A **Titan 3C rocket** was launched into orbit with a total thrust of 2,400,000 lbs., the greatest thrust of any rocket ever to leave Earth's surface. The launching was the first to use large solid fuel rockets.

July 15: Mariner 4 began transmission of 21 pictures of the surface of Mars taken at a range of between 7000 and 10,500 miles. Continually transmitting data to Earth since its launch on Nov. 28, 1964, the craft flew within 5700 miles of Mars.

Aug 21: Gemini 5, piloted by Lt. Col. Gordon Cooper and Lt. Commander Charles Conrad, was launched on an eight-day, 120-orbit mission. The flight took as long as a round trip to the moon. There was some difficulty with a new fuel cell system.

Oct 12: The **Sealab 2** U.S. Navy research program, a series of 15-day stays 205 feet below the surface of the Pacific Ocean, was completed. The purpose was to study the effects on humans of living underwater and to conduct equipment tests.

Oct 21: The **Nobel Prize in Physics** was awarded jointly to Richard P. Feynman of the California Institute of Technology, Julian S. Schwinger of Harvard University, and Shinichero Tomonaga of Tokyo Education University in Japan for their work in quantum electrodynamics.

Oct 21: The **Nobel Prize in Chemistry** was awarded to Robert Burns Woodward of Harvard University for his work in synthesizing complex organic compounds.

Dec 4: Gemini 7, piloted by Lt. Col. Frank Borman and Commander James A. Lovell, Jr., was launched from Cape Kennedy on a 14-day, 206-orbit mission and rendezvous in space with Gemini 6.

Dec 15: Gemini 6, piloted by Capt. Walter Schirra and Maj. Thomas Stafford, was launched. It made the first successful space rendezvous, with Gemini 7, some 185 miles above Earth. During its 14-orbit flight, it came within six feet of Gemini 7 and traveled in close formation with the sister ship.

IV. Fashion
Folkways
Holidays
Social Issues and Crime
Sports

In clothing and hairstyles, the trend was toward sexual ambiguity. Young men sprouted shoulder-length hair, and girls wore bangs and shingles, a style designed by London hairdresser Vidal Sassoon. The Mod look, also emanating from London, put the young of both sexes into tight, bell-bottom trousers. For dress-up, women wore skirts two inches above the knee and blouses ruffled at the throat and wrist. The Courrèges look was the high-fashion sensation. It featured a solid color A-line dress trimmed with contrasting bands, high white boots, and often a helmet-type hat. Art-inspired fashions included the Mondrian dresses of Yves St. Laurent and op art fabrics favored by Capucci. In sports Muhammad Ali defied World Boxing Association (WBA) rules against rematches and met Sonny Liston in a short and sweet, successful title defense. Nonetheless, the WBA stripped Ali of his title and declared the championship vacant. In golf the top money winners were Jack Nicklaus, $142,752, and Kathy Whitworth, $32,937. Deaths of this year included John Leonard "Pepper" Martin, of the St. Louis Cardinals, Mar. 5, at 61; Branch W. Rickey, baseball executive, Dec. 9, at 84; Helena Rubinstein, founder of a cosmetics empire, Apr. 1, at about 89; and Amos Alonzo Stagg, college football coach for more than 60 years, 41 of them at the University of Chicago, Mar. 17, at 102.

Mar 20: The **NCAA basketball championship** was won by UCLA, which defeated Michigan 91 to 80.

Apr 18-25: The **NBA basketball championship** was won for the seventh straight year by the Boston Celtics, who defeated the Los Angeles Lakers four games to one.

May 25: The **world heavyweight boxing championship** was successfully defended by Muhammad Ali, who knocked out Sonny Liston about a minute into the first round of a rematch. Few fans saw the punch that floored Liston. Despite Ali's win, the World Boxing Association maintained that its heavyweight title belonged to Ernie Terrell, who had outpointed Eddie Machen on Mar. 5. Ali retained the National Boxing Association title.

June 21: The **U.S. Open golf tournament** was won by Gary Player of South Africa. He became the third man to win golf's four top pro titles; only Gene Sarazen and Ben Hogan had previously taken the U.S. and British Opens, the Masters, and the PGA.

Aug 15: The **PGA golf tournament** was won by Dave Marr.

Sep 9: A **perfect baseball game** was pitched by Sandy Koufax of the Los Angeles Dodgers (NL) against the Chicago Cubs. Koufax fanned 14 batters in the 1 to 0 victory. It was the fourth no-hit game of his career, a major league record, and only the eighth perfect game in baseball history.

Oct 6-14: The 62nd annual **World Series** was won by the Los Angeles Dodgers (NL), defeating the Minnesota Twins (AL) four games to three. In the seventh game, on Oct. 14, Sandy Koufax pitched his second World Series shutout, blanking the Twins 2 to 0.

Oct 17: The **New York World's Fair closed** after two years, drawing its largest crowd, 446,953, on the last day. The final days of the fair were marred by vandalism and looting by souvenir hunters. In its two-year run, the fair had the largest total attendance of any international exposition in history, 51,607,037, but not the predicted 70,000,000. Declared an "artistic, cultural, and educational success" by Robert Moses, president of the fair corporation, it was a financial disappointment; backers faced a return of 39 cents on the dollar of the $30,000,000 they had invested.

Nov 17: **William D. Eckert** was elected baseball commissioner. He succeeded Ford Frick, who retired after having held the post since 1952.

Nov 22: **Muhammad Ali** stopped ex-champ Floyd Patterson in the 12th round of what had been billed as a fight for the heavyweight championship. Although the bout had been set up by Jim Deskin, new head of the World Boxing Association, that organization afterward classified Ali as merely the top contender for the crown the WBA had given to Ernie Terrell on Mar. 5.

Dec 26: The **AFL football championship** was won by the Buffalo Bills, who defeated the San Diego Chargers 23 to 0.

1966

I. Civil Rights
Exploration and Settlement
Government
Statistics
Wars

Steadily escalating participation in the Vietnamese war resulted in 5008 U.S. troop deaths and 30,093 wounded in 1966, bringing total casualties since Jan. 1, 1961, to 6664 killed and 37,738 wounded. By the end of the year, the U.S. had almost 400,000 troops in Southeast Asia. Among the antiwar demonstrations were the International Days of Protest (Mar. 25–27), during which parades and rallies were held in seven U.S. and seven foreign cities. The proposed budget for fiscal 1967 set expenditures at $112,800,000,000, with a predicted deficit of $1,800,000,000, the smallest in seven years. Congress turned down the administration's proposed civil rights bill, largely because

of its open housing provisions, but it did pass measures giving the government a major role in determining automobile and highway safety standards, in attacking urban decay, and in controlling air and water pollution. Notables who died this year included Christian A. Herter, secretary of state under Pres. Eisenhower from 1959 to 1961, Dec. 30, at 71; and Chester W. Nimitz, commander in chief of the U.S. Pacific fleet during World War II, Feb. 20, at 80.

Jan 17: **Robert C. Weaver** was unanimously confirmed as secretary of the newly created Department of Housing and Urban Development. He was the first black to hold a Cabinet position.

Jan 17: A **military aircraft collision** involving a U.S. B-52 bomber and a KC-135 jet tanker over Spain's Mediterranean coast killed seven of the 11 men aboard the planes. The B-52 was refueling. Four hydrogen bombs fell from the B-52, three on land. The fourth bomb was recovered from the Mediterranean Sea on Apr. 7.

Jan 29-31: The worst **blizzard** in 70 years struck an area stretching from North Carolina to New England, killing 165 people.

Jan 31: Pres. Johnson announced resumption of **bombing raids on North Vietnam.** They had been suspended on Dec. 24. The bombing had been halted in hope of furthering negotiations, but no move toward peace had been made by North Vietnam.

Feb 21: The first **air strike against North Vietnam** since the Jan. 31 resumption of bombing was made against a training center at the old French military base at Dien Bien Phu.

Feb 22: **Operation White Wing,** a month-long search and destroy mission by more than 20,000 U.S., South Vietnamese, and South Korean troops in Quang Ngai Province in South Vietnam, ended after enemy resistance collapsed. Communist troop deaths were reported at 1130.

Mar 2: **U.S. troop strength in Vietnam** was reported by Sec. of Defense Robert S. McNamara to have reached 215,000. Another 20,000 U.S. troops were said to be on the way.

Mar 10: A **Green Beret camp was overrun** by about 2000 North Vietnamese troops after a 72-hour siege. About 200 U.S. and South Vietnamese troops were killed or captured at the Special Forces base in the Ashau Valley.

Mar 25: **Poll taxes** were declared unconstitutional by the Supreme Court on grounds that they represented an economic barrier to voting.

Apr 12: **B-52 strategic bombers** were used for the first time on targets in North Vietnam.

Apr 23: **North Vietnamese aircraft** for the first time attacked U.S. aircraft flying over North Vietnam.

May 1: The **first intentional shelling of Cambodian targets** occurred when U.S. artillery fired on forces attacking U.S. troops operating along the Caibac R.

May 15: In an **antiwar demonstration in Washington, D.C.,** more than 10,000 persons picketed the White House. At a rally at the Washington Monument, 63,000 voters' pledges to vote only for antiwar candidates were displayed.

May 30: In the heaviest **air raids on North Vietnam** to date, more than 300 U.S. planes bombed targets. On May 31 an important North Vietnamese arsenal was virtually destroyed by U.S. bombers.

June 3-13: A **major battle was fought in Kontum province,** in the Central Highlands of South Vietnam. No figures on U.S. casualties were announced.

June 6: **James Meredith was shot** and wounded while on a lone march from Memphis, Tenn., to Jackson, Miss., to encourage black voter registration. On June 26 groups from across the country joined with Meredith to complete the march, which was highlighted by a debate between Martin Luther King, Jr., the leading advocate of nonviolence, and Stokely Carmichael and Floyd McKissick, militant advocates of political confrontation.

June 11: **U.S. troop strength in Vietnam** would be increased by 18,000 within 45 days, Sec. of Defense McNamara reported, bringing total troop strength to 285,000. U.S. dead since Jan. 1 were placed at 2100.

June 13: In the landmark case of *Miranda v. Arizona,* the U.S. Supreme Court ruled that the provision in the Fifth Amendment to the Constitution against self-incrimination applied to police interrogation of a criminal suspect. Among other guidelines, the Court specified that suspects must be told they have the right to have a lawyer present while being questioned and that, if suspects choose to make a confession without a lawyer and are subsequently put on trial, the prosecution must prove that the defendants understood their rights when they confessed.

June 29: **Hanoi and Haiphong were bombed** for the first time in the Vietnam War. Oil storage and loading installations, highways, railroads, bridges, and ships were attacked. Approximately two-thirds of North Vietnam's oil supply was destroyed within a week.

July 30: The **demilitarized zone (DMZ)** separating North and South Vietnam was bombed by U.S. planes for the first time.

Aug 1: In what was called the **Texas tower massacre,** Charles J. Whitman, 25, barricaded himself in a tower at the University of Texas at Austin, Tex., and shot and killed 13 and wounded 31 before police killed him. Earlier he had killed his wife and mother.

Aug 6: **Demonstrations against the Vietnam War** were held across the country on the anniversary of the atomic bombing of Hiroshima in 1945. In Washington, D.C., pickets demonstrated in front of the White House and the church where Pres. Johnson's daughter Luci was being married. In New York City 5000 marched to Times Square. On Aug. 9, the anniversary of the atomic bombing of Nagasaki, 200 demonstrators attempted a sit-in at the New York office of the Dow Chemical Company, a manufacturer of napalm.

Sep 18-24: **U.S. weekly casualties** in the Vietnam War hit a record 970: 142 killed, 825 wounded, 3 missing. During the same period South Vietnamese losses were 98 killed, 280 wounded, 71 missing.

Sep 23: **Aerial defoliation** of areas immediately south of the Demilitarized Zone (DMZ) between North and South Vietnam had begun, the U.S. military command announced, to deprive infiltrating North Vietnamese of protective cover.

Oct 5: The **conviction of Jack Ruby** for the 1963 murder of Lee Harvey Oswald, alleged assassin of Pres. John F. Kennedy, was reversed by the Texas Court of Appeals on the grounds of improperly submitted evidence.

Oct 13: The heaviest **air strike on North Vietnam** to date was made by 173 U.S. bombers. The next day 175 bombers renewed the raid. On Oct. 15 it was announced that 403 U.S. planes and three helicopters had been lost over North Vietnam since Feb. 7, 1965.

Oct 26: A **fire at sea** on the U.S. carrier *Oriskany,* in the Gulf of Tonkin, killed 43 men and injured 16.

Nov 8: In **congressional elections** the Republicans gained three Senate seats and 47 House seats, but the Democrats still held a 64–36 Senate majority and a 248–187 House majority. One of the new Republican senators was Edward W. Brooke of Massachusetts, the first black elected to the Senate since Reconstruction.

II. Architecture
Arts and Music
Popular Entertainment
Publishing
Theater

American theater this year offered a number of literate and entertaining productions. The strongest of these appeared to be the musicals, among them *Mame* and *Cabaret.* One of the year's highlights was the Broadway revival of Hal Holbrook's one-man show *Mark Twain Tonight!.* The New York City Opera moved into its new home in the Lincoln Center for the Performing Arts. The Metropolitan Opera announced in December that its two-year-old touring company, the Metropolitan Opera National Company, would be disbanded in 1967 for financial reasons. Among the year's top motion pictures were *Who's Afraid of Virginia Woolf?; Dr. Zhivago; Torn Curtain,* Alfred Hitchcock's 50th film; and *Thunderball,* the fourth of the James Bond films and a box office smash. By the time the fall television season began, nearly all network shows were being broadcast in color. Nearly half the 11,000,000 TV sets sold this year were color sets. In architecture, the use of steel and glass in conservatively designed structures continued to be the rule. The leader in this trend was Ludwig Mies van der Rohe. Notables who died in 1966 included Russel Crouse, playwright, Apr. 3, at 73; Walt Disney, pioneer in motion picture animation, Dec. 15, at 65; Hans Hofmann, abstract expressionist, Feb. 17, at 85; Buster Keaton, comedian, Feb. 1, at 69; Kathleen Norris, novelist, Jan. 18, at 85; Maxfield Parrish, painter, Mar. 30, at 95; Billy Rose, theatrical producer, Feb. 10, at 66; Mari Sandoz, novelist, Mar. 10, at about 65; Delmore Schwartz, poet, July 11, at 52; Deems Taylor, composer and music critic, July 3, at 80; Sophie Tucker, the Last of the Red Hot Mamas, Jan. 13, at about 79; and Ed Wynn, comedian and actor, June 19, at 79.

Among **books published** this year was *In Cold Blood* by Truman Capote. Described as nonfiction, the book employed fictional techniques to recreate the 1959 murder of a farm family in Holcomb, Kans. The book became a best seller. Other books published this year included *The Embezzler* by Louis Auchincloss, a novel; *Tai-Pan* by James Clavell, a novel about Japan in the mid-nineteenth century; *Papa Hemingway* by A.E. Hotchner, a biography; *Rush to Judgment* by Mark Lane, one of a spate of books criticizing the investigation of the Kennedy assassination; *The Fixer* by Bernard Malamud, a novel; *Valley of the Dolls* by Jacqueline Susann, a novel that critics hated but readers turned into a runaway best seller; and *Ariel* by Sylvia Plath, a collection of poems that further increased the posthumous recognition of the poet, a suicide in 1963.

Apr 16: At the end of the last performance of the **Metropolitan Opera** in its venerable house at Broadway and 39th St. in New York City, performers and audience joined hands and sang "Auld Lang Syne." The fabulous gold curtain later was cut into small patches and packaged with souvenir recordings of the occasion. A committee was formed to preserve the old house but failed to prevent its demolition.

May 2: Pulitzer prizes were awarded for the following: fiction, *The Collected Stories of Katherine Anne Porter;* biography, *A Thousand Days* by Arthur M. Schlesinger, Jr.; history, *The Life of the Mind in America* by Perry Miller; general nonfiction, *Wandering Through Winter* by Edwin Way Teale; poetry, *Selected Poems* by Richard Eberhart.

III. Business and Industry
Education
Philosophy and Religion
Science

The movement for school integration showed signs of division, as did the entire civil rights movement. Pacifist followers of the Southern Christian Leadership Conference of Martin Luther King, Jr., differed with militants such as Stokely Carmichael of SNCC and Floyd McKissick of CORE. Carmichael and others used the term *black power* which, depending on the context of its use, meant anything from blacks taking control of their own political and economic destinies to the destruction of western capitalism. A corollary catch phrase, *white backlash,* came into use to describe the vocal and sometimes violent reaction to this emerging militancy and to continuing efforts by local and federal governments to end discrimination in education, housing, and jobs. Proposals to end de facto school segregation by redrawing district lines and busing children to and from black neighborhoods provoked bitter controversy At the same time, the Gemini space program came to a successful conclusion, and NASA began preparations for Apollo, a program to put U.S. astronauts on the moon. Notables who died this year included Gilbert H. Grosvenor, longtime president of the National Geographic Society, Feb. 4, at 90; and Sebastian Spering Kresge, founder of the S. S. Kresge store chain, Oct. 18, at 99.

Feb 9: The **New York Stock Exchange** reached the peak of a three-and-one-half-year bull market as the Dow Jones industrial average hit an all-time high of 995. A downturn in stock prices for most of the rest of the year set market analysts to worrying about a recession. A low of 744 was reached Oct. 7.

Mar 16: Gemini 8, manned by astronauts Neil Armstrong and David Scott, was launched and made the first successful space docking, closing on its target vehicle after a six-and-one-half-hour chase. A yaw thruster rocket on the Gemini malfunctioned, throwing the connected crafts into a frightening tumble and bringing the projected 71-hour flight to an end in less than 11 hours.

Apr 6: Cesar Chavez's **National Farm Workers Union,** which had started a strike against California grape growers Sept. 8, 1965, scored its first victory when it was recognized as the bargaining agent for farm workers of Schenley Industries, a major grower.

Apr 24: The **longest newspaper strike** in a major city began. Fearing loss of jobs as a result of a merger of three ailing New York City papers—the *World-Telegram and Sun,* the *Journal-American,* and the *Herald Tribune*—the Newspaper Guild struck the new World-Journal-Tribune Inc. The strike lasted until Sept. 11.

May 13: Federal funding for education was denied to 12 school districts in the deep South, the first such action against violators of the desegregation guidelines of the 1964 Civil Rights Act.

May 17: The **Gemini 9** launch was postponed because of the failure of an Atlas booster rocket to launch an Agena target vehicle into orbit.

June 2: Surveyor 1, launched May 30, made the first U.S. soft landing on the moon after a flight of 231,483 miles in 63 hrs., 36 min. It immediately began televising pictures of the moon's surface; by July 14, when its batteries went dead, it had sent more than 11,000 back to Earth. Shots of indentations made by the craft's legs showed that the surface was strong enough to support an astronaut.

June 3: Gemini 9, manned by astronauts Thomas Stafford and Eugene Cernan, was successfully launched and attempted to rendezvous with a target vehicle orbited several hours earlier. The astronauts found the target vehicle's nose shroud only partially detached, gaping open like the "jaws of an angry alligator" and making docking impossible. On the second day of the flight, Cernan spent a record 2 hrs., 5 min. in a space walk, but found his equipment so troublesome that he terminated his extravehicular activity early. Gemini 9 splashed down on June 6 after 70 hrs., 20 min. aloft.

July 1: The **Medicare** insurance program for the elderly was inaugurated. The new health plan, condemned by some as the first step toward socialized medicine, covered the cost of care in hospitals and, after Jan. 1, 1967, in nursing homes.

July 8: An **airline strike** that grounded the planes of all major airlines until Aug. 19 was called by the International Association of Machinists.

July 18: Gemini 10, manned by astronauts John Young and Michael Collins, was successfully launched and docked in space with an Agena target vehicle. Both astronauts suffered eye irritation when lithium hydroxide leaked from their life-support system. Gemini 10 splashed down on July 21 in full view of TV cameras after a 71-hour flight.

Aug 8: The **first successful artificial heart pump,** a left ventricle bypass, was installed in a patient at Methodist Hospital in Houston, Tex., by a team headed by heart surgeon Michael DeBakey. It was removed ten days later.

Aug 10: Lunar Orbiter 1, designed to photograph possible landing sites on the moon, was launched from Cape Kennedy. It went into lunar orbit on Aug. 14 and televised 215 pictures. On Oct. 29 it was crashed into the moon, lest its radio signals interfere with Lunar Orbiter 2, scheduled for launch on Nov. 6.

Aug 22: The **Consumer Price Index** hit a record high in July, making 1966 the most inflationary year since 1957.

Sep 12: Gemini 11, manned by astronauts Charles Conrad and Richard Gordon, was successfully launched and docked with an Agena target vehicle. On Sept. 14 the joined crafts achieved a record altitude of 851 miles. Gemini 11 landed Sept. 15, its descent controlled entirely by on-board instruments—a space first.

Sep 12: School violence broke out at two newly integrated public schools in Grenada, Miss. Police stood by as white mobs assaulted black children and their parents with ax handles, pipes, and chains, injuring 40.

Sep 22: Surveyor 2, launched two days earlier, crashed into the moon as attempts to correct its tumbling flight failed.

Oct 7: Stock prices hit the year's low, with the Dow Jones industrial average down to 744 from a February high of 995. It was the worst decline since the one-day crash of May 28, 1962.

Nov 6: Lunar Orbiter 2 was launched. On Nov. 17 it went into orbit, photographing possible landing sites along the lunar equator. NASA scientists said that photographs of domelike formations indicated that the moon formerly had volcanic activity.

Nov 11: Gemini 12, manned by astronauts James Lovell and Edwin Aldrin, was successfully launched and rendezvoused with an Agena target vehicle. This was the last mission of the Gemini program. On Nov. 12 the astronauts took pictures of a solar eclipse. Aldrin spent a total of five and a half hours in extravehicular activity, without the fatigue and equipment difficulties that had marked earlier Gemini flights. Gemini 12 landed safely on Nov. 15.

Nov 18: Abstinence from meat on Fridays would no longer be required of U.S. Roman Catholics, except during Lent. The change became effective Dec. 2.

Dec 10: The **Nobel Prize in Chemistry** was awarded to Robert S. Mulliken of the University of Chicago for his work on the chemical bond of atoms in a molecule.

Dec 10: The **Nobel Prize in Physiology or Medicine** was awarded jointly to Charles B. Huggins of the University of Chicago and Francis Peyton Rous, a member emeritus of the Rockefeller Institute, in recognition of their pioneer discoveries of the causes of specific types of cancer.

IV. Fashion
Folkways
Holidays
Social Issues and Crime
Sports

Southpaw Sandy Koufax made the Los Angeles Dodgers pay $130,000 for the use of his pitching arm for the season. He demonstrated its worth by winning 27 games and the National League pennant for his club, even though he had to take cortisone shots before each game for his arthritic arm. But the Baltimore Orioles swept the World Series in four straight games. After the season Koufax retired. The San Francisco Giants' Willie Mays hit 37 home runs for a career total of 542, second only to Babe Ruth's 714. Muhammad Ali consolidated his world heavyweight boxing championship by beating five contenders, the last being Cleveland Williams at the Houston Astrodome (Nov. 14) before 34,420 spectators, largest indoor crowd in boxing history. In golf the top money winners were Billy Casper, $121,944, and Kathy Whitworth, $33,517. In fashion the year's rage was the miniskirt, which put hemlines four or five—and occasionally a daring seven—inches above the knee. This year also saw a fad for paper throwaway clothes, especially inexpensive one-wearing dresses. The use of drugs became a national phenomenon, with the emphasis on LSD and other hallucinogens. The word *psychedelic,* first used to describe such drugs or their effects in the 1950s, came into popular use. The high priest of LSD was Timothy Leary, a psychologist fired from Harvard in 1963. Notables who died this year included James "Sunny Jim" Fitzsimmons, active in horse racing for 78 years, Mar. 11, at 91; Hedda Hopper, born Elda Furry, the Hollywood gossip columnist, Feb. 1, at 75; Tony Lema, golfer, July 24, at 32; Margaret Sanger, the pioneer in family planning, Sept. 6, at 82; and Abe Saperstein, founder of the Harlem Globetrotters, Mar. 15, at 63.

Jan 2: The 1965 **NFL championship** was won by the Green Bay Packers, who defeated the Cleveland Browns 23 to 12.

Mar 5: A new indoor **pole vault record** of 17 ft., 1/4 in. was set by Bob Seagren in Albuquerque, N. Mex.

Mar 12: Bobby Hull of the Chicago Black Hawks scored his 51st hockey goal of the season against the New York Rangers in Chicago. Hull thus became the first player to score more than 50 in a season; he later ran the total to 54.

Mar 12: Jockey **Johnny Longden,** 59, retired after 40 years of racing and after riding his 6,032nd winner—the most ever for a jockey—in the San Juan Capistrano Handicap at Santa Anita.

Mar 19: The **NCAA basketball championship** was won by Texas Western College, which defeated Kentucky 72 to 65.

Apr 17-28: The **NBA basketball championship** was won by the Boston Celtics, who beat the Los Angeles Lakers four games to three, thus enabling coach Red Auerbach to retire with his eighth successive championship. Auerbach was replaced by Bill Russell, Celtic center, the first black to coach a major U.S. sports team.

May 30: At the 50th annual **Indianapolis 500** auto race, nearly half of the 33 starters were involved in a first-lap crash, but only one driver was hurt. Graham Hill led the six finishers, completing the course in 3 hrs., 27 min., 52.53 sec., for an average speed of 144.317 mph.

June 8: A **merger** of the National and American football leagues, effective in 1970, was announced. The move provided for a common draft of college players in 1967, putting an end to costly competition between the leagues. It also set up a Super Bowl game between the league champions of the 1966–1967 season.

June 20: The **U.S. Open golf tournament** was won by Billy Casper, who beat Arnold Palmer in a playoff.

June 25: Buckpasser set a new world record of 1:32 3/5 for the mile in winning the Arlington Classic. He also became the first three-year-old to win more than $1,000,000. Kauai King, the Derby and Preakness winner this year, went lame in the race; his retirement from racing was announced three days later.

July 2: At the **Wimbledon** tennis championships in England, Billie Jean King beat Maria Bueno of Brazil to win the women's singles championship.

July 2-3: The **world decathlon record** of 8089 points, held by C.K. Yang, was bested twice at Salina, Kans., by Russ Hodge (8130) and Bill Toomey (8234).

July 9: Jack Nicklaus won the British Open, joining Gene Sarazen, Ben Hogan, and Gary Player as the only men to have won the four major golf championships of the world. (The other events are the PGA, Masters, and U.S. Open.)

July 17: A new **record for the mile run,** 3:51.3, was set by Jim Ryun, a 19-year-old college freshman, trimming 2.3 sec. from the world record.

July 23: A new outdoor **pole vault record** of 17 ft., 6 1/4 in. was set by John Pennel of Los Angeles, Calif.

July 24: The **PGA golf tournament** was won by Al Geiberger.

Oct 5-9: The 63rd annual **World Series** was won by the Baltimore Orioles (AL), who swept the Los Angeles

Dodgers (NL) in four straight games, the last three being shutouts.

1967

I. Civil Rights
Exploration and Settlement
Government
Statistics
Wars

By mid-November this year, more than 17,000 Americans had died in Vietnam since 1961, 2000 more in the first ten months of 1967 than in the period 1961–1966. U.S. and UN efforts to achieve peace were entirely unsuccessful, with UN Secretary General U Thant asserting that the impasse was caused by the U.S. bombing of North Vietnam. In South Vietnam, in the first election since the 1963 coup, Nguyen Van Thieu and Nguyen Cao Ky were elected president and vice president amid charges of election fraud. At home, Pres. Johnson got a $69,900,000,000 defense appropriation for the 1967–1968 fiscal year, the largest single appropriation ever passed by Congress. But he was unsuccessful in his request for an income tax surcharge that he said was needed to fight the war, to conduct the Great Society programs, and to fight inflation. Congress passed bills providing for increased Social Security benefits, aid to education, and antipoverty funds. Administration legislation requests included the smallest appropriation for foreign aid in 20 years, a Civil Rights Act that would end discrimination in housing by 1969 and prevent discrimination in selecting juries, and revision of the Selective Service System through substitution of a lottery to select draftees. In what was called the long hot summer, the U.S. suffered the worst race riots in its history, with trouble in no fewer than 100 American cities. Notables who died this year included John Nance Garner, vice president of the United States from 1933 to 1941, Nov. 7, at 98; and Jack Ruby, convicted killer of Lee Harvey Oswald, alleged assassin of Pres. John F. Kennedy. Ruby died in Dallas, Tex., Jan. 3, at 55, while awaiting retrial after his conviction was overturned.

Jan 10: Lester Maddox, the Georgia restaurant owner who made headlines in 1964 by passing out ax handles to white customers to prevent desegregation of his eatery, was sworn in as governor of Georgia.

Jan 16: The **first black southern sheriff** since Reconstruction, former paratrooper Lucius Amerson, was sworn in at Tuskegee, Ala.

Jan 27: A 63-nation **space demilitarization treaty** was signed by the U.S. and the U.S.S.R. The treaty prohibited the orbiting of nuclear weapons and forbade territorial claims on celestial bodies. It became effective on Oct. 10.

Jan 29: Robert G. "Bobby" Baker, former secretary to the Senate Democratic majority, was convicted of income tax evasion, theft, and conspiracy to defraud the government. He was sentenced Apr. 7 to from one to three years in prison.

Mar 1: Rep. **Adam Clayton Powell,** Democrat of New York, was denied his seat in the 90th Congress by a vote of 307 to 116. This was the third time the House had taken such action against a duly elected member. A committee investigating Powell's activities found that he had "wrongfully and willfully" misused approximately $46,000 of government money for private purposes and had "improperly maintained" his wife on his office payroll.

Apr 4: Military authorities announced that the **500th U.S. plane** had been shot down over North Vietnam since bombing began in 1964.

Apr 15: In an **antiwar demonstration** in New York City, some 100,000 to 400,000 persons marched from New York's Central Park to UN headquarters. A similar protest in San Francisco drew about 50,000.

Apr 20: The North Vietnamese port city of **Haiphong was bombed** by U.S. planes, which destroyed two power plants and struck at North Vietnamese Mig airfields for the first time.

Apr 21: Svetlana Aliluyeva, daughter of Joseph Stalin, the late premier of the U.S.S.R., arrived in New York City after receiving political asylum at the U.S. Embassy in New Delhi, India.

May 19: The **first U.S. air strike on central Hanoi,** North Vietnam's capital, was launched by U.S. planes.

June 1: U.S. casualties in Vietnam for the week of May 21–27 were reported as 313 killed and 2616 wounded, the greatest weekly casualty toll of the war.

June 8: The **U.S. communications ship *Liberty*** was attacked by Israeli torpedo boats and planes in international waters 15 miles north of the Sinai Peninsula; 34 seamen were killed and 75 were wounded. Israel apologized for the accidental attack.

June 12: State laws forbidding **interracial marriages** were ruled unconstitutional by the U.S. Supreme Court.

June 23 and 25: Ten hours of **U.S.-Soviet talks at Glassboro,** N.J., were held by Pres. Johnson and Premier Aleksei Kosygin. Kosygin had headed his nation's delegation to the UN during its attempt to have Israel branded the aggressor in the Six Day War (June 5–10) against Egypt, Syria, and Jordan.

June 30: The **General Agreement on Tariffs and Trade** (GATT), the result of four years of negotiations begun during the Kennedy administration, was signed in Geneva by the U.S. and 45 other nations.

July 2-7: U.S. Marines at **Con Thien,** just south of the DMZ in South Vietnam, suffered heavy casualties in fierce fighting with North Vietnamese units.

July 12-17: A **race riot in Newark,** N.J., left 26 dead and more than 1300 injured before police and National Guard troops restored order.

July 22: It was announced that **U.S. troop strength in Vietnam** was to be increased to 525,000 by the end of 1968.

July 23: Puerto Rico voted to remain a commonwealth of the U.S. Some 60.5% of the votes cast rejected statehood or full independence.

July 23: The **worst race riot** in U.S. history erupted in Detroit, Mich., killing 43 people and causing some $200,000,000 in damage in five days of violence.

July 25: A **riot in Cambridge,** Md., followed a speech by H. Rap Brown, chairman of SNCC. Brown was arrested by the FBI in Alexandria, Va., the next day. On Aug. 14 he was indicted in Cambridge for arson, inciting to riot, and disturbing the public peace.

July 29: An **aircraft carrier fire** aboard the U.S.S. *Forrestal* in the Gulf of Tonkin, caused by a punctured fuel tank, killed 134 people and injured 62.

Aug 21: The Defense Department announced that **two U.S. Navy jets had been shot down** over the People's Republic of China after straying off course from a bombing mission over North Vietnam.

Sep 1-Oct 4: A siege of the U.S. Marine base at **Con Thien,** just south of the DMZ in South Vietnam, raged for more than a month before U.S. firepower forced North Vietnamese gunners to withdraw from their artillery positions in the DMZ.

Sep 28: Walter Washington was sworn in as commissioner of the District of Columbia, the first black to head a major city government.

Oct 2: Thurgood Marshall was sworn in as the first black Supreme Court justice in U.S. history.

Oct 20: Seven **Ku Klux Klan members were convicted** of conspiracy in the 1964 murders of three civil rights workers, James Chaney, Andrew Goodman, and Michael Schwerner, in Mississippi. The federal jury acquitted eight others and could reach no verdict on three others.

Oct 21-22: An **antiwar march in Washington,** D.C., drew some 50,000 participants. At least 647 were arrested, most after a clash with police and troops at the Pentagon.

Oct 26: Cancellation of draft deferments of college students who violated draft laws or interfered with recruiting was ordered by Lewis Hershey, director of the Selective Service.

Oct 30-Nov 4: A North Vietnamese assault on **Loc Ninh,** on the Cambodian border about 90 miles north of Saigon, was broken after six days by U.S. artillery and air strikes. The attack on the town and the U.S. Special Forces camp there was unusually determined, possibly because the communists wanted a victory to offset the Oct. 31 inauguration of Nguyen Van Thieu as president of South Vietnam.

Nov 7: Carl B. Stokes, a Democrat, was elected the first black mayor of Cleveland, Ohio, the eighth largest city in the U.S.

Nov 20: The U.S. **population** reached 200,000,000, despite the lowest yearly birthrate in history, 17.8 per 1000.

Dec 5: More than 1000 **antiwar protesters** attempted to close down a New York City induction center. Among the 264 arrested were Dr. Benjamin Spock and the poet Allen Ginsberg.

Dec 15: A **collapse of the Silver Bridge** on the Ohio R. between Point Pleasant, W. Va., and Kanauga, Ohio, killed 46 people. The collapse occurred during rush hour.

Dec 20: U.S. troop strength in Vietnam reached 474,300.

II. Architecture
Arts and Music
Popular Entertainment
Publishing
Theater

The most important art news this year was the effort to save the cultural treasures damaged by a flood that struck Florence, Italy, on Nov. 4, 1966. U.S. art conservationists and concerned nonprofessionals volunteered their services, and many organizations helped raise money for salvage and restoration work. In theater, the 1966–1967 season was marked by scarcity of good new plays. Welcome visitors from abroad were the Old Vic, which began a 17-week tour of the U.S. in January; and the Jewish State Theater of Poland, which began a U.S. tour in October. In popular music a new element, Indian music, as popularized by the sitarist Ravi Shankar, appeared in the work of rock groups, notably the Beatles, whose new album *Sgt. Pepper's Lonely Hearts Club Band,* also showed signs of the growing influence of the drug culture. Notables who died this year included John Coltrane, jazz musician and composer, July 17, at 40; Nelson Eddy, singer and movie actor, Mar. 6, at 65; Mischa Elman, violinist, Apr. 5, at 76; Woodrow Wilson "Woody" Guthrie, folk singer, Oct. 3, at 55; Edward Hopper, realist painter, May 15, at 84; Langston Hughes, poet and writer, May 22, at 65; Bert Lahr, comedian and actor, Dec. 4, at 72; Henry R. Luce, founder of *Time* and *Life*, Feb. 28, at 68; Carson McCullers, writer, Sept. 29, at 50; Paul Muni, actor, Aug. 25, at 71; Dorothy Parker, writer, June 7, at 73; Claude Rains, actor, May 30, at 77; Basil Rathbone, actor, July 21, at 75; Carl Sandburg, poet, biographer, and folklorist, July 22, at 89; Alice B. Toklas, longtime companion of Gertrude Stein, Mar. 7, at 89; Spencer Tracy, actor, June 10, at 67; and Paul Whiteman, king of jazz, Dec. 29, at 77.

Among **books published** this year was *The Death of a President* by William Manchester, about the assassination of Pres. Kennedy. The Kennedy family had sought to halt publication on the grounds that they had not given final approval of the manuscript, as had been agreed with the author. The book was published after the Kennedys won the right to delete from it some particularly sensitive material. Other books published this year included *Tales of Manhattan* by Louis Auchincloss, short stories; *The Arrangement* by Elia Kazan, a novel; *Death at an Early Age* by Jonathan Kozol, dealing with conditions in ghetto schools; *Rosemary's Baby* by Ira Levin, a shocker that was the basis for an enormously successful movie; *The Medium Is the Massage* by Marshall McLuhan and Quentin Fiore, a study of the impact of technology and communication on society; *Nicholas and Alexandra* by Robert K. Massie, a biography of the last czar and czarina of Russia; *The Complete Poems of Marianne Moore*; *The Instrument* by John O'Hara, a novel; *The Chosen* by Chaim Potok, a first novel that became a best seller; *The Confessions of Nat Turner* by William Styron, a novel based on an 1831 slave revolt; and *Pulitzer* by W. A. Swanberg, a biography.

Feb 5: The **Bollingen Prize** for poetry was awarded to Robert Penn Warren for his 1966 collection *Selected Poems, New and Old, 1923–1966.*

Apr 26: A new **art auction record** was set by David Mann, a New York City art dealer, who bought Pablo Picasso's painting *Mother and Child* at Sotheby's in London for $532,000, the highest price ever paid for a work by a living artist.

May 1: Pulitzer prizes were awarded for the following: fiction, *The Fixer* by Bernard Malamud; biography, *Mr. Clemens and Mark Twain* by Justin Kaplan; history, *Exploration and Empire* by William H. Goetzmann; general nonfiction, *The Problem of Slavery in Western Culture* by David Brion Davis; poetry, *Live or Die* by Anne Sexton; drama, *A Delicate Balance* by Edward Albee.

June 25: The **first global TV broadcast**, *Our World*, originated live from 19 countries on five continents, and was seen in 39 nations via satellite.

Nov 7: A law creating the **Corporation for Public Broadcasting**, a nonprofit public corporation to aid noncommercial television, was signed by Pres. Johnson.

Dec 6: At a seminar on **art forgery** at New York City's Metropolitan Museum of Art, the museum revealed that one of its most prized pieces was a forgery. It was an elegant statue of a horse, estimated to be 2400 years old when it was acquired in 1923 and since then widely reproduced in casts and used as an illustration in many books on Greek art. A gamma-ray shadowgraph confirmed that the forgery had been cast by a technique developed in the fourteenth century but was probably no more than 50 years old.

III. Business and Industry
Education
Philosophy and Religion
Science

The space program suffered a setback when three astronauts were killed in a fire while taking their Apollo vehicle through tests at Cape Kennedy, Fla. Space exploration news was not all bad. The U.S. made three successful soft landings on the moon to obtain data about the lunar surface and possible landing sites for manned flights. Mariner 5 sent back information about the atmosphere of Venus, and the new Saturn 5 rocket, the world's largest launch vehicle, orbited Earth in a test to determine its use for eventual manned flights to the moon. The economy showed signs of vigor despite civil unrest in U.S. cities. School integration progressed, but campus violence continued, a reminder that change is rarely easy. Notables who died this year included Henry Kaiser, industrialist, Aug. 24, at 85; J. Robert Oppenheimer, nuclear physicist known as the father of the atomic bomb, Feb. 18, at 62; and Francis Cardinal Spellman, archbishop of New York, Dec. 2, at 78.

Jan 27: A **launch pad fire** during Apollo tests at Cape Kennedy, Fla., killed astronauts Virgil I. "Gus" Grissom, Edward H. White, II, and Roger B. Chaffee. An investigation concluded that a faulty electrical wire was the probable cause.

Feb 4: Lunar Orbiter 3 was launched from Cape Kennedy, Fla., on its 92-hour mission to the moon. The spacecraft relayed pictures of possible landing sites for manned space vehicles.

Mar 7: James R. Hoffa, president of the International Brotherhood of Teamsters, began an eight-year prison sentence for jury tampering after the Supreme Court refused to review his 1964 conviction.

Apr 2: A report on **school desegregation** by the Southern Education Reporting Service stated that 16% of black students in 11 southern states were attending desegregated schools in 1967, an increase of 10% over 1966.

Apr 17: Surveyor 3 was successfully launched from Cape Kennedy, Fla. The second U.S. spacecraft to make a soft landing on the moon, it studied the lunar surface and sent back more than 6300 pictures.

May 11: Ceremonies marking installation of the **100,000,000th telephone** in the U.S. were attended by Pres. Johnson and representatives of the Bell System and the U.S. Independent Telephone Association. The U.S. had approximately half the telephones in the world.

May 29: A **California property law** giving owners "absolute discretion" in housing rental or sales was ruled unconstitutional by the U.S. Supreme Court on the grounds that it was discriminatory and violated the Fourteenth Amendment.

June 14: Mariner 5 was successfully launched toward Venus.

June 19: De facto **school segregation in Washington, D.C.,** was ordered ended by autumn by U.S. District Judge J. Skelly Wright.

July 17: Surveyor 4, launched from Cape Kennedy on July 14 and programed to land in Sinus Medii in the center of the near side of the moon, lost radio contact with Earth moments before it landed.

Sep 8: Surveyor 5 was launched from Cape Kennedy and made a soft landing on the moon 65 hours later. By Sept. 24 it had transmitted a total of 18,006 pictures to Earth along with other important information.

Oct 18: The **Nobel Prize in Physiology or Medicine** was awarded jointly to Dr. Haldan Keffer Hartline of Rockefeller University, Dr. George Wald of Harvard University, and Dr. Ragnar Granit of Sweden for research on the eye and its transmission of sensory information to the brain.

Oct 18: The **Nobel Prize in Physics** was awarded to Dr. Hans Albrecht Bethe of Cornell University for his study of energy generation in stars.

Oct 19: Mariner 5 passed within 2480 miles of the planet Venus and sent back data indicating that the planet had no magnetic field and that its surface was unfit for human habitation.

Nov 7: Surveyor 6 was launched. On Nov. 9 it made a soft landing on the moon and began transmitting pictures and soil analysis data. On Nov. 17 it lifted off the moon's surface and landed a few feet away. Surveyor 6 then took pictures of its original landing site. It was the first spacecraft to lift off the moon.

Nov 9: The unmanned **Apollo 9** space vehicle completed an 8-hr., 37-min. test orbit of Earth. The capsule was recovered in the Pacific Ocean just ten miles from its target area. It had been launched from Cape Kennedy by the Saturn 5 rocket, the world's largest launch vehicle, designed for eventual manned flights to the moon. It was the first time Saturn 5 was used.

IV. Fashion
Folkways
Holidays
Social Issues and Crime
Sports

In baseball the Boston Red Sox outfielder Carl Yastrzemski led the American League in three batting categories. He finished the year with an average of .326, batted in 121 runs, and tied Harmon Killebrew in home runs, 44 for the season. The Kansas City Athletics moved to Oakland for the 1968 season, and the American League decided to expand to 12 teams in 1969 by creating a new Kansas City franchise and awarding a franchise to Seattle. The NFL granted a franchise to the New Orleans Saints, and split the league into two conferences and four divisions: Eastern Conference (Century and Capitol divisions) and Western Conference (Central and Coastal divisions). This year the AFL and NFL played the first Super Bowl game, the World Series of professional football. In boxing Muhammad Ali continued to support his claim to be the greatest of all time by successfully defending the world heavyweight crown against Ernie Terrell in a 15-round decision (Feb. 6) and Zora Folley in a seventh-round knockout (Mar. 22). When Ali refused to be drafted into the Army on religious grounds, the World Boxing Association again stripped him of his title. In golf the top money winners were Jack Nicklaus, $188,998, and Kathy Whitworth, $32,937. In fashion there was little new, but women began to wear maxis, which were ankle-length coats, over their miniskirts. A British model, named Twiggy caused a sensation with her closely cropped hair and tomboyish appeal. Notables who died this year included James E. "Jimmy" Foxx, a great hitter with a lifetime record of 534 home runs, July 21, at 59; John J. "Johnny" Keane, of the St. Louis Cardinals, Jan. 6, at 55; and Reese "Goose" Tatum, of the Harlem Globetrotters, Jan. 18, at 45.

Jan 15: The first annual **Super Bowl** was won by the Green Bay Packers (NFL), who defeated the Kansas City Chiefs (AFL) 35 to 10. The Packers had won the NFL championship Jan. 1 by beating the Dallas Cowboys 34 to 27. The same day the Chiefs won the AFL championship over the Buffalo Bills, 31 to 7.

Jan 18: Albert De Salvo, self-confessed **Boston strangler,** who allegedly murdered 13 women between June 1962 and Jan. 1964, was sentenced to life imprisonment for armed robbery, assault, and sex offenses. For lack of evidence, he was not tried for the murders.

Feb 2: Formation of the **American Basketball Association** (ABA), a second pro basketball league, with former NBA star George Mikan as commissioner, was announced. The new league, with 11 teams, failed to lure stars from the NBA.

Mar 25: The **NCAA basketball championship** was won for the third time in four years by undefeated UCLA, which beat Dayton 79 to 64. UCLA's center, sophomore Lew Alcindor, had an all-time high season field goal percentage of .667 in this, his first varsity year.

Apr 14-24: The **NBA basketball championship** was won by the Philadelphia 76ers, who defeated the San Francisco Warriors four games to two.

May 14: New York Yankee outfielder **Mickey Mantle** hit his 500th career home run at Yankee Stadium, becoming the sixth player to reach that mark.

June 18: The **U.S. Open golf tournament** was won by Jack Nicklaus with a score of 275, one stroke better than the record set by Ben Hogan in 1948.

June 20: Muhammad Ali was given a five-year sentence and fined $10,000 for refusing to be drafted into the Army. Boxing authorities had earlier stripped him of his world title, rejecting his claim to exemption as a minister of the Nation of Islam.

June 23: A new **world record for the mile** was set by Jim Ryun, who shaved two-tenths of a second from his old record with a run of 3:51.1 in the AAU championships at Bakersfield, Calif. At the same meet, Paul Wilson cleared 17 ft. 7¾ in., a new world record for the outdoor pole vault.

July 8: At the **Wimbledon** tennis championships in England, Billie Jean King swept the women's singles; the women's doubles, with Rosemary Casals; and the mixed doubles, with Owen Davidson of Australia.

July 14: Eddie Mathews of the Houston Astros became the seventh player to hit 500 home runs.

July 24: The **PGA golf tournament** was won by Don January in a playoff with Don Massengale.

Sep 12-18: The **America's Cup** was successfully defended by the U.S. yacht *Intrepid,* which swept the Australian challenger *Dame Pattie* in four straight races.

Oct 4-12: The 64th annual **World Series** was won by the St. Louis Cardinals (NL), who defeated the Boston Red Sox (AL) four games to three.

Dec 31: The **NFL championship** was won by the Green Bay Packers, who defeated the Dallas Cowboys 21 to 17 with a touchdown scored from the one-yard line by Bart Starr with 13 seconds remaining in the game.

Dec 31: The **AFL championship** was won by the Oakland Raiders, who routed the Houston Oilers 40 to 7.

1968

I. Civil Rights
Exploration and Settlement
Government
Statistics
Wars

Dissent and doubt regarding the war in Vietnam and the economy at home prompted several Democratic leaders to challenge Pres. Johnson in the run for the presidential nomination, and stimulated the third-party candidacy of George C. Wallace of Alabama. In March, in the wake of the enemy offensive in Vietnam that came to be known as the Tet offensive, Pres. Johnson announced he would not seek another term. Later, the country was shocked by the assassinations of Martin Luther King, Jr., and Sen. Robert F. Kennedy, and by violence surrounding the Democratic National Convention in Chicago. The Republican candidate, Richard M. Nixon, pledging to end the war in Vietnam and restore law and order in the U.S., narrowly won the presidency. Although inflation had become critical, Pres. Johnson's budget was a record $186,000,000,000, with the year's expenditure on Vietnam about $25,000,000,000. In August the U.S.S.R. and other Warsaw Pact forces invaded Czechoslovakia and ended that country's movement toward liberalism. Notables who died this year included Husband Edward Kimmel, commander of the U.S. Pacific Fleet at the time of the Japanese attack on Pearl Harbor in 1941, May 14, at 86; Joseph Martin, Jr., Speaker of the House from 1946–1948 and 1952–1954, Mar. 6, at 83; Norman Thomas, head of the U.S. Socialist Party from 1926–1955, Dec. 19, at 84; and Lurleen Burns Wallace, who in 1966 succeeded her husband George C. Wallace as governor of Alabama, May 7, at 41.

Jan 5: Indictments for conspiracy to aid and abet draft evasion were handed down against Dr. Benjamin Spock, the eminent pediatrician, the Rev. William Sloane Coffin of Yale, and three other antiwar activists. On June 14 Spock, Coffin, and two others were convicted; the fifth defendant was acquitted.

Jan 17: In his **State of the Union** message, Pres. Johnson called for a 10% income tax surcharge to reduce the budget deficit estimated at $20,000,000,000 for fiscal 1968 and to curb inflation.

Jan 21: A nuclear-armed **B-52 bomber crashed** near Greenland. Some radiation was released from its four hydrogen bombs, which broke up in the crash.

Jan 23: The *Pueblo* incident began when the Navy intelligence ship U.S.S. *Pueblo* was seized off the coast of North Korea by North Korean patrol boats. It was claimed that the *Pueblo* had been caught within North Korean waters. Its crew of 83 were subjected to harsh treatment until their release on Dec. 23.

Jan 30-Feb 24: The **Tet offensive,** timed to coincide with the Vietnamese New Year, was a massive assault by enemy forces throughout South Vietnam. U.S. forces were surprised by the scope and size of the operation, whose key targets included Saigon, the Marine base at Khe Sanh, and the provincial capital Hue. Enemy forces suffered a devastating setback, but the offensive increased antiwar sentiment in the U.S.

Feb 1: Former Vice Pres. **Richard M. Nixon announced his candidacy** for the Republican presidential nomination.

Feb 8: Former Gov. of Alabama **George C. Wallace announced his candidacy** for president as a third-party candidate on a law-and-order platform.

Feb 14: In the *Pueblo* incident, talks intended to resolve the issue began at Panmunjom between the U.S. and North Korea.

Feb 24: Hue was recaptured by U.S. forces in Vietnam.

Feb 29: The **Kerner Commission report** was released by the President's National Advisory Committee on Civil Disorders. The report condemned racism in the U.S. and called for aid to black communities to avert further racial polarization and violence.

Mar 12: Sen. **Eugene J. McCarthy** of Minnesota won the majority of convention delegates selected in the New Hampshire Democratic presidential primary. Campaigning on an antiwar platform and aided by student volunteers, McCarthy won 42% of the vote. Although Pres. Johnson won 48% of the vote, McCarthy won 20 of the 24 delegates.

Mar 13: It was announced that **nerve gas testing** by the Army at Dugway Proving Grounds in Utah might have caused the deaths of some 6400 sheep in the area.

Mar 16: Sen. **Robert F. Kennedy announced his candidacy** for the Democratic presidential nomination.

Mar 28: Violence in Memphis, Tenn., erupted during a march led by Dr. Martin Luther King in support of a sanitation workers' strike. One black marcher was killed. Dr. King urged calm as National Guard troops were called to restore order. He promised to return in April to attend another march.

Mar 31: Pres. **Johnson announced he would not seek the presidency again.** Addressing the nation on television, the president also called for a partial halt to the bombing of North Vietnam and the opening of peace negotiations.

Apr 2: The **Wisconsin Democratic primary** was won by Sen. McCarthy.

Apr 4: Dr. **Martin Luther King, Jr., was assassinated** at age 39 by a sniper in Memphis, Tenn. The event was followed by a week of rioting in urban black ghettos. New York City remained calm but Washington, D.C., was seriously disrupted. King's funeral in Atlanta, Ga., on Apr. 9 was attended by an estimated 75,000 people.

Apr 5: The **siege of Khe Sanh,** site of a U.S. Marine base in Vietnam, was lifted.

Apr 8: Operation Complete Victory, involving 100,000 allied troops in Vietnam, was begun. It aimed to drive enemy forces from the provinces around Saigon.

Apr 11: The **1968 Civil Rights Act** was signed by Pres. Johnson. Discrimination in housing was made illegal for almost all types of dwellings.

Apr 27: Vice Pres. **Hubert H. Humphrey announced his candidacy** for the Democratic presidential nomination.

Apr 30: New York's Gov. **Nelson A. Rockefeller announced his candidacy** for the Republican presidential nomination.

May 2: The **Poor People's March on Washington,** planned by Dr. Martin Luther King, Jr., before his death, got under way. It was led by the Rev. Ralph Abernathy. Later in the month some 3000 marchers camped on a muddy site, dubbed Resurrection City, near the Washington Monument.

May 3: Agreement to hold **peace talks in Paris** was reached between the U.S. and North Vietnam.

May 5: Another **major enemy offensive** was launched in South Vietnam against allied strongholds. Although Saigon came under attack from mortar and sniper fire, the assault was judged to be not as severe as the Tet offensive.

May 10: Peace talks opened in Paris with W. Averell Harriman representing the U.S. and Xan Thuy representing North Vietnam.

May 28: The **Oregon Democratic primary** was won by Sen. McCarthy.

May 29: The U.S. nuclear submarine *Scorpion* was reported missing off the Azores with 99 men aboard.

June 5: Sen. **Robert F. Kennedy was shot** in Los Angeles at 12:15 A.M., shortly after delivering a speech acknowledging his victory in the June 4 California Democratic primary. Sirhan B. Sirhan, a Jordanian, was seized for the shooting. Kennedy died June 6 and Sirhan was indicted for murder on June 7.

June 8: Ex-convict **James Earl Ray was arrested** in London for the murder of Martin Luther King, Jr., on Apr. 4.

June 10: Gen. **William C. Westmoreland** turned over command of U.S. forces in Vietnam to Gen. Creighton W. Abrams. Gen. Westmoreland had been appointed chief of staff by Pres. Johnson on Mar. 22 in a move interpreted as reflecting disappointment with the conduct of the war.

June 13: Chief Justice **Earl Warren submitted his resignation** to Pres. Johnson, effective on the approval of a successor.

June 23: The war in Vietnam became the **longest war in U.S. history.**

June 24: **Resurrection City** in Washington, D.C., was cleared by police, who arrested 124 people after expiration of their camping permit.

June 26: Associate Justice **Abe Fortas was nominated** by Pres. Johnson as chief justice of the Supreme Court.

July 1: The **nuclear nonproliferation treaty** was signed by the U.S., U.S.S.R., and 59 other nations, concluding four years of negotiations.

July 23: A **sniper attack** on police in Cleveland, Ohio, initiated four days of rioting, during which four civilians and three policemen were killed.

Aug 7: **Rioting in Miami,** Fla., broke out in the city's black section. Three people were killed and hundreds injured before National Guard troops could restore order.

Aug 8: The **Republican National Convention nominated Richard M. Nixon** for the presidency over Gov. Ronald Reagan of California and Gov. Nelson A. Rockefeller of New York. Gov. Spiro T. Agnew of Maryland was nominated for the vice presidency on Aug. 9 at the convention in Miami Beach, Fla.

Aug 10: Sen. **George McGovern of South Dakota announced his candidacy** for the Democratic presidential nomination.

Aug 28: **John Gordon Mein,** U.S. ambassador to Guatemala, was killed by terrorists.

Aug 29: In Chicago the **Democratic National Convention nominated Vice Pres. Hubert H. Humphrey** for the presidency. Sen. Edmund S. Muskie of Maine was named the vice presidential candidate. The convention, which began Aug. 26, was the most violent in U.S. history. Antiwar protestors clashed with police and national guardsmen. Hundreds of people, including bystanders and members of the press, were beaten by police, some in full view of television cameras.

Oct 2: Justice **Abe Fortas** asked to be withdrawn from consideration for confirmation as chief justice. The Senate had objected to his advisory services to the president while on the Court.

Oct 3: George Wallace named his running mate in his third-party bid for the presidency, former Air Force chief of staff Gen. Curtis E. LeMay.

Oct 31: Bombing of North Vietnam was ordered stopped by Pres. Johnson.

Nov 5: Richard M. Nixon was elected president of the United States, defeating his Democratic opponent Vice Pres. Hubert H. Humphrey in a close race. Spiro T. Agnew, Republican of Maryland, was elected vice president. The electoral vote was Nixon, 302; Humphrey, 191; George C. Wallace, third-party candidate, 45. One Nixon elector later cast his vote for Wallace. The popular vote was Nixon, 31,785,480; Humphrey, 31,275,166; Wallace, 9,906,473. The Republicans gained four seats in the House and five in the Senate, but the Democrats still held majorities of 58–42 in the Senate and 243–192 in the House. The Republicans gained five governorships in the election.

Dec 1: Condemning as a **police riot** the actions of Chicago police during the Democratic Convention in August, the National Commission on the Causes and Prevention of Violence warned against a national tendency toward violence.

II. Architecture
Arts and Music
Popular Entertainment
Publishing
Theater

This year several new theatrical companies opened, notably the Negro Ensemble Company and Theatre Atlanta. The motion picture industry adopted a new voluntary film rating code to restrict viewing of inappropriate films by the young. The year in architecture was marked by the opening in Chicago of the John Hancock Building, a 100-story structure crisscrossed with diagonal exterior braces and tapered for stability. Among the notables who died this year were Tallulah Bankhead, stage and screen star, Dec. 12, at 65; Edna Ferber, novelist, Feb. 23, at 78; Dorothy Gish, actress, June 4, at 70; Harold Gray, creator of the *Little Orphan Annie* comic strip, May 9, at 74; Fannie Hurst, novelist, Feb. 23, at 78; Howard Lindsay, playwright, Feb. 11, at 78; Thomas Merton, Trappist monk and writer, Dec. 10, at 53; Charles Münch, conductor of the Boston Symphony from 1949 to 1962, Nov. 6, at 77; Edwin O'Connor, novelist, Mar. 23, at 49; Conrad Richter, novelist, Oct. 30, at 78; Ruth St. Denis, choreographer of modern dance, July 21, at about 90; Upton Sinclair, author, Nov. 25, at 90; John Steinbeck, Nobel Prize-winning author, Dec. 20, at 66; and Walter Wanger, Hollywood producer, Nov. 18, at 74.

Among **books published** this year were two nonfiction works by Norman Mailer. His *The Armies of the Night* was a personal account of the antiwar demonstrations in Washington, D.C., in Oct. 1967 that culminated in a march on the Pentagon. *Miami and the Siege of Chicago* was Mailer's equally personal view of the 1968 political conventions. Other books published this year included *Tell Me How Long the Train's Been Gone* by James Baldwin, a novel; *Lost in the Funhouse* by John Barth, a collection of stories; *A Brand New Life* by James T. Farrell, a sequel to his *Studs Lonigan* trilogy; *The Algiers Motel Incident* by John Hersey, dealing with the murder of three blacks by police during riots in Detroit; *A Small Town in Germany* by John Le Carré, a master of the spy novel; *The Salzburg Connection* by Helen MacInnes, another master of the genre; *The Naked Ape* by Desmond Morris, a nonfiction study of human beings; *The First Circle* and *Cancer Ward* by Alexander Solzhenitsyn, the Russian writer's second and third novels; and *Couples* by John Updike, a novel.

Apr 6: San Antonio, Tex., celebrated its 200th anniversary with the **opening of HemisFair 68,** an attractive world's fair that featured many permanent buildings, including the 622-ft.-high Tower of the Americas, the largest construction of its type since the Eiffel Tower. One of the permanent buildings, the Theater for Performing Arts, opened with a performance of Verdi's *Don Carlo.*

May 8: Pulitzer prizes were awarded for the following: fiction, *The Confessions of Nat Turner* by William Styron; biography, *Memoirs 1925–1950* by George F. Kennan; history, *The Ideological Origins of the American Revolution* by Bernard Bailyn; general nonfiction, *Rousseau and Revolution* by Will and Ariel Durant; poetry, *The Hard Hours* by Anthony Hecht.

May 25: The **Gateway Arch** in St. Louis, Mo., designed by Eero Saarinen, was formally dedicated.

Oct 9: A record **art auction price** was paid at a Parke-Bernet auction in New York City by Norton Simon, the California industrialist. He bid $1,550,000 for Pierre Auguste Renoir's *Le Pont des Arts,* a record for an impressionist painting.

III. Business and Industry
Education
Philosophy and Religion
Science

The economy was seriously threatened by inflation, while unemployment remained low, averaging 3.6% of the labor force for the year. A record 9% increase brought the GNP to $860,000,000,000. In April and June William McChesney Martin, chairman of the Federal Reserve Board, warned that unless weaknesses in the economy were corrected, particularly inflation and the balance-of-payments deficit, the nation would face a serious crisis. Following passage of the income tax surcharge bill in June and exercise of fiscal restraints, interest rates dropped. By December, however, the prime rate had risen again, to a record 6.75%. Labor made strong gains, but they were offset in part by inflation and increased taxes. In education, major strikes by teachers hit New York City and Florida. On many campuses college students demanded reforms, including separation of universities from government defense research projects, greater student participation in college administration, increased enrollment of black and impoverished students, and introduction of black-studies programs. Students pressed their demands with calls for strikes, in some cases met by police action. In medicine, new progress was made in organ transplants. Dr. Denton Cooley of Texas, the most successful in the field, performed 17 heart transplant operations. This year Americans noted the deaths of Francis Cardinal Brennan of Philadelphia July 2, at 74; Chester F. Carlson, inventor of xerography, Sept. 19, at 62; Donald L. Hall, who designed the *Spirit of St. Louis,* flown across the Atlantic by Charles A. Lindbergh in 1927, May 2, at 69; Helen A. Keller, who although deaf, blind, and mute from childhood learned to read, write, and speak and became a leader in the drive for educational aid for the handicapped, June 1, at 87; Charles W. Mayo, the son and nephew of the founders of the Mayo Clinic and a noted surgeon, July 28, at 70; and Robert Reynolds "Bob" Jones, founder of Bob Jones University, Jan. 16, at 84.

Jan 9: Surveyor 7 made a soft landing on the moon and began sending back data, including photographs. This was the last flight of the Surveyor series.

Jan 22: The unmanned **Apollo 5** spacecraft was successfully launched into Earth orbit. During the flight its Lunar Excursion Module (LEM) was tested.

Feb 8: Four days of **student disorder in Orangeburg,** S.C., culminated in the deaths of three black students in a clash between police and students at South Carolina State College. The trouble began when students from the college and nearby Claflin College protested the barring of blacks from a local bowling alley.

Feb 19: The **first statewide teachers' strike** in U.S. history began when more than half of Florida's public school teachers walked off the job. The strike lasted until Mar. 8.

Mar 17: A two-tiered **gold price system** was negotiated in Washington, D.C. by representatives of the U.S. and six European nation members of the London Gold Pool. All gold transactions between governments would be at the official price of $35 an ounce, but the private market would be allowed to fluctuate. This resolved a critical rush on gold that had threatened to disrupt the international economy.

Apr 4: Apollo 6 was launched in an unmanned mission designed to test, for the second and last time, the Saturn 5 rocket prior to manned flight.

Apr 18: The **Bell Telephone System was struck,** for the first time in its history, by 178,000 members of the Communications Workers Union. The strike hardly affected telephone service, but the record-breaking settlement on May 5, amounting to an increase of 19.58% over three years, set a high standard for other unions to reach for in their wage negotiations.

Apr 23: A **sit-in at Columbia University** was begun by students protesting university plans to build a gymnasium on land used by the neighboring community. The sit-in, involving several university buildings, led to the closing of the university on Apr. 26. On the night of Apr. 30, the police cleared all buildings occupied by the students. In the police action, some 150 students and police were injured. The university did not resume normal operations until the opening of the fall semester.

June 13: A new **stock trading record** was set on the New York Stock Exchange, with 2,350,000 shares traded. The marked upsurge in business that had begun in April was attributed to general optimism that the war in Vietnam was coming to an end. The volume of paperwork became so great in this period that, starting on June 12, the exchange closed down trading on Wednesdays.

July 1: The **United Auto Workers formally separated from the AFL-CIO.** The split followed years of conflict during which UAW head Walter Reuther accused AFL-CIO head George Meany of blocking labor reforms and allowing the movement to stagnate. Three weeks later, the UAW joined with the Teamsters to form the Alliance for Labor Action.

July 4: Explorer 38, a giant radio astronomy satellite, was launched into Earth orbit. With its antennas extended, the satellite was 1500 feet in diameter.

July 15: The **first direct U.S.-U.S.S.R. commercial flights began** when a Soviet Aeroflot jet landed at Kennedy Airport in New York City. On the same day, a U.S. commercial jet took off for Moscow.

July 31: A statement on **birth control** was issued by the National Council of Catholic Bishops. It supported Pope Paul VI's encyclical of July 25, which reiterated condemnation of artificial methods of birth control. Nevertheless, some Catholic priests and laymen publicly disagreed with the pope's position.

Aug 8: In a **stock manipulation** case, financier Louis E. Wolfson and three associates were convicted of violating SEC regulations in connection with the liquidation of Merrit-Chapman & Scott Corp.

Oct 11: The **first manned Apollo mission,** Apollo 7, manned by Commander Walter M. Schirra, Jr., Donn F. Eisele, and Walter Cunningham, was successfully launched and began an 11-day Earth orbit during which the crew transmitted live television broadcasts from the spaceship. The men successfully performed a docking maneuver with the lunar module.

Oct 16: The **Nobel Prize in Physiology or Medicine** was awarded jointly to Dr. Robert W. Holley of the Salk Institute, Dr. H. Gobind Khorana of the University of Wisconsin, and Dr. Marshall W. Nirenberg of the National Institutes of Health for their studies of the genetic code.

Oct 30: The **Nobel Prize in Chemistry** was awarded to Lars Onsager of Yale University for his work in thermodynamic theory.

Oct 30: The **Nobel Prize in Physics** was awarded to Luis W. Alvarez of the University of California at Berkeley for his work in the field of subatomic particles, particularly his development of the bubble chamber.

Nov 6: A **student strike** was begun by dissident students at San Francisco State College. The students called for reforms, especially in the area of black-studies programs. This initiated almost four months of turmoil, during which the president of the school, S. I. Hayakawa, called in police to help end the strike.

Dec 4: A new **medical definition of death** was formulated by the American Medical Association in an effort to resolve controversy arising from organ-transplant operations. The AMA declared that a death had to be declared irreversible by two independent physicians before an organ could be removed from an apparently dead patient for transplanting. The term *brain death* was introduced by Dr. Henry K. Beecher of Harvard on Dec. 12 to denote irreversible death.

Dec 21-27: Apollo 8, manned by Commander Frank Borman, James Lovell, Jr., and William Anders, was launched from Cape Kennedy, Fla. It completed a pioneering five-day mission that included ten orbits of the moon (Dec. 24–25) and yielded spectacular photographs of Earth and the moon.

IV. Fashion
Folkways
Holidays
Social Issues and Crime
Sports

In fashion, hemlines remained high, and efforts to introduce the so-called midi length (hemline at mid-calf) were unsuccessful. Pantsuits for evening wear, with full flowing lines, gained wide acceptance. More and more men favored bold, extravagant fashions, and both men and women were wearing leather garments. For the first time the Gallup Poll reported that crime ranked number one among the issues that concerned the public. Another serious problem was the rising use of heroin by middle-class and upper-class youths along with an increase in drug abuse throughout American society. In sports, the National League added two new baseball franchises, San Diego and Montreal. Both the National and American leagues formed two divisions, Eastern and Western, with league championships to be determined by five-game playoffs beginning in 1969. In football, the NFL Players Association campaigned for better pensions. In golf there was a split between the PGA and the new American Professional Golfers, with both groups struggling for control of the ever more lucrative tournaments. A compromise agreement was reached on Dec. 13. The year's top golf money winners were Billy Casper, $121,944, and Kathy Whitworth, $48,380. In boxing, Jimmy Ellis became the World Boxing Association champion by outpointing Jerry Quarry in a bout on Apr. 27. New York State, Massachusetts, and Illinois recognized Joe Frazier, who had knocked out Buster Mathis in a title bout on Mar. 4. The new American Basketball Association concluded its first season with a $2,500,000 loss. This year tennis tournaments were opened to professionals as well as amateurs for the first time. Among the notables who died this year were Tommy Bridges, Detroit Tigers pitcher, Apr. 19, at 61; Samuel Earl "Wahoo Sam" Crawford, outfielder for the Detroit Tigers and Cincinnati Reds, June 15, at 88; Lawson Little, golfer, Feb. 1, at 57; Earl Sande, one of racing's most successful jockeys, Aug. 20, at 69; and Jess Willard, world heavyweight boxing champion from 1915 to 1919, Dec. 15, at 86.

Jan 14: **Super Bowl II** was won by the Green Bay Packers (NFL), who defeated the Oakland Raiders (AFL) 33–14 for their second Super Bowl victory. Shortly thereafter the Packers' coach, Vince Lombardi, retired to an executive post with the team. The Packers had won the NFL title on Dec. 31, 1967, by beating the Dallas Cowboys 21 to 17. The same day the Raiders had clinched the AFL title by beating the Houston Oilers 40 to 7.

Feb 6-18: At the 1968 **Winter Olympics** in Grenoble, France, the unofficial team championship was won by Norway. The U.S. won only one gold medal, the one taken by figure skater Peggy Fleming.

Mar 23: The **NCAA basketball championship** was won by UCLA, which defeated North Carolina 78–55. The day before, UCLA had beaten its archrival, the University of Houston, in the NCAA semifinals.

Apr 18-May 4: The **first ABA basketball championship** was won by the Pittsburgh Pipers, who beat the New Orleans Buccaneers four games to three.

Apr 21-May 2: The **NBA basketball championship** was won by the Boston Celtics, who defeated the Los Angeles Lakers four games to two.

May 4: The 94th annual **Kentucky Derby** was won by Dancer's Image, with a time of 2:02⅕. The jockey was Bob Ussery. Three days later Dancer's Image was disqualified when traces of a pain-killing drug were found in tests, and Forward Pass, ridden by Ismael Valenzuela, was declared the winner. This was the first recalled race in Derby history. Peter Fuller, owner of Dancer's Image, challenged the recall. Finally, on Dec. 23, the Kentucky Racing Commission ruled that Dancer's Image had won the race but not the purse.

May 8: A **perfect baseball game** was pitched by Jim "Catfish" Hunter of the Oakland Athletics, in leading his team to a 4 to 0 victory over the Minnesota Twins. This was the first American League perfect game since 1922.

June 16: The **U.S. Open golf tournament** was won by Lee Trevino, who beat Jack Nicklaus by four strokes and became the first person in the tournament's history to play all four rounds under par.

July 6: At the **Wimbledon** tennis championships in England, Billie Jean King won the women's singles title for the third straight year. King and Rosemary Casals won the women's doubles title for the second year running.

July 21: The **PGA golf tournament** was won by Julius Boros, who beat Arnold Palmer and Bob Charles by one stroke.

Aug 24: A new **horse racing record** for the mile was set by Dr. Fager, who ran the distance in 1:32⅕ at Arlington Park in Arlington, Ill. This year Dr. Fager was voted horse of the year and then was retired to stud.

Sep 9: The **first U.S. Open tennis championships** were won by Arthur Ashe in the men's singles division and by Virginia Wade of England (Sept. 8) in the women's singles division.

Oct 2-10: The 65th annual **World Series** was won for the first time since 1945 by the Detroit Tigers (AL), who beat the St. Louis Cardinals (NL) four games to three.

Oct 12-27: At the **Summer Olympics** in Mexico City, the U.S. won 45 gold medals and took first place in the unofficial team standings. Despite the altitude, many records were broken, and spectacular performances were turned in by Bob Beamon, who broke the world broad jump record by 21 in. with a jump of 29 ft., 2½ in., and Dick Fosbury, who won the high jump at 7 ft., 4½ in., going over the bar backward. On Oct. 18 two U.S. track stars, Tommy Smith and John Carlos, were suspended from competition after giving the black power salute, a clenched fist raised high over the head, at an awards ceremony. Smith and Carlos had won the gold and bronze medals for the 200-meter dash.

Nov 17: In what became known as the **Heidi game,** a critical football game between the New York Jets and the Oakland Raiders televised on NBC, the network cut away the last minute of the game to broadcast a production of a children's program, *Heidi.* Oakland, behind at the time, scored twice in nine seconds to win 43 to 32.

Dec 26-28: In Australia, the **Davis Cup** international tennis round was won, for the first time since 1963, by the U.S., which beat Australia four matches to one.

1969

I. Civil Rights
Exploration and Settlement
Government
Statistics
Wars

Richard Milhous Nixon assumed the presidency, carrying the burden of the most unpopular war in U.S. history. At the Paris peace talks little progress was made to end the Vietnam War. After Pres. Nixon made the first moves toward U.S. troop reductions in June, Sen. Charles Goodell, Republican of New York, demanded a complete pullout by the end of 1970. In October and November mammoth peace demonstrations were held in the nation's capital and other major cities. These rallies sparked prowar marches by what the president called "the great silent majority." As the year progressed, the new administration came under increasing criticism for allegedly pursuing a so-called southern strategy, a plan purportedly

devised by Attorney General John Mitchell to frame policies and make appointments that would mollify the South and encourage Republican victories there in coming years. Congress voted a $5,000,000,000 cut in military spending, but failed by one vote to defeat construction of the Safeguard antiballistic missile system. This year skyjackers made off with 65 planes, a number that exceeded the total for all years since the first such seizure in 1952. Notables who died this year included Sen. Everett McKinley Dirksen, Senate Republican leader since 1959, Sept. 7, at 73; Allen W. Dulles, diplomat and director of the CIA from 1953 to 1961, Jan. 29, at 75; Joseph P. Kennedy, father of John F. and Robert Kennedy, Nov. 18, at 81; and Adm. Raymond A. Spruance, USN (ret.), who commanded the U.S. fleet at the Battle of Midway in 1942 during World War II, Dec. 13, at 83.

Jan-Mar: Torrential **rains,** the heaviest in 100 years, caused vast mud slides in southern California, killed more than 100, and destroyed nearly 10,000 homes. Damage exceeded $60,000,000. The worst storms hit on Jan. 18–26 and Feb. 23–26.

Jan 3: The House voted to seat Rep. **Adam Clayton Powell** of New York in the 91st Congress, but fined him $25,000 for improper use of government funds and stripped him of seniority.

Jan 16: At the **Paris peace talks,** U.S. and North Vietnamese delegates finally agreed on the shape of the table to be used when the South Vietnamese and the National Liberation Front joined the negotiations. Four-party talks began Jan. 18.

Jan 20: Richard M. Nixon was inaugurated president of the United States. Spiro T. Agnew was inaugurated vice president. The inaugural ceremonies were marked by antiwar demonstrations.

Jan 20: At the **Paris peace talks,** Henry Cabot Lodge replaced W. Averell Harriman as chief U.S. negotiator.

Mar 4: Regular rail shipments of **nerve gas** were revealed by the Department of Defense, which reported it was spending $350,000,000 a year on chemical and biological weapons.

Mar 10: James Earl Ray, convicted assassin of Dr. Martin Luther King, Jr., was sentenced to 99 years in prison.

Apr 3: U.S. combat deaths in Vietnam since Jan. 1, 1961, reached 33,641, topping the 33,629 killed in the Korean War.

Apr 15: A **U.S. reconnaissance plane was shot down** by North Korean Mig jets over the Sea of Japan; 31 crewmen were lost.

Apr 23: Sirhan Sirhan was sentenced to death for the murder of Sen. Robert Kennedy.

Apr 24: In the **heaviest bombing raid** to date in the Vietnam War, U.S. B-52's dropped nearly 3000 tons of bombs on enemy positions near the Cambodian border northwest of Saigon.

May 14: An eight-point **Vietnam peace plan** was proposed by Pres. Nixon. It included pullout of most foreign troops within a year and elections supervised by an international body.

May 15: Supreme Court Justice **Abe Fortas** announced his resignation. He had been criticized for accepting a fee from the family foundation of Louis E. Wolfson, who was jailed for stock manipulation.

May 16: The $50,000,000 **nuclear submarine** *Guitarro* sank at dockside in San Francisco while undergoing final fitting. A House report later charged the Navy with "inexcusable carelessness."

May 20: U.S. and South Vietnamese troops captured **Hamburger Hill** after ten days of bloody battle. Sen. Edward M. Kennedy of Massachusetts criticized such assaults as senseless. The hill was abandoned May 27 and later was reoccupied by North Vietnamese troops.

June 6: Court testimony revealed that the **FBI had tapped the phones of Martin Luther King, Jr.,** despite a 1965 order by Pres. Johnson to tap only for purposes of national security. The testimony was taken in a federal court in Houston, Tex.

June 23: **Earl Warren retired** as chief justice of the U.S. after swearing in Warren Burger as his successor.

July 11: The convictions of Dr. **Benjamin Spock** and three codefendants for conspiring to counsel draft evasion were overturned by a U.S. court of appeals.

July 18: Sen. **Edward M. Kennedy** was involved in an auto accident when the car he was driving crashed off a bridge into the waters off Chappaquiddick Island, Mass. Kennedy was unable to rescue his passenger, Mary Jo Kopechne, who drowned. He reported the accident to Edgartown, Mass., police on July 19. On July 25 he pleaded guilty to leaving the scene of an accident. That evening, in a television statement, he called his actions in delaying the report of the accident "indefensible." He asked his constituents to help him decide on whether to continue his political career. Supported by a favorable response, he resumed his Senate duties on July 31.

Sep 9: An **air collision** of a passenger jet and a light plane near Indianapolis, Ind., killed 83 people.

Sep 21: **Operation Intercept,** a U.S. drive to halt drug traffic from Mexico, brought border traffic to a virtual halt. Travel eased considerably on Oct. 10 after complaints by the Mexican government.

Sep 24: The trial of the **Chicago Eight** began. Eight radical leaders had been indicted on Mar. 20 on charges of conspiring to incite riots during the 1968 Democratic convention in Chicago. The eight—Rennie Davis, David Dellinger, John Froines, Tom Hayden, Abbie Hoffman, Jerry Rubin, Bobby Seale, and Lee Weiner—claimed they were being tried for their political views. The trial was marked by numerous disruptions by the defendants, and on Oct. 29 Judge Julius J. Hoffman ordered Seale bound and gagged. On Nov. 5 Seale was sentenced to four years in prison on 16 counts of contempt, and his case was severed from that of the others, who then became known as the Chicago Seven. On Oct. 9–11 National Guard troops were called into Chicago to control demonstrators outside the courtroom.

Oct 15: The **first Vietnam Moratorium Day** was observed by millions with prayer vigils, candlelight processions, mass meetings, and black armbands. Pres. Nixon ignored it. Vice Pres. Agnew on Oct. 19 called protest leaders "an effete corps of impudent snobs."

Oct 28: Charges that an **illegal war in Laos** was being conducted without congressional knowledge or consent were leveled against the administration and the Pentagon by Sen. J. William Fulbright, chairman of the Senate Foreign Relations Committee.

Nov 3: Pres. Nixon said that **secret U.S. peace proposals had been rejected** by the North Vietnamese. Nixon asked the nation to support his plans to Vietnamize the war, that is, encourage Vietnam to pursue the war on its own, and withdraw U.S. troops.

Nov 11: **Pro-America demonstrations** in support of U.S. policy in Vietnam by U.S. citizens whom Pres. Nixon called "the great silent majority" marked this year's Veterans' Day observances.

Nov 14: The **second Vietnam Moratorium Day** began with a long, single-file "March Against Death" in Washington, D.C. On the next day 250,000 people marched there against the war. A San Francisco protest against U.S. participation in the war drew 100,000 demonstrators.

Nov 16: News reports charged a U.S. infantry unit with **massacre at My Lai 4,** a village in the Songmy district in South Vietnam, on Mar. 16, 1968. More than 450 villagers, including many women and babies, were said to have been slain. Pending an investigation, Lt. William L. Calley, Jr., in charge of the U.S. unit at that time, was kept on active duty beyond his official tour.

Nov 17: The first round of **Strategic Arms Limitation Talks** (SALT) between the U.S. and U.S.S.R. opened in Helsinki, Finland. The conference ended on Dec. 22 with an agreement to resume talks in Vienna on Apr. 16, 1970.

Nov 20: Henry Cabot Lodge resigned as chief U.S. negotiator at the Paris peace talks.

Nov 21: The nomination of **Clement Haynsworth** to the Supreme Court was rejected by the Senate after three months of consideration.

Nov 24: The **nuclear nonproliferation treaty** was signed by the U.S. and U.S.S.R., the 23rd and 24th signatories.

Dec 4: Fred Hampton, Illinois chairman of the Black Panther Party, was shot and killed along with another party member in a predawn police raid in Chicago. On the next day the Illinois ACLU demanded an investigation of the Panthers' charge that Hampton had been murdered in his bed.

Dec 8: An early morning police **raid on Black Panther headquarters** in Los Angeles led to a four-hour shootout before 11 party members surrendered.

Dec 15: U.S. troop strength in Vietnam would be cut to 434,000 by Apr. 12, Pres. Nixon announced. This would represent a total reduction of about 110,000 since he took office.

Dec 22: The most far-reaching **tax reform bill** in U.S. history was passed by Congress. Although it removed 9,000,000 of the very poor from federal tax rolls, it was criticized as a measure that aided the rich. The bill, signed by Pres. Nixon on Dec. 30, reduced the tax surcharge from 10% to 5% and extended it for six months, reduced the oil depletion allowance from 27.5% to 22%, closed numerous tax loopholes, and increased Social Security benefits by 15%.

II. Architecture
Arts and Music
Popular Entertainment
Publishing
Theater

Most of the year's theatrical excitement was generated on off-Broadway stages, where patrons saw an unusual number of works by black playwrights, including Lorraine Hansberry, LeRoi Jones, and Lonne Elder, III. *Ché,* a play about Guevara, the Latin American revolutionist, opened in New York on Mar. 22; two days later its cast and production staff were arrested on obscenity charges. *Oh! Calcutta!* by Kenneth Tynan was panned by critics but soon became one of the season's hits. In December seven cast members and the producer of its Los Angeles troupe were arrested for indecent exposure and lewdness. A strike by opera performers and musicians postponed the opening of the Metropolitan Opera's season until Dec. 29. In art, Pres. Lyndon B. Johnson presided over the groundbreaking ceremonies for the Joseph H. Hirshhorn Museum and Sculpture Garden in Washington, D.C., in January. The museum was to house the art collection Hirshhorn donated to the U.S. in 1966. Also in January, the New York Museum of Modern Art announced it had acquired the art collection of Gertrude Stein, valued at more than $6,000,000. In May Gov. Nelson A. Rockefeller of New York announced he had donated his collection of primitive art to the Metropolitan Museum of Art in New York City. In September, the Metropolitan announced that its late chairman, Robert Lehman, who had died on Aug. 9, had bequeathed his collection, valued at more than $100,000,000, to the museum. Other notables who died this year included Max Eastman, poet and author, Mar. 25, at 86; Judy Garland, singer and actress, June 22, at 47; Walter Gropius, founder of the Bauhaus school of design, July 5, at 86; Jack Kerouac, Beat novelist, Oct. 21, at 47; Frank Loesser, songwriter and composer, July 28, at 59; Giovanni Martinelli, tenor for the Metropolitan Opera for 33 years, Feb. 22, at 83; Ludwig Mies van der Rohe, architect, Aug. 17, at 83; Drew Pearson, columnist, Sept. 1, at 71, Ben Shahn, painter, Mar. 14, at 70; and Gladys Swarthout, mezzo-soprano for the Metropolitan Opera from 1929 to 1945, July 7, at 64.

Among **books published** this year was *Naked Came the Stranger* by Penelope Ashe, a randy novel actually written in collaboration by 24 writers of the Long Island, N.Y., newspaper *Newsday.* Deliberately written as trash, it nonetheless made the best-seller list. Other books published this year included *Ernest Hemingway: A Life Story* by Carlos Baker; *Bullet Park* by John Cheever, a novel; *Henry James: The Treacherous Years 1895–1901* by Leon Edel, volume four in Edel's biography of James; *In This House of Brede* by Rumer Godden, a novel of life in an English convent; *An Unfinished Woman* by Lillian Hellman, autobiography; *Ada* by Vladimir Nabokov, a novel; *The Godfather* by Mario Puzo; *Portnoy's Complaint* by Philip Roth, a novel that became the year's publishing sensation; *Slaughterhouse-Five* by Kurt Vonnegut, Jr., a novel dealing with the Allied bombing of Dresden during World War II; and *The Making of the President 1968* by Theodore White.

Jan 5: The **Bollingen Prize** for poetry was awarded jointly to John Berryman for his 1968 collection *His Toy, His Dream, His Rest* and to Karl Shapiro for his 1968 volume of *Selected Poems.*

Feb 8: The last issue of the *Saturday Evening Post* was published. The magazine was first published on Aug. 4, 1821, but Cyrus H. K. Curtis, after acquiring it in 1898, claimed it had been "founded in 1728 by B. Franklin." In the 1970s the magazine was resurrected and issued nine times a year. The new publication lacked many of its predecessor's most attractive qualities.

Apr 7: Obscenity laws prohibiting the private possession of obscene materials were ruled unconstitutional by the U.S. Supreme Court. Justice Thurgood Marshall wrote: "Our whole constitutional heritage rebels at the thought of giving government the power to control men's minds."

May 5: Pulitzer prizes were awarded for the following: fiction, *House Made of Dawn* by N. Scott Momaday; general nonfiction, *So Human an Animal* by René Dubos and *The Armies of the Night* by Norman Mailer; biography, *The Man from New York: John Quinn and His Friends* by B. L. Reid; history, *Origins of the Fifth Amendment* by Leonard W. Levy; poetry, *Of Being Numerous* by George Oppen; drama, *The Great White Hope* by Howard Sackler.

III. Business and Industry
Education
Philosophy and Religion
Science

The U.S. economy continued to show danger signs. Inflation had not been adequately checked, and a recession threatened. The GNP rose to $932,300,000,000, about a 7.7% increase. Averaged over the year, the Consumer Price Index rose a sharp 7.2%. In an effort to fight inflation, the Federal Reserve Board acted to impose monetary restraint; by June 9 the prime lending rate had reached a record high of 8.5%. In science, the flights of Apollo 11 and Apollo 12 to the moon dwarfed all other achievements. These manned missions, exploring for the first time a heavenly body other than Earth, caused 1969 to be popularly called the year of the moon. The year in education was marked by increased unrest on college campuses as students watched the government's failure to bring the Vietnam War to an end or to address domestic problems. Notables who died this year included John L. Lewis, president of the United Mine Workers from 1920 to 1960, June 11, at 79; Willy Ley, science writer, June 24, at 62; and Bishop James A. Pike, the controversial Episcopal leader who was charged with heresy in 1966 and left the church in Apr. 1969. Pike died, probably on Sept. 3, after his car broke down in the desert in Israel. He was 56.

Jan 16: The **first synthesized enzyme,** ribonuclease, was announced by Merck Laboratories and Rockefeller University. It was produced by teams of scientists working independently at the two institutions.

Jan 20: The first optical identification of a **pulsar,** a dense neutron star, was announced by astronomers at the University of Arizona, who located such a body in the Crab Nebula.

Jan 29: The federal deadline for **school desegregation** was extended 60 days for five southern school districts before federal funds would be cut off. This reprieve was widely interpreted as a sign that the Nixon administration was not committed to enforcing integration.

Feb 14: The longest **dock strike** to date, a 57-day strike of Port of New York dock workers, which had begun on Dec. 20, 1968, was ended with agreement on a new three-year contract. But 43,000 other members of the International Longshoremen's Association continued to strike, closing ports along the Atlantic and Gulf coasts until Apr. 2.

Feb 25: Mariner 6 was successfully launched toward Mars. On July 30 it passed within 2120 miles of the Martian surface, sending back 74 photographs.

Mar 3: Apollo 9, manned by James A. McDivitt, Russell L. Schweickart, and David R. Scott, was successfully launched into Earth orbit on a ten-day mission to test the Lunar Excursion Module (LEM). Apollo 9 splashed down on Mar. 13.

Mar 27: Mariner 7 was successfully launched toward Mars. On Aug. 5 it passed over the planet's south pole and sent back 91 photographs.

Apr 4: The world's **first totally artificial heart**—made of Dacron and plastic—was implanted in a human by Dr. Denton A. Cooley in Houston, Tex. The patient died Apr. 8.

May 15: In Berkeley, Calif., the makeshift **People's Park** established by students and area residents on property owned by the University of California was attacked by police and National Guardsmen. Shotguns and tear gas were used. Five days later a National Guard helicopter dropped a stinging chemical powder on demonstrators, including faculty members.

May 18: Apollo 10, the first manned mission to the moon, was successfully launched. Manned by Thomas P. Stafford, Eugene A. Cernan, and John W. Young, Apollo 10 went into lunar orbit. On May 22 the Lunar Excursion Module (LEM) descended to within ten miles of the moon's surface before returning to the Command Module. Apollo 10 returned to Earth and splashed down on May 26.

July 1: A federal **Truth-in-Lending Law** went into effect, requiring that charges for credit and loans be made clear to debtors.

July 3: It was announced that the Sept. 1969 **school desegregation deadline** would be enforced for all southern school districts except those with "bona fide educational and administrative problems." The next day, the National Education Association voted overwhelmingly to demand restoration of the deadline without modification.

July 16: Apollo 11, manned by Neil A. Armstrong, Edwin E. Aldrin, Jr., and Michael Collins, was successfully launched toward the moon. On July 20 Armstrong and Aldrin entered the Lunar Excursion Module *Eagle* and began the descent to a landing site near the Sea of Tranquillity. Touching down at 4:17 P.M. EDT, it became the first manned vehicle to land on the moon. Armstrong radioed "Houston, Tranquillity Base here. The *Eagle* has landed." About six and a half hours later, Armstrong became the first person to set foot on the moon, saying "That's one small step for [a] man, one giant leap for mankind." Aldrin joined Armstrong. The two spoke via telephone link to Pres. Nixon, set up experiments, and gathered samples of moon rocks during a two-hour moon walk. On July 21 *Eagle* lifted off and docked with the Command Module *Columbia*. Apollo 11 splashed down in the Pacific Ocean on July 24 at 12:50 P.M. EDT.

Aug 8: Pres. Nixon called for a guaranteed **minimum income** for families with children as part of a comprehensive reform of the welfare system.

Sep 14: The **first large vessel to navigate the Northwest Passage** was the SS *Manhattan,* an icebreaking tanker that sailed through the Prince of Wales Strait. The ship, the first commercial vessel to make the journey, had left Chester, Pa., on Aug. 24 and arrived at Point Barrow, Alaska, on Sept. 21. The project tested the feasibility of transporting crude oil by sea from northern Alaska. It cost the three sponsoring oil companies $40,000,000.

Oct 16: The **Nobel Prize for Physiology or Medicine** was awarded jointly to Dr. Max Delbruck of the California Institute of Technology, Dr. Alfred D. Hershey of the Carnegie Institute, Cold Spring Harbor, N.Y., and Dr. Salvador E. Luria of the Massachusetts Institute of Technology for their work on the genetic structure of viruses.

Oct 18: The use of **cyclamates,** artificial sweeteners, was banned by the Department of Health, Education, and Welfare. The ban was modified on Dec. 20 to permit use of specified amounts, except in soft drinks.

Oct 29: The Supreme Court ordered **immediate school desegregation** of the 33 Mississippi school districts for which the federal government had asked a delay. It was the first decision handed down by Chief Justice Warren Burger, who had been appointed by Pres. Nixon.

Oct 30: The **Nobel Prize in Physics** was awarded to Dr. Murray Gell-Mann of the California Institute of Technology for his contribution to the theory of elementary particles.

Nov 14: Apollo 12, manned by Charles Conrad, Jr., Richard F. Gordon, Jr., and Alan L. Bean, was launched on a lunar flight in rainy weather. Some 36.5 sec. after liftoff, it was hit by an electric charge, which briefly knocked out power in the spacecraft but not in the rocket. On Nov. 19 Conrad and Bean became the third and fourth humans to land on the moon when they brought down the *Intrepid,* their Lunar Excursion Module, on the plain of the Ocean of Storms. They made two moon walks, and the next day successfully blasted off to rejoin Gordon in the command ship, the *Yankee Clipper.* Apollo 12 splashed down on Nov. 24, only three miles from the carrier *Hornet.*

Nov 20: In the first step toward total **ban of DDT** by 1971, the U.S. Department of Agriculture ordered a halt to its use in residential areas.

Nov 22: Isolation of a single gene, the basic unit of heredity, was announced by scientists at Harvard University. Their feat promised to facilitate study of the mechanism of gene control.

Dec 2: The **Boeing 747,** which cost $21,400,000 to develop, made its first public flight, from Seattle, Wash., to New York City.

IV. Fashion
Folkways
Holidays
Social Issues and Crime
Sports

Major league baseball's 100th anniversary was a year of change and excitement. The National League added two teams, San Diego and Montreal, to its roster, and the American League added Kansas City and Seattle. Each league was split into divisions, and playoffs for league pennants were inaugurated. Players refused to report for spring training until owners increased their pension benefits. The outfields of six ball parks were shortened to make it easier to hit home runs and, in a further attempt to spark offensive play, the strike zone was narrowed and the pitcher's mound lowered. Mickey Mantle and Don Drysdale retired. The New York Mets astounded everyone with their first World Series victory. In soccer, the North American Soccer League continued to suffer organizational and financial growing pains. The league championship was won, on the basis of final team standings, by the Kansas City Spurs. In boxing, Joe Frazier twice defended his world heavyweight title, but Jimmy Ellis, recognized champion of the World Boxing Association, fought no championship bouts. In golf, the top money winners were Frank Beard, $175,223, and Carol Mann, $49,153. In fashion, bell-bottom pants were in vogue for women and men. Unisex fashions also became popular. People in the news who died this year included Vito Genovese, considered the head of U.S. organized crime, Feb. 14, at 71; Walter Hagen, five-time PGA title winner, Oct. 5, at 76; Rocky Marciano, former world heavyweight boxing champion, in a plane crash on Aug. 31, at 46; and Tom Zachary, pitcher for the Washington Senators, Jan. 24, at 72.

Jan 12: Super Bowl III was won by the New York Jets (AFL), who defeated the Baltimore Colts (NFL) 16 to 7 to gain the first AFL victory. On Dec. 31, 1968, the Jets had won the AFL championship by beating the Oakland Raiders 27 to 23. The same day the Colts had won the NFL title from the Cleveland Browns, 34 to 0.

Feb 7: The **first woman jockey** to race at a U.S. pari-mutuel track was Diana Crump. At Hialeah, Fla., she rode her first mount to a tenth-place finish in a field of 12.

Feb 22: The **first winning woman jockey** at a U.S. thoroughbred track was Barbara Jo Rubin, with a victory at Charles Town, W. Va.

Mar 22: The **NCAA basketball championship** was won by UCLA, sparked by center Lew Alcindor, defeating Purdue 97 to 92. Alcindor became the first player to win the tourney's Most Valuable Player award three years in a row. Later, the Milwaukee Bucks were reported to have paid $1,200,000 for Alcindor's services during the next five years.

Apr 23-May 5: The **NBA basketball championship** was won by the Boston Celtics, who beat the Los Angeles Lakers four games to three. Following this, his tenth victory in 11 years, Celtics player-coach Bill Russell announced his retirement.

Apr 30-May 7: The **ABA basketball championship** was won by the Oakland Oaks, who beat the Indiana Pacers four games to one.

May 10: Plans for the 1970 **pro football merger** of the AFL and NFL were completed. The new National Football League was to have two conferences of 13 teams each. The old NFL was renamed the National Football Conference (NFC), and three of its teams (Baltimore, Cleveland, and Pittsburgh) were shifted to the new American Football Conference.

June 15: The **U.S. Open golf tournament** was won by Orville Moody by a single stroke over Deane Beman, Al Geiberger, and Bob Rosburg.

June 21: A new **world pole vault record** was set by John Pennel, who cleared the bar at 17 ft., $10\frac{1}{2}$ in. at a meet at Sacramento, Calif.

Aug 9: Sharon Tate and four others were found, apparently murder victims, at the Los Angeles home of the actress. In December, Charles Manson and several members of his nomadic hippie cult were indicted for the murders.

Aug 13: Bowie Kuhn, temporary commissioner of baseball since February, was formally appointed to that post with a seven-year contract.

Aug 15-18: At the **Woodstock Music and Art Fair,** a weekend folk-rock festival, inadequate planning and bad weather threatened for a time to make a disaster area of the site, Max Yasgur's farm near Bethel. The crowd was estimated at 300,000 to 400,000, and many more failed to reach the fair when traffic jams clogged all roads leading to the Catskill area. Helicopters were pressed into service to supply food, water, and medicine. Rains made a quagmire of the festival grounds. Drugs circulated freely, and a number of people were treated for bad drug reactions. Almost miraculously, there were only three deaths. The police adopted a hands-off posture, and the youths present enjoyed themselves in a general spirit of peace, cooperation, and enthusiasm. While many treated the affair as an idyll, others expressed alarm at the incontrovertible evidence of a mass drug culture.

Aug 17: The **PGA golf tournament** was won by Ray Floyd. The tournament was marred by the behavior of civil rights demonstrators, who harassed Gary Player of South Africa on Aug. 16.

Sep 7-8: The **U.S. Open tennis singles championships** were won by Margaret Smith Court of Australia (Sept. 7) in the women's division and Rod Laver of Australia (Sept. 8) in the men's division. With his victory, Laver completed the grand slam of tennis by winning the top four international championships— the Australian, French, Wimbledon, and U.S. singles titles. Laver had won the grand slam once before, in 1962.

Sep 19-21: The **Davis Cup** was successfully defended by the U.S., defeating Rumania in five straight matches.

Sep 22: San Francisco Giants outfielder **Willie Mays hit his 600th home run,** becoming the only player other than Babe Ruth to reach that mark.

Oct 11-16: The **World Series** was won by the New York Mets (NL), who won four straight games from the Baltimore Orioles (AL) after losing the opener to the Orioles. The Mets had beaten the Atlanta Braves in three straight games to take the National League pennant. The Orioles had swept three games from the Minnesota Twins for the American League pennant.

Oct 18: A new **football field goal record** was set by Chester Marcol of Hillsdale College in Michigan, who kicked a 62-yard field goal, the longest on record for either amateur or pro football.

Dec 11-12: A new **world record decathlon score** of 8417 points was set by Bill Toomey at the Southern Pacific AAU meet at UCLA.

1970

I. Civil Rights
   Exploration and Settlement
   Government
   Statistics
   Wars

One of the major problems confronting Pres. Richard M. Nixon and the nation was the faltering economy. Pres. Nixon countered rising inflation and joblessness with fiscal austerity, marked by severe cuts in U.S. aerospace programs. He also proposed a coordinated plan to improve the natural environment. The president was disappointed in his second attempt to secure Senate approval of a so-called strict constructionist, and a southerner, to fill a vacant Supreme Court seat. Perhaps the most damaging event for the administration was the U.S. military invasion of Cambodia, which Pres. Nixon announced to the American people on Apr. 30. The incident sparked a nationwide shutdown of colleges and universities, violent demonstrations, and deaths on two college campuses. By late December U.S. troop strength in Vietnam had dropped to 340,000. By year's end, the total death toll of U.S. personnel had passed 44,000. Among notables who died this year were Brig. Gen. Benjamin O. Davis, Sr., the first black to attain the rank of general, Nov. 26, at 93; and Rep. L. Mendel Rivers, Democrat of South Carolina, chairman of the House Armed Services Committee, Dec. 28, at 65.

Jan 6: A **heroin-control agreement with France** was announced. It was aimed at halting the illegal production of the drug in France. The diplomatic agreement was part of an effort to halt heroin smuggling into the U.S.

Feb 14: Pres. Nixon, discussing **chemical warfare,** stated that the U.S. would not be the first to use lethal and incapacitating chemicals. He had previously renounced U.S. use of biological weapons.

Feb 26: The Army announced it would discontinue **surveillance of civilian demonstrations** and maintenance of files on civilians who might be involved in civil disturbances.

Mar 5: The **nuclear nonproliferation treaty,** ratified by the U.S., U.S.S.R., and 41 other nations, went into effect.

Apr 1: The 19th U.S. **Census** recorded a preliminary population count approaching 205,000,000.

Apr 8: The nomination of **G. Harrold Carswell** to the U.S. Supreme Court was rejected by the Senate after a prolonged debate. In 1969 the Senate had rejected the nomination of Clement F. Haynsworth, Jr., to the same vacant seat.

Apr 16: The second round of **Strategic Arms Limitation Talks** (SALT) opened in Vienna, Austria. The talks recessed on Aug. 14, both sides agreeing to resume in Helsinki, Finland, on Nov. 2. The third round (Nov. 2-Dec. 8) ended on a less optimistic note than the Vienna round, but a fourth round was scheduled to begin in Vienna on Mar. 15, 1971.

Apr 29: A military **invasion of Cambodia,** called an *incursion* by the White House, was launched by some 50,000 U.S. and South Vietnamese troops. The operation, aimed at destroying Vietcong and North Vietnamese sanctuaries, was announced by Pres. Nixon in a televised address on Apr. 30.

May 4: At **Kent State University** in Kent, Ohio, four students were killed when National Guard troops fired at some 600 antiwar demonstrators, some of whom had been throwing rocks at the guardsmen and taunting them.

May 9: An **antiwar rally in Washington,** D.C., drew some 100,000 protesters to the nation's capital. Similar demonstrations were held in many parts of the country.

May 12: The nomination of Judge **Harry A. Blackmun** of Minnesota to the Supreme Court was approved by the Senate.

May 15: At **Jackson State College** in Jackson, Miss., two students were killed when city and state police opened fire on demonstrators.

June 15: The claim of **conscientious objector status** on moral grounds alone was found constitutional by the Supreme Court in the case of *Welsh v. United States.* Previously such status was granted only on the basis of long-standing religious belief and training.

July 4: Honor America Day was observed in Washington, D.C., as thousands gathered to show support for the administration's war policies.

Sep 22: A bill authorizing **congressional representation for the District of Columbia** through a nonvoting delegate to the House of Representatives was signed by Pres. Nixon. The district had not been represented in Congress since 1875.

Oct 13: Angela Davis, former faculty member at UCLA, black militant, and self-proclaimed communist, was seized in New York City in connection with an Aug. 7 courtroom shootout in San Raphael, Calif., in which a judge and three others were killed. She was wanted on kidnaping, murder, and conspiracy charges.

Oct 15: The **Organized Crime Control Act** was signed by Pres. Nixon, who pledged "total war against organized crime."

Oct 21: The **Nobel Peace Prize** was awarded to Dr. Norman E. Borlaug for his work on high-yield grains to help Third World nations boost food production and overcome the cycle of hunger and poverty.

Nov 2: **Strategic Arms Limitation Talks** (SALT) between the U.S. and U.S.S.R. were resumed at Helsinki, Finland.

Nov 3: In **congressional elections** the Democrats lost four seats in the Senate but maintained a majority of 54–44, with two seats going to independent and Conservative candidates. In the House the Democrats picked up 12 seats for a 255–180 majority.

Nov 12: The **court-martial of Lt. William L. Calley, Jr.,** a key figure in the massacre of some 102 South Vietnamese civilians at My Lai (Songmy), began at Fort Benning, Ga.

Nov 27: Testimony that an antiwar group called the **East Coast Conspiracy to Save Lives** was planning to kidnap a high government official and blow up the underground heating system for federal buildings in Washington, D.C., was given to a Senate subcommittee by FBI director J. Edgar Hoover. Hoover named Philip and Daniel Berrigan, both priests, as leaders in the plot. The government official was later identified as presidential adviser Henry Kissinger.

Dec 2: The **Environmental Protection Agency,** established in July by executive order, was activated. William D. Ruckelshaus was confirmed the same day as its director.

Dec 21: Reduction of the **voting age** in national elections to 18 years was ruled constitutional by the Supreme Court.

Dec 23: Plans for a speedy **phase-out of herbicide operations** in Indochina were announced by the Nixon administration.

II. Architecture
Arts and Music
Popular Entertainment
Publishing
Theater

The Broadway theater season was marked by the openings of a few outstanding serious plays, accompanied by an increased interest by both producers and theatergoers in comedies and musicals. The motion picture industry, suffering a financial pinch, reduced its offerings by 25%, but presented viewers with a number of excellent films, including *Catch-22, The Graduate, Patton,* and the rock documentaries *Woodstock,* which recounted the 1969 festival in upstate New York, and *Gimme Shelter,* about the ultimately disastrous 1969 U.S. tour of the Rolling Stones. This year the Metropolitan Museum of Art celebrated its centennial, and George Balanchine, director of the New York City Ballet, celebrated his 50th anniversary as a choreographer. The art world saw another year of record art prices. At the Parke-Bernet Galleries in New York City, Vincent van Gogh's *Le Cyprès et l'Arbe en Fleur* fetched $1,300,000, a record for a van Gogh work. On Nov. 27 Wildenstein Gallery of New York City paid $5,544,000, a record price for a single painting, for a Velázquez portrait. On May 12, 1971, the painting was acquired by the Metropolitan Museum of Art in New York City. On Dec. 10 Parke-Bernet sold Thomas Eakins' *Cowboys in the Badlands* for $210,000, a record for a U.S. painting. Notables who died this year included John Dos Passos, the novelist, Sept. 28, at 74; Erle Stanley Gardner, creator of Perry Mason, Mar. 11, at 80; Reuben Lucius "Rube" Goldberg, whose zany drawings of impossibly complex devices gave birth to the phrase *Rube Goldberg contraption,* Dec. 7, at 87; John Gunther, the author, May 29, at 68; James Marshall "Jimi" Hendrix, rock guitarist, Sept. 18, at 27; Richard Hofstadter, historian, Oct. 24, at 54; Janis Joplin, rock singer, Oct. 4, at 27; Gypsy Rose Lee, real name Rose Louise Hovick, celebrated striptease artist and author, Apr. 26, at 56; John O'Hara, author, Apr. 11, at 65; Erich Maria Remarque, German-born novelist, Sept. 25, at 72; Mark Rothko, painter, Feb. 25, at 66; and George Szell, conductor of the Cleveland Orchestra from 1946, July 30, at 73.

Among **books published** this year was *Everything You Always Wanted to Know About Sex* by Dr. David Reuben, just one of a number of books about sex that became best sellers, including *The Sensuous Woman* by "J.," *Sexual Politics* by Kate Millett, a feminist treatment of the battle of the sexes, and *Human Sexual Inadequacy* by the research team of Dr. William H. Masters and Virginia Johnson. Other books published this year included *Mr. Sammler's Planet* by Saul Bellow, a novel; *Ball Four* by Jim Bouton, which took the baseball establishment to task; *Deliverance* by James Dickey, the poet's first novel; *Islands in the*

Stream, a posthumous novel by Ernest Hemingway; *You Might as Well Live: The Life and Times of Dorothy Parker* by John Keats; *The Art of His Life* by Jay Martin, a biography of Nathanael West; *Culture and Commitment* by Margaret Mead; *Zelda* by Nancy Milford, a biography of Zelda Fitzgerald; *The Greening of America* by Charles A. Reich; *Hard Times, An Oral History of the Great Depression* by Studs Terkel; *Bech: A Book* by John Updike, a novel; and *QB VII* by Leon Uris, a novel.

May 4: Pulitzer prizes were awarded for the following: fiction, *Collected Stories* by Jean Stafford; biography, *Huey Long* by T. Harry Williams; history, *Present at the Creation: My Years in the State Department* by Dean G. Acheson; general nonfiction, *Gandhi's Truth: On the Origins of Militant Non-violence* by Erik H. Erikson; poetry, *Untitled Subjects* by Richard Howard.

Oct 11: Natalia Makarova, the prima ballerina with the Leningrad Kirov Ballet who defected from the U.S.S.R. in September, joined the American Ballet Theater.

Dec 23: The north tower of the **World Trade Center** in New York City was topped out, making it the tallest building in the world. At 1350 ft., it was 100 ft. taller than the Empire State Building.

III. Business and Industry
Education
Philosophy and Religion
Science

The word *recession* crept back into the public vocabulary. The economic policies of Pres. Richard Nixon sought a controlled contraction in the economy, accompanied by reduced industrial output and temporarily higher unemployment to break the inflationary spiral that began some three years earlier. By year's end it was apparent that the brakes had been applied too strongly. On Dec. 4 it was announced that unemployment had risen to 5.8%. Officials began to move to reduce interest rates as a means of stimulating the economy. The space program suffered major cuts in the budget squeeze, and some of the best-known astronauts left the program to pursue other careers. NASA was hurt further by the near-disastrous Apollo 13 lunar mission in April. In education, the year was marked by explosive campus unrest. Pres. Nixon established a Commission on Campus Unrest, which reported that student disorders reflected student opposition to U.S. military activities,

concern over racial injustice, and general dissatisfaction with American life. The commission urged Pres. Nixon to use his leadership to bring the nation together. Notables who died this year included Richard Cardinal Cushing of Boston, Nov. 2, at 75; Joseph Wood Krutch, naturalist and author, May 22, at 76; Walter Reuther, president of the United Auto Workers, who died with his wife and four others in a plane crash, May 9, at 62; John T. Scopes, Dayton, Tenn., central figure in the so-called Scopes monkey trial in 1925, Oct. 21, at 70; and Blanche Stuart Scott, a pioneer woman aviator, Jan. 12, at 84.

Jan 5: Joseph Yablonski, unsuccessful candidate for president of the United Mine Workers, was found murdered in his home along with his wife and daughter.

Jan 14: A Feb. 1, 1970, **deadline for desegregation** of public schools in Alabama, Florida, Georgia, Louisiana, Mississippi, and Tennessee was issued by the Supreme Court, overruling the Sept. 1970 deadline set by a lower court.

Feb 4: An **ion propulsion engine** was launched into orbit aboard the satellite Sert 2 (for Space Electric Rocket Test). The engine was burned continuously for six months.

Feb 18: The **Chicago Seven** were acquitted of conspiracy charges in connection with riots during the 1968 Democratic convention in Chicago. Five were found guilty of crossing a state line with intent to incite a riot. On Feb. 20 they were sentenced to five-year prison terms.

Mar 16: The *New English Bible* was published in its entirety. Translated directly from ancient texts, it was the work of British scholars of the major Protestant churches, who were assisted by a panel of literary experts. It was the subject of debate because its language departed radically from the rich sonorities of the King James Bible.

Mar 18: The **first major postal workers' strike** in U.S. history began. On Mar. 23 Pres. Nixon ordered the National Guard to help alleviate mail delays. The strike ended on Mar. 25.

Apr 1: A **bill banning cigarette advertising** on radio and television, effective Jan. 1, 1971, was signed by Pres. Nixon.

Apr 11: Apollo 13 was successfully launched, carrying astronauts James A. Lovell, Jr., John L. Swigert, Jr., and Fred W. Haise, Jr., toward a lunar landing. The mission seemed to be going perfectly, but on Apr. 13 a tank of liquid oxygen exploded, damaging the spacecraft. The crippled spacecraft continued to the moon, circled it and returned to Earth on Apr. 17. Months later scientists reported that faulty design had caused the problem.

June 4: Use of the drug **L-dopa** for treatment of Parkinson's disease was approved by the Food and Drug Administration.

July 3: No **deaths from polio** were recorded in 1969, the National Communicable Disease Center reported. It was the first year without fatalities since record-keeping began in 1955.

Aug 11: The Rev. **Daniel J. Berrigan,** a Jesuit priest who was a fugitive for four months, was seized by FBI agents. Berrigan, his brother the Rev. Philip F. Berrigan, and seven others had been convicted of burning draft records at Catonsville, Md., in 1968. They were known collectively as the Catonsville Nine.

Sep 6: A **TWA airliner was hijacked** to Jordan by Palestinian terrorists. On Sept. 12 it was blown up along with two other western-owned airplanes.

Sep 30: The *New American Bible* was published in its entirety for the first time. It was the first Roman Catholic-sponsored translation in English created directly from original sources.

Oct 15: The **Nobel Prize in Physiology or Medicine** was awarded jointly to Dr. Julius Axelrod of the National Institute of Mental Health in Bethesda, Md., Sir Bernard Katz of Great Britain, and Ulf von Euler of Sweden for their study of the chemistry of nerves in controlling the vascular system.

Oct 16: The **Nobel Prize in Economics** was awarded to Paul A. Samuelson of MIT. It was the second such award, and the first won by an American.

Nov 18: Linus Pauling, the Nobel Prize-winning scientist, reported that high doses of vitamin C could ward off the common cold and the flu. Other scientists held that such doses given over a long period of time could be harmful.

Dec 31: The **National Air Quality Control Act** was signed by Pres. Nixon. It tightened air pollution standards and penalties and called for a 90% reduction in pollution from automobile exhausts by 1975.

IV. Fashion
   Folkways
   Holidays
   Social Issues and Crime
   Sports

The year in sports was marked by unrest. Curt Flood, of the St. Louis Cardinals, objected to being traded to the Philadelphia Phillies and brought an antitrust suit against organized baseball over the so-called reserve clause. The sports year was also marked by ever-increasing salaries for top athletes and record cash purses for major sports events. In golf, the top money winners were Lee Trevino, $157,037, and Kathy Whitworth, $30,235. In boxing, Joe Frazier was recognized as the world heavyweight champion, and Muhammad Ali, who had been stripped of the title in 1967, made a comeback with victories over Jerry Quarry (Oct. 26) and Oscar Bonavena (Dec. 7). In soccer the North American Soccer League (NASL) split into two divisions and added New York City and Toronto franchises for the 1971 season. In football, the American Football League added three franchises and became the American Conference of the National Football League. The old NFL roster was reorganized into the National Conference, each conference organized into three divisions. Winners of division playoffs in each conference would go to the Super Bowl. In fashion, many designers pushed the midi style, which dropped the hemline to mid-calf. Youth's influence in dress styles was reflected in such apparel as tie-dyed garments, granny dresses, and secondhand military attire. Americans mourned the passing of Charles "Sonny" Liston, 38, heavyweight boxing champion from 1962 to 1964, about Dec. 28; Vincent Thomas "Vince" Lombardi, celebrated coach of the Green Bay Packers, Sept. 3, at 57; and John J. "Johnny" Murphy, former pitcher for the New York Yankees, Jan. 14, at 61.

Jan 11: Super Bowl IV was won by the Kansas City Chiefs (AFL), who defeated the Minnesota Vikings (NFL) 23 to 7. On Jan. 4 the Chiefs had won the AFL championship by beating the Oakland Raiders 17 to 7. The same day the Vikings took the NFL title by beating the Cleveland Browns 27 to 7.

Feb 16: The **world heavyweight boxing championship** was awarded to Joe Frazier, who knocked out Jimmy Ellis in the fifth round in New York City.

Mar 21: The **NCAA basketball championship** was won for the fourth straight time by UCLA, which defeated Jacksonville University 80 to 69.

Apr 24-May 8: The **NBA basketball championship** was won for the first time in 24 years by the New York Knickerbockers, who beat the Los Angeles Lakers four games to three.

May 15-25: The **ABA basketball championship** was won by the Indiana Pacers, who beat the Los Angeles Stars four games to two.

June 18-20: A new **world 440-yard hurdles record** of 48.8 sec. was set at the NCAA outdoor championships by Ralph Mann of Brigham Young University.

June 21: The **U.S. Open golf tournament** was won by Tony Jacklin of Great Britain, beating Dave Hill by five strokes to become the first Englishman to win the tournament in 50 years.

July 4: At the **Wimbledon** tennis championships, the women's doubles title was won by Billie Jean King and Rosemary Casals for the third time in four years. Casals teamed with Ilie Nastase of Rumania to win the mixed doubles title.

Aug 16: The **PGA golf tournament** was won by Dave Stockton, who topped Arnold Palmer and Bob Murphy by two strokes.

Aug 29-31: The **Davis Cup** international tennis challenge round was won by the U.S., which swept West Germany in five straight matches.

Sep 2-13: The **U.S. Open tennis singles championships** were won by Ken Rosewall of Australia in the men's division and Margaret Court of Australia in the women's division.

Sep 7: A new **world record for winning mounts** was set by Willie Shoemaker, who broke Johnny Longden's record by winning his 6033rd race, at Del Mar, Calif.

Sep 12: Dr. **Timothy Leary,** the former educator who became a leading proponent of LSD use, escaped from prison near San Luis Obispo, Calif., and fled to Algeria.

Sep 15-28: The **America's Cup** was successfully defended by the U.S. yacht *Intrepid,* which beat the British challenger *Gretel II* four races to one. In the second race *Gretel II* was disqualified because it collided with *Intrepid* at the beginning of the race, the first such forfeit in the yachting classic's history.

Oct 2: Fourteen members of the **Wichita State University football team** were killed when their chartered plane crashed in the Rocky Mts.

Oct 10-15: The 67th **World Series** was won by the Baltimore Orioles (AL), defeating the Cincinnati Reds four games to one. On Oct. 5 the Orioles had clinched the American League pennant by sweeping the Minnesota Twins in three games; the Reds had taken the National League pennant by beating the Pittsburgh Pirates three straight.

Oct 23: A new **land speed record** of 622.407 mph was set by Gary Gabelich of Long Beach, Calif. He drove a rocket-powered car at the Bonneville Salt Flats in Utah.

Nov 8: A new **football field goal record** of 63 yards was set by Tom Dempsey of the New Orleans Saints in a two-point win over the Detroit Lions.

Nov 14: Forty-three players and coaches of the **Marshall University football team** died when their chartered plane crashed in Kenova, W. Va.

1971

I. Civil Rights
Exploration and Settlement
Government
Statistics
Wars

Pres. Richard Nixon announced in July that he would visit the People's Republic of China and the U.S.S.R. in 1972. The indication that the U.S. and China would move toward normalizing relations profoundly effected international relations. The U.S. continued to disengage from combat in Vietnam, and by December U.S. troop strength in South Vietnam had dropped to 184,000. Opposition to continued American involvement there made itself felt in Washington, D.C., in March, when a bomb planted by the radical Weather Underground exploded in the Capitol. In May thousands of people protesting the war were arrested by police when they attempted to shut down the government by blocking all traffic in the city. In other war-related events, Lt. William L. Calley, Jr. was convicted for his role in the My Lai massacre of 1968. His superiors were exonerated, prompting some to claim Calley was being used as a scapegoat. Pres. Nixon sought funds for the treatment and rehabilitation of Vietnam era veterans who suffered from drug addiction. As the 1972 presidential election approached, Pres. Nixon was faced with challenges for the Republican nomination from Rep. Paul N. McCloskey, Jr., of California, a liberal who sought more rapid deescalation of the war, and Rep. John M. Ashbrook of Ohio, a conservative campaigning to cut deficit spending and eliminate wage and price controls introduced in August. Eleven Democrats were registered for Democratic primaries. The Senate confirmed the nomination of Lewis F. Powell and William H. Rehnquist to the Supreme Court. Notables who died this year included Dean Acheson, former secretary of state, Oct. 12, at 78; Ralph Bunche, diplomat and winner of the 1950 Nobel Peace Prize, Oct. 11, at 67; Thomas E. Dewey, former governor of New York, Mar. 16, at 68; Adm. Thomas C. Hart, USN (ret.), commander in chief of the U.S. Pacific Fleet when Pearl Harbor was bombed, July 4, at 94; Audie Murphy, the most decorated U.S. soldier of World War II, May 28, at 46; Sen. Richard B. Russell, Democrat of Georgia, Jan. 21, at 73; Arthur B. Springarn, president of the NAACP from 1940–1965,

Dec. 1, at 93; and Whitney M. Young, Jr., head of the National Urban League from 1961, Mar. 11, at 49.

Jan 12: The Rev. **Philip F. Berrigan** was indicted with five others for conspiring to kidnap presidential adviser Henry Kissinger and to bomb the heating systems of federal buildings in Washington, D.C. Berrigan was serving a sentence for burning draft cards.

Feb 9: An **earthquake** in southern California caused more than $500,000,000 in damage and killed 65 people, including 47 at a Veterans Administration hospital in Sylmar, near San Fernando.

Feb 11: A **treaty banning nuclear weapons from the seabed** beyond the standard 12-mile coastal limit was signed by the U.S. and 62 other nations at ceremonies in Washington, D.C., London, and Moscow. It was to become effective after ratification by 22 nations.

Feb 24: The Supreme Court ruled that **illegally obtained evidence,** generally inadmissible in a criminal trial, could be used to contradict a defendant's voluntary testimony. The decision marked a significant alteration of the Miranda ruling of 1966.

Mar 1: In Washington, D.C., the **Capitol was bombed** by the radical Weather Underground. The device, planted in a restroom in the Senate wing, caused some $300,000 in damage but no injuries.

Mar 8: Draft exemption for conscientious objectors, the Supreme Court ruled, must be based on opposition to all war, not just to the Vietnam War.

Mar 15: The fourth round of **Strategic Arms Limitation Talks** (SALT) between the U.S. and U.S.S.R. began in Vienna, Austria. On May 28 the conference ended with an agreement to resume talks on July 8 in Helsinki, Finland.

Mar 29: Lt. **William L. Calley, Jr.,** was convicted of the premeditated murder of 22 people during the 1968 massacre of South Vietnamese civilians at My Lai. On Mar. 31 he was sentenced to life imprisonment. Exoneration on Sept. 22 of Calley's superior, Capt. Ernest L. Medina, coupled with the earlier dropping of charges against 11 superior officers, fueled the public outcry that Calley was being used as a scapegoat. On Apr. 1 Pres. Nixon ordered Calley released from the stockade and moved to his quarters at Fort Benning, Ga., pending the appeal process. Nixon announced that he would review Calley's case before sentence was carried out. On Aug. 20 Calley's sentence was reduced to 20 years' imprisonment.

May 3: In what was called the **Mayday antiwar protest** in Washington, D.C., the culmination of several weeks of antiwar activities in the nation's capital, thousands of demonstrators were arrested and confined when they tried to stop government activities by blocking traffic in the city. Most charges were dropped.

June 23: Claude E. Vealey confessed to the Dec. 1969 murders of dissident United Mine Workers leader **Joseph A. Yablonski** and his wife and daughter. In a Washington, Pa., court hearing, he stated he would testify against four others indicted for the murders, including Aubran W. Martin and Paul E. Gilly. On Nov. 12 Martin was convicted; he was sentenced to death the next day. Gilly was convicted on Mar. 1, 1972, and was sentenced to death the following day.

June 30: The **Twenty-sixth Amendment** to the U.S. Constitution, lowering the voting age for all elections to 18, went into effect when Ohio became the 38th state to ratify it.

July 8: The fifth round of the **Strategic Arms Limitation Talks** (SALT) convened in Helsinki, Finland. The talks recessed on Sept. 23 with unofficial reports that the U.S. and U.S.S.R. were approaching agreement on limitation of antiballistic missile (ABM) systems. The talks resumed in Vienna on Nov. 15. On Sept. 30 the two powers signed agreements on ways to reduce the risk of accidental nuclear war.

July 15: A projected **presidential visit to China** before May 1972 was announced by Pres. Nixon. He would be the first president to be received by a Chinese government.

Aug 2: Admission of the People's Republic of China to the UN would not be opposed by the U.S., it was announced. The U.S. also stated it would not agree to depriving Nationalist China of its representation. On Oct. 25 the UN General Assembly voted to admit the People's Republic of China and expel Nationalist China.

Sep 4: In the **worst single airplane crash** to date in the U.S., 111 people were killed when an Alaska Airlines Boeing 727 crashed into a mountain west of Juneau, Alaska.

Sep 9-13: A **prison riot at Attica** State Correctional Facility, Attica, N.Y., led to the deaths of 43 people. Nine prison guards held hostage and 28 prisoners were killed when some 1500 state police and other law enforcement officers staged an air and ground assault to end the uprising.

Sep 26: Japanese Emperor **Hirohito** was greeted by Pres. Nixon at Anchorage, Alaska, in the first foreign trip ever undertaken by a Japanese emperor. It was also the first meeting of a U.S. president and a Japanese monarch.

Dec 6: The nomination of **Lewis F. Powell, Jr.,** to the Supreme Court was approved by the Senate. Powell succeeded Justice Hugo L. Black, who resigned on Sept. 17 and died a week later.

Dec 10: The nomination of **William H. Rehnquist** to the Supreme Court was approved by the Senate.

Rehnquist succeeded Justice John M. Harlan, who had resigned on Sept. 23.

Dec 26-30: Massive air bombardment of military installations in North Vietnam resumed. The heaviest attack since the Nov. 1968 bombing halt was conducted by U.S. Navy and Air Force planes.

II. Architecture
   ## Arts and Music
   ## Popular Entertainment
   ## Publishing
   ## Theater

The Broadway season offered few new shows, and museums reduced their hours of operation. The big publishing story of the year was the leak to *The New York Times* of a top secret Pentagon study of U.S. involvement in Vietnam. The series of excerpts that came to be known as the Pentagon Papers prompted heated debate over the newspaper's right to publish sensitive documents and the federal government's need to protect the documents. The motion picture industry continued to experience hard times as fewer pictures were produced by the major studios, even though more independent productions were filmed on location throughout the country. Film makers reported that sexually explicit films, which had been the rage for a time, were losing their box office appeal. Americans mourned the deaths of Duane Allman, rock guitarist, Oct. 29, at 24; Louis Daniel "Satchmo" Armstrong, the gravel-voiced jazz singer and trumpeter, July 6, at 71; Margaret Bourke-White, internationally renowned photographer, Aug. 27, at 67; Walter Van Tilburg Clark, author of *The Ox-Bow Incident* (1940), Nov. 10, at 62; Rockwell Kent, artist and illustrator, Mar. 13, at 88; Ted Lewis, real name Theodore L. Friedman, band leader and entertainer, Aug. 25, at 80; Harold Lloyd, comic genius of the silent film, Mar. 8, at 77; James Douglas "Jim" Morrison, rock singer, July 3, at 27; Ogden Nash, poet, known best for his humorous verse, May 19, at 68; Elmo Roper, pioneer pollster, Apr. 30, at 70; and Igor Stravinsky, the Russian-born composer, Apr. 6, at 88.

Among **books published** this year was *The Vantage Point* by former Pres. Lyndon Johnson. In these memoirs, Johnson recalled the events of his years in the White House and discussed many of the details that were revealed this year by *The New York Times* in the Pentagon Papers scandal. Other books published this year included *The Exorcist* by William Peter Blatty, a shocker that was the basis for an enormously successful motion picture; *Bury My Heart at Wounded Knee* by Dee Brown, an account of the virtual destruction of American Indian society between 1860 and 1890; *The Book of Daniel* by E. L. Doctorow, a novel based on the Rosenberg spy case; *Eleanor and Franklin: The Story of Their Relationship Based on Eleanor Roosevelt's Private Papers* by Joseph P. Lash; *The Tenants* by Bernard Malamud, a novel; *Wonderland,* a novel by Joyce Carol Oates; *Honor Thy Father* by Gay Talese, a firsthand account of the life of an organized crime family; *The Other* by Thomas Tryon, a novel of the supernatural; *Rabbit Redux* by John Updike, a sequel to *Rabbit Run* (1960); *Meet Me in the Green Glen* by Robert Penn Warren, a novel; and *The Winds of War* by Herman Wouk, a massive novel of the early years of World War II.

Jan 10: The **Bollingen Prize** for poetry was awarded jointly to Richard Wilbur and to Mona Van Duyn for their contributions to American poetry.

May 3: Pulitzer prizes were awarded for the following: biography, *Robert Frost: The Years of Triumph, 1915–1938* by Lawrence R. Thompson; history, *Roosevelt, The Soldier of Freedom* by James McGregor Burns; general nonfiction, *The Rising Sun* by John Toland; poetry, *The Carriers of Ladders* by W.S. Merwin; drama, *The Effect of Gamma Rays on Man-in-the-Moon Marigolds* by Paul Zindel.

June 13: The first installment of what came to be known as the **Pentagon Papers,** excerpts from the Pentagon study *History of the U.S. Decision-making Process on Vietnam Policy,* was published in *The New York Times.* Publication of the documents was halted in federal court, but the decision was reversed on June 30 by the Supreme Court. On June 28 a former Defense Department official, Dr. Daniel Ellsberg, admitted that he had given the documents to the *Times.* He was subsequently indicted for theft and possession of secret documents.

July 21: *Fiddler on the Roof* became the longest-running Broadway musical, its 2845 performances surpassing the record set by *Hello, Dolly!*

III. Business and Industry
   ## Education
   ## Philosophy and Religion
   ## Science

Projected GNP figures were off, unemployment was up to 6%, and inflation rose above 4% for the year. For the first time in the twentieth century imports exceeded exports. In August Pres. Richard M. Nixon announced a plan to control wages and prices, coupled with devaluation of the dollar to improve the U.S. balance of trade. In education, the National Science Foundation reported federal aid to colleges and universities was the lowest since 1966 and forecast an oversupply of scientists and engineers with Ph.D. degrees by 1980. The National Education Association reported that teacher demand was the lowest in 20 years. Despite serious cuts in NASA's budget, the U.S. completed two more manned lunar landings and launched Mariner 9 on its way to a Mars orbit. Late in the year Mariner sent back the first of many photographs of the surface of the planet. Back on Earth, underwater research produced a practical system for the recovery of manganese nodules from the ocean bottom, and at the California Institute of Technology, scientists reported they had successfully tested Albert Einstein's General Theory of Relativity. Notables who died this year included Philo T. Farnsworth, pioneer in the development of television, Mar. 11, at 64; Reinhold Niebuhr, Protestant theologian, June 1, at 78; James Cash Penney, founder of the J. C. Penney department store chain, Feb. 12, at 95; and David Sarnoff, a pioneer in television broadcasting, Dec. 12, at 80.

Jan 25: In its first decision on **sex discrimination in hiring** practices, the Supreme Court upheld the equal hiring provisions of the 1964 Civil Rights Act by ruling that businesses could not deny employment to women with preschool children unless they applied the same hiring criteria to men.

Jan 31: Apollo 14, manned by Alan B. Shepard, Jr., Edgar D. Mitchell, and Stuart A. Roosa, was successfully launched. After initial problems in docking the lunar and command modules, the mission proceeded to a successful lunar landing (Feb. 5–6). Apollo 14 returned to Earth on Feb. 9, bringing back more than 100 lbs. of rock for study.

Mar 2: William A. "Tony" Boyle, president of the United Mine Workers, was indicted on charges of conspiracy, embezzlement, and illegal campaign contributions.

Mar 29: Development of an apparently effective **serum hepatitis vaccine** for children was announced by the New York University Research Center.

Apr 14: Pres. Nixon announced the lifting of a **trade embargo** with the People's Republic of China, which had existed for more than 20 years.

Apr 20: The use of **school busing** to end racial segregation in public school systems was ruled constitutional by the Supreme Court.

May 1: Amtrak, also known as the National Railroad Passenger Corporation, began operation. It was to provide service by 182 trains to more than 300 cities.

May 8: Mariner 8 fell into the Atlantic Ocean after the launch vehicle's second-stage booster failed.

May 30: Mariner 9 was successfully launched from Cape Kennedy, Fla., toward a Mars orbit on Nov. 12.

After achieving orbit, it began to send back spectacular pictures of the Martian surface as well as shots of the two moons of Mars.

June 28: State programs to underwrite **nonreligious instruction in parochial schools** were ruled unconstitutional by the Supreme Court.

July 1: The **U.S. Postal Service,** the semi- independent corporation organized to replace the Post Office Department, was officially inaugurated at the White House in Washington, D.C.

July 26: Apollo 14, manned by astronauts David R. Scott, James B. Irwin, and Alfred M. Worden, was successfully launched. Scott and Irwin were the fourth team to land on the moon (July 30-Aug. 2). They traveled 17.3 miles on the lunar surface using a four-wheeled lunar rover and collected what appeared to be a fragment of the moon's original crust. Nicknamed Genesis rock, it was later found to be about 4,000,000,000 years old. Apollo 14 splashed down in the Pacific on Aug. 7.

Aug 2: A federal bailout of Lockheed Aircraft Corporation was authorized by Congress, which passed by a narrow margin a $250,000,000 loan guarantee for the aerospace giant's TriStar airbus program. The guarantee was officially approved by the administration on Sept. 9.

Sep 29: The **Orbiting Solar Observatory VII** was launched to study a solar flare through x-ray observations.

Oct 14: The **Nobel Prize in Physiology or Medicine** was awarded to Dr. Earl W. Sutherland of Vanderbilt University for his work with hormones.

Oct 15: The **Nobel Prize in Economics** was awarded to Simon Kuznets, formerly a professor at Harvard University, who pioneered the use of the gross national product as a means of measuring economic output.

IV. Fashion
Folkways
Holidays
Social Issues and Crime
Sports

Sports and politics found common ground this year when a team of U.S. table tennis players was invited to China in April for an impromptu tournament. They lost to the Chinese players but their presence in China, combined with the relaxation of U.S. foreign policy toward the People's Republic, led many to speak hopefully of an era of Ping-Pong diplomacy. This year Billie Jean King became the first woman athlete in history to win more than $100,000 in a year. In golf the top money winners were Jack Nicklaus, $244,490, and Kathy Whitworth, $41,182. Lee Trevino became the fourth U.S. golfer to win both the U.S. and British Open tournaments in the same year. In fashion, skirt lengths settled at just below the knee for daytime and just above the ankle for evening. Both blue denim and leather were popular, and short-shorts were jazzed up and renamed *hot pants*. A fad for 1940s styles reflected nostalgia for what some thought of as a simpler time. Among those who died this year were Robert T. "Bobby" Jones, great golfer, Dec. 18, at 69; Nathan Leopold, who was convicted with Richard Loeb for the "thrill murder" of Bobby Franks in 1924, Aug. 28, at 66; and Joseph Valachi, the crime figure who testified in Senate hearings in 1963 about the workings of Cosa Nostra, Apr. 3, at 66.

Jan 17: **Super Bowl V** was won in the last five seconds by the Baltimore Colts (AFC), who beat the Dallas Cowboys (NFC) 16–13 on a field goal by Jim O'Brien. On Jan. 3 the Colts had beaten the Oakland Raiders 27–17 to win the AFC championship and the Cowboys had topped the San Francisco 49ers 17–10 for the NFC championship.

Jan 25: **Charles Manson** was convicted, along with Susan Atkins, Leslie Van Houten, and Patricia Krenwinkel, of the 1969 murders of actress Sharon Tate and six others. On Apr. 19 they were sentenced to death. On Oct. 21 Charles Watson was also sentenced to death for the murders.

Feb 28: The **PGA golf tournament** was won by Jack Nicklaus, beating Billy Casper by three strokes.

Mar 8: The **world heavyweight boxing championship** was defended by Joe Frazier in a unanimous 15-round decision over Muhammad Ali. The fight, one of the richest sports events in history, grossed nearly $20,000,000, largely through receipts from closed-circuit television.

Mar 27: The **NCAA basketball championship** was won for the fifth straight year by UCLA, who beat Villanova 68 to 62.

Apr 8: The first legal **off-track betting** (OTB) system in the U.S. went into operation in New York City.

Apr 30: The **NBA basketball championship** was won by the Milwaukee Bucks in a four-game sweep over the Baltimore Bullets.

May 18: The **ABA basketball championship** was won by the Utah Stars, who beat the Kentucky Colonels four games to three.

June 21: The **U.S. Open golf tournament** was won by Lee Trevino, who beat Jack Nicklaus by two strokes in a playoff. On July 10 Trevino won the British Open,

becoming the fourth U.S. player to win both championships in the same year.

June 28: **Muhammad Ali** won a four-year legal battle when the Supreme Court overturned his 1967 conviction for draft evasion.

July 3: At the **Wimbledon** tennis championships, the women's doubles title was won for the second year in a row by Billie Jean King and Rosemary Casals. King teamed with Owen Davidson of Australia to win the mixed doubles title.

Aug 21: **George Jackson,** 29, one of three black convicts known as the Soledad Brothers after being charged with the murder of a guard at Soledad prison in California, was killed while attempting to escape from San Quentin. Two convicts and three guards were also killed in the attempted mass breakout. Jackson's prison writings had been collected in *Soledad Brother* (1970).

Sep 5-15: The **U.S. Open tennis singles championships** were won by Stan Smith in the men's division and Billie Jean King in the women's division. It was the first time in 16 years both titles were won by U.S. players.

Sep 21: The **Washington Senators,** often fondly described by baseball fans as "first in war, first in peace, and last in the American League," would move to Texas for the 1972 season, it was announced. The team would be renamed the Texas Rangers.

Oct 8-11: The **Davis Cup** international tennis challenge round was won by the U.S., defeating Rumania three matches to two. This year it was decided to abolish the challenge round. Beginning in 1972, the defending team would be required to play through the entire competition.

Oct 9-17: The 68th annual **World Series** was won by the underdog Pittsburgh Pirates (NL), who beat the Baltimore Orioles (AL) four games to three. On Oct. 5 Baltimore had completed a three-game sweep over the Oakland Athletics to take the American League championship. On Oct. 6 the Pirates had clinched the National League pennant, beating the San Francisco Giants three games to one.

Oct 26: **Bobby Fischer** became the first U.S. chess player to make his way through the elimination matches for the world chess championship. Fischer defeated Tigran Petrosian of the U.S.S.R. in Buenos Aires, Argentina, thus qualifying for competition against Boris Spassky, the world champion, in 1972.

Oct 30: A new **college football rushing record** was set by Ed Marinaro of Cornell University, who scored a three-year career total of 4132 yards.

1972

I. Civil Rights
Exploration and Settlement
Government
Statistics
Wars

Pres. Richard M. Nixon enhanced his already substantial chances for reelection with trips to the People's Republic of China in February and to the U.S.S.R. in May. These successes were capped in October when two key strategic arms (SALT) agreements were signed. The Paris peace talks stalled when U.S. representatives walked out, claiming the North Vietnamese were not working for a settlement. On Mar. 30 North Vietnam moved into South Vietnam through the DMZ and from Cambodia. This was met by heavy air bombardment of North Vietnam. After initial losses, South Vietnamese forces began to turn back the North Vietnamese. On Apr. 27 the Paris talks resumed. Despite stepped-up air support for South Vietnamese military actions, U.S. disengagement continued. The last U.S. ground combat troops were withdrawn in August. On the eve of the presidential election, Henry Kissinger, security adviser to Pres. Nixon, reported that a Vietnam peace settlement was close. The Democratic Party proved unable to support its candidate, Sen. George S. McGovern of South Dakota, who had vowed to end the U.S. military presence in Vietnam within 90 days of his inauguration. McGovern also supported cuts in defense spending and proposed amnesty for those who had chosen prison or exile over military service in Vietnam. McGovern's charges of corruption in the Nixon administration, including the role of administration officials in the Watergate affair, failed to influence the electorate. Notables who died this year included J. Edgar Hoover, head of the FBI from 1924, May 2, at 77; and the Rev. Adam Clayton Powell, Jr., controversial Baptist minister and congressman from New York (1945–1970), Apr. 4, at 63.

Feb 4: The sixth round of the **Strategic Arms Limitation Talks** (SALT) in Vienna, Austria, begun on Nov. 15, 1971, ended with indications of progress. The seventh round opened in Helsinki, Finland, on Mar. 28 and led to the strategic arms agreements signed in Moscow on May 26.

Feb 21-28: A historic **presidential visit to China** was undertaken by Pres. Nixon. In the Shanghai Communiqué (Feb. 27), the two nations agreed to work to lessen the risk of war, to normalize relations, and to increase scientific and cultural ties. The Chinese held that Taiwan was part of China. The U.S. acknowledged that there was one China and stated that its policy was to withdraw U.S. military forces from Taiwan as tensions in the area decreased.

Mar 22: The **Twenty-seventh, or Equal Rights, Amendment** to the Constitution, prohibiting discrimination on the basis of sex, was passed by the Senate and sent to the states for ratification. Hawaii was the first to ratify. By the end of the year, 22 of the required 38 states had ratified it.

Mar 22: The **National Commission on Marijuana and Drug Abuse** urged an end to criminal penalties for the private possession and use of marijuana.

Apr 7: The **Federal Election Campaign Act** went into effect. The law set limits on advertising budgets and on candidates' financing of their own campaigns. It also required disclosure of contributors of more than $100.

Apr 10: A treaty banning **biological warfare** was signed by the U.S. and some 120 other nations.

May 8: The **mining of Haiphong harbor** and other major North Vietnamese ports was ordered by Pres. Nixon.

May 15: Alabama Gov. **George C. Wallace was shot** in Laurel, Md., by Arthur Bremer, 21, while campaigning in Maryland's Democratic presidential primary. Wallace was paralyzed from the waist down; three others were seriously injured.

May 22-30: The **first presidential visit to Moscow** in history was made by Pres. Nixon. U.S. and Soviet officials signed a number of agreements, including one for a joint space flight in 1975. On May 26 Pres. Nixon and secretary Leonid I. Brezhnev signed a treaty on antiballistic missile systems and an interim agreement on limitation of strategic missiles.

June 4: Angela Davis, the black militant, was acquitted in San Jose, Calif., of abetting a 1970 courtroom escape attempt that left four people dead.

June 17: In what became known as the **Watergate affair,** police arrested five men involved in a burglary of Democratic Party headquarters in the Watergate apartment complex in Washington, D.C. Among the five was James McCord, a former CIA agent then working for the Republican National Committee and the Committee to Reelect the President. Democratic Party Chairman Larry O'Brien, charging Pres. Nixon's campaign staff with "political espionage," filed a $1,000,000 civil suit on June 20.

June 19-23: Hurricane Agnes swept the East Coast, killing 127 and causing more than $1,000,000,000 in damage.

June 29: State death penalties were ruled unconstitutional by the Supreme Court, which held that they constituted cruel and unusual punishment.

July 10-14: The **Democratic National Convention nominated Sen. George S. McGovern** of South Dakota for president and Sen. Thomas F. Eagleton of Missouri for vice president. On July 25 Eagleton confirmed rumors that he had received psychiatric treatment three times from 1960 to 1966 for nervous exhaustion and fatigue. On July 31 Eagleton withdrew from the campaign. On Aug. 8, R. Sargent Shriver, former head of the Peace Corps, succeeded Eagleton on the ticket.

Aug 3: The **Strategic Arms Limitation Treaty** (SALT I) was passed by the U.S. Senate. The treaty limited the U.S. and U.S.S.R. to two antiballistic missile systems of 100 missiles each, one for defense of each nation's capital, one for defense of a portion of its ICBM system. A five-year interim agreement on limitation of strategic arms was approved by the House on Aug. 18 and by the Senate on Sept. 14. The two accords were signed in ceremonies at the White House on Oct. 3.

Aug 4: Arthur Bremer was convicted on nine counts in the May 15 shootings of Gov. George C. Wallace of Alabama and three others. He was sentenced to 63 years in prison.

Aug 12: The **last U.S. ground combat forces** in Vietnam were withdrawn.

Aug 21-23: The **Republican National Convention nominated Pres. Nixon** and Vice Pres. Spiro T. Agnew for reelection.

Aug 29: Pres. Nixon announced that a **White House investigation** of the Watergate break-in, conducted by White House counsel John Dean, revealed that administration officials were not involved in the burglary.

Sep 5: In what was known as the **trial of the Harrisburg Seven,** federal prosecutors moved to drop all conspiracy charges against the Rev. Philip F. Berrigan and six others accused of plotting to kidnap Henry Kissinger and blow up heating tunnels in Washington, D.C. The trial against the seven in Harrisburg, Pa., had ended in a hung jury.

Sep 15: In the **Watergate break-in** case, a federal grand jury indicted the five originally accused of burglary and former White House aides G. Gordon Liddy and E. Howard Hunt.

Oct 12-13: A **racial brawl on the carrier** *Kitty Hawk* off the coast of Vietnam left some 46 sailors injured.

In November the carrier *Constellation* returned to port after more than 100 seamen protested what they termed racist actions by officers. On Nov. 10 Adm. Elmo R. Zumwalt, chief of naval operations, reprimanded some 90 naval officers and demanded an end to racist behavior in the Navy.

Nov 7: Richard M. Nixon was reelected president of the United States in the greatest Republican landslide in history. Spiro T. Agnew was reelected vice president. The electoral vote was Nixon, 521; Sen. George S. McGovern, Democrat, 17. The popular vote was Nixon, 45,767,218; McGovern 28,357,668. The Democrats picked up two Senate seats for a 57–43 majority. The Republicans gained 13 seats in the House, but the Democrats still led 255–179, with one seat going to an independent.

Nov 22: A 22-year-old **ban on travel to China** was lifted.

Dec 18: Full-scale bombing of North Vietnam was resumed after the Paris peace negotiations reached an impasse. The bombing was again halted on Dec. 30. Private talks were to resume on Jan. 8, 1973.

II. Architecture
Arts and Music
Popular Entertainment
Publishing
Theater

This year the publishing world was rocked by a hoax. The giant McGraw-Hill Company had paid Clifford Irving $750,000 for *The Autobiography of Howard Hughes,* supposedly based on some 100 talks with the reclusive billionaire. After telephone calls by a person claiming to be Hughes, the scheme began to unravel. Irving and his wife pleaded guilty to the hoax on Mar. 14, two weeks before the planned, but aborted, publication date of the book. In the art world, museum management came under fire for a practice called deaccessioning, the selling or trading of art works. Thomas Hoving of the Metropolitan Museum in New York City defended the practice as a way to improve collections. Critics charged the transactions put into private hands works that artists and donors had intended for public view. This year's theater season was noted for its numerous revivals, among them *A Funny Thing Happened on the Way to the Forum.* The music world also offered revivals, with a reemergence of '50s rock 'n' roll, ragtime music, and the big band sound of Benny Goodman and Duke Ellington. Many of Hollywood's film offerings were noted for their brutality, among them *The French Connection* and *The Godfather.* Notables who died this year included the poet John Berryman, a suicide, Jan. 7, at 57; Rudolf Friml, composer, Nov. 12, at 93; Ferde Grofé, composer of the *Grand Canyon Suite,* Apr. 3, at 80; Gabriel Heatter, the newscaster, Mar. 30, at 81; Mahalia Jackson, gospel singer, Jan. 27, at 60; José Limón, dancer, Dec. 2, at 64; Marianne Moore, poet, Feb. 5, at 84; Kenneth Patchen, poet, Jan. 1, at 60; Ezra Pound, poet, Nov. 1, at 87; Ted Shawn, dancer, Jan. 9, at 80; Helen Traubel, Wagnerian soprano, July 28, at 69; Edmund Wilson, author and critic, June 12, at 77; and Walter Winchell, columnist and broadcaster, Feb. 20, at 74.

Among **books published** this year was *August 1914* by Alexander Solzhenitsyn, a novel of the first weeks of World War I and culminating in the Russian defeat in the Battle of Tannenberg. Other books published included a slim volume by Richard Bach entitled *Jonathan Livingston Seagull,* a phenomenal best seller; *Delusions, Etc.,* poems by John Berryman; *The Late John Marquand* by Stephen Birmingham, a biography; *Captains and the Kings* by Taylor Caldwell, a novel; *The Best and the Brightest* by David Halberstam, an account of the Kennedy administration and the early years of American involvement in the Vietnam War; *The Boys of Summer* by Roger Kahn, a nostalgic look at the old Brooklyn Dodgers; *Eleanor and Franklin* by Joseph P. Lash, a study of the Roosevelts; *The Human Season: Selected Poems, 1926–1972* by Archibald MacLeish; and *The Optimist's Daughter* by Eudora Welty, a novel.

Jan 17: A report on TV violence by the surgeon general found little effect on children but found it harmful to people predisposed to aggressive behavior. Critics said the report was slanted in favor of the TV industry.

May 1: Pulitzer prizes were awarded for the following: fiction, *Angle of Repose* by Wallace Stegner; biography, *Eleanor and Franklin: The Story of Their Relationship* by Joseph P. Lash; history, *Neither Black nor White* by Carl N. Degler; general nonfiction, *Stilwell and the American Experience in China* by Barbara W. Tuchman; poetry, *Collected Poems* by James Wright.

June 29: In a landmark decision bearing on **freedom of the press,** the Supreme Court ruled that journalists have no right to withhold confidential information from grand juries. On Oct. 4 Peter Bridge of the Newark *News* became the first reporter to be jailed under this decision.

July 8-9: The largest **rock festival** since the 1969 Woodstock event drew some 200,000 rock music lovers to Pocono International Raceway at Long Pond, Pa.

Dec 29: *Life* magazine, a pioneer in photojournalism, suspended publication after 36 years of weekly publication.

III. Business and Industry
Education
Philosophy and Religion
Science

The inflationary spiral appeared to be coming under control. Unemployment was down, as was inflation, and economic growth was up. The economy's record was the best since 1967, and in November the Dow Jones average hit 1000 for the first time in history. The number of government employees had not risen and, for the first time in a decade, the number of agricultural workers had not dropped. Nevertheless, businessmen worried about the federal deficit, and many labor leaders withdrew from the Federal Pay Board, charging that wages were being more carefully monitored than prices. The big economic news was the $750,000,000 wheat sale to the U.S.S.R., prompting charges that grain dealers had known about the impending sale and had bought up grain at low prices, thus making big profits at farmers' expense. In medicine the leading topic was acupuncture, the Chinese practice of achieving anesthesia by inserting needles at specific points on the body. In transportation, the rise in airline hijackings sparked an international strike by pilots, which prompted U.S. officials to institute stricter airport screening procedures. Notables who died this year included Saul Alinsky, social activist, June 12, at 63; Lillian Gilbreth, a pioneer in time-motion studies, Jan. 2, at 93; Paul Goodman, writer and social critic, Aug. 2, at 60; Howard Johnson, founder of the restaurant chain bearing his name, June 20, at 75; Igor Sikorsky, developer of the helicopter, Oct. 26, at 83; Harlow Shapley, astronomer, Oct. 20, at 86; and Joseph F. Smith, Jr., president of the Church of Jesus Christ of Latter Day Saints, July 2, at 95.

Jan 11: A stock-ordering scandal rocked Wall Street when Abraham Treff, a college student, revealed he had violated a New York Stock Exchange "know your customer" rule by placing more than $200,000 in telephone orders through six member firms in Philadelphia without depositing any cash for the transactions.

Jan 14: Plans were announced for the **first breeder reactor,** a nuclear reactor that produces more fuel than it consumes. It was to be built in Tennessee by a consortium of government and private organizations.

Feb 5: In a move to prevent **airplane hijacking,** screening of passengers and their luggage became mandatory on all domestic and foreign flights by U.S. scheduled airlines.

Mar 1: The Supreme Court ruled that the **Federal Trade Commission** could extend its traditional authority in antitrust cases and bar unfair or deceptive marketing practices.

Mar 1: In the **Yablonski murder case,** Paul Gilly was convicted for the 1970 murders of United Mine Workers (UMW) dissident Joseph Yablonski, his wife, and his daughter. Gilly was sentenced to death the next day. On Apr. 11 Gilly's wife pleaded guilty and implicated several UMW leaders, including its president, William A. "Tony" Boyle. On May 2 Albert Pass, a union official, was arrested; on the following day, Tennessee local president Silous Huddleston confessed to his role in the killings. On Aug. 23 a federal grand jury indicted four union officials—Pass, Chester Philpot, William Prater, and Ernest Stults—and named three others as unindicted co-conspirators.

Mar 2: Pioneer 10 was successfully launched on a 22-month voyage that would take it past Jupiter.

Mar 27: In the wake of a huge **defense contract cost overrun, Sen.** William Proxmire, Democrat of Wisconsin, asked the Justice Department to investigate a report that the Air Force had overpaid $400,000,000 to Lockheed to build the C5-A cargo plane.

Apr 16: Apollo 16, manned by astronauts John W. Young, Charles M. Duke, and Thomas K. Mattingly, was successfully launched into orbit around the moon. On Apr. 20 Duke and Young descended to the moon's surface, remaining there until Apr. 23 to conduct tests and collect rock samples Apollo 16 splashed down on Apr. 27.

May 1: The 1969 election of **William A. "Tony" Boyle** as president of the United Mine Workers was declared void by a federal judge because union funds and facilities had been used in Boyle's campaign. On Dec. 19 Boyle resigned after Arnold Miller, a reform candidate, won a new election.

June 3: The **first woman rabbi in the U.S.,** Sally J. Priesand, 25, was ordained in Cincinnati, Ohio.

July 20: An agreement limiting **railroad featherbedding** settled the longstanding dispute over the use of firemen on railroads. A new contract allowed drastic reductions in the number of jobs, to be achieved by attrition.

July 23: ERTS-1, the first Earth Resources Technology Satellite, was successfully launched into Earth orbit. On July 25 it began sending photographic information about Earth's resources back to scientists on the ground.

Aug 21: Copernicus, an orbiting astronomical observatory designed to study the stars and the nature of the universe, was successfully launched into orbit.

Oct 12: The **Nobel Prize in Physiology or Medicine** was awarded jointly to Gerald M. Edelman of Rockefeller University and Rodney R. Porter of Great Britain for their studies of antibodies.

Oct 18: The **Water Pollution Control Act** was passed by Congress over Pres. Nixon's veto. It required industry to halt discharges by 1985, set industry-wide standards, and provided massive federal funding for building and improving sewage plants.

Oct 20: The **Nobel Prize in Physics** was awarded jointly to John Bardeen of the University of Illinois, Leon N. Cooper of Brown University, and John R. Schrieffer of the University of Pennsylvania for their development of the theory of superconductivity.

Oct 20: The **Nobel Prize in Chemistry** was awarded jointly to Christian B. Anfinsen of the National Institutes of Health, and Stanford Moore and William H. Stein of the Rockefeller Institute for their work in enzyme chemistry, particularly their studies of ribonuclease.

Oct 25: The **Nobel Prize in Economics** was awarded jointly to Kenneth J. Arrow of Harvard University and John R. Hicks of Great Britain.

Nov 13: An international convention to control **oceanic pollution** was signed by the U.S. and 90 other nations.

Nov 14: The **Dow Jones Index** of 30 industrial stocks closed above 1000 on the New York Stock Exchange for the first time in history.

Dec 7: Apollo 17, the sixth and last of the Apollo lunar landing missions, was successfully launched. It was crewed by Eugene Cernan, Ronald Evans, and Harrison Schmitt. During their lunar excursion (Dec. 11–14), Cernan and Schmitt found what they described as orange soil, which was taken to be a possible indication of volcanic activity, and collected some 249 lbs. of rock and soil samples. Apollo 17 splashed down in the Pacific Ocean on Dec. 19.

Dec 31: A near-total **ban on DDT use,** ordered by the Environmental Protection Agency, went into effect.

IV. Fashion
Folkways
Holidays
Social Issues and Crime
Sports

Professional sports were beset this year by organizational feuds. The new World Hockey Association attracted some of the NHL's best players with big contracts. After several months of conflict, the International Lawn Tennis Federation came to terms with Lamar Hunt's World Championship Tennis (WCT) group by dividing control over the scheduling of tournaments. Because the agreement was not approved until July, professionals under contract to the WCT were barred from playing in many major tournaments, including Wimbledon. In basketball, the American Basketball Association filed a $300,000,000 antitrust suit against the National Basketball Association, charging it with seeking to eliminate competition by encouraging ABA players to jump leagues. For the first time in history, major league baseball players struck, returning to play only after team owners agreed to an increase in players' pensions. Americans became interested in chess this year because of Bobby Fischer's antics in Reykjavik, Iceland. Fischer and the defending world chess champion, Boris Spassky of the U.S.S.R., argued for months about details leading up to the showdown. During play, Fischer made demands of match officials that kept him in the headlines for months. In golf the top money winners were Jack Nicklaus, $320,542, and Kathy Whitworth, $65,063. This year Americans mourned the deaths of Charles Atlas, real name Angelo Siciliano, body builder, Dec. 24, at 79; Roberto Clemente, star outfielder of the Pittsburgh Pirates, who was killed in the crash of a cargo plane taking relief supplies to earthquake victims in Managua, Nicaragua, Dec. 31, at 38; Gilbert R. "Gil" Hodges, former Brooklyn Dodgers star, Apr. 2, at 47; Norman Norell, real name Norman Levinson, fashion designer, Oct. 25, at 72; Jackie Robinson, first black to play in the major leagues, Oct. 24, at 53; Harold J. "Pie" Traynor, in 1969 voted greatest third baseman of all time, Mar. 16, at 72; and George Weiss, former baseball executive, Aug. 13, at 78.

Jan 16: Super Bowl VI was won by the Dallas Cowboys (NFC), who defeated the Miami Dolphins (AFC) 24 to 3. On Jan. 2 the Cowboys had stopped the San Francisco 49ers 14 to 3 for the NFC championship, and the Dolphins had defeated the Baltimore Colts 21 to 0 for the AFC title.

Feb 3-13: At the **Winter Olympics** at Sapporo, Japan, U.S. athletes won three gold medals. The U.S.S.R. was first, with eight gold medals, followed by East Germany, Switzerland, and the Netherlands, all with four.

Mar 25: The **NCAA basketball championship** was won by UCLA, defeating Florida State 81 to 76 and maintaining its 45-game winning streak.

Mar 27: In the trial of the two remaining **Soledad Brothers,** John Cluchette and Fleeta Drumgo were found innocent by a San Francisco jury of slaying a prison guard at Soledad state prison in 1970. The third convict charged, George Jackson, was killed during a prison break attempt in Aug. 1971.

Apr 7: Reputed Mafia kingpin **Joseph "Crazy Joe" Gallo,** 43, was murdered by four gunmen at his birthday party in a New York City restaurant.

Apr 28: In a settlement of the **1968 Kentucky Derby controversy,** a Kentucky court of appeals awarded the prize money to the second-place winner, Forward Pass. The winner, Dancer's Image, was disqualified from the money, but not the win, because the horse had been given a pain-killing drug before the race.

May 7: The **NBA basketball championship** was won by the Los Angeles Lakers, who defeated the New York Knicks four games to one.

May 20: The **ABA basketball championship** was won by the Indiana Pacers, who beat the New York Nets four games to two.

June 18: The **U.S. Open golf tournament** was won for the third time by Jack Nicklaus, tying Bobby Jones's record of 13 major golf titles.

June 19: In a decision bearing on **baseball's reserve clause,** the Supreme Court ruled major league baseball exempt from antitrust statutes, thus ending Curt Flood's 1970 suit against organized baseball. The Court called the exemption an "anomaly" and called on Congress to correct the situation through legislation.

July 2: A new **world pole vault record** of 18 feet, 5¾ inches was set by Bob Seagren using a fiberglass pole in a meet at Eugene, Oreg.

July 7: The **first women FBI agents,** Susan Lynn Roley, a former U.S. Marine, and Joanne E. Pierce, a former nun, were sworn in.

July 7: At the **Wimbledon** tennis championships in England, Billie Jean King won the women's singles title. On July 9 Stan Smith won the men's singles title, completing the first U.S. singles sweep since 1955. King teamed with Betty Stove of the Netherlands to win the women's doubles, and Rosemary Casals teamed with Ilie Nastase of Rumania to take the mixed doubles title.

July 11-Sep 1: The **world chess championship** was won by Bobby Fischer, who triumphed over the defending champion, Boris Spassky of the U.S.S.R., in competition at Reykjavik, Iceland.

Aug 6: The **PGA golf tournament** was won by Gary Player.

Aug 26-Sep 11: At the **Summer Olympics** in Munich, West Germany, the U.S. won 33 gold medals to the Soviet Union's 50. Swimmer Mark Spitz set an Olympic record by winning seven gold medals. Frank Shorter was the first U.S. athlete in 64 years to win the gold medal for the marathon, and the U.S. basketball team lost for the first time since the game was introduced in 1936. On Sept. 5 Arab terrorists entered the Olympic village, killed two Israeli coaches and took nine Israeli athletes hostage. All nine were killed, along with a number of terrorists, in a shootout at a nearby airport. The Olympic Games were suspended for the first time in modern history. They were resumed on Sept. 6 after a memorial service for the dead athletes.

Sep 9-10: The **U.S. Open tennis singles championships** were won by Billie Jean King, for the third time, in the women's division and Ilie Nastase of Rumania in the men's division.

Oct 13-15: The **Davis Cup tennis championship** was successfully defended by the U.S., defeating Rumania three matches to two in Bucharest.

Oct 14-22: The **World Series** was won by the Oakland Athletics (AL), defeating the Cincinnati Reds (NL) four games to three. On Oct. 11 the Reds had won the National League pennant by beating the Pittsburgh Pirates three games to two. The next day the Athletics won the American League title over the Detroit Tigers, three games to two.

1973

I. **Civil Rights**
   Exploration and Settlement
   Government
   Statistics
   Wars

The landslide victory of Pres. Richard M. Nixon in Nov. 1972 was interpreted by some as a vote of confidence in the Nixon administration's policies. U.S. involvement in Vietnam seemed to be drawing to a close. As the year progressed, however, the story of the Watergate break-in was uncovered by journalists and by the Senate Select Committee on Presidential Campaign Activities. Pres. Nixon's attempts to use executive privilege or national security as reasons to withhold evidence and limit testimony by administration aides caused further friction between the White House and investigators. The revelation that Pres. Nixon had had his official conversations recorded since 1971 set off a struggle for the tapes of conversations relating to Watergate. Key tapes became unavailable, and a portion of one was mysteriously erased. In August Vice Pres. Spiro T. Agnew revealed he was under investigation in connection with official corruption in Maryland that took place while he served as Baltimore County executive and

governor of Maryland. By year's end the Nixon administration was in deep trouble. Nixon came under pressure to resign, and the House began an investigation to determine whether impeachment proceedings were in order. The year was marked also by the deaths of several national figures. Lyndon Baines Johnson, 36th president of the United States, whose efforts to realize the Great Society were overwhelmed by the tragedy of Vietnam, died on Jan. 22, at 64. Other notables who died this year included Earl Browder, head of the U.S. Communist Party from 1930 to 1945, June 27, at 82; Jeannette Rankin, who as Republican congresswoman from Montana (1917–1919 and 1941–1943) was the first woman elected to Congress and the only member to vote against U.S. entry into both world wars, May 18, at 92; and Winthrop Rockefeller, philanthropist, governor of Arkansas from 1967–1971, and grandson of John D. Rockefeller, Feb. 22, at 60.

Jan 22: A **Vietnam peace agreement** was signed in Paris by representatives of the U.S., North and South Vietnam, and the Vietcong. Its key provisions included a cease-fire throughout North and South Vietnam; withdrawal of U.S. forces and dismantling of U.S. installations within 60 days; release of North Vietnamese, Vietcong, and U.S. prisoners of war within 60 days; and reunification of the North and South through peaceful means. The South Vietnamese government was to remain until new elections were held. North Vietnamese forces in the South would remain in place, but could not be replaced or reinforced.

Jan 30: In the continuing **Watergate** scandal, James W. McCord and G. Gordon Liddy, former members of the Nixon reelection campaign, were convicted of breaking into and illegally wiretapping Democratic Party headquarters in 1972. Five others involved had earlier pleaded guilty.

Feb 28: Wounded Knee, S.D., was occupied by militant members of the American Indian Movement (AIM) to dramatize the group's demands for free elections of tribal leaders, investigation of the Bureau of Indian Affairs, and review of all U.S.-Indian treaties. The group surrendered on May 8 after officials promised to investigate the complaints.

Apr 11: In Mississippi, the **Mississippi R.** reached its highest flood level, 50.3 feet, in 30 years. By May 4 more than 35,000 in nine states had fled their homes, 11 had died, and damages had reached $500,000,000.

Apr 27: Acting FBI director **L. Patrick Gray resigned** following revelations he had destroyed records involving Watergate given him by White House counsel John Dean.

Apr 30: In a televised **address on Watergate,** Pres. Nixon announced he had accepted the resignations of his chief of staff H. R. Haldeman, domestic policy assistant John Ehrlichman, counsel John Dean, and Attorney Gen. Richard G. Kleindienst. He denied any involvement in the Watergate break-in or any subsequent cover-up.

May 14: In a major **equal rights decision,** the Supreme Court ruled that women in the armed forces were entitled to the same benefits for their spouses as those accorded male servicemen.

May 17: The **Senate Select Committee on Presidential Campaign Activities,** headed by Sen. Sam J. Ervin, Democrat of North Carolina, opened public hearings to explore the alleged cover-up of administration involvement in the Watergate affair.

May 25: **Archibald Cox,** a professor at Harvard Law School, was sworn in as special Watergate prosecutor.

June 16-25: U.S.S.R. Party Sec. **Leonid I. Brezhnev** visited the U.S. He signed agreements to reduce the risk of accidental nuclear war, increase air travel, and promote scientific exchanges between the U.S. and U.S.S.R.

June 25-29: John Dean testified before the Senate committee investigating Watergate. He implicated himself, H. R. Haldeman, John Ehrlichman, Pres. Nixon, John Mitchell, and others in a cover-up. Dean testified that Nixon had discussed the use of executive privilege as a means of avoiding personal involvement in Watergate, and so-called hush money. Dean also produced what was described as a White House enemies list, naming scores of administration foes.

July 16: The existence of what were to be called the **Watergate tapes,** recordings of White House conversations, was revealed by former White House aide Alexander P. Butterfield. On July 23 special prosecutor Archibald Cox and the Senate committee subpoenaed the tapes. On July 26 Pres. Nixon refused to release them, appealing the case through the courts until Oct. 19, when he offered a summary of requested tapes in return for no further requests for tapes or papers. This was rejected by Cox.

Aug 6: Vice Pres. **Agnew** revealed he was being investigated by the Justice Department on charges of receiving kickbacks while serving as Baltimore County executive and governor of Maryland. He denied any wrongdoing on Aug. 8.

Sep 4: **John Ehrlichman and G. Gordon Liddy were indicted** along with two White House officials in connection with the burglary of the office of Daniel Ellsberg's psychiatrist in 1971. The action had been instigated by the so-called White House plumbers' unit, created to stop security leaks, following Ellsberg's release of Pentagon documents to the press.

Oct 10: Vice Pres. **Agnew resigned** and pleaded nolo contendere (no contest) to one charge of income tax evasion in return for the dropping of other charges. Agnew was fined and given three years' probation. He was only the second vice president to resign. John C. Calhoun resigned in 1832 to take a Senate seat.

Oct 12: Rep. **Gerald R. Ford,** Republican of Michigan, was nominated by Pres. Nixon for the vice presidency.

Oct 16: The **first black mayor of a major southern city,** Maynard Jackson, was elected to office in Atlanta, Ga.

Oct 16: The **Nobel Peace Prize** was awarded jointly to Sec. of State Henry A. Kissinger and to Le Duc Tho of North Vietnam for their efforts in ending the Vietnam War. Tho declined the award.

Oct 20: In what came to be called the **Saturday night massacre,** Attorney General Elliot Richardson resigned after refusing to fire special Watergate prosecutor Archibald Cox. Deputy Attorney General William Ruckelshaus was fired after refusing also. Solicitor General Robert Bork then fired Cox, who had earlier in the day announced he would not accept White House summaries of the Watergate tapes.

Oct 23: Eight **impeachment resolutions** were introduced in the House, even as Pres. Nixon announced he would turn over the subpoenaed Watergate tapes.

Nov 1: Leon A. Jaworski was appointed special Watergate prosecutor by Pres. Nixon, who pledged to seek congressional approval before interfering with his investigation.

Nov 7: The **War Powers Act,** requiring congressional approval for commitment of U.S. forces in combat abroad longer than 60 days, was passed by Congress over Pres. Nixon's veto.

Nov 21: An **18½-minute gap** in a key Watergate tape was revealed by the White House. The tapes requested were turned over to Judge John J. Sirica. On Nov. 27 Rose Mary Woods, Pres. Nixon's personal secretary, testified she had accidentally caused about five minutes of the erasure. The remaining gap was unexplained.

Dec 4: In the **Chicago Seven** conspiracy case, David Dellinger, Abbie Hoffmann, Jerry Rubin, and their attorney William Kunstler were convicted of contempt of court, but no sentence was imposed.

Dec 6: Gerald R. Ford was sworn in as vice president, the first to take office under the terms of the Twenty-fifth Amendment.

II. Architecture
Arts and Music
Popular Entertainment
Publishing
Theater

Broadway show revenues dropped to a ten-year low during the 1972–1973 season. To avoid the financial disaster accompanying a closing on opening night, a number of producers made Broadway their last stop on extensive national tours. *Lorelei,* starring Carol Channing, was scheduled to arrive in New York City in 1974 after a long 13-city tour. Joseph Papp, director of the New York Shakespeare Festival, took over the Vivian Beaumont Theater in Lincoln Center. By year's end he controlled productions on some ten stages, a reflection of the importance of resident, noncommercial theater. In motion pictures nostalgia was popular with audiences, as evidenced by the success of such films as *American Graffiti,* about growing up in the early 1960s, *Paper Moon, The Sting,* and *Dillinger.* Nostalgia carried the day with television audiences as well. The surprise hit was *The Waltons,* a warm view of southern family life during the Great Depression. A view of contemporary family life was offered by a documentary called *An American Family,* about the Loud family of California. Notables who died this year included Conrad Aiken, author and poet, Aug. 17, at 84; W. H. Auden, one of the great poets of the twentieth century, Sept. 28, at 66; S. N. Behrman, playwright, Sept. 9, at 80; Pearl S. Buck, Nobel Prize-winning novelist, Mar. 6, at 80; Lon Chaney, Jr., actor, July 12, at 67; Eddie Condon, jazz guitarist, Aug. 14, at 67; John Ford, director, Aug. 31, at 78; Betty Grable, 1940s pinup girl, July 2, at 56; William Inge, playwright, June 10, at 60; Gene Krupa, big band musician known for his drum solos, Oct. 16, at 64; Jacques Lipchitz, pioneer of cubist sculpture, May 26, at 81; Lauritz Melchior, leading Wagnerian tenor of the 1930s and 1940s, Mar. 18, at 80; Edward G. Robinson, actor, Jan. 26, at 79; Robert Ryan, actor, July 11, at 63; Edward Steichen, photographer, Mar. 25, at 93; and Max Yasgur, whose 600-acre Sullivan County, N.Y., farm had been the site of the 1969 Woodstock rock festival, Feb. 9, at 53.

Among **books published** this year was *Gravity's Rainbow* by Thomas Pynchon, a massive novel that explored the themes of sexuality, death, and warfare and their relationship to the development of twentieth-century history. Other books published this year included *Recovery* by John Berryman, an unfinished novel; *The Ascent of Man* by Jacob Bronowski, nonfiction; *The World of Apples* by John Cheever, stories; *Economics and the Public Purpose* by John Kenneth Galbraith; *The Taking of Pelham One Two Three* by John Godey, a novel about the hijacking of a New York City subway train; *Serpico* by Peter Maas, the true story of a policeman's struggle to overcome police corruption; *Marilyn* by Norman Mailer, another nonfiction novel; *Rembrandt's Hat* by Bernard Malamud, stories; *Do With Me What You Will* by Joyce Carol Oates, a novel; *The Implosion Conspiracy* by Louis Nizer, an account of the spy trial of Julius and Ethel Rosenberg; *The Great American Novel* by Philip Roth, a novel about a third baseball league, made up of misfits; *Breakfast of Champions* by Kurt Vonnegut, an example of the comic novel of despair; and *The Onion Field* by Joseph Wambaugh, a police novel based on fact.

Jan 7: The **Bollingen Prize** for poetry was awarded to James Merrill.

May 3: The 110-story **Sears Tower** in Chicago, Ill., was topped out at 1450 feet, making it the world's tallest building.

May 7: Pulitzer prizes were awarded for the following: fiction, *The Optimist's Daughter* by Eudora Welty; biography, *Luce and His Empire* by W. A. Swanberg; history, *People of Paradox: An Inquiry Concerning the Origin of American Civilization* by Michael Kammen; general nonfiction, *Fire in the Lake: The Vietnamese and the Americans in Vietnam* by Frances Fitzgerald and *Children of Crisis,* volumes two and three, by Robert Coles; drama, *That Championship Season* by Jason Miller.

May 11: In the **Pentagon Papers** trial of Daniel Ellsberg and Anthony Russo, Jr., charges of espionage, theft, and conspiracy in connection with release of sensitive Pentagon documents to the press were dismissed. Federal Judge William Byrne, Jr., cited "improper government conduct," including the burglary of the office of Ellsberg's psychiatrist.

May 26: In a major decision on **radio and TV advertising,** the Supreme Court ruled that stations were not obligated to sell equal air time for political or controversial issues.

June 21: In a series of decisions on **obscenity,** the Supreme Court ruled that juries could establish the prurient appeal of materials on the basis of prevailing attitudes in their own communities.

July 29: A rock festival at **Watkins Glen,** N.Y., drew some 600,000 fans to hear music by such groups as the Allman Brothers Band, the Grateful Dead, and The Band.

Sep 21: A new **record art price** for a painting by a U.S. artist, $2,000,000, was paid by the Australian National Gallery in Canberra for Jackson Pollock's *Blue Poles.*

III. Business and Industry
Education
Philosophy and Religion
Science

Record levels of retail sales, factory output, new car sales, employment, and personal incomes balanced against inflation of 8.5% and the second dollar devaluation in 14 months, added up to what a consumer columnist described as joyless prosperity. As food prices climbed, consumer groups organized a meat boycott. Toward the end of the year the situation was aggravated by an oil embargo imposed on the U.S. and other industrialized nations by members of the Organization of Arab Petroleum Exporting Countries (OAPEC). The oil shortage caused long lines at gas stations and shut down factories. The federal government organized an emergency gas rationing system, but it was not implemented. In education, the end of the military draft, skyrocketing tuition costs, and increasing competition among degree holders for jobs and for admittance to graduate and professional schools led students to question the value of a college education. Enrollment was up only 2%, but enrollment at less expensive public institutions was strong. Notables who died this year included Harvey S. Firestone, Jr., an industrialist, June 1, at 75; Harold B. Lee, president of the Church of Jesus Christ of Latter Day Saints, Dec. 26, at 74; Marjorie Post, a philanthropist whose wealth was estimated at some $200,000,000, Sept. 12, at 86; and Selman A. Waksman, winner of the 1952 Nobel Prize for Medicine for his discovery of streptomycin, Aug. 16, at 85.

Jan 18: In a **job discrimination** case, the American Telephone & Telegraph Company agreed to pay $15,000,000 to women and minority employees who had been treated unfairly, and to set up job-training programs and establish hiring quotas.

Jan 22: In a decision on **abortion,** the Supreme Court struck down state laws restricting abortions during the first six months of pregnancy.

Mar 22: The **National Commission on Marijuana and Drug Abuse** urged treatment for drug users and recognition that alcoholism is a drug problem.

Apr 2: Political intervention by big business was highlighted by the admission by International Tele-

phone and Telegraph that it had offered funds to the CIA to oppose the election of Salvador Allende Gossens, a Marxist, to the presidency of Chile in 1970. Allende was elected, but on Sept. 11, 1973, his government was overthrown by a military junta and he was killed.

Apr 5: Pioneer 11 was launched toward a December rendezvous with the planet Jupiter.

Apr 15: The signing of **contracts with California grape growers** by the International Brotherhood of Teamsters was announced. It prompted a strike by César Chávez's United Farm Workers Union, which charged the Teamsters with union busting by taking over contracts held by the UFW.

May 14: Skylab, the first U.S. space station, was launched into Earth orbit, but a launch mishap damaged one of its solar-power panels and jammed the other. On May 25, Skylab 2 carried astronauts Charles Conrad, Joseph Kerwin, and Paul Weitz to a rendezvous with the station. The crew deployed the stuck panel, made further repairs, and conducted scientific experiments before splashing down in the Pacific on June 22.

June 25: Several programs for **state aid to parochial schools** were declared unconstitutional by the Supreme Court.

June 29: Establishment of a **Federal Energy Office** to promote conservation and research into alternative sources of energy was announced by Pres. Nixon. It later assumed responsibility for mandatory fuel allocations and potential gasoline rationing.

June 30: The **largest merchant ship** built in the U.S., the 1094-foot, 230,000-ton supertanker *Brooklyn,* was christened at the Brooklyn, N.Y., Navy Yard.

July 28: Skylab 3 carried astronauts Alan Bean, Owen Garriott, and Jack Lousma to a rendezvous with the Skylab orbiting laboratory. They made repairs to the station and performed a number of experiments before returning to Earth on Sept. 25.

Sep 1: The nation's strongest **drug control law** went into effect in New York State. It imposed mandatory life sentences for those convicted of trafficking in hard drugs and for addicts who commit violent crimes.

Sep 6: Former United Mine Workers president **W. A. "Tony" Boyle was indicted** on charges of ordering the 1969 murders of labor dissident Joseph Yablonski, his wife, and his daughter.

Oct 17: An **embargo on oil** shipped to the U.S. and other nations supporting Israel was instituted by 11 Middle Eastern oil-exporting states.

Oct 18: The **Nobel Prize in Economics** was awarded to Wassily Leontief of Harvard University.

Oct 23: The **Nobel Prize in Physics** was awarded jointly to Ivar Giaver of the General Electric Company in Schenectady, N.Y.; Leo Esaki, a Japanese citizen working for IBM in Yorktown Heights, N.Y.; and Brian D. Josephson of Great Britain for their theoretical work in the field of microelectronics.

Nov 3: Mariner 10, the first U.S. probe of the planet Mercury, was launched. It was to fly by Venus on its way to Mercury.

Nov 7: A **call for energy self-sufficiency** by 1980 was made by Pres. Nixon. He also asked for extension of Daylight Savings Time (passed Dec. 14) and reduction of the highway speed limit to 55 mph (passed Dec. 22); set heating oil allocations for homes, schools, and industries; reduced jet fuel allocations; and ordered lower temperatures in federal buildings. On Nov. 25 he called for a Sunday ban on gasoline sales. On Dec. 27 the Federal Energy Office outlined a standby gasoline rationing program.

Nov 13. Plans for a **trans-Alaska oil pipeline**, designed to supply 2,000,000 barrels of oil a day, were approved by Congress.

Dec 15: Homosexuality was not a mental illness, the American Psychiatric Association announced, overturning its 100-year-old position on the subject.

IV. Fashion
Folkways
Holidays
Social Issues and Crime
Sports

Salaries increased and attendance declined for football, basketball, and baseball, to the benefit of other sports, notably hockey, soccer, and tennis. In September the ban on local television coverage of football games was lifted for events sold out in advance, and many ticket-holders stayed home to watch the games. In baseball the American League adopted the designated hitter rule—which provided for a tenth player in the lineup to hit for the pitcher without forcing the pitcher to leave the game—in the hope of increasing scoring and boosting attendance. In hockey the NHL drew 9,299,028 fans for the 1972–1973 season, an increase of more than 1,000,000 over the previous year. In golf the top money winners were Jack Nicklaus, $308,362, and Kathy Whitworth, $82,864. As professional sports were changing and growing, so was the national passion for physical fitness. Some 60,000,000 Americans were involved in sports for exercise, including some 18,000,000 cyclists. Another carefully observed trend was the national crime rate. On Mar. 28 a preliminary report showed the 1972 crime rate was down 2%, but an FBI report released on Dec. 27 showed the rate for the first nine months of 1973 to be up 1%, and violent crime up 3%. Among those who died this year were Frank Costello, a leading underworld figure, Feb. 18, at 82; Walt Kelly, creator of the comic strip *Pogo*, Oct. 18, at 60; Edward V. "Eddie" Rickenbacker, World War I flying ace, July 23, at 82; and Murat B. "Chic" Young, creator of the comic strip *Blondie*, Mar. 14, at 72.

Jan 14: Super Bowl VII was won by the Miami Dolphins (AFC), defeating the Washington Redskins (NFC) 14 to 7. On Dec. 31, 1972, the Dolphins had defeated the Pittsburgh Steelers 21 to 17 for the AFC championship and the Redskins had beaten the Dallas Cowboys 26 to 3 for the NFC title.

Jan 22: The **world heavyweight boxing championship** was won by George Foreman, who defeated Joe Frazier in a second-round knockout. On Sept. 1 he defended the title with a one-round knockout of Joe Roman in Tokyo, Japan.

Feb 25: Juan Corona was sentenced to 25 consecutive life terms after being convicted for the 1971 murders of 25 migrant workers in California. In 1978 his conviction was overturned, on the grounds his lawyer did not defend him competently, and a new trial was ordered. He was convicted again on Sept. 23, 1982.

Mar 1: Robyn Smith became the first woman jockey to win a stakes race when she rode North Sea to victory in the Paumonok Handicap at Aqueduct Raceway.

Mar 1: The **birthrate** for the last six months of 1972 was reported at 1.98 children per couple, below the 2.1 rate for zero population growth.

Mar 26: The **NCAA basketball championship** was won for the seventh consecutive year by UCLA, defeating Memphis State 87 to 66.

Apr 28-May 12: The **ABA basketball championship** was won by the Indiana Pacers, who defeated the Kentucky Colonels four games to three.

May 5: The 99th annual **Kentucky Derby** was won by Secretariat, with a record time of 1:59^{2}/$_{5}$. The jockey was Ron Turcotte.

May 10: The **NBA basketball championship** was won by the New York Knicks, who beat the Los Angeles Lakers four games to one.

May 19: The 98th annual **Preakness Stakes** was won by Secretariat, with a time of 1:55. The jockey was Ron Turcotte.

May 21: The **first athletic scholarship awarded to a woman** was given to Lynn Genesko, a swimmer from Woodbridge, N.J., by the University of Miami (Fla.).

May 27: A new **track record** for the 880-yd. run was set by Rick Wohlhuter, who ran the distance in 1:44.6 at the AAU meet in Los Angeles, Calif.

June 9: The 105th annual **Belmont Stakes** was won by Secretariat, with a time of 2:24, thus becoming the ninth horse to win racing's Triple Crown. The jockey was Ron Turcotte.

June 17: The **U.S. Open golf tournament** was won by Johnny Miller.

July 7-8: At the **Wimbledon** tennis championships in England, Billie Jean King won the women's singles title for the second straight year. King teamed with Rosemary Casals to win the women's doubles, and with Owen Davidson of Australia to win the mixed doubles. Jimmy Connors teamed with Ilie Nastase of Rumania to take the men's doubles. Many tennis professionals boycotted the championship because of the International Lawn Tennis Federation's suspension of Yugoslavian player Nikki Pilic for refusing to play on the Yugoslavian Davis Cup team.

Aug 12: The **PGA golf tournament** was won by Jack Nicklaus.

Aug 29-Sep 9: The **U.S. Open tennis singles championships** were won by John Newcombe of Australia in the men's division and Margaret Smith Court of Australia, for the fifth time, in the women's division.

Sep 20: In a nationally televised tennis mismatch billed as the "**Battle of the Sexes**," Billie Jean King beat Bobby Riggs in three straight sets and went home $100,000 richer.

Oct 13-21: The **World Series** was won for the second year in a row by the Oakland Athletics (AL), defeating the New York Mets (NL) four games to three. The Mets had won the National League pennant on Oct. 10 by beating the Cincinnati Reds three games to two. The Athletics had won the American League title Oct. 11, beating the Baltimore Orioles three games to two.

Nov 30-Dec 2: The **Davis Cup** tennis championship was won in Cleveland, Ohio, by Australia, beating the U.S. in five straight matches.

Dec 1: Jack Nicklaus won the Disney World Open, becoming the first professional golfer to hit a career total of $2,000,000.

Dec 16: A new **NFL rushing record** was set by O.J. Simpson, running back for the Buffalo Bills, who broke Jim Brown's 1963 total of 1863 yds. Simpson later set a new pro record of 2003 yds.

1974

I. Civil Rights
Exploration and Settlement
Government
Statistics
Wars

The scandals revealed by the Watergate affair continued to cripple the Nixon presidency. The climax came when the Supreme Court ordered the White House to release transcriptions of recorded presidential conversations; the tapes indicated that Nixon had been involved in the cover-up of the Watergate burglary. The House Judiciary Committee, after several months of hearings, voted three articles of impeachment, and it seemed likely an impeachment trial would take place in the Senate. As Nixon's base of support disappeared, he made a tour of the Middle East (June 10–18) and traveled to the U.S.S.R. (June 25-July 3) to sign a limited accord on nuclear weapons testing. These trips were not enough to restore his popular support and in August, faced with impeachment, Nixon became the first U.S. president to resign. Meanwhile, Sec. of State Henry Kissinger followed a policy of shuttle diplomacy, flying from one capital to another in the Middle East. By year's end he had obtained agreement in principle by all parties to resume peace talks in Geneva. This success contrasted with disclosures that the FBI had carried out counterintelligence operations against civil rights groups in the U.S. and that the CIA had been involved in the destabilization or overthrow of foreign governments, particularly the elected Marxist government of Chile. Notables who died this year included Gen. Creighton W. Abrams, Army chief of staff, Sept. 4, at 59; former Sen. Wayne L. Morse of Oregon, July 22, at 73; Gen. Carl A. Spaatz, the first chief of staff of the United States Air Force, in 1947, July 14, at 83; Lewis L. Strauss, head of the Atomic Energy Commission from 1953–1958, Jan. 21, at 78; and Earl Warren, former chief justice of the Supreme Court, July 19, at 83.

Jan 15: In testimony on the **White House tapes,** an expert stated the 18½-minute gap in a critical tape had been caused by deliberate and repeated erasures.

Feb 6: An **impeachment inquiry** against Pres. Nixon by the House Judiciary Committee was approved by the House of Representatives.

Feb 28: The $6,400,000 **lawsuit against the Committee to Reelect the President** for its involvement in the

Watergate break-in was settled. The Democratic National Committee accepted $775,000.

May 23: Following revelation of **cheating by Annapolis midshipmen,** some 900 were ordered by the U.S. Naval Academy to retake an examination .

July 24: In a decision on the **White House tapes,** the Supreme Court ordered that special prosecutor Leon Jaworski's subpoena of tapes and documents be honored by the White House. It ruled that presidential privilege did not apply to evidence required in prosecuting Watergate-related crimes. Pres. Nixon turned over the materials on July 30 and Aug. 5.

July 30: Three articles of impeachment were voted against Pres. Nixon by the House Judiciary Committee: for blocking the investigation of the Watergate affair, for abuse of presidential powers, and for hindering the impeachment process by not complying with the committee's subpoena for taped White House conversations.

Aug 5: Pres. **Nixon released tape transcripts** revealing he had impeded the Watergate investigation. One example of the evidence was an order to H. R. Haldeman on June 23, 1972, to tell the FBI: "Don't go any further in this case, period!"

Aug 8: Pres. **Nixon announced in a televised address that he would resign.** Nixon told an audience of some 100,000,000 he had made some wrong decisions but that he was resigning because he no longer had enough support in Congress.

Aug 9: Pres. **Nixon resigned.** Gerald R. Ford was sworn in as the 38th president of the United States.

Aug 20: Nelson A. Rockefeller, former governor of New York, was nominated for the vice presidency by Pres. Ford.

Sep 7: In a revelation of **CIA covert operations,** it was disclosed that in April CIA director William Colby had told a congressional committee that from 1970 to 1973 some $8,000,000 had been budgeted for operations against Chile's Marxist government.

Sep 8: Pres. **Nixon was pardoned** by Pres. Ford for any crimes he may have committed or may have participated in while in office. On Oct. 17 Ford defended this action before the House Judiciary Committee, saying he wanted to end the national divisions created by the Watergate affair.

Sep 16: Mary Louise Smith of Iowa became the first woman to head the Republican National Committee.

Sep 16: A limited **amnesty proclamation** was issued by Pres. Ford, offering clemency to thousands of Vietnam-era draft resisters and military deserters if they swore allegiance to the U.S. and performed up to two years of public service work.

Sep 16: Charges stemming from the 1973 **occupation of Wounded Knee,** S.D., against Russell Means and Dennis Banks, leaders of the American Indian Movement (AIM), were dismissed in federal court. The judge criticized the government's handling of witnesses and evidence.

Oct 10: Legislation providing for **public funding of presidential primaries and elections** was passed by Congress. It set limits on donations and outlays for congressional and presidential campaigns.

Nov 5: In **congressional elections** the Democrats gained a 61–37 majority in the Senate, with two seats held by independents. In the House the Democrats gained 43 seats, for a 291–144 majority. The Democrats also won four governorships, for a total of 36. Among the new Democratic governors was Ella Grasso of Connecticut, the first elected woman governor. In this election voters in the District of Columbia chose for the first time a mayor and a 14-member city council, posts previously filled by presidential appointment.

Nov 8: Charges against eight Ohio National Guardsmen stemming from the 1970 **Kent State** tragedy were dropped in federal court.

Nov 21: The **Freedom of Information Act,** providing expanded public access to government files, was passed by Congress over Pres. Ford's veto. The law provided that secrecy classification could be challenged in court and had to be justified by federal authorities.

Dec 10: Rep. **Wilbur D. Mills,** Democrat of Arkansas, resigned his chairmanship of the Ways and Means Committee. Several well-publicized incidents had linked him with Fanne Fox, a burlesque performer.

Dec 21: Allegations of illegal CIA activities were leveled by *The New York Times.* The newspaper reported that during the Nixon administration, the agency had maintained files on some 10,000 U.S. citizens and had engaged in illegal domestic operations against opponents of U.S. policy in Vietnam as well as other dissidents. On Dec. 26 CIA director William Colby acknowledged the truth of the allegations in a letter to Pres. Ford.

II. Architecture
Arts and Music
Popular Entertainment
Publishing
Theater

The year in theater was dominated again by British imports, notably works by Tom Stoppard and Alan Ayckbourn. In motion pictures nostalgia maintained its box office appeal. *That's Entertainment,* a pastiche of musicals from the 1930s to the 1950s, grossed $18,000,000, and *Chinatown* was reminiscent of the classic 1940s detective films. Disaster films such as *Towering Inferno* were also popular. In the art world, a study entitled *Museums USA* indicated the gravity of U.S. museums' financial woes. The report showed that 36% of the nation's museums had been forced to cut personnel and services since 1966, 37% had been forced to charge admission, and almost 57% of museum staffs were volunteers. Americans mourned the deaths this year of William A. "Bud" Abbott, straight man of the comedy team Abbott and Costello, Apr. 24, at 78; Jack Benny, the comedian, Dec. 26, at 80; Edward Kennedy "Duke" Ellington, the jazz composer and musician, May 24, at 75; Cassandra "Mama Cass" Elliot, the entertainer, July 29, at 33; Dorothy Fields, composer of such song hits as "I'm in the Mood for Love" and "The Way You Look Tonight," Mar. 28, at 68; Samuel Goldwyn, real name Goldfish, the Hollywood producer, Jan. 31, at 91; Adolph Gottlieb, the artist and pioneer in abstract expressionism, Mar. 4, at 71; Chester R. "Chet" Huntley, who was co-anchorman of NBC's nightly *Huntley-Brinkley Report* from 1956–1970, Mar. 20, at 62; Solomon I. "Sol" Hurok, the impresario, Mar. 5, at 85; Louis I. Kahn, the architect, Mar. 17, at 73; Walter Lippmann, the journalist, Dec. 14, at 85; John Crowe Ransom, the poet, July 3, at 86; Cornelius Ryan, known for his books about World War II, Nov. 23, at 54; Anne Sexton, the poet, Oct. 4, at 45; Edward V. "Ed" Sullivan, newspaper columnist and television host, Oct. 13, at 73; and Jacqueline Susann, the best-selling novelist, Sept. 21, at 53.

Among **books published** this year was *Something Happened* by Joseph Heller, the long-awaited second novel by the author of the 1961 classic *Catch-22.* In this new work Heller presented the perspective of a middle-aged man examining his life and finding it to be a mixture of stifled hopes, disillusionment, minor victories, and a sense of loss. Other books published this year included *Watership Down* by Richard Adams, an allegory of life, death, and continuity in the form of a touching animal story; *If Beale Street Could Talk* by James Baldwin, a novel; *Jaws* by Peter Benchley, a novel; *All the President's Men* by Carl Bernstein and Robert Woodward, a study of the people around Pres. Richard Nixon in the shadow of Watergate; *The Hawkline Monster* by Richard Brautigan, described as a Gothic western; *Fear of Flying* by Erica Jong, a novel; *The CIA and the Cult of Intelligence* by Victor Marchetti and John D. Marks, a study of the U.S. intelligence community; *Centennial* by James Michener, a novel examining the history of Colorado and Wyoming from prehistoric to recent times; *Plain Speaking, An Oral Biography of Harry S*

Truman by Merle Miller; and *My Life as a Man* by Philip Roth, a novel.

Apr 1: In a decision on **censorship for national security,** a federal court ruled that *The CIA and the Cult of Intelligence* by Victor Marchetti and John D. Marks could be published with only 15 deletions made in the original text. The CIA had asked for 168 cuts.

May 7: Pulitzer prizes were awarded for the following: biography, *O'Neill, Son and Artist* by Louis Sheaffer; history, *The Americans: The Democratic Experience* by Daniel J. Boorstin; general nonfiction, *The Denial of Death* by Ernest Becker; poetry, *The Dolphin* by Robert Lowell.

Sep 27: A **record price for an American painting** was set with the sale of Willem de Kooning's *Woman V* to the Australian National Gallery for $850,000. The painting had been sold in 1953 for $30,000.

Nov 2: J. D. Salinger, ending a 21-year public silence, announced he was suing a publisher and several major bookstores for unauthorized publication and distribution of short stories he had written early in his career.

III. Business and Industry
Education
Philosophy and Religion
Science

The economy slid into crisis. Inflation hit 10.3%, auto sales were off 20%, and housing starts were down 40%. Unemployment soared to 7.2% by December. Nevertheless, the economic depression feared by many did not occur. Foreign trade did not decline, and the international banking system withstood the impact of a dramatic rise in oil prices. In education, community control surfaced as a burning issue in the fall. In Kanawha County, W. Va., parents protested their schools' use of books reflecting contemporary sexual mores and dissident views about the U.S. In Boston, the busing of students to achieve integration led to violence and to a confrontation between a citizens group and the federal judge who ordered integration of the city's schools. In science, there were questions regarding the safety of modern genetic research and warnings of possible environmental problems, such as depletion of the ozone layer in the atmosphere. In religion, even as membership in major church denominations declined, attendance at fundamentalist churches continued to climb. Notables who died this year included Vannevar Bush, who pioneered the development of electronic analog computers, June 28, at 84; Adelle Davis, the nutritionist, May 31, at 70; Haroldson Lafayette Hunt, one of the world's wealthiest men, Nov. 29, at 75; Charles A.

Lindbergh, the pioneer aviator, Aug. 26, at 72; Alexander P. Seversky, an early advocate of strategic air power, Aug. 24, at 80; Stephen Gill Spottswood, bishop of the African Methodist Episcopal Zion Church and chairman of the NAACP from 1961, Dec. 1, at 77; Earl W. Sutherland, the Nobel Prize-winning pharmacologist, Mar. 9, at 58; and Arthur K. Watson, a key figure in the phenomenal growth of IBM in the 1950s and 1960s, July 26, at 55.

Mar 7: The Civil War ironclad *Monitor,* which had sunk in a gale in 1862, was reported found off Hatteras, N.C.

Mar 18: The **Arab oil embargo** against the U.S. was officially lifted following Sec. of State Henry Kissinger's efforts to mediate between Egypt and Israel.

Apr 8: A bill extending the **minimum wage** to some 8,000,000 additional workers, and gradually raising it to $2.30 an hour, was signed by Pres. Richard M. Nixon.

Apr 11: William A. "Tony" Boyle, former president of the United Mine Workers, was found guilty by a Media, Pa., jury of ordering the 1969 murders of Joseph Yablonski and Yablonski's wife and daughter.

Apr 30: Federal **wage and price controls were lifted.** A number of price increases by the steel and copper industries followed.

May 2: Legislation for a **Federal Energy Administration,** to be established by July 1975, was passed by Congress. The new agency would be responsible for gas rationing, emergency planning, conservation measures, curbing exorbitant profits, and shaping foreign trade policies.

July 6: Heart disease, chief cause of death in the U.S., had declined 10% since 1963, according to a report by the National Center for Health Statistics.

July 29: The **first women Episcopal priests** were ordained by four bishops in Philadelphia, Pa. The ordination of the 11 women was ruled invalid by the House of Bishops on Aug. 15, but on Oct. 17 the same body approved in principle the ordination of women as priests.

Sep 2: The **Employee Retirement Income Security Act** was signed by Pres. Gerald R. Ford. It was to bring some 300,000 private pension plans under federal regulation by Jan. 1976, when uniform standards would become enforceable and a federal reinsurance program would go into effect to protect benefits if private plans should fail.

Sep 12: Opposition to **court-ordered school busing** in Boston turned into violence on opening day of classes. Subsequent violence prompted mobilization of the National Guard on Oct. 15.

Sep 29: Controversy over the accepted treatment **of breast cancer** was heightened by a report from the National Cancer Institute indicating that radical mastectomy, the prevailing treatment, was too drastic in many cases. The study pressed for surgery that was less deforming and that reduced the lingering pain, weakness, and other effects associated with radical mastectomy.

Oct 8: A program to control inflation, called **WIN (Whip Inflation Now),** was proposed by Pres. Ford. It called for voluntary energy conservation measures to help combat spiraling oil prices. Pres. Ford also asked for a 5% tax surcharge on corporate profits and on personal incomes of more than $15,000.

Oct 8: In the **biggest bank failure in U.S. history** to date, the Franklin National Bank, of New York, was declared insolvent. On Oct. 17 the Securities and Exchange Commission filed fraud charges against the bank's holding company and nine members of the firm.

Oct 10: The **Nobel Prize in Physiology or Medicine** was awarded jointly to Albert Claude, formerly of the Rockefeller Institute and currently director of the Institut Jules Bordet in Belgium, Emil Palade of Yale University Medical School, and Christian de Duve of Belgium, associated with the Rockefeller Institute and the University of Louvain, for their research into the inner workings of cells.

Oct 15: The **Nobel Prize in Chemistry** was awarded to Paul J. Flory of Stanford University for his research on macromolecules, which led to development of new plastics and other synthetic materials.

Nov 13: Blueprint for Project Independence, a plan to reduce U.S. reliance on oil imports, was released by the Federal Energy Administration. The study called for a federal tax of 15 cents a gallon on gasoline; a mandatory fuel standard of 20 miles a gallon for autos; tax credits for insulating homes and buildings; efficiency criteria for electrical appliances; and national standards for heating, cooling, and lighting.

Nov 15: The **retail price of sugar** soared to 65 cents a pound following the sixth major price increase by two leading U.S. refiners since Oct. 9. On Jan. 1 the price of a pound of sugar had been about 18 cents.

Nov 27: The **longest surviving heart transplant patient,** Louis B. Russell, Jr., died in Richmond, Va., at 49. He had received his new heart in 1968.

Dec 30: The **Boston School Committee was fined** by federal Judge W. Arthur Garrity, and its members were barred from participation in school integration matters unless they backed a new public school desegregation plan by Jan. 7, 1975.

Dec 31: A 41-year ban on **private possession of gold** was lifted. Early sales of bullion were light.

IV. Fashion
  Folkways
  Holidays
  Social Issues and Crime
  Sports

A Harris survey showed that tennis claimed 26% of 1974 sports audiences, compared with a 17.7% share in 1973. A Nielsen poll showed that 33,900,000 Americans played the game in 1974, a jump of 68% over the previous year. In golf the top money winners were Johnny Miller, $353,201, and JoAnne Carner, $87,094. In baseball Frank Robinson became the first black manager in major league baseball, Henry Aaron topped the home-run record set by Babe Ruth, and Lou Brock broke the record for stolen bases set by Maury Wills in 1962. Motorcycle stunt driving became a high-paying occupation this year as Robert Craig "Evel" Knievel managed (Sept. 8) to jump the Snake R. Canyon in Twin Falls, Idaho. The year's top fad was streaking, or running naked through a variety of settings. College students were especially fond of the new, short-lived sport. Among the notables who died this year were Jay Hanna "Dizzy" Dean, the baseball pitcher, July 17, at 63; Anne Klein, the fashion designer, Mar. 19, at 51; Peter Revson, a top U.S. race car driver, Mar. 22, at 35; Daniel R. Topping, New York Yankees baseball executive, May 18, at 61; and Amy Vanderbilt, writer on etiquette, Dec. 27, at 66.

Jan 13: Super Bowl VIII was won by the Miami Dolphins, defeating the Minnesota Vikings 24 to 7 for their second consecutive Super Bowl win. On Dec. 30, 1973, the Dolphins had defeated the Oakland Raiders 27 to 10 for the NFC championship, and the Vikings had defeated the Dallas Cowboys 27 to 10 for the AFC championship.

Feb 5: Patricia Hearst, daughter of publisher Randolph Hearst, was kidnaped from her Berkeley, Calif., apartment by members of a group calling itself the Symbionese Liberation Army. On Feb. 12 a ransom message from her abductors demanded $70 in food for every needy person in California. The Hearst family started a $2,000,000 food giveaway on Feb. 22.

Mar 24: The NCAA basketball championship was won by North Carolina State University, defeating Marquette University 76 to 64.

Apr 3: Patricia Hearst, in a tape to authorities sent by her abductors, declared she was joining the Symbionese Liberation Army of her own free will. On Apr. 15 a camera took a picture of her participating in the robbery of a San Francisco bank. On June 6 she was indicted by a federal grand jury for her role in the crime.

Apr 8: Henry "Hank" Aaron of the Atlanta Braves (NL) hit his 715th career home run in Atlanta against the Los Angeles Dodgers, breaking the record set decades earlier by the great Babe Ruth. Aaron finished the year with a career total of 733 homers.

Apr 28-May 12: The **NBA basketball championship** was won by the Boston Celtics, who took their 12th title win in 18 years by beating the Milwaukee Bucks four games to three.

Apr 30-May 10: The **ABA basketball championship** was won by the New York Nets, who beat the Utah Stars four games to one.

May 4: Expo '74 opened in Spokane, Wash. Its focus was environmental issues and solutions. The 100-acre site of the mini-world's fair was designed for future use as a park. Washington State's pavilion was intended to serve after Expo '74 as an opera house and convention center.

May 16: In a serial murder case known as the **Zebra killings,** four Black Muslims were indicted in San Francisco for the murder of three persons and attempted murder of six others. Twelve people, all of them white, had been killed, apparently at random, over a five-month period.

May 17: A shootout with the **Symbionese Liberation Army** in Los Angeles left six of eight known members of the terrorist group dead after police opened fire on their headquarters and the building caught fire. Among the dead were the group's leader, Donald D. DeFreeze, self-styled General Field Marshall Cinque. Patty Hearst and William and Emily Harris, wanted for bank robbery, were not in the building at the time of the attack.

June 12: Little League baseball announced that its teams would be open to girls.

June 16: The **U.S. Open golf tournament** was won by Hale Irwin, beating Forrest Fezler by two strokes.

July 5: At the **Wimbledon** tennis championships in England, Chris Evert won the women's singles title. On July 6 Jimmy Connors won the men's singles title. Peggy Michel teamed with Evonne Goolagong of Australia to win the women's doubles, and Billie Jean King teamed with Owen Davidson of Australia to win the mixed doubles.

Aug 11: The **PGA golf tournament** was won by Lee Trevino, beating Jack Nicklaus by one stroke.

Sep 9: The **U.S. Open tennis singles championships** were won by Jimmy Connors in the men's division and Billie Jean King in the women's division.

Sep 10: Lou Brock of the St. Louis Cardinals (NL) broke the major league record for stolen bases in a season, set by Maury Wills in 1962, when he stole base number 105 in a home game against the Philadelphia Phillies. Brock finished the year with a National League career record of 753 stolen bases.

Sep 10-17: The **America's Cup** was successfully defended by the U.S. yacht *Courageous,* which won four straight races from the Australian challenger *Southern Cross.*

Oct 3: Frank Robinson became the first black manager in major league baseball when he signed a $175,000-a-year contract as player-manager with the Cleveland Indians (AL).

Oct 12-17: The **World Series** was won for the third straight year by the Oakland Athletics (AL), who beat the Los Angeles Dodgers four games to one. On Oct. 9 the Athletics had won the American League pennant, beating the Baltimore Orioles three games to one. The same day the Dodgers took the National League pennant from the Pittsburgh Pirates, winning three games to one.

Oct 30: The **world heavyweight boxing championship** was regained by Muhammad Ali, who triumphed over George Foreman with an eighth-round knockout in Kinshasa, Zaire.

1975

I. Civil Rights
Exploration and Settlement
Government
Statistics
Wars

The Vietnam War reached its conclusion this year. In January the North Vietnamese stepped up military actions in South Vietnam. In mid-March the South Vietnamese army began a withdrawal from northern South Vietnam that soon became a full-scale retreat. On Apr. 30 the last U.S. citizens were airlifted out of Saigon. On the same day, Gen. Duong Van Minh, who had been installed as president two days earlier, surrendered to the Vietcong. In March the new government of Thailand announced it would seek complete U.S. withdrawal from that country within a year, conditions permitting. In mid-April Cambodia fell to the Khmer Rouge. The agony of Vietnam would continue for the U.S. The war had divided the nation politically and philosophically for more than a decade, and its end prompted disillusionment and a new spirit of isolationism. Thus, Congress and the nation proved unwilling to commit itself against in-

surgents in Angola and Ethiopia. At home further revelations in the Watergate scandal, investigations of illegal FBI and CIA activities, and growing concern over the faltering national economy continued to erode Americans' faith in their government and in themselves. Notables who died this year included Hannah Arendt, the political philosopher noted for her writings on totalitarianism, Dec. 5, at 69; Gen. Anthony C. McAuliffe, acting commander of the 101st Airborne Division at Bastogne, Belgium, during the Battle of the Bulge in 1944, Aug. 11, at 77; and Raymond Moley, a member of Pres. Roosevelt's so-called Brain Trust, Feb. 18, at 88.

Jan 5: A **commission on CIA domestic activities** was appointed by Pres. Gerald R. Ford to investigate whether the agency had violated its charter by engaging in domestic intelligence operations. Headed by Vice Pres. Nelson A. Rockefeller, the commission reported on June 10 that the CIA had undertaken unlawful surveillance of some 300,000 persons or organizations and had supplied Pres. Nixon with information to use against political foes.

Jan 24: Fraunces Tavern was bombed in New York City, killing four persons and injuring 53. A terrorist group seeking Puerto Rican independence claimed responsibility.

Jan 27: A bipartisan **Senate investigation of FBI and CIA activities,** headed by Sen. Frank Church of Idaho, was begun. On Nov. 20 the committee released its report. It charged both agencies with illegal surveillance of U.S. citizens and the CIA with plotting to assassinate foreign leaders and maintaining a secret stockpile of poisons despite a presidential order to destroy the poisons.

Jan 31: Pres. Ford's **clemency program** for Vietnam-era military resisters was extended to Mar. 1.

Feb 21: For their parts in the **Watergate** cover-up, former White House aides H. R. Haldeman and John D. Ehrlichman, and former attorney general John Mitchell were each sentenced to 30 months' imprisonment.

Apr 4: A U.S. **C-5A transport plane crashed** shortly after takeoff from Saigon, South Vietnam. Some 200 of the refugees being airlifted to the U.S., most of them children, were killed.

May 12: The U.S. merchant ship **Mayaguez** was seized by Cambodian forces and its crew charged with spying within Cambodia's territorial waters. The crew of 39 was freed on May 14 in a U.S. military rescue operation. Fifteen U.S. soldiers died and 50 were wounded. The operation received virtually unanimous approval by U.S. citizens.

June 24: One hundred and thirteen people were killed when their **jet crashed while attempting to land** in a thunderstorm at Kennedy International Airport in New York City.

July 14: Allegations of **FBI burglaries and break-ins** were confirmed by agency director Clarence B. Kelley, who stated that such activities occurred in national-security cases. On July 16 the Washington *Post* revealed that some of the incidents involved ordinary criminal cases.

July 29: U.S. bases in Turkey were seized by the Turkish government after a U.S. embargo on military aid to Turkey. The embargo had been imposed because of a stalemate in negotiations between Turkey and Greece over Cyprus.

Aug 5: Alger Hiss was ordered reinstated to the Massachusetts bar 25 years after he lost his right to practice law because of a conviction for perjury before a grand jury investigating espionage against the U.S.

Aug 6: Literacy requirements for voting were abolished and a number of linguistic minorities were brought under the protection of the Voting Rights Act of 1965. The act itself was extended for seven years.

Sep 5: An **assassination attempt** against Pres. Ford in Sacramento, Calif., was ended when a Secret Service agent wrested a pistol from Lynette A. "Squeaky" Fromme, a follower of Charles Manson.

Sep 22: In a second **assassination attempt** against Pres. Ford, this time in San Francisco, Calif., the president was shot at by Sara Jane Moore, a police and FBI informer.

Sep 28: A bill authorizing **admission of women to the military academies** for the three major services by the fall of 1976 was passed by Congress.

Oct 22: Air Force Sgt. **Leonard Matlovich,** a much-decorated Vietnam veteran, was given a general discharge after publicly declaring his homosexuality. His intent was to challenge the ban against homosexuals in the military. His discharge was later upgraded to honorable.

Nov 3: In an **administration shakeup** that came to be known as the Halloween massacre, Sec. of State Henry Kissinger resigned his second post as head of the National Security Council, and Sec. of Defense James R. Schlesinger and CIA director William E. Colby were dismissed by Pres. Ford. The president subsequently nominated Donald Rumsfeld for secretary of defense and George Bush for CIA director.

Nov 12: William O. Douglas, 77, suffering from effects of a stroke incurred in 1974, announced his retirement from the Supreme Court after 36 years of service. During his tenure, longest of any Supreme Court justice in history, he earned a reputation as a civil libertarian.

Nov 18: Eldridge Cleaver, a former leader of the Black Panther Party, returned to the U.S. after seven years of exile to face criminal charges stemming from a shoot-out with Oakland, Calif., police.

Dec 4: A staff report of the Senate Committee investigating **illegal CIA activities** absolved the agency of direct participation in the 1973 military overthrow and subsequent murder of Chilean president Salvador Allende Gossens. The CIA was reported to have spent some $13,400,000 from 1963 on Chilean operations, mostly for anti-Allende activities.

Dec 19: U.S. covert aid to factions in Angola was cut by the Senate, despite warnings that U.S. security was at stake in the resolution of the civil war. The war had broken out after Portugal granted independence to Angola.

Dec 20: The last of some 130,000 **Indochinese refugees** resettling in the U.S. left the processing center at Fort Chaffee, Ark.

Dec 29: An **airport bombing** in the main passenger terminal at LaGuardia Airport in New York City killed 11 people and injured 70.

II. Architecture
Arts and Music
Popular Entertainment
Publishing
Theater

In New York City, hard times notwithstanding, Broadway revenues for the 1974–1975 season hit $57,400,000, almost 25% more than the preceding year. Inflation and recession, however, did take their toll on museums. As the value of endowments fell, museums attempted to reduce operating deficits. They fired employees, curtailed services, shortened schedules, and instituted or increased admission fees. By contrast, the motion picture industry enjoyed a second straight year of record revenues, some $2,000,000,000. Fewer films were made, but income from such blockbusters as *Jaws* and *The Godfather, Part II,* as well as such slick sex films as *Emmanuelle* and *The Story of O* helped boost the box office take. This year Americans mourned the passing of Julian E. "Cannonball" Adderley, the jazz musician, Aug. 8, at 46; Josephine Baker, the cabaret singer, Apr. 10, at 68; Thomas Hart Benton, the artist, Jan. 19, at 85; Walker Evans, the photographer known best for his stark portraits of Depression-era subjects, Apr. 10, at 71; Susan Hayward, the actress, Mar. 14, at 55; Vincent Lopez, the band leader and pianist, Sept. 20, at 80; Fredric March, the actor, Apr. 14, at 77; Ozzie Nelson, the radio and television performer, June 3, at 68; Rod Serling, the author and screenwriter, June 28, at 50; George Stevens, the film director, Mar. 8, at 70; Rex Stout, the creator of fictional detective Nero

Wolfe, Oct. 27, at 88; Richard Tucker, the opera tenor, Jan. 8, at 60; Charles Weidman, the modern dancer and choreographer, July 15, at 73; Thornton Wilder, the author, Dec. 7, at 78; and P.G. Wodehouse, the English-born author and humorist, Feb. 14, at 93.

Among **books published** this year was *Ragtime* by E. L. Doctorow, a novel set in the U.S. at the turn of the century. The novel carefully intermingled its fictional characters with such real figures as Henry Ford, Harry Houdini, and Stanford White. Other books published this year included *Humboldt's Gift* by Saul Bellow, a novel; *Thurber* by Burton Bernstein, a biography; *How the Good Guys Finally Won* by Jimmy Breslin, one of several books published this year dealing with the Watergate scandal and the Nixon administration; *Against Our Will: Men, Women and Rape* by Susan Brownmiller; *The Lonely Hunter: A Biography of Carson McCullers* by Virginia Spencer Carr; *Shogun, A Novel of Japan* by James Clavell; *Poems: Selected and New, 1950–1974* by Adrienne Rich; *Looking for Mr. Goodbar* by Judith Rossner, a novel that became one of the year's best sellers; *Passions*, stories by Isaac Bashevis Singer; *Breach of Faith* by Theodore H. White, a study of Richard M. Nixon and the Watergate scandal; *A Time to Die* by Tom Wicker, a study of the 1971 Attica prison riot; and *The Twenties*, a posthumous publication from the notebooks of Edmund Wilson.

Jan 7: The **Bollingen Prize** for poetry was awarded to A. R. Ammons for his work *Sphere: The Form of a Motion* (1974).

Apr 8: The principle of **family viewing time** was adopted by the directors of the National Association of Broadcasters, representing two-thirds of all television stations. For two hours in the early evening, stations were to avoid broadcasting shows with strong themes of violence or sex.

May 5: Pulitzer prizes were awarded for the following: fiction, *The Killer Angels* by Michael Shaara; biography, *The Power Broker: Robert Moses and the Fall of New York* by Robert Caro; history, *Thomas Jefferson and His Times* by Dumas Malone; general nonfiction, *Pilgrim at Tinker Creek* by Annie Dillard; poetry, *Turtle Island* by Gary Snyder; drama, *Seascape* by Edward Albee.

May 27: In a landmark case dealing with **government censorship,** the Supreme Court let stand a lower court ruling requiring former CIA agent Victor Marchetti to submit all writings about the CIA to the agency for prior approval. It was the first such ruling on record.

Aug 1: The **New Orleans Superdome,** the world's largest indoor sports and entertainment center, was dedicated. It cost $162,000,000 and seated 97,000 people.

Sep 25: The FCC lifted the **equal time ruling** that required radio and television stations to offer equal broadcast time for all political candidates.

III. Business and Industry
Education
Philosophy and Religion
Science

Soaring prices prompted many to turn to gardening and home canning to trim food expenses, which were at an eight-year high as a percentage of take-home pay. There were as many as 6,000,000 new gardeners, according to estimates by the Department of Agriculture. Recovery from the recession began in spring but was hampered by steep interest rates and record high savings levels. Pres. Ford secured a federal tax cut but was unsuccessful in trimming the federal deficit. The budget for 1976 included a deficit of about $52,000,000,000, about 11.5% more than in 1975. This year a Senate committee and the Securities and Exchange Commission investigated illegal payoffs by U.S. businesses overseas. In medicine the increasing number of malpractice suits and high court awards produced skyrocketing insurance premiums, and in some cases withdrawal of malpractice coverage. In a number of states physicians threatened job actions if legislative remedies were not taken. This year also saw publication of a landmark religious work, *The Torah—A Modern Commentary,* Reform Judaism's first comprehensive and authorized commentary on the first five books of the Old Testament. Notables who died this year included John R. Dunning, the physicist, Aug. 25, at 67; Euell Gibbons, the naturalist and author, Dec. 29, at 64; Elijah Muhammad, leader of the Nation of Islam for 41 years, Feb. 25, at 77; Charles H. Revson, the business executive, Aug. 24, at 69; and Henry P. Van Dusen, the Protestant theologian, Feb. 13, at 77.

Mar 11: The **proportion of blacks in predominantly white schools** was higher in the South than in the North, according to a report by the Commission on Civil Rights.

Mar 17-20: In the first major **doctors' strike** in U.S. history, some 2000 interns and resident physicians successfully struck New York City's 21 metropolitan hospitals. They achieved their goal of securing shorter work shifts.

Mar 28: Authorization for so-called **no-frills airline fares** was given for the first time, to National Airlines, by the Civil Aeronautics Board. The fares were for travelers willing to forego such amenities as free meals and drinks.

May: Exxon Corporation was listed as the nation's wealthiest company in the annual *Fortune* magazine listing of 500 top industrial firms. Exxon bumped General Motors, number one in the listing for 40 years. Of the top 20 corporations, ten were oil companies.

May 22: A bill providing broad **securities industry reforms** was passed by Congress. It abolished fixed brokerage fees and ordered the Securities and Exchange Commission to set up a national securities clearance system that would give investors up-to-date information on dealings across the country.

May 27: The number of **abortion-related deaths** had been drastically reduced by liberal abortion laws, a report by the National Academy of Sciences revealed. Compared with 320 deaths in 1961, when illegal abortions were common, there had been only 47 deaths in 1973, including 16 linked to illegal operations.

June 4: Discovery of the **oldest animal fossils** in the U.S., large marine worms dating back some 620,000,000 years, was reported by paleontologists in North Carolina.

June 26: Forced confinement of mental patients was barred by the Supreme Court, provided that the patients could care for themselves and did not endanger others.

June 30: The **discovery of a galaxy** approximately 8,000,000,000 light-years away from Earth, identified as Galaxy 3C123, was announced by astronomers at the University of California. The farthest known galaxy from Earth, 3C123 was estimated to be five to ten times larger than the Milky Way.

July 15: The **Apollo-Soyuz** joint space mission began with the launch of Soyuz 19 from the U.S.S.R. and the launch of Apollo, carrying astronauts Thomas P. Stafford, Donald K. Slayton, and Vance D. Brand, from Kennedy Space Center in Florida. On July 17 the craft docked with one another. During their 44-hour linkup, the crews performed a number of experiments. Soyuz returned to Earth on July 21, and Apollo splashed down on July 24.

July 31: Former Teamsters president **James R. Hoffa** was reported missing by his family. Hoffa, who had served a prison term for jury tampering and mail fraud, had been trying to regain leadership of the Teamsters. It was speculated that he had been murdered by organized crime figures.

July 31: The **cancer death rate** was placed at 176.3 persons per 100,000 by the National Center for Health Statistics. The rate was 105.9 in 1933 and 169.5 in 1974.

Sep 4: The first court-ordered **cross-district school busing** in a metropolitan area began in Louisville and adjacent Jefferson County in Kentucky. The National Guard was called in on Sept. 6 because of violence in two working-class suburbs.

Sep 11: Former United Mine Workers president **William A. "Tony" Boyle** was sentenced to three consecutive life terms in Media, Pa., for ordering the 1969 murders of union opponent Joseph Yablonski and Yablonski's wife and daughter.

Sep 14: Mother **Elizabeth Ann Bayley Seton** was canonized in Rome by Pope Paul VI. She was the first U.S.-born saint.

Oct 14: The **Nobel Prize in Economics** was awarded jointly to Tjalling C. Koopmans of Yale University and to Leonid Kantorovich of the U.S.S.R.

Oct 16: The **Nobel Prize in Physiology or Medicine** was awarded jointly to David Baltimore of the Center for Cancer Research at MIT, Howard M. Temin of the University of Wisconsin, and Dr. Renato Dulbecco of Italy for their studies of tumor viruses and the effect of the viruses on genetic material.

Oct 17: The **Nobel Prize in Physics** was awarded jointly to James Rainwater of Columbia University and to Aage N. Bohr and Ben Mottelson of Copenhagen, Denmark, for their work on the asymmetry of the atomic nucleus.

Oct 20: In a decision on **corporal punishment,** the Supreme Court ruled that teachers could spank students if the students were told in advance of the behavior that would warrant such punishment.

Nov 10: The parents of **Karen Anne Quinlan,** a young woman who had been comatose in a hospital for seven months, lost a bid in New Jersey Superior Court to have the respirator believed to be keeping their daughter alive turned off. The court ruled that although her condition was irreversible, she was not dead according to legal or medical criteria. On Mar. 31, 1976, the New Jersey Supreme Court gave its approval for disconnecting the respirator. Quinlan proved able to breathe without assistance.

Dec 2: A federal law prohibiting the **mailing** of **firearms** that could be hidden on one's person was upheld by the Supreme Court.

Dec 6: Creation of the **first artificial animal gene** was reported by a team of four Harvard scientists.

Dec 9: South Boston High School was placed under federal court receivership by Judge W. Arthur Garrity after charging the Boston School Committee with failing to implement a court-ordered busing plan to desegregate the school.

Dec 11: Legislation for **voluntary conversion to the metric system** within ten years was passed by Congress.

IV. Fashion
Folkways
Holidays
Social Issues and Crime
Sports

Declining attendance and failure to secure a profitable television contract led to the demise of the World Football League. The American Basketball Association, reduced from eleven teams to eight by season's end, also faced collapse. Increasing violence in hockey led to the first criminal trial of a player for conduct during a game. New federal guidelines requiring equal access for women in school sports were criticized by officials as burdening schools with oppressive costs. Athletics for females traditionally had been neglected in sports budgets. For example, in 1974–1975 UCLA spent $180,000 of its $3,000,000 sports budget for women's athletics. At the University of Nebraska, women's athletics was allocated $45,000 of a $4,000,000 sports budget. In professional golf the top money winners were Jack Nicklaus, $323,149, and Sandra Palmer, $94,805. This year many Americans found recreation in discothèques, where they could dance to music they enjoyed and be treated to colorful lighting effects. Jewelry for men became popular this year. Among the most fashionable items were pendants, rings, bracelets, and neck chains with shark teeth, a fad sparked by the motion picture *Jaws.* Notables who died this year included Avery Brundage, president of the International Olympic Committee from 1952–1972, May 8, at 87; Ezzard Charles, world heavyweight boxing champion from 1949–1951, May 27, at 53; Leland Stanford "Larry" MacPhail, the baseball executive, Oct. 1, at 85; Perle Mesta, the Washington hostess with the mostest, Mar. 16, at 85; Joan Whitney Payson, owner of the New York Mets, Oct. 4, at 72; and Charles Dillon "Casey" Stengel, who managed the New York Yankees and later the New York Mets and mismanaged the English language to the endless delight of sports fans, Sept. 29, at 85.

Jan 12: Super Bowl IX was won by the Pittsburgh Steelers (AFC), who defeated the Minnesota Vikings (NFC) 16–6 for their first Super Bowl win. On Dec. 29, 1974, the Steelers had beaten the Oakland Raiders 24 to 13 for the AFC championship and the Vikings had defeated the Los Angeles Rams 14 to 10 for the NFC title.

Feb 1: Otis Francis Tabler, a computer scientist, became the first declared **homosexual to get security clearance** for work on a Defense Department contracts.

Mar 31: The **NCAA basketball championship** was won for the tenth time in 12 years by UCLA, defeating the University of Kentucky 92 to 85. On Mar. 29 UCLA coach John Wooden had announced he was retiring, after compiling a 620–147 career record.

Apr 3: Bobby Fischer was stripped of his world chess title after he failed to accept a match with U.S.S.R. challenger Anatoly Karpov. Karpov became champion by default.

May 13-22: The **ABA basketball championship** was won by the Kentucky Colonels, who defeated the Indiana Pacers four games to one.

May 18-25: The **NBA basketball championship** was won by the Golden State Warriors, who swept the Washington Bullets in four games.

June 3: It was reported that **Pelé,** the Brazilian soccer star (born Edson Arantes do Nascimento), would come out of retirement to play for the New York Cosmos. His three-year, $7,000,000 contract made him the highest-paid team athlete in the world.

June 23: The **U.S. Open golf tournament** was won by Lou Graham, who beat John Mahaffey in a playoff.

July 4-5: At the **Wimbledon** tennis championships in England, Billie Jean King won the women's singles title and Arthur Ashe became the first black to win the men's singles title. The men's doubles was won by Vitas Gerulaitis and Sandy Mayer. Ann Kiyomura teamed with Kazuko Sawamatsu of Japan to win the women's doubles, and Marty Riessen teamed with Margaret Court of Australia to win the mixed doubles.

Aug 10: Betty Ford, wife of Pres. Gerald R. Ford, created an uproar when she said during a television interview that she suspected all four of her children had tried marijuana, that she would not be surprised if her 18-year-old daughter Susan told her she was having an affair, and that the Supreme Court had made a "great, great decision" in legalizing abortion.

Aug 10: The **PGA golf tournament** was won by Jack Nicklaus, who beat Bruce Crampton and Tom Weiskopf by two strokes.

Sep 1: Tom Seaver, pitcher for the New York Mets (NL), set a new major league record of eight consecutive years with 200 strikeouts or more in a season.

Sep 6-7: The **U.S. Open tennis singles championships** were won by Chris Evert Lloyd in the women's division and Manuel Orantes of Spain in the men's division.

Sep 18: Patricia Hearst was captured in a San Francisco apartment, ending a 19-month FBI search for the kidnaped newspaper heiress who subsequently joined her abductors, the terrorist Symbionese Liberation Army. Hearst and William and Emily Harris were indicted by a Los Angeles jury on Oct. 2 on charges of assault, robbery, and kidnaping in connection with a 1974 shoplifting incident.

Oct 1: In what he called the **Thriller in Manila,** the Philippines, heavyweight champion Muhammad Ali defeated Joe Frazier in 14 rounds in his fourth title defense of the year.

Oct 11-22: The **World Series** was won for the first time in 35 years by the Cincinnati Reds (NL), who beat the Boston Red Sox (AL) four games to three. On Oct. 7 the Reds had beaten the Pittsburgh Pirates in three straight games for the National League pennant, and the Red Sox had swept the Oakland Athletics in three straight.

1976

I. Civil Rights
Exploration and Settlement
Government
Statistics
Wars

Former governor James Earl "Jimmy" Carter of Georgia pulled off a clear-cut victory in the presidential election by sweeping the South and carrying four of the most populous northern industrial states. Having served only one term as governor, Carter made his neophyte status an asset by appealing to voters' mistrust of politicians, particularly those in Washington, D.C. Voters appeared to believe he would keep his promises. "I'll never tell you a lie," he pledged. In Washington, Rep. Wayne Hays was forced to resign in the wake of a sex scandal, and influential congressmen admitted to receiving illegal donations from Gulf Oil Corporation, although they denied having known the source of the donations. The Justice Department conducted a probe of a scheme by South Korean lobbyists to secure support for the government of Park Chung Hee with lavish gifts and political contributions to congressmen. The scandal almost predictably became known as Koreagate. Notables who died this year included Richard J. Daley, longtime mayor and political boss of Chicago, Dec. 20, at 74; James A. Farley, a leading political figure during the first two terms of Pres. Franklin D. Roosevelt, June 9, at 88; Sen. Philip A. Hart, Democrat of Michigan (1958–1976), Dec. 26, at 64; and Martha Mitchell, wife of former attorney general John Mitchell, who herself made headlines during

Watergate by providing information of the scandal to the press, May 31, at 56.

Jan 30: Ruling on the **Federal Election Campaign Act** of 1974, the Supreme Court upheld the provisions for government financing of presidential campaigns, disclosure of campaign contributions, and a ceiling on contributions. The court struck down limits on campaign expenditures except those placed on funds spent by candidates accepting federal subsidies. It declared unconstitutional the Federal Election Commission as set up, stating that its officers would have to be appointed by the executive branch, not the legislative.

Feb 10: U.S. officials confirmed that **microwave radiation** had been trained on the U.S. Embassy in Moscow. Soviet officials later contended that the emissions had been intended to incapacitate U.S. listening devices.

Feb 17: In a move to **restructure the U.S. intelligence community,** Pres. Gerald R. Ford announced creation of an independent board to oversee U.S. foreign intelligence operations. The next day he issued an executive order curtailing domestic surveillance of U.S. citizens and proscribing burglaries, illegal use of federal tax returns, and drug tests of unsuspecting subjects. Political assassination in foreign covert operations was also forbidden.

Apr 26 and 28: The heavily censored, two-part report of the **Senate Select Committee on Intelligence** was issued. It urged stricter guidelines for intelligence activities, closer congressional oversight, and more stringent safeguards against violation of civil liberties.

May 28: A **nuclear test pact** was signed by the U.S. and U.S.S.R. It limited underground tests to devices of no more than 150 kiloton yields and permitted examination of Soviet test sites by the U.S..

June 5: In Idaho, the **Teton R. Dam collapsed** as it was being filled for the first time, flooding an area of 300 sq. mi. Fourteen people were killed, and estimated damage was $1,000,000,000.

June 16: The **U.S. ambassador to Lebanon was assassinated.** Francis E. Meloy, Jr., and an aide were killed in Beirut by unidentified gunmen. Meloy and his aide were en route to a meeting with president-elect Elias Sarkis.

July 2: **Death penalty laws** in Georgia, Florida, and Texas were upheld by the Supreme Court, but those in North Carolina and Louisiana, which prescribed death sentences for specific crimes, were struck down.

July 14: The **Democratic National Convention nominated Jimmy Carter** for the presidency on the first ballot. The next day Sen. Walter F. Mondale of Minnesota was nominated for the vice presidency.

July 20: The last **U.S. forces in Thailand** were withdrawn at the Thai government's request.

July 27: Some 160 **Americans were evacuated from Beirut,** Lebanon, along with 148 other foreigners, by the U.S. Navy acting in conjunction with the Palestine Liberation Organization and the Lebanese Army.

Aug 18: Two U.S. soldiers were killed by North Korean troops, who attacked a work party setting out to prune a tree that blocked surveillance of the demilitarized zone between North and South Korea. The U.S. protested the slayings. On Aug. 21 North Korea called the incident regrettable but did not accept responsibility.

Aug 19: The **Republican National Convention nominated Pres. Ford** for reelection in a narrow victory over former governor Ronald Reagan of California. Sen. Robert J. Dole of Kansas was nominated for the vice presidency.

Sep 10-12: An **airplane was hijacked** at La Guardia Airport in New York City by five Croatian terrorists, who forced the crew of the TWA 727 to fly the airplane to Paris. There the Croatians surrendered on Sept. 12. On the day before, a bomb left in New York by the terrorists exploded, killing a police bomb expert and wounding three others. The five terrorists were returned to the U.S. to face charges of air piracy and murder.

Sep 27: In the **first presidential TV debate** between an incumbent and a challenger, Pres. Ford and Democratic candidate Jimmy Carter discussed domestic issues before a television audience estimated at 90,000,000. Two more debates were held on Oct. 6 and Oct. 22. A fourth debate was held between vice-presidential candidates Walter Mondale and Robert Dole (Oct. 15). It was the first televised debate between candidates for vice president.

Oct 20: In what came to be called **Koreagate,** the Justice Department reported that a major probe was under way concerning the activities of a South Korean lobby, led by businessman Tongsun Park. The purpose of the lobby was to influence congressmen and other government officials through cash grants and campaign contributions estimated at $500,000 to $1,000,000 annually.

Nov 2: James Earl "Jimmy" Carter, Jr., was elected president of the United States. Walter F. Mondale was elected vice president. The electoral vote was Carter, 297; Pres. Ford, 240. The popular vote was Carter, 40,828,929; Ford, 39,148,940. In congressional elections the Democrats kept a 2–1 Senate majority, 61–38, with one seat going to an independent, and a House majority of 292–143.

II. Architecture
Arts and Music
Popular Entertainment
Publishing
Theater

The year in theater was noteworthy for its excellent revivals of *Porgy and Bess, My Fair Lady, Guys and Dolls,* and *Fiddler on the Roof.* In film the year was highlighted by such foreign works as Ingmar Bergman's version of Mozart's *The Magic Flute* and Lina Wertmuller's *Seven Beauties.* But in Hollywood, the biggest success came with *Rocky,* starring Sylvester Stallone as a small-time boxer given an improbable shot at the championship. The movie made Stallone a star and led to several sequels. Television hits included the miniseries *Rich Man, Poor Man,* the lightweight series *Charlie's Angels,* featuring three eye-catching private investigators, and the soap opera spoof *Mary Hartman, Mary Hartman.* Notables who died this year included Busby Berkeley, real name William Berkeley Enos, the Hollywood choreographer, Mar. 14, at 80; Alexander Calder, the sculptor, Nov. 11, at 78; Lee J. Cobb, the actor, Feb. 11, at 64; Paul Gallico, the writer, July 15, at 78; Bobby Hackett, the jazz cornetist, June 7, at 61; Fritz Lang, the motion picture director, Aug. 2, at 85; Lotte Lehmann, the German-born soprano, Aug. 26, at 88; Johnny Mercer, writer of such songs as "Moon River" and "That Old Black Magic," June 25, at 66; Samuel Eliot Morison, the historian, May 15, at 89; Phil Ochs, songwriter and folk singer, Apr. 9, at 35; Walter Piston, the composer, Nov. 12, at 82; Lily Pons, the French-born Metropolitan Opera star for some 25 years, Feb. 13, at 71; Man Ray, the artist and leading exponent of Dada, Nov. 18, at 86; Paul Robeson, the singer and actor, Jan. 23, at 77; Rosalind Russell, the actress, Nov. 28, at 63; Mark Tobey, the abstract painter, Apr. 24, at 85; Dalton Trumbo, the novelist and screenwriter who was blacklisted in the late 1940s, Sept. 10, at 70; and Adolph Zukor, the motion picture executive who founded Paramount Pictures, June 10, at 103.

Among **books published** this year was *Roots* by Alex Haley, a fictionalized account of the author's discovery of his lineage in Africa. The book became a best seller and was the basis for an enormously popular television miniseries. Other books published this year included *The Black Family in Slavery and Freedom* by Herbert Gutman, which attacked the notion that blacks lacked strong family units in the past; *Scoundrel Time* by Lillian Hellman, memoirs; *World of Our Fathers* by Irving Howe, a study of the lives of Jews who emigrated from eastern Europe; *Lyndon*

Johnson and the American Dream by Doris Kearns, a sympathetic portrait of the former president; *Agent in Place* by Helen MacInnes, a spy thriller; *The Russians* by Hedrick Smith, nonfiction; *Spandau* by Albert Speer, memoirs; *Adolf Hitler* by John Toland, biography; *Trinity* by Leon Uris, a novel; *Slapstick* by Kurt Vonnegut, a novel; and *The Final Days* by Robert Woodward and Carl Bernstein, an account of the end of the Nixon presidency.

Feb 11-18: The New York City weekly ***The Village Voice*** published major portions of a secret House of Representatives report on intelligence agencies. CBS news reporter Daniel Schorr admitted on Feb. 12 that he had provided the *Voice* with a copy of the report. Schorr was suspended by CBS on Feb. 23, after the House ordered an inquiry to determine how he obtained the document. The inquiry proved unsuccessful and was halted on Sept. 22.

Apr 22: Barbara Walters became the first anchorwoman of a network television news program and the highest-paid journalist in history when she accepted a five-year, $5,000,000 contract with ABC.

May 3: Pulitzer prizes were awarded for the following: fiction, *Humboldt's Gift* by Saul Bellow; biography, *Edith Wharton: A Biography* by R. W. B. Lewis; history, *Lamy of Santa Fe* by Paul Horgan; general nonfiction, *Why Survive? Being Old in America* by Robert N. Butler; poetry, *Self-Portrait in a Convex Mirror* by John Ashbery; drama, *A Chorus Line* by Michael Bennett, Nicholas Dante, Marvin Hamlisch, James Kirkwood, and Edward Kleban.

May 18: What was billed as the **Concert of the Century** was presented at Carnegie Hall in New York City to benefit a $6,500,000 fund drive for the concert hall. Among the musical greats who participated were Leonard Bernstein, Yehudi Menuhin, Mstislav Rostropovich, Vladimir Horowitz, and Isaac Stern.

June 2: A **journalist's car was bombed** in Phoenix, Ariz. Don Bolles, an investigative reporter for the *Arizona Republic*, had been probing the role of leading politicians in land swindles. He died on June 13.

Sep 29: A new **record art price** for a painting by Rembrandt, $3,250,000, was set by the industrialist Armand Hammer, who announced acquisition of Rembrandt's *Juno*.

Sep 30: In the first major attempt at **copyright reform** since 1909, Congress approved legislation, effective Jan. 1, 1978, extending copyright protection for 50 years after the death of an author, artist, or composer. It also restricted reproduction of copyrighted material and set royalty rates for phonograph records played by broadcasters or used in jukeboxes.

Oct 6: The last privately owned painting by **Jackson Pollock**, *Lavender Mist*, was reported to have been acquired by the National Gallery of Art in Washington, D.C., for $2,000,000. It had been bought in 1950 for about $1500.

Oct 21: The **Nobel Prize in Literature** was awarded to Saul Bellow "for the human understanding and subtle analysis of contemporary culture that are combined in his work."

III. Business and Industry
Education
Philosophy and Religion
Science

The state of the economy was probably a major contributor to Jimmy Carter's election to the presidency this year. Voters were wary of inflation, which fluctuated between 5% and 6%, and unemployment, which was about 8%. In this year, business ethics came under scrutiny following revelations of corporate payoffs to win sales abroad. Lockheed and Northrop were two major firms that were strongly criticized. Public indignation was also kindled by reports that a number of multinational corporations were cooperating with an Arab embargo on trade with Israel. Congress sought to discourage such behavior by eliminating tax incentives to participating firms. Census Bureau reports indicated that the number of Americans with high-school diplomas had doubled since 1950, but public concern about the quality of education was reflected in calls for greater emphasis on traditional educational skills. A number of states began to require high-school students to pass a comprehensive test before receiving diplomas. The year in science was highlighted by a clean sweep of Nobel Prizes by Americans. Notables who died this year included Jean Paul Getty, the billionaire oil tycoon, June 6, at 83; Howard R. Hughes, Jr., the reclusive billionaire, Apr. 5, at 72; Gerald L. K. Smith, the anti-Semitic, anti-Catholic founder of the so-called National Christian Crusade, Apr. 15, at 78; and Luther Allan Weigle, the biblical scholar who oversaw compilation of the Revised Standard Version of the Bible, Sept. 2, at 96.

Jan 12: The **first report on national health** issued by the Department of Health, Education, and Welfare indicated that Americans were generally healthy. Infant mortality rates had dropped from their 1950 level of 29.2 per 1000 births to 16.5. Heart disease among those 55 to 64 years of age had declined by almost 15% since 1970. The role of insurance companies in medical payments expanded. In 1950 they paid one-third of all health bills, but in 1975 they paid two-thirds.

Feb 12: Production of **Red Dye No. 2,** most frequently used in drugs, foods, and cosmetics, was banned by the Food and Drug Administration after studies indicated that the dye was carcinogenic.

Apr 1: Conrail, a federally funded corporation, took over operation of six bankrupt northeastern railroads. Federal subsidies were slated to end after five years.

Apr 21: Production of convertibles by the U.S. auto industry halted as General Motors rolled the last of its Cadillac Eldorado convertibles off the assembly line. The move was made in response to declining sales.

Apr 22: Widespread **cheating at West Point** was reported. By September, 700 cadets at the U.S. Military Academy were implicated in violations of the academy's honor code.

May 24: Concorde supersonic jet service between the U.S. and Europe was inaugurated when two Anglo-French Concorde jets arrived from Paris and London at Dulles International Airport, near Washington, D.C.

June 25: Discrimination by private nonsectarian schools was ruled unconstitutional by the Supreme Court.

July 9: The tranquilizer **Valium and alcohol** were the leading causes of drug-related ailments, according to a report of the National Institute on Drug Abuse. Valium, used by some 65,000,000 Americans, was the most often prescribed drug. The report stated that alcohol surpassed all other drugs in social costs.

July 18: Discovery of **Lyme arthritis,** a new, infectious strain of arthritis, was reported by researchers at Yale University's School of Medicine. Some 51 cases of the disease, apparently caused by an insect-borne virus, were recorded in and around Lyme, Conn.

July 20: **Viking 1,** launched on Aug. 20, 1975, landed on Mars. It was the first spacecraft to reach the planet. Data collected by Viking 1 and by **Viking 2,** launched on Sept. 9, 1975, and landed on Mars on Sept. 3, 1976, showed Mars to be a barren, rocky planet. Tests to detect the presence of life there were inconclusive.

July 27-Aug 31: What came to be called **Legionnaires' disease** claimed the lives of 29 people who had attended an American Legion convention in Philadelphia, Pa., on July 21–24. Another 151 were hospitalized for high fever and respiratory problems, symptoms of the disease.

Aug 28: Synthesis of a bacterial gene had been accomplished for the first time, scientists at the Massachusetts Institute of Technology reported. The gene functioned properly when implanted in a living cell.

Aug 30: Medicaid waste from fraud, abuse, and government bungling devoured some 25–50% of the $15,000,000,000 Medicaid budget, a Senate study reported. About half the $3,000,000,000 spent on physicians, dentists, pharmacies, and laboratories went for substandard or unnecessary care provided by Medicaid mills, privately owned clinics usually located in poor urban neighborhoods.

Sep 16: The **ordination of women** was approved by the 65th triennial General Convention of the Episcopal Church. By year's end, some of those who disapproved of the change were preparing to break with the church.

Sep 18: The Rev. **Sun Myung Moon,** head of the evangelical Unification Church, presided over a "God Bless America" rally in Washington, D.C., that drew some 50,000 persons. Moon, who advocated U.S. defense of South Korea, was denounced by established church leaders for perverting Christian doctrine. He was also under attack from parents who claimed brainwashing tactics had been used to recruit young people into the church. The converts, who solicited contributions in public places, were frequently referred to as *Moonies.*

Sep 28: The **Toxic Substances Control Act,** was passed by Congress. It prohibited the marketing of new chemical compounds before testing their impact on human health and the environment. The law also forbade production of polychlorinated biphenyls, or PCBs, after 1979. Studies of PCBs had shown they did not break down in the environment and were linked to cancer.

Sep 30: The first state **right-to-die law** was passed in California. It granted to adult patients the right to authorize a physician to shut off their life-support equipment when death was imminent. The law went into effect on Jan. 1, 1977.

Oct 14: The **Nobel Prize in Physiology or Medicine** was awarded jointly to Dr. Baruch S. Blumberg of the University of Pennsylvania Medical School and to Dr. D. Carleton Gajdusek of the National Institute for Neurological Diseases for their work on infectious diseases.

Oct 14: The **Nobel Prize in Economics** was awarded to Milton Friedman of the University of Chicago.

Oct 18: The **Nobel Prize in Chemistry** was awarded to William N. Lipscomb, Jr., of Harvard University for his studies of the structure and bonding of chemical compounds known as boranes.

Oct 18: The **Nobel Prize in Physics** was awarded jointly to Burton Richter of Stanford University and to Samuel C. C. Ting of MIT for their discovery of the psi, or J, particle.

Dec 15: A major **oil spill** began when the Liberian-registered tanker *Argo Merchant* ran aground near Nantucket Island, Mass., and its 7,700,000-gallon oil cargo leaked.

IV. Fashion
Folkways
Holidays
Social Issues and Crime
Sports

Professional athletes in baseball, basketball, and football gained greater freedom as team owners revised reserve and option clauses. The issue centered on the tying of players to clubs until retirement or disposal by the team. Owners' fears that so-called free agents would cripple sports proved groundless. Only 24 football players and 24 baseball players chose free-agent status. In basketball, free trading was slated to start in 1980. In boxing, Muhammad Ali defended his heavyweight title in three bouts and then announced his retirement. In golf the top money winners were Jack Nicklaus, $266,438, and Judy Rankin, $150,734. This year Americans found new sources of amusement in Citizen Band radios and in electronic games that hooked up to television sets. Among the year's deaths was that of Carlo Gambino, reportedly a leading figure in organized crime, Oct. 15, at 74.

Jan 9: A new amateur **pole vault record** of 18 ft. 1¼ in. was set by Dan Ripley at a National Invitational Indoor Track meet in College Park, Md.

Jan 18: Super Bowl X was won by the Pittsburgh Steelers (AFC), who defeated the Dallas Cowboys (NFC) 21 to 17 to pick up their second straight victory. On Jan. 4 the Steelers had beaten the Oakland Raiders 16–10 for the AFC championship and the Cowboys had beaten the Los Angeles Rams 37 to 7 for the NFC title.

Feb 4-15: At the **Winter Olympics** in Innsbruck, Austria, the U.S. won three gold medals and tied with West Germany for third place, behind the U.S.S.R. and East Germany. Dorothy Hamill, who won a gold medal on Feb. 13, emerged from the games as an Olympic star.

Mar 20: Patricia Hearst was convicted by a San Francisco jury of taking part in a 1974 bank robbery. She was sentenced to seven years in jail on Sept. 24 and released on bail pending appeal.

Mar 29: The **NCAA basketball championship** was won by Indiana, defeating Michigan 86 to 68.

May 1-13: The **ABA basketball championship** was won by the New York Nets, who defeated the Denver Nuggets four games to two to take their second championship in three years.

May 23-June 6: The **NBA basketball championship** was won for the 13th time by the Boston Celtics, defeating the Phoenix Suns four games to two.

June 17: In a **basketball merger,** the 18 teams of the NBA merged with four of the six remaining teams of the ABA.

June 20: The **U.S. Open golf tournament** was won in an upset by golf rookie Jerry Pate, who beat Tom Weiskopf and Al Geiberger by two strokes.

July 2-3: At the **Wimbledon** tennis championships in England, Chris Evert Lloyd won the women's singles title. Brian Gottfried teamed with Paul Ramirez of Mexico to win the men's doubles, and Evert Lloyd teamed with Martina Navratilova of Czechoslovakia to win the women's doubles.

July 4: A year of festivities celebrating the **bicentennial of U.S. independence** was capped at 2 P.M. by the ringing of bells nationwide. Among the special events this day were Operation Sail, a parade in New York harbor of more than 50 warships and 16 windjammers from many nations; convergence at Valley Forge, Pa., of six wagon trains that had trekked across the country; sealing of time capsules; and a 76-hour vigil (starting July 2) at the National Archives to honor the signing of the Declaration of Independence.

July 12: A change in the baseball **reserve clause** was agreed to by major league owners and players. The new rule allowed players to become free agents after five years.

July 17-Aug 1: At the **Summer Olympics** in Montreal, Canada, the U.S. won 34 gold medals and finished second in unofficial team standings behind the U.S.S.R. Among the stars of the games was decathlon champion Bruce Jenner.

Aug 16: The **PGA golf tournament** was won by Dave Stockton for the second time.

Aug 27: A new type of **sexual discrimination** in sports was highlighted when transsexual Renee Richards, formerly Richard Raskind, an eye surgeon, was barred from competing at the U.S. Open tennis championships at Forest Hills, N.Y., after refusing to submit to a chromosome qualification test.

Sep 11-12: The **U.S. Open tennis singles championships** were won by Chris Evert Lloyd in the women's division and Jimmy Connors in the men's division.

Oct 16-21: The **World Series** was won in a four-game sweep by the Cincinnati Reds (NL) over the New York Yankees (AL). On Oct. 12 the Reds had won the National League pennant over the Philadelphia Phillies in a three-game sweep, and the Yankees had taken the American League pennant from the Kansas City Royals three games to two.

Nov 4: In major league baseball's **first free-agent draft,** 24 players from 13 clubs participated. Reggie Jackson signed the most lucrative contract, calling for $2,900,000 over five years with the New York Yankees (AL).

1977

I. Civil Rights
Exploration and Settlement
Government
Statistics
Wars

In the first months of Pres. Jimmy Carter's administration, most Vietnam-era draft resisters were pardoned, the planned pullout of U.S. forces from South Korea was announced, and administration officials spoke out against human rights violations worldwide. Pres. Carter also established guidelines to prevent conflict of interest among officials, opened communication between the White House and ordinary citizens, ended U.S. opposition to the admission of Vietnam to the UN, and signed two treaties returning control of the Panama Canal to Panama. The new president suffered setbacks when Congress challenged the financial dealings of Bert Lance, director of the Office of Management and Budget, and opposed passage of Carter's energy conservation program. Vernon Jordan of the National Urban League charged the administration with not doing enough to reduce unemployment among blacks. Notables who died this year included Lewis B. Hershey, director of the Selective Service System from 1941 to 1973, May 20, at 83; Sen. John L. McClellan, chairman of the Senate Appropriations Committee, Nov. 27, at 81; and Francis Gary Powers, the pilot shot down over the U.S.S.R. in 1960, Aug. 1, at 48.

Jan 19: Tokyo Rose, real name Iva Toguri D'Aquino, was pardoned by Pres. Gerald R. Ford 27 years after her conviction for treason. She had made propaganda broadcasts from Japan during World War II in an attempt to demoralize U.S. troops.

Jan 21: A **presidential pardon** for most of the nation's Vietnam draft resisters was issued by Pres. Carter.

Jan 28-29: A **blizzard** paralyzed much of the East and Midwest, worsening a severe shortage of natural gas. Among the hardest hit cities was Buffalo, N.Y., which already had a cumulative snowfall of 160 inches.

Feb 28: A longstanding **land suit** against the state of Maine by the Passamaquoddy and Penobscot Indians prompted the federal government to warn that it would sue Maine if the state did not reach a settlement quickly.

Mar 2: A new **House ethics code** was adopted. It limited outside income for members of the House of Representatives, broadened financial disclosure requirements, and restricted gifts by lobbyists. The Senate adopted a similar code on Apr. 1.

Mar 9: U.S. ground forces in Korea would be withdrawn within five years, Pres. Carter announced.

Mar 18: U.S. **travel restrictions** to Cuba, Vietnam, North Korea, and Cambodia were lifted.

Apr 27: A **task force on illegal aliens** reported to Pres. Carter that 6,000,000 to 8,000,000 illegal aliens were living in the U.S. About 876,000 had been caught in 1976, compared with 89,000 in 1961.

Apr 28: In a major **espionage** case, a U.S. citizen named Christopher J. Boyce was convicted of supplying data on satellites and CIA codes to the U.S.S.R. in complicity with another American, Andrew Lee. On Sept. 12 Boyce was sentenced to 40 years in prison. Lee was convicted on May 14 and sentenced on July 18 to life imprisonment.

May 3: Normalization talks between the U.S. and Vietnam began in Paris. On the next day, the U.S. agreed to stop blocking Vietnam's request for admission to the UN.

May 4: Richard M. Nixon, in the first of five television interviews with David Frost, for which the former president was paid, acknowledged that he had "let the American people down" through his actions in the Watergate cover-up. In the May 19 interview, Nixon argued that sanctioning burglary and other illegal activities taken against dissidents is not illegal "when the president does it."

May 23: The end of the road in the **Watergate** scandal came for three former U.S. officials, John Ehrlichman, H. R. Haldeman, and John Mitchell, when the Supreme Court refused to hear their appeals. On June 22 Mitchell became the first former attorney general to begin serving a prison sentence.

June 6: Development of a **neutron bomb** by the U.S. was reported by the Washington *Post.* The weapon was designed to kill people but cause minimal destruction of property.

June 30: A halt in production of the **B-1 bomber** was announced by Pres. Carter.

July 13-14: A 25-hour **power failure** struck New York City and suburban Westchester County, leading to extensive looting and arson in the city. Some 3776 looters were arrested and 100 policemen injured. Property damage was estimated at $135,000,000.

July 19: Flooding struck the Johnstown, Pa., area, killing 76 people and causing some $200,000,000 in damage.

July 20: In the so-called **Koreagate** lobbying scandal, former Watergate prosecutor Leon Jaworski agreed to lead a House Ethics Committee probe into alleged congressional influence-buying by South Korean lobbyists. On Dec. 30 the Justice Department announced that South Korean businessman Tongsun Park had agreed to testify in return for immunity from prosecution.

Aug 4: Legislation creating the **Department of Energy,** the twelfth Cabinet-level department and the first new one since 1966, was signed by Pres. Carter. James R. Schlesinger was nominated and quickly confirmed as the first secretary of energy.

Aug 20: The **Republican Party** was reported by a Gallup poll to have the support of 20% of U.S. voters, the worst showing in 40 years.

Sep 7: Two **Panama Canal treaties,** transferring control of the canal to Panama by the year 2000, were signed by Pres. Carter and Panama's head of state, Brig. Gen. Omar Torrijos Herrera. The accords, capping 13 years of negotiations, were subject to ratification by each nation's legislature.

Sep 21: Bert Lance resigned as director of the Office of Management and Budget following severe criticism of his past financial practices as a banker in Georgia.

Nov 18-21: The first **National Women's Conference,** the largest feminist gathering since the Seneca Falls, N.Y., convention in 1848, drew 1442 delegates to Houston, Tex., to call for passage of the Equal Rights Amendment and elimination of institutional discrimination. Opponents of ERA and abortion held a so-called pro-family rally five miles away.

Dec 20: Legislation authorizing a **Social Security tax increase** was signed by Pres. Carter. The tax revision was expected to cost workers and employers $227,000,000,000 in the next ten years.

II. Architecture
Arts and Music
Popular Entertainment
Publishing
Theater

Even as the nation's interest in the arts boomed, the top 200 nonprofit performing arts groups were sinking under a $125,000,000 deficit incurred during the 1976–1977 season. The Metropolitan Opera in New York City confronted a $14,000,000 deficit; museums in New York, Chicago, and San Diego cut viewing hours to save costs. The American Shakespeare Festival in Stratford, Conn., failed to open for the season, and the City Center Joffrey Ballet in New York scrapped its spring season. In contrast, motion picture revenues were up to a record $2,300,000,000, largely because of such phenomenally successful films as *Star Wars* and *Close Encounters of the Third Kind*. Television's hit show of the year was the miniseries *Roots*, based on the book by Alex Haley. Americans mourned the passing this year of James M. Cain, the novelist, Oct. 27, at 85; Maria Callas, the opera singer, Sept. 16, at 53; Joan Crawford, the actress, May 10, at 69; Harry Lillis "Bing" Crosby, Oct. 14, at 73; Howard Hawks, the motion picture director, Dec. 26, at 81; James Jones, the novelist, May 9, at 55; Guy Lombardo, the band leader, Nov. 5, at 75; Robert Lowell, the poet, Sept. 12, at 60; Alfred Lunt, who performed with his wife Lynn Fontanne in numerous Broadway plays, Aug. 3, at 83; Julius Henry "Groucho" Marx, Aug. 19, at 86, and his brother, Milton "Gummo" Marx, Apr. 21, at 84; Samuel J. "Zero" Mostel, the actor, Sept. 8, at 62; Vladimir Nabokov, the writer, July 2, at 78; Elvis Presley, the king of rock 'n' roll, Aug. 16, at 42; and Ethel Waters, the blues singer and actress, Sept. 1, at 80.

Among **books published** this year was *A Rumor of War* by Philip Caputo. The book was hailed as one of the year's best of several works dealing with the Vietnam War. Other books published this year included *Falconer* by John Cheever, a novel examining the soul of a convict; *Six Men* by Alistair Cooke, essays on six well-known figures of the twentieth century; *A Book of Common Prayer* by Joan Didion, a novel dealing with the inability of its middle-aged characters to find meaning in their lives; *The Immigrants* by Howard Fast, a novel; *The Age of Uncertainty* by John Kenneth Galbraith; *The Thorn Birds* by Colleen McCullough, a novel that became a runaway best seller; *Coming into the Country* by John McPhee, an excellent book about Alaska and Alaskans; and *Ring* by Jonathan Yardley, a biography of Ring Lardner.

Jan 11: The **Bollingen Prize** for poetry was awarded to David Ignatow.

Feb 8: Larry Flynt, publisher of the sexually explicit magazine *Hustler*, was convicted in Cincinnati of promoting obscenity and involvement in organized crime.

Apr 18: Pulitzer prizes were awarded for the following: biography, *A Prince of Our Disorder* by John E. Mack; history, *The Impending Crisis: 1841–1861* by David M. Potter; general nonfiction, *Beautiful Swimmers* by William W. Warner; poetry, *Divine Comedies* by James Merrill; drama, *The Shadow Box* by Michael Cristofer. A special award was given for *Roots,* written by Alex Haley.

June 30: The **Newport Jazz Festival,** citing prohibitive costs and acoustical problems, announced it was ending its six-year tenure in New York City and moving in 1978 to Saratoga Springs, N.Y.

Nov 13: The final installment of *Li'l Abner,* the comic strip created by Al Capp in 1934, marked Capp's retirement.

Nov 22: What was said to be a **record price for sculpture**—between $3,500,000 and $5,000,000—was reported to have been paid by the J. Paul Getty Museum in California for a fourth-century B.C. bronze.

III. Business and Industry
Education
Philosophy and Religion
Science

The U.S. faced a high trade deficit, primarily because of oil imports and the falling value of the dollar. Uncertainty about Pres. Carter's legislative program for tax reform and concern about new, inflationary social programs slowed investment by the private sector. The Dow Jones average declined more than 165 points during the year, and unemployment remained at 7% of the work force. The retail price of a pound of coffee hit $5.00, mainly because of a killing frost in Brazil in 1975. Many consumers struck back by switching to tea. Tea imports rose by nearly 30%, and tea prices rose as well. In transportation, the year was marked by sharp air fare reductions on domestic and transatlantic routes as airlines began offering no-frills flights. Transportation Sec. Brock Adams ruled that airbags or safety belts would be required automotive equipment beginning in 1984. In education, amendments to the Rehabilitation Act of 1973 required that handicapped children be included in regular school settings. Notables who died this year included Wernher von Braun, the German-born rocket pioneer, June 16, at 65; Loren C. Eiseley, the anthropologist and author, July 9, at 69; and John R. Powers, founder of the Powers modeling agency, July 19, at 80.

Jan 1: The **first woman Episcopal priest** in the U.S., Jacqueline Means, was ordained.

Jan 11: Henry Ford, II, resigned as trustee of the Ford Foundation, criticizing its staff for ingratitude for the capitalist wealth that made its work possible.

Jan 11: Discriminatory zoning laws, enabling suburbs to block racially integrated housing for low- and middle-income families, were upheld by the Supreme Court. The Court ruled that the refusal of a suburb to change zoning laws was not inherently unconstitutional.

Feb 23: The **Environmental Protection Agency** was held by the Supreme Court to have the authority to establish industry-wide standards to control discharge of pollutants into waterways.

Mar 1: The U.S. extended its **fishing limits** to 200 miles offshore to protect depleted fisheries against the activities of foreign fishing fleets.

Mar 9: A ban on **saccharin** was proposed by the Food and Drug Administration after tests suggested that the artificial sweetener might be carcinogenic. Consumer resistance and intense lobbying led the FDA to allow saccharin to be sold as an over-the-counter drug. On Nov. 4 Congress postponed the ban for 18 months, pending new tests.

Apr 18: An all-out campaign for **energy conservation** was called for by Pres. Carter, who called the effort "the moral equivalent of war." On Apr. 20 he asked Congress for new legislation designed to discourage energy waste and encourage conservation measures.

Apr 30: Some 2000 **opponents of nuclear energy** occupied the construction site of a nuclear generating plant at Seabrook, N.H. By May 2 some 1414 protesters had been arrested for trespassing.

May 1: Controversy over **Laetrile,** a purported anticancer compound derived primarily from apricot pits, continued as the state of Indiana passed the first law legalizing its manufacture, sale, and use.

May 30: Viking 1 and 2 biological experiments on the planet Mars, which had proven inconclusive, were terminated by NASA scientists.

June 19: Bishop **John N. Neumann** of Philadelphia, known for his development of the parochial school system, was canonized by the Roman Catholic Church. He became the first American male to achieve sainthood.

June 20: Medicaid funding for elective abortions was ruled by the Supreme Court to be not obligatory under the Constitution or federal law.

June 27: Legal advertising of fees for specific, routine services was upheld by the Supreme Court in a decision with wide-ranging implications for a number of professions.

July 28: The 799-mile **trans-Alaska pipeline** went into full operation as the first oil from Alaska's Prudhoe

Bay fields arrived at the loading port of Valdez at 11:02 P.M. (4:02 A.M. July 29, EST). Pumping operations had begun on June 20.

Aug 12: The **space shuttle** *Enterprise,* with astronauts C. Gordon Fullerton and Fred W. Haise, Jr., aboard, made its first free flight at Edwards Air Force Base after being lifted to 25,000 feet on the back of a Boeing 747.

Aug 23: The 77-pound aircraft *Gossamer Condor,* powered by its pilot, was flown by Bryan Allen over a one-mile, figure-eight course at Shafter, Calif. The craft won for its designer, Paul MacCready, the $86,000 Kremer prize for human-powered aircraft.

Sep 13: The **first U.S. diesel automobiles** were introduced by General Motors. The cars, Oldsmobile 88 and 98 models, were said to have 40% greater fuel efficiency than gasoline-powered cars.

Oct 11: The **Nobel Prize in Physics** was awarded jointly to John H. Van Vleck of Harvard University, Philip W. Anderson of Bell Laboratories and Princeton University, and Nevill F. Mott of Great Britain for their contributions to the field of solid state electronic circuitry.

Oct 13: The **Nobel Prize in Physiology or Medicine** was awarded jointly to Rosalyn S. Yalow of the Veterans Administration Hospital, Bronx, N.Y., Roger C. L. Guillemin of the Salk Institute, and Andrew V. Schally of Veterans Administration Hospital, New Orleans, La., and Tulane University for their independent studies of the production of peptide hormones in the brain and the relation of the hypothalamus in controlling the pituitary gland.

Oct 19: The **Concorde SST** made its first flight from France to Kennedy Airport in New York two days after the Supreme Court refused to stay a lower court ruling authorizing the flights. Concorde flights to Washington, D.C., had begun in May 1976.

Nov 1: A law raising the **minimum wage** from $2.30 to $3.35 an hour by 1981 was signed by Pres. Carter.

Dec 10: A nationwide **farmers' strike** was launched by the American Agriculture Movement, which held rallies in 30 state capitals in a drive to raise farmers' falling incomes.

IV. Fashion
   Folkways
   Holidays
   Social Issues and Crime
   Sports

With star player Pelé in action with an American professional team, soccer became the fastest growing team sport in the U.S. Growth of soccer (some 350,000 persons under 18 years of age were playing the game) was enhanced further by availability of inexpensive equipment, low injury rate, and accessibility for women players. The price of a professional soccer franchise had risen tenfold since 1971, when the going price was $10,000. Baseball attendance leaped 24% over 1976 levels, and basketball attendance edged the 10,000,000 mark. In horse racing 17-year-old Steve Cauthen drew wide attention for his remarkable achievements as a jockey. In boxing, Muhammad Ali decided not to retire and defended his heavyweight crown twice. In golf the top money winners were Tom Watson, $310,653, and Judy Rankin, $122,890. Also this year, skateboards became a new activity for vast numbers of youngsters. Notables who died this year included Robert Calvin "Cal" Hubbard, the baseball umpire, Oct. 17, at 77; Bernard "Toots" Shor, the celebrated New York City barkeeper, Jan. 23, at 73; and Philip K. Wrigley, owner of the Chicago Cubs baseball team, Apr. 12, at 82.

Jan 9: Super Bowl XI was won by the Oakland Raiders (AFC), who defeated the Minnesota Vikings (NFC) 32 to 14. On Dec. 26, 1976, the Raiders had beaten the Pittsburgh Steelers 24 to 7 for the NFC championship, and the Vikings had beaten the Los Angeles Rams 24 to 13 for the AFC title.

Jan 17: Convicted murderer **Gary Gilmore** was executed by a Utah firing squad, ending a ten-year halt on capital punishment in the U.S.

Mar 9-11: A **terrorist raid** was staged in Washington, D.C., by 12 Hanafi Muslim gunmen. The terrorists seized three buildings and demanded custody of five Black Muslims who had been imprisoned for the 1973 murder of seven Hanafis and of three more Black Muslims who had been imprisoned for the 1965 murder of Malcolm X. One person was killed during the raid, and 139 were held prisoner for 39 hours before the terrorists surrendered.

Mar 28: The **NCAA basketball championship** was won by Marquette University, defeating North Carolina 67 to 59.

May 7: The 103rd **Kentucky Derby** was won by Seattle Slew, with a time of 2:02⅕. The jockey was Jean Cruguet.

May 9: Patricia Hearst, serving a prison sentence for a 1974 robbery, was released on probation.

May 21: The 102nd **Preakness Stakes** was won by Seattle Slew, with a time of 1:54⅖. The jockey was Jean Cruguet.

May 22-June 5: The **NBA basketball championship** was won by the Portland Trail Blazers, who beat the

Philadelphia 76ers four games to two after losing the first two games of the series.

May 26: One of the towers of the **World Trade Center was scaled** by George Willig, a toy designer, who climbed the south tower in three and a half hours. He was fined $1.10, one cent for each story of the building.

June 11: The 109th annual **Belmont Stakes** was won by Seattle Slew, finishing in 2:29³⁄₅ to take the race and become the tenth horse to win racing's Triple Crown. The jockey was Jean Cruguet.

June 19: The **U.S. Open golf tournament** was won by Hubert Green, beating Lou Graham by one stroke.

June 29: Capital punishment for rape was ruled unconstitutional by the Supreme Court.

July 2: At the **Wimbledon** tennis championships in England, the only U.S. player to win in finals play was Joanne Russell, who teamed with Helen Gourlay Cawley of Australia to win the women's doubles championship.

Aug 1: A return to **bell-bottom trousers,** white caps, and jumpers for sailors' uniforms was announced by the Navy after an experiment with coat-and-shirt uniforms.

Aug 10: The so-called **Son of Sam** serial murder case in New York City culminated in the arrest of David Berkowitz, 24, suspected of murdering six people and wounding seven more over a 13-month period.

Aug 14: The **PGA golf tournament** was won by Lanny Wadkins, who beat Gene Littler on the third hole of a sudden-death playoff.

Sep 10-11: The **U.S. Open tennis singles championships** were won by Chris Evert Lloyd, for the third straight time, in the women's division and Guillermo Vilas of Argentina in the men's division.

Sep 13-18: The **America's Cup** was successfully defended by the U.S. yacht *Courageous,* which beat the challenger *Australia* in four straight races.

Oct 1: The soccer superstar **Pelé** played his farewell game, playing the first half with the New York Cosmos and the second half with his former team, the Santos of Brazil.

Oct 11-18: The **World Series** was won by the New York Yankees (AL), defeating the Los Angeles Dodgers (NL) four games to two. On Oct. 8 the Dodgers had won the National League pennant over the Philadelphia Phillies, three games to one, and the following day the Yankees had clinched the American League pennant from the Kansas City Royals, three games to two.

Dec 10: Steve Cauthen became the first jockey to win more than $5,000,000 in purse money in one year. Cauthen ended 1977 with 488 wins.

1978

I. Civil Rights
Exploration and Settlement
Government
Statistics
Wars

Pres. Jimmy Carter returned on Jan. 6 from a nine-day, seven-nation tour of Europe, the Middle East, and India to a U.S. that was beset by grave domestic problems. The availability of energy was a major concern for the government and for business, and short supplies were reflected in rising inflation. To deal with inflation Carter announced (Apr. 11) that wage increases for federal employees would be held to 5.5% and asked (Oct. 24) for voluntary compliance on guidelines for wage and price increases. In the Koreagate lobbying scandal, Tongsun Park, a South Korean businessman, told the Justice Department he had given some $750,000 to members of Congress and political groups to influence legislation from 1970 to 1975. Americans mourned the passing of Gen. Lucius D. Clay, military governor of the U.S. zone in Berlin after World War II, Apr. 16, at 80; and Hubert Horatio Humphrey, former senator from Minnesota and vice president from 1965 to 1969 under Lyndon B. Johnson, Jan. 13, at 66.

Jan 6: A precedent-setting **Indian land claim suit** was lost by the Wampanoag Indians of Mashpee, Mass., who had gone to court to recover some 13,700 acres on Cape Cod. The jury decided the Indians did not legally constitute a tribe in 1870, when the land was supposedly taken from them, or in Aug. 1976, when they filed their lawsuit. The decision was expected to affect similar cases pending in the Northeast.

Jan 19: William H. Webster was appointed director of the FBI. A U.S. appeals court judge in St. Louis, Mo., Webster succeeded Clarence M. Kelley.

Feb 8: Pres. **Anwar el-Sadat** of Egypt began a six-day visit to the U.S. He conferred at length with Pres. Carter, urging the U.S. to exert pressure on Israel to negotiate a Middle East peace settlement.

Feb 22: Two days after a **train derailment** in Waverly, Tenn., two tank cars containing liquid propane exploded, killing 15 people and leveling two blocks of Waverly's business district.

Mar 16: A **Panama Canal treaty,** the first of two Canal treaties negotiated in 1977, was ratified by the Senate. The treaty guaranteed neutrality of the canal after Panama assumes control at the end of 1999.

Apr 6: A **retirement age bill,** giving most workers the option of retiring at age 70 rather than 65, was signed by Pres. Carter.

Apr 7: Production of the **neutron bomb** was deferred by Pres. Carter pending final decision on its construction and deployment.

Apr 18: The second **Panama Canal treaty** was ratified by the Senate. The treaty stated conditions for the operation and defense of the canal until 1999, when control of the canal passes to Panama. Ratification of both treaties was a triumph for Pres. Carter over strong opposition.

Apr 27: A **construction accident** at the site of a nuclear power plant at Willow Island, W. Va., killed 51 workers when a scaffolding collapsed inside a cooling tower. The workers, including 11 members of one family, fell 170 feet and were buried under tons of concrete.

May 11: The **first woman Marine Corps general,** Margaret A. Brewer, 47, was appointed.

June 6: Proposition 13, a California constitutional amendment that would reduce property taxes by 57%, was approved by 65% of the Californians who voted on the controversial proposal.

June 28: The concept of **racial quotas** came under fire when the Supreme Court ruled in the case of *Bakke v. the University of California* that the university had to admit Allan P. Bakke to its medical school. Bakke, who was white, claimed his civil rights had been violated when he was refused admission because of racial quotas designed to increase the number of minority students in the medical school.

Aug 7: The **Love Canal** area of Niagara Falls, N.Y., considered to be environmentally unfit for human habitation, was declared a disaster area by Pres. Carter. Evacuation of the area, which had been used as a toxic waste dump from 1947 to 1952, had begun on Aug. 4.

Sep 6-17: A **Middle East peace conference** at Camp David, Md., was attended by Pres. Carter, Pres. Anwar el-Sadat of Egypt, and Prime Minister Menachem Begin of Israel. On Sept. 17 Sadat and Begin signed an agreement at the White House to conclude a peace treaty between Egypt and Israel within three months.

Sep 25: A **midair collision** over San Diego, Calif., of a Southwest Airlines jet and a private plane killed all 137 people aboard the two craft and at least ten more on the ground.

Oct 6: The deadline for ratification of the **Equal Rights Amendment** was extended to June 30, 1982, by Congress. Since its passage in 1972, all but three of the required 38 states had ratified the measure. This was the first extension granted for ratification of a pro-posed constitutional amendment since 1917, when Congress set seven years as the limit for the process.

Oct 15: The **National Energy Act of 1978** was passed by Congress. The bill regulated natural gas prices, encouraged use of coal by utilities, set fuel efficiency standards, and provided tax credits for energy conservation. It was signed by Pres. Carter on Nov. 9.

Oct 30: In an **espionage case,** two Soviet citizens, former employees of the UN convicted for attempting to buy U.S. military secrets, were sentenced to 50 years in prison by a federal judge in Newark, N.J. The sentences were considered unusually severe.

Nov 7: In **congressional elections** the Republicans gained three Senate seats, but the Democrats still held a majority of 58–41, with one seat held by an independent. In the House the Republicans gained 12 seats, but the Democrats led 276–159.

Nov 18: A grisly **mass suicide in Guyana** was prefaced by the murder of Rep. Leo J. Ryan of California and four others visiting the People's Temple on a fact-finding mission to the country. When Jim Jones, leader of the religious sect, learned of the event he led the group in a mass suicide by poison. The final count was 911 dead, including more than 200 children. Most of Jones's followers, like Jones himself, were American citizens.

Nov 27: George Moscone and Harvey Milk, the mayor and city supervisor of San Francisco, respectively, were shot to death in City Hall by Dan White, a former supervisor.

Dec 15: The city of **Cleveland, Ohio, defaulted** on $15,500,000 in short-term notes, thus becoming the first major U.S. city to default on its obligations since the 1930s.

Dec 15: The **People's Republic of China** and the U.S. announced the two nations would initiate full diplomatic relations on Jan. 1, 1979. The U.S. was to sever diplomatic ties with the Republic of China (Taiwan).

II. Architecture
Arts and Music
Popular Entertainment
Publishing
Theater

The year in theater was disappointing despite a handful of above average plays. The year's biggest hit was the musical *Ain't Misbehavin'.* In May Mikhail Baryshnikov left the American Ballet and joined the New York City Ballet. Both companies had severe financial problems this year but managed to stay afloat. Art auction prices continued to climb. George Caleb Bingham's *The Jolly Flatboatmen* brought $980,000, the highest price paid to date for an American painting. Notables who died this year included Faith Baldwin, a writer known for her romantic novels, Mar. 18, at 84; Edgar Bergen, ventriloquist, Sept. 30, at 75; Charles Boyer, actor, Aug. 26, at 79; Maybelle "Mother" Carter, grand old lady of the Grand Ole Opry and matriarch of the musical Carter family, Oct. 23, at 69; Bruce Catton, author and historian known for his books on the Civil War, Aug. 28, at 78; James Gould Cozzens, Pulitzer Prize-winning novelist, Aug. 9, at 74; Charles Eames, designer known best for his molded plywood, form-fitting chairs, Aug. 21, at 71; Ruth Etting, Ziegfeld Follies girl and popular singer, Sept. 24, at 80; Phyllis McGinley, Pulitzer Prize-winning poet, Feb. 22, at 72; Jack Oakie, comedian, Jan. 23, at 74; Norman Rockwell, artist known best for his cover illustrations for the *Saturday Evening Post,* Nov. 9, at 84; Edward Durrell Stone, architect, Aug. 6, at 76; and Jack L. Warner, motion picture producer, Sept. 9, at 86.

Among **books published** this year was *The Stories of John Cheever,* a collection that won the Pulitzer Prize. Other books published this year included *The World According to Garp* by John Irving, a novel; *American Caesar* by William Manchester, a biography of Douglas MacArthur; *Chesapeake* by James Michener, a novel; *In Search of History: A Personal Adventure* by Theodore H. White; and *War and Remembrance,* a novel by Herman Wouk.

Apr 7: A **record book auction price** was set in New York City when The Stuttgart Museum bought a Gutenberg Bible for $2,000,000.

Apr 17: Pulitzer prizes were awarded for the following: fiction, *Elbow Room* by James A. McPherson; biography, *Samuel Johnson* by Walter Jackson Bate; history, *The Visible Hand* by Alfred D. Chandler, Jr.; poetry, *Collected Poems* by Howard Nemerov; general nonfiction, *The Dragons of Eden* by Carl Sagan; drama, *The Gin Game* by Donald L. Coburn.

July 7: The **censorship** controversy involving former CIA employees continued. On this date, Frank W. Snepp, III, who wrote an unauthorized book about the agency, was held by a federal judge to have violated his contract with the CIA. Snepp was ordered to hand over his earnings from the book to the federal government.

Oct 5: The **Nobel Prize for Literature** was awarded to Isaac Bashevis Singer, the Polish-born author who writes in Yiddish. He was cited for his "impassioned narrative art."

Oct 17: Congress voted the contralto **Marian Anderson** a special gold medal for her "unselfish devotion to the promotion of the arts" and her "untiring efforts on behalf of the Brotherhood of Man." In 1939 the black singer had been refused the use of Constitution Hall by the Daughters of the American Revolution. She subsequently performed before 75,000 at the Lincoln Memorial in Washington, D.C.

III. Business and Industry
Education
Philosophy and Religion
Science

The nation's economic woes continued. Inflation rose to 8%, productivity increased only 0.4%, the smallest rise since 1974, and the annual U.S. trade deficit reached $28,450,000. Pres. Jimmy Carter was not successful in pushing labor law reforms through Congress, nor was he able to get Congress to move toward a national health plan to be phased in during the 1980s. Health costs continued to rise, prompting the Department of Health, Education, and Welfare to ask hospitals to hold to a 9.7% increase in 1979. Congress voted a five-year, $50,000,000,000 extension of the Elementary and Secondary Education Act. This year the Mormon Church ended its 148-year ban on the ordination of black men. Notables who died this year included James Bryant Conant, longtime president of Harvard University, Feb. 11, at 84; John Donald MacArthur, billionaire insurance company tycoon, Jan. 6, at 80; Margaret Mead, anthropologist, Nov. 15, at 76; John D. Rockefeller, III, eldest of John D. Rockefeller's five grandsons and a noted philanthropist, Jan. 10, at 72; and Harry Winston, jeweler to the rich and famous, Dec. 28, at 82.

Jan 13: Japan agreed to some opening of its domestic market to U.S. products in order to reduce Japan's export trade surplus. Tariffs on some 300 items were to be reduced, and quotas on 12 items, 11 of them agricultural, were to be removed.

Mar 25: A 110-day **coal miners' strike,** longest in the industry's history, ended when miners accepted a new three-year contract and went back to work. The strike had caused fears of power shortages and industrial layoffs, but stockpiling before the strike prevented them.

Apr 17: A new **stock trading record** was set by the New York Stock Exchange, which saw 63,500,000 shares change hands.

Apr 19: The **first black woman pilot** for a major U.S. airline, Jill E. Brown, 27, from Baltimore, Md., began working for Texas International Airlines.

May 5: Organized medicine was declared by Pres. Carter to be the major obstacle to better health care. Carter affirmed that doctors care about their patients, but said the American Medical Association was concerned only with doctors' interests.

May 8: The **largest U.S. corporation,** according to *Fortune* magazine, was General Motors, with annual sales of $54,000,000,000. Exxon Corporation was rated second largest.

May 20: Pioneer Venus 1 was launched toward Venus. On Dec. 4 it went into orbit around Venus and began sending back data on the planet's atmosphere.

June 15: The $100,000,000 **Tellico Dam** project in Tennessee was halted indefinitely when the Supreme Court ruled that the snail darter, a rare species of perch, was protected by the Endangered Species Act of 1973 and that construction of the dam threatened its extinction.

June 22: In studying photos of **Pluto,** James W. Christy of the U.S. Naval Observatory discovered a hitherto unknown small moon of Pluto in orbit around it, only 12,000 miles from the planet.

Aug 8: Pioneer Venus 2 was successfully launched toward a December rendezvous with Venus. On Dec. 9 it sent four probes to the planet's surface and began relaying data about atmosphere and surface conditions of Venus.

Aug 11: The bacterium causing **legionnaires' disease** had been isolated, the Centers for Disease Control in Atlanta, Ga., announced. Previously it could only be studied in the tissue of a victim.

Oct 6: The **first woman university president** in the U.S., Hannah H. Gray, was inaugurated at the University of Chicago.

Oct 15: The **Humphrey-Hawkins full employment bill,** named for the late Hubert H. Humphrey of Minnesota and Rep. Augustus F. Hawkins, Democrat of California, was passed by Congress. A watered-down version of the original 1976 bill, it called for a national policy of reducing unemployment to 4% and inflation to 3% by 1983. It was signed by Pres. Carter on Oct. 27.

Oct 16: The **Nobel Prize in Economics** was awarded to Herbert A. Simon of Carnegie-Mellon University.

Oct 17: The **Nobel Prize in Physics** was awarded jointly to Arno A. Penzias and Robert W. Wilson of Bell Laboratories for their discovery of weak electromagnetic radiation existing throughout the universe, and to Per Kapitsa of the U.S.S.R. for his studies of liquid helium.

IV. Fashion
Folkways
Holidays
Social Issues and Crime
Sports

Professional sports prospered this year. Major league baseball drew a record 40,000,000 fans, and the Los Angeles Dodgers (NL) drew 3,347,776 customers to become the first team to break the 3,000,000 mark. In basketball, David Thompson of the Denver Nuggets negotiated an $800,000 contract for the year, highest to date for any professional athlete. Pro football increased its regular season from 14 to 16 games. In golf the top money winners were Tom Watson, $362,429, and Nancy Lopez, $153,097. The boom in jogging and physical fitness activities was good news for sportswear manufacturers, and even the fashion world began paying attention to Americans' interest in fitness and health. Americans also burned up the calories on the dance floors of discothèques, which became enormously popular in the wake of the hit film *Saturday Night Fever.* Notables who died this year included Ford C. Frick, former president of the National League (1934–1951), Apr. 8, at 83; Joseph V. McCarthy, who managed the New York Yankees to eight American League championships and seven World Series victories between 1931 and 1946, Jan. 13, at 90; and James Joseph "Gene" Tunney, undefeated heavyweight champion of the world from 1926 to 1928, Nov. 17, at 80.

Jan 9: In a major ruling on **coeducational sports,** a federal judge in Dayton, Ohio, ruled against preventing high-school girls from playing on the same sports teams as boys.

Jan 15: Super Bowl XII was won by the Dallas Cowboys (NFC), defeating the Denver Broncos (AFC) 27–10. On Jan. 1 the Cowboys had beaten the Minnesota Vikings 23 to 6 for the NFC championship and the Broncos had defeated the Oakland Raiders 20 to 17 to take the AFC title.

Feb 15: The **world heavyweight boxing championship** was won by Leon Spinks in a 15-round decision over Muhammad Ali at Las Vegas, Nev.

Mar 27: The **NCAA basketball championship** was won by the University of Kentucky, beating Duke University 94 to 88.

May 5: Pete Rose of the Cincinnati Reds (NL) made his 3000th base hit. He was the 13th player in baseball history to do so and, at 37, the youngest.

May 6: The 104th **Kentucky Derby** was won by Affirmed, with a time of 2:01 $1/5$. The jockey was Steve Cauthen.

May 20: The 103rd **Preakness Stakes** was won by Affirmed, with a time of 1:54 $2/5$. The jockey was Steve Cauthen.

May 21-June 7: The **NBA basketball championship** was won by the Washington Bullets, who beat the Seattle Supersonics four games to three.

May 26: The **first legal casino** in the U.S. outside Nevada was opened in Atlantic City, N.J., by Resorts International Hotel Casino.

June 9: The World Boxing Council **heavyweight boxing championship** was won by Larry Holmes, in a 15-round decision over Ken Norton.

June 10: The 110th **Belmont Stakes** was won by Affirmed, with a time of 2:26⅘ to become the 11th horse to win racing's Triple Crown. The jockey, once again, was Steve Cauthen. As in the Kentucky Derby and Preakness, Alydar finished second. This was the first time there were Triple Crown winners in consecutive years, Seattle Slew having won in 1977.

June 18: The **U.S. Open golf tournament** was won by Andy North, beating J. C. Snead and Dave Stockton on the last hole after seeing a substantial lead vanish.

Aug 6: The **PGA golf tournament** was won by John Mahaffey, beating Tom Watson and Jerry Pate on the second hole of a sudden-death playoff.

Aug 11-17: The first successful **transatlantic balloon crossing** was made by Max Anderson, Ben Abruzzo, and Larry Newman, who flew from Presque Isle, Maine, to Paris, France, in 137 hrs., 18 min.

Sep 10: The **U.S. Open tennis singles championships** were won by Chris Evert in the women's division and Jimmy Connors in the men's division.

Sep 15: The World Boxing Association **heavyweight boxing championship** was won by Muhammad Ali, who beat Leon Spinks in 15 rounds to regain the title for an unprecedented third time.

Oct 10-17: The **World Series** was won by the New York Yankees (AL), defeating the Los Angeles Dodgers (NL) four games to two. On Oct. 7 the Yankees had won the American League pennant, beating the Kansas City Royals three games to one, and the Dodgers had taken the National League title, downing the Philadelphia Phillies three games to one.

Dec 8-10: The **Davis Cup** international tennis challenge round was won by the U.S., defeating Great Britain four matches to one.

1979

I. Civil Rights
Exploration and Settlement
Government
Statistics
Wars

The nation's attention was focused this year on events in Iran, where in January a wave of revolutionary unrest toppled the regime of Shah Moham-

mad Reza Pahlavi and installed a fundamentalist Islamic dictatorship under the Ayatollah Ruhollah Khomeini. In November Islamic revolutionaries seized the U.S. embassy in Teheran, taking many hostages and demanding that the Shah, then in the U.S. for medical reasons, be returned to Iran to stand trial for alleged crimes. Pres. Jimmy Carter refused the terrorists' demands and retaliated by banning the import of Iranian oil, freezing Iranian assets in the U.S., and threatening military action to free the hostages. Thus began a diplomatic nightmare that came to be known as the hostage crisis. Notables who died this year included Nelson A. Rockefeller, four times governor of New York, and vice president of the United States from 1974 to 1977, Jan. 26, at 70.

Jan 4: The legal battle over the **Kent State** University shootings in Ohio in 1970 ended when an out-of-court settlement was reached. The parents of the four students killed by National Guardsmen and the nine wounded by the guardsmen were awarded a total of $675,000.

Feb 8: Military ties with **Nicaragua** had been severed, Pres. Carter announced, adding that economic aid to the repressive regime of Anastasio Somoza DeBayle would be reduced as well. The moves were intended to force Somoza to negotiate with the revolutionary Sandinista movement threatening to topple the Nicaraguan government.

Feb 14: The U.S. **ambassador to Afghanistan was kidnaped** in Kabul and then killed when Afghan government forces attempted to free him.

Mar 5: **Alimony laws** requiring payments by divorced husbands but not by divorced wives were ruled unconstitutional by the Supreme Court, which struck down an Alabama law as violating the Fourteenth Amendment.

Mar 26: An **Egyptian-Israeli peace treaty** ended the 30-year state of war between the two nations. The treaty was signed by Pres. Anwar el-Sadat of Egypt and Prime Minister Menachem Begin of Israel at the White House.

Apr 3: Jane Byrne was elected the first woman mayor of Chicago by the largest majority in that city since 1901.

Apr 27: A **prisoner exchange** with the U.S.S.R. was effected in New York City. The U.S. traded two Soviets convicted in 1978 of spying for five Soviet dissidents, including Alexander Ginsburg, who had helped found a committee to monitor human rights violations in the U.S.S.R.

May 25: An **airline crash** of an American Airlines DC-10 jet shortly after takeoff in Chicago killed all 272 passengers and three people on the ground.

June 13: An **Indian land claim suit** was settled, granting the Sioux nation $17,500,000 for an area of the Black Hills of South Dakota taken from them in 1877. Including interest, the award was estimated to exceed $100,000,000. It was the largest award ever received by an Indian group.

June 18: The **SALT 2** strategic arms limitation treaty was signed in Vienna, Austria, by Pres. Carter and Pres. Leonid Brezhnev of the U.S.S.R.

July 2: Attendance at **criminal pretrial proceedings** is not a constitutional right of the public or the press, the Supreme Court ruled. The decision left open the possibility that public access to criminal trials could be limited as well.

July 19: In a major **Cabinet reorganization,** Pres. Carter dismissed four members, including the secretaries of the treasury and of energy; a fifth resigned. At a meeting of his Cabinet and staff, Carter had bluntly expressed his dissatisfaction, prompting the tendering of resignations by all his Cabinet members and by his senior White House staff.

July 25: Paul Volcker was appointed chairman of the Federal Reserve Board by Pres. Carter. He was confirmed on Aug. 2 and sworn in on Aug. 6.

Aug 15: Andrew Young resigned as U.S. ambassador to the UN following controversy over his unauthorized meeting with representatives of the Palestine Liberation Organization in July.

Sep 12-14: Hurricane Frederic struck the Gulf Coast, causing some $1,500,000,000 in damage with winds of up to 130 mph. Only eight people were killed, but some 500,000 were forced to evacuate.

Nov 3: A **shootout in Greensboro,** N.C., between Ku Klux Klan members and participants in an anti-Klan rally left five demonstrators dead and eight wounded. Fourteen Klansmen were arrested and 12 of them were charged with first-degree murder.

Nov 4: The **U.S. embassy in Teheran** was seized by Iranian revolutionaries, so-called students, who took some 90 hostages, including about 65 Americans. The revolutionaries released the non-U.S. hostages and 13 U.S. hostages, all women or blacks, but kept about 50. The revolutionaries demanded that the U.S. return the deposed Shah to Iran to stand trial. He was in the U.S. undergoing medical treatment. The U.S. refused to comply.

Nov 21: The **U.S. embassy in Islamabad,** Pakistan, was besieged for five hours before Pakistani soldiers restored order. One U.S. Marine was killed.

Dec 2: The **U.S. embassy in Tripoli,** Libya, was attacked by a mob. Two floors were damaged but the 21 people in the building escaped unharmed.

II. Architecture
Arts and Music
Popular Entertainment
Publishing
Theater

The Broadway theater prospered this year, with 119 productions generating $40,600,000 in profits, up 10% over the previous season. There were 46 off-Broadway shows. Among the year's hits were The *Elephant Man* and the musical *Sugar Babies.* On Dec. 8 the musical *Grease* gave its 3243rd performance and became the longest-running Broadway musical in history. The music industry faced hard times as oil price hikes translated into higher prices for records. Sales of recordings showed a decided drop after 25 years of steady growth. A new art auction price for an American work was set when *Icebergs,* a painting by Frederick Church that had hung unnoticed in England since 1863, sold for $2,500,000. Notables who died this year included Elizabeth Bishop, Pulitzer Prize-winning poet, Oct. 6, at 68; Al Capp, cartoonist, Nov. 11, at 70; James T. Farrell, author of the *Studs Lonigan* trilogy, Aug. 22, at 75; Arthur Fiedler, conductor of the Boston Pops Orchestra for 50 years, July 10, at 84; Emmett Kelly, clown, Mar. 28, at 80; Peggy Guggenheim, art collector and patron, Dec. 23, at 81; Roy Harris, composer, Oct. 1, at 81; S. J. Perelman, humorist, Oct. 17, at 75; Mary Pickford, first major star of silent movies, May 29, at 86; Richard Rodgers, composer, Dec. 30, at 77; Jean Stafford, writer, Mar. 26, at 63; and John Wayne, actor, June 11, at 72.

Among **books published** this year, the most talked-about work was Norman Mailer's nonfiction novel *The Executioner's Song,* a treatment of the life and death of Gary Gilmore, who was executed in 1977. The book became a best seller and won a Pulitzer Prize. Other books published this year included *A Streak of Luck* by Robert Conot, a biography of Thomas Edison; *Hanta Yo* by Ruth Beebe Hill, a historical novel that drew fire from some American Indians but became a best seller; *The Poems of Stanley Kunitz,* a collection of the poet's work over 50 years; *The Rise of Theodore Roosevelt* by Edmund Morris; *The Ghost Writer* by Philip Roth, fiction; *Sophie's Choice* by William Styron, a novel; and *Jailbird* by Kurt Vonnegut, a novel panned by critics but kept firmly on the best-seller lists by the public.

Jan 9: The **Bollingen Prize** for poetry was awarded to W. S. Merwin.

Feb 9: In the first major **art theft** from the Metropolitan Museum of Art in its 110-year history, thieves stole an ancient Greek marble head valued at $250,000.

Apr 16: Pulitzer prizes were awarded for the following: fiction, *The Stories of John Cheever;* biography, *Days of Sorrow and Pain* by Leonard Baker; history, *The Dred Scott Case* by Don E. Fehrenbacker; general nonfiction, *On Human Nature* by Edward O. Wilson; poetry, *Now and Then Poems* by Robert Penn Warren; drama, *Buried Child* by Sam Shepard.

Dec 3: A **rock concert disaster** claimed the lives of 11 youths who were trampled to death at Riverfront Coliseum in Cincinnati, Ohio. Fans were scrambling to get seats at a concert by The Who.

III. Business and Industry
Education
Philosophy and Religion
Science

The economic news continued bad: interest rates, inflation, and the foreign trade deficit all were higher. The Consumer Price Index was up 13.3%, the largest jump in 33 years. In December United States Steel announced it would close 13 plants, putting 13,000 steelworkers out of work and causing further unemployment in other industries. The Dow Jones Average of industrial stocks closed out the year at 838.4, up 4.2% over 1978. Trading was heavy, and a new record of shares traded was set: 8,155,915,314. Consumption of petroleum products declined 1.8%, the first drop since 1975. In education, costs were up and enrollment was down to 58,400,000, a full 3,000,000 fewer students than in 1975. Several events of religious significance highlighted the year. Reader's Digest announced it would publish a condensed version of the Bible, using the Revised Standard Version and reducing it by 40%. In September the Dalai Lama, religious leader of some 6,000,000 Tibetan Buddhists, came to the U.S. on a month-long visit. In October Pope John Paul II visited the U.S. Notables who died this year included Charles E. Coughlin, conservative, anti-Semitic "radio priest" of the 1930s, Oct. 27, at 88; Cyrus S. Eaton, Canadian-born multimillionaire, May 9, at 95; Conrad Hilton, founder of the Hilton hotel chain, Jan. 3, at 91; James Francis Cardinal McIntyre, Roman Catholic archbishop of Los Angeles, July 16, at 93; Samuel I. Newhouse, founder of the Newhouse publishing and broadcasting conglomerate, Aug. 29, at 84; Talcott Parsons, sociologist, May 8, at 76; A. Philip Randolph, labor and civil rights leader, May 16, at 90; Bishop Fulton J. Sheen, who reached millions through his radio and television broadcasts, Dec. 9, at 84; and Rexford Guy Tugwell, a leading figure in Franklin D. Roosevelt's so-called Brain Trust in the 1930s, July 21, at 88.

Jan 11: Cigarette smoking was labeled the "single most important environmental factor contributing to early death," in a report issued by U.S. Surgeon General Julius B. Richmond.

Feb 13: A report on **school desegregation** by the U.S. Civil Rights Commission stated that 46% of the nation's minority children were attending segregated schools 25 years after the Supreme Court declared segregation unconstitutional.

Mar 5: Voyager 1, launched in 1977, made its closest approach to Jupiter, coming within 172,000 miles of the planet's turbulent cloud cover.

Mar 28: A **nuclear near-disaster** occurred at Three Mile Island, near Harrisburg, Pa., when a power plant malfunctioned and its operators were unable to deal with the situation. The plant's containment building was flooded and a disaster of enormous magnitude was averted. However, two days later the governor of Pennsylvania advised pregnant women and preschool children living within five miles of the plant to leave the area.

May 5: The **largest U.S. corporation** in 1978, according to *Fortune* magazine's annual survey, was General Motors, with sales of more than $63,000,000,000.

June 27: The Supreme Court ruled that **black employees** could be promoted ahead of whites with greater work experience provided the move was part of an affirmative action program intended to offset racial discrimination.

July 11: Skylab, the 77-ton U.S. orbiting laboratory, reentered Earth's atmosphere and broke up, showering debris over the Indian Ocean and Australia. No one was hurt.

Sep 1: Pioneer 2, launched in 1973, flew past Saturn, discovering two new rings and an eleventh moon.

Oct 1-7: Pope John Paul II paid a six-day visit to the U.S., stopping at Boston, New York City, Philadelphia, Des Moines, Chicago, and Washington, D.C. On Oct. 6 he became the first pope to meet a U.S. president at the White House.

Oct 6: A **financial and stock panic** was sparked when the Federal Reserve Board announced—on a Saturday night—a raise in its discount rate from 11% to 12% and took stiff actions to tighten control of the money supply. In the next few days bond prices plunged, stock prices dropped in the heaviest trading since 1929, and banks raised their prime rates to 14.5%. By Oct. 11 the markets regained their balance and recovered most of their losses.

Oct 12: The **Nobel Prize in Physiology or Medicine** was awarded jointly to Allan M. Cormack of Tufts University and Geoffrey N. Hounsfield of Great Britain for their development of the CAT scan, an advanced type of x-ray equipment.

Oct 16: The **Nobel Prize in Chemistry** was awarded jointly to Herbert C. Brown of Purdue University and Georg Wittig of West Germany for their discoveries in the chemistry of boron and phosphorus.

Oct 16: The **Nobel Prize in Physics** was awarded jointly to Steven Weinberg and Sheldon L. Glashow of Harvard University, and to Abdus Salam of Pakistan for their contributions to the development of a unified field theory.

Oct 17: The **Nobel Prize in Economics** was awarded jointly to Theodore W. Schultz of the University of Chicago and Arthur Lewis of Princeton University for their work on the economic problems of developing nations.

Oct 17: A bill creating the **Department of Education,** the 13th Cabinet-level agency, was signed by Pres. Carter. On Oct. 30 the president appointed Shirley Hufstedler, a U.S. Court of Appeals judge in Louisiana, to head the new agency. The Department of Health, Education, and Welfare became the Department of Health and Human Services.

Dec 21: A bill authorizing a **federal bailout for Chrysler Corporation** by providing $1,500,000,000 in federal loan guarantees for the ailing automotive company was passed by Congress. It was signed by Pres. Carter on Jan. 7, 1980.

IV. Fashion
Folkways
Holidays
Social Issues and Crime
Sports

One incident reflecting the changes American society had undergone in the last several decades was the so-called palimony case involving the actor Lee Marvin and his former companion Michelle Triola Marvin. The couple had broken up in 1970, but Miss Marvin sued the actor for half of the $3,600,000 he had earned during their six-year relationship. In April a judge ruled against Michelle Marvin but awarded her $104,000 for purposes of rehabilitation. In sports, Muhammad Ali retired from boxing, leaving the World Boxing Association heavyweight crown up for grabs. John Tate won the heavyweight championship in October. In golf the top money winners were Tom Watson, $462,636, and Nancy Lopez, $215,987.

Jan 21: Super Bowl XIII was won by the Pittsburgh Steelers (AFC), defeating the Dallas Cowboys (NFC) 35 to 31. On Jan. 7 the Steelers had beaten the Houston Oilers 34 to 5 for the AFC championship and the Cowboys had defeated the Los Angeles Rams 28 to 0 for the NFC title.

Mar 26: The **NCAA basketball championship** was won by Michigan State, defeating Indiana State 75 to 64.

May 20-June 1: The **NBA basketball championship** was won by the Seattle Supersonics, who defeated the Washington Bullets four games to one after losing the opening game.

June 17: The **U.S. Open golf tournament** was won by Hale Irwin, repeating his 1974 victory.

Aug 6: The **PGA golf tournament** was won by David Graham of Australia, beating Ben Crenshaw on the third hole of a playoff.

Sep 9: The **U.S. Open tennis singles championships** were won by John McEnroe in the men's division and Tracy Austin, 16, in the women's division. Austin became the youngest player to win the women's singles title.

Oct 10-17: The **World Series** was won by the Pittsburgh Pirates (NL), defeating the Baltimore Orioles (AL) four games to three. On Oct. 5 the Pirates completed a three-game sweep of the Cincinnati Reds for the National League pennant. The following day the Orioles had taken the American League championship from the California Angels, three games to one.

Oct 21: The World Boxing Association **heavyweight boxing championship** was won in Pretoria, South Africa, by John Tate, who took a 15-round decision over Gerrie Coetzee.

1980

I. Civil Rights
Exploration and Settlement
Government
Statistics
Wars

It was a heartbreaking year for Pres. Jimmy Carter, whose administration seemed unable to achieve significant successes in domestic or foreign affairs. The national economy slumped under skyrocketing inflation and rising unemployment. The Carter administration was unable to bring the Iranian hostage crisis to a conclusion, and the Soviet invasion of Afghanistan in Dec. 1979 chilled U.S.-Soviet relations to the freezing point. Meanwhile, the Republican Party, solidly behind Ronald Reagan, expended great energy and vast resources in the presidential election campaign and swept their candidate into power in a Republican landslide. Another factor in U.S. politics was the 1980 Census, which reported a population of 226,504,825 and indicated a shift of 17 seats in the House of Representatives from the Northeast and Midwest to the South and West. This year Americans mourned the deaths of Helen Gahagan Douglas, former actress and Democratic congresswoman from 1944 to 1950 who lost her House seat to Richard M. Nixon in a bitterly fought campaign, June 28, at 79; and William O. Douglas, who had served on the Supreme Court for 36 years beginning in 1939, longer than any other justice in the Court's history, Jan. 19, at 81.

Jan 4: In a protest against the **Soviet invasion of Afghanistan** in December, Pres. Carter announced that the 17,000,000 metric tons of grain ordered by the U.S.S.R. would not be delivered. Carter also suspended the sale of high-technology equipment, postponed the opening of new consulates in the two countries, and curtailed Soviet fishing privileges in U.S. waters. Carter also entertained the idea of a U.S. boycott of the 1980 Summer Olympics in Moscow, a move he announced on Jan. 20.

Jan 23: In his **State of the Union** message, Pres. Carter said that Persian Gulf oil supply routes would be defended by force if necessary.

Jan 29: Six Americans escaped from Iran with the aid of Canadian embassy personnel, it was revealed. The U.S. citizens, who had posed as Canadians, had not been among those held in the U.S. embassy in Teheran.

Feb 2: Details of **Abscam,** an FBI sting operation to uncover official corruption, were released. Some 31 public officials were named as targets of the investigation, including Sen. Harrison Williams, Republican of New Jersey, and six members of the House of Representatives. In the operation an FBI agent posed as an Arab sheik and offered bribes for political favors.

Mar 15: An **Indian land claim suit** was settled when the Penobscot Indian tribe in Maine accepted an $81,500,000 settlement for land taken from it in violation of the Indian Non-Intercourse Act of 1790.

Mar 17: The **Refugee Act of 1980** was signed by Pres. Carter. It broadened the definition of the term *refugee* to include people from any part of the world, and increased the maximum annual number to be admitted to the U.S. from 290,000 to 320,000.

Apr 7: The U.S. broke **diplomatic relations with Iran** in the wake of the continuing hostage crisis. All exports to Iran were banned and Iranian diplomats in the U.S. were expelled.

Apr 11: Regulations prohibiting **sexual harassment of women** by their superiors in government or business were issued by the Equal Opportunity Commission.

Apr 24: A U.S. **hostage rescue mission** in Iran ended in disaster. During the operation, three of the eight helicopters of the airborne operation failed. At the staging area inside Iran, the mission was canceled, but during the withdrawal one of the remaining helicopters collided with one of six C-130 transports, killing eight and injuring five.

Apr 26: Sec. of State **Cyrus Vance resigned,** stating his opposition to the U.S. military rescue attempt in Iran. He was succeeded by Sen. Edmund Muskie, Democrat of Maine.

May 9: A **marine accident** killed at least 35 people when the freighter *Summit Venture* rammed the Sunshine Skyway Bridge over Tampa Bay, Fla., collapsing one of its twin highway spans. On Jan. 28 a Coast Guard cutter had struck an oil tanker near the bridge, killing 23 sailors.

May 17-19: Race riots in Miami, Fla., left at least 14 dead and more than 300 injured, and caused some $100,000,000 in damage. Nearly 1000 people were arrested in the violence, which erupted after an all-white jury acquitted four former Miami policemen charged with the fatal beating of a black man.

May 18: The eruption of **Mt. St. Helens** in southwestern Washington State blew the top of the mountain into the atmosphere, leveled some 120 sq. mi., and set off a series of fires, mudslides, and floods. About 400 people had been evacuated before the eruption, but a count in July showed 15 others dead and about 40 missing. The volcano had been dormant since 1857.

June 3: A total of 101,476 **Cuban refugees** had fled to the U.S. since mid-April with the tacit approval of Fidel Castro's government, it was reported. At first the refugees had been welcomed by the U.S., but by mid-May steps were taken to slow the tide and screen the refugees. It was feared Castro was using the exodus as a way to empty his prisons of criminals.

June 23-Aug 15: A summer-long **heat wave and drought** devastated crops and livestock and left 1272 people dead in 20 states. The mid-Mississippi R. Valley, the Southwest, and the South were hardest hit in the worst drought since the Dust Bowl days of the 1930s.

June 27: A law requiring **draft registration** by men 19 to 20 years of age was signed by Pres. Carter. Registration was to begin in July, but no actual draft was contemplated.

July 14-17: The **Republican National Convention** nominated Ronald W. Reagan for the presidency by a nearly unanimous vote. George Bush of Texas, former ambassador to the UN and former director of the CIA, was nominated for the vice presidency.

Aug 11-14: The **Democratic National Convention nominated Pres. Carter** and Vice Pres. Walter F. Mondale for reelection. Carter defeated Sen. Edward M. Kennedy of Massachusetts by a margin of nearly two to one.

Sep 19: A **fuel explosion** at a Titan 2 missile site near Damascus, Ark., killed one Air Force employee and injured 21. The blast left a crater 250-feet wide and forced the evacuation of 1400 people from the area for 12 hours.

Oct 2: In the **first House expulsion** since 1861, the House of Representatives expelled Michael Joseph Myers, Democrat of Pennsylvania. Myers had been convicted on Aug. 31 of bribery and conspiracy in connection with the Abscam investigation.

Nov 4: Ronald Reagan was elected president of the United States, carrying 44 states. The electoral vote was Reagan 489, Pres. Jimmy Carter 49. The popular vote was Reagan, 42,797,153; Carter, 34,434,100; John Anderson, independent candidate, 5,533,927. In congressional elections the Republicans picked up 12 Senate seats for a 53–46 majority, with one independent seat. In the House the Democrats lost 33 seats but kept a majority of 242–192, with one seat going to an independent.

II. Architecture
Arts and Music
Popular Entertainment
Publishing
Theater

The Broadway theater season was marked by revivals of such former hits as *West Side Story, The Music Man,* and *Brigadoon.* The American Ballet Theater celebrated its 40th anniversary this year, and Mikhail Baryshnikov became its director. Conflicts between the Metropolitan Opera Company and its orchestra led to cancellation of its 1980–1981 season. After a last-minute settlement on Dec. 10, the season was begun two months late. Plans for the long-awaited New York City Exposition and Convention Center were finally approved. The single structure would cover five blocks, have 500,000 sq. ft. of exhibition space, and be the largest structure of its kind. This year viewers crowded New York City's Museum of Modern Art to see more than 1000 works by Pablo Picasso. In May a Picasso painting brought $3,000,000 at auction. This sale soon was eclipsed by a $3,900,000 bid for a painting by Paul Cézanne, and

$5,200,000 for a painting by Vincent Van Gogh. In music, digitally recorded LP records were widely marketed for the first time. In publishing, two of the nation's most respected magazines, *Harper's* and *Atlantic,* nearly failed but were saved at the last minute. Americans mourned the deaths this year of Gower Champion, choreographer, who died hours before his last show, *42nd Street,* opened, Aug. 25, at 61; Harold E. Clurman, director, drama critic, and author, Sept. 9, at 78; Jimmy Durante, entertainer, Jan. 29, at 86; Jane Froman, big band singer of the 1930s and 1940s, Apr. 23, at 72; José Iturbi, Spanish-born pianist, June 28, at 84; Andre Kostelanetz, conductor, Jan 13, at 78; Henry Miller, author of *Tropic of Cancer* and other controversial works, June 7, at 88; Katherine Anne Porter, Pulitzer Prize-winning author, Sept. 18, at 90; and Mae West, sex queen of the movies for 60 years, Nov. 22, at 87.

Among **books published** was *A Confederacy of Dunces* by John Kennedy Toole, who committed suicide after being unable to find a publisher for his work. Years later his mother found a publisher for his novel, which went on to win a Pulitzer Prize. Other books published this year included *Creek Mary's Blood* by Dee Brown, a novel; *Loon Lake* by E. L. Doctorow, a novel; *Walt Whitman,* a biography by Justin Kaplan; *The White House Years* by Henry Kissinger, which focused on the Vietnam War and prompted much debate; *The Covenant,* another blockbuster by James Michener; and *The Second Coming* by Walker Percy, the author's fifth novel.

Mar 6: Marguerite Yourcenar became the first woman to be elected to the French Academy. A naturalized U.S. citizen, the author had resided in Maine for more than 30 years.

Apr 14: Pulitzer prizes were awarded for the following: fiction, *The Executioner's Song* by Norman Mailer; biography, *The Rise of Theodore Roosevelt* by Edmund Morris; history, *Been in the Storm So Long* by Leon F. Litwack; general nonfiction, *Gödel, Escher, Bach* by Douglas R. Hofstadter; poetry, *Selected Poems* by Donald R. Justice; drama, *Talley's Folly* by Lanford Wilson.

May 1: The first **American Book Awards,** formerly known as the National Book Awards, were presented for the following: fiction, *Sophie's Choice* by William Styron; general nonfiction, *The Right Stuff* by Tom Wolfe; biography, *The Rise of Theodore Roosevelt* by Edmund Morris; history, *The White House Years* by Henry Kissinger; poetry, *Ashes* by Philip Levine. The National Medal for Literature was presented to Eudora Welty.

May 29: A **world auction record** for a painting was set when J. M. W. Turner's *Juliet and Her Nurse* was sold in New York City for $6,400,000.

Oct 9: The **Nobel Prize in Literature** was awarded to Czeslaw Milosz, a self-exiled Pole living and teaching in California.

Nov 21: The so-called **Who Shot J.R.?** episode of the TV evening soap *Dallas* was seen by more U.S. viewers than any other television program in history. More than half the nation's audience watched to see who had tried to kill J.R. Ewing, a question unanswered at the end of the spring season.

Dec 8: **John Lennon was shot** and killed outside his apartment building in New York City. Mark David Chapman, 25, a former mental patient, was held for the shooting.

III. Business and Industry
Education
Philosophy and Religion
Science

Inflation reached 12.4% by year's end, marking the second successive year of double-digit inflation. The Federal Reserve raised its discount rate to 13%, and unemployment hit an average of 7.1% for the year. Sales of U.S. automobiles were at a 19-year low, down 20% from 1979 levels, and the Ford Motor Co. reported a third-quarter loss of $595,000,000, the biggest ever for a U.S. corporation. This year the federal government took steps to deregulate the trucking industry and railroads. On July 1 Pres. Jimmy Carter signed a bill giving truckers more freedom to raise or lower rates without having to seek ICC permission. On Oct. 14 Pres. Carter signed a bill giving the railroads greater flexibility in setting rates. New federal assistance for railroads in financial trouble was also provided. A noteworthy development was the decline in computer prices. Sales of personal computers were up, although the expected production boom was hurt by short supply of integrated circuit chips. Notables who died this year included Jacqueline Cochran, first woman to fly faster than the speed of sound, Aug. 8, at 70; George Meany, president of the AFL-CIO from 1955 to 1979, Jan. 10, at 85; and Harland "Colonel" Sanders, founder of the Kentucky Fried Chicken food chain, Dec. 16, at 90.

Jan 16: The successful **synthesis of human interferon,** thought to be effective against viral diseases and possibly against some types of cancer, was announced by a group of scientists in Boston.

Feb 14: The 1500-lb. **Solar Maximum Observatory,** designed to study solar flares, was successfully launched into orbit.

Mar 13: In the **first criminal trial of a U.S. corporation** in a product defect case, the Ford Motor Company was found not guilty by a jury in Winimac, Ind., of reckless homicide. The case involved the 1978 deaths of three women killed in a Ford Pinto.

Apr 2: The **Crude Oil Windfall Profits Tax** bill was signed by Pres. Carter. It was expected to produce $227,000,000,000 in tax revenues from the nation's oil companies by 1990.

Apr 28: A report on **cancer death rates** issued by the American Cancer Society projected that 8,500,000 Americans would die from cancer in the 1980s, at least 2,000,000 more than had died in the 1970s.

May 5: The **largest U.S. corporation,** according to the annual report by *Fortune* magazine, was Exxon, with sales of $79,106,471,000 in 1979. Exxon moved from second to first place, dropping General Motors to number two.

June 16: In a landmark ruling on **genetic engineering,** the Supreme Court ruled that organisms created in the laboratory could be patented.

Sep 22: The risk of **toxic shock syndrome** led to recall of a tampon product manufactured by Procter and Gamble. Federal studies had linked use of the tampon with the deaths of 25 women.

Oct 10: The **Nobel Prize in Physiology or Medicine** was awarded jointly to Baruj Benacerraf of Harvard University, George Snell of the Jackson Laboratory in Maine, and Jean Dausset of France for their studies of antigens, protein-carbohydrate complexes found in the body.

Oct 14: The **Nobel Prize in Chemistry** was awarded jointly to Paul Berg of Stanford University for his studies of the manipulation of gene structures, and to Walter Gilbert of Harvard University and Frederick Sanger of England for their work on reading the fine details of the structure of DNA.

Oct 14: The **Nobel Prize in Physics** was awarded jointly to James Cronin of the University of Chicago and Val L. Fitch of Princeton University for their discoveries concerning the symmetry of subatomic particles.

Oct 15: The **Nobel Prize in Economics** was awarded to Lawrence R. Klein of the Wharton School of the University of Pennsylvania for his development of models for forecasting economic trends.

Nov 12: Voyager 1, launched in Sept. 1977, flew within 77,000 miles of Saturn and found far more rings around the planet than had been previously identified, some with eccentric orbits. The spacecraft also found three new moons, making 15 known in all.

IV. Fashion
Folkways
Holidays
Social Issues and Crime
Sports

On Jan. 20 Pres. Carter announced U.S. withdrawal from the Summer Olympics, to be held in Moscow in July, in response to the Soviet invasion of Afghanistan in 1979. Some 50 nations followed suit, but many athletes who had trained for years for the games felt great bitterness at the move. In February Americans witnessed an athletic miracle as the U.S. Olympic hockey team defeated the favored Finnish and Russian hockey teams to take the gold medal and become national heroes. Another top story this year was Muhammad Ali's attempt to win the world heavyweight boxing title for an unprecedented fourth time. Ali had retired from boxing in 1979 after defeating Michael Spinks. On Oct. 2 he faced off against WBA champion Larry Holmes in Las Vegas, but his dream of victory was not to become reality. Nonetheless, the former champ earned $8,000,000 for his part in what many considered a terrible match. In golf, the year's top money winners were Tom Watson, $530,808, and Beth Daniel, $231,000. The year's fashion rage was the bulky coat, down-filled, quilted, and often reaching almost to the ground. Among those who died in 1980 were Alice Longworth Roosevelt, last surviving child of Theodore Roosevelt, Feb. 20, at 96; Richard "Rube" Marquard, one of baseball's all-time great pitchers, June 1, at 90; and Jesse Owens, track star who won four gold medals at the 1936 Olympics in Germany and shattered the Nazi myth of racial superiority, Mar. 30, at age 66.

Jan 20: **Super Bowl XIV** was won by the Pittsburgh Steelers (AFC), defeating the Los Angeles Rams (NFC) 31 to 19. On Jan. 6 the Steelers had beaten the Houston Oilers 27 to 13 for the AFC title and the Rams had defeated the Tampa Bay Buccaneers 9 to 0 for the NFC championship.

Feb 12-24: At the **Winter Olympics** in Lake Placid, N.Y., the U.S. won six gold medals and finished third behind the U.S.S.R. and East Germany. The U.S. hockey team scored a major upset over the U.S.S.R. team, which had been favored to win the gold medal. Eric Heiden swept the speed skating events, becoming the first athlete to win five gold medals in the Winter Olympics.

Mar 14: Twenty-two members of a **U.S. amateur boxing team died** when the Polish airliner they were traveling on crashed near Warsaw. The crash killed 87.

Mar 24: The **NCAA basketball championship** was won by the University of Louisville, beating UCLA 59 to 54.

Mar 31: The World Boxing Association **heavyweight boxing championship** was won by Mike "Hercules" Weaver, who knocked out John Tate in the 15th round at Knoxville, Tenn.

May 4-16: The **NBA basketball championship** was won by the Los Angeles Lakers, who defeated the Philadelphia 76ers four games to two.

May 12: The first nonstop **transcontinental balloon flight** was completed by Maxie Anderson and his son Kris, who flew 3100 miles from Fort Baker, Calif., to Matane, Quebec, on the Gaspé Peninsula, in four days aboard the balloon *Kitty Hawk*.

June 15: the **U.S. Open golf tournament** was won by Jack Nicklaus. It was his fourth U.S. Open win.

Aug 10: The **PGA golf tournament** was won for the fifth time by Jack Nicklaus.

Sep 6-7: The **U.S. Open tennis singles championships** were won by John McEnroe in the men's division and Chris Evert Lloyd in the women's division.

Sep 16-25: The **America's Cup** was successfully defended by the U.S. yacht *Freedom*, which beat the challenger *Australia* four races to one.

Oct 14-21: The **World Series** was won by the Philadelphia Phillies (NL), defeating the Kansas City Royals (AL) four games to two. On Oct. 10 the Royals completed a three-game sweep of the New York Yankees to win the American League pennant. On Oct. 12 the Phillies won the National League pennant, beating the Houston Astros three games to two.

1981

I. **Civil Rights**
Exploration and Settlement
Government
Statistics
Wars

The UN Conference on the Law of the Sea, which had worked for several years on the question of how to apportion underseas resources, met in New York City on Mar. 9 in what was expected to be its final session. However, the fledgling administration of Pres. Ronald Reagan, reversing the position of the previous administration, objected to some of the terms of the proposed treaty, and the U.S. did not sign it. In domestic matters, the Bureau of the Census estimated the nation's population as 230,500,000 at year's end, an increase of 2,200,000 over 1980. Divorces in 1981 hit a record 1,210,000, the government reported. Notables who died this year included Roger Baldwin, a founder of the American Civil Liberties Union, Aug. 26, at 97; Gen. Omar N. Bradley, called the "GI's general" during World War II, Apr. 8, at 88; Emanuel Celler, Democrat of New York, who served 50 years (1923–1973) in the House of Representatives, Jan. 15, at 92; David E. Lilienthal, former chairman of the Tennessee Valley Authority and first chairman of the Atomic Energy Commission, Jan. 15, at 81; Carl Vinson, Democrat of Georgia, who served 50 years (1914–1964) in the House of Representatives, June 1, at 97; and Roy Wilkins, leader of the NAACP from 1931 to 1977, Sept. 8, at 80.

Jan 20: **Ronald Reagan was inaugurated president** of the United States. A Republican, he was at 69 the oldest person ever to assume the presidency. George Bush was inaugurated vice president.

Jan 20: The Iranian **hostage crisis** ended when Iran released the 52 U.S. captives seized at the U.S. embassy in Teheran in Nov. 1979. The release was accomplished with the help of Algeria minutes after Ronald Reagan succeeded Jimmy Carter as president. On Jan. 21 Carter flew to Wiesbaden, West Germany, to greet the freed Americans.

Feb 18: In his first **State of the Union** message, Pres. Reagan called for cuts of $41,000,000,000 in the budget Pres. Carter had submitted. He also proposed a 10% income tax cut in each of the next three years, an increase of about $5,000,000,000 in defense spending, and more liberal depreciation rules for business.

Mar 30: Pres. **Reagan was shot** by John W. Hinckley, Jr., 25, outside a Washington, D.C., hotel. Reagan underwent two hours of surgery for a wound in his left lung. Presidential press secretary James Brady was shot in the head but survived. Also wounded were Secret Service agent Timothy J. McCarthy and Washington police officer Thomas K. Delahanty. Reagan returned to the White House on Apr. 11.

Apr 4: The **first Mexican-American mayor** of a major U.S. city, Henry Gabriel Cisneros, 33, was elected in San Antonio, Tex.

Apr 21: A major **Saudi arms sale** was announced. The U.S. agreed to sell $1,000,000,000 worth of military equipment to Saudi Arabia, including five AWACS electronic surveillance aircraft. Israel protested the sale.

Apr 24: The 15-month **embargo on grain** shipments to the U.S.S.R. would be lifted, Pres. Reagan announced, thus fulfilling a campaign pledge he had made.

June 8: In a ruling on **wage discrimination,** the Supreme Court ruled women could sue for equal pay even if the work they did was not identical with that of male employees.

June 25: The Supreme Court ruled that **draft registration** and, by extension, a military draft, could exclude women without violating the Constitution.

July 7: Sandra Day O'Connor, a judge of the Arizona Court of Appeals, was nominated by Pres. Reagan to become the first woman member of the Supreme Court. She was confirmed by the Senate on Sept. 21 and sworn in on Sept. 25.

July 17: A **hotel disaster** in Kansas City, Mo., in which two indoor aerial walkways collapsed, killed 111 people and injured 190. About 1500 persons were attending a tea dance when the steel and concrete structures plunged to the floor below.

Aug 4: Pres. Reagan's **income tax reduction plan** was passed by Congress with only a slight modification. The bill reduced income taxes by 5% (rather than the requested 10%) as of Oct. 1, 10% as of July 1, 1982, and 10% as of July 1, 1983.

Aug 10: Production of the **neutron bomb** as a warhead for missiles and artillery was authorized by Pres. Reagan. The decision reversed U.S. policy set by Pres. Carter in 1978. The weapons were to be kept in the U.S.

Aug 19: Two **Libyan jets were shot down** by U.S. Navy fighters about 60 miles from the Libyan coast after the Libyan fighters opened fire on the U.S. jets. Libya claimed control of all of the Gulf of Sidra, where the Navy was holding military exercises. The U.S. maintained that the gulf was an international body of water.

Dec 4: Covert domestic intelligence operations by the CIA and other agencies were authorized for the first time in an executive order issued by Pres. Reagan.

II. Architecture
Arts and Music
Popular Entertainment
Publishing
Theater

The worldwide recession weakened the art market, and a strong U.S. dollar discouraged foreign buyers. Nevertheless, in May a Picasso self-portrait sold in New York City for $5,300,000, a new auction record for a twentieth-century painting. The Joffrey Ballet celebrated its 25th anniversary in October. In the same month, theatergoers greeted the opening of a British import, *The Life and Adventures of Nicholas Nickleby,* which coincided with publication of new paperback editions of the Dickens novel. Tickets for the play cost $100. An advertisement for a $5 edition of the novel suggested buying the book and saving $95. Among the year's top motion pictures were *Superman II* and *Raiders of the Lost Ark.* In music, videocassettes became an important part of the marketing strategy for many rock groups, who found that airtime on MTV, a rock music channel carried by 252 cable television stations, translated into big sales in record stores. In architecture, increasing attention was being paid to preserving and restoring old buildings. A restoration of particular interest was that of the elaborate terra cotta facade of the Woolworth Building in New York City. Americans mourned the deaths of Nelson Algren, known best for his 1949 novel *The Man With the Golden Arm,* May 9, at 72; Samuel Barber, Pulitzer Prize-winning composer, Jan. 23, at 70; Hoagy Carmichael, popular composer, Dec. 27, at 82; Ariel and Will Durant, husband and wife authors of the 11-volume *The Story of Civilization,* she on Oct. 25, at 83, and he on Nov. 7, at 96; Howard Hanson, composer and director of the Eastman School of Music for 40 years, Feb. 26, at 84; Joseph H. Hirshhorn, millionaire art collector and founder in 1974 of the Hirshhorn Museum in Washington, D.C., Aug. 31, at 82; George Jessel, comedian, May 24, at 83; Anita Loos, novelist and playwright, Aug. 18, at 88; Rosa Ponselle, first U.S.-trained singer to star at the Metropolitan Opera, May 25, at 84; Robert Montgomery, actor, Sept. 27, at 77; William Saroyan, author and playwright, May 18, at 72; and Dewitt Wallace, founder in 1922 of *Reader's Digest,* Mar. 30, at 91.

Among **books published** this year was Dumas Malone's six-volume life of *Thomas Jefferson,* a work 40 years in the making. Its publication was greeted with unanimous acclaim. Other books published this year included *The Company of Women* by Mary Gordon, her second novel; *The Hotel New Hampshire* by John Irving, a novel that disappointed many who had praised his earlier novel *The World According to Garp; Tar Baby* by Toni Morrison, fiction; *The Collected Poems* of the late Sylvia Plath; and *Rabbit Is Rich* by John Updike, the author's third novel about Harry "Rabbit" Angstrom.

Jan 13: The **Bollingen Prize** for poetry was awarded jointly to May Swenson and Howard Nemerov.

Jan 14: Broadcasting regulations for radio stations were eased by the FCC, freeing stations to air as many commercials an hour as they pleased and removing any obligation to allocate time for news or public affairs programing.

Apr 13: Pulitzer prizes were awarded for the following: fiction, *A Confederacy of Dunces* by John Kennedy Toole; biography, *Peter the Great* by Robert K. Massie; history, *American Education: The National Experience, 1783–1876* by Lawrence A. Cremin; general nonfiction, *Fin-de-Siècle Vienna: Politics and Culture* by Carl E. Schorske; poetry, *The Morning of the Poem* by James Schuyler; drama, *Crimes of the Heart* by Beth Henley.

June 6: A nationwide competition to design a **Vietnam War Memorial** for Washington, D.C., was won by Maya Yang Lin, a 21-year-old Yale undergraduate in architecture. The winning design consisted of two long, low granite walls in the form of an open V, on which the names of all the U.S. war dead in the Vietnam War would be inscribed.

III. Business and Industry
Education
Philosophy and Religion
Science

The economy continued to falter in 1981. Inflation hit an annual rate of 14%. Unemployment hit 7.4% and continued to rise. The Census Bureau reported that average household income before taxes had declined 2.6%. Automobile production was at its lowest level in 20 years, with Detroit producing only 6,200,000 passenger cars. The cost of medical care climbed 12.5% and was the highest since records were begun in 1935. In January, Pres. Ronald Reagan lifted oil price controls. Crude oil and oil product prices shot up at once, but an oversupply of crude soon brought them back down. The U.S. imported 40% less oil than in the peak importing year of 1978. The ten major airlines reported a total operating loss of $577,000,000, more than double their losses in 1980. In July a potentially devastating pest, the Mediterranean fruit fly, was found in California. An area of 550 square miles was quarantined, and Gov. Jerry Brown ordered ground spraying and the stripping of fruit from trees. In September, threatened with a federal quarantine of the state's produce, Gov. Brown ordered aerial spraying in spite of protests from environmentalists. The last outbreak of fruit flies was reported in August. By October it appeared a disaster had been averted. Probably the year's brightest news concerned the introduction of a personal computer by IBM, a development that lent legitimacy to the growing personal computer industry and that was to turn it into a major economic force in a few short years. Among those who died this year were Donald W. Douglas, airplane designer, Feb. 2, at 88; John S. Knight, founder of the Knight newspaper empire, June 16, at 87; Lowell Thomas, broadcast pioneer, Aug. 30, at 89; and Harold C. Urey, winner of the

Nobel Prize for his discovery of heavy hydrogen, Jan. 5, at 87.

Jan 7: A **stock market run** began when Joe Granville, a popular market forecaster, advised investors to "sell everything." The Dow Jones average of industrial stocks fell 23.8 points, and trading on the New York Stock Exchange set a new daily record of 93,700,000 shares. By Jan. 19 the situation had stabilized and stocks had rebounded.

Jan 8: An increase in the risk of **coronary death** was linked to consumption of large amounts of cholesterol, according to a report in the *New England Journal of Medicine.* The report was based on a 20-year study of 1900 men.

Mar 5: Teaching evolution in public schools did not violate the rights of religious fundamentalists, a Superior Court judge ruled in a California case. He said, however, that dogmatic teaching about the origin of life was not to be permitted.

Apr 12-14: The **space shuttle** *Columbia,* with Robert L. Crippen and John W. Young aboard, was launched from Cape Canaveral, Fla., on its maiden flight. After a flight of 54 hrs., 20 min., 48 sec., including 36 orbits of Earth, *Columbia* touched down at Edwards Air Force Base, Calif., making the first wheels-down landing by any spacecraft.

May 4: The **largest U.S. corporation,** according to the annual survey by *Fortune* magazine, was Exxon, with sales in 1980 of $103,142,834,000. Mobil was second with $59,610,000,000. General Motors dropped to third place.

June 18: A vaccine produced by **genetic engineering** and effective against hoof and mouth disease was announced. The vaccine was believed to be the first product of gene splicing to provide protection against disease in animals or humans.

July 9: The **herpes simplex virus** had been successfully suppressed by an experimental drug, acyclovir, it was reported in the *New England Journal of Medicine.* Genital herpes, caused by the virus, was identified as the most rapidly spreading sexually transmitted disease in the U.S.

Aug 3: A nationwide **air traffic controllers' strike** was begun by the 13,000 members of the traffic controllers' union, PATCO. Pres. Reagan announced that the strikers had to return to work by Aug. 5 or face dismissal. Many stayed home and were fired. On Aug. 17 the Federal Aviation Administration began accepting applications for new air controllers. On Oct. 22 the federal Labor Relations Authority decertified PATCO, removing any possibility of a negotiated settlement with striking air controllers.

Aug 25: Voyager 2, launched in 1977, flew within 63,000 miles of Saturn. Data sent back by the spacecraft showed thousands of rings around the planet, many more than the several hundred previously believed to exist.

Oct 9: The **Nobel Prize in Physiology or Medicine** was awarded jointly to David H. Hubel and Tlosten N. Wiesel of Harvard University for their studies of the way the brain processes visual information; and to Roger W. Sperry of the California Institute of Technology for demonstrating the different functions of the right and left hemispheres of the brain.

Oct 13: The **Nobel Prize in Economics** was awarded to James Tobin of Yale University for his development of the portfolio selection theory of investment.

Oct 19: The **Nobel Prize in Chemistry** was awarded jointly to Ronald Hoffman of Cornell University and Kenichi Fukui of Japan for applying theories of quantum mechanics to predict the course of chemical reactions.

Oct 19: The **Nobel Prize in Physics** was awarded jointly to Nicolaas Bloembergen of Harvard University and Arthur Schawlow of Stanford University for their contribution to the development of laser spectroscopy.

Nov 14: The **space shuttle** *Columbia* completed its second mission, the second flight ever of a reusable spacecraft. The mission was cut short by the failure of a fuel cell.

Dec 8: The constitutionality of **religious services in campus buildings** by student organizations at public colleges and universities was upheld by the Supreme Court. Many considered this to be the most significant ruling on the issue of separation of church and state in years.

IV. Fashion
Folkways
Holidays
Social Issues and Crime
Sports

A trend toward dullness that had prevailed in fashion gave way to a new freshness, characterized by a simple, sexy look. A touch of opulence also became stylish, perhaps inspired by the dress of Nancy Reagan, wife of the president. This year a maintenance worker won $5,000,000 in the New York State Lottery, the largest lottery payoff to date. State lotteries in the U.S. were estimated to take in $3,600,000,000 annually. Crime continued to be a concern. The Burns Detective Agency estimated that white collar crime in 1981 would amount to between $1,200,000,000 and $1,800,000,000 and that only 15% of such crimes would be detected. Divorces in the U.S. totaled a record 1,200,000 this year, the government reported. In sports, the National Football League set a new attendance record of 13,392,000, an average of about 60,000 fans present at a game. In boxing Larry Holmes successfully defended his World Boxing Association heavyweight title in a three-round bout (June 12) against Leon Spinks. In pro golf the top money winners were Tom Kite, $375,699, and Beth Daniel, $206,977. Notables who died included John Kieran, sportswriter who became a star of the radio show *Information Please* in the 1930s and 1940s, Dec. 10, at 89; and Joe Louis, the "Brown Bomber," who held the heavyweight boxing title from 1937 to 1949, the longest reign ever, Apr. 12, at 66.

Jan 25: Super Bowl XV was won by the Oakland Raiders (AFC), defeating the Philadelphia Eagles (NFC) 27 to 10. On Jan. 11 the Raiders had beaten the San Diego Chargers 34 to 27 for the AFC championship and the Eagles had defeated the Dallas Cowboys 20 to 7 for the NFC title.

Mar 30: The **NCAA basketball championship** was won by Indiana, which defeated North Carolina 63 to 50.

May 5-14: The **NBA basketball championship** was won by the Boston Celtics, who defeated the Houston Rockets four games to two.

May 24: The 65th **Indianapolis 500** auto race ended in controversy. A day after the race, Mario Andretti, who had finished second, was named winner over Bobby Unser because Unser had broken a rule during a slowdown period near the end of the race. On Oct. 8 the U.S. Auto Club (USAC) reversed the decision and gave the victory to Unser, but fined him $40,000 for his infraction. Unser had completed the race in 3 hrs., 35 min., 41.78 sec., with an average speed of 139.085 mph.

June 21: The **U.S. Open golf tournament** was won by David Graham of Australia, the fifth foreign player to win this title.

July 3-4: At the **Wimbledon** tennis championships in England, John McEnroe won the men's singles title and Chris Evert Lloyd won the women's singles. McEnroe teamed with Peter Fleming to win the men's doubles, and Pam Shriver teamed with Martina Navratilova to win the women's doubles.

Aug 9: The **PGA golf tournament** was won by Larry Nelson, beating Fuzzy Zoeller by three strokes.

Sep 9-13: The **U.S. Open Tennis singles championships** were won by John McEnroe in the men's division and Tracy Austin in the women's division.

Oct 20: What came to be called the **Brinks robbery,** a bungled armored-car holdup in Nanuet, N.Y., ended with two policemen and one guard dead and two guards wounded. Four persons were arrested, including three members of the terrorist Weather Underground group.

Oct 20-28: The **World Series** was won by the Los Angeles Dodgers (NL), defeating the New York Yankees (AL) four games to two. On Oct. 15 the Yankees had won the American League pennant over the Oakland Athletics in a three-game sweep. On Oct. 19 the Dodgers won the National League pennant, defeating the Montreal Expos three games to two.

Dec 11-13: The **Davis Cup** international tennis competition was won by the U.S., defeating Argentina three matches to one in Cincinnati, Ohio.

1982

I. Civil Rights
Exploration and Settlement
Government
Statistics
Wars

In January Pres. Ronald Reagan predicted that the recession, which had begun in 1981, would be short and followed by a strong recovery. His prediction proved overly optimistic, but at year's end there were encouraging signs in the economy. In foreign affairs the freeze in U.S.-Soviet relations continued as the U.S.S.R. stepped up its war in Afghanistan. The declaration of martial law in Poland on Dec. 13, 1981, viewed as a response to Soviet pressure, contributed to the broadening in June of a U.S. embargo on goods to the U.S.S.R. The Middle East again became a battleground as Israeli forces advanced into Lebanon in June in response to continued Palestinian attacks on Israel from Lebanon. Attempts by the U.S. to bring peace to the region were complex and generally fruitless, but the president decided to commit U.S. Marines as a peacekeeping force in Beirut, an action that provoked much controversy. Americans mourned the deaths this year of former Supreme Court Justice Abe Fortas, Apr. 5, at 71, and Bess Truman, widow of Pres. Harry S Truman, Oct. 18, at 97.

Jan 13: An Air Florida **jet crashed** into a bridge over the Potomac R. in Washington, D.C., shortly after taking off from National Airport, killing 78 people, including seven who were on the bridge.

Feb 6: Pres. Reagan's **proposed budget** for fiscal 1982 of $757,600,000,000 included a projected deficit of $91,500,000,000. Reagan called for deep cuts in domestic spending but asked for an 18% increase in the defense budget.

Mar 10: Economic sanctions against Libya were announced by the Reagan administration in response to Libya's involvement with international terrorist organizations. The sanctions included an embargo on Libyan oil shipments to the U.S. and a ban on export of high-technology products to Libya.

June 18: Exports to the U.S.S.R. of equipment to be used to build or operate the Siberian gas pipeline were banned. The ban also applied to the sale of such equipment produced by foreign subsidiaries or licensees of U.S. corporations. The move was protested four days later by the European Economic Community, but the ban was not lifted until Nov. 13.

June 21: John W. Hinckley, Jr., was found not guilty by reason of insanity in the Mar. 30, 1981, shooting of Pres. Reagan and three others. The verdict caused widespread shock and demands for revision of laws governing insanity pleas.

June 24: In a ruling on **presidential liability,** the Supreme Court ruled that a president could not be sued for damages for actions he took while in office. The decision was made in ruling on a suit brought against former president Richard M. Nixon by a government employee.

June 25: Alexander M. Haig, Jr., resigned as secretary of state following disagreements with Pres. Reagan and some of his advisers. George P. Shultz, a former Cabinet member and a businessman, was appointed to succeed Haig. Shultz was confirmed on July 15 and sworn in the next day.

June 30: The **Equal Rights Amendment** failed to achieve ratification despite an extension granted by Congress in 1978. At that time 35 of the required 38 states had ratified, but no others had done so in the intervening years.

July 9: A Pan American **jet crashed** after takeoff in New Orleans, La., killing 154 people. It was the second worst single-plane disaster in U.S. history.

Aug 20: About 800 **U.S. Marines landed in Beirut,** Lebanon, as part of a multinational force to oversee withdrawal of PLO fighters from the city. The Marines were withdrawn on Sept. 10, but they returned to Beirut on Sept. 29 following massacres of Palestinians in the Sabra and Shattila refugee camps by so-called Christian militiamen (Sept. 16–18) and a Lebanese request (Sept. 20) for assistance. On Sept. 30 one Marine was killed and three others wounded while attempting to defuse a bomb.

Sep 29-Oct 1: Cyanide placed in Tylenol capsules caused the deaths of seven persons in the Chicago area. By Oct. 6 a nationwide alert was sounded. Suspicious deaths in other parts of the country were reported but none appeared to be related to the Chicago murders. The makers of Tylenol, a pain reliever, recalled 264,000 bottles of the drug. The killer was never found.

Nov 2: In **congressional elections** the Republicans kept their 54–46 Senate majority, but the Democrats picked up 26 House seats for a 269–166 majority.

Nov 22: Construction of the **MX missile** was proposed by Pres. Reagan, who called for deployment of 100 of the multiple-warhead missiles in "dense pack mode," a relatively small area thought to be easier to defend against an enemy's first strike. The cost of the proposal was put at $26,000,000,000.

II. Architecture
Arts and Music
Popular Entertainment
Publishing
Theater

The Broadway season was relatively quiet. Biggest hits of the year were the musicals *Nine* and *Cats*. The cost of Broadway productions continued to climb. Cost of producing a musical approached $5,000,000. Opera companies and orchestras continued to have financial problems. The American Ballet Theater's season was shortened by a two-month lockout of its dancers in the fall. The dancers were finally given large salary increases. The Joffrey Ballet, in a move to gain a wider audience, decided to become a resident company in Los Angeles for part of the year while keeping its New York City season. This year movie theaters grossed $3,449,000,000, up 16% over 1981. The most successful film of the year was *E.T.: The Extraterrestrial,* which captured the hearts of millions. The recession was reflected in a softening of art auction prices, but a Henry Moore sculpture, *Reclining Figure,* brought $1,265,000. The 58-year-old *Saturday Review* suspended publication this year after losing $3,000,000 in the previous two years. Notables who died this year included Stringfellow Barr, educator known for his curriculum based on "100 Great Books," Feb. 2, at 85; Ingrid Bergman, actress, Aug. 29, at 67; John Cheever, writer, June 19, at 70; Frederick Dannay, who with his cousin Manfred B. Lee wrote the popular Ellery Queen mystery stories, Sept. 3, at 76; Babette Deutsch, poet, Nov. 13, at 87; Henry Fonda, actor, Aug. 12, at 77; John Gardner, novelist, Sept. 14, at 49; Melville Bell Grosvenor, president of the National Geographic Society, Apr. 22, at 80; Archibald MacLeish, poet, Apr. 20, at 89; Thelonius Monk, jazz pianist and composer, Feb. 17, at 64; Ayn Rand, novelist and champion of a controversial form of individualism, Mar. 6, at 77; Lee

Strasberg, proponent of the method theory of acting, Feb. 17, at 80; King Vidor, pioneer film director, Nov. 1, at 87; and John Hay Whitney, millionaire horse breeder, Feb. 8, at 77.

Among **books published** this year were a number of volumes on the arms race and the threat of nuclear war. Perhaps the best was *The Fate of the Earth* by Jonathan Schell, which caused much discussion and gained a wide readership. Other books published this year included *The Dean's December* by Saul Bellow, a novel; *Oh, What a Paradise It Seems* by John Cheever, the author's last novel; *God's Grace* by Bernard Malamud, a novel; and *The Mosquito Coast* by Paul Theroux, the story of a modern, unsuccessful Swiss Family Robinson. This year the Library of America, embarking on a program to issue uniform, quality editions of works of major U.S. authors, issued volumes of the works of Nathaniel Hawthorne, Herman Melville, Harriet Beecher Stowe, and Mark Twain.

Mar 12: Pulitzer prizes were awarded for the following: fiction, *Rabbit Is Rich* by John Updike; biography, *Grant, A Biography* by William S. McFeeley; history, *Mary Chestnut's Civil War* by C. Vann Woodward; general nonfiction, *The Soul of a New Machine* by Tracy Kidder; poetry, *The Collected Poems* of Sylvia Plath; drama, *A Soldier's Play* by Charles Fuller.

July 10: A painting by **Samuel F. B. Morse,** *The Gallery of the Louvre,* brought $3,250,000 in a private sale, the most ever paid for an American work of art to date. The painting had been owned since 1884 by Syracuse University.

III. Business and Industry
Education
Philosophy and Religion
Science

The recession that began in the summer of 1981 had run its course by November of this year. In 1982 the rate of inflation dropped to 6% and the Consumer Price Index rose only 3.9% for the year, smallest increase since 1972. The gross national product fell 1.8%, largest decrease since 1946. Unemployment rose to 10.8% by December and averaged 9.7% for the year. Some 4,600,000 people were receiving unemployment compensation by October, the largest number since such payments began in the 1930s. More than 30 banks failed, and high interest rates crippled new housing starts. Yet there were signs that U.S. business was on the rebound. Boeing introduced a new jet, the 767, said to be 35% more fuel efficient than older aircraft. Kodak introduced the disc camera, its most important new product in nearly 20 years. The camera was about the size of a pack of cigarettes. In September IBM introduced its 3084 computer, almost twice as powerful as its predecessor and able to process instructions at the rate of 26,000,000 a second. The largest solar plant yet built, expected to produce 10,000 kilowatts of electricity, was completed in the Mojave Desert. The U.S. Institute of Medicine estimated that of the fatalities caused by the ten leading causes of death, fully 50% could be traced to their victims' styles of living, and that some 320,000 deaths a year were caused by smoking. The spread of genital herpes alarmed the nation. It was estimated that 20,000,000 Americans had the disease, and that 300,000 to 500,000 new cases were occurring every year. In education, there were 520,000 fewer students in all U.S. schools than in the previous school year. The College Board reported that black students on average scored 100 points lower on both verbal and math Scholastic Aptitude Tests than white students. Notables who died this year included William Bernbach, founder in 1939 of the Doyle Dane Bernbach advertising firm, Oct. 2, at 71; John Cardinal Cody, Roman Catholic archbishop of Chicago since 1965 and an outspoken advocate of integration, Apr. 25, at 74; and René Dubos, biologist, environmentalist, and author, Feb. 20, at 81.

Jan 5: An Arkansas law requiring the teaching of **creation science,** a theory of creation based on the Bible, in schools in which the theory of evolution was taught was struck down by a federal judge in Arkansas. The court ruled that the teaching of creation science violated the constitutional requirement of separation of church and state.

Jan 8: The **American Telephone and Telegraph Company** agreed to divest itself of its 22 Bell Telephone operating systems. The agreement ended an eight-year antitrust suit by the Justice Department that charged AT&T with monopolizing U.S. telephone service.

May 3: The **largest U.S. corporation,** according to the annual *Fortune* magazine survey, remained Exxon, with 1981 sales of $108,107,688,000. Mobil Oil was second.

May 13: Braniff International Corporation, operator of the nation's eighth-largest airline, filed for bankruptcy. Braniff was the first major U.S. airline to go bankrupt.

June 29: A major **Protestant church merger** brought together the United Presbyterian Church and the Presbyterian Church in the United States. The new church would have 3,000,000 members.

July 5: The **Penn Square Bank** in Oklahoma City, Okla., was closed by federal regulators. The bank had suffered heavy losses through loans to depressed energy-based businesses in the Southwest. Some of the bank's $2,000,000,000 in loans had been bought by other banks, causing tremors throughout the banking industry.

July 16: The Rev. **Sun Myung Moon,** leader of the controversial Unification Church, was sentenced to 18 months in prison and fined $25,000 after being convicted of tax fraud and conspiracy to obstruct justice.

Sep 8: Agreement on a Lutheran church **merger of three Lutheran denominations** was announced. The American Lutheran Church, the Association of Evangelist Lutheran Churches, and the Lutheran Church in America voted to form a single denomination, which would have 5,500,000 members.

Oct 15: A new **weekly stock trading record** was set by the New York Stock Exchange, 592,460,000 shares. On Oct. 7 the NYSE had reached a new one-day high of 147,070,000 shares.

Oct 18: The **Nobel Prize in Physics** was awarded to Kenneth G. Wilson of Cornell University for development of a mathematical system explaining changes in the behavior of matter at critical points of pressure and temperature.

Oct 20: The **Nobel Prize in Economics** was awarded to George Stigler of the University of Chicago for his study of government regulation and its effect on the economy.

Nov 11-16: The **first operational space shuttle flight** was completed by the shuttle *Columbia,* which successfully carried two satellites into orbit.

Dec 2: The first successful **artificial heart transplant** was completed at the University of Utah Medical Center. The recipient was Barney C. Clark, 61, who had been near death at the time of the operation.

IV. Fashion
   Folkways
   Holidays
   Social Issues and Crime
   Sports

This year the NCAA sponsored for the first time a major college basketball championship for women. The Association for Intercollegiate Athletics for Women (AIAW), which had been holding championship games since 1972, held its annual game this year, but it was clearly at the end of its existence and disgruntled at the NCAA takeover after years of lack of interest in women's competition. Major league baseball set an attendance record of 44,500,000. Tom Watson was the outstanding golfer of the year, winning both the British and U.S. Open championships. The top pro golf money winners were Craig Stadler, $446,462, and JoAnne Carner, $320,399. Fashions showed a tendency toward greater elegance. Women's winter styles included ponchos and knickers. Sports fans mourned the passing of Leroy "Satchel" Paige, one of the great pitchers of all time, June 8, at 75; and Walter W. "Red" Smith, Pulitzer Prize-winning sportswriter, Jan. 15, at 76.

Jan 24: Super Bowl XVI was won by the San Francisco 49ers (NFC), defeating the Cincinnati Bengals (AFC) 26 to 21. On Jan. 10 the 49ers had beaten the Dallas Cowboys 28 to 27 for the NFC title, and Cincinnati had beaten the San Diego Chargers 27 to 7 for the AFC championship.

Mar 29: The **NCAA men's basketball championship** was won by North Carolina, which defeated Georgetown 63 to 62.

May 27-June 8: The **NBA basketball championship** was won by the Los Angeles Lakers, who defeated the Philadelphia 76ers four games to two.

June 20: The **U.S. Open golf tournament** was won by Tom Watson, who beat Jack Nicklaus by two strokes.

July 3-4: At the **Wimbledon** tennis championships in England, Jimmy Connors won the men's singles title and Martina Navratilova won the women's singles. Navratilova teamed with Pam Shriver to win the women's doubles, and Anne Smith teamed with Kevin Curran of South Africa to win the mixed doubles.

Aug 8: The **PGA golf tournament** was won by Raymond Floyd, who posted a record opening round score of 63.

Sep 11-12: The **U.S. Open tennis singles championships** were won by Jimmy Connors in the men's division and by Chris Evert Lloyd in the women's division.

Oct 12-20: The **World Series** was won by the St. Louis Cardinals (NL), defeating the Milwaukee Brewers four games to three. On Oct. 10 the Cardinals had won the National League pennant over the Atlanta Braves in three straight games. The same day the Brewers won the American League pennant over the California Angels, three games to two. The Brewers became the first team to win a playoff after losing the first two games.

Nov 26-28: The **Davis Cup** international tennis championship was won in Grenoble, France, by the U.S., defeating France four matches to one.

Dec 10: The **WBA heavyweight boxing championship** was won by Michael Dokes, who knocked out Mike Weaver in the first round of a bout at Las Vegas, Nev.

Dec 12: The **largest cash robbery** in U.S. history occurred when thieves in New York City made off with $9,800,000 from an armored truck company.

1983

I. Civil Rights
Exploration and Settlement
Government
Statistics
Wars

Pres. Ronald Reagan's administration faced a difficult year in foreign relations. In Lebanon the U.S. was unsuccessful in its attempt to secure withdrawal of Syrian and Israeli forces and to aid the Lebanese government in its struggle to assert authority over the many political and religious factions fighting in Beirut. Disaster struck the U.S. peacemaking effort in April when the U.S. embassy in Beirut was bombed. The crushing blow came in October when terrorists blew up U.S. Marine headquarters in Beirut. In Central America the U.S. sent military aid to the government of El Salvador in its long and bloody civil war. Pres. Reagan described the Salvadoran insurgents as terrorists. Meanwhile the U.S. sent aid to the anti-Sandinista, anticommunist "freedom fighters" in Nicaragua. Politicians and private citizens alike called for a consistent foreign policy for both the Middle East and Central America and voiced concern that U.S. policies would eventually involve the country in a war. In October U.S. forces were committed in an invasion of the island of Grenada, ostensibly to protect U.S. citizens there after a coup by Marxist radicals. In domestic affairs, the Census Bureau reported that the number of Americans living in poverty grew from 34,400,000 in 1982 to 35,300,000 in 1983, boosting the poverty rate to its highest level in 18 years. Even the weather was dismal in 1983. Heat, cold, and storms killed some 700 people, nearly twice the 1982 total, and caused an estimated $27,000,000,000 in damage. Among the notables who died this year were Benjamin V. Cohen, who wrote much of the precedent-setting legislation of the New Deal of the early 1930s, Aug. 15, at 88; Gen. Alfred M. Gruenther, a principal aide to Gen. Dwight D. Eisenhower in

World War II and NATO commander from 1953 to 1956, May 30, at 84; and Sen. Henry M. "Scoop" Jackson, Democrat of Washington, who had served in Congress for nearly 43 years, Sept. 1, at 71.

Jan 15: Changes in the **Social Security system** were recommended by the National Commission on Social Security Reform. The changes, calculated to produce $168,700,000,000 by 1989 and make the system solvent, included tax increases, a reduction in the growth rate of benefits, and an eventual raising of the retirement age. A bill incorporating these modifications was passed by Congress on Mar. 25 and signed by Pres. Reagan on Apr. 20.

Apr 11: A presidential panel reviewing the **MX missile** recommended that 100 of the ICBMs be installed in existing missile silos in Wyoming and Nebraska. The panel also recommended development of a smaller, single-warheaded missile, dubbed Midgetman.

Apr 12: The **first black mayor of Chicago,** Harold Washington, a Democratic congressman, was elected to office by a narrow margin.

Apr 18: The **U.S. embassy in Beirut,** Lebanon, was almost totally destroyed by a car-bomb explosion that killed 63 people, including 17 Americans. Pro-Iranian terrorists were blamed but the perpetrators were not found.

May 24: MX missile research and development funds, totaling $625,000,000, were authorized by Congress. Some Democrats supported Republicans on the measure after Pres. Reagan promised to be more flexible in arms control negotiations.

June 15: In a ruling on **legal abortions** involving five different cases, the Supreme Court curbed the power of state and local governments to limit access to such operations. The decision reaffirmed the 1973 ruling giving women unrestricted rights to abortions during the first three months of pregnancy.

June 23: The so-called **legislative veto,** by which Congress overruled actions of federal agencies, was ruled unconstitutional by the Supreme Court as an invasion of executive authority by the legislative branch.

June 28: A proposed **abortion amendment,** allowing legislation to curb or ban abortions, was rejected by the Senate. The vote was 50–49 in favor, but a two-thirds majority was required.

July 28: Soviet grain purchases were increased by at least 50% as a result of a new five-year agreement. The U.S.S.R. was to buy a minimum of 9,000,000 metric tons a year, up from 6,000,000, and could purchase as much as 12,000,000 tons.

Aug 27: A **march on Washington,** D.C., commemorating the famous 1963 civil rights march led by the Rev.

Martin Luther King, Jr., brought some 250,000 persons to the nation's capital.

Sep 5: Sanctions against the U.S.S.R., in response to the Sept. 1 downing of a South Korean airliner by a Soviet fighter, were announced by Pres. Reagan. The largely token measures included suspension of negotiations for a U.S. consulate in Kiev. The airliner had been shot down after violating Soviet airspace, killing all 269 people aboard.

Sep 20: A resolution reaffirming the **War Powers Act of 1973,** the Multinational Force in Lebanon Resolution, was passed by Congress. The measure authorized U.S. Marines to remain in Lebanon for another 18 months as a peacekeeping force.

Oct 23: The **U.S. Marine headquarters in Beirut,** Lebanon, was destroyed when an explosive-laden truck evaded security measures and blew up outside the building. The driver of the truck was killed in the blast, which took the lives of 241 Marine and Navy personnel.

Oct 25: An **invasion of Grenada,** an island nation in the Caribbean, was launched by U.S. forces a week after a bloody coup by pro-Cuban Marxists. The guerrillas murdered Grenada's top leaders. By Nov. 2 the Department of Defense reported the end of hostilities. U.S. casualties were listed as 18 dead, 115 wounded. The action was taken to restore order and protect the 1100 U.S. citizens, mostly students, on the island.

Nov 11: The first U.S. **cruise missiles** arrived in Great Britain. In all, 572 of the intermediate-range missiles were to be deployed in Europe, including 160 in Great Britain.

Nov 23: The U.S.S.R. withdrew from **arms limitation talks** aimed at reducing the number of intermediate-range missiles in Europe. The action was in response to deployment of such weapons by the U.S.

Dec 4: Carrier-based **U.S. warplanes attacked Syrian positions** near Beirut, Lebanon, for the first time. Two planes were shot down. One pilot was killed and one captured. Syrian forces had fired on U.S. reconnaissance planes on the previous day, prompting the strike.

Dec 28: U.S. withdrawal from UNESCO, the United Nations Educational, Scientific, and Cultural Organization, as of Dec. 31, 1984, was announced. The reasons for the withdrawal included UNESCO's increasing political bias and financial mismanagement. The U.S. deferred withdrawing pending attempts to achieve improvements in UNESCO operations and management, but on Dec. 19, 1984, the decision to withdraw was reaffirmed.

II. Architecture
Arts and Music
Popular Entertainment
Publishing
Theater

Americans all over the country this year celebrated the 100th anniversaries of New York City's Metropolitan Opera and the Brooklyn Bridge. The celebrations at the Brooklyn Bridge on May 24, witnessed by an estimated 2,100,000 persons, were climaxed by a spectacular fireworks display staged by the master pyrotechnicians, the Grucci family. The year's major art exhibitions included *The Vatican Collections: The Papacy and Art,* which was seen in New York City, Chicago, and San Francisco; and a comprehensive exhibit of the works of Grant Wood, which was organized by the Minneapolis Institute of Art. A collection of 16 French impressionist works collected by Mr. and Mrs. H. O. Havemayer sold at auction for $16,800,000. Mark Rothko's *Black, Maroon, and White* sold for $1,815,000 and Willem de Kooning's *Two Women* fetched $1,200,000. Movie theaters had record attendance for the third consecutive year, with revenues of nearly $3,700,000,000. The two most popular films were *The Return of the Jedi,* the third completed film in George Lucas's projected nine-film *Star Wars* series; and *Never Say Never Again,* featuring Sean Connery as the super agent James Bond. Television offered two highly successful miniseries, *The Thorn Birds* and *The Winds of War,* both based on best-selling novels. The number of cable television subscribers reached 25,000,000. This year some 4,100,000 videocassette recorders were sold, auguring a strong new electronics market and promising a fundamental change in TV viewing habits. Sales of rock videos, records, and tapes were all up, but the craze for arcade video games came to a sudden halt in 1983. Rupert Murdoch, the Australian newspaper magnate, made headlines of his own by buying the Chicago *Sun-Times* for $90,000,000. Notables who died this year included George Balanchine, choreographer, Apr. 30, at 79; Eubie Blake, ragtime composer and pianist, Feb. 12, at 100; John Cowles, Sr., head of the Cowles publishing empire, Feb. 25, at 84; George Cukor, a leading film director for over 50 years, Jan. 24, at 83; Lynn Fontanne, who with her late husband Alfred Lunt starred in numerous Broadway plays, July 30, at 95; Ira Gershwin, celebrated lyricist, Aug. 17, at 86; Earl "Fatha" Hines, father of modern jazz piano, Apr. 22, at 77; Harry James, trumpeter and band leader, July 6, at 67; Raymond Massey, Canadian-born actor, July 29, at 86; José Luis Sert, architect, Mar. 15, at 80; Norma Shearer, actress, June 12, at 80; Gloria Swanson, film star, Apr. 4, at 84; and Tennessee Williams, playwright, Feb. 25, at 71.

Among **books published** this year was *Ironweed* by William Kennedy, a novel showing the seamier side of the author's hometown, Albany, N.Y. Kennedy had great difficulty securing publication for his book, but its release to enthusiastic reviews was accompanied by the reissue of two of Kennedy's earlier books, *Legs* (1975) and *Billy Phelan's Greatest Game* (1978). *Ironweed* went on to win the Pulitzer Prize. Other books published this year included *During the Reign of the Queen of Sheba* by Joan Chase, a novel; *Ancient Evenings* by Norman Mailer, a novel of ancient Egypt that received mixed reviews; *The Cannibal Galaxy* by Cynthia Ozick, a novel; *In Search of Excellence* by Thomas J. Peters and Robert H. Waterman, Jr., a best-selling study of what the authors considered to be the best-run companies in the U.S.; and *The Anatomy Lesson* by Philip Roth, a novel.

Jan 21: The **Bollingen Prize** for poetry was awarded jointly to Anthony E. Hecht and John Hollander.

Mar 2: The **final episode of** *M*A*S*H,* a long-running series on U.S. medics in the Korean War, was seen by the largest television audience to date for a nonsports program, 125,000,000 viewers.

Apr 18: Pulitzer prizes were awarded for the following: fiction, *The Color Purple* by Alice Walker; biography, *Growing Up* by Russell Baker; history, *The Transformation of Virginia, 1740–1790* by Rhys L. Isaac; general nonfiction, *Is There No Place on Earth for Me?* by Susan Sheehan; poetry, *Selected Poems* by Galway Kinnell; drama, *'Night, Mother* by Marsha Norman.

III. Business and Industry
Education
Philosophy and Religion
Science

The economy showed strong signs of improvement this year. Consumer prices rose only 3.8%, slightly less than in 1982, and personal income was up 6.3%, slightly more than in 1982. Orders for manufactured goods rose 10.6%, the largest increase in four years. Automobile production increased 10.2%, and major appliance production was up 21.3%. The greatest increase of all was in new home construction, which jumped 60% over 1982. The country's top executives did spectacularly well. Forty-six captains of industry had cash compensation of more than $1,000,000, and the leader in total compensation took home $13,229,000. The New York Stock Exchange set a new record of 21,589,000,000 shares traded in 1982, and

the Dow Jones industrial average closed the year at 1258.64, about 200 points ahead of the 1982 closing mark. The nation's airlines continued to have problems, however, and the foreign trade deficit hit a record for the year of $60,600,000,000. The worst drought since 1936 devastated the South and Midwest, wiping out crops and raising food prices. Elementary school enrollment was down for the eighth year in a row, but gifts to institutions of higher education were up 6.2% to a record $5,100,000,000. Hospital costs rose 10.7%. At the end of August the administration announced a new schedule of Medicare fees for hospital and medical costs in a move to slow the increase in medical bills. This year the number of persons killed in auto accidents dropped to 43,028, the lowest figure in 20 years, in part because of increased use of safety belts and a growing campaign against drunk driving. Notables who died this year included Terence Cardinal Cooke, Roman Catholic archbishop of New York and vicar of the U.S. armed forces, Oct. 6, at 62; R. Buckminster Fuller, architect and inventor of the geodesic dome, July 3, at 87; Herman Kahn, futurist and nuclear stragetist, July 7, at 71; and Humberto Cardinal Madeiros, Roman Catholic archbishop of Boston since 1973 and a noted conservative, Sept. 17, at 67.

Feb 2: Bishop **Joseph L. Bernardin,** archbishop of Chicago, was among 18 new cardinals invested by Pope John Paul II.

Mar 23: Barney Clark, 62, the first recipient of a permanent artificial heart, died 112 days after receiving the device.

Mar 30: The first **California condor chick** born in captivity was hatched at the San Diego Zoo. A second one was hatched on Apr. 5.

Apr 4-9: The **space shuttle** *Challenger,* the second U.S. space shuttle, made its maiden voyage into orbit with astronauts Paul Weitz, Donald Peterson, Karol Bobko, and Story Musgrave aboard.

Apr 13: The **largest U.S. corporation,** according to the annual survey by *Fortune* magazine, was Exxon, with sales of $97,172,523,000 in 1982. General Motors moved up from third to second place.

Apr 26: The **quality of American education** is so poor that it "threatens our very future as a nation and a people," a federal report announced. It decried what it called a "rising tide of mediocrity," which was reflected in high school test scores that were lower than those of 1957. It calculated that some 23,000,000 Americans were functionally illiterate.

May 3: The nuclear **arms race was condemned** in a pastoral letter issued by the Roman Catholic bishops of the U.S.

June 18-24: Sally K. Ride became the first U.S. woman astronaut in space as a member of the crew of the space shuttle *Challenger* in its second flight.

June 25: The **Washington Public Power Supply System** defaulted on debts of $2,250,000,000, becoming the largest governmental unit to fail in U.S. history. Of the five nuclear power plants it set out to build in Washington State, only one was ever completed.

Aug 9: The first direct evidence supporting the existence of **stellar systems** was reported by the Jet Propulsion Laboratory in Pasadena, Calif. An orbiting satellite had detected solid objects orbiting the star Vega. This was the first time that solid objects of any size had been identified in orbit around a star other than the sun.

Aug 30-Sep 5: The **first black astronaut in space,** Lt. Col. Guion S. Bluford, USAF, was part of the crew on space shuttle *Challenger's* third mission. On Sept. 5 *Challenger* made the first nighttime shuttle landing.

Oct 10: The **Nobel Prize in Physiology or Medicine** was awarded to Barbara McClintock, a botanist at the Cold Spring Harbor Laboratory, Long Island, N.Y., for her studies of gene shifting on plant chromosomes and their effect on hereditary factors.

Oct 17: The **Nobel Prize in Economics** was awarded to Gerard Debreu, a French-born professor at the University of California, Berkeley, for his study of the way prices in a free-market economy work to balance consumer and producer forces.

Oct 19: The **Nobel Prize in Physics** was awarded jointly to Subrahmanyan Chandrasekhar of the University of Chicago for his work on the density of stars, and to William Fowler of the California Institute of Technology for his theory of the formation of the elements in the universe.

Dec 22: A joint **U.S.-Japanese auto venture** by General Motors and Toyota of Japan was approved by the Federal Trade Commission. The new plant, in Fremont, Calif., was expected to produce from 200,000 to 250,000 autos a year. Ford and Chrysler had both opposed the plan.

IV. Fashion
   Folkways
   Holidays
   Social Issues and Crime
   Sports

Baseball was the top spectator sport in 1983, drawing 78,051,343 fans and dropping horse racing, with 75,784,430 fans, to second place. In golf the year's top money winners were Hal Sutton, $426,668, and JoAnne Carner, $291,404. In fashion the key words were clean lines and classic shapes. Black was the favorite color, but winter brought a craze for brightly colored leg warmers. This year's top craze, however, was the Cabbage Patch doll, a soft cloth doll made by hand, so no two were exactly alike. The supply was nowhere near the demand, and by Christmas many a parent could not find one for sale at any price. Price was no object for some furniture buyers this year. A Rhode Island Chippendale dining table brought $687,000 at auction in 1983, a new record for American furniture. Notables who died this year included Paul "Bear" Bryant of the University of Alabama, the winningest football coach in history, Jan. 26, at 69; Jack Dempsey, world heavyweight boxing champion from 1919 to 1926, May 31, at 86; George Halas, longtime coach of the Chicago Bears, Oct. 31, at 88; and Meyer Lansky, reputed to have been for 40 years the top boss of organized crime, Jan. 15, at 80.

Jan 30: Super Bowl XVII was won by the Washington Redskins (NFC), defeating the Miami Dolphins (AFC) 27 to 17. On Jan. 22 the Redskins had beaten the Dallas Cowboys 31 to 17 for the NFC championship and the Dolphins had shut out the New York Jets 14 to 0 for the AFC title.

Apr 4: The **NCAA men's basketball championship** was won by North Carolina State, defeating the University of Houston 54 to 52.

May 22-31: The **NBA basketball championship** was won by the Philadelphia 76ers, who swept the Los Angeles Lakers in four straight games.

June 20: The **U.S. Open golf tournament** was won by Larry Nelson, who beat Tom Watson by one stroke.

July 2-3: At the **Wimbledon** tennis championships in England, John McEnroe won the men's singles title and Martina Navratilova won the women's singles. McEnroe teamed with Peter Fleming to win the men's doubles, and Navratilova teamed with Pam Shriver to win the women's doubles.

Aug 7: The **PGA golf tournament** was won by Hal Sutton, beating Jack Nicklaus by one stroke.

Sep 11: The **U.S. Open tennis singles championships** were won by Jimmy Connors in the men's division, and by Martina Navratilova in the women's division.

Sep 14-26: The **America's Cup** was lost by the U.S. for the first time in the yachting classic's 132-year history. The Australian challenger *Australia II* defeated the U.S. yacht *Liberty* four races to three.

Sep 23: The **World Boxing Association heavyweight boxing championship** was won by Gerrie Coatzee of South Africa, who knocked out Michael Dokes in ten rounds at Richfield, Ohio.

Oct 11-16: The **World Series** was won by the Baltimore Orioles (AL), defeating the Philadelphia Phillies (NL) four games to one. On Oct. 8 the Orioles won the American League pennant over the Chicago White

Sox, three games to one, and the Phillies won the National League pennant from the Los Angeles Dodgers, three games to one.

Nov 2: A federal holiday honoring Dr. **Martin Luther King, Jr.,** the slain civil rights leader, was designated for observance on the third Monday of January in a bill signed by Pres. Reagan. King was the first person honored with a federal holiday since George Washington's birthday was so named.

1984

I. Civil Rights
Exploration and Settlement
Government
Statistics
Wars

The year's top domestic story was the presidential campaign, a race between former vice president Walter F. Mondale and Pres. Ronald Reagan, a highly popular incumbent and master of the media campaign. The Democrats tried unsuccessfully to challenge Reagan's ability to manage the government, even to comprehend the major issues of the day. The Republicans pointed to the booming national economy and assailed the Democrats for their free-spending ways and lack of political vision. In foreign affairs the U.S. and U.S.S.R. jockeyed for position in the debate over resuming nuclear arms limitation talks, so no progress was made. The U.S. appeared also to have lost the initiative in seeking peace in the Middle East. Congress and Pres. Reagan clashed on aid for El Salvador, where the established government was fighting insurgents, and on aid for the so-called *contras* in Nicaragua. There insurgents were fighting the established government, led by the Marxist-dominated Sandinistas. At home in midyear the Census Bureau estimated the U.S. population at 236,158,000. Almost all the population growth of the previous four years had been in the South and West. Two other items of current demographic information were also remarkable: Seven states had more than 1,000,000 residents aged 65 or older, and 454,136 people were in prison, almost double the total of ten years earlier. This year Los Angeles displaced Chicago as the nation's second largest city.

Notables who died this year included George D. Aiken, Republican senator from Vermont from 1941 to 1975, Nov. 19, at 92; Ellsworth Bunker, a diplomat who served under six presidents, Sept. 30, at 90; Sen. Frank Church, Democrat of Ohio from 1957 to 1981, Apr. 7, at 59; Gen. Mark W. Clark, a top U.S. commander during World War II, Apr. 17, at 87; and Glen H. Taylor, former senator from Idaho who was Henry A. Wallace's vice presidential running mate on the Progressive ticket in 1948, Apr. 28, at 80.

Jan 10: Restoration of full **diplomatic relations with the Vatican** after a period of 117 years was announced in Washington, D.C. The move came at a time when the Vatican apparently was taking much interest in international affairs.

Feb 7: **Withdrawal of U.S. Marines from Beirut,** Lebanon was announced by Pres. Reagan. The troops were completely redeployed to Navy ships offshore by Feb. 29.

Mar 5: In a major decision on **separation of church and state,** the Supreme Court ruled that a city may make a Nativity scene part of an official Christmas display without violating the constitutional separation of government and organized religion.

Mar 20: A constitutional **school prayer amendment,** permitting organized spoken prayer in public schools, was rejected by the U.S. Senate. The 56–44 vote fell 11 short of the required two-thirds majority.

Apr 26-May 1: A **presidential trip to China** was made by Pres. Reagan. He was party to formal agreements on scientific and cultural exchanges, economic cooperation, and development of nuclear energy.

May 7: Establishment of an **Agent Orange victims' fund** of $180,000,000 was announced. The fund, provided by Dow Chemical Company and six other manufacturers of the herbicide, was intended to provide assistance for Vietnam veterans suffering from exposure to Agent Orange and for the families of victims.

May 22: In a decision on **job discrimination,** the Supreme Court ruled that law firms may not discriminate on the basis of sex, race, religion, or national origin in promoting associates to partnership. The decision affirmed that partnerships are covered by federal laws against discrimination, as are other forms of businesses.

June 6: On the **40th anniversary of D-Day,** Pres. Reagan joined with representatives from Great Britain, Canada, and other nations in ceremonies at Normandy, where Allied armies landed first in the invasion of France in 1944.

June 11: In a ruling on **admissibility of evidence,** the Supreme Court declared that illegally obtained evidence may be admitted at a trial provided it could be proved that the evidence would have been discovered inevitably by lawful means. On July 5 the Court ruled that some evidence obtained with defective search warrants could be used in a trial.

July 16-19: The **Democratic National Convention** nominated **Walter F. Mondale** of Minnesota for the presidency and Rep. Geraldine Ferraro of New York for the vice presidency.

July 17: To promote raising of the **legal drinking age** to 21, Pres. Reagan signed a bill giving states until Oct. 1, 1986, to do so or face a 5% cut in federal highway funds.

July 18: The **Deficit Reduction Act of 1984,** raising taxes by about $50,000,000,000 and cutting spending by $13,000,000,000 through 1987, was signed by Pres. Reagan.

Aug 20-23: The **Republican National Convention** nominated **Pres. Reagan** for reelection. George Bush was renominated for the vice presidency.

Sep 20: The **U.S. Embassy in Beirut was bombed.** A suicide car-bomb exploded outside the Embassy, killing at least 23, including two Americans.

Oct 3: The **first FBI agent charged with espionage,** Richard W. Miller, was arrested. He was accused of passing a classified document to two Soviet émigrés.

Oct 14: A bill introducing **major changes in U.S. criminal law** was signed by Pres. Reagan. The new law, permitting detention without bail for the first time in peacetime, was denounced by some as a threat to civil liberty.

Nov 2: In the first **execution of a woman** in 22 years, Margie Velma Barfield, 52, convicted of murder, was put to death in North Carolina.

Nov 6: Ronald Reagan was reelected president of the United States in the greatest Republican landslide in history. Reagan carried 49 states. Walter F. Mondale carried Minnesota and the District of Columbia. The electoral vote was Reagan, 525; Mondale 13. The popular vote was Reagan, 54,455,075; Mondale, 37,577,185. In congressional elections the Republicans gained two Senate seats for a 53–47 majority. In the House the Democrats lost 14 seats but kept a majority of 253–182.

Nov 26: The **World Court** declared it had jurisdiction in a case brought by Nicaragua to have the U.S. declared an aggressor nation. On May 10 the court had ruled unanimously that the U.S. should halt any attempts to blockade or mine Nicaraguan ports. The U.S. had stated it would not be bound by the decision of the World Court.

II. Architecture
Arts and Music
Popular Entertainment
Publishing
Theater

Although at year's end almost half of Broadway's 37 theaters were dark, prospects for the theater were promising. Gross receipts were up, and the 1983–1984 season had produced three sellout musicals, *La Cage aux Folles, Cats,* and *Sunday in the Park With George.* The American Academy of Dramatic Arts celebrated its centennial this year, and the Long Wharf Theater in New Haven, Conn., its 20th year anniversary. Major museum exhibits included the *Van Gogh at Arles* exhibit at the Metropolitan Museum in New York City, a complete sellout; an extensive James McNeill Whistler show at the Freer Gallery in Washington, D.C.; and a showing of works of traditional art of the Maori people of New Zealand at the Metropolitan Museum. In mid-May the Museum of Modern Art in New York City opened its new and greatly enlarged facilities. In the fall the Indianapolis Symphony Orchestra moved to a renovated movie palace, but orchestras in St. Louis, Pittsburgh, and Miami moved into new homes. Of the year's top films, *Indiana Jones and the Temple of Doom* earned $42,267,345 in its first six days of release, and went on to break virtually every box office record. The top recording artist of the year was Michael Jackson, whose album *Thriller* sold more than 20,000,000 copies worldwide in 1983 and 1984. Among those who died this year were Ansel Adams, photographer, Apr. 22, at 82; Brooks Atkinson, the drama critic, Jan. 13, at 89; William "Count" Basie, jazz pianist and band leader, Apr. 26, at 79; Richard Burton, the actor, Aug. 5, at 58; Truman Capote, the author, Aug. 25, at 59; Jackie Coogan, first major child star in U.S. film history, Mar. 1, at 69; Janet Gaynor, winner of the first Academy Award for best actress, Sept. 14, at 77; Lillian Hellman, the playwright, June 30, at 79; Alfred A. Knopf, founder of the publishing house bearing his name, Aug. 11, at 91; Mabel Mercer, a singer whose style greatly influenced popular music, Apr. 20, at 84; Ethel Merman, star of musical comedy, Feb. 15, at 76; Jan Peerce, tenor with the Metropolitan Opera for 27 years, Dec. 15, at 80; Lee Krasner Pollock, abstract expressionist painter, June 19, at 75; William Powell, the movie star, Mar. 5, at 91; Irwin Shaw, the author, May 16, at 71; Fred Waring, the band leader, July 29, at 84; Johnny Weissmuller, Olympic star and movie Tarzan, Jan. 20, at 79; and

Meredith Willson, Broadway composer and lyricist, June 15, at 82.

Among **books published** this year was a reissue of George Orwell's 1949 classic novel of totalitarianism, *1984.* Critics noted that Orwell had intended the novel to be a warning of things that might occur, not a prediction of the inevitable. Readers put the book firmly on the best-seller lists. Other books published this year included *Him With His Foot in His Mouth and Other Stories* by Saul Bellow; *Lives of the Poets* by E.L. Doctorow, six stories and a novella; *Iacocca* by Lee Iacocca with William Novak, an autobiography of the man credited with returning Chrysler Corporation to prosperity from virtual bankruptcy; *The Aquitaine Progression* by Robert Ludlum, a spy thriller that topped the hardcover best-seller lists; and *Walt Whitman,* a biography by Paul Zweig.

Mar 4: A **Television Academy Hall of Fame** was established. Its first inductees were Lucille Ball, Milton Berle, Paddy Chayefsky, Norman Lear, Edward R. Murrow, William S. Paley, and David Sarnoff.

Apr 16: **Pulitzer prizes** were awarded for the following: fiction, *Ironweed* by William Kennedy; general nonfiction, *Social Transformation of American Medicine* by Paul Starr; biography, *Booker T. Washington* by Louis R. Harlan; poetry, *American Primitive* by Mary Oliver; drama, *Glengarry Glen Ross* by David Mamet.

May 9: A sculpture by **Alexander Calder,** a 24-foot-high mobile entitled *Big Crinkly,* sold at auction in New York City for $852,000, a new record for sculpture by an American.

June 9: Donald Duck's 50th birthday was celebrated at Disneyland in California. Donald's career began in 1934 with a bit part in the animated film *Wise Little Men.*

Nov 1: A 1953 painting by **Willem de Kooning,** *Two Women,* sold at auction for $1,980,000, the highest auction price ever paid for a post-World War II artwork.

III. Business and Industry
Education
Philosophy and Religion
Science

The year was excellent for businesses and consumers. The economy expanded 6.8%, its best performance since 1951. The rise in consumer prices was only 4%, and personal income rose 6.8%. New housing starts hit 1,700,000, the highest number since 1979. Americans bought 14,100,000 cars and light trucks, the largest volume since 1979. This helped put Detroit back on its feet, and the big three automobile makers earned $9,810,000,000, a new record. Not all the news was good, however. The foreign trade deficit hit a record $107,600,000,000, the Dow Jones average finished the year about 60 points below its opening price, and 79 banks failed, the largest number since 1938. Although employment was up, the unemployment rate stood at 7.1% in December, down only 0.3% from a year earlier. Organized labor's membership declined to 18.8% of wage and salary workers, compared with 23% in 1980. For the third year in a row, the value of farmland dropped, with the largest declines registered in Iowa and Nebraska. This was bad news for farmers, many of whom had borrowed heavily on their land and now were faced with bankruptcy. Medical costs continued to rise, contributing to the growth of prepaid medical plans and health maintenance organizations, known as HMOs. In November the Great American Smokeout saw more than 5,000,000 smokers kick the habit, according to the American Cancer Society; another 15,000,000 cut back their smoking. In education, this year's high-school graduates scored an average of four points higher on scholastic aptitude tests than the year before. Black students continued to improve their scores faster than white students but remained below the national averages. A study by the National Council of Churches showed members of the clergy to be among the lowest-paid professionals in the country, and women in the clergy to be the lowest paid. Among notables who died this year were the Rev. Martin Luther King, Sr., father of the slain civil rights leader, Nov. 11, at 84; John Rock, who helped develop the birth control pill, Dec. 4, at 94; and George G. Simpson, a world authority on vertebrate paleontology, Oct. 6, at 82.

Jan 13: A **nuclear operating license was withheld** from a nearly completed power plant in Illinois. It was the first time the Nuclear Regulatory Commission had refused to license a nuclear power facility that was close to completion.

Feb 3: In the first case of **surrogate conception,** the birth of a baby conceived in one woman's womb and brought to term by another woman was announced by a team of California physicians.

Feb 7: The **first human satellites** floated in space, two astronauts powered by jet packs and without lifelines connected to their spacecraft. The astronauts were Bruce McCandless and Robert Stewart, crew members on the fourth orbital flight (Feb. 3–11) of the space shuttle *Challenger.*

Feb 13: The **first heart and liver transplant** was performed on a six-year-old Texas girl, Stormie Jones.

Apr 11: The **largest U.S. corporation,** according to the annual survey by *Fortune* magazine, was Exxon, with 1983 sales of $88,561,134,000. General Motors was second.

Apr 23: Identification of a virus thought to **cause acquired immune deficiency syndrome** (AIDS) was announced by federal researchers. The disease, which destroys the body's natural immune system and is considered to be ultimately fatal, was estimated to have afflicted 4000 Americans to date.

May 9: **Ordination of noncelibate homosexuals** was prohibited by the General Conference of the United Methodist Church.

May 23: Kristine Holderied became the **first woman midshipman** to graduate at the top of her class at the U.S. Naval Academy at Annapolis, Md.

May 30: Scientists reported that an effective **chicken pox vaccine** had been developed. The disease claimed some 100 to 150 lives in the U.S. each year.

June 4: Successful **cloning of DNA** from an extinct animal was reported by scientists at the University of California. The gene fragments, cloned from an animal related to the zebra and the horse, were the first to be extracted from a vanished animal species.

June 12: In a decision supporting the **last hired, first fired** policy of many businesses, the Supreme Court ruled that courts could not overrule seniority programs to prevent layoffs of employees hired under affirmative action programs. Labor leaders applauded the decision, but civil rights groups and others condemned it.

June 14: A resolution opposing the **ordination of women** was passed by the Southern Baptist Convention. The resolution was nonbinding on local congregations and did not apply to women already ordained for the Baptist ministry.

June 21: In the **largest single stock transaction** in the history of the New York Stock Exchange, 10,000,000 shares of Superior Oil stock were sold for $423,800,000.

July 26: In the **largest federal loan guarantee** to a private enterprise, the U.S. government committed itself to $4,500,000,000 in loan guarantees to the Continental Illinois National Bank and Trust Company.

Aug 3: A new **daily volume record** of 236,600,000 shares was set by the New York Stock Exchange. It was the first time the volume exceeded 200,000,000 shares.

Aug 11: A bill protecting **student meetings** for religious or political purposes outside of normal school hours was signed by Pres. Reagan.

Aug 30-Sep 5: The **space shuttle** *Discovery,* the third of four U.S. space shuttles, made its maiden flight. Its crew of six included Judith Resnick, the second U.S. woman astronaut in space.

Oct 11: Dr. Kathryn D. Sullivan became the **first U.S. woman astronaut to walk in space.** She was one of seven crew members on the sixth flight of the space shuttle *Challenger* (Oct. 5–13). Also aboard in addition to the crew was the first Canadian astronaut, Marc Garneau.

Oct 16: A **baboon heart transplant to a human,** the first operation of its kind, was performed on a 15-day-old baby girl, identified only as Baby Fae, at Loma Linda University Medical Center in California. Baby Fae lived until Nov. 15.

Oct 17: The **Nobel Prize in Chemistry** was awarded to Dr. Bruce Merrifield of Rockefeller University for protein research offering promise of development of important new drugs.

Nov 11: In a **pastoral letter on economic justice,** a committee of Roman Catholic bishops called for sweeping economic changes to aid the poor, stating that the level of inequality between the wealthy and the poor was "morally unacceptable."

Nov 12: The **first space salvage operation** was performed during the second flight (Nov. 8–16) of the space shuttle *Discovery.* Astronauts Joseph Allen and Dale Gardner retrieved a nonfunctioning satellite and brought it into the shuttle's cargo bay. A second retrieval was accomplished on Nov. 14.

Nov 25: The **second artificial heart transplant** was performed at Humana Heart Institute International in Louisville, Ky. The recipient was William J. Schroeder, 52, of Jasper, Ind.

Nov 30: The basis for a **Protestant church merger** by nine major Protestant denominations was reached by the Consultation on Church Union, after 22 years of effort. The nine denominations were: African Methodist Episcopal Church; African Methodist Episcopal Zion Church; Christian Church (Disciples of Christ); Christian Methodist Episcopal Church; Episcopal Church; International Council of Community Churches; Presbyterian Church (U.S.A.); United Methodist Church; and United Church of Christ.

Dec 10: Discovery was announced of what was thought to be the **first planet detected outside the solar system.** U.S. astronomers had discovered a huge, gaseous object orbiting a star in the constellation Ophiuchus.

Dec 11-12: Discovery of **7000-year-old human skulls with brains virtually intact** was reported by archeologists in Florida. The skulls were found buried in peat at the bottom of a lake. They were described as the oldest skulls from which it had thus far been possible to extract and analyze DNA.

IV. Fashion
Folkways
Holidays
Social Issues and Crime
Sports

This year saw the centennial of the American Kennel Club, on Sept. 17. Another institution celebrating its centennial was the roller coaster, first put in operation at Coney Island, N.Y., on June 16, 1884. A different kind of celebration was held in Chicago, where a 28-year-old printer won $40,000,000 in the Illinois state lottery. It was the largest lottery win by one person in North America. The divorce rate dropped for the third year in a row, down to 4.9% of marriages. After three years of decline, traffic fatalities were up. Safety experts thought the increase was associated with the booming economy, which meant traffic was heavier than in recent years. Sales of home exercise equipment passed the $1,000,000,000 mark in 1984, and the growing U.S. mania for fitness and personal appearance also helped the cosmetics industry. It sold $10,000,000,000 worth of skin care products. The mania for Cabbage Patch dolls and their accessories continued. In fashion, the introduction of oversize men's clothing for women triggered a boom for used clothing stores, where women snapped up men's coats at bargain prices. In sports the NFL reported an increase in attendance at football games, but major league baseball showed a drop in attendance. A Gallup poll showed that swimming, bicycling, and fishing were the most popular activities of adult Americans. This year the memory of track star Jesse Owens, star of the 1936 Olympics in Berlin, was honored in West Berlin with the naming of an avenue after him. In professional golf, the year's top money winners were Tom Watson, $476,200, and Betsy King, $266,771. Americans mourned the deaths this year of Walter Alston, manager of the Los Angeles Dodgers for 23 years, Oct. 1, at 72; Joe Cronin, former star shortstop and later president of the American League, Sept. 7, at 77; Jim Fixx, whose books about running fueled the American passion for jogging, July 20, at 52; Waite Hoyt, former pitching great, Aug. 25, at 84; Oswald Jacoby, one of the great contract bridge players of all time, July 27, at 81; and Al Schacht, a player and coach who entertained fans at baseball games with pantomime antics that won him the title of Clown Prince of Baseball, July 14, at 91.

Jan 22: Super Bowl XVIII was won by the Los Angeles Raiders (AFC), defeating the Washington Redskins (NFC) 38 to 9. On Jan. 8 the Raiders had defeated the Seattle Seahawks 30 to 14 to win the AFC championship, and the Redskins had beaten the San Francisco 49ers 24 to 21 for the NFC title.

Mar 3: Peter V. Ueberroth, president of the Los Angeles Olympic Organizing Committee, was elected commissioner of baseball by the major league team owners.

Mar 9: The World Boxing Council **heavyweight boxing championship** was won by Tim Witherspoon, who outpointed Greg Page in a 12-round bout at Las Vegas, Nev.

Apr 2: The **NCAA men's basketball championship** was won by Georgetown, which defeated Houston 84 to 75.

May 8: The **U.S.S.R. withdrew from the 1984 Olympics.** The U.S.S.R. Olympic Committee said Soviet athletes could not compete because of "gross flouting" of Olympic ideals by the U.S. The move was seen in some quarters as revenge for the boycott of the 1980 games in Moscow by the U.S. and some other Western nations.

May 27-June 12: The **NBA basketball championship** was won by the Boston Celtics, who beat the Los Angeles Lakers four games to three.

June 18: The **U.S. Open golf tournament** was won by Fuzzy Zoeller in an 18-hole playoff with Greg Norman.

July 7-8: At the **Wimbledon** tennis championships in England, John McEnroe won the men's singles title and Martina Navratilova won the women's singles. McEnroe teamed with Peter Fleming to win the men's doubles, and Navratilova teamed with Pam Shriver to win the women's doubles.

July 18: A **gunman killed 21 people** in and near a McDonald's restaurant in San Ysidro, Calif. James Humberty, heavily armed, walked into the fast food store and began shooting, then continued killing people on the street before he was shot and killed by police officers.

July 28-Aug 12: At the **Summer Olympics** in Los Angeles, Calif., the U.S. won 83 gold medals and finished first in unofficial team standings. Carl Lewis won four gold medals in track and field events, and Mary Lou Retton won four in gymnastics. Joan Benoit won the first Olympic women's marathon.

Aug 19: The **PGA golf tournament** was won by Lee Trevino, who shot a 15 under par 273 to finish four strokes ahead of Gary Player and Lanny Wadkins.

Aug 31: The World Boxing Council **heavyweight boxing championship** was won by Pinklon Thomas, who outpointed Tim Witherspoon in a 12-round bout in Las Vegas, Nev.

Sep 8-9: The **U.S. Open tennis singles championships** were won by John McEnroe in the men's division and Martina Navratilova in the women's division.

Sep 14-18: The **first transatlantic solo balloon flight** was completed by Joe W. Kittinger, who flew 3535 miles from Caribou, Maine, to near Savona, Italy. He made the flight in the gondola of his ten-story-tall, helium-lifted craft named *Rosie O'Grady's Balloon of Peace.*

Oct 9-14: The **World Series** was won by the Detroit Tigers (AL), defeating the San Diego Padres (NL) four games to one. On Oct. 5 the Tigers had won the American League pennant over the Kansas City Royals in a three-game sweep, and on Oct. 7 the Padres had taken the National League pennant over the Chicago Cubs, three games to two.

Nov 9: The first world heavyweight boxing match under the auspices of the **International Boxing Federation** (IBF) was won by Larry Holmes, who knocked out James "Bonecrusher" Smith in the 12th round of a bout in Las Vegas, Nev. Holmes had vacated his WBC title when arrangements to fight Greg Page, the top contender, were not completed.

Dec 1: The WBA **heavyweight boxing championship** was won by Greg Page, who knocked out Gerrie Coetzee of South Africa in the eighth round of a bout in Sun City, Bophuthatswana.

Dec 16-18: The **Davis Cup** international tennis championship was won by Sweden, defeating the U.S. four matches to one at Göteborg, Sweden.

1985

I. **Civil Rights**
   Exploration and Settlement
   Government
   Statistics
   Wars

The nation was stunned by what appeared to be an epidemic of spying. Thirteen Americans were charged with espionage in the course of the year. Of those charged, most were past or present CIA or Navy personnel and one was an FBI agent. Most of those accused were said to have turned to spying not for reasons of ideology but for money. One of the accused had been supplying Israel, an ally, with information, much to the discomfiture of the U.S. and Israel. Late in November *The New York Times* reported that since 1968 U.S. citizens had been attacked by terrorists in 72 countries. In 1985 seventeen Americans were killed in terrorist attacks and 154 had been wounded. The government reported that 90 planned terrorist attacks had been foiled in a 12-month period. The Social Security system celebrated its 50th anniversary on Aug. 14, having paid $1,800,000,000 in benefits and carrying 36,700,000 people on its rolls. Americans mourned the passing of former Sen. Sam J. Ervin, Jr., Democrat of North Carolina, who headed the Senate Watergate investigation that led to Pres. Richard Nixon's resignation, Apr. 23, at 88; Patricia Roberts Harris, who served in two Cabinet posts under Pres. Jimmy Carter, Mar. 23, at 60; Henry Cabot Lodge, former Republican senator from Massachusetts and diplomat, Feb. 27, at 82; former Sen. John J. Sparkman, Democrat of Alabama, who served 42 years in Congress, Nov. 16, at 85; Potter Stewart, who served on the Supreme Court from 1958 to 1981, Dec. 7, at 70; and Robert H. W. Welch, Jr., who in 1958 founded the John Birch Society and headed it until 1983, Jan. 6, at 85.

Jan 18: The **U.S withdrew from World Court proceedings** in a case brought against it by Nicaragua, stating that the court had overextended its jurisdiction. Nicaragua had charged the U.S. with conducting a secret war by aiding rebel *contra* forces and mining Nicaraguan harbors. On Oct. 7 the U.S. announced it no longer would comply automatically with World Court decisions because its procedures had been "abused for political ends."

Jan 20-21: A record **cold wave** hit much of the U.S., killing at least 40 people in 15 states. A record temperature of −27° F was reached in Chicago.

May 28: A plan for a **major tax revision** was unveiled by Pres. Reagan, who called for an income tax system that was "clear, simple, and fair for all." The new plan would reduce taxes for many Americans, but would increase corporate taxes. A bill along these lines passed the House in December, but no further action was taken on it in 1985.

June 14: A **TWA jetliner was hijacked in Athens,** Greece, by two Shiite Muslim terrorists, who forced the plane to Beirut, Lebanon, and demanded the release of 766 Shiites held in Israel. Some of the hostages were released, but 39 Americans were removed from the plane and kept hostage. Complicated negotiations led to their release on June 30, after Israel independently began to release the interned Shiites.

July 13: Pres. **Reagan underwent surgery** to remove a cancerous tumor from his colon. For eight hours Vice Pres. George Bush exercised the powers of the presidency.

Aug 2: An **airplane crash** of a Delta Airlines L-1011 at the Dallas-Fort Worth Airport killed 133 people. The plane crashed during an attempted landing in a violent thunderstorm.

Sep 1: The **wreck of the *Titanic*,** the luxury liner that sank on its maiden voyage in 1912, was found by a U.S.-French exploratory team. The wreck was found about 500 miles south of Newfoundland, but its exact location was kept secret to discourage salvage attempts.

Sep 9: Sanctions against South Africa were announced by Pres. Reagan to protest that country's policy of apartheid. Sale of computers was banned, and imports of the Kruggerand were halted. The sanctions, which were relatively mild, were viewed as an effort to head off demands by Congress for sterner measures.

Sep 18: A **U.S. hostage in Lebanon,** the Rev. Benjamin Weir, was back in the U.S., Pres. Reagan announced. Weir had been held prisoner in Lebanon for 16 months. Six other Americans, kidnaped between Mar. 1984 and June 1985, were still in the hands of terrorists in Lebanon.

Sep 26-27: Hurricane Gloria struck off the coast of North Carolina, then moved north to the New York metropolitan region. The storm forced evacuation of some 280,000 coastal residents, but only three people were killed. Winds of up to 130 mph caused massive power line damage. Repairs on Long Island continued for more than a week after the storm.

Oct 7-10: The Italian liner *Achille Lauro* was hijacked in the Mediterranean by four members of the Palestinian Liberation Front (PLF). En route to Port Said, Egypt, the terrorists shot and killed a wheelchair-bound American, Leon Klinghoffer, 69, and dumped his body overboard. The hijackers surrendered in Egypt on Oct. 9. On the next day an Egyptian airliner flew them out of the country. The jet was intercepted by U.S. fighters and forced to land in Italy, where the four were arrested by Italian authorities. Also with them were Muhammad Abbas, head of the PLF, and another PLF representative, who had joined the others after the hijacking. Abbas was subsequently released and fled to Yugoslavia. The four original hijackers were convicted in Italy on Nov. 19 and imprisoned for possession of guns and explosives.

Oct 11: The **Nobel Peace Prize** was awarded to the International Physicians for the Prevention of Nuclear War, a Boston-based group founded by doctors from the U.S. and U.S.S.R. The cofounders were Dr. Bernard Lown of the Harvard School of Public Health and Dr. Yevgeny I. Chazov of the U.S.S.R.

Oct 27-Nov 7: Hurricane Juan struck the Gulf Coast, killing seven people and causing some $1,000,000,000 in damage in Louisiana. Downgraded to a tropical storm, Juan moved north, dumping heavy rains on West Virginia, Virginia, Maryland, and Pennsyl-

vania, causing great damage and killing 42 more people.

Nov 4: A **Soviet defector changed his mind** and decided to return to the U.S.S.R. Vitaly Yurchenko, described as a senior KGB official, had defected in late July but on Nov. 2 escaped from CIA custody in Washington, D.C., and went to the Soviet Embassy there. He returned to the U.S.S.R. on Nov. 6.

Nov 20-21: A **summit meeting in Geneva,** Switzerland, was conducted by Pres. Reagan and Mikhail Gorbachev, Communist Party secretary of the U.S.S.R. The meeting was characterized as friendly. No major breakthroughs were reached, but both sides agreed to work toward strategic arms reductions and planned to hold another summit meeting in the U.S. in 1986.

Dec 11: The so-called **Gramm-Rudman bill** to eliminate the federal deficit by 1991 was passed by Congress. Pres. Reagan signed it the following day. The bill called on the president to impose automatic spending reductions if Congress did not meet each year's deficit ceiling. Social Security, interest on the national debt, and some programs for the poor were exempted from cuts.

Dec 12: An Arrow Airlines **charter jet crashed** in Gander, Newfoundland, killing all 248 U.S. Army soldiers aboard and the plane's crew of eight. The soldiers, members of the 101st Airborne Division, were on their way to Fort Campbell, Ky., after a tour of duty in the Sinai Peninsula. It was reported that the DC-8 had a history of mechanical problems.

Dec 27: A **terrorist attack at Rome airport** in Italy, and an almost simultaneous attack at the Vienna, Austria, airport left 18 dead and 110 wounded, including five U.S. citizens.

II. Architecture
Arts and Music
Popular Entertainment
Publishing
Theater

On Broadway, fewer shows were staged than in any other year in the century. After two good seasons, attendance and ticket sales were down. Only musicals seemed to attract patrons. A surprise hit of the season was the musical *Tango Argentino,* which opened in October for a projected five-week run and made it big. The Dance Theater of Harlem celebrated its tenth anniversary this year, and the Metropolitan Opera Guild observed its 50th anniversary. The Boston Pops celebrated its centennial with a performance before a full house of 2000. Sales of compact discs and compact disc players far exceeded supply. Music lovers seemed to hover in record stores and buy up the discs as fast as they were unpacked. Manufacturers and audiophiles predicted that the CD would eventually replace the LP record. Books on cassettes were big sellers as well. Book lovers found they could enjoy literature while doing other things, even while driving to work. In art, Rembrandt Peale's portrait of his younger brother, *Rubens Peale With a Geranium,* sold for $4,070,000, the most ever paid at auction for an American painting. Museums across the country opened or planned new facilities. The Arthur M. Sackler Museum opened at Harvard in October. The Whitney Museum planned an addition, the design of which sparked instant controversy. The Metropolitan Museum proposed a new wing, the Dallas Art Museum opened one, and Ft. Lauderdale was finishing work on its first art museum. A landmark in book publishing was reached this year when Shel Silverstein's 1981 collection of poems and drawings, *A Light in the Attic,* made the best-seller list of *The New York Times* for the 112th week in a row, longer than any other book in the list's 59-year history. The movie industry suffered a 7% drop in ticket sales in 1985. Among the top films of the year were *Back to the Future, Rambo: First Blood Part II,* and *Rocky IV.* Videocassette recorder sales began to skyrocket, producing a new form of competition for movie houses. Notables who died this year included Yul Brynner, known for his almost nonstop acting role in *The King and I,* Oct. 10, at 65; Marc Chagall, the artist, Mar. 28, at 97; Stepin Fetchit, born Lincoln Theodore Perry, the first well-known black Hollywood actor, Nov. 19, at 83; Ruth Gordon, the stage and screen actress, Aug. 28, at 88; Rock Hudson, a movie actor who became the first major public figure known to have died of AIDS, Oct. 2, at 59; Eugene List, the concert pianist, Mar. 1, at 66; Helen MacInnes, master of the spy novel, Sept. 30, at 77; Robert Nathan, the author, May 25, at 91; Eugene Ormandy, musical director of the Philadelphia Orchestra for 44 years, Mar. 12, at 85; Roger Sessions, one of America's foremost composers, Mar. 16, at 88; Eric Sloane, the artist, Mar. 6, at 80; Orson Welles, director and actor, Oct. 10, at 70; E. B. White, author and longtime contributor to *The New Yorker* magazine, Oct. 1, at 86; and Efrem Zimbalist, internationally renowned violinist, Feb. 22, at 94.

Among **books published** this year was *Yeager* by Chuck Yeager with Leo Janos. The autobiography of the celebrated test pilot became a best seller. Other books published this year included *The Kingdom of the Wicked* by Anthony Burgess, a novel; *Chapterhouse: Dune* by Frank Herbert, the sixth novel in the author's science fiction epic; *The Cider House Rules* by John Irving, a novel; *Lake Wobegon Days* by Garri-

son Keillor, the witty host of the radio show *Prairie Home Companion; Skeleton Crew* by Stephen King, stories in the horror fiction genre; *Masters of Atlantis* by Charles Portis, a novel; *All Fall Down: America's Tragic Encounter with Iran* by Gary Sick; *Family Album* by Danielle Steel, a novel that became a best seller; *Dashiell Hammett* by Julian Symons, a biography of the celebrated mystery writer; *The Old Forest and Other Stories* by Peter Taylor; *Gods of War* by John Toland, the author's first novel; and *Galapagos* by Kurt Vonnegut, a novel.

Jan 15: The **Bollingen Prize** for poetry was awarded jointly to John Ashbery and Fred Chapell.

Apr 24: Pulitzer prizes were awarded for the following: fiction, *Foreign Affairs* by Alison Lurie; general nonfiction, *The Good War: An Oral History of World War II* by Studs Terkel; biography, *The Life and Times of Cotton Mather* by Kenneth Silverman; history, *Prophets of Regulation* by Thomas K. McCraw; poetry, *Yin* by Carolyn Kizer; drama, *Sunday in the Park With George* by Stephen Sondheim and James Lapine.

June 20: The **Metropolitan Opera** announced that it would abandon its national tour after 1986 because of rising costs and other considerations. The Met had gone on tour each year ever since its founding in 1883.

Nov 26: The rights to **Ronald Reagan's autobiography** were acquired by Random House for $3,000,000. The bid was believed to be the highest ever for a single book. The biography was to be written by Edmund Morris for completion early in 1991.

III. Business and Industry
Education
Philosophy and Religion
Science

The economy continued to expand, but at the low rate of 2.3%. The unemployment rate at the end of the year was 6.8%, lowest in nearly five years. Consumer prices rose only 3.8% and personal income rose 5.95%. Consumer spending rose by 6.6%. Americans bought a record 15,600,000 automobiles and light trucks. All this good news was balanced by some distressing statistics. The federal deficit hit a record $211,900,000,000 for the fiscal year ending Sept. 30, and the trade deficit for calendar 1985 climbed to a record $148,500,000,000. By mid-September the U.S. for the first time since World War I became a debtor nation, owing more to other countries than was owed to it. To alleviate this imbalance, the U.S., Great Britain, France, West Germany, and Japan agreed on Sept. 22 to take steps to lower the value of the dollar.

On the next day the dollar fell in value by 4.29% against other major currencies. In business 1985 was the year of the corporate merger, with about $125,000,000,000 changing hands in buy-out transactions. There were 24 mergers involving $1,000,000,000 or more each. A government report released in October said that at least 6928 accidents involving toxic chemicals had occurred in the past five years, killing more than 135 people. The American Medical Association reported that nearly three times as many medical malpractice suits were being filed compared with ten years earlier. According to a congressional investigation, more than 500,000 persons had obtained false degrees or other credentials in fields ranging from architecture to medicine to zoology. Notables who died this year included Eugene Carson Blake, general secretary of the World Council of Churches from 1966 to 1972, July 31, at 78; Sarah G. Blanding, president of Vassar College from 1946 to 1964, the first woman to hold the position, Mar. 3, at 86; Stuart Chase, the economist and semanticist, Nov. 16, at 97; Archibald M. Crossley, a founder of modern public opinion polling, May 1, at 88; Gardner Cowles, Jr., head of the Cowles publishing and communications empire, July 8, at 82; Milton S. Eisenhower, diplomat, presidential adviser, and brother of Dwight D. Eisenhower, May 2, at 85; Spencer Kimball, president of the Mormon Church since 1973, Nov. 15, at 90; Simon Kuznets, Nobel Prize-winning economist, July 8, at 84; Charles F. Richter, for whom the Richter scale of earthquake measurement is named, Sept. 30, at 85; and Robert W. Woodruff, who turned the Coca-Cola Company into an international business giant, Mar. 7, at 95.

Jan 24-27: The **first secret space shuttle flight** was made by the shuttle *Discovery.* Even the launch time had been kept secret for the mission, which was devoted entirely to achieving military objectives.

Feb 17: A $120,000,000 **libel suit against CBS** was dropped by Gen. William C. Westmoreland, former commander of U.S. forces in Vietnam, after 18 weeks of court testimony. The case involved a 1982 CBS documentary that claimed Westmoreland had withheld important information on enemy troop strength.

Mar 4: A virtual **ban on leaded gasoline** was ordered by the Environmental Protection Agency, which required removal of 90% of the lead in automobile fuel by the end of the year. The agency contemplated ordering a total ban by 1988.

Mar 8: After having had **three heart implants** within 46 hours, Thomas Creighton, a 33-year-old Arizona man, died at the University Medical Center in Tucson, Ariz. Creighton had been given a human heart.

When that failed he was given an untried artificial heart, then a second human heart.

Mar 18: The **largest U.S. corporation,** according to *The New York Times,* was Exxon, with 1984 sales of $97,276,000,000. General Motors was second.

Mar 18: The **American Broadcasting Company** was bought by Capital Cities Communications, Inc., for $3,500,000,000. It was the first time one of the three major networks had been sold.

Apr 8: The **Union Carbide Corporation was sued** by the government of India in connection with a plant disaster at Bhopal, India, on Dec. 3, 1984, that killed some 1700 persons and injured as many as 200,000.

Apr 24: Two new **U.S. Roman Catholic cardinals** were named by Pope John Paul II. They were Archbishop John J. O'Connor of New York and Archbishop Bernard F. Law of Boston.

May 12: The **first woman Conservative rabbi,** Amy Eilberg, 30, was ordained during graduation ceremonies at Jewish Theological Seminary in New York City.

May 21: In the **largest multiple birth** on record in the U.S., Patricia Frustaci gave birth to seven children, one stillborn, in California. Three died within a short time. The last of the three survivors did not leave the hospital until Oct. 4. On Dec. 3 the Frustacis filed a $3,200,000 malpractice suit against the physicians and the clinic that had given her fertility drugs.

June 4: In a decision on **school prayers** the Supreme Court struck down an Alabama law permitting one minute of prayer or meditation in public schools. The ruling suggested that other state laws might be found constitutional if they did not have as their sole purpose the fostering of religious activity.

July 1: In a decision on **separation of church and state,** the Supreme Court ruled that public school teachers could not enter parochial school classrooms to provide remedial or enrichment instruction. The ruling applied specifically to programs in New York City and Grand Rapids, Mich.

July 19: Christa McAuliffe, 36, a high-school teacher and mother of two from Concord, N.H., was selected from 11,000 applicants to become the first teacher to fly aboard a space shuttle.

Aug 23: The **TVA shut down its last nuclear plant,** the Sequoyah facility at Daisy, Tenn., because of doubts about the safety of nuclear power.

Oct 14: The **Nobel Prize in Physiology or Medicine** was awarded to Michael S. Brown and Joseph L. Goldstein of the University of Texas Health Center in Dallas for their discoveries in the field of cholesterol metabolism and contributions to the treatment of diseases linked to presence of the substance.

Oct 15: The **Nobel Prize in Economics** was awarded to Franco Modigliani of MIT for his work in analyzing the behavior of household savers and the functioning of financial markets.

Oct 16: The **Nobel Prize in Chemistry** was awarded jointly to Herbert A. Hauptman of the Medical Foundation of Buffalo, N.Y., and Jerome Karle of the Naval Research Laboratory, Washington, D.C., for developing techniques for determining the structures of molecules vital to life.

Dec 10: The **highest award for damages** in U.S. history was upheld by a Texas state judge. A jury had ordered Texaco, Inc., to pay $11,100,000,000 to the Pennzoil Company because it had interfered with an agreement for Pennzoil to acquire the Getty Oil Company in 1984. Texaco announced it would appeal the decision.

Dec 10: A complete **ban on tobacco advertising,** including smokeless tobacco products, was urged by the American Medical Association. On Dec. 19 the surgeon general of the U.S. said that cigarette smoking was a greater health threat to most Americans than hazards of the workplace.

Dec 16: A new **stock record** was set by the Dow Jones industrial average, which closed at 1553.10. It had gained 17.89 points in one day.

Dec 23: The **costliest farm bill** in history was signed by Pres. Reagan. Estimated to cost $169,000,000,000 over five years, it nonetheless reduced income and price supports to farmers for the first time since 1933.

IV. Fashion
Folkways
Holidays
Social Issues and Crime
Sports

The Coca-Cola Company shocked the public on Apr. 23 when it announced it was doing away with its 99-year-old recipe for the famous soft drink and offering a new formula. Faithful Coke drinkers responded so forcefully against the change that on July 10 Coca-Cola was forced to reintroduce the old Coke under a new name, Coca-Cola Classic. In fashion elegance continued to gain favor. Career women were beginning to wear more colorful suits, not just feminized copies of men's traditional wear. Meanwhile, the U.S. Army ruled that its male officers were not allowed to carry umbrellas. The national craze for Cabbage Patch dolls continued, and the classic Barbie doll was given a new French-designed wardrobe as well as a business suit with attaché case. In sports the North American Soccer League went out of business after heavy financial losses. Professional basketball and major league baseball, however, reported record attendance in 1985. This year the major league baseball playoffs were extended to best-of-seven series. Critics of the move said it would detract from the importance of the World Series. In golf the top money winners were Curtis Strange, $542,321, and Nancy Lopez, $416,472. Notables who died this year included James Beard, authority on cooking, Jan. 23, at 81; Rudi Gernreich, avant-garde fashion designer who introduced the topless bathing suit for women in the 1960s, Apr. 21, at 62; Burleigh Grimes, pitcher and member of the Baseball Hall of Fame, Dec. 6, at 92; John B. Kelly, Jr., president of the U.S. Olympic Committee, Mar. 2, at 57; Roger Maris, Yankee batting champ who broke Babe Ruth's home run record in 1961, Dec. 14, at 51; John Scarne, international authority on games and gambling, July 7, at 82; and Joseph "Smoky Joe" Wood, a pitcher who won 34 games for the Boston Red Sox in 1912, July 27, at 95.

Jan 20: **Super Bowl XIX** was won by the San Francisco 49ers (NFC), defeating the Miami Dolphins (AFC) 38 to 16. On Jan. 6 the 49ers had shut out the Chicago Bears 23 to 0 for the NFC championship, and the Dolphins had beaten the Pittsburgh Steelers 45 to 28 for the AFC title.

Mar 3: The **first jockey to win $100,000,000** in career purse money was Willie Shoemaker, who rode Lord at War to victory in the Santa Anita Handicap in Arcadia, Calif.

Apr 1: The **NCAA men's basketball championship** was won by Villanova, which beat Georgetown 66 to 64.

Apr 29: The **WBA heavyweight boxing championship** was won by Tony Tubbs in a 15-round decision over Greg Page at Buffalo, N.Y.

May 27-June 9: The **NBA basketball championship** was won by the Los Angeles Lakers, who defeated the Boston Celtics four games to two.

June 16: The **U.S. Open golf tournament** was won by Andy North, who came from behind to beat Tze-Chung Chen of Taiwan by one stroke.

July 6-7: At the **Wimbledon** tennis championships in England, Martina Navratilova won the women's singles title. Navratilova teamed with Paul McNamee of Australia to win the mixed doubles, and Kathy Jordan teamed with Elizabeth Smylie of Australia to win the women's doubles.

July 11: **Nolan Ryan** of the Houston Astros (NL) became the first pitcher in major league history to strike out 4000 batters when he fanned Danny Heep of the New York Mets on three pitches in the sixth inning at Houston. The Astros won 4 to 3.

July 23: A new **record auction price for a thoroughbred** was set at Lexington, Ky., when a yearling son of Nijinsky II and My Charmer sold for $13,100,000.

Aug 11: The **PGA golf tournament** was won by Hubert Green, who beat defending champion Lee Trevino by two strokes.

Sep 7-8: The **U.S. Open tennis singles championships** were won by Ivan Lendl of Czechoslovakia in the men's division and Hana Mandlikova of Czechoslovakia in the women's division.

Sep 11: Pete Rose of the Cincinnati Reds (NL) set a new major league baseball record of 4192 career hits in a 2 to 0 win over the San Diego Padres at Cincinnati. The old record of 4191 hits was set by Ty Cobb in 1928.

Sep 21: The International Boxing Federation **heavyweight boxing championship** was won by Michael Spinks in a 15-round decision over Larry Holmes in Las Vegas, Nev.

Oct 5: Eddie Robinson of Grambling State University became the **"winningest" college football coach** in history when his team picked up its 324th win in his 44-year career. During that time Grambling State had lost 106 games and tied 15.

Oct 19-27: The **World Series** was won by the Kansas City Royals (AL), defeating the St. Louis Cardinals (NL) four games to three. On Oct. 16 the Royals had won the American League pennant against the Toronto Blue Jays four games to three, and the Cardinals had won the National League pennant against the Los Angeles Dodgers four games to two.

1986

I. **Civil Rights**
   Exploration and Settlement
   Government
   Statistics
   Wars

On New Year's Day Pres. Ronald Reagan appeared on television in the U.S.S.R., and Soviet leader Mikhail S. Gorbachev appeared on U.S. television. Both leaders expressed their hopes for world peace. Despite this apparent warming of U.S.-Soviet relations, the Reagan administration continued its tough policy toward the U.S.S.R. A statement of policy issued Mar. 14 committed the U.S. to "democratic revolution" around the world and implied a lessening of support for dictatorships based simply on the fact that they were anticommunist. On Jan. 28 Jonas Savimbi, leader of a rebel military group seeking to overthrow the Marxist government of Angola, was given a warm welcome in Washington. On Feb. 7 President-for-life Jean-Claude Duvalier of Haiti was forced to flee his country; he was flown to France aboard a U.S. jet. On Feb. 26 Pres. Ferdinand Marcos of the Philippines was forced out of office by a bloodless popular uprising. The Reagan administration had urged him to resign following his victory in a rigged election. On Mar. 12 the administration criticized the right-wing government of Chile for its abuses of human rights. In April a *New York Times*/CBS poll showed that 51% of Republicans, 74% of Democrats, and 59% of independents opposed a proposed $100,000,000 of aid to the Nicaraguan Contras. The Office of Management and Budget announced on Oct. 23 that the federal deficit for the year ended Sept. 30 reached $220,700,000,000, the fourth record figure in five years. Notables who died this year included Rep. Joseph P. Addabbo, Democrat of New York, a powerful figure in the shaping of defense policy, Apr. 10, at 61; Chester Bowles, senator, ambassador, and advertising executive, May 25, at 85; Sen. John P. East, Republican of North Carolina, June 29, at 55; James O. Eastland, Democratic senator from Mississippi for 36 years, Feb. 19, at 81; Charles A. Halleck, Republican of Indiana, who served 16 terms in the House of Representatives and was both minority and majority leader, Mar. 3, at 85; W. Averell Harriman, adviser to four presidents, July 26, at 94; Jacob J. Javits, Republican senator from New York from 1954 to 1981, Mar. 7, at 81; Philip C. Jessup, an authority in the field of international law who served on the International Court of Justice from 1960 to 1969, Jan. 31, at 89; and Adm. Hyman G. Rickover, the "father of the nuclear navy," July 8, at 86.

Jan 7: Economic sanctions against Libya were ordered by Pres. Reagan in retaliation for alleged Libyan involvement in terrorist attacks on Dec. 27, 1985, at the Rome and Vienna airports. Five U.S. citizens had been among the victims. All Libyan assets in the U.S. were frozen, and all U.S. citizens in Libya were ordered home.

Feb 19: A United Nations **treaty outlawing genocide** was ratified by the Senate. The treaty had been signed by the U.S. in 1948, but the Senate had never acted on it.

Mar 20: A controversial $100,000,000 **Contra aid bill** for Nicaraguan rebel forces was voted down by the House of Representatives, 222 to 210.

Mar 24: An **armed clash with Libya** occurred in the Gulf of Sidra after Libyan shore installations launched missiles at a U.S. fleet on maneuvers in the gulf. U.S. missiles damaged the Libyan missile site and destroyed two patrol boats advancing on the fleet.

Mar 25: Military aid to Honduras amounting to $20,000,000 was approved by Congress following reports of a Nicaraguan military incursion to destroy rebel Contra bases just inside the Honduran border.

Mar 25: A constitutional **amendment to require a balanced federal budget** was defeated in the Senate. The 66 to 34 vote in favor was one vote short of the two-thirds vote required for passage.

Apr 2: A **terrorist bombing** aboard a TWA jet flying from Rome, Italy, to Athens, Greece, killed four American passengers, including one infant. Nine other passengers were injured. An Arab terrorist group claimed responsibility.

Apr 5: A **terrorist bombing** in a West Berlin discothèque killed a U.S. soldier and a Turkish woman and wounded 155 other persons, including about 60 Americans. U.S. officials later stated they had firm evidence that Libya was involved in the crime.

Apr 14: A **U.S. air strike against Libya** was launched in retaliation for Libya's involvement in the West Berlin bombing of Apr. 5 and other terrorist acts. Sixteen U.S. F-111s flying from Great Britain were joined by U.S. carrier-based planes in attacks on five military bases and terrorist centers near Tripoli and Benghazi.

May 19: A new **gun control law,** weakening the 1968 federal gun control law, was signed by Pres. Reagan. Among other provisions, the new law allowed interstate retail sales of rifles. Police organizations had been among the groups that had lobbied against the bill.

May 27: Pres. Reagan announced that **U.S. strategic arms policy** would no longer be bound by the terms of the unratified SALT II arms agreement. At the same time, he announced that two Poseidon submarines would be dismantled to make room for a new Trident submarine and keep the U.S. in step with the treaty's provisions.

June 5: Ronald W. Pelton was convicted of espionage. The former National Security Agency employee had been charged with selling intelligence secrets to the U.S.S.R.

June 11: Constitutional protection for the **right to abortion** was narrowly reaffirmed by the Supreme Court. The decision voided a Pennsylvania law because some of its provisions were designed to deter women from having abortions and others would require doctors to risk the health of pregnant women.

June 17: Pres. Reagan announced that **Warren E. Burger** would retire as chief justice of the Supreme Court, effective July 10. The president named Associate Justice William H. Rehnquist as Burger's successor, and also named Antonin Scalia, of the U.S. Court of Appeals for the District of Columbia, to the Court. The changes were interpreted as a gain for conservative judicial philosophy.

June 18: A **midair collision** between a plane and a helicopter over the Grand Canyon killed all 25 persons aboard the two aircraft.

June 19: Richard W. Miller became the first FBI agent ever to be convicted of espionage. He was charged was passing information to the U.S.S.R.

June 19: Cyanide poisoning was declared the cause of death of two persons in the Seattle, Wash., area. Both had taken Extra-Strength Excedrin capsules containing the poison. Bristol-Meyers, the maker of Excedrin, announced the next day it was withdrawing all its nonprescription capsule drugs from sale.

June 27: U.S. actions against Nicaragua, including aid to antigovernment rebels, was ruled a violation of national law by the International Court of Justice. The U.S. was ordered to stop arming and training the insurgents and to pay Nicaragua for damages. U.S. officials had withdrawn from the case, stating the court had no jurisdiction.

June 30: The Supreme Court ruled that **homosexual relations,** even in private between consenting adults, are not protected by the Constitution. The decision upheld an 1816 Georgia law banning sodomy.

July 2: The use of **affirmative action** to remedy job discrimination was upheld by the Supreme Court, 6-3. The decision meant that it was legal to use numerical goals to increase minority representation among workers. The Reagan administration had opposed this interpretation of the law.

July 7: Part of the **Gramm-Rudman budget balancing act** of Dec. 1985 was found unconstitutional by the Supreme Court, 7–2. The court said the provision for automatic spending cuts violated the separation of powers within the federal government. The decision left standing a fall-back provision of the act requiring Congress to make budget cuts under certain conditions.

Aug 13: Congressional action on **Contra aid** supplied $100,000,000 to the Nicaraguan rebels. Pres. Reagan had requested the appropriation, which also added $300,000,000 for four neighboring Central America nations.

Aug 31: The **collision of two planes** near Los Angeles left all 67 persons aboard the two craft dead, and at least 15 others on the ground were believed killed also. One plane was an Aeromexico DC-9, the other a single-engine private plane. Ten houses were also demolished.

Oct 2: Pres. Reagan's **veto of a sanctions bill against South Africa** was overridden by Congress. The Senate vote was 78–21. On Sept. 29 the House had voted to override, 313–83. The law banned new investment by Americans in South Africa, prohibited the importation of such items as iron and steel, and cancelled landing rights in the U.S. for South African airlines.

Oct 9: The **Senate convicted federal judge Harry E. Clairborne** on three of four articles of impeachment, thus removing him from office. Clairborne had previously been convicted of tax evasion but had refused to resign his judgeship. It was the first impeachment trial in the Senate in 50 years.

Oct 11-12: No agreement on **arms control** was reached by Pres. Ronald Reagan and General Secretary Mikhail S. Gorbachev of the U.S.S.R. after two days of talks at a summit meeting in Reykjavik, Iceland. Reagan refused to accede to the Soviet insistence that the U.S. abandon its plan for a space-based missile defense system, popularly known as "Star Wars."

Oct 14: The **Nobel Peace Prize** was awarded to Elie Wiesel, author and human rights activist. He was cited as a "spiritual leader" against "violence, repression, and racism."

Oct. 22: A revised **federal income tax law** was signed by Pres. Ronald Reagan. The most complete revision of the tax code in more than 40 years, the new law lowered tax rates for almost everyone while eliminating many previous deductions and other tax preferences. The top rate for individuals was lowered from 50% to 38.5%. Most of the changes were to take place on Jan. 1, 1987. The total amount of taxes to be collected was expected to remain about the same.

Nov 2: One **American hostage,** David P. Jacobsen, director of the American Hospital in Beirut, Lebanon, held by kidnapers for 18 months, was freed. Another kidnap victim of Moslem terrorists, the Rev. Lawrence M. Jenco, had been released on July 26. However, on Apr. 17 another kidnap victim, Peter Kilburn, a librarian at the American University of Beirut, was found dead. The terrorists subsequently seized Frank Reed, an American educator, on Sept. 9; Joseph J. Cicippio, chief accountant at the American University, on Sept. 12; and Edward A. Tracy, an author, on Oct. 21.

Nov 3: What became known as the **Iran-Contra affair** began when a Lebanese magazine revealed that the U.S. had been secretly selling arms to Iran in the hope of securing the release of hostages held in Lebanon. American intelligence sources on Nov. 6 confirmed that the operation had taken place. On Nov. 12 Pres. Reagan admitted that he knew of the arms sale,

but on Nov. 25 he said he had not been fully informed of all that went on. That same day it was revealed that some of the money received from the sale of arms to Iran had been secretly diverted to the Nicaraguan rebels, known as Contras. Also on Nov. 25 the two officials who were the major planners and overseers of the scheme left office: Vice Adm. John M. Poindexter, national security adviser, resigned, and his assistant, Marine Lt. Col. Oliver L. North, was dismissed. On Nov. 26 the president appointed a three-member panel, headed by former Sen. John G. Tower, to investigate the actions of the National Security Council staff. Meanwhile, Congress prepared to carry out its own investigation, and on Dec. 19 an independent counsel was named to head another inquiry into what was becoming a national scandal.

Nov 4: In the biennial **Congressional elections** the Democrats won control of the Senate, 53–47, with a gain of eight seats. They retained control of the House of Representatives, 253–182, a loss of five seats.

Nov 6: Pres. Reagan signed into law an **immigration act** that established new and drastically changed policies concerning aliens in the U.S. Employers were to be prohibited from employing illegal aliens, but many such persons would be given an opportunity to secure legal status, by showing that they entered the U.S. before Jan. 1, 1982, and had resided here continuously "in an illegal status."

Dec 31: At least **95 persons died in a fire** in a high-rise hotel in San Juan, Puerto Rico. It was later determined that the fire was caused by a disgruntled employee who probably did not intend to do more than shake up the management.

II. Architecture
Arts and Music
Popular Entertainment
Publishing
Theater

For the second year in a row, the Broadway theater set a new record for fewest productions: 26, of which only six were very successful. One of the latter was a revival of an old-fashioned musical, *Me and My Girl*. The movies continued to cater generally to teenagers over other age groups with such films as *Ferris Bueller's Day Off*. Major movies of the year included Woody Allen's amusing *Hannah and Her Sisters; Top Gun*, featuring the exploits of a fighter pilot; and *The Color of Money*, with the ever-popular Paul Newman. In art, the Brooklyn Museum presented *From Courbet to Cezanne: A New 19th Century*, a show exhibiting 130 works from the new Musée D'Orsay in Paris,

France. Brooklyn, N.Y., was also the site of the first U.S. performance by the Central Ballet of China. After the company's final appearance at the Brooklyn Academy of Music on Mar. 16, the young dancers from the People's Republic of China began a tour of other U.S. cities. In publishing, the Louisville (Ky.) *Times* and *Courier-Journal* newspapers, owned by the Bingham family for nearly 70 years, were acquired by the Gannett newspaper group on May 19 for $305,000,000. On May 28 the Baltimore *Sun* and *Evening Sun* papers were purchased by the Times Mirror Company of Los Angeles for some $450,000,000. In the newspaper world in general, the trend to abandon the publishing of evening papers continued, with 26 of them shifting to the morning field. In book publishing, the year was marked by the purchase on Sept. 28 of Doubleday & Co. by Bertelsmann AG, a large West German publisher, for $475,000,000. In November Bertelsmann sold the 95% interest Doubleday held in the Mets, New York's NL baseball team, to Nelson Doubleday, Jr., and Fred Wilpon for $95,000,000. Of magazines, one survey showed that the most popular among college students was *Cosmopolitan*. Notables who died this year included Harold Arlen, composer of such hit songs as "Over the Rainbow," Apr. 23, at 81; Desi Arnaz, prominent television actor, musician, and producer, Dec. 2, at 69; Cass Canfield, a leading book publisher for 40 years, Mar. 27, at 88; Lucia Chase, who helped found the American Ballet Theater in 1940, Jan. 9, at 88; John Ciardi, the poet and translator, Mar. 30, at 69; Broderick Crawford, the actor, Apr. 26, at 74; Benny Goodman, the "King of Swing," June 13, at 77; Cary Grant, suave leading man of the movies for 30 years, Nov. 29, at 82; Frank Herbert, the writer known best for his *Dune* series of science fiction novels, Feb. 11, at 65; L. Ron Hubbard, science fiction writer and founder of Scientology, Jan. 24, at 71; Joseph Kraft, the Washington columnist whose work appeared in some 200 newspapers, Jan. 10, at 61; Alan Jay Lerner, the lyricist and playwright known best for his collaboration with Frederick Loewe on *My Fair Lady* and other hits, June 14, at 67; Raymond Loewy, the father of "streamlining" and industrial design, July 14, at 92; Bernard Malamud, the Pulitzer Prize-winning novelist and short-story writer, Mar. 18, at 71; Una Merkel, one of the few silent film stars able to make the transition to sound films, Jan. 2, at 82; Gordon McRae, the movie actor and singer known best for his performance in *Oklahoma*, Jan. 24, at 64; Ray Milland, the actor, Mar. 10, at 81; Vincente Minnelli, producer of some of Hollywood's best musicals, July 25, at 76; Reuben Nakian, distinguished sculptor, Dec. 4, at 89; Georgia O'Keeffe, the artist, known for her desert paintings and exotic, colorful studies of flowers, Mar. 6, at 98; Otto Preminger, the movie director and producer, Apr. 23, at 80; Kate Smith, one of the most popular singers of the twentieth century, who made "God Bless America" an unofficial national anthem, June 17, at 79; Blanche Sweet, early film star who appeared in D. W. Griffith movies, Sept. 6, at 90; Rudy Vallee, an enormously popular singer and band leader in the 1920s and 1930s, July 3, at 84; Hal B. Wallis, producer of some 400 movies, including *The Maltese Falcon*, Oct. 5, at 88; Theodore H. White, the Pulitzer Prize-winning writer and acknowledged dean of political journalism, May 15, at 71; and Teddy Wilson, jazz pianist with a 50-year career, July 31, at 73.

Among **books published** this year was *The Garden of Eden*, a posthumous novel by Ernest Hemingway that received mixed reaction from critics. Another novel, *Gone With the Wind* by Margaret Mitchell, turned 50 on June 30 with publication of a facsimile edition of 50,000. The novel, which sold 25,000,000 copies in its first half century, hit the best-seller list once again. Among novels praised and popular were *Kate Vaiden* by Reynolds Price, *The Beet Queen* by Louise Erdrich, *A Summons to Memphis* by Peter Taylor, and *Roger's Version* by John Updike. Representative of an excellent array of nonfiction titles were *The Man Who Mistook His Wife for a Hat*, the recounting of a number of curious medical cases, by Dr. Oliver Sacks; *Ford: The Men and the Machine* by Robert Lacey; *Crabgrass Frontier: The Suburbanization of America*, winner of two prestigious history prizes, by Kenneth T. Jackson; *Tombee: Portrait of a Cotton Planter* by Theodore Rosengarten; and *The Triumph of Politics: Why the Reagan Revolution Failed* by David A. Stockman, former director of the Office of Management and Budget. None of these matched in sales Bill Cosby's *Fatherhood* or Tom Clancy's thriller *Red Storm Rising*.

Jan 11: A new **record book price** was set when William Morrow & Company and Avon Books bid $5,000,000 for North American hardbound and paperback rights to James Clavell's novel *Whirlwind*.

Feb 26: Robert Penn Warren became the first official poet laureate of the U.S. Daniel Boorstin, the Librarian of Congress, made the appointment.

Apr 17: Pulitzer prizes were awarded for the following: fiction, *Lonesome Dove* by Larry McMurtry; general nonfiction, *Move Your Shadow: South Africa, Black and White* by Joseph Lelyveld and *Common Ground: A Turbulent Decade in the Lives of Three American Families* by J. Anthony Lukas; biography, *Louise Bogan: A Portrait* by Elizabeth Frank; poetry,

The Flying Change by Henry Taylor. No award was given for drama.

Apr 27: A **video pirate** interrupted the showing of a cable TV movie by Home Box Office by overriding the broadcast with a message saying he would not pay for his cable service. The FCC and commercial users of satellite transmissions expressed dismay that an unknown person could override the HBO signal.

Apr 29: Probably the worst **library fire** in U.S. history destroyed or damaged some 800,000 books at the Los Angeles Central Library. On May 5 officials reported that the fire, which caused $22,000,000 in damage, had been deliberately set.

May 6: A new record **auction price for a contemporary sculpture,** $1,300,000, was bid by a New York City art dealer for David Smith's 1963 welded-steel work *Voltri-Bolton XXIII.*

June 1: Television coverage of Senate proceedings was begun, in a test that was to continue until July 15. The House of Representatives had allowed such coverage since Mar. 19, 1979.

June 27: A **record auto auction price** of $6,500,000 was bid in Reno, Nev., by Jerry J. Moore, a Houston shopping center builder, for a 1931 Bugatti Royale. The French-built auto, one of seven built, had originally cost $42,000.

Aug 9: The popular artist **Andrew Wyeth** revealed for the first time 240 works of art secretly painted by him over 15 years. All but one of them were of a woman known only as Helga but later revealed to be a Wyeth neighbor. The collection was bought for an estimated $10,000,000 or more by a collector, Leonard E. B. Andrews.

Dec 15: America's most famous music auditorium, **Carnegie Hall** in New York City, reopened with a gala concert featuring many noted musicians. It had been closed for seven months for a $50,000,000 remodeling.

III. Business and Industry
Education
Philosophy and Religion
Science

The year's top story was the tragic loss of the NASA space shuttle *Challenger* and the deaths of all seven persons aboard. Investigations led to the conclusion that failure of a seal on one of the shuttle's solid-fuel booster rockets had caused the disaster. NASA records showed that agency officials had been warned of problems with the rocket joints. The disaster prompted fresh debate on the U.S. space program, particularly over use of the space shuttle as opposed to unmanned vehicles. For the most part it was a successful year for the national economy. Car and truck sales set a record of 16,000,000, with 28.2% of the vehicles imported. The price of oil fell as low as $12 a barrel in July, lowering the price of gasoline but damaging the domestic oil industry. By late December the price was back up to $16.90 as OPEC threatened to cut production. Hot weather and drought in some mid-Atlantic and southern states did great damage to crops and livestock, so that by the end of July losses were estimated at $2,000,000,000. At the year's end unemployment was down to 6.6%, the lowest figure in six years, while producer prices fell 2.5% for the year, the first decline since 1963. On the other hand the GNP grew only 2.5%, the worst showing in four years, but the CPI rose only 1.1%, the smallest increase since 1961. The foreign trade deficit, however, rose to $169,780,000,000, a record. The Labor Department reported that in February the number of women professionals in the U.S. topped for the first time the number of men holding professional jobs, by a margin of 29,000. A National Science Board report in March revealed that programs in college-level science, mathematics, and engineering had so declined as to constitute a "grave long-term threat" to the country. The Educational Testing Service of Princeton, N.J., announced it would spend $30,000,000 over 15 years to develop new tests that would focus less on absolute scores and concentrate more on what the test-taker knows and does not know. In June the federal government reported 21,915 cases of the disease AIDS in the U.S. and that 12,008 of these persons had already died. The sale of videocassette recorders continued to boom, with a total of 13,174,000 in 1986. Sales of compact discs reached $930,000,000, compared with $17,000,000 in 1983, while sales of LPs declined in the same period from $1,689,000,000 to $983,000,000. Notables who died this year included Herbert W. Armstrong, founder of the Worldwide Church of God, Jan. 15, at 93; Harrison Brown, pioneer in producing plutonium and later a foe of nuclear weapons, Dec. 8, at 69; Arthur F. Burns, Federal Reserve Board chairman and ambassador to West Germany, June 26, at 83; Edwin T. Dahlberg, former president of the National Council of Churches, Sept. 6, at 93; Edward Doisy, Sr., Nobel Prize winner who isolated vitamin K, Oct. 23, at 92; Dana McLean Greeley, president of the Unitarian Universalist Association, June 13, at 77; Fritz A. Lipman, joint Nobel Prize winner for the discovery of coenzyme, important in the body's metabolism, July 24, at 87; Robert S. Mulliken, Nobel Prize winner for his study of the chemistry of atoms, Oct. 31, at 90; James Rainwater, the Nobel Prize-winning physicist, May 31, at 68; Albert Szent-Györgyi,

Nobel Prize winner for isolating vitamin C, Oct. 22, at 93; and Helen Taussig, the founder of pediatric cardiology, May 20, at 87.

Jan 12-18: The **space shuttle** *Columbia* completed its seventh orbital mission after liftoff had been postponed a record seven times. Its landing was postponed twice.

Jan 14: Local laws forbidding **backyard satellite dish antennas,** as distinct from other types of antennas, were banned by the FCC.

Jan 24: The spacecraft *Voyager 2* flew within 50,679 miles of the planet Uranus, discovering new moons and rings and obtaining the first evidence of a magnetic field around the planet.

Jan 28: The **space shuttle** *Challenger* exploded 74 seconds after liftoff at Cape Canaveral, Fla., killing all seven astronauts aboard, including Christa McAuliffe, 37, a Concord, N.H., schoolteacher, the first private citizen chosen for a space shuttle flight. On June 9 a presidential commission report identified failure of a seal on a solid-fuel booster rocket as the cause of the explosion and criticized NASA for a long history of managerial and engineering mistakes. On July 2 NASA announced it would modify the faulty booster rocket joints to eliminate the danger of further booster failures.

Mar 11: In a controversy over the **teaching of Roman Catholic doctrine,** the Rev. Charles E. Curran, a liberal theologian at the Catholic University of America in Washington, D.C., was ordered by the Vatican to retract his views on birth control and other sexual issues or lose the right to teach Roman Catholic doctrine. On Aug. 18 Father Curran's right to teach theology was revoked, and on Apr. 12, 1988, the trustees of Catholic University barred him from teaching in the theology department.

Mar 15: In a statement on the **treatment of terminal patients,** the American Medical Association said it was ethical for doctors to withhold "all means of life-prolonging medical treatment."

Apr 3: The **U.S. national debt** exceeded $2,000,000,000,000, having doubled in five years.

Apr 16: The first **surrogate birth of a test-tube baby,** a girl, was announced by spokesmen at Mount Sinai Hospital in Cleveland, Ohio.

Apr 17: Computers using the **megabit memory chip,** capable of storing more than 1,000,000 bits of electronic data, were being manufactured for the first time, IBM officials announced.

Apr 18: An Air Force **Titan rocket exploded** moments after launch. On May 4 a Delta rocket failed soon after launch and had to be destroyed. These failures, combined with the *Challenger* disaster, were seen as major setbacks for the U.S. space program.

Apr 22: The first **genetically altered virus** to be released into the environment was approved by the Department of Agriculture. It was to be used to fight a form of herpes affecting swine, which caused an annual $60,000,000 in damage.

Apr 28: The **largest U.S. corporation,** according to the annual *Fortune* magazine survey, was General Motors, with 1985 sales of $96,371,700,000. Exxon was second with sales of $86,673,000,000.

Apr 29: "Clear and unconditional" **opposition to use of nuclear weapons** was voted unanimously by the Council of Bishops of the United Methodist Church.

Apr 29: Settling a dispute over **AIDS virus research,** the Patent and Trademark Office designated the Pasteur Institute of Paris as the "senior party," rather than the U.S. National Institutes of Health, in the matter of which developed the first AIDS blood test. At stake were millions of dollars in royalties to be earned by the use of the test.

May 6: The **first American Indian to become a Roman Catholic bishop,** the Rev. Donald E. Pelotte, 41, was ordained in Gallup, N. Mex.

May 30: The first outdoor test of **genetically engineered plants** was begun when genetically altered tobacco was planted on a Wisconsin farm. The field test opened up the possibility of creating high-yield crops that would reduce farmers' dependence on toxic chemicals to control pests.

June 9: The **Dow Jones average** of industrial stocks marked a record one-day loss of 45.75 points.

June 12: The number of **deaths from AIDS** (acquired immune deficiency syndrome) would increase more than tenfold in five years, federal health officials predicted. By 1991 the disease would afflict some 270,000, causing 179,000 deaths, at a health cost of up to $16,000,000,000 annually.

June 19: The **third artificial heart recipient,** Murray P. Haydon, died at 59 in a Louisville, Ky., hospital. He had received the heart on Feb. 17, 1985.

July 2: Affirmative action programs to cure past discrimination in the work place were upheld by the Supreme Court, ruling in cases involving a New York City labor union and the Cleveland Fire Department.

Aug 2: Leslie Alexander became the first woman to take part in a service as a rabbi of a major Conservative Jewish congregation. Two days earlier she had been appointed assistant rabbi of Congregation Adat Ari El in Los Angeles. There were now reported to be 130 women rabbis in the U.S., mostly in Reform congregations.

Aug 6: The **longest-lived recipient of an artificial heart,** William J. Schroeder, died at age 54. He had suffered a series of strokes. Schroeder received the implant on Nov. 25, 1984, and lived 620 days. He was the second recipient and the last survivor of five persons to have had permanent artificial hearts implanted.

Aug 29: The **Evangelical Lutheran Church** in America was established by the merging of the Lutheran Church in America, the American Lutheran Church, and the Association of Evangelical Lutheran Churches. The new church, with 5,300,000 members, represented about two-thirds of all Lutherans in the U.S.

Sep 4: In an unusual action, **the Vatican** ordered an American archbishop to turn over to an auxiliary bishop authority in five areas involving such social issues as birth control and homosexuality. Archbishop Raymond Hunthausen of Seattle had previously been criticized for his liberal position on certain issues. The next day 140 Catholic leaders in the diocese protested in a letter to the Vatican. On May 27, 1987, full authority was restored to Archbishop Hunthausen.

Sep 11: On the **New York Stock Exchange** the Dow Jones average of industrial stocks fell 88.61 points, a record to this date, and closed at 1792.89. The volume of trading for the day was also a record at 237,600,000 shares. That record, however, lasted only until the next day, when 240,500,000 shares were traded.

Oct 13: The **Nobel Prize in Physiology or Medicine** was awarded to Rita Levi-Montalcini, holder of dual U.S. and Italian citizenship, of the Institute of Cell Biology in Rome and Stanley Cohen of Vanderbilt University. They were honored for their discovery of substances that influence cell growth.

Oct 15: The **Nobel Prize in Chemistry** was awarded to Dudley R. Herschback of Harvard University, Yuan T. Lee of the University of California, and John C. Polanyi of the University of Toronto for their discovery of a method of studying chain reactions molecule by molecule.

Oct 16: The **Nobel Prize in Economics** was awarded to James M. Buchanan of George Mason University for his studies in applying economic principles to political decision making.

Oct 20: Withdrawal from South Africa was announced by General Motors, the largest American company with business interests there. It said it was selling its operations. On Oct. 21 International Business Machines made a similar announcement, followed by Eastman Kodak on Nov. 19 and Citibank, formerly opposed to such action, on June 16, 1987.

Nov 3: Poverty in the U.S. was called a "social and moral scandal" in a pastoral letter adopted by America's Roman Catholic bishops. In preparation for over five years, the document said the government must do more to create jobs and help poor people. Less military spending, more economic planning, and an increase in the minimum wage were among the recommendations.

Dec 23: The **first nonstop flight around the world without refueling** was completed when the experimental airplane *Voyager* landed at Edwards Air Force Base, California, after a journey of 25,012 miles that took 9 days, 3 min., 44 sec. Made of plastic and stiffened paper, the fragile-looking plane carried five times its weight in fuel. The pilot was Richard G. Rutan and the copilot Jeana Yeager.

Dec 31: The production of alloys that provide **superconductivity** at much higher temperatures than ever before was announced by Bell Laboratories and by University of Houston researchers. The Bell Labs material was reported to achieve full superconductivity at 36 K (0 on the Kelvin scale is equal to $-460°$, or absolute zero, on the Fahrenheit scale).

Dec 31: On the **New York Stock Exchange** the Dow Jones average of industrial stocks closed the year at 1895.95. On Dec. 2 it had reached a record high of 1955.57, and on Dec. 19 a record 244,700,000 shares were traded.

IV. Fashion
Folkways
Holidays
Social Issues and Crime
Sports

Drug use by professional athletes became an issue this year following 1985 courtroom revelations by baseball players concerning cocaine use in the major leagues. In February Michael Ray Richardson of the New York Nets basketball team was banned from playing in the NBA after his third drug violation, and John Lucas of the Houston Rockets was released after he failed a drug test. On June 19 Len Bias, a University of Maryland basketball star, died of cocaine poisoning, and on June 27 Don Rogers of the Cleveland Browns football team also died after using cocaine. In football, the major television networks announced they were dropping one-third of the 18 scheduled college bowl game broadcasts for lack of advertising support. A panel of medical experts said handball, squash, and swimming were the most effective sports in promoting fitness. This year marked the hundredth anniversary of the tuxedo, first worn by Griswold Lorillard to a ball in Tuxedo Park, N.Y., in the fall of 1886. A rise in tux sales and rentals this year was fueled, no doubt, by the growing popularity of weekend weddings, three-day affairs including dinners, brunches, barbecues, sports activities and, of course, the wedding ceremony itself. The Statue of Liberty also turned 100 this year. Its centennial celebration in New York City in July included a breathtaking parade of tall ships from around the world. Texas celebrated the 150th anniversary of its independence from Mexico with 10,000 different events, including the "World's Largest Rattlesnake Roundup." The Oreo cookie marked its 75th anniversary this year. The ever-popular Popsicle underwent a change, as the manufacturer announced the frozen treat in future would sport only one stick. The company, which began manufacturing Popsicles more than 50 years ago, reported annual sales of 100,000,000 dozen. Vanilla was reported to be the nation's favorite flavor of ice cream. Bloomingdale's, the trendy New York City department store, offered eight rules on how to eat caviar properly (it should be eaten with a fork, and never put lemon on it). The Census Bureau reported there were 2,220,000 unwed couples in the U.S., compared with 523,000 in 1970. In fashion, dress design was more relaxed in comparison with the spare style of 1985. The lean silhouette was in. Notables who died this year included James H. "Jim" Crowley, last surviving member of the so-called Four Horsemen of Notre Dame, the backfield that made football history in the 1920s under coach Knute Rockne, Jan. 15, at 83; Vincent Paul "Vince" DiMaggio, oldest of the three DiMaggio brothers in major league baseball, who played ten seasons in the NL, Oct. 3, at 74; Henry "Hank" Greenberg, slugging first baseman for the Detroit Tigers and member of the Baseball Hall of Fame, Sept. 4, at 75; William "Billy" Haughton, top harness racing driver, after a racing accident, July 15, at 62; Robert L. "Bobby" Layne, star quarterback of the Detroit Lions and member of the Pro Football Hall of Fame, Dec. 1, at 59; Theodore H. "Ted" Lyons, pitcher for 21 years for the Chicago White Sox and member of the Baseball Hall of Fame, July 25, at 85; and William "Bill" Veeck, the maverick baseball team owner known as the "Barnum of Baseball," Jan. 1, at 71.

Jan 17: The **WBA heavyweight boxing championship** was won by Tim Witherspoon in a 15-round decision over Tony Tubbs in Atlanta, Ga.

Jan 26: Super Bowl XX was won by the Chicago Bears (NFC), who defeated the New England Patriots (AFC) 46 to 10. The Bears had beaten the Los Angeles Rams 24 to 0 for the NFC title on Jan. 11. On the next day the Patriots had defeated the Miami Dolphins 31 to 14 for the AFC title.

Mar 22: The **WBC heavyweight boxing championship** was won by Trevor Berbick in a 12-round decision over Pinklon Thomas in Las Vegas, Nev.

Mar 31: The **NCAA men's basketball championship** was won by Louisville, defeating Duke 72 to 69.

Apr 2: The **three-point field goal** in men's basketball, made from a minimum distance of 16 ft., 9 in. from the basket, was adopted by the NCAA. The association also approved use of instant TV replays to check scoring and timing decisions.

Apr 11: A new **sailing record** for a solo nonstop circumnavigation of the globe was set by Dodge Morgan, 54, who arrived in St. George, Bermuda, aboard his 60-foot sloop *American Promise.* Morgan, the first American to complete such a voyage, had left Bermuda on Nov. 12, 1985, and had sailed 27,000 miles in 150 days. The previous record had been 292 days.

May 2: An **expedition to the North Pole** was completed by six U.S. and Canadian adventurers, the first expedition since 1909 to reach the pole assisted only by dogs. They made the 500-mile trek from Ward Hunt Island, Canada, in 56 days and returned from the pole by airplane.

May 3: The 112th **Kentucky Derby** was won by Ferdinand, with a time of 2:02⅘. The jockey was Willie Shoemaker, 54, who picked up his fourth Derby win and became the oldest jockey to win the annual racing classic.

May 25: In an event called **Hands Across America,** nearly 6,000,000 people linked hands in a chain that stretched 4150 miles from New York City to Long Beach, Calif., broken only along a few desert stretches. Sponsors hoped to raise $50,000,000 to aid the hungry and homeless in the U.S.

May 26-June 8: The **NBA basketball championship** was won by the Boston Celtics, beating the Houston Rockets four games to two for their 16th NBA title.

June 8: In the **longest nine-inning game** in American League baseball history, the Baltimore Orioles beat the New York Yankees 18 to 9 at Yankee Stadium in 4 hrs., 16 min.

June 15: The **U.S. Open golf tournament** was won by Raymond Floyd, 43, who beat Chip Beck and Lanny Wadkins by two strokes to become the oldest golfer to win the championship.

June 19: Len Bias, star forward for the U. of Maryland's basketball team, died of a heart attack, reported to have been brought on by using cocaine at a party celebrating his signing of a lucrative contract with the Boston Celtics.

June 21: Roger Clemens, Boston Red Sox (AL) ace pitcher, became the seventh pitcher in major league history to start a season with 13 straight wins, beating the Baltimore Orioles 7 to 2 at Boston. On Apr. 29 Clemens had struck out 20, a major league record, in a Boston win over the Seattle Mariners.

July 3-6: Liberty Weekend, a gala national celebration, capped a three-year, $70,000,000 restoration of the Statue of Liberty. On July 3 Pres. Reagan relighted the statue's torch, and new citizens were sworn in around the country. The next day a squadron of tall ships from around the world made its way up New York harbor. That evening saw the greatest fireworks display ever attempted, totaling some 40,000 pieces.

July 5-6: At the **Wimbledon** tennis championships in England, Martina Navratilova bested Hana Mandlikova of Czechoslovakia to win the women's singles title, her fifth consecutive and seventh career win in this event. Navratilova teamed with Pam Shriver to win the women's doubles. Ken Flach and Kathy Jordan won the mixed doubles.

July 27: Greg LeMond became the **first American to win the Tour de France,** the best-known bicycle racing event in the world. LeMond covered the 2500-mile over-the-road route in 110 hrs., 35 min., 19 sec., beating his nearest competitor by 3 min., 10 sec. The race began on July 4.

Aug 11: The **PGA golf tournament** was won by Bob Tway, who sank a spectacular bunker shot on the final hole to edge out Greg Norman.

Aug 20: The third worst **mass murder** in U.S. history took place in Edmond, Okla. Patrick Henry Sherrill, described as always lonely and who had lost his post-office job for lack of competence, shot and killed 14 of his former coworkers, wounded 6 others, and then killed himself.

Sep 7: The **U.S. Open tennis singles championships** were won by Martina Navratilova over Helena Sukova of Czechoslovakia in the women's division and by Ivan Lendl of Czechoslovakia over his countryman, Miloslav Mecir, in the men's division.

Sept 23: Congress voted to make the rose the **official national flower** of the U.S. The subject had been debated off and on for about 100 years.

Oct 18-27: The **World Series** was won by the New York Mets (NL), who defeated the Boston Red Sox (AL) four games to three. New York lost the first two games at home, and the Sox lost the next two in Boston before winning game five to take a 3–2 advantage. The sixth game, played in New York, went to the Mets 6–5 in the tenth.

Nov 14: In one of the nation's **biggest financial scandals,** Ivan F. Boesky agreed to pay the government $100,000,000 as a penalty for illegal insider trading. The Securities and Exchange Commission announced that Boesky was barred for life from participating in the securities business, but he was allowed to liquidate stocks in order to pay off $1,400,000,000 of debt owed by his firm. On Apr. 23, 1987, he pleaded guilty to one charge of conspiracy to file false documents with the federal government; on Dec. 18 he was sentenced to three years in prison; and on Mar. 24, 1988, he began to serve his sentence.

Nov 22: The WBC **heavyweight boxing championship** was won by Mike Tyson, who knocked out Trevor Berbick in the second round at Las Vegas, Nev. Tyson, 20 years old, became the youngest heavyweight champion in boxing history.

Dec 12: The WBA **heavyweight boxing championship** was won by James "Bonecrusher" Smith, who knocked out Tim Witherspoon in the first round of a bout in New York City.

1987

I. Civil Rights
Exploration and Settlement
Government
Statistics
Wars

The nation celebrated the 200th anniversary of its Constitution with two separate ceremonies in Philadelphia, where it was written in 1787. On May 25 delegates who had gathered from the 13 original states on May 22 held a ceremony on Independence Mall. On July 16, 200 members of Congress assembled in the Quaker City, ending their visit the next day with an observance of the signing of the document that featured the ringing of a replica of the Liberty Bell. In Washington the *Post* reported that in fiscal 1987 the U.S. gave $660,000,000 in military aid to the Afghans resisting the Soviet invasion. About the same time, in Waukee, Iowa, the plight of some farmers was dramatized when a bank foreclosed the mortgage on the home of Ann Zimmerman, who had been the state's first woman lieutenant governor. Back in Washington, it was revealed that for over 50 years the FBI had been busy keeping a number of America's leading authors under surveillance, including John Steinbeck, Gertrude Stein, Norman Mailer, and William F. Buckley, Jr. Also in Washington, in March, the "Grate American Sleep-Out" took place to publicize the distress of the homeless in the nation's capital. Taking part were actor Martin Sheen, Mayor Marion Barry, Jr., and Congressman Tony Coelho. The Hispanic population, the Census Bureau reported, had grown by 30% since 1980 and stood at 18,800,000. In the good old summertime a heat wave in the Midwest and East was blamed for nearly 100 deaths, with some areas suffering temperatures near or above 100° for 17 days. Notable people who died during the year included William J. Casey, director of the CIA and former chairman of the Securities and Exchange Commission, May 6, at 74; Ira C. Eaker, who was commander of U.S. air forces in Europe in World War II and helped establish the Air Force as a separate service, Aug. 6, at 91; Alfred M. Landon, Republican candidate for president in 1936, Oct. 12, at 100; Bayard Rustin, longtime civil rights leader, Aug. 24, at 77; and Maxwell D. Taylor, commander of airborne troops in World War II, Apr. 19, at 85.

Jan 4: The **crash of a 12-car Amtrak passenger train** with three Conrail freight engines near Chase, Md., killed 15 people and injured more than 175. It was the worst accident in Amtrak's history and occurred when the train and engines were mistakenly merged onto the same track.

Jan 22: An **East Coast blizzard** raged from Maine to Florida, causing at least 37 deaths. Parts of North Carolina received 20 inches of snow.

Jan 24: Three American members of the faculty of Beirut University College were **kidnaped by gunmen** in West Beirut, Lebanon. They were Allen Steen, Jesse Turner, and Robert Polhill. On June 17 another American, Charles Glass, a journalist, was kidnaped, but on Aug. 18 he either escaped or was allowed to escape. At this time five other Americans were being held captive by Moslem terrorists.

Feb 4: Pres. Ronald Reagan's veto of a **Clean Water Act** was overridden by Congress, the Senate acting today and the House having taken action the previous day. The law authorized the spending of $20,000,000,000 through 1994 for sewer construction and the cleaning up of estuaries and toxic "hot spots" and for other purposes. Reagan said the bill was "loaded with waste and larded with pork."

Feb 19: **Trade sanctions against Poland** were lifted by Pres. Reagan after the Communist regime freed political prisoners. The action removed the ban on trade credits and restored Poland's "most favored nation" status for export-import purposes.

Feb 26: The **Tower Commission report** on the Iran-Contra affair was critical of Pres. Reagan for failing to understand or control the secret attempt to trade arms to Iran for the release of American hostages being held in Lebanon that ended with profits from the sale being improperly diverted to the Nicaraguan Contras. The commission, appointed by the president in Nov. 1986, said Reagan must take responsibility for the policy, which ended in "chaos" and caused the U.S. much embarrassment abroad. Blame was placed also on Donald T. Regan, the White House chief of staff, whom the president replaced with former Senator Howard H. Baker, Jr., on Feb. 27. In a television address on Mar. 4, the president said he took "full responsibility," but he did not admit that the plan for dealing with Iran was basically wrong.

Apr 27: **Kurt Waldheim** will not be allowed to enter the U.S., the Justice Dept. announced. The president of Austria and former secretary general of the United Nations was banned because he had "participated in activities amounting to persecution" of Jews and others while he was serving with the German army in the Balkans from 1942 to 1945. Waldheim was the first head of state ever put on a list of persons excluded from the U.S.

May 17: **A missile attack on a U.S. frigate** in the Persian Gulf killed 37 sailors and badly damaged the USS *Stark*. An Iraqi warplane fired two missiles by mistake and Iraq apologized for the attack. On July 22 U.S. warships began escorting Kuwaiti tankers re-registered under the American flag through the gulf to protect them from possible Iranian attacks. On Sept. 22 an American helicopter attacked and damaged an Iranian minelayer, and on Oct. 19 U.S. naval forces shelled two offshore installations in retaliation for Iranian attacks on Persian Gulf shipping.

Aug 16: The **crash of a Northwest Airlines jet** on take-off from the Detroit Metropolitan Airport killed 156 of the 157 persons on board. The only survivor was a four-year-old girl, who was injured but recovered. On May 10, 1988, a federal investigative report blamed the crash on the failure of the two pilots to follow required checklist procedures before takeoff.

Oct 1: A **severe earthquake** shook the Los Angeles area, killing at least 8 people and injuring more than 100. It was the strongest quake in the region since 1971 and registered 6.1 on the Richter scale. Glass fell from skyscraper windows and in Whittier 30 buildings collapsed.

Oct 23: The **Senate rejected the nomination of Robert H. Bork** to the Supreme Court by a vote of 58–42. Bork, a member of the federal Appeals Court in Washington, had been nominated by Pres. Reagan to fill the vacancy caused by the resignation of Justice Lewis F. Powell, Jr., on July 1. Lobbying against Bork by many liberal groups, who accused him of extreme right-wing views on issues of civil rights and individual privacy, was intense. After two weeks of hearings in September, the Senate Judiciary Committee on Oct. 6 voted to recommend rejection of the nomination by a 9–5 tally. On Oct. 29 Reagan nominated Douglas H. Ginsburg, also an Appeals Court judge. Ginsburg withdrew on Nov. 7 after charges of a conflict of interest in the past and the admission that he used marijuana while teaching at Harvard Law School. The president then nominated Anthony Kennedy, a federal judge in California, on Nov. 11. Finally, on Feb. 3, 1988, the Senate unanimously confirmed Kennedy by a vote of 97–0.

Nov 15: Taking off in a snowstorm, a **Continental Airlines jet crashed** at Denver's Stapleton Airport, flipping over and breaking into three pieces. Of the 81 persons aboard, 28 were killed and more than 50 injured.

Nov 18: The **Congressional committees' report on the Iran-Contra affair** blamed Pres. Reagan for failing in his constitutional duty and said he bore "the ultimate responsibility" for the wrongdoing of his aides. The committees' 690-page report also said "the rule of law was subverted" and that if the president did not know what his national security advisers were up to, he should have. The report provided the most complete accounting to date of what became of the nearly $48,000,000 that was raised by the sale of arms to Iran. The two committees had held joint hearings from May 5 to Aug. 15, during which they heard more than 250 hours of testimony from 28 witnesses. The chief witnesses were John M. Poindexter, national security adviser at the time of the affair, and his assistant, Lt. Col. Oliver L. North. The latter was briefly somewhat of a hero, with his gung-ho defense of his actions, which, in his view, had put his patriotic duty above the law.

Nov 20: Pres. Reagan and Congressional leaders agreed on **a plan to reduce the federal budget deficit** by $30,000,000,000 for the fiscal year that had begun on Oct. 1 and by $46,000,000,000 in the following year. On Dec. 22 Reagan signed budget bills totalling $603,900,000,000, a record that would presumably reduce the deficit by $3,400,000,000 more than previously agreed on.

Nov 21: A **federal prison riot** at Oakdale, La., by about 1000 Cuban refugees being held for possible deportation began with the seizure of 30 hostages. On Nov. 23 a similar group of 1392 detainees at the federal prison in Atlanta, Ga., also took action, seizing the prison and 75 hostages. The detainees were aroused by reports of a new agreement between the U.S. and Cuba whereby Cuba would take back more than 2000 "undesirables." After negotiations and without violence, the riot ended at Oakdale on Nov. 29 and at Atlanta on Dec. 4. The detainees were assured they would receive individual and full reviews of their status. By late Apr. 1988, 1153 of the detainees had been released, ten times more than in the previous five months.

Dec 8: The **first treaty that would reduce nuclear arsenals** was signed in Washington by Pres. Reagan and General Secretary Mikhail S. Gorbachev of the U.S.S.R. Under the terms of the treaty 2611 U.S. and Soviet medium- and short-range missiles sited in Europe would be destroyed. The pact provided for on-site verification in both countries. The agreement was seen as a first step toward agreement on the reduction of U.S. and Soviet long-range missiles.

Dec 16: Michael K. Deaver was found guilty on three of five counts of perjury stemming from his lobbying activities after he left the position of aide to Pres. Reagan. He had been tried on charges of having lied to a House subcommittee about efforts to arrange a meeting between the president and a South Korean trade representative and also of having lied to a federal grand jury. At the base of Deaver's troubles were accusations that he violated the 1978 Ethics in Government Act, which regulates lobbying by former government officials. White House deputy chief of staff until May 1985, Deaver was the highest-ranking Reagan administration official to be convicted of a crime.

Dec 22: Aid to the **Nicaraguan Contras** of $14,000,000 for nonlethal use was approved by Pres. Reagan when he signed a bill just passed by Congress as a compromise with the executive branch.

II. Architecture
Arts and Music
Popular Entertainment
Publishing
Theater

Successful Broadway musicals were bigger, if not better, than ever. *Les Misérables* (from England) had advance ticket sales (some as high as $50) of $11,000,000, and *Starlight Express*, a show whose main features were its setting and gadgetry, cost $8,000,000 to stage, a record. The only successful drama was *Fences* by August Wilson. The movies provided a varied fare, including such comedies as *Three Men and a Baby*, *Raising Arizona*, and *Moonstruck*. *Full Metal Jacket* and *Good Morning, Vietnam* concerned the war there. Also popular and worthy were

Broadcast News, The Last Emperor, and *Empire of the Sun.* An unusual art exhibit opened in March in Leningrad, displaying 116 works by the three Wyeths—N.C., son Andrew, and grandson James. As another sign, perhaps, of more cordial relations between the U.S. and the U.S.S.R., a temporary exchange of masterpieces was arranged with the National Gallery of Art, sending an El Greco to the Hermitage in Leningrad, which in turn sent a Titian to Washington. Back home in Philadelphia, the Museum of Art staged the largest display of Chinese ceramic sculpture ever seen outside China, and in New York the Metropolitan Museum held the most important exhibit ever to come out of Israel, "Treasures of the Holy Land: Ancient Art from the Israel Museum." Both these exhibits were to go to Houston and Los Angeles. In North Adams, Mass., 28 vacant factory buildings were about to be taken over to house one of the largest collections of contemporary art, on loan from Count Giuseppe Pahza di Biumo. On the West Coast, Norton Simon, the industrialist, and the University of California at Los Angeles reached an agreement calling for the transfer of the large art collections owned by Simon to the school. The gift was said to be worth $750,000,000. At auction, artworks by Americans commanded higher prices than ever: a Georgia O'Keefe work selling for $1,900,000, a record for the artist; an Elie Nadelman sculpture going for $2,000,000; a Willem de Kooning painting bringing $3,600,000; and a George Caleb Bingham oil topping all with a reported price of $6,000,000 in a private sale. The American Ballet Theater sold $6,200,000 worth of tickets for its new production of *Sleeping Beauty,* but the dancers of the Dallas Ballet had to raise $500,000 or else disband. Publishing mergers continued to make news. In March media tycoon Rupert Murdoch, who owned newspapers and book publishing houses in Britain, Australia, and the U.S., acquired Harper & Row for $300,000,000. In June British publishing entrepreneur and corporate raider Robert Maxwell attempted to buy Harcourt Brace Jovanovich for $1,730,000,000, but HBJ fought back with a reorganization plan that saved the company from Maxwell but burdened it with an enormous debt. The circulation of daily newspapers dropped by a slight 0.4% and the number of papers from 1676 to 1657. In July it was estimated that 43,260,000 U.S. households, 49.5% of the total, had cable TV. This was an increase of about 2,000,000 in a year. Noteworthy persons who died included Fred Astaire, the popular dancer, June 22, at 88; the actress Mary Astor, Sept. 25, at 81; Bil Baird, master puppeteer, Mar. 18, at 82; James Baldwin, whose writings spurred the civil rights movement, Dec. 1, at 63; Mi-

chael Bennett, Broadway choreographer and winner of eight Tony Awards, July 2, at 44; Ray Bolger, actor best known as the Scarecrow in the movie *The Wizard of Oz,* Jan. 15, at 83; James Burnham, founding editor of the conservative *National Review,* July 28, at 82; Erskine Caldwell, author of novels about the South, such as *Tobacco Road,* Apr. 11, at 83; Jackie Gleason, comedian whose TV show of the 1950s, *The Honeymooners,* developed a cult following, June 24, at 71; Rita Hayworth, glamorous movie star, May 14, at 68; Jascha Heifetz, violin virtuoso, Dec. 10, at 86; Woody Herman, popular leader of big bands, Oct. 29, at 74; John Huston, noted movie director, Aug. 28, at 81; Danny Kaye, comedian, dancer, and singer, Mar. 3, at 74; Nora Kaye, ballerina who created a new, contemporary look among dancers, Feb. 28, at 67; Sammy Kaye, popular musician noted for the music of his "sweet bands," June 2, at 77; Mervyn LeRoy, who directed 75 films over 40 years, including *Little Caesar,* Sept. 13, at 86; Clare Boothe Luce, sharp-tongued playwright, ambassador, and politician, Oct. 9, at 84; Rouben Mamoulian, director of *Porgy and Bess* and *Oklahoma!* for the stage and of inventive films, Dec. 4, at 90; Pola Negri, exotic vamp of the movies of the 1920s and 1930s, Aug. 1, at 88; Geraldine Page, stage and screen actress, June 13, at 62; Andrés Segovia, who restored the guitar to top rank in classical music, June 2, at 94; Myron Stout, abstract artist of minimal black and white compositions, Aug. 2, at 79; Antony Tudor, who introduced psychological motivation in his choreography, Apr. 20, at 78 or 79; Andy Warhol, founder of Pop Art, Feb. 22, at 58; Glenway Wescott, novelist, acclaimed at age 26 for *The Grandmothers,* Feb. 22, at 85; and Marguerite Yourcenar, author, holder of dual French and U.S. citizenship, known particularly for *Memoirs of Hadrian,* an imaginary autobiography, and for being the first woman elected to the Académie Française, Dec. 17, at 84.

Among **books published** this year, most talked about novels were Toni Morrison's *Beloved,* the story of a woman escaped from slavery, and Tom Wolfe's *The Bonfire of the Vanities,* an account of a New York yuppie in big trouble. Other important novels were *The Counterlife,* the fourth in Philip Roth's Zuckerman series, and *Crossing to Safety,* Wallace Stegner's account of the friendship of two couples. The most popular suspense and thriller entries were *Patriot Games* by Tom Clancy and *Presumed Innocent* by Scott Turow. Among autobiographical works were *Man of the House* by former Speaker Thomas P. O'Neill, Jr., and *Trump: The Art of the Deal* by the successful New York real estate developer, Donald Trump. Two conservative critics of American education had their say in *The Closing of the American Mind* by Allan Bloom and *Cultural Literacy* by E. D. Hirsch, Jr.

Mar 30: Acquisition of the **Arturo Toscanini Archives** was announced by the New York Public Library. The large collection of scores, recordings, letters, and memorabilia of the late conductor, valued at $2,000,000, had been inaccessible since 1970 while negotiations went on.

Apr 6: The first American to win the **Ritz Paris Hemingway Award,** worth $50,000, was Peter Taylor for his novel *A Summons to Memphis.*

Apr 7: The **National Museum of Women in the Arts** opened in Washington, D.C., the first museum devoted entirely to women artists. It already held more than 500 examples of such art from the Renaissance to the 20th century. Some feminists felt it would segregate women's artistic work rather than promoting it.

Apr 16: Pulitzer prizes were awarded for the following: fiction, *A Summons to Memphis* by Peter Taylor; general nonfiction, *Arab and Jew: Wounded Spirits in a Promised Land* by David K. Shipler; biography, *Bearing the Cross: Martin Luther King, Jr., and the Southern Christian Leadership Conference* by David J. Garrow; history, *Voyagers to the West: A Passage in the Peopling of America on the Eve of the Revolution* by Bernard Bailyn; poetry, *Thomas and Beulah* by Rita Dove; drama, *Fences* by August Wilson.

Apr 17: Richard Wilbur was appointed the second **poet laureate** of the U.S. by the Librarian of Congress.

Sep 14: A new method of **measuring TV audiences** was introduced by the A. C. Nielsen Co., which for 20 years had relied on a system of diaries kept by a sampling of households. The new system featured "people meters," which registered opinion by viewers' pushing buttons. Early results of the new method made the TV networks unhappy, as it seemed to register fewer viewers than the diary system.

Sep 28: Two new museums opened in Washington, D.C., as part of the Smithsonian Institution. One was the National Museum of African Art, which had existed since 1964 but was now greatly expanded; the other was the all-new Arthur M. Sackler Museum for Asian and Near East Art. The museums, 96% underground, were on three levels and cost $73,000,000. They exhibited 6000 objects of African and 2500 of Asian art.

Oct 22: The **Nobel Prize for Literature** was awarded to Joseph Brodsky, Soviet-born exile, now a citizen of the U.S. A poet and essayist, in both English and Russian, Brodsky at 47 was the second youngest to win this award.

Nov 11: The **highest price ever paid for a painting,** $53,900,000, was bid at auction in New York for *Irises* by Vincent Van Gogh. The painting had been owned by John Whitney Payson, a member of a wealthy family. Some of the proceeds were to go to the Payson Foundation and to Westbrook College, Portland, Me. *Irises* was painted in 1889 soon after Van Gogh entered the asylum at Saint-Rémy, France.

III. Business and Industry
Education
Philosophy and Religion
Science

In spite of staging in October the greatest stock market crash in history, the national economy had a more or less successful year. Unemployment was down to 5.7%, the lowest since mid-1979, and the GNP rose 3.8%, increasing for the sixth consecutive year. On the other hand, the CPI was up 4.4%, the highest rate of inflation since 1981, and the trade deficit, at $171,220,000,000, set a record for the fifth year in a row, although the December deficit was the lowest in 11 months. The dollar weakened, ending the year at 121.05 to the Japanese yen, down 23% compared with the previous year end. Black-owned industrial and service businesses set a record, with $4,100,000,000 of sales. The TLC group, an investment concern, with $1,800,000,000 in sales, became the first such minority concern to pass the $1,000,000,000 mark. The recorded-music business prospered again. Unit sales of compact discs were up 93% to 102,000,000, with a value of $1,600,000,000. Sales of cassette tapes rose 19% to 410,000,000, worth about $2,900,000,000. However, sales of record albums and LPs declined 15% to 107,000,000, worth $793,000,000. *Forbes* magazine declared that Sam Moore Walton, 69, the founder of the Wal-Mart discount stores, was, for the third year in a row, the richest American, worth $8,500,000,000. But Albert J. Lowry, former supermarket butcher who had written widely on how to become a millionaire by dealing in real estate, filed for bankruptcy. During the year 30 states, compared with only five in 1983, appropriated money to fight the disease AIDS, and one estimate of what it would cost to battle AIDS nationwide in 1991 was $8,500,000,000. A report from the federal government said 40,000,000 Americans had blood cholesterol high enough to put them at risk of heart disease. The Mathematical Science Education Board found that, compared with 21 other countries, the achievement of American students was "lackluster." In 1987, 17% of college students were from minority groups, which comprise 21% of the U.S. population. Among notable persons who died were I. W. Abel, a founder of the United Steel Workers of America and its president from 1965 to 1977, Aug. 10, at 78; Walter H. Brattain, cowinner of the 1956 Nobel Prize in Physics for the invention of the transistor, Oct. 13, at 85; Henry Ford II, grandson of the founder of the giant automaking company, whose management brought the concern back from a sharp decline, Sept. 29, at 70; and Walter W. Heller, economic adviser to presidents Kennedy and Johnson, June 15, at 71.

Mar 19: The Rev. **Jim Bakker,** a successful TV evangelist, resigned his ministry, admitting that he had an extramarital sexual encounter with a church secretary seven years earlier. The founder of PTL (Praise the Lord, or People That Love) said he had paid what he called blackmail to the woman involved. His wife, Tammy, had also been active in the ministry and had her own line of cosmetics for sale. PTL operated a $172,000,000, 2300-acre theme park, Heritage USA, in Fort Mill, S.C., and in 1986 Bakker was paid $1,600,000 in salary and bonuses. On May 6 the Assemblies of God dismissed Bakker as a minister. On June 12 the new management of PTL filed for bankruptcy, noting $71,000,000 of debt, and on Feb. 1, 1988, sued Bakker for $52,800,000, charging mismanagement and unjustified compensation.

Mar 20: The **first drug to benefit AIDS patients** was approved by the federal government. The drug was azidothymidine, or AZT, and while it would not cure AIDS, tests showed it would let victims of the disease live longer. Because AZT could have severe side effects, its use was to be limited to selected categories of patients, totalling about 15,000. The drug was estimated to cost as much as $10,000 per patient per year. On Aug. 18 the Food and Drug Administration approved the trial use, for the first time on humans, of a possible AIDS vaccine. Similar tests were already being carried out in France. The test vaccine used a protein, CD4, that seemed to attract the AIDS virus, thus preventing it from entering nearby body cells.

Apr 4: Introduced by the nation's Roman Catholic bishops, a **New Testament avoids the use of the word "man"** when the reference is to both men and women. A passage that read "Not on bread alone is man to live" had been changed to "One does not live by bread alone." Known as the Revised New Testament of the American Bible, it was now the authorized version for America's 50,000,000 Catholics.

Apr 16: The **patenting of new forms of animal life** created through gene splicing would be allowed, the federal government announced. The U.S. was the first country to take such a step. The policy allowed the patenting of animals with new traits created by recently devised reproductive technologies, includ-

ing genetic engineering. Specifically banned was the patenting of new genetic characteristics in human beings.

Apr 27: The **largest U.S. corporation** in 1986, according to *Fortune* magazine, was General Motors, with sales of $102,813,700,000. Second was Exxon, whose sales were $69,888,000,000.

Apr 28: In the **third-largest U.S. takeover deal,** Standard Oil agreed to sell to British Petroleum for $7,800,000,000 the 45% of Standard not already owned by BP. The deal made BP the third-largest oil company in the world, behind Exxon and the Royal Dutch/Shell Group.

May 12: A **three-way heart and lung transplant,** believed to be a medical first, was performed in Baltimore, Md. A healthy heart was taken from a living person and transplanted to another. The heart donor then received the heart and lungs of an accident victim who had died in a nearby hospital. On May 14 a spokesman for a British hospital said similar operations had been performed there the last week in April and the first week in May.

June 2: A **new chairman of the Federal Reserve Board,** economist Alan Greenspan, was named by Pres. Ronald Reagan. He succeeded Paul A. Volcker, who had held the post for eight years and who was noted for the strong measures he had taken to quell the high inflation in the economy when he took office. In financial markets, where it had been expected Volcker would serve a third term, there was a sharp drop in bond prices. Greenspan, who had worked in both business and government, was known for his free-market sympathies and was not expected to change noticeably the policies Volcker had followed.

June 19: Teaching the **creationist theory** of human origin may not be required in public schools alongside the theory of evolution when the intent is to promote religious belief, according to the Supreme Court. Thus, by a 7–2 vote, the Court held unconstitutional a Louisiana law of 1984. The decision was seen as a serious blow to the efforts of fundamentalist Christians to mold public school curriculums to fit their beliefs.

June 30: By adopting the declaration **"Judaism has not been superseded by Christianity,"** The United Church of Christ became the first major U.S. Protestant denomination to so affirm the position of the Jewish religion. The declaration, adopted at the convention of the church in Cleveland, Ohio, also stated "God has not rejected the Jewish people."

Aug 25: On the New York Stock Exchange a **new record, 2722.42, was set by the Dow Jones industrial average.** The Dow had closed above the 2000 mark, at 2002.25, for the first time on Jan. 8. On Jan. 15 the exchange had set a new record for volume with 253,100,000 shares traded. On Sept. 22 the Dow Jones average scored its largest one-day gain, 75.23 points.

Sep 5-7: Infant **twins joined at the head** were separated in a lengthy and unusual operation at the Johns Hopkins University Hospital in Baltimore, Md. Metal plates were implanted over the skull holes caused by the operation. On Apr. 7, 1988, the hospital announced the twins would be discharged in a few days to return to West Germany, where they were born. They suffered some brain damage and might have vision problems but otherwise seemed likely to lead normal lives.

Oct 12: The **Nobel Prize in Medicine** was awarded to Susumu Tonegawa, a Japanese scientist working at the Massachusetts Institute of Technology. He had discovered how the human body marshals its immunological defenses against many different diseases it has never met before. Dr. Tonegawa was the first Japanese to win the Nobel Prize in this category.

Oct 14: The **Nobel Prize in Chemistry** was awarded jointly to Donald J. Cram of the University of California at Los Angeles, Charles J. Pedersen, formerly a research chemist with E. I. du Pont de Nemours & Co., and Jean-Marie Lehn, a French professor of chemistry. The three had carried out varied researches that included the creation of artificial molecules that mimic vital chemical reactions of life processes.

Oct 16: A baby only three hours old became the **youngest person to undergo a heart transplant.** The operation was performed at the Linda Loma (Calif.) Medical Center after the baby was delivered by Caesarean section. The donor of the heart was an infant who had been declared legally dead a few days earlier.

Oct 19: The **worst stock crash** in the history of the New York Stock Exchange occurred when the Dow Jones industrial average fell 508 points, closing at 1738.74, a decline of 22.6%, nearly double the decline in 1929 that ushered in the Great Depression. The volume of stocks traded, 604,330,000, was nearly twice the previous record of 338,500,000, set on Oct. 16. Computerized program trading, as well as various factors in the national and international economy, was blamed for the collapse of a market that had exhibited a case of the jitters in recent weeks. On Oct. 20 the Dow Jones rose 102.27 points and trading set another new record for volume with 608,120,000 shares traded. In spite of the gain, largely confined to blue chip issues, many more stocks fell than rose. The Dow gained another 186 points the following day but dropped 77.42 points on Oct. 22. The major markets set temporarily shorter hours in hopes of easing the tension, but on Oct. 26 there was another drop of 156.83

points. After a short period of relative quiet, the Dow fell 50.56 on Nov. 3, ending a five-day rally, and on Nov. 9 the average was down another 58.85 points, closing at 1900.20.

Oct 21: The **Nobel Prize in Economics** was awarded to Robert M. Solow of the Massachusetts Institute of Technology for his contributions to the theory of economic growth.

Nov 20: An agreement to reduce the **federal budget deficit** by $30,000,000,000 in the fiscal year that began on Oct. 1 was reached by Pres. Reagan and Congressional leaders after four weeks of complicated and sometimes rancorous negotiations, spurred by the stock market debacle of Oct. 19. Legislation would be required to make the agreement effective. Among steps to be taken were a reduction of $6,600,000,000 in domestic spending and a $5,000,000,000 cut in the defense budget.

Dec 2: A **free trade agreement** was signed by Pres. Reagan and Prime Minister Brian Mulroney of Canada. The pact, which included a mechanism for settling disputes, would eliminate tariffs and lower other trade barriers by the end of the century. All agricultural tariffs would be dropped within ten years. Approval by the legislative bodies of both countries was required before the agreement takes effect.

Dec 10: Teaching about the use of condoms in the battle against the disease AIDS was given qualified support by the Roman Catholic bishops of the U.S. in spite of the church's opposition to birth control. The bishops' position paper called on all Catholic schools to teach AIDS prevention.

Dec 11: To cover possible claims resulting from the use of the **Dalkon Shield birth control device,** a federal judge ordered the A. H. Robins Co., producer of the IUD, to establish a fund of $2,475,000,000 as part of its reorganization plan. The company had filed for bankruptcy in Aug. 1985 because of the thousands of claims against it by women who said they became infertile or suffered injuries as a result of using the shield. About 9500 women had already received compensation.

Dec 19: In the **largest cash settlement in U.S. corporate history,** Texaco agreed to pay Pennzoil $3,000,000,000 to settle a bitter lawsuit. In 1985 a Texas court had ordered Texaco to pay $10,100,000,000, plus interest, to Pennzoil for having illegally interfered with the latter's attempt to take over the Getty Oil Co. In its battle to overturn this decision, and in its very unfriendly negotiations to reach a less costly settlement with Pennzoil, Texaco filed for bankruptcy on Apr. 12, 1987. The agreed-upon settlement was paid to Pennzoil on Apr. 7, 1988.

That same day Texaco ended 361 days in bankruptcy. On Apr. 15 Texaco, announcing it would sell at least $5,000,000,000 of its assets to recover its financial strength, said it would resume paying a quarterly dividend.

Dec 31: The **Dow Jones** average of industrial stocks closed the year at 1938.83. Although it was off 29% from its August peak, it was up 2.26% for the year in spite of the shattering crash of Oct. 19.

IV. Fashion
Folkways
Holidays
Social Issues and Crime
Sports

As in other years, Americans faced new problems, tried new or unusual things, set records, committed crimes. A commercial for condoms, a protection against the disease AIDS, first appeared on TV in a major market on Jan. 16, on KRON in San Francisco. Detroit and Indianapolis TV channels soon followed suit. In California an epidemic of random shooting at vehicles on its freeways resulted in four deaths, 16 injuries, and increased highway patrolling. Manufacturers, the Justice Department, and the Consumer Products Safety Commission agreed to a ban on the sale of three-wheeled all-terrain vehicles (ATVs), blamed for about 900 deaths since the early 1980s. Bob Barker, host for 20 years of the Miss Universe Pageant and an animal rights activist, refused to emcee this year's affair unless the contestants wore fake rather than real furs. In a case begun in California, where a wife can be entitled to half of an estate, the Supreme Court let stand a divorce settlement of $76,000,000 against Sheik Mohammed al-Fassi. In the suburbs the now adult baby boomers were interested in backyard gardening. Sales of lawn and garden materials and equipment reached $17,490,000,000, an increase of 47% since 1983. In fashion, for men of all ages there was good news, and for older women, bad: the miniskirt was back for the first time since the early 1970s. Many women refused to exhibit their thighs, and this time, more than before, the mini raised the question of appropriate wear at work for women aspiring to reach the executive suite. Noteworthy people who died included Wayne W. "Woody" Hayes, successful football coach at Ohio State, Mar. 12, at 74; Richard D. "Dick" Howser, baseball player and manager who led the Kansas City Royals to their only World Series victory, in 1985, June 18, at 51; Travis Jackson, shortstop for the New York Giants for 15 years and a member of the Baseball Hall of Fame, July 27, at 83; Thomas G.

Lanphier, Jr., who in World War II shot down the plane carrying Adm. Isoroku Yamamoto, commander of the Japanese navy, Nov. 26, at 71; and William M. Masland, who in 1943 commanded the first round-the-world flight by a commercial aircraft, Feb. 20, at 79.

Jan 1-2: In **college football bowl games,** the results were Ohio State 28, Texas A&M 12 in the Cotton Bowl; Oklahoma 42, Arkansas 8 in the Orange Bowl; Arizona State 22, Michigan 15 in the Rose Bowl; and Nebraska 30, Louisiana State 15 in the Sugar Bowl. Both the AP and UPI polls chose Penn State as national champion for 1986 after Pennsylvania's Nittany Lions, in a battle of previously undefeated teams, triumphed over Miami (Fla.) 14–10 in the Fiesta Bowl on Jan. 2.

Jan 13: One of the **most successful prosecutions of organized crime figures** resulted in the conviction of eight key men, called "the board of directors." Seven of the Mafia leaders were given 100-year sentences in federal court. On Jan. 16 nine other racketeers were given shorter terms.

Jan 25: Super Bowl XXI was won by the New York Giants (NFC), defeating the Denver Broncos (AFC) 39–20. On Jan. 11, the Giants had won the NFC title by defeating the Washington Redskins 17–0 and Denver had won the AFC championship by defeating the Cleveland Browns 23–20 in overtime.

Jan 31-Feb 4: The **America's Cup** was regained by the U.S. when the American challenger *Stars & Stripes*, skippered by Dennis Connor of San Diego, Calif., defeated the Australian yacht *Kookaburra III* in four straight races at Fremantle, Australia. Connor, the losing skipper in 1983, thus became the first American skipper to lose and regain the yachting trophy.

Feb 24: A **world record ice-fishing catch** was made by Omer J. Lebel of Van Buren, Me., when he caught a brook trout weighing 8 lbs., 4 oz.

Feb 25: The NCAA ruled that **Southern Methodist U.** could not field a football team this year because athletic officials had violated NCAA rules by paying about $61,000 to players. This, the stiffest penalty ever imposed on a football program, also provided that in 1988 SMU could play only seven games, all away from home and thus earning no revenue for SMU.

Feb 26: Michael Spinks was **stripped of his IBF heavyweight championship.** The action was taken because he failed to defend his title within nine months of winning the crown from Larry Holmes on Apr. 19, 1986, thus failing to live up to IBF rules.

Mar 7: The **combined WBA and WBC heavyweight boxing championship** was won by Mike Tyson, who defeated James "Bonecrusher" Smith by a unanimous decision in a 15-round bout at Las Vegas, Nev.

Mar 28: Setting a new **college basketball attendance record** before 64,959 fans, Indiana defeated the U. of Nevada, Las Vegas, 97–93 in the semifinals of the NCAA championship in the New Orleans Superdome.

Mar 29: The **NCAA women's basketball championship,** held in Austin, Tex., was won by Tennessee over Louisiana Tech 67–44.

Mar 30: The **NCAA men's basketball championship** was won by Indiana, defeating Syracuse 74–73.

Mar 31: After a grueling and precedent-setting legal battle, **custody of a baby born to a surrogate mother** was awarded to the father. Baby M, as the girl was known during the trial before a New Jersey judge, was born Mar. 27, 1986, the result of the artificial insemination of Mary Beth Whitehead by William Stern. Stern and his wife, Elizabeth, agreed to pay the mother $10,000 and she in turn would relinquish all rights to the child. Mrs. Whitehead, however, refused to give up the baby, and a suit brought by the Sterns to enforce the contract began on Jan. 5, 1987. Saying he was creating law, the judge in his decision upheld the legality of such a surrogate agreement and stripped the mother of all parental rights. On Feb. 3, 1988, however, the Supreme Court of New Jersey ruled unanimously that commercial surrogate motherhood contracts were illegal. It was the first ruling by a state's highest court in such a case and would probably influence courts and legislatures in other states. The Baby M dispute went back to a lower court, and on Apr. 6, 1988, the mother was granted broad rights to see the child, although the Sterns retained custody.

Apr 12: The **Masters golf tournament** was won by Larry Mize on the second hole of a three-way playoff, when he sank a 50-yard wedge shot to defeat Greg Norman and Seve Ballesteros.

Apr 18: An **unconscious sky diver was rescued** by another jumper. Debbie Williams was knocked out by colliding with another sky diver. Noticing her plight, Gregory Robertson dived to reach her and yanked open her ripcord when she was less than 3500 ft. from the ground. Williams was seriously injured, but Robertson resumed sky diving the same day.

May 2: The 113th **Kentucky Derby** was won by Alysheba, with a time of 2:03²⁄₅. The jockey was Chris McCarron.

May 3: The **richest prize in PGA tour history,** $225,000, was won by Paul Azinger when he captured the Panasonic Las Vegas golf tournament. In addi-

tion, Scott Hoch received a $118,299 Rolls-Royce for a hole-in-one at the 17th hole.

May 4: **Women must be admitted to Rotary Clubs,** hitherto all male, the Supreme Court ruled, 7–0. On July 4 the Lions Club International voted to admit women and on July 7 Kiwanis International followed suit.

May 10-18: The **NHL Stanley Cup** championship was won by the Edmonton Oilers, who beat the Philadelphia Flyers four games to three.

May 14: An **1873 Colt revolver sold for $242,000,** a record, at auction. The single-action, .45-caliber weapon was the first six-shooter of the type known as the "Peacemaker" and the most famous gun ever produced in the U.S. The revolver was discovered in a New Hampshire farmhouse in 1925 and bought from the widow of an army major for $4.

May 16: The 112th **Preakness Stakes** was won by Alysheba, with a time of 1:55⁴⁄₅. The jockey was Chris McCarron.

May 24: A record **10,000th winning harness race** was won by Hervé Filion, a French-Canadian driver, at Yonkers Raceway, N.Y.

May 24: The 71st **Indianapolis 500 auto race** was won by Al Unser, completing the 500-mi. course in 3 hrs., 4 min., 59.147 sec. In winning this race for the fourth time, Unser became the oldest Indy winner, five days short of his 48th birthday.

June 2-14: The **NBA basketball championship** was won by the Los Angeles Lakers over the Boston Celtics four games to two.

June 4: The **longest winning streak in track history** ended when Edwin Moses lost a 400-m. hurdles race in Madrid to Danny Harris, another American. Moses had won 122 consecutive races, his last loss coming on Aug. 26, 1977, when he was beaten by Harald Schmid of West Germany. Moses holds the world record of 47.02 sec. for the 400-m. hurdle event.

June 6: The **119th Belmont Stakes** was won by Bet Twice by 14 lengths, with a time of 2:28²⁄₅. The jockey was Craig Perret. In addition, Bet Twice won $1,000,000 in the first Triple Crown participation bonus. Bet Twice finished second in both the Kentucky Derby and the Preakness Stakes. Alysheba had won those two races but finished fourth in the Belmont. On a 5-3-1 point basis, Bet Twice earned 11 points to Alysheba's 10. Had one horse won all three races, and thereby the Triple Crown, the bonus would have been $5,000,000.

June 15: In a bout promoted as deciding the **heavyweight championship,** Michael Spinks knocked out

Gerry Cooney in the fifth round of a scheduled 15-round fight. The WBA and the WBC said they would not recognize the winner as champion, but several state boxing commissions said they would.

June 16: For the first time in a single meet, **three long jumpers cleared 28 ft.,** at the USA/Mobil Outdoor Track and Field Championships at San Jose, Calif. The winner, with a jump of 28 ft., 4½ in., was Carl Lewis. He thus extended his winning streak in track and field to 50 in six years. Lewis also won the 200-m. dash.

June 21: The **U.S. Open golf tournament** was won by Scott Simpson, who defeated Tom Watson by one stroke.

June 23: The **oldest living Olympic medalist in the U.S.** celebrated his 95th birthday by jogging along Fifth Ave. in New York City. He was Abel Kiviat, who won the silver medal in the 1500-m. race at the 1912 Olympics. He once held the records for 600 yards, 1000 yards, and the mile, all at the same time.

July 21: Lady's Secret became the **richest filly or mare in racing history** when she won a race at Monmouth Park, Oceanport, N.J. The victory brought total winnings to $3,015,764, surpassing the record set by All Along. Lady's Secret was sired by Secretariat, the Triple Crown winner in 1973.

July 22: Television sports fans favored pro football over baseball, the second most popular sport among watchers, according to a 1986 survey by Simmons Market Research. Pro football was watched frequently by 63,200,000 people, with baseball close behind at 62,700,000. The two leaders were followed by college football, 48,900,000; boxing, 37,200,000; and college basketball, 36,200,000.

July 29: The Dallas Cowboys became the first NFL team to **test its personnel for AIDS.** The testing was described as voluntary and the results as confidential. All tests administered were reported to be negative.

Aug 1: Mary R. Stout, a former U.S. Army nurse, became the **first woman to head a national veterans' organization.** She was elected president of the Vietnam Veterans of America, which had 35,000 members, only about 300 of whom were women.

Aug 1: The unified **heavyweight boxing championship** was won by Mike Tyson, who earned a unanimous 12-round decision over Tony Tucker at Las Vegas, Nev. Tyson held the World Boxing Association and World Boxing Council titles, and Tucker was the champion of the International Boxing Federation. Tyson thus became the first undisputed titleholder

since Feb. 1978, when Leon Spinks beat Muhammad Ali.

Aug 2: In the **fastest race in Indy car history,** Michael Andretti won the Marlboro 500 at Michigan International Speedway in Brooklyn, Mich., with an average speed of 171.490 mph. This bettered the mark of 170.722 mph set by Bobby Rahal when he won the Indianapolis 500 in 1986. One of the drivers who lost to Andretti was his father, Mario.

Aug 8-23: At the tenth **Pan-American Games,** in Indianapolis, Ind., the U.S. won 369 medals, including 168 gold medals. Cuba was second with 75 gold medals and 175 in all, and Canada was third with 30 and 162. For the U.S., track star Jackie Joyner-Kersee tied the world record for the long jump at 24 ft., 5.5 in., and Jeff Kubiak set a record for the games of 2 min., 17.62 sec. in the 200-m. breaststroke.

Aug 9: The **PGA championship** was won by Larry Nelson, who defeated Lanny Wadkins on the first hole of a sudden death playoff. The two had tied at 287 for the four rounds, only one under par, the highest winning score since the event became a stroke-play, 72-hole tournament in 1958.

Aug 16: The **tenth anniversary of the death of Elvis Presley,** rock-and-roll idol, was marked by the pilgrimage of 20,000 or so fans to his home, Graceland, in Memphis, Tenn. Carrying lighted candles, the singer's worshippers gathered at his grave, where a spotlight shone on a statue of Jesus Christ.

Aug 18: Donald Harvey, 35, was **found guilty of killing 24 people** since 1983 by a jury in Ohio. Of them 21 died, mostly by poison, in a Cincinnati hospital where he was an orderly. Harvey was sentenced to three consecutive life terms.

Aug 27: Edward W. Gillet, 36, **paddled a kayak alone from California to Hawaii,** arriving at Kahului after 63 days at sea. He left Monterey on June 25 expecting to make the 2200-mile crossing in 40 days. He ran out of food four days before landing and lost 25 pounds on the voyage.

Aug 29: Little League baseball celebrated the 40th anniversary of its world series. It claims 2,500,000 participants in 16,000 chartered programs. The world championship was won by Hua Lian, the Taiwanese team, beating the Irvine, Calif., team 21-1 at Williamsport, Pa. Teams from the Far East had won 17 Little League championships in the last 21 years. It was Taiwan's seventh win in 11 years. Taiwanese teams had won 12 championships since 1969.

Sep 12: The women's division of the **U.S. Open tennis singles championship** was won by Martina Navratilova over Steffi Graf of West Germany. It was

Navratilova's fourth victory in this event in five years. After a 24-hour rain delay, Ivan Lendl on Sept. 14 defeated Mats Wilander of Sweden for the men's title.

Sep 29: A new **major league record for grand slam home runs** was set by Don Mattingly of the New York Yankees when he hit his sixth of the season. The opposing pitcher was Bruce Hurst of the Boston Red Sox. In July, Mattingly had tied a major league record by hitting home runs in eight consecutive games.

Oct 9: A **world record price for a single postage stamp** was paid when a Japanese bank bought for $1,100,000 a stamp that had sold in Pittsburgh, Pa., in 1852 for two cents. The stamp was from a wedding invitation mailed to a Rev. and Mrs. McGill and is known as the Lady McGill. The previous highest price paid for a stamp was $935,000 in 1980.

Oct 17-25: The **World Series** was won by the Minnesota Twins (AL), who defeated the St. Louis Cardinals four games to three. In every game played, the home team won. Thus, with the Series opening in Minnesota, the Twins jumped out to a two-game lead. The next three games, played in St. Louis, were won by the Cardinals. On the teams' return to the Twins domed stadium, which provides a poor background against which to track high fly balls and with loyal hometown fans in full voice creating a din, the Cardinals folded in games six and seven. On Oct. 12, the Twins had won the American League pennant against the Detroit Tigers four games to one, and two days later the Cardinals won the National League pennant against the San Francisco Giants four games to three.

Nov 1: The **richest prize in tournament golf history,** $384,000, was won by Tom Watson at the $3,000,000 Nabisco Championship at San Antonio, Tex. The first place money brought Watson's total PGA tournament earnings to $4,701,629 in 17 years on the PGA tour. Although Curtis Strange finished last in this tournament, he won the title for highest golf earnings in 1987, a record $925,941.

Nov 5: A **27,000-mile solo voyage around the world** was completed by Tanis Aebi, 21, at Sandy Hook, N.J. She had sailed from New York on May 25, 1985, in a 26-foot sloop, *Varuna*. Her record as a solo sailor will not go into the record books, however, because she gave an acquaintance an 80-mile ride between two Pacific islands.

Nov 18: Paying the **highest price ever for such a car,** a Providence, R.I., business partnership paid $1,600,000 at auction for a 1963 Ferrari 250 GTO racing car. The vehicle, a red, two-seat hardtop made in Italy, of which only 32 exist, had been confiscated by the federal government from a murdered drug dealer's estate.

1988

I. Civil Rights
Exploration and Settlement
Government
Statistics
Wars

The nation entered another presidential election year with the certainty that it would be selecting a new tenant for the White House since Ronald Reagan would have served the maximum two terms allowed by the Constitution. More citizens than ever would be eligible to vote, the Census Bureau noting on Apr. 4 that as of July 1, 1987, there were 90,031,000 households. Within those households, the median age of Americans was increasing, exceeding 32 for the first time: 32.1 on July 1, 1987. Since there were so many baby boomers born in the early post-World War II years, they were now producing children in large numbers. The government reported in August that there were 3,829,000 births in 1987, the most in nearly a quarter of a century. Whether baby boomers or not, Americans were deserting their farms. About 240,000 left such rural places in 1987, bringing the nation's farm population to its lowest level since before the Civil War. Notables who died this year included Burnita S. Matthews, the first woman to serve as a federal district court judge, appointed in 1949, Apr. 25, at 93; Franklin D. Roosevelt, Jr., son of the late president, a U.S. representative, Aug. 17, at 74; J. Skelly Wright, federal judge who was a pioneer in the desegregation of schools and transportation in New Orleans, Aug. 6, at 77.

Jan 2: One of the **largest inland oil spills** ever, 20 miles up the Monongahela River from Pittsburgh, Pa., dumped 860,000 gallons into the stream when a 40-year-old tank of the Ashland Oil Co. collapsed. Flowing into the Ohio River, the spill caused extensive damage to water supplies and wildlife before dissipating.

Feb 5: Gen. **Manuel Antonio Noriega,** the most powerful figure in the government of Panama since he became commander of the armed forces on Aug. 12, 1983, was indicted by a federal grand jury in Miami, Fla., in connection with illegal drug dealings. It was charged that he had received more than $4,600,000 in payoffs for allowing large-scale drug dealers to use airstrips under his protection. The president of Panama, Eric Arturo Delvalle, on Feb. 25 tried to remove him from his post, but the general's armed forces drove the president from office. On Mar. 2 the U.S. government said it had asked New York banks not to distribute any government funds to Noriega. This and other economic measures caused great distress in Panama but did not dislodge Noriega. It was announced on Mar. 19 that the general had refused an American offer to leave the country with a promise of no attempt to extradite him. On May 25 the Reagan administration admitted it had failed to oust Noriega and said it would not carry on any further negotiations with him.

Feb 11: A federal jury convicted **Lyn Nofziger,** former White House political director, on three counts of illegal lobbying under the 1978 Ethics in Government Act. The law forbids lobbying a federal agency for a year after a person has left it. Nofziger was charged with violating this law on behalf of the Wedtech Corp., which sought defense contracts, and two other clients. On Apr. 8 he was sentenced to 90 days in jail and fined $30,000.

Feb 17: U.S. Marine Lt. Col. **William R. Higgins was kidnaped** in southern Lebanon, presumably by Palestinian terrorists. His abduction brought to nine the number of Americans missing in Lebanon. One of them, Terry A. Anderson, a journalist, had been held since March 16, 1985.

Feb 24: The **right to criticize public figures** was strongly endorsed by the Supreme Court, 8–0, when it overturned a $200,000 award to the Rev. Jerry Falwell, founder of the Moral Majority. The award had been made on the basis of an insulting parody in *Hustler* magazine. The court said such free speech was to be protected even when it is "outrageous." Civil libertarians and press organizations hailed the decision.

Mar 16: In the **Iran-Contra affair** two key figures were indicted on charges of conspiracy to defraud the U.S. by illegally providing the Nicaraguan rebels with profits from the sale of American weapons to Iran. They were Vice Adm. John M. Poindexter and Marine Lt. Col. Oliver L. North. Indicted with them on 23 counts were two others involved in the scheme. The indictments came after a 14-month grand jury investigation conducted by independent prosecutor Lawrence E. Walsh. The indictments said that weapon sales to Iran totaled about $30,000,000 and that the U.S. government received $12,000,000. On June 8 the judge in the case ruled that the four defendants must be tried separately. The ruling permitted each defendant to use the testimony his codefendants gave to Congress. The ruling was seen as making it more difficult for the special prosecutor to obtain convictions. On June 9 Walsh announced he would bring North to trial first.

Mar 16: U.S. troops were ordered to Honduras on the basis of reports that 1500 or more Nicaraguan troops had made an incursion into Honduras to attack Contra bases there. The Nicaraguan government denied this. The American troops, four battalions of about 3200 men, were not involved in any fighting and were returned to the U.S. by Mar. 28.

Mar 22: The **Civil Rights Restoration Act** became law when both houses of Congress overrode a presidential veto. The new law stemmed from a Supreme Court decision of Feb. 28, 1984, known as the Grove City College case, in which the court held that if civil rights laws were violated in connection with a specific program receiving federal funds, other such programs at the same institution need not suffer. The new law said, in effect, that violations in connection with one program affected all parts of the institution receiving federal money.

Apr 1: Pres. Ronald Reagan signed legislation that provided $47,900,000 of **humanitarian aid for the Nicaraguan Contras.** The bill included $17,700,000 for children who were victims of the civil war. On Feb. 3, by a vote of 219–211, the House had rejected an administration proposal for $36,250,000 of aid that would have included money for military equipment.

Apr 4: The **governor of Arizona was convicted** of misconduct and removed from office by a vote of 21–9 in the state senate. It was the first impeachment trial of a governor in 60 years. Evan Mecham was found guilty of two charges of misconduct, one of which involved his lending $80,000 of state money to his auto dealership. He was also convicted of obstructing justice by trying to prevent an inquiry into charges that one of his aides had made a death threat against a grand jury witness. On June 16 a state jury found Mecham and his brother Willard not guilty of concealing a $350,000 campaign loan.

Apr 14: The **withdrawal of Soviet troops from Afghanistan,** which had invaded that country in Dec. 1979, was provided for in agreements signed by the U.S., the U.S.S.R., Afghanistan, and Pakistan. The U.S. and the Soviet Union agreed not to interfere in Afghan and Pakistani affairs, and Afghanistan and Pakistan would not interfere in each other's internal affairs. The troop withdrawal began on May 15.

Apr 18: The **U.S. Navy attacked Iranian forces** in the southern half of the Persian Gulf. The Americans destroyed two Iranian oil platforms and crippled or sank six armed Iranian ships. One American helicopter and its crew of two were lost. The U.S. said this strike was in retaliation for Iranian mining of gulf waters that resulted in damage to a Navy ship. On

Apr. 29 the government announced that U.S. forces in the gulf would broaden their mission and protect all neutral ships attacked by Iran.

Apr 28: An **explosionlike rupture of the fuselage** of an Aloha Airlines Boeing 737 jet flying at 24,000 feet between Hilo and Honolulu, Hawaii, resulted in the death of a flight attendant, swept to her death, and injuries to 60 of the 94 other persons aboard. The plane made an emergency landing safely. Investigators said the cause of the disaster was apparently structural failure.

May 4: An **explosion in a chemical plant** near Henderson, Nev., injured about 200 people. The shock of the explosion was felt for 15 miles and hundreds of windows were shattered in nearby Las Vegas. The plant, which was leveled by four blasts, made fuel for the NASA space shuttles. On June 7 military and space agency officials said the loss of the plant would cause severe fuel shortage in 1989 that would remain a problem into the 1990s.

May 14: The **head-on, fiery crash** of a pickup truck and a bus carrying 67 people near Carrollton, Ky., took the lives of 27, mostly teenagers, returning from a church youth outing. The driver of the truck, who was traveling the wrong way on an interstate highway, was charged two days later with 27 counts of capital murder. Police said he was drunk at the time of the accident.

May 23: Maryland became the **first state to ban the sale of cheap pistols,** effective Jan. 1, 1990. The ban covered the manufacture and sale of pistols that were determined to be easily concealed, inaccurate, unsafe, or poorly made. Provision was made to ban plastic guns also.

May 24: Pres. **Ronald Reagan vetoed a trade bill** that Congress had been working on for three years. The House overrode the veto the same day, 308–113, but on June 8 the Senate failed to register a two-thirds vote to override, 61–37. The president objected particularly to a provision that would require businesses to give 60 days' notice of plant closings or large-scale layoffs. In general the bill was protectionist, intending to defend the nation's industries against what were considered by its supporters unfair trading practices of other countries.

May 27: By a vote of 95–3, the **Senate ratified the Intermediate-Range Nuclear Forces Treaty,** which called for the elimination of land-based medium-range and short-range missiles now installed in Europe by the U.S. and the Soviet Union. It was the first U.S.-Soviet arms accord approved by the Senate since 1972. The official documents were rushed to Moscow so that formal ratifications could be ex-

changed by Pres. Reagan and General Secretary Gorbachev at their forthcoming summit meeting.

May 29-June 1: Their **fourth summit meeting** was held in Moscow by Pres. Reagan and General Secretary Gorbachev. The meeting was notable chiefly for the extent to which Reagan pushed Gorbachev on the matter of human rights in the Soviet Union and the irritation publicly expressed in return by the Communist leader. Although some progress was made on a number of issues, there was no movement on arms reductions.

June 21: The **annual economic summit conference** of the Group of Seven—the leading industrial democracies Canada, France, Great Britain, Italy, Japan, the U.S., and West Germany—ended in Toronto, Can., with the heads of government expressing satisfaction with and confidence in the economic outlook. They called on the rapidly industrializing nations of Asia to do more for the world economy. The seven nations could not agree on how to reduce the enormous subsidies paid their farmers to help them export their products. The seven leaders agreed to set up a high-level task force to coordinate the fight against the illegal drug traffic.

June 29: The constitutionality of a federal law providing for **independent prosecutors** to investigate high-ranking government officials suspected of criminal activities was upheld by the Supreme Court, 7–1. The decision was a sharp rebuff for the Reagan administration, which had argued that the law was unconstitutional because it encroached on the executive power of the president. The law, enacted in 1978 as a result of the Watergate scandal, allowed the special prosecutors to be appointed by a three-judge federal appellate court.

July 3: An **Iranian passenger jet was shot down** by a U.S. Navy warship at the southern end of the Persian Gulf when it was mistaken for an Iranian F-14 fighter plane. A missile fired from the cruiser *Vincennes* resulted in the death of all 290 persons aboard the Airbus A300. The cruiser at the time was fighting off attacks by Iranian gunboats. There was confusion over what sort of signals, if any, were received from the passenger jet that led the commander of the *Vincennes*, Capt. Will C. Rogers 3d, to believe that his ship was about to be attacked. On Aug. 2 it was revealed that the report of an investigation by the military blamed crew error caused by psychological stress on men in combat for the first time.

July 5: Attorney General **Edwin Meese 3d,** under criticism for some time for alleged criminal or ethical wrongdoing, announced he would resign later in the summer. He asserted that the report of an independent prosecutor, who had been investigating the high official for 14 months, "vindicated" him because it recommended that no criminal charges be brought. The report, made public on July 18, said that Meese had willfully filed a false income tax return but had intended to pay. It also said there was insufficient evidence to seek indictments in two other matters. One concerned Meese's ties to the Wedtech Corp. of New York City, which had apparently tried to bribe its way into government defense contracts. The other involved an aborted plan to build a $1,000,000,000 oil pipeline in Iraq, the negotiations for which might have violated the Foreign Corrupt Practices Act.

July 18-21: The **Democratic National Convention** nominated Gov. Michael S. Dukakis of Massachusetts for president and Sen. Lloyd M. Bentsen, Jr., of Texas for vice president.

Aug 4: Rep. **Mario Biaggi** of New York City was convicted in federal court on 15 felony counts as the Wedtech racketeering trial ended. The case arose through the use of the Wedtech Corp. of the Bronx, New York City, as a source for extorted bribes paid to the defendants, who had lobbied in Washington on behalf of Wedtech, which was seeking contracts as, originally, a minority-owned business. Five other defendants were also convicted. On Aug. 5 Biaggi announced he would resign his House seat but would appeal his conviction.

Aug 10: Interned Japanese-Americans who were forced into relocation camps during World War II would receive compensation for their ordeal, according to a bill signed by Pres. Reagan. The 120,000 surviving internees, about half the original number, and their beneficiaries would each receive $20,000 tax-free and an apology from the U.S. government.

Aug 15-18: The **Republican National Convention** nominated Vice Pres. George Bush of Texas for president and Sen. James Daniel Quayle of Indiana for vice president.

Aug 27: A **settlement of Indian land claims,** one of the largest in U.S. history, was confirmed by a vote of the tribe concerned, the Puyallup. The settlement gave the tribe $162 million in cash, land, and jobs, in return for surrendering further claims to land and buildings in Tacoma, Wash., valued at more than $750,000,000. Each adult member received $20,000 in cash at once; younger members would receive this sum when they reached 21.

Aug 31: So far this year 66,895 **forest fires** had burned 3.4 million acres in the U.S. It was the worst record since 1919 and approached the record of 1910, when more than 5 million acres were destroyed.

Sep 6: The **Hispanic population** of the U.S. had increased 34% since the 1980 census, the Census Bureau reported. There were now approximately 19.4 million people of Hispanic background, and they represented 8.1% of the total population. More than half of them lived in California and Texas.

Sep 14: The explosion of a **Soviet nuclear device** in Central Asia was witnessed for the first time by American officials. The U.S. government was in the process of deciding whether to agree to proposals that would allow each country to verify the other's underground tests.

Sep 22: Forest fires in Yellowstone National Park had by now burned half the park's 2.2 million acres in summer-long blazes. Controversy arose because park officials followed a policy of allowing naturally caused fires to burn themselves out.

Sep 30: Accidents in government-operated nuclear reactors at the Savannah River plant in South Carolina had been kept secret for as long as 31 years, Congressional committees reported. On Oct. 10 the Energy Dept. announced that it was shutting down the plutonium-processing plant near Boulder, Colo., because of safety problems. On Oct. 14 it was revealed that officials at a plant near Fernald, Ohio, knew for decades that it was releasing tons of radioactive uranium waste into the air. All the plants produced material for the nation's nuclear weapons.

Oct 3: Kidnapers released one hostage in Lebanon. He was Mithileshwar Singh, an Indian with resident alien status in the U.S. Nine Americans were still being held by terrorists.

Oct 13: A **welfare reform bill** was signed into law by Pres. Reagan. The most revolutionary change it made was to require single parents on welfare with children over three years old to get regular jobs. If they could not find work, they had to enroll in job training or educational courses. The law provided $3.34 billion for the first five years to carry out the law's provisions.

Oct 17: American military bases in the Philippines would continue to operate through Sept. 1991 by the terms of a modified agreement. The U.S. would provide the Philippines with $481 million a year in military and economic aid in 1990 and 1991. This was an increase over the current $180 million a year. The Subic Bay Naval Station and Clark Air Force Base were the two principal American installations.

Oct 18: Congress completed action on a bill to raise the **Veterans Administration** to Cabinet level. Pres. Reagan was expected to sign the measure. The Department of Veterans Affairs was to be officially established on Mar. 15, 1989. It would be the fifth addition to the Cabinet since 1953.

Nov 8: Vice President **George Bush,** the Republican candidate, was elected president of the United States, carrying 40 states. He defeated Governor Michael

Dukakis of Massachusetts, the Democratic candidate. The electoral college vote was Bush 426, Dukakis 112. The popular vote was Bush 47,917,341, Dukakis 41,013,030.

II. Architecture
Arts and Music
Popular Entertainment
Publishing
Theater

In box office receipts, the 1987–1988 Broadway theater season was the best ever. Theaters took in $253 million, an increase of 21% over the previous year. Musicals—such as *The Phantom of the Opera, Les Misérables, Starlight Express,* and *Me and My Girl*—accounted for most of the ticket sales. Dramas like *Speed-the-Plow, Joe Turner's Come and Gone,* and *Walk in the Woods* were critical successes. The catastrophe of the season was the musical *Carrie,* on which work began seven years before and which closed after 16 previews and 5 regular performances with a loss of $7,000,000. The most talked about movie of the year received most of its attention before the public saw it. This was *The Last Temptation of Christ,* based on the novel by Nikos Kazantzakis and directed by Martin Scorsese. It was vociferously condemned by fundamentalist Protestants and some Roman Catholics, who had not yet viewed it, as being blasphemous and sacrilegious. Many viewers found it a well-meant but not overly successful cinematic effort to show how Christ might have been tempted to give up the role of messiah and live an ordinary family life. Hollywood was said to be making more movies to appeal to older audiences, but the year's production did not attest to that except perhaps for such different films as *Broadcast News,* a comedy, and *The Unbearable Lightness of Being,* a love story from the novel by Milan Kundera. On the other hand there was the popular *Who Framed Roger Rabbit,* which cleverly used both animated and live characters. Other box office successes included *Coming to America,* in which comedian Eddie Murphy played an African prince; *Crocodile Dundee II,* again starring Paul Hogan as a he-man from the outback; and *Bull Durham,* a baseball comedy with sex. In television there were both bright and dim spots. With the start of its reruns *The Cosby Show* sold $60,000,000 worth of commercials immediately. But there was a falling off of network viewing by children, costing millions in lost advertising revenue. The continued growth of cable television was also a factor in the loss of revenue, with 45 million American homes now subscribing. VCR and videocassettes also affected the home

viewing market. Cassette sales continued to boom and were expected to reach nearly $7,000,000,000 in 1988, but there were so many videocassette stores selling and renting cassettes—25,000—that competition was driving profits down. A new recording by the group Run-D.M.C., *Tougher Than Leather,* was said to show that rap music was now in the mainstream of American culture. Rap began among young urban blacks, but now its rhymed chanting to a driving beat and its culture, known as hip-hop, were widely acceptable if not always respectable. The book publishing industry prospered, which perhaps accounted for the number of mergers, takeovers, and offers in the works. The big takeover news was the sale of the Crown Publishing Group to Random House on Aug. 15. No price was announced. One estimate projected the growth of book sales at an annual rate of 3.3% through 1992. Sales of children's books were increasing and might reach more than $800 million in 1988, double their sales of five years earlier. Export sales of American books were also expanding, to $739,000,000 in 1987, an increase in one year of 22%. Only in mass market paperbacks did the situation not seem rosy. Dollar sales were going up, but unit sales were down. Newspaper publishing was not as upbeat as book publishing. Although the number of households increased 41.4% from 1970 to 1987, weekday newspaper circulation rose only 1% and Sunday circulation 22.4%. Among notable persons who died were the poet Leonie Adams, June 27, at 88; Romare Bearden, collagist, Mar. 12, at 75; Barry Bingham, Sr., newspaper publisher, Aug. 15, at 82; Milton A. Caniff, comic strip artist, creator of *Terry and the Pirates,* Apr. 3, at 81; singer and actress Hazel Dawn, Aug. 28, at 98; Dennis Day, singer and comic with the Jack Benny radio show, June 22, at 71; Florence Eldridge, stage and movie star, Aug. 1, at 86; Gil Evans, jazz composer and arranger, Mar. 20, at 75; Robert A. Heinlein, science fiction writer, May 8, at 80; Robert Joffrey, founder and artistic director of the ballet troupe bearing his name, Mar. 25, at 57; Jim Jordan, star of the radio show *Fibber McGee and Molly,* Apr. 1, at 91; Louis L'Amour, author of best-selling westerns, June 10, at 80; composer Frederick Loewe, Feb. 14, at 86; Joshua L. Logan, Broadway director, July 12, at 79; James McCracken, dramatic tenor, Apr. 30, at 61; Colleen Moore, who in the silent movies was the personification of the 1920s flapper, Jan. 25, at 87; Louise Nevelson, pioneering artist in creating environmental sculpture, Apr. 17, at 88; Melvin James "Cy" Oliver, jazz composer and orchestra leader, May 27, at 77; Irene Rich, star of silent movies, Apr. 22, at 96; Adela Rogers St. John, journalist, author, and screenwriter, Aug. 10, at 94; Max Shulman, humorist and creator of the TV character Dobie Gillis, Aug. 28, at 69.

Among **books published** this year were *A Brief History of Time* by Stephen W. Hawking and *Chaos: Making a New Science* by James Gleick. Biographies included *Freud: A Life for Our Times* by Peter Gay and *Oscar Wilde* by Richard Ellmann. Historians offered *Battle Cry of Freedom* by James M. McPherson, a vivid account of the Civil War, and *Reconstruction: America's Unfinished Revolution* by Eric Foner. Fiction as usual offered a wide range of subject matter: *The Tenants of Time*, about 19th-century Ireland, by Thomas Flanagan; *Libra*, a recounting of the Kennedy Assassination by Don DeLillo; *Quinn's Book*, set in 19th-century Albany, N.Y., by William Kennedy; and *The Mysteries of Pittsburgh*, a coming-of-age first novel by Michael Chabon. There were, too, the usual assortment of readable suspense and mystery stories, such as *Freaky Deaky* by Elmore Leonard and *The Cardinal of the Kremlin* by Tom Clancy.

Mar 20: An exhibition of **art treasures from the Hermitage Museum** in Leningrad opened at the Metropolitan Museum in New York, consisting of 51 Dutch and Flemish paintings from the 17th century, most of which had never been seen in the U.S. The exhibit was to go to the Art Institute of Chicago, which was the joint organizer with the Metropolitan of the exhibit. In exchange, the two American museums arranged a display of 51 19th- and early-20th-century French paintings that will be seen at the Hermitage and later in Moscow.

Mar 31: Pulitzer prizes were awarded for the following: fiction, *Beloved* by Toni Morrison; general nonfiction, *The Making of the Atomic Bomb* by Richard Rhodes; biography, *Look Homeward: A Life of Thomas Wolfe* by David Herbert Donald; history, *The Launching of Modern American Science, 1846–1876* by Robert V. Bruce; poetry, *Partial Accounts: New and Selected Poems* by William Meredith; drama, *Driving Miss Daisy* by Alfred Uhry.

Apr 1: The **first nightly news anchorman** in American broadcasting retired. He was Douglas Edwards, who joined the CBS radio network in 1942 and held the anchor position for 20 years.

Apr 8: Grolier, Inc., an American publisher of educational and reference materials, agreed to be taken over by Hachette S. A., a French book and magazine publisher, for about $450,000,000. On Apr. 13 Hachette became the largest magazine publisher in the world, with 74 publications in ten countries, by acquiring an American company, Diamandis Communications, Inc., for $712,000,000.

Apr 25: Publishing rights to a **sequel to *Gone With the Wind*** by Margaret Mitchell, one of the most popular novels of all time, were sold to Warner Books in an auction for $4,940,000. The sequel, which was scheduled for publication in 1990, was to be written by Alexandra Ripley, author of four novels. *Gone With the Wind* was published in 1936 and had sold about 25,000,000 copies.

May 2: A **Jackson Pollock painting,** *Search* (1955), was purchased at auction in New York for $4,800,000, a record for the artist and for any post-World War II work of art. The purchaser was a Tokyo art dealer. On May 3, also at auction, Jasper Johns's *Diver* (1962), sold for $4,200,000, a record for the artist. The buyer was not identified.

May 3: Andy Warhol's collection of art and other objects sold for a total of $25,300,000 over a ten-day period of auctions. About 10,000 items were disposed of in the largest auction ever held by Sotheby's in New York. Warhol, who died in 1987, had an enormous collection of cookie jars, which brought $247,030. Other items included paintings, pottery, antiques, folk art, and American Indian art.

May 10: A **record price for any work of sculpture** was paid at auction in New York when *Little Dancer at 14 Years of Age* by Edgar Degas was sold for $10,120,000. An unidentified European was the purchaser. The bronze of Degas's 1881 wax sculpture is 37½ inches tall.

May 11: The **100th birthday of Irving Berlin,** America's most prolific and popular song writer, was celebrated with a gala concert at Carnegie Hall in New York City. Among the well-known performers paying tribute were Frank Sinatra, Willie Nelson, Ray Charles, Marilyn Horne, and Leonard Bernstein. Mr. Berlin could not attend but planned to watch the taped telecast.

May 18: Howard Nemerov, 68, was named the third **poet laureate** of the U.S., having been appointed by the Librarian of Congress.

June 7: Papers of Saul Bellow, consisting of notebooks, typescripts, and other materials relating to his novel *Mr. Sammler's Planet* (1969), were sold in New York City for $66,000, a record at auction for a work by a living author. It was the first manuscript the author, winner of the Nobel Prize for Literature in 1976, had sold. The items were bought as an anonymous gift to be presented to the Berg Collection of the New York Public Library.

June 15: A **new edition of James Joyce's *Ulysses*** published four years earlier became the center of a lively literary controversy. The edition, prepared by a team of German scholars, was claimed to correct some 5000 omissions, transpositions, and other errors in earlier editions. But John Kidd of the University of Virginia, in an 8000-word article in *The New York Review of Books,* said the edition had more flaws than its predecessors. Other scholars supported Kidd. As a result Random House, publisher of *Ulysses* in the U.S. since 1933, asked a textual scholar, G. Thomas Tanselle of Columbia University, to organize a committee to decide which edition it should publish.

Aug 7: The **sale of Triangle Publications,** Inc., publisher of *TV Guide,* the *Daily Racing Form,* and *Seventeen* magazine, to Rupert Murdoch, Australian publishing magnate with interests in the U.S., Great Britain, and Australia, was announced. At $3,000,000,000 the deal was the largest takeover ever in publishing.

Sep 17: The **Art Institute of Chicago** opened a large new gallery of 66,640 square feet. Limestone-sheathed, it was designed to blend with the original Beaux-Arts building of the Institute. The new building cost $23 million.

Sep 27: Soviet and American curators for the first time organized jointly a museum exhibition. It was entitled "Crossroads of Continents: Cultures of Siberia and Alaska" and opened for a six-month stay at the Smithsonian Institution, Washington, D.C. The exhibit contained nearly 600 objects showing the prehistoric life of peoples in those parts of the world.

Sep 29: Union Station in Washington, D.C., reopened after renovations that cost $160 million. The 81-year-old classical-style station was appropriate in its grandeur to a period when railroad travel was at its peak and when the U.S. capital was becoming an imperial city. It had been neglected and had gone to ruin since a failed attempt to renew it in 1976. It now had shops, restaurants, and theaters.

Oct 8: A very large collection of **Italian Renaissance manuscripts** and other documents had been acquired by Yale University. The material comprised the 500-year-old archives of the Spinelli banking family of Florence. The approximately 150,000 documents included business records as well as correspondence with a number of popes and such major figures as Lorenzo de' Medici.

III. Business and Industry
Education
Philosophy and Religion
Science

More than halfway through 1988, the national economy showed strong growth but also an increase in inflation. As a result, the Federal Reserve on Aug. 9 raised its discount rate a half point, to 6.5%. Banks in turn increased their prime rate to 10%, the highest since June 1985. In July the nation's factories, mines, and utilities operated at their highest level in eight years, aiding economic growth but also causing inflationary pressures. In June the unemployment rate, at 5.2%, was at its lowest since May 1974. It rose to 5.5% in August, but this in turn reduced fears of rising inflation. The most serious problem facing the economy was the Midwest and Southwest drought, with conditions not seen since the Dust Bowl years of the 1930s. In August the Department of Agriculture estimated that the grain harvest would be 31% lower than in 1987. Farmers were losing income and consumers could expect to pay higher prices for food. The government appropriated $3.9 billion for farm relief. In foreign trade, there was considerable improvement because the decrease in the value of the dollar stimulated exports of American goods. Imports, however, did not decrease as much as expected, so that the foreign trade deficit was not lowered very much. The environment was not in as good shape as the economy. In June a NASA scientist said global warming had begun, the earth having been warmer in the first five months of 1988 than in any comparable period in the past 130 years. The Environmental Protection Agency reported that clean air standards for ozone were violated in 1987 in more areas than before. The Fish and Wildlife Service revealed that the development of oil fields in northern Alaska had done far more environmental damage than the government originally predicted. For education, the report card showed mixed grades. At the college level the demand for admission was so great that some students near the top in high school were not being admitted anywhere. At the public school level, the children of the baby boomers were forcing the reopening of schools closed in the 1970s and early 1980s when the school population dropped. Young Americans who made it to college were revealed to be sadly lacking in geographical knowledge. In a survey of nine countries they ranked lowest. A bright spot was the growing interest young people were showing in the teaching profession. Education schools reported increases of up to 50% in applications. More racial unrest at predominantly white universities was noticeable and black students reported they were not welcome. Secretary of Education William J. Bennett stirred controversy when he said in April that the overall performance of American schools was "unacceptably low," an evaluation at once challenged by a number of educators. Charitable donations for religious, educational, and other purposes were a record $93.6 billion in 1987, but the rate of increase was the lowest in 12 years, which was blamed on the stock market collapse and the new income tax law. On July

27 the surgeon general of the U.S., in the most comprehensive report on nutrition and health ever issued by the government, said fat was a leading cause of disease and that its overconsumption was a major American health problem. In the business world, a boom in facsimile-transmission machines marked the year. Documents were being sent across the country in 20 seconds. American business was active in the Soviet Union. Pepsico, Inc., producer of Pepsi-Cola, claimed the honor of being the first American company to buy commercial time on Soviet TV, as of May 17. McDonald's in April prepared to open 20 stores in Moscow to sell the Big Mac—*Bolshoi Mak* in Russian. Notable persons who died in 1988 included Luis W. Alvarez, Nobel Prize-winning physicist, Sept. 1, at 77; John Cardinal Dearden, liberal Catholic prelate and archbishop of Detroit, Aug. 1, at 80; Richard F. Feynman, Nobel Prize-winning theoretical physicist, Feb. 15, at 69; Raymond W. Goldsmith, economist, July 12, at 83; James R. Killian, Jr., in 1957 the first presidential assistant for science and technology and president of MIT, Jan. 29, at 83; Gardiner C. Means, economist, Feb. 15, at 91; Jackie Presser, president of the International Brotherhood of Teamsters, July 9, at 61; Isidor Isaac Rabi, pioneer atomic scientist and Nobel Prize winner Jan. 11, at 89; Sewall Wright, geneticist who established a mathematical basis for evolution, Mar. 3, at 98.

Jan 8: The **stock market plunge of Oct. 19, 1987,** was blamed on automatic trading programs of large money management firms, which generated huge sell orders, in a report of the Presidential Task Force on Market Mechanisms. The task force recommended that the Federal Reserve Board be made responsible for regulating trading. On Feb. 2 a staff report of the Securities and Exchange Commission said the crash was accelerated by trading in stock futures. It recommended that certain computerized trading in such futures be limited and that higher margins be required. The NYSE announced on Feb. 4 that it would curb the use of its electronic trading system when the Dow Jones average of industrial stocks rose or fell more than 50 points in a day.

Jan 13: The **oldest and most distant objects ever seen in the universe** were detected by astronomers, according to a report made before the American Astronomical Society. The objects appeared to be beyond any observed quasar and, being perhaps 17,000,000,000 years old, their radiations were coming from the creation of some of the universe's first galaxies.

Jan 28: The **risk of heart attack among men** could be sharply reduced by taking one aspirin tablet every other day, according to a report in *The New England Journal of Medicine.* The report was the result of a nationwide study carried on over a five-year period. On Jan. 30 a report involving 5000 British doctors found no strong evidence of this effect.

Jan 28: Controversy over a **nuclear power plant** caused the Public Service Co. of New Hampshire to file for bankruptcy. The Seabrook plant, 15 years in construction, was completed in July 1986 at a cost of $5,200,000,000 but had never been granted an operating license because of disputes over emergency evacuation plans. On May 27, in a similar dispute about emergency evacuation, the Long Island Lighting Co. agreed with New York State to abandon plans to operate its Shoreham nuclear plant, which over 20 years had cost $5,300,000,000 without ever being put to use.

Mar 14: A **treaty to protect the earth's ozone shield** was ratified by the Senate, 83–0, making the U.S. the first major user and producer of chlorofluorocarbons to approve an international agreement reached in Montreal in Sept. 1987. The agreement first froze and then called for a rollback of the use of such chemicals, which are believed to damage the ozone in the upper atmosphere. On Mar. 24 E. I. du Pont de Nemours & Co., the world's largest producer of chlorofluorocarbons, announced plans to phase out all production of such chemicals.

Mar 15: The **first black Catholic archbishop** in the U.S. was named by Pope John Paul II. Eugene Antonio Marino was installed on May 5 as head of the Archdiocese of Atlanta.

Apr 1: The **largest department store takeover** in the U.S. was completed when Federated Department Stores, Inc., accepted a bid of $6,600,000,000 from the Campeau Corp. of Canada. The deal was the fifth largest acquisition in U.S. history. Fifteen months earlier Campeau had purchased another American department store chain, Allied Stores Corp., for $3,600,000,000.

Apr 6: Matthew Alexander Henson, the black American who reached the North Pole with Robert E. Peary 79 years earlier on this date, was reburied in Arlington National Cemetery. Henson spent most of his life after 1909 in obscurity as a clerk in the Customs House in New York City, and when he died in 1955 at 88 he was buried in Woodlawn Cemetery, New York City.

Apr 8: Television evangelist the Rev. **Jimmy Swaggart was defrocked** as a minister of the Assemblies of God after he rejected punishment ordered by the church. He had been directed to stop preaching for a year after he publicly confessed "moral failure" on Feb. 21 following reports that he had committed lewd acts with a prostitute. He left his pulpit on Feb. 21 but on

May 22 Swaggart appeared in the pulpit of his Family Worship Center in Baton Rouge, La., preaching without ministerial credentials.

Apr 11: Expansion of the **roles of women in the Roman Catholic Church** was recommended by a committee of Catholic bishops. Women's leadership roles would be expanded at almost all levels of the church except the priesthood. The report also condemned the "sin of sexism." Women should be encouraged to preach and to distribute communion, and the possibility of ordaining women as deacons should be studied.

Apr 12: The **world's first patent for a higher form of life,** a mouse, was issued to Harvard University. The patent for "transgenic nonhuman mammals" was in the names of two scientists, Dr. Philip Leder and Dr. Timothy A. Stewart, who injected a gene that causes cancer in many mammals into fertilized mouse eggs and so developed a new breed of genetically altered mice. The patented mouse was a more effective model for studying how genes contribute to the development of cancer.

Apr 13: Christian, Moslem, and Jewish **fundamentalism was rejected** by the Conservative movement of Judaism in the first statement of principles in its 143-year history. Conservative Judaism, the report said, should follow a moderate course, with loyalty to tradition but "without resigning from the 20th century." The report was the work of 35 scholars, rabbis, and laypeople.

Apr 22: A popular **antiacne drug caused severe birth defects,** according to the Food and Drug Administration. The drug, Accutane, was estimated to have caused defects in 900 to 1300 babies between 1982 and 1986. The drug's use may also have caused 700 to 1000 spontaneous abortions. Hoffmann-La Roche, maker of the drug, asserted that only 62 cases of birth defects were the result of taking Accutane. On Apr. 26 the FDA recommended that distribution of Accutane be greatly restricted.

Apr 23: A **ban on smoking** in passenger planes went into effect. The no-smoking rule applied to all flights of two hours or less, except for travel clubs, charter trips, and flights to foreign destinations. Northwest Airlines announced it would ban smoking on all domestic flights regardless of their duration.

Apr 25: The **largest U.S. corporation** in 1987, according to *Fortune* magazine, was General Motors, with sales of $101,781,900,000. Exxon was second, with sales of $76,416,000,000.

May 1: The Reagan administration announced an **increase in arms sales abroad.** Its aim was to sell $15,000,000,000 worth, which would be $3,000,000,000 more than it sold in the previous fiscal year. In that year another $2,000,000,000 worth was sold for export directly by manufacturers.

May 13: A **second genetic code** had been deciphered, according to a report in *Nature* by two scientists at MIT. This code directed one of several steps in the synthesis of proteins inside cells. Solution to the problem had been sought by molecular biologists for 20 years. It was a step in providing scientists a way to make proteins to order.

May 13: The **drug AZT** prolonged the lives of AIDS patients, according to the company that produced it. Of 144 patients who participated in the first human trials of azidothymidine (AZT), 84.5% were alive after one year. So far, however, experiments seeking a vaccine were discouraging. With nearly 35,000 Americans reported to have died of AIDS, Congress and Pres. Reagan approved a $1 billion program for education, treatment, and research.

May 16: Only slight changes in the **operations of stock markets** was recommended by the White House Working Group, the third federal government body to study the stock market crash of Oct. 19, 1987. The principal proposal was that trading be halted for one hour on all U.S. markets if any one of them fell or rose the equivalent of 250 points on the Dow Jones industrial average. Most experts were surprised that the group had so little to suggest and felt that the recommendations did not go far enough to prevent another crash.

May 26: A **health advisory about AIDS,** in the form of a pamphlet, was mailed by the federal government to every American with a mailing address. No such mailing had ever been made before. Written in language the 12-to-13-year level, the pamphlet was printed in an edition of 110 million copies in English and 4 million in Spanish.

May 29: Two **new American cardinals** of the Roman Catholic Church were among 25 prelates named to the high posts by Pope John Paul II. The Americans, who were officially installed on June 28, were James Aloysius Hickey of Washington and Edmund Casimir Szoka of Detroit. The appointments brought to ten the number of U.S. cardinals.

June 13: A **cigarette manufacturer** was found guilty for the first time in the cancer death of a longtime smoker. A federal jury in New Jersey awarded $400,000 damages to Antonio Cipollone, whose wife, Rose, died in 1984 and had smoked heavily for 40 years. However, the Liggett Group, found liable, and other tobacco companies were found not guilty of the charge that they had fraudulently misrepresented the risks of smoking and had conspired to misrepresent facts. The suit was the first of more than 300 since 1954 in which any tobacco company had lost a case.

June 14: The **Southern Baptist Convention** for the tenth consecutive year elected a conservative as its president. The victor was the Rev. Jerry Vines of Jacksonville, Fla., but he won by only 692 votes out of 31,274 cast by delegates. One of the most divisive issues was control of teaching at the denomination's seminaries. On June 16 the delegates voted to condemn homosexuality as "a manifestation of a depraved nature" and "a perversion of divine standards."

June 14: The **General Assembly of the Presbyterian Church** (U.S.A.) adopted a statement on Christian responsibilities in the nuclear age that declared nuclear war immoral. The statement said that under some circumstances noncooperation or disobedience to civil authority "has been deemed an appropriate Christian response." On June 25 the Roman Catholic bishops of the U.S. approved a report that questioned the morality of deploying a system of space-based defenses against missiles.

June 15: More than half of all **new mothers remained in the job market** for the first time in the nation's history, the Census Bureau reported. The figure reached 50.8% in 1987. Of new mothers with college degrees, 63% remained in the work force, compared with 38% of those with only a high school education. It was noted that women who had more education and more work experience before having children were better able to afford child care.

June 17: A federal law to **ban discrimination** against AIDS victims was recommended by a divided presidential commission appointed to consider all aspects of the spread of the disease. The Reagan administration did not at once accept this recommendation. In all, the commission's report contained almost 600 recommendations. One of them said "a top national priority" should be given to the problem of intravenous drug users.

June 20: Agreement was reached on a **new U.S.-Japanese trade pact** concerning the import of American beef and citrus products into Japan. Although under the arrangement U.S. exports will increase only about $1,000,000,000 a year, the dispute over these two items had been a symbolic one in America's effort to break down Japan's stiff barriers to trade. Under the terms of the agreement, Japan's import quotas on beef and fresh oranges will be abolished in three years and the quota on orange juice in four.

June 21: No cavities or other tooth decay were reported by half the nation's school children, according to a federal government survey. The increase to 49.9% of those with no decay, compared with 36.6% in a 1979–1980 survey, was attributed to the widespread use of fluoride and the high level of dental care. Officials said that if the situation continued to improve it would mean the end of dental disease as a major public health problem.

June 27: Surrogate motherhood was banned by a state for the first time when Gov. James J. Blanchard of Michigan signed a bill that outlawed commercial contracts for women to bear children for others. Other state legislatures were considering similar measures.

July 1: A **catastrophic health care bill** was signed by Pres. Reagan. Effective Jan. 1, 1989, it provided the first major expansion of the Medicare program. Among its provisions were unlimited free hospital care after the recipient pays the first $564 annually; unlimited free physician care after the first $1400 annually; and an increase in payments for nursing-home care. Premiums were increased to pay the new costs.

July 3: A 19th-century **American woman was canonized** by Pope John Paul II at the Vatican. Sister Rose Philippine Duchesne, born in France in 1769 and who immigrated to the U.S. in 1818, was the fourth American to attain sainthood in the Roman Catholic Church. Sister Duchesne, who died in 1852, founded dozens of schools and a convent for young women as well as directing the American branch of her order, the Society of the Sacred Heart. Most of her work was done on the midwestern frontier, where she also nursed Indians and tried to spread Christianity among them. She opened in St. Charles, Mo., a free school that was the first such institution in the West.

July 11: The **General Convention of the Episcopal Church** closed in an atmosphere of compromise on several issues. On the subject of sexual morality, the delegates reaffirmed "the biblical and traditional teaching of chastity and fidelity," but also called for "an open dialogue" on human sexuality. Anticipating the likelihood of women becoming bishops, the convention provided for bishops to come in from outside a diocese where churches were at odds with their local bishop over women as clergy.

Aug 2: A bill requiring **notice of plant closings** became law without Pres. Reagan's signature. He opposed the bill but heeded Republican appeals that vetoing it would hurt the party's election chances in the fall. Under the bill's terms, a company with 100 or more full-time employees must give 60 days notice of plans to close a plant. The same notice must be given if 500, or a third, of a plant's workers are to be laid off.

Aug 17: The first joint American-Soviet **nuclear test verification experiment** took place in Nevada. Teams of U.S. and Soviet scientists used different methods to determine the strength of a nuclear blast of an American device.

Aug 17: The **first hair growth drug** was approved for marketing by the Food and Drug Administration. It was a prescription drug called Rogaine and beneficial only under certain circumstances. A study of 1833 men found that 15% to 20% had cosmetically significant hair growth by using it.

Aug 23: A **foreign trade bill** with protectionist overtones was signed by Pres. Reagan. Covering a large number of areas, the new law was aimed particularly at what was alleged to be unfair trading practices of other nations. A most important provision allowed the president to negotiate international agreements to enlarge the markets for goods and services such as banking and insurance.

Sep 1: Colon and rectal cancer, in more than half such cases, could be traced to genetic predisposition, according to a new study. In the U.S. colon and rectal cancer cause more cancer deaths than any other form except lung cancer in men and breast cancer in women. The study showed that about a third of white Americans have this genetic disposition.

Sep 19: A **free trade agreement** with Canada was approved by the Senate, 83–9, completing U.S. action. The agreement would do away with almost all trade barriers and tariffs by 1999. The Canadian House of Commons had previously approved the agreement.

Sep 20: The **first Hispanic member** of the president's Cabinet took office as secretary of education. He was Lauro F. Cavazos, since 1980 president of Texas Tech University.

Sep 24: The **first woman to be elected a bishop** of the Episcopal Church was chosen to be suffragan bishop of the Diocese of Massachusetts. She was the Rev. Barbara C. Harris, a black who had been a priest for eight years.

Sep 28: A **bill to limit textile imports** was vetoed by Pres. Reagan. The bill would have limited the increase of textile imports to 1% per year and would have frozen at current levels the importation of footwear not made of rubber. On Oct. 4 the House of Representatives failed to override the veto by a vote of 272–152.

Sep 29-Oct 3: The **first U.S. manned space flight in 32 months** took place with five astronauts aboard the space shuttle *Discovery.* In the course of its journey the *Discovery* successfully launched a $100 million communications satellite. It was the first American manned flight in space since the *Challenger* blew up shortly after blastoff, on Jan. 28, 1986.

Oct 17: The **largest consumer products company in the world** would be formed by a proposed takeover of Kraft Inc. by Philip Morris Companies Inc. The latter offered $11.5 billion for Kraft. It would be the largest takeover in history after the $13.3 billion takeover of Gulf Oil Corp. by Chevron Corp. in 1984.

Oct 17: The **Nobel Prize in Physiology or Medicine** was awarded jointly to two Americans, Gertrude B. Elion and George H. Hitchings of the Burroughs Wellcome Co., and a Briton, James Black of London. The award was given for discoveries of "important principles for drug treatment." The winners developed drugs for treating such ailments as heart disease, gout, leukemia, and peptic ulcers.

Oct 19: The **Nobel Prize in Physics** was awarded to three Americans: Leon M. Lederman, of the Fermi National Accelerator Laboratory; Melvin Schwartz, of Digital Pathways Inc.; and Jack Steinberger, of the European Center for Nuclear Research. They received the award for their experiments in the early 1960s that produced the first laboratory-made beam of neutrinos. This work made possible detailed studies of radioactive decay involving the "weak" nuclear force.

IV. Fashion
Folkways
Holidays
Social Issues and Crime
Sports

Statistics reported in April for 1987 showed that baseball was still the national game. It attracted 88,200,000 spectators. Horse racing came in second with attendance at 73,600,000, followed by football with 50,000,000 fans. By opening day of the 1988 baseball season, the game had set a salary record: major league owners were paying their players a total of $300,511,924 for the season. The men who officiated at professional sports did not do as well. Major league umpires and NBA referees earned a maximum of $100,000, while the NFL paid $1,800 per regular game. "Tomboy" was an obsolete word, said a Penn State professor in reporting that 82% of today's young women participated in sports. The 100th anniversary of golf in the U.S. was observed on June 20 at the St. Andrews Golf Club in Hastings-on-Hudson, N.Y., near where the first match was played. On the consumer front Americans had new, if not better, products to rush out and buy. Among them was a fake automobile telephone, of which 40,000 had been sold at $9.95; a vending machine that cooked french fries while you wait; perfume and other cosmetics for babies, under such names as Eau de Senteur; a stopper to keep champagne corks on a four-inch leash; chocolate that would not melt in hot weather; and gourmet dog food for overweight pooches. In a more practical way of life, a survey found that teenagers were into cooking, and not just with microwave ovens. One survey of 2200 young people found that 80% said they had cooked a meal for themselves in the previous week. On the crime front, the Justice Department reported that there were 581,609 inmates in state and federal prisons, an increase of 6.7% in a year and more than double the 1970 prison population. Notable persons who died included Alan Ameche, Baltimore Colts running back, Aug. 8, at 55; Gregory "Pappy" Boyington, Marine ace of World War II who shot down 28 Japanese planes and won the Medal of Honor, Jan. 11, at 75; Glenn Cunningham, world-record holder for the mile, Mar. 10, at 78; Robert Lee "Bobby" Dodd, famed football coach at the Georgia Institute of Technology, June 21, at 79; Ted Kluszewski, slugging first baseman, Mar. 29, at 63; Peter Press "Pete" Maravich, college and professional basketball star whose 3667 points in his college career remained a record, Jan. 5, at 40; Arthur Joseph Rooney, Sr., a leading American sportsman and founder of the Pittsburgh Steelers of the NFL, Aug. 25, at 87; Edd Roush, twice batting champion of the National League, 1917 and 1919, Mar. 21, at 94.

Jan 31: Super Bowl XXII was won by the Washington Redskins (NFC), who defeated the Denver Broncos (AFC) 42–10. On Jan. 17 the Redskins had defeated the Minnesota Vikings 17–10 to win the NFC championship and the Broncos had beaten the Cleveland Browns 38–33 for the AFC title.

Feb 9: New York City's largest single **art theft** occurred when 18 paintings and 10 drawings valued at $6,000,000 were taken from the Colnaghi Ltd. gallery on the Upper East Side. The most valuable items taken were two paintings by Fra Angelico.

Feb 13-28: The **XVth Olympic Winter Games,** held in Calgary, Can., saw the U.S. win only six medals: two gold, one silver, and three bronze. The two American gold medalists were Brian Boitano, men's figure skating champion, and Bonnie Blair, winner of the women's 500-meter speed skating event. The Soviet Union took the most medals, 29, including 11 gold. East Germany was second with a total of 25.

Feb 27: A **new round-the-world speed record** was set by a Gulfstream IV jet when it landed in Houston after a flight of 36 hrs., 8 min. The former record had been set as recently as Jan. 30 by a Boeing 747SP, which made the flight in 36 hrs., 54 min., 15 sec.

Mar 31: The U.S. and Italy joined in a **drug case** that brought charges against 233 suspected members of a Sicilian Mafia drug ring. More than 100 suspects were under arrest. The investigation had been underway for more than two years. Italian officials said it showed that all three of Italy's major underworld organizations were involved in the drug trade and that New York's Mafia families had had more contact with them than previously thought.

Apr 4: The **NCAA men's basketball championship** was won by Kansas, which defeated Oklahoma 83 to 79.

Apr 20: The New York Yankees became the first team to hit more than 10,000 **home runs** in the major leagues when Jack Clark hit no. 10,001. It was his first home run of the season.

Apr 22: For the first time in its 37 years, the **Little 500,** a bicycle race held on the Indiana University campus in Bloomington, included an event for women's teams. Hitherto women had been restricted to a tricycle race and cheering the men. The Willkie Sprint team, representing a dormitory quadrangle, won this first women's event.

Apr 28: By **losing 21 consecutive games** at the start of the baseball season, the Baltimore Orioles set an American League record. They then won a game, but followed that with two more losses. The previous mark of 20 losses was set by Boston in 1906 and tied in 1916 and 1943 by Philadelphia.

May 2: The **most severe penalty** ever imposed on a major league baseball manager for an on-field incident was handed Pete Rose of the Cincinnati Reds by the president of the NL. Rose was suspended for 30 days for an incident in a game on Apr. 30 when he disputed a call by an umpire and pushed him. Aroused by comments of broadcasters of the game, fans threw a variety of things onto the field and forced one umpire to flee to safety.

May 3: The **largest cocaine seizure** in U.S. history was made by officials at Tarpon Springs, Fla., when they found 9200 pounds of the drug in hollowed-out lumber that had been shipped from Colombia. The cocaine was estimated to have a street value of more than $2,000,000,000. The largest previous cocaine seizure occurred in Fort Lauderdale, Fla., in Nov. 1987, when 8700 pounds were found.

May 4: Anthony "Fat Tony" Salerno, reputed to be the boss of the Genovese crime family, was convicted with eight other men of racketeering. The numerous crimes he was charged with included a multimillion-dollar scheme to rig bids in the construction industry. Those convicted faced up to 20 years in prison on the racketeering charge. Salerno was already serving a 100-year sentence for his conviction as a member of the Mafia's ruling "commission."

May 18: "Casey at the Bat," a poetic baseball classic and one of the most often recited poems in the English language, marked its 100th anniversary. On May 18, 1888, at Wallack's Theater in New York City, it was first recited by the popular actor William De Wolfe Hopper, who went on to repeat his performance about 10,000 times over the years. The saga of the mighty baseball hero who failed in the clutch was written by a 25-year-old Harvard graduate, Ernest L. Thayer. It was first published on June 3, 1888, in the San Francisco *Examiner* and Thayer was paid $5.

May 19: Carlos Lehder Rivas was convicted of smuggling tons of cocaine into the U.S. Lehder was the reputed leader of a violent Colombian drug ring and, with a codefendant, was found guilty of conspiring to bring 3.3 tons of cocaine into the U.S. between 1978 and 1980. Lehder could be sentenced to life plus 150 years in prison and fined up to $350,000.

June 7-21: The **NBA basketball championship** was won by the Los Angeles Lakers, defeating the Detroit Pistons four games to three. It was the first time since 1969 that a team had won the title two years in succession.

June 12: The **Tour of Italy bicycle race** was won by an American for the first time since the race was first held in 1909. The winner was Andy Hampsten, 26, who dropped out of the University of North Dakota to take up bicycling. He defeated 198 other cyclists and finished 1 min., 43 sec. ahead of his nearest challenger. The Tour of Italy is considered second only to the Tour de France in importance in professional bike racing.

June 20: A law to force the **admission of women to private clubs** was upheld unanimously by the Supreme Court. At issue was a New York City law requiring women to be admitted to large, private clubs that are said to play important roles in business and professional life. In New York the University Club had already voted to admit women. By the end of August the Union League Club, the Century Association, and the Friars Club in New York agreed to admit women. The Friars Club in California admitted its first female member in 1987. On June 18 the exclusive Cosmos Club in Washington, D.C., unassailably male for 110 years, voted by a large majority to accept women. It too had been threatened with legal action.

June 20: The **U.S. Open golf tournament** was won by Curtis Strange, who defeated Nick Faldo by four strokes in an 18-hole playoff.

June 25: "Axis Sally" died. Mildred E. Gillars (see Mildred Elizabeth Sisk) received her nickname during World War II, when, although an American citizen, she broadcast Nazi propaganda to U.S. troops fighting in Europe. Ms. Gillars was said to have been influenced by her lover, Max O. Koischwitz, a German

citizen and foreign-office official, who had at one time taught at Hunter College in New York City. After the war Ms. Gillars was arrested and tried for treason. Convicted, she was sentenced to 10 to 30 years in prison and fined $10,000. Ms. Gillars was released after 12 years and later taught music in a convent school in Columbus, Ohio, having earned a bachelor's degree in music in 1973.

June 27: The **heavyweight boxing championship** of the world was retained by Mike Tyson when he knocked out Michael Spinks in 1 min., 31 sec. of the first round of a bout in Atlantic City, N.J. This was Tyson's third defense of his title in 1988. On Jan. 22 he knocked out Larry Holmes, a former champion, in the fourth round, and on Mar. 21 he knocked out Tony Tubbs in the second round.

July 11: Unrestricted free agency for 280 members of the NFL Players Association was denied by a federal judge in Minneapolis. The players had sought an injunction that would free them to negotiate with any team they chose because there was no collective bargaining agreement between the NFL owners and the players at the time the players' contracts expired in February. The decision meant players must sign with their own teams or not at all. The players' association said it would continue to press an antitrust suit against the owners.

July 11: His **4000th career victory as a harness racing driver** was registered by John Campbell at the Meadowlands in New Jersey. He became the 15th driver in harness racing history to record that many wins. Campbell also led in career earnings, with $60 million in purses.

July 13: The **oldest U.S. veteran died.** He was Samuel Leroy Mendel, 104, of Galva, Ill. At 14 he attempted to enlist in the army to serve in the Spanish-American War of 1898 but was turned down. He served three years after 1901. His death left Nathan E. Cook, 102, of Tempe, Ariz., as the oldest U.S. veteran.

July 16: A new **world record for the women's heptathlon** was set by Jackie Joyner-Kersee, with a total of 7,215 points for the seven events. The record she broke was her own. Florence Griffith Joyner, Joyner-Kersee's sister-in-law, set a new world record of 10.49 sec. for the women's 100-meter dash. Both records were made at the Olympic trials in Indianapolis, Ind.

July 16: The **longest scoreless game** in professional baseball ended in the bottom of the 26th inning. The game was won by the San Antonio Missions over the Jackson Mets by 1–0 in a Texas League (Class AA) game in San Antonio. The game took 7 hrs., 23 min. to play.

July 31: The **last Playboy Club,** in Lansing, Mich., closed. The first opened in Chicago in 1960, and by

1972 a million men had joined 22 clubs. Daringly risqué for their time, the clubs featured as waitresses pretty girls barely stuffed into costumes that included bunny ears and tails.

Aug 8: The **first night baseball game at Wrigley Field,** Chicago, was played 53 years after the first major league night baseball game took place in Cincinnati, Ohio. Light for night games had never been installed until now. The game, however, was called after four innings because of heavy rain. For many years Wrigley Field was the only major league baseball park without lights.

Aug 9: The **largest trade in professional sports** occurred when the Edmonton Oilers of the NHL sent Wayne Gretzky, superstar of ice hockey, to the Los Angeles Kings for $15,000,000. The deal also sent two other Oiler players to the Kings, which in turn sent three of its skaters to Edmonton.

Aug 14: The **PGA golf tournament** was won by Jeff Sluman by three strokes. It was his first victory after six years on the pro tour.

Aug 20: Jack Nicklaus became the first professional golfer to win more than $5 million in tournament play. A small prize of $5275 in the International Golf Tournament at Castle Rock, Colo., brought his total to $5,002,825.

Aug 20: All **20 defendants were acquitted** in a racketeering trial that lasted 21 months, one of the longest trials in federal court history. Those acquitted constituted all the members of the Lucchese family, an alleged criminal organization of New Jersey. The jury apparently did not believe the government's witnesses, many of whom were convicted criminals. It was also thought that the jury felt the prosecution had needlessly prolonged the trial.

Aug 31: Guilty of conspiring against free agents was the finding of an arbitrator against the owners of the major league baseball clubs. These owners, the ruling said, violated baseball's collective bargaining agreement in relation to 79 players who became free agents at the end of the 1986 season. Almost none of the clubs attempted to sign such players from other clubs. Monetary damages if any were to be determined later. A similar finding was made in 1987 with regard to players who became free agents in 1985.

Sep 8: A **new commissioner of baseball,** A. Bartlett Giamatti, was named to take office on Apr. 1, 1989. He would succeed Peter Ueberroth. Giamatti, then president of the National League, was formerly presi-

denaissa

Sep 9: ersity and a professor there of Renwhen ttwo stratest for t **Cup** was retained by the U.S.
The *Stars* es defeated the *New Zealand* in
and the *Ne* as the most unorthodox con
A sharp dis 7-year history of the event.
this odd con 60-foot-long catamaran,
sailed. 132-foot-long monohull.

Sep 16: The **14t** d in court, resulted in
ball history wa the races would be
Cincinnati Reds.
ers 1–0.

Sep 17-Oct 2: At t ajor league base
South Korea, the U rowning of the
nings, taking 36 gol Angeles Dodgfirst, with 55 and 132,
and 102. Among A s in Seoul,
Biondi, who won 7 me edal winming events; Greg Lou S.R. was
man to win the three-met with 37
secutive Olympics; Jackie Matt
the heptathlon and the bro imlaw Florence Griffith Joyner st
and 200-meter dashes, settinformer.

Sep 23: José Canseco of the Oakthe first major league baseball
home runs and steal 40 bases in

Oct 4: A new major league baseba
nings of scoreless pitching ended
of the Los Angeles Dodgers when thscored on him in the ninth inning of
the 1988 National League playoffs.

Oct 8: The **longest losing streak** in major
ball came to an end when Columbia defeateton, 16–13. The Lions had lost 44 games oveyears before winning this one. The next week thlost again.

Oct 15: The **World Series** was won by the Los Angeles Dodgers (NL) who defeated the Oakland Athletics (AL) four games to one. On Oct. 12 the Dodgers had won the National League pennant over the New York Mets, four games to three. On Oct. 9 the Athletics took the American League pennant by defeating the Boston Red Sox, four games to none.

1989

I. Civil Rights
Exploration
Government
Statistics
Wars

For the [...] ars the nation had a new [...] o had been vice president [...] preme Court decided states [...] victed criminals as young as [...] retarded persons, although it [...] be taken into account in sen- [...] the government announced that [...] e Hispanic population of the U.S. [...] ,000,000 mark, constituting 8.2% of [...] red with 6.5% in 1980. It was also [...] the number of babies born each year [...] e 4,000,000 mark, a figure not reached [...] espite a much–publicized war on drugs, [...] Americans used illicit drugs at least once [...] During the year Americans gave [...] ,000,000 to charitable causes, an increase of [...] real terms over the 1955 figure. Public fig- [...] ho died in 1989 included August A. Busch, Jr., [...] of the country's largest brewing company and [...] er of the St. Louis Cardinals baseball team, Sept. [...] at 90; Michael Harrington, a leading spokesman [...] r socialist ideas and ideals, July 31, at 61; Huey [...] Newton, black activist and a founder of the Black Panther party, murdered in Oakland, Calif., Aug. 22, at 47; and Claude Pepper, long-time congressman and chief legislative spokesman for the elderly, May 30, at 88.

Jan 4: Two **Libyan fighter planes were shot down** by American warplanes from the carrier *John F. Kennedy.* The U.S. pilots encountered the soviet-built MIG-23 fighters in international waters off the Libyan coast. Libya claimed its planes were unarmed and on routine patrol; the American pilots claimed they had been trailed in a hostile manner, and the U.S. government said on Jan. 5 it had visual evidence that the Libyan planes were armed with missiles.

Jan 11: Use of chemical weapons was condemned by representatives of 140 nations, including the U.S., at a meeting in Paris. They urged greater efforts to complete a treaty that would ban development, production, and possession of such weapons. The U.S. and France, which had convoked the conference, did so partly because of their alarm at the large-scale use of chemical weapons in the Iraq-Iran War of 1980—1988.

Jan 20: George Bush was inaugurated president of the United States, the nation's 41st president. Dan Quayle was inaugurated vice president.

Jan 23: A Richmond, Va., law favoring **minority-owned construction companies** was ruled invalid by the Supreme Court, 6–3. The rule provided that 30% of public works funds must go to such businesses. The court said such a law could be enforced only if it reduced "identifiable discrimination."

Jan 28: At an **unusual gathering in Moscow** of American, Cuban, and Soviet officials who had been involved in the superpower showdown over Russian nuclear weapons in Cuba in Oct., 1962, the Russians revealed that, unknown to the U.S., there were 20 nuclear warheads in Cuba before Pres. John F. Kennedy declared a naval blockade of Cuba on Oct. 23, 1962. The warheads had not been attached to missiles but the Soviets said that could have been done in a matter of hours.

Jan 31: The **U.S. population,** the Census Bureau projected, would peak at about 302,000,000 in 2038 and would then gradually decline to 292,000,000 by 2080. The bureau estimated that by 2030 there would be 66,000,000 persons 65 years and older, compared with 30,000,000 this year.

Mar 24: The worst **oil spill** in U.S. territory began when the supertanker *Exxon Valdez,* owned by the Exxon Corp., ran aground in Prince William Sound in southeastern Alaska, dumping 240,000 barrels of oil into the water. Wind and currents spread the oil more than 50 miles from its source, and 730 miles of coastline were affected. It was estimated that as many as 400,000 birds and animals suffered. It was alleged that the captain of the tanker, Joseph J. Hazelwood, had been drinking and that an uncertified officer was at the helm. On Mar. 22, 1990, Hazelwood was convicted of misdemeanor negligence, fined $50,000, and ordered to perform 1000 hours of community service. His captain's license was suspended on July 25, 1990. Exxon was also blamed by the National Transportation Safety Board and on Mar. 13, 1991, Exxon agreed with Alaska and the federal government to pay a penalty of $100,000,000 and provide $1,000,000,000 over a period of ten years to continue the cleanup. However, on May 3, 1991, both Alaska and Exxon changed their minds and rejected the agreement. The matter was finally settled on Oct. 8, 1991, when Exxon agreed to pay an extra $25,000,000 penalty. On July 10, 1992, an Alaska court overturned Hazelwood's conviction, citing a federal statute that grants immunity from prosecution to those who report oil spills.

Apr 19: An **explosion at sea** aboard the battleship *Iowa* in one of its 16-inch gun turrets killed 47 sailors. The warship was about 300 miles north of Puerto Rico at the time. An initial Navy investigation asserted that the blast had been caused when a sailor attempted to commit suicide. The outcry against this verdict was such that another Navy investigation took place and the Navy apologized on Oct. 17, 1991, to the family of the accused sailor, saying the cause of the blast could not be determined.

May 4: A federal jury convicted **Oliver L. North,** a former official of the National Security Council, on charges stemming from his part in the IranContra affair in which arms were sold secretly to Iran and money from the operation was funneled to the Nicaraguan Contra rebels. North was found guilty on three charges concerning the destruction of documents, and aiding and abetting the obstruction of Congress. He was acquitted of nine other charges. On July 20, 1990, a federal appeals court suspended North's conviction and overturned one count. Richard V. Secord, a former air force general, who had organized the operation that shipped arms to Iran, pleaded guilty Nov. 8, 1989, to a charge of making false statements to Congress. On Sept. 16, 1991, all charges against North were dropped by a federal judge because the trial testimony used to convict him had been affected by testimony he had given Congress under immunity.

May 31: James C. Wright, Jr., announced his resignation as Speaker of the House of Representatives and retired from the House. The House Ethics Committee had accused him on Apr. 17 of having violated rules concerning the acceptance of gifts and outside income. Wright denied the charges. He was succeeded on June 6 as Speaker by Thomas S. Foley of the state of Washington.

June 12: Burning the American flag as a political protest is protected by the First Amendment's guarantee of free speech, the Supreme Court ruled, 5–4. On Oct. 12 Pres. Bush said he would let a bill passed by Congress banning such burning become law without his signature. He wanted a constitutional amendment. The Supreme Court, 5–4, declared on June 11, 1990, that the law was unconstitutional.

July 3: A restrictive **Missouri law on abortion** was upheld by the Supreme Court, 5–4. The law forbade public employees to perform abortions; banned the use of public buildings for abortions; and required doctors treating women 20 weeks or more pregnant to determine whether the fetus could survive if born.

July 19: A United Airlines DC-10 **jet crashed** short of the runway at Sioux City, Iowa, and 112 of the 296 persons aboard died. The pilot had struggled for 45 minutes to control the plane after an explosion in its tail engine. On Nov. 1, 1990, the National Transportation Safety Board blamed the airline for failure to detect the flaw in the engine that caused it to disintegrate.

Sep 18–24: Hurricane Hugo, one of the worst storms of the century, struck Puerto Rico, the U.S. Virgin Islands, and the east coast of the mainland where Charleston, S.C., was hardest hit. On St. Croix 97% of the buildings were destroyed; in Charleston many landmark structures were destroyed and thousands of trees felled. Damage in South Carolina was estimated at $3,700,000,000 and in Puerto Rico at $1,000,000,000. In the storm 24 Americans lost their lives.

Oct 17: An **earthquake** struck the San Francisco area, registering 6.9 on the Richter scale, with its epicenter near Santa Cruz. The quake killed 66 persons, most of whom died in the collapse of a section of a double-deck freeway in Oakland. Damage was estimated at $10,000,000,000. The tremor struck just as the third game of the 1989 World Series was to get underway in Candlestick Park in San Francisco. The stadium, with more than 60,000 people in it, was only slightly damaged and spectators were evacuated without incident.

Nov 8: L. Douglas Wilder became **the first black elected governor** of a state when he won the Virginia election.

Nov 21: Pres. Bush signed **an anti-drug law** that appropriated $3,180,000,000 for treatment facilities, federal prison expansion, education, and law enforcement.

Dec 3: The first **summit meeting** of Pres. Bush and Mikhail S. Gorbachev, president of the U.S.S.R., took place on ships of the two nations in the harbor of Valetta, Malta. In closing statements both presidents said in effect that the Cold War was over. The two leaders also discussed nuclear disarmament and improvement of trade relations between the countries.

Dec 20: American armed forces invaded Panama in an attempt to overthrow and capture Manuel Antonio Noriega, the military dictator of the country who had been indicted in the U.S. on drug trafficking charges. The invasion force numbered about 24,000, half of whom had been stationed in Panama. After fairly stiff resistance by Noriega's Panama Defense Forces, he surrendered on Jan. 3, 1990, and was flown to the U.S. to stand trial. American casualties were 23 killed and 323 wounded. Panamanian forces suffered 314 killed and 124 wounded. In addition some 200 non–combatants died.

II. Architecture
Arts and Music
Popular Entertainment
Publishing
Theater

The 1988–1989 Broadway theater season set a record for box office receipts at $262,000,000, an increase of 3.6% over the previous season. However, attendance dropped by 100,000 from 8,100,000 in 1987–1988, perhaps because the 30 fewer productions were a new low. *The Heidi Chronicles* by Wendy Wasserstein, peopled by women who went to college together in the 1970s, was favorably received by critics and theatergoers. Musicals did better, including *Grand Hotel,* based on a hit movie of 1932; *Gypsy,* a revival featuring a mother intent on making a star of her daughter; and *Jerome Robbins' Broadway,* a potpourri of music from hit shows directed and choreographed by Robbins. Moviegoers spent more than $5,000,000,000 at the box office, breaking the previous record set in 1988 of $4,450,000,000, and total attendance was 1,120,000,000, the most in five years. *Batman,* which sold more than $251,000,000 worth of tickets, made its sponsors happy. Other box office successes included *Indiana Jones and the Last Crusade,* another wild adventure of its protagonist; and *Ghostbusters II,* not up to the original. *Dead Poets Society* concerned an unconventional teacher and his students; *Do the Right Thing,* with Spike Lee as director and actor, had a rather unusual slant on racial violence. Steven Soderbergh's *sex, lies, and videotape* won the top prize at the Cannes Film Festival. *Parenthood* was the most popular comedy; *Pet Sematary* was another scary Stephen King production; and *Field of Dreams* showed that faith could even bring back long-dead baseball players. Among serious fare were *Driving Miss Daisy,* about an elderly widow and her long suffering chauffeur; and *Glory,* the story of the first black regiment to fight in the Civil War. As to entertainment in the home, 56.4% of households now had cable TV, while 62% of households had VCRs. The Denver, Detroit, and Cleveland symphony orchestras faced financial problems, but the Dallas Symphony moved into a new home that cost $81,500,000. The JVC Jazz Festival (at one time the Newport and at another the Kool) took place in New York City and marked its 35th anniversary. Among a number of serious book-length studies of jazz, *The Swing Era: The Development of Jazz, 1930–1945* by Gunther Schuller, was outstanding. A major art exhibit at the National Gallery in Washington during the winter of 1988–1989 marked the 400th anniversary of the Venetian painter, Paolo Veronese, with 50 paintings and 55 drawings on display. A praiseworthy addition to the New York City skyline was Rockefeller Plaza West, on Seventh Avenue, a 57-story office building that went well with the older, neighboring Rockefeller Center. It was stepped back in design, built of limestone, stainless steel, and glass, and featured a 10-story glass section at its southeast corner. Mass market paperbacks increased at a rate of 6.5% per year from 1982 to 1989 while adult hardbound books did even better, with a 12.4% annual increase. In dollar sales, the growth in hardbounds was from $770,800,000 to $1,700,000,000, and paperbacks went from $703,000,000 to $1,100,000,000. Magazine publishing did not prosper, with advertising revenue falling as the year went on, and with the competition of 500 to 600 new ones each year—of which eight out of ten would fail. Unique among new ones was *UpTime: The Disk Monthly,* about computers, was published as a disk, and required a computer to be read. It was offered at $720 a year. Among notable persons who died were Alvin Ailey, founder of the American Dance Theater, Dec. 1, at 58; Joseph Alsop, Jr., political columnist and art collector, Aug. 28, at 78; Lucille Ball, comedienne of movies and television, Apr. 26, at 77; Donald Barthelme, author who wrote with wry humor, July 23, at 58; Irving Berlin, America's all-time greatest song writer, Sept. 22, at 101; Mel Blanc, the voice of Bugs Bunny and other such characters, July 10, at 81; Malcolm Cowley, liberal literary and social critic, Mar. 27, at 90; Bette Davis, one of the movies' greats, Oct. 6, at 81; Vladimir Horowitz, world leader as a pianist, Nov. 5, at 85; Mary McCarthy, outspoken critic and novelist, Oct. 25, at 77; Zinka Milanov, dramatic soprano, May 30, at 83; Richard B. Morris, historian of Colonial America, Mar. 3, at 84; Frederic Prokosch, novelist, June 1, at 81; I. F. Stone, liberal and iconoclastic columnist, June 18, at 81; Virgil G. Thomson, composer and critic, Sept. 30, at 92; Barbara W. Tuchman, historian, Feb. 6, at 77; Robert Penn Warren, the first U.S. poet laureate, Sept. 15, at 84.

Among **books published** in 1989 were a number of worthy works of fiction: Two novellas by Saul Bellow, *A Theft* and *The Bellarossa Connection; Billy Bathgate* by E. L. Doctorow, about a young man and his fascination with gangsters; *Oldest Living Confederate Widow Tells All* by Allan Gurganus, which lived up to its title; *The Mambo Kings Play Songs of Love* by Oscar Hijuelos, telling of the somewhat wild way of life of some Cuban-Americans; *A Prayer for Owen Meany* by John Irving, about a misfit and the life he made; *The Russia House* by John le Carré; *Some Can Whistle* by Larry McMurtry, more Texas goings-on; *American Appetites,* Joyce Carol Oates's 19th book;

Polar Star by Martin Cruz Smith; and *The Joy Luck Club* by Amy Tan, a first novel concerning Chinese-American families. Nonfiction of the year included three substantial books about blacks: *And the Walls Came Tumbling Down,* Ralph David Abernathy's account of his part in the civil rights movement; *Paul Robeson* by Martin Bauml Duberman, a biography of the singer, actor, and radical; and *Jazz Cleopatra: Josephine Baker in Her Time* by Phyllis Rose, the life of Josephine Baker whose career was made mostly in France. Volumes of poetry included *Human Wishes* by Robert Haas and *Time's Power, Poems 1985–1988* by Adrienne Rich. In a category by itself was *The Good Times,* more "aw shucks" recollections by Russell Baker.

Jan 8: *42nd Street,* the **second longest-running musical** in the history of the New York theater, closed after 3486 performances. Its run was exceeded only by that of *A Chorus Line,* which was still being performed. *42nd Street* opened on Aug. 25, 1980, and was based on a 1933 movie. A London production closed Jan. 7 after 1823 performances.

Feb 22: Grammy Awards were presented for the following: best album of 1988, *Faith* by George Michael; best song and best record, "Don't Worry, Be Happy," by Bobby McFerrin; best new artist and best female pop vocalist, Tracy Chapman for "Fast Car"; best male rock vocalist, Robert Palmer for *Simply Irresistible;* best female rock vocalist, Tina Turner for *Tina Live in Europe.*

Mar 29: Academy Awards were presented to *Rain Man* as outstanding motion picture of 1988; Dustin Hoffman as best actor for *Rain Man;* Jodie Foster as best actress for *The Accused;* Kevin Kline as best supporting actor for *A Fish Called Wanda;* and Geena Davis as best supporting actress for *The Accidental Tourist.*

Mar 30: Pulitzer prizes were awarded for the following: fiction, *Breathing Lessons* by Anne Tyler; general nonfiction, *A Bright Shining Lie: John Paul Vann and America in Vietnam* by Neil Sheehan; biography, *Oscar Wilde* by Richard Ellmann; history, *Parting the Waters: America in the King Years, 1954–1963* by Taylor Branch, and *Battle Cry of Freedom: The Civil War Years* by James M. McPherson; poetry, *New and Collected Poems* by Richard Wilbur; drama *The Heidi Chronicles* by Wendy Wasserstein.

June 4: Tony awards for the 1988–1989 theatrical season were presented for the following: best play, *The Heidi Chronicles* by Wendy Wasserstein; best musical, *Jerome Robbins' Broadway;* best actor in a play, Philip Bosco for *Lend Me a Tenor;* best actress, Pauline Collins for *Shirley Valentine;* best actor in a musical, Jason Alexander for *Jerome Robbins' Broadway;*

best actress in a musical, Ruth Brown for *Black and Blue.*

June 13: In an **obscenity** controversy, an exhibition of photographs by Robert Mapplethorpe was cancelled by the Corcoran Gallery of Art, Washington, in the face of controversy in Congress and the National Endowment for the Arts because of the homoerotic and sadomasochistic content of the late photographer's work. The Washington Project for the Arts, a private group, took over the exhibit and opened it July 20.

Sep 17: Emmy Awards were presented for the following: best dramatic series, *L. A. Law;* best comedy series, *Cheers;* best actor in a dramatic series, Carroll O'Connor for *In the Heat of the Night;* best actor in a comedy series, Richard Mulligan for *Empty Nest;* best actress in a dramatic series, Dana Delany for *China Beach;* best actress in a comedy series, Candice Bergen for *Murphy Brown.*

Nov 29: National Book Awards were presented for the following: fiction, *Spartina* by John Casey; nonfiction, *From Beirut to Jerusalem* by Thomas L. Friedman.

Nov 30: With the **art auction** in New York City of Pablo Picasso's *Pierrette's Wedding* for $51,300,000, six of the ten highest prices ever paid for paintings were registered in 1989 and the Picasso sale was the second highest price so far recorded. Also in 1989 *Yo Picasso,* a self-portrait, went for $47,900,000; a third Picasso, *Au Lapin Agile,* for $40,700,000; *Halberdier,* by Jacopo Pontormo, $35,100,000; *Rue Mosnier, Paris, Decorated with Flags on June 30, 1887,* by Edouard Manet, $26,400,000; and *Mirror,* by Picasso, also $26,400,000. In addition, Willem de Kooning's *Interchange* was sold on Nov. 8 for $10,700,000, a record at the time at auction for a living artist, while Jackson Pollock's *No. 8, 1950* was sold on May 2 for $11,000,000, the most so far paid for a work by this artist.

III. Business and Industry
Education
Philosophy and Religion
Science

The American economy did not prosper during the year. Although the unemployment rate at year's end was 5.3%, a decline of 0.2%, and 2,500,000 new jobs had been created, almost all of them were in the service industries rather than manufacturing where higher wages prevailed on the whole. Industrial production was up only 1.7%, while retail sales increased 5.0% and producer prices rose 4.8%. Nevertheless, the U.S. continued to attract foreign investments. There were 343 such transactions, valued at $51,200,000,000, compared with 299 with a value of $50,000,000,000 in 1988. In the field of education, the government reported that 4,200,000 young adults were not high school graduates and that of them 15% were white, 22% black, and 28% Hispanic. Two-year community colleges had been growing for a decade and 6,000,000 students were expected to be enrolled in them for the 1989–1990 school year. The Roman Catholic Church continued to be the largest religious denomination with 54,000,000 members, followed by the Southern Baptist Convention at 14,800,000 and the United Methodist Church at 9,100,000. The largest black denomination, the National Baptist Convention, U.S.A., Inc., built its own headquarters for the first time, a $10,000,000 structure in Nashville, Tenn. The Christian Church (Disciples of Christ) sent 50,000 Russian-language Bibles to Moscow in April and planned on shipping 450,000 more by 1991. The Salvation Army expanded its activities to a 91st country, El Salvador. Noteworthy people who died included Salo Wittmayer Baron, much respected for his life's work devoted to Jewish history, Nov. 25, at 94; George W. Beadle, Nobel prize winner for his work in genetics, June 9, at 85; William M. Fairbank, physicist who pursued the elusive quark, Sept. 30, at 72; Sidney Hook, political philosopher and enemy of communism, July 12, at 96; Walter Hoving, who revived from its doldrums the jewel of jewelry stores, Tiffany & Co., Nov. 27, at 91; Timothy Cardinal Manning, archbishop of Los Angeles, June 23, at 79; Owen Lattimore, scholar of Far Eastern affairs, May 31, at 88; Charles J. Pedersen, Nobel prize winner in chemistry, Oct. 26, at 85; Emilio G. Segre, Nobel prize winning nuclear physicist, Apr. 22, at 84; J. C. Street, co-discoverer of the muon, Nov. 7, at 83.

Jan 2: A comprehensive **free trade agreement** between the U.S. and Canada was signed by Pres. Ronald Reagan and Prime Minister Brian Mulroney of Canada. The agreement will eliminate tariffs and reduce other barriers to trade and investment by the end of the century. The legislatures of both countries ratified the agreement before the end of the year.

Jan 31: Thirteen-year-old **American students rank last** in math and science, according to the Education Testing Service. The comparison was with students from South Korea, Great Britain, Ireland, Spain, and four Canadian provinces. The Korean students ranked first in math and, with British Columbia students, first in science.

Feb 3: In the **largest business takeover ever** RJR Nabisco agreed to be acquired for $25,000,000,000 by Kohlberg Kravis and Roberts & Co., an investment firm specializing in mergers and buyouts. With the Beatrice Companies, which had been acquired in a leveraged buyout in 1986, the combined concerns accounted for about 13% of all U.S. food manufacturing.

Mar 23: A claim to having achieved **nuclear fusion at room temperature** was made by two chemists working at the University of Utah. They were B. Stanley Pons and Martin Fleischmann. Fusion ordinarily takes place at temperatures of several hundred million degrees and had not yet become a practical source of energy. Most scientists were skeptical of the PonsFleischmann process as to whether it existed at all or, if it did, whether it could produce enough energy to be practical. A federal conference in May, which brought together hundreds of scientists in different fields, delivered a strong negative verdict.

May 4: The unmanned spacecraft **Magellan** was launched by the space shuttle *Atlantis* to begin a voyage to Venus. It reached Venus orbit Aug. 10, 1990, and began sending back new and astounding information. Active volcanoes, fractured landscapes, and a thin plastic crust were revealed, unlike anything hitherto seen in the solar system. Other photographs showed pancake-shaped lava domes about half a mile high and ten miles in diameter.

May 22: The first successful **transfer of cells containing foreign genes** into a human being was performed at the National Institutes of Health, Bethesda, Maryland. The altered cancer-fighting cells were placed in the blood stream of a cancer patient. Although the patient was not expected to benefit, doctors hoped that tracking the cells would eventually help them develop techniques for transplanting foreign genes in such a way as to cure or control disease.

June: Nearly 106,000 cases of AIDS had been reported to date in the U.S. and of these sufferers 61,000 had died. It was estimated that by the end of 1992 there would be between 179,000 and 208,000 more cases. Departing from the usual practice, federal drug officials announced Sept. 28 that they would allow an experimental drug to be prescribed while it was still being tested. The drug was dideoxyinosine (DDI). Meanwhile first tests of an earlier approved drug, AZT, showed improvement in patients using it.

June 10: The disbanding of **Moral Majority,** the conservative Protestant political action group established in 1979, was announced by its founder, the Rev. Jerry Falwall, a Baptist clergyman. He said its goal of getting fundamentalist Christians into politics had been achieved. At its peak Moral Majority claimed a membership of 6,500,000 and in 1984 raised $11,000,000 for political lobbying.

1989 ■ *PRES.* GEORGE BUSH

July 9: The **richest man in the U.S.,** according to *Forbes* magazine, was Sam Moore Walton, founder of the Wal-Mart Stores, said to be worth $8,700,000,000.

July 24: The world's **largest media and entertainment conglomerate** was created by the merger of Warner Communications, Inc., into Time, Inc. As Time Warner, Inc., the new corporation had a stock market value of $15,200,000,000 and annual revenues of $10,000,000,000. Time was chiefly a magazine and book publishing company and Warner was a producer of movies and recordings. Both also had sizable cable television operations.

Aug 9: A bill to bail out **savings and loan associations** was signed into law by Pres. George Bush. It provided $166,000,000,000, of which 75% would come from taxes over a ten-year period. It was expected that the total cost would be some $300,000,000,000. A new government body, the Resolution Trust Corporation, was established to merge or liquidate the institutions in trouble so as to protect depositors. Many of the thrift institutions got in financial trouble through bad loans, investments in junk bonds, bad management, and criminal acts of executives. The Federal Deposit Insurance Corporation (FDIC) had already seized 261 institutions with assets of $104,000,000,000.

Sep 27: In the **largest Japanese acquisition** to date of an American company, Sony Corp., producer of electronic products, arranged to buy Columbia Pictures Entertainment, Inc., for $3,400,000,000.

Sep 28: A compromise on the **ordination of women** in the Episcopal Church was the substance of a statement issued by the House of Bishops meeting in Philadelphia. The statement, which seemed likely to remove the danger of a split within the church, noted that opposition to the ordination of women continued to be "a recognized theological position" and that church leaders should be "pastorally sensitive" to those who will not accept women as priests.

Oct 9: The **Dow Jones industrial average** closed at a new high of 2791.41, breaking the previous record set Aug. 24, 1987. However, on Oct. 13 the index fell 190.58 points, the second largest decline ever, although only the 12th worst in terms of percentage. The Dow Jones closed at 2569.26.

Oct 9: The **Nobel Prize in Physiology or Medicine** was awarded jointly to J. Michael Bishop and Harold E. Warmus, both of the University of California at San Francisco, for their discovery of how normal cell growth can change so as to cause cancer.

Oct 12: The **Nobel Prize in Chemistry** was awarded to Sidney Altman of Yale University and Thomas R. Cech of the University of Colorado for their determination that RNA is not only a passive carrier of ge-

netic information but can also process such information, promote chain reactions, and reproduce itself.

Oct 12: The **Nobel Prize in Physics** was awarded to Norman F. Ramsey of Harvard University for his development of the atomic clock, and to Hans Dehmelt of the University of Washington and Wolfgang Paul of West Germany for their method of isolating atomic and subatomic particles for prolonged study.

Oct 18: The unmanned spacecraft **Galileo** was launched on a roundabout trip to Jupiter by astronauts aboard the space shuttle *Atlantis*. It was due to reach Jupiter on Dec. 7, 1995, and to collect gravitational acceleration it flew by Venus Feb. 16, 1990. During its passage there it took photographs of Venusian cloud and wind patterns. Galileo next headed for a swing around the earth to give it a further gravitational push and it came within 600 miles of its home planet on Dec. 8, 1990. On this part of its long journey it made photographs on Dec. 7, 1990, of areas of the far side of the moon never seen before. On Oct. 29, 1991, Galileo took the first photographs of a rocky asteroid, Gaspra, a body about 12 miles long.

Oct 30: A controlling interest in **Rockefeller Center** in New York City was sold by the Rockefeller Group to the Mitsubishi Estate Co. of Tokyo, which bought 51% of the skyscraper complex for $864,000,000.

Nov 17: A new **minimum wage bill** that increased the rate from $3.35 an hour to $3.80 on Apr. 1, 1990, and to $4.25 on Apr. 1, 1991, was signed into law by Pres. Bush. The law also established a "training wage" minimum of $3.35 an hour for 16–19-year-olds for the first three months of employment.

Nov 19: American astronomers announced they had detected a source of **light coming from the edge of the universe** and the beginning of time.

Nov 27: The first U.S. **liver transplant** using a live donor was successfully completed at the University of Chicago Medical Center. Four other such operations had been performed in other countries. In the operation a mother gave a third of her liver to her 21-month-old daughter. A second operation took place successfully at the same medical center on Dec. 8.

Dec 31: The **Dow Jones industrial average** ended the year at 2753.20, up 584.63 for a gain of 27%.

IV. Fashion
Folkways
Holidays
Social Issues and Crime
Sports

In sports, Ty Murray of Odessa, Tex., became at age 20 the youngest person to win the all-around championship of professional cowboys; Georgia Southern University, playing in the NCAA's Division I-AA, became the first school in the 20th century to win 15 football games in a season; Sunday Silence set a thoroughbred horse racing record for earnings in one season with $4,578,454; at the Henley Regatta in England 60 of the 400 competing crews were from the U.S.; Tom Kite set a record for annual winnings on the PGA tour with $1,395,278; and Tom Watson became the second professional golfer to pass the $5,000,000 mark in winnings. The designers of high fashion brought forth clothes with softer and gentler lines, abandoning the mannish silhouette. Deep and bright colors were featured but most young women seemed to prefer to go around in black. In men's fashions the double-breasted suit made a comeback. The population of federal prisons reached 48,017 compared with 24,162 in 1980. This left the 70 available facilities 50% over their rated capacity. One of every 42 registered automobiles was stolen or looted in the course of the year. Prominent people who died included Earl "Red" Blaik, football coach at West Point from 1941 to 1958, May 6, at 92; John "Jocko" Conlan, feisty major league baseball umpire, as well liked by fans as any ump could be, Apr. 16, at 89; Lily Daché, designer noted for her hats, especially turbans, Dec. 31, at 97; A. Bartlett Giamatti, Renaissance scholar, president of Yale University, and commissioner of Major League Baseball, Sept. 1, at 51; Vernon "Lefty" Gomez, pitcher for 14 years for the New York Yankees, winner of six World Series games without a loss, and member of the Baseball Hall of Fame, Feb. 17, at 80; William "Billy" Martin, bad boy of baseball and manager at five different times of the New York Yankees, Dec. 25, at 61; William "Bill" Terry, New York Giants player and manager with a .341 batting average over 14 seasons, Jan. 9, at 90; Sugar Ray Robinson, five times middleweight boxing champion, Apr. 12, at 67; Valentina Nicholaevna Sanina Schlee, fashion designer known professionally by her first name only, who dressed many stars of the theater, Sept. 14, age uncertain; Glenna Collett Vare, a pioneer of women's golf and a charter member of the Women's Golf Hall of Fame, Feb. 3, at 89; Diana Vreeland, the most influential fashion editor of her time, Aug. 22, at 86.

Jan 2: In **college football bowl games** the results were UCLA 10, Arkansas 2 in the Cotton Bowl; Miami 23, Nebraska 3 in the Orange Bowl; Michigan 22, USC 14 in the Rose Bowl; and Florida State 13, Auburn 7 in the Sugar Bowl. Both the AP and the UPI polls chose Notre Dame as the 1988 national champion. Notre Dame defeated West Virginia, 34 to 12, in the Fiesta Bowl.

Jan 22: Super Bowl XXIII was won by the San Francisco 49ers (NFC) who defeated the Cincinnati Bengals (AFC) 20 to 16. On Jan. 8 San Francisco had won the NFC title by defeating the Chicago Bears 28 to 3 and Cincinnati had taken the AFC title by defeating the Buffalo Bills 21 to 10.

Feb 3: The **National League** of major league baseball elected Bill White as president. A player for 14 years and then a sports broadcaster, he was the first black elected to head a major sports organization.

Feb 11–12: U.S. figure skating championships were won in Baltimore, Md., by Jill Trenary, women's singles; Christopher Bowman, men's singles; Kristi Yamaguchi and Rudi Galindo, pairs; and Susan Wynne and Joseph Druar, dance.

Apr 2: The **NCAA women's basketball championship** was won by Tennessee which defeated Auburn 76 to 60.

Apr 3: The **NCAA men's basketball championship** was won by Michigan which defeated Seton Hall 80 to 79 in overtime.

Apr 9: The **Masters golf tournament** was won by Nick Faldo of England on the second hole of a playoff with Scott Hoch.

Apr 17: The 93rd **Boston Marathon** was won in the men's division by Abebe Mekonnen of Ethiopia in a time of 2 hrs., 9 min., 6 sec. The women's division was won by Ingrid Kristiansen of Norway in 2 hrs., 24 min., 33 sec.

May 6: The 115th **Kentucky Derby** was won by Sunday Silence with a time of 2:05. The jockey was Pat Valenzuela.

May 20: The 114th **Preakness Stakes** was won by Sunday Silence with a time of 1:53 4/5. The jockey was Pat Valenzuela.

May 21: The **LPGA golf tournament** was won by Nancy Lopez by three strokes.

May 25: The **NHL Stanley Cup** was won by the Calgary Flames who defeated the Montreal Canadiens four games to two.

May 28: The 73rd **Indianapolis 500** auto race was won by Emerson Fittipaldi of Brazil with an average speed of 167.581 mph.

June 10: The 121st **Belmont Stakes** was won by Easy Goer, with a time of 2:26. The jockey was Pat Day.

June 13: The **NBA basketball championship** was won by the Detroit Pistons who defeated the Los Angeles Lakers four games to none.

June 18: The **U.S. Open golf tournament** was won by Curtis Strange who became the first player since 1950–1951 to win the title two years in succession.

July 11: The **baseball All-Star Game** was won by the American League, which beat the National League 5 to 3.

July 16: The **U.S. Women's Open golf tournament** was won by Betsy King by a margin of four strokes.

July 23: The **British Open golf tournament** was won by Mark Calcavecchia of the U.S. who defeated Greg Norman and Wayne Grady in a four-hole playoff.

July 23: An American won the **Tour de France** for the second time when Greg Lemond triumphed in the cross-country bicycle race by the smallest victory margin ever, eight seconds. In 1986 Lemond became the first American to win the event.

July 23: The **Baseball Hall of Fame** inducted Johnny Bench, catcher, Carl Yastrzemski, outfielder, Al Barlick, umpire, and Albert F. "Red" Schoendienst, infielder.

Aug 13: The **PGA golf tournament** was won by Payne Stewart who birdied four of the last five holes.

Aug 22: The **first pitcher to strike out 5000 batters,** Nolan Ryan of the Texas Rangers (AL), reached this mark in a game against the Oakland Athletics (AL).

Aug 24: Pete Rose, one of the game's superstars, was banned from baseball for life by A. Bartlett Giamatti, commissioner of Major League Baseball, for having bet on games, allegedly including those of his own team, the Cincinnati Reds (NL), for whom he played and managed.

Aug 30: Wealthy hotel owner **Leona Helmsley** was found guilty in federal court in New York City on 33 counts of tax evasion, fraud, and conspiracy. She was acquitted on eight other counts. On Dec. 12 she was sentenced to four years in prison, fined $7,200,000, and ordered to perform 750 hours of community service.

Sep 9–10: The **U.S. Open tennis singles championships** were won in the men's division by Boris Becker and in the women's by Steffi Graf, both of West Germany.

Sep 13: Francis F. "Fay" Vincent was named **commissioner of Major League Baseball,** in succession to A. Bartlett Giamatti, who died Sept. 1. Vincent had recently been deputy commissioner.

Sep 17: The **Miss America** title was won by Debbye Turner, 23, of Columbia, Mo., at the annual pageant in Atlantic City, N.J.

Sep 20: The murderer known as the **"Night Stalker"** for his method of operation, Richard Ramirez, a drifter from Texas, was found guilty in Los Angeles of 30 murders and 30 other crimes. He had terrorized Southern California in the summer of 1985 with a series of killings.

Sep 29: Law officers **seized 20 tons of cocaine** in a raid on a warehouse in Los Angeles. They also found $10,000,000 in cash in what was said to be the largest drug seizure in history. Four persons were arrested. The cocaine had a wholesale value of $2,000,000,000 and a street sale value of up to $7,000,000,000.

Oct 14–28: The **World Series** was won by the Oakland Athletics (AL) when they defeated the San Francisco Giants (NL) four games to none. The last two games had been postponed since Oct. 17 when an earthquake shook Candlestick Park in San Francisco just as the third game of the series was about to start. On Oct. 8 the Athletics had won the American League championship by beating the Toronto Blue Jays four games to one and the next day the Giants had won the National League title, beating the Chicago Cubs four games to one.

Oct 15: Wayne Gretzky became the **highest scorer in NHL history** when, playing for the Los Angeles Kings against the Edmonton Oilers, he registered his 1850th point. The record broken had been set by Gordie Howe over 26 seasons. This was Gretzky's 11th season.

Oct 26: Paul Tagliabue was named **commissioner of the National Football League,** succeeding Pete Rozelle who had retired after 30 years. Tagliabue as a lawyer was associated with a law firm that was outside counsel to the NFL.

Nov 5: The 20th **New York City Marathon** was won in the men's division by Juma Ikangaa of Tanzania with a time of 2 hrs., 8 min., 1 sec. The women's division was won by Ingrid Kristiansen of Norway with a time of 2 hrs., 25 min., 30 sec.

Nov 21: For the **exclusive right to broadcast all NCAA tournaments** for a seven-year period CBS agreed to pay the college sports organization $1,000,000,000. Seventeen sports were included but the chief prize was the annual national basketball championship.

Nov 22: Kirby Puckett, a centerfielder, became the **first $3,000,000-a-year baseball player** when he signed a three-year contract with the Minnesota Twins of the American League for $9,000,000. This figure was exceeded Dec. 1 when Mark Langston, a left-handed pitcher, agreed to a five-year contract with the California Angels for $16,000,000, or $3,200,000 a year. Mark Davis, a left-handed relief pitcher, signed on Dec. 11 with the Kansas City Royals for $13,000,000 for four years, or $3,250,000 a year.

1990

I. Civil Rights
Exploration and Settlement
Government
Statistics
Wars

By the second half of the year the nation faced the start of a recession at home and a war abroad, the latter the result of Iraq's invasion of Kuwait Aug. 2. Pres. George Bush's handling of foreign policy, especially his skill in building an international coalition to oppose Iraq's Pres. Saddam Hussein, was widely praised. Bush showed less interest in domestic affairs, and the year was notable chiefly for a protracted, acrimonious debate between the Republican-controlled executive branch and the Democratic-controlled Congress over the federal budget deficit. The result was a plan intended to cut that deficit nearly $500,000,000,000 over five years. In mid-term elections the Democratic party made small gains and with its Republican opponents managed to spend $203,000,000 on congressional and state elections, an increase of 26% over 1986, the last comparable year. On Dec. 27 the Census Bureau reported that the population of the country as of Apr. 1 was 249,632,692, an increase of 23,000,000 over 1980. The largest relative increases occurred in the southern and sun belt states, especially California, Florida, and Texas. Also notable in population change was the fact that the number of Asians and Pacific islanders in the U.S. increased from 3,834,000 in 1980 to 6,880,000 in 1990. Among notable persons who died were James M. Gavin, a top combat commander in World War II, Feb. 23, at 82; Arthur J. Goldberg, former Supreme Court justice, Jan. 19, at 81; Curtis E. LeMay, commander of the air forces that bombed Japan in World War II, Oct. 1, at 83; Louella Luhrman, an army nurse in World War I and the oldest living veteran, Jan. 26, at 108; Spark M. Matsunaga, Democratic senator from Hawaii, 1977–1990, Apr. 15, at 73; Edwin O. Reischauer, East Asian scholar and ambassador to Japan, Sept. 1, at 79.

Jan 2–Sep 27: Six oil spills dumped 670,000 gallons of oil and petroleum products into the Arthur Kill and the Kill van Kull, two narrow waterways between Staten Island, New York, and New Jersey. The New Jersey side of the waterways is lined with refineries and tanks that can hold nearly 2,000,000,000 gallons of oil products. Also, on the west coast, off Hunting-ton Beach in southern California, a tanker that hit an underwater object on Feb. 7 spilled about 400,000 gallons of crude oil into the Pacific Ocean.

Apr 7: For his part in the **Iran-Contra affair** John M. Poindexter, a former national security adviser, was found guilty of five criminal charges involving conspiracy, obstruction of Congress, and making false statements. He was sentenced June 11 to six months in prison. On Nov. 15, 1991, a federal appeals court reversed his conviction because testimony he had given before a congressional committee under a promise of immunity had been used against him.

June 1: At a **summit meeting** in Washington, D.C., Pres. Bush and Pres. Mikhail Gorbachev of the U.S.S.R. signed an agreement to make large cuts in nuclear weapons. The U.S. would reduce its arsenal of missiles from about 12,000 to about 9500; the Soviets would reduce theirs from about 11,300 to about 6900. To achieve these totals both sides would scrap missile submarines and bombers as well as missiles. An agreement concerning chemical weapons called for the destruction of at least 50% of stocks by 1999.

June 4: The **use of high school facilities** by student political and religious groups was upheld by the Supreme Court, 8–1. The decision meant that a federal law requiring high schools to permit such use was constitutional. The case involved a high school in Omaha, Neb.

June 14: Flash floods set off by heavy thunderstorms swept through central and eastern Ohio, northern West Virginia, and western Pennsylvania driving hundreds of people from their homes. Shadyside, Ohio, was especially hard hit with 23 dead and ten others missing.

June 25: In a case concerning the **right to die,** the Supreme Court decided, 8–1, that if a person's wishes are clearly known, he or she has a constitutional right to have life-sustaining procedures ended. However, the justices also upheld, 5–4, a Missouri law allowing the sustaining of life of a woman, comatose for more than seven years, because there was no "clear and convincing evidence" that she wanted treatment stopped.

July 20: William J. Brennan, Jr., announced his resignation from the Supreme Court, where he had served for nearly 34 years. He was the acknowledged leader of the liberal bloc on the court.

July 26: A landmark act protecting the **rights of disabled persons** was signed by Pres. Bush. Estimated to affect 43,000,000 Americans, the law forbade discrimination in employment, public accommodations, and transportation.

Aug 2–Dec 31: Iraqi armed forces invaded Kuwait and overran it in hours. Iraq laid claim to Kuwait's territory, saying it had been stealing from its part of an oil field lying in both countries. The United Nations Security Council demanded Iraq's withdrawal and on Aug. 6 ordered a trade and financial boycott. The U.S., asserting that Saudi Arabia, Kuwait's neighbor to the south, was also threatened, on Aug. 7 ordered troops, armor, and aircraft to the Saudi kingdom. By Aug. 9 a naval blockade was formed and all export of oil from Iraq and Kuwait was cut off. On Aug. 10 at a meeting in Cairo, 12 of the 21 member nations of the Arab League voted to support the UN and U.S. actions. By Nov. 8 some 230,000 American troops were in Saudi Arabia and Pres. Bush announced that 150,000 more would be sent. The UN Security Council on Nov. 29 voted to authorize the U.S. and its allies to use force to expel Iraq from Kuwait if Iraqi troops did not leave by Jan. 15, 1991. By year's end 580,000 Iraqi troops were believed to be in Kuwait or southern Iraq. Facing them were 485,000 troops of 17 allied countries.

Oct 22: Pres Bush vetoed a **civil rights bill** and two days later the Senate upheld the veto. Bush said the act would have imposed racial and other quotas in employment. It would have put on employers the burden of defending themselves when charged with discrimination.

Nov 1: An agreement to end all **dumping of industrial waste at sea** by 1995 was made by 43 nations, including the U.S. and all the leading industrial countries of the world at a meeting in London. The measure was legally binding on all 64 nations that had signed the 20-year-old treaty known as the London Dumping Convention.

Nov 5: Pres. Bush signed a **budget law** intended to reduce the federal budget by $492,000,000,000 over the next five years. This act ended a bitter three-month controversy between the Republican president and Congress, controlled by the Democrats. The law included $140,000,000,000 in new taxes over a five-year period in spite of Bush's campaign promise in 1988 that he would never approve new taxes.

Nov 6: In **congressional elections** the Democrats gained one seat in the Senate to give them a 56–44 majority, and eight seats in the House for a 267–167 majority, with one place going to an independent.

Nov 15: The **Clean Air Act of 1990,** which updated and tightened air pollution standards for the first time since 1977, was signed into law by Pres. Bush. The aim of the law was to cut acid rain pollutants by half, reduce urban smog, and eliminate industrial emissions of toxic chemicals by the end of the century. The cost was expected to be $25,000,000,000 a year.

Nov 19: The most extensive **arms control treaty** in history was signed in Paris by 20 European nations, the U.S., and Canada. NATO and the Warsaw Pact would each be limited to 20,000 tanks, 20,000 artillery pieces, 30,000 armored vehicles, 6800 airplanes, and 2000 helicopters. Current levels of these items ranged from about 10% higher to more than double. In addition the U.S. and Germany agreed to a level of no more than 195,000 American troops in Central Europe and no more than 370,000 personnel in the German armed forces.

Nov 29: The **Immigration Act of 1990,** the most far-ranging revision in 66 years, was signed into law by Pres. Bush. It set a total of 700,000 persons to be admitted per year. Of these, 465,000 were to be relatives of American citizens or permanently residing aliens. Another 140,000 places were reserved for skilled workers.

Dec 7: Negotiations concerning the **General Agreement on Tariffs and Trade** (GATT) broke down after four years of discussion among 107 nations. Failure came to the Brussels, Belgium, session when the European Community refused to cut its farm subsidies as much as the U.S. demanded. The negotiators also failed to reach agreements to protect drug and software companies whose patents were not recognized in the developing world, and American music and movie companies from copyright pirates.

Dec 11: Two chain reaction collisions of a total of 75 vehicles in southeastern Tennessee on Interstate Highway 75 killed 15 people and injured more than 50. Heavy fog was blamed for the disaster which involved cars and trucks on both sides of the highway.

II. Architecture
Arts and Music
Popular Entertainment
Publishing
Theater

The 1989–1990 Broadway theater season set a record for box office receipts for the third year in a row: $283,000,000, up from $262,000,000. Attendance was 8,030,000, up from 7,970,000 and there were 35 new productions compared with 30. Generally judged the best new American plays of the year were *Six Degrees of Separation, The Piano Lesson,* and *Prelude to a Kiss.* The movies had box office receipts at nearly $5,000,000,000 for their second best year ever, but with the total number of screens now nearly 23,000, not enough hit movies were being produced to keep the seats filled. For 1990 the movies with the highest gross sales were *Ghost, Pretty Woman,* and *Home Alone.* Mostly praised but not all hits were *Dances*

With Wolves, Dick Tracy, Alice, The Godfather, Part III, and *Goodfellas. Bonfire of the Vanities* was a flop, but *Teenage Mutant Ninja Turtles* did more than well. In the world of dance there was a festival of Jerome Robbins's ballets, and the American Ballet Theater celebrated its 50th anniversary. From the U.S.S.R. the Georgia State Dance Company was warmly welcomed. Among the many musical events of the year, the New York City Opera's production of Arnold Schoenberg's *Moses and Aaron* was a high point, as was the debut of Yevgeny Kissin, a young Russian pianist, with the New York Philharmonic. Although two new television series, *Twin Peaks* and *The Simpsons,* were far from run of the mill and became hits, the most popular series were old ones: *Cheers,* in its ninth year, *60 Minutes,* and *Murder She Wrote.* The outstanding production by far was *The Civil War,* 11 hours in length on PBS. Newspaper circulation in large cities showed a tendency to decline as that of suburban papers increased. In 1950 New Yorkers bought 9,200,000 copies of the Sunday papers; in 1990 the figure was a little under 3,200,000. In the magazine field 3100 were being published, of which 536 began publication this year. Paperback books showed a greater sales increase than hardbound books: about 7.2% compared with 4.4%. In the Christmas season 36% of adult Americans received one or more books as gifts, an increase of 17.5% over 1989. Notable people who died included Eve Arden, comedienne, particularly known as *Our Miss Brooks* on TV, Nov. 12, at 83; Pearl Bailey, a singer with a warm and mischievous style, Aug. 17, at 72; Joan Bennett, star of the movies and the stage, Dec. 7, at 80; Leonard Bernstein, conductor, composer, and pianist, Oct. 14, at 72; Gordon Bunshaft, a leader among International Style architects, Aug. 6, at 81; Aaron Copland, composer noted for his treatment of American themes, Dec. 2, at 90; Norman Cousins, magazine editor and author, Nov. 30, at 75; Sammy Davis, Jr., black singer, dancer, and actor, May 16, at 74; Hedley Donovan, editor-in-chief of Time, Inc., from 1964 to 1979, June 29, at 74; Irene Dunne, actress in both sophisticated and humorous roles, Sept. 4, at 91; Douglas Edwards, the first TV anchorman, Oct. 13, at 73; Charles Farrell, movie star of the 1930s and 1940s, May 6, at 82; Stuart Berg Flexner, a leading lexicographer, Dec. 3, at 62; Greta Garbo, movie actress of magnetic and elusive beauty, Apr. 15, at 84; Ava Gardner, a most seductive screen star, Jan. 25, at 77; Paulette Goddard, film actress in both sultry and comedy roles, Apr. 23, at 78; Dexter Gordon, jazz saxophonist and pioneer of be-bop, Apr. 25, at 67; Jim Henson, creator of the delightful puppets, the Muppets, May 16, at 53; Werner Janssen, conductor and composer who made use of jazz idioms, Sept. 19, at 91; Eric Larrabee, editor and author, best known as a champion of the arts, Dec. 4, at 68; Mary Martin, vivacious star of musical comedy and of *Peter Pan,* Nov. 3, at 78; Lewis Mumford, critic in various fields and a pioneer advocate of city planning, Jan. 26, at 94; Walker Percy, novelist who wrote of the present-day South, May 10, at 73; George Nakashima, a master of woodworking and design, June 15, at 85; Johnny Ray, a popular singer of great emotion, Feb. 24, at 63; Anya Seton, author of popular historical novels and biographies, Nov. 8, at 86; Bella Spewack, writer, with her husband, of the books for many plays and movies, Apr. 27, at 91; Barbara Stanwyck, accomplished in varied roles on the stage and in the movies, Jan. 20, at 82; Eleanor Steber, soprano, noted for her roles in Mozart and Strauss operas, Oct. 3, at 76; Iphigene Ochs Sulzberger, who behind the scenes had great influence on the development of *The New York Times* for three generations, Feb. 26, at 97; Sarah Vaughan, a jazz singer with a rich and impressive voice, Apr. 3, at 76; Irving Wallace, author of 33 books that sold millions of copies, June 29, at 74.

Books published in 1990 displayed the usual diversity of subject matter. In fiction there was *The Plains of Passage,* more adventures in prehistoric times by Jean M. Auel; *Buffalo Girls,* Larry McMurtry's view of the Old West; *Friend of My Youth,* short stories by Alice Munro; *Because It Is Bitter, and Because It Is My Heart,* Joyce Carol Oates's account of a young girl coming of age; *The Things They Carried,* short stories by Tim O'Brien, set among soldiers in Vietnam; *Burden of Proof* by Scott Turow, a complicated tale of financial misdoings; *Rabbit at Rest,* John Updike's ending of the life and times of Harry 'Rabbit' Angstrom; and *Hollywood* by Gore Vidal, the sixth of his novels chronicling American history. Nonfiction was marked by two books reflecting the Reagan era just ended: *Barbarians at the Gate: The Fall of RJR Nabisco* by Bryan Burrough and John Helyar was an account of the finagling that accompanied the buyout of RJR Nabisco, and *The Politics of Rich and Poor* by Kevin Phillips showed how well the wealthy fared compared with the poor. Other nonfiction offerings included *A Life on the Road* by Charles Kuralt; *Captain Sir Richard Francis Burton* by Edward Rice, the life of the man most remembered for translating the *Arabian Nights* but who did much, much more; *Baseball: The People's Game,* the third volume of Harold Seymour's erudite history of the pastime; *Father, Son & Co.: My Life at IBM and Beyond* by Thomas J. Watson, Jr., indicating it was not easy to follow in the footsteps of his father, the founder; and *Men at Work* by George F. Will, the columnist's tribute to the skill of baseball players. Finally, in a class by itself, was *Millie's Book: As Dictated to Barbara Bush*, in which the First Dog told of life in the White House.

Feb 21: Grammy Awards were presented for the following: best album of 1989, *Nick of Time* by Bonnie Raitt, who also won the awards for best female pop and rock vocalist; best song, "Wind Beneath My Wings" by Bette Midler; best male rock vocalist, Don Henley for *The End of Innocence;* best male pop vocalist, Michael Bolton for "How Am I Supposed to Live Without You."

Mar 18: In a nighttime **art theft** at the Isabella Stewart Gardner Museum in Boston, thieves made off with 12 works of art, including paintings by Degas, Rembrandt, Renoir, and Vermeer, valued at about $100,000,000.

Mar 26: Academy Awards were presented to *Driving Miss Daisy* as outstanding motion picture of 1989; Daniel Day-Lewis as best actor for *My Left Foot;* Jessica Tandy as best actress for *Driving Miss Daisy;* Denzel Washington as best supporting actor for *Glory;* and Brenda Fricker as best supporting actress for *My Left Foot.*

Mar 29: The major producing companies agreed to put a **warning label on recordings** that contain lyrics which might offend some people. Some companies had already been attaching warnings about lyrics that were explicit about violence and sex.

Apr 7: Indictments for **obscenity** were lodged against the Contemporary Art Center, Cincinnati, Ohio, and its director in connection with an exhibit of photographs by the late Robert M. Mapplethorpe, known for his homoerotic themes. Officials seized 175 of the pictures on exhibit. On Oct. 5 a jury acquitted the museum and the director.

Apr 12: Pulitzer prizes were awarded for the following: fiction, *The Mambo Kings Play Song of Love* by Oscar Hijuelos; biography, *Machiavelli in Hell* by Sebastian de Grazia; history, *In Our Image: America's Empire in the Philippines* by Stanley Karnow; general nonfiction, *And Their Children After Them* by Dale Maharidge and Michael Williamson; poetry, *The World Doesn't End* by Charles Simic; drama, *The Piano Lesson* by August Wilson.

Apr 28: The **longest running show on Broadway, A Chorus Line,** closed after 6237 performances. It opened July 25, 1975, and on Sept. 29, 1983, became the longest running production when it surpassed *Grease* with its 3389th performance. In its run *A Chorus Line* was seen by about 6,543,000 people and had 510 different members of the cast.

May 15: In New York the **highest art auction price** ever paid, $82,500,000, was brought by Vincent Van Gogh's painting *Portrait of Dr. Gachet.* On May 17 the second highest price ever paid for a painting was registered when *At the Moulin de la Galette* by Pierre Auguste Renoir went for $78,100,000. The purchaser of both paintings was Ryoei Saito, a Japanese industrialist, who had been an art collector for 40 years.

May 25: Mark Strand was named the fourth **poet laureate** of the U.S. Strand was born in Canada.

June 3: Tony awards for the 1989–1990 season were presented for the following: best play, *The Grapes of Wrath* adapted by James Galati; best musical, *City of Angels* by Larry Gelbart, Cy Coleman, and David Zippel; best actor in a play, Robert Morse for *Tru;* best actress in a play, Maggie Smith for *Lettice and Lovage;* best actor in a musical, James Naughton for *City of Angels;* best actress in a musical, Tyne Daly for *Gypsy.*

Sep 16: Emmy Awards were presented for the following: best drama series, *L. A. Law;* best comedy series, *Murphy Brown;* best actor in a drama series, Peter Falk for *Columbo;* best actress in a drama series, Patricia Wettig for *Thirtysomething;* best actor in a comedy series, Ted Danson for *Cheers;* best actress in a comedy series, Candice Bergen for *Murphy Brown.*

Nov 27: National Book Awards were presented for the following: fiction, *The Middle Passage* by Charles Johnson; nonfiction, *The House of Morgan: An American Banking Dynasty and the Rise of Modern Finance* by Ron Chernow.

III. Business and Industry
Education
Philosophy and Religion
Science

The national economy without doubt was in a recession by year's end. GNP rose only 0.9% for the year and declined by 2.1% in the last quarter. Unemployment rose to 6.1%, its highest level since mid-1987, but the consumer price index rose 6.1%, the most since 1981. Sales of new homes fell by 17.5% to the lowest level since 1981 and sales of motor vehicles dropped 5.1% to the lowest figure since 1983. On the financial front merger deals amounted to $412,500,000,000, down from $518,800,000,000 in 1989, while the rating of $510,000,000,000 of corporate debt was downgraded. The recession helped narrow the trade deficit by reducing imports so that the imbalance for the year was $100,000,000,000, the smallest in seven years, and personal income rose 6.08%, almost matching the inflation rate. For the first time in seven years the consumption of petroleum fell, by 2.1% to 16,960,000 barrels a day, but domestic production decreased by 5.1% to 7,200,000 barrels a day. By 1990 the number of fast food outlets had risen since 1980 to 119,000 from 67,290, while the number of book stores had grown, from 10,200 to 17,620. Also on the rise was the temperature around the U.S. It averaged 53.94° F in 1990, the seventh highest on record. The 96-year average was 52.5° F, the record having been set in 1934 at 54.67° F. Notable people who died in 1990 included Ralph David Abernathy, pioneer in the civil rights movement, successor to Martin Luther King, Jr., Apr. 17, at 74; Bruno Bettelheim, psychoanalyst who specialized in the emotional problems of children, Mar. 13, at 86; Harry Bridges, left-wing labor leader who led a general strike that tied up San Francisco in 1934, Mar. 30, at 88; Harold E. Edgerton, inventor of the electronic flash for photography, Jan. 4, at 86; Malcolm S. Forbes, flamboyant millionaire magazine publisher, Feb. 24, at 70; Armand Hammer, oil executive known for his business relations with the U.S.S.R. in spite of the Cold War, Dec. 10, at 92; Robert Hofstadter, Nobel prize physicist who explored nuclear particles, Nov. 17, at 75; Samuel Noah Kramer, the leading authority on ancient Sumeria, Nov. 26, at 93; Karl A. Menninger, innovative psychiatrist, one of the founders of the Menninger Clinic, July 18, at 96; Robert N. Noyce, coinventor of the integrated circuit, which revolutionized the electronics industry, June 3, at 62; William S. Paley, founder and builder of the Columbia Broadcasting System, Oct. 26, at 89; Albert Rose, whose research made possible the television picture tube, July 26, at 80; B. F. Skinner, psychologist whose theories of behavior control were alarming to some, Aug. 18, at 86; Nathaniel C. Wyeth, inventor of the plastic soda bottle, July 4, at 80.

Jan 11: Approval of the **Jarvik-7 artificial heart** was withdrawn by the Food and Drug Administration saying there were manufacturing problems and reports of adverse reactions. In 1982 it was the first artificial heart in the world and by now had been used about 150 times.

Jan 22: In the growing **savings and loan crisis,** the Justice Department reported that 403 people had been convicted of fraud in the past two years in connection with misdeeds in 506 savings and loan institutions. Losses from the frauds totalled $6,400,000,000 and 79% of those convicted had received prison terms.

Feb 27: Federal health officials recommended a **reduction in the fat content of diets** whether or not a person had a high cholesterol level.

Mar 3: A gift of $50,000,000 to the **United Negro College Fund** was announced by Walter H. Annenberg, wealthy publisher and a former ambassador to Great Britain. The Fund represents 41 predominately black institutions and this gift was the largest ever in this field.

Apr: Officials of the **Mormon Church** confirmed that the church dropped a vow in which women pledged obedience to their husbands and also a requirement that they veil their faces at a point in a ceremony.

Apr 22: The **20th anniversary of Earth Day** was celebrated around the world and organizers said 200,000,000 people in 140 countries had participated. In the U.S. in cities and towns there were demonstrations, tree plantings, recycling exhibits, workshops on endangered species, and other events.

Apr 25: Seven years behind schedule, the **Hubble Space Telescope** was launched by the space shuttle *Discovery* into an orbit 381 miles above the earth. The $1,500,000,000 instrument, weighing 12 tons, was expected to enlarge the vision of astronomers tenfold and to bring into view up to 10,000,000,000,000 objects in the universe. However after the instrument was opened to the heavens with some difficulty it was discovered on June 27 that there was a serious flaw in its main light-gathering mirror. It would not be able to carry out the major part of its planned observations until and unless replacement instruments were installed. Nevertheless, the Hubble Telescope produced some valuable observations: an unexpected concentration of stars around what had been thought to be an ordinary galaxy; new views of Saturn and Pluto; the first sighting of a faint quasar billions of light years from earth; and an unusually clear picture of a storm around Saturn.

June 5: The Presbyterian Church (U.S.A.) adopted a **new statement of faith.** While reaffirming the basic Christian beliefs of the denomination, the statement declared that everyone was equal "in God's image, male and female, of every race and people, to live as one community."

June 12: Conservatives retained control of the Southern Baptist Convention for the 12th year in succession, electing a fundamentalist, Morris Chapman, a clergyman of Wichita Falls, Tex., as president with 58% of the votes of the delegates.

June 25: The Central Conference of American Rabbis voted to **admit active homosexuals to the rabbinate.** The conference represented Reform Judaism, and with 1,500,000 members was the largest branch of American Judaism. The issue had been before reform rabbis for 15 years.

June 30: The **AIDS epidemic** was spreading to new groups in society, including black and Hispanic women, the National Academy of Science said. Men and women enlisting in the military were equally infected. By now 16,000 persons had died of AIDS in New York City.

July 18: In a controversy over **homosexuals in the clergy,** the Evangelical Lutheran Church in America suspended two congregations for having ordained an openly gay man and two lesbian women. The church had previously accepted the ordination of gay clergy who were silent about their sexual orientation.

July 31: Experiments in **gene therapy** by the insertion of new genes into body cells were approved for the first time by an advisory committee of the National Institutes of Health. One gene therapy procedure would treat children with adenosine deaminase (ADA), an immune disorder in which there is a lack of an enzyme necessary to break down certain dangerous byproducts that can destroy immune cells.

Sep 30: The **New Revised Standard Version of the Bible,** successor to the Revised Standard Version of 1952, the Bible used officially by the major Protestant denominations, was published. The new edition made several notable changes: although God is still "our Father," elsewhere masculine terms were changed, as "man" to "one"; "dark, but comely" became "black and beautiful"; and archaic "thees" were modernized.

Oct 6: The unmanned spacecraft **Ulysses** was put into orbit from the space shuttle *Discovery.* It was intended to survey the southern hemisphere of the Sun from May to September, 1994. Its course was to take it 500,000,000 miles to Jupiter before it used that planet's gravity to head toward the solar orbit.

Oct 8: The **Nobel Prize for Medicine or Physiology** was awarded jointly to Joseph E. Murray of the Brigham and Women's Hospital in Boston, Mass., and to E. Donnall Thomas of the Fred Hutchinson Cancer Center in Seattle, Wash. In the early 1950s they performed, respectively, the first kidney and the first bone-marrow transplants.

Oct 12: The **largest award in a patent infringement case** resulted from an order in a federal court that the Eastman Kodak Company pay the Polaroid Corporation $909,400,000. Kodak had been found guilty in 1985 of infringing Polaroid's instant photography patents. On Jan. 11, 1991, a judge reduced the award by $36,000,000.

Oct 16: The **Nobel Prize in Physics** was awarded to Jerome I. Friedman and Henry W. Kendall, both of the Massachusetts Institute of Technology, and to Richard E. Taylor, a Canadian at Stanford University. All three were honored for their research that confirmed the existence of quarks.

Oct 16: The **Nobel Prize in Chemistry** was awarded to Elias James Corey of Harvard University who developed methods for synthesizing complex substances.

Oct 16: The **Nobel Prize in Economics** was awarded to Harry M. Markowitz of the City University of New York for his investment theories; to Merton H. Miller of the University of Chicago for his work on the best ways to evaluate a corporation's value; and to William F. Sharpe of William F. Sharpe Associates for his explanation of how stock markets move in relation to investors' decisions.

Oct 25: A historic **transplant operation** was performed at the Stanford University Medical School when part of a mother's lung was transferred into that of her 12-year-old daughter who was dying as a result of severe scarring of the lungs. Hitherto such operations had been performed using organs from persons who had recently died.

Nov 11: The first recipient of a **heart and liver transplant** in the same operation died. Stormie Jones was not quite seven years old when the operation was performed on her in a Pittsburgh hospital Feb. 14, 1984.

Nov 16: The world's **first superconducting transistors** able to operate at relatively high temperatures have been built at the Sandia National Laboratories in Albuquerque, New Mexico, it was announced. The new devices were said to be useful mostly in assisting further research in the field.

Nov 21: The creator of the "junk bond," **Michael R. Milken,** was sentenced to ten years in prison for violating federal securities laws and for other crimes. He had pleaded guilty on Apr. 24, 1990, to six criminal charges and agreed to pay $600,000,000 in fines and other penalties.

Dec 10: The **first essentially new contraceptive device** in 25 years was approved by the Food and Drug Administration. It is a set of small soft tubes that are implanted under a woman's skin and which then release progestin, a hormone that can prevent conception for five years.

Dec 31: The **Dow Jones industrial stock average** closed the year at 2633.66, down 4.3%.

IV. Fashion
Folkways
Holidays
Social Issues and Crime
Sports

A poll showed that football continued to be America's favorite sport with a following of 35%. Baseball stayed in second place with a 16% following, but basketball's fans had increased from 10% to 15% in the last decade. Baseball had reason to worry: its most faithful followers were over 50 years of age. Basketball, on the other hand, had a following made up of younger fans and blacks. As to active participation in athletics, 158,000 women now took part in intercollegiate sports, an increase from the 34,000 cited 18 years earlier. On the PGA Seniors tour, Lee Trevino won $1,190,518, topping Greg Norman's $1,165,477 on the regular tour, the first time a Seniors pro was the top PGA money-winner. Meanwhile, on the LPGA tour, Pat Bradley became the first woman golfer to pass the $3,000,000 mark, her winnings in the year's tournaments putting her at $3,059,718. Most of the nation's cities set new records for homicides, among them Dallas, Memphis, Milwaukee, New York, Phoenix, San Antonio, and Washington. Figures released this year showed that the homicide rate among black men, ages 15 to 24, rose by two-thirds from 1985 through 1988. On the downward trend were drinking and smoking. In 1979 76% of those 18 to 25 years of age said they had used alcohol in the past month; now it was 63%; those who smoked cigarettes decreased to 32% compared with a high of 50% in 1976. Deaths of notable persons included George Allen, a successful football coach, Dec. 31, at 72; Spurgeon F. "Spud" Chandler, a winning pitcher for the New York Yankees in the 1940s, Jan. 10, at 82; "Rocky" Graziano (Thomas Rocco Barbella), middleweight boxing champion, popular for his brawling style, May 22, at 71; Halston (Roy Halston Frowick), an influential fashion designer of the 1970s, Mar. 26, at 57; Tom Harmon, Michigan's All-American running back who scored 33 touchdowns in 24 games, Mar. 15, at 70; Charley Keller, hard-hitting outfielder for the New York Yankees in the 1940s and 1950s, May 23, at 73; Lester J. Maitland, who made the first flight from the U.S. mainland to Hawaii in 1927, Mar. 29, at 91; Alice Marble, champion tennis player of the late 1930s who four times won the U.S. title, Dec. 13, at 77; Bronislaw "Bronko" Nagurski, a daunting running back in college and in the pros in the 1920s and 1930s, Jan. 7, at 81; Joe Sewell, member of the Baseball Hall of Fame who batted .312 over a 14-season career, Mar. 6, at 91; George P. Stavropoulos, fashion designer, Dec. 10, at 70; Horace C. Stoneham, owner of the New York Giants baseball team who in 1958 moved the team to San Francisco Giants, Jan. 7, at 86.

Jan 1: In **college football bowl games** the results were Tennessee 31, Arkansas 27 in the Cotton Bowl; Notre Dame 14, Colorado 0 in the Orange Bowl; USC 17, Michigan 10 in the Rose Bowl; and Miami 33, Alabama 25 in the Sugar Bowl. Both the AP and UPI picked Miami as the national collegiate champions of 1989.

Jan 28: Super Bowl XXIV was won by the San Francisco Forty-Niners, who defeated the Denver Broncos 55 to 10 and whose total points and victory margin set records. On Jan. 14 San Francisco had won the NFC title by defeating the Los Angeles Rams 30 to 3,

and Denver won the AFC by beating the Cleveland Browns 37 to 21.

Feb 3: Jockey **Bill Shoemaker** retired, having ridden to 8833 victories, including four Kentucky Derby triumphs, five in the Belmont Stakes, and two in the Preakness Stakes.

Feb 10–11: U.S. figure skating championships were won at Salt Lake City, Utah, by Jill Trenary, for the third time, in women's singles; Todd Eldredge, men's singles; Kristi Yamaguchi and Rudi Galindo, pairs; and Susan Wynne and Joseph Druar, dance.

Feb 11: The **world heavyweight boxing championship** was won by James "Buster" Douglas when he knocked out the titleholder Mike Tyson in the tenth round of a bout in Tokyo. However, Douglas lost his title Oct. 25 in Los Vegas when he was knocked out in the third round of a fight with Evander Holyfield.

Mar 25: In one of the worst **mass murders** in U.S. history, a fire in a crowded illegal social club, the Happy Land Social Club in the Bronx, New York City, took 87 lives after a man who had been ejected from the club for quarreling with a former girlfriend, returned, threw gasoline near the door and set it afire. The flash fire took its toll by asphyxiation and burns within minutes. The arsonist, Julio Gonzalez, 36, a Cuban refugee, was convicted of all 87 murders as well as arson and assault on Aug. 19, 1991, and on September 19, 1991, he was sentenced to 25 years to life in prison.

Apr 1: The **NCAA women's basketball championship** was won by Stanford which defeated Auburn 88 to 81.

Apr 2: The **NCAA men's basketball championship** was won by the University of Nevada, Las Vegas, which defeated Duke 103 to 73. It was the first time more than 100 points had been scored by a team in this championship game.

Apr 8: The **Masters golf tournament** was won by Nick Faldo of England who defeated Raymond Floyd on the second hole of a playoff. Faldo became only the second player to win this event two years in succession.

Apr 16: The 94th **Boston Marathon** was won by Gelindo Bordin of Italy in the men's division with a time of 2 hrs., 8 min., 19 sec. The women's division was won by Rosa Mota of Portugal with a time of 2 hrs., 23 min., 24 sec.

May 5: The 116th **Kentucky Derby** was won by Unbridled with a time of 2:02. The jockey was Craig Perret.

May 19: The 115th **Preakness Stakes** was won by Summer Squall with a time of 1:53 3/5. The jockey was Pat Day.

May 24: The **NHL Stanley Cup** was won by the Edmonton Oilers for the fifth time in seven years when they defeated the Boston Bruins four games to one.

May 27: The 74th **Indianapolis 500** auto race was won by Arie Luyendyk of the Netherlands with an average speed of 185.984 mph, a new record.

June 9: The 122nd **Belmont Stakes** was won by Go and Go, an Irish colt, with a time of 2:27 2/5. The jockey was Michael Kinane.

June 14: The **NBA basketball championship** was won for the second consecutive year by the Detroit Pistons, who defeated the Portland Trail Blazers four games to one.

June 18: The **U.S. Open golf tournament** was won by Hale Irwin in a 19-hole playoff. It was the third time he had won this event and he was the oldest player ever to do so.

June 27: Becoming the **highest paid player in professional baseball,** José Canseco of the Oakland Athletics signed a contract that would earn him $23,500,000 over a five-year period. By the end of 1990 23 players had signed contracts giving them more than $3,000,000 a year.

July 2: **Imelda Marcos** was acquitted of four charges of racketeering and fraud in a federal court in New York City. The widow of the former president of the Philippines, she had been accused with her husband Ferdinand of stealing more than $200,000,000 from the government they once headed and using it to buy art, jewelry, and real estate in the U.S. Ferdinand Marcos had also been indicted on Apr. 6, 1989, but had been declared too ill to stand trial. He died on Sept. 28, 1989.

July 7: At the **Wimbledon** tennis championships in England, the women's singles tennis title was won by Martina Navratilova for a record ninth time. She won her other eight titles in 1978–1979 and 1982–1987. Navratilova had been tied with Helen Wills Moody, who won the last of her eight championships in 1938.

July 10: The **baseball All-Star Game** was won for the third straight year by the American League, which defeated the National League 2 to 0.

July 15: The **U.S. Women's Open golf tournament** was won by Betsy King for the second consecutive year, by one stroke.

July 30: **George Steinbrenner,** the general partner of the New York Yankees (AL), was banned by Commissioner of Major League Baseball Fay Vincent from any further involvement in the management of the team. Vincent found that Steinbrenner had violated a major league rule by becoming involved with a known gambler for the past three years. He was allowed to retain his partial ownership of the club. On Aug. 15 Robert E. Nederlander, of a theatrical management family, was named to run the Yankees.

July 31: **Nolan Ryan** of the Texas Rangers (AL) became the 10th major league pitcher to win 300 games in his career when he pitched his team to an 11 to 3 victory over the Milwaukee Brewers.

Aug 6: The **Baseball Hall of Fame** inducted Joe Morgan, a second baseman who had played for five teams, and Jim Palmer, star pitcher of the Baltimore Orioles. Both had been elected in their first year of eligibility.

Aug 11: The **PGA golf tournament** was won by Wayne Grady of Australia by three strokes.

Sep 2: A **major league pitching record** of nine no-hit games in a season was set when Dave Stieb of the Toronto Blue Jays (AL) pitched such a game against the Cleveland Indians. Seven of the no–hitters were pitched in the American League and set a record there.

Sep 8: **Ellis Island,** in New York Harbor, through which 12,000,000 immigrants entered the U.S. between 1892 and 1924, reopened as a museum of immigration. Passage through the island's facilities ended in 1954 and the ten buildings, badly deteriorated, had now been restored at a cost of $156,000,000 through private contributions.

Sep 8: The **Miss America** title was won by Marjorie Judith Vincent, 25, a law student from Oak Park, Ill., and the fourth black to win, at the annual pageant in Atlantic City, N.J.

Sep 8–9: The **U.S. Open tennis singles championships** were won by Gabriela Sabatini in the women's division and by Pete Sampras, only 19 years old, in the men's division.

Oct 16–20: The **World Series** was won by the Cincinnati Reds (NL) over the Oakland Athletics (AL), four games to none, in an upset. On Oct. 12 the Reds had won the National League Pennant by defeating the Pittsburgh Pirates four games to two, and on Oct. 10 the Athletics had won the American League title over the Boston Red Sox in four straight games.

Dec 13: **Serial murderer** Arthur J. Shawcross was convicted of killing ten women in the Rochester, N.Y., area between 1988 and 1990. Shawcross was on parole for having strangled two children in 1972. On Feb. 1, 1991, he was sentenced to a minimum of 250 years in prison.

Dec 21: In the case of **collusion against free agents,** major league baseball club owners agreed to pay certain players $280,000,000 to compensate them for what they presumably lost between 1986 and 1990 when the owners in collusion dealt with free agent players in such a way as to reduce their salaries. As part of the agreement, 15 players became "new–look" free agents, allowed to negotiate with any club.

1991

I. Civil Rights
   Exploration and Settlement
   Government
   Statistics
   Wars

The nation began the year with apprehension over imminent war in the Persian Gulf, became euphoric when victory was quickly achieved, but relapsed into apprehension again when an economic recession hung on and seemed to get worse. The year saw a continued shift of population to the South and the West with a considerable part of the movement accounted for by blacks leaving the northern cities. The number of persons identifying themselves as Native American had tripled to 1,800,000 since 1960; the number of Asian Americans had increased by 107.8% and Hispanics by 53.0% since 1980. Other data this year revealed that about 5,500,000 children under 12 were going hungry; that nearly one out of four babies was born out of wedlock; that in the 1980s more than 900 male farmers in the upper Middle West committed suicide; that while black-white marriages had more than tripled since 1970, such couples still faced considerable social ostracism; and that women held only 31.3% of high-level state and local government positions, while occupying 43.5% of lower-level jobs. Notable persons who died included Virginia Mae Brown, first woman to be chairman of the Interstate Commerce Commission, Feb. 24, at 67; John Sherman Cooper, liberal Republican senator for more than 20 years, Feb. 21, at 89; Hamilton Fish, an isolationist and bitter enemy of Pres. Franklin D. Roosevelt who served in Congress for 24 years, Jan. 18, at 102; Lloyd K. Garrison, a lawyer who championed liberal social causes, Oct. 2, at 93; James Roosevelt, eldest son of Pres. Roosevelt, a combat Marine and congressman, Aug. 13, at 83; John G. Tower, Republican senator from Texas for 24 years, Apr. 5, at 65; and Robert F. Wagner, Mayor of New York City from 1954 to 1965, Feb. 12, at 80.

Jan 7: Cancellation of the **largest weapons program ever terminated** was announced by the Defense Dept. Involved was the A-12 Avenger, a navy plane of the radar-evading stealth type. The planes were to have cost $57,000,000,000 but the program was already 16 months behind schedule and more than $2,700,000,000 over budget.

Jan. 15: In a **school desegregation case,** the Supreme Court, 5–2, ruled that districts may be released from court-ordered busing when they have taken all "practicable" steps to eliminate segregation. The case concerned the Oklahoma City, Okla., schools.

Jan. 15–Feb. 27: The **Persian Gulf War,** codenamed Operation Desert Storm, authorized by the U.N. and led by the U.S., began with an all-out air war against Iraq. Its objective was to drive Iraqi forces out of Kuwait, which Iraq had occupied since Aug. 2, 1990. Ground action began Feb. 24 and three days later Pres. George Bush halted the fighting with Iraqi forces routed. Iraq agreed to destroy its facilities for making chemical, nuclear, and biological weapons, but stalled the actual carrying out of the relevant UN resolutions. American casualties were 146 dead and 467 wounded.

Feb 1: The State Department's annual report on **human rights** around the world said Iraq had an "abysmal record" of torture and summary executions, but it also criticized Kuwait, Saudi Arabia, Syria, and Turkey, all U.S. allies in the Persian Gulf War.

Feb 1: A head-on **airplane crash** at the Los Angeles airport, involving a USAir Boeing 737 about to land and a SkyWest commuter craft about to take off from the same runway, killed 22 of 69 persons aboard the former and all 12 on the latter. The planes were mistakenly cleared to use the same runway.

Feb 3: A **postal rate increase** for first class postage, from 25 to 29 cents for the first ounce, was announced by the U.S. Postal Service. Other rates were to go up in proportion.

Feb 6: An **act to benefit Vietnam War veterans** who were exposed to the herbicide Agent Orange, which was used to defoliate jungle cover, was signed by Pres. Bush. The law extended disability benefits to those suffering from two kinds of cancer, Non-Hodgkin's lymphoma and soft-tissue sarcoma.

Mar. 20: In a unanimous decision affecting **women in the workplace,** the Supreme Court ruled that employers may not exclude women from jobs that might expose a fetus to toxic substances. The court said such action would be a violation of the federal Civil Rights Act of 1964 which prohibits sex discrimination in employment.

Apr 1: The use of **racial criteria in jury selection** is unconstitutional, regardless of the race of the defendant or the jurors excluded, the Supreme Court ruled, 7–2. The decision broadened the right of defendants to object to the use of race by prosecutors in jury selection.

Apr 16: More than 79 **tornadoes** struck seven states in the Midwest and Southwest, killing 23 people, 14 of them in Andover, Kans., where 290 trailer homes and 110 houses were demolished.

June 3: In another ruling on **racial criteria in jury selection,** the Supreme Court voted, 6–3, that jurors may not be excluded from civil lawsuits because of race. The decision extended a 1986 decision that barred prosecutors in criminal cases from excluding jurors on the basis of race.

June 27: Thurgood Marshall resigned as a justice of the Supreme Court. A hero of the civil rights movement and a strong liberal voice on the court, he had served since 1967, and was the first black to become a justice.

July 10: Most **economic sanctions against South Africa** were lifted by order of Pres. Bush. He said the movement to end apartheid was now "irreversible." The sanctions had been imposed by a law passed in 1986.

July 31: A **nuclear arms reduction treaty** was signed in Moscow by Pres. Bush and Mikhail S. Gorbachev, president of the U.S.S.R. The treaty called for the Soviet Union to cut its nuclear warheads from 10,841 to 8040 within seven years while the U.S. would reduce its total to 10,395 from 12,081.

Aug 8–Dec 4: The last **six American hostages in Lebanon,** who had been held for varying lengths of time, were released by Islamic terrorists. One, Terry Anderson, had been a prisoner since Mar. 16, 1985.

Sep 2: Full **diplomatic recognition of the Baltic states,** Estonia, Latvia, and Lithuania, was granted by the U.S., signifying their freedom from rule by the U.S.S.R.

Sep 3: A **fire in a chicken processing plant** killed 25 people in Hamlet, N.C., and injured 45 others. Exits were either blocked or locked.

Sep 19: A **military alliance** was signed by the U.S. and Kuwait. It allowed the U.S. to use Kuwaiti ports and other facilities, and to store military equipment over a ten-year period, but there was not to be a permanent American military garrison.

Sep 27: A large unilateral **cut in nuclear weapons** was announced by Pres. Bush. All tactical weapons in Europe and Asia and on ships would be eliminated; long-range bombers and intercontinental missiles would no longer be on 24-hour alert status. On Oct. 5 Pres. Gorbachev of the U.S.S.R. announced a similar reduction.

Oct 7: Elliott Abrams pleaded guilty to withholding information from Congress in 1986, while serving as assistant secretary of state, in connection with hearings about secret efforts to aid the Nicaraguan Contras. On Nov. 15 a federal judge sentenced Abrams to two years' probation and 100 hours of community service.

Oct 15: Clarence Thomas, the second black to be appointed to the Supreme Court, was narrowly confirmed by the Senate, 52–48, after bitter confirmation hearings. Besides being opposed by liberals, Thomas was accused of sexual harassment by Anita F. Hill, a black professor of law, whose testimony was savagely attacked by several senators.

Oct 20–23: The **worst fire in California's history,** started in brush in a hilly section of Oakland, took 23 lives, destroyed 2777 single-family homes and 433 apartment units, and did damage estimated at $5,000,000,000.

Nov 4: The **Ronald Reagan Presidential Library** was dedicated at Simi Valley, Calif., with all five living presidents on hand. Besides Reagan, present were George Bush, Jimmy Carter, Gerald Ford, and Richard Nixon. The new library contains 47,000,000 documents.

Nov 21: The **Civil Rights Act of 1991** was signed by Pres. Bush. The new law overturned a Supreme Court decision of 1989 by making it easier for employees to sue employers on grounds of discrimination. The burden of defense was now put on the employer.

Nov 27: Seeking **extradition of suspected terrorists,** Great Britain and the U.S. demanded that Libya turn over to them two intelligence agents they said were responsible for the bombing Dec. 21, 1988, of Pan Am flight 103 over Scotland with the loss of 270 lives. The U.S. had indicted the pair Nov. 14.

Dec 3: Pres. Bush's chief of staff **John Sununu resigned** after months of controversy over his dictatorial style and his use of military aircraft for personal and political trips. He was succeeded by Samuel K. Skinner, transportation secretary.

Dec 27: Amid strained **U.S.-Philippine relations,** the Philippine government ordered the U.S. to close its Subic Bay naval base near Manila by Jan. 12, 1992. An attempt to negotiate a new treaty ended Sept. 16 when the Philippine Senate rejected a new lease. However, on Nov. 5, 1992, the two nations agreed that U.S. forces would continue to have access to military installations in the Philippines.

II. Architecture
Arts and Music
Popular Entertainment
Publishing
Theater

The Broadway theater did not prosper during the 1990–1991 season. There were 28 productions, a decline of two; attendance was 7,360,000, down from 8,030,000; and ticket sales totalled $267,000,000, down from $283,000,000. The most talked about show of the season was the musical *Miss Saigon,* first because of a controversy as to whether or not its stars from the London production would be allowed to take the stage in New York, and then for establishing a new high for a seat at $100. Other hits included *Lost in Yonkers* by Neil Simon, and *The Will Rogers Follies.* The movie industry suffered a summer of letdowns with admissions the lowest in nearly 20 years, dropping from 390,000,000 in 1990 to 329,000,000 this year. High-tech violence did all right in the case of *Terminator 2: Judgment Day,* which at $85,000,000 was the most expensive film ever made. *Hudson Hawk,* even though it starred Bruce Willis, was a flop. On the other hand, *Hook,* somewhat of a sequel to *Peter Pan,* did well, as did the animated version of *Beauty and the Beast.* The field of dance marked the year with both new and old events and attractions: the Guangdong Modern Dance Company of China made its American debut, and a new staging of *The Sleeping Beauty* at a cost of $2,800,000 was deemed worth the price. Television had its high and low spots. Most impressive was the PBS six-and-a-half-hour production of the Sanskrit epic, *The Mahabharata.* More down to earth was *Sarah, Plain and Tall,* in which Glenn Close portrayed a determined pioneer in the Midwest. The usual number of new comedy series began and quickly ended. An exception was *Brooklyn Bridge,* about family life in the 1950s. Most spectacular on the home screen, though, were real-life events, in particular the Persian Gulf War and the Clarence Thomas-Anita Hill controversy in the Senate concerning the Thomas's nomination to the Supreme Court. The recession hit museums, forcing them to close galleries and shorten visiting hours. Among those affected were the Brooklyn Museum and the Detroit Institute of Arts. Two noted artists had retrospective shows: Stuart Davis at the Metropolitan Museum in New York, and Robert Rauschenberg at both the Whitney Museum in New York and the Corcoran Gallery of Art in Washington. Notable persons who died included Berenice Abbott, a pioneer of modern photography, Dec. 10, at 93; Jean Arthur, a most charming actress in comedy dramas, June 19, at 90; Charlie Barnet, jazz saxophonist of the swing era, Sept. 4, at 77; Ralph Bellamy, a character actor who appeared in more than 100 movies, Nov. 29, at 87; Homer Bigart, war correspondent who won two Pulitzer prizes, Apr. 16, at 83; Niven Busch, novelist and screen writer, best known for *Duel in the Sun,* Aug. 25, at 88; Frank Capra, Academy Award winning movie director, noted for his films in praise of the common man, Sept. 3, at 94; Oona O'Neill Chaplin, daughter of playwright Eugene O'Neill and wife of the movie actor Charlie Chaplin, Sept. 27, at

66; John Charles Daly, Jr., popular host of the television quiz show *What's My Line,* Feb. 25, at 77; Miles Davis, jazz trumpeter and protagonist of cool jazz, Sept. 28, at 65; George T. Delacorte, publisher and philanthropist who was especially fond of donating fountains, May 4, at 97; Colleen Dewhurst, a foremost star of the American theater, closely identified with the plays of Eugene O'Neill, Aug. 22, at 67; Mildred Dunnock, stage and movie actress, remembered particularly for her role in *Death of a Salesman,* July 5, at 90; Sumner Locke Elliott, novelist and playwright who came to the U.S. from Australia, June 24, at 73; Paul Engle, poet, editor, and teacher, Mar. 22, at 82; Tennessee Ernie Ford, whose homespun manner made him popular as a host and as a country and Western singer, Oct. 17, at 72; Redd Foxx, black comedian whose humor was bawdy and who was at his best in the television series *Sanford and Son,* Oct. 11 at 68; Stan Getz, who had great influence on jazz with his tenor saxophone, June 6 at 64; Martha Graham, one of the greatest dancers and choreographers the world has known, Apr. 1, at 96; A. B. Guthrie, Jr., a leading novelist of the American West, Apr. 26, at 90; Eva Le Gallienne, innovative actress, producer, and director, June 3, at 92; Fred MacMurray, a pleasant and popular movie and television star, Nov. 5, at 83; Jimmy McPartland, cornetist and exponent of Chicago-style jazz, Mar. 13, at 83; Robert Motherwell, a giant of the abstract-expressionist school, July 16, at 76; Howard Nemerov, poet laureate of the U.S. and Pulitzer prize winner, July 5, at 71; Joseph Papp, one of the most influential theatrical producers of his time, Oct. 31, at 70; Lee Remick, attractive and versatile actress, able to portray an assortment of characters, July 2, at 55; Gene Roddenberry, creator of *Star Trek,* the television and movie success that developed a cult following, Oct. 24, at 70; Rudolph Serkin, one of the most admired pianists of the century, May 8, at 88; Theodor Seuss Geisel, who as Dr. Seuss delighted children with his fantastic stories, Sept. 24, at 87; Elie Siegmeister, composer of the contemporary American symphonic school, Mar. 10, at 82; Isaac Bashevis Singer, master of portraying the life of his native Poland, July 24, at 87; Danny Thomas, comedian and philanthropist, best remembered for his television show *Make Room for Daddy,* Feb. 6, at 79; and Frank Yerby, historical novelist whose 32 books sold millions of copies, Nov. 29, at 76.

Dollar sales of **books published** this year (not including mass market paperbacks) were up by 9.1%. Aiding this increase was *Scarlett* by Alexandra Ripley, a deliberately planned sequel to Margaret Mitchell's eternally popular *Gone With the Wind.* It became a number one bestseller and occupied the same position on the critics' thumbs-down list. Other works of fiction included Norman Mailer's 1328-page novel *Harlot's Ghost,* about the CIA; *How to Make an American Quilt* by Whitney Otto, a novel concerning a women's quilting circle in California; and *The Kitchen God's Wife* by Amy Tan, in which a Chinese matriarch in San Francisco tells the story of her hard life. Nonfiction titles included *The Journals of John Cheever,* the rather sad account of life and its problems the writer noted down over 35 years; and *Final Exit* by Derek Humphry, a how-to book for would-be suicides. Simon and Schuster cancelled publication of *American Psycho* by Bret Easton Ellis, considering the fictional tale of an amoral psychopath unfit for its list. Vintage took it over, but the book was damned in print even before publication. Writers of spy novels also had their troubles with the fall of the Soviet Union denying them the usual villains of the KGB. New ones were found in drug dealers, terrorists, and even people who committed crimes via computer. More black authors were being published, especially writers of fiction. In addition two volumes of the writings of Richard Wright, who died in 1960, were issued, including a revised version of *Native Son,* which originally had been heavily censored. The largest prize ever given for a single novel, the Turner Tomorrow Award, presented by Ted Turner, a communications magnate, went to Daniel Quinn for *Ishmael,* consisting of philosophical conversations between a man and an ape. Also in the big money was Gen. H. Norman Schwarzkopf, Jr., the victorious commander in the Persian Gulf War, who accepted $5,000,000 for the rights to his memoirs.

Jan 27: Observance of the **bicentennial of Wolfgang Amadeus Mozart's death** began on the anniversary of his birth in 1756. In the U.S. the occasion was to be marked by the performance at Lincoln Center, New York City, of all 835 of his surviving works.

Feb 13: The long-lost manuscript of the first half of Mark Twain's **Huckleberry Finn,** which had been discovered some months earlier in an attic in Los Angeles, was authenticated. It had disappeared a century earlier from a library in Buffalo, N.Y. The 665-page manuscript was handwritten by Twain between 1876 and 1883.

Feb 20: The 33rd **Grammy Awards** were presented for the following: best album of 1990, *Back on the Block* by Quincy Jones; best record, "Another Day in Paradise" by Phil Collins; best male rock vocalist, Eric Clapton for "Bad Love"; best female rock vocalist, Alannah Myles for "Black Velvet"; best male pop vocalist, Roy Orbison for "Oh Pretty Woman"; best female pop vocalist, Mariah Carey for "Vision of Love."

Mar 11: One of the largest **art donations** ever was announced by Walter H. Annenberg, a wealthy publisher and philanthropist, who said he would bequeath his collection, valued at at least $1,000,000,000, to the Metropolitan Museum of Art, New York City. The collection is especially strong in the works of the French impressionists and post-impressionists.

Mar 17: To celebrate the **National Gallery of Art's 50th anniversary,** the museum opened an exhibit in Washington, D.C., featuring some of the more than 500 works solicited by it to observe the event. The exhibit included paintings, drawings, sculptures, and photographs, among them works by Titian, Albert Bierstadt, Winslow Homer, and Claes Oldenburg.

Mar 25: Academy Awards were presented to *Dances With Wolves* as the outstanding motion picture of 1990; Jeremy Irons as best actor for *Reversal of Fortune;* Kathy Bates as best actress for *Misery;* Joe Pesci as best supporting actor for *Goodfellas;* and Whoopie Goldberg as best supporting actress for *Ghost.*

Apr 9: Pulitzer prizes were awarded for the following: fiction, *Rabbit at Rest* by John Updike; general nonfiction, *The Ants* by Berthold K. Holldobler and Edward O. Wilson; history, *A Midwife's Tale: The Life of Martha Ballard, Based on Her Diary 1785–1812* by Laurel Thatcher Ulrich; biography, *Jackson Pollock: An American Saga* by Steven Naifeh and Gregory White Smith; poetry, *Near Changes* by Mona Van Duyn; drama, *Lost in Yonkers* by Neil Simon.

May 10: Joseph Brodsky was appointed the fifth poet laureate of the U.S. A one-time inmate of a Soviet prison camp, he emigrated to America in 1972.

May 28: After 13 years **Zubin Mehta retired** as musical director of the New York Philharmonic Orchestra. His tenure was the longest in modern times.

June 2: Tony awards for the 1990–1991 theater season were presented for the following: best play, *Lost in Yonkers* by Neil Simon; best musical, *The Will Rogers Follies* by Cy Coleman, Betty Comden, Adolph Green, and Peter Stone; best actor in a play, Nigel Hawthorne for *Shadowlands;* best actress in a play, Mercedes Ruehl for *Lost in Yonkers;* best actor in a musical, Jonathan Pryce for *Miss Saigon;* best actress in a musical, Lea Salonga for *Miss Saigon.*

June 9: The **100th anniversary of the birth of Cole Porter,** the composer of some of the most tuneful and sophisticated popular music of his time, was marked by a concert featuring 40 stars, at Carnegie Hall, New York City.

Aug 5: Emmy Awards were presented for the following: best drama series, *L.A. Law;* best comedy series, *Cheers;* best actor in a drama series, James Earl Jones for *Gabriel's Fire;* best actress in a drama series, Patricia Wettig for *Thirtysomething;* best actor in a comedy series, Burt Reynolds for *Evening Shade;* best actress in a comedy series, Kirstie Alley for *Cheers.*

Nov 20: National Book Awards were presented for the following: fiction, *Mating* by Norman Rush; nonfiction, *Freedom* by Orlando Patterson; poetry, *What Work Is,* by Philip Levine.

Dec 5: The $62,000,000 **Seattle Art Museum** opened its doors and was now able to display most of its entire collection, strong in the field of artifacts of the Indians of the Northwest. The 155,000-square-foot, five-story building was designed by Robert Venturi.

III. Business and Industry
   Education
   Philosophy and Religion
   Science

Early in the year the recession that began in May, 1990, seemed to be easing, but as the year went on the economy worsened. By the end of the year unemployment was up to 7.1%, a 5.5 year high; industrial production dropped 1.9%; sales of new homes were down 5.6%, the third straight year of declines; auto sales fared even worse, being down 11.2%, the worst year since 1983; orders for durable goods followed suit, being off 4.6%, the worst since 1982; the total of installment credit fell 1.0%, the first time it had shrunk since 1958; employers' health costs rose 12.1%; and ten large industries announced in the course of the second half of the year that they would lay off 161,000 workers, with General Motors accounting for 70,000 and International Business Machines 20,000. The economic news was not all bad: the consumer price index was up only 3.1%, a five-year low; the international trade deficit of $8,620,000,000 was the lowest for a decade; and nonfarm productivity showed a gain of 0.3%, the first in three years. Even the troubled savings and loan institutions did better, the 2096 that had not needed government help showing an overall profit of almost $2,000,000,000, although by now 700 other institutions had been seized by the government. Not everyone was faring badly: the Census Bureau reported that the income of the top 20% of households rose by 14% from 1984 to 1988, but the median for all households in that period dropped from $37,012 to $35,752 per year. Among the affluent, according to *Forbes* magazine were 71 billionaires, an increase of 5 for the year. The number of owners of farm land, 2,950,000 people, was the smallest this century, and 47% of such land was held by only 124,000 owners. In March the 5,000,000th patent was issued, for an up-to-the-minute product, a genetically engineered

microbe. A poll showed that 61% of women had met with some form of sexual harassment at work, but only 4.0% reported such incidents. More than 400,000 Americans were dying each year from smoking, according to the Federal Centers for Disease Controls. Late in the year there was a decrease in the number of births for the first time in five years and it was blamed on the recession. Another government report said life expectancy for blacks was improving, but that they still died about six years younger than whites. Hispanic Americans suffer more than others from diabetes, high blood pressure, kidney disease, and some cancers. The infant mortality rate dropped in 1990 by the largest amount in nearly ten years, from 9.7 deaths per 1000 live births to 9.1. Liberal Protestant denominations lost membership while the Roman Catholic Church and some conservative Protestant denominations gained. The 32 denominations belonging to the National Council of Churches saw membership drop 100,000 to 41,800,000; Catholic membership grew by 2,000,000 to 57,000,000; and the Southern Baptist Convention gained 100,000 to 14,900,000. Overall, reported a 1990 survey, Protestants made up 60.2% of the American population, Catholics 26.2%; non-Christian faiths 3.7%; and those professing no religion 7.5%. Following a series of scandals, the leading television evangelists lost large numbers of followers. Jimmy Swaggart, for example, now had only 20% of his one-time 2,200,000 viewers. General economic conditions were troubling all churches because, while giving rose, expenses, especially for medical and other insurance, and for work for the poor and the homeless, outstripped contributions. In general, education did not do well this year either. Verbal scores on the Scholastic Aptitude Test fell to an all-time low, while math scores fell for the first time since 1980. The proportion of whites taking the test had declined from 87% to 72% since 1972 while the nonwhite proportion rose from 13% to 28%. College enrollment was up in spite of the recession, but more students were selecting colleges on the basis of cost as tuition fees continued to rise. The report card for elementary and secondary schools was not encouraging. The percentage of pupils earning high school diplomas was no higher than 15 years earlier. Notable persons who died in 1991 included Carl D. Anderson, Nobel Prize winner in physics for his discovery of the positron, Jan. 11, at 85; John Bardeen, co-inventor of the transistor, for which he received the Nobel Prize in physics, Jan. 30, at 82; John Sloan Dickey, president of Dartmouth College, 1945 to 1970, Feb. 9, at 83; John K. Fairbank, most influential scholar of his time in China studies, Sept. 14, at 84; Louis Finkelstein, the dominant figure of the 20th century in Conservative Judaism, Nov. 21, at 96; James L. Knight, a builder of the Knight-Ridder newspaper chain, Feb. 5, at 81; Edwin H. Land, inventor of instant photography, Mar. 1, at 81; Salvador E. Luria, Nobel Prize winner in medicine and physiology for his work in genetics, Feb. 6, at 78; William A. Lewis, winner of the Nobel Prize in economics, June 15, at 76; Thomas D. Nicholson, director of the American Museum of Natural History from 1969 to 1989, July 9, at 68; Harold R. Perry, the first black to be consecrated a Roman Catholic Bishop in the 20th century, July 17, at 74; and Sylvia Porter, widely read business and financial news columnist, June 5, at 77.

Jan 8: Pan American World Airways, one of the largest U.S. airlines, filed for bankruptcy but would keep flying pending the sale of its planes and routes to other airlines. On Jan. 18 Eastern Airlines, already in bankruptcy, shut down its operations.

Jan 25: The **death toll from AIDS** had now reached 100,777 and 161,073 cases had been reported since 1981, federal health officials reported. More than 215,000 persons were expected to die of the disease in the next three years.

Feb 1: Installed as president of the **Teamsters Union,** long noted for its corruption and mob influence, was Ronald R. Carey, a reformer. The insurgent head of a local in New York City, Carey in a Dec. election received 48.5% of the votes in a contest with two insiders.

Feb 11: Carter Hawley Hale Stores, Inc., the largest department store chain on the West Coast, filed for bankruptcy. Much of the chain's financial problems stemmed from the $1,600,000,000 debt in junk bonds it issued in 1987 to prevent a hostile takeover by the Limited, Inc., a chain of women's specialty stores.

Feb 21: A new type of **genetically engineered drug** for fighting infections that often affect cancer patients undergoing chemotherapy was approved by the Food and Drug Administration. It was hoped that the drug, granulocyte colony stimulating factor (G-CSF), would also prove effective as a treatment for other types of infections.

Apr 4: The ozone layer over the U.S. is being depleted more than twice as fast as previously thought, the Environmental Protection Agency announced.

Apr 7: The space shuttle *Atlantis* launched into orbit the **Gamma Ray Observatory,** weighing 17 tons and costing $600,000,000. It was to study gamma ray emissions that result from violent explosions in other space when stars collapse and matter and antimatter collide.

Apr 26: Discovery of the **first catacombs** known to have been used by American Indians for burial and sacred rites was reported by archaeologists. The catacombs were under a 15-acre settlement in eastern Arizona known as Casa Malpais. The natural spaces had been enlarged.

May 6: The question of **who first discovered the AIDS virus** was somewhat cleared up when French and American scientists agreed that laboratory mixups had caused the dispute. The French and U.S. strains were contaminated by a third strain of the genetically variable virus.

May 25: The **first person to receive a fully portable heart pump,** Larry Heinsohn, died in Houston, Tex. He had received the device May 9. Connected with a battery pack that could be slung over the shoulder, the pump was intended to be used only until a human heart donor was available.

May 29: Two Americans were among 23 **new cardinals** of the Roman Catholic Church appointed by Pope John Paul II. They were Anthony J. Bevilacqua of Philadelphia, Pa., and Roger M. Mahony of Los Angeles, Calif. These appointments brought to ten the number of American cardinals.

June 5: In Washington, D.C., the **ordination of a homosexual woman** living in an openly lesbian relationship caused controversy within the Episcopal Church. The woman, Elizabeth L. Carl, was not the first acknowledged homosexual to be ordained but the candor of church officials as well as the candidate was unusual.

June 6: The **Greek Orthodox Church** suspended its ties with the National Council of Churches, the largest ecumenical organization, saying that it was troubled by the "extreme liberalism" shown by the council in the positions it had taken regarding abortion and homosexuality.

June 11: A policy on **sexual misconduct** was adopted by the Presbyterian Church (U.S.A.). The General Assembly's first statement of detailed policy on the subject, it prohibited sexual contact between a parishioner and a clergyman or church employee regardless of who sought to initiate it. Church bodies were urged to establish "sexual misconduct response teams."

July 5: The **Bank of Credit and Commerce International (BCCI),** controlled by the emir of Abu Dhabi, was seized by bank regulators in the U.S., Great Britain, and other countries. The bank, supposedly with assets of $20,000,000,000, was bankrupt as the result of false accounting and fictitious loans. It had secretly acquired control of two American banks. BCCI agreed Dec. 19 to pay the U.S. $550,000,000 in penalties.

July 15–Nov. 20: A wave of **bank mergers** created the second, third, and fourth largest banks in the U.S. The third largest was formed July 15 by the merger of Chemical Bank and Manufacturers Hanover Trust of New York, with assets of $139,000,000,000; the second largest Aug. 15 when BankAmerica Corp. and Security Pacific Corp. of California announced a merger with assets of $190,000,000,000; and the fourth largest by the merger Nov. 20 of a North Carolina and a Georgia bank, NCNB Corp. and C&S/Sovran Corp., with assets of $115,000,000,000.

July 19: A **compromise statement on homosexual relationships** was adopted by the General Convention of the Episcopal Church. It reaffirmed the church teaching that sexual relations should be limited to matrimony, but it admitted that many church members did not agree. The statement avoided a decision on the divisive question of ordaining homosexuals.

Aug 18: The Treasury Dept. suspended **Salomon Brothers** from bidding at its auctions of government securities. However, it changed its mind the same day and said it would allow Salomon, one of Wall Street's largest investment houses, to bid on federal securities for its own account but not for clients. Salomon had admitted that for more than a year it had been buying more than the maximum share allowed any one firm.

Oct 15: The **Nobel Prize in Economics** was awarded to Ronald H. Coase, a British-born retired professor of the University of Chicago for his theories of why companies, rather than individual businesses, came into being.

Dec 3: In the continuing **savings and loan crisis,** Pres. Bush signed a bill appropriating $25,000,000,000 to cover losses in the failure of savings and loan institutions. In March $30,000,000,000 had been voted, and the total since the fall of 1988 was now $105,000,000,000.

Dec 31: On the last day of the year the **Dow Jones average** of industrial stocks set a new all-time high mark on the New York Stock Exchange at 3168.83, about 20% above the Jan. 1 figure.

IV. Fashion
Folkways
Holidays
Social Issues and Crime
Sports

Thanks to Title IX of the Educational Amendments Act of 1972, many more young women were participating in sports at all levels. This law prohibited sexual discrimination in programs in schools receiving federal financing. As a result, high schools now reported an increase of participation from 7% to 36%, while in colleges where previously all NCAA activities were male, women now accounted for 33% of participants. In spite of the recession the National

Football League recorded its third consecutive year of gains in attendance, to 17,752,139, up about 100,000. Thoroughbred horse racing, however, began the year with decreases in both attendance and betting, attributed to the recession and the Persian Gulf War. Hard times also hit Las Vegas, Nev., heart of the gambling industry, where some of the games were down as much as a third in Oct., the busiest month, and two casinos went bankrupt. Rodeo, on the other hand, was prospering. In four years the number of rodeos increased by 25% to 800, while prize money now totalled $2,600,000 at the National Rodeo Finals, compared with about $150,000 in 1970. In professional golf Corey Pavin was the leading money winner at $979,430. At the beginning of the year there were 695,000 inmates in state prisons and 60,000 in federal penitentiaries, an increase in one year of 80,000, the most ever. After five years of mostly miniskirts, the fashion world began to offer some longer hemlines, to the calf or beyond. Of course many women had ignored fashion's decrees and wore whatever length skirt they thought suited them. Among people of note who died were Luke Appling, Hall of Famer, shortstop for 20 years, Jan. 3, at 83; Laz Berrera, trainer of the Triple Crown winner Affirmed, Apr. 25, at 66; James "Cool Papa" Bell, legendary figure of the Negro Baseball League, Mar. 7, at 87; Paul Brown, innovative pro football coach, Aug. 5, at 82; A. B. "Happy" Chandler, commissioner of baseball from 1945 to 1951, June 15, at 92; Leo Durocher, fiery baseball manager known as "Leo the Lip," Oct. 7, at 86; Charles H. Goren, deviser of the most popular contract bridge bidding system, Apr. 3, at 90; Harold "Red" Grange, star college and pro football running back of the 1920s, Jan. 28, at 87; and Arthur Murray, the best-known teacher of ballroom dancing, Mar. 3, at 95.

Jan 1: In **college football bowl games** the results were Miami 46, Texas 3 in the Cotton Bowl; Colorado 10, Notre Dame 9 in the Orange Bowl; Washington 46, Iowa 34 in the Rose Bowl; and Tennessee 23, Virginia 22 in the Sugar Bowl. The AP picked Colorado as the 1990 national champion, but the UPI selected Georgia Tech, which defeated Nebraska, 45 to 21, in the Citrus Bowl.

Jan 5: A new **basketball record** for individual scoring in a game was set by Kevin Bradshaw of United States International University of San Diego, Calif., when he registered 72 points in an NCAA Division I game. The feat broke a 21-year-old record.

Jan 21: The **exclusion of women** from Princeton's eating clubs was finally ended when the Supreme Court let stand a rule that the Tiger Inn, the last holdout, must admit women. By Feb. 10, some 27 female students had been taken in. The case began in 1979 when a woman student filed a civil rights complaint.

Jan 27: Super Bowl XXV was won by the New York Giants (NFC) who defeated the Buffalo Bills (AFC) 20 to 19. On Jan. 20 the Giants had won the NFC championship by defeating the San Francisco Forty-Niners 15 to 13 and Buffalo won the AFC title by beating the Los Angeles Raiders 51 to 3.

Feb 2: The **500th basketball victory** of his career was registered by Lou Carnesecca of St. John's University when his basketball team defeated Seton Hall 81 to 65. St. John's coach for 23 years, Carnesecca became the 30th major college coach to achieve 500 wins.

Feb 4: The board of directors of the **Baseball Hall of Fame** voted to exclude any player who had been banned from the game. The move was triggered by the 1989 banning for life of Pete Rose, star player and manager of the Cincinnati Reds, for having bet on games.

Feb 14: A law allowing the **registration of "domestic partnerships"** by homosexual and unmarried heterosexual couples went into effect in San Francisco. Although the law granted no legal rights, about 200 couples registered the first day.

Feb 15–17: U.S. figure skating championships were won in Minneapolis, Minn., by Tonya Harding, women's singles; Todd Eldredge, for the second consecutive year, men's singles; Natasha Kuchiki and Todd Sand, pairs; Elizabeth Punsalan and Jerod Swallow, dance.

Mar 16: Three American women set a **figure skating record** when they finished one, two, three in the world championships at Munich, Germany. It was the first time in the 73-year history of the event that skaters from the same country accomplished this. The three, in order, were Kristi Yamaguchi, Tonya Harding, and Nancy Kerrigan.

Mar 31: The **NCAA women's basketball championship** was won by Tennessee, which defeated Virginia 70 to 67 in overtime.

Apr 1: The **NCAA men's basketball championship** was won by Duke, which defeated Kansas 72 to 65.

Apr 14: The **Masters golf tournament** was won by Ian Woosnam of Wales by one stroke on the last hole.

Apr 15: The 95th **Boston Marathon** was won in the men's division by Ibrahim Hussein of Kenya with a time of 2 hrs., 11 min., 6 sec. The winner of the women's division was Wanda Panfil of Poland with a time of 2 hrs., 24 min., 18 sec.

May 4: The 117th **Kentucky Derby** was won by Strike the Gold with a time of 2:03. The jockey was Chris Antley.

May 18: The 116th **Preakness Stakes** was won by Hansel with a time of 1:54. The jockey was Jerry Bailey.

May 25: The **NHL Stanley Cup** was won by the Pittsburgh Penguins who defeated the Minnesota North Stars four games to two. It was the first such victory for the Penguins.

May 26: The **Indianapolis 500** auto race was won by Rick Mears, who became only the third racing driver to win the event four times. His average speed was 176.460 mph, and the time was 2 hrs., 50 min., 0.791 sec.

June 8: The 123rd **Belmont Stakes** was won by Hansel with a time of 2:28. The jockey was Jerry Bailey.

June 9: The first championship of the **World League of American Football** was won by the London Monarchs, who defeated the Barcelona Dragons 21 to 0. The league began its first season Mar. 23 with ten teams. Three of them represented European cities (Barcelona, Frankfurt, and London), and seven North American localities (Birmingham, Montreal, New York/New Jersey, Orlando, Raleigh-Durham, Sacramento, and San Antonio).

June 12: The **NBA basketball championship** was won by the Chicago Bulls, who defeated the Los Angeles Lakers four games to two. It was the first time the Bulls had won the title.

June 17: The **U.S. Open golf tournament** was won by Payne Stewart by two strokes in an 18-hole playoff. On the first day of the tournament, June 13, lightning killed one spectator and injured five others.

June 30: The **LPGA golf tournament** was won by Meg Mallon by one stroke with a birdie putt on the final hole.

July 5: National League expansion beginning in 1993, with two new baseball teams, was announced. Owners of the present clubs approved the addition of a Denver team to be known as the Colorado Rockies and a Miami team to be called the Florida Marlins. The additions brought to 28 the total number of major league teams, with 14 in each league.

July 14: The **U.S. Women's Open golf tournament** was won by Meg Mallon by two strokes. She was the only player to finish with an under par score.

July 21: The **Baseball Hall of Fame** inducted Rod Carew, a batting champion; two pitchers, Gaylord Perry and Ferguson Jenkins; Bill Veeck, owner of three different clubs; and Tony Lazzeri, a New York Yankee second baseman.

July 25: Jeffrey L. Dahmer was arrested in Milwaukee, Wis., for the serial murder and dismemberment of as many as 17 people. Dahmer later confessed to sexually-motivated-murder charges and on Feb. 17, 1992, was sentenced to 15 consecutive life terms in prison.

July 28: The 15th **perfect baseball game** in major league history was pitched by Dennis Martinez of the Montreal Expos (NL), who retired all 27 Los Angeles

Dodgers batters without any reaching base. The first such game was pitched June 12, 1880.

Aug 2–18: At the 11th **Pan-American Games** in Havana, Cuba, the U.S. won the most medals, 352 to Cuba's 265, but Cuba took the most gold medals, 140 to 130; Canada was third with 22 gold and 127 overall.

Aug 11: The **PGA golf championship** was won by John Daly by three strokes. He was only the sixth player whose first tournament victory was a major championship.

Aug 25: A new **world track record** for the 100-meter dash, 9.86 sec., was set by Carl Lewis at the Tokyo World Championships. He bettered the old mark by .04 sec. On Aug. 30 Mike Powell set a new world record for the long jump of 29 ft., 4.5 in., exceeding the old mark by 2 in.

Sep 7–8: The **U.S. Open tennis singles championships** were won by Monica Seles in the women's division and by Stefan Edberg in the men's division. Both won in straight sets.

Sep 14: The **Miss America** title was won by Carolyn Suzanne Sapp, 20, of Hawaii, at the annual pageant in Atlantic City, N.J.

Oct 16: A bloody **mass killing** occurred at Killeen, Tex., when George Jo Hennard rammed his pickup truck into a restaurant and began firing with a semi–automatic pistol, killing 22 people and wounding 20. He then shot himself. No motive was known.

Oct 19–27: The **World Series** was won by the Minnesota Twins (AL), defeating the Atlanta Braves (NL) four games to three. The Twins had won the American League pennant on Oct. 13 by beating the Toronto Blue Jays four games to one; the Braves had won the National League pennant on Oct. 17, defeating the Pittsburgh Pirates four games to three.

Nov 3: The 22nd **New York City Marathon** was won in the men's division by Salvador Garcia of Mexico with a time of 2 hrs., 9 min., 28 sec. The women's division was won by Liz McColgan of Scotland with a time of 2 hrs., 27 min., 32 sec.

Nov 7: Earvin "Magic" Johnson, a star of the Los Angeles Lakers basketball team, announced his retirement because he was infected with the HIV virus that causes AIDS. A professional basketball player for 12 seasons, Johnson admitted to having had many unprotected sexual contacts. Johnson changed his mind and signed a one-year, $14,600,000 contract with the Lakers, but retired again on Nov. 2, 1992.

Nov 30: The **first world championship of women's soccer** was won in Guangzhou, China, by the U.S. which defeated Norway, 2 to 1.

Dec 2: Bobby Bonilla became the **highest paid player in professional team sports** when he signed a contract with the New York Mets of the National League that would pay him $29,000,000 over five years. The highest paid pitcher in baseball was Jack Morris of the Toronto Blue Jays, who signed a two-year contract Dec. 18 for $10,850,000. In all, six players were now being paid more than $5,000,000 a year.

1992

I. Civil Rights
Exploration and Settlement
Government
Statistics
Wars

The national elections, besides ending 12 years of Republican control of the executive branch, had several unusual aspects. An independent candidate, H. Ross Perot, a self-made Texas billionaire who entered the race for president, withdrew, and then reentered, polled 19% of the popular vote, an unusually high rating for a third party candidate. Four women were elected to the Senate, bringing the total to six, the most ever; one of these women was the first black female ever elected to the Senate. Also elected to the Senate was the first American Indian, a male. The total turnout of voters was about 55% of those eligible, an increase of about 5% from 1988. Voters in 14 states approved the application of limits to the number of terms senators and representatives may serve. Winning and losing candidates alike spent a great deal of money. A month before the election the average House incumbent had spent about $293,000, while the average for senators seeking reelection was about $2,350,000. One Senate candidate had raised nearly $9,000,000; the top money raiser among those running for House seats had amassed $4,200,000. Those who won would find in Washington that the federal budget deficit had not eased: for the year ending Sept. 30 it was a record $290,000,000,000. The 50 state governments had their financial problems also. Though they had a combined estimated surplus of $825,000,000, that was less than 1% of their total spending. The cost of the Medicaid program was alarming governors and state legislators as it presently accounted for 15% of total spending and was expected to rise to 28% by 1995. The nation observed, rather mildly, the 500th anniversary of Christopher Columbus's first voyage to the Western Hemisphere.

Native Americans were now vocal in pointing out that their ancestors had "discovered" America and had lived in it for thousands of years before Columbus. As a result, the anniversary witnessed such events as changing the name of Columbus Day to Indigenous People's Day by the city council of Berkeley, Calif., and the canceling of a parade in Denver, Colo., for fear of a clash between paraders and American Indians. Other anniversaries were less controversial. The Alaska Highway, the 1500-mile road from British Columbia to Fairbanks, Alaska, that was rushed to completion in 1942 during World War II, marked its 50th anniversary. The battleship *Missouri*, on which Japan's surrender in 1945 was received, was decommissioned for the third time. On May 18 an amendment to the Constitution first proposed 203 years ago, prohibiting Congress from voting itself immediate pay raises, was finally ratified. Meanwhile Americans remained much as in days of yore. A survey showed that 80% of us still thought a single-family detached home with a yard was the ideal, but many people were finding it hard to come up with the necessary down payment. Americans were also concerned about the state of race relations, brought only too bloodily to their attention by rioting in Los Angeles in April. A survey showed that the majority believed too little money was being spent on the problems of inner cities and on securing justice and equality for black Americans. Among cities a new study rated Tulsa, Okla., the most typical, with Charleston, W. Va., second, and Midland, Tex., third. In New York City the landmark Pan Am Building, opened in 1963, was renamed the Met Life Building. The insurance company had owned the skyscraper since 1981 and Pan American World Airways, a pioneer in air transportation, had gone into bankruptcy. Whether a result of the recession or not, the nation's well-to-do citizens were not giving as big a share of their incomes to charity, in spite of the riches that accrued to them during the 1980s. The more than 7% of the after-tax income they gave in 1979 had declined to less than 4%. On the other hand the number of millionaires increased so greatly over the decade that the total they gave rose to a record level. Ironically, more than a third of the chief executives of the 100 largest charitable foundations had salaries of $200,000 or more in 1991. The highest was the $624,500 paid to Howard B. Keck, chairman of the Keck Foundation; the lowest was $18,500. One item of good news for most people: the winter that ended in March was the warmest in the 97 years such records have been kept. For the period Dec., 1991, through Feb., 1992, the nationwide average temperature was 4°F above normal. Eastern Montana was 11° above normal, but cities in the Northeast registered only 2° above normal. Notable persons who died his year included Quentin N. Burdick, Democratic senator from North Dakota for 32 years, Sept. 8, at 84; Millicent H. Fenwick, Republican representative from New Jersey from 1964 to 1982, known for her political independence, Sept. 16, at 82; Philip C. Habib, diplomat for nearly three decades and an accomplished trouble-shooter, May 25, at 72; Wilbur D. Mills, a leading Democrat in the House of Representatives for more than 20 years, May 2, at 82; Joseph L. Rauh, Jr., a foremost civil rights lawyer for nearly 50 years, Sept. 3, at 81; John Joseph Sirica, federal judge whose decisions during the Watergate scandal of the early 1970s did much to end the presidency of Richard M. Nixon, Aug. 14, at 88; James A. Van Fleet, four-decade veteran of the Army, who led major campaigns in both World War II and the Korean War, Sept. 23, at 100; and Ted Weiss, Democratic congressman since 1976 and one of the most outspoken liberals in Congress, Sept. 14, at 64.

Jan 16: An **agreement on patents, copyrights, and trade secrets** was reached by the U.S. and China to provide protection for American books, music recordings, pharmaceuticals, and computer software. In effect China agreed to adopt international standards, ending what was estimated to be more than $800,000,000 of income lost annually by American firms.

Jan 26: Provisions of a **federal law to aid the disabled** went into effect, with other rules due to be implemented in July. The new regulations were expected to be of special assistance to those confined to wheelchairs, but would also benefit the visually impaired. The law also called for enhanced employment opportunities and better transportation facilities.

Jan 31: The State Department's annual **report on human rights** was especially critical of China, India, Peru, and Syria, even though the last had been an ally in the Persian Gulf War.

Feb 1: The **end of the Cold War** was proclaimed in Washington by Pres. George Bush and Pres. Boris Yeltsin of Russia. On May 23 the U.S. signed with Russia, Belarus, Kazakhstan, and Ukraine an agreement to abide by the nuclear arms reduction treaty negotiated with the U.S.S.R. before its collapse in late 1991. On June 16 Pres. Bush and Pres. Yeltsin announced an agreement to further control nuclear armaments. Each nation was to reduce its nuclear warheads to between 3000 and 3500 by the year 2003 from the present combined total of about 22,500.

Mar 8: In the continuing **savings and loan scandal,** a large law firm agreed to pay the federal government $41,000,000 to settle charges that it had improperly withheld damaging information about a savings association it had represented. The firm was Kaye, Scholer, Fierman, Hays, and Handler of New York City, and its client was the Lincoln Savings and Loan Association of Irvine, Calif.

Mar 31: A Supreme Court decision, 8–0, concerning **school desegregation** would make it easier for educational institutions to take back local control from federal judges. The justices said this could come about as different aspects of school operations were desegregated, rather than having to wait until all was accomplished.

Apr 5: A **march to support abortion rights** drew an estimated 500,000 people to Washington, D.C. Thought to be the largest ever protest march in the nation's capital, it came as the Supreme Court was about to consider a Pennsylvania law that limited access to abortion.

Apr 13: A **flood in Chicago,** caused by water surging through tunnnels beneath buildings in the Loop, the main business section, shut down stores, courts, and commodity exchanges for a week. The flood was caused by 250,000,000 gallons of water that flowed from a leak in the Chicago River into a series of tunnels once used to transport freight and coal. Electricity was shut off in a 12-block area.

Apr 16: In a **congressional banking scandal,** a list of U.S. representatives who overdrew their checking accounts in the House bank was released, showing that 252 current and 51 former members of Congress had done so. Former Rep. Tommy Robinson of Arkansas was reported to have made the most overdrafts, 996, but he denied that he had made so many.

May 4: State prison inmates' appeals to federal courts were made more difficult by a Supreme Court decision, 5–4, which overturned a precedent. Federal courts would no longer be obliged to grant a hearing because a prisoner showed that his lawyer had not properly presented his case.

June 1: In a ruling on the use of **frozen embryos,** Tennessee's highest court said that a divorced man could deny his former wife the use of such an embryo that had been fertilized with his sperm. The court held in effect that a man cannot be forced to become a father against his will.

June 12: Speaking at the **Earth Summit** in Rio de Janeiro, Brazil, Pres. Bush said the U.S. would not sign a treaty agreed to by most of the 172 nations present, which was designed to protect rare and endangered animals and plants. He claimed it would "retard technology and undermine the protection of ideas." The U.S. did sign a treaty aimed at preventing further global warming.

June 18: In a decision on **racism in jury selection,** the Supreme Court ruled, 7–2, that criminal defendants cannot exclude jurors on the basis of race. Basing its decision on constitutional guarantees of equal protection under the law, the court extended a rule it had laid down six years earlier concerning prosecutors and broadened in a case last year.

June 22: A **law to aid inner cities** was signed by Pres. Bush. Spurred in part by the recent rioting in Los Angeles (see Col. IV, Apr. 29), the law provided $1,300,000,000 for relief of that disaster in the form of grants and loans for housing and business, plus a summer employment program for 75 cities.

June 22: Laws criminalizing "hate speech" or "bias crimes" were unconstitutional, the Supreme Court ruled. The decision was based on a St. Paul, Minn., ordinance that the court found violated the First Amendment. Although the decision formally came on a 5–4 vote, all the justices found the law unconstitutional on some grounds.

June 28: The most powerful **earthquake** to strike California in 40 years registered 7.4 on the Richter scale. The quake was centered in the Yucca Valley, east of Los Angeles, and was felt as far north as Idaho and Washington. Considerable damage was done to stores and houses but there was only one fatality.

June 29: The constitutional **right to abortion** was reaffirmed by the Supreme Court, 5–4. At the same time the court permitted states to impose some restrictions. The case involved a Pennsylvania law and the court upheld its provisions for a 24-hour waiting period, and the consent of one parent of a teenager or of a judge, among other points.

July 15–16: The **Democratic National Convention** nominated Gov. **William Clinton** of Arkansas for the presidency and Sen. Albert Gore of Tennessee for the vice presidency.

Aug: Forest fires destroyed hundreds of thousands of acres of woodland in many parts of California, Colorado, Idaho, Nevada, Oregon, and Washington. At least 9000 fire-fighters, including National Guardsmen, fought the blazes, most of which were caused by lightning striking trees suffering from severe drought. Many homes were destroyed.

Aug 19–20: The **Republican National Convention,** meeting in Houston, Tex., nominated Pres. George Bush and Vice Pres. Dan Quayle for reelection.

Aug 23: James A. Baker, III, resigned as secretary of state and was appointed chief of staff to Pres. Bush. In his new post Baker was to take over command of Bush's reelection campaign, which was seen as floundering.

Aug 24: Hurricane Andrew, the most powerful hurricane ever to strike the continental U.S., ravaged southern Florida with winds of up to 150 mph. Although only 38 persons were killed, either directly or in the storm's aftermath, 85,000 homes were damaged or destroyed, and 250,000 persons were made homeless. Damage was estimated as high as $30,000,000,000, including the destruction of Homestead Air Force Base. Andrew struck southern Louisiana on Aug. 26, leaving at least 25,000 people homeless. More than 20,000 federal troops and National Guardsmen were called in to assist in relief efforts.

Aug 25: In a new **sanction against Iraq,** the U.S. and its allies ordered Iraq to stop all military flights over the southern part of the country below the 32nd parallel, to prevent armed repression of large numbers of dissident Shiite Muslims. With support from France and Great Britain, allied warplanes flew their first missions over the area Aug. 28 without meeting any resistance.

Aug 28: Typhoon Omar struck the U.S. territory of Guam in the Pacific with winds of 150 mph. Military installations were damaged and about 4300 of the island's 32,000 homes were destroyed or damaged. Total damage was estimated at $250,000,000.

Sep 11: Hurricane Iniki, the most powerful storm to strike Hawaii in the 20th century, blasted the island of Kauai. With gusts up to 160 mph, Iniki killed two persons and injured 98, also destroying or damaging 10,000 homes on the island, which has a population of 55,000.

Sep 24: An inquiry into the **Tailhook sexual assault scandal** at a naval aviators' convention reported that high ranking officers had deliberately covered up the affair to avoid unfavorable publicity for the U.S. Navy. As a result, two admirals who supervised the inquiry were forced to retire and a third was reassigned. The affair took place in 1991 at a convention, in Las Vegas, Nev., of the Tailhook Association, an organization of past and present naval aviators, at which 26 women naval personnel were harassed and had clothing torn off.

Oct 14: Alger Hiss never spied for the Soviet Union, according to the chairman of the Russian government's military intelligence archives. He based his finding on a review of newly accessible files. Hiss, a former State Department employee, had been convicted of perjury in 1951 in connection with testimony before a federal grand jury considering spy charges leveled against him.

Oct 24: Pres. Bush signed a new **energy bill** that promoted competition between utilities in generating power, made it easier to license nuclear power plants, and took steps to promote gasoline substitutes. However, a provision in the original bill to allow oil drilling in the Arctic National Wildlife Refuge was removed before final passage of the bill by Congress.

Oct 30: An **Omnibus Water Bill,** authorizing diversion of some water formerly reserved for farmers in California to environmentally endangered areas, was signed by Pres. Bush. The new law would also allow farmers to sell some of the water from irrigation projects to California cities.

Nov 3: William "Bill" Clinton was elected president of the United States. Sen. Albert "Al" Gore, Jr. was elected vice president. Clinton defeated the Republican candidate, Pres. George Bush, by 370 to 168 electoral votes. Independent candidate H. Ross Perot received no electoral votes. The popular vote was Clinton, 43,728,375; Bush, 38,167,416; and Perot, 18,237,247. The Democrats held their 57–43 majority in the Senate. In the House the Democrats lost nine seats but retained a majority of 259–175, with one independent. Including the first black woman ever elected to the Senate, four women won seats, bringing the total number to six, the most ever.

Nov 20: An agreement to reduce government subsidies of farm products was reached by the U.S. and the European Community. It called for a reduction of 21% in the tonnage of subsidized grain exports. France called the terms "unacceptable."

Nov 21–23: About **45 freak tornadoes** struck 11 states from Texas north to Ohio and in the South. At least 25 persons were killed, hundreds injured, and much damage done, especially in trailer parks.

Dec 9: The **first contingent of U.S. troops** landed in Mogadishu, capital of Somalia, to begin relief operations, under a UN mandate, to distribute goods in a land wracked by starvation, civil war, and drought.

Dec 24: Pres. Bush pardoned **six former federal officials.** During the administration of Presidents Reagan and Bush they had been involved in an arms-for-hostage scandal concerning the illegal supply of arms to Iran. The six include Caspar W. Weinberger, former secretary of defense, and Robert C. McFarlane, former national security adviser.

II. Architecture
Arts and Music
Popular Entertainment
Publishing
Theater

At the box office the Broadway theater season of 1991–1992 was the best ever, with receipts of $292,000,000. Thirty–seven shows were produced, compared with 28 of the previous season, and more than any in the past five seasons. Attendance was up slightly to 7,352,005. Old and new shows and revivals all contributed to the good times. *Miss Saigon* and *The Phantom of the Opera* continued to be popular, but revivals were most talked about, including *Guys and Dolls,* the musical based on Damon Runyon's tales of New York City's night people, and *Man of La Mancha,* a musical version of *Don Quixote.* A new musical with old music was *Crazy for You,* with a generous collection of George Gershwin's melodies, as was *Jelly's Last Jam,* starring Gregory Hines and remembering "Jelly Roll" Morton of jazz fame. *The Secret Garden* was billed as a "family musical" that children would enjoy. There was a new staging of *A Streetcar Named Desire,* and Judd Hirsch was hailed in *Conversations with My Father.* As usual, Neil Simon's latest play, *Lost in Yonkers,* was a success, and what was billed as the "world's longest running musical," *The Fantasticks,* was in its fourth decade. The first hit of the 1992–1993 season was *The Sisters Rosensweig* by Wendy Wasserstein, a comedy of three women seeking love as well as self-definition. Another new play was David Mamet's *Oleanna,* a drama about sexual politics. The movies, as usual, presented a mixed bag of products. *Batman Returns* was an obvious hit, and vampires were in style, including a new filming of *Bram Stoker's Dracula,* by Francis Ford Coppola. James Fenimore Cooper's *The Last of the Mohicans* was presented with rich historical pageantry and romance. Babe Ruth was the subject of a mythical filmed version of his mythical life, *The Babe. White Men Can't Jump* dealt with racism, but it also pictured two men who didn't want to grow up. Robert Redford's direction of *A River Runs Through It* was an enthralling view of both fly fishing and father-son relationships. If *1492* was supposed to be a tribute to the 500th anniversary of Christopher Columbus's first voyage, it missed the mark with its soap opera style dialogue. Among other failures were *Man Trouble,* in which Jack Nicholson, usually a drawing card, played a dog trainer; and *Boomerang,* in which Eddie Murphy played a womanizing advertising executive. The latter did not do nearly as well as Murphy's earlier movies. More popular films included *Unforgiven,* in which Clint Eastwood was a reformed killer facing his past; *Sister Act,* with Whoopi Goldberg as a night club singer who flees to a convent to escape mobsters; and *A League of Their Own,* about a women's baseball team during World War II. Overall, movie attendance was down, being 10,000,000 tickets behind normal by mid-August. Many of America's orchestras were in financial trouble as costs of all kinds continued to increase. In the past five years they had gone up by 42%. On the positive side, orchestras were playing to about 1500 people per performance, an increase of 300 from ten

years earlier. The Metropolitan Opera marked the 500th anniversary of the first voyage of Columbus to the Western Hemisphere with a new work commissioned from the composer Philip Glass. Called *The Voyage,* it ran for three and a half hours and cost $2,000,000 to stage. Actually, Columbus figured in only a small part of the work, since it began with a landing of aliens on earth in the Ice Age and concluded with the U.S. finding life on another planet. Another new opera was *McTeague,* based on the 1899 novel by Frank Norris about a greedy San Francisco dentist. The composer was William Bolcom and the work had its world premier at the Lyric Opera, Chicago, Ill. An unusual musical event was the appearance on a North American tour for the first time of the Red Star Red Army Chorus and Dance, 130 members strong. The fall television season got off to a disappointing start so far as the networks were concerned. Shows seen early on Saturday evening, for example, were drawing only a 56% share of the total audience, compared with 66% a year earlier. Older shows, such as *The Simpsons* and *Doogie Howser, M.D.,* had fewer viewers, and new shows, such as *Angel Street* and *Final Appeal,* were doing poorly compared with their predecessors. On the whole the networks seemed to be less and less interested in older people. Typical of the new shows that were popular were *Love and War,* a sitcom about an oddly matched young couple; and *Mad About You,* involving newlyweds whose personalities were not on the same wavelength. A further indication of changing times was seen in the arrival of a series such as *Middle Ages,* intended to appeal to the "baby boomers" who were now into their forties. It was pointed out that there was now a generation of TV viewers who, via cable and satellite, had a much wider range of choices than their elders. But a study by two economists found that average American workers had less time to enjoy the arts and sports than two decades ago because they worked 140 hours more a year. Also, paid days off had dwindled as vacation, sick leave, and personal days fell by about 15% during the 1980s. Americans were spending more time working and less time on leisure pursuits in part because real wages had declined. Deaths of notable people this year included Roy Acuff, country music singer and fiddler, Nov. 23, at 89; Stella Adler, actress and teacher, Dec. 21, at 91; Peter Allen, concert entertainer and winner of both a Grammy and an Academy Award for his songwriting, June 18, at 48; Judith Anderson, Australian-born stage, screen and television actress, Jan. 3, at 93; Isaac Asimov, prolific author of nearly 500 books, Apr. 6, at 72; Freddie Bartholomew, child movie star of the 1930s, best known in *Little Lord Fauntleroy*, Jan. 23, at 69/70; Shirley Booth, star of stage and screen, radio and TV, noted for her role in *Come Back, Little Sheba*, Oct. 16, at 94; Kay Boyle, popular author of four dozen books, Dec. 27, at 89; John Cage, minimalist composer who also influenced choreography, Aug. 12, at 79; Morris Carnovsky, character actor known especially for his Shakespearean roles, Sept. 1, at 94; Mae Clarke, movie actress, remembered forever for the scene in which James Cagney shoved a grapefruit in her face, Apr. 29, at 81; Kevin "Chuck" Connors, tough man star of TV and the movies, Nov. 1, at 71; Sandy Dennis, actress who won two Tony Awards as well as an Academy Award, Mar. 2, at 54; Helen Deutsch, screenwriter of the hit movie *Lili* and co-author of *National Velvet,* Mar. 15, at 85; Pietro di Donato, author remembered for *Christ in Concrete* (1938), Jan. 19, at 80; Marlene Dietrich, perhaps the most glamorous star and singer the movies have known, May 6, at 90; Alfred Drake, baritone who was a sensational hit in the lead role in *Oklahoma!* (1943), and other Broadway shows, July 25, at 77; José Ferrer, writer, actor, and director, famous for his role as Cyrano de Bergerac, Jan. 26, at 80; M. F. K. Fisher, short story writer and author of cookbooks that set a new style for the genre, June 22, at 83; Alex Haley, author of the best-selling novel *Roots* (1976), Feb. 10, at 70; Paul Henreid, actor and director of many TV dramas, remembered most of all for his role in the movie *Casablanca,* Mar. 29, at 84; Hanya Holm, choreographer, Nov. 3, at 99; Lou Jacobs, leading clown of the Ringling Brothers and Barnum and Bailey Circus for some 60 years, Sept. 13, at 89; Allan Jones, romantic tenor who sang in many films, most notably in *Show Boat* (1936), June 27, at 84; Dorothy Kirsten, longtime leading lyric soprano of the Metropolitan Opera, Nov. 18, at 82; Oscar Lewis, historian, July 11, at 99; Pare Lorentz, writer and director of socially conscious documentary films such as *The River,* Mar. 4, at 86; Max Lerner, educator and journalist with strong liberal views, June 5, at 89; Cleavon Little, Tony award winning actor of the stage, screen, and TV, Oct. 22, at 53; Nathan Milstein, Russian-born American violinist, Dec. 21, at 87; Joan Mitchell, important among the second generation of American abstract expressionists, Oct. 30, at 66; Bert Parks, television host who emceed the Miss America pageant for 25 years, Feb. 2, at 77; Anthony Perkins, versatile actor known best for his role as a psychopath in *Psycho* (1960), Sept. 12, at 60; Molly Picon, comedienne who starred in the Yiddish theater, Apr. 6, at 94; Harold "Hal" Roach, pioneer movie producer and director, Nov. 2, at 100; William Schuman, composer and president of the Juilliard School of Music, Feb. 15, at

81; Eric Sevareid, outstanding radio and television reporter and commentator, July 9, at 79; William Shawn, legendary editor for 35 years of *The New Yorker,* Dec. 8, at 85; William A. Swanberg, author who specialized in biographies, Sept. 17, at 84; Nancy Walker, actress who portrayed wild and brassy characters on stage and in the movies, Mar. 25, at 69; and Lawrence Welk, folksy bandleader, May 17 at 89.

Affected by the number of **books published** in relation to the public's ability to buy them, and also by the recession, a number of publishers announced they were cutting back on the size of their lists. Yet a number of very lucrative contracts were signed. Barbara Taylor Bradford was to get about $24,000,000 for three novels in the romance genre; Magic Johnson, the basketball star with AIDS, about $5,000,000 for three books; and Kitty Kelley $4,000,000 for a book about the British royal family. This being a presidential election year, books about politics, politicians, and government in general, were numerous. In the last category the leader was *United We Stand* by H. Ross Perot, outlining the nation's core problems and detailing what he would do to solve them if elected to the presidency. Close on his heels was *Putting People First* by Bill Clinton and Al Gore, the Democratic party candidates for president and vice president. Senator Gore also had a best-selling book on the environment, *Earth in the Balance.* Among the year's fiction offerings were *Vox* by Nicholson Baker, consisting entirely of an erotic telephone conversation between a man and a woman; *Rising Sun* by Michael Crichton, as much an attack on Japan as a murder mystery; *"I" Is for Innocent* by Sue Grafton, continuing alphabetically the adventures of Kinsey Milhone, private detective; *Fatherland* by Robert Harris, a believable account of events after Hitler won World War II; *Gerald's Game* by Stephen King, the tale of a woman handcuffed to a bed for more than a day; *Jazz* by Toni Morrison, with Harlem of the 1920s as background; *Black Water* by Joyce Carol Oates, a retelling of the tragedy of Sen. Edward Kennedy at Chappaquiddick; *The Tale of the Body Thief* by Anne Rice, extending her chronicles of vampires; *Red Square* by Martin Cruz Smith, again featuring Moscow detective Arkady Renko; and *The Volcano Lover* by Susan Sontag, which took an unusual approach to the story of admiral Horatio Nelson and Lady Hamilton. Nonfiction titles included *America: What Went Wrong?* by Donald L. Bartlett and James B. Steel; *The End of History and the Last Man* by Francis Fukuyama, in which the author claimed that achieving liberal democracy would mean the end of history; *The Government Racket* by Martin L. Gross; *Woodrow Wilson,* a biography by August Heckscher; *Kissinger: A Biography* by Walter Isaacson; *Truman* by David McCullough; *The Making of Middlebrow Culture* by Joan Shelley Rubin, explaining how publishers and others have tried to sell culture to almost everyone; *It Doesn't Take a Hero*, a highly successful autobiography by Gen. H. Norman Schwarzkopf, Jr., the commanding general in the Persian Gulf War; *The Silent Passage* by Gail Sheehy, on the significance of menopause for modern women; *The Diversity of Life* by Edward O. Wilson, which argued that human beings were their own worst enemies by their disregard for other species; and *The Radicalism of the American Revolution* by Gordon S. Wood, which argued that the war for independence was indeed much more radical than is usually thought. Finally, in a class by itself, was *Sex*, a sensational collection of photographs of the superstar Madonna.

Feb 2: The **William S. Paley Collection,** consisting of nearly 80 paintings, drawings, and sculptures, went on exhibit at the Museum of Modern Art, New York City. Featuring works of the modern French masters, the collection of the late founder of the Columbia Broadcasting System was the most significant gift the museum had received in recent years.

Feb 26: Grammy Awards were presented for the following: best album of 1991, *Unforgettable* by Natalie Cole; best record, 'Unforgettable' by Natalie Cole; best male pop vocalist, Michael Bolton for 'When a Man Loves a Woman'; best female pop and rock vocalist, Bonnie Raitt for 'Something to Talk About' and 'Luck of the Draw.'

Mar 31: Academy Awards were presented to *The Silence of the Lambs* as the outstanding motion picture of 1991; Anthony Hopkins as best actor for *The Silence of the Lambs;* Jodie Foster as best actress for *The Silence of the Lambs;* Jack Palance as best supporting actor for *City Slickers;* and Mercedes Ruehl as best supporting actress for *The Fisher King.*

Apr 7: Pulitzer Prizes were awarded for the following: fiction, *A Thousand Acres* by Jane Smiley; general nonfiction, *The Prize: The Epic Quest for Oil, Money and Power* by Daniel Yergin; biography, *Fortunate Son: The Healing of a Vietnam Vet* by Lewis B. Puller, Jr.; history, *The Fate of Liberty: Abraham Lincoln and Civil Liberties* by Mark E. Neely, Jr.; poetry, *Selected Poems* by James Tate; drama, *The Kentucky Cycle* by Robert Schenkkan.

Apr 30: *The Cosby Show,* the most popular situation comedy ever to appear on TV, presented its last weekly episode. The comedy series had begun on Sept. 20, 1984. Starring the comedian Bill Cosby as a physician with a large and active family, including a wife who was a lawyer, the program held first place in the ratings for 69 consecutive weeks.

June 1: Tony Awards for the 1991–1992 theater season were presented for the following: best play, *Dancing at Lughnasa* by Brian Friel; best musical, *Crazy for You* by George Gershwin, Ira Gershwin, and Ken Ludwig; best actor in a play, Judd Hirsch for *Conversations With My Father;* best actress in a play, Glenn Close for *Death and the Maiden;* best actor in a musical, Gregory Hines for *Jelly's Last Jam;* best actress in a musical, Faith Prince for *Guys and Dolls.*

June 14: Mona Van Duyn was appointed the **sixth poet laureate** of the U.S. She was the first woman so named.

June 28: The **Guggenheim Museum** in New York City opened a new ten-story addition and its renovated Frank Lloyd Wright original landmark building. The changes nearly tripled, to 80,000 sq. ft., the amount of exhibit space.

July 7: The **National Gallery of Art** announced that more than 2444 works of art had been promised to it in 1991 when it celebrated its 50th anniversary. The largest and most important gift to the Washington institution was the collection of Herbert and Dorothy Vogel, consisting of more than 2000 works of minimalist, conceptual, and post-1960 art.

Aug 30: Emmy Awards were presented for the following: best drama series, *Northern Exposure;* best comedy series, *Murphy Brown;* best actor in a drama series, Christopher Lloyd for *Avonlea;* best actress in a drama series, Dana Delany for *China Beach;* best actor in a comedy series, Craig T. Nelson for *Coach;* best actress in a comedy series, Candice Bergen for *Murphy Brown.*

Sep 5: The pop artist **Prince,** it was announced, had signed a $100,000,000 recording contract with Warner Brothers, making him the highest paid performer in his field.

Sep 16: The New York Philharmonic Orchestra, founded in 1842 and the oldest orchestra in the U.S., began the observance of its 150th year with a gala benefit concert at Avery Fisher Hall, New York City. The orchestra made its debut on Dec. 7, 1842.

Sep 24: The largest exhibit of the art of **Henri Matisse** opened at the Museum of Modern Art, New York City. It included 300 paintings, as well as drawings and sculptures, and was assembled from public collections in Russia and France and also private collectors from around the world. It was the most expensive show the museum had ever mounted, and the art shown was valued at about $1,000,000,000.

Oct 2: The **musical collection of Irving Berlin,** the late composer, will be donated by his heirs to the Library of Congress in Washington, D.C. Amounting to

750,000 items, the collection included original scores, manuscripts, scrapbooks, and other materials recording the 60-year career of Berlin.

Oct 8: A new **postage stamp series** honoring rock-and–roll and country musicians would be issued in 1993, the U.S. Postal Service announced. Foremost among those included would be Elvis Presley. Among others would be Patsy Cline, Buddy Holly, Dinah Washington, and Hank Williams.

Nov 18: National Book Awards were presented to: fiction, *All the Pretty Horses* by Cormac McCarthy; nonfiction, *Becoming a Man: Half a Life Story* by Paul Monette; poetry, *New and Selected Poems* by Mary Oliver.

III. Business and Industry
Education
Philosophy and Religion
Science

The recession that began in the spring of 1990 refused to go away, although the third quarter report for the Gross Domestic product (GDP) showed an encouraging gain of 3.9%. A report on consumer confidence indicated it rose 0.4% in October after having in September reached its lowest point since February. The unemployment picture remained rather bleak although the jobless rate fell to 7.4% in October, from a peak of 7.8% earlier in the year. Payroll jobs increased overall by 27,000 in the month but there was a drop of 55,000 in factory jobs. Fear of bad times was reflected in the report that for seven consecutive months consumers had reduced their debts instead of taking on new obligations. But in October retail sales rose 0.9% and automobile sales in early November were up by 21.6% compared with the previous year. The stock market reflected unease, with the Dow Jones industrial average reaching its low for the year to date at 3136.58 on Oct. 9. Further reflecting a weak economy was a government report that the poverty rate rose for the second year to 14.2%. "Cents-off" coupons were perhaps another indicator, with 4,100,000,000 redeemed in the first six months, an increase over 1991 of 10%. On the health front there was good, bad, and indifferent news. Ordinary people were puzzled by a study which found that 98.6°F is not necessarily a person's normal body temperature; it may vary from 96° to 99.9°. On the news front, smoking in the U.S. reached its lowest level in 37 years. This good news was countered by a steep rise in cases of tuberculosis, a disease which once had been virtually eradicated. In religion, a poll showed that two-thirds of American Roman Catholics thought women should be allowed to become priests, while 70% believed priests should be allowed to marry. The recession did not stop the cost of a college education from going up. In public colleges the year's increase was 10%; in private colleges, 7%. Average tuition fees at the former were $2253; at the latter, $8879. The range was all the way from $321 for a year's education to $24,380. In high schools dropout rates were declining for blacks and whites, but not for Hispanics. Another survey reported that the use of standardized tests may hinder efforts to improve math and science education by leading teachers to emphasize memorization rather than reasoning. Noteworthy persons who died this year included Marguerite Ross Barnett, president of the University of Houston since 1990 and the first black woman to head a major American university, Feb. 26, at 49; Eugene R. Black, president of the World Bank from 1949 to 1962, Feb. 20, at 93; Allan Bloom, conservative critic of American universities whose book *The Closing of the American Mind* (1987) caused controversy, Oct. 7, at 62; S. I. Hayakawa, language scholar, college president, and Republican senator from California, Feb. 27, at 85; Timothy S. Healy, president of Georgetown University and the New York Public Library, Dec. 30, at 69; Daniel K. Ludwig, self-made ship owner and real estate developer, and one of the richest men in the world, Aug. 27, at 95; Barbara McClintock, a leader in genetic research and a Nobel prize winner, Sept. 2, at 90; William McGowan, long-time head of MCI Communications Corp., June 8, at 64; Stephen Ross, head of Time Warner, Inc., the largest media and entertainment company in the world, Dec. 20, at 65; Lee Salk, child psychologist and authority on family relationships, May 2, at 65; Marc H. Tanenbaum, popular rabbi who contributed greatly to furthering Christian-Jewish relations, July 3, at 66; Willard L. Thorp, economist who helped draft the Marshall Plan for European recovery after World War II, May 10, at 92; Sam Walton, founder of the Wal-Mart store chain that made his family the richest in the U.S., Apr. 5, at 74; and James E. Webb, head of the National Aeronautics and Space Administration during the period when men first reached the moon, Mar. 27, at 85.

Jan 6: In a wave of **department store closings,** the Woolworth Corp. announced it would close, sell, or reformat 900 of its 6500 stores because of the recession. On Jan. 27 R.H. Macy & Co., one of the largest department store operators in the country, with 251 stores, filed for bankruptcy, saddled by $3,500,000,000 of debt incurred in a management-led buyout in 1986. On May 20 Macy announced that it would close eight stores in the New York City area, having already shut 64 shops around the country that it operated under other names. On May 15 Alexander's closed all 11 of its stores in the New York area.

Jan 8: At a **summit meeting** in Tokyo, Pres. George Bush and Prime Minister Kiichi Miyazawa of Japan announced some general plans for battling the current recession by creating momentum for expansion and by fighting inflation. On Jan. 9 Bush announced that Japan had agreed to buy more American cars and $10,000,000,000 more in auto parts by 1995. The heads of the three major American auto manufacturers, who participated in the meetings, denounced the agreement as inadequate.

Feb 24: The **closing of 21 auto plants** in the U.S. and Canada over the next several years was announced by General Motors. Twelve plants, affecting 16,300 workers, were to be shut down within three years. At the same time the nation's largest auto manufacturer reported a loss in 1991 of $4,445,000,000, the largest in American corporate history.

Mar 9: The resignation of the chairman of the **Christian Science Church** was announced amid a controversy within the church concerning its direction and its finances. The outgoing chairman, Harvey W. Wood, had been the leader in the establishment of the Monitor Channel, a TV outlet that had lost millions of dollars and had borrowed $41,500,000 from the church's pension fund.

Mar 12: A **warning about a dangerous heart valve** that had been implanted in more than 20,000 Americans was issued by the Food and Drug Administration. It said there was such a high rate of sudden fatal failure that recipients of this particular type of valve should consider having it replaced. The company that produced the valves admitted that worldwide about 500 had failed, killing two-thirds or more of the patients.

Mar 24: Donna Redel was elected the **first woman chairperson of the New York Commodity Exchange.** The 39-year-old Redel was an executive vice president of the Redel Trading Co.

Apr 1: A **Russian aid plan,** to provide $24,000,000,000 to further democratization and a free market economy in Russia, was announced by Pres. Bush and Chancellor Helmut Kohl of Germany. The seven leading industrial nations were to take part and the U.S. share was to be nearly $4,500,000,000.

Apr 16: Sharp restrictions on the use of **silicone gel breast implants** were ordered by the Food and Drug Administration. A panel of experts had concluded that there was not enough evidence to show that the implants were safe or effective. The Dow Corning Corp., the largest maker of the implants, first denied

any danger, then admitted it had some evidence to the contrary, and announced it was stopping their production.

May 12: Homosexual behavior conflicts with Christian teaching, the General Conference of the United Methodist Church declared. On June 10 the Southern Baptist Convention voted to banish two of its churches for accepting homosexuals and began a process to change its by-laws to exclude any church that accepted homosexuals. On July 1 the Roman Catholic Church urged its bishops in the U.S. to oppose any laws that promote public acceptance of homosexual conduct.

May 13: Two **"firsts" in space activity** were registered by American astronauts. Three astronauts from the shuttle *Endeavour* walked in space at the same time, and they used only their gloved hands to wrestle a damaged satellite inside the shuttle for repairs. They were some 230 miles above the earth when they captured the 17–foot, 4.5-ton satellite.

May 26: In an announcement concerning **foods produced through genetic engineering,** the federal government said that new and varied products should result and that no more regulation was required than for ordinary foodstuffs. Although some critics had argued that there could be safety risks in such foods, the government held that except in special cases no extraordinary testing was needed.

June 1: The **Dow Jones average** of industrial stocks passed the 3400 mark for the first time ever, ending the day at 3413.21.

June 24: Affirming its previous ruling on state sponsored **prayer in public schools,** the Supreme Court, 5–4, again held that such practices are unconstitutional and violate the First Amendment.

June 26: The Supreme Court ruled, 8–1, that **Mississippi had failed to end racial segregation** in its state university system as required to meet constitutional standards. Although the state's eight public universities were nominally open to all, five remained largely white and three mostly black.

June 28: A **baboon's liver was transplanted into a human** for the first time. The 11.5-hour operation was performed at a Pittsburgh, Pa., hospital on a 35-year-old man who was dying of hepatitis B.

July 6: The **largest educational gift** ever made to a public university or college by an individual was announced by Henry M. Rowan, a wealthy founder of a manufacturing company. The recipient of the $100,000,000 donation was Glassboro State College, Glassboro, N.J., which then changed its name to Rowan College of New Jersey.

July 9: Ending the **longest space shuttle flight** to date, the *Columbia* landed at Cape Canaveral, Fla., after two weeks in orbit. The craft traveled 5,760,000 miles and circled the earth 221 times.

Sep: The **oldest DNA** ever recovered from fossils was reported to have been found in gene fragments extracted from insects preserved in amber for up to 40,000,000 years. Scientists said that this showed DNA could survive far longer than had been believed possible.

Sep 20: The **first space flight devoted to Japanese research** ended when the space shuttle *Endeavor* landed after an eight-day mission. Thirty-four experiments had been carried out on behalf of Japanese scientists. The flight also carried the first married couple, first black woman, and first Japanese astronaut into space.

Sep 21: The American branch of the ancient **Ethiopian Orthodox Church** declared itself independent of the mother church in Addis Ababa. Church leaders claimed that the recently appointed Patriarch Abuna Paulos was named illegally.

Sep 25: The 5,700-pound **Mars Observer** was launched on an 11-month voyage to Mars. The first U.S. spacecraft to head for Mars in 17 years, it was intended to map the planet and explore its geological and climatological history after its arrival on Aug. 24, 1993.

Oct 7: Heart disease may be promoted by oils used in the manufacture of margarine, the Department of Agriculture reported. Some vegetable oils found in margarine and other products can in the manufacturing process create, at room temperature, trans-fatty acids which act like saturated fats.

Oct 9: A major **U.S.-Chinese trade agreement** was signed. By its terms, China would reduce barriers that hinder the importation of such U.S. produced goods as computers, cameras, and chemicals. In Aug. the U.S. had threatened to impose restrictive tariffs on many Chinese goods if such an agreement were not reached.

Oct 9: The spacecraft **Pioneer 12** ceased operation after 14 years of service. Launched on May 30, 1978, it originally had been expected to send back data about Venus over a one-year period only. It had by now sent 400,000,000,000 bits of data.

Oct 12: The **Nobel Prize in Physiology or Medicine** was shared by two scientists at the University of Washington, Edmond H. Fischer and Edwin G. Krebs. They were honored for their discovery of the way proteins are altered or switched to perform functions within cells.

Oct 12: The most concentrated **search for life on other worlds** began when programs directed to the world's largest radio telescope in Puerto Rico and another in California were activated. The ten-year, $100,000,000 project was to search more than 10,000,000 different frequency channels for possible signals from extraterrestrials.

Oct 13: The **Nobel Prize in Economics** was awarded to Gary S. Becker of the University of Chicago for his studies of the economic bases of decisions people make in such areas as education, family size, and crime. This was the third successive year in which a University of Chicago economist won this prize.

Oct 14: The **Nobel Prize in Chemistry** was awarded to Rudolph A. Marcus, a Canadian-born scientist at the California Institute of Technology, for providing a mathematical explanation for puzzling chemical interactions involving the transfer of electrons between molecules.

Oct 29: An **injectable contraceptive** that prevents pregnancy for three months was approved by the FDA. The drug contains synthetic progesterone, which inhibits ovulation. Controversy over the drug's use had gone on in the U.S. for two decades, although the drug has been available in more than 90 other countries.

Oct 30: Women need not submit to abusive husbands, a statement by the nation's Roman Catholic bishops declared. There is nothing in the Bible requiring such submission, they said, and added: "Violence in any form—physical, sexual, psychological, or verbal—is sinful."

Nov 18: A **pastoral letter on the place of women** in the church and society was rejected by the National Conference of Catholic Bishops after nine years of drafting and debating. The vote failed to reach the two-thirds majority requirement. The letter affirmed the equality of men and women but opposed the ordaining of women into the priesthood.

Dec 31: On the New York Stock Exchange the **Dow Jones industrial average** closed at 3301.11, up 132.28 points from the previous year's close.

IV. Fashion
Folkways
Holidays
Social Issues and Crime
Sports

According to a report by the federal General Accounting Office total earnings of a head coach of men's basketball were more than twice that of a head coach of women's basketball. In addition, few blacks were found to hold key positions in athletic departments. In professional sports a survey showed that football is now the favorite sport to watch on TV, with 38% favoring it, compared with 16% for baseball and 12% for basketball. Baseball viewership fell 24% among young men aged 12 to 17, while NBA viewership was up 31% and NFL 16%. This trend was also evident in attendance at major league baseball games in the 1992 season, with a drop of nearly 600,000 in the National League and about 325,000 in the American League. On the other hand, owners of teams in professional sports seemed to be doing all right. The New York Yankees baseball franchise was at the top of the list, being valued at $200,000,000. For the first time the average salary of a major league baseball player passed the $1,000,000 mark. Crime figures were also impressive—or depressing. The U.S. held in prison a higher percentage of its population than any other nation. The 1,100,000 inmates represented an incarceration rate of 455 people per 100,000. In late October the 27th execution in the U.S. this year took place in North Carolina, marking the highest number of executions since 1962, when 47 convicts were put to death. News of weapons was not all in the lethal category. More powerful water guns, able to throw a stream 50 feet, became the rage. All was not peaceful in the field of fashion, either. The New York City consumer affairs commissioner attacked designers and producers of beauty products for not using enough members of minority groups in their advertising. The designers, meanwhile, solved the problem of skirt length by featuring pants for women; but while the women covered up, men bared almost all when they modeled underwear at a fashion show of a leading designer. Notable persons who died during the year included Sandy Amoros, hero of the 1955 World Series as starter of a spectacular double play, June 27, at 62; Walter "Red" Barber, most popular of sports broadcasters over a 33-year career, Oct. 27, at 84; Danny Biasone, professional basketball team owner who devised the 24-second shot clock to make the game more exciting, May 25, at 83; Easley Blackwood, leading contract bridge expert who invented the Blackwood convention as a bidding device in 1933, Mar. 27, at 89; Anita Colby, called the first "supermodel" and who wrote on beauty, Mar. 27, at 77; Mel Hein, iron man center and linebacker of the pro football Giants in the 1930s and 1940s, Jan. 31, at 82; Billy Herman, second baseman of the Brooklyn Dodgers and a member of the Baseball Hall of Fame, Sept. 5, at 83; Eddie Lopat, star pitcher for the New York Yankees for five championship years, June 15, at 73; Salvatore "Sal" Maglie, pitcher, mostly for the

New York Giants, much feared by batters, Dec. 28, at 75; Mollie Parnis, designer whose dresses were worn by several First Ladies, July 18, at 90+; Samuel Reshevsky, chess grandmaster, Apr. 4, at 80; Anthony "Fat Tony" Salerno, boss of the Genovese crime family, in prison since 1989, July 27, at 80; Carl Stotz, who founded Little League baseball in 1938, June 4, at 82; and Jean R. Yawkey, majority owner of the Boston Red Sox and a philanthropist, Feb. 26, at 83.

Jan 1: In **college football bowl games,** the results were Florida State 10, Texas A&M 2 in the Cotton Bowl; Miami 22, Nebraska 0 in the Orange Bowl; Washington 34, Michigan 14 in the Rose Bowl; and Notre Dame 30, Florida 28 in the Sugar Bowl. The AP and *The New York Times* selected Miami as the national collegiate champions of 1991, but the UPI and *USA Today/*CNN polls chose Washington.

Jan 8: The **NCAA adopted stricter academic standards** for athletes. The changes would require incoming freshman athletes to have a higher grade-point average than before in core subjects in high school, and would strengthen the requirement that athletes show progress toward a degree.

Jan 9–11: U.S. figure skating championships were won in Orlando, Fla., by Christopher Bowman, men's singles; Kristi Yamaguchi, women's singles; Calla Urbanski and Rocky Marval, pairs; April Sargent-Thomas and Russ Witherby, dance.

Jan 18: Pat Bradley became only the 12th member of the LPGA Hall of Fame, having won the required 30 tournament victories during her career. Bradley had also won more prize money—$4,109,165—than any other female golfer.

Jan 26: Super Bowl XXVI was won by the Washington Redskins (NFC) who defeated the Buffalo Bills (AFC) 37 to 24. On Jan. 12 the Redskins had beaten the Detroit Lions 41 to 10 for the NFC title and the Bills defeated the Denver Broncos 10 to 7 for the AFC title.

Feb 8–23: At the **XVIth Winter Olympic Games,** held in Albertville, France, the U.S. finished sixth in the medal standings, winning five gold medals and 11 in total. All the gold medals were won by women: Bonnie Blair, two in speed skating; Kristi Yamaguchi, figure skating; Cathy Turner, 500-meter race; and Donna Weinbrecht, mogul skiing.

Feb 10: Former heavyweight boxing champion **Mike Tyson was convicted of rape** in Indianapolis, Ind., and on Mar. 26 was sentenced to six years in prison. He had been charged with raping an 18-year-old beauty pageant contestant on July 19, 1991.

Feb 17: Martina Navratilova won her 158th tennis title, more than any other player, male or female. She took her first championship in Czechoslovakia in 1973.

Mar 2: Ryne Sandberg became the **highest paid player in professional baseball** when he signed a contract with the Chicago Cubs (NL) worth $28,400,000 over four years. On Aug. 24 Cal Ripken, Jr., of the Baltimore Orioles (AL) became the second-highest paid player when he signed a five-year contract worth $30,500,000.

Apr 5: The **NCAA women's basketball championship** was won by Stanford, which defeated Western Kentucky 78 to 62.

Apr 6: The NCAA men's basketball championship was won by Duke, which defeated Michigan 71 to 51.

Apr 8: Arthur Ashe, the black tennis champion and rights activist, revealed that he had contracted AIDS, apparently from a blood transfusion. In 1968 Ashe had become the first and only black man to win the U.S. tennis championship, and in 1975, the British title.

Apr 9: Manuel Antonio Noriega, the former dictator of Panama, was convicted in a federal court on eight counts of cocaine trafficking, racketeering, and money laundering. He had surrendered to U.S. forces Jan. 3, 1990, during an invasion of Panama by American troops. On July 10 he was sentenced to 40 years in prison.

Apr 10: The key figure in a major **savings and loan scandal,** Charles H. Keating, Jr., was sentenced to ten years in prison for having duped about 23,000 depositors of the Lincoln Savings and Loan Association, which he headed, into buying high-risk junk bonds. On July 10 a federal jury ordered Keating to pay $3,300,000,000 in damage claims. On Mar. 30 an accounting firm and a law firm, involved in the financial scandal, had agreed to pay $87,000,000 in damages.

Apr 10: The **first professional hockey strike** in the history of the NHL, a ten–day walkout, ended with an agreement between the owners and the Players Association effective through the 1992–1993 season. Among the terms of the new agreement were the establishment of a minimum salary of $100,000, up from $25,000, and an increase in regular season games from 80 to 84.

Apr 12: The **Masters golf tournament** was won by Fred Couples by two strokes. It was his first major title in his 12–year career.

Apr 20: The 96th **Boston Marathon** was won in the men's division by Ibrahim Hussein of Kenya, with a time of 2 hrs., 8 min., 14 sec. Olga Markova of Russia won the women's division with a time of 2 hrs., 23

min., 43 sec. Both times were the second fastest ever run on the course.

Apr 22: In a major **sexual abuse case,** the operator of a day care center in Edenton, N.C., was convicted on 99 charges of sexually abusing children. The trial of Robert F. Kelly, Jr., operator of the Little Rascals Day Care Center, lasted eight months, the longest and costliest ever in North Carolina.

Apr 29: A bloody and destructive **riot** in south central Los Angeles broke out after four policemen were acquitted of beating a black man while making an arrest, even though the incident had been videotaped by a bystander. In all, 51 persons died, 30 of them homicide victims. Nearly 1800 people were injured, and 6345 were arrested. In the three days of disorder 3767 buildings were burned.

May 1: The 118th **Kentucky Derby** was won by Lil. E. Tee with a time of 2:03. The jockey was Pat Day.

May 9–16: The **America's Cup** was successfully defended by *America 3,* which defeated the Italian yacht *Moro di Venezia* four races to one, off San Diego, Calif.

May 16: The 117th **Preakness Stakes** was won by Pine Bluff, with a time of 1:55 3/5. The jockey was Chris McCarron.

May 17: The **LPGA golf tournament** was won by Betsy King, whose four round total of 267 was the lowest ever for this event.

May 24: The 76th **Indianapolis 500 auto race** was won by Al Unser, Jr., completing the 500-mile course in 3 hrs., 43 min., 4.991 sec., with an average speed of 134.479 mph. Unser won by only .043 sec., a record margin, and his was the eighth victory by a member of his family.

June 1: The **NHL Stanley Cup** was won for the second consecutive year by the Pittsburgh Penguins, who defeated the Chicago Blackhawks in four straight games.

June 6: The 124th **Belmont Stakes** was won by A. P. Indy, with a time of 2:26. The jockey was Eddie Delahoussaye.

June 6: The second **World League of American Football championship** was won by the Sacramento Surge, defeating the Orlando Thunder 21 to 17.

June 11: The first **foreign ownership of a major league baseball team** by non–North Americans came about when the Seattle Mariners (AL) were sold for $125,000,000 to a seven-member group that included the president of the Nintendo Co. of Japan.

June 14: The **NBA basketball championship** was won for the second consecutive year by the Chicago Bulls, who defeated the Portland Trail Blazers four games to two.

June 21: The **U.S. Open golf tournament** was won by Tom Kite by two strokes.

June 23: **John Gotti,** head of the Gambino crime family, was sentenced to life imprisonment in federal court in Brooklyn, N.Y. He had been convicted on Apr. 2 on 13 counts, including murder, conspiracy, tax fraud, and obstruction of justice.

July 5: At the **Wimbledon** tennis championships in England, Andre Agassi won the title in five sets over Goran Ivaniasevic of Croatia. Agassi was the first American to win this title since 1984.

July 11: **Tracy Austin,** 29, became the youngest inductee of the International Tennis Hall of Fame in a ceremony at Newport, R.I. Austin, at age 16, had in 1979 become the youngest U.S. Open champion. However, an injury suffered in an auto accident halted her career in 1989.

July 14: The **baseball All-Star Game** was won by the American League over the National League, 13 to 6.

July 23: **Judit Polgar,** the youngest person ever to earn the rank of chess grandmaster, celebrated her 16th birthday. She had achieved this ranking the previous Dec. There were only 401 active grandmasters in the world.

July 24: **George Steinbrenner** was returned to control of the New York Yankee baseball club as of Mar. 1, 1993. The principal owner of the team, he had been banned from major league baseball on July 30, 1990 by Fay Vincent, commissioner of major league baseball, for having paid a known gambler to try to secure discrediting information about a Yankee player, Dave Winfield. Settlement of a number of legal and other matters led Vincent to rescind the ban.

July 25–Aug 9: At the **25th Summer Olympic Games** in Barcelona, Spain, the U.S. finished second in medal winnings with 37 gold and 108 in all. The Unified Team, representing 12 of the former U.S.S.R. republics, was first with 45 gold and 112 in all. Among American winners were: Gail Devers, who won the gold medal in the 100-meter dash 18 months after she came near having her feet amputated as a result of radiation treatment for Graves' disease; Jackie Joyner-Kersee, who for the second time won the gold in the heptathlon; Mike Conley, who set an Olympic record of 57 ft., 10.5 in. in the triple jump; and Carl Lewis, who won his eighth gold medal in three Olympics as part of the 400-meter relay team. The Americans who attracted the most attention were the members of the basketball "Dream Team," composed for the first time almost entirely of professionals from the NBA. They defeated all their opponents by an average of almost 44 points a game. They were also considered arrogant and selfish, enjoying

such luxuries as chartered planes and lavish hotel rooms.

July 27: The **U.S. Women's Open golf tournament** was won by Betsy Sheehan, who defeated Juli Inkster by two strokes in an 18-hole playoff.

Aug 2: The **Baseball Hall of Fame** inducted pitcher Tom Seaver; Rollie Fingers, pitcher; Hal Newhouser, pitcher; and Bill McGowan, umpire. Seaver, in his first year of eligibility, received the highest percentage (98.8%) of the votes ever cast for a player.

Aug 16: The **PGA championship** was won by Nick Price of Zimbabwe by three strokes. It was his first major title.

Sep 5: A **world record in the decathlon** of 8891 points was set by Dan O'Brien at a meet in Talence, France. He bettered the previous 1984 record by 44 points.

Sep 7: **Baseball commissioner Fay Vincent resigned,** bowing to the demands of the club owners. On Sept. 3 the owners had voted, 18–9 with one abstention, to ask him to leave office. On Sept. 9 Bud Selig of the Milwaukee Brewers (AL) was chosen by the owners to be chairman of the executive council, in effect taking over from Vincent temporarily.

Sep 9: **Robin Yount** of the Milwaukee Brewers (AL) made his 3000th career hit, becoming the 17th player in the history of major league baseball to achieve this feat. On Oct. 1 George Brett of the Kansas City Royals (AL) joined this exclusive group.

Sep 10: The NFL **free-agent system** was ruled illegal by a federal court jury. Under the so-called Plan B, the teams were able to prevent their best players from joining other teams for more money. Damages totalling $1,629,000 were awarded to four of the plaintiffs under the antitrust laws. The outlawed rule had meant that the best players never achieved free agency during the peaks of their careers.

Sep 12–13: The **U.S. Open tennis championships** were won by Monica Seles in the women's division and by Stefan Edberg in the men's division. Both repeated their 1991 victories.

Sep 17: **Little League Baseball** stripped a Philippine team of the title it had won in the league's World Series on Aug. 29. The Zamboanga team was forced to forfeit its championship because in the series it had used players from other teams. Such a decision, never before made, gave the title to the team from Long Branch, Calif., which represented the U.S. and had lost the final game to Zamboanga, 15 to 4.

Sep 17: Operation of the **World League of American football** was suspended by the NFL for one year after two years of play. Expansion of the NFL by two teams was also delayed until at least 1994. Both decisions were based on labor unrest, with owners and players at odds on several issues.

Sep 19: The **Miss America** title was won by Leanza Cornett, 21, of Jacksonville, Fla., at the annual pageant in Atlantic City, N.J.

Sep 20: Ray Floyd became the first golfer to win tournaments in the same year on both the regular and the Senior PGA tour when he was the victor in a Senior tournament played in Indianapolis, Ind. He had won the Doral–Ryder tournament on the regular tour on Mar. 8.

Sep 20: The first **unassisted triple play** in the National League in 65 years was made by Mickey Morandini, second baseman of the Philadelphia Phillies, in a game against the Pirates at Pittsburgh.

Sep 23: In an advance for **women in professional sports,** Manon Rheaume became the first woman to play in one of the four major professional sports (baseball, football, basketball, ice hockey) when she appeared as goaltender for the Tampa Bay Lightning in an exhibition ice hockey game. She played one period, faced nine shots, and allowed two goals.

Oct 11: LeRoy Walker became the **first black president of the U.S. Olympic Committee.** Walker had been treasurer of the U.S.O.C., head coach of the men's track and field team for the 1976 Olympics, and chancellor of North Carolina Central University.

Oct 17–24: The **World Series** was won by the Toronto Blue Jays (AL), who defeated the Atlanta Braves (NL) four games to two. On Oct. 14 the Blue Jays had won the American League pennant, beating the Oakland Athletics four games to two, and the Braves had won the National League championship, defeating the Pittsburgh Pirates four games to three. For the first time a team located outside the U.S. won the series, although no player on the Blue Jays was a Canadian.

Nov 1: The 23rd **New York City Marathon** was won in the men's division by Willi Mtolo of South Africa, with a time of 2 hrs., 9 min., 29 sec. The women's division was won by Lisa Ondieki of Australia, with a time of 2 hrs., 24 min., 40 sec., a new course record for women.

Nov 13: The **world heavyweight boxing championship** was won by Riddick Bowe of Las Vegas, Nevada, when he earned a unanimous 12-round decision over the defending champion Evander Holyfield.

Dec 6: The **U.S. won the Davis Cup** in international tennis competition by defeating Switzerland three matches to one.

Dec 10: The NHL voted to expand by adding teams in Miami, Florida, and Anaheim, California, bringing the number of teams in the league to 25. The new teams paid $50,000,000 each to join and were to begin play in the 1993–1994 season.

1993

I. **Civil Rights**
  Exploration and Settlement
  Government
  Statistics
  Wars

With the inauguration in January of William Jefferson Clinton as president, the executive and legislative branches of the federal government were, for the first time in 12 years, controlled by the same party, the Democratic. Clinton's accession also marked a generational change, he being the first chief executive born after World War II. In his first year in office, Clinton, unlike his predecessor, George Bush, emphasized domestic matters, pushing for deficit control, health care reform, and gun control. Nevertheless, he was forced by circumstances to pay more attention than he would have liked to foreign affairs, especially the explosive situations in Haiti, Somalia, Bosnia and Herzegovina, Russia, and North Korea. The Census Bureau estimated that as of July 1, the nation's population stood at 257,900,000, an increase of nearly 2,800,000 in a year. Another report showed that, unlike the 1980s, the early 1990s were marked by a small increase in the number of people moving to rural areas. It was also noted that the number of poor people had increased by 1,200,000 to 36,900,000 in 1992. Among notable persons who died were John B. Connally, former governor of Texas who was seriously wounded at the time of John F. Kennedy's assassination in 1963, June 15, at 76; James H. Doolittle, aviation pioneer and air force general who led the first daylight raid on Tokyo in World War II, Sept. 27, at 96; H. R. Haldeman, White House chief of staff who served a prison term for his part in the Watergate scandal, Nov. 12, at 67; Thurgood Marshall, the first black justice on the Supreme Court and a leader of the civil rights movement, Jan. 25, at 84; Matthew B. Ridgway, combat commander in World War II and the Korean War, July 26, at 98.

Jan 3: The second **Strategic Arms Reduction Treaty** was signed in Moscow by Pres. George Bush and Russian Pres. Boris Yeltsin. Both the U.S. and Russia are to cut their nuclear arsenals to about one-third their present levels within a decade.

Jan 13: Negotiations on a treaty concerning chemical warfare, attended by 120 nations, including the U.S., began in Paris. To take effect Jan. 15, 1995, the treaty would outlaw the manufacture, stockpiling, and use of chemical weapons.

Jan 13: Iraqi missile batteries and radar stations were attacked by more than 100 U.S., British, and French warplanes. The raids were in response to violations by Iraq of UN resolutions stemming from the Persian Gulf War and Iraq's activities in a southern no-fly zone.

Jan 17: The **100th anniversary of the end of Hawaiian independence** was observed in Honolulu. On Jan. 17, 1883, a coup led by white businessmen overthrew the regime of Queen Liliuokalani, Hawaii's last monarch.

Jan 20: William Jefferson Clinton was inaugurated as the 42nd president of the U.S. Albert Gore, Jr. was inaugurated as vice president.

Jan 25: Five restrictions on abortion established during recent Republican administrations were overturned by executive order of Pres. Clinton. One rule that was eliminated banned even the discussion of abortion at federally funded clinics.

Jan 30: The **first subway in Los Angeles,** a 4.4-mile underground stretch, opened for service with five stations. At a cost of $183,000,000,000, the system was planned to total 22.7 miles of track by 2001 and to reduce smog and traffic congestion.

Feb 5: The **Family and Medical Leave Act** was signed by Pres. Clinton. The law would require large companies to allow up to 12 weeks of unpaid leave for family and medical emergencies.

Feb 26: A **bomb explosion in the World Trade Center** in New York City killed 6 persons and injured more than 1000. The massive explosion took place in a parking garage underneath one of the Center's twin towers. By the end of June, 9 persons had been arrested in connection with the crime.

Feb 28–Mar 3: U.S. Air Force planes began dropping emergency food supplies to Muslims who were under siege by Serbian forces in Bosnia-Herzegovina. The one-ton crates carried medical supplies as well as military-style rations.

Mar 4: A bill providing **six months' additional unemployment benefits** for the longtime jobless was signed by Pres. Clinton. The cost was to be $5,700,000,000.

Mar 11: Janet Reno, the **first woman to be attorney general of the U.S.,** was confirmed by the Senate. She had been prosecuting attorney of Dade County, Fla.

Mar 13-14: An **unusually powerful snowstorm** struck the East Coast of the U.S. from Florida to Maine. Hurricane-force winds of up to 109 mph cut off power to about 3,000,000 homes and flooded coastal areas. In all, 213 deaths, including a few in Cuba and Canada, were reported, and damage was estimated at $800,000,000.

Apr-July: Unprecedented **flooding of the Mississippi R.** and many of its tributaries caused great damage in the midwestern states. About 16,000,000 acres of land were flooded, 33 deaths were caused, and at least 40,000 homes and businesses were destroyed. Damage was estimated at more than $10,000,000,000. On Aug. 12, Pres. Clinton signed a bill appropriating $6,200,000,000 for flood relief.

Apr 4: Aid in the amount of $1,600,000,000 was promised to Russia at a summit meeting of Pres. Clinton and Pres. Boris Yeltsin. There were also agreements to relax restrictions on trade that had been in effect during the Cold War.

Apr 17: A **federal jury convicted two Los Angeles police officers** of violating the civil rights of a black man who had been beaten by police in March, 1991. Two others were acquitted. The acquittal of the same officers on state charges in April, 1992, led to the worst urban rioting in the century.

Apr 19: A **religious cult's compound was destroyed by fire** near Waco, Tex., after cult members had been involved in a 51-day standoff with federal law enforcement officials. Believed to be a case of mass suicide, the fire killed at least 75 persons, about a third of them children. Nine escaped. Federal officials had originally sought to seize firearms believed to be in the compound, which was ruled by a self-styled messiah, David Koresh.

Apr 22: The **U.S. Holocaust Memorial Museum** was dedicated in Washington, D.C., in honor of the more than 6,000,000 Jews and others who were systematically killed by the Nazi rulers of Germany during World War II. The exhibits included photographs, documents, and artifacts. Private donations paid the $168,000,000 cost of the museum.

Apr 28: Women will be allowed to serve in aerial combat according to a ruling of the Defense Department. They will also be able to serve in combat positions aboard most Navy vessels.

May 11: A **bill to increase voter registration** was approved and sent to Pres. Clinton, who promised to sign it. The new law requires states to provide registration forms in motor vehicle offices, military recruiting stations, and welfare offices.

May 13: The Pentagon announced that research on the **Strategic Defense Initiative,** popularly known as Star Wars, will be discontinued. Intended as a shield against enemy missiles, work had begun in 1983 and cost $30,000,000,000.

June 6: A **ship with nearly 300 illegal Chinese immigrants aboard** ran aground off the New York City coast. At least six of the passengers died, and the captain and ten crew members were arrested.

June 8: The Equal Employment Opportunity Commission ruled that **employers may not refuse to hire persons with disabilities** because they are concerned about the effect on health insurance costs. Such workers must be given "equal access" to health insurance programs.

June 22: The status of a full-time government official was granted to **Hillary Rodham Clinton,** Pres. Clinton's wife, by a federal appeals court. The ruling resulted from a case that challenged the Task Force on National Health Care Reform, which she headed, to conduct its business in public.

June 26: U.S. Navy ships fired 23 Tomahawk missiles at a building in a suburb of Baghdad, Iraq, that was the headquarters of Iraqi intelligence operations. About eight persons were reported killed and a dozen injured, some of them civilians. The attack was in retaliation for an alleged Iraqi plot to kill former Pres. George Bush when he visited Kuwait in April.

July 19: A new policy concerning homosexuals in the **armed forces,** effective Oct. 1, was announced by Pres. Clinton. The policy was described as "don't ask, don't tell." Previously, known homosexuals had not been allowed to join the armed forces and were discharged if discovered. On Dec. 22 the Pentagon issued detailed guidelines for the new policy. Homosexual feelings could be acknowledged but homosexual acts would be banned.

Aug 3: The **Senate confirmed Ruth Bader Ginsburg as a member of the Supreme Court,** making her the second woman ever to achieve that position. Ginsburg had served on a federal appeals court. She succeeded Byron R. White, who retired in June after 31 years on the High Court.

Aug 10: The **Omnibus Budget Reconciliation Act** was signed by Pres. Clinton. Its intent was to reduce the federal budget deficit by a total of $496,000,000,000 through fiscal 1998. Spending was to to be cut by $225,000,000,000 and new taxes were to provide $241,000,000,000.

Sep 13: The **first agreement between Jews and Palestinians** was signed in a ceremony in Washington, D.C. With Pres. Clinton presiding, Prime Minister Yitzhak Rabin of Israel and Yasir Arafat, chairman of the Palestine Liberation Organization, shook hands. The Declaration of Principles provided for Palestinian self-government in the Gaza Strip and in Jericho on the occupied West Bank.

Sep 18: To commemorate the laying of the cornerstone of the Capitol in Washington, D.C., 200 years ago, a new cornerstone was set in place. At the same

ceremony the refurbished bronze statue of Freedom was replaced atop the Capitol dome.

Sep 20: A **plan to close 130 domestic military bases** and to scale down 45 more became effective when Congress refused to overturn the recommendations of the Base Closure and Realignment Commission.

Sep 21: Legislation creating a **National Service Program** was signed by Pres. Clinton. The law provided $1,500,000,000 over three years to permit young people to repay federal educational assistance through community service.

Sep 22: A **proposal to guarantee health care for every American** was presented by Pres. Clinton in a speech before Congress that was televised nationally. Large-scale health maintenance organizations were expected to be the basis of the plan, with employers, employees, and the government paying the costs.

Sep 22: Of 206 passengers and crew, 47 were killed when an Amtrak train on its way to Miami, Fla., hurtled off a bridge over a bayou near Chickasaw, Ala. A string of barges had apparently hit the bridge shortly before the disaster.

Oct 7: Pres. Clinton announced that **all American forces in Somalia** will be brought home by Mar. 31, 1994. The move came four days after 18 Americans were killed and 75 wounded in clashes with a Somalian warlord's supporters. The U.S. had originally sent troops to Somalia Dec. 9, 1992, on a humanitarian mission, but they and other UN forces had become involved in clashes with Somalian guerrillas. At year's end, 9135 American troops were in Somalia or on ships offshore.

Oct 11: U.S. troops on a mission to Haiti on behalf of the UN were kept from landing by armed demonstrators. Forced to turn back, the ship carried 125 Americans and 25 Canadians, mostly engineers. They represented part of a yearlong failed attempt to restore the democratically elected president of Haiti, Jean-Bertrand Aristide, who had been overthrown by the military on Sept. 30, 1991.

Oct 14: The **most expensive piece of road ever built** in America opened in Los Angeles, Calif. The cost was $2,200,000,000 for 17.3 miles of freeway. Expected to be the last road of its kind built in the area, its cost included providing housing for 25,500 displaced persons.

Oct 15: Three admirals were censured and 30 senior Navy officers were reprimanded by the Pentagon for their failure to properly supervise a convention in Las Vegas, Nev., in 1991 of the Tailhook Association, composed of naval aviators. Allegedly, scores of women were sexually harassed during a night of debauchery. Earlier, 140 fliers had been accused of indecent exposure, assault, and lying under oath.

Oct 18: In Los Angeles, Calif., **two black men were acquitted** of most charges in the beating of a white truck driver during rioting in April, 1992, that followed the acquittal of white police officers charged with having beaten a black man while arresting him. The jury returned seven acquittals and convicted the defendants on six less serious charges.

Oct 27–Nov 3: Brushfires swept through much of southern California, destroying more than 1000 homes, blackening about 200,000 acres, causing three deaths, and doing about $1,000,000,000 of damage. Especially hard hit were Altadena, Laguna Beach, and Malibu. Some of the fires were believed to be the work of arsonists.

Nov 9: A **broader definition of sexual harassment** was announced by a unanimous Supreme Court. By the new standard, workers could win their cases without having to prove the offensive behavior had damaged them psychologically or had made them unable to do their jobs properly.

Nov 11: A **bronze sculpture dedicated to the women who served in the armed forces during the Vietnam War** was unveiled in Washington, D.C. The statue depicts two nurses and a wounded soldier. In all, 280,000 women served during the war, 11,500 of them in Vietnam.

Nov 14: In a nonbinding referendum, **Puerto Rican voters opted for the continuance of their commonwealth status.** The vote was 48.4% for commonwealth status, 46.2% for statehood, and 4.4% for independence.

Nov 16: The **Religious Freedom Restoration Act** was signed by Pres. Clinton. The new law, which overturned a 1990 ruling of the Supreme Court, requires the government to abide by strict standards before doing anything that might restrict religious practices.

Nov 20: A **meeting of leaders of 13 Asian-Pacific nations** was held in Seattle, Wash., with Pres. Clinton as host. The intention was to explore ways of opening markets for goods and services. Clinton said the gathering had laid the basis for a Pacific Rim "community." On Nov. 19 Clinton met separately with Jiang Zemin, president of China, to discuss both trade and human rights.

Nov 30: The **Brady handgun control bill** was signed into law by Pres. Clinton. First introduced in Congress Feb. 4, 1987, and named for James S. Brady, who was seriously wounded in the 1981 attempt to assassinate Pres. Ronald Reagan, the law required a would-be buyer of a handgun to wait five business days while his or her background is checked by authorities.

Dec 7: The federal government announced that **204 previously undisclosed nuclear weapons tests** had been conducted between 1963 and 1969 in Nevada. These were part of the total of 1051 such tests.

Dec 8: The **North American Free Trade Agreement** (NAFTA) was signed by Pres. Clinton. NAFTA would eventually end almost all trade barriers between Canada, Mexico, and the U.S., and would create the world's largest free trade zone. It was to take effect Jan. 1, 1994.

Dec 14: A **world trade agreement** was settled by 117 nations, including the U.S., under the General Agreement on Tariffs and Trade (GATT). After seven years of negotiations the nations agreed to cut tariffs by a third, on average, over six years. However, agreement was not reached on trade issues concerning movies, civil aircraft, financial services, and various other matters.

II. Architecture
Arts and Music
Popular Entertainment
Publishing
Theater

With box office sales of $327,700,000, the 1992–1993 Broadway theater season set a new record, while touring productions took in another $621,000,000. Broadway attendance was 7,900,000 and there were 33 new productions, four fewer than in 1991–1992. Tony Kushner's *Angels in America* was by far the longest theatrical experience, its two parts each running three and a half hours. Shortest in terms of number of performances was *The Red Shoes,* which lasted only five days (after 51 previews); at a cost of $8,000,000 to stage, it became the most expensive Broadway failure ever. The three best movies of the year were quietly intense dramas set in the past: *The Age of Innocence, The Remains of the Day,* and *The Piano.* They offset such thrillers as *The Pelican Brief,* about the search for the murderer of two Supreme Court justices, and *Jurassic Park,* about a theme park with cloned dinosaurs, which at $350,000,000 became the highest grossing film in history. In a class by itself was *Schindler's List,* the story of a man who saved the lives of more than 1000 Jews during World War II. Country music, with its headquarters in Nashville, Tenn., was booming, with sales of recordings increasing from $425,000,000 in 1988 to $1,500,000,000 in 1992 and 2200 radio stations using country music formats. The late George Balanchine was honored and remembered by the New York City Ballet, which presented 73 ballets by the master choreographer. The most impressive and popular exhibition of art was the Joan Miró retrospective at the Museum of Modern Art, New York City. This museum also received $1,200,000 from the estate of the pioneer movie actress Lillian Gish to acquire and preserve the many movies in which she and her sister Dorothy appeared. The Studio Museum in Harlem celebrated its 25th anniversary of presenting the works of black artists. At the same time, New York City was to get a new museum dedicated to Austrian and German expressionist art. In Chicago the Art Institute celebrated its 100th anniversary with a special exhibition. Among notables who died were Don Ameche, versatile in the movies as both a leading man and character actor, Dec. 6, at 85; Marian Anderson, superb contralto and the first black to be a permanent member of the Metropolitan Opera Co., Apr. 6, at 96; Clarence L. Barnhart, lexicographer and dictionary editor, Oct. 24, at 92; Kenneth Burke, influential philosopher and critic, Nov. 19, at 96; Raymond Burr, movie and TV actor, best known for his portrayal of the lawyer-sleuth Perry Mason, Sept. 12, at 76; Lillian de la Torre, writer of masterful mystery stories for nearly half a century, Sept. 13, at 91; Agnes de Mille, choreographer, whose talents revolutionized American dance, Oct. 7, at 88; Peter De Vries, author, popular for his comic talents, Sept. 28, at 83; William "Billy" Eckstine, baritone and bandleader, Mar. 8, at 78; John "Dizzy" Gillespie, trumpeter and innovator of bebop, Jan. 6, at 75; Lillian Gish, unequaled presence on stage and in the movies for more than 85 years, Feb. 7, at 99; Moses Gunn, actor for more than 30 years, remembered for his Othello, Dec. 17, at 64; Erskine Hawkins, trumpeter and bandleader of the swing era, Nov. 11, at 79; Helen Hayes, whose 65-year career made her the first lady of the American theater, Mar. 17, at 92; Audrey Hepburn, actress, whose grace and elegance charmed millions, Jan. 20, at 63; John Hersey, journalist and novelist, best known for *Hiroshima,* Mar. 24, at 78; Irving Howe, social and literary critic, May 5, at 72; Ruby Keeler, talented dancer in Hollywood musicals, Feb. 28, at 82; Irving "Swifty" Lazar, feisty agent for numerous entertainment and literary stars, Dec. 30, at 86; Erich Leinsdorf, conductor with a worldwide reputation, Sept. 11, at 81; Myrna Loy, urbane actress, remembered especially for *The Thin Man* movie, Dec. 14, at 88; Joseph L. Mankiewicz, prolific as movie scriptwriter, director, and producer, Feb. 5, at 83; Garry Moore, cheerful host of pioneer TV variety and game shows, Nov. 28, at 78; Helen O'Connell, the ideal big band singer of the 1930s and 1940s, Sept. 9, at 73; Vincent Price, master of the suave menace in many movies, Oct. 25, at 82; Harrison Salisbury, noted foreign correspondent and author of insightful books, July 5, at 84; William L. Shirer, journalist, historian, author of *The Rise and Fall of the Third Reich,* Dec. 28, at 89; Wallace Stegner, novelist, biographer, and essayist, Apr. 13, at 84; C. L. Sulzberger, foreign affairs columnist and correspondent, Sept. 20, at 80; Alice Tully, singer and generous patron of the arts, Dec. 10, at 91; Frank Zappa, composer, bandleader, and guitarist in various styles, Dec. 4, at 52.

Among **books published** this year were some noteworthy fiction but also some that were spurned by critics. The latter category was marked especially by two novels by Robert James Waller that topped the bestseller lists: *Slow Waltz in Cedar Bend* and *The Bridges of Madison County,* difficult to tell apart. More acceptable to the critics were *The Collected Stories* by Reynolds Price and *The Oracle at Stoneleigh Court* by Peter Taylor. Among novels were *The Road to Wellville* by T. Coraghessan Boyle, an antiromance set in 1907; *The Streets of Laredo* by Larry McMurtry, a sequel to *Lonesome Dove; Foxfire: Confessions of a Girl Gang* by Joyce Carol Oates. The late Edith Wharton also appeared on the fiction list with *The Buccaneers,* an unfinished novel completed by Marion Mainwaring. Attracting attention in the field of nonfiction was *Case Closed* by Gerald Posner, published in the 30th anniversary year of the assassination of John F. Kennedy, and perhaps coming closer to the truth than any other of the 2200 or so books on the subject. The year also produced *The Beginning of the Journey* by Diana Trilling, an account of her life with the critic and teacher Lionel Trilling; *The Age of Federalism* by Stanley Elkins and Eric McKittrick; *The Fifties* by David Halberstam; *The Morning After: Sex, Fear and Feminism on Campus* by Katie Roiphe; and *The Fountain of Age* by Betty Friedan, which was meant to do for aging what *The Feminine Mystique* did for feminism 30 years earlier. Two veteran reference books appeared in new editions: *Bartlett's Familiar Quotations* and *The Columbia Encyclopedia.*

Jan 8: Elvis Presley became the first rock star to be honored with a U.S. postage stamp on what would have been his 58th birthday. The stamp, of which 500,000,000 were printed, shows him as a young man.

Feb 24: Grammy Awards were presented for the following: best album of 1992, *Unplugged* by Eric Clapton, who also won awards for the best male pop vocal, "Tears in Heaven," and the best male rock vocal for *Unplugged;* best female pop vocal, k. d. lang for "Constant Craving"; best female rock vocal, Melissa Etheridge for "Ain't It Heavy."

Mar 29: Academy Awards were presented to *Unforgiven* as the best motion picture of 1992; Al Pacino as best actor for *Scent of a Woman;* Emma Thompson as best actress for *Howards End;* Gene Hackman as best supporting actor for *Unforgiven;* and Marisa

Tomei as best supporting actress for *My Cousin Vinny.*

Apr 13: Pulitzer Prizes were awarded for the following: fiction, *A Good Scent from a Strange Mountain* by Robert Olen Butler; biography, *Truman* by David McCullough; history, *The Radicalism of the American Revolution* by Gordon S. Wood; general nonfiction, *Lincoln at Gettysburg: The Words That Remade America* by Garry Wills; poetry, *The Wild Iris* by Louise Gluck; drama, *Angels in America: Millennium Approaches* by Tony Kushner.

June 6: Tony Awards for the 1992-1993 season were presented for the following: best play, *Angels in America: Millennium Approaches* by Tony Kushner; best musical, *Kiss of the Spider Woman;* best actor in a play, Ron Leibman for *Angels in America;* best actress in a play, Madeline Kahn for *The Sisters Rosensweig;* best actor in a musical, Brent Carver for *Kiss of the Spider Woman;* best actress in a musical, Chita Rivera for *Kiss of the Spider Woman.*

Sep 19: Emmy Awards were presented for the following: best drama series, *Picket Fences;* best comedy series, *Seinfeld;* best actor in a drama series, Tom Skerritt for *Picket Fences;* best actress in a drama series, Kathy Baker for *Picket Fences;* best actor in a comedy series, Ted Danson for *Cheers;* best actress in a comedy series, Roseanne Arnold for *Roseanne.*

Sep 23: A **hoard of antique gold, silver, and bronze objects** will be returned to the Turkish government by the Metropolitan Museum of Art, New York City, after a six-year legal struggle. The more than 200 vessels, jewels, and other objects dated from the reign of King Croesus of Lydia in the seventh and sixth centuries B.C. Turkey claimed they had been looted in the 1960s.

Oct 7: The **Nobel Prize in Literature** was awarded to Toni Morrison. The first black woman to receive this award, she is known for her novels of black American life. The awarding committee said, "She delves into the language itself, a language she wants to liberate from the fetters of race."

Oct 8: The **highest price ever paid at auction for a photograph**, $398,500, was offered in New York City for a 1920 photograph by Alfred Stieglitz of the hands of his wife, the painter Georgia O'Keeffe. The previous record for a photograph was $193,895.

Nov 8: The **archives of the late Leonard Bernstein**, conductor and composer, enormous in extent, will be donated to the Library of Congress, Washington, D.C. To make the material widely available, the correspondence, musical manuscripts, recordings, and photographs will be digitally copied as the Leonard Bernstein Multi-Media Archive.

Nov 10: Paramount Communications agreed to buy Macmillan, Inc. for $553,000,000. The merger would create one of the largest book publishing entities in the world, second only to Bertelsmann, A.G. of Germany.

Nov 17: National Book Awards were presented for the following: fiction, *Shipping News* by E. Annie Proulx; nonfiction, *United States: Essays 1952-1992* by Gore Vidal; poetry, *Garbage* by A. R. Ammons.

III. Business and Industry
Education
Philosophy and Religion
Science

In 1993 the nation's economy improved slowly but steadily, with a 2.9% growth rate, the best showing since 1988. In November the jobless rate fell to 6.4%, showing the largest month-to-month improvement in 10 years. At this time civilian employment reached 120,400,000, an increase of about 2,000,000 in a year. There were, though, 8,300,000 unemployed. The overall inflation rate was 2.7%, the smallest increase in 7 years. Automobile sales were up and the hotel industry expected to show a profit for the first time in 11 years. In November sales of existing homes were the highest ever recorded. The world of science was at odds with itself over the ethics of cloning human embryos after scientists at the George Washington Medical Center split single embryos into identical twins or triplets. Bad news on the medical front included reports that AIDS had become the leading killer of American men age 15-44; that the increase of tuberculosis by 20% since 1985 was caused by the federal government's failure to spend enough money; that substance abuse (alcohol, drugs, and tobacco) was to blame for more than 500,000 deaths a year; and that obese women are less likely to marry and more likely to be poor and to earn less than those of normal weight. There was also worry that a 25-year decline in smoking was ending, and that the use of Prozac, an antidepressant drug introduced in 1988, was becoming too widespread. As to food, the Department of Agriculture said school lunches contained too much fat and salt; and the Defense Department announced a new field ration, meatless, nutritious, and culturally correct. There was some good news: Americans have lower blood cholesterol than in the past, and a record number of drivers were using seat belts. In the field of education there were mixed reports. The number of blacks and Hispanics in schools with mostly minority students was rising, but the Pentagon reported that the number of new recruits with high school educations declined this year by 4%.

An international report, however, said that the U.S. does a respectable job in preparing its students compared with other nations, and a federal report showed that scores in math tests improved somewhat in 1992. At the university level there were serious financial problems, with costs increasing and endowment income down. Meanwhile, an effort by many colleges to hire more minority faculty members made little progress, partly because of the comparatively small number of such persons earning doctoral degrees. The university presidents who had to worry about such matters were 88.2% male and 90.4% white. A Gallup poll revealed that more teenagers go to church than do adults, half of them, some 10% more than their parents. Overall, the number of adults who attend church once a week has remained steady since World War II at about 40%. Among notable persons who died were Dave Beck, tough and powerful head of the International Brotherhood of Teamsters, who served a prison term for income tax evasion, Dec. 26, at 99; César E. Chávez, labor leader who struggled to organize migrant farm workers, Apr. 23, at 66; Julio Gallo, who made the E. & J. Gallo Winery the largest in the country, May 2, at 83; William Randolph Hearst, Jr., head of the publishing empire his father established, May 4, at 85; Eliot Janeway, writer and commentator on economic matters, Mar. 8, at 80; Polykarp Kusch, physicist and Nobel Prize winner, Mar. 20, at 82; Alexander D. Langmuir, public health leader whose efforts helped control epidemics, Nov. 22, at 83; Norman Vincent Peale, popular clergyman whose philosophy was summed up in his bestseller *The Power of Positive Thinking*, Dec. 24, at 95; Joseph Pulitzer, Jr., chief of the publishing enterprise originated by his grandfather, May 26, at 80; Albert B. Sabin, deviser of the oral vaccine for polio, Mar. 3, at 86; Norton W. Simon, industrialist, art collector, and patron, June 2, at 86; Donald K. "Deke" Slayton, one of the seven original astronauts, June 13, at 69; Lewis Thomas, known as the poet-philosopher of medicine, Dec. 3, at 80; Thomas J. Watson, Jr., who headed International Business Machines when it led the way into the computer age and became the largest corporation in the world, Dec. 31, at 79.

Jan 8: Other people's tobacco smoke has a "serious and substantial public health impact" on nonsmokers, according to a report of the Environmental Protection Agency. Among other findings, the agency said passive smoking caused lung cancer in 3000 nonsmokers annually.

Jan 14: Deaths caused by AIDS will total between 330,000 and 385,000 by 1995, the Centers for Disease Control estimated.

Jan 21: Failure of the unmanned spacecraft Galileo was acknowledged by mission officials. The main antenna on the craft, which was launched in 1989 and was due to reach Jupiter in December, 1995, could not be deployed. A weaker, smaller antenna was still expected to send back data.

Jan 25: The **end of publication of its well-known mail order catalog** was announced by Sears, Roebuck & Co. First issued in 1896, the catalog was the cornerstone of what became a nationwide retailing giant.

Feb 11: The **largest one-year loss in corporate history** was announced by General Motors, which said its 1992 deficit reached $23,500,000,000.

Apr 20: The **French abortion pill RU-486** was licensed for manufacture in the U.S. by Roussel-Uclaf, holder of the patent. The license was granted to the nonprofit Population Council of New York City. On Nov. 14 it was announced that a group of American scientists had also made arrangements to manufacture the pill in the U.S. It was unclear, however, as to when the pill might be on the market. The Food and Drug Administration said on Nov. 18 that it had authorized tests of RU-486 as a possible treatment for women with advanced breast cancer.

June 7: Religious groups must be granted the use of school facilities on the same basis as other community groups, the Supreme Court ruled in a unanimous decision. The case involved a New York State church group and in effect overturned a state law forbidding such use.

June 11: Animal sacrifices by religious groups are permissible, the Supreme Court ruled unanimously. The decision declared unconstitutional a Hialeah, Fla., ordinance banning such rites. Adherents of Santeria, which combines elements of Roman Catholicism with beliefs brought to the Caribbean region by Yoruba slaves from West Africa, were pleased with the ruling.

July 23: The **first drug approved for treating multiple sclerosis (MS)** in the U.S. was announced by the Food and Drug Administration. Known as interferon beta 1B, it was genetically engineered to treat those patients who at times have "relapsing-remitting" symptoms. The new drug would not cure MS, but was expected to reduce those symptoms.

Aug 12-15: Pope John Paul II, making a three-day visit to the Denver, Col., area, celebrated World Youth Day by addressing 90,000 young people in Denver's Mile High Stadium. The pope also met with Pres. Clinton during his visit.

Aug 21: Contact with the spacecraft Mars Observer failed and the craft was presumed lost. Launched in September, 1992, at a cost of $980,000,000, Mars Observer was within three days of going into orbit around the planet, whose surface it was to have mapped.

Sep 2: The **U.S. and Russia agreed to build jointly a manned space station,** ending years of rivalry in space exploration. It was hoped to combine by 1997 components from both countries in a jointly manned station.

Sep 23: A **multibillion-dollar auction of airwaves** to provide a new system of wireless communications was announced by the Federal Communications Commission. With the U.S. divided into 51 regions and 492 subdivisions, the auction, to take place in June, 1994, was expected to bring $10,200,000,000.

Sep 25: A **new but separate program for women students** was announced by the Virginia Military Institute in an attempt to meet court orders stemming from a suit that charged its all-male policy violated the civil rights of females. The school proposed to establish at a nearby women's college a program to be called the Virginia Women's Institute for Leadership.

Sep 28: The **sale of *The Boston Globe*,** the newspaper with the largest circulation in New England, to *The New York Times* was approved by stockholders of both companies. The $1,000,000,000 merger made *The Globe* the biggest property of *The Times*, which also owned other newspapers, magazines, and radio and television stations.

Sep 28: A **New York law firm agreed to pay the federal government $45,000,000** for its role in a bank operation that cost taxpayers more than $1,500,000,000. The firm, Paul, Weiss, Rifkind, Wharton & Garrison, was involved in events that led to the bankruptcy of the Centrust Savings Bank of Miami, Fla.

Oct 2: The **largest investor-owned hospital chain in the world** was expected to be formed under the announced merger of Columbia Healthcare Corp. and HCA-Hospital Corp. The deal involved 190 hospitals with 48,000 beds in 26 states, and was valued at $10,250,000,000.

Oct 5: **Plans to develop the deepest offshore oil field** ever attempted were announced by Shell Oil Co. A rig was planned to extract oil at a depth of 2933 feet from the Gulf of Mexico. The project was expected to cost $1,200,000,000.

Oct 6: The **Women's Equity Mutual Fund,** with plans to invest in "woman friendly" companies, was formed. It was intended to invest in companies that are oustanding in the ways they hire, promote, and compensate women. Included in the first ten selected was one that boasted 8 women among its 25 highest paid officers.

Oct 11: The **Nobel Prize in Physiology or Medicine** was awarded to Philip A. Sharp of the Massachusetts Institute of Technology and Richard J. Roberts of New England Biolabs for their discovery, independently in 1977, of "split genes."

Oct 12: The **Nobel Prize in Economic Science** was awarded to Robert W. Fogel of the University of Chicago and Douglass C. Worth of Washington University for their work in economic history.

Oct 12: An **unusually large merger in the communications industry** was announced by the Bell Atlantic Corp., one of the "baby Bells," which agreed to buy Tele-Communications Inc., the largest cable operator in the U.S. The deal was valued at more than $23,000,000,000 and would give the merged concern access to 42% of all American homes.

Oct 13: **Tax exemption was granted to the Church of Scientology** by the Internal Revenue Service, ending nearly 40 years of disputes over the matter. The "church" was founded in the 1950s by L. Ron Hubbard, an author of science fiction books. His bestseller *Dianetics* expounds on how individuals can overcome mental obstacles. At this time the church was worth about $400,000,000.

Oct 13: The **Nobel Prize in Chemistry** was awarded to Kary B. Mullis, formerly of Cetus Corp., and Michael Smith of the University of British Columbia. The former invented a method for making copies of a single gene fragment; the latter developed a way of splicing foreign components into genetic molecules.

Oct 13: The **Nobel Prize in Physics** was awarded to Joseph H. Taylor of Princeton University and Russell A. Hulse of the Princeton Plasma Physics Laboratory. They were recognized for their investigation of gigantic gravitational forces exerted by ultradense stars.

Oct 29: A **law to end construction of the Superconducting Supercollider** was signed by Pres. Clinton. Estimated to cost at least $11,000,000,000, the project in the field of high-energy physics, approved four and a half years earlier, was about one-fifth completed in Texas. Fourteen miles of a tunnel that was to have been 54 miles in circumference had been built.

Nov 1: The **first woman to lead a diocese of the Episcopal Church,** Bishop Mary Adelia McLeod, became head of the diocese of Vermont. The church's other two bishops were assistants to diocesan bishops in Massachusetts and Washington State.

Nov 5: A **genetically engineered drug to increase the production of dairy cows** was approved by the Food and Drug Administration. This action made milk the first food to be allowed to use a genetically produced drug. Experiments indicated the drug increased milk production by 10 to 20%.

Nov 17: Ricki R. Tigert was **nominated to be the first woman chairperson** of the Federal Deposit Insurance Corp. A Washington lawyer, she had had experience in banking in both private and government sectors.

Nov 17: The Roman Catholic bishops of the U.S. voted unanimously at a conference in Washington, D.C., that **men should share fully in child rearing and household duties.** The bishops also stated that husbands and wives should treat each other as equals. In another area, the bishops asked the Vatican to make it easier to dismiss priests who sexually abuse minors.

Nov 26: **A gene responsible for resistance to disease** in tomatoes was isolated and cloned for the first time in a major plant, scientists at Cornell University announced. The gene can be transferred into plants through genetic engineering.

Dec 2-10: The **malfunctioning Hubble Space Telescope** was repaired by astronauts aboard the space shuttle *Endeavour.* At a height of 357 miles above Earth, a record five space walks were needed to replace damaged and faulty parts. Launched in April, 1990, the telescope was to explore the farthest reaches of the universe, but its primary mirror turned out to be improperly ground. After repairs it was expected to take weeks of tests to determine whether all the faults had been corrected.

Dec 3: **Isolation of a gene that predisposes people** to a common type of colon cancer (hereditary nonpolyposis colorectal cancer) was announced by scientists at several laboratories. It was predicted that a genetic test for people known to be at risk could be available in six months. Colon cancer is the second most fatal malignancy in the U.S.

Dec 3: **Guidelines for breast cancer screening** were changed by the National Cancer Institute, which announced it was dropping its recommendation that women under 50 have regular mammograms. The institute said experts agreed that mammograms every year or two reduce the death rate from cancer in women over 50 by a third.

Dec 3: Imam Abdul Rasheed Muhammad, the **first Muslim chaplain in the U.S. military,** was sworn in at the Pentagon. There were about 2500 Muslims in the armed services.

Dec 6: Judith Rodin, **the first woman to head an Ivy League school,** was named president of the University of Pennsylvania. She had previously been acting president and provost of Yale University.

Dec 9: **New records toward achieving practical hydrogen fusion** were reported by scientists at the Princeton Plasma Physics Laboratory. The Tokamak Fusion Test Reactor registered a seven-second burst of fusion power equal to 3,000,000 watts. Two days later a peak of 5,300,000 watts was achieved, but practical application of fusion power was expected to be at least several decades away.

Dec 17: The **single largest gift to public education** in the U.S. was announced by Walter H. Annenberg, publisher and philanthropist, who said he would award grants totaling $500,000,000 over five years to educational groups involved in school reform.

Dec 29: On the New York Stock Exchange the **Dow Jones industrial average** reached an all-time high at 3794.33. The Dow ended the year at 3754.09.

IV. Fashion
Folkways
Holidays
Social Issues and Crime
Sports

Both owners and players enjoyed a very good year of major league baseball. Attendance set a record at 70,257,938, aided by two new teams, one of which, the Colorado Rockies, set a single club record of 4,483,450. The average salary of players was $1,120,254 and 99 of them were being paid $3,000,000 or more. Among the clubs, the payroll of the New York Yankees was the highest at $46,761,000. By winning the World Series each player on the Toronto Blue Jays received $121,920, about $21,000 for each of the six games. Professional football also set a record with NFL attendance at 13,967,272, slightly higher than the previous record set in 1990. A poll in November showed that somewhat more than 15% of Americans thought crime and violence were the most important problems facing the nation. Presumably, much of this feeling stemmed from the great number of murders and other crimes in which guns played a part. Mass shootings by "loners" shocked the country. Some of them occurred in workplaces, where in the past nine years there were 125 such incidents, with 393 deaths and 214 wounded. There were also serial killers, such as the Long Island man who, police said, admitted to having murdered 17 women. Crime reached into the schools with one in four students and one in ten teachers saying they had been victims. More cases of alleged sexual abuse came to light, with 1800 scoutmasters being suspected, over 20 years, of having molested Boy Scouts. More approval of gun control was evidenced, one example being the decision of Wal-Mart stores to stop selling handguns in its 2000 outlets. Life-styles continued to change. Fathers were now taking care of one of every five preschool children, while gay parents were visible as well. A survey of male sexuality found that only

1% of them were exclusively homosexual, a considerably lower figure than previous surveys had reported. Legalized gambling was prospering, thanks to the Indian Gaming Regulatory Act of 1988, which allowed American Indian tribes to operate casinos on their reservations. By now there were 170 such casinos, taking in $5,800,000,000 a year. Notable persons who died included Arthur Ashe, top-rated tennis player and the first black to win the Wimbledon championship, Feb. 6, at 49; Roy Campanella, Baseball Hall of Fame catcher for the Brooklyn Dodgers, June 26, at 71; Bill Dickey, New York Yankee catcher and manager and member of the Baseball Hall of Fame, Nov. 12, at 86; Don Drysdale, Baseball Hall of Fame pitcher for the Los Angeles Dodgers, July 3, at 56; Doris Duke, tobacco heiress and philanthropist who had a "poor little rich girl" life, Oct. 28, at 80; Charlie Gehringer, Baseball Hall of Fame second baseman for 18 years with the Detroit Tigers, Jan. 21, at 89; Johnny Mize, first baseman for several teams and member of the Baseball Hall of Fame, June 2, at 80; Willie Mosconi, one of the greatest among pocket billiard players, Sept. 16, at 80; John Pennel, pole vaulter who in 1963 became the first to clear 17 feet, Sept. 26, at 53; Samuel M. Stayman, champion contract bridge player whose Stayman Convention is widely used in bidding, Dec. 11, at 84; Jim Valvano, colorful and successful basketball coach at North Carolina State, Apr. 28, at 47.

Jan 1: In **college football bowl games** the results were: Notre Dame 28, Texas A&M 3 in the Cotton Bowl; Florida State 27, Nebraska 14 in the Orange Bowl; Michigan 38, Washington 31 in the Rose Bowl; and Alabama 34, Miami 13 in the Sugar Bowl. Both the AP and the *USA Today*/CNN polls picked Alabama as the 1992 national champion.

Jan 5: The **Baseball Hall of Fame** elected Reggie Jackson, a star outfielder and slugger for 21 seasons, to membership in his first year of eligibility.

Jan 6: A **seven-year labor agreement** was approved by players and owners of the NFL teams. Players would become unrestricted free agents after five years. Under certain conditions, a salary cap on total compensation per team would go into effect.

Jan 23-24: **U.S. figure skating championships** were won by Nancy Kerrigan in the women's division and Scott Davis in the men's.

Jan 31: **Super Bowl XXVII** was won by the Dallas Cowboys (NFC), who defeated the Buffalo Bills (AFC) 52-17. On Jan. 17 the Cowboys had beaten the San Francisco 49ers 30-20 for the NFC title and the Bills defeated the Miami Dolphins 29-10 for the AFC title.

Feb 3: **Marge Schott, owner of the Cincinnati Reds, was suspended** for a year by the executive council of Major League Baseball for making racist and anti-Semitic remarks. She was also fined $25,000.

Feb 28: **Tom Kite became the first golfer of the PGA to earn more than $8,000,000** when he won the Nissan Los Angeles Open and brought his winnings to $8,075,279.

Apr 4: The **NCAA women's basketball championship** was won by Texas Tech, which defeated Ohio State 84-82.

Apr 5: The **NCAA men's basketball championship** was won by North Carolina, which defeated Michigan 77-71.

Apr 11: The **Masters golf tournament** was won by Bernhard Langer of Germany by four strokes.

Apr 19: The 97th **Boston Marathon** was won in the men's division by Cosmas N'Deti of Kenya, with a time of 2 hrs., 9 min., 33 sec. Olga Markova of Russia won the women's division for the second year in a row with a time of 2 hrs., 25 min., 27 sec.

May 1: The 119th **Kentucky Derby** was won by Sea Hero with a time of 2:02 2/5. The jockey was Jerry Bailey.

May 15: The 118th **Preakness Stakes** was won by Prairie Bayou with a time of 1:56 2/5. The jockey was Mike Smith.

May 30: The 77th **Indianapolis 500 auto race** was won by Emerson Fittipaldi, who completed the course with an average speed of 157.207 mph.

June 5: The 125th **Belmont Stakes** was won by Colonial Affair with a time of 2:29 4/5. The jockey was Julie Krone, who became the first woman to win a Triple Crown race.

June 9: The **NHL Stanley Cup** was won by the Montreal Canadiens, who defeated the Los Angeles Kings four games to one.

June 13: The **LPGA golf championship** was won by Patty Sheehan by one stroke.

June 20: The **NBA basketball championship was won by the Chicago Bulls** for the third straight year by defeating the Phoenix Suns four games to two.

June 20: The **U.S. Men's Open golf tournament** was won by two strokes by Lee Janzen, who registered his first victory in a major golf event.

June 30: A **warning to parents concerning violence on television** was announced by four networks. In the face of threatened federal action, the networks said they would put such notices on the air just before shows of that type and would make the information available to newspapers and magazines.

July 4: The **Wimbledon men's tennis championship** was won by Pete Sampras, who defeated his fellow American Jim Courier.

July 13: The **All-Star baseball game** was won by the American League over the National League, 9-3. It was the sixth straight victory for the AL.

July 25: The **U.S. Women's Open golf tournament** was won by Laurie Merten by one stroke.

Aug 15: The **PGA golf tournament** was won by Paul Azinger on the second hole of a playoff.

Sep 11-12: The **U.S. Open tennis** championships were won in the women's division by Steffi Graf of Germany and in the men's division by Pete Sampras of the U.S.

Sep 16: **Dave Winfield became the 19th hitter in major league baseball** to achieve 3000 hits. An outfielder for several teams, Winfield also ranked 18th in home runs.

Sep 18: The **Miss America** title for 1994 was won by Kimberly Aiken of South Carolina at the annual pageant in Atlantic City, N.J.

Sep 21: Becoming the highest paid player in the NHL, Wayne Gretzky signed a contract with the Los Angeles Kings that would pay him $25,000,000 over three years.

Sep 22: Nolan Ryan, extraordinary major league baseball pitcher, ended his career with a record number of strikeouts, 5714. He also ranked first in number of seasons played, 27; in number of walks given, 2795; and in number of no-hitters pitched, 7.

Sep 23: Vicki Van Meter, 11 years old, became **the youngest girl to pilot a plane across the country** when she landed her single-engine Cessna 172 in San Diego, Calif. The flight took four days.

Oct 6: Michael Jordan, superstar of professional basketball, announced his retirement after nine seasons. Besides guiding the Chicago Bulls to three consecutive NBA championships, he led the league in scoring for seven years of the nine he played.

Oct 8: After 23 years as a convicted fugitive from justice, Katherine Ann Power was sentenced to 8 to 12 years in a Massachusetts prison for her part in the murder of a Boston police officer during a 1970 bank robbery. Ms. Power, who turned herself in, had been a member of a radical antiwar group at the time of the crime.

Oct 16-23: The **World Series** was won by the Toronto Blue Jays (AL), who defeated the Philadelphia Phillies (NL) four games to two. The Blue Jays had won the American League pennant by beating the Chicago White Sox four games to two, while the Phillies had won the National League title over the Atlanta Braves by the same margin.

Oct 26: A **new NFL franchise** was awarded to Charlotte, N.C.; on Nov. 30 a similar franchise was granted to Jacksonville, Fla. Bringing the number of NFL teams to 30, the Carolina Panthers and the Jacksonville Jaguars were each expected to pay a franchise fee of $140,000,000 and begin play in 1995.

Oct 30: The **first women's amateur boxing match** sanctioned by U.S. Amateur Boxing Inc. occurred in Lynwood, Wash., when 16-year-old Dallas Malloy won a three-round decision over Heather Poyner.

Nov 4: The **NBA awarded a new franchise** to Toronto, Canada, with play to begin in the 1995-1996 season. The 28th team in the league paid $125,000,000 for the franchise.

Nov 6: The **world heavyweight boxing championship was rewon by Evander Holyfield** over Riddick Bowe in 12 rounds at Las Vegas, Nev., by the judges' decisions, two in his favor and one a draw. Holyfield had lost the title to Bowe Nov. 13, 1992. The fight was disrupted for 21 minutes during the seventh round when a parachutist landed in the ring and was injured.

Nov 9: A **9391-mile run around the perimeter of the U S** was completed by nine members of a musical group known as Japan's Demon Drummers. They began their run, which took them through 28 states, Nov. 15, 1990.

Nov 14: The **24th New York City Marathon** was won in the men's division by Andres Espinosa of Mexico with a time of 2 hrs., 10 min., 4 sec. The women's division was won by Uta Pippig of Germany with a time of 2 hrs., 26 min., 24 sec.

Nov 14: Don Shula became the coach with the most wins in NFL history when the Miami Dolphins beat the Philadelphia Eagles 19-14. It was Shula's 325th victory, one more than the previous record set by George Halas of the Chicago Bears.

Nov 30: Dozens of boys were sexually molested over the course of more than 20 years by 11 friars at St. Anthony's Seminary, Santa Barbara, Calif., an inquiry by the Franciscan order of the Roman Catholic Church revealed. At least 34 boys had been molested between 1964 and 1987.

Dec 7: Six people were killed and 19 wounded when a gunman sprayed bullets from a semiautomatic handgun in a crowded car of a commuter train of New York's Long Island Railroad. Arrested in the incident was Colin Ferguson, an immigrant from Jamaica, who had previously expressed his hatred for, among others, whites, Asians, and "Uncle Tom Negroes."

Dec 23: Troy Aikman became the **highest paid player in professional football history** when he signed an eight-year $50,000,000 contract with the Dallas Cowboys. The star quarterback was to be paid an average of $6,250,000 a year.

1994

I. Civil Rights
Exploration and Settlement
Government
Statistics
Wars

The economy prospered, but Americans felt considerable dissatisfaction with their government, as shown in the November elections, which put the Republican Party in control of both houses of Congress and gained the party 11 governorships. The most noticeable area in which no action was taken was health care reform, in spite of a comprehensive, perhaps overelaborate, plan presented by the Clinton administration. With or without government action, Americans in increasing numbers were signing up for some kind of managed health care arrangement: 65% in 1994 compared with 47% 3 years earlier. Among such health care businesses, for-profit organizations now outnumbered nonprofit health maintenance organizations (HMOs). On the whole, both American women and men were living longer (overall average life expectancy in 1992 was 75.7 years), smoking less, and eating more vegetables. They were, however, gaining too much weight, an average of 8 pounds in the past decade. Thirty percent of the population were now classified as obese. Also in the bad news category was the finding that heterosexual transmission of AIDS accounted for 9% of new cases, up from 1.9% in 1985. The Census Bureau estimated that the U.S. population in 1994 reached 260,300,000, an increase of 2,600,000 in a year. This year Texas, with 18,378,000 people, passed New York, with 18,200,000 people, to become the second most populous state. California, at 31,400,000, remained by far the most populous state, while Florida, with 13,953,000, was now fourth. Connecticut, Rhode Island, and the District of Columbia registered small losses. The Census Bureau also reported that by 1992 there were only 1,925,300 farms in the U.S., the smallest number since 1850. In addition, the bureau noted that the 1990 census had revealed that the Hispanic population now outnumbered the black population in four of the ten largest cities, and overall had increased by 53% since 1980. Looking ahead, the bureau estimated that in 2020 the nation's population would reach 325,900,000, and would be older, less white, less female, and less northern. The median age was also increasing, now being 33.7 years, up from 32.8 in

1990. A study reported that Americans were giving less time and money to charitable causes than previously: 3.4% fewer did volunteer work in 1993 than in 1991, and households were giving $19 less per year than before. Nature, in the form of both cold and warm weather, was unkind to much of the country. The 1993–1994 winter struck the East and Southeast with 16 major snow and ice storms that cost insurance companies about $1,000,000,000. These storms also caused 113 deaths, but in Trenton, N.J., a drop in crime was credited to the cold weather. New York City had 50.3 inches of snow, the most in 16 years. When summer came it was the turn of 11 Western states to feel nature's power, in the form of forest fires. By September 3,500,000 acres had been burned over, and 25 firefighters had been killed, 12 of them in a single blast of flame in Colorado. More than 20,000 firefighters battled the blazes, including a contingent of U.S. Marines. Among notable people who died were George W. Ball, undersecretary of state in the Kennedy and Johnson administrations and forceful opponent of involvement in the Vietnam War, May 26, at 84; Laurence C. Craigie, who on Oct. 2, 1942, flew the first U.S. military jet plane, Feb. 27, at 92; Orval E. Faubus, who, as governor of Arkansas in 1957, led the South's losing fight against school desegregation, Dec. 14, at 84; Mildred McAfee Horton, president of Wellesley College, who, in World War II, became the first director of the WAVES, Sept. 2, at 94; William H. Natcher, who set a record of 18,401 consecutive roll-call votes in the House of Representatives, Mar. 29, at 84; Richard M. Nixon, president of the U.S. (1969–1974), forced to resign the office because of the Watergate scandal, Apr. 22, at 81; Louis Nizer, shrewd lawyer who represented well-known people in spectacular cases, Nov. 10, at 92; Jacqueline Kennedy Onassis, glamorous first lady (1961–1963), environmentalist, and patron of the arts, May 19, at 64; Thomas P. O'Neill, Jr., colorful politician, speaker of the House of Representatives (1977–1987), Jan. 5, at 81; Jerry Rubin, a flamboyant founder of the radical Yippies of the 1960s and later a successful businessman, Nov. 28, at 56; Dean Rusk, secretary of state (1961–1969), defender of U.S. involvement in the Vietnam War, Dec. 20, at 85.

Jan 1–Sep 9: More than 30,000 Cubans sought refuge in the U.S. but most of them were settled in internment camps at Guantanamo Bay or in Panama. The flow stopped only after Cuba and the U.S. agreed on Sept. 9 that the former would prevent its citizens from fleeing the country and the latter would accept at least 20,000 legal Cuban immigrants a year.

Jan 17: An earthquake struck Los Angeles and the surrounding area, registering 6.6 on the Richter scale, and killing 51 persons, injuring nearly 5500, leaving 15,000 homeless, and causing damage estimated at least $15,000,000,000.

Jan 17: A final **report on the Iran-Contra arms scandal**, released by the independent prosecutor Lawrence E. Walsh, criticized former presidents Ronald Reagan and George Bush and asserted that in 1986 and 1987 senior administration officials had made a concerted effort to deceive Congress and the public. But the report found no evidence that Reagan or Bush had engaged in any criminal activity.

Feb 3: The 19-year-old **trade embargo against Vietnam** was ended by Pres. Clinton, who said that Vietnam was cooperating in trying to locate 2238 Americans still listed as missing in the Vietnam War. On May 26 the U.S. and Vietnam agreed to take first steps toward resuming diplomatic relations.

Feb 26: Eleven members of the **Branch Davidian Sect**, involved in an attack on their compound near Waco, Tex., by federal officers on Feb. 28, 1993, were acquitted by a federal court jury of the murder of four agents and of conspiracy charges. Seven of the members were convicted of other charges, and on June 17 five of them were sentenced to 40 years in prison.

Feb 28: U.S. fighter planes, in the **first military action in the 44-year history of NATO**, shot down four Serbian warplanes after they had bombed a Bosnian munitions plant. In the continuing civil war in part of former Yugoslavia, American planes joined other NATO aircraft on Apr. 10 and 11, and on Nov. 21 and 23, in other strikes at Bosnian Serb military positions and airfields.

Mar 4: On trial for **bombing the World Trade Center** in New York City on Feb. 26, 1993, four men were convicted by a federal court jury and on May 24 sentenced to life in prison with no possibility of parole. The four terrorists, whose deed killed six people and injured hundreds, were Mohammed A. Salameh, Ahmad M. Ajaj, Nidal A. Ayyad, and Mahmud Abouhalima.

Mar 23: Two **U.S. Air Force planes**, a C-130 and a F-16D, collided while attempting to land at Pope Air Force Base in Fayetteville, N.C., killing 23 soldiers and injuring 85. The casualties occurred among troops on the ground when the C-130 struck and ignited a C-141 near which the soldiers were gathered.

Mar 25: The **last American troops in Somalia**, 1100 Marines, left that country. American forces had first landed under UN auspices on Dec. 9, 1992, on a mission of mercy to a nation starving and torn by civil strife. The U.S. troops became involved in a seemingly endless battle with armed groups contending for power.

Mar 30: Most **export controls** on the sale of telecommunication equipment and computers to China, Russia, and other former Soviet bloc nations imposed during the Cold War were ended by the Clinton administration.

Apr 14: Two **U.S. Army helicopters were shot down** by mistake by two Air Force fighter planes over a no-flight zone in northern Iraq. The incident, in which the helicopters were mistaken for Russian aircraft, resulted in the deaths of all 26 persons aboard, 15 Americans and 11 of other nations. After an investigation, charges against those involved were dropped, except for those against one person who faced a court-martial.

Apr 19: In a **decision on jury selection**, the Supreme Court ruled, 6-3, that the exclusion of potential jurors on the basis of gender was unconstitutional.

Apr 28: A **turncoat CIA agent** who had spied for the Soviet Union for 10 years was sentenced to life imprisonment. Aldrich H. Ames's activities, which went undetected in spite of his eccentric behavior and lavish lifestyle, may have resulted in the deaths of 10 Soviet bloc spies working for the CIA.

May 26: **China's most favored nation trade status** was renewed by Pres. Clinton despite his acknowledgment that the country had not made as much progress in ensuring human rights as had been hoped.

May 26: A **law to protect abortion clinics** was signed by Pres. Clinton. The act made it a federal crime to attack or blockade such clinics, their operators, or their patrons.

June 6: The **50th anniversary of D-Day**, the Allied invasion of France in World War II, was observed in Normandy with Pres. Clinton attending ceremonies in the presence of many veterans of the landing.

June 30: The Clinton administration announced that the **Law of the Sea Treaty** was expected to be signed by the U.S. because changes in its original form made it more friendly to business. Pres. Reagan had rejected the treaty in 1982. It was to take effect in November.

June 30: The **American bald eagle** was removed from the endangered species list and placed on the threatened list. In the lower 48 states there were now about 4000 adult nesting pairs compared with 791 counted in 1974. The Endangered Species Act of 1973 was credited with the change.

July 2: A **USAir DC-9 crashed** in Charlotte, N.C., as it tried to abort a landing in a heavy thunderstorm. Thirty-seven of the 57 persons aboard were killed.

July 5–13: **Floods in Georgia**, resulting from unusually heavy rainstorms, caused 31 deaths, left 50,000 homeless, flooded 300,000 acres, and did great damage to roads and bridges.

July 25: Israel and Jordan, represented by Prime Minister Yitzhak Rabin and King Hussein, met with Pres. Clinton at the White House and agreed in principle to establish peace between their two countries after nearly 50 years of official antagonism. They were to work toward normal diplomatic relations and a formal peace treaty.

Aug 11: The **Exxon Corporation** was ordered by a federal jury in Anchorage, Alaska, to pay $286,800,000 in compensatory damages to about 34,000 fishermen and others because of the harm caused by the *Exxon Valdez* oil spill of Mar. 24, 1989. On Sept. 16 the jury ordered Exxon to pay a further $5,000,000,000 in punitive damages to the same group.

Aug 15: The **Social Security Administration** became an independent agency when Pres. Clinton signed an act separating it from the Department of Health and Human Services. The law was intended to shield the agency, established in 1935, from political manipulation.

Sep 8: A **USAir Boeing 737-300 crashed** near Pittsburgh, Pa., as it was attempting to land, killing all 132 persons aboard.

Sep 12: A **small airplane crashed onto the White House lawn** without detection or interference. The pilot of the Cessna 150, Frank Eugene Corder, was killed in the crash. Pres. and Mrs. Clinton were not in the White House at the time. Corder's motive was not known.

Sep 13: The **Violent Crime Control and Law Enforcement Act** was signed by Pres. Clinton. Among the many provisions of the $30,000,000,000 law were expansion of the death penalty to cover more than 50 federal crimes; money for communities to hire 100,000 policemen; and various drug treatment and educational programs.

Sep 18: Haiti's military government, under pressure from the Clinton administration, agreed, after negotiating with an American delegation led by former president Jimmy Carter, to give up office by Oct. 15. On Sept. 19 American troops landed unopposed in Haiti to begin the process of restoring to office the democratically elected president, Jean-Bertrand Aristide. Raoul Cédras, leader of the military government, resigned Oct. 10, and on Oct. 15 Aristide returned to Haiti and reassumed the presidency.

Sep 22: New **reductions in nuclear weapons** were ordered by Pres. Clinton, who said he hoped Russia would follow suit. The cuts included bombers and submarines.

Oct 9: Plans to send 36,000 troops to the Persian Gulf were announced by the Clinton administration as the result of the movement, beginning Oct. 2, of Iraqi forces toward the Kuwaiti border. Hundreds of aircraft were also to be sent. By Oct. 12 a major part of the Iraqi troops had been pulled back from the border. Most of the American troops sent to the region were brought home by Christmas.

Oct 15–19: Floods in southeastern Texas, brought on by heavy rains, killed 19 persons and left thousands homeless. East of Houston the floodwaters ruptured a gasoline pipeline, which caught fire and burned boats, a railroad trestle, and homes on the banks of the San Jacinto River. Sixty-nine people were injured.

Oct 21: The **U.S. and North Korea** signed an agreement aimed at ending the latter's apparent attempt to produce nuclear weapons. The U.S. had threatened to seek UN sanctions against North Korea, but talks between former president Jimmy Carter and North Korea's dictator Kim Il Sung eased the situation and led to the agreement. Over a period of 10 years, Korea's plutonium fuel rods were to be impounded and inspection of its nuclear sites allowed, while South Korea and Japan would finance two nuclear reactors to provide electric energy. North Korea announced on Nov. 20 that it had frozen its nuclear reactor program.

Oct 31: An **American Eagle ATR-72 crashed** in a field south of Gary, Ind., on a flight from Indianapolis to Chicago, killing all 68 persons aboard. The twin-engine commuter plane may have suffered ice buildup on its wings.

Nov 8: In **two unusual referendums**, voters in California and Oregon approved hotly debated proposals. Proposition 187 in California, if judged constitutional, was to make all illegal immigrants ineligible for welfare services, schooling, and non-emergency medical care. The Oregon measure was to allow patients with six months to live to ask a doctor, who would be subject to certain procedural steps, to prescribe a lethal dose of drugs to end unbearable suffering.

Nov 8: In **congressional elections**, the Republican Party won control of both houses of Congress for the first time in 40 years. The 104th Congress consisted of 53 Republicans and 47 Democrats in the Senate, and 230 Republicans, 214 Democrats, and one independent in the House of Representatives.

Nov 10: Breaking ranks with its NATO allies, the U.S. announced it was no longer enforcing the UN arms embargo against Bosnia. The other NATO nations refused to go along with this action. However, on Dec. 10, Pres. Clinton said that the U.S. was prepared to supply as many as 25,000 troops to assist in the withdrawal of UN peacekeeping forces in Bosnia if that became necessary. On Dec. 23 the Muslim-led Bosnian government and the Bosnian Serbs signed a cease-fire agreement that had been negotiated by former president Jimmy Carter and that on Dec. 31 formally established a four-month truce in the warfare.

Dec 5: The **Strategic Arms Reduction Treaty** came into force when Pres. Clinton and the presidents of Belarus, Kazakhstan, Russia, and Ukraine signed it in Budapest, Hungary. The treaty called for the elimination of 9000 of the 21,000 warheads that the U.S. and the former Soviet Union declared they had when negotiations began more than a decade earlier.

II. Architecture
Arts and Music
Popular Entertainment
Publishing
Theater

The Broadway theater season of 1993–1994 was the best in 6 years with total attendance of 8,100,000 in 35 theaters. Gross receipts were $356,000,000, while road companies added another $688,000,000. There were 37 new productions, 4 more than in the previous season. Helping make this good news was the musical *Cats*, which on Sept. 28 celebrated its 5000th performance. Also contributing was the lavish Disney production of *Beauty and the Beast,* which cost at least $12,000,000 to stage. Other successes of the season were a revival of *Carousel*, with a brilliant setting; *Medea,* starring Diana Rigg; and *Three Tall Women,* an impressive return effort of playwright Edward Albee. Launching the new season in the fall were 2 more spectacular shows: *Show Boat* and *Sunset Boulevard.* The former was a revival of a classic, but with a new approach: emphasis on racial problems. In its first week of performances, *Show Boat* sold $842,636 worth of tickets, a record. *Sunset Boulevard* is a musical based on the classic movie of 1950 that starred Gloria Swanson. Among movies of the year, some that stood out were the very popular *Forrest Gump,* about 40 years in the life of a mentally retarded but likable man; *Pulp Fiction,* called imaginative by most critics; *Mrs. Parker and the Vicious Circle,* a biography of the witty writer Dorothy Parker; *Quiz Show,* about the 1960 scandal surrounding one of television's most popular programs; *Interview with the Vampire,* one more time around with the living dead; and, at the end of the year, *Nobody's Fool,* starring Paul Newman and Jessica Tandy in her last role; and a nearly perfect version of Louisa May Alcott's *Little Women.* A new staging of *Sleeping Beauty* at New York's Metropolitan Opera House, with a fresh and dizzying setting, and a revival of Merce Cunningham's *Sounddance* marked the dance season. The Berkshire Music Festival, near Lenox,

Mass., opened a concert hall and named it for the conductor Seiji Ozawa. In April Carlo Bergonzi, a tenor who made his debut in 1948, appeared in his New York farewell recital. Also in April, the Metropolitan Museum of Art in New York City opened its Irving Galleries for the Arts of South and Southeast Asia, while the New York Public Library staged a documentary exhibit of gay life entitled "Becoming Visible: The Legacy of Stonewall." The most successful of the new television programs was *E.R.,* which takes place in the emergency room of a big-city hospital. Just as much of an attraction, but with a real-life setting, was the daily showing of the trials and tribulations of former football star O.J. Simpson, charged with the murder of his former wife and her friend. Millions watched live TV as it followed the chase of Simpson by the Los Angeles police along a freeway. Notable persons who died included Robert Bloch, author of many mysteries, including the classic *Psycho,* Sept. 23, at 77; Cleanth Brooks, Southern literary critic and a leader of the New Criticism movement, May 10, at 87; Cab(ell) Calloway, flamboyant jazz band leader and composer of the 1930s and 1940s, Nov. 18, at 86; John Candy, outsized comedian and star of a number of successful movies, Mar. 4, at 43; Marchette Chute, biographer of such figures as Shakespeare and Chaucer, May 6, at 84; Amy Clampitt, late-blooming poet, known for her ornate and allusive style, Sept. 10, at 74; Kurt Cobain, a creator of the grunge rock sound, who committed suicide, Apr. 8, at 27; Joseph Cotten, stage and movie actor, known for his subtly menacing roles, Feb. 6, at 88; Lily Damita, a Hollywood actress noted for her glamorous personality, Mar. 21, at 90; Ralph Ellison, whose novel *Invisible Man* (1952) sharply reminded readers of America's race problems, Apr. 16, at 80; Tom Ewell, character actor and comedian of the stage and movies, Sept. 12, at 85; Leonard Feather, a composer and musician who was also the dean of American jazz critics, Sept. 22, at 80; Rudolf Firkusny, Czech-born pianist, known for the elegance of his style, July 19, at 82; Avery Fisher, who gave millions to arts organizations, especially Lincoln Center in New York City, Feb. 26, at 87; Clement Greenberg, art critic who championed Abstract Expressionism, May 7, at 85; Erick Hawkins, a pioneer in American choreography, Nov. 23, at 85; Julie Haydon, actress, remembered especially for her role in *The Glass Menagerie* (1945), Dec. 24, at 84; Raul Julia, distinguished actor both in classics on the stage and in popular movies, Oct. 24, at 54; Russell Kirk, author and a founder of the modern conservative movement, Apr. 29, at 75; Arthur B. Krim, lawyer who became the producer of more than 1000 movies, and who was active in Democratic politics, Sept. 21, at 84; Burt Lancaster, versatile movie actor, Oct. 20, at 80; Robert Lansing, deep-voiced, craggy actor of stage, movies, and television, Oct. 23, at 66; Joe Layton, producer, director, and choreographer, known especially for his Broadway musicals, May 4, at 64; Harry Levin, Harvard literary critic and leading figure in the development of comparative literature as a discipline, May 29, at 81; Henry Mancini, whose music for movies and television won four Academy Awards, June 14, at 70; Margaret Millar, master author of psychological mysteries, Mar. 26, at 79; Henry Morgan, radio star of the 1940s, known for his satirical wit, May 19, at 79; Mildred Natwick, who played eccentric and whimsical characters on stage, in the movies, and on television for 60 years, Oct. 25, at 89; Harriet Nelson, for 14 years a star of the popular TV family comedy *The Adventures of Ozzie and Harriet,* Oct. 2, at 85; George Peppard, known first as a movie actor, then as a tough guy in television's *The A-Team,* May 8, at 65; John Pope-Hennessy, first a British museum director, then (1977–1986) chief of European painting at the Metropolitan Museum of Art, New York City, Oct. 31, at 80; Pearl Primus, who as dancer, choreographer, and teacher helped establish dance by and about black Americans, Oct. 29, at 74; Martha Raye, singer and comic actress, noted for both her big mouth and her big heart, Oct. 19, at 78; Gilbert Roland, first a leading man in the days of silent movies, then a character actor, May 15, at 88; Lawrence E. Spivak, originator of the trend-setting radio and television news program *Meet the Press,* Mar. 9, at 93; Francis Steegmuller, prolific biographer, novelist, and translator, Oct. 20, at 88; Jule Styne, composer of many popular songs, among them "Three Coins in the Fountain," Sept. 20, at 88; Jessica Tandy, one of the best loved actresses to grace the American theater and movies, Sept. 11, at 85; Peter Taylor, novelist, but more praised for his short stories, Nov. 2, at 77; Marion Williams, pioneer gospel singer, July 2, at 66; Igor Youskevitch, Ukrainian-born master dancer in the classical style, June 13, at 82.

The number of **books published** and sold in 1994 left little cause for complaint, but quality was, perhaps, another matter. The fiction bestseller list was dominated by such books as *The Celestine Prophecy* by James Redfield, the story of an ancient manuscript, and, with more than 2 years on the list, Robert James Waller's romance, *The Bridges of Madison County.* Some old hands at storytelling were active, with William Gaddis presenting *A Frolic of His Own,* described as both "misanthropic" and "hilarious"; Joseph Heller offering *Closing Time,* a sequel to *Catch-22;* E. L. Doctorow telling a gothic tale of New York

City in 1871, *The Waterworks;* and the late Peter Taylor represented by his last novel, *In the Tennessee Country.* There was an impressive first novel by John Dufresne, *Louisiana Power and Light,* concerning an orphan with problems, and a humorous novel by Christopher Buckley, *Thank You for Smoking.* Two experts in the short story category were on hand: John Updike with *The Afterlife and Other Stories,* and Grace Paley with her *Collected Stories.* Two veteran poets published collections: John Ashbery with *And the Stars Were Shining,* and Amy Clampitt with *A Silence Opens.* Best rewarded poet of the year was W. S. Merwin, who won the first Tanning Prize, worth $100,000. Two unusual books on American history were *Paul Revere's Ride* by David Hackett Fischer, emphasizing not thc ride itself but the events surrounding it, and *The Unredeemed Captive* by John Demos, which focuses on a little girl captured in the Indian raid on Deerfield, Mass., in 1704, who chooses never to return to white civilization. Most of the books in the field of public affairs aroused controversy. Chief among them was *The Bell Curve* by Richard J. Herrnstein and Charles Murray, apparently arguing that IQ is produced by genes and accounts for most of one's success and, by implication, that blacks' IQs are generally lower than those of other groups. *Strange Justice: The Selling of Clarence Thomas* by Jane Mayer and Jill Abramson reopened Thomas's bitter Supreme Court confirmation struggle, accusing the religious right for the part it played. More amusing was *Politically Correct Bedtime Stories* by James Finn Garner, a tongue-in-cheek retelling of some classic tales. In a category by itself and selling very well was *Crossing the Threshold of Hope,* in which Pope John Paul II discussed his beliefs.

Mar 1: Grammy Awards were presented for the following: best album of 1993, *The Bodyguard* by Whitney Houston; best record, "I Will Always Love You" by Whitney Houston; best male pop vocalist, Sting for "If I Ever Lose My Faith in You"; best rock vocalist, solo, Meat Loaf for "I'd Do Anything for Love"; best rock duo or group with vocal, Aerosmith for "Livin' on the Edge."

Mar 4: A two-day **auction of Barbra Streisand's collection** of 358 art deco and art nouveau art, furniture, and other objects in New York brought $6,200,000.

Mar 7: Freeing parody from the constraints of federal copyright law, the Supreme Court ruled unanimously that the rap group 2 Live Crew had not infringed the copyright of a rock classic, "Oh, Pretty Woman," with its bawdy version.

Mar 21: Academy Awards were presented to *Schindler's List* as the outstanding motion picture of 1993; Tom Hanks as best actor for *Philadelphia;* Holly

Hunter as best actress for *The Piano;* Tommy Lee Jones as best supporting actor for *The Fugitive;* and Anna Paquin as best supporting actress for *The Piano.*

Apr 12: Pulitzer Prizes were awarded for the following: fiction, *The Shipping News* by E. Annie Proulx; general nonfiction, *Lenin's Tomb: The Last Days of the Soviet Empire* by David Remnick; biography, *W.E.B. Du Bois: Biography of a Race, 1868–1919* by David Levering Lewis; drama, *Three Tall Women* by Edward Albee. No award was given for history.

June 12: Tony Awards for the 1993–1994 theater season were presented for the following: best play, *Angels in America: Perestroika* by Tony Kushner; best musical, *Passion;* leading actor in a play, Stephen Spinella for *Angels in America;* leading actress in a play, Diana Rigg for *Medea;* leading actor in a musical, Boyd Gaines for *She Loves Me;* leading actress in a musical, Donna Murphy for *Passion.*

Sep 11: Emmy Awards were presented for the following: best drama series, *Picket Fences;* best comedy series, *Frasier;* leading actor in a drama series, Dennis Franz for *N.Y.P.D. Blue;* leading actress in a drama series, Sela Ward for *Sisters;* leading actor in a comedy series, Kelsey Grammer for *Frasier;* leading actress in a comedy series, Candice Bergen for *Murphy Brown.*

Oct 30: The National Museum of the American Indian opened in New York City, the first such institution to give federal government recognition to Native American culture. More than 500 objects were on display. A central headquarters for the museum was to be erected in Washington, D.C., by 2001.

Nov 11: A rare **Leonardo da Vinci notebook** was sold at auction in New York City for $30,800,000, a record for an auctioned manuscript. The buyer was William H. Gates, chairman of Microsoft Corp. The 72-page work contained more than 300 illustrations and some scientific writings.

Nov 16: National Book Awards were presented for the following: fiction, *A Frolic of His Own* by William Gaddis; nonfiction, *How We Die: Reflections on Life's Final Chapter* by Sherwin B. Nuland; poetry, *Worshipful Company of Fletchers* by James Tate.

III. Business and Industry
   Education
   Philosophy and Religion
   Science

The economy grew steadily, the inflation rate was low, 2.7%, and the unemployment rate fell to 5.4% in December, the lowest since July, 1990, with 3,500,000 jobs added during the year. However, not everything was onward and upward for many Americans. The Census Bureau reported that the percentage of those working full time but earning less than the poverty level of about $13,000 a year for a family of four had increased 50% in the past 13 years. And in 1993 a million households dropped below the poverty level. A survey in March revealed that 39% of workers worried that they might be laid off within the next 2 years. On the other hand, most of the jobs created recently were in occupations paying more than the average of $15.43 an hour, which was an increase of almost $2 since 1990. A federal government survey showed, however, that many women felt they were not getting the pay, benefits, or recognition they deserved. Among these women were those in their 50s who had entered the workplace in increasing numbers in the last 10.5 years. There were now 8,100,000 of them, or 65% of their age group, including about 80% of those aged 50 to 60 who were college graduates. Among working women of all ages, many took jobs full time or part time because their husbands' earnings had declined and they saw work as a way of holding families together. One person who did not need to worry about such matters was Michael Eisner, chairman of the Walt Disney Co., who in 1993 was paid $203,100,000, the highest figure ever recorded for the chief executive of a public corporation. The number of corporate mergers increased, a top example for the year being the takeover for $9,700,000,000 of American Cyanamid by American Home Products. Throughout the year the dollar fared poorly against the Japanese yen, falling on June 21 below the 100 level for the first time since currency trading resumed after World War II. A favorable development was the transformation of the recycling movement from a concern chiefly with the environment to a substantial business as the demand for raw materials increased. Some astronomers were now convinced there was evidence that other planets exist besides those in our solar system. They found three planets orbiting a pulsar known as PSRB1257+12. Other scientists, looking closer to home, described how in about 1,500,000,000 years the sun's brightness and temperature will have risen so as to make life on Earth impossible. In August the College Board reported that the gap between the sexes in SAT scores continued to narrow, by six points since 1987, with men only slightly ahead of women. At the same time a Department of Education analysis found a gain since 1983 of almost a full grade in science proficiency among elementary and secondary school students, but no gain in reading and writing skills. More black students were completing high school, 75% in 1993 compared with 67% 20 years earlier, but overall the dropout rate for minority students continued to increase. Among leading colleges the total cost of a four-year degree broke the $100,000 mark. The average annual tuition at a private four-year college was $11,709, at a public college, $2686. Many college presidents were well paid, the top figure of $776,963 going to John Silber of Boston University. National student of the year honors went to Harry Kloor, who at Purdue University became the first ever to earn two doctorates at the same time. Some bad news from the health front: The American Lung Association said nearly 23,000,000 people lived in regions where air pollution in the form of particles violated federal standards; a report from the American Medical Association found that nearly one in every five American adults was suffering from pain that had lasted at least six months. Almost as soon as farmers were allowed to use a genetically engineered dairy hormone to increase milk production, a fierce war of words broke out between manufacturers of the hormone and consumers who feared it was unsafe. But no subject was more controversial than the one over the dangers of tobacco smoking. Although all seven top executives of the largest tobacco companies swore before Congress that smoking was not addictive, a survey of the public found that 91% believed cigarettes to be addictive. Later the Federal Trade Commission reported smokers were getting more tar and nicotine than package labels claimed, while the head of the Food and Drug Administration said cigarette manufacturers had secretly developed a tobacco with more than double the current amount of nicotine. A national survey in 1993 found that 23% of women smoked, down from 25% the previous year. Smokers found their lives increasingly difficult: The Pentagon banned smoking in all offices and other indoor work areas; California and Maryland outlawed it in public buildings; Michigan voters chose to triple the tax on cigarettes; and, among many other places, Vermont, Washington State, and Aspen, Col., took antismoking action. Supporting such bans was a government report that in 1993 smoking-related illnesses cost the nation at least $50,000,000,000. A number of Protestant church groups were worried by a drop in giving for national and missionary purposes, with more money being held at the local level. Both the Episcopal Church and the Presbyterian Church (U.S.A.) were forced to cut their headquarters staffs, while the Southern Baptists' Cooperative Program and the United Church of Christ had to get along on smaller donations. Notable persons who died included Ezra Taft Benson, president (1985–1994) of the Church of Jesus Christ of Latter-Day Saints, May 30, at 94; Erik H. Erikson, psychoanalyst,

whose theories changed viewpoints on human development, May 12, at 91; Rollo May, psychologist whose writings emphasized the positive aspects of human beings, Oct. 22, at 85; Linus C. Pauling, winner of Nobel prizes for both chemistry and peace, Aug. 19, at 93; Menachen Mendel Schneerson, rabbi and leader of the Lubavitch Hasidic movement, hailed by some as the Messiah, June 12, at 92; Julian Schwinger, theoretical physicist who won a Nobel Prize for his work in electrodynamics, July 16, at 76; Jerome B. Wiesner, science adviser to Pres. John F. Kennedy, and president for nine years of the Massachusetts Institute of Technology, Oct. 21, at 79.

Mar 11: Viacom, Inc., won control of Paramount Communications, Inc., for $6,600,000,000 for 50.1% of the latter's stock. Holders of Paramount stock were also to receive various Viacom securities, bringing the total price of the acquisition to about $10,000,000,000. The merged companies owned cable TV channels, a movie studio, sports teams, a publishing house, and a film library.

Mar 18: Colon cancer, in a large percentage of cases that stem from hereditary factors, is caused by a genetic defect that destroys a cell's quality control system, according to a report by two separate teams of scientific investigators. It was expected that within a year blood tests could be used to screen for the defective gene.

Apr 4: Two large military contractors merged when Northrop Corp. acquired Grumman Corp. for $2,100,000,000. The two companies had combined sales in 1993 of more than $8,000,000,000. On Aug. 30 two other leading military contractors, Lockheed and Martin Marietta, with combined revenues of $23,000,000,000, announced plans to merge. Martin Marietta was expected to pay about $10,000,000,000. Both mergers were attributed to the decline in U.S. military purchases following the end of the Cold War.

Apr 26: Discovery of the top quark, the last of the 12 subatomic building blocks that were thought to make up all of the material world, was announced by the Fermi National Accelerator Laboratory of Batavia, Ill., where an international team of 439 scientists had worked on the project.

May 8: New nutrition labels on food products were required by the Food and Drug Administration. The new labels included not only the amount of nutrients in absolute terms, but also the percentage of recommended daily consumption of a given item, such as fat, contained in the food package.

May 16: The **French abortion pill RU-486** could be available to American women by 1996, according to an agreement between the manufacturer and the

Population Council, a nonprofit contraceptive research organization in New York City. Clinical trials were to begin in the fall.

May 18: A **genetically altered tomato** that was to remain fresh longer was approved for sale to the public by the Food and Drug Administration. It was expected to ripen longer on the vine and remain firm for picking and shipping.

May 23: The **Fox television network** significantly altered the nation's TV alignment when it secured the defection of eight important CBS stations to Fox, as well as three from ABC and one from NBC. Fox had earlier outbid CBS to get the National Football Conference (NFC) of the National Football League (NFL) to switch the telecasts of its games to Fox.

May 25: Evidence of the existence of **black holes** that are so powerful gravitationally that they suck in everything around them, including light and matter, was discovered by astronomers using the Hubble Space Telescope. They found an unusually powerful black hole, weighing as much as 3,000,000,000 suns, about 50,000,000 light-years away.

May 27: A new **Catechism of the Catholic Church**, the first such manual of doctrine in 400 years, was published. Its four sections covered such topics as belief in God, marriage, morality, and prayer.

June 6: Eighty-six-year-old Howard W. Hunter was elected the **14th president of the Mormon Church** (Church of Jesus Christ of Latter-Day Saints). The former corporate lawyer, who succeeded the late Ezra Taft Benson, became the supreme authority and "prophet" of the denomination.

July 14: Federated Department Stores agreed to pay $4,100,000,000 for R.H. Macy, a nationwide chain in bankruptcy. The merged corporation was to operate 460 stores under nine different names.

Aug 2: Dante II, an eight-legged walking robot, completed a five-day exploration of the bottom of an Alaskan volcano, 650 feet deep, where it was too dangerous for humans to go. Damaged by falling rocks on its way back, the robot when 400 feet down had to be lifted out by a helicopter on Aug. 13.

Aug 24: The bishops of the **Episcopal Church** approved a statement that affirmed marriage as the standard for sexual relations, but that also said the church should "respond pastorally" to homosexuals. A statement by conservative bishops, calling for chastity outside marriage and refusing to condone homosexuality, was added to the document.

Sep 1: A class-action lawsuit concerning **silicone breast implants** ended with an agreement by some 60 companies that manufactured the implants to pay to the more than 90,500 women who claimed the implants had injured them a total of $4,250,000,000.

It was the largest product liability settlement in U.S. history.

Sep 10: The unmanned **spacecraft Magellan**, launched May 4, 1989, was about to end its four-year mapping of 98% of the surface of Venus. It was to be sent plunging into Venus's atmosphere, where friction would burn it up.

Sep 15: A gene whose mutation causes **hereditary breast cancer** had been discovered, it was announced by the leader of a team of 45 scientists who worked on the project. No diagnostic test was available as yet. About 600,000 women in the U.S. may carry this defective gene.

Sep 16: Two astronauts walked in space without lifelines, spending 7 hours outside the space shuttle *Discovery* 150 miles above Earth, and using a jet pack that cost $7,000,000. It was the first such space walk in a decade.

Sep 19: The **purchase of McCaw Cellular Communications** by AT&T for $12,600,000,000 joined the world's largest telecommunications company with the largest operator of cellular phones. AT&T planned to integrate the cellular network with its long-distance telephone network.

Sep 29: An **interstate banking bill** that was to allow banks to operate branches across the country was signed into law by Pres. Clinton. It abolished barriers that dated to the 1920s.

Oct 1: Agreement on a trade pact between the U.S. and Japan was announced. It was to open Japan's markets in insurance, glass, medical supplies, and telecommunications, thus increasing America's exports. However, negotiators failed to reach agreement on terms to increase Japanese imports of American cars and car parts.

Oct 3: The nation's **first entire school system under private management** was established in Hartford, Ct., by action of its school board, which voted to turn over the troubled system to Education Alternatives, a for-profit business of Minneapolis, Minn.

Oct 4: The **largest for-profit hospital chain**, Columbia/HCA Healthcare Corp., became even bigger when it merged with Healthtrust, Inc., in a deal valued at $3,600,000,000. The combined firms had annual revenues of $15,000,000,000 and operated 311 hospitals with 60,000 beds.

Oct 10: The **Nobel Prize in Physiology or Medicine** was awarded jointly to Alfred G. Gilman, of the University of Texas, and Martin Rodbell, formerly of the National Institute of Environmental Health Sciences, for their discovery of G-proteins and the ways in which they help cells convert signals from the environment and within the body into cellular reactions that control life processes.

Oct 11: The **Nobel Prize in Economic Science** was awarded jointly to two Americans, John F. Nash of Princeton University and John C. Harsanyi of the University of California, Berkeley, and to a German, Reinhard Selten of the University of Bonn. The three were pioneers in the field of game theory, providing foundations for analyzing interactions among businesses and other groups.

Oct 12: The **Nobel Prize in Physics** was awarded jointly to an American and a Canadian, Clifford G. Shull, formerly of the Massachusetts Institute of Technology, and Bertram N. Brockhouse, of McMaster University. They devised powerful neutron probes used to explore atomic structures.

Oct 12: The **Nobel Prize in Chemistry** was awarded to George A. Olah of the University of Southern California for his research into hydrocarbons that are important in the development of new fuels.

Oct 19: Black and white Pentecostal groups, split mostly along racial lines since the 1920s, agreed to form a national association to bring about interracial congregations. The new association was to be called the Pentecostal-Charismatic Churches of North America.

Oct 21: A **giant laser machine** to generate miniature blasts of thermonuclear fusion energy will be built at the Lawrence Livermore National Laboratory in California, the Energy Department announced. The world's largest and most powerful assemblage of lasers was to study fusion without large-scale blast tests underground.

Oct 30: Pope John Paul II announced that **two new American cardinals** were among 30 worldwide appointments as princes of the Roman Catholic Church. They were William Henry Keeler, archbishop of Baltimore, and Adam Joseph Maida, archbishop of Detroit.

Nov 2: Cholesterol levels in elderly people were not seen to be linked to heart disease to the extent they appeared to be in middle-aged people, according to a study carried out at Yale University.

Nov 7: A new record for power generated by a fusion reactor was announced by the Plasma Physics Laboratory of Princeton University. The experimental Tokamak Fusion Test Reactor generated 10,700,000 watts of power in a one-second burst of energy.

Nov 11: New standards for **teaching world history** were proposed by a federal education panel. They were intended to put more emphasis on cultures other than Western civilization, including understanding the development of early mankind in Africa, the unification of China, and the spread of Islam in southwest Asia.

Nov 15: An agreement to work toward **free trade by 2020** was reached by 18 nations, including the U.S., members of the Asia-Pacific Economic Cooperation (APEC) group. Meeting in Jakarta, Indonesia, the forum also agreed that industrialized nations such as Canada, Japan, and the U.S. should set 2010 as their goal.

Nov 15: The **Federal Reserve**, determined to hold down inflation in the face of an expanding economy, raised short-term interest rates for the sixth time in 1994. The total increase was from 3% to 5.5%. Other interest rates, such as banks' prime interest rates, rose correspondingly.

Nov 16: The **expansion of women's roles** in the Roman Catholic Church so that they could attain leadership positions should be explored, a meeting of American bishops decided. The bishops agreed that sexism remained persistent among "some members."

Dec 8: Eleven Orthodox Christian churches with 6,000,000 members agreed for the first time to establish an administratively united church in order to have one voice on social, political, and religious issues. Greek, Russian, Serbian, and other churches had grown separately in the U.S. for 200 years.

Dec 8: An expanded **General Agreement on Tariffs and Trade** (GATT) was signed by Pres. Clinton. The 124-nation revision was to cut tariffs worldwide by 38% and to abolish other trade barriers. To carry out the agreement a new group, the World Trade Organization (WTO), was to replace GATT on Jan. 1, 1995.

Dec 10: Creation of a Western Hemisphere **free trade zone** by 2005 was agreed on by 34 nations, including the U.S., at a meeting in Miami, Fla. On Dec. 11 Canada, Mexico, and the U.S. invited Chile to join them in the North American Free Trade Agreement (NAFTA).

Dec 31: The **Dow Jones industrial average** closed the year at 3,834.44, up 2.1%, or 80.35 points.

IV. Fashion
Folkways
Holidays
Social Issues and Crime
Sports

It was not a good year for sports fans, with a major league baseball strike that ended the season in midsummer, and an ice hockey season that never got started in 1994. Pro athletes, however, did not seem to suffer: The highest paid football quarterback was Troy Aikman of the Dallas Cowboys, at $6,400,000; the average New York Yankee was being paid $1,721,744. While some sports suffered, ice figure skating prospered, in both public interest and prizes that went as high as $200,000. Professional football, to make itself more entertaining, adopted new rules, including the two-point conversion after touchdowns. Attendance at the 1994 regular season games was 14,034,977, setting a record for the second year in a row. A few more blacks were being hired to fill college athletic administrative jobs; they now held 8.7% of the more than 29,000 positions in the 1993–1994 academic year. On Apr. 8 Chan Ho Park became the first Korean ever to play major league baseball when he pitched for the Los Angeles Dodgers. The number of robberies, assaults, and murders in almost all the large cities declined, according to the New York Police Department. Meanwhile, the U.S. Justice Department announced that in June the number of men and women in state and federal prisons reached 1,012,851, a record. Most disturbing were the number of violent crimes committed by the very young and by teenagers. Between 1985 and 1991 the annual rate at which men 15 to 19 years of age were killed rose 154%. In western New York, a 14-year-old boy was convicted of murdering a four-year-old; in Chicago a five-year-old was thrown from a 14th-floor window by two older boys because he refused to steal candy; in Cincinnati a 12-year-old girl admitted she had killed a 13-month-old cousin when she was three. In Brooklyn, N.Y., a 13-year-old boy was killed by police when his toy gun appeared to be real. This and other incidents led to a demand for ending the sale of such realistic looking toys. Justice came to some serial killers: Joel Rifkin was convicted in a Long Island court after confessing to the murders of 17 women; Henry Louis Wallace was charged in Charlotte, N.C., with the deaths of 10 women; and in Joliet, Ill., John Wayne Gacy was put to death for murdering 13 young men and boys. Among more unusual events in the world of crime: A gang of about 12 men stole 9 luxury cars at one time from a New York City parking garage; a man confessed to having robbed 56 banks in Seattle, some of them with the aid of his wife; and, most tragic, a South Carolina mother drowned her two young sons by letting her car with them in it sink in a lake. In another aspect of American life, a mammoth report on sex by the National Opinion Research Center at the University of Chicago found that 85% of married women and 75% of married men said they had been faithful to their spouses; more than half the men, but only 19% of the women, said they thought about sex every day; about one man in four and one woman in ten masturbated at least once a week; and 2.8% of the men and 1.4% of the women identified themselves as homosexual or bisexual. Though the fashion world decreed that the waif look was out and glamour was in, most young

women wore, day in and day out, high black leggings or stockings. Sales of Barney the dinosaur fell off, while those of Mighty Morphin Power Rangers were on the way to capturing more than 40% of the action toy market. Also, trivial or otherwise, these events reflected the U.S. of 1994: One survey found that minorities—blacks, Hispanics, and Asians—resented each other as much as they did whites; a mock slave auction in Williamsburg, Va., was widely denounced; products with alleged magic powers—cosmetics, food, etc.—were increasingly popular; vanilla was the year's favorite flavor; the Fort Worth, Tex., public library had thousands of its books damaged after a radio station as a promotion stunt said it had put $5 and $10 bills in volumes in the fiction section; the baby boomers were becoming backyard gardeners with 68,000,000 Americans spending $22,000,000,000 a year on plants and equipment; and, finally, Tabitha, a cat, flew 30,000 miles around the country for 12 days, lost somewhere in a Boeing 747 jet, before being rescued, little the worse for her experience. Deaths of notable people included those of Barry Bishop, a member of the first American team to scale Mount Everest (1963), Sept. 24, at 62; Julius Boros, popular and successful professional golfer, winner of 18 tournaments, May 28, at 74; Charles S. Feeney, baseball executive, president of the National League, Jan. 10, at 72; Vitas Gerulaitis, once the third-ranked men's tennis player, Sept. 18, at 40; Fred Lebow, creator of the New York City Marathon, who saw it grow to become the largest such race in the world, Oct. 9, at 62; Albert Pierce "Allie" Reynolds, whose pitching helped the New York Yankees win six World Series in the 1940s and 1950s, Dec. 27, at 79; Wilma Rudolph, sprinter, who at the 1960 Olympics became the first woman to win three gold medals in track and field, Nov. 12, at 54; Jack Sharkey, world heavyweight boxing champion (1932–1933), Aug. 17, at 91; Ellsworth Vines, tennis star of the 1930s, Mar. 17, at 82; Charles "Bud" Wilkinson, football coach whose University of Oklahoma teams won national championships in 1950, 1955, and 1956, Feb. 9, at 77.

Jan 1: In **college football bowl games** the results were: Florida State 18, Nebraska 16 in the Orange Bowl; Notre Dame 24, Texas A&M 21 in the Cotton Bowl; Florida 21, West Virginia 7 in the Sugar Bowl; Wisconsin 21, UCLA 16 in the Rose Bowl. The AP and the *USA Today/*CNN polls voted Florida State the national collegiate champions of 1993.

Jan 6 & 8: **U.S. figure skating championships** were won by Scott Boitano, men's singles, and Tonya Harding, women's singles.

Jan 12: Elected to the **Baseball Hall of Fame** was left-handed pitcher Steve Carlton in his first year of eligibility. On Jan. 25 the veterans committee elected Phil Rizzuto, longtime New York Yankee shortstop, and the late Leo Durocher, fiery manager of several major league teams.

Jan 19: A **realignment of major league baseball** was approved by the club owners. The National and American leagues were each divided into three divisions instead of two. There would thus be an additional round of playoff games before the World Series.

Jan 21: Charged with cutting off her husband's penis, Lorena Bobbitt was acquitted by reason of temporary insanity by a Manassas, Va., jury. She had admitted the charge, saying it was in retaliation for John Bobbitt's sexual assaults. The organ had been successfully reattached.

Jan 30: Super Bowl XXVIII was won by the Dallas Cowboys (NFC), who defeated the Buffalo Bills (AFC) 30-13. The Bills had won the AFC championship by defeating the Kansas City Chiefs 30-13, while the Cowboys defeated the San Francisco 49ers 38-21 for the NFC title. It was the Cowboys' second successive Super Bowl victory, while the Bills lost for the fourth time in a row.

Feb 5: A self-proclaimed **white supremacist was convicted** of a murder committed in 1963. The victim was Medgar Evers, a black civil rights leader in Mississippi. Sentenced to life imprisonment was Byron De La Beckwith, whose two previous trials had resulted in deadlocked juries. Since then new evidence had been found.

Feb 10: An **NBA franchise was granted to Toronto**, Canada, with play to start in the 1995–1996 season. On Apr. 27 a similar franchise was granted to Vancouver, Canada.

Feb 12–27: At the **XVIIth Winter Olympic Games**, held in Lillehammer, Norway, the U.S. finished fifth, winning six gold medals and 13 in all. Bonnie Blair won two gold medals in speed skating, giving her a record-setting six gold for her career.

Feb 15: The **first woman to pitch** in an NCAA college baseball game was Ila Borders, a freshman left-hander. She won, but lost for the first time on Mar. 3.

Mar 5: The **killing of an abortion doctor** in Pensacola, Fla., on Mar. 10, 1993, resulted in the conviction on a charge of first-degree murder of Michael F. Griffin, an anti-abortionist. He was sentenced to life imprisonment.

Mar 11: The **Boston St. Patrick's Day parade**, scheduled for Mar. 20, was canceled by the organizers after Massachusetts's highest court ruled that a gay and lesbian group had a right to be in the parade.

Mar 16: Star **figure skater Tonya Harding** pleaded guilty to a charge of conspiracy in connection with an assault on a rival, Nancy Kerrigan, on Jan. 6. Three others, including Harding's former husband, also admitted they had been involved in the attack, in which Kerrigan was hit on the knee with a metal baton.

Mar 23: Wayne Gretzky of the NHL became the league's career leading goal scorer with 802. The previous record was held by Gordie Howe.

Apr 3: The **NCAA women's basketball championship** was won by North Carolina, which defeated Louisiana Tech 60-59.

Apr 4: The **NCAA men's basketball championship** was won by Arkansas, which defeated Duke 76-72.

Apr 6: A **record amount for an NFL franchise**, $185,000,000, was paid for the Philadelphia Eagles. The team had last changed hands in 1985 for $65,000,000.

Apr 10: The **Masters golf tournament** was won by José Maria Olazabal of Spain by two strokes.

Apr 18: The **98th Boston Marathon** was won in the men's division by Cosmas N'Deti of Kenya with a time of 2 hrs., 7 min., 15 sec., a record for the event. The women's division was won by Uta Pippig of Germany with a time of 2 hrs., 21 min., 45 sec., also a record.

Apr 22: The **heavyweight boxing championship** of the world was won at Las Vegas, Nev., by Michael Moorer with a unanimous decision over Evander Holyfield, the defending champion.

May 7: The 120th **Kentucky Derby** was won by Go for Gin with a time of 2:03 $^3/_5$. The jockey was Chris McCarron.

May 15: The **LPGA golf championship** was won by Laura Davies of Great Britain by three strokes.

May 21: The 119th **Preakness Stakes** was won by Tobasco Cat with a time of 1:56 $^2/_5$. The jockey was Pat Day.

May 29: The 78th **Indianapolis 500 auto race** was won by Al Unser, Jr., with an average speed of 160.872 mph. It was Unser's second Indy victory.

June 11: The 126th **Belmont Stakes** was won by Tobasco Cat with a time of 2:26 $^4/_5$. The jockey was Pat Day.

June 14: The **NHL Stanley Cup** was won by the New York Rangers, who defeated the Vancouver Canucks four games to three. It was the Rangers' first championship in 54 years.

June 17: O(renthal) J(ames) Simpson, former college and professional football superstar, was charged with the murder on June 12 of his former wife, Nicole Brown Simpson, and her friend, Ronald L. Goldman. By the end of the year a jury had been selected, but arguments between the defense and the prosecution became so prolonged that the actual trial had not begun.

June 20: The **U.S. Men's Open golf tournament** was won by Ernie Els of South Africa in a three-way playoff.

June 22: The **NBA basketball championship** was won by the Houston Rockets, who defeated the New York Knicks four games to three. It was the first title for the Rockets.

July 3: The **Wimbledon men's tennis championship** was won by Pete Sampras of the U.S. for the second year in a row. He defeated Ivan Ivanisevic in straight sets.

July 6: The **100-meter dash record** was broken in Lausanne, Switzerland, by Leroy Burrell with a time of 9.85 sec., one hundredth of a second better than the previous record.

July 12: The **All-Star baseball game** was won by the National League, which defeated the American League 8-7 for its first victory since 1987.

July 12: The **youngest teenage pilot** to fly solo across the country completed the feat at Long Beach, Cal. He was Jimmy Mathis, 16, who began his trip June 30 and made seven stops on the way.

July 17: The **World Cup of soccer**, played for in the U.S. for the first time, was won at Pasadena, Cal., by Brazil, which defeated Italy 3-2 with penalty kicks after 120 minutes of scoreless regular playing time and overtime.

July 24: The **U.S. Women's Open golf tournament** was won by Patty Sheehan by one stroke.

Aug 13: The **PGA championship tournament** was won by Nick Price of South Africa by six strokes.

Aug 14: Celebration of the 25th anniversary of the Woodstock festival ended at Saugerties, N.Y., as some 300,000 to 350,000 people left the muddy, littered grounds. Numerous rock bands and other performers entertained the throng, of which 1600 were treated in the festival's hospital.

Aug 28: The **U.S. amateur golf championship** was won by Tiger Woods who, at 18 years of age, became the youngest winner in the 99-year history of the event. He was also the first black to take the title.

Sep 4: The world-renowned **Tiffany's jewelry store** in New York City was robbed of $1,000,000 worth of jewels late at night by thieves who seemed to know their way around. Six men, including a security supervisor of the store, were arrested Sept. 10 and about half the loot was recovered.

Sep 10–11: The **U.S. Open tennis championships** were won in the women's division by Arantxa Sánchez Vicario of Spain, and in the men's division by Andre Agassi.

Sep 14: The remainder of the **major league baseball season**, including divisional playoffs and the World Series, was canceled by the team owners. The cancellation came after the players had been on strike since Aug. 12. Neither side had been able to agree to a new contract. It was the first time since 1904 that no World Series was played.

Sep 17: The **Miss America** title was won by Heather Whitestone, 21, of Birmingham, Ala., at the annual pageant in Atlantic City. Deaf since she was 18 months old, Ms. Whitestone was the first contestant with a major disability to win the crown.

Sep 30: The **National Hockey League** postponed the start of the 1994–1995 season because of the failure of the league and the players' union to reach agreement on a new contract. On Dec. 29, with no agreement in sight, the league said that if no settlement was reached by Jan. 15, 1995, the entire season was to be canceled.

Oct 29: The **north face of the White House** was attacked by Martin Duran of Colorado, who fired more than a score of bullets from a semiautomatic weapon at the building. Pres. Clinton was at home at the time, but no one was injured and little damage done. Duran was charged with various offenses, including attempting to assassinate the president. On Dec. 17 four bullets struck the south side of the White House, doing little damage. The perpetrator and the reason for the attack were unknown.

Nov 5: The **world heavyweight boxing championship** was won at Las Vegas, Nev., by George Foreman, who knocked out the titleholder, Michael Moorer, in the tenth round. Foreman, at 45, became the oldest fighter ever to win the title, which he had held once before and had lost 20 years earlier.

Nov 6: The 25th **New York City Marathon** was won in the men's division, by only two seconds, by German Silva of Mexico with a time of 2 hrs., 11 min., 21 sec. The women's division was won by Tegla Loroupe of Kenya with a time of 2 hrs., 27 min., 37 sec. She was the first black African woman to win a major marathon.

Nov 15: Martina Navratilova retired as the generally rated finest woman tennis player in the history of the sport. During her 22-year career she won 55 Grand Slam titles, including 18 singles championships and 1443 matches while losing only 210. She earned a total of $20,100,000.

Nov 28: Jeffrey L. Dahmer, a mass murderer convicted of killing and dismembering at least 15 men and boys, was beaten to death in a Wisconsin prison by a fellow inmate. Dahmer was serving 15 consecutive life terms, having been sentenced on Feb. 17, 1992.

Dec 6: Paul Hill, the **killer of an abortion doctor** and his escort, was sentenced to death by a judge in a state court in Pensacola, Fla., where the murders occurred. On Dec. 2 a federal court judge had sentenced him to two life sentences.

Dec 10: A **pro football record** for catching passes in consecutive games was set by Art Monk, formerly of the Washington Redskins and currently with the New York Jets: 178 from 1983 to 1994.

Dec 21: A **homemade firebomb** exploded in a New York City subway car, injuring 45 people, some of them critically. Edward J. Leary, an unemployed computer expert, one of those badly hurt, was indicted on Dec. 27 on charges of causing the incident. It was believed that the bomb went off prematurely.

Dec 23: Major league baseball club owners unilaterally implemented a salary cap to set a limit on each team's total of players' salaries. The action came after negotiations between the owners and the players' union, which began the strike in August, had failed to agree on a new contract. On Dec. 27 both sides filed unfair labor practice charges with the National Labor Relations Board.

Dec 30: Shootings at two abortion clinics in Brookline, Mass., left two receptionists dead and five people wounded, all of them employees or volunteers. A suspect, John C. Salvi 3d, 22, of Hampton, N.H., was arrested in Norfolk, Va., on Dec. 31 after he fired shots at an abortion clinic there. No one was injured.

1995

I. Civil Rights
Exploration and Settlement
Government
Statistics
Wars

Veterans Day, Nov. 11, was marked with special fervor to observe the 50th anniversary of the end of World War II. New York City's parade, with half a million spectators, was the largest since the end of hostilities. There were smaller parades around the country, as well as wreath layings and religious observances. In Los Angeles special tribute was paid to Japanese-American veterans. Also celebrated in 1995 was the 25th anniversary of Earth Day, with observances around the country, but with considerable worry by environmentalists about the great amount of effort still needed to clean up the environment. One of the worst hurricane seasons brought death and damage to various areas, but particularly on the American Virgin Island of St. Thomas and in the Florida Panhandle. On Sept. 16 the former was struck by Hurricane Marilyn, which left 8 persons dead and destroyed or damaged 80% of the homes on the island. Hurricane Opal hit Florida on Oct. 4, killing 18 persons there and in nearby states, as well as causing $1,500,000,000 damage in the Panhandle alone. The Census Bureau reported that 8.7% of the American population, or 22,600,000 persons, were foreign-born, the highest percentage since World War II. Another Census Bureau report said that in the 1994 congressional elections, 60.1% of those with incomes over $50,000 voted, but only 23.3% of those with incomes of $5000 to $10,000 went to the polls. Overall, only 44.6% of eligible Americans voted. The 75th anniversary of the ratification of the 19th Amendment, which gave women the right to vote in 1920, was marked by women's groups. However, the Inter-Parliamentary Union said that of the nations with freely elected legislative assemblies, the U.S. ranked 43rd, with only 10.9% of national seats held by women. Both men and women, the Census Bureau found, were less likely to move out of state than at any time since 1950. About 16.7% of Americans changed state residences in a one-year period ending Mar., 1994, whereas the figure had been about 20% in the 1950s and the 1960s. The number of births in 1994 was estimated at 3,949,000, falling below the 4,000,000 mark for the first time in seven years. There were 2,294,000 deaths, the most in the nation's history. Even so, people over the age of 85 constituted the fastest-growing segment of the population, increasing by 232% in the past 35 years. On the other hand, traffic deaths in 1994 rose for the second year in a row, reaching 43,000. Donations to charities increased in 1994 by 3.6% to $130,000,000,000. At the same time, the heads of charitable and other nonprofit organizations were well paid, the top earner being the head of the J. Paul Getty Trust at $610,001. Notable persons who died included Leslie Aspin, Jr., Democratic representative from Wisconsin for 22 years and briefly secretary of defense in the Clinton administration, May 21, at 56; Warren E. Burger, chief justice of the U.S. for 17 years ending in 1986, June 25, at 87; Angier Biddle Duke, diplomat and chief of protocol for two presidents, Apr. 29, at 79; J. William Fulbright, Democratic senator from Arkansas for 39 years ending in 1974 and creator of the Fulbright fellowships for international study, Feb. 9, at 89; Oveta Culp Hobby, first head of the Women's Auxiliary Army Corps and first secretary of the Dept.

of Health, Education, and Welfare, Aug. 16, at 90; Rose Fitzgerald Kennedy, matriarch of the politically powerful Kennedy family, Jan. 22, at 104; William Kunstler, controversial radical lawyer, defender of unpopular people and causes, Sept. 4, at 76; George W. Romney, automobile executive who was for a time a Republican presidential candidate in 1968, July 26, at 88; Margaret Chase Smith, of Maine, the first woman to be elected to both houses of Congress, May 29, at 97; John C. Stennis, Mississippi Democrat who served for 41 years in the Senate, longer than all but one other person, Apr. 23, at 93; James L. Whitten, Mississippi congressman whose 51 years set a record for service in the House of Representatives, Sept. 9, at 85.

Jan 12: The **U.S. and India** signed a military accord intended to mark an end to disagreements that arose between the two nations during the Cold War era. The pact called for joint military exercises and consultations between the two nations' defense departments.

Jan 20: Trade restrictions imposed on North Korea since 1950 were relaxed by the U.S. Some imports would be allowed and direct telephone calls between the two countries were permitted.

Jan 23: The **Congressional Accountability Act** was signed into law by Pres. Clinton. It required Congress to abide by the same laws governing the workplace, such as those having to do with discrimination, that applied throughout the rest of the country.

Feb 1: In its annual survey of human rights the State Department claimed that China had made no progress during the past year. The report was a setback for the Clinton administration, which had made several attempts to push China toward more lenient policies.

Feb 18: The **National Association for the Advancement of Colored People** ousted its chairman, William F. Gibson, and replaced him with Myrlie Evers-Williams, widow of Medgar Evers, a civil rights leader who was murdered in 1963. Gibson had been accused of spending the NAACP's money lavishly, and even using some of it for private purposes.

Mar: Rainstorms and floods in northern and central California killed at least 15 people and caused $2,000,000,000 in damage, including $500,000,000 to crops and livestock.

Mar 3: The last **U.S. Marines left Mogadishu**, Somalia. Eighteen hundred marines had gone ashore on Feb. 28 to evacuate 2500 UN troops, the final contingent of the force that since Dec., 1992, had been trying without success to end civil strife in Somalia.

Mar 22: States could no longer be required to carry out **mandates from Congress** unless Congress provides federal funds to pay for them, according to an act signed into law by Pres. Clinton.

Mar 31: At a **ceremony in Port-au-Prince**, Haiti, Pres. Clinton formally handed over responsibility for the security of the recently restored regime of Pres. Jean-Bertrand Aristide from American troops to a UN peacekeeping force. American soldiers had landed in Haiti about six months earlier to put an end to the military dictatorship.

Apr 10: Carol Bellamy, director of the Peace Corps, was chosen executive director of the United Nations Children's Fund. In 1976 Bellamy became the first woman to be elected president of the New York City Council. The top job at UNICEF (formerly known as the United Nations International Children's Emergency Fund) had been held by an American since its founding in 1946 as an emergency operation.

Apr 19: A tremendous **blast from a truck bomb killed 168 persons** and ruined a federal office building in Oklahoma City, Okla. Many other buildings in the neighborhood were damaged. On Aug. 10, a federal grand jury indicted Timothy J. McVeigh and Terry L. Nichols on charges of having engineered the crime. At one time close friends in the Army, they apparently hated the federal government. McVeigh and Nichols were to be tried in May, 1996.

Apr 26: A **law banning possession of a gun** within 1000 feet of a school was declared unconstitutional by a 5–4 vote of the Supreme Court. The decision said that the federal government was unlawfully invading local rights.

Apr 30: An **embargo against all trade and investment** with Iran was announced by Pres. Clinton. His goal was to discourage Iran from acquiring nuclear weapons and supporting terrorism. America's European allies and Japan declined to join the move.

May 2: In a **reversal of policy toward Cuba**, the Clinton administration announced that it would hereafter return all Cuban boat people to their country after admitting about 20,000 who were being held at the Guantanamo Bay Naval Station. For about 30 years such Cuban refugees had received special status, permitting them to reside in the U.S.

May 3: Former Pres. **George Bush resigned** from the National Rifle Association. In his letter of resignation, Bush angrily denounced the NRA for distributing fund-raising material that described federal law enforcement agents as "jackbooted government thugs."

May 6: Ron Kirk, a Democrat, became the **first black mayor** of a major Texas city. He was elected with 62% of the vote in Dallas.

May 8–9: The **50th anniversary of the Allied victory** over Nazi Germany was marked in Moscow by a gathering of world leaders, including Pres. Clinton. Earlier ceremonies had been held in Berlin, London, Paris, and Washington.

May 8–10: Floods covered the New Orleans, La., area with up to 2 feet of water from torrential rains. The storm caused 6 deaths and inflicted damage estimated at $3,000,000,000.

May 10: An agreement on some aspects of **European security** was reached by Pres. Clinton and Pres. Boris Yeltsin of Russia at a meeting in Moscow. Yeltsin agreed to end his opposition to an early stage of NATO expansion, while Clinton agreed to oppose the withholding of aid to Russia.

May 11: A **treaty to limit the spread of nuclear arms** was approved by more than 170 nations, including the U.S., at a meeting in the UN. The treaty, in effect for 25 years, was now extended in perpetuity.

May 20: A section of **Pennsylvania Avenue** in front of the White House was permanently closed to traffic after several recent incidents. In one a light plane crashed on the lawn, and in two others shots were fired at the president's home. Three days after the closing an armed man jumped onto the lawn and was shot.

May 22: The **number of terms a member of Congress** may serve cannot, in the absence of a constitutional amendment, be limited, the Supreme Court decided in a 5–4 decision. Twenty-three states had adopted term-limit laws.

June 7: Exercising the first veto of his administration, Pres. Clinton killed a Republican-sponsored bill that ostensibly would cut $16,400,000,000 from government spending in the current fiscal year. Clinton claimed that the measure would harm educational programs. On Aug. 11 he used his second veto to strike down a measure that would have required the U.S. to lift its part of the UN arms embargo against Bosnia.

June 12: Affirmative action programs that classify people by race, even though intended to achieve benign purposes, are probably unconstitutional, the Supreme Court decided by a 5–4 vote. Such programs must be "narrowly tailored" and have a "compelling governmental interest" to be permissible.

June 16: Leaders of the **Group of Seven** industrialized powers (Canada, France, Germany, Great Britain, Italy, Japan, and the U.S.) at an economic summit meeting in Halifax, Nova Scotia, asked that steps be taken to prevent currency crises, such as the recent one in Mexico. They called on the International Monetary Fund to exercise closer supervision over national economic policies and to find a new source for emergency funds.

June 19: The **right to reject parade marchers** whose beliefs and programs are objected to by the private sponsors of the parade is constitutional, the Supreme Court ruled unanimously. The case concerned Boston's St. Patrick's Day parade; sponsors there had refused to allow gay and lesbian organizations to march with them.

June 21: The **Supreme Court upheld a Florida law** that required lawyers to wait 30 days before soliciting an accident victim's business. The 5–4 vote was a departure from earlier decisions that had upheld the right of lawyers to advertise.

June 26: Random drug testing of school athletes was upheld by the Supreme Court, 6–3. The ruling stressed that such athletes serve as role models.

June 29: A program developed under the 1973 **Endangered Species Act** was upheld by the Supreme Court, 6–3. The ruling applied to a program that protected endangered species by barring the destruction of essential habitats on private land.

June 29: Race as a "predominant factor" in drawing congressional district lines can be presumed unconstitutional, the Supreme Court decided, 5–4. The decision was based on a dispute over the boundaries of the 11th District in Georgia, which had created a majority-black district.

June 29: More governmental **financial support for religious organizations** became possible when the Supreme Court, voting 5–4, held that the University of Virginia must subsidize a student religious magazine on the same basis as other student publications.

July 11: Full diplomatic recognition of Vietnam was granted by the Clinton administration 22 years after U.S. military forces withdrew from that country following 10 years of war. Pres. Clinton said that he would continue to urge Vietnam to give an accounting of the 2202 U.S. military personnel still listed as missing.

July 12: A **heat wave** that had begun in the Midwest and had spread to the East killed about 1000 people, 733 of them in Chicago, Ill., before the weather changed. Most of the deaths were among the elderly.

Aug 15: The federal government agreed to pay **$3,100,000 to the family of a white separatist** whose wife and teenage son were shot to death by federal agents. The killings had occurred Aug. 21–22, 1992, at the cabin of Randall C. Weaver, located on a remote Idaho mountainside.

Aug 25: An **American human rights activist,** Harry Wu, was expelled and ordered deported to the U.S. one day after he had been found guilty in a Chinese court of spying and stealing state secrets. A sentence of 15 years in prison was cancelled by the deportation. Wu had spent 19 years in Chinese prisons and labor camps before leaving China in 1985 and becoming an American citizen. Deporting Wu instead of inflicting prison time was seen in some quarters as a Chinese gesture to please the U.S.

Sep 2: The **surrender of Japan in 1945**, which ended World War II, was marked by ceremonies in Honolulu, Hawaii. Pres. Clinton praised the heroism of those Americans who fought in the "most destructive conflict in all human history."

Sep 5: Hillary Rodham Clinton, the first lady, spoke vigorously in support of human rights at the Fourth World Conference on Women in Beijing, China. She particularly criticized China for trying to prevent free discussion of women's issues.

Sep 7: Sen. Bob Packwood, Republican of Oregon, announced that he would resign his seat one day after the Senate Ethics Committee voted 6–0 to recommend his expulsion on grounds of sexual and official misconduct. His retirement was set for Oct. 1.

Sep 10: For the first time, **NATO used both cruise missiles and long-range bombs** to attack Serbian air defenses in northwestern Bosnia. The missiles were fired from a U.S. Navy cruiser. On Aug. 30 and earlier in September, NATO planes had bombed Serbian-held positions.

Sep 12: Two American balloonists were shot down and killed over Belarus by combat aircraft as they participated in a race that had begun in Switzerland. The victims were Alan Fraenckel and John Stuart-Jervis. Four other Americans were forced down and held captive for a time.

Sep 19: A 35,000-word **manifesto written by the Unabomber**, whose mail bombings over the previous 17 years had resulted in 3 deaths and 23 injuries in various parts of the country, was printed in both *The New York Times* and *The Washington Post*. In June the mysterious bomber had promised to stop the killings if the manifesto, which called for a revolution against modern industrial and technological society, was printed. As of the end of 1995 no further bombings had occurred.

Sep 22: A U.S. Air Force **E-3B AWACS jet crashed** shortly after takeoff in Anchorage, Alaska, killing all 24 persons aboard—22 Americans and 2 Canadians. The accident may have been caused by geese being sucked into one of the four engines. It was the first crash of an American AWACS plane in more than 100,000 missions.

Sep 28: An **accord between Israel and the Palestine Liberation Organization**, which would eventually transfer control of much of the West Bank to its Arab residents, was signed in Washington by Yitzhak Rabin, prime minister of Israel, and Yasir Arafat, chairman of the PLO. The agreement, witnessed by

Pres. Clinton, made specific the basic agreement that had been reached two years earlier, also signed at a White House ceremony.

Oct 1: Ten militant Muslims were convicted in federal court in New York City of conspiring to carry out a terrorist campaign of bombings and assassinations that would have destroyed the United Nations building and many New York landmarks, as well as killing hundreds of people. One object of the planned attacks was to force the U.S. to abandon its support of Israel and Egypt. The leading figure among those convicted on 48 of 50 charges was Sheik Omar Abdel Rahman, a blind cleric and an Egyptian, who was the spiritual leader of a fundamentalist group.

Oct 4–8: Pope John Paul II, on an enthusiastically acclaimed visit to the U.S., addressed the UN, where he urged all nations to live up to their moral responsibilities, and celebrated three masses in the New York area and in Baltimore before enormous crowds.

Oct 5: Restrictions on travel to Cuba were eased by Pres. Clinton's executive order. Also, human rights groups would be allowed to expand their work in Cuba, and news organizations could open bureaus in that country.

Oct 9: In Arizona, the **derailment of an Amtrak train** en route from Miami to Los Angeles killed 1 crew member and injured 77. The track had been sabotaged. A note at the scene referred to the attack by federal officers on the Branch Davidian sect's compound near Waco, Tex., in Apr., 1993. The note was signed "Sons of the Gestapo," an organization never heard of before.

Oct 16: The so-called **Million Man March** on Washington brought 400,000 or more black men to the capital to express their solidarity and to promise stronger leadership in their communities. The rally was called by Louis Farrakhan, leader of the Nation of Islam, whose previous anti-Semitic and other racist remarks made the event controversial.

Oct 23: An **American-Russian summit meeting** between presidents Clinton and Boris N. Yeltsin stressed continued friendly relations between the two countries, but did not solve the problem of integrating Russian troops into any peacekeeping force that might be sent to Bosnia. The meeting was held at Hyde Park, N.Y., at the home of Pres. Franklin D. Roosevelt.

Oct 24: At a **summit meeting** in New York City, presidents Clinton and Jiang Zemin of China reached no concrete agreements, but both sides said that they were making strong efforts to settle their differences over such issues as U.S. criticism of China's human rights record.

Oct 25: In New York City the **UN observed its 50th anniversary** with a series of weekend-long meetings and speeches in which a record 185 heads of state and government, along with other high officials, participated. There were 201 speeches during the three-day event.

Nov 14: **Explosions at an American-run military training center** in Riyadh, Saudi Arabia, killed six people, including five Americans, and wounded 37 other Americans. The bombers were unknown, but authorities believed that the incident was an attempt to drive Americans out of the country.

Nov 16: **Aimed at curtailing lobbyists,** the House of Representatives voted to prohibit its members and their staffs from accepting such gifts as free meals and free travel from anyone except personal friends and family members. Earlier in the year the Senate had banned gifts worth more than $100. The rules for both houses were to become effective on Jan. 1, 1996.

Nov 29-Dec 2: On a **major European tour** Pres. Clinton addressed the British Parliament in London; he pressed for a continuation of the peace efforts in Northern Ireland during visits to Ulster and Dublin; and explained to American troops stationed in in Germany why they were being sent to Bosnia as peacekeepers. He also met with European leaders in Madrid.

Dec 14: Meeting in Paris, the **leaders of Bosnia, Croatia, and Serbia**, with Pres. Clinton presiding, signed a peace agreement that had been reached in principle Nov. 21 after negotiations held at Wright-Patterson Air Force Base in Dayton, Ohio. Under the terms of the agreement, a Bosnian-Croat federation would control about 51% of Bosnia, while the Serb Republic would occupy 49% of the country; a constitution would create a central government; troops would be withdrawn behind cease-fire lines; and a NATO-led peacekeeping force of 60,000 troops would enforce the agreement. During the negotiations Pres. Clinton had pledged that the U.S. would contribute 20,000 members to this force. He contended that as president he had the right to order this deployment whether or not Congress approved, and on Dec. 3 he announced that the first American troops would arrive at a staging area in Hungary the next day. By year's end 2000 U.S. troops were in Bosnia. On Dec. 13 the Senate passed, 69–30, a resolution supporting the deployment, but on the condition that the U.S. head an international effort to arm and train Bosnian Muslims.

Dec 20: The **crash of an American Airlines Boeing 757**, en route from Miami, Fla., to Cali, Colombia, killed 160 of the 164 persons aboard. The accident occurred when the plane crashed into a mountain about 40 miles north of Cali.

Dec 22: A **bill restricting securities litigation** became law when the Senate, following the House, overrode a veto by Pres. Clinton. The new law would make it more difficult for individual stockholders to sue underwriters, brokers, company officials, and accountants in case of securities fraud.

Dec 23: An act that stiffened the punishment for **sex offenses involving children** was signed into law by Pres. Clinton. The new law would increase the length of prison terms for those convicted of various crimes involving child pornography.

Dec 24: A **fire at the Philadelphia Zoo** killed 10 lemurs, 6 West African lowland gorillas, 4 white-handed gibbons, and 3 Bornean orangutans. All of the animals were among endangered species. The youngest was an 11-month-old female gorilla.

Dec 31: The **Interstate Commerce Commission** went out of existence by an act of Congress. Established in 1887, the ICC was created to rein in the excesses of the robber barons who controlled the nation's railroads at the time. Deregulation of the transportation industry in the 1980s had left the commission with little to do.

Dec 31: The **federal government was largely shut down** at year's end because of a dispute between Pres. Clinton and the Republican-controlled Congress over how to balance the budget by the year 2002. Some 260,000 federal employees had been on furlough since Dec. 15 and many services, such as the issuance of passports, were halted. The main issues in the dispute centered on the welfare program, Medicare, Medicaid, and tax cuts.

II. Architecture
Arts and Music
Popular Entertainment
Publishing
Theater

Attendance at Broadway theaters during the 1994–1995 season totaled 9,000,000, an increase of 12% over the previous season and the highest in 12 years. Only 28 new shows opened, but ticket sales were a record $406,000,000, while shows on tour around the country took in another $695,000,000. One unusual production was *Having Our Say*, based on the memoir of two feisty sisters, Sarah and Bessie Delany, both over 100 years old. Very pleasant was the return to Broadway after 30 years of Julie Andrews in a musical, *Victor/Victoria*. Revivals of *How to Succeed in Business Without Really Trying* and *The Rose Tattoo* were welcomed. Movie producers for the most part spent the year showing how easy it was to spend millions on films few wanted to see. *Waterworld*, costing $235,000,000, making it the most expensive movie ever, was the prime example. Based on Nathaniel Hawthorne's novel, *The Scarlet Letter*, probably the worst movie of the year, had a scene in which the sinning couple went skinny-dipping. But there was also good news for moviegoers: Disney's *Toy Story* charmed and excited viewers with its state-of-the-art animation; *Apollo 13* was a letter-perfect reprise of the actual near-fatal adventure of that spacecraft; two other films, *Sense and Sensibility* and *Persuasion*, caught the drama and atmosphere of Jane Austen's novels. On the other hand, sleaze and violence dominated several films, notably *Showgirls*, which many critics claimed exploited sex at the expense of a storyline, and *Seven*, in which a woman's nose was sliced off. In the end, *Batman Forever* was, judging by box office receipts, the most successful film of the year, taking in $184,000,000. The Metropolitan Museum of Art in New York City observed its 125th anniversary with a founders' ball and other events. The museum's "Origins of Impressionism" exhibit was the most popular of the 1994–1995 season, drawing 794,108 viewers. Next in popularity was "The Italian Metamorphosis" at the Guggenheim Museum, which attracted 216,000 persons. Somewhat off the beaten path of museum exhibits was "Beat Culture and the New America, 1950–1965" at the Whitney Museum in New York City. The 18th-century American painter John Singleton Copley was honored with two exhibits, one at the Metropolitan featuring his work done in America, and another at the National Gallery of Art in Washington, D.C., featuring paintings done in England. The Cincinnati Symphony Orchestra celebrated its 100th birthday. Rock music continued to enthrall the younger generation, but there was much criticism of gangsta rap, which featured lyrics exploiting violence and sex. The most successful album of the year was *Cracked Rear View* by Hootie and the Blowfish, which sold 7,000,000 copies; the bestselling single was "Gangsta's Paradise" by Coolio with sales of 2,500,000 copies. The Beatles returned with an anthology album that passed the million mark in sales. Academics and others gathered in Oxford, Miss., in August for a conference called "In Search of Elvis/Music, Race, Religion, Art, Performance." Entertainment on the television networks was more or less at a standstill, with the continuing medical drama *E.R.* being the most popular weekly show. Viewers were more taken by the many hours devoted to real life events, such as the Oklahoma City bombing and the O.J. Simpson murder trial. Business support for arts organizations totaled $875,000,000 in 1994, up from $518,000,000 in 1991, the last time this figure was calculated. Among notable persons who died were George Abbott, a leading playwright, producer, director, and actor for 80 years, Jan. 31, at 107; Maxene Andrews of the Andrews Sisters trio, a popular singing group best remembered for their entertainment of servicemen during World War II, Oct. 21, at 79; Vivian Blaine, actress, who created the role of Miss Adelaide in *Guys and Dolls*, Dec. 9, at 74; Jeremy Brett, English actor well known in the U.S. for his television portrayal of Sherlock Holmes, Sept. 12, at 69; Anne Elizabeth (Bessie) Delany, who joined with her sister Sarah to write their memoir, *Having Our Say*, which met with great success both on the stage and the bestseller lists, Sept. 25, at 104; Eazy-E (Eric Wright), who made a commercial success of gangsta rap, Mar. 26, at 31; Alfred Eisenstaedt, German-born photographer whose work defined photojournalism, Aug. 23, at 96; Jack Finney, science fiction writer, noted for his novel *Time and Again*, Nov. 14, at 84; Eva Gabor, actress and youngest of the three glamorous Gabor sisters, July 4, at 74; Jerry Garcia, guitarist who led an extremely popular band, the Grateful Dead, for 30 years, Aug. 9, at 53; Gale Gordon, popular character actor in television sitcoms opposite Eve Arden Ball, June 30, at 89; Charles Gordone, who in 1970 became the first black playwright to win the Pulitzer Prize for drama, Nov. 17, at 70; Phil Harris, brash bandleader whose noisy style made him a star on the Jack Benny radio show, Aug. 11, at 91; Patricia Highsmith, author of 20 novels, most of which were tales of murder with a strong psychological background, Feb. 4, at 74; Paul Horgan, known for his writings, both fiction and nonfiction, about the American Southwest, Mar. 8, at 91; Burl Ives, internationally popular folksinger and actor, Apr. 14, at 85; Helene Johnson, a poet of the Harlem Renaissance of the 1920s, July 7, at 89; Sidney Kingsley, playwright, remembered for *Dead End* and other dramas, Mar. 20, at 88; Louis Krasner, Russian-born violinist who was a champion of 20th-century music, May 4, at 91; Corliss Lamont, philosopher, teacher, and socialist activist, Apr. 26, at 93; Ida Lupino, movie actress and director, renowned for her roles as villainesses, Aug. 3, at 77; Louis Malle, French film director who also made controversial movies in the U.S., Nov. 23, at 63; Dean Martin, singer, comedian, and movie actor noted for his jaunty, tongue-in-cheek portrayals of James Bond-like characters, Dec. 25, at 78; Butterfly McQueen, who won screen immortality as the slave girl with the high-pitched voice in *Gone With the Wind*, Dec. 22, at 84; James Merrill, poet, who won many prizes for his 14 volumes of verse, Feb. 6, at 68; Elizabeth Montgomery, actress, who had an enthusiastic following as the star of the 1960s television series *Bewitched*, May 18, at 57; Erica Morini, Austrian-born violinist of international renown, Nov. 1, at 91; Elting E. Morison, historian and biographer of military leaders, Apr. 20, at 85; Tessie O'Shea, lively music hall singer and actress in both the U.S. and Great Britain, Apr. 21, at 83; George Price, cartoonist, whose odd slants on life were for many years a feature of *The New Yorker*, Jan. 12, at 93; Selena Quintanilla, star of the Tejano music form, murdered Mar. 31, at 23; James Reston of *The New York Times*, generally acclaimed the most influential journalist of his time, Dec. 6, at 86; Ginger Rogers, actress, whose vivacity as she danced with Fred Astaire made her the symbol of an era, Apr. 25, at 83; Norman Rosten, playwright, novelist, and poet, whose work often featured his native Brooklyn, Mar. 7, at 81; Henry Roth, novelist, known for his much praised *Call It Sleep*, Oct. 13, at 89; May Sarton, poet and novelist, July 16, at 83; Nicolas Slonimsky, Russian-born musicologist, lexicographer, composer, conductor, and pianist, Dec. 25, at 101; Page Smith, historian, who worked mostly in the field of American history, writing for both scholars and the general public, Aug. 28, at 77; Terry Southern, novelist and screenwriter, whose most enduring work was the film *Dr. Strangelove*, Oct. 29, at 71; John Cameron Swayze, one of the first television news anchormen, Aug. 15, at 89; Lana Turner, who began as a pinup girl but earned a reputation as a serious movie actress, June 29, at 75; Benay Venuta, whose career as a dancer, singer, and sculptor extended from 1925 to 1993, Sept. 1, at 84; David Wayne, who played many different character roles on stage, in the movies, and on television, Feb. 9, at 81; René Wellek, longtime Yale University professor and a founder of the study of comparative literature in the U.S., Nov. 10, at 92; Calder Willingham, author and screenwriter, noted for his novel *End As a Man*, Feb. 19, at 72; Gay Allen Wilson, biographer and authority on Walt Whitman, Aug. 6, at 92; José Yglesias, novelist, playwright, and journalist, who wrote mainly about Latin Americans, Nov. 7, at 75; Marguerite Young, known for her 1198-page novel *Miss MacIntosh, My Darling*, Nov. 17, at 87.

In midyear a **book publishing** industry report projected sales for the year at about $26,000,000,000, which would buy about 2,300,000,000 books. The average cost of a hardcover book was $18.30 and was expected to go up to $22 by 1999. At the retail level, chain stores were taking an increasing part of the business. Superstores led the chains' advance, with Barnes & Noble planning to open 75 such units in 1995. Another growth area in the book industry involved audio books. Retail sales had now reached $1,400,000,000 a year, with large publishers issuing up to 100 titles a year on tape. Books of literary importance did not lead the bestseller lists. Attracting the most attention and sales were *My American Journey*, Gen. Colin Powell's autobiography, for which he had received a $6,500,000 advance; *Miss America* by the radio talk show host Howard Stern, as distinct in its typography as in its freewheeling language; and *The Road Ahead* by Bill Gates, the billionaire genius of the computer world's Microsoft Corp. Notable among works of fiction were *Independence Day* by Richard Ford, about a man and his troubled teenage son; *Sabbath's Theater* by Philip Roth, the story of an aging man leaving his wife; *The Promise of Rest* by Reynolds Price, the final volume of a trilogy about a family; *All the Days and Nights*, the collected short stories of William Maxwell; and *From Time to Time*, another unusual science fiction tale by Jack Finney. Less notable from the point of view of quality, but a sturdy bestseller, was *The Christmas Box* by Richard Paul Evans, in which a young family learns the real significance of Christmas. In the nonfiction field there was, as usual, a wide variety of titles. History offered *Democracy on Trial* by Page Smith, a candid account of the forced relocation of Japanese-Americans during World War II; *Terrible Honesty* by Ann Douglas, a vivid look at Manhattan in the 1920s; and *Autopsy on an Empire* by Jack F. Matlock, Jr., a former ambassador's inside view of the collapse of the Soviet Union. Americans wrote excellent biographies of British authors: *George Eliot* by Frederick R. Karl; *Lewis Carroll* by Morton N. Cohen; and *The Brontës* by Juliet Barker. Readers showed an interest in religion and the spiritual life by buying such books as *God: A Biography* by Jack Miles; *The Origin of Satan* by Elaine Pagels; and *Brush of an Angel's Wings* by Charlie W. Shedd. A somewhat new fiction genre that might be called Christian thrillers combined adventure with conservative theology. Examples were *Gideon's Torch* by Charles Colson and *The Oath* by Frank E. Peretti. The O.J. Simpson murder trial resulted in the publication of at least 30 books focusing on the sensational case, with more to follow. Marcia Clark, chief of the unsuccessful prosecution, was offered $4,200,000 for her version of events, while a leading defense lawyer, Johnnie Cochran, received more than $2,500,000 for his side. Books might be selling well, but People for the American Way reported that more books were banned from public school libraries in 1994 than the year before.

Jan 12–13: The contents of Rudolf **Nureyev's apart-**

ment in Manhattan brought nearly $8,000,000 at auction. The late dancer's ballet slippers, costumes, paintings, and furniture went on the block. One bidder paid $9200 for a pair of pink slippers.

Jan 13: The **manuscripts of the late composer John Cage**, consisting of 26,000 pages of scores, musical writings, and other material, were acquired by the New York Public Library. The papers were purchased from the composer's estate for an undisclosed sum.

Jan 20: The **comedian George Burns** marked his 99th birthday. The previous day a Los Angeles street was named for his late wife and partner, Gracie Allen. It intersected already-named George Burns Road.

Jan 25: The **San Francisco Museum of Modern Art** opened its new home in a $60,000,000 building with 225,000 sq. ft. of space. The new facility was designed by the Swiss architect Mario Botto.

Mar 1: Grammy Awards were presented for the following: best album of 1994, *MTV Unplugged* by Tony Bennett; best single record, "All I Wanna Do" by Sheryl Crow; best male pop vocalist, Elton John for "Can You Feel the Love Tonight"; best female pop vocalist, Sheryl Crow for "All I Wanna Do"; best male rock vocalist, Bruce Springsteen for "Streets of Philadelphia"; best female rock vocalist, Melissa Etheridge for "Come to My Window."

Mar 14: *The New York Times* published its 50,000th single issue. It was part of Vol. CXLIV, appearing 143 years and 177 days after the first issue.

Mar 27: Academy Awards were presented to *Forrest Gump* as the oustanding motion picture of 1994; Tom Hanks as best actor for *Forrest Gump*; Jessica Lange as best actress for *Blue Sky*; Martin Landau as best supporting actor for *Ed Wood*; and Dianne Wiest as best supporting actress for *Bullets Over Broadway*.

Apr 18: Pulitzer Prizes were awarded for the following: fiction, *The Stone Diaries* by Carol Shields; general nonfiction, *The Beak of the Finch: A Story of Evolution in Our Time* by Jonathan Weiner; biography, *Harriet Beecher Stowe: A Life* by Joan D. Hedrick; history, *No Ordinary Time: Franklin and Eleanor Roosevelt: The Home Front in World War II* by Doris Kearns Goodwin; poetry, *Simple Truth* by Philip Levine; drama, *The Young Man from Atlanta* by Horton Foote; music, *Stringmusic* by Morton Gould.

Apr 22: A **Tiffany lamp** was sold at auction in New York City for a record-breaking $1,100,000. The purchaser was the Louis Tiffany Museum of Nagoya, Japan.

May 8: Robert Hass was named poet laureate of the U.S. for a one-year term. Hass's poetry included such collections as *Field Guide* and *Human Wishes*.

May 8: The **highest price paid for a painting** since 1990 was offered at auction in New York City for a Pablo Picasso portrait of the artist Angel Fernandez de Soto. The painting sold for $29,100,000. At the same time, Henri Matisse's *Hindu Pose* was sold for $14,800,000, the highest price ever paid for a work by that artist.

May 23: The **New York Public Library** celebrated the 100th anniversary of the opening of its magnificent main building on Fifth Avenue with a gala party for 500 guests and the showing of such exhibits as "Books of the Century" and "What Price Freedom."

June 4: Tony Awards for the 1994–1995 theater season were presented for the following: best play, *Love! Valor! Compassion!* by Terrence McNally; best musical, *Sunset Boulevard*; leading actor in a play, Ralph Fiennes for *Hamlet*; leading actress in a play, Cherry Jones for *The Heiress*; leading actor in a musical, Matthew Broderick for *How to Succeed in Business Without Really Trying*; leading actress in a musical, Glenn Close for *Sunset Boulevard*.

Sep 1: The **Rock-and-Roll Hall of Fame and Museum** opened its new $92,000,000 home in Cleveland, Ohio, with a concert in which many famous figures in the field participated. The new building, designed by I.M. Pei, was an assemblage of geometrical shapes with 150,000 sq. ft. of space.

Sep 5: **"Creating French Culture,"** an exhibit intended to display the growth of French culture over the centuries, opened at the Library of Congress in Washington, D.C. The exhibit included more than 200 manuscripts, books, maps, and prints, beginning with a ninth-century illuminated manuscript, from the French National Library.

Sep 7: The **Joffrey Ballet**, founded in New York City in 1956 by Robert Joffrey and Gerald Arpino, announced that it was moving its headquarters to Chicago, Ill. The ballet had been in financial difficulties for several years.

Sep 10: Emmy Awards were presented for the following: best drama series, *N.Y.P.D. Blue*; best comedy series, *Frasier*; leading actor in a drama series, Mandy Patinkin for *Chicago Hope*; leading actress in a drama series, Kathy Baker for *Picket Fences*; leading actor in a comedy series, Kelsey Grammer for *Frasier*; leading actress in a comedy series, Candice Bergen for *Murphy Brown*.

Sep 29: Eighty-five works of art valued at more than $50,000,000 were donated to the National Gallery of Art, Washington, D.C., by Mr. and Mrs. Paul Mellon, collectors and philanthropists. The gift included paintings by many major artists, such as Cézanne, Manet, and Degas.

Oct 2: The **Metropolitan Opera** of New York City unveiled its new system for translating the text of on-stage operas. The system consisted of individual display screens placed on seat backs. The 3989 screens cost $1,200,000 to install.

Nov 15: National Book Awards were presented for the following: fiction, *Sabbath's Theater* by Philip Roth; nonfiction, *The Haunted Land: Facing Europe's Ghosts After Communism* by Tina Rosenberg; poetry, *Passing Through: The Later Poems, New and Selected* by Stanley Kunitz.

Nov 21: The **first major exhibit of the work of Jan Vermeer**, Dutch genre and landscape painter, since his death in 1675, opened at the National Gallery of Art in Washington, D.C. The exhibit, which included 21 of the 35 paintings that Vermeer was known to have done, attracted large crowds.

Dec 1: Various **belongings of Frank Sinatra**, the popular singer, were sold at auction in New York City, bringing $2,070,000. Among the objects purchased were a metal mailbox ($13,800) and a gold, diamond-set shoehorn ($5520).

Dec 18: *Encyclopædia Britannica*, the internationally noted 32-volume reference work, was sold for an undisclosed amount to an investment group headed by Jacob E. Safra, a financier based in Switzerland. Proceeds from the sale would go to the University of Chicago via the William Benton Foundation, the current owner. *Britannica* was first published in Scotland from 1768 to 1771; it became American-owned in 1920 when bought by Julius Rosenwald, founder of Sears, Roebuck & Co.

III. Business and Industry
Education
Philosophy and Religion
Science

The economy grew modestly in 1995. Inflation was only 2.6%, but some indicators were not encouraging. Consumer credit was at a high level ($911,200,000,000 in December), and many people seemed reluctant to take on more obligations. Sales of the big three auto manufacturers (Chrysler, Ford, and General Motors) declined by 1.7% from 1994 to 15,115,079 vehicles, while retailers had a disappointing Christmas season. Same store sales in December were up only 2.0% from a year earlier, compared with a 5.4% increase in 1994 over 1993. Though business and industry on the whole made healthy profits, and the stock market surged, shareholders and workers did not see much of the gains. In the 12 months

ending Oct. 31 wages rose only 2.7%, the smallest increase on record. It was, though, a banner year for mergers. More than 9000 deals, worth about $470,000,000,000, were registered. Among the most noteworthy deals, Cadbury Schweppes of Great Britain bought the Dr Pepper/Seven-Up companies for $1,700,000,000; two railroads, the Sante Fe Pacific Corp. and the Burlington Northern Corp., agreed to a $1,100,000,000 merger; and the Kimberly-Clark Corp. took over the Scott Paper Co. in a $7,000,000,000 deal, creating the second-largest consumer products company. In another deal the last U.S. manufacturer of television sets, the Zenith Electronics Corp., agreed to sell a controlling interest to a South Korean electronics firm. At a different economic level, government figures showed that 27,000,000 persons were receiving food stamps in late 1994; the number of persons receiving Aid to Families with Dependent Children was about 11,000,000. Another study found that poor children in the U.S. were worse off than poor children in 16 other industrialized nations. At another extreme, the average lawyer made $1,116 a week, but child care workers were paid only $158. The "glass ceiling" still existed for women and minorities: a federal survey found that white men, who made up 43% of the workforce, held about 95 out of every 100 senior management positions. Correspondingly, in another survey 84% of women polled said they faced more restrictions in life than men. At the same time, other data revealed that more than half of employed women provided about half their families' incomes. A major problem in higher education was the cost of college tuition, which went up about 6% in the 1994–1995 academic year; the average tuition for elite schools was now nearly $30,000 a year. At least partly as a result, the number of loans given through the Federal Family Education Loan Program rose to 6,700,000 in 1994, with the dollar total reaching $23,000,000,000. Meanwhile, college presidents seemed to be well paid, with John R. Silber of Boston University at the top with $564,020. In other developments, Harvard, Stanford, and the University of California at Berkeley were rated the leaders in the quality of their doctorate programs; a record 45,365 persons applied for admission to medical schools in 1994; only 10% of high school seniors read proficiently, a drop of 10% in two years. These same seniors did not know basic facts about American history, such as the meaning of the Monroe Doctrine. After a revision of the Scholastic Assessment Test in 1994, high school students in 1995 had the best scores in years; though males still outscored females, the gap narrowed to only three points in the verbal test. For the first time a woman cadet ranked first scholastically at the U.S. Military Academy. Jury awards for medical malpractice dropped in 1994 to an average of $977,000 from nearly $1,500,000 in the 1988–1993 period. But the number of Americans without health insurance reached 43,000,000, an increase of a million from the year before. The American Heart Association reported that 42.5% of all deaths in the U.S. were caused by heart disease or stroke, but a 1995 report said that the death rate from breast cancer dropped by nearly 5% during the 1989–1992 period. The proportion of American children who were overweight more than doubled in the last three decades. Three-quarters of American women did not get enough exercise, and in an index measuring maternal health, the U.S. ranked 18th internationally. The situation in the battle against AIDS did not improve: the disease was now the leading killer of Americans aged 24 to 44; it was spreading among men in the suburbs and rural areas; cases among women were increasing at a rate of about 17% a year; and three-quarters of new infections were among drug addicts. A survey found that the typical member of the Christian Coalition, the largest organization of religious conservatives, was a married white woman at least 55 years old; 68% of the members of the coalition were Republicans and only 4% were Democrats. In August the Clinton administration issued guidelines, or recommendations, on what kind of religious activities should be allowed in public schools: student prayer, if not organized by teachers or administrators; the wearing of religious clothing or symbols; saying grace before meals; providing school facilities for religious groups if such facilities are available to other private organizations. Not approved was teaching a particular religion, rather than teaching about religion, and "harassing" students to participate in prayer. In June the launching of the space shuttle *Discovery* was delayed for over a month when it was discovered that woodpeckers had drilled at least six dozen holes into the foam insulation that protected the external fuel tank. Among notable persons who died were Edward L. Bernays, leading opinion maker, called the "father of public relations," Mar. 9, at 103; Ernest L. Boyer, innovative educator who served as U.S. commissioner of education and president of the Carnegie Foundation for the Advancement of Teaching, Dec. 7, at 67; Subrahmanyan Chandrasekhar, Indian-born scientist who won a Nobel Prize in Physics for his discovery concerning the evolution of stars, Aug. 21, at 84; Georgia Neese Clark, who in 1949 became the first woman to be named U.S. treasurer, Oct. 26, at 95; William A. Fowler, astrophysicist and Nobel laureate who helped develop a theory concerning the creation of the elements, Mar. 14, at 83; Laurence McKinley Gould, Antarctic explorer and an innovative president of Carleton College, June 20, at 98; Herschel H. Hobbs, former president of the Southern Baptist Convention and chairman of the panel that in 1963 drafted a revised statement of the church's doctrine, Nov. 28, at 88; Carl H. Mau, Jr., clergyman, general secretary of the Lutheran World Federation (1974–1985), Mar. 31, at 72; Orville Redenbacher, who revolutionized the American popcorn industry, Sept. 19, at 88; Jonas Salk, who developed the first successful vaccine against poliomyelitis, June 23, at 80; Mar Athanasius Yeshue Samuel, archbishop and primate of the Syrian Orthodox Church in the U.S., Apr. 16, at 87; Jerome Theisen, the second American to lead the Benedictine order as abbot primate, Sept. 10, at 64; Eugene Wigner, winner of the Nobel Prize in Physics for advances he made in nuclear physics and quantum theory, Jan. 1, at 92.

Jan 11: "Compelling evidence" for the existence of **black holes** was announced by a team of American and Japanese scientists. The evidence consisted of a gigantic concentration of mass, equal to 40,000,000 suns, which was detected in the heart of a distant galaxy. Jets of gas were emerging at speeds of 400 miles a second.

Jan 30: The National Institutes of Health announced the development of the **first treatment for sickle cell anemia** that fights the underlying cause of the disease rather than merely combating the painful symptoms. The drawback was that the drug, hydroxyurea, should be considered for adult patients only. In the U.S. the disease primarily afflicts African Americans.

Feb 6: Two space shuttles flew within 37 feet of each other high above Earth when the U.S. *Discovery* and the Russian *Mir* met during the first American–Russian rendezvous in space since 1975. On board the *Discovery* was Eileen M. Collins, who became the first woman to pilot a NASA spacecraft.

Feb 20: Two large apparel unions, the International Ladies Garment Workers Union and the Amalgamated Clothing and Textile Workers Union, announced they would merge. The new organization, with more than 350,000 members, would be known as the Union of Needletrades, Industrial, and Textile Employees (UNITE).

Feb 21: The **Mexican economy** was rescued from collapse after the peso plunged and private Mexican banks came close to failing. By agreement, the U.S. provided Mexico with a $20,000,000,000 aid program. Additional international assistance in the form of loan guarantees brought the total aid package to $50,000,000,000.

Feb 26: A **trade agreement between the U.S. and China** ended threats of a trade war in which the U.S. would have levied sanctions amounting to $1,000,000,000 against Chinese goods. The agreement was intended to end Chinese piracy of intellectual property, such as movies, computer software, and compact disks. There was to be a tough six-month crackdown on suspected violators.

Feb 28: The **nation's first new major airport** in 21 years opened in Denver, Colo., 16 months behind schedule. The cost, $4,900,000,000, was $2,000,000,000 over budget; part of the excess was caused by trying to cure the faults in an ultramodern baggage system that chewed up bags.

Mar 8: The **longest shuttle flight** ended when the spacecraft *Endeavour* landed in California. During the 16-day, 15-hour mission 7 astronauts traveled 6,900,000 miles and circled Earth 262 times.

Mar 12: The **Church of Jesus Christ of Latter-day Saints** ordained Gordon B. Hinckley as its 15th president. Hinckley, 84, succeeded Howard W. Hunter, 87, who died on Mar. 3 after nine months in office.

Mar 17: The **first vaccine to prevent chicken pox** was approved by the Food and Drug Administration. The varicella zoster virus (VZV) vaccine would be given to children one year of age or older. About 4,000,000 persons catch the disease each year in the U.S.

Mar 26: **Six wolves** were set loose in Yellowstone National Park. The animals, which had been bought from Canadian trappers for $2000 each, were the first free-roaming wolves to live in the park in more than 50 years. Officials hoped that the wolves would multiply and keep down the growing population of elks and other animals, but ranchers, farmers, and some environmentalists protested.

Apr 9: It was announced that the **Seagram Company would buy 80% of MCA, Inc.** from the Matsushita Electric Industrial Company for $5,700,000,000. MCA was a dominant factor in movies, television, recordings, publishing, and theme parks. Seagram owned a large liquor business as well as a 15% stake in Time Warner, Inc. Matsushita had paid $6,600,000,000 for MCA in 1990.

Apr 26: The **New York Zoological Society** observed the 100th anniversary of its founding by Theodore Roosevelt and other wealthy hunters. The society, which had been active in conserving wildlife, opened the Bronx Zoo on Nov. 8, 1899.

May 19: The **world's youngest medical school graduate**, Balamurali Ambati, 17, received his diploma from Mount Sinai School of Medicine in New York City. He had graduated from college in two years at age 13.

May 24: Two scientists announced that the **entire DNA sequence** of a free-living organism had been deciphered for the first time. The organism was the bacterium known as *Hemophilus influenzae*.

May 25: A record for distance by a **battery-powered vehicle**, without recharging, was set at 238 miles at a road rally in New England. The car was a four-passenger vehicle manufactured by the Solectria Corp. of Wilmington, Mass.

June 14: The **source of the comets** that move among the planets was discovered, a team of scientists announced. The Hubble Space Telescope had detected icy, comet-sized objects on the fringes of the solar system in the Kulper Belt, the existence of which had previously been theoretical.

June 20: The **Southern Baptist Convention**, representing the largest Protestant denomination in the U.S., and which was founded in part in defense of slavery in 1845, voted to "repent racism of which we have been guilty." The resolution also asked forgiveness from "all African-Americans."

June 21: The **first black president of the American Medical Association** took office. He was Lonnie R. Bristow, M.D., a native of New York City.

June 26: The **largest health care organization** in the U.S. was created when the United Healthcare Corp. bought Metrohealth Companies in a $1,650,000,000 deal. The combined company would serve 14,140,000 people and have a combined revenue of more than $2,000,000,000 annually.

June 28: A **trade dispute with Japan** was settled after the U.S. threatened to place $5,900,000,000 in tariffs on Japanese luxury cars. The agreement called for Japan to buy more U.S. auto parts; to encourage U.S. car dealers in Japan; and to open its market to repair parts.

July 5: The **World Congress of the Seventh-Day Adventist Church**, meeting in Utrecht, the Netherlands, voted to reject a move to permit the ordination of women. However, on Sept. 23 The Sligo Seventh-Day Adventist Church of Takoma Park, Md., challenged the rule by ordaining three women. The church was established in the U.S. in 1863; one of its chief founders was a woman, Ellen White.

July 7: **After nearly two months in space,** American astronaut Norman E. Thagard returned to Earth. Thagard had spent the time, which set a record for Americans in space, aboard the Russian space station *Mir*. He returned aboard the American shuttle *Atlantis*, which had linked up with *Mir*.

July 13: A **bizarre kind of matter** that had been postulated by Albert Einstein had finally been created, scientists announced. Known as the Bose-Einstein condensate, the substance was a gas consisting of atoms chilled to such a low temperature that their motion was virtually halted.

July 20: Affirmative action came to an end at the University of California when the regents voted to stop admitting students, hiring professors, or awarding contracts on the basis of race and sex. In 1994 student enrollment was 49% white, 29% Asian, and 4% black.

July 27: Three large industrial unions, the steelworkers, the automobile workers, and the machinists, announced that they would merge. Their combined membership was about 2,000,000.

July 31: The **most powerful entertainment and media company** in the world to date was created when Capital Cities/ABC Inc. was acquired by the Walt Disney Company for $19,000,000,000. The combined firm would have revenues of nearly $17,000,000,000 a year.

Aug 1: The **Westinghouse Electric Corp. agreed to acquire CBS, Inc.,** the last independent television network, for $5,400,000,000. Though primarily an industrial manufacturing giant, Westinghouse already owned television and radio stations and produced programs. In recent years CBS had dropped to third place among the networks and had lost some of its most valuable affiliated stations.

Aug 18: The **first female ever admitted to The Citadel,** a South Carolina military academy, withdrew after four days because of illness. Shannon R. Faulkner fought a legal battle for more than two years against virulent opposition but became ill from heat on her first day. She had successfully contended that a school receiving government money could not discriminate on the basis of gender.

Aug 23: New computer software, **Windows 95,** was put on sale by Microsoft Corp. amid a frenzy of promotion and public anticipation. A million copies were sold within the first four days, at about $85 a copy, but then sales began to fall off and there was some criticism of the quality of the product.

Aug 28: The **largest bank in the U.S.** was created by the merger of the Chemical Banking Corp. and the Chase Manhattan Corp., both of New York. The deal was valued at almost $10,000,000,000, and the combined bank would have assets of $297,000,000,000.

Aug 31: A **new method for performing abortions** in early pregnancy was reported in *The New England Journal of Medicine.* The procedure used the drugs methotrexate and misoprostol, each of which was easily available by prescription.

Sep 20: AT&T announced that it would split into three separate companies in what would be the largest dismantling of a corporation in U.S. history. AT&T stock was valued at more than $101,000,000,000. The three new companies would

be involved in the operation of long-distance and wireless communications, the making and marketing of telephones and other equipment, and the manufacturing and selling of computer systems.

Sep 22: The **world's largest communications company** would result from the announced merger of the Turner Broadcasting System into Time Warner, Inc., with the latter securing 82% of the former for stock worth $7,500,000,000. The combined operation would have revenues of $19,800,000,000 and would own such well-known entities as *Time* magazine, CNN, and Warner Brothers.

Sep 30: Bishops of the Episcopal Church must allow women to be ordained in their dioceses, a conference of the bishops decided. The action was aimed at four bishops who had refused such ordination. The church had allowed the ordination of female priests since 1976.

Oct 2: The **largest single gift to medical research** was announced by Jon M. Huntsman, a billionaire chemical industry executive, who gave $100,000,000 for cancer research at the University of Utah.

Oct 9: The **Nobel Prize in Physiology or Medicine** was awarded jointly to two Americans, Edward B. Lewis of the California Institute of Technology and Eric F. Wieschaus of Princeton University, and to a German, Christiane Nüsslein-Volhard of the Max Planck Institute. They were honored for discovering how genes control the early structural development of the body.

Oct 10: The **Nobel Prize in Economic Science** was awarded to Robert E. Lucas of the University of Chicago for his influence on macroeconomic research. Lucas was the fifth member of the University of Chicago faculty to win this prize in the past six years.

Oct 11: The **Nobel Prize in Chemistry** was awarded jointly to two Americans, F. Sherwood Rowland of the University of California at Irvine and Mario Molina of the Massachusetts Institute of Technology, and to Paul Crutzen, a Dutch citizen working in Germany at the Max Planck Institute. The three were honored for their work in explaining the chemical processes that deplete Earth's ozone shield.

Oct 11: The **Nobel Prize in Physics** was awarded jointly to Martin L. Perl, of the Stanford Linear Accelerator Center, and Frederick Reines, an emeritus professor of the University of California at Irvine, for their discovery of two elusive subatomic particles, the tau and the neutrino.

Oct 18: John J. Sweeney was elected president of the AFL-CIO. An insurgent candidate for the post, Sweeney, who had been president of the Service Employees International Union for 15 years, promised more aggressive organizing efforts.

Nov 9: The **largest cash gift by a foreigner** to an American university was announced by Princeton University, which was to receive $100,000,000 from a graduate, Gordon Y.S. Wu, a Hong Kong businessman. The donation was to go to the School of Engineering and Applied Science.

Nov 19: Eighteen Pacific Rim nations, including the U.S., approved a plan for achieving free trade in the region by the year 2020 at a meeting of the Asia-Pacific Economic Cooperation Group (APEC) in Osaka, Japan. China announced that in 1996 it would cut tariffs on more than 4000 items by an average of at least 30%.

Nov 30: The **first photograph of a brown star** was announced by astronomers at the Palomar Observatory in California. The object photographed is a companion to the small star Gliese 229, 19 light-years away in the constellation Lepus. A brown star, theorized for three decades, is a brown dwarf that does not emit light like a star but is too massive and hot to be a planet.

Dec 7: Saquinavir, the first of a new class of drugs designed to fight the AIDS virus, was approved by the Food and Drug Administration (FDA). It was a member of a group of drugs called protease inhibits that attack the ability of the human immunodeficiency virus (HIV), which causes AIDS, to produce.

Dec 7: The spacecraft **Galileo** entered the orbit of Jupiter and launched an instrument-laden capsule into the planet's atmosphere. On Dec. 10 the first message from the probe was relayed to Earth from Galileo, which had taken six years to reach Jupiter and which was expected to orbit the planet for at least two more years. Release of the computerized messages was planned for the following summer.

Dec 13: Bone marrow from a baboon was injected into a 38-year-old man with AIDS in a cross-species experiment acknowledged to be extremely risky. The injected cells were thought to be resistant to the AIDS virus and so might save the man's damaged immune system.

Dec 14: A **new treatment for stroke** that in some cases could prevent irreversible brain damage was announced. The clot-dissolving drug, T.P.A., was to be given intravenously and would cost $2000 to administer.

Dec 21: The **remains of a nesting dinosaur** that died 80,000,000 years ago while sitting on its eggs was found in the Gobi Desert of Mongolia, scientists from the American Museum of Natural History, New York City, reported. The fossil remains were those of an Oviraptor, and resembled a small ostrich with a tail. There were at least 15 eggs. The discovery provided strong support for an evolutionary link between dinosaurs and modern birds.

Dec 22: The halfway point in **mapping human genes** was reached by researchers at the Whitehead Institute for Biomedical Research in Cambridge, Mass., and at Genethon in France. The researchers were in the process of identifying markers to guide them in locating the approximately 100,000 human genes.

Dec 31: The **Dow Jones industrial stock average** closed the year at 5117.12, an increase of 33.5%. In the course of 1995 the average passed both the 4000 and the 5000 marks, and on Dec. 13 reached an all-time high of 5216.47. On Dec. 15 the NYSE registered its largest trading volume ever when 653,200,000 shares changed hands.

IV. Fashion
Folkways
Holidays
Social Issues and Crime
Sports

The NBA set an attendance record of 18,516,484 for the 1994–1995 season, but otherwise sports news in 1995 mostly concerned money: Super Bowl XXIX sponsors paid an average of $1,000,000 for each of the 60 30-second commercial spots; the New York Yankees had a total payroll of $54,889,849, which meant an average salary of just over $2,000,000 per player; two members of the Baseball Hall of Fame, Duke Snider and Willie McCovey, pleaded guilty to federal charges of tax fraud for failing to report money earned for signing autographs; the New York Knicks of the NBA doubled the price of seats for a game viewed from the VIP row to $1000; Mike Tyson's comeback prizefight, which lasted only 89 seconds, had a worldwide gross of more than $96,000,000; in August Greg Norman became the leading career money winner on the PGA tour when his earnings reached $9,493,579. As usual there was sensational crime news: in California Lester Suff was convicted of having murdered 12 prostitutes; also in California, nine people were shot to death in two days, five by hooded gunmen in a bar robbery, four when a disgruntled electrician went after his superiors. On the whole, though, figures for 1994 showed a decrease of 3% nationally in major crimes; for the first half of 1995 the number of homicides reported in major cities dropped by 12%. Fifty-six persons were executed for murder in 1995. Bad news came in the form of a Justice Dept. report that stated that the number of arrests of juveniles for violent crimes would double by the year 2010 because of the expected increase of 20% in the juvenile population. In 1994 the number of persons in federal and state prisons and local jails reached 1,500,000, with 3,500,000 convicted criminals out on parole. There was an increase in inmates' assaults on prison guards, up 20% in 1994. Prison inmates accounted for nearly 7% of all black males, but only 1% of all adult white males. The Brady law, intended to restrict the sale of handguns, seemed to be having some effect: 45,000 felons were not allowed to buy guns after their records were reviewed. In 1994 alcohol-related traffic deaths dropped to 16,884, the lowest figure in a dozen years. In August Tommy Lee Farmer went to prison for life; he was the first person to be sentenced under a new federal law that called for such a term if a person were convicted of three violent crimes. Antismoking activity increased, but the tobacco industry battled back. Though Philip Morris, the world's largest tobacco company, fought regulation, it was revealed in June that it had sponsored studies showing that nicotine affected the body, brain, and behavior of smokers. Partly as a result, Pres. Clinton proposed that the FDA begin a process aimed at declaring nicotine a drug and so pave the way for government regulation. A poll showed that a large majority of Americans favored government action to prevent children from smoking. Philip Morris, which in May had recalled 8,000,000,000 cigarettes because of imperfect filters that caused throat irritation, announced on June 27 a $5,000,000 campaign, called "Action Against Access," to curb cigarette sales to young people. The company had also agreed to remove from stadiums and sports arenas cigarette advertising that might be seen on television. Nevertheless, a survey of 8th-, 10th-, and 12th-graders found that smoking among these age groups had increased by 30% from 1991 to 1994. Meanwhile, cigar smoking enjoyed new popularity, largely among affluent males, imports of premium cigars having increased 29% in three years to more than 120,000,000. Hollywood celebrities, regardless of the occasion, were said to favor for footwear Hush Puppies, J.P. Tod's, and Gucci. Also popular in the fashion world were black ankle boots, worn half-laced. The use of sexuality to sell clothes reached a new low when a new Calvin Klein promotional campaign featured teenagers in tasteless poses. On Aug. 28 Klein withdrew the ads and posters and apologized. Sexually active teenagers were decreasing in number, leveling off at 53%. Among them only 52.8% were using condoms. Two-thirds of Americans now use seat belts. The suicide rate among children 10 to 14 years of age was increasing. Forty-two percent of mothers surveyed said they had spanked their children that week. Snack—or junk—food consumption was high, with Americans eating 5,700,000,000 pounds of salty snacks, such as potato chips, at a cost of $15,000,000,000 a year. Notable persons who died included Al Barlick, National League umpire for 32 years and only the sixth umpire to be admitted to the Baseball Hall of Fame, Dec. 27, at 80; Margaret Gorman Cahill, who became the first Miss America in 1921, Oct. 1, at 9?; Florence Chadwick, long-distance swimmer, who crossed the English Channel four times, setting records, Mar. 15, at 76; Douglas "Wrong-Way" Corigan, aviator, who in 1938 flew from Brooklyn to Ireland, but claimed that he had intended to fly to California, Dec. 9, at 88; Howard Cosell, for 30 years an outspoken and controversial sports broadcaster, Apr. 23, at 77; Rick Ferrell, major league baseball catcher for 18 years, member of the Hall of Fame, July 27, at 89; Pancho Gonzalez, two-time national tennis champion, July 3, at 67; Nat Holman, star basketball player and coach of championship teams at C.C.N.Y., Feb. 12, at 98; Jim Lee Howell, who as player and coach led the Giants of the NFL to seven titles, Jan. 4, at 80; Ron Luciano, major league baseball umpire, known for his flamboyant style and his entertaining reminiscences, Jan. 18, at 57; Mickey Mantle of the New York Yankees, one of baseball's greatest all-time sluggers and fielders, Aug. 13, at 63; Vera Maxwell, pioneer designer of sportswear for women, Jan. 15, at 93; Lindsey Nelson, broadcast voice of the New York Mets for 17 years, June 10, at 76; Alice Greenough Orr, for two decades rodeo queen of the bronco riders, Aug. 20, at 93; Harvey Penick, golf instructor whose witty book about the game became the bestselling sports book of all time, Apr. 2, at 90; Bobby Riggs, tennis champion, but best remembered for his three-set loss in 1973 to Billie Jean King, Oct. 25, at 77; Adele Simpson, a leading fashion designer after World War II, Aug. 23, at 91; Marion Tinsley, who held the world checkers championship from 1955 to 1994, Apr. 3, at 68; Zoilo Versalles, Cuban-born shortstop who in 1965 became the first Latin American to be named most valuable player in either of the major leagues, June 9, at 55.

Jan 1: In **college football bowl games** the results were: Nebraska 24, Miami 17 in the Orange Bowl; Southern California 55, Texas Tech 14 in the Cotton Bowl; Florida State 23, Florida 17 in the Sugar Bowl; Penn State 38, Oregon 20 in the Rose Bowl. The AP and the *USA Today/*CNN polls voted Nebraska the national collegiate champion of 1994.

Jan 6: Lenny Wilkens became the winningest coach in NBA history when his Atlanta Hawks beat the

Washington Bullets, giving him his 939th victory. The previous record had been held by Red Auerbach, who coached the Boston Celtics for 20 seasons.

Jan 9: Elected to the **Baseball Hall of Fame** was Michael Jack Schmidt, Philadelphia Phillies third baseman, in his first year of eligibility and with the largest number of votes ever cast for one player. On Mar. 7 the Veterans Committee elected Richie Ashburn, hard-hitting center fielder. The committee also chose Leon Day, a star of the onetime Negro League; Vic Willis, a turn-of-the-century pitcher; and William Hulbert, an organizer of the National League.

Jan 11: A **NHL lockout** of the league's players ended after 103 days when the owners and the players reached a collective bargaining agreement. The 1994–1995 season was to consist of 48 games instead of the usual 84.

Jan 25: The **International Tennis Hall of Fame** elected Chris Evert. Evert, the holder of 18 grand slam championships, became only the fourth person to be elected unanimously.

Jan 29: Super Bowl XXIX was won by the San Francisco 49ers (NFC), who defeated the San Diego Chargers (AFC) 49–26. The 49ers had won the NFC championship by defeating the Dallas Cowboys 38–28, while the Chargers had won the AFC title by beating the Pittsburgh Steelers 17–13.

Feb 9: Darryl Strawberry, baseball star noted for his home runs, pleaded guilty in a federal court to having evaded more than $100,000 in income taxes. Although he was not sentenced to prison, he was penalized by having restrictions placed on his personal activities.

Feb 11: U.S. figure skating championships were won by Todd Eldredge, men's singles, and Nicole Bobek, women's singles.

Feb 21: The **distance record for balloons** was broken by Steve Fossett when he landed in Canada, about 250 miles northeast of Helena, Mont. He had left Seoul, South Korea, on Feb. 18; his craft covered about 5430 miles during the flight.

Mar 9: Major League Baseball voted to create two new teams to begin play in 1998. They were to be called the Tampa Bay Devil Rays and the Arizona Diamondbacks; each would pay an entrance fee of $130,000,000.

Mar 9–26: At the **Pan American Games** in Mar del Plata, Argentina, the U.S. won 169 gold medals and 424 in all. Cuba was second with 112 and 238. The U.S. sent 750 of the more than 7000 athletes who participated in the games.

Mar 22: Colin Ferguson, who on Dec. 7, 1993, shot to death 6 persons and wounded 19 others on a Long Island Railroad commuter train, was sentenced to the maximum term of 200 years to life.

Mar 31: A **234-day strike of major league baseball players** ended when a federal judge issued an injunction against the club owners. The 1995 season was to start on Apr. 26 and consist of 144 games instead of the normal 162.

Apr 2: The **NCAA women's basketball championship** was won by Connecticut, which defeated Tennessee 70–64. Connecticut ended an undefeated season with 35 victories.

Apr 3: The **NCAA men's basketball championship** was won by UCLA, which defeated Arkansas 89–78.

Apr 9: The **Masters golf tournament** was won by Ben Crenshaw by one stroke. The victory was his second in the event.

Apr 12: The **NFL team owners** voted to allow the Rams, who were playing in Anaheim, Calif., to move to St. Louis, Mo. The Rams were to pay $46,000,000 to the NFL in a step intended to improve their attendance and their finances.

Apr 17: Wayne Gretzky, star hockey player of the Los Angeles Kings, became the first NHL player to score 2500 career points.

Apr 17: The 99th **Boston Marathon** was won in the men's division for the third time in succession by Cosmas N'Deti of Kenya with a time of 2 hrs., 9 min., 22 sec. The women's division was won for the second successive year by Uta Pippig of Germany with a time of 2 hrs., 25 min., 11 sec.

Apr 18: Joe Montana, generally acknowledged to be the greatest quarterback in pro football history, announced his retirement. He had played for 16 seasons for the San Francisco 49ers and the Kansas City Chiefs. Montana had passed for a total of 40,551 yards, including 273 touchdowns, in regular season play.

May 8: The 121st **Kentucky Derby** was won by Thunder Gulch with a time of 2:01 1/5. The jockey was Gary Stevens.

May 13: The **America's Cup** was won by the New Zealand yacht *Black Magic I* with a 5–0 sweep of the U.S. yacht *Young America*. The victory marked only the second time in the 144-year history of the cup that it had not been won by an American boat.

May 14: The **LPGA championship** was won by Kelly Robbins by one stroke.

May 20: The 120th **Preakness Stakes** was won by Timber Country with a time of 1:54 2/5. The jockey was Pat Day.

May 25: The **Quebec Nordiques** of the NHL were sold for $75,000,000; later in the year the franchise would move to Denver, Colo.

May 28: A **major league record** was set by the Chicago White Sox and the Detroit Tigers when their batters combined to hit 12 home runs in one game. An American League record of 21 extra-base hits was also set.

May 28: The **Indianapolis 500 auto race** was won by Jacques Villeneuve of Canada, who finished with an average speed of 153.616 mph. It was only Villeneuve's second attempt to win the event.

June 8: Faster major league baseball games were the object of a number of new rules and suggestions. Among them were less time for TV commercials; keeping batters from wandering in and out of the batter's box; and ordering umpires to call the "high strike."

June 14: The **NBA basketball championship** was won by the Houston Rockets, who defeated the Orlando Magic four games to none. It was the Rocket's second successive title.

June 18: The **U.S. Men's Open golf championship** was won by Corey Pavin by two strokes. Pavin finished the event at even par, the highest winning score since 1979.

June 21: An **ex-convict was shot and killed** by police after a five-day murderous rampage in New Jersey and New York, during which he killed seven people and injured three others. Darnell Collins had been released from prison on parole after having served 10 years for armed robbery.

June 24: The **NHL Stanley Cup** was won by the New Jersey Devils, who swept the Detroit Red Wings four games to none. It was the Devils first Stanley Cup victory.

June 25: With her 30th tournament victory, Betsy King entered the **LPGA Hall of Fame.** She automatically joined 13 others already in the hall.

June 27: The 127th **Belmont Stakes** was won by Thunder Gulch with a time of 2:32, the slowest since 1970. The jockey was Gary Stevens.

June 29: A **man who fired at the White House** on Oct. 29, 1994, was sentenced to 40 years in prison by a federal judge. Francisco Martin Duran, an upholsterer from Colorado Springs, Colo., had shot at least two dozen bullets.

June 30: Eddie Murray of the Cleveland Indians became the 20th player in major league baseball history to record 3000 hits. Murray's first hit was on Sept. 7, 1977.

July 9: The **Wimbledon men's tennis championship** was won for the third straight year by Pete Sampras of the U.S. He defeated Boris Becker of Germany in four sets.

July 11: The **All-Star baseball game** was won by the National League, which defeated the American League 3–2 for its second victory in a row.

July 16: The **U.S. Women's Open golf tournament** was won by Annika Sorenstam of Sweden by one stroke. The victory was her first tournament victory in the U.S.

July 21: The **NFL voted to allow the Raiders** to move from Los Angeles back to Oakland, Calif., which the team had left 13 years before.

July 23: The **British Open golf tournament** was won by John Daly of the U.S. in a four-hole playoff.

July 28: A **South Carolina mother,** Susan Smith, was sentenced to life imprisonment after having been convicted of murdering her two small sons by drowning them. She had claimed at first that the boys had been abducted.

Aug 13: The **PGA championship** was won by Steve Elkington by one stroke. Elkington finished with a record low 267 strokes for this event.

Aug 19: Mike Tyson, former heavyweight boxing champion, in his first fight since his release from jail where he had served a three-year term for rape, knocked out Peter McNeeley in 89 seconds of the first round. Of the $70,000,000 the bout took in, Tyson received $25,000,000.

Aug 23: Phil Rizzuto, former New York Yankee star and member of the Baseball Hall of Fame, announced that he was retiring as a radio and television announcer of Yankee games after 39 years at the microphone.

Sep 6: By playing in his **2131st consecutive game,** Cal Ripken, Baltimore Orioles shortstop, broke a record held for 56 years by Lou Gehrig of the New York Yankees. By the end of the season Ripken's total was 2153. His streak began on May 30, 1982.

Sep 9–10: The **U.S. Open tennis championships** were won in the women's division by Steffi Graf of Germany, and in the men's division by Pete Sampras.

Sep 11: In Owega, N.Y., Waneta D. Hoyt was convicted of having **smothered to death** five of her children between 1965 and 1971. Hoyt was sentenced to at least 75 years in prison.

Sep 16: The **Miss America title** was won by Shawntel Smith, 24, Miss Oklahoma, at the annual pageant in Atlantic City. In a ballot conducted among TV viewers, the vote favored continuing the swimsuit competition, which had been criticized in recent years in feminist circles.

Sep 18: The **NBA team owners lockout** of the league's players ended following the ratification by the players on Sept. 15 of a new six-year labor agreement. The lockout began on June 30.

Sep 29: The **Benevolent and Protective Order of Elks** changed the wording of its constitution to make women eligible for membership. The BPOE had 2230 lodges with 1,300,000 members, all men.

Oct 3: O(renthal) J(ames) Simpson, former star athlete and actor, was acquitted of the murder of his former wife, Nicole Brown Simpson, and her friend, Ronald L. Goldman, by a Los Angeles jury that deliberated for less than four hours. Simpson had been held in prison for 474 days, and the jury had been sequestered for the 264 days of the unusually long trial.

Oct 7: Eddie Robinson of Grambling State University became the first football coach to win 400 games when his team defeated Mississippi Valley State, 42–6. Robinson had been Grambling's head coach since 1941 and had compiled a 400–145–15 record.

Oct 10: The **world chess championship** was retained by Gary Kasparov of Russia when he defeated Viswanathan Anand of India, 10 1/2 to 7 1/2 games in a match that began Sept. 11 in New York City. Kasparov's winner's purse was $900,000.

Oct 18: For dropping a 5-year-old boy from the 14th floor of a building in Chicago and killing him, an 11-year-old boy and a 12-year-old boy were found guilty of murder. They said they did it because the victim refused to steal candy for them. On Jan. 29, 1996, both were sentenced to maximum security juvenile prisons, the younger child, now 12 years old, becoming the youngest person in the country confined in a maxiumum-security prison.

Oct 18: The **Winnipeg Jets of the NHL** were sold for $68,000,000 and were to move to Phoenix, Ariz., for the 1996–1997 season.

Oct 21–28: The **World Series** was won by the Atlanta Braves (NL), who defeated the Cleveland Indians (AL) four games to two. The Braves had won the National League championship by beating the Cincinnati Reds, while the Indians took the American League title by defeating the Seattle Mariners. Atlanta's victory marked the first time that a baseball franchise had won the series while playing in three different cities; the other titles had been won by the Boston Braves (1914) and the Milwaukee Braves (1957).

Oct 27: A **sniper shot and killed one soldier** at Fort Bragg, N.C., and wounded 18 others. The incident occurred as troops of the 82nd Airborne Division were starting an early morning run. The suspect in the shooting was identified as Sgt. William Kreutzer, a member of the division.

Oct 28: A **single-season earnings record** for a thoroughbred racehorse was set by Cigar when he won the Breeders' Cup Classic at Belmont Park, N.Y. The victory brought his total to $4,819,800.

Oct 29: A **career record for pass receiving yardage** in the NFL was set by Jerry Rice of the San Francisco 49ers in a game with the New Orleans Saints, when his total reached 14,040 yards.

Nov 6: The **Cleveland Browns of the NFL** announced that they would move to Baltimore, Md., beginning with the 1996 season. The team was promised a new $200,000,000 stadium. In 1984 the Baltimore Colts moved to Indianapolis, Ind.

Nov 7: Three American servicemen pleaded guilty at Naha, Okinawa, Japan, in a case involving charges of abducting and raping a 12-year-old Okinawan schoolgirl. Seaman Marcus D. Gill admitted his guilt on all counts, while two marines, Kendrick M. Ledet and Rodrico Harp, denied raping and beating the girl but admitted guilt on other charges. The incident fueled the long-standing resentment of Okinawans against the overwhelming presence on the island of the American military.

Nov 12: The 26th **New York City Marathon** was won in the men's division by German Silva of Mexico with a time of 2 hrs., 11 min. The women's division was won by Tegla Loroupe of Kenya with a time of 2 hrs., 28 min., 6 sec. Both runners repeated their triumphs of 1994.

Nov 13: A **record for winning the Cy Young Award** was set by Greg Maddux, right-handed pitcher for the Atlanta Braves, who was voted the honor for the fourth consecutive year. His record for the 1995 season was 19 wins and 2 losses, with an earned run average of 1.63.

Dec 3: The **Davis Cup**, emblematic of international tennis supremacy, was won by the U.S. for the first time since 1992 when the American team defeated the Russian team in Moscow three matches to two.

Dec 12: NBC agreed to pay $2,300,000,000 for **broadcast and cable rights to future Olympic games.** The agreement covered the 2004 Summer Olympics, the 2006 Winter Olympics, and the 2008 Summer Olympics. The deal was the most expensive in television sports history.

1996

I. Civil Rights
Exploration and Settlement
Government
Statistics
Wars

A wave of burnings of black churches, attributed to arson with racist overtones, struck the South. By midyear there had been at least 30 such incidents in the previous 18 months. On June 8, Pres. Bill Clinton increased federal efforts to investigate these fires. Forest fires flared in most of the Western states and Alaska; by fall, more than 6,000,000 acres had been destroyed, the most since 1952. More than 150 homes burned down in Alaska and 100 or more in California. The fires damaged ancient Indian sites in Colorado and for a time threatened the Los Alamos National Laboratory in New Mexico. At the same time, drought severely damaged crops in the Southwest. Oklahoma suffered its second driest period in 101 years. The Census Bureau reported that the quality of life was improving for many black families: family income of blacks was rising faster than that of white households, as blacks in 1995 earned 87% as much as whites, up from 79% in 1989. Meanwhile, Americans were filing for bankruptcy at a record rate: 1,100,000 were expected in 1996, an increase of 25% in one year. The average amount owed by bankrupts rose from about $90,000 in 1992 to nearly $130,000 in 1996. Some people, though, were not suffering. *Worth* magazine found Rolling Hills, Calif., a suburb of Los Angeles, to be the wealthiest town in the U.S., followed by Hewlett Bay Park on Long Island. Some of those not-so-well-off owed the federal government, for loans in various categories, a total of $126,000,000,000, an increase of $26,000,000,000 in 2 years. The American Bar Association found that women were still not being treated on an equal basis with men in the nation's law firms. Though 23% of all lawyers were now women, they were not as likely to be promoted, nor did they earn as much, as men. Only 12% of federal judges were women. The Census Bureau issued some predictions for the year 2050: the nation's population was expected to rise to 364,000,000, and only 53% of the people were to be non-Hispanic whites, compared with 73% in 1996. Hispanics were expected to comprise 24.9% of the population, up from the present 10.2%, while the black population was likely to increase only to 13.6%,

up from the current 12.0%. The nation was also getting older: there were now 1,370,000 people over 90, an increase of 23% in 4 years. Working Americans spent an average of 22.4 minutes getting to work, with 86.5% of them using autos. Donations to charity increased by 11% to $143,900,000,000 in 1995, the largest increase since 1986. Religion was by far the favorite charity, receiving $63,450,000,000, followed by education at $17,940,000,000. Notable persons who died included Spiro T. Agnew, 39th vice president of the U.S., who resigned the office in 1973 in the face of income tax invasion charges, Sept. 17, at 77; Melvin Belli, flamboyant lawyer who won many notable lawsuits, July 9, at 88; Edmund G. "Pat" Brown, twice (1959-1967) governor of California, Feb. 16, at 90; Herbert Brownell Jr., who, as attorney general under Pres. Eisenhower, speeded school integration in the 1950s, May 1, at 92; McGeorge Bundy, foreign policy adviser to Kennedy and Johnson in the 1960s, who advocated increased involvement in the Vietnam War, Sept. 16, at 77; Arleigh A. Burke, admiral, a hero of the war against Japan in the South Pacific, Jan. 1, at 94; William E. Colby, director of the CIA at a time of upheaval in the 1970s, Apr. 27, at 76; J. Edward Day, former U.S. postmaster general, who introduced the five-digit ZIP code in 1963, Oct. 29, at 82; Eleanor Lansing Dulles, State Department economist who largely planned the reconstruction of West Berlin after World War II, Oct. 30, at 101; Hamilton Fish Jr., New York Republican, fourth generation of his family to serve in Congress (1969–1994), July 23, at 70; Alger Hiss, central figure in one of the abiding mysteries of the Cold War, convicted of perjury in an espionage case, Nov. 15, at 92; Barbara Jordan, black congresswoman, first of her race elected from Texas since the Reconstruction era, Jan. 17, at 59; Edmund S. Muskie, Maine Democrat who served as state's governor and as U.S. senator and secretary of state, Mar. 26, at 81; Loret Ruppe, who revived the Peace Corps after her appointment as its head in 1981, Aug. 6, at 60; Carl B. Stokes, who became in 1967 the first black elected mayor of a major U.S. city, Cleveland, Apr. 4, at 68; Elbert P. Tuttle, federal appeals judge who played a major role in extending civil rights to black southerners, June 23, at 98; Ralph Yarborough, Texas Democrat, the only senator from the deep South to vote for the 1964 Civil Rights Act, Jan.. 27, at 92.

Jan 7: The **Blizzard of 1996**, a main component of the long, hard winter of 1995–1996, struck the eastern U.S., leaving more than two feet of snow in major cities and crippling transportation and business. Several dozen persons died. A second storm, almost as severe, struck the New York City metropolitan area on Jan. 12. Other parts of the country were not spared: a blizzard hit the northern Plains states on Jan. 18, while melting snow and ice as well as heavy rains brought devastating floods to Washington State, Idaho and, especially, Oregon. Meanwhile, the Northeast also suffered floods when the blizzards' snows melted. Most of Wilkes-Barre, Pa., had to be evacuated. In early February bitter cold swept most of the country from the Rockies to the Great Lakes, and then moved into the South, threatening citrus crops. At the same time, the Northeast had its third big snowstorm of the winter.

Jan 17: Sheik Omar Abdel Rahman, a blind Islamic cleric, was sentenced in federal court in New York City to life imprisonment after having been convicted of plotting bombings and assassinations meant to end U.S. support for Israel and Egypt. Nine codefendants were given sentences ranging from 25 years to life.

Jan 19: A **spill of 820,000 gallons of heating oil** near a Rhode Island beach caused the closing of a 105-sq.-mi. area to fishing. The accident occurred when a barge carrying 4,000,000 gallons of oil ran aground after a fire broke out on its tugboat.

Jan 26: Start II, a major arms reduction treaty, signed three years before by U.S. Pres. George Bush and Pres. Boris Yeltsin of Russia, was finally approved by the Senate, 87-4. The pact had not yet been ratified by the Russian parliament.

Feb 8: Major changes in the telecommunications industry were assured when Pres. Clinton signed into law a bill to bring wide open competition among telephone companies, long-distance carriers, cable television operators, and even electric utilities. One result was expected to be a wave of mergers and acquisitions, and the end of monopolies such as those enjoyed by local telephone companies and cable TV operators.

Feb 10: Pres. Clinton signed a $265,000,000 defense bill, but said that he was not going to enforce a provision in it that required the Pentagon to discharge service people who had the virus that causes AIDS.

Feb 12: A **westbound Amtrak train** collided with a local commuter train just outside Washington, D.C., killing 12 and injuring 20 people. The commuter train was supposed to have stopped until the Amtrak express passed it.

Feb 24: Cuban jet fighter aircraft shot down two small planes that belonged to a Cuban refugee and exile assistance group based in Miami, Fla. The flight of the aircraft was a protest against the Castro regime. Pres. Clinton suspended all air charter travel between the U.S. and Cuba and said that he was going to ask Congress to approve a bill that would tighten economic sanctions against Cuba.

Mar 7: Three American servicemen, two from the Marine Corps and one from the navy, were convicted in Okinawa, Japan, by a Japanese court of the abduction and rape of a 12-year-old Japanese girl. Two of them were sentenced to 7 years in prison and the other to 6 1/2.

Mar 8: Strom Thurmond, Republican senator of South Carolina, at the age of 93 years and 94 days, became the oldest person ever to serve in the U.S. Senate.

Mar 13: More than two dozen **world leaders,** including Pres. Clinton, met in Egypt to encourage the peace process in the Middle East, especially the ongoing negotiations between Israel and the Palestinian Authority. The meeting was also meant to isolate those states, such as Iran, Iraq, Libya, and the Sudan, that were regarded as encouraging terrorism.

Apr 3: Ronald H. Brown, the U.S. secretary of commerce, and 34 others, mostly American corporate executives, were killed when their military plane crashed into a mountain as it approached the airport at Dubrovnik, Croatia. An investigation found that U.S. Air Force commanders had not carried out a safety inspection of the airport.

Apr 9: A **line-item veto bill** became law when it was signed by Pres. Clinton. It gave the president power to veto specific items in spending and tax bills without rejecting the whole measure. However, Congress retained its power to overturn such vetoes.

Apr 10: A bill intended to outlaw a certain type of **late-term abortion** was vetoed by Pres. Clinton. The procedure, only performed after 20 weeks of gestation, is known as "partial birth" abortion.

Apr 21: At a **summit meeting** in Moscow, Pres. Clinton and Pres. Boris Yeltsin of Russia spoke enthusiastically of the American-Russian partnership, but avoided settling a number of differences in policies.

Apr 24: A bill to **fight terrorism** was signed into law by Pres. Clinton. It provided new tools and new penalties to be used against terrorism. The law also provided that inmates on death row must initiate their final state proceedings within six months before filing federal habeous corpus petitions.

Apr 25: A **long battle over the budget** for the fiscal year that had begun on Oct. 1, 1995, was finally settled when Congress passed a spending bill that Pres. Clinton said he intended to sign the next day. Both the Democrats and the Republicans gained and lost some of the measures they had sought. Early in the year, much of the federal government had been shut down twice when Congress and the White House could not agree on temporary spending measures.

May 2: An omnibus measure concerning **AIDS** was approved by both Congress and Pres. Clinton. It extended federal assistance for five years and was intended to increase the voluntary testing of pregnant women for the AIDS virus, HIV.

May 11: A **Valujet Airlines DC-9 crashed** into the Florida Everglades shortly after taking off from Miami, killing all 109 persons on board. The water and mire into which the plane plunged made it impossible to recover all the bodies. Some chemical devices, put aboard the plane by mistake, were believed to have started a fire and explosion.

May 13: A **ban on advertising liquor prices** was struck down by the Supreme Court, 9-0. The court said that a Rhode Island law violated the First Amendment's guarantee of freedom of speech.

May 15: Sen. **Robert Dole**, assured of the Republican party nomination for president later in the year, announced that he was going to resign from the Senate, where he was majority leader, by June 11 in order to devote all his time to running for the presidency. He had been in Congress for 35 years.

May 15: U.S. troops were likely to stay in **Bosnia**, Pres. Clinton said, for an additional 18 months after 20,000 peace-keeping troops had been sent there for a tour of about one year. On Dec. 17, NATO defense ministers approved a new American-led force, to consist of troops from the U.S. and 24 other countries.

May 16: Admiral **Jeremy Boorda,** chief of naval operations, committed suicide after he learned that he was to be accused of not having earned two Vietnam War combat decorations he had been wearing. Boorda had been the first sailor to climb from the lowest enlisted ranks to four-star admiral.

May 17: A bill requiring that states issue warnings to communities when **convicted sex offenders** settle in them was signed into law by Pres. Clinton.

May 20: Future laws protecting the **rights of homosexuals** cannot be banned in advance, the Supreme Court decided, 6-3. The ruling nullified a 1992 amendment to the Colorado constitution which was to have both killed any such existing laws and banned future ones.

May 20: A **punitive damage award** was overturned for the first time by the Supreme Court, 5-4. The court found that a $2,000,000 award to an Alabama man was "grossly excessive" enough to violate the constitutional requirement of due process of law.

June 3: The **death penalty in the military** was upheld by the Supreme Court, 9-0. A suit had questioned the constitutionality of an executive order Pres. Ronald Reagan had issued in 1984.

June 13: The use of **race as a criterion in legislative districting** was found unconstitutional by the Supreme Court, 5-4. One congressional district in North Carolina and three in Texas were affected. These district lines had been drawn after the 1990 census to give minority voters more influence.

June 13: After resisting for 81 days, the last 16 members of **the Freemen**, a right-wing group in Montana, surrendered to federal officials. Fourteen members of the antigovernment group were to face charges of threatening federal officers and of defrauding banks and businesses of more than $1,800,000. Government agents had gone out of their way to avoid the use of force during the confrontation.

June 17 An **agreement to curb piracy** of music, movies, and computer materials in China was reached by that country and the U.S. Compact disc factories were to be closed and attempted exports more closely controlled. The U.S. had threatened China with the imposition of $2,000,000,000 in import penalties if an agreement was not reached.

June 24: **Seizure of property** of someone accused of a crime does not violate the constitutional ban on double jeopardy, even though the accused is also prosecuted on criminal charges, the Supreme Court ruled, 8-1 and 9-0 in two cases involving this matter.

June 25: A **truck bomb** exploded near Dhahran, Saudi Arabia, killing 19 American military personnel and wounding more than 300 people. Bombed was an apartment complex that housed about 2500 Americans. There were no solid clues about the identity of the perpetrators.

June 28: **Strict limits on federal courts appeals** by state prisoners, as embodied in a recently enacted law, was unanimously upheld by the Supreme Court. The case in question involved a section of the law that limited the right of state prisoners who had filed one habeas corpus petition in federal court to file more.

July 12: Two hurricanes, Bertha and Fran (Sept. 6), struck the same stretch of coastal North Carolina. Fran killed at least 28 people, and both storms did great damage to property, crops, and the region's infrastructure. Bertha also struck Puerto Rico (July 8), killing at least 5 people.

July 17: A **Trans World Airlines Boeing 747 jet blew up** over the Atlantic Ocean a few minutes after taking off from Kennedy International Airport in New York City. All 230 persons aboard were killed. A long investigation did not clear up the question of the cause of the blast; speculation focused on the possibility of a missile, a bomb on board, or an internal explosion of a fuel tank.

July 27: The **Summer Olympic Games** in Atlanta, Ga., were disrupted by a bomb explosion in Centennial Olympic Park that killed 1 person and injured more than 100. Thousands of persons were watching a concert.

Aug 5: A bill intended to impose **sanctions on foreign companies** that make large investments in Iran or Libya was signed into law by Pres. Clinton. Aimed at the two countries as "dangerous supporters of terrorism," the law denied certain forms of U.S. assistance to foreign countries that invested heavily in either of the two countries. Germany and France at once protested the measure.

Aug 6: A bill to help states **upgrade water systems** was signed by Pres. Clinton. The measure created a fund of $9,600,000,000 for grants and loans, and revised federal drinking water standards.

Aug 20: The **minimum wage** was to rise eventually to $5.15 per hour under a new law signed by Pres. Clinton. On Oct. 1, the new rate was to rise to $4.75 an hour, up from $4.25, and was to increase to $5.15 on Sept. 1, 1997.

Aug 21: Access to **health insurance** was expected to expand as a result of a bill signed into law by Pres. Clinton. The legislation enabled workers to keep their health insurance coverage when they changed or lost their jobs. Insurance companies could not deny insurance to people who had preexisting medical conditions.

Aug 22: A bill intended to reform radically the nation's **welfare system** was signed by Pres. Clinton. The states were to receive block grants; the guarantee of assistance for poor children was to end; work was to be required of welfare recipients after two years; and lifetime welfare benefits were to be limited to five years.

Aug 22: Destruction of an enormous stockpile of **chemical weapons** began at an army depot in Utah. A total of 11,000 tons of mustard and nerve gas at eight bases was to be destroyed over a seven-year period.

Aug 23: Restrictions intended to discourage **smoking by young people** were announced by Pres. Clinton. The new rules banned vending machines in many locations; prohibited brand-name sponsorship of sporting events; and outlawed advertising billboards located within 1000 ft. of schools.

Sep 3: Two **cruise missile attacks** on military targets in Iraq were staged by the U.S. in retaliation for an advance by Iraqi troops into a northern Kurdish enclave in support of one faction of Kurds fighting another. The next day, the Iraqi troops were reported to have pulled back from the excluded zone. The U.S. expanded the "no-fly zone" (the area in southern Iraq forbidden to Iraqi military aircraft) northward by 60 miles, or nearly to Baghdad.

Sep 21: States could ignore **same-sex marriages** permitted by other states under a bill signed into law by Pres. Clinton. Also, federal benefits could be denied to married people of the same sex.

Sep 24: A treaty to ban all **nuclear weapons tests** was signed at the United Nations by Pres. Clinton. A large majority of the nations of the world had agreed (Sept. 10) to the treaty, but it was not to go into effect for at least two years.

Oct 9: **Airport security** would be heightened under a bill signed by Pres. Clinton. Measures included new baggage and passenger screening methods and steps to prevent terrorism.

Oct 12: A **$3,800,000,000 federal water projects bill** was signed by Pres. Clinton. The money was to be spent on such projects as park and wildlife refuge maintenance, and included $75,000,000 to preserve and restore the Florida Everglades.

Nov 5: William "Bill" Clinton was reelected president of the U.S., running on the Democratic ticket and defeating the Republican candidate, Robert "Bob" Dole, by 379 to 159 electoral college votes. The Reform party candidate, Ross Perot, received no electoral votes. The popular vote was Clinton, 45,628,667; Dole, 37,869,436; and Perot, 7,874,283. The Republicans gained two Senate seats for a 55-45 majority. The Republicans remained in control in the House, but their majority was reduced from 37 to 19, with 227 Republicans, 207 Democrats and 1 independent.

Dec 5: Madeleine K. Albright, U.S. representative to the UN, was selected to become secretary of state in his second adminstration by Pres. Clinton, making her the first woman ever to hold this top cabinet post. Albright, the daughter of a Czech diplomat, fled her native land in World War II to escape the Nazis.

II. Architecture
Arts and Music
Popular Entertainment
Publishing
Theater

Attendance at Broadway theaters during the 1995–1996 season was 9,450,000, an increase of nearly half a million over the previous season. Ticket sales were $436,000,000, an increase of $30,000,000, while the 38 new productions represented an increase of 9 productions. U.S. and Canadian road tours grossed $810,000,000, a healthy rise of $108,000,000. The sensation of the theatrical season was the rock musical *Rent*, inspired by the opera *La Bohéme*. Opening in a small East Village theater, *Rent* soon moved to Broadway and box office success; however, this achievement was marred by the death of its author, Jonathan Larson, the night of the final dress rehearsal. Another surprise was the revival of the musical *Chicago*, first seen in the mid-1970s. New and loud was *Bring in da Noise/Bring in da Funk*. There was also the musical *Big*, based on the movie, which closed after a six-month run during which it lost its entire $10,300,000 investment. Art museums around the country offered an array of exhibits: "Discovery and Deceit: Archaeology and the Forger's Craft" at the Nelson-Atkins Museum in Kansas City, Mo.; a retrospective of the works of Jasper Johns at the Museum of Modern Art in New York City; "From Court Jews to the Rothschilds: Art, Patronage and Power 1600-1800" at the Jewish Museum in New York City; "American Schoolgirl Needlework," 50 examples of Needlework at the Metropolitan Museum, New York City; and "Ancient Art of Olmec Mexico" at the National Gallery of Art in Washington, D.C. The year also saw the publication of the new *Grove's Dictionary of Art*, comprised of 34 volumes and 26,300,000 words, and priced at $8,000. A major cultural event was Lincoln Center Festival '96, a new summertime program in New York City that featured, besides music, puppets and Samuel Beckett's works, and attracted 83,500 people to the various events, which cost $8,500,000 to stage. In money terms, though, the leaders in the music world were three tenors, Luciano Pavarotti, Placido Domingo, and José Carreras, the first of whom was estimated to have earned between $16,000,000 and $18,000,000, the other two $10,000,000 each in the 1995–1996 season. James Levine celebrated his 25th anniversary as artistic director of the Metropolitan Opera in New York City. The year also marked the 100th anniversary of the composition of John Philip Sousa's most popular march, "The Stars and Stripes Forever." In the world of pop and rock, Alanis Morissette ranked high with sales of her album *Jagged Little Pill*, which reached more than 11,000,000 sets. A group known as Kiss led the way in receipts from concerts at $44,000,000. The highlight of the dance season was the appearance in New York City of the Paris Opera Ballet. The Hollywood movie industry did not have a good year, though *Independence Day*, in which just about everything, including the White House, was blown up, set a record of $11,100,000 in first-day receipts. *A Time to Kill*, a courtroom drama based on a novel by John Grisham, was another major success. Contrasts in movie fare were represented near the end of the year by a four-hour production of *Hamlet*, and the pop goddess Madonna starring in *Evita*, a fictionalized musical about the life of the late Argentinian political figure Eva Perón. Network television produced only one sitcom of hit quality, *Third Rock from the Sun*, about some aliens who come to Earth and find its ways peculiar. A study by the Center for Communications Policy at UCLA found that violence on network television had declined in the past year; only 5 of 114

network series in 1995–1996 raised concern about the violence depicted, compared with 9 the previous year. Among notables who died were Morey Amsterdam, popular comedian of vaudeville, radio, and television, Oct. 18, at 81; Lew Ayres, movie actor, who won early fame in *All Quiet on the Western Front* (1930), Dec. 30, at 88; Martin Balsam, talented character actor, Feb. 13, at 76; Pandro Berman, Hollywood producer, who masterminded films with such stars as Fred Astaire, Ginger Rogers, and Elizabeth Taylor, July 13, at 91; Erma Bombeck, whose humorous columns about ordinary life made her a top-ranking journalist, Apr. 22, at 69; Albert Broccoli, producer of the James Bond (Agent 007) movies, June 26, at 87; Harold Brodkey, novelist and essayist, Jan. 26, at 65; Joseph Brodsky, Russian-born, Nobel Prize winner for poetry, Jan. 28, at 55; George Burns, the famous and ageless comedian, Mar. 9, at 100; Irving Caesar, lyricist of such hit songs as "Tea for Two," Dec. 17, at 101; John Chancellor, long-time correspondent and anchor for NBC News, July 12, at 68; Richard M. Clurman, leading editor at *Time* and *Newsday*, May 15, at 72; Claudette Colbert, whose comedy roles had made her one of the most popular film stars, July 30, at 92; Richard Condon, author of novels of political conspiracy, Apr. 9, at 81; Merle Eugene Curti, who won a Pulitzer Prize for his intellectual history of the U.S., Mar. 9 at 98; Marcia Davenport, biographer of Mozart and others, Jan. 16, at 92; Paul Draper, who brought style to tap dancing, Sept. 20, at 86; Mignon G. Eberhart, whose many mystery stories combined suspense and romance, Oct. 8, at 97; Vince Edwards, handsome surgeon of TV's *Ben Casey*, Mar. 11, at 67; Lonne Elder 3d, black playwright who wrote *Ceremonies in Dark Old Men*, June 11, at 69; Mercer Ellington, who led his father's band after the Duke's death, Feb. 7, at 76; Ella Fitzgerald, the foremost jazz singer of her generation, June 15, at 79; Greer Garson, actress, remembered especially for *Mrs. Miniver*, Apr. 6, at 92; Morton Gould, composer and conductor, Feb. 21, at 82; Margaux Hemingway, glamorous actress and model, July 1, at 41; Bernard B. Jacobs, one of the most powerful men in the American theater as head of the Shubert Organization, Aug. 27, at 80; Gene Kelly, dancer whose work was both graceful and athletic, Feb. 2, at 83; Harry Kemelman, author of the mystery novels featuring Rabbi David Small, Dec. 15, at 88; Walter Kerr, influential theater critic, Oct. 9, at 83; Lincoln Kirstein, a founder of the New York City Ballet, Jan. 5, at 88; Dorothy Lamour, sultry film star, Sept. 22, at 81; Otto Leuning, composer, conductor, and advocate of contemporary music, Sept. 2, at 96; Henry Lewis, the first black conductor of a major American orchestra, Jan. 26, at 63; Dorothy Maynor, soprano and founder of the Harlem School of the Arts, Feb. 19, at 85; Audrey Meadows, wife and foil to Jackie Gleason in TV's *The Honeymooners*, Feb. 3, at 71; Jessica Mitford, British-born author of *The American way of Death*, July 23, at 78; Gerry Mulligan, saxophonist and pioneer of "cool" jazz, Jan. 20, at 68; Vance Packard, social critic who warned of excesses in advertising, Dec. 12, at 82; Minnie Pearl, star of *The Grand Ole Opry* for over 50 years, Mar. 4, at 83; Orville Prescott, influential book critic of *The New York Times* for 24 years, Apr. 28, at 89; M. L. Rosenthal, poet and leading critic of 20th-century poetry, July 21, at 79; Vermont Royster, editor who helped make *The Wall Street Journal* the country's leading business newspaper, July 22, at 82; Meyer Schapiro, art historian, Mar. 3, at 91; Jerry Siegel, creator of Superman, Jan. 28, at 81; McLean Stevenson, TV star of the popular *M*A*S*H* series, Feb. 15, at 66; Tiny Tim (Herbert Khaury), whose ukulele and falsetto voice put him in the musical spotlight, Nov. 30, at 64; Tamara Toumanova, glamorous ballerina, May 29, at 77; and Diana Trilling, cultural, social, and literary critic, Oct. 23, at 91. In October, *Books in Print* reported that 49,040 publishers had 1,352,929 different books in print, most of them hard to find and in little demand. In some cases, though, there were too many copies, which were being returned unsold to publishers at a rate as high as 40% of gross sales. Publishers also had a new worry: piracy of copyrighted titles on the Internet. A further concern was the absence of blacks in professional publishing positions; U.S. government statistics showed that blacks occupied only 3.4% of such jobs. An impetus to reading was provided by talk show host Oprah Winfrey, who started an on-the-air book club. When she recommended a 19-year-old book, *Song of Solomon*, by Toni Morrison, thousands of Winfrey's followers bought it. Christian bookstores were departing from staid and conservative ways to embrace espresso bars and pop music. Books with spiritual themes sold well in secular stores as well as Christian bookstores, among them *How to Be a Perfect Stranger: A Guide to Other People's Religious Ceremonies*. Notable books of the year were a varied lot: *The Collected Stories of Mavis Gallant; Selected Stories* by Alice Munro; *At a Century's Ending: Reflections, 1982–1995* by the distinguished diplomat George F. Kennan; *Grand Expectations: The United States, 1945–1974* by James T. Patterson; *Pearl S. Buck: A Cultural Biography* by Peter Conn; and *Great Books: My Adventures with Homer, Rousseau, Woolf, and Other Indestructible Writers of the Western World* by David Denby. Among bestsellers were *Primary Colors*, a thinly disguised takeoff on the Clinton primary campaign, by "Anonymous," who turned out to be the columnist Joe Klein and who was castigated for having lied about his authorship; and *The Green Mile* by Stephen King, a thriller published in six separate parts. Inspirational bestsellers included *The Seven Habits of Highly Effective People* by Stephen R. Covey and *The Seven Spiritual Laws of Success* by Deepak Chopra.

Jan 9: The first **Truman Capote Lifetime Achievement Award** in Literary Criticism was presented to Alfred Kazin, a pioneer in the serious study of American literature. The award, worth $100,000, and which was to be given every four years, was presented by the estate of the late author Truman Capote.

Jan 17: Phil Donahue, the originator of the audience-participation television talk show, announced that he would retire in May, only half a season away from the 30th anniversary of his show. Donahue was credited with bringing to public discussion such charged subjects as sex and child abuse.

Jan 18: An exhibition of works by the sculptor **Constantin Brancusi** opened at the Museum of Modern Art in New York City. It included 14 works from the Georges Pompidou Center in Paris and 14 works from MOMA's own collection. A larger retrospective of Brancusi's sculptures, exhibited at the Philadelphia Museum of Art, had closed on Dec. 31, 1995.

Jan 20: The highest price ever for a **piece of needlework**, $1,000,000, was paid at an auction in New York City. It was a needlepoint chimney piece made in 1750 by Hannah Otis, a schoolgirl. It depicted the Boston of the time and was bought on behalf of the Museum of Fine Arts in Boston.

Feb 2: The **Museum of Modern Art,** located in New York City, was enabled to increase its space by 250,000 sq. ft., nearly double its current cramped quarters, as the result of the purchase of an adjoining hotel and two brownstones at a cost of $50,000,000.

Feb 12: The most comprehensive collection of **Lincoln memorabilia** went on exhibit at the Chicago Historical Society. Entitled "The Last Best Hope of Earth: Abraham Lincoln and the Promise of America," the exhibit included more than 200 objects, such as a Gettysburg Address manuscript and the gloves Lincoln wore the night he was assassinated.

Feb 28: Grammy Awards were presented for the following: best album of 1995, *Jagged Little Pill* by Alanis Morissette; best single record, "Kiss from a Rose" by Seal; best male pop vocalist, Seal; best female pop vocalist, Annie Lennox; best male rock vocalist, Tom Petty; best female rock vocalist, Alanis Morissette.

Feb 29: A promise to establish a **television program rating system** by Jan. 1, 1997, was made to Pres.

Clinton by leaders of the entertainment industry. Earlier in the month, the four broadcast networks, in the face of growing criticism of violence on TV, had agreed to establish a rating system somewhat like the one governing the motion-picture industry.

Feb 29: Author **Joan Collins** was awarded $1,000,000, to be paid by her publisher, Random House, by a judge in New York City. The award was part of an advance against a book Ms. Collins wrote under contract, but which Random House claimed was unpublishable.

Mar 17: A West Coast **Museum of Television and Radio** opened in Beverly Hills, Calif., joining the one founded in New York City in 1975. The new museum was housed in a $16,000,000 building, giving access to 750,000 TV and radio programs heard and seen over seven decades.

Mar 21: "Splendors of Imperial China," an exhibition of about 450 treasures from the National Palace Museum in Taipei, Taiwan, opened at the Metropolitan Museum of Art in New York City. The items, including paintings, porcelains, bronzes, and jade carvings, covered about 3000 years of imperial history.

Mar 25: **Academy Awards** were presented to *Braveheart* as the outstanding motion picture of 1995; Nicholas Cage as best actor for *Leaving Las Vegas*; Susan Sarandon as best actress for *Dead Man Walking*; Kevin Spacey as best supporting actor for *The Usual Suspects*; and Mira Sorvino as best supporting actress for *Mighty Aphrodite*.

Apr 9: **Pulitzer Prizes** were awarded for the following: fiction, *Independence Day* by Richard Ford; general nonfiction, *The Haunted Land: Facing Europe's Ghosts After Communism* by Tina Rosenberg; biography, *God: A Biography* by Jack Miles; history, *William Cooper's Town: Power and Persuasion on the Frontier of the Early American Republic* by Alan Taylor; poetry, *The Dream of the Unified Field* by Jorie Graham; drama, *Rent* by Jonathan Larson; music, *Lilacs* by George Walker.

Apr 10: An exhibit of **Currier and Ives prints** opened at the Museum of the City of New York. The 80 prints on display showed life in America in the mid-19th century; idealized home life; the Civil War; and racist satires of the lifestyle of blacks.

Apr 11: Treasures of the **Saxon State Library** of Dresden, Germany, went on exhibit at the Library of Congress in Washington, D.C. The exhibit included manuscripts of the composers Robert Schumann and Richard Wagner; material relating to Martin Luther; and a Jewish Holy Day Prayer Book dating from about 1290. These treasures survived the Allied fire bombing of Dresden in World War II and subsequent Russian looting.

Apr 23–26: An auction in New York City of possessions of **Jacqueline Kennedy Onassis** brought wild bidding for all kinds of items owned by her or her first husband, Pres. John Fitzgerald Kennedy. Total receipts amounted to $34,400,000, with bids reaching $772,500 for a set of his golf clubs, and $112,500 for two simulated pearl necklaces which belonged to her.

Apr 28: "Picasso and Portraiture," an exhibit of the artist's work in this field, opened at the Museum of Modern Art in New York City. Covering Picasso's long lifetime, the exhibit showed works from all the periods of his various styles.

May 20: Thirteen works of **20th century art** were given to New York City's Metropolitan Museum of Art by Klaus G. and Amelia Perls, who had been art dealers and collectors for more than 60 years. The works, by such masters as Picasso, Braque, and Léger, were valued at $60,000,000 or more.

May 30: "Cézanne," the first retrospective of the artist's work in 60 years, opened at the Philadelphia Museum of Art. The exhibit included 170 works by the Impressionist master and attracted about 700,000 visitors, a record for the museum.

June 2: **Tony Awards** for the 1995–1996 theater season were presented for the following: best play, *Master Class* by Terrence McNally; best musical, *Rent*; leading actor in a play, George Grizzard for *A Delicate Balance*; leading actress in a play, Zoe Caldwell for *Master Class*; leading actor in a musical, Nathan Lane for *A Funny Thing Happened on the Way to the Forum*; leading actress in a musical, Donna Murphy for *The King and I.*

June 12: The J. Paul Getty Museum, located in Malibu, Calif., announced that Lawrence A. and Barbara Fleischman would give the museum one of the best private collections of **ancient Greek and Roman art.** About 300 objects, dating from 2000 B.C. to A.D. 400 and valued at about $80,000,000, were included.

June 16: "Masterpieces from the Palazzo Doria Pamphili," located in Rome, opened at the National Gallery of Art in Washington, D.C., as an exhibit of selections from the collection begun in 1651 by Pope Innocent X. The European paintings, which date from the 16th to the 18th century, included Velásquez' famous portrait of the pope.

June 20: A **film storage and preservation center** was opened at Hamlin, Pa., by the Museum of Modern Art. The two-building installation, costing $11,200,000, can house and keep safe more than 13,000 titles, from kinetoscope subjects of the 1890s to the latest movies.

June 20: A retrospective exhibit of the works of **Winslow Homer** opened at the Metropolitan Museum of

Art in New York City. About 180 paintings, drawings, and watercolors examined the artist's career from his first oil painting of a Civil War scene to his later seascapes.

June 26: Four exhibitions observing the **100th anniversary of the purchase of the** *New York Times* **by Adolph S. Ochs** opened simultaneously at the New York Public Library, the Museum of Modern Art, the American Museum of Natural History, and the Pierpont Morgan Library. Each exhibit tied the history of the *Times* to the purpose of the institution where it was to be seen.

July 1: Jazz at Lincoln Center officially became a full-fledged constituent of that home of the performing arts, which consists of ten other organizations, including the Metropolitan Opera and the New York Philharmonic Orchestra. Jazz at Lincoln Center planned to expand its concert programs as well as its educational efforts, national tours, and broadcasts.

July 2: The **Museum of Contemporary Art** in Chicago, Ill., officially opened a new building and a sculpture garden. The new structure, which cost $46,000,000, increased the museum's gallery space fourfold, to 45,000 sq. ft.

July 8: Philip Johnson, the dominant figure in American architecture for more than a generation, observed his 90th birthday without any indication of retiring. From skyscrapers to glass houses, Johnson had spread his work over a large area, both physically and stylistically.

July 11: The **Arnold Schoenberg collection** of musical scores, writings, and tapes, housed at the University of Southern California in Los Angeles, Calif., since 1973, and valued at about $50,000,000, had to be returned to the composer's heirs. The family had charged that the university had violated its pledge not to use the building housing the collection for purposes unrelated to Schoenberg's music. Where the collection was to go remained uncertain.

July 29: Three hours of **children's programming** a week was promised by the broadcast industry after negotiations with federal officials. Each TV station would have to prove that it had complied with this standard when applying for a renewal of its license.

Sep 8: Emmy Awards were presented for the following: best drama series, *E.R.*; best comedy series, *Frasier*; best actor in a drama series, Dennis Franz for *N.Y.P.D. Blue*; best actress in a drama series, Kathy Baker for *Picket Fences*; best actor in a comedy series, John Lithgow for *Third Rock from the Sun*; best actress in a comedy series, Helen Hunt for *Mad About You.*

Sep 19: One hundred pieces of **Chinese furniture** brought a total of $11,200,000 at an auction in New York City. A carved 17th-century screen with an image showing a craggy mountain range went for $1,100,000.

Sep 30: "Degas: Beyond Impressionism," an exhibit of about 100 works of the artist's later years, opened at the Chicago Art Institute. Degas, who always concentrated on dancers and bathers, emphasized color and forms during this period.

Oct 9: The most highly regarded example of **Pop Art,** Andy Warhol's *Campbell's Soup Cans*, was acquired by the Museum of Modern Art in New York City, along with an early painting by Ellsworth Kelly. The works were valued at about $15,000,000, one of the highest prices ever listed for contemporary art.

Oct 26: "Leonardo's Codex Leicester: A Masterpiece of Science" was the title of an exhibit of the work of the great artist and scientist that opened at the American Museum of Natural History in New York City. The 78-page manuscript was a miscellany of ideas and sketches that Leonardo set down between 1506 and 1510 and had recently sold at auction for $30,800,000. It was bought by Bill Gates, founder of Microsoft and thought to be the richest man in the U.S.

Oct 31: Although cracked down one side, a **Korean dragon jar** from the 17th century sold at auction in New York City for $8,600,000, the highest price ever paid at auction for an Asian art object. At 19 inches, it was the tallest known of this type of ceramic vessel.

Nov 3: "The Peale Family: Creation of an American Legacy, 1770–1870" opened at the Philadelphia Museum of Art, showing the work of the leading family of artists of that city. Included were works by the father, Charles Willson Peale, who painted more than 1000 portraits, and works by his sons, Raphaelle, Rembrandt, and Titian.

Nov 3: "Corot," a showing of 150 paintings by the artist known as the supreme landscapist of his time, opened at the Metropolitan Museum of Art in New York City. The exhibit attempted to show the variety of Corot's work, not just his best.

Nov 6: National Book Awards were presented for the following: fiction, *Ship Fever and Other Stories* by Andrea Barrett; nonfiction, *An American Requiem: God, My Father and the War That Came Between Us* by James Carroll; poetry, *Scrambled Eggs and Whiskey: Poems, 1991–1995* by Hayden Carruth; children's literature, *Parrot in the Oven: Mi Vida* by Victor Martinez.

Nov 12: An **Edouard Manet pastel portrait** of a woman sold at auction in New York City for $2,900,000, the most ever paid for this type of Manet's work. Also sold was Edgar Degas's *Young Dancer at 14*, for $11,900,000. These and other items were sold by the Shelburne Museum of Shelburne, Vt., to relieve its financial problems.

Nov 13: A **French silver tureen** sold for $10,300,000 at auction in New York City, the highest price ever paid for a work of the French decorative arts. The tureen, made in the 1730s in the rococo style, weighed 30 pounds.

Nov 20: The **highest price for an artwork** at auction in 1996 was paid in New York City for Willem de Kooning's *Woman*, which was sold for $15,600,000.

Nov 25: Art works with a value of more than $150,000,000 were left to the Metropolitan Museum of Art and the Museum of Modern Art, both in New York City, by Florence May Schoenborn, an heiress and longtime collector. The 32 works included paintings and sculptures by such artists as Brancusi, Braque, and Picasso.

Nov 26: A **book publishing merger** in which the Penguin Group was to acquire the Putnam Berkley Group for $336,000,000 was expected to establish a firm representing about 12% of all book sales in the U.S.

Dec 19: A **rating system for television** was proposed by network executives. It was intended to rate programs from "TV-Y (all children)" to "TV-M (mature audiences only)." Critics complained that such a system was not specific enough to be useful.

III. Business and Industry
Education
Philosophy and Religion
Science

In September, the Census Bureau reported that U.S. household income rose in 1995 for the first time in six years. Half the households in the nation had incomes of at least $34,074, an increase of 2.7% over 1994. The economy, however, grew only 2.1%, the smallest gain since 1991. Productivity, on the other hand, grew 1.1% in 1995, the largest gain since 1992. The Internet grew faster than ever. Beginning in 1960 as a network connecting three computers, it consisted by 1996 of about 2000 networks and nearly 40,000,000 computers. One of the most popular uses of the Internet was for sending and receiving E(for electronic)-mail, with 1,000,000,000,000 messages recorded in 1995. Another gainer was the cellular phone industry, which signed up 9,600,000 new customers in 1995, bringing the total to 33,800,000. The Census Bureau reported that the income gap between the richest and the poorest Americans by 1994 was the widest since the end of World War II. Contributing to the gap were many CEOs: the average compensation for heads of large companies rose 23% in 1995 to $4,370,000,

while Bill Gates of Microsoft, the computer software giant, was reported to be the wealthiest man in the world with assets of $18,000,000,000. Cigarette manufacturers received a setback when the Minnesota Mining and Manufacturing Co., the third-largest outdoor billboard advertising company, announced that after 1996 it would no longer accept tobacco advertising. By the end of 1996 Big Macs were being sold at 18,700 McDonald's in 100 countries. The National Long Term Care Surveys found that not only were Americans living longer, they were developing fewer chronic diseases and other disabilities. However, the suicide rate among the elderly increased by 9% from 1980 to 1992. The federal government reported that AIDS had become the third-leading cause of death among American women 25 to 44 years of age, and the leading cause of death among white men in that age group. A record number of blacks were earning Ph.D.s; in 1995, 1,287 such degrees were awarded to blacks, an increase of almost 100 over 1994. Blacks were also closing the gap with whites in high school diplomas, with 86.5% of blacks between the ages of 25 and 29 holding diplomas, compared with 87.4% of whites. Attempts to set standards for teaching history and English were made. Proposed history standards, strongly attacked by conservatives, were amended to decrease the attention paid to controversial issues. The English language report simply called for students to have read a "wide assortment of literature." The American Association of University Professors reported that men in the academic world were paid about 30% more than women. The National Commission on Teaching and America's Future found that more than a quarter of all new teachers had inadequate training or teaching skills. Radio stations broadcasting 15 or more hours of weekly religious programs increased 10% in 1995 to 1463. The United Church of Christ published a new hymnal that updated traditional language, changing especially the old emphasis on masculine titles. The hymn "Dear Lord and Father of Mankind" became "Dear God, Embracing Humankind." The number of police officers killed in the line of duty dropped to 117 in 1996, compared with 162 in 1995. Fifty-five of the 117 were killed by firearms. The automobile industry marked its 100th anniversary, it having been 1896 when Charles and Frank Duryea built in Springfield, Mass., 13 two-passenger, two-cylinder runabouts. Notable persons who died included Joseph Cardinal Bernardin, archbishop of Chicago, a moderate leader of the Roman Catholic Church, Nov. 14, at 68; Seymour Cray, a pioneer of the computer industry and father of the supercomputer, Oct. 5, at 71; Ray W. Fuller, codiscoverer of Prozac, the most widely used antidepressant drug, Aug. 11, at 60; William E. Hanford, industrial chemist who developed the first liquid household detergent as well as polyurethanes, Jan. 27, at 87; Julian W. Hill, research chemist who discovered nylon, Jan. 28, at 91; John Cardinal Krol, archbishop of Philadelphia, a leading figure in Roman Catholic Church affairs, Mar. 3, at 85; Arthur J. Lelyveld, rabbi, a leader of Reform Judaism, Apr. 15, at 83; Ray McIntire, chemical engineer, who by accident invented styrofoam, Feb. 2, at 77; David Packard, a founder of the Hewlett-Packard Co., a pioneer in electronics, Mar. 26, at 83; Roger Tory Peterson, whose field guides to birds were used worldwide, July 28, at 87; Carl Sagan, astronomer, whose work popularized science, Dec. 20, at 62; George Davis Snell, who shared a Nobel Prize for research that helped make human organ transplants possible, June 6, at 92; Walter Sullivan, newspaper reporter on nearly every aspect of science, Mar. 19, at 78.

Jan 5: A **merger of two large military contractors** was announced by Lockheed Martin, which said that it would acquire the Loral Corp. in a deal valued at $10,000,000,000. The merger would make Lockheed the largest producer of military hardware, with annual sales of about $30,000,000,000.

Jan 15–31: The **number of galaxies** in the universe was now estimated at 50,000,000,000, five times as many as previously estimated, as a result of discoveries made by the Hubble Space Telescope. On Jan. 16 other astronomers said that they thought they had accounted for about half of the missing mass of the universe and that it probably consisted of many unseen, burned-out stars known as white dwarfs. Two California astronomers reported on Jan. 17 that they had found two planets that were orbiting Sun-like stars and were possibly warm enough to produce life. Astronomers in Hawaii said on Jan. 31 that they had detected a galaxy 14,000,000,000 light-years away, the most distant ever observed.

Jan 24: Approval of a **fat substitute, Olestra,** was announced by the Food and Drug Administration, but for use only in such snack foods as potato chips. Some scientists warned of possible adverse effects on health and disapproved its use.

Feb 17: An **unmanned spacecraft was launched** from Cape Canaveral, Fla., bound for Eros, an asteroid orbiting the sun and relatively close to the Earth. Called Near, the craft was to reach Eros in Feb., 1999, after traveling 1,300,000,000 miles.

Feb 25: An **experiment with a satellite on a cable** failed when the cable broke after nearly 12 of its 13-mile extent had been paid out from the space shuttle *Columbia.* The experiment was a joint venture of NASA and the Italian Space Agency, and cost nearly $450,000,000.

Mar 1: The **transmission of information** at the rate of 1,000,000,000,000 bits of information a second, using optical fiber, had been achieved, announced three research teams that worked jointly on the project. The feat amounted to transmitting the entire contents of 300 years of daily newspapers in one second.

Mar 7: The **first views of the surface of Pluto,** the smallest and most distant planet of the solar system, were recorded through the Hubble Space Telescope. Pluto was shown to have icy polar caps and clusters of features, some of which were bright and some dark.

Mar 13: The **tobacco industry** was stunned when the Liggett Group, the smallest of the nation's five major tobacco companies, became the first to settle a class action lawsuit concerning the effect of smoking on health. On Mar. 15, Liggett announced that it had also agreed to a settlement with five states which sought reimbursement for Medicaid spending on smoking-related illnesses.

Mar 25: **Virtual marriage of same-sex couples** was carried out en masse in San Francisco, Calif., when Mayor Willie L. Brown, Jr. officiated at a "domestic partnership ceremony" for nearly 200 gay and lesbian couples. The ceremonies had no legal status.

Mar 28: Civil **marriage for gay and lesbian couples** was approved by the Central Conference of American Rabbis. The rabbis also voted to oppose governmental efforts to forbid such unions.

Apr 1: The **largest medical benefits company** in the U.S. was created by the purchase, for $8,800,000,000, by the Aetna Life and Casualty Co. of U.S. Healthcare, Inc. The combined operation was to provide coverage for 23,000,000 people.

Apr 1: Two **regional Bell telephone companies** agreed to merge, with SBC Communications acquiring the Pacific Telesis Group for $17,000,000,000. The merged firm would serve 30,000,000 residential and business customers in 7 states west of the Mississippi River, including California and Texas. In the East, two other regional phone companies agreed on Apr. 21 to merge. They were NYNEX and Bell Atlantic, which between them had 36,000,000 customers in 12 eastern states from Maine to Virginia.

May 9: Explorer **Richard E. Byrd's** claim to having been the first person to fly over the North Pole (May 9, 1926) was possibly false, according to experts who recently found the diary Byrd kept on the flight. They said that he was well short of his goal and that he knew it.

May 15: A retired Episcopal bishop, Walter C. Righter, was cleared of a charge of **heresy** by a church court.

The court found that he had not violated the church's "core doctrine" by ordaining a gay man as a deacon.

May 21: Trinity Church, surrounded by the skyscrapers of New York City's Wall Street area, observed the 150th anniversary of its opening in 1846. The Episcopal edifice, of chocolate-colored brownstone, was the tallest structure in the city until 1876.

June 20: The **two largest radio broadcasting companies** announced that they would merge, with the Westinghouse Electric Corp. acquiring the Infinity Broadcasting Corp. for $3,700,000,000. With limits on the number of radio stations one company may own lifted by a new federal communications law, the combined firms now operated 83 stations.

June 26: Women cannot be denied admittance to a state-supported military school, the Supreme Court ruled, 7-1. The Virginia Military Institute did not agree to abide by the court's decision until Sept. 1, but then it said that it was requiring women to meet the same standards as men. Meanwhile, on June 28, The Citadel, a similar school in South Carolina, announced that it was going to admit women, and on July 24 four were accepted.

July 2: A model for a new type of **space vehicle** was approved by NASA. Wedge-shaped and reusable, it was to be built by the Lockheed Martin Corp. The first major new spacecraft in 25 years, the full-scale ship was designed to be 127 ft. long, be cheaper to operate, and be a replacement for the present shuttle.

July 3: A merger creating the nation's **largest railroad** was approved by the Surface Transportation Board. The takeover of the Southern Pacific Railroad by the Union Pacific was accomplished for $5,400,000,000. The new rail unit was expected to be one of two that together could handle 90% of all freight west of the Mississippi River.

July 5: The **ordination of homosexuals,** so long as they remained celibate and disavowed their past sexuality, was approved by the governing body of the Presbyterian Church (U.S.A.). The policy also called for ordained unmarried heterosexuals to refrain from having sex.

July 10: Close-up photographs of **Ganymede,** the huge satellite of the planet Jupiter, taken by the spacecraft Galileo, showed it to have a deeply wrinkled surface and, unlike other moons, a magnetic field of its own.

July 17: The **Earth's inner core** rotates slightly faster than the rest of the Earth, scientists at Columbia University announced. The core moves fast enough to make one more rotation than does the Earth about every 400 years. The discovery was expected to increase knowledge of how heat flows through the Earth.

July 30: Metropolitan Spyridon (George Papageorgiou), serving in Italy, was elected to head the Greek Orthodox Church in the U.S. The American-born prelate, who succeeded Archbishop Iakovo, had been made a bishop in 1985.

Aug 6: Evidence of **primitive life on Mars** was found in a meteorite that originated from that planet, according to scientists at the Johnson Space Center in Houston, Tex. The scientists said that molecules of organic compounds discovered in the meteorite indicated fossil traces of past biological activity. Other scientists were skeptical of the claim.

Sep 12: Remains of the first successful **English settlement** in what is now the U.S. were discovered on Jamestown Island, Va., archaeologists announced. Traces of the original fort, founded in 1607, included wood stains showing where the original wall was, the skeleton of a settler, and glass beads used for trading with the local Indians.

Sep 26: A **record for time in space** was set by Shannon Lucid, a scientist and astronaut, who came back to earth after 188 days aboard the Russian space station *MIR*. She set the record for any American astronaut and, worldwide, for a woman.

Oct 7: The **Nobel Prize in Physiology or Medicine** was awarded to Peter C. Doherty, an Australian long associated with St. Jude's Children's Research Hospital in Memphis, Tenn., and to Rolf M. Zinkernagel of Switzerland. They were cited for their discovery of how the body's immune system recognizes cells infected with viruses.

Oct 8: The **Nobel Prize in Economics** was awarded to William Vickrey of Columbia University and James A. Mirrlees of Cambridge University, England. They were cited for "their fundamental contributions to the economic theory of incentives." Vickrey, 82, died suddenly of cardiac arrest three days later (Oct. 11).

Oct 9: The **Nobel Prize in Chemistry** was awarded to Richard E. Smalley and Robert F. Curl, Jr. of Rice University, and Harold W. Kroto of England. The award went to them for the discovery of a hitherto unknown class of carbon molecules.

Oct 9: The **Nobel Prize in Physics** was awarded to David M. Lee and Robert C. Richardson of Cornell University, and Douglas D. Osheroff of Stanford University. They had discovered a phenomenon known as superfluidity while studying a rare form of helium.

Oct 17: A direct scientific link between **smoking and lung cancer** was found, a team of researchers announced. This first evidence from the level of cell biology found a chemical in cigarettes that causes genetic damage to lung cells.

Oct 24: The first national **labor union for physicians** was formed by most of the country's podiatrists and was to be affiliated with the A.F.L.-C.I.O. Organized to deal with the changes brought about by managed health care, the new group was to be known as the First National Guild for Health Care Providers of the Lower Extremities.

Nov 1: A **$22,000,000,000 offer** by British Telecommunications to buy the 80% it did not already own of MCI Telecommunications, America's second largest long-distance phone company, was announced. If approved by the federal government, the deal was intended to establish the first transatlantic phone company.

Nov 7: The **Mars Global Explorer**, an unmanned spacecraft, was launched at Cape Canaveral, Fla., on a voyage planned to reach Mars in Sept. 1997. Once established in a 235-mile-high orbit, the spacecraft was to study with its scientific instruments the planet's atmosphere and surface for one Martian year, which consists of 687 Earth days.

Nov 12: **The National Conference of Catholic Bishops approved a 10-point "Catholic Framework for Economic Life"** which said that economic life must be subject to moral principles. People, it declared, have a right to basic necessities, including health care and a safe environment.

Nov 13: Approving a **set of norms** that colleges and universities should follow, the National Conference of Catholic Bishops acted to make sure that Roman Catholic institutions keep their religious identity. They should, first of all, acknowledge their Catholic identity.

Nov 15: The largest settlement ever in a **racial discrimination case** was reached when Texaco, Inc., agreed to pay more than $140,000,000 to end a lawsuit brought by its minority employees. The company also agreed to revise its personnel operations.

Dec 3: There may be **water on the moon**, according to findings by American scientists based on radar signals from a spacecraft. The signals indicated that there might be water ice in the cold shadow of a deep basin near the moon's south pole.

Dec 4: An unmanned spacecraft, Pathfinder, was started on a **voyage to Mars**, where it was scheduled to launch a roving vehicle, Sojourner, that was to land on the planet to photograph rocks to determine their composition.

Dec 7: The **longest flight of any space shuttle** ended when the *Columbia* landed at Cape Canaveral, Fla., after 17 days, 15 hours, and 54 minutes in space. The shuttle and its five astronauts traveled 7,000,000 miles.

Dec 15: The largest merger in the **aerospace industry** was expected by the offer of the Boeing Co. to acquire the McDonnell Douglas Corp. for $13,300,000,000.

Boeing was to become the only manufacturer of commercial jet planes in the U.S., as well as the world's largest aerospace company.

Dec 31: The **Dow Jones industrial stock average** closed the year at 6,448.27, compared with a close of 5,117.12 in 1995. The average reached a new high of 6,560.91 on Dec. 27, and set a record for shares traded of 683,000,000 on July 16.

IV. Fashion
Folkways
Holidays
Social Issues and Crime
Sports

In the sports world, everything seemed to be bigger than ever in 1996. A new record for major league home runs–4962–was registered, about 500 more than the previous record. The Baltimore Orioles set a new single-season team record with 257 homers. Average attendance at games was 26,889, a gain of 6.5%. On Jan. 28, Super Bowl XXX had the highest television rating in 10 years. Advertisers paid about $1,200,000 for a 30-second commercial. Professional athletes had bigger than ever paychecks. The New York Yankees' payroll was the largest in major league baseball at $52,189,370; however, the average Baltimore Oriole player was the best paid, at $1,949,073. Professional basketball players did even better. Shaquille O'Neal signed a 7-year, $120,000,000 contract to play for the Los Angeles Lakers, while Michael Jordan was to be paid $25,000,000 for playing for 1 year for the Chicago Bulls. Not in money but in numbers, young women were in the news. The NCAA reported that 110,524 of them competed in college sports in 1994–1995, compared with only 29,977 in 1971-1972. Crime, on the other hand, was decreasing. The Justice Department reported that violent crime fell more than 9% in 1995. For the second year in a row homicides by juveniles decreased, down 22.8% from a 1993 peak. Some of the homicides that did occur were unusual. In Moses Lake, Wash., a 14-year-old boy with a rifle killed a teacher and two students; in Fort Lauderdale, Fla., a onetime beach cleaner shot and killed 5 of his former colleagues; in San Diego, Calif., a graduate student, shot and killed 3 of his professors during an oral exam; in Brooklyn, N.Y., a 10-year-old shot and killed another 10-year-old, his best friend; and in New York City a mother was convicted of killing her 6-year-old daughter. Several reports indicated that the use of tobacco, marijuana, and other drugs was on the rise among youths. Of teenagers age 17 and under, 34.8% said that they had smoked tobacco, compared with just over 30% in 1993. Marijuana's use by teenagers jumped 141% between 1994 and 1995. In fashion, casual clothing prevailed, especially for business-women for whom the power suit and high heels were no longer so necessary. Even wedgies, favorite shoes during World War II, were making a comeback. The Population Reference Bureau said that the traditional American family–two parents and children–was also staging a comeback. The number of such households increased by 700,000 from 1990 to 1995, while the divorce rate fell per 1000 women from 23 in 1980 to 20.5 in 1994. Baylor University, a Baptist institution in Waco, Tex., said that it would allow dancing for the first time in its 151 year history. The year ended with the incident of the hair-eating doll. Cabbage Patch Snacktime Kids, a popular Christmas gift for young children, had a mechanism that allowed it to appear to eat plastic carrots and French fries. But then the doll took to nibbling at the hair and fingers of its young female owners, with about 100 such incidents reported by year's end. Notable Americans who died during the year included Mel Allen, sports broadcaster, the "voice of the Yankees" from 1939 to 1964, June 16, at 83; Ewell Blackwell, star fastball pitcher of the late 1940s and early 1950s, Oct. 29, at 74; Charlie Conerly, quarterback and star of the New York Giants football team in the 1950s, Feb. 13, at 74; Ellsworth "Babe" Dahlgren, who succeeded Lou Gehrig at first base for the New York Yankees when Gehrig's record consecutive game streak ended, Sept. 4, at 84; Sarah Palfrey Danzig, graceful and stylish tennis champion, Feb. 27, at 83; Del Ennis, star outfielder for the Philadelphia Phillies in the 1950s, Feb. 8, at 70; Max Factor Jr., cosmetics company executive who popularized makeup, June 7, at 91; Charles O. Finley, colorful former owner of the Oakland A's, whose ideas for change upset other owners, Feb. 19, at 77; Pierre Franey, legendary chef and author, Oct. 15, at 75; Frank Howard, football coach who made Clemson University a football power, Jan. 26, at 86; Timothy Leary, clinical psychologist who became noted for his experiments with psychedelic drugs, May 31, at 75; Del Miller, hall of fame harness racing driver, Aug. 19, at 83; F. Don Miller, longtime head of the United States Olympic Committee, Jan. 17, at 75; Martha Phillips, for more than 60 years a notable figure in luxury fashion retailing, Sept. 7, at 98; Theodora Ayer Randolph, Virginia resident known as the first lady of fox hunting, June 12, at 90; Pete Rozelle, commissioner for 29 years of the National Football League, who made the NFL the top professional sports organization, Dec. 6, at 70; Jimmy "the Greek" Snyder, who brought gambling to televised sports, Apr. 21, at 76; Mary Thompson,

daughter of slaves and thought to be the oldest American, Aug. 3, at 120; Helen Wallenda, last of the famous high wire troupe, May 9, at 85; Rudolf Walter Wanderone, who as "Minnesota Fats" was a hustler in many fields, not just pool, Jan. 18, at 83(?).

Jan 1: In **college football bowl games,** the results were Nebraska 62, Florida 24 in the Fiesta Bowl; Florida State 31, Notre Dame 26 in the Orange Bowl; Colorado 38, Oregon 6 in the Cotton Bowl; and Southern California (USC) 41, Northwestern 31 in the Rose Bowl. The AP and *USA Today/*CNN polls voted Nebraska collegiate champion for 1995, its second title in a row.

Jan 5: Don Shula, the winningest coach in National Football League history, announced his resignation. His teams had won 347 games while losing 173 and tying 6. He had spent 26 of his 43 years of association with the NFL as head coach of the Miami Dolphins.

Jan 8: The **Baseball Writers Association** failed to elect anyone to the Baseball Hall of Fame, only the seventh time this had occurred. However, on Mar. 5 the Veterans Committee elected Jim Bunning, a pitcher; Earl Weaver, a former manager; Ned Hanlon, a turn-of-the-century manager; and Bill Foster, a pitcher in the Negro leagues.

Jan 9: A CBS golf analyst, **Ben Wright,** was suspended by the network for allegedly having used pejorative remarks about the effect of lesbianism on the women's professional golf tour. Wright, who was to receive pay covering his four-year contract, was said to have first made such remarks in May and to have made similar comments in November, 1995.

Jan 10: An attempt to be the first to fly a **balloon** nonstop around the world ended on a frozen lake in Canada when Steve Fosset, an American commodities broker, was forced by storms to abandon his effort, which had begun when his balloon, the *Solo Challenger,* left the ground near Rapid City, S.D., on Jan. 8.

Jan 18: The owners of **major league baseball teams** voted to begin interleague play in 1997. Each team in the American and National Leagues would play 15 or 16 games against teams in the other league. Details remained to be worked out and approval by the players' union was needed.

Jan 20: U.S. figure skating championships were won by Rudy Galindo, the first such champion to be openly gay, and 15-year-old Michelle Kwan, the youngest women's champion in 32 years.

Jan 28: Super Bowl XXX was won by the Dallas Cowboys (NFC), who defeated the Pittsburgh Steelers (AFC) 27-17. The Cowboys had won the NFC title by defeating the Green Bay Packers 38-27, while the

Steelers won the AFC championship by defeating the Indianapolis Colts 20-16.

Jan 30: Two boys, 12 and 13 years old, were sentenced to serve time in a maximum security juvenile prison for having dropped a 5-year-old boy from a 14-story window when he refused to steal candy for them. The boys were 10 and 11 years old at the time. Their release was scheduled for when they reach the age of 21.

Jan 31: The **richest contract in baseball history** was signed by Ken Griffey, Jr., outfielder of the Seattle Mariners. It called for payments of $34,000,000 over four years, an average of $8,500,000 a year.

Feb 9: Moving the **Cleveland Browns** of the NFL to Baltimore was approved by the owners of the other NFL teams. In return, Cleveland was promised a new NFL franchise by 1999. On Apr. 30, the owners agreed to allow the Houston Oilers to transfer the team to Nashville in 1998, when a new $292,000,000 stadium was to be ready.

Feb 17: In a **six-game chess match,** Gary Kasparov, the world champion, defeated a computer, four games to two. The computer, known as Deep Blue, was managed by a team of computer scientists from IBM.

Mar 16: The **world heavyweight boxing championship** was rewon by Mike Tyson, who defeated Frank Bruno in three rounds. The referee stopped the bout with Bruno nearly knocked out.

Mar 19: Ending a week's suspension from the NBA, **Mahmoud Abdul-Rauf** of the Denver Nuggets agreed to stand and pray while the national anthem was being played. He had previously refused to stand. His refusal, he said, was based on personal and religious beliefs.

Mar 31: The **NCAA women's basketball championship** was won by Tennessee, which defeated Georgia 83-65.

Apr 1: The **NCAA men's basketball championship** was won by Kentucky, which defeated Syracuse 76-67.

Apr 3: Theodore J. Kaczynski, 53, was arrested and charged with being the so-called Unabomber, whose mail bombings between May, 1978, and Apr., 1995, had killed 3 persons and wounded 23. A number of his targets were people who worked on computers or in genetic research.

Apr 11: In an attempt to become the youngest **cross-country airplane pilot,** seven-year-old Jessica Dubroff was killed shortly after her plane crashed on take-off from Cheyenne, Wyo. Her father, Lloyd, and her flight instructor were also killed.

Apr 14: Nick Faldo won the **Masters golf tournament** by five strokes. He defeated Greg Norman, who had held a six-stroke lead going into the final round.

Apr 15: The 100th **Boston Marathon** was won in the men's division by Moses Tanui of Kenya with a time of 2 hrs., 9 min., 16 sec. The women's division was won for the third year in a row by Uta Pippig of Germany with a time of 2 hrs., 27 min., 12 sec.

May 2: A computer analyst who had lost his job was sentenced to 94 years in prison for **firebombing two New York City subway trains**. The most serious of the bombings occurred on Dec. 21, 1994, and injured 48 people, 14 of them seriously.

May 4: The 122nd **Kentucky Derby** was won by Grindstone with a time of 2:01. The jockey was Jerry Bailey.

May 12: Laura Davies won the **LPGA championship** by one stroke at even par.

May 18: The 121st **Preakness Stakes** was won by Louis Quatorze with a time of 1:53²⁄₅. The jockey was Pat Day.

May 26: The **Indianapolis 500 auto race** was won by Buddy Lazier by 0.695 of a second. His average speed was 147.956 mph.

June 2: The **U.S. Women's Open golf tournament** was won by Annika Sorenstam of Sweden by six strokes. She won for the second year in a row and set a scoring record for the event of 272.

June 8: The 128th **Belmont Stakes** was won by Editor's Note with a time of 2:28⁴⁄₅. The jockey was Rene Douglas.

June 11: The **NHL Stanley Cup** was won by the Colorado Avalanche with a four-game sweep of the Florida Panthers.

June 12: Control of the **Cincinnati Reds** of baseball's National League was given up through the 1998 season by Marge Schott, managing general partner, after she made disturbing comments with racial and ethnic content. The other team owners had been prepared to take further action if she did not act voluntarily.

June 16: The **NBA championship** was won by the Chicago Bulls, who defeated the Seattle Supersonics four games to two. The Bulls had had the best regular season in NBA history, winning 72 games while losing only 10.

June 16: The **U.S. Men's Open golf tournament** was won by Steve Jones by one stroke.

July 9: The **All-Star baseball game** was won by the National League, which defeated the American League 6-0 for its third consecutive victory.

July 11: The **International Chess Federation** crowned Anatoly Karpov of Russia its world champion after he defeated Gata Kamsky of the U.S. with 10.5 points to Kamsky's 7.5 in a match played in Elista, Russia. Karpov collected $937,500 for his victory.

July 17: A **baseball museum** opened in Louisville, Ky., in connection with the completion of a new factory for Hillerich & Bradsby, long the makers of "Louisville Sluggers," the bats used by most professional players as well as by thousands of amateurs. The museum was to show its links to such stars as Ty Cobb, Babe Ruth, and Jackie Robinson.

July 19–Aug 4: At the **XXVIth Summer Olympic Games,** hosted by Atlanta, Ga., in which 10,700 athletes from 197 nations participated, the U.S. finished first in medals with 44 gold, 32 silver, and 25 bronze. Germany was second with 65 medals. Amy Van Dyken won four gold medals in swimming; Michael Johnson won both the 200- and the 400-meter sprints, the former in world record time of 19.32 sec.; Dan O'Brien became the first American since Bruce Jenner in 1976 to win the decathlon; the women's soccer team won the first soccer tournament in Olympic history; and Carl Lewis won the long jump for the fourth consecutive time.

July 21: The **British Open** golf tournament was won by an American, Tom Lehman, by two strokes.

July 25: **Amanda Wallace** was given life in prison without parole in a Chicago court after she was convicted of killing her three-year-old son by hanging him from a transom with an extension cord around his neck.

Aug 11: The **PGA championship tournament** was won by Mark Brooks on the first hole of a sudden-death playoff.

Aug 26: The **U.S. Amateur golf tournament** was won for an unprecedented third consecutive year by Tiger Woods, a Stanford University junior, on the second hole of a sudden-death playoff. On Aug. 28 Woods turned professional, signing a five-year, $40,000,000 contract with Nike, a manufacturer of sneakers. Woods was also the first black to win this tournament.

Sep 6: **Eddie Murray** of the Baltimore Orioles became only the third player in major league baseball history to achieve both 500 home runs and 3000 hits when he homered in the seventh inning of a game. He joined Hank Aaron and Willie Mays in this category.

Sep 8: The **U.S. Open tennis championships** were won by Pete Sampras in the men's division, and by Steffi Graf in the women's division.

Sep 14: The **Miss America** title was won by Tara Dawn Holland of Kansas at the annual pageant in Atlantic City, N.J.

Sep 21: The rarest of all **baseball cards** was sold at auction in New York City for a record-breaking $640,500. Dating from 1910, it depicts a star player, Honus Wagner of the Pittsburgh Pirates, often called the greatest player ever.

Oct 20–26: The **World Series** was won by the New York Yankees (AL) who defeated the Atlanta Braves (NL) four games to two. The Yankees had won the American League championship by defeating the Baltimore Orioles four games to one, while the Braves took the National League title by defeating the St. Louis Cardinals four games to three.

Nov 3: The 27th **New York City Marathon** was won in the men's division by Giacomo Leone of Italy with a time of 2 hrs., 9 min., 54 sec. The women's division was won by Anuta Catuna of Romania with a time of 2 hrs., 28 min., 18 sec.

Nov 9: The **world heavyweight boxing championship** was won by Evander Holyfield with an 11th-round TKO of Mike Tyson, the defending titleholder.

Nov 19: Albert Belle became the **highest paid player** in major league baseball when he signed a five-year contract with the Chicago White Sox that guaranteed him $55,000,000. The slugging outfielder had hit 98 home runs and driven in 274 runs in his previous two seasons with the Cleveland Indians.

Dec 5: The **longest labor dispute** in baseball history ended when the players' union ratified an agreement that club owners had approved on Nov. 26. Among other provisions, the new agreement called for revenue sharing by the clubs, a payroll tax on players, a luxury tax on teams, and interleague play.

How to Use the Index

Each index entry includes a date and section number. When a subject appears more than once in the book, the index supplies a date and section number for each instance.

When a text entry is dated by month and day, this information appears in the index. The citation

Adams, Leonie, 1955 Jan. 9, II

directs the reader to the time period 1955 and the entry dated January 9 in section II.

Introductory paragraphs, which appear at the beginning of each section for every time period, are identified in the index solely by year and section number. For example,

Acupuncture, 1972, III

means that information on acupuncture is to be found in the section III introductory paragraph of the time period 1972.

Undated text entries appear directly *after* the introductory paragraphs and are identified in the index by consecutive numbers in parentheses. Thus,

Actinomycin, 1940(1), III

directs the reader to the first undated entry *after* the introductory paragraph in section III of the time period 1940. Similarly, parenthetical numbers are used to identify multiple entries having the same date. The index entry

Adams, Sherman, 1958 Sept. 22(2), I

directs the reader to the time period 1958 and the second entry dated September 22 in section I.

The early time periods—from the beginning through 1799—are organized in multiple-year blocks. Therefore, for the index entry

Adultery: colonial divorce grounds, 1660(1), IV

the reader, realizing there is no discrete time period for the year 1660, turns to the time period 1660–1669, then locates the first entry dated 1660 in section IV.

Edwards, Douglas, 1988 Apr. 1, II; 1990, II

Edwards, Jonathan:
  Great Awakening, 1730-1734, III
  Great Awakening sermon, 1741(1), III
  resignation ended Great Awakening, 1750, III

Edwards, Vince, 1996, II

Eggleston, Edward, 1871(1), II; 1873(1), II

Egypt *see* Israeli-Arab conflict

Ehrlichman, John, 1973 Apr. 30, I; 1973 June 25-29, I; 1973 Sept. 4, I; 1975 Feb. 21, I; 1977 May 23, I

Eilberg, Amy, 1985 May 12, III

Einstein, Albert, 1930, III; 1971, III; 1995 July 13, III

Eisele, Donn F., 1968 Oct. 11, III

Eiseley, Loren C., 1977, III

Eisenhower, Dwight David:
  Adams resigned, 1958 Sept. 22(2), I
  atomic weapon use, 1955 Mar. 16, I
  backed Adams in Goldfine case, 1958 June 17, I
  Crusade in Europe, 1948(1), II
  Doctrine, 1957, I; 1957 Jan. 5, I
  domestic policies, 1954, I
  elected president, 1952, I; 1952 Nov. 4, I
  Far East tour, 1960 June 26, I
  flew to Korea, 1952 Nov. 29, I
  foreign policy, 1954, I
  general of Army rank, 1944 Dec. 15, I
  heart attack, 1955 Sept. 26, III
  Japanese tour canceled, 1960 June 16, I
  legislation signed, 1954 May 13, III; 1954 Sept. 3, I; 1958 July 7, I
  meeting with Khrushchev, 1959 Sept. 15-27, I
  named Supreme Allied commander, 1943 Dec. 24, I
  nominated for second term, 1956 Aug. 20-24, I
  Normandy invasion, 1944 June 6, I
  North African invasion, 1942 Nov. 7, I
  nuclear policy, 1954, I
  presidential candidacy, 1952 July 11, I
  problems of presidency, 1953, I
  proposed military information exchanges with Soviets, 1955, I
  reelected president, 1956 Nov. 6, I
  sent troops to Little Rock (Ark.), 1957 Sept. 24, I
  SHAPE command, 1951 Apr. 4, I
  Social Security proposals, 1953 Aug. 1, I
  steel strike, 1959, III
  on subversion, 1954, I
  vetoed housing bill, 1959 July 7, I
  vowed to go to Korea, 1952 Oct. 24, I

Eisenhower, Milton S., 1985, III

Eisenstaedt, Alfred, 1995, II

Eisner, Michael, 1994, III

Elder, Lonne, III, 1996, II

Elderly (*see also* Medicare):
  cholesterol link to heart disease less pronounced than in middle-aged people, 1994 Nov. 2, II

fastest growing population segment increase in over age 90, 1996, I

suicide rate rise, 1996, III

Thurmond oldest senator, 1996 Mar. 8, I

Eldredge, Todd, 1990 Feb. 10-11, IV; 1991 Feb. 15-17, IV; 1995 Feb. 11, IV

Election Campaign Act, 1972 Apr. 7, I; 1976 Jan. 30, I

Elections (*see also* Campaign financing; Electoral college and vote count; Presidential elections; Voting rights):
  campaign spending, 1990, I
  congressional, 1788 Sept. 30-1790 Aug. 31, I; 1790-1791, I; 1792-1793, I; 1794-1795, I; 1796-1797, I; 1798-1799, I; 1800-1801, I; 1802-1803, I; 1804-1805, I; 1806-1807, I; 1808-1809, I; 1810-1811, I; 1812-1813, I; 1814-1815, I; 1816-1817, I; 1818-1819, I; 1820-1821, I; 1822-1823, I; 1824-1825, I; 1826-1827, I; 1828-1829, I; 1830-1831, I; 1832-1833, I; 1834-1835, I; 1836-1837, I; 1838-1839, I; 1840-1841, I; 1842-1843, I; 1844-1845, I; 1844 Dec. 4, I; 1846-1847, I; 1848-1849, I; 1850-1851, I; 1852-1853, I; 1854-1855, I; 1856-1857, I; 1858-1859, I; 1860-1861, I; 1862-1863, I; 1864-1865, I; 1866-1867, I; 1868-1869, I; 1870-1871, I; 1872-1873, I; 1874-1875, I; 1876-1877, I; 1878(1), I; 1880 Nov. 2, I; 1882 Nov. 7, I; 1884 Nov. 4, I; 1886 Nov. 2, I; 1888 Nov. 6, I; 1890 Nov. 4, I; 1894 Nov. 6, I; 1896 Nov. 3, I; 1898 Nov. 8, I; 1900 Nov. 6, I; 1902 Nov. 4, I; 1904 Nov. 8, I; 1906 Nov. 6, I; 1908 Nov. 3, I; 1910 Nov. 8, I; 1912 Nov. 5, I; 1914 Nov. 3, I; 1916 Nov. 7, I; 1918 Nov. 5, I; 1920 Nov. 2, I; 1922 Nov. 7, I; 1924 Nov. 4, I; 1926 Nov. 2, I; 1928 Nov. 6, I; 1930 Nov. 4, I; 1932 Nov. 8, I; 1934 Nov. 6, I; 1936 Nov. 3, I; 1938 Nov. 8, I; 1940 Nov. 5, I; 1942 Nov. 3, I; 1944 Nov. 7, I; 1946 Nov. 5, I; 1948 Nov. 2, I; 1950 Nov. 7, I; 1952 Nov. 4, I; 1954 Nov. 2, I; 1956 Nov. 6, I; 1958 Nov. 4, I; 1960 Nov. 8, I; 1962 Nov. 6, I; 1964 Nov. 3, I; 1966 Nov. 8, I; 1968 Nov. 5, I; 1970 Nov. 3, I; 1972 Nov. 7, I; 1974 Nov. 5, I; 1976 Nov. 2, I; 1978 Nov. 7, I; 1980 Nov. 4, I; 1982 Nov. 2, I; 1984 Nov. 6, I; 1986 Nov. 4, I; 1990, I; 1990 Nov. 6, I; 1992, I; 1992 Nov. 3, I; 1994, I; 1994 Nov 8, I; 1995, I; 1996 Nov. 5, I
  Crump campaign song (Tenn.), 1909, II
  Democratic congressional sweep, 1958, I; 1958 Nov. 4, I
  direct, of senators, 1913 May 31, I
  federal supervision of city, 1871 Feb. 28, I
  first Kansas, 1855 Mar. 30, I
  first nominating convention (Utica, N.Y.), 1824 Aug., I
  reapportionment act, 1842 June 25, I
  Republican sweep, 1994, I; Nov. 8, I

voter turnout increased, 1992, I

Electoral college and vote count, 1792 Dec. 5, I; 1796 Dec., I; 1800, I; 1804 Dec. 5, I; 1808 Dec. 7, I; 1812 Dec. 2, I; 1816 Dec. 4, I; 1820 Dec. 6, I; 1824 Dec. 1, I; 1828 Dec. 3, I; 1832 Dec. 5, I; 1836 Dec. 7, I; 1840 Dec. 2, I; 1844 Dec. 4, I; 1848 Nov. 7, I; 1852 Nov. 2, I; 1856 Nov. 4, I; 1860 Nov. 6, I; 1864 Nov. 8, I; 1868 Nov. 3, I; 1872 Nov. 5, I; 1876 Nov. 7, I; 1880 Nov. 2, I; 1884 Nov. 4, I; 1888 Nov. 6, I; 1892 Nov. 8, I; 1896 Nov. 3, I; 1900 Nov. 6, I; 1904 Nov. 8, I; 1908 Nov. 3, I; 1912 Nov. 5, I; 1916 Nov. 7, I; 1920 Nov. 2, I; 1924 Nov. 4, I; 1928 Nov. 6, I; 1932 Nov. 8, I; 1936 Nov. 3, I; 1940 Nov. 5, I; 1944 Nov. 7, I; 1948 Nov. 2, I; 1952 Nov. 4, I; 1956 Nov. 6, I; 1960 Nov. 8, I; 1964 Nov. 3, I; 1968 Nov. 5, I; 1972 Nov. 7, I; 1976 Nov. 2, I; 1980 Nov. 4, I; 1984 Nov. 6, I

Electoral Count Act, 1887 Feb. 3, I
  proposed reforms, 1965 Jan. 28, I
  separate ballots for president and vice president, 1804 Sept. 25, I
  Tilden-Hayes dispute, 1877, I

Electra plane, 1960 May 12, III

Electricity (*see also* Blackouts and dimouts; Hydroelectric power; Lighting; Public utilities):
  first alternating current motor, 1892(5), III
  first central power plant, 1881(1), III
  first sewing machine, 1889(5), III
  Franklin kite experiment, 1752 June, III
  motors, 1834(1), III
  Rural Electrification Administration established, 1935 May 11, I
  Tesla's inventions, 1888, III

E (electronic)-mail, 1996 III

Electronics, 1964 Oct. 29, III; 1973 Oct. 23, III; 1977 Oct. 11, III

Electron microscope, 1940 Apr. 20, III

Elementary and Secondary Education Act, 1978, III

Elevators:
  first (N.Y.C.), 1852, III
  first in hotel (N.Y.C.), 1859(2), III

Elion, Gertrude B., 1988 Oct. 17, III

Eliot, Charles W., 1869, III

Eliot, Jared (Rev.), 1735-1739, III

Eliot, John (Rev.), 1631 Nov. 3, III; 1639, II; 1653, II; 1660, III; 1661, II

Eliot, T. S., 1922(1), II; 1948 Nov. 4, II; 1965, II

Elizabeth I (Queen of England), 1584, II

Elkington, Steve, 1995 Aug. 13, IV

Elkins, Stanley, 1993, II

Elkins, Stephen B., 1903, I; 1910, I

Elkins Act, 1903, I

Elks, Benevolent Protective Order of, 1868(2), III
  women made eligible for membership, 1995 Sept. 29, IV

Ellington, Duke, 1962 May 31-June 3, II; 1974, II

Freemasons (*see also* Anti-Masonic Party):
first military lodge, 1738, IV
first settler, 1682, IV
Imperial Council of the Ancient Arabic Order of Nobles of the Mystic Shrine, 1876 June 6, IV
Freemen:
surrendered, 1996 June 13(2), I
Freer Gallery (Wash., D.C.), 1984, II
Free-Soil Party, 1852 Aug. 11, I
Free trade *see* Trade; specific agreements
Frelinghuysen, Theodore, 1844 May 1, I
Frémont, Jesse, 1944(1), II
Frémont, John C.:
first expedition, 1842(1), I
presidential nomination, 1856 June 2, I
Republican presidential candidate, 1856 June 17-19, I
second expedition, 1843 May 29, I
third expedition, 1845 Spring, I
French and Indian War (*see also* Paris, Treaty of; Queen Anne's War; Seven Year's War):
Braddock mortally wounded, 1755 July 9, I
Detroit surrendered by French, 1760 Nov. 29, I
first refugees, 1755 Nov. 30, I
first skirmish, 1754 May 28, I
Ft. Duquesne captured, 1758 Nov. 25, I
Ft. Loudon surrender, 1760 Aug. 7, I
Ft. Necessity surrendered, 1754 July 4, I
Ft. Oswego (N.Y.) captured, 1756 Aug. 14, I
Ft. Ticonderoga, 1758 July 8, I; 1759 July 26, I
Ft. William Henry (N.Y.) captured, 1757 Aug. 9, I
French defeated on Plains of Abraham, 1759 Sept. 13, I
French surrendered Louisbourg (Nova Scotia), 1758 July 26, I
Montreal surrendered by French, 1760 Sept. 8, I
Freneau, Philip, 1775-1779, II; 1788, II; 1815, II
Frick, Ford C., 1978, IV
Fricker, Brenda, 1990 Mar. 26, II
Friedan, Betty, 1993, II
Friedman, Jerome I., 1990 Oct. 16(1), III
Friedman, Milton, 1976 Oct. 14(2), III
Friedman, Thomas L., 1989 Nov. 29, II
Friel, Brian, 1992 June 1, II
Friml, Rudolf, 1924, II; 1972, II
Frings, Ketti, 1958 May 5, II
Frobisher, Martin (Sir), 1600-1609, I
Froebel, Friedrich, 1860, III
Froman, Jane, 1980, II
Fromme, Lynette (Squeaky), 1975 Sept. 5, I
Frontier (*see also* Cowboys; Homestead Act; Westward expansion; specific forts):
Colt revolver, 1833, III
folk heroes, 1833, IV

plays about, 1870 Feb. 14, II
rough sports, 1819, IV
tough image, 1820, IV
Turner on, 1893(1), III
Frontier Day (Wyo.), 1897(1), IV
Frost, David, 1977 May 4, I
Frost, Robert, 1914(1), II; 1923(1), II; 1928(1), II; 1930(1), II; 1936(1), II; 1939(1), II; 1945(1), II; 1962(1), II
aided Pound, 1958 Apr. 18, I
Bollingen Prize, 1963(3), II
died, 1963, II
Pulitzer Prize, 1924 May 11, II; 1931 May 4, II; 1937 May 3, II; 1943 May 3, II
Fruits and vegetables *see* specific types
Frustaci, Patricia, 1985 May 21, III
Fry, Shirley, 1951 July 6-7, IV; 1952 July 5, IV; 1953 July 3, IV; 1956 July 7, IV
Fry, William Henry, 1855, II
Fuel *see* Energy and power; Heating; specific types
Fugitive slave laws, 1802, IV; 1850 Sept. 18, I; 1851, I; 1851 Feb. 15, I; 1859, I
Fukui, Kenichi, 1981 Oct. 19(1), III
Fukuyama, Francis, 1992(1), II
Fulbright, J. William:
on U.S. involvement in Laos, 1969 Oct. 28, I
death of, 1995, I
Fuller, Charles, 1982 Mar. 12, II
Fuller, Margaret, 1840, II; 1846(1), II
Fuller, Ray W., 1996, III
Fuller, R. Buckminster, 1983, III
Fullerton, C. Gordon, 1977 Aug. 12, III
Fulton, Robert, 1807 Aug. 11, III
Fundamental Constitutions (Locke), 1660-1669, III
Fundamentalism (*see also* Evolution):
growth, 1974, III
modernist controversy with, 1892(2), III
Moral Majority disbanded, 1989 June 10, II
rejected by Conservative Judaism, 1988 Apr. 13, III
Sunday's advocacy, 1896, III
Southern Baptist Convention, 1990 June 12, III
Fund for the Republic, 1953(1), III
Funerals:
colonial customs, 1735-1739, IV
Furgol, Ed, 1954 June 19, IV
Furniture and home furnishings:
auction of Chinese, 1996 Sept. 19, II
chief colonial designers, 1780-1784, IV
colonial manufacturers, 1650-1659, IV
Empire style, 1804, IV
high-backed settle, 1640, IV
Queen Anne style, 1725, IV
record auction prices, 1983, IV; 1996 Nov. 13, II
Sheraton and Directoire styles, 1800(2), IV
slat-back chair, c1700, IV
Fur trading:
Ashley's expedition, 1822, IV

Astor's enterprises, 1808, III; 1811 Apr. 12, I
Monts's monopoly, 1603, III
U.S.-British competition (Ore.), 1827, I
Fusion *see* Cold fusion; Nuclear energy

Gabor, Eva, 1995, II
Gacy, John Wayne, 1994, IV
Gaddis, William, 1994, II; 1994 Nov. 16, II
Gadsden Purchase, 1853 Dec. 30, I
Gaines, Boyd, 1994 June 12, II
Gajdusek, D. Carleton, 1976 Oct. 14(1), III
Galbraith, John Kenneth, 1958(1), II; 1960(1), II; 1973(1), II; 1977(1), II
Galileo (spacecraft), 1989 Oct. 18, III; 1993 Jan. 21, III; 1995 Dec. 7, III
Galindo, Rudy, 1996 Jan. 20, IV
Gallaudet, Thomas, 1852 Oct., III
Gallaudet College (Wash., D.C.), 1864, III
Gallico, Paul, 1976, II
Gallo, Joseph ("Crazy Joe"), 1972 Apr. 7, IV
Gallo, Julio, 1993, III
Gambino, Carlo, 1976, IV
Gambling (*see also* Horse racing; Lotteries):
baseball, 1990 July 30, IV; 1992 July 24, IV
decreased, 1991, IV
colonial, 1699 June, IV
first legal casino (outside Nev.) opened (N.J.), 1978 May 26, IV
first legalized horse racing (N.H.), 1964 Sept. 12, IV
Native American casinos proliferated, 1993, IV
riverboat, 1856, IV
Rose banned from baseball, 1989 Aug. 24, IV
Gamma Ray Observatory, 1991 Apr. 7, III
Games and recreation (*see also* Sports; specific games and sports):
arcade video craze, 1983, II
card playing suppressed (Mass.), 1699 June, IV
coaching and fox-hunting, 1879, IV
colonial, 1610-1619, IV; 1660-1669, IV
craps, 1813, IV
electronic, 1976, IV
mid-eighteenth century, 1750-1754, IV
most popular activities, 1984, IV
pioneer farmers, 1801, IV
Plymouth strictures, 1621 Dec. 25, IV
popular N.Y.C. colonial, 1766, IV
Game theory, 1994 Oct. 11, III
Gangsta rap, 1995, II
Gangsters *see* Organized crime
Gantt, Harvey B., 1963 Jan. 28, III
Garbo, Greta, 1990, II
Garcia, Jerry, 1995, II
Gardens *see* Horticulture
Gardner, Ava, 1990, II
Gardner, Dale, 1984 Nov. 12, III
Gardner, Erle Stanley, 1970, II

INDEX

Supreme Court *(cont.)*
immigration, 1882, I
income tax constitutional, 1881 Jan. 24, I; 1916 Jan. 24, III
independent prosecutor upheld, 1988 June 29, I
interception of communist propaganda banned, 1965 May 24, III
interracial marriages upheld, 1967 June 12, I
interstate commerce, 1898 June 1, III
job discrimination ruling, 1984 May 22, I
judicial review doctrine, 1803, I
jury rulings, 1991 Apr. 1, I; 1991 June 3, I; 1992 June 18, I; 1994 Apr. 19, I
Kennedy nomination confirmed, 1987 Oct. 23, I
last hired, first fired policy upheld, 1984 June 12, III
lawyer solicitation of accident liability business ruling, 1995 June 27, I
legal fee advertising upheld, 1977 June 27, III
Legal Tender Act, 1871 May 1, III
legislative veto struck down, 1983 June 23, I
liquor advertising ban ruled illegal, 1996 May 13, I
longest justice's tenure, 1980, I
Marshall resigned, 1991 June 27, I
Marshall's contribution, 1801 Jan. 20, I
Medicaid-funded abortion not mandatory, 1977 June 20, III
mental patients' forced confinement barred, 1975 June 26, III
military death penalty upheld, 1996 June 3, I
minority-owned construction company preference law invalid, 1989 Jan. 23, I
Miss. school desegregation ordered, 1969 Oct. 29, III
Mississippi university system ruled still segregated, 1992 June 26, III
movie censorship, 1961 Jan. 23, II
National Labor Relations Act upheld, 1937 Apr. 12, III
Nativity display upheld, 1984 Mar. 5, I
Nev. divorces, 1942 Dec. 21, IV
New Deal measures, 1933 May 12, I; 1935, I; 1935 May 27, I
Nixon nominees, 1970 May 12, I
Nixon nominees approved, 1971, I; 1971 Dec. 6, I; 1971 Dec. 10, I
Nixon nominees rejected, 1970, I; 1970 Apr. 8, I
obscenity rulings, 1973 June 21, II
parochial school aid barred, 1973 June 25, III
parochial school aid rulings, 1971 June 28, III
poll taxes unconstitutional, 1966 Mar. 25, I
Powell approved, 1971, I; 1971 Dec. 6, I
presidential liability ruling, 1982 June 24, I
prisoners' appeals restricted, 1992 May 4, I

private nonsectarian school discrimination banned, 1976 June 25, III
private possession of obscene material allowed, 1969 Apr. 7, II
Prohibition decisions, 1930 May 26, I
public school religious education barred, 1948 Mar. 8, III
Puerto Rican citizenship, 1904 Jan. 4, I
punitive damage award overturned, 1996 May 20(2), I
race as factor in congressional district lines ruled illegal, 1995 June 29, I
racial criterion in legislative redistricting overturned, 1996 June 13(1), I
Rehnquist approved, 1971, I; 1971 Dec. 10, I
religious services in public universities upheld, 1981 Dec. 8, III
right to criticize public figures upheld, 1988 Feb. 24, I
right-to-die rulings, 1990 June 25, I
school busing to desegregate ruling, 1971 Apr. 20, III
school desegregation issues, 1954 May 17, I; 1955 May 31, III; 1964 May 25, III; 1991 Jan. 15(1), I; 1992 Mar. 31, I
school facilities' use by religious groups allowed, 1993 June 7, III
school facilities' use by student political/religious groups upheld, 1990 June 4, I
school prayer banned (N.Y.), 1962 June 25, III
school prayer law struck down, 1985 June 4, III
school prayer law struck down again, 1992 June 24(2), III
school religious publication allowed government funds, 1995 June 29, I
second woman justice, 1993 Aug. 3, I
segregation in transportation banned, 1962 Feb. 26, I
seizure of defendant's property upheld, 1996 June 24, I
separate but equal doctrine, 1896 May 18, I
sex hiring discrimination ruling, 1971 Jan. 25, III
sexual harassment broadly defined, 1993 Nov. 9, I
slavery, 1857, I; 1859, I
southern school desegregation deadline, 1970 Jan. 14, III
steel mill seizure, 1952, III; 1952 June 2, III
steel strike, 1959 Nov. 7, III
subversion decisions, 1952 Mar. 2, III
Taney as chief justice, 1834 June 24, I
Teapot Dome ruling, 1927 Oct. 10, I
televising criminal trials, 1965 June 7(2), I
Tellico Dam (Tenn.) halted, 1978 June 15, III
Thomas confirmed, 1991 Oct. 15, I
travel restrictions overturned, 1964 June 22, I

travel restrictions upheld, 1959 Dec. 7, I
unfair marketing practices, 1972 Mar. 1(1), III
wage and hour law upheld, 1941 Feb. 3, I
Warren resigned, 1968 June 13, I
Warren retired, 1969 June 23, I
Watergate appeals rejected, 1977 May 23, I
White House tapes subpoenaed, 1974, I; 1974 July 24, I
women in workplace ruling, 1991 Mar. 20(1), I
women lawyers permitted to argue cases, 1879 Feb. 15, I
women's admission to all-male clubs ruled, 1987 May 4, IV
women's admittance to state-supported military schools upheld, 1996 June 26, III
women's exclusion from draft upheld, 1981 June 25, I
women's minimum wage law upheld, 1937 Mar. 29, III
women's suffrage, 1922 Feb. 27, I
women's wage discrimination ruling, 1981 June 8, I
working hours limitations, 1905 Apr. 17, III
zoning laws upheld, 1977 Jan. 11(2), III
Surrogate-mother cases, 1987 Mar. 31, IV; 1988 June 27, III
Surveyor 1, 1966 June 2, III
Surveyor 2, 1966 Sept. 22, III
Surveyor 3, 1967 Apr. 17, III
Surveyor 4, 1967 July 17, III
Surveyor 5, 1967 Sept. 8, III
Surveyor 6, 1967 Nov. 7, III
Surveyor 7, 1968 Jan. 9, III
Susann, Jacqueline, 1966(1), II; 1974, II
Susman, Karen Hantze, 1962 July 7, IV
Sutherland, Earl W., 1971 Oct. 14, III; 1974, III
Sutherland, Joan, 1961, II
Sutter, John, 1848 Jan. 24, IV
Sutton, Hal, 1983, IV; 1983 Aug. 7, IV
Sutton, May G., 1905(4), IV; 1907(1), IV
Swaggart, Jimmy, 1988 Apr. 8, III
Swallow, Silas C., 1904 Nov. 8, I
Swanberg, W. A., 1967(1), II; 1973 May 7, II; 1992, II
Swanson, Gloria, 1983, II
Swarthout, Gladys, 1969, II
Swayze, John Cameron, 1995, II
Swedenborg, Emanuel, 1800, IV
Sweeney, John J., 1995 Oct. 18, III
Swenson, May, 1981 Jan. 13, II
Swift, Gustavus Franklin, 1870(2), III
Swigert, John L., Jr., 1970 Apr. 11, III
Swimming:
first school (Boston, Mass.), 1827 July 23, IV
first woman across English Channel, 1926 Aug. 6, IV
two-minute mark freestyle record, 1963 Aug. 24(1), IV
world record, 1958 June 28, IV

WHY SHOULD I STUDY?

ENGLISH

- The ability to write is a tremendous asset in the working world. As your responsibilities rise, the amount of writing and reading you do will also increase. Don't let your achievements be limited by an inability to express yourself properly!
- A love letter can be a powerful thing. So can a letter of complaint, or a letter to the editor of your local newspaper. Writing, reading, and thinking well will benefit you in very practical ways.

CALCULUS

- Considering our rapidly changing, technological world, you may be training for a job which does not even exist yet. A solid background in and understanding of calculus will not only broaden your career options, but will put you in a position to be a leader in change and development.
- Many of the more complex processes of physics, biology, and chemistry would require pages and pages of algebra to describe, when the application of calculus would simplify this to one page. Calculus also allows you to understand some very complex behaviors in business and economics.

ECONOMICS

- Economics helps improve your decision-making skills as you explore the opportunity costs of real-life choices.
- The study of economics provides insight into how goods and services are priced, which is useful as you negotiate through life as a consumer, businessperson, or wage earner.

HISTORY OF WESTERN CIVILIZATION

- You can learn from history how confusing, discouraging, and inspiring human affairs can be. By studying the past, you will gain insight into the present and the future.
- The study of history pays off because it introduces you to other ways of thinking and acting, and in so doing, teaches you more about yourself.

BUSINESS ADMINISTRATION

- Learning about the different elements of running a business will help you determine if you would like to work for a small or large company and if you would like to run your own business someday. Success in your business career is not an accident—it builds on the practical skills you learn.
- By studying the staffing process, you can learn interview techniques—not only those needed to make a good impression, but also those needed to determine if the company is a good match for you.

NATURAL SCIENCES

- Learning about human organ systems will help you understand how your body will respond to factors in your environment, such as food, weather, and stress.
- Being aware of the impact of obtaining and using natural resources helps you learn to take better care of the environment.

SOCIAL SCIENCES

- When you study the roots of behavior and techniques of self control, you will be able to make better choices about your actions. You will be able to act, instead of react.
- More American businesses are becoming international and hiring people with knowledge of the world. Cultural anthropology and the other social sciences can help prepare you to live and work in areas outside the United States.

ALL SUBJECTS

- Studying different disciplines helps you shape your career goals.
- Successful study habits lead to successful work habits.
- Staying on schedule reduces stress.
- Staying on schedule frees up your time for other school, work, and leisure activities.
- Effective studying puts you in charge.
- Learning to focus on a topic will help you strengthen both personal and professional relationships.